Mutual Fund 500

MORNINGSTAR

Morningstar's Product Support, Circulation, Shipping and Receiving, and Accounting departments help bring you *Morningstar Mutual Fund 500.*

Morningstar Mutual Fund 500 (ISSN #0-7863-0431-6) is published annually. The subscription rate is $35 per year.

Table of Contents

Introduction

The *Morningstar Mutual Fund 500* represents a real improvement over last year's model. It is easier to read and offers new features that we hope make it a more useful tool for the mutual-fund investor.

We've reorganized the book and redesigned the mutual-fund page to give you quicker access to information. These changes should make the *Morningstar Mutual Fund 500* more efficient for longtime Morningstar readers. For the investor new to Morningstar, we hope the book provides a friendly, understandable introduction to our mutual-fund information.

The redesigned *Morningstar Mutual Fund 500* includes four new features on the data pages: Manager's Investment Style offers an inside scoop on the strategies of a fund; Manager Experience gives background on the portfolio manager's track record; Diversification Value for Portfolio Types can help investors judge if a fund belongs in their current portfolio; and the Bear Market Performance indicator can help investors assess how funds do during down markets—something that may be of particular interest to investors who weathered 1994.

Another new addition is a listing of category overviews, which provide summaries of groups of similar funds; categories are established based on the historical risk or investment mandate of each fund. The overviews feature year-end commentary by a Morningstar analyst as well as various statistics—such as Best 3-Year Return Percentage and Lowest 3-Year Morningstar Risk—to help identify standouts in each category.

This year's book also features more tables and charts that furnish across-the-board information for the mutual-fund market and for the funds in the *Morningstar Mutual Fund 500*. Included are performance summaries, manager changes, and a 1994 timeline that offers a quarter-by-quarter analysis. To make sense of it all, the new user's guide helps any investor, whether an experienced veteran or an unseasoned rookie, get a grasp of key definitions needed to understand mutual-fund information.

In the *Morningstar Mutual Fund 500* all the information you need to make intelligent investments in mutual funds is at your fingertips.

Kurt Kunert
Jim Raker
Editors

Good Returns–If You Can Get 'Em

It's a lower-return era, and welcome to it.

Prognosticators have predicted since the dawn of this decade that returns on investments will be lower in the 1990s than they were in the 1980s and, perhaps, than in many other decades. After a couple of death-defying climbs in 1991 and 1993, the stock and bond markets seem to finally be succumbing to this prediction. In 1994, returns were not only weak, but also sporadic and unpredictable. Who could have foreseen, for example, that a municipal-bond-market rally in late 1994 would be crushed by the financial woes of a single California county? Who would have thought that the price of Chrysler's stock would fall, even as its profits climbed?

In such a challenging environment, keeping one's financial head above water isn't as simple as tossing coins at the market, as was often true during the raging bull market of the 1980s. To maximize whatever return the markets may be willing to offer, it now falls to the investor not only to find well-managed funds, but also to employ good management themselves. The data provided on the following pages offers the tools that allows any investor to diversify, control risk and costs, limit tax liability, and maintain a long-term focus—the basic tenets of any rational search for good investment return.

It would be most rewarding to start the portfolio-building process by determining where the best place to find returns in the coming year will be. Unfortunately, it's an impossible question to answer. According to historical studies of long-term asset-class performance by Ibbotson Associates and others, the average bond has provided more return than cash, the average stock has walloped the average bond, and the typical small-cap stock has surpassed the standard large-cap issue. In a single market year, however, those rules can change swiftly, especially in a market as tumultuous as 1994's.

Where Will It Come From?

Because it's not possible to know exactly where returns will come from, the next best thing is to be everywhere that returns are likely to be. In other words, when in doubt, diversify. A number of tools provided on the Morningstar 500 pages are specifically designed to guide the investor in their hunt for diversification— whether their portfolio may be of two funds or 20.

As a snapshot of a fund's investment positioning, for example, the Style Box in the Investment Style section gives investors a powerful first screen for determining diversification. A portfolio of funds from different squares of the style box offers exposure to a variety of domestic-equity and fixed-income markets. Furthermore, investors can determine how consistently a fund has stuck to a single style in recent years by checking the Investment Style History section at the top of each page. An individual comparing hybrid funds, for example, could see that **Stagecoach Asset Allocation**, which invests primarily in S&P 500 stocks and long-term Treasuries, has a far more consistent style box history than has, say, **Founders Balanced**, which favors a high-turnover approach.

By its nature, the style box is a single average of all a portfolio's holdings: Investors don't have to stop there. The nitty-gritty of diversification is in knowing the actual types of stocks and bonds a fund owns. Is **ABT Emerging Growth** a mid-cap growth fund because it owns a small number of midsize stocks with specific growth characteristics? Or is its style-box positioning the result of a broadly diversified portfolio that tends in the aggregate toward a midsize market cap and a growth approach? The Portfolio, Index Allocation, and Sector Weightings sections of the page help to answer that question. Moreover, the Manager's Investment Style area provides investors with detail about how the manager interprets a fund's investment mandate. In ABT's case, manager Harold Ireland does focus specifically on mid-cap stocks with heavily growth-oriented fundamentals, and doesn't often stray from his chosen investment universe.

These specifics are important for helping investors maximize their diversification, no matter how many funds they may own. An investor could enjoy significant diversification, for example, simply by owning **Franklin Income** (which invests in Treasuries, junk bonds, large-cap equities, and gold) and **Strong Opportunity** (which owns small- and mid-cap stocks with high growth rates but low prices, as well as a near-20% stake in foreign stocks). The investor with a broader palette of funds, on the other hand, must work to eliminate excessive crossover in his or her portfolio—such as similar style-box positioning or single market exposures repeated across numerous funds—by choosing funds such as **Vanguard Preferred Stock**, **Benham Treasury Note**, or **PBHG Growth** (to name just a few) that consistently restrict their focus to specific market segments.

Most Similar Funds and Diversification Value by Portfolio Types provide two performance-based takes on diversification. Most Similar Funds allows investors to recognize the names of (and, ideally, avoid) funds that are highly similar to funds they already own, based upon their actual performance patterns over the past three years. It might also reveal whether a fund' strategy is mimicked by other, possibly better performing, funds, and it allows investors to compare the portfolios of funds that have performed similarly in the past. Diversification Value by Portfolio Types analyzes past performance to illustrate what type of portfolio would have received the biggest diversification benefit from a given fund.

Choose Your Steps Carefully

Another key element of building a successful portfolio is taking on only as much risk as one is prepared to accept. Luckily, while returns are impossible to gauge, risk levels tend to be highly predictable. The segments on the page that analyze risk—the Morningstar Risk-Adjusted Rating and Other Measures—provide clear guidance as to what level of risk a manager has taken on in the past and is likely to in the future, either in terms of total volatility (standard deviation and beta) or, more specifically, in terms of downside risk (Morningstar Risk). Although both funds are distinguished, for example, exceedingly cautious investors are likely to be happier with Fidelity Short-Term Bond's three-year Morningstar risk score of 0.50 and its 2.53 standard deviation than they are with Fidelity Government Securities' 1.26 Morningstar risk score and 5.61 standard deviation.

The new Bear-Market Performance indicator provides two views of bear-market performance. It ranks each fund's total performance during months when the index to which it is compared (the S&P 500 or the Lehman Brothers Aggregate Bond) struggles. But it also lists the fund's own worst consecutive three-month performance, to identify those instances when a fund's worst losses come during better markets. A gold fund that holds up well when the S&P 500 drops, for example, is not really a low-risk choice if its own worst three-month performance bottoms out worse than the S&P's does.

The Objective listing and the previously mentioned Manager's Investment Style segment, along with the plethora of portfolio information, provides other clues on what kind of markets a manager is investing in, and therefore what kind of risks it is assuming. For example, despite the similarity of name, **Scudder Global** by mandate invests substantially greater portions of its assets in U.S. stocks than does its sibling, **Scudder International**.

Performance statistics that stand out from those of similar funds may also provide clues as to where a fund is taking risks. **Strong Advantage**, for example, is to be applauded for posting a higher 1994 SEC yields than nearly all of its very-short-term bond-fund competitors. Investors can be sure, however, that the fund does not pull its income from Treasury bills. To generate that yield, the fund has long emphasized callable corporate bonds and bonds with low to moderate credit quality. The strategy has proven itself a winner in good market environments and bad, but investors comfortable only with exposure to more-sedate Treasuries aren't a good match for the rewards, and risks, that Strong Advantage has to offer.

Lord of the Realm

Perhaps the best way to maximize returns in an uncertain environment is to be sure to hold on to gains already made. If overall returns continue to be moderate going forward, losing more of one's gains to fund expenses will become increasingly intolerable. Despite growing competition among mutual funds, costs have not consistently declined; in fact, with 12B-1 fees and increasingly costly services being tucked back into fund expense ratios, the average dollar invested in equity and muni funds is actually being eroded faster by costs than it has in the past.

The Morningstar 500 favors funds that maintain reasonable expenses, but we nevertheless provide voluminous cost information—an Expense Ratio history in the History section, as well as an Expenses & Fees listing in the Operations section—to help investors make up their own minds about what they consider reasonable. **Dreyfus Global Growth** has an interesting global strategy, but is it worth the approximately 90 basis points in brokerage costs the fund incurs annually with its rapid-turnover approach? These pages will allow investors to consider such difficult questions.

Even more important, however, is gaining a clue about how much of a particular investment an investor will be forced to share with Uncle Sam. Funds that regularly pay out income or that constantly realize gains and pay them out to shareholders without making any attempt to offset those gains with occasional fund losses expose investors to significant tax bills over time. In a low-return environment, unnecessarily high taxes can shave needless percentage points off total returns. Funds that have a low tax efficiency as indicated by a low percentage of pretax return in the Tax Analysis section, such as Berwyn Income, are often better choices for tax-advantaged accounts. Taxable accounts, on the other hand, can avoid the April 16 hangover by preferring funds like Vanguard Index 500, which have high tax efficiencies (or a higher percentage of pretax return).

Choose Wisely and Forever Hold Your Peace

These simple concepts—diversify, avoid unexpected risks, shy away from high costs and big tax bills—aren't absolutely necessary to make money in mutual funds. Over time, however, they have shown themselves to be the surest means of making, and keeping, the most money out of a fund portfolio. With the S&P 500 providing only a 1.3% return in 1994, it's a good idea to own the kind of portfolio that can make lemonade out of the market's lemons. Such portfolios not only comfort the wallet, but they also comfort the mind—a vital factor in promoting the disciplined, long-term investment approach that survives, and prospers from, short-term volatility.

The best advice that Alliance Growth manager Tyler Smith ever received, he has said, was that "the object is not to be right; the object is to make money." These tenets guide the investor to long-term portfolio success—in all market climates.

Kylelane Purcell,
Editor, 5-Star Investor

Performance Summary

Net Assets ($Million)	Investment Objective	1994 Total Return %										Average Annual Return %					
		1st Qtr	# of Funds	2nd Qtr	# of Funds	3rd Qtr	# of Funds	4th Qtr	# of Funds	Year End	# of Funds	3Yr	# of Funds	5Yr	# of Funds	10Yr	# of Funds
Equity																	
31152.3	Aggressive Growth	-4.03	71	-6.41	76	8.72	80	-0.47	81	-3.31	71	7.09	49	11.07	43	13.37	27
45872.5	Equity-Income	-3.78	86	0.34	89	3.94	91	-2.44	95	-1.99	86	6.74	54	7.34	43	11.59	16
6168.2	Europe Stock	1.41	29	-1.89	33	3.22	35	-1.10	37	1.30	29	5.40	24	2.72	11	—	—
76699.2	Foreign Stock	-1.62	177	-0.56	204	6.46	236	-6.78	255	-2.91	177	9.11	85	5.46	50	15.72	16
242561.9	Growth	-3.35	625	-2.72	652	5.77	682	-1.52	708	-2.06	625	5.86	356	8.84	284	12.75	164
198567.9	Growth and Income	-3.37	343	-0.51	352	4.10	361	-1.63	379	-1.47	343	5.83	227	7.75	176	11.77	104
14049.1	Pacific Stock	-8.03	48	3.46	58	5.21	62	-8.17	67	-8.20	48	11.84	22	3.15	13	16.35	4
46453.9	Small Company	-2.77	222	-5.36	233	8.19	242	-0.37	253	-0.74	222	9.39	119	11.81	92	13.29	39
2416.3	Specialty	-2.16	25	-2.64	28	1.61	34	-1.76	34	-5.27	25	8.45	22	9.68	18	13.54	4
2011.8	Specialty–Financial	-3.08	13	5.96	13	0.48	15	-5.53	15	-2.65	13	14.82	12	15.17	10	13.43	3
4342.0	Specialty–Health	-4.06	15	0.86	16	14.03	16	-0.79	16	4.26	15	-3.51	11	9.91	10	16.29	5
3242.2	Specialty–Nat Res	-3.35	27	3.98	28	4.84	31	-6.77	32	-2.64	27	6.68	20	3.52	18	8.71	7
5507.2	Specialty–Prec Metals	-4.41	33	-7.01	34	15.97	35	-14.59	36	-11.67	33	10.46	29	-0.46	26	5.50	13
5552.0	Specialty–Technology	1.01	22	-6.77	24	13.12	28	4.50	29	10.49	22	14.15	17	14.63	16	11.78	11
24496.2	Specialty–Utilities	-6.59	65	-2.73	74	2.55	77	-1.64	80	-8.30	65	5.16	28	6.84	19	10.96	8
45586.0	World Stock	-2.00	111	-1.31	118	5.10	126	-4.75	137	-3.12	111	7.67	57	5.60	35	13.29	16
564608.5	**U.S. Diversified Equity Avg**	**-3.32**	**1347**	**-2.61**	**1402**	**5.81**	**1456**	**-1.36**	**1516**	**-1.75**	**1347**	**6.51**	**805**	**9.02**	**638**	**12.51**	**350**
754678.8	**Equity Fund Average**	**-3.20**	**1912**	**-2.10**	**2032**	**5.87**	**2151**	**-2.63**	**2254**	**-2.32**	**1912**	**7.06**	**1132**	**8.26**	**864**	**12.43**	**437**
Hybrid																	
38168.6	Asset Allocation	-2.81	97	-1.34	111	2.81	129	-1.61	139	-3.17	97	5.68	59	7.07	48	10.13	8
67042.3	Balanced	-3.19	183	-1.34	199	2.78	206	-1.07	216	-2.81	183	5.08	82	7.83	59	11.52	28
3868.1	Convertible Bond	-2.10	26	-2.23	28	3.23	28	-3.06	29	-4.11	26	7.98	24	9.13	21	10.90	3
42385.5	Corp Bond–High Yield	-1.06	91	-1.33	97	-0.13	102	-1.46	104	-3.86	91	10.55	63	10.52	60	9.92	31
44042.7	Income	-3.37	57	-1.33	62	1.36	75	-1.37	79	-4.51	57	5.84	38	8.14	34	10.45	14
16154.5	World Bond	-4.60	101	-1.48	117	1.76	123	-1.42	125	-5.77	101	3.77	50	7.49	33	9.47	2
211661.7	**Hybrid Fund Average**	**-3.00**	**555**	**-1.41**	**614**	**2.01**	**663**	**-1.42**	**692**	**-3.82**	**555**	**6.39**	**316**	**8.42**	**255**	**10.57**	**86**
Taxable Bond																	
57497.4	Corp Bond–General	-2.71	287	-1.37	307	0.57	317	-0.18	333	-3.65	287	4.59	122	7.29	86	9.46	33
31558.0	Corp Bond–High Quality	-1.88	140	-0.93	144	0.53	149	0.10	158	-2.16	140	4.02	92	6.64	68	8.84	27
9325.8	Govt Bond–Adj-Rate Mtg	-0.07	66	-0.52	67	0.11	69	-1.56	69	-2.12	66	1.77	31	5.07	5	—	—
61728.5	Govt Bond–General	-2.55	282	-1.35	307	0.27	319	0.05	330	-3.55	282	3.38	147	6.36	113	8.29	25
57648.1	Govt Bond–Mortgage	-2.58	107	-1.51	110	0.37	116	-0.07	127	-3.62	107	3.08	66	6.55	55	8.32	22
8309.9	Govt Bond–Treasury	-3.18	59	-1.39	59	-0.02	59	0.32	65	-4.10	59	3.87	39	6.70	31	8.17	5
5541.3	Short-Term World Income	-2.02	30	-0.93	31	0.76	32	-2.24	33	-4.53	30	0.41	20	-0.64	2	—	—
231609.0	**Taxable-Bond Fund Avg**	**-2.36**	**971**	**-1.25**	**1025**	**0.40**	**1061**	**-0.18**	**1115**	**-3.35**	**971**	**3.57**	**517**	**6.64**	**360**	**8.77**	**112**
Municipal Bond																	
34225.8	Muni Bond–California	-5.60	120	0.41	128	0.50	129	-2.23	137	-6.78	120	4.28	68	6.04	54	8.22	17
123165.0	Muni Bond–National	-4.97	364	0.70	384	0.47	400	-1.38	421	-5.20	364	4.57	211	6.17	174	8.43	80
21174.1	Muni Bond–New York	-5.52	90	0.58	95	0.17	102	-1.90	110	-6.64	90	4.71	62	6.37	44	8.41	14
49928.5	Muni Bond–Single State	-5.60	625	0.65	695	0.39	740	-1.66	789	-6.18	625	4.74	269	6.33	165	8.23	24
228493.4	**Municipal-Bond Fund Avg**	**-5.40**	**1199**	**0.64**	**1302**	**0.41**	**1371**	**-1.65**	**1457**	**-5.98**	**1199**	**4.62**	**610**	**6.23**	**437**	**8.37**	**135**
1426442.9	**Total Fund Average**	**-3.57**	**4637**	**-1.12**	**4973**	**2.85**	**5246**	**-1.72**	**5518**	**-3.66**	**4637**	**5.70**	**2575**	**7.51**	**1916**	**10.98**	**770**
Index Benchmarks																	
	Standard & Poor's 500 Index	-3.78		0.42		4.88		-0.02		1.32		6.27		8.69		14.38	
	First Boston High Yield	-1.06		-1.44		1.60		-0.04		-0.98		11.16		13.07		—	
	Lehman Brothers ARM Index	-0.64		-0.39		0.30		0.16		-0.58		—		—		—	
	Lehman Brothers Aggregate Bond Index	-2.87		-1.03		0.61		0.38		-2.92		4.55		7.63		9.94	
	Lehman Brothers Corporate Bond Index	-3.52		-1.57		0.73		0.44		-3.92		5.41		8.26		10.63	
	Lehman Brothers Government Bond Index	-3.01		-1.15		0.42		0.36		-3.37		4.66		7.53		9.57	
	Lehman Brothers Mortgage Backed Bond Index	-2.32		-0.56		0.87		0.43		-1.61		3.98		7.57		10.34	
	Lehman Brothers Municipal Bond Index	-5.49		1.14		0.19		-1.44		-5.60		4.87		6.77		9.43	
	Morgan Stanley EAFE Index	3.50		5.11		0.10		-1.02		7.78		7.86		1.50		17.55	
	Morgan Stanley Europe Index	-1.50		-1.33		4.27		0.93		2.28		8.01		6.51		18.46	
	Morgan Stanley Pacific Index	8.13		10.30		-2.94		-2.54		12.83		7.70		-1.83		16.84	
	Morgan Stanley World Index	0.61		3.00		2.14		-0.73		5.08		6.85		3.67		14.84	
	Salomon Brothers Non-$ World Govt Bond	1.94		2.38		1.65		0.57		6.70		8.77		11.52		15.11	
	Wilshire 4500 Index	-3.62		-3.07		6.87		-2.50		-2.66		7.61		9.09		12.63	
	Treasury (3 Month) Index	0.80		0.99		1.11		1.30		4.27		3.58		4.72		5.76	
	Consumer Price Index	0.96		0.54		0.95		0.20		2.68		2.77		3.49		3.58	

Performance Summary 1980-1994

Category	1980 TR%	# of Funds	1981 TR%	# of Funds	1982 TR%	# of Funds	1983 TR%	# of Funds	1984 TR%	# of Funds	1985 TR%	# of Funds
Equity												
Aggressive Growth	48.59	15	-7.67	16	29.04	19	19.39	19	-14.44	21	29.25	27
Equity-Income	20.65	13	5.13	13	27.15	13	23.61	13	8.05	15	27.38	16
Europe Stock	—	—	—	—	—	—	—	—	—	—	—	—
Foreign Stock	32.16	5	-2.84	6	4.73	9	27.98	11	-4.86	12	46.25	16
Growth	38.25	113	-1.46	119	27.70	125	21.58	133	-1.69	148	29.23	164
Growth and Income	27.25	77	-0.49	79	23.04	84	21.18	89	4.24	94	27.41	104
Pacific Stock	35.79	3	17.14	3	-2.63	3	35.14	3	-0.55	3	28.93	4
Small Company	40.47	17	-1.09	18	25.53	20	25.80	25	-6.66	34	29.84	39
Specialty							13.46	1	-0.30	1	35.01	4
Specialty—Financial	13.54	2	16.34	2	18.65	3	26.42	3	15.73	3	39.79	3
Specialty—Health	—	—	—	—	45.34	1	6.11	2	-3.56	3	39.92	5
Specialty—Nat Res	56.09	1	17.04	2	10.81	4	22.36	4	-10.77	5	15.10	7
Specialty—Prec Metals	64.23	6	24.23	6	48.62	7	1.87	7	-26.86	9	-9.35	13
Specialty—Technology	39.05	5	12.34	5	28.29	6	26.28	7	-9.44	9	18.94	11
Specialty—Utilities	4.01	2	11.86	2	21.68	5	11.52	5	19.76	7	25.56	8
World Stock	33.55	8	-1.94	8	15.13	10	26.84	10	-4.74	12	41.17	16
U.S. Diversified Equity Average	**34.49**	**235**	**-1.17**	**245**	**26.11**	**261**	**21.77**	**279**	**-0.83**	**312**	**28.68**	**350**
Equity Fund Average	**34.89**	**267**	**-1.63**	**279**	**24.84**	**309**	**21.70**	**332**	**-1.55**	**376**	**28.39**	**437**
Hybrid												
Asset Allocation	27.90	2	4.59	2	31.19	3	21.39	4	0.22	6	24.74	8
Balanced	20.13	25	3.84	25	28.48	26	16.81	28	7.40	28	27.68	28
Convertible Bond	33.31	3	3.80	3	36.49	3	22.28	3	2.06	3	24.54	3
Corp Bond—High Yield	3.42	22	6.33	24	31.08	24	15.99	24	8.53	26	22.43	31
Income	15.31	12	8.40	12	27.09	12	16.06	12	10.09	13	22.26	14
World Bond	—	—	—	—	29.46	1	1.55	1	5.13	2	25.43	2
Hybrid Fund Average	**14.34**	**64**	**5.60**	**66**	**29.62**	**69**	**16.68**	**72**	**7.41**	**78**	**24.47**	**86**
Taxable Bond												
Corp Bond—General	1.33	21	4.85	23	32.24	24	8.95	24	12.69	25	21.61	33
Corp Bond—High Quality	2.22	14	6.22	17	31.10	17	8.24	20	13.23	23	19.37	27
Govt Bond—Adj-Rate Mtg	—	—	—	—	—	—	—	—	—	—	—	—
Govt Bond—General	6.00	5	7.74	5	26.51	7	7.14	13	12.83	15	18.23	25
Govt Bond—Mortgage	-4.21	4	2.41	5	32.13	5	8.49	8	13.29	9	18.51	22
Govt Bond—Treasury	—	—	10.64	1	17.53	1	7.52	1	13.09	3	17.91	5
Short-Term World Income	—	—	—	—	—	—	—	—	—	—	—	—
Taxable-Bond Fund Average	**1.64**	**44**	**5.47**	**51**	**30.86**	**54**	**8.30**	**66**	**12.97**	**75**	**19.54**	**112**
Municipal Bond												
Muni Bond—California	-10.05	1	-6.32	1	26.39	1	6.23	1	6.92	9	18.78	17
Muni Bond—National	-10.47	37	-5.83	41	35.61	47	9.81	52	8.96	58	18.01	80
Muni Bond—New York	—	—	—	—	20.41	1	10.04	2	8.57	6	19.78	14
Muni Bond—Single State	-19.13	2	-6.97	2	28.42	2	11.95	2	7.75	8	17.71	24
Municipal-Bond Fund Average	**-10.89**	**40**	**-5.89**	**44**	**34.85**	**51**	**9.83**	**57**	**8.58**	**81**	**18.24**	**135**
Total Fund Average	**23.78**	**415**	**-0.15**	**440**	**27.25**	**483**	**18.05**	**527**	**2.73**	**610**	**24.89**	**770**
Index Name												
Standard & Poor 500 Index	32.22		-5.08		21.46		22.47		6.27		31.74	
First Boston High Yield	—		—		—		—		—		—	
Morgan Stanley EAFE Index	22.58		-2.28		-1.86		23.69		7.38		56.16	
Morgan Stanley Europe Index	—		—		3.97		20.96		0.62		78.93	
Morgan Stanley Pacific Index	—		—		-6.66		25.98		13.14		39.03	
Morgan Stanley World Index	—		—		9.71		21.93		4.72		40.57	
Wilshire 4500 Index	—		—		—		—		-1.72		32.02	
Salomon Brothers Non-$ World Govt Bond	—		—		—		—		—		35.01	
Lehman Brothers Corporate Bond Index	-0.30		2.97		39.22		9.27		16.62		24.06	
Lehman Brothers Government Bond Index	5.19		9.36		27.75		7.39		14.50		20.43	
Lehman Brothers Aggregate Bond Index	2.71		6.26		32.64		8.37		15.15		22.13	
Lehman Brothers Municipal Bond Index	-8.92		-10.23		40.86		8.05		10.55		20.02	
Lehman Brothers ARM Index	—		—		—		—		—		—	
Lehman Brothers Mortgage Backed Bond Index	0.65		0.07		43.04		10.13		15.79		25.21	
Treasury (3 Month) Index	11.58		14.01		10.70		8.62		9.57		7.49	
Consumer Price Index	12.52		8.92		3.83		3.79		3.95		3.80	

1986 TR%	# of Funds	1987 TR%	# of Funds	1988 TR%	# of Funds	1989 TR%	# of Funds	1990 TR%	# of Funds	1991 TR%	# of Funds	1992 TR%	# of Funds	1993 TR%	# of Funds	1994 TR%	# of Funds
12.03	28	-2.97	34	15.89	42	27.45	42	-8.73	43	54.51	47	8.20	49	18.79	51	-3.31	71
17.64	19	-1.95	23	17.02	31	21.39	40	-6.24	43	27.20	48	9.30	54	13.58	63	-1.99	86
17.17	2	10.12	5	7.20	8	22.62	10	-6.68	11	6.55	21	-8.24	24	26.16	25	1.30	29
45.90	20	8.16	26	16.93	35	22.14	41	-11.63	50	12.90	62	-4.33	85	40.05	125	-2.91	177
15.04	188	2.90	214	15.00	245	26.90	264	-4.79	283	36.71	314	8.45	356	11.71	478	-2.06	625
15.83	116	2.01	132	15.08	152	23.64	165	-4.61	176	28.66	200	8.26	227	11.09	273	-1.47	343
72.00	6	32.42	8	22.66	10	27.70	11	-19.78	13	13.68	18	-4.10	22	58.48	31	-8.20	48
10.33	47	-2.57	60	19.33	74	23.59	85	-9.46	92	50.27	99	13.71	119	17.07	154	-0.74	222
17.29	8	-2.77	13	24.58	14	22.80	14	-11.84	18	33.96	21	11.64	22	21.55	22	-5.27	25
15.14	7	-11.35	10	19.03	10	24.84	10	-15.66	10	58.98	10	35.08	12	16.75	13	-2.65	13
17.07	7	0.27	8	11.61	8	38.50	9	14.99	9	63.76	10	-14.54	11	3.76	13	4.26	15
10.87	9	9.33	9	9.80	16	29.41	17	-8.60	18	6.26	19	2.89	20	21.86	23	-2.64	27
34.06	16	36.79	19	-17.72	20	25.59	26	-23.78	26	-3.89	28	-15.15	29	84.97	30	-11.67	33
6.66	14	0.44	15	4.89	16	24.01	16	-5.10	16	44.55	17	12.63	17	23.96	20	10.49	22
20.26	9	-1.97	10	14.41	12	31.32	17	-2.07	19	20.37	24	9.79	28	15.52	40	-8.30	65
33.68	17	4.86	21	13.54	29	21.79	34	-10.16	35	20.53	48	-1.10	57	31.46	75	-3.12	111
14.62	**398**	**1.26**	**463**	**15.79**	**544**	**25.19**	**596**	**-5.78**	**637**	**36.87**	**708**	**9.21**	**805**	**12.82**	**1019**	**-1.75**	**1347**
17.66	**513**	**3.04**	**609**	**14.60**	**722**	**25.21**	**801**	**-7.02**	**863**	**31.92**	**986**	**6.47**	**1132**	**19.35**	**1436**	**-2.32**	**1912**
21.44	12	8.39	17	8.14	27	16.66	42	-1.09	48	20.91	52	6.11	59	15.44	67	-3.17	97
16.39	33	1.46	36	12.34	46	19.29	54	-0.47	60	26.25	68	6.96	82	10.82	126	-2.81	183
15.38	7	-3.96	11	11.92	14	14.47	20	-5.46	21	27.85	23	13.78	24	15.33	25	-4.11	26
13.46	34	1.97	44	12.87	55	-0.59	58	-10.23	60	36.85	62	17.69	63	19.19	69	-3.86	91
13.21	16	-0.72	21	12.77	26	12.74	29	0.28	34	24.06	35	9.19	38	13.33	48	-4.51	57
18.03	2	17.99	10	4.39	15	6.14	24	14.03	33	13.10	37	2.01	50	15.93	70	-5.77	101
15.49	**104**	**2.90**	**139**	**11.26**	**183**	**11.07**	**227**	**-1.31**	**256**	**25.72**	**277**	**8.94**	**316**	**14.47**	**405**	**-3.82**	**555**
14.36	37	2.21	42	8.69	59	11.01	76	6.21	86	16.43	98	7.42	122	10.38	196	-3.65	287
13.32	28	2.43	34	7.19	46	11.52	54	7.62	68	14.11	77	6.28	92	8.29	116	-2.16	140
8.81	1	-1.24	2	5.91	4	12.33	5	8.27	5	10.53	6	4.45	31	3.80	53	-2.12	66
12.14	41	1.44	63	6.63	90	11.93	106	8.38	112	14.01	121	6.10	146	8.07	191	-3.55	282
11.00	32	2.17	41	7.63	51	12.87	54	9.43	55	14.65	61	6.38	66	7.06	85	-3.62	107
28.21	12	-0.03	16	9.85	23	14.73	28	6.47	31	15.55	33	6.38	39	10.70	51	-4.10	59
—	—	-9.26	1	10.15	1	14.29	1	-1.40	2	7.72	12	-0.41	20	6.51	27	-4.53	30
13.92	**151**	**1.72**	**199**	**7.63**	**274**	**11.97**	**324**	**7.66**	**359**	**14.59**	**408**	**6.15**	**516**	**8.43**	**719**	**-3.35**	**971**
17.23	26	-2.40	38	10.96	42	9.67	48	6.58	54	11.00	61	8.40	68	12.12	86	-6.78	120
16.75	104	-0.15	129	10.40	152	9.30	167	6.19	174	11.36	192	8.36	211	11.28	257	-5.20	364
16.67	18	-1.76	28	10.64	36	9.32	41	5.21	44	12.93	52	9.43	62	12.27	70	-6.64	90
16.27	44	-1.38	77	11.43	131	9.46	150	6.15	165	11.27	210	8.68	269	12.10	373	-6.18	625
16.70	192	-0.98	272	10.86	361	9.41	406	6.12	437	11.44	515	8.61	610	11.85	786	-5.98	1199
16.64	**960**	**1.91**	**1219**	**12.09**	**1540**	**17.29**	**1758**	**-0.51**	**1915**	**23.07**	**2186**	**7.22**	**2574**	**14.65**	**3346**	**-3.66**	**4637**
18.68		5.26		16.61		31.68		-3.12		30.48		7.62		10.06		1.32	
15.64		6.53		11.43		0.39		-6.38		43.75		16.66		18.90		-0.98	
69.44		24.63		28.27		10.54		-23.45		12.13		-12.17		32.56		7.78	
43.85		3.66		15.81		28.51		-3.85		13.11		-4.71		29.28		2.28	
93.44		39.66		34.99		2.53		-34.42		11.30		-18.40		35.69		12.83	
41.89		16.16		23.29		16.61		-17.02		18.28		-5.23		22.50		5.08	
11.76		-3.51		20.54		23.94		-13.56		43.45		11.76		14.54		-2.66	
31.35		35.15		2.36		-3.43		15.29		16.24		4.77		15.12		6.70	
16.53		2.56		9.22		13.98		7.15		18.51		8.70		12.17		-3.92	
15.32		2.20		7.03		14.23		8.72		15.32		7.23		10.66		-3.37	
15.25		2.76		7.88		14.54		8.95		16.00		7.24		9.75		-2.92	
19.32		1.50		10.16		10.79		7.30		12.14		8.82		12.28		-5.60	
—		—		—		—		—		—		—		5.98		-0.58	
13.43		4.29		8.72		15.35		10.72		15.72		6.96		6.84		-1.61	
5.97		5.83		6.67		8.11		7.51		5.41		3.46		3.02		4.27	
1.10		4.43		4.42		4.65		6.11		3.06		2.90		2.75		2.68	

The equity style box is a nine-box matrix that displays both the fund's investment methodology and the size of the companies in which it invests. Combining these two variables offers a broad view of a fund's holdings and risk.

Risk		Median Market Capitalization	Investment Style		
			Value	Blend	Growth
Low	○	Large	Large-cap Value	Large-cap Blend	Large-cap Growth
Moderate	◐	Medium	Mid-cap Value	Mid-cap Blend	Mid-cap Growth
High	●	Small	Small-cap Value	Small-cap Blend	Small-cap Growth

Criteria vary slightly for international–equity style boxes.
Please see User's Guide for a complete explanation.

Value
Combined relative P/E and P/B ratio of less than 1.75

Blend
Combined relative P/E and P/B ratio of greater than or equal to 1.75, but less than or equal to 2.25

Growth
Combined relative P/E and P/B ratio of greater than 2.25

Large Capitalization
Median market cap of greater than $5 billion

Medium Capitalization
Median market cap of greater than or equal to $1 billion, but less than or equal to $5 billion

Small Capitalization
Median market cap of less than $1 billion

The following tables break down the Morningstar Mutual Fund universe by individual style box squares. The top five and lowest five funds are shown, based on their five-year annualized total returns.

Obj	Fund (Ranked by 5Yr Total Return)	5Yr Star Rating	Morningstar		Average Annual Return %				Sales Charge	Net Assets ($Mil)
			Return	Risk	1Yr	3Yr	5Yr	10Yr		
Large-Cap/Value Average (130 funds)		★★★	0.62	0.82	-1.64	6.89	7.57	11.70	—	1279.09
	Highest									
EI	Invesco Industrial Income	★★★★	2.00	0.69	-3.88	4.24	12.20	15.53	None	3695.4
GI	Neuberger & Berman Guardian	★★★★	1.96	0.85	1.42	11.37	12.08	14.32	None	2423.8
GI	Dreman High Return	★★★★	1.88	1.10	-1.18	9.01	11.80	—	None	35.0
AA	Merrill Lynch Global Allocation A	★★★★	1.52	0.56	-2.00	9.99	11.78	—	5.25%	1307.8
G	New York Venture A	★★★★	1.54	0.98	-1.93	8.45	11.72	16.75	4.75%	1090.5
	Lowest									
GI	Steadman American Industry	★	-3.14	2.13	-37.18	-13.80	-14.93	-9.57	Closed	1.5
GI	Steadman Investment	★	-2.13	1.68	-33.80	-14.43	-6.71	-3.65	Closed	2.2
GI	Steadman Associated	★	-1.51	1.49	-20.48	-2.40	-2.78	1.23	Closed	5.5
WF	Quantitative International Eqty Ord	★	-1.09	1.30	9.05	7.60	-0.31	—	1.00%d	28.9
WF	Dreyfus/Laurel International Inv	★	-0.98	1.35	3.55	4.94	0.09	—	None	5.1

| | | | Morningstar | | Average Annual Return % | | | | Sales | Net Assets |
Obj	Fund (Ranked by 5Yr Total Return)	5Yr Star Rating	Return	Risk	1Yr	3Yr	5Yr	10Yr	Charge	($Mil)
Large-Cap/Blend Average (217 funds)		★★	0.52	0.85	-1.36	5.46	7.38	12.61	—	851.06
	Highest									
G	Fidelity Destiny II	★★★★★	2.61	0.90	4.48	15.23	16.10	—	8.24%	1468.2
G	Fidelity Destiny I	★★★★★	2.38	0.86	4.43	14.96	15.39	17.41	8.24%	3207.8
G	Phoenix Capital Appreciation A	★★★★★	2.64	0.73	-3.84	4.63	15.34	—	4.75%	410.5
G	Fidelity Advisor Growth Opport A	★★★★★	2.59	0.90	2.86	13.07	15.19	—	4.75%	4826.6
G	Fidelity Growth Company	★★★★	2.19	1.03	-2.22	7.04	13.51	17.02	3.00%	2993.4
	Lowest									
G	Excel Centurion T.A.A.	★	-2.70	1.40	-25.11	-12.78	-10.20	2.04	4.50%	0.5
AA	API Special Markets	★	-1.40	1.50	-6.91	-1.01	-2.17	—	None	1.0
GI	Monitrend Summation	★	-1.50	0.68	-1.98	-5.20	-1.82	—	4.50%	1.6
WF	Invesco International Growth	★	-0.89	1.32	0.60	4.00	0.59	—	None	108.6
WW	Smith Barney Global Opportunities A	★	-0.96	1.00	-3.80	2.09	1.23	8.98	5.00%	45.9
Large-Cap/Growth Average (51 funds)		★★★	1.14	0.96	-1.80	5.04	9.59	13.71	—	1081.82
	Highest									
ST	Fidelity Select Technology	★★★★★	5.36	1.16	11.13	15.84	22.25	10.56	3.00%	227.4
AG	Twentieth Century Ultra Investors	★★★★★	4.49	1.43	-3.62	5.94	19.38	18.78	None	9850.8
SH	Fidelity Select Health Care	★★★★★	3.91	1.11	21.43	0.89	18.58	21.53	3.00%	796.1
G	Fidelity Advisor Instl Equity Growth	★★★★★	3.79	1.03	-0.04	8.38	17.52	19.72	None	432.5
WP	Newport Tiger	★★★★	2.52	1.21	-11.99	23.49	15.03	—	5.00%	455.9
	Lowest									
I	MIM Bond Income	★★	-0.13	0.57	-3.61	1.95	4.17	—	None	1.9
WW	John Hancock Global B	★★	-0.08	1.21	-5.44	8.07	4.55	—	5.00%d	29.3
G	Beacon Hill Mutual	★★	-0.04	0.87	0.27	-2.27	4.56	8.90	None	4.0
G	Reynolds Blue Chip Growth	★★	0.09	0.99	-0.57	-1.92	5.11	—	None	23.7
WF	International Equity	★★	0.13	1.14	-0.27	12.10	5.28	—	None	174.6
Mid-Cap/Value Average (112 funds)		★★★	0.69	0.83	-3.39	7.52	7.64	11.12	—	420.34
	Highest									
SF	John Hancock Regional Bank B	★★★★★	4.00	0.83	-0.20	21.03	18.19	—	5.00%d	477.2
SF	Invesco Strategic Financial Services	★★★★★	3.95	1.07	-5.89	12.24	17.96	—	None	236.4
SF	Fidelity Select Regional Banks	★★★★★	3.28	1.29	0.23	18.28	16.83	—	3.00%	108.4
S	Fidelity Select Automotive	★★★★★	3.16	0.91	-12.77	18.70	16.46	—	3.00%	64.0
G	AIM Value A	★★★★★	2.72	0.89	3.28	12.45	15.76	16.65	5.50%	1358.3
	Lowest									
ST	Steadman Ocean Technology & Growth	★	-3.33	2.47	-37.10	-18.10	-16.96	-12.44	Closed	0.9
WE	GAM Europe	★	-1.41	1.14	-3.11	4.17	-1.19	—	5.00%	31.4
WE	G.T. Global Europe Growth A	★	-1.35	1.34	-5.80	2.36	-0.93	—	4.75%	647.3
GI	Gintel ERISA	★	-0.94	1.03	-21.30	-1.92	0.33	7.97	None	30.1
WF	Flag Investors International	★	-1.02	1.32	-7.40	7.68	0.80	—	4.50%	13.8
Mid-Cap/Blend Average (177 funds)		★★	0.74	0.93	-3.14	6.34	7.87	12.39	—	732.95
	Highest									
ST	Fidelity Select Computers	★★★★★	6.10	1.41	20.45	23.71	23.99	—	3.00%	175.4
ST	Fidelity Select Electronics	★★★★★	5.70	1.20	17.17	25.41	23.07	—	3.00%	156.6
GI	Oppenheimer Main St Income & Growth A	★★★★★	5.06	0.83	-1.53	20.45	22.23	—	5.75%	1268.8
SC	Strong Common Stock	★★★★★	4.34	0.82	-0.50	14.58	19.00	—	Closed	790.1
G	Fidelity Contrafund	★★★★★	3.52	0.71	-1.12	11.64	17.51	18.55	3.00%	8682.4
	Lowest									
WP	Capstone Nikko Japan	★	-2.26	2.46	24.27	3.46	-6.70	—	4.75%	3.3
G	Progressive Value	★	-1.68	1.41	-11.30	-6.90	-2.99	—	4.00%	0.3
WW	Bailard, Biehl & Kaiser Intl Equity	★	-1.47	1.33	-12.58	2.21	-2.56	11.46	None	148.8
SP	MainStay Natural Resources/Gold B	★	-1.23	1.67	-8.85	6.30	-1.01	—	5.00%d	20.7
WP	Japan	★	-1.09	1.92	10.03	4.24	-0.47	15.64	None	586.0

Obj	Fund (Ranked by 5Yr Total Return)	5Yr Star Rating	Morningstar		Average Annual Return %				Sales Charge	Net Assets ($Mil)
			Return	Risk	1Yr	3Yr	5Yr	10Yr		
Mid-Cap/Growth Average (106 funds)		★★★	1.03	1.23	-4.14	8.01	8.69	13.35	—	528.73
	Highest									
ST	Invesco Strategic Technology	★★★★★	5.80	1.29	5.27	12.89	22.54	18.90	None	310.1
ST	T. Rowe Price Science & Technology	★★★★★	5.55	1.41	15.79	19.55	21.98	—	None	915.1
ST	Alliance Technology A	★★★★★	5.11	1.41	28.51	21.76	21.97	17.11	4.25%	215.7
ST	Fidelity Select Software & Computer	★★★★★	5.08	1.44	0.39	21.78	21.58	—	3.00%	211.5
G	Fidelity Blue Chip Growth	★★★★★	3.84	0.78	9.85	13.24	18.40	—	3.00%	3287.0
	Lowest									
SP	Monitrend Gold	★	-3.60	2.61	-50.25	-24.77	-19.37	—	4.50%	0.7
SN	Invesco Strategic Energy	★	-1.94	1.57	-7.25	-2.07	-5.42	4.82	None	46.9
WP	G.T. Global Japan Growth A	★	-2.02	1.74	6.56	3.73	-5.01	—	4.75%	100.3
SP	MFS Gold & Natural Resources B	★	-1.36	1.76	-17.70	7.20	-1.73	—	4.00%d	29.6
SN	United Services Global Resources	★	-1.31	1.14	-9.69	1.34	-1.68	4.69	None	20.4
Small-Cap/Value Average 77 funds)		★★★	1.23	0.88	-2.01	9.43	9.55	11.87	—	233.62
	Highest									
SF	Fidelity Select Home Finance	★★★★★	5.93	1.18	2.67	27.30	23.59	—	3.00%	130.2
G	Crabbe Huson Special	★★★★★	4.53	1.03	11.72	26.10	19.48	—	None	377.5
SC	Fidelity Low-Priced Stock	★★★★★	4.02	0.63	4.81	17.56	18.88	—	3.00%	2354.5
SC	Skyline Special Equities	★★★★★	4.06	0.87	-1.17	20.02	18.25	—	Closed	202.8
SC	Regis ICM Small Company	★★★★★	4.01	0.85	3.41	18.62	18.11	—	None	126.4
	Lowest									
AG	Prudent Speculator	★	-1.12	2.05	-8.93	-1.77	-0.63	—	None	2.5
WE	DFA Continental Small Company	★	-0.90	1.15	11.00	3.72	0.51	—	None	345.0
B	Rea-Graham Balanced	★	-0.93	0.72	-5.26	-0.34	1.36	6.23	4.75%	15.0
EI	Eaton Vance Equity-Income	★★	-0.72	0.68	-6.40	0.49	1.56	—	6.00%d	27.7
S	United Services Real Estate	★★	-0.40	1.29	-11.63	-2.50	2.92	—	None	11.0
Small-Cap/Blend Average (47 funds)		★★★	1.25	1.12	-2.73	8.61	9.54	12.17	—	287.19
	Highest									
AG	AIM Aggressive Growth	★★★★★	5.63	1.28	17.18	23.37	23.54	15.96	Closed	714.7
SC	Cowen Opportunity A	★★★★★	3.29	1.25	3.89	12.77	17.28	—	4.75%	33.6
SC	Founders Discovery	★★★★★	3.49	1.20	-7.75	5.59	16.72	—	None	187.5
SC	RSI Retirement Trust Emerg Grth Eqty	★★★★★	3.39	1.42	3.53	15.65	16.43	14.47	None	48.9
S	Fidelity Select Retailing	★★★★★	2.97	1.20	-5.01	9.44	15.92	—	3.00%	35.5
	Lowest									
S	Fidelity Select Environmental Svcs	★	-1.37	1.39	-9.55	-3.94	-1.42	—	3.00%	32.1
SN	Fidelity Select Energy Service	★	-1.19	1.80	0.56	7.96	-0.41	—	3.00%	50.8
G	Eagle Growth	★	-1.39	1.09	-15.57	-2.42	-0.35	6.44	8.50%	2.3
WW	Alliance Global Small Cap A	★	-1.07	1.35	-4.55	2.91	0.51	8.76	4.25%	55.8
AG	Bull & Bear Special Equities	★	-0.56	1.87	-16.54	7.63	2.19	—	None	45.5
Small-Cap/Growth Average (64 funds)		★★★	1.67	1.45	-0.65	7.44	10.53	12.44	—	356.24
	Highest									
ST	Seligman Communications&Information A	★★★★★	6.00	1.56	35.30	28.96	24.22	22.20	4.75%	307.6
SC	Twentieth Century Giftrust Investors	★★★★★	5.56	1.56	13.49	20.74	22.00	25.58	None	274.2
SC	PBHG Growth	★★★★★	5.56	1.46	4.75	25.42	21.98	—	None	745.8
SC	John Hancock Special Equities A	★★★★★	4.97	1.36	2.02	16.79	21.83	—	Closed	310.9
SC	MFS Emerging Growth B	★★★★★	5.26	1.45	4.00	12.95	21.38	—	4.00%d	801.4
	Lowest									
SH	Merrill Lynch Healthcare B	★	-2.56	1.94	-4.99	-23.57	-9.86	—	4.00%d	63.0
SH	Merrill Lynch Healthcare A	★	-2.48	1.89	-4.30	-21.83	-8.22	2.06	5.25%	62.8
WP	DFA Japanese Small Company	★	-1.85	2.73	29.49	2.98	-4.86	—	None	342.0
SP	Invesco Strategic Gold	★	-1.71	2.28	-27.85	4.56	-3.97	1.94	None	222.0
SP	Lexington Strategic Silver	★	-1.84	2.49	-8.37	12.68	-3.65	-2.91	5.75%	50.0

Fixed-Income Style Box Performance Summary

Morningstar Mutual Fund
Universe

The fixed-income style box is a nine-box matrix that display both the credit quality on a fund's bonds and the maturity of those bonds in which it invests. Combining these two variables offers a broad view of a fund's holdings and risk.

Risk		Quality	Maturity		
			Short-term	Intermediate-term	Long-term
Low	○	High	Short-term High Quality	Interm-term High Quality	Long-term High Quality
Moderate	◐	Medium	Short-term Medium Quality	Interm-term Medium Quality	Long-term Medium Quality
High	●	Low	Short-term Low Quality	Interm-term Low Quality	Long-term Low Quality

Short Maturity
Average effective maturity of less than or equal to four years

Intermediate Maturity
Average effective maturity of greater than four years, but less than or equal to four years

Long Maturity
Average effective maturity of greater than four years

High Quality
Average credit rating greater than or equal to AA

Medium Quality
Average credit rating of AA or BBB

Low Quality
Average credit rating of BBB or below

The following tables break down the Morningstar Mutual Fund universe by individual style box squares. The top five and lowest five funds are shown, based on their five-year annualized total returns.

	Obj	Fund (Ranked by 5Yr Total Return)	5Yr Star Rating	Morningstar		Average Annual Return %				Sales Charge	Net Assets ($Mil)
				Return	Risk	1Yr	3Yr	5Yr	10Yr		
High Quality/Short Maturity Average (59 funds)			★★★	0.32	0.56	-0.91	3.24	5.94	7.12	—	398.10
		Highest									
	GG	Sit U.S. Government Securities	★★★★★	0.71	0.49	1.79	4.84	7.61	—	None	36.3
	GG	DFA Five-Year Government	★★★★	0.66	0.80	-3.16	4.01	7.41	—	None	222.0
	CQ	Franklin Investment Grade Income	★★★★	0.41	0.74	-1.16	4.60	7.38	—	4.25%	28.0
	GG	Dreyfus Short-Intermediate Government	★★★★★	0.63	0.55	-0.75	4.46	7.32	—	None	472.1
	CQ	American AAdvantage Ltd-Term Inc Inst	★★★★★	0.59	0.40	1.29	4.62	7.16	—	None	73.6
		Lowest									
	GG	Capstone Government Income	★	-0.46	0.77	1.15	2.67	2.65	7.08	None	8.4
	GA	Putnam Adjustable Rate U.S. Govt A	★★	-0.34	0.54	-0.18	1.39	3.89	—	3.25%	101.9
	MN	Managers Short Municipal	★★★★	0.35	0.14	0.36	2.80	3.93	5.07	None	2.3
	GA	Franklin Adjustable U.S. Govt Secs	★★★	-0.22	0.42	-1.95	1.12	4.24	—	2.25%	684.0
	MN	Short-Term Municipal Instl	★★★★	0.51	0.21	0.12	3.07	4.55	5.11	None	243.5

1995 Morningstar Mutual Fund 500

13

Obj	Fund (Ranked by 5Yr Total Return)	5Yr Star Rating	Morningstar		Average Annual Return %				Sales Charge	Net Assets ($Mil)
			Return	Risk	1Yr	3Yr	5Yr	10Yr		
High Quality/Interm Maturity Average (162 funds)		★★★	0.49	0.95	-3.63	3.82	6.63	8.47	—	666.24
	Highest									
WB	Scudder International Bond	★★★★★	1.64	0.54	-8.61	4.44	11.00	—	None	1086.2
WB	T. Rowe Price International Bond	★★★★	1.50	0.68	-1.84	6.46	10.52	—	None	738.1
CG	FPA New Income	★★★★★	1.03	0.62	1.46	7.49	9.85	10.97	4.50%	129.9
CG	Harbor Bond	★★★★★	1.02	0.97	-3.76	5.69	8.80	—	None	167.0
GG	Strong Government Securities	★★★★★	0.96	0.79	-3.37	5.97	8.58	—	None	276.8
	Lowest									
CQ	Parkstone Bond Inv A	★	-0.98	1.86	-3.64	-0.45	0.93	—	4.00%	16.7
CQ	IDS Strategy Short-Term Income	★★	-0.09	0.97	-2.21	2.30	4.48	—	5.00%d	215.3
GG	Fortis Advantage Govt Total Return A	★	-0.19	1.15	-7.72	1.69	4.83	—	4.50%	66.3
GM	PaineWebber U.S. Government Income A	★	-0.13	1.22	-10.50	0.41	5.02	7.59	4.00%	413.8
GG	PIMCo Advisors U.S. Government C	★★	0.09	1.16	-5.29	1.32	5.12	—	1.00%d	311.6
High Quality/Long Maturity Average (325 funds)		★★★	0.49	0.95	-3.63	3.82	6.63	8.47	—	666.24
	Highest									
WB	IDS Global Bond	★★★★	0.84	0.54	-6.26	6.10	9.25	—	5.00%	449.8
CG	MAS Domestic Fixed-Income	★★★★★	1.14	1.18	-3.98	6.06	9.23	—	None	9.7
CG	PIMCo Total Return Instl	★★★★★	1.07	0.96	-3.58	5.99	8.99	—	None	6554.8
CQ	Vanguard F/I Long-Term Corporate Bond	★★★	1.04	1.42	-5.30	5.98	8.86	10.41	None	2552.3
CG	MAS Fixed-Income	★★★★	1.01	1.25	-5.43	5.29	8.75	10.71	None	1167.4
	Lowest									
MS	First Hawaii Municipal Bond	★	0.23	1.21	-6.17	4.09	3.38	—	None	46.1
MN	PIMCo Advisors Tax-Exempt C	★	0.57	1.48	-9.54	2.99	4.77	—	1.00%d	58.5
GT	Benham Target Maturities 2015	★	0.03	4.92	-14.15	3.29	4.85	—	None	122.7
MN	SunAmerica Tax-Exempt Insured A	★★	0.54	0.72	-3.99	3.40	4.94	—	4.75%	135.9
MS	Prudential Municipal MN B	★★	0.76	1.12	-5.95	3.50	4.98	7.39	5.00%d	21.7
Medium Quality/Short Maturity Average (12 funds)		★★★★	0.52	0.41	-0.59	4.33	6.49	6.99	—	851.86
	Highest									
CG	PIMCo Low Duration Instl	★★★★★	0.72	0.32	0.63	5.32	7.64	—	None	2215.6
CG	Strong Advantage	★★★★★	0.66	0.19	3.55	6.68	7.43	—	None	910.5
CG	Vanguard F/I Short-Term Corporate	★★★★★	0.61	0.48	-0.08	4.67	7.21	8.48	None	2905.8
CG	Prudential Structured Maturity A	★★★★	0.34	0.57	-1.39	4.03	6.86	—	3.25%	91.8
CG	Connecticut Mutual Income	★★★★	0.37	0.57	-0.96	4.44	6.69	—	2.00%	46.5
	Lowest									
MN	Merrill Lynch Municipal Ltd Maturity A	★★★★★	0.55	0.11	1.27	3.81	4.98	5.50	1.00%	638.5
MN	Dreyfus Short-Intermediate Muni Bond	★★★★★	0.75	0.20	-0.32	4.29	5.54	—	None	426.8
MN	Fidelity Spartan Short-Interm Muni	★★★★★	0.80	0.29	-0.08	4.47	5.73	—	None	913.1
CG	AmSouth Limited Maturity	★★★★	0.22	0.56	-1.80	3.72	6.28	—	3.00%	48.0
CQ	Neuberger & Berman Ltd Mat Bond	★★★★	0.39	0.52	-0.34	3.83	6.36	—	None	293.9
Medium Quality/Interm Maturity Average (24 funds)		★★★	0.63	1.00	-3.97	4.75	6.97	9.10	—	520.56
	Highest									
CG	Fortress Bond	★★★★★	1.65	1.70	-3.36	9.23	11.25	—	1.00%	142.3
CG	Bond Fund of America	★★★	0.69	1.08	-5.02	6.48	8.58	10.58	4.75%	4941.2
CG	SteinRoe Income	★★★★	0.84	0.99	-4.06	5.87	8.10	—	None	152.8
CG	Putnam Income A	★★★	0.54	1.00	-3.29	5.93	7.98	9.65	4.75%	764.4
CG	New England Bond Income A	★★★	0.53	1.06	-4.24	4.84	7.91	9.32	4.50%	155.8
	Lowest									
CG	PIMCo Advisors High-Income C	★	-0.15	1.47	-7.14	2.21	4.07	6.81	1.00%d	148.5
MC	Thornburg Limited-Term Muni CA A	★★★★★	0.91	0.33	-2.15	4.43	5.50	—	2.50%	109.7
MS	Dupree KY Tax-Free Short-to-Medium	★★★★★	0.82	0.18	1.02	4.52	5.53	—	None	61.9
CG	Merrill Lynch Corp Investment Grade B	★★	0.28	1.32	-6.01	2.56	5.88	—	4.00%d	471.9
WB	Fidelity Global Bond	★★★	0.28	0.61	-16.70	1.73	5.92	—	None	382.9

	Obj	Fund (Ranked by 5Yr Total Return)	5Yr Star Rating	Morningstar		Average Annual Return %				Sales Charge	Net Assets ($Mil)
				Return	Risk	1Yr	3Yr	5Yr	10Yr		
Medium Quality/Long Maturity Average (122 funds)			★★★	1.01	1.06	-6.74	4.84	6.56	8.89	—	641.03
		Highest									
	CG	Alliance Bond Corporate Bond A	★★	1.10	1.96	-12.75	9.01	10.04	10.93	4.25%	212.9
	CG	IDS Bond	★★★★	0.80	1.14	-4.32	6.91	9.07	10.75	5.00%	2135.5
	CG	Invesco Select Income	★★★★★	0.97	0.79	-1.20	6.70	8.62	10.00	None	136.7
	CG	PaineWebber Investment Grade Income A	★★★	0.58	1.07	-5.60	5.22	8.00	9.50	4.00%	265.0
	CG	Smith Barney Investment Grade Bond B	★	0.79	1.95	-9.33	5.07	7.91	10.21	4.50%d	215.3
		Lowest									
	MC	California Muni	★	0.57	1.52	-20.01	0.05	2.60	4.77	None	10.6
	MY	New York Muni	★	0.39	2.07	-20.39	0.07	2.81	6.29	None	213.2
	MN	Van Kampen Merritt Tax-Fr High-Inc A	★★	0.58	0.74	-4.87	3.29	4.30	—	4.65%	601.4
	MC	EV Marathon CA Municipals	★	0.87	1.34	-9.09	2.45	4.31	—	5.00%d	396.4
	MN	Bull & Bear Municipal Income	★	0.55	1.51	-9.73	1.92	4.57	8.24	None	15.9
Low Quality/Short Maturity Average (0 funds)			—	—	—	—	—	—	—	—	—
		Highest									
		None									
		Lowest									
		None									
Low Quality/Interm Maturity Average (57 funds)			★★★★	1.26	0.57	-4.40	9.93	10.38	9.85	—	602.77
		Highest									
	CY	Fidelity Advisor High-Yield A	★★★★★	2.83	0.35	-2.08	13.05	15.91	—	4.75%	682.8
	CY	Liberty High-Income Bond A	★★★★★	2.11	0.61	-1.68	10.59	13.59	11.51	4.50%	421.2
	CY	Oppenheimer Champion High-Yield A	★★★★★	2.06	0.29	-0.09	12.13	13.50	—	4.75%	174.9
	CY	MainStay High-Yield Corporate Bond B	★★★★★	2.16	0.48	1.50	14.52	12.86	—	5.00%d	1122.1
	CY	Putnam High Yield Advantage A	★★★★★	1.84	0.55	-5.15	10.84	12.77	—	4.75%	666.4
		Lowest									
	CY	Venture Income (+) Plus A	★★	0.05	0.63	1.63	13.75	5.96	5.97	4.75%	57.0
	CY	Princor High-Yield A	★★★	0.28	0.54	-1.35	7.23	7.00	—	5.00%	19.7
	CY	Keystone Custodian B-4	★★★	0.74	0.93	-12.19	9.39	7.73	6.92	4.00%d	669.4
	CY	GIT Maximum Income	★★★★	0.77	0.51	-2.66	7.86	7.84	7.99	None	6.7
	CY	Invesco High-Yield	★★★★	0.87	0.45	-4.98	8.03	8.25	10.13	None	210.8
Low Quality/Long Maturity Average (2 funds)			★★★★★	2.12	0.74	-6.31	12.59	12.59	0.00	—	156.65
		Highest									
	CY	Advantage High-Yield Bond	★★★★★	2.30	0.68	-2.18	14.05	13.17	—	4.00%d	136.3
	CY	MAS High-Yield	★★★★★	1.94	0.80	-7.06	11.12	12.00	—	None	177.0
		Lowest									
	CY	MAS High-Yield	★★★★★	1.94	0.80	-7.06	11.12	12.00	—	None	177.0
	CY	Advantage High-Yield Bond	★★★★★	2.30	0.68	-2.18	14.05	13.17	—	4.00%d	136.3

Time Line 1994

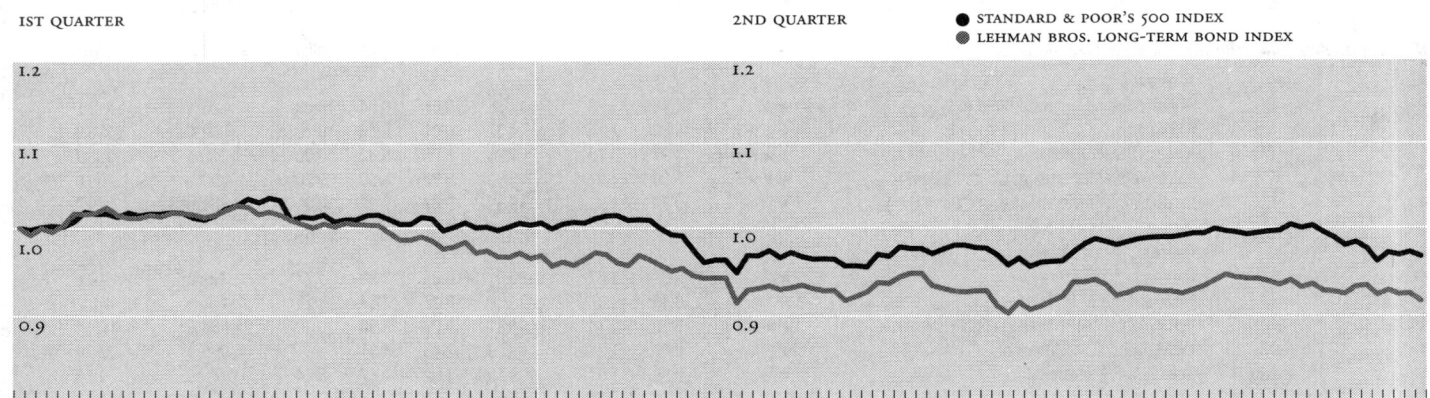

Nineteen ninety four's first quarter was a study in contrasts. The new year got off to a great start, with the S&P 500 enjoying a 3.4% gain in January. Markets around the world posted gains, as well; in fact, a number of smaller markets in the Pacific region, including Hong Kong, hit all-time highs. The domestic bond market managed to eke out a 1.35% return, as well. The municipal-bond market was even able to absorb unexpectedly high issuance without much ado, finishing the month up 1.14%.

On February 4, however, the party came to an end: The Federal Reserve caught the markets unawares, as it fired a preemptive strike against inflation by hiking short-term rates 25 basis points—the first tightening in over five years. Not surprisingly, the markets suffered losses during the month, with the worst performers being interest-rate sensitive utilities and large-cap value stocks. Munis were among the hardest hit sector of the bond market. Emerging market debt suffered sympathy pains, as well. The bright spots for the month were less-rate-sensitive junk bonds and mid- to small-cap growth stocks, which managed to eke out gains.

No sector of the markets was left untouched by the Fed's second rate hike on March 22—which raised rates by another 25 basis points. Selloff in the stock and bond markets induced lenders to call in some of their loans to heavily leveraged investors, thus resulting heightened losses on an international scope. Emerging market stocks fell more than 8% in March, and emerging-market Brady bonds slid a whopping 12%. Growth stocks that has withstood the first rate hike tumbled after the second, and the formerly resilient junk bonds took a drubbing, too.

The first-quarter snapshot thus ends up looking pretty grim, despite some early-year gains: The S&P finished the quarter off 3.78%, and the Lehman Brothers Aggregate Index ended 2.87% in the red. There were few upbeat performers for the quarter. Japan was a big winner, and U.S. investors multiplied their gains, thanks to a strong yen. REITs, often thought of as rate sensitive, managed to defy the odds and ended the quarter in the black, too.

A preoccupation with inflation continued to be a dominant theme in the second quarter—the Fed added fuel to the fire by hiking rates once again on April 18—but the stock market ended the quarter essentially in the same place where it began. The S&P 500 was up 0.42% for the quarter. REITs continued to exhibit abnormal behavior, rising 1.4% during the quarter, and emerging-market stocks tread water. The U.S. dollar made news almost constantly during this time, hitting post-World War II lows against the Yen. The Japanese market continued to show strength, despite the resignation of prime minister Hata in June and the island's first socialist prime minister in over 40 years.

Not all stock-market segments were buoyant during the quarter, though. Although value stocks managed to stay on an even keel, growth stocks got taken to the cleaners. Small-cap growth issues were hit the hardest, shedding nearly 8% during the quarter. Much of that carnage came in late June, when a selloff of technology names dominated trading. Utility stocks fared even worse, losing more than 8% during the quarter; increased competition in the industry coupled with rising interest rates made utilities the worst performers during the first half.

Except for a respite in the municipal-bond market, the broader fixed-income market ended the quarter in the red. Treasuries continued to lose ground in the face of rising rates, mortgage-backeds lengthened as prepayments subsided, and even less-rate-sensitive junk bonds couldn't post gains. World bonds didn't fare any better. Brady bonds felt sympathy pains with the U.S. market, and sank another 1.5% during the quarter, while high-quality bonds stumbled, too. Japanese bonds, however, thrived, pushing the Salomon Brothers Non-Dollar World Bond Index up 2.4%.

The big headline-grabber for much of the quarter, however, was derivatives, particularly of the exotic mortgage-backed variety. Victims to ill-understood derivatives transactions include Gibson Greetings, Metallgesellschaft, and Proctor & Gamble, as well as a handful of mutual funds.

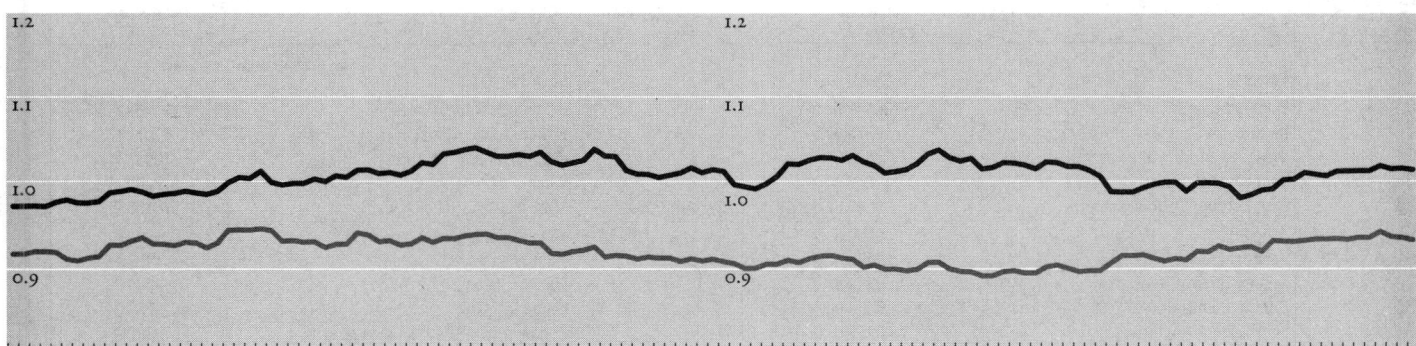

The third quarter saw an almost across-the-board reversal:
The s&p 500 ended up 4.88% and the Lehman Brothers Aggregate
Bond Index eked out a .61% gain after two quarters of losses.
More striking, some of the areas hardest hit during the year's first
half staged turnarounds: Technology stocks rallied, while the
demise of the Clinton health plan revived biotech and other health
stocks. These sectors, largely, boosted the Russell 2000 to
a 6.94% gain. Led by Latin America, emerging markets harked
back to 1993, with a 21% gain in the broad Morgan Stanley
emerging-markets index. Pummeled utilities perked up; the Dow
Jones Utility Average, rose 4.22% by the quarter's end.

The few first-half winners, meanwhile, toppled. Japan slumped
for the quarter, though its year-to-date performance was
still strong. Real estate investment trusts (REITs), happier in
an inflationary market, didn't take well to the possibility
of a slowing economy and ended the third quarter down 2.46%.

The quarter's relative success stories did little to calm the skittish
markets. Conflicting economic trends, more than anything,
caused wide swings in both stocks and bonds: Home sales slowed
and consumer confidence dropped while new job growth
remained strong mid-August producer prices showed their largest
gain in 18 months. Reports of solid second-quarter earnings
fed fears of an overheating economy and Fed responded with its
5th rate hike on August 16.

Currency movement also influenced the markets. The dollar
hit new lows against the yen and the mark early in the quarter.
In September, however, trade talks between the U.S. and
Japan boosted the greenback over the 100-yen mark for first
time in a month.

Finally, on September 27 derivatives took the blame as Community Bankers U.S. Government Money-Market became the
first money-market fund to have its NAV fall below a dollar.

Thus in spite of offering some hopeful signs to investors the third
quarter could not undo the year's difficult first half.

The fourth quarter finished off a decidedly unpleasant year.
The Lehman Brothers Aggregate Index ended down 2.92%, while
many bonds such as long Treasuries and zeros did much worse.
While broad indices like the s&p 500 ended the year with a slight
gain, the majority of equity mutual funds did not.

The fourth quarter set off on a rocky path when, early on,
inflation fears triggered dramatic downturns in the Dow Jones
Industrial Average, the Russell 2000, and the Treasury market.
In many cases, European markets joined in the decline,
with French and German markets reaching new lows for the year.

By mid-October strong third-quarter earning reports injected
life into the stock market—with technology stocks making
significant gains. No surefooted climber, however, the market fell
when fear of an overcharged economy outweighed the benefits
of solid earnings. In October, the yield on the benchmark 30-year
Treasury surpassed 8% for the first time in two-and-a-half years.

This set the tone for the remainder of the year. In November,
the Fed intervened to prop up the sagging dollar and on the 15th
it raised short-term rates by .75%. The Dow Jones Industrial
Average fell 91.52% on November 22—its biggest one-day drop
in nine months. Meanwhile, the November election brought
a record number of Republicans into office, and the lame-duck
Congress ended the month with approval for GAAT.

December was full of surprises. At the month's start, Orange
County, California announced a paper loss of $1.5 billion
in its over-leveraged, derivatives-laden investment fund. Stocks
and bonds sank as the county declared bankruptcy. Fidelity
stunned markets worldwide on December 5th when it announced
its Magellan fund would not make a year-end distribution,
despite earlier reports to the contrary. Topping off the year, the
Mexican government eliminated the floor on the peso. The
currency declined sharply while financial markets across Latin
America were shaken.

Investors thus bid a relieved adieu to 1994.

Equity

Obj	Fund	Net Assets ($Million)
	Largest	
G	Fidelity Magellan	36441.5
GI	Investment Company of America	19279.6
GI	Washington Mutual Investors	12668.3
GI	Vanguard/Windsor	10672.9
AG	20th Century Ultra Investors	9850.8
G	Janus	9400.6
GI	Vanguard Index 500	9356.4
GI	Fidelity Growth & Income	9344.9
G	Fidelity Contrafund	8682.4
WF	EuroPacific Growth	8269.5
GI	Vanguard/Windsor II	7959.0
EI	Fidelity Equity-Income II	7697.5
EI	Fidelity Equity-Income	7412.8
GI	Dean Witter Dividend Growth	6696.0
WW	New Perspective	6540.2
GI	Putnam Fund for Growth & Inc A	5848.1
WF	T. Rowe Price Intl Stock	5786.9
WW	Templeton Growth	5475.7
WF	Templeton Foreign	5305.8
GI	American Mutual	5278.6
G	Growth Fund of America	5274.2
G	Fidelity Advisor Growth Opport A	4826.6
G	IDS New Dimensions	4458.4
G	20th Century Growth Investors	4158.0
GI	Affiliated	4081.6
	Smallest	
SC	Schooner	4.7
SH	Franklin Global Health Care	10.9
G	Papp America-Abroad	11.5
G	SteinRoe Young Investor	12.0
G	Bramwell Growth	13.4
SP	Gabelli Gold	17.5
SC	Fasciano	17.7
SC	Oak Hall Equity	20.2
G	Westcore Midco Growth Ret	21.9
GI	Dreyfus Disciplined Stock Inv	23.8
GI	Seven Seas Growth & Income	26.0
GI	Quantitative Growth & Inc Ord	34.5
G	Tweedy, Browne American Value	35.7
G	L. Roy Papp Stock	36.5
SC	Babson Enterprise II	36.8
SU	Lindner Utility	43.4
G	Mutual Benefit	43.9
SP	SoGen Gold	47.7
SC	Quantitative Numeric Ord	47.8
GI	Analytic Optioned Equity	48.2
EI	Gabelli Equity-Income	48.3
G	Greenspring	50.3
GI	FPA Perennial	51.9
GI	T. Rowe Price Dividend Growth	53.5
AG	Wasatch Aggressive Equity	55.5
	Average Net Assets ($Million)	**1559.0**

Hybrid

Obj	Fund	Net Assets ($Million)
	Largest	
B	Fidelity Puritan	11769.4
AA	Fidelity Asset Manager	11075.6
I	Income Fund of America	10502.7
B	Vanguard/Wellington	8809.4
AA	Merrill Lynch Global Alloc B	6155.3
I	Vanguard/Wellesley Income	5680.6
B	Fidelity Balanced	4999.1
I	Franklin Income	4789.3
B	Vanguard STAR	3766.2
I	Oppenheimer Strategic Income A	2986.9
B	IDS Mutual	2924.8
AA	Fidelity Asset Manager: Growth	2852.9
B	Phoenix Balanced A	2415.7
CY	Kemper High-Yield A	2249.5
CY	Vanguard Fixed-Inc High-Yld Corp	2120.7
B	American Balanced	2081.9
CY	Fidelity Capital & Income	2039.8
B	MFS Total Return A	1825.1
AA	SoGen International	1822.5
CY	Franklin AGE High-Income	1719.6
I	USAA Mutual Income	1611.8
I	Lindner Dividend	1605.2
CY	IDS Extra Income	1526.0
I	Putnam Diversified Income A	1439.3
B	Keystone Custodian K-1	1286.3
	Smallest	
AA	Overland Express Asset Alloc A	40.3
CV	Value Line Convertible	45.1
B	Pasadena Balanced Return A	53.0
AA	MIMLIC Asset Allocation A	53.9
I	Berwyn Income	55.8
CV	SBSF Convertible Securities	57.9
CY	Seligman High-Yield Bond A	59.0
I	Advantage Income	73.8
AA	Flex-funds Muirfield	81.8
AA	Lindner Bulwark	83.1
B	Founders Balanced	95.9
AA	Crabbe Huson Asset Allocation	107.0
CV	Gabelli Convertible Securities	112.1
AA	Fortis Advantage Asset Alloc A	116.3
B	USAA Investment Balanced	124.6
I	Value Line Income	131.6
CY	Nicholas Income	140.9
AA	Zweig Managed Assets A	154.4
I	Phoenix Multi-Sector Fixed-Inc A	162.4
AA	Quest for Value Opportunity A	166.4
CV	Vanguard Convertible Securities	170.6
AA	Connecticut Mutual Total Return	177.9
WB	Fidelity New Markets Income	179.5
CV	MainStay Convertible B	180.1
WB	Templeton Income	198.5
	Average Net Assets ($Million)	**1279.5**

Taxable Bond

Obj	Fund	Net Assets ($Million)
	Largest	
GM	Franklin U.S. Government	10984.6
GM	Vanguard Fixed-Inc GNMA	5777.8
CG	Bond Fund of America	4941.2
CG	Vanguard Fixed-Inc S/T Corporate	2905.8
GG	American Capital Govt Secs A	2580.4
CQ	Vanguard Fixed-Inc L/T Corp Bond	2552.3
CQ	Scudder Short-Term Bond	2138.8
CQ	Fidelity Intermediate Bond	2127.4
CG	Vanguard Bond Idx Total Bond Mkt	1730.7
CG	Fidelity Short-Term Bond	1514.8
GG	Vanguard Fixed-Inc S/T Federal	1504.8
GM	Dreyfus GNMA	1427.9
CQ	T. Rowe Price New Income	1367.8
GG	U.S. Government Securities	1290.1
GA	Overland Express Var Rate Govt A	1215.5
CG	Strong Short-Term Bond	1041.1
GM	Benham GNMA Income	952.3
CG	Strong Advantage	910.5
GT	Vanguard Fixed-Inc I/T US Treas	844.2
GG	Fidelity Spartan Lim Mat Govt	830.6
CG	Putnam Income A	764.4
GM	T. Rowe Price GNMA	752.2
GT	Vanguard Fixed-Inc S/T US Treas	704.0
GG	Fidelity Government Securities	611.2
GM	Alliance Mortgage Secs Income A	553.4
	Smallest	
CG	Loomis Sayles Bond	82.5
CQ	Neuberger & Berman Ultra Short	90.7
CG	Prudential Structured Maturity A	91.7
CG	FPA New Income	129.9
GM	Lexington GNMA Income	132.3
CQ	Babson Bond L	138.9
CG	SteinRoe Income	152.8
CG	New England Bond Income A	155.8
CG	American Capital Corp Bond A	161.0
CG	Harbor Bond	167.0
GG	Gradison-McDonald Govt Income	184.0
CG	Alliance Bond Corporate Bond A	212.8
GG	WPG Government Securities	216.3
CQ	Portico Bond Immdex Ret	249.4
CQ	Columbia Fixed-Income Securities	252.0
CG	PaineWebber Invmt Grade Income A	264.9
GG	Strong Government Securities	276.8
GT	Benham Treasury Note	296.2
GM	Fidelity Spartan Ginnie Mae	347.8
GM	Scudder GNMA	417.0
CG	MFS Bond A	434.5
CQ	Scudder Income	464.1
GG	Dreyfus Short-Interm Government	472.1
CQ	T. Rowe Price Short-Term Bond	474.9
SW	Scudder Short-Term Global Income	496.9
	Average Net Assets ($Million)	**1167.7**

Municipal Bond

Obj	Fund	Net Assets ($Million)
	Largest	
MN	Franklin Federal Tax-Free Income	6561.4
MN	IDS High-Yield Tax-Exempt	5604.9
MN	Vanguard Muni Bond Interm-Term	4585.0
MN	Dreyfus Municipal Bond	3625.8
MN	Franklin High-Yield T/F Income	3124.5
MN	Colonial Tax-Exempt A	2837.5
MN	Nuveen Municipal Bond	2590.8
MN	MFS Municipal Bond A	1886.6
MN	Vanguard Muni Bond Insured L/T	1738.0
MN	USAA Tax-Exempt Long-Term	1661.2
MN	Vanguard Muni Bond Limited-Term	1629.5
MN	Franklin Insured Tax-Free Income	1621.4
MN	Vanguard Muni Bond High-Yield	1572.6
MN	Vanguard Muni Bond Short-Term	1483.5
MN	Dreyfus Intermediate Muni Bond	1447.6
MN	USAA Tax-Exempt Interm-Term	1416.1
MN	First Investors Insured Tax-Ex A	1297.4
MN	Van Kampen Insured T/F Income A	1186.6
MN	Thornburg Ltd-Term Muni Natl A	1019.2
MN	Fidelity Municipal Bond	1005.6
MN	Fidelity Spartan Sh-Interm Muni	913.1
MN	General Municipal Bond	829.1
MN	USAA Tax-Exempt Short-Term	810.8
MN	T. Rowe Price Tax-Fr High-Yield	802.2
MN	Fidelity Aggressive Tax-Free	793.8
	Smallest	
MN	Vista Tax-Free Income A	82.0
MN	SunAmerica Tax-Exempt Insured A	135.9
MN	Flagship All-American Tax-Ex A	168.0
MN	SteinRoe Intermediate Municipals	215.5
MN	Value Line Tax-Exempt High-Yield	225.8
MN	Sit Tax-Free Income	243.3
MN	Scudder High-Yield Tax-Free	259.7
MN	Strong Municipal Bond	279.8
MN	American Capital Muni Bond A	295.7
MN	Fidelity Insured Tax-Free	318.3
MN	Alliance Muni Income National A	318.9
MN	United Municipal High-Income	339.4
MN	Fortress Municipal Income	413.6
MN	Dreyfus Short-Interm Muni Bond	426.7
MN	Safeco Municipal Bond	434.4
MN	T. Rowe Price Tax-Fr Short-Intrm	451.1
MN	Fidelity Advisor High-Inc Muni A	506.4
MN	Oppenheimer Tax-Free Bond A	541.1
MN	Calvert Tax-Free Res Lim-Term A	547.6
MN	SteinRoe Managed Municipals	604.6
MN	Lord Abbett Tax-Free Income Natl	614.5
MN	Merrill Lynch Muni Ltd MaturityA	638.5
MN	Scudder Medium-Term Tax-Free	703.1
MN	Smith Barney Tax-Exempt Income B	731.3
MN	Putnam Municipal Income A	784.2
	Average Net Assets ($Million)	**1246.5**

Equity

Obj	Fund	Expense Ratio %
	Highest	
AG	Kaufmann	2.48
AG	American Heritage	2.41
WP	Merrill Lynch Dragon B	2.35
SP	SoGen Gold	2.27
G	Tweedy, Browne American Value	2.26
SC	MFS Emerging Growth B	2.23
WF	Govett Emerging Markets	2.18
SC	Alger Small Capitalization	2.17
WF	Templeton Developing Markets	2.17
WW	Calvert World Values Glob Eqty A	2.10
SF	Hancock Regional Bank B	2.01
WF	Scudder Latin America	2.01
SC	Oak Hall Equity	2.01
SC	Legg Mason Special Invmnt	1.94
GI	Legg Mason Total Return	1.94
WP	Morgan Stanley Asian Growth A	1.90
GI	MainStay Value B	1.90
G	PIMCo Adv Growth C	1.90
AG	PIMCo Adv Opportunity C	1.90
WF	20th Century Intl Equity	1.90
WP	Strong Asia Pacific	1.90
WF	Montgomery Emerging Markets	1.85
G	Fidelity Advisor Strat Opp A	1.84
SU	G.T. Global Telecommunications A	1.83
SC	Quantitative Numeric Ord	1.83
	Lowest	
SH	Franklin Global Health Care	0.10
SN	Vanguard Special Energy	0.17
SH	Vanguard Special Health Care	0.19
GI	Vanguard Index 500	0.19
GI	Vanguard Index Total Stock Mkt	0.20
SC	Vanguard Index Extended Market	0.20
SP	Vanguard Special Gold & Prec Met	0.26
GI	Vanguard/Windsor II	0.39
SU	Vanguard Special Utilities Inc	0.42
EI	Vanguard Equity-Income	0.43
GI	Vanguard/Windsor	0.45
WF	Vanguard Intl Growth	0.46
G	Vanguard U.S. Growth	0.52
GI	Merrill Lynch Capital A	0.53
GI	American Mutual	0.60
GI	Lexington Corporate Leaders	0.62
GI	Affiliated	0.63
SC	Acorn	0.63
SU	Franklin Utilities	0.64
G	Lindner	0.65
GI	Fidelity	0.65
EI	Fidelity Equity-Income	0.66
SC	Nicholas II	0.67
GI	Washington Mutual Investors	0.69
GI	Massachusetts Investors A	0.69
	Average Expense Ratio %	**1.21**

Hybrid

Obj	Fund	Expense Ratio %
	Highest	
AA	Robertson Stephens Contrarian	2.22
B	Pasadena Balanced Return A	2.00
AA	Prudential Allocation Conserv B	2.00
WB	PaineWebber Global Income B	1.96
CV	MainStay Convertible B	1.90
AA	Merrill Lynch Global Alloc B	1.86
AA	Quest For Value Opportunity A	1.78
B	Keystone Custodian K-1	1.71
B	MainStay Total Return B	1.70
I	Advantage Income	1.69
CY	MainStay Hi-Yield Corp Bond B	1.60
AA	Zweig Managed Assets A	1.60
WB	MFS World Governments A	1.58
AA	Fortis Advantage Asset Alloc A	1.53
AA	Crabbe Huson Asset Allocation	1.47
CV	Gabelli Convertible Securities	1.36
B	Founders Balanced	1.33
CV	American Capital Harbor A	1.32
I	Hancock Strategic Income A	1.32
CV	SBSF Convertible Securities	1.32
AA	Overland Express Asset Alloc A	1.31
I	Blanchard Flexible Income	1.30
WB	G.T. Global Government Income A	1.29
WB	Putnam Global Governmental Inc A	1.29
WB	Fidelity New Markets Income	1.28
	Lowest	
CY	Vanguard Fixed-Inc High-Yld Corp	0.32
I	Vanguard/Wellesley Income	0.35
B	Vanguard/Wellington	0.39
I	USAA Mutual Income	0.41
I	Vanguard Preferred Stock	0.45
CV	Pacific Horizon Capital Income	0.46
AA	Vanguard Asset Allocation	0.50
CY	Merrill Lynch Corp High-Income A	0.52
B	Dodge & Cox Balanced	0.58
CY	Nicholas Income	0.59
CY	Franklin AGE High-Income	0.59
I	Income Fund of America	0.63
I	Lindner Dividend	0.64
I	Franklin Income	0.64
AA	Lindner Bulwark	0.66
CV	Vanguard Convertible Securities	0.73
I	Merrill Lynch World Income A	0.75
B	MFS Total Return A	0.79
B	IDS Mutual	0.79
CY	IDS Extra Income	0.79
B	Fidelity Puritan	0.79
AA	Stagecoach Asset Allocation A	0.82
B	USAA Investment Balanced	0.84
CY	T. Rowe Price High-Yield	0.85
CY	Kemper High-Yield A	0.86
	Average Expense Ratio %	**1.09**

Taxable Bond		
Obj	Fund	Expense Ratio %
	Highest	
CG	Alliance Bond Corporate Bond A	1.30
CG	American Capital Corp Bond A	1.09
CG	PaineWebber Invmt Grade Income A	1.09
CG	New England Bond Income A	1.08
GG	American Capital Govt Secs A	1.03
SW	Scudder Short-Term Global Income	1.00
GM	Alliance Mortgage Secs Income A	0.98
GM	Lexington GNMA Income	0.97
CG	MFS Bond A	0.96
CQ	Scudder Income	0.96
GM	Dreyfus GNMA	0.95
GG	Strong Government Securities	0.90
CG	Strong Short-Term Bond	0.90
GG	Gradison-McDonald Govt Income	0.89
CG	Loomis Sayles Bond	0.88
GM	Scudder GNMA	0.87
CQ	T. Rowe Price New Income	0.82
CG	SteinRoe Income	0.82
CG	Prudential Structured Maturity A	0.81
CG	Fidelity Short-Term Bond	0.80
CG	Strong Advantage	0.80
GA	Overland Express Var Rate Govt A	0.79
CG	Putnam Income A	0.79
GG	WPG Government Securities	0.78
GG	U.S. Government Securities	0.78
	Lowest	
CG	Vanguard Bond Idx Total Bond Mkt	0.18
GG	Vanguard Fixed-Inc S/T Federal	0.26
CG	Vanguard Fixed-Inc S/T Corporate	0.26
GT	Vanguard Fixed-Inc S/T US Treas	0.26
GT	Vanguard Fixed-Inc I/T US Treas	0.26
GM	Vanguard Fixed-Inc GNMA	0.28
CQ	Vanguard Fixed-Inc L/T Corp Bond	0.30
GG	Dreyfus Short-Interm Government	0.42
CQ	Portico Bond Immdex Ret	0.49
GT	Benham Treasury Note	0.51
GM	Benham GNMA Income	0.54
GM	Franklin U.S. Government	0.55
CQ	Fidelity Intermediate Bond	0.64
GM	Fidelity Spartan Ginnie Mae	0.65
CQ	Neuberger & Berman Ultra Short	0.65
GG	Fidelity Spartan Lim Mat Govt	0.65
CQ	Columbia Fixed-Income Securities	0.66
GG	Fidelity Government Securities	0.69
CQ	Scudder Short-Term Bond	0.72
CQ	T. Rowe Price Short-Term Bond	0.74
CG	FPA New Income	0.74
GM	T. Rowe Price GNMA	0.77
CG	Harbor Bond	0.77
GG	U.S. Government Securities	0.78
GG	WPG Government Securities	0.78
	Average Expense Ratio %	**0.73**

Municipal Bond		
Obj	Fund	Expense Ratio %
	Highest	
MN	Smith Barney Tax-Exempt Income B	1.33
MN	SunAmerica Tax-Exempt Insured A	1.28
MN	First Investors Insured Tax-Ex A	1.21
MN	Fortress Municipal Income	1.09
MN	Colonial Tax-Exempt A	1.01
MN	Putnam Municipal Income A	0.97
MN	Thornburg Ltd-Term Muni Natl A	0.95
MN	American Capital Muni Bond A	0.93
MN	Fidelity Advisor High-Inc Muni A	0.89
MN	Oppenheimer Tax-Free Bond A	0.88
MN	Lord Abbett Tax-Free Income Natl	0.86
MN	General Municipal Bond	0.82
MN	Scudder High-Yield Tax-Free	0.80
MN	Strong Municipal Bond	0.80
MN	T. Rowe Price Tax-Fr High-Yield	0.79
MN	Van Kampen Insured T/F Income A	0.79
MN	Sit Tax-Free Income	0.77
MN	United Municipal High-Income	0.76
MN	Dreyfus Short-Interm Muni Bond	0.74
MN	SteinRoe Intermediate Municipals	0.71
MN	Dreyfus Intermediate Muni Bond	0.70
MN	Dreyfus Municipal Bond	0.68
MN	Calvert Tax-Free Res Lim-Term A	0.65
MN	SteinRoe Managed Municipals	0.65
MN	Fidelity Aggressive Tax-Free	0.64
	Lowest	
MN	Vanguard Muni Bond Short-Term	0.20
MN	Vanguard Muni Bond Interm-Term	0.20
MN	Vanguard Muni Bond High-Yield	0.20
MN	Vanguard Muni Bond Limited-Term	0.20
MN	Vanguard Muni Bond Insured L/T	0.20
MN	USAA Tax-Exempt Long-Term	0.38
MN	USAA Tax-Exempt Interm-Term	0.40
MN	Merrill Lynch Muni Ltd MaturityA	0.40
MN	USAA Tax-Exempt Short-Term	0.43
MN	Fidelity Spartan Sh-Interm Muni	0.47
MN	Vista Tax-Free Income A	0.48
MN	Safeco Municipal Bond	0.52
MN	Franklin Insured Tax-Free Income	0.52
MN	Franklin Federal Tax-Free Income	0.52
MN	Franklin High-Yield T/F Income	0.53
MN	Fidelity Municipal Bond	0.54
MN	Scudder Medium-Term Tax-Free	0.56
MN	Value Line Tax-Exempt High-Yield	0.58
MN	MFS Municipal Bond A	0.59
MN	IDS High-Yield Tax-Exempt	0.59
MN	Fidelity Insured Tax-Free	0.59
MN	Alliance Muni Income National A	0.59
MN	T. Rowe Price Tax-Fr Short-Intrm	0.60
MN	Nuveen Municipal Bond	0.62
MN	Flagship All-American Tax-Ex A	0.62
	Average Expense Ratio %	**0.66**

Equity

Obj	Fund	Potential Capital Gain Exposure %
	Highest	
SF	Century Shares	51
G	Salomon Bros Opportunity	42
GI	Sentinel Common Stock	38
SC	FPA Capital	35
GI	Lexington Corporate Leaders	35
SC	Acorn	34
G	Sequoia	32
SC	Nicholas Limited Edition	31
SC	Nicholas II	31
SC	MFS Emerging Growth B	31
SC	Evergreen	29
AG	ABT Emerging Growth	28
EI	United Income	27
AG	PIMCo Adv Opportunity C	26
GI	FPA Perennial	25
G	Franklin Growth	25
G	Nicholas	23
G	Growth Fund of America	23
AG	Kaufmann	22
AG	Value Line Leveraged Growth Inv	22
ST	T. Rowe Price Science & Tech	21
SC	Pennsylvania Mutual	21
WP	Newport Tiger	20
GI	Evergreen Growth & Income	20
GI	Dean Witter Dividend Growth	20
	Lowest	
AG	American Heritage	-86
SC	Oak Hall Equity	-26
EI	Stratton Monthly Dividend	-23
EI	Evergreen Total Return	-20
SU	Vanguard Special Utilities Inc	-15
GI	Seven Seas Growth & Income	-11
WF	Oakmark International	-10
WP	Strong Asia Pacific	-10
WF	Govett Emerging Markets	-8
G	CGM Capital Development	-7
SU	Franklin Utilities	-7
WF	Scudder Latin America	-7
S	Templeton Real Estate Securities	-6
SC	Monetta	-6
WF	Strong International Stock	-6
WF	GAM International	-6
WP	T. Rowe Price New Asia	-6
AG	Rydex Nova	-5
SN	Vanguard Special Energy	-5
SU	Fortress Utility	-5
GI	Analytic Optioned Equity	-5
EI	Royce Equity-Income	-5
AG	Strong Discovery	-4
GI	20th Century Value	-4
GI	Franklin Rising Dividends	-4
	Average Potential Capital Gain Exposure %	**8**

Hybrid

Obj	Fund	Potential Capital Gain Exposure %
	Highest	
AA	Fortis Advantage Asset Alloc A	10
AA	SoGen International	9
B	Vanguard/Wellington	8
B	MFS Total Return A	8
B	Dodge & Cox Balanced	7
B	Calvert Social Invmnt Managed A	6
B	Keystone Custodian K-1	6
B	MainStay Total Return B	5
B	Sentinel Balanced	5
AA	Quest For Value Opportunity A	5
B	20th Century Balanced Investors	5
AA	USAA Investment Cornerstone	4
B	Pasadena Balanced Return A	3
AA	Lindner Bulwark	3
B	T. Rowe Price Balanced	3
AA	Crabbe Huson Asset Allocation	2
B	American Balanced	2
B	Delaware A	2
B	Fidelity Puritan	1
B	Vanguard STAR	1
I	Advantage Income	1
AA	MIMLIC Asset Allocation A	1
AA	Prudential Allocation Conserv B	0
AA	Connecticut Mutual Total Return	0
AA	Flex-funds Muirfield	0
	Lowest	
CY	Phoenix High-Yield A	-81
CY	MFS High-Income A	-40
CY	Franklin AGE High-Income	-40
I	Colonial Strategic Income A	-35
WB	Fidelity Global Bond	-30
CY	T. Rowe Price High-Yield	-28
CY	IDS Extra Income	-28
WB	G.T. Global Government Income A	-27
CY	Delaware Delchester A	-24
CY	Oppenheimer High-Yield A	-24
CY	Seligman High-Yield Bond A	-22
CY	Northeast Investors	-21
CY	Putnam High Yield Advantage A	-20
CY	Liberty High-Income Bond A	-19
CY	Lord Abbett Bond-Debenture	-19
WB	Fidelity New Markets Income	-18
WB	Putnam Global Governmental Inc A	-18
WB	Scudder International Bond	-17
CY	AIM High-Yield A	-17
I	Vanguard Preferred Stock	-17
I	Hancock Strategic Income A	-16
I	Blanchard Flexible Income	-16
CY	Nicholas Income	-16
CY	Colonial High-Yield Securities A	-15
I	Phoenix Multi-Sector Fixed-Inc A	-15
	Average Potential Capital Gain Exposure %	**-8**

Taxable Bond

Obj	Fund	Potential Capital Gain Exposure %
	Highest	
CG	FPA New Income	0
CG	Strong Advantage	-1
CQ	T. Rowe Price New Income	-4
CQ	Fidelity Intermediate Bond	-4
GT	Vanguard Fixed-Inc S/T US Treas	-5
GM	Vanguard Fixed-Inc GNMA	-5
CG	Vanguard Fixed-Inc S/T Corporate	-5
CQ	Vanguard Fixed-Inc L/T Corp Bond	-5
GG	Vanguard Fixed-Inc S/T Federal	-6
CG	Vanguard Bond Idx Total Bond Mkt	-6
CQ	Neuberger & Berman Ultra Short	-6
CQ	Portico Bond Immdex Ret	-6
GT	Benham Treasury Note	-7
CG	Bond Fund of America	-8
CG	New England Bond Income A	-8
GM	Benham GNMA Income	-8
CQ	Columbia Fixed-Income Securities	-8
CG	Prudential Structured Maturity A	-8
CQ	Scudder Income	-8
CG	Putnam Income A	-8
GM	Lexington GNMA Income	-9
GG	Strong Government Securities	-9
CG	SteinRoe Income	-9
CG	Harbor Bond	-9
GG	Fidelity Spartan Lim Mat Govt	-10
	Lowest	
CG	Alliance Bond Corporate Bond A	-49
GG	American Capital Govt Secs A	-43
GG	WPG Government Securities	-22
CG	PaineWebber Invmt Grade Income A	-20
GM	Alliance Mortgage Secs Income A	-19
GM	Dreyfus GNMA	-17
CG	American Capital Corp Bond A	-16
SW	Scudder Short-Term Global Income	-14
CQ	Babson Bond L	-14
GA	Overland Express Var Rate Govt A	-14
GM	Scudder GNMA	-13
CG	Loomis Sayles Bond	-13
CG	Fidelity Short-Term Bond	-13
GM	Franklin U.S. Government	-13
CG	MFS Bond A	-12
GG	Gradison-McDonald Govt Income	-12
GM	Fidelity Spartan Ginnie Mae	-12
CQ	T. Rowe Price Short-Term Bond	-11
CG	Strong Short-Term Bond	-11
CQ	Scudder Short-Term Bond	-10
GT	Vanguard Fixed-Inc I/T US Treas	-10
GG	Dreyfus Short-Interm Government	-10
GG	Fidelity Government Securities	-10
GG	U.S. Government Securities	-10
GM	T. Rowe Price GNMA	-10
	Average Potential Capital Gain Exposure %	**-11**

Municipal Bond

Obj	Fund	Potential Capital Gain Exposure %
	Highest	
MN	Franklin Insured Tax-Free Income	1
MN	MFS Municipal Bond A	0
MN	Calvert Tax-Free Res Lim-Term A	-1
MN	Nuveen Municipal Bond	-1
MN	American Capital Muni Bond A	-1
MN	Van Kampen Insured T/F Income A	-1
MN	T. Rowe Price Tax-Fr Short-Intrm	-1
MN	Vanguard Muni Bond Short-Term	-1
MN	IDS High-Yield Tax-Exempt	-1
MN	Vanguard Muni Bond Interm-Term	-1
MN	SteinRoe Intermediate Municipals	-1
MN	First Investors Insured Tax-Ex A	-1
MN	SteinRoe Managed Municipals	-2
MN	Safeco Municipal Bond	-2
MN	Franklin Federal Tax-Free Income	-2
MN	Thornburg Ltd-Term Muni Natl A	-2
MN	Dreyfus Intermediate Muni Bond	-2
MN	Merrill Lynch Muni Ltd MaturityA	-2
MN	Vanguard Muni Bond Insured L/T	-2
MN	Franklin High-Yield T/F Income	-2
MN	USAA Tax-Exempt Short-Term	-2
MN	Vanguard Muni Bond Limited-Term	-2
MN	Flagship All-American Tax-Ex A	-2
MN	USAA Tax-Exempt Interm-Term	-3
MN	T. Rowe Price Tax-Fr High-Yield	-3
	Lowest	
MN	Alliance Muni Income National A	-12
MN	Vista Tax-Free Income A	-11
MN	Fidelity Advisor High-Inc Muni A	-10
MN	Fidelity Municipal Bond	-10
MN	Putnam Municipal Income A	-9
MN	Lord Abbett Tax-Free Income Natl	-9
MN	Strong Municipal Bond	-9
MN	SunAmerica Tax-Exempt Insured A	-9
MN	Fidelity Insured Tax-Free	-8
MN	Scudder High-Yield Tax-Free	-7
MN	Oppenheimer Tax-Free Bond A	-7
MN	Fidelity Aggressive Tax-Free	-7
MN	Value Line Tax-Exempt High-Yield	-7
MN	Fortress Municipal Income	-7
MN	USAA Tax-Exempt Long-Term	-6
MN	Colonial Tax-Exempt A	-6
MN	Vanguard Muni Bond High-Yield	-5
MN	General Municipal Bond	-4
MN	Dreyfus Municipal Bond	-4
MN	Smith Barney Tax-Exempt Income B	-4
MN	Scudder Medium-Term Tax-Free	-4
MN	Sit Tax-Free Income	-3
MN	United Municipal High-Income	-3
MN	Fidelity Spartan Sh-Interm Muni	-3
MN	Dreyfus Short-Interm Muni Bond	-3
	Average Potential Capital Gain Exposure %	**-4**

Highest/Lowest Yield

Equity

Obj	Fund	Yield	SEC Yield
	Highest		
EI	Stratton Monthly Dividend	8.1	7.5
EI	Evergreen Total Return	6.2	4.9
SU	Franklin Utilities	6.2	6.0
SU	Vanguard Special Utilities Inc	5.9	6.0
SU	Fortress Utility	5.4	5.1
EI	Capital Income Builder	5.2	4.9
EI	Safeco Income	4.8	5.0
EI	Vanguard Equity-Income	4.5	4.9
GI	Burnham A	4.3	4.9
GI	Merrill Lynch Capital A	4.2	4.0
GI	American Mutual	4.0	3.8
SU	Fidelity Utilities	3.9	5.1
EI	Invesco Industrial Income	3.7	3.9
G	Greenspring	3.7	1.0
GI	Washington Mutual Investors	3.6	3.4
EI	T. Rowe Price Equity-Income	3.5	3.2
GI	Vanguard/Windsor II	3.4	3.6
GI	Mutual Beacon	3.3	3.1
GI	Vanguard/Windsor	3.3	3.6
GI	Hancock Sovereign Investors A	3.2	3.2
SU	Flag Investors Telephone Inc A	3.1	3.0
GI	Putnam Fund for Growth & Inc A	3.0	3.6
GI	Mutual Shares	3.0	3.0
EI	Fidelity Equity-Income	3.0	4.4
WW	Capital World Growth & Income	2.9	3.2
	Lowest		
G	Weitz Value	0.0	0.5
G	PIMCo Adv Target A	0.0	0.0
AG	PIMCo Adv Opportunity C	0.0	0.0
SC	PBHG Emerging Growth	0.0	0.0
SC	Robertson Stephens Value + Grth	0.0	5.1
WW	Putnam Global Growth A	0.0	9.8
SC	PBHG Growth	0.0	0.0
G	Berger 100	0.0	1.8
WW	Dreyfus Global Growth	0.0	3.5
SC	Warburg Pincus Emerging Gr Comm	0.0	-0.6
G	Warburg Pincus Captl Appr Comm	0.1	0.4
G	Vista Capital Growth A	0.3	0.7
SC	Evergreen	0.5	0.6
SH	Franklin Global Health Care	0.5	0.7
G	Growth Fund of America	0.6	0.9
GI	Warburg Pincus Growth & Income	0.8	0.2
SC	Nicholas II	0.8	7.8
SC	Acorn	0.9	1.3
GI	Evergreen Growth & Income	0.9	1.0
G	Franklin Growth	0.9	1.1
G	Schafer Value	0.9	4.3
G	New York Venture A	1.0	5.0
G	Vanguard U.S. Growth	1.2	1.6
WF	Vanguard Intl Growth	1.3	1.4
G	Wayne Hummer Growth	1.4	5.7
	Average Yield %	**2.4**	

Hybrid

Obj	Fund	Yield	SEC Yield
	Highest		
CY	Delaware Delchester A	12.1	10.9
CY	IDS Extra Income	11.6	8.9
CY	Putnam High Yield Advantage A	11.3	10.2
CY	AIM High-Yield A	10.8	11.2
CY	Oppenheimer High-Yield A	10.5	9.6
CY	Northeast Investors	10.3	9.0
CY	Invesco High-Yield	10.2	10.8
CY	Franklin AGE High-Income	10.2	10.0
CY	Seligman High-Yield Bond A	10.1	10.3
CY	Phoenix High-Yield A	10.1	9.8
CY	Kemper High-Yield A	10.1	10.5
CY	Lord Abbett Bond-Debenture	10.1	9.0
CY	Liberty High-Income Bond A	10.0	10.5
CY	Colonial High-Yield Securities A	10.0	9.4
CY	T. Rowe Price High-Yield	9.7	10.3
CY	American High-Income	9.7	10.2
CY	Merrill Lynch Corp High-Income A	9.6	9.8
I	Hancock Strategic Income A	9.5	8.8
CY	Vanguard Fixed-Inc High-Yld Corp	9.4	10.4
CY	Nicholas Income	9.4	9.5
I	Oppenheimer Strategic Income A	9.2	9.7
CY	MFS High-Income A	9.2	10.0
I	Colonial Strategic Income A	9.1	8.7
CY	MainStay Hi-Yield Corp Bond B	9.0	8.9
I	Putnam Diversified Income A	8.8	10.0
	Lowest		
AA	Robertson Stephens Contrarian	0.0	2.7
WB	MFS World Governments A	1.4	6.5
AA	Phoenix Total Return A	2.1	2.8
B	Pasadena Balanced Return A	2.2	1.4
AA	Prudential Allocation Conserv B	2.3	2.5
B	Founders Balanced	2.3	3.2
AA	MIMLIC Asset Allocation A	2.6	3.6
B	20th Century Balanced Investors	2.8	3.3
B	Phoenix Balanced A	3.2	3.7
B	Fidelity Balanced	3.3	5.6
B	Evergreen Foundation	3.3	3.8
B	Fidelity Puritan	3.5	4.0
B	T. Rowe Price Balanced	3.8	4.8
B	Dodge & Cox Balanced	3.9	4.5
B	USAA Investment Balanced	3.9	4.5
B	Keystone Custodian K-1	4.0	3.4
AA	Connecticut Mutual Total Return	4.0	4.5
B	Vanguard STAR	4.0	4.6
B	Sentinel Balanced	4.1	4.1
B	MFS Total Return A	4.3	4.6
B	George Putnam Fund of Boston A	4.3	5.1
CV	Pacific Horizon Capital Income	4.4	4.9
B	Vanguard/Wellington	4.5	5.0
B	American Balanced	4.6	4.6
CV	Vanguard Convertible Securities	4.8	5.7
	Average Yield %	**7.1**	

Equity

Obj	Fund	Yield	SEC Yield
	Highest		
CG	Alliance Bond Corporate Bond A	9.6	9.1
CG	Loomis Sayles Bond	8.6	9.8
CG	Bond Fund of America	8.3	8.0
SW	Scudder Short-Term Global Income	8.2	8.3
GG	U.S. Government Securities	8.0	6.5
CG	Putnam Income A	8.0	7.9
CG	PaineWebber Invmt Grade Income A	7.9	7.8
GM	Franklin U.S. Government	7.8	7.3
GM	T. Rowe Price GNMA	7.6	7.1
CQ	Vanguard Fixed-Inc L/T Corp Bond	7.6	8.3
CG	American Capital Corp Bond A	7.5	7.2
CG	SteinRoe Income	7.5	8.3
CG	MFS Bond A	7.4	7.5
GM	Alliance Mortgage Secs Income A	7.4	6.8
CQ	Babson Bond L	7.3	7.0
GG	WPG Government Securities	7.3	7.2
GM	Lexington GNMA Income	7.2	7.7
GG	Dreyfus Short-Interm Government	7.2	7.1
GM	Vanguard Fixed-Inc GNMA	7.1	7.4
GM	Benham GNMA Income	7.0	7.7
GG	American Capital Govt Secs A	7.0	5.5
CQ	Scudder Short-Term Bond	6.9	7.7
GM	Scudder GNMA	6.8	6.9
GM	Dreyfus GNMA	6.8	6.7
CQ	Columbia Fixed-Income Securities	6.8	7.6
	Lowest		
CQ	Neuberger & Berman Ultra Short	3.9	5.5
GA	Overland Express Var Rate Govt A	4.7	4.8
GT	Benham Treasury Note	5.2	7.3
GT	Vanguard Fixed-Inc S/T US Treas	5.3	7.6
CG	Strong Advantage	5.5	6.8
GG	Vanguard Fixed-Inc S/T Federal	5.6	7.5
CG	Vanguard Fixed-Inc S/T Corporate	5.7	7.7
CG	Harbor Bond	5.9	7.2
CG	Prudential Structured Maturity A	5.9	6.8
GG	Fidelity Spartan Lim Mat Govt	5.9	7.1
CQ	T. Rowe Price Short-Term Bond	6.0	7.1
CQ	Scudder Income	6.2	7.2
GT	Vanguard Fixed-Inc I/T US Treas	6.2	7.8
GG	Gradison-McDonald Govt Income	6.2	6.7
CQ	Portico Bond Immdex Ret	6.5	7.9
CQ	Fidelity Intermediate Bond	6.5	6.8
GG	Strong Government Securities	6.5	7.4
CG	New England Bond Income A	6.6	7.5
CG	Fidelity Short-Term Bond	6.6	7.1
CG	Strong Short-Term Bond	6.7	8.3
GM	Fidelity Spartan Ginnie Mae	6.7	7.8
GG	Fidelity Government Securities	6.7	7.0
CG	Vanguard Bond Idx Total Bond Mkt	6.8	7.8
CQ	T. Rowe Price New Income	6.8	7.3
CQ	Columbia Fixed-Income Securities	6.8	7.6
	Average Yield %	**7.4**	

Hybrid

Obj	Fund	Yield	SEC Yield
	Highest		
MN	Franklin High-Yield T/F Income	7.2	6.9
MN	Fidelity Aggressive Tax-Free	7.1	7.2
MN	Franklin Federal Tax-Free Income	6.9	6.0
SW	IDS High-Yield Tax-Exempt	6.9	6.2
MN	Lord Abbett Tax-Free Income Natl	6.8	5.5
MN	T. Rowe Price Tax-Fr High-Yield	6.5	6.5
MN	Putnam Municipal Income A	6.5	6.7
MN	Alliance Muni Income National A	6.4	6.2
MN	Dreyfus Municipal Bond	6.4	6.1
MN	Vanguard Muni Bond High-Yield	6.4	6.6
MN	Colonial Tax-Exempt A	6.3	6.0
MN	Fidelity Advisor High-Inc Muni A	6.3	6.5
MN	Flagship All-American Tax-Ex A	6.3	5.9
MN	USAA Tax-Exempt Long-Term	6.3	6.5
MN	General Municipal Bond	6.2	6.3
MN	Oppenheimer Tax-Free Bond A	6.2	5.7
MN	Franklin Insured Tax-Free Income	6.2	5.5
MN	Safeco Municipal Bond	6.2	6.1
MN	Vanguard Muni Bond Insured L/T	6.1	6.2
MN	Scudder High-Yield Tax-Free	6.1	6.5
MN	Strong Municipal Bond	6.0	6.2
MN	Fortress Municipal Income	6.0	6.6
MN	Van Kampen Insured T/F Income A	6.0	5.4
MN	American Capital Muni Bond A	6.0	5.2
MN	Sit Tax-Free Income	6.0	6.3
	Lowest		
MN	Vanguard Muni Bond Short-Term	3.6	4.5
MN	Calvert Tax-Free Res Lim-Term A	3.6	4.4
MN	Merrill Lynch Muni Ltd Maturity A	3.7	3.5
MN	T. Rowe Price Tax-Fr Short-Intrm	4.2	4.7
MN	USAA Tax-Exempt Short-Term	4.4	4.8
MN	Vanguard Muni Bond Limited-Term	4.4	4.9
MN	Dreyfus Short-Interm Muni Bond	4.5	4.5
MN	Fidelity Spartan Sh-Interm Muni	4.5	4.8
MN	SteinRoe Intermediate Municipals	4.8	5.1
MN	Thornburg Ltd-Term Muni Natl A	4.9	4.7
MN	Vista Tax-Free Income A	5.2	5.5
MN	Scudder Medium-Term Tax-Free	5.3	5.3
MN	First Investors Insured Tax-Ex A	5.4	5.8
MN	MFS Municipal Bond A	5.4	5.7
MN	Vanguard Muni Bond Interm-Term	5.5	5.7
MN	Fidelity Municipal Bond	5.6	6.1
MN	SunAmerica Tax-Exempt Insured A	5.6	5.3
MN	Dreyfus Intermediate Muni Bond	5.7	5.6
MN	USAA Tax-Exempt Interm-Term	5.7	5.9
MN	Value Line Tax-Exempt High-Yield	5.7	5.9
MN	Fidelity Insured Tax-Free	5.8	6.2
MN	SteinRoe Managed Municipals	5.8	5.8
MN	Nuveen Municipal Bond	5.8	5.6
MN	Smith Barney Tax-Exempt Income B	5.9	5.9
MN	Sit Tax-Free Income	6.0	6.3
	Average Yield %	**5.7**	

Highest/Lowest Bear Market Performance

Equity

Obj	Fund	Bear Market	Worst 3-Month Period 1990–94
	Highest		
SP	Vanguard Special Gold & Prec Met	1	-21.36
G	Greenspring	1	-10.80
I	Oppenheimer Strategic Income A	1	-6.20
I	Merrill Lynch World Income A	1	-5.32
I	Phoenix Multi-Sector Fixed-Inc A	1	-5.77
I	USAA Mutual Income	1	-6.07
G	Merger	1	-10.04
I	Putnam Diversified Income A	1	-5.33
I	Berwyn Income	1	-5.48
AA	Stagecoach Asset Allocation A	1	-6.96
AA	Flex-funds Muirfield	1	-6.19
SU	Franklin Utilities	1	-9.94
I	Lindner Dividend	1	-6.13
AA	Overland Express Asset Alloc A	1	-6.03
I	Vanguard Preferred Stock	1	-6.90
B	T. Rowe Price Balanced	1	-4.99
I	Colonial Strategic Income A	1	-8.51
WW	Dreyfus Global Growth	1	-7.52
I	Hancock Strategic Income A	1	-12.08
I	Janus Flexible Income	1	-8.47
I	Pioneer Income	1	-5.70
AA	Strong Asset Allocation	1	-4.68
I	Vanguard/Wellesley Income	1	-6.17
SU	Fidelity Utilities	1	-5.84
GI	Gateway Index Plus	1	-4.84
	Lowest		
SC	PBHG Growth	10	-29.05
G	CGM Capital Development	10	-23.19
AG	Delaware Trend A	10	-32.67
SC	Hancock Emerging Growth B	10	-23.09
AG	PIMCo Adv Opportunity C	10	-19.55
ST	T. Rowe Price Science & Tech	10	-29.53
SC	FPA Capital	10	-32.19
SC	Columbia Special	10	-29.30
G	T. Rowe Price New America Growth	10	-25.21
G	Pasadena Growth A	10	-24.96
SC	MFS Emerging Growth B	10	-30.83
SC	Hancock Special Equities A	10	-25.94
ST	Invesco Strategic Technology	10	-28.55
AG	AIM Constellation	10	-26.24
WP	Japan	10	-22.44
AG	Wasatch Aggressive Equity	10	-25.48
AG	Founders Special	10	-18.25
SC	Founders Frontier	10	-18.07
SC	Alger Small Capitalization	10	-22.41
AG	Putnam Voyager A	9	-19.59
AG	20th Century Ultra Investors	9	-16.25
SC	Oppenheimer Discovery A	9	-17.11
AG	Kaufmann	9	-28.26
S	Invesco Strategic Leisure	9	-25.04
SC	Ariel Growth	9	-25.39
	Average Value		**-14.49**

Bond

Obj	Fund	Bear Market	Worst 3-Month Period 1990–94
	Highest		
MN	Calvert Tax-Free Res Lim-Term A	1	0.36
CV	Gabelli Convertible Securities	1	-2.66
MN	Merrill Lynch Muni Ltd Maturity A	1	-0.40
CQ	Neuberger & Berman Ultra Short	1	-0.51
CG	Strong Advantage	1	-0.20
MN	Vanguard Muni Bond Short-Term	1	-0.24
MN	Dreyfus Short-Interm Muni Bond	1	-1.36
MN	T. Rowe Price Tax-Fr Short-Intrm	1	-1.61
MN	USAA Tax-Exempt Short-Term	1	-1.32
MN	Vanguard Muni Bond Limited-Term	1	-1.43
MN	Fidelity Spartan Sh-Interm Muni	1	-2.37
CQ	Scudder Short-Term Bond	1	-2.77
GG	Fidelity Spartan Lim Mat Govt	1	-2.69
CY	Merrill Lynch Corp High-Income A	1	-13.53
GG	Dreyfus Short-Interm Government	1	-1.98
CY	Fidelity Capital & Income	1	-8.02
CG	Fidelity Short-Term Bond	1	-3.50
CY	Northeast Investors	1	-7.51
CQ	T. Rowe Price Short-Term Bond	1	-2.39
MN	Thornburg Ltd-Term Muni Natl A	1	-2.45
CY	Fidelity Advisor High-Yield A	1	-7.14
CG	Vanguard Fixed-Inc S/T Corporate	1	-2.18
CG	FPA New Income	1	-1.65
CY	MainStay Hi-Yield Corp Bond B	1	-11.40
GG	Vanguard Fixed-Inc S/T Federal	1	-2.42
	Lowest		
CG	Alliance Bond Corporate Bond A	10	-13.61
CQ	Vanguard Fixed-Inc L/T Corp Bond	10	-7.05
MN	Safeco Municipal Bond	10	-7.80
MN	Vanguard Muni Bond Insured L/T	10	-6.50
CV	American Capital Harbor A	10	-9.54
MN	MFS Municipal Bond A	9	-6.89
WB	Fidelity Global Bond	9	-13.98
MN	Vanguard Muni Bond High-Yield	9	-6.18
MN	Scudder High-Yield Tax-Free	9	-7.56
MN	Lord Abbett Tax-Free Income Natl	9	-7.48
MN	Fidelity Insured Tax-Free	9	-8.03
MN	Fidelity Municipal Bond	9	-7.53
MN	Vista Tax-Free Income A	9	-7.42
MN	Flagship All-American Tax-Ex A	9	-6.52
MN	Oppenheimer Tax-Free Bond A	8	-8.30
CQ	Scudder Income	8	-6.72
CG	MFS Bond A	8	-6.59
MN	General Municipal Bond	8	-7.04
MN	Value Line Tax-Exempt High-Yield	8	-7.57
MN	Alliance Muni Income National A	8	-8.50
MN	USAA Tax-Exempt Long-Term	7	-6.48
MN	SteinRoe Managed Municipals	7	-5.91
CV	Pacific Horizon Capital Income	7	-15.30
CG	PaineWebber Invmt Grade Income A	7	-7.02
CY	Franklin AGE High-Income	7	-19.19
	Average Value		**-6.79**

Highest/Lowest Foreign Percentage

Equity

Obj	Fund	Foreign%	S&P 500%	S&P Mid-Cap 400 %	U.S. Small-Cap %
	Highest				
WF	EuroPacific Growth	100.0	0.4	0.0	0.0
WF	GAM International	100.0	0.0	0.0	0.0
WF	Govett Emerging Markets	100.0	0.0	0.0	0.0
WF	Harbor International	100.0	0.0	0.0	0.0
WP	Merrill Lynch Dragon B	100.0	0.0	0.0	0.0
WF	Oakmark International	100.0	0.0	0.0	0.0
WF	Scudder International	100.0	0.0	0.0	0.0
WP	Japan	100.0	0.0	0.0	0.0
WF	20th Century Intl Equity	100.0	0.0	0.0	0.0
WF	Vanguard Intl Growth	99.7	0.2	0.0	0.4
WF	Templeton Foreign	99.3	0.0	0.0	0.7
WF	Templeton Developing Markets	99.1	0.0	0.0	0.9
WF	Strong International Stock	99.1	0.7	0.0	0.2
WP	Morgan Stanley Asian Growth A	98.7	0.0	0.0	1.3
WP	Newport Tiger	98.6	0.0	0.0	1.4
WF	T. Rowe Price Intl Stock	98.4	0.4	0.0	1.4
WP	Strong Asia Pacific	98.3	0.0	0.0	1.7
WP	T. Rowe Price New Asia	98.2	0.9	0.0	0.9
WE	Invesco European	98.0	1.3	1.0	0.0
WF	Acorn International	96.4	0.3	0.0	3.4
WF	Montgomery Emerging Markets	96.3	1.2	0.3	2.2
WF	SoGen Overseas	95.3	0.4	2.3	2.0
WF	Scudder Latin America	94.8	0.0	0.0	5.2
SP	Vanguard Special Gold & Prec Met	92.3	9.9	0.0	3.1
SP	Gabelli Gold	87.3	17.9	0.0	3.8
	Lowest				
SC	PBHG Emerging Growth	0.0	0.0	0.0	100.0
SC	Schooner	0.0	0.0	25.2	74.8
I	Phoenix Multi-Sector Fixed-Inc A	0.0	0.0	0.0	0.0
SC	Skyline Special Equities II	0.0	9.1	21.4	69.5
GI	Washington Mutual Investors	0.0	92.7	3.9	3.4
G	Yacktman	0.0	67.1	12.5	20.4
EI	USAA Mutual Income Stock	0.0	70.6	13.9	15.5
I	USAA Mutual Income	0.0	55.3	31.4	13.3
B	USAA Investment Balanced	0.0	89.4	10.6	0.0
G	UMB Stock	0.0	88.3	8.5	3.2
G	Third Avenue Value	0.0	15.0	8.3	76.8
SC	Skyline Special Equities	0.0	1.6	1.3	97.1
G	Sequoia	0.0	40.6	26.1	33.3
GI	Selected American	0.0	70.3	13.5	16.2
G	Reich & Tang Equity	0.0	45.1	37.5	17.4
SC	Robertson Stephens Value + Grth	0.0	28.7	24.9	46.4
I	Putnam Diversified Income A	0.0	0.0	0.0	100.0
B	Pax World	0.0	73.9	10.1	16.1
G	L. Roy Papp Stock	0.0	70.5	11.5	18.0
AG	Keystone Amer Omega A	0.0	47.3	23.5	29.2
G	IAI Regional	0.0	45.5	18.5	36.0
I	Pioneer Income	0.0	57.2	15.7	27.1
SC	Meridian	0.0	15.1	17.4	67.4
I	Merrill Lynch World Income A	0.0	28.7	0.0	71.3
GI	Lexington Corporate Leaders	0.0	100.0	0.0	0.0
	Average Foreign %	**18.7**			

Bond

Obj	Fund	Foreign%	S&P 500%	S&P Mid-Cap 400 %	U.S. Small-Cap %
	Highest				
WB	Fidelity New Markets Income	100.0	0.0	0.0	0.0
CY	Oppenheimer High-Yield A	14.2	3.9	0.0	82.0
CY	Fidelity Capital & Income	12.3	11.6	0.0	76.1
CY	T. Rowe Price High-Yield	9.5	16.7	0.0	73.8
CY	MainStay Hi-Yield Corp Bond B	8.6	27.1	14.3	50.0
CV	SBSF Convertible Securities	7.5	43.5	16.2	32.8
CY	Lord Abbett Bond-Debenture	6.7	0.0	0.0	93.3
CV	American Capital Harbor A	4.9	85.4	8.9	0.8
CV	Phoenix Convertible A	4.9	71.7	23.7	4.6
CV	Fidelity Convertible Securities	3.8	56.1	2.3	40.9
CV	Putnam Convertible Income Grth A	3.2	83.6	7.4	7.4
CY	Fidelity Advisor High-Yield A	1.5	0.0	0.0	98.5
CY	Liberty High-Income Bond A	0.0	0.0	0.0	100.0
CY	Putnam High Yield Advantage A	0.0	0.0	0.0	100.0
CY	Franklin AGE High-Income	0.0	0.0	0.0	100.0
CY	American High-Income	0.0	21.4	0.0	78.7
CG	Bond Fund of America	0.0	0.0	0.0	100.0
WB	Capital World Bond	0.0	0.0	0.0	100.0
CY	AIM High-Yield A	0.0	0.0	0.0	0.0
CY	Colonial High-Yield Securities A	0.0	5.7	0.0	94.3
CY	Delaware Delchester A	0.0	0.0	0.0	100.0
CV	Gabelli Convertible Securities	0.0	26.1	22.3	51.6
CY	IDS Extra Income	0.0	0.0	0.0	100.0
CY	Kemper High-Yield A	0.0	0.0	0.0	100.0
CV	MainStay Convertible B	0.0	32.5	21.6	45.9
	Lowest				
CG	New England Bond Income A	0.0	100.0	0.0	0.0
WB	Putnam Global Governmental Inc A	0.0	0.0	0.0	100.0
CQ	Scudder Income	0.0	100.0	0.0	0.0
CG	PaineWebber Invmt Grade Income A	0.0	0.0	0.0	0.0
CG	Strong Short-Term Bond	0.0	0.0	0.0	0.0
CY	Invesco High-Yield	0.0	0.0	0.0	100.0
CG	American Capital Corp Bond A	0.0	100.0	0.0	0.0
CV	Pacific Horizon Capital Income	0.0	96.1	0.0	3.9
WB	Templeton Income	0.0	27.0	0.0	73.0
CV	Vanguard Convertible Securities	0.0	0.0	23.6	76.4
CV	Value Line Convertible	0.0	0.0	0.0	0.0
CY	Phoenix High-Yield A	0.0	0.0	0.0	0.0
CY	Northeast Investors	0.0	57.2	15.4	27.4
CY	Nicholas Income	0.0	0.0	0.0	100.0
CY	Merrill Lynch Corp High-Income A	0.0	0.0	0.0	100.0
CY	MFS High-Income A	0.0	0.0	0.0	100.0
CG	MFS Bond A	0.0	0.0	0.0	100.0
CV	MainStay Convertible B	0.0	32.5	21.6	45.9
CY	Kemper High-Yield A	0.0	0.0	0.0	100.0
CY	IDS Extra Income	0.0	0.0	0.0	100.0
CV	Gabelli Convertible Securities	0.0	26.1	22.3	51.6
CY	Delaware Delchester A	0.0	0.0	0.0	100.0
CY	Colonial High-Yield Securities A	0.0	5.7	0.0	94.3
CY	AIM High-Yield A	0.0	0.0	0.0	0.0
WB	Capital World Bond	0.0	0.0	0.0	100.0
	Average Foreign %	**4.2**			

Manager Changes During 1994

Fund	Old Manager	New Manager	Date
Acorn International	Greenberg/Zell/Wanger	Leah Zell/Ralph Wanger	1994
Alliance Growth & Income A	Thomas M. Perkins	Paul Rissman	11/01/94
American Leaders A	Donnelly/Anderson	Tim Keefe	12/01/94
Benham GNMA Income	Jeffrey R. Tyler	Casey Colton/Jeffrey R. Tyler	1994
Berger 100	Linafelter/Berger	Rodney L. Linafelter	1994
Berwyn Income	Robert E. Killen	Edward Killen	06/30/94
Burnham A	I. W. Burnham/Paul J. Ferguson	I. W. Burnham	1994
Clipper	James H. Gipson	Gipson/Sandler	01/01/94
Colonial Tax-Exempt A	Boatman/Hardie	Bonny E. Boatman	1994
Columbia Special	Alan J. Folkman	Robert A. Unger	06/30/94
Dreyfus Short-Interm Government	Barbara L. Kenworthy	Gerald E. Thunelius	06/01/94
Fidelity Advisor High-Inc Muni A	Peter J. Allegrini	Guy E. Wickwire	07/18/94
Fidelity Capital & Income	Daniel Harmetz/David Breazzano	David Breazzano	1994
Fidelity OTC	Alan R. Radlo	Abigail Johnson	04/01/94
Fortress Utility	Christopher H. Wiles	Wiles/Duessel	12/01/94
Founders Balanced	Borgen/Hooper, Jr./Keely/Haines/Adams/Schoelzel	Borgen/Hooper, Jr./Keely/Haines/Cleworth/Adams	1994
Founders Blue Chip	Hooper, Jr./Keely/Haines/Gerding/Cleworth/Adams	Borgen/Hooper, Jr./Keely/Haines/Gerding/Cleworth	1994
Founders Frontier	Borgen/Hooper, Jr./Keely/Demmitt/Haines/Gerding	Borgen/Hooper, Jr./Keely/Haines/Gerding/Cleworth	1994
Founders Special	Borgen/Hooper, Jr./Keely/Haines/Gerding	Borgen/Hooper, Jr./Keely/Haines/Gerding/Cleworth	1994
Franklin High-Yield T/F Income	Jennings, Sr./Johnson/Harrington	Johnson/Harrington/Amoroso	08/01/94
G.T. Global Worldwide Growth A	Wignall/Andrews/Eadon-Clarke/Selfslagh/Betterton	Wignall/Andrews/Eadon-Clarke/Yates/Selfslagh/Bette	1994
Gabelli Growth	Mario Gabelli	Howard F. Ward	1994
IAI Regional	Julian P. Carlin	Carlin/Hoonsbeen	07/01/94
Invesco High-Yield	William B. Veronda	Jerry Paul	05/01/94
Invesco Industrial Income	Mayer/Kaweske/Lout	Charles P. Mayer/Jerry Paul	05/31/94
Kemper Growth A	Arends/Lewis	C. Beth Cotner	04/25/94
Lexington Corporate Leaders	William S. Stack	Alan H. Wapnick	07/29/94
Longleaf Partners	O. Mason Hawkins	Cates/Hawkins	1994
MFS High-Income A	Joan S. Batchelder	Robert J. Manning	06/01/94
Neuberger & Berman Partners	Michael Kassen	Kassen/Gendelman	10/03/94
Oppenheimer Discovery A	Jay W. Tracey III	Jay W. Tracey III	09/20/94
Pacific Horizon Capital Income	William S. Hensel	Ed Cassens	11/01/94
PaineWebber Global Income B	Nimrod Fachler/Stuart Waugh	Stuart Waugh	1994
Phoenix Growth A	Catherine Dudley/Robert Chesek	Catherine Dudley	1994
T. Rowe Price Equity-Income	Rogers/Broadus, Jr.	Brian C. Rogers	1994
T. Rowe Price High-Yield	Richard S. Swingle	Catherine H. Bray	09/30/94
T. Rowe Price Tax-Fr High-Yield	William T. Reynolds	C. Stephen Wolfe	03/31/94
Prudential Allocation Conserv B	McHugh/Guidone/Felice/Fetch/Ford/Schaefer/Rodriguez	Stumpp/Ford/Rodriguez	1994
Putnam Diversified Income A	Saef/Leichter	Kohli/Leichter/Powers	1994
Putnam Global Governmental Inc A	Jallits/Daly	Kohli/Turner/Francis	04/14/94
Putnam Voyager A	Matthew A. Weatherbie	Swanberg/Weatherbie	1994
Reich & Tang Equity	Delafield/Hoerle/Wilson/Sellecchia/Baker	Hoerle/Wilson	1994
Rydex Nova	Skip Viragh	Thomas G. Michael	04/01/94
Schooner	James H. Gipson	Douglas Grey/James H. Gipson	1994
Scudder Global	Garrett/Holzer	Ho/Bratt/Holzer	1994
Scudder Income	William M. Hutchinson	Wohler/Hutchinson	1994
Scudder International	Franklin/Cheng/Bratt	Franklin/Rodrigo III/Cheng/Bratt	1994
Scudder Latin America	Games, Jr./Rathnam/Truscott	Games, Jr./Cornell/Truscott	1994
Scudder Short-Term Bond	Gootkind/Martland/Poor	Gootkind/Dolan/Poor	1994
Sentinel Balanced	Rodney A. Buck	Pender/Buck	1994
Sentinel Common Stock	Christopher E. Martin	Merrill/Pender/Lee	09/30/94
Seven Seas Growth & Income	Brenton Dickson	Management Team	11/01/94
Smith Barney Appreciation A	Williamson, Jr./Cohen	Hersh Cohen	1994
Smith Barney Income & Growth A	Bruce D. Sargent	Weissman/Sargent	1994
SteinRoe Prime Equities	Ralph Segall	Hurwitz/Christensen	08/01/94

Manager Changes During 1994 (continued)

Fund	Old Manager	New Manager	Date
Strong Common Stock	Ziegler/Carlson/Weiss	Carlson/Weiss	1994
Strong Opportunity	Ziegler/Carlson/Weiss	Carlson/Weiss	1994
SunAmerica Tax-Exempt Insured A	John C. Keogh	John C. Mooney	08/01/94
20th Century Balanced Investors	Duboc/Fogle/Stowers III/Puff, Jr./Honour	Duboc/Prial/Puff, Jr.	1994
20th Century Heritage Investors	Duboc/Fogle/Stowers III/Puff, Jr./Honour	Duboc/Prial/Puff, Jr.	1994
USAA Investment Balanced	Miller/Saunders, Jr./Willmann	Gladson/Saunders, Jr./Willmann/Klaffke	01/01/94
USAA Investment Cornerstone	Miller/Saunders, Jr.	Saunders, Jr./Johnson/Klaffke/Selmier II	01/01/94
USAA Tax-Exempt Short-Term	David G. Miller	Clifford A. Gladson	04/01/94
Vanguard Fixed-Inc GNMA	Paul G. Sullivan	Paul D. Kaplan	03/31/94
Vanguard Fixed-Inc L/T Corp Bond	Paul G. Sullivan	Earl E. McEvoy	03/31/94
Vanguard Special Utilities Inc	John R. Ryan	John R. Ryan/Paul D. Kaplan	05/15/94
Vanguard/Wellington	Sullivan/Bajakian	Vincent Bajakian	1994
Warburg Pincus Captl Appr Comm	Andrew H. Massie, Jr.	Susan L. Black	09/30/94
First Philippine	Rodrigo III/Clemente	Roberto Ticzon	04/01/94
Global Health Sci	John J. Kaweske	Barry Kurokawa	01/05/94
Global Income Plus	Nimrod Fachler/Stuart Waugh	Stuart Waugh	1994
Growth Fund Spain	Suarez/Milans/Wilson	Ferro/Suarez/Milans	1994
GT Greater Europe	Nigel Ledeboer/Stephen Pearson	James Dickson/John R. Legat	03/01/94
Irish Investment	Harry Hartford	Jane Neill	06/01/94
Jakarta Growth	Haruo Sawada/Iwao Komatsu	Iwao Komatsu	1994
Japan OTC Equity	Haruo Sawada/Iwao Komatsu	Iwao Komatsu	1994
Putnam Mgd Muni Inc	Erickson/Reeves	Howard Manning	02/01/94
Swiss Helvetia	Wilkinson/de Montebello/Grimm	Georges L. de Montebello	1994

Name Changes

Old Name	New Name	Date
Calvert-Ariel Appreciation A	Ariel Appreciation A	09/06/94
Calvert-Ariel Growth	Ariel Growth	09/06/94
Dreyfus Strategic World Investing	Dreyfus Global Growth	02/07/94
Evergreen Value Timing	Evergreen Growth & Income Y	08/01/94
Fidelity Utilities Income	Fidelity Utilities	09/08/94
G.T. Worldwide Growth A	G.T. Global Worldwide Growth A	05/01/94
Laurel Stock Inv	Dreyfus Disciplined Stock Inv	10/17/94
Pilgrim Baxter Emerging Growth	PBHG Emerging Growth	05/31/94
Prudential FlexiFund Conserv Mgd B	Prudential Allocation Conserv B	08/02/94
Quantitative Boston Grth & Income Ord	Quantitative Growth & Inc Ord	08/01/94
Quantitative Boston Numeric Ord	Quantitative Numeric Ord	08/01/94
Robertson Stephens Value Plus	Robertson Stephens Value + Grth	10/14/94
Smith Barney Shearson Appreciation A	Smith Barney Appreciation A	11/07/94
Smith Barney Shearson Tax-Ex Income B	Smith Barney Tax-Exempt Income B	11/07/94
Southeastern Asset Mgmt Value	Longleaf Partners	07/22/94
TNE Bond Income A	New England Bond Income A	04/18/94
Thomson Growth B	PIMCo Adv Growth C	11/14/94
Thomson Opportunity B	PIMCo Adv Opportunity C	11/14/94
Thomson Target A	PIMCo Adv Target A	11/14/94
Transamerica Emerging Growth B	Hancock Emerging Growth B	12/22/94
Tweedy, Browne Value	Tweedy, Browne American Value	10/04/94
Vanguard Bond Index	Vanguard Bond Idx Total Bond Mkt	01/19/94

No Indexing Here

Last year wasn't awful for the S&P 500, but core funds that found the most success shied away from the index.

A prime, if inappropriately named, example is **Fidelity Blue Chip Growth**. It posted a big 1994 gain by ignoring the blue chips of the S&P in favor of what manager Michael Gordon calls "the blue chips of tomorrow"—cheap smaller-cap issues, especially technology winners and turnaround energy stocks, with lofty earnings-growth rates.

Longleaf Partners (formerly Southeastern Asset Management Value) scored big when merger-and-acquisition activity propelled its favorite subset of the broad market—firms selling at discounts to their free-market value. **Strong Opportunity** comanagers Dick Weiss and Carlene Ziegler hit on stocks with positive earnings surprises. The duo's success makes it all the sadder that they broke up at year-end: Ziegler decided to start her own firm with husband (and former Strong president) Andy Ziegler.

A number of funds excelled with well-placed bets overseas. For example, **Fidelity Value**'s Jeffrey Ubben rode economic recovery in Europe and Japan with a few cyclicals in both regions.

There were also funds that would have been better off sticking with the S&P: Rising rates and costly natural disasters hurt **Century Shares**' insurance-heavy portfolio, and **Legg Mason Special Investment** battled with ill-fated shifts into Mexico, casinos, and financials.

Nonetheless, core funds' moderate success at a time when both aggressive and conservative funds struggled proves their mettle in—and their appropriateness for—shaky market environments.

Kylelane Purcell

Growth of $10,000
- Core Category ($000)
- Wilshire 5000 ($000)

Net Assets ($bil)

	1983	1984	1985	1986	1987	1988	1989	1990	1991	1992	1993	1994	History
	39.14	16.92	68.64	61.29	24.73	40.08	56.85	16.80	66.37	48.90	40.11	9.93	High
	25.53	3.12	33.23	19.47	2.59	18.85	28.54	-4.78	34.81	11.40	16.45	-0.10	Total Return %
	13.22	-8.59	14.43	1.40	-18.36	3.96	11.66	-20.57	0.28	-3.47	-1.45	-13.07	Low
	3.07	-3.15	1.49	0.79	-2.67	2.24	-3.15	-1.66	4.32	3.78	6.40	-1.41	+/- S&P 500
	2.07	0.07	0.66	3.37	0.22	0.91	-0.64	1.41	0.60	2.43	5.17	-0.03	+/- Wilshire 5000
	3.25	3.02	2.62	1.99	2.54	2.54	2.59	2.45	1.97	1.46	1.31	1.24	Income Return %
	21.39	0.65	26.76	16.26	-1.04	15.76	24.44	-6.81	32.34	9.94	15.14	-1.34	Capital Return %
	0.36	0.35	0.30	0.28	0.38	0.33	0.38	0.37	0.28	0.25	0.24	0.23	Income $
	0.96	0.99	0.99	1.04	1.14	1.22	1.19	1.22	1.21	1.18	1.13	1.08	Expense Ratio
	3.31	3.41	3.07	2.46	1.93	2.33	2.48	2.60	2.15	1.59	1.35	1.23	Income Ratio
	77.36	66.02	63.47	74.62	83.69	81.24	75.96	80.52	76.39	68.99	71.23	76.70	Turnover Ratio
	12.46	13.24	19.43	31.46	34.55	38.10	52.33	54.72	88.57	121.92	177.20	212.07	Total Net Assets ($bil)

Style Box Analysis

Number of Funds (Large / Med / Small)

Value	Blend	Growth
9	22	11
10	24	7
9	8	0

1 Yr Total Return % (Large / Med / Small)

Value	Blend	Growth
-0.59	0.00	0.99
-1.90	0.75	0.93
-3.00	0.72	NMF

5 Yr Total Return % (Large / Med / Small)

Value	Blend	Growth
9.21	9.25	9.90
10.80	11.02	11.21
10.05	11.14	NMF

Average Mstar Risk (Large / Med / Small)

Value	Blend	Growth
0.79	0.79	0.91
0.80	0.79	0.90
0.75	0.84	NMF

1.00 = Equity Average

Risk Analysis

	Load-Adj Return	Morningstar[1] Return	Risk	Morningstar Risk-Adj Rating
1 Yr	-2.00			
3 Yr	8.19	1.45[2]	0.78	★★★★
5 Yr	9.86	1.36[2]	0.83	★★★★
10 Yr	14.26	1.36	0.86	★★★★

[1]1.00=Equity Average [2]1.00=90-day T-bill return

Other Measures

			Standard Index S&P 500
Standard Deviation	9.32	Alpha	2.94
Mean	8.89	Beta	0.88
Sharpe Ratio	0.57	R-Squared	60.19

Performance 12-31-94

	Total Return%	+/- S&P	+/- Wil 5000
3 Mo	-1.78	-1.76	-1.01
6 Mo	2.90	-1.96	-1.72
1 Yr	-0.10	-1.41	-0.03
3 Yr Average	8.86	2.60	2.25
5 Yr Average	10.28	1.59	1.46
10 Yr Average	14.52	0.14	0.66
15 Yr Average	15.05	0.57	1.07

Portfolio

Total Equity: 5369
Total Fixed-Income: 694

Amount 000		Value $000	% Net Assets
25842	IBM	1786169	0.89
22683	FNMA	1764461	0.88
30424	Motorola	1641791	0.82
26509	Intel	1632404	0.81
25405	General Electric	1273384	0.63
22158	Philip Morris	1273264	0.63
25958	Oracle Systems	1097107	0.55
17478	Caterpillar	1028111	0.51
26765	Sears Roebuck	1026747	0.51
24237	Columbia/HCA Healthcare	1001133	0.50
18650	AT & T	979428	0.49
13868	CSX	977227	0.49
12209	Pfizer	912332	0.45
11402	British Petroleum (ADR)	866667	0.43
16057	FHLMC	861988	0.43
20206	Citicorp	846873	0.42
11633	Texas Instruments	833364	0.42
8898	Hewlett-Packard	831282	0.41
21908	Lowe's	817700	0.41
12827	Exxon	783004	0.39

Composition %

Cash	8.83	Preferreds	0.50
Stocks	87.75	Convertibles	1.21
Bonds	1.63	Other	0.07

Tax Analysis

	Tax-Adj Hist Return %	% Pretax Return
3 Yr Avg	7.19	76.00
5 Yr Avg	8.39	80.36
10 Yr Avg	11.72	80.33

Sector Weightings

	% of Stocks	Rel S&P500
Utilities	4.2	0.34
Energy	6.7	0.66
Financials	21.5	2.03
Industrial Cyclicals	15.6	0.95
Consumer Durables	7.6	1.22
Consumer Staples	6.7	0.53
Services	11.9	1.46
Retail	5.4	0.93
Health	8.7	1.01
Technology	11.7	1.28

Worst Three Months

	Worst 3 Month Performance 1990-1994
Hancock Regional Bank B	-22.94
Century Shares	-22.51
Ariel Appreciation A	-22.44
Templeton Smaller Company Growth	-21.95
Schafer Value	-21.43

Category Leaders

Lowest 3 Yr Morningstar Risk

Royce Equity-Income	0.38
Longleaf Partners	0.43
Oakmark	0.44
Reich & Tang Equity	0.47
Crabbe Huson Equity	0.48
Fidelity Equity-Income II	0.50
Fidelity Value	0.50
Fidelity Low-Priced Stock	0.51
Third Avenue Value	0.53
Sound Shore	0.54

Top Rated Funds

Oakmark	8.60
Oppenheimer Main St Inc&Gr A	5.09
Hancock Regional Bank B	4.91
Fidelity Low-Priced Stock	4.50
Fidelity Blue Chip Growth	3.64
Fidelity Equity-Income II	3.63
Warburg Pincus Growth & Inc	3.61
Longleaf Partners	3.54
Crabbe Huson Equity	3.44
Janus Worldwide	3.26

Best 3 Yr Return %

Oakmark	26.15
Hancock Regional Bank B	21.03
Oppenheimer Main St Inc&Gr A	20.45
Fidelity Low-Priced Stock	17.56
Warburg Pincus Growth & Inc	17.18
Longleaf Partners	17.08
Fidelity Value	17.03
Safeco Equity	16.29
Crabbe Huson Equity	14.23
Third Avenue Value	13.91

Stock Funds–Core

Fund / Ticker	Obj	Style Box	NAV	Total Return % through 12-31-94		Annualized			Trailing 12 Mo Yield %	Morningstar Risk 1.00=Equity Average			Rtn % Rank Obj			Bear Mkt Indicator (Worst 3 mo)	Star Rating	Avg Star Rating
				YTD	1Yr	3Yr	5Yr	10Yr		3Yr	5Yr	10Yr	3Yr	5Yr	10Yr			
S&P 500 Index				1.31	1.31	6.27	8.69	14.38										
Affiliated LAFFX	GI		9.99	3.95	3.95	9.82	8.89	13.10	2.9	0.57	0.71	0.80	12	26	33	5 (-13)	★★★	3.5
AIM Charter CHTRX	GI		8.14	-4.26	-4.26	2.05	9.64	13.98	2.4	0.78	0.68	0.80	88	16	15	3 (-8)	★★★★	3.6
AIM Weingarten WEINX	G		15.21	-0.34	-0.34	-0.07	9.12	15.91	0.4	1.13	0.99	1.05	89	42	7	6 (-16)	★★★	4.1
Alliance Growth & Income A CABDX	GI		2.13	-4.20	-4.20	3.25	6.58	12.53	2.3	0.82	0.82	0.82	83	80	46	6 (-14)	★★★	3.8
American Leaders A FALDX	GI		14.39	0.05	0.05	7.68	9.96	11.94	1.7	0.75	0.80	0.79	24	14	57	5 (-17)	★★★	3.7
Ariel Appreciation A CAAPX	G		19.51	-8.39	-8.39	3.85	7.99		0.3	0.83	0.90		66	62		7 (-22)	★★★	2.8
Bartlett Basic Value MBBVX	GI		14.10	0.42	0.42	7.32	7.08	10.53	1.6	0.68	0.81	0.69	27	71	84	5 (-19)	★★★	3.3
William Blair Growth Shares WBGSX	G		9.60	6.45	6.45	9.79	13.36	14.36	0.2	0.83	0.89	0.97	19	9	22	6 (-15)	★★★★	3.4
Century Shares CENSX	SF		21.77	-3.90	-3.90	6.74	8.07	13.32	2.0	0.95	1.03	1.02	91	90	66	7 (-23)	★★★	3.6
Clipper CFIMX	G		46.09	-2.51	-2.51	7.93	9.03	13.33	1.5	0.93	0.89	0.84	32	45	40	5 (-16)	★★★★	3.8
Columbia Growth CLMBX	G		24.84	-0.64	-0.64	7.93	10.33	14.31	1.0	0.94	0.92	0.93	31	26	24	6 (-16)	★★★★	3.9
Crabbe Huson Equity CHEYX	G		15.69	1.60	1.60	14.23	14.67	—	0.9	0.48	0.67	—	4	6		3 (-17)	★★★★★	4.6
Dean Witter Dividend Growth DWDVX	GI		29.23	-3.18	-3.18	5.37	7.25	13.23	2.8	0.64	0.75	0.74	60	68	30	5 (-15)	★★★★	4.2
Delaware Value A DEVLX	G		18.87	-6.98	-6.98	8.26	10.72	—	0.3	0.62	0.85	—	28	23		8 (-18)	★★★★	3.8
Dreyfus Appreciation DGAGX	G		15.17	3.62	3.62	2.86	8.14	13.56	1.8	0.97	0.88	0.94	75	60	36	4 (-15)	★★★	3.7
Dreyfus New Leaders DNLDX	SC		31.33	-0.15	-0.15	8.55	10.39	—	0.2	0.80	0.89		55	62		8 (-19)	★★★★	3.5
Enterprise Capital Appreciation ENCAX	AG		28.54	-3.46	-3.46	2.60	12.27	—	0.0	1.23	1.02		85	34		7 (-18)	★★★	4.3
EuroPacific Growth AEPGX	WF		21.13	1.13	1.13	11.94	10.69	17.64	1.5	0.83	0.79	0.75	22	10	18	4 (-14)	★★★★★	4.4
Evergreen EVGRX	SC		12.03	0.73	0.73	5.21	7.56	13.03	0.5	0.90	1.01	0.98	81	86	43	8 (-21)	★★★	3.7
Evergreen Growth & Income EV VTX	GI		14.52	1.70	1.70	9.83	9.75		0.9	0.68	0.79		11	15		5 (-14)	★★★★	4.0
FAM Value FAMVX	SC		21.04	6.83	6.83	10.21	13.33		0.6	0.65	0.72		39	29		3 (-18)	★★★★★	4.4
Fasciano FASCX	SC		17.18	3.68	3.68	6.46	10.00		0.0	0.69	0.80		73	66		4 (-17)	★★★★	3.7
Fidelity Advisor Growth Opport A FAGOX	G		24.40	2.86	2.86	13.07	15.20		1.1	0.62	0.90		7	6		9 (-21)	★★★★★	4.4
Fidelity Blue Chip Growth FBGRX	G		25.95	9.85	9.85	13.24	18.40		0.0	0.68	0.78		7	1		6 (-15)	★★★★★	5.0
Fidelity Contrafund FCNTX	G		30.28	-1.12	-1.12	11.64	17.51	18.55	0.0	0.68	0.71	0.81	11	2	2	6 (-13)	★★★★★	3.9
Fidelity Disciplined Equity FDEQX	G		17.94	3.01	3.01	9.94	12.39		1.4	0.74	0.81		18	12		7 (-16)	★★★★	4.5
Fidelity Equity-Income II FEQTX	EI		17.72	3.16	3.16	13.45	—	—	2.1	0.50			2			7 (—)	★★★★★	5.0
Fidelity FFIDX	GI		18.48	2.58	2.58	9.61	9.18	13.65	1.7	0.64	0.75	0.82	13	20	20	5 (-12)	★★★★	3.9
Fidelity Growth & Income FGRIX	GI		21.09	2.27	2.27	10.89	12.51		1.8	0.55	0.73		8	4		7 (-14)	★★★★	4.6
Fidelity Low-Priced Stock FLPSX	SC		16.00	4.81	4.81	17.56	18.88		0.5	0.51	0.64		7	7		4 (-15)	★★★★★	5.0
Fidelity Magellan FMAGX	G		66.80	-1.81	-1.81	9.42	12.02	17.95	0.2	0.76	0.85	0.87	22	14	4	8 (-17)	★★★★★	5.0
Fidelity OTC FOCPX	G		23.27	-2.70	-2.70	6.61	11.48	18.07	0.9	0.93	0.93	0.96	43	15	3	6 (-15)	★★★★	3.9
Fidelity Real Estate Investment FRESX	S		13.20	2.04	2.04	11.12	11.76		4.8	0.92	0.78		40	38	—	2 (-14)	★★★★	3.4
Fidelity Stock Selector FDSSX	G		17.91	0.78	0.78	9.85	—		0.8	0.85			19	—		7 (—)	★★★★	4.2
Fidelity Value FDVLX	G		40.81	7.63	7.63	17.03	12.02	13.61	0.4	0.51	0.74	0.87	2	14	35	7 (-14)	★★★★	3.3
Founders Blue Chip FRMUX	GI		6.16	0.53	0.53	4.71	8.15	13.30	0.9	0.82	0.77	0.85	67	45	27	5 (-11)	★★★★	3.6
Franklin Growth FKGRX	G		15.00	2.93	2.93	4.32	7.99	13.19	0.9	0.78	0.74	0.75	63	63	43	4 (-13)	★★★	3.6
Fundamental Investors ANCFX	GI		17.50	1.33	1.33	9.68	10.03	14.77	2.5	0.65	0.80	0.88	12	14	7	6 (-17)	★★★★	4.0
G.T. Global Worldwide Growth A GTWGX	WW		15.53	-6.65	-6.65	7.14	5.28		0.0	1.00	0.96		62	45	—	8 (-17)	★★	3.0
Gabelli Growth GABGX	G		19.68	-3.40	-3.40	3.94	8.13		0.4	0.91	0.84		66	60		5 (-12)	★★★	4.4
Gabelli Small Cap Growth GABSX	SC		15.84	-2.93	-2.93	12.74	—	—	0.0	0.66			25	—	—	— (—)	★★★★	4.0
Growth Fund of America AGTHX	G		25.53	0.02	0.02	7.14	9.88	14.66	0.6	0.84	0.93	0.95	38	31	18	7 (-18)	★★★★	3.7
Guardian Park Avenue GPAFX	G		26.89	-1.44	-1.44	12.62	11.10	15.17	1.1	0.73	0.86	0.91	8	19	14	6 (-18)	★★★★	4.3
Hancock Freedom Regional Bank B FRBFX	SF		19.62	-0.20	-0.20	21.03	18.19	—	1.2	0.65	0.83	—	8	10	—	4 (-23)	★★★★★	4.2
IAI Regional IARGX	G		20.15	0.69	0.69	4.34	8.92	15.84	0.9	0.82	0.80	0.81	62	47	8	4 (-14)	★★★★	4.5
IDS New Dimensions INNDX	G		13.29	-2.98	-2.98	5.21	13.09	17.28	0.9	1.04	0.88	0.91	54	11	5	5 (-14)	★★★★	4.5
Janus JANSX	G		18.78	-1.10	-1.10	5.44	10.69	15.13	0.0	0.72	0.77	0.74	52	24	15	4 (-14)	★★★★	4.5
Janus Growth & Income JAGIX	GI		13.88	-4.87	-4.87	2.26	—		0.7	1.05			87	—	—	— (—)	★★	3.0
Janus Worldwide JAWWX	WW		24.39	3.61	3.61	13.19	—		2.1	0.78			9	—	—	— (—)	★★★★★	5.0
Legg Mason Special Invmnt LMASX	SC		19.03	-13.07	-13.07	7.57	11.78	—	0.0	1.23	1.02	—	59	46	—	6 (-16)	★★★★	3.7

Bold numbers indicate *highest* return for the listed time period in each category.

Stock Funds—Core

Fund / Ticker	Obj	Style Box	NAV	Total Return % through 12-31-94		Annualized			Trailing 12 Mo Yield %	Morningstar Risk 1.00=Equity Average			Rtn % Rank Obj			Bear Mkt Indicator (Worst 3 mo)	Star Rating	Avg Star Rating
				YTD	1Yr	3Yr	5Yr	10Yr		3Yr	5Yr	10Yr	3Yr	5Yr	10Yr			
S&P 500 Index				1.31	1.31	6.27	8.69	14.38										
Legg Mason Total Return LMTRX	GI	▦	12.15	-7.12	-7.12	6.60	7.20	—	2.3	0.81	0.86	—	36	69	—	7(-19)	★★★	2.6
Lexington Corporate Leaders LEXCX	GI	▦	10.51	-0.77	-0.77	8.55	7.91	14.86	3.7	0.78	0.77	0.80	17	51	6	5(-12)	★★★★	4.2
Longleaf Partners LLPFX	G	▦	17.13	8.97	8.97	17.08	13.25	—	0.9	0.43	0.76	—	2	9	—	5(-21)	★★★★★	4.0
MainStay Value B MKVAX	GI	▦	14.66	-0.22	-0.22	10.64	12.44	—	0.6	0.62	0.71	—	10	4	—	3(-12)	★★★★	3.6
Massachusetts Investors A MITTX	GI	▦	10.07	-1.02	-1.02	5.36	8.33	13.40	2.2	0.78	0.77	0.83	60	40	26	5(-12)	★★★	3.4
Neuberger & Berman Guardian NGUAX	GI	▦	18.23	1.42	1.42	11.37	12.08	14.32	2.2	0.64	0.85	0.90	6	5	11	7(-17)	★★★★	3.9
Neuberger & Berman Partners NPRTX	G	▦	18.52	-1.89	-1.89	10.32	9.29	13.16	0.6	0.76	0.81	0.82	16	40	44	6(-14)	★★★★	4.4
New Perspective ANWPX	WW	▦	14.37	2.97	2.97	10.78	10.30	15.95	1.5	0.77	0.79	0.74	22	8	12	5(-14)	★★★★★	4.1
New York Venture A NYVTX	G	▦	11.16	-1.93	-1.93	8.45	11.73	16.75	1.0	1.04	0.98	0.89	16	11	5	7(-15)	★★★★	4.8
Nicholas NICSX	G	▦	48.03	-2.84	-2.84	5.04	9.39	12.71	1.4	0.75	0.85	0.76	55	38	55	6(-19)	★★★★	4.5
Nicholas II NCTWX	SC	▦	24.46	1.03	1.03	5.64	9.06	12.98	0.8	0.73	0.82	0.81	78	72	48	4(-20)	★★★★	3.8
Oakmark OAKMX	G	▦	22.97	3.32	3.32	**26.15**	—	—	1.0	0.45	—	—	1	—	—	(—)	★★★★★	5.0
Oppenheimer Main St Inc & Grth A MSIGX	GI	▦	20.98	-1.53	-1.53	20.45	**22.23**	—	2.1	0.92	0.83	—	1	1	—	3(-13)	★★★★★	4.7
Papp America-Abroad	G	▦	12.24	7.78	7.78	4.88	—	—	0.8	0.95	—	—	58	—	—	(—)	★★★	3.0
L. Roy Papp Stock LRPSX	G	▦	14.63	-1.45	-1.45	4.38	9.29	—	0.9	0.74	0.81	—	61	40	—	6(-17)	★★★★	3.5
PIMCo Adv Growth C PGWCX	G	▦	20.01	-0.75	-0.75	3.79	9.73	15.27	0.0	1.02	0.91	0.89	68	33	13	6(-13)	★★★★	4.4
T. Rowe Price Intl Stock PRITX	WF	▦	11.32	-0.76	-0.76	10.31	7.22	18.00	1.0	1.04	1.05	0.90	35	30	6	8(-19)	★★★★	4.4
T. Rowe Price New Era PRNEX	SN	▦	20.15	5.17	5.17	7.38	5.33	11.61	1.8	0.64	0.77	0.83	45	22	14	3(-15)	★★★	3.2
Putnam Global Growth A PEQUX	WW	▦	9.22	-0.85	-0.85	9.43	7.01	16.60	0.4	0.86	0.89	0.80	34	25	6	8(-18)	★★★★	4.2
Quantitative Growth & Inc Ord USBOX	GI	▦	12.62	-0.66	-0.66	5.72	8.38	—	1.2	0.72	0.79	—	56	37	—	5(-14)	★★★	4.0
Quest for Value A QFVFX	G	▦	11.20	0.85	0.85	8.22	9.41	12.18	0.7	0.73	0.80	0.78	29	37	63	6(-17)	★★★	3.7
Reich & Tang Equity RCHTX	G	▦	15.39	1.69	1.69	10.63	9.43	—	1.4	0.47	0.72	—	15	36	—	5(-16)	★★★★	3.5
Royce Equity-Income RYEQX	EI	▦	5.12	-3.26	-3.26	9.30	7.57	—	3.5	0.38	0.59	—	17	39	—	3(-19)	★★★	4.0
Safeco Equity SAFQX	GI	▦	13.68	**9.94**	**9.94**	16.29	12.96	16.16	1.9	0.86	0.97	0.95	2	2	1	8(-17)	★★★★★	3.5
Salomon Bros Opportunity SAOPX	G	▦	28.39	0.82	0.82	9.00	7.28	12.09	1.2	0.68	0.91	0.84	24	72	65	7(-19)	★★★	4.0
Schafer Value SCHVX	G	▦	33.23	-4.28	-4.28	12.09	12.28	—	1.0	0.72	0.93	—	10	12	—	9(-21)	★★★★	3.9
Scudder Global SCOBX	WW	▦	23.33	-4.20	-4.20	9.50	7.55	—	0.5	0.64	0.73	—	30	22	—	5(-14)	★★★	4.2
Scudder International SCINX	WF	▦	40.37	-2.99	-2.99	8.84	5.59	16.19	0.0	0.98	1.06	0.90	45	44	43	8(-18)	★★★★	4.1
Selected American SLASX	GI	▦	13.09	-3.26	-3.26	2.59	8.70	13.29	1.6	1.04	1.03	0.90	85	32	28	7(-19)	★★★	4.1
Sentinel Common Stock SENCX	GI	▦	27.38	-1.24	-1.24	4.53	7.76	12.93	2.9	0.75	0.75	0.85	70	54	35	5(-12)	★★★	4.0
Smith Barney Appreciation A SHAPX	G	▦	10.15	-0.77	-0.77	4.48	7.62	13.81	1.7	0.68	0.71	0.76	61	66	30	4(-11)	★★★	4.2
Sound Shore SSHFX	G	▦	15.46	0.30	0.30	10.81	9.96	—	1.3	0.54	0.76	—	14	30	—	5(-19)	★★★★	3.6
SteinRoe Prime Equities SRPEX	GI	▦	13.78	-0.14	-0.14	7.43	10.04	—	1.3	0.65	0.69	—	26	13	—	4(-13)	★★★★	3.9
SteinRoe Special SRSPX	G	▦	21.72	-3.35	-3.35	9.90	10.88	15.70	0.6	0.73	0.85	0.91	19	21	9	6(-17)	★★★★	4.6
Strong Opportunity SOPFX	G	▦	27.71	3.18	3.18	13.63	11.38	—	0.5	0.69	0.77	—	6	17	—	5(-13)	★★★★	3.6
Templeton Foreign TEMFX	WF	▦	8.82	0.35	0.35	11.18	9.53	17.73	1.7	0.83	0.76	0.67	30	14	12	3(-14)	★★★★	4.5
Templeton Real Estate Securities TEMRX	S	▦	12.49	-7.70	-7.70	8.53	8.35	—	1.7	0.74	0.80	—	59	61	—	5(-19)	★★★	3.3
Templeton Smaller Company Growth TEMGX	WW	▦	7.43	-4.59	-4.59	9.26	8.95	12.33	1.4	0.81	0.89	0.88	37	11	68	7(-22)	★★★	3.2
Third Avenue Value TAVFX	G	▦	16.97	-1.46	-1.46	13.91	—	—	1.5	0.53	—	—	6	—	—	(—)	★★★★★	4.3
20th Century Heritage Investors TWHIX	G	▦	9.35	-6.32	-6.32	7.51	8.95	—	0.3	1.11	1.05	—	35	46	—	9(-18)	★★★	3.7
United Income UNCMX	EI	▦	23.34	-1.80	-1.80	8.07	9.12	15.30	1.5	0.67	0.84	0.86	32	20	6	7(-18)	★★★★	4.1
Vanguard Index Extended Market VEXMX	SC	▦	18.52	-1.76	-1.76	8.15	9.07	—	1.5	0.86	0.96	—	57	71	—	8(-20)	★★★	3.0
Vanguard Index 500 VFINX	GI	▦	42.97	1.18	1.18	6.10	8.50	14.05	2.7	0.74	0.80	0.86	46	35	14	6(-14)	★★★★	4.0
Vanguard Special Energy VGENX	SN	▦	14.29	-1.63	-1.63	9.71	5.49	12.02	1.7	1.28	1.15	1.05	20	16	1	4(-12)	★★	3.5
Vanguard Special Health Care VGHCX	SH	▦	35.47	9.54	9.54	6.43	15.55	**20.00**	1.5	1.16	0.90	0.89	18	30	40	4(-11)	★★★★★	4.7
Vanguard U.S. Growth VWUSX	G	▦	15.33	3.88	3.88	1.71	10.06	12.83	1.2	0.84	0.86	0.93	82	29	52	5(-16)	★★★	3.2
Vanguard/Windsor II VWNFX	GI	▦	15.82	-1.17	-1.17	7.94	7.81	—	3.4	0.69	0.83	—	22	52	—	5(-15)	★★★	3.7
Vista Growth & Income A VGRIX	GI	▦	29.09	-3.41	-3.41	7.90	14.89	—	1.8	0.67	0.75	—	22	1	—	4(-14)	★★★★	4.9
Warburg Pincus Captl Appr Comm CUCAX	G	▦	12.66	-2.74	-2.74	6.64	7.68	—	0.1	0.88	0.89	—	43	65	—	7(-14)	★★★	3.3
Warburg Pincus Growth & Income RBEGX	GI	▦	13.64	7.57	7.57	17.18	13.60	—	0.8	0.63	0.65	—	1	2	—	2 (-9)	★★★★★	4.1

Bold numbers indicate *highest* return for the listed time period in each category.

Concentration Yields Success

Few are the victors in the aggressive group this year.

Through the end of December, only about one fifth of all funds in the aggressive group—those with Morningstar risk scores of 1.00 or higher—beat the S&P 500's 1.3% total return, but twice that number have lost 3.0% or more. The difference between the two wasn't explained by levels of risk, however. Some of the riskiest, most-concentrated funds came out ahead.

Fidelity Select Health Care led the way with a mind-blowing 21.4% gain. The death of health-care reform earlier this fall gave the fund a lift, as did its sizable stake in American Cyanamid—recently taken over by American Home Products. Shareholders earned those gains, though: The fund's extremely concentrated portfolio sent it spiraling to a 7% loss in the first quarter.

Small-cap wunderkind **Kaufmann** has also delivered this year. The fund's very small ($471 million) median market cap, its high multiples, and its large sector overweightings were a painful mix in the first and second quarters. When technology stocks rebounded in the third, though, this fund came roaring back with a near 12.5% gain.

Making big bets in the U.S. market wasn't the only profitable strategy this year. While funds that homed in on emerging markets got clobbered, those that favored Japan rose to prominence in the international crowd. Aided by the yen's strong gains, the Japanese market rallied, lifting the **Japan Fund** to a 10% gain through the month of December.

Daniel O'Keefe

Growth of $10,000
■ Aggressive Category ($000)
— Russell 2000 ($000)

Net Assets ($bil)

	1983	1984	1985	1986	1987	1988	1989	1990	1991	1992	1993	1994	History
	43.06	0.24	59.44	77.55	38.73	58.57	64.53	24.32	96.59	33.38	93.36	21.43	High
	22.57	-9.23	30.22	21.25	2.53	15.98	32.52	-4.68	55.18	8.51	25.88	-2.17	Total Return %
	6.43	-25.00	-13.55	-25.73	-37.16	-14.19	-2.80	-30.77	3.11	-19.41	-5.87	-35.33	Low
	0.11	-15.49	-1.52	2.57	-2.73	-0.63	0.84	-1.57	24.70	0.90	15.83	-3.49	+/- S&P 500
	-6.56	-1.93	-0.83	15.57	11.30	-8.92	16.28	14.83	9.13	-9.90	6.98	-0.35	+/- Russell 2000
	1.06	0.96	0.86	0.88	0.74	0.92	1.04	0.89	0.64	0.56	0.43	0.58	Income Return %
	20.25	-10.1	27.03	15.94	1.23	15.08	30.97	-5.31	50.98	7.95	25.45	-2.76	Capital Return %
	0.12	0.09	0.07	0.10	0.15	0.11	0.13	0.11	0.08	0.15	0.11	0.20	Income $
	1.54	1.54	1.67	2.00	1.72	1.82	1.75	1.78	1.63	1.47	1.40	1.25	Expense Ratio
	0.75	0.90	0.95	0.00	-0.11	0.55	0.61	0.55	0.15	0.51	-0.12	0.05	Income Ratio
	100.7	116.0	106.5	122.0	154.2	143.4	138.6	141.7	149.7	136.2	110.3	113.4	Turnover Ratio
	2.92	2.71	3.30	4.26	4.58	4.67	6.47	7.59	18.62	27.98	44.82	53.46	Total Net Assets ($bil)

Style Box Analysis

Number of Funds	Value	Blend	Growth
	1	2	8
	0	5	16
	5	3	10

1 Yr Total Return %

	Value	Blend	Growth
	-3.05	-0.37	-1.62
	NMF	-0.97	-3.17
	3.33	-6.59	-3.33

5 Yr Total Return %

	Value	Blend	Growth
	3.95	7.27	13.93
	NMF	9.44	14.92
	17.78	13.15	14.60

Average Mstar Risk

	Value	Blend	Growth
	1.19	1.13	1.19
	NMF	1.23	1.24
	0.88	1.31	1.28

1.00 = Equity Average

Risk Analysis

	Load-Adj Return	Morningstar[1] Return	Risk	Morningstar Risk-Adj Rating
1 Yr	-4.01			
3 Yr	8.89	1.73[2]	1.25	★★★
5 Yr	13.26	2.46[2]	1.22	★★★★
10 Yr	15.50	1.77	1.25	★★★★

[1]1.00=Equity Average [2]1.00=90-day T-bill return

Other Measures

				Standard Index S&P 500
Standard Deviation	14.67	Alpha		3.93
Mean	10.11	Beta		1.00
Sharpe Ratio	0.45	R-Squared		34.49

Performance 12-31-94

	Total Return%	+/- S&P	+/- Russ 2000
3 Mo	-1.08	-1.06	0.79
6 Mo	7.01	2.15	2.07
1 Yr	-2.17	-3.49	-0.35
3 Yr Average	9.53	3.27	-1.86
5 Yr Average	13.66	4.97	3.46
10 Yr Average	15.75	1.37	4.21
15 Yr Average	13.76	-0.72	0.70

Portfolio

Amount 000	Total Equity: 3305 Total Fixed-Income: 112	Value $000	% Net Assets
14792	Oracle Systems	635761	1.25
9462	Motorola	510416	1.00
8212	Microsoft	470244	0.92
12400	Compaq Computer	426350	0.84
8426	3Com	341883	0.67
10801	DSC Communications	339683	0.67
6544	United HealthCare	337545	0.66
6895	Sybase	320494	0.63
5892	AT & T	314980	0.62
6623	Applied Materials	311403	0.61
5594	Amgen	303231	0.60
350	BBC Brown Boveri (Reg)	301280	0.59
6735	Home Depot	290837	0.57
5460	Johnson & Johnson	282479	0.56
13410	Nomura Securities	275077	0.54
3877	IBM	272261	0.54
12750	Toyota Motor	262901	0.52
5387	Cabletron Systems	259553	0.51
6289	Columbia/HCA Healthcare	254061	0.50
7285	Philips Electronics	222336	0.44

Worst Three Months

	Worst 3 Month Performance 1990-1994
Delaware Trend A	-32.67
FPA Capital	-32.19
T. Rowe Price Science & Tech	-29.53
Columbia Special	-29.30
PBHG Growth	-29.05

Composition %

Cash	9.40	Preferreds	0.22
Stocks	88.44	Convertibles	0.41
Bonds	1.12	Other	0.43

Tax Analysis

	Tax-Adj Hist Return %	% Pretax Return
3 Yr Avg	9.28	83.63
5 Yr Avg	12.30	86.66
10 Yr Avg	14.21	85.11

Sector Weightings

	% of Stocks	Rel S&P500
Utilities	2.4	0.19
Energy	3.0	0.29
Financials	10.8	1.03
Industrial Cyclicals	13.4	0.82
Consumer Durables	7.7	1.24
Consumer Staples	2.4	0.19
Services	14.8	1.82
Retail	8.0	1.37
Health	11.2	1.29
Technology	26.3	2.87

Category Leaders

Lowest 3 Yr Morningstar Risk		Top Rated Funds		Best 3 Yr Return %	
Royce Premier	0.25	PBHG Growth	5.99	Crabbe Huson Special	26.10
Invesco Strat Leisure	0.76	Crabbe Huson Special	5.90	PBHG Growth	25.42
20th Century Intl Equity	0.89	T. Rowe Price Science & Tech	5.11	Newport Tiger	23.49
Babson Enterprise II	0.90	T. Rowe Price New Asia	4.04	T. Rowe Price Science & Tech	19.55
Columbia Special	0.91	Newport Tiger	3.70	GAM International	18.53
Vista Capital Growth A	0.91	Kaufmann	3.62	T. Rowe Price New Asia	17.15
Vanguard Intl Growth	0.97	Royce Premier	3.55	Invesco Strat Leisure	16.75
Meridian	1.01	Invesco Strat Leisure	3.36	FPA Capital	16.14
GAM International	1.02	Invesco Strat Technology	3.21	Vanguard Spec Gold&Prec Mets	13.80
Fidelity Growth Company	1.02	Brandywine	2.97	Templeton Developing Markets	12.91

Stock Funds—Aggressive

Fund / Ticker	Obj	Style Box	NAV	Total Return % through 12-31-94		Annualized			Trailing 12 Mo Yield %	Morningstar Risk 1.00=Equity Average			Rtn % Rank Obj			Bear Mkt Indicator (Worst 3 mo)	Star Rating	Avg Star Rating
				YTD	1Yr	3Yr	5Yr	10Yr		3Yr	5Yr	10Yr	3Yr	5Yr	10Yr			
S&P 500 Index				1.31	1.31	6.27	8.69	14.38										
ABT Emerging Growth ABEGX	AG		13.44	-9.31	-9.31	6.79	15.56	15.71	0.0	1.56	1.34	1.45	44	20	25	9(-20)	★★★	2.8
AIM Constellation CSTGX	AG		17.19	1.30	1.30	10.98	17.44	19.82	0.0	1.22	1.24	1.35	20	11	1	10(-26)	★★★★★	3.6
Alger Small Capitalization ALSCX	SC		22.43	-4.62	-4.62	3.82	13.03	—	0.0	1.67	1.41	—	87	34	—	10(-22)	★★★	4.5
American Heritage AHERX	AG		0.85	-35.33	-35.33	2.82	8.15	-2.68	NMF	1.71	1.42	1.65	75	72	96	8(-29)	★★	1.3
Babson Enterprise II BAETX	SC		16.19	-7.39	-7.39	9.15	—	—	0.1	0.90	—	—	48	—	—	—(—)	★★★★	3.8
Berger 100 BEONX	G		15.69	-6.66	-6.66	7.08	16.95	19.14	0.0	1.41	1.24	1.18	39	2	2	9(-21)	★★★★★	3.2
Brandywine BRWIX	G		23.50	0.02	0.02	12.35	16.31	—	0.0	1.18	1.12	—	9	4	—	8(-19)	★★★★★	4.2
Columbia Special CLSPX	SC		18.69	2.26	2.26	12.26	13.28	—	0.4	0.91	1.23	—	27	30	—	10(-29)	★★★★	4.4
Crabbe Huson Special CHSPX	G		13.34	11.72	11.72	**26.10**	19.48	—	0.3	1.03	1.03	—	1	1	—	7(-16)	★★★★★	4.1
Delaware Trend A DELTX	AG		11.75	-9.97	-9.97	10.48	12.15	15.39	0.0	1.25	1.38	1.40	24	37	37	10(-33)	★★★	2.8
Fidelity Emerging Growth FDEGX	AG		16.99	-0.18	-0.18	9.04	—	—	0.0	1.25	—	—	40	—	—	—(—)	★★★	3.4
Fidelity Growth Company FDGRX	G		27.26	-2.23	-2.23	7.04	13.51	17.02	0.8	1.02	1.03	1.09	39	9	6	9(-21)	★★★★	3.7
Fidelity Select Health Care FSPHX	SH		70.80	**21.43**	**21.43**	0.89	18.58	**21.53**	0.8	1.63	1.11	1.13	45	1	1	3(-17)	★★★★	4.1
Founders Frontier FOUNX	SC		26.50	-2.81	-2.81	7.25	11.26	—	0.0	1.22	1.21	—	65	54	—	10(-18)	★★★★	4.5
Founders Special FRSPX	AG		7.01	-4.90	-4.90	6.12	11.87	14.80	0.0	1.33	1.20	1.17	51	41	40	10(-18)	★★★★	3.4
FPA Capital FPPTX	SC		20.61	10.37	10.37	16.14	17.31	18.14	0.2	1.08	1.35	1.27	10	12	2	10(-32)	★★★★★	3.0
GAM International GAMNX	WF		172.06	-10.22	-10.22	18.53	12.27	—	3.1	1.02	0.91	—	1	1	—	2(-13)	★★★★	4.0
Hancock Emerging Growth B TSEGX	SC		25.16	-1.49	-1.49	7.29	14.16	—	0.0	1.39	1.33	—	64	26	—	10(-23)	★★★★	4.3
Harbor Capital Appreciation HACAX	G		16.71	3.37	3.37	8.43	14.14	—	0.2	1.11	1.09	—	27	7	—	8(-21)	★★★★	4.1
Invesco European FEURX	WE		12.29	-3.05	-3.05	3.72	3.95	—	1.3	1.30	1.12	—	62	45	—	5(-15)	★★	2.4
Invesco Strategic Leisure FLISX	S		21.21	-4.98	-4.98	16.75	16.69	19.88	0.0	0.76	0.98	1.05	13	1	1	9(-25)	★★★★★	4.4
Invesco Strategic Technology FTCHX	ST		24.04	5.27	5.27	12.89	**22.54**	18.90	0.0	1.40	1.30	1.42	64	18	9	10(-29)	★★★★★	3.4
Japan SJPNX	WP		10.51	10.03	10.03	4.24	-0.47	15.64	0.0	1.94	1.92	1.35	81	69	50	10(-22)	★★★	3.9
Kaufmann KAUFX	AG		3.76	8.99	8.99	12.76	19.28	—	0.0	1.21	1.17	—	10	6	—	9(-28)	★★★★★	4.4
Kemper Growth A KGRAX	G		12.68	-5.91	-5.91	-2.00	10.28	13.66	0.0	1.38	1.07	1.03	96	27	34	5(-15)	★★★	3.4
Keystone Amer Omega A OMGAX	AG		15.54	-5.66	-5.66	5.40	12.05	15.71	0.0	1.12	1.08	1.07	59	39	29	9(-16)	★★★★	3.0
Loomis Sayles Small Cap LSSCX	SC		12.85	-8.31	-8.31	8.95	—	—	0.0	1.23	—	—	51	—	—	—(—)	★★★	4.1
MainStay Capital Appreciation B MCSCX	G		19.11	-1.52	-1.52	7.62	16.92	—	0.0	1.39	1.17	—	34	3	—	6(-12)	★★★★	3.5
Meridian MERDX	SC		25.12	0.55	0.55	9.51	16.59	14.95	0.7	1.01	0.93	1.11	44	17	23	6(-18)	★★★★	3.3
Newport Tiger NWTRX	WP		10.80	-11.99	-11.99	23.49	15.03	—	0.3	1.30	1.21	—	4	1	—	9(-24)	★★★★	3.8
Oppenheimer Discovery A OPOCX	SC		33.37	-11.18	-11.18	6.88	12.30	—	0.0	1.52	1.31	—	68	42	—	9(-17)	★★★	4.0
Pasadena Growth A PASGX	G		15.40	-3.75	-3.75	-2.52	8.22	—	0.0	1.29	1.26	—	97	58	—	10(-25)	★★	3.8
PBHG Growth PBHGX	SC		15.91	4.75	4.75	25.42	21.98	—	0.0	1.41	1.46	—	1	2	—	10(-29)	★★★★★	3.6
T. Rowe Price New America Growth PRWAX	G		25.42	-7.43	-7.43	6.11	11.17	—	0.0	1.22	1.19	—	48	18	—	10(-25)	★★★★	3.4
T. Rowe Price New Asia PRASX	WP		8.01	-19.15	-19.15	17.15	—	—	0.8	1.41	—	—	22	—	—	—(—)	★★★★★	4.7
T. Rowe Price Science & Tech PRSCX	ST		21.64	15.79	15.79	19.55	21.98	—	0.0	1.31	1.41	—	35	31	—	10(-30)	★★★★★	4.9
Putnam Voyager A PVOYX	AG		11.52	0.44	0.44	9.28	13.77	18.06	0.0	1.04	1.08	1.08	38	27	11	10(-20)	★★★★	3.8
Royce Premier RYPRX	SC		6.48	3.28	3.28	12.49	—	—	0.8	0.25	—	—	27	—	—	—(—)	★★★★★	5.0
Sit Growth NBNGX	G		11.51	-0.47	-0.47	1.88	11.38	15.37	0.0	1.39	1.18	1.16	81	16	12	8(-18)	★★★★	3.3
Strong Discovery STDIX	AG		15.67	-5.68	-5.68	5.52	13.88	—	4.2	1.20	1.00	—	57	25	—	5(-10)	★★★★	4.4
Templeton Developing Markets TEDMX	WF		13.42	-8.58	-8.58	12.91	—	—	0.9	1.02	—	—	15	—	—	—(—)	★★★★	4.0
20th Century Growth Investors TWCGX	G		18.74	-1.49	-1.49	-0.73	9.72	15.46	0.2	1.32	1.17	1.23	92	33	11	8(-19)	★★★	3.8
20th Century Intl Equity TWIEX	WF		6.96	-4.76	-4.76	12.51	—	—	0.0	0.89	—	—	18	—	—	—(—)	★★★★	4.8
20th Century Ultra Investors TWCUX	AG		19.95	-3.62	-3.62	5.94	19.38	18.78	0.0	1.67	1.43	1.52	53	4	3	9(-16)	★★★★	3.2
Value Line Leveraged Growth Inv VALLX	AG		23.18	-3.71	-3.71	2.96	9.45	13.54	0.5	1.31	1.11	1.10	73	58	59	7(-16)	★★★	3.3
Vanguard Intl Growth VWIGX	WF		13.43	0.76	0.76	11.17	4.83	17.17	1.3	0.97	1.16	0.97	31	54	25	8(-18)	★★★★	4.3
Vanguard Special Gold & Prec Met VGPMX	SP		12.72	-5.42	-5.42	13.80	4.27	10.54	2.4	1.89	1.70	1.75	31	7	7	1(-21)	★★	2.0
Vista Capital Growth A VCAGX	G		30.53	-1.31	-1.31	10.24	16.55	—	0.3	0.91	0.99	—	17	4	—	6(-19)	★★★★★	5.0
Warburg Pincus Emerging Gr Comm CUEGX	SC		21.99	-1.43	-1.43	9.29	12.92	—	0.0	1.20	1.18	—	47	35	—	9(-19)	★★★★	3.6
Wasatch Aggressive Equity WAAEX	AG		19.06	5.50	5.50	10.88	17.21	—	0.0	1.13	1.14	—	22	13	—	10(-25)	★★★★★	3.7

Bold numbers indicate *highest* return for the listed time period in each category.

	Funds in Category	Yield	SEC Yield	Assets ($bil)
	50	3.28%	3.64%	104.76

What Conservative Landslide?

In 1994, it was better to be a conservative Congressman than it was to be a conservative investor. Although the typical conservative fund slightly outperformed the typical aggressive fund, it lagged well behind the averages for core funds and rookies, as well as the S&P 500 index.

Nearly all conservative funds have a taste for income, and most like to play with blue chips. This has led to over-weightings in some painfully rate-sensitive sectors. The worst sector by far in 1994 were utilities. For example, the group's most ailing member, **Stratton Monthly Dividend**, which lost 12.1% by year-end, held a weighty 75% utilities stake.

The group's top 20 performers, on the other hand, held utilities to a weighting of less than 9%. The funds in this group favored either financials, industrial cyclicals, or a little of both. Like utilities, financials suffered from rate hikes, but the sector also offered attractive opportunities in mergers and acquisitions that funds such as the aptly named **Merger** were able to grab. Industrial cyclicals were the most robust of the conservative group's top three sectors, but only one fund, **FPA Paramount**, put more than half of its equity assets into those companies. That fund's fat cyclical stake wasn't the only factor contributing to its double-digit return; small- and mid-cap issues led the market in 1994, and FPA Paramount has kept one of the lowest median market caps in the group.

The disappointing showing of the conservative group in 1994 serves as a lesson: Low risk does not a bear-market performer make.

Pat Regnier

Growth of $10,000
- ■ Conservative Category ($000)
- — Wil Large Value ($000)

Net Assets ($bil)

	1983	1984	1985	1986	1987	1988	1989	1990	1991	1992	1993	1994	History
	40.50	38.72	34.55	32.64	21.91	31.12	49.67	10.32	46.28	22.92	32.70	9.40	High
	23.75	9.44	27.10	17.92	2.79	17.96	23.37	-2.87	24.52	9.96	14.21	-1.31	**Total Return %**
	11.87	-1.94	15.89	4.42	-11.40	6.95	10.55	-14.02	13.33	-2.73	-3.50	-12.13	Low
	1.29	3.17	-4.64	-0.76	-2.47	1.35	-8.32	0.25	-5.97	2.34	4.15	-2.63	+/- S&P 500
	-1.65	-21.11	-3.12	-4.30	-0.80	-4.84	-1.78	4.72	-1.12	-4.43	0.75	3.03	+/- Wil Large Value
	4.61	5.22	5.52	4.12	4.28	4.77	5.24	4.58	4.45	3.41	2.92	3.16	Income Return %
	17.46	4.59	21.13	12.49	-1.84	13.05	17.79	-7.44	20.07	6.55	11.28	-4.47	Capital Return %
	0.59	0.59	0.68	0.63	0.66	0.64	0.79	0.76	0.63	0.57	0.52	0.59	Income $
	1.17	1.08	1.02	0.98	0.96	1.03	1.04	1.06	1.05	1.03	1.00	0.97	Expense Ratio
	5.13	5.39	5.18	4.31	3.85	4.35	4.60	4.50	4.04	3.38	2.91	3.28	Income Ratio
	72.64	74.49	76.76	80.58	98.55	71.06	67.80	69.99	65.15	59.20	53.16	46.14	Turnover Ratio
	9.68	11.64	16.54	25.55	28.88	33.51	44.60	44.17	61.71	80.90	104.16	104.76	Total Net Assets ($bil)

Style Box Analysis

Number of Funds

	Value	Blend	Growth	
	12	12	0	Large
	12	8	1	Med
	4	1	0	Small

1 Yr Total Return %

	Value	Blend	Growth	
	-1.15	-1.23	NMF	Large
	-3.30	0.15	-0.17	Med
	0.54	-0.66	NMF	Small

5 Yr Total Return %

	Value	Blend	Growth	
	8.40	7.81	NMF	Large
	8.15	8.95	9.23	Med
	8.61	8.00	NMF	Small

Average Mstar Risk

	Value	Blend	Growth	
	0.67	0.60	NMF	Large
	0.62	0.65	0.60	Med
	0.48	0.59	NMF	Small

1.00 = Equity Average

Risk Analysis

	Load-Adj Return	Morningstar[1] Return	Morningstar Risk	Morningstar Risk-Adj Rating
1 Yr	-3.60			
3 Yr	6.52	0.92[2]	0.60	★★★
5 Yr	7.82	0.78[2]	0.62	★★★
10 Yr	12.37	0.97	0.64	★★★★

[1]1.00=Equity Average [2]1.00=90-day T-bill return

Other Measures

			Standard Index S&P 500
Standard Deviation	7.20	Alpha	1.78
Mean	7.33	Beta	0.72
Sharpe Ratio	0.55	R-Squared	66.07

Performance 12-31-94

	Total Return%	+/- S&P	+/- Wil Lg Val
3 Mo	-1.62	-1.61	-1.17
6 Mo	2.23	-2.63	1.47
1 Yr	-1.31	-2.63	3.03
3 Yr Average	7.34	1.08	-0.13
5 Yr Average	8.31	-0.38	0.72
10 Yr Average	12.66	-1.72	-1.17
15 Yr Average	13.97	-0.51	-2.08

Portfolio

Amount 000	Total Equity: 2474 / Total Fixed-Income: 1128	Value $000	% Net Assets
20604	Philip Morris	1189242	1.13
36670	GTE	1133652	1.08
8408	Royal Dutch Petroleum	913565	0.87
8717	Xerox	890692	0.84
15071	El duPont de Nemours	882818	0.84
17282	General Electric	850312	0.81
14169	AT & T	762685	0.72
12378	Amoco	760936	0.72
19828	US West	760780	0.72
9932	Warner-Lambert	753553	0.71
11606	American Home Products	722297	0.69
24686	American Express	714854	0.68
19869	Merck	708542	0.67
11387	Eli Lilly	702884	0.67
9982	IBM	698802	0.66
11979	Bristol-Myers Squibb	692442	0.66
16244	Ameritech	655725	0.62
10190	United Technologies	640372	0.61
8076	FNMA	633629	0.60
14413	BankAmerica	629361	0.60

Composition %

Cash	9.52	Preferred	1.11
Stocks	77.04	Convertibles	4.79
Bonds	7.46	Other	0.09

Tax Analysis

	Tax-Adj Hist Return %	% Pretax Return
3 Yr Avg	5.42	66.54
5 Yr Avg	6.08	72.20
10 Yr Avg	9.62	75.52

Sector Weightings

	% of Stocks	Rel S&P500
Utilities	18.8	1.52
Energy	8.2	0.81
Financials	21.1	1.99
Industrial Cyclicals	13.9	0.85
Consumer Durables	5.5	0.88
Consumer Staples	6.2	0.50
Services	10.1	1.24
Retail	4.1	0.70
Health	7.0	0.80
Technology	5.2	0.57

Worst Three Months

	Worst 3 Month Performance 1990-1994
Pennsylvania Mutual	-19.80
Templeton Growth	-18.89
Vanguard Equity-Income	-16.52
Fidelity Equity-Income	-16.15
Lindner	-15.22

Category Leaders

Lowest 3 Yr Morningstar Risk

Merger	0.22
Greenspring	0.28
Gateway Index Plus	0.29
T. Rowe Price Capital Apprec	0.31
Mutual Beacon	0.37
Analytic Optioned Equity	0.42
Mutual Qualified	0.42
Mutual Benefit	0.42
Mutual Shares	0.46
T. Rowe Price Equity-Income	0.47

Top Rated Funds

Mutual Beacon	2.72
Mutual Qualified	2.66
Mutual Shares	2.43
Merger	2.21
T. Rowe Price Equity-Income	2.16
Gabelli Asset	2.11
T. Rowe Price Capital Apprec	2.05
FPA Paramount	1.99
Greenspring	1.84
Scudder Growth & Income	1.75

Best 3 Yr Return %

Mutual Beacon	16.86
Mutual Qualified	16.76
Mutual Shares	15.35
FPA Paramount	13.16
Gabelli Asset	11.80
Fidelity Equity-Income	11.72
Templeton Growth	11.71
Greenspring	11.19
T. Rowe Price Equity-Income	11.07
Lindner	10.31

Stock Funds—Conservative

Fund / Ticker	Obj	Style Box	NAV	Total Return % through 12-31-94		Annualized			Trailing 12 Mo Yield %	Morningstar Risk 1.00=Equity Average			Rtn % Rank Obj			Bear Mkt Indicator (Worst 3 mo)	Star Rating	Avg Star Rating
				YTD	1Yr	3Yr	5Yr	10Yr		3Yr	5Yr	10Yr	3Yr	5Yr	10Yr			
S&P 500 Index				1.31	1.31	6.27	8.69	14.38										
American Mutual AMRMX	GI		20.11	0.34	0.34	7.33	8.17	12.97	4.0	0.58	0.61	0.64	27	45	34	3 (-9)	★★★★	4.0
Analytic Optioned Equity ANALX	GI		11.12	2.47	2.47	5.10	5.96	9.36	2.8	0.42	0.49	0.51	64	86	92	2 (-8)	★★★	3.1
Burnham A BURHX	GI		19.88	-1.77	-1.77	4.98	6.04	12.20	4.3	0.58	0.52	0.53	66	85	51	2 (-5)	★★★★	3.9
Capital Income Builder CAIBX	EI		31.72	-2.26	-2.26	7.42	10.11	—	5.3	0.59	0.52	—	47	9	—	2 (-7)	★★★★	3.9
Colonial A COLFX	GI		7.34	-2.10	-2.10	8.17	8.06	12.62	2.3	0.64	0.72	0.69	20	47	43	5(-14)	★★★	3.9
Dreyfus DREVX	GI		11.93	-4.26	-4.26	2.43	5.87	10.95	1.7	0.81	0.76	0.68	86	86	76	4(-13)	★★★	3.4
Dreyfus Global Growth DSWIX	WW		32.99	-7.28	-7.28	3.15	6.41	—	0.0	0.83	0.51	—	86	40	—	1 (-8)	★★★	3.9
Evergreen Total Return EVTRX	EI		17.03	-6.42	-6.42	5.15	6.03	10.04	6.3	0.63	0.67	0.65	69	74	68	3(-11)	★★★	4.0
Fidelity Advisor Strat Opp A FASPX	G		18.71	-7.12	-7.12	8.08	7.60	—	1.9	0.66	0.67	—	30	67	—	3 (-8)	★★★	3.7
Fidelity Equity-Income FEQIX	EI		30.70	0.24	0.24	11.72	9.18	12.50	3.0	0.57	0.76	0.74	4	18	25	6(-16)	★★★★	4.1
Fidelity Utilities FIUIX	SU		13.06	-5.29	-5.29	6.69	8.43	—	3.9	0.74	0.59	—	17	10	—	1 (-6)	★★★★	4.3
Flag Investors Telephone Inc A TISHX	SU		12.30	-6.33	-6.33	7.55	7.24	15.40	3.1	0.90	0.80	0.74	7	36	1	3(-11)	★★★★	4.5
Fortress Utility FEUTX	SU		11.72	-7.95	-7.95	4.90	7.97	—	5.4	0.70	0.56	—	50	21	—	2 (-7)	★★★	4.2
FPA Paramount FPRAX	GI		14.41	**9.40**	**9.40**	13.17	**12.85**	15.16	1.6	0.69	0.63	0.65	4	3	3	3 (-9)	★★★★	4.3
FPA Perennial FPPFX	GI		21.97	-0.04	-0.04	5.75	7.76	11.15	2.0	0.55	0.57	0.57	56	55	73	2(-12)	★★★	3.2
Franklin Rising Dividends FRDPX	GI		14.29	-5.17	-5.17	0.34	6.61	—	2.0	0.78	0.70	—	95	79	—	3(-14)	★★	3.6
Franklin Utilities FKUTX	SU		8.47	-11.66	-11.66	2.41	6.01	10.46	6.2	0.89	0.68	0.72	82	63	50	1(-10)	★★	3.6
Gabelli Asset GABAX	G		22.21	-0.17	-0.17	11.80	9.23	—	1.1	0.57	0.63	—	11	41	—	3(-10)	★★★★	4.4
Gateway Index Plus GATEX	GI		15.48	5.57	5.57	6.03	9.15	10.57	1.6	0.29	0.30	0.36	48	20	83	1 (-5)	★★★★	3.3
Greenspring GRSPX	G		13.39	2.88	2.88	11.19	8.93	11.58	3.7	0.28	0.42	0.34	13	46	71	1(-11)	★★★★	4.0
Hancock Sovereign Investors A SOVIX	GI		14.24	-1.85	-1.85	3.62	8.67	12.76	3.2	0.60	0.56	0.66	80	32	39	2(-10)	★★★	3.8
Wayne Hummer Growth WHGRX	G		21.34	-0.90	-0.90	4.14	8.85	12.16	1.4	0.64	0.65	0.82	65	48	64	4(-12)	★★★	3.4
Invesco Industrial Income FIIIX	EI		10.52	-3.88	-3.88	4.24	12.20	**15.53**	3.7	0.72	0.70	0.72	80	1	1	4(-13)	★★★★	4.5
Investment Company of America AIVSX	GI		17.67	0.15	0.15	6.15	8.79	14.37	2.6	0.70	0.69	0.71	45	28	10	4(-11)	★★★★	4.2
Lindner LDNRX	G		20.89	-0.66	-0.66	10.31	8.00	12.26	1.5	0.58	0.66	0.57	17	62	62	4(-15)	★★★★	4.5
Merger MERFX	G.		13.17	7.13	7.13	9.92	9.42	—	0.0	0.22	0.32	—	18	37	—	1(-10)	★★★★	3.4
Merrill Lynch Capital A MACPX	GI		25.70	0.91	0.91	6.42	8.72	13.54	4.2	0.57	0.58	0.59	40	31	23	3 (-9)	★★★★	4.0
Mutual Beacon BEGRX	GI		31.03	5.62	5.62	**16.86**	11.50	15.40	3.3	0.37	0.52	0.49	1	8	2	2(-13)	★★★★★	3.8
Mutual Benefit MUBFX	G		16.67	2.80	2.80	7.30	8.40	14.35	2.0	0.42	0.61	0.68	37	55	22	3(-15)	★★★★	3.8
Mutual Qualified MQIFX	GI		26.67	5.73	5.73	16.76	11.63	15.13	2.8	0.42	0.57	0.51	2	8	4	3(-14)	★★★★★	4.8
Mutual Shares MUTHX	GI		78.69	4.53	4.53	15.35	10.86	14.77	3.0	0.46	0.59	0.52	3	9	8	3(-14)	★★★★★	4.7
Oppenheimer Equity-Income A OPPEX	EI		9.14	-2.79	-2.79	5.96	6.59	11.87	5.2	0.58	0.58	0.59	63	62	31	2 (-9)	★★★	3.9
Pennsylvania Mutual PENNX	SC		7.41	-0.72	-0.72	8.83	8.50	12.06	1.4	0.51	0.67	0.64	53	78	56	4(-20)	★★★★	4.0
Phoenix Growth A PHGRX	G		19.60	-1.60	-1.60	2.31	7.77	13.27	1.4	0.64	0.64	0.71	78	64	41	3 (-9)	★★★	4.4
T. Rowe Price Capital Apprec PRWCX	G		12.10	3.80	3.80	9.50	9.53	—	2.7	0.31	0.47	—	21	35	—	2(-13)	★★★★	4.4
T. Rowe Price Equity-Income PRFDX	EI		15.98	4.53	4.53	11.07	9.86	—	3.5	0.47	0.62	—	8	11	—	3(-14)	★★★★	3.9
Prudential Utility B PRUTX	SU		8.26	-8.51	-8.51	4.78	5.07	13.32	2.8	0.83	0.68	0.72	57	78	25	2 (-8)	★★★	4.5
Putnam Fund for Growth & Inc A PGRWX	GI		12.72	-0.28	-0.28	8.45	9.26	13.88	3.0	0.58	0.62	0.66	18	19	18	3(-11)	★★★★	4.0
Safeco Income SAFIX	EI		16.54	-1.09	-1.09	7.46	6.42	11.16	4.8	0.53	0.67	0.70	43	67	50	3(-13)	★★★	4.0
SBSF SBFFX	GI		13.82	-5.64	-5.64	6.63	7.03	11.40	1.4	0.62	0.62	0.66	35	72	65	3 (-9)	★★★	3.6
Scudder Growth & Income SCDGX	GI		16.27	2.60	2.60	9.12	10.22	14.26	2.9	0.62	0.65	0.70	15	12	12	4(-10)	★★★★	4.0
Smith Barney Income & Growth A SBCIX	GI		12.18	-4.21	-4.21	6.12	6.38	11.53	3.6	0.65	0.71	0.66	46	83	63	4(-13)	★★★	3.8
SteinRoe Total Return SRFBX	EI		24.30	-4.12	-4.12	5.13	8.16	11.04	4.8	0.55	0.57	0.58	71	30	56	3(-11)	★★★	3.2
Stratton Monthly Dividend STMDX	EI		23.78	-12.13	-12.13	1.11	6.07	9.27	8.1	0.89	0.66	0.67	95	72	93	2 (-8)	★★	3.6
Templeton Growth TEPLX	WW		16.23	0.82	0.82	11.71	10.74	14.95	1.7	0.74	0.79	0.77	16	5	25	6(-19)	★★★★	3.8
UMB Stock UMBSX	G		15.01	2.76	2.76	6.79	8.20	11.38	2.4	0.56	0.62	0.72	41	58	74	3(-12)	★★★	3.2
USAA Mutual Income Stock USISX	EI		13.06	-0.70	-0.70	6.09	8.43	—	5.7	0.67	0.64	—	62	27	—	3 (-8)	★★★★	4.2
Vanguard Equity-Income VEIPX	EI		12.77	-1.59	-1.59	7.20	6.35	—	4.5	0.64	0.79	—	49	69	—	5(-17)	★★★	3.0
Washington Mutual Investors AWSHX	GI		16.84	0.49	0.49	7.42	8.04	13.88	3.6	0.65	0.76	0.78	26	47	19	5(-13)	★★★★	4.0
Weitz Value WVALX	G		14.43	-9.82	-9.82	7.14	8.27	—	0.0	0.69	0.67	—	38	56	—	3(-12)	★★★	4.2

Bold numbers indicate *highest* return for the listed time period in each category.

But Can These Rookies Play Ball?

Although funds in the Rookie category performed differently in 1994, one theme united them: potential.

The Rookie list is, by nature, a mixed bag. Pacific funds, such as **Morgan Stanley Asian Growth**, stand beside blue-chip domestic players such as **Vanguard Index Total Stock Market**. Not surprisingly, then, the group yielded disparate 1994 results. **Franklin Global Healthcare** rode that sector's resurgence to a 14.2% gain by year-end. Burgeoning technology stocks drove **Janus Mercury** to double-digit gains, too. Not all rookies fared as well, however. Rising interest rates and deregulation among electric utilities walloped **Vanguard Special Utilities**' utility-laden portfolio and the fallout of the Hong Kong stock market buried **Merrill Lynch Dragon**'s return.

These funds all share one of two common traits. Either they're headed by outstanding managers or they practice off-the-beaten-path strategies. Indeed, the group showcases top-notch investors: Jean-Marie Eveillard, Don Yacktman, Elizabeth Bramwell, Charles Royce, and Mario Gabelli—all of whom have proven their expertise with established funds. Nonconventional approaches also make the rookie list unlike other categories. For instance, rookie **Scudder Latin America** allows investors access to Scudder's highly regarded international talent pool and provides a strictly Latin American focus. Those looking for an uncommon investor might find upstart **Robertson Stephens Contrarian** to their liking.

The funds that fill the rookie ranks may be too untested for some tastes, but given their dynamic potential, they're at least worth watching.

Susan Paluch

Worst Three Months

Worst 3 Month Performance
1990-1994

Category Leaders

Lowest 3 Yr Morningstar Risk   **Top Rated Funds**   **Best 3 Yr Return %**

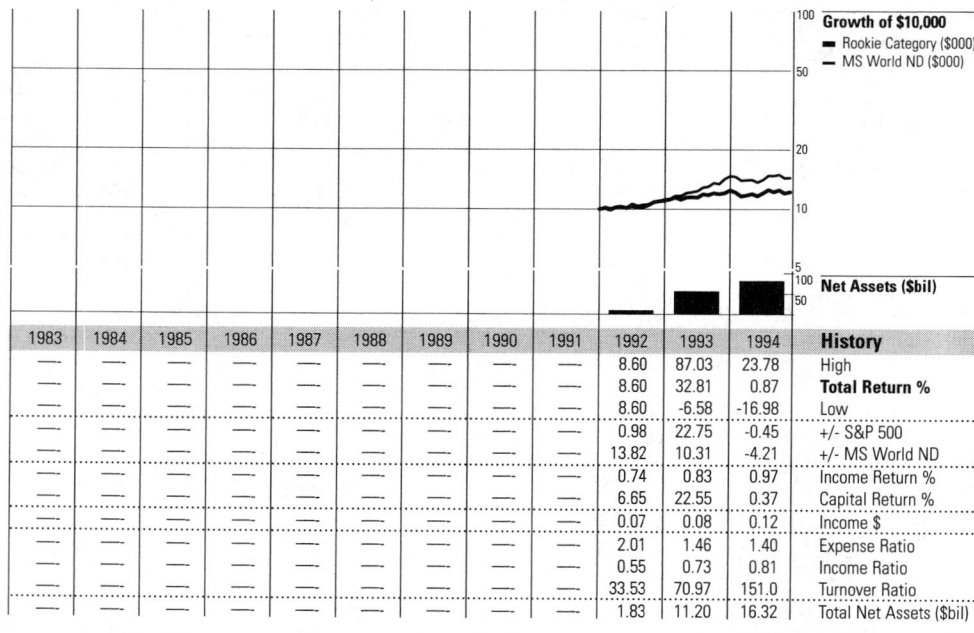

Growth of $10,000
- Rookie Category ($000)
- MS World ND ($000)

Net Assets ($bil)

History	1983	1984	1985	1986	1987	1988	1989	1990	1991	1992	1993	1994
High	—	—	—	—	—	—	—	—	—	8.60	87.03	23.78
Total Return %	—	—	—	—	—	—	—	—	—	8.60	32.81	0.87
Low	—	—	—	—	—	—	—	—	—	8.60	-6.58	-16.98
+/- S&P 500	—	—	—	—	—	—	—	—	—	0.98	22.75	-0.45
+/- MS World ND	—	—	—	—	—	—	—	—	—	13.82	10.31	-4.21
Income Return %	—	—	—	—	—	—	—	—	—	0.74	0.83	0.97
Capital Return %	—	—	—	—	—	—	—	—	—	6.65	22.55	0.37
Income $	—	—	—	—	—	—	—	—	—	0.07	0.08	0.12
Expense Ratio	—	—	—	—	—	—	—	—	—	2.01	1.46	1.40
Income Ratio	—	—	—	—	—	—	—	—	—	0.55	0.73	0.81
Turnover Ratio	—	—	—	—	—	—	—	—	—	33.53	70.97	151.0
Total Net Assets ($bil)	—	—	—	—	—	—	—	—	—	1.83	11.20	16.32

Style Box Analysis

Number of Funds

	Value	Blend	Growth
Large	1	6	3
Med	8	4	13
Small	2	3	7

1 Yr Total Return %

	Value	Blend	Growth
Large	1.22	-0.02	-9.29
Med	-1.11	-1.51	5.35
Small	-0.60	-7.47	6.69

5 Yr Total Return %

	Value	Blend	Growth
Large	NMF	NMF	NMF
Med	NMF	NMF	NMF
Small	NMF	NMF	NMF

Average Mstar Risk

	Value	Blend	Growth
Large	NMF	NMF	NMF
Med	NMF	NMF	NMF
Small	NMF	NMF	NMF

1.00 = Equity Average

Risk Analysis

	Load-Adj Return	Morningstar[1] Return	Risk	Morningstar Risk-Adj Rating
1 Yr	-0.70			
3 Yr	—	—	—	—
5 Yr	—	—	—	—
10 Yr	—	—	—	—

[1]1.00=Equity Average [2]1.00=90-day T-bill return

Other Measures

			Standard Index S&P 500
Standard Deviation	—	Alpha	—
Mean	—	Beta	—
Sharpe Ratio	—	R-Squared	—

Performance 12-31-94

	Total Return%	+/- S&P	+/- MS Wld ND
3 Mo	-2.35	-2.33	-1.62
6 Mo	5.45	0.59	4.05
1 Yr	0.87	-0.45	-4.21
3 Yr Average	—	—	—
5 Yr Average	—	—	—
10 Yr Average	—	—	—
15 Yr Average	—	—	—

Portfolio

Amount 000	Total Equity: 3938 / Total Fixed-Income: 383	Value $000	% Net Assets
1525	Telefonos de Mexico L (ADR)	80370	0.53
499	Nokia Cl K	73701	0.49
57975	US Treasury Bill	57825	0.38
6252	Reckitt & Colman	57069	0.38
986	Motorola	56859	0.38
998	Exide	55928	0.37
1340	Intl Nederlander Groep	55290	0.37
624	Telefonos de Chile (ADR)	54919	0.37
21820	Pioneer International	54144	0.36
1204378	Telebras Pfd	52672	0.35
20894	Saatchi & Saatchi	48713	0.32
5278	Grupo Carso Cl A1	48425	0.32
843	Philip Morris	47118	0.31
1013	Kvaerner	45838	0.30
1255	US West	45069	0.30
45823	GNMA 8%	44287	0.29
10488	Union Electrica Fenosa	44025	0.29
2262	Banco Espirito Santo & Com	43807	0.29
22649	Lion Nathan	43778	0.29
353	Banco Popular Espanol (Reg)	42008	0.28

Composition %

Cash	12.05	Preferreds	1.32
Stocks	79.57	Convertibles	1.42
Bonds	3.85	Other	1.80

Tax Analysis

	Tax-Adj Hist Return %	% Pretax Return
3 Yr Avg	—	—
5 Yr Avg	—	—
10 Yr Avg	—	—

Sector Weightings

	% of Stocks	Rel S&P500
Utilities	8.5	0.69
Energy	4.6	0.45
Financials	14.2	1.35
Industrial Cyclicals	20.3	1.24
Consumer Durables	8.6	1.39
Consumer Staples	6.7	0.53
Services	10.5	1.29
Retail	5.6	0.95
Health	7.7	0.89
Technology	13.3	1.45

Stock Funds—Rookies

Fund / Ticker	Obj	Style Box	NAV	Since Inception	3Mo	6Mo	1Yr	Anticipated Risk Category	Inception Date
S&P 500 Index					-0.02	4.86	1.31		
Blanchard Flexible Income BLFIX	I		4.55	8.49	-0.81	-0.85	-5.54	Hybrid	11/02/92
Bramwell Growth BRGRX	G	▦	10.25	2.59	0.39	—	—	Core	08/01/94
Calvert World Values Glob Eqty A CWVGX	WW	▦	16.14	17.60	-5.54	-3.29	-2.73	Core	07/02/92
Capital World Growth & Income CWGIX	WW	▦	17.47	23.72	-0.30	5.15	1.22	Hybrid	03/26/93
Dreyfus Disciplined Stock Inv	GI	▦	17.31	0.18	-1.98	2.99	—	Core	04/06/94
Fidelity Fifty FFTYX	AG	▦	10.88	10.13	-0.79	8.19	4.00	Core	09/20/93
Fidelity New Millennium FMILX	G	▦	12.11	26.71	-0.63	8.91	0.83	Aggressive	12/28/92
Fidelity Small Cap Stock FDSCX	SC	▦	10.45	5.20	-0.76	6.52	-3.33	Aggressive	06/28/93
Franklin Global Health Care FKGHX	SH	▦	10.99	21.94	-1.03	15.43	14.20	Aggressive	02/14/92
G.T. Global Telecommunications A GTTCX	SU	▦	15.58	40.97	-5.34	2.01	-4.40	Aggressive	01/27/92
Gabelli Equity-Income GABEX	EI	▦	10.72	29.40	-0.69	4.15	1.08	Core	01/02/92
Gabelli Gold GOLDX	SP	▦	11.07	10.70	-10.51	—	—	Aggressive	07/11/94
Govett Emerging Markets GIEMX	WF		13.29	68.21	-16.48	0.15	-12.70	Aggressive	01/07/92
IAI Midcap Growth IAMCX	G	▦	14.05	49.24	2.72	10.52	5.65	Core	04/06/92
Janus Enterprise JAENX	G	▦	22.98	63.44	4.35	16.63	8.92	Aggressive	09/01/92
Janus Mercury JAMRX	G	▦	13.61	38.80	2.43	17.33	15.86	Aggressive	05/03/93
Lindner Bulwark LDNBX	AA	▦	7.45	7.18	4.42	4.64	—	Hybrid	02/11/94
Lindner Utility LDUTX	SU	▦	10.27	-0.39	-2.36	4.68	-0.95	Aggressive	10/04/93
Merrill Lynch Dragon B MBDRX	WP	▦	15.03	57.68	-9.59	0.81	-16.98	Aggressive	05/29/92
Montgomery Emerging Markets MNEMX	WF	▦	13.65	46.81	-10.65	5.10	-7.72	Aggressive	03/01/92
Montgomery Growth MNGFX	G	▦	16.93	43.09	3.34	11.80	20.91	Aggressive	09/30/93
Morgan Stanley Asian Growth A MSAAX	WP	▦	15.26	31.45	-10.68	1.77	-14.18	Aggressive	06/23/93
Oak Hall Equity OHEFX	SC	▦	11.38	34.91	-6.94	-0.64	-11.62	Aggressive	07/13/92
Oakmark International OAKIX	WF	▦	12.41	40.26	-8.19	-2.26	-9.06	Core	09/30/92
PBHG Emerging Growth PBEGX	SC	▦	15.10	64.11	10.91	35.05	23.78	Aggressive	06/15/93
PIMCo Adv Target A PTAAX	G	▦	12.89	31.79	-0.57	10.17	3.86	Core	12/17/92
T. Rowe Price Dividend Growth PRDGX	GI	▦	11.04	21.99	0.53	4.44	2.16	Conservative	12/31/92
T. Rowe Price Mid-Cap Growth RPMGX	G	▦	14.85	57.67	-0.56	6.46	0.29	Core	06/30/92
Quantitative Numeric Ord USBNX	SC	▦	14.92	**73.02**	0.56	13.11	4.31	Core	08/01/92
Robertson Stephens Contrarian RSCOX	AA	▦	10.53	5.68	-4.61	-9.03	-5.53	Hybrid	06/30/93
Robertson Stephens Value + Grth RSVPX	SC	▦	15.88	60.71	5.86	24.07	23.12	Aggressive	05/12/92
Rydex Nova RYNVX	AG		9.99	-0.20	-3.29	2.25	-6.72	Aggressive	07/12/93
Schooner	SC	▦	25.25	3.04	1.76	2.28	0.32	Core	06/24/93
Scudder Latin America SLAFX	WF	▦	18.88	64.50	-22.19	-1.31	-9.41	Aggressive	12/08/92
Seven Seas Growth & Income SSGWX	GI	▦	9.89	1.04	-2.41	3.58	-0.26	Core	09/01/93
Skyline Special Equities II SPEQX	SC	▦	10.14	8.41	-3.92	2.08	-1.52	Aggressive	02/09/93
SoGen Gold SGGDX	SP	▦	11.20	13.24	-9.92	3.51	-0.84	Aggressive	08/31/93
SoGen Overseas SGOVX	WF	▦	11.70	17.71	-2.08	1.73	7.79	Aggressive	08/31/93
SteinRoe Young Investor SRYIX	G	▦	10.66	7.49	4.87	10.71	—	Core	05/02/94
Strong Asia Pacific SASPX	WP	▦	9.35	-5.28	-6.36	-3.73	-5.28	Aggressive	12/31/93
Strong Growth SGROX	G	▦	11.61	17.27	2.38	10.26	17.27	Aggressive	12/31/93
Strong International Stock STISX	WF	▦	12.65	42.22	-3.87	-1.06	-1.56	Aggressive	03/04/92
Tweedy, Browne American Value TWEBX	G	▦	9.82	-1.16	-3.67	0.65	-0.56	Core	12/08/93
Tweedy, Browne Global Value TBGVX	WW	▦	11.88	20.43	-2.09	-1.37	4.36	Aggressive	06/15/93
20th Century Value TWVLX	GI	▦	4.92	7.18	-0.22	4.37	3.99	Core	09/01/93
Vanguard Index Total Stock Mkt VTSMX	GI	▦	11.37	21.93	-0.95	4.62	-0.17	Core	04/27/92
Vanguard Special Utilities Inc VGSUX	SU	▦	9.94	18.01	-0.79	0.60	-8.56	Conservative	05/15/92
Westcore Midco Growth Ret WMGRX	G	▦	16.07	1.93	-1.60	8.92	-1.13	Core	10/08/93
Yacktman YACKX	G	▦	10.05	6.44	0.55	10.08	8.80	Core	07/02/92
Zweig Managed Assets A ZMAAX	AA	▦	11.76	8.70	-0.17	-0.59	-2.93	Hybrid	02/08/93

Bold numbers indicate *highest* return for the listed time period in each category.

Doubly Frustrated: Hybrid Funds Battle Weak Stock and Bond Markets

Rising interest rates turned the hybrid world on its ear in 1994.

Even those with foresight fell victim to reeling U.S. stock and bond markets this year. For example, **Fidelity Balanced** manager Robert Haber moved money into foreign bonds, only to watch the Canadian and French bond markets slide in sympathy with the United States'. **CGM Mutual**'s fortunes turned upside down as well. Manager Ken Heebner hoarded too many 30-year Treasury bonds from 1993, then chose to shift the fund's assets into REITs just as they began to languish in the second quarter. With so many pitfalls afoot, it took strokes of luck as well as genius to win in 1994's market. **Fidelity Puritan**'s Richard Fentin, for example, boosted his fund into the black by starting the year positioned defensively with short-duration bonds, then shifting to rebounding large-cap stocks.

Income funds were hurt the worst in the hybrid group. Their reliance on dividends from utility companies and preferred stock caused them to suffer double-digit losses: In many cases, a move toward deregulation eroded the value of these issues in a climate of higher interest rates and stagnant stock prices. However, yields have held up for funds that supplemented stakes in utilities with high-yield or convertible bonds, such as **Franklin Income** and **Lindner Dividend**.

Despite 1994's disappointing results, hybrid funds are still appealing for the one-stop diversification convenience that they offer—hybrids rarely perform as poorly as the weakest market in which they invest.

Andrew Lohmeier

Growth of $10,000
— Hybrid Category ($000)
— LB Agg ($000)

Net Assets ($bil)

	1983	1984	1985	1986	1987	1988	1989	1990	1991	1992	1993	1994	History
	45.23	16.64	34.44	40.81	13.70	24.23	32.98	10.53	51.46	21.71	26.32	4.92	High
	17.45	9.71	25.69	18.40	2.43	11.47	19.51	0.63	26.02	9.14	13.48	-2.57	Total Return %
	6.74	-2.22	12.71	8.45	-7.71	2.89	10.23	-10.29	14.68	-6.06	-1.06	-9.73	Low
	-5.02	3.44	-6.05	-0.28	-2.83	-5.14	-12.17	3.75	-4.46	1.52	3.43	-3.88	+/- S&P 500
	9.08	-5.45	3.57	3.15	-0.33	3.59	4.97	-8.32	10.02	1.89	3.73	0.35	+/- LB Aggregate
	7.81	8.03	7.71	5.89	-21.1	5.84	6.04	5.64	5.68	4.50	3.89	3.76	Income Return %
	9.63	1.30	17.09	10.52	-29.1	4.68	12.97	-5.01	19.82	4.64	9.59	-6.33	Capital Return %
	0.83	0.82	0.80	0.73	0.68	0.66	0.69	0.71	0.64	0.61	0.56	0.57	Income $
	0.86	0.87	0.88	0.87	0.91	1.00	1.12	1.16	1.16	1.13	1.06	0.97	Expense Ratio
	7.41	8.13	7.15	5.83	5.47	6.14	5.97	5.70	5.14	4.62	3.85	4.06	Income Ratio
	89.32	78.73	84.36	90.34	102.9	104.4	92.22	95.51	90.87	99.69	89.05	96.87	Turnover Ratio
	4.79	4.91	6.61	11.32	14.44	16.02	20.53	21.77	32.51	51.51	88.08	96.44	Total Net Assets ($bil)

Style Box Analysis

Number of Funds

	Value	Blend	Growth
Large	13	10	4
Med	6	13	1
Small	1	0	0

1 Yr Total Return %

	Value	Blend	Growth
Large	-2.85	-3.67	-2.80
Med	-3.01	-1.16	-0.83
Small	-1.10	NMF	NMF

5 Yr Total Return %

	Value	Blend	Growth
Large	8.81	8.58	7.86
Med	9.29	8.60	8.46
Small	11.74	NMF	NMF

Average Mstar Risk

	Value	Blend	Growth
Large	0.68	0.67	0.91
Med	0.69	0.68	0.82
Small	0.40	NMF	NMF

1.00 = Equity Average

Risk Analysis

	Load-Adj Return	Morningstar[1] Return	Risk	Morningstar Risk-Adj Rating
1 Yr	-4.87			
3 Yr	5.63	0.63[2]	0.71	★★★
5 Yr	8.24	0.89[2]	0.69	★★★★
10 Yr	11.40	0.95	0.65	★★★★

[1]1.00=Equity Average [2]1.00=90-day T-bill return

Other Measures

			Standard Index S&P 500
Standard Deviation	6.18	Alpha	1.13
Mean	6.39	Beta	0.62
Sharpe Ratio	0.46	R-Squared	63.21

Portfolio

Amount 000	Total Equity: 2276 / Total Fixed-Income: 3407	Value $000	% Net Assets
2052432	US Treasury Note 6.25%	1889788	1.94
99372	Vanguard/Windsor II Fund	1572071	1.61
631509	US Treasury Bond 8.125%	698159	0.72
11045	Philip Morris	633057	0.65
2666244	Govt of France 8.5%	528517	0.54
9074	Bristol-Myers Squibb	506642	0.52
476698	US Treasury Bond 7.125%	490366	0.50
472382	Vanguard Prime Portfolio Fd	472382	0.48
49281	Vanguard F/I GNMA Fund	472109	0.48
58560	Vanguard F/I L-T Corp Fund	471411	0.48
506853	US Treasury Bond 7.25%	469978	0.48
8689	General Electric	390792	0.40
4563	Mobil	383186	0.39
6238	American Home Products	375847	0.39
567952	United Mexican States 6.25%	371967	0.38
419511	US Treasury Note 5.75%	367730	0.38
6130	El DuPont de Nemours	351508	0.36
345170	US Treasury Bond 7.875%	339893	0.35
5681	Schlumberger	328354	0.34
11994	Baxter International	327021	0.34

Worst Three Months

	Worst 3 Month Performance 1990-1994
Quest for Value Opportunity A	-16.75
Pasadena Balanced Return A	-16.28
Franklin Income	-14.97
Seligman Income A	-13.79
Evergreen Foundation	-11.96

Performance 12-31-94

	Total Return%	+/- S&P	+/- LB Agg
3 Mo	-1.10	-1.09	-1.48
6 Mo	1.38	-3.48	0.39
1 Yr	-2.57	-3.88	0.35
3 Yr Average	6.41	0.14	1.86
5 Yr Average	8.71	0.02	1.08
10 Yr Average	11.67	-2.72	1.72
15 Yr Average	12.94	-1.55	2.13

Composition %

Cash	11.51	Preferreds	2.34
Stocks	45.54	Convertibles	4.70
Bonds	35.91	Other	0.00

Tax Analysis

	Tax-Adj Hist Return %	% Pretax Return
3 Yr Avg	4.50	61.68
5 Yr Avg	6.39	72.77
10 Yr Avg	8.45	72.16

Sector Weightings

	% of Stocks	Rel S&P500
Utilities	14.1	1.14
Energy	8.5	0.84
Financials	17.4	1.65
Industrial Cyclicals	16.7	1.02
Consumer Durables	6.5	1.04
Consumer Staples	7.2	0.58
Services	8.6	1.05
Retail	5.3	0.90
Health	8.2	0.94
Technology	7.7	0.84

Category Leaders

Lowest 3 Yr Morningstar Risk		Top Rated Funds		Best 3 Yr Return %	
Berwyn Income	0.39	Evergreen Foundation	2.91	Fidelity Puritan	12.58
Lindner Dividend	0.42	Berwyn Income	2.78	Berwyn Income	12.08
Flex-funds Muirfield	0.48	Fidelity Asset Manager: Grth	2.77	Fidelity Asset Manager: Grth	11.98
Merrill Lynch Global Alloc B	0.51	Fidelity Asset Manager	2.07	Evergreen Foundation	11.14
Income Fund of America	0.52	Merrill Lynch Global Alloc B	2.00	Lindner Dividend	10.40
Franklin Income	0.53	Fidelity Puritan	1.95	Quest for Value Opport A	10.23
Crabbe Huson Asset Alloc	0.54	Crabbe Huson Asset Alloc	1.89	Crabbe Huson Asset Alloc	9.55
Phoenix Total Return A	0.55	Lindner Dividend	1.88	Franklin Income	9.46
Seligman Income A	0.56	Dodge & Cox Balanced	1.79	Dodge & Cox Balanced	9.39
American Balanced	0.57	Quest for Value Opport A	1.75	USAA Investment Cornerstone	9.20

Hybrid Funds

Fund / Ticker	Obj	Style Box	NAV	Total Return % through 12-31-94					Trailing 12 Mo Yield %	Morningstar Risk 1.00=Equity Average			Rtn % Rank Obj			Bear Mkt Indicator (Worst 3 mo)	Star Rating	Avg Star Rating
				YTD	1Yr	Annualized 3Yr	5Yr	10Yr		3Yr	5Yr	10Yr	3Yr	5Yr	10Yr			
S&P 500 Index				**1.31**	**1.31**	**6.27**	**8.69**	**14.38**										
Advantage Income ADGIX	I		11.54	-5.33	-5.33	5.28	7.34	—	4.8	0.73	0.66	—	55	73	—	2 (-6)	★★★	3.5
American Balanced ABALX	B		12.00	0.34	0.34	6.92	8.45	12.44	4.7	0.57	0.68	0.66	25	31	25	2(-10)	★★★★	3.9
Berwyn Income BERIX			10.74	-1.10	-1.10	12.08	11.74		6.8	0.39	0.40	—	1	2	—	1 (-6)	★★★★★	4.4
Calvert Social Invmnt Managed A CSIFX	B		27.87	-4.74	-4.74	2.74	5.39	10.40	3.3	0.71	0.65	0.65	80	94	78	2 (-6)	★★★	3.3
CGM Mutual LOMMX	B		25.05	-9.73	-9.73	5.27	10.69	**14.85**	4.2	1.19	1.11	1.02	48	6	3	6(-11)	★★★★	4.3
Connecticut Mutual Total Return CNMTX	AA		13.44	-2.11	-2.11	7.62	9.79	—	4.0	0.65	0.68	—	23	14	—	2 (-9)	★★★★	3.5
Crabbe Huson Asset Allocation CHAAX	AA		12.17	-0.84	-0.84	9.56	9.61	—	2.5	0.54	0.61	—	7	18	—	2 (-7)	★★★★	3.8
Delaware A DELFX	B		17.23	-1.35	-1.35	6.73	7.90	11.78	3.6	0.66	0.79	0.95	30	53	46	3 (-9)	★★★	3.1
Dodge & Cox Balanced DODBX	B		45.21	2.05	2.05	9.39	9.79	13.96	3.9	0.64	0.76	0.71	3	12	7	3(-11)	★★★★★	4.2
Evergreen Foundation EFONX	B		12.27	-1.12	-1.12	11.14	**14.99**		3.3	0.77	0.76	—	2	1	—	2(-12)	★★★★★	5.0
Fidelity Asset Manager FASMX	AA		13.83	-6.60	-6.60	9.09	11.09	—	2.9	0.62	0.59	—	11	4	—	2 (-8)	★★★★	4.9
Fidelity Asset Manager: Growth FASGX	AA		12.84	-7.39	-7.39	11.98	—		1.5	0.86	—	—	2	—	—	— (—)	★★★★★	5.0
Fidelity Balanced FBALX	B		12.29	-5.31	-5.31	6.83	9.00	—	3.3	0.62	0.60	—	29	21	—	2 (-7)	★★★★	4.6
Fidelity Puritan FPURX	B		14.81	1.78	1.78	**12.58**	10.71	13.70	3.5	0.60	0.80	0.67	1	4	10	3(-12)	★★★★★	4.6
Flex-funds Muirfield FLMFX	AA		5.34	2.70	2.70	6.12	9.66	—	2.6	0.48	0.52	—	36	16	—	1 (-6)	★★★★	3.9
Fortis Advantage Asset Alloc A FAAAX	AA		14.03	-0.83	-0.83	5.46	8.47	—	2.8	0.90	0.78	—	51	37	—	2 (-9)	★★★	3.4
Founders Balanced FRINX	B		8.56	-1.94	-1.94	8.21	8.14	10.48	2.3	0.68	0.70	0.63	8	36	67	2 (-7)	★★★★	3.6
Franklin Income FKINX	I		2.10	-6.37	-6.37	9.47	11.05	11.90	8.5	0.53	0.63	0.53	7	5	7	2(-15)	★★★★	4.1
IDS Mutual INMUX	B		11.02	-2.97	-2.97	7.02	8.00	12.05	4.9	0.70	0.76	0.70	24	39	39	3(-10)	★★★★	4.0
Income Fund of America AMECX	I		13.14	-2.50	-2.50	7.58	8.39	12.11	6.3	0.52	0.61	0.57	18	38	1	2 (-8)	★★★★	4.0
Keystone Custodian K-1 KKONX	B		8.99	-4.68	-4.68	2.86	5.80	10.43	4.0	0.79	0.80	0.75	77	87	71	3 (-9)	★★★	3.5
Lindner Dividend LDDVX	I		23.97	-3.31	-3.31	10.40	9.89	11.69	7.7	0.42	0.47	0.42	5	11	21	1 (-6)	★★★★	4.9
MainStay Total Return B MKTRX	B		14.76	-2.41	-2.41	3.77	9.94	—	2.5	1.12	0.97	—	70	11	—	2 (-7)	★★★	3.8
Merrill Lynch Global Alloc B MBLOX	AA		12.12	-2.89	-2.89	8.98	10.72	—	2.5	0.51	0.58	—	12	6	—	2 (-8)	★★★★	4.7
MFS Total Return A MSFRX	B		12.44	-2.69	-2.69	7.24	7.94	12.80	4.3	0.64	0.71	0.70	21	46	14	2 (-8)	★★★★	4.0
MIMLIC Asset Allocation A MIAAX	AA		12.78	-2.14	-2.14	3.15	7.77	—	2.6	0.90	0.76	—	85	47	—	2 (-7)	★★★	3.6
Overland Express Asset Alloc A OEAAX	AA		10.67	-0.68	-0.68	6.29	9.18	—	2.7	0.84	0.58	—	29	27	—	1 (-6)	★★★★	3.8
Pasadena Balanced Return A PABRX	B		20.54	-4.43	-4.43	0.78	7.19	—	2.2	1.01	1.09	—	93	67	—	6(-16)	★★	3.7
Pax World PAXWX	B		13.39	2.65	2.65	0.73	6.38	10.26	3.7	0.83	0.66	0.71	94	82	82	1 (-5)	★★★	3.4
Phoenix Balanced A PHBLX	B		14.83	-4.55	-4.55	2.73	7.94	12.40	3.2	0.66	0.62	0.63	81	45	32	2 (-5)	★★★	4.5
Phoenix Total Return A PTRFX	AA		14.82	-2.26	-2.26	6.01	9.87	—	2.1	0.55	0.58	—	43	12	—	2 (-5)	★★★★	3.4
Pioneer Income MOMIX	I		9.11	-4.31	-4.31	4.31	6.88	10.11	7.4	0.60	0.54	0.48	73	82	57	1 (-6)	★★★	3.3
T. Rowe Price Balanced RPBAX	B		11.14	-2.05	-2.05	6.00	9.25	12.47	3.8	0.71	0.58	0.69	38	19	21	1 (-5)	★★★★	3.6
Prudential Allocation Conserv B PRFCX	AA		10.63	-3.59	-3.59	5.37	7.89	—	2.3	0.68	0.63	—	53	45	—	2 (-6)	★★★★	3.8
George Putnam Fund of Boston A PGEOX	B		12.91	-0.38	-0.38	6.05	7.73	12.40	4.3	0.68	0.76	0.75	36	58	35	3(-10)	★★★★	3.2
Quest for Value Opportunity A QVOPX	AA		18.30	**4.92**	**4.92**	10.23	12.72	—	0.6	0.75	0.95	—	4	1	—	4(-17)	★★★★	4.6
Seligman Income A SINFX	I		13.05	-5.44	-5.44	8.85	9.00	10.83	5.8	0.56	0.68	0.59	10	26	35	2(-14)	★★★★	3.3
Sentinel Balanced SEBLX	B		14.09	-3.56	-3.56	3.94	7.12	10.99	4.1	0.68	0.62	0.65	69	68	57	2 (-6)	★★★	3.8
Stagecoach Asset Allocation A SFAAX	AA		16.73	-2.82	-2.82	6.11	9.46	—	4.4	0.78	0.53	—	39	22	—	1 (-7)	★★★★	4.0
Strong Asset Allocation STAAX	AA		17.91	-1.51	-1.51	5.21	7.44	9.31	3.9	0.61	0.52	0.50	56	54	50	1 (-5)	★★★	3.7
20th Century Balanced Investors TWBIX	B		15.27	-0.07	-0.07	0.22	8.52	—	2.8	1.22	1.07	—	96	28	—	3(-11)	★★	3.6
USAA Investment Balanced USBLX	B		11.64	-2.62	-2.62	5.13	6.20	—	4.0	0.61	0.57	—	54	85	—	1 (-4)	★★★	3.0
USAA Investmnt Cornerstone USCRX	AA		21.24	-1.05	-1.05	9.20	6.56	12.34	2.6	0.73	0.85	0.71	9	66	25	2(-11)	★★★★	3.8
USAA Mutual Income USAIX	I		11.19	-5.22	-5.22	4.13	7.73	9.94	7.7	0.63	0.45	0.42	78	55	64	1 (-6)	★★★★	3.9
Value Line Income VALIX	I		6.21	-4.36	-4.36	1.75	6.67	10.36	3.4	0.87	0.78	0.75	92	85	50	2 (-7)	★★★	3.6
Vanguard Asset Allocation VAAPX	AA		13.54	-2.32	-2.32	6.03	8.59	—	4.2	0.82	0.78	—	41	35	—	2 (-8)	★★★★	4.0
Vanguard Preferred Stock VQIIX	I		8.15	-7.95	-7.95	4.11	7.74	10.77	8.0	0.63	0.50	0.50	81	52	42	1 (-7)	★★★★	3.7
Vanguard STAR VGSTX	B		12.60	-0.29	-0.29	6.91	7.91	—	4.1	0.63	0.77	—	26	51	—	3(-11)	★★★	3.8
Vanguard/Wellesley Income VWINX	I		17.05	-4.44	-4.44	5.99	8.47	11.80	6.4	0.70	0.57	0.53	39	35	14	1 (-6)	★★★★	4.5
Vanguard/Wellington VWELX	B		19.39	-0.49	-0.49	6.83	7.94	12.40	4.5	0.75	0.84	0.79	27	43	28	3(-10)	★★★★	4.1

Bold numbers indicate *highest* return for the listed time period in each category.

	Funds in Category	Yield	SEC Yield	Assets ($bil)
	50	8.07%	8.73%	35.09

Junk Rules Specialty-Bond Fund Roost in 1994

The specialty-bond group selectively rewarded risks in 1994.

Funds in this group assume risks outside of the investment mainstream. Corporate high-yield funds (nearly half the specialty-bond group), for example, dip into the lowest credit strata in search of the higher yields offered there. Fortunately for these funds, credit concerns were not an issue in 1994's market as the economy grew strongly in spite of rising interest rates.

Convertible funds experienced a varied year, with returns largely dependent on where their market allegiances lay. For funds that took on the higher risks of stock-like performance, such as **Putnam Convertible Income Growth**, 1994 wasn't too bad. Such funds were rewarded with considerable third-quarter bounce, especially those with smaller-cap and technology-laden portfolios. Conversely, more bond-like funds suffered, such as **Value Line Convertible**.

The saddest of the specialty-bond lot were the world-bond funds. These global travelers fell with a thud last year after a stellar 1993, hurt not only by a collapsing domestic-debt market, but by gloomy results abroad. Losses were exacerbated by dollar hedges. This tactic, a defensive play against currency fluctuations, backfired when the dollar plummeted against the yen and Deutschemark through 1994's first half. A firmer second-half dollar wasn't enough to lift the funds out of their funk.

Even with variations in returns, 1994 was not a scrapbook year. Most funds finished 1994 in the red, leaving managers looking for redemption in the new year.

Jason Windawi

Growth of $10,000

- Specialty Bond Category ($000)
- LB Agg ($000)

Net Assets ($bil)

	1983	1984	1985	1986	1987	1988	1989	1990	1991	1992	1993	1994	History
	26.75	13.07	29.91	30.05	24.42	17.91	27.08	21.11	60.34	28.05	25.52	2.20	High
	16.79	7.40	22.88	15.01	3.05	12.73	5.77	-1.68	29.76	13.57	17.64	-4.43	**Total Return %**
	1.55	-4.38	18.84	4.76	-10.62	2.72	-5.04	-16.73	10.75	0.38	9.92	-16.70	Low
	8.42	-7.75	0.76	-0.24	0.29	4.85	-8.77	-10.62	13.75	6.32	7.89	-1.52	+/- LB Agg
	1015.8	1006.4	1021.9	-0.63	-3.48	1.30	5.38	4.70	-14.00	-3.09	-1.26	-3.46	+/- FB High-Yield
	11.17	11.94	12.53	9.17	9.19	-12.2	9.41	10.23	12.42	9.33	8.63	7.06	Income Return %
	4.83	-4.34	9.68	3.01	-5.70	-20.6	-3.84	-11.8	17.33	4.24	9.42	-11.4	Capital Return %
	1.02	0.99	1.00	0.85	0.92	0.92	0.91	0.95	0.87	0.82	0.77	0.72	Income $
	0.99	0.94	0.94	0.88	1.02	1.08	1.08	1.15	1.16	1.11	1.05	1.04	Expense Ratio
	10.98	11.41	11.41	10.36	9.41	9.92	10.34	10.88	10.39	8.90	7.85	7.42	Income Ratio
	101.1	76.10	94.13	101.0	119.6	116.5	123.3	124.5	132.9	125.5	141.3	151.3	Turnover Ratio
	3.62	4.51	6.45	13.29	15.71	18.69	16.77	13.74	20.10	27.73	40.48	35.09	Total Net Assets ($bil)

Style Box Analysis

Number of Funds	Short	Interm	Long		1 Yr Total Return %	Short	Interm	Long		5 Yr Total Return %	Short	Interm	Long		Average Mstar Risk	Short	Interm	Long
High	0	1	1		High	NMF	-8.61	-1.43		High	NMF	11.00	8.35		High	NMF	0.63	0.54
Med	1	1	0		Med	-2.92	-16.70	NMF		Med	8.56	5.92	NMF		Med	0.45	0.76	NMF
Low	3	22	0		Low	-4.51	-2.85	NMF		Low	8.97	11.28	NMF		Low	0.45	0.45	NMF

1.00=Hybrid Average

Risk Analysis

	Load-Adj Return	Morningstar[1] Return	Risk	Morningstar Risk-Adj Rating
1 Yr	-7.52			
3 Yr	7.40	1.18[2]	0.51	★★★★
5 Yr	9.46	1.23[2]	0.55	★★★★
10 Yr	10.40	0.74	0.49	★★★★

[1]1.00=Hybrid Average [2]1.00=90-day T-bill return

Other Measures

			Standard Index LB Agg
Standard Deviation	5.35	Alpha	4.18
Mean	8.32	Beta	0.65
Sharpe Ratio	0.93	R-Squared	28.82

Portfolio

Amount 000	Total Equity: 521 Total Fixed-Income: 3039	Value $000	% Net Assets
162296	US Treasury Note 8.75%	169092	0.46
16533	T Rowe Price High-Yield Fund	135078	0.37
128988	US Treasury Bond 7.875%	127295	0.35
813521	Kingdom of Denmark 7%	118446	0.32
13241	T Rowe Price New Income Fund	113743	0.31
11492	T Rowe Price Intl Bond Fund	112510	0.31
167427	PanAmSat Capital 11.375%	107518	0.29
100759	Kaiser Aluminium/Chem 12.75%	100930	0.28
114968	Flagstar 11.25%	99591	0.27
110877	K & F Industries 13.75%	99328	0.27
6092	T Rowe Price Eqty Income Fd	98020	0.27
517171	Kingdom of Denmark 9%	97774	0.27
102574	Stone Container 9.875%	96437	0.26
97901	Adelphia Communications 12.5%	95788	0.26
150157	Govt of Canada 8%	93560	0.26
10250	T Rowe Price GNMA Fund	92760	0.25
107314	Gaylord Container 12.75%	92422	0.25
91849	AK Steel 10.75%	91592	0.25
100997	Westpoint Stevens 9.375%	90977	0.25
207270	NEXTEL Communications 0%	89288	0.24

Worst Three Months

	Worst 3 Month Performance 1990-1994
Franklin AGE High-Income	-19.19
Kemper High-Yield A	-18.58
Putnam Convertible Income Grth A	-18.21
Vanguard Convertible Securities	-17.76
Liberty High-Income Bond A	-17.76

Performance 12-31-94

	Total Return%	+/- LB Agg	+/- FB High-Yld
	-1.50	-1.88	-1.46
3 Mo	0.09	-0.90	-1.46
6 Mo	-4.43	-1.52	-3.46
1 Yr	8.52	3.98	-2.64
3 Yr Average	10.15	2.52	-2.93
5 Yr Average	10.80	0.86	—
10 Yr Average	11.73	0.92	—

Composition %

Cash	7.68	Preferreds	1.05
Stocks	4.43	Convertibles	17.22
Bonds	69.37	Other	0.24

Tax Analysis

	Tax-Adj Hist Return %	% Pretax Return
3 Yr Avg	5.61	57.82
5 Yr Avg	6.54	63.22
10 Yr Avg	6.35	58.49

Coupon Range

	% of Bonds
0%	6.3
0 to 8.5%	39.9
8.5 to 9.5%	24.1
9.5 to 11%	10.4
More than 11%	12.2
Not Applicable	7.0

Category Leaders

Lowest 3 Yr Morningstar Risk		Top Rated Funds		Best 3 Yr Return %	
MainStay Hi-Yield Corp Bd B	0.23	Fidelity Adv High-Yield A	3.30	Fidelity Capital & Income	14.71
Nicholas Income	0.23	MainStay Hi-Yield Corp Bd B	3.25	MainStay Hi-Yield Corp Bd B	14.52
Seligman High-Yield Bond A	0.27	Fidelity Convertible Secs	2.81	Northeast Investors	14.07
Colonial High-Yield Secs A	0.27	MainStay Convertible B	2.70	Colonial High-Yield Secs A	13.06
Gabelli Convertible Secs	0.29	Seligman High-Yield Bond A	2.52	Fidelity Adv High-Yield A	13.05
Franklin AGE High-Income	0.33	Fidelity Capital & Income	2.51	Seligman High-Yield Bond A	12.99
Northeast Investors	0.34	Putnam High Yield Adv A	2.27	Fidelity Convertible Secs	12.19
Fidelity Adv High-Yield A	0.34	Northeast Investors	2.23	Pacific Horizon Capital Inc	11.91
AIM High-Yield A	0.35	Pacific Horizon Capital Inc	2.19	Putnam Convert Income Grth A	11.60
Oppenheimer High-Yield A	0.37	Merrill Lynch Corp Hi-Inc A	1.95	MainStay Convertible B	11.57

Bond Funds—Specialty

Fund / Ticker	Obj	Style Box	NAV	Total Return % through 12-31-94 YTD	1Yr	Annualized 3Yr	5Yr	10Yr	Trailing 12 Mo Yield %	Morningstar Risk 1.00=Hybrid Average 3Yr	5Yr	10Yr	Rtn % Rank Obj 3Yr	5Yr	10Yr	Bear Mkt Indicator (Worst 3 mo)	Star Rating	Avg Star Rating
Lehman Bros. Aggregate Bond Index				-2.92	-2.92	4.55	7.63	9.94										
AIM High-Yield A AMHYX	CY	⊞	8.93	-1.68	-1.68	11.35	12.30	12.00	10.8	0.35	0.55	0.43	24	16	3	2 (-15)	★★★★	3.7
American Capital Harbor A ACHBX	CV		13.24	-6.43	-6.43	5.25	7.23	10.50	4.6	0.79	0.76	0.76	83	61	66	10 (-10)	★★★	3.1
American High-Income AHITX	CY	⊞	13.13	-5.11	-5.11	8.33	10.99	—	9.7	0.43	0.48	—	89	37	—	5 (-11)	★★★★	3.9
Capital World Bond CWBFX	WB	⊞	15.12	-1.43	-1.43	5.07	8.35	—	6.4	0.62	0.48	—	24	24	—	3 (-5)	★★★★	3.1
Colonial High-Yield Securities A COLHX	CY	⊞	6.30	-0.34	-0.34	13.06	12.11	11.31	10.0	0.27	0.57	0.42	12	17	22	4 (-16)	★★★★	3.6
Colonial Strategic Income A COSIX	I	⊞	6.53	-3.68	-3.68	6.72	7.73	9.30	9.1	0.41	0.48	0.67	28	58	78	1 (-9)	★★★	2.5
Delaware Delchester A DETWX	CY	⊞	6.05	-4.57	-4.57	9.22	10.40	10.86	12.1	0.39	0.58	0.46	77	47	29	4 (-15)	★★★★	3.4
Fidelity Advisor High-Yield A FAHYX	CY	⊞	10.84	-2.08	-2.08	13.05	**15.91**	—	7.0	0.34	0.35	—	13	1	—	1 (-7)	★★★★★	4.4
Fidelity Capital & Income FAGIX	CY	⊞	8.63	-5.09	-5.09	**14.71**	13.51	11.91	8.7	0.42	0.46	0.44	4	4	6	1 (-8)	★★★★★	4.1
Fidelity Convertible Securities FCVSX	CV		15.36	-1.76	-1.76	12.19	13.73	—	5.2	0.71	0.79	—	4	4	—	4 (-13)	★★★★★	4.8
Fidelity Global Bond FGBDX	WB	⊞	9.88	-16.70	-16.70	1.73	5.92	—	6.5	0.97	0.61	—	84	84	—	9 (-14)	★★★	3.9
Fidelity New Markets Income FNMIX	WB		10.20	-16.47	-16.47	—	—	—	5.4	—	—	—	—	—	—	— (—)		
Franklin AGE High-Income AGEFX	CY	⊞	2.60	-1.55	-1.55	10.53	11.37	9.87	10.2	0.33	0.64	0.55	45	32	54	7 (-19)	★★★★	2.9
G.T. Global Government Income A GGINX	WB		8.31	-14.39	-14.39	3.09	6.24	—	7.5	0.95	0.65	—	64	75	—	7 (-11)	★★★	3.2
Gabelli Convertible Securities GACSX	CV		10.60	-0.17	-0.17	8.44	8.79	—	5.2	0.29	0.25	—	25	57	—	1 (-3)	★★★★	4.0
Hancock Strategic Income A JHFIX	I	⊞	6.81	-3.05	-3.05	5.84	7.40	—	9.5	0.40	0.56	—	44	67	—	1 (-12)	★★★	2.6
IDS Extra Income INEAX	CY	⊞	3.78	-7.57	-7.57	9.81	10.39	9.69	11.6	0.53	0.61	0.53	61	49	61	5 (-12)	★★★★	3.0
Invesco High-Yield FHYPX	CY	⊞	6.38	-4.99	-4.99	8.03	8.25	10.14	10.2	0.40	0.45	0.38	91	92	48	3 (-9)	★★★★	3.8
Janus Flexible Income JAFIX	I	⊞	8.75	-2.92	-2.92	7.90	8.56	—	8.2	0.38	0.50	—	13	32	—	1 (-8)	★★★★	3.4
Kemper High-Yield A KHYAX	CY	⊞	7.56	-1.72	-1.72	11.44	12.08	12.25	10.1	0.38	0.66	0.49	23	19	1	6 (-19)	★★★★	3.9
Liberty High-Income Bond A FHIIX	CY	⊞	10.23	-1.68	-1.68	10.59	13.59	11.51	10.0	0.38	0.62	0.51	40	2	12	4 (-18)	★★★★	3.5
Lord Abbett Bond-Debenture LBNDX	CY	⊞	8.71	-3.86	-3.86	8.96	10.59	10.43	10.1	0.39	0.53	0.46	81	46	41	5 (-14)	★★★★	3.3
MainStay Convertible B MCSVX	CV		11.67	-1.34	-1.34	11.57	13.98	—	4.0	0.69	0.76	—	16	1	—	6 (-10)	★★★★★	3.1
MainStay Hi-Yield Corp Bond B MKHCX	CY	⊞	7.44	1.50	1.50	14.52	12.86	—	9.0	0.23	0.48	—	5	9	—	1 (-11)	★★★★★	3.2
Merrill Lynch Corp High-Income A MAHIX	CY	⊞	7.31	-3.98	-3.98	10.76	12.62	11.87	9.6	0.37	0.50	0.40	37	12	9	1 (-14)	★★★★	3.9
Merrill Lynch World Income A MAWIX	I		8.20	-4.25	-4.25	5.05	9.41	—	8.5	0.44	0.38	—	57	20	—	1 (-5)	★★★★	4.1
MFS High-Income A MHITX	CY	⊞	4.82	-2.61	-2.61	10.82	11.03	9.69	9.2	0.37	0.65	0.53	35	36	64	5 (-16)	★★★★	3.2
MFS World Governments A MWGTX	WB		10.91	-6.57	-6.57	3.88	8.43	**13.45**	1.4	0.78	0.57	0.60	48	21	1	4 (-7)	★★★★	4.0
Nicholas Income NCINX	CY		3.21	-0.17	-0.17	7.55	8.66	9.30	9.4	0.23	0.32	0.30	94	89	67	2 (-7)	★★★★	3.4
Northeast Investors NTHEX	CY	⊞	9.55	**2.20**	**2.20**	14.07	11.24	11.40	10.3	0.34	0.52	0.39	7	34	19	1 (-8)	★★★★★	3.7
Oppenheimer High-Yield A OPPHX	CY	⊞	12.83	-2.33	-2.33	10.27	10.78	10.50	10.5	0.37	0.38	0.34	53	41	38	2 (-7)	★★★★	3.3
Oppenheimer Strategic Income A OPSIX	I		4.55	-4.70	-4.70	7.06	9.86	—	9.2	0.51	0.36	—	26	14	—	1 (-6)	★★★★	4.0
Pacific Horizon Capital Income PACIX	CV		13.28	-5.85	-5.85	11.91	13.14	—	4.4	0.73	0.86	—	8	9	—	7 (-15)	★★★★★	4.6
PaineWebber Global Income B PGBBX	WB		9.87	-4.74	-4.74	2.72	7.16	—	5.8	0.61	0.43	—	70	57	—	2 (-6)	★★★★	3.8
Phoenix Convertible A PHCVX	CV		16.55	-3.81	-3.81	6.09	7.00	10.80	4.8	0.42	0.51	0.55	66	49	33	4 (-6)	★★★	3.9
Phoenix High-Yield A PHCHX	CY	⊞	7.73	-7.97	-7.97	9.35	10.03	9.97	10.1	0.53	0.49	0.43	74	61	51	3 (-7)	★★★★	3.4
Phoenix Multi-Sector Fixed-Inc A NAMFX	I	⊞	11.53	-6.77	-6.77	6.37	10.20	—	8.2	0.56	0.40	—	34	8	—	1 (-6)	★★★★	4.3
T. Rowe Price High-Yield PRHYX	CY	⊞	7.75	-8.00	-8.00	8.74	8.43	9.72	9.7	0.54	0.61	0.48	86	91	58	4 (-12)	★★★★	3.6
T. Rowe Price Spectrum Income RPSIX	I		10.11	-1.93	-1.93	5.92	—	—	6.7	0.38	—	—	42	—	—	— (—)	★★★★	4.0
Putnam Convertible Income Grth A PCONX	CV		17.13	-1.92	-1.92	11.60	10.11	11.39	5.3	0.50	0.82	0.82	12	33	1	7 (-18)	★★★★	3.2
Putnam Diversified Income A PDINX	I		11.23	-5.60	-5.60	7.08	9.77	—	8.8	0.40	0.37	—	23	17	—	1 (-5)	★★★★	4.1
Putnam Global Governmental Inc A PGGIX	WB		12.92	-9.98	-9.98	2.22	7.43	—	7.0	0.84	0.55	—	74	48	—	5 (-7)	★★★	3.8
Putnam High Yield Advantage A PHYIX	CY	⊞	9.00	-5.15	-5.15	10.84	12.77	—	11.3	0.43	0.55	—	34	11	—	3 (-11)	★★★★★	3.4
SBSF Convertible Securities SBFCX	CV		10.41	-6.45	-6.45	7.73	8.80	—	5.5	0.58	0.64	—	37	52	—	3 (-10)	★★★★	3.9
Scudder International Bond SCIBX	WB	⊞	11.38	-8.61	-8.61	4.44	11.00	—	8.7	0.77	0.54	—	38	1	—	2 (-6)	★★★★	4.7
Seligman High-Yield Bond A SHYBX	CY	⊞	6.35	0.78	0.78	12.99	11.82	—	10.1	0.27	0.42	—	15	26	—	2 (-11)	★★★★★	3.5
Templeton Income TPINX	WB		8.82	-3.58	-3.58	3.14	6.74	—	7.6	0.78	0.54	—	62	63	—	3 (-6)	★★★	3.4
Value Line Convertible VALCX	CV		11.01	-5.28	-5.28	7.38	8.94	—	6.6	0.74	0.85	—	41	47	—	3 (-14)	★★★★	2.8
Vanguard Convertible Securities VCVSX	CV		10.55	-5.68	-5.68	8.42	9.47	—	4.8	0.88	1.05	—	29	38	—	6 (-18)	★★★★	2.8
Vanguard Fixed-Inc High-Yld Corp VWEHX	CY	⊞	7.20	-1.71	-1.71	9.91	10.03	10.57	9.4	0.41	0.51	0.41	59	59	35	7 (-13)	★★★★	3.6

Bold numbers indicate *highest* return for the listed time period in each category.

Investment Bombs

Investors who thought putting money in bonds meant steady income without risk were in for a nasty surprise in 1994.

After years of falling interest rates, investors had grown accustomed to seeing their assets rise (most bonds appreciate as interest rates decline). When the Fed lifted short-term interest rates in February, however, investment bonds got hammered. Only three out of 50 investment bond funds finished 1994 with a positive total return.

The funds that did fare well were short-maturity funds. **Strong Advantage** manager Jeffrey Koch, who keeps his fund's maturity below one year, propelled the fund to the top of the investment-bond fund group with a 3.6% gain. **FPA New Income**, though not forced by charter to shorten maturity, also kept its head above water. Manager Bob Rodriguez astutely shifted from longer maturity bonds into securities with less than three-year maturities. Although he has re-extended the fund's maturity since then, most of the market damage has already been done.

Bonds biggest blow, though, came in the form of derivatives—securities created by chopping up and reconfiguring straight bonds. Among the stricken was **WPG Government Securities**. Manager David Hoyle tried skirting the effect of rising interest rates by scorning rate-sensitive principal-only bonds and scooping up more-defensive interest-only strips. The market abused derivative issues so badly, though, that liquidity dried up, and even many cautious derivatives plummeted in value.

Historically, these funds have offered lower risk than stock funds, and produced dependable income streams as well.

Jennifer Newport

Worst Three Months

	Worst 3 Month Performance 1990-1994
Alliance Bond Corporate Bond A	-13.61
Vanguard Fixed-Inc L/T Corp Bond	-7.05
PaineWebber Invmt Grade Income A	-7.02
Alliance Mortgage Secs Income A	-6.76
Scudder Income	-6.72

Category Leaders

Lowest 3 Yr Morningstar Risk		Top Rated Funds		Best 3 Yr Return %	
Strong Advantage	0.14	Loomis Sayles Bond	2.03	Loomis Sayles Bond	10.25
Neuberger&Berman Ultra Sh	0.23	Strong Advantage	1.60	Alliance Bond Corp Bond A	9.01
FPA New Income	0.38	FPA New Income	1.44	FPA New Income	7.49
Strong Short-Term Bond	0.56	Vanguard F/I Short-Trm Corp	1.08	Strong Advantage	6.68
Vanguard F/I Short-Trm Corp	0.57	Strong Government Securities	0.99	Bond Fund of America	6.48
Fidelity Spartan Lim Mat Gov	0.57	Harbor Bond	0.91	Vanguard F/I L/T Corp Bond	5.98
Overland Exp Var Rate Govt A	0.60	Vanguard F/I GNMA	0.88	Strong Government Securities	5.97
Scudder Short-Term GlobalInc	0.62	Fidelity Intermediate Bond	0.88	Putnam Income A	5.93
Vanguard F/I Short-Trm US Tr	0.63	Dreyfus Short-Intrm Govt	0.88	SteinRoe Income	5.87
Vanguard F/I Short-Trm Fed	0.66	Scudder Short-Term Bond	0.86	Harbor Bond	5.69

Growth of $10,000
— Investment Bond Category ($000)
— LB Agg ($000)

Net Assets ($bil)

	1983	1984	1985	1986	1987	1988	1989	1990	1991	1992	1993	1994	History
	11.47	16.43	26.53	15.97	7.87	12.86	15.60	11.01	21.04	14.29	31.09	3.55	High
	8.78	12.94	20.15	12.53	2.33	7.81	11.96	8.27	15.25	7.47	9.93	-3.02	Total Return %
	5.35	9.11	12.79	8.95	-1.56	5.22	3.99	3.27	7.42	3.64	3.22	-12.75	Low
	0.41	-2.21	-1.97	-2.72	-0.43	-0.07	-2.58	-0.67	-0.75	0.23	0.18	-0.10	+/- LB Agg
	0.79	-2.08	-1.16	-3.08	0.03	0.23	-2.27	-0.01	-0.88	-0.10	-1.13	0.49	+/- LB Govt/Corp
	11.21	11.28	10.67	8.59	8.30	8.65	9.20	8.69	8.55	7.57	6.81	6.14	Income Return %
	-2.51	0.88	7.20	2.35	-5.95	-1.11	2.29	-0.72	6.02	-0.09	3.12	-9.15	Capital Return %
	1.00	0.93	0.91	0.85	0.83	0.83	0.86	0.85	0.82	0.79	0.72	0.68	Income $
	0.87	0.87	0.86	0.87	0.83	0.83	0.82	0.79	0.77	0.75	0.72	0.71	Expense Ratio
	10.96	11.35	10.96	9.36	8.56	8.82	9.00	8.85	8.39	7.62	6.85	6.43	Income Ratio
	105.3	96.71	123.1	149.2	156.6	202.3	160.8	141.3	152.0	153.7	160.1	150.0	Turnover Ratio
	2.51	5.67	12.89	35.41	31.81	29.85	30.81	32.69	50.57	63.88	71.70	58.39	Total Net Assets ($bil)

Style Box Analysis

Number of Funds

	Short	Interm	Long	
High	9	21	3	
Med	4	4	5	
Low	0	0	0	

1 Yr Total Return %

	Short	Interm	Long	
High	-1.85	-2.90	-4.00	
Med	0.07	-4.15	-6.23	
Low	NMF	NMF	NMF	

5 Yr Total Return %

	Short	Interm	Long	
High	6.35	7.43	7.92	
Med	7.05	8.14	8.41	
Low	NMF	NMF	NMF	

Average Mstar Risk

	Short	Interm	Long	
High	0.62	0.90	1.14	
Med	0.46	1.01	1.21	
Low	NMF	NMF	NMF	

1.00=Taxable-Bond Avg

Risk Analysis

	Load-Adj Return	Morningstar[1] Return	Risk	Morningstar Risk-Adj Rating
1 Yr	-4.21			
3 Yr	4.16	0.18[2]	0.90	★★★★
5 Yr	7.11	0.58[2]	0.86	★★★★
10 Yr	9.06	0.85	0.98	★★★★

[1]1.00=Taxable-Bond Average [2]1.00=90-day T-bill return

Other Measures

			Standard Index LB Agg
Standard Deviation	3.75	Alpha	0.20
Mean	4.58	Beta	0.86
Sharpe Ratio	0.25	R-Squared	82.64

Performance 12-31-94

	Total Return%	+/- LB Agg	+/- LB Gvt/Corp
3 Mo	-0.09	-0.47	-0.46
6 Mo	0.67	-0.33	-0.20
1 Yr	-3.02	-0.10	0.49
3 Yr Average	4.61	0.06	-0.25
5 Yr Average	7.41	-0.21	-0.30
10 Yr Average	9.29	-0.65	-0.55
	10.23	-0.57	-0.48

Portfolio

Amount 000	Total Equity: 3 Total Fixed-Income: 3672	Value $000	% Net Assets
608093	GNMA 8.5%	602056	0.99
457454	FNMA ARM CMT	463670	0.76
428042	FHLMC ARM COF	432436	0.71
395701	US Treasury Note 9.375%	413841	0.68
371915	GNMA 10.5%	403379	0.66
363947	Repurchase Agreement 4.78%	363899	0.60
370387	GNMA 7.5%	342278	0.56
324116	GNMA 9.5%	334011	0.55
289151	GNMA 12%	327032	0.54
320395	US Treasury Bond 8.125%	322406	0.53
318301	FHLMC CMO REMIC FRN	309778	0.51
250572	GNMA 12.5%	286214	0.47
228045	US Treasury Bond 10.375%	272318	0.45
260400	US Treasury Note 8.5%	269952	0.44
282750	US Treasury Note 5.125%	266878	0.44
254922	US Treasury Note 8.875%	263565	0.43
262630	GNMA ARM CMT	252762	0.41
219906	GNMA 13%	251868	0.41
224280	US Treasury Note 9.25%	242365	0.40
168200	US Treasury Bond 11.625%	217802	0.36

Composition %

Cash	7.69	Preferred	0.25
Stocks	0.11	Convertibles	0.90
Bonds	93.85	Other	-0.19

Tax Analysis

	Tax-Adj Hist Return %	% Pretax Return
3 Yr Avg	1.95	38.34
5 Yr Avg	4.61	61.82
10 Yr Avg	5.78	62.04

Coupon Range

	% of Bonds
0%	2.9
0 to 8.5%	50.6
8.5 to 9.5%	20.1
9.5 to 11%	11.0
More than 11%	8.8
Not Applicable	6.7

Bond Funds–Investment

Fund / Ticker	Obj	Style Box	NAV	Total Return % through 12-31-94		Annualized			Trailing 12 Mo Yield %	Morningstar Risk 1.00=Bond Average			Rtn % Rank Obj			Bear Mkt Indicator (Worst 3 mo)	Star Rating	Avg Star Rating
				YTD	1Yr	3Yr	5Yr	10Yr		3Yr	5Yr	10Yr	3Yr	5Yr	10Yr			
Lehman Bros. Aggregate Bond Index				-2.92	-2.92	4.55	7.63	9.94										
Alliance Bond Corporate Bond A CBFAX	CG	▦	11.88	-12.75	-12.75	9.01	**10.04**	10.93	9.6	2.15	1.96	1.52	2	2	3	10 (-14)	★★★	3.1
Alliance Mortgage Secs Income A ALMSX	GM		8.13	-6.14	-6.14	3.66	7.37	8.68	7.4	1.05	0.95	0.90	31	13	45	5 (-7)	★★★	3.3
American Capital Corp Bond A ACCBX	CG	▦	6.36	-4.27	-4.27	5.07	7.70	9.75	7.6	1.04	1.01	0.93	31	28	36	5 (-6)	★★★★	3.1
American Capital Govt Secs A ACGVX	GG	▦	9.67	-4.26	-4.26	3.33	6.88	8.14	7.0	1.02	1.03	1.17	54	29	56	7 (-6)	★★	1.8
Babson Bond L BABIX	CQ	▦	1.47	-3.29	-3.29	5.09	7.54	9.34	7.3	1.01	0.98	0.98	9	15	29	4 (-5)	★★★★	4.0
Benham GNMA Income BGNMX	GM	▦	9.90	-1.51	-1.51	4.19	7.56	—	7.0	0.76	0.74	—	11	8	—	3 (-4)	★★★★★	4.4
Benham Treasury Note CPTNX	GT	▦	9.76	-2.35	-2.35	3.94	6.88	8.00	5.2	0.90	0.81	1.29	51	48	40	3 (-4)	★★★	1.6
Bond Fund of America ABNDX	CG	▦	12.69	-5.02	-5.02	6.48	8.58	10.58	8.3	1.00	1.08	1.03	7	11	12	6 (-7)	★★★★	3.9
Columbia Fixed-Income Securities CFISX	CQ	▦	12.16	-3.36	-3.36	4.87	7.85	9.42	6.8	1.09	1.03	1.03	14	9	25	6 (-5)	★★★★	3.6
Dreyfus GNMA DRGMX	GM	▦	13.79	-2.78	-2.78	3.47	6.84	—	6.9	0.84	0.77	—	43	44	—	4 (-4)	★★★★	3.4
Dreyfus Short-Interm Government DSIGX	GG	▦	10.53	-0.75	-0.75	4.46	7.32	—	7.2	0.69	0.55	—	9	14	—	1 (-2)	★★★★★	4.8
Fidelity Government Securities FGOVX	GG	▦	9.17	-5.21	-5.21	4.74	7.86	9.08	6.7	1.24	1.07	1.03	7	5	8	7 (-6)	★★★	3.3
Fidelity Intermediate Bond FTHRX	CQ	▦	9.83	-2.01	-2.01	5.19	7.46	9.12	6.5	0.82	0.80	0.88	8	17	44	3 (-4)	★★★★	4.4
Fidelity Short-Term Bond FSHBX	CG	▦	8.60	-4.09	-4.09	3.97	6.27	—	6.6	0.66	0.63	—	68	84	—	1 (-4)	★★★★	4.4
Fidelity Spartan Ginnie Mae SGNMX	GM	▦	9.32	-1.51	-1.51	3.55	—	—	6.7	0.86	—	—	37	—	—	— (—)	★★★	3.7
Fidelity Spartan Lim Mat Govt FSTGX	GG	▦	9.35	-0.95	-0.95	3.69	6.37	—	5.9	0.58	0.47	—	39	54	—	1 (-3)	★★★★★	4.7
FPA New Income FPNIX	CG	▦	10.40	1.46	1.46	7.50	9.85	**10.98**	6.7	0.39	0.62	0.76	4	3	1	1 (-2)	★★★★★	3.9
Franklin U.S. Government FKUSX	GM	▦	6.42	-2.68	-2.68	3.77	7.08	9.02	7.8	0.79	0.66	0.70	28	28	27	2 (-4)	★★★★	3.3
Gradison-McDonald Govt Income GGIFX	GG	▦	12.02	-3.69	-3.69	3.25	6.44	—	6.2	1.01	0.97	—	57	50	—	5 (-5)	★★★	3.1
Harbor Bond HABDX	CG	▦	10.28	-3.76	-3.76	5.69	8.80	—	5.9	0.93	0.97	—	16	7	—	5 (-5)	★★★★★	4.5
Lexington GNMA Income LEXNX	GM	▦	7.60	-2.08	-2.08	3.64	7.07	8.79	7.2	0.96	0.99	1.07	32	30	36	6 (-4)	★★★	2.5
Loomis Sayles Bond LSBDX	CG	▦	10.05	-4.07	-4.07	**10.25**	—	—	8.6	1.02	—	—	1	—	—	— (—)	★★★★★	5.0
MFS Bond A MFBFX	CG	▦	12.13	-4.46	-4.46	4.95	7.88	9.94	7.4	1.15	1.13	1.12	34	25	24	8 (-7)	★★★	3.0
Neuberger & Berman Ultra Short NBMMX	CQ	▦	9.45	2.23	2.23	3.03	4.95	—	3.9	0.23	0.18	—	91	95	—	1 (-1)	★★★★	4.5
New England Bond Income A NEFRX	CG	▦	10.95	-4.24	-4.24	4.84	7.91	9.32	6.6	1.15	1.06	1.00	35	23	63	6 (-6)	★★★	2.6
Overland Express Var Rate Govt A OEVGX	GA	▦	9.19	-3.81	-3.81	1.68	—	—	4.7	0.60	—	—	61	—	—	— (—)	★★	2.4
PaineWebber Invmt Grade Income A PIGAX	CG	▦	9.70	-5.60	-5.60	5.22	8.00	9.50	7.9	1.19	1.07	1.16	28	19	57	7 (-7)	★★★	2.6
Portico Fixed Immdex Ret POBIX	CQ	▦	25.29	-3.06	-3.06	4.98	7.86	—	6.5	0.98	0.95	—	11	6	—	6 (-5)	★★★★	4.8
T. Rowe Price GNMA PRGMX	GM	▦	8.88	-1.64	-1.64	3.58	7.06	—	7.6	0.82	0.80	—	35	31	—	4 (-4)	★★★★	3.9
T. Rowe Price New Income PRCIX	CQ	▦	8.39	-2.21	-2.21	3.84	7.06	8.79	6.8	0.97	0.95	0.92	62	34	59	4 (-4)	★★★	4.2
T. Rowe Price Short-Term Bond PRWBX	CQ	▦	4.63	-2.92	-2.92	2.81	5.60	7.01	6.0	0.71	0.61	0.52	95	87	92	1 (-2)	★★★	4.1
Prudential Structured Maturity A PBSMX	CG	▦	10.97	-1.39	-1.39	4.03	6.86	—	5.9	0.69	0.57	—	52	45	—	2 (-3)	★★★★	3.4
Putnam Income A PINCX	CG	▦	6.47	-3.30	-3.30	5.93	7.98	9.65	8.0	0.85	1.00	0.99	10	20	45	5 (-5)	★★★	3.2
Scudder GNMA SGMSX	GM	▦	13.66	-3.11	-3.11	3.18	6.83	—	6.9	1.02	0.92	—	66	46	—	5 (-5)	★★★	3.5
Scudder Income SCSBX	CQ	▦	12.32	-4.50	-4.50	4.72	7.86	9.70	6.9	1.18	1.11	1.07	17	8	18	8 (-7)	★★★★	3.7
Scudder Short-Term Bond SCSTX	CQ	▦	10.92	-2.87	-2.87	3.40	6.78	8.91	6.9	0.67	0.55	0.75	80	53	48	1 (-3)	★★★★★	4.2
Scudder Short-Term Global Income SSTGX	SW	▦	10.54	-1.13	-1.13	3.64	—	—	8.2	0.62	—	—	1	—	—	— (—)	★★★★	3.9
SteinRoe Income SRHBX	CG	▦	9.06	-4.06	-4.06	5.88	8.10	—	7.5	1.01	1.00	—	12	18	—	7 (-6)	★★★★	3.7
Strong Advantage STADX	CG	▦	9.98	**3.55**	**3.55**	6.68	7.43	—	5.5	0.14	0.19	—	6	39	—	1 (0)	★★★★★	4.7
Strong Government Securities STVSX	GG	▦	9.63	-3.37	-3.37	5.97	8.58	—	6.5	0.99	0.79	—	1	1	—	3 (-5)	★★★★★	4.9
Strong Short-Term Bond SSTBX	CG	▦	9.42	-1.79	-1.79	4.63	6.69	—	6.7	0.56	0.57	—	39	74	—	2 (-3)	★★★★	4.0
U.S. Government Securities AMUSX	GG	▦	12.69	-4.65	-4.65	4.25	7.23	—	8.0	1.09	0.92	—	14	17	—	5 (-6)	★★★	2.9
Vanguard Bond Idx Total Bond Mkt VBMFX	CG	▦	9.17	-2.65	-2.65	4.59	7.45	—	6.8	0.94	0.92	—	23	20	—	6 (-5)	★★★★	3.8
Vanguard Fixed-Inc GNMA VFIIX	GM	▦	9.58	-0.95	-0.95	3.87	7.62	9.52	7.1	0.79	0.78	0.89	17	2	1	4 (-3)	★★★★★	4.2
Vanguard Fixed-Inc I/T US Treas VFITX	GT	▦	9.63	-4.33	-4.33	4.74	—	—	6.2	1.22	—	—	7	—	—	— (—)	★★★	3.7
Vanguard Fixed-Inc L/T Corp Bond VWESX	CQ	▦	8.05	-5.30	-5.30	5.98	8.86	10.41	7.6	1.36	1.43	1.35	2	1	1	10 (-7)	★★★★	3.6
Vanguard Fixed-Inc S/T Corporate VFSTX	CG	▦	10.30	-0.08	-0.08	4.67	7.21	8.48	5.7	0.57	0.48	0.48	18	28	66	1 (-2)	★★★★★	4.9
Vanguard Fixed-Inc S/T Federal VSGBX	GG	▦	9.69	-0.94	-0.94	4.02	6.67	—	5.6	0.66	0.55	—	24	38	—	1 (-2)	★★★★	4.7
Vanguard Fixed-Inc S/T US Treas VFISX	GT	▦	9.79	-0.48	-0.48	4.14	—	—	5.3	0.63	—	—	43	—	—	— (—)	★★★★	4.0
WPG Government Securities WPGVX	GG	▦	8.82	-8.83	-8.83	2.34	5.88	—	7.2	1.32	1.12	—	88	78	—	4 (-7)	★★	4.1

Bold numbers indicate *highest* return for the listed time period in each category.

	Funds in Category	Yield	SEC Yield	Assets ($bil)
	50	5.75%	5.79%	62.32

1994: A Haunted House for Municipal Bond Funds

Tax-free bond funds got walloped by rising interest rates in 1994, more so than any other category save utilities funds.

Municipal bonds bear long maturities in general, but the longest of the long naturally suffered most. **General Municipal Bond**, for example, has one of the group's most aggressive yield-curve postures, and, not surprisingly, suffered twice as much as its typical peer for the year. A handful of funds, however, like **Putnam Municipal Income**, curbed their losses somewhat by hedging with short futures.

On top of interest-rate sensitivity, many tax-free funds felt the pangs of illiquidity. The muni market is illiquid as it is, but 1994's inflation fears exacerbated problems by triggering sales by both individual bond holders and mutual funds. The California Orange County debacle did not help matters, either. That municipality, which engaged in a high degree of ill-advised leverage, caused a panic in the muni market when it filed for bankruptcy. The net result of illiquidity and the Orange County scare was that prices on municipal bonds plummeted to historic lows.

Yields, on the other hand, were at historic highs. In 1994, **Franklin High-Yield Tax-Free Income** offered, on average, a distributed yield more than 300 basis points in excess of inflation. Manager Sheila Amoroso achieved that payout through lower-tier credits and nonrated paper, which helped temper the fund's interest-rate sensitivity.

Those shareholders who haven't fled the muni-fund market have suffered many a bellyache. The good news is that such low prices and top notch yields make tax-free funds an attractive buy for 1995.

Kim Rebecca

Growth of $10,000
- Municipal Bond Category ($000)
- LB Agg ($000)

Net Assets ($bil)

	1983	1984	1985	1986	1987	1988	1989	1990	1991	1992	1993	1994	History
	16.92	16.26	23.43	23.35	4.49	13.99	13.09	10.29	14.75	12.83	15.02	2.42	High
	10.07	9.36	17.52	15.97	0.54	10.22	9.29	6.55	11.35	8.67	11.02	-4.55	Total Return %
	5.06	6.80	6.70	7.39	-5.80	4.89	6.00	4.63	6.46	4.71	3.82	-9.64	Low
	1.70	-5.79	-4.61	0.72	-2.21	2.34	-5.25	-2.40	-4.66	1.42	1.27	-1.63	+/- LB Agg
	2.02	-1.19	-2.51	-3.35	-0.96	0.06	-1.50	-0.75	-0.80	-0.15	-1.26	1.06	+/- LB Muni
	7.10	7.83	7.89	7.26	6.54	7.21	7.26	7.14	7.12	6.39	5.85	5.12	Income Return %
	1.50	0.50	7.54	7.31	-5.88	2.66	1.93	-0.59	4.22	2.28	5.17	-9.67	Capital Return %
	0.64	0.71	0.73	0.73	0.72	0.72	0.75	0.74	0.73	0.68	0.64	0.61	Income $
	0.84	0.73	0.64	0.63	0.69	0.69	0.69	0.66	0.64	0.63	0.65	0.65	Expense Ratio
	8.26	8.21	8.45	7.28	6.89	7.00	6.91	6.90	6.76	6.26	5.64	5.36	Income Ratio
	109.5	126.7	101.9	62.60	74.86	84.82	77.62	73.53	67.39	63.60	55.17	52.37	Turnover Ratio
	6.69	8.31	13.84	24.34	24.81	28.76	33.70	37.27	47.68	59.45	73.22	62.32	Total Net Assets ($bil)

Style Box Analysis

Number of Funds	Short	Interm	Long			1 Yr Total Return %	Short	Interm	Long			5 Yr Total Return %	Short	Interm	Long			Average Mstar Risk	Short	Interm	Long		
	5	5	20	High			1.05	-3.04	-6.68	High			5.18	6.64	6.41	High			0.20	0.69	1.09	High	
	3	1	15	Med			0.29	-4.03	-5.17	Med			5.42	6.60	6.87	Med			0.21	0.76	0.92	Med	
	0	0	0	Low			NMF	NMF	NMF	Low			NMF	NMF	NMF	Low			NMF	NMF	NMF	Low	

1.00=Muni Average

Risk Analysis

	Load-Adj Return	Morningstar[1] Return	Risk	Morningstar Risk-Adj Rating
1 Yr	-6.44			
3 Yr	4.09	1.03[2]	0.86	★★★
5 Yr	6.00	0.99[2]	0.84	★★★
10 Yr	8.12	0.93	0.84	★★★

[1]1.00=Muni Average [2]1.00=90-day T-bill return

Other Measures

				Standard Index LB Agg
Standard Deviation	4.99	Alpha		0.36
Mean	4.82	Beta		0.93
Sharpe Ratio	0.27	R-Squared		54.25

Performance 12-31-94

	Total Return%	+/- LB Agg	+/- LB Muni
3 Mo	-1.29	-1.66	0.15
6 Mo	-0.78	-1.77	0.47
1 Yr	-4.55	-1.63	1.06
3 Yr Average	4.79	0.24	-0.08
5 Yr Average	6.42	-1.21	-0.36
10 Yr Average	8.33	-1.62	-1.10
15 Yr Average	8.13	-2.67	-0.34

Portfolio

Amount 000	Total Equity: 0 Total Fixed-Income: 10439	Value $000	% Net Assets
139128	CO Denver Arpt Sys 8.5%	142432	0.22
159242	CA San Joaquin Hills Transp Toll 6.75%	137419	0.21
115700	DE Econ Dev Hosp Bill/Collection Svc DMD	115700	0.18
113000	CA Sacramento Transp 4.5%	112340	0.17
105000	GA Burke Dev Poll Cntrl Pwr 6.6%	102194	0.16
102221	NJ Tpk 6.5%	102015	0.16
99000	TX Dallas/Ft Worth Intl Arpt Fac 8%	101573	0.16
101245	TX Alliance Arpt Spcl Fac American 7.5%	97265	0.15
98396	IL Metro Pier/Expo McCormick Expsn 6.5%	91936	0.14
77708	FL Broward Resource Rec North 7.95%	83797	0.13
94695	WA Pub Pwr Sply Sys Proj #1 6%	83306	0.13
73000	IN Indianapolis GO Local Pub Impr 8.5%	82878	0.13
71489	MS Claiborne Poll Cntrl Engy 9.875%	81012	0.12
77385	NH Indl Dev Poll Cntrl Pub Svc 7.65%	78717	0.12
85340	NC East Muni Pwr Sys 6.25%	77349	0.12
76985	NH Indl Dev Poll Cntrl Pub Svc 7.5%	76773	0.12
71005	LA St Charles Poll Cntrl Pwr 8.25%	76392	0.12
75825	MA New England Educ Loan Mktg 5.8%	75234	0.12
70025	NC East Muni Pwr Sys 7.75%	74618	0.11
86780	WA Pub Pwr Sply Sys Proj #3 5.375%	73411	0.11

Worst Three Months

	Worst 3 Month Performance 1990-1994
Alliance Muni Income National A	-8.50
Oppenheimer Tax-Free Bond A	-8.30
Fidelity Insured Tax-Free	-8.03
Safeco Municipal Bond	-7.80
Value Line Tax-Exempt High-Yield	-7.57

Composition

Cash	6.15	Preferreds	0.00
Stocks	0.00	Convertibles	0.00
Bonds	93.85	Other	0.00

Tax Analysis

	Tax-Adj Hist Return %	% Pretax Return
3 Yr Avg	4.57	95.48
5 Yr Avg	6.25	97.54
10 Yr Avg	8.17	98.24

Coupon Range

	% of Bonds
0%	3.3
0 to 8.5%	50.3
8.5 to 9.5%	16.4
9.5 to 11%	12.2
More than 11%	11.4
Not Applicable	6.4

Category Leaders

Lowest 3 Yr Morningstar Risk

Calvert Tax-Fr Res Lim-TermA	0.02
Vanguard Muni Short-Term	0.10
Merrill Lynch Muni Ltd Mat A	0.12
Dreyfus Short-Intrm Muni Bd	0.21
USAA Tax-Exempt Short-Term	0.22
T. Rowe Price Tax-Fr Sh-Intm	0.28
Vanguard Muni Limited-Term	0.29
Fidelity Spartan Sh-Int Muni	0.31
Thornburg Ltd-Term Natl A	0.43
Sit Tax-Free Income	0.54

Top Rated Funds

Sit Tax-Free Income	1.90
Franklin High-Yld T/F Income	1.70
T. Rowe Price Tax-Fr Hi-Yld	1.67
United Municipal High-Income	1.66
Fidelity Aggressive Tax-Free	1.62
Dreyfus Short-Intrm Muni Bd	1.61
Fidelity Spartan Sh-Int Muni	1.58
Vanguard Muni Limited-Term	1.54
Strong Municipal Bond	1.45
Thornburg Ltd-Term Natl A	1.40

Best 3 Yr Return %

United Municipal High-Income	6.50
Franklin High-Yld T/F Income	6.36
Vista Tax-Free Income A	6.23
Strong Municipal Bond	5.98
Flagship All-American T/E A	5.98
Vanguard Muni Intermed-Term	5.93
T. Rowe Price Tax-Fr Hi-Yld	5.78
Sit Tax-Free Income	5.74
Franklin Insured T/F Income	5.60
Vanguard Muni High-Yield	5.53

Bond Funds—Municipal

Fund / Ticker	Obj	Style Box	NAV	YTD	1Yr	3Yr	5Yr	10Yr	Trailing 12 Mo Yield %	3Yr	5Yr	10Yr	3Yr	5Yr	10Yr	Bear Mkt Indicator (Worst 3 mo)	Star Rating	Avg Star Rating
Lehman Bros. Municipal Bond Index				-5.60	-5.60	4.87	6.77	9.43										
Alliance Muni Income National A ALTHX	MN		9.29	-9.64	-9.64	4.18	6.31	—	6.4	1.23	1.15	—	69	45	—	8 (-9)	★★	4.0
American Capital Muni Bond A ACMBX	MN		9.57	-3.52	-3.52	5.27	6.60	8.90	3.6	0.79	0.91	1.10	18	26	43	6 (-5)	★★★	2.5
Calvert Tax-Free Res Lim-Term A CTFLX	MN		10.59	2.42	2.42	3.84	4.89	5.87	3.6	0.02	0.03	0.10	83	96	93	1 (0)	★★★★★	3.9
Colonial Tax-Exempt A COLTX	MN		12.44	-6.27	-6.27	3.97	5.97	8.35	6.3	1.01	0.94	0.81	77	60	66	6 (-6)	★★★	4.1
Dreyfus Intermediate Muni Bond DITEX	MN		13.14	-4.57	-4.57	4.99	6.55	8.13	5.7	0.86	0.81	0.75	29	29	73	4 (-5)	★★★★	3.9
Dreyfus Municipal Bond DRTAX	MN		11.63	-6.92	-6.92	4.38	6.27	8.58	6.4	1.13	1.01	0.99	58	48	59	7 (-7)	★★★	3.5
Dreyfus Short-Interm Muni Bond DSIBX	MN		12.70	-0.33	-0.33	4.29	5.54	—	4.5	0.21	0.20	—	64	84	—	1 (-1)	★★★★★	4.7
Fidelity Advisor High-Inc Muni A FAHIX	MN		11.00	-8.05	-8.05	5.18	7.56	—	6.3	1.05	0.91	—	21	3	—	5 (-7)	★★★★	4.8
Fidelity Aggressive Tax-Free FATFX	MN		10.81	-5.90	-5.90	5.36	7.04	—	7.1	0.88	0.79	—	15	12	—	4 (-6)	★★★★★	5.0
Fidelity Insured Tax-Free FMUIX	MN		10.69	-7.73	-7.73	4.32	6.29	—	5.8	1.24	1.21	—	61	46	—	9 (-8)	★★	2.4
Fidelity Municipal Bond FMBDX	MN		7.36	-9.08	-9.08	3.96	6.10	8.86	5.6	1.28	1.22	1.15	78	55	46	9 (-8)	★★	2.9
Fidelity Spartan Sh-Interm Muni FSTFX	MN		9.66	-0.08	-0.08	4.48	5.73	—	4.6	0.32	0.29	—	54	75	—	1 (-2)	★★★★★	3.9
First Investors Insured Tax-Ex A FITAX	MN		9.42	-6.07	-6.07	3.70	5.45	8.22	5.4	0.90	0.87	0.81	88	88	69	5 (-6)	★★	3.6
Flagship All-American Tax-Ex A FLAAX	MN		10.03	-5.89	-5.89	5.98	7.58	—	6.3	1.07	1.14	—	6	3	—	9 (-7)	★★★	3.2
Fortress Municipal Income FHTFX	MN		10.02	-5.75	-5.75	4.17	5.97	—	6.0	1.01	0.94	—	70	61	—	6 (-6)	★★★	4.2
Franklin Federal Tax-Free Income FKTIX	MN		11.29	-3.73	-3.73	5.47	6.99	9.30	6.9	0.72	0.79	0.94	12	14	27	4 (-5)	★★★★	3.4
Franklin High-Yield T/F Income FRHIX	MN		10.35	-2.58	-2.58	6.37	7.29	—	7.2	0.60	0.68	—	2	7	—	4 (-4)	★★★★★	4.9
Franklin Insured Tax-Free Income FTFIX	MN		11.54	-3.58	-3.58	5.60	6.92	—	6.2	0.77	0.84	—	10	15	—	5 (-5)	★★★★	2.4
General Municipal Bond GMBDX	MN		13.72	-7.32	-7.32	4.88	7.33	9.13	6.2	1.20	1.12	1.17	34	6	33	8 (-7)	★★★	3.2
IDS High-Yield Tax-Exempt INHYX	MN		4.25	-5.05	-5.05	4.22	5.93	9.04	6.9	0.86	0.91	0.93	66	63	39	7 (-6)	★★★★	4.0
Lord Abbett Tax-Free Income Natl LANSX	MN		10.22	-7.94	-7.94	4.29	6.48	9.33	6.8	1.25	1.24	1.16	63	33	26	9 (-7)	★★	2.9
Merrill Lynch Muni Ltd MaturityA MALMX	MN		9.77	1.27	1.27	3.81	4.98	5.50	3.7	0.12	0.11	0.15	84	95	96	1 (0)	★★★★	3.9
MFS Municipal Bond A MMBFX	MN		10.17	-6.94	-6.94	4.99	6.78	9.45	5.4	1.20	1.32	1.15	29	20	18	10 (-7)	★★	3.4
Nuveen Municipal Bond NUVBX	MN		8.65	-1.85	-1.85	4.96	6.24	9.36	5.9	0.58	0.67	0.78	30	50	23	3 (-3)	★★★★	3.5
Oppenheimer Tax-Free Bond A OPTAX	MN		8.93	-9.30	-9.30	4.07	6.00	8.83	6.2	1.28	1.22	1.09	73	60	47	9 (-8)	★★	3.4
T. Rowe Price Tax-Fr High-Yield PRFHX	MN		11.16	-4.38	-4.38	5.78	7.21	—	6.5	0.80	0.76	—	8	9	—	4 (-5)	★★★★★	5.0
T. Rowe Price Tax-Fr Short-Intrm PRFSX	MN		5.18	0.33	0.33	4.19	5.29	5.89	4.2	0.29	0.28	0.36	68	92	92	1 (-2)	★★★★	3.2
Putnam Municipal Income A PTFHX	MN		8.25	-6.40	-6.40	5.28	6.94	—	6.5	0.95	0.84	—	17	14	—	5 (-6)	★★★★	4.7
Safeco Municipal Bond SFCOX	MN		12.46	-8.25	-8.25	4.02	6.43	9.59	6.2	1.38	1.43	1.23	75	38	14	10 (-8)	★★★	3.5
Scudder High-Yield Tax-Free SHYTX	MN		10.86	-8.38	-8.38	4.97	6.83	—	6.1	1.21	1.20	—	30	17	—	9 (-8)	★★★	3.3
Scudder Medium-Term Tax-Free SCMTX	MN		10.39	-3.50	-3.50	5.26	6.81	7.02	5.3	0.81	0.64	0.55	18	18	86	2 (-4)	★★★★	3.5
Sit Tax-Free Income SNTIX	MN		9.43	-0.63	-0.63	5.74	6.75	—	6.0	0.54	0.42	—	9	22	—	2 (-3)	★★★★★	5.0
Smith Barney Tax-Exempt Income B SXMTX	MN		16.33	-6.53	-6.53	4.34	5.82	—	5.9	1.01	1.01	—	60	69	—	6 (-6)	★★★	3.3
SteinRoe Intermediate Municipals SRIMX	MN		10.70	-3.51	-3.51	4.83	6.51	—	4.8	0.84	0.85	—	38	31	—	4 (-5)	★★★	3.1
SteinRoe Managed Municipals SRMMX	MN		8.36	-5.55	-5.55	4.35	6.70	**10.18**	5.8	1.03	1.05	1.25	59	23	2	8 (-7)	★★★★	3.0
Strong Municipal Bond SXFIX	MN		9.23	-4.55	-4.55	6.16	7.25	—	6.1	0.95	1.06	—	5	7	—	6 (-6)	★★★★	3.0
SunAmerica Tax-Exempt Insured A STEAX	MN		11.56	-3.99	-3.99	3.40	4.94	—	5.6	0.82	0.72	—	93	95	—	3 (-5)	★★	3.1
Thornburg Ltd-Term Muni Natl A LTMFX	MN		12.92	-1.49	-1.49	4.92	5.96	7.33	4.9	0.43	0.38	0.31	32	61	82	1 (-2)	★★★★★	5.0
United Municipal High-Income UMUHX	MN		4.93	-3.11	-3.11	**6.50**	7.70	—	6.9	0.71	0.67	—	1	2	—	3 (-5)	★★★★★	5.0
USAA Tax-Exempt Interm-Term USATX	MN		12.02	-4.03	-4.03	5.09	6.60	8.08	5.7	0.81	0.77	0.73	24	27	74	4 (-5)	★★★★	3.9
USAA Tax-Exempt Long-Term USTEX	MN		12.22	-7.93	-7.93	4.51	6.45	8.90	6.3	1.12	1.11	1.06	52	36	44	8 (-6)	★★★	3.6
USAA Tax-Exempt Short-Term USSTX	MN		10.33	0.82	0.82	4.07	5.14	6.01	4.4	0.22	0.19	0.23	73	94	91	1 (-1)	★★★★★	4.0
Value Line Tax-Exempt High-Yield VLHYX	MN		9.89	-6.91	-6.91	3.82	6.01	8.25	5.7	1.24	1.17	0.95	84	59	67	8 (-8)	★★★	4.3
Van Kampen Insured T/F Income A VKMTX	MN		17.57	-6.31	-6.31	4.85	6.42	9.34	6.0	1.25	1.22	1.15	36	40	24	7 (-7)	★★★	2.6
Vanguard Muni Bond High-Yield VWAHX	MN		9.66	-5.07	-5.07	5.53	7.39	9.97	6.4	1.20	1.32	1.22	11	6	3	9 (-6)	★★★★	3.2
Vanguard Muni Bond Insured L/T VILPX	MN		11.23	-5.59	-5.59	5.24	7.02	9.52	6.1	1.28	1.40	1.23	19	13	17	10 (-6)	★★★	3.2
Vanguard Muni Bond Interm-Term VWITX	MN		12.39	-2.12	-2.12	5.93	7.40	9.13	5.5	0.78	0.82	0.87	6	5	32	4 (-4)	★★★★★	3.1
Vanguard Muni Bond Limited-Term VMLTX	MN		10.37	0.07	0.07	4.21	5.81	—	4.4	0.29	0.30	—	67	69	—	1 (-1)	★★★★★	4.5
Vanguard Muni Bond Short-Term VWSTX	MN		15.33	1.63	1.63	3.38	4.77	5.49	3.6	0.11	0.09	0.13	94	96	97	1 (0)	★★★★	3.8
Vista Tax-Free Income A VTFIX	MN		11.05	-7.64	-7.64	6.23	**7.95**	—	5.2	1.14	1.22	—	4	1	—	9 (-7)	★★★	2.5

Bold numbers indicate *highest* return for the listed time period in each category.

Funds in Category	Yield	SEC Yield	Assets ($bil)
20	0.80%	3.58%	29.37

Closed Funds Are Not an Open-and-Shut Case

Closed-fund activity in 1994 proved nothing is certain.

After 1993 saw a record number of funds close to new investors, several members of the Closed Fund Hall of Fame reconsidered their off-limits status in 1994. **FAM Value** manager Thomas Putnam reopened his small-cap fund in March, following Michael Price's decision to throw open the portals of growth-and-income funds **Mutual Shares** and **Mutual Qualified**. Growth-and-income offering **FPA Paramount** and small-company fund **Pennsylvania Mutual** reopened as well. In the year's most-telling development, ultra-hot sector fund **Hancock Freedom Regional Bank B** closed and reopened during the course of 1994.

Unfortunately for several opened funds, 1994 was not an encouraging year. Few funds generated the kind of shareholder response they once received. The $450 million FPA Paramount, for example, set a new closing target of $500 million in assets, but had not yet met this goal as of December 31, 1994.

Amid the rash of reopenings, however, a few funds shut their doors in 1994. After 1993's surge in international investing, overseas funds were flooded with shareholder monies. **Acorn International** closed after a scant 17 months of operation. Similarly, international asset-allocation fund **SoGen International** closed early in the year. Small-cap **MFS Emerging Growth A** issued a final boarding call as well.

Of course, if 1994 is any indication, investors needn't rule out investing in these or other Hall of Famers; they may be back again.

Alice Lowenstein

Growth of $10,000
- Hall of Fame
- Category ($000)
- Wil 5000 ($000)

Net Assets ($bil)

	1983	1984	1985	1986	1987	1988	1989	1990	1991	1992	1993	1994	History
	30.06	19.47	46.15	28.44	15.89	39.93	50.85	11.38	99.08	42.41	49.11	5.46	High
	24.47	5.46	33.57	14.62	2.53	21.87	25.70	-5.92	51.44	16.60	22.39	-1.65	**Total Return %**
	15.36	-7.27	27.96	-4.28	-18.34	-0.30	15.03	-17.54	18.82	-0.20	0.49	-22.92	Low
	2.00	-0.80	1.84	-4.06	-2.73	5.26	-5.98	-2.81	20.96	8.98	12.33	-2.97	+/- S&P 500
	1.00	2.41	1.01	-1.48	0.16	3.92	-3.47	0.26	17.24	7.63	11.11	-1.58	+/- Wilshire 5000
	4.00	2.99	2.57	2.30	1.78	2.46	1.67	1.53	2.41	1.23	0.79	0.81	Income Return %
	16.25	3.38	25.79	9.04	-1.26	17.89	24.04	-7.46	49.04	14.86	21.60	-2.47	Capital Return %
	0.64	0.48	0.43	0.45	0.32	0.39	0.28	0.26	0.35	0.28	0.21	0.15	Income $
	0.96	1.02	1.33	1.30	1.35	1.39	1.36	1.42	1.36	1.34	1.21	1.09	Expense Ratio
	4.08	3.33	2.80	1.96	1.49	1.78	1.59	1.45	1.08	0.65	0.51	0.65	Income Ratio
	67.88	50.28	92.25	99.60	120.9	110.9	98.00	97.88	220.9	72.40	63.35	56.88	Turnover Ratio
	2.37	3.19	5.03	6.45	6.25	7.74	10.92	9.64	14.96	20.69	29.55	29.37	Total Net Assets ($bil)

Style Box Analysis

Number of Funds	Value	Blend	Growth		1 Yr Total Return %	Value	Blend	Growth		5 Yr Total Return %	Value	Blend	Growth		Average Mstar Risk	Value	Blend	Growth	
Large	3	0	1		Large	3.00	NMF	-6.73		Large	10.31	NMF	10.86		Large	0.85	NMF	1.21	
Med	0	2	0		Med	NMF	-3.35	NMF		Med	NMF	15.27	NMF		Med	NMF	0.93	NMF	
Small	5	2	7		Small	-0.14	-0.26	-3.92		Small	11.93	11.11	18.11		Small	0.78	0.61	1.23	

1.00 = Equity Average

Risk Analysis

	Load-Adj Return	Morningstar[1] Return	Risk	Morningstar Risk-Adj Rating
1 Yr	-2.30			
3 Yr	10.73	2.31[2]	0.95	★★★★
5 Yr	13.82	2.63[2]	0.98	★★★★
10 Yr	16.04	1.83	0.92	★★★★

[1]1.00=Equity Average [2]1.00=90-day T-bill return

Other Measures

			Standard Index S&P 500
Standard Deviation	11.77	Alpha	5.17
Mean	11.08	Beta	0.92
Sharpe Ratio	0.67	R-Squared	39.53

Performance 12-31-94

	Total Return%	+/- S&P	+/- Wil 5000
3 Mo	-2.29	-2.28	-1.52
6 Mo	4.37	-0.49	-0.25
1 Yr	-1.65	-2.97	-1.58
3 Yr Average	10.96	4.69	4.35
5 Yr Average	13.94	5.25	5.12
10 Yr Average	16.10	1.72	2.24
15 Yr Average	17.14	2.65	3.16

Portfolio

Amount 000	Total Equity: 1992 / Total Fixed-Income: 187	Value $000	% Net Assets
19069	Citicorp	789664	2.67
13635	Chrysler	668117	2.26
21372	Ford Motor	598427	2.03
5799	Atlantic Richfield	590089	2.00
355	US Treasury Bond 12%	472040	1.60
21	Berkshire Hathaway	429094	1.45
8599	Aetna Life & Casualty	405208	1.37
6269	CIGNA	396483	1.34
24027	USX-Marathon Group	393445	1.33
6937	Bankers Trust New York	389154	1.32
10077	Burlington Resources	353279	1.20
8449	First Union	349569	1.18
3910	ALCOA	338660	1.15
8189	BankAmerica	323468	1.10
5821	FHLMC	293955	1.00
240	US Treasury Bond 10.375%	285600	0.97
11221	Unicom	269316	0.91
5338	Reynolds Metals	262119	0.89
245	US Treasury Note 7.25%	242590	0.82
6716	Chemical Banking	240487	0.81

Worst Three Months

	Worst 3 Month Performance 1990-1994
MFS Emerging Growth B	-30.83
Hancock Special Equities A	-25.94
Ariel Growth	-25.39
Babson Enterprise	-25.27
Acorn	-24.48

Composition %

Cash	8.44	Preferreds	1.04
Stocks	88.80	Convertibles	0.51
Bonds	1.19	Other	0.02

Tax Analysis

	Tax-Adj Hist Return %	% Pretax Return
3 Yr Avg	10.52	80.62
5 Yr Avg	12.09	85.09
10 Yr Avg	12.91	79.82

Sector Weightings

	% of Stocks	Rel S&P500
Utilities	1.9	0.16
Energy	3.9	0.38
Financials	18.1	1.71
Industrial Cyclicals	17.7	1.08
Consumer Durables	10.3	1.66
Consumer Staples	4.5	0.36
Services	15.6	1.92
Retail	6.9	1.19
Health	6.9	0.79
Technology	14.2	1.55

Category Leaders

Lowest 3 Yr Morningstar Risk

SoGen International	0.38
T. Rowe Price Small-Cap Val	0.51
Skyline Special Equities	0.56
Babson Enterprise	0.63
Sequoia	0.67
Nicholas Limited Edition	0.71
Vanguard/Windsor	0.73
Strong Common Stock	0.73
Janus Venture	0.75
Ariel Growth	0.80

Top Rated Funds

Skyline Special Equities	4.91
Strong Common Stock	4.24
Hancock Special Equities A	3.99
MFS Emerging Growth B	3.76
PIMCo Adv Opportunity C	3.44
T. Rowe Price Small-Cap Val	2.81
Harbor International	2.48
Acorn	2.47
CGM Capital Development	2.28
SoGen International	2.24

Best 3 Yr Return %

Skyline Special Equities	20.02
PIMCo Adv Opportunity C	18.56
Hancock Special Equities A	16.79
Harbor International	15.23
Acorn	15.00
Strong Common Stock	14.58
Babson Enterprise	14.05
T. Rowe Price Small-Cap Val	13.70
MFS Emerging Growth B	12.95
SoGen International	12.07

Closed Fund Hall of Fame

Categ	Fund	Obj	Style Box	NAV	Total Return % through 12-31-94		Annualized			Trailing 12 Mo Yield %	Morningstar Risk 1.00=Equity Average			Rtn % Rank Obj			Bear Mkt Indicator (Worst 3 mo)	Star Rating	Avg Star Rating
					YTD	1Yr	3Yr	5Yr	10Yr		3Yr	5Yr	10Yr	3Yr	5Yr	10Yr			
S&P 500 Index					**1.31**	**1.31**	**6.27**	**8.69**	**14.38**										
Core	Acorn ACRNX	SC		12.24	-7.45	-7.45	15.00	13.07	16.56	0.9	0.85	0.95	0.85	16	33	12	9(-24)	★★★★★	4.3
Aggr.	Acorn International ACINX	WF		15.24	-3.80	-3.80	—	—	—	0.6	—	—	—	—	—	—	— (—)		3.0
Core	Ariel Growth ARGFX	SC		26.98	-4.22	-4.22	5.19	5.33	—	0.8	0.80	1.00	—	82	93	—	9(-25)	★★	3.0
Core	Babson Enterprise BABEX	SC		15.15	2.42	2.42	14.06	12.29	14.80	0.2	0.63	0.84	0.89	21	43	25	7(-25)	★★★★	3.2
Aggr.	CGM Capital Development LOMCX	G		20.58	-22.92	-22.92	5.23	18.68	**19.64**	0.3	1.70	1.46	1.38	54	1	1	10(-23)	★★★★	4.7
Aggr.	Hancock Special Equities A JHNSX	SC		16.15	2.02	2.02	16.79	**21.83**	—	0.0	1.54	1.36	—	8	3	—	10(-26)	★★★★★	2.9
Core	Harbor International HAINX	WF		24.45	5.43	5.43	15.23	10.90	—	1.0	1.01	0.98	—	5	6	—	7(-17)	★★★★	3.7
Core	Janus Twenty JAVLX	G		22.71	-6.73	-6.73	-0.54	10.86	—	0.3	1.34	1.12	—	91	21	—	9(-18)	★★★	4.0
Consv.	Janus Venture JAVTX	SC		48.68	**5.46**	**5.46**	7.32	12.72	—	0.1	0.75	0.75	—	63	40	—	5(-15)	★★★★	4.8
Aggr.	MFS Emerging Growth B MEGBX	SC		18.89	4.00	4.00	12.95	21.38	—	0.0	1.51	1.45	—	23	4	—	10(-31)	★★★★★	3.8
Core	Monetta MONTX	SC		14.52	-6.20	-6.20	-0.19	11.54	—	0.0	1.22	1.00	—	98	52	—	7(-20)	★★★	4.3
Core	Mutual Discovery MDISX	SC		12.55	3.62	3.62	—	—	—	1.2	—	—	—	—	—	—	— (—)		
Consv.	Nicholas Limited Edition NCLEX	SC		17.09	-3.04	-3.04	7.27	11.68	—	0.6	0.71	0.80	—	64	49	—	4(-20)	★★★★	4.3
Aggr.	PIMCo Adv Opportunity C POPCX	AG		27.48	-4.73	-4.73	18.56	21.01	18.76	1.0	1.49	1.34	1.30	4	2	7	10(-20)	★★★★★	3.7
Core	T. Rowe Price Small-Cap Value PRSVX	SC		13.40	-1.38	-1.38	13.70	11.84	—	1.0	0.51	0.69	—	22	45	—	4(-21)	★★★★	3.7
Consv.	Sequoia SEQUX	G		55.59	3.71	3.71	8.49	11.46	14.30	1.1	0.67	0.73	0.61	26	16	25	4(-16)	★★★★	5.0
Core	Skyline Special Equities SKSEX	SC		15.64	-1.17	-1.17	**20.03**	18.25	—	0.0	0.56	0.87	—	2	9	—	9(-24)	★★★★★	4.5
Hybr.	SoGen International SGENX	AA		22.68	2.52	2.52	12.07	10.54	15.37	0.7	0.38	0.47	0.49	1	8	1	1 (-8)	★★★★★	4.7
Core	Strong Common Stock STCSX	SC		16.74	-0.50	-0.50	14.58	19.00	—	0.3	0.73	0.82	—	19	6	—	8(-16)	★★★★★	5.0
Aggr.	Vanguard/Windsor VWNDX	GI		12.59	-0.15	-0.15	11.56	8.57	13.28	3.3	0.73	0.99	0.92	5	33	29	9(-22)	★★★	4.3

Bold numbers indicate *highest* return for the listed time period in each category.

Funds in Category	Yield	Avg Prem/Disc	Assets ($bil)
13	9.00%	-2.35	4.02

Derivatives Didn't Color Income Funds Blue

Luckily, one bad apple hasn't spoiled the whole closed-end income-fund bunch.

Inflation fears and rising long-term interest rates stung income portfolios in 1994. **American Government Income Portfolio**'s 26% loss was by far the worst of the lot. The fund—along with a handful of other Piper Jaffray-managed offerings—grabbed headlines with huge mortgage-backed-derivative losses. NAV growth is unlikely unless rates pull back and investor participation in the beleaguered derivatives market revives.

The income category didn't suffer as badly as Piper Jaffray's woes might indicate, though. A handful of unconventional funds handled rising rates with aplomb. The income shares of dual-purpose funds **Convertible Holdings Income** and **Gemini II Income** racked up nice gains, thanks to meaty income streams and solid NAVs. Convertible-laden **AIM Strategic Income** did well by shorting some of the common stock underlying each convertible in the portfolio. Finally, by investing in less-liquid commercial mortgages, **PIMCo Commercial Mortages** warded off the rising-rate demon.

Some more-conventional income funds also withstood rising rates well. **John Hancock Investors'** losses were limited by a dual-barbell strategy, designed to simultaneously control interest-rate and credit risk. **Allmerica Securities** held its own, as well, because management focused on middle-tier credits, pulled in duration, and raised cash.

The silver lining behind all this was that prices of many defensive funds have gotten pummeled. Savvy investors may thus find value among the rubble.

Susan Paluch

Worst Three Months

	Worst 3 Month Performance 1990-1994
Amer Govt Inc Port	-24.88
High Yield Plus	-16.43
Lincoln Natl Convert	-11.27
Transamerica Income	-7.44
Putnam Mgd Muni Inc	-6.65

Category Leaders

Lowest 3 Yr Morningstar Risk		Top Rated Funds		Best 3 Yr Return %	
AIM Strategic Inc	0.28	High Yield Plus	2.22	Lincoln Natl Convert	11.59
High Yield Plus	0.46	Lincoln Natl Convert	2.18	High Yield Plus	11.34
Nuv Muni Value	0.46	AIM Strategic Inc	1.56	AIM Strategic Inc	7.31
Lincoln Natl Convert	0.61	Putnam H/Y Muni	1.39	Putnam Mgd Muni Inc	7.27
Allmerica Sec Trust	0.63	Pacific American Inc	1.36	Allmerica Sec Trust	7.00
Pacific American Inc	0.66	Allmerica Sec Trust	1.27	Putnam H/Y Muni	6.68
Putnam H/Y Muni	0.67	Nuv Muni Value	1.23	Pacific American Inc	6.64
J Hancock Inc	0.74	Putnam Mgd Muni Inc	1.17	J Hancock Inc	6.38
Global Income Plus	0.82	Transamerica Income	1.12	Transamerica Income	6.06
Transamerica Income	0.82	J Hancock Inc	1.08	Nuv Muni Value	5.04

Growth of $10,000
- Closed-End Income ($000)
- Index ($000)

Net Assets ($bil)

	1983	1984	1985	1986	1987	1988	1989	1990	1991	1992	1993	1994	History
	9.89	16.42	24.36	14.86	3.38	15.28	27.20	18.19	42.73	18.46	27.97	1.20	High
	9.89	16.42	22.79	13.88	1.23	11.48	12.16	5.62	21.55	10.85	15.31	-4.60	NAV Total Return %
	9.89	16.42	21.23	12.91	-4.71	9.17	-2.14	-7.13	10.55	1.71	8.33	-25.86	Low
	1.52	1.27	0.67	-1.37	-1.53	3.60	-2.38	-3.32	5.54	3.61	5.56	-1.69	+/- LB Agg
	1.84	5.87	2.77	-5.43	-0.28	1.32	1.38	-1.68	9.40	2.03	3.03	1.00	+/- LB Muni
	12.17	13.48	13.19	10.57	10.23	9.76	10.04	10.44	10.68	8.59	8.55	7.47	Income Return %
	-1.33	2.40	11.57	3.29	-9.00	1.72	2.12	-4.82	10.86	2.26	6.76	-12.0	Capital Return %
	1.60	1.62	1.65	1.36	1.45	1.05	1.05	1.15	1.09	1.03	0.98	0.97	Income $
	0.88	0.87	0.83	0.78	0.79	0.93	1.27	1.28	1.25	1.09	1.10	1.07	Expense Ratio
	10.91	11.72	10.74	9.57	9.00	9.22	9.59	9.68	9.11	8.55	10.02	8.78	Income Ratio
	55.43	61.52	81.07	86.01	48.65	38.64	77.66	58.04	61.80	77.71	55.74	53.80	Turnover Ratio
	0.27	0.39	0.43	0.57	1.98	2.72	3.52	3.48	3.76	3.90	4.22	4.02	Total Net Assets ($bil)

Style Box Analysis

Number of Funds	Short	Interm	Long			1 Yr Total Return %	Short	Interm	Long		5 Yr Total Return %	Short	Interm	Long		Average Mstar Risk	Short	Interm	Long
High	0	0	1				NMF	NMF	-25.86			NMF	NMF	6.48			NMF	NMF	2.03
Med	0	4	1				NMF	-1.80	-4.45			NMF	9.00	8.76			NMF	0.75	0.78
Low	0	1	0				NMF	-5.04	NMF			NMF	12.84	NMF			NMF	0.58	NMF

1.00 = Bond Average

Risk Analysis

	Load-Adj Return	Morningstar[1] Return	Risk	Morningstar Risk-Adj Rating
1 Yr	N/A			
3 Yr	N/A	0.37[2]	1.00	★★★
5 Yr	N/A	0.93[2]	0.93	★★★
10 Yr	N/A	1.00	0.85	★★★★

[1] 1.00=Bond Average [2] 1.00=90-day T-bill return

Other Measures

			Standard Index LB Agg
Standard Deviation	5.78	Alpha	1.94
Mean	6.52	Beta	1.03
Sharpe Ratio	0.59	R-Squared	64.31

Performance 12-31-94

	Total Return%	+/- S&P	+/-LB Muni
3 Mo	-0.36	-0.74	1.08
6 Mo	1.35	0.36	2.60
1 Yr	-4.60	-1.69	1.00
3 Yr Average	6.55	2.00	1.68
5 Yr Average	9.08	1.46	2.31
10 Yr Average	10.43	0.48	1.00
15 Yr Average	—	—	—

Portfolio

Amount 000	Total Equity: 4 / Total Fixed-Income: 1018	Value $000	% Net Assets
51930	SC Piedmont Muni Pwr Elec 7.25%	52600	1.28
45015	UT Intermountain Pwr Spcl Obl 7.875%	47164	1.14
41590	CO Denver Arpt Sys 8.5%	42158	1.02
24265	TX Austin Combined Util Sys 12.5%	38001	0.92
37625	NC East Muni Pwr Sys 7.25%	37883	0.92
41205	CO Denver Arpt Sys 7%	36374	0.88
30640	MA Muni Whlse Elec Pwr Sply Sys 8.75%	33568	0.81
28845	TX Houston Wtr/Swr Sys 8.125%	31522	0.76
29750	UT Intermountain Pwr Sply 7%	30118	0.73
28105	GA Burke Dev Poll Cntrl Pwr 10.5%	29899	0.73
28070	MA Hsg Fin Multi-Fam 8.8%	29661	0.72
26815	NC Muni Pwr #1 Catawba Elec 8.5%	28196	0.68
25710	TX Muni Pwr 8%	27346	0.66
31025	CO Denver Arpt Sys 6.75%	26687	0.65
22865	LA Pub Fac South Baptist Hosp 8%	25609	0.62
23610	NC East Muni Pwr Sys 7.75%	24926	0.60
3023860	Govt of Spain 10.9-13.45%	24646	0.60
22800	CA Metro Wtr Dist South Wtrwks 6.75%	24624	0.60
22755	UT Intermountain Pwr Sply 7.75%	24013	0.58
22390	KY Dev Fin Good Samaritan Hosp 10.25%	23861	0.58

Composition %

Cash	2.90	Preferreds	0.05
Stocks	0.0	Convertibles	14.97
Bonds	81.86	Other	0.23

Tax Analysis

	Tax-Adj Hist Return %	% Pretax Return
3 Yr Avg	N/A	N/A
5 Yr Avg	N/A	N/A
10 Yr Avg	N/A	N/A

Coupon Range

	% of Bonds
0%	1.5
0 to 8.5%	32.6
8.5 to 9.5%	21.8
9.5 to 11%	18.6
More than 11%	13.9
Not Applicable	11.5

Closed-End Income Funds

Fund / Ticker	Obj	Mkt Price	Prem/ Disc	Total Return % through 12-31-94		Annualized			Trailing 12 Mo Yield %	Morningstar Risk 1.00=Bond Average			Rtn % Rank Obj			Bear Mkt Indicator (Worst 3 mo)	Star Rating	Avg Star Rating
				YTD	1Yr	3Yr	5Yr	10Yr		3Yr	5Yr	10Yr	3Yr	5Yr	10Yr			
Lehman Bros. Aggregate Bond Index				**-2.92**	**-2.92**	**4.55**	**7.63**	**9.94**										
Lehman Bros. Municipal Bond Index				**-5.60**	**-5.60**	**4.87**	**6.77**	**9.43**										
Specialized Bond Funds										1.00=Clsd-End Hybrid Avg								
AIM Strategic Income AST	CV	8.000	-12.9	0.26	0.26	7.31	9.02	—	5.6	0.22	0.21	—	66	66	—	1 (-4)	★★★★	3.8
American Govt Inc Port AAF	GB	7.250	8.5	-25.87	-25.87	-1.25	6.48	—	14.6	2.44	1.86	—	80	44	—	10 (-25)	★	4.1
Convertible Holdings Inc CNVpr	I	10.000	7.5	11.89	11.89	11.91	12.40	—	11.9	0.02	0.01	—	20	25	—	1 (2)	★★★★★	4.6
Gemini II Income GMIpr	I	10.500	7.5	**22.14**	**22.14**	**16.68**	**15.51**	—	16.5	0.15	0.12	—	1	1	—	1 (2)	★★★★★	4.5
Global Income Plus GLI	IB	8.000	-7.2	-3.64	-3.64	4.51	8.91	—	8.3	0.85	0.79	—	22	28	—	1 (-6)	★★★★	3.3
High Yield Plus HYP	CY	7.250	-5.8	-5.04	-5.04	11.34	12.84	—	11.9	0.48	0.72	—	60	6	—	8 (-16)	★★★★	3.3
Lincoln National Conv LNV	CV	15.375	-9.0	-0.24	-0.24	12.05	14.20	—	6.1	0.62	0.78	—	11	11	—	9 (-11)	★★★★	4.3
PIMCo Commercial Mtg Sec PCM	CB	11.125	-14.2	1.11	1.11	—	—	—	10.1	—	—	—	—	—	—	— (—)		
Investment Bond Funds										1.00=Clsd-End Bond Avg								
Allmerica Securities Trust ALM	CB	9.375	-11.9	-2.05	-2.05	6.97	9.09	10.21	9.1	0.66	0.77	0.79	23	20	56	5 (-5)	★★★★	3.8
John Hancock Income JHS	CB	13.750	-9.0	-2.63	-2.63	6.38	8.70	**10.64**	9.2	0.70	0.64	0.89	34	40	25	5 (-5)	★★★★	3.7
Pacific American Inc Shs PAI	CB	13.125	-7.7	-3.57	-3.57	6.72	9.23	—	9.1	0.70	0.73	—	26	12	—	4 (-5)	★★★★	3.8
Transamerica Income TAI	CB	21.125	-6.0	-4.45	-4.45	6.06	8.76	—	9.1	0.85	0.76	—	50	32	—	6 (-7)	★★★	4.4
Municipal Bond Funds										1.00=Clsd-End Muni Avg								
Nuveen Muni Value NUV	MN	9.375	-4.2	-1.61	-1.61	5.04	6.64	—	7.0	0.47	0.69	—	71	53	—	4 (-3)	★★★	2.5
Putnam High Yield Muni PYM	MN	8.625	-0.1	-4.43	-4.43	6.64	6.93	—	8.7	0.67	0.77	—	18	36	—	3 (-5)	★★★★	4.5
Putnam Managed Muni Inc PMM	MN	9.500	1.9	-6.55	-6.55	7.27	8.45	—	8.0	0.95	1.19	—	6	3	—	7 (-7)	★★★	3.9

Bold numbers indicate *highest* return for the listed time period in each category.

Today's Ugly Ducklings— Tomorrow's Swans?

Two words characterize closed-end equity funds in 1994: deflated prices.

After the worldwide market rallies of 1993, 1994 was a sobering experience for closed-end-fund investors. Inflation jitters, a weak dollar, and rising interest rates stalled the domestic stock market, and stocks around the world followed suit. Only a couple of markets—namely Brazil's and India's—turned substantial profits.

Not only did global markets retreat, but the premiums many funds had once commanded collapsed in 1994. For example, despite an ebullient Indian market that drove NAV up 23.2% for the year, **India Growth** stuck its shareholders with a market-price loss. Domestic blue-chip-laden **Liberty All-Star Equity** saw its persistent premium shrivel to a discount by the end of the year, as well.

Market prices of closed-end funds are typically more volatile than their underlying NAV performance; as such, a poor year for equities would naturally bode ill for equity-fund share prices. When these markets do kick back into gear, however, investors who bought these funds at fire-sale prices could reap generous rewards.

Diminishing premiums and widening discounts thus provide investment opportunities. Large-cap growth die-hard **General American Investors** was trading at a double-digit discount by year-end; the fund had already ridden the revival in growth stocks, posting a 4.6% NAV gain in 1994's second half. **Global Health Sciences**, at a near-20% markdown, is an excellent way to play reviving health-care stocks. Finally, shares of many European and Pacific/Asia funds were trading at double-digit discounts by year-end.

Susan Paluch

Growth of $10,000
- Closed-End Equity Category ($000)
- MS World ND ($000)

Net Assets ($bil)

	1983	1984	1985	1986	1987	1988	1989	1990	1991	1992	1993	1994	History
	43.22	31.62	35.00	85.24	74.19	77.85	219.01	28.27	131.16	74.50	107.57	60.98	High
	20.96	6.76	27.60	27.40	9.44	26.42	45.24	-9.43	31.55	9.38	43.15	1.37	NAV Total Return %
	-0.42	-7.09	21.67	9.79	-7.55	-10.76	8.85	-68.03	-27.86	-5.43	-43.33	Low
	-1.51	0.50	-4.14	8.73	4.18	9.81	13.55	-6.31	1.07	1.76	33.09	0.05	+/- S&P 500
	-0.97	2.04	-12.97	-14.49	-6.73	3.14	28.63	7.59	13.27	14.61	20.64	-3.71	+/- MS World ND
	7.90	5.49	5.51	5.25	4.60	3.81	5.61	3.47	2.37	1.76	1.58	1.63	Income Return %
	13.06	1.27	22.09	22.16	4.84	22.61	39.63	-12.9	29.18	7.63	41.57	-0.26	Capital Return %
	0.98	0.81	0.55	0.54	0.51	0.50	0.80	0.42	0.31	0.25	0.24	0.25	Income $
	0.77	0.93	1.23	1.17	1.28	1.41	1.39	3.27	2.45	2.05	1.50	2.01	Expense Ratio
	3.51	3.49	4.25	3.68	2.24	2.28	2.27	0.01	1.97	0.27	-0.26	-0.80	Income Ratio
	35.33	28.97	31.25	33.79	55.82	44.34	40.92	19.00	7.52	24.31	35.77	29.18	Turnover Ratio
	1.15	1.24	1.99	2.89	3.18	5.79	5.06	5.68	7.28	7.94	11.29	10.86	Total Net Assets ($bil)

Style Box Analysis

Number of Funds	Value	Blend	Growth			1 Yr Total Return %	Value	Blend	Growth			5 Yr Total Return %	Value	Blend	Growth			Average Mstar Risk	Value	Blend	Growth	
Large	3	4	2				3.27	-7.18	5.59				10.57	11.46	12.33				0.60	0.82	1.32	
Med	6	4	10				-2.10	-15.92	8.68				12.35	12.58	16.88				0.57	0.99	1.07	
Small	3	1	1				6.61	-15.11	-11.45				19.11	NMF	25.45				0.71	1.07	0.78	

1.00 = Equity Average

Risk Analysis

	Load-Adj Return	Morningstar[1] Return	Risk	Morningstar Risk-Adj Rating
1 Yr	N/A			
3 Yr	N/A	1.99[2]	0.90	★★★★
5 Yr	N/A	2.42[2]	0.92	★★★★
10 Yr	N/A	1.73	0.85	★★★★

[1]1.00=Equity Average [2]1.00=90-day T-bill return

Other Measures

				Standard Index S&P 500
Standard Deviation	18.78		Alpha	11.93
Mean	16.37		Beta	0.72
Sharpe Ratio	0.88		R-Squared	23.80

Performance 12-31-94

	Total Return%	+/- S&P	+/- MS Wld ND
3 Mo	-5.80	-5.78	-5.07
6 Mo	4.07	-0.79	2.68
1 Yr	1.37	0.05	-3.71
3 Yr Average	15.55	9.29	8.70
5 Yr Average	14.36	5.67	10.69
10 Yr Average	17.68	3.29	2.84
15 Yr Average	14.79	0.30	—

Portfolio

Amount 000	Total Equity: 2492 Total Fixed-Income: 314	Value $000	% Net Assets
43698	Cifra Cl B	124424	0.96
576	Samsung Electronics	108458	0.83
11971	Cemex Cl A	107152	0.82
101	Korea Mobile Telecom	94115	0.72
466724	Petrobras	89746	0.69
4258	Kimberly-Clark de Mexico A	84553	0.65
7126	Grupo Carso Cl A1	75924	0.58
7951	Apasco Cl A	74224	0.57
5008	Consolidated Tomoka Land	61970	0.48
6958	Grupo Industrial Bimbo Cl A	56522	0.44
3616	Tolmex Cl B2	52651	0.41
585	American International Group	51947	0.40
1024	United HealthCare	51584	0.40
1209	Home Depot	50757	0.39
815976	Telebras	48528	0.37
6968	Grupo Fin Banamex Accival C	47879	0.37
17085	Telefonos de Mexico Cl L	47653	0.37
1018	First Union	44029	0.34
16233	Cifra Cl C	43763	0.34
808	FHLMC	43127	0.33

Composition %

Cash	4.91	Preferreds	0.43
Stocks	86.98	Convertibles	5.21
Bonds	2.79	Other	-0.29

Tax Analysis

	Tax-Adj Hist Return %	% Pretax Return
3 Yr Avg	N/A	N/A
5 Yr Avg	N/A	N/A
10 Yr Avg	N/A	N/A

Sector Weightings

	% of Stocks	Rel S&P500
Utilities	10.2	0.82
Energy	4.3	0.43
Financials	25.3	2.40
Industrial Cyclicals	19.6	1.20
Consumer Durables	7.7	1.24
Consumer Staples	7.9	0.63
Services	8.8	1.08
Retail	3.9	0.66
Health	7.2	0.82
Technology	5.1	0.56

Worst Three Months

	Worst 3 Month Performance 1990-1994
Brazil Fund	-52.71
Mexico Fund	-42.48
Gemini II Cap	-38.97
Taiwan Fund	-36.30
Thai Fund	-35.40

Category Leaders

Lowest 3 Yr Morningstar Risk		Top Rated Funds		Best 3 Yr Return %	
Conv Hold Inc	0.01	Chile Fund	9.28	First Financial	41.67
Gemini II Inc	0.12	First Financial	6.80	Brazil Fund	38.24
Royce Value	0.27	First Philippine	5.55	First Philippine	37.29
Source Capital	0.33	Templtn Em Mkts	4.62	Thai Fund	32.01
Central Secs	0.40	Morgan Stan Em Mkts	4.02	Chile Fund	30.20
Adams Express	0.49	Gemini II Inc	3.65	Morgan Stan Em Mkts	27.86
First Financial	0.49	Thai Fund	3.34	Korea Fund	26.20
Quest For Val Cap	0.54	Mexico Fund	2.91	Central Secs	24.49
Baker Fentress	0.54	Conv Hold Inc	2.77	Malaysia Fund	23.89
Swiss Helvetia	0.55	Brazil Fund	2.69	Asia Pacific	22.34

Closed-End Equity Funds

Fund / Ticker	Obj	Mkt Price	Prem/ Disc	NAV Total Return % through 12-31-94		Annualized			Trailing 12 Mo Yield %	Morningstar Risk 1.00=Equity Average			Rtn % Rank Obj			Bear Mkt Indicator (Worst 3 mo)	Star Rating	Avg Star Rating
				YTD	1Yr	3Yr	5Yr	10Yr		3Yr	5Yr	10Yr	3Yr	5Yr	10Yr			
S&P 500 Index				1.31	1.31	6.27	8.69	14.38										
MSCI EAFE				7.78	7.78	7.86	1.50	17.55										
Aggressive Funds										1.00=Clsd-End Equity Avg								
Asia Pacific APB	WP	13.750	-1.0	-21.70	-21.70	22.34	13.82	—	0.1	1.28	1.26	—	33	40	—	10(-29)	★★★★	4.1
Brazil BZF	WL	33.000	7.1	**60.82**	**60.82**	38.19	14.29	—	0.0	1.46	2.42	—	1	66	—	9(-53)	★★★★	1.6
Chile CH	WL	46.125	-12.2	33.57	33.57	30.21	**40.12**	—	2.0	1.04	0.80	—	12	1	—	2(-15)	★★★★★	4.9
Emerging Mkts Infrastruct EMG	WW	10.250	-21.3	-5.97	-5.97			—	0.4	—	—	—	—	—	—	—(—)		
First Financial FF	DE	12.750	-10.9	13.79	13.79	**41.67**	27.21	—	0.3	0.52	0.99	—	1	1	—	10(-28)	★★★★★	3.1
First Philippine FPF	WP	19.375	-17.9	2.65	2.65	37.29	24.23	—	0.0	0.88	0.77	—	1	1	—	5(-14)	★★★★★	4.4
France Growth FRF	WE	9.125	-16.8	-5.79	-5.79	4.44	—	—	0.3	0.86	—	—	47	—	—	—(—)	★★★	2.7
Gemini II Capital GMI	DE	17.625	-10.3	-11.13	-11.13	9.19	5.56	—	0.0	0.81	1.32	—	21	68	—	10(-39)	★★	2.8
Global Health Sciences GHS	DE	9.875	-20.8	2.21	2.21	—	—	—	0.0	—	—	—	—	—	—	—(—)		
Greater China GCH	WP	12.125	-15.2	-36.54	-36.54	—	—	—	0.8	—	—	—	—	—	—	—(—)		
Growth Fund of Spain GSP	WE	9.500	-16.5	3.19	3.19	0.56	—	—	4.7	1.15	—	—	78	—	—	—(—)	★★	2.0
India Growth IGF	WP	19.250	-9.1	23.20	23.20	16.70	14.16	—	0.0	2.17	1.79	—	40	20	—	1(-35)	★★★★	3.0
Jakarta Growth JGF	WP	9.000	4.4	-15.11	-15.11	12.40	—	—	0.3	1.06	—	—	66	—	—	—(—)	★★★	2.0
Japan OTC Equity JOF	WP	9.750	-3.8	13.18	13.18	-0.03	—	—	0.0	1.91	—	—	93	—	—	—(—)	★	1.2
Korea KF	WP	22.750	10.2	24.84	24.84	26.20	7.12	26.07	0.0	1.33	1.45	1.11	20	60	1	6(-24)	★★★★	3.6
Latin American Discovery LDF	WL	18.250	6.4	0.81	0.81	—	—	—	0.0	—	—	—	—	—	—	—(—)		
Malaysia MF	WP	17.375	-6.6	-23.70	-23.70	23.89	13.86	—	0.0	1.21	1.26	—	26	30	—	10(-29)	★★★★	3.5
Mexico MXF	WL	22.625	6.9	-42.89	-42.89	4.72	20.45	**30.38**	1.0	1.78	1.24	1.51	62	33	1	6(-42)	★★★★★	4.1
Morgan Stan Africa Inv AFF	WW	11.375	-20.8			—	—	—		—	—	—	—	—	—	—(—)		
Morgan Stan Emerg Mkts MSF	WW	21.500	7.4	-6.88	-6.88	27.84	—	—	0.0	0.64	—	—	1	—	—	—(—)	★★★★★	5.0
New Germany GF	WE	11.500	-20.9	3.85	3.85	6.27	—	—	1.4	0.89	—	—	42	—	—	—(—)	★★	2.3
Swiss Helvetia SWZ	WE	18.875	-4.6	1.10	1.10	16.42	10.94	—	1.4	0.59	0.70	—	5	1	—	7(-15)	★★★	2.6
Taiwan TWN	WP	28.875	-8.9	22.00	22.00	15.17	-2.60	—	0.1	0.98	1.53	—	60	90	—	7(-36)	★★	2.4
Templeton Emerg Mkts EMF	WW	19.500	9.2	-11.50	-11.50	21.45	25.44	—	0.4	0.85	0.74	—	12	1	—	8(-19)	★★★★★	4.8
Thai TTF	WP	22.375	-20.9	-13.66	-13.66	32.01	17.54	—	1.3	1.29	1.48	—	13	10	—	10(-35)	★★★★	4.1
Core Funds																		
Baker Fentress BKF	DE	13.750	-21.4	-3.21	-3.21	5.14	4.32	10.29	2.3	0.56	0.69	0.66	46	82	61	8(-19)	★★★	2.8
Central Securities CET	DE	15.750	-7.1	8.71	8.71	24.49	17.24	16.34	1.3	0.42	0.59	0.68	6	6	7	6(-13)	★★★★	3.1
G.T. Greater Europe GTF	WE	11.875	-15.8	-0.50	-0.50	9.07	—	—	0.2	0.72	—	—	31	—	—	—(—)	★★★	2.8
General American Inv GAM	DE	19.000	-14.7	-2.93	-2.93	-0.40	11.17	15.54	0.3	0.81	0.79	0.80	81	27	15	8(-19)	★★★	3.0
Irish Investment IRL	WE	8.625	-16.0	5.43	5.43	3.46	—	—	0.0	1.07	—	—	57	—	—	—(—)	★★	2.0
Quest For Value Cap KFV	DE	23.000	-10.8	-3.17	-3.17	10.66	12.71	—	0.0	0.52	0.65	—	18	17	—	9(-19)	★★★★	4.3
Royce Value RVT	DE	11.000	-10.9	0.62	0.62	12.15	11.01	—	0.1	0.28	0.51	—	12	31	—	7(-20)	★★★★	3.1
Conservative Funds																		
Adams Express ADX	DE	15.625	-13.1	0.02	0.02	5.92	9.82	13.51	3.0	0.51	0.56	0.62	34	37	30	7(-11)	★★★	3.3
Liberty All-Star Equity USA	DE	8.375	-9.7	-1.32	-1.32	4.69	10.73	—	5.4	0.60	0.63	—	53	34	—	8(-13)	★★★★	3.7
Source Capital SOR	DE	37.000	-4.0	0.60	0.60	6.60	7.41	11.73	3.7	0.35	0.46	0.45	28	62	46	6(-13)	★★★	4.1

Bold numbers indicate *highest* return for the listed time period in each category.

Review Pages

ABT Emerging Growth

ABT Emerging Growth Fund seeks long-term capital appreciation. The fund normally invests at least 65% of its assets in the common stocks of emerging-growth companies. These companies are considered to be in the developing stage of their business life cycles and are expected to achieve rapid growth in sales and earnings. While some emerging-growth companies may be larger and more established, most tend to be small to medium-sized (typically with sales of $1 billion or less).

Prior to Sept. 1, 1984, The First National Bank in Palm Beach served as the fund's advisor.

Manager's Investment Style

The fund's true growth manager, Harold Ireland, likes to make qualitative decisions, seeking earnings or sales growth of at least 20% annually (and paying high prices for it). A modest trader, Ireland typically keeps a concentrated portfolio (20 to 30 issues) and likes low debt and high ROE, though he does not have a distinct market cap preference. Recent favorites include technology and consumer stocks.

Fund Manager(s)

Harold J. Ireland, Jr., since 04-83. Birthdate: 02-39.

Manager Experience

	Dates Managed	Invest Obj	Std Dev	+/- Index
Harold J. Ireland, Jr.				
ABT Growth & Income	01/91 - 08/91	GI	14.58	-1.12

Ticker	Load	NAV	Yield	SEC Yield	Assets	Objective
ABEGX	4.75%	13.44	0.0%	N/A	62.2	Aggr. Growth

Historical Profile
Return Above Average
Risk High
Rating ★★★ Neutral

98% 96% 97% 88% 92% 97% 96% 95%

Investment Style History
Equity
Average % Stocks Held in Portfolio

Growth of $10,000
|||| Value of Fund ($000)
— Value of Index ($000)
SPMid400
▼ Manager Change
▽ Partial Manager Change
► Mgr Unknown After
◄ Mgr Unknown Before

Performance Quartile (Within Objective)

	1983	1984	1985	1986	1987	1988	1989	1990	1991	1992	1993	1994	History
NAV	5.49	5.43	7.75	8.77	7.07	7.99	8.96	7.89	11.46	12.79	14.82	13.44	NAV
	-8.65 *	-1.09	46.04	13.16	-16.51	13.01	33.88	-4.51	77.23	13.90	17.88	-9.31	Total Return %
	-15.90 *	-7.36	14.30	-5.52	-21.77	-3.60	2.19	-1.39	46.75	6.28	7.83	-10.63	+/- S&P 500
	---	0.63	14.02	1.40	-13.00	-7.52	9.93	9.05	33.78	2.14	3.35	-6.66	+/- Wilshire 4500
	0.00	0.00	0.00	0.00	0.00	0.00	0.00	0.00	0.00	0.00	0.00	0.00	Income Return %
	-8.65	-1.09	46.04	13.16	-16.51	13.01	33.87	-4.51	77.23	13.90	17.88	-9.31	Capital Return %
	---	69	3	66	99	37	8	69	1	12	21	91	Total Rtn % Rank All
	---	9	7	39	82	52	28	37	6	28	55	85	Total Rtn % Rank Obj
	0.00	0.00	0.00	0.00	0.00	0.00	0.00	0.00	0.00	0.00	0.00	0.00	Income $
	0.00	0.00	0.18	0.00	0.25	0.00	1.63	0.66	2.20	0.26	0.24	0.00	Capital Gains $
	---	2.36	2.34	1.65	1.57	2.02	1.78	1.86	1.59	1.44	1.31	1.22	Expense Ratio %
	---	-0.38	-1.29	-0.90	-1.05	-1.36	-1.19	-0.49	-0.71	-0.93	-0.92	-1.00	Income Ratio %
	---	42	101	49	65	45	120	100	108	46	48	51	Turnover Rate %
	4.3	9.4	16.1	37.3	25.8	19.6	19.9	16.2	27.5	35.2	60.7	62.2	Net Assets ($mil)

Performance 12-31-94

	1st Qtr	2nd Qtr	3rd Qtr	4th Qtr	Total
1987	33.41	-8.80	-6.56	-26.56	-16.51
1988	10.75	11.75	-5.26	-3.62	13.01
1989	12.14	7.25	16.86	-4.75	33.88
1990	-3.79	9.86	-19.85	12.73	-4.51
1991	21.55	2.29	19.78	19.01	77.23
1992	-3.40	-8.58	9.59	17.70	13.90
1993	3.05	1.37	7.78	4.70	17.88
1994	-3.58	-12.88	8.84	-0.81	-9.31

Bear Market Performance

Decile Rank (5-year period)

Worst			Best

	Worst 3 Mo Period 1985-89	Worst 3 Mo Period 1990-94
ABT Emerging Growth	-41.11	-19.85
+/- S&P 500	-11.53	-6.11
+/- Best Fit Index : SPMid400	-12.31	-2.07

Trailing Returns

	Total Return %	+/- S&P 500	+/- Wil 4500	% Rank All	% Rank Obj	Growth of $10,000
3 Mo	-0.81	-0.79	1.69	40	54	9,919
6 Mo	7.95	3.09	3.76	6	49	10,795
1 Yr	-9.31	-10.63	-6.66	91	85	9,069
3 Yr Avg	6.78	0.52	-0.82	28	44	12,177
5 Yr Avg	15.56	6.87	6.47	4	20	20,608
10 Yr Avg	15.71	1.33	3.07	7	25	43,019
15 Yr Avg	---	---	---	---	---	---

Operations

Address and Telephone	340 Royal Palm Way
	Palm Beach, FL 33480
	800-553-7838 / 407-655-7255
Advisor	Palm Beach Capital Management
Subadvisor	None
Distributor	ABT Financial Services
States Available	All
Report Grade	B+
Income Distrib	Paid Annually
* Date of Inception	04-15-83
Fiscal Year End	October

Min Initial Purchase	$1000 (Addt'l: $50)
Min IRA Purchase	$250 (Addt'l: $50)
Min Auto Invest Plan	$1000 (Systematic Inv: $50)

Expenses & Fees
Sales Fees	4.75% front
	0.00% deferred
	0.25% 12b-1
Management Fee	0.60% flat fee, 0.07%A
3-,5-,10-yr Expense Projections	$87, $116, $199
Annual Brokerage Cost	0.10%

Risk Analysis

Time Period	Load-Adj Return %	Risk % Rank [1] All	Risk % Rank [1] Obj	Morningstar [2] Return	Morningstar Risk	Morningstar Risk-Adj Rating
1 Yr	-13.62					
3 Yr	5.07	97	79	0.44 [3]	1.56	★★
5 Yr	14.44	95	60	2.71 [3]	1.34	★★★★★
10 Yr	15.15	97	81	1.52	1.45	★★★
Average Historical Rating (105 months)					2.8	★s

[1] 1 = low, 100 = high [2] 1.00 = Equity Avg [3] 1.00 = 90-day T-bill return

Other Measures

	Standard S&P 500	Best Fit SPMid400
Standard Deviation	17.70	
Mean	8.14	
Sharpe Ratio	0.26	
Alpha	0.5	-1.4
Beta	1.43	1.56
R-Squared	41	76

Investment Style

	Stock Portfolio Avg	Relative S&P 500
Price/Earnings Ratio	23.7	1.28
Price/Book Ratio	4.9	1.44
5 Yr Earnings Gr %	48.6#	8.75
Return on Assets %	14.3	1.91
Debt % Total Cap	20.6	0.73
Med Mkt Cap ($mil)	1013	0.08

figure is based on 50% or less of stocks

Style
Value Blend Growth
Size Large/Med Small

Diversification Value for Portfolio Types

Large Cap: Medium	Small Cap: Low	Bond: High	Balanced: Medium	Diversified: Medium

Portfolio 04-30-94

Total Stocks: 29
Total Fixed-Income: 0

Share Chg (10-93) 000	Amount 000		Value $000	% Net Assets
0	81	Home Depot	3402	5.41
55	110	Hospitality Franchise System	3286	5.23
75	75	Breed Technologies	3216	5.11
60	110	AutoZone	3190	5.07
0	90	Office Depot	3173	5.04
0	125	Discount Auto Parts	3016	4.80
30	90	Sensormatic Electronics	2948	4.69
77	77	John Alden Financial	2907	4.62
70	150	Tech Data	2681	4.26
65	65	Danka Business Systems (ADR)	2543	4.04
0	55	First Data	2393	3.80
0	100	Snapple Beverage	2350	3.74
130	130	Nature's Bounty	2340	3.72
80	80	Gentex	2330	3.71
0	100	American Power Conversion	2225	3.54
-40	80	Blockbuster Entertainment	2170	3.45
20	70	cisco Systems	2122	3.37
80	80	Physician of America	1925	3.06
0	60	Fastenal	1920	3.05
35	35	Ramsay-HMO	1916	3.05
30	100	EMC	1788	2.84
50	50	Parametric Technology	1425	2.27
11	56	Clayton Homes	1202	1.91
28	28	Health Management Assoc Cl A	1026	1.63
30	60	Westcott Communications	990	1.57

Composition % 12-31-94

Cash	5.9	Preferreds	0.0
Stocks	94.2	Convertibles	0.0
Bonds	0.0	Other	0.0

Tax Analysis

	Tax-Adj Historical Return %	% Pretax Return
3 Yr Avg	6.43	94.5
5 Yr Avg	13.71	84.9
10 Yr Avg	14.03	82.2
Potential Capital Gain Exposure (% of assets)		28%

Most Similar Funds in MF500

20th Century Ultra Investors	Fair Fit
Berger 100	Fair Fit
T. Rowe Price New America G	Weak Fit

Index Allocation

	% of Stocks
S&P 500	13.0
S&P MidCap 400	22.3
U.S. Small Cap	60.6
Foreign	4.2

Sector Weightings

	% of Stocks	Relative S&P 500
Utilities	0.0	0.00
Energy	0.0	0.00
Financials	4.8	0.45
Industrial Cyclicals	15.2	0.92
Consumer Durables	0.0	0.00
Consumer Staples	3.9	0.31
Services	22.0	2.70
Retail	18.9	3.25
Health	13.9	1.60
Technology	21.5	2.35

Acorn

	Ticker	Load	NAV	Yield	SEC Yield	Assets	Objective
	ACRNX	Clsd	12.24	0.9%	N/A	1982.8	Small Company

Acorn Fund seeks capital growth; income is a consideration.
The fund invests primarily in common stocks that may benefit from favorable economic trends for a number of years. It particularly seeks smaller companies (with market caps of less than $800 million) that have superior growth potential. Adequate capitalization, strategic market niches, and fundamental value are primary components in the selection process. The fund may invest up to 33% of its assets in foreign securities.

Historical Profile

Return	High
Risk	Average
Rating	★★★★★
	Closed

Investment Style History
Equity
Average % Stocks Held in Portfolio

85% 90% 94% 85% 90% 93% 95% 91%

Growth of $10,000

- |||| Value of Fund ($000)
- — Value of Index ($000) S&P 500
- ▼ Manager Change
- ▽ Partial Manager Change
- ◄– Mgr Unknown After
- –► Mgr Unknown Before

Performance Quartile (Within Objective)

Manager's Investment Style

Manager Ralph Wanger invests in small-cap firms with high growth potential that he anticipates will benefit from broad investment themes. He is especially interested in information technology and the potential of small-cap stocks in foreign, especially emerging, markets. Wanger hopes to find stocks capable of 10-fold increases; as such he holds issues for long time periods and maintains a diversified portfolio.

Fund Manager(s)

Ralph Wanger CFA(1967), since 06-70. Birthdate: 06-34. BS, MIT 1955 MS, MIT 1958

Manager Experience

	Dates Managed	Invest Obj	Std Dev	+/- Index
Ralph Wanger				
Acorn International	09/92 - 12/94	WF	11.09	13.60

1983	1984	1985	1986	1987	1988	1989	1990	1991	1992	1993	1994	History
6.36	6.18	7.56	7.45	6.48	7.27	8.58	6.51	9.32	11.06	13.95	12.24	NAV
25.29	4.28	31.55	16.97	4.50	24.70	24.98	-17.54	47.35	24.18	32.32	-7.45	Total Return %
2.82	-1.98	-0.19	-1.71	-0.76	8.09	-6.71	-14.42	16.86	16.56	22.27	-8.76	+/- S&P 500
---	6.00	-0.47	5.21	8.01	4.16	1.03	-3.98	3.90	12.43	17.79	-4.79	+/- Wilshire 4500
3.97	1.93	1.65	1.30	2.00	2.33	1.44	1.72	1.45	1.38	0.49	0.86	Income Return %
21.32	2.35	29.90	15.67	2.50	22.37	23.54	-19.26	45.90	22.80	31.84	-8.31	Capital Return %
23	53	21	41	25	6	23	95	9	2	7	83	Total Rtn % Rank All
37	8	30	14	21	23	41	85	57	11	3	89	Total Rtn % Rank Obj
0.21	0.11	0.10	0.10	0.15	0.16	0.11	0.13	0.10	0.14	0.06	0.11	Income $
0.21	0.33	0.37	1.22	1.09	0.64	0.36	0.44	0.15	0.34	0.59	0.56	Capital Gains $
0.85	0.85	0.78	0.79	0.82	0.80	0.73	0.82	0.72	0.67	0.65	0.63	Expense Ratio %
1.94	2.31	1.73	1.71	1.85	1.52	1.59	1.60	1.30	0.72	0.30	0.58	Income Ratio %
22	33	32	34	52	36	26	36	25	25	20	19	Turnover Rate %
173.8	210.2	317.5	414.0	418.2	562.7	854.1	769.5	1150.3	1449.0	2042.6	1982.8	Net Assets ($mil)

Performance 12-31-94

	1st Qtr	2nd Qtr	3rd Qtr	4th Qtr	Total
1987	17.14	2.90	9.44	-20.78	4.50
1988	11.51	6.64	2.12	2.70	24.70
1989	7.87	6.23	10.90	-1.66	24.98
1990	-2.45	5.73	-23.77	4.88	-17.54
1991	19.25	3.42	8.68	9.93	47.35
1992	8.43	-4.99	3.91	16.00	24.18
1993	9.64	6.73	9.16	3.60	32.32
1994	-5.52	-3.72	6.64	-4.60	-7.45

Bear Market Performance

Decile Rank (5-year period)

Worst   Best

	Worst 3 Mo Period 1985-89	Worst 3 Mo Period 1990-94
Acorn	-26.01	-24.48
+/- S&P 500	3.57	-10.64
+/- Best Fit Index : Wil 4500	4.13	-5.08

Trailing Returns

	Total Return %	+/- S&P 500	+/- Wil 4500	% Rank All	% Rank Obj	Growth of $10,000
3 Mo	-4.60	-4.58	-2.09	90	91	9,540
6 Mo	1.74	-3.12	-2.45	29	84	10,174
1 Yr	-7.45	-8.76	-4.79	83	89	9,255
3 Yr Avg	15.00	8.73	7.39	4	16	15,208
5 Yr Avg	13.07	4.37	3.97	7	33	18,478
10 Yr Avg	16.56	2.18	3.93	6	12	46,306
15 Yr Avg	15.46	0.97	---	9	1	86,348

Operations

Address and Telephone	227 West Monroe Street Ste 3000 Chicago, IL 60606 800-922-6769
Advisor	Wanger Asset Management
Subadvisor	None
Distributor	Acorn Investment Trust
States Available	All
Report Grade	B+
Income Distrib	Paid Annually
Date of Inception	06-10-70
Fiscal Year End	December

Risk Analysis

Time Period	Load-Adj Return %	Risk % Rank[1] All	Obj	Morningstar[2] Return	Morningstar Risk	Morningstar Risk-Adj Rating
1 Yr	-7.45					
3 Yr	15.00	75	33	3.68[3]	0.85	★★★★★
5 Yr	13.07	78	27	2.27[3]	0.95	★★★★
10 Yr	16.56	61	7	1.87	0.85	★★★★★

Average Historical Rating (109 months)   4.3 ★s

[1] = low, 100 = high   [2] 1.00 = Equity Avg   [3] 1.00 = 90-day T-bill return

Other Measures

		Standard S&P 500	Best Fit Wil 4500
Standard Deviation	11.66	Alpha	8.8	6.7
Mean	14.73	Beta	0.94	1.10
Sharpe Ratio	0.96	R-Squared	41	85

Investment Style

	Stock Portfolio Avg	Relative S&P 500
Price/Earnings Ratio	26.2	1.42
Price/Book Ratio	3.6	1.05
5 Yr Earnings Gr %	17.3#	3.12
Return on Assets %	8.1	1.09
Debt % Total Cap	30.4	1.08
Med Mkt Cap ($mil)	689	0.05

figure is based on 50% or less of stocks

Style: Value Blend Growth / Size Large Med Small

Diversification Value for Portfolio Types

Large Cap: Medium	Small Cap: Low	Bond: High	Balanced: Low	Diversified: Medium

Portfolio 12-30-94

Total Stocks: 354
Total Fixed-Income: 7

Share Chg (09-94) 000	Amount 000		Value $000	% Net Assets
-100	3800	Tele-Communications Cl A	82650	4.17
-105	4050	Intl Game Technology	62775	3.17
10	1250	Harley-Davidson	35000	1.77
200	1200	Solectron	33000	1.66
0	1400	Newell	29400	1.48
690	1380	Carnival Cl A	29325	1.48
5	525	Thermo Electron	23559	1.19
0	900	Teva Pharmaceutical (ADR)	21769	1.10
-880	1120	Rouse	21560	1.09
0	570	Harman International	21090	1.06
160	800	ADVANTA Cl A	21008	1.06
0	1030	Worthington Industries	20600	1.04
0	2250	Genting	19297	0.97
0	579	First USA	19035	0.96
0	400	Telephone & Data Systems	18450	0.93
880	880	Rouse (Restricted)	16940	0.85
0	950	ADVO	16388	0.83
0	440	United Asset Management	16225	0.82
0	300	Cellular Communications Cv Pfd	16050	0.81
22	22	Systems Applied Productions	14685	0.74
0	700	Systems & Computer Tech	14613	0.74
-45	730	Arctco	14144	0.71
21	1016	Mercury Finance	13208	0.67
-150	523	ADVANTA Cl B	13198	0.67
0	600	Expeditors Intl Washington	13050	0.66

Composition % 12-31-94

Cash	7.3	Preferreds	1.3
Stocks	90.9	Convertibles	0.5
Bonds	0.0	Other	0.0

Tax Analysis

	Tax-Adj Historical Return %	% Pretax Return
3 Yr Avg	13.44	88.3
5 Yr Avg	11.36	84.1
10 Yr Avg	13.94	74.0
Potential Capital Gain Exposure (% of assets)		34%

Most Similar Funds in MF500

Oppenheimer Main St Inc&Gr	Fair Fit
Columbia Special	Fair Fit
Vista Capital Growth A	Fair Fit

Min Initial Purchase / Expenses & Fees

Min Initial Purchase	Closed (Addt'l: $100)
Min IRA Purchase	$200 (Addt'l: $100)
Min Auto Invest Plan	$1000 (Systematic Inv: $100)

Expenses & Fees

Sales Fees	0.00% front
	0.00% deferred
	0.00% 12b-1
Management Fee	0.75% max./0.40% min.
3-,5-,10-yr Expense Projections	$21, $36, $81
Annual Brokerage Cost	0.11%

Index Allocation

	% of Stocks
S&P 500	8.3
S&P MidCap 400	14.6
U.S. Small Cap	51.5
Foreign	25.7

Sector Weightings

	% of Stocks	Relative S&P 500
Utilities	3.9	0.31
Energy	3.7	0.36
Financials	17.1	1.62
Industrial Cyclicals	12.3	0.75
Consumer Durables	9.1	1.47
Consumer Staples	1.7	0.13
Services	25.8	3.17
Retail	4.8	0.82
Health	7.1	0.82
Technology	14.6	1.59

MORNINGSTAR 1995 Mutual Fund 500

Acorn International

	Ticker	Load	NAV	Yield	SEC Yield	Assets	Objective
	ACINX	Clsd	15.24	0.6%	N/A	1364.8	Foreign Stock

Acorn International seeks long-term growth of capital.
The fund normally invests at least 75% of its assets in equity and debt securities of small- and mid-cap, non-United States securities. It invests in a minimum of three countries with developed or emerging markets. Companies with superior growth potential, financial strength and stability, strong management, and fundamental value are particularly attractive. The fund may invest up to 20% of assets in debt securities rated below investment grade.

Historical Profile
Return ---
Risk ---
Rating
Closed

Investment Style History
Equity

Average % Stocks Held in Portfolio

84% 90% 81%

Growth of $10,000

|||| Value of Fund ($000)
— Value of Index ($000)
    S&P 500
▼ Manager Change
▽ Partial Manager Change
► Mgr Unknown After
◄ Mgr Unknown Before

Performance Quartile
(Within Objective)

Manager's Investment Style

Following the theme-oriented approach used at sibling Acorn Fund, management attempts to find small-cap companies in developed and developing markets that have the potential to ride emerging industry themes to fast-paced earnings growth and lofty stock-price gains. Firms exploiting niches with low competition are especially attractive. Turnover is low, and diversification is high.

Fund Manager(s)

Ralph Wanger et al. Birthdate: 06-34 BS, MIT 1955 MS, MIT 1958

Manager Experience

	Dates Managed	Invest Obj	Std Dev	+/- Index
Ralph Wanger				
Acorn	06/70 - 12/94	SC	16.94	6.09

1983	1984	1985	1986	1987	1988	1989	1990	1991	1992	1993	1994	History
---	---	---	---	---	---	---	---	---	10.69	15.94	15.24	NAV
---	---	---	---	---	---	---	---	---	6.90 *	49.11	-3.80	Total Return %
---	---	---	---	---	---	---	---	---	1.51 *	39.05	-5.11	+/- S&P 500
---	---	---	---	---	---	---	---	---	---	16.55	-11.58	+/- MSCI EAFE
---	---	---	---	---	---	---	---	---	0.00	0.00	0.54	Income Return %
---	---	---	---	---	---	---	---	---	6.90	49.11	-4.33	Capital Return %
---	---	---	---	---	---	---	---	---	---	3	51	Total Rtn % Rank All
---	---	---	---	---	---	---	---	---	---	20	60	Total Rtn % Rank Obj
---	---	---	---	---	---	---	---	---	0.00	0.00	0.09	Income $
---	---	---	---	---	---	---	---	---	0.00	0.00	0.01	Capital Gains $
---	---	---	---	---	---	---	---	---	2.40	1.20	1.20	Expense Ratio %
---	---	---	---	---	---	---	---	---	-1.40	0.10	0.60	Income Ratio %
---	---	---	---	---	---	---	---	---	20	19	20	Turnover Rate %
---	---	---	---	---	---	---	---	---	29.6	901.4	1364.8	Net Assets ($mil)

Performance 12-31-94

	1st Qtr	2nd Qtr	3rd Qtr	4th Qtr	Total
1987	---	---	---	---	---
1988	---	---	---	---	---
1989	---	---	---	---	---
1990	---	---	---	---	---
1991	---	---	---	---	---
1992	---	---	---	6.79	6.90 *
1993	12.25	7.67	7.66	14.59	49.11
1994	-0.56	-1.89	6.05	-7.02	-3.80

Bear Market Performance

Decile Rank (5-year period)

Worst ———————————————— Best

	Worst 3 Mo Period 1985-89	Worst 3 Mo Period 1990-94
Acorn International	---	---
+/- S&P 500	---	---
+/- Best Fit Index :	---	---

Trailing Returns

	Total Return %	+/- S&P 500	+/- MSCI EAFE	% Rank All	Obj	Growth of $10,000
3 Mo	-7.02	-7.00	-6.00	95	67	9,298
6 Mo	-1.39	-6.25	-0.46	80	52	9,861
1 Yr	-3.80	-5.11	-11.58	51	60	9,620
3 Yr Avg	---	---	---	---	---	---
5 Yr Avg	---	---	---	---	---	---
10 Yr Avg	---	---	---	---	---	---
15 Yr Avg	---	---	---	---	---	---

Operations

Address and Telephone	227 West Monroe Street Ste 3000 Chicago, IL 60606 800-922-6769	
Advisor	Wanger Asset Management	
Subadvisor	None	
Distributor	Acorn Investment Trust	
States Available	All	
Report Grade	B+	
Income Distrib	Paid Annually	
* Date of Inception	09-23-92	
Fiscal Year End	December	

Risk Analysis

Time Period	Load-Adj Return %	Risk % Rank [1]		Morningstar [2]		Morningstar Risk-Adj Rating [3]
		All	Obj	Return	Risk	
1 Yr	-3.80					
3 Yr	---	---	---	---	---	---
5 Yr	---	---	---	---	---	---
10 Yr	---	---	---	---	---	---
Average Historical Rating ---					---	

[1] 1 = low, 100 = high [2] 1.00 = Equity Avg [3] 1.00 = 90-day T-bill return

Other Measures

		Standard S&P 500	Best Fit
Standard Deviation	---	Alpha	---	---
Mean	---	Beta	---	---
Sharpe Ratio	---	R-Squared	---	---

Investment Style

	Stock Portfolio Avg	Rel MSCI EAFE	Rel Obj	Style V B G
Price/Earnings Ratio	24.7#	0.67	0.88	
Price/Cash Flow	14.9#	0.96	1.11	
Price/Book Ratio	3.7#	1.42	1.25	
5 Yr Earnings Gr %	---	---	---	
Return on Assets %	10.8#	2.36	1.49	
Debt % Total Cap	22.3#	0.66	0.81	
Med Mkt Cap ($mil)	570#	0.05	0.11	

figure is based on 50% or less of stocks

Size L M S

Diversification Value for Portfolio Types

Large Cap: Small Cap: Bond: Balanced: Diversified:

Portfolio 12-31-94

Total Stocks: 288
Total Fixed-Income: 8

Share Chg (09-94) 000	Amount 000		Value $000	% Net Assets
0	303	Security Patrols	18833	1.38
-145	800	Allgon Cl B	15067	1.10
0	265	Sony Music Entertainment	14877	1.09
0	19	Korea Mobile Telecom	13369	0.98
	6400	Village Roadshow Pfd	13147	0.96
0	40	Benefon	13087	0.96
0	240	Hennes & Mauritz Cl B Free	12301	0.90
0	800	William Data Nordic	11515	0.84
20	20	Systems Applied Productions	11333	0.83
0	114	Sanyo Shinpan	10983	0.80
-180	350	TOSTEM	10211	0.75
0	1155	Genting	9906	0.73
0	2430	Television Broadcasts	9704	0.71
0	255	Getronics	9305	0.68
0	7	Generale de Surveillance	9087	0.67
0	173	Promise	8828	0.65
0	316	Komori	8458	0.62
-100	300	Intl CableTel	8325	0.61
0	328	Heiwa	8253	0.60
0	450	Arjo Wiggins Appleton	8233	0.60

Regional Exposure 12-31-94

% of Stocks

Europe	10	Pacific Rim	19
Japan	9	Other	13
Latin Amer	6		

Composition % 12-31-94

Cash	10.2	Preferreds	4.1
Stocks	85.1	Convertibles	0.4
Bonds	0.0	Other	0.2

Tax Analysis

	Tax-Adj Historical Return %	% Pretax Return
3 Yr Avg	---	---
5 Yr Avg	---	---
10 Yr Avg	---	---
Potential Capital Gain Exposure (% of assets)		5%

Most Similar Funds in MF500

Fund lacks three-year record

Min Initial Purchase / Expenses & Fees

Min Initial Purchase	Closed (Addt'l: $100)
Min IRA Purchase	$200 (Addt'l: $100)
Min Auto Invest Plan	$1000 (Systematic Inv: $100)

Expenses & Fees

Sales Fees	0.00% front
	0.00% deferred
	0.00% 12b-1
Management Fee	1.25% max./0.80% min.
3-,5-,10-yr Expense Projections	$38, $66, $145
Annual Brokerage Cost	0.98%

Country Exposure 12-31-94

% of Stocks

Japan	10
United Kingdom	9
Sweden	6
Hong Kong	5
Switzerland	4

Total Number of Countries: 40
Hedging Policy: Occasional

Sector Weightings

	% of Stocks	Relative S&P 500
Utilities	5.1	0.57
Energy	3.3	0.81
Financials	15.7	0.83
Industrial Cyclicals	15.8	0.63
Consumer Durables	10.2	0.95
Consumer Staples	9.0	1.31
Services	21.7	1.99
Retail	8.1	1.40
Health	6.7	1.87
Technology	4.5	0.87

Adams Express

	Ticker	NAV	Mkt Price	Prem/Disc	Yield	Objective
	ADX	$17.98	$15.63	-13.1%	3.0%	Domestic Eq

Adams Express Company's principal objective is preservation of capital. Income and capital appreciation are secondary objectives.

The fund generally holds a diversified portfolio of equity securities from industries that management believes to be defensive.

The fund owns approximately 9% of partner fund Petroleum & Resources Corporation.

In July 1969, the fund completed a 5:1 transferable rights offering of 1,909,380 shares, which raised approximately $23.9 million. The fund held a 5:1 rights offering in September 1993, which raised approximately $117 million.

-7.2	-3.9	-4.4	6.8	2.0	-3.4	-9.7	-8.4	91.6	-1.3	3.8	-7.6	Highest Prem/Disc
-13.2	-10.0	-7.7	-13.5	-10.5	-10.7	-17.5	-16.4	-14.6	-8.0	-10.8	-14.5	Lowest Prem/Disc

Historical Profile

Return	Average
Risk	Below Average
Rating	★★★ Neutral

Growth of $10,000
— at NAV ($000)
— at Market Price ($000)

Premium Discount %

	1983	1984	1985	1986	1987	1988	1989	1990	1991	1992	1993	1994	History
	19.27	17.96	20.54	19.51	15.92	16.11	18.35	16.82	20.21	20.48	19.78	17.98	NAV
	18.66	4.61	27.66	18.49	-0.03	13.67	29.36	2.36	31.29	9.82	8.19	0.08	NAV Total Return %
	-3.80	-1.65	-4.07	-0.19	-5.29	-2.94	-2.33	5.47	0.81	2.21	-1.87	-1.24	+/- S&P 500
	1.26	1.65	-5.28	3.03	-4.77	-1.53	-5.86	2.02	-15.33	3.89	8.72	-2.90	+/- Wil Large Growth
	6.12	4.01	4.55	3.83	4.24	3.36	4.81	4.28	3.31	2.44	2.28	2.94	Income Return %
	12.55	0.61	23.11	14.66	-4.28	10.31	24.55	-1.92	27.99	7.38	5.90	-2.87	Capital Return %
	35	57	25	24	70	39	16	56	21	47	89	13	Total Rtn % Rank All
	72	15	46	21	54	65	37	20	54	34	61	37	Total Rtn % Rank Obj
	14.48	4.39	30.09	23.14	-4.72	11.39	20.30	5.42	40.76	14.08	0.11	-3.76	Market Total Rtn %
	-9.7	-7.0	-6.2	-6.7	-3.3	-7.9	-14.8	-12.3	-8.4	-4.9	-3.3	-11.4	Avg Prem/Disc %
	0.92	0.66	0.72	0.71	0.78	0.50	0.70	0.66	0.54	0.46	0.45	0.50	Income $
	0.81	1.33	1.20	3.74	2.66	1.32	1.36	1.06	1.09	1.16	1.18	1.10	Capital Gains $
	0.52	0.54	0.54	0.53	0.48	0.55	0.51	0.50	0.58	0.49	0.36	0.32	Expense Ratio %
	4.30	4.15	3.81	2.81	2.68	3.20	3.87	3.57	2.74	2.30	2.33	2.53	Income Ratio %
	18	19	31	35	28	18	26	25	18	18	21	---	Turnover Rate %
	370.0	364.9	437.8	468.3	427.2	455.8	550.1	529.5	661.9	696.9	840.6	798.3	Net Assets ($mil)

Manager's Investment Style

Because the fund's primary goal is capital preservation, management takes a defensive approach to equity investing. It typically steers clear of high-multiple--and thus high-flying--sectors, such as technology and healthcare. Instead, the portfolio is usually heavy on more-staid utilities and energy stocks. Management also holds more than 100 names in the portfolio for diversification purposes.

Fund Manager(s)

Douglas G. Ober, CFA. Since 1986. BSE'68 Princeton U.; MF'79 Loyola C.

Manager Experience

	Dates Managed	Invest Obj	Std Dev	+/- Index
Douglas G. Ober				
Petrol & Resources	01/86 - 12/94	DE	16.52	-0.95

NAV Performance % 12-30-94

	1st Qtr	2nd Qtr	3rd Qtr	4th Qtr	Total
1987	18.04	1.99	3.31	-19.62	-0.03
1988	6.12	6.53	-1.33	1.91	13.67
1989	6.50	7.04	9.46	3.67	29.36
1990	-2.10	6.78	-11.12	10.16	2.36
1991	14.43	-0.18	5.97	8.48	31.29
1992	-2.56	-0.24	4.51	8.10	9.82
1993	3.20	-0.78	3.96	1.64	8.19
1994	-3.91	0.21	4.86	-0.89	0.08

Bear Market Performance

Decile Rank (5-year period)

Worst | Best

	Worst 3 Mo Period 1985-89	Worst 3 Mo Period 1990-94
Adams Express	-26.18	-11.12
+/- S&P 500	3.40	2.63

Trailing Returns

	NAV Total Return %	+/- S&P 500	+/- Wil Lg Grow	% Rank All	% Rank Obj	Mkt Total Return %
3 Mo	-0.89	-0.87	-2.50	31	37	-1.58
6 Mo	3.92	-0.94	-4.48	11	26	-0.91
1 Yr	0.08	-1.24	-2.90	13	37	-3.76
3 Yr Avg	5.94	-0.32	3.19	51	34	3.20
5 Yr Avg	9.83	1.14	0.02	26	37	10.28
10 Yr Avg	13.52	-0.87	-1.35	17	30	12.80

Operations

Address and Telephone	7 Saint Paul Street, Ste. 1140 Baltimore, MD 21202 410-752-5900 / 800-638-2479
Advisor	Adams Express
Subadvisor	N/A
Administrator	Internally Administered
Transfer Agent	Bank of New York
Custodian	Bank of New York
Auditor	Coopers & Lybrand
Legal Counsel	Chadbourne & Parke

Risk Analysis

	Risk % Rank[1] All	Obj	Morningstar[2] Return	Risk	Morningstar Risk-Adj Rating
3 Yr	67	31	0.31	0.49	★★★
5 Yr	70	20	0.98	0.53	★★★
10 Yr	57	7	0.80	0.61	★★★
Average Historical Rating (145 months)				3.3 ★s	

[1] = Low, 100 = High [2] 1.00 = Equity Avg [3] 1.00 = 90-day T-bill Return

Other Measures

				S&P 500
Standard Deviation	8.25	Alpha		-0.09
Mean	6.12	Beta		0.93
Sharpe Ratio	0.32	R-Squared		81

Investment Style

	Stock Portfolio Avg	Relative S&P 500
Price/Earnings Ratio	18.9	1.02
Price/Cash Flow Ratio	13.0	1.12
Price/Book Ratio	3.2	0.95
5 Yr Earnings Gr %	5.7	1.03
Return on Assets %	6.1	0.82
Debt % Total Cap	26.7	0.94
Med Mkt Cap ($mil)	5744	0.44

figure is based on less than 50% of stocks

Style: Value Blend Growth; Size Large/Med/Small

Index Allocation

	% of Stocks
Dow 30	13.3
S&P 500	63.1
S&P Mid-Cap 400	10.2
US Small-Cap	19.0
Foreign	9.1

Diversification Value for Portfolio Types

Large Cap: Low	Small Cap: Medium	Bond: High	Balanced: Low	Diversified: Low

Portfolio 09-30-94

Share Chg (06-94)	Amount	Total Equity: 111 Total Fixed-Income: 16	Value $000	% Total Invest
0	1145570	Petroleum & Resources	32362	3.90
0	154000	American International Group	13687	1.65
0	280000	General Electric	13475	1.62
-61900	300000	Intl Flavors & Fragrances	12488	1.51
0	201000	Texaco	12060	1.45
---	9700000	Home Depot Cv 4.5%	11252	1.36
-25000	470000	Wal-Mart Stores	10986	1.32
0	300000	Merck	10688	1.29
0	300000	Toys 'R' Us	10688	1.29
---	210000	American Express 6.25%	9345	1.13
0	160000	General Mills	9240	1.11
0	210000	First Union	9083	1.10
10000	280000	Wachovia	9030	1.09
0	330000	McDonald's	8704	1.05
-20000	80000	Royal Dutch Petroleum	8590	1.04
0	215000	Campbell Soup	8493	1.02
0	190000	Weyerhaeuser	8479	1.02
0	160000	Motorola	8440	1.02
10000	150000	Mellon Bank	8438	1.02
81400	100000	First Interstate Bancorp	8113	0.98
-50000	150000	LM Ericsson Telephone	8063	0.97
0	135000	Kimberly-Clark	7931	0.96
0	100000	Intl Paper	7850	0.95
0	100000	Dow Chemical	7825	0.94
---	6675000	Integrated Hlth Svcs Cv 5.75%	7676	0.93

Composition % 12-31-94

Cash	9.8	Preferreds	0.0
Stocks	80.6	Convertibles	8.4
Bonds	1.2	Other	0.0

Tax Analysis

	Tax-Adj Historical Return %	% Pretax Return
3 Yr Avg	3.65	50.8
5 Yr Avg	7.09	63.3
10 Yr Avg	9.62	56.7
Potential Capital Gain Exposure (% of assets)	22	

Sector Weightings

	% of Stocks	Relative S&P 500
Utilities	13.9	1.12
Energy	11.1	1.09
Financials	15.7	1.48
Industrial Cyclicals	18.6	1.14
Consumer Durables	1.9	0.31
Consumer Staples	7.2	0.57
Services	11.0	1.35
Retail	5.9	1.01
Health	8.3	0.96
Technology	6.4	0.70

Most Similar Funds in MF500

Warburg Pincus Cap Appr	Fair Fit
Liberty All-Star	Fair Fit
Vanguard Index 500	Fair Fit

Income Distrib Schedule	Paid Quarterly
Management Fee	0.00%
Reinvestment Plan	Yes
Direct Purchase Plan	No
Shares Outstanding	44,389,990
Exchange	NYSE
Date of Inception	10-01-29
Shareholder Report	B-

MORNINGSTAR 1995 Mutual Fund 500

Advantage Income

	Ticker	Load	NAV	Yield	SEC Yield	Assets	Objective
	ADGIX	4.00%d	11.54	4.8%	5.63%	73.8	Income

Advantage Income Fund seeks income. Capital appreciation is a secondary objective.

The fund normally invests at least 65% of its assets in income-producing securities. These may be investment-grade debt securities, common and preferred stocks, and convertible securities. Up to 10% of the fund's assets may be invested in lower-rated or unrated debt. The fund may also invest up to 10% of assets in guaranteed investment contracts issued by insurance companies, and it may write covered call options.

Historical Profile

Return	Average
Risk	Below Average
Rating	★★★
	Neutral

Manager's Investment Style

Management maintains positions in several income-producing securities, including convertibles, junk bonds, dividend-paying stocks, and REITs. Compared with other income funds, this fund often holds more stocks; management also seeks some growth potential in its stock choices. As a result, the fund's payout is relatively low.

Fund Manager(s)

Susann Stauffer, since 02-86. Birthdate: 10-48.
Music, Boston U. 1970   MBA, Boston U.

Manager Experience	Dates Managed	Invest Obj	Std Dev	+/- Index
Not available.				

Investment Style History
Fixed Income

Income Rtn % Rank Obj

Growth of $10,000

‖‖ Value of Fund ($000)
— Value of Index ($000)
      LB L-T
▼ Manager Change
▽ Partial Manager Change
► Mgr Unknown After
◄ Mgr Unknown Before

Performance Quartile
(Within Objective)

	1983	1984	1985	1986	1987	1988	1989	1990	1991	1992	1993	1994	History
	---	---	---	10.39	9.11	9.71	10.71	10.13	11.66	12.05	12.94	11.54	NAV
	---	---	---	10.74 *	-5.38	13.39	17.71	0.79	21.17	8.06	14.08	-5.33	Total Return %
	---	---	---	-6.07 *	-10.64	-3.22	-13.98	3.90	-9.31	0.44	4.02	-6.64	+/- S&P 500
	---	---	---	---	-8.13	5.51	3.17	-8.16	5.17	0.81	4.33	-2.41	+/- LB Aggregate
	---	---	---	3.99	5.20	6.80	7.41	6.20	6.07	4.71	4.03	4.39	Income Return %
	---	---	---	6.75	-10.58	6.59	10.30	-5.42	15.10	3.34	10.05	-9.72	Capital Return %
	---	---	---	---	89	35	41	53	43	44	33	67	Total Rtn % Rank All
	---	---	---	---	80	42	24	52	65	52	41	60	Total Rtn % Rank Obj
	---	---	---	0.40	0.56	0.60	0.68	0.65	0.57	0.52	0.49	0.56	Income $
	---	---	---	0.28	0.23	0.00	0.00	0.00	0.00	0.00	0.31	0.16	Capital Gains $
	---	---	---	2.15	1.98	2.10	2.04	2.10	2.06	2.02	1.77	1.69	Expense Ratio %
	---	---	---	5.72	5.70	6.30	6.38	5.73	5.21	4.73	3.99	4.10	Income Ratio %
	---	---	---	79	46	25	56	57	77	59	38	39	Turnover Rate %
	---	---	---	49.4	58.8	57.5	58.0	44.8	49.4	56.8	80.8	73.8	Net Assets ($mil)

Performance 12-31-94

	1st Qtr	2nd Qtr	3rd Qtr	4th Qtr	Total
1987	6.35	-0.48	0.41	-10.96	-5.38
1988	7.07	3.19	1.13	1.48	13.39
1989	3.81	6.25	5.98	0.69	17.71
1990	-3.55	4.29	-5.36	5.87	0.79
1991	8.39	-1.75	7.05	6.29	21.17
1992	-2.53	3.34	3.75	3.40	8.06
1993	7.32	2.07	4.96	-0.79	14.08
1994	-3.25	-1.13	1.19	-2.19	-5.33

Bear Market Performance

Decile Rank (5-year period)

	Worst 3 Mo Period 1985-89	Worst 3 Mo Period 1990-94
Advantage Income	---	-5.94
+/- S&P 500	---	-0.19
+/- Best Fit Index : LB L-T	---	3.45

Trailing Returns

	Total Return %	+/- S&P 500	+/- LB Aggregate	% Rank All	% Rank Obj	Growth of $10,000
3 Mo	-2.19	-2.18	-2.57	72	74	9,781
6 Mo	-1.03	-5.89	-2.02	74	74	9,898
1 Yr	-5.33	-6.64	-2.41	67	60	9,467
3 Yr Avg	5.28	-0.98	0.74	42	55	11,670
5 Yr Avg	7.34	-1.35	-0.28	43	73	14,252
10 Yr Avg	---	---	---	---	---	---
15 Yr Avg	---	---	---	---	---	---

Operations

Address and Telephone	280 Trumbull Street
	Hartford, CT 06103
	800-241-2039 / 203-241-2030
Advisor	Boston Security Counsellors
Subadvisor	None
Distributor	Advest
States Available	All
Report Grade	C+
Income Distrib	Paid Quarterly
* Date of Inception	02-03-86
Fiscal Year End	December

Min Initial Purchase	$500 (Addt'l: $250)
Min IRA Purchase	$500 (Addt'l: $250)
Min Auto Invest Plan	$25 (Systematic Inv: $25)

Expenses & Fees

Sales Fees	0.00% front
	4.00% deferred
	0.95% 12b-1
Management Fee	0.65% flat fee
3-,5-,10-yr Expense Projections	$76, $96, $208
Annual Brokerage Cost	0.07%

Risk Analysis

Time Period	Load-Adj Return %	Risk % Rank[1] All	Obj	Morningstar[2] Return	Morningstar Risk	Morningstar Risk-Adj Rating
1 Yr	-8.00					
3 Yr	4.98	52	84	0.41[3]	0.73	★★★
5 Yr	7.34	49	76	0.64[3]	0.66	★★★
10 Yr	---					
Average Historical Rating (71 months)				3.5 ★s		

[1] 1 = low, 100 = high   [2] 1.00 = Hybrid Avg   [3] 1.00 = 90-day T-bill return

Other Measures

			Standard S&P 500	Best Fit LB L-T
Standard Deviation	5.91	Alpha	0.2	0.5
Mean	5.33	Beta	0.57	0.64
Sharpe Ratio	0.31	R-Squared	58	70

Investment Style

Stocks	Port Avg	Rel S&P 500
Price/Earnings Ratio	15.2	0.82
Price/Book Ratio	2.8	0.82
5 Yr Earnings Gr %	3.3	0.60
Med Mkt Cap ($mil)	4472	0.34

Bonds	
Avg Effective Duration	7.3 Yrs
Avg Effective Maturity	9.1 Yrs
Avg Credit Quality	A
Avg Weighted Coupon	7.29%

Diversification Value for Portfolio Types

Large Cap: Low	Small Cap: Medium	Bond: Low	Balanced: Low	Diversified: Low

Portfolio 09-30-94

Total Stocks: 38
Total Fixed-Income: 47

Share Chg (03-94)000	Amount 000		Date of Maturity	Value $000	% Net Assets
	2000	US Treasury Note 6.5%	08-15-97	1981	2.53
4	18	Dow Chemical		1409	1.80
	1490	GNMA 6.5%	10-15-28	1283	1.64
-10	40	Cedar Fair		1275	1.63
	1000	Federal Express 10%	09-01-98	1075	1.37
0	34	Sonat		1067	1.36
-10	33	Meditrust		1050	1.34
	1000	General Electric Cap 8.375%	03-01-01	1026	1.31
	1000	Sears Roebuck 8.6%	03-26-02	1026	1.31
0	30	Union Carbide		1020	1.30
0	7	Wells Fargo		1016	1.30
	1000	Valassis Comm 8.875%	03-15-99	1005	1.28
	1000	Rouse 8.5%	01-15-03	995	1.27
	1000	Sun 7.95%	12-15-01	987	1.26
	2800	Freeport-McMoRan Cv 0%	08-05-06	977	1.25
	1000	Hertz 7.625%	08-01-02	958	1.22
0	32	Health Care Pptys Invst Tr		956	1.22
	1000	English China Clays 7.375%	10-01-02	947	1.21
	1000	ConAgra 7.4%	09-15-04	942	1.20
	25	Citicorp 7.125%	06-01-03	929	1.18

Index Allocation

	% of Stocks
S&P 500	57.6
S&P MidCap 400	3.5
U.S. Small Cap	33.3
Foreign	5.6

Composition % 09-30-94

Cash	12.1	Preferreds	0.8
Stocks	38.6	Convertibles	10.6
Bonds	37.8	Other	0.1

Tax Analysis

	Tax-Adj Historical Return %	% Pretax Return
3 Yr Avg	3.32	61.6
5 Yr Avg	5.39	70.7
10 Yr Avg	---	---
Potential Capital Gain Exposure (% of assets)	1%	

Most Similar Funds in MF500

SteinRoe Total Return	Strong Fit
Vanguard/Wellesley Income	Strong Fit
Oppenheimer Equity-Inc A	Strong Fit

Bond Credit Analysis 09-30-94
% of Bonds

US Govt	15	BB	11
AAA	6	B	0
AA	0	Below B	4
A	23	NR/NA	0
BBB	42		

Stock Sector Weightings	% of Stocks	Relative S&P 500
Utilities	19.1	1.54
Energy	9.0	0.89
Financials	32.0	3.03
Industrial Cyclicals	21.2	1.29
Consumer Durables	0.0	0.00
Consumer Staples	8.6	0.69
Services	4.8	0.59
Retail	0.0	0.00
Health	5.3	0.61
Technology	0.0	0.00

Affiliated

	Ticker	Load	NAV	Yield	SEC Yield	Assets	Objective
	LAFFX	5.75%	9.99	2.9%	2.88%	4081.6	Growth/Inc.

Affiliated Fund seeks long-term growth of capital and income, consistent with low volatility.

The fund normally invests in common stocks of large, seasoned companies. It sells stocks judged to be overpriced relative to risks assumed and reinvests the proceeds in securities that offer better values. The fund may write covered call options, but it does not intend to do so with respect to more than 10% of its total assets.

Historical Profile
Return	Average
Risk	Below Average
Rating	★★★
	Neutral

Investment Style History
Equity
Average % Stocks Held in Portfolio

91% 86% 92% 89% 86% 82% 83% 87%

Growth of $10,000
|||| Value of Fund ($000)
— Value of Index ($000)
S&P 500
■ Manager Change
▽ Partial Manager Change
► Mgr Unknown After
◄ Mgr Unknown Before

Manager's Investment Style

Affiliated's management seeks large, well-established companies with P/Es that are below their historical averages. Management complements its value screens with a macroeconomic outlook, which attempts to take advantage of secular market trends. Believing there has been a shift toward capital investment, management has been investing heavily in cyclicals for many years.

Fund Manager(s)

Thomas S. Henderson CFA(1967), since 04-91.
Birthdate: 01-32. BA, Williams C. 1954 MBA, Harvard 1956

Manager Experience

	Dates Managed	Invest Obj	Std Dev	+/- Index
Not available.

Performance Quartile
(Within Objective)

	1983	1984	1985	1986	1987	1988	1989	1990	1991	1992	1993	1994	History
NAV	9.41	8.98	9.91	10.50	8.93	9.20	10.49	8.95	10.13	10.27	10.67	9.99	NAV
	25.54	6.91	26.71	23.14	3.01	12.62	23.61	-5.27	22.00	12.51	13.23	3.95	Total Return %
	3.07	0.64	-5.03	4.46	-2.25	-3.99	-8.07	-2.15	-8.48	4.89	3.18	2.63	+/- S&P 500
	2.08	3.86	-5.86	7.04	0.65	-5.32	-5.56	0.92	-12.21	3.54	1.95	4.02	+/- Wilshire 5000
	5.95	6.21	6.25	5.24	5.27	5.41	5.12	4.44	4.54	3.93	3.22	3.08	Income Return %
	19.59	0.69	20.45	17.90	-2.26	7.21	18.50	-9.71	17.46	8.58	10.01	0.87	Capital Return %
	22	42	39	11	35	40	27	72	41	14	38	5	Total Rtn % Rank All
	26	30	58	7	42	69	51	65	85	17	33	6	Total Rtn % Rank Obj
	0.52	0.53	0.56	0.55	0.58	0.48	0.47	0.43	0.40	0.39	0.33	0.32	Income $
	0.82	0.48	0.81	1.14	1.34	0.36	0.36	0.53	0.33	0.68	0.60	0.77	Capital Gains $
	0.33	0.32	0.32	0.32	0.37	0.43	0.42	0.50	0.58	0.60	0.63	0.63	Expense Ratio %
	5.48	6.10	5.89	4.90	4.18	5.00	4.64	4.37	4.22	3.73	2.95	2.91	Income Ratio %
	41	35	49	54	43	27	34	32	56	42	45	51	Turnover Rate %
	2053.1	2058.1	2332.6	3211.3	3235.8	3267.0	3671.5	3210.5	3605.2	3805.8	4156.6	4081.6	Net Assets ($mil)

Performance 12-31-94

	1st Qtr	2nd Qtr	3rd Qtr	4th Qtr	Total
1987	16.71	4.88	5.68	-20.36	3.01
1988	3.19	8.19	-1.50	2.41	12.62
1989	3.79	6.94	7.96	3.16	23.61
1990	-1.73	1.65	-12.52	8.41	-5.27
1991	9.50	-0.41	6.25	5.29	22.00
1992	-0.50	4.48	2.80	5.28	12.51
1993	5.47	0.94	4.27	2.01	13.23
1994	-3.49	1.47	6.11	0.03	3.95

Bear Market Performance

Decile Rank (5-year period)

Worst ———— Best

	Worst 3 Mo Period 1985-89	Worst 3 Mo Period 1990-94
Affiliated	-26.86	-12.70
+/- S&P 500	2.73	1.14
+/- Best Fit Index : S&P 500	2.73	1.14

Trailing Returns

	Total Return %	+/- S&P 500	+/- Wil 5000	% Rank All	% Rank Obj	Growth of $10,000
3 Mo	0.03	0.05	0.80	21	14	10,003
6 Mo	6.14	1.28	1.52	8	5	10,614
1 Yr	3.95	2.63	4.02	5	6	10,395
3 Yr Avg	9.81	3.55	3.20	14	12	13,243
5 Yr Avg	8.89	0.19	0.07	25	26	15,306
10 Yr Avg	13.10	-1.28	-0.76	26	33	34,247
15 Yr Avg	13.95	-0.53	-0.02	24	29	70,935

Operations

Address and Telephone	General Motors Bld. 767 Fifth Ave New York, NY 10153-0203 800-874-3733 / 212-848-1800
Advisor	Lord Abbett
Subadvisor	None
Distributor	Lord Abbett
States Available	All
Report Grade	B-
Income Distrib	Paid Quarterly
Date of Inception	05-01-34
Fiscal Year End	October

Risk Analysis

Time Period	Load-Adj Return %	Risk % Rank [1] All	Obj	Morningstar [2] Return	Morningstar Risk	Morningstar Risk-Adj Rating
1 Yr	-2.03					
3 Yr	7.67	53	11	1.23 [3]	0.57	★★★★
5 Yr	7.60	60	26	0.71 [3]	0.71	★★★
10 Yr	12.43	55	43	0.96	0.80	★★★
Average Historical Rating (109 months)					3.5	★s

[1] 1 = low, 100 = high [2] 1.00 = Equity Avg [3] 1.00 = 90-day T-bill return

Other Measures

			Standard S&P 500	Best Fit S&P 500
Standard Deviation	7.46	Alpha	3.7	3.7
Mean	9.68	Beta	0.88	0.88
Sharpe Ratio	0.82	R-Squared	88	88

Investment Style

	Stock Portfolio Avg	Relative S&P 500
Price/Earnings Ratio	16.2	0.88
Price/Book Ratio	2.3	0.68
5 Yr Earnings Gr %	-0.9	-0.15
Return on Assets %	5.5	0.74
Debt % Total Cap	27.2	0.96
Med Mkt Cap ($mil)	9348	0.72

Style
Value Blend Growth
Size Large Med Small

Diversification Value for Portfolio Types

Large Cap: None	Small Cap: Medium	Bond: Medium	Balanced: None	Diversified: Low

Expenses & Fees

Sales Fees	5.75% front
	0.00% deferred
	0.25% 12b-1
Management Fee	0.50% max./0.30% min.
3-,5-,10-yr Expense Projections	$77, $91, $132
Annual Brokerage Cost	0.15%

Min Initial Purchase
Min Initial Purchase	$250 (Addt'l: None)
Min IRA Purchase	$250 (Addt'l: None)
Min Auto Invest Plan	$250 (Systematic Inv: $50)

Portfolio 10-31-94

Share Chg (04-94) 000	Amount 000	Total Stocks: 63 Total Fixed-Income: 4	Value $000	% Net Assets
250	1500	Hewlett-Packard	146625	3.47
0	2400	Minnesota Mining & Mfg	132900	3.14
4084	4484	Archer-Daniels-Midland	128352	3.03
750	2000	Exxon	125750	2.97
0	3500	Merck	125125	2.96
2100	2750	Chevron	123750	2.93
50	1650	Dow Chemical	121275	2.87
-110	1540	AMP	116447	2.75
400	2400	Boeing	105300	2.49
0	1415	TRW	100819	2.38
750	2000	Sears Roebuck	99000	2.34
-506	1245	Intl Paper	92715	2.19
-265	2735	Union Carbide	90597	2.14
1000	2500	TOTAL (ADR)	82500	1.95
1626	1626	Anheuser-Busch	82494	1.95
0	2000	Chemical Banking	76000	1.80
1027	2277	Browning-Ferris Industries	72307	1.71
0	1000	Deere	71750	1.70
350	1000	CIGNA	65875	1.56
-144	756	British Petroleum (ADR)	64252	1.52
500	1300	General Electric	63538	1.50
1250	1250	VF	63281	1.50
0	1200	Textron	61200	1.45
2000	2000	SmithKline Beecham (ADR)	61000	1.44
0	1233	Eastman Kodak	59355	1.40

Composition % 12-31-94

Cash	7.7	Preferreds	0.0
Stocks	86.8	Convertibles	3.2
Bonds	2.3	Other	0.0

Tax Analysis

	Tax-Adj Historical Return %	% Pretax Return
3 Yr Avg	6.69	66.1
5 Yr Avg	5.87	62.2
10 Yr Avg	9.35	59.6
Potential Capital Gain Exposure (% of assets)		13%

Most Similar Funds in MF500

Putnam Fund for Grth & Inc A	Strong Fit
Scudder Growth & Income	Strong Fit
Washington Mutual Investors	Strong Fit

Index Allocation

	% of Stocks
S&P 500	91.6
S&P MidCap 400	3.9
U.S. Small Cap	0.0
Foreign	4.5

Sector Weightings

	% of Stocks	Relative S&P 500
Utilities	4.1	0.33
Energy	8.7	0.86
Financials	15.8	1.50
Industrial Cyclicals	29.6	1.80
Consumer Durables	2.1	0.34
Consumer Staples	9.4	0.75
Services	9.9	1.21
Retail	5.2	0.89
Health	6.1	0.70
Technology	9.3	1.01

MORNINGSTAR 1995 Mutual Fund 500

AIM Charter

	Ticker	Load	NAV	Yield	SEC Yield	Assets	Objective
	CHTRX	5.50%	8.14	2.4%	N/A	1475.1	Growth/Inc.

AIM Charter Fund seeks capital growth and current income.

The fund invests a substantial portion of its assets in dividend-paying common stocks. Non-dividend-paying stocks may comprise no more than 10% of the fund's equity holdings. The fund may invest in various short-term debt securities for liquidity or defensive purposes. It may invest up to 10% of its assets in ADRs, and another 10% in direct foreign securities.

Prior to 1987, capital appreciation was the fund's sole stated objective. Prior to October 1, 1988, the fund was named Charter Fund.

Manager's Investment Style

In seeking out dividend-paying stocks, management emphasizes firms with large market caps and earnings momentum. Management takes a defensive approach, though, and therefore has maintained significant positions in both cash and convertible bonds.

Historical Profile
Return	Average
Risk	Below Average
Rating	★★★★ Above Average

Investment Style History
Equity
Average % Stocks Held in Portfolio

81% 93% 85% 80% 72% 68% 59% 54%

Growth of $10,000
|||| Value of Fund ($000)
— Value of Index ($000) S&P 500
▼ Manager Change
▽ Partial Manager Change
► Mgr Unknown After
◄ Mgr Unknown Before

Performance Quartile (Within Objective)

1983	1984	1985	1986	1987	1988	1989	1990	1991	1992	1993	1994	History
6.56	6.18	7.55	6.22	5.19	5.21	6.51	6.58	8.64	8.57	9.05	8.14	NAV
19.31	-5.75	25.86	17.10	10.42	3.96	38.09	8.23	37.77	1.13	9.76	-4.26	Total Return %
-3.16	-12.02	-5.88	-1.58	5.17	-12.65	6.41	11.35	7.28	-6.49	-0.30	-5.57	+/- S&P 500
-4.15	-8.80	-6.71	1.00	8.06	-13.98	8.92	14.41	3.56	-7.84	-1.52	-4.19	+/- Wilshire 5000
2.66	0.00	3.69	2.48	4.44	3.58	4.35	2.32	2.31	1.94	1.86	2.28	Income Return %
16.66	-5.75	22.17	14.62	5.98	0.39	33.74	5.91	35.46	-0.81	7.90	-6.54	Capital Return %
42	82	43	39	10	94	5	13	16	88	69	56	Total Rtn % Rank All
64	96	65	46	8	94	1	1	10	95	58	81	Total Rtn % Rank Obj
0.17	0.00	0.18	0.17	0.26	0.19	0.26	0.15	0.17	0.17	0.16	0.20	Income $
0.65	0.00	0.00	2.38	1.40	0.00	0.42	0.31	0.23	0.00	0.19	0.33	Capital Gains $
1.10	1.08	1.09	1.21	1.15	1.46	1.35	1.35	1.30	1.17	1.17	1.17	Expense Ratio %
2.60	3.03	2.39	1.91	1.57	2.83	3.73	2.51	2.14	2.14	1.89	2.32	Income Ratio %
68	106	68	75	225	247	131	215	144	95	144	126	Turnover Rate %
77.1	75.4	75.6	75.2	89.3	63.2	77.4	122.9	586.9	1358.1	1652.3	1475.1	Net Assets ($mil)

Fund Manager(s)

Lanny H. Sachnowitz, since 01-91. Birthdate: 02-65. BS, U. of Southern California 1987 MBA, U. of Houston 1991

Julian A. Lerner, since 11-68. Birthdate: 11-24.

Manager Experience	Dates Managed	Invest Obj	Std Dev	+/- Index
Julian A. Lerner				
Atlas Growth & Income A	12/90 - 10/93	GI	10.50	0.95
Lanny H. Sachnowitz				
AIM Balanced A	10/89 - 10/93	B	13.99	4.47

Performance 12-31-94

	1st Qtr	2nd Qtr	3rd Qtr	4th Qtr	Total
1987	22.61	3.88	7.09	-19.04	10.42
1988	-0.19	3.09	-0.37	1.42	3.96
1989	10.36	9.22	12.58	1.76	38.09
1990	-2.61	11.04	-7.53	8.23	8.23
1991	16.72	-0.91	8.94	9.35	37.77
1992	-4.05	-1.57	0.49	6.55	1.13
1993	4.08	1.36	5.84	-1.70	9.76
1994	-3.00	-1.39	3.25	-3.06	-4.26

Bear Market Performance

Decile Rank (5-year period)

Worst — Best

	Worst 3 Mo Period 1985-89	Worst 3 Mo Period 1990-94
AIM Charter	-25.99	-8.26
+/- S&P 500	3.59	5.58
+/- Best Fit Index : S&P 500	3.59	5.58

Trailing Returns

	Total Return %	+/- S&P 500	+/- Wil 5000	% Rank All	% Rank Obj	Growth of $10,000
3 Mo	-3.06	-3.04	-2.29	83	85	9,694
6 Mo	0.09	-4.77	-4.53	55	87	10,009
1 Yr	-4.26	-5.57	-4.19	56	81	9,574
3 Yr Avg	2.05	-4.22	-4.56	92	88	10,627
5 Yr Avg	9.64	0.95	0.83	19	16	15,845
10 Yr Avg	13.98	-0.40	0.12	18	15	37,021
15 Yr Avg	13.31	-1.17	-0.66	34	45	65,178

Operations

Address and Telephone	11 Greenway Plaza Suite 1919
	Houston, TX 77046-1173
	800-347-1919 / 713-626-1919
Advisor	AIM Advisors
Subadvisor	AIM Capital Management
Distributor	AIM Distributors
States Available	All plus PR
Report Grade	B
Income Distrib	Paid Quarterly
Date of Inception	11-26-68
Fiscal Year End	October

Min Initial Purchase	$500 (Addt'l: $50)
Min IRA Purchase	$500 (Addt'l: $50)
Min Auto Invest Plan	$50 (Systematic Inv: $50)

Expenses & Fees
Sales Fees	5.50% front
	0.00% deferred
	0.30% 12b-1
Management Fee	1.00% max./0.63% min.
3-,5-,10-yr Expense Projections	$90, $116, $189
Annual Brokerage Cost	0.34%

Risk Analysis

Time Period	Load-Adj Return %	Risk % Rank[1] All	Risk % Rank[1] Obj	Morningstar[2] Return	Morningstar Risk	Morningstar Risk-Adj Rating
1 Yr	-9.52					
3 Yr	0.14	70	66	-0.96[3]	0.78	★★
5 Yr	8.41	58	18	0.92[3]	0.68	★★★★
10 Yr	13.34	55	45	1.13	0.80	★★★★
Average Historical Rating (109 months)					3.6	★s

[1] 1 = low, 100 = high [2] 1.00 = Equity Avg [3] 1.00 = 90-day T-bill return

Other Measures
			Standard S&P 500	Best Fit S&P 500
Standard Deviation	7.43	Alpha	-3.6	-3.6
Mean	2.31	Beta	0.84	0.84
Sharpe Ratio	-0.16	R-Squared	80	80

Investment Style
	Stock Portfolio Avg	Relative S&P 500
Price/Earnings Ratio	18.2	0.98
Price/Book Ratio	3.5	1.03
5 Yr Earnings Gr %	6.9	1.24
Return on Assets %	7.8	1.05
Debt % Total Cap	29.5	1.04
Med Mkt Cap ($mil)	8617	0.66

Style: Value Blend Growth / Large Med Small

Diversification Value for Portfolio Types
Large Cap: Low	Small Cap: Medium	Bond: Medium	Balanced: None	Diversified: Low

Tax Analysis
	Tax-Adj Historical Return %	% Pretax Return
3 Yr Avg	0.75	36.0
5 Yr Avg	8.05	80.9
10 Yr Avg	10.91	67.3
Potential Capital Gain Exposure (% of assets)		0%

Most Similar Funds in MF500
Alliance Growth & Income A	Strong Fit
Dreyfus	Fair Fit
Massachusetts Inv A	Fair Fit

Portfolio 10-31-94

Share Chg (04-94) 000	Amount 000	Total Stocks: 103 / Total Fixed-Income: 66	Value $000	% Net Assets
400	640	General Electric	31280	1.95
-20	400	FNMA	30400	1.90
400	400	IBM	29800	1.86
360	480	AT & T	26400	1.65
80	320	First Interstate Bancorp	25600	1.60
400	400	Johnson & Johnson	21850	1.36
200	200	Xerox	20500	1.28
220	300	Procter & Gamble	18750	1.17
240	640	Equifax	18640	1.16
120	600	Abbott Laboratories	18600	1.16
80	240	Gillette	17850	1.11
240	240	Dow Chemical	17640	1.10
320	320	FHLMC	17440	1.09
0	200	Mobil	17200	1.07
160	400	Southwestern Bell	16750	1.05
	14000	Home Depot Cv 4.5%	16520	1.03
160	560	Williams	16240	1.01
-40	320	JC Penney	16200	1.01
260	260	Philip Morris	15925	0.99
220	320	Sears Roebuck	15840	0.99
280	480	Sprint	15660	0.98
600	600	Baxter International	15600	0.97
	100	Chrysler Cl A Cv Pfd $4.625	13618	0.85
0	240	Mellon Bank	13350	0.83
200	200	Microsoft	12600	0.79

Composition % 12-31-94
Cash	4.1	Preferreds	0.0
Stocks	69.5	Convertibles	20.8
Bonds	5.5	Other	0.0

Index Allocation
	% of Stocks
S&P 500	86.4
S&P MidCap 400	5.6
U.S. Small Cap	5.6
Foreign	4.1

Sector Weightings
	% of Stocks	Relative S&P 500
Utilities	7.2	0.58
Energy	4.2	0.42
Financials	18.3	1.73
Industrial Cyclicals	21.2	1.29
Consumer Durables	3.9	0.63
Consumer Staples	7.3	0.58
Services	3.7	0.45
Retail	5.0	0.86
Health	9.4	1.08
Technology	19.8	2.16

AIM Constellation

AIM Constellation Fund seeks capital appreciation; interest and dividend income is incidental.

The fund invests primarily in common stocks, emphasizing small- to medium-size emerging-growth companies. Companies in which the fund invests typically fall into two categories: "core" companies that have experienced above-average and consistent long-term earnings growth and exhibit favorable prospects for future growth, and "earnings acceleration" companies that are currently experiencing a dramatic increase in profits.

Prior to Oct. 1, 1988, the fund was named Constellation Growth Fund.

Manager's Investment Style

Management emphasizes earnings momentum with its stock picks, preferring small- to mid-cap issues with 20% or greater five-year earnings growth rates. Usually, about 25% of assets are devoted to cheaper earnings surprise plays. The fund made its name under the leadership of long-time manager Heinz Hutzler; its current management team has maintained Hutzler's philosophy and, so far, his success.

Fund Manager(s)

Jonathan C. Schoolar CFA, since 05-87.
David P. Barnard, since 08-90.
Robert M. Kippes, since 08-93.

Manager Experience

	Dates Managed	Invest Obj	Std Dev	+/- Index
Jonathan C. Schoolar				
AIM Balanced A	09/89 - 10/93	B	13.99	4.21
David P. Barnard				
AIM Strategic Inc	03/89 - 12/94	CV	3.26	0.18

Performance 12-31-94

	1st Qtr	2nd Qtr	3rd Qtr	4th Qtr	Total
1987	36.10	0.61	2.79	-26.92	2.85
1988	8.03	13.70	-5.26	-0.04	16.34
1989	9.27	8.49	20.09	-3.04	38.02
1990	2.98	11.57	-26.24	13.18	-4.09
1991	27.68	-0.91	16.05	16.06	70.41
1992	0.00	-9.33	6.12	19.55	15.03
1993	0.87	5.32	7.38	2.82	17.29
1994	-1.54	-6.62	10.19	-0.02	1.30

Bear Market Performance

Decile Rank (5-year period)

	Worst 3 Mo Period 1985-89	Worst 3 Mo Period 1990-94
AIM Constellation	-41.61	-26.24
+/- S&P 500	-12.03	-12.50
+/- Best Fit Index : Wil 4500	-11.47	-8.01

Trailing Returns

	Total Return %	+/- S&P 500	+/- Wil 4500	% Rank All	Obj	Growth of $10,000
3 Mo	-0.02	0.00	2.49	22	40	9,998
6 Mo	10.18	5.31	5.98	4	38	11,018
1 Yr	1.30	-0.02	3.95	12	19	10,130
3 Yr Avg	10.98	4.71	3.37	11	20	13,668
5 Yr Avg	17.44	8.75	8.35	2	11	22,338
10 Yr Avg	19.82	5.43	7.18	1	1	60,971
15 Yr Avg	17.84	3.35	---	2	1	117,271

Operations

Address and Telephone	11 Greenway Plaza Suite 1919
	Houston, TX 77046-1173
	800-347-1919 / 713-626-1919
Advisor	AIM Advisors
Subadvisor	AIM Capital Management
Distributor	AIM Distributors
States Available	All plus PR
Report Grade	C+
Income Distrib	Paid Annually
Date of Inception	04-30-76
Fiscal Year End	October

Min Initial Purchase	$500 (Addt'l: $50)
Min IRA Purchase	$500 (Addt'l: $50)
Min Auto Invest Plan	$50 (Systematic Inv: $50)

Expenses & Fees

Sales Fees	5.50% front
	0.00% deferred
	0.30% 12b-1
Management Fee	1.00% max./0.63% min.
3-,5-,10-yr Expense Projections	$92, $118, $195
Annual Brokerage Cost	0.24%

Ticker	Load	NAV	Yield	SEC Yield	Assets	Objective
CSTGX	5.50%	17.19	0.0%	N/A	3703.5	Aggr. Growth

Historical Profile
Return	High
Risk	Above Average
Rating	★★★★★ Highest

Investment Style History
Equity

Average % Stocks Held in Portfolio

Growth of $10,000
IIII Value of Fund ($000)
— Value of Index ($000) S&P 500
▼ Manager Change
▽ Partial Manager Change
► Mgr Unknown After
◄ Mgr Unknown Before

Performance Quartile (Within Objective)

1983	1984	1985	1986	1987	1988	1989	1990	1991	1992	1993	1994	History
10.75	8.48	10.90	10.58	6.35	7.01	8.06	7.73	12.97	14.92	17.50	17.19	NAV
24.57	-15.23	28.56	28.56	2.85	16.34	38.02	-4.09	70.41	15.03	17.29	1.30	Total Return %
2.10	-21.50	-3.18	9.88	-2.41	-0.27	6.34	-0.98	39.93	7.42	7.24	-0.02	+/- S&P 500
---	-13.51	-3.46	16.80	6.36	-4.20	14.08	9.46	26.96	3.28	2.76	3.95	+/- Wilshire 4500
0.00	0.00	0.00	0.00	0.00	0.00	0.13	0.00	0.00	0.00	0.00	0.00	Income Return %
24.57	-15.23	28.55	28.56	2.85	16.34	37.90	-4.09	70.41	15.03	17.29	1.30	Capital Return %
25	94	31	7	36	23	5	68	2	10	22	12	Total Rtn % Rank All
15	52	48	1	35	35	11	32	21	24	59	19	Total Rtn % Rank Obj
0.00	0.00	0.00	0.00	0.00	0.00	0.01	0.00	0.00	0.00	0.00	0.00	Income $
0.00	0.63	0.00	3.38	4.54	0.37	1.58	0.00	0.19	0.00	0.00	0.52	Capital Gains $
1.30	1.10	1.10	1.10	1.10	1.30	1.40	1.40	1.40	1.20	1.20	1.20	Expense Ratio %
-1.00	-0.20	-0.20	-0.50	-0.40	-0.60	0.10	-0.40	-0.40	-0.40	-0.30	-0.50	Income Ratio %
90	132	117	107	135	131	149	192	109	62	70	---	Turnover Rate %
126.0	97.7	101.9	78.9	71.9	74.9	83.6	108.6	486.9	1298.7	2924.8	3703.5	Net Assets ($mil)

Risk Analysis

Time Period	Load-Adj Return %	Risk % Rank All	Obj	Morningstar Return	Morningstar Risk	Morningstar Risk-Adj Rating
1 Yr	-4.27					
3 Yr	8.90	91	40	1.62 [3]	1.22	★★★
5 Yr	16.12	93	48	3.28 [3]	1.24	★★★★★
10 Yr	19.14	94	44	2.60	1.35	★★★★★

Average Historical Rating (109 months) 3.6 ★ s

[1] = low, 100 = high [2] 1.00 = Equity Avg [3] 1.00 = 90-day T-bill return

Other Measures

	Standard S&P 500	Best Fit Wil 4500
Standard Deviation	14.42	
Mean	11.50	
Sharpe Ratio	0.55	
Alpha	4.6	2.1
Beta	1.22	1.37
R-Squared	45	87

Investment Style

	Stock Portfolio Avg	Relative S&P 500
Price/Earnings Ratio	24.5	1.32
Price/Book Ratio	4.5	1.34
5 Yr Earnings Gr %	22.5	4.06
Return on Assets %	12.5	1.66
Debt % Total Cap	22.0	0.78
Med Mkt Cap ($mil)	1589	0.12

Style
Value Blend Growth / Large Med Small

Diversification Value for Portfolio Types

Large Cap: Medium	Small Cap: Low	Bond: High	Balanced: Low	Diversified: Medium

Tax Analysis

	Tax-Adj Historical Return %	% Pretax Return
3 Yr Avg	10.67	96.9
5 Yr Avg	17.15	97.8
10 Yr Avg	16.71	72.4
Potential Capital Gain Exposure (% of assets)		17%

Most Similar Funds in MF500

Fidelity Emerging Growth	Strong Fit
Invesco Strat Technology	Strong Fit
MainStay Capital Apprec B	Strong Fit

Portfolio 10-31-94

Share Chg (06-94)000	Amount 000		Value $000	% Net Assets
		Total Stocks: 286		
		Total Fixed-Income: 0		
525	875	Cabletron Systems	43969	1.17
172	1969	EMC	42325	1.12
468	1118	Adobe Systems	40241	1.07
0	750	Applied Materials	39000	1.04
0	1545	Humana	37659	1.00
75	500	Texas Instruments	37438	0.99
0	700	United HealthCare	36925	0.98
0	737	US Healthcare	34842	0.93
84	750	Oracle Systems	34500	0.92
100	800	LSI Logic	34000	0.90
0	675	Computer Associates Intl	33497	0.89
300	1000	Teradyne	32875	0.87
100	1000	DSC Communications	30750	0.82
175	500	LM Ericsson Telephone (ADR)	30469	0.81
-500	750	Compaq Computer	30094	0.80
0	800	Atmel	29500	0.78
50	500	Motorola	29438	0.78
250	800	Analog Devices	28600	0.76
400	700	3Com	28175	0.75
125	625	Lam Research	28125	0.75
97	497	Novellus Systems	27092	0.72
800	800	Sun Microsystems	26200	0.70
375	1125	Staples	25875	0.69
-200	700	Parametric Technology	25200	0.67
600	600	Callaway Golf	22950	0.61

Composition % 12-31-94

	%		%
Cash	4.5	Preferreds	0.0
Stocks	87.5	Convertibles	0.0
Bonds	8.0	Other	0.0

Index Allocation

	% of Stocks
S&P 500	23.5
S&P MidCap 400	33.0
U.S. Small Cap	34.9
Foreign	9.1

Sector Weightings

	% of Stocks	Relative S&P 500
Utilities	0.8	0.07
Energy	0.2	0.02
Financials	4.5	0.42
Industrial Cyclicals	9.9	0.60
Consumer Durables	9.4	1.51
Consumer Staples	1.1	0.09
Services	7.6	0.93
Retail	7.2	1.23
Health	14.9	1.72
Technology	44.5	4.85

MORNINGSTAR 1995 Mutual Fund 500

AIM High-Yield A

AIM High-Yield Fund - Class A seeks a high level of current income. Potential for capital appreciation is also considered.

The fund normally invests at least 80% of its assets in debt securities, including convertible debt securities and cash instruments. It invests primarily in securities rated BBB, BB, or B, or unrated securities of comparable quality. The fund may also invest in preferred stocks.

Prior to July 1, 1992, the fund was named CIGNA High-Yield Fund. On October 15, 1993, AIM High-Yield Securities merged into this fund.

Manager's Investment Style

This fund's management duo largely restricts itself to high-yield bonds with B ratings. The belief is that B rated bonds limit both the interest-rate sensitivity of higher-rated issues and the credit problems of lower-rated junk bonds.

Fund Manager(s)

Alan C. Petersen, since 01-82. Business Administration, Valparaiso U. MBA, Northwestern U.
John L. Pessarra, since 07-92. Birthdate: 11-60. BBA, Sam Houston State U. 1984

Manager Experience	Dates Managed	Invest Obj	Std Dev	+/- Index
Alan C. Petersen				
CIGNA High-Income	08/88 - 12/94	CY	12.26	0.58
John L. Pessarra				
AIM Income A	08/93 - 12/94	CG	6.27	-4.03

Performance 12-31-94

	1st Qtr	2nd Qtr	3rd Qtr	4th Qtr	Total
1987	5.74	-1.18	-2.08	0.73	3.06
1988	6.91	3.57	2.53	2.53	16.41
1989	1.77	3.81	-0.84	-3.42	1.18
1990	-4.05	5.65	-9.71	-0.61	-9.04
1991	14.35	8.55	7.74	6.32	42.18
1992	9.00	2.45	5.06	1.10	18.60
1993	6.62	4.74	1.68	4.27	18.39
1994	-0.18	-0.74	0.09	-0.85	-1.68

Bear Market Performance

Decile Rank (5-year period)

Worst   Best

	Worst 3 Mo Period 1985-89	Worst 3 Mo Period 1990-94
AIM High-Yield A	-5.81	-15.04
+/- LB Aggregate	-6.63	-15.79
+/- Best Fit Index : FB HY	---	-0.94

Trailing Returns

	Total Return %	+/- LB Aggregate	+/- FB High-Yield	% Rank All	% Rank Obj	Growth of $10,000
3 Mo	-0.85	-1.23	-0.81	41	41	9,915
6 Mo	-0.76	-1.76	-2.32	69	46	9,924
1 Yr	-1.68	1.24	-0.70	31	20	9,832
3 Yr Avg	11.35	6.81	0.19	9	24	13,807
5 Yr Avg	12.30	4.67	-0.78	8	16	17,857
10 Yr Avg	11.99	2.05	---	37	3	31,044
15 Yr Avg	12.31	1.50	---	50	9	57,044

Operations

Address and Telephone	11 Greenway Plaza Suite 1919
	Houston, TX 77046-1173
	800-347-1919 / 713-626-1919
Advisor	AIM Advisors
Subadvisor	Cigna Investments
Distributor	AIM Distributors
States Available	All
Report Grade	B
Income Distrib	Paid Monthly
Date of Inception	07-11-78
Fiscal Year End	December

Min Initial Purchase	$500 (Addt'l: $50)
Min IRA Purchase	$500 (Addt'l: $50)
Min Auto Invest Plan	$50 (Systematic Inv: $50)

Expenses & Fees

Sales Fees	4.75% front
	0.00% deferred
	0.25% 12b-1
Management Fee	0.63% max./0.45% min.
3-,5-,10-yr Expense Projections	$81, $106, $177

Ticker	Load	NAV	Yield	SEC Yield	Assets	Objective
AMHYX	4.75%	8.93	10.8%	11.22%	575.6	Corp Hi Yld

Historical Profile

Return	Above Average
Risk	Low
Rating	★★★★ Above Average

Investment Style History
Fixed Income

Income Rtn % Rank Obj

Growth of $10,000
IIII Value of Fund ($000)
— Value of Index ($000) LB Agg
▼ Manager Change
▽ Partial Manager Change
► Mgr Unknown After
◄ Mgr Unknown Before

Performance Quartile (Within Objective)

	1983	1984	1985	1986	1987	1988	1989	1990	1991	1992	1993	1994	History
NAV	9.84	9.43	10.21	10.54	9.67	10.01	8.94	7.07	8.86	9.40	10.05	8.93	NAV
Total Return %	17.46	9.78	23.49	15.97	3.06	16.41	1.18	-9.04	42.18	18.60	18.39	-1.68	Total Return %
+/- LB Aggregate	9.08	-5.37	1.36	0.72	0.31	8.53	-13.36	-17.98	26.18	11.36	8.64	1.24	+/- LB Aggregate
+/- FB High-Yield	---	---	---	0.34	-3.46	4.98	0.79	-2.66	-1.57	1.94	-0.51	-0.70	+/- FB High-Yield
Income Return %	14.09	13.95	15.21	12.74	11.32	12.89	11.87	11.88	16.87	12.51	11.48	9.47	Income Return %
Capital Return %	3.36	-4.17	8.27	3.23	-8.25	3.52	-10.69	-20.92	25.32	6.09	6.91	-11.14	Capital Return %
Total Rtn % Rank All	49	28	52	49	35	23	98	82	12	6	20	31	Total Rtn % Rank All
Total Rtn % Rank Obj	29	30	19	20	31	10	38	44	28	35	53	20	Total Rtn % Rank Obj
Income $	1.28	1.28	1.28	1.24	1.20	1.18	1.21	1.12	1.04	1.05	1.01	0.96	Income $
Capital Gains $	0.00	0.00	0.00	0.00	0.00	0.00	0.00	0.00	0.00	0.00	0.00	0.00	Capital Gains $
Expense Ratio %	0.99	0.91	0.94	0.92	0.92	0.96	0.99	1.21	1.22	1.15	1.12	1.05	Expense Ratio %
Income Ratio %	12.43	13.44	12.91	11.84	11.21	11.84	12.40	13.59	12.67	11.00	9.82	9.70	Income Ratio %
Turnover Rate %	65	137	79	86	81	76	36	27	61	56	53	---	Turnover Rate %
Net Assets ($mil)	70.2	89.7	147.1	246.0	242.9	274.6	261.9	204.9	259.7	324.5	547.8	575.6	Net Assets ($mil)

Risk Analysis

Time Period	Load-Adj Return %	Risk % Rank All	Risk % Rank Obj	Morningstar [2] Return	Morningstar [2] Risk	Morningstar Risk-Adj Rating
1 Yr	-6.35					
3 Yr	9.56	7	31	1.83 [3]	0.35	★★★★
5 Yr	11.21	44	46	1.70 [3]	0.55	★★★★★
10 Yr	11.45	30	25	0.94	0.43	★★★★
Average Historical Rating (109 months)				3.7 ★s		

[1] 1 = low, 100 = high   [2] 1.00 = Hybrid Avg   [3] 1.00 = 90-day T-bill return

Other Measures

			Standard LB Agg	Best Fit FB HY
Standard Deviation	5.13	Alpha	7.1	-0.5
Mean	10.93	Beta	0.51	1.10
Sharpe Ratio	1.44	R-Squared	16	86

Investment Style

Interest-Rate Stance

Avg Effective Duration	4.4 Yrs
Avg Effective Maturity	8.2 Yrs

Quality

Avg Credit Quality	B

Avg Weighted Coupon	11.52%
Avg Weighted Price	92.57% of Par

Diversification Value for Portfolio Types

Large Cap: High	Small Cap: High	Bond: High	Balanced: High	Diversified: High

Portfolio 06-30-94

Total Stocks: 2
Total Fixed-Income: 99

Amount 000	Date of Maturity		Value $000	% Net Assets
18138	12-15-02	Silgan Holdings 13.25%	14510	2.50
16261	12-15-98	GPA Delaware 8.75%	13172	2.27
15448	08-01-01	K & F Industries 13.75%	13131	2.26
14177	11-01-04	Flagstar 11.25%	12688	2.18
10841	02-01-03	Kaiser Aluminium/Chem 12.75%	10949	1.88
12926	05-01-03	Neodata Services 12%	10341	1.78
11174	10-15-03	Harris Chemical 10.75%	10280	1.77
10007	02-15-99	Calmar Spraying Systems 14%	9957	1.71
9840	08-15-99	Stone Container 11%	9791	1.68
10007	02-01-04	USA Mobile Communications 9.5%	9231	1.59
9173	08-01-99	Seven-Up/RC Bottlg So CA 11.5%	9127	1.57
13092	10-01-00	Horizon Cellular Tel 11.375%	9099	1.57
8339	09-30-03	Agricultural Min/Chem 10.75%	8423	1.45
8339	07-15-02	Polymer Group 12.25%	8360	1.44
8777	03-01-02	Interlake 12.125%	8250	1.42
13343	09-01-03	Cellular 11.75%	8139	1.40
7922	10-01-03	Ackerley Communication 10.75%	7883	1.36
7088	12-15-02	KENETECH 12.75%	7868	1.35
12621	12-01-03	Indspec Chemical 11.5%	7857	1.35
8727	12-15-03	Dan River 10.125%	7854	1.35
8339	12-15-03	Bally's Grand 10.375%	7589	1.31
7505	04-01-02	Applied Extrusion Tech 11.5%	7580	1.30
9181	05-01-97	Americold 11%	7529	1.30
7922	02-01-04	Allied Waste Industry 10.75%	7486	1.29
7505	04-01-02	Empress River Casino 10.75%	7243	1.25

Composition % 12-31-94

Cash	5.9	Preferreds	0.0
Stocks	0.3	Convertibles	0.0
Bonds	93.8	Other	0.0

Tax Analysis

	Tax-Adj Historical Return %	% Pretax Return
3 Yr Avg	7.25	61.4
5 Yr Avg	7.96	59.4
10 Yr Avg	7.18	47.5
Potential Capital Gain Exposure (% of assets)		-17%

Most Similar Funds in MF500

Liberty High-Income Bond A	Strong Fit
Kemper High-Yield A	Strong Fit
MFS High-Income A	Strong Fit

Coupon Range

	% of Bonds	Rel Obj
0%, PIK	1.7	0.23
0% to 11%	32.3	0.66
11% to 13%	50.1	1.50
13% to 14.5%	14.3	2.63
More than 14.5%	0.5	0.31
Not applicable	1.1	0.35

Credit Analysis 12-31-94

% of Bonds

US Govt	0	BB	16
AAA	0	B	68
AA	0	Below B	14
A	0	NR/NA	3
BBB	0		

AIM Strategic Income

	Ticker	NAV	Mkt Price	Prem/Disc	Yield	Objective
	AST	$9.18	$8.00	-12.9%	5.6%	Convertible

AIM Strategic Income Fund seeks high current income consistent with stability of principal.

The fund invests 65% to 100% of its assets in income-producing securities, mainly convertibles. Its strategy involves investing in convertible securities and employing short selling against the common stock underlying them. The fund then receives interest income on the proceeds of the short sale during the period in which the short position remains open. Options strategies may also be employed.

Antitakeover provisions include staggered board terms and supermajority voting requirements.

Beginning Jan. 1, 1994, and each fiscal year thereafter, if the fund's shares are trading at an average discount of more than 10% during the 12 weeks prior to December 31, the board may submit a proposal to shareholders to open-end the fund.

| | | | | | | | 9.7 | 4.7 | -0.1 | 1.7 | 0.4 | -6.8 | Highest Prem/Disc |
| | | | | | | | 5.0 | -11.5 | -10.7 | -7.9 | -8.1 | -15.2 | Lowest Prem/Disc |

Historical Profile

Return Average
Risk Low
Rating ★★★★ Above Average

Growth of $10,000
■ at NAV ($000)
— at Market Price ($000)

Premium Discount %

	1983	1984	1985	1986	1987	1988	1989	1990	1991	1992	1993	1994	History
	---	---	---	---	---	---	9.12	8.62	9.15	9.28	9.76	9.18	NAV
	---	---	---	---	---	---	6.39*	6.37	17.16	10.49	11.54	0.26	NAV Total Return %
	---	---	---	---	---	---	---	-2.57	1.16	3.25	1.78	3.18	+/- LB Aggregate
	---	---	---	---	---	---	---	9.49	-13.33	2.88	1.48	-1.05	+/- S&P 500
	---	---	---	---	---	---	8.33*	11.42	10.32	7.19	5.86	5.12	Income Return %
	---	---	---	---	---	---	-1.94*	-5.04	6.84	3.31	5.68	-4.85	Capital Return %
	---	---	---	---	---	---	---	34	53	41	78	13	Total Rtn % Rank All
	---	---	---	---	---	---	---	1	88	77	88	1	Total Rtn % Rank Obj
	---	---	---	---	---	---	5.78*	-9.10	19.13	16.96	4.60	-5.25	Market Total Rtn %
	---	---	---	---	---	---	7.3	-5.3	-5.2	-3.8	-4.9	-11.9	Avg Prem/Disc %
	---	---	---	---	---	---	0.77	0.98	0.80	0.61	0.50	0.46	Income $
	---	---	---	---	---	---	0.00	0.04	0.05	0.17	0.04	0.11	Capital Gains $
	---	---	---	---	---	---	1.40	1.58	1.60	1.66	1.51	1.54	Expense Ratio %
	---	---	---	---	---	---	10.86	10.96	9.04	6.50	5.17	4.91	Income Ratio %
	---	---	---	---	---	---	162	92	89	90	117	---	Turnover Rate %
	---	---	---	---	---	---	62.1	59.6	63.1	64.1	68.1	64.0	Net Assets ($mil)

Manager's Investment Style

Management takes a defensive approach to the convertible-bond market. In an attempt to reduce the portfolio's overall volatility, management shorts the underlying common stock of the convertibles in its portfolio, which hedges against stock-price movements. This strategy also allows the fund to profit from rising rates, because it earns interest on the cash balance that results from its short sales. This strategy generally limits upside potential, but makes the fund a winner when the going gets tough.

Fund Manager(s)

David P. Barnard. Since 3-89. BBA Western Michigan U.; MBA Western Michigan U.

Manager Experience

	Dates Managed	Invest Obj	Std Dev	+/- Index
David P. Barnard				
AIM Weingarten	08/90 - 12/94	G	13.79	-1.34
AIM Constellation	08/90 - 12/94	AG	18.46	10.46

NAV Performance % 12-30-94

	1st Qtr	2nd Qtr	3rd Qtr	4th Qtr	Total
1987	---	---	---	---	---
1988	---	---	---	---	---
1989	-0.75*	2.79	2.20	2.05	6.39*
1990	2.53	1.26	2.02	0.43	6.37
1991	3.56	2.70	4.67	5.24	17.16
1992	2.24	1.89	2.74	3.23	10.49
1993	3.10	4.09	4.13	-0.19	11.54
1994	0.16	-2.42	3.07	-0.47	0.26

Bear Market Performance

Decile Rank (5-year period)

Worst — Best

	Worst 3 Mo Period 1985-89	Worst 3 Mo Period 1990-94
AIM Strategic Inc	---	-3.93
+/- LB Aggregate	---	-0.67

Trailing Returns

	NAV Total Return %	+/- LB Agg	+/- S&P 500	% Rank All	% Rank Obj	Mkt Total Return %
3 Mo	-0.47	-0.85	-0.46	25	1	-0.44
6 Mo	2.59	1.59	-2.28	16	22	2.44
1 Yr	0.26	3.18	-1.05	13	1	-5.25
3 Yr Avg	7.31	2.76	1.04	31	66	5.05
5 Yr Avg	9.02	1.39	0.33	33	66	4.65
Incept Avg	8.92*	---	---	---	---	5.03*

Operations

Address and Telephone	Eleven Greenway Plaza, Ste. 1919
	Houston, TX 77046
	713-626-1919
Advisor	AIM Advisors, Inc.
Subadvisor	N/A
Administrator	N/A
Transfer Agent	State Street Bank and Trust Co.
Custodian	State Street Bank and Trust Co.
Auditor	KPMG Peat Marwick
Legal Counsel	Ballard, Spahr, Andrews & Ingersoll

Income Distrib Schedule	Paid Monthly
Management Fee	0.80%
Reinvestment Plan	Yes
Direct Purchase Plan	No
Shares Outstanding	6,974,488
Exchange	AMEX
*Date of Inception	03-23-89
Shareholder Report	C+

Risk Analysis

	Risk % Rank[1]		Morningstar[2]		Morningstar
	All	Obj	Return	Risk	Risk-Adj Rating
3 Yr	8	1	0.75	0.25	★★★
5 Yr	11	1	0.92	0.22	★★★★
10 Yr	---	---	---	---	

Average Historical Rating (34 months)   3.8 ★s

[1] = Low, 100 = High   [2] 1.00 = Hybrid Avg   [3] 1.00 = 90-day T-bill Return

Other Measures

				LB Aggregate
Standard Deviation	3.56	Alpha		3.25
Mean	7.14	Beta		0.41
Sharpe Ratio	1.01	R-Squared		21

Investment Style

Interest-Rate Stance

	Fund	Relative Objective
Avg Effective Maturity	9.6 Yrs	0.88
Avg Weighted Coupon	5.34%	0.82
Avg Weighted Price	105.3% Par	1.08

Quality

Avg Credit Quality   BB

Credit Analysis 12-31-94

	% of Bonds		% of Bonds
US Govt	0	BB	13
AAA	0	B	53
AA	0	Below B	0
A	12	NR/NA	8
BBB	15		

Diversification Value for Portfolio Types

Large Cap: High   Small Cap: Medium   Bond: High   Balanced: Medium   Diversified: High

Portfolio 06-30-94

Amount 000	Total Equity: 1 Total Fixed-Income: 50	Maturity	Value $000	% Total Invest
650	EMC Cv 6.25%	04-01-02	2868	4.60
4000	Office Depot Cv 0%	12-11-07	2675	4.29
40	General Motors Cv Pfd $3.25		2263	3.63
15	Chrysler Cv Pfd $4.625		1975	3.17
1600	Arrow Electronics Cv 5.75%	10-15-02	1936	3.11
1400	General Instrument Cv 5%	06-15-00	1831	2.94
1500	Pogo Producing Cv 5.5%	03-15-04	1815	2.91
1000	Home Depot Cv 4.5%	02-15-97	1748	2.80
15	Citicorp Cv Pfd $5.375		1688	2.71
30	Beverly Enterprise Cv Pfd $2.75		1684	2.70
1500	Petrie Stores Cv 8%	12-15-10	1673	2.68
2000	Motorola Cv 0%	09-07-09	1635	2.62
1300	Genesis Health Ventures Cv 6%	11-30-03	1573	2.52
1500	Thermo Electron Cv 5%	04-15-01	1508	2.42
1300	Quantum Hlth Resource Cv 4.75%	10-01-00	1488	2.39
1200	Omnicare Cv 5.75%	10-01-03	1482	2.38
1300	Integrated Health Svcs Cv 6%	01-01-03	1389	2.23
1000	Mark IV Industries Cv 6.25%	02-15-07	1375	2.21
1200	Telefonos de Chile Cv 4.5%	01-15-03	1365	2.19
1000	Carnival Cv 4.5%	07-01-97	1358	2.18
25	Bethlehem Steel Cv Pfd $5.00		1344	2.16
2000	Motorola Cv 2.25%	09-27-13	1265	2.03
1000	Lam Research Cv 6%	05-01-03	1251	2.01
1100	American Stores Cv 7.25%	09-15-01	1249	2.00
1000	LSI Logic Cv 5.5%	03-15-01	1168	1.87

Composition % 12-31-94

Cash	0.0	Preferreds	0.0
Stocks	0.0	Convertibles	100.0
Bonds	0.0	Other	0.0

Tax Analysis

	Tax-Adj Historical Return %	% Pretax Return
3 Yr Avg	4.75	63.3
5 Yr Avg	5.97	62.3
10 Yr Avg	---	---

Potential Capital Gain Exposure (% of assets)   0

Coupon Range

	% of Bonds	Relative Objective
0%	7.1	1.5
0% to 6%	48.2	1.9
6% to 7%	11.9	0.6
7% to 8.5%	10.3	0.6
More than 8.5%	1.5	0.1
Not applicable	21.0	0.9

1.0 = Objective Average

Most Similar Funds in MF500

Connecticut Mutual Total	Weak Fit
Value Line Convertible	Weak Fit
Phoenix Convertible A	Weak Fit

MORNINGSTAR 1995 Mutual Fund 500

AIM Weingarten

	Ticker	Load	NAV	Yield	SEC Yield	Assets	Objective
	WEINX	5.50%	15.21	0.4%	N/A	3667.6	Growth

AIM Weingarten Fund seeks long-term capital appreciation. Current income is not an important criterion of investment selection.

The fund invests primarily in common stocks; these issues do not have to be listed on an exchange. It may invest in foreign securities, but such investments normally comprise less than 10% of the fund's assets. The fund may write covered call options listed on an organized securities exchange with up to 25% of its assets.

Prior to Oct. 1, 1988, the fund was named Weingarten Fund.

Manager's Investment Style

The fund's management typically seeks larger firms with rapid growth rates, though it is also partial to companies with potential earnings surprises. Although management will make large sector bets, it keeps the portfolio diversified and seeks to keep the fund's price multiples from climbing too much higher than the market's.

Historical Profile

Return	Average
Risk	Average
Rating	★★★
	Neutral

Average % Stocks Held in Portfolio: 97% 96% 97% 94% 94% 92% 90% 88%

Investment Style History Equity
Average % Stocks Held in Portfolio

Growth of $10,000
||| Value of Fund ($000)
— Value of Index ($000) SPMid400
▼ Manager Change
▽ Partial Manager Change
► Mgr Unknown After
◄ Mgr Unknown Before

Performance Quartile (Within Objective)

1983	1984	1985	1986	1987	1988	1989	1990	1991	1992	1993	1994	History
9.67	6.73	9.10	8.82	8.36	9.19	11.79	12.14	17.66	17.33	17.15	15.21	NAV
28.88	-6.06	36.12	25.06	9.75	11.29	36.04	5.55	46.86	-1.37	1.53	-0.34	Total Return %
6.42	-12.33	4.38	6.38	4.49	-5.32	4.36	8.66	16.38	-8.99	-8.52	-1.65	+/- S&P 500
5.42	-9.11	3.56	8.96	7.39	-6.65	6.87	11.73	12.66	-10.34	-9.75	-0.27	+/- Wilshire 5000
0.00	0.33	0.88	0.92	0.91	1.36	0.57	0.76	0.50	0.50	0.65	0.45	Income Return %
28.88	-6.39	35.24	24.14	8.83	9.93	35.47	4.79	46.36	-1.87	0.88	-0.79	Capital Return %
12	83	9	9	10	51	6	39	9	91	98	22	Total Rtn % Rank All
14	75	12	4	14	67	14	3	19	93	90	37	Total Rtn % Rank Obj
0.00	0.02	0.05	0.09	0.09	0.11	0.06	0.09	0.07	0.09	0.11	0.07	Income $
0.00	2.13	0.00	2.39	1.27	0.00	0.64	0.21	0.09	0.00	0.33	1.78	Capital Gains $
1.20	1.10	1.00	1.00	1.00	1.10	1.19	1.30	1.20	1.10	1.10	1.20	Expense Ratio %
0.10	0.80	1.00	0.80	0.70	0.90	0.96	0.80	0.70	0.60	0.60	0.40	Income Ratio %
118	130	99	113	108	93	87	79	46	37	109	---	Turnover Rate %
117.6	119.1	168.5	171.1	286.5	291.0	435.7	803.1	3293.2	5608.8	4712.4	3667.6	Net Assets ($mil)

Fund Manager(s)

Jonathan C. Schoolar CFA, since 05-87.
David P. Barnard, since 08-90.
Robert M. Kippes, since 08-93.

Manager Experience	Dates Managed	Invest Obj	Std Dev	+/- Index
Jonathan C. Schoolar				
AIM Balanced A	09/89 - 10/93	B	13.99	4.21
David P. Barnard				
AIM Strategic Inc	03/89 - 12/94	CV	3.26	0.18

Performance 12-31-94

	1st Qtr	2nd Qtr	3rd Qtr	4th Qtr	Total
1987	23.90	4.93	7.88	-21.76	9.75
1988	5.62	6.00	-2.35	1.79	11.29
1989	8.05	8.36	16.54	-0.30	36.04
1990	-1.36	14.10	-15.75	11.31	5.55
1991	19.28	-1.31	8.61	14.88	46.86
1992	-7.59	-3.68	3.44	7.12	-1.37
1993	-2.83	-0.24	4.23	0.49	1.53
1994	-1.52	-4.38	7.12	-1.20	-0.34

Bear Market Performance

Decile Rank (5-year period)

Worst ———————————————— Best

	Worst 3 Mo Period 1985-89	Worst 3 Mo Period 1990-94
AIM Weingarten	-30.82	-15.75
+/- S&P 500	-1.24	-2.00
+/- Best Fit Index : SPMid400	-2.01	2.03

Trailing Returns

	Total Return %	+/- S&P 500	+/- Wil 5000	% Rank All	% Rank Obj	Growth of $10,000
3 Mo	-1.20	-1.19	-0.43	49	50	9,880
6 Mo	5.83	0.97	1.21	9	26	10,583
1 Yr	-0.34	-1.65	-0.27	22	37	9,966
3 Yr Avg	-0.07	-6.33	-6.68	96	89	9,980
5 Yr Avg	9.12	0.43	0.30	23	42	15,470
10 Yr Avg	15.91	1.52	2.05	6	7	43,757
15 Yr Avg	16.58	2.10	2.61	4	11	99,912

Operations

Address and Telephone	11 Greenway Plaza Suite 1919
	Houston, TX 77046-1173
	800-347-1919 / 713-626-1919
Advisor	AIM Advisors
Subadvisor	AIM Capital Management
Distributor	AIM Distributors
States Available	All plus PR
Report Grade	B-
Income Distrib	Paid Annually
Date of Inception	06-17-69
Fiscal Year End	October

Min Initial Purchase	$500 (Addt'l: $50)
Min IRA Purchase	$500 (Addt'l: $50)
Min Auto Invest Plan	$50 (Systematic Inv: $50)

Expenses & Fees

Sales Fees	5.50% front
	0.00% deferred
	0.30% 12b-1
Management Fee	1.00% max./0.63% min.
3-,5-,10-yr Expense Projections	$89, $114, $185
Annual Brokerage Cost	0.32%

Risk Analysis

Time Period	Load-Adj Return %	Risk % Rank All	Risk % Rank Obj	Morningstar Return	Morningstar Risk	Morningstar Risk-Adj Rating
1 Yr	-5.82					
3 Yr	-1.93	88	78	-1.51[3]	1.13	★
5 Yr	7.89	82	69	0.78[3]	0.99	★★★
10 Yr	15.25	82	71	1.55	1.05	★★★★
Average Historical Rating (109 months)				4.1	★s	

[1] 1 = low, 100 = high [2] 1.00 = Equity Avg [3] 1.00 = 90-day T-bill return

Other Measures

			Standard S&P 500	Best Fit SPMid400
Standard Deviation	9.90	Alpha	-5.9	-6.3
Mean	0.42	Beta	1.03	0.88
Sharpe Ratio	-0.31	R-Squared	68	77

Investment Style

	Stock Portfolio Avg	Relative S&P 500
Price/Earnings Ratio	22.0	1.19
Price/Book Ratio	3.9	1.14
5 Yr Earnings Gr %	13.3	2.39
Return on Assets %	10.6	1.41
Debt % Total Cap	24.5	0.87
Med Mkt Cap ($mil)	3755	0.29

Diversification Value for Portfolio Types

Large Cap: Low	Small Cap: Low	Bond: High	Balanced: Low	Diversified: Low

Portfolio 10-31-94

Share Chg (04-94) 000	Amount 000	Total Stocks: 236 Total Fixed-Income: 1	Value $000	% Net Assets
-164	993	Texas Instruments	74321	1.86
950	1250	Cabletron Systems	62813	1.57
0	800	FNMA	60800	1.52
0	1600	Philips Electronics	52400	1.31
150	900	Applied Materials	46800	1.17
-525	875	United HealthCare	46156	1.15
1378	1378	Bank of New York	43755	1.05
0	700	Philip Morris	42875	1.07
-30	1746	Humana	42547	1.06
115	845	Nordstrom	41631	1.04
-250	700	Motorola	41213	1.03
280	1000	Compaq Computer	40125	1.00
-250	750	Computer Associates Intl	37219	0.93
-205	777	US Healthcare	36723	0.92
450	800	Premark International	35800	0.89
107	957	Adobe Systems	34456	0.86
140	800	Columbia/HCA Healthcare	33300	0.83
340	400	Capital Cities/ABC	33250	0.83
835	835	Lowe's	33191	0.83
-297	403	First Interstate Bancorp	32208	0.80
50	650	Citicorp	31038	0.77
500	1000	DSC Communications	30750	0.77
359	559	Novellus Systems	30482	0.76
650	650	Oracle Systems	29900	0.75
653	653	Thermo Electron	29798	0.74

Composition % 12-31-94

Cash	6.3	Preferreds	0.1
Stocks	90.6	Convertibles	0.4
Bonds	2.7	Other	0.0

Tax Analysis

	Tax-Adj Historical Return %	% Pretax Return
3 Yr Avg	-1.41	NMF
5 Yr Avg	8.01	85.9
10 Yr Avg	13.98	80.0
Potential Capital Gain Exposure (% of assets)	8%	

Most Similar Funds in MF500

Janus Twenty	Strong Fit
20th Century Growth Investor	Strong Fit
Kemper Growth A	Fair Fit

Index Allocation

	% of Stocks
S&P 500	54.1
S&P MidCap 400	21.8
U.S. Small Cap	14.1
Foreign	11.2

Sector Weightings

	% of Stocks	Relative S&P 500
Utilities	1.1	0.09
Energy	0.6	0.06
Financials	12.1	1.14
Industrial Cyclicals	17.9	1.09
Consumer Durables	11.7	1.89
Consumer Staples	4.1	0.32
Services	4.6	0.57
Retail	7.5	1.29
Health	10.1	1.17
Technology	30.3	3.30

Alger Small Capitalization

	Ticker	Load	NAV	Yield	SEC Yield	Assets	Objective
	ALSCX	5.00%d	22.43	0.0%	N/A	294.3	Small Company

Alger Small Capitalization Portfolio seeks long-term capital appreciation. Income is a consideration in the selection of investments, but it is not an objective of the fund.

The fund invests primarily in companies traded in the over-the-counter market. These may be companies still in the developmental stage, older companies that appear to be entering a new stage of growth, or companies that provide products or services with high unit-volume growth. The fund may also invest up to 35% of its net assets in companies with market capitalizations of $1 billion and above.

Historical Profile
Return	Average
Risk	High
Rating	★★★
	Neutral

Manager's Investment Style

Management uses a true earnings momentum strategy, favoring stocks that display earnings growth rates greater than 35%, no matter what their price. Manager David Alger trades frequently to catch momentum-based gains in the stock market.

Investment Style History
Equity
Average % Stocks Held in Portfolio

59% 89% 87% 85% 88% 89% 88% 89%

Growth of $10,000
IIII Value of Fund ($000)
— Value of Index ($000)
SPMid400
▼ Manager Change
▽ Partial Manager Change
► Mgr Unknown After
◄ Mgr Unknown Before

Performance Quartile (Within Objective)

	1983	1984	1985	1986	1987	1988	1989	1990	1991	1992	1993	1994	History
	---	---	---	9.71	9.56	11.23	14.58	15.28	22.53	23.43	23.53	22.43	NAV
	---	---	---	-2.90 *	-1.55	17.47	64.53	6.69	54.57	4.00	12.81	-4.62	Total Return %
	---	---	---	-1.47 *	-6.80	0.86	32.85	9.80	24.08	-3.62	2.75	-5.93	+/- S&P 500
	---	---	---	---	1.97	-3.07	40.59	20.24	11.12	-7.76	-1.73	-1.96	+/- Wilshire 4500
	---	---	---	0.00	0.00	0.00	0.00	0.00	0.00	0.00	0.00	0.00	Income Return %
	---	---	---	-2.90	-1.54	17.47	64.53	6.69	54.57	3.99	12.81	-4.62	Capital Return %
	---	---	---	---	72	20	1	25	6	81	43	60	Total Rtn % Rank All
	---	---	---	---	42	61	1	4	36	87	69	77	Total Rtn % Rank Obj
	---	---	---	0.00	0.00	0.00	0.00	0.00	0.00	0.00	0.00	0.00	Income $
	---	---	---	0.00	0.00	0.00	3.79	0.27	1.07	0.00	2.76	0.01	Capital Gains $
	---	---	---	3.00	3.01	3.25	2.66	2.23	2.17	2.13	2.17	Expense Ratio %
	---	---	---	-2.02	-2.07	-1.92	-1.17	-1.37	-1.64	-1.52	-1.62	Income Ratio %
	---	---	---	268	228	441	253	171	121	148	---	Turnover Rate %
	---	---	---	1.1	2.8	3.7	13.6	29.5	80.9	230.2	287.6	294.3	Net Assets ($mil)

Fund Manager(s)

David Alger, since 11-86. Birthdate: 12-43. BA, Harvard 1966 MBA, U. of Michigan 1968

Manager Experience	Dates Managed	Invest Obj	Std Dev	+/- Index
David Alger				
Alger Growth	11/86 - 12/94	G	18.84	1.59
Alger Income & Growth	11/86 - 12/94	GI	12.64	-4.52

Performance 12-31-94

	1st Qtr	2nd Qtr	3rd Qtr	4th Qtr	Total
1987	25.64	0.74	5.86	-26.52	-1.55
1988	10.15	7.03	-3.73	3.50	17.47
1989	20.21	18.44	19.14	-3.01	64.53
1990	3.02	12.92	-22.41	18.20	6.69
1991	26.18	-5.91	12.73	15.49	54.57
1992	-8.61	-10.93	7.85	18.45	4.00
1993	-8.37	7.27	12.24	2.25	12.81
1994	-9.56	-6.44	9.54	2.91	-4.62

Bear Market Performance

Decile Rank (5-year period)

Worst ─────────────────────────── Best

	Worst 3 Mo Period 1985-89	Worst 3 Mo Period 1990-94
Alger Small Capitalization	---	-22.41
+/- S&P 500	---	-8.66
+/- Best Fit Index : SPMid400	---	-4.63

Trailing Returns

	Total Return %	+/- S&P 500	+/- Wil 4500	% Rank All	Obj	Growth of $10,000
3 Mo	2.91	2.92	5.41	3	19	10,291
6 Mo	12.73	7.86	8.53	3	21	11,273
1 Yr	-4.62	-5.93	-1.96	60	77	9,538
3 Yr Avg	3.82	-2.45	-3.79	74	87	11,190
5 Yr Avg	13.03	4.34	3.94	7	34	18,452
10 Yr Avg	---	---	---	---	---	---
15 Yr Avg	---	---	---	---	---	---

Operations

Address and Telephone	75 Maiden Lane
	New York, NY 10038
	800-992-3863 / 201-547-8320
Advisor	Fred Alger Management
Subadvisor	None
Distributor	Fred Alger & Company
States Available	All
Report Grade	C+
Income Distrib	Paid Annually
* Date of Inception	11-11-86
Fiscal Year End	October

Risk Analysis

Time Period	Load-Adj Return %	Risk % Rank [1] All	Obj	Morningstar [2] Return	Morningstar Risk	Morningstar Risk-Adj Rating
1 Yr	-8.43					
3 Yr	3.20	98	90	-0.11 [3]	1.67	★★
5 Yr	12.91	96	80	2.22 [3]	1.41	★★★★
10 Yr	---	---	---	---	---	

Average Historical Rating (62 months)   4.5 ★s

[1] 1 = low, 100 = high   [2] 1.00 = Equity Avg   [3] 1.00 = 90-day T-bill return

Other Measures

				Standard S&P 500	Best Fit SPMid400
Standard Deviation	16.95	Alpha		-1.9	-4.0
Mean	5.20	Beta		1.23	1.48
Sharpe Ratio	0.10	R-Squared		33	75

Investment Style

	Stock Portfolio Avg	Relative S&P 500
Price/Earnings Ratio	28.5	1.54
Price/Book Ratio	4.6	1.35
5 Yr Earnings Gr %	37.5#	6.75
Return on Assets %	13.9	1.86
Debt % Total Cap	18.9	0.67
Med Mkt Cap ($mil)	851	0.07

Style: Value Blend Growth / Size Large Med Small

figure is based on 50% or less of stocks

Diversification Value for Portfolio Types

Large Cap: Medium	Small Cap: Low	Bond: High	Balanced: Medium	Diversified: Medium

Expenses & Fees

Sales Fees	0.00% front
	5.00% deferred
	1.00% 12b-1
Management Fee	0.85% flat fee
3-,5-,10-yr Expense Projections	$97, $134, $246
Annual Brokerage Cost	0.20% (aggregate)

Min Initial Purchase	None (Addt'l: None)
Min IRA Purchase	None (Addt'l: None)
Min Auto Invest Plan	$25 (Systematic Inv: $25)

Portfolio 12-31-94

Share Chg (09-94) 000	Amount 000	Total Stocks: 87 Total Fixed-Income: 0	Value $000	% Net Assets
125	225	Maxim Integrated Products	7875	2.68
-71	182	Altera	7621	2.59
0	133	Tellabs	7409	2.52
10	313	Adaptec	7383	2.51
0	158	Telephone & Data Systems	7292	2.48
5	133	Linear Technology	6559	2.23
0	175	DSC Communications	6278	2.13
0	199	Viking Office Products	6101	2.07
90	154	Integrated Health Services	6083	2.07
0	186	Informix	5975	2.03
-18	207	Landry's Seafood Restaurants	5865	1.99
17	292	Lone Star Steakhouse/Saloon	5848	1.99
0	191	Century Telephone Enterprise	5635	1.91
0	222	QUALCOMM	5328	1.81
-55	176	Dollar General	5265	1.79
55	215	Network Equipment Technology	5148	1.75
9	197	Sports & Recreation	5060	1.72
10	145	Charles Schwab	5057	1.72
25	293	Western Digital	4899	1.67
0	187	Merix	4745	1.61
15	81	Glenayre Technologies	4678	1.59
25	140	Callaway Golf	4638	1.58
0	133	Atmel	4456	1.51
16	197	Players International	4433	1.51
150	150	OfficeMax	3975	1.35

Composition % 12-31-94

Cash	10.3	Preferreds	0.0
Stocks	89.7	Convertibles	0.0
Bonds	0.0	Other	0.0

Tax Analysis

	Tax-Adj Historical Return %	% Pretax Return
3 Yr Avg	2.79	72.3
5 Yr Avg	11.94	89.7
10 Yr Avg	---	---
Potential Capital Gain Exposure (% of assets)		14%

Most Similar Funds in MF500

20th Century Ultra Investors	Fair Fit
Oppenheimer Discovery A	Fair Fit
Hancock Emerging Growth B	Weak Fit

Index Allocation

	% of Stocks
S&P 500	2.7
S&P MidCap 400	29.8
U.S. Small Cap	65.0
Foreign	2.5

Sector Weightings

	% of Stocks	Relative S&P 500
Utilities	2.5	0.20
Energy	0.6	0.06
Financials	2.6	0.15
Industrial Cyclicals	2.5	0.15
Consumer Durables	10.2	1.64
Consumer Staples	0.0	0.00
Services	17.9	2.19
Retail	10.5	1.80
Health	6.4	0.74
Technology	46.8	5.11

MORNINGSTAR 1995 Mutual Fund 500

Alliance Bond Corp Bond A

	Ticker	Load	NAV	Yield	SEC Yield	Assets	Objective
	CBFAX	4.25%	11.88	9.6%	9.11%	212.9	Corp General

Alliance Bond Fund Corporate Bond Portfolio - Class A seeks income.

The fund normally invests at least 65% of its assets in investment-grade debt. It may hold corporate bonds, convertibles, U.S. government debt, stocks, and foreign securities.

Class A shares have front loads and lower 12b-1 fees; Class B shares have deferred loads and conversion features; Class C shares have no loads. Prior to March 2, 1987, the fund was named Bullock Monthly Income Shares. From then until Jan. 4, 1993, it was named Alliance Bond Fund Monthly Income Shares. Alliance Bond Fund High-Yield merged into the fund on that date.

Manager's Investment Style

Manager Wayne Lyski takes an aggressive approach with this fund. He prefers bonds at the lower-quality end of investment grade, and typically keeps a portion of assets in noninvestment-grade and nonrated debt in an effort to find bonds with credit-upgrade potential. Lyski prefers especially long bonds--those with 14- to 17-year maturities--because he believes that these issues benefit the most from credit upgrades. He also maintains a stake (as much as 25% of assets) in emerging-market debt. High turnover is common.

Fund Manager(s)

Wayne D. Lyski, since 10-86. BA, Seattle Pacific U. MBA, Wharton

Manager Experience

	Dates Managed	Invest Obj	Std Dev	+/- Index
Wayne D. Lyski				
Alliance Mtg Secs Inc A	02/84 - 03/93	GM	4.43	-1.18
Alliance Bond U.S. Govt A	12/85 - 03/92	GG	4.09	-1.70

Performance 12-31-94

	1st Qtr	2nd Qtr	3rd Qtr	4th Qtr	Total
1987	3.45	-2.11	-2.56	4.14	2.76
1988	3.66	0.60	2.68	0.85	7.98
1989	0.26	9.07	-0.50	3.91	13.06
1990	-3.09	3.06	-1.49	7.23	5.51
1991	2.39	1.43	7.40	5.86	18.07
1992	-0.41	3.67	8.88	0.75	13.26
1993	10.77	6.67	5.28	5.38	31.09
1994	-8.43	-4.11	5.33	-5.67	-12.75

Bear Market Performance

Decile Rank (5-year period)

Worst | Best

	Worst 3 Mo Period 1985-89	Worst 3 Mo Period 1990-94
Alliance Bond Corp Bond A	-2.56	-13.61
+/- LB Aggregate	0.17	-8.68
+/- Best Fit Index : LB Corp	1.07	-7.35

Trailing Returns

	Total Return %	+/- LB Aggregate	+/- LB Corp	% Rank All	% Rank Obj	Growth of $10,000
3 Mo	-5.67	-6.05	-6.11	93	99	9,433
6 Mo	-0.64	-1.63	-1.82	67	90	9,936
1 Yr	-12.75	-9.83	-8.83	97	98	8,725
3 Yr Avg	9.01	4.47	3.60	17	2	12,954
5 Yr Avg	10.04	2.42	1.78	17	2	16,137
10 Yr Avg	10.93	0.99	0.31	48	3	28,223
15 Yr Avg	11.13	0.32	-0.20	64	9	48,705

Operations

Address and Telephone	P.O. Box 1520
	Secaucus, NJ 07096-1520
	800-227-4618 / 201-319-4000
Advisor	Alliance Capital Management
Subadvisor	None
Distributor	Alliance Fund Distributors
States Available	All
Report Grade	C+
Income Distrib	Paid Monthly
Date of Inception	03-11-74
Fiscal Year End	June

Min Initial Purchase	$250 (Addt'l: $50)
Min IRA Purchase	$250 (Addt'l: $50)
Min Auto Invest Plan	$250 (Systematic Inv: $25)

Expenses & Fees

Sales Fees	4.25% front
	0.00% deferred
	0.30% 12b-1
Management Fee	0.63% max./0.50% min.
3-,5-,10-yr Expense Projections	$82, $111, $193

Historical Profile

Return	High
Risk	High
Rating	★★★
	Neutral

38	29	10	3	8	1	2	4

Growth of $10,000

|||| Value of Fund ($000)
— Value of Index ($000) LB Corp
▼ Manager Change
▽ Partial Manager Change
► Mgr Unknown After
◄ Mgr Unknown Before

Performance Quartile (Within Objective)

	1983	1984	1985	1986	1987	1988	1989	1990	1991	1992	1993	1994	History
	10.84	11.08	12.16	12.62	11.81	11.64	11.96	11.32	12.17	12.49	14.86	11.88	NAV
	9.88	15.19	22.33	13.96	2.76	7.98	13.06	5.51	18.07	13.26	31.09	-12.75	Total Return %
	1.51	0.04	0.20	-1.29	0.01	0.10	-1.48	-3.44	2.07	6.02	21.34	-9.83	+/- LB Aggregate
	0.61	-1.43	-1.74	-2.57	0.21	-1.24	-0.92	-1.65	-0.44	4.56	18.93	-8.83	+/- LB Corporate
	11.51	12.98	12.58	10.18	9.18	9.42	10.31	10.86	10.56	10.63	9.86	7.30	Income Return %
	-1.63	2.21	9.75	3.78	-6.42	-1.44	2.75	-5.35	7.51	2.63	21.24	-20.05	Capital Return %
	80	5	58	61	37	73	54	39	48	13	8	97	Total Rtn % Rank All
	33	16	42	51	30	65	25	73	27	2	1	98	Total Rtn % Rank Obj
	1.25	1.26	1.26	1.17	1.15	1.08	1.14	1.23	1.08	1.21	1.14	1.14	Income $
	0.00	0.00	0.00	0.00	0.00	0.00	0.00	0.00	0.00	0.00	0.25	0.00	Capital Gains $
	1.04	1.18	1.15	1.08	1.27	1.81	1.84	1.51	1.44	1.48	1.39	1.30	Expense Ratio %
	11.32	11.88	11.00	9.80	9.17	9.24	9.53	10.70	9.84	8.98	9.29	7.76	Income Ratio %
	27	10	142	240	95	98	104	480	357	610	579	372	Turnover Rate %
	39.4	36.4	40.6	44.0	38.9	37.0	73.1	69.8	64.6	68.7	249.4	212.9	Net Assets ($mil)

Risk Analysis

Time Period	Load-Adj Return %	Risk % Rank All	Risk % Rank Obj	Morningstar Return [2]	Morningstar Risk	Morningstar Risk-Adj Rating
1 Yr	-16.46					
3 Yr	7.45	72	100	1.16 [3]	2.15	★★★
5 Yr	9.09	51	99	1.10 [3]	1.96	★★
10 Yr	10.45	37	93	1.27 [3]	1.52	★★★
Average Historical Rating (109 months)					3.1	★ s

[1] = low, 100 = high   [2] 1.00 = Taxable Avg   [3] 1.00 = 90-day T-bill return

Other Measures

			Standard LB Agg	Best Fit LB Corp
Standard Deviation	9.59	Alpha	3.7	2.7
Mean	9.12	Beta	1.91	1.53
Sharpe Ratio	0.58	R-Squared	64	65

Investment Style

Interest-Rate Stance

Avg Effective Duration	6.3 Yrs
Avg Effective Maturity	16.4 Yrs

Quality

Avg Credit Quality	BBB
Avg Weighted Coupon	8.74%
Avg Weighted Price	84.79% of Par

Diversification Value for Portfolio Types

Large Cap: Medium | Small Cap: High | Bond: Low | Balanced: Low | Diversified: Medium

Portfolio 06-30-94

Amount 000	Date of Maturity	Total Stocks: 0 Total Fixed-Income: 31	Value $000	% Net Assets
13271	04-15-21	AMR 10%	13120	5.99
12548	02-01-13	News America Holdings 9.25%	12568	5.73
14911	08-01-22	Paramount Comm 8.25%	11840	5.40
12065	07-15-21	United Air Lines 10.25%	11180	5.10
9652	04-15-18	Chrysler 10.95%	10850	4.95
11148	08-01-12	Westinghouse Electric 8.625%	10285	4.69
24613	04-15-14	Republic of Brazil 8%	10183	4.65
9652	06-02-04	Phillipine Long Dist 10.625%	9724	4.44
9652	03-15-23	Time Warner Entertnmnt 8.375%	8525	3.89
7649	10-30-07	TKR Cable I 10.5%	8164	3.72
9652	12-15-03	Banco Rio La Plata 8.75%	8115	3.70
7238	06-01-16	DQU II Funding 8.7%	7098	3.24
354		Santander Finl A Cv Pfd 7.375%	7081	3.23
6961	02-10-96	Lehman Brothers FRN	6620	3.02
13513		Republic of Peru N/A	6554	2.99
7239	05-15-03	Transport Maritima 9.25%	6334	2.89
7239	07-01-13	Turner Broadcasting Sys 8.375%	6189	2.82
7239	02-01-24	Turner Broadcasting Sys 8.4%	6072	2.77
7239	02-17-01	Mexicano de Desarrollo 8.25%	5864	2.68
42469	11-15-21	US Treasury Bond 0%	5299	2.42
5593	12-15-03	Home Holdings 7.875%	5152	2.35
4725	01-15-13	USX 9.125%	4648	2.12
9169	09-15-13	Republic of Brazil FRN	4424	2.02
4826	08-15-23	US Treasury Bond 6.25%	4055	1.85
4826	07-15-19	Long Island Lighting 8.9%	4038	1.84

Composition % 12-30-94

Cash	53.1	Preferreds	0.0
Stocks	5.1	Convertibles	0.0
Bonds	42.5	Other	-0.7

Tax Analysis

	Tax-Adj Historical Return %	% Pretax Return
3 Yr Avg	5.45	58.5
5 Yr Avg	6.57	61.1
10 Yr Avg	7.10	54.1
Potential Capital Gain Exposure (% of assets)		-14%

Most Similar Funds in MF500

Bond Fund of America	Weak Fit
Stagecoach Asset Alloc A	Weak Fit
Phoenix Multi-Sector F/I A	Weak Fit

Coupon Range

	% of Bonds	Rel Obj
0%	2.5	1.16
0% to 8.5%	34.7	0.55
8.5% to 9.5%	26.5	1.63
9.5% to 11%	25.3	2.73
More than 11%	0.0	0.00
Not applicable	11.0	2.20

Credit Analysis 12-30-94

% of Bonds

US Govt	0	BB	12
AAA	5	B	0
AA	0	Below B	0
A	18	NR/NA	13
BBB	52		

Investment Style History

Fixed Income

Income Rtn % Rank Obj

Alliance Growth & Income A

	Ticker	Load	NAV	Yield	SEC Yield	Assets	Objective
	CABDX	4.25%	2.13	2.3%	N/A	387.8	Growth/Inc.

Alliance Growth & Income Fund - Class A seeks reasonable income and capital appreciation.

The fund invests primarily in dividend paying common stocks. It may invest in high-quality foreign issues.

Class A shares have front loads and lower 12b-1 fees; Class B shares have deferred loads and conversion features; Class C shares have level loads. The fund was named Bullock Dividend Shares and had a different investment advisor prior to March 2, 1987. From that date until October 20, 1989, it was called Alliance Dividend Shares. On July 22, 1993, Equitable Growth and Income Fund Front-Load merged into this fund.

Manager's Investment Style

Management invests in dividend-paying, very-large-cap stocks. Although it does invest in traditional income-paying issues, management prefers stocks with above-market earnings growth, and often holds popular growth issues selling well-below their former highs.

Fund Manager(s)

Paul Rissman, since 11-94. PhD, U. of Pennsylvania MBA, Columbia U.

Manager Experience

	Dates Managed	Invest Obj	Std Dev	+/- Index
Not available.				

Historical Profile
Return	Average
Risk	Below Average
Rating	★★★
	Neutral

91% 94% 90% 88% 88% 87% 85% 80%

Investment Style History
Equity

Average % Stocks Held in Portfolio

Growth of $10,000
‖‖‖ Value of Fund ($000)
— Value of Index ($000)
S&P 500
▼ Manager Change
▽ Partial Manager Change
► Mgr Unknown After
◄ Mgr Unknown Before

Performance Quartile
(Within Objective)

1983	1984	1985	1986	1987	1988	1989	1990	1991	1992	1993	1994	History
3.20	2.96	3.35	3.53	2.65	2.52	2.62	2.17	2.52	2.41	2.40	2.13	NAV
20.98	6.67	31.70	21.56	0.86	16.76	25.56	-1.70	27.08	4.50	9.96	-4.20	Total Return %
-1.49	0.40	-0.04	2.88	-4.40	0.15	-6.12	1.42	-3.41	-3.12	-0.10	-5.51	+/- S&P 500
-2.49	3.62	-0.86	5.46	-1.50	-1.18	-3.61	4.49	-7.13	-4.47	-1.32	-4.13	+/- Wilshire 5000
3.97	4.37	4.46	3.63	3.97	2.96	3.65	4.10	3.14	2.50	2.50	2.28	Income Return %
17.00	2.29	27.25	17.93	-3.11	13.80	21.91	-5.79	23.93	2.00	7.46	-6.48	Capital Return %
36	44	20	15	52	22	22	60	32	79	67	55	Total Rtn % Rank All
50	36	23	16	60	39	41	29	60	84	53	81	Total Rtn % Rank Obj
0.12	0.13	0.13	0.13	0.14	0.08	0.10	0.10	0.07	0.06	0.06	0.05	Income $
0.23	0.31	0.35	0.40	0.78	0.48	0.43	0.30	0.15	0.16	0.18	0.12	Capital Gains $
0.91	0.99	0.95	0.81	0.86	1.09	1.08	1.09	1.14	1.09	1.07	1.03	Expense Ratio %
4.24	4.54	3.78	3.31	2.77	3.09	3.49	3.40	2.74	2.63	2.38	2.36	Income Ratio %
8	14	15	11	60	66	79	76	84	104	91	68	Turnover Rate %
279.8	258.6	276.1	344.7	314.9	327.2	362.6	330.5	426.6	427.0	445.8	387.8	Net Assets ($mil)

Performance 12-31-94

	1st Qtr	2nd Qtr	3rd Qtr	4th Qtr	Total
1987	15.34	3.02	6.57	-20.35	0.86
1988	5.66	7.19	0.00	3.08	16.76
1989	7.55	6.69	9.48	-0.04	25.56
1990	-2.29	5.51	-12.41	8.87	-1.70
1991	11.52	-0.43	5.70	8.27	27.08
1992	-2.19	-0.60	2.27	5.10	4.50
1993	4.78	-0.19	4.63	0.49	9.96
1994	-3.99	-1.20	2.78	-1.73	-4.20

Bear Market Performance

Decile Rank (5-year period)

Worst | Best

	Worst 3 Mo Period 1985-89	Worst 3 Mo Period 1990-94
Alliance Growth & Income A	-26.91	-13.87
+/- S&P 500	2.67	-0.03
+/- Best Fit Index : S&P 500	2.67	-0.03

Trailing Returns

	Total Return %	+/- S&P 500	+/- Wil 5000	% Rank All	% Rank Obj	Growth of $10,000
3 Mo	-1.73	-1.72	-0.96	63	55	9,827
6 Mo	1.00	-3.86	-3.63	37	75	10,100
1 Yr	-4.20	-5.51	-4.13	55	81	9,580
3 Yr Avg	3.25	-3.01	-3.36	83	83	11,008
5 Yr Avg	6.58	-2.11	-2.24	61	80	13,751
10 Yr Avg	12.53	-1.85	-1.33	32	46	32,553
15 Yr Avg	13.33	-1.15	-0.65	33	41	65,319

Operations

Address and Telephone	P.O. Box 1520 Secaucus, NJ 07096-1520 800-227-4618 / 201-319-4000
Advisor	Alliance Capital Management
Subadvisor	None
Distributor	Alliance Fund Distributors
States Available	All
Report Grade	B-
Income Distrib	Paid Annually
Date of Inception	07-01-32
Fiscal Year End	October

Risk Analysis

Time Period	Load-Adj Return %	Risk % Rank All	Obj	Morningstar Return	Morningstar Risk	Morningstar Risk-Adj Rating
1 Yr	-8.27					
3 Yr	1.77	72	74	-0.52[3]	0.82	★★
5 Yr	5.66	69	65	0.22[3]	0.82	★★
10 Yr	12.04	57	48	0.89	0.82	★★★
Average Historical Rating (109 months)				3.8		★ s

[1] 1 = low, 100 = high   [2] 1.00 = Equity Avg   [3] 1.00 = 90-day T-bill return

Other Measures

				Standard S&P 500	Best Fit S&P 500
Standard Deviation	8.28	Alpha		-2.7	-2.7
Mean	3.55	Beta		0.96	0.96
Sharpe Ratio	0.00	R-Squared		85	85

Investment Style

	Stock Portfolio Avg	Relative S&P 500	Style
Price/Earnings Ratio	17.0	0.92	Value Blend Growth
Price/Book Ratio	3.3	0.97	
5 Yr Earnings Gr %	9.0	1.62	
Return on Assets %	6.6	0.88	
Debt % Total Cap	32.4	1.15	
Med Mkt Cap ($mil)	10213	0.79	

Diversification Value for Portfolio Types

Large Cap: None	Small Cap: Low	Bond: High	Balanced: None	Diversified: Low

Expenses & Fees

Sales Fees	4.25% front
	0.00% deferred
	0.30% 12b-1
Management Fee	0.63% max./0.45% min.
3-,5-,10-yr Expense Projections	$75, $99, $168
Annual Brokerage Cost	0.28%

Min Initial Purchase	$250 (Addt'l: $50)
Min IRA Purchase	$250 (Addt'l: $50)
Min Auto Invest Plan	$250 (Systematic Inv: $25)

Portfolio 10-31-94

Share Chg (04-94) 000	Amount 000	Total Stocks: 99 Total Fixed-Income: 56	Value $000	% Net Assets
266	386	Sprint	12591	3.04
-11	338	Travelers	11728	2.83
118	240	General Electric	11706	2.83
-52	69	Royal Dutch Petroleum	8038	1.94
17	211	May Department Stores	7951	1.92
37	120	Philip Morris	7338	1.77
	4771	General Instrument Cv 5%	7133	1.72
-2	70	American International Group	6569	1.59
51	92	Shell Trans/Trading UK (ADR)	6535	1.58
77	133	Chevron	5994	1.45
96	199	McDonald's	5731	1.38
	59	Ford Motor Cl A Cv Pfd 4.25%	5719	1.38
-10	144	Merrill Lynch	5653	1.36
-19	94	Motorola	5563	1.34
-55	171	Abbott Laboratories	5312	1.28
-2	60	ITT	5284	1.28
	135	Salomon (Elks) Cv Pfd 7.25%	5121	1.24
-14	189	Astra Cl B	5053	1.22
-54	83	Rohm & Haas	5033	1.21
-25	75	Texaco	4932	1.19
-44	150	American Express	4621	1.12
60	60	Monsanto	4544	1.10
	62	Chemical Banking Cv Pfd 10%	4528	1.09
	4250	Legg Mason Cv 7%	4526	1.09
-24	115	Weyerhaeuser	4519	1.09

Composition % 12-31-94
Cash	6.1	Preferreds	6.0
Stocks	77.3	Convertibles	5.1
Bonds	5.5	Other	0.0

Tax Analysis
	Tax-Adj Historical Return %	% Pretax Return
3 Yr Avg	0.61	18.2
5 Yr Avg	3.33	47.4
10 Yr Avg	7.78	49.5
Potential Capital Gain Exposure (% of assets)		0%

Most Similar Funds in MF500
Liberty All-Star	Strong Fit
Dreyfus	Strong Fit
PIMCo Adv Growth C	Strong Fit

Index Allocation
	% of Stocks
S&P 500	79.5
S&P MidCap 400	4.0
U.S. Small Cap	8.5
Foreign	11.2

Sector Weightings
	% of Stocks	Relative S&P 500
Utilities	4.7	0.38
Energy	11.7	1.16
Financials	24.2	2.29
Industrial Cyclicals	14.2	0.86
Consumer Durables	6.8	1.09
Consumer Staples	5.6	0.45
Services	9.2	1.13
Retail	5.3	0.91
Health	11.2	1.29
Technology	7.0	0.77

MORNINGSTAR **1995 Mutual Fund 500**

Alliance Mortgage Secs Inc

	Ticker	Load	NAV	Yield	SEC Yield	Assets	Objective
	ALMSX	4.25%	8.13	7.4%	6.78%	553.4	Gvt Mortgage

Alliance Mortgage Securities Income Fund - Class A seeks income.

The fund normally invests at least 65% of its assets in mortgage-related securities that provide funds for mortgage loans made to U.S. homebuyers. These loans are originated primarily by S&L institutions, mortgage bankers, commercial banks, and other mortgage lenders, and are grouped into pools by various government, government-related, and private organizations.

Class A shares have front loads and lower 12b-1 fees; Class B shares have deferred loads and conversion features; Class C shares have no loads.

Manager's Investment Style

Management takes a high-turnover approach with this fund, trading back and forth between Treasuries and mortgages (depending on yield spreads) and executing mortgage dollar rolls (sometimes leveraging as much as 30% of the portfolio to do so) when the market environment is positive. Management also prefers bonds with longer durations for their higher yields and capital-gains potential. The comanagers will shorten duration and turn to cash and cash surrogates for defensive purposes.

Fund Manager(s)

Paul A. Ullman, since 02-92. BS, Washington U.
Patricia J. Young, since 02-92. BA, Indiana U. MBA, Wharton

Manager Experience

	Dates Managed	Invest Obj	Std Dev	+/- Index
Patricia J. Young				
Managers Short Govt	09/90 - 05/93	GG	1.70	-5.90
Paul A. Ullman				
Managers Short Govt	08/90 - 05/93	GG	1.66	-5.87

Historical Profile

Return	Average
Risk	Average
Rating	★★★ Neutral

	1983	1984	1985	1986	1987	1988	1989	1990	1991	1992	1993	1994	History
	---	9.54	9.97	9.74	9.03	8.81	8.76	8.79	9.21	9.08	9.29	8.13	NAV
	---	12.19 *	18.36	9.12	3.40	8.64	10.98	11.01	15.44	7.73	10.15	-6.14	Total Return %
	---	---	-3.77	-6.13	0.65	0.76	-3.56	2.06	-0.56	0.49	0.39	-3.23	+/- LB Aggregate
	---	---	-6.86	-4.32	-0.89	-0.08	-4.37	0.29	-0.28	0.78	3.31	-4.54	+/- LB Mortgage
	---	11.76	13.85	11.22	10.45	11.07	11.55	10.67	10.66	9.15	7.83	6.34	Income Return %
	---	0.42	4.51	-2.10	-7.04	-2.44	-0.57	0.34	4.78	-1.41	2.31	-12.49	Capital Return %
	---	---	81	87	33	70	65	3	55	49	66	73	Total Rtn % Rank All
	---	---	45	81	24	18	88	2	28	7	8	89	Total Rtn % Rank Obj
	---	1.02	1.22	1.06	0.99	0.98	0.97	0.87	0.87	0.81	0.69	0.60	Income $
	---	0.00	0.00	0.02	0.03	0.00	0.00	0.00	0.00	0.00	0.00	0.00	Capital Gains $
	---	0.66	0.87	1.00	1.15	1.11	1.13	1.12	1.16	1.18	1.00	0.98	Expense Ratio %
	---	12.86	12.30	10.86	10.79	10.80	11.03	10.09	9.92	8.56	7.20	6.68	Income Ratio %
	---	---	164	190	211	239	328	393	439	555	622	---	Turnover Rate %
	---	316.6	609.6	756.7	679.6	619.5	556.1	495.3	541.5	789.9	845.3	553.4	Net Assets ($mil)

Investment Style History
Fixed Income
Income Rtn % Rank Obj

2	1	1	1	2	2	16	38

Growth of $10,000
|||| Value of Fund ($000)
— Value of Index ($000) LB Agg
▼ Manager Change
▽ Partial Manager Change
► Mgr Unknown After
◄ Mgr Unknown Before

Performance Quartile (Within Objective)

Performance 12-31-94

	1st Qtr	2nd Qtr	3rd Qtr	4th Qtr	Total
1987	2.27	-1.44	-2.60	5.32	3.40
1988	5.39	1.50	1.63	-0.06	8.64
1989	0.86	4.86	1.09	3.80	10.98
1990	-0.37	3.43	1.72	5.90	11.01
1991	2.72	1.99	5.62	4.32	15.44
1992	-0.45	3.48	4.02	0.55	7.73
1993	4.51	2.84	1.41	1.06	10.15
1994	-4.30	-1.63	-0.40	0.10	-6.14

Bear Market Performance

Decile Rank (5-year period)

	Worst 3 Mo Period 1985-89	Worst 3 Mo Period 1990-94
Alliance Mortgage Secs Inc	-2.60	-6.76
+/- LB Aggregate	0.13	-1.82
+/- Best Fit Index : LB Agg	0.13	-1.82

Trailing Returns

	Total Return %	+/- LB Aggregate	+/- LB Mortgage	% Rank All	% Rank Obj	Growth of $10,000
3 Mo	0.10	-0.28	-0.33	19	45	10,010
6 Mo	-0.30	-1.29	-1.61	62	87	9,970
1 Yr	-6.14	-3.23	-4.54	73	89	9,386
3 Yr Avg	3.66	-0.89	-0.33	76	31	11,137
5 Yr Avg	7.37	-0.25	-0.20	42	13	14,272
10 Yr Avg	8.68	-1.27	-1.67	78	45	22,979
15 Yr Avg	---	---	---	---	---	---

Operations

Address and Telephone	P.O. Box 1520
	Secaucus, NJ 07096-1520
	800-227-4618 / 201-319-4000
Advisor	Alliance Capital Management
Subadvisor	None
Distributor	Alliance Fund Distributors
States Available	All
Report Grade	C
Income Distrib	Paid Monthly
* Date of Inception	02-29-84
Fiscal Year End	December

Risk Analysis

Time Period	Load-Adj Return %	Risk % Rank [1] All	Obj	Morningstar [2] Return	Morningstar Risk	Morningstar Risk-Adj Rating
1 Yr	-10.13					
3 Yr	2.17	26	78	-0.40 [3]	1.05	★★
5 Yr	6.44	19	68	0.41 [3]	0.95	★★★
10 Yr	8.21	10	31	0.60 [3]	0.90	★★★
Average Historical Rating (95 months)				3.3	★ s	

[1] = low, 100 = high   [2] 1.00 = Taxable Avg   [3] 1.00 = 90-day T-bill return

Other Measures

			Standard LB Agg	Best Fit LB Agg
Standard Deviation	4.27	Alpha	-0.8	-0.8
Mean	3.69	Beta	0.98	0.98
Sharpe Ratio	0.04	R-Squared	85	85

Investment Style

Interest-Rate Stance
Avg Effective Duration	5.9 Yrs
Avg Effective Maturity	10.9 Yrs

Quality
Avg Credit Quality	AAA
Avg Weighted Coupon	7.26%
Avg Weighted Price	94.80% of Par

Diversification Value for Portfolio Types

Large Cap: High	Small Cap: High	Bond: None	Balanced: Medium	Diversified: High

Portfolio 06-30-94

Total Stocks: 0
Total Fixed-Income: 51

Amount 000	Date of Maturity		Value $000	% Net Assets
141064	02-15-24	GNMA 7.5%	134540	19.20
122418	04-01-24	GNMA 7%	112700	16.08
88371		FHLMC TBA 7%	82323	11.75
85572		FNMA TBA 7%	79635	11.37
65546		FHLMC TBA 6.5%	59114	8.44
30241	12-31-00	Lehman Card Account Tr 4.575%	30204	4.31
22490	03-15-17	GNMA 15yr 8%	22778	3.25
15218	05-15-08	FHLMC CMO PAC 6.4%	13715	1.96
11268	07-25-24	DLJ Mortgage CMO FRN Libor	11381	1.62
12515	07-15-07	FHLMC CMO PAC 6%	11196	1.60
10481		FNMA TBA 6.5%	9439	1.35
7808	01-15-08	FHLMC CMO PAC 6.4%	7157	1.02
4418	10-15-20	GNMA 11%	4926	0.70
5232	06-25-08	FNMA CMO 6%	4673	0.67
3998	02-01-18	GNMA 12.5%	4598	0.66
4317	07-25-23	FHLMC CMO FRN	4388	0.63
3355	07-01-20	FHLMC 12%	3730	0.53
3154	06-15-19	FHLMC 12.5%	3599	0.51
2515	06-01-20	FHLMC 11.5%	2771	0.40
3005	09-25-07	FNMA CMO PAC 6%	2622	0.37
2232	04-01-19	FNMA 12.5%	2547	0.36
4158	10-25-08	FNMA CMO PAC Ifrn	2518	0.36
2335	05-25-08	FNMA CMO PAC 6.5%	2116	0.30
1802	09-01-21	FNMA 12%	2039	0.29
1508	04-15-19	FHLMC 11.75%	1658	0.24

Composition % 09-30-94

Cash	-6.7	Preferreds	0.0
Stocks	0.0	Convertibles	0.0
Bonds	106.7	Other	0.0

Tax Analysis

	Tax-Adj Historical Return %	% Pretax Return
3 Yr Avg	0.80	21.3
5 Yr Avg	4.34	55.4
10 Yr Avg	4.76	45.6
Potential Capital Gain Exposure (% of assets)		-19%

Most Similar Funds in MF500

U.S. Government Securities	Strong Fit
American Cap Govt Secs A	Strong Fit
SteinRoe Income	Strong Fit

Coupon Range

	% of Bonds	Rel Obj
0%	0.0	0.00
0% to 8%	91.0	1.66
8% to 9%	0.0	0.00
9% to 10%	0.1	0.02
More than 10%	6.0	0.91
Not applicable	2.9	0.40

Sector Analysis 06-30-94
% of Bonds

US Treas	0	CMOs	10
GNMA mtgs	45	ARMs	0
FNMA mtgs	16	Other	5
FHLMC mtgs	25		

Expenses & Fees

Min Initial Purchase	$250 (Addt'l: $50)
Min IRA Purchase	$250 (Addt'l: $50)
Min Auto Invest Plan	$250 (Systematic Inv: $25)

Sales Fees	
	4.25% front
	0.00% deferred
	0.30% 12b-1
Management Fee	0.55% max./0.50% min.
3-,5-,10-yr Expense Projections	$73, $95, $160

Alliance Muni Income National A

	Ticker	Load	NAV	Yield	SEC Yield	Assets	Objective
	ALTHX	4.25%	9.29	6.4%	6.24%	318.9	Muni Nat

Alliance Municipal Income Fund National Portfolio - Class A seeks current income.

The fund normally invests at least 75% of its assets in investment-grade intermediate- to long-term municipal obligations. The majority of the debt is AMT-subject. The portfolio's average weighted maturity ranges from 10 to 25 years.

Class A shares have front loads and lower 12b-1 fees; Class B shares have deferred loads and conversion features; Class C shares have no loads and no conversion features. Prior to Sept. 27, 1988, this fund was named Alliance Tax-Free Income High-Income Tax-Free. Equitable Tax-Exempt Front-Load merged into this fund on July 22, 1993.

Manager's Investment Style

This fund is one of the municipal-bond category's more-aggressive members. Management maintains high interest-rate sensitivity by holding long-maturity bonds and lower-coupon issues. It often buys bonds on bad news or when credit quality is under scrutiny and holds them for a potential turnaround. Management also owns numerous private-activity bonds and other issues subject to the alternative minimum tax because of their above-average payouts.

Fund Manager(s)

Susan G. Peabody, since 12-86. Birthdate: 02-57. History, U. of California-Berkeley 1980 Finance, U. of Michigan 1989

Manager Experience

	Dates Managed	Invest Obj	Std Dev	+/- Index
Susan G. Peabody				
Sierra CA Municipal A	07/89 - 04/92	MC	3.50	-2.67

Historical Profile
Return	Below Average
Risk	Above Average
Rating	★★
	Below Average

	15	14	15	20	25	21	24	21

Growth of $10,000
|||| Value of Fund ($000)
— Value of Index ($000) LB Muni
▼ Manager Change
▽ Partial Manager Change
► Mgr Unknown After
◄ Mgr Unknown Before

Investment Style History
Fixed Income
Income Rtn % Rank Obj

Performance Quartile (Within Objective)

	1983	1984	1985	1986	1987	1988	1989	1990	1991	1992	1993	1994	History
	---	---	---	9.60	9.00	9.41	9.61	9.62	10.06	10.43	10.92	9.29	NAV
	---	---	---	0.00 *	1.29	12.80	10.10	7.39	11.84	10.43	13.32	-9.64	Total Return %
	---	---	---	---	-1.47	4.92	-4.44	-1.55	-4.16	3.19	3.57	-6.72	+/- LB Aggregate
	---	---	---	---	-0.21	2.64	-0.69	0.09	-0.30	1.61	1.05	-4.04	+/- LB Muni
	---	---	---	0.00	7.54	8.25	7.79	7.29	7.27	6.70	6.16	5.29	Income Return %
	---	---	---	0.00	-6.25	4.56	2.31	0.10	4.57	3.73	7.17	-14.93	Capital Return %
	---	---	---	---	48	39	72	18	77	20	38	93	Total Rtn % Rank All
	---	---	---	---	28	19	30	6	41	6	17	96	Total Rtn % Rank Obj
	---	---	---	0.00	0.71	0.70	0.70	0.67	0.66	0.64	0.62	0.60	Income $
	---	---	---	0.00	0.00	0.00	0.02	0.00	0.00	0.00	0.24	0.00	Capital Gains $
	---	---	---	---	0.50	0.40	0.38	0.60	0.75	0.83	0.65	0.59	Expense Ratio %
	---	---	---	---	7.71	7.71	7.25	7.06	6.81	6.35	5.69	5.42	Income Ratio %
	---	---	---	---	---	261	216	105	64	86	233	---	Turnover Rate %
	---	---	---	---	20.7	71.1	135.5	189.0	211.1	284.3	394.0	318.9	Net Assets ($mil)

Performance 12-31-94

	1st Qtr	2nd Qtr	3rd Qtr	4th Qtr	Total
1987	2.18	-3.97	-1.83	5.16	1.29
1988	3.28	2.50	3.15	3.30	12.80
1989	0.80	5.78	-0.05	3.31	10.10
1990	1.14	1.99	0.29	3.81	7.39
1991	2.07	2.76	3.75	2.78	11.84
1992	1.24	4.26	2.41	2.15	10.43
1993	3.52	3.84	3.75	1.61	13.32
1994	-7.66	0.41	0.36	-2.90	-9.64

Bear Market Performance

Decile Rank (5-year period)

Worst ———————————— Best

	Worst 3 Mo Period 1985-89	Worst 3 Mo Period 1990-94
Alliance Muni Income National	---	-8.50
+/- LB Aggregate	---	-3.57
+/- Best Fit Index : LB Muni	---	-2.74

Trailing Returns

	Total Return %	+/- LB Aggregate	+/- LB Muni	% Rank All	% Rank Obj	Growth of $10,000
3 Mo	-2.90	-3.28	-1.46	82	97	9,710
6 Mo	-2.55	-3.54	-1.30	92	94	9,745
1 Yr	-9.64	-6.72	-4.04	93	96	9,036
3 Yr Avg	4.18	-0.36	-0.69	65	69	11,308
5 Yr Avg	6.31	-1.31	-0.46	68	45	13,582
10 Yr Avg	---	---	---	---	---	---
15 Yr Avg	---	---	---	---	---	---

Operations

Address and Telephone	P.O. Box 1520
	Secaucus, NJ 07096-1520
	800-227-4618 / 201-319-4000
Advisor	Alliance Capital Management
Subadvisor	None
Distributor	Alliance Fund Distributors
States Available	All
Report Grade	C
Income Distrib	Paid Monthly
* Date of Inception	12-29-86
Fiscal Year End	October

Risk Analysis

Time Period	Load-Adj Return %	Risk % Rank All	Obj	Morningstar Return	Morningstar Risk	Morningstar Risk-Adj Rating
1 Yr	-13.48					
3 Yr	2.69	46	79	0.68	1.23	★
5 Yr	5.39	30	64	0.88	1.15	★★
10 Yr	---	---	---	---	---	

Average Historical Rating (61 months) 4.0 ★s

[1] 1 = low, 100 = high [2] 1.00 = Muni Avg [3] 1.00 = 90-day T-bill return

Other Measures

			Standard LB Agg	Best Fit LB Muni
Standard Deviation	6.72	Alpha	-0.4	-0.8
Mean	4.33	Beta	1.21	1.19
Sharpe Ratio	0.12	R-Squared	52	95

Investment Style

Interest-Rate Stance
Avg Effective Maturity 21.0 Yrs

Quality
Avg Credit Quality AA
Avg Weighted Coupon 5.61%
Avg Weighted Price 85.51% of Par

Diversification Value for Portfolio Types

Large Cap: Medium | Small Cap: High | Bond: Low | Balanced: Medium | Diversified: High

Portfolio 12-30-94

Amount 000	Date of Maturity	Total Stocks: 0 / Total Fixed-Income: 124	Value $000	% Net Assets
13316	11-15-21	CO Denver Arpt Sys 7.75%	12733	3.99
13906	06-01-05	KY Higher Educ Student Loan 5.3%	12655	3.97
34171	01-01-10	GA Atlanta Arpt Fac 0%	12515	3.92
13571	06-01-23	CA Poll Cntrl Fin Pacific Gas 5.875%	11468	3.60
9812	12-01-29	TX Alliance Arpt Spcl Fac American 7.5%	9309	2.92
11332	12-01-28	NY Engy Rsrch/Dev Elec Fac Edison 5.7%	9264	2.90
10857	08-01-23	WA Pilchuck Dev Pub Spcl Fac Arpt 6%	8794	2.76
7822	05-01-23	IN Warrick Envir Impr 6%	6697	2.10
7125	07-01-05	MA New England Educ Loan Mktg 5.7%	6519	2.04
6786	11-01-25	TX Dallas/Ft Worth Intl Arpt Impr 7.5%	6429	2.02
6786	06-01-11	MI Kalamazoo Hosp Fin Bronson IFRN	5946	1.86
5793	12-01-05	TX Central Higher Educ Student Loan 5.5%	5286	1.66
5619	03-01-05	TX Panhandle/Plains Higher Educ 5.55%	5169	1.62
4976	08-01-19	NY New York City GO 7.25%	5014	1.57
5429	07-01-04	MA New England Educ Loan Mktg 5.625%	4967	1.56
5295	06-01-14	NE Higher Educ Loan Prog Student 5.875%	4779	1.50
9118	11-15-04	CO Denver Arpt Sys 0%	4479	1.40
5383	11-01-23	UT Emery Poll Cntrl Pacific Proj 5.625%	4475	1.40
5021	06-01-28	NE Higher Educ Loan Prog Student 6%	4444	1.39
5087	02-15-28	IN Envir Dev Fin 5.75%	4394	1.38

Credit Analysis % of Bonds 12-31-94

				Coupon Range	% Bonds	Rel Obj
US Govt	0	BB	0	0%	7.0	2.81
AAA	96	B	0	0% to 6.8%	70.0	1.16
AA	4	Below B	0	6.8% to 7.5%	8.8	0.57
A	0	NR/NA	0	7.5% to 8.3%	7.8	0.89
BBB	0			More than 8.3%	2.5	0.28
				Not applicable	3.9	0.99

Composition % of Assets 12-31-94

Cash	0.4	Preferreds	0.0
Stocks	0.0	Convertibles	0.0
Bonds	99.6	Other	0.0

Tax Analysis

	Tax-Adj Historical Return %	% Pretax Return
3 Yr Avg	3.97	94.7
5 Yr Avg	6.18	97.7
10 Yr Avg	---	---
Potential Capital Gain Exposure (% of assets)		-12%

Most Similar Funds in MF500

Oppenheimer Tax-Fr Bond A	Strong Fit
Fidelity Insured Tax-Free	Strong Fit
Fidelity Municipal Bond	Strong Fit

Sector Weightings

	% Bonds	Rel Obj
General Obl	6.87	0.33
Utilities	1.84	0.15
Health	6.76	0.51
Water/Waste	2.11	0.33
Housing	7.99	1.09
Education	24.47	3.82
Transportation	27.50	2.70
COP/Lease	0.29	0.09
Private	20.97	1.80
Misc Revenue	1.20	0.24
Demand	0.00	0.00

Top 5 States % of Bonds

TX	10.84	CO	6.28
MA	7.51	NY	6.02
MI	6.33		

Min Initial Purchase	$250 (Addt'l: $50)
Min IRA Purchase	N/A
Min Auto Invest Plan	$250 (Systematic Inv: $25)

Expenses & Fees

Sales Fees	4.25% front
	0.00% deferred
	0.30% 12b-1
Management Fee	0.63% flat fee
3-,5-,10-yr Expense Projections	$62, $77, $120

MORNINGSTAR 1995 Mutual Fund 500

Allmerica Securities Trust

	Ticker	NAV	Mkt Price	Prem/Disc	Yield	Objective
	ALM	$10.64	$9.38	-11.9%	9.1%	Corp General

Allmerica Securities Trust seeks high current income. Capital appreciation is a secondary objective.

The fund will invest at least 40% of assets in marketable debt securities, including investment-grade straight-debt securities; securities of the U.S. government and its agencies or instrumentalities; securities guaranteed by the government of Canada; and cash or cash equivalents. It may hold up to 50% of assets in restricted securities acquired through direct placements. The fund may use short-term trading to achieve its investment objectives.

Prior to June 1, 1994, the fund was known as State Mutual Securities.

-5.3	0.0	9.7	12.4	6.1	3.9	3.0	1.8	5.2	4.3	-2.6	Highest Prem/Disc
-9.0	-5.0	-2.2	-5.8	-2.3	-6.8	-15.3	-6.3	-4.4	-7.1	-18.7	Lowest Prem/Disc

Historical Profile

Return	Above Average
Risk	Below Average
Rating	★★★★ Above Average

Growth of $10,000
■ at NAV ($000)
― at Market Price ($000)

Premium Discount %

Manager's Investment Style

In its quest for yield, management delves into lower-quality issues than some of its corporate-general rivals: The majority of the fund's assets are stashed in BBB and BB rated fare. Management dedicates some assets to higher-yielding nonrated securities, as well. The fund has also dabbled in Treasuries and mortgage-backed bonds.

Fund Manager(s)

John G. Grant, CFA. Since 1-90. BA'83 Boston U.; MBA'86 Northeastern U.

1983	1984	1985	1986	1987	1988	1989	1990	1991	1992	1993	1994	History
---	10.57	11.48	11.70	10.85	10.67	10.68	10.11	11.08	11.30	11.77	10.64	NAV
---	---	21.23	12.91	3.38	9.17	10.72	4.90	20.33	11.09	12.51	-1.97	NAV Total Return %
---	---	-0.90	-2.34	0.62	1.29	-3.82	-4.04	4.33	3.84	2.76	0.95	+/- LB Aggregate
---	---	-2.84	-3.62	0.82	-0.06	-3.26	-2.25	1.82	2.39	0.34	1.96	+/- LB Corp
---	---	12.65	11.03	9.95	10.82	10.62	10.24	10.73	9.10	8.35	7.63	Income Return %
---	---	8.58	1.88	-6.57	-1.66	0.09	-5.34	9.59	1.99	4.16	-9.60	Capital Return %
---	---	74	63	36	79	56	46	43	37	72	21	Total Rtn % Rank All
---	---	75	64	25	76	64	56	40	26	66	17	Total Rtn % Rank Obj
7.88	16.14	24.37	28.46	-2.76	8.51	10.61	-1.92	21.20	20.46	6.87	-12.62	Market Total Rtn %
---	-7.4	-3.3	5.2	0.6	0.7	-1.9	-5.2	-3.1	-1.4	-0.4	-9.4	Avg Prem/Disc %
1.20	1.23	1.20	1.20	1.12	1.13	1.09	1.04	0.97	0.97	0.91	0.85	Income $
0.00	0.00	0.00	0.00	0.08	0.00	0.00	0.00	0.00	0.00	0.00	0.00	Capital Gains $
1.06	1.10	1.01	0.90	0.81	0.81	0.84	0.82	0.77	0.76	0.74	0.77	Expense Ratio %
11.03	11.78	11.01	10.11	10.11	10.50	10.14	10.00	9.29	8.49	7.72	7.47	Income Ratio %
15	21	32	52	21	10	31	39	43	55	55	---	Turnover Rate %
83.3	83.7	91.7	96.1	89.7	89.5	89.6	85.4	91.1	95.4	101.2	91.4	Net Assets ($mil)

Manager Experience

	Dates Managed	Invest Obj	Std Dev	+/- Index

Not available.

NAV Performance % 12-30-94

	1st Qtr	2nd Qtr	3rd Qtr	4th Qtr	Total
1987	2.41	-1.83	-2.04	4.97	3.38
1988	3.61	1.67	2.13	1.46	9.17
1989	1.21	5.47	1.22	2.48	10.72
1990	-0.18	3.65	-2.82	4.33	4.90
1991	5.23	2.47	6.21	5.06	20.33
1992	1.18	4.55	4.92	0.09	11.09
1993	5.59	3.21	2.54	0.68	12.51
1994	-2.24	-1.33	1.37	0.26	-1.97

Bear Market Performance

Decile Rank (5-year period)

Worst |-----------------| Best

	Worst 3 Mo Period 1985-89	Worst 3 Mo Period 1990-94
Allmerica Sec Trust	-3.02	-5.30
+/- LB Aggregate	0.53	-0.37

Trailing Returns

	NAV Total Return %	+/- LB Agg	+/- LB Corp	% Rank All	% Rank Obj	Mkt Total Return %
3 Mo	0.26	-0.12	-0.18	17	61	2.15
6 Mo	1.63	0.64	0.46	22	32	-5.91
1 Yr	-1.97	0.95	1.96	21	17	-12.62
3 Yr Avg	7.00	2.46	1.59	37	23	4.00
5 Yr Avg	9.11	1.49	0.85	32	20	5.98
10 Yr Avg	10.22	0.27	-0.41	62	56	9.57

Risk Analysis

	Risk % Rank[1]		Morningstar[2]		Morningstar
	All	Obj	Return	Risk	Risk-Adj Rating
3 Yr	19	23	1.02[3]	0.62	★★★★
5 Yr	29	36	1.11[3]	0.76	★★★★
10 Yr	2	6	0.97	0.79	★★★★

Average Historical Rating (96 months)   3.8 ★s

[1] 1 = Low, 100 = High [2] 1.00 = Fixed-Inc Avg [3] 1.00 = 90-day T-bill Return

Other Measures

			LB Aggregate
Standard Deviation	4.36	Alpha	2.36
Mean	6.88	Beta	1.02
Sharpe Ratio	0.77	R-Squared	88

Investment Style

Interest-Rate Stance

	Fund	Relative Objective
Avg Eff Duration	5.2 Yrs	0.82
Avg Eff Maturity	9.4 Yrs	0.60
Avg Wtd Coupon	9.13%	1.02
Avg Wtd Price	98.6% Par	1.00

Duration Short Intm Long
Quality High Med Low

Quality

Avg Cred Quality   BB

Credit Analysis 12-31-94

	% of Bonds		% of Bonds
US Govt	10	BB	29
AAA	2	B	14
AA	0	Below B	0
A	3	NR/NA	17
BBB	25		

Diversification Value for Portfolio Types

Large Cap: High	Small Cap: High	Bond: None	Balanced: Medium	Diversified: High

Operations

Address and Telephone	440 Lincoln Street Worcester, MA 01605 508-855-1000
Advisor	Allmerica Asset Mgmt., Inc.
Subadvisor	N/A
Administrator	N/A
Transfer Agent	Bank of New York
Custodian	Citibank N.A.
Auditor	Ernst & Young LLP
Legal Counsel	Ropes & Gray

Income Distrib Schedule	Paid Quarterly
Management Fee	0.30%
Reinvestment Plan	Yes
Direct Purchase Plan	Yes
Shares Outstanding	8,592,306
Exchange	NYSE
Date of Inception	02-28-73
Shareholder Report	A-

Portfolio 09-30-94

Amount 000	Total Equity: 0 Total Fixed-Income: 62	Maturity	Value $000	% Total Invest
5632	US Treasury Bond 7.125%	02-15-23	5118	5.49
2850	US Treasury Note 5.75%	08-15-03	2513	2.70
2000	Lehman Brothers 10%	05-15-99	2130	2.28
2000	ANR Pipeline 9.625%	11-01-21	2111	2.26
2000	USX 8.875%	09-15-97	2055	2.20
2100	Arkla 8.9%	12-15-06	2037	2.18
2000	Westinghouse Electric 8.875%	06-01-01	2021	2.17
2000	Bethlehem Steel 10.375%	09-01-03	1993	2.14
2000	Sithe Energies 9%	12-30-13	1912	2.05
2000	Usinor Sacilor 7.26%	01-31-04	1898	2.04
2000	Fort Howard 8.25%	02-01-02	1820	1.95
1710	Wilmington Trust 9.23%	07-02-02	1772	1.90
1500	Texas Eastern Transmsn 10%	08-15-01	1632	1.75
1500	Amax 9.875%	06-13-01	1611	1.73
1500	Continental Cablevsn 12.875%	11-01-04	1598	1.71
1500	Boise Cascade 10.125%	12-15-97	1580	1.70
1500	Transcontinental Gas PL 9%	11-15-96	1538	1.65
1500	Texas-New Mexico Power 9.25%	09-15-00	1504	1.61
1500	Southwest Gas 9.375%	02-01-17	1452	1.56
1500	North Atlantic Energy 9.05%	06-01-02	1427	1.53
1453	United Air Lines 9.3%	03-22-08	1310	1.41
1320	USAir 10.3%	01-15-00	1243	1.33
1500	Republic of Argentina 8.375%	12-20-03	1230	1.32
1250	US Treasury Note 6.375%	08-15-02	1165	1.25
1326	Stone Container Cv 6.75%	02-15-07	1154	1.24

Composition % 12-31-94

Cash	6.0	Preferreds	0.0
Stocks	0.0	Convertibles	0.0
Bonds	94.0	Other	0.0

Tax Analysis

	Tax-Adj Historical Return %	% Pretax Return
3 Yr Avg	3.89	53.9
5 Yr Avg	5.85	60.1
10 Yr Avg	6.20	50.2

Potential Capital Gain Exposure (% of assets)   -6

Most Similar Funds in MF500

Bond Fund of America	Strong Fit
J Hancock Inc	Strong Fit
Putnam Income A	Strong Fit

Coupon Range

	% of Bonds	Relative Objective
0%, PIK	0.0	0.0
0% to 8.5%	30.7	0.9
8.5% to 9.5%	29.1	1.1
9.5% to 11%	28.8	1.3
More than 11%	11.4	1.3
Not applicable	0.0	0.0

1.0 = Objective Average

American Balanced

	Ticker	Load	NAV	Yield	SEC Yield	Assets	Objective
	ABALX	5.75%	12.00	4.6%	4.62%	2081.9	Balanced

American Balanced Fund seeks capital preservation, current income, and long-term growth of capital and income.

The fund normally invests in a diversified array of equities, debt, and cash instruments. These purchases may include common stocks, preferred stocks, corporate bonds, or U.S. government securities. The equity portion includes foreign and domestic issues. Fixed-income securities must be rated investment grade at the time of purchase. The fund primarily seeks issues that demonstrate fundamental values at reasonable prices.

Historical Profile
Return	Average
Risk	Below Average
Rating	★★★★ Above Average

Equity ... 59% 56% 55% 54% 50% 47% 48% 51%

Investment Style History
Equity

Average % Stocks Held in Portfolio

Growth of $10,000
- |||| Value of Fund ($000)
- — Value of Index ($000) S&P 500
- ▼ Manager Change
- ▽ Partial Manager Change
- ► Mgr Unknown After
- ◄ Mgr Unknown Before

Performance Quartile (Within Objective)

Manager's Investment Style
The fund has used Capital Research and Management's team-management approach to create a highly diversified portfolio including large-cap, income-paying stocks bought at moderate prices and high-quality premium bonds. Management has also shown a willingness to change the fund's asset allocation in response to market movements. The goal is to provide investors with the optimal single core fund.

Fund Manager(s)
Abner D. Goldstine, since 09-75.
George A. Miller, since 12-65.
Robert G. O'Donnell, since 04-86.

	1983	1984	1985	1986	1987	1988	1989	1990	1991	1992	1993	1994	History
	10.91	10.06	11.65	10.83	10.13	10.46	11.41	10.32	12.05	12.28	12.57	12.00	NAV
	16.11	9.37	29.11	16.87	4.02	12.87	21.53	-1.57	24.69	9.48	11.27	0.34	Total Return %
	-6.36	3.10	-2.63	-1.81	-1.24	-3.74	-10.15	1.55	-5.79	1.86	1.22	-0.98	+/- S&P 500
	7.73	-5.79	6.99	1.62	1.26	5.00	6.99	-10.52	8.69	2.24	1.52	3.25	+/- LB Aggregate
	7.87	7.61	6.94	5.79	6.04	6.33	6.50	5.77	6.43	5.22	5.02	4.50	Income Return %
	8.23	1.75	22.17	11.08	-2.02	6.55	15.03	-7.34	18.27	4.27	6.25	-4.16	Capital Return %
	53	30	29	42	27	38	32	60	36	27	57	17	Total Rtn % Rank All
	42	35	39	51	19	39	34	61	45	26	46	10	Total Rtn % Rank Obj
	0.76	0.71	0.64	0.64	0.67	0.62	0.67	0.63	0.62	0.60	0.60	0.56	Income $
	0.00	0.98	0.50	2.02	0.48	0.32	0.58	0.27	0.13	0.27	0.46	0.05	Capital Gains $
	0.77	0.75	0.70	0.67	0.68	0.76	0.78	0.84	0.82	0.74	0.71	---	Expense Ratio %
	6.76	6.37	6.18	5.71	5.17	5.54	5.80	5.95	5.56	5.19	4.74	---	Income Ratio %
	83	48	63	59	42	42	37	26	25	17	28	---	Turnover Rate %
	114.5	121.9	148.2	166.8	193.0	218.1	275.2	370.4	642.0	1066.5	1709.5	2081.9	Net Assets ($mil)

Manager Experience

	Dates Managed	Invest Obj	Std Dev	+/- Index
George A. Miller				
Endowments	07/75 - 12/94	GI	11.60	0.35
Income Fund of America	02/76 - 12/94	I	9.18	-0.36

Performance 12-31-94

	1st Qtr	2nd Qtr	3rd Qtr	4th Qtr	Total
1987	11.32	2.18	2.30	-10.61	4.02
1988	5.24	4.85	0.78	1.50	12.87
1989	4.60	8.10	6.27	1.13	21.53
1990	-1.90	2.47	-9.62	8.34	-1.57
1991	9.80	1.52	5.12	6.42	24.69
1992	-0.51	3.50	4.09	2.14	9.48
1993	4.18	2.32	2.99	1.35	11.27
1994	-3.72	0.91	3.44	-0.17	0.34

Bear Market Performance
Decile Rank (5-year period)

Worst — Best

	Worst 3 Mo Period 1985-89	Worst 3 Mo Period 1990-94
American Balanced	-16.41	-9.62
+/- S&P 500	13.17	4.12
+/- Best Fit Index : S&P 500	13.17	4.12

Trailing Returns

	Total Return %	+/- S&P 500	+/- LB Aggregate	% Rank All	% Rank Obj	Growth of $10,000
3 Mo	-0.17	-0.15	-0.54	27	21	9,983
6 Mo	3.27	-1.59	2.28	19	12	10,327
1 Yr	0.34	-0.98	3.25	17	10	10,034
3 Yr Avg	6.92	0.66	2.38	27	25	12,223
5 Yr Avg	8.45	-0.24	0.82	28	31	15,002
10 Yr Avg	12.44	-1.94	2.50	33	25	32,302
15 Yr Avg	13.10	-1.39	2.29	38	36	63,346

Operations

Address and Telephone	4 Embarcadero Cntr P.O. Box 7650 San Francisco, CA 94120 800-421-4120 / 415-421-9360	
Advisor	Capital Research & Management	
Subadvisor	None	
Distributor	American Funds Distributors	
States Available	All plus GU,PR,VI	
Report Grade	A	
Income Distrib	Paid Quarterly	
Date of Inception	01-01-33	
Fiscal Year End	December	

Min Initial Purchase	$500 (Addt'l: $50)
Min IRA Purchase	$250 (Addt'l: $50)
Min Auto Invest Plan	$50 (Systematic Inv: $50)

Expenses & Fees
Sales Fees	5.75% front
	0.00% deferred
	0.25% 12b-1
Management Fee	0.42% flat fee
3-,5-,10-yr Expense Projections	$79, $95, $141
Annual Brokerage Cost	0.10%

Risk Analysis

Time Period	Load-Adj Return %	Risk % Rank All	Obj	Morningstar Return	Morningstar Risk	Morningstar Risk-Adj Rating
1 Yr	-5.43					
3 Yr	4.83	32	7	0.37[3]	0.57	★★★
5 Yr	7.17	50	26	0.60[3]	0.68	★★★
10 Yr	11.78	41	28	1.01	0.66	★★★★
Average Historical Rating (109 months)				3.9	★s	

[1] 1 = low, 100 = high [2] 1.00 = Hybrid Avg [3] 1.00 = 90-day T-bill return

Other Measures

			Standard S&P 500	Best Fit S&P 500
Standard Deviation	5.35	Alpha	1.6	1.6
Mean	6.85	Beta	0.61	0.61
Sharpe Ratio	0.62	R-Squared	81	81

Investment Style

Stocks
	Port Avg	Rel S&P 500	Style
Price/Earnings Ratio	17.0	0.92	V B G
Price/Book Ratio	2.7	0.78	
5 Yr Earnings Gr %	0.6	0.11	
Med Mkt Cap ($mil)	10325	0.80	

Bonds
		Maturity
Avg Effective Duration	4.4 Yrs**	S I L
Avg Effective Maturity	7.90	
Avg Credit Quality	AA	
Avg Weighted Coupon	8.92%	

**figure provided by fund

Diversification Value for Portfolio Types
Large Cap: None	Small Cap: High	Bond: Low	Balanced: None	Diversified: Low

Portfolio 06-30-94

Total Stocks: 67
Total Fixed-Income: 112

Share Chg (12-93)000	Amount 000		Date of Maturity	Value $000	% Net Assets
	32000	US Treasury Note 8.5%	04-15-97	33615	1.84
50	550	American Home Products		31213	1.71
350	630	Minnesota Mining & Mfg		31185	1.71
0	800	Melville		31000	1.70
0	500	Eli Lilly		28438	1.56
-130	620	BankAmerica		28365	1.55
	27000	US Treasury Note 8.875%	02-15-96	28194	1.54
0	400	Warner-Lambert		26400	1.44
0	900	First Hawaiian		25200	1.38
50	450	Dun & Bradstreet		24975	1.37
50	250	Xerox		24438	1.34
0	740	American Brands		23403	1.28
0	400	EI DuPont de Nemours		23350	1.28
750	750	Honeywell		23250	1.27
-50	350	Dow Chemical		22881	1.25
100	810	American General		22376	1.22
20	420	Philip Morris		21630	1.18
	20000	US Treasury Note 7.25%	08-31-96	20394	1.12
300		Ameritech		19125	1.05
	15300	US Treasury Bond 10.75%	02-15-03	18635	1.02

Index Allocation
	% of Stocks
S&P 500	93.6
S&P MidCap 400	1.0
U.S. Small Cap	4.3
Foreign	2.7

Composition % 12-31-94
Cash	20.8	Preferreds	0.0
Stocks	51.7	Convertibles	1.6
Bonds	25.9	Other	0.0

Tax Analysis
	Tax-Adj Historical Return %	% Pretax Return
3 Yr Avg	4.54	64.0
5 Yr Avg	6.01	67.8
10 Yr Avg	9.05	61.8
Potential Capital Gain Exposure (% of assets)		2%

Most Similar Funds in MF500
George Putnam of Boston A	Strong Fit
Vanguard STAR	Strong Fit
IDS Mutual	Strong Fit

Bond Credit Analysis 12-31-94
% of Bonds
US Govt	63	BB	1
AAA	1	B	0
AA	1	Below B	0
A	9	NR/NA	0
BBB	25		

Stock Sector Weightings
	% of Stocks	Relative S&P 500
Utilities	13.3	1.07
Energy	9.3	0.92
Financials	19.2	1.82
Industrial Cyclicals	23.2	1.42
Consumer Durables	1.3	0.21
Consumer Staples	5.8	0.47
Services	6.4	0.78
Retail	3.4	0.58
Health	14.4	1.66
Technology	3.7	0.40

 **1995 Mutual Fund 500**

American Capital Corp Bond A

	Ticker	Load	NAV	Yield	SEC Yield	Assets	Objective
	ACCBX	4.75%	6.36	7.5%	N/A	161.0	Corp General

American Capital Corporate Bond Fund - Class A seeks income.
The fund typically invests 60% to 100% of its assets in investment-grade corporate bonds, U.S. government obligations, and cash equivalents; up to 40% in BB-rated debt securities; and up to 20% in securities rated B or below.

Class A shares have front loads; Class B shares have deferred loads, higher 12b-1 fees, and conversion features; Class C shares have level loads and longer periods until conversion. Prior to Sept. 9, 1983, the fund was named American General Capital Bond Fund.

Historical Profile
Return Above Average
Risk Average
Rating ★★★★ Above Average

Investment Style History
Fixed Income
Income Rtn % Rank Obj

4 2 16 5 23 15 21 14

Growth of $10,000
||| Value of Fund ($000)
— Value of Index ($000)
LB Corp
▼ Manager Change
▽ Partial Manager Change
► Mgr Unknown After
◄ Mgr Unknown Before

Performance Quartile (Within Objective)

1983	1984	1985	1986	1987	1988	1989	1990	1991	1992	1993	1994	History
6.77	6.53	7.31	7.29	6.90	7.02	6.59	6.38	6.84	6.86	7.14	6.36	NAV
11.03	9.11	26.12	11.28	6.23	12.86	3.99	7.04	16.73	8.50	11.68	-4.27	Total Return %
2.66	-6.05	4.00	-3.97	3.48	4.98	-10.55	-1.90	0.73	1.25	1.92	-1.35	+/- LB Aggregate
1.76	-7.52	2.06	-5.25	3.68	3.63	-9.99	-0.11	-1.77	-0.20	-0.49	-0.35	+/- LB Corporate
11.47	12.65	14.18	11.56	11.58	11.12	10.12	10.23	9.52	8.20	7.59	6.65	Income Return %
-0.44	-3.55	11.94	-0.27	-5.35	1.74	-6.13	-3.19	7.21	0.29	4.08	-10.92	Capital Return %
75	31	42	78	18	38	96	21	52	39	53	56	Total Rtn % Rank All
16	88	6	72	9	2	95	46	42	22	28	63	Total Rtn % Rank Obj
0.76	0.80	0.83	0.81	0.83	0.74	0.71	0.64	0.56	0.54	0.51	0.48	Income $
0.00	0.00	0.00	0.00	0.00	0.00	0.00	0.00	0.00	0.00	0.00	0.00	Capital Gains $
0.76	0.80	0.76	0.72	0.72	0.74	0.75	0.94	1.00	1.00	1.05	1.09	Expense Ratio %
11.23	12.10	12.29	11.17	10.63	10.46	10.21	10.07	9.03	7.90	7.24	7.06	Income Ratio %
49	28	62	30	28	56	18	54	15	37	19	0	Turnover Rate %
95.6	81.4	91.3	111.0	185.6	221.4	225.2	188.8	189.4	186.3	184.6	161.0	Net Assets ($mil)

Manager's Investment Style
This was a junk-bond fund several years ago. Management now runs it as a high-quality corporate fund, however, and continues to maintain its highest weightings in BBB bonds--those at the lowest end of investment grade. The portfolio is often concentrated by sector. Management will change the portfolio's duration and shift assets to cash depending on the market environment, but this fund's real benefits stem from its thorough credit research.

Fund Manager(s)
David R. Troth, since 05-79. Birthdate: 12-33.
BS, St. Peter's C. 1955 MBA, New York U. 1961

Manager Experience

	Dates Managed	Invest Obj	Std Dev	+/- Index
David R. Troth				
Amer Cap Bond	06/86 - 12/94	CB	5.65	-0.90

Performance 12-31-94

	1st Qtr	2nd Qtr	3rd Qtr	4th Qtr	Total
1987	4.59	-0.76	-0.13	2.48	6.23
1988	5.63	3.16	2.27	1.27	12.86
1989	1.71	3.20	-2.18	1.27	3.99
1990	-0.91	3.02	0.62	4.21	7.04
1991	3.40	2.09	5.39	4.93	16.73
1992	-0.21	3.85	4.79	-0.09	8.50
1993	4.80	3.25	4.17	-0.93	11.68
1994	-2.56	-2.35	0.44	0.16	-4.27

Bear Market Performance
Decile Rank (5-year period)

Worst ▬ Best

	Worst 3 Mo Period 1985-89	Worst 3 Mo Period 1990-94
American Capital Corp Bond A	-2.18	-5.57
+/- LB Aggregate	-3.31	-0.64
+/- Best Fit Index : LB Corp	-3.48	0.70

Trailing Returns

	Total Return %	+/- LB Aggregate	+/- LB Corp	% Rank All	% Rank Obj	Growth of $10,000
3 Mo	0.16	-0.22	-0.27	18	35	10,016
6 Mo	0.60	-0.39	-0.57	45	42	10,060
1 Yr	-4.27	-1.35	-0.35	56	63	9,573
3 Yr Avg	5.07	0.52	-0.35	47	31	11,599
5 Yr Avg	7.70	0.08	-0.56	37	28	14,493
10 Yr Avg	9.75	-0.19	-0.87	60	36	25,360
15 Yr Avg	9.86	-0.95	-1.47	80	66	40,957

Operations

Address and Telephone	2800 Post Oak Boulevard	Min Initial Purchase	$500 (Addt'l: $25)
	Houston, TX 77056	Min IRA Purchase	$500 (Addt'l: $25)
	800-421-5666 / 713-993-0500	Min Auto Invest Plan	$25 (Systematic Inv: $25)
Advisor	American Capital Asset Management	**Expenses & Fees**	
Subadvisor	None	Sales Fees	4.75% front
Distributor	American Capital Marketing		0.00% deferred
States Available	All plus PR,GU		0.25% 12b-1
Report Grade	B	Management Fee	0.50% max./0.35% min.
Income Distrib	Paid Monthly	3-,5-,10-yr Expense Projections	$79, $103, $170
Date of Inception	09-23-71		
Fiscal Year End	August		

Risk Analysis

Time Period	Load-Adj Return %	Risk % Rank [1] All	Risk % Rank [1] Obj	Morningstar [2] Return	Morningstar [2] Risk	Morningstar Risk-Adj Rating
1 Yr	-8.82					
3 Yr	3.38	25	54	-0.06 [3]	1.04	★★★
5 Yr	6.66	25	47	0.47 [3]	1.01	★★★
10 Yr	9.22	13	21	0.89 [3]	0.93	★★★★
Average Historical Rating (109 months)					3.1	★s

[1] 1 = low, 100 = high [2] 1.00 = Taxable Avg [3] 1.00 = 90-day T-bill return

Other Measures

	Standard LB Agg		Best Fit LB Corp
Standard Deviation	4.59	Alpha	0.4	-0.2
Mean	5.06	Beta	1.10	0.89
Sharpe Ratio	0.33	R-Squared	92	95

Investment Style

Interest-Rate Stance
Avg Effective Duration 6.3 Yrs
Avg Effective Maturity 14.3 Yrs

Quality
Avg Credit Quality BBB

Avg Weighted Coupon 9.12%
Avg Weighted Price 98.37% of Par

Maturity
Short Intm Long
Quality High Med Low

Diversification Value for Portfolio Types

Large Cap: High Small Cap: High Bond: None Balanced: Medium Diversified: High

Portfolio 09-30-94

Total Stocks: 0
Total Fixed-Income: 54

Amount 000	Date of Maturity		Value $000	% Net Assets
8899	12-01-07	Unicom 8.25%	9227	5.93
7718	06-15-06	Coastal 11.75%	8487	5.46
8172	07-01-99	Occidental Petroleum 9.625%	8446	5.43
5644	02-01-98	Columbia Pictures Ent 9.875%	6012	3.86
5721	11-15-12	Ashland Oil 8.8%	5665	3.64
5721	08-01-03	PDV America 7.875%	5089	3.27
5448	04-26-23	News America Holdings 8.875%	5008	3.22
4540	11-01-98	Deere 9.625%	4803	3.09
4540	05-15-22	Phillips Petroleum 8.86%	4365	2.81
4086	05-15-01	Ryder System 9.25%	4274	2.75
4540	03-22-14	United Air Lines 10.02%	4239	2.73
4540	06-15-13	IBM 7.5%	4001	2.57
4086	01-15-14	First PV Funding 10.3%	3964	2.55
4222	07-30-22	Province Nova Scotia 8.25%	3899	2.51
3632	02-15-06	Union Oil of California 9.125%	3757	2.42
3632	10-15-21	Province Newfoundland 9%	3630	2.33
3632	07-01-12	Federal Paper Board 8.875%	3538	2.27
154		IBM Pfd 7.5%	3531	2.27
3632	05-01-21	Long Island Lighting 9.75%	3487	2.24
4540	06-01-17	Beaver Valley II Fdg 9%	3382	2.17
3468	11-30-06	PNPP Funding 8.51%	3316	2.13
3632	04-15-23	Crown Cork & Seal 8%	3242	2.08
2724	02-01-03	Union Oil of California 9.25%	2854	1.83
2724	05-15-01	AMR 9.5%	2828	1.82
2724	02-15-18	Georgia-Pacific 9.5%	2679	1.72

Composition % 10-31-94

Cash	10.7	Preferreds	0.0
Stocks	0.0	Convertibles	0.0
Bonds	89.3	Other	0.0

Tax Analysis

	Tax-Adj Historical Return %	% Pretax Return
3 Yr Avg	2.30	44.2
5 Yr Avg	4.80	58.8
10 Yr Avg	5.91	50.5
Potential Capital Gain Exposure (% of assets)		-16%

Most Similar Funds in MF500
New England Bond Income A Strong Fit
Columbia Fixed-Income Secs Strong Fit
MFS Bond A Strong Fit

Coupon Range

	% of Bonds	Rel Obj
0%	0.0	0.00
0% to 8.5%	28.3	0.45
8.5% to 9.5%	40.3	2.48
9.5% to 11%	23.2	2.51
More than 11%	6.9	1.78
Not applicable	1.3	0.27

Credit Analysis 10-31-94
% of Bonds

US Govt	0	BB	6
AAA	0	B	0
AA	3	Below B	0
A	24	NR/NA	0
BBB	66		

American Capital Govt Secs A

	Ticker	Load	NAV	Yield	SEC Yield	Assets	Objective
	ACGVX	4.75%	9.67	7.0%	N/A	2580.4	Gvt General

American Capital Government Securities Fund - Class A seeks current income consistent with preservation of capital.

The fund normally invests at least 80% of its assets in U.S. government securities. The balance of assets may be invested in real-estate mortgage investment conduits, collateralized mortgage obligations, and other mortgage-related securities. The fund's average weighted maturity normally varies between three and eight years.

Class A shares have front loads and lower 12b-1 fees; Class B shares have deferred loads and conversion features; Class C shares have lower deferred loads and longer periods until conversion.

Manager's Investment Style

Management shifts between current or discount mortgages and Treasuries in seeking bonds that offer good prices and yields. It usually keeps duration between four and six years, often by barbelling the portfolio. Because NAV stability is important to management, the fund typically avoids NAV-eroding premium bonds, and therefore can be interest-rate sensitive.

Fund Manager(s)

John R. Reynoldson, since 01-88. Birthdate: 05-53. BBA, U. of Wisconsin 1975   MBA, U. of Wisconsin 1977

Manager Experience

	Dates Managed	Invest Obj	Std Dev	+/- Index
John R. Reynoldson				
American Cap U.S. Govt A	10/92 - 06/94	GG	4.16	-2.65
American Cap Fed Mortg C	08/93 - 06/94	GA	1.42	2.49

Performance 12-31-94

	1st Qtr	2nd Qtr	3rd Qtr	4th Qtr	Total
1987	1.85	-3.42	-5.07	5.43	-1.56
1988	3.74	0.95	1.26	0.84	6.94
1989	0.87	8.98	0.71	3.80	14.91
1990	-2.28	3.56	1.56	5.77	8.71
1991	2.61	1.62	5.90	5.31	16.28
1992	-1.34	3.50	3.72	0.61	6.56
1993	3.53	2.43	2.03	-0.05	8.15
1994	-3.52	-1.30	0.15	0.39	-4.26

Bear Market Performance

Decile Rank (5-year period)

Worst   Best

	Worst 3 Mo Period 1985-89	Worst 3 Mo Period 1990-94
American Capital Govt Secs A	-5.30	-5.68
+/- LB Aggregate	-1.74	-0.75
+/- Best Fit Index : LB Agg	-1.74	-0.75

Trailing Returns

	Total Return %	+/- LB Aggregate	+/- LB Govt	% Rank All	% Rank Obj	Growth of $10,000
3 Mo	0.39	0.01	0.03	13	22	10,039
6 Mo	0.54	-0.45	-0.25	46	40	10,054
1 Yr	-4.26	-1.34	-0.89	56	68	9,574
3 Yr Avg	3.33	-1.21	-1.33	81	54	11,034
5 Yr Avg	6.88	-0.75	-0.65	53	29	13,947
10 Yr Avg	8.14	-1.80	-1.43	85	56	21,876
15 Yr Avg	---	---	---	---	---	---

Operations

Address and Telephone	2800 Post Oak Boulevard
	Houston, TX 77056
	800-421-5666 / 713-993-0500
Advisor	American Capital Asset Management
Subadvisor	None
Distributor	American Capital Marketing
States Available	All plus PR,GU
Report Grade	B-
Income Distrib	Paid Monthly
* Date of Inception	07-16-84
Fiscal Year End	December

Historical Profile

Return	Below Average
Risk	Above Average
Rating	★★
	Below Average

72	8	4	12	12	8	10	22

Growth of $10,000

‖‖‖ Value of Fund ($000)
— Value of Index ($000)
LB Agg
▼ Manager Change
▽ Partial Manager Change
► Mgr Unknown After
◄ Mgr Unknown Before

Performance Quartile (Within Objective)

Investment Style History
Fixed Income
Income Rtn % Rank Obj

	1983	1984	1985	1986	1987	1988	1989	1990	1991	1992	1993	1994	History
	---	11.90	12.04	11.69	10.31	9.98	10.37	10.27	10.95	10.75	10.80	9.67	NAV
	---	6.52 *	17.26	10.58	-1.56	6.94	14.91	8.71	16.28	6.56	8.15	-4.26	Total Return %
	---		-4.87	-4.67	-4.32	-0.94	0.37	-0.24	0.27	-0.68	-1.60	-1.34	+/- LB Aggregate
	---		-3.17	-4.73	-3.76	-0.09	0.68	-0.01	0.96	-0.67	-2.51	-0.89	+/- LB Government
	---	3.55	11.20	8.02	7.62	10.14	11.00	9.67	9.65	8.39	7.69	6.20	Income Return %
	---	2.97	6.05	2.57	-9.18	-3.20	3.91	-0.96	6.62	-1.83	0.47	-10.46	Capital Return %
	---		85	82	72	81	47	11	53	63	78	56	Total Rtn % Rank All
	---		56	68	86	35	4	54	15	29	42	68	Total Rtn % Rank Obj
	---	0.40	1.20	0.90	0.85	1.02	1.02	0.93	0.90	0.88	0.80	0.68	Income $
	---	0.10	0.53	0.64	0.35	0.00	0.00	0.00	0.00	0.00	0.00	0.00	Capital Gains $
	---		1.08	0.67	0.69	0.82	0.90	0.93	0.96	0.97	0.98	1.03	Expense Ratio %
	---		9.75	9.06	8.54	9.74	9.88	9.56	8.65	8.42	7.73	7.46	Income Ratio %
	---		---	411	52	34	9	177	131	239	239	---	Turnover Rate %
	---	770.4	1681.1	8944.9	6854.6	5238.1	4664.2	3888.8	3871.1	3635.9	3419.6	2580.4	Net Assets ($mil)

Risk Analysis

Time Period	Load-Adj Return %	Risk % Rank [1] All	Risk % Rank [1] Obj	Morningstar [2] Return	Morningstar [2] Risk	Morningstar Risk-Adj Rating
1 Yr	-8.81					
3 Yr	1.67	24	52	-0.54 [3]	1.02	★★
5 Yr	5.84	26	57	0.27 [3]	1.03	★★
10 Yr	7.62	29	76	0.44 [3]	1.17	★

Average Historical Rating (91 months)   1.8 ★s

[1] 1 = low, 100 = high   [2] 1.00 = Taxable Avg   [3] 1.00 = 90-day T-bill return

Other Measures

			Standard LB Agg	Best Fit LB Agg
Standard Deviation	3.91	Alpha	-1.1	-1.1
Mean	3.36	Beta	0.96	0.96
Sharpe Ratio	-0.04	R-Squared	97	97

Investment Style

Interest-Rate Stance
		Maturity
Avg Effective Duration	2.4 Yrs **	Short Intm Long
Avg Effective Maturity	6.0 Yrs	

Quality
Avg Credit Quality	AAA
Avg Weighted Coupon	8.13%
Avg Weighted Price	96.50% of Par

** figure provided by fund

Diversification Value for Portfolio Types

Large Cap: Medium	Small Cap: High	Bond: None	Balanced: Low	Diversified: Medium

Portfolio 09-30-94

Amount 000	Date of Maturity	Total Stocks: 0 / Total Fixed-Income: 32	Value $000	% Net Assets
370387	11-15-24	GNMA 7.5%	342278	12.58
266882		GNMA Forward 8.5%	262463	9.64
274664	08-15-24	GNMA 8%	262215	9.64
258878	05-15-21	GNMA 9%	262194	9.63
177922	02-15-96	US Treasury Note 8.875%	183092	6.73
177922		FNMA Forward 8%	170860	6.28
177922		FNMA Forward 7.5%	166079	6.10
88961		FHLMC Forward 8.5%	87404	3.21
88961		FNMA Forward 8.5%	87238	3.21
88832	10-01-24	FNMA 8%	86546	3.18
88961		GNMA Forward 8%	84930	3.12
89709	09-01-24	FHLMC 7.5%	83794	3.08
88961		FHLMC Forward 7.5%	82895	3.05
88690	08-15-24	GNMA 7%	79045	2.90
44925	10-01-24	FHLMC 8%	43198	1.59
44480		FHLMC Forward 8%	42771	1.57
45850	09-01-24	FHLMC 7%	41537	1.53
44876	08-01-24	FNMA 7%	40627	1.49
32044	03-15-23	GNMA 8.5%	31514	1.16
15273	04-15-19	GNMA 11.5%	17021	0.63
10394	01-15-16	GNMA 12%	11615	0.43
7780	01-01-16	FNMA 12%	8592	0.32
4342	07-15-18	GNMA 12.5%	4944	0.18
519	05-01-19	FNMA 11.5%	570	0.02
472	11-15-20	GNMA 11%	517	0.02

Composition % 09-30-94

Cash	-27.4	Preferreds	0.0
Stocks	0.0	Convertibles	0.0
Bonds	127.4	Other	0.0

Tax Analysis

	Tax-Adj Historical Return %	% Pretax Return
3 Yr Avg	0.61	17.7
5 Yr Avg	4.06	55.8
10 Yr Avg	4.53	46.9

Potential Capital Gain Exposure (% of assets)   -43%

Most Similar Funds in MF500

Gradison-McDonald Govt Inc	Strong Fit
Vanguard Bond Indx Total Bd	Strong Fit
Scudder GNMA	Strong Fit

Coupon Range

	% of Bonds	Rel Obj
0%	0.0	0.00
0% to 8%	61.5	0.98
8% to 9%	36.8	2.39
9% to 10%	0.0	0.00
More than 10%	1.7	0.28
Not applicable	0.0	0.00

Sector Analysis 09-30-94
% of Bonds

US Treas	7	CMOs	0
GNMA mtgs	55	ARMs	0
FNMA mtgs	23	Other	0
FHLMC mtgs	15		

Min Initial Purchase / Expenses

Min Initial Purchase	$500 (Addt'l: $25)
Min IRA Purchase	$500 (Addt'l: $25)
Min Auto Invest Plan	$25 (Systematic Inv: $25)

Expenses & Fees
Sales Fees	4.75% front
	0.00% deferred
	0.25% 12b-1
Management Fee	0.50% max./0.20% min.
3-,5-,10-yr Expense Projections	$77, $99, $162

 **1995 Mutual Fund 500**

American Capital Harbor A

	Ticker	Load	NAV	Yield	SEC Yield	Assets	Objective
	ACHBX	5.75%	13.24	4.6%	N/A	369.9	Convrt. Bond

American Capital Harbor Fund - Class A seeks current income and capital appreciation consistent with preservation of capital.

The fund invests primarily in fixed-income securities of various ratings. At least 50% of the fund's assets are typically invested in convertible securities. The fund may invest up to 45% of its assets in common stocks.

Class A shares have front loads and lower 12b-1 fees; Class B shares have deferred loads and conversion features; Class C shares have deferred loads and longer periods until conversion. Prior to Sept. 9, 1983, the fund was named American General Harbor Fund.

Manager's Investment Style

Although this fund will hold small stakes in stocks and cash, its management emphasizes convertibles, preferring large-cap issues with high credit quality and avoiding smaller and more-speculative issues. Management keeps the fund well-diversified by issue and sector.

Fund Manager(s)

James H. Behrmann CFA(1977), since 10-84. MS, George Washington U. MBA, Southern Illinois U.

Manager Experience

	Dates Managed	Invest Obj	Std Dev	+/- Index
James H. Behrmann				
Common Sense G & I	04/87 - 02/89	GI	19.61	-4.38

Historical Profile

Return	Below Average
Risk	Below Average
Rating	★★★ Neutral

	27	14	25	28	26	25	36	34	Income Rtn % Rank Obj

Growth of $10,000

|||| Value of Fund ($000)
— Value of Index ($000)
LB Agg
▼ Manager Change
▽ Partial Manager Change
► Mgr Unknown After
◄ Mgr Unknown Before

Performance Quartile (Within Objective)

1983	1984	1985	1986	1987	1988	1989	1990	1991	1992	1993	1994	History
16.42	12.10	13.99	13.43	11.48	12.39	14.06	12.93	14.91	14.95	15.13	13.24	NAV
26.75	-4.38	24.25	13.73	-3.77	16.76	20.59	-1.23	23.08	9.72	13.56	-6.43	Total Return %
18.38	-19.53	2.12	-1.52	-6.52	8.88	6.05	-10.18	7.08	2.48	3.81	-3.51	+/- LB Aggregate
4.29	-10.65	-7.49	-4.95	-9.02	0.15	-11.09	1.89	-7.41	2.10	3.51	-7.74	+/- S&P 500
6.72	6.80	7.75	6.14	5.86	7.59	7.11	6.24	7.76	5.93	4.48	4.19	Income Return %
20.03	-11.18	16.50	7.59	-9.63	9.18	13.48	-7.47	15.31	3.79	9.09	-10.62	Capital Return %
17	79	48	63	84	22	34	59	40	25	36	76	Total Rtn % Rank All
1	66	33	71	27	1	15	9	65	75	52	69	Total Rtn % Rank Obj
0.82	0.84	0.84	0.84	0.84	0.84	0.84	0.87	0.92	0.84	0.66	0.62	Income $
0.00	2.87	0.08	1.56	0.72	0.13	0.00	0.09	0.00	0.51	1.12	0.33	Capital Gains $
0.65	0.68	0.63	0.64	0.60	0.71	0.76	0.89	0.91	0.99	1.02	1.32	Expense Ratio %
5.51	6.44	5.78	4.88	4.87	6.82	6.52	7.29	5.86	5.00	4.37	4.68	Income Ratio %
49	37	89	83	83	95	94	71	91	85	134	---	Turnover Rate %
185.2	171.0	208.9	316.7	349.4	342.3	387.1	337.0	385.1	393.8	432.1	369.9	Net Assets ($mil)

Performance 12-31-94

	1st Qtr	2nd Qtr	3rd Qtr	4th Qtr	Total
1987	13.47	0.70	5.78	-20.38	-3.77
1988	7.30	4.96	-0.14	3.82	16.76
1989	6.29	7.79	4.80	0.43	20.59
1990	-1.48	4.34	-8.45	4.96	-1.23
1991	8.60	-0.38	6.71	6.60	23.08
1992	-0.13	0.40	3.92	5.30	9.72
1993	5.37	2.48	4.03	1.09	13.56
1994	-3.82	-2.90	2.54	-2.29	-6.43

Bear Market Performance

Decile Rank (5-year period)

Worst .... Best

	Worst 3 Mo Period 1985-89	Worst 3 Mo Period 1990-94
American Capital Harbor A	-24.06	-9.54
+/- LB Aggregate	-26.23	-10.28
+/- Best Fit Index : Wil 4500	6.08	9.86

Trailing Returns

	Total Return %	+/- LB Aggregate	+/- S&P 500	% Rank All	% Rank Obj	Growth of $10,000
3 Mo	-2.29	-2.67	-2.27	74	17	9,771
6 Mo	0.19	-0.80	-4.67	53	42	10,019
1 Yr	-6.43	-3.51	-7.74	76	69	9,357
3 Yr Avg	5.25	0.71	-1.01	43	83	11,659
5 Yr Avg	7.22	-0.40	-1.47	45	61	14,173
10 Yr Avg	10.50	0.55	-3.88	53	66	27,139
15 Yr Avg	12.65	1.85	-1.83	46	66	59,729

Operations

Address and Telephone	2800 Post Oak Boulevard
	Houston, TX 77056
	800-421-5666 / 713-993-0500
Advisor	American Capital Asset Management
Subadvisor	None
Distributor	American Capital Marketing
States Available	All plus PR,GU
Report Grade	B-
Income Distrib	Paid Quarterly
Date of Inception	11-15-56
Fiscal Year End	December

Min Initial Purchase	$500 (Addt'l: $25)
Min IRA Purchase	$500 (Addt'l: $25)
Min Auto Invest Plan	$25 (Systematic Inv: $25)

Expenses & Fees

Sales Fees	5.75% front
	0.00% deferred
	0.25% 12b-1
Management Fee	0.55% max./0.40% min.
3-,5-,10-yr Expense Projections	$88, $111, $175

Risk Analysis

Time Period	Load-Adj Return %	Risk % Rank All [1]	Risk % Rank Obj	Morningstar [2] Return	Morningstar Risk	Morningstar Risk-Adj Rating
1 Yr	-11.81					
3 Yr	3.19	56	62	-0.11[3]	0.79	★★★
5 Yr	5.96	52	33	0.29[3]	0.76	★★★
10 Yr	9.85	44	33	0.63	0.76	★★★
Average Historical Rating (109 months)				3.1	★s	

[1] = low, 100 = high [2] 1.00 = Hybrid Avg [3] 1.00 = 90-day T-bill return

Other Measures

			Standard LB Agg	Best Fit Wil 4500
Standard Deviation	6.51	Alpha	0.7	-0.7
Mean	5.34	Beta	1.06	0.59
Sharpe Ratio	0.28	R-Squared	42	78

Investment Style

Interest-Rate Stance

Avg Effective Maturity   11.4 Yrs

Quality

Avg Credit Quality	---
Avg Weighted Coupon	4.99%
Avg Weighted Price	89.75% of Par

Not Applicable

Diversification Value for Portfolio Types

Large Cap: Low	Small Cap: Low	Bond: Medium	Balanced: None	Diversified: Low

Portfolio 09-30-94

Amount 000	Date of Maturity	Total Stocks: 29 Total Fixed-Income: 87	Value $000	% Net Assets
9628	01-10-15	Time Warner Cv 8.75%	9507	2.43
7951	04-11-05	American Brands Cv 5.75%	9064	2.32
14395	02-20-12	Automatic Data Process Cv 0%	5830	1.49
105		Sears Roebuck A Cv Pfd $3.75	5806	1.48
4729	08-15-10	SFP Pipeline Holdings Cv FRN	5674	1.45
5315	12-15-15	Consolidated Nat Gas Cv 7.25%	5328	1.36
5335	03-01-01	Price/Costco Cv 6.75%	5149	1.32
84		Philip Morris	5147	1.32
11173	07-24-06	Rite Aid Cv 0%	5084	1.30
6172	09-01-02	Potomac Electric Power Cv 5%	5000	1.28
39		Citicorp Cv Pfd $5.375	4766	1.22
87		Olin Cl A Cv Pfd $3.64	4461	1.14
4478	08-02-98	SAB Finance Cv 7.5%	4444	1.14
4277	12-15-14	USLICO Cv 8.5%	4384	1.12
54		Mobil	4366	1.12
71		Exxon	4233	1.08
4185	05-15-98	Chubb Cv 6%	4185	1.07
4090	04-15-07	Alexander & Alexander Cv 11%	4141	1.06
4352	09-29-02	Texas Instruments Euro 2.75%	4091	1.05
115		Rockwell International	4086	1.04
50		British Petroleum (ADR)	4011	1.03
3934	03-05-01	American Brands Cv 7.625%	3973	1.02
67		El DuPont de Nemours	3959	1.01
109		Dean Witter Discover	3917	1.00
78		WHX Cv Pfd $3.75	3864	0.99

Composition % 11-29-94

Cash	11.0	Preferreds	0.0
Stocks	16.0	Convertibles	73.0
Bonds	0.0	Other	0.0

Tax Analysis

	Tax-Adj Historical Return %	% Pretax Return
3 Yr Avg	2.28	42.1
5 Yr Avg	4.51	59.1
10 Yr Avg	7.28	59.4
Potential Capital Gain Exposure (% of assets)		-3%

Most Similar Funds in MF500

Fortis Advant Asset Alloc A	Strong Fit
SteinRoe Total Return	Fair Fit
Invesco Industrial Income	Fair Fit

Coupon Range

	% of Bonds	Rel Obj
0%	16.9	1.98
0% to 6%	24.7	0.73
6% to 7%	12.5	0.84
7% to 8.5%	12.9	1.10
More than 8.5%	7.1	1.29
Not applicable	26.0	1.01

Credit Analysis 03-31-94

% of Bonds

US Govt	0	BB	16
AAA	0	B	11
AA	12	Below B	0
A	22	NR/NA	15
BBB	26		

American Capital Muni Bond A

	Ticker	Load	NAV	Yield	SEC Yield	Assets	Objective
	ACMBX	4.75%	9.57	6.0%	N/A	295.8	Muni Nat

American Capital Municipal Bond Fund - Class A seeks income exempt from federal income tax.

The fund normally invests at least 80% of its assets in municipal bonds. No more than 50% of the fund's assets may be invested in municipal bonds rated below A or unrated; up to 20% of assets may be invested in bonds rated B or BB. The fund may invest up to 20% of its assets in AMT-subject bonds.

Class A shares have front loads and lower 12b-1 fees; Class B shares have deferred loads and conversion features; Class C shares have level loads. Prior to Sept. 9, 1983, the fund was named American General Municipal Bond Fund.

Manager's Investment Style

Under current manager Robert Evans, the fund emphasizes yield and thus holds bonds with longer maturities, a broad variety of credit ratings (including noninvestment-grade issues), and a notable stake in nonrated bonds (which he estimates to be comparable to investment grade). He attempts to mitigate volatility by maintaining a core position in stable essential-services issues.

Fund Manager(s)

Robert B. Evans, since 01-88. Birthdate: 11-40.
BA, Pennsylvania State U. 1962

Manager Experience

	Dates Managed	Invest Obj	Std Dev	+/- Index
Robert B. Evans				
American T-E H/Y MunA	06/89 - 07/91	MN	2.15	-2.50

Historical Profile

Return	Average
Risk	Average
Rating	★★★
	Neutral

| | 5 | 8 | 25 | 35 | 28 | 24 | 18 | 17 |

Investment Style History
Fixed Income
Income Rtn % Rank Obj

Growth of $10,000
||| Value of Fund ($000)
— Value of Index ($000) LB Muni
▼ Manager Change
▽ Partial Manager Change
► Mgr Unknown After
◄ Mgr Unknown Before

Performance Quartile (Within Objective)

1983	1984	1985	1986	1987	1988	1989	1990	1991	1992	1993	1994	History
8.62	8.70	9.83	10.62	8.74	9.21	9.52	9.37	9.81	10.02	10.51	9.57	NAV
9.64	10.54	22.90	16.30	-5.80	13.99	11.04	5.49	11.89	8.77	11.16	-3.52	Total Return %
1.26	-4.61	0.78	1.06	-8.56	6.12	-3.50	-3.46	-4.12	1.53	1.41	-0.60	+/- LB Aggregate
1.59	-0.01	2.88	-3.01	-7.31	3.83	0.25	-1.82	-0.26	-0.05	-1.11	2.08	+/- LB Muni
9.29	9.62	9.92	8.32	8.15	8.61	7.61	7.06	7.19	6.63	6.27	5.42	Income Return %
0.35	0.93	12.99	7.99	-13.96	5.38	3.42	-1.58	4.70	2.14	4.89	-8.94	Capital Return %
81	23	55	46	90	32	64	39	77	36	58	49	Total Rtn % Rank All
49	14	6	70	97	5	10	82	39	41	60	28	Total Rtn % Rank Obj
0.78	0.78	0.78	0.78	0.83	0.71	0.67	0.65	0.63	0.62	0.60	0.58	Income $
0.00	0.00	0.00	0.00	0.45	0.00	0.00	0.00	0.00	0.00	0.00	0.00	Capital Gains $
0.80	0.80	0.72	0.68	0.64	0.69	0.71	0.86	0.89	0.90	0.91	0.93	Expense Ratio %
8.95	8.80	9.20	8.10	7.29	7.47	7.05	6.84	6.71	6.29	5.82	5.76	Income Ratio %
28	153	197	69	164	33	32	17	10	6	3	6	Turnover Rate %
56.4	68.9	100.5	159.2	165.0	198.6	241.6	245.3	274.6	301.4	335.6	295.8	Net Assets ($mil)

Performance 12-31-94

	1st Qtr	2nd Qtr	3rd Qtr	4th Qtr	Total
1987	2.07	-7.34	-4.68	4.49	-5.80
1988	3.29	2.91	3.51	3.60	13.99
1989	0.96	6.21	-0.28	3.84	11.04
1990	-0.50	2.40	-0.85	4.42	5.49
1991	1.89	1.99	4.12	3.41	11.89
1992	0.17	4.02	2.38	1.97	8.77
1993	3.70	3.03	2.81	1.20	11.16
1994	-3.72	0.53	0.74	-1.05	-3.52

Bear Market Performance

Decile Rank (5-year period)

Worst ———————————— Best

	Worst 3 Mo Period 1985-89	Worst 3 Mo Period 1990-94
American Capital Muni Bond A	-10.96	-4.72
+/- LB Aggregate	-7.41	0.21
+/- Best Fit Index : LB Muni	-4.47	1.04

Trailing Returns

	Total Return %	+/- LB Aggregate	+/- LB Muni	% Rank All	% Rank Obj	Growth of $10,000
3 Mo	-1.05	-1.43	0.38	45	32	9,895
6 Mo	-0.32	-1.31	0.93	62	26	9,968
1 Yr	-3.52	-0.60	2.08	49	28	9,648
3 Yr Avg	5.27	0.72	0.40	42	18	11,666
5 Yr Avg	6.60	-1.02	-0.17	60	26	13,768
10 Yr Avg	8.90	-1.04	-0.52	74	43	23,464
15 Yr Avg	7.83	-2.98	-0.65	94	59	30,967

Operations

Address and Telephone	2800 Post Oak Boulevard
	Houston, TX 77056
	800-421-5666 / 713-993-0500
Advisor	American Capital Asset Management
Subadvisor	None
Distributor	American Capital Marketing
States Available	All plus PR,GU
Report Grade	B
Income Distrib	Paid Monthly
Date of Inception	12-06-76
Fiscal Year End	September

Risk Analysis

Time Period	Load-Adj Return %	Risk % Rank[1] All	Obj	Morningstar[2] Return	Morningstar Risk	Morningstar Risk-Adj Rating
1 Yr	-8.10					
3 Yr	3.58	14	26	0.93	0.79	★★★
5 Yr	5.57	15	37	0.91	0.91	★★★
10 Yr	8.37	19	54	1.01	1.10	★★

Average Historical Rating (109 months) 2.5 ★s

[1] 1 = low, 100 = high [2] 1.00 = Muni Avg [3] 1.00 = 90-day T-bill return

Other Measures

			Standard LB Agg	Best Fit LB Muni
Standard Deviation	4.84	Alpha	0.8	0.5
Mean	5.26	Beta	0.91	0.86
Sharpe Ratio	0.36	R-Squared	57	94

Investment Style

Interest-Rate Stance

		Maturity Short Intm Long	
Avg Effective Maturity	20.0 Yrs		Quality High Med Low

Quality

Avg Credit Quality A

Avg Weighted Coupon 7.25%

Avg Weighted Price 99.38% of Par

Diversification Value for Portfolio Types

| Large Cap: Medium | Small Cap: High | Bond: Low | Balanced: Medium | Diversified: High |

Portfolio 09-30-94

Total Stocks: 0
Total Fixed-Income: 263

Amount 000	Date of Maturity		Value $000	% Net Assets
8449	06-01-12	OK Grand Rvr Dam 5%	7046	2.29
7472	09-01-13	TX Muni Pwr 5.5%	6585	2.14
6979	07-01-08	KY Tpk Resource Rec 5%	6091	1.98
6713	01-01-24	NC East Muni Pwr Sys 4.5%	5237	1.70
4615	01-01-28	AZ Salt Rvr Agri Impr/Pwr Dist 7.875%	5058	1.64
3206	10-01-17	TX Brazos Rvr Poll Cntrl Lt/Pwr 9.875%	3601	1.17
3184	07-01-20	UT Intermountain Pwr Sply Ser B 7.75%	3438	1.12
2835	05-15-12	NY Dorm State Univ Educ Fac 7.7%	3202	1.04
2617	06-15-15	NY New York City Muni Wtr Fin Swr 7.25%	2892	0.94
2792	01-01-20	NJ Tpk 6.5%	2817	0.91
3577	06-15-17	NY NY City Muni Wtr Fin Swr Sys 5%	2814	0.91
2486	01-01-19	NC Muni Pwr #1 Catawba Elec 7.875%	2725	0.88
2704	09-01-10	MS Panola DMD	2704	0.88
2325	01-01-21	NC East Muni Pwr Sys 8%	2557	0.83
2617	01-01-21	GA Atlanta Arpt Fac 6.25%	2412	0.78
2181	10-01-16	FL Orlando Aviation Arpt Fac 8.375%	2395	0.78
2181	01-01-15	NH Higher Educ/Hlth Fac Hosp 8.5%	2376	0.77
9553	08-15-14	KY Jefferson Cap Proj Lease 0%	2335	0.76
2181	05-15-18	PA Emmaus Genl Local Govt Pool Prog 7.9%	2328	0.76
2181	01-01-18	NY Pwr Genl Purp 7.375%	2291	0.74

Credit Analysis % of Bonds 10-10-94

US Govt	0	BB	1
AAA	22	B	1
AA	17	Below B	1
A	30	NR/NA	17
BBB	12		

Composition % of Assets 10-10-94

Cash	5.0	Preferreds	0.0
Stocks	0.0	Convertibles	0.0
Bonds	95.0	Other	0.0

Tax Analysis

	Tax-Adj Historical Return %	% Pretax Return
3 Yr Avg	5.27	100.0
5 Yr Avg	6.60	100.0
10 Yr Avg	8.76	97.6
Potential Capital Gain Exposure (% of assets)		-1%

Most Similar Funds in MF500

Franklin Insured T/F Income	Strong Fit
T. Rowe Price Tax-Fr Hi-Yld	Strong Fit
Dreyfus Intermediate Muni	Strong Fit

Coupon Range

	% Bonds	Rel Obj
0%	0.8	0.31
0% to 6.8%	34.6	0.57
6.8% to 7.5%	17.4	1.12
7.5% to 8.3%	27.8	3.14
More than 8.3%	16.2	1.83
Not applicable	3.1	0.80

Sector Weightings

	% Bonds	Rel Obj
General Obl	6.21	0.30
Utilities	28.76	2.30
Health	16.74	1.27
Water/Waste	4.82	0.76
Housing	4.71	0.64
Education	3.39	0.53
Transportation	10.62	1.04
COP/Lease	3.45	1.08
Private	14.64	1.26
Misc Revenue	3.54	0.71
Demand	3.12	1.27

Top 5 States % of Bonds

TX	15.55	IL	6.19
NY	7.75	FL	5.26
PA	7.44		

Min Purchases

Min Initial Purchase	$500 (Addt'l: $25)
Min IRA Purchase	$500 (Addt'l: $25)
Min Auto Invest Plan	$25 (Systematic Inv: $25)

Expenses & Fees

Sales Fees	4.75% front
	0.00% deferred
	0.25% 12b-1
Management Fee	0.50% flat fee
3-,5-,10-yr Expense Projections	$75, $96, $154

MORNINGSTAR 1995 Mutual Fund 500

American Government Income Portfolio

	Ticker	NAV	Mkt Price	Prem/Disc	Yield	Objective
	AAF	$6.45	$7.25	12.4%	14.6%	Govt Bond

American Government Income Portfolio seeks a high level of current income consistent with preservation of capital.

The fund invests at least 65% of assets in U.S. government securities and repurchase agreements. The fund may also invest in U.S.-dollar-denominated Canadian governments or investment-grade corporates, and may employ futures and options for hedging purposes.

The fund may leverage its assets through internal borrowing.

Commencing with the fiscal year beginning Nov. 1, 1992, if the fund's shares have consistently traded at a discount and if 10% of existing shareholders request to open-end the fund, the board must submit a proposal to shareholders to open-end the fund.

The fund may retain excess income and pay an excise tax.

| | | | | | | 9.9 | 10.1 | 11.4 | 8.5 | 9.0 | 10.9 | 25.2 | Highest Prem/Disc |
| | | | | | | 5.6 | 4.8 | -0.9 | -1.5 | -2.6 | 2.5 | 2.8 | Lowest Prem/Disc |

Historical Profile
Return Below Average
Risk High
Rating ★ Lowest

Growth of $10,000
— at NAV ($000)
— at Market Price ($000)

Premium Discount %

	1983	1984	1985	1986	1987	1988	1989	1990	1991	1992	1993	1994	History
	---	---	---	---	---	8.87	9.14	8.99	10.38	10.32	9.93	6.45	NAV
	---	---	---	---	---	-1.19*	15.70	10.67	28.44	15.53	12.45	-25.86	NAV Total Return %
	---	---	---	---	---	---	1.16	1.73	12.44	8.29	2.70	-22.95	+/- LB Aggregate
	---	---	---	---	---	---	0.36	-0.05	12.72	8.58	5.61	-24.26	+/- LB Mortgage
	---	---	---	---	---	3.43*	11.99	12.31	12.23	10.51	14.93	9.18	Income Return %
	---	---	---	---	---	-4.62*	3.71	-1.64	16.21	5.02	-2.48	-35.05	Capital Return %
	---	---	---	---	---	---	28	11	26	16	73	97	Total Rtn % Rank All
	---	---	---	---	---	---	1	66	1	1	7	90	Total Rtn % Rank Obj
	---	---	---	---	---	1.01*	10.85	12.52	22.80	23.04	14.27	-24.78	Market Total Rtn %
	---	---	---	---	---	---	7.0	5.1	2.7	3.6	7.1	11.9	Avg Prem/Disc %
	---	---	---	---	---	0.33	1.01	1.07	1.02	1.08	1.65	1.06	Income $
	---	---	---	---	---	0.00	0.06	0.00	0.06	0.60	0.14	0.00	Capital Gains $
	---	---	---	---	---	2.83	2.59	3.19	2.76	1.25	0.95	1.28	Expense Ratio %
	---	---	---	---	---	7.42	8.06	8.80	11.25	13.12	17.42	10.84	Income Ratio %
	---	---	---	---	---	---	66	49	94	100	79	106	Turnover Rate %
	---	---	---	---	---	294.3	206.5	210.5	243.0	241.7	238.8	159.3	Net Assets ($mil)
	---	---	---	---	---	15.6	26.0	51.0	61.0	101.8	103.6	0.0	Pfd/Debt Leverage ($mil)

Manager's Investment Style
Manager Worth Bruntjen and his team take an aggressive approach to the bond market. Although they invest in liquid Treasuries and straight mortgage-backeds, Bruntjen and his team have invested a large portion of the fund's assets in mortgage-backed derivatives, including such complex and long-duration instruments as principal-only strips, inverse floaters, and z-tranche bonds. They have typically used mortgage dollar rolls and reverse-repurchase agreements to boost yield.

Fund Manager(s)
Worth Bruntjen. Since 9-88. BBA'61 U. of Minnesota.
Marijo Goldstein. Since 9-88. BS U. of Maryland; MBA U. of Minnesota.
Marcy K. Winson. Since 3-93. BSE'87 Wharton; MS'90 Northwestern U.

Manager Experience	Dates Managed	Invest Obj	Std Dev	+/- Index
Marijo Goldstein				
Piper Jaffray Instl Govt	07/88 - 01/94	GM	3.88	2.14
Worth Bruntjen				
Managers Interm Mtg	05/86 - 10/94	GM	7.24	-1.35

NAV Performance % 12-30-94

	1st Qtr	2nd Qtr	3rd Qtr	4th Qtr	Total
1987	---	---	---	---	---
1988	---	---	0.00*	-1.19	-1.19*
1989	-0.23	9.23	1.06	5.06	15.70
1990	-2.31	4.26	0.55	8.07	10.67
1991	5.29	1.92	10.09	8.71	28.44
1992	-2.21	7.48	9.64	0.26	15.53
1993	9.25	3.53	2.11	-2.63	12.45
1994	-7.69	-18.13	1.08	-2.95	-25.87

Bear Market Performance
Decile Rank (5-year period)

Worst ... Best

	Worst 3 Mo Period 1985-89	Worst 3 Mo Period 1990-94
Amer Govt Inc Port	---	-24.88
+/- LB Aggregate	---	-21.62

Trailing Returns

	NAV Total Return %	+/- LB Agg	+/- LB Mortgage	% Rank All	% Rank Obj	Mkt Total Return %
3 Mo	-2.95	-3.33	-3.38	68	94	6.08
6 Mo	-1.90	-2.89	-3.21	66	85	-9.39
1 Yr	-25.86	-22.95	-24.26	97	90	-24.78
3 Yr Avg	-1.25	-5.79	-5.23	95	80	1.88
5 Yr Avg	6.48	-1.14	-1.09	72	44	7.88
Incept Avg	7.42*	---	---	---	---	8.19*

Operations

Address and Telephone	Piper Jaffray Tower, 222 S. 9th St. Minneapolis, MN 55402 612-342-6223 / 800-333-6000
Advisor	Piper Capital Management, Inc.
Subadvisor	N/A
Administrator	Piper Capital Management, Inc.
Transfer Agent	Investors Fiduciary Trust Co.
Custodian	Investors Fiduciary Trust Co.
Auditor	KPMG Peat Marwick
Legal Counsel	Dorsey & Whitney

Income Distrib Schedule	Paid Monthly
Management Fee	1.00%, 0.20%A
Reinvestment Plan	Yes
Direct Purchase Plan	No
Shares Outstanding	24,711,524
Exchange	NYSE
*Date of Inception	09-29-88
Shareholder Report	B+

Risk Analysis

	Risk % Rank[1] All	Obj	Morningstar[2] Return	Risk	Morningstar Risk-Adj Rating
3 Yr	80	80	-1.33[3]	2.33	★
5 Yr	68	66	0.42[3]	1.84	★
10 Yr	---	---	---	---	---

Average Historical Rating (40 months) 4.0 ★s

[1] 1 = Low, 100 = High [2] 1.00 = Fixed-Inc Avg [3] 1.00 = 90-day T-bill Return

Other Measures

				LB Aggregate
Standard Deviation	12.31	Alpha		-6.20
Mean	-0.46	Beta		2.37
Sharpe Ratio	-0.32	R-Squared		60

Investment Style

Interest-Rate Stance	Fund	Relative Objective
Avg Eff Duration	12.0 Yrs**	2.81
Avg Eff Maturity	11.6 Yrs	1.09
Avg Wtd Coupon	6.47%	0.97
Avg Wtd Price	76.7% Par	0.86

Duration Short Intm Long

Quality
Avg Cred Quality AAA
** figure provided by fund

Sector Analysis 10-31-94

	% of Bonds		% of Bonds
US Treasury	17	POs	10
Straight Mtgs	12	ARMs	0
CMOs	18	Inv Floaters	37
IOs	1	Other	5

Diversification Value for Portfolio Types

Large Cap: High | Small Cap: High | Bond: Low | Balanced: Medium | Diversified: High

Portfolio 10-31-94

Amount 000	Total Equity: 0 Total Fixed-Income: 81	Maturity	Value $000	% Total Invest
16000	FNMA 7.5%	01-01-00	15795	8.18
15000	US Treasury Note 5.875%	05-31-96	14839	7.69
19189	FNMA CMO Z	09-25-21	14818	7.68
15000	US Treasury Note 5.75%	08-15-03	13096	6.78
9292	FNMA CMO Z	04-25-18	9383	4.86
5923	FNMA CMO LIBOR IFRN	12-25-21	4883	2.53
7050	FNMA CMO COFI IFRN	01-25-09	4865	2.52
6234	FNMA CMO LIBOR FRN	10-25-21	4862	2.52
5851	FHLMC CMO COFI IFRN	05-15-08	3819	1.98
4000	FNMA 7%	01-01-08	3799	1.97
7520	FNMA CMO PO	11-25-23	3154	1.63
---	Int Rate Cap JP Morgan LIBOR	02-15-98	3049	1.58
4527	FHLMC CMO COFI IFRN	05-15-08	2767	1.43
4816	FHLMC CMO COFI IFRN	12-15-08	2730	1.41
---	FHLMC CMO IO LIBOR IFRN	11-15-18	2615	1.35
3000	FHLMC CMO PO	06-15-21	2169	1.12
3771	FHLMC CMO COFI IFRN	11-15-23	2112	1.09
4992	FNMA CMO PO	11-25-23	2047	1.06
3383	FHLMC CMO COFI IFRN	09-15-23	1941	1.01
2880	FHLMC CMO PO	10-15-08	1800	0.93
3954	Westam Mtg Fin CMO PO	07-26-18	1705	0.88
---	FHLMC CMO IO LIBOR IFRN	09-15-21	1516	0.79
---	FNMA CMO IO LIBOR IFRN	04-25-23	1488	0.77
4540	FNMA CMO PO	06-25-21	1476	0.76
---	Int Rate Cap Goldman Sachs	09-10-97	1400	0.73

Composition % 12-31-94

Cash	0.2	Preferreds	0.0
Stocks	0.0	Convertibles	0.0
Bonds	94.6	Other	5.2
Leverage factor: 1.00			

Coupon Range

	% of Bonds	Relative Objective
0%	0.0	0.0
0% to 8%	29.0	0.6
8% to 9%	0.0	0.0
9% to 10%	0.0	0.0
More than 10%	0.0	0.0
Not applicable	71.0	2.5

1.0 = Objective Average

Tax Analysis

	Tax-Adj Historical Return %	% Pretax Return
3 Yr Avg	-6.26	NMF
5 Yr Avg	1.74	24.4
10 Yr Avg	---	---

Potential Capital Gain Exposure (% of assets) -57

Most Similar Funds in MF500

WPG Government Securities	Weak Fit
Vanguard Preferred Stock	Weak Fit
Gradison-McDonald Govt	Weak Fit

American Heritage

American Heritage Fund seeks growth of capital. Current income is incidental.

The fund invests primarily in common stocks and convertibles. To maximize returns, it uses various speculative techniques, including short-term trading, hedging, and leveraging. Through these techniques, the fund attempts to take advantage of investment opportunities in both rising and declining markets. It tries to remain substantially or fully invested in common stocks at all times. The fund may also purchase securities of relatively small and lesser-known companies.

Manager's Investment Style

Under current manager Heiko Thieme, American Heritage has taken on more risk than nearly any other open-end mutual fund. In its goal to produce 15% to 25% total returns annually, the fund seeks out compelling investment stories. It prefers tiny-cap stocks and private placements that are selling below their market value, but will also buy beaten-down large caps and foreign issues. About 10% of the portfolio is dedicated to rapid, speculative trading. Short selling, option writing, and leverage also play a role in the fund's volatile performance.

Fund Manager(s)

Heiko H. Thieme, since 02-90. Birthdate: 09-43.
JD, U. of Hamburg

Manager Experience

	Dates Managed	Invest Obj	Std Dev	+/- Index
Heiko H. Thieme				
American Heritage Growth	06/94 - 12/94	AG	7.21	10.23

Ticker	Load	NAV	Yield	SEC Yield	Assets	Objective
AHERX	None	0.85	NMF	N/A	57.0	Aggr. Growth

Historical Profile
Return	Below Average
Risk	High
Rating	★★ Below Average

Investment Style History
Equity

Average % Stocks Held in Portfolio

97% --- --- --- 71% 77% 78% 87%

Growth of $10,000
- IIII Value of Fund ($000)
- — Value of Index ($000) Russ 2000
- ▼ Manager Change
- ▽ Partial Manager Change
- ► Mgr Unknown After
- ◄ Mgr Unknown Before

Performance Quartile (Within Objective)

1983	1984	1985	1986	1987	1988	1989	1990	1991	1992	1993	1994	History
3.64	2.73	2.36	1.42	1.05	1.07	1.04	0.72	1.02	1.13	1.53	0.85	NAV
6.43	-25.00	-13.55	-25.73	-18.98	1.91	-2.80	-30.77	96.59	18.88	41.39	-35.33	Total Return %
-16.03	-31.27	-45.29	-44.41	-24.24	-14.71	-34.49	-27.65	66.10	11.26	31.33	-36.65	+/- S&P 500
---	-23.28	-45.57	-37.49	-15.47	-18.63	-26.75	-17.21	53.14	7.13	26.85	-32.68	+/- Wilshire 4500
0.00	0.00	0.00	0.00	0.00	0.00	0.00	0.00	0.00	0.00	0.00	9.11	Income Return %
6.43	-25.00	-13.55	-25.73	-18.98	1.90	-2.80	-30.77	96.59	18.88	41.39	-44.44	Capital Return %
94	98	100	100	100	100	99	100	1	6	4	100	Total Rtn % Rank All
94	85	96	96	91	88	97	93	1	12	1	99	Total Rtn % Rank Obj
0.00	0.00	0.00	0.00	0.00	0.00	0.00	0.00	0.00	0.00	0.00	0.00	Income $
0.00	0.00	0.00	0.36	0.09	0.00	0.00	0.00	0.38	0.08	0.07	0.14	Capital Gains $
7.50	7.20	11.30	22.70	11.80	11.90	13.02	11.04	6.79	2.23	2.10	2.41	Expense Ratio %
-5.50	-5.30	-8.30	-20.4	-9.30	-8.70	-8.00	-5.80	-3.72	21.50	-0.46	3.40	Income Ratio %
5	7	7	98	287	189	81	76	607	776	278	434	Turnover Rate %
0.7	0.4	0.3	0.6	1.1	0.8	0.7	1.0	5.2	24.7	149.8	57.0	Net Assets ($mil)

Performance 12-31-94

	1st Qtr	2nd Qtr	3rd Qtr	4th Qtr	Total
1987	19.72	-2.94	0.00	-30.27	-18.98
1988	9.52	1.74	-5.13	-3.60	1.91
1989	0.93	3.70	0.89	-7.96	-2.80
1990	-1.92	1.96	-28.85	-2.70	-30.77
1991	54.17	-0.90	12.73	14.15	96.59
1992	17.65	-6.67	-7.14	16.60	18.88
1993	18.58	9.70	4.76	3.74	41.39
1994	-17.65	-13.49	-0.92	-8.39	-35.33

Bear Market Performance

Decile Rank (5-year period)

Worst | | | | | Best

	Worst 3 Mo Period 1985-89	Worst 3 Mo Period 1990-94
American Heritage	-35.33	-28.85
+/- S&P 500	-5.75	-15.10
+/- Best Fit Index : Russ 2000	0.22	-4.31

Trailing Returns

	Total Return %	+/- S&P 500	+/- Wil 4500	% Rank All	% Rank Obj	Growth of $10,000
3 Mo	-8.39	-8.37	-5.88	97	98	9,161
6 Mo	-9.23	-14.09	-13.42	100	98	9,077
1 Yr	-35.33	-36.65	-32.68	100	99	6,467
3 Yr Avg	2.82	-3.45	-4.79	87	75	10,870
5 Yr Avg	8.15	-0.54	-0.94	31	72	14,794
10 Yr Avg	-2.68	-17.06	-15.31	100	96	7,622
15 Yr Avg	-1.14	-15.62	---	100	93	8,425

Operations

Address and Telephone	1370 Avenue of the Americas
	New York, NY 10019
	800-828-5050 / 212-397-3900
Advisor	American Heritage Management
Subadvisor	None
Distributor	American Heritage Group
States Available	All except AR,NE,NH,WI
Report Grade	C+
Income Distrib	Paid Annually
Date of Inception	05-01-52
Fiscal Year End	May

Risk Analysis

Time Period	Load-Adj Return %	Risk % Rank All	Risk % Rank Obj	Morningstar Return	Morningstar Risk	Morningstar Risk-Adj Rating
1 Yr	-35.33					
3 Yr	2.82	98	89	-0.22[3]	1.71	★★
5 Yr	8.15	96	72	0.85[3]	1.41	★★
10 Yr	-2.68	98	96	-0.64	1.65	★
Average Historical Rating (109 months)					1.3	★s

[1] = low, 100 = high   [2] 1.00 = Equity Avg   [3] 1.00 = 90-day T-bill return

Other Measures

		Standard S&P 500	Best Fit Russ 2000
Standard Deviation	18.09	Alpha	-1.9	-7.0
Mean	4.40	Beta	0.97	1.01
Sharpe Ratio	0.05	R-Squared	18	43

Investment Style

	Stock Portfolio Avg	Relative S&P 500
Price/Earnings Ratio	17.1#	0.93
Price/Book Ratio	4.7	1.38
5 Yr Earnings Gr %	---	---
Return on Assets %	8.3#	1.11
Debt % Total Cap		
Med Mkt Cap ($mil)	159	0.01

Style: Value Blend Growth / Size Large Med Small

figure is based on 50% or less of stocks

Diversification Value for Portfolio Types

Large Cap: High	Small Cap: Medium	Bond: High	Balanced: High	Diversified: High

Tax Analysis

	Tax-Adj Historical Return %	% Pretax Return
3 Yr Avg	-0.12	---
5 Yr Avg	4.61	52.8
10 Yr Avg	-4.89	NMF
Potential Capital Gain Exposure (% of assets)	-86%	

Most Similar Funds in MF500

Oppenheimer Discovery A	Weak Fit
Loomis Sayles Small Cap	Weak Fit
Mexico Fund	Weak Fit

Expenses & Fees

Sales Fees	0.00% front
	0.00% deferred
	0.00% 12b-1
Management Fee	1.25% max./1.00% min., 0.01% A
3-,5-,10-yr Expense Projections	$86, $146, $310
Annual Brokerage Cost	1.39%

Min Initial Purchase / IRA

Min Initial Purchase	$5000 (Addt'l: $1000)
Min IRA Purchase	$2000 (Addt'l: None)
Min Auto Invest Plan	N/A

Portfolio 12-09-94

Share Chg (05-94) 000	Amount 000	Total Stocks: 93 / Total Fixed-Income: 0	Value $000	% Net Assets
0	200	Kouri Capital Group (Rest)	8000	13.11
1905	2903	Senetek (ADR)	5625	9.22
7	58	Philip Morris	3270	5.36
22	1400	Spectrum Information Tech	1531	2.51
25	25	Motorola	1384	2.27
-135	363	MTC Electronic Technology	1201	1.97
30	30	Compaq Computer	1200	1.97
0	4250	ADM Tronics	1195	1.96
11	80	Woolworth	1100	1.80
-8	37	Millicom Intl Cellular	1040	1.71
15	15	Caterpillar	763	1.25
200	200	Extreme Technologies	762	1.25
10	10	Texas Instruments	720	1.18
-10	71	Box Energy Cl B	692	1.13
0	100	Immune Response	675	1.11
0	45	Navistar International	630	1.03
10	20	GTE	613	1.00
-25	50	Westinghouse Electric	606	0.99
25	25	Advanced Micro Devices	594	0.97
-10	194	Interdigital Communications	582	0.95
0	15	General Motors	559	0.92
30	30	Bethlehem Steel	529	0.87
0	196	Acorn Intl (Rest)	501	0.82
0	300	Medcom Electronics (Rest)	500	0.82
10	10	AT & T	490	0.80

Composition % 12-31-94

Cash	16.5	Preferreds	0.0
Stocks	68.5	Convertibles	0.0
Bonds	0.0	Other	15.0

Index Allocation

	% of Stocks
S&P 500	43.0
S&P MidCap 400	0.7
U.S. Small Cap	33.8
Foreign	22.6

Sector Weightings

	% of Stocks	Relative S&P 500
Utilities	4.0	0.32
Energy	9.1	0.89
Financials	0.4	0.04
Industrial Cyclicals	9.1	0.55
Consumer Durables	10.1	1.63
Consumer Staples	11.1	0.88
Services	23.1	2.84
Retail	3.7	0.64
Health	6.7	0.77
Technology	22.8	2.49

American High-Income

	Ticker	Load	NAV	Yield	SEC Yield	Assets	Objective
	AHITX	4.75%	13.13	9.7%	10.24%	798.2	Corp Hi Yld

American High-Income Trust seeks a high level of current income; capital appreciation is secondary.

The fund normally invests at least 65% of its assets in lower-rated or unrated corporate bonds. It may, however, maintain assets in cash or cash equivalents under certain market conditions. In addition, the fund may invest up to 25% of its assets in common stocks, convertibles, and preferred stocks, and up to 25% in foreign or foreign-denominated issues.

Historical Profile
Return	Above Average
Risk	Low
Rating	★★★★ Above Average

Investment Style History
Fixed Income
Income Rtn % Rank Obj

Growth of $10,000
- |||| Value of Fund ($000)
- — Value of Index ($000) FB HY
- ▼ Manager Change
- ▽ Partial Manager Change
- ► Mgr Unknown After
- ◄ Mgr Unknown Before

Performance Quartile (Within Objective)

	1983	1984	1985	1986	1987	1988	1989	1990	1991	1992	1993	1994	History
	---	---	---	---	---	14.10	13.30	11.72	13.92	14.37	15.24	13.13	NAV
	---	---	---	---	---	8.37 *	5.63	0.07	32.36	14.30	17.22	-5.11	Total Return %
	---	---	---	---	---	---	-8.91	-8.87	16.36	7.05	7.47	-2.20	+/- LB Aggregate
	---	---	---	---	---	---	5.25	6.45	-11.39	-2.37	-1.68	-4.14	+/- FB High-Yield
	---	---	---	---	---	9.63	11.31	11.95	13.59	10.09	9.25	8.31	Income Return %
	---	---	---	---	---	-1.26	-5.67	-11.88	18.77	4.20	7.97	-13.42	Capital Return %
	---	---	---	---	---	---	95	55	23	11	22	65	Total Rtn % Rank All
	---	---	---	---	---	---	6	7	67	83	74	76	Total Rtn % Rank Obj
	---	---	---	---	---	1.32	1.58	1.58	1.43	1.33	1.26	1.29	Income $
	---	---	---	---	---	0.00	0.00	0.00	0.00	0.13	0.26	0.08	Capital Gains $
	---	---	---	---	---	---	0.97	1.00	1.00	0.94	0.87	0.86	Expense Ratio %
	---	---	---	---	---	---	11.49	12.42	11.41	9.58	8.60	8.63	Income Ratio %
	---	---	---	---	---	---	46	38	44	58	44	42	Turnover Rate %
	---	---	---	---	---	88.0	125.5	147.0	284.7	454.7	788.9	798.2	Net Assets ($mil)

Manager's Investment Style
This fund's management team typically emphasizes the higher-quality end of the noninvestment-grade market. While income is important, management is willing to sacrifice some yield in return for capital appreciation. In looking for long-term appreciation plays, management has devoted a significant amount of assets recently to the multimedia sectors.

Fund Manager(s)
Richard T. Schotte, since 02-88. BA, Amherst C. MA, Columbia U.
David C. Barclay, since 1990.

Manager Experience
	Dates Managed	Invest Obj	Std Dev	+/- Index
Richard T. Schotte				
Income Fund of America	11/78 - 12/94	I	9.32	-1.37
Bond Fund of America	01/80 - 12/94	CG	7.10	0.28

Performance 12-31-94
	1st Qtr	2nd Qtr	3rd Qtr	4th Qtr	Total
1987	---	---	---	---	---
1988	---	3.78	2.11	2.47	8.37 *
1989	1.95	4.97	0.23	-1.53	5.63
1990	-1.36	6.03	-6.81	2.68	0.07
1991	13.95	4.40	5.71	5.25	32.36
1992	4.10	2.52	5.13	1.88	14.30
1993	5.69	4.23	2.11	4.22	17.22
1994	-2.87	-0.44	0.82	-2.67	-5.11

Bear Market Performance
Decile Rank (5-year period)

Worst ————————— Best

	Worst 3 Mo Period 1985-89	Worst 3 Mo Period 1990-94
American High-Income	---	-10.55
+/- LB Aggregate	---	-11.29
+/- Best Fit Index : FB HY	---	3.56

Trailing Returns
	Total Return %	+/- LB Agg	+/- FB High-Yield	% Rank All	% Rank Obj	Growth of $10,000
3 Mo	-2.67	-3.05	-2.63	79	74	9,733
6 Mo	-1.87	-2.86	-3.43	86	60	9,813
1 Yr	-5.11	-2.20	-4.14	65	76	9,489
3 Yr Avg	8.33	3.78	-2.83	19	89	12,713
5 Yr Avg	10.98	3.36	-2.09	12	37	16,839
10 Yr Avg	---	---	---	---	---	---
15 Yr Avg	---	---	---	---	---	---

Operations
Address and Telephone	333 S. Hope Street
	Los Angeles, CA 90071
	800-421-4120 / 213-486-9200
Advisor	Capital Research & Management
Subadvisor	None
Distributor	American Funds Distributors
States Available	All plus GU,PR,VI
Report Grade	A+
Income Distrib	Paid Monthly
* Date of Inception	02-19-88
Fiscal Year End	September

Risk Analysis
Time Period	Load-Adj Return %	Risk % Rank[1] All	Risk % Rank[1] Obj	Morningstar[2] Return	Morningstar Risk	Morningstar Risk-Adj Rating
1 Yr	-9.62					
3 Yr	6.59	14	78	0.89[3]	0.43	★★★★
5 Yr	9.91	41	21	1.33[3]	0.48	★★★★
10 Yr	---	---	---	---	---	

Average Historical Rating (47 months)   3.9 ★s

[1] 1 = low, 100 = high   [2] 1.00 = Hybrid Avg   [3] 1.00 = 90-day T-bill return

Other Measures
			Standard LB Agg	Best Fit FB HY
Standard Deviation	4.78	Alpha	3.9	-2.4
Mean	8.14	Beta	0.77	0.98
Sharpe Ratio	0.97	R-Squared	42	78

Investment Style
Interest-Rate Stance
Avg Effective Duration	4.8 Yrs**
Avg Effective Maturity	6.4 Yrs

Quality
Avg Credit Quality	B
Avg Weighted Coupon	9.61%
Avg Weighted Price	86.30% of Par

**figure provided by fund

Diversification Value for Portfolio Types
Large Cap: High	Small Cap: High	Bond: Medium	Balanced: Medium	Diversified: High

Most Similar Funds in MF500
Invesco High-Yield	Strong Fit
Vanguard F/I High-Yield Corp	Strong Fit
Phoenix High-Yield A	Strong Fit

Portfolio 09-30-94
Total Stocks: 8
Total Fixed-Income: 119

Amount 000	Date of Maturity		Value $000	% Net Assets
24330	11-01-01	Rogers Cantel Mobile 10.75%	25060	3.00
33000	2004	California Energy Step 10.25%	24090	2.89
36850	2004	MFS Communications Step 9.375%	21373	2.56
2017		Nortel Inversora Cl A Pfd	20160	2.41
20000	1999	US Treasury Note 6.875%	19675	2.36
20250	04-15-03	Container of America 9.75%	19541	2.34
32500	2004	Dial Call Comm Step 12.25%	17225	2.06
30500	09-01-03	NEXTEL Communications 0%	16928	2.03
14900	12-15-99	Global Marine 12.75%	16167	1.94
13950	06-15-00	Riverwood Intl 10.75%	14570	1.75
16000	11-01-01	Centennial Cellular 8.875%	14560	1.74
14750	07-15-02	Ralphs Grocery 10.25%	14160	1.70
24500	2004	Bell Cablemedia Step 11.95%	14026	1.68
25500	2004	Videotron Hldgs Step 11.125%	14025	1.68
13250	05-15-02	Paging Network 11.75%	13913	1.67
14250	03-15-01	Fort Howard 9.25%	13823	1.66
16813	11-01-02	Dr Pepper/Seven-Up 11.5%	13387	1.60
25550	2004	OneComm Step 10.125%	12839	1.54
12500	04-01-00	Coltec Industries 9.75%	12625	1.51
13750	2000	Inda Kiat Intl 8.875%	12375	1.48
13500	03-01-99	Foodmaker 9.25%	12353	1.48
21675	2003	Intl CableTel Step 10.875%	12138	1.45
18500	04-15-98	Marvel 0%	11655	1.40
19150	2003	MobileMedia Comm Step 10.5%	11107	1.33
10700	11-15-98	MagneTek 10.75%	11021	1.32

Composition % 12-31-94
Cash	3.6	Preferreds	0.0
Stocks	2.8	Convertibles	0.3
Bonds	93.3	Other	0.0

Tax Analysis
	Tax-Adj Historical Return %	% Pretax Return
3 Yr Avg	4.60	53.3
5 Yr Avg	7.10	59.8
10 Yr Avg	---	---

Potential Capital Gain Exposure (% of assets)   -10%

Coupon Range
	% of Bonds	Rel Obj
0%, PIK	6.3	0.85
0% to 11%	65.6	1.34
11% to 13%	24.2	0.72
13% to 14.5%	0.8	0.14
More than 14.5%	0.0	0.00
Not applicable	3.2	1.04

Credit Analysis 12-31-94
% of Bonds
US Govt	4	BB	28
AAA	0	B	60
AA	0	Below B	7
A	0	NR/NA	0
BBB	1		

Expenses & Fees
Sales Fees	4.75% front
	0.00% deferred
	0.30% 12b-1
Management Fee	0.30% max./0.21% min.+3.00%I
3-,5-,10-yr Expense Projections	$74, $93, $150

| | |
|---|---|
| Min Initial Purchase | $1000 (Addt'l: $50) |
| Min IRA Purchase | $250 (Addt'l: $50) |
| Min Auto Invest Plan | $50 (Systematic Inv: $50) |

American Leaders A

	Ticker	Load	NAV	Yield	SEC Yield	Assets	Objective
	FALDX	5.50%	14.39	1.6%	1.79%	242.5	Growth/Inc.

American Leaders Fund - Class A seeks growth of capital and income.

The fund normally invests at least 65% of its assets in equity and debt securities of companies included on The Leaders List - a list developed by the fund that includes 100 blue-chip companies and that is subject to continuous review.

Class A shares have front loads; Class B shares have deferred loads; Class C shares have level loads; Fortress shares have low front and deferred loads. Purchases made with the proceeds of a mutual fund share redemption may be subject to a redemption fee.

Manager's Investment Style

American Leaders' management chooses from a list of 100 blue-chip firms, seeking the stocks with the lowest valuations compared with earnings and book value. It also seeks issues that are capable of near-term earnings surprises. The goal is to own inexpensive firms with a high chance of being noticed by the market.

Fund Manager(s)

Tim Keefe CFA(1990), since 12-94. Birthdate: 08-92. BS, Boston C. 1984 MBA, U. of Pittsburgh 1992

Manager Experience

	Dates Managed	Invest Obj	Std Dev	+/- Index
Not available.				

Historical Profile

Return	Average
Risk	Below Average
Rating	★★★
	Neutral

Investment Style History
Equity

Average % Stocks Held in Portfolio: 77% 77% 72% 89% 90% 86% 87% 89%

Growth of $10,000
|||| Value of Fund ($000)
— Value of Index ($000) S&P 500
▼ Manager Change
▽ Partial Manager Change
► Mgr Unknown After
◄ Mgr Unknown Before

Performance Quartile (Within Objective)

	1983	1984	1985	1986	1987	1988	1989	1990	1991	1992	1993	1994	History
	11.30	10.88	12.39	12.49	12.20	12.59	12.26	11.34	13.87	14.09	14.98	14.39	NAV
	26.12	15.47	27.71	14.86	4.66	12.10	11.68	-1.77	31.04	11.68	11.75	0.05	Total Return %
	3.65	9.20	-4.03	-3.82	-0.60	-4.51	-20.00	1.35	0.56	4.06	1.69	-1.27	+/- S&P 500
	2.66	12.42	-4.85	-1.24	2.30	-5.84	-17.49	4.42	-3.17	2.71	0.47	0.12	+/- Wilshire 5000
	5.58	5.38	4.91	3.92	3.25	3.81	4.78	3.62	2.08	2.08	1.72	1.63	Income Return %
	20.53	10.08	22.81	10.94	1.41	8.29	6.90	-5.38	28.96	9.60	10.03	-1.59	Capital Return %
	20	5	34	55	24	45	60	61	25	16	53	19	Total Rtn % Rank All
	23	6	47	60	26	70	94	31	30	21	41	39	Total Rtn % Rank Obj
	0.56	0.55	0.52	0.50	0.43	0.46	0.60	0.43	0.26	0.28	0.25	0.24	Income $
	0.86	1.35	0.84	1.23	0.47	0.59	1.18	0.30	0.65	1.04	0.49	0.35	Capital Gains $
	1.45	1.37	1.06	1.09	1.00	1.00	1.01	1.01	1.02	1.02	1.13	1.18	Expense Ratio %
	6.36	5.14	3.18	4.42	3.44	3.35	3.85	4.23	3.06	2.12	2.07	1.48	Income Ratio %
	58	42	32	31	28	65	27	50	57	67	39	27	Turnover Rate %
	47.9	47.9	78.1	121.6	160.9	148.9	148.2	132.7	161.1	188.5	229.8	242.5	Net Assets ($mil)

Performance 12-31-94

	1st Qtr	2nd Qtr	3rd Qtr	4th Qtr	Total
1987	14.58	3.03	3.96	-14.72	4.66
1988	3.65	6.54	-0.13	1.64	12.10
1989	4.70	3.97	6.22	-3.41	11.68
1990	0.43	3.87	-14.45	10.08	-1.77
1991	16.72	-0.59	4.48	8.10	31.04
1992	0.57	1.96	2.73	6.01	11.68
1993	6.25	1.66	2.81	0.64	11.75
1994	-2.30	1.30	4.03	-2.83	0.05

Bear Market Performance

Decile Rank (5-year period)

Worst —— Best

	Worst 3 Mo Period 1985-89	Worst 3 Mo Period 1990-94
American Leaders A	-21.09	-16.81
+/- S&P 500	8.49	-2.97
+/- Best Fit Index : S&P 500	8.49	-2.97

Trailing Returns

	Total Return %	+/- S&P 500	+/- Wil 5000	% Rank All	% Rank Obj	Growth of $10,000
3 Mo	-2.83	-2.81	-2.06	81	82	9,717
6 Mo	1.09	-3.77	-3.53	36	73	10,109
1 Yr	0.05	-1.27	0.12	19	39	10,005
3 Yr Avg	7.68	1.42	1.07	23	24	12,486
5 Yr Avg	9.96	1.26	1.14	17	14	16,072
10 Yr Avg	11.94	-2.44	-1.92	38	57	30,893
15 Yr Avg	14.09	-0.39	0.11	23	26	72,218

Operations

Address and Telephone	Liberty Center Federated Inv Twr
	Pittsburgh, PA 15222-3779
	800-245-5051 / 412-288-1900
Advisor	Federated Advisers
Subadvisor	None
Distributor	Federated Securities
States Available	All plus PR
Report Grade	B
Income Distrib	Paid Quarterly
Date of Inception	02-26-69
Fiscal Year End	March

Risk Analysis

Time Period	Load-Adj Return %	Risk % Rank [1] All	Obj	Morningstar [2] Return	Risk	Morningstar Risk-Adj Rating
1 Yr	-5.95					
3 Yr	5.67	67	56	0.62 [3]	0.75	★★★
5 Yr	8.72	67	54	1.00 [3]	0.80	★★★
10 Yr	11.31	54	38	0.76	0.79	★★★
Average Historical Rating (109 months)					3.7	★ s

[1] 1 = low, 100 = high [2] 1.00 = Equity Avg [3] 1.00 = 90-day T-bill return

Other Measures

			Standard S&P 500	Best Fit S&P 500
Standard Deviation	8.36	Alpha	1.5	1.5
Mean	7.77	Beta	0.95	0.95
Sharpe Ratio	0.51	R-Squared	82	82

Investment Style

	Stock Portfolio Avg	Relative S&P 500
Price/Earnings Ratio	16.4	0.89
Price/Book Ratio	3.1	0.92
5 Yr Earnings Gr %	6.4	1.15
Return on Assets %	6.2	0.83
Debt % Total Cap	32.6	1.15
Med Mkt Cap ($mil)	6253	0.48

Style: Value/Blend/Growth — Large/Med/Small — Size

Diversification Value for Portfolio Types

Large Cap: None	Small Cap: Medium	Bond: Medium	Balanced: None	Diversified: Low

Min Purchases / Expenses

Min Initial Purchase	$500 (Addt'l: $100)
Min IRA Purchase	$50 (Addt'l: $50)
Min Auto Invest Plan	$500 (Systematic Inv: $100)

Expenses & Fees

Sales Fees	5.50% front
	0.00% deferred
	0.25% 12b-1
Management Fee	0.55% flat fee+4.50%I, 0.15%A
3-,5-,10-yr Expense Projections	$91, $117, $191
Annual Brokerage Cost	0.06%

Portfolio 09-30-94

Share Chg (08-94) 000	Amount 000	Total Stocks: 51 Total Fixed-Income: 4	Value $000	% Net Assets
4	115	Phelps Dodge	7159	2.93
4	113	Philip Morris	6922	2.83
11	252	Mattel	6834	2.80
5	138	Sears Roebuck	6626	2.71
4	123	AT & T	6624	2.71
3	71	Hewlett-Packard	6168	2.52
3	95	Raytheon	6096	2.49
4	117	Textron	5968	2.44
4	156	General Motors Cl E	5931	2.43
4	92	FMC	5696	2.33
6	121	US Healthcare	5620	2.30
3	125	Martin Marietta	5543	2.27
5	131	Chevron	5457	2.23
2	91	Texaco	5456	2.23
3	104	Eastman Kodak	5390	2.21
2	89	American Home Products	5357	2.19
0	151	Rockwell International	5170	2.11
4	201	American Stores	5076	2.08
3	88	Bristol-Myers Squibb	5070	2.07
1	89	Mellon Bank	5012	2.05
1	113	Citicorp	4813	1.97
7	194	Praxair	4725	1.93
5	128	Reebok International	4578	1.87
5	202	Tele-Communications Cl A	4477	1.83
0	75	Avon Products	4475	1.83

Composition % 09-30-94

Cash	6.1	Preferreds	2.1
Stocks	90.2	Convertibles	1.6
Bonds	0.0	Other	0.0

Tax Analysis

	Tax-Adj Historical Return %	% Pretax Return
3 Yr Avg	5.76	73.6
5 Yr Avg	7.95	76.7
10 Yr Avg	9.11	66.6
Potential Capital Gain Exposure (% of assets)		13%

Most Similar Funds in MF500

Investment Comp of America	Fair Fit
Vanguard Index 500	Fair Fit
Clipper	Fair Fit

Index Allocation

	% of Stocks
S&P 500	91.1
S&P MidCap 400	7.0
U.S. Small Cap	1.9
Foreign	0.0

Sector Weightings

	% of Stocks	Relative S&P 500
Utilities	6.7	0.54
Energy	12.2	1.21
Financials	17.3	1.64
Industrial Cyclicals	19.5	1.19
Consumer Durables	8.7	1.40
Consumer Staples	5.2	0.41
Services	4.0	0.49
Retail	5.3	0.91
Health	9.3	1.07
Technology	11.9	1.30

MORNINGSTAR 1995 Mutual Fund 500

American Mutual

American Mutual Fund seeks a balance of three investment objectives: current income, capital growth, and stability.

The fund invests chiefly in equity securities, such as common stocks or preferred stock. The securities are issued by companies domiciled in the United States and/or listed on the S&P 500. The fund may also invest in high-quality convertible and debt obligations. Its purchases are limited to a preapproved list of securities reviewed by the board of directors. The fund does not attempt to seek all of its objectives in one type of security.

		Ticker	Load	NAV	Yield	SEC Yield	Assets	Objective
		AMRMX	5.75%	20.11	4.0%	3.78%	5278.6	Growth/Inc.

Historical Profile
Return	Average
Risk	Low
Rating	★★★★ Above Average

Investment Style History
Equity
Average % Stocks Held in Portfolio

68% 73% 69% 67% 77% 76% 73% 70%

Growth of $10,000
‖‖ Value of Fund ($000)
— Value of Index ($000)
   S&P 500
▼ Manager Change
▽ Partial Manager Change
► Mgr Unknown After
◄ Mgr Unknown Before

Performance Quartile (Within Objective)

Manager's Investment Style
This fund uses Capital Research and Management's multimanagement system, here dividing assets among five different managers plus a team of analysts. As a result, the portfolio is well diversified. Overall, management tends to invest in well-known large-cap stocks that offer both income and potential for growth, buying when those stocks are selling at below-market multiples.

Fund Manager(s)
Management Team

	1983	1984	1985	1986	1987	1988	1989	1990	1991	1992	1993	1994	History
	15.41	14.94	17.74	17.99	17.05	17.59	20.20	18.67	21.05	20.79	21.77	20.11	NAV
	24.13	6.43	30.60	18.61	4.45	12.85	25.25	-1.62	21.72	7.83	14.28	0.33	Total Return %
	1.67	0.17	-1.14	-0.07	-0.81	-3.76	-6.43	1.50	-8.76	0.22	4.23	-0.98	+/- S&P 500
	0.67	3.39	-1.96	2.52	2.09	-5.09	-3.92	4.56	-12.49	-1.14	3.00	0.40	+/- Wilshire 5000
	6.00	5.11	5.37	4.32	5.74	5.62	5.50	5.02	4.87	4.34	3.99	4.02	Income Return %
	18.13	1.32	25.23	14.29	-1.29	7.23	19.76	-6.64	16.85	3.49	10.29	-3.69	Capital Return %
	27	45	23	29	25	38	23	60	42	48	31	17	Total Rtn % Rank All
	36	37	30	32	28	67	44	28	86	45	27	36	Total Rtn % Rank Obj
	0.76	0.70	0.72	0.74	1.06	0.96	0.98	0.99	0.88	0.88	0.84	0.84	Income $
	0.48	0.64	0.70	2.08	0.71	0.67	0.79	0.20	0.66	0.97	1.11	0.87	Capital Gains $
	0.49	0.49	0.46	0.45	0.47	0.54	0.59	0.60	0.63	0.60	0.59	0.60	Expense Ratio %
	5.10	5.21	4.83	4.46	4.26	4.77	5.20	5.00	4.47	4.15	3.83	4.07	Income Ratio %
	20	21	24	18	13	17	23	12	24	37	22	18	Turnover Rate %
	844.8	1038.7	1419.8	2162.8	2339.3	2568.7	3308.5	3426.4	4328.9	4709.6	5194.3	5278.6	Net Assets ($mil)

Manager Experience
	Dates Managed	Invest Obj	Std Dev	+/- Index
James K. Dunton				
Washington Mutual Inv	01/78 - 12/94	GI	13.96	1.04
Robert G. O'Donnell				
American Balanced	04/86 - 12/94	B	9.53	-1.72

Performance 12-31-94
	1st Qtr	2nd Qtr	3rd Qtr	4th Qtr	Total
1987	11.28	3.52	4.38	-13.12	4.45
1988	5.10	6.10	-0.10	1.30	12.85
1989	5.80	7.54	7.48	2.42	25.25
1990	-1.44	2.24	-8.68	6.91	-1.62
1991	8.09	1.65	4.18	6.33	21.72
1992	-1.43	3.46	2.90	2.76	7.83
1993	6.49	2.88	4.21	0.09	14.28
1994	-3.22	1.19	3.35	-0.87	0.33

Bear Market Performance
Decile Rank (5-year period)

Worst ———————————————— Best

	Worst 3 Mo Period 1985-89	Worst 3 Mo Period 1990-94
American Mutual	-18.36	-8.68
+/- S&P 500	11.22	5.07
+/- Best Fit Index : S&P 500	11.22	5.07

Trailing Returns
	Total Return %	+/- S&P 500	+/- Wil 5000	% Rank All	% Rank Obj	Growth of $10,000
3 Mo	-0.87	-0.86	-0.10	41	39	9,913
6 Mo	2.45	-2.42	-2.18	24	52	10,245
1 Yr	0.33	-0.98	0.40	17	36	10,033
3 Yr Avg	7.33	1.07	0.72	25	27	12,365
5 Yr Avg	8.17	-0.53	-0.65	31	45	14,806
10 Yr Avg	12.97	-1.41	-0.89	28	34	33,864
15 Yr Avg	14.71	0.23	0.73	17	15	78,348

Operations
Address and Telephone	333 S. Hope Street
	Los Angeles, CA 90071
	800-421-4120 / 213-486-9200
Advisor	Capital Research & Management
Subadvisor	None
Distributor	American Funds Distributors
States Available	All plus GU,PR,VI
Report Grade	A
Income Distrib	Paid Quarterly
Date of Inception	02-21-50
Fiscal Year End	October

Risk Analysis
Time Period	Load-Adj Return %	Risk % Rank[1] All	Obj	Morningstar[2] Return	Morningstar Risk	Morningstar Risk-Adj Rating
1 Yr	-5.43					
3 Yr	5.23	54	13	0.49[3]	0.58	★★★
5 Yr	6.89	55	10	0.52[3]	0.61	★★★
10 Yr	12.31	44	9	0.94	0.64	★★★★
Average Historical Rating (109 months)					4.0	★s

[1] 1 = low, 100 = high [2] 1.00 = Equity Avg [3] 1.00 = 90-day T-bill return

Other Measures
			Standard S&P 500	Best Fit S&P 500
Standard Deviation	6.93	Alpha	1.5	1.5
Mean	7.34	Beta	0.81	0.81
Sharpe Ratio	0.55	R-Squared	85	85

Investment Style
	Stock Portfolio Avg	Relative S&P 500
Price/Earnings Ratio	16.2	0.88
Price/Book Ratio	2.6	0.76
5 Yr Earnings Gr %	-0.4	-0.06
Return on Assets %	5.3	0.71
Debt % Total Cap	29.7	1.05
Med Mkt Cap ($mil)	10325	0.80

Style: Value Blend Growth / Size Large Med Small

Diversification Value for Portfolio Types
Large Cap: None	Small Cap: High	Bond: Medium	Balanced: None	Diversified: Low

Portfolio 10-31-94
Total Stocks: 96
Total Fixed-Income: 27

Share Chg (06-94) 000	Amount 000		Value $000	% Net Assets
0	2030	AT & T	111628	2.07
-200	1090	American Cyanamid	107637	1.99
0	2650	Ameritech	106994	1.98
0	3300	GTE	101475	1.88
0	1600	Amoco	101400	1.88
0	854	Royal Dutch Petroleum	99526	1.84
-640	1620	El duPont de Nemours	96593	1.79
0	1175	IBM	87537	1.62
	75000	US Treasury Note 7.5%	75961	1.41
0	2100	Merck	75075	1.39
-150	2300	Sprint	75037	1.39
0	2200	Wachovia	73700	1.37
	50000	US Treasury Bond 12.375%	65093	1.21
	60000	US Treasury Note 8.5%	62569	1.16
	60000	US Treasury Note 8.25%	61772	1.14
	60000	US Treasury Note 8.125%	61585	1.14
0	410	Wells Fargo	60936	1.13
	50000	US Treasury Bond 11.75%	60343	1.12
0	955	Norfolk Southern	60165	1.11
0	925	Exxon	58159	1.08
	60000	US Treasury Note 6%	58097	1.08
0	2440	PNC Bank	57340	1.06
0	1800	Pacific Telesis Group	56925	1.05
	60000	US Treasury Note 5.125%	56072	1.04
70	950	Dun & Bradstreet	55694	1.03

Composition % 12-31-94
Cash	15.7	Preferreds	0.0
Stocks	69.2	Convertibles	2.4
Bonds	12.6	Other	0.0

Tax Analysis
	Tax-Adj Historical Return %	% Pretax Return
3 Yr Avg	4.50	59.7
5 Yr Avg	5.57	64.8
10 Yr Avg	9.86	65.4
Potential Capital Gain Exposure (% of assets)		15%

Most Similar Funds in MF500
Washington Mutual Investors	Strong Fit
Vanguard Equity-Income	Strong Fit
Vanguard/Wellington	Strong Fit

Index Allocation
	% of Stocks
S&P 500	92.6
S&P MidCap 400	1.8
U.S. Small Cap	5.6
Foreign	2.8

Sector Weightings
	% of Stocks	Relative S&P 500
Utilities	21.7	1.75
Energy	9.9	0.98
Financials	18.2	1.72
Industrial Cyclicals	18.8	1.15
Consumer Durables	3.4	0.55
Consumer Staples	2.7	0.21
Services	8.3	1.02
Retail	0.9	0.15
Health	10.5	1.21
Technology	5.7	0.62

Expenses & Fees
Sales Fees	5.75% front
	0.00% deferred
	0.25% 12b-1
Management Fee	0.39% max./0.28% min.
3-,5-,10-yr Expense Projections	$75, $89, $127
Annual Brokerage Cost	0.06%

Min Initial Purchase / IRA / Auto Invest
Min Initial Purchase	$250 (Addt'l: $50)
Min IRA Purchase	$250 (Addt'l: $50)
Min Auto Invest Plan	$50 (Systematic Inv: $50)

Analytic Optioned Equity

	Ticker	Load	NAV	Yield	SEC Yield	Assets	Objective
	ANALX	None	11.12	2.8%	N/A	48.2	Growth/Inc.

Analytic Optioned Equity Fund seeks total return.
    The fund invests primarily in dividend-paying common stocks and in convertibles. It attempts to limit its share volatility by hedging virtually all of these holdings. The fund also sells covered call options and secured put options and enters into closing purchase transactions with respect to certain options. The fund attempts to maintain a diversified portfolio of common stocks selected to correspond closely to the industry-group weightings of the S&P 500 Index.

Historical Profile

Return Below Average
Risk   Low
Rating ★★★
        Neutral

Average % Stocks Held in Portfolio: 85% 91% 94% 92% 90% 75% 71% 90%

Investment Style History
Equity

Growth of $10,000

‖‖‖ Value of Fund ($000)
— Value of Index ($000)
    S&P 500
▼ Manager Change
▽ Partial Manager Change
► Mgr Unknown After
◄ Mgr Unknown Before

Performance Quartile (Within Objective)

Manager's Investment Style

Manager Charles Dobson uses an unusual strategy in which he purchases S&P 500 stocks and then writes options on them. The strategy is designed to limit the price volatility the fund is exposed to in any one stock, and Dobson can also use S&P puts to further protect the portfolio from losses. This approach limits the fund's potential for capital gains but boosts the fund's distributable income above its peers'.

Fund Manager(s)

Charles L. Dobson, since 07-78. Birthdate: 12-41.
BA, U. of California-Irvine 1970   MS, U. of California-Irvine 1979

Manager Experience	Dates Managed	Invest Obj	Std Dev	+/- Index
Not available.				

	1983	1984	1985	1986	1987	1988	1989	1990	1991	1992	1993	1994	History
	13.86	14.31	14.89	13.70	11.38	12.06	13.00	11.92	12.29	11.97	11.96	11.12	NAV
	19.18	6.77	16.98	10.39	4.24	15.60	17.72	1.50	13.33	6.13	6.76	2.47	Total Return %
	-3.29	0.51	-14.76	-8.29	-1.02	-1.01	-13.96	4.62	-17.15	-1.48	-3.30	1.15	+/- S&P 500
	-4.28	3.72	-15.58	-5.71	1.87	-2.34	-11.45	7.68	-20.87	-2.84	-4.52	2.54	+/- Wilshire 5000
	5.06	3.32	3.59	3.17	3.39	3.63	4.20	3.90	3.33	2.40	2.71	9.49	Income Return %
	14.12	3.45	13.39	7.22	0.85	11.98	13.52	-2.40	10.01	3.74	4.04	-7.02	Capital Return %
	43	44	87	83	26	26	40	51	67	67	85	9	Total Rtn % Rank All
	66	35	96	87	29	50	81	9	98	67	81	11	Total Rtn % Rank Obj
	0.60	0.44	0.48	0.45	0.46	0.42	0.51	0.48	0.40	0.29	0.33	0.31	Income $
	0.24	0.02	1.20	2.20	2.48	0.66	0.66	0.78	0.80	0.78	0.49	0.82	Capital Gains $
	1.23	1.30	1.23	1.18	1.17	1.13	1.09	1.11	1.10	1.02	1.07	1.01	Expense Ratio %
	3.71	3.65	3.30	2.90	2.68	3.44	3.74	3.68	3.05	2.33	2.51	4.81	Income Ratio %
	49	45	54	64	84	66	61	72	76	82	36	44	Turnover Rate %
	54.3	76.7	85.5	77.1	75.0	103.1	106.9	107.3	102.1	92.9	64.7	48.2	Net Assets ($mil)

Performance 12-31-94

	1st Qtr	2nd Qtr	3rd Qtr	4th Qtr	Total
1987	9.18	3.47	3.99	-11.27	4.24
1988	4.92	5.09	1.79	3.00	15.60
1989	4.23	4.75	6.59	1.16	17.72
1990	-0.38	2.18	-7.38	7.67	1.50
1991	6.82	0.08	3.67	2.26	13.33
1992	1.06	1.13	1.21	2.60	6.13
1993	3.59	0.73	1.62	0.68	6.76
1994	-1.92	1.29	3.75	-0.58	2.47

Bear Market Performance

Decile Rank (5-year period)

Worst [ ] Best

	Worst 3 Mo Period 1985-89	Worst 3 Mo Period 1990-94
Analytic Optioned Equity	-15.96	-7.51
+/- S&P 500	13.62	6.33
+/- Best Fit Index : S&P 500	13.62	6.33

Trailing Returns

	Total Return %	+/- S&P 500	+/- Wil 5000	% Rank All	% Rank Obj	Growth of $10,000
3 Mo	-0.58	-0.56	0.19	36	34	9,942
6 Mo	3.15	-1.71	-1.48	20	41	10,315
1 Yr	2.47	1.15	2.54	9	11	10,247
3 Yr Avg	5.10	-1.16	-1.51	46	64	11,610
5 Yr Avg	5.96	-2.73	-2.86	77	86	13,356
10 Yr Avg	9.36	-5.02	-4.50	66	92	24,467
15 Yr Avg	10.41	-4.07	-3.57	72	88	44,172

Operations

Address and Telephone	2222 Martin Street Suite 230
	Irvine, CA 92715-1454
	800-374-2633 / 714-833-0294
Advisor	Analytic Investment Management
Subadvisor	None
Distributor	Analytic Optioned Equity Fund
States Available	All except ND,VT
Report Grade	B-
Income Distrib	Paid Quarterly
Date of Inception	07-01-78
Fiscal Year End	December

Min Initial Purchase	$5000 (Addt'l: None)
Min IRA Purchase	None (Addt'l: None)
Min Auto Invest Plan	N/A

Expenses & Fees

Sales Fees	0.00% front
	0.00% deferred
	0.00% 12b-1
Management Fee	0.75% max./0.55% min.
3-,5-,10-yr Expense Projections	$34, $59, $131
Annual Brokerage Cost	---

Risk Analysis

Time Period	Load-Adj Return %	Risk % Rank [1] All	Obj	Morningstar [2] Return	Morningstar Risk	Morningstar Risk-Adj Rating
1 Yr	2.47					
3 Yr	5.10	28	2	0.45 [3]	0.42	★★★
5 Yr	5.96	49	2	0.29 [3]	0.49	★★★
10 Yr	9.36	39	2	0.45	0.51	★★★
Average Historical Rating (109 months)					3.1	★s

[1] 1 = low, 100 = high   [2] 1.00 = Equity Avg   [3] 1.00 = 90-day T-bill return

Other Measures

		Standard S&P 500	Best Fit S&P 500
Standard Deviation	4.75	Alpha	0.0	0.0
Mean	5.10	Beta	0.56	0.56
Sharpe Ratio	0.33	R-Squared	87	87

Investment Style

	Stock Portfolio Avg	Relative S&P 500
Price/Earnings Ratio	17.3	0.94
Price/Book Ratio	3.4	1.00
5 Yr Earnings Gr %	3.2	0.58
Return on Assets %	7.1	0.94
Debt % Total Cap	30.4	1.08
Med Mkt Cap ($mil)	9994	0.77

Style: Value Blend Growth / Size Large Med Small

Diversification Value for Portfolio Types

Large Cap: None	Small Cap: Medium	Bond: Medium	Balanced: None	Diversified: Low

Portfolio 09-30-94

Total Stocks: 129
Total Fixed-Income: 2

Share Chg (06-94) 000	Amount 000		Value $000	% Net Assets
	2000	US Treasury Note 8.5%	2082	3.35
0	23	IBM	1578	2.54
	1400	US Treasury Note 7.75%	1428	2.30
-6	28	General Electric	1343	2.16
0	20	Philip Morris	1223	1.97
0	16	FNMA	1221	1.96
0	23	JC Penney	1162	1.87
0	13	Hewlett-Packard	1092	1.76
6	19	Exxon	1066	1.71
0	30	Merck	1065	1.71
0	20	AT & T	1053	1.69
-12	23	Chevron	957	1.54
0	18	General Motors	853	1.37
5	11	Georgia-Pacific	842	1.35
0	28	GTE	835	1.34
-7	15	Bell Atlantic	784	1.26
0	20	Duke Power	780	1.25
14	28	Harley-Davidson	774	1.24
0	23	Upjohn	768	1.23
5	10	Quaker Oats	765	1.23
0	9	First Interstate Bancorp	746	1.20
0	40	Southern	745	1.20
0	14	Eastman Kodak	725	1.17
0	11	Telefonos de Mexico L (ADR)	688	1.11
2	8	ALCOA	678	1.09

Composition % 12-31-94

Cash	2.2	Preferreds	0.0
Stocks	97.3	Convertibles	0.5
Bonds	0.0	Other	0.0

Tax Analysis

	Tax-Adj Historical Return %	% Pretax Return
3 Yr Avg	2.22	42.4
5 Yr Avg	2.97	47.0
10 Yr Avg	5.72	51.4
Potential Capital Gain Exposure (% of assets)		-5%

Most Similar Funds in MF500

George Putnam of Boston A	Strong Fit
Vanguard STAR	Fair Fit
Prudential Alloc Cons Mgd B	Fair Fit

Index Allocation

	% of Stocks
S&P 500	86.4
S&P MidCap 400	5.0
U.S. Small Cap	3.8
Foreign	7.0

Sector Weightings

	% of Stocks	Relative S&P 500
Utilities	15.6	1.26
Energy	10.8	1.06
Financials	12.2	1.15
Industrial Cyclicals	17.6	1.08
Consumer Durables	8.0	1.28
Consumer Staples	10.1	0.80
Services	5.5	0.68
Retail	4.7	0.81
Health	8.5	0.98
Technology	7.1	0.77

MORNINGSTAR 1995 Mutual Fund 500

Ariel Appreciation A

	Ticker	Load	NAV	Yield	SEC Yield	Assets	Objective
	CAAPX	None	19.51	0.3%	N/A	128.5	Growth

Ariel Appreciation Fund - Class A seeks long-term capital appreciation.

The fund invests primarily in common stocks of companies with market capitalizations between $200 million and $5 billion. It actively seeks environmentally-responsible companies and may not invest in issuers engaged in manufacturing weapons systems or producing nuclear energy.

Prior to Sept. 6, 1994, the fund was named Calvert-Ariel Appreciation Fund - Class A. Other funds that have merged into this fund: Washington Area Growth Fund on Sept. 16, 1991, Calvert Capital Value Fund on June 12, 1992, and Ariel Appreciation Fund C on Dec. 8, 1994.

Manager's Investment Style

In addition to screening stocks for social responsibility, management also seeks issues selling at a 20% discount to their future growth rates. Issuers must have good cash flow, solid management, and low debt. Management's goal is to find good growth companies that are being overlooked by Wall Street.

Fund Manager(s)

Eric T. McKissack CFA(1987), since 12-89.
Birthdate: 12-53. BS, MIT 1976 MBA, U. of California-Berkeley 1981

Manager Experience	Dates Managed	Invest Obj	Std Dev	+/- Index
Not available.				

Historical Profile

Return	Average
Risk	Average
Rating	★★★
	Neutral

Investment Style History
Equity
Average % Stocks Held in Portfolio

| | 89% | 88% | 88% | 95% | 99% |

Growth of $10,000

|||| Value of Fund ($000)
— Value of Index ($000)
    SPMid400
▼ Manager Change
▽ Partial Manager Change
► Mgr Unknown After
◄ Mgr Unknown Before

Performance Quartile
(Within Objective)

	1983	1984	1985	1986	1987	1988	1989	1990	1991	1992	1993	1994	History
	---	---	---	---	---	---	15.00	14.53	19.15	21.60	22.89	19.51	NAV
	---	---	---	---	---	---	0.00 *	-1.51	33.16	13.24	7.95	-8.39	Total Return %
	---	---	---	---	---	---	-1.04 *	1.61	2.68	5.62	-2.10	-9.71	+/- S&P 500
	---	---	---	---	---	---	---	4.67	-1.05	4.27	-3.33	-8.32	+/- Wilshire 5000
	---	---	---	---	---	---	0.00	1.13	1.17	0.45	0.25	0.32	Income Return %
	---	---	---	---	---	---	0.00	-2.64	31.99	12.79	7.71	-8.71	Capital Return %
	---	---	---	---	---	---	---	60	22	13	79	88	Total Rtn % Rank All
	---	---	---	---	---	---	---	31	56	22	68	91	Total Rtn % Rank Obj
	---	---	---	---	---	---	0.00	0.17	0.17	0.08	0.05	0.06	Income $
	---	---	---	---	---	---	0.00	0.08	0.02	0.00	0.35	1.40	Capital Gains $
	---	---	---	---	---	---	---	0.70	1.50	1.44	1.37	1.35	Expense Ratio %
	---	---	---	---	---	---	---	2.23	1.61	0.57	0.33	0.17	Income Ratio %
	---	---	---	---	---	---	---	4	20	2	56	12	Turnover Rate %
	---	---	---	---	---	---	0.1	26.2	90.1	179.3	219.3	128.5	Net Assets ($mil)

Performance 12-31-94

	1st Qtr	2nd Qtr	3rd Qtr	4th Qtr	Total
1987	---	---	---	---	---
1988	---	---	---	---	---
1989	---	---	---	---	0.00 *
1990	4.07	6.21	-22.44	14.88	-1.51
1991	22.57	-0.22	3.43	5.27	33.16
1992	2.04	-3.43	2.91	11.67	13.24
1993	-2.55	-1.85	4.89	7.60	7.95
1994	-4.85	-0.37	0.55	-3.90	-8.39

Bear Market Performance

Decile Rank (5-year period)

Worst — Best

	Worst 3 Mo Period 1985-89	Worst 3 Mo Period 1990-94
Ariel Appreciation A	---	-22.44
+/- S&P 500	---	-8.69
+/- Best Fit Index : SPMid400	---	-4.66

Trailing Returns

	Total Return %	+/- S&P 500	+/- Wil 5000	% Rank All	% Rank Obj	Growth of $10,000
3 Mo	-3.90	-3.88	-3.13	88	88	9,610
6 Mo	-3.37	-8.23	-7.99	95	98	9,663
1 Yr	-8.39	-9.71	-8.32	88	91	9,161
3 Yr Avg	3.85	-2.42	-2.77	73	66	11,199
5 Yr Avg	7.99	-0.70	-0.83	33	62	14,687
10 Yr Avg	---	---	---	---	---	---
15 Yr Avg	---	---	---	---	---	---

Operations

Address and Telephone	307 N. Michigan Avenue Suite 500 Chicago, IL 60601 800-292-7435 / 301-951-4820
Advisor	Ariel Capital Management
Subadvisor	None
Distributor	Ariel Capital Management
States Available	All
Report Grade	B+
Income Distrib	Paid Annually
* Date of Inception	12-01-89
Fiscal Year End	September

Risk Analysis

Time Period	Load-Adj Return %	Risk % Rank [1] All	Obj	Morningstar [2] Return	Morningstar Risk	Morningstar Risk-Adj Rating
1 Yr	-8.39					
3 Yr	3.85	73	38	0.08 [3]	0.83	★★★
5 Yr	7.99	76	48	0.81 [3]	0.90	★★★
10 Yr	---					

Average Historical Rating (25 months)   2.8 ★s

[1] 1 = low, 100 = high   [2] 1.00 = Equity Avg   [3] 1.00 = 90-day T-bill return

Other Measures

			Standard S&P 500	Best Fit SPMid400
Standard Deviation	9.20	Alpha	-1.6	-2.3
Mean	4.20	Beta	0.79	0.78
Sharpe Ratio	0.07	R-Squared	46	69

Investment Style

	Stock Portfolio Avg	Relative S&P 500
Price/Earnings Ratio	15.0	0.81
Price/Book Ratio	2.9	0.86
5 Yr Earnings Gr %	8.3	1.50
Return on Assets %	8.2	1.09
Debt % Total Cap	25.8	0.91
Med Mkt Cap ($mil)	649	0.05

Style: Value Blend Growth / Size Large Med Small

Diversification Value for Portfolio Types

Large Cap: Medium	Small Cap: Low	Bond: High	Balanced: Medium	Diversified: Medium

Expenses & Fees

Min Initial Purchase	$1000 (Addt'l: $50)
Min IRA Purchase	$1000 (Addt'l: $50)
Min Auto Invest Plan	$50 (Systematic Inv: $50)

Sales Fees	0.00% front
	0.00% deferred
	0.30% 12b-1
Management Fee	0.25% flat fee, 0.50%A
3-,5-,10-yr Expense Projections	$43, $75, $104
Annual Brokerage Cost	0.00%

Portfolio 09-30-94

Share Chg (03-94) 000	Amount 000	Total Stocks: 45 Total Fixed-Income: 0	Value $000	% Net Assets
-74	456	Interco	6500	4.01
-93	319	Rouse	6141	3.78
-22	109	Omnicom Group	5472	3.37
2	163	Russell	4986	3.07
-114	177	Vivra	4823	2.97
0	166	American Greetings Cl A	4796	2.96
-80	258	Juno Lighting	4699	2.90
0	159	Hasbro	4699	2.90
-8	134	Leggett & Platt	4673	2.88
3	134	Stanhome	4566	2.81
3	425	Payless Cashways	4519	2.78
-184	208	Shorewood Packaging	4480	2.76
1	184	Watts Industries Cl A	4452	2.74
4	268	Duff & Phelps	4314	2.66
-21	210	Merry Land & Investment	4122	2.54
-37	119	Sybron International	4088	2.52
0	68	MBIA	4084	2.52
-19	121	Universal Foods	3588	2.21
-15	154	Armor All Products	3576	2.20
-31	87	Houghton Mifflin	3572	2.20
11	183	Harte-Hanks Communications	3543	2.18
0	100	Longs Drug Stores	3457	2.13
-56	73	Carnival Cl A	3181	1.96
-43	104	Invacare	3065	1.89
-88	187	Bergen Brunswig Cl A	3058	1.88

Composition % 12-31-94

Cash	-5.6	Preferreds	0.0
Stocks	105.6	Convertibles	0.0
Bonds	0.0	Other	0.0

Tax Analysis

	Tax-Adj Historical Return %	% Pretax Return
3 Yr Avg	2.94	75.7
5 Yr Avg	7.24	89.3
10 Yr Avg	---	---
Potential Capital Gain Exposure (% of assets)		10%

Most Similar Funds in MF500

Ariel Growth	Fair Fit
Enterprise Capital Apprec	Weak Fit
Babson Enterprise II	Weak Fit

Index Allocation

	% of Stocks
S&P 500	20.8
S&P MidCap 400	27.6
U.S. Small Cap	51.6
Foreign	0.0

Sector Weightings

	% of Stocks	Relative S&P 500
Utilities	0.0	0.00
Energy	0.0	0.00
Financials	12.3	1.16
Industrial Cyclicals	15.4	0.94
Consumer Durables	19.1	3.07
Consumer Staples	7.9	0.63
Services	20.4	2.50
Retail	6.9	1.19
Health	14.7	1.69
Technology	3.4	0.37

Ariel Growth

	Ticker	Load	NAV	Yield	SEC Yield	Assets	Objective
	ARGFX	Clsd	26.98	0.8%	N/A	130.8	Small Company

Ariel Growth Fund seeks long-term capital appreciation.

The fund normally invests at least 80% of its assets in equities, emphasizing companies with capitalizations under $1.5 billion. The balance may be invested in investment-grade debt securities and U.S. government obligations. The fund favors securities with low P/E ratios and companies that have demonstrated long-term performance through various economic cycles. The fund may not invest in weapons systems manufacturers or nuclear energy producers.

Prior to June 30, 1988, the fund was named Ariel Growth Fund. From that date until Sept. 6, 1994, it was named Calvert-Ariel Growth Fund.

Manager's Investment Style

Management seeks smaller firms with earnings-growth rates of at least 12% per year and good management. It has typically found such stocks in the consumer-goods arena, where it has maintained a significant long-term weighting. The fund is highly concentrated, and sells only rarely.

Fund Manager(s)

John W. Rogers, Jr., since 09-86. Birthdate: 03-58. BA, Princeton U. 1980

Manager Experience

	Dates Managed	Invest Obj	Std Dev	+/- Index
Not available.				

Historical Profile

Return	Below Average
Risk	Average
Rating	★★
	Closed

Average % Stocks Held in Portfolio: 97% 96% 82% 93% 94% 99% 99% 101%

Investment Style History Equity

Average % Stocks Held in Portfolio

Growth of $10,000

IIII Value of Fund ($000)
— Value of Index ($000) Wil 4500
▼ Manager Change
▽ Partial Manager Change
► Mgr Unknown After
◄ Mgr Unknown Before

Performance Quartile (Within Objective)

1983	1984	1985	1986	1987	1988	1989	1990	1991	1992	1993	1994	History
---	---	---	15.53	16.50	22.55	27.68	22.94	29.10	29.74	30.19	26.98	NAV
---	---	---	3.60 *	11.40	39.93	25.11	-16.08	32.72	11.73	8.75	-4.22	Total Return %
---	---	---	-2.94 *	6.14	23.32	-6.58	-12.97	2.24	4.11	-1.30	-5.54	+/- S&P 500
---	---	---	---	14.91	19.39	1.16	-2.53	-10.73	-0.03	-5.78	-1.57	+/- Wilshire 4500
---	---	---	0.07	0.34	0.77	1.69	1.04	1.91	2.63	1.03	0.86	Income Return %
---	---	---	3.53	11.06	39.16	23.41	-17.12	30.81	9.10	7.72	-5.08	Capital Return %
---	---	---	---	9	1	23	94	23	16	75	56	Total Rtn % Rank All
---	---	---	---	4	2	39	79	89	60	84	75	Total Rtn % Rank Obj
---	---	---	0.01	0.06	0.15	0.39	0.28	0.47	0.75	0.30	0.23	Income $
---	---	---	0.00	0.74	0.38	0.13	0.00	0.79	1.92	1.73	1.70	Capital Gains $
---	---	---	0.22	1.23	1.56	1.41	1.31	1.25	1.23	1.16	1.25	Expense Ratio %
---	---	---	---	0.54	-1.47	2.32	1.28	1.72	0.83	0.72	0.56	Income Ratio %
---	---	---	---	60	22	14	20	39	19	13	9	Turnover Rate %
---	---	---	2.6	6.5	36.1	179.8	207.5	262.3	254.7	225.8	130.8	Net Assets ($mil)

Performance 12-31-94

	1st Qtr	2nd Qtr	3rd Qtr	4th Qtr	Total
1987	15.45	3.46	13.10	-17.54	11.40
1988	20.30	12.91	-0.22	3.24	39.93
1989	7.23	7.73	6.95	1.26	25.11
1990	-4.77	5.50	-25.39	11.94	-16.08
1991	18.88	1.25	4.27	5.75	32.72
1992	2.41	-2.62	1.96	9.88	11.73
1993	2.72	-5.60	5.62	6.18	8.75
1994	-5.33	-0.59	1.48	0.29	-4.22

Bear Market Performance

Decile Rank (5-year period)

Worst | | Best

	Worst 3 Mo Period 1985-89	Worst 3 Mo Period 1990-94
Ariel Growth	---	-25.39
+/- S&P 500	---	-11.64
+/- Best Fit Index : Wil 4500	---	-7.16

Trailing Returns

	Total Return %	+/- S&P 500	+/- Wil 4500	% Rank All	% Rank Obj	Growth of $10,000
3 Mo	0.29	0.31	2.80	15	34	10,029
6 Mo	1.78	-3.08	-2.42	28	84	10,178
1 Yr	-4.22	-5.54	-1.57	56	75	9,578
3 Yr Avg	5.19	-1.08	-2.42	44	82	11,638
5 Yr Avg	5.33	-3.37	-3.77	86	93	12,962
10 Yr Avg	---	---	---	---	---	---
15 Yr Avg	---	---	---	---	---	---

Operations

Address and Telephone	307 N. Michigan Avenue Suite 500 Chicago, IL 60601 800-292-7435 / 301-951-4820
Advisor	Ariel Capital Management
Subadvisor	None
Distributor	Ariel Capital Management
States Available	All
Report Grade	B+
Income Distrib	Paid Annually
* Date of Inception	09-29-86
Fiscal Year End	September

Risk Analysis

Time Period	Load-Adj Return %	Risk % Rank All	Obj	Morningstar Return	Morningstar Risk	Morningstar Risk-Adj Rating
1 Yr	-4.22					
3 Yr	5.19	71	27	0.47[3]	0.80	★★★
5 Yr	5.33	82	39	0.14[3]	1.00	★★
10 Yr	---	---	---	---	---	

Average Historical Rating (64 months) 3.0 ★s

[1] 1 = low, 100 = high [2] 1.00 = Equity Avg [3] 1.00 = 90-day T-bill return

Other Measures

				Standard S&P 500	Best Fit Wil 4500
Standard Deviation	9.36	Alpha		0.0	-1.2
Mean	5.51	Beta		0.69	0.75
Sharpe Ratio	0.21	R-Squared		35	62

Investment Style

	Stock Portfolio Avg	Relative S&P 500
Price/Earnings Ratio	15.9	0.86
Price/Book Ratio	3.0	0.88
5 Yr Earnings Gr %	1.4	0.25
Return on Assets %	8.4	1.12
Debt % Total Cap	24.2	0.86
Med Mkt Cap ($mil)	723	0.06

Style Value Blend Growth — Size Large Med Small

Diversification Value for Portfolio Types

Large Cap: Medium	Small Cap: Low	Bond: High	Balanced: Medium	Diversified: Medium

Expenses & Fees

Sales Fees	
	0.00% front
	0.00% deferred
	0.30% 12b-1
Management Fee	0.25% flat fee, 0.40%A
3-,5-,10-yr Expense Projections	$40, $68, $151
Annual Brokerage Cost	0.00%

Min Initial Purchase	Closed (Addt'l: $50)
Min IRA Purchase	$1000 (Addt'l: $50)
Min Auto Invest Plan	$50 (Systematic Inv: $50)

Portfolio 09-30-94

Share Chg (03-94) 000	Amount 000	Total Stocks: 34 Total Fixed-Income: 0	Value $000	% Net Assets
-78	201	Longs Drug Stores	6961	4.66
-66	407	Enquirer/Star Group Cl A	6860	4.59
-54	132	Clorox	6860	4.59
-91	199	First Brands	6661	4.46
-77	216	Russell	6599	4.41
-68	341	Rouse	6564	4.39
-24	223	Central Newspapers Cl A	6342	4.24
-35	285	Ecolab	6206	4.15
-6	201	Hasbro	5937	3.97
-91	262	Shorewood Packaging	5636	3.77
-75	112	Omnicom Group	5634	3.77
0	165	T Rowe Price Associates	5542	3.71
-69	330	Bergen Brunswig Cl A	5409	3.62
-59	155	Stanhome	5285	3.53
0	466	Payless Cashways	4948	3.31
-48	228	General Binding	4699	3.14
-60	351	Interface Cl A	4568	3.06
-35	162	Angelica	4507	3.01
92	92	Caesars World	4006	2.68
48	190	McCormick	3767	2.52
-60	335	United Stationers	3430	2.29
-40	221	Sealright	3423	2.29
-24	117	American Greetings Cl A	3388	2.27
-13	125	Johnson Worldwide Cl A	3314	2.22
-75	201	Hunt Manufacturing	3308	2.21

Composition % 12-31-94

Cash	-4.6	Preferreds	0.0
Stocks	104.6	Convertibles	0.0
Bonds	0.0	Other	0.0

Tax Analysis

	Tax-Adj Historical Return %	% Pretax Return
3 Yr Avg	3.01	56.7
5 Yr Avg	3.67	66.7
10 Yr Avg	---	---
Potential Capital Gain Exposure (% of assets)		20%

Most Similar Funds in MF500

Ariel Appreciation A	Fair Fit
T. Rowe Price New America G	Weak Fit
Nicholas II	Weak Fit

Index Allocation

	% of Stocks
S&P 500	25.0
S&P MidCap 400	30.9
U.S. Small Cap	44.1
Foreign	0.0

Sector Weightings

	% of Stocks	Relative S&P 500
Utilities	0.0	0.00
Energy	0.0	0.00
Financials	6.1	0.57
Industrial Cyclicals	21.0	1.28
Consumer Durables	23.8	3.84
Consumer Staples	18.9	1.51
Services	15.7	1.93
Retail	10.7	1.85
Health	3.8	0.44
Technology	0.0	0.00

MORNINGSTAR 1995 Mutual Fund 500

Asia Pacific

	Ticker	NAV	Mkt Price	Prem/Disc	Yield	Objective
	APB	$13.89	$13.75	-1.0%	0.1%	Pacific/Asia

Asia Pacific Fund seeks long-term capital appreciation.

The fund normally invests at least 80% of its assets in companies in Hong Kong, Korea, Malaysia, the Philippines, Singapore, Taiwan, and Thailand. There is no limit to the percentage of assets that may be invested in any one country. The fund may engage in hedging transactions.

Shareholders have the option to open-end the fund if, during the 12 weeks preceding May 15 of each year, the fund's average discount from NAV is more than 5%. Approval to open-end, liquidate, or amend the articles of incorporation requires the approval of two thirds of the outstanding shares.

The fund may leverage its assets with a credit facility provided through Deutche Bank.

The fund held two rights offerings in 1993; both were oversubscribed. In January, the fund raised $26 million. In December, it raised $49.5 million.

Historical Profile
Return — Above Average
Risk — Above Average
Rating ★★★★ — Above Average

| | 7.1 | -10.8 | 12.5 | 29.4 | 4.7 | 23.6 | 34.9 | 27.7 | Highest Prem/Disc |
| | -34.7 | -28.6 | -24.9 | -17.2 | -13.4 | 0.0 | -5.6 | -6.3 | Lowest Prem/Disc |

Growth of $10,000
— at NAV ($000)
— at Market Price ($000)

Premium Discount %

Manager's Investment Style

Management takes a top-down approach to the Pacific Rim's emerging markets. It first considers the growth, liquidity, and valuations of the region's markets, and then zeros in on particular sectors and themes. Management has shown a willingness to take large positions in only a few markets: The portfolio's Hong Kong position, for example, has swelled over 40% of assets in the past. Additionally, the fund regularly borrows to take advantage of market opportunities, which exacerbates risk.

Fund Manager(s)
David Brennan. Since 5-87. MA'79 Oxford U.; '82 New York U.

1983	1984	1985	1986	1987	1988	1989	1990	1991	1992	1993	1994	History
---	---	---	---	6.70	8.90	15.78	12.04	12.22	12.46	21.29	13.89	NAV
---	---	---	---	-27.96*	34.13	78.90	-15.25	23.10	13.58	105.88	-21.70	NAV Total Return %
---	---	---	---	-15.17*	17.52	47.22	-12.13	-7.39	5.96	95.83	-23.02	+/- S&P 500
---	---	---	---	---	5.86	68.37	8.20	10.97	25.75	73.32	-29.48	+/- MSCI EAFE
---	---	---	---	---	-29.12	41.16	16.34	9.98	7.39	19.87	-12.80	+/- MSCI FE ex Jpn
---	---	---	---	0.00*	1.29	0.22	4.78	1.30	0.60	0.00	0.18	Income Return %
---	---	---	---	-27.96*	32.84	78.68	-20.03	21.80	12.97	105.88	-21.88	Capital Return %
---	---	---	---	---	6	2	85	37	21	1	95	Total Rtn % Rank All
---	---	---	---	---	33	25	50	26	26	5	72	Total Rtn % Rank Obj
---	---	---	---	-56.25*	47.13	180.94	-36.64	52.73	31.05	106.56	-35.29	Market Total Rtn %
---	---	---	---	-9.4	-22.6	-9.2	-8.5	-3.7	10.2	17.2	11.9	Avg Prem/Disc %
---	---	---	---	0.00	0.07	0.04	0.71	0.16	0.09	0.00	0.02	Income $
---	---	---	---	0.00	0.00	0.14	0.58	2.32	1.65	3.30	3.10	Capital Gains $
---	---	---	---	2.30	2.91	2.41	2.13	2.19	2.57	2.37	3.71	Expense Ratio %
---	---	---	---	-0.20	0.67	-0.12	0.56	0.70	0.76	-0.33	0.10	Income Ratio %
---	---	---	---	---	39	46	37	63	105	101	---	Turnover Rate %
---	---	---	---	100.0	69.3	127.2	105.9	107.6	110.5	298.2	196.1	Net Assets ($mil)
---	---	---	---	7.7	6.4	5.0	3.5	1.8	20.0	26.0	10.0	Pfd/Debt Leverage ($mil)

Manager Experience

	Dates Managed	Invest Obj	Std Dev	+/- Index
Not available.				

NAV Performance % 12-30-94

	1st Qtr	2nd Qtr	3rd Qtr	4th Qtr	Total
1987	---	4.19*	20.02	-42.39	-27.96*
1988	20.00	8.71	-8.24	12.05	34.13
1989	22.81	7.87	24.26	8.69	78.90
1990	-0.57	8.79	-28.93	10.25	-15.25
1991	18.27	-1.39	-0.75	6.34	23.10
1992	9.74	12.90	-9.86	1.70	13.58
1993	7.60	6.20	17.75	53.01	105.88
1994	-23.49	0.37	12.64	-9.48	-21.70

Bear Market Performance

Decile Rank (5-year period)

Worst — Best

	Worst 3 Mo Period 1985-89	Worst 3 Mo Period 1990-94
Asia Pacific	---	-28.93
+/- S&P 500	---	-15.18

Trailing Returns

	NAV Total Return %	+/- S&P 500	+/- MSCI FE ex Jpn	% Rank All	% Rank Obj	Mkt Total Return %
3 Mo	-9.48	-9.47	-1.22	93	67	-20.36
6 Mo	1.96	-2.91	-3.40	20	33	-16.95
1 Yr	-21.70	-23.02	-12.80	95	72	-35.29
3 Yr Avg	22.34	16.07	0.71	5	33	20.55
5 Yr Avg	13.82	5.13	6.97	9	40	11.13
Incept Avg	16.87*	---	---	---	---	15.74*

Operations

Address and Telephone	One Seaport Plaza New York, NY 10292 212-214-3334 / 800-451-6788	Income Distrib Schedule	Paid Irregularly
		Management Fee	1.10%, 0.25%A
Advisor	Baring International Investment	Reinvestment Plan	Yes
Subadvisor	N/A	Direct Purchase Plan	No
Administrator	Prudential Mutual Fund Mgmt., Inc.	Shares Outstanding	8,660,000
Transfer Agent	State Street Bank and Trust Co.	Exchange	NYSE
Custodian	State Street Bank and Trust Co.	*Date of Inception	05-04-87
Auditor	Deloitte & Touche	Shareholder Report	A
Legal Counsel	Sullivan & Cromwell		

Risk Analysis

	Risk % Rank[1] All	Obj	Morningstar[2] Return	Risk	Morningstar[3] Risk-Adj Rating
3 Yr	92	46	2.87	1.27	★★★★
5 Yr	92	30	1.89	1.22	★★★★
10 Yr	---	---	---	---	
Average Historical Rating (56 months)				4.1	★s

[1] = Low, 100 = High [2] 1.00 = Equity Avg [3] 1.00 = 90-day T-bill Return

Other Measures

			S&P 500
Standard Deviation	27.28	Alpha	18.59
Mean	23.86	Beta	1.10
Sharpe Ratio	0.75	R-Squared	10

Investment Style

	Stock Portfolio Avg	Rel WS Pac ex Jpn	Rel WS Foreign
Price/Earnings Ratio	23.7	0.81	0.48
Price/Cash Flow Ratio	22.8#	1.21	1.56
Price/Book Ratio	2.9	0.70	0.96
5 Yr Earnings Gr %	18.1#	0.78	NMF
Return on Assets %	8.7#	0.81	1.89
Debt % Total Cap	21.2	1.09	0.66
Med Mkt Cap ($mil)	7114	1.56	1.13

figure is based on less than 50% of stocks

Country Exposure (top five) 01-04-95

Securities %		Currency %	
Hong Kong	30	Hong Kong	30
Thailand	21	Thailand	21
Singapore	14	Singapore	14
South Korea	11	South Korea	11
India	6	India	6

Diversification Value for Portfolio Types

Large Cap: High | Small Cap: High | Bond: High | Balanced: High | Diversified: High

Portfolio 09-30-94

Total Equity: 102
Total Fixed-Income: 4

Share Chg (03-94)	Amount		Value $000	% Total Invest
0	2387000	Hutchison Whampoa	11275	4.81
13761	62310	Samsung Electronics	10525	4.49
0	88000	Pohang Iron & Steel	9773	4.17
0	1876000	Cheung Kong Holdings	9128	3.90
625000	957000	Swire Pacific Cl A	7493	3.20
269000	728470	Siam Commercial Bank	7059	3.01
359000	948000	Sun Hung Kai Properties	7054	3.01
0	993000	Hang Seng Bank	6972	2.98
160000	624200	HSBC Holdings (HK)	6967	2.98
0	123000	Siam Cement	6402	2.73
208000	772670	Thai Farmers Bank	6095	2.60
1495000	1755000	New World Development	6053	2.58
119324	357972	Manila Electric Cl B	4629	1.98
50524	218939	Regional Container Lines	4383	1.87
0	7450000	Great Eagle Holdings	4319	1.84
410000	410000	Development Bank Singapore	4314	1.84
0	722000	Tenaga National	3802	1.62
0	184000	Land & House	3654	1.56
1132000	1132000	Citic Pacific	3501	1.50
0	425000	Telekom Malaysia	3332	1.42
780000	2730000	Indah Kiat Pulp & Paper	3293	1.41
470000	470000	Malayan Banking	3135	1.34
2165000	2165000	Marco Polo Developments	3038	1.30
288000	288000	United Overseas Bank	2895	1.24
0	601000	Television Broadcasts	2792	1.19

Composition % 12-31-94

Cash	5.5	Preferreds	0.1
Stocks	94.0	Convertibles	0.5
Bonds	0.0	Other	0.0
Leverage factor: 1.05			

Tax Analysis

	Tax-Adj Historical Return %	% Pretax Return
3 Yr Avg	18.00	72.5
5 Yr Avg	9.48	59.2
10 Yr Avg	---	---

Potential Capital Gain Exposure (% of assets) 17

Most Similar Funds in MF500

T. Rowe Price New Asia	Fair Fit
Newport Tiger	Weak Fit
Malaysia Fund	Weak Fit

Sector Weightings

	% of Stocks
Utilities	8.1
Energy	0.3
Financials	44.8
Industrial Cyclicals	19.1
Consumer Durables	15.3
Consumer Staples	0.5
Services	10.6
Retail	0.1
Health	0.5
Technology	0.7

Babson Bond L

	Ticker	Load	NAV	Yield	SEC Yield	Assets	Objective
	BABIX	None	1.47	7.3%	N/A	139.0	Corp Hi Qlty

Babson Bond Trust Portfolio L seeks current income and reasonable stability of principal.

The fund normally invests at least 80% of its assets in direct or guaranteed obligations of the U.S. government and its agencies, and in investment-quality debt securities issued by corporations or other business organizations. The fund usually invests in bonds rated A or better. Up to 25% of its assets, however, may be invested in securities rated BBB.

Prior to March 31, 1988, the fund was named Babson Bond Trust.

Manager's Investment Style

Management typically maintains neutral credit and interest-rate exposures by keeping its average credit quality in the AA range and its average duration close to that of the Lehman Brothers Aggregate Bond Index. It tries to pick up added yield by keeping hefty stakes in lower-rated investment-grade bonds (barbelled against a large stake in governments) and investing portions of assets in more-unusual issues, such as Canadian Yankee bonds, mortgage issues, and a few derivatives. It is management's policy to remain fully invested.

Fund Manager(s)

Edward L. Martin CFA, since 1984. Birthdate: 1949. BA, Washington U. 1971 MBA, Suffolk U. (MA) 1977

Manager Experience

	Dates Managed	Invest Obj	Std Dev	+/- Index
Edward L. Martin				
Babson Bond S	04/88 - 12/94	CQ	3.12	-1.18

Historical Profile	
Return	Above Average
Risk	Average
Rating	★★★★
	Above Average

Investment Style History
Fixed Income
Income Rtn % Rank Obj

| | 17 | 4 | 13 | 21 | 19 | 15 | 9 | 8 |

Growth of $10,000

- ||| Value of Fund ($000)
- — Value of Index ($000) LB Govt
- ▼ Manager Change
- ▽ Partial Manager Change
- ► Mgr Unknown After
- ◄ Mgr Unknown Before

Performance Quartile (Within Objective)

1983	1984	1985	1986	1987	1988	1989	1990	1991	1992	1993	1994	History
1.49	1.50	1.63	1.69	1.56	1.51	1.56	1.54	1.63	1.62	1.63	1.47	NAV
9.63	12.97	20.65	13.88	1.94	7.17	13.13	7.78	14.99	7.97	11.15	-3.29	Total Return %
1.26	-2.18	-1.47	-1.37	-0.82	-0.71	-1.42	-1.16	-1.01	0.72	1.39	-0.37	+/- LB Aggregate
0.36	-3.65	-3.41	-2.66	-0.62	-2.05	-0.86	0.63	-3.51	-0.73	-1.02	0.64	+/- LB Corporate
11.60	12.30	11.99	10.20	9.63	10.38	9.81	9.07	9.15	7.91	7.33	6.53	Income Return %
-1.97	0.67	8.67	3.68	-7.69	-3.21	3.31	-1.28	5.84	0.06	3.82	-9.82	Capital Return %
82	13	69	62	43	79	53	16	58	46	58	46	Total Rtn % Rank All
21	47	44	42	55	50	21	58	47	9	17	61	Total Rtn % Rank Obj
0.17	0.17	0.16	0.16	0.16	0.16	0.14	0.13	0.13	0.12	0.12	0.11	Income $
0.00	0.00	0.00	0.00	0.00	0.00	0.00	0.00	0.00	0.01	0.05	0.00	Capital Gains $
0.75	0.92	0.98	0.97	0.97	0.97	0.97	0.97	0.98	0.99	0.98	---	Expense Ratio %
11.08	11.31	10.45	9.42	9.29	9.99	9.19	8.81	8.42	7.67	7.00	---	Income Ratio %
49	42	39	41	54	42	51	51	75	54	80	---	Turnover Rate %
37.1	42.1	54.7	62.0	64.2	66.7	77.1	91.1	114.8	145.0	160.4	139.0	Net Assets ($mil)

Performance 12-31-94

	1st Qtr	2nd Qtr	3rd Qtr	4th Qtr	Total
1987	2.23	-2.64	-2.70	5.25	1.94
1988	3.19	0.14	1.82	1.87	7.17
1989	1.06	7.82	0.93	2.86	13.13
1990	-0.41	2.90	0.90	4.24	7.78
1991	2.83	0.82	6.04	4.60	14.99
1992	-1.14	4.54	4.37	0.09	7.97
1993	4.30	3.00	2.89	0.55	11.15
1994	-2.67	-1.50	1.08	-0.19	-3.29

Bear Market Performance

Decile Rank (5-year period)

Worst ———————————— Best

	Worst 3 Mo Period 1985-89	Worst 3 Mo Period 1990-94
Babson Bond L	-3.85	-5.09
+/- LB Aggregate	-0.29	-0.16
+/- Best Fit Index : LB Govt	-0.39	-0.01

Trailing Returns

	Total Return %	+/- LB Aggregate	+/- LB Corporate	% Rank All	% Rank Obj	Growth of $10,000
3 Mo	-0.19	-0.57	-0.63	27	78	9,981
6 Mo	0.88	-0.11	-0.29	40	33	10,088
1 Yr	-3.29	-0.37	0.64	46	61	9,671
3 Yr Avg	5.09	0.54	-0.33	46	9	11,605
5 Yr Avg	7.54	-0.08	-0.72	40	15	14,384
10 Yr Avg	9.34	-0.60	-1.29	66	29	24,424
15 Yr Avg	10.08	-0.73	-1.25	76	42	42,216

Operations

Address and Telephone	Three Crown Cntr 2440 Pershing Rd. Kansas City, MO 64108 800-422-2766 / 816-471-5200
Advisor	Jones & Babson
Subadvisor	David L. Babson & Company
Distributor	Jones & Babson
States Available	All plus PR
Report Grade	B
Income Distrib	Paid Monthly
Date of Inception	04-01-45
Fiscal Year End	November

Risk Analysis

Time Period	Load-Adj Return %	Risk % Rank [1] All	Obj	Morningstar [2] Return	Morningstar Risk	Morningstar Risk-Adj Rating
1 Yr	-3.29					
3 Yr	5.09	23	61	0.44 [3]	1.01	★★★★
5 Yr	7.54	22	61	0.69 [3]	0.98	★★★★
10 Yr	9.34	16	37	0.92 [3]	0.98	★★★★

Average Historical Rating (109 months)   4.0 ★s

[1] 1 = low, 100 = high   [2] 1.00 = Taxable Avg   [3] 1.00 = 90-day T-bill return

Other Measures

			Standard LB Agg	Best Fit LB Govt
Standard Deviation	4.22	Alpha	0.5	0.5
Mean	5.06	Beta	1.01	0.94
Sharpe Ratio	0.36	R-Squared	92	93

Investment Style

Interest-Rate Stance

Avg Effective Duration	4.9 Yrs
Avg Effective Maturity	8.2 Yrs

Maturity Short Intm Long

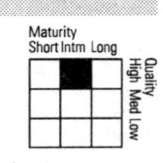

Quality

Avg Credit Quality	AA
Avg Weighted Coupon	9.14%
Avg Weighted Price	100.95% of Par

Diversification Value for Portfolio Types

Large Cap: High	Small Cap: High	Bond: None	Balanced: Medium	Diversified: High

Portfolio 12-31-94

		Total Stocks: 0		

Amount 000	Date of Maturity	Total Fixed-Income: 65	Value $000	% Net Assets
6050	12-15-20	Province Saskatchewan 9.375%	6327	4.55
4885	11-15-12	US Treasury Bond 10.375%	5813	4.18
5475	07-15-98	US Treasury Note 8.25%	5543	3.99
5000	08-01-00	CSX 9.5%	5226	3.76
4250	03-15-12	Province of Ontario 15.75%	5062	3.64
5000	11-18-98	Cooper Industries 7.87%	4929	3.55
4650	07-29-03	Chemical Bank FRN	4493	3.23
4500	11-17-97	GMAC 7.85%	4418	3.18
5000	03-15-23	Time Warner Entertnmnt 8.375%	4151	2.99
4000	12-15-06	FHLMC CMO 8.5%	4005	2.88
3500	02-15-97	Long Island Lighting 8.75%	3495	2.51
3250	06-15-10	Hydro-Quebec 10.75%	3415	2.46
3250	01-15-97	Comdisco 9.75%	3320	2.39
3650	02-15-03	US Treasury Note 6.25%	3301	2.38
4000	02-09-24	Province of Quebec 7.125%	3214	2.31
2850	02-15-16	US Treasury Bond 9.25%	3207	2.31
2500	06-15-05	Columbia Gas System 9.62%	3050	2.19
3000	05-15-97	US Treasury Note 8.5%	3045	2.19
3000	05-15-97	US Treasury Note 6.5%	2917	2.10
2450	11-15-11	British Col Hydro Pwr 15.5%	2892	2.08
2750	05-25-19	FNMA CMO 9.3%	2765	1.99
3000	03-01-23	Georgia-Pacific 8.25%	2682	1.93
2500	11-15-00	Ford Capital BV 10.125%	2668	1.92
2750	10-15-17	Green Tree Finl CMO REMIC 6.7%	2521	1.81
2500	07-22-03	First Union FRN	2431	1.75

Composition % 12-31-94

Cash	3.0	Preferreds	0.0
Stocks	0.0	Convertibles	0.0
Bonds	97.1	Other	0.0

Tax Analysis

	Tax-Adj Historical Return %	% Pretax Return
3 Yr Avg	2.05	39.0
5 Yr Avg	4.57	57.2
10 Yr Avg	5.76	52.1

Potential Capital Gain Exposure
(% of assets)   -14%

Most Similar Funds in MF500

Portico Bond Immdex Ret	Strong Fit
Columbia Fixed-Income Secs	Strong Fit
Strong Government Securities	Strong Fit

Coupon Range

	% of Bonds	Rel Obj
0%	0.6	0.28
0% to 8.5%	45.7	0.65
8.5% to 9.5%	21.4	1.63
9.5% to 11%	18.1	3.95
More than 11%	8.8	3.79
Not applicable	5.4	0.71

Credit Analysis 12-31-94

% of Bonds

US Govt	34	BB	0
AAA	3	B	0
AA	11	Below B	2
A	25	NR/NA	0
BBB	25		

Expenses & Fees

Sales Fees	0.00% front
	0.00% deferred
	0.00% 12b-1
Management Fee	0.95% flat fee
3-,5-,10-yr Expense Projections	$31, $54, $120

Min Initial Purchase	$500 (Addt'l: $50)
Min IRA Purchase	$250 (Addt'l: $50)
Min Auto Invest Plan	$100 (Systematic Inv: $100)

 **1995 Mutual Fund 500**

Babson Enterprise

	Ticker	Load	NAV	Yield	SEC Yield	Assets	Objective
	BABEX	Clsd	15.15	0.2%	N/A	190.5	Small Company

Babson Enterprise Fund seeks long-term growth of capital.

The fund normally invests at least 80% of its assets in common stocks of small, fast-growing companies. The fund uses three primary criteria when selecting its investments: 1) small market capitalization (total market value of outstanding shares), usually $15 million to $300 million; 2) potential for strong earnings stemming from favorable sales gains and superior return-on-equity capital; and 3) reasonable stock valuation. Preferred stocks, bonds, or other issues may also be acquired for defensive purposes.

Manager's Investment Style

Management seeks tiny stocks that are not well known by the market. It buys firms with good sales or returns on equity because of their high earnings-growth potential, and focuses primarily on inexpensive stocks, especially in the industrial or computer-products sectors. It maintains a five-year time horizon for its purchases.

Fund Manager(s)

Peter C. Schliemann, since 01-85. Birthdate: 1945. BA, Amherst C. 1967 MBA, Harvard 1969

Manager Experience

	Dates Managed	Invest Obj	Std Dev	+/- Index
Peter C. Schliemann				
Shadow Stock	08/87 - 12/94	SC	15.55	-2.96
Babson Enterprise II	08/91 - 12/94	SC	10.77	2.24

Historical Profile

Return	Above Average
Risk	Average
Rating	★★★★
	Closed

93% 90% 92% 93% 93% 94% 93% 96%

Investment Style History
Equity
Average % Stocks Held in Portfolio

Growth of $10,000
- IIII Value of Fund ($000)
- — Value of Index ($000) Russ 2000
- ▼ Manager Change
- ▽ Partial Manager Change
- ► Mgr Unknown After
- ◄ Mgr Unknown Before

Performance Quartile (Within Objective)

1983	1984	1985	1986	1987	1988	1989	1990	1991	1992	1993	1994	History
9.92	9.22	12.78	12.12	9.22	11.39	13.06	10.55	14.19	15.22	16.51	15.15	NAV
-0.80 *	-4.99	38.61	9.01	-9.19	32.47	22.46	-15.87	43.04	24.59	16.27	2.42	Total Return %
-0.85 *	-11.26	6.87	-9.67	-14.45	15.86	-9.22	-12.75	12.56	16.97	6.21	1.11	+/- S&P 500
---	-3.27	6.59	-2.75	-5.68	11.93	-1.48	-2.31	-0.41	12.83	1.73	5.08	+/- Wilshire 4500
0.00	0.76	0.00	0.37	0.74	0.50	1.49	1.15	0.61	0.58	0.34	0.25	Income Return %
-0.80	-5.75	38.61	8.64	-9.93	31.97	20.97	-17.02	42.43	24.01	15.93	2.17	Capital Return %
---	80	7	87	95	2	30	93	11	2	25	9	Total Rtn % Rank All
---	38	15	53	77	6	51	77	68	11	52	25	Total Rtn % Rank Obj
0.00	0.07	0.00	0.05	0.08	0.06	0.19	0.13	0.08	0.09	0.05	0.04	Income $
0.00	0.13	0.00	1.73	1.68	0.76	0.69	0.31	0.76	2.33	1.11	1.69	Capital Gains $
---	1.67	1.58	1.37	1.35	1.37	1.24	1.22	1.17	1.11	1.09	---	Expense Ratio %
---	0.73	0.62	0.42	0.23	0.50	1.74	1.08	0.66	0.57	0.33	---	Income Ratio %
---	14	38	32	24	41	15	10	15	28	17	---	Turnover Rate %
0.6	7.3	34.5	46.9	35.7	53.4	86.9	79.5	133.3	184.3	197.3	190.5	Net Assets ($mil)

Performance 12-31-94

	1st Qtr	2nd Qtr	3rd Qtr	4th Qtr	Total
1987	21.81	-1.84	5.76	-28.18	-9.19
1988	18.22	10.73	2.07	-0.86	32.47
1989	10.27	5.02	9.93	-3.80	22.46
1990	-1.84	4.76	-21.74	4.54	-15.87
1991	24.55	1.07	6.85	6.35	43.04
1992	13.81	-4.27	3.10	10.91	24.59
1993	6.83	-0.86	5.21	4.34	16.27
1994	-2.24	-0.68	5.37	0.12	2.42

Bear Market Performance

Decile Rank (5-year period)

Worst ▬ Best

	Worst 3 Mo Period 1985-89	Worst 3 Mo Period 1990-94
Babson Enterprise	-33.05	-25.27
+/- S&P 500	-3.47	-11.42
+/- Best Fit Index : Russ 2000	2.50	0.63

Trailing Returns

	Total Return %	+/- S&P 500	+/- Wil 4500	% Rank All	% Rank Obj	Growth of $10,000
3 Mo	0.12	0.14	2.62	18	36	10,012
6 Mo	5.49	0.63	1.30	10	50	10,549
1 Yr	2.42	1.11	5.08	9	25	10,242
3 Yr Avg	14.05	7.79	6.45	5	21	14,837
5 Yr Avg	12.29	3.60	3.20	8	43	17,855
10 Yr Avg	14.80	0.41	2.16	12	25	39,746
15 Yr Avg	---	---	---	---	---	---

Operations

Address and Telephone	Three Crown Cntr 2440 Pershing Rd. Kansas City, MO 64108 800-422-2766 / 816-471-5200
Advisor	Jones & Babson
Subadvisor	David L. Babson & Company
Distributor	Jones & Babson
States Available	All
Report Grade	B
Income Distrib	Paid Annually
* Date of Inception	12-02-83
Fiscal Year End	November

Risk Analysis

Time Period	Load-Adj Return %	Risk % Rank [1] All	Risk % Rank [1] Obj	Morningstar [2] Return	Morningstar Risk	Morningstar Risk-Adj Rating
1 Yr	2.42					
3 Yr	14.06	57	10	3.34 [3]	0.63	★★★★★
5 Yr	12.29	70	16	2.03 [3]	0.84	★★★★
10 Yr	14.80	67	10	1.44	0.89	★★★★

Average Historical Rating (97 months)   3.2 ★s

[1] 1 = low, 100 = high   [2] 1.00 = Equity Avg   [3] 1.00 = 90-day T-bill return

Other Measures

				Standard S&P 500	Best Fit Russ 2000
Standard Deviation	9.67	Alpha		8.8	4.4
Mean	13.68	Beta		0.58	0.73
Sharpe Ratio	1.05	R-Squared		23	79

Investment Style

	Stock Portfolio Avg	Relative S&P 500
Price/Earnings Ratio	18.9	1.02
Price/Book Ratio	1.7	0.50
5 Yr Earnings Gr %	-0.2	-0.04
Return on Assets %	5.6	0.75
Debt % Total Cap	28.6	1.01
Med Mkt Cap ($mil)	113	0.01

Style Value Blend Growth
Size Large Med Small

Diversification Value for Portfolio Types

Large Cap: High	Small Cap: Low	Bond: High	Balanced: Medium	Diversified: High

Min Initial Purchase Closed (Addt'l: $100)
Min IRA Purchase $250 (Addt'l: $50)
Min Auto Invest Plan $100 (Systematic Inv: $100)

Expenses & Fees

Sales Fees	0.00% front
	0.00% deferred
	0.00% 12b-1
Management Fee	1.50% max./1.00% min.
3-,5-,10-yr Expense Projections	$35, $60, $133
Annual Brokerage Cost	0.07%

Portfolio 12-31-94

Share Chg (11-94) 000	Amount 000	Total Stocks: 89 Total Fixed-Income: 0	Value $000	% Net Assets
0	269	Anthony Industries	4305	2.26
0	205	CDI	4082	2.14
0	234	Apogee Enterprises	4031	2.12
0	183	Furon	4019	2.11
0	209	Raymond	3861	2.03
0	338	Perry Drug Stores	3713	1.95
0	88	Pacific Scientific	3576	1.88
-27	211	GoodMark Foods	3486	1.83
0	386	Jason	3478	1.83
0	287	Brenco	3405	1.79
0	70	WH Brady Cl A	3390	1.78
0	195	Helen of Troy	3323	1.74
0	140	ABM Industries	3255	1.71
0	77	TCF Financial	3156	1.66
0	177	SyQuest Technology	3149	1.65
0	106	Toro	3050	1.60
0	111	American Filtrona	2992	1.57
0	248	Falcon Products	2908	1.53
0	189	Intl Recovery	2882	1.51
0	146	Alltrista	2876	1.51
0	217	Nichols Research	2769	1.45
0	98	West	2687	1.41
0	166	Material Sciences	2634	1.38
0	149	Norstan	2615	1.37
0	324	Schwitzer	2553	1.34

Composition % 12-31-94

Cash	4.2	Preferreds	0.0
Stocks	95.8	Convertibles	0.0
Bonds	0.0	Other	0.0

Tax Analysis

	Tax-Adj Historical Return %	% Pretax Return
3 Yr Avg	10.78	74.3
5 Yr Avg	9.71	75.0
10 Yr Avg	12.14	72.1
Potential Capital Gain Exposure (% of assets)		14%

Most Similar Funds in MF500

Columbia Special	Weak Fit
Strong Common Stock	Weak Fit
Pennsylvania Mutual	Weak Fit

Index Allocation

	% of Stocks
S&P 500	0.0
S&P MidCap 400	0.0
U.S. Small Cap	100.0
Foreign	0.0

Sector Weightings

	% of Stocks	Relative S&P 500
Utilities	0.0	0.00
Energy	3.5	0.35
Financials	5.9	0.56
Industrial Cyclicals	31.4	1.92
Consumer Durables	17.6	2.83
Consumer Staples	7.3	0.58
Services	15.8	1.94
Retail	6.2	1.07
Health	0.0	0.00
Technology	12.2	1.34

Babson Enterprise II

Babson Enterprise Fund II seeks long-term growth of capital.
The fund normally invests at least 80% of its assets in common stocks of small, fast-growing companies whose securities are considered to be realistically valued at the time of purchase. Valuation of such securities is based on price/earnings ratios, price relative to sales, and price/book ratios. Under normal conditions, the fund intends to invest at least 65% of its assets in companies that have market capitalizations of $250 million to $1 billion.

	Ticker	Load	NAV	Yield	SEC Yield	Assets	Objective
	BAETX	None	16.19	0.1%	N/A	36.8	Small Company

Historical Profile

Return	Above Average
Risk	Average
Rating	★★★★ Above Average

Investment Style History
Equity
Average % Stocks Held in Portfolio

| --- | --- | --- | --- | --- | 95% | 94% | 96% |

Growth of $10,000
|||| Value of Fund ($000)
— Value of Index ($000)
Russ 2000
▼ Manager Change
▽ Partial Manager Change
► Mgr Unknown After
◄ Mgr Unknown Before

Performance Quartile (Within Objective)

Manager's Investment Style

Management seeks small-cap stocks (though not as small as its closed older sibling Babson Enterprise) that are selling cheaply in the market, then holds them for long periods. Management also tends to favor cyclical firms and seeks to avoid popular small-cap-stock stories.

Fund Manager(s)

Lance F. James, since 08-91. Birthdate: 1954. AB, Princeton U. 1976 MBA, Wharton 1978

Peter C. Schliemann, since 08-91. Birthdate: 1945. BA, Amherst C. 1967 MBA, Harvard 1969

Manager Experience	Dates Managed	Invest Obj	Std Dev	+/- Index
Peter C. Schliemann				
Babson Enterprise	01/85 - 12/94	SC	16.90	-0.52
Shadow Stock	08/87 - 12/94	SC	15.55	-2.96

	1983	1984	1985	1986	1987	1988	1989	1990	1991	1992	1993	1994	History
	---	---	---	---	---	---	---	---	12.80	14.97	17.60	16.19	NAV
	---	---	---	---	---	---	---	---	5.32 *	17.21	19.80	-7.39	Total Return %
	---	---	---	---	---	---	---	---	-4.56 *	9.59	9.74	-8.70	+/- S&P 500
	---	---	---	---	---	---	---	---	---	5.46	5.26	-4.74	+/- Wilshire 4500
	---	---	---	---	---	---	---	---	0.31	0.00	0.00	0.14	Income Return %
	---	---	---	---	---	---	---	---	5.00	17.21	19.80	-7.53	Capital Return %
	---	---	---	---	---	---	---	---	---	7	17	82	Total Rtn % Rank All
	---	---	---	---	---	---	---	---	---	32	34	88	Total Rtn % Rank Obj
	---	---	---	---	---	---	---	---	0.04	0.00	0.00	0.02	Income $
	---	---	---	---	---	---	---	---	0.00	0.03	0.33	0.09	Capital Gains $
	---	---	---	---	---	---	---	---	1.49	1.83	1.60	---	Expense Ratio %
	---	---	---	---	---	---	---	---	0.76	-0.11	-0.14	---	Income Ratio %
	---	---	---	---	---	---	---	---	---	14	18	---	Turnover Rate %
	---	---	---	---	---	---	---	---	3.3	12.3	31.0	36.8	Net Assets ($mil)

Performance 12-31-94

	1st Qtr	2nd Qtr	3rd Qtr	4th Qtr	Total
1987	---	---	---	---	---
1988	---	---	---	---	---
1989	---	---	---	---	---
1990	---	---	---	---	---
1991	---	---	---	6.36	5.32 *
1992	7.50	-6.32	2.87	13.15	17.21
1993	4.54	-0.26	6.34	8.04	19.80
1994	-2.33	-3.66	2.54	-4.01	-7.39

Bear Market Performance

Decile Rank (5-year period)

Worst			Best

		Worst 3 Mo Period 1985-89	Worst 3 Mo Period 1990-94
Babson Enterprise II		---	---
+/- S&P 500		---	---
+/- Best Fit Index :		---	---

Trailing Returns

	Total Return %	+/- S&P 500	+/- Wil 4500	% Rank All Obj	Growth of $10,000
3 Mo	-4.01	-3.99	-1.51	89 89	9,599
6 Mo	-1.57	-6.44	-5.77	83 98	9,843
1 Yr	-7.39	-8.70	-4.74	82 88	9,261
3 Yr Avg	9.15	2.89	1.54	17 48	13,004
5 Yr Avg	---	---	---	--- ---	---
10 Yr Avg	---	---	---	--- ---	---
15 Yr Avg	---	---	---	--- ---	---

Operations

Address and Telephone	Three Crown Cntr 2440 Pershing Rd. Kansas City, MO 64108 800-422-2766 / 816-471-5200
Advisor	Jones & Babson
Subadvisor	David L. Babson & Company
Distributor	Jones & Babson
States Available	All
Report Grade	B
Income Distrib	Paid Annually
* Date of Inception	08-05-91
Fiscal Year End	November

Risk Analysis

Time Period	Load-Adj Return %	Risk % Rank [1] All Obj	Morningstar [2] Return Risk	Morningstar Risk-Adj Rating
1 Yr	-7.39	--- ---	--- ---	---
3 Yr	9.15	77 39	1.70[3] 0.90	★★★★
5 Yr	---	--- ---	--- ---	---
10 Yr	---	--- ---	--- ---	---

Average Historical Rating (5 months)   3.8 ★s

[1] 1 = low, 100 = high   [2] 1.00 = Equity Avg   [3] 1.00 = 90-day T-bill return

Other Measures

			Standard S&P 500	Best Fit Russ 2000
Standard Deviation	10.35	Alpha	3.6	-0.6
Mean	9.32	Beta	0.78	0.80
Sharpe Ratio	0.56	R-Squared	36	83

Investment Style

	Stock Portfolio Avg	Relative S&P 500
Price/Earnings Ratio	17.7	0.96
Price/Book Ratio	2.0	0.60
5 Yr Earnings Gr %	7.9	1.41
Return on Assets %	7.6	1.02
Debt % Total Cap	27.2	0.96
Med Mkt Cap ($mil)	527	0.04

Style
Value Blend Growth
Size: Large / Med / Small

Diversification Value for Portfolio Types

Large Cap: Medium	Small Cap: None	Bond: High	Balanced: Medium	Diversified: Medium

Expenses & Fees

Sales Fees	0.00% front
	0.00% deferred
	0.00% 12b-1
Management Fee	1.50% max./1.00% min.
3-,5-,10-yr Expense Projections	$51, $87, $190
Annual Brokerage Cost	---

Min Initial Purchase	$1000 (Addt'l: $100)
Min IRA Purchase	$250 (Addt'l: $50)
Min Auto Invest Plan	$100 (Systematic Inv: $100)

Portfolio 12-31-94

Share Chg (11-94) 000	Amount 000	Total Stocks: 48 Total Fixed-Income: 0	Value $000	% Net Assets
0	48	Baldor Electric	1286	3.49
0	31	Carlisle	1120	3.04
0	39	Modine Manufacturing	1110	3.01
0	61	Juno Lighting	1086	2.95
0	109	Cash America International	1078	2.93
0	31	First Brands	1068	2.90
0	34	Trinity Industries	1055	2.87
0	56	Consolidated Stores	1043	2.83
0	57	Waban	1012	2.75
0	32	La-Z-Boy Chair	1004	2.73
0	34	Wallace Computer Services	986	2.68
0	19	Omnicom Group	968	2.63
0	61	California Energy	950	2.58
0	38	Arvin Industries	884	2.40
0	25	Lee Enterprises	878	2.38
0	27	FirsTier Financial	854	2.32
0	35	MA Hanna	831	2.26
0	52	Fingerhut	809	2.20
0	35	First Commercial	803	2.18
0	38	Armor All Products	789	2.14
0	31	Hannaford Brothers	787	2.14
30	30	Mosinee Paper	776	2.11
0	53	Southdown	763	2.07
0	38	TriMas	760	2.06
0	31	Kennametal	757	2.06

Composition % 12-31-94

Cash	2.3	Preferreds	0.0
Stocks	97.7	Convertibles	0.0
Bonds	0.0	Other	0.0

Tax Analysis

	Tax-Adj Historical Return %	% Pretax Return
3 Yr Avg	8.87	96.7
5 Yr Avg	---	---
10 Yr Avg	---	---
Potential Capital Gain Exposure (% of assets)		7%

Most Similar Funds in MF500

Vanguard Index Extended Mkt	Fair Fit
Columbia Growth	Fair Fit
Dreyfus New Leaders	Fair Fit

Index Allocation

	% of Stocks
S&P 500	1.9
S&P MidCap 400	48.5
U.S. Small Cap	48.9
Foreign	0.7

Sector Weightings

	% of Stocks	Relative S&P 500
Utilities	2.7	0.22
Energy	2.3	0.22
Financials	4.7	0.44
Industrial Cyclicals	28.5	1.74
Consumer Durables	20.5	3.29
Consumer Staples	4.8	0.38
Services	16.2	1.99
Retail	12.8	2.21
Health	3.3	0.37
Technology	4.4	0.48

MORNINGSTAR **1995 Mutual Fund 500**

Baker Fentress

	Ticker	NAV	Mkt Price	Prem/Disc	Yield	Objective
	BKF	$17.47	$13.75	-21.3%	2.3%	Domestic Eq

Baker, Fentress & Company seeks capital appreciation and income consistent with this goal.

The fund is nondiversified and invests mainly in equity securities. It may also purchase debt securities without equity features. A 79% interest in Consolidated-Tomoka Land Co., a Florida real estate, agriculture, and resort company, constitutes a substantial part of the fund's portfolio.

Open-ending, merging, or liquidating the fund requires approval by at least 80% of outstanding shares or two thirds of directors. Directors serve staggered terms.

In 1990, the fund repurchased 100,000 shares with market value totaling $1,971,750. On October 26, 1993, the fund completed a fully subscribed 5:1 rights offering that raised $68,207,672 in new assets.

The fund has an annual 8% payout policy.

| -16.1 | -3.3 | -12.9 | -4.3 | -13.8 | -14.5 | -14.6 | -14.8 | -12.2 | -11.9 | -12.7 | -13.4 | Highest Prem/Disc |
| -26.7 | -19.9 | -16.9 | -19.9 | -28.1 | -24.6 | -21.1 | -24.4 | -22.4 | -21.0 | -18.9 | -21.4 | Lowest Prem/Disc |

Historical Profile

Return	Below Average
Risk	Below Average
Rating	★★★ Neutral

Growth of $10,000
— at NAV ($000)
— at Market Price ($000)

Premium Discount %

	1983	1984	1985	1986	1987	1988	1989	1990	1991	1992	1993	1994	History
	20.85	20.70	25.25	25.17	23.29	24.08	25.18	18.66	21.49	20.82	20.42	17.47	NAV
	19.31	4.66	31.10	11.24	4.85	15.74	21.76	-16.30	26.99	5.35	13.97	-3.61	NAV Total Return %
	-3.16	-1.61	-0.64	-7.44	-0.41	-0.87	-9.92	-13.18	-3.49	-2.27	3.92	-4.93	+/- S&P 500
	-2.66	9.25	0.95	-3.52	10.23	0.67	-0.22	-3.39	-28.42	-6.94	-1.78	-4.52	+/- Wil Mid Growth
	3.34	3.83	3.52	2.82	3.53	3.52	3.28	3.91	3.58	2.17	2.83	2.17	Income Return %
	15.97	0.83	27.58	8.42	1.31	12.22	18.48	-20.21	23.41	3.18	11.15	-5.78	Capital Return %
	29	54	17	68	25	30	23	86	27	73	63	29	Total Rtn % Rank All
	63	7	30	64	18	53	59	79	67	53	32	72	Total Rtn % Rank Obj
	30.96	3.16	38.07	9.69	-9.60	28.95	25.96	-23.83	34.03	4.88	14.50	-7.51	Market Total Rtn %
	-20.7	-15.9	-15.4	-14.2	-20.5	-19.2	-18.0	-18.5	-17.2	-15.9	-16.4	-17.9	Avg Prem/Disc %
	0.50	0.63	0.60	0.64	0.70	0.67	0.72	0.70	0.58	0.39	0.48	0.35	Income $
	0.17	0.25	0.76	1.91	1.63	1.59	2.72	1.25	1.15	1.13	1.76	1.46	Capital Gains $
	0.44	0.75	0.65	0.53	0.49	0.64	0.64	0.68	0.84	0.76	0.83	0.86	Expense Ratio %
	2.42	3.12	2.81	2.33	2.37	2.78	2.49	3.03	2.53	2.01	2.42	1.02	Income Ratio %
	5	5	9	15	29	53	35	26	51	28	31	---	Turnover Rate %
	166.3	306.3	379.7	396.6	378.3	486.5	456.2	350.2	417.4	419.8	516.9	461.9	Net Assets ($mil)

Manager's Investment Style

Management takes advantage of the fixed-asset base that the closed-end structure affords by holding a basket of private placements. At times, the portfolio's private placements have taken up 15% of assets. Despite the fact that it features more than 50 issues, the portfolio is somewhat concentrated because its top five positions consume more than a fourth of the fund's assets. The publicly traded portion of the portfolio showcases management's dedication to a handful of themes, which have included the shift in the economy from consumption to investment in capital goods.

Fund Manager(s)

Steven C. Carhart. Since 9-91. SB'70 MIT; SM'72 MIT.

Scott E. Smith. Since 1991. BS'77 U. of Missouri; MBA'79 Indiana U.

Manager Experience	Dates Managed	Invest Obj	Std Dev	+/- Index

Not available.

NAV Performance % 12-30-94

	1st Qtr	2nd Qtr	3rd Qtr	4th Qtr	Total
1987	15.32	3.72	11.06	-21.07	4.85
1988	7.16	2.75	2.75	2.32	15.74
1989	9.32	8.14	3.65	-0.63	21.76
1990	-4.97	4.71	-19.19	4.09	-16.30
1991	10.02	3.82	1.95	9.06	26.99
1992	2.23	-1.14	-1.58	5.92	5.35
1993	1.83	3.86	6.43	1.26	13.97
1994	1.08	-5.81	4.37	-3.00	-3.61

Bear Market Performance

Decile Rank (5-year period)

Worst | Best

	Worst 3 Mo Period 1985-89	Worst 3 Mo Period 1990-94
Baker Fentress	-24.64	-19.19
+/- S&P 500	4.94	-5.44

Trailing Returns

	NAV Total Return %	+/- S&P 500	+/- Wil Mid Grow	% Rank All	% Rank Obj	Mkt Total Return %
3 Mo	-3.00	-2.98	-2.52	69	62	-5.75
6 Mo	1.24	-3.62	-8.57	24	57	-7.18
1 Yr	-3.61	-4.93	-4.52	29	72	-7.51
3 Yr Avg	4.99	-1.28	-4.47	66	46	3.56
5 Yr Avg	4.23	-4.46	-7.93	92	82	2.55
10 Yr Avg	10.24	-4.14	-3.18	57	61	9.69

Operations

Address and Telephone	200 W. Madison St., Suite 3510
	Chicago, IL 60606
	312-236-9190
Advisor	Baker Fentress
Subadvisor	N/A
Administrator	Internally Administered
Transfer Agent	Harris Trust & Savings
Custodian	United Missouri Bank N.A.
Auditor	Ernst & Young LLP
Legal Counsel	Bell, Boyd & Lloyd

Income Distrib Schedule	Paid Irregularly
Management Fee	0.00%
Reinvestment Plan	Yes
Direct Purchase Plan	No
Shares Outstanding	26,441,682
Exchange	NYSE
Date of Inception	01-01-71
Shareholder Report	A-

Risk Analysis

	Risk % Rank[1] All	Obj	Morningstar[2] Return	Risk	Morningstar Risk-Adj Rating
3 Yr	71	43	0.18	0.55	★★★
5 Yr	78	48	-0.08	0.66	★★★
10 Yr	60	15	0.40	0.66	★★★
Average Historical Rating (145 months)				2.8 ★s	

[1] = Low, 100 = High [2] 1.00 = Equity Avg [3] 1.00 = 90-day T-bill Return

Other Measures

				S&P 500
Standard Deviation	9.07	Alpha		-0.60
Mean	5.29	Beta		0.82
Sharpe Ratio	0.19	R-Squared		51

Investment Style

	Stock Portfolio Avg	Relative S&P 500
Price/Earnings Ratio	20.3	1.10
Price/Cash Flow Ratio	19.4	1.68
Price/Book Ratio	3.0	0.87
5 Yr Earnings Gr %	6.7	1.20
Return on Assets %	8.3	1.11
Debt % Total Cap	15.0	0.53
Med Mkt Cap ($mil)	1519	0.12

figure is based on less than 50% of stocks

Index Allocation

	% of Stocks
Dow 30	2.4
S&P 500	47.8
S&P Mid-Cap 400	22.0
US Small-Cap	30.3
Foreign	3.3

Diversification Value for Portfolio Types

Large Cap: Low	Small Cap: Low	Bond: High	Balanced: Low	Diversified: Low

Portfolio 09-30-94

Share Chg (06-94)	Amount	Total Equity: 60 Total Fixed-Income: 13	Value $000	% Total Invest
0	5000000	Consolidated Tomoka Land	61875	12.17
0	1400000	MCI Communications	35525	6.99
0	470611	United HealthCare	22267	4.38
0	400000	Barnett Banks	17700	3.48
0	500000	American Barrick Resources	13313	2.62
0	517266	Wausau Paper Mills	12156	2.39
0	450000	Cincinnati Milacron	11588	2.28
0	180000	Great Lakes Chemical	10575	2.08
-50000	150000	Nucor	10444	2.05
0	180000	MAPCO	10080	1.98
---	10000000	Earth Technology 12.5%	10000	1.97
0	250000	Walt Disney	9688	1.91
170000	170000	Bandag	9201	1.81
0	270000	Aon	9011	1.77
200000	400000	Newell	8900	1.75
0	300000	Cisco Systems	8213	1.62
200000	200000	Cooper Industries	8050	1.58
0	400000	Giddings & Lewis	7125	1.40
0	250000	Cirrus Logic	7000	1.38
---	7000000	Citadel Comm Cl A 12%	7000	1.38
0	1511374	AEC	6809	1.34
0	90000	Autodesk	5625	1.11
---	5240000	Champion Healthcare 11%	5240	1.03
0	350000	Joy Technologies Cl A	5075	1.00
0	125000	Department 56	4875	0.96

Composition % 12-31-94

Cash	1.0	Preferreds	0.0
Stocks	85.0	Convertibles	13.0
Bonds	0.0	Other	1.0

Tax Analysis

	Tax-Adj Historical Return %	% Pretax Return
3 Yr Avg	2.04	34.0
5 Yr Avg	1.10	21.8
10 Yr Avg	6.69	53.1
Potential Capital Gain Exposure (% of assets)		45

Most Similar Funds in MF500

IDS New Dimensions	Weak Fit
Keystone Amer Omega A	Weak Fit
Fidelity Growth Company	Weak Fit

Sector Weightings

	% of Stocks	Relative S&P 500
Utilities	8.7	0.70
Energy	7.9	0.78
Financials	10.1	0.95
Industrial Cyclicals	19.7	1.20
Consumer Durables	10.3	1.66
Consumer Staples	15.2	1.21
Services	6.4	0.79
Retail	0.9	0.16
Health	6.0	0.69
Technology	14.8	1.61

Bartlett Basic Value

Bartlett Basic Value Fund seeks capital appreciation; current income is a secondary consideration.

The fund invests in securities that management believes to have market-appreciation potential because their basic value, with respect to the issuer's assets and earning power, is not adequately reflected in their market price. The fund invests primarily in common stocks or securities convertible into common stock. The fund's investments may include foreign securities.

Manager's Investment Style

Management focuses on firms selling below book value that also carry low price to cash-flow ratios. The fund typically has large weightings in financials and foreign investments.

Fund Manager(s)

James A. Miller CFA(1981), since 01-90.
Birthdate: 03-49. BA, U. of Michigan 1971 MBA, Harvard 1974
Woodrow H. Uible CFA(1980), since 04-93.
Birthdate: 06-53. BA, U. of Cincinnati 1975

Manager Experience	Dates Managed	Invest Obj	Std Dev	+/- Index
Not available.				

	Ticker	Load	NAV	Yield	SEC Yield	Assets	Objective
	MBBVX	None	14.10	1.6%	N/A	93.2	Growth/Inc.

Historical Profile
Return	Average
Risk	Below Average
Rating	★★★ Neutral

76% 63% 67% 77% 78% 85% 85% 86%

Investment Style History
Equity
Average % Stocks Held in Portfolio

Growth of $10,000
|||| Value of Fund ($000)
— Value of Index ($000) S&P 500
▼ Manager Change
▽ Partial Manager Change
► Mgr Unknown After
◄ Mgr Unknown Before

Performance Quartile (Within Objective)

	1983	1984	1985	1986	1987	1988	1989	1990	1991	1992	1993	1994	History
	10.28	10.53	12.37	12.20	11.01	12.18	12.58	10.87	13.28	14.02	15.28	14.10	NAV
	5.44 *	8.41	25.30	13.67	-3.76	26.28	11.66	-9.60	25.96	10.24	11.66	0.42	Total Return %
	2.17 *	2.14	-6.44	-5.01	-9.02	9.67	-20.02	-6.49	-4.52	2.62	1.60	-0.89	+/- S&P 500
	---	5.36	-7.27	-2.43	-6.12	8.34	-17.51	-3.42	-8.24	1.27	0.37	0.49	+/- Wilshire 5000
	2.64	5.97	5.64	3.59	3.41	4.52	6.93	3.99	3.79	2.43	1.58	1.64	Income Return %
	2.80	2.43	19.66	10.08	-7.17	21.76	4.73	-13.59	22.17	7.81	10.07	-1.22	Capital Return %
	---	35	45	63	84	5	60	83	34	21	53	17	Total Rtn % Rank All
	---	24	69	69	88	5	95	83	66	27	42	35	Total Rtn % Rank Obj
	0.26	0.59	0.55	0.45	0.45	0.52	0.84	0.52	0.39	0.32	0.22	0.24	Income $
	0.00	0.00	0.18	1.41	0.39	1.15	0.18	0.00	0.00	0.28	0.14	1.03	Capital Gains $
	---	1.99	1.78	1.56	1.28	1.57	1.23	1.19	1.21	1.22	1.21	1.20	Expense Ratio %
	---	5.71	6.01	4.05	3.49	2.75	4.57	4.81	3.87	2.77	2.14	1.48	Income Ratio %
	---	8	36	82	58	97	99	77	92	49	43	33	Turnover Rate %
	12.0	12.4	30.6	74.6	73.2	95.6	109.5	84.8	90.4	98.9	100.5	93.2	Net Assets ($mil)

Performance 12-31-94

	1st Qtr	2nd Qtr	3rd Qtr	4th Qtr	Total
1987	10.82	4.40	4.17	-20.14	-3.76
1988	13.71	4.90	2.86	2.91	26.28
1989	4.11	4.78	5.22	-2.71	11.66
1990	-0.72	3.65	-18.78	8.16	-9.60
1991	16.74	-2.22	6.06	4.04	25.96
1992	1.88	3.71	1.37	2.92	10.24
1993	5.56	-1.22	3.79	3.16	11.66
1994	-2.23	1.01	4.63	-2.81	0.42

Bear Market Performance

Decile Rank (5-year period)

Worst | Best

	Worst 3 Mo Period 1985-89	Worst 3 Mo Period 1990-94
Bartlett Basic Value	-22.45	-18.78
+/- S&P 500	7.13	-5.04
+/- Best Fit Index : S&P 500	7.13	-5.04

Trailing Returns

	Total Return %	+/- S&P 500	+/- Wil 5000	% Rank All	% Rank Obj	Growth of $10,000
3 Mo	-2.81	-2.80	-2.04	81	82	9,719
6 Mo	1.69	-3.18	-2.94	29	64	10,169
1 Yr	0.42	-0.89	0.49	17	35	10,042
3 Yr Avg	7.32	1.06	0.71	25	27	12,361
5 Yr Avg	7.07	-1.62	-1.74	48	71	14,075
10 Yr Avg	10.53	-3.86	-3.33	53	84	27,204
15 Yr Avg	---	---	---	---	---	---

Operations

Address and Telephone	36 E. Fourth Street Cincinnati, OH 45202 800-800-4612 / 513-621-4612	
Advisor	Bartlett	
Subadvisor	None	
Distributor	Bartlett Capital Trust	
States Available	All except AK	
Report Grade	B	
Income Distrib	Paid Quarterly	
* Date of Inception	05-05-83	
Fiscal Year End	March	

Risk Analysis

Time Period	Load-Adj Return %	Risk % Rank [1] All	Obj	Morningstar [2] Return	Risk	Morningstar Risk-Adj Rating
1 Yr	0.42					
3 Yr	7.32	62	34	1.12 [3]	0.68	★★★★
5 Yr	7.07	68	61	0.57 [3]	0.81	★★★
10 Yr	10.53	48	21	0.63	0.69	★★★
Average Historical Rating (104 months)					3.3 ★s	

[1] 1 = low, 100 = high [2] 1.00 = Equity Avg [3] 1.00 = 90-day T-bill return

Other Measures

				Standard S&P 500	Best Fit S&P 500
Standard Deviation	7.66	Alpha		1.5	1.5
Mean	7.38	Beta		0.81	0.81
Sharpe Ratio	0.50	R-Squared		71	71

Investment Style

	Stock Portfolio Avg	Relative S&P 500	Style
Price/Earnings Ratio	15.6	0.85	Value Blend Growth
Price/Book Ratio	2.3	0.68	Size Large/Med/Small
5 Yr Earnings Gr %	6.4	1.15	
Return on Assets %	4.7	0.63	
Debt % Total Cap	28.1	0.99	
Med Mkt Cap ($mil)	2487	0.19	

Diversification Value for Portfolio Types

Large Cap: Low	Small Cap: Medium	Bond: High	Balanced: Low	Diversified: Low

Expenses & Fees

Sales Fees	0.00% front
	0.00% deferred
	0.00% 12b-1
Management Fee	2.00% max./1.00% min.
3-,5-,10-yr Expense Projections	$38, $66, $146
Annual Brokerage Cost	0.13%

Min Initial Purchase	$5000 (Addt'l: $100)
Min IRA Purchase	$250 (Addt'l: $100)
Min Auto Invest Plan	N/A

Portfolio 11-30-94

Share Chg (10-94) 000	Amount 000	Total Stocks: 53 Total Fixed-Income: 5	Value $000	% Net Assets
0	90	Potash of Saskatchewan	3206	3.37
0	256	Royce Value Trust	3099	3.26
0	65	Martin Marietta	2819	2.96
2	40	Philip Morris	2390	2.51
0	10	Bayer (ADR)	2226	2.34
-7	65	Phillips Petroleum	2145	2.25
8	55	General Motors	2088	2.20
0	50	National Presto Industries	2063	2.17
10	70	Multimedia	2021	2.12
-3	114	Security Capital Bancorp	2002	2.10
	2000	Merrill Lynch 0%	1972	2.07
0	28	IBM	1954	2.05
20	95	Kellwood	1948	2.05
-6	61	TOTAL Cl B (ADR)	1906	2.00
	2000	Goldman Sachs Group 7.8%	1900	2.00
0	104	Hanson (ADR)	1893	1.99
0	75	British Steel (ADR)	1884	1.98
0	29	Raytheon	1823	1.92
0	54	Time Warner	1823	1.92
0	21	Loews	1814	1.91
0	25	FNMA	1778	1.87
10	106	Cabot Oil & Gas Cl A	1770	1.86
0	22	ITT	1762	1.85
0	60	NIPSCO Industries	1755	1.84
0	45	Merck	1676	1.76

Composition % 12-31-94
Cash	3.8	Preferreds	0.8
Stocks	87.9	Convertibles	1.1
Bonds	6.5	Other	0.0

Tax Analysis
	Tax-Adj Historical Return %	% Pretax Return
3 Yr Avg	5.68	76.4
5 Yr Avg	5.57	76.5
10 Yr Avg	8.06	68.0
Potential Capital Gain Exposure (% of assets)		12%

Most Similar Funds in MF500
Investment Comp of America	Fair Fit
Scudder Growth & Income	Fair Fit
Merrill Lynch Capital A	Fair Fit

Index Allocation
	% of Stocks
S&P 500	35.0
S&P MidCap 400	14.9
U.S. Small Cap	28.0
Foreign	22.1

Sector Weightings
	% of Stocks	Relative S&P 500
Utilities	8.1	0.65
Energy	9.6	0.94
Financials	32.5	3.07
Industrial Cyclicals	9.6	0.59
Consumer Durables	11.8	1.90
Consumer Staples	3.1	0.25
Services	11.9	1.46
Retail	0.4	0.06
Health	4.7	0.54
Technology	8.5	0.93

MORNINGSTAR 1995 Mutual Fund 500

Benham GNMA Income

	Ticker	Load	NAV	Yield	SEC Yield	Assets	Objective
	BGNMX	None	9.90	7.0%	7.71%	952.3	Gvt Mortgage

Benham GNMA Income Fund seeks current income consistent with safety of principal and maintenance of liquidity.

The fund normally invests at least 65% of its assets in mortgage-backed GNMA certificates guaranteed by the Government National Mortgage Association and backed by the full faith and credit of the U.S. government. The balance of the fund's assets may be invested in other U.S. government securities.

Historical Profile
Return   Above Average
Risk   Below Average
Rating   ★★★★★ Highest

Investment Style History
Fixed Income
Income Rtn % Rank Obj

56 61 47 39 41 34 58 33

Growth of $10,000
|||| Value of Fund ($000)
— Value of Index ($000) LB Mtg
▼ Manager Change
▽ Partial Manager Change
► Mgr Unknown After
◄ Mgr Unknown Before

Performance Quartile (Within Objective)

Manager's Investment Style
Management attempts to offer a moderate play on GNMA securities only, and eschews other mortgage types. Durations and coupons are often laddered to provide diversification. Management attempts to add value by seeking out GNMA securities with unusual but attractive characteristics (such as graduated payment mortgages), and by researching pools to determine prepayment rates.

Fund Manager(s)
Jeffrey R. Tyler, since 11-92. Birthdate: 11-57.
BA, U. of California-Santa Barbara 1979 MM, Northwestern U. 1981
Casey Colton CFA(1991), since 01-94. BS, San Jose

Manager Experience	Dates Managed	Invest Obj	Std Dev	+/- Index
Jeffrey R. Tyler				
Benham Treasury Note	02/88 - 01/92	GT	3.78	-1.91
Benham Target Mat 2005	03/89 - 07/90	GT	15.17	2.42

1983	1984	1985	1986	1987	1988	1989	1990	1991	1992	1993	1994	History
---	---	10.34	10.45	9.78	9.69	10.08	10.15	10.80	10.78	10.76	9.90	NAV
---	---	5.71 *	11.37	2.87	8.29	13.89	10.16	15.57	7.73	6.59	-1.51	Total Return %
---	---	---	-3.88	0.11	0.42	-0.65	1.21	-0.43	0.49	-3.16	1.41	+/- LB Aggregate
---	---	---	-2.06	-1.42	-0.43	-1.46	-0.56	-0.15	0.78	-0.25	0.10	+/- LB Mortgage
---	---	2.31	10.31	8.68	9.21	9.86	9.46	9.16	7.92	6.64	6.48	Income Return %
---	---	3.40	1.06	-5.81	-0.92	4.02	0.69	6.40	-0.19	-0.05	-7.99	Capital Return %
---	---	---	77	36	72	50	4	55	49	85	30	Total Rtn % Rank All
---	---	---	37	29	26	25	31	23	8	50	24	Total Rtn % Rank Obj
---	---	0.23	1.01	0.88	0.88	0.90	0.89	0.86	0.82	0.70	0.70	Income $
---	---	0.00	0.00	0.07	0.00	0.00	0.00	0.00	0.00	0.01	0.00	Capital Gains $
---	---	---	0.29	0.74	0.73	0.75	0.75	0.72	0.62	0.56	0.54	Expense Ratio %
---	---	---	10.52	8.79	8.94	9.11	9.04	8.85	8.18	7.31	6.12	Income Ratio %
---	---	---	---	566	497	497	433	207	97	71	49	Turnover Rate %
---	---	65.1	255.7	247.5	257.3	281.1	353.6	702.8	1006.1	1257.0	952.3	Net Assets ($mil)

Performance 12-31-94
	1st Qtr	2nd Qtr	3rd Qtr	4th Qtr	Total
1987	1.76	-2.39	-2.99	6.76	2.87
1988	4.10	1.60	2.08	0.30	8.29
1989	0.99	7.68	1.05	3.64	13.89
1990	-0.04	3.50	1.31	5.10	10.16
1991	2.69	1.92	5.41	4.75	15.57
1992	-0.62	3.94	3.27	0.99	7.73
1993	2.71	1.93	0.81	1.00	6.59
1994	-2.23	-0.43	0.75	0.42	-1.51

Bear Market Performance
Decile Rank (5-year period)
Worst —— Best

	Worst 3 Mo Period 1985-89	Worst 3 Mo Period 1990-94
Benham GNMA Income	---	-3.61
+/- LB Aggregate	---	1.32
+/- Best Fit Index : LB Mtg	---	0.39

Trailing Returns
	Total Return %	+/- LB Aggregate	+/- LB Mortgage	% Rank All	% Rank Obj	Growth of $10,000
3 Mo	0.42	0.05	0.00	13	23	10,042
6 Mo	1.18	0.19	-0.12	35	19	10,118
1 Yr	-1.51	1.41	0.10	30	24	9,849
3 Yr Avg	4.19	-0.36	0.21	65	11	11,310
5 Yr Avg	7.56	-0.06	-0.01	39	8	14,399
10 Yr Avg	---	---	---	---	---	---
15 Yr Avg	---	---	---	---	---	---

Operations
Address and Telephone	1665 Charleston Road Mountain View, CA 94043 800-331-8331 / 415-965-4274
Advisor	Benham Management
Subadvisor	None
Distributor	Benham Distributors
States Available	All
Report Grade	A
Income Distrib	Paid Monthly
* Date of Inception	09-23-85
Fiscal Year End	March

Risk Analysis
Time Period	Load-Adj Return %	Risk % Rank All	Risk % Rank Obj	Morningstar Return	Morningstar Risk	Morningstar Risk-Adj Rating
1 Yr	-1.51					
3 Yr	4.19	10	17	0.18 [3]	0.76	★★★★
5 Yr	7.56	9	24	0.70 [3]	0.74	★★★★★
10 Yr	---	---	---	---	---	

Average Historical Rating (76 months) 4.4 ★ s

[1] 1 = low, 100 = high [2] 1.00 = Taxable Avg [3] 1.00 = 90-day T-bill return

Other Measures
			Standard LB Agg	Best Fit LB Mtg
Standard Deviation	3.12	Alpha	-0.1	0.2
Mean	4.16	Beta	0.72	0.95
Sharpe Ratio	0.20	R-Squared	84	97

Investment Style
Interest-Rate Stance
Avg Effective Duration 5.2 Yrs
Avg Effective Maturity 8.7 Yrs
Quality
Avg Credit Quality AAA
Avg Weighted Coupon 8.34%
Avg Weighted Price 98.51% of Par

Maturity: Short Intm Long
Quality: High Med Low

Diversification Value for Portfolio Types
Large Cap: Medium | Small Cap: High | Bond: None | Balanced: Medium | Diversified: Medium

Expenses & Fees
Sales Fees
0.00% front
0.00% deferred
0.00% 12b-1
Management Fee 0.50% flat fee, 0.11%A
3-,5-,10-yr Expense Projections $17, $30, $68

Min Initial Purchase $1000 (Addt'l: $100)
Min IRA Purchase $1000 (Addt'l: $100)
Min Auto Invest Plan $1000 (Systematic Inv: $25)

Portfolio 09-30-94
Total Stocks: 0 Total Fixed-Income: 52
Amount 000	Date of Maturity		Value $000	% Net Assets
142928	08-20-24	GNMA 9%	146238	14.21
128593	04-15-24	GNMA 7.5%	121092	11.77
116015	05-15-31	GNMA 8.5%	115608	11.23
88662	11-15-33	GNMA 8%	86133	8.37
63377	03-15-23	GNMA 8.25%	61751	6.00
55827	01-15-29	GNMA 7%	50549	4.91
47870		GNMA TBA 8%	46432	4.51
36146	08-15-25	GNMA 8.75%	36025	3.50
35036	11-15-25	GNMA 9.25%	35863	3.48
25000	04-30-99	US Treasury Note 6.5%	24297	2.36
22965	08-20-24	GNMA 9.5%	23927	2.33
24344	06-20-23	GNMA 7.75%	22991	2.23
19798		GNMA TBA 9%	20301	1.97
16003	11-20-21	GNMA 9.75%	16736	1.63
15142	09-20-24	GNMA ARM	15262	1.48
15140	09-20-23	GNMA 7.25%	13813	1.34
13887	12-15-20	GNMA 8.35%	13768	1.34
15000		GNMA TBA 7%	13617	1.32
12492	02-15-21	GNMA 10.25%	13284	1.29
12543	02-15-18	GNMA 7.65%	11796	1.15
12550	04-20-24	GNMA 6.5%	11002	1.07
10000	05-15-97	US Treasury Note 6.5%	9928	0.96
9000		GNMA TBA ARM	8961	0.87
8930	01-15-21	GNMA 7.77%	8452	0.82
7875	02-20-22	GNMA 10%	8385	0.81

Composition % 12-31-94
Cash	7.0	Preferreds	0.0
Stocks	0.0	Convertibles	0.0
Bonds	93.0	Other	0.0

Tax Analysis
	Tax-Adj Historical Return %	% Pretax Return
3 Yr Avg	1.60	37.1
5 Yr Avg	4.85	60.8
10 Yr Avg	---	---
Potential Capital Gain Exposure (% of assets)		-8%

Most Similar Funds in MF500
Franklin U.S. Government Sec Strong Fit
Vanguard F/I GNMA Strong Fit
T. Rowe Price GNMA Strong Fit

Coupon Range
	% of Bonds	Rel Obj
0%	0.0	0.00
0% to 8%	44.0	0.80
8% to 9%	40.7	1.86
9% to 10%	8.8	1.02
More than 10%	4.1	0.63
Not applicable	2.4	0.33

Sector Analysis 09-30-94
% of Bonds
US Treas	4	CMOs	0
GNMA mtgs	94	ARMs	2
FNMA mtgs	0	Other	0
FHLMC mtgs	0		

Benham Treasury Note

	Ticker	Load	NAV	Yield	SEC Yield	Assets	Objective
	CPTNX	None	9.76	5.2%	7.28%	296.2	Gvt Treasury

Benham Treasury Note Fund seeks current income consistent with the preservation of assets.

The fund may invest at least 65% of its net assets in Treasury notes. The remaining 35% may be invested in any combination of Treasury bills and bonds. The fund may not invest in repurchase agreements, making it solely a Treasury fund. Its average portfolio maturity ranges between 13 months and 10 years.

Prior to April 17, 1989, the fund was known as Capital Preservation Treasury Note Trust.

Historical Profile

Return	Average
Risk	Above Average
Rating	★★★
	Neutral

Investment Style History
Fixed Income

Income Rtn % Rank Obj

68 47 46 51 57 66 59 48

Growth of $10,000

|||| Value of Fund ($000)
— Value of Index ($000)
LB Int
▼ Manager Change
▽ Partial Manager Change
► Mgr Unknown After
◄ Mgr Unknown Before

Performance Quartile
(Within Objective)

Manager's Investment Style

Management benchmarks the fund's performance to the Merrill Lynch One- to 10-Year Treasury Index. It tries to beat that index's performance by managing duration and by determining which maturity ranges offer the best relative yields. When bullish, management will hold Treasury bonds with maturities longer than 10 years.

1983	1984	1985	1986	1987	1988	1989	1990	1991	1992	1993	1994	History
10.19	10.40	11.20	11.01	9.97	9.74	10.09	10.22	10.85	10.46	10.51	9.76	NAV
7.52	12.32	17.67	12.88	-1.01	5.22	11.92	9.20	13.74	6.56	7.91	-2.35	Total Return %
-0.86	-2.83	-4.46	-2.37	-3.77	-2.66	-2.62	0.26	-2.26	-0.69	-1.84	0.57	+/- LB Aggregate
0.12	-2.18	-2.76	-2.43	-3.21	-1.81	-2.30	0.49	-1.57	-0.67	-2.74	1.03	+/- LB Government
9.82	10.26	9.98	7.85	6.84	7.53	8.33	7.91	7.58	5.72	4.75	4.79	Income Return %
-2.30	2.06	7.69	5.03	-7.85	-2.31	3.59	1.29	6.16	0.84	3.17	-7.14	Capital Return %
90	16	84	68	67	91	59	8	64	63	80	37	Total Rtn % Rank All
1	66	40	58	62	95	64	12	66	51	59	41	Total Rtn % Rank Obj
0.97	0.96	0.94	0.86	0.73	0.74	0.77	0.75	0.72	0.60	0.49	0.51	Income $
0.00	0.00	0.00	0.78	0.19	0.00	0.00	0.00	0.00	0.48	0.28	0.00	Capital Gains $
1.00	1.00	1.00	1.00	0.93	0.75	0.75	0.75	0.73	0.59	0.53	0.51	Expense Ratio %
9.97	9.44	9.76	8.42	6.26	7.36	7.67	7.66	7.49	6.55	5.18	4.50	Income Ratio %
0	0	53	294	396	465	386	217	70	149	299	213	Turnover Rate %
11.1	9.2	12.5	39.9	42.5	66.3	95.2	129.4	301.7	360.0	388.9	296.2	Net Assets ($mil)

Fund Manager(s)

David W. Schroeder, since 01-92. Birthdate: 07-55. BA, Pomona C. 1977

Manager Experience

	Dates Managed	Invest Obj	Std Dev	+/- Index
David W. Schroeder				
Benham Target Mat 2020	07/90 - 12/94	GT	18.43	-0.55
Benham Target Mat 2005	07/90 - 12/94	GT	10.81	1.60

Performance 12-31-94

	1st Qtr	2nd Qtr	3rd Qtr	4th Qtr	Total
1987	0.30	-2.96	-3.88	5.80	-1.01
1988	3.25	0.54	1.19	0.16	5.22
1989	0.86	6.67	0.79	3.21	11.92
1990	-0.33	3.05	1.97	4.26	9.20
1991	1.86	1.54	4.77	4.97	13.74
1992	-1.56	4.07	4.60	-0.55	6.56
1993	3.79	1.91	1.97	0.04	7.91
1994	-2.04	-0.74	0.79	-0.35	-2.35

Bear Market Performance

Decile Rank (5-year period)

Worst ———————————— Best

	Worst 3 Mo Period 1985-89	Worst 3 Mo Period 1990-94
Benham Treasury Note	-5.51	-3.81
+/- LB Aggregate	-1.95	1.12
+/- Best Fit Index : LB Int	-3.36	0.42

Trailing Returns

	Total Return %	+/- LB Aggregate	+/- LB Govt	% Rank All	% Rank Obj	Growth of $10,000
3 Mo	-0.35	-0.73	-0.71	31	70	9,965
6 Mo	0.43	-0.56	-0.35	48	58	10,043
1 Yr	-2.35	0.57	1.03	37	41	9,765
3 Yr Avg	3.94	-0.61	-0.72	71	51	11,229
5 Yr Avg	6.88	-0.74	-0.65	53	48	13,948
10 Yr Avg	8.00	-1.94	-1.57	87	40	21,597
15 Yr Avg	---	---	---	---	---	---

Operations

Address and Telephone	1665 Charleston Road Mountain View, CA 94043 800-331-8331 / 415-965-4274	
Advisor	Benham Management	
Subadvisor	None	
Distributor	Benham Distributors	
States Available	All	
Report Grade	A	
Income Distrib	Paid Monthly	
Date of Inception	05-16-80	
Fiscal Year End	March	

Risk Analysis

Time Period	Load-Adj Return %	Risk % Rank All	Risk % Rank Obj	Morningstar Return	Morningstar Risk	Morningstar Risk-Adj Rating
1 Yr	-2.35					
3 Yr	3.94	16	28	0.10[3]	0.90	★★★★
5 Yr	6.88	12	22	0.52[3]	0.81	★★★★
10 Yr	8.00	33	60	0.54[3]	1.29	★

Average Historical Rating (109 months)　1.6 ★s

[1] = low, 100 = high　[2] 1.00 = Taxable Avg　[3] 1.00 = 90-day T-bill return

Other Measures

				Standard LB Agg	Best Fit LB Int
Standard Deviation	3.43	Alpha		-0.4	-0.1
Mean	3.93	Beta		0.83	0.99
Sharpe Ratio	0.12	R-Squared		92	98

Investment Style

Interest-Rate Stance

Avg Effective Duration	2.8 Yrs
Avg Effective Maturity	2.9 Yrs

Quality

Avg Credit Quality	AAA
Avg Weighted Coupon	4.12%
Avg Weighted Price	91.35% of Par

Maturity Short Intm Long
Quality High Med Low

Diversification Value for Portfolio Types

● Large Cap: High　● Small Cap: High　○ Bond: None　◢ Balanced: Medium　● Diversified: High

Min Initial Purchase	$1000 (Addt'l: $100)
Min IRA Purchase	$1000 (Addt'l: $100)
Min Auto Invest Plan	$1000 (Systematic Inv: $25)

Expenses & Fees

Sales Fees	0.00% front
	0.00% deferred
	0.00% 12b-1
Management Fee	0.50% flat fee, 0.11%A
3-,5-,10-yr Expense Projections	$16, $29, $64

Portfolio 09-30-94

Amount 000	Date of Maturity	Total Stocks: 0 / Total Fixed-Income: 15	Value $000	% Net Assets
38300	05-15-96	US Treasury Note 0%	34577	10.59
47100	02-15-99	US Treasury Note 0%	34482	10.56
33800	08-31-96	US Treasury Note 7.25%	34223	10.48
44200	11-15-98	US Treasury Note 0%	33014	10.11
31900	07-31-96	US Treasury Note 7.875%	32638	9.99
19000	02-15-99	US Treasury Note 8.875%	20188	6.18
20500	12-31-96	US Treasury Note 5.125%	18975	5.81
19000	07-31-96	US Treasury Note 6.125%	18881	5.78
19100	01-31-96	US Treasury Note 5%	17566	5.38
16800	11-30-96	US Treasury Note 6.5%	16753	5.13
17300	08-15-96	US Treasury Note 4.375%	16657	5.10
15600	05-15-96	US Treasury Note 4.25%	15093	4.62
14800	11-15-96	US Treasury Note 7.25%	14980	4.59
19000	08-15-03	US Treasury Note 0%	9673	2.96
8500	11-15-96	US Treasury Note 0%	7407	2.27

Composition % 12-31-94

Cash	0.1	Preferreds	0.0
Stocks	0.0	Convertibles	0.0
Bonds	99.9	Other	0.0

Tax Analysis

	Tax-Adj Historical Return %	% Pretax Return
3 Yr Avg	1.40	34.6
5 Yr Avg	4.39	60.7
10 Yr Avg	4.93	53.2
Potential Capital Gain Exposure (% of assets)		-7%

Most Similar Funds in MF500

T. Rowe Price New Income	Strong Fit
Vanguard Bond Indx Total Bd	Strong Fit
Fidelity Intermediate Bond	Strong Fit

Coupon Range

	% of Bonds	Rel Obj
0%	36.7	2.14
0% to 8%	57.1	1.13
8% to 9%	6.2	0.91
9% to 10%	0.0	0.00
More than 10%	0.0	0.00
Not applicable	0.0	0.00

Maturity Breakdown 09-30-94

% of Bonds

1 to 3 Yrs	59	10 to 15 Yrs	0
3 to 5 Yrs	38	15 to 20 Yrs	0
5 to 7 Yrs	0	20 to 30 Yrs	0
7 to 10 Yrs	3	Non-Treas	0

MORNINGSTAR 1995 Mutual Fund 500

Berger 100

	Ticker	Load	NAV	Yield	SEC Yield	Assets	Objective
	BEONX	None	15.69	0.0%	N/A	2113.0	Growth

Berger 100 Fund seeks long-term capital appreciation. Income is incidental.

The fund invests primarily in common stocks of established companies. It may also purchase other types of securities, such as convertibles, government issues, senior debt, and preferred stocks. The fund may purchase put and call options on stock indexes with up to 1% of fund assets. Foreign issues may be purchased by the fund without a specified limit. The fund may invest in zero coupon bonds and strips.

Prior to Nov. 27, 1989, the fund was named One Hundred Fund.

Manager's Investment Style

Management seeks mid-cap stocks with high growth rates and with returns on assets that are either unknown or that are suffering temporary market weakness, then holds these issues for the long term. The fund has recently heavily emphasized technology stocks.

Fund Manager(s)

Rodney L. Linafelter, since 11-90. Birthdate: 09-59. Economics/Management, U. of South Dakota 1981 Management, U. of South Dakota

Manager Experience	Dates Managed	Invest Obj	Std Dev	+/- Index
Rodney L. Linafelter				
Berger 101	10/91 - 12/94	GI	11.40	0.47
New England Star Adv A	07/94 - 12/94	G	9.56	3.59

Performance 12-31-94

	1st Qtr	2nd Qtr	3rd Qtr	4th Qtr	Total
1987	25.98	-0.21	-0.57	-7.47	15.67
1988	0.45	3.39	-0.69	-1.40	1.69
1989	10.51	10.18	22.42	-0.50	48.31
1990	-3.01	8.53	-20.71	13.08	-5.63
1991	31.15	0.78	22.58	16.54	88.81
1992	-2.90	-10.56	5.68	18.24	8.53
1993	0.22	8.20	9.97	1.63	21.20
1994	-4.40	-10.83	11.37	-1.69	-6.66

Bear Market Performance

Decile Rank (5-year period)

Worst ▬▬▬▬▬▬▬▬▬▬ Best

	Worst 3 Mo Period 1985-89	Worst 3 Mo Period 1990-94
Berger 100	-19.95	-20.76
+/- S&P 500	9.63	-6.92
+/- Best Fit Index : Wil 4500	10.18	-1.36

Trailing Returns

	Total Return %	+/- S&P 500	+/- Wil 5000	% Rank All	% Rank Obj	Growth of $10,000
3 Mo	-1.69	-1.67	-0.92	62	59	9,831
6 Mo	9.49	4.63	4.87	5	10	10,949
1 Yr	-6.66	-7.98	-6.59	77	83	9,334
3 Yr Avg	7.08	0.81	0.46	26	39	12,277
5 Yr Avg	16.95	8.26	8.13	3	2	21,876
10 Yr Avg	19.14	4.76	5.28	2	2	57,626
15 Yr Avg	14.97	0.49	1.00	13	26	81,094

Operations

Address and Telephone	210 University Boulevard Ste 900
	Denver, CO 80206
	800-333-1001 / 303-329-0200
Advisor	Berger Associates
Subadvisor	None
Distributor	Berger Associates
States Available	All
Report Grade	C+
Income Distrib	Paid Annually
Date of Inception	08-01-66
Fiscal Year End	September

Min Initial Purchase	$250 (Addt'l: $50)
Min IRA Purchase	$250 (Addt'l: $50)
Min Auto Invest Plan	$50 (Systematic Inv: $50)

Expenses & Fees

Sales Fees	0.00% front
	0.00% deferred
	0.25% 12b-1
Management Fee	0.75% max./0.50% min.
3-,5-,10-yr Expense Projections	$45, $78, $170
Annual Brokerage Cost	0.12%

Historical Profile

Return	High
Risk	Above Average
Rating	★★★★★
	Highest

94% 91% 90% 81% 81% 83% 82% 85%

Performance Quartile (Within Objective)

	1983	1984	1985	1986	1987	1988	1989	1990	1991	1992	1993	1994	History
	5.90	4.60	5.79	6.57	5.97	5.99	7.98	6.87	12.78	13.87	16.81	15.69	NAV
	16.99	-20.11	25.72	20.10	15.67	1.69	48.31	-5.63	88.81	8.53	21.20	-6.66	Total Return %
	-5.47	-26.37	-6.02	1.42	10.41	-14.92	16.62	-2.51	58.33	0.91	11.14	-7.98	+/- S&P 500
	-6.47	-23.16	-6.84	4.01	13.31	-16.25	19.13	0.56	54.61	-0.44	9.92	-6.59	+/- Wilshire 5000
	0.00	1.88	0.00	0.00	0.00	0.00	0.13	0.00	0.00	0.00	0.00	0.00	Income Return %
	16.99	-21.98	25.72	20.10	15.67	1.69	48.18	-5.63	88.81	8.53	21.20	-6.66	Capital Return %
	51	97	44	19	6	96	2	72	1	39	15	77	Total Rtn % Rank All
	69	99	72	15	5	96	1	59	1	45	12	83	Total Rtn % Rank Obj
	0.00	0.11	0.00	0.00	0.00	0.00	0.01	0.00	0.00	0.00	0.00	0.00	Income $
	0.00	0.00	0.00	0.39	1.58	0.08	0.89	0.59	0.17	0.00	0.00	0.00	Capital Gains $
	1.70	1.90	2.00	1.71	1.61	1.72	1.62	2.13	2.24	1.89	1.69	1.70	Expense Ratio %
	-0.51	1.95	-0.59	-0.47	-0.27	-0.57	-0.54	-0.71	-1.06	-0.75	-1.00	-0.74	Income Ratio %
	155	272	130	122	106	166	83	145	78	51	74	64	Turnover Rate %
	14.4	9.6	8.9	10.1	10.4	10.1	14.6	15.0	192.1	760.5	1648.7	2113.0	Net Assets ($mil)

Investment Style History
Equity

Average % Stocks Held in Portfolio

Growth of $10,000

|||| Value of Fund ($000)
— Value of Index ($000)
    S&P 500
▼ Manager Change
▽ Partial Manager Change
► Mgr Unknown After
◄ Mgr Unknown Before

Risk Analysis

Time Period	Load-Adj Return %	Risk % Rank [1] All	Obj	Morningstar [2] Return	Morningstar Risk	Morningstar Risk-Adj Rating
1 Yr	-6.66					
3 Yr	7.08	95	95	1.04 [3]	1.41	★★★
5 Yr	16.95	93	92	3.58 [3]	1.23	★★★★★
10 Yr	19.14	91	91	2.60	1.18	★★★★★
Average Historical Rating (109 months)				3.2 ★s		

[1] = low, 100 = high [2] 1.00 = Equity Avg [3] 1.00 = 90-day T-bill return

Other Measures

				Standard S&P 500	Best Fit Wil 4500
Standard Deviation	14.88	Alpha		1.3	-1.4
Mean	7.96	Beta		1.10	1.37
Sharpe Ratio	0.30	R-Squared		34	81

Investment Style

	Stock Portfolio Avg	Relative S&P 500
Price/Earnings Ratio	26.2	1.42
Price/Book Ratio	5.0	1.49
5 Yr Earnings Gr %	44.8	4.85
Return on Assets %	13.2	1.76
Debt % Total Cap	25.9	0.92
Med Mkt Cap ($mil)	1785	0.14

figure is based on 50% or less of stocks

Diversification Value for Portfolio Types

Large Cap: Medium	Small Cap: Low	Bond: High	Balanced: Medium	Diversified: Medium

Portfolio 09-30-94

Share Chg (06-94) 000	Amount 000	Total Stocks: 91 Total Fixed-Income: 1	Value $000	% Net Assets
0	900	Oracle Systems	38700	1.74
100	700	Motorola	36925	1.66
0	1000	Grupo Tribasa (ADR)	36750	1.65
100	800	Columbia/HCA Healthcare	34800	1.56
0	1000	HBO	34000	1.53
800	800	Citicorp	34000	1.53
900	900	Dell Computer	33694	1.51
250	1000	Parametric Technology	33250	1.49
200	1000	CUC International	33000	1.48
0	1000	Healthtrust	32875	1.48
700	700	Sybase	32113	1.44
300	300	Xerox	32025	1.44
400	600	Medtronic	31725	1.43
0	1000	Atmel	31375	1.41
100	500	Telefonos de Mexico L (ADR)	31250	1.40
150	900	Williams-Sonoma	30769	1.38
800	800	General Motors Cl E	30400	1.37
0	1500	EMC	30188	1.36
500	500	Nokia (ADR)	29250	1.31
0	750	Lowe's	28969	1.30
0	600	PeopleSoft	28950	1.30
400	400	Gillette	28300	1.27
200	500	Microsoft	28063	1.26
250	750	Magna International Cl A	27656	1.24
1000	1000	cisco Systems	27375	1.23

Composition % 12-31-94

Cash	10.9	Preferreds	0.0
Stocks	89.1	Convertibles	0.0
Bonds	0.0	Other	0.0

Tax Analysis

	Tax-Adj Historical Return %	% Pretax Return
3 Yr Avg	7.08	100.0
5 Yr Avg	16.26	94.6
10 Yr Avg	17.49	84.3
Potential Capital Gain Exposure (% of assets)		10%

Most Similar Funds in MF500

Oppenheimer Discovery A	Strong Fit
Hancock Emerging Growth B	Strong Fit
T. Rowe Price New America G	Strong Fit

Index Allocation

	% of Stocks
S&P 500	25.5
S&P MidCap 400	23.8
U.S. Small Cap	37.8
Foreign	13.0

Sector Weightings

	% of Stocks	Relative S&P 500
Utilities	1.7	0.13
Energy	5.6	0.56
Financials	6.5	0.61
Industrial Cyclicals	5.2	0.31
Consumer Durables	9.8	1.58
Consumer Staples	1.2	0.09
Services	7.9	0.97
Retail	8.3	1.43
Health	16.0	1.84
Technology	38.0	4.15

Berwyn Income

Ticker	Load	NAV	Yield	SEC Yield	Assets	Objective
BERIX	None	10.74	6.8%	8.56%	55.8	Income

Berwyn Income Fund seeks current income consistent with reasonable risk and preservation of capital. Capital appreciation is also considered.

The fund generally invests at least 80% of its assets in income-producing securities. These may include U.S. government obligations, corporate debt securities, convertible bonds, and income-producing equity securities. The fund may invest without limit in high-yield, high-risk corporate debt securities. It may invest up to 25% of its assets in common stocks paying cash dividends, and may invest in preferred stocks.

Manager's Investment Style

Management attempts to provide a high income payout while also giving the portfolio exposure to the equity markets and potential for capital growth. As such, the fund typically focuses on convertibles, with additional positions in junk bonds (the fund typically has a lower average-credit quality than its peers). Its stocks are mainly small-caps that are underfollowed by the market and that are selling at single-digit price multiples. Management has also maintained notable positions in foreign stocks.

Fund Manager(s)

Edward Killen, since 06-94. Birthdate: 09-51.
BA, Hunter C. 1972 MS, U. of Colorado 1977

Manager Experience

	Dates Managed	Invest Obj	Std Dev	+/- Index

Not available.

Historical Profile

Return	Above Average
Risk	Low
Rating	★★★★★ Highest

Investment Style History
Fixed Income

Income Rtn % Rank Obj

Growth of $10,000
- ‖‖ Value of Fund ($000)
- — Value of Index ($000) FB HY
- ▼ Manager Change
- ▽ Partial Manager Change
- ► Mgr Unknown After
- ◄ Mgr Unknown Before

Performance Quartile (Within Objective)

	1983	1984	1985	1986	1987	1988	1989	1990	1991	1992	1993	1994	History
	---	---	---	---	9.50	9.84	10.03	9.14	10.20	11.12	11.63	10.74	NAV
	---	---	---	---	---	12.38	10.81	-0.15	23.91	21.71	16.96	-1.10	Total Return %
	---	---	---	---	---	-4.23	-20.88	2.97	-6.57	14.10	6.91	-2.41	+/- S&P 500
	---	---	---	---	---	4.50	-3.73	-9.09	7.91	14.47	7.21	1.82	+/- LB Aggregate
	---	---	---	---	---	8.25	8.26	8.36	10.73	6.88	5.92	6.28	Income Return %
	---	---	---	---	---	4.13	2.55	-8.51	13.18	14.84	11.04	-7.38	Capital Return %
	---	---	---	---	---	42	66	56	38	3	23	27	Total Rtn % Rank All
	---	---	---	---	---	46	55	61	40	1	10	4	Total Rtn % Rank Obj
	---	---	---	---	0.04	0.77	0.79	0.83	0.93	0.70	0.65	0.73	Income $
	---	---	---	---	0.00	0.05	0.06	0.04	0.13	0.55	0.68	0.03	Capital Gains $
	---	---	---	---	---	5.98	1.75	1.50	1.46	1.34	1.34	1.07	1.00	Expense Ratio %
	---	---	---	---	---	1.84	8.29	8.00	8.59	8.40	6.14	6.15	6.30	Income Ratio %
	---	---	---	---	---	---	17	3	14	14	46	83	28	Turnover Rate %
	---	---	---	---	---	0.9	2.6	3.9	4.0	5.4	12.5	30.3	55.8	Net Assets ($mil)

Performance 12-31-94

	1st Qtr	2nd Qtr	3rd Qtr	4th Qtr	Total
1987	---	---	---	-1.14	
1988	6.00	2.43	2.21	1.26	12.38
1989	0.91	6.47	2.44	0.68	10.81
1990	-1.10	2.27	-4.83	3.73	-0.15
1991	8.97	2.34	5.72	5.09	23.91
1992	10.59	2.98	4.64	2.13	21.71
1993	5.67	3.88	4.06	2.40	16.96
1994	0.34	-2.34	3.52	-2.51	-1.10

Bear Market Performance

Decile Rank (5-year period)

Worst ▮ Best

	Worst 3 Mo Period 1985-89	Worst 3 Mo Period 1990-94
Berwyn Income	---	-5.48
+/- S&P 500	---	8.36
+/- Best Fit Index : FB HY	---	8.63

Trailing Returns

	Total Return %	+/- S&P 500	+/- LB Aggregate	% Rank All	% Rank Obj	Growth of $10,000
3 Mo	-2.51	-2.50	-2.89	77	83	9,749
6 Mo	0.92	-3.94	-0.07	39	27	10,092
1 Yr	-1.10	-2.41	1.82	27	4	9,890
3 Yr Avg	12.08	5.81	7.53	8	1	14,079
5 Yr Avg	11.74	3.05	4.11	10	2	17,420
10 Yr Avg	---	---	---	---	---	---
15 Yr Avg	---	---	---	---	---	---

Operations

Address and Telephone	1189 Lancaster Avenue Berwyn, PA 19312 800-824-2249 / 215-640-4330
Advisor	Killen Group
Subadvisor	None
Distributor	Berwyn Income Fund
States Available	All except MS,ND,SD,WV
Report Grade	B-
Income Distrib	Paid Quarterly
* Date of Inception	04-02-87
Fiscal Year End	December

Risk Analysis

Time Period	Load-Adj Return %	Risk % Rank [1] All	Risk % Rank [1] Obj	Morningstar [2] Return	Morningstar Risk	Morningstar Risk-Adj Rating
1 Yr	-1.10					
3 Yr	12.08	10	7	2.66 [3]	0.39	★★★★★
5 Yr	11.74	31	20	1.86 [3]	0.40	★★★★★
10 Yr	---					

Average Historical Rating (53 months)   4.4 ★s

[1] 1 = low, 100 = high   [2] 1.00 = Hybrid Avg   [3] 1.00 = 90-day T-bill return

Other Measures

			Standard S&P 500	Best Fit FB HY
Standard Deviation	6.13	Alpha	7.3	1.1
Mean	11.64	Beta	0.38	0.97
Sharpe Ratio	1.32	R-Squared	24	48

Investment Style

Stocks

	Port Avg	Rel S&P 500
Price/Earnings Ratio	22.0	1.19
Price/Book Ratio	1.4	0.42
5 Yr Earnings Gr %	1.8#	0.32
Med Mkt Cap ($mil)	442	0.03

figure is based on 50% or less of stocks

Bonds

Avg Effective Duration	3.8 Yrs **
Avg Effective Maturity	10.8 Yrs
Avg Credit Quality	B
Avg Weighted Coupon	8.66%

**figure provided by fund

Diversification Value for Portfolio Types

Large Cap: High	Small Cap: Medium	Bond: High	Balanced: Medium	Diversified: High

Min Initial Purchase, etc.

Min Initial Purchase	$10000 (Addt'l: $250)
Min IRA Purchase	$1000 (Addt'l: None)
Min Auto Invest Plan	$10000 (Systematic Inv: $50)

Expenses & Fees

Sales Fees	0.00% front
	0.00% deferred
	0.00% 12b-1
Management Fee	0.50% flat fee
3-,5-,10-yr Expense Projections	$34, $59, $131
Annual Brokerage Cost	0.47%

Portfolio 09-30-94

Share Chg (03-94)000	Amount 000	Total Stocks: 28 / Total Fixed-Income: 69	Date of Maturity	Value $000	% Net Assets
1285	1285	Acme Metals 12.5%	08-01-02	1298	2.47
1450	1450	Data General Cv 7.75%	06-01-01	1254	2.39
1300	1300	OMI International 10.25%	11-01-03	1147	2.19
1358	1358	Ducommun Cv 7.75%	03-31-11	1107	2.11
1150	1150	Geneva Steel 9.5%	01-15-04	1035	1.97
1055	1055	Wainoco Oil Cv 7.75%	06-01-14	997	1.90
1046	1046	M/A-Communications Cv 9.25%	05-15-06	991	1.89
1300	1300	Dixie Yarns Cv 7%	05-15-12	982	1.87
1250	1250	Rohr Industries Cv 7%	10-01-12	919	1.75
1000	1000	Gulf Canada Resources Cv 9.25%	01-15-04	918	1.75
1200	1200	Standard Commercial Cv 7.25%	03-31-07	905	1.72
1250	1250	Zenith Electronics Cv 6.25%	04-01-11	891	1.70
1000	1000	Kaiser Aluminum 9.875%	02-15-02	885	1.69
801	801	Western Digital Cv 9%	06-01-14	883	1.68
850	850	Computer Products Cv 9.5%	05-15-97	878	1.67
903	903	Brown & Sharp Mfg Cv 9.25%	12-15-05	869	1.66
24	24	National Intergroup Pfd		851	1.62
1000	1000	Seagate Technology Cv 6.75%	05-01-12	841	1.60
1100	1100	Cray Research Cv 6.125%	02-01-11	831	1.58
800	800	Gaylord Container 11.5%	05-15-01	816	1.55

Index Allocation

	% of Stocks
S&P 500	19.9
S&P MidCap 400	21.6
U.S. Small Cap	48.1
Foreign	11.7

Composition % 12-31-94

Cash	4.8	Preferreds	3.3
Stocks	15.6	Convertibles	47.6
Bonds	28.7	Other	0.0

Tax Analysis

	Tax-Adj Historical Return %	% Pretax Return
3 Yr Avg	8.59	68.8
5 Yr Avg	8.33	66.2
10 Yr Avg	---	---
Potential Capital Gain Exposure (% of assets)		-6%

Most Similar Funds in MF500

Lindner	Weak Fit
Schafer Value	Weak Fit
Neuberger&Berman Partners	Weak Fit

Bond Credit Analysis 12-31-94

% of Bonds			
US Govt	0	BB	11
AAA	0	B	55
AA	0	Below B	7
A	0	NR/NA	23
BBB	4		

Stock Sector Weightings

	% of Stocks	Relative S&P 500
Utilities	18.2	1.46
Energy	13.0	1.28
Financials	10.9	1.03
Industrial Cyclicals	35.3	2.15
Consumer Durables	3.6	0.57
Consumer Staples	0.0	0.00
Services	15.1	1.86
Retail	0.0	0.00
Health	4.0	0.46
Technology	0.0	0.00

MORNINGSTAR   1995 Mutual Fund 500

William Blair Growth Shares

	Ticker	Load	NAV	Yield	SEC Yield	Assets	Objective
	WBGSX	None	9.60	0.2%	N/A	182.2	Growth

William Blair Growth Shares seeks long-term capital appreciation. Increasing income is secondary.

The fund invests primarily in common stocks of well-managed companies in growing industries. To qualify for consideration, a company should be a leader in its field, be a unique or specialty company, produce quality products or services, demonstrate distinctive marketing capability, show value to customers, have the potential to achieve above-average return on equity, and maintain conservative financial policies and accounting practices.

Prior to April 30, 1991, the fund was named Growth Industry Shares.

Manager's Investment Style

Although the fund's prospectus outlines many specific investment policies, management has had (and has taken) the liberty to alter the fund's median market cap and to shift from growth to more-value-oriented cyclical stocks when it deems appropriate. Management will also take concentrated positions in stocks and sectors.

Fund Manager(s)

Rocky Barber CFA(1981), since 05-93. Birthdate: 10-51. MS, Stanford U. 1973 MBA, Stanford U. 1975
Mark Fuller, since 05-93. Birthdate: 03-57. BA, Northwestern U. 1979 MBA, Northwestern U. 1983

Manager Experience	Dates Managed	Invest Obj	Std Dev	+/- Index
Rocky Barber				
William Blair Income	09/90 - 01/93	CQ	3.81	-0.87

Historical Profile

Return	Above Average
Risk	Average
Rating	★★★★ Above Average

Investment Style History
Equity

86% 91% 89% 85% 91% 89% 87% 90%

Average % Stocks Held in Portfolio

Growth of $10,000
- ‖‖ Value of Fund ($000)
- — Value of Index ($000) SPMid400
- ▼ Manager Change
- ▽ Partial Manager Change
- ► Mgr Unknown After
- ◄ Mgr Unknown Before

Performance Quartile (Within Objective)

	1983	1984	1985	1986	1987	1988	1989	1990	1991	1992	1993	1994	History
	11.69	10.29	11.82	9.10	8.21	7.81	7.84	6.97	9.49	9.39	9.73	9.60	NAV
	13.45	-4.22	23.34	9.79	7.99	7.12	30.45	-2.02	44.37	7.61	15.51	6.45	Total Return %
	-9.02	-10.48	-8.39	-8.89	2.73	-9.49	-1.23	1.10	13.88	-0.01	5.46	5.14	+/- S&P 500
	-10.01	-7.27	-9.22	-6.30	5.62	-10.82	1.28	4.17	10.16	-1.36	4.23	6.52	+/- Wilshire 5000
	1.67	2.14	2.25	2.07	1.36	1.97	1.61	1.70	0.87	0.52	0.37	0.26	Income Return %
	11.78	-6.36	21.10	7.72	6.62	5.15	28.84	-3.72	43.50	7.09	15.14	6.19	Capital Return %
	65	78	53	85	13	80	12	62	11	50	27	3	Total Rtn % Rank All
	86	63	80	85	19	84	32	35	22	52	31	5	Total Rtn % Rank Obj
	0.19	0.22	0.23	0.22	0.14	0.16	0.13	0.13	0.07	0.05	0.04	0.03	Income $
	0.34	0.67	0.57	3.52	1.37	0.80	2.14	0.58	0.45	0.77	1.05	0.71	Capital Gains $
	0.87	0.92	0.95	0.90	0.87	0.92	0.91	0.87	0.90	0.83	0.78	0.72	Expense Ratio %
	1.76	2.06	1.96	1.69	1.46	1.46	1.36	1.70	0.83	1.34	0.38	0.25	Income Ratio %
	10	13	43	26	22	18	45	34	33	27	55	---	Turnover Rate %
	63.5	58.4	72.2	68.6	66.3	59.8	67.4	62.9	91.4	111.1	149.8	182.2	Net Assets ($mil)

Performance 12-31-94

	1st Qtr	2nd Qtr	3rd Qtr	4th Qtr	Total
1987	18.35	3.48	4.89	-15.93	7.99
1988	4.11	4.37	-1.52	0.10	7.12
1989	3.33	11.49	11.79	1.30	30.45
1990	-1.66	9.60	-14.61	6.46	-2.02
1991	19.94	-2.87	9.70	12.97	44.37
1992	-4.95	-1.66	5.59	9.03	7.61
1993	0.32	0.64	9.52	4.47	15.51
1994	-4.62	1.94	9.26	0.21	6.45

Bear Market Performance

Decile Rank (5-year period)

Worst ————————— Best

	Worst 3 Mo Period 1985-89	Worst 3 Mo Period 1990-94
William Blair Growth Shares	-25.37	-14.86
+/- S&P 500	4.21	-1.02
+/- Best Fit Index : SPMid400	3.44	3.56

Trailing Returns

	Total Return %	+/- S&P 500	+/- Wil 5000	% Rank All	% Rank Obj	Growth of $10,000
3 Mo	0.21	0.23	0.98	17	18	10,021
6 Mo	9.49	4.63	4.87	5	10	10,949
1 Yr	6.45	5.14	6.52	3	5	10,645
3 Yr Avg	9.79	3.52	3.17	14	19	13,233
5 Yr Avg	13.36	4.67	4.54	6	9	18,718
10 Yr Avg	14.36	-0.03	0.50	15	22	38,250
15 Yr Avg	14.65	0.17	0.68	17	33	77,782

Operations

Address and Telephone	222 W. Adams Street 34th Floor
	Chicago, IL 60606
	800-742-7272 / 312-853-2424
Advisor	William Blair & Company
Subadvisor	None
Distributor	William Blair & Company
States Available	All
Report Grade	B
Income Distrib	Paid Semiannually
Date of Inception	03-20-46
Fiscal Year End	December

Risk Analysis

Time Period	Load-Adj Return %	Risk % Rank [1] All	Risk % Rank [1] Obj	Morningstar [2] Return	Morningstar Risk	Morningstar Risk-Adj Rating
1 Yr	6.45					
3 Yr	9.79	73	40	1.90 [3]	0.83	★★★★
5 Yr	13.36	75	44	2.36 [3]	0.89	★★★★★
10 Yr	14.36	75	55	1.35	0.97	★★★★
Average Historical Rating (109 months)					3.4	★s

[1] 1 = low, 100 = high [2] 1.00 = Equity Avg [3] 1.00 = 90-day T-bill return

Other Measures

			Standard S&P 500	Best Fit SPMid400
Standard Deviation	10.38	Alpha	3.4	2.8
Mean	9.91	Beta	1.07	0.93
Sharpe Ratio	0.62	R-Squared	67	79

Investment Style

	Stock Portfolio Avg	Relative S&P 500
Price/Earnings Ratio	28.3	1.53
Price/Book Ratio	4.0	1.17
5 Yr Earnings Gr %	17.6#	3.18
Return on Assets %	9.4	1.26
Debt % Total Cap	22.2	0.78
Med Mkt Cap ($mil)	1290	0.10

figure is based on 50% or less of stocks

Style: Value Blend Growth / Large Med Small

Diversification Value for Portfolio Types

Large Cap: Low	Small Cap: Low	Bond: High	Balanced: Low	Diversified: Low

Expenses & Fees

Sales Fees	0.00% front
	0.00% deferred
	0.00% 12b-1
Management Fee	0.63% max./0.50% min.
3-,5-,10-yr Expense Projections	$25, $46, $97
Annual Brokerage Cost	0.17%

Portfolio 12-31-94

Total Stocks: 68
Total Fixed-Income: 0

Share Chg (11-94) 000	Amount 000		Value $000	% Net Assets
30	130	Alco Standard	8158	4.48
24	124	FHLMC	6262	3.44
10	120	Home Depot	5520	3.03
20	80	Microsoft	4890	2.68
30	130	Elan (ADR)	4631	2.54
28	118	Household International	4381	2.40
30	150	AirTouch Communications	4369	2.40
26	96	Air Products & Chemicals	4262	2.34
20	140	Green Tree Financial	4253	2.33
25	108	Canandaigua Wine Cl A	4112	2.26
40	165	Heilig-Meyers	4099	2.25
0	100	Department 56	3975	2.18
20	110	Cintas	3905	2.14
40	130	Minerals Technologies	3803	2.09
25	135	Acxiom	3746	2.06
20	100	HEALTHSOUTH Rehabilitation	3700	2.03
20	110	CUC International	3658	2.01
0	74	Vishay Intertechnology	3612	1.98
40	190	Digi International	3563	1.95
30	100	Norand	3550	1.95
35	135	Mattel	3392	1.86
0	55	First Financial Management	3389	1.86
25	113	Heartland Express	3375	1.85
40	180	MCI Communications	3308	1.82
0	75	Omnicare	3281	1.80

Composition % 12-31-94

Cash	13.0	Preferreds	0.0
Stocks	87.0	Convertibles	0.0
Bonds	0.0	Other	0.0

Tax Analysis

	Tax-Adj Historical Return %	% Pretax Return
3 Yr Avg	7.18	71.5
5 Yr Avg	10.71	76.0
10 Yr Avg	10.22	58.2
Potential Capital Gain Exposure (% of assets)		20%

Most Similar Funds in MF500

Putnam Voyager A	Fair Fit
Harbor Capital Appreciation	Fair Fit
Vanguard Index Extended Mkt	Fair Fit

Index Allocation

	% of Stocks
S&P 500	30.6
S&P MidCap 400	18.2
U.S. Small Cap	46.0
Foreign	5.2

Sector Weightings

	% of Stocks	Relative S&P 500
Utilities	1.8	0.14
Energy	0.0	0.00
Financials	8.6	0.82
Industrial Cyclicals	14.2	0.87
Consumer Durables	12.7	2.05
Consumer Staples	4.3	0.34
Services	12.0	1.48
Retail	10.8	1.86
Health	7.4	0.85
Technology	28.2	3.08

Blanchard Flexible Income

	Ticker	Load	NAV	Yield	SEC Yield	Assets	Objective
	BLFIX	None	4.55	7.1%	7.87%	272.1	Income

Blanchard Flexible Income Fund seeks current income; capital appreciation is secondary.

The fund normally invests at least 65% of its assets in income-producing securities, including domestic and foreign government, mortgage, and corporate securities. It may participate in options and futures transactions to seek high current income. The fund does not typically invest more than 35% of its assets in securities rated below investment grade. It may not invest more than 15% of its assets in emerging-market fixed-income securities.

A one-time account opening fee of $75 is levied on all initial investments regardless of size.

Manager's Investment Style

Management uses a multimarket approach, dividing assets among high-quality domestic bonds, domestic junk bonds, and foreign-government bonds. It may also invest up to 15% of assets (a mandated maximum) in emerging-market debt. Turnover to date has been very high.

Fund Manager(s)

Jack Burks, since 11-92. Birthdate: 04-51. BA, Indiana U. 1972 MBA, Indiana U. 1978

Manager Experience

	Dates Managed	Invest Obj	Std Dev	+/- Index
Jack Burks				
Blanchard Short-Term Bond	04/93 - 12/94	CG	1.39	1.95

Historical Profile

Return	---
Risk	---
Rating	Not Rated

Investment Style History
Fixed Income

Income Rtn % Rank Obj

Growth of $10,000

|||| Value of Fund ($000)
— Value of Index ($000)
    S&P 500
▼ Manager Change
▽ Partial Manager Change
► Mgr Unknown After
◄ Mgr Unknown Before

Performance Quartile
(Within Objective)

History	1983	1984	1985	1986	1987	1988	1989	1990	1991	1992	1993	1994
NAV	---	---	---	---	---	---	---	---	---	4.98	5.15	4.55
Total Return %	---	---	---	---	---	---	---	---	---	0.87 *	13.86	-5.54
+/- S&P 500	---	---	---	---	---	---	---	---	---	-2.79 *	3.81	-6.85
+/- LB Aggregate	---	---	---	---	---	---	---	---	---	---	4.11	-2.62
Income Return %	---	---	---	---	---	---	---	---	---	1.27	8.98	6.11
Capital Return %	---	---	---	---	---	---	---	---	---	-0.40	4.88	-11.65
Total Rtn % Rank All	---	---	---	---	---	---	---	---	---	---	34	69
Total Rtn % Rank Obj	---	---	---	---	---	---	---	---	---	---	50	71
Income $	---	---	---	---	---	---	---	---	---	0.06	0.43	0.32
Capital Gains $	---	---	---	---	---	---	---	---	---	0.00	0.07	0.00
Expense Ratio %	---	---	---	---	---	---	---	---	---	---	0.20	1.30
Income Ratio %	---	---	---	---	---	---	---	---	---	---	9.02	7.10
Turnover Rate %	---	---	---	---	---	---	---	---	---	---	---	346
Net Assets ($mil)	---	---	---	---	---	---	---	---	---	32.0	690.5	272.1

Performance 12-31-94

	1st Qtr	2nd Qtr	3rd Qtr	4th Qtr	Total
1987	---	---	---	---	---
1988	---	---	---	---	---
1989	---	---	---	---	---
1990	---	---	---	---	---
1991	---	---	---	---	---
1992	---	---	---	---	0.87 *
1993	4.69	3.21	2.58	2.73	13.86
1994	-2.63	-2.15	-0.05	-0.81	-5.54

Bear Market Performance

Decile Rank (5-year period)

Worst   Best

	Worst 3 Mo Period 1985-89	Worst 3 Mo Period 1990-94
Blanchard Flexible Income	---	---
+/- S&P 500	---	---
+/- Best Fit Index :	---	---

Trailing Returns

	Total Return %	+/- S&P 500	+/- LB Aggregate	% Rank All	% Rank Obj	Growth of $10,000
3 Mo	-0.81	-0.79	-1.18	40	37	9,919
6 Mo	-0.85	-5.71	-1.84	71	65	9,915
1 Yr	-5.54	-6.85	-2.62	69	71	9,446
3 Yr Avg	---	---	---	---	---	---
5 Yr Avg	---	---	---	---	---	---
10 Yr Avg	---	---	---	---	---	---
15 Yr Avg	---	---	---	---	---	---

Risk Analysis

Time Period	Load-Adj Return %	Risk % Rank [1] All	Obj	Morningstar [2] Return	Morningstar Risk	Morningstar Risk-Adj Rating
1 Yr	-5.54					
3 Yr	---	---	---	---	---	---
5 Yr	---	---	---	---	---	---
10 Yr	---	---	---	---	---	---

Average Historical Rating ---   ---

[1] = low, 100 = high   [2] 1.00 = Hybrid Avg   [3] 1.00 = 90-day T-bill return

Other Measures

			Standard S&P 500	Best Fit
Standard Deviation	---	Alpha	---	---
Mean	---	Beta	---	---
Sharpe Ratio	---	R-Squared	---	---

Investment Style

Stocks

	Port Avg	Rel S&P 500
Price/Earnings Ratio	---	---
Price/Book Ratio	---	---
5 Yr Earnings Gr %	---	---
Med Mkt Cap ($mil)	---	---

Not Available

Bonds

		Maturity S I L
Avg Effective Duration	4.3 Yrs	
Avg Effective Maturity	6.3 Yrs	
Avg Credit Quality	A	
Avg Weighted Coupon	8.31%	

Diversification Value for Portfolio Types

Large Cap: Small Cap: Bond: Balanced: Diversified:

Portfolio 10-31-94

Share Chg ---000	Amount 000	Total Stocks: 0 Total Fixed-Income: 81	Date of Maturity	Value $000	% Net Assets
	45823	GNMA 8%	06-15-24	44287	13.38
	25000	US Treasury Note 7.875%	04-15-98	25469	7.69
	25000	US Treasury Note 6.875%	10-31-96	25023	7.56
	25000	US Treasury Note 7.5%	05-15-02	24773	7.48
	25000	US Treasury Note 7%	04-15-99	24617	7.44
	10000	FNMA Debenture 8.625%	04-10-01	10019	3.03
	14720	Republic of Germany 7%	12-12-97	9842	2.97
	14420	Republic of Germany 7.25%	10-20-97	9726	2.94
	9000	FNMA Debenture 8.2%	08-10-98	9032	2.73
	4550	Leucadia National 10.375%	06-15-02	4783	1.44
	4251	Republic of Argentina 16.04%	05-01-01	4658	1.41
	4000	RJR Nabisco 8%	01-15-00	3750	1.13
	4265	Tucson Electric Power 10.21%	01-01-09	3668	1.11
	3000	Owens-Illinois 10%	08-01-02	2970	0.90
	3000	Sequa 8.75%	12-15-01	2715	0.82
	4000	Rogers Cablesystems 9.65%	01-15-14	2628	0.79
	2506	Omega Healthcare 7.11%	07-15-00	2444	0.74
	2656	Resolution Trust 7.1%	12-25-24	2357	0.71
	2500	Stone Container 9.875%	02-01-01	2350	0.71
	2500	UNC 9.125%	07-15-03	2213	0.67

Index Allocation

	% of Stocks
S&P 500	---
S&P MidCap 400	---
U.S. Small Cap	---
Foreign	---

Composition % 12-31-94

Cash	1.3	Preferreds	0.1
Stocks	0.0	Convertibles	0.0
Bonds	98.6	Other	0.0

Tax Analysis

	Tax-Adj Historical Return %	% Pretax Return
3 Yr Avg	---	---
5 Yr Avg	---	---
10 Yr Avg	---	---

Potential Capital Gain Exposure
(% of assets)   -16%

Most Similar Funds in MF500

Fund lacks three-year record

Bond Credit Analysis 12-31-94

% of Bonds

US Govt	54	BB	11
AAA	4	B	24
AA	1	Below B	1
A	0	NR/NA	0
BBB	5		

Stock Sector Weightings

	% of Stocks	Relative S&P 500
Utilities	---	---
Energy	---	---
Financials	---	---
Industrial Cyclicals	---	---
Consumer Durables	---	---
Consumer Staples	---	---
Services	---	---
Retail	---	---
Health	---	---
Technology	---	---

Operations

Address and Telephone	41 Madison Avenue 24th Floor New York, NY 10010 800-922-7771 / 212-779-7979
Advisor	Sheffield Management
Subadvisor	Offitbank
Distributor	Sheffield Investments
States Available	All
Report Grade	C+
Income Distrib	Paid Monthly
* Date of Inception	11-02-92
Fiscal Year End	April

Min Initial Purchase	$3000 (Addt'l: $200)
Min IRA Purchase	$2000 (Addt'l: $200)
Min Auto Invest Plan	$3000 (Systematic Inv: $100)

Expenses & Fees

Sales Fees	0.00% front
	0.00% deferred
	0.25% 12b-1
Management Fee	0.75% flat fee
3-,5-,10-yr Expense Projections	$70, $103, $195
Annual Brokerage Cost	---

MORNINGSTAR   1995 Mutual Fund 500

Bond Fund of America

Bond Fund of America seeks current income consistent with the preservation of capital.

The fund invests in a diversified portfolio consisting primarily of marketable fixed-income debt securities, government obligations, and money-market instruments. At least 60% of the fund's assets are invested in high-grade (A or better) straight debt securities, government securities, or high-grade short-term investments. The balance of assets may be invested in other debt securities, but any security rated below BBB is subject to special review.

Manager's Investment Style

The fund's management team emphasizes diversification, holding government and corporate bonds of various maturities and credit qualities. Management has invested a relatively large stake in zero-coupon bonds and lower-quality credits compared with its average peer, adding potential for downmarket volatility. Lower-quality bonds and a sizable stake in higher-coupon debt from years ago help keep the fund's yield high, which often mitigates volatility.

Fund Manager(s)

Abner D. Goldstine, since 05-74.
John H. Smet, since 01-89.
Richard T. Schotte, since 01-80.

Manager Experience	Dates Managed	Invest Obj	Std Dev	+/- Index
Abner D. Goldstine				
Income Fund of America	11/73 - 12/94	I	9.53	-0.15
Bond Port for Endowments	01/75 - 12/94	CG	6.65	0.13

Performance 12-31-94

	1st Qtr	2nd Qtr	3rd Qtr	4th Qtr	Total
1987	4.01	-2.99	-3.84	5.07	1.96
1988	5.22	1.92	2.31	0.89	10.70
1989	1.48	5.82	0.85	1.69	10.13
1990	-1.02	3.69	-2.15	2.84	3.27
1991	5.63	2.78	5.83	5.35	21.04
1992	0.80	4.23	5.22	0.72	11.34
1993	5.58	3.61	3.37	0.95	14.15
1994	-3.71	-1.53	0.77	-0.59	-5.02

Bear Market Performance

Decile Rank (5-year period)

Worst ———————————— Best

	Worst 3 Mo Period 1985-89	Worst 3 Mo Period 1990-94
Bond Fund of America	-4.62	-6.54
+/- LB Aggregate	-1.07	-1.60
+/- Best Fit Index : LB Corp	-0.51	-0.27

Trailing Returns

	Total Return %	+/- LB Aggregate	+/- LB Corp	% Rank All	% Rank Obj	Growth of $10,000
3 Mo	-0.59	-0.97	-1.03	36	83	9,941
6 Mo	0.17	-0.82	-1.00	54	72	10,017
1 Yr	-5.02	-2.10	-1.09	64	78	9,498
3 Yr Avg	6.48	1.93	1.07	30	7	12,072
5 Yr Avg	8.58	0.95	0.31	27	11	15,090
10 Yr Avg	10.58	0.63	-0.05	52	12	27,332
15 Yr Avg	11.19	0.38	-0.14	63	4	49,090

Operations

Address and Telephone	333 S. Hope Street	
	Los Angeles, CA 90071	
	800-421-4120 / 213-486-9200	
Advisor	Capital Research & Management	
Subadvisor	None	
Distributor	American Funds Distributors	
States Available	All plus GU,PR,VI	
Report Grade	A-	
Income Distrib	Paid Monthly	
Date of Inception	05-28-74	
Fiscal Year End	December	

Min Initial Purchase	$1000 (Addt'l: $50)
Min IRA Purchase	$250 (Addt'l: $50)
Min Auto Invest Plan	$50 (Systematic Inv: $50)

Expenses & Fees

Sales Fees	
	4.75% front
	0.00% deferred
	0.25% 12b-1
Management Fee	0.30% max./0.16% min.+3.00%I
3-,5-,10-yr Expense Projections	$69, $85, $132

Ticker	Load	NAV	Yield	SEC Yield	Assets	Objective
ABNDX	4.75%	12.69	8.3%	7.95%	4941.2	Corp General

Historical Profile

Return	High
Risk	Average
Rating	★★★★ Above Average

Investment Style History
Fixed Income
Income Rtn % Rank Obj

26	21	14	14	9	5	11	7

Growth of $10,000

IIII Value of Fund ($000)
— Value of Index ($000) LB Corp
▼ Manager Change
▽ Partial Manager Change
► Mgr Unknown After
◄ Mgr Unknown Before

Performance Quartile (Within Objective)

1983	1984	1985	1986	1987	1988	1989	1990	1991	1992	1993	1994	History
12.41	12.34	14.01	14.21	13.14	13.24	13.23	12.39	13.70	13.99	14.45	12.69	NAV
9.41	11.93	26.53	15.16	1.96	10.70	10.13	3.27	21.04	11.34	14.15	-5.02	Total Return %
1.04	-3.22	4.40	-0.09	-0.80	2.82	-4.41	-5.68	5.04	4.10	4.40	-2.10	+/- LB Aggregate
0.14	-4.69	2.47	-1.37	-0.60	1.48	-3.85	-3.89	2.54	2.65	1.99	-1.09	+/- LB Corporate
11.54	12.50	13.00	10.79	9.49	9.94	10.20	9.62	10.47	8.93	7.95	7.16	Income Return %
-2.13	-0.56	13.53	4.37	-7.53	0.76	-0.08	-6.35	10.57	2.42	6.20	-12.18	Capital Return %
83	18	40	53	43	55	72	48	43	17	32	64	Total Rtn % Rank All
45	64	1	32	45	14	67	89	6	4	12	78	Total Rtn % Rank Obj
1.44	1.44	1.44	1.44	1.34	1.27	1.30	1.24	1.18	1.16	1.08	1.05	Income $
0.00	0.00	0.00	0.40	0.00	0.00	0.00	0.00	0.00	0.04	0.39	0.00	Capital Gains $
0.63	0.66	0.61	0.58	0.59	0.66	0.76	0.76	0.77	0.73	0.71	---	Expense Ratio %
11.43	11.66	10.80	9.39	9.45	9.54	9.73	9.70	9.28	8.36	7.53	---	Income Ratio %
121	128	142	108	93	93	64	60	56	50	45	---	Turnover Rate %
319.3	355.3	450.7	694.3	825.0	1021.3	1480.8	1944.8	2858.5	3917.3	5284.6	4941.2	Net Assets ($mil)

Risk Analysis

Time Period	Load-Adj Return %	Risk % Rank[1] All	Obj	Morningstar[2] Return	Morningstar Risk	Morningstar Risk-Adj Rating
1 Yr	-9.53					
3 Yr	4.77	22	47	0.35[3]	1.00	★★★★
5 Yr	7.53	29	60	0.69[3]	1.08	★★★
10 Yr	10.04	19	39	1.14[3]	1.03	★★★★★
Average Historical Rating (109 months)					3.9	★ s

[1] 1 = low, 100 = high [2] 1.00 = Taxable Avg [3] 1.00 = 90-day T-bill return

Other Measures

			Standard LB Agg	Best Fit LB Corp
Standard Deviation	4.72	Alpha	1.8	1.2
Mean	6.41	Beta	1.13	0.91
Sharpe Ratio	0.61	R-Squared	91	93

Investment Style

Interest-Rate Stance

Avg Effective Duration	4.8 Yrs
Avg Effective Maturity	7.6 Yrs

Quality

Avg Credit Quality	A
Avg Weighted Coupon	8.50%
Avg Weighted Price	97.45% of Par

Diversification Value for Portfolio Types

Large Cap: Medium	Small Cap: High	Bond: None	Balanced: Low	Diversified: Medium

Portfolio 06-30-94

Amount 000	Date of Maturity	Total Stocks: 2 / Total Fixed-Income: 434	Value $000	% Net Assets
162114	2024	GNMA 4.5%	152472	3.04
114750	11-15-04	US Treasury Bond 11.625%	149318	2.98
108000	08-15-98	US Treasury Note 9.25%	117282	2.34
79500	02-15-10	US Treasury Bond 11.75%	103797	2.07
65000	11-15-02	US Treasury Bond 11.625%	82530	1.65
60500	08-15-17	US Treasury Bond 8.875%	67646	1.35
63000	01-15-97	US Treasury Note 8%	65343	1.30
66849	2024	GNMA 5%	64140	1.28
65691	2024	GNMA 7%	60540	1.21
58137	2024	GNMA 7.5%	55458	1.11
50000	03-01-21	General Motors 8.8%	53380	1.07
50000	04-15-97	US Treasury Note 8.5%	52524	1.05
45000	02-15-98	US Treasury Note 8.125%	47018	0.94
43475	11-01-01	Rogers Cantel Mobile 10.75%	44779	0.89
42000	02-15-96	US Treasury Note 8.875%	43857	0.88
37500	10-15-12	News America Holdings 10.125%	39435	0.79
25500	11-15-11	US Treasury Bond 14%	38561	0.77
56000	09-01-03	NEXTEL Communications 0%	35000	0.70
39245	2024	GNMA 6.5%	34743	0.69
60000	2004	NEXTEL Communications 0%	34200	0.68
35429	2023	FNMA 7%	32981	0.66
30000	11-15-00	US Treasury Note 8.5%	32114	0.64
29000	08-15-00	US Treasury Note 8.75%	31379	0.63
52900	2000	Comcast 0%	31211	0.62
30000	04-30-96	US Treasury Note 7.625%	30773	0.61

Composition % 12-31-94

Cash	11.9	Preferreds	0.0
Stocks	0.4	Convertibles	2.9
Bonds	84.8	Other	0.0

Tax Analysis

	Tax-Adj Historical Return %	% Pretax Return
3 Yr Avg	3.22	48.2
5 Yr Avg	5.35	58.5
10 Yr Avg	6.74	53.1
Potential Capital Gain Exposure (% of assets)		-8%

Most Similar Funds in MF500

SteinRoe Income	Strong Fit
J Hancock Inc	Strong Fit
Putnam Income A	Strong Fit

Coupon Range

	% of Bonds	Rel Obj
0%	7.0	3.20
0% to 8.5%	30.9	0.49
8.5% to 9.5%	25.3	1.56
9.5% to 11%	18.1	1.96
More than 11%	16.5	4.24
Not applicable	2.3	0.46

Credit Analysis 12-31-94

% of Bonds

US Govt	44	BB	10
AAA	7	B	14
AA	4	Below B	1
A	6	NR/NA	0
BBB	14		

Bramwell Growth

	Ticker	Load	NAV	Yield	SEC Yield	Assets	Objective
	BRGRX	None	10.25	N/A	N/A	13.4	Growth

Bramwell Growth Fund seeks long-term capital growth; current income is a secondary objective.

The fund invests primarily in common stock and high-quality convertible securities. Its investment approach incorporates both top-down and bottom-up analysis, targeting companies positioned to realize long-term unit and earnings growth. No more than 5% of the fund's assets may be invested in securities of companies having records of less than three years of continuous operation. The fund may invest up to 25% of its assets in foreign securities, either directly or through American depositary receipts. It may also invest up to 5% of its assets in warrants or rights.

Manager's Investment Style

In this fund, manager Elizabeth Bramwell is implementing the investment style that won her accolades as manager of Gabelli Growth. She typically takes a flexible approach to growth investing, seeking not only traditional mid-cap-growth names, but also stocks of other firms that are actively improving productivity, gaining international exposure, or releasing new products.

Fund Manager(s)

Elizabeth R. Bramwell CFA(1973), since 08-94.
Birthdate: 12-40. BA, Bryn Mawr C. 1962   MBA, Columbia U. 1967

Manager Experience

	Dates Managed	Invest Obj	Std Dev	+/- Index
Elizabeth R. Bramwell				
Gabelli Growth	04/87 - 02/94	G	15.59	5.40

Historical Profile

Return ---
Risk ---
Rating Not Rated

Investment Style History
Equity

Average % Stocks Held in Portfolio 92%

Growth of $10,000

‖‖ Value of Fund ($000)
— Value of Index ($000) S&P 500
▼ Manager Change
▽ Partial Manager Change
► Mgr Unknown After
◄ Mgr Unknown Before

Performance Quartile (Within Objective)

	1983	1984	1985	1986	1987	1988	1989	1990	1991	1992	1993	1994	History
	---	---	---	---	---	---	---	---	---	---	---	10.25	NAV
	---	---	---	---	---	---	---	---	---	---	---	2.59 *	Total Return %
	---	---	---	---	---	---	---	---	---	---	---	1.67 *	+/- S&P 500
	---	---	---	---	---	---	---	---	---	---	---	---	+/- Wilshire 5000
	---	---	---	---	---	---	---	---	---	---	---	0.09	Income Return %
	---	---	---	---	---	---	---	---	---	---	---	2.50	Capital Return %
	---	---	---	---	---	---	---	---	---	---	---	---	Total Rtn % Rank All
	---	---	---	---	---	---	---	---	---	---	---	---	Total Rtn % Rank Obj
	---	---	---	---	---	---	---	---	---	---	---	0.01	Income $
	---	---	---	---	---	---	---	---	---	---	---	0.00	Capital Gains $
	---	---	---	---	---	---	---	---	---	---	---	---	Expense Ratio %
	---	---	---	---	---	---	---	---	---	---	---	---	Income Ratio %
	---	---	---	---	---	---	---	---	---	---	---	---	Turnover Rate %
	---	---	---	---	---	---	---	---	---	---	---	13.4	Net Assets ($mil)

Performance 12-31-94

	1st Qtr	2nd Qtr	3rd Qtr	4th Qtr	Total
1987	---	---	---	---	---
1988	---	---	---	---	---
1989	---	---	---	---	---
1990	---	---	---	---	---
1991	---	---	---	---	---
1992	---	---	---	---	---
1993	---	---	---	---	---
1994	---	---	---	0.39	2.59 *

Bear Market Performance

Decile Rank (5-year period)

Worst — Best

	Worst 3 Mo Period 1985-89	Worst 3 Mo Period 1990-94
Bramwell Growth	---	---
+/- S&P 500	---	---
+/- Best Fit Index :	---	---

Trailing Returns

	Total Return %	+/- S&P 500	+/- Wil 5000	% Rank All	Obj	Growth of $10,000
3 Mo	0.39	0.40	1.16	13	16	10,039
6 Mo	---	---	---	---	---	---
1 Yr	---	---	---	---	---	---
3 Yr Avg	---	---	---	---	---	---
5 Yr Avg	---	---	---	---	---	---
10 Yr Avg	---	---	---	---	---	---
15 Yr Avg	---	---	---	---	---	---

Risk Analysis

Time Period	Load-Adj Return %	Risk % Rank All	Obj	Morningstar Return	Morningstar Risk	Morningstar Risk-Adj Rating
1 Yr	---					
3 Yr	---	---	---	---	---	
5 Yr	---	---	---	---	---	
10 Yr	---	---	---	---	---	

Average Historical Rating ---

[1] 1 = low, 100 = high   [2] 1.00 = Equity Avg   [3] 1.00 = 90-day T-bill return

Other Measures

				Standard S&P 500	Best Fit
Standard Deviation	---	Alpha		---	---
Mean	---	Beta		---	---
Sharpe Ratio	---	R-Squared		---	---

Investment Style

	Stock Portfolio Avg	Relative S&P 500
Price/Earnings Ratio	21.9	1.18
Price/Book Ratio	3.6	1.06
5 Yr Earnings Gr %	8.3	1.49
Return on Assets %	9.0	1.20
Debt % Total Cap	27.0	0.95
Med Mkt Cap ($mil)	1757	0.14

Style Value Blend Growth
Size Large Med Small

Diversification Value for Portfolio Types

Large Cap: Small Cap: Bond: Balanced: Diversified:

Operations

Address and Telephone	745 Fifth Avenue New York, NY 10151 800-272-6227
Advisor	Bramwell Capital Management
Subadvisor	None
Distributor	Bramwell Capital Management
States Available	All
Report Grade	N/A
Income Distrib	Paid Annually
* Date of Inception	08-01-94
Fiscal Year End	

Min Initial Purchase	$1000 (Addt'l: $100)
Min IRA Purchase	$500 (Addt'l: $100)
Min Auto Invest Plan	$1000 (Systematic Inv: $50)

Expenses & Fees

Sales Fees	0.00% front
	0.00% deferred
	0.25% 12b-1
Management Fee	1.00% flat fee, 0.15%A
3-,5-,10-yr Expense Projections	$57, N/A, N/A
Annual Brokerage Cost	---

Portfolio 12-31-94

Total Stocks: 64
Total Fixed-Income: 0

Share Chg (09-94) 000	Amount 000		Value $000	% Net Assets
55	55	Terra Industries	571	4.25
9	11	Loral	417	3.10
5	9	JC Penney	379	2.82
6	7	AT & T	352	2.62
4	10	Chesapeake	330	2.46
15	15	Enron	330	2.46
12	12	Community Health Systems	327	2.44
9	20	On Assignment	320	2.38
9	9	Charles Schwab	314	2.34
15	15	Archer-Daniels-Midland	309	2.30
5	13	Cooper Tire & Rubber	307	2.29
2	7	Illinois Tool Works	306	2.28
20	20	Colonial Data Technologies	303	2.25
8	8	Homedco Group	301	2.24
18	18	Guidant	288	2.14
5	5	Nucor	277	2.06
1	4	Dow Chemical	269	2.00
10	10	OfficeMax	265	1.97
18	20	Santa Fe Pacific Gold	260	1.94
3	8	ALLTEL	241	1.79
10	10	Robert Half International	240	1.79
0	5	Telephone & Data Systems	231	1.72
9	9	Coca-Cola FEMSA (ADR)	229	1.71
2	10	Huntco	220	1.64
70	70	Talbots	219	1.63

Composition % 12-31-94

Cash	6.4	Preferreds	0.0
Stocks	93.6	Convertibles	0.0
Bonds	0.0	Other	0.0

Tax Analysis

	Tax-Adj Historical Return %	% Pretax Return
3 Yr Avg	---	---
5 Yr Avg	---	---
10 Yr Avg	---	---
Potential Capital Gain Exposure (% of assets)	---	

Most Similar Funds in MF500

Fund lacks three-year record

Index Allocation

	% of Stocks
S&P 500	39.8
S&P MidCap 400	15.3
U.S. Small Cap	36.3
Foreign	8.6

Sector Weightings

	% of Stocks	Relative S&P 500
Utilities	4.5	0.36
Energy	4.6	0.46
Financials	2.7	0.25
Industrial Cyclicals	27.1	1.65
Consumer Durables	7.6	1.22
Consumer Staples	7.1	0.57
Services	9.4	1.16
Retail	9.6	1.64
Health	7.3	0.84
Technology	20.1	2.19

MORNINGSTAR   1995 Mutual Fund 500

Brandywine

Brandywine Fund seeks long-term capital appreciation. Current income is a secondary consideration.

The fund invests principally in common stocks of well-financed companies that have proven records of profitability and strong earnings momentum. These stocks are likely to be issues of smaller, lesser-known companies moving from a lower to a higher market share within their industry group. The fund may also invest, however, in stocks of larger, better-researched companies.

	Ticker	Load	NAV	Yield	SEC Yield	Assets	Objective
	BRWIX	None	23.50	0.0%	N/A	2299.3	Growth

Historical Profile
Return High
Risk Above Average
Rating ★★★★★
Highest

Investment Style History
Equity
Average % Stocks Held
in Portfolio

94% 93% 93% 66% 78% 90% 89% 77%

Growth of $10,000
|||| Value of Fund ($000)
— Value of Index ($000)
Wil 4500
▼ Manager Change
▽ Partial Manager Change
► Mgr Unknown After
◄ Mgr Unknown Before

Performance Quartile
(Within Objective)

Manager's Investment Style

Management's bottom-up strategy looks for good companies--smaller- to mid-sized firms with earnings growth between 20% and 30%, low debt, and high sales growth--and is willing to pay a high price for them. The fund also seeks firms capable of positive earnings surprises. The fund often makes concentrated sector bets, especially in technology, and will raise cash in what management considers to be especially risky markets.

Fund Manager(s)

Foster S. Friess et al. Birthdate: 04-40 BBA, U. of Wisconsin 1962 International Economics, U. of Oslo

	1983	1984	1985	1986	1987	1988	1989	1990	1991	1992	1993	1994	History
	---	---	10.00	11.61	10.97	12.87	16.40	15.17	20.17	22.74	24.97	23.50	NAV
	---	---	0.00 *	19.03	2.64	17.66	32.88	0.62	49.18	15.68	22.58	0.02	Total Return %
	---	---	-2.53 *	0.35	-2.62	1.05	1.19	3.74	18.69	8.06	12.52	-1.30	+/- S&P 500
	---	---	---	2.94	0.28	-0.28	3.70	6.80	14.97	6.71	11.30	0.09	+/- Wilshire 5000
	---	---	0.00	2.93	0.00	0.34	0.20	1.87	0.69	0.05	0.00	0.00	Income Return %
	---	---	0.00	16.10	2.64	17.32	32.68	-1.25	48.49	15.63	22.58	0.02	Capital Return %
	---	---	---	26	38	19	9	54	8	9	13	19	Total Rtn % Rank All
	---	---	---	23	52	38	23	20	15	14	10	33	Total Rtn % Rank Obj
	---	---	0.00	0.30	0.00	0.04	0.03	0.28	0.13	0.01	0.00	0.00	Income $
	---	---	0.00	0.00	0.88	0.00	0.68	1.00	2.12	0.54	2.87	1.45	Capital Gains $
	---	---	---	1.29	1.17	1.15	1.13	1.12	1.09	1.10	1.10	1.10	Expense Ratio %
	---	---	---	0.71	-0.18	0.34	0.23	0.93	1.50	0.20	-0.10	0.10	Income Ratio %
	---	---	---	58	147	107	91	158	188	189	150	190	Turnover Rate %
	---	---	---	66.5	91.2	124.7	165.8	312.1	623.6	839.7	1527.5	2299.3	Net Assets ($mil)

Manager Experience

	Dates Managed	Invest Obj	Std Dev	+/- Index
Foster S. Friess				
Brandywine Blue	01/91 - 12/94	G	13.86	5.44
William F. D'Alonzo				
Brandywine Blue	01/91 - 12/94	G	13.86	5.44

Performance 12-31-94

	1st Qtr	2nd Qtr	3rd Qtr	4th Qtr	Total
1987	30.75	2.04	9.75	-29.90	2.64
1988	8.11	15.43	-5.84	0.14	17.66
1989	9.95	8.48	16.42	-4.30	32.88
1990	5.98	11.57	-18.62	4.58	0.62
1991	27.09	-6.33	13.62	10.28	49.18
1992	-0.50	-8.57	5.50	20.52	15.68
1993	1.58	5.97	14.54	-0.59	22.58
1994	-0.12	-6.01	5.67	0.83	0.02

Bear Market Performance

Decile Rank (5-year period)

Worst ——————————— Best

	Worst 3 Mo Period 1985-89	Worst 3 Mo Period 1990-94
Brandywine	---	-18.62
+/- S&P 500	---	-4.87
+/- Best Fit Index : Wil 4500	---	-0.39

Trailing Returns

	Total Return %	+/- S&P 500	+/- Wil 5000	% Rank All	% Rank Obj	Growth of $10,000
3 Mo	0.83	0.84	1.60	8	11	10,083
6 Mo	6.55	1.69	1.92	8	22	10,655
1 Yr	0.02	-1.30	0.09	19	33	10,002
3 Yr Avg	12.35	6.09	5.74	7	9	14,183
5 Yr Avg	16.31	7.62	7.50	3	4	21,289
10 Yr Avg	---	---	---	---	---	---
15 Yr Avg	---	---	---	---	---	---

Operations

Address and Telephone	P.O. Box 4166 Greenville, DE 19807 800-656-3017 / 302-656-6200	
Advisor	Friess Associates	
Subadvisor	None	
Distributor	Brandywine Fund	
States Available	All	
Report Grade	A+	
Income Distrib	Paid Annually	
* Date of Inception	12-12-85	
Fiscal Year End	September	

Risk Analysis

Time Period	Load-Adj Return %	Risk % Rank [1] All	Obj	Morningstar [2] Return	Risk	Morningstar Risk-Adj Rating
1 Yr	0.02					
3 Yr	12.35	89	83	2.76 [3]	1.18	★★★★
5 Yr	16.31	88	86	3.35 [3]	1.12	★★★★★
10 Yr	---	---	---	---	---	

Average Historical Rating (73 months) 4.2 ★s

[1] 1 = low, 100 = high [2] 1.00 = Equity Avg [3] 1.00 = 90-day T-bill return

Other Measures

			Standard S&P 500	Best Fit Wil 4500
Standard Deviation	13.60	Alpha	6.2	3.7
Mean	12.62	Beta	1.05	1.26
Sharpe Ratio	0.67	R-Squared	37	82

Investment Style

	Stock Portfolio Avg	Relative S&P 500
Price/Earnings Ratio	24.1	1.31
Price/Book Ratio	3.9	1.16
5 Yr Earnings Gr %	22.5	4.05
Return on Assets	10.8	1.45
Debt % Total Cap	24.3	0.86
Med Mkt Cap ($mil)	1668	0.13

Diversification Value for Portfolio Types

Large Cap: Medium	Small Cap: Low	Bond: High	Balanced: Medium	Diversified: Medium

Expenses & Fees

Sales Fees	0.00% front
	0.00% deferred
	0.00% 12b-1
Management Fee	1.00% flat fee
3-,5-,10-yr Expense Projections	$35, $61, $134
Annual Brokerage Cost	0.40%

Min Initial Purchase $25000 (Addt'l: $1000)
Min IRA Purchase $25000 (Addt'l: $1000)
Min Auto Invest Plan N/A

Portfolio 12-31-94

Share Chg (09-94)000	Amount 000	Total Stocks: 227 Total Fixed-Income: 0	Value $000	% Net Assets
985	2663	DSC Communications	95532	4.15
2114	2264	cisco Systems	79537	3.46
334	886	Scott Paper	61272	2.66
0	1558	Columbia/HCA Healthcare	56852	2.47
82	728	AMP	52991	2.30
124	872	Premark International	39004	1.70
1004	1004	Arrow Electronics	36022	1.57
-1133	843	LSI Logic	34016	1.48
729	729	Cabletron Systems	33912	1.47
1400	1400	Rite Aid	32727	1.42
473	947	Informix	30413	1.32
304	786	HEALTHSOUTH Rehabilitation	29075	1.26
1044	1044	Fruit of the Loom Cl A	28185	1.23
-141	360	Dayton Hudson	25477	1.11
0	715	Sun Microsystems	25375	1.10
0	698	Varian Associates	24430	1.06
606	606	Apple Computer	23650	1.03
-23	787	Dollar General	23613	1.03
0	515	Parker-Hannifin	23414	1.02
0	552	Nordstrom	23188	1.01
478	478	Cardinal Health	22186	0.96
362	362	Cordis	21901	0.95
292	292	IBM	21477	0.93
263	780	FHP International	20095	0.87
0	771	Bank of Boston	19952	0.87

Composition % 12-31-94

Cash	13.3	Preferreds	0.0
Stocks	86.7	Convertibles	0.0
Bonds	0.0	Other	0.0

Tax Analysis

	Tax-Adj Historical Return %	% Pretax Return
3 Yr Avg	10.40	82.6
5 Yr Avg	13.84	80.8
10 Yr Avg	---	---
Potential Capital Gain Exposure (% of assets)		7%

Most Similar Funds in MF500

AIM Constellation	Strong Fit
Kaufmann	Strong Fit
Invesco Strat Technology	Fair Fit

Index Allocation

	% of Stocks
S&P 500	38.5
S&P MidCap 400	23.9
U.S. Small Cap	37.1
Foreign	0.5

Sector Weightings

	% of Stocks	Relative S&P 500
Utilities	0.0	0.00
Energy	0.0	0.00
Financials	1.6	0.15
Industrial Cyclicals	13.4	0.82
Consumer Durables	3.8	0.61
Consumer Staples	0.3	0.02
Services	3.6	0.44
Retail	11.9	2.04
Health	17.4	2.00
Technology	48.2	5.26

Brazil Fund

	Ticker	NAV	Mkt Price	Prem/Disc	Yield	Objective
	BZF	$31.09	$33.00	6.1%	0.0%	Latin America

Brazil Fund seeks long-term capital appreciation.

Normally, the fund intends to invest at least 70% of its assets in common and preferred stocks of companies registered with the Brazilian Securities Commission. The balance is held in debt securities of the Brazilian government, Brazilian corporations, and U.S.-dollar-denominated money-market accounts. The fund may engage in futures and options transactions for hedging purposes.

To discourage takeover attempts, board members serve staggered terms, and 75% of outstanding shares are required to replace a director or to approve any proposal to open-end the fund.

Historical Profile

Return: Above Average
Risk: High
Rating: ★★★★ Above Average

-10.3	-31.7	13.1	31.1	19.9	3.9	12.7	Highest Prem/Disc
-39.0	-54.8	-39.3	-10.2	-13.0	-13.7	-13.3	Lowest Prem/Disc

Growth of $10,000
■ at NAV ($000)
— at Market Price ($000)

Premium/Discount %

History	1983	1984	1985	1986	1987	1988	1989	1990	1991	1992	1993	1994	
NAV	---	---	---	---	---	12.90	18.84	5.97	13.80	14.12	20.98	31.09	
NAV Total Return %	---	---	---	---	---	14.53*	63.97	-68.03	131.16	6.44	54.19	60.98	
+/- S&P 500	---	---	---	---	---	8.52*	32.29	-64.91	100.67	-1.18	44.13	59.66	
+/- MSCI EAFE	---	---	---	---	---	---	53.43	-44.58	119.03	18.61	21.63	53.20	
+/- MSCI Brazil	---	---	---	---	---	---	29.99	-2.50	-41.98	13.71	-44.36	-2.84	
Income Return %	---	---	---	---	---	3.52*	7.40	0.28	0.00	0.00	0.35	0.00	
Capital Return %	---	---	---	---	---	11.02*	56.57	-68.31	131.16	6.44	53.84	60.98	
Total Rtn % Rank All	---	---	---	---	---	---	3	100	1	70	7	1	
Total Rtn % Rank Obj	---	---	---	---	---	---	50	66	1	75	40	1	
Market Total Rtn %	---	---	---	---	---	-35.01*	83.56	-48.09	122.64	-3.91	60.89	69.69	
Avg Prem/Disc %	---	---	---	---	---	-24.5	-43.4	-9.7	9.3	3.3	-5.7	0.4	
Income $	---	---	---	---	---	0.41	0.89	0.12	0.00	0.00	0.08	0.00	
Capital Gains $	---	---	---	---	---	0.00	0.93	0.00	0.00	0.00	0.66	0.74	2.46
Expense Ratio %	---	---	---	---	---	1.90	2.01	2.25	2.15	2.22	1.84	1.74	
Income Ratio %	---	---	---	---	---	4.70	4.76	11.27	8.13	1.13	0.56	-0.34	
Turnover Rate %	---	---	---	---	---	1	14	4	13	8	5	---	
Net Assets ($mil)	---	---	---	---	---	271.0	226.9	72.0	166.6	170.6	253.7	376.4	

Manager's Investment Style

As the fund's modest turnover ratio suggests, management takes a buy-and-hold approach to the volatile Brazilian stock market. Although the fund does own such widely held government-run utilities stocks such as Telebras, management prefers private second-tier blue chips, which aren't as prone to downdrafts in investor sentiment.

Fund Manager(s)

Edmund B. Games, Jr. Since 4-88. BA'59 Harvard.
Nicholas Bratt. Since 1989. BA Oxford U.; MBA Columbia U.
William F. Truscott. Since 10-93. BA'83 Middlebury C.; MBA'91 New York U.

Manager Experience	Dates Managed	Invest Obj	Std Dev	+/- Index
Edmund B. Games, Jr.				
Scudder Latin America	01/93 - 12/94	WF	26.02	21.74
Nicholas Bratt				
Scudder International	01/76 - 12/94	WF	15.38	0.54

NAV Performance % 12-30-94

	1st Qtr	2nd Qtr	3rd Qtr	4th Qtr	Total
1987	---	---	---	---	---
1988	---	0.69*	8.12	5.20	14.53*
1989	37.22	-6.55	26.37	1.18	63.97
1990	-3.02	-45.33	-3.23	-37.68	-68.03
1991	62.81	44.34	4.26	4.86	131.16
1992	42.39	-26.40	14.01	-10.91	6.44
1993	17.08	12.39	14.23	2.58	54.19
1994	33.15	-18.74	67.29	-11.07	60.98

Bear Market Performance

Decile Rank (5-year period)

Worst ▮ Best

	Worst 3 Mo Period 1985-89	Worst 3 Mo Period 1990-94
Brazil Fund	---	-52.71
+/- S&P 500	---	-62.56

Trailing Returns

	NAV Total Return %	+/- S&P 500	+/- MSCI Brazil	% Rank All	% Rank Obj	Mkt Total Return %
3 Mo	-11.07	-11.05	5.12	95	10	0.62
6 Mo	48.78	43.92	4.26	1	1	47.26
1 Yr	60.98	59.66	-2.84	1	1	69.69
3 Yr Avg	38.24	31.97	-6.24	1	1	37.92
5 Yr Avg	14.32	5.62	-8.89	6	66	24.84
Incept Avg	21.29*	---	---	---	---	21.05*

Operations

Address and Telephone	345 Park Avenue New York, NY 10154 617-330-5602 / 800-349-4281	Income Distrib Schedule	Paid Irregularly
		Management Fee	1.25%
		Reinvestment Plan	Yes
Advisor	Scudder, Stevens & Clark	Direct Purchase Plan	Yes
Subadvisor	Banco Icatu	Shares Outstanding	12,107,722
Administrator	N/A	Exchange	NYSE
Transfer Agent	First National Bank of Boston	*Date of Inception	04-08-88
Custodian	Brown Brothers Harriman & Co.	Shareholder Report	A-
Auditor	Price Waterhouse LLP		
Legal Counsel	Debevoise & Plimpton		

Risk Analysis

	Risk % Rank[1]		Morningstar[2]		Morningstar
	All	Obj	Return	Risk	Risk-Adj Rating
3 Yr	96	62	6.10	1.51	★★★★★
5 Yr	99	66	2.01	2.35	★★★
10 Yr	---	---	---	---	

Average Historical Rating (45 months) 1.7 ★s

[1] 1 = Low, 100 = High [2] 1.00 = Equity Avg [3] 1.00 = 90-day T-bill Return

Other Measures

				S&P 500
Standard Deviation	39.29	Alpha		40.14
Mean	40.47	Beta		0.94
Sharpe Ratio	0.94	R-Squared		4

Investment Style

	Stock Portfolio Avg	Rel WS Brazil	Rel WS Foreign
Price/Earnings Ratio	135.7	1.12	2.76
Price/Cash Flow Ratio	---	---	---
Price/Book Ratio	23.7	1.22	7.86
5 Yr Earnings Gr %	---	---	---
Return on Assets %	---	---	---
Debt % Total Cap	---	---	---
Med Mkt Cap ($mil)	2125	0.23	0.34

figure is based on less than 50% of stocks

Country Exposure (top five) 12-31-94

	Securities %		Currency %
Brazil	93	Brazil	93
		US	7

Diversification Value for Portfolio Types

Large Cap: High	Small Cap: High	Bond: High	Balanced: High	Diversified: High
●	●	●	●	●

Portfolio 09-30-94

Total Equity: 40
Total Fixed-Income: 0

Share Chg (06-94)	Amount		Value $000	% Total Invest
-23.000M	247.740M	Petrobras	49080	10.91
-70.000M	581.257M	Telebras	36252	8.06
-1000000	136.888M	Vale do Rio Doce	28565	6.35
-2500000	81794208	Banco Itau	27808	6.18
0	47070689	Telecom de Sao Paolo PN	26764	5.95
-400000	14811430	Sadia Concordia Indl & Com	22226	4.94
-200000	61096254	Cervejaria Brahma	18623	4.14
20000	2008543	Souza Cruz Industria/Coml	17425	3.87
20000000	1176.72M	White Martins	15450	3.43
3700000	145.408M	Energetica de Minas Gerais	15342	3.41
10000	22366000	Suzano Papel Celulose	14946	3.32
20000	2310236	Vidraria Santa Marina	12458	2.77
-112000	4798700	Aracruz Cl B	12433	2.76
3080.0M	6980.00M	Usinas Siderurgicas de Minas	11456	2.55
-5550000	11529400	Copene-Petro do Nordeste A	11083	2.46
500000	5199792	Industrias Klabin Papel	9510	2.11
-63.900M	470.967M	Hering	8829	1.96
-710000	17006600	WEG	8354	1.86
0	242.238M	Lojas Americanas	7494	1.67
83900000	160.600M	Siderurgica Nacional	7060	1.57
-400000	30659465	Mesbla	6602	1.47
-500000	32629600	Sao Paulo Alpargatas	6178	1.37
-200000	14818000	Brasmotor	5906	1.31
-50000	1182600	Moinho Santista Industrias	5878	1.31
3750000	103.762M	Metal Leve Indl Com	5839	1.30

Composition % 12-31-94

Cash	7.2	Preferreds	0.0
Stocks	92.8	Convertibles	0.0
Bonds	0.0	Other	0.0

Tax Analysis

	Tax-Adj Historical Return %	% Pretax Return
3 Yr Avg	36.21	93.0
5 Yr Avg	13.24	90.6
10 Yr Avg	---	---
Potential Capital Gain Exposure (% of assets)		33

Most Similar Funds in MF500

France Growth	Weak Fit
Mexico Fund	Weak Fit
American Heritage	Weak Fit

Sector Weightings

	% of Stocks
Utilities	19.6
Energy	11.9
Financials	6.7
Industrial Cyclicals	31.1
Consumer Durables	6.5
Consumer Staples	16.6
Services	0.0
Retail	4.3
Health	0.0
Technology	3.4

MORNINGSTAR 1995 Mutual Fund 500

Burnham A

	Ticker	Load	NAV	Yield	SEC Yield	Assets	Objective
	BURHX	3.00%	19.88	4.3%	4.85%	101.8	Growth/Inc.

Burnham Fund - Class A seeks capital appreciation; income is a secondary consideration.

The fund primarily purchases common stocks and other equity securities. It may invest without limit in fixed-income securities when market conditions warrant. The fund may invest up to 15% of its assets in foreign securities.

Class A shares have front loads; Class B shares have low deferred loads and higher 12b-1 fees; Class C shares have no loads and are designed for financial planners.

Prior to Sept. 7, 1989, the fund was called Drexel Burnham Fund and was managed by Drexel Management Corp.

Manager's Investment Style

Management emphasizes income, typically holding one third of assets in government and corporate bonds, and a large portion of its equity portfolio in income-paying large-cap stocks. Longtime manager I.W. Burnham recently returned to the fund after a two-year hiatus, and has since shifted the fund's equity portion to a slightly more growth-oriented focus.

Fund Manager(s)

I. W. Burnham, since 06-75. Birthdate: 01-09.
BS, U. of Pennsylvania 1931

Manager Experience

	Dates Managed	Invest Obj	Std Dev	+/- Index

Not available.

Historical Profile
Return	Average
Risk	Low
Rating	★★★★ Above Average

Investment Style History
Equity

Average % Stocks Held in Portfolio

69%	49%	50%	44%	52%	55%	53%	49%

Growth of $10,000
|||| Value of Fund ($000)
— Value of Index ($000) S&P 500
▼ Manager Change
▽ Partial Manager Change
► Mgr Unknown After
◄ Mgr Unknown Before

Performance Quartile (Within Objective)

1983	1984	1985	1986	1987	1988	1989	1990	1991	1992	1993	●994	History
17.38	17.57	21.95	21.28	19.58	20.89	23.62	20.01	22.16	21.95	21.86	19.88	NAV
12.11	7.24	32.13	21.81	6.70	11.89	22.75	-1.76	17.98	7.70	9.35	-1.77	Total Return %
-10.36	0.97	0.40	3.13	1.44	-4.72	-8.93	1.36	-12.50	0.08	-0.71	-3.09	+/- S&P 500
-11.36	4.19	-0.43	5.71	4.33	-6.05	-6.42	4.42	-16.23	-1.27	-1.93	-1.70	+/- Wilshire 5000
6.20	5.24	5.92	3.73	4.74	3.95	6.61	6.03	5.89	5.49	4.35	4.26	Income Return %
5.91	2.00	26.21	18.07	1.95	7.94	16.14	-7.79	12.09	2.21	5.01	-6.03	Capital Return %
70	40	18	14	17	46	29	61	48	49	71	32	Total Rtn % Rank All
91	29	16	13	17	72	55	30	94	47	67	60	Total Rtn % Rank Obj
0.98	0.86	0.91	0.80	1.07	0.75	1.25	1.24	1.06	1.12	0.90	0.88	Income $
0.00	0.15	0.16	4.23	2.15	0.22	0.50	1.94	0.22	0.66	1.11	0.71	Capital Gains $
1.10	1.10	1.10	1.00	1.00	1.10	1.20	1.20	1.14	1.20	1.50	1.50	Expense Ratio %
5.30	5.50	4.60	3.80	3.90	5.60	5.30	5.60	5.00	4.10	3.70	3.40	Income Ratio %
80	101	114	114	121	94	93	107	121	69	54	83	Turnover Rate %
75.1	71.4	99.8	160.6	200.6	184.7	160.8	123.7	125.4	117.2	118.5	101.8	Net Assets ($mil)

Performance 12-31-94

	1st Qtr	2nd Qtr	3rd Qtr	4th Qtr	Total
1987	13.34	3.61	2.91	-11.70	6.70
1988	5.08	2.43	1.53	2.39	11.89
1989	5.48	5.48	5.78	4.30	22.75
1990	-3.43	1.77	-3.78	3.88	-1.76
1991	5.70	-0.84	5.05	7.15	17.98
1992	-1.36	0.06	4.74	4.18	7.70
1993	3.38	2.17	4.44	-0.87	9.35
1994	-4.92	0.02	3.76	-0.45	-1.77

Bear Market Performance

Decile Rank (5-year period)

Worst ▮ Best

	Worst 3 Mo Period 1985-89	Worst 3 Mo Period 1990-94
Burnham A	-16.09	-5.28
+/- S&P 500	13.50	0.47
+/- Best Fit Index : S&P 500	13.50	0.47

Trailing Returns

	Total Return %	+/- S&P 500	+/- Wil 5000	% Rank All	% Rank Obj	Growth of $10,000
3 Mo	-0.45	-0.43	0.32	33	32	9,955
6 Mo	3.29	-1.57	-1.33	19	38	10,329
1 Yr	-1.77	-3.09	-1.70	32	60	9,823
3 Yr Avg	4.98	-1.29	-1.64	49	66	11,568
5 Yr Avg	6.04	-2.65	-2.78	75	85	13,408
10 Yr Avg	12.20	-2.18	-1.66	35	51	31,625
15 Yr Avg	12.77	-1.72	-1.21	43	62	60,621

Operations

Address and Telephone	1325 Ave of the Americas 17th Fl
	New York, NY 10019
	800-874-3863 / 212-262-3100
Advisor	Burnham Asset Management
Subadvisor	None
Distributor	Burnham Securities
States Available	All
Report Grade	B-
Income Distrib	Paid Quarterly
Date of Inception	06-13-75
Fiscal Year End	December

Risk Analysis

Time Period	Load-Adj Return %	Risk % Rank All	Risk % Rank Obj	Morningstar Return	Morningstar Risk	Morningstar Risk-Adj Rating
1 Yr	-4.72					
3 Yr	3.92	54	12	0.10[3]	0.58	★★★
5 Yr	5.40	51	3	0.16[3]	0.52	★★★
10 Yr	11.86	41	5	0.85	0.53	★★★★

Average Historical Rating (109 months) 3.9 ★s

[1] 1 = low, 100 = high [2] 1.00 = Equity Avg [3] 1.00 = 90-day T-bill return

Other Measures

		Standard S&P 500	Best Fit S&P 500
Standard Deviation	6.28	Alpha	-0.5	-0.5
Mean	5.06	Beta	0.70	0.70
Sharpe Ratio	0.25	R-Squared	77	77

Investment Style

	Stock Portfolio Avg	Relative S&P 500
Price/Earnings Ratio	20.8	1.12
Price/Book Ratio	2.8	0.83
5 Yr Earnings Gr %	4.3	0.77
Return on Assets %	6.9	0.93
Debt % Total Cap	26.8	0.95
Med Mkt Cap ($mil)	13820	1.06

Style Value Blend Growth / Size Large Med Small

Diversification Value for Portfolio Types

Large Cap: Low	Small Cap: Medium	Bond: Medium	Balanced: None	Diversified: Low

Expenses & Fees

Sales Fees	3.00% front
	0.00% deferred
	0.25% 12b-1
Management Fee	0.63% flat fee
3-,5-,10-yr Expense Projections	$77, $111, $207
Annual Brokerage Cost	0.12%

Portfolio 12-31-94

Share Chg (11-94) 000	Amount 000	Total Stocks: 52 Total Fixed-Income: 51	Value $000	% Net Assets
0	140	Contel Cellular Cl A	3488	3.43
0	50	Exxon	3027	2.97
0	50	AT & T	2504	2.46
0	70	AirTouch Communications	2032	2.00
	1993	Texaco Capital 8.65%	2018	1.98
0	50	Southwestern Bell	2012	1.98
	1993	General Electric 7.875%	1994	1.96
	1993	Ford Motor Credit 8%	1992	1.96
0	100	Caremark International	1707	1.68
0	20	Mobil	1679	1.65
	1495	Johnson & Johnson 8.5%	1511	1.48
	1495	USG 8%	1491	1.46
	997	Bank of New York Cv 7.5%	1485	1.46
0	30	Chrysler	1465	1.44
	1495	US Treasury Note 6.5%	1454	1.43
0	25	Motorola	1442	1.42
0	50	Morton International	1420	1.39
0	20	Hilton Hotels	1343	1.32
0	40	Travelers	1296	1.27
0	20	Intel	1271	1.25
0	30	General Motors	1263	1.24
0	30	Citicorp	1237	1.22
	997	Riverwood Intl 10.75%	1196	1.17
0	20	Amoco	1179	1.16
0	15	Pfizer	1155	1.13

Composition % 12-31-94

Cash	4.9	Preferreds	0.0
Stocks	53.5	Convertibles	2.3
Bonds	39.2	Other	0.1

Tax Analysis

	Tax-Adj Historical Return %	% Pretax Return
3 Yr Avg	2.26	44.2
5 Yr Avg	3.04	47.3
10 Yr Avg	8.86	61.8
Potential Capital Gain Exposure (% of assets)		5%

Most Similar Funds in MF500

Evergreen Total Return Y	Strong Fit
Dean Witter Dividend Growth	Fair Fit
Investment Comp of America	Fair Fit

Index Allocation

	% of Stocks
S&P 500	67.0
S&P MidCap 400	9.8
U.S. Small Cap	20.4
Foreign	2.8

Sector Weightings

	% of Stocks	Relative S&P 500
Utilities	17.5	1.41
Energy	12.9	1.28
Financials	11.8	1.12
Industrial Cyclicals	8.0	0.49
Consumer Durables	8.5	1.36
Consumer Staples	1.0	0.08
Services	10.3	1.27
Retail	3.4	0.58
Health	11.1	1.28
Technology	15.5	1.69

Min Initial / IRA Purchase

Min Initial Purchase	$1000 (Addt'l: $250)
Min IRA Purchase	None (Addt'l: None)
Min Auto Invest Plan	$1000 (Systematic Inv: $50)

Calvert Social Invmnt Managed A

Ticker	Load	NAV	Yield	SEC Yield	Assets	Objective
CSIFX	4.75%	27.87	3.3%	N/A	489.7	Balanced

Calvert Social Investment Fund Managed Growth Portfolio - Class A seeks a total return above the rate of inflation.

The fund invests in stocks, bonds, and money-market instruments. Up to 20% of fund assets may be invested in debt securities rated below BBB. All potential investments are first screened for financial soundness. Also, the fund may only invest in companies with solid social values and employee relations. It will not invest in companies engaged in nuclear-energy production or weapons manufacture.

Class A shares have front loads and lower 12b-1 fees; Class C shares have level loads.

Historical Profile

Return	Below Average
Risk	Below Average
Rating	★★★
	Neutral

62% 49% 48% 36% 46% 46% 45% 53%

Investment Style History
Equity
Average % Stocks Held in Portfolio

Growth of $10,000
|||| Value of Fund ($000)
— Value of Index ($000)
S&P 500
▼ Manager Change
▽ Partial Manager Change
► Mgr Unknown After
◄ Mgr Unknown Before

Performance Quartile
(Within Objective)

	1983	1984	1985	1986	1987	1988	1989	1990	1991	1992	1993	1994	History
	17.05	17.21	20.61	23.48	23.26	24.33	27.49	25.85	29.22	29.86	30.42	27.87	NAV
	11.29	6.79	26.90	18.11	4.97	10.73	18.72	1.76	17.79	7.46	5.95	-4.74	Total Return %
	-11.18	0.52	-4.84	-0.57	-0.29	-5.88	-12.96	4.88	-12.70	-0.16	-4.11	-6.06	+/- S&P 500
	2.91	-8.37	4.77	2.86	2.21	2.86	4.18	-7.18	1.79	0.22	-3.80	-1.82	+/- LB Aggregate
	2.83	5.85	6.00	2.64	3.09	5.61	3.68	4.99	4.69	3.81	3.28	3.01	Income Return %
	8.46	0.94	20.90	15.47	1.87	5.13	15.04	-3.23	13.09	3.65	2.67	-7.75	Capital Return %
	73	44	39	32	22	55	38	51	49	52	88	61	Total Rtn % Rank All
	85	50	57	45	16	60	52	21	92	47	88	79	Total Rtn % Rank Obj
	0.44	0.93	0.92	0.56	0.73	1.28	0.86	1.31	1.14	1.05	0.96	0.92	Income $
	0.00	0.00	0.16	0.29	0.64	0.12	0.46	0.75	0.01	0.41	0.23	0.21	Capital Gains $
	0.85	1.50	1.30	1.30	1.29	1.34	1.29	1.30	1.31	1.28	1.25	1.23	Expense Ratio %
	4.75	6.58	5.96	3.42	2.82	4.30	4.49	4.85	4.73	3.90	3.25	3.19	Income Ratio %
	179	54	54	24	14	46	34	24	25	14	33	---	Turnover Rate %
	5.7	10.4	25.6	104.6	149.0	173.9	222.0	263.1	365.1	448.5	541.3	489.7	Net Assets ($mil)

Manager's Investment Style

Management interprets its socially conscious mandate by avoiding weapons manufacturers and seeking firms that promote good workplace conditions and humanitarian values. The fund's performance, however, has mostly been driven by a fondness for bonds, which take up the majority of assets, except in periods when management is especially bullish on stocks or sees unusual equity values. Management typically favors high-quality bonds and the stocks of well-established firms.

Fund Manager(s)

Domenic Colasacco CFA(1979), since 01-84.
Birthdate: 11-48. BS, Babson C. 1969 MBA, Babson C. 1982

Manager Experience

	Dates Managed	Invest Obj	Std Dev	+/- Index
Domenic Colasacco				
Calvert Social Inv Eq A	08/87 - 06/92	G	15.87	3.95

Performance 12-31-94

	1st Qtr	2nd Qtr	3rd Qtr	4th Qtr	Total
1987	11.16	2.68	3.59	-11.22	4.97
1988	7.70	1.63	0.36	0.81	10.73
1989	2.79	8.10	4.72	2.02	18.72
1990	-3.24	4.37	-5.72	6.88	1.76
1991	5.76	0.48	3.46	7.14	17.79
1992	-2.51	0.86	5.10	3.98	7.46
1993	2.26	0.22	3.20	0.17	5.95
1994	-3.38	-1.78	2.08	-1.67	-4.74

Bear Market Performance

Decile Rank (5-year period)

Worst ———————————————— Best

	Worst 3 Mo Period 1985-89	Worst 3 Mo Period 1990-94
Calvert Social Invmnt Managed	-15.75	-5.72
+/- S&P 500	13.83	8.03
+/- Best Fit Index : S&P 500	13.83	8.03

Trailing Returns

	Total Return %	+/- S&P 500	+/- LB Aggregate	% Rank All	% Rank Obj	Growth of $10,000
3 Mo	-1.67	-1.65	-2.05	61	72	9,833
6 Mo	0.37	-4.49	-0.62	49	77	10,037
1 Yr	-4.74	-6.06	-1.82	61	79	9,526
3 Yr Avg	2.74	-3.52	-1.80	87	80	10,846
5 Yr Avg	5.39	-3.30	-2.24	86	94	13,000
10 Yr Avg	10.40	-3.99	0.45	54	78	26,887
15 Yr Avg	---	---	---	---	---	---

Operations

Address and Telephone	4550 Montgomery Ave Ste 1000N Bethesda, MD 20814 800-368-2748 / 301-951-4820
Advisor	Calvert Asset Management
Subadvisor	United States Trust of Boston
Distributor	Calvert Securities
States Available	All
Report Grade	B
Income Distrib	Paid Quarterly
Date of Inception	10-21-82
Fiscal Year End	September

Risk Analysis

Time Period	Load-Adj Return %	Risk % Rank All	Obj	Morningstar Return	Morningstar Risk	Morningstar Risk-Adj Rating
1 Yr	-9.27					
3 Yr	1.09	50	52	-0.70[3]	0.71	★★
5 Yr	4.37	48	19	-0.08[3]	0.64	★★
10 Yr	9.86	41	25	0.63	0.65	★★★
Average Historical Rating (109 months)					3.3	★s

[1] = low, 100 = high [2] 1.00 = Hybrid Avg [3] 1.00 = 90-day T-bill return

Other Measures

			Standard S&P 500	Best Fit S&P 500
Standard Deviation	5.25	Alpha	-2.3	-2.3
Mean	2.85	Beta	0.57	0.57
Sharpe Ratio	-0.13	R-Squared	74	74

Investment Style

Stocks

	Port Avg	Rel S&P 500
Price/Earnings Ratio	17.4	0.94
Price/Book Ratio	3.1	0.92
5 Yr Earnings Gr %	6.6	1.19
Med Mkt Cap ($mil)	3911	0.30

Bonds

Avg Effective Duration	4.4 Yrs**
Avg Effective Maturity	7.5 Yrs
Avg Credit Quality	AAA
Avg Weighted Coupon	7.41%

**figure provided by fund

Diversification Value for Portfolio Types

Large Cap: Low	Small Cap: Medium	Bond: Low	Balanced: None	Diversified: Low

Portfolio 09-30-94

Total Stocks: 71
Total Fixed-Income: 65

Share Chg (03-94)000	Amount 000		Date of Maturity	Value $000	% Net Assets
	20923	FNMA Debenture 6.05%	01-12-98	20208	3.95
	14945	FNMA Debenture 8.15%	05-11-98	15328	2.99
	14646	FNMA Debenture 8.2%	03-10-16	14601	2.85
	12454	FNMA Debenture 9.55%	11-10-97	13229	2.58
	12454	FNMA CMO REMIC 7%	04-25-22	11187	2.18
-1	249	May Department Stores		9808	1.92
0	149	WW Grainger		8855	1.73
	299	Albertson's		8705	1.70
-1	199	Illinois Tool Works		8519	1.66
	9963	FNMA Debenture 5.49%	10-02-03	8404	1.64
0	149	Automatic Data Processing		8388	1.64
25	75	Xerox		7977	1.56
0	100	FNMA		7846	1.53
24	249	Equitable Resources		7472	1.46
0	125	Emerson Electric		7426	1.45
104	139	Medtronic		7375	1.44
9	249	American Greetings Cl A		7192	1.40
49	199	Toys 'R' Us		7099	1.39
100	100	Schering-Plough		7074	1.38
25	125	Consolidated Papers		6445	1.26

Index Allocation

	% of Stocks
S&P 500	63.9
S&P MidCap 400	22.8
U.S. Small Cap	13.3
Foreign	0.0

Composition % 10-31-94

Cash	7.0	Preferreds	0.0
Stocks	55.0	Convertibles	0.0
Bonds	38.0	Other	0.0

Tax Analysis

	Tax-Adj Historical Return %	% Pretax Return
3 Yr Avg	1.26	45.1
5 Yr Avg	3.69	66.3
10 Yr Avg	8.52	75.0
Potential Capital Gain Exposure (% of assets)		6%

Most Similar Funds in MF500

Prudential Alloc Cons Mgd B	Fair Fit
SteinRoe Total Return	Fair Fit
Sentinel Balanced	Fair Fit

Bond Credit Analysis 09-30-94
% of Bonds

US Govt	80	BB	0
AAA	6	B	0
AA	7	Below B	0
A	4	NR/NA	1
BBB	2		

Stock Sector Weightings

	% of Stocks	Relative S&P 500
Utilities	6.0	0.49
Energy	0.5	0.05
Financials	15.1	1.42
Industrial Cyclicals	28.3	1.73
Consumer Durables	3.9	0.62
Consumer Staples	8.3	0.66
Services	11.0	1.35
Retail	11.3	1.94
Health	8.7	1.00
Technology	7.0	0.77

Operations (continued)

Min Initial Purchase	$1000 (Addt'l: $250)
Min IRA Purchase	$1000 (Addt'l: $100)
Min Auto Invest Plan	$100 (Systematic Inv: $50)

Expenses & Fees

Sales Fees	4.75% front 0.00% deferred 0.35% 12b-1
Management Fee	0.70% flat fee
3-,5-,10-yr Expense Projections	$85, $113, $191
Annual Brokerage Cost	---

Morningstar 1995 Mutual Fund 500

Calvert Tax-Free Res Lim-Term A

	Ticker	Load	NAV	Yield	SEC Yield	Assets	Objective
	CTFLX	2.00%	10.59	3.6%	4.44%	547.6	Muni Nat

Calvert Tax-Free Reserves Limited-Term Portfolio - Class A seeks tax-exempt interest income consistent with prudent investment management and preservation of capital.

The fund invests primarily in a diversified portfolio of medium- and higher-grade municipal obligations. Fixed-rate investments are limited to obligations with remaining maturities of three years or less; variable-rate investments may have longer maturities. The fund expects to maintain an average weighted maturity of between one and two years.

Class A shares have front loads and lower 12b-1 fees; Class C shares have level loads.

Manager's Investment Style

Management interprets the fund's charter very conservatively. It maintains the lowest average duration in the municipal-national group and emphasizes higher-quality bonds. To keep yield competitive, management focuses on tender-option bonds (older bonds with higher coupons and attached put options), which pay a slightly enhanced yield because they are somewhat less liquid than straightforward muni issues. Management also keeps a stake in private-activity bonds, which are subject to the alternative minimum tax.

Fund Manager(s)

David R. Rochat, since 03-81.
Reno J. Martini, since 01-83.
John P. Nichols CFA, since 04-93.

Manager Experience	Dates Managed	Invest Obj	Std Dev	+/- Index
David R. Rochat				
Calvert Tax-Fr Res L-T A	08/83 - 12/94	MN	6.72	-2.11
Calvert T-F Res VT Muni A	04/91 - 12/94	MS	4.43	-0.88

Historical Profile
Return Low
Risk Low
Rating ★★★★★ Highest

	94	93	79	72	87	97	97	94

Investment Style History
Fixed Income
Income Rtn % Rank Obj

Growth of $10,000
‖‖‖ Value of Fund ($000)
— Value of Index ($000)
LB Muni
▼ Manager Change
▽ Partial Manager Change
► Mgr Unknown After
◄ Mgr Unknown Before

Performance Quartile (Within Objective)

1983	1984	1985	1986	1987	1988	1989	1990	1991	1992	1993	1994	History
10.29	10.33	10.48	10.67	10.45	10.55	10.61	10.61	10.65	10.68	10.72	10.59	NAV
6.35	7.36	8.52	8.48	3.47	6.80	7.12	6.50	6.46	5.08	4.02	2.42	Total Return %
-2.03	-7.80	-13.61	-6.77	0.71	-1.08	-7.42	-2.44	-9.54	-2.17	-5.73	5.34	+/- LB Aggregate
-1.70	-3.20	-11.51	-10.83	1.97	-3.36	-3.66	-0.80	-5.68	-3.74	-8.25	8.03	+/- LB Muni
6.44	6.87	6.79	6.32	5.53	5.84	6.55	6.50	6.08	4.80	3.65	3.63	Income Return %
-0.10	0.49	1.73	2.16	-2.06	0.96	0.57	0.00	0.38	0.28	0.37	-1.21	Capital Return %
95	40	97	89	32	82	93	28	97	76	94	9	Total Rtn % Rank All
87	78	91	95	7	83	91	41	99	98	99	1	Total Rtn % Rank Obj
0.65	0.68	0.68	0.64	0.58	0.60	0.67	0.67	0.63	0.50	0.38	0.39	Income $
0.01	0.01	0.03	0.04	0.00	0.00	0.00	0.00	0.00	0.00	0.00	0.00	Capital Gains $
1.00	0.96	0.88	0.81	0.76	0.81	0.78	0.77	0.73	0.71	0.67	0.65	Expense Ratio %
6.37	6.84	6.65	6.00	5.59	5.71	6.35	6.35	5.99	4.58	3.59	3.41	Income Ratio %
79	155	90	67	52	68	21	12	1	5	14	---	Turnover Rate %
55.7	52.3	77.8	189.4	204.8	145.4	132.2	151.5	291.3	567.0	653.8	547.6	Net Assets ($mil)

Performance 12-31-94

	1st Qtr	2nd Qtr	3rd Qtr	4th Qtr	Total
1987	1.46	0.56	-0.03	1.44	3.47
1988	2.49	1.47	1.31	1.36	6.80
1989	1.54	2.20	1.40	1.80	7.12
1990	1.40	1.74	1.24	1.97	6.50
1991	1.48	1.54	1.69	1.61	6.46
1992	1.29	1.23	1.29	1.18	5.08
1993	0.99	1.02	1.07	0.89	4.02
1994	0.45	0.67	0.81	0.47	2.42

Bear Market Performance

Decile Rank (5-year period)

Worst _____ Best

	Worst 3 Mo Period 1985-89	Worst 3 Mo Period 1990-94
Calvert Tax-Free Res Lim-Term	-0.60	0.36
+/- LB Aggregate	-1.41	5.29
+/- Best Fit Index : LB Muni	2.53	6.12

Trailing Returns

	Total Return %	+/- LB Aggregate	+/- LB Muni	% Rank All	% Rank Obj	Growth of $10,000
3 Mo	0.47	0.09	1.90	12	2	10,047
6 Mo	1.28	0.29	2.53	33	2	10,128
1 Yr	2.42	5.34	8.03	9	1	10,242
3 Yr Avg	3.84	-0.71	-1.03	73	83	11,195
5 Yr Avg	4.89	-2.74	-1.89	90	96	12,693
10 Yr Avg	5.87	-4.08	-3.56	97	93	17,688
15 Yr Avg	---	---	---	---	---	---

Operations

Address and Telephone	4550 Montgomery Ave Ste 1000N
	Bethesda, MD 20814
	800-368-2748 / 301-951-4820
Advisor	Calvert Asset Management
Subadvisor	None
Distributor	Calvert Securities
States Available	All
Report Grade	C+
Income Distrib	Paid Monthly
Date of Inception	03-04-81
Fiscal Year End	December

Min Initial Purchase	$2000 (Addt'l: $250)
Min IRA Purchase	$1000 (Addt'l: $100)
Min Auto Invest Plan	$100 (Systematic Inv: $50)

Expenses & Fees
Sales Fees	2.00% front
	0.00% deferred
	0.00% 12b-1
Management Fee	0.60% flat fee
3-,5-,10-yr Expense Projections	$41, $57, $102

Risk Analysis

Time Period	Load-Adj Return %	Risk % Rank[1] All	Risk % Rank[1] Obj	Morningstar[2] Return	Morningstar[2] Risk	Morningstar Risk-Adj Rating
1 Yr	0.37					
3 Yr	3.14	1	1	0.49	0.02	★★★★
5 Yr	4.46	1	1	0.49	0.03	★★★★★
10 Yr	5.66	1	1	0.38	0.10	★★★★★
Average Historical Rating (109 months)				3.9		★s

[1] 1 = low, 100 = high [2] 1.00 = Muni Avg [3] 1.00 = 90-day T-bill return

Other Measures

				Standard LB Agg	Best Fit LB Muni
Standard Deviation	0.47	Alpha		0.2	0.2
Mean	3.77	Beta		0.07	0.06
Sharpe Ratio	0.52	R-Squared		24	36

Investment Style

Interest-Rate Stance
Avg Effective Maturity	0.9 Yrs

Maturity Short Intm Long
Quality High Med Low

Quality
Avg Credit Quality	AA
Avg Weighted Coupon	5.30%
Avg Weighted Price	100.50% of Par

Diversification Value for Portfolio Types

Large Cap: High	Small Cap: High	Bond: High	Balanced: High	Diversified: High

Portfolio 06-30-94

Amount 000	Date of Maturity	Total Stocks: 0 / Total Fixed-Income: 158	Value $000	% Net Assets
38772	03-01-06	IL Oakbrook Terrace Hsg Multi-Fam 5.4%	38873	5.84
22788	11-01-13	NM Farmington Poll Cntrl DMD	22809	3.42
17835	09-01-17	CA Redlands COP Swr Fac 4.5%	17835	2.68
14927	11-01-08	CA San Juan Capistrano GO Sch Dist DMD	14927	2.24
14733	12-01-25	CA Los Angeles Regl Arpt Impr DMD	14733	2.21
14540	12-01-27	CO Pueblo Sngl Fam Mtg 5%	14659	2.20
13473	11-01-16	NH Indl Dev DMD	13473	2.02
12601	08-01-94	RI Solid Waste Mgmt Landfill 3.25%	12605	1.89
12116	12-01-95	CA Cathedral City 4.5%	12185	1.83
12062	12-01-02	FL Hsg Fin Multi-Fam Mtg 4.75%	12074	1.81
11922	12-01-17	IL Chicago O'Hare Intl Arpt 4%	11922	1.79
11632	09-01-05	FL Dade Hsg Fin Multi-Fam Fairgreen DMD	11632	1.75
9693	05-15-95	FL COP Const Equip Fin Prog 5.75%	9810	1.47
9693	06-01-11	IL Lakemoor Multi-Fam Hsg 4.35%	9769	1.47
9693	10-15-95	MA Wtr Resource 4.125%	9732	1.46
9693	11-01-04	HI State GO DMD	9693	1.45
9645	08-15-94	CO Pueblo Urban Renewal 6.5%	9685	1.45
9014	09-01-18	OH Wtr Dev Poll Cntrl Edison 3.125%	9015	1.35
7754	06-15-95	NJ State COP 4.45%	7774	1.17
7754	05-01-18	PA Westmoreland Indl Dev 4.375%	7730	1.16

Credit Analysis % of Bonds 09-30-94

US Govt	0	BB	0
AAA	47	B	0
AA	22	Below B	0
A	16	NR/NA	0
BBB	15		

Composition % of Assets 09-30-94

Cash	6.0	Preferreds	0.0
Stocks	0.0	Convertibles	0.0
Bonds	94.0	Other	0.0

Tax Analysis

	Tax-Adj Historical Return %	% Pretax Return
3 Yr Avg	3.84	100.0
5 Yr Avg	4.89	100.0
10 Yr Avg	5.86	99.7
Potential Capital Gain Exposure (% of assets)		-1%

Most Similar Funds in MF500

Vanguard Muni Short-Term	Weak Fit
Merrill Lynch Muni Ltd Mat A	Weak Fit
USAA Tax-Exempt Short-Term	Weak Fit

Coupon Range

	% Bonds	Rel Obj
0%	0.0	0.00
0% to 6.8%	52.4	0.87
6.8% to 7.5%	5.3	0.34
7.5% to 8.3%	0.5	0.06
More than 8.3%	2.0	0.22
Not applicable	39.8	10.24

Sector Weightings

	% Bonds	Rel Obj
General Obl	6.33	0.30
Utilities	3.28	0.26
Health	1.16	0.09
Water/Waste	2.00	0.31
Housing	16.52	2.25
Education	5.04	0.79
Transportation	4.88	0.48
COP/Lease	10.66	3.34
Private	9.88	0.85
Misc Revenue	3.71	0.75
Demand	36.53	14.85

Top 5 States % of Bonds

CA	16.51	PA	6.01
IL	11.72	CO	5.65
FL	8.73		

Calvert World Values Glob Eqty A

	Ticker	Load	NAV	Yield	SEC Yield	Assets	Objective
	CWVGX	4.75%	16.14	4.2%	N/A	176.6	World Stock

Calvert World Values Global Equity Fund - Class A seeks total return consistent with reasonable risk.

The fund normally invests at least 65% of its assets in equities issued by established U.S. and foreign companies; it invests in at least three countries. The balance may be invested in debt securities. The fund actively seeks environmentally sound companies and may not invest in issuers engaged in the manufacture of weapons systems or the production of nuclear energy. Up to 30% of the fund's assets may be invested in developing countries.

Class A shares have front loads; Class C shares have level loads.

Manager's Investment Style

As one of the first socially responsible global funds, this fund looks for companies with environmental friendliness, fair employee practices, and good human-rights records. Management also uses top-down considerations to find liquid markets with low inflation and good potential for a market rally. Management then looks at stocks in those markets from the bottom up to identify well-managed firms that have growth potential and dominant positioning, and that are selling cheaply to the market.

Fund Manager(s)

Andrew Preston, since 07-92. Birthdate: 08-48 BA, U. of Melbourne 1971
Rodger Scullion, since 07-92. Birthdate: 01-48

Manager Experience

	Dates Managed	Invest Obj	Std Dev	+/- Index
Rodger Scullion				
Voyageur Intl Equity A	05/94 - 12/94	WF	10.01	-9.82

Historical Profile

Return	---
Risk	---
Rating	
	Not Rated

Investment Style History: Equity

Average % Stocks Held in Portfolio: 91% / 88%

Growth of $10,000
- |||| Value of Fund ($000)
- — Value of Index ($000) S&P 500
- ▼ Manager Change
- ▽ Partial Manager Change
- ► Mgr Unknown After
- ◄ Mgr Unknown Before

Performance Quartile (Within Objective)

1983	1984	1985	1986	1987	1988	1989	1990	1991	1992	1993	1994	History
---	---	---	---	---	---	---	---	---	14.32	17.47	16.14	NAV
---	---	---	---	---	---	---	---	---	-3.88 *	25.79	-2.73	Total Return %
---	---	---	---	---	---	---	---	---	-11.27 *	15.73	-4.05	+/- S&P 500
---	---	---	---	---	---	---	---	---	---	3.28	-7.81	+/- MSCI World
---	---	---	---	---	---	---	---	---	0.37	3.41	4.00	Income Return %
---	---	---	---	---	---	---	---	---	-4.25	22.38	-6.73	Capital Return %
---	---	---	---	---	---	---	---	---	---	11	41	Total Rtn % Rank All
---	---	---	---	---	---	---	---	---	---	71	49	Total Rtn % Rank Obj
---	---	---	---	---	---	---	---	---	0.05	0.46	0.68	Income $
---	---	---	---	---	---	---	---	---	0.03	0.04	0.18	Capital Gains $
---	---	---	---	---	---	---	---	---	1.01	1.50	2.10	Expense Ratio %
---	---	---	---	---	---	---	---	---	1.23	0.80	-0.54	Income Ratio %
---	---	---	---	---	---	---	---	---	---	35		Turnover Rate %
---	---	---	---	---	---	---	---	---	15.5	80.6	176.6	Net Assets ($mil)

Performance 12-31-94

	1st Qtr	2nd Qtr	3rd Qtr	4th Qtr	Total
1987	---	---	---	---	---
1988	---	---	---	---	---
1989	---	---	---	---	---
1990	---	---	---	---	---
1991	---	---	---	---	---
1992	---	---	0.69	-3.88 *	
1993	4.82	1.67	7.14	10.17	25.79
1994	1.83	-1.24	2.39	-5.54	-2.73

Bear Market Performance

Decile Rank (5-year period)

Worst ——————— Best

	Worst 3 Mo Period 1985-89	Worst 3 Mo Period 1990-94
Calvert World Values Glob Eqty	---	---
+/- S&P 500	---	---
+/- Best Fit Index :	---	---

Trailing Returns

	Total Return %	+/- S&P 500	+/- MSCI World	% Rank All	% Rank Obj	Growth of $10,000
3 Mo	-5.54	-5.53	-4.81	93	68	9,446
6 Mo	-3.29	-8.15	-4.68	95	85	9,671
1 Yr	-2.73	-4.05	-7.81	41	49	9,727
3 Yr Avg	---	---	---	---	---	---
5 Yr Avg	---	---	---	---	---	---
10 Yr Avg	---	---	---	---	---	---
15 Yr Avg	---	---	---	---	---	---

Operations

Address and Telephone	4550 Montgomery Ave Ste 1000N
	Bethesda, MD 20814
	800-368-2748 / 301-951-4820
Advisor	Calvert Asset Management
Subadvisor	Murray Johnstone International
Distributor	Calvert Securities
States Available	All
Report Grade	A-
Income Distrib	Paid Annually
* Date of Inception	07-02-92
Fiscal Year End	September

Risk Analysis

Time Period	Load-Adj Return %	Risk % Rank [1] All	Obj	Morningstar [2] Return	Risk	Morningstar Risk-Adj Rating
1 Yr	-7.35					
3 Yr	---	---	---	---	---	---
5 Yr	---	---	---	---	---	---
10 Yr	---	---	---	---	---	---

Average Historical Rating ---

[1] = low, 100 = high [2] 1.00 = Equity Avg [3] 1.00 = 90-day T-bill return

Other Measures

		Standard S&P 500	Best Fit
Standard Deviation	---	Alpha	---	---
Mean	---	Beta	---	---
Sharpe Ratio	---	R-Squared	---	---

Investment Style

	Stock Portfolio Avg	Rel MSCI EAFE	Rel Obj
Price/Earnings Ratio	26.7	0.72	1.08
Price/Cash Flow	14.1	0.91	1.04
Price/Book Ratio	2.7	1.04	0.92
5 Yr Earnings Gr %	0.7	---	0.14
Return on Assets %	5.0	1.11	0.73
Debt % Total Cap	33.6	0.99	1.17
Med Mkt Cap ($mil)	3243	0.27	0.64

Diversification Value for Portfolio Types

Large Cap: Small Cap: Bond: Balanced: Diversified:

Expenses & Fees

Sales Fees   4.75% front / 0.00% deferred / 0.35% 12b-1
Management Fee   1.00% max./0.93% min., 0.10%A
3-,5-,10-yr Expense Projections $112, $161, $305
Annual Brokerage Cost   ---

Min Purchase
Min Initial Purchase $2000 (Addt'l: $250)
Min IRA Purchase $1000 (Addt'l: $100)
Min Auto Invest Plan $100 (Systematic Inv: $50)

Portfolio 09-30-94

Share Chg (03-94)000	Amount 000	Total Stocks: 91 / Total Fixed-Income: 0	Value $000	% Net Assets
865	1313	Hysan Development	3670	2.09
25	55	Telefonos de Mexico L (ADR)	3429	1.95
441	441	National Australia Bank	3368	1.92
980	980	Telecom New Zealand	3110	1.77
90	205	Pryca	3101	1.77
217	217	Telefonica de Espana	2928	1.67
78	122	Grupo Finan Bancomer (ADR)	2925	1.67
562	980	Cifra (ADR)	2893	1.65
982	982	Telecom Italia	2769	1.58
308	637	Wharf Holdings	2563	1.46
343	343	Italcementi	2530	1.44
5	5	Linde	2523	1.44
490	490	Glynwed International	2503	1.43
71	117	Aguas de Barcelona	2503	1.43
22	22	Unilever	2500	1.42
3	8	Douglas Holdings	2486	1.42
17	17	Deutsche Babcock/Wilcox	2472	1.41
209	209	Kuraray	2443	1.39
111	111	Tsukishima Kikai	2424	1.38
39	73	Healthtrust	2416	1.38

Regional Exposure 09-30-94
% of Stocks

Europe	23	Pacific Rim	0
Japan	16	U.S.	25
Latin Amer	0	Other	36

Composition % 09-30-94

Cash	6.0	Preferreds	0.0
Stocks	94.0	Convertibles	0.0
Bonds	0.0	Other	0.0

Tax Analysis

	Tax-Adj Historical Return %	% Pretax Return
3 Yr Avg	---	---
5 Yr Avg	---	---
10 Yr Avg	---	---

Potential Capital Gain Exposure (% of assets)   -2%

Most Similar Funds in MF500
Fund lacks three-year record

Top 5 Countries 09-30-94
% of Stocks

Hong Kong	2
U.S.	2
Australia	2
New Zealand	2
Spain	2

Total Number of Countries: 17
Hedging Policy: Occasional

Sector Weightings

	% of Stocks	Relative S&P 500
Utilities	9.2	1.11
Energy	1.1	0.22
Financials	18.2	1.10
Industrial Cyclicals	34.2	1.47
Consumer Durables	1.8	0.17
Consumer Staples	1.8	0.36
Services	13.9	1.18
Retail	11.9	2.05
Health	1.8	0.34
Technology	6.1	0.69

MORNINGSTAR 1995 Mutual Fund 500

Capital Income Builder

	Ticker	Load	NAV	Yield	SEC Yield	Assets	Objective
	CAIBX	5.75%	31.72	5.2%	4.85%	3596.5	Equity-Inc.

Capital Income Builder seeks current income and growth of income.

The fund normally invests at least 50% of its assets in common stocks, and at least 90% in income-producing securities. Common stocks are selected on the basis of both current dividend yield and the potential for increasing dividend payments. Up to 40% of the fund's assets may be invested in foreign securities.

Historical Profile

Return	Average
Risk	Low
Rating	★★★★ Above Average

Average % Stocks Held in Portfolio

66% 52% 52% 63% 65% 56% 55% 60%

Investment Style History
Equity

Growth of $10,000

- ▐▐▐▐ Value of Fund ($000)
- — Value of Index ($000) S&P 500
- ▼ Manager Change
- ▽ Partial Manager Change
- ► Mgr Unknown After
- ◄ Mgr Unknown Before

Performance Quartile (Within Objective)

	1983	1984	1985	1986	1987	1988	1989	1990	1991	1992	1993	1994	History
	---	---	---	---	21.13	22.56	25.72	25.31	30.00	31.31	34.30	31.72	NAV
	---	---	---	---	-4.41 *	12.45	19.94	3.89	25.70	10.00	15.29	-2.26	Total Return %
	---	---	---	---	16.65 *	-4.16	-11.74	7.01	-4.79	2.38	5.23	-3.57	+/- S&P 500
	---	---	---	---	---	-5.49	-9.23	10.08	-8.51	1.03	4.01	-2.19	+/- Wilshire 5000
	---	---	---	---	2.17	5.69	5.93	5.49	6.07	5.25	5.32	4.99	Income Return %
	---	---	---	---	-6.59	6.77	14.01	-1.59	19.63	4.75	9.96	-7.25	Capital Return %
	---	---	---	---		42	35	46	35	22	27	36	Total Rtn % Rank All
	---	---	---	---		74	58	2	55	39	32	53	Total Rtn % Rank Obj
	---	---	---	---	0.50	1.17	1.26	1.35	1.43	1.51	1.59	1.67	Income $
	---	---	---	---	0.00	0.00	0.00	0.00	0.23	0.11	0.12	0.10	Capital Gains $
	---	---	---	---	---	1.16	1.11	1.01	0.98	0.81	0.72	---	Expense Ratio %
	---	---	---	---	---	5.24	5.44	5.70	5.09	4.71	4.69	---	Income Ratio %
	---	---	---	---	---	36	16	25	14	17	11	---	Turnover Rate %
	---	---	---	---	68.4	130.6	208.7	236.4	656.8	1452.8	3040.2	3596.5	Net Assets ($mil)

Manager's Investment Style

Management seeks income, emphasizing domestic utilities and financials, dividend-paying foreign stocks, and a 35% position in short-term bonds. The goal is to create a fund that can raise its dividends to shareholders each quarter, which it has done for the past 27 quarters.

Fund Manager(s)

Management Team

Manager Experience

	Dates Managed	Invest Obj	Std Dev	+/- Index
Thierry Vandeventer				
New Perspective	01/78 - 12/94	WW	13.89	2.40
EuroPacific Growth	04/84 - 12/94	WF	14.38	2.39

Performance 12-31-94

	1st Qtr	2nd Qtr	3rd Qtr	4th Qtr	Total
1987	---	---	---	-4.63	-4.41 *
1988	5.20	2.91	1.87	1.97	12.45
1989	3.56	6.03	5.58	3.46	19.94
1990	-2.10	2.54	-7.04	11.32	3.89
1991	10.71	0.25	6.12	6.73	25.70
1992	-2.57	7.54	3.42	1.52	10.00
1993	5.46	0.08	5.89	3.15	15.29
1994	-5.77	0.24	3.37	0.11	-2.26

Bear Market Performance

Decile Rank (5-year period)

Worst ———————————————— Best

	Worst 3 Mo Period 1985-89	Worst 3 Mo Period 1990-94
Capital Income Builder	---	-7.04
+/- S&P 500	---	6.71
+/- Best Fit Index : S&P 500	---	6.71

Trailing Returns

	Total Return %	+/- S&P 500	+/- Wil 5000	% Rank All	% Rank Obj	Growth of $10,000
3 Mo	0.11	0.12	0.88	19	8	10,011
6 Mo	3.48	-1.38	-1.15	18	9	10,348
1 Yr	-2.26	-3.57	-2.19	36	53	9,774
3 Yr Avg	7.42	1.16	0.81	24	47	12,395
5 Yr Avg	10.11	1.42	1.30	16	9	16,187
10 Yr Avg	---	---	---	---	---	---
15 Yr Avg	---	---	---	---	---	---

Operations

Address and Telephone	333 S. Hope Street
	Los Angeles, CA 90071
	800-421-4120 / 213-486-9200
Advisor	Capital Research & Management
Subadvisor	None
Distributor	American Funds Distributors
States Available	All plus GU,PR,VI
Report Grade	A+
Income Distrib	Paid Quarterly
* Date of Inception	07-30-87
Fiscal Year End	October

Risk Analysis

Time Period	Load-Adj Return %	Risk % Rank [1] All	Risk % Rank [1] Obj	Morningstar [2] Return	Morningstar [2] Risk	Morningstar Risk-Adj Rating
1 Yr	-7.88					
3 Yr	5.32	55	45	0.51 [3]	0.59	★★★
5 Yr	8.82	51	1	1.03 [3]	0.52	★★★★
10 Yr	---	---	---	---	---	

Average Historical Rating (54 months) 3.9 ★s

[1] = low, 100 = high [2] 1.00 = Equity Avg [3] 1.00 = 90-day T-bill return

Other Measures

			Standard S&P 500	Best Fit S&P 500
Standard Deviation	7.09	Alpha	1.9	1.9
Mean	7.43	Beta	0.69	0.69
Sharpe Ratio	0.55	R-Squared	59	59

Investment Style

	Stock Portfolio Avg	Relative S&P 500
Price/Earnings Ratio	14.7	0.80
Price/Book Ratio	2.3	0.67
5 Yr Earnings Gr %	3.7	0.67
Return on Assets %	6.7	0.89
Debt % Total Cap	30.6	1.08
Med Mkt Cap ($mil)	5744	0.44

Style: Value Blend Growth / Size Large Med Small

Diversification Value for Portfolio Types

Large Cap: Low	Small Cap: High	Bond: Low	Balanced: Low	Diversified: Low

Min Initial Purchase	$1000 (Addt'l: $50)
Min IRA Purchase	$250 (Addt'l: $50)
Min Auto Invest Plan	$50 (Systematic Inv: $50)

Expenses & Fees

Sales Fees	5.75% front
	0.00% deferred
	0.30% 12b-1
Management Fee	0.30% max./0.18% min.+5.00%l
3-,5-,10-yr Expense Projections	$79, $95, $142
Annual Brokerage Cost	0.13%

Portfolio 09-30-94

Total Stocks: 106
Total Fixed-Income: 44

Share Chg (06-94) 000	Amount 000		Value $000	% Net Assets
100	1320	American Home Products	79200	2.22
300	2925	Entergy	68006	1.91
0	3300	Hanson (ADR)	59813	1.68
-70	1950	GTE	59231	1.66
-100	6630	Thames Water	52959	1.49
700	4645	Southern Electric (ADR)	52947	1.49
0	915	Bristol-Myers Squibb	52498	1.47
3950	3950	Eastern Group	46176	1.30
0	6496	B-A-T Industries	44671	1.25
0	4357	Welsh Water	44138	1.24
75	1000	Ameritech	40250	1.13
0	12240	Telecom New Zealand (144A)	38832	1.09
0	4420	North West Water	38335	1.08
0	620	Philip Morris	37898	1.06
225	875	First Union	37844	1.06
0	3960	Southern Water	35937	1.01
400	2125	Long Island Lighting	34531	0.97
-100	320	Royal Dutch Petroleum	34360	0.96
-150	3005	East Midlands Electric	33993	0.95
0	1859	Property Trust America	32757	0.92
0	1370	Pacific Gas & Electric	31168	0.88
0	1400	Central & Southwest	31150	0.87
0	800	American Brands	29000	0.81
0	1395	Hong Kong Telecom (ADR)	28074	0.79
0	800	Signet Banking	27600	0.77

Composition % 12-31-94

Cash	16.4	Preferreds	0.2
Stocks	60.6	Convertibles	1.5
Bonds	21.3	Other	0.0

Tax Analysis

	Tax-Adj Historical Return %	% Pretax Return
3 Yr Avg	5.45	72.0
5 Yr Avg	8.16	77.7
10 Yr Avg	---	---
Potential Capital Gain Exposure (% of assets)		2%

Most Similar Funds in MF500

Vanguard Equity-Income	Fair Fit
Washington Mutual Investors	Fair Fit
Fidelity Utilities	Fair Fit

Index Allocation

	% of Stocks
S&P 500	48.8
S&P MidCap 400	4.0
U.S. Small Cap	13.8
Foreign	35.3

Sector Weightings

	% of Stocks	Relative S&P 500
Utilities	35.5	2.87
Energy	4.9	0.48
Financials	31.6	2.99
Industrial Cyclicals	1.3	0.08
Consumer Durables	0.6	0.10
Consumer Staples	8.6	0.69
Services	6.3	0.78
Retail	0.0	0.00
Health	10.7	1.23
Technology	0.4	0.05

Capital World Bond

	Ticker	Load	NAV	Yield	SEC Yield	Assets	Objective
	CWBFX	4.75%	15.12	6.3%	7.14%	563.2	World Bond

Capital World Bond Fund seeks total return consistent with prudent investment management.

The fund intends to invest primarily in investment-grade fixed-income obligations denominated in various currencies, including U.S. dollars, or in multinational currency units such as European currency units (ECUs). Under normal conditions, the fund invests at least 65% of its assets in the bonds of issuers in at least three countries. Issuers of any one country may not represent more than 40% of the fund's assets. The fund may engage in currency futures and options thereon.

Manager's Investment Style

Management invests this fund's assets in a broad set of global bond markets, including that of the United States. Preferring high-quality investments, management largely avoids developing markets and limits its corporate holdings. It does occasionally hedge currency risk.

Fund Manager(s)
James R. Mulally, since 08-87.
Mark H. Dalzell, since 04-91.

Manager Experience
	Dates Managed	Invest Obj	Std Dev	+/- Index
Not available.				

Historical Profile
Return Average
Risk Low
Rating ★★★★
Above Average

Investment Style History
Fixed Income

Income Rtn % Rank Obj

| --- | 60 | 58 | 69 | 64 | 76 | 59 | 38 |

Growth of $10,000
|||| Value of Fund ($000)
— Value of Index ($000) LB Corp
▼ Manager Change
▽ Partial Manager Change
► Mgr Unknown After
◄ Mgr Unknown Before

Performance Quartile (Within Objective)

	1983	1984	1985	1986	1987	1988	1989	1990	1991	1992	1993	1994	History
	---	---	---	---	15.89	14.87	14.38	14.81	15.89	14.94	16.33	15.12	NAV
	---	---	---	---	14.00 *	2.72	4.57	11.65	15.28	0.82	16.73	-1.43	Total Return %
	---	---	---	---	---	-5.16	-9.97	2.70	-0.72	-6.43	6.98	1.49	+/- LB Aggregate
	---	---	---	---	---	0.36	8.00	-3.64	-0.96	-3.96	1.61	-8.13	+/- SB World Govt
	---	---	---	---	2.63	7.15	7.86	8.66	7.99	5.84	6.84	5.98	Income Return %
	---	---	---	---	11.38	-4.43	-3.30	2.99	7.29	-5.02	9.89	-7.41	Capital Return %
	---	---	---	---	---	96	96	2	56	89	23	29	Total Rtn % Rank All
	---	---	---	---	---	60	75	66	27	66	32	19	Total Rtn % Rank Obj
	---	---	---	---	0.37	1.10	1.14	1.18	1.10	0.93	0.98	0.96	Income $
	---	---	---	---	0.01	0.33	0.00	0.00	0.00	0.16	0.08	0.00	Capital Gains $
	---	---	---	---	---	1.38	1.30	1.52	1.42	1.38	1.19	1.11	Expense Ratio %
	---	---	---	---	---	6.84	7.69	8.40	7.54	6.88	6.25	6.88	Income Ratio %
	---	---	---	---	---	94	62	76	81	95	28	77	Turnover Rate %
	---	---	---	---	---	12.2	36.3	37.7	50.7	94.0	255.0	525.5	563.2	Net Assets ($mil)

Performance 12-31-94
	1st Qtr	2nd Qtr	3rd Qtr	4th Qtr	Total
1987	---	---	---	14.32	14.00 *
1988	1.95	-3.55	0.66	3.77	2.72
1989	-2.22	1.22	2.68	2.90	4.57
1990	-3.20	4.71	3.51	6.42	11.65
1991	1.28	0.74	6.92	5.67	15.28
1992	-2.14	4.79	1.01	-2.68	0.82
1993	5.29	3.81	3.84	2.84	16.73
1994	-2.58	-1.90	1.05	2.06	-1.43

Bear Market Performance
Decile Rank (5-year period)

Worst ———— Best

	Worst 3 Mo Period 1985-89	Worst 3 Mo Period 1990-94
Capital World Bond	---	-5.11
+/- LB Aggregate	---	-0.17
+/- Best Fit Index : LB Corp	---	1.16

Trailing Returns
	Total Return %	+/- LB Aggregate	+/- SB World	% Rank All	Obj	Growth of $10,000
3 Mo	2.06	1.69	1.50	3	5	10,206
6 Mo	3.14	2.15	0.91	20	12	10,314
1 Yr	-1.43	1.49	-8.13	29	19	9,857
3 Yr Avg	5.07	0.53	-3.70	46	24	11,600
5 Yr Avg	8.35	0.72	-3.17	30	24	14,930
10 Yr Avg	---	---	---	---	---	---
15 Yr Avg	---	---	---	---	---	---

Operations
Address and Telephone	333 S. Hope Street
	Los Angeles, CA 90071
	800-421-4120 / 213-486-9200
Advisor	Capital Research & Management
Subadvisor	None
Distributor	American Funds Distributors
States Available	All plus GU,PR,VI
Report Grade	A+
Income Distrib	Paid Quarterly
* Date of Inception	08-04-87
Fiscal Year End	September

Min Initial Purchase	$1000 (Addt'l: $50)
Min IRA Purchase	$250 (Addt'l: $50)
Min Auto Invest Plan	$50 (Systematic Inv: $50)

Expenses & Fees
Sales Fees	4.75% front
	0.00% deferred
	0.30% 12b-1
Management Fee	0.70% max./0.50% min.
3-,5-,10-yr Expense Projections	$83, $110, $185

Risk Analysis
Time Period	Load-Adj Return %	Risk % Rank [1] All	Obj	Morningstar [2] Return	Risk	Morningstar Risk-Adj Rating
1 Yr	-6.11					
3 Yr	3.38	40	24	-0.06 [3]	0.62	★★★
5 Yr	7.30	41	12	0.63 [3]	0.48	★★★★
10 Yr	---	---	---	---	---	---

Average Historical Rating (53 months) 3.1 ★s

[1] 1 = low, 100 = high [2] 1.00 = Hybrid Avg [3] 1.00 = 90-day T-bill return

Other Measures
			Standard LB Agg	Best Fit LB Corp
Standard Deviation	5.10	Alpha	0.7	0.2
Mean	5.09	Beta	0.87	0.70
Sharpe Ratio	0.31	R-Squared	47	48

Investment Style
Interest-Rate Stance
Avg Effective Maturity	11.2 Yrs

Quality
Avg Credit Quality	AAA
Avg Weighted Coupon	8.49%

Maturity: Short Intm Long
Quality: High Med Low

Diversification Value for Portfolio Types
● Large Cap: High ● Small Cap: High ▨ Bond: Medium ● Balanced: High ▨ Diversified: Medium

Portfolio 09-30-94
Total Stocks: 0
Total Fixed-Income: 68

Amount 000	Date of Maturity		Value $000	% Net Assets
79300	2023	Govt of Netherlands 7.5%	43246	7.51
195000	2004	Republic of Finland 9.5%	38191	6.63
2820000	2001	European Investment Bk 6.75%	31783	5.52
2600000	2003	Export-Import Bk Japan 4.375%	25699	4.46
3350000	2003	Kingdom of Spain 10.5%	24900	4.33
44550	2000	Govt of New Zealand 6.5%	23831	4.14
120900	2023	Govt of France 8.5%	22775	3.96
124000	1998	Kingdom of Netherlands 9%	20552	3.57
2020	1998	Kingdom of Spain 11.45%	15935	2.77
28000	2004	Govt of New Zealand 8%	15489	2.69
10200	1999	Republic of Ireland 6.25%	14399	2.50
97000	1999	Kingdom of Sweden 11%	13076	2.27
18000000	2003	Republic of Italy 11.5%	11396	1.98
13000	2009	Govt of Canada 10.75%	11056	1.92
48000	1996	Republic of Finland 11.75%	10396	1.81
13000	2010	Govt of Canada 9.5%	10092	1.75
16500	2003	Govt of Netherlands 6.75%	10059	1.75
17000	2004	New South Wales Treasury 7%	9911	1.72
8000	2022	Govt of France 8.25%	9093	1.58
7250	11-15-09	US Treasury Bond 10.375%	8538	1.48
15000	2006	Republic of Australia 6.75%	8297	1.44
5000	1999	United Kingdom Treasury 9.5%	8087	1.40
7500	03-01-21	ConAgra 9.75%	8069	1.40
4500	2003	Republic of Ireland 9.25%	7088	1.23
7000	1996	Czech National Bank 7%	6990	1.21

Composition % 12-31-94
Cash	6.1	Preferreds	0.0
Stocks	0.0	Convertibles	0.0
Bonds	93.9	Other	0.0

Tax Analysis
	Tax-Adj Historical Return %	% Pretax Return
3 Yr Avg	2.64	50.7
5 Yr Avg	5.86	66.8
10 Yr Avg	---	---

Potential Capital Gain Exposure (% of assets) -7%

Most Similar Funds in MF500
PaineWebber Global Inc B	Fair Fit
MFS World Governments A	Fair Fit
Templeton Income	Weak Fit

Country Exposure 09-30-94
	% of Bonds
Japan	12
U.S.	11
Finland	9
Netherlands	8
Spain	7

Currency Exposure 03-31-94
	% of Net Assets
U.S.	46
Japan	12
Canada	10
Finland	6
Denmark	5

MORNINGSTAR **1995 Mutual Fund 500**

Capital World Growth & Inc

	Ticker	Load	NAV	Yield	SEC Yield	Assets	Objective
	CWGIX	5.75%	17.47	2.9%	3.21%	2827.1	World Stock

Capital World Growth and Income Fund seeks long-term capital appreciation.

The fund invests in foreign and domestic equities, debt obligations, and money-market instruments. The portfolio is allocated according to long-term economic and market trends; the fund does not anticipate frequent shifts among asset classes. The fund invests principally in equity securities. The debt portion concentrates on intermediate- and long-term fixed-income securities; foreign debt consists mostly of governmental obligations. Up to 10% of assets may be invested in low-quality debt. No more than 40% of fund assets may be invested in any one country.

Manager's Investment Style

Despite a broad prospectus, management has so far divided assets between global stocks and a healthy cash stake. Management has emphasized larger, dividend-paying stocks from both developed and developing markets.

Historical Profile

Return ---
Risk ---
Rating Not Rated

Investment Style History
Equity

Average % Stocks Held in Portfolio

71% 79%

Growth of $10,000

|||| Value of Fund ($000)
— Value of Index ($000) S&P 500
▼ Manager Change
▽ Partial Manager Change
◄ Mgr Unknown After
◄ Mgr Unknown Before

Performance Quartile (Within Objective)

	1983	1984	1985	1986	1987	1988	1989	1990	1991	1992	1993	1994	History
	---	---	---	---	---	---	---	---	---	---	18.07	17.47	NAV
	---	---	---	---	---	---	---	---	---	---	22.22 *	1.22	Total Return %
	---	---	---	---	---	---	---	---	---	---	15.60 *	-0.09	+/- S&P 500
	---	---	---	---	---	---	---	---	---	---	---	-3.85	+/- MSCI World
	---	---	---	---	---	---	---	---	---	---	2.39	2.94	Income Return %
	---	---	---	---	---	---	---	---	---	---	19.83	-1.72	Capital Return %
	---	---	---	---	---	---	---	---	---	---	---	12	Total Rtn % Rank All
	---	---	---	---	---	---	---	---	---	---	---	22	Total Rtn % Rank Obj
	---	---	---	---	---	---	---	---	---	---	0.32	0.52	Income $
	---	---	---	---	---	---	---	---	---	---	0.00	0.29	Capital Gains $
	---	---	---	---	---	---	---	---	---	---	---	---	Expense Ratio %
	---	---	---	---	---	---	---	---	---	---	---	---	Income Ratio %
	---	---	---	---	---	---	---	---	---	---	---	---	Turnover Rate %
	---	---	---	---	---	---	---	---	---	---	1761.6	2827.1	Net Assets ($mil)

Fund Manager(s)

Management Team

Manager Experience

Manager Experience	Dates Managed	Invest Obj	Std Dev	+/- Index
Thierry Vandeventer				
New Perspective	01/78 - 12/94	WW	13.89	2.40
EuroPacific Growth	04/84 - 12/94	WF	14.38	2.39

Performance 12-31-94

	1st Qtr	2nd Qtr	3rd Qtr	4th Qtr	Total
1987	---	---	---	---	---
1988	---	---	---	---	---
1989	---	---	---	---	---
1990	---	---	---	---	---
1991	---	---	---	---	---
1992	---	---	---	---	---
1993	---	1.79	7.93	10.95	22.22 *
1994	-2.88	-0.87	5.47	-0.30	1.22

Bear Market Performance

Decile Rank (5-year period)

	Worst 3 Mo Period 1985-89	Worst 3 Mo Period 1990-94
Capital World Growth & Inc	---	---
+/- S&P 500	---	---
+/- Best Fit Index :	---	---

Worst ... Best

Trailing Returns

	Total Return %	+/- S&P 500	+/- MSCI World	% Rank All	% Rank Obj	Growth of $10,000
3 Mo	-0.30	-0.29	0.43	30	5	9,970
6 Mo	5.15	0.29	3.75	11	8	10,515
1 Yr	1.22	-0.09	-3.85	12	22	10,122
3 Yr Avg	---	---	---	---	---	---
5 Yr Avg	---	---	---	---	---	---
10 Yr Avg	---	---	---	---	---	---
15 Yr Avg	---	---	---	---	---	---

Operations

Address and Telephone	333 S. Hope Street Los Angeles, CA 90071 800-421-4120 / 213-486-9200	
Advisor	Capital Research & Management	
Subadvisor	None	
Distributor	American Funds Distributors	
States Available	All plus GU,PR	
Report Grade	A+	
Income Distrib	Paid Quarterly	
* Date of Inception	03-26-93	
Fiscal Year End	November	

Min Initial Purchase	$1000 (Addt'l: $50)
Min IRA Purchase	$250 (Addt'l: $50)
Min Auto Invest Plan	$50 (Systematic Inv: $50)

Expenses & Fees

Sales Fees	5.75% front
	0.00% deferred
	0.30% 12b-1
Management Fee	0.60% max./0.40% min.
3-,5-,10-yr Expense Projections	$85, N/A, N/A
Annual Brokerage Cost	---

Risk Analysis

Time Period	Load-Adj Return %	Risk % Rank All	Risk % Rank Obj	Morningstar Return	Morningstar Risk	Morningstar Risk-Adj Rating
1 Yr	-4.60					
3 Yr	---	---	---	---	---	---
5 Yr	---	---	---	---	---	---
10 Yr	---	---	---	---	---	---

Average Historical Rating ---

[1] = low, 100 = high [2] 1.00 = Equity Avg [3] 1.00 = 90-day T-bill return

Other Measures

	Standard S&P 500	Best Fit
Standard Deviation	---	Alpha --- ---
Mean	---	Beta --- ---
Sharpe Ratio	---	R-Squared --- ---

Investment Style

	Stock Portfolio Avg	Rel MSCI EAFE	Rel Obj
Price/Earnings Ratio	16.0	0.43	0.65
Price/Cash Flow	11.4	0.73	0.84
Price/Book Ratio	2.3	0.87	0.78
5 Yr Earnings Gr %	1.4	---	0.28
Return on Assets %	6.7	1.48	0.98
Debt % Total Cap	30.2	0.89	1.05
Med Mkt Cap ($mil)	5581	0.47	1.11

Style V B G / Size L M S

Diversification Value for Portfolio Types

Large Cap: Small Cap: Bond: Balanced: Diversified:

Portfolio 05-31-94

Total Stocks: 229
Total Fixed-Income: 27

Share Chg (11-93)000	Amount 000		Value $000	% Net Assets
445	1222	Intl Nederlander Groep	50202	2.10
105	2136	Thorn-Emi	33119	1.39
4162	5403	Commonwealth Bank Australia	32278	1.35
-1237	10448	Telecom New Zealand	30735	1.29
625	625	First Union	29219	1.22
103	384	Telefonos de Mexico L (ADR)	23838	1.00
-1080	5094	Hutchison Whampoa	22419	0.94
298	684	ABN AMRO Holdings	22343	0.93
14038	29231	Brierley Investments	22236	0.93
90	193	Akzo	21722	0.91
1076	2786	Advance Bank of Australia	20138	0.84
437	547	Telebras (ADR)	20113	0.84
1400	1400	Jefferson Smurfit Group	19250	0.81
1210	2170	Southern Electric	18978	0.79
	21200	Bangkok Bank Cv 3.25%	18656	0.78
665	1875	Eastern Electricity	16922	0.71
550	1875	Reckitt & Colman	16866	0.71
550	2245	North West Water	16752	0.70
0	5195	Tesco	16538	0.69
	9044	TNT Cv Pfd	16344	0.68

Regional Exposure 12-31-94

% of Stocks

Europe	46	Pacific Rim	20
Japan	1	U.S.	28
Latin Amer	2	Other	4

Composition % 12-31-94

Cash	12.0	Preferreds	0.0
Stocks	81.0	Convertibles	4.0
Bonds	3.0	Other	0.0

Tax Analysis

	Tax-Adj Historical Return %	% Pretax Return
3 Yr Avg	---	---
5 Yr Avg	---	---
10 Yr Avg	---	---
Potential Capital Gain Exposure (% of assets)		4%

Most Similar Funds in MF500

Fund lacks three-year record

Top 5 Countries 12-31-94

	% of Stocks
U.S.	28
United Kingdom	18
Netherlands	8
Australia	8
New Zealand	6

Total Number of Countries: 23
Hedging Policy: Never

Sector Weightings

	% of Stocks	Relative S&P 500
Utilities	15.8	1.90
Energy	5.7	1.18
Financials	26.9	1.63
Industrial Cyclicals	16.6	0.72
Consumer Durables	8.2	0.79
Consumer Staples	6.9	1.35
Services	8.2	0.69
Retail	3.1	0.54
Health	6.3	1.21
Technology	2.4	0.27

Central Securities

Ticker	NAV	Mkt Price	Prem/Disc	Yield	Objective
CET	$16.82	$15.75	-6.4%	1.3%	Domestic Eq

Central Securities Corporation seeks capital appreciation. Income is a secondary consideration.

The fund invests primarily in common stocks but may invest in convertibles, preferreds, and debt securities. The fund does not restrict itself as to the types of securities in which it invests or the proportion of the value of its assets invested in any type of securities.

The fund is leveraged with convertible-preferred stock.

The Christian A. Johnson Endeavor Foundation (of which Mrs. Wilmot Kidd is president) owns 39.9% of the fund's voting stock. Mrs. Christian A. Johnson (Mrs. Kidd's mother) owns 9.4% of the voting stock, and manager Wilmot Kidd owns 6.9%.

Although the fund does not have a dividend-reinvestment plan, it issues year-end distributions in the form of stock, unless shareholders elect to receive them in cash.

1983	1984	1985	1986	1987	1988	1989	1990	1991	1992	1993	1994	
-10.7	-4.3	3.6	-7.2	-8.5	-13.5	-16.9	-16.0	-15.2	-14.1	1.4	-2.3	Highest Prem/Disc
-24.6	-14.5	-12.3	-12.6	-29.6	-21.6	-21.3	-22.0	-22.5	-22.3	-16.3	-12.2	Lowest Prem/Disc

Historical Profile
Return Above Average
Risk Below Average
Rating ★★★★ Above Average

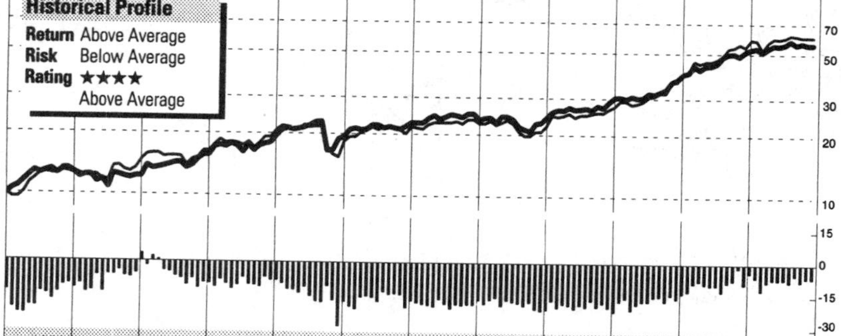

Growth of $10,000
at NAV ($000)
at Market Price ($000)

Premium Discount %

1983	1984	1985	1986	1987	1988	1989	1990	1991	1992	1993	1994	History
16.23	13.51	15.24	12.98	11.18	11.54	11.96	9.93	11.61	13.85	17.10	16.82	NAV
43.22	-5.71	27.71	15.07	4.67	15.76	15.13	-9.08	26.30	29.77	36.75	8.71	NAV Total Return %
20.76	-11.97	-4.03	-3.61	-0.59	-0.85	-16.56	-5.97	-4.19	22.15	26.69	7.40	+/- S&P 500
17.12	-6.89	-7.87	-1.14	6.71	-5.11	-20.41	-3.97	-23.77	17.87	22.82	12.30	+/- S&P Mid 400
4.02	3.26	1.69	1.86	2.18	1.71	3.84	2.52	1.67	1.04	1.26	1.42	Income Return %
39.20	-8.97	26.02	13.21	2.49	14.04	11.29	-11.60	24.63	28.74	35.49	7.29	Capital Return %
1	78	22	34	26	28	30	78	29	3	11	4	Total Rtn % Rank All
1	53	38	35	22	50	74	62	70	9	2	2	Total Rtn % Rank Obj
65.40	-0.40	22.09	16.68	-19.41	29.95	17.17	-11.83	28.93	36.71	47.68	12.30	Market Total Rtn %
-17.6	-9.1	-5.0	-9.9	-15.0	-17.1	-19.3	-18.7	-19.5	-17.5	-9.4	-7.1	Avg Prem/Disc %
0.44	0.42	0.21	0.23	0.22	0.16	0.35	0.20	0.14	0.10	0.18	0.22	Income $
1.31	1.28	1.36	3.47	1.55	0.92	0.65	0.50	0.56	0.76	1.42	1.39	Capital Gains $
0.69	0.91	0.92	0.84	0.87	0.89	0.92	0.98	0.96	0.88	0.77	0.57	Expense Ratio %
2.66	2.19	1.89	1.61	1.74	1.88	1.83	2.11	1.78	1.42	1.17	1.64	Income Ratio %
16	16	25	35	33	9	14	7	17	19	15	---	Turnover Rate %
98.1	85.9	105.9	106.5	100.5	108.8	119.3	101.1	121.6	155.6	208.9	222.4	Net Assets ($mil)
3.8	5.6	5.5	10.2	10.1	10.1	10.0	10.0	10.0	10.0	10.0	9.7	Pfd/Debt Leverage ($mil)

Manager's Investment Style

Management buys firms that operate on different business cycles in an effort to diversify. The portfolio, nevertheless, tends to favor economically sensitive issues. Management buys individual companies and is willing to dedicate a substantial portion of assets to each one: The portfolio typically features between 25 and 40 names. Usually about 10 securities take up 50% of assets.

Fund Manager(s)

Wilmot H. Kidd. Since 5-73. BA'64 Washington & Lee U.; MBA'65 Northwestern U.

Manager Experience Dates Managed / Invest Obj / Std Dev / +/- Index

Not available.

NAV Performance % 12-30-94

	1st Qtr	2nd Qtr	3rd Qtr	4th Qtr	Total
1987	17.80	1.07	6.68	-17.59	4.67
1988	12.70	3.95	-1.82	0.64	15.76
1989	3.47	4.37	4.30	2.22	15.13
1990	-4.26	1.43	-13.23	7.90	-9.08
1991	15.51	0.26	-0.53	9.64	26.30
1992	3.88	1.52	6.93	15.09	29.77
1993	16.17	0.75	13.79	2.67	36.75
1994	-0.12	7.29	1.54	-0.10	8.71

Bear Market Performance

Decile Rank (5-year period)

Worst ... Best

	Worst 3 Mo Period 1985-89	Worst 3 Mo Period 1990-94
Central Secs	-26.84	-13.23
+/- S&P 500	2.74	0.52

Trailing Returns

	NAV Total Return %	+/- S&P 500	+/- S&P Mid 400	% Rank All	% Rank Obj	Mkt Total Return %
3 Mo	-0.10	-0.08	2.48	21	30	-1.43
6 Mo	1.44	-3.42	-2.56	24	60	2.22
1 Yr	8.71	7.40	12.30	4	2	12.30
3 Yr Avg	24.49	18.22	17.37	4	6	31.37
5 Yr Avg	17.24	8.55	5.40	4	6	20.85
10 Yr Avg	16.34	1.95	0.30	8	7	16.25

Risk Analysis

	Risk % Rank[1] All	Risk % Rank[1] Obj	Morningstar[2] Return	Morningstar[2] Risk	Morningstar Risk-Adj Rating
3 Yr	54	15	3.26	0.40	★★★★
5 Yr	72	24	2.77	0.56	★★★★
10 Yr	62	23	1.24	0.67	★★★★

Average Historical Rating (145 months) 3.1 ★s

[1] 1 = Low, 100 = High [2] 1.00 = Equity Avg [3] 1.00 = 90-day T-bill Return

Other Measures S&P 500

Standard Deviation	11.31	Alpha	17.68
Mean	22.73	Beta	0.98
Sharpe Ratio	1.70	R-Squared	47

Investment Style

	Stock Portfolio Avg	Relative S&P 500
Price/Earnings Ratio	16.3	0.88
Price/Cash Flow Ratio	12.5	1.08
Price/Book Ratio	2.3	0.68
5 Yr Earnings Gr %	5.7	1.03
Return on Assets %	6.5	0.86
Debt % Total Cap	20.5	0.72
Med Mkt Cap ($mil)	1592	0.12

Style: Value Blend Growth; Size: Large Med Small

figure is based on less than 50% of stocks

Index Allocation % of Stocks

Dow 30	0.0
S&P 500	24.2
S&P Mid-Cap 400	52.9
US Small-Cap	21.4
Foreign	1.6

Diversification Value for Portfolio Types

Large Cap: Medium | Small Cap: Low | Bond: High | Balanced: Low | Diversified: Medium

Portfolio 12-31-94

Total Equity: 38
Total Fixed-Income: 4

Share Chg (06-94)	Amount		Value $000	% Total Invest
0	70000	Plymouth Rock Cl A	31500	13.90
-190000	550000	Analog Devices	19319	8.53
-100000	670000	Reynolds & Reynolds Cl A	16750	7.39
0	480000	MA Hanna	11400	5.03
0	200000	WH Brady Cl A	9700	4.28
0	150000	Intel	9581	4.23
0	300000	Bank of New York	8700	3.84
0	185000	Murphy Oil	7863	3.47
270000	270000	Signet Banking	7729	3.41
-20000	200000	Household International	7425	3.28
0	200000	Chemical Banking	7175	3.17
122500	367500	American Management Systems	7074	3.12
-20000	450000	NEXTEL Communications Cl A	6469	2.85
0	100000	Rohm & Haas	5713	2.52
0	175000	Measurex	4134	1.82
0	480000	Santa Fe Energy Resources	3840	1.69
-177920	533757	Transport of America Cl B	3803	1.68
0	112600	Vesta Insurance Group	3209	1.42
0	100000	GTE	3038	1.34
---	3080000	Steuart Petroleum 9%	3028	1.34
0	100000	Media General Cl A	2838	1.25
0	150000	Tidewater	2775	1.22
100000	100000	Mutual Risk Management	2625	1.16
30000	130000	Caremark International	2226	0.98
100000	100000	Provident Life & Accident B	2175	0.96

Composition % 12-31-94

Cash	9.7	Preferreds	0.0
Stocks	87.4	Convertibles	1.1
Bonds	1.3	Other	0.5

Leverage factor: 1.04

Tax Analysis

	Tax-Adj Historical Return %	% Pretax Return
3 Yr Avg	21.17	83.8
5 Yr Avg	14.21	77.4
10 Yr Avg	12.39	62.3

Potential Capital Gain Exposure (% of assets) 46

Most Similar Funds in MF500

Oppenheimer Main St	Weak Fit
Strong Opportunity	Weak Fit
Strong Common Stock	Weak Fit

Sector Weightings

	% of Stocks	Relative S&P 500
Utilities	1.9	0.15
Energy	7.2	0.71
Financials	22.5	2.13
Industrial Cyclicals	10.3	0.63
Consumer Durables	7.7	1.24
Consumer Staples	0.3	0.03
Services	12.1	1.48
Retail	0.0	0.00
Health	1.7	0.20
Technology	36.3	3.96

Operations

Address and Telephone	375 Park Avenue New York, NY 10152 212-688-3011
Advisor	Central Securities
Subadvisor	N/A
Administrator	Internally Administered
Transfer Agent	First Chicago Trust Co. New York
Custodian	United States Trust Co. New York
Auditor	KPMG Peat Marwick
Legal Counsel	Chadbourne & Parke

Income Distrib Schedule	Paid Irregularly
Management Fee	0.40%
Reinvestment Plan	No
Direct Purchase Plan	No
Shares Outstanding	12,324,766
Exchange	AMEX
Date of Inception	10-01-29
Shareholder Report	C-

Century Shares

Century Shares Trust seeks growth of principal and income.
The fund invests in equity securities of banks, trusts, and insurance companies. It may also purchase debt constituting a legal investment for Massachusetts savings banks. The fund maintains no restriction on the relative amounts invested in the banking and insurance industries, and it may invest in all types of insurance companies: property and casualty, life, health, multiline, and specialty insurers. Also, various types of bank securities, such as commercial or investment, may be purchased.

Manager's Investment Style

Manager Allan Fulkerson has a preference for insurance firms, and invests almost exclusively in a limited number of high-quality insurance providers. He holds these issues for the long-term, rarely trading.

Fund Manager(s)

Allan W. Fulkerson, since 01-76. Birthdate: 09-33. BA, Williams C. 1954

Manager Experience

	Dates Managed	Invest Obj	Std Dev	+/- Index

Not available.

	Ticker	Load	NAV	Yield	SEC Yield	Assets	Objective
	CENSX	None	21.77	2.0%	N/A	206.1	Sp.-Financ'l

Historical Profile
Return Average
Risk Average
Rating ★★★
Neutral

| | 97% | 97% | 96% | 94% | 94% | 89% | 91% | 97% |

Investment Style History
Equity
Average % Stocks Held in Portfolio

Growth of $10,000
|||| Value of Fund ($000)
— Value of Index ($000) LB L-T
▼ Manager Change
▽ Partial Manager Change
► Mgr Unknown After
◄ Mgr Unknown Before

Performance Quartile (Within Objective)

1983	1984	1985	1986	1987	1988	1989	1990	1991	1992	1993	1994	History
13.62	14.02	18.22	18.30	14.76	14.62	19.42	16.82	21.03	25.68	24.04	21.77	NAV
21.00	15.48	43.40	9.61	-8.02	15.69	41.64	-7.84	31.51	26.99	-0.36	-3.90	Total Return %
-1.47	9.22	11.67	-9.07	-13.28	-0.92	9.95	-4.73	1.02	19.37	-10.42	-5.21	+/- S&P 500
---	---	---	1.60	8.74	-2.67	8.99	13.59	-19.23	3.62	-11.46	-0.36	+/- S&P Financial
5.21	4.87	3.53	2.66	2.89	3.41	3.20	2.70	2.71	1.97	1.77	1.96	Income Return %
15.79	10.61	39.87	6.95	-10.91	12.28	38.43	-10.55	28.80	25.01	-2.13	-5.86	Capital Return %
36	4	4	86	94	26	3	79	24	2	99	52	Total Rtn % Rank All
66	33	1	57	30	70	1	10	90	66	92	69	Total Rtn % Rank Obj
0.64	0.60	0.54	0.51	0.50	0.54	0.50	0.51	0.47	0.42	0.45	0.45	Income $
0.45	0.91	0.91	1.11	1.61	1.90	0.71	0.58	0.57	0.56	1.10	0.88	Capital Gains $
0.94	0.95	0.84	0.77	0.81	0.87	0.94	1.03	0.95	0.84	0.82	1.02	Expense Ratio %
4.57	4.30	3.14	2.57	2.60	3.45	2.78	2.82	2.28	1.84	1.72	1.77	Income Ratio %
4	4	6	6	2	3	3	3	0	5	19	---	Turnover Rate %
74.4	76.9	123.2	141.5	109.4	110.4	150.4	130.0	157.9	260.3	233.8	206.1	Net Assets ($mil)

Performance 12-31-94

	1st Qtr	2nd Qtr	3rd Qtr	4th Qtr	Total
1987	10.05	-2.26	4.37	-18.07	-8.02
1988	7.38	4.04	7.02	-3.24	15.69
1989	11.97	7.51	11.58	5.45	41.64
1990	-5.25	3.53	-18.83	15.75	-7.84
1991	17.06	-0.73	-0.16	13.34	31.51
1992	-1.47	7.02	10.38	9.11	26.99
1993	5.30	-2.47	6.15	-8.60	-0.36
1994	-5.66	0.39	1.55	-0.08	-3.90

Bear Market Performance

Decile Rank (5-year period)

Worst ▮ Best

	Worst 3 Mo Period 1985-89	Worst 3 Mo Period 1990-94
Century Shares	-22.30	-22.51
+/- S&P 500	7.28	-8.67
+/- Best Fit Index : LB L-T	-24.89	-21.61

Trailing Returns

	Total Return %	+/- S&P 500	+/- S&P Financial	% Rank All	% Rank Obj	Growth of $10,000
3 Mo	-0.08	-0.06	3.03	24	1	9,992
6 Mo	1.47	-3.39	6.19	31	6	10,147
1 Yr	-3.90	-5.21	-0.36	52	69	9,610
3 Yr Avg	6.74	0.47	-3.02	28	91	12,160
5 Yr Avg	8.06	-0.63	-1.32	32	90	14,737
10 Yr Avg	13.32	-1.06	---	23	66	34,913
15 Yr Avg	13.77	-0.71	---	27	50	69,238

Operations

Address and Telephone	1 Liberty Square
	Boston, MA 02109
	800-321-1928 / 617-482-3060
Advisor	Century Capital Management
Subadvisor	None
Distributor	Century Shares Trust
States Available	All
Report Grade	A-
Income Distrib	Paid Semiannually
Date of Inception	03-01-28
Fiscal Year End	December

Risk Analysis

Time Period	Load-Adj Return %	Risk % Rank All	Risk % Rank Obj	Morningstar Return	Morningstar Risk	Morningstar Risk-Adj Rating
1 Yr	-3.90					
3 Yr	6.74	80	41	0.94[3]	0.95	★★★
5 Yr	8.06	84	20	0.83[3]	1.03	★★★
10 Yr	13.32	80	1	1.13	1.02	★★★

Average Historical Rating (109 months) 3.6 ★s

[1] 1 = low, 100 = high [2] 1.00 = Equity Avg [3] 1.00 = 90-day T-bill return

Other Measures

			Standard S&P 500	Best Fit LB L-T
Standard Deviation	10.25	Alpha	1.5	1.8
Mean	7.06	Beta	0.72	0.86
Sharpe Ratio	0.35	R-Squared	31	43

Investment Style

	Stock Portfolio Avg	Relative S&P 500
Price/Earnings Ratio	11.6	0.63
Price/Book Ratio	1.6	0.48
5 Yr Earnings Gr %	9.4	1.70
Return on Assets %	3.0	0.40
Debt % Total Cap	22.1	0.78
Med Mkt Cap ($mil)	3113	0.24

Style
Value Blend Growth
Size Large Med Small

Diversification Value for Portfolio Types

Large Cap: Medium	Small Cap: High	Bond: Medium	Balanced: Medium	Diversified: High

Portfolio 09-30-94

Share Chg (06-94) 000	Amount 000	Total Stocks: 28 / Total Fixed-Income: 4	Value $000	% Net Assets
0	120	General Re	12705	5.97
0	140	American International Group	12443	5.85
0	170	Chubb	12091	5.68
0	230	Cincinnati Financial	12018	5.65
0	265	Torchmark	11627	5.47
0	195	MBIA	11627	5.47
0	345	Aon	11514	5.41
0	220	SAFECO	11330	5.33
-5	355	Ohio Casualty	11094	5.22
0	300	Progressive	10688	5.02
0	250	Saint Paul	10156	4.77
0	320	Providian	10080	4.74
-10	135	JP Morgan	8201	3.86
0	167	GEICO	8162	3.84
0	400	AVEMCO	6101	2.87
0	125	UNUM	5750	2.70
-25	200	American General	5425	2.55
0	150	Wachovia	4838	2.27
0	110	Hartford Steam Boiler Ins	4826	2.27
-11	100	Protective Life	4400	2.07
0	225	American Heritage Life	4134	1.94
0	150	Liberty	3994	1.88
0	100	USLIFE	3313	1.56
0	120	Horace Mann Educators	2925	1.38
	450	USF & G CI C Cv Pfd	2590	1.22

Composition % 12-31-94

Cash	1.5	Preferreds	0.0	
Stocks	96.9	Convertibles	1.1	
Bonds	0.5	Other	0.0	

Tax Analysis

	Tax-Adj Historical Return %	% Pretax Return
3 Yr Avg	5.00	73.0
5 Yr Avg	6.26	74.9
10 Yr Avg	10.61	69.9
Potential Capital Gain Exposure (% of assets)		51%

Most Similar Funds in MF500

New York Venture A	Weak Fit
Calvert Social Inv Managed A	Weak Fit
Selected American	Weak Fit

Index Allocation

	% of Stocks
S&P 500	53.1
S&P MidCap 400	13.2
U.S. Small Cap	33.8
Foreign	0.0

Sector Weightings

	% of Stocks	Relative S&P 500
Utilities	0.0	0.00
Energy	0.0	0.00
Financials	94.6	8.95
Industrial Cyclicals	0.0	0.00
Consumer Durables	0.0	0.00
Consumer Staples	0.0	0.00
Services	5.4	0.66
Retail	0.0	0.00
Health	0.0	0.00
Technology	0.0	0.00

Expenses & Fees

Sales Fees	0.00% front
	0.00% deferred
	0.00% 12b-1
Management Fee	0.70% max./0.60% min.
3-,5-,10-yr Expense Projections	$27, $47, $105
Annual Brokerage Cost	0.03%

Min Purchases

Min Initial Purchase	$500 (Addt'l: $25)
Min IRA Purchase	$500 (Addt'l: $25)
Min Auto Invest Plan	N/A

CGM Capital Development

	Ticker	Load	NAV	Yield	SEC Yield	Assets	Objective
	LOMCX	Clsd	20.58	0.3%	N/A	401.7	Growth

CGM Capital Development Fund seeks long-term capital appreciation.

The fund normally invests substantially all of its assets in common stocks and convertible securities. It may invest in well-established companies; companies likely to benefit from internal innovations, changes in consumer demand, or trends in basic economic forces; and smaller companies with good management and attractive prospects.

Prior to March 1, 1990, the fund was named Loomis-Sayles Capital Development Fund.

Manager's Investment Style

Manager Ken Heebner is renowned for his willingness to make fast-paced calls on particular sectors and stocks. He does not restrict the fund to specific market-cap or price parameters. Rather, he builds up concentrated positions in issues with high earnings-growth potential and modest prices, especially if he can foresee a coming improvement in market sentiment toward the stock or the sector that the stock is in.

Fund Manager(s)

G. Kenneth Heebner CFA, since 1977. Birthdate: 09-40. BS, Amherst C. 1962 MBA, Harvard 1965

Manager Experience

	Dates Managed	Invest Obj	Std Dev	+/- Index
G. Kenneth Heebner				
New England Value A	01/77 - 03/90	GI	19.09	0.84
New England Balanced A	01/79 - 01/89	B	16.32	-0.89

Historical Profile
Return	High
Risk	High
Rating	★★★★
	Closed

Investment Style History
Equity
Average % Stocks Held in Portfolio

98% 53% 94% 100% 99% 99% 100% 100%

Growth of $10,000

|||| Value of Fund ($000)
— Value of Index ($000)
SPMid400
▼ Manager Change
▽ Partial Manager Change
◄– Mgr Unknown After
–► Mgr Unknown Before

Performance Quartile (Within Objective)

	1983	1984	1985	1986	1987	1988	1989	1990	1991	1992	1993	1994	History
	25.21	17.28	25.02	23.12	16.56	15.87	18.37	18.55	25.80	27.43	27.71	20.58	NAV
	15.36	-7.27	46.15	28.44	15.89	-0.30	17.71	1.50	99.08	17.48	28.66	-22.92	Total Return %
	-7.11	-13.53	14.41	9.76	10.63	-16.91	4.61	68.60	9.86	18.60	-24.23	+/- S&P 500
	-8.11	-10.32	13.59	12.34	13.53	-18.24	-11.47	7.68	64.88	8.51	17.38	-22.85	+/- Wilshire 5000
	2.20	0.62	1.36	0.80	0.65	3.78	1.95	0.52	0.23	0.73	0.25	0.31	Income Return %
	13.16	-7.88	44.79	27.64	15.24	-4.08	15.75	0.98	98.85	16.74	28.41	-23.23	Capital Return %
	57	85	3	8	5	97	40	51	1	7	9	100	Total Rtn % Rank All
	80	79	1	2	5	98	86	14	1	10	3	100	Total Rtn % Rank Obj
	0.47	0.11	0.18	0.16	0.14	0.62	0.31	0.10	0.06	0.20	0.07	0.07	Income $
	2.50	6.15	0.00	7.46	10.09	0.02	0.00	0.00	11.07	2.68	7.51	0.71	Capital Gains $
	0.76	0.70	0.79	0.74	0.82	0.92	0.92	0.94	0.88	0.86	0.85	0.84	Expense Ratio %
	0.44	1.18	0.66	0.45	0.70	3.89	1.26	0.40	0.21	0.79	0.23	0.15	Income Ratio %
	174	129	209	208	187	301	254	226	272	163	143	153	Turnover Rate %
	143.7	130.9	170.5	210.4	231.8	194.2	189.9	140.1	326.0	394.9	523.8	401.7	Net Assets ($mil)

Performance 12-31-94

	1st Qtr	2nd Qtr	3rd Qtr	4th Qtr	Total
1987	37.46	-3.70	13.51	-22.87	15.89
1988	-5.56	6.91	-3.17	1.98	-0.30
1989	0.82	9.69	16.92	-8.97	17.71
1990	-0.54	17.30	-23.19	13.27	1.50
1991	33.91	5.07	24.56	13.60	99.08
1992	-1.59	-5.47	3.79	21.68	17.48
1993	6.09	3.23	7.76	9.02	28.66
1994	-3.61	-11.98	6.64	-14.80	-22.92

Bear Market Performance

Decile Rank (5-year period)

Worst _____ Best

	Worst 3 Mo Period 1985-89	Worst 3 Mo Period 1990-94
CGM Capital Development	-31.11	-23.19
+/- S&P 500	-1.53	-9.45
+/- Best Fit Index : SPMid400	-2.31	-5.41

Trailing Returns

	Total Return %	+/- S&P 500	+/- Wil 5000	% Rank All	% Rank Obj	Growth of $10,000
3 Mo	-14.80	-14.78	-14.03	99	100	8,520
6 Mo	-9.14	-14.01	-13.77	100	100	9,086
1 Yr	-22.92	-24.23	-22.85	100	100	7,708
3 Yr Avg	5.23	-1.04	-1.39	43	54	11,651
5 Yr Avg	18.68	9.99	9.86	2	1	23,542
10 Yr Avg	19.64	5.26	5.78	2	1	60,103
15 Yr Avg	20.70	6.22	6.72	1	1	168,064

Operations

Address and Telephone	P.O. Box 449
	Boston, MA 02117
	800-345-4048 / 617-859-7714
Advisor	Capital Growth Management
Subadvisor	None
Distributor	CGM Trust
States Available	All
Report Grade	B-
Income Distrib	Paid Annually
Date of Inception	06-22-61
Fiscal Year End	December

Min Initial Purchase	Closed (Addt'l: $50)
Min IRA Purchase	$1000 (Addt'l: $50)
Min Auto Invest Plan	$2500 (Systematic Inv: $50)

Expenses & Fees
Sales Fees	0.00% front
	0.00% deferred
	0.00% 12b-1
Management Fee	0.75% max./0.65% min.
3-,5-,10-yr Expense Projections	$27, $47, $105
Annual Brokerage Cost	---

Risk Analysis

Time Period	Load-Adj Return %	Risk % Rank[1] All	Obj	Morningstar[2] Return	Morningstar Risk	Morningstar Risk-Adj Rating
1 Yr	-22.92					
3 Yr	5.23	98	100	0.48[3]	1.70	★★
5 Yr	18.68	97	100	4.22[3]	1.46	★★★★★
10 Yr	19.64	96	100	2.76	1.38	★★★★★
Average Historical Rating (109 months)				4.7	★s	

[1] = low, 100 = high [2] 1.00 = Equity Avg [3] 1.00 = 90-day T-bill return

Other Measures

			Standard S&P 500	Best Fit SPMid400
Standard Deviation	17.38	Alpha	-1.4	-2.6
Mean	6.62	Beta	1.55	1.49
Sharpe Ratio	0.18	R-Squared	50	71

Investment Style

	Stock Portfolio Avg	Relative S&P 500
Price/Earnings Ratio	16.5	0.89
Price/Book Ratio	4.6	1.36
5 Yr Earnings Gr %	-10.0#	-1.81
Return on Assets %	3.9	0.52
Debt % Total Cap	32.8	1.16
Med Mkt Cap ($mil)	880	0.07

figure is based on 50% or less of stocks

Style: Value Blend Growth / Large Med Small (Size)

Diversification Value for Portfolio Types

Large Cap: Medium — Small Cap: Low — Bond: High — Balanced: Low — Diversified: Medium

Portfolio 09-30-94

Share Chg (06-94) 000	Amount 000	Total Stocks: 26 / Total Fixed-Income: 0	Value $000	% Net Assets
0	2014	Stone Container	39273	8.11
0	1840	LTV	37720	7.79
-23	962	National Gypsum	36556	7.55
0	1097	Geon	32919	6.80
0	1758	WHX	30097	6.22
0	409	Bankers Trust New York	27301	5.64
20	1227	Southdown	25775	5.32
268	601	Citicorp	25543	5.28
394	394	Telefonos de Mexico L (ADR)	24625	5.09
56	657	Chemical Banking	22995	4.75
45	3004	Standard-Pacific	21777	4.50
575	575	AK Steel Holding	18688	3.86
1033	1033	Rexene	16915	3.49
895	895	Northwest Airlines	16222	3.35
225	540	Rouge Steel	15863	3.28
650	650	National Steel	12513	2.58
219	219	Temple-Inland	12100	2.50
10	510	Compass Bancshares	12049	2.49
320	640	Geneva Steel Cl A	11520	2.38
194	194	Potash of Saskatchewan	7930	1.64
-887	366	USG	7557	1.56
55	251	Whitney Holding	6777	1.40
228	228	Bank of New York	6755	1.40
355	355	Continental Airlines Cl A	6124	1.27
137	137	Tektronix	5309	1.10

Composition % 09-30-94

				% of Stocks
Cash	0.2	Preferreds	0.0	
Stocks	99.8	Convertibles	0.0	
Bonds	0.0	Other	0.0	

Tax Analysis

	Tax-Adj Historical Return %	% Pretax Return
3 Yr Avg	1.77	32.8
5 Yr Avg	14.25	69.9
10 Yr Avg	15.09	61.4
Potential Capital Gain Exposure (% of assets)		-7%

Most Similar Funds in MF500

Strong Discovery	Weak Fit
Sit Growth	Weak Fit
Janus Growth & Income	Weak Fit

Index Allocation

	% of Stocks
S&P 500	29.4
S&P MidCap 400	7.2
U.S. Small Cap	53.5
Foreign	10.0

Sector Weightings

	% of Stocks	Relative S&P 500
Utilities	5.5	0.44
Energy	0.0	0.00
Financials	22.5	2.12
Industrial Cyclicals	69.6	4.25
Consumer Durables	0.0	0.00
Consumer Staples	0.0	0.00
Services	1.4	0.17
Retail	0.0	0.00
Health	0.0	0.00
Technology	1.2	0.13

MORNINGSTAR 1995 Mutual Fund 500

CGM Mutual

	Ticker	Load	NAV	Yield	SEC Yield	Assets	Objective
	LOMMX	None	25.05	4.2%	N/A	1063.4	Balanced

CGM Mutual Fund seeks long-term capital appreciation without undue risk. Current income is a consideration.

The fund invests in both equities and fixed-income securities. It is flexibly managed; the percentage of assets invested in each type of security may vary according to the economic and investment outlook. At least 25% of its assets are invested in fixed-income securities.

Prior to March 1, 1990, the fund was named Loomis-Sayles Mutual Fund.

Manager's Investment Style

Manager Ken Heebner is well known for his opportunistic, high-turnover approach to the stock market. Historically, Heebner has held expensive, fast-growing stocks and maintained high sector concentrations. He has also been willing to make aggressive plays on interest rates. True to his efforts to keep up with the market's dominant trends, however, Heebner has recently attempted to buy and hold equities that should perform well in a slow-growth economy, specifically financials.

Fund Manager(s)

G. Kenneth Heebner CFA, since 1980. Birthdate: 09-40. BS, Amherst C. 1962 MBA, Harvard 1965

Manager Experience

Manager Experience	Dates Managed	Invest Obj	Std Dev	+/- Index
G. Kenneth Heebner				
New England Value A	01/77 - 03/90	GI	19.09	0.84
New England Balanced A	01/79 - 01/89	B	16.32	-0.89

Historical Profile

Return	Above Average	
Risk	Above Average	
Rating	★★★★	
	Above Average	

72% 50% 70% 79% 58% 57% 62% 71%

Investment Style History
Equity
Average % Stocks Held in Portfolio

Growth of $10,000

- IIII Value of Fund ($000)
- — Value of Index ($000) S&P 500
- ▼ Manager Change
- ▽ Partial Manager Change
- ► Mgr Unknown After
- ◄ Mgr Unknown Before

Performance Quartile (Within Objective)

	1983	1984	1985	1986	1987	1988	1989	1990	1991	1992	1993	1994	History
	18.81	17.01	21.53	22.86	20.40	19.94	22.34	21.64	26.80	26.02	28.88	25.05	NAV
	10.00	6.45	34.44	25.22	13.70	3.18	21.66	1.11	40.88	6.07	21.83	-9.73	Total Return %
	-12.47	0.18	2.70	6.54	8.44	-13.43	-10.03	4.22	10.39	-1.55	11.78	-11.05	+/- S&P 500
	1.63	-8.71	12.31	9.97	10.94	-4.70	7.12	-7.84	24.88	-1.17	12.08	-6.81	+/- LB Aggregate
	6.42	6.01	7.86	4.47	4.45	5.43	4.53	4.24	3.99	3.66	3.09	3.53	Income Return %
	3.58	0.44	26.57	20.75	9.25	-2.25	17.12	-3.13	36.88	2.41	18.75	-13.26	Capital Return %
	79	45	13	9	7	95	32	52	13	68	14	93	Total Rtn % Rank All
	96	53	3	1	1	95	30	31	9	64	1	99	Total Rtn % Rank Obj
	1.09	0.95	1.08	0.94	1.06	1.10	0.93	0.93	0.97	0.93	0.86	1.04	Income $
	0.00	1.86	0.00	2.75	4.52	0.00	0.95	0.00	2.64	1.42	1.93	0.00	Capital Gains $
	0.87	0.85	0.86	0.84	0.94	1.01	0.97	0.97	0.93	0.93	0.93	---	Expense Ratio %
	5.14	6.67	5.10	3.81	3.69	5.25	4.26	4.00	3.80	3.74	3.45	---	Income Ratio %
	194	135	186	127	197	218	218	159	201	121	97	---	Turnover Rate %
	95.5	90.6	121.1	203.3	303.1	292.8	312.1	260.6	401.9	549.4	947.1	1063.4	Net Assets ($mil)

Performance 12-31-94

	1st Qtr	2nd Qtr	3rd Qtr	4th Qtr	Total
1987	17.83	4.09	8.30	-14.39	13.70
1988	0.05	4.10	-3.74	2.91	3.18
1989	2.56	8.90	12.22	-2.93	21.66
1990	-5.33	10.84	-11.39	8.74	1.11
1991	17.24	-0.67	11.48	8.51	40.88
1992	-5.26	2.61	1.12	7.90	6.07
1993	8.95	4.82	6.41	0.25	21.83
1994	-4.78	-2.56	0.79	-3.47	-9.73

Bear Market Performance

Decile Rank (5-year period)

Worst ——————— Best

	Worst 3 Mo Period 1985-89	Worst 3 Mo Period 1990-94
CGM Mutual	-22.04	-11.39
+/- S&P 500	7.54	2.36
+/- Best Fit Index : S&P 500	7.54	2.36

Trailing Returns

	Total Return %	+/- S&P 500	+/- LB Aggregate	% Rank All	% Rank Obj	Growth of $10,000
3 Mo	-3.47	-3.45	-3.85	86	95	9,653
6 Mo	-2.71	-7.57	-3.70	93	100	9,729
1 Yr	-9.73	-11.05	-6.81	93	99	9,027
3 Yr Avg	5.27	-1.00	0.72	42	48	11,665
5 Yr Avg	10.69	2.00	3.06	14	6	16,615
10 Yr Avg	14.85	0.46	4.90	12	3	39,917
15 Yr Avg	14.44	-0.04	3.63	20	4	75,617

Operations

Address and Telephone	P.O. Box 449 Boston, MA 02117 800-345-4048 / 617-859-7714
Advisor	Capital Growth Management
Subadvisor	None
Distributor	CGM Trust
States Available	All
Report Grade	B+
Income Distrib	Paid Quarterly
Date of Inception	11-05-29
Fiscal Year End	December

Risk Analysis

Time Period	Load-Adj Return %	Risk % Rank All	Obj	Morningstar Return	Morningstar Risk	Morningstar Risk-Adj Rating
1 Yr	-9.73					
3 Yr	5.27	77	97	0.50[3]	1.19	★★★
5 Yr	10.69	68	97	1.55[3]	1.10	★★★★
10 Yr	14.85	58	89	1.75	1.02	★★★★★

Average Historical Rating (109 months) 4.3 ★s

[1] = low, 100 = high   [2] 1.00 = Hybrid Avg   [3] 1.00 = 90-day T-bill return

Other Measures

			Standard S&P 500	Best Fit S&P 500
Standard Deviation	9.14	Alpha	-0.5	-0.5
Mean	5.57	Beta	0.88	0.88
Sharpe Ratio	0.22	R-Squared	58	58

Investment Style

Stocks

	Port Avg	Rel S&P 500
Price/Earnings Ratio	12.9	0.70
Price/Book Ratio	2.8	0.84
5 Yr Earnings Gr %	-6.5	-1.17
Med Mkt Cap ($mil)	6255	0.48

Style

Bonds

Avg Effective Duration	8.3 Yrs
Avg Effective Maturity	22.4 Yrs
Avg Credit Quality	BB
Avg Weighted Coupon	8.54%

Diversification Value for Portfolio Types

Large Cap: Low   Small Cap: Medium   Bond: Medium   Balanced: Low   Diversified: Low

Min Initial Purchase	$2500 (Addt'l: $50)
Min IRA Purchase	$1000 (Addt'l: $50)
Min Auto Invest Plan	$2500 (Systematic Inv: $50)

Expenses & Fees

Sales Fees	
	0.00% front
	0.00% deferred
	0.00% 12b-1
Management Fee	0.75% max./0.65% min.
3-,5-,10-yr Expense Projections	$30, $51, $114
Annual Brokerage Cost	0.31%

Portfolio 06-30-94

Total Stocks: 34
Total Fixed-Income: 17

Share Chg (03-94)000	Amount 000		Date of Maturity	Value $000	% Net Assets
75	1595	Chemical Banking		61408	5.44
10	1483	Citicorp		59115	5.23
45	827	Bankers Trust New York		55099	4.88
367	910	Telefonos de Mexico L (ADR)		50846	4.50
0	806	Ford Motor		47554	4.21
0	924	General Motors		46431	4.11
10	742	JP Morgan		45911	4.06
	42000	USX 8.125%	07-15-23	36602	3.24
	35500	AMR 10%	04-15-21	35081	3.11
	39000	News America Holdings 8.25%	08-10-18	35020	3.10
498	1898	USG		34401	3.04
0	1758	Lafarge		34057	3.01
0	1547	Avalon Properties		32867	2.91
136	696	Chrysler		32799	2.90
	33500	Georgia-Pacific 8.125%	06-15-23	30635	2.71
281	281	Xerox		27419	2.43
	31500	Fruit of the Loom 7.375%	11-15-23	26866	2.38
105	579	Chase Manhattan		22147	1.96
100	838	Oasis Residential		20733	1.84
0	661	Equity Residential Ppty Tr		19665	1.74

Index Allocation

	% of Stocks
S&P 500	50.0
S&P MidCap 400	1.8
U.S. Small Cap	37.6
Foreign	10.7

Composition % 09-30-94

Cash	1.0	Preferreds	0.0
Stocks	68.6	Convertibles	5.1
Bonds	25.3	Other	0.0

Tax Analysis

	Tax-Adj Historical Return %	% Pretax Return
3 Yr Avg	2.85	52.8
5 Yr Avg	8.08	71.8
10 Yr Avg	11.47	65.6
Potential Capital Gain Exposure (% of assets)		-2%

Most Similar Funds in MF500

Warburg Pincus Cap Apr Com	Weak Fit
New York Venture A	Weak Fit
Flag Inv Telephone Income A	Weak Fit

Bond Credit Analysis 09-30-94

% of Bonds

US Govt	0	BB	19
AAA	0	B	20
AA	0	Below B	3
A	1	NR/NA	0
BBB	57		

Stock Sector Weightings

	% of Stocks	Relative S&P 500
Utilities	6.4	0.52
Energy	0.0	0.00
Financials	65.4	6.18
Industrial Cyclicals	12.1	0.74
Consumer Durables	16.1	2.59
Consumer Staples	0.0	0.00
Services	0.0	0.00
Retail	0.0	0.00
Health	0.0	0.00
Technology	0.0	0.00

Chile Fund

	Ticker	NAV	Mkt Price	Prem/Disc	Yield	Objective
	CH	$52.52	$46.13	-12.2%	2.0%	Latin America

26.4	27.6	-0.9	6.6	10.6	13.1	Highest Prem/Disc
4.6	-26.3	-22.1	-17.0	-9.5	-18.4	Lowest Prem/Disc

Chile Fund seeks total return, consisting of capital appreciation and income.

The fund invests at least 75% of assets in Chilean equity and debt securities. It may invest up to 25% in U.S. securities for temporary purposes and no more than 20% may be invested in unlisted Chilean equities. The fund may engage in futures, options, and other hedging transactions.

The fund may use a credit agreement with the First National Bank of Boston for leveraging purposes.

Directors serve staggered terms in order to discourage takeover attempts.

The fund held a rights offering in the third quarter of 1993 that raised $40.3 million.

Historical Profile
Return High
Risk Average
Rating ★★★★★ Highest

Growth of $10,000
■ at NAV ($000)
— at Market Price ($000)

Premium Discount %

Manager's Investment Style
As the fund's low turnover strategy illustrates, management takes a buy-and-hold approach to Chilean stocks. Management overweights the most-visible infrastructure, utilities, and telecommunications names that tend to dominate the market.

Fund Manager(s)
Emilio Bassini. Since 9-89. BS U. of Pennsylvania; MBA Wharton.

History	1983	1984	1985	1986	1987	1988	1989	1990	1991	1992	1993	1994	
	---	---	---	---	---	---	14.76	17.54	29.68	31.08	40.25	52.52	NAV
	---	---	---	---	---	---	5.81*	28.27	90.71	16.31	42.12	33.54	NAV Total Return %
	---	---	---	---	---	---	2.29*	31.38	60.22	8.69	32.06	32.23	+/- S&P 500
	---	---	---	---	---	---	---	51.72	78.58	28.48	9.56	25.76	+/- MSCI EAFE
	---	---	---	---	---	---	---	8.06	-14.87	-1.57	10.72	-7.63	+/- MSCI Chile
	---	---	---	---	---	---	0.00*	9.43	1.61	2.84	1.90	2.61	Income Return %
	---	---	---	---	---	---	5.81*	18.84	89.10	13.47	40.22	30.94	Capital Return %
	---	---	---	---	---	---	---	1	2	15	10	1	Total Rtn % Rank All
	---	---	---	---	---	---	---	1	33	37	90	20	Total Rtn % Rank Obj
	---	---	---	---	---	---	4.17*	7.07	73.60	54.10	47.42	6.08	Market Total Rtn %
	---	---	---	---	---	---	---	-1.1	-14.6	-7.5	-0.1	-3.7	Avg Prem/Disc %
	---	---	---	---	---	---	0.00	1.25	0.38	0.87	0.70	0.93	Income $
	---	---	---	---	---	---	0.00	0.00	2.77	2.35	0.75	0.13	Capital Gains $
	---	---	---	---	---	---	1.98	2.04	1.75	1.71	1.72	1.48	Expense Ratio %
	---	---	---	---	---	---	1.44	9.56	3.97	2.61	2.47	2.11	Income Ratio %
	---	---	---	---	---	---	10	13	19	6	11	---	Turnover Rate %
	---	---	---	---	---	---	79.5	320.1	164.0	168.3	282.5	367.1	Net Assets ($mil)

Manager Experience

	Dates Managed	Invest Obj	Std Dev	+/- Index
Emilio Bassini				
Portugal Fund	11/89 - 12/94	WE	19.40	-7.69
Latin Amer Invest	07/90 - 12/94	WL	22.86	25.88

NAV Performance % 12-30-94

	1st Qtr	2nd Qtr	3rd Qtr	4th Qtr	Total
1987	---	---	---	---	---
1988	---	---	---	---	---
1989	---	---	-1.43*	7.35	5.81*
1990	16.40	-4.89	-3.49	20.05	28.27
1991	34.55	21.91	35.72	-14.34	90.71
1992	31.47	3.10	-13.04	-1.32	16.31
1993	3.12	3.78	8.75	22.12	42.12
1994	1.42	12.18	14.65	2.38	33.54

Bear Market Performance
Decile Rank (5-year period)

Worst — Best

	Worst 3 Mo Period 1985-89	Worst 3 Mo Period 1990-94
Chile Fund	---	-14.52
+/- S&P 500	---	-15.52

Trailing Returns

	NAV Total Return %	+/- S&P 500	+/- MSCI Chile	% Rank All	Obj	Mkt Total Return %
3 Mo	2.38	2.40	-1.45	4	1	-2.42
6 Mo	17.38	12.52	-5.95	2	20	9.78
1 Yr	33.54	32.23	-7.63	1	20	6.08
3 Yr Avg	30.20	23.94	0.41	3	12	34.07
5 Yr Avg	40.11	31.42	-0.02	1	1	34.97
Incept Avg	39.28*	---	---	---	---	34.02*

Operations

Address and Telephone	One Citicorp Center, 58th Flr. New York, NY 10022 212-832-2626
Advisor	BEA Associates
Subadvisor	Celsius Agente de Valores Limitada
Administrator	Provident Financial Process. Corp.
Transfer Agent	Provident National Bank
Custodian	Chase Manhattan Bank N.A.
Auditor	Coopers & Lybrand
Legal Counsel	Willkie Farr & Gallagher

Income Distrib Schedule	Paid Annually
Management Fee	1.20%, 0.10%A
Reinvestment Plan	Yes
Direct Purchase Plan	Yes
Shares Outstanding	6,989,326
Exchange	NYSE
*Date of Inception	09-27-89
Shareholder Report	B

Risk Analysis

	Risk % Rank[1] All	Obj	Morningstar[2] Return	Risk	Morningstar Risk-Adj Rating
3 Yr	88	1	4.37	1.03	★★★★★
5 Yr	83	1	12.01	0.80	★★★★★
10 Yr	---	---	---	---	

Average Historical Rating (28 months) 4.9 ★s
[1] 1 = Low, 100 = High [2] 1.00 = Equity Avg [3] 1.00 = 90-day T-bill Return

Other Measures

				S&P 500
Standard Deviation	24.42	Alpha		26.53
Mean	29.56	Beta		0.79
Sharpe Ratio	1.07	R-Squared		7

Investment Style

	Stock Portfolio Avg	Rel WS Chile	Rel WS Foreign
Price/Earnings Ratio	21.9#	0.73	0.44
Price/Cash Flow Ratio	18.3#	1.20	1.25
Price/Book Ratio	4.2#	1.19	1.39
5 Yr Earnings Gr %	---	---	---
Return on Assets %	13.6#	1.23	2.95
Debt % Total Cap	27.2#	1.31	0.84
Med Mkt Cap ($mil)	3424#	1.26	0.54
figure is based on less than 50% of stocks

Country Exposure (top five) 09-30-94

	Securities %		Currency %
Chile	95	Chile	95
		US	5

Diversification Value for Portfolio Types

Large Cap: High	Small Cap: High	Bond: High	Balanced: High	Diversified: High

Portfolio 06-30-94

Share Chg (12-93)	Amount	Total Equity: 85 / Total Fixed-Income: 0	Value $000	% Total Invest
0	52527708	Endesa de Chile	38655	12.00
0	7515737	Telefonos de Chile Cl A	37837	11.74
0	50637422	Enersis	21557	6.69
0	4931691	Chilectra Metro	21219	6.59
0	4863505	Copec de Chile	17331	5.38
0	2570395	Chilgener	15891	4.93
0	3952506	Embotelladora Andina	14935	4.64
0	192.273M	CTI	11496	3.57
0	1047197	Cartones	11270	3.50
0	2258304	Cervezas	10019	3.11
0	774113	Entel	9275	2.88
0	1594008	CAP	8768	2.72
1357200	1696500	Antofagasta Holdings (UK)	8485	2.63
0	9316048	Masisa	7352	2.28
0	512964	Emelsa	5091	1.58
0	117000	Chilectra Metro (ADR)	5045	1.57
0	1502814	Gral Electricidad	3774	1.17
0	635009	Fosforos	3341	1.04
0	691164	Elecmetal	3256	1.01
0	1446507	Quimica y Minera Chile Cl A	3114	0.97
0	316132	Cordillera	3024	0.94
0	721628	Credito	2330	0.72
0	24600	Telefonos de Chile (ADR)	2103	0.65
0	8266362	Banmedica	1937	0.60
0	85000	Cerveceras Unidas (ADR)	1870	0.58

Composition % 09-30-94

Cash	4.8	Preferreds	0.0
Stocks	95.3	Convertibles	0.0
Bonds	0.0	Other	0.0

Tax Analysis

	Tax-Adj Historical Return %	% Pretax Return
3 Yr Avg	29.28	86.8
5 Yr Avg	37.93	84.6
10 Yr Avg	---	---
Potential Capital Gain Exposure (% of assets)		68

Most Similar Funds in MF500

India Growth	Weak Fit
G.T. Global Worldwide Grth	Weak Fit
Mexico Fund	Weak Fit

Sector Weightings

	% of Stocks
Utilities	38.9
Energy	0.0
Financials	3.7
Industrial Cyclicals	44.8
Consumer Durables	0.0
Consumer Staples	11.1
Services	0.3
Retail	0.0
Health	1.2
Technology	0.0

MORNINGSTAR 1995 Mutual Fund 500

Clipper

	Ticker	Load	NAV	Yield	SEC Yield	Assets	Objective
	CFIMX	None	46.09	1.5%	N/A	247.1	Growth

Clipper Fund seeks long-term growth of capital.

The fund invests primarily in undervalued equity securities, including common stock, convertible debt, convertible preferred stock, and warrants. It generally examines dividend discounting models, relative price-earnings ratios, and comparisons with sales of comparable assets to help determine the fundamental worth of an enterprise. The fund purchases shares when the market price appears to be below the fundamental worth of the securities. It may invest up to 25% of its assets in fixed-income and convertible securities, and up to 15% of its assets in foreign issues.

Manager's Investment Style

Management looks for firms that it believes have strong fundamentals, judged by their profit margins, ROE, cash flows, and name recognition, and seeks to buy those firms at low costs or below their intrinsic worth. Management also emphasizes domestic or multinational firms with significant exposure to overseas markets. Management tends to concentrate its positions, and keeps turnover low.

Fund Manager(s)

James H. Gipson, since 02-84. Birthdate: 10-42.
MA, U. of California-Los Angeles 1964   MBA, Harvard 1973
Michael C. Sandler, since 01-94. Birthdate: 01-55. MBA, U. of Iowa 1981   JD, U. of Iowa 1981

Manager Experience	Dates Managed	Invest Obj	Std Dev	+/- Index
James H. Gipson				
Schooner	06/93 - 12/94	SC	4.36	-2.16

Historical Profile
Return	Average
Risk	Average
Rating	★★★★
	Above Average

Investment Style History Equity

Average % Stocks Held in Portfolio

Growth of $10,000
|||| Value of Fund ($000)
— Value of Index ($000)
S&P 500
▼ Manager Change
▽ Partial Manager Change
► Mgr Unknown After
◄ Mgr Unknown Before

Performance Quartile (Within Objective)

	1983	1984	1985	1986	1987	1988	1989	1990	1991	1992	1993	1994	History
% Stocks		56%	78%	72%	73%	65%	77%	87%	96%				
	---	29.58	36.17	41.55	33.76	37.74	43.45	38.80	48.10	51.74	50.05	46.09	NAV
	---	20.27 *	26.42	18.74	3.41	19.67	22.11	-7.57	32.57	15.90	11.26	-2.51	Total Return %
	---	9.50 *	-5.32	0.06	-1.85	3.06	-9.57	-4.45	2.09	8.28	1.21	-3.82	+/- S&P 500
	---	---	-6.15	2.64	1.05	1.73	-7.06	-1.39	-1.63	6.93	-0.02	-2.44	+/- Wilshire 5000
	---	1.97	2.69	0.00	8.94	2.65	2.52	2.69	2.84	1.90	1.51	1.50	Income Return %
	---	18.30	23.73	18.74	-5.53	17.01	19.59	-10.26	29.73	14.00	9.76	-4.01	Capital Return %
	---	---	41	28	33	15	31	79	23	9	57	38	Total Rtn % Rank All
	---	---	70	24	48	27	73	74	59	13	51	56	Total Rtn % Rank Obj
	---	0.49	0.84	0.00	3.42	0.95	1.00	1.14	1.18	0.96	0.75	0.71	Income $
	---	0.00	0.38	1.41	5.95	1.68	1.55	0.21	1.97	3.02	6.73	2.00	Capital Gains $
	---	1.50	1.50	1.28	1.25	1.24	1.17	1.15	1.15	1.12	1.11	1.13	Expense Ratio %
	---	6.59	5.19	4.26	4.00	2.44	2.54	2.71	2.67	2.02	1.41	1.45	Income Ratio %
	---	---	28	15	40	140	33	26	23	42	46	64	40	Turnover Rate %
	---	2.8	35.1	73.5	75.6	85.4	128.4	125.1	161.3	209.9	239.8	247.1	Net Assets ($mil)

Performance 12-31-94

	1st Qtr	2nd Qtr	3rd Qtr	4th Qtr	Total
1987	12.17	-0.29	-0.27	-7.29	3.41
1988	9.03	4.65	4.80	0.07	19.67
1989	7.13	10.36	6.95	-3.43	22.11
1990	-7.46	5.77	-15.64	11.93	-7.57
1991	12.76	-0.46	6.54	10.86	32.57
1992	-1.27	4.46	4.37	7.66	15.90
1993	4.17	-0.37	1.47	5.65	11.26
1994	-4.82	0.23	2.16	0.03	-2.51

Bear Market Performance

Decile Rank (5-year period)

Worst ———————— Best

	Worst 3 Mo Period 1985-89	Worst 3 Mo Period 1990-94
Clipper	-16.01	-15.64
+/- S&P 500	13.57	-1.89
+/- Best Fit Index : S&P 500	13.57	-1.89

Trailing Returns

	Total Return %	+/- S&P 500	+/- Wil 5000	% Rank All	% Rank Obj	Growth of $10,000
3 Mo	0.03	0.05	0.80	21	21	10,003
6 Mo	2.19	-2.67	-2.43	25	69	10,219
1 Yr	-2.51	-3.82	-2.44	38	56	9,749
3 Yr Avg	7.93	1.66	1.32	22	32	12,572
5 Yr Avg	9.03	0.34	0.21	23	45	15,406
10 Yr Avg	13.33	-1.05	-0.53	23	40	34,944
15 Yr Avg	---	---	---	---	---	---

Operations

Address and Telephone	9601 Wilshire Blvd Suite 828
	Beverly Hills, CA 90210
	800-776-5033 / 310-247-3940
Advisor	Pacific Financial Research
Subadvisor	None
Distributor	Clipper Fund
States Available	All
Report Grade	A
Income Distrib	Paid Annually
* Date of Inception	02-29-84
Fiscal Year End	December

Risk Analysis

Time Period	Load-Adj Return %	Risk % Rank[1] All	Risk % Rank[1] Obj	Morningstar[2] Return	Morningstar Risk	Morningstar Risk-Adj Rating
1 Yr	-2.51					
3 Yr	7.93	79	56	1.31[3]	0.93	★★★
5 Yr	9.03	75	45	1.08[3]	0.89	★★★
10 Yr	13.33	60	24	1.13	0.84	★★★★
Average Historical Rating (95 months)				3.8 ★s		

[1] 1 = low, 100 = high   [2] 1.00 = Equity Avg   [3] 1.00 = 90-day T-bill return

Other Measures

			Standard S&P 500	Best Fit S&P 500
Standard Deviation	10.36	Alpha	1.4	1.4
Mean	8.19	Beta	1.15	1.15
Sharpe Ratio	0.45	R-Squared	77	77

Investment Style

	Stock Portfolio Avg	Relative S&P 500
Price/Earnings Ratio	13.3	0.72
Price/Book Ratio	3.3	0.96
5 Yr Earnings Gr %	12.9	2.32
Return on Assets %	6.6	0.88
Debt % Total Cap	30.3	1.07
Med Mkt Cap ($mil)	9240	0.71

Style Value Blend Growth
Size Large Med Small

Diversification Value for Portfolio Types

Large Cap: Low	Small Cap: Medium	Bond: Medium	Balanced: Low	Diversified: Low

Operations — (continued)

Min Initial Purchase	$5000 (Addt'l: $1000)
Min IRA Purchase	$1000 (Addt'l: $200)
Min Auto Invest Plan	N/A

Expenses & Fees
Sales Fees	0.00% front
	0.00% deferred
	0.00% 12b-1
Management Fee	1.00% flat fee
3-,5-,10-yr Expense Projections	$35, $61, $135
Annual Brokerage Cost	0.12%

Portfolio 10-31-94

Share Chg (09-94) 000	Amount 000	Total Stocks: 26 Total Fixed-Income: 0	Value $000	% Net Assets
0	319	FNMA	24221	9.44
41	440	FHLMC	23964	9.34
0	569	PepsiCo	19926	7.76
-103	310	Philip Morris	18969	7.39
0	289	Morgan Stanley Group	18920	7.37
-47	235	Johnson & Johnson	12826	5.00
181	757	Bear Stearns	12298	4.79
0	115	Loews	10105	3.94
0	251	Salomon	9867	3.84
0	117	Pfizer	8658	3.37
0	202	Tambrands	8294	3.23
0	277	McDonald's	8004	3.12
0	165	Tyco International	7961	3.10
0	221	Merck	7873	3.07
0	274	Fruit of the Loom Cl A	7846	3.06
0	183	Merrill Lynch	7206	2.81
0	177	Honeywell	5702	2.22
0	112	Anheuser-Busch	5679	2.21
0	274	Old Republic International	5575	2.17
213	213	DeBeers Consolidated Mines	5085	1.98
0	320	PaineWebber Group	4876	1.90
0	292	MagneTek	4336	1.69
0	538	Service Merchandise	3225	1.26
0	87	Stanhome	2909	1.13
0	81	First Brands	2707	1.05

Composition % 12-31-94
Cash	2.1	Preferreds	0.0
Stocks	92.0	Convertibles	0.0
Bonds	5.9	Other	0.0

Tax Analysis
	Tax-Adj Historical Return %	% Pretax Return
3 Yr Avg	5.21	63.9
5 Yr Avg	6.74	71.4
10 Yr Avg	10.63	70.0
Potential Capital Gain Exposure (% of assets)		5%

Most Similar Funds in MF500
Massachusetts Inv A	Weak Fit
Investment Comp of America	Weak Fit
Vanguard Index 500	Weak Fit

Index Allocation
	% of Stocks
S&P 500	65.5
S&P MidCap 400	24.3
U.S. Small Cap	8.2
Foreign	2.0

Sector Weightings
	% of Stocks	Relative S&P 500
Utilities	0.0	0.00
Energy	0.0	0.00
Financials	49.9	4.72
Industrial Cyclicals	7.2	0.44
Consumer Durables	4.2	0.68
Consumer Staples	27.5	2.20
Services	3.2	0.39
Retail	1.3	0.22
Health	6.6	0.76
Technology	0.0	0.00

Colonial A

	Ticker	Load	NAV	Yield	SEC Yield	Assets	Objective
	COLFX	5.75%	7.34	2.3%	2.81%	538.1	Growth/Inc.

Colonial Fund - Class A seeks income and capital appreciation; capital preservation is a secondary consideration.

The fund invests primarily in domestic and foreign common stocks that meet certain quantitative standards that management feels indicate above-average financial soundness and high intrinsic value in relation to risk. The issuer must have consolidated net worth in excess of total consolidated debt, except for banking or electric-utility companies. The fund may invest the balance of its assets in U.S. government debt obligations.

Class A shares have front loads; Class B shares have deferred loads and higher 12b-1 fees.

Manager's Investment Style

The heart of this fund is management's focus on stocks with strong balance sheets, more equity than debt, and either low price multiples or high dividends. Management has maintained a high level of sector and issue diversification, and has kept turnover low, both of which decrease risk. More recently, management has established positions in intermediate-term bonds and foreign dividend-paying stocks.

Fund Manager(s)

Daniel Rie, since 04-93. Birthdate: 08-40. BS, MIT 1963 PhD, MIT 1974

Elizabeth A. Palmer, since 04-93. Birthdate: 04-54. BA, Mount Holyoke C. 1976 MBA, Columbia U. 1982

Manager Experience	Dates Managed	Invest Obj	Std Dev	+/- Index
Daniel Rie				
Colonial Growth Shares A	04/86 - 12/94	G	16.90	-1.00
Colonial Int Fund for GrA	12/93 - 12/94	WF	10.95	-8.91

Performance 12-31-94

	1st Qtr	2nd Qtr	3rd Qtr	4th Qtr	Total
1987	13.60	-0.32	4.34	-16.32	-1.13
1988	11.31	4.89	1.38	2.81	21.69
1989	6.39	5.57	7.46	-0.60	19.97
1990	-1.87	1.72	-11.99	5.23	-7.55
1991	12.99	1.70	5.85	3.50	25.89
1992	2.86	1.96	1.24	6.38	12.95
1993	7.58	0.46	4.39	1.47	14.46
1994	-2.43	-1.43	2.87	-1.05	-2.10

Bear Market Performance

Decile Rank (5-year period)

Worst			Best

	Worst 3 Mo Period 1985-89	Worst 3 Mo Period 1990-94
Colonial A	-21.69	-13.85
+/- S&P 500	7.89	-0.01
+/- Best Fit Index : S&P 500	7.89	-0.01

Trailing Returns

	Total Return %	+/- S&P 500	+/- Wil 5000	% Rank All	Obj	Growth of $10,000
3 Mo	-1.05	-1.04	-0.28	45	42	9,895
6 Mo	1.78	-3.08	-2.84	28	62	10,178
1 Yr	-2.10	-3.42	-2.03	35	63	9,790
3 Yr Avg	8.17	1.90	1.56	20	20	12,657
5 Yr Avg	8.05	-0.64	-0.76	32	47	14,730
10 Yr Avg	12.62	-1.77	-1.24	31	43	32,809
15 Yr Avg	13.15	-1.34	-0.83	37	51	63,761

Operations

Address and Telephone	One Financial Center
	Boston, MA 02111
	800-248-2828 / 617-426-3750
Advisor	Colonial Management Associates
Subadvisor	None
Distributor	Colonial Investment Services
States Available	All plus PR
Report Grade	B-
Income Distrib	Paid Quarterly
Date of Inception	01-01-04
Fiscal Year End	October

Historical Profile

Return	Average
Risk	Below Average
Rating	★★★
	Neutral

Performance Quartile (Within Objective)

	1983	1984	1985	1986	1987	1988	1989	1990	1991	1992	1993	1994	History
	4.65	4.70	5.46	5.93	5.40	6.08	6.84	5.90	7.08	7.52	8.20	7.34	NAV
	25.13	7.99	26.76	21.73	-1.13	21.69	19.97	-7.55	25.89	12.95	14.46	-2.10	Total Return %
	2.67	1.72	-4.98	3.05	-6.39	5.08	-11.72	-4.43	-4.59	5.33	4.41	-3.42	+/- S&P 500
	1.67	4.94	-5.81	5.64	-3.49	3.75	-9.21	-1.37	-8.32	3.98	3.18	-2.03	+/- Wilshire 5000
	7.80	6.85	6.83	4.75	4.82	4.98	4.80	4.15	3.25	2.50	2.01	2.28	Income Return %
	17.34	1.14	19.92	16.99	-5.95	16.72	15.17	-11.70	22.65	10.45	12.46	-4.39	Capital Return %
	23	38	39	15	68	10	35	78	34	13	31	35	Total Rtn % Rank All
	29	27	57	15	79	18	72	75	67	15	24	63	Total Rtn % Rank Obj
	0.28	0.30	0.30	0.27	0.31	0.29	0.29	0.27	0.19	0.18	0.16	0.18	Income $
	0.00	0.00	0.15	0.44	0.19	0.20	0.15	0.16	0.14	0.28	0.25	0.50	Capital Gains $
	0.94	0.96	1.05	1.06	0.97	0.92	0.97	1.04	1.06	1.09	1.10	1.14	Expense Ratio %
	6.67	7.13	6.32	4.70	3.99	4.92	4.34	4.05	3.35	2.52	1.94	2.07	Income Ratio %
	12	13	69	48	47	27	27	41	36	37	14	54	Turnover Rate %
	85.9	89.5	104.9	173.8	238.7	245.0	323.3	303.3	377.9	438.9	530.6	538.1	Net Assets ($mil)

Risk Analysis

Time Period	Load-Adj Return %	Risk % Rank All	Obj	Morningstar Return	Morningstar Risk	Morningstar Risk-Adj Rating
1 Yr	-7.73					
3 Yr	6.06	59	23	0.73[3]	0.64	★★★
5 Yr	6.78	60	27	0.50[3]	0.72	★★★
10 Yr	11.95	48	20	0.87	0.86	★★★
Average Historical Rating (109 months)					3.9	★s

[1] = low, 100 = high   [2] 1.00 = Equity Avg   [3] 1.00 = 90-day T-bill return

Other Measures

			Standard S&P 500	Best Fit S&P 500
Standard Deviation	7.64	Alpha	2.2	2.2
Mean	8.17	Beta	0.86	0.86
Sharpe Ratio	0.61	R-Squared	79	79

Investment Style

	Stock Portfolio Avg	Relative S&P 500	Style Value Blend Growth
Price/Earnings Ratio	12.4	0.67	
Price/Book Ratio	1.8	0.53	
5 Yr Earnings Gr %	5.4	0.97	
Return on Assets %	6.7	0.90	
Debt % Total Cap	23.9	0.84	
Med Mkt Cap ($mil)	3755	0.29	

Diversification Value for Portfolio Types

Large Cap: Low	Small Cap: Low	Bond: Medium	Balanced: None	Diversified: Low

Expenses & Fees

Sales Fees	5.75% front
	0.00% deferred
	0.25% 12b-1
Management Fee	0.55% flat fee
3-,5-,10-yr Expense Projections	$92, $117, $188
Annual Brokerage Cost	0.06%

Min Initial Purchase $1000 (Addt'l: $50)
Min IRA Purchase $25 (Addt'l: $25)
Min Auto Invest Plan $50 (Systematic Inv: $50)

Portfolio 12-30-94

Total Stocks: 180
Total Fixed-Income: 2

Share Chg (10-94) 000	Amount 000		Value $000	% Net Assets
	47511	FNMA 15yr 6.5%	43472	8.08
	23610	US Treasury Note 7.875%	23632	4.39
-29	266	Martin Marietta	11813	2.20
-2	307	NYNEX	11299	2.10
40	191	Textron	9637	1.79
27	116	Texas Instruments	8712	1.62
30	190	Cummins Engine	8617	1.60
13	130	Deere	8609	1.60
-273	30	Baxter International	8500	1.58
-3	336	PECO Energy	8238	1.53
119	218	American Brands	8161	1.52
-1	177	Southwestern Bell	7129	1.32
100	231	Upjohn	7089	1.32
-3	392	Waban	6960	1.29
50	152	JC Penney	6787	1.26
70	143	Aetna Life & Casualty	6748	1.25
-1	151	Gas & Electricidad	6432	1.20
-2	336	Dresser Industries	6337	1.18
-5	737	North West Water	6260	1.16
-104	309	Southern	6190	1.15
143	221	Louisiana Pacific	6027	1.12
67	171	Goodyear Tire & Rubber	5754	1.07
-1	137	E-Systems	5711	1.06
-1	148	AMBAC	5500	1.02
-1	157	Lincoln National	5485	1.02

Composition % 12-31-94

Cash	5.9	Preferreds	0.0
Stocks	81.6	Convertibles	0.0
Bonds	12.5	Other	0.0

Tax Analysis

	Tax-Adj Historical Return %	% Pretax Return
3 Yr Avg	6.04	72.4
5 Yr Avg	5.99	71.4
10 Yr Avg	9.96	69.4
Potential Capital Gain Exposure (% of assets)		7%

Most Similar Funds in MF500

American Leaders A	Strong Fit
Fundamental Investors	Strong Fit
Bartlett Basic Value	Fair Fit

Investment Style History

Equity

Average % Stocks Held in Portfolio

Growth of $10,000

|||| Value of Fund ($000)
— Value of Index ($000)
   S&P 500
▼ Manager Change
▽ Partial Manager Change
► Mgr Unknown After
◄ Mgr Unknown Before

Index Allocation

	% of Stocks
S&P 500	63.9
S&P MidCap 400	8.0
U.S. Small Cap	13.3
Foreign	14.8

Sector Weightings

	% of Stocks	Relative S&P 500
Utilities	18.0	1.45
Energy	3.9	0.38
Financials	19.6	1.85
Industrial Cyclicals	17.4	1.06
Consumer Durables	7.1	1.15
Consumer Staples	2.8	0.23
Services	4.4	0.53
Retail	6.7	1.16
Health	6.0	0.69
Technology	14.2	1.55

MORNINGSTAR 1995 Mutual Fund 500

Colonial High-Yield Secs A

	Ticker	Load	NAV	Yield	SEC Yield	Assets	Objective
	COLHX	4.75%	6.30	10.0%	9.42%	389.6	Corp Hi Yld

Colonial High-Yield Securities Fund - Class A seeks high current income; capital appreciation is secondary.

The fund invests at least 80% of its assets in high-yield securities rated as low as D; some may be convertible into common stock. The fund may purchase bonds of any maturity, and may also invest up to 20% of its assets in common stocks.

Class A shares have front loads; Class B shares have deferred loads and higher 12b-1 fees.

On June 5, 1992, Colonial Value Investing Portfolio High-Income Fund merged into this fund.

Investment Style History
Fixed Income
Income Rtn % Rank Obj

Historical Profile

Return	Above Average
Risk	Low
Rating	★★★★
	Above Average

70 57 1 44 34 43 29 25

Manager's Investment Style

New lead manager Andrea Feingold attempts to maximize total return and is willing to trade the fund's portfolio to achieve it. Currently, the portfolio emphasizes the highest-yielding junk bonds for their income and interest-rate defensiveness. The portfolio is typically well diversified.

Growth of $10,000

|||| Value of Fund ($000)
— Value of Index ($000)
LB Agg
▼ Manager Change
▽ Partial Manager Change
► Mgr Unknown After
◄ Mgr Unknown Before

Performance Quartile
(Within Objective)

1983	1984	1985	1986	1987	1988	1989	1990	1991	1992	1993	1994	History
7.33	7.07	7.55	7.69	7.18	7.21	6.34	4.64	5.86	6.40	6.95	6.30	NAV
20.39	10.51	21.78	13.77	4.23	12.66	1.31	-14.85	43.89	21.16	19.69	-0.34	Total Return %
12.02	-4.64	-0.35	-1.48	1.48	4.78	-13.23	-23.79	27.88	13.91	9.94	2.58	+/- LB Aggregate
---	---	---	-1.87	-2.29	1.23	0.93	-8.47	0.13	4.50	0.79	0.63	+/- FB High-Yield
14.62	14.06	14.99	11.92	10.87	12.24	13.16	11.97	17.59	11.94	11.10	9.01	Income Return %
5.77	-3.55	6.79	1.85	-6.63	0.42	-11.84	-26.81	26.29	9.22	8.59	-9.35	Capital Return %
38	23	61	62	26	40	97	92	11	4	18	22	Total Rtn % Rank All
4	15	54	50	20	55	37	77	21	16	35	11	Total Rtn % Rank Obj
0.96	0.96	0.96	0.86	0.84	0.85	0.84	0.83	0.71	0.66	0.66	0.63	Income $
0.00	0.00	0.00	0.00	0.00	0.00	0.02	0.00	0.00	0.00	0.00	0.00	Capital Gains $
1.03	1.03	1.08	1.11	1.18	1.17	1.21	1.33	1.36	1.26	1.23	1.23	Expense Ratio %
12.92	13.79	13.06	11.41	11.56	11.91	12.71	14.32	13.41	10.64	9.55	8.83	Income Ratio %
107	76	63	52	51	40	22	9	37	66	122	152	Turnover Rate %
75.3	95.0	132.4	442.1	430.2	463.6	365.4	234.5	299.3	346.5	440.6	389.6	Net Assets ($mil)

Fund Manager(s)

Andrea S. Feingold et al. BA, Columbia U.

Manager Experience

	Dates Managed	Invest Obj	Std Dev	+/- Index
Andrea S. Feingold				
Colonial Int H/I	06/93 - 12/94	CY	5.16	4.70
Helen Frame Peters				
Colonial Federal SecsB	10/92 - 12/94	GG	5.30	-0.90

Performance 12-31-94

	1st Qtr	2nd Qtr	3rd Qtr	4th Qtr	Total
1987	5.91	-0.76	-0.85	0.02	4.23
1988	5.91	3.18	2.09	0.99	12.66
1989	2.01	2.75	-1.22	-2.14	1.31
1990	-5.93	5.22	-10.66	-3.70	-14.85
1991	13.89	9.61	8.04	6.68	43.89
1992	9.26	3.61	4.54	2.37	21.16
1993	5.50	5.12	1.84	5.98	19.69
1994	-0.52	-0.65	0.23	0.60	-0.34

Bear Market Performance

Decile Rank (5-year period)

Worst ━━━━ Best

	Worst 3 Mo Period 1985-89	Worst 3 Mo Period 1990-94
Colonial High-Yield Secs A	-5.11	-16.06
+/- LB Aggregate	-5.93	-16.80
+/- Best Fit Index : FB HY	---	-1.95

Trailing Returns

	Total Return %	+/- LB Aggregate	+/- FB High-Yield	% Rank All	% Rank Obj	Growth of $10,000
3 Mo	0.60	0.22	0.64	10	5	10,060
6 Mo	0.84	-0.16	-0.72	40	16	10,084
1 Yr	-0.34	2.58	0.63	22	11	9,966
3 Yr Avg	13.06	8.51	1.90	6	12	14,452
5 Yr Avg	12.11	4.48	-0.97	8	17	17,707
10 Yr Avg	11.31	1.36	---	45	22	29,187
15 Yr Avg	11.57	0.76	---	59	36	51,665

Operations

Address and Telephone	One Financial Center
	Boston, MA 02111
	800-248-2828 / 617-426-3750
Advisor	Colonial Management Associates
Subadvisor	None
Distributor	Colonial Investment Services
States Available	All plus PR
Report Grade	C
Income Distrib	Paid Monthly
Date of Inception	11-04-71
Fiscal Year End	December

Risk Analysis

Time Period	Load-Adj Return %	Risk % Rank All	Risk % Rank Obj	Morningstar[2] Return	Morningstar Risk	Morningstar Risk-Adj Rating
1 Yr	-5.08					
3 Yr	11.24	4	12	2.38[3]	0.27	★★★★★
5 Yr	11.02	46	54	1.65[3]	0.57	★★★★
10 Yr	10.77	28	19	0.80	0.13	★★★★
Average Historical Rating (109 months)					3.6	★s

[1] 1 = low, 100 = high [2] 1.00 = Hybrid Avg [3] 1.00 = 90-day T-bill return

Other Measures

		Standard LB Agg	Best Fit FB HY
Standard Deviation	4.34	Alpha	8.8	2.3
Mean	12.43	Beta	0.48	0.93
Sharpe Ratio	2.05	R-Squared	19	85

Investment Style

Interest-Rate Stance

Avg Effective Duration	4.2 Yrs
Avg Effective Maturity	7.9 Yrs

Maturity Short Intm Long

Quality High Med Low

Quality

Avg Credit Quality	B
Avg Weighted Coupon	9.85%
Avg Weighted Price	93.05% of Par

Diversification Value for Portfolio Types

Large Cap:	Small Cap:	Bond:	Balanced:	Diversified:
High	High	High	High	High

Expenses & Fees

Sales Fees	4.75% front
	0.00% deferred
	0.25% 12b-1
Management Fee	0.60% flat fee
3-,5-,10-yr Expense Projections	$85, $112, $190

Min Initial Purchase	$1000 (Addt'l: $50)
Min IRA Purchase	$25 (Addt'l: $25)
Min Auto Invest Plan	$50 (Systematic Inv: $50)

Portfolio 12-30-94

Total Stocks: 17
Total Fixed-Income: 139

Amount 000	Date of Maturity		Value $000	% Net Assets
9895	10-15-97	US Treasury Note 8.75%	10117	2.60
6364	06-30-05	SCI Television 11%	6427	1.65
6667	01-15-04	Gulf Canada Resources 9.25%	6117	1.57
5455	04-15-04	Huntsman 11%	5673	1.46
5455	05-01-07	Host Marriott 11%	5455	1.40
8485	06-01-05	American Standard 0%	5452	1.40
5152	09-30-03	Agricultural Min & Chem 10.75%	5203	1.34
5758	02-01-02	Repap Wisconsin 9.25%	5182	1.33
7424	07-15-03	Eagle Industries 10.5%	4826	1.24
4849	04-01-04	AK Steel 10.75%	4800	1.23
6061	11-01-97	Triton Energy 0%	4455	1.14
4242	06-01-07	Continental Cablevision 11%	4306	1.11
3939	12-15-01	Magma Copper 12%	4255	1.09
4242	07-15-04	Integrated Health Svcs 10.75%	4242	1.09
4242	04-01-04	Cablevision Systems 10.75%	4242	1.09
4091	02-01-00	Overhead Door 12.25%	4132	1.06
4000	12-15-02	USG 10.25%	4070	1.04
3939	08-01-04	Aftermarket Tech 12%	4058	1.04
4242	12-15-00	TRISM 10.75%	4030	1.03
3939	05-15-04	Santa Fe Energy 11%	3999	1.03
3939	09-01-01	Hillhaven 10.125%	3939	1.01
3939	02-15-03	Atlantis Plastics 11%	3821	0.98
3470	08-15-01	American Medical Intl 13.5%	3782	0.97
3939	06-15-02	Pathmark Stores 11.625%	3782	0.97
3636	04-15-01	Domtar 12%	3782	0.97

Composition % 12-31-94

Cash	1.5	Preferreds	1.4
Stocks	0.7	Convertibles	0.0
Bonds	96.4	Other	0.0

Tax Analysis

	Tax-Adj Historical Return %	% Pretax Return
3 Yr Avg	9.16	67.6
5 Yr Avg	7.78	58.9
10 Yr Avg	6.50	45.8
Potential Capital Gain Exposure (% of assets)		-15%

Most Similar Funds in MF500

Seligman High-Yield Bond A	Strong Fit
Merrill Lynch Corp Hi-Inc A	Fair Fit
MainStay Hi-Yield Corp Bd B	Fair Fit

Coupon Range

	% of Bonds	Rel Obj
0%, PIK	11.7	1.57
0% to 11%	48.5	0.99
11% to 13%	36.3	1.09
13% to 14.5%	3.0	0.56
More than 14.5%	0.2	0.12
Not applicable	0.3	0.09

Credit Analysis 12-31-94

% of Bonds

US Govt	10	BB	7
AAA	0	B	73
AA	0	Below B	6
A	0	NR/NA	3
BBB	0		

Colonial Strategic Income A

Ticker	Load	NAV	Yield	SEC Yield	Assets	Objective
COSIX	4.75%	6.53	9.1%	8.70%	637.1	Income

Colonial Strategic Income Fund - Class A seeks high income; principal stability is secondary.

The fund invests in U.S. government securities, foreign government securities, and high-yield high-risk securities rated as low as D. The allocation among each of these types varies.

Class A shares have front loads; Class B shares have deferred loads and higher 12b-1 fees.

Prior to 1988, the fund was managed as an option-income vehicle. On Oct. 1, 1990, Colonial Income Plus Fund merged into this fund. Prior to Aug. 16, 1991, the fund was named Colonial Diversified Income Fund.

Manager's Investment Style

This fund attempts to succeed through moderation. Management maintains a constant asset-allocation approach, in which each of its three favored markets--junk bonds, U.S. governments, and foreign debt--receive between 20% and 50% of assets each. Management also prefers market-like durations, emphasizes mature-market debt in its foreign stake (though it does maintain a small emerging-market stake), and focuses on junk bonds with B ratings.

Fund Manager(s)

Carl C. Ericson CFA(1976), since 01-91.
Birthdate: 04-43. BA, Harvard 1965 MBA, Stanford U. 1969

Manager Experience	Dates Managed	Invest Obj	Std Dev	+/- Index
Carl C. Ericson				
Colonial Income A	02/91 - 12/94	CG	4.61	1.02
Colonial Intermkt	06/93 - 12/94	MB	5.09	-2.58

Historical Profile
Return	Average
Risk	Below Average
Rating	★★★
	Neutral

Investment Style History
Fixed Income
Income Rtn % Rank Obj

	85	76	44	44	17	10	6	6

Growth of $10,000
IIII Value of Fund ($000)
— Value of Index ($000)
   LB L-T
▼ Manager Change
▽ Partial Manager Change
► Mgr Unknown After
◄ Mgr Unknown Before

Performance Quartile
(Within Objective)

1983	1984	1985	1986	1987	1988	1989	1990	1991	1992	1993	1994	History
9.10	8.04	8.29	7.58	6.89	7.27	7.25	6.06	7.02	7.01	7.39	6.53	NAV
19.10	4.50	20.28	4.76	3.74	16.66	9.94	-6.89	28.20	9.77	14.95	-3.67	Total Return %
-3.36	-1.77	-11.46	-13.92	-1.52	0.05	-21.75	-3.77	-2.28	2.16	4.89	-4.99	+/- S&P 500
10.73	-10.66	-1.84	-10.49	0.98	8.78	-4.60	-15.84	12.20	2.53	5.19	-0.76	+/- LB Aggregate
2.70	3.46	3.22	2.13	3.32	6.19	9.39	9.36	12.36	9.92	9.52	7.96	Income Return %
16.40	1.04	17.06	2.62	0.42	10.46	0.55	-16.25	15.84	-0.14	5.42	-11.64	Capital Return %
43	53	71	96	29	22	74	77	30	24	29	50	Total Rtn % Rank All
8	69	50	87	19	19	58	82	17	31	33	34	Total Rtn % Rank Obj
0.24	0.28	0.25	0.17	0.25	0.42	0.66	0.71	0.68	0.68	0.63	0.59	Income $
1.38	1.12	1.01	0.93	0.81	0.32	0.06	0.02	0.00	0.00	0.00	0.00	Capital Gains $
0.90	0.88	0.93	0.99	1.00	1.07	1.10	1.12	1.12	1.18	1.19	1.21	Expense Ratio %
3.25	3.26	2.64	2.21	3.31	5.33	8.94	10.27	10.27	9.39	8.42	8.12	Income Ratio %
171	89	121	134	82	28	32	2	48	96	138	62	Turnover Rate %
1108.3	1441.9	1382.4	1069.7	784.0	632.6	499.0	411.0	425.2	436.9	660.3	637.1	Net Assets ($mil)

Performance 12-31-94

	1st Qtr	2nd Qtr	3rd Qtr	4th Qtr	Total
1987	16.42	2.50	3.93	-16.36	3.74
1988	9.67	4.30	-1.33	3.35	16.66
1989	2.88	3.03	3.30	0.41	9.94
1990	-3.02	3.51	-6.48	-0.82	-6.89
1991	8.61	4.68	6.44	5.93	28.20
1992	1.49	4.48	3.64	-0.11	9.77
1993	4.53	3.34	2.19	4.13	14.95
1994	-3.30	-1.31	0.24	0.70	-3.68

Bear Market Performance

Decile Rank (5-year period)

Worst _____ Best

	Worst 3 Mo Period 1985-89	Worst 3 Mo Period 1990-94
Colonial Strategic Income A	-21.49	-8.51
+/- S&P 500	8.09	5.33
+/- Best Fit Index : LB L-T	-24.08	-7.62

Trailing Returns

	Total Return %	+/- S&P 500	+/- LB Aggregate	% Rank All	% Rank Obj	Growth of $10,000
3 Mo	0.70	0.72	0.32	9	4	10,070
6 Mo	0.94	-3.93	-0.06	38	26	10,094
1 Yr	-3.67	-4.99	-0.76	50	34	9,633
3 Yr Avg	6.72	0.45	2.17	28	28	12,154
5 Yr Avg	7.73	-0.96	0.10	37	58	14,508
10 Yr Avg	9.29	-5.09	-0.65	68	78	24,321
15 Yr Avg	9.96	-4.53	-0.85	79	91	41,518

Operations

Address and Telephone	One Financial Center
	Boston, MA 02111
	800-248-2828 / 617-426-3750
Advisor	Colonial Management Associates
Subadvisor	None
Distributor	Colonial Investment Services
States Available	All plus PR
Report Grade	C+
Income Distrib	Paid Monthly
Date of Inception	04-21-77
Fiscal Year End	December

Min Initial Purchase	$1000 (Addt'l: $50)
Min IRA Purchase	$25 (Addt'l: $25)
Min Auto Invest Plan	$50 (Systematic Inv: $50)

Expenses & Fees
Sales Fees	4.75% front
	0.00% deferred
	0.25% 12b-1
Management Fee	0.65% flat fee
3-,5-,10-yr Expense Projections	$84, $111, $188
Annual Brokerage Cost	---

Risk Analysis

Time Period	Load-Adj Return %	Risk % Rank All [1]	Risk % Rank Obj [1]	Morningstar [2] Return	Morningstar Risk	Morningstar Risk-Adj Rating
1 Yr	-8.25					
3 Yr	5.00	12	15	0.42 [3]	0.41	★★★
5 Yr	6.68	41	44	0.47 [3]	0.48	★★★
10 Yr	8.76	41	71	0.44	0.67	★★
Average Historical Rating (109 months)				2.5	★s	

[1] 1 = low, 100 = high   [2] 1.00 = Hybrid Avg   [3] 1.00 = 90-day T-bill return

Other Measures
			Standard S&P 500	Best Fit LB L-T
Standard Deviation	4.12	Alpha	2.3	2.3
Mean	6.61	Beta	0.27	0.40
Sharpe Ratio	0.75	R-Squared	27	56

Investment Style
Stocks	Port Avg	Rel S&P 500
Price/Earnings Ratio	13.2	0.71
Price/Book Ratio	2.2	0.66
5 Yr Earnings Gr %	---	---
Med Mkt Cap ($mil)	313	0.02

figure is based on 50% or less of stocks

Bonds		
Avg Effective Duration	4.0 Yrs	
Avg Effective Maturity	10.1 Yrs	
Avg Credit Quality	BBB	
Avg Weighted Coupon	9.99%	

Diversification Value for Portfolio Types

Large Cap: Medium   Small Cap: High   Bond: Low   Balanced: Medium   Diversified: Medium

Portfolio 06-30-94

Share Chg (12-93)000	Amount 000	Total Stocks: 18 / Total Fixed-Income: 223	Date of Maturity	Value $000	% Net Assets
	61894	Republic of Italy 11%	06-01-03	39075	5.80
	33769	US Treasury Note 9.25%	01-15-96	35415	5.26
	194428	Kingdom of Denmark 9%	11-15-00	32648	4.85
	38261	Western Australia Treas 12%	08-01-01	30657	4.55
	20302	US Treasury Note 7.875%	04-15-98	21053	3.13
	19895	US Treasury Note 8.5%	04-15-97	20899	3.10
	14279	US Treasury Bond 9.875%	11-15-15	17425	2.59
	15463	US Treasury Note 8.625%	10-15-95	16007	2.38
	14784	US Treasury Note 7.625%	05-31-96	15179	2.25
	10680	US Treasury Bond 11.875%	11-15-03	13904	2.06
	14315	Victoria Treasury 12.5%	07-15-00	11639	1.73
	10411	US Treasury Note 8.875%	07-15-95	10766	1.60
	7680	US Treasury Bond 11.5%	11-15-95	8259	1.23
	15617	Republic of Argentina 5.792%	03-31-23	7886	1.17
	5206	US Treasury Note 6.75%	05-31-99	5160	0.77
	4164	Fairfield Mfg 11.375%	07-01-01	4206	0.62
	3904	Container of America 11.25%	05-01-04	4002	0.59
	2910	US Treasury Bond 12%	08-15-13	3986	0.59
	6767	Videotron 11.125%	07-01-04	3947	0.59
	3904	Collins & Aikman 7.5%	01-31-05	3865	0.57

Index Allocation
	% of Stocks
S&P 500	0.0
S&P MidCap 400	0.0
U.S. Small Cap	100.0
Foreign	0.0

Composition % 12-31-94
Cash	2.8	Preferreds	1.5
Stocks	0.0	Convertibles	0.0
Bonds	95.7	Other	0.0

Tax Analysis
	Tax-Adj Historical Return %	% Pretax Return
3 Yr Avg	3.34	48.1
5 Yr Avg	4.28	51.7
10 Yr Avg	5.64	51.1
Potential Capital Gain Exposure (% of assets)		-35%

Most Similar Funds in MF500
Bond Fund of America	Strong Fit
Oppenheimer Strat Income A	Fair Fit
T. Rowe Price Spectrum Inc	Fair Fit

Bond Credit Analysis 12-31-94
% of Bonds
US Govt	21	BB	2
AAA	8	B	42
AA	22	Below B	4
A	0	NR/NA	1
BBB	0		

Stock Sector Weightings
	% of Stocks	Relative S&P 500
Utilities	0.0	0.00
Energy	0.0	0.00
Financials	0.0	0.00
Industrial Cyclicals	35.1	2.15
Consumer Durables	0.0	0.00
Consumer Staples	2.6	0.21
Services	0.0	0.00
Retail	53.4	9.17
Health	8.9	1.03
Technology	0.0	0.00

MORNINGSTAR 1995 Mutual Fund 500

Colonial Tax-Exempt A

	Ticker	Load	NAV	Yield	SEC Yield	Assets	Objective
	COLTX	4.75%	12.44	6.3%	5.97%	2837.5	Muni Nat

Colonial Tax-Exempt Fund - Class A seeks current income exempt from federal income tax. Capital preservation is a secondary objective.

The fund normally invests at least 65% of its assets in investment-grade tax-exempt obligations; the balance may be invested in lower-quality debt.

Class A shares have front loads; Class B shares have deferred loads and higher 12b-1 fees. Prior to Sept. 18, 1984, the fund was named Colonial Tax-Managed Trust. From that date until Jan. 11, 1990, it was named Colonial Tax-Exempt High-Yield Trust, and its initial series of shares were called Colonial Tax-Exempt High-Yield Fund.

Manager's Investment Style

Management attempts to maintain a moderate, index-like interest-rate stance, and to hold a broad variety of credits (including nonrateds). It seeks to add value by finding issues that have better credit quality than the ratings agencies believe, and also by analyzing macroeconomic factors, such as supply and demand, that may affect municipal-market performance.

Fund Manager(s)

Bonny E. Boatman, since 06-93. Birthdate: 01-50.
M, Harvard MBA, Wharton 1984

Manager Experience

	Dates Managed	Invest Obj	Std Dev	+/- Index
Bonny E. Boatman				
Colonial MA Tax-Exempt A	04/87 - 04/88	MS	8.38	-2.34

Historical Profile

Return	Below Average
Risk	Average
Rating ★★★	Neutral

Investment Style History
Fixed Income
Income Rtn % Rank Obj

	18	11	11	6	11	11	9	14

Growth of $10,000
|||| Value of Fund ($000)
— Value of Index ($000) LB Muni
▼ Manager Change
▽ Partial Manager Change
► Mgr Unknown After
◄ Mgr Unknown Before

Performance Quartile (Within Objective)

	1983	1984	1985	1986	1987	1988	1989	1990	1991	1992	1993	1994	History
	12.34	11.82	12.85	13.73	12.77	13.03	13.05	12.86	13.36	13.53	14.10	12.44	NAV
	12.18	16.26	19.73	16.30	0.46	10.40	8.08	6.44	11.74	8.27	10.73	-6.27	Total Return %
	3.81	1.11	-2.39	1.06	-2.30	2.52	-6.46	-2.51	-4.27	1.02	0.98	-3.35	+/- LB Aggregate
	4.13	5.71	-0.29	-3.01	-1.04	0.24	-2.71	-0.86	-0.41	-0.55	-1.54	-0.66	+/- LB Muni
	0.00	5.64	11.02	8.75	7.45	8.36	7.92	7.89	7.85	7.00	6.52	5.51	Income Return %
	12.18	10.62	8.71	7.56	-6.99	2.04	0.15	-1.46	3.89	1.27	4.21	-11.77	Capital Return %
	69	3	74	46	56	58	90	29	78	43	62	74	Total Rtn % Rank All
	22	1	52	69	40	59	81	43	45	58	68	62	Total Rtn % Rank Obj
	0.00	0.64	1.20	1.07	1.02	1.03	1.00	0.99	0.96	0.90	0.85	0.79	Income $
	0.00	1.78	0.00	0.08	0.00	0.00	0.00	0.00	0.00	0.00	0.00	0.00	Capital Gains $
	1.84	1.22	1.11	1.05	1.08	1.06	1.03	1.05	1.03	1.05	1.02	1.01	Expense Ratio %
	8.72	8.06	9.37	8.10	7.79	7.77	7.67	7.64	7.29	6.81	6.06	5.85	Income Ratio %
	74	512	68	26	20	22	9	10	10	14	28	60	Turnover Rate %
	428.8	292.0	759.9	1342.2	1273.3	1412.8	1555.4	1924.7	2550.7	2960.8	3435.3	2837.5	Net Assets ($mil)

Performance 12-31-94

	1st Qtr	2nd Qtr	3rd Qtr	4th Qtr	Total
1987	2.51	-2.96	-2.22	3.29	0.46
1988	3.22	2.52	2.28	2.00	10.40
1989	0.76	4.29	0.22	2.63	8.08
1990	0.54	2.11	0.45	3.21	6.44
1991	1.71	2.18	3.74	3.64	11.74
1992	-0.08	3.48	2.58	2.08	8.27
1993	2.77	2.69	3.26	1.61	10.73
1994	-5.85	0.44	0.43	-1.30	-6.27

Bear Market Performance

Decile Rank (5-year period)

Worst | Best

	Worst 3 Mo Period 1985-89	Worst 3 Mo Period 1990-94
Colonial Tax-Exempt A	-5.62	-6.18
+/- LB Aggregate	-2.06	-1.25
+/- Best Fit Index : LB Muni	0.88	-0.42

Trailing Returns

	Total Return %	+/- LB Aggregate	+/- LB Muni	% Rank All	% Rank Obj	Growth of $10,000
3 Mo	-1.30	-1.68	0.13	52	48	9,870
6 Mo	-0.88	-1.88	0.36	71	49	9,912
1 Yr	-6.27	-3.35	-0.66	74	62	9,373
3 Yr Avg	3.97	-0.58	-0.90	70	77	11,238
5 Yr Avg	5.97	-1.65	-0.80	76	60	13,365
10 Yr Avg	8.35	-1.59	-1.07	82	66	22,308
15 Yr Avg	10.90	0.09	2.43	67	2	47,205

Operations

Address and Telephone	One Financial Center Boston, MA 02111 800-248-2828 / 617-426-3750
Advisor	Colonial Management Associates
Subadvisor	None
Distributor	Colonial Investment Services
States Available	All plus PR
Report Grade	C+
Income Distrib	Paid Monthly
Date of Inception	11-21-78
Fiscal Year End	November

Risk Analysis

Time Period	Load-Adj Return %	Risk % Rank [1] All	Obj	Morningstar [2] Return	Morningstar Risk	Morningstar Risk-Adj Rating
1 Yr	-10.72					
3 Yr	2.29	30	49	0.62	1.01	★★
5 Yr	4.95	16	42	0.83	0.93	★★★
10 Yr	7.83	6	22	0.95	0.81	★★★★

Average Historical Rating (109 months) 4.1 ★s

[1] 1 = low, 100 = high [2] 1.00 = Muni Avg [3] 1.00 = 90-day T-bill return

Other Measures

				Standard LB Agg	Best Fit LB Muni
Standard Deviation	5.50	Alpha		-0.5	-0.8
Mean	4.05	Beta		1.02	0.98
Sharpe Ratio	0.10	R-Squared		56	95

Investment Style

Interest-Rate Stance

Avg Effective Maturity	23.7 Yrs

Quality

Avg Credit Quality	A
Avg Weighted Coupon	6.48%
Avg Weighted Price	87.12% of Par

Diversification Value for Portfolio Types

Large Cap: Medium	Small Cap: High	Bond: Low	Balanced: Medium	Diversified: Medium

Portfolio 12-30-94

Total Stocks: 0
Total Fixed-Income: 483

Amount 000	Date of Maturity		Value $000	% Net Assets
47047	07-01-09	PR Commonwealth GO 5.5%	42096	1.48
45153	05-15-25	TN Nashville/Davidson Metro Govt 6.15%	41711	1.47
37004	02-01-23	TN Chattanooga Hlth Educ/Hsg Fac 8.5%	33674	1.19
33722	01-01-20	GA Muni Elec Pwr 5.5%	28664	1.01
25724	12-01-24	TN Nashville/Davidson Metro Govt 6.875%	25981	0.92
310463	10-01-23	GA De Kalb Wtr/Swr 5.25%	24901	0.88
30683	02-15-25	NY Med Care Fac Fin 5.375%	24853	0.88
29230	05-15-13	NY Dorm State Univ Educ Fac 5.5%	24773	0.87
31647	07-01-21	CA Los Angeles Metro Transp Sales Tax 5%	24289	0.86
24211	12-01-16	MI Strategic Fund 10.25%	24150	0.85
31301	03-01-22	MA Wtr Resource 5%	23946	0.84
30264	01-01-21	NY Urban Dev Crtnl Cap Fac Lease 5.25%	23303	0.82
26783	06-15-24	NY New York City Muni Wtr Fin Swr 5.5%	22732	0.80
27121	07-01-20	UT Intermountain Pwr Sply 5.5%	22408	0.79
25759	07-01-09	PR Hwy/Transp 5.5%	22206	0.78
28314	04-01-21	NY Local Govt Assist 5%	22014	0.78
24202	07-01-20	NY Dorm City Univ 6%	21009	0.74
26602	01-01-20	MA Tpk 5%	20683	0.73
21989	01-01-13	NC Muni Pwr #1 Catawba Elec 5.5%	19982	0.70
172936	08-15-18	AL Daphne Spcl Care Fac Fin 0%	19888	0.70

Credit Analysis % of Bonds 12-31-94

US Govt	0	BB	1
AAA	38	B	0
AA	18	Below B	0
A	15	NR/NA	18
BBB	10		

Composition % of Assets 12-31-94

Cash	2.5	Preferreds	0.0
Stocks	0.0	Convertibles	0.0
Bonds	97.5	Other	0.0

Tax Analysis

	Tax-Adj Historical Return %	% Pretax Return
3 Yr Avg	3.97	100.0
5 Yr Avg	5.97	100.0
10 Yr Avg	8.34	99.8
Potential Capital Gain Exposure (% of assets)		-6%

Most Similar Funds in MF500

Smith Barney Tax-Ex IncB	Strong Fit
Fortress Municipal Income	Strong Fit
Dreyfus Muni Bond	Strong Fit

Coupon Range

	% Bonds	Rel Obj
0%	5.1	2.05
0% to 6.8%	43.0	0.71
6.8% to 7.5%	15.0	0.97
7.5% to 8.3%	10.5	1.18
More than 8.3%	23.6	2.67
Not applicable	2.8	0.72

Sector Weightings

	% Bonds	Rel Obj
General Obl	11.15	0.53
Utilities	16.20	1.29
Health	18.61	1.41
Water/Waste	6.89	1.08
Housing	11.40	1.56
Education	7.04	1.10
Transportation	8.43	0.83
COP/Lease	2.24	0.70
Private	10.47	0.90
Misc Revenue	6.72	1.35
Demand	0.85	0.35

Top 5 States % of Bonds

NY	16.67	TX	6.14
MA	7.04	PA	6.07
CA	6.82		

Min Initial Purchase / Expenses

Min Initial Purchase	$1000 (Addt'l: $50)
Min IRA Purchase	N/A
Min Auto Invest Plan	$50 (Systematic Inv: $50)

Expenses & Fees

Sales Fees	4.75% front
	0.00% deferred
	0.25% 12b-1
Management Fee	0.60% max./0.55% min.
3-,5-,10-yr Expense Projections	$78, $101, $166

Columbia Fixed-Income Secs

	Ticker	Load	NAV	Yield	SEC Yield	Assets	Objective
	CFISX	None	12.16	6.8%	7.62%	252.1	Corp Hi Qlty

Columbia Fixed-Income Securities Fund seeks income consistent with capital preservation.

The fund normally invests at least 95% of its assets in investment-grade debt securities. It may also invest in unrated securities of similar quality. Up to 5% of the fund's assets may be invested in securities rated below investment grade at the time of purchase. The fund ordinarily invests a portion of its assets in U.S. government obligations, including GNMAs and FNMAs. The portfolio maturity varies in reponse to anticipated changes in interest rates. Generally, the fund purchases securities with intermediate- and long-term maturities.

Manager's Investment Style

Management avoids interest-rate calls, maintaining a market-like duration, and instead seeks bonds offering the best price and yield combination. In doing so, the fund will own corporate bonds, Treasuries, and mortgages. In recent years, management has kept its largest weightings in mortgages, including CMOs.

Fund Manager(s)

Thomas L. Thomsen et al.

Manager Experience

	Dates Managed	Invest Obj	Std Dev	+/- Index
Thomas L. Thomsen				
Columbia Municipal Bond	07/84 - 12/94	MS	5.96	-2.09
Columbia U.S. Govt Secs	11/86 - 12/94	GT	2.49	-1.43

Historical Profile

Return	High
Risk	Average
Rating	★★★★ Above Average

Investment Style History
Fixed Income
Income Rtn % Rank Obj

61	50	52	46	38	31	29	18

Growth of $10,000

|||| Value of Fund ($000)
— Value of Index ($000) LB Govt
▼ Manager Change
▽ Partial Manager Change
► Mgr Unknown After
◄ Mgr Unknown Before

Performance Quartile (Within Objective)

	1983	1984	1985	1986	1987	1988	1989	1990	1991	1992	1993	1994	History
NAV	12.21	12.14	13.05	13.37	12.23	12.11	12.75	12.72	13.59	13.28	13.44	12.16	NAV
Total Return %	7.19 *	12.26	20.19	12.31	1.36	7.72	14.35	8.30	16.85	8.01	10.49	-3.36	Total Return %
	---	-2.89	-1.94	-2.94	-1.40	-0.16	-0.19	-0.65	0.85	0.76	0.73	-0.44	+/- LB Aggregate
	---	-4.36	-3.87	-4.22	-1.20	-1.51	0.37	1.14	-1.66	-0.69	-1.68	0.56	+/- LB Corporate
Income Return %	10.59	12.84	12.69	9.86	8.14	8.70	9.07	8.53	8.50	7.33	6.50	6.16	Income Return %
Capital Return %	-3.40	-0.57	7.50	2.45	-6.78	-0.98	5.28	-0.24	8.35	0.67	3.99	-9.52	Capital Return %
	---	16	72	72	47	75	49	13	51	45	63	47	Total Rtn % Rank All
	---	69	51	64	64	26	8	39	19	7	25	63	Total Rtn % Rank Obj
Income $	1.28	1.44	1.40	1.21	1.03	1.04	1.04	1.03	1.00	0.95	0.85	0.83	Income $
Capital Gains $	0.00	0.00	0.00	0.00	0.27	0.00	0.00	0.00	0.18	0.40	0.36	0.00	Capital Gains $
Expense Ratio %	1.22	1.05	0.88	0.79	0.82	0.77	0.74	0.73	0.69	0.66	0.66	0.66	Expense Ratio %
Income Ratio %	11.30	12.17	11.03	9.15	8.21	8.44	8.27	8.20	7.63	7.03	6.14	6.16	Income Ratio %
Turnover Rate %	47	98	94	97	114	133	114	132	159	196	119	161	Turnover Rate %
Net Assets ($mil)	24.5	38.1	83.2	102.0	100.3	102.6	110.5	133.9	207.3	262.6	300.5	252.1	Net Assets ($mil)

Performance 12-31-94

	1st Qtr	2nd Qtr	3rd Qtr	4th Qtr	Total
1987	2.15	-3.00	-3.28	5.77	1.36
1988	3.59	1.37	2.07	0.50	7.72
1989	1.27	8.03	0.87	3.63	14.35
1990	-0.88	3.48	0.69	4.85	8.30
1991	2.61	1.73	6.16	5.44	16.85
1992	-1.40	4.74	5.01	-0.42	8.01
1993	4.78	2.90	3.03	-0.54	10.49
1994	-3.04	-1.05	0.41	0.32	-3.36

Bear Market Performance

Decile Rank (5-year period)

Worst 3 Mo Period 1985-89	Worst 3 Mo Period 1990-94
Columbia Fixed-Income Secs	-4.81	-5.13
+/- LB Aggregate	-1.25	-0.20
+/- Best Fit Index : LB Govt	-1.35	-0.05

Trailing Returns

	Total Return %	+/- LB Aggregate	+/- LB Corporate	% Rank All	% Rank Obj	Growth of $10,000
3 Mo	0.32	-0.06	-0.12	14	37	10,032
6 Mo	0.73	-0.26	-0.44	43	43	10,073
1 Yr	-3.36	-0.44	0.56	47	63	9,664
3 Yr Avg	4.87	0.32	-0.55	51	14	11,532
5 Yr Avg	7.85	0.23	-0.41	35	9	14,593
10 Yr Avg	9.42	-0.53	-1.21	65	25	24,594
15 Yr Avg	---	---	---	---	---	---

Operations

Address and Telephone	1301 SW Fifth Ave P.O. Box 1350
	Portland, OR 97207-1350
	800-547-1707 / 503-222-3606
Advisor	Columbia Funds Management
Subadvisor	None
Distributor	Columbia Financial Center
States Available	All except NH
Report Grade	C
Income Distrib	Paid Monthly
* Date of Inception	02-25-83
Fiscal Year End	December

Risk Analysis

Time Period	Load-Adj Return %	Risk % Rank [1] All	Risk % Rank [1] Obj	Morningstar [2] Return	Morningstar Risk	Morningstar Risk-Adj Rating
1 Yr	-3.36					
3 Yr	4.87	28	71	0.38 [3]	1.09	★★★★
5 Yr	7.85	26	67	0.77 [3]	1.03	★★★★
10 Yr	9.42	19	48	0.94 [3]	1.03	★★★★
Average Historical Rating (107 months)					3.6	★ s

[1] 1 = low, 100 = high   [2] 1.00 = Taxable Avg   [3] 1.00 = 90-day T-bill return

Other Measures

				Standard LB Agg	Best Fit LB Govt
Standard Deviation	4.56	Alpha		0.2	0.2
Mean	4.86	Beta		1.13	1.04
Sharpe Ratio	0.29	R-Squared		98	99

Investment Style

Interest-Rate Stance

Avg Effective Duration	5.7 Yrs
Avg Effective Maturity	6.4 Yrs

Quality

Avg Credit Quality	AA
Avg Weighted Coupon	7.77%
Avg Weighted Price	95.45% of Par

Diversification Value for Portfolio Types

●	●	○	▨	●
Large Cap: High	Small Cap: High	Bond: None	Balanced: Medium	Diversified: High

Expenses & Fees

Sales Fees	0.00% front
	0.00% deferred
	0.00% 12b-1
Management Fee	0.50% flat fee
3-,5-,10-yr Expense Projections	$21, $37, $82

Portfolio 12-31-94

Total Stocks: 0
Total Fixed-Income: 84

Amount 000	Date of Maturity		Value $000	% Net Assets
21705	08-15-13	US Treasury Bond 12%	28813	11.43
13270	11-15-16	US Treasury Bond 7.5%	12571	4.99
11138	06-15-24	GNMA 7.5%	9676	3.84
10170	07-31-98	US Treasury Note 5.25%	9360	3.71
9565	02-28-98	US Treasury Note 5.125%	8849	3.51
9416	04-25-19	FNMA CMO REMIC PAC 7%	8487	3.37
10386	09-01-22	FHA Project Loan 7.43%	7877	3.12
7075	05-28-99	GMAC 7.375%	6743	2.67
5925	02-15-16	US Treasury Bond 9.25%	6655	2.64
5745	02-15-96	US Treasury Note 4.625%	5573	2.21
5625	06-04-02	Province of Ontario 7.75%	5433	2.16
5282	09-15-24	GNMA 8.5%	5176	2.05
4660	07-21-03	Financial Assistance 9.375%	5049	2.00
5200	11-15-99	Mellon Financial 7.625%	5046	2.00
4900	08-15-19	US Treasury Bond 8.125%	4956	1.97
5550	01-25-07	Prudential Home Mtg CMO 6.9%	4930	1.96
3800	05-25-24	Nomura Asset Secs 7%	3633	1.44
3350	03-20-97	Temple-Inland 8.85%	3397	1.35
3380	12-01-02	RJR Nabisco 8.625%	3135	1.24
3125	12-01-06	Eli Lilly 8.375%	3113	1.23
3480	10-09-00	Pacific Gas/Electric 5.63%	3040	1.21
7349	02-01-24	FHA Project Loan 9.68%	2942	1.17
2805	06-01-96	Deere 8.25%	2818	1.12
4400	11-25-23	FNMA CMO REMIC PAC Z 0%	2797	1.11
2999	05-25-24	Prudential Home Mtg CMO 7.425%	2745	1.09

Composition % 12-31-94

Cash	4.1	Preferreds	0.0
Stocks	0.0	Convertibles	0.0
Bonds	95.9	Other	0.0

Tax Analysis

	Tax-Adj Historical Return %	% Pretax Return
3 Yr Avg	1.86	37.1
5 Yr Avg	4.90	58.9
10 Yr Avg	5.91	53.2
Potential Capital Gain Exposure (% of assets)		-8%

Most Similar Funds in MF500

Portico Bond Immdex Ret	Strong Fit
New England Bond Income A	Strong Fit
U.S. Government Securities	Strong Fit

Coupon Range

	% of Bonds	Rel Obj
0%	0.6	0.25
0% to 8.5%	79.6	1.13
8.5% to 9.5%	7.6	0.58
9.5% to 11%	5.6	1.22
More than 11%	6.6	2.85
Not applicable	0.0	0.00

Credit Analysis 12-31-94

% of Bonds

US Govt	64	BB	4
AAA	9	B	1
AA	5	Below B	0
A	10	NR/NA	0
BBB	8		

Min Initial Purchase

Min Initial Purchase	$1000 (Addt'l: $100)
Min IRA Purchase	$1000 (Addt'l: $100)
Min Auto Invest Plan	$1000 (Systematic Inv: $50)

MORNINGSTAR 1995 Mutual Fund 500

Columbia Growth

	Ticker	Load	NAV	Yield	SEC Yield	Assets	Objective
	CLMBX	None	24.84	1.0%	N/A	591.7	Growth

Columbia Growth Fund seeks capital appreciation.
The fund invests primarily in common stocks. In selecting its investments, the fund considers sales trends, earnings, and profit margins, the potential for new product development, the dynamics of the industry in which the company operates, the ability of management, and investment for the future in research and facilities. These fundamental factors are judged within the framework of general economic conditions and market action in order to finalize investment decisions.

Historical Profile

Return	Above Average
Risk	Average
Rating	★★★★
	Above Average

Investment Style History
Equity
Average % Stocks Held in Portfolio

84% 79% 87% 85% 88% 95% 97% 95%

Growth of $10,000

|||| Value of Fund ($000)
— Value of Index ($000) S&P 500
▼ Manager Change
▽ Partial Manager Change
► Mgr Unknown After
◄ Mgr Unknown Before

Performance Quartile (Within Objective)

Manager's Investment Style
Top-down economic considerations guide management's investment choices. Once management decides which sectors will benefit most from their macroeconomic forecast, they employ a bottom-up analysis to pick the individual stocks based on valuations and earnings growth.

Fund Manager(s)
Alexander S. Macmillan III et al.

Manager Experience

	Dates Managed	Invest Obj	Std Dev	+/- Index

Not available.

1983	1984	1985	1986	1987	1988	1989	1990	1991	1992	1993	1994	History
25.45	21.52	28.02	22.88	20.19	21.21	23.40	21.68	26.26	26.18	26.38	24.84	NAV
21.51	-5.62	32.07	7.06	14.81	10.89	29.46	-3.27	34.43	11.91	13.09	-0.64	Total Return %
-0.95	-11.88	0.33	-11.62	9.56	-5.72	-2.22	-0.15	3.94	4.29	3.03	-1.96	+/- S&P 500
-1.95	-8.67	-0.50	-9.04	12.45	-7.06	0.29	2.91	0.22	2.94	1.81	-0.57	+/- Wilshire 5000
0.56	0.84	1.86	1.63	2.86	2.55	2.42	2.16	1.56	0.77	0.69	1.04	Income Return %
20.95	-6.46	30.20	5.44	11.96	8.34	27.05	-5.43	32.87	11.14	12.40	-1.68	Capital Return %
34	81	19	93	6	54	14	65	20	15	40	24	Total Rtn % Rank All
49	70	34	92	7	69	38	42	52	27	43	39	Total Rtn % Rank Obj
0.12	0.19	0.33	0.40	0.61	0.52	0.54	0.48	0.39	0.20	0.18	0.26	Income $
2.42	2.41	0.00	6.48	5.33	0.64	3.40	0.46	2.44	2.98	3.02	1.11	Capital Gains $
1.10	1.18	1.06	1.00	1.04	1.04	0.96	0.96	0.90	0.86	0.82	0.83	Expense Ratio %
1.48	1.78	1.81	0.78	1.46	2.33	2.14	2.08	1.50	0.77	0.66	0.92	Income Ratio %
95	90	93	131	197	179	166	172	164	116	106	90	Turnover Rate %
145.5	155.1	250.6	200.9	193.5	204.4	266.9	270.7	431.5	518.4	605.4	591.7	Net Assets ($mil)

Performance 12-31-94

	1st Qtr	2nd Qtr	3rd Qtr	4th Qtr	Total
1987	22.63	5.06	7.11	-16.80	14.81
1988	5.94	4.96	-1.87	1.62	10.89
1989	7.78	7.92	9.65	1.51	29.46
1990	-1.58	6.95	-12.75	5.33	-3.27
1991	17.53	-2.00	5.81	10.31	34.43
1992	0.27	-5.43	4.94	12.46	11.91
1993	3.67	0.74	5.74	2.41	13.09
1994	-3.41	-2.47	5.59	-0.11	-0.65

Bear Market Performance
Decile Rank (5-year period)

Worst — Best

	Worst 3 Mo Period 1985-89	Worst 3 Mo Period 1990-94
Columbia Growth	-23.17	-15.52
+/- S&P 500	6.42	-1.68
+/- Best Fit Index : Wil 4500	6.97	3.88

Trailing Returns

	Total Return %	+/- S&P 500	+/- Wil 5000	% Rank All	% Rank Obj	Growth of $10,000
3 Mo	-0.11	-0.10	0.66	25	23	9,989
6 Mo	5.47	0.61	0.85	10	29	10,547
1 Yr	-0.64	-1.96	-0.57	24	39	9,936
3 Yr Avg	7.93	1.67	1.32	22	31	12,574
5 Yr Avg	10.33	1.64	1.52	15	26	16,350
10 Yr Avg	14.31	-0.07	0.45	16	24	38,103
15 Yr Avg	15.47	0.99	1.50	9	18	86,553

Operations

Address and Telephone	1301 SW Fifth Ave P.O. Box 1350
	Portland, OR 97207-1350
	800-547-1707 / 503-222-3606
Advisor	Columbia Funds Management
Subadvisor	None
Distributor	Columbia Financial Center
States Available	All except NH
Report Grade	C
Income Distrib	Paid Annually
Date of Inception	06-16-67
Fiscal Year End	December

Min Initial Purchase	$1000 (Addt'l: $100)
Min IRA Purchase	$1000 (Addt'l: $100)
Min Auto Invest Plan	$1000 (Systematic Inv: $50)

Expenses & Fees

Sales Fees	0.00% front
	0.00% deferred
	0.00% 12b-1
Management Fee	0.75% max./0.50% min.
3-,5-,10-yr Expense Projections	$26, $46, $101
Annual Brokerage Cost	0.24%

Risk Analysis

Time Period	Load-Adj Return %	Risk % Rank [1] All	Risk % Rank [1] Obj	Morningstar [2] Return	Morningstar [2] Risk	Morningstar Risk-Adj Rating
1 Yr	-0.64					
3 Yr	7.93	79	57	1.31 [3]	0.94	★★★
5 Yr	10.33	77	51	1.45 [3]	0.92	★★★★
10 Yr	14.31	71	44	1.34	0.93	★★★★
Average Historical Rating (109 months)					3.9	★s

[1] 1 = low, 100 = high [2] 1.00 = Equity Avg [3] 1.00 = 90-day T-bill return

Other Measures

		Standard S&P 500	Best Fit Wil 4500
Standard Deviation	10.59	Alpha	1.6	0.3
Mean	8.22	Beta	1.09	1.03
Sharpe Ratio	0.44	R-Squared	66	91

Investment Style

	Stock Portfolio Avg	Relative S&P 500
Price/Earnings Ratio	21.3	1.15
Price/Book Ratio	4.2	1.24
5 Yr Earnings Gr %	14.6	2.63
Return on Assets %	8.4	1.12
Debt % Total Cap	31.4	1.11
Med Mkt Cap ($mil)	4517	0.35

Style
Value Blend Growth
Large Med Small (Size)

Diversification Value for Portfolio Types

Large Cap: Low	Small Cap: Low	Bond: High	Balanced: Low	Diversified: Low

Tax Analysis

	Tax-Adj Historical Return %	% Pretax Return
3 Yr Avg	5.13	62.9
5 Yr Avg	7.69	70.6
10 Yr Avg	10.70	62.7
Potential Capital Gain Exposure (% of assets)		6%

Most Similar Funds in MF500

Fidelity Growth Company	Strong Fit
Vanguard Index Extended Mkt	Strong Fit
20th Century Heritage Invest	Strong Fit

Portfolio 12-31-94

Total Stocks: 104
Total Fixed-Income: 3

Share Chg (08-94)000	Amount 000		Value $000	% Net Assets
-13	596	Sunbeam-Oster	15350	2.59
37	331	Sears Roebuck	15203	2.57
0	195	FNMA	14189	2.40
-86	222	Philip Morris	12788	2.16
15	165	Gillette	12334	2.08
180	533	Abbey Healthcare Group	12188	2.06
23	219	LM Ericsson Telephone (ADR)	12045	2.04
0	230	General Electric	11730	1.98
186	326	Time Warner	11454	1.94
57	180	Avon Products	10755	1.82
0	355	Equity Residential Ppty Tr	10650	1.80
0	443	Circus Circus Enterprises	10300	1.74
0	171	Amgen	10095	1.71
-115	361	UST (Inc)	10015	1.69
75	150	Emerson Electric	9375	1.58
0	156	Motorola	9029	1.53
-35	180	Mead	8753	1.48
101	268	Fred Meyer	8226	1.39
25	160	Computer Sciences	8160	1.38
-75	289	Ford Motor	8084	1.37
49	400	Federated Department Stores	7700	1.30
0	225	Vodafone Group (ADR)	7566	1.28
0	121	First Financial Management	7444	1.26
0	350	JP Realty	7350	1.24
0	200	Columbia/HCA Healthcare	7300	1.23

Composition % 12-31-94

Cash	5.0	Preferreds	0.0
Stocks	93.0	Convertibles	2.0
Bonds	0.0	Other	0.0

Index Allocation

	% of Stocks
S&P 500	56.3
S&P MidCap 400	10.6
U.S. Small Cap	25.9
Foreign	7.1

Sector Weightings

	% of Stocks	Relative S&P 500
Utilities	0.3	0.02
Energy	7.5	0.74
Financials	15.2	1.44
Industrial Cyclicals	7.1	0.44
Consumer Durables	7.7	1.24
Consumer Staples	8.7	0.69
Services	14.7	1.81
Retail	12.6	2.17
Health	10.0	1.16
Technology	16.1	1.76

Columbia Special

		Ticker	Load	NAV	Yield	SEC Yield	Assets	Objective
		CLSPX	None	18.69	0.4%	N/A	889.5	Small Company

Columbia Special Fund seeks capital appreciation.
The fund intends to invest primarily in smaller companies. It expects to select securities of companies that are more aggressive than the market as a whole and, therefore, carry greater than average risk. It does, however, invest in larger companies when management believes that they offer special capital-appreciation opportunities or that such investments are needed to stabilize the portfolio. The fund may invest in new issues, companies involved in tender offers, leveraged buyouts or mergers, and foreign securities.

Historical Profile

Return	Above Average
Risk	Above Average
Rating	★★★★
	Above Average

Investment Style History
Equity
Average % Stocks Held in Portfolio

Top row: 96% 92% 96% 95% 94% 96% 90% 86%

Growth of $10,000

|||| Value of Fund ($000)
— Value of Index ($000)
     Russ 2000
▼ Manager Change
▽ Partial Manager Change
► Mgr Unknown After
◄ Mgr Unknown Before

Performance Quartile (Within Objective)

Manager's Investment Style

Management places about half the fund's assets into stable small- and mid-cap growth stocks with high earnings-growth rates and noteworthy insider-ownership levels. The remainder of assets is used to make shorter-term top-down sector bets, and to invest in special-situation stocks. Former manager Alan Folkman was especially successful with this formula; current lead manager Robert Unger has been with Columbia for many years, and will maintain this fund's tripartite approach.

Fund Manager(s)

Robert A. Unger et al.

	Dates Managed	Invest Obj	Std Dev	+/- Index
Manager Experience				
Robert A. Unger				
Columbia Growth	01/87 - 01/91	G	16.39	0.77

	1983	1984	1985	1986	1987	1988	1989	1990	1991	1992	1993	1994	History
	---	---	7.99	8.99	9.26	11.32	13.85	12.12	17.45	18.79	19.51	18.69	NAV
	---	---	11.75 *	17.08	3.04	42.56	31.92	-12.39	50.46	13.70	21.69	2.26	Total Return %
	---	---	4.88 *	-1.60	-2.22	25.95	0.23	-9.27	19.98	6.08	11.63	0.94	+/- S&P 500
	---	---	---	5.32	6.55	22.02	7.97	1.17	7.01	1.94	7.15	4.91	+/- Wilshire 4500
	---	---	0.00	0.00	0.00	0.00	0.07	0.12	0.00	0.00	0.05	0.37	Income Return %
	---	---	11.75	17.08	3.04	42.56	31.84	-12.51	50.46	13.70	21.64	1.88	Capital Return %
	---	---	---	39	35	1	10	88	7	12	15	9	Total Rtn % Rank All
	---	---	---	12	26	1	19	59	45	52	30	26	Total Rtn % Rank Obj
	---	---	0.00	0.00	0.00	0.00	0.01	0.02	0.00	0.00	0.01	0.07	Income $
	---	---	0.00	0.37	0.00	1.87	1.05	0.00	0.77	1.04	3.32	1.19	Capital Gains $
	---	---	1.24	1.54	1.44	1.38	1.35	1.32	1.22	1.19	1.12	1.11	Expense Ratio %
	---	---	0.94	-0.47	-0.63	0.06	0.18	0.05	-0.16	-0.25	0.01	0.31	Income Ratio %
	---	---	---	112	203	333	244	124	147	115	117	155	125	Turnover Rate %
	---	---	3.1	20.4	20.6	30.5	95.9	121.6	264.4	470.7	772.7	889.5	Net Assets ($mil)

Performance 12-31-94

	1st Qtr	2nd Qtr	3rd Qtr	4th Qtr	Total
1987	30.07	4.96	5.19	-28.25	3.04
1988	16.45	10.23	5.55	5.22	42.56
1989	10.51	8.29	11.63	-1.26	31.92
1990	1.44	6.26	-29.30	14.96	-12.39
1991	24.36	-0.62	9.70	10.97	50.46
1992	4.70	-8.65	-0.66	19.67	13.70
1993	2.66	5.65	8.34	3.56	21.69
1994	0.41	-3.93	6.06	-0.05	2.26

Bear Market Performance

Decile Rank (5-year period)

Worst   Best

	Worst 3 Mo Period 1985-89	Worst 3 Mo Period 1990-94
Columbia Special	---	-29.30
+/- S&P 500	---	-15.56
+/- Best Fit Index : Russ 2000	---	-4.77

Trailing Returns

	Total Return %	+/- S&P 500	+/- Wil 4500	% Rank All	% Rank Obj	Growth of $10,000
3 Mo	-0.05	-0.03	2.45	23	38	9,995
6 Mo	6.00	1.14	1.81	9	48	10,600
1 Yr	2.26	4.94	4.91	9	26	10,226
3 Yr Avg	12.26	6.00	4.65	7	27	14,148
5 Yr Avg	13.28	4.58	4.18	6	30	18,650
10 Yr Avg	---	---	---	---	---	---
15 Yr Avg	---	---	---	---	---	---

Operations

Address and Telephone	1301 SW Fifth Ave P.O. Box 1350
	Portland, OR 97207-1350
	800-547-1707 / 503-222-3606
Advisor	Columbia Funds Management
Subadvisor	None
Distributor	Columbia Financial Center
States Available	All except NH
Report Grade	C
Income Distrib	Paid Annually
* Date of Inception	11-20-85
Fiscal Year End	December

Risk Analysis

Time Period	Load-Adj Return %	Risk % Rank [1] All	Obj	Morningstar [2] Return	Risk	Morningstar Risk-Adj Rating
1 Yr	2.26					
3 Yr	12.26	78	42	2.73 [3]	0.91	★★★★
5 Yr	13.28	93	68	2.33 [3]	1.23	★★★★
10 Yr	---	---	---	---	---	

Average Historical Rating (74 months)   4.4 ★s

[1] 1 = low, 100 = high   [2] 1.00 = Equity Avg   [3] 1.00 = 90-day T-bill return

Other Measures

				Standard S&P 500	Best Fit Russ 2000
Standard Deviation	11.86	Alpha		6.4	1.4
Mean	12.32	Beta		0.90	0.93
Sharpe Ratio	0.74	R-Squared		36	85

Investment Style

	Stock Portfolio Avg	Relative S&P 500
Price/Earnings Ratio	26.1	1.41
Price/Book Ratio	3.5	1.03
5 Yr Earnings Gr %	16.0#	2.88
Return on Assets %	8.7	1.16
Debt % Total Cap	29.2	1.03
Med Mkt Cap ($mil)	920	0.07

figure is based on 50% or less of stocks

Style: Value Blend Growth / Size Large Med Small

Diversification Value for Portfolio Types

Large Cap: Medium	Small Cap: None	Bond: High	Balanced: Medium	Diversified: Medium

Expenses & Fees

Sales Fees	0.00% front
	0.00% deferred
	0.00% 12b-1
Management Fee	1.00% max./0.75% min.
3-,5-,10-yr Expense Projections	$36, $62, $136
Annual Brokerage Cost	0.39%

Portfolio 12-31-94

Share Chg (08-94)000	Amount 000	Total Stocks: 193 / Total Fixed-Income: 2	Value $000	% Net Assets
175	375	cisco Systems	13172	1.48
75	250	Sybase	13000	1.46
300	400	AirTouch Communications	11650	1.31
315	315	Elan (ADR)	11222	1.26
0	350	Fred Meyer	10772	1.21
-35	140	Nokia (ADR)	10500	1.18
415	515	Orbital Sciences	9914	1.11
25	700	Biomet	9800	1.10
60	260	Sun Microsystems	9230	1.04
-50	350	WMX Technologies	9188	1.03
25	150	Microsoft	9169	1.03
75	350	Sun Healthcare Group	8881	1.00
0	360	Thomas Nelson	8640	0.97
0	190	Houghton Mifflin	8621	0.97
275	275	Bed Bath & Beyond	8250	0.93
0	225	Louisiana Land & Exploration	8184	0.92
0	320	Applied Power Cl A	8120	0.91
0	450	Novell	7706	0.87
0	275	Ventritex	7425	0.83
290	290	Merix	7359	0.83
50	175	Biogen	7306	0.82
66	250	Titan Wheel International	6938	0.78
200	200	HBO	6875	0.77
28	178	Anadarko Petroleum	6861	0.77
-25	125	Tribune	6844	0.77

Composition % 12-31-94

Cash	9.7	Preferreds	2.2
Stocks	88.1	Convertibles	0.0
Bonds	0.0	Other	0.0

Tax Analysis

	Tax-Adj Historical Return %	% Pretax Return
3 Yr Avg	9.50	75.4
5 Yr Avg	11.32	82.0
10 Yr Avg	---	---
Potential Capital Gain Exposure (% of assets)		6%

Most Similar Funds in MF500

Brandywine	Strong Fit
Vista Capital Growth A	Fair Fit
AIM Constellation	Fair Fit

Index Allocation

	% of Stocks
S&P 500	26.1
S&P MidCap 400	19.3
U.S. Small Cap	47.1
Foreign	8.1

Sector Weightings

	% of Stocks	Relative S&P 500
Utilities	0.4	0.03
Energy	5.8	0.58
Financials	7.9	0.74
Industrial Cyclicals	17.0	1.04
Consumer Durables	5.7	0.91
Consumer Staples	0.0	0.00
Services	15.1	1.86
Retail	8.5	1.46
Health	11.6	1.33
Technology	28.0	3.05

Min Initial Purchase / IRA / Auto

Min Initial Purchase	$2000 (Addt'l: $100)
Min IRA Purchase	$2000 (Addt'l: $100)
Min Auto Invest Plan	$2000 (Systematic Inv: $50)

Morningstar 1995 Mutual Fund 500

Connecticut Mutual Total Ret

	Ticker	Load	NAV	Yield	SEC Yield	Assets	Objective
	CNMTX	5.00%	13.44	4.0%	4.49%	177.9	Asset Alloc.

Connecticut Mutual Total Return Account seeks capital appreciation and income.

The fund allocates its assets among stocks, bonds, and money-market instruments. Although the portfolio normally includes some combination of these three asset classes, it may from time to time be fully invested in only one asset class. The allocation process uses quantitative asset-allocation tools that measure value relationships among the three asset classes in conjunction with the subadvisor's judgment of current market dynamics. The fund may invest in foreign securities.

Manager's Investment Style

Management uses a computer model to determine its asset allocation. The portfolio typically consists of bonds with durations within 20% (plus or minus) of the Lehman Brothers Aggregate Bond Index's, and inexpensive stocks with a recently reported earnings surprise.

Fund Manager(s)

Peter M. Antos et al. Birthdate: 06-45 BA, Tufts U. 1967 MBA, Columbia U. 1969

Manager Experience

	Dates Managed	Invest Obj	Std Dev	+/- Index
Stephen F. Libera				
Connecticut Mutual Inc	09/85 - 12/94	CG	3.64	-1.50
Connecticut Mut Gov Sec	09/85 - 12/94	GG	4.61	-0.60

Historical Profile

Return	Above Average
Risk	Below Average
Rating	★★★★ Above Average

Investment Style History
Equity
Average % Stocks Held in Portfolio

| | | | | | | 86% | | | 57% | 46% | 50% | 43% |

Growth of $10,000

|||| Value of Fund ($000)
— Value of Index ($000) S&P 500
▼ Manager Change
▽ Partial Manager Change
◄■ Mgr Unknown After
■► Mgr Unknown Before

Performance Quartile (Within Objective)

1983	1984	1985	1986	1987	1988	1989	1990	1991	1992	1993	1994	History
---	---	10.91	11.87	10.91	11.51	12.69	11.94	14.02	13.81	14.54	13.44	NAV
---	---	10.56 *	11.88	3.92	10.40	22.61	-0.21	28.21	9.88	15.89	-2.11	Total Return %
---	---	-6.55 *	-6.80	-1.34	-6.21	-9.08	2.91	-2.27	2.26	5.83	-3.42	+/- S&P 500
---	---	---	-3.37	1.16	2.52	8.07	-9.15	12.21	2.63	6.14	0.81	+/- LB Aggregate
---	---	1.24	2.72	3.06	4.90	6.48	5.17	4.40	3.66	3.39	3.87	Income Return %
---	---	9.32	9.16	0.86	5.50	16.13	-5.38	23.81	6.22	12.50	-5.98	Capital Return %
---	---	74	28	58	30	56	30	23	25	35	Total Rtn % Rank All
---	---	75	70	37	16	50	18	17	33	40	Total Rtn % Rank Obj
---	---	0.12	0.30	0.39	0.53	0.76	0.66	0.54	0.50	0.48	0.55	Income $
---	---	0.00	0.04	1.09	0.00	0.63	0.07	0.71	1.07	0.97	0.24	Capital Gains $
---	---	1.50	1.26	1.08	1.11	1.20	1.24	1.20	1.11	1.02	0.92	Expense Ratio %
---	---	4.46	3.22	3.15	4.61	5.90	5.31	4.02	3.61	3.40	3.48	Income Ratio %
---	---	50	143	198	224	149	115	122	178	155	102	Turnover Rate %
---	---	12.1	54.0	44.7	54.3	65.0	66.4	86.5	109.7	171.2	177.9	Net Assets ($mil)

Performance 12-31-94

	1st Qtr	2nd Qtr	3rd Qtr	4th Qtr	Total
1987	15.25	2.40	4.50	-15.73	3.92
1988	4.03	4.43	-0.51	2.14	10.40
1989	5.73	6.34	7.50	1.43	22.61
1990	-1.10	4.11	-8.60	6.04	-0.21
1991	9.97	1.41	7.08	7.37	28.21
1992	1.64	0.32	2.51	5.12	9.88
1993	6.01	3.25	4.93	0.91	15.89
1994	-2.54	-1.71	2.81	-0.59	-2.11

Bear Market Performance

Decile Rank (5-year period)

Worst _____ Best

	Worst 3 Mo Period 1985-89	Worst 3 Mo Period 1990-94
Connecticut Mutual Total Ret	---	-8.60
+/- S&P 500	---	5.15
+/- Best Fit Index : S&P 500	---	5.15

Trailing Returns

	Total Return %	+/- S&P 500	+/- LB Aggregate	% Rank All	% Rank Obj	Growth of $10,000
3 Mo	-0.59	-0.58	-0.97	36	42	9,941
6 Mo	2.20	-2.66	1.21	25	35	10,220
1 Yr	-2.11	-3.42	0.81	35	40	9,789
3 Yr Avg	7.62	1.36	3.08	23	23	12,465
5 Yr Avg	9.79	1.09	2.16	18	14	15,949
10 Yr Avg	---	---	---	---	---	---
15 Yr Avg	---	---	---	---	---	---

Operations

Address and Telephone	140 Garden Street
	Hartford, CT 06154
	800-234-5606
Advisor	G.R. Phelps & Company
Subadvisor	None
Distributor	G.R. Phelps & Company
States Available	All plus PR
Report Grade	D
Income Distrib	Paid Semiannually
* Date of Inception	09-16-85
Fiscal Year End	December

Risk Analysis

Time Period	Load-Adj Return %	Risk % Rank All	Obj	Morningstar Return	Morningstar Risk	Morningstar Risk-Adj Rating
1 Yr	-7.00					
3 Yr	5.80	43	33	0.65[3]	0.65	★★★
5 Yr	8.67	50	47	0.99[3]	0.68	★★★★
10 Yr	---	---	---	---	---	

Average Historical Rating (76 months) 3.5 ★s

[1] 1 = low, 100 = high [2] 1.00 = Hybrid Avg [3] 1.00 = 90-day T-bill return

Other Measures

			Standard S&P 500	Best Fit S&P 500
Standard Deviation	5.95	Alpha	2.2	2.2
Mean	7.55	Beta	0.63	0.63
Sharpe Ratio	0.68	R-Squared	70	70

Investment Style

Stocks

	Port Avg	Rel S&P 500
Price/Earnings Ratio	15.2	0.82
Price/Book Ratio	2.5	0.73
5 Yr Earnings Gr %	7.3	1.32
Med Mkt Cap ($mil)	4708	0.36

Bonds

Avg Effective Duration	5.4 Yrs
Avg Effective Maturity	8.1 Yrs
Avg Credit Quality	AA
Avg Weighted Coupon	7.39%

Diversification Value for Portfolio Types

Large Cap: Low	Small Cap: Low	Bond: Low	Balanced: None	Diversified: Low

Portfolio 11-30-94

Share Chg (09-94)000	Amount 000		Date of Maturity	Value $000	% Net Assets
		Total Stocks: 68 Total Fixed-Income: 126			
	11750	US Treasury Bond 8.75%	05-15-17	12506	6.40
	8000	US Treasury Note 6.375%	08-15-02	7319	3.75
	6650	US Treasury Note 8%	01-15-97	6718	3.44
	2500	US Treasury Note 3.875%	04-30-95	2477	1.27
	2550	US Treasury Note 5.125%	11-30-98	2321	1.19
0	67	Safeway		2053	1.05
0	75	Mattel		1996	1.02
	2000	US Treasury Note 5.125%	03-31-96	1948	1.00
0	49	Ameritech		1928	0.99
0	35	Columbia/HCA Healthcare		1918	0.98
16	49	Compaq Computer		1909	0.98
	1996	GNMA 7%	03-15-24	1774	0.91
5	49	American Brands		1737	0.89
0	41	Citicorp		1719	0.88
	1994	GNMA 6.5%	04-15-24	1708	0.87
0	61	Archer-Daniels-Midland		1691	0.87
-14	65	Baxter International		1676	0.86
0	79	Panhandle Eastern		1675	0.86
0	23	IBM		1634	0.84
4	36	Computer Associates Intl		1615	0.83

Index Allocation

	% of Stocks
S&P 500	77.9
S&P MidCap 400	14.0
U.S. Small Cap	7.3
Foreign	4.4

Composition % 12-31-94

Cash	7.8	Preferreds	0.0
Stocks	41.6	Convertibles	0.0
Bonds	50.6	Other	0.0

Tax Analysis

	Tax-Adj Historical Return %	% Pretax Return
3 Yr Avg	4.76	60.8
5 Yr Avg	7.08	68.6
10 Yr Avg	---	---
Potential Capital Gain Exposure (% of assets)		0%

Most Similar Funds in MF500

MFS Total Return A	Strong Fit
Oppenheimer Equity-Inc A	Strong Fit
IDS Mutual	Strong Fit

Min Initial Purchase / Expenses

Min Initial Purchase	$1000 (Addt'l: $50)
Min IRA Purchase	$250 (Addt'l: $50)
Min Auto Invest Plan	$100 (Systematic Inv: $100)

Expenses & Fees

Sales Fees	5.00% front
	0.00% deferred
	0.00% 12b-1
Management Fee	0.63% max./0.45% min.
3-,5-,10-yr Expense Projections	$81, $104, $169
Annual Brokerage Cost	0.21%

Bond Credit Analysis 12-31-94

% of Bonds

US Govt	49	BB	7
AAA	1	B	2
AA	3	Below B	0
A	17	NR/NA	2
BBB	19		

Stock Sector Weightings

	% of Stocks	Relative S&P 500
Utilities	9.1	0.73
Energy	8.1	0.80
Financials	8.7	0.82
Industrial Cyclicals	18.1	1.10
Consumer Durables	6.3	1.01
Consumer Staples	13.9	1.11
Services	2.0	0.25
Retail	10.2	1.75
Health	10.3	1.19
Technology	13.4	1.46

Convertible Holdings Income

	Ticker	NAV	Mkt Price	Prem/Disc	Yield	Objective
	CNVpr	$9.30	$10.00	7.5%	11.9%	Income

Convertible Holdings has the dual objective of long-term capital appreciation and current and long-term growth of income.

The fund seeks to meet its objectives by investing at least 70% of assets in convertible debt securities and convertible preferred stocks. It may invest up to 20% of assets in cash equivalents and up to 10% in common stocks.

The fund's income shares are entitled to all net income from fund holdings. The fund maintains a minimum rate of income return equal to 85% of the yield of the Value Line Convertible Index. The income shares are not entitled to capital gains from fund holdings, except as necessary to maintain a minimum annual distribution of $1 per share.

All income shares will be redeemed on July 31, 1997, for $9.30 per share plus any unpaid dividends.

Prior to 1987, the fund was named Merrill Lynch Convertible Securities, Inc.

Manager's Investment Style

To feed the income shares of this dual-purpose fund the yield that they require, management invests the bulk of assets in high-paying convertibles. Management's fine picks have kept this fund's yield well above its minimum $1 per share. Additionally, shareholders have received a leveraged level of income without NAV volatility, because all the capital gains and losses of the portfolio are absorbed by the fund's capital shares.

Fund Manager(s)

Vincent T. Lathbury III, CFA. Since 8-85. BA'62 Washington & Lee U.; MBA'76 Temple U.

Manager Experience

	Dates Managed	Invest Obj	Std Dev	+/- Index
Vincent T. Lathbury III				
Merrill Lynch World Inc B	11/91 - 12/94	I	4.19	-5.11
Corp High Yield	06/93 - 12/94	CY	7.00	0.13

NAV Performance % 12-30-94

	1st Qtr	2nd Qtr	3rd Qtr	4th Qtr	Total
1987	2.19	2.83	2.49	2.84	10.75
1988	3.41	3.02	3.91	2.11	13.04
1989	3.86	3.18	2.82	2.02	12.42
1990	3.76	3.24	3.17	2.75	13.55
1991	3.76	2.97	3.31	2.12	12.72
1992	3.76	2.97	1.85	2.83	11.89
1993	3.44	2.77	2.58	2.66	11.95
1994	3.23	2.61	2.77	2.79	11.89

Bear Market Performance

Decile Rank (5-year period)

Worst _____ Best

	Worst 3 Mo Period 1985-89	Worst 3 Mo Period 1990-94
Conv Hold Inc	---	1.85
+/- S&P 500	---	-1.31

Trailing Returns

	NAV Total Return %	+/- S&P 500	+/- LB Agg	% Rank All	% Rank Obj	Mkt Total Return %
3 Mo	2.79	2.80	2.41	4	12	3.41
6 Mo	5.64	0.78	4.65	9	12	1.23
1 Yr	11.89	10.58	14.81	3	6	5.31
3 Yr Avg	11.91	5.65	7.37	14	20	3.58
5 Yr Avg	12.40	3.71	4.77	12	25	9.30
Incept Avg	10.53*	---	---	---	---	10.53*

Operations

Address and Telephone	633 3rd Avenue
	New York, NY 10017
	609-282-2800 / 800-543-6217
Advisor	Merrill Lynch Asset Mgmt, Inc.
Subadvisor	N/A
Administrator	N/A
Transfer Agent	State Street Bank and Trust Co.
Custodian	National Westminster Bank NJ
Auditor	Deloitte & Touche
Legal Counsel	Brown, Wood, Ivey, Mitchell & Petty

Historical Profile

Return	Above Average
Risk	Low
Rating	★★★★★ Highest

	23.7	44.8	46.0	23.4	25.8	22.1	35.6	33.1	25.9	19.6	Highest Prem/Disc
	15.7	30.0	7.7	13.0	17.8	5.9	15.3	17.3	13.5	3.0	Lowest Prem/Disc

Growth of $10,000
■ at NAV ($000)
— at Market Price ($000)

Premium Discount %

1983	1984	1985	1986	1987	1988	1989	1990	1991	1992	1993	1994	History
---	---	9.64	9.63	9.38	9.32	9.30	9.30	9.31	9.30	9.30	9.30	NAV
---	---	-8.34*	10.69	10.75	13.04	12.42	13.55	12.72	11.89	11.95	11.89	NAV Total Return %
---	---	-20.58*	-7.99	5.49	-3.57	-19.27	16.67	-17.77	4.27	1.90	10.58	+/- S&P 500
---	---	---	-4.56	7.99	5.16	-2.12	4.61	-3.28	4.64	2.20	14.81	+/- LB Aggregate
---	---	1.57*	10.80	13.34	13.68	12.63	13.55	12.61	12.00	11.95	11.89	Income Return %
---	---	-9.91*	-0.10	-2.60	-0.64	-0.22	0.00	0.11	-0.11	0.00	0.00	Capital Return %
---	---	---	80	15	41	44	6	75	30	75	3	Total Rtn % Rank All
---	---	---	1	1	1	50	12	77	40	75	6	Total Rtn % Rank Obj
---	---	5.06*	24.81	-10.74	24.60	12.66	7.38	30.72	-0.19	5.73	5.31	Market Total Rtn %
---	---	---	38.9	25.8	18.3	21.7	14.6	21.0	26.9	19.3	11.9	Avg Prem/Disc %
---	---	0.20	1.35	1.55	1.47	1.41	1.38	1.40	1.36	1.20	1.19	Income $
---	---	0.00	0.00	0.00	0.00	0.00	0.00	0.00	0.00	0.00	0.00	Capital Gains $
---	---	---	0.72	0.83	0.79	0.80	0.86	0.83	0.80	0.80	0.90	Expense Ratio %
---	---	---	6.71	6.37	7.55	7.15	7.39	7.24	6.34	5.10	5.20	Income Ratio %
---	---	---	37	23	49	50	40	55	77	116	---	Turnover Rate %
---	---	131.2	131.0	127.6	126.9	126.5	126.6	126.6	121.4	113.7	108.6	Net Assets ($mil)

Risk Analysis

	Risk % Rank[1]		Morningstar[2]		Morningstar
	All	Obj	Return	Risk	Risk-Adj Rating
3 Yr	1	10	1.74	0.01	★★★★★
5 Yr	1	1	1.76	0.01	★★★★★
10 Yr	---	---	---	---	---
Average Historical Rating (76 months)					4.6 ★s

[1] 1 = Low, 100 = High [2] 1.00 = Hybrid Avg [3] 1.00 = 90-day T-bill Return

Other Measures

				S&P 500
Standard Deviation	1.24	Alpha	8.20	
Mean	11.31	Beta	-0.04	
Sharpe Ratio	6.30	R-Squared	6	

Investment Style

	Stock Portfolio Avg	Relative S&P 500
Price/Earnings Ratio	12.1	0.66
Price/Cash Flow Ratio	7.8	0.67
Price/Book Ratio	1.9	0.57
5 Yr Earnings Gr %	7.8	1.40
Return on Assets %	5.3	0.71
Debt % Total Cap	20.0	0.71
Med Mkt Cap ($mil)	1243	0.10

figure is based on less than 50% of stocks

Style
Value Blend Growth — Size Large Med Small

Index Allocation

	% of Stocks
Dow 30	0.0
S&P 500	29.7
S&P Mid-Cap 400	23.9
US Small-Cap	44.0
Foreign	2.5

Diversification Value for Portfolio Types

Large Cap: High	Small Cap: High	Bond: High	Balanced: High	Diversified: High

Portfolio 06-30-94

Total Equity: 13
Total Fixed-Income: 94

Share Chg (12-93)	Amount		Value $000	% Total Invest
0	100000	Bristol-Myers Squibb	5363	2.14
0	155211	BB & T Financial	4850	1.94
---	4000000	Mediplex Group Cv 6.5%	4600	1.84
0	128479	Trinity Industries	4513	1.80
---	135900	Southern Natl Cv Pfd $1.6875	4213	1.68
---	84000	AGCo Cv Pfd $1.625	4158	1.66
---	4000000	Pioneer Financial Svcs Cv 8%	4080	1.63
---	3550000	Integrated Health Svcs Cv 6%	3852	1.54
-111900	210955	Hudson Foods Cl A	3744	1.50
0	140584	Baxter International	3690	1.47
---	138200	ONBANCorp Cv Pfd $1.6875	3610	1.44
---	4000000	Genzyme Cv 6.75%	3570	1.43
---	3388000	Ingles Markets Cv 10%	3524	1.41
---	3560000	Seacor Holdings Cv 6%	3462	1.38
0	96848	First of America Bank	3450	1.38
---	3500000	Avnet Cv 6%	3430	1.37
---	3656000	GIANT Group Cv 7%	3400	1.36
---	3052000	Big B Cv 6.5%	3281	1.31
---	3500000	Masco Cv 5.25%	3150	1.26
---	2889000	Quixote Cv 8%	3120	1.25
---	3730000	Continental Hms Hldg Cv 6.875%	3115	1.24
---	3000000	Kroger Cv 8.25%	3030	1.21
---	3200000	Interface Cv 8%	3008	1.20
---	2751000	Storage Technology Cv 8%	2902	1.16
---	200000	Masco Tech Cv Pfd	2850	1.14

Composition % 09-30-94

Cash	16.4	Preferreds	0.0
Stocks	13.4	Convertibles	72.6
Bonds	0.7	Other	-3.1

Tax Analysis

	Tax-Adj Historical Return %	% Pretax Return
3 Yr Avg	7.41	59.5
5 Yr Avg	7.97	58.8
10 Yr Avg	---	---

Potential Capital Gain Exposure (% of assets) -3

Most Similar Funds in MF500

Warburg Pincus Emg Gr	Weak Fit
MainStay Capital App B	Weak Fit
Templeton Devlp Mkts	Weak Fit

Sector Weightings

	% of Stocks	Relative S&P 500
Utilities	0.0	0.00
Energy	0.0	0.00
Financials	32.6	3.08
Industrial Cyclicals	21.1	1.29
Consumer Durables	2.5	0.39
Consumer Staples	11.2	0.90
Services	0.0	0.00
Retail	0.1	0.02
Health	32.5	3.75
Technology	0.0	0.00

Income Distrib Schedule	Paid Quarterly
Management Fee	0.60%, 0.00%P
Reinvestment Plan	Yes
Direct Purchase Plan	No
Shares Outstanding	11,695,600
Exchange	NYSE
*Date of Inception	08-02-85
Shareholder Report	B+

MORNINGSTAR 1995 Mutual Fund 500

Crabbe Huson Asset Allocation

Ticker	Load	NAV	Yield	SEC Yield	Assets	Objective
CHAAX	None	12.17	2.5%	N/A	107.1	Asset Alloc.

Crabbe Huson Asset Allocation Fund seeks capital preservation, capital appreciation, and income.

The fund adheres to a flexible policy of investing in a portfolio of common stocks, fixed-income securities, and cash or cash equivalents. Normally, the fund will invest between 20% and 75% of its net assets in common stocks. Management will constantly monitor and adjust its weighting of investments in any particular area, adapting to changing market and economic conditions. The fund may engage in certain futures and options strategies, enter into repurchase agreements, and invest up to 35% of its net assets in foreign securities.

Manager's Investment Style

As they do with Crabbe Huson Equity, this fund's management team seeks the stocks of high-quality firms that are selling at depressed prices, but that have the potential, either through an internal strategy or an external event, to return to higher prices. Management matches that equity portfolio with a healthy stake in high-quality bonds, usually Treasuries. Management does trade the fund's bond portfolio to manage its interest-rate exposure.

Fund Manager(s)

Richard S. Huson CFA(1972), since 01-89.
Stephen D. Laveson, since 10-91.
John E. Maack, Jr. CFA(1984), since 10-91.

Manager Experience

	Dates Managed	Invest Obj	Std Dev	+/- Index
Richard S. Huson				
Crabbe Huson Equity	01/89 - 12/94	G	11.92	1.71
John E. Maack, Jr.				
Crabbe Huson Equity	10/91 - 12/94	G	8.66	6.51

Performance 12-31-94

	1st Qtr	2nd Qtr	3rd Qtr	4th Qtr	Total
1987	---	---	---	---	---
1988	---	---	---	---	---
1989	---	4.85	1.98	-3.11	4.73 *
1990	-1.35	2.35	-6.90	5.57	-0.76
1991	8.64	0.46	5.82	4.96	21.22
1992	2.47	1.70	3.65	3.85	12.18
1993	5.15	3.55	3.02	5.38	18.21
1994	-1.97	-1.38	3.49	-0.88	-0.84

Bear Market Performance

Decile Rank (5-year period)

Worst ——————————————— Best

	Worst 3 Mo Period 1985-89	Worst 3 Mo Period 1990-94
Crabbe Huson Asset Allocation	---	-7.14
+/- S&P 500	---	6.70
+/- Best Fit Index : S&P 500	---	6.70

Trailing Returns

	Total Return %	+/- S&P 500	+/- LB Aggregate	% Rank All	% Rank Obj	Growth of $10,000
3 Mo	-0.88	-0.86	-1.26	41	47	9,912
6 Mo	2.58	-2.29	1.58	23	26	10,258
1 Yr	-0.84	-2.16	2.08	26	22	9,916
3 Yr Avg	9.55	3.29	5.01	15	7	13,149
5 Yr Avg	9.60	0.91	1.98	19	18	15,818
10 Yr Avg	---	---	---	---	---	---
15 Yr Avg	---	---	---	---	---	---

Operations

Address and Telephone	P.O. Box 6559
	Portland, OR 97228-6559
	800-541-9732 / 503-295-0919
Advisor	Crabbe Huson Group
Subadvisor	None
Distributor	Crabbe Huson Securities
States Available	All
Report Grade	B-
Income Distrib	Paid Quarterly
* Date of Inception	01-31-89
Fiscal Year End	October

Historical Profile

Return	Above Average
Risk	Below Average
Rating	★★★★
	Above Average

	100%	40%	47%	48%	50%

Investment Style History
Equity
Average % Stocks Held in Portfolio

Growth of $10,000
|||| Value of Fund ($000)
— Value of Index ($000) S&P 500
▼ Manager Change
▽ Partial Manager Change
► Mgr Unknown After
◄ Mgr Unknown Before

Performance Quartile (Within Objective)

	1983	1984	1985	1986	1987	1988	1989	1990	1991	1992	1993	1994	History
NAV	---	---	---	---	---	---	10.34	9.78	11.15	11.87	13.07	12.17	NAV
	---	---	---	---	---	---	4.73 *	-0.76	21.22	12.18	18.21	-0.84	Total Return %
	---	---	---	---	---	---	-17.97 *	2.35	-9.26	4.56	8.16	-2.16	+/- S&P 500
	---	---	---	---	---	---		-9.71	5.22	4.93	8.46	2.08	+/- LB Aggregate
	---	---	---	---	---	---	0.53	4.65	4.98	2.92	1.77	2.49	Income Return %
	---	---	---	---	---	---	4.21	-5.42	16.25	9.25	16.44	-3.33	Capital Return %
	---	---	---	---	---	---	---	58	43	15	20	26	Total Rtn % Rank All
	---	---	---	---	---	---	---	58	52	9	27	22	Total Rtn % Rank Obj
	---	---	---	---	---	---	0.05	0.46	0.47	0.32	0.22	0.32	Income $
	---	---	---	---	---	---	0.08	0.00	0.19	0.30	0.72	0.47	Capital Gains $
	---	---	---	---	---	---	1.91	1.90	1.76	1.52	1.46	1.47	Expense Ratio %
	---	---	---	---	---	---	5.02	4.51	3.97	3.02	1.85	1.94	Income Ratio %
	---	---	---	---	---	---	---	162	158	155	116	---	Turnover Rate %
	---	---	---	---	---	---	12.7	13.7	26.2	55.4	92.0	107.1	Net Assets ($mil)

Risk Analysis

Time Period	Load-Adj Return %	Risk % Rank[1] All	Obj	Morningstar[2] Return	Risk	Morningstar Risk-Adj Rating
1 Yr	-0.84					
3 Yr	9.55	27	14	1.83[3]	0.54	★★★★
5 Yr	9.60	47	29	1.24[3]	0.61	★★★★
10 Yr	---	---	---	---	---	

Average Historical Rating (36 months) 3.8 ★s

[1] 1 = low, 100 = high [2] 1.00 = Hybrid Avg [3] 1.00 = 90-day T-bill return

Other Measures

			Standard S&P 500	Best Fit S&P 500
Standard Deviation	5.95	Alpha	4.0	4.0
Mean	9.34	Beta	0.64	0.64
Sharpe Ratio	0.98	R-Squared	73	73

Investment Style

Stocks

	Port Avg	Rel S&P 500
Price/Earnings Ratio	16.8	0.91
Price/Book Ratio	3.1	0.93
5 Yr Earnings Gr %	3.4#	0.60
Med Mkt Cap ($mil)	1900	0.15

figure is based on 50% or less of stocks

Bonds

Avg Effective Duration	5.7 Yrs
Avg Effective Maturity	10.1 Yrs
Avg Credit Quality	AAA
Avg Weighted Coupon	7.23%

Diversification Value for Portfolio Types

Large Cap: Low	Small Cap: Medium	Bond: Medium	Balanced: Low	Diversified: Low

Portfolio 10-31-94

Total Stocks: 46
Total Fixed-Income: 21

Share Chg (04-94)000	Amount 000		Date of Maturity	Value $000	% Net Assets
	5500	US Treasury Note 8%	01-15-97	5620	5.10
	4970	US Treasury Note 7.875%	07-31-96	5064	4.60
	3900	US Treasury Bond 8.125%	08-15-21	3912	3.55
	3830	US Treasury Note 5.125%	03-31-98	3585	3.25
	3500	US Treasury Bond 7.625%	11-15-22	3329	3.02
	2085	Intermountain Power Agcy 9%	07-01-19	2168	1.97
0	107	HF Ahmanson		2046	1.86
	2000	US Treasury Note 8%	08-15-99	2045	1.86
	2000	FHLMC 8.02%	10-02-01	2000	1.82
55	89	Consolidated Freightways		1991	1.81
0	26	IBM		1915	1.74
42	90	Equitable		1763	1.60
101	101	Norfolk Southern		1758	1.60
0	44	WR Grace		1747	1.59
39	130	Mentor Graphics		1733	1.57
	1700	FNMA Debenture 8.65%	12-10-99	1704	1.55
22	37	Apple Computer		1589	1.44
-38	71	Occidental Petroleum		1553	1.41
77	77	USG		1513	1.37
39	106	ENSERCH		1511	1.37

Index Allocation

	% of Stocks
S&P 500	64.2
S&P MidCap 400	13.1
U.S. Small Cap	18.9
Foreign	3.8

Composition % 12-31-94

Cash	5.1	Preferreds	0.0
Stocks	54.6	Convertibles	0.0
Bonds	40.3	Other	0.0

Tax Analysis

	Tax-Adj Historical Return %	% Pretax Return
3 Yr Avg	7.51	77.1
5 Yr Avg	7.68	77.0
10 Yr Avg	---	---

Potential Capital Gain Exposure (% of assets) 2%

Most Similar Funds in MF500

Dodge & Cox Balanced	Fair Fit
Crabbe Huson Equity	Fair Fit
Putnam Fund for Grth & Inc A	Fair Fit

Bond Credit Analysis 12-31-94

% of Bonds

US Govt	91	BB	0
AAA	1	B	0
AA	5	Below B	0
A	1	NR/NA	0
BBB	3		

Stock Sector Weightings

	% of Stocks	Relative S&P 500
Utilities	7.5	0.60
Energy	8.4	0.83
Financials	12.6	1.19
Industrial Cyclicals	10.0	0.61
Consumer Durables	5.3	0.86
Consumer Staples	11.4	0.91
Services	19.6	2.40
Retail	3.8	0.66
Health	7.6	0.88
Technology	13.8	1.50

Min Initial Purchase / Fees

Min Initial Purchase	$2000 (Addt'l: $500)
Min IRA Purchase	$2000 (Addt'l: $500)
Min Auto Invest Plan	$2000 (Systematic Inv: $100)

Expenses & Fees

Sales Fees	0.00% front
	0.00% deferred
	0.25% 12b-1
Management Fee	1.00% max./0.60% min.
3-,5-,10-yr Expense Projections	$47, $83, $188
Annual Brokerage Cost	---

Crabbe Huson Equity

	Ticker	Load	NAV	Yield	SEC Yield	Assets	Objective
	CHEYX	None	15.69	0.9%	N/A	155.5	Growth

Crabbe Huson Equity Fund seeks long-term capital appreciation and the preservation of capital.

The fund invests at least 65% of its assets in a diversified portfolio of common stocks that are widely and actively traded. It employs a value approach, emphasizing income-statement and balance-sheet analysis and the relationship between the market price of a security and its underlying value. The fund may invest up to 35% of its assets in foreign securities.

Historical Profile
Return	High
Risk	Low
Rating	★★★★★
	Highest

Investment Style History
Equity

Average % Stocks Held in Portfolio

| | | | | | 75% | 80% | 74% | 73% |

Growth of $10,000

||||| Value of Fund ($000)
— Value of Index ($000)
SPMid400
▼ Manager Change
▽ Partial Manager Change
► Mgr Unknown After
◄ Mgr Unknown Before

Performance Quartile
(Within Objective)

Manager's Investment Style
Richard Huson leads a management team that searches both large- and small-cap markets for once-sucessful stocks that have been badly beaten down. Management then evaluates the stock's turnaround potential. This approach results in a small, but diverse, selection of issues for the portfolio, many of which boast low price multiples and sound earnings growth. The fund also tends raise large cash positions during times of market instability.

1983	1984	1985	1986	1987	1988	1989	1990	1991	1992	1993	1994	History
---	---	---	---	---	---	10.14	9.64	12.00	13.27	15.84	15.69	NAV
---	---	---	---	---	---	2.76 *	-1.54	35.12	16.43	26.00	1.60	Total Return %
---	---	---	---	---	---	-19.94 *	1.57	4.63	8.82	15.94	0.28	+/- S&P 500
---	---	---	---	---	---	---	4.64	0.91	7.46	14.71	1.67	+/- Wilshire 5000
---	---	---	---	---	---	0.16	3.39	1.21	1.18	0.47	0.94	Income Return %
---	---	---	---	---	---	2.60	-4.93	33.91	15.25	25.53	0.65	Capital Return %
---	---	---	---	---	---	---	60	19	8	11	11	Total Rtn % Rank All
---	---	---	---	---	---	---	31	47	13	5	20	Total Rtn % Rank Obj
---	---	---	---	---	---	0.02	0.34	0.13	0.15	0.07	0.15	Income $
---	---	---	---	---	---	0.12	0.00	0.83	0.55	0.79	0.25	Capital Gains $
---	---	---	---	---	---	1.69	1.93	1.84	1.55	1.49	1.49	Expense Ratio %
---	---	---	---	---	---	3.98	2.56	1.60	1.57	0.67	0.78	Income Ratio %
---	---	---	---	---	---	---	265	172	181	114	---	Turnover Rate %
---	---	---	---	---	---	4.8	3.1	7.1	15.8	41.3	155.5	Net Assets ($mil)

Fund Manager(s)
Richard S. Huson CFA(1972), since 01-89.
Stephen D. Laveson, since 01-90.
John E. Maack, Jr. CFA(1984), since 10-91.

Manager Experience	Dates Managed	Invest Obj	Std Dev	+/- Index
Richard S. Huson				
Crabbe Huson Asset Alloc	01/89 - 12/94	AA	7.14	-2.17
Stephen D. Laveson				
Crabbe Huson Asset Alloc	10/91 - 12/94	AA	6.58	2.13

Performance 12-31-94
	1st Qtr	2nd Qtr	3rd Qtr	4th Qtr	Total
1987	---	---	---	---	---
1988	---	---	---	---	---
1989	---	3.55	4.19	-6.16	2.76 *
1990	0.20	3.54	-14.92	11.55	-1.54
1991	18.98	1.31	5.68	6.07	35.12
1992	4.50	0.72	3.33	7.07	16.43
1993	7.69	4.06	3.30	8.85	26.00
1994	-0.69	-0.95	5.26	-1.87	1.60

Bear Market Performance
Decile Rank (5-year period)

Worst ▮ Best

	Worst 3 Mo Period 1985-89	Worst 3 Mo Period 1990-94
Crabbe Huson Equity	---	-17.09
+/- S&P 500	---	-3.25
+/- Best Fit Index : SPMid400	---	1.33

Trailing Returns
	Total Return %	+/- S&P 500	+/- Wil 5000	% Rank All	% Rank Obj	Growth of $10,000
3 Mo	-1.87	-1.86	-1.10	66	61	9,813
6 Mo	3.29	-1.57	-1.33	19	58	10,329
1 Yr	1.60	0.28	1.67	11	20	10,160
3 Yr Avg	14.23	7.96	7.61	5	4	14,904
5 Yr Avg	14.67	5.98	5.85	4	6	19,827
10 Yr Avg	---	---	---	---	---	---
15 Yr Avg	---	---	---	---	---	---

Operations
Address and Telephone	P.O. Box 6559
	Portland, OR 97228-6559
	800-541-9732 / 503-295-0919
Advisor	Crabbe Huson Group
Subadvisor	None
Distributor	Crabbe Huson Securities
States Available	All
Report Grade	B-
Income Distrib	Paid Annually
* Date of Inception	01-31-89
Fiscal Year End	October

Risk Analysis
Time Period	Load-Adj Return %	Risk % Rank [1] All	Obj	Morningstar [2] Return	Morningstar Risk	Morningstar Risk-Adj Rating
1 Yr	1.60					
3 Yr	14.23	41	3	3.40 [3]	0.48	★★★★★
5 Yr	14.67	58	8	2.79 [3]	0.67	★★★★★
10 Yr	---					

Average Historical Rating (36 months)   4.6 ★s

[1] 1 = low, 100 = high   [2] 1.00 = Equity Avg   [3] 1.00 = 90-day T-bill return

Other Measures
			Standard S&P 500	Best Fit SPMid400
Standard Deviation	8.03	Alpha	8.1	7.8
Mean	13.70	Beta	0.83	0.69
Sharpe Ratio	1.27	R-Squared	67	71

Investment Style
	Stock Portfolio Avg	Relative S&P 500
Price/Earnings Ratio	17.4	0.94
Price/Book Ratio	3.3	0.98
5 Yr Earnings Gr %	3.5#	0.63
Return on Assets %	5.2	0.69
Debt % Total Cap	32.3	1.14
Med Mkt Cap ($mil)	1772	0.14

figure is based on 50% or less of stocks

Style Value Blend Growth
Size Large Med Small

Diversification Value for Portfolio Types
Large Cap:	Small Cap:	Bond:	Balanced:	Diversified:
Low	Low	High	Low	Low

Expenses & Fees
Sales Fees	0.00% front
	0.00% deferred
	0.25% 12b-1
Management Fee	1.00% max./0.60% min.
3-,5-,10-yr Expense Projections	$48, $84, $192
Annual Brokerage Cost	---

Min Initial Purchase	$2000 (Addt'l: $500)
Min IRA Purchase	$2000 (Addt'l: $500)
Min Auto Invest Plan	$2000 (Systematic Inv: $100)

Portfolio 10-31-94
Share Chg (04-94) 000	Amount 000	Total Stocks: 46 Total Fixed-Income: 0	Value $000	% Net Assets
172	224	Equitable	4370	2.85
152	190	Consolidated Freightways	4240	2.77
191	191	USG	3748	2.45
212	212	Southern Pacific Rail	3687	2.41
56	56	Dun & Bradstreet	3277	2.14
148	223	ENSERCH	3175	2.07
53	166	HF Ahmanson	3171	2.07
27	58	CPC International	3092	2.02
59	59	Delta Air Lines	3068	2.00
21	138	Occidental Petroleum	3010	1.97
96	215	Zenith Electronics	3010	1.97
166	166	Portland General	2891	1.89
23	71	WR Grace	2817	1.84
100	151	The Limited	2778	1.81
85	85	Times Mirror Cl A	2776	1.81
14	37	IBM	2719	1.78
43	43	Exxon	2710	1.77
117	202	Mentor Graphics	2704	1.77
78	115	Ryder System	2703	1.77
24	62	Apple Computer	2695	1.76
91	128	Spieker Properties	2554	1.67
123	123	McCormick	2419	1.58
48	81	American Greetings Cl A	2228	1.46
66	66	Bausch & Lomb	2135	1.39
25	38	Telefonos de Mexico L (ADR)	2111	1.38

Composition % 12-31-94
Cash	20.2	Preferreds	0.0
Stocks	79.9	Convertibles	0.0
Bonds	0.0	Other	0.0

Tax Analysis
	Tax-Adj Historical Return %	% Pretax Return
3 Yr Avg	12.81	88.8
5 Yr Avg	13.07	86.3
10 Yr Avg	---	---
Potential Capital Gain Exposure (% of assets)		2%

Most Similar Funds in MF500
Fidelity Adv Growth Opport A	Strong Fit
Crabbe Huson Asset Alloc	Strong Fit
Gabelli Asset	Fair Fit

Index Allocation
	% of Stocks
S&P 500	61.8
S&P MidCap 400	13.7
U.S. Small Cap	20.6
Foreign	3.9

Sector Weightings
	% of Stocks	Relative S&P 500
Utilities	8.4	0.67
Energy	8.6	0.84
Financials	13.5	1.27
Industrial Cyclicals	10.4	0.63
Consumer Durables	6.5	1.05
Consumer Staples	10.8	0.86
Services	19.3	2.37
Retail	4.1	0.70
Health	6.6	0.76
Technology	12.0	1.31

MORNINGSTAR 1995 Mutual Fund 500

Crabbe Huson Special

Ticker	Load	NAV	Yield	SEC Yield	Assets	Objective
CHSPX	None	13.34	0.3%	N/A	377.5	Growth

Crabbe Huson Special Fund seeks long-term capital appreciation and preservation of purchasing power.

The fund invests in a diversified portfolio of carefully selected securities, principally common stocks, but also preferred stocks and bonds. It uses a basic value approach, emphasizing balance-sheet and cash-flow analysis, and the relationship between the market price of a security and its value as an ongoing business. It may invest no more than 35% of its assets in foreign securities.

Prior to Feb. 23, 1993, the fund was named Crabbe Huson Growth Fund.

Manager's Investment Style

Management takes a contrarian approach to very small-cap investing. It prefers well-managed, cash-rich firms carrying severely depressed market prices. It will take extremely concentrated positions in both sectors and stocks.

Fund Manager(s)

James E. Crabbe, since 01-90. Birthdate: 06-45. BS, U. of Oregon 1967

Manager Experience

	Dates Managed	Invest Obj	Std Dev	+/- Index
Not available.				

Historical Profile
Return	High
Risk	Average
Rating	★★★★★ Highest

Investment Style History Equity

Average % Stocks Held in Portfolio: 82% 93% 92% 64%

Growth of $10,000

|||| Value of Fund ($000)
— Value of Index ($000) Russ 2000
▼ Manager Change
▽ Partial Manager Change
► Mgr Unknown After
◄ Mgr Unknown Before

Performance Quartile (Within Objective)

	1983	1984	1985	1986	1987	1988	1989	1990	1991	1992	1993	1994	History
	---	---	---	---	8.26	9.87	9.92	9.45	7.10	9.47	12.40	13.34	NAV
	---	---	---	---	-16.90 *	19.49	14.66	3.78	17.00	33.38	34.55	11.72	Total Return %
	---	---	---	---	-3.29 *	2.88	-17.02	6.90	-13.49	25.76	24.50	10.40	+/- S&P 500
	---	---	---	---	1.55	-14.51	9.97	-17.21	24.41	23.27	11.79	+/- Wilshire 5000
	---	---	---	---	0.00	0.00	0.00	1.66	0.71	0.00	0.00	0.31	Income Return %
	---	---	---	---	-16.90	19.49	14.66	2.13	16.29	33.38	34.55	11.41	Capital Return %
	---	---	---	---		15	48	47	51	1	6	2	Total Rtn % Rank All
	---	---	---	---		28	93	8	97	1	1	2	Total Rtn % Rank Obj
	---	---	---	---	0.00	0.00	0.00	0.16	0.05	0.00	0.00	0.04	Income $
	---	---	---	---	0.00	0.00	1.40	0.68	3.74	0.00	0.33	0.45	Capital Gains $
	---	---	---	---		3.94	2.00	2.00	1.92	1.74	1.57	1.48	Expense Ratio %
	---	---	---	---		3.34	1.96	1.55	0.32	-0.25	-0.73	-0.40	Income Ratio %
	---	---	---	---		155	276	315	257	102	73	---	Turnover Rate %
	---	---	---	---	1.9	4.4	3.5	3.2	3.1	7.2	29.0	377.5	Net Assets ($mil)

Performance 12-31-94

	1st Qtr	2nd Qtr	3rd Qtr	4th Qtr	Total
1987	---	---	1.39	-19.26	-16.90 *
1988	11.86	4.00	-1.46	4.22	19.49
1989	4.76	7.35	7.57	-5.22	14.66
1990	0.30	6.53	-13.40	12.15	3.78
1991	19.79	-1.41	5.65	-6.22	17.00
1992	19.30	-7.32	3.95	16.05	33.38
1993	11.62	1.32	4.76	13.57	34.55
1994	3.06	-0.78	8.83	0.38	11.72

Bear Market Performance

Decile Rank (5-year period)

Worst ▬ Best

	Worst 3 Mo Period 1985-89	Worst 3 Mo Period 1990-94
Crabbe Huson Special	---	-15.74
+/- S&P 500	---	-1.90
+/- Best Fit Index : Russ 2000	---	10.16

Trailing Returns

	Total Return %	+/- S&P 500	+/- Wil 5000	% Rank All	% Rank Obj	Growth of $10,000
3 Mo	0.38	0.40	1.15	13	16	10,038
6 Mo	9.25	4.39	4.63	5	10	10,925
1 Yr	11.72	10.40	11.79	2	2	11,172
3 Yr Avg	26.10	19.83	19.48	1	1	20,049
5 Yr Avg	19.48	10.78	10.66	1	1	24,345
10 Yr Avg	---	---	---	---	---	---
15 Yr Avg	---	---	---	---	---	---

Operations

Address and Telephone	P.O. Box 6559 Portland, OR 97228-6559 800-541-9732 / 503-295-0919	Min Initial Purchase	$2000 (Addt'l: $500)
		Min IRA Purchase	$2000 (Addt'l: $500)
		Min Auto Invest Plan	$2000 (Systematic Inv: $100)
Advisor	Crabbe Huson Group	**Expenses & Fees**	
Subadvisor	None	Sales Fees	0.00% front
Distributor	Crabbe Huson Securities		0.00% deferred
States Available	All		0.25% 12b-1
Report Grade	B-	Management Fee	1.00% max./0.60% min.
Income Distrib	Paid Annually	3-,5-,10-yr Expense Projections	$51, $89, $202
* Date of Inception	04-09-87	Annual Brokerage Cost	---
Fiscal Year End	October		

Risk Analysis

Time Period	Load-Adj Return %	Risk % Rank [1] All	Risk % Rank [1] Obj	Morningstar [2] Return	Morningstar [2] Risk	Morningstar Risk-Adj Rating
1 Yr	11.72					
3 Yr	26.10	83	67	8.02 [3]	1.03	★★★★★
5 Yr	19.48	84	76	4.53 [3]	1.03	★★★★★
10 Yr	---	---	---	---	---	---
Average Historical Rating (57 months)				4.1 ★s		

[1] 1 = low, 100 = high   [2] 1.00 = Equity Avg   [3] 1.00 = 90-day T-bill return

Other Measures

			Standard S&P 500	Best Fit Russ 2000
Standard Deviation	18.03	Alpha	20.1	12.0
Mean	24.97	Beta	1.04	1.26
Sharpe Ratio	1.19	R-Squared	21	68

Investment Style

	Stock Portfolio Avg	Relative S&P 500
Price/Earnings Ratio	18.0	0.97
Price/Book Ratio	2.0	0.58
5 Yr Earnings Gr %	18.9#	3.41
Return on Assets %	7.8	1.04
Debt % Total Cap	24.6#	0.87
Med Mkt Cap ($mil)	416	0.03

figure is based on 50% or less of stocks

Style Value Blend Growth / Size Large Med Small

Diversification Value for Portfolio Types

Large Cap: High	Small Cap: Low	Bond: High	Balanced: High	Diversified: High

Portfolio 10-31-94

Share Chg (04-94) 000	Amount 000	Total Stocks: 47 Total Fixed-Income: 1	Value $000	% Net Assets
1618	2188	Rollins Environmental Svcs	12853	4.02
822	945	VLSI Technology	12280	3.84
566	566	Cray Research	10827	3.39
533	533	Airborne Freight	10192	3.19
687	687	Snapple Beverage	9617	3.01
613	716	Mentor Graphics	9581	3.00
573	573	Giddings & Lewis	8885	2.78
201	201	Apple Computer	8698	2.72
286	582	Zenith Electronics	8151	2.55
840	840	Payless Cashways	7872	2.46
777	777	MK Rail	7576	2.37
753	753	Cato Cl A	7060	2.21
277	407	Sofamor/Danek Group	6814	2.13
145	145	BMC Software	6539	2.04
370	370	Prime Residential	5874	1.84
158	158	Parametric Technology	5702	1.78
412	823	Catellus Development	5449	1.70
86	200	US Bancorp (OR)	4945	1.55
276	276	Oregon Steel Mills	4725	1.48
352	352	Burlington Coat Factory Whse	4577	1.43
200	200	Landmark Graphics	4100	1.28
89	164	American Prem Underwriters	4095	1.28
27	225	Lattice Semiconductor	3788	1.18
297	297	20th Century Industries	3605	1.13
288	677	Olympic Financial	3385	1.06

Composition % 12-31-94

Cash	30.2	Preferreds	0.0
Stocks	69.4	Convertibles	0.4
Bonds	0.0	Other	0.0

Tax Analysis

	Tax-Adj Historical Return %	% Pretax Return
3 Yr Avg	25.36	96.5
5 Yr Avg	16.04	77.0
10 Yr Avg	---	---
Potential Capital Gain Exposure (% of assets)		3%

Most Similar Funds in MF500

FPA Capital	Weak Fit
Babson Enterprise	Weak Fit
Vanguard Convertible Secs	Weak Fit

Index Allocation

	% of Stocks
S&P 500	28.8
S&P MidCap 400	21.4
U.S. Small Cap	49.6
Foreign	0.2

Sector Weightings

	% of Stocks	Relative S&P 500
Utilities	0.6	0.05
Energy	0.0	0.00
Financials	12.7	1.20
Industrial Cyclicals	12.2	0.75
Consumer Durables	8.2	1.32
Consumer Staples	4.8	0.38
Services	12.9	1.58
Retail	7.5	1.29
Health	3.4	0.39
Technology	37.7	4.12

Dean Witter Dividend Growth

	Ticker	Load	NAV	Yield	SEC Yield	Assets	Objective
	DWDVX	5.00%d	29.23	2.3%	N/A	6696.0	Growth/Inc.

Dean Witter Dividend Growth Securities seeks current income and long-term growth of income and capital.

The fund invests primarily in common stocks of companies that have a record of paying dividends and a potential for increasing dividends. It avoids speculative securities. Management uses a risk screen, a dividend-growth model, and a five-year dividend-growth screen in conjunction with fundamental research to select stocks.

Historical Profile

Return	Average	
Risk	Below Average	
Rating	★★★★ Above Average	

Investment Style History
Equity

Average % Stocks Held in Portfolio

70%	80%	84%	87%	---	83%	84%	86%

Growth of $10,000

- ‖‖‖ Value of Fund ($000)
- — Value of Index ($000) S&P 500
- ▼ Manager Change
- ▽ Partial Manager Change
- ► Mgr Unknown After
- ◄ Mgr Unknown Before

Performance Quartile (Within Objective)

1983	1984	1985	1986	1987	1988	1989	1990	1991	1992	1993	1994	History
12.50	12.93	16.35	18.48	17.41	19.24	23.74	21.24	26.84	27.65	30.87	29.23	NAV
20.27	8.47	31.93	19.26	-0.66	18.82	31.50	-7.17	30.64	5.81	14.20	-3.18	Total Return %
-2.19	2.20	0.19	0.58	-5.92	2.21	-0.19	-4.05	0.15	-1.81	4.14	-4.49	+/- S&P 500
-3.19	5.42	-0.63	3.16	-3.02	0.88	2.32	-0.99	-3.57	-3.16	2.92	-3.11	+/- Wilshire 5000
4.95	4.82	3.89	3.08	3.71	3.47	3.88	3.36	3.83	2.64	2.55	2.14	Income Return %
15.32	3.65	28.04	16.18	-4.36	15.35	27.62	-10.53	26.80	3.17	11.65	-5.31	Capital Return %
38	35	19	24	65	17	11	78	25	71	32	45	Total Rtn % Rank All
56	23	21	31	75	28	11	75	32	72	27	73	Total Rtn % Rank Obj
0.52	0.56	0.47	0.52	0.73	0.62	0.76	0.80	0.76	0.69	0.68	0.66	Income $
0.07	0.02	0.15	0.48	0.30	0.08	0.64	0.00	0.07	0.04	0.00	0.00	Capital Gains $
1.38	1.17	1.24	1.55	1.52	1.55	1.55	1.41	1.51	1.42	1.40	1.37	Expense Ratio %
5.65	5.08	6.20	4.73	3.35	3.47	3.44	3.46	3.62	2.91	2.67	2.31	Income Ratio %
7	3	10	6	12	7	8	3	5	5	8	13	Turnover Rate %
23.7	40.5	284.1	1261.9	1700.0	1731.0	2780.7	2785.9	3500.0	5035.8	6549.6	6696.0	Net Assets ($mil)

Manager's Investment Style

Management takes a long-term approach to investing, and the fund has a correspondingly low turnover. Manager Paul Vance buys firms that pass four quantitative screens relating to earnings growth, dividend growth, and risk, and establishes price targets at which he will sell a stock.

Fund Manager(s)

Paul Vance CFA, since 03-81.

Manager Experience

	Dates Managed	Invest Obj	Std Dev	+/- Index
Paul Vance				
Dean Witter Capital Grth	04/90 - 12/94	G	13.96	-3.64
Dean Witter Glob Div Gr	06/93 - 12/94	WW	11.99	4.56

Performance 12-31-94

	1st Qtr	2nd Qtr	3rd Qtr	4th Qtr	Total
1987	13.05	3.08	3.41	-17.56	-0.66
1988	8.09	4.78	0.83	4.04	18.82
1989	8.97	8.46	8.95	2.12	31.50
1990	-3.78	3.09	-14.79	9.83	-7.17
1991	12.30	1.89	5.79	7.93	30.64
1992	-0.71	1.17	2.78	2.49	5.81
1993	5.68	2.86	2.49	2.51	14.20
1994	-4.81	0.30	3.49	-2.01	-3.18

Bear Market Performance

Decile Rank (5-year period)

Worst ———————————————— Best

	Worst 3 Mo Period 1985-89	Worst 3 Mo Period 1990-94
Dean Witter Dividend Growth	-23.31	-14.79
+/- S&P 500	6.27	-1.04
+/- Best Fit Index : S&P 500	6.27	-1.04

Trailing Returns

	Total Return %	+/- S&P 500	+/- Wil 5000	% Rank All	% Rank Obj	Growth of $10,000
3 Mo	-2.01	-2.00	-1.24	69	64	9,799
6 Mo	1.41	-3.45	-3.21	32	69	10,141
1 Yr	-3.18	-4.49	-3.11	45	73	9,682
3 Yr Avg	5.37	-0.89	-1.24	41	60	11,699
5 Yr Avg	7.25	-1.45	-1.57	44	68	14,188
10 Yr Avg	13.23	-1.15	-0.63	25	30	34,647
15 Yr Avg	---	---	---	---	---	---

Operations

Address and Telephone	Two World Trade Center 72nd Fl New York, NY 10048 800-869-3863 / 212-392-2550
Advisor	Dean Witter InterCapital
Subadvisor	None
Distributor	Dean Witter Distributors
States Available	All
Report Grade	C+
Income Distrib	Paid Quarterly
Date of Inception	03-30-81
Fiscal Year End	February

Risk Analysis

Time Period	Load-Adj Return %	Risk % Rank[1] All	Obj	Morningstar[2] Return	Morningstar Risk	Morningstar Risk-Adj Rating
1 Yr	-6.96					
3 Yr	4.77	59	24	0.35[3]	0.64	★★★
5 Yr	7.09	62	35	0.58[3]	0.75	★★★
10 Yr	13.23	51	31	1.11	0.74	★★★★
Average Historical Rating (109 months)					4.2	★s

[1] = low, 100 = high   [2] 1.00 = Equity Avg   [3] 1.00 = 90-day T-bill return

Other Measures

			Standard S&P 500	Best Fit S&P 500
Standard Deviation	7.15	Alpha	-0.5	-0.5
Mean	5.50	Beta	0.85	0.85
Sharpe Ratio	0.28	R-Squared	88	88

Investment Style

	Stock Portfolio Avg	Relative S&P 500
Price/Earnings Ratio	16.2	0.87
Price/Book Ratio	3.2	0.95
5 Yr Earnings Gr %	1.3	0.24
Return on Assets %	6.6	0.89
Debt % Total Cap	32.0	1.13
Med Mkt Cap ($mil)	10699	0.82

Style: Value Blend Growth / Large Med Small (Size)

Diversification Value for Portfolio Types

Large Cap: None	Small Cap: Medium	Bond: Medium	Balanced: None	Diversified: Low

Portfolio 12-31-94

Share Chg (08-94) 000	Amount 000	Total Stocks: 72 Total Fixed-Income: 8	Value $000	% Net Assets
	250000	US Treasury Bond 6.25%	203008	3.03
-25	1775	IBM	130463	1.95
-100	1550	Gillette	115863	1.73
0	1335	ALCOA	115644	1.73
-50	2200	Coca-Cola	113300	1.69
-25	1825	Procter & Gamble	113150	1.69
0	1500	Schering-Plough	111000	1.66
-100	3980	Sprint	109948	1.64
0	1950	El duPont de Nemours	109688	1.64
0	1300	Mobil	109525	1.64
0	3300	Abbott Laboratories	107663	1.61
0	975	Royal Dutch Petroleum	104813	1.57
-50	1550	Dow Chemical	104238	1.56
0	2175	Eastman Kodak	103856	1.55
0	3700	Ford Motor	103600	1.55
0	1750	Amoco	103469	1.55
0	1675	Exxon	101756	1.52
0	1000	Atlantic Richfield	101750	1.52
-50	1025	Xerox	101475	1.52
0	1600	American Home Products	100400	1.50
0	1875	Minnesota Mining & Mfg	100078	1.49
-20	1405	Monsanto	99053	1.48
0	1550	United Technologies	97456	1.46
0	1675	Bristol-Myers Squibb	96941	1.45
0	1900	General Electric	96900	1.45

Composition % 12-31-94

Cash	2.2	Preferreds	0.0
Stocks	85.3	Convertibles	0.0
Bonds	12.5	Other	0.0

Tax Analysis

	Tax-Adj Historical Return %	% Pretax Return
3 Yr Avg	4.48	82.6
5 Yr Avg	6.24	84.4
10 Yr Avg	11.61	81.1
Potential Capital Gain Exposure (% of assets)		20%

Most Similar Funds in MF500

Smith Barney Inc & Grth A	Strong Fit
Vanguard Index 500	Strong Fit
Investment Comp of America	Strong Fit

Min Initial Purchase / IRA / Auto

Min Initial Purchase	$1000 (Addt'l: $100)
Min IRA Purchase	$1000 (Addt'l: $100)
Min Auto Invest Plan	$1000 (Systematic Inv: $100)

Expenses & Fees

Sales Fees	0.00% front
	5.00% deferred
	1.00% 12b-1
Management Fee	0.63% max./0.33% min.
3-,5-,10-yr Expense Projections	$74, $97, $168
Annual Brokerage Cost	0.03%

Index Allocation

	% of Stocks
S&P 500	97.4
S&P MidCap 400	0.8
U.S. Small Cap	0.1
Foreign	4.5

Sector Weightings

	% of Stocks	Relative S&P 500
Utilities	12.3	1.00
Energy	12.2	1.20
Financials	8.3	0.78
Industrial Cyclicals	28.2	1.72
Consumer Durables	5.6	0.90
Consumer Staples	7.7	0.62
Services	4.2	0.51
Retail	2.4	0.41
Health	12.0	1.38
Technology	7.3	0.79

MORNINGSTAR 1995 Mutual Fund 500

Delaware Delchester A

	Ticker	Load	NAV	Yield	SEC Yield	Assets	Objective
	DETWX	4.75%	6.05	12.1%	10.90%	948.1	Corp Hi Yld

Delaware Delchester Fund - Class A seeks high current income.
The fund normally invests at least 80% of its assets in corporate bonds rated BBB or lower, government securities, or commercial paper. It invests any remaining assets in income-producing securities.

Retail shares have front loads and 12b-1 fees; Institutional shares are offered to institutional investors. Prior to June 1, 1992, the fund was named Delaware Group Delchester High-Yield Bond Fund Delchester II. Before June 15, 1988, it was named Delchester Bond Fund Delchester II. On June 1, 1992, Delaware Group Delchester High-Yield Bond Fund Delchester I merged into this fund.

Manager's Investment Style

This fund's management duo maintains a core portfolio of standard high-yield fare, usually bonds with B ratings, then seeks to add value by making modest sector plays in lower-rated debt. Management also diversifies assets across issues and sectors, and keeps the fund's maturity below average.

Fund Manager(s)

Paul A. Matlack, since 12-90. BA, U. of Pennsylvania MBA, George Washington U.
Gerald T. Nichols, since 12-90. BS, U. of Kansas MS, U. of Kansas

Manager Experience

	Dates Managed	Invest Obj	Std Dev	+/- Index
Paul A. Matlack				
Delaware Group Div	03/93 - 12/94	I	6.51	0.17

Historical Profile

Return	Above Average
Risk	Low
Rating	★★★★ Above Average

	45	70	61	59	38	26	12	2

Investment Style History
Fixed Income
Income Rtn % Rank Obj

Growth of $10,000
IIII Value of Fund ($000)
— Value of Index ($000) LB Agg
▼ Manager Change
▽ Partial Manager Change
► Mgr Unknown After
◄ Mgr Unknown Before

Performance Quartile (Within Objective)

	1983	1984	1985	1986	1987	1988	1989	1990	1991	1992	1993	1994	History
NAV	7.77	7.37	7.83	8.05	7.51	7.59	6.76	5.14	6.48	6.78	7.09	6.05	NAV
	12.60	8.34	23.19	16.22	4.67	13.19	0.75	-12.24	43.45	17.19	16.50	-4.57	Total Return %
	4.22	-6.81	1.06	0.97	1.91	5.31	-13.80	-21.18	27.45	9.95	6.75	-1.65	+/- LB Aggregate
	---	---	---	0.58	-1.86	1.76	0.36	-5.86	-0.30	0.53	-2.40	-3.60	+/- FB High-Yield
	12.34	13.49	16.95	13.41	11.38	12.13	11.68	11.73	17.38	12.56	11.93	10.10	Income Return %
	0.26	-5.15	6.24	2.81	-6.71	1.07	-10.94	-23.96	26.07	4.63	4.57	-14.67	Capital Return %
	68	36	54	47	24	36	98	88	11	7	24	59	Total Rtn % Rank All
	83	57	29	17	13	48	42	61	23	48	87	69	Total Rtn % Rank Obj
	0.92	0.98	1.13	0.99	0.91	0.88	0.91	0.85	0.79	0.77	0.76	0.73	Income $
	0.00	0.00	0.00	0.00	0.00	0.00	0.00	0.00	0.00	0.00	0.00	0.00	Capital Gains $
	1.23	1.23	1.26	1.14	1.23	1.17	1.15	1.15	1.20	1.08	1.04	1.05	Expense Ratio %
	11.90	13.02	13.45	12.37	11.29	11.88	12.00	13.17	14.15	11.58	11.17	10.48	Income Ratio %
	131	117	104	137	149	139	66	72	38	101	72	92	Turnover Rate %
	39.9	39.7	58.7	128.0	16.0	75.1	85.1	77.6	130.5	802.9	1006.8	948.1	Net Assets ($mil)

Performance 12-31-94

	1st Qtr	2nd Qtr	3rd Qtr	4th Qtr	Total
1987	7.45	-1.68	-2.51	1.63	4.67
1988	6.41	2.39	1.90	1.95	13.19
1989	1.82	3.64	-1.01	-3.55	0.75
1990	-4.44	3.91	-8.25	-3.67	-12.24
1991	18.33	8.19	6.20	5.52	43.45
1992	7.36	4.06	3.78	1.08	17.19
1993	6.07	3.82	1.30	4.43	16.50
1994	-0.58	-1.09	-2.44	-0.54	-4.57

Bear Market Performance

Decile Rank (5-year period)

Worst | Best

	Worst 3 Mo Period 1985-89	Worst 3 Mo Period 1990-94
Delaware Delchester A	-5.21	-14.59
+/- LB Aggregate	-6.02	-15.33
+/- Best Fit Index : FB HY	---	-0.48

Trailing Returns

	Total Return %	+/- LB Aggregate	+/- FB High-Yield	% Rank All	% Rank Obj	Growth of $10,000
3 Mo	-0.54	-0.91	-0.49	35	27	9,947
6 Mo	-2.96	-3.95	-4.52	94	74	9,704
1 Yr	-4.57	-1.65	-3.60	59	69	9,543
3 Yr Avg	9.22	4.67	-1.94	16	77	13,029
5 Yr Avg	10.40	2.78	-2.67	15	47	16,403
10 Yr Avg	10.86	0.91	---	49	29	28,029
15 Yr Avg	10.92	0.12	---	67	54	47,359

Operations

Address and Telephone	1818 Market Street
	Philadelphia, PA 19103-3682
	800-523-4640 / 215-988-1333
Advisor	Delaware Management
Subadvisor	None
Distributor	Delaware Distributors
States Available	All plus PR
Report Grade	B+
Income Distrib	Paid Monthly
Date of Inception	08-20-70
Fiscal Year End	July

Min Initial Purchase	$250 (Addt'l: $25)
Min IRA Purchase	$250 (Addt'l: $25)
Min Auto Invest Plan	$250 (Systematic Inv: $25)

Expenses & Fees

Sales Fees	4.75% front
	0.00% deferred
	0.30% 12b-1
Management Fee	0.60% max./0.55% min.
3-,5-,10-yr Expense Projections	$79, $103, $170

Risk Analysis

Time Period	Load-Adj Return %	Risk % Rank All	Risk % Rank Obj	Morningstar Return	Morningstar Risk	Morningstar Risk-Adj Rating
1 Yr	-9.11					
3 Yr	7.46	10	59	1.16 [3]	0.39	★★★★
5 Yr	9.33	46	56	1.17 [3]	0.58	★★★★
10 Yr	10.32	33	48	0.72	0.46	★★★★
Average Historical Rating (109 months)					3.4 ★s	

[1] 1 = low, 100 = high   [2] 1.00 = Hybrid Avg   [3] 1.00 = 90-day T-bill return

Other Measures

			Standard LB Agg	Best Fit FB HY
Standard Deviation	4.59	Alpha	5.0	-1.6
Mean	8.96	Beta	0.56	0.98
Sharpe Ratio	1.18	R-Squared	24	84

Investment Style

Interest-Rate Stance

Avg Effective Duration	4.2 Yrs
Avg Effective Maturity	7.3 Yrs

Quality

Avg Credit Quality	BB
Avg Weighted Coupon	11.30%
Avg Weighted Price	93.43% of Par

Maturity Short Intm Long
Quality High Med Low

Diversification Value for Portfolio Types

Large Cap: High	Small Cap: High	Bond: High	Balanced: High	Diversified: High

Portfolio 07-31-94

Total Stocks: 3
Total Fixed-Income: 109

Amount 000	Date of Maturity		Value $000	% Net Assets
51032	08-15-95	US Treasury Note 10.5%	53679	5.48
27523	05-01-03	Kloster Cruise 13%	28624	2.92
27620	06-30-03	American Standard 14.25%	28449	2.91
11979	11-26-05	American Medical Intl 15%	21142	2.16
31181	10-01-98	G-I Holdings 0%	18630	1.90
16825	05-01-02	MGM Grand Hotel Finance 12%	18423	1.88
23020	06-15-01	Trump Plaza Funding 10.875%	18301	1.87
16368	12-31-03	American Standard 12.75%	16531	1.69
13533	11-01-02	Bankers Life Holding 13%	16003	1.63
14950	12-15-00	Stone Savannah River 14.125%	15922	1.63
18425	01-15-03	Bally's Health & Tennis 13%	15385	1.57
13670	11-01-00	Anacomp 15%	15311	1.56
28826	1999	New World Holdings 0%	15206	1.55
13716	12-01-01	Container of America 14%	15019	1.53
17145	08-01-01	K & F Industries 13.75%	14916	1.52
16413	08-15-03	Specialty Foods 11.75%	14526	1.48
14630	05-15-02	Adelphia Communications 12.5%	14521	1.48
12609	1997	Unisys 13.5%	13948	1.42
13350	10-15-03	NL Industries 11.75%	13851	1.42
13716	03-01-01	Stater Brothers 11%	13510	1.38
12344	10-01-97	Acadia Partners 13%	12745	1.30
9144	05-01-20	Auburn Hills Trust 15.375%	12640	1.29
15682	12-15-02	Silgan Holdings 13%	12193	1.25
11266	04-15-00	Georgia Gulf 15%	11956	1.22
10927	02-01-00	Sullivan Graphics 15%	11419	1.17

Composition % 12-31-94

Cash	2.1	Preferreds	0.0
Stocks	1.4	Convertibles	0.0
Bonds	96.5	Other	0.0

Tax Analysis

	Tax-Adj Historical Return %	% Pretax Return
3 Yr Avg	4.90	51.0
5 Yr Avg	5.89	51.8
10 Yr Avg	5.86	42.6
Potential Capital Gain Exposure (% of assets)		-24%

Most Similar Funds in MF500

Putnam High Yield Adv A	Strong Fit
Liberty High-Income Bond A	Strong Fit
AIM High-Yield A	Strong Fit

Coupon Range

	% of Bonds	Rel Obj
0%, PIK	8.6	1.16
0% to 11%	21.7	0.44
11% to 13%	42.7	1.28
13% to 14.5%	16.9	3.09
More than 14.5%	8.1	5.02
Not applicable	2.0	0.67

Credit Analysis 12-31-94

% of Bonds

US Govt	0	BB	18
AAA	8	B	67
AA	0	Below B	1
A	0	NR/NA	4
BBB	1		

Delaware A

	Ticker	Load	NAV	Yield	SEC Yield	Assets	Objective
	DELFX	5.75%	17.23	3.6%	N/A	442.2	Balanced

Delaware Fund - Class A seeks capital appreciation and income consistent with capital preservation.

The fund invests primarily in equities issued by established companies. It normally invests at least 25% of its assets in investment-grade fixed-income securities, including U.S. government obligations, various convertible securities, and corporate debt. This portion of the portfolio maintains an average maturity that ranges from five to 30 years. The fund may also invest in money-market instruments.

Class A shares have front loads; Class B shares have deferred loads, higher 12b-1 fees, and conversion features; Institutional shares are offered to institutional investors.

Manager's Investment Style

Management attempts to maintain a fairly consistent 60% to 40% ratio of stocks to bonds, and emphasizes yield. George Burwell manages the fund's equity portion, and seeks firms with a strong dividend history or with the potential for consistent future dividend growth. Dorothea Dutton, who manages the fund's bond section, typically seeks high-quality, intermediate-term bonds.

Fund Manager(s)

George H. Burwell CFA(1988), since 03-92.
Birthdate: 10-61. BA, U. of Virginia 1983
Dorothea M. Dutton CFA, since 1988. Birthdate: 09-46. U. of Washington 1969

Manager Experience	Dates Managed	Invest Obj	Std Dev	+/- Index
Dorothea M. Dutton				
Delaware U.S. Govt A	10/86 - 01/93	GG	3.85	-0.88
Delaware Treas Res Int A	01/86 - 01/90	GG	1.56	-2.73

Historical Profile
Return	Average
Risk	Average
Rating	★★★
	Neutral

Stocks held: 88% 73% 59% 51% 63% 61% 60% 60%

Investment Style History
Equity
Average % Stocks Held in Portfolio

Growth of $10,000
- |||| Value of Fund ($000)
- — Value of Index ($000) SPMid400
- ▼ Manager Change
- ▽ Partial Manager Change
- ► Mgr Unknown After
- ◄ Mgr Unknown Before

Performance Quartile (Within Objective)

1983	1984	1985	1986	1987	1988	1989	1990	1991	1992	1993	1994	History
19.47	18.07	20.78	18.34	12.84	14.81	17.74	16.48	17.64	18.41	18.36	17.23	NAV
14.63	2.48	31.55	11.04	-6.17	21.02	25.55	-0.47	20.84	12.68	9.39	-1.35	Total Return %
-7.83	-3.78	-0.19	-7.64	-11.43	4.41	-6.13	2.64	-9.64	5.06	-0.67	-2.67	+/- S&P 500
6.26	-12.67	9.42	-4.21	-8.93	13.14	11.01	-9.42	5.43	5.43	-0.36	1.57	+/- LB Aggregate
4.42	4.56	3.77	2.53	1.75	5.67	5.77	5.07	4.11	3.80	3.25	3.49	Income Return %
10.21	-2.07	27.78	8.51	-7.92	15.34	19.78	-5.54	16.74	8.87	6.14	-4.84	Capital Return %
60	58	21	79	91	12	22	57	44	14	71	29	Total Rtn % Rank All
57	78	21	84	88	1	6	52	76	8	68	28	Total Rtn % Rank Obj
0.91	0.80	0.70	0.55	0.32	0.71	0.81	0.88	0.70	0.66	0.60	0.63	Income $
2.83	1.01	2.00	4.31	4.09	0.00	0.00	0.29	1.54	0.77	1.16	0.25	Capital Gains $
0.73	0.76	0.75	0.69	0.73	0.77	0.76	0.75	0.71	0.79	0.89	0.94	Expense Ratio %
3.93	4.64	3.71	2.53	1.64	4.01	4.73	4.99	4.29	3.64	3.27	3.25	Income Ratio %
78	75	132	104	205	180	129	147	212	144	160	---	Turnover Rate %
307.2	304.4	341.3	370.5	311.9	306.2	384.5	370.8	458.4	483.5	489.7	442.2	Net Assets ($mil)

Performance 12-31-94

	1st Qtr	2nd Qtr	3rd Qtr	4th Qtr	Total
1987	21.10	1.18	5.25	-27.25	-6.17
1988	6.22	7.09	3.61	2.68	21.02
1989	5.74	8.99	7.47	1.37	25.55
1990	-2.99	7.27	-9.11	5.23	-0.47
1991	9.95	-0.91	5.44	5.20	20.84
1992	2.44	0.84	4.07	4.81	12.68
1993	4.56	0.05	3.11	1.41	9.39
1994	-2.07	-0.11	2.21	-1.33	-1.35

Bear Market Performance

Decile Rank (5-year period)

Worst ———————————— Best

	Worst 3 Mo Period 1985-89	Worst 3 Mo Period 1990-94
Delaware A	-34.30	-9.11
+/- S&P 500	-4.72	4.63
+/- Best Fit Index : SPMid400	-5.50	8.67

Trailing Returns

	Total Return %	+/- S&P 500	+/- LB Aggregate	% Rank All	% Rank Obj	Growth of $10,000
3 Mo	-1.33	-1.32	-1.71	52	63	9,867
6 Mo	0.85	-4.02	-0.15	40	70	10,085
1 Yr	-1.35	-2.67	1.57	29	28	9,865
3 Yr Avg	6.73	0.47	2.19	28	30	12,159
5 Yr Avg	7.90	-0.79	0.27	35	53	14,623
10 Yr Avg	11.78	-2.60	1.83	40	46	30,451
15 Yr Avg	13.85	-0.64	3.04	26	12	69,951

Operations

Address and Telephone	1818 Market Street
	Philadelphia, PA 19103-3682
	800-523-4640 / 215-988-1333
Advisor	Delaware Management
Subadvisor	None
Distributor	Delaware Distributors
States Available	All plus PR
Report Grade	B-
Income Distrib	Paid Quarterly
Date of Inception	04-25-38
Fiscal Year End	October

Risk Analysis

Time Period	Load-Adj Return %	Risk % Rank All	Risk % Rank Obj	Morningstar[2] Return	Morningstar[2] Risk	Morningstar Risk-Adj Rating
1 Yr	-7.02					
3 Yr	4.65	43	31	0.31[3]	0.66	★★★
5 Yr	6.63	54	59	0.46[3]	0.79	★★★
10 Yr	11.12	53	82	0.81[3]	0.95	★★★
Average Historical Rating (109 months)					3.1	★s

[1] 1 = low, 100 = high   [2] 1.00 = Hybrid Avg   [3] 1.00 = 90-day T-bill return

Other Measures

		Standard S&P 500	Best Fit SPMid400
Standard Deviation	5.99	Alpha	1.4	1.1
Mean	6.71	Beta	0.64	0.54
Sharpe Ratio	0.53	R-Squared	70	80

Investment Style

Stocks	Port Avg	Rel S&P 500	Style
Price/Earnings Ratio	15.8	0.86	V B G
Price/Book Ratio	2.9	0.84	
5 Yr Earnings Gr %	12.6	2.27	
Med Mkt Cap ($mil)	2343	0.18	

Bonds		Maturity S I L
Avg Effective Duration	4.2 Yrs **	
Avg Effective Maturity	4.5 Yrs	
Avg Credit Quality	AA	
Avg Weighted Coupon	6.63%	
**figure provided by fund		

Diversification Value for Portfolio Types

Large Cap: Low	Small Cap: Low	Bond: High	Balanced: Low	Diversified: Low

Portfolio 05-31-94

Share Chg (04-94)000	Amount 000	Total Stocks: 79 / Total Fixed-Income: 77	Date of Maturity	Value $000	% Net Assets
-1	567	MBNA		14963	3.19
71	189	Procter & Gamble		10659	2.27
0	124	FNMA		10352	2.21
18	268	Singer		9295	1.98
22	120	CSX		9212	1.96
	9111	US Treasury Note 5.625%	01-31-98	8843	1.88
	6159	Banco Nacional de Mex Cv 7%	12-15-99	7144	1.52
	6866	US Treasury Note 6.875%	04-30-97	6963	1.48
0	175	Nationwide Health Properties		6935	1.48
0	213	Health Care REIT		6612	1.41
0	200	Supervalu		6399	1.36
0	219	Unocal		6042	1.29
60	120	General Electric		5976	1.27
	6117	US Treasury Note 4.375%	08-15-96	5907	1.26
	6088	GNMA 6.5%	10-15-08	5775	1.23
0	192	First Security (UT)		5674	1.21
0	183	Developers Diversified Rlty		5527	1.18
151	229	Reynolds & Reynolds Cl A		5212	1.11
22	130	May Department Stores		5033	1.07
0	126	Danaher		4930	1.05

Index Allocation

	% of Stocks
S&P 500	50.4
S&P MidCap 400	17.7
U.S. Small Cap	22.1
Foreign	11.4

Composition % 12-31-94

Cash	4.5	Preferreds	0.0
Stocks	57.9	Convertibles	0.9
Bonds	36.7	Other	0.0

Tax Analysis

	Tax-Adj Historical Return %	% Pretax Return
3 Yr Avg	4.32	62.6
5 Yr Avg	5.23	62.8
10 Yr Avg	8.27	59.4
Potential Capital Gain Exposure (% of assets)		2%

Most Similar Funds in MF500

Merrill Lynch Capital A	Strong Fit
SteinRoe Prime Equities	Strong Fit
American Cap Harbor A	Fair Fit

Min Initial Purchase	$250 (Addt'l: $25)
Min IRA Purchase	$250 (Addt'l: $25)
Min Auto Invest Plan	$250 (Systematic Inv: $25)

Expenses & Fees

Sales Fees	5.75% front
	0.00% deferred
	0.30% 12b-1
Management Fee	0.60% max./0.48% min.
3-,5-,10-yr Expense Projections	$84, $104, $161
Annual Brokerage Cost	0.20%

Bond Credit Analysis 12-31-94
% of Bonds

US Govt	22	BB	0
AAA	49	B	0
AA	1	Below B	0
A	12	NR/NA	4
BBB	13		

Stock Sector Weightings

	% of Stocks	Relative S&P 500
Utilities	5.4	0.43
Energy	7.0	0.69
Financials	28.8	2.72
Industrial Cyclicals	5.8	0.35
Consumer Durables	11.3	1.82
Consumer Staples	12.1	0.97
Services	11.8	1.45
Retail	5.6	0.96
Health	4.4	0.51
Technology	7.9	0.86

Morningstar 1995 Mutual Fund 500

Delaware Trend A

	Ticker	Load	NAV	Yield	SEC Yield	Assets	Objective
	DELTX	5.75%	11.75	0.0%	N/A	268.0	Aggr. Growth

Delaware Trend Fund - Class A seeks long-term capital appreciation; income is not an objective.

The fund invests primarily in common stocks and convertible securities of emerging and growth-oriented companies that are responsive to changes within the marketplace and have the fundamental characteristics to support growth. It looks for changing and dominant trends within the economy, the political arena, and society at large, and purchases securities of companies that may benefit from these trends.

Class A shares have front loads; Class B shares have deferred loads. Prior to June 15, 1988, the fund was known as Delta Trend Fund.

Manager's Investment Style

Management seeks out tiny, growth-oriented companies with the potential to take advantage of major market or economic trends, and generally attempts to buy such firms at a 25% discount to their projected growth rates. Management is also willing to invest in newer firms without established track records.

Historical Profile

Return	Above Average
Risk	High
Rating	★★★ Neutral

94% 97% 86% 85% 97% 89% 85% 90%

Investment Style History
Equity

Average % Stocks Held in Portfolio

Growth of $10,000

IIII Value of Fund ($000)
— Value of Index ($000) Russ 2000
▼ Manager Change
▽ Partial Manager Change
► Mgr Unknown After
◄ Mgr Unknown Before

Performance Quartile (Within Objective)

1983	1984	1985	1986	1987	1988	1989	1990	1991	1992	1993	1994	History
6.88	5.43	6.82	7.18	6.62	8.06	9.68	6.86	11.81	13.13	13.95	11.75	NAV
37.77	-19.83	28.04	5.28	-7.80	26.83	49.69	-24.61	74.49	22.40	22.37	-9.97	Total Return %
15.30	-26.09	-3.69	-13.40	-13.06	10.22	18.01	-21.49	44.01	14.78	12.31	-11.28	+/- S&P 500
---	-18.11	-3.97	-6.48	-4.29	6.29	25.75	-11.05	31.04	10.64	7.83	-7.31	+/- Wilshire 4500
0.49	1.19	2.54	0.00	0.00	0.00	0.52	0.55	0.00	0.00	0.00	0.00	Income Return %
37.27	-21.02	25.51	5.28	-7.80	26.83	49.17	-25.15	74.49	22.40	22.37	-9.97	Capital Return %
4	97	33	95	93	5	1	99	1	3	14	94	Total Rtn % Rank All
1	76	55	78	70	16	1	83	10	6	24	88	Total Rtn % Rank Obj
0.04	0.08	0.13	0.00	0.00	0.00	0.05	0.05	0.00	0.00	0.00	0.00	Income $
1.55	0.00	0.00	0.00	0.00	0.32	2.22	0.52	0.16	1.15	1.94	0.79	Capital Gains $
1.19	1.25	1.28	1.20	1.18	1.20	1.28	1.27	1.29	1.18	1.33	1.37	Expense Ratio %
1.09	1.52	2.23	-0.57	-0.64	-0.51	0.19	0.82	-0.24	-0.43	-0.61	-0.72	Income Ratio %
280	148	85	113	93	63	48	80	67	76	75	67	Turnover Rate %
57.4	71.6	87.0	73.5	51.8	54.3	79.5	63.5	104.0	169.6	277.6	268.0	Net Assets ($mil)

Fund Manager(s)

Edward N. Antoian CFA(1985), since 1984.
Birthdate: 12-55. BS, SUNY-Albany 1977 MBA, Wharton 1982

Manager Experience

	Dates Managed	Invest Obj	Std Dev	+/- Index
Edward N. Antoian				
Delaware DelCap A	03/86 - 12/94	G	23.73	9.53

Performance 12-31-94

	1st Qtr	2nd Qtr	3rd Qtr	4th Qtr	Total
1987	27.58	-0.44	5.59	-31.26	-7.80
1988	14.80	6.97	-0.49	3.78	26.83
1989	18.36	13.94	13.76	-2.43	49.69
1990	-6.10	9.68	-32.67	8.72	-24.61
1991	29.15	0.68	18.50	13.25	74.49
1992	6.18	-9.25	6.10	19.72	22.40
1993	2.36	4.02	14.32	0.53	22.37
1994	-5.73	-7.15	6.62	-3.53	-9.97

Bear Market Performance

Decile Rank (5-year period)

Worst ▬▬▬ Best

	Worst 3 Mo Period 1985-89	Worst 3 Mo Period 1990-94
Delaware Trend A	-42.60	-32.67
+/- S&P 500	-13.02	-18.92
+/- Best Fit Index : Russ 2000	-7.05	-8.13

Trailing Returns

	Total Return %	+/- S&P 500	+/- Wil 4500	% Rank All	% Rank Obj	Growth of $10,000
3 Mo	-3.53	-3.51	-1.03	86	89	9,647
6 Mo	2.86	-2.00	-1.33	21	82	10,286
1 Yr	-9.97	-11.28	-7.31	94	88	9,003
3 Yr Avg	10.48	4.21	2.87	12	24	13,484
5 Yr Avg	12.15	3.45	3.05	8	37	17,738
10 Yr Avg	15.39	1.01	2.76	9	37	41,855
15 Yr Avg	16.14	1.65	---	6	13	94,301

Operations

Address and Telephone	1818 Market Street
	Philadelphia, PA 19103-3682
	800-523-4640 / 215-988-1333
Advisor	Delaware Management
Subadvisor	None
Distributor	Delaware Distributors
States Available	All plus PR
Report Grade	A-
Income Distrib	Paid Semiannually
Date of Inception	10-03-68
Fiscal Year End	June

Min Initial Purchase	$250 (Addt'l: $25)
Min IRA Purchase	$250 (Addt'l: $25)
Min Auto Invest Plan	$250 (Systematic Inv: $25)

Expenses & Fees

Sales Fees	5.75% front
	0.00% deferred
	0.30% 12b-1
Management Fee	0.75% flat fee
3-,5-,10-yr Expense Projections	$98, $128, $213
Annual Brokerage Cost	0.12%

Risk Analysis

Time Period	Load-Adj Return %	Risk % Rank [1] All	Risk % Rank [1] Obj	Morningstar [2] Return	Morningstar Risk	Morningstar Risk-Adj Rating
1 Yr	-15.15					
3 Yr	8.32	92	46	1.43 [3]	1.24	★★★
5 Yr	10.83	96	65	1.59 [3]	1.38	★★★
10 Yr	14.71	96	66	1.42	1.40	★★★
Average Historical Rating (109 months)				2.8	★ s	

[1] 1 = low, 100 = high [2] 1.00 = Equity Avg [3] 1.00 = 90-day T-bill return

Other Measures

				Standard S&P 500	Best Fit Russ 2000
Standard Deviation	14.64	Alpha		4.8	-1.6
Mean	11.07	Beta		0.98	1.14
Sharpe Ratio	0.52	R-Squared		28	84

Investment Style

	Stock Portfolio Avg	Relative S&P 500
Price/Earnings Ratio	27.0	1.46
Price/Book Ratio	3.6	1.07
5 Yr Earnings Gr %	---	---
Return on Assets %	8.2	1.10
Debt % Total Cap	24.0	0.85
Med Mkt Cap ($mil)	256	0.02

Style Value Blend Growth — Size Large Med Small

Diversification Value for Portfolio Types

Large Cap: Medium	Small Cap: None	Bond: High	Balanced: Medium	Diversified: Medium

Portfolio 12-31-94

Share Chg (06-94) 000	Amount 000	Total Stocks: 142 Total Fixed-Income: 2	Value $000	% Net Assets
92	234	HBO	8047	2.70
146	360	Consolidated Stores	6712	2.25
5	268	Broadway & Seymour	5938	1.99
109	287	Mirage Resorts	5892	1.98
10	200	Pittston Services Group	5300	1.78
7	140	CUC International	4680	1.57
79	150	General Instrument	4500	1.51
5	100	Oracle Systems	4425	1.48
8	150	General Nutrition	4313	1.45
157	375	Central Sprinkler	4221	1.42
197	197	Cadence Design Systems	4059	1.36
6	215	WMS Industries	4024	1.35
165	165	British Sky Broadcasting	3960	1.33
26	199	Schultz Sav-O Stores	3934	1.32
244	244	Guidant	3907	1.31
246	246	Comcast CI A	3816	1.28
154	154	Dreyer's Grand Ice Cream	3800	1.27
89	170	Scientific-Atlanta	3570	1.20
43	114	Fred Meyer	3518	1.18
5	100	Sierra On-Line	3400	1.14
-40	150	PLATINUM technology	3375	1.13
152	280	Rio Hotel & Casino	3362	1.13
140	140	ITI Technology	3178	1.07
7	146	Renal Treatment Centers	3121	1.05
125	296	Playboy Enterprises CI B	3105	1.04

Composition % 12-31-94

Cash	5.8	Preferreds	0.0
Stocks	93.5	Convertibles	0.0
Bonds	0.7	Other	0.0

Tax Analysis

	Tax-Adj Historical Return %	% Pretax Return
3 Yr Avg	7.70	71.6
5 Yr Avg	9.79	76.9
10 Yr Avg	13.16	76.7
Potential Capital Gain Exposure (% of assets)		6%

Most Similar Funds in MF500

Loomis Sayles Small Cap	Strong Fit
Hancock Emerging Growth B	Fair Fit
Invesco Strat Technology	Fair Fit

Index Allocation

	% of Stocks
S&P 500	9.5
S&P MidCap 400	10.7
U.S. Small Cap	77.2
Foreign	2.6

Sector Weightings

	% of Stocks	Relative S&P 500
Utilities	0.0	0.00
Energy	1.7	0.17
Financials	3.6	0.34
Industrial Cyclicals	4.1	0.25
Consumer Durables	15.8	2.55
Consumer Staples	1.6	0.19
Services	30.1	3.70
Retail	11.8	2.02
Health	6.4	0.74
Technology	24.9	2.72

Delaware Value A

	Ticker	Load	NAV	Yield	SEC Yield	Assets	Objective
	DEVLX	5.75%	18.87	0.8%	N/A	174.8	Growth

Delaware Value Fund - Class A seeks capital appreciation.
The fund invests primarily in common stocks and convertible securities. These equities have market values that appear low relative to the underlying value and growth potential of the company. The fund may also invest in companies where current or anticipated changes within the company provide an opportunity for capital appreciation.
Class A shares have front loads; Class B shares have deferred loads, higher 12b-1 fees, and conversion features; Institutional shares are designed for institutional investors.

Historical Profile
Return: Above Average
Risk: Average
Rating: ★★★★ Above Average

83% 81% 84% 61% 68% 68%

Investment Style History
Equity
Average % Stocks Held in Portfolio

Growth of $10,000
IIII Value of Fund ($000)
— Value of Index ($000) Wil 4500
▼ Manager Change
▽ Partial Manager Change
► Mgr Unknown After
◄ Mgr Unknown Before

Performance Quartile (Within Objective)

Manager's Investment Style
Management looks for value in a variety of places. Although it takes the traditional value approach of buying assets cheaply, and therefore maintains low multiples, it also buys a few stocks that are selling below their earnings growth. Among growth stocks, it prefers smaller, little-recognized firms that are posting modest but stable growth.

Fund Manager(s)
Edward A. Trumpbour, since 06-87. Birthdate: 11-57. BS, Georgetown U. 1979 MBA, Wharton 1985

	1983	1984	1985	1986	1987	1988	1989	1990	1991	1992	1993	1994	History
NAV	---	---	---	---	8.68	10.90	13.50	11.32	16.10	17.62	20.73	18.87	NAV
	---	---	---	---	-8.45 *	26.41	31.87	-13.15	50.97	14.78	18.83	-6.98	Total Return %
	---	---	---	---	9.53 *	9.80	0.19	-10.03	20.49	7.17	8.77	-8.29	+/- S&P 500
	---	---	---	---	---	8.47	2.70	-6.96	16.77	5.81	7.54	-6.91	+/- Wilshire 5000
	---	---	---	---	0.47	0.83	1.10	1.29	0.00	0.23	0.18	0.83	Income Return %
	---	---	---	---	-8.92	25.58	30.78	-14.43	50.97	14.55	18.65	-7.80	Capital Return %
	---	---	---	---			5	11	90	7	10	19	80	Total Rtn % Rank All
	---	---	---	---			7	26	90	13	17	18	85	Total Rtn % Rank Obj
	---	---	---	---	0.05	0.07	0.14	0.16	0.00	0.04	0.04	0.16	Income $
	---	---	---	---	0.00	0.00	0.72	0.25	0.99	0.82	0.17	0.25	Capital Gains $
	---	---	---	---	1.50	2.02	1.98	1.79	2.26	1.93	1.64	1.44	Expense Ratio %
	---	---	---	---	1.74	0.35	1.14	1.12	-0.07	0.39	0.25	0.48	Income Ratio %
	---	---	---	---	---	---	60	66	103	69	99	68	32	---	Turnover Rate %
	---	---	---	---	5.0	7.0	11.3	8.0	14.0	43.6	160.0	174.8	Net Assets ($mil)

Performance 12-31-94
	1st Qtr	2nd Qtr	3rd Qtr	4th Qtr	Total
1987	---	---	14.48	-20.03	-8.45 *
1988	9.45	12.11	-2.82	6.01	26.41
1989	13.12	9.25	8.46	-1.61	31.87
1990	-8.07	5.64	-16.40	6.98	-13.15
1991	15.55	1.38	18.17	9.06	50.97
1992	2.36	-3.22	3.57	11.86	14.78
1993	8.63	-0.68	5.79	4.11	18.83
1994	-2.80	-2.48	3.21	-4.91	-6.98

Bear Market Performance
Decile Rank (5-year period)

Worst ———— Best

	Worst 3 Mo Period 1985-89	Worst 3 Mo Period 1990-94
Delaware Value A	---	-17.76
+/- S&P 500	---	-3.92
+/- Best Fit Index : Wil 4500	---	1.64

Trailing Returns
	Total Return %	+/- S&P 500	+/- Wil 5000	% Rank All	% Rank Obj	Growth of $10,000
3 Mo	-4.91	-4.90	-4.14	91	93	9,509
6 Mo	-1.87	-6.73	-6.49	86	96	9,813
1 Yr	-6.98	-8.29	-6.91	80	85	9,302
3 Yr Avg	8.26	1.99	1.64	20	28	12,687
5 Yr Avg	10.72	2.02	1.90	14	23	16,636
10 Yr Avg	---	---	---	---	---	---
15 Yr Avg	---	---	---	---	---	---

Operations
Address and Telephone	1818 Market Street Philadelphia, PA 19103-3682 800-523-4640 / 215-988-1333
Advisor	Delaware Management
Subadvisor	None
Distributor	Delaware Distributors
States Available	All plus PR
Report Grade	B+
Income Distrib	Paid Annually
* Date of Inception	06-24-87
Fiscal Year End	November

Risk Analysis
Time Period	Load-Adj Return %	Risk % Rank All	Risk % Rank Obj	Morningstar Return	Morningstar Risk	Morningstar Risk-Adj Rating
1 Yr	-12.33					
3 Yr	6.14	57	10	0.76 [3]	0.62	★★★
5 Yr	9.41	71	32	1.19 [3]	0.85	★★★★
10 Yr	---	---	---	---	---	

Average Historical Rating (55 months) 3.8 ★s
[1] 1 = low, 100 = high [2] 1.00 = Equity Avg [3] 1.00 = 90-day T-bill return

Other Measures
				Standard S&P 500	Best Fit Wil 4500
Standard Deviation	7.66	Alpha		3.1	1.8
Mean	8.25	Beta		0.57	0.69
Sharpe Ratio	0.62	R-Squared		34	77

Investment Style
	Stock Portfolio Avg	Relative S&P 500	Style Value Blend Growth
Price/Earnings Ratio	18.2	0.99	
Price/Book Ratio	2.3	0.67	
5 Yr Earnings Gr %	10.9#	1.96	Size Large Med Small
Return on Assets %	7.4	0.99	
Debt % Total Cap	30.8	1.09	
Med Mkt Cap ($mil)	358	0.03	

figure is based on 50% or less of stocks

Diversification Value for Portfolio Types
Large Cap: Medium
Small Cap: Low
Bond: High
Balanced: Medium
Diversified: Medium

Portfolio 05-31-94
Total Stocks: 162
Total Fixed-Income: 1

Share Chg (11-93) 000	Amount 000		Value $000	% Net Assets
29	135	Geneva Steel Cl A	2421	1.37
44	87	Reynolds & Reynolds Cl A	1981	1.12
1	1	Sig Schweiz Industrie	1891	1.07
19	77	ROC Communities	1857	1.05
0	64	Arctco	1773	1.00
29	39	Willamette Industries	1736	0.98
0	68	Grupo Radio Centro (ADR)	1693	0.96
8	68	Custom Chrome	1684	0.95
0	48	Champion Enterprises	1548	0.88
0	48	ALC Communications	1536	0.87
34	51	Mid Ocean	1533	0.87
20	116	INDRESCO	1523	0.86
11	97	Delhi Group	1511	0.85
12	56	Camden Property Trust	1461	0.83
1	319	Grupo Sidek Cl B	1454	0.82
0	35	IDEX	1394	0.79
1	232	Americredit	1393	0.79
61	61	Istituto Mobiliare Italiano	1389	0.79
0	77	Musicland Stores	1383	0.78
91	91	Tom Brown	1358	0.77
0	47	Cherry	1343	0.76
0	48	Factory Stores of America	1306	0.74
0	84	Methode Electronics Cl A	1294	0.73
0	44	Horizon Outlet Centers	1246	0.70
0	1	Bobst (Br)	1229	0.69

Composition % 12-31-94
Cash	35.7	Preferreds	0.0
Stocks	64.3	Convertibles	0.0
Bonds	0.0	Other	0.0

Tax Analysis
	Tax-Adj Historical Return %	% Pretax Return
3 Yr Avg	7.43	89.2
5 Yr Avg	9.60	87.6
10 Yr Avg	---	---
Potential Capital Gain Exposure (% of assets)		3%

Most Similar Funds in MF500
Vanguard Index Extended Mkt	Fair Fit
Vista Capital Growth A	Fair Fit
Dreyfus New Leaders	Fair Fit

Index Allocation
	% of Stocks
S&P 500	2.9
S&P MidCap 400	14.3
U.S. Small Cap	67.3
Foreign	15.5

Sector Weightings
	% of Stocks	Relative S&P 500
Utilities	1.3	0.11
Energy	8.7	0.86
Financials	21.2	2.01
Industrial Cyclicals	34.5	2.10
Consumer Durables	9.0	1.46
Consumer Staples	1.9	0.15
Services	11.8	1.45
Retail	0.6	0.10
Health	2.4	0.27
Technology	8.7	0.95

Expenses & Fees
Sales Fees	5.75% front
	0.00% deferred
	0.30% 12b-1
Management Fee	0.75% flat fee
3-,5-,10-yr Expense Projections	$106, $142, $241
Annual Brokerage Cost	0.13%

Min Initial Purchase	$250 (Addt'l: $25)
Min IRA Purchase	$250 (Addt'l: $25)
Min Auto Invest Plan	$250 (Systematic Inv: $25)

Manager Experience
Dates Managed | Invest Obj | Std Dev | +/- Index
Not available.

MORNINGSTAR 1995 Mutual Fund 500

Dodge & Cox Balanced

	Ticker	Load	NAV	Yield	SEC Yield	Assets	Objective
	DODBX	None	45.21	3.9%	4.47%	725.3	Balanced

Dodge & Cox Balanced Fund seeks income, conservation of principal, and long-term growth of principal and income.

The fund may invest up to 75% of its assets in common stocks and convertible securities. Prospective earnings and dividends are major considerations in these purchases. Individual securities are selected with regard to financial strength and economic background. The balance of the fund's assets are invested in investment-grade fixed-income securities; unrated debt must be judged to be equivalent to those rated at least A. The fund may retain securities that have been downgraded below BBB.

Manager's Investment Style

With its stock picks, management seeks equities that have high growth prospects and that are temporarily depressed in price. Its holdings are well diversified across sectors, and turnover is typically very low. On the bond side, management has attempted to maintain market-like interest-rate exposure and high quality, while pursuing incremental yield. As such, it often holds agency debt and corporate bonds in addition to Treasuries.

Fund Manager(s)

Management Team

Manager Experience

	Dates Managed	Invest Obj	Std Dev	+/- Index
Charles F. Pohl				
Dodge & Cox Stock	01/91 - 12/94	GI	11.09	1.58
Dodge & Cox Income	01/91 - 12/94	CG	4.78	1.11

Performance 12-31-94

	1st Qtr	2nd Qtr	3rd Qtr	4th Qtr	Total
1987	14.27	3.00	3.76	-12.24	7.18
1988	4.94	4.41	-0.06	1.86	11.54
1989	4.51	7.46	6.37	2.99	23.02
1990	-1.28	4.45	-9.26	7.89	0.94
1991	9.67	0.83	4.55	4.42	20.72
1992	0.64	3.21	2.67	3.70	10.59
1993	6.60	4.17	3.12	1.28	15.98
1994	-1.21	-0.09	3.42	-0.02	2.05

Bear Market Performance

Decile Rank (5-year period)

	Worst 3 Mo Period 1985-89	Worst 3 Mo Period 1990-94
Dodge & Cox Balanced	-17.40	-10.55
+/- S&P 500	12.18	3.29
+/- Best Fit Index : S&P 500	12.18	3.29

Trailing Returns

	Total Return %	+/- S&P 500	+/- LB Aggregate	% Rank All	% Rank Obj	Growth of $10,000
3 Mo	-0.02	0.00	-0.40	23	17	9,998
6 Mo	3.40	-1.46	2.41	18	10	10,340
1 Yr	2.05	0.74	4.97	10	4	10,205
3 Yr Avg	9.39	3.12	4.84	15	3	13,089
5 Yr Avg	9.79	1.10	2.16	18	12	15,950
10 Yr Avg	13.96	-0.43	4.01	18	7	36,926
15 Yr Avg	13.59	-0.90	2.78	30	28	67,588

Operations

Address and Telephone	One Sansome Street 35th Floor San Francisco, CA 94104 800-621-3979 / 415-434-0311
Advisor	Dodge & Cox
Subadvisor	None
Distributor	Dodge & Cox
States Available	Selected states
Report Grade	B+
Income Distrib	Paid Quarterly
Date of Inception	06-26-31
Fiscal Year End	December

Historical Profile

Return	Above Average
Risk	Below Average
Rating	★★★★★ Highest

62%	61%	62%	59%	58%	58%	58%	57%	

Investment Style History Equity

Average % Stocks Held in Portfolio

Growth of $10,000

- IIII Value of Fund ($000)
- — Value of Index ($000) S&P 500
- ▼ Manager Change
- ▽ Partial Manager Change
- ► Mgr Unknown After
- ◄ Mgr Unknown Before

Performance Quartile (Within Objective)

1983	1984	1985	1986	1987	1988	1989	1990	1991	1992	1993	1994	History
27.33	25.92	31.93	32.62	30.72	32.09	36.85	35.03	40.09	42.44	46.40	45.21	NAV
16.88	4.71	32.50	18.81	7.18	11.54	23.02	0.94	20.72	10.59	15.98	2.05	Total Return %
-5.59	-1.55	0.76	0.13	1.92	-5.07	-8.66	4.06	-9.76	2.97	5.92	0.74	+/- S&P 500
8.51	-10.44	10.37	3.56	4.42	3.66	8.48	-8.01	4.72	3.35	6.22	4.97	+/- LB Aggregate
7.04	6.87	7.31	5.12	4.86	5.52	5.70	5.02	5.30	4.52	3.95	3.86	Income Return %
9.84	-2.16	25.19	13.70	2.32	6.02	17.32	-4.08	15.42	6.07	12.02	-1.81	Capital Return %
52	52	18	27	15	49	29	52	44	19	25	10	Total Rtn % Rank All
39	67	17	39	11	52	28	34	77	14	9	4	Total Rtn % Rank Obj
1.72	1.73	1.70	1.62	1.70	1.68	1.76	1.81	1.76	1.73	1.67	1.79	Income $
0.31	0.83	0.37	3.55	2.67	0.46	0.71	0.33	0.29	0.08	1.07	0.36	Capital Gains $
0.76	0.76	0.75	0.73	0.72	0.77	0.72	0.70	0.65	0.63	0.60	0.58	Expense Ratio %
6.31	6.76	6.03	4.86	4.69	5.19	4.98	5.24	4.78	4.27	3.67	3.74	Income Ratio %
10	7	26	14	15	9	12	10	10	6	15	---	Turnover Rate %
19.6	19.1	24.5	27.5	34.4	39.0	51.0	82.6	179.4	268.8	486.8	725.3	Net Assets ($mil)

Risk Analysis

Time Period	Load-Adj Return %	Risk % Rank [1] All	Risk % Rank [1] Obj	Morningstar [2] Return	Morningstar [2] Risk	Morningstar Risk-Adj Rating
1 Yr	2.05					
3 Yr	9.39	42	22	1.77 [3]	0.64	★★★★
5 Yr	9.79	53	47	1.29 [3]	0.76	★★★★
10 Yr	13.96	43	53	1.52	0.71	★★★★★

Average Historical Rating (109 months) 4.2 ★s

[1] 1 = low, 100 = high [2] 1.00 = Hybrid Avg [3] 1.00 = 90-day T-bill return

Other Measures

		Standard S&P 500	Best Fit S&P 500
Standard Deviation	6.32	Alpha	3.6	3.6
Mean	9.21	Beta	0.73	0.73
Sharpe Ratio	0.90	R-Squared	83	83

Investment Style

Stocks	Port Avg	Rel S&P 500
Price/Earnings Ratio	15.8	0.86
Price/Book Ratio	2.2	0.65
5 Yr Earnings Gr %	-0.5	-0.09
Med Mkt Cap ($mil)	7292	0.56

Bonds	
Avg Effective Duration	5.7 Yrs
Avg Effective Maturity	11.7 Yrs
Avg Credit Quality	AA
Avg Weighted Coupon	8.01%

Diversification Value for Portfolio Types

Large Cap: None	Small Cap: Medium	Bond: Medium	Balanced: None	Diversified: Low

Portfolio 09-30-94

Share Chg (06-94)000	Amount 000	Total Stocks: 73 Total Fixed-Income: 46	Date of Maturity	Value $000	% Net Assets
	26000	FNMA CMO 6.5%	09-25-23	22552	3.23
	19500	US Treasury Note 7.875%	07-31-96	19948	2.85
	17242	FNMA 7.5%	06-01-11	16915	2.42
	14701	FNMA CMO 5%	01-25-06	13341	1.91
0	173	IBM		12024	1.72
10	143	Dayton Hudson		10940	1.57
0	351	American Express		10662	1.53
	9900	US Treasury Note 9.125%	05-15-99	10625	1.52
	12300	FNMA CMO 6%	03-25-09	10455	1.50
	7000	US Treasury Bond 14%	11-15-11	10362	1.48
20	166	Procter & Gamble		9898	1.42
22	200	General Motors		9375	1.34
	10000	FHLMC CMO 7%	01-15-06	9325	1.33
-2	104	ALCOA		8839	1.26
0	110	Intl Paper		8635	1.24
0	285	RR Donnelley & Sons		8550	1.22
	8000	Canadian Pacific 9.45%	08-01-21	8435	1.21
0	107	Dow Chemical		8373	1.20
73	223	Melville		7944	1.14
0	325	James River		7881	1.13

Index Allocation

	% of Stocks
S&P 500	93.9
S&P MidCap 400	1.8
U.S. Small Cap	0.2
Foreign	5.8

Composition % 12-31-94

Cash	4.3	Preferreds	0.0
Stocks	57.4	Convertibles	0.0
Bonds	38.3	Other	0.0

Tax Analysis

	Tax-Adj Historical Return %	% Pretax Return
3 Yr Avg	7.56	79.1
5 Yr Avg	7.93	78.1
10 Yr Avg	11.24	70.6
Potential Capital Gain Exposure (% of assets)		7%

Most Similar Funds in MF500

Putnam Fund for Grth & Inc A	Strong Fit
Affiliated	Strong Fit
American Mutual	Strong Fit

Bond Credit Analysis 12-31-94

% of Bonds

US Govt	64	BB	3
AAA	5	B	0
AA	1	Below B	0
A	19	NR/NA	0
BBB	8		

Stock Sector Weightings

	% of Stocks	Relative S&P 500
Utilities	5.5	0.44
Energy	8.6	0.85
Financials	19.8	1.87
Industrial Cyclicals	22.6	1.38
Consumer Durables	7.8	1.26
Consumer Staples	3.4	0.27
Services	8.8	1.08
Retail	6.6	1.14
Health	5.9	0.68
Technology	11.1	1.21

Expenses & Fees

Sales Fees	0.00% front
	0.00% deferred
	0.00% 12b-1
Management Fee	0.50% flat fee
3-,5-,10-yr Expense Projections	$19, $33, $75
Annual Brokerage Cost	0.06%

Min Purchase

Min Initial Purchase	$2500 (Addt'l: $100)
Min IRA Purchase	$1000 (Addt'l: $100)
Min Auto Invest Plan	$2500 (Systematic Inv: $100)

Dreyfus Appreciation

	Ticker	Load	NAV	Yield	SEC Yield	Assets	Objective
	DGAGX	None	15.17	1.8%	N/A	233.9	Growth

Dreyfus Appreciation Fund seeks long-term growth consistent with the preservation of capital. Current income is secondary.

The fund invests primarily in common stocks of domestic and foreign issuers, common stocks with warrants attached, and debt securities of foreign governments. Up to 10% of the fund's assets may be invested in foreign securities not traded in the United States. Up to 2% may be invested in unattached warrants.

The fund adopted Fayez Sarofim & Company as subadvisor on Oct. 31, 1990. Prior to Dec. 30, 1991, the fund was named General Aggressive Growth Fund.

Manager's Investment Style

Management has a high level of allegiance to blue-chip growth stocks. It screens specifically for companies with solid overseas operations, assuming that companies facing pricing pressure in the United States can rely on their foreign growth prospects.

Fund Manager(s)

Fayez Sarofim, since 10-90. BS, U. of California-Berkeley 1949 MBA, Harvard 1951
Russell Hawkins, since 10-90. BA, Cornell U. 1977 MBA, Harvard 1979

Manager Experience	Dates Managed	Invest Obj	Std Dev	+/- Index
Fayez Sarofim				
GAM North America	09/90 - 12/94	G	11.47	-5.55
Premier Growth A	07/93 - 12/94	WW	8.59	2.13

Historical Profile

Return	Average
Risk	Average
Rating	★★★
	Neutral

Investment Style History
Equity

Average % Stocks Held in Portfolio

82% 75% 88% 80% 93% 90% 90% 95%

Growth of $10,000

|||| Value of Fund ($000)
— Value of Index ($000)
S&P 500
▼ Manager Change
▽ Partial Manager Change
► Mgr Unknown After
◄ Mgr Unknown Before

Performance Quartile (Within Objective)

	1983	1984	1985	1986	1987	1988	1989	1990	1991	1992	1993	1994	History
	---	6.42	8.52	9.67	9.03	10.28	12.20	10.95	14.67	15.15	14.92	15.17	NAV
	---	13.83 *	35.19	15.03	4.54	16.61	27.20	-1.83	38.43	4.28	0.71	3.62	Total Return %
	---	9.23 *	3.45	-3.65	-0.72	0.00	-4.48	1.29	7.95	-3.34	-9.35	2.31	+/- S&P 500
	---	---	2.63	-1.06	2.17	-1.33	-1.97	4.35	4.23	-4.69	-10.58	3.69	+/- Wilshire 5000
	---	0.00	2.32	0.22	1.48	1.81	1.44	2.11	1.73	0.67	1.81	1.88	Income Return %
	---	13.83	32.87	14.82	3.05	14.80	25.77	-3.94	36.70	3.62	-1.10	1.74	Capital Return %
	---	---	11	54	25	23	18	61	16	80	98	6	Total Rtn % Rank All
	---	---	18	46	39	43	49	34	38	75	93	11	Total Rtn % Rank Obj
	---	0.00	0.12	0.02	0.14	0.17	0.17	0.24	0.20	0.10	0.27	0.28	Income $
	---	0.00	0.01	0.10	0.96	0.08	0.69	0.78	0.25	0.05	0.06	0.01	Capital Gains $
	---	---	1.51	1.50	1.63	1.74	1.18	1.24	1.30	1.14	1.07	---	Expense Ratio %
	---	---	1.15	0.65	0.65	1.41	1.38	2.21	1.69	1.46	1.66	---	Income Ratio %
	---	---	198	183	179	137	130	179	13	3	10	---	Turnover Rate %
	---	1.1	5.4	27.4	39.5	41.3	45.7	40.4	80.9	207.6	237.0	233.9	Net Assets ($mil)

Performance 12-31-94

	1st Qtr	2nd Qtr	3rd Qtr	4th Qtr	Total
1987	22.40	3.33	9.75	-24.69	4.54
1988	9.80	9.13	-2.30	-0.39	16.61
1989	6.08	7.52	10.11	1.29	27.20
1990	-1.56	7.58	-14.70	8.68	-1.83
1991	15.66	-1.62	7.06	13.63	38.43
1992	-3.75	0.28	4.45	3.44	4.28
1993	-3.50	-1.78	0.14	6.10	0.71
1994	-5.23	0.50	6.85	1.82	3.62

Bear Market Performance

Decile Rank (5-year period)

Worst — Best

	Worst 3 Mo Period 1985-89	Worst 3 Mo Period 1990-94
Dreyfus Appreciation	-29.19	-14.70
+/- S&P 500	0.39	-0.96
+/- Best Fit Index : S&P 500	0.39	-0.96

Trailing Returns

	Total Return %	+/- S&P 500	+/- Wil 5000	% Rank All	% Rank Obj	Growth of $10,000
3 Mo	1.82	1.84	2.59	4	7	10,182
6 Mo	8.80	3.94	4.18	5	12	10,880
1 Yr	3.62	2.31	3.69	6	11	10,362
3 Yr Avg	2.86	-3.41	-3.75	87	75	10,882
5 Yr Avg	8.14	-0.55	-0.68	32	60	14,789
10 Yr Avg	13.56	-0.82	-0.30	21	36	35,663
15 Yr Avg	---	---	---	---	---	---

Operations

Address and Telephone	One Exchange Place
	Boston, MA 02109
	800-645-6561 / 718-895-1206
Advisor	Dreyfus
Subadvisor	Fayez Sarofim & Company
Distributor	Premier Mutual Fund Services
States Available	All plus PR
Report Grade	B+
Income Distrib	Paid Annually
* Date of Inception	01-18-84
Fiscal Year End	December

Min Initial Purchase	$2500 (Addt'l: $100)
Min IRA Purchase	$750 (Addt'l: None)
Min Auto Invest Plan	$2500 (Systematic Inv: $100)

Expenses & Fees

Sales Fees	
	0.00% front
	0.00% deferred
	0.20% 12b-1
Management Fee	0.44% max./0.28% min.
3-,5-,10-yr Expense Projections	$34, $59, $131
Annual Brokerage Cost	0.04%

Risk Analysis

Time Period	Load-Adj Return %	Risk % Rank [1] All	Risk % Rank [1] Obj	Morningstar [2] Return	Morningstar Risk	Morningstar Risk-Adj Rating
1 Yr	3.62					
3 Yr	2.86	81	61	-0.21 [3]	0.97	★★
5 Yr	8.14	74	39	0.85 [3]	0.88	★★★
10 Yr	13.56	73	51	1.18	0.94	★★★

Average Historical Rating (96 months) 3.7 ★s

[1] 1 = low, 100 = high [2] 1.00 = Equity Avg [3] 1.00 = 90-day T-bill return

Other Measures

	Standard S&P 500	Best Fit S&P 500
Standard Deviation	9.03	
Mean	3.23	
Sharpe Ratio	-0.03	
Alpha	-3.2	-3.2
Beta	1.01	1.01
R-Squared	80	80

Investment Style

	Stock Portfolio Avg	Relative S&P 500
Price/Earnings Ratio	18.8	1.02
Price/Book Ratio	4.4	1.30
5 Yr Earnings Gr %	7.4	1.34
Return on Assets %	9.1	1.22
Debt % Total Cap	25.3	0.90
Med Mkt Cap ($mil)	28414	2.19

Diversification Value for Portfolio Types

Large Cap: Low	Small Cap: Medium	Bond: High	Balanced: Low	Diversified: Low

Portfolio 06-30-94

Total Stocks: 54
Total Fixed-Income: 2

Share Chg (12-93) 000	Amount 000		Value $000	% Net Assets
0	250	Philip Morris	12875	6.10
0	300	Coca-Cola	12188	5.77
100	200	General Electric	9325	4.42
	75	Ford Motor Cl A Cv Pfd $4.20	7275	3.44
0	65	Royal Dutch Petroleum	6801	3.22
0	100	Pfizer	6313	2.99
0	75	Mobil	6122	2.90
0	90	Gillette	5861	2.78
0	190	Merck	5653	2.68
0	105	Procter & Gamble	5604	2.65
0	100	AT & T	5438	2.57
0	175	PepsiCo	5359	2.54
-15	125	Nestle (Reg) (ADR)	5234	2.48
-10	115	Johnson & Johnson	4931	2.33
-50	100	Roche Holding (ADR)	4744	2.25
0	80	El duPont de Nemours	4670	2.21
0	75	Rohm & Haas	4669	2.21
45	90	Minnesota Mining & Mfg	4455	2.11
10	110	Citicorp	4386	2.08
0	75	Exxon	4247	2.01
0	50	FNMA	4175	1.98
0	40	Unilever	4030	1.91
0	35	HSBC Holdings (ADR)	3798	1.80
40	80	Motorola	3560	1.69
-15	70	Anheuser-Busch	3553	1.68

Composition % 09-30-94

Cash	0.8	Preferreds	0.0	
Stocks	95.3	Convertibles	4.0	
Bonds	0.0	Other	0.0	

Tax Analysis

	Tax-Adj Historical Return %	% Pretax Return
3 Yr Avg	2.23	77.5
5 Yr Avg	6.94	83.3
10 Yr Avg	12.11	83.2
Potential Capital Gain Exposure (% of assets)		11%

Most Similar Funds in MF500

Vanguard U.S. Growth	Fair Fit
Dreyfus	Fair Fit
Papp America-Abroad	Fair Fit

Index Allocation

	% of Stocks
S&P 500	89.3
S&P MidCap 400	0.0
U.S. Small Cap	2.5
Foreign	13.5

Sector Weightings

	% of Stocks	Relative S&P 500
Utilities	2.9	0.23
Energy	11.0	1.09
Financials	8.0	0.75
Industrial Cyclicals	16.2	0.99
Consumer Durables	4.8	0.78
Consumer Staples	28.5	2.27
Services	7.8	0.96
Retail	6.4	1.10
Health	14.4	1.66
Technology	0.0	0.00

MORNINGSTAR 1995 Mutual Fund 500

Dreyfus Disciplined Stock Inv

	Ticker	Load	NAV	Yield	SEC Yield	Assets	Objective
	N/A	None	17.31	N/A	N/A	23.8	Growth/Inc.

Dreyfus Disciplined Stock Fund - Investor Shares seeks growth and income.

The fund normally invests at least 65% of its assets in equities, primarily dividend-paying stocks. The candidate universe is generated by applying quantitative security selection and risk-control techniques. The fund's economic sector and industry exposure is similar to the S&P 500 Index.

Investor shares have a 0.25% 12b-1 fee and are sold primarily to retail investors; R shares are sold primarily to bank trust departments and other financial service providers. Prior to Oct. 17, 1994, the fund was named Laurel Stock Portfolio - Investor Shares.

Manager's Investment Style

Management uses both quantitative models and qualitative analysis in an attempt to stay one step ahead of the S&P 500. The quantitative model ranks stocks on 15 criteria, which include both value and growth screens. Although it generally keeps the portfolio's sector exposure in line with that of the S&P 500, management tries to get an edge by picking cheaply priced stocks in each sector that are experiencing upward price and earnings momentum.

Fund Manager(s)

Bert J. Mullins et al. Birthdate: 03-42 BS, Indiana U. 1965

Manager Experience	Dates Managed	Invest Obj	Std Dev	+/- Index
Not available.				

Historical Profile
Return ---
Risk ---
Rating
Not Rated

Investment Style History
Equity
96%
Average % Stocks Held in Portfolio

Growth of $10,000
|||| Value of Fund ($000)
— Value of Index ($000) S&P 500
▼ Manager Change
▽ Partial Manager Change
►■ Mgr Unknown After
◄■ Mgr Unknown Before

Performance Quartile
(Within Objective)

	1983	1984	1985	1986	1987	1988	1989	1990	1991	1992	1993	1994	History
	---	---	---	---	---	---	---	---	---	---	---	17.31	NAV
	---	---	---	---	---	---	---	---	---	---	---	0.18 *	Total Return %
	---	---	---	---	---	---	---	---	---	---	---	-4.59 *	+/- S&P 500
	---	---	---	---	---	---	---	---	---	---	---	---	+/- Wilshire 5000
	---	---	---	---	---	---	---	---	---	---	---	1.01	Income Return %
	---	---	---	---	---	---	---	---	---	---	---	-0.83	Capital Return %
	---	---	---	---	---	---	---	---	---	---	---	---	Total Rtn % Rank All
	---	---	---	---	---	---	---	---	---	---	---	---	Total Rtn % Rank Obj
	---	---	---	---	---	---	---	---	---	---	---	0.18	Income $
	---	---	---	---	---	---	---	---	---	---	---	0.47	Capital Gains $
	---	---	---	---	---	---	---	---	---	---	---	1.15	Expense Ratio %
	---	---	---	---	---	---	---	---	---	---	---	1.29	Income Ratio %
	---	---	---	---	---	---	---	---	---	---	---	---	Turnover Rate %
	---	---	---	---	---	---	---	---	---	---	---	23.8	Net Assets ($mil)

Performance 12-31-94

	1st Qtr	2nd Qtr	3rd Qtr	4th Qtr	Total
1987	---	---	---	---	---
1988	---	---	---	---	---
1989	---	---	---	---	---
1990	---	---	---	---	---
1991	---	---	---	---	---
1992	---	---	---	---	---
1993	---	---	---	---	---
1994	---	---	5.08	-1.98	0.18 *

Bear Market Performance

Decile Rank (5-year period)

Worst | Best

	Worst 3 Mo Period 1985-89	Worst 3 Mo Period 1990-94
Dreyfus Disciplined Stock Inv	---	---
+/- S&P 500	---	---
+/- Best Fit Index :	---	---

Trailing Returns

	Total Return %	+/- S&P 500	+/- Wil 5000	% Rank All	% Rank Obj	Growth of $10,000
3 Mo	-1.98	-1.97	-1.21	68	63	9,802
6 Mo	2.99	-1.87	-1.63	21	43	10,299
1 Yr	---	---	---	---	---	---
3 Yr Avg	---	---	---	---	---	---
5 Yr Avg	---	---	---	---	---	---
10 Yr Avg	---	---	---	---	---	---
15 Yr Avg	---	---	---	---	---	---

Operations

Address and Telephone	One Exchange Place Boston, MA 02109 800-645-6561 / 718-895-1206
Advisor	Dreyfus
Subadvisor	None
Distributor	Premier Mutual Fund Services
States Available	All plus PR
Report Grade	C
Income Distrib	Paid Quarterly
* Date of Inception	04-06-94
Fiscal Year End	October

Risk Analysis

Time Period	Load-Adj Return %	Risk % Rank [1] All	Obj	Morningstar [2] Return	Morningstar Risk	Morningstar Risk-Adj Rating
1 Yr	---	---	---	---	---	
3 Yr	---	---	---	---	---	---
5 Yr	---	---	---			
10 Yr	---	---	---			

Average Historical Rating ---   ---

[1] 1 = low, 100 = high   [2] 1.00 = Equity Avg   [3] 1.00 = 90-day T-bill return

Other Measures

			Standard S&P 500	Best Fit
Standard Deviation	---	Alpha	---	---
Mean	---	Beta	---	---
Sharpe Ratio	---	R-Squared	---	---

Investment Style

	Stock Portfolio Avg	Relative S&P 500
Price/Earnings Ratio	17.4	0.94
Price/Book Ratio	3.2	0.95
5 Yr Earnings Gr %	6.4	1.15
Return on Assets %	7.3	0.98
Debt % Total Cap	29.6	1.05
Med Mkt Cap ($mil)	10620	0.82

Style: Value Blend Growth — Size Large/Med/Small

Diversification Value for Portfolio Types

Large Cap: | Small Cap: | Bond: | Balanced: | Diversified:

Expenses & Fees

Sales Fees	
	0.00% front
	0.00% deferred
	0.25% 12b-1
Management Fee	0.90% flat fee
3-,5-,10-yr Expense Projections	$37, N/A, N/A
Annual Brokerage Cost	---

Min Initial Purchase	$2500 (Addt'l: $100)
Min IRA Purchase	$750 (Addt'l: N/A)
Min Auto Invest Plan	$2500 (Systematic Inv: $100)

Portfolio 10-31-94

Share Chg (04-94) 000	Amount 000	Total Stocks: 178 Total Fixed-Income: 0	Value $000	% Net Assets
9	9	Exxon	544	2.78
9	10	AT & T	525	2.68
10	10	General Electric	501	2.56
6	6	Philip Morris	385	1.97
7	7	Coca-Cola	364	1.86
5	5	Procter & Gamble	329	1.68
5	5	El duPont de Nemours	319	1.63
3	3	Royal Dutch Petroleum	304	1.55
12	12	Wal-Mart Stores	293	1.50
5	5	Amoco	292	1.49
8	8	Merck	280	1.43
4	4	Motorola	246	1.26
3	3	IBM	239	1.22
4	4	Johnson & Johnson	234	1.20
4	4	Chrysler	217	1.11
5	5	Southwestern Bell	210	1.08
3	3	Intel	205	1.05
7	7	Archer-Daniels-Midland	188	0.96
2	2	Pfizer	183	0.94
9	9	Southern	182	0.93
6	6	Abbott Laboratories	180	0.92
5	5	PepsiCo	180	0.92
2	2	Intl Paper	173	0.88
3	3	BellSouth	172	0.88
3	3	Bell Atlantic	167	0.85

Composition % 06-30-94

Cash	4.5	Preferreds	0.0
Stocks	95.5	Convertibles	0.0
Bonds	0.0	Other	0.0

Tax Analysis

	Tax-Adj Historical Return %	% Pretax Return
3 Yr Avg	---	---
5 Yr Avg	---	---
10 Yr Avg	---	---
Potential Capital Gain Exposure (% of assets)		-3%

Most Similar Funds in MF500

Fund lacks three-year record

Index Allocation

	% of Stocks
S&P 500	84.6
S&P MidCap 400	7.8
U.S. Small Cap	4.5
Foreign	6.5

Sector Weightings

	% of Stocks	Relative S&P 500
Utilities	11.5	0.93
Energy	9.6	0.95
Financials	11.0	1.04
Industrial Cyclicals	17.0	1.04
Consumer Durables	6.4	1.04
Consumer Staples	12.4	0.99
Services	6.6	0.82
Retail	7.4	1.27
Health	8.4	0.97
Technology	9.7	1.06

Dreyfus

	Ticker	Load	NAV	Yield	SEC Yield	Assets	Objective
	DREVX	None	11.93	1.7%	N/A	2447.9	Growth/Inc.

Dreyfus Fund seeks long-term capital growth consistent with the preservation of capital; current income is a secondary consideration.

The fund invests primarily in the securities of seasoned companies. In periods of market strength, the fund tries to be fully invested in common stocks. At other times, it may hold fixed-income securities. To a limited extent, the fund may purchase put and call options. The fund may also invest up to 20% of its assets in foreign securities not publicly traded in the United States.

Manager's Investment Style

Management invests in large-cap classic-growth firms and cyclicals that have growth potential, seeking firms trying to improve their margins or increase their earnings power. The fund often holds significant cash stakes to ameliorate volatility.

Fund Manager(s)

Wolodymyr Wronskyj, since 1990. BA, City C. of New York MA, New York U.

Manager Experience

	Dates Managed	Invest Obj	Std Dev	+/- Index
Not available.				

Historical Profile

Return	Below Average
Risk	Below Average
Rating ★★★	Neutral

Investment Style History
Equity
Average % Stocks Held in Portfolio

67% 47% 57% 61% 81% 84% 83% 88%

Growth of $10,000

|||| Value of Fund ($000)
— Value of Index ($000) S&P 500
▼ Manager Change
▽ Partial Manager Change
► Mgr Unknown After
◄ Mgr Unknown Before

Performance Quartile (Within Objective)

1983	1984	1985	1986	1987	1988	1989	1990	1991	1992	1993	1994	History
15.40	12.45	13.86	12.55	10.28	10.55	12.07	10.80	13.14	13.27	13.10	11.93	NAV
19.77	3.22	25.07	16.32	8.62	8.74	23.64	-3.33	28.01	5.53	6.37	-4.26	Total Return %
-2.70	-3.04	-6.66	-2.36	3.36	-7.87	-8.05	-0.21	-2.47	-2.09	-3.69	-5.57	+/- S&P 500
-3.70	0.17	-7.49	0.22	6.25	-9.20	-5.54	2.85	-6.19	-3.44	-4.91	-4.19	+/- Wilshire 5000
5.54	5.94	4.23	4.80	6.64	4.49	5.52	4.44	3.25	1.93	2.53	1.70	Income Return %
14.23	-2.72	20.84	11.52	1.97	4.26	18.12	-7.78	24.76	3.60	3.84	-5.96	Capital Return %
40	56	46	46	12	69	27	66	30	73	86	56	Total Rtn % Rank All
59	51	71	53	12	85	51	47	52	77	84	82	Total Rtn % Rank Obj
0.73	0.75	0.49	0.59	0.77	0.46	0.59	0.51	0.35	0.24	0.33	0.22	Income $
1.52	2.66	0.98	2.70	2.57	0.16	0.36	0.37	0.28	0.34	0.66	0.40	Capital Gains $
0.74	0.76	0.75	0.74	0.71	0.77	0.75	0.77	0.78	0.74	0.74	---	Expense Ratio %
5.09	3.99	4.24	3.77	3.51	4.62	4.73	4.20	2.65	2.08	1.67	---	Income Ratio %
80	50	83	149	110	179	104	99	80	55	39	---	Turnover Rate %
1650.5	1922.0	2166.0	2308.6	2364.1	2258.4	2536.0	2525.4	2996.7	3148.9	2850.5	2447.9	Net Assets ($mil)

Performance 12-31-94

	1st Qtr	2nd Qtr	3rd Qtr	4th Qtr	Total
1987	13.83	5.36	5.31	-14.01	8.62
1988	3.91	3.81	-1.47	2.32	8.74
1989	4.37	7.66	7.28	2.56	23.64
1990	-3.15	7.39	-12.57	6.31	-3.33
1991	11.20	-1.34	6.83	9.22	28.01
1992	-2.89	-1.10	4.49	5.16	5.53
1993	2.49	-2.33	2.35	3.82	6.37
1994	-2.88	-2.29	2.73	-1.79	-4.26

Bear Market Performance

Decile Rank (5-year period)

Worst | Best

	Worst 3 Mo Period 1985-89	Worst 3 Mo Period 1990-94
Dreyfus	-20.33	-12.57
+/- S&P 500	9.25	1.17
+/- Best Fit Index : S&P 500	9.25	1.17

Trailing Returns

	Total Return %	+/- S&P 500	+/- Wil 5000	% Rank All	% Rank Obj	Growth of $10,000
3 Mo	-1.79	-1.77	-1.02	64	57	9,821
6 Mo	0.89	-3.97	-3.73	39	78	10,089
1 Yr	-4.26	-5.57	-4.19	56	82	9,574
3 Yr Avg	2.43	-3.83	-4.18	89	86	10,747
5 Yr Avg	5.87	-2.82	-2.95	79	86	13,300
10 Yr Avg	10.95	-3.44	-2.91	48	76	28,256
15 Yr Avg	12.02	-2.46	-1.95	54	72	54,895

Operations

Address and Telephone	One Exchange Place Boston, MA 02109 800-645-6561 / 718-895-1206
Advisor	Dreyfus
Subadvisor	None
Distributor	Dreyfus Service
States Available	All plus PR
Report Grade	B
Income Distrib	Paid Quarterly
Date of Inception	05-24-51
Fiscal Year End	December

Risk Analysis

Time Period	Load-Adj Return %	Risk % Rank [1] All	Obj	Morningstar [2] Return	Risk	Morningstar Risk-Adj Rating
1 Yr	-4.26					
3 Yr	2.43	71	71	-0.33 [3]	0.81	★★
5 Yr	5.87	63	39	0.27 [3]	0.76	★★★
10 Yr	10.95	47	18	0.70	0.68	★★★
Average Historical Rating (109 months)				3.4	★ s	

[1] 1 = low, 100 = high [2] 1.00 = Equity Avg [3] 1.00 = 90-day T-bill return

Other Measures

			Standard S&P 500	Best Fit S&P 500
Standard Deviation	8.03	Alpha	-3.5	-3.5
Mean	2.73	Beta	0.95	0.95
Sharpe Ratio	-0.10	R-Squared	87	87

Investment Style

	Stock Portfolio Avg	Relative S&P 500
Price/Earnings Ratio	15.0	0.81
Price/Book Ratio	3.0	0.87
5 Yr Earnings Gr %	9.5	1.71
Return on Assets %	6.2	0.83
Debt % Total Cap	32.4	1.15
Med Mkt Cap ($mil)	7197	0.55

Style
Value Blend Growth
Size Large Med Small

Diversification Value for Portfolio Types

○ Large Cap: None
◨ Small Cap: Low
● Bond: High
○ Balanced: None
◨ Diversified: Low

Portfolio 06-30-94

Total Stocks: 80
Total Fixed-Income: 9

Share Chg (12-93) 000	Amount 000		Value $000	% Net Assets
0	1500	Chrysler	70688	2.77
1000	2000	Lowe's	68500	2.69
0	1140	Conrail	62415	2.45
0	1176	Colgate-Palmolive	61152	2.40
1000	2000	McDonald's	57750	2.26
0	983	Mellon Bank	55299	2.17
0	1140	Roche Holding (ADR)	54293	2.13
0	1000	Procter & Gamble	53375	2.09
0	800	Gillette	52100	2.04
0	1000	Philip Morris	51500	2.02
545	1090	General Electric	50821	1.99
750	2250	MBNA	50625	1.98
0	1250	AMBAC	49063	1.92
300	1000	Sears Roebuck	48000	1.88
0	800	Ford Motor	47200	1.85
0	1525	PepsiCo	46703	1.83
800	1600	Bank of New York	46200	1.81
0	600	CSX	45300	1.78
0	600	Hewlett-Packard	45225	1.77
0	1000	Dial	42750	1.68
0	500	ITT	40813	1.60
0	700	AT & T	38063	1.49
0	700	Burlington Northern	37363	1.46
0	750	Eastman Kodak	36094	1.42
0	950	Sprint	33131	1.30

Composition % 09-30-94

Cash	17.0	Preferreds	0.3	
Stocks	82.5	Convertibles	0.2	
Bonds	0.0	Other	0.0	

Tax Analysis

	Tax-Adj Historical Return %	% Pretax Return
3 Yr Avg	0.70	28.1
5 Yr Avg	3.97	65.1
10 Yr Avg	7.64	59.6
Potential Capital Gain Exposure (% of assets)		19%

Most Similar Funds in MF500

Alliance Growth & Income A	Strong Fit
Liberty All-Star	Strong Fit
Dreyfus Appreciation	Strong Fit

Index Allocation

	% of Stocks
S&P 500	83.0
S&P MidCap 400	6.3
U.S. Small Cap	7.5
Foreign	4.2

Sector Weightings

	% of Stocks	Relative S&P 500
Utilities	2.8	0.22
Energy	0.0	0.00
Financials	15.6	1.48
Industrial Cyclicals	11.4	0.70
Consumer Durables	19.0	3.05
Consumer Staples	14.5	1.16
Services	14.5	1.79
Retail	8.0	1.37
Health	3.4	0.39
Technology	10.9	1.19

Expenses & Fees

Min Initial Purchase	$2500 (Addt'l: $100)
Min IRA Purchase	$750 (Addt'l: None)
Min Auto Invest Plan	$2500 (Systematic Inv: $100)

Sales Fees
	0.00% front
	0.00% deferred
	0.00% 12b-1
Management Fee	0.65% max./0.55% min.
3-,5-,10-yr Expense Projections	$24, $41, $92
Annual Brokerage Cost	0.10%

MORNINGSTAR 1995 Mutual Fund 500

Dreyfus Global Growth

	Ticker	Load	NAV	Yield	SEC Yield	Assets	Objective
	DSWIX	3.00%	32.99	0.0%	N/A	134.2	World Stock

Dreyfus Global Growth Fund seeks capital growth.

The fund may invest in foreign and domestic securities, normally investing in the securities of at least three countries. All publicly issued common stocks of foreign and domestic issuers may be purchased, without limitation as to the type, size, operating history, or dividend record of the issuers. It may also invest in debt securities rated at least CCC when they appear to offer the potential for capital growth. The fund may leverage, engage in arbitrage, sell short, and use a number of futures and options strategies.

Prior to Feb. 7, 1994, the fund was named Dreyfus Strategic World Investing.

Manager's Investment Style

Because this fund is technically a limited partnership, it has the freedom to leverage its assets and make short-term bets without limit. Typically, management has used various hedging instruments to limit the risks in international markets, and has often held large stakes in cash. New manager Kelly McDermott has changed the fund focus recently from top-down country allocation to bottom-up stockpicking, and has invested more fund assets in stocks.

Fund Manager(s)

Kelly McDermott, since 10-93. International Economics, London School of Economics

Manager Experience	Dates Managed	Invest Obj	Std Dev	+/- Index
Kelly McDermott				
Dreyfus Strategic Growth	10/93 - 12/94	AG	8.04	3.57
Dreyfus Global InvB(Prem)	10/93 - 12/94	WW	11.60	-0.32

Historical Profile

Return	Below Average
Risk	Below Average
Rating ★★★	Neutral

Average % Stocks Held in Portfolio: 81% 68% 79% 42% 42% 27% 53% 80%

Investment Style History Equity

Growth of $10,000

||||Value of Fund ($000)
— Value of Index ($000) MSPacxJp
▼ Manager Change
▽ Partial Manager Change
► Mgr Unknown After
◄ Mgr Unknown Before

Performance Quartile (Within Objective)

	1983	1984	1985	1986	1987	1988	1989	1990	1991	1992	1993	1994	History
	---	---	---	---	17.30	19.98	24.18	25.58	30.06	29.24	35.58	32.99	NAV
	---	---	---	---	33.08 *	15.49	21.02	5.79	17.51	-2.73	21.68	-7.28	Total Return %
	---	---	---	---	46.58 *	-1.12	-10.66	8.91	-12.97	-10.35	11.63	-8.59	+/- S&P 500
	---	---	---	---	---	-7.80	4.41	22.81	-0.77	2.50	-0.82	-12.36	+/- MSCI World
	---	---	---	---	0.00	0.00	0.00	0.00	0.00	0.00	0.00	0.00	Income Return %
	---	---	---	---	33.08	15.49	21.02	5.79	17.51	-2.73	21.68	-7.28	Capital Return %
	---	---	---	---	---	26	33	37	49	93	15	82	Total Rtn % Rank All
	---	---	---	---	---	34	52	5	41	62	85	83	Total Rtn % Rank Obj
	---	---	---	---	0.00	0.00	0.00	0.00	0.00	0.00	0.00	0.00	Income $
	---	---	---	---	0.00	0.00	0.00	0.00	0.00	0.00	0.00	0.00	Capital Gains $
	---	---	---	---	---	1.74	1.50	1.78	1.62	1.61	1.50	---	Expense Ratio %
	---	---	---	---	---	2.62	1.37	3.73	2.39	1.67	0.96	---	Income Ratio %
	---	---	---	---	---		452	452	566	420	439	187	Turnover Rate %
	---	---	---	---	9.8	18.2	17.2	25.3	54.5	111.4	159.4	134.2	Net Assets ($mil)

Performance 12-31-94

	1st Qtr	2nd Qtr	3rd Qtr	4th Qtr	Total
1987	---	21.08	11.50	-1.42	33.08 *
1988	8.96	1.49	-0.16	4.61	15.49
1989	2.60	4.20	11.14	1.85	21.02
1990	3.35	2.32	-1.80	1.87	5.79
1991	7.19	-0.18	6.72	2.91	17.51
1992	0.50	1.03	-2.59	-1.65	-2.73
1993	3.63	2.64	3.25	10.81	21.68
1994	-4.81	-0.77	2.62	-4.35	-7.28

Bear Market Performance

Decile Rank (5-year period)

Worst — Best

	Worst 3 Mo Period 1985-89	Worst 3 Mo Period 1990-94
Dreyfus Global Growth	---	-7.52
+/- S&P 500	---	-1.76
+/- Best Fit Index : MSPacxJp	---	3.57

Trailing Returns

	Total Return %	+/- S&P 500	+/- MSCI World	% Rank All	% Rank Obj	Growth of $10,000
3 Mo	-4.35	-4.33	-3.62	90	45	9,565
6 Mo	-1.84	-6.71	-3.24	86	77	9,816
1 Yr	-7.28	-8.59	-12.36	82	83	9,272
3 Yr Avg	3.15	-3.12	-3.70	84	86	10,975
5 Yr Avg	6.41	-2.28	2.74	66	40	13,644
10 Yr Avg	---	---	---	---	---	---
15 Yr Avg	---	---	---	---	---	---

Operations

Address and Telephone	One Exchange Place Boston, MA 02109 800-645-6561 / 718-895-1206
Advisor	Dreyfus
Subadvisor	None
Distributor	Premier Mutual Fund Services
States Available	All plus PR
Report Grade	B-
Income Distrib	Paid Annually
* Date of Inception	04-10-87
Fiscal Year End	December

Min Initial Purchase	$2500 (Addt'l: $500)
Min IRA Purchase	N/A
Min Auto Invest Plan	$2500 (Systematic Inv: $100)

Expenses & Fees

Sales Fees	3.00% front
	0.00% deferred
	0.25% 12b-1
Management Fee	0.75% flat fee
3-,5-,10-yr Expense Projections	$76, $109, $204
Annual Brokerage Cost	0.91%

Risk Analysis

Time Period	Load-Adj Return %	Risk % Rank All	Risk % Rank Obj	Morningstar Return	Morningstar Risk	Morningstar Risk-Adj Rating
1 Yr	-10.06					
3 Yr	2.11	73	30	-0.42[3]	0.83	★★
5 Yr	5.76	50	1	0.25[3]	0.51	★★★
10 Yr	---					

Average Historical Rating (58 months)   3.9 ★ s

[1] 1 = low, 100 = high   [2] 1.00 = Equity Avg   [3] 1.00 = 90-day T-bill return

Other Measures

				Standard S&P 500	Best Fit MSPacxJp
Standard Deviation	9.78	Alpha		-1.6	-5.7
Mean	3.57	Beta		0.56	0.39
Sharpe Ratio	0.01	R-Squared		21	68

Investment Style

	Stock Portfolio Avg	Rel MSCI EAFE	Rel Obj	Style
Price/Earnings Ratio	33.8	0.91	1.37	V B G
Price/Cash Flow	12.8	0.82	0.95	
Price/Book Ratio	2.8	1.06	0.95	Size L M S
5 Yr Earnings Gr %	3.9	---	0.81	
Return on Assets %	6.4	1.40	0.93	
Debt % Total Cap	22.4	0.66	0.78	
Med Mkt Cap ($mil)	5129	0.43	1.02	

Diversification Value for Portfolio Types

Large Cap: High	Small Cap: High	Bond: High	Balanced: High	Diversified: Medium

Portfolio 06-30-94

Total Stocks: 88
Total Fixed-Income: 1

Share Chg (12-93)000	Amount 000		Value $000	% Net Assets
330	330	Mitsubishi Heavy Industries	2643	1.79
0	1	Roche Holding (Gen)	2638	1.78
245	245	Hitachi	2562	1.73
49	49	TDK	2433	1.64
260	260	New Japan Securities	2376	1.60
3	3	BBC Brown Boveri Cl A	2357	1.59
0	0	DDI Pharmaceuticals	2343	1.58
170	170	Yamato Transport	2261	1.53
45	45	Boeing	2081	1.41
-102	371	Malayan Banking	2077	1.40
90	90	Toyota Motor	2019	1.36
0	8	Mannesmann (Germany)	2012	1.36
225	225	Jurong Shipyard	1990	1.34
130	130	Toppan Printing	1980	1.34
250	250	Jardine Matheson Holdings	1924	1.30
125	125	Sumitomo Electric Industries	1916	1.29
90	90	Nippondenso	1891	1.28
0	13	Deutsche Babcock/Wilcox	1861	1.26
0	98	Kimberly-Clark	1815	1.23
0	307	Resorts World	1768	1.19

Regional Exposure 04-12-94
% of Stocks

Europe	32	Pacific Rim	19
Japan	16	U.S.	28
Latin Amer	6	Other	0

Composition % 09-30-94

Cash	17.8	Preferreds	0.0
Stocks	82.2	Convertibles	0.0
Bonds	0.0	Other	0.0

Tax Analysis

	Tax-Adj Historical Return %	% Pretax Return
3 Yr Avg	3.15	100.0
5 Yr Avg	6.41	100.0
10 Yr Avg	---	---
Potential Capital Gain Exposure (% of assets)		15%

Most Similar Funds in MF500

Scudder International	Weak Fit
T. Rowe Price Intl Stock	Weak Fit
G.T. Global Worldwide Grth A	Weak Fit

Top 5 Countries 09-14-94

	% of Stocks
Japan	18
U.S.	15
Germany	8
Malaysia	8
France	4

Total Number of Countries: 14
Hedging Policy: Active

Sector Weightings

	% of Stocks	Relative S&P 500
Utilities	4.1	0.49
Energy	2.2	0.45
Financials	13.9	0.84
Industrial Cyclicals	26.0	1.12
Consumer Durables	15.0	1.45
Consumer Staples	2.8	0.54
Services	10.0	0.84
Retail	7.8	1.34
Health	7.3	1.38
Technology	11.1	1.25

Dreyfus GNMA

	Ticker	Load	NAV	Yield	SEC Yield	Assets	Objective
	DRGMX	None	13.79	6.8%	6.74%	1427.9	Gvt Mortgage

Dreyfus GNMA Fund seeks current income consistent with preservation of capital.

The fund normally invests at least 65% of its assets in Government National Mortgage Association (GNMA) certificates. It may also invest in other securities issued or guaranteed by the U.S. government or issued by its agencies or instrumentalities that are backed by the full faith and credit of the U.S. government. The fund may invest in repurchase agreements on these securities. The fund may also write and sell covered call option contracts on up to 20% of its assets.

Manager's Investment Style

Management prefers straightforward GNMA securities with intermediate durations. It will make moderate interest-rate bets, using non-GNMA government issues, with small portions of assets. The fund has held a large stake in older superpremium mortgages for several years, which has helped boost the fund's yield.

Fund Manager(s)

Garitt Kono, since 12-92. Birthdate: 08-40. BBA, U. of Notre Dame 1962

Manager Experience

	Dates Managed	Invest Obj	Std Dev	+/- Index
Garitt Kono				
Premier GNMA A	12/92 - 12/94	GM	3.36	-0.72
Dreyfus Investors GNMA	12/92 - 12/94	GM	3.08	0.51

Historical Profile

Return	Above Average
Risk	Below Average
Rating	★★★★ Above Average

Investment Style History
Fixed Income

| | | | | | | | | 21 | 71 | 63 | 46 | 43 | 51 | 48 | 47 | Income Rtn % Rank Obj |

Growth of $10,000
|||| Value of Fund ($000)
— Value of Index ($000) LB Mtg
▼ Manager Change
▽ Partial Manager Change
► Mgr Unknown After
◄ Mgr Unknown Before

Performance Quartile (Within Objective)

1983	1984	1985	1986	1987	1988	1989	1990	1991	1992	1993	1994	History
---	---	15.73	15.70	14.59	14.21	14.49	14.54	15.32	15.12	15.15	13.79	NAV
---	---	14.17 *	9.71	2.57	6.38	11.56	9.75	14.50	6.34	7.16	-2.78	Total Return %
---	---	---	-5.54	-0.18	-1.50	-2.98	0.81	-1.51	-0.91	-2.59	0.13	+/- LB Aggregate
---	---	---	-3.72	-1.72	-2.34	-3.79	-0.97	-1.23	-0.62	0.33	-1.18	+/- LB Mortgage
---	---	5.69	9.90	9.49	8.99	9.59	9.40	9.13	7.64	6.96	6.19	Income Return %
---	---	8.48	-0.19	-6.91	-2.60	1.97	0.35	5.36	-1.31	0.20	-8.98	Capital Return %
---	---	---	85	38	86	61	6	60	65	83	41	Total Rtn % Rank All
---	---	---	75	41	81	82	53	58	51	37	58	Total Rtn % Rank Obj
---	---	0.78	1.47	1.46	1.29	1.29	1.29	1.23	1.13	1.03	0.94	Income $
---	---	0.00	0.00	0.03	0.00	0.00	0.00	0.00	0.00	0.00	0.00	Capital Gains $
---	---	0.96	1.01	1.01	0.99	0.97	0.97	0.95	0.94	0.94	0.95	Expense Ratio %
---	---	---	10.27	8.87	8.98	8.89	8.98	8.81	8.05	7.20	6.54	Income Ratio %
---	---	---	245	257	288	473	272	26	61	156	211	Turnover Rate %
---	---	402.0	2178.2	1977.4	1762.3	1565.6	1545.2	1823.8	1837.1	1792.7	1427.9	Net Assets ($mil)

Performance 12-31-94

	1st Qtr	2nd Qtr	3rd Qtr	4th Qtr	Total
1987	2.33	-2.04	-2.39	4.83	2.57
1988	3.70	1.48	1.15	-0.06	6.38
1989	0.36	6.12	1.32	3.38	11.56
1990	-0.02	3.53	1.54	4.42	9.75
1991	2.70	1.67	4.96	4.47	14.50
1992	-1.32	3.38	3.82	0.41	6.34
1993	3.06	2.02	1.20	0.72	7.16
1994	-2.36	-0.58	0.18	-0.03	-2.78

Bear Market Performance

Decile Rank (5-year period)

Worst .... Best

	Worst 3 Mo Period 1985-89	Worst 3 Mo Period 1990-94
Dreyfus GNMA	---	-3.78
+/- LB Aggregate	---	1.15
+/- Best Fit Index : LB Mtg	---	0.22

Trailing Returns

	Total Return %	+/- LB Aggregate	+/- LB Mortgage	% Rank All	% Rank Obj	Growth of $10,000
3 Mo	-0.03	-0.41	-0.46	23	56	9,997
6 Mo	0.14	-0.85	-1.16	54	68	10,014
1 Yr	-2.78	0.13	-1.18	41	58	9,722
3 Yr Avg	3.47	-1.07	-0.51	79	43	11,078
5 Yr Avg	6.84	-0.79	-0.73	54	44	13,921
10 Yr Avg	---	---	---	---	---	---
15 Yr Avg	---	---	---	---	---	---

Operations

Address and Telephone	One Exchange Place
	Boston, MA 02109
	800-645-6561 / 718-895-1206
Advisor	Dreyfus
Subadvisor	None
Distributor	Premier Mutual Fund Services
States Available	All plus PR
Report Grade	B-
Income Distrib	Paid Monthly
* Date of Inception	05-29-85
Fiscal Year End	April

Risk Analysis

Time Period	Load-Adj Return %	Risk % Rank All	Risk % Rank Obj	Morningstar[2] Return	Morningstar Risk	Morningstar Risk-Adj Rating
1 Yr	-2.78					
3 Yr	3.47	13	37	-0.03[3]	0.84	★★★
5 Yr	6.84	10	30	0.51[3]	0.77	★★★★
10 Yr	---	---	---	---	---	---

Average Historical Rating (80 months)   3.4 ★s

[1] 1 = low, 100 = high   [2] 1.00 = Taxable Avg   [3] 1.00 = 90-day T-bill return

Other Measures

		Standard LB Agg	Best Fit LB Mtg
Standard Deviation	3.26	Alpha	-0.8	-0.5
Mean	3.47	Beta	0.78	0.99
Sharpe Ratio	-0.02	R-Squared	90	95

Investment Style

Interest-Rate Stance

Avg Effective Duration	5.4 Yrs
Avg Effective Maturity	9.5 Yrs

Quality

Avg Credit Quality	AAA
Avg Weighted Coupon	8.44%
Avg Weighted Price	99.11% of Par

Diversification Value for Portfolio Types

| Large Cap: Medium | Small Cap: High | Bond: None | Balanced: Medium | Diversified: Medium |

Portfolio 10-31-94

Amount 000	Date of Maturity	Total Stocks: 0 / Total Fixed-Income: 20	Value $000	% Net Assets
344707	07-15-24	GNMA 8%	332763	22.59
280182	08-15-24	GNMA 8.5%	277030	18.81
198490	08-15-24	GNMA 7%	185596	12.60
100000		GNMA TBA 9%	101843	6.92
90968	05-15-09	GNMA 7.5%	88437	6.00
60888	09-15-19	GNMA 11%	67287	4.57
55852	10-15-20	GNMA 10%	59849	4.06
52257	06-15-21	GNMA 10.5%	56770	3.85
50000		GNMA TBA 7%	44859	3.05
23772	07-15-19	GNMA 11.5%	26609	1.81
7040	10-15-23	GNMA 7.25%	7084	0.48
4307	03-20-16	GNMA 9%	4354	0.30
3439	01-20-16	GNMA GPM 11.25%	3754	0.25
2131	12-20-15	GNMA 12%	2333	0.16
1422	06-20-15	GNMA 13.5%	1604	0.11
1450	04-15-16	GNMA GPM 10.75%	1572	0.11
749	03-15-11	GNMA GPM 11%	813	0.06
437	01-20-16	GNMA GPM 11.75%	478	0.03
407	10-15-18	GNMA GPM 10.25%	438	0.03
71	03-15-15	GNMA GPM 12.25%	78	0.01

Composition % 09-30-94

Cash	14.0	Preferreds	0.0
Stocks	0.0	Convertibles	0.0
Bonds	86.1	Other	0.0

Tax Analysis

	Tax-Adj Historical Return %	% Pretax Return
3 Yr Avg	0.91	25.5
5 Yr Avg	4.15	57.5
10 Yr Avg	---	---

Potential Capital Gain Exposure (% of assets)   -17%

Most Similar Funds in MF500

Vanguard F/I GNMA	Strong Fit
T. Rowe Price GNMA	Strong Fit
Benham GNMA Income	Strong Fit

Coupon Range

	% of Bonds	Rel Obj
0%	0.0	0.00
0% to 8%	52.1	0.95
8% to 9%	30.3	1.39
9% to 10%	4.7	0.55
More than 10%	12.8	1.95
Not applicable	0.0	0.00

Sector Analysis 10-31-94

% of Bonds

US Treas	0	CMOs	0
GNMA mtgs	100	ARMs	0
FNMA mtgs	0	Other	0
FHLMC mtgs	0		

Expenses & Fees

Sales Fees	
	0.00% front
	0.00% deferred
	0.20% 12b-1
Management Fee	0.60% flat fee
3-,5-,10-yr Expense Projections	$30, $53, $117

Min Initial Purchase	$2500 (Addt'l: $100)
Min IRA Purchase	$750 (Addt'l: None)
Min Auto Invest Plan	$2500 (Systematic Inv: $100)

136

MORNINGSTAR 1995 Mutual Fund 500

Dreyfus Intermediate Muni Bond

Ticker	Load	NAV	Yield	SEC Yield	Assets	Objective
DITEX	None	13.14	5.7%	5.61%	1447.6	Muni Nat

Dreyfus Intermediate Municipal Bond Fund seeks current income exempt from federal income tax, consistent with preservation of capital.

The fund normally invests at least 80% of its assets in high-quality municipal obligations. It expects to maintain an average weighted portfolio maturity between three and 10 years. The fund may invest up to 5% of its assets in zero-coupon or pay-in-kind bonds and may invest an unlimited amount in bonds subject to the Alternative Minimum Tax.

Prior to Sept. 12, 1990, the fund was named Dreyfus Intermediate Tax-Exempt Bond Fund.

Manager's Investment Style

The fund's intermediate mandate limits the fund's overall potential for volatility, but management prefers to take aggressive positions within its mandate. Average maturity is typically at the long end of the fund's three- to 10-year range, with lower-rated investment-grade issues and nonrated bonds typically taking up large portions of assets. The fund is less volatile than the average muni fund, but more volatile than the average intermediate muni fund.

Fund Manager(s)

Monica S. Wieboldt, since 05-85. BA, SUNY-New Paltz

Manager Experience	Dates Managed	Invest Obj	Std Dev	+/- Index
Monica S. Wieboldt				
Dreyfus NY Tax-Ex Bond	09/85 - 12/94	MY	5.92	-1.48
Dreyfus NY Tax-Ex Int Bd	06/87 - 12/94	MY	4.57	-1.78

Historical Profile

Return	Average
Risk	Below Average
Rating ★★★★	Above Average

Investment Style History
Fixed Income
Income Rtn % Rank Obj

47 52 34 27 37 42 44 28

Growth of $10,000

|||| Value of Fund ($000)
— Value of Index ($000)
LB Muni
▼ Manager Change
▽ Partial Manager Change
► Mgr Unknown After
◄ Mgr Unknown Before

Performance Quartile (Within Objective)

	1983	1984	1985	1986	1987	1988	1989	1990	1991	1992	1993	1994	History
NAV	12.42	12.28	13.16	14.12	13.30	13.37	13.54	13.48	13.95	13.97	14.61	13.14	NAV
	2.57 *	7.46	16.06	15.43	1.15	8.04	8.72	6.75	11.13	8.71	11.56	-4.57	Total Return %
	---	-7.69	-6.06	0.18	-1.61	0.16	-5.82	-2.19	-4.87	1.47	1.80	-1.65	+/- LB Aggregate
	---	-3.09	-3.96	-3.89	-0.36	-2.13	-2.06	-0.55	-1.01	-0.11	-0.72	1.04	+/- LB Muni
	3.21	8.59	8.90	8.13	6.95	7.51	7.45	7.19	7.05	6.30	5.74	5.11	Income Return %
	-0.64	-1.13	7.17	7.29	-5.81	0.53	1.27	-0.44	4.08	2.41	5.81	-9.67	Capital Return %
	---	39	89	51	49	73	86	24	83	37	55	59	Total Rtn % Rank All
	---	76	78	72	30	77	71	28	62	44	52	38	Total Rtn % Rank Obj
	0.40	1.02	1.02	1.01	0.97	0.97	0.96	0.94	0.90	0.85	0.77	0.75	Income $
	0.00	0.00	0.00	0.00	0.00	0.00	0.00	0.00	0.08	0.31	0.16	0.06	Capital Gains $
	---	0.69	0.81	0.75	0.71	0.73	0.71	0.71	0.69	0.70	0.71	0.70	Expense Ratio %
	---	8.31	8.23	7.76	7.07	7.21	7.27	7.01	6.84	6.47	5.68	5.22	Income Ratio %
	---	---	21	34	50	49	34	40	31	48	60	36	Turnover Rate %
	68.6	228.5	548.7	920.2	983.9	1048.1	1110.2	1143.5	1379.0	1570.6	1832.8	1447.6	Net Assets ($mil)

Performance 12-31-94

	1st Qtr	2nd Qtr	3rd Qtr	4th Qtr	Total
1987	2.77	-2.75	-1.31	2.54	1.15
1988	2.57	1.73	1.84	1.66	8.04
1989	0.78	4.19	0.79	2.74	8.72
1990	0.78	1.91	0.76	3.15	6.75
1991	2.08	2.06	3.49	3.06	11.13
1992	0.43	3.82	2.54	1.68	8.71
1993	3.10	3.30	3.50	1.21	11.56
1994	-4.45	1.07	0.37	-1.53	-4.57

Bear Market Performance

Decile Rank (5-year period)

Worst — Best

	Worst 3 Mo Period 1985-89	Worst 3 Mo Period 1990-94
Dreyfus Intermediate Muni Bon	-4.92	-5.10
+/- LB Aggregate	-1.36	-0.17
+/- Best Fit Index : LB Muni	1.57	0.66

Trailing Returns

	Total Return %	+/- LB Aggregate	+/- LB Muni	% Rank All	% Rank Obj	Growth of $10,000
3 Mo	-1.53	-1.91	-0.10	58	60	9,847
6 Mo	-1.17	-2.17	0.07	76	60	9,883
1 Yr	-4.57	-1.65	1.04	59	38	9,543
3 Yr Avg	4.99	0.45	0.12	48	29	11,574
5 Yr Avg	6.55	-1.08	-0.23	61	29	13,730
10 Yr Avg	8.13	-1.81	-1.30	85	73	21,854
15 Yr Avg	---	---	---	---	---	---

Operations

Address and Telephone	One Exchange Place
	Boston, MA 02109
	800-645-6561 / 718-895-1206
Advisor	Dreyfus
Subadvisor	None
Distributor	Premier Mutual Fund Services
States Available	All plus PR
Report Grade	C
Income Distrib	Paid Monthly
* Date of Inception	08-11-83
Fiscal Year End	May

Risk Analysis

Time Period	Load-Adj Return %	Risk % Rank All	Risk % Rank Obj	Morningstar Return	Morningstar Risk	Morningstar Risk-Adj Rating
1 Yr	-4.57					
3 Yr	4.99	19	34	1.27	0.86	★★★★
5 Yr	6.55	10	28	1.10	0.81	★★★★
10 Yr	8.13	4	18	0.92	0.92	★★★★
Average Historical Rating (102 months)					3.9	★ s

1 = low, 100 = high   ² 1.00 = Muni Avg   ³ 1.00 = 90-day T-bill return

Other Measures

			Standard LB Agg	Best Fit LB Muni
Standard Deviation	5.04	Alpha	0.5	0.2
Mean	5.01	Beta	0.95	0.91
Sharpe Ratio	0.29	R-Squared	57	97

Investment Style

Interest-Rate Stance

Avg Effective Maturity   10.0 Yrs

Maturity: Short Intm Long
Quality: High Med Low

Quality

Avg Credit Quality	AA
Avg Weighted Coupon	6.49%
Avg Weighted Price	102.83% of Par

Diversification Value for Portfolio Types

Large Cap: Medium	Small Cap: High	Bond: Low	Balanced: Medium	Diversified: High

Portfolio 05-31-94

Total Stocks: 0
Total Fixed-Income: 288

Amount 000	Date of Maturity		Value $000	% Net Assets
27000		WA Pub Pwr Sply Sys Proj #3 DMD	27000	1.57
23500	07-01-04	FL Tpk 5.9%	24757	1.44
20000	11-15-06	CA Sacramento MUD Elec 5.4%	19452	1.13
16745	07-01-02	WA Pub Pwr Sply Sys Proj #1 7.7%	19263	1.12
17500	01-01-08	IN Muni Pwr Sply Sys IFRN	17200	1.00
16800	12-15-03	LA Crtnl Fac IFRN	17154	0.99
16400		KY Jefferson Alliant Hlth Sys DMD	16400	0.95
16200		LA Crtnl Fac Lease DMD	16200	0.94
15910	06-01-03	CA Sacramento Sch Ins Compensation 5.75	16179	0.94
16000	08-01-09	TX San Antonio GO 5.75%	15839	0.92
14485	11-15-05	CO Denver Arpt Sys 8.75%	15775	0.91
15000		LA Offshore Term Deepwtr Port DMD	15000	0.87
13750	06-15-09	PA Philadelphia Hosp/Higher Educ 8.875%	14996	0.87
15000	10-01-98	TX Bell Hlth Fac Dev 4.75%	14568	0.84
15300	09-27-07	HI Honolulu GO IFRN	14459	0.84
15350	01-01-04	DE Rvr/Bay 3.75%	14257	0.83
13455	01-01-06	NC East Muni Pwr Sys 6%	13588	0.79
12400	08-01-00	NY New York City GO 7.875%	13522	0.78
13000	05-15-08	TX North Central Hlth Fac Dev 9%	13516	0.78
11995	05-15-03	NY Dorm State Univ Educ Fac 7.25%	13406	0.78

Credit Analysis % of Bonds 10-12-94

US Govt	0	BB	0
AAA	36	B	0
AA	21	Below B	0
A	26	NR/NA	7
BBB	10		

Composition % of Assets 10-12-94

Cash	2.0	Preferreds	0.0
Stocks	0.0	Convertibles	0.0
Bonds	98.0	Other	0.0

Tax Analysis

	Tax-Adj Historical Return %	% Pretax Return
3 Yr Avg	4.63	92.4
5 Yr Avg	6.29	95.6
10 Yr Avg	8.00	97.8
Potential Capital Gain Exposure (% of assets)		-2%

Most Similar Funds in MF500

USAA Tax-Exempt Int-Term	Strong Fit
SteinRoe Intermediate Munis	Strong Fit
T. Rowe Price Tax-Fr Hi-Yld	Strong Fit

Coupon Range

	% Bonds	Rel Obj
0%	0.0	0.00
0% to 6.8%	57.2	0.95
6.8% to 7.5%	17.8	1.15
7.5% to 8.3%	8.4	0.95
More than 8.3%	7.1	0.81
Not applicable	9.4	2.43

Sector Weightings

	% Bonds	Rel Obj
General Obl	12.09	0.57
Utilities	7.99	0.64
Health	18.29	1.39
Water/Waste	3.81	0.60
Housing	2.92	0.40
Education	20.75	3.24
Transportation	7.70	0.76
COP/Lease	4.09	1.28
Private	11.37	0.98
Misc Revenue	6.03	1.21
Demand	4.97	2.02

Top 5 States % of Bonds

TX	7.37	CA	6.71
PA	7.08	LA	6.05
NY	6.91		

Operations (continued)

Min Initial Purchase	$2500 (Addt'l: $100)
Min IRA Purchase	N/A
Min Auto Invest Plan	$2500 (Systematic Inv: $100)

Expenses & Fees

Sales Fees	
	0.00% front
	0.00% deferred
	0.00% 12b-1
Management Fee	0.60% flat fee
3-,5-,10-yr Expense Projections	$22, $39, $87

Dreyfus Municipal Bond

	Ticker	Load	NAV	Yield	SEC Yield	Assets	Objective
	DRTAX	None	11.63	6.4%	6.13%	3625.8	Muni Nat

Dreyfus Municipal Bond Fund seeks current income exempt from federal income tax, consistent with the preservation of capital.

The fund normally invests at least 80% of its assets in municipal obligations. At least 65% of the fund's assets are invested in bonds and debentures, and at least 75% of assets consist of high-quality debt obligations. The fund may invest without limitation in municipal securities that may be subject to the Alternative Minimum Tax.

Prior to April 20, 1992, the fund was named Dreyfus Tax-Exempt Bond Fund.

Historical Profile

Return	Average
Risk	Average
Rating	★★★
	Neutral

Manager's Investment Style

Management keeps the portfolio highly diversified by issue, coupon, maturity, sector, state, and credit quality. It attempts to increase the fund's payout by maintaining stakes in average-quality credits and higher-paying sectors and states. Management has also owned derivatives in an effort to boost yield.

Fund Manager(s)

Richard J. Moynihan, since 10-76. BS, Rider C. MBA, New York U.

Manager Experience	Dates Managed	Invest Obj	Std Dev	+/- Index
Richard J. Moynihan				
Dreyfus Strat Munis	09/87 - 12/94	MN	3.60	-0.59
Dreyfus Strat Mn Bd	11/89 - 12/94	MN	4.26	-1.24

Investment Style History
Fixed Income
Income Rtn % Rank Obj

38	22	22	14	23	24	21	11

Growth of $10,000

‖‖ Value of Fund ($000)
— Value of Index ($000)
LB Muni
▼ Manager Change
▽ Partial Manager Change
► Mgr Unknown After
◄ Mgr Unknown Before

Performance Quartile
(Within Objective)

1983	1984	1985	1986	1987	1988	1989	1990	1991	1992	1993	1994	History
11.07	10.95	11.97	13.01	11.86	12.27	12.48	12.35	12.92	12.87	13.36	11.63	NAV
11.58	8.64	19.42	17.34	-1.72	11.50	9.40	6.43	11.95	8.42	12.71	-6.92	Total Return %
3.21	-6.52	-2.70	2.10	-4.48	3.62	-5.14	-2.52	-4.05	1.18	2.95	-4.00	+/- LB Aggregate
3.53	-1.91	-0.60	-1.97	-3.22	1.34	-1.39	-0.87	-0.19	-0.40	0.43	-1.32	+/- LB Muni
9.46	9.72	10.11	8.66	7.12	8.04	7.68	7.47	7.34	6.63	6.21	5.56	Income Return %
2.12	-1.08	9.32	8.69	-8.84	3.46	1.71	-1.04	4.62	1.79	6.50	-12.49	Capital Return %
71	34	76	37	73	50	80	29	76	40	44	79	Total Rtn % Rank All
26	61	56	58	76	39	53	44	37	52	29	71	Total Rtn % Rank Obj
0.99	1.02	1.02	0.97	0.92	0.91	0.91	0.90	0.86	0.82	0.78	0.75	Income $
0.00	0.00	0.00	0.00	0.00	0.00	0.00	0.00	0.00	0.28	0.33	0.07	Capital Gains $
0.73	0.71	0.69	0.69	0.68	0.71	0.68	0.67	0.67	0.68	0.69	0.68	Expense Ratio %
9.05	9.22	9.11	8.16	7.34	7.68	7.41	7.23	7.05	6.49	5.96	5.80	Income Ratio %
37	22	28	53	67	51	36	28	36	68	45	36	Turnover Rate %
1891.1	2156.7	2949.5	3703.9	3107.8	3346.6	3562.0	3684.7	4117.4	4325.7	4571.9	3625.8	Net Assets ($mil)

Performance 12-31-94

	1st Qtr	2nd Qtr	3rd Qtr	4th Qtr	Total
1987	2.22	-4.94	-3.49	4.80	-1.72
1988	2.82	2.50	3.10	2.62	11.50
1989	0.81	5.36	0.20	2.79	9.40
1990	0.70	2.15	0.33	3.13	6.43
1991	2.28	2.49	3.69	3.00	11.95
1992	0.32	4.00	2.35	1.54	8.42
1993	3.77	3.78	3.85	0.77	12.71
1994	-5.93	0.45	0.20	-1.70	-6.92

Bear Market Performance

Decile Rank (5-year period)

Worst ———————————————— Best

	Worst 3 Mo Period 1985-89	Worst 3 Mo Period 1990-94
Dreyfus Municipal Bond	-7.27	-6.92
+/- LB Aggregate	-3.72	-1.98
+/- Best Fit Index : LB Muni	-0.78	-1.16

Trailing Returns

	Total Return %	+/- LB Aggregate	+/- LB Muni	% Rank All	% Rank Obj	Growth of $10,000
3 Mo	-1.70	-2.08	-0.26	62	69	9,830
6 Mo	-1.50	-2.49	-0.26	82	77	9,850
1 Yr	-6.92	-4.00	-1.32	79	71	9,308
3 Yr Avg	4.38	-0.16	-0.49	61	58	11,373
5 Yr Avg	6.27	-1.36	-0.51	69	48	13,552
10 Yr Avg	8.57	-1.37	-0.85	79	59	22,766
15 Yr Avg	7.53	-3.28	-0.94	96	81	29,715

Operations

Address and Telephone	One Exchange Place
	Boston, MA 02109
	800-645-6561 / 718-895-1206
Advisor	Dreyfus
Subadvisor	None
Distributor	Premier Mutual Fund Services
States Available	All plus PR
Report Grade	C+
Income Distrib	Paid Monthly
Date of Inception	10-04-76
Fiscal Year End	August

Risk Analysis

Time Period	Load-Adj Return %	Risk % Rank[1] All	Obj	Morningstar[2] Return	Morningstar Risk	Morningstar Risk-Adj Rating
1 Yr	-6.92					
3 Yr	4.38	39	63	1.17	1.13	★★★
5 Yr	6.27	20	47	1.09	1.01	★★★
10 Yr	8.57	12	37	1.05	0.99	★★★
Average Historical Rating (109 months)					3.5	★s

[1] 1 = low, 100 = high [2] 1.00 = Muni Avg   [3] 1.00 = 90-day T-bill return

Other Measures

		Standard LB Agg	Best Fit LB Muni
Standard Deviation	6.15	Alpha	-0.2	-0.6
Mean	4.49	Beta	1.19	1.11
Sharpe Ratio	0.16	R-Squared	60	98

Investment Style

Interest-Rate Stance

Avg Effective Maturity 23.1 Yrs

Quality

Avg Credit Quality AA

Avg Weighted Coupon 6.80%

Avg Weighted Price 100.12% of Par

Diversification Value for Portfolio Types

Large Cap: Medium	Small Cap: High	Bond: Low	Balanced: Medium	Diversified: Medium

Portfolio 08-31-94

Total Stocks: 0
Total Fixed-Income: 373

Amount 000	Date of Maturity		Value $000	% Net Assets
73000	02-01-18	IN Indianapolis GO Local Pub Impr 8.5%	82878	2.07
65200	10-01-19	DC Metro Washington Arpt 6.625%	67154	1.68
51300	10-01-22	KS Wichita Hosp RIB	51769	1.29
50600	01-15-33	CA Los Angeles Dept Wtr/Pwr Elec 6.125%	48063	1.20
50200	10-01-15	WA State GO 5.7%	47661	1.19
42000	02-01-07	NY New York City GO 7.5%	46506	1.16
43600	06-01-17	WA State GO 6.4%	44974	1.12
44000	07-01-11	UT Intermountain Pwr Sply 5.55%	41253	1.03
37000	09-01-23	CA Pub Wks Brd Univ Lease 6.75%	40827	1.02
40000	06-01-23	FL GO Brd Educ Cap 5.875%	38261	0.95
33000	12-01-14	LA West Feliciana Poll Cntrl Util 7.7%	35867	0.89
34000	04-01-24	MD Comnty Dev Admin Sngl Fam Prog 6.8%	34499	0.86
37000	08-01-25	AK Valdez Marine Term BP Pipeline 5.85%	33358	0.83
34295	07-01-25	NH Hsg Fin Sngl Fam Mtg 6.05%	32773	0.82
28755	07-01-08	NY Dorm City Univ Sys Ser D 8.125%	32028	0.80
30500	11-15-23	CO Denver Arpt Sys 8.5%	31840	0.79
30975	06-01-25	MA Hsg Fin Sngl Fam Mtg 7.125%	31547	0.79
35710	07-01-15	WA Pub Pwr Sply Sys Proj #3 5.375%	31304	0.78
30800		WA Pub Pwr Sply Sys Proj #2 DMD	30800	0.77
26915	12-01-25	FL Orange Hlth Fac Ser A 7.875%	28530	0.71

Credit Analysis % of Bonds 09-30-94

US Govt	0	BB	1
AAA	27	B	0
AA	30	Below B	1
A	18	NR/NA	5
BBB	20		

Composition % of Assets 09-30-94

Cash	0.1	Preferreds	0.0
Stocks	0.0	Convertibles	0.0
Bonds	99.9	Other	0.0

Tax Analysis

	Tax-Adj Historical Return %	% Pretax Return
3 Yr Avg	3.89	88.3
5 Yr Avg	5.96	94.6
10 Yr Avg	8.42	97.5
Potential Capital Gain Exposure (% of assets)		-4%

Most Similar Funds in MF500

USAA Tax-Exempt Long-Term	Strong Fit
General Municipal Bond	Strong Fit
Smith Barney Tax-Ex Inc B	Strong Fit

Coupon Range

	% Bonds	Rel Obj
0%	2.0	0.79
0% to 6.8%	46.7	0.77
6.8% to 7.5%	16.5	1.07
7.5% to 8.3%	12.9	1.46
More than 8.3%	10.7	1.21
Not applicable	11.1	2.87

Sector Weightings

	% Bonds	Rel Obj
General Obl	15.18	0.72
Utilities	7.95	0.64
Health	18.39	1.39
Water/Waste	3.96	0.62
Housing	11.72	1.60
Education	5.01	0.78
Transportation	12.81	1.26
COP/Lease	4.10	1.29
Private	15.49	1.33
Misc Revenue	0.77	0.15
Demand	4.53	1.84

Top 5 States % of Bonds

NY	8.13	TX	6.88
FL	7.32	IN	6.65
CA	6.96		

Operations (Purchase / Fees)

Min Initial Purchase	$2500 (Addt'l: $100)
Min IRA Purchase	N/A
Min Auto Invest Plan	$2500 (Systematic Inv: $100)

Expenses & Fees

Sales Fees	0.00% front
	0.00% deferred
	0.00% 12b-1
Management Fee	0.60% flat fee
3-,5-,10-yr Expense Projections	$22, $38, $86

 **1995 Mutual Fund 500**

Dreyfus New Leaders

	Ticker	Load	NAV	Yield	SEC Yield	Assets	Objective
	DNLDX	None	31.33	0.2%	N/A	392.8	Small Company

Dreyfus New Leaders Fund seeks capital appreciation.
The fund seeks smaller companies that the advisor judges to be new leaders; that is, the fund seeks to invest in emerging companies with new or innovative products, services, or processes that should enhance prospects for growth or future earnings. Up to 25% of the fund's assets may be invested in foreign companies' common stocks or foreign governments' debt securities. The fund may adopt a defensive posture in declining markets.

Historical Profile

Return	Above Average
Risk	Average
Rating	★★★★
	Above Average

Investment Style History
Equity
Average % Stocks Held in Portfolio

85% 76% 85% 75% 81% 84% 84% 83%

Growth of $10,000

|||| Value of Fund ($000)
— Value of Index ($000)
Wil 4500
▼ Manager Change
▽ Partial Manager Change
► Mgr Unknown After
◄ Mgr Unknown Before

Performance Quartile (Within Objective)

Manager's Investment Style

Management emphasizes sector themes and turnaround plays (especially low-priced firms that are reorganizing), as well as firms that can generate high returns off their own cash flow. In the case of turnaround plays, management looks for companies with a catalyst to propel them to profitability in addition to good value.

Fund Manager(s)

Thomas A. Frank et al. Birthdate: 10-41 BA, Williams C. 1963 Columbia U.

	1983	1984	1985	1986	1987	1988	1989	1990	1991	1992	1993	1994	History
	---	---	18.11	20.36	19.16	23.41	29.27	24.25	32.29	32.17	34.13	31.33	NAV
	---	---	16.69 *	12.51	-5.12	23.35	31.29	-11.86	45.39	9.43	17.07	-0.15	Total Return %
	---	---	-6.27 *	-6.17	-10.38	6.74	-0.39	-8.74	14.90	1.81	7.01	-1.46	+/- S&P 500
	---	---	---	0.75	-1.61	2.81	7.35	1.70	1.94	-2.33	2.53	2.51	+/- Wilshire 4500
	---	---	0.00	0.05	0.77	1.17	1.38	1.86	0.71	0.45	0.21	0.25	Income Return %
	---	---	16.69	12.46	-5.89	22.18	29.91	-13.71	44.68	8.98	16.85	-0.40	Capital Return %
	---	---	71	89	7	12	88	10	28	23	21		Total Rtn % Rank All
	---	---	40	62	32	21	58	61	71	48	41		Total Rtn % Rank Obj
	---	---	0.00	0.01	0.17	0.22	0.38	0.48	0.22	0.14	0.07	0.08	Income $
	---	---	0.00	0.01	0.00	0.00	1.09	1.08	2.74	2.93	3.34	2.61	Capital Gains $
	---	---	1.30	1.41	1.50	1.37	1.42	1.29	1.21	1.22	---		Expense Ratio %
	---	---	0.66	0.35	0.90	1.60	1.31	0.76	0.43	0.19	---		Income Ratio %
	---	---	195	177	120	114	129	108	119	128	---		Turnover Rate %
	---	---	5.1	65.0	79.6	112.2	195.9	102.3	194.0	233.6	339.0	392.8	Net Assets ($mil)

Manager Experience

	Dates Managed	Invest Obj	Std Dev	+/- Index

Not available.

Performance 12-31-94

	1st Qtr	2nd Qtr	3rd Qtr	4th Qtr	Total
1987	21.45	2.27	6.50	-28.28	-5.12
1988	15.03	9.66	-1.49	-0.74	23.35
1989	6.62	8.77	10.13	2.79	31.29
1990	-4.17	7.24	-16.72	2.99	-11.86
1991	18.76	1.42	10.37	9.36	45.39
1992	2.73	-7.08	3.83	10.42	9.43
1993	4.82	0.27	11.64	-0.22	17.07
1994	-2.61	-0.87	5.53	-1.99	-0.15

Bear Market Performance

Decile Rank (5-year period)

Worst ▬ Best

	Worst 3 Mo Period 1985-89	Worst 3 Mo Period 1990-94
Dreyfus New Leaders	---	-18.56
+/- S&P 500	---	-4.72
+/- Best Fit Index : Wil 4500	---	0.84

Trailing Returns

	Total Return %	+/- S&P 500	+/- Wil 4500	% Rank All	% Rank Obj	Growth of $10,000
3 Mo	-1.99	-1.98	0.51	68	68	9,801
6 Mo	3.43	-1.44	-0.77	18	69	10,343
1 Yr	-0.15	-1.46	2.51	21	41	9,985
3 Yr Avg	8.55	2.29	0.94	19	55	12,791
5 Yr Avg	10.39	1.70	1.30	15	62	16,392
10 Yr Avg	---	---	---	---	---	---
15 Yr Avg	---	---	---	---	---	---

Operations

Address and Telephone	One Exchange Place
	Boston, MA 02109
	800-645-6561 / 718-895-1206
Advisor	Dreyfus
Subadvisor	None
Distributor	Premier Mutual Fund Services
States Available	All plus PR
Report Grade	B+
Income Distrib	Paid Annually
* Date of Inception	01-29-85
Fiscal Year End	December

Risk Analysis

Time Period	Load-Adj Return %	Risk % Rank [1] All	Risk % Rank [1] Obj	Morningstar [2] Return	Morningstar Risk	Morningstar Risk-Adj Rating
1 Yr	-0.15					
3 Yr	8.55	71	28	1.51 [3]	0.80	★★★★
5 Yr	10.39	75	21	1.46 [3]	0.89	★★★★
10 Yr	---	---	---	---	---	---

Average Historical Rating (84 months) 3.5 ★s

[1] 1 = low, 100 = high [2] 1.00 = Equity Avg [3] 1.00 = 90-day T-bill return

Other Measures

				Standard S&P 500	Best Fit Wil 4500
Standard Deviation	9.76	Alpha		3.1	1.2
Mean	8.71	Beta		0.74	0.93
Sharpe Ratio	0.53	R-Squared		37	86

Investment Style

	Stock Portfolio Avg	Relative S&P 500
Price/Earnings Ratio	20.4	1.10
Price/Book Ratio	2.2	0.64
5 Yr Earnings Gr %	11.9#	2.15
Return on Assets %	6.1	0.82
Debt % Total Cap	26.3	0.93
Med Mkt Cap ($mil)	299	0.02

figure is based on 50% or less of stocks

Style Value Blend Growth
Size Large Med Small

Diversification Value for Portfolio Types

Large Cap: Medium Small Cap: None Bond: High Balanced: Low Diversified: Low

Portfolio 06-30-94

Share Chg (12-93)000	Amount 000	Total Stocks: 124 Total Fixed-Income: 1	Value $000	% Net Assets
350	350	NovaCare	5600	1.58
158	158	Georgia Gulf	5394	1.52
195	195	Crescent Real Estate	5265	1.49
70	195	Canandaigua Wine Cl A	4875	1.38
45	190	Parker & Parsley Petroleum	4845	1.37
150	150	Precision Castparts	4763	1.34
50	175	Universal Health Services B	4572	1.29
135	205	Colonial Bankgroup Cl A	4484	1.27
3	128	Coastal Healthcare Group	4303	1.21
-30	160	Airgas	4220	1.19
0	275	Baldwin & Lyons Cl B	4056	1.14
111	135	Talbots	4050	1.14
150	150	A Schulman	3881	1.10
100	550	Coda Energy	3781	1.07
355	355	T2 Medical	3683	1.04
-18	87	Danaher	3632	1.02
75	325	Dual Drilling	3616	1.02
0	135	IBP	3594	1.01
85	300	Community Psychiatric Cntrs	3563	1.01
-109	183	Flair	3559	1.00
175	175	Cytec Industries	3478	0.98
-60	150	Dr Pepper/Seven-Up	3450	0.97
500	500	Presidential Life	3438	0.97
-33	105	Equitable of Iowa	3321	0.94
5	170	Albany International Cl A	3209	0.91

Composition % 09-30-94

Cash	17.4	Preferreds 0.0
Stocks	82.5	Convertibles 0.1
Bonds	0.0	Other 0.0

Index Allocation

	% of Stocks
S&P 500	2.4
S&P MidCap 400	20.0
U.S. Small Cap	74.5
Foreign	3.1

Tax Analysis

	Tax-Adj Historical Return %	% Pretax Return
3 Yr Avg	5.92	67.5
5 Yr Avg	7.82	71.5
10 Yr Avg	---	---
Potential Capital Gain Exposure (% of assets)		7%

Most Similar Funds in MF500

Vanguard Index Extended Mkt	Strong Fit
Vista Capital Growth A	Fair Fit
20th Century Heritage Invest	Fair Fit

Sector Weightings

	% of Stocks	Relative S&P 500
Utilities	0.0	0.00
Energy	9.6	0.95
Financials	16.6	1.57
Industrial Cyclicals	28.6	1.74
Consumer Durables	3.3	0.54
Consumer Staples	6.7	0.53
Services	6.9	0.84
Retail	1.6	0.27
Health	18.3	2.10
Technology	8.5	0.93

Expenses & Fees

Min Initial Purchase	$2500 (Addt'l: $100)
Min IRA Purchase	$750 (Addt'l: $100)
Min Auto Invest Plan	$2500 (Systematic Inv: $100)

Sales Fees	0.00% front
	0.00% deferred
	0.25% 12b-1
Management Fee	0.75% flat fee
3-,5-,10-yr Expense Projections	$40, $69, $152
Annual Brokerage Cost	0.34%

Dreyfus Short-Interm Govt

	Ticker	Load	NAV	Yield	SEC Yield	Assets	Objective
	DSIGX	None	10.53	7.2%	7.10%	472.1	Gvt General

Dreyfus Short-Intermediate Government Fund seeks current income consistent with preservation of capital.

The fund invests in U.S. government obligations and related repurchase agreements. These investments include U.S. Treasury obligations, Government National Mortgage Association pass-through certificates, Federal Home Loan Bank obligations, Federal National Mortgage obligations, and Student Loan Marketing Association debt. The maximum remaining maturity of any security in the fund's portfolio may not exceed 3.5 years.

Manager's Investment Style

Since taking over for longtime Dreyfus standout, Barbara Kenworthy, head manager Gerald Thunelius has kept a conservative stance. He has kept down average effective maturity and duration to about two years or less. He has also remained conservative on issue selection. The fund has stuck primarily with Treasuries. He says that with the volatility in 1994's market, he has been comfortable holding only the most-liquid securities. For Thunelius, the key is upholding the fund's two most important qualities: low risk and high relative yield.

Fund Manager(s)

Gerald E. Thunelius, since 06-94. BBA, Dowling C.

Manager Experience	Dates Managed	Invest Obj	Std Dev	+/- Index
Gerald E. Thunelius				
Dreyfus 100% US Tres L-T	06/94 - 12/94	GT	5.85	-3.20
Dreyfus 100% US Tres I-T	06/94 - 12/94	GT	2.46	-1.48

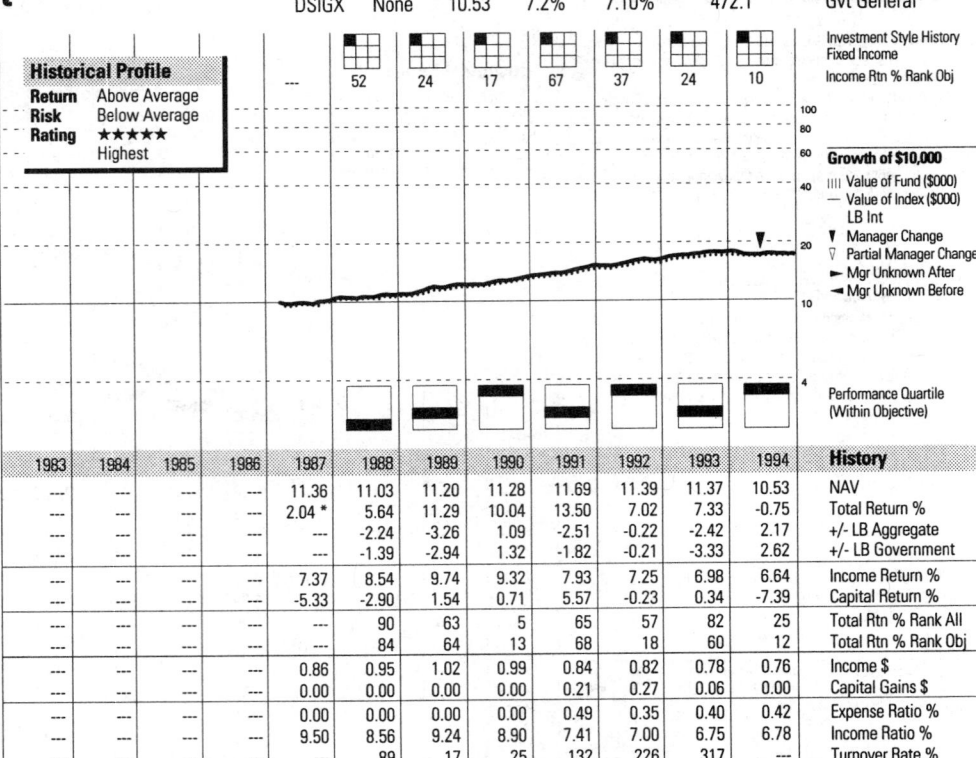

Historical Profile
Return: Above Average
Risk: Below Average
Rating: ★★★★★ Highest

Investment Style History
Fixed Income
Income Rtn % Rank Obj

Growth of $10,000
|||| Value of Fund ($000)
— Value of Index ($000) LB Int
▼ Manager Change
▽ Partial Manager Change
► Mgr Unknown After
◄ Mgr Unknown Before

Performance Quartile (Within Objective)

	1983	1984	1985	1986	1987	1988	1989	1990	1991	1992	1993	1994	History
												52 24 17 67 37 24 10	(style boxes)
	---	---	---	---	11.36	11.03	11.20	11.28	11.69	11.39	11.37	10.53	NAV
	---	---	---	---	2.04 *	5.64	11.29	10.04	13.50	7.02	7.33	-0.75	Total Return %
	---	---	---	---	---	-2.24	-3.26	1.09	-2.51	-0.22	-2.42	2.17	+/- LB Aggregate
	---	---	---	---	---	-1.39	-2.94	1.32	-1.82	-0.21	-3.33	2.62	+/- LB Government
	---	---	---	---	7.37	8.54	9.74	9.32	7.93	7.25	6.98	6.64	Income Return %
	---	---	---	---	-5.33	-2.90	1.54	0.71	5.57	-0.23	0.34	-7.39	Capital Return %
	---	---	---	---	---	90	63	5	65	57	82	25	Total Rtn % Rank All
	---	---	---	---	---	84	64	13	68	18	60	12	Total Rtn % Rank Obj
	---	---	---	---	0.86	0.95	1.02	0.99	0.84	0.82	0.78	0.76	Income $
	---	---	---	---	0.00	0.00	0.00	0.00	0.21	0.27	0.06	0.00	Capital Gains $
	---	---	---	---	0.00	0.00	0.00	0.00	0.49	0.35	0.40	0.42	Expense Ratio %
	---	---	---	---	9.50	8.56	9.24	8.90	7.41	7.00	6.75	6.78	Income Ratio %
	---	---	---	---	---	89	17	25	132	226	317	---	Turnover Rate %
	---	---	---	---	6.0	19.3	34.7	74.0	137.0	350.1	541.9	472.1	Net Assets ($mil)

Performance 12-31-94

	1st Qtr	2nd Qtr	3rd Qtr	4th Qtr	Total
1987	---	-1.73	-0.42	4.28	2.04 *
1988	2.75	0.71	1.32	0.76	5.64
1989	1.00	5.52	1.47	2.90	11.29
1990	1.00	2.73	2.48	3.48	10.04
1991	1.92	1.82	4.33	4.83	13.50
1992	-1.04	4.15	4.44	-0.57	7.02
1993	3.50	1.62	1.74	0.31	7.33
1994	-0.97	-0.07	0.58	-0.28	-0.75

Bear Market Performance

Decile Rank (5-year period)

Worst ————————————————— Best

	Worst 3 Mo Period 1985-89	Worst 3 Mo Period 1990-94
Dreyfus Short-Interm Govt	---	-1.98
+/- LB Aggregate	---	2.96
+/- Best Fit Index : LB Int	---	2.25

Trailing Returns

	Total Return %	+/- LB Aggregate	+/- LB Govt	% Rank All	% Rank Obj	Growth of $10,000
3 Mo	-0.28	-0.66	-0.64	30	76	9,972
6 Mo	0.29	-0.70	-0.49	51	58	10,029
1 Yr	-0.75	2.17	2.62	25	12	9,925
3 Yr Avg	4.46	-0.08	-0.20	59	9	11,400
5 Yr Avg	7.32	-0.31	-0.21	43	14	14,237
10 Yr Avg	---	---	---	---	---	---
15 Yr Avg	---	---	---	---	---	---

Risk Analysis

Time Period	Load-Adj Return %	Risk % Rank [1] All	Obj	Morningstar [2] Return	Morningstar Risk	Morningstar Risk-Adj Rating
1 Yr	-0.75					
3 Yr	4.46	7	14	0.26 [3]	0.69	★★★★
5 Yr	7.32	4	9	0.63 [3]	0.55	★★★★★
10 Yr	---					

Average Historical Rating (58 months) 4.8 ★s

[1] 1 = low, 100 = high [2] 1.00 = Taxable Avg [3] 1.00 = 90-day T-bill return

Other Measures

			Standard LB Agg	Best Fit LB Int
Standard Deviation	2.90	Alpha	0.3	0.5
Mean	4.42	Beta	0.62	0.78
Sharpe Ratio	0.31	R-Squared	73	84

Investment Style

Interest-Rate Stance
Avg Effective Duration	1.5 Yrs
Avg Effective Maturity	2.2 Yrs

Maturity: Short Intm Long
Quality: High Med Low

Quality
Avg Credit Quality	AAA
Avg Weighted Coupon	8.16%
Avg Weighted Price	103.52% of Par

Diversification Value for Portfolio Types

● Large Cap: High
● Small Cap: High
▨ Bond: Low
● Balanced: High
● Diversified: High

Portfolio 05-31-94

Total Stocks: 0
Total Fixed-Income: 12

Amount 000	Date of Maturity		Value $000	% Net Assets
172000	04-15-96	US Treasury Note 9.375%	182213	34.64
55000	04-15-97	US Treasury Note 8.5%	58059	11.04
40000	05-31-96	US Treasury Note 5.875%	39913	7.59
40000	08-15-95	US Treasury Note 4.625%	39581	7.53
30000	11-15-95	US Treasury Note 8.5%	31167	5.93
25000	02-15-96	US Treasury Note 8.875%	26203	4.98
25000	01-25-96	FNMA Debenture FRN	25015	4.76
25000	10-04-96	FHLMC Debenture FRN	24969	4.75
20000	08-15-95	US Treasury Note 8.5%	20678	3.93
12000	04-15-95	US Treasury Note 8.375%	12309	2.34
10000	05-15-97	US Treasury Note 6.5%	10041	1.91
10000	04-07-97	Federal Home Loan Bank Step 5%	9806	1.86

Composition % 09-30-94

Cash	2.4	Preferreds	0.0
Stocks	0.0	Convertibles	0.0
Bonds	97.6	Other	0.0

Tax Analysis

	Tax-Adj Historical Return %	% Pretax Return
3 Yr Avg	1.60	34.8
5 Yr Avg	4.40	56.8
10 Yr Avg	---	---
Potential Capital Gain Exposure (% of assets)		-10%

Most Similar Funds in MF500

Vanguard F/I Short-Trm Fed	Strong Fit
Prudential Struct Maturity A	Strong Fit
Vanguard F/I Short-Trm US Tr	Strong Fit

Coupon Range

	% of Bonds	Rel Obj
0%	0.0	0.00
0% to 8%	20.7	0.33
8% to 9%	30.9	2.01
9% to 10%	38.0	4.73
More than 10%	0.0	0.00
Not applicable	10.4	1.76

Sector Analysis 05-31-94
% of Bonds

US Treas	88	CMOs	0
GNMA mtgs	0	ARMs	0
FNMA mtgs	0	Other	12
FHLMC mtgs	0		

Operations

Address and Telephone	One Exchange Place Boston, MA 02109 800-645-6561 / 718-895-1206
Advisor	Dreyfus
Subadvisor	None
Distributor	Dreyfus Service
States Available	All plus PR
Report Grade	C
Income Distrib	Paid Monthly
* Date of Inception	04-06-87
Fiscal Year End	November

Min Initial Purchase	$2500 (Addt'l: $100)
Min IRA Purchase	$750 (Addt'l: $100)
Min Auto Invest Plan	$2500 (Systematic Inv: $100)

Expenses & Fees
Sales Fees	0.00% front
	0.00% deferred
	0.00% 12b-1
Management Fee	0.50% flat fee
3-,5-,10-yr Expense Projections	$24, $42, $93

MORNINGSTAR **1995 Mutual Fund 500**

Dreyfus Short-Interm Muni Bond

	Ticker	Load	NAV	Yield	SEC Yield	Assets	Objective
	DSIBX	None	12.70	4.5%	4.45%	426.8	Muni Nat

Dreyfus Short-Intermediate Municipal Bond Fund seeks current income exempt from federal income tax, consistent with capital preservation.

The fund invests primarily in tax-exempt municipal obligations with remaining maturities of five years or less; at least 80% of assets are invested in high-quality municipal bonds and notes. The dollar-weighted average maturity of the portfolio is usually two to three years. The fund may temporarily invest up to 20% of its assets in short-term taxable instruments. No more than 20% of assets may be AMT-subject.

Prior to Sept. 30, 1993, the fund was named Dreyfus Short-Intermediate Tax-Exempt Bond Fund.

Manager's Investment Style

Management typically stays well within its two- to three-year maturity mandate to limit interest-rate volatility. The fund does take modest credit risk by owning some lower-quality bonds, and has invested in municipal-bond derivatives.

Historical Profile

Return	Below Average	
Risk	Low	
Rating	★★★★★	
	Highest	

Investment Style History
Fixed Income

Income Rtn % Rank Obj

| --- | 89 | 84 | 77 | 92 | 86 | 86 | 76 |

Growth of $10,000

|||| Value of Fund ($000)
— Value of Index ($000)
   LB Muni
▼ Manager Change
▽ Partial Manager Change
► Mgr Unknown After
◄ Mgr Unknown Before

Performance Quartile
(Within Objective)

History

	1983	1984	1985	1986	1987	1988	1989	1990	1991	1992	1993	1994	
	---	---	---	---	12.58	12.54	12.55	12.58	12.88	13.05	13.31	12.70	NAV
	---	---	---	---	4.52 *	5.76	6.51	6.66	8.26	6.68	6.66	-0.32	Total Return %
	---	---	---	---	---	-2.12	-8.03	-2.29	-7.74	-0.56	-3.09	2.59	+/- LB Aggregate
	---	---	---	---	---	-4.40	-4.27	-0.64	-3.88	-2.13	-5.61	5.28	+/- LB Muni
	---	---	---	---	3.88	6.08	6.43	6.42	5.88	5.24	4.56	4.26	Income Return %
	---	---	---	---	0.64	-0.32	0.08	0.24	2.38	1.44	2.10	-4.58	Capital Return %
	---	---	---	---	---	89	94	26	95	61	85	22	Total Rtn % Rank All
	---	---	---	---	---	93	96	32	96	90	95	6	Total Rtn % Rank Obj
	---	---	---	---	0.48	0.75	0.78	0.78	0.71	0.65	0.58	0.57	Income $
	---	---	---	---	0.00	0.00	0.00	0.00	0.00	0.02	0.01	0.00	Capital Gains $
	---	---	---	---	---	0.00	0.43	0.50	0.59	0.72	0.75	0.74	Expense Ratio %
	---	---	---	---	---	5.81	6.01	6.29	6.07	5.42	4.76	4.35	Income Ratio %
	---	---	---	---	---	---	126	100	67	64	32	35	Turnover Rate %
	---	---	---	---	34.0	61.4	61.3	77.4	157.8	341.5	575.8	426.8	Net Assets ($mil)

Fund Manager(s)

Samuel J. Weinstock, since 12-87. BS, U. of Florida

Manager Experience

	Dates Managed	Invest Obj	Std Dev	+/- Index
Samuel J. Weinstock				
Premier State Muni MA A	08/87 - 12/94	MS	5.40	-0.99
Premier Municipal Bond A	08/87 - 12/94	MN	6.41	-0.62

Performance 12-31-94

	1st Qtr	2nd Qtr	3rd Qtr	4th Qtr	Total
1987	---	2.17	0.09	2.23	4.52 *
1988	1.87	0.97	1.36	1.44	5.76
1989	0.57	2.57	1.48	1.74	6.51
1990	1.33	1.64	1.38	2.15	6.66
1991	1.81	1.50	2.41	2.30	8.26
1992	1.10	2.30	1.77	1.36	6.68
1993	2.34	1.44	1.47	1.26	6.66
1994	-1.12	0.70	0.63	-0.52	-0.33

Bear Market Performance

Decile Rank (5-year period)

Worst ———————————————— Best

	Worst 3 Mo Period 1985-89	Worst 3 Mo Period 1990-94
Dreyfus Short-Interm Muni	---	-1.36
+/- LB Aggregate	---	3.58
+/- Best Fit Index : LB Muni	---	4.40

Trailing Returns

	Total Return %	+/- LB Aggregate	+/- LB Muni	% Rank All	% Rank Obj	Growth of $10,000
3 Mo	-0.52	-0.89	0.92	35	14	9,948
6 Mo	0.11	-0.88	1.36	55	14	10,011
1 Yr	-0.32	2.59	5.28	22	6	9,968
3 Yr Avg	4.29	-0.26	-0.58	63	64	11,342
5 Yr Avg	5.54	-2.08	-1.23	84	84	13,097
10 Yr Avg	---	---	---	---	---	---
15 Yr Avg	---	---	---	---	---	---

Operations

Address and Telephone	One Exchange Place
	Boston, MA 02109
	800-645-6561 / 718-895-1206
Advisor	Dreyfus
Subadvisor	None
Distributor	Premier Mutual Fund Services
States Available	All plus PR
Report Grade	C+
Income Distrib	Paid Monthly
* Date of Inception	04-30-87
Fiscal Year End	March

Risk Analysis

Time Period	Load-Adj Return %	Risk % Rank [1] All	Obj	Morningstar [2] Return	Morningstar Risk	Morningstar Risk-Adj Rating
1 Yr	-0.32					
3 Yr	4.29	1	2	0.90	0.21	★★★★★
5 Yr	5.54	1	3	0.75	0.20	★★★★★
10 Yr	---	---	---	---	---	---

Average Historical Rating (58 months)   4.7 ★s

[1] 1 = low, 100 = high   [2] 1.00 = Muni Avg   [3] 1.00 = 90-day T-bill return

Other Measures

			Standard LB Agg	Best Fit LB Muni
Standard Deviation	1.77	Alpha	0.4	0.3
Mean	4.22	Beta	0.32	0.30
Sharpe Ratio	0.39	R-Squared	50	80

Investment Style

Interest-Rate Stance
Avg Effective Maturity   2.2 Yrs

Maturity: Short Intm Long
Quality: High Med Low

Quality

Avg Credit Quality	A
Avg Weighted Coupon	5.47%
Avg Weighted Price	100.22% of Par

Diversification Value for Portfolio Types

Large Cap: Medium	Small Cap: High	Bond: Low	Balanced: Medium	Diversified: High

Portfolio 09-30-94

Total Stocks: 0
Total Fixed-Income: 120

Amount 000	Date of Maturity		Value $000	% Net Assets
22700	10-01-98	TX Bell Hlth Fac Dev IFRN	22082	4.29
20000	08-01-97	NY New York City GO 5.25%	20200	3.93
17455	07-01-96	MS Higher Educ Assist Student Loan 5.4%	17556	3.41
11915	08-01-96	NY State GO 6.625%	12223	2.38
11845	07-01-97	PA Philadelphia Gas Wks 5.2%	11856	2.31
11300	02-01-97	NY New York City GO 6.8%	11737	2.28
10215	10-01-95	FL Hsg Fin Multi-Fam Mtg 6.375%	10444	2.03
10000	08-01-97	OH Air Qlty Dev Poll Cntrl Edison 4.25%	9929	1.93
9200	11-01-96	ME Student Loan Educ Mktg 6.35%	9450	1.84
8100	12-01-97	VA Fairfax Redev/Hsg Shenandoah 5.25%	8118	1.58
8250	07-15-96	OH Cuyahoga Hosp IFRN	8106	1.58
7500	12-01-94	CO Denver Arpt Sys 6.35%	7502	1.46
7000	09-01-97	MS Higher Educ Assist Student Loan 4.6%	6895	1.34
7640	01-01-99	GA Burke Dev Poll Cntrl Oglethorpe DMD	6716	1.31
6620	10-01-98	TX Bell Hlth Fac Dev 4.75%	6447	1.25
6110	06-01-96	CA Vallejo Multi-Fam Hsg Apt Proj 5.75%	6162	1.20
6000	09-01-95	TX Dept Hsg/Comnty Affairs Mtg 6.25%	6139	1.19
7035	06-15-97	IL Metro Pier/Expo Dedicated Tax 0%	6119	1.19
6400	01-01-97	VA Winchester Indl Dev M/C IFRN	5997	1.17
5975	04-01-97	CT Hsg Fin Mtg Prog 4.6%	5940	1.16

Credit Analysis % of Bonds 09-30-94

US Govt	0	BB	0
AAA	13	B	0
AA	20	Below B	15
A	48	NR/NA	3
BBB	2		

Composition % of Assets 10-11-94

Cash	18.0	Preferreds	0.0
Stocks	0.0	Convertibles	0.0
Bonds	82.0	Other	0.0

Tax Analysis

	Tax-Adj Historical Return %	% Pretax Return
3 Yr Avg	4.27	99.5
5 Yr Avg	5.53	99.7
10 Yr Avg	---	---

Potential Capital Gain Exposure
(% of assets)   -3%

Most Similar Funds in MF500

USAA Tax-Exempt Short-Term	Strong Fit
T. Rowe Price Tax-Fr Sh-Intm	Strong Fit
Vanguard Muni Limited-Term	Strong Fit

Min Initial Purchase $2500 (Addt'l: $100)
Min IRA Purchase $750 (Addt'l: None)
Min Auto Invest Plan $2500 (Systematic Inv: $100)

Expenses & Fees

Sales Fees	0.00% front
	0.00% deferred
	0.10% 12b-1
Management Fee	0.50% flat fee
3-,5-,10-yr Expense Projections	$24, $41, $92

Coupon Range

	% Bonds	Rel Obj
0%	1.3	0.51
0% to 6.8%	78.6	1.30
6.8% to 7.5%	6.5	0.42
7.5% to 8.3%	2.8	0.31
More than 8.3%	0.0	0.00
Not applicable	10.9	2.81

Sector Weightings

	% Bonds	Rel Obj
General Obl	20.97	1.00
Utilities	5.55	0.44
Health	12.56	0.95
Water/Waste	0.00	0.00
Housing	12.66	1.73
Education	18.66	2.92
Transportation	3.64	0.36
COP/Lease	3.95	1.24
Private	17.39	1.49
Misc Revenue	2.26	0.45
Demand	2.35	0.96

Top 5 States % of Bonds

NY	19.18	MS	6.47
TX	9.94	CO	5.91
CA	6.67		

Emerging Markets Infrastructure

	Ticker	NAV	Mkt Price	Prem/Disc	Yield	Objective
	EMG	$13.02	$10.25	-21.3%	0.4%	World Stock

Emerging Markets Infrastructure Fund seeks long-term capital appreciation.

The fund invests at least 70% of assets in the equity securities of infrastructure companies in emerging countries. It may invest up to 30% of assets in equity securities of companies that service or manufacture products for infrastructure companies. A portion of fund assets will be invested in privatizations. The fund may invest up to 30% of assets in private placements of equity securities. To supplement income, the fund may lend securities worth up to one third of its assets. Forward currency transactions may be used for hedging purposes.

To discourage takeover attempts, board members serve staggered terms and supermajority voter approval is required to merge, open-end, or liquidate the fund.

Historical Profile

Return Not Rated
Risk Not Rated
Rating

Manager's Investment Style

Given that management's expertise is in Latin America, it's not surprising that this portfolio features large telephone and energy companies from that region. Management has, however, moved beyond Latin markets, by establishing positions in Hong Kong and India. Because management targets the most-visible infrastructure and telecommunications names, the fund is a reasonable way to get exposure to the blue chips of emerging markets.

Fund Manager(s)

Piers Playfair. Since 12-93. BA U. of London; Polytechnic of Central London.
Emilio Bassini. Since 12-93. BS U. of Pennsylvania; MBA Wharton.

Manager Experience	Dates Managed	Invest Obj	Std Dev	+/- Index
Piers Playfair				
Latin Amer Equity	10/91 - 01/94	WL	22.69	22.96
Emerg Mkts Telecom	06/92 - 01/93	WW	10.81	-10.09

NAV Performance % 12-30-94

	1st Qtr	2nd Qtr	3rd Qtr	4th Qtr	Total
1987	---	---	---	---	---
1988	---	---	---	---	---
1989	---	---	---	---	---
1990	---	---	---	---	---
1991	---	---	---	---	---
1992	---	---	---	---	---
1993	---	---	---	-0.36*	-0.36*
1994	-7.27	-6.21	22.58	-11.81	-5.97

Bear Market Performance

Decile Rank (5-year period)

Worst | Best

	Worst 3 Mo Period 1985-89	Worst 3 Mo Period 1990-94
Emerg Mkts Infra	---	---
+/- S&P 500	---	---

Trailing Returns

	NAV Total Return %	+/- S&P 500	+/- MSCI Emerging	% Rank All	% Rank Obj	Mkt Total Return %
3 Mo	-11.81	-11.79	0.30	96	77	-22.35
6 Mo	8.10	3.24	2.08	6	22	-8.54
1 Yr	-5.97	-7.29	-3.56	46	41	-35.69
3 Yr Avg	---	---	---	---	---	---
5 Yr Avg	---	---	---	---	---	---
Incept Avg	-6.16*	---	---	---	---	-30.78*

Operations

Address and Telephone	One Citicorp Center, 58th Flr. New York, NY 10022 212-832-2626
Advisor	BEA Associates
Subadvisor	N/A
Administrator	Bear Stearns Funds Management, Inc.
Transfer Agent	ABD Securities Corp.
Custodian	Brown Brothers Harriman & Co.
Auditor	Coopers & Lybrand
Legal Counsel	Willkie Farr & Gallagher

Income Distrib Schedule	Paid Annually
Management Fee	1.30%, 0.15%A
Reinvestment Plan	Yes
Direct Purchase Plan	Yes
Shares Outstanding	16,107,169
Exchange	NYSE
*Date of Inception	12-21-93
Shareholder Report	B

												1993	1994	History
													11.7	Highest Prem/Disc
													-21.3	Lowest Prem/Disc
1983	1984	1985	1986	1987	1988	1989	1990	1991	1992	1993	1994			History
---	---	---	---	---	---	---	---	---	---	---	13.90	13.02		NAV
---	---	---	---	---	---	---	---	---	---	-0.36*	-5.97			NAV Total Return %
---	---	---	---	---	---	---	---	---	---	-0.80*	-7.29			+/- S&P 500
---	---	---	---	---	---	---	---	---	---	---	-13.75			+/- MSCI EAFE
---	---	---	---	---	---	---	---	---	---	---	-3.56			+/- MSCI Emerging
---	---	---	---	---	---	---	---	---	---	0.00*	0.36			Income Return %
---	---	---	---	---	---	---	---	---	---	-0.36*	-6.33			Capital Return %
---	---	---	---	---	---	---	---	---	---	---	46			Total Rtn % Rank All
---	---	---	---	---	---	---	---	---	---	---	41			Total Rtn % Rank Obj
---	---	---	---	---	---	---	---	---	---	6.67*	-35.69			Market Total Rtn %
---	---	---	---	---	---	---	---	---	---	---	-6.4			Avg Prem/Disc %
---	---	---	---	---	---	---	---	---	---	0.00	0.04			Income $
---	---	---	---	---	---	---	---	---	---	0.00	0.00			Capital Gains $
---	---	---	---	---	---	---	---	---	---	---	1.99			Expense Ratio %
---	---	---	---	---	---	---	---	---	---	---	-0.11			Income Ratio %
---	---	---	---	---	---	---	---	---	---	---	---			Turnover Rate %
---	---	---	---	---	---	---	---	---	---	205.8	209.7			Net Assets ($mil)

Growth of $10,000
■ at NAV ($000)
— at Market Price ($000)

Premium Discount %

Risk Analysis

	Risk % Rank All	Risk % Rank Obj	Morningstar Return	Morningstar Risk	Morningstar Risk-Adj Rating
3 Yr	---	---	---	---	---
5 Yr	---	---	---	---	---
10 Yr	---	---	---	---	---

[1] 1 = Low, 100 = High [2] 1.00 = Equity Avg [3] 1.00 = 90-day T-bill Return

Other Measures

	S&P 500		
Standard Deviation	---	Alpha	---
Mean	---	Beta	---
Sharpe Ratio	---	R-Squared	---

Investment Style

	Stock Portfolio Avg	Rel WS Foreign	Rel WS World
Price/Earnings Ratio	57.7#	1.17	1.40
Price/Cash Flow Ratio	---	---	---
Price/Book Ratio	11.1#	3.68	3.55
5 Yr Earnings Gr %	---	---	---
Return on Assets %	---	---	---
Debt % Total Cap	---	---	---
Med Mkt Cap ($mil)	2816#	0.45	0.37

figure is based on less than 50% of stocks

Country Exposure (top five) 08-31-94

	Securities %		Currency %
Brazil	19	Brazil	19
Chile	14	Chile	14
Argentina	11	Argentina	11
Mexico	11	Mexico	11
Hong Kong	8	Hong Kong	8

Diversification Value for Portfolio Types

Large Cap: | Small Cap: | Bond: | Balanced: | Diversified:

Portfolio 08-31-94

Share Chg (05-94)	Amount	Total Equity: 109 Total Fixed-Income: 1	Value $000	% Total Invest
0	68016000	Energetica de Minas Gerais	7830	3.30
0	122300	Telefonos de Mexico A (ADR)	7674	3.24
0	1770000	Technology Resources	7401	3.12
113700	113700	India Magnum Fund CI A	7277	3.07
0	154900	Distrib Chilectra Metro 144A	7144	3.01
0	108200	Philippine Lg Dist Tel (ADR)	7141	3.01
0	806600	Telecom Argentina Stet CI A	5890	2.49
0	87200	Siam Cement	5175	2.18
0	11847600	Electrobras	4881	2.06
0	64837500	Paulista de Forca E Luz	4702	1.98
0	2304800	Consolid Electric Power Asia	4459	1.88
0	48000	Telefonos de Chile (ADR)	4380	1.85
0	73000000	Telebras	4309	1.82
0	833000	China Light & Power	4301	1.81
0	162500	YPF (ADR)	4205	1.77
0	9540000	Eletrobras CI B	4027	1.70
0	21248266	Petrobras	3765	1.59
0	151041	Millicom	3625	1.53
0	250000	Tolmex	3472	1.46
0	1729347	Camuzzi Argentina	3290	1.39
0	325000	Cementos Apasco	3185	1.34
0	166171	Argentine Cellular Comm	2991	1.26
0	1155000	Italiana Esercizio Telecom	2846	1.20
0	116000	Enersis (ADR)	2828	1.19
0	100000	Tele Danmark CI B (ADR)	2713	1.14

Composition % 08-31-94

Cash	1.5	Preferreds	0.0
Stocks	98.6	Convertibles	0.0
Bonds	0.0	Other	0.0

Tax Analysis

	Tax-Adj Historical Return %	% Pretax Return
3 Yr Avg	---	---
5 Yr Avg	---	---
10 Yr Avg	---	---
Potential Capital Gain Exposure (% of assets)		-8

Most Similar Funds in MF500

Fund lacks 3-year record

Sector Weightings

	% of Stocks
Utilities	57.6
Energy	7.8
Financials	9.4
Industrial Cyclicals	16.9
Consumer Durables	0.6
Consumer Staples	0.8
Services	3.4
Retail	0.0
Health	0.0
Technology	3.5

Enterprise Capital Appreciation

	Ticker	Load	NAV	Yield	SEC Yield	Assets	Objective
	ENCAX	4.75%	28.54	0.0%	N/A	101.2	Aggr. Growth

Enterprise Group Capital Appreciation Portfolio seeks capital appreciation; income is incidental.

The fund invests primarily in common stocks of companies with steadily increasing earnings and an average five-year performance record for sales, earnings, dividend growth, pretax margins, return on equity, and earnings reinvestment that is 1.5 times the average performance of the S&P 500 for the same period. The companies in the fund's portfolio tend to have an average market capitalization lower than the average capitalization of the S&P 500.

Prior to January 1, 1990, the fund was named Enterprise Group Aggressive Growth Portfolio.

Manager's Investment Style

This fund's very specific charter leads management to hold a concentrated portfolio of relatively large firms with consistent records of sales and earnings growth.

Historical Profile
Return	Average
Risk	Average
Rating	★★★
	Neutral

Investment Style History Equity
Average % Stocks Held in Portfolio

--- --- 82% 79% 84% 82% 89% 90%

Growth of $10,000
- Value of Fund ($000)
- Value of Index ($000) SPMid400
- ▼ Manager Change
- ▽ Partial Manager Change
- ► Mgr Unknown After
- ◄ Mgr Unknown Before

Performance Quartile (Within Objective)

	1983	1984	1985	1986	1987	1988	1989	1990	1991	1992	1993	1994	History
NAV	---	---	---	---	12.28	13.01	16.94	17.49	27.80	29.42	31.10	28.54	NAV
	---	---	---	---	2.50 *	5.95	34.27	3.90	58.95	5.83	5.71	-3.46	Total Return %
	---	---	---	---	0.20 *	-10.67	2.59	7.01	28.46	-1.79	-4.35	-4.78	+/- S&P 500
	---	---	---	---	---	-14.59	10.33	17.45	15.50	-5.93	-8.83	-0.81	+/- Wilshire 4500
	---	---	---	---	0.17	0.00	0.00	0.65	0.00	0.00	0.00	0.00	Income Return %
	---	---	---	---	2.33	5.94	34.27	3.25	58.95	5.83	5.71	-3.46	Capital Return %
	---	---	---	---	---	88	8	46	5	71	89	48	Total Rtn % Rank All
	---	---	---	---	---	76	26	11	44	59	93	57	Total Rtn % Rank Obj
	---	---	---	---	0.02	0.00	0.00	0.11	0.00	0.00	0.00	0.00	Income $
	---	---	---	---	0.00	0.00	0.53	0.00	0.00	0.00	0.00	1.48	Capital Gains $
	---	---	---	---	2.50	2.50	2.50	1.75	1.75	1.72	1.64	1.70	Expense Ratio %
	---	---	---	---	0.20	0.00	-0.50	0.70	-0.10	-0.20	-0.60	-0.70	Income Ratio %
	---	---	---	---	---	49	66	61	40	33	62	115	Turnover Rate %
	---	---	---	---	1.1	2.8	8.4	12.6	33.2	72.4	103.2	101.2	Net Assets ($mil)

Fund Manager(s)

Jeffrey J. Miller CFA, since 11-87. Birthdate: 1950. BS, U. of Southern California 1972 MBA, U. of Southern California 1973

Manager Experience	Dates Managed	Invest Obj	Std Dev	+/- Index
Jeffrey J. Miller				
Managers Special Equity	06/84 - 10/94	SC	17.63	-0.14

Performance 12-31-94

	1st Qtr	2nd Qtr	3rd Qtr	4th Qtr	Total
1987	---	---	---	---	2.50 *
1988	3.18	4.10	-2.88	1.56	5.95
1989	8.84	11.51	13.87	-2.84	34.27
1990	-0.71	14.15	-17.81	11.53	3.90
1991	21.61	0.89	12.86	14.78	58.95
1992	-4.03	-3.34	6.44	7.18	5.83
1993	-1.46	0.69	7.71	-1.08	5.71
1994	-4.37	-3.36	6.99	-2.36	-3.46

Bear Market Performance

Decile Rank (5-year period)

Worst ———————— Best

	Worst 3 Mo Period 1985-89	Worst 3 Mo Period 1990-94
Enterprise Capital Appreciation	---	-17.81
+/- S&P 500	---	-4.07
+/- Best Fit Index : SPMid400	---	-0.03

Trailing Returns

	Total Return %	+/- S&P 500	+/- Wil 4500	% Rank All	% Rank Obj	Growth of $10,000
3 Mo	-2.36	-2.35	0.14	75	73	9,764
6 Mo	4.46	-0.40	0.27	13	69	10,446
1 Yr	-3.46	-4.78	-0.81	48	57	9,654
3 Yr Avg	2.60	-3.67	-5.01	88	85	10,800
5 Yr Avg	12.27	3.58	3.18	8	34	17,835
10 Yr Avg	---	---	---	---	---	---
15 Yr Avg	---	---	---	---	---	---

Operations

Address and Telephone	1200 Ashwood Parkway Suite 290 Atlanta, GA 30338 800-432-4320 / 404-396-8118
Advisor	Enterprise Capital Management
Subadvisor	Provident Investment Counsel
Distributor	Enterprise Fund Distributors
States Available	All
Report Grade	C+
Income Distrib	Paid Annually
* Date of Inception	11-17-87
Fiscal Year End	December

Risk Analysis

Time Period	Load-Adj Return %	Risk % Rank [1] All	Obj	Morningstar [2] Return	Morningstar Risk	Morningstar Risk-Adj Rating
1 Yr	-8.05					
3 Yr	0.95	91	42	-0.74 [3]	1.23	★★
5 Yr	11.18	83	20	1.69 [3]	1.02	★★★★
10 Yr	---					

Average Historical Rating (50 months) 4.3 ★s

[1] = low, 100 = high [2] 1.00 = Equity Avg [3] 1.00 = 90-day T-bill return

Other Measures

			Standard S&P 500	Best Fit SPMid400
Standard Deviation	12.07	Alpha	-3.6	-4.4
Mean	3.30	Beta	1.19	1.10
Sharpe Ratio	-0.02	R-Squared	61	81

Investment Style

	Stock Portfolio Avg	Relative S&P 500
Price/Earnings Ratio	24.7	1.33
Price/Book Ratio	5.0	1.47
5 Yr Earnings Gr %	24.6	4.43
Return on Assets %	11.7	1.56
Debt % Total Cap	22.3	0.79
Med Mkt Cap ($mil)	7171	0.55

Style Value Blend Growth / Size Large Med Small

Diversification Value for Portfolio Types

Large Cap: Low	Small Cap: Low	Bond: High	Balanced: Low	Diversified: Low

Expenses & Fees

Sales Fees	4.75% front
	0.00% deferred
	0.45% 12b-1
Management Fee	0.75% flat fee
3-,5-,10-yr Expense Projections	$100, $138, $244
Annual Brokerage Cost	0.17%

Min Initial Purchase	$1000 (Addt'l: $50)
Min IRA Purchase	$250 (Addt'l: $25)
Min Auto Invest Plan	$100 (Systematic Inv: $50)

Portfolio 12-31-94

Share Chg (11-94) 000	Amount 000	Total Stocks: 57 Total Fixed-Income: 0	Value $000	% Net Assets
0	98	Motorola	5666	5.60
0	75	Microsoft	4560	4.50
0	97	Home Depot	4450	4.40
0	86	Oracle Systems	3812	3.77
0	92	US Healthcare	3781	3.73
0	58	LM Ericsson Telephone (ADR)	3208	3.17
0	66	United HealthCare	2992	2.96
0	97	Enron	2952	2.92
0	34	Capital Cities/ABC	2899	2.86
0	59	First Data	2786	2.75
0	119	MBNA	2785	2.75
0	37	FNMA	2711	2.68
-25	122	Wal-Mart Stores	2601	2.57
0	56	Compaq Computer	2228	2.20
0	84	AutoZone	2042	2.02
0	20	Hewlett-Packard	1978	1.95
0	62	Equity Residential Ppty Tr	1869	1.85
0	77	Office Depot	1840	1.82
0	43	Applied Materials	1796	1.77
0	48	Sensormatic Electronics	1742	1.72
0	51	MGIC Investment	1699	1.68
0	29	Automatic Data Processing	1697	1.68
0	45	Lowe's	1560	1.54
0	45	First USA	1463	1.45
19	63	Humana	1425	1.41

Composition % 12-31-94

Cash	9.0	Preferreds	0.0
Stocks	91.0	Convertibles	0.0
Bonds	0.0	Other	0.0

Tax Analysis

	Tax-Adj Historical Return %	% Pretax Return
3 Yr Avg	2.12	81.3
5 Yr Avg	11.91	96.4
10 Yr Avg	---	---
Potential Capital Gain Exposure (% of assets)		14%

Most Similar Funds in MF500

Sit Growth	Fair Fit
20th Century Growth Investor	Fair Fit
Value Line Leveraged Gr Inv	Fair Fit

Index Allocation % of Stocks

S&P 500	63.5
S&P MidCap 400	10.3
U.S. Small Cap	19.5
Foreign	6.6

Sector Weightings

	% of Stocks	Relative S&P 500
Utilities	0.9	0.08
Energy	3.3	0.32
Financials	14.7	1.39
Industrial Cyclicals	3.9	0.24
Consumer Durables	8.1	1.30
Consumer Staples	0.0	0.00
Services	11.3	1.39
Retail	12.8	2.19
Health	11.6	1.33
Technology	33.6	3.66

EuroPacific Growth

EuroPacific Growth Fund seeks long-term growth of capital. The fund normally invests at least 65% of its assets in equity securities of issuers domiciled in Europe or the Pacific Basin. There is no limit as to the percentage of assets the fund may invest in companies and governments of either developing or developed countries. A portion of the fund's assets may be invested in countries that are considered to be developing and have emerging securities markets.

	Ticker	Load	NAV	Yield	SEC Yield	Assets	Objective
	AEPGX	5.75%	21.13	1.5%	1.85%	8269.5	Foreign Stock

Historical Profile
Return   High
Risk   Below Average
Rating   ★★★★★
          Highest

Investment Style History
Equity
Average % Stocks Held in Portfolio

81% 83% 75% 75% 82% 81% 82% 79%

Growth of $10,000
|||| Value of Fund ($000)
— Value of Index ($000)
MSEASEA
▼ Manager Change
▽ Partial Manager Change
► Mgr Unknown After
◄ Mgr Unknown Before

Performance Quartile (Within Objective)

Manager's Investment Style

The fund's management team takes a conservative approach, often holding large cash stakes and restricting the majority of fund assets to developed global economies. The fund will hold modest stakes in emerging markets. Management also follows a typical Capital Research & Management theme with its emphasis on telecommunications and media services though it maintains a highly diversified approach.

Fund Manager(s)

Management Team

Manager Experience

	Dates Managed	Invest Obj	Std Dev	+/- Index
Thierry Vandeventer				
New Perspective	01/78 - 12/94	WW	13.89	2.40
Capital Income Builder	07/87 - 12/94	EI	8.31	1.93

History	1983	1984	1985	1986	1987	1988	1989	1990	1991	1992	1993	1994
NAV	---	6.92	9.32	12.29	11.48	12.81	14.62	14.12	16.43	16.55	22.11	21.13
Total Return %	---	1.59 *	35.13	39.89	7.53	20.95	24.26	-0.11	18.59	2.30	35.60	1.13
+/- S&P 500	---	-7.88 *	3.39	21.21	2.27	4.34	-7.42	3.00	-11.90	-5.32	25.55	-0.19
+/- MSCI EAFE	---	---	-21.03	-29.55	-17.10	-7.32	13.72	23.34	6.46	14.47	3.04	-6.65
Income Return %	---	0.72	0.45	0.75	2.84	1.46	2.11	2.17	2.19	1.57	1.49	1.51
Capital Return %	---	0.87	34.68	39.13	4.68	19.49	22.15	-2.29	16.40	0.73	34.12	-0.39
Total Rtn % Rank All	---	---	12	5	15	12	25	56	47	86	5	13
Total Rtn % Rank Obj	---	---	75	75	53	20	39	1	20	10	56	29
Income $	---	0.05	0.03	0.09	0.33	0.18	0.28	0.33	0.30	0.26	0.24	0.32
Capital Gains $	---	0.00	0.00	0.63	1.35	0.86	0.92	0.18	0.00	0.00	0.07	0.90
Expense Ratio %	---	---	1.80	1.31	1.27	1.21	1.30	1.24	1.28	1.24	1.10	0.99
Income Ratio %	---	---	1.81	1.88	1.63	1.56	1.87	2.29	2.23	1.85	1.40	1.13
Turnover Rate %	---	---	5	34	22	29	36	26	9	10	10	21
Net Assets ($mil)	---	17.6	26.0	183.3	184.7	208.4	405.2	929.9	1716.7	2623.4	5803.0	8269.5

Performance 12-31-94

	1st Qtr	2nd Qtr	3rd Qtr	4th Qtr	Total
1987	9.52	10.85	9.63	-19.21	7.53
1988	10.24	1.38	-0.69	8.98	20.95
1989	4.49	0.61	14.24	3.47	24.26
1990	-1.57	10.31	-13.85	6.79	-0.11
1991	7.51	-1.33	7.17	4.32	18.59
1992	1.28	4.02	-3.76	0.90	2.30
1993	6.62	3.54	10.93	10.73	35.60
1994	-0.72	-0.98	5.28	-2.29	1.13

Bear Market Performance

Decile Rank (5-year period)

Worst   Best

	Worst 3 Mo Period 1985-89	Worst 3 Mo Period 1990-94
EuroPacific Growth	-24.90	-13.85
+/- S&P 500	4.68	-0.11
+/- Best Fit Index : MSEASEA	-0.58	2.77

Trailing Returns

	Total Return %	+/- S&P 500	+/- MSCI EAFE	% Rank All	% Rank Obj	Growth of $10,000
3 Mo	-2.29	-2.28	-1.27	74	15	9,771
6 Mo	2.87	-1.99	3.79	21	9	10,287
1 Yr	1.13	-0.19	-6.65	13	29	10,113
3 Yr Avg	11.94	5.68	4.08	8	22	14,028
5 Yr Avg	10.69	2.00	9.19	14	10	16,617
10 Yr Avg	17.64	3.26	0.09	4	18	50,764
15 Yr Avg	---	---	---	---	---	---

Operations

Address and Telephone	333 S. Hope Street
	Los Angeles, CA 90071
	800-421-4120 / 213-486-9200
Advisor	Capital Research & Management
Subadvisor	None
Distributor	American Funds Distributors
States Available	All plus GU,PR,VI
Report Grade	A+
Income Distrib	Paid Semiannually
* Date of Inception	04-16-84
Fiscal Year End	March

Risk Analysis

Time Period	Load-Adj Return %	Risk % Rank[1] All	Risk % Rank[1] Obj	Morningstar[2] Return	Morningstar Risk	Morningstar Risk-Adj Rating
1 Yr	-4.69					
3 Yr	9.76	73	3	1.89[3]	0.83	★★★★
5 Yr	9.39	66	2	1.18[3]	0.79	★★★★
10 Yr	16.95	52	6	1.97	0.75	★★★★★
Average Historical Rating (93 months)					4.4 ★s	

[1] 1 = low, 100 = high   [2] 1.00 = Equity Avg   [3] 1.00 = 90-day T-bill return

Other Measures

	Standard S&P 500		Best Fit MSEASEA
Standard Deviation	10.42	Alpha	6.3	3.7
Mean	11.87	Beta	0.77	0.74
Sharpe Ratio	0.80	R-Squared	34	88

Investment Style

	Stock Portfolio Avg	Rel MSCI EAFE	Rel Obj
Price/Earnings Ratio	24.3	0.66	0.87
Price/Cash Flow	13.9	0.89	1.04
Price/Book Ratio	2.9	1.13	0.99
5 Yr Earnings Gr %	-0.1#	---	-0.03
Return on Assets %	6.6#	1.44	0.91
Debt % Total Cap	30.5	0.90	1.10
Med Mkt Cap ($mil)	5523	0.46	1.08

Style V B G / Size L M S

figure is based on 50% or less of stocks

Diversification Value for Portfolio Types

Large Cap: Medium / Small Cap: High / Bond: High / Balanced: Medium / Diversified: Low

Expenses & Fees

Sales Fees	5.75% front
	0.00% deferred
	0.25% 12b-1
Management Fee	0.69% max./0.47% min.
3-,5-,10-yr Expense Projections	$87, $109, $172
Annual Brokerage Cost	0.18%

Min Initial Purchase $250 (Addt'l: $50)
Min IRA Purchase $250 (Addt'l: $50)
Min Auto Invest Plan $50 (Systematic Inv: $50)

Portfolio 09-30-94

Share Chg (03-94)000	Amount 000	Total Stocks: 298 Total Fixed-Income: 34	Value $000	% Net Assets
15432	22752	Eurotunnel (Paris)	94398	1.18
0	798	Nokia	92992	1.16
0	1453	Telefonos de Mexico L (ADR)	90812	1.13
0	99	Nestle	90059	1.12
2160	3740	Astra Cl A	89743	1.12
534	2040	Intl Nederlander Groep	88108	1.10
	1376213	Telebras Pfd	85832	1.07
38	339	Mannesmann (Germany)	85010	1.06
28685	28685	Telecom Italia Spa	81253	1.01
5	42	Munchener Ruckvers (Reg)	76694	0.96
1015	4855	Rogers Comm Cl B	73766	0.92
2640	5928	Svenska Handelsbanken Group	72905	0.91
14423	23513	ANZ Banking Group	68052	0.85
0	1425	Polygram (Netherlands)	61796	0.77
10660	19091	Telecom New Zealand	60568	0.76
0	1182	News (ADR)	59819	0.75
0	5701	Bangkok Bank	58904	0.74
66	1705	ABN AMRO Holdings	57060	0.71
0	3590	Tolmex Cl B2	54490	0.68
10579	17409	Westpac Banking	54251	0.68

Regional Exposure 12-31-94
% of Stocks

Europe	11	Pacific Rim	20
Japan	11	Other	5
Latin Amer	9		

Composition % 12-31-94

Cash	18.5	Preferreds	0.0
Stocks	79.4	Convertibles	1.2
Bonds	0.9	Other	0.0

Tax Analysis

	Tax-Adj Historical Return %	% Pretax Return
3 Yr Avg	10.93	90.7
5 Yr Avg	9.72	89.1
10 Yr Avg	15.89	82.7
Potential Capital Gain Exposure (% of assets)		11%

Most Similar Funds in MF500

Templeton Foreign	Strong Fit
New Perspective	Strong Fit
Putnam Global Growth A	Strong Fit

Country Exposure 12-31-94
% of Stocks

United Kingdom	11
Japan	11
Germany	9
Sweden	8
Netherlands	8

Total Number of Countries: 27
Hedging Policy: Occasional

Sector Weightings

	% of Stocks	Relative S&P 500
Utilities	10.0	1.12
Energy	2.1	0.51
Financials	19.0	1.01
Industrial Cyclicals	23.6	0.94
Consumer Durables	13.0	1.21
Consumer Staples	3.1	0.45
Services	17.0	1.56
Retail	4.2	0.73
Health	4.2	1.17
Technology	3.7	0.73

MORNINGSTAR **1995 Mutual Fund 500**

Evergreen Foundation

	Ticker	Load	NAV	Yield	SEC Yield	Assets	Objective
	EFONX	None	12.27	3.3%	3.75%	331.5	Balanced

Evergreen Foundation Fund seeks income, conservation of capital, and capital appreciation.

The fund invests in a combination of dividend-paying common stocks, preferred stocks, convertible securities, corporate and U.S. debt obligations, and short-term debt instruments. Normally, at least 25% of the fund's assets are in fixed-income securities; the balance is invested in income-producing equity securities. In order to generate additional income and to offset expenses, the fund may lend portfolio securities.

Historical Profile

Return	High
Risk	Below Average
Rating	★★★★★ Highest

Investment Style History
Equity

Average % Stocks Held in Portfolio

Growth of $10,000

||| Value of Fund ($000)
— Value of Index ($000)
S&P 500
▼ Manager Change
▽ Partial Manager Change
► Mgr Unknown After
◄ Mgr Unknown Before

Manager's Investment Style

Manager Stephen Lieber allocates the fund's assets based on his overall view of the prices of various markets, looking specifically at interest rates. He seeks stocks, and often whole sectors, that are suffering from price weakness because of a lack of attention, or because of short-term market panics. He has often favored financials. In addition, Lieber holds high-quality bonds, but does make interest-rate calls.

Performance Quartile
(Within Objective)

Fund Manager(s)

Stephen A. Lieber, since 01-90. Birthdate: 08-25. BA, Williams C. 1946

	1983	1984	1985	1986	1987	1988	1989	1990	1991	1992	1993	1994	History
	---	---	---	---	---	---	10.00	8.95	10.75	11.98	13.12	12.27	NAV
	---	---	---	---	---	---	---	6.60 *	37.38	19.97	15.73	-1.12	Total Return %
	---	---	---	---	---	---	---	11.41 *	6.90	12.35	5.67	-2.43	+/- S&P 500
	---	---	---	---	---	---	---	---	21.38	12.73	5.98	1.80	+/- LB Aggregate
	---	---	---	---	---	---	---	12.25	4.55	2.15	2.56	3.32	Income Return %
	---	---	---	---	---	---	---	-5.66	32.83	17.82	13.17	-4.43	Capital Return %
	---	---	---	---	---	---	---	---	17	5	26	27	Total Rtn % Rank All
	---	---	---	---	---	---	---	---	15	1	13	25	Total Rtn % Rank Obj
	---	---	---	---	---	---	---	1.17	0.41	0.24	0.31	0.42	Income $
	---	---	---	---	---	---	---	0.52	0.97	0.63	0.41	0.28	Capital Gains $
	---	---	---	---	---	---	---	0.00	1.20	1.40	1.20	1.17	Expense Ratio %
	---	---	---	---	---	---	---	15.07	2.86	2.93	2.81	3.21	Income Ratio %
	---	---	---	---	---	---	---	---	178	127	60	---	Turnover Rate %
	---	---	---	---	---	---	---	2.2	10.5	63.7	239.8	331.5	Net Assets ($mil)

Manager Experience

	Dates Managed	Invest Obj	Std Dev	+/- Index
Stephen A. Lieber				
Evergreen	10/71 - 12/94	SC	19.30	5.96
Evergreen Tax Strategic	11/93 - 12/94	B	9.21	3.52

Performance 12-31-94

	1st Qtr	2nd Qtr	3rd Qtr	4th Qtr	Total
1987	---	---	---	---	---
1988	---	---	---	---	---
1989	---	---	---	---	---
1990	0.80	8.04	-11.96	11.19	6.60
1991	10.92	1.97	10.14	10.28	37.38
1992	5.02	2.53	4.06	7.06	19.97
1993	6.93	1.62	6.29	0.20	15.73
1994	-3.66	-0.08	2.63	0.08	-1.12

Bear Market Performance

Decile Rank (5-year period)

Worst — Best

	Worst 3 Mo Period 1985-89	Worst 3 Mo Period 1990-94
Evergreen Foundation	---	-11.96
+/- S&P 500	---	1.78
+/- Best Fit Index : S&P 500	---	1.78

Trailing Returns

	Total Return %	+/- S&P 500	+/- LB Aggregate	% Rank All	% Rank Obj	Growth of $10,000
3 Mo	0.08	0.10	-0.29	20	13	10,008
6 Mo	2.72	-2.15	1.72	22	25	10,272
1 Yr	-1.12	-2.43	1.80	27	25	9,888
3 Yr Avg	11.14	4.88	6.60	10	2	13,729
5 Yr Avg	14.99	6.30	7.37	4	1	20,106
10 Yr Avg	---	---	---	---	---	---
15 Yr Avg	---	---	---	---	---	---

Operations

Address and Telephone	237 Park Avenue New York, NY 10017 800-235-0064 / 914-694-2020
Advisor	Evergreen Asset Management
Subadvisor	Lieber & Company
Distributor	Evergreen Funds Distributor
States Available	All
Report Grade	B+
Income Distrib	Paid Quarterly
* Date of Inception	01-02-90
Fiscal Year End	December

Risk Analysis

Time Period	Load-Adj Return %	Risk % Rank [1] All	Risk % Rank [1] Obj	Morningstar [2] Return	Morningstar Risk	Morningstar Risk-Adj Rating
1 Yr	-1.12					
3 Yr	11.14	54	60	2.35 [3]	0.77	★★★★★
5 Yr	14.99	52	46	2.90 [3]	0.76	★★★★★
10 Yr	---					

Average Historical Rating (25 months) 5.0 ★s

[1] 1 = low, 100 = high   [2] 1.00 = Hybrid Avg   [3] 1.00 = 90-day T-bill return

Other Measures

			Standard S&P 500	Best Fit S&P 500
Standard Deviation	7.59	Alpha	5.2	5.2
Mean	10.90	Beta	0.79	0.79
Sharpe Ratio	0.97	R-Squared	68	68

Investment Style

Stocks

	Port Avg	Rel S&P 500
Price/Earnings Ratio	16.0	0.87
Price/Book Ratio	2.6	0.77
5 Yr Earnings Gr %	8.8	1.59
Med Mkt Cap ($mil)	3553	0.27

Bonds

Avg Effective Duration	10.1 Yrs
Avg Effective Maturity	16.9 Yrs
Avg Credit Quality	AAA
Avg Weighted Coupon	7.78%

Diversification Value for Portfolio Types

Large Cap: Low	Small Cap: Low	Bond: Medium	Balanced: Low	Diversified: Low

Portfolio 09-30-94

Total Stocks: 123
Total Fixed-Income: 24

Share Chg (06-94)000	Amount 000		Date of Maturity	Value $000	% Net Assets
	30000	US Treasury Bond 7.25%	05-15-16	27741	8.71
	21000	US Treasury Bond 7.125%	02-15-23	19090	5.99
	11000	US Treasury Bond 8.125%	08-15-19	11138	3.50
0	76	McKesson		7692	2.42
	7000	US Treasury Bond 8.375%	08-15-08	7236	2.27
0	136	General Electric		6545	2.05
5	85	Intel		5228	1.64
5	66	FNMA		5190	1.63
0	5000	US Treasury Bond 8%	11-15-21	5017	1.58
0	139	Household International		4980	1.56
	5000	US TVA 7.25%	07-15-43	4208	1.32
20	170	Caremark International		3974	1.25
0	41	American International Group		3662	1.15
27	55	JP Morgan		3341	1.05
20	120	Bank of Boston		3195	1.00
55	55	Eli Lilly		3183	1.00
22	61	Whirlpool		3118	0.98
23	43	Schering-Plough		3053	0.96
10	101	MGIC Investment		3031	0.95
0	55	BayBanks		3025	0.95

Index Allocation

	% of Stocks
S&P 500	56.6
S&P MidCap 400	7.8
U.S. Small Cap	35.7
Foreign	0.0

Composition % 12-31-94

Cash	8.6	Preferreds	0.0
Stocks	60.4	Convertibles	2.2
Bonds	28.8	Other	0.0

Tax Analysis

	Tax-Adj Historical Return %	% Pretax Return
3 Yr Avg	9.05	79.6
5 Yr Avg	11.66	72.8
10 Yr Avg	---	---
Potential Capital Gain Exposure (% of assets)		-3%

Most Similar Funds in MF500

Neuberger&Berman Guardian	Fair Fit
Evergreen Growth & Income	Fair Fit
Colonial A	Fair Fit

Bond Credit Analysis 12-31-94
% of Bonds

US Govt	93	BB	2
AAA	0	B	0
AA	0	Below B	1
A	1	NR/NA	2
BBB	1		

Stock Sector Weightings

	% of Stocks	Relative S&P 500
Utilities	1.4	0.11
Energy	1.3	0.12
Financials	48.2	4.56
Industrial Cyclicals	13.5	0.82
Consumer Durables	7.3	1.18
Consumer Staples	1.9	0.15
Services	4.7	0.58
Retail	0.3	0.06
Health	16.9	1.95
Technology	4.6	0.50

Expenses & Fees

Sales Fees	
	0.00% front
	0.00% deferred
	0.00% 12b-1
Management Fee	0.88% flat fee
3-,5-,10-yr Expense Projections	$38, $66, $145
Annual Brokerage Cost	0.20%

Min Initial Purchase	$500 (Addt'l: None)
Min IRA Purchase	None (Addt'l: None)
Min Auto Invest Plan	$500 (Systematic Inv: $50)

Evergreen

	Ticker	Load	NAV	Yield	SEC Yield	Assets	Objective
	EVGRX	None	12.03	0.5%	0.61%	454.9	Small Company

Evergreen Fund seeks capital appreciation; income is not a consideration.

The fund looks for little-known companies, small companies, and special situations. A little-known company is one that is limited to a regional market or has only a small portion of its outstanding shares traded publicly. Small companies are small in size or serve a limited market. Special-situation companies may be large or small firms whose outlook is enhanced due to recent or anticipated changes. The balance of the fund's assets may be invested in large-cap companies with the potential for growth.

Manager's Investment Style

Fund management has a broader investment scope than most of its pure small-cap peers. Manager Stephen Lieber emphasizes stocks with low prices compared with their projected growth rates. Although the portfolio is dominated by small-company stocks, Lieber has held a few large caps, usually ones that fit into a specific investment theme that he has developed.

Fund Manager(s)

Stephen A. Lieber, since 10-71. Birthdate: 08-25.
BA, Williams C. 1946

Manager Experience

	Dates Managed	Invest Obj	Std Dev	+/- Index
Stephen A. Lieber				
Evergreen Foundation	01/90 - 12/94	B	10.95	5.20
Evergreen Tax Strategic	11/93 - 12/94	B	9.21	3.52

Historical Profile

Return	Average
Risk	Average
Rating	★★★
	Neutral

90% 98% 93% 88% 86% 94% 95% 100%

1983	1984	1985	1986	1987	1988	1989	1990	1991	1992	1993	1994	History
11.28	9.94	12.67	12.47	9.97	11.49	12.21	10.34	13.54	14.03	14.20	12.03	NAV
30.07	-0.02	52.51	13.00	-3.05	23.06	14.98	-11.72	40.05	8.77	6.30	0.73	Total Return %
7.60	-6.29	20.77	-5.68	-8.31	6.45	-16.70	-8.60	9.57	1.15	-3.76	-0.59	+/- S&P 500
---	1.70	20.49	1.24	0.46	2.52	-8.96	1.84	-3.40	-2.99	-8.24	3.38	+/- Wilshire 4500
2.65	1.66	1.82	1.15	3.50	1.93	3.11	1.63	1.46	0.49	0.65	0.62	Income Return %
27.42	-1.68	50.69	11.85	-6.56	21.13	11.87	-13.35	38.59	8.27	5.64	0.11	Capital Return %
10	65	2	67	80	8	47	87	14	36	87	15	Total Rtn % Rank All
25	17	5	36	51	34	83	57	73	74	91	35	Total Rtn % Rank Obj
0.19	0.17	0.16	0.14	0.38	0.21	0.36	0.18	0.17	0.07	0.09	0.07	Income $
0.05	1.20	1.66	1.66	1.68	0.56	0.61	0.26	0.69	0.62	0.61	2.16	Capital Gains $
1.11	1.10	1.08	1.04	1.03	1.03	1.11	1.15	1.15	1.13	1.12	1.23	Expense Ratio %
1.95	1.83	1.73	1.41	1.32	1.70	2.46	1.83	1.45	0.56	0.60	0.36	Income Ratio %
78	53	59	48	46	42	40	39	35	32	21	---	Turnover Rate %
210.4	238.9	334.2	643.8	588.1	709.4	792.4	580.1	826.0	782.2	629.7	454.9	Net Assets ($mil)

Investment Style History
Equity

Average % Stocks Held in Portfolio

Growth of $10,000

||| Value of Fund ($000)
— Value of Index ($000)
   Wil 4500
▼ Manager Change
▽ Partial Manager Change
► Mgr Unknown After
◄ Mgr Unknown Before

Performance Quartile (Within Objective)

Performance 12-31-94

	1st Qtr	2nd Qtr	3rd Qtr	4th Qtr	Total
1987	18.47	0.83	3.42	-21.53	-3.05
1988	17.95	4.51	1.46	-1.61	23.06
1989	6.88	5.94	7.69	-5.70	14.98
1990	-5.81	6.78	-21.34	11.59	-11.72
1991	19.63	1.05	6.56	8.72	40.05
1992	2.07	-5.14	-0.08	12.42	8.77
1993	1.21	-1.41	3.29	3.14	6.30
1994	-2.04	0.29	4.80	-2.17	0.73

Bear Market Performance

Decile Rank (5-year period)

Worst — Best

	Worst 3 Mo Period 1985-89	Worst 3 Mo Period 1990-94
Evergreen	-29.28	-21.34
+/- S&P 500	0.30	-7.59
+/- Best Fit Index : Wil 4500	0.86	-3.11

Trailing Returns

	Total Return %	+/- S&P 500	+/- Wil 4500	% Rank All	% Rank Obj	Growth of $10,000
3 Mo	-2.17	-2.15	0.34	71	70	9,783
6 Mo	2.53	-2.33	-1.66	23	77	10,253
1 Yr	0.73	-0.59	3.38	15	35	10,073
3 Yr Avg	5.21	-1.06	-2.40	44	81	11,646
5 Yr Avg	7.56	-1.13	-1.53	39	86	14,399
10 Yr Avg	13.03	-1.35	0.40	27	43	34,037
15 Yr Avg	14.57	0.08	---	18	23	76,895

Risk Analysis

Time Period	Load-Adj Return %	Risk % Rank [1] All	Risk % Rank [1] Obj	Morningstar [2] Return	Morningstar [2] Risk	Morningstar Risk-Adj Rating
1 Yr	0.73					
3 Yr	5.21	78	41	0.48 [3]	0.90	★★★
5 Yr	7.56	82	40	0.70 [3]	1.01	★★★
10 Yr	13.03	77	30	1.07	0.98	★★★
Average Historical Rating (109 months)				3.7	★s	

[1] = low, 100 = high [2] 1.00 = Equity Avg [3] 1.00 = 90-day T-bill return

Other Measures

			Standard S&P 500	Best Fit Wil 4500
Standard Deviation	9.38	Alpha	-0.5	-1.8
Mean	5.53	Beta	0.89	0.89
Sharpe Ratio	0.21	R-Squared	56	85

Investment Style

	Stock Portfolio Avg	Relative S&P 500	Style
Price/Earnings Ratio	16.6	0.90	Value Blend Growth
Price/Book Ratio	2.5	0.73	
5 Yr Earnings Gr %	13.6	2.46	
Return on Assets %	7.2	0.96	
Debt % Total Cap	20.1	0.71	
Med Mkt Cap ($mil)	821	0.06	

Size: Large/Med/Small

Diversification Value for Portfolio Types

Large Cap: Low	Small Cap: None	Bond: High	Balanced: Low	Diversified: Medium

Portfolio 09-30-94

Share Chg (06-94) 000	Amount 000	Total Stocks: 207 / Total Fixed-Income: 0	Value $000	% Net Assets
0	127	First Empire State	19241	3.66
-105	500	Merck	17750	3.38
-55	167	FNMA	13112	2.49
0	273	Barnett Banks	12094	2.30
0	118	McKesson	11996	2.28
-25	219	Clear Channel Communications	11238	2.14
0	190	BayBanks	10450	1.99
74	298	Lancaster Colony	10422	1.98
-51	200	Johnson & Johnson	10325	1.96
0	350	A Schulman	9438	1.79
0	178	Tecumseh Products Cl A	8797	1.67
0	279	MGIC Investment	8393	1.60
-10	237	Stryker	8218	1.56
0	300	Dillard Department Stores A	8025	1.53
-16	214	Household International	7651	1.45
0	139	Alexander's	7562	1.44
0	890	Hibernia Cl A	7116	1.35
0	189	AMBAC	7008	1.33
-41	127	FHLMC	6773	1.29
-63	160	First Fidelity Bancorp (NJ)	6699	1.27
0	264	Fingerhut	6067	1.15
0	261	First Michigan Bank	6065	1.15
0	193	Fort Wayne National	5970	1.14
-2	98	MBIA	5855	1.11
-40	100	First Financial Management	5760	1.10

Composition % 12-31-94

Cash	-5.0	Preferreds	0.0
Stocks	105.0	Convertibles	0.0
Bonds	0.0	Other	0.0

Tax Analysis

	Tax-Adj Historical Return %	% Pretax Return
3 Yr Avg	2.70	50.5
5 Yr Avg	5.37	67.9
10 Yr Avg	10.14	67.7
Potential Capital Gain Exposure (% of assets)		29%

Most Similar Funds in MF500

Nicholas	Fair Fit
IDS New Dimensions	Fair Fit
Columbia Growth	Fair Fit

Index Allocation

	% of Stocks
S&P 500	23.9
S&P MidCap 400	16.3
U.S. Small Cap	59.4
Foreign	0.4

Sector Weightings

	% of Stocks	Relative S&P 500
Utilities	0.0	0.00
Energy	0.0	0.00
Financials	38.6	3.65
Industrial Cyclicals	14.3	0.87
Consumer Durables	7.1	1.14
Consumer Staples	2.3	0.18
Services	8.9	1.09
Retail	5.3	0.92
Health	16.6	1.92
Technology	6.8	0.74

Operations

Address and Telephone	237 Park Avenue
	New York, NY 10017
	800-235-0064 / 914-694-2020
Advisor	Evergreen Asset Management
Subadvisor	None
Distributor	Evergreen Funds Distributor
States Available	All plus GU,PR,VI
Report Grade	B+
Income Distrib	Paid Annually
Date of Inception	10-01-71
Fiscal Year End	September

Min Initial Purchase	$2000 (Addt'l: None)
Min IRA Purchase	None (Addt'l: None)
Min Auto Invest Plan	$2000 (Systematic Inv: $50)

Expenses & Fees

Sales Fees	0.00% front
	0.00% deferred
	0.00% 12b-1
Management Fee	1.00% flat fee
3-,5-,10-yr Expense Projections	$36, $62, $136
Annual Brokerage Cost	---

MORNINGSTAR 1995 Mutual Fund 500

Evergreen Growth & Income

	Ticker	Load	NAV	Yield	SEC Yield	Assets	Objective
	EVVTX	None	14.52	0.9%	0.98%	73.5	Growth/Inc.

Evergreen Growth and Income Fund seeks capital appreciation and current income.

The fund may invest in equity securities as well as in convertible and nonconvertible debt securities. It emphasizes securities management believes to be undervalued, as measured by assets, breakup value, earnings, or potential earnings growth. Management favors securities as they become less popular and sells them as they grow in favor with the market.

Class Y shares are closed to new investors; Class A shares have front loads; Class B shares have deferred loads; Class C shares have level loads. Prior to Aug. 1, 1994, the fund was named Evergreen Value Timing Fund.

Manager's Investment Style

Originally called Evergreen Value Timing, the fund's new name better reflects management's strategy. Since the fund's inception, the manager has focused on stock selection, picking up equities selling at a low price relative to earnings, book value, or cash flow. Rather than waiting for the market to recognize these picks, management also looks for stocks that have a catalyst (such as management change) for improved earnings.

Fund Manager(s)

Edmund H. Nicklin, Jr. CFA(1986), since 10-86.
Birthdate: 12-46. MS, Rensselaer Polytechnic Institute 1970

Manager Experience

	Dates Managed	Invest Obj	Std Dev	+/- Index
Not available.				

Historical Profile

Return	Above Average
Risk	Below Average
Rating	★★★★
	Above Average

87% 90% 86% 77% 81% 94% 90% 93%

Investment Style History
Equity

Average % Stocks Held in Portfolio

Growth of $10,000
|||| Value of Fund ($000)
— Value of Index ($000)
  SPMid400
▼ Manager Change
▽ Partial Manager Change
► Mgr Unknown After
◄ Mgr Unknown Before

Performance Quartile (Within Objective)

	1983	1984	1985	1986	1987	1988	1989	1990	1991	1992	1993	1994	History
	---	---	---	10.05	9.38	10.62	12.03	10.72	12.99	14.18	15.41	14.52	NAV
	---	---	---	0.50 *	-4.32	24.55	25.41	-4.47	25.82	13.84	14.45	1.69	Total Return %
	---	---	---	-1.77 *	-9.58	7.94	-6.27	-1.36	-4.66	6.22	4.39	0.38	+/- S&P 500
	---	---	---	---	-6.69	6.61	-3.76	1.71	-8.39	4.87	3.17	1.76	+/- Wilshire 5000
	---	---	---	0.00	2.34	1.87	4.60	2.68	1.60	1.04	0.93	0.96	Income Return %
	---	---	---	0.50	-6.67	22.69	20.81	-7.15	24.22	12.80	13.52	0.74	Capital Return %
	---	---	---	---	86	6	22	69	35	12	31	11	Total Rtn % Rank All
	---	---	---	---	90	9	42	57	68	12	25	15	Total Rtn % Rank Obj
	---	---	---	0.00	0.24	0.19	0.52	0.30	0.19	0.15	0.14	0.14	Income $
	---	---	---	0.00	0.00	0.86	0.76	0.47	0.31	0.46	0.68	1.01	Capital Gains $
	---	---	---	1.73	1.76	1.56	1.54	1.50	1.41	1.33	1.26	1.37	Expense Ratio %
	---	---	---	3.23	1.90	1.70	4.13	2.62	1.55	1.18	0.99	0.94	Income Ratio %
	---	---	---	4	48	41	53	41	23	30	28	---	Turnover Rate %
	---	---	---	20.7	21.5	23.9	31.5	36.3	45.9	63.8	78.0	73.5	Net Assets ($mil)

Performance 12-31-94

	1st Qtr	2nd Qtr	3rd Qtr	4th Qtr	Total
1987	11.43	0.54	4.92	-18.60	-4.32
1988	13.75	4.87	0.80	3.57	24.55
1989	6.31	6.82	9.20	1.13	25.41
1990	-2.00	2.80	-13.04	9.03	-4.47
1991	13.06	-0.41	4.47	6.96	25.82
1992	2.39	-2.11	3.76	9.46	13.84
1993	5.57	0.87	4.97	2.39	14.45
1994	-4.22	1.02	7.24	-1.99	1.70

Bear Market Performance

Decile Rank (5-year period)

Worst _____ Best

	Worst 3 Mo Period 1985-89	Worst 3 Mo Period 1990-94
Evergreen Growth & Income	---	-13.56
+/- S&P 500	---	0.29
+/- Best Fit Index : SPMid400	---	4.86

Trailing Returns

	Total Return %	+/- S&P 500	+/- Wil 5000	% Rank All	% Rank Obj	Growth of $10,000
3 Mo	-1.99	-1.98	-1.22	68	64	9,801
6 Mo	5.10	0.24	0.48	11	8	10,510
1 Yr	1.69	0.38	1.76	11	15	10,169
3 Yr Avg	9.83	3.57	3.22	14	11	13,250
5 Yr Avg	9.75	1.06	0.94	18	15	15,926
10 Yr Avg	---	---	---	---	---	---
15 Yr Avg	---	---	---	---	---	---

Operations

Address and Telephone	237 Park Avenue New York, NY 10017 800-235-0064 / 914-694-2020	Min Initial Purchase	$2000 (Addt'l: None)
		Min IRA Purchase	None (Addt'l: None)
		Min Auto Invest Plan	$2000 (Systematic Inv: $50)
Advisor	Evergreen Asset Management		
Subadvisor	Lieber & Company	**Expenses & Fees**	
Distributor	Evergreen Funds Distributor	Sales Fees	0.00% front
States Available	All plus PR,VI,GU		0.00% deferred
Report Grade	B+		0.00% 12b-1
Income Distrib	Paid Annually	Management Fee	1.00% flat fee
* Date of Inception	10-15-86	3-,5-,10-yr Expense Projections	$42, $73, $160
Fiscal Year End	December	Annual Brokerage Cost	0.11%

Risk Analysis

Time Period	Load-Adj Return %	Risk % Rank [1] All	Risk % Rank [1] Obj	Morningstar [2] Return	Morningstar [2] Risk	Morningstar Risk-Adj Rating
1 Yr	1.69					
3 Yr	9.83	62	32	1.92 [3]	0.68	★★★★
5 Yr	9.75	66	50	1.28 [3]	0.79	★★★★
10 Yr	---	---	---	---	---	

Average Historical Rating (63 months)   4.0 ★s

[1] 1 = low, 100 = high   [2] 1.00 = Equity Avg   [3] 1.00 = 90-day T-bill return

Other Measures

				Standard S&P 500	Best Fit SPMid400
Standard Deviation	8.43	Alpha		3.6	3.4
Mean	9.77	Beta		0.94	0.75
Sharpe Ratio	0.74	R-Squared		77	77

Investment Style

	Stock Portfolio Avg	Relative S&P 500
Price/Earnings Ratio	17.2	0.93
Price/Book Ratio	3.5	1.04
5 Yr Earnings Gr %	8.9#	1.61
Return on Assets %	7.5	1.00
Debt % Total Cap	27.3	0.96
Med Mkt Cap ($mil)	2301	0.18

figure is based on 50% or less of stocks

Style: Value Blend Growth / Size Large Med Small

Diversification Value for Portfolio Types

Large Cap: Low	Small Cap: Low	Bond: High	Balanced: None	Diversified: Low

Portfolio 09-30-94

Share Chg (06-94) 000	Amount 000	Total Stocks: 80 Total Fixed-Income: 7	Value $000	% Net Assets
0	116	Reynolds & Reynolds Cl A	2915	3.95
0	43	FHLMC	2295	3.11
0	22	American Cyanamid	2189	2.97
0	28	Schering-Plough	1988	2.70
0	80	Praxair	1950	2.64
0	67	AirTouch Communications	1904	2.58
0	25	Great Lakes Chemical	1469	1.99
35	53	Morton International	1444	1.96
0	28	Tecumseh Products Cl A	1356	1.84
0	25	CPC International	1266	1.72
13	45	Coastal	1254	1.70
0	30	WR Grace	1245	1.69
0	48	Associated Communications A	1231	1.67
0	30	Policy Management Systems	1196	1.62
0	22	Union Pacific	1180	1.60
0	145	Hibernia Cl A	1160	1.57
0	20	First Financial Management	1150	1.56
0	15	Michigan National	1144	1.55
0	50	Santa Fe Pacific	1131	1.53
0	14	FNMA	1103	1.50
0	53	Washington Mutual	1070	1.45
0	30	Time Warner	1054	1.43
0	23	Air Products & Chemicals	1052	1.43
0	8	LIN Broadcasting	1043	1.42
0	50	Chicago & North West Transp	1031	1.40

Composition % 12-31-94

Cash	3.6	Preferreds	0.0
Stocks	94.2	Convertibles	0.0
Bonds	2.2	Other	0.0

Tax Analysis

	Tax-Adj Historical Return %	% Pretax Return
3 Yr Avg	8.06	80.6
5 Yr Avg	7.97	78.8
10 Yr Avg	---	---
Potential Capital Gain Exposure (% of assets)		20%

Most Similar Funds in MF500

Neuberger&Berman Partners	Strong Fit
SteinRoe Special	Strong Fit
Fidelity Stock Selector	Fair Fit

Index Allocation

	% of Stocks
S&P 500	46.4
S&P MidCap 400	18.7
U.S. Small Cap	34.8
Foreign	0.2

Sector Weightings

	% of Stocks	Relative S&P 500
Utilities	11.1	0.90
Energy	1.5	0.15
Financials	14.3	1.35
Industrial Cyclicals	18.6	1.14
Consumer Durables	0.5	0.09
Consumer Staples	3.9	0.31
Services	17.4	2.13
Retail	3.0	0.52
Health	16.0	1.85
Technology	13.6	1.48

Evergreen Total Return

	Ticker	Load	NAV	Yield	SEC Yield	Assets	Objective
	EVTRX	None	17.03	6.2%	4.85%	943.7	Equity-Inc.

Evergreen Total Return Fund seeks current income and capital appreciation.

Normally, the fund purchases primarily equity securities and convertibles; the balance may consist of debt securities. The proportions of equity and debt vary according to market conditions. The fund generally places equal emphases on income and growth. The fund may engage in short-term trading on occasion. A significant portion of these equity securities are income producing. The fund may lend up to 30% of its portfolio to brokers. Also, the fund may borrow up to 5% of its assets.

Manager's Investment Style

Management has invested the fund's assets heavily in midsize utilities (especially electric utilities) and financials, and has kept a large stake in convertibles to provide shareholders with NAV stability and a high payout. Recently, management has begun to add dividend-paying cyclicals for diversification.

Fund Manager(s)

Nola M. Falcone CFA(1980), since 08-78.
Birthdate: 07-39. BA, Duke U. 1961 MBA, Wharton 1966

Manager Experience

	Dates Managed	Invest Obj	Std Dev	+/- Index
Nola M. Falcone				
RSI Retrmnt Emerging Grth	01/83 - 09/90	SC	17.25	-5.86

Historical Profile

Return	Below Average
Risk	Low
Rating ★★★	Neutral

	66%	73%	76%	83%	84%	82%	73%	73%

Growth of $10,000
||| Value of Fund ($000)
— Value of Index ($000) S&P 500
▼ Manager Change
▽ Partial Manager Change
► Mgr Unknown After
◄ Mgr Unknown Before

Investment Style History Equity

Average % Stocks Held in Portfolio

Performance Quartile (Within Objective)

1983	1984	1985	1986	1987	1988	1989	1990	1991	1992	1993	1994	History
15.90	15.52	17.87	19.18	15.66	17.01	18.76	16.49	19.12	19.43	19.62	17.03	NAV
30.54	14.00	29.89	20.19	-7.99	15.74	16.83	-6.30	22.99	10.03	12.93	-6.42	Total Return %
8.08	7.73	-1.85	1.51	-13.24	-0.87	-14.85	-3.18	-7.49	2.41	2.87	-7.73	+/- S&P 500
7.08	10.95	-2.67	4.09	-10.35	-2.20	-12.34	-0.12	-11.21	1.06	1.64	-6.35	+/- Wilshire 5000
6.51	6.85	6.91	6.26	6.70	7.01	6.54	5.80	7.04	5.96	5.58	5.65	Income Return %
24.03	7.14	22.98	13.93	-14.68	8.74	10.29	-12.10	15.95	4.07	7.35	-12.07	Capital Return %
9	10	26	19	94	25	42	75	40	22	42	75	Total Rtn % Rank All
15	6	37	26	82	51	78	47	81	35	47	92	Total Rtn % Rank Obj
0.84	0.95	0.97	1.09	1.33	1.08	1.09	1.08	1.08	1.08	1.08	1.08	Income $
0.73	1.32	0.98	1.11	0.88	0.02	0.00	0.00	0.00	0.46	1.20	0.25	Capital Gains $
1.29	1.09	1.31	1.11	1.02	1.01	1.02	1.18	1.23	1.21	1.18	1.18	Expense Ratio %
6.94	6.21	6.18	6.06	5.68	5.80	6.36	5.64	5.90	5.73	5.65	5.29	Income Ratio %
113	67	82	65	44	81	86	89	137	137	164	106	Turnover Rate %
32.9	47.4	230.9	1059.3	1277.2	1297.7	1367.0	1101.5	1122.1	1077.9	1195.4	943.7	Net Assets ($mil)

Performance 12-31-94

	1st Qtr	2nd Qtr	3rd Qtr	4th Qtr	Total
1987	7.66	-1.38	0.29	-13.59	-7.99
1988	9.26	4.37	1.34	0.16	15.74
1989	5.35	6.89	4.87	-1.07	16.83
1990	-2.67	0.46	-11.12	7.82	-6.30
1991	9.88	0.62	7.22	3.74	22.99
1992	-1.57	3.19	3.90	4.26	10.03
1993	7.57	0.85	5.00	-0.86	12.93
1994	-6.78	-0.75	4.77	-3.46	-6.42

Bear Market Performance

Decile Rank (5-year period)

Worst ▬ Best

	Worst 3 Mo Period 1985-89	Worst 3 Mo Period 1990-94
Evergreen Total Return	-19.37	-11.12
+/- S&P 500	10.21	2.63
+/- Best Fit Index : S&P 500	10.21	2.63

Trailing Returns

	Total Return %	+/- S&P 500	+/- Wil 5000	% Rank All	Obj	Growth of $10,000
3 Mo	-3.46	-3.44	-2.69	86	73	9,654
6 Mo	1.14	-3.72	-3.48	35	54	10,114
1 Yr	-6.42	-7.73	-6.35	75	92	9,358
3 Yr Avg	5.15	-1.11	-1.46	45	69	11,627
5 Yr Avg	6.03	-2.66	-2.79	76	74	13,399
10 Yr Avg	10.04	-4.34	-3.82	57	68	26,028
15 Yr Avg	13.55	-0.93	-0.42	30	30	67,299

Operations

Address and Telephone	237 Park Avenue New York, NY 10017 800-235-0064 / 914-694-2020
Advisor	Evergreen Asset Management
Subadvisor	Lieber & Company
Distributor	Evergreen Funds Distributor
States Available	All
Report Grade	A
Income Distrib	Paid Quarterly
Date of Inception	08-31-78
Fiscal Year End	March

Risk Analysis

Time Period	Load-Adj Return %	Risk % Rank[1] All	Obj	Morningstar[2] Return	Risk	Morningstar Risk-Adj Rating
1 Yr	-6.42					
3 Yr	5.15	57	52	0.46[3]	0.63	★★★
5 Yr	6.03	57	39	0.31[3]	0.67	★★★
10 Yr	10.04	45	18	0.55	0.65	★★★
Average Historical Rating (109 months)					4.0	★ s

[1] 1 = low, 100 = high [2] 1.00 = Equity Avg [3] 1.00 = 90-day T-bill return

Other Measures

			Standard S&P 500	Best Fit S&P 500
Standard Deviation	7.15	Alpha	-0.4	-0.4
Mean	5.29	Beta	0.76	0.76
Sharpe Ratio	0.25	R-Squared	72	72

Investment Style

	Stock Portfolio Avg	Relative S&P 500
Price/Earnings Ratio	15.4	0.83
Price/Book Ratio	2.5	0.74
5 Yr Earnings Gr %	-0.6	-0.10
Return on Assets %	5.3	0.71
Debt % Total Cap	32.8	1.16
Med Mkt Cap ($mil)	4417	0.34

Style: Value Blend Growth / Size: Large Med Small

Diversification Value for Portfolio Types

Large Cap: Low	Small Cap: Medium	Bond: Medium	Balanced: Low	Diversified: Low

Expenses & Fees

Sales Fees	
	0.00% front
	0.00% deferred
	0.00% 12b-1
Management Fee	1.00% flat fee
3-,5-,10-yr Expense Projections	$37, $65, $143
Annual Brokerage Cost	0.28%

Portfolio 09-30-94

Share Chg (06-94) 000	Amount 000	Total Stocks: 118 Total Fixed-Income: 46	Value $000	% Net Assets
94	912	Bell Atlantic	48347	4.67
150	563	Bristol-Myers Squibb	32325	3.13
64	64	Cadbury Schweppes (ADR)	30451	2.94
	434	General Motors E Cv Pfd $3.25	24944	2.41
421	471	JC Penney	24290	2.35
215	215	Royal Dutch Petroleum	23086	2.23
120	515	Hartford Steam Boiler Ins	22604	2.19
276	667	Texas Utilities	21767	2.10
0	577	Southern New England Telecom	19398	1.88
	249	Magma Copper E Cv Pfd 6%	17423	1.68
-100	776	Unicom	17264	1.67
900	900	Glaxo Holdings (ADR)	16425	1.59
455	606	Simon Property Group	15534	1.50
	225	Magma Copper D Cv Pfd 5.625%	15042	1.45
-157	563	Carolina Power & Light	14846	1.44
-16	286	Transamerica	14366	1.39
-253	407	Houston Industries	14350	1.39
	500	Freeport-McMoRan C/G Cv Pfd 7%	13878	1.34
	231	Burlington Northern Pfd 6%	13831	1.34
0	403	FPL Group	13081	1.26
220	220	General Mills	12705	1.23
50	453	Shared Medical Systems	12444	1.20
-153	612	Kranzco Realty Trust	12081	1.17
-50	327	Springs Industries Cl A	11768	1.14
	452	Freeport-McMoRan C/G Cv Pfd 5%	11072	1.07

Composition % 12-31-94

Cash	1.5	Preferreds	0.0
Stocks	71.4	Convertibles	24.0
Bonds	3.2	Other	0.0

Tax Analysis

	Tax-Adj Historical Return %	% Pretax Return
3 Yr Avg	2.12	39.9
5 Yr Avg	3.39	53.4
10 Yr Avg	6.95	59.7
Potential Capital Gain Exposure (% of assets)		-20%

Most Similar Funds in MF500

USAA Mutual Income Stock	Strong Fit
Fortress Utility	Fair Fit
Vanguard Equity-Income	Fair Fit

Index Allocation

	% of Stocks
S&P 500	54.6
S&P MidCap 400	12.2
U.S. Small Cap	21.1
Foreign	15.2

Sector Weightings

	% of Stocks	Relative S&P 500
Utilities	31.3	2.53
Energy	5.0	0.49
Financials	27.9	2.64
Industrial Cyclicals	2.9	0.18
Consumer Durables	3.4	0.55
Consumer Staples	5.8	0.47
Services	4.4	0.54
Retail	5.4	0.93
Health	9.5	1.09
Technology	4.3	0.47

Min Purchase

Min Initial Purchase	$2000 (Addt'l: None)
Min IRA Purchase	None (Addt'l: None)
Min Auto Invest Plan	$2000 (Systematic Inv: $50)

FAM Value

	Ticker	Load	NAV	Yield	SEC Yield	Assets	Objective
	FAMVX	None	21.04	0.6%	N/A	210.3	Small Company

FAM Value Fund seeks to maximize total return.
The fund invests primarily in undervalued common stocks. The companies in which the fund invests may have some or all of the following characteristics: low price/earnings multiples in relation to the market as a whole, based on current and/or potential future earnings; high total return on capital and low debt structure; and a market price-per-share that is near or at a discount to the company's per-share book value. From time to time, the fund may purchase convertible securities rated B or higher.

Manager's Investment Style

Management seeks value by focusing on cheap stocks (usually 12 times projected earnings) and companies with low debt and solid return on equity. Some recent favorites have been small regional banks and niche insurance companies. Management generally holds its stocks until they are recognized by the market, as illustrated by the fund's extremely low turnover.

Fund Manager(s)

Thomas O. Putnam, since 01-87. Birthdate: 05-44.
BA, U. of Rochester 1966 MBA, Tulane U. 1968
Diane C. Van Buren, since 01-87. Birthdate: 02-58. BA, SUNY-Oneonta 1980

Manager Experience	Dates Managed	Invest Obj	Std Dev	+/- Index
Not available.				

Historical Profile
Return: Above Average
Risk: Below Average
Rating: ★★★★★ Highest

87% 90% 94% 94% 93% 90% 88% 94%

Growth of $10,000
|||| Value of Fund ($000)
— Value of Index ($000)
Russ 2000
▼ Manager Change
▽ Partial Manager Change
► Mgr Unknown After
◄ Mgr Unknown Before

Investment Style History
Equity
Average % Stocks Held in Portfolio

Performance Quartile (Within Objective)

	1983	1984	1985	1986	1987	1988	1989	1990	1991	1992	1993	1994	History
	---	---	---	9.97	8.14	10.78	12.85	12.06	16.87	20.50	20.40	21.04	NAV
	---	---	---	---	-18.36 *	37.50	20.24	-5.39	47.63	25.04	0.21	6.83	Total Return %
	---	---	---	---	-23.61 *	20.89	-11.45	-2.28	17.15	17.42	-9.85	5.52	+/- S&P 500
	---	---	---	---	---	16.97	-3.70	8.16	4.18	13.28	-14.33	9.49	+/- Wilshire 4500
	---	---	---	---	0.00	4.67	0.43	0.62	0.54	0.50	0.45	0.58	Income Return %
	---	---	---	---	-18.36	32.83	19.81	-6.01	47.10	24.54	-0.24	6.25	Capital Return %
	---	---	---	---	---	1	35	72	9	2	99	3	Total Rtn % Rank All
	---	---	---	---	---	3	59	29	54	9	98	8	Total Rtn % Rank Obj
	---	---	---	---	0.00	0.35	0.05	0.08	0.08	0.10	0.09	0.12	Income $
	---	---	---	---	0.00	0.02	0.06	0.02	0.82	0.48	0.05	0.63	Capital Gains $
	---	---	---	---	1.54	1.48	1.51	1.53	1.49	1.50	1.39	1.37	Expense Ratio %
	---	---	---	---	1.47	2.89	0.56	0.72	0.66	0.81	0.57	0.47	Income Ratio %
	---	---	---	---	16	12	15	9	14	10	5	---	Turnover Rate %
	---	---	---	---	1.2	2.0	4.8	6.5	13.9	42.0	220.0	210.3	Net Assets ($mil)

Performance 12-31-94

	1st Qtr	2nd Qtr	3rd Qtr	4th Qtr	Total
1987	12.24	0.00	3.66	-29.83	-18.36
1988	18.55	6.31	5.44	3.47	37.50
1989	8.26	8.40	7.11	-4.34	20.24
1990	-2.26	7.80	-15.51	6.27	-5.39
1991	20.81	11.46	4.86	4.55	47.63
1992	12.27	-4.86	-0.83	18.04	25.04
1993	0.63	-2.62	3.14	-0.86	0.21
1994	-3.92	1.22	5.70	3.93	6.83

Bear Market Performance

Decile Rank (5-year period)

Worst --- Best

	Worst 3 Mo Period 1985-89	Worst 3 Mo Period 1990-94
FAM Value	---	-17.84
+/- S&P 500	---	-4.00
+/- Best Fit Index : Russ 2000	---	8.05

Trailing Returns

	Total Return %	+/- S&P 500	+/- Wil 4500	% Rank All	% Rank Obj	Growth of $10,000
3 Mo	3.93	3.94	6.43	2	13	10,393
6 Mo	9.85	4.99	5.65	5	34	10,985
1 Yr	6.83	5.52	9.49	3	8	10,683
3 Yr Avg	10.21	3.94	2.60	13	39	13,385
5 Yr Avg	13.33	4.64	4.24	6	29	18,695
10 Yr Avg	---	---	---	---	---	---
15 Yr Avg	---	---	---	---	---	---

Operations

Address and Telephone	111 N. Grand Street P.O. Box 399 Cobleskill, NY 12043 800-932-3271 / 518-234-7000
Advisor	Fenimore Asset Management
Subadvisor	None
Distributor	Fenimore Asset Management
States Available	All except AR,NE,RI
Report Grade	B-
Income Distrib	Paid Annually
* Date of Inception	01-01-87
Fiscal Year End	December

Risk Analysis

Time Period	Load-Adj Return %	Risk % Rank [1] All	Obj	Morningstar [2] Return	Morningstar Risk	Morningstar Risk-Adj Rating
1 Yr	6.83					
3 Yr	10.21	60	11	2.04 [3]	0.65	★★★★
5 Yr	13.33	60	6	2.35 [3]	0.72	★★★★★
10 Yr	---					

Average Historical Rating (61 months) 4.4 ★ s

[1] 1 = low, 100 = high [2] 1.00 = Equity Avg [3] 1.00 = 90-day T-bill return

Other Measures

				Standard S&P 500	Best Fit Russ 2000
Standard Deviation	9.75	Alpha		5.2	1.5
Mean	10.22	Beta		0.56	0.65
Sharpe Ratio	0.69	R-Squared		21	61

Investment Style

	Stock Portfolio Avg	Relative S&P 500
Price/Earnings Ratio	21.3	1.15
Price/Book Ratio	2.2	0.66
5 Yr Earnings Gr %	12.0	2.16
Return on Assets %	5.7	0.77
Debt % Total Cap	13.5	0.48
Med Mkt Cap ($mil)	274	0.02

Style Value Blend Growth — Size Large Med Small

Diversification Value for Portfolio Types

 Large Cap: High
Small Cap: Low
 Bond: High
Balanced: Medium
 Diversified: High

Portfolio 12-31-94

Share Chg (06-94) 000	Amount 000	Total Stocks: 54 Total Fixed-Income: 0	Value $000	% Net Assets
278	833	Conmed	16547	7.87
0	286	Fourth Financial	8875	4.22
-42	269	C-COR Electronics	8345	3.97
0	300	CR Bard	8100	3.85
0	382	Namic USA	7163	3.41
0	298	Kaydon	7140	3.40
0	352	Hawkeye Bancorp	6784	3.23
0	233	NWNL	6760	3.21
0	90	Fund American Enterpr Hldg	6481	3.08
0	220	American Express	6475	3.08
0	248	Hannaford Brothers	6296	2.99
0	270	First Colony	6048	2.88
0	157	Salomon	5888	2.80
22	290	Scherer Healthcare	5835	2.77
0	230	ONBANCorp	5348	2.54
0	155	Stanhome	4902	2.33
58	356	Versa Technologies	4892	2.33
0	101	Tennant	4859	2.31
0	589	Intercargo	4858	2.31
0	238	Jostens	4438	2.11
0	430	Mail Boxes Etc	4300	2.04
0	101	Blair	4032	1.92
0	144	Allied Group	3575	1.70
0	146	Centura Banks	3565	1.70
0	120	Zurich Reinsurance Centre	3465	1.65

Composition % 12-31-94

Cash	6.7	Preferreds	0.0
Stocks	93.3	Convertibles	0.0
Bonds	0.0	Other	0.0

Tax Analysis

	Tax-Adj Historical Return %	% Pretax Return
3 Yr Avg	9.46	92.0
5 Yr Avg	12.48	92.1
10 Yr Avg	---	---
Potential Capital Gain Exposure (% of assets)		7%

Most Similar Funds in MF500

Warburg Pincus Emerg Gr Con	Weak Fit
Wasatch Aggressive Equity	Weak Fit
Columbia Special	Weak Fit

Index Allocation

	% of Stocks
S&P 500	14.9
S&P MidCap 400	9.6
U.S. Small Cap	75.5
Foreign	0.0

Sector Weightings

	% of Stocks	Relative S&P 500
Utilities	0.0	0.00
Energy	0.0	0.00
Financials	43.1	4.08
Industrial Cyclicals	6.3	0.39
Consumer Durables	16.0	2.58
Consumer Staples	2.5	0.20
Services	5.3	0.65
Retail	5.3	0.91
Health	19.6	2.26
Technology	1.9	0.21

Expenses & Fees

Sales Fees	0.00% front
	0.00% deferred
	0.00% 12b-1
Management Fee	1.00% flat fee
3-,5-,10-yr Expense Projections	$44, $76, $167
Annual Brokerage Cost	0.23%

Min Initial Purchase	$2000 (Addt'l: $100)
Min IRA Purchase	$100 (Addt'l: $50)
Min Auto Invest Plan	$500 (Systematic Inv: $100)

Fasciano

	Ticker	Load	NAV	Yield	SEC Yield	Assets	Objective
	FASCX	None	17.18	0.0%	N/A	17.7	Small Company

Fasciano Fund seeks long-term capital growth; current income is secondary.

The fund invests primarily in publicly traded common stocks of small companies (with total market values of $500 million or less) that have superior potential to increase sales and earnings; are conservatively managed, especially with respect to the use of financial leverage; and are undervalued. The fund may also invest in foreign issues or unseasoned companies. Preferred stocks and debt securities may be purchased if these types of investments present opportunities for long-term capital growth.

Manager's Investment Style

Manager Michael Fasciano's style is distinctive. A bottom-up stock picker, Fasciano focuses on easily understood businesses, with low debt, management ownership of at least 10%, and a midwestern headquarters. Management prefers earnings growth rates of 15% to 20% though he will not take on excessive price risk. High sector concentrations and a cash stake of 10% to 20% of assets are also characteristic.

Fund Manager(s)

Michael F. Fasciano CFA(1986), since 08-87.
Birthdate: 06-55. BS, U. of Wisconsin-Parkside 1978 MBA, U. of Wisconsin-Milwaukee 1983

Manager Experience

	Dates Managed	Invest Obj	Std Dev	+/- Index
Not available.				

Historical Profile

Return	Above Average
Risk	Below Average
Rating	★★★★ Above Average

Investment Style History
Equity

Average % Stocks Held in Portfolio

Growth of $10,000

|||| Value of Fund ($000)
— Value of Index ($000) Wil 4500
▼ Manager Change
▽ Partial Manager Change
► Mgr Unknown After
◄ Mgr Unknown Before

Performance Quartile (Within Objective)

	1983	1984	1985	1986	1987	1988	1989	1990	1991	1992	1993	1994	History
	---	---	---	---	9.55	11.45	13.16	12.50	16.49	17.29	17.68	17.18	NAV
	---	---	---	---	-3.40 *	20.16	22.45	-1.18	35.08	7.67	8.08	3.68	Total Return %
	---	---	---	---	17.73 *	3.55	-9.24	1.94	4.60	0.05	-1.98	2.37	+/- S&P 500
	---	---	---	---		-0.38	-1.49	12.38	-8.37	-4.09	-6.46	6.34	+/- Wilshire 4500
	---	---	---	---	1.03	0.26	1.94	0.92	0.10	0.00	0.00	0.00	Income Return %
	---	---	---	---	-4.43	19.90	20.51	-2.10	34.98	7.67	8.08	3.68	Capital Return %
	---	---	---	---		13	30	59	19	50	79	6	Total Rtn % Rank All
	---	---	---	---		49	52	22	86	77	87	19	Total Rtn % Rank Obj
	---	---	---	---	0.10	0.03	0.24	0.12	0.02	0.00	0.00	0.00	Income $
	---	---	---	---	0.01	0.00	0.59	0.38	0.36	0.46	1.00	1.14	Capital Gains $
	---	---	---	---		0.60	2.00	1.90	1.70	1.70	1.70	1.70	Expense Ratio %
	---	---	---	---		3.30	0.90	0.70	0.20	-0.30	-0.30	Income Ratio %
	---	---	---	---			57	8	29	43	99	Turnover Rate %
	---	---	---	---	2.6	4.5	5.2	9.6	13.0	17.4	17.7	Net Assets ($mil)

Performance 12-31-94

	1st Qtr	2nd Qtr	3rd Qtr	4th Qtr	Total
1987	---	---	---	-3.59	-3.40 *
1988	10.16	6.27	1.11	1.51	20.16
1989	8.65	7.70	7.86	-2.98	22.45
1990	-0.08	7.98	-15.99	9.01	-1.18
1991	22.00	2.75	2.42	5.21	35.08
1992	2.49	-3.67	-0.80	9.93	7.67
1993	0.93	1.66	4.79	0.52	8.08
1994	-1.87	-0.06	3.81	1.84	3.68

Bear Market Performance

Decile Rank (5-year period)

	Worst 3 Mo Period 1985-89	Worst 3 Mo Period 1990-94
Fasciano	---	-16.96
+/- S&P 500	---	-3.11
+/- Best Fit Index : Wil 4500	---	2.45

Trailing Returns

	Total Return %	+/- S&P 500	+/- Wil 4500	% Rank All	% Rank Obj	Growth of $10,000
3 Mo	1.84	1.85	4.34	4	21	10,184
6 Mo	5.71	0.85	1.52	9	48	10,571
1 Yr	3.68	2.37	6.34	6	19	10,368
3 Yr Avg	6.46	0.19	-1.15	30	73	12,065
5 Yr Avg	10.00	1.31	0.91	17	66	16,106
10 Yr Avg	---	---	---	---	---	---
15 Yr Avg	---	---	---	---	---	---

Operations

Address and Telephone	190 S. LaSalle Street Suite 2800
	Chicago, IL 60603
	800-848-6050 / 312-444-6050
Advisor	Fasciano Company
Subadvisor	None
Distributor	Fasciano Fund
States Available	Selected states
Report Grade	B-
Income Distrib	Paid Annually
* Date of Inception	08-03-87
Fiscal Year End	June

Risk Analysis

Time Period	Load-Adj Return %	Risk % Rank [1] All	Obj	Morningstar [2] Return	Morningstar Risk	Morningstar Risk-Adj Rating
1 Yr	3.68					
3 Yr	6.46	62	13	0.85 [3]	0.69	★★★
5 Yr	10.00	67	10	1.35 [3]	0.80	★★★★
10 Yr	---					
Average Historical Rating (53 months)				3.7 ★s		

[1] 1 = low, 100 = high [2] 1.00 = Equity Avg [3] 1.00 = 90-day T-bill return

Other Measures

			Standard S&P 500	Best Fit Wil 4500
Standard Deviation	7.85	Alpha	1.6	0.3
Mean	6.58	Beta	0.52	0.64
Sharpe Ratio	0.39	R-Squared	28	63

Investment Style

	Stock Portfolio Avg	Relative S&P 500
Price/Earnings Ratio	19.0	1.03
Price/Book Ratio	3.0	0.89
5 Yr Earnings Gr %	14.9#	2.69
Return on Assets %	11.1	1.49
Debt % Total Cap	22.4	0.79
Med Mkt Cap ($mil)	284	0.02

figure is based on 50% or less of stocks

Diversification Value for Portfolio Types

Large Cap: Medium	Small Cap: Low	Bond: High	Balanced: Medium	Diversified: Medium

Expenses & Fees

Sales Fees	0.00% front
	0.00% deferred
	0.00% 12b-1
Management Fee	1.00% flat fee
3-,5-,10-yr Expense Projections	$53, $92, $200
Annual Brokerage Cost	0.16%

Min Initial Purchase	$1000 (Addt'l: $100)
Min IRA Purchase	$1000 (Addt'l: $100)
Min Auto Invest Plan	$50 (Systematic Inv: $50)

Portfolio 11-30-94

Share Chg (06-94) 000	Amount 000	Total Stocks: 48 Total Fixed-Income: 0	Value $000	% Net Assets
40	40	Keane	900	5.16
0	30	Vivra	859	4.92
0	8	Intl Speedway	769	4.41
0	20	CDW Computer Centers	680	3.90
5	20	DENTSPLY International	580	3.32
0	15	Regal Cinemas	572	3.28
0	15	Zebra Technologies Cl A	563	3.22
20	20	Astoria Financial	555	3.18
0	40	Personnel Management	530	3.04
0	30	Coral Gables Fedcorp	510	2.92
0	30	Information Resources	450	2.58
10	30	Material Sciences	428	2.45
2	9	Cardinal Health	427	2.44
0	15	Liberty Bancorp	356	2.04
5	15	Concord EFS	353	2.02
0	20	Landauer	340	1.95
-20	20	Digi International	335	1.92
0	15	McClatchy Newspapers Cl A	334	1.91
20	30	Code Alarm	319	1.83
0	8	Pulitzer Publishing	282	1.62
10	20	Medar	270	1.55
0	20	Mercury Finance	260	1.49
0	20	ADESA	255	1.46
0	15	Intl Dairy Queen Cl A	255	1.46
0	13	Schultz Sav-O Stores	254	1.45

Composition % 12-31-94

Cash	5.3	Preferreds	0.0
Stocks	94.8	Convertibles	0.0
Bonds	0.0	Other	0.0

Tax Analysis

	Tax-Adj Historical Return %	% Pretax Return
3 Yr Avg	5.05	77.1
5 Yr Avg	8.71	84.9
10 Yr Avg	---	---
Potential Capital Gain Exposure (% of assets)		15%

Most Similar Funds in MF500

Nicholas II	Fair Fit
Fidelity OTC	Weak Fit
Columbia Growth	Weak Fit

Index Allocation

	% of Stocks
S&P 500	0.0
S&P MidCap 400	9.0
U.S. Small Cap	91.0
Foreign	0.0

Sector Weightings

	% of Stocks	Relative S&P 500
Utilities	0.0	0.00
Energy	0.0	0.00
Financials	17.2	1.63
Industrial Cyclicals	10.2	0.62
Consumer Durables	7.0	1.12
Consumer Staples	0.0	0.00
Services	21.4	2.63
Retail	1.9	0.33
Health	16.0	1.84
Technology	26.3	2.87

MORNINGSTAR 1995 Mutual Fund 500

Fidelity Advisor Growth Opport A

	Ticker	Load	NAV	Yield	SEC Yield	Assets	Objective
	FAGOX	4.75%	24.40	1.1%	N/A	4826.6	Growth

Fidelity Advisor Growth Opportunities Fund - Class A seeks capital growth.

The fund invests primarily in common stocks and convertible securities. At least 65% of the portfolio is invested in securities of companies with long-term growth potential. The fund may invest in all types of securities, including foreign securities, debt securities, warrants, rights, and options.

Prior to Jan. 29, 1992, the fund was named Plymouth Growth Opportunities Portfolio.

Manager's Investment Style

Management's strategy combines flexibility and moderation. It highlights stocks with improving earnings and that still sell at moderate price/book and price/earnings multiples. Careful sector research is also typical of the strategy, with management's emphasis on capacity utilization and industry pricing patterns. This stock-picking style typically results in a portfolio that shifts between core growth holdings and cyclical issues.

Fund Manager(s)

George Vanderheiden CFA(1976), since 11-87.
Birthdate: 12-45. BA, Colby C. 1968 MBA, Boston U. 1971

Manager Experience	Dates Managed	Invest Obj	Std Dev	+/- Index
George Vanderheiden				
Fidelity Destiny I	11/80 - 12/94	G	17.46	5.10
Fidelity Destiny II	12/85 - 12/94	G	19.75	8.56

Historical Profile
Return	High
Risk	Average
Rating	★★★★★ Highest

Performance Quartile (Within Objective)

	1983	1984	1985	1986	1987	1988	1989	1990	1991	1992	1993	1994	History
	---	---	---	---	10.76	13.54	15.55	15.12	19.77	21.32	25.12	24.40	NAV
	---	---	---	---	7.60 *	33.28	24.14	-1.65	42.68	15.03	22.17	2.86	Total Return %
	---	---	---	---	6.35 *	16.67	-7.54	1.47	12.20	7.41	12.12	1.54	+/- S&P 500
	---	---	---	---		15.34	-5.03	4.54	8.48	6.06	10.89	2.93	+/- Wilshire 5000
	---	---	---	---	0.00	0.23	0.33	1.12	0.52	0.63	0.29	1.11	Income Return %
	---	---	---	---	7.60	33.05	23.81	-2.77	42.17	14.40	21.89	1.75	Capital Return %
	---	---	---	---		2	26	60	12	10	14	8	Total Rtn % Rank All
	---	---	---	---		2	64	32	25	16	10	15	Total Rtn % Rank Obj
	---	---	---	---	0.00	0.03	0.05	0.17	0.09	0.13	0.07	0.27	Income $
	---	---	---	---	0.00	0.76	1.17	0.00	1.53	1.26	0.84	1.16	Capital Gains $
	---	---	---	---		2.52	2.45	2.00	1.73	1.60	1.64	1.62	Expense Ratio %
	---	---	---	---		0.82	0.31	1.49	0.47	0.80	0.43	1.12	Income Ratio %
	---	---	---	---		143	163	136	142	94	69	43	Turnover Rate %
	---	---	---	---	2.0	9.1	39.6	69.5	264.4	715.5	2340.6	4826.6	Net Assets ($mil)

Investment Style History Equity — Average % Stocks Held in Portfolio: 97%, 93%, 94%, 96%, 89%, 83%, 79%

Growth of $10,000
- IIII Value of Fund ($000)
- — Value of Index ($000) S&P 500
- ▼ Manager Change
- ▽ Partial Manager Change
- ► Mgr Unknown After
- ◄ Mgr Unknown Before

Performance 12-31-94

	1st Qtr	2nd Qtr	3rd Qtr	4th Qtr	Total
1987	---	---	---	---	7.60 *
1988	18.22	11.08	0.28	1.20	33.28
1989	7.53	8.72	8.46	-2.10	24.14
1990	-2.51	8.84	-20.91	17.19	-1.65
1991	25.40	0.05	8.65	4.67	42.68
1992	3.95	1.80	0.86	7.78	15.03
1993	7.18	3.37	4.15	5.88	22.17
1994	-0.48	0.40	3.94	-0.97	2.86

Bear Market Performance

Decile Rank (5-year period)

	Worst 3 Mo Period 1985-89	Worst 3 Mo Period 1990-94
Fidelity Advisor Growth Opport	---	-20.91
+/- S&P 500	---	-7.16
+/- Best Fit Index : S&P 500	---	-7.16

Trailing Returns

	Total Return %	+/- S&P 500	+/- Wil 5000	% Rank All	% Rank Obj	Growth of $10,000
3 Mo	-0.97	-0.95	-0.20	43	42	9,903
6 Mo	2.94	-1.92	-1.68	21	63	10,294
1 Yr	2.86	1.54	2.93	8	15	10,286
3 Yr Avg	13.07	6.80	6.45	6	7	14,455
5 Yr Avg	15.19	6.50	6.38	4	6	20,284
10 Yr Avg	---	---	---	---	---	---
15 Yr Avg	---	---	---	---	---	---

Operations

Address and Telephone	82 Devonshire Street
	Boston, MA 02109
	800-522-7297 / 617-439-6793
Advisor	Fidelity Management & Research
Subadvisor	None
Distributor	Fidelity Distributors
States Available	All
Report Grade	A
Income Distrib	Paid Annually
* Date of Inception	11-18-87
Fiscal Year End	October

Min Initial Purchase	$2500 (Addt'l: $250)
Min IRA Purchase	$500 (Addt'l: $100)
Min Auto Invest Plan	$1000 (Systematic Inv: $100)

Expenses & Fees

Sales Fees	4.75% front
	0.00% deferred
	0.65% 12b-1
Management Fee	0.30% flat fee+0.52%G+(-)0.20%P
3-,5-,10-yr Expense Projections	$97, $132, $233
Annual Brokerage Cost	0.21%

Risk Analysis

Time Period	Load-Adj Return %	Risk % Rank All	Risk % Rank Obj	Morningstar Return	Morningstar Risk	Morningstar Risk-Adj Rating
1 Yr	-2.03					
3 Yr	11.25	57	11	2.38 [3]	0.62	★★★★
5 Yr	14.08	75	46	2.59 [3]	0.90	★★★★★
10 Yr	---					
Average Historical Rating (50 months)					4.4	★s

[1] 1 = low, 100 = high [2] 1.00 = Equity Avg [3] 1.00 = 90-day T-bill return

Other Measures

			Standard S&P 500	Best Fit S&P 500
Standard Deviation	8.94	Alpha	6.6	6.6
Mean	12.74	Beta	0.96	0.96
Sharpe Ratio	1.03	R-Squared	73	73

Investment Style

	Stock Portfolio Avg	Relative S&P 500
Price/Earnings Ratio	17.6	0.95
Price/Book Ratio	2.9	0.85
5 Yr Earnings Gr %	11.6	2.10
Return on Assets %	7.0	0.94
Debt % Total Cap	29.9	1.06
Med Mkt Cap ($mil)	10207	0.79

Style: Value Blend Growth / Large Med Small — (blend/large)

Diversification Value for Portfolio Types

Large Cap: Low	Small Cap: Low	Bond: High	Balanced: Low	Diversified: Low

Portfolio 10-31-94

Total Stocks: 238
Total Fixed-Income: 8

Share Chg (04-94)000	Amount 000		Value $000	% Net Assets
	325	US Treasury Bond 8.125%	325000	7.07
1091	2884	FNMA	219220	4.77
1323	2910	Philip Morris	178219	3.88
1790	2783	Compaq Computer	111684	2.43
1298	2279	Chrysler	111092	2.42
394	1580	Intel	98158	2.13
378	1019	IBM	75923	1.65
1276	1920	Vodafone Group (ADR)	66734	1.45
159	1123	Motorola	66087	1.44
564	885	Pfizer	65578	1.43
782	913	Texaco	59687	1.30
819	819	Deere	58742	1.28
-392	659	British Petroleum (ADR)	55986	1.22
302	920	Schlumberger	54062	1.18
131	476	Atlantic Richfield	51532	1.12
624	2203	Shawmut National	45445	0.99
354	755	Caterpillar	45087	0.98
1285	2087	Federated Department Stores	44308	0.94
821	1402	Solectron	39086	0.85
214	711	FHLMC	38750	0.84
25	973	General Motors	38438	0.84
722	837	UNUM	38416	0.84
630	907	Burlington Resources	38333	0.83
295	1677	Tele-Communications Cl A	37933	0.82
256	530	Schering-Plough	37784	0.82

Composition % 11-30-94

Cash	12.0	Preferreds	0.0
Stocks	76.0	Convertibles	0.0
Bonds	12.0	Other	0.0

Tax Analysis

	Tax-Adj Historical Return %	% Pretax Return
3 Yr Avg	11.40	85.9
5 Yr Avg	13.60	86.8
10 Yr Avg	---	---
Potential Capital Gain Exposure (% of assets)		0%

Most Similar Funds in MF500

Fidelity Contrafund	Fair Fit
Schafer Value	Fair Fit
Fidelity	Fair Fit

Index Allocation

	% of Stocks
S&P 500	77.0
S&P MidCap 400	5.5
U.S. Small Cap	12.1
Foreign	5.7

Sector Weightings

	% of Stocks	Relative S&P 500
Utilities	6.7	0.54
Energy	11.2	1.11
Financials	21.0	1.99
Industrial Cyclicals	7.2	0.44
Consumer Durables	8.1	1.31
Consumer Staples	8.2	0.65
Services	6.1	0.75
Retail	7.7	1.32
Health	5.3	0.69
Technology	18.6	2.03

Fidelity Advisor High-Inc Muni A

Ticker	Load	NAV	Yield	SEC Yield	Assets	Objective
FAHIX	4.75%	11.00	6.3%	6.45%	506.4	Muni Nat

Fidelity Advisor High-Income Municipal Fund - Class A seeks high current yield. Stability and growth of principal are also considered.

The fund normally invests at least 80% of its net assets in municipal obligations whose interest is exempt from federal income tax. It may invest without limit in bonds subject to the Alternative Minimum Tax, and may purchase municipal obligations rated as low as CCC or of comparable quality.

Class A shares have front loads; Class B shares have deferred loads and higher 12b-1 fees. Prior to Jan. 29, 1992, the fund was named Plymouth High-Income Municipal Portfolio.

Manager's Investment Style

Management keeps more than 75% of assets in issues rated BBB or below, including a large stake in nonrated issues. Because management takes an income orientation, the fund's BBB and below stake may increase in the future. Management has also been willing to make aggressive interest-rate calls, and has, on occasion, owned a few municipal derivatives.

Historical Profile

Return	Above Average
Risk	Below Average
Rating ★★★★	Above Average

Investment Style History
Fixed Income
Income Rtn % Rank Obj

Growth of $10,000
llll Value of Fund ($000)
— Value of Index ($000)
LB Muni
▼ Manager Change
▽ Partial Manager Change
► Mgr Unknown After
◄ Mgr Unknown Before

Performance Quartile (Within Objective)

History	1983	1984	1985	1986	1987	1988	1989	1990	1991	1992	1993	1994
NAV	---	---	---	---	10.06	10.41	10.81	10.95	11.44	11.87	12.70	11.00
Total Return %	---	---	---	---	2.84 *	11.80	13.09	10.29	12.18	11.09	13.90	-8.05
+/- LB Aggregate	---	---	---	---	---	3.92	-1.45	1.34	-3.82	3.84	4.15	-5.13
+/- LB Muni	---	---	---	---	---	1.64	2.31	2.99	0.04	2.27	1.62	-2.44
Income Return %	---	---	---	---	2.24	7.81	8.25	7.85	7.61	7.05	6.27	5.34
Capital Return %	---	---	---	---	0.60	3.99	4.84	2.43	4.57	4.03	7.63	-13.39
Total Rtn % Rank All	---	---	---	---	---	47	53	4	74	17	34	86
Total Rtn % Rank Obj	---	---	---	---	---	33	1	1	29	3	10	86
Income $	---	---	---	---	0.22	0.75	0.82	0.80	0.79	0.77	0.71	0.70
Capital Gains $	---	---	---	---	0.00	0.05	0.10	0.12	0.01	0.03	0.07	0.00
Expense Ratio %	---	---	---	---	0.80	0.89	0.90	0.90	0.90	0.90	0.92	0.89
Income Ratio %	---	---	---	---	7.24	7.33	7.60	7.37	7.08	6.59	5.59	5.78
Turnover Rate %	---	---	---	---	0	19	27	11	10	13	27	38
Net Assets ($mil)	---	---	---	---	1.0	3.4	7.7	25.6	77.2	198.5	538.6	506.4

Fund Manager(s)

Guy E. Wickwire, since 07-94. Birthdate: 05-47. Business/Psychology, Northwestern U. 1969

Manager Experience	Dates Managed	Invest Obj	Std Dev	+/- Index
Guy E. Wickwire				
Fidelity High-Yld T-F	09/81 - 10/93	MN	7.21	-1.01
Fidelity Adv High-Inc A	09/87 - 02/92	MN	2.77	0.18

Performance 12-31-94

	1st Qtr	2nd Qtr	3rd Qtr	4th Qtr	Total
1987	---	---	---	3.77	2.84 *
1988	3.61	2.87	2.19	2.64	11.80
1989	2.14	5.15	1.96	3.27	13.09
1990	1.51	2.31	1.57	4.55	10.29
1991	2.54	3.12	3.41	2.59	12.18
1992	2.17	3.20	3.32	1.97	11.09
1993	4.27	3.55	4.07	1.36	13.90
1994	-6.76	0.89	0.37	-2.61	-8.05

Bear Market Performance

Decile Rank (5-year period)

Worst ——————— Best

	Worst 3 Mo Period 1985-89	Worst 3 Mo Period 1990-94
Fidelity Advisor High-Inc Muni A	---	-7.22
+/- LB Aggregate	---	-2.29
+/- Best Fit Index : LB Muni	---	-1.46

Trailing Returns

	Total Return %	+/- LB Aggregate	+/- LB Muni	% Rank All	% Rank Obj	Growth of $10,000
3 Mo	-2.61	-2.98	-1.17	78	95	9,739
6 Mo	-2.25	-3.24	-1.00	90	92	9,775
1 Yr	-8.05	-5.13	-2.44	86	86	9,195
3 Yr Avg	5.18	0.63	0.31	45	21	11,635
5 Yr Avg	7.56	-0.07	0.78	39	3	14,394
10 Yr Avg	---	---	---	---	---	---
15 Yr Avg	---	---	---	---	---	---

Operations

Address and Telephone	82 Devonshire Street
	Boston, MA 02109
	800-522-7297 / 617-439-6793
Advisor	Fidelity Management & Research
Subadvisor	None
Distributor	Fidelity Distributors
States Available	All
Report Grade	A
Income Distrib	Paid Monthly
* Date of Inception	09-16-87
Fiscal Year End	October

Min Initial Purchase	$2500 (Addt'l: $250)
Min IRA Purchase	$500 (Addt'l: $100)
Min Auto Invest Plan	$1000 (Systematic Inv: $100)

Expenses & Fees
Sales Fees	4.75% front
	0.00% deferred
	0.25% 12b-1
Management Fee	0.25% flat fee+0.37%G
3-,5-,10-yr Expense Projections	$75, $96, $155

Risk Analysis

Time Period	Load-Adj Return %	Risk % Rank [1] All	Obj	Morningstar [2] Return	Morningstar Risk	Morningstar Risk-Adj Rating
1 Yr	-12.42					
3 Yr	3.48	32	51	0.92	1.05	★★★
5 Yr	6.51	15	37	1.16	0.91	★★★★
10 Yr	---					

Average Historical Rating (52 months)   4.8 ★s

[1] 1 = low, 100 = high   [2] 1.00 = Muni Avg   [3] 1.00 = 90-day T-bill return

Other Measures

			Standard LB Agg	Best Fit LB Muni
Standard Deviation	6.16	Alpha	0.6	0.2
Mean	5.25	Beta	1.13	1.09
Sharpe Ratio	0.28	R-Squared	54	95

Investment Style

Interest-Rate Stance
Avg Effective Maturity	20.7 Yrs

Maturity Short Intm Long

Quality
Avg Credit Quality	BBB
Avg Weighted Coupon	6.86%
Avg Weighted Price	91.38% of Par

Diversification Value for Portfolio Types

Large Cap: Medium	Small Cap: High	Bond: Low	Balanced: Low	Diversified: Medium

Tax Analysis

	Tax-Adj Historical Return %	% Pretax Return
3 Yr Avg	5.10	98.4
5 Yr Avg	7.43	98.0
10 Yr Avg	---	---
Potential Capital Gain Exposure (% of assets)		-10%

Most Similar Funds in MF500
Dreyfus Muni Bond	Strong Fit
Smith Barney Tax-Exempt IncE	Strong Fit
Putnam Municipal Income A	Strong Fit

Portfolio 10-31-94

Amount 000	Date of Maturity	Total Stocks: 0 / Total Fixed-Income: 251	Value $000	% Net Assets
14035	05-15-13	NY Dorm State Univ Educ Fac 5.5%	11895	2.15
12000	08-01-17	CA San Bernardino COP M/C Cap Fac 5.5%	9525	1.72
8500	11-01-24	VA Loudoun Indl Dev Falcons Landing 7.5%	8071	1.46
8840	02-01-21	KY Kenton Arpt Brd Spcl Fac Delta 7.125%	7967	1.44
8000	04-01-11	IL Dev Fin Solid Waste Disp 7.875%	7780	1.40
7500	08-15-22	LA Lake Charles Harbor/Term Dist 7.75%	7753	1.40
8325	12-01-33	NV Clark Indl Dev SW Gas 6.5%	7055	1.27
6750	12-01-20	MI Detroit Hosp Fin Hlth Care 10%	6910	1.25
7000	10-01-14	OH Solid Waste Republic Engineered 8.25%	6764	1.22
6400	12-01-15	MI Wayne Arpt Spcl Fac Republic 10.375%	6760	1.22
7500	06-15-07	PA Philadelphia Wtr/Wastewtr 5.5%	6709	1.21
7500	04-01-17	NY Local Govt Assist 5.5%	6384	1.15
7170	07-01-13	NY Dorm City Univ 5.75%	6256	1.13
7180	07-01-18	PA Philadelphia Hosp/Higher Educ 6.25%	6219	1.12
7000	11-01-17	MN St Paul Hsg/Redev Healtheast 6.625%	6134	1.11
6700	02-01-22	CO Hlth Fac Rocky Mtn Adventist 6.625%	6044	1.09
6000	06-01-15	MD Baltimore Poll Cntrl Bethlehem 7.5%	5948	1.07
6000	10-15-16	MD Engy Fin Admin Solid Waste Disp 9%	5895	1.06
6500	11-01-25	TX Tyler Hlth Fac Dev East M/C 6.75%	5736	1.03
6100	08-15-15	TX Harris Cultural/Educ Fac Fin 9.25%	5704	1.03

Credit Analysis % of Bonds 09-30-94
US Govt	0	BB	7
AAA	8	B	3
AA	4	Below B	0
A	12	NR/NA	42
BBB	24		

Composition % of Assets 09-30-94
Cash	3.1	Preferreds	0.0
Stocks	0.0	Convertibles	0.0
Bonds	96.9	Other	0.0

Coupon Range
	% Bonds	Rel Obj
0%	4.6	1.82
0% to 6.8%	46.3	0.77
6.8% to 7.5%	15.2	0.98
7.5% to 8.3%	11.1	1.26
More than 8.3%	13.4	1.52
Not applicable	9.4	2.43

Sector Weightings
	% Bonds	Rel Obj
General Obl	2.82	0.13
Utilities	3.96	0.32
Health	24.85	1.88
Water/Waste	4.16	0.65
Housing	3.05	0.42
Education	7.40	1.16
Transportation	8.90	0.87
COP/Lease	6.42	2.01
Private	28.75	2.47
Misc Revenue	3.69	0.74
Demand	6.01	2.44

Top 5 States % of Bonds
PA	11.49	MI	7.78
NY	8.33	IL	5.37
CA	7.79		

MORNINGSTAR 1995 Mutual Fund 500

Fidelity Advisor High-Yield A

	Ticker	Load	NAV	Yield	SEC Yield	Assets	Objective
	FAHYX	4.75%	10.84	7.0%	8.29%	682.8	Corp Hi Yld

Fidelity Advisor High-Yield Fund - Class A seeks income and capital appreciation.

The fund invests primarily in high-yielding bonds, debentures, notes, convertible securities, and preferred stocks. Up to 50% of its assets may be invested in zero-coupon bonds, and up to 35% in equities. The fund may also purchase foreign government obligations and other foreign securities.

Prior to Dec. 31, 1988, the fund was named Plymouth Aggressive Income Portfolio. From that date until Jan. 29, 1992, the fund was named Plymouth High-Yield Portfolio.

Historical Profile

Return	High
Risk	Low
Rating	★★★★★
	Highest

Investment Style History
Fixed Income
Income Rtn % Rank Obj

| --- | 26 | 4 | 22 | 62 | 61 | 92 | 97 |

Growth of $10,000

‖‖ Value of Fund ($000)
— Value of Index ($000) FB HY
∇ Manager Change
▽ Partial Manager Change
► Mgr Unknown After
◄ Mgr Unknown Before

Performance Quartile (Within Objective)

Manager's Investment Style

Management seeks undiscovered opportunities among high-yield bonds. Inexpensive issues of firms that display improving or already strong fundamentals are given the most consideration, especially if the issues have reliable asset coverage and good bondholder protection. As a result, the portfolio is often a diversified blend of higher- to lower-quality issues, as well as nonrated bonds; the portfolio will sometimes also include foreign government (especially emerging-market) debt.

Fund Manager(s)

Margaret Eagle CFA(1987), since 01-87. Birthdate: 08-49. BA, U. of Chicago 1971 PhD, U. of Chicago 1981

Manager Experience

	Dates Managed	Invest Obj	Std Dev	+/- Index
Margaret Eagle				
Fidelity Spartan Hi-Inc	08/90 - 04/93	CY	6.34	10.57

	1983	1984	1985	1986	1987	1988	1989	1990	1991	1992	1993	1994	History
	---	---	---	---	9.40	9.77	8.86	8.40	10.00	10.91	11.83	10.84	NAV
	---	---	---	---	4.52 *	17.24	3.63	7.30	34.96	23.02	19.93	-2.08	Total Return %
	---	---	---	---	---	9.37	-10.91	-1.65	18.96	15.77	10.18	0.84	+/- LB Aggregate
	---	---	---	---	---	5.81	3.24	13.68	-8.79	6.36	1.03	-1.10	+/- FB High-Yield
	---	---	---	---	10.52	13.31	12.94	12.49	15.91	11.40	8.92	6.29	Income Return %
	---	---	---	---	-6.00	3.94	-9.31	-5.19	19.05	11.61	11.01	-8.37	Capital Return %
	---	---	---	---	---	---	20	96	19	19	3	17	35	Total Rtn % Rank All
	---	---	---	---	---	4	21	1	54	10	32	26	Total Rtn % Rank Obj
	---	---	---	---	1.05	1.19	1.27	1.07	1.21	1.09	0.92	0.76	Income $
	---	---	---	---	0.00	0.00	0.00	0.00	0.00	0.23	0.26	0.00	Capital Gains $
	---	---	---	---	1.24	1.10	1.10	1.10	1.10	1.10	1.11	1.22	Expense Ratio %
	---	---	---	---	10.74	11.86	12.98	12.72	12.20	9.95	8.09	7.33	Income Ratio %
	---	---	---	---	166	135	131	90	103	100	79	126	Turnover Rate %
	---	---	---	---	9.1	12.2	13.7	17.2	43.8	161.8	549.5	682.8	Net Assets ($mil)

Performance 12-31-94

	1st Qtr	2nd Qtr	3rd Qtr	4th Qtr	Total
1987	---	-1.66	-2.35	1.01	---
1988	7.91	4.31	1.71	2.41	17.24
1989	2.42	5.01	-1.42	-2.26	3.63
1990	-0.25	7.59	-2.71	2.77	7.30
1991	12.23	6.94	6.37	5.71	34.96
1992	12.00	3.55	4.80	1.21	23.02
1993	7.48	4.45	2.30	4.44	19.93
1994	-0.67	-0.68	1.62	-2.32	-2.08

Bear Market Performance

Decile Rank (5-year period)

| Worst | | | | | Best |

	Worst 3 Mo Period 1985-89	Worst 3 Mo Period 1990-94
Fidelity Advisor High-Yield A	---	-7.14
+/- LB Aggregate	---	-7.88
+/- Best Fit Index : FB HY	---	6.97

Trailing Returns

	Total Return %	+/- LB Aggregate	+/- FB High-Yield	% Rank All	% Rank Obj	Growth of $10,000
3 Mo	-2.32	-2.69	-2.27	74	74	9,768
6 Mo	-0.74	-1.73	-2.29	69	45	9,926
1 Yr	-2.08	0.84	-1.10	35	26	9,792
3 Yr Avg	13.05	8.50	1.89	6	13	14,446
5 Yr Avg	15.91	8.28	2.83	4	1	20,920
10 Yr Avg	---	---	---	---	---	---
15 Yr Avg	---	---	---	---	---	---

Operations

Address and Telephone	82 Devonshire Street
	Boston, MA 02109
	800-522-7297 / 617-439-6793
Advisor	Fidelity Management & Research
Subadvisor	None
Distributor	Fidelity Distributors
States Available	All
Report Grade	A-
Income Distrib	Paid Monthly
* Date of Inception	01-05-87
Fiscal Year End	October

Risk Analysis

Time Period	Load-Adj Return %	Risk % Rank [1] All	Risk % Rank [1] Obj	Morningstar [2] Return	Morningstar Risk	Morningstar Risk-Adj Rating
1 Yr	-6.73					
3 Yr	11.23	7	29	2.38 [3]	0.34	★★★★★
5 Yr	14.79	22	7	2.83 [3]	0.35	★★★★★
10 Yr	---					
Average Historical Rating (60 months)				4.4 ★s		

[1] 1 = low, 100 = high [2] 1.00 = Hybrid Avg [3] 1.00 = 90-day T-bill return

Other Measures

			Standard LB Agg	Best Fit FB HY
Standard Deviation	5.29	Alpha	8.7	0.7
Mean	12.46	Beta	0.60	1.14
Sharpe Ratio	1.69	R-Squared	20	87

Investment Style

Interest-Rate Stance

Avg Effective Duration	4.7 Yrs
Avg Effective Maturity	6.0 Yrs

Maturity Short Intm Long
Quality High Med Low

Quality

Avg Credit Quality	B
Avg Weighted Coupon	9.37%
Avg Weighted Price	87.03% of Par

Diversification Value for Portfolio Types

| Large Cap: High | Small Cap: High | Bond: High | Balanced: High | Diversified: High |

Expenses & Fees

Sales Fees	4.75% front
	0.00% deferred
	0.25% 12b-1
Management Fee	0.45% flat fee+0.37%G
3-,5-,10-yr Expense Projections	$81, $106, $176

Min Initial Purchase	$2500 (Addt'l: $250)
Min IRA Purchase	$500 (Addt'l: $100)
Min Auto Invest Plan	$1000 (Systematic Inv: $100)

Portfolio 10-31-94

Total Stocks: 31
Total Fixed-Income: 189

Amount 000	Date of Maturity		Value $000	% Net Assets
40392	03-15-98	Revlon Worldwide 0%	22317	3.28
14410	07-07-06	Viacom International 8%	12519	1.84
1605		RJR Nabisco A Cv Pfd	11234	1.65
10586	04-01-97	Robin Media Group 11.125%	10215	1.50
466		Carson Pirie Scott	8969	1.32
18411	06-01-04	Echostar Communications 0%	8745	1.29
8459	11-01-04	Star Markets 13%	8522	1.25
7927	02-15-04	Citicasters 9.75%	7729	1.14
7630	02-01-03	Kaiser Aluminium/Chem 12.75%	7591	1.12
7298	08-01-01	Tjiwi Kimia 13.25%	7535	1.11
12201	12-17-02	Univision Network 7%	7503	1.10
7795	04-01-01	Revlon Consumer Prods 9.375%	6938	1.02
255		Atlantic-Richfield Cv Pfd	6928	1.02
5395	08-01-11	Columbia Gas System 10.25%	6852	1.01
6878	12-01-03	Specialty Equipment 11.375%	6775	1.00
6508	10-01-04	Stone Container 11.5%	6556	0.96
5171	06-01-12	Columbia Gas System 10.5%	6515	0.96
6820	12-15-03	Red Roof Inns 9.625%	6291	0.93
7166	05-01-06	Repap Wisconsin 9.875%	6270	0.92
10508	01-15-04	MFS Communications 0%	6186	0.91
7064	12-15-03	Bally's Grand 10.375%	6145	0.90
6508	10-01-02	OSI Specialties 9.25%	5954	0.88
5971	08-01-96	NWA 8.625%	5822	0.86
6586	07-15-01	Fair Lanes 9.5%	5476	0.81
5854	09-03-03	Boyd Gaming 10.75%	5459	0.80

Composition % 09-30-94

Cash	14.3	Preferreds	6.3
Stocks	5.7	Convertibles	0.4
Bonds	73.3	Other	0.0

Tax Analysis

	Tax-Adj Historical Return %	% Pretax Return
3 Yr Avg	9.42	69.7
5 Yr Avg	11.95	69.5
10 Yr Avg	---	---
Potential Capital Gain Exposure (% of assets)		-5%

Most Similar Funds in MF500

Fidelity Capital & Income	Strong Fit
AIM High-Yield A	Strong Fit
Putnam High Yield Adv A	Strong Fit

Coupon Range

	% of Bonds	Rel Obj
0%, PIK	6.2	0.84
0% to 11%	58.4	1.19
11% to 13%	27.0	0.81
13% to 14.5%	2.9	0.54
More than 14.5%	1.0	0.65
Not applicable	4.4	1.45

Credit Analysis 09-30-94

% of Bonds

US Govt	0	BB	7
AAA	0	B	42
AA	0	Below B	7
A	0	NR/NA	44
BBB	0		

Fidelity Advisor Strat Opp A

	Ticker	Load	NAV	Yield	SEC Yield	Assets	Objective
	FASPX	4.75%	18.71	1.8%	N/A	376.7	Growth

Fidelity Advisor Strategic Opportunities Fund - Class A seeks capital appreciation.

The fund invests primarily in companies in special situations that may involve technological advances, new products or services, changes in consumer demand, changes in competitive outlook or growth potential, changes in management and corporate structure, or significant economic or political occurrences. The fund may invest up to 30% of its assets in foreign securities.

Prior to Jan. 29, 1992, the Advisor Class was named the Plymouth Class. Prior to Aug. 31, 1993, the fund was named Fidelity Special Situations Fund: Advisor Class.

Manager's Investment Style

Management has a broad mandate to seek potential investment opportunities, and invests in everything from long-term Treasuries to Hong Kong stocks. Management often makes concentrated sector bets, recently favoring utilities and financials, and trades frequently.

Fund Manager(s)

Daniel R. Frank, since 08-86. Birthdate: 01-57.
BS, Boston U. 1979

Manager Experience

	Dates Managed	Invest Obj	Std Dev	+/- Index
Not available.				

Historical Profile

Return	Average
Risk	Low
Rating	★★★
	Neutral

Investment Style History
Equity
Average % Stocks Held in Portfolio

--- | 96% | 88% | 75% | 83% | 77% | 74% | 76%

Growth of $10,000

- |||| Value of Fund ($000)
- — Value of Index ($000) S&P 500
- ▼ Manager Change
- ▽ Partial Manager Change
- ► Mgr Unknown After
- ◄ Mgr Unknown Before

Performance Quartile (Within Objective)

	1983	1984	1985	1986	1987	1988	1989	1990	1991	1992	1993	1994	History
	---	---	---	16.21	13.02	15.36	19.81	17.65	18.49	19.05	20.80	18.71	NAV
	---	---	---	-3.49 *	-6.33	22.25	32.60	-7.12	23.01	12.87	20.44	-7.12	Total Return %
	---	---	---	-1.83 *	-11.59	5.64	0.91	-4.00	-7.48	5.25	10.38	-8.43	+/- S&P 500
	---	---	---	---	-8.70	4.31	3.42	-0.94	-11.20	3.90	9.15	-7.05	+/- Wilshire 5000
	---	---	---	0.54	1.81	4.28	3.63	3.79	3.59	3.09	2.11	1.76	Income Return %
	---	---	---	-4.03	-8.15	17.97	28.97	-10.90	19.42	9.78	18.33	-8.88	Capital Return %
	---	---	---	---	91	10	9	77	40	13	16	80	Total Rtn % Rank All
	---	---	---	---	91	16	24	72	89	24	15	85	Total Rtn % Rank Obj
	---	---	---	0.09	0.24	0.56	0.55	0.75	0.62	0.57	0.43	0.35	Income $
	---	---	---	0.97	1.91	0.00	0.00	0.00	2.42	1.21	1.71	0.26	Capital Gains $
	---	---	---	1.50	1.67	1.71	1.51	1.59	1.56	1.46	1.57	1.84	Expense Ratio %
	---	---	---	2.77	2.36	3.10	3.23	3.70	3.61	3.22	2.06	1.89	Income Ratio %
	---	---	---	0	225	160	89	114	223	211	183	159	Turnover Rate %
	---	---	---	22.1	199.9	179.9	204.6	178.6	197.6	205.4	310.0	376.7	Net Assets ($mil)

Performance 12-31-94

	1st Qtr	2nd Qtr	3rd Qtr	4th Qtr	Total
1987	12.52	1.04	3.36	-20.30	-6.33
1988	9.60	9.39	-0.51	2.49	22.25
1989	7.49	9.39	8.25	4.18	32.60
1990	-6.11	0.00	-7.47	6.91	-7.12
1991	12.80	1.66	5.63	1.55	23.01
1992	-0.49	5.22	0.88	6.86	12.87
1993	8.08	1.07	8.22	1.88	20.44
1994	-6.49	1.03	1.53	-3.16	-7.12

Bear Market Performance

Decile Rank (5-year period)

Worst |████| Best

	Worst 3 Mo Period 1985-89	Worst 3 Mo Period 1990-94
Fidelity Advisor Strat Opp A	---	-7.77
+/- S&P 500	---	6.07
+/- Best Fit Index : S&P 500	---	6.07

Trailing Returns

	Total Return %	+/- S&P 500	+/- Wil 5000	% Rank All	% Rank Obj	Growth of $10,000
3 Mo	-3.16	-3.15	-2.39	84	81	9,684
6 Mo	-1.68	-6.55	-6.31	84	95	9,832
1 Yr	-7.12	-8.43	-7.05	80	85	9,288
3 Yr Avg	8.08	1.82	1.47	21	30	12,626
5 Yr Avg	7.60	-1.09	-1.21	38	67	14,426
10 Yr Avg	---	---	---	---	---	---
15 Yr Avg	---	---	---	---	---	---

Operations

Address and Telephone	82 Devonshire Street
	Boston, MA 02109
	800-522-7297 / 617-439-6793
Advisor	Fidelity Management & Research
Subadvisor	FMR (U.K.)/FMR (Far East)
Distributor	Fidelity Distributors
States Available	All
Report Grade	A
Income Distrib	Paid Annually
* Date of Inception	08-20-86
Fiscal Year End	September

Risk Analysis

Time Period	Load-Adj Return %	Risk % Rank¹ All	Obj	Morningstar² Return	Morningstar Risk	Morningstar Risk-Adj Rating
1 Yr	-11.53					
3 Yr	6.34	60	16	0.82³	0.66	★★★
5 Yr	6.56	57	7	0.44³	0.67	★★★
10 Yr	---	---	---	---	---	---
Average Historical Rating (65 months)					3.7	★ s

¹ 1 = low, 100 = high ² 1.00 = Equity Avg ³ 1.00 = 90-day T-bill return

Other Measures

		Standard S&P 500	Best Fit S&P 500
Standard Deviation	8.25	Alpha	2.3	2.3
Mean	8.14	Beta	0.80	0.80
Sharpe Ratio	0.56	R-Squared	58	58

Investment Style

	Stock Portfolio Avg	Relative S&P 500
Price/Earnings Ratio	14.3	0.78
Price/Book Ratio	2.2	0.66
5 Yr Earnings Gr %	4.1	0.74
Return on Assets %	3.0	0.40
Debt % Total Cap	28.8	1.02
Med Mkt Cap ($mil)	982	0.08

Style Value Blend Growth / Size Large Med Small

Diversification Value for Portfolio Types

Large Cap:	Small Cap:	Bond:	Balanced:	Diversified:
Low	Medium	Medium	Low	Low

Expenses & Fees

Sales Fees	4.75% front
	0.00% deferred
	0.65% 12b-1
Management Fee	0.30% flat fee+0.52%G+(-)0.20%P
3-,5-,10-yr Expense Projections	$95, $129, $225
Annual Brokerage Cost	0.49%

Min Initial Purchase	$2500 (Addt'l: $250)
Min IRA Purchase	$500 (Addt'l: $100)
Min Auto Invest Plan	$1000 (Systematic Inv: $100)

Portfolio 09-30-94

Share Chg (03-94) 000	Amount 000	Total Stocks: 209 Total Fixed-Income: 14	Value $000	% Net Assets
	121	US Treasury Bond 0%	29815	7.74
	19	US Treasury Bond 9.125%	20823	5.40
24	308	BellSouth	17165	4.45
79	420	Ameritech	16899	4.39
719	1020	i-STAT	16700	4.33
53	289	Bell Atlantic	15329	3.98
-14	317	Southwestern Bell	13482	3.50
57	336	NYNEX	12931	3.36
-98	261	US West	10123	2.63
200	243	Viacom Cl A	9643	2.50
66	350	Regis	5161	1.34
52	308	Kinder Care Learning Ctr	4387	1.14
92	205	American Savings of FL FSB	3772	0.98
4	61	MAPCO	3396	0.88
83	168	Coral Gables Fedcorp	3212	0.83
-3	191	Anchor Bancorp	3084	0.80
336	336	Showscan Entertainment	2855	0.74
-12	196	Joy Technologies Cl A	2841	0.74
119	271	Riggs National	2756	0.72
98	98	First Commerce	2621	0.68
11	75	Southern New England Telecom	2510	0.65
96	96	United Carolina Bancshares	2499	0.65
57	57	CCB Financial	2476	0.64
63	91	Commercial Federal (NE)	2263	0.59
70	70	Intl CableTel	2239	0.58

Composition % 11-30-94

Cash	25.1	Preferreds	0.0
Stocks	74.9	Convertibles	0.0
Bonds	0.0	Other	0.0

Tax Analysis

	Tax-Adj Historical Return %	% Pretax Return
3 Yr Avg	5.78	69.9
5 Yr Avg	5.07	63.4
10 Yr Avg	---	---
Potential Capital Gain Exposure (% of assets)		-4%

Most Similar Funds in MF500

Warburg Pincus Cap Appr Con	Fair Fit
Prudential Alloc Cons Mgd B	Weak Fit
Flag Inv Telephone Income A	Weak Fit

Index Allocation

	% of Stocks
S&P 500	36.3
S&P MidCap 400	7.7
U.S. Small Cap	53.8
Foreign	2.3

Sector Weightings

	% of Stocks	Relative S&P 500
Utilities	30.3	2.44
Energy	4.3	0.43
Financials	45.9	4.34
Industrial Cyclicals	1.5	0.09
Consumer Durables	1.8	0.29
Consumer Staples	1.8	0.14
Services	8.4	1.03
Retail	0.2	0.03
Health	5.8	0.67
Technology	0.0	0.00

MORNINGSTAR **1995 Mutual Fund 500**

Fidelity Aggressive Tax-Free

	Ticker	Load	NAV	Yield	SEC Yield	Assets	Objective
	FATFX	None	10.81	7.1%	7.15%	793.8	Muni Nat

Fidelity Aggressive Tax-Free Portfolio seeks high current yield exempt from federal income tax.

The fund normally invests at least 65% of its assets in municipal obligations rated A or lower. At least 80% of the fund's assets are invested in municipal obligations whose interest is exempt from federal taxes; up to 20% of the fund's assets may be subject to the Alternative Minimum Tax. The fund normally expects to purchase securities with maturities of 20 years or more. It may buy and sell futures contracts and options with respect to 25% of its assets. The fund may invest up to 10% of its assets in municipal securities that are in default.

Manager's Investment Style

Because of the fund's aggressive mandate, management maintains the majority of assets in lower-quality bonds, especially nonrated bonds. Management does, however, concern itself with total return as much as with yield, seeking out bonds in sectors or states that it believes are undervalued.

Fund Manager(s)

Anne Punzak CFA, since 09-85. Birthdate: 12-58.
BS, Boston C. 1980 MBA, Wharton 1984

Manager Experience	Dates Managed	Invest Obj	Std Dev	+/- Index
Anne Punzak				
Fidelity Insured Tax-Free	10/89 - 10/93	MN	4.33	-0.46

Historical Profile

Return	High	
Risk	Below Average	
Rating	★★★★★ Highest	

Investment Style History
Fixed Income
Income Rtn % Rank Obj

Growth of $10,000

- |||| Value of Fund ($000)
- — Value of Index ($000) LB Muni
- ▼ Manager Change
- ▽ Partial Manager Change
- ► Mgr Unknown After
- ◄ Mgr Unknown Before

Performance Quartile (Within Objective)

	1983	1984	1985	1986	1987	1988	1989	1990	1991	1992	1993	1994	History
	---	---	10.66	11.56	10.82	11.33	11.49	11.43	11.80	11.88	12.34	10.81	NAV
	---	---	9.26 *	17.63	1.42	13.33	9.51	7.48	11.77	9.20	13.83	-5.90	Total Return %
	---	---	---	2.38	-1.34	5.45	-5.04	-1.46	-4.23	1.95	4.08	-2.98	+/- LB Aggregate
	---	---	---	-1.69	-0.08	3.17	-1.28	0.18	-0.37	0.38	1.56	-0.29	+/- LB Muni
	---	---	2.66	9.19	7.82	8.62	8.09	8.01	7.99	7.39	6.94	6.19	Income Return %
	---	---	6.60	8.44	-6.40	4.71	1.41	-0.52	3.78	1.80	6.89	-12.09	Capital Return %
	---	---	---	35	47	36	79	17	78	30	34	71	Total Rtn % Rank All
	---	---	---	53	26	13	49	5	43	25	11	57	Total Rtn % Rank Obj
	---	---	0.26	0.92	0.90	0.89	0.88	0.88	0.86	0.84	0.79	0.77	Income $
	---	---	0.00	0.00	0.00	0.00	0.00	0.00	0.06	0.13	0.34	0.05	Capital Gains $
	---	---	0.60	0.65	0.74	0.73	0.69	0.66	0.69	0.64	0.64	0.64	Expense Ratio %
	---	---	10.17	8.17	8.06	7.98	7.68	7.79	7.46	7.01	6.37	6.52	Income Ratio %
	---	---	4	17	68	46	46	46	30	43	54	45	Turnover Rate %
	---	---	106.2	329.5	352.0	452.9	543.2	548.2	650.4	758.5	948.1	793.8	Net Assets ($mil)

Performance 12-31-94

	1st Qtr	2nd Qtr	3rd Qtr	4th Qtr	Total
1987	4.38	-3.28	-1.16	1.63	1.42
1988	4.39	2.52	3.02	2.79	13.33
1989	1.28	5.29	0.76	1.91	9.51
1990	1.08	1.71	1.66	2.84	7.48
1991	1.74	2.39	4.20	2.97	11.77
1992	0.88	3.60	2.57	1.87	9.20
1993	4.28	3.52	3.71	1.67	13.83
1994	-5.50	0.90	0.69	-1.98	-5.90

Bear Market Performance

Decile Rank (5-year period)

Worst		Best

	Worst 3 Mo Period 1985-89	Worst 3 Mo Period 1990-94
Fidelity Aggressive Tax-Free	---	-6.01
+/- LB Aggregate	---	-1.07
+/- Best Fit Index : LB Muni	---	-0.25

Trailing Returns

	Total Return %	+/- LB Aggregate	+/- LB Muni	% Rank All	% Rank Obj	Growth of $10,000
3 Mo	-1.98	-2.36	-0.55	68	82	9,802
6 Mo	-1.31	-2.30	-0.06	79	66	9,869
1 Yr	-5.90	-2.98	-0.29	71	57	9,410
3 Yr Avg	5.36	0.82	0.50	41	15	11,697
5 Yr Avg	7.04	-0.58	0.27	49	12	14,053
10 Yr Avg	---	---	---	---	---	---
15 Yr Avg	---	---	---	---	---	---

Operations

Address and Telephone	82 Devonshire Street
	Boston, MA 02109
	800-544-8888
Advisor	Fidelity Management & Research
Subadvisor	None
Distributor	Fidelity Distributors
States Available	All
Report Grade	A-
Income Distrib	Paid Monthly
* Date of Inception	09-13-85
Fiscal Year End	December

Min Initial Purchase	$2500 (Addt'l: $250)
Min IRA Purchase	None (Addt'l: None)
Min Auto Invest Plan	$2500 (Systematic Inv: $100)

Expenses & Fees

Sales Fees	0.00% front
	0.00% deferred
	0.00% 12b-1
Management Fee	0.30% flat fee+0.37%G
3-,5-,10-yr Expense Projections	$20, $36, $80

Risk Analysis

Time Period	Load-Adj Return %	Risk % Rank [1] All	Obj	Morningstar [2] Return	Morningstar Risk	Morningstar Risk-Adj Rating
1 Yr	-5.90					
3 Yr	5.36	20	36	1.57	0.88	★★★★★
5 Yr	7.04	9	25	1.36	0.79	★★★★★
10 Yr	---					
Average Historical Rating (76 months)				5.0	★ s	

[1] 1 = low, 100 = high [2] 1.00 = Muni Avg [3] 1.00 = 90-day T-bill return

Other Measures

				Standard LB Agg	Best Fit LB Muni
Standard Deviation	5.39	Alpha		0.8	0.5
Mean	5.38	Beta		1.02	0.97
Sharpe Ratio	0.34	R-Squared		57	97

Investment Style

Interest-Rate Stance

Avg Effective Maturity   20.2 Yrs

Quality

Avg Credit Quality   BBB

Avg Weighted Coupon   7.19%
Avg Weighted Price   95.01% of Par

Diversification Value for Portfolio Types

Large Cap: Medium	Small Cap: High	Bond: Low	Balanced: Low	Diversified: Medium

Portfolio 06-30-94

Total Stocks: 0
Total Fixed-Income: 262

Amount 000	Date of Maturity		Value $000	% Net Assets
14900	08-15-22	LA Lake Charles Harbor/Term 7.75%	15794	1.80
14750	05-15-19	NY Dorm State Univ Educ Fac 5.5%	13191	1.50
11900	05-15-20	MI Strategic Fund Ltd Obl Mercy Svc 9.4%	12733	1.45
12000	11-01-15	AZ Hlth Fac St Luke Hosp 10.125%	12645	1.44
15500	04-01-21	NY Local Govt Assist 5%	12613	1.44
12000	04-01-11	IL Dev Fin Poll Cntrl Pwr 7.875%	12165	1.39
12100	02-01-13	CO Hlth Fac Rocky Mtn Adventist 6.625%	11752	1.34
10000	01-01-18	MA Indl Fin Emerson Clg 8.9%	11100	1.26
10000		CA Ventura DMD	10073	1.15
9365	03-01-20	MI Highland Park Hosp Fin Lakeside 10%	9763	1.11
8500	01-01-17	GA Muni Elec Spcl Obl 6.5%	8617	0.98
10000	05-15-15	NY Dorm State Univ Educ Fac 5.25%	8500	0.97
7500	12-15-16	NJ Econ Dev Holt Hauling/Warehouse 9.75	8175	0.93
8500	01-01-19	NY New York City GO 6%	7894	0.90
8735	01-01-17	NY Triborough Bridge/Tunnel Genl 5.5%	7818	0.89
10000	07-01-12	WA Pub Pwr Sply Sys Proj #3 IFRN	7613	0.87
7350	12-01-19	MI Highland Park Hosp Fin 9.875%	7598	0.87
9000	10-01-23	FL Orlando Util Com Wtr/Elec 5.25%	7571	0.86
6195	12-01-14	MS Claiborne Poll Cntrl Engy 9.875%	7101	0.81
6750	12-01-14	LA West Feliciana Poll Cntrl Util 7.7%	7096	0.81

Credit Analysis % of Bonds 10-31-94

US Govt	0	BB	8
AAA	13	B	0
AA	6	Below B	2
A	11	NR/NA	47
BBB	14		

Composition % of Assets 10-31-94

Cash	4.8	Preferreds	0.0
Stocks	0.0	Convertibles	0.0
Bonds	95.2	Other	0.0

Tax Analysis

	Tax-Adj Historical Return %	% Pretax Return
3 Yr Avg	4.95	92.0
5 Yr Avg	6.76	95.5
10 Yr Avg	---	---
Potential Capital Gain Exposure (% of assets)		-7%

Most Similar Funds in MF500

Putnam Municipal Income A	Strong Fit
Smith Barney Tax-Exempt I B	Strong Fit
Dreyfus Intermediate Muni	Strong Fit

Coupon Range

	% Bonds	Rel Obj
0%	6.0	2.40
0% to 6.8%	32.2	0.53
6.8% to 7.5%	9.3	0.60
7.5% to 8.3%	10.2	1.16
More than 8.3%	34.0	3.86
Not applicable	8.2	2.10

Sector Weightings

	% Bonds	Rel Obj
General Obl	8.28	0.39
Utilities	8.02	0.64
Health	26.18	1.98
Water/Waste	2.92	0.46
Housing	2.25	0.31
Education	4.87	0.76
Transportation	10.01	0.98
COP/Lease	5.72	1.79
Private	23.30	2.00
Misc Revenue	3.65	0.73
Demand	4.80	1.95

Top 5 States % of Bonds

NY	11.33	MA	7.26
CA	10.49	PA	6.35
MI	8.38		

Fidelity Asset Manager

	Ticker	Load	NAV	Yield	SEC Yield	Assets	Objective
	FASMX	None	13.83	2.9%	N/A	11075.6	Asset Alloc.

Fidelity Asset Manager seeks total return with reduced risk over the long term.

The fund normally allocates its assets within the following investment parameters: 10%-60% in stocks; 20%-60% in bonds; and 0%-70% in short-term fixed-income instruments. A neutral mix consists of 40% stocks, 40% bonds, and 20% money-market instruments. The bond portion consists of debt of varying quality; maturities are greater than three years. A single reallocation may not involve more than 10% of assets. The fund may purchase foreign issues.

Manager's Investment Style

Management is known for its bold moves, relative to other asset-allocation funds. This includes expeditions into unpopular or underfollowed areas of the market. For example, it has dabbled in commodities, junk bonds, a wide array of smaller domestic stocks, emerging-market debt, and foreign stocks. Conversely, in more difficult climates such as that of 1994, management has turned to Treasuries and cash, with fewer foreign and domestic stocks.

Fund Manager(s)

Robert A. Beckwitt, since 12-88. Birthdate: 11-55. BA, Princeton U. 1981. MS, MIT 1986.

Manager Experience

	Dates Managed	Invest Obj	Std Dev	+/- Index
Robert A. Beckwitt				
Fidelity Spartan Govt Inc	12/88 - 10/93	GG	3.98	-0.50
Fidelity Spartan L-T Gov	09/90 - 10/93	GG	5.75	5.56

Historical Profile

Return	Above Average
Risk	Below Average
Rating	★★★★ Above Average

Investment Style History Equity

Average % Stocks Held in Portfolio

32% 34% 37% 38% 51% 43%

Growth of $10,000

|||| Value of Fund ($000)
— Value of Index ($000) S&P 500
▼ Manager Change
▽ Partial Manager Change
► Mgr Unknown After
◄ Mgr Unknown Before

Performance Quartile (Within Objective)

	1983	1984	1985	1986	1987	1988	1989	1990	1991	1992	1993	1994	History
	---	---	---	---	---	10.03	10.94	10.87	12.46	13.37	15.40	13.83	NAV
	---	---	---	---	---	0.30 *	15.28	5.38	23.64	12.75	23.29	-6.60	Total Return %
	---	---	---	---	---	-0.21 *	-16.41	8.50	-6.85	5.13	13.23	-7.92	+/- S&P 500
	---	---	---	---	---	---	0.74	-3.57	7.64	5.50	13.54	-3.68	+/- LB Aggregate
	---	---	---	---	---	0.00	3.68	6.02	3.98	3.82	4.53	2.58	Income Return %
	---	---	---	---	---	0.30	11.60	-0.64	19.65	8.92	18.76	-9.18	Capital Return %
	---	---	---	---	---	---	46	40	38	14	13	77	Total Rtn % Rank All
	---	---	---	---	---	---	66	8	43	6	11	85	Total Rtn % Rank Obj
	---	---	---	---	---	0.00	0.38	0.65	0.45	0.48	0.59	0.40	Income $
	---	---	---	---	---	0.00	0.24	0.00	0.50	0.19	0.43	0.17	Capital Gains $
	---	---	---	---	---	---	1.58	1.17	1.17	1.17	1.09	1.04	Expense Ratio %
	---	---	---	---	---	---	5.88	5.89	5.74	5.58	4.28	3.63	Income Ratio %
	---	---	---	---	---	---	167	105	134	134	98	109	Turnover Rate %
	---	---	---	---	---	5.5	299.7	372.0	1016.3	3392.7	9094.4	11075.6	Net Assets ($mil)

Performance 12-31-94

	1st Qtr	2nd Qtr	3rd Qtr	4th Qtr	Total
1987	---	---	---	---	---
1988	---	---	---	---	0.30 *
1989	3.09	6.77	3.17	1.51	15.28
1990	-1.46	4.36	-5.42	8.35	5.38
1991	11.78	1.89	5.17	3.22	23.64
1992	3.37	2.41	2.35	4.06	12.75
1993	6.15	3.85	4.36	7.17	23.29
1994	-4.84	-1.46	3.09	-3.38	-6.60

Bear Market Performance

Decile Rank (5-year period)

Worst — Best

	Worst 3 Mo Period 1985-89	Worst 3 Mo Period 1990-94
Fidelity Asset Manager	---	-7.89
+/- S&P 500	---	-2.14
+/- Best Fit Index : S&P 500	---	-2.14

Trailing Returns

	Total Return %	+/- S&P 500	+/- LB Aggregate	% Rank All	% Rank Obj	Growth of $10,000
3 Mo	-3.38	-3.37	-3.76	85	85	9,662
6 Mo	-0.40	-5.26	-1.39	63	78	9,960
1 Yr	-6.60	-7.92	-3.68	77	85	9,340
3 Yr Avg	9.09	2.83	4.55	17	11	12,983
5 Yr Avg	11.08	2.39	3.46	12	4	16,915
10 Yr Avg	---	---	---	---	---	---
15 Yr Avg	---	---	---	---	---	---

Operations

Address and Telephone	82 Devonshire Street
	Boston, MA 02109
	800-544-8888
Advisor	Fidelity Management & Research
Subadvisor	None
Distributor	Fidelity Distributors
States Available	All
Report Grade	A
Income Distrib	Paid Quarterly
* Date of Inception	12-28-88
Fiscal Year End	September

Risk Analysis

Time Period	Load-Adj Return %	Risk % Rank All [1]	Risk % Rank Obj [1]	Morningstar [2] Return	Morningstar [2] Risk	Morningstar Risk-Adj Rating
1 Yr	-6.60					
3 Yr	9.09	39	24	1.68 [3]	0.62	★★★★
5 Yr	11.08	46	27	1.67 [3]	0.59	★★★★
10 Yr	---	---	---	---	---	

Average Historical Rating (37 months) 4.9 ★s

[1] 1 = low, 100 = high [2] 1.00 = Hybrid Avg [3] 1.00 = 90-day T-bill return

Other Measures

			Standard S&P 500	Best Fit S&P 500
Standard Deviation	6.57	Alpha	3.7	3.7
Mean	8.95	Beta	0.62	0.62
Sharpe Ratio	0.83	R-Squared	55	55

Investment Style

Stocks

	Port Avg	Rel S&P 500
Price/Earnings Ratio	20.7	1.12
Price/Book Ratio	2.8	0.81
5 Yr Earnings Gr %	8.0	1.44
Med Mkt Cap ($mil)	5559	0.43

Style V B G / Size L M S

Bonds

Avg Effective Duration	4.0 Yrs
Avg Effective Maturity	---
Avg Credit Quality	---
Avg Weighted Coupon	8.02%

Not Available

Diversification Value for Portfolio Types

 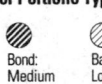 

Large Cap: Low	Small Cap: Medium	Bond: Medium	Balanced: Low	Diversified: Low

Portfolio 09-30-94

Share Chg (03-94)000	Amount 000	Total Stocks: 935 Total Fixed-Income: 214	Date of Maturity	Value $000	% Net Assets
	1356260	US Treasury Note 6.25%	02-15-03	1246281	10.57
	358750	United Mexican States 6.25%	12-31-19	232291	1.97
	212400	US Treasury Note 5.75%	08-15-03	187277	1.59
	134400	US Treasury Bond 12.75%	11-15-10	183267	1.55
	209131	Republic of Argentina 6.5%	03-31-05	159462	1.35
503	1817	Philip Morris		111064	0.94
50	1314	FNMA		103454	0.88
	65000	US Treasury Bond 14%	11-15-11	96220	0.82
	62000	US Treasury Bond 11.875%	11-15-03	79098	0.67
-436	982	British Petroleum (ADR)		74354	0.63
146	962	IBM		66887	0.57
	62180	Cemex 8.875%	06-10-98	61403	0.52
	63406	Republic of Brazil 8.75%	01-01-01	52785	0.45
271	920	Schlumberger		50001	0.42
114	4097	Grupo Carso CI A1		46208	0.39
-613	746	Intel		45885	0.39
633	1403	Compaq Computer		45766	0.39
292	651	Pfizer		45014	0.38
	80430	Govt of New Zealand 8%	04-15-04	44582	0.38
670	1078	Ameritech		43369	0.37

Index Allocation

	% of Stocks
S&P 500	53.2
S&P MidCap 400	7.6
U.S. Small Cap	11.2
Foreign	29.4

Composition % 11-30-94

Cash	24.1	Preferreds	0.0
Stocks	36.3	Convertibles	0.0
Bonds	39.6	Other	0.0

Tax Analysis

	Tax-Adj Historical Return %	% Pretax Return
3 Yr Avg	7.24	78.3
5 Yr Avg	9.08	78.7
10 Yr Avg	---	---
Potential Capital Gain Exposure (% of assets)		-3%

Most Similar Funds in MF500

Fidelity Asset Manager: Grth	Fair Fit
Scudder Growth & Income	Fair Fit
Scudder Global	Fair Fit

Bond Credit Analysis 06-30-94

% of Bonds

US Govt	0	BB	16
AAA	30	B	14
AA	5	Below B	0
A	6	NR/NA	28
BBB	1		

Stock Sector Weightings

	% of Stocks	Relative S&P 500
Utilities	12.4	1.00
Energy	9.8	0.97
Financials	15.6	1.47
Industrial Cyclicals	14.1	0.86
Consumer Durables	8.2	1.31
Consumer Staples	7.4	0.59
Services	7.0	0.86
Retail	5.9	1.02
Health	6.9	0.80
Technology	12.8	1.39

Expenses & Fees

Sales Fees	0.00% front
	0.00% deferred
	0.00% 12b-1
Management Fee	0.40% flat fee+0.52%G
3-,5-,10-yr Expense Projections	$35, $60, $133
Annual Brokerage Cost	0.19%

Purchase info

Min Initial Purchase	$2500 (Addt'l: $250)
Min IRA Purchase	$500 (Addt'l: $250)
Min Auto Invest Plan	$2500 (Systematic Inv: $100)

MORNINGSTAR 1995 Mutual Fund 500

Fidelity Asset Manager: Grth

	Ticker	Load	NAV	Yield	SEC Yield	Assets	Objective
	FASGX	None	12.84	1.5%	N/A	2852.9	Asset Alloc.

Fidelity Asset Manager: Growth seeks total return over the long term.

The fund allocates its assets among domestic and foreign stocks, bonds, and short-term instruments. It considers a "neutral" asset mix to consist of roughly 65% stocks, 30% bonds, and 5% short-term instruments, but it regularly reviews its asset allocations to provide the most favorable return. Usually, reallocations are gradual; a single reallocation does not involve more than 20% of the fund's assets. The fund may invest up to 15% of its assets in precious metals, and may engage in various options and futures strategies.

Manager's Investment Style

Management's strategy is partly influenced by the fund's role as the most-aggressive of the Fidelity Asset Manager trio. As would be expected from this charter, management's holdings can be unusual and aggressive such as its recently acquired structured notes linked to Russia's emerging stocks. Junk bonds, emerging-markets debt and equity, European bonds, and various types of structured notes have all shown up here. Generally, cash is kept to a minimum, though if necessary management will use it to gain a safe haven.

Fund Manager(s)

Robert A. Beckwitt, since 12-91. Birthdate: 11-55. BA, Princeton U. 1981 MS, MIT 1986

Manager Experience	Dates Managed	Invest Obj	Std Dev	+/- Index
Robert A. Beckwitt				
Fidelity Spartan Govt Inc	12/88 - 10/93	GG	3.98	-0.50
Fidelity Spartan L-T Gov	09/90 - 10/93	GG	5.75	5.56

Historical Profile
Return	High
Risk	Average
Rating	★★★★★ Highest

Investment Style History
Equity

Average % Stocks Held in Portfolio

| | 67% | 74% | 60% |

Growth of $10,000

|||| Value of Fund ($000)
— Value of Index ($000)
SPMid400
▽ Manager Change
▽ Partial Manager Change
► Mgr Unknown After
◄ Mgr Unknown Before

Performance Quartile (Within Objective)

	1983	1984	1985	1986	1987	1988	1989	1990	1991	1992	1993	1994	History
NAV	---	---	---	---	---	---	---	---	10.00	11.77	14.25	12.84	NAV
Total Return %	---	---	---	---	---	---	---	---	0.00 *	20.03	26.32	-7.39	Total Return %
+/- S&P 500	---	---	---	---	---	---	---	---	-0.72 *	12.41	16.26	-8.70	+/- S&P 500
+/- LB Aggregate	---	---	---	---	---	---	---	---	---	12.79	16.56	-4.47	+/- LB Aggregate
Income Return %	---	---	---	---	---	---	---	---	0.00	1.44	0.67	1.39	Income Return %
Capital Return %	---	---	---	---	---	---	---	---	0.00	18.59	25.65	-8.78	Capital Return %
Total Rtn % Rank All	---	---	---	---	---	---	---	---	---	5	10	82	Total Rtn % Rank All
Total Rtn % Rank Obj	---	---	---	---	---	---	---	---	---	1	5	89	Total Rtn % Rank Obj
Income $	---	---	---	---	---	---	---	---	0.00	0.15	0.09	0.19	Income $
Capital Gains $	---	---	---	---	---	---	---	---	0.00	0.08	0.51	0.17	Capital Gains $
Expense Ratio %	---	---	---	---	---	---	---	---	---	1.64	1.19	1.15	Expense Ratio %
Income Ratio %	---	---	---	---	---	---	---	---	---	3.50	3.02	2.64	Income Ratio %
Turnover Rate %	---	---	---	---	---	---	---	---	---	693	97	104	Turnover Rate %
Net Assets ($mil)	---	---	---	---	---	---	---	---	9.0	236.7	1795.0	2852.9	Net Assets ($mil)

Performance 12-31-94

	1st Qtr	2nd Qtr	3rd Qtr	4th Qtr	Total
1987	---	---	---	---	---
1988	---	---	---	---	---
1989	---	---	---	---	---
1990	---	---	---	---	---
1991	---	---	---	---	0.00 *
1992	5.20	1.24	4.79	7.56	20.03
1993	6.71	3.90	5.52	7.97	26.32
1994	-4.35	-2.35	4.51	-5.12	-7.39

Bear Market Performance

Decile Rank (5-year period)

Worst   Best

	Worst 3 Mo Period 1985-89	Worst 3 Mo Period 1990-94
Fidelity Asset Manager: Grth	---	---
+/- S&P 500	---	---
+/- Best Fit Index :	---	---

Trailing Returns

	Total Return %	+/- S&P 500	+/- LB Aggregate	% Rank All	% Rank Obj	Growth of $10,000
3 Mo	-5.12	-5.11	-5.50	92	95	9,488
6 Mo	-0.85	-5.71	-1.84	71	83	9,915
1 Yr	-7.39	-8.70	-4.47	82	89	9,261
3 Yr Avg	11.98	5.71	7.43	8	2	14,042
5 Yr Avg	---	---	---	---	---	---
10 Yr Avg	---	---	---	---	---	---
15 Yr Avg	---	---	---	---	---	---

Operations

Address and Telephone	82 Devonshire Street
	Boston, MA 02109
	800-544-8888
Advisor	Fidelity Management & Research
Subadvisor	FMR (U.K.)/FMR (Far East)/FMR (Texas)
Distributor	Fidelity Distributors
States Available	All plus GU,PR,VI except WI
Report Grade	A
Income Distrib	Paid Annually
* Date of Inception	12-30-91
Fiscal Year End	September

Min Initial Purchase	$2500 (Addt'l: $250)
Min IRA Purchase	$500 (Addt'l: $250)
Min Auto Invest Plan	$2500 (Systematic Inv: $100)

Expenses & Fees

Sales Fees	0.00% front
	0.00% deferred
	0.00% 12b-1
Management Fee	0.40% flat fee+0.52%G
3-,5-,10-yr Expense Projections	$38, $66, $145
Annual Brokerage Cost	0.36%

Risk Analysis

Time Period	Load-Adj Return %	Risk % Rank [1] All	Obj	Morningstar [2] Return	Risk	Morningstar Risk-Adj Rating
1 Yr	-7.39					
3 Yr	11.98	60	70	2.63 [3]	0.86	★★★★★
5 Yr	---					
10 Yr	---					

Average Historical Rating (1 month)   5.0 ★s

[1] 1 = low, 100 = high [2] 1.00 = Hybrid Avg [3] 1.00 = 90-day T-bill return

Other Measures

	Standard S&P 500	Best Fit SPMid400
Standard Deviation	8.72	Alpha	6.0	5.5
Mean	11.75	Beta	0.81	0.74
Sharpe Ratio	0.94	R-Squared	54	69

Investment Style

Stocks	Port Avg	Rel S&P 500
Price/Earnings Ratio	22.2	1.20
Price/Book Ratio	3.1	0.90
5 Yr Earnings Gr %	7.5	1.35
Med Mkt Cap ($mil)	5539	0.43

Bonds	
Avg Effective Duration	4.7 Yrs
Avg Effective Maturity	---
Avg Credit Quality	---
Avg Weighted Coupon	7.88%

Not Available

Diversification Value for Portfolio Types

Large Cap: Low	Small Cap: Low	Bond: High	Balanced: Low	Diversified: Low

Portfolio 09-30-94

Total Stocks: 907
Total Fixed-Income: 195

Share Chg (03-94)000	Amount 000		Date of Maturity	Value $000	% Net Assets
329855		US Treasury Note 6.25%	02-15-03	303108	9.87
97750		United Mexican States 6.25%	12-31-19	63294	2.06
42400		US Treasury Bond 12.75%	11-15-10	57816	1.88
49200		Republic of Argentina FRN	03-31-05	35228	1.15
59350		Republic of Argentina FRN	03-31-23	29452	0.96
230	477	Philip Morris		29157	0.95
-11	358	IBM		24852	0.81
651	2140	Grupo Carso Cl A1		24142	0.79
32	260	FNMA		20507	0.67
	16000	US Treasury Bond 11.875%	11-15-03	20412	0.66
1531	2068	Cemex Cl B		19097	0.62
-31	237	British Petroleum (ADR)		17950	0.58
	114277	Siderugica Brasileiras Cv 6%	08-15-99	17785	0.58
-60	237	Telefonos de Mexico L (ADR)		14812	0.48
0	625	Daehan Korean Bluechip		14062	0.46
243	428	Compaq Computer		13966	0.45
23700		Telesp Pfd		13475	0.44
16170		Republic of Brazil 8.75%	01-01-01	13462	0.44
117	236	Schlumberger		12839	0.42
341	472	Alcan Aluminium		12431	0.40

Index Allocation

	% of Stocks
S&P 500	42.6
S&P MidCap 400	7.1
U.S. Small Cap	11.6
Foreign	40.7

Composition % 11-30-94

Cash	5.0	Preferreds	0.0
Stocks	60.9	Convertibles	0.0
Bonds	34.1	Other	0.0

Tax Analysis

	Tax-Adj Historical Return %	% Pretax Return
3 Yr Avg	10.97	90.7
5 Yr Avg	---	---
10 Yr Avg	---	---
Potential Capital Gain Exposure (% of assets)		-6%

Most Similar Funds in MF500

Fidelity Asset Manager	Fair Fit
Neuberger&Berman Partners	Fair Fit
SteinRoe Special	Fair Fit

Bond Credit Analysis 03-31-94

% of Bonds

US Govt	0	BB	22
AAA	0	B	0
AA	10	Below B	1
A	0	NR/NA	65
BBB	2		

Stock Sector Weightings

	% of Stocks	Relative S&P 500
Utilities	6.9	0.55
Energy	7.5	0.74
Financials	15.3	1.45
Industrial Cyclicals	17.1	1.04
Consumer Durables	9.2	1.48
Consumer Staples	7.9	0.63
Services	8.4	1.03
Retail	5.3	0.91
Health	5.2	0.60
Technology	17.4	1.89

Fidelity Balanced

	Ticker	Load	NAV	Yield	SEC Yield	Assets	Objective
	FBALX	None	12.29	3.3%	5.58%	4999.1	Balanced

Fidelity Balanced Fund seeks income consistent with preservation of capital.

The fund invests in a broadly diversified portfolio of high-yielding securities, including common stocks, preferred stocks, and bonds. At least 25% of total assets will always be invested in fixed-income senior securities rated BBB or higher. The fund may write covered call options and buy put options.

Historical Profile
Return	Above Average
Risk	Below Average
Rating ★★★★	Above Average

Investment Style History
Equity

Average % Stocks Held in Portfolio

54% 46% 43% 36% 45% 26% 34% 27%

Growth of $10,000
||| Value of Fund ($000)
— Value of Index ($000)
S&P 500
▼ Manager Change
▽ Partial Manager Change
► Mgr Unknown After
◄ Mgr Unknown Before

Performance Quartile (Within Objective)

Manager's Investment Style

Management has generally kept equity exposure low in an effort to reduce volatility. It also limits risk through a value orientation, which involves cutting back on asset classes--whether equity or fixed income--it deems overvalued. Management also ventures into foreign markets, picking up stocks and bonds, thus adding further diversification to the portfolio and muting volatility.

Fund Manager(s)

Robert J. Haber CFA, since 06-88. Birthdate: 01-58. MS, Tufts U. 1980 MBA, Harvard 1985

Manager Experience	Dates Managed	Invest Obj	Std Dev	+/- Index
Robert J. Haber				
Fidelity Adv Inc & Gr A	01/87 - 12/94	B	10.39	0.85
Fidelity Global Balanced	02/93 - 12/94	I	12.12	3.55

	1983	1984	1985	1986	1987	1988	1989	1990	1991	1992	1993	1994	History
	---	---	---	10.16	9.72	10.55	11.37	10.63	12.35	12.29	13.39	12.29	NAV
	---	---	---	1.60 *	1.95	15.78	19.71	-0.47	26.78	7.95	19.28	-5.31	Total Return %
	---	---	---	2.55 *	-3.31	-0.83	-11.98	2.65	-3.70	0.33	9.22	-6.63	+/- S&P 500
	---	---	---	---	-0.81	7.90	5.17	-9.41	10.78	0.70	9.53	-2.40	+/- LB Aggregate
	---	---	---	0.00	5.67	7.24	9.71	6.04	5.75	5.51	4.85	2.90	Income Return %
	---	---	---	1.60	-3.72	8.54	10.00	-6.51	21.03	2.43	14.43	-8.22	Capital Return %
	---	---	---	---	43	25	36	57	32	46	18	67	Total Rtn % Rank All
	---	---	---	---	50	23	45	49	33	40	4	83	Total Rtn % Rank Obj
	---	---	---	0.00	0.60	0.68	1.00	0.68	0.60	0.66	0.60	0.40	Income $
	---	---	---	0.00	0.07	0.00	0.22	0.00	0.45	0.36	0.64	0.00	Capital Gains $
	---	---	---	---	1.19	1.30	1.13	0.97	0.98	0.96	0.93	1.01	Expense Ratio %
	---	---	---	---	6.03	6.29	8.90	6.74	5.93	5.68	5.07	4.09	Income Ratio %
	---	---	---	---	161	213	168	223	238	242	162	157	Turnover Rate %
	---	---	---	56.6	121.8	123.2	196.3	293.1	725.2	1754.5	4684.5	4999.1	Net Assets ($mil)

Performance 12-31-94

	1st Qtr	2nd Qtr	3rd Qtr	4th Qtr	Total
1987	9.75	-0.91	0.93	-7.12	1.95
1988	6.77	5.21	1.33	1.72	15.78
1989	3.79	7.13	4.64	2.89	19.71
1990	-2.20	2.37	-5.54	5.25	-0.47
1991	10.92	2.99	5.88	4.82	26.78
1992	0.81	2.77	3.67	0.50	7.95
1993	8.31	4.95	3.60	1.28	19.28
1994	-3.25	-1.73	2.15	-2.52	-5.31

Bear Market Performance

Decile Rank (5-year period)

Worst ▮ Best

	Worst 3 Mo Period 1985-89	Worst 3 Mo Period 1990-94
Fidelity Balanced	---	-6.59
+/- S&P 500	---	-0.83
+/- Best Fit Index : MSAllCtry	---	-2.72

Trailing Returns

	Total Return %	+/- S&P 500	+/- LB Aggregate	% Rank All	% Rank Obj	Growth of $10,000
3 Mo	-2.52	-2.50	-2.90	77	90	9,748
6 Mo	-0.42	-5.28	-1.41	64	93	9,958
1 Yr	-5.31	-6.63	-2.40	67	83	9,469
3 Yr Avg	6.83	0.56	2.28	28	29	12,191
5 Yr Avg	9.00	0.31	1.37	24	21	15,384
10 Yr Avg	---	---	---	---	---	---
15 Yr Avg	---	---	---	---	---	---

Operations

Address and Telephone	82 Devonshire Street
	Boston, MA 02109
	800-544-8888
Advisor	Fidelity Management & Research
Subadvisor	None
Distributor	Fidelity Distributors
States Available	All
Report Grade	A
Income Distrib	Paid Quarterly
* Date of Inception	11-06-86
Fiscal Year End	July

Risk Analysis

Time Period	Load-Adj Return %	Risk % Rank [1] All	Risk % Rank [1] Obj	Morningstar [2] Return	Morningstar Risk	Morningstar Risk-Adj Rating
1 Yr	-5.31					
3 Yr	6.83	38	15	0.97 [3]	0.62	★★★★
5 Yr	9.00	47	12	1.08 [3]	0.59	★★★★
10 Yr	---	---	---	---	---	---

Average Historical Rating (62 months)   4.6 ★s

[1] 1 = low, 100 = high   [2] 1.00 = Hybrid Avg   [3] 1.00 = 90-day T-bill return

Other Measures

				Standard S&P 500	Best Fit MSAllCtry
Standard Deviation	5.72	Alpha		2.0	2.3
Mean	6.79	Beta		0.45	0.40
Sharpe Ratio	0.57	R-Squared		38	54

Investment Style

Stocks	Port Avg	Rel S&P 500
Price/Earnings Ratio	29.5	1.60
Price/Book Ratio	1.8	0.54
5 Yr Earnings Gr %	-8.5#	-1.53
Med Mkt Cap ($mil)	2415	0.19

figure is based on 50% or less of stocks

Bonds	
Avg Effective Duration	6.0 Yrs
Avg Effective Maturity	13.3 Yrs
Avg Credit Quality	AA
Avg Weighted Coupon	7.57%

Diversification Value for Portfolio Types

Large Cap: Medium	Small Cap: High	Bond: Low	Balanced: Low	Diversified: Low

Portfolio 07-31-94

Total Stocks: 139
Total Fixed-Income: 251

Share Chg (01-94)000	Amount 000		Date of Maturity	Value $000	% Net Assets
	2252900	Govt of France 8.5%	04-25-23	446497	8.28
	236585	US Treasury Bond 8.125%	08-15-19	253330	4.70
	102030	US Treasury Note 6.25%	02-15-03	96642	1.79
	147000	Govt of Canada 6.5%	06-01-04	87908	1.63
	330600	Govt of France 8.5%	11-25-03	65845	1.22
	66000	US Treasury Note 5.5%	04-30-96	65577	1.22
4390	4390	Methanex		64131	1.19
	1144	Unocal Cv Pfd $3.50		63206	1.17
	47771	Thermo Electron Cv 4.625%	08-01-97	63058	1.17
	40371	Carnival Cv 4.5%	07-01-97	57932	1.07
	91500	Govt of Canada 8%	06-01-23	57359	1.06
615	3161	Stone Container		52150	0.97
60	997	Temple-Inland		50972	0.95
	45650	US Treasury Note 9.25%	08-15-98	49922	0.93
	82800	Govt of New Zealand 8%	04-15-04	49625	0.92
	77600	Republic of Italy 11%	06-01-03	48179	0.89
-28	931	Pennzoil		46884	0.87
	35000	US Treasury Bond 9.875%	11-15-15	43876	0.81
8017	8017	Jefferson Smurfit Group		43511	0.81
	43000	US Treasury Note 5.125%	03-31-98	41105	0.76

Index Allocation	% of Stocks
S&P 500	32.3
S&P MidCap 400	8.0
U.S. Small Cap	6.8
Foreign	54.1

Composition % 11-30-94
Cash	32.0	Preferreds	0.0
Stocks	13.8	Convertibles	14.4
Bonds	39.8	Other	0.0

Tax Analysis

	Tax-Adj Historical Return %	% Pretax Return
3 Yr Avg	4.49	64.3
5 Yr Avg	6.61	70.0
10 Yr Avg	---	---
Potential Capital Gain Exposure (% of assets)		-6%

Most Similar Funds in MF500
USAA Invest Cornerstone	Weak Fit
Smith Barney Inc & Grth A	Weak Fit
Oppenheimer Equity-Inc A	Weak Fit

Min Initial Purchase	$2500 (Addt'l: $250)
Min IRA Purchase	$500 (Addt'l: $250)
Min Auto Invest Plan	$2500 (Systematic Inv: $100)

Expenses & Fees
Sales Fees	0.00% front
	0.00% deferred
	0.00% 12b-1
Management Fee	0.20% flat fee+0.52%G
3-,5-,10-yr Expense Projections	$32, $56, $124
Annual Brokerage Cost	0.31%

Bond Credit Analysis 08-31-94
% of Bonds
US Govt	0	BB	4
AAA	58	B	0
AA	4	Below B	0
A	6	NR/NA	0
BBB	27		

Stock Sector Weightings	% of Stocks	Relative S&P 500
Utilities	9.8	0.79
Energy	13.2	1.30
Financials	7.6	0.72
Industrial Cyclicals	38.6	2.36
Consumer Durables	4.4	0.71
Consumer Staples	2.5	0.20
Services	3.4	0.42
Retail	3.8	0.64
Health	1.7	0.19
Technology	15.3	1.67

MORNINGSTAR 1995 Mutual Fund 500

Fidelity Blue Chip Growth

	Ticker	Load	NAV	Yield	SEC Yield	Assets	Objective
	FBGRX	3.00%	25.95	0.0%	N/A	3287.0	Growth

Fidelity Blue Chip Growth Fund seeks long-term capital appreciation.

The fund normally invests at least 65% of its assets in the common stocks of blue-chip companies. These companies have market capitalizations of at least $200 million and are included in the Dow Jones Industrial Average or the S&P 500 Index. The fund seeks companies expected to demonstrate high long-term earnings growth. It also attempts to maintain representation in as many market sectors as possible, but may concentrate in the strongest sectors of the market.

Manager's Investment Style

Current management (in place since 1993) has tended to deviate more from a strict blue-chip portfolio than past management did. At present, management seeks stocks with accelerating earnings and that sell at low prices relative to their projected growth rates. Its choices have been known to stray into small-cap or mid-cap territory, though the charter mandates a 65% weighting in Dow Jones Industrials or S&P 500 names. Management justifies its unusual approach to blue chips by stating its willingness to hold the blue chips of the future.

Fund Manager(s)

Michael Gordon, since 01-93. BA, Tufts U.

Manager Experience

	Dates Managed	Invest Obj	Std Dev	+/- Index
Michael Gordon				
Fidelity Sel Biotech	05/90 - 08/92	SH	25.43	25.83
Fidelity Sel Chemicals	08/92 - 01/93	S	5.54	-1.97

Historical Profile

Return	High
Risk	Below Average
Rating	★★★★★ Highest

	1983	1984	1985	1986	1987	1988	1989	1990	1991	1992	1993	1994	History
						97%	96%	93%	95%	94%	90%	92%	Average % Stocks Held in Portfolio
	---	---	---	---	10.00	10.56	14.09	14.43	22.25	22.83	24.17	25.95	NAV
	---	---	---	---	---	5.91	36.24	3.50	54.81	6.17	24.50	9.85	Total Return %
	---	---	---	---	---	-10.70	4.55	6.62	24.33	-1.45	14.45	8.54	+/- S&P 500
	---	---	---	---	---	-12.03	7.06	9.68	20.60	-2.80	13.22	9.92	+/- Wilshire 5000
	---	---	---	---	---	0.31	1.00	1.09	0.62	0.63	0.04	0.00	Income Return %
	---	---	---	---	---	5.60	35.24	2.41	54.19	5.54	24.46	9.85	Capital Return %
	---	---	---	---	---	89	6	47	6	67	12	2	Total Rtn % Rank All
	---	---	---	---	---	89	14	10	11	63	7	3	Total Rtn % Rank Obj
	---	---	---	---	0.00	0.03	0.12	0.15	0.08	0.14	0.01	0.00	Income $
	---	---	---	---	0.00	0.00	0.17	0.00	0.00	0.62	4.12	0.58	Capital Gains $
	---	---	---	---	---	2.74	1.56	1.26	1.26	1.27	1.25	1.22	Expense Ratio %
	---	---	---	---	---	0.14	0.97	1.14	0.80	0.55	0.46	0.21	Income Ratio %
	---	---	---	---	---	40	83	68	99	71	319	271	Turnover Rate %
	---	---	---	---	---	38.2	64.3	131.4	390.0	567.4	1094.7	3287.0	Net Assets ($mil)

Investment Style History
Equity

Growth of $10,000
IIII Value of Fund ($000)
— Value of Index ($000)
SPMid400
▼ Manager Change
▽ Partial Manager Change
► Mgr Unknown After
◄ Mgr Unknown Before

Performance Quartile (Within Objective)

Performance 12-31-94

	1st Qtr	2nd Qtr	3rd Qtr	4th Qtr	Total
1987	---	---	---	---	---
1988	1.20	5.53	-1.87	1.06	5.91
1989	6.63	9.77	15.16	1.07	36.24
1990	-1.21	12.79	-14.98	9.25	3.50
1991	21.97	-1.08	11.78	14.79	54.81
1992	-5.35	0.43	4.39	6.99	6.17
1993	4.38	7.93	8.43	1.92	24.50
1994	0.79	0.66	7.75	0.49	9.85

Bear Market Performance

Decile Rank (5-year period)

Worst ——————————— Best

	Worst 3 Mo Period 1985-89	Worst 3 Mo Period 1990-94
Fidelity Blue Chip Growth	---	-14.98
+/- S&P 500	---	-1.23
+/- Best Fit Index : SPMid400	---	2.80

Trailing Returns

	Total Return %	+/- S&P 500	+/- Wil 5000	% Rank All	% Rank Obj	Growth of $10,000
3 Mo	0.49	0.51	1.26	12	14	10,049
6 Mo	8.28	3.42	3.66	6	14	10,828
1 Yr	9.85	8.54	9.92	2	3	10,985
3 Yr Avg	13.24	6.97	6.63	6	7	14,521
5 Yr Avg	18.40	9.71	9.58	2	1	23,266
10 Yr Avg	---	---	---	---	---	---
15 Yr Avg	---	---	---	---	---	---

Operations

Address and Telephone	82 Devonshire Street Boston, MA 02109 800-544-8888	Min Initial Purchase	$2500 (Addt'l: $250)
		Min IRA Purchase	$500 (Addt'l: $250)
Advisor	Fidelity Management & Research	Min Auto Invest Plan	$2500 (Systematic Inv: $100)
Subadvisor	FMR (U.K.)/FMR (Far East)		
Distributor	Fidelity Distributors	Expenses & Fees	
States Available	All	Sales Fees	3.00% front
Report Grade	A		0.00% deferred
Income Distrib	Paid Annually		0.00% 12b-1
* Date of Inception	12-31-87	Management Fee	0.30% flat fee+0.52%G+(-)0.20%P
Fiscal Year End	July	3-,5-,10-yr Expense Projections	$68, $95, $173
		Annual Brokerage Cost	0.62%

Risk Analysis

Time Period	Load-Adj Return %	Risk % Rank [1] All	Risk % Rank [1] Obj	Morningstar [2] Return	Morningstar Risk	Morningstar Risk-Adj Rating
1 Yr	6.55					
3 Yr	12.10	62	19	2.67 [3]	0.68	★★★★
5 Yr	17.68	64	17	3.84 [3]	0.78	★★★★★
10 Yr	---					
Average Historical Rating (49 months)				5.0 ★s		

[1] 1 = low, 100 = high   [2] 1.00 = Equity Avg   [3] 1.00 = 90-day T-bill return

Other Measures

			Standard S&P 500	Best Fit SPMid400
Standard Deviation	9.96	Alpha	6.7	6.4
Mean	12.99	Beta	1.04	0.84
Sharpe Ratio	0.95	R-Squared	68	69

Investment Style

	Stock Portfolio Avg	Relative S&P 500
Price/Earnings Ratio	28.1	1.52
Price/Book Ratio	4.3	1.25
5 Yr Earnings Gr %	15.2#	2.74
Return on Assets %	8.2	1.09
Debt % Total Cap	25.1	0.89
Med Mkt Cap ($mil)	4234	0.33

figure is based on 50% or less of stocks

Diversification Value for Portfolio Types

Large Cap: Low	Small Cap: Medium	Bond: High	Balanced: Low	Diversified: Low

Portfolio 07-31-94

Total Stocks: 299
Total Fixed-Income: 0

Share Chg (01-94)000	Amount 000		Value $000	% Net Assets
1948	1960	Oracle Systems	74974	3.38
1441	1865	Lowe's	67154	3.02
1031	1157	Motorola	61321	2.76
897	983	IBM	60706	2.73
415	783	British Petroleum (ADR)	59485	2.68
932	932	Oxford Health Plans	54528	2.46
792	997	Compuware	39253	1.77
958	963	Dean Witter Discover	38634	1.74
777	796	Sears Roebuck	37630	1.69
434	537	Nucor	37074	1.67
902	918	Sybase	36150	1.63
376	376	FNMA	32653	1.47
930	932	Travelers	30875	1.39
559	566	LM Ericsson Telephone (ADR)	30831	1.39
496	498	General Instrument	30161	1.36
521	577	Amerada Hess	29994	1.35
2237	2237	Suzuki Motor	29334	1.32
127	962	Unocal	27907	1.26
1125	1133	Silicon Graphics	26774	1.21
2520	2520	Hitachi	24342	1.10
383	402	FHLMC	23889	1.08
451	490	Broderbund Software	23775	1.07
-275	389	Intel	23072	1.04
557	705	Adobe Systems	21867	0.98
1022	1022	Toyota Motor	21688	0.98

Composition % 12-31-94

Cash	10.2	Preferreds	0.0
Stocks	84.1	Convertibles	0.0
Bonds	5.7	Other	0.0

Tax Analysis

	Tax-Adj Historical Return %	% Pretax Return
3 Yr Avg	11.05	81.7
5 Yr Avg	16.91	89.3
10 Yr Avg	---	---
Potential Capital Gain Exposure (% of assets)		7%

Most Similar Funds in MF500

Fidelity Magellan	Fair Fit
William Blair Growth	Weak Fit
SteinRoe Special	Weak Fit

Index Allocation

	% of Stocks
S&P 500	44.3
S&P MidCap 400	12.3
U.S. Small Cap	24.8
Foreign	19.1

Sector Weightings

	% of Stocks	Relative S&P 500
Utilities	0.2	0.02
Energy	13.4	1.32
Financials	17.7	1.67
Industrial Cyclicals	10.1	0.62
Consumer Durables	12.1	1.94
Consumer Staples	0.0	0.00
Services	5.1	0.63
Retail	10.3	1.77
Health	1.6	0.19
Technology	29.5	3.22

Fidelity Capital & Income

	Ticker	Load	NAV	Yield	SEC Yield	Assets	Objective
	FAGIX	None	8.63	8.7%	8.71%	2039.8	Corp Hi Yld

Fidelity Capital and Income Fund seeks income and capital growth.

The fund typically invests the majority of its assets in debt obligations, emphasizing securities rated below investment grade. It may invest without limit, however, in common and preferred stocks and convertible securities. The fund may invest in equity and debt securities of foreign and domestic companies involved in special situations such as bankruptcy proceedings, reorganizations, or financial restructurings.

Prior to Dec. 27, 1990, the fund was named Fidelity High-Income Fund.

Manager's Investment Style

Although this fund does maintain a core of standard, midquality junk bonds, management attempts to stay ahead of the pack by seeking bonds selling at depressed prices because of market disdain, severe business troubles, or bankruptcy. As such, it holds a large stake in unrated debt. Management has been willing to take an active role in turning around the firms from which it buys debt.

Fund Manager(s)

David Breazzano, since 11-90. BA, Union C. MBA, Cornell U.

Manager Experience

	Dates Managed	Invest Obj	Std Dev	+/- Index
Not available.				

Historical Profile

Return	Above Average
Risk	Low
Rating	★★★★★ Highest

	59	59	45	94	86	93	77	87

Investment Style History
Fixed Income
Income Rtn % Rank Obj

Growth of $10,000

- |||| Value of Fund ($000)
- — Value of Index ($000) LB Agg
- ▼ Manager Change
- ▽ Partial Manager Change
- ► Mgr Unknown After
- ◄ Mgr Unknown Before

Performance Quartile (Within Objective)

1983	1984	1985	1986	1987	1988	1989	1990	1991	1992	1993	1994	History
8.90	8.59	9.51	9.72	8.53	8.56	7.26	6.23	7.28	8.61	9.86	8.63	NAV
18.54	10.50	25.54	17.99	1.31	12.59	-3.22	-3.85	29.82	28.05	24.19	-5.09	Total Return %
10.17	-4.65	3.42	2.74	-1.45	4.71	-17.76	-12.79	13.82	20.81	14.44	-2.17	+/- LB Aggregate
---	---	---	2.35	-5.22	1.16	-3.60	2.54	-13.93	11.39	5.29	-4.11	+/- FB High-Yield
13.71	13.99	14.83	12.29	11.00	12.24	11.97	10.34	12.97	9.78	9.67	7.39	Income Return %
4.83	-3.48	10.71	5.69	-9.68	0.35	-15.19	-14.19	16.85	18.27	14.52	-12.47	Capital Return %
45	24	44	32	48	41	99	67	27	2	12	65	Total Rtn % Rank All
12	19	9	5	56	57	69	17	76	1	6	75	Total Rtn % Rank Obj
1.10	1.16	1.15	1.10	1.05	1.00	1.08	0.76	0.74	0.66	0.78	0.75	Income $
0.00	0.00	0.00	0.31	0.28	0.00	0.00	0.00	0.00	0.00	0.00	0.00	Capital Gains $
0.87	0.85	0.83	0.80	0.88	0.88	0.77	0.81	0.81	0.80	0.91	0.97	Expense Ratio %
12.45	13.51	12.54	11.30	10.99	11.38	11.96	12.70	11.26	9.77	7.45	6.78	Income Ratio %
129	71	157	104	116	68	72	95	108	132	102	100	Turnover Rate %
256.9	390.4	839.3	1671.8	1308.9	1689.2	1288.9	814.6	1155.5	1670.3	2745.7	2039.8	Net Assets ($mil)

Performance 12-31-94

	1st Qtr	2nd Qtr	3rd Qtr	4th Qtr	Total
1987	6.07	-1.53	-2.45	-0.57	1.31
1988	5.40	2.79	2.18	1.71	12.59
1989	1.79	3.55	-2.92	-5.41	-3.22
1990	-4.16	4.73	-2.92	-1.33	-3.85
1991	10.21	6.74	6.04	4.07	29.82
1992	15.23	4.46	3.99	2.29	28.05
1993	9.34	6.81	2.30	3.94	24.19
1994	0.29	-2.93	0.54	-3.03	-5.09

Bear Market Performance

Decile Rank (5-year period)

Worst									Best

	Worst 3 Mo Period 1985-89	Worst 3 Mo Period 1990-94
Fidelity Capital & Income	-7.40	-8.02
+/- LB Aggregate	-8.86	-8.77
+/- Best Fit Index : FB HY	---	6.09

Trailing Returns

	Total Return %	+/- LB Aggregate	+/- FB High-Yield	% Rank All	% Rank Obj	Growth of $10,000
3 Mo	-3.03	-3.41	-2.99	83	82	9,697
6 Mo	-2.51	-3.50	-4.06	92	68	9,749
1 Yr	-5.09	-2.17	-4.11	65	75	9,491
3 Yr Avg	14.71	10.16	3.55	4	4	15,093
5 Yr Avg	13.51	5.88	0.43	6	4	18,840
10 Yr Avg	11.91	1.97	---	39	6	30,809
15 Yr Avg	12.82	2.01	---	42	4	61,088

Operations

Address and Telephone	82 Devonshire Street Boston, MA 02109 800-544-8888	
Advisor	Fidelity Management & Research	
Subadvisor	FMR (Far East)/FMR (U.K.)	
Distributor	Fidelity Distributors	
States Available	All	
Report Grade	A	
Income Distrib	Paid Monthly	
Date of Inception	11-01-77	
Fiscal Year End	April	

Min Initial Purchase	$2500 (Addt'l: $250)
Min IRA Purchase	$500 (Addt'l: $250)
Min Auto Invest Plan	$2500 (Systematic Inv: $100)

Expenses & Fees

Sales Fees	0.00% front
	0.00% deferred
	0.00% 12b-1
Management Fee	0.55% flat fee+0.37%G
3-,5-,10-yr Expense Projections	$31, $54, $119

Risk Analysis

Time Period	Load-Adj Return %	Risk % Rank [1] All	Risk % Rank [1] Obj	Morningstar [2] Return	Morningstar Risk	Morningstar Risk-Adj Rating
1 Yr	-6.59					
3 Yr	14.71	13	74	3.57 [3]	0.42	★★★★★
5 Yr	13.51	39	17	2.41 [3]	0.46	★★★★★
10 Yr	11.91	32	35	1.04	0.44	★★★★

Average Historical Rating (109 months)   4.1 ★ s

[1] = low, 100 = high   [2] 1.00 = Hybrid Avg   [3] 1.00 = 90-day T-bill return

Other Measures

				Standard LB Agg	Best Fit FB HY
Standard Deviation	6.44	Alpha		10.3	1.0
Mean	14.00	Beta		0.62	1.32
Sharpe Ratio	1.63	R-Squared		15	78

Investment Style

Interest-Rate Stance

Avg Effective Duration	4.7 Yrs
Avg Effective Maturity	6.6 Yrs

Maturity Short Intm Long

Quality

Avg Credit Quality	---
Avg Weighted Coupon	9.10%
Avg Weighted Price	82.93% of Par

Diversification Value for Portfolio Types

Large Cap: High	Small Cap: High	Bond: High	Balanced: High	Diversified: High

Portfolio 10-31-94

Total Stocks: 46
Total Fixed-Income: 160

Amount 000	Date of Maturity		Value $000	% Net Assets
184555	08-15-04	NEXTEL Communications 0%	81204	3.50
112804	06-15-99	NWCG Holdings 0%	59786	2.57
53189	11-01-03	Thermadyne Industries 10.75%	51593	2.22
17862		Gulf Canada Resources ARP	46887	2.02
39969	05-01-02	Thermadyne Industries 10.25%	38770	1.67
1417		Dr Pepper/Seven-Up	35961	1.55
52015	06-15-98	Bally's Casino Holding 10.5%	31209	1.34
30732	07-30-00	Zale Delaware 11%	29810	1.28
29500	09-03-03	Boyd Gaming 10.75%	27508	1.18
2253		Thermadyne Holdings	26750	1.15
26692	12-22-00	Barry's Jewelers 11%	26158	1.13
25820	05-01-03	Berg Electronics 11.375%	26143	1.13
25680	02-01-03	Kaiser Aluminium/Chem 12.75%	25552	1.10
27022	09-15-01	USG 9.25%	25536	1.10
41840	02-01-01	USAir 9.625%	24999	1.08
26750	02-15-03	Revlon Consumer Prods 10.5%	24747	1.07
27100	03-03-97	GPA Delaware 8.5%	24051	1.04
24610	04-01-97	Robin Media Group 11.125%	23748	1.02
23980	04-01-01	Revlon Consumer Prods 9.375%	21341	0.92
24870	11-01-04	Flagstar 11.25%	21077	0.91
22700	07-01-02	Trans-Resources 11.875%	20430	0.88
39440	04-01-13	El Paso Funding 10.75%	19917	0.86
18590	09-15-02	Hat Brands 12.625%	19752	0.85
20000	12-01-03	Specialty Equipment 11.375%	19700	0.85
29027	09-15-03	Resorts Intl Financing 11%	19448	0.84

Composition % 11-30-94

Cash	9.2	Preferreds	14.3
Stocks	0.0	Convertibles	2.1
Bonds	68.1	Other	6.3

Tax Analysis

	Tax-Adj Historical Return %	% Pretax Return
3 Yr Avg	11.43	75.3
5 Yr Avg	10.03	69.3
10 Yr Avg	7.40	50.1
Potential Capital Gain Exposure (% of assets)		-13%

Most Similar Funds in MF500

Fidelity Adv High-Yield A	Fair Fit
IDS Extra Income	Fair Fit
Putnam High Yield Adv A	Fair Fit

Coupon Range

	% of Bonds	Rel Obj
0%, PIK	3.7	0.50
0% to 11%	67.3	1.37
11% to 13%	20.4	0.61
13% to 14.5%	2.4	0.45
More than 14.5%	2.5	1.56
Not applicable	3.6	1.20

Credit Analysis 11-30-94

% of Bonds

US Govt	0	BB	3
AAA	0	B	28
AA	0	Below B	1
A	0	NR/NA	69
BBB	0		

MORNINGSTAR **1995 Mutual Fund 500**

Fidelity Contrafund

	Ticker	Load	NAV	Yield	SEC Yield	Assets	Objective
	FCNTX	3.00%	30.28	0.0%	N/A	8682.4	Growth

Fidelity Contrafund seeks capital appreciation.

The fund invests primarily in undervalued common stocks and securities convertible into common stock. It also may invest in preferred stocks, warrants, and other debt securities. The fund seeks companies currently out of favor with the investing public that may have favorable long-term outlooks due to termination of unprofitable operations, changes in management, industry or products, or a possible merger/acquisition. However, these issues are considered speculative. The fund may invest up to 5% of its assets in lower-quality debt obligations.

Manager's Investment Style

Although management has typically posted very high turnovers, management is now placing more emphasis on holdings it can stick with. Management's habit of rotating through small-cap stocks is being curtailed by the fund's ballooning asset base. Still, management's style remains eclectic, as illustrated by its combination of contrarian picks and more-popular names, as well as its tendency toward diversification among individual stocks, though it may concentrate more-heavily in sectors.

Fund Manager(s)

Will Danoff, since 10-90. BA, Harvard 1982 MBA, Wharton 1986

Manager Experience

	Dates Managed	Invest Obj	Std Dev	+/- Index
Not available.				

Historical Profile
Return	High
Risk	Below Average
Rating	★★★★★ Highest

Investment Style History Equity
Average % Stocks Held in Portfolio

Growth of $10,000
|||| Value of Fund ($000)
— Value of Index ($000) SPMid400
▼ Manager Change
▽ Partial Manager Change
► Mgr Unknown After
◄ Mgr Unknown Before

Performance Quartile (Within Objective)

	1983	1984	1985	1986	1987	1988	1989	1990	1991	1992	1993	1994	History
	12.73	9.77	12.16	11.29	10.72	12.65	16.78	17.35	25.60	27.47	30.84	30.28	NAV
	23.28	-8.27	27.06	13.32	-1.90	21.02	43.15	3.94	54.92	15.89	21.43	-1.12	Total Return %
	0.81	-14.54	-4.67	-5.36	-7.16	4.41	11.47	7.05	24.43	8.28	11.37	-2.44	+/- S&P 500
	-0.19	-11.32	-5.50	-2.78	-4.26	3.08	13.98	10.12	20.71	6.92	10.14	-1.05	+/- Wilshire 5000
	3.97	2.99	2.60	2.22	0.00	3.02	1.59	0.54	0.49	0.74	0.60	0.00	Income Return %
	19.30	-11.26	24.46	11.10	-1.90	18.00	41.56	3.40	54.43	15.15	20.82	-1.12	Capital Return %
	29	87	37	65	74	12	2	46	6	9	15	27	Total Rtn % Rank All
	41	83	66	65	78	21	4	7	11	14	12	44	Total Rtn % Rank Obj
	0.45	0.29	0.25	0.25	0.00	0.32	0.25	0.09	0.11	0.20	0.18	0.00	Income $
	0.38	1.69	0.00	2.15	0.43	0.00	1.07	0.00	1.06	1.92	2.25	0.22	Capital Gains $
	0.96	0.99	0.95	0.88	0.92	0.98	0.95	1.06	0.89	0.87	1.06	1.03	Expense Ratio %
	3.61	2.82	3.84	1.68	1.26	3.01	4.01	3.02	1.01	1.19	0.46	0.64	Income Ratio %
	452	234	135	190	196	250	266	320	217	297	255	275	Turnover Rate %
	86.2	79.6	86.8	84.4	87.7	105.0	296.6	332.1	1002.4	1958.3	6193.3	8682.4	Net Assets ($mil)

(Investment Style History percentages: 97% 89% 79% 66% 92% 87% 86% 89%)

Performance 12-31-94

	1st Qtr	2nd Qtr	3rd Qtr	4th Qtr	Total
1987	23.45	4.82	6.51	-28.82	-1.90
1988	11.47	5.44	2.54	0.41	21.02
1989	11.62	11.26	14.45	0.72	43.15
1990	-1.25	9.72	-13.31	10.66	3.94
1991	24.96	0.97	12.79	8.86	54.92
1992	3.31	-0.31	2.33	9.97	15.89
1993	8.81	4.70	6.23	0.34	21.43
1994	-1.64	-3.22	4.87	-0.95	-1.12

Bear Market Performance

Decile Rank (5-year period)

Worst		Best

	Worst 3 Mo Period 1985-89	Worst 3 Mo Period 1990-94
Fidelity Contrafund	-34.16	-13.31
+/- S&P 500	-4.58	0.44
+/- Best Fit Index : SPMid400	-5.35	4.47

Trailing Returns

	Total Return %	+/- S&P 500	+/- Wil 5000	% Rank All	% Rank Obj	Growth of $10,000
3 Mo	-0.95	-0.93	-0.18	43	42	9,905
6 Mo	3.88	-0.99	-0.75	16	50	10,388
1 Yr	-1.12	-2.44	-1.05	27	44	9,888
3 Yr Avg	11.64	5.38	5.03	9	11	13,915
5 Yr Avg	17.51	8.82	8.69	2	2	22,405
10 Yr Avg	18.55	4.17	4.69	2	2	54,827
15 Yr Avg	16.40	1.92	2.42	5	13	97,548

Operations

Address and Telephone	82 Devonshire Street Boston, MA 02109 800-544-8888
Advisor	Fidelity Management & Research
Subadvisor	None
Distributor	Fidelity Distributors
States Available	All
Report Grade	A
Income Distrib	Paid Annually
Date of Inception	05-17-67
Fiscal Year End	December

Risk Analysis

Time Period	Load-Adj Return %	Risk % Rank [1] All	Risk % Rank [1] Obj	Morningstar [2] Return	Morningstar Risk	Morningstar Risk-Adj Rating
1 Yr	-4.09					
3 Yr	10.51	62	18	2.14 [3]	0.68	★★★★
5 Yr	16.79	60	10	3.52 [3]	0.71	★★★★★
10 Yr	18.19	56	15	2.32	0.81	★★★★★

Average Historical Rating (109 months)   3.9 ★s

[1] = low, 100 = high   [2] 1.00 = Equity Avg   [3] 1.00 = 90-day T-bill return

Other Measures

			Standard S&P 500	Best Fit SPMid400
Standard Deviation	9.03	Alpha	5.5	4.8
Mean	11.47	Beta	0.91	0.83
Sharpe Ratio	0.88	R-Squared	63	83

Investment Style

	Stock Portfolio Avg	Relative S&P 500
Price/Earnings Ratio	22.5	1.22
Price/Book Ratio	3.5	1.02
5 Yr Earnings Gr %	8.5	1.54
Return on Assets %	8.6	1.14
Debt % Total Cap	28.5	1.01
Med Mkt Cap ($mil)	3195	0.25

Style: Value Blend Growth — Size Large/Med/Small

Diversification Value for Portfolio Types

Large Cap: Low	Small Cap: Low	Bond: High	Balanced: Low	Diversified: Low

Portfolio 06-30-94

Share Chg (12-93) 000	Amount 000	Total Stocks: 554 Total Fixed-Income: 18	Value $000	% Net Assets
2005	2230	Intel	130467	1.72
1229	1404	Texas Instruments	111586	1.47
-255	1762	IBM	103500	1.36
1395	1395	NationsBank	71681	0.94
1870	1870	Oracle Systems	70125	0.92
1227	1227	Amoco	69962	0.92
830	830	FNMA	69305	0.91
-33	968	United Technologies	62162	0.82
883	1200	Microsoft	61800	0.81
1000	1000	FHLMC	60500	0.80
559	869	Nucor	59499	0.78
995	995	El DuPont de Nemours	58082	0.77
2575	2575	Toyota Motor	57745	0.76
1225	2000	Philips	57500	0.76
-197	789	British Petroleum (ADR)	56611	0.75
983	983	General Instrument	56008	0.74
1177	1702	Compaq Computer	54880	0.72
280	725	Federal Express	54066	0.71
1516	1516	Micron Technology	52285	0.69
-238	974	Anadarko Petroleum	49786	0.66
639	699	Capital Cities/ABC	49682	0.65
1833	1833	AirTouch Communications	43300	0.57
887	887	Sears Roebuck	42581	0.56
920	975	Southwestern Bell	42413	0.56
4030	4030	Hitachi	42120	0.55

Composition % 11-30-94

Cash	9.1	Preferreds	0.0
Stocks	90.8	Convertibles	0.0
Bonds	0.1	Other	0.0

Tax Analysis

	Tax-Adj Historical Return %	% Pretax Return
3 Yr Avg	10.01	84.6
5 Yr Avg	16.15	89.8
10 Yr Avg	16.72	82.4

Potential Capital Gain Exposure (% of assets)   3%

Most Similar Funds in MF500

Fidelity Magellan	Strong Fit
Fidelity	Strong Fit
Neuberger&Berman Partners	Strong Fit

Index Allocation

	% of Stocks
S&P 500	47.8
S&P MidCap 400	12.9
U.S. Small Cap	26.9
Foreign	12.9

Sector Weightings

	% of Stocks	Relative S&P 500
Utilities	2.1	0.17
Energy	10.6	1.05
Financials	11.7	1.10
Industrial Cyclicals	13.1	0.80
Consumer Durables	9.4	1.51
Consumer Staples	2.8	0.22
Services	12.3	1.51
Retail	6.0	1.03
Health	7.8	0.90
Technology	24.3	2.65

Expenses & Fees

Min Initial Purchase	$2500 (Addt'l: $250)
Min IRA Purchase	$500 (Addt'l: $250)
Min Auto Invest Plan	$2500 (Systematic Inv: $100)

Sales Fees	3.00% front
	0.00% deferred
	0.00% 12b-1
Management Fee	0.30% flat fee+0.52%G+(-)0.20%P
3-,5-,10-yr Expense Projections	$63, $87, $156
Annual Brokerage Cost	0.50%

Fidelity Convertible Securities

	Ticker	Load	NAV	Yield	SEC Yield	Assets	Objective
	FCVSX	None	15.36	5.2%	N/A	891.3	Convrt. Bond

Fidelity Convertible Securities Fund seeks total return through a combination of current income and capital appreciation.

The fund normally invests at least 65% of its assets in convertible securities. The balance of assets may be invested in corporate or U.S. debt securities, common stocks, preferred stocks, and money-market instruments. The fund may invest in lower-quality, high-yielding securities, although the fund currently expects that its fixed-income securities are primarily rated B or better. It may write covered call options or buy put options.

Manager's Investment Style

The fund's manager takes an aggressive approach to the convertibles market. He mainly buys convertibles of small-cap firms with very little market visibility, especially if they are weak performers just beginning to turn around. Management generally prefers issues with the potential for high growth, and is willing to hold a notable percentage of assets in the stocks into which the convertibles convert. The manager trades frequently, and recently has increased the fund's overall concentration.

Fund Manager(s)

Andrew Offit, since 03-92. Birthdate: 07-60.
BBA, Emory U. 1982 MBA, Wharton 1987

Manager Experience	Dates Managed	Invest Obj	Std Dev	+/- Index
Andrew Offit				
Fidelity Sel Health Care	05/90 - 03/92	SH	21.86	33.37

Historical Profile

Return	High
Risk	Average
Rating	★★★★★
	Highest

	1983	1984	1985	1986	1987	1988	1989	1990	1991	1992	1993	1994	History
	---	---	---	---	9.12	9.83	11.60	10.65	13.67	15.55	16.45	15.36	NAV
	---	---	---	---	-4.88 *	15.89	26.28	-2.89	38.74	22.02	17.79	-1.76	Total Return %
	---	---	---	---	---	8.01	11.74	-11.84	22.74	14.78	8.04	1.16	+/- LB Aggregate
	---	---	---	---	-6.20 *	-0.72	-5.40	0.22	8.25	14.40	7.73	-3.07	+/- S&P 500
	---	---	---	---	3.92	8.11	8.28	5.30	6.13	5.04	4.68	4.87	Income Return %
	---	---	---	---	-8.80	7.79	18.01	-8.19	32.61	16.98	13.11	-6.63	Capital Return %
	---	---	---	---	---	25	20	64	15	3	21	32	Total Rtn % Rank All
	---	---	---	---	---	14	5	19	13	4	20	23	Total Rtn % Rank Obj
	---	---	---	---	0.42	0.72	0.77	0.62	0.64	0.67	0.73	0.80	Income $
	---	---	---	---	0.00	0.00	0.00	0.00	0.37	0.40	1.09	0.00	Capital Gains $
	---	---	---	---	1.60	1.60	1.38	1.31	1.17	0.96	0.92	0.87	Expense Ratio %
	---	---	---	---	5.45	6.20	7.48	5.63	4.99	4.82	4.62	4.55	Income Ratio %
	---	---	---	---	233	191	207	223	152	258	312	401	Turnover Rate %
	---	---	---	---	38.9	40.0	63.2	59.7	133.4	480.4	1063.9	891.3	Net Assets ($mil)

Income Rtn % Rank Obj: --- 1 5 61 60 58 28 19

Growth of $10,000
- ||| Value of Fund ($000)
- — Value of Index ($000)
  - Russ 2000
- ▼ Manager Change
- ▽ Partial Manager Change
- ► Mgr Unknown After
- ◄ Mgr Unknown Before

Performance Quartile (Within Objective)

Performance 12-31-94

	1st Qtr	2nd Qtr	3rd Qtr	4th Qtr	Total
1987	---	-0.08	6.62	-16.78	---
1988	9.43	5.42	-0.87	1.33	15.89
1989	8.46	6.94	8.01	0.81	26.28
1990	-0.67	4.32	-11.82	6.29	-2.89
1991	16.06	2.60	9.79	6.13	38.74
1992	6.66	2.16	3.15	8.57	22.02
1993	6.60	3.29	4.60	2.27	17.79
1994	-3.56	-2.11	6.52	-2.30	-1.76

Bear Market Performance

Decile Rank (5-year period)

Worst ————————————— Best

	Worst 3 Mo Period 1985-89	Worst 3 Mo Period 1990-94
Fidelity Convertible Securities	---	-12.96
+/- LB Aggregate	---	-13.70
+/- Best Fit Index : Russ 2000	---	12.94

Trailing Returns

	Total Return %	+/- LB Aggregate	+/- S&P 500	% Rank All	% Rank Obj	Growth of $10,000
3 Mo	-2.30	-2.68	-2.28	74	20	9,770
6 Mo	4.07	3.08	-0.79	15	3	10,407
1 Yr	-1.76	1.16	-3.07	32	23	9,824
3 Yr Avg	12.19	7.64	5.92	8	4	14,120
5 Yr Avg	13.72	6.10	5.03	5	4	19,023
10 Yr Avg	---	---	---	---	---	---
15 Yr Avg	---	---	---	---	---	---

Operations

Address and Telephone	82 Devonshire Street
	Boston, MA 02109
	800-544-8888
Advisor	Fidelity Management & Research
Subadvisor	None
Distributor	Fidelity Distributors
States Available	All
Report Grade	A
Income Distrib	Paid Quarterly
* Date of Inception	01-05-87
Fiscal Year End	November

Min Initial Purchase	$2500 (Addt'l: $250)
Min IRA Purchase	$500 (Addt'l: $250)
Min Auto Invest Plan	$2500 (Systematic Inv: $100)

Expenses & Fees

Sales Fees	0.00% front
	0.00% deferred
	0.00% 12b-1
Management Fee	0.20% flat fee+0.52%G
3-,5-,10-yr Expense Projections	$29, $51, $113

Risk Analysis

Time Period	Load-Adj Return %	Risk % Rank [1] All	Risk % Rank [1] Obj	Morningstar [2] Return	Morningstar Risk	Morningstar Risk-Adj Rating
1 Yr	-1.76					
3 Yr	12.19	50	50	2.70 [3]	0.71	★★★★★
5 Yr	13.72	54	42	2.48 [3]	0.79	★★★★★
10 Yr	---	---	---	---	---	

Average Historical Rating (60 months) 4.8 ★s

[1] 1 = low, 100 = high [2] 1.00 = Hybrid Avg [3] 1.00 = 90-day T-bill return

Other Measures

	Standard LB Agg	Best Fit Russ 2000
Standard Deviation	7.74	
Mean	11.85	
Sharpe Ratio	1.08	
Alpha	7.9	4.0
Beta	0.66	0.55
R-Squared	12	69

Investment Style

Interest-Rate Stance

Avg Effective Maturity ---

Not Applicable

Quality

Avg Credit Quality ---

Avg Weighted Coupon 4.77%

Avg Weighted Price 85.97% of Par

Diversification Value for Portfolio Types

Large Cap: Medium	Small Cap: Low	Bond: High	Balanced: Low	Diversified: Medium

Portfolio 11-30-94

Total Stocks: 24
Total Fixed-Income: 48

Amount 000	Date of Maturity		Value $000	% Net Assets
8671		RJR Nabisco	54192	6.00
73530	11-17-00	Chiron 1.9%	53309	5.90
46247	11-15-01	IVAX Cv 6.5%	42085	4.66
1469		US Surgical Cv Pfd $2.20	38186	4.23
39300	07-27-99	Cellular Communications Cv 0%	32029	3.55
100	06-25-11	US WEST Cv 0%	30750	3.40
427		IBM	30231	3.35
24450	09-01-13	Amoco Canada Petro A Cv 7.375%	29096	3.22
334		Warner-Lambert	25874	2.86
21575	11-30-99	Thomas Nelson Cv 5.75%	23732	2.63
23925	05-15-01	Benson Eyecare Cv 8%	23327	2.58
22400	12-01-99	Horace Mann Educators Cv 4%	20664	2.29
21950	12-01-01	Synetic Cv 7%	20633	2.28
23950	11-30-02	WMS Industries Cv 5.75%	20597	2.28
18500	07-22-02	Mentor Cv 6.75%	19980	2.21
16225	12-01-02	Abbey Healthcare Group 6.5%	19794	2.19
17000	04-11-05	American Brands Cv 5.75%	19423	2.15
754		Barr Laboratories	19416	2.15
353		Fieldcrest Cannon A Cv Pfd $3	18340	2.03
366		Occidental Petro A Cv Pfd $3	18158	2.01
408		Maxicare Health A Cv Pfd $2.25	17675	1.96
38000	10-16-12	Elan Intl Finance Cv 0%	15675	1.74
196		Pfizer	15196	1.68
40000	05-14-11	Whirlpool Cv 0%	14950	1.65
23915	01-15-02	Advanced Medical Cv 7.25%	13871	1.54

Composition % 12-05-94

Cash	7.0	Preferreds	0.0
Stocks	20.0	Convertibles	73.0
Bonds	0.0	Other	0.0

Tax Analysis

	Tax-Adj Historical Return %	% Pretax Return
3 Yr Avg	9.47	75.6
5 Yr Avg	11.17	77.4
10 Yr Avg	---	---

Potential Capital Gain Exposure (% of assets) -4%

Most Similar Funds in MF500

Pacific Horizon Capital Inc	Fair Fit
Vanguard Convertible Secs	Fair Fit
Fidelity Contrafund	Fair Fit

Coupon Range

	% of Bonds	Rel Obj
0%	6.0	0.70
0% to 6%	32.9	0.98
6% to 7%	13.0	0.87
7% to 8.5%	16.0	1.37
More than 8.5%	11.0	2.01
Not applicable	21.1	0.82

Credit Analysis
% of Bonds

US Govt	---	BB	---
AAA	---	B	---
AA	---	Below B	---
A	---	NR/NA	---
BBB	---		

MORNINGSTAR 1995 Mutual Fund 500

Fidelity Disciplined Equity

Ticker	Load	NAV	Yield	SEC Yield	Assets	Objective
FDEQX	None	17.94	1.4%	N/A	1160.1	Growth

Fidelity Disciplined Equity Fund seeks capital growth.

The fund normally invests at least 65% of its assets in domestic common stocks of companies with market capitalizations exceeding $100 million, systematically reviewing factors such as a company's historical earnings, dividend yield, market price relative to book value, earnings per share, payout ratio, and financial leverage. It attempts to maintain representation in as many sectors as possible, although sector emphasis shifts as a result of changes in the outlook for earnings among market sectors.

Manager's Investment Style

The management of this fund is single minded: Brad Lewis aims to beat the S&P 500 in every calendar year. Management keeps the portfolio's industry weightings at roughly that of the index, while using a set of quantitative models to choose individual stocks. Lewis' proprietary models combine three elements: A neural-network program that focuses on how the market is currently valuing stocks and which features it finds attractive; another program evaluates traditional fundamental factors including earnings, quality, and valuation; while the third program builds an optimal portfolio based on output from the other two.

Fund Manager(s)

Brad Lewis CFA(1978), since 12-88. Birthdate: 01-55. BS, Naval Academy 1977 MBA, Wharton 1985

Manager Experience

	Dates Managed	Invest Obj	Std Dev	+/- Index
Brad Lewis				
Fidelity Stock Selector	09/90 - 12/94	G	12.92	6.44
Fidelity Small Cap Stock	06/93 - 12/94	SC	11.81	-0.74

Historical Profile

Return	Above Average
Risk	Below Average
Rating ★★★★	Above Average

Investment Style History
Equity

Average % Stocks Held in Portfolio

97% 96% 95% 93% 84% 86%

Growth of $10,000

|||| Value of Fund ($000)
— Value of Index ($000) SPMid400
▼ Manager Change
▽ Partial Manager Change
► Mgr Unknown After
◄ Mgr Unknown Before

Performance Quartile (Within Objective)

	1983	1984	1985	1986	1987	1988	1989	1990	1991	1992	1993	1994	History
	---	---	---	---	---	10.11	13.52	13.11	16.14	17.07	18.18	17.94	NAV
	---	---	---	---	---	1.10 *	36.34	-0.78	36.02	13.23	13.94	3.01	Total Return %
	---	---	---	---	---	0.59 *	4.66	2.34	5.54	5.61	3.88	1.69	+/- S&P 500
	---	---	---	---	---	---	7.17	5.40	1.82	4.26	2.65	3.08	+/- Wilshire 5000
	---	---	---	---	---	0.00	1.14	2.25	1.61	1.15	1.19	1.42	Income Return %
	---	---	---	---	---	1.10	35.20	-3.03	34.41	12.08	12.75	1.59	Capital Return %
	---	---	---	---	---	---	6	58	18	13	34	7	Total Rtn % Rank All
	---	---	---	---	---	---	13	26	44	23	38	14	Total Rtn % Rank Obj
	---	---	---	---	---	0.00	0.13	0.30	0.23	0.19	0.21	0.25	Income $
	---	---	---	---	---	0.00	0.13	0.00	1.32	0.99	1.04	0.52	Capital Gains $
	---	---	---	---	---	---	1.94	1.24	1.19	1.16	1.09	1.05	Expense Ratio %
	---	---	---	---	---	---	2.04	2.29	2.05	1.79	1.39	1.43	Income Ratio %
	---	---	---	---	---	---	118	171	210	255	279	139	Turnover Rate %
	---	---	---	---	---	---	112.2	106.8	175.0	448.4	795.8	1160.1	Net Assets ($mil)

Performance 12-31-94

	1st Qtr	2nd Qtr	3rd Qtr	4th Qtr	Total
1987	---	---	---	---	---
1988	---	---	---	---	1.10 *
1989	12.07	7.24	12.59	0.76	36.34
1990	-0.89	7.24	-15.17	10.05	-0.78
1991	17.09	-0.65	7.08	9.20	36.02
1992	3.22	0.42	2.93	6.12	13.23
1993	4.39	1.46	7.30	0.25	13.94
1994	-1.54	-0.56	4.61	0.57	3.01

Bear Market Performance

Decile Rank (5-year period)

Worst ▬ Best

	Worst 3 Mo Period 1985-89	Worst 3 Mo Period 1990-94
Fidelity Disciplined Equity	---	-16.06
+/- S&P 500	---	-2.22
+/- Best Fit Index : SPMid400	---	2.36

Trailing Returns

	Total Return %	+/- S&P 500	+/- Wil 5000	% Rank All	% Rank Obj	Growth of $10,000
3 Mo	0.57	0.59	1.34	10	13	10,057
6 Mo	5.21	0.34	0.58	10	33	10,521
1 Yr	3.01	1.69	3.08	7	14	10,301
3 Yr Avg	9.94	3.68	3.33	13	18	13,288
5 Yr Avg	12.39	3.70	3.58	8	12	17,934
10 Yr Avg	---	---	---	---	---	---
15 Yr Avg	---	---	---	---	---	---

Operations

Address and Telephone	82 Devonshire Street
	Boston, MA 02109
	800-544-8888
Advisor	Fidelity Management & Research
Subadvisor	FMR (U.K.)/FMR (Far East)
Distributor	Fidelity Distributors
States Available	All
Report Grade	A
Income Distrib	Paid Annually
* Date of Inception	12-28-88
Fiscal Year End	October

Risk Analysis

Time Period	Load-Adj Return %	Risk % Rank All	Risk % Rank Obj	Morningstar [2] Return	Morningstar Risk	Morningstar Risk-Adj Rating
1 Yr	3.01					
3 Yr	9.94	66	26	1.95[3]	0.74	★★★★
5 Yr	12.39	68	23	2.06[3]	0.81	★★★★
10 Yr	---					

Average Historical Rating (37 months) 4.5 ★s

[1] 1 = low, 100 = high [2] 1.00 = Equity Avg [3] 1.00 = 90-day T-bill return

Other Measures

				Standard S&P 500	Best Fit SPMid400
Standard Deviation	9.06	Alpha		3.7	3.3
Mean	9.92	Beta		0.97	0.82
Sharpe Ratio	0.71	R-Squared		72	81

Investment Style

	Stock Portfolio Avg	Relative S&P 500
Price/Earnings Ratio	16.4	0.89
Price/Book Ratio	3.3	0.96
5 Yr Earnings Gr %	2.3	0.41
Return on Assets %	8.1	1.08
Debt % Total Cap	29.9	1.06
Med Mkt Cap ($mil)	8063	0.62

Style: Value Blend Growth / Large Med Small

Diversification Value for Portfolio Types

Large Cap: Low	Small Cap: Low	Bond: High	Balanced: Low	Diversified: Low

Portfolio 10-31-94

Share Chg (04-94)000	Amount 000	Total Stocks: 197 / Total Fixed-Income: 0	Value $000	% Net Assets
215	475	Amoco	30103	2.78
0	336	Mobil	28887	2.67
0	379	Schering-Plough	26975	2.49
277	358	IBM	26649	2.46
414	414	El DuPont de Nemours	24685	2.28
204	588	Ameritech	23732	2.19
458	458	Coca-Cola	23015	2.13
283	373	Philip Morris	22846	2.11
174	336	Procter & Gamble	21000	1.94
152	273	Pfizer	20236	1.87
228	428	Southwestern Bell	17923	1.66
0	234	Monsanto	17828	1.65
178	328	BellSouth	17466	1.61
173	173	American Cyanamid	17084	1.58
153	153	Atlantic Richfield	16581	1.53
0	493	Sprint	16091	1.49
23	295	JC Penney	14929	1.38
0	201	Clark Equipment	14067	1.30
-4	255	Johnson & Johnson	13929	1.29
74	342	General Motors	13524	1.25
346	454	Ford Motor	13393	1.24
153	364	Chase Manhattan	13114	1.21
389	389	Upjohn	12837	1.19
-3	86	Wells Fargo	12782	1.18
193	193	CIGNA	12714	1.17

Composition % 11-30-94

Cash	20.5	Preferreds	0.0
Stocks	79.5	Convertibles	0.0
Bonds	0.0	Other	0.0

Tax Analysis

	Tax-Adj Historical Return %	% Pretax Return
3 Yr Avg	8.08	79.9
5 Yr Avg	10.53	81.9
10 Yr Avg	---	---
Potential Capital Gain Exposure (% of assets)		3%

Most Similar Funds in MF500

Fidelity Stock Selector	Strong Fit
Vanguard Index Extended Mkt	Fair Fit
Neuberger&Berman Partners	Fair Fit

Index Allocation

	% of Stocks
S&P 500	78.0
S&P MidCap 400	8.0
U.S. Small Cap	13.5
Foreign	0.5

Sector Weightings

	% of Stocks	Relative S&P 500
Utilities	12.0	0.97
Energy	11.3	1.12
Financials	12.3	1.16
Industrial Cyclicals	15.4	0.94
Consumer Durables	5.8	0.94
Consumer Staples	13.6	1.09
Services	3.9	0.48
Retail	3.9	0.68
Health	11.4	1.31
Technology	10.3	1.13

Expenses & Fees

Min Initial Purchase	$2500 (Addt'l: $250)
Min IRA Purchase	$500 (Addt'l: $250)
Min Auto Invest Plan	$2500 (Systematic Inv: $100)
Sales Fees	
	0.00% front
	0.00% deferred
	0.00% 12b-1
Management Fee	0.30% flat fee+0.52%G+(-)0.20%P
3-,5-,10-yr Expense Projections	$35, $66, $133
Annual Brokerage Cost	0.39%

Fidelity Emerging Growth

	Ticker	Load	NAV	Yield	SEC Yield	Assets	Objective
	FDEGX	3.00%	16.99	0.0%	N/A	635.2	Aggr. Growth

Fidelity Emerging Growth Fund seeks capital appreciation.

The fund normally invests at least 65% of its assets in equity securities of emerging-growth companies; these companies are in a development stage and have demonstrated or are expected to achieve rapid growth in earnings and/or revenues. The fund invests in both small companies and large established companies with strong growth prospects. It may also invest a portion of its assets in debt securities and foreign securities, enter into currency-exchange contracts, and invest in stock-index futures and options.

Historical Profile

Return	Average
Risk	Above Average
Rating	★★★
	Neutral

Investment Style History
Equity
Average % Stocks Held in Portfolio

				88%	90%	91%	93%

Growth of $10,000

- |||| Value of Fund ($000)
- — Value of Index ($000) SPMid400
- ▼ Manager Change
- ▽ Partial Manager Change
- ► Mgr Unknown After
- ◄ Mgr Unknown Before

Performance Quartile (Within Objective)

1983	1984	1985	1986	1987	1988	1989	1990	1991	1992	1993	1994	History
---	---	---	---	---	---	---	10.06	16.38	17.58	17.33	16.99	NAV
---	---	---	---	---	---	---	0.60 *	67.10	8.36	19.88	-0.18	Total Return %
---	---	---	---	---	---	---	-0.16 *	36.62	0.74	9.82	-1.49	+/- S&P 500
---	---	---	---	---	---	---	---	23.65	-3.40	5.34	2.48	+/- Wilshire 4500
---	---	---	---	---	---	---	0.00	0.00	0.12	0.00	0.00	Income Return %
---	---	---	---	---	---	---	0.60	67.10	8.24	19.88	-0.18	Capital Return %
---	---	---	---	---	---	---	---	3	41	17	21	Total Rtn % Rank All
---	---	---	---	---	---	---	---	29	48	44	31	Total Rtn % Rank Obj
---	---	---	---	---	---	---	0.00	0.00	0.02	0.00	0.00	Income $
---	---	---	---	---	---	---	0.00	0.39	0.14	3.57	0.31	Capital Gains $
---	---	---	---	---	---	---	---	1.31	1.09	1.19	1.11	Expense Ratio %
---	---	---	---	---	---	---	---	-0.10	0.56	-0.20	-0.57	Income Ratio %
---	---	---	---	---	---	---	---	326	531	332	204	Turnover Rate %
---	---	---	---	---	---	---	2.3	724.3	641.3	652.6	635.2	Net Assets ($mil)

Manager's Investment Style

Manager Lawrence Greenberg believes strongly in top- and bottom-line growth, and pays little attention to a company's size. His search for potent growth rates has led him to place a large amount of the fund's portfolio in technology stocks. Greenberg says the fund will always have the highest P/E ratio at Fidelity. He trades actively.

Fund Manager(s)

Lawrence D. Greenberg, since 10-93. Birthdate: 05-63. BS, U. of Pennsylvania 1985. MBA, Wharton 1986.

Manager Experience

	Dates Managed	Invest Obj	Std Dev	+/- Index

Not available.

Performance 12-31-94

	1st Qtr	2nd Qtr	3rd Qtr	4th Qtr	Total
1987	---	---	---	---	---
1988	---	---	---	---	---
1989	---	---	---	---	---
1990	---	---	---	---	0.60 *
1991	29.62	-1.23	18.09	10.52	67.10
1992	-7.57	-6.72	4.78	19.94	8.36
1993	2.07	9.01	5.11	2.50	19.88
1994	-3.12	-10.22	10.85	3.54	-0.18

Bear Market Performance

Decile Rank (5-year period)

Worst _____ Best

	Worst 3 Mo Period 1985-89	Worst 3 Mo Period 1990-94
Fidelity Emerging Growth	---	---
+/- S&P 500	---	---
+/- Best Fit Index :	---	---

Trailing Returns

	Total Return %	+/- S&P 500	+/- Wil 4500	% Rank All	% Rank Obj	Growth of $10,000
3 Mo	3.54	3.55	6.04	2	12	10,354
6 Mo	14.77	9.91	10.58	3	22	11,477
1 Yr	-0.18	-1.49	2.48	21	31	9,982
3 Yr Avg	9.04	2.78	1.44	17	40	12,966
5 Yr Avg	---	---	---	---	---	---
10 Yr Avg	---	---	---	---	---	---
15 Yr Avg	---	---	---	---	---	---

Operations

Address and Telephone	82 Devonshire Street
	Boston, MA 02109
	800-544-8888
Advisor	Fidelity Management & Research
Subadvisor	FMR (U.K.)/FMR (Far East)
Distributor	Fidelity Distributors
States Available	All
Report Grade	A
Income Distrib	Paid Annually
* Date of Inception	12-28-90
Fiscal Year End	November

Risk Analysis

Time Period	Load-Adj Return %	Risk % Rank [1] All	Risk % Rank [1] Obj	Morningstar [2] Return	Morningstar Risk	Morningstar Risk-Adj Rating
1 Yr	-3.17					
3 Yr	7.94	92	48	1.31 [3]	1.25	★★★
5 Yr	---					
10 Yr	---					

Average Historical Rating (13 months)   3.4 ★s

[1] 1 = low, 100 = high [2] 1.00 = Equity Avg [3] 1.00 = 90-day T-bill return

Other Measures

	Standard S&P 500	Best Fit SPMid400
Standard Deviation	14.21	Alpha	2.7	1.2
Mean	9.70	Beta	1.23	1.29
Sharpe Ratio	0.43	R-Squared	47	81

Investment Style

	Stock Portfolio Avg	Relative S&P 500
Price/Earnings Ratio	29.4	1.59
Price/Book Ratio	6.5	1.92
5 Yr Earnings Gr %	30.9#	5.57
Return on Assets %	14.8	1.98
Debt % Total Cap	17.1	0.61
Med Mkt Cap ($mil)	2250	0.17

figure is based on 50% or less of stocks

Style: Value Blend Growth / Size Large Med Small

Diversification Value for Portfolio Types

Large Cap: Medium	Small Cap: Low	Bond: High	Balanced: Low	Diversified: Low

Portfolio 11-30-94

Total Stocks: 240
Total Fixed-Income: 0

Share Chg (05-94) 000	Amount 000		Value $000	% Net Assets
-25	650	Oracle Systems	26813	4.39
-150	725	DSC Communications	22656	3.71
105	430	Lowe's	16071	2.63
35	270	Motorola	15221	2.49
225	500	Vanguard Cellular Systems A	13250	2.17
100	475	AirTouch Communications	12884	2.11
75	325	Compaq Computer	12716	2.08
63	250	Cabletron Systems	11875	1.94
50	350	Newbridge Networks	11769	1.93
105	250	Home Depot	11563	1.89
-15	335	Silicon Graphics	10301	1.69
51	172	3Com	7499	1.23
45	95	Pfizer	7351	1.20
-25	150	Applied Materials	7181	1.18
52	52	Nokia Cl B	7116	1.16
239	299	Sunglass Hut International	6457	1.06
125	250	Office Depot	5944	0.97
-40	260	EMC	5850	0.96
125	200	Informix	5750	0.94
-90	90	Intel	5681	0.93
53	80	Nokia (ADR)	5590	0.91
175	200	Lincare Holdings	5450	0.89
-11	114	United HealthCare	5429	0.89
65	165	cisco Systems	5321	0.87
-25	125	Micron Technology	5188	0.85

Composition % 10/31/94

Cash	4.3	Preferreds	0
Stocks	95.7	Convertibles	0
Bonds	0	Other	0

Tax Analysis

	Tax-Adj Historical Return %	% Pretax Return
3 Yr Avg	6.97	75.6
5 Yr Avg	---	---
10 Yr Avg	---	---
Potential Capital Gain Exposure (% of assets)		10%

Most Similar Funds in MF500

Berger 100	Strong Fit
Fidelity Growth Company	Strong Fit
AIM Constellation	Fair Fit

Index Allocation

	% of Stocks
S&P 500	33.1
S&P MidCap 400	18.6
U.S. Small Cap	40.7
Foreign	7.6

Sector Weightings

	% of Stocks	Relative S&P 500
Utilities	0.5	0.04
Energy	0.0	0.00
Financials	0.6	0.05
Industrial Cyclicals	4.5	0.28
Consumer Durables	8.1	1.31
Consumer Staples	0.6	0.05
Services	8.6	1.05
Retail	12.3	2.11
Health	9.1	1.05
Technology	55.6	6.07

Min Initial Purchase / Expenses & Fees

Min Initial Purchase	$2500 (Addt'l: $250)
Min IRA Purchase	$500 (Addt'l: $250)
Min Auto Invest Plan	$2500 (Systematic Inv: $100)

Expenses & Fees

Sales Fees	3.00% front
	0.00% deferred
	0.00% 12b-1
Management Fee	0.35% flat fee+0.52%G+(-)0.20%P
3-,5-,10-yr Expense Projections	$67, $93, $170
Annual Brokerage Cost	---

MORNINGSTAR 1995 Mutual Fund 500

Fidelity Equity-Income

Ticker	Load	NAV	Yield	SEC Yield	Assets	Objective
FEQIX	2.00%	30.70	3.0%	4.38%	7412.8	Equity-Inc.

Fidelity Equity-Income Fund seeks income. The potential for capital appreciation is also a consideration.

The fund normally invests at least 80% of its assets in income-producing equity securities that have demonstrated a yield higher than the composite yield on the stocks in the S&P 500 Index. The remainder of the portfolio may be invested in debt obligations. The majority of these instruments are convertible into common stocks. The fund does not intend to invest in securities of companies without proven earnings or credit.

Historical Profile
Return	Average
Risk	Below Average
Rating	★★★★ Above Average

Investment Style History
Equity
Average % Stocks Held in Portfolio

79% 78% 76% 79% 78% 74% 73% 75%

Growth of $10,000
|||| Value of Fund ($000)
— Value of Index ($000)
    S&P 500
▼ Manager Change
▽ Partial Manager Change
► Mgr Unknown After
◄ Mgr Unknown Before

Performance Quartile (Within Objective)

Manager's Investment Style
More conservative than other Fidelity offerings, this fund's management seeks stocks with dividends greater than that of the S&P 500, and also holds cash, bonds, and convertibles. Management employs significant diversification among and within sectors, and holds a broad portfolio, to minimize risks.

Fund Manager(s)
Stephen R. Petersen CFA, since 08-93. BA, U. of Wisconsin MS, U. of Wisconsin

Manager Experience

	Dates Managed	Invest Obj	Std Dev	+/- Index
Not available.				

1983	1984	1985	1986	1987	1988	1989	1990	1991	1992	1993	1994	History
26.53	23.95	27.51	27.29	21.85	25.20	26.90	21.34	26.31	29.01	29.01	30.70	NAV
29.24	10.53	25.06	17.07	-1.64	22.49	18.67	-14.02	29.40	14.68	21.31	0.24	Total Return %
6.78	4.27	-6.68	-1.61	-6.90	5.88	-13.01	-10.90	-1.08	7.06	11.25	-1.07	+/- S&P 500
5.78	7.48	-7.50	0.97	-4.00	4.55	-10.50	-7.84	-4.80	5.71	10.03	0.31	+/- Wilshire 5000
7.48	7.49	7.51	6.38	5.71	7.16	6.93	5.76	6.11	4.41	4.18	3.06	Income Return %
21.77	3.05	17.55	10.70	-7.34	15.33	11.74	-19.79	23.29	10.26	17.13	-2.81	Capital Return %
12	23	46	39	72	9	38	91	28	11	15	18	Total Rtn % Rank All
23	20	81	57	43	19	65	88	32	10	7	21	Total Rtn % Rank Obj
1.70	1.63	1.70	1.70	1.51	1.51	1.75	1.55	1.20	1.08	1.15	0.98	Income $
1.42	3.12	0.52	3.08	3.92	0.00	1.16	0.30	0.00	0.00	0.12	2.22	Capital Gains $
0.82	0.80	0.72	0.66	0.65	0.66	0.63	0.71	0.70	0.68	0.67	0.66	Expense Ratio %
8.50	7.00	7.90	7.10	5.80	5.50	6.50	6.10	6.21	4.81	4.02	3.55	Income Ratio %
138	118	123	118	110	120	68	92	107	111	84	70	Turnover Rate %
743.5	1185.9	2238.7	3360.0	3476.0	4064.9	5037.7	3925.5	4413.7	4976.0	6641.9	7412.8	Net Assets ($mil)

Performance 12-31-94

	1st Qtr	2nd Qtr	3rd Qtr	4th Qtr	Total
1987	14.88	0.89	3.55	-18.04	-1.64
1988	10.32	8.37	0.69	1.75	22.49
1989	7.48	6.53	6.49	-2.67	18.67
1990	-5.92	2.02	-15.66	6.21	-14.02
1991	13.86	1.13	7.19	4.85	29.40
1992	2.66	3.18	1.25	6.92	14.68
1993	8.91	2.82	4.79	3.37	21.31
1994	-3.25	2.11	3.93	-2.37	0.24

Bear Market Performance
Decile Rank (5-year period)

Worst ▭ Best

	Worst 3 Mo Period 1985-89	Worst 3 Mo Period 1990-94
Fidelity Equity-Income	-22.96	-16.15
+/- S&P 500	6.62	-2.31
+/- Best Fit Index : S&P 500	6.62	-2.31

Trailing Returns

	Total Return %	+/- S&P 500	+/- Wil 5000	% Rank All	% Rank Obj	Growth of $10,000
3 Mo	-2.37	-2.36	-1.60	75	45	9,763
6 Mo	1.46	-3.40	-3.16	31	49	10,146
1 Yr	0.24	-1.07	0.31	18	21	10,024
3 Yr Avg	11.72	5.46	5.11	9	4	13,945
5 Yr Avg	9.18	0.49	0.37	22	18	15,515
10 Yr Avg	12.50	-1.88	-1.36	32	25	32,480
15 Yr Avg	15.81	1.33	1.83	7	1	90,401

Operations

Address and Telephone	82 Devonshire Street Boston, MA 02109 800-544-8888
Advisor	Fidelity Management & Research
Subadvisor	FMR (U.K.)/FMR (Far East)
Distributor	Fidelity Distributors
States Available	All
Report Grade	A
Income Distrib	Paid Quarterly
Date of Inception	05-16-66
Fiscal Year End	January

Min Initial Purchase	$2500 (Addt'l: $250)
Min IRA Purchase	$500 (Addt'l: $250)
Min Auto Invest Plan	$2500 (Systematic Inv: $100)

Expenses & Fees
Sales Fees	2.00% front
	0.00% deferred
	0.00% 12b-1
Management Fee	0.12% flat fee+0.52%G
3-,5-,10-yr Expense Projections	$23, $42, $96
Annual Brokerage Cost	0.14%

Risk Analysis

Time Period	Load-Adj Return %	Risk % Rank [1] All	Obj	Morningstar [2] Return	Morningstar Risk	Morningstar Risk-Adj Rating
1 Yr	-1.76					
3 Yr	10.97	54	38	2.29 [3]	0.57	★★★★
5 Yr	8.74	63	72	1.01 [3]	0.76	★★★★
10 Yr	12.28	51	50	0.93	0.74	★★★
Average Historical Rating (109 months)					4.1	★s

[1] 1 = low, 100 = high [2] 1.00 = Equity Avg [3] 1.00 = 90-day T-bill return

Other Measures

				Standard S&P 500	Best Fit S&P 500
Standard Deviation	7.67	Alpha		5.5	5.5
Mean	11.43	Beta		0.87	0.87
Sharpe Ratio	1.03	R-Squared		80	80

Investment Style

	Stock Portfolio Avg	Relative S&P 500
Price/Earnings Ratio	18.4	0.99
Price/Book Ratio	2.3	0.69
5 Yr Earnings Gr %	2.6	0.46
Return on Assets %	4.3	0.57
Debt % Total Cap	32.7	1.16
Med Mkt Cap ($mil)	7292	0.56

Style: Value Blend Growth / Size Large Med Small

Diversification Value for Portfolio Types

Large Cap: Low	Small Cap: Medium	Bond: Medium	Balanced: None	Diversified: Low

Portfolio 07-31-94

Share Chg (01-94) 000	Amount 000	Total Stocks: 275 Total Fixed-Income: 195	Value $000	% Net Assets
2501	3833	General Electric	193098	2.72
1550	2372	Philip Morris	130465	1.84
2998	3800	American Express	100708	1.42
	794	Citicorp Cv Pfd $5.375	91321	1.29
	158376	Republic of Argentina 4.25%	83150	1.17
129	1264	IBM	78077	1.10
-4	1310	NationsBank	73031	1.03
749	1502	Ameritech	61586	0.87
0	1446	WR Grace	60017	0.85
-165	1265	First Fidelity Bancorp (NJ)	59146	0.83
0	575	Xerox	58812	0.83
-10	756	British Petroleum (ADR)	57426	0.81
0	680	CSX	52808	0.74
251	884	Schlumberger	52127	0.74
-60	1984	Entergy	50602	0.71
20	181	Mannesman (ADR)	50251	0.71
-52	1381	Household International	47292	0.67
1027	1215	Chemical Banking	46626	0.66
273	745	Pfizer	46159	0.65
617	1457	Bank of New York	46093	0.65
0	1136	Beneficial	45148	0.64
-49	736	United Technologies	44344	0.63
15	135	Veba	44279	0.62
492	665	Warner-Lambert	43218	0.61
527	1107	AlliedSignal	42358	0.60

Composition % 11-30-94
Cash	6.2	Preferreds	0.0
Stocks	76.0	Convertibles	11.5
Bonds	6.3	Other	0.0

Tax Analysis
	Tax-Adj Historical Return %	% Pretax Return
3 Yr Avg	9.63	80.5
5 Yr Avg	7.06	73.8
10 Yr Avg	9.14	62.2
Potential Capital Gain Exposure (% of assets)		8%

Most Similar Funds in MF500
Fidelity Growth & Income	Strong Fit
Fidelity Equity-Income II	Strong Fit
Fundamental Investors	Strong Fit

Index Allocation
	% of Stocks
S&P 500	68.0
S&P MidCap 400	7.7
U.S. Small Cap	6.5
Foreign	18.8

Sector Weightings
	% of Stocks	Relative S&P 500
Utilities	11.9	0.96
Energy	10.9	1.08
Financials	23.6	2.24
Industrial Cyclicals	18.6	1.14
Consumer Durables	8.5	1.37
Consumer Staples	6.7	0.53
Services	5.5	0.67
Retail	3.6	0.61
Health	6.4	0.74
Technology	4.4	0.47

Fidelity Equity-Income II

	Ticker	Load	NAV	Yield	SEC Yield	Assets	Objective
	FEQTX	None	17.72	2.1%	N/A	7697.5	Equity-Inc.

Fidelity Equity-Income II Fund seeks income. Potential for capital appreciation is a consideration.

The fund normally invests at least 65% of its assets in income-producing equity securities. It seeks a yield that exceeds the composite yield of the S&P 500 Index. The balance of the fund's assets may be invested in debt securities of any type or credit quality. The fund may invest in foreign securities, enter into currency-exchange contracts, or invest in stock-index futures and options.

Historical Profile

Return	High
Risk	Low
Rating	★★★★★ Highest

Investment Style History

Equity

Average % Stocks Held in Portfolio

	71%	68%	74%	79%

Growth of $10,000

||||| Value of Fund ($000)
— Value of Index ($000) S&P 500
▼ Manager Change
▽ Partial Manager Change
► Mgr Unknown After
◄ Mgr Unknown Before

Performance Quartile (Within Objective)

Manager's Investment Style

Management emphasizes total return and an aggregate payout that tops the S&P 500's. It steps outside the typical equity-income group to look at a wide stock universe, from which it focuses on companies that are selling at discounted multiples, yet have some catalyst for improved earnings growth. This bottom-up, value-driven approach leads management to what it calls unrecognized growth stocks, which may or may not resemble typical equity-income favorites.

1983	1984	1985	1986	1987	1988	1989	1990	1991	1992	1993	1994	History
---	---	---	---	---	---	---	10.39	14.52	16.51	18.41	17.72	NAV
---	---	---	---	---	---	---	4.51 *	46.60	19.06	18.89	3.16	Total Return %
---	---	---	---	---	---	---	0.18 *	16.11	11.44	8.83	1.85	+/- S&P 500
---	---	---	---	---	---	---		12.39	10.09	7.60	3.23	+/- Wilshire 5000
---	---	---	---	---	---	---	0.61	4.68	2.63	2.65	2.11	Income Return %
---	---	---	---	---	---	---	3.90	41.91	16.42	16.24	1.05	Capital Return %
---	---	---	---	---	---	---	---	9	5	19	7	Total Rtn % Rank All
---	---	---	---	---	---	---	---	1	4	13	9	Total Rtn % Rank Obj
---	---	---	---	---	---	---	0.06	0.46	0.38	0.45	0.39	Income $
---	---	---	---	---	---	---	0.00	0.17	0.36	0.73	0.88	Capital Gains $
---	---	---	---	---	---	---	2.50	1.52	1.01	0.88	0.84	Expense Ratio %
---	---	---	---	---	---	---	3.89	3.83	3.09	2.69	2.48	Income Ratio %
---	---	---	---	---	---	---	167	206	89	55	81	Turnover Rate %
---	---	---	---	---	---	---	6.2	370.9	2169.8	5021.9	7697.5	Net Assets ($mil)

Fund Manager(s)

Brian S. Posner, since 04-92. Birthdate: 09-61.
BA, Northwestern U. 1983 MBA, U. of Chicago 1987

Manager Experience

	Dates Managed	Invest Obj	Std Dev	+/- Index
Brian S. Posner				
Fidelity Value	09/90 - 07/92	G	11.81	1.96
Fidelity Sel Energy	11/91 - 01/92	SN	0.00	-10.53

Performance 12-31-94

	1st Qtr	2nd Qtr	3rd Qtr	4th Qtr	Total
1987	---	---	---	---	---
1988	---	---	---	---	---
1989	---	---	---	---	---
1990	---	---	---	6.75	4.51 *
1991	18.89	5.48	10.31	5.98	46.60
1992	5.74	2.63	2.25	7.29	19.06
1993	8.52	2.77	3.91	2.60	18.89
1994	-1.43	3.15	3.77	-2.22	3.16

Bear Market Performance

Decile Rank (5-year period)

Worst | Best

	Worst 3 Mo Period 1985-89	Worst 3 Mo Period 1990-94
Fidelity Equity-Income II	---	---
+/- S&P 500	---	---
+/- Best Fit Index :	---	---

Trailing Returns

	Total Return %	+/- S&P 500	+/- Wil 5000	% Rank All	% Rank Obj	Growth of $10,000
3 Mo	-2.22	-2.21	-1.45	72	43	9,778
6 Mo	1.47	-3.39	-3.16	31	48	10,147
1 Yr	3.16	1.85	3.23	7	9	10,316
3 Yr Avg	13.45	7.18	6.84	6	2	14,601
5 Yr Avg	---	---	---	---	---	---
10 Yr Avg	---	---	---	---	---	---
15 Yr Avg	---	---	---	---	---	---

Operations

Address and Telephone	82 Devonshire Street Boston, MA 02109 800-544-8888
Advisor	Fidelity Management & Research
Subadvisor	None
Distributor	Fidelity Distributors
States Available	All
Report Grade	A
Income Distrib	Paid Quarterly
* Date of Inception	08-21-90
Fiscal Year End	November

Risk Analysis

Time Period	Load-Adj Return %	Risk % Rank [1] All	Risk % Rank [1] Obj	Morningstar [2] Return	Morningstar Risk	Morningstar Risk-Adj Rating
1 Yr	3.16					
3 Yr	13.45	44	12	3.13 [3]	0.50	★★★★★
5 Yr	---	---	---	---	---	
10 Yr	---	---	---	---	---	

Average Historical Rating (17 months)   5.0 ★s

[1] 1 = low, 100 = high [2] 1.00 = Equity Avg [3] 1.00 = 90-day T-bill return

Other Measures

			Standard S&P 500	Best Fit S&P 500
Standard Deviation	7.54	Alpha	7.3	7.3
Mean	12.97	Beta	0.82	0.82
Sharpe Ratio	1.25	R-Squared	74	74

Investment Style

	Stock Portfolio Avg	Relative S&P 500
Price/Earnings Ratio	18.9	1.02
Price/Book Ratio	2.0	0.59
5 Yr Earnings Gr %	4.7	0.84
Return on Assets %	4.0	0.54
Debt % Total Cap	32.3	1.14
Med Mkt Cap ($mil)	5161	0.40

Style
Value Blend Growth
Size Large Med Small

Diversification Value for Portfolio Types

Large Cap: Low	Small Cap: Low	Bond: High	Balanced: Low	Diversified: Low

Portfolio 11-30-94

Total Stocks: 190
Total Fixed-Income: 60

Share Chg (05-94) 000	Amount 000		Value $000	% Net Assets
3826	9174	American Express	271771	3.57
128	2961	British Petroleum (ADR)	235048	3.09
1304	3550	Schlumberger	188610	2.48
1339	2076	FNMA	147677	1.94
2158	4395	Travelers	144473	1.90
1663	4845	Alcan Aluminium	119291	1.57
11764	17062	RJR Nabisco	106638	1.40
-401	1764	Philip Morris	105399	1.39
597	1487	Total Petroleum Cl B	93087	1.22
528	1048	Loews	90556	1.19
2374	2374	NYNEX	89326	1.17
834	1685	Great Lakes Chemical	89279	1.17
1092	1821	Sears Roebuck	86038	1.13
884	1935	Western Atlas	84404	1.11
2908	2908	Seagram	84282	1.11
2674	2674	Dillard Department Stores A	75206	0.99
405	1660	Murphy Oil	74281	0.98
894	1379	El DuPont de Nemours	74272	0.98
208	1597	Amerada Hess	72659	0.96
743	1234	United Technologies	72206	0.95
1427	3682	The Limited	71341	0.94
1851	1851	General Motors	70577	0.93
752	2230	Union Carbide	63845	0.84
980	1543	Ameritech	60941	0.80
-623	2141	Bank of New York	59682	0.78

Composition % 11-30-94

Cash	13.3	Preferreds	0.0
Stocks	78.9	Convertibles	4.1
Bonds	3.7	Other	0.0

Index Allocation

	% of Stocks
S&P 500	58.1
S&P MidCap 400	10.1
U.S. Small Cap	10.5
Foreign	22.9

Tax Analysis

	Tax-Adj Historical Return %	% Pretax Return
3 Yr Avg	11.41	83.2
5 Yr Avg	---	---
10 Yr Avg	---	---
Potential Capital Gain Exposure (% of assets)		1%

Most Similar Funds in MF500

Fidelity Equity-Income	Strong Fit
Fidelity Growth & Income	Strong Fit
Fidelity Value	Strong Fit

Sector Weightings

	% of Stocks	Relative S&P 500
Utilities	5.5	0.45
Energy	15.4	1.52
Financials	27.5	2.60
Industrial Cyclicals	18.8	1.15
Consumer Durables	5.2	0.84
Consumer Staples	8.0	0.64
Services	7.3	0.89
Retail	5.7	0.98
Health	3.7	0.43
Technology	2.9	0.32

Expenses & Fees

Min Initial Purchase	$2500 (Addt'l: $250)
Min IRA Purchase	$500 (Addt'l: $250)
Min Auto Invest Plan	$2500 (Systematic Inv: $100)

Expenses & Fees

Sales Fees	0.00% front
	0.00% deferred
	0.00% 12b-1
Management Fee	0.20% flat fee+0.52%G
3-,5-,10-yr Expense Projections	$28, $49, $108
Annual Brokerage Cost	0.14%

MORNINGSTAR 1995 Mutual Fund 500

Fidelity Fifty

	Ticker	Load	NAV	Yield	SEC Yield	Assets	Objective
	FFTYX	3.00%	10.88	0.2%	N/A	60.6	Aggr. Growth

Fidelity Fifty Fund seeks capital appreciation.
The fund normally invests in common stocks, preferred stocks, and convertibles issued by 50 to 60 companies. In addition to fundamental, qualitative research, it uses statistical models to evaluate growth potential, valuation, liquidity, and investment risk of equity securities being considered for investment. The fund may invest in foreign securities and in options and futures contracts. No limitation is placed on the amount of the fund's assets that may be invested in foreign securities or in any one country or currency.

Manager's Investment Style

Management uses a variety of computer models that identify inexpensive stocks that may have better future earnings than Wall Street expects, then hand picks 50 or 60 of these with good earnings or turnaround potential for the portfolio. Management also uses a customized BARRA computer model that analyzes potential portfolio risks through 68 different variables.

Fund Manager(s)

Scott Stewart, since 09-93. Birthdate: 10-58.
MBA, Cornell U. 1983 PhD, Cornell U. 1985

Manager Experience

	Dates Managed	Invest Obj	Std Dev	+/- Index

Not available.

Historical Profile

Return ---
Risk ---
Rating Not Rated

Investment Style History
Equity

Average % Stocks Held in Portfolio

83% 84%

Growth of $10,000

|||| Value of Fund ($000)
— Value of Index ($000)
   S&P 500
▼ Manager Change
▽ Partial Manager Change
► Mgr Unknown After
◄ Mgr Unknown Before

Performance Quartile
(Within Objective)

	1983	1984	1985	1986	1987	1988	1989	1990	1991	1992	1993	1994	History
	---	---	---	---	---	---	---	---	---	---	10.58	10.88	NAV
	---	---	---	---	---	---	---	---	---	---	5.90 *	4.00	Total Return %
	---	---	---	---	---	---	---	---	---	---	2.47 *	2.68	+/- S&P 500
	---	---	---	---	---	---	---	---	---	---	---	6.65	+/- Wilshire 4500
	---	---	---	---	---	---	---	---	---	---	0.10	0.19	Income Return %
	---	---	---	---	---	---	---	---	---	---	5.80	3.81	Capital Return %
	---	---	---	---	---	---	---	---	---	---	---	5	Total Rtn % Rank All
	---	---	---	---	---	---	---	---	---	---	---	8	Total Rtn % Rank Obj
	---	---	---	---	---	---	---	---	---	---	0.01	0.02	Income $
	---	---	---	---	---	---	---	---	---	---	0.00	0.10	Capital Gains $
	---	---	---	---	---	---	---	---	---	---	---	1.58	Expense Ratio %
	---	---	---	---	---	---	---	---	---	---	---	0.23	Income Ratio %
	---	---	---	---	---	---	---	---	---	---	---	320	Turnover Rate %
	---	---	---	---	---	---	---	---	---	---	---	60.6	Net Assets ($mil)

Performance 12-31-94

	1st Qtr	2nd Qtr	3rd Qtr	4th Qtr	Total
1987	---	---	---	---	---
1988	---	---	---	---	---
1989	---	---	---	---	---
1990	---	---	---	---	---
1991	---	---	---	---	---
1992	---	---	---	---	---
1993	---	---	---	3.01	5.90 *
1994	-2.74	-1.17	9.05	-0.79	4.00

Bear Market Performance

Decile Rank (5-year period)

Worst ——————————————— Best

	Worst 3 Mo Period 1985-89	Worst 3 Mo Period 1990-94
Fidelity Fifty	---	---
+/- S&P 500	---	---
+/- Best Fit Index :	---	---

Trailing Returns

	Total Return %	+/- S&P 500	+/- Wil 4500	% Rank All	Obj	Growth of $10,000
3 Mo	-0.79	-0.77	1.71	40	51	9,921
6 Mo	8.19	3.33	3.99	6	48	10,819
1 Yr	4.00	2.68	6.65	5	8	10,400
3 Yr Avg	---	---	---	---	---	---
5 Yr Avg	---	---	---	---	---	---
10 Yr Avg	---	---	---	---	---	---
15 Yr Avg	---	---	---	---	---	---

Operations

Address and Telephone	82 Devonshire Street
	Boston, MA 02109
	800-544-8888
Advisor	Fidelity Management & Research
Subadvisor	FMR (U.K.)/FMR (Far East)
Distributor	Fidelity Distributors
States Available	All
Report Grade	A
Income Distrib	Paid Semiannually
* Date of Inception	09-20-93
Fiscal Year End	June

Risk Analysis

Time Period	Load-Adj Return %	Risk % Rank All	Obj	Morningstar [2] Return	Morningstar Risk	Morningstar Risk-Adj Rating
1 Yr	0.88					
3 Yr	---	---	---	---	---	---
5 Yr	---	---	---	---	---	---
10 Yr	---	---	---	---	---	---
Average Historical Rating	---			---		

[1] 1 = low, 100 = high   [2] 1.00 = Equity Avg   [3] 1.00 = 90-day T-bill return

Other Measures

				Standard S&P 500	Best Fit
Standard Deviation	---	Alpha		---	---
Mean	---	Beta		---	---
Sharpe Ratio	---	R-Squared		---	---

Investment Style

	Stock Portfolio Avg	Relative S&P 500	Style Value Blend Growth
Price/Earnings Ratio	20.7	1.12	
Price/Book Ratio	3.9	1.14	
5 Yr Earnings Gr %	8.1#	1.46	
Return on Assets %	8.0	1.07	
Debt % Total Cap	31.7	1.12	
Med Mkt Cap ($mil)	3548	0.27	

figure is based on 50% or less of stocks

Diversification Value for Portfolio Types

Large Cap: Small Cap: Bond: Balanced: Diversified:

Expenses & Fees

Min Initial Purchase	$2500 (Addt'l: $250)
Min IRA Purchase	$500 (Addt'l: $250)
Min Auto Invest Plan	$2500 (Systematic Inv: $100)

Sales Fees	3.00% front
	0.00% deferred
	0.00% 12b-1
Management Fee	0.30% flat fee+0.52%G+(-)0.20%P
3-,5-,10-yr Expense Projections	$78, $113, $212
Annual Brokerage Cost	---

Portfolio 06-30-94

Share Chg (12-93)000	Amount 000	Total Stocks: 53 Total Fixed-Income: 0	Value $000	% Net Assets
25	25	Olin	1336	2.76
5	21	AMR	1259	2.60
49	49	MA Hanna	1251	2.59
18	18	Nucor	1240	2.56
22	22	Amoco	1226	2.53
29	29	Compuware	1200	2.48
55	55	Manpower	1145	2.37
20	20	American Cyanamid	1114	2.30
54	54	Washington Mutual Savings Bk	1106	2.29
23	23	Sears Roebuck	1085	2.24
21	21	Fluor	1079	2.23
47	47	Rochester Telephone	1068	2.21
22	22	LM Ericsson Telephone (ADR)	1066	2.20
1	14	CSX	1065	2.20
21	21	3Com	1058	2.19
18	18	General Instrument	1020	2.11
26	26	Oracle Systems	979	2.02
13	13	Federal Express	970	2.01
-3	16	IBM	940	1.94
13	13	McKesson	938	1.94
-4	35	Union Carbide	931	1.92
23	23	Chemical Banking	886	1.83
33	33	Baxter International	866	1.79
22	22	State Street Boston	850	1.76
17	17	Kendall International	847	1.75

Composition % 11-30-94

Cash	13.0	Preferreds	0.0
Stocks	87.0	Convertibles	0.0
Bonds	0.0	Other	0.0

Tax Analysis

	Tax-Adj Historical Return %	% Pretax Return
3 Yr Avg	---	---
5 Yr Avg	---	---
10 Yr Avg	---	---
Potential Capital Gain Exposure (% of assets)	3%	

Most Similar Funds in MF500

Fund lacks three-year record

Index Allocation

	% of Stocks
S&P 500	47.9
S&P MidCap 400	16.6
U.S. Small Cap	28.3
Foreign	7.3

Sector Weightings

	% of Stocks	Relative S&P 500
Utilities	6.1	0.49
Energy	6.1	0.60
Financials	7.3	0.69
Industrial Cyclicals	11.9	0.73
Consumer Durables	8.8	1.42
Consumer Staples	1.2	0.10
Services	22.6	2.77
Retail	3.3	0.56
Health	15.3	1.76
Technology	17.5	1.91

Fidelity

	Ticker	Load	NAV	Yield	SEC Yield	Assets	Objective
	FFIDX	None	18.48	1.7%	N/A	1886.1	Growth/Inc.

Fidelity Fund seeks long-term capital growth. Current return is also a consideration.

The fund invests primarily in common stocks and convertible securities. It may also purchase debt securities for current income. The percentage of its assets in any one type of security may vary. The fund diversifies in two ways: by investing in several types of securities at the same time and by investing in different industries. The fund may invest up to 5% of its assets in lower-quality debt and may also purchase restricted securities. It may also make foreign investments, and engage in options and futures contracts.

Manager's Investment Style

A 1993 management change has led to only a slight retuning of the strategy. Current management continues to emphasize industrial-cyclical names, with across-the-board attention to stocks that show signs of fundamental improvement, but haven't yet been bid up to high prices. Nonetheless, under Beth Terrana, the individual stocks of the portfolio were almost altogether shifted, resulting in a slightly more growth-oriented approach, with increased foreign holdings, and increased attention to capital returns, as well as yield.

Fund Manager(s)

Beth F. Terrana CFA(1989), since 08-93.
Birthdate: 09-57. BS, SUNY-Binghamton 1978 MBA, Harvard 1983

Manager Experience	Dates Managed	Invest Obj	Std Dev	+/- Index
Beth F. Terrana				
Fidelity Equity-Income	10/90 - 08/93	EI	9.42	5.79
Fidelity Adv Inst Eq Inc	10/90 - 07/93	EI	10.08	5.34

Historical Profile
Return	Above Average
Risk	Below Average
Rating	★★★★ Above Average

Investment Style History
Equity
Average % Stocks Held in Portfolio

| 92% | 89% | 87% | 76% | 85% | 81% | 85% | 81% |

Growth of $10,000
- |||| Value of Fund ($000)
- — Value of Index ($000) SPMid400
- ▼ Manager Change
- ▽ Partial Manager Change
- ► Mgr Unknown After
- ◄ Mgr Unknown Before

Performance Quartile (Within Objective)

	1983	1984	1985	1986	1987	1988	1989	1990	1991	1992	1993	1994	History
	19.89	14.82	18.08	16.05	13.58	15.42	17.93	16.29	18.46	18.94	19.27	18.48	NAV
	22.42	1.61	27.66	15.76	3.28	17.85	28.80	-5.10	24.15	8.46	18.36	2.58	Total Return %
	-0.04	-4.66	-4.08	-2.92	-1.98	1.24	-2.88	-1.98	-6.34	0.84	8.31	1.27	+/- S&P 500
	-1.04	-1.44	-4.90	-0.33	0.92	-0.09	-0.37	1.09	-10.06	-0.51	7.08	2.65	+/- Wilshire 5000
	4.64	5.15	5.22	3.86	2.87	4.30	4.22	4.05	2.88	2.63	2.30	1.76	Income Return %
	17.78	-3.55	22.44	11.91	0.41	13.55	24.58	-9.15	21.26	5.83	16.06	0.82	Capital Return %
	31	61	34	50	34	19	16	71	37	40	20	8	Total Rtn % Rank All
	41	66	48	55	39	31	25	62	74	40	10	10	Total Rtn % Rank Obj
	0.84	0.72	0.72	0.66	0.48	0.56	0.68	0.74	0.50	0.48	0.44	0.33	Income $
	1.97	4.40	0.05	4.08	2.72	0.00	1.17	0.00	1.15	0.58	2.55	0.94	Capital Gains $
	0.71	0.66	0.66	0.60	0.67	0.67	0.64	0.66	0.68	0.67	0.66	0.65	Expense Ratio %
	4.34	5.06	4.25	3.48	2.75	3.69	3.76	4.04	2.84	2.37	2.94	1.85	Income Ratio %
	210	200	215	214	211	175	191	259	267	151	261	207	Turnover Rate %
	668.9	618.5	761.5	782.4	873.1	895.2	1085.5	1065.9	1309.7	1353.2	1546.2	1886.1	Net Assets ($mil)

Performance 12-31-94

	1st Qtr	2nd Qtr	3rd Qtr	4th Qtr	Total
1987	21.47	2.80	6.95	-22.67	3.28
1988	7.13	7.80	-0.37	2.43	17.85
1989	5.97	10.10	10.27	0.11	28.80
1990	-1.50	4.04	-12.17	5.44	-5.10
1991	16.03	-0.66	5.29	2.30	24.15
1992	1.28	0.22	1.08	5.72	8.46
1993	6.61	2.61	5.71	2.36	18.36
1994	-2.47	-0.12	5.51	-0.19	2.58

Bear Market Performance

Decile Rank (5-year period)

Worst ———————————————— Best

	Worst 3 Mo Period 1985-89	Worst 3 Mo Period 1990-94
Fidelity	-29.02	-12.29
+/- S&P 500	0.56	1.55
+/- Best Fit Index : SPMid400	-0.21	6.13

Trailing Returns

	Total Return %	+/- S&P 500	+/- Wil 5000	% Rank All	% Rank Obj	Growth of $10,000
3 Mo	-0.19	-0.18	0.58	27	25	9,981
6 Mo	5.30	0.44	0.68	10	7	10,530
1 Yr	2.58	1.27	2.65	8	10	10,258
3 Yr Avg	9.61	3.34	3.00	15	13	13,169
5 Yr Avg	9.18	0.49	0.37	22	20	15,515
10 Yr Avg	13.65	-0.73	-0.21	20	20	35,945
15 Yr Avg	14.66	0.18	0.69	17	16	77,867

Operations

Address and Telephone	82 Devonshire Street
	Boston, MA 02109
	800-544-8888
Advisor	Fidelity Management & Research
Subadvisor	FMR (U.K.)/FMR (Far East)
Distributor	Fidelity Distributors
States Available	All
Report Grade	A
Income Distrib	Paid Quarterly
Date of Inception	04-30-30
Fiscal Year End	December

Risk Analysis

Time Period	Load-Adj Return %	Risk % Rank [1] All	Risk % Rank [1] Obj	Morningstar [2] Return	Morningstar Risk	Morningstar Risk-Adj Rating
1 Yr	2.58					
3 Yr	9.61	58	22	1.85[3]	0.64	★★★★
5 Yr	9.18	63	36	1.13[3]	0.75	★★★★
10 Yr	13.65	58	50	1.20	0.82	★★★★
Average Historical Rating (109 months)					3.9	★s

[1] 1 = low, 100 = high [2] 1.00 = Equity Avg [3] 1.00 = 90-day T-bill return

Other Measures

			Standard S&P 500	Best Fit SPMid400
Standard Deviation	8.05	Alpha	3.5	3.3
Mean	9.53	Beta	0.88	0.73
Sharpe Ratio	0.75	R-Squared	75	79

Investment Style

	Stock Portfolio Avg	Relative S&P 500
Price/Earnings Ratio	20.5	1.11
Price/Book Ratio	2.9	0.87
5 Yr Earnings Gr %	8.2	1.47
Return on Assets %	6.8	0.91
Debt % Total Cap	29.8	1.05
Med Mkt Cap ($mil)	5270	0.41

Style
Value Blend Growth
Size Large/Med/Small

Diversification Value for Portfolio Types

Large Cap: Low	Small Cap: Low	Bond: High	Balanced: None	Diversified: Low

Portfolio 06-30-94

Share Chg (12-93) 000	Amount 000	Total Stocks: 266 / Total Fixed-Income: 35	Value $000	% Net Assets
43	525	British Petroleum (ADR)	37633	2.36
361	748	General Electric	34880	2.19
21	356	Xerox	34799	2.19
128	329	CSX	24870	1.56
-30	430	Philip Morris	22166	1.39
74	207	Caterpillar	20740	1.30
308	308	IBM	18095	1.14
120	264	Schlumberger	15609	0.98
275	275	American Cyanamid	15417	0.97
32	176	FNMA	14679	0.92
77	366	GFC Financial	12205	0.77
125	461	La Quinta Inns	12046	0.76
98	156	Premark International	11754	0.74
47	164	Warner-Lambert	10804	0.68
188	188	Eli Lilly	10704	0.67
29	219	Sears Roebuck	10531	0.66
	190	Unocal Cv Pfd $3.50	10307	0.65
33	33	Elektrizetaets & Bergwerks	10268	0.64
-3	382	Union Carbide	10216	0.64
93	93	General Re	10148	0.64
-157	232	Murphy Oil	9914	0.62
20	20	BMW	9849	0.62
123	192	NationsBank	9841	0.62
120	120	Mobil	9828	0.62
167	167	El duPont de Nemours	9743	0.61

Composition % 11-30-94

Cash	14.1	Preferreds	0.0
Stocks	74.5	Convertibles	3.4
Bonds	8.0	Other	0.0

Tax Analysis

	Tax-Adj Historical Return %	% Pretax Return
3 Yr Avg	6.77	68.5
5 Yr Avg	6.64	68.8
10 Yr Avg	10.22	63.5
Potential Capital Gain Exposure (% of assets)		4%

Most Similar Funds in MF500

Fundamental Investors	Strong Fit
Fidelity Disciplined Equity	Strong Fit
Fidelity Magellan	Strong Fit

Index Allocation
	% of Stocks
S&P 500	57.1
S&P MidCap 400	10.2
U.S. Small Cap	22.1
Foreign	11.5

Sector Weightings
	% of Stocks	Relative S&P 500
Utilities	1.7	0.14
Energy	10.6	1.05
Financials	14.9	1.41
Industrial Cyclicals	20.7	1.26
Consumer Durables	8.6	1.38
Consumer Staples	5.7	0.46
Services	13.0	1.60
Retail	7.7	1.31
Health	9.4	1.08
Technology	7.7	0.84

Min Initial Purchase / Expenses

Min Initial Purchase	$2500 (Addt'l: $250)
Min IRA Purchase	$500 (Addt'l: $250)
Min Auto Invest Plan	$2500 (Systematic Inv: $100)

Expenses & Fees

Sales Fees	0.00% front
	0.00% deferred
	0.00% 12b-1
Management Fee	0.09% flat fee+0.52%G
3-,5-,10-yr Expense Projections	$21, $36, $81
Annual Brokerage Cost	0.42%

MORNINGSTAR 1995 Mutual Fund 500

Fidelity Global Bond

	Ticker	Load	NAV	Yield	SEC Yield	Assets	Objective
	FGBDX	None	9.88	6.5%	8.36%	382.9	World Bond

Fidelity Global Bond Fund seeks high total investment return. The fund invests primarily in debt securities (including convertibles) issued anywhere in the world. It considers both yield and potential capital appreciation in making investment selections. The fund allocates its assets among countries, geographic regions, and currency denominations in an attempt to achieve high total investment return. The average weighted maturity of the fund may not exceed 15 years. The fund may engage in futures and options transactions with respect to both the securities in its portfolio and currencies.

Historical Profile

Return	Below Average
Risk	Below Average
Rating	★★★
	Neutral

Investment Style History
Fixed Income
Income Rtn % Rank Obj

					59	28	35	70
60	40	79	60					

Growth of $10,000

|||| Value of Fund ($000)
— Value of Index ($000) LB Agg
▼ Manager Change
▽ Partial Manager Change
► Mgr Unknown After
◄ Mgr Unknown Before

Performance Quartile (Within Objective)

Manager's Investment Style

Over the long-term, management has ventured into lesser-followed and emerging-market debt, all while placing more emphasis on choosing a good market than on making currency bets. (Most of the holdings are dollar denominated.) Since taking over in late 1993 John Kelly has maintained the overall strategy, while working to reduce the fund's volatility. He has, for example, balanced the emerging-markets stake by putting assets into more established markets as well. Further, management dilutes risk through his preference for moderately priced bonds.

Fund Manager(s)

Jonathan Kelly, since 10-93. Birthdate: 1963.
BA, Dartmouth C. 1985 MBA, Wharton 1991

Manager Experience

	Dates Managed	Invest Obj	Std Dev	+/- Index
Not available.				

1983	1984	1985	1986	1987	1988	1989	1990	1991	1992	1993	1994	History
---	---	---	10.05	11.21	10.72	11.08	11.38	11.90	11.34	12.61	9.88	NAV
---	---	---	0.50 *	19.07	3.67	7.93	12.28	12.77	3.69	21.91	-16.70	Total Return %
---	---	---		16.32	-4.21	-6.61	3.33	-3.23	-3.56	12.15	-13.78	+/- LB Aggregate
---	---	---		-16.08	1.31	11.36	-3.01	-3.47	-1.09	6.79	-23.40	+/- SB World Govt
---	---	---	0.00	7.53	8.04	4.57	9.57	8.20	8.39	8.20	4.86	Income Return %
---	---	---	0.50	11.54	-4.37	3.36	2.71	4.57	-4.71	13.70	-21.56	Capital Return %
---	---	---		4	95	91	2	69	82	14	99	Total Rtn % Rank All
---	---	---		60	53	25	54	56	22	13	91	Total Rtn % Rank Obj
---	---	---	0.00	0.69	0.90	0.49	1.05	0.90	1.00	0.86	0.64	Income $
---	---	---	0.00	0.00	0.00	0.00	0.00	0.00	0.25	0.02	Capital Gains $
---	---	---		0.95	1.14	1.50	1.40	1.35	1.37	1.17	1.20	Expense Ratio %
---	---	---		7.14	7.61	7.56	7.82	7.92	6.92	6.79	6.17	Income Ratio %
---	---	---		297	227	150	154	228	142	198	289	Turnover Rate %
---	---	---		105.8	83.0	74.9	134.7	184.0	274.9	681.1	382.9	Net Assets ($mil)

Performance 12-31-94

	1st Qtr	2nd Qtr	3rd Qtr	4th Qtr	Total
1987	6.88	-1.03	-1.33	14.09	19.07
1988	0.36	-1.60	0.54	4.41	3.67
1989	-1.40	1.70	2.98	4.52	7.93
1990	-0.36	3.53	4.20	4.45	12.28
1991	1.67	1.47	4.31	4.79	12.77
1992	-0.76	4.51	1.54	-1.55	3.69
1993	4.98	4.87	4.68	5.78	21.91
1994	-11.29	-6.11	3.09	-2.98	-16.70

Bear Market Performance

Decile Rank (5-year period)

Worst ————————————— Best

	Worst 3 Mo Period 1985-89	Worst 3 Mo Period 1990-94
Fidelity Global Bond	---	-13.98
+/- LB Aggregate	---	-9.05
+/- Best Fit Index : LB Agg	---	-9.05

Trailing Returns

	Total Return %	+/- LB Aggregate	+/- SB World	% Rank All	% Rank Obj	Growth of $10,000
3 Mo	-2.98	-3.36	-3.55	83	82	9,702
6 Mo	0.02	-0.98	-2.21	57	50	10,002
1 Yr	-16.70	-13.78	-23.40	99	91	8,330
3 Yr Avg	1.73	-2.81	-7.04	93	84	10,529
5 Yr Avg	5.92	-1.71	-5.60	78	84	13,332
10 Yr Avg	---	---	---	---	---	---
15 Yr Avg	---	---	---	---	---	---

Operations

Address and Telephone	82 Devonshire Street Boston, MA 02109 800-544-8888	
Advisor	Fidelity Management & Research	
Subadvisor	FMR (U.K.)/FMR (Far East)/Fidelity Intl In	
Distributor	Fidelity Distributors	
States Available	All	
Report Grade	A-	
Income Distrib	Paid Monthly	
* Date of Inception	12-30-86	
Fiscal Year End	December	

Risk Analysis

Time Period	Load-Adj Return %	Risk % Rank All [1]	Risk % Rank Obj	Morningstar [2] Return	Morningstar Risk	Risk-Adj Rating
1 Yr	-16.70					
3 Yr	1.73	66	82	-0.52[3]	0.97	★★
5 Yr	5.92	47	54	0.28[3]	0.61	★★★
10 Yr	---	---	---	---		

Average Historical Rating (61 months) 3.9 ★s

[1] 1 = low, 100 = high [2] 1.00 = Hybrid Avg [3] 1.00 = 90-day T-bill return

Other Measures

				Standard LB Agg	Best Fit LB Agg
Standard Deviation	7.87	Alpha		-2.8	-2.8
Mean	2.04	Beta		1.29	1.29
Sharpe Ratio	-0.19	R-Squared		44	44

Investment Style

Interest-Rate Stance

Avg Effective Maturity 8.3 Yrs

Maturity Short Intm Long

Quality

Avg Credit Quality BBB

Avg Weighted Coupon 6.83%

Quality High Med Low

Diversification Value for Portfolio Types

Large Cap: High	Small Cap: High	Bond: Medium	Balanced: Medium	Diversified: Medium

Expenses & Fees

Sales Fees	0.00% front
	0.00% deferred
	0.00% 12b-1
Management Fee	0.55% flat fee+0.37%G
3-,5-,10-yr Expense Projections	$37, $64, $142

Min Initial Purchase	$2500 (Addt'l: $250)
Min IRA Purchase	$500 (Addt'l: $250)
Min Auto Invest Plan	$2500 (Systematic Inv: $100)

Portfolio 06-30-94

Total Stocks: 0
Total Fixed-Income: 51

Amount 000	Date of Maturity		Value $000	% Net Assets
59896	03-31-05	Republic of Argentina 5%	42751	8.23
20500	11-20-98	United Kingdom Treasury 12%	35698	6.87
34550	01-01-01	Republic of Brazil IDU 6.0625%	24012	4.62
25000	01-03-09	Govt of Morocco 4.5%	17938	3.45
24018	04-01-01	Republic of Argentina 4.5%	16445	3.17
21350	04-15-04	Govt of New Zealand 8%	12939	2.49
15000	12-31-19	United Mexican States 5.8125%	12300	2.37
20550	01-01-99	Republic of Italy 8.5%	12117	2.33
20000	06-01-04	Govt of Canada 6.5%	11885	2.29
20818	04-01-01	Republic of Argentina 3.25%	11274	2.17
93250	12-31-19	United Mexican States 6.63%	10449	2.01
810000	12-19-08	Canon 1.3%	9740	1.88
18000	01-04-24	Republic of Germany 6.25%	9555	1.84
45000	03-15-04	Republic of Finland 9.5%	8431	1.62
50000	12-15-04	Kingdom of Denmark 7%	7268	1.40
530000	05-31-02	Matsushita Elec Works 2.7%	6736	1.30
11200	04-01-99	Republic of Italy 8.5%	6579	1.27
9000	03-15-02	Govt of New Zealand 10%	6038	1.16
10000	07-15-98	Govt of New Zealand 8%	5999	1.16
12000	03-31-23	Republic of Argentina 4.25%	5925	1.14
9000	12-08-03	Province of Ontario 7.75%	5758	1.11
5400	09-10-97	Province of Chaco 11.875%	5454	1.05
36149	08-15-99	Siderurgica Brasileiras 6%	4385	0.84
6250	07-30-98	Softe 4.25%	4354	0.84
20000	05-15-14	US Treasury Bond 0%	4154	0.80

Composition % 09-30-94

Cash	6.8	Preferreds	0.0
Stocks	0.0	Convertibles	0.0
Bonds	93.2	Other	0.0

Tax Analysis

	Tax-Adj Historical Return %	% Pretax Return
3 Yr Avg	-1.06	---
5 Yr Avg	3.11	49.7
10 Yr Avg	---	---

Potential Capital Gain Exposure (% of assets) -30%

Most Similar Funds in MF500

Global Income Plus	Weak Fit
G.T. Global Govt Income A	Weak Fit
PaineWebber Global Inc B	Weak Fit

Country Exposure 11-30-94

	% of Bonds
Argentina	24
Mexico	18
U.S.	16
United Kingdom	7
Germany	6

Currency Exposure 11-30-94

	% of Net Assets
U.S.	62
Mexico	10
New Zealand	10
Singapore	6
Thailand	6

Fidelity Government Securities

	Ticker	Load	NAV	Yield	SEC Yield	Assets	Objective
	FGOVX	None	9.17	6.7%	7.03%	611.2	Gvt General

Fidelity Government Securities Fund seeks current income consistent with preservation of principal.

The fund invests in tax-exempt U.S. government securities. It may invest a significant portion of assets in securities issued by agencies or instrumentalities, such as Federal Home Loan Bank debt and Student Loan Marketing Association debt. The portfolio's average maturity shifts in response to anticipated changes in interest rates. The fund may hedge up to 25% of its assets by selling futures, buying puts, and writing calls.

The fund was organized as a Nebraska limited partnership prior to Jan. 1, 1992.

Investment Style History
Fixed Income
Income Rtn % Rank Obj

43	32	61	20	20	30	31	32

Historical Profile
Return: Above Average
Risk: Average
Rating: ★★★ Neutral

Growth of $10,000
IIII Value of Fund ($000)
— Value of Index ($000)
LB Govt
▼ Manager Change
▽ Partial Manager Change
► Mgr Unknown After
◄ Mgr Unknown Before

Manager's Investment Style
Manager Curtis Hollingsworth follows a contrarian duration-averaging strategy, which leads him to extend duration when real interest rates rise, and to pull it back when rates fall. He has, however, tied the fund's benchmark yield to the average long-bond rate over the past 40 years, rather than adjusting it based on Fidelity's economic outlook. While not allowed to hold mortgage-backed securities, management shifts between Treasury bonds with varying coupons to build a laddered or barbelled portfolio for example.

Performance Quartile (Within Objective)

1983	1984	1985	1986	1987	1988	1989	1990	1991	1992	1993	1994	History
9.28	9.24	9.80	10.28	9.52	9.27	9.61	9.64	10.30	10.10	10.34	9.17	NAV
6.05	11.29	17.74	14.63	1.06	6.36	12.62	9.53	15.96	7.93	12.32	-5.21	Total Return %
-2.32	-3.87	-4.39	-0.62	-1.70	-1.52	-1.92	0.59	-0.04	0.69	2.57	-2.29	+/- LB Aggregate
-1.34	-3.21	-2.69	-0.69	-1.13	-0.67	-1.61	0.82	0.65	0.70	1.67	-1.83	+/- LB Government
10.10	11.72	11.68	9.73	8.45	8.99	8.95	9.22	9.11	7.43	6.77	5.94	Income Return %
-4.05	-0.43	6.06	4.90	-7.39	-2.63	3.67	0.31	6.85	0.50	5.55	-11.15	Capital Return %
96	20	83	57	50	86	55	6	54	46	48	66	Total Rtn % Rank All
81	80	52	14	62	59	32	20	17	10	6	82	Total Rtn % Rank Obj
0.94	1.01	0.98	0.91	0.85	0.84	0.79	0.83	0.80	0.73	0.67	0.62	Income $
0.28	0.00	0.00	0.00	0.00	0.00	0.00	0.00	0.00	0.25	0.31	0.02	Capital Gains $
0.88	0.85	0.81	0.84	0.87	0.79	0.73	0.66	0.70	0.70	0.69	0.69	Expense Ratio %
9.92	11.14	10.46	8.72	8.68	8.87	8.29	8.84	8.23	7.31	6.40	6.26	Income Ratio %
---	---	137	138	253	283	312	302	257	219	323	402	Turnover Rate %
84.9	87.5	266.9	745.3	678.3	567.0	557.6	464.4	523.3	568.1	753.4	611.2	Net Assets ($mil)

Fund Manager(s)
Curtis Hollingsworth, since 02-90. Birthdate: 05-57. BA, Boston U. 1983

Manager Experience

	Dates Managed	Invest Obj	Std Dev	+/- Index
Curtis Hollingsworth				
Fidelity Instl Sh-Int Gov	01/87 - 12/94	GG	2.32	-0.84
Fidelity Spartan Ltd Mat	05/88 - 12/94	GG	2.15	-1.83

Performance 12-31-94

	1st Qtr	2nd Qtr	3rd Qtr	4th Qtr	Total
1987	0.79	-1.84	-2.09	4.33	1.06
1988	3.32	0.61	1.62	0.69	6.36
1989	1.18	6.68	0.80	3.51	12.62
1990	-0.79	3.13	1.50	5.47	9.53
1991	1.94	1.21	6.21	5.82	15.96
1992	-2.16	4.45	5.30	0.30	7.93
1993	5.44	3.06	3.85	-0.47	12.32
1994	-4.03	-1.56	0.17	0.17	-5.21

Bear Market Performance

Decile Rank (5-year period)

Worst — Best

	Worst 3 Mo Period 1985-89	Worst 3 Mo Period 1990-94
Fidelity Government Securities	-3.61	-6.45
+/- LB Aggregate	-0.06	-1.52
+/- Best Fit Index : LB Govt	-0.15	-1.37

Trailing Returns

	Total Return %	+/- LB Aggregate	+/- LB Govt	% Rank All	% Rank Obj	Growth of $10,000
3 Mo	0.17	-0.21	-0.19	17	39	10,017
6 Mo	0.34	-0.65	-0.44	50	53	10,034
1 Yr	-5.21	-2.29	-1.83	66	82	9,479
3 Yr Avg	4.74	0.20	0.08	54	7	11,492
5 Yr Avg	7.86	0.23	0.33	35	5	14,596
10 Yr Avg	9.08	-0.86	-0.49	71	8	23,848
15 Yr Avg	10.02	-0.79	-0.54	77	20	41,871

Risk Analysis

Time Period	Load-Adj Return %	Risk % Rank[1] All	Obj	Morningstar[2] Return	Morningstar Risk	Morningstar Risk-Adj Rating
1 Yr	-5.21					
3 Yr	4.74	39	81	0.34[3]	1.24	★★★
5 Yr	7.86	28	61	0.77[3]	1.07	★★★★
10 Yr	9.08	19	64	0.84[3]	1.03	★★★

Average Historical Rating (109 months)   3.3 ★s

[1] = low, 100 = high   [2] 1.00 = Taxable Avg   [3] 1.00 = 90-day T-bill return

Other Measures

		Standard LB Agg	Best Fit LB Govt
Standard Deviation	5.24	Alpha	0.0	-0.1
Mean	4.78	Beta	1.28	1.20
Sharpe Ratio	0.24	R-Squared	96	99

Investment Style

Interest-Rate Stance
Avg Effective Duration   5.6 Yrs
Avg Effective Maturity   10.8 Yrs

Maturity: Short Intm Long
Quality: High Med Low

Quality
Avg Credit Quality   AAA
Avg Weighted Coupon   8.99%
Avg Weighted Price 111.49% of Par

Diversification Value for Portfolio Types

Large Cap: Medium
Small Cap: High
Bond: None
Balanced: Medium
Diversified: Medium

Portfolio 09-30-94

Amount 000	Date of Maturity	Total Stocks: 0 / Total Fixed-Income: 25	Value $000	% Net Assets
94500	11-15-10	US Treasury Bond 12.75%	128859	21.00
100000	07-30-98	Federal Home Loan Bank 4.55%	92703	15.11
68195	08-15-19	US Treasury Bond 8.125%	68941	11.24
50400	08-15-23	US Treasury Bond 12%	67591	11.02
52225	07-06-01	Federal Home Loan Bank 7.31%	51050	8.32
37568	10-01-99	Tennessee Valley Auth 8.375%	39223	6.39
34000	08-15-17	US Treasury Bond 8.875%	36996	6.03
27000	11-15-96	US Treasury Note 7.25%	27312	4.45
13230	10-25-99	Federal Home Loan Bank 8.375%	13767	2.24
11095	11-02-18	FICO 9.65%	12718	2.07
10000	11-01-95	SLMA 10.5%	10420	1.70
8500	04-15-42	Tennessee Valley Auth 8.25%	8123	1.32
9800	08-15-23	US Treasury Bond 6.25%	7953	1.30
7035	01-20-97	Twelve Federal Land Bks 7.35%	7090	1.16
6000	02-08-18	FICO 9.4%	6761	1.10
5000	04-07-99	Federal Farm Credit Bk 9%	5275	0.86
3580	10-01-99	Federal Farm Credit Bk 8.65%	3791	0.62
4500	12-15-43	Tennessee Valley Auth 6.875%	3619	0.59
3475	11-15-99	Tennessee Valley Auth 8.25%	3568	0.58
3000	03-18-99	Federal Home Loan Bank 5.92%	2834	0.46
1900	11-01-01	Federal Home Loan Bank 7.93%	1913	0.31
1500	10-21-96	Twelve Federal Land Bks 7.95%	1534	0.25
1250	12-13-00	Federal Farm Credit Bk 8.35%	1294	0.21
1000	04-05-19	FICO 9.7%	1153	0.19
1800	02-25-04	Federal Home Loan Bank P/O 0%	851	0.14

Composition % 12-22-94

Cash	6.7	Preferreds	0.0
Stocks	0.0	Convertibles	0.0
Bonds	93.3	Other	0.0

Tax Analysis

	Tax-Adj Historical Return %	% Pretax Return
3 Yr Avg	1.73	35.3
5 Yr Avg	4.91	58.9
10 Yr Avg	5.66	53.0
Potential Capital Gain Exposure (% of assets)		-10%

Most Similar Funds in MF500
Vanguard F/I Interm-Term US   Strong Fit
Scudder Income   Strong Fit
New England Bond Income A   Strong Fit

Coupon Range

	% of Bonds	Rel Obj
0%	0.1	0.10
0% to 8%	32.4	0.51
8% to 9%	29.9	1.95
9% to 10%	3.4	0.42
More than 10%	34.2	5.46
Not applicable	0.0	0.00

Sector Analysis 09-30-94
% of Bonds

US Treas	56	CMOs	0
GNMA mtgs	0	ARMs	0
FNMA mtgs	0	Other	44
FHLMC mtgs	0		

Operations

Address and Telephone	82 Devonshire Street Boston, MA 02109 800-544-8888
Advisor	Fidelity Management & Research
Subadvisor	None
Distributor	Fidelity Distributors
States Available	All
Report Grade	A
Income Distrib	Paid Monthly
Date of Inception	04-04-79
Fiscal Year End	September

Min Initial Purchase	$2500 (Addt'l: $250)
Min IRA Purchase	$500 (Addt'l: $250)
Min Auto Invest Plan	$2500 (Systematic Inv: $100)

Expenses & Fees

Sales Fees	0.00% front
	0.00% deferred
	0.00% 12b-1
Management Fee	0.30% flat fee+0.37%G
3-,5-,10-yr Expense Projections	$22, $38, $86

MORNINGSTAR 1995 Mutual Fund 500

Fidelity Growth & Income

	Ticker	Load	NAV	Yield	SEC Yield	Assets	Objective
	FGRIX	3.00%	21.09	1.8%	N/A	9344.9	Growth/Inc.

Fidelity Growth and Income Portfolio seeks long-term growth, current income, and growth of income, consistent with reasonable investment risk.

The fund invests primarily in dividend-paying common stocks with growth potential. Generally, the fund sells securities whose dividends fall below the yield of the S&P 500 Index. Some common-stock selections, however, may be made in securities not paying dividends but offering prospects for capital growth or future income. The fund's fixed-income investments are generally in corporate bonds.

Manager's Investment Style

The most-recent management change has somewhat tamed a wilder strategy. Previous management was known for an adventurous style (relative to the objective) that could include foreign stocks, high-yield bonds, rapid trading, and large sector bets. Current management has raised median market cap and focused more heavily on S&P 500 names. Manager Steven Kaye looks for stocks that show improved earnings, but still sell at low prices. Recent sector exposure has been broad. Convertibles and bonds can also show up in the portfolio.

Fund Manager(s)

Steven Kaye, since 01-93. BA, Johns Hopkins U.
MBA, Wharton

Manager Experience	Dates Managed	Invest Obj	Std Dev	+/- Index
Steven Kaye				
Fidelity Blue Chip Growth	10/90 - 01/93	G	15.42	9.46

Historical Profile

Return	Above Average
Risk	Below Average
Rating ★★★★	
	Above Average

Average % Stocks Held in Portfolio: 78% 88% 81% 78% 89% 67% 72% 81%

Investment Style History Equity

Growth of $10,000
IIII Value of Fund ($000)
— Value of Index ($000)
SPMid400
▼ Manager Change
▽ Partial Manager Change
► Mgr Unknown After
◄ Mgr Unknown Before

Performance Quartile (Within Objective)

	1983	1984	1985	1986	1987	1988	1989	1990	1991	1992	1993	1994	History
NAV	---	---	9.65	13.33	12.60	14.85	17.17	15.22	20.49	19.71	22.22	21.09	NAV
Total Return %	---	---	-3.50 *	39.80	5.77	22.98	29.60	-6.80	41.84	11.54	19.53	2.27	Total Return %
+/- S&P 500	---	---	-4.10 *	21.12	0.52	6.37	-2.08	-3.68	11.36	3.92	9.47	0.95	+/- S&P 500
+/- Wilshire 5000	---	---	---	23.70	3.41	5.04	0.43	-0.61	7.64	2.57	8.25	2.34	+/- Wilshire 5000
Income Return %	---	---	0.00	1.67	2.93	5.12	4.85	3.40	2.29	2.93	2.59	1.84	Income Return %
Capital Return %	---	---	-3.50	38.13	2.85	17.86	24.75	-10.19	39.56	8.61	16.94	0.43	Capital Return %
Total Rtn % Rank All	---	---	---	5	19	8	14	77	13	16	18	9	Total Rtn % Rank All
Total Rtn % Rank Obj	---	---	---	1	21	12	21	74	5	22	6	12	Total Rtn % Rank Obj
Income $	---	---	0.00	0.16	0.45	0.62	0.75	0.58	0.38	0.57	0.52	0.40	Income $
Capital Gains $	---	---	0.00	0.00	1.35	0.00	1.27	0.22	0.64	2.40	0.77	1.24	Capital Gains $
Expense Ratio %	---	---	---	1.21	1.09	1.02	0.89	0.87	0.87	0.86	0.83	0.82	Expense Ratio %
Income Ratio %	---	---	---	3.12	2.96	3.69	4.76	3.43	2.62	2.49	2.67	2.09	Income Ratio %
Turnover Rate %	---	---	---	69	165	135	97	108	215	221	87	92	Turnover Rate %
Net Assets ($mil)	---	---	---	793.5	1125.7	1145.1	1532.5	1729.5	3355.5	4828.6	7684.0	9344.9	Net Assets ($mil)

Performance 12-31-94

	1st Qtr	2nd Qtr	3rd Qtr	4th Qtr	Total
1987	20.93	3.93	6.82	-21.21	5.77
1988	9.50	7.69	2.34	1.90	22.98
1989	8.37	9.90	8.44	1.95	29.60
1990	-2.10	4.13	-14.41	6.82	-6.80
1991	24.85	-0.08	8.25	5.03	41.84
1992	2.49	0.61	2.04	6.00	11.54
1993	7.77	3.51	5.26	1.79	19.53
1994	-2.68	0.55	5.58	-1.01	2.27

Bear Market Performance

Decile Rank (5-year period)

Worst ———————— Best

	Worst 3 Mo Period 1985-89	Worst 3 Mo Period 1990-94
Fidelity Growth & Income	---	-14.41
+/- S&P 500	---	-0.67
+/- Best Fit Index : SPMid400	---	3.37

Trailing Returns

	Total Return %	+/- S&P 500	+/- Wil 5000	% Rank All	% Rank Obj	Growth of $10,000
3 Mo	-1.01	-1.00	-0.24	45	42	9,899
6 Mo	4.51	-0.35	-0.11	13	21	10,451
1 Yr	2.27	0.95	2.34	9	12	10,227
3 Yr Avg	10.89	4.62	4.27	11	8	13,634
5 Yr Avg	12.51	3.81	3.69	8	4	18,024
10 Yr Avg	---	---	---	---	---	---
15 Yr Avg	---	---	---	---	---	---

Operations

Address and Telephone	82 Devonshire Street
	Boston, MA 02109
	800-544-8888
Advisor	Fidelity Management & Research
Subadvisor	None
Distributor	Fidelity Distributors
States Available	All
Report Grade	A
Income Distrib	Paid Quarterly
* Date of Inception	12-30-85
Fiscal Year End	July

Risk Analysis

Time Period	Load-Adj Return %	Risk % Rank [1] All	Obj	Morningstar [2] Return	Morningstar Risk	Morningstar Risk-Adj Rating
1 Yr	-0.80					
3 Yr	9.77	51	8	1.90 [3]	0.55	★★★★
5 Yr	11.82	61	28	1.88 [3]	0.73	★★★★
10 Yr						

Average Historical Rating (73 months)   4.6 ★s

[1] 1 = low, 100 = high   [2] 1.00 = Equity Avg   [3] 1.00 = 90-day T-bill return

Other Measures

			Standard S&P 500	Best Fit SPMid400
Standard Deviation	7.38	Alpha	4.9	4.7
Mean	10.65	Beta	0.80	0.65
Sharpe Ratio	0.97	R-Squared	74	76

Investment Style

	Stock Portfolio Avg	Relative S&P 500
Price/Earnings Ratio	19.0	1.03
Price/Book Ratio	2.7	0.81
5 Yr Earnings Gr %	8.1	1.45
Return on Assets %	6.2	0.83
Debt % Total Cap	31.0	1.10
Med Mkt Cap ($mil)	6235	0.48

Style Value Blend Growth / Size Large Med Small

Diversification Value for Portfolio Types

 Large Cap: Low   Small Cap: Low   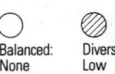 Bond: High   Balanced: None   Diversified: Low

Expenses & Fees

Sales Fees	3.00% front
	0.00% deferred
	0.00% 12b-1
Management Fee	0.20% flat fee+0.52%G
3-,5-,10-yr Expense Projections	$55, $74, $128
Annual Brokerage Cost	0.16%

Min Purchases

Min Initial Purchase	$2500 (Addt'l: $250)
Min IRA Purchase	$500 (Addt'l: $250)
Min Auto Invest Plan	$2500 (Systematic Inv: $100)

Portfolio 07-31-94

Share Chg (01-94)000	Amount 000	Total Stocks: 353 Total Fixed-Income: 69	Value $000	% Net Assets
2616	4857	General Electric	244671	2.79
1199	2614	Philip Morris	143792	1.64
556	1712	British Petroleum (ADR)	130074	1.49
1177	2530	Columbia/HCA Healthcare	102452	1.17
1146	1640	Schlumberger	96772	1.11
89	1088	FNMA	94401	1.08
207	2155	Ameritech	88367	1.01
170	2039	Southwestern Bell	85646	0.98
1278	2615	American Express	69300	0.79
1094	1119	Intel	66289	0.76
419	2192	Union Carbide	61930	0.71
1039	1039	El duPont de Nemours	61661	0.70
1964	1964	Browning-Ferris Industries	60896	0.70
1013	1013	Great Lakes Chemical	60268	0.69
594	1272	Sears Roebuck	60107	0.69
983	983	American Cyanamid	59594	0.68
50	692	ITT	59348	0.68
-30	762	CSX	59142	0.68
657	918	BellSouth	57350	0.65
631	936	United Technologies	56418	0.64
1139	1542	Toys 'R' Us	52993	0.61
766	857	IBM	52889	0.60
-74	498	Xerox	50951	0.58
1188	1188	Becton Dickinson	50040	0.57
97	962	Amerada Hess	50029	0.57

Composition % 11-30-94

Cash	0.0	Preferreds	0.0
Stocks	100.0	Convertibles	0.0
Bonds	0.0	Other	0.0

Tax Analysis

	Tax-Adj Historical Return %	% Pretax Return
3 Yr Avg	7.96	71.1
5 Yr Avg	10.03	76.4
10 Yr Avg	---	---
Potential Capital Gain Exposure (% of assets)		6%

Most Similar Funds in MF500

Fidelity Equity-Income	Strong Fit
Fidelity	Strong Fit
Fundamental Investors	Strong Fit

Index Allocation

	% of Stocks
S&P 500	63.9
S&P MidCap 400	9.2
U.S. Small Cap	14.9
Foreign	13.7

Sector Weightings

	% of Stocks	Relative S&P 500
Utilities	6.1	0.49
Energy	10.8	1.07
Financials	15.0	1.42
Industrial Cyclicals	20.6	1.26
Consumer Durables	5.6	0.91
Consumer Staples	8.3	0.66
Services	10.0	1.23
Retail	6.0	1.04
Health	9.5	1.10
Technology	8.1	0.88

Fidelity Growth Company

	Ticker	Load	NAV	Yield	SEC Yield	Assets	Objective
	FDGRX	3.00%	27.26	0.8%	N/A	2993.4	Growth

Fidelity Growth Company Fund seeks capital appreciation.

The fund invests primarily in common stocks and convertible securities of companies with above-average growth characteristics. Growth can be measured by earnings or gross sales. Most often, these characteristics are found in smaller, lesser-known companies in emerging areas of the economy. However, the fund may also seek growth characteristics in revitalized or well-positioned larger companies in mature industries.

The fund was formerly named Fidelity Mercury Fund.

Historical Profile

Return	Above Average
Risk	Above Average
Rating	★★★★ Above Average

Investment Style History
Equity

Average % Stocks Held in Portfolio

Growth of $10,000

		93%	87%	85%	86%	84%	87%	86%	88%			

IIII Value of Fund ($000)
— Value of Index ($000)
    SPMid400
▼ Manager Change
▽ Partial Manager Change
► Mgr Unknown After
◄ Mgr Unknown Before

Performance Quartile
(Within Objective)

1983	1984	1985	1986	1987	1988	1989	1990	1991	1992	1993	1994	History
13.11	12.10	16.83	14.11	13.02	15.00	18.92	19.60	27.09	27.64	29.06	27.26	NAV
31.10 *	-5.50	39.91	13.03	-1.70	16.06	41.64	3.59	48.33	7.94	16.19	-2.22	Total Return %
13.70 *	-11.77	8.17	-5.65	-6.96	-0.55	9.96	6.71	17.85	0.33	6.13	-3.54	+/- S&P 500
---	-8.55	7.34	-3.07	-4.06	-1.88	12.47	9.78	14.12	-1.03	4.91	-2.15	+/- Wilshire 5000
0.00	0.23	0.81	0.47	0.08	0.86	0.79	0.00	0.33	0.33	0.25	0.81	Income Return %
31.10	-5.73	39.09	12.56	-1.78	15.21	40.85	3.59	48.00	7.61	15.94	-3.04	Capital Return %
---	81	6	67	73	24	3	47	8	46	25	36	Total Rtn % Rank All
---	67	5	67	76	46	6	9	16	49	28	53	Total Rtn % Rank Obj
0.00	0.03	0.07	0.07	0.01	0.11	0.14	0.00	0.08	0.09	0.07	0.22	Income $
0.00	0.28	0.00	4.65	0.83	0.00	2.00	0.00	1.73	1.48	2.92	0.92	Capital Gains $
1.24	1.17	1.18	1.11	1.02	1.03	0.95	1.14	1.07	1.09	1.07	1.08	Expense Ratio %
0.81	0.62	0.55	0.23	0.00	0.70	1.42	1.51	0.75	0.52	0.43	0.41	Income Ratio %
136	143	129	120	212	257	269	189	174	250	159	143	Turnover Rate %
133.8	108.5	155.2	172.5	145.3	138.4	298.7	601.7	1376.4	1810.7	2542.7	2993.4	Net Assets ($mil)

Manager's Investment Style

Manager Robert Stansky looks beyond earnings growth and to such top-line considerations as revenue and unit growth to find growth potential before the rest of the market does. Stansky has a mid- to large-cap bias.

Fund Manager(s)

Robert E. Stansky CFA, since 04-87. Nichols C. 1978 MBA, New York U. 1983

Manager Experience

	Dates Managed	Invest Obj	Std Dev	+/- Index
Robert E. Stansky				
Fidelity Emerging Growth	12/90 - 04/91	AG	14.20	15.09

Performance 12-31-94

	1st Qtr	2nd Qtr	3rd Qtr	4th Qtr	Total
1987	21.69	-2.46	8.90	-23.95	-1.70
1988	7.76	6.70	-0.80	1.76	16.06
1989	10.48	11.00	14.23	1.11	41.64
1990	1.64	10.14	-20.87	16.95	3.59
1991	24.90	-2.66	11.92	9.01	48.33
1992	-3.28	-5.52	2.33	15.44	7.94
1993	3.12	4.85	5.29	2.06	16.19
1994	-3.15	-4.03	5.35	-0.15	-2.22

Bear Market Performance

Decile Rank (5-year period)

Worst								Best

	Worst 3 Mo Period 1985-89	Worst 3 Mo Period 1990-94
Fidelity Growth Company	-35.78	-20.87
+/- S&P 500	-6.20	-7.12
+/- Best Fit Index : SPMid400	-6.97	-3.09

Trailing Returns

	Total Return %	+/- S&P 500	+/- Wil 5000	% Rank All	% Rank Obj	Growth of $10,000
3 Mo	-0.15	-0.14	0.62	26	24	9,985
6 Mo	5.19	0.33	0.57	10	33	10,519
1 Yr	-2.22	-3.54	-2.15	36	53	9,778
3 Yr Avg	7.04	0.77	0.42	27	39	12,263
5 Yr Avg	13.51	4.82	4.69	6	9	18,843
10 Yr Avg	17.02	2.64	3.16	5	6	48,156
15 Yr Avg	---	---	---	---	---	---

Operations

Address and Telephone	82 Devonshire Street Boston, MA 02109 800-544-8888
Advisor	Fidelity Management & Research
Subadvisor	FMR (U.K.)/FMR (Far East)
Distributor	Fidelity Distributors
States Available	All
Report Grade	A
Income Distrib	Paid Annually
* Date of Inception	01-17-83
Fiscal Year End	November

Risk Analysis

Time Period	Load-Adj Return %	Risk % Rank All	Risk % Rank Obj	Morningstar[2] Return	Morningstar Risk	Morningstar Risk-Adj Rating
1 Yr	-5.16					
3 Yr	5.96	83	67	0.70[3]	1.02	★★★
5 Yr	12.82	84	76	2.19[3]	1.03	★★★★
10 Yr	16.67	85	80	1.90	1.09	★★★★★

Average Historical Rating (108 months) 3.7 ★s

[1] 1 = low, 100 = high [2] 1.00 = Equity Avg [3] 1.00 = 90-day T-bill return

Other Measures

			Standard S&P 500	Best Fit SPMid400
Standard Deviation	10.97	Alpha	0.9	-0.1
Mean	7.42	Beta	1.04	1.05
Sharpe Ratio	0.36	R-Squared	56	89

Investment Style

	Stock Portfolio Avg	Relative S&P 500
Price/Earnings Ratio	19.8	1.07
Price/Book Ratio	3.9	1.14
5 Yr Earnings Gr %	16.2	2.92
Return on Assets %	10.8	1.44
Debt % Total Cap	24.1	0.85
Med Mkt Cap ($mil)	6253	0.48

Style
Value Blend Growth
Size Large Med Small

Diversification Value for Portfolio Types

Large Cap: Low	Small Cap: Low	Bond: High	Balanced: Low	Diversified: Low

Expenses & Fees

Sales Fees	3.00% front
	0.00% deferred
	0.00% 12b-1
Management Fee	0.30% flat fee+0.52%G+(-)0.20%P
3-,5-,10-yr Expense Projections	$63, $87, $157
Annual Brokerage Cost	0.20%

Min Initial Purchase	$2500 (Addt'l: $250)
Min IRA Purchase	$500 (Addt'l: $250)
Min Auto Invest Plan	$2500 (Systematic Inv: $100)

Portfolio 11-30-94

Share Chg (05-94) 000	Amount 000	Total Stocks: 333 Total Fixed-Income: 7	Value $000	% Net Assets
-80	1268	General Electric	58342	1.96
182	1469	Compaq Computer	57475	1.93
529	1488	Lowe's	55621	1.87
659	1222	Oracle Systems	50399	1.69
538	874	Motorola	49272	1.65
483	798	Philip Morris	47669	1.60
156	581	Warner-Lambert	44939	1.51
86	604	IBM	42754	1.44
376	898	Sears Roebuck	42426	1.42
123	540	Pfizer	41806	1.40
528	1828	EMC	41128	1.38
237	770	Johnson & Johnson	41077	1.38
544	816	Cabletron Systems	38758	1.30
211	1225	DSC Communications	38272	1.28
192	808	Home Depot	37379	1.25
49	774	Applied Materials	37074	1.24
-373	437	Texas Instruments	33024	1.11
132	442	FNMA	31445	1.06
106	750	Micron Technology	31144	1.05
441	441	Nokia (ADR)	30787	1.03
147	614	Chrysler	29712	1.00
836	1085	Ford Motor	29425	0.99
106	583	FHLMC	29057	0.98
-28	455	Intel	28690	0.96
-188	431	Microsoft	27074	0.91

Composition % 11-30-94

Cash	4.6	Preferreds	0.0
Stocks	95.4	Convertibles	0.0
Bonds	0.0	Other	0.0

Tax Analysis

	Tax-Adj Historical Return %	% Pretax Return
3 Yr Avg	5.11	71.3
5 Yr Avg	11.89	85.2
10 Yr Avg	14.89	78.8
Potential Capital Gain Exposure (% of assets)		3%

Most Similar Funds in MF500

Harbor Capital Appreciation	Strong Fit
IDS New Dimensions	Strong Fit
Fidelity Emerging Growth	Strong Fit

Index Allocation

	% of Stocks
S&P 500	62.9
S&P MidCap 400	14.1
U.S. Small Cap	16.0
Foreign	7.0

Sector Weightings

	% of Stocks	Relative S&P 500
Utilities	3.0	0.24
Energy	3.1	0.31
Financials	11.7	1.10
Industrial Cyclicals	9.6	0.59
Consumer Durables	7.9	1.27
Consumer Staples	3.0	0.24
Services	8.7	1.07
Retail	12.2	2.10
Health	7.7	0.89
Technology	33.0	3.61

MORNINGSTAR 1995 Mutual Fund 500

Fidelity Insured Tax-Free

	Ticker	Load	NAV	Yield	SEC Yield	Assets	Objective
	FMUIX	None	10.69	5.8%	6.21%	318.3	Muni Nat

Fidelity Insured Tax-Free Portfolio seeks income exempt from federal taxes, consistent with preservation of capital.

The fund normally invests at least 80% of its net assets in municipals whose interest is exempt from federal taxes; these obligations are primarily insured either by the issuer or by the fund. It may also invest up to 35% of its assets in uninsured, investment-grade municipal obligations. The fund may invest in unrated obligations and may at times purchase obligations rated below BBB.

Historical Profile

Return	Average
Risk	Above Average
Rating ★★	Below Average

80 70 66 61 57 47 37 27

Investment Style History
Fixed Income
Income Rtn % Rank Obj

Growth of $10,000
- |||| Value of Fund ($000)
- — Value of Index ($000) LB Muni
- ▼ Manager Change
- ▽ Partial Manager Change
- ► Mgr Unknown After
- ◄ Mgr Unknown Before

Manager's Investment Style

Management accentuates the interest-rate sensitivity it gains from its heavy exposure to modest-yielding insured bonds by holding large stakes in zero-coupon and discount bonds. The fund has correspondingly shown significant volatility.

Performance Quartile (Within Objective)

	1983	1984	1985	1986	1987	1988	1989	1990	1991	1992	1993	1994	History
	---	---	10.23	11.33	10.36	10.78	11.05	11.09	11.63	11.72	12.37	10.69	NAV
	---	---	2.36 *	18.43	-2.09	11.19	9.45	7.08	11.58	7.97	13.95	-7.73	Total Return %
	---	---	---	3.18	-4.85	3.31	-5.09	-1.86	-4.43	0.72	4.20	-4.81	+/- LB Aggregate
	---	---	---	-0.88	-3.60	1.03	-1.34	-0.22	-0.57	-0.85	1.67	-2.12	+/- LB Muni
	---	---	0.06	7.68	6.40	7.14	6.94	6.72	6.71	6.23	5.86	5.12	Income Return %
	---	---	2.30	10.75	-8.49	4.05	2.50	0.36	4.87	1.74	8.09	-12.84	Capital Return %
	---	---	---	29	76	52	80	21	79	46	34	84	Total Rtn % Rank All
	---	---	---	45	81	45	51	14	51	64	10	82	Total Rtn % Rank Obj
	---	---	0.01	0.74	0.72	0.71	0.72	0.71	0.70	0.70	0.67	0.63	Income $
	---	---	0.00	0.00	0.01	0.00	0.00	0.00	0.00	0.11	0.28	0.12	Capital Gains $
	---	---	0.60	0.60	0.62	0.70	0.70	0.67	0.65	0.63	0.61	0.59	Expense Ratio %
	---	---	7.89	6.52	6.73	6.64	6.57	6.52	6.23	5.91	5.31	5.34	Income Ratio %
	---	---	0	23	57	35	51	66	62	69	78	71	Turnover Rate %
	---	---	9.5	146.2	145.0	153.7	174.7	197.8	301.3	368.8	446.7	318.3	Net Assets ($mil)

Fund Manager(s)

Guy E. Wickwire, since 10-93. Birthdate: 05-47.
Business/Psychology, Northwestern U. 1969

Manager Experience	Dates Managed	Invest Obj	Std Dev	+/- Index
Guy E. Wickwire				
Fidelity High-Yld T-F	09/81 - 10/93	MN	7.21	-1.01
Fidelity Adv High-Inc A	09/87 - 02/92	MN	2.77	0.18

Performance 12-31-94

	1st Qtr	2nd Qtr	3rd Qtr	4th Qtr	Total
1987	2.16	-6.10	-4.15	6.48	-2.09
1988	2.59	2.57	2.81	2.78	11.19
1989	0.45	6.12	-0.54	3.24	9.45
1990	0.44	2.00	0.35	4.16	7.08
1991	1.84	1.93	3.95	3.40	11.58
1992	-0.15	3.81	2.30	1.82	7.97
1993	4.85	3.37	3.70	1.39	13.95
1994	-7.22	0.48	0.69	-1.71	-7.73

Bear Market Performance

Decile Rank (5-year period)

Worst ──────────── Best

	Worst 3 Mo Period 1985-89	Worst 3 Mo Period 1990-94
Fidelity Insured Tax-Free	---	-8.03
+/- LB Aggregate	---	-3.10
+/- Best Fit Index : LB Muni	---	-2.27

Trailing Returns

	Total Return %	+/- LB Aggregate	+/- LB Muni	% Rank All	% Rank Obj	Growth of $10,000
3 Mo	-1.71	-2.09	-0.27	62	71	9,829
6 Mo	-1.03	-2.02	0.22	74	55	9,897
1 Yr	-7.73	-4.81	-2.12	84	82	9,227
3 Yr Avg	4.32	-0.23	-0.55	63	61	11,352
5 Yr Avg	6.29	-1.34	-0.49	69	46	13,563
10 Yr Avg	---	---	---	---	---	---
15 Yr Avg	---	---	---	---	---	---

Operations

Address and Telephone	82 Devonshire Street Boston, MA 02109 800-544-8888
Advisor	Fidelity Management & Research
Subadvisor	None
Distributor	Fidelity Distributors
States Available	All
Report Grade	A
Income Distrib	Paid Monthly
* Date of Inception	11-13-85
Fiscal Year End	December

Risk Analysis

Time Period	Load-Adj Return %	Risk % Rank[1] All	Obj	Morningstar[2] Return	Morningstar Risk	Morningstar Risk-Adj Rating
1 Yr	-7.73					
3 Yr	4.32	47	81	1.09	1.24	★★★
5 Yr	6.29	34	70	1.02	1.21	★★
10 Yr	---					

Average Historical Rating (74 months) 2.4 ★s

[1] 1 = low, 100 = high [2] 1.00 = Muni Avg [3] 1.00 = 90-day T-bill return

Other Measures

			Standard LB Agg	Best Fit LB Muni
Standard Deviation	6.80	Alpha	-0.3	-0.7
Mean	4.47	Beta	1.28	1.22
Sharpe Ratio	0.14	R-Squared	57	97

Investment Style

Interest-Rate Stance
Avg Effective Maturity 18.4 Yrs

Maturity
Short Intm Long
Quality High Med Low

Quality
Avg Credit Quality AAA

Avg Weighted Coupon 5.23%
Avg Weighted Price 88.15% of Par

Diversification Value for Portfolio Types

Large Cap: Medium	Small Cap: High	Bond: Low	Balanced: Low	Diversified: Medium

Portfolio 06-30-94

Amount 000	Date of Maturity	Total Stocks: 0 Total Fixed-Income: 187	Value $000	% Net Assets
8000	07-15-10	AZ Pima Indl Dev Tucson Elec 7.25%	8540	2.24
10000	11-15-18	MN Minneapolis/St Paul Hsg/Redev 4.75%	7913	2.08
10000	09-01-18	CA State GO 4.75%	7838	2.06
8000	07-01-17	MA Muni Whlse Elec Pwr Sply Sys Rfdg 5%	6598	1.73
7250	07-01-11	CA West/Central Basin Fin 5%	6092	1.60
13475	12-01-08	CO Denver GO Sch Dist #1 0%	5892	1.55
7145	08-01-15	CA Rancho Wtr Dist Fin 4.875%	5850	1.54
5000	06-01-12	CO Adams Sngl Fam Mtg 8.7%	5544	1.46
5500	07-01-11	KY Tpk Econ Dev 5.5%	5234	1.38
43080	12-01-16	IL Chicago Sngl Fam Mtg Cap 0%	5223	1.37
5090	12-15-10	CO Adams GO Sch Dist #12 Thornton 6.2%	5108	1.34
6000	06-01-17	NY Suffolk Wtr Wtrwks 5%	5093	1.34
5960	07-01-17	MA Muni Whls Elec Pwr Sply Sys Ser A 5%	5012	1.32
13500	11-15-10	TX Austin Combined Util Sys 0%	4742	1.25
5600	01-01-12	TN Nashville/Davidson Metro Govt Wtr 0%	4669	1.23
4550	01-01-13	GA Muni Elec Spcl Obl 6.4%	4613	1.21
4250	06-01-08	OK Grand Rvr Dam 5.75%	4202	1.10
3940	07-01-12	NM Mtg Fin Local Hsg 6.85%	4024	1.06
4000	11-01-11	NC Muni Pwr #1 Catawba Elec 6%	3970	1.04
4000	02-15-21	CO Hlth Fac PSL Sys 6.25%	3955	1.04

Credit Analysis % of Bonds 10-31-94

US Govt	0	BB	0
AAA	84	B	0
AA	7	Below B	0
A	4	NR/NA	5
BBB	0		

Composition % of Assets 10-31-94

Cash	3.6	Preferreds	0.0
Stocks	0.0	Convertibles	0.0
Bonds	96.4	Other	0.0

Tax Analysis

	Tax-Adj Historical Return %	% Pretax Return
3 Yr Avg	3.91	90.2
5 Yr Avg	6.04	95.6
10 Yr Avg	---	---
Potential Capital Gain Exposure (% of assets)		-8%

Most Similar Funds in MF500

Lord Abbett T/F Income Natl	Strong Fit
Fidelity Municipal Bond	Strong Fit
Safeco Municipal Bond	Strong Fit

Min Initial Purchase $2500 (Addt'l: $250)
Min IRA Purchase N/A
Min Auto Invest Plan $2500 (Systematic Inv: $100)

Expenses & Fees

Sales Fees	0.00% front
	0.00% deferred
	0.00% 12b-1
Management Fee	0.25% flat fee+0.37%G
3-,5-,10-yr Expense Projections	$20, $34, $76

Coupon Range % Bonds Rel Obj

0%	10.2	4.07
0% to 6.8%	66.5	1.10
6.8% to 7.5%	9.9	0.64
7.5% to 8.3%	3.6	0.40
More than 8.3%	3.2	0.36
Not applicable	6.6	1.70

Sector Weightings % Bonds Rel Obj

General Obl	14.98	0.71
Utilities	13.95	1.12
Health	24.77	1.88
Water/Waste	10.48	1.65
Housing	8.88	1.21
Education	3.92	0.61
Transportation	5.11	0.50
COP/Lease	4.34	1.36
Private	7.08	0.61
Misc Revenue	5.53	1.11
Demand	0.97	0.39

Top 5 States % of Bonds

CA	14.92	IL	7.12
MA	7.25	TX	4.83
CO	7.13		

Fidelity Intermediate Bond

	Ticker	Load	NAV	Yield	SEC Yield	Assets	Objective
	FTHRX	None	9.83	6.5%	6.78%	2127.4	Corp Hi Qlty

Fidelity Intermediate Bond Fund seeks current income.
The fund invests in high-quality corporate obligations, U.S. government securities, obligations of major U.S. banks, prime commercial paper, and other instruments that the fund's advisor believes to be of comparable quality. The fund's weighted maturity is expected to be 10 years or less.
Prior to Oct. 6, 1987, the fund was named Fidelity Thrift Fund.

Historical Profile

Return	Above Average
Risk	Below Average
Rating	★★★★ Above Average

| | 1 | 43 | 30 | 45 | 45 | 21 | 7 | 22 |

Investment Style History
Fixed Income
Income Rtn % Rank Obj

Growth of $10,000

|||| Value of Fund ($000)
— Value of Index ($000) LB Govt
▼ Manager Change
▽ Partial Manager Change
► Mgr Unknown After
◄ Mgr Unknown Before

Manager's Investment Style

Manager Michael Gray is flexible, within the fund's interest-rate constraints (as an intermediate fund, maturity is limited to 10 years or less). He has tended to keep the fund slightly longer than the Lehman Brothers Intermediate Bond Index, though he will scale back as necessary, such as he did in 1994 and going forward. Typically, management also places between 20% and 30% of its assets into foreign bonds. Further, since shareholders voted to allow the fund to hold bonds rated BBB, Gray has built up a stake there.

Fund Manager(s)

Michael S. Gray, since 09-87. Birthdate: 11-56.
BA, Union C. 1978 MBA, Wharton 1982

Manager Experience	Dates Managed	Invest Obj	Std Dev	+/- Index
Michael S. Gray				
Fidelity Adv Govt Inv A	01/87 - 01/92	GM	4.30	-1.82

Performance Quartile
(Within Objective)

	1983	1984	1985	1986	1987	1988	1989	1990	1991	1992	1993	1994	History
	9.72	9.83	11.03	11.55	10.04	9.87	10.10	10.00	10.62	10.41	10.78	9.83	NAV
	8.46	13.59	20.78	13.08	2.00	7.22	11.82	7.54	14.50	6.08	11.96	-2.01	Total Return %
	0.09	-1.57	-1.35	-2.17	-0.75	-0.66	-2.72	-1.40	-1.50	-1.17	2.21	0.91	+/- LB Aggregate
	-0.81	-3.04	-3.29	-3.46	-0.55	-2.01	-2.16	0.39	-4.01	-2.62	-0.21	1.92	+/- LB Corporate
	9.88	12.46	8.57	6.26	14.40	8.91	9.49	8.53	8.30	7.50	7.51	6.05	Income Return %
	-1.42	1.13	12.21	6.82	-12.39	-1.69	2.33	-0.99	6.20	-1.42	4.45	-8.06	Capital Return %
	87	11	68	67	43	79	59	17	60	68	51	34	Total Rtn % Rank All
	52	34	40	50	52	47	45	64	50	62	11	39	Total Rtn % Rank Obj
	0.95	1.10	0.74	0.66	1.61	0.87	0.89	0.82	0.77	0.77	0.75	0.64	Income $
	0.00	0.00	0.00	0.22	0.10	0.00	0.00	0.00	0.00	0.06	0.09	0.09	Capital Gains $
	0.69	0.73	0.79	0.75	0.86	0.87	0.62	0.72	0.66	0.63	0.61	0.64	Expense Ratio %
	10.43	11.62	10.73	9.27	9.17	8.76	9.35	8.57	8.05	7.45	7.44	6.88	Income Ratio %
	238	80	68	101	67	59	101	82	73	80	51	81	Turnover Rate %
	113.1	149.5	243.4	368.0	367.3	499.7	626.6	806.7	1172.1	1454.6	1840.2	2127.4	Net Assets ($mil)

Performance 12-31-94

	1st Qtr	2nd Qtr	3rd Qtr	4th Qtr	Total
1987	1.40	-1.72	-1.95	4.39	2.00
1988	3.48	0.80	1.80	0.98	7.22
1989	1.34	5.81	1.13	3.11	11.82
1990	-0.71	2.92	1.27	3.92	7.54
1991	2.25	1.40	5.07	5.10	14.50
1992	-1.43	3.62	3.94	-0.07	6.08
1993	4.88	2.69	3.50	0.45	11.96
1994	-2.64	-0.49	0.66	0.48	-2.01

Bear Market Performance

Decile Rank (5-year period)

| | | Worst | | | Best |

	Worst 3 Mo Period 1985-89	Worst 3 Mo Period 1990-94
Fidelity Intermediate Bond	-3.44	-4.19
+/- LB Aggregate	0.12	0.74
+/- Best Fit Index : LB Govt	0.02	0.89

Trailing Returns

	Total Return %	+/- LB Aggregate	+/- LB Corporate	% Rank All	% Rank Obj	Growth of $10,000
3 Mo	0.48	0.10	0.04	12	28	10,048
6 Mo	1.14	0.15	-0.03	35	23	10,114
1 Yr	-2.01	0.91	1.92	34	39	9,799
3 Yr Avg	5.19	0.64	-0.23	44	8	11,638
5 Yr Avg	7.46	-0.16	-0.80	41	17	14,330
10 Yr Avg	9.12	-0.83	-1.51	70	44	23,933
15 Yr Avg	10.67	-0.14	-0.66	70	14	45,749

Risk Analysis

Time Period	Load-Adj Return %	Risk % Rank All	Risk % Rank Obj	Morningstar[2] Return	Morningstar Risk	Morningstar Risk-Adj Rating
1 Yr	-2.01					
3 Yr	5.19	12	39	0.47[3]	0.82	★★★★★
5 Yr	7.46	12	39	0.67[3]	0.80	★★★★
10 Yr	9.12	9	22	0.86[3]	0.87	★★★★
Average Historical Rating (109 months)					4.4	★s

[1] 1 = low, 100 = high   [2] 1.00 = Taxable Avg   [3] 1.00 = 90-day T-bill return

Other Measures

			Standard LB Agg	Best Fit LB Govt
Standard Deviation	3.79	Alpha	0.7	0.6
Mean	5.14	Beta	0.91	0.85
Sharpe Ratio	0.43	R-Squared	91	95

Investment Style

Interest-Rate Stance

Avg Effective Duration	4.3 Yrs
Avg Effective Maturity	6.5 Yrs

Quality

Avg Credit Quality	AA
Avg Weighted Coupon	7.75%
Avg Weighted Price	94.49% of Par

Maturity: Short Intm Long
Quality: High Med Low

Diversification Value for Portfolio Types

●	●	○	◐	●
Large Cap: High	Small Cap: High	Bond: None	Balanced: Medium	Diversified: High

Operations

Address and Telephone	82 Devonshire Street Boston, MA 02109 800-544-8888
Advisor	Fidelity Management & Research
Subadvisor	FMR (U.K.)/FMR (Far East)
Distributor	Fidelity Distributors
States Available	All
Report Grade	A
Income Distrib	Paid Monthly
Date of Inception	05-23-75
Fiscal Year End	April

Min Initial Purchase	$2500 (Addt'l: $250)
Min IRA Purchase	$500 (Addt'l: $250)
Min Auto Invest Plan	$2500 (Systematic Inv: $100)

Expenses & Fees

Sales Fees	0.00% front
	0.00% deferred
	0.00% 12b-1
Management Fee	0.15% flat fee+0.37%G
3-,5-,10-yr Expense Projections	$20, $36, $80

Portfolio 10-31-94

Amount 000	Date of Maturity	Total Stocks: 0 Total Fixed-Income: 153	Value $000	% Net Assets
156280	08-15-19	US Treasury Bond 8.125%	156280	7.64
69300	05-15-97	US Treasury Note 6.5%	68477	3.35
59200	03-31-98	US Treasury Note 5.125%	55454	2.71
65000	02-15-98	US Treasury Note 0%	51414	2.51
50070	11-15-96	US Treasury Note 7.25%	50454	2.46
42900	02-15-19	US Treasury Bond 8.875%	46278	2.26
44000	04-15-96	US Treasury Note 9.375%	45684	2.23
54000	11-01-95	Govt of Canada 8.25%	40404	1.97
40500	02-15-21	US Treasury Bond 7.875%	39430	1.93
23812	09-15-23	GNMA 8%	22897	1.12
105000	04-25-03	Govt of France 8.5%	20723	1.01
30000	09-22-97	Republic of Germany 8%	20587	1.01
20500	05-15-21	US Treasury Bond 8.125%	20526	1.00
20000	02-25-97	GMAC 7.75%	20059	0.98
20000	01-15-22	Hydro-Quebec 8.4%	18706	0.91
17000	02-15-99	US Treasury Note 8.875%	17898	0.87
17500	09-15-02	Province of Manitoba 6.875%	16135	0.79
1500	03-20-03	Intl Bank Reconstr/Dev 4.5%	15255	0.75
14703	10-15-18	GNMA 9%	15011	0.73
15000	11-15-20	Province of Manitoba 8.8%	14910	0.73
15000	05-01-99	Soc Natl Elf Aquitane 7.75%	14896	0.73
14110	06-01-04	RailCar Trust 7.75%	13987	0.68
85000	05-15-03	Kingdom of Denmark 8%	13583	0.66
90000	12-15-04	Kingdom of Denmark 7%	13312	0.65
12500	08-31-99	US Treasury Note 6.875%	12201	0.60

Composition % 11-30-94			
Cash	32.4	Preferreds	0.0
Stocks	0.0	Convertibles	0.0
Bonds	76.3	Other	-8.7

Tax Analysis	Tax-Adj Historical Return %	% Pretax Return
3 Yr Avg	2.40	44.9
5 Yr Avg	4.73	60.1
10 Yr Avg	5.81	54.4

Potential Capital Gain Exposure (% of assets) -4%

Most Similar Funds in MF500

Vanguard Bond Indx Total Bd	Strong Fit
Harbor Bond	Strong Fit
Portico Bond Immdex Ret	Strong Fit

Coupon Range	% of Bonds	Rel Obj
0%	4.9	2.13
0% to 8.5%	65.7	0.94
8.5% to 9.5%	20.9	1.60
9.5% to 11%	4.2	0.92
More than 11%	4.1	1.75
Not applicable	0.2	0.02

Credit Analysis 11-30-94
% of Bonds

US Govt	46	BB	0
AAA	0	B	0
AA	7	Below B	0
A	9	NR/NA	28
BBB	11		

Investment Style History
Fixed Income
Income Rtn % Rank Obj

MORNINGSTAR 1995 Mutual Fund 500

Fidelity Low-Priced Stock

	Ticker	Load	NAV	Yield	SEC Yield	Assets	Objective
	FLPSX	3.00%	16.00	0.5%	N/A	2354.5	Small Company

Fidelity Low-Priced Stock Fund seeks capital appreciation; current income is not emphasized.

The fund normally invests at least 65% of its assets in equity securities that are trading at $25 per share or less. It may hold securities that have appreciated beyond the low-priced limit and still satisfy the 65% requirement. The low-priced stocks purchased are considered to be undervalued; these purchases are made on the basis of a contrarian approach. Issuers of low-priced securities often have market capitalizations under $100 million, and some have a negative net worth.

Manager's Investment Style

Management favors low-priced stocks of companies that have strong current earnings, new products, or turnaround potential. Foreign positions can often be substantial, consuming more than 20% of invested assets. Dealing with a massive asset base--the fund is the largest in the small-company objective--management has often plied the mid- and large-cap fields; many of the fund's biggest holdings are in larger-cap issues. In an attempt to control cash flows, Fidelity has, on occasion, closed this fund's doors. Nevertheless, the fund has sported a 20% or higher cash cushion during much of the past few years.

Fund Manager(s)

Joel C. Tillinghast CFA(1987), since 12-89.
Birthdate: 06-58. BA, Wesleyan U. 1980 MBA, Northwestern U. 1983

Manager Experience

	Dates Managed	Invest Obj	Std Dev	+/- Index

Not available.

Historical Profile

Return	High
Risk	Low
Rating	★★★★★ Highest

Historical data

	1983	1984	1985	1986	1987	1988	1989	1990	1991	1992	1993	1994	History
								79%	81%	71%	81%	80%	Average % Stocks Held in Portfolio
NAV	---	---	---	---	---	---	9.89	9.47	13.05	15.96	17.30	16.00	NAV
	---	---	---	---	---	---	-1.10 *	-0.08	46.26	28.95	20.21	4.81	Total Return %
	---	---	---	---	---	---	-2.67 *	3.04	15.78	21.33	10.16	3.49	+/- S&P 500
	---	---	---	---	---	---	---	13.48	2.81	17.20	5.68	7.46	+/- Wilshire 4500
	---	---	---	---	---	---	0.00	1.50	1.31	0.70	0.97	0.56	Income Return %
	---	---	---	---	---	---	-1.10	-1.58	44.95	28.25	19.24	4.25	Capital Return %
	---	---	---	---	---	---	---	56	9	1	17	4	Total Rtn % Rank All
	---	---	---	---	---	---	---	19	58	6	32	14	Total Rtn % Rank Obj
	---	---	---	---	---	---	0.00	0.14	0.15	0.10	0.16	0.09	Income $
	---	---	---	---	---	---	0.00	0.26	0.60	0.69	1.62	2.05	Capital Gains $
	---	---	---	---	---	---	---	1.92	1.36	1.20	1.12	1.13	Expense Ratio %
	---	---	---	---	---	---	---	3.77	2.14	1.27	1.00	0.51	Income Ratio %
	---	---	---	---	---	---	---	126	84	82	47	54	Turnover Rate %
	---	---	---	---	---	---	---	88.8	375.3	2240.4	2060.1	2354.5	Net Assets ($mil)

Investment Style History Equity

Growth of $10,000
IIII Value of Fund ($000)
— Value of Index ($000) Russ 2000
▼ Manager Change
▽ Partial Manager Change
► Mgr Unknown After
◄ Mgr Unknown Before

Performance Quartile (Within Objective)

Performance 12-31-94

	1st Qtr	2nd Qtr	3rd Qtr	4th Qtr	Total
1987	---	---	---	---	---
1988	---	---	---	---	---
1989	---	---	---	---	-1.10 *
1990	2.33	6.72	-14.39	6.88	-0.08
1991	26.82	-0.92	9.52	6.27	46.26
1992	11.80	-0.82	3.81	12.03	28.95
1993	4.76	1.50	5.74	6.92	20.21
1994	0.52	-0.92	6.60	-1.28	4.81

Bear Market Performance

Decile Rank (5-year period)

	Worst 3 Mo Period 1985-89	Worst 3 Mo Period 1990-94
Fidelity Low-Priced Stock	---	-15.37
+/- S&P 500	---	-1.53
+/- Best Fit Index : Russ 2000	---	10.52

Trailing Returns

	Total Return %	+/- S&P 500	+/- Wil 4500	% Rank All	% Rank Obj	Growth of $10,000
3 Mo	-1.28	-1.26	1.22	51	56	9,872
6 Mo	5.23	0.37	1.04	10	51	10,523
1 Yr	4.81	3.49	7.46	4	14	10,481
3 Yr Avg	17.56	11.29	9.95	2	7	16,247
5 Yr Avg	18.88	10.19	9.79	2	7	23,744
10 Yr Avg	---	---	---	---	---	---
15 Yr Avg	---	---	---	---	---	---

Operations

Address and Telephone	82 Devonshire Street Boston, MA 02109 800-544-8888
Advisor	Fidelity Management & Research
Subadvisor	FMR (U.K.)/FMR (Far East)
Distributor	Fidelity Distributors
States Available	All
Report Grade	A
Income Distrib	Paid Annually
* Date of Inception	12-27-89
Fiscal Year End	July

Risk Analysis

Time Period	Load-Adj Return %	Risk % Rank [1] All	Risk % Rank [1] Obj	Morningstar [2] Return	Morningstar Risk	Morningstar Risk-Adj Rating
1 Yr	1.66					
3 Yr	16.37	44	5	4.17 [3]	0.51	★★★★★
5 Yr	18.16	56	3	4.02 [3]	0.63	★★★★★
10 Yr						

Average Historical Rating (25 months) 5.0 ★s

[1] 1 = low, 100 = high [2] 1.00 = Equity Avg [3] 1.00 = 90-day T-bill return

Other Measures

			Standard S&P 500	Best Fit Russ 2000
Standard Deviation	9.81	Alpha	11.7	7.5
Mean	16.76	Beta	0.74	0.74
Sharpe Ratio	1.35	R-Squared	36	80

Investment Style

	Stock Portfolio Avg	Relative S&P 500
Price/Earnings Ratio	14.0	0.76
Price/Book Ratio	1.9	0.55
5 Yr Earnings Gr %	11.9#	2.14
Return on Assets %	7.9	1.06
Debt % Total Cap	26.8	0.95
Med Mkt Cap ($mil)	130	0.01

figure is based on 50% or less of stocks

Diversification Value for Portfolio Types

Large Cap: Medium Small Cap: Low Bond: High Balanced: Medium Diversified: Medium

Expenses & Fees

Sales Fees	3.00% front
	0.00% deferred
	0.00% 12b-1
Management Fee	0.35% flat fee+0.52%G+(-)0.20%P
3-,5-,10-yr Expense Projections	$65, $90, $163
Annual Brokerage Cost	0.15%

Min Initial Purchase	$2500 (Addt'l: $250)
Min IRA Purchase	$500 (Addt'l: $250)
Min Auto Invest Plan	$2500 (Systematic Inv: $100)

Portfolio 07-31-94

Share Chg (01-94) 000	Amount 000	Total Stocks: 728 / Total Fixed-Income: 17	Value $000	% Net Assets
-70	1117	Universal Health Services B	31000	1.43
-3045	305	Welsh Water	29221	1.35
16	2600	Northumbrian Water Group	25372	1.17
25	577	Exar	17587	0.81
-338	1460	National Health Lab Hldgs	16607	0.77
-3	898	Libbey	15034	0.69
-550	5400	Industrias Penoles Cl A2	14717	0.68
187	1121	Castle Energy	14159	0.65
-1277	21400	Evered Bardon	13546	0.63
0	400	Astoria Financial	13450	0.62
0	671	Devon Group	13412	0.62
1724	18446	Brierley Investments	13331	0.62
100	525	GP Financial	12403	0.57
-682	495	DeBeers Consol Mines (ADR)	11763	0.54
377	377	Rayonier	11643	0.54
0	2000	Northern Ireland Electric	11086	0.51
-8	518	Quixote	10886	0.50
113	594	First Federal Svgs Bk (PR)	10402	0.48
291	404	Cytec Industries	10205	0.47
316	316	Syds-Sonderjylland Holding	9884	0.46
-2700	1800	Seeboard	9783	0.45
-302	348	Seagate Technology	9266	0.43
207	566	Stewart Information Services	9260	0.43
-83	316	BMC Industries	8992	0.42
0	1174	Giant Industries	8952	0.41

Composition % 12-31-94

Cash	26.4	Preferreds	0.0
Stocks	73.6	Convertibles	0.0
Bonds	0.0	Other	0.0

Tax Analysis

	Tax-Adj Historical Return %	% Pretax Return
3 Yr Avg	14.60	80.8
5 Yr Avg	16.39	82.6
10 Yr Avg	---	---
Potential Capital Gain Exposure (% of assets)		8%

Most Similar Funds in MF500

Skyline Special Equities	Fair Fit
Strong Common Stock	Fair Fit
Babson Enterprise	Fair Fit

Index Allocation

	% of Stocks
S&P 500	1.7
S&P MidCap 400	5.1
U.S. Small Cap	71.3
Foreign	22.0

Sector Weightings

	% of Stocks	Relative S&P 500
Utilities	6.0	0.48
Energy	8.6	0.85
Financials	15.7	1.49
Industrial Cyclicals	22.6	1.38
Consumer Durables	11.9	1.92
Consumer Staples	0.9	0.07
Services	11.1	1.36
Retail	4.2	0.71
Health	5.5	0.63
Technology	13.6	1.49

Fidelity Magellan

	Ticker	Load	NAV	Yield	SEC Yield	Assets	Objective
	FMAGX	3.00%	66.80	0.2%	N/A	36441.5	Growth

Fidelity Magellan Fund seeks capital appreciation.
The fund invests primarily in common stocks and convertible securities, with up to 20% of its assets invested in debt securities of all types and qualities. It features domestic corporations operating primarily in the United States, domestic corporations that have significant activities and interests outside the U.S., and foreign companies. No limitations are placed on total foreign investment, but no more than 40% of assets will be invested in companies operating exclusively in one foreign country.
Fund shares were not publicly sold until 1981.

Investment Style History
Equity

Average % Stocks Held in Portfolio

Manager's Investment Style

Legendary Peter Lynch left the fund in 1990; after a brief stint under Morris Smith, the fund landed in the hands of Jeff Vinik in 1992. Vinik maintains the flexibility and against-the-grain approach that helped make Magellan the largest mutual fund around. He tempers higher-priced, earnings-momentum plays with cheap, underfollowed names--and he isn't afraid to move in and out of concentrated sector bets rather rapidly. Despite the fund's massive size, Vinik refuses to limit himself to large-cap stocks; the fund often falls in the mid-cap range of the style box.

Fund Manager(s)

Jeffrey N. Vinik CFA, since 07-92. Birthdate: 03-59. BS, Duke U. 1981 MBA, Harvard 1985

Manager Experience	Dates Managed	Invest Obj	Std Dev	+/- Index
Jeffrey N. Vinik				
Fidelity Growth & Income	10/90 - 07/92	GI	14.76	7.53
Fidelity Contrafund	01/89 - 10/90	G	15.28	9.55

Historical Profile
Return — High
Risk — Average
Rating — ★★★★★
 — Highest

Growth of $10,000
|||| Value of Fund ($000)
— Value of Index ($000) SPMid400
▼ Manager Change
▽ Partial Manager Change
► Mgr Unknown After
◄ Mgr Unknown Before

Performance Quartile (Within Objective)

| 97% | 95% | 92% | 90% | 97% | 81% | 84% | 93% | |

1983	1984	1985	1986	1987	1988	1989	1990	1991	1992	1993	1994	History
37.33	33.69	45.21	48.69	40.10	48.32	59.85	53.93	68.61	63.01	70.85	66.80	NAV
38.59	2.03	43.11	23.74	1.00	22.77	34.58	-4.51	41.03	7.02	24.66	-1.81	Total Return %
16.12	-4.24	11.37	5.07	-4.26	6.16	2.90	-1.39	10.54	-0.60	14.60	-3.13	+/- S&P 500
15.13	-1.02	10.55	7.65	-1.36	4.82	5.41	1.67	6.82	-1.96	13.38	-1.74	+/- Wilshire 5000
0.73	1.18	1.94	0.90	1.65	2.27	2.22	1.51	2.18	2.00	1.12	0.19	Income Return %
37.86	0.85	41.17	22.85	-0.65	20.50	32.36	-6.02	38.85	5.01	23.54	-2.00	Capital Return %
4	60	5	11	51	9	7	69	13	57	11	32	Total Rtn % Rank All
4	30	2	6	62	14	19	50	31	58	7	50	Total Rtn % Rank Obj
0.26	0.37	0.65	0.46	0.72	0.90	1.24	0.83	1.30	1.25	0.75	0.13	Income $
1.88	3.69	1.78	6.84	9.02	0.90	3.82	2.42	5.43	8.82	6.50	2.64	Capital Gains $
0.85	1.04	1.12	1.08	1.08	1.14	1.08	1.03	1.06	1.05	1.00	0.99	Expense Ratio %
2.56	1.47	2.79	1.95	1.18	1.33	2.13	2.54	2.47	1.57	2.11	1.07	Income Ratio %
120	85	126	96	96	101	87	82	135	172	155	132	Turnover Rate %
1606.9	1954.4	4136.0	7405.5	7800.1	8971.1	12699.6	12325.7	19257.1	22268.9	31705.1	36441.5	Net Assets ($mil)

Performance 12-31-94

	1st Qtr	2nd Qtr	3rd Qtr	4th Qtr	Total
1987	22.92	2.57	6.42	-24.73	1.00
1988	9.98	8.46	0.23	2.69	22.77
1989	9.52	9.61	13.16	-0.93	34.58
1990	-2.09	6.61	-16.48	9.53	-4.51
1991	20.23	-0.14	9.06	7.70	41.03
1992	-0.70	0.65	1.73	5.25	7.02
1993	8.62	6.42	8.21	-0.34	24.66
1994	-1.59	-4.49	5.43	-0.90	-1.81

Bear Market Performance

Decile Rank (5-year period)

Worst — Best

	Worst 3 Mo Period 1985-89	Worst 3 Mo Period 1990-94
Fidelity Magellan	-33.09	-16.57
+/- S&P 500	-3.51	-2.72
+/- Best Fit Index : SPMid400	-4.29	1.85

Trailing Returns

	Total Return %	+/- S&P 500	+/- Wil 5000	% Rank All	% Rank Obj	Growth of $10,000
3 Mo	-0.90	-0.89	-0.14	42	40	9,910
6 Mo	4.47	-0.39	-0.15	13	42	10,447
1 Yr	-1.81	-3.13	-1.74	32	50	9,819
3 Yr Avg	9.41	3.15	2.80	15	22	13,099
5 Yr Avg	12.02	3.33	3.20	9	14	17,640
10 Yr Avg	17.95	3.57	4.09	3	4	52,130
15 Yr Avg	22.73	8.25	8.75	1	1	215,931

Risk Analysis

Time Period	Load-Adj Return %	Risk % Rank[1] All	Risk % Rank[1] Obj	Morningstar[2] Return	Morningstar Risk	Morningstar Risk-Adj Rating
1 Yr	-4.76					
3 Yr	8.31	68	31	1.43[3]	0.76	★★★★
5 Yr	11.34	71	31	1.74[3]	0.85	★★★★
10 Yr	17.59	63	29	2.15	0.87	★★★★★

Average Historical Rating (109 months)   5.0 ★s

[1] 1 = low, 100 = high [2] 1.00 = Equity Avg [3] 1.00 = 90-day T-bill return

Other Measures

	Standard S&P 500	Best Fit SPMid400
Standard Deviation	9.35	Alpha 3.1 / 2.8
Mean	9.47	Beta 1.01 / 0.82
Sharpe Ratio	0.64	R-Squared 73 / 74

Investment Style

	Stock Portfolio Avg	Relative S&P 500
Price/Earnings Ratio	20.4	1.10
Price/Book Ratio	3.7	1.09
5 Yr Earnings Gr %	16.7	3.01
Return on Assets %	9.0	1.21
Debt % Total Cap	26.4	0.93
Med Mkt Cap ($mil)	2604	0.20

Style
Value Blend Growth
Size: Large Med Small

Diversification Value for Portfolio Types

| Large Cap: Low | Small Cap: Low | Bond: Medium | Balanced: Low | Diversified: Low |

Portfolio 09-30-94

Total Stocks: 506
Total Fixed-Income: 91

Share Chg (03-94) 000	Amount 000		Value $000	% Net Assets
9152	16251	Motorola	857224	2.37
12590	15298	Oracle Systems	657823	1.82
2882	9091	IBM	631845	1.75
3536	12808	Lowe's	494690	1.37
-4759	7962	Intel	489681	1.35
719	10599	Columbia/HCA Healthcare	461043	1.27
1519	5686	FNMA	447804	1.24
3279	7053	Caterpillar	381744	1.06
94	5441	CSX	372722	1.03
111	4993	Texas Instruments	341417	0.94
2227	7105	Sears Roebuck	341035	0.94
	2797	Nokia Pfd	324909	0.90
85	3711	Hewlett-Packard	324249	0.90
7416	9190	Merrill Lynch	318200	0.88
3480	6597	Applied Materials	308428	0.85
5589	5589	AT & T	301779	0.83
2885	14299	EMC	287767	0.80
5655	7529	Dean Witter Discover	283295	0.78
1155	9349	Advanced Micro Devices	278130	0.77
7673	9720	General Instrument	277023	0.77
8793	9629	Silicon Graphics	247947	0.69
1446	3460	Nucor	240882	0.67
5294	5294	Computer Associates Intl	235561	0.65
3220	4429	United HealthCare	234710	0.65
4770	6653	Micron Technology	229515	0.63

Composition % 11-30-94

Cash	3.3	Preferreds	0.0
Stocks	96.1	Convertibles	0.0
Bonds	0.6	Other	0.0

Tax Analysis

	Tax-Adj Historical Return %	% Pretax Return
3 Yr Avg	6.51	67.2
5 Yr Avg	9.23	72.6
10 Yr Avg	14.88	71.3
Potential Capital Gain Exposure (% of assets)		9%

Most Similar Funds in MF500

Fidelity	Fair Fit
Fidelity Contrafund	Fair Fit
Fidelity Stock Selector	Fair Fit

Index Allocation

	% of Stocks
S&P 500	53.4
S&P MidCap 400	20.1
U.S. Small Cap	20.6
Foreign	6.6

Sector Weightings

	% of Stocks	Relative S&P 500
Utilities	1.8	0.14
Energy	4.8	0.47
Financials	10.4	0.98
Industrial Cyclicals	18.2	1.11
Consumer Durables	10.2	1.64
Consumer Staples	0.7	0.05
Services	10.6	1.30
Retail	6.5	1.12
Health	4.9	0.56
Technology	32.1	3.50

Operations

Address and Telephone	82 Devonshire Street Boston, MA 02109 800-544-8888
Advisor	Fidelity Management & Research
Subadvisor	FMR (U.K.)/FMR (Far East)
Distributor	Fidelity Distributors
States Available	All
Report Grade	A
Income Distrib	Paid Semiannually
Date of Inception	05-02-63
Fiscal Year End	March

Min Initial Purchase	$2500 (Addt'l: $250)
Min IRA Purchase	$500 (Addt'l: $250)
Min Auto Invest Plan	$2500 (Systematic Inv: $100)

Expenses & Fees

Sales Fees	3.00% front
	0.00% deferred
	0.00% 12b-1
Management Fee	0.30% flat fee+0.52%G+(-)0.20%P
3-,5-,10-yr Expense Projections	$61, $83, $148
Annual Brokerage Cost	0.24%

MORNINGSTAR 1995 Mutual Fund 500

Fidelity Municipal Bond

	Ticker	Load	NAV	Yield	SEC Yield	Assets	Objective
	FMBDX	None	7.36	5.6%	6.14%	1005.6	Muni Nat

Fidelity Municipal Bond Portfolio seeks interest income exempt from federal income tax, consistent with preservation of capital.

The fund invests primarily in municipal bonds judged by the advisor to be of at least upper-medium quality (A or higher), but may invest up to one third of its assets in bonds rated BBB. Although the fund has no restriction on portfolio maturity, the average maturity is currently expected to be greater than 20 years.

Historical Profile

Return	Average
Risk	Above Average
Rating ★★	Below Average

Investment Style History
Fixed Income
Income Rtn % Rank Obj

68 46 40 45 48 31 29 43

Growth of $10,000

IIII Value of Fund ($000)
— Value of Index ($000)
      LB Muni
▼ Manager Change
▽ Partial Manager Change
► Mgr Unknown After
◄ Mgr Unknown Before

Performance Quartile
(Within Objective)

1983	1984	1985	1986	1987	1988	1989	1990	1991	1992	1993	1994	History
6.72	6.70	7.42	8.28	7.60	7.95	8.13	8.13	8.47	8.50	8.69	7.36	NAV
9.24	9.02	20.09	19.54	-1.56	12.30	9.56	6.91	11.91	9.04	13.32	-9.08	Total Return %
0.87	-6.14	-2.04	4.29	-4.32	4.42	-4.98	-2.04	-4.09	1.80	3.57	-6.16	+/- LB Aggregate
1.19	-1.54	0.07	0.22	-3.06	2.14	-1.22	-0.39	-0.23	0.23	1.05	-3.48	+/- LB Muni
9.09	9.31	9.34	7.95	6.65	7.70	7.30	6.91	6.83	6.51	6.03	4.81	Income Return %
0.15	-0.30	10.75	11.59	-8.21	4.61	2.26	0.00	5.09	2.53	7.30	-13.89	Capital Return %
84	31	72	22	72	43	79	23	76	32	38	91	Total Rtn % Rank All
54	51	46	25	71	27	47	22	38	29	18	94	Total Rtn % Rank Obj
0.60	0.59	0.58	0.55	0.55	0.56	0.56	0.54	0.53	0.53	0.50	0.42	Income $
0.00	0.00	0.00	0.00	0.00	0.00	0.00	0.00	0.07	0.18	0.41	0.14	Capital Gains $
0.59	0.53	0.46	0.51	0.57	0.51	0.50	0.50	0.50	0.49	0.49	0.54	Expense Ratio %
8.74	8.98	8.06	6.90	7.03	7.11	6.90	6.71	6.35	6.11	5.51	5.54	Income Ratio %
52	93	145	72	72	46	64	49	33	53	74	91	Turnover Rate %
699.4	738.0	902.0	1154.0	909.4	980.2	1050.2	1066.9	1159.5	1186.3	1258.1	1005.6	Net Assets ($mil)

Manager's Investment Style

Manager Gary Swayze maintains a relatively standard municipal-bond portfolio, focusing primarily on straightforward essential-services bonds. He does, however, make bets on interest rates, typically erring toward a long duration (and thus higher interest-rate sensitivity). He will also own bonds from higher-paying states, such as New York, and has recently decided to take greater advantage of the prospectus' allowance of a one third stake in bonds with BBB ratings.

Fund Manager(s)

Gary Swayze, since 08-85. U. of Missouri-Kansas City 1974

Manager Experience

	Dates Managed	Invest Obj	Std Dev	+/- Index
Gary Swayze				
Fidelity NY T-F Hi-Yld	01/85 - 10/93	MY	5.85	-1.52
Fidelity NY T-F Insured	10/85 - 09/92	MY	6.41	-2.09

Performance 12-31-94

	1st Qtr	2nd Qtr	3rd Qtr	4th Qtr	Total
1987	2.45	-5.27	-3.56	5.17	-1.56
1988	3.51	2.59	2.97	2.70	12.30
1989	0.38	6.39	-0.36	2.96	9.56
1990	0.44	2.45	0.18	3.70	6.91
1991	1.87	2.22	3.83	3.51	11.91
1992	0.14	4.09	2.20	2.35	9.04
1993	4.18	3.61	3.67	1.28	13.32
1994	-6.81	0.67	0.15	-3.23	-9.08

Bear Market Performance

Decile Rank (5-year period)

Worst _____ Best

	Worst 3 Mo Period 1985-89	Worst 3 Mo Period 1990-94
Fidelity Municipal Bond	-7.30	-7.53
+/- LB Aggregate	-3.75	-2.60
+/- Best Fit Index : LB Muni	-0.81	-1.77

Trailing Returns

	Total Return %	+/- LB Aggregate	+/- LB Muni	% Rank All	Obj	Growth of $10,000
3 Mo	-3.23	-3.61	-1.79	85	99	9,677
6 Mo	-3.08	-4.07	-1.83	95	99	9,692
1 Yr	-9.08	-6.16	-3.48	91	94	9,092
3 Yr Avg	3.96	-0.59	-0.91	70	78	11,235
5 Yr Avg	6.09	-1.53	-0.68	73	55	13,442
10 Yr Avg	8.86	-1.08	-0.57	75	46	23,373
15 Yr Avg	7.26	-3.55	-1.21	97	91	28,625

Operations

Address and Telephone	82 Devonshire Street
	Boston, MA 02109
	800-544-8888
Advisor	Fidelity Management & Research
Subadvisor	None
Distributor	Fidelity Distributors
States Available	All
Report Grade	A
Income Distrib	Paid Monthly
Date of Inception	08-19-76
Fiscal Year End	December

Min Initial Purchase	$2500 (Addt'l: $250)
Min IRA Purchase	N/A
Min Auto Invest Plan	$2500 (Systematic Inv: $100)

Expenses & Fees

Sales Fees	
	0.00% front
	0.00% deferred
	0.00% 12b-1
Management Fee	0.25% flat fee+0.37%G
3-,5-,10-yr Expense Projections	$17, $30, $68

Risk Analysis

Time Period	Load-Adj Return %	Risk % Rank[1] All	Obj	Morningstar[2] Return	Risk	Morningstar Risk-Adj Rating
1 Yr	-9.08					
3 Yr	3.96	49	88	0.99	1.28	★★
5 Yr	6.09	34	72	0.99	1.21	★★
10 Yr	8.86	23	68	1.05	1.15	★★
Average Historical Rating (109 months)					2.9	★s

[1] 1 = low, 100 = high   [2] 1.00 = Muni Avg   [3] 1.00 = 90-day T-bill return

Other Measures

			Standard LB Agg	Best Fit LB Muni
Standard Deviation	6.72	Alpha	-0.7	-1.1
Mean	4.12	Beta	1.26	1.21
Sharpe Ratio	0.09	R-Squared	57	98

Investment Style

Interest-Rate Stance

Avg Effective Maturity   17.4 Yrs

Quality

Avg Credit Quality	AA
Avg Weighted Coupon	5.84%
Avg Weighted Price	91.15% of Par

Maturity: Short Intm Long
Quality: High Med Low

Diversification Value for Portfolio Types

Large Cap: Medium	Small Cap: High	Bond: Low	Balanced: Low	Diversified: Medium

Portfolio 06-30-94

Total Stocks: 0
Total Fixed-Income: 288

Amount 000	Date of Maturity		Value $000	% Net Assets
26350	04-01-21	NY Local Govt Assist 5%	21442	1.97
16910	09-01-23	CA Univ Brd Regents Multi Purp Proj 5%	13741	1.26
15500	01-01-16	IL Chicago O'Hare Intl Arpt Ser A 5%	13114	1.20
14430	07-01-18	NY Dorm City Univ Sys 5.75%	13020	1.20
15335	09-01-16	PA Pittsburgh Wtr/Swr Sys 4.75%	12499	1.15
13075	01-01-17	NY Triborough Bridge/Tunnel Genl 5.5%	11702	1.07
13500	01-01-18	MI Pub Pwr Belle Rvr Proj 5.25%	11627	1.07
13500	07-01-16	FL Tpk Bridge Tollway 5%	11379	1.04
11600	02-01-13	CO Hlth Fac Rocky Mtn Adventist 6.625%	11267	1.03
9815	10-01-20	DC Howard Univ 7.25%	10551	0.97
26500	02-01-10	TX San Antonio Elec/Gas Sys 0%	10425	0.96
10000	07-31-95	CA San Bernardino DMD	10068	0.92
10000	01-01-26	GA Muni Elec Pwr Spcl Obl 6.5%	10038	0.92
12000	10-01-23	FL Orlando Util Com Wtr/Elec 5%	9750	0.90
11100	01-01-17	NE Pub Pwr Dist Elec Sply Sys 5%	9450	0.87
10000	06-01-10	OK Grand Rvr Dam 5.5%	9237	0.85
12000	09-01-23	CA State GO 4.75%	9075	0.83
11145	08-01-24	CA San Jose Redev Mrgd Area Tax 4.75%	8545	0.78
10400	07-01-24	MD Hlth/Higher Educ Fac Doctors 5.5%	8541	0.78
9000	06-15-07	PA Philadelphia Wtr/Wastewtr 5.5%	8471	0.78

Credit Analysis % of Bonds 10-31-94

US Govt	0	BB	0
AAA	33	B	0
AA	21	Below B	0
A	26	NR/NA	11
BBB	10		

Composition % of Assets 10-31-94

Cash	7.1	Preferreds	0.0
Stocks	0.0	Convertibles	0.0
Bonds	92.9	Other	0.0

Tax Analysis

	Tax-Adj Historical Return %	% Pretax Return
3 Yr Avg	3.14	78.7
5 Yr Avg	5.55	94.0
10 Yr Avg	8.58	95.5
Potential Capital Gain Exposure (% of assets)		-10%

Most Similar Funds in MF500

Fidelity Insured Tax-Free	Strong Fit
Lord Abbett T/F Income Natl	Strong Fit
Safeco Municipal Bond	Strong Fit

Coupon Range

	% Bonds	Rel Obj
0%	3.0	1.20
0% to 6.8%	70.1	1.16
6.8% to 7.5%	10.7	0.69
7.5% to 8.3%	4.5	0.50
More than 8.3%	5.1	0.58
Not applicable	6.6	1.71

Sector Weightings

	% Bonds	Rel Obj
General Obl	11.10	0.53
Utilities	17.86	1.43
Health	18.33	1.39
Water/Waste	9.51	1.49
Housing	4.02	0.55
Education	9.35	1.46
Transportation	11.52	1.13
COP/Lease	3.19	1.00
Private	4.67	0.40
Misc Revenue	7.82	1.57
Demand	2.64	1.07

Top 5 States % of Bonds

CA	15.33	MA	7.35
NY	11.71	TX	5.77
PA	7.54		

Fidelity New Markets Income

	Ticker	Load	NAV	Yield	SEC Yield	Assets	Objective
	FNMIX	None	10.20	5.4%	9.80%	179.5	World Bond

Fidelity New Markets Income Funds seeks high current income; capital appreciation is a secondary objective.

The fund normally invests at least 65% of its assets in debt securities issued by companies and governments in emerging markets. The fund expects to emphasize investment in Latin America, and to a lesser extent, Asia, Africa, and emerging European nations. The debt securities held by the fund may be below investment grade; some securities are poor quality or in default. The fund invests in at least three countries; it actively manages the asset allocation with regard to country, geographic region, and currency denomination.

Manager's Investment Style

Manager-since-inception Rob Citrone takes an aggressive approach--even among the emerging-markets players. The fund's country allocations showcase this bold streak. Management has no qualms about venturing into smaller markets--such as Russia and Bulgaria recently--as long as he has confidence that their fortunes will eventually improve. Citrone does, however, make efforts to mitigate this strategy's risks. His recent emphasis on floating-rate debt, for example, has muted interest-rate sensitivity. In addition, he avoids currency plays by mainly holding dollar-denominated bonds, and he adds diversification through a small equity stake.

Fund Manager(s)

Robert K. Citrone, since 05-93. BA, Hampden-Sydney C. 1987 MBA, U. of Virginia 1990

Manager Experience

	Dates Managed	Invest Obj	Std Dev	+/- Index
Robert K. Citrone				
Fidelity Adv Emerg Mkts A	03/94 - 12/94	WB	18.60	6.82

Historical Profile
Return ---
Risk ---
Rating
Not Rated

History	1983	1984	1985	1986	1987	1988	1989	1990	1991	1992	1993	1994	
												71	Income Rtn % Rank Obj
NAV	---	---	---	---	---	---	---	---	---	---	13.07	10.20	
Total Return %	---	---	---	---	---	---	---	---	---	---	38.28 *	-16.47	
+/- LB Aggregate	---	---	---	---	---	---	---	---	---	---	---	-13.55	
+/- SB World Govt	---	---	---	---	---	---	---	---	---	---	---	-23.17	
Income Return %	---	---	---	---	---	---	---	---	---	---	5.50	4.56	
Capital Return %	---	---	---	---	---	---	---	---	---	---	32.78	-21.03	
Total Rtn % Rank All	---	---	---	---	---	---	---	---	---	---	---	99	
Total Rtn % Rank Obj	---	---	---	---	---	---	---	---	---	---	---	90	
Income $	---	---	---	---	---	---	---	---	---	---	0.49	0.57	
Capital Gains $	---	---	---	---	---	---	---	---	---	---	0.17	0.20	
Expense Ratio %	---	---	---	---	---	---	---	---	---	---	1.24	1.28	
Income Ratio %	---	---	---	---	---	---	---	---	---	---	6.29	5.17	
Turnover Rate %	---	---	---	---	---	---	---	---	---	---	324	472	
Net Assets ($mil)	---	---	---	---	---	---	---	---	---	---	283.9	179.5	

Growth of $10,000
|||| Value of Fund ($000)
— Value of Index ($000) LB Agg
▼ Manager Change
▽ Partial Manager Change
► Mgr Unknown After
◄ Mgr Unknown Before

Performance Quartile (Within Objective)

Performance 12-31-94

	1st Qtr	2nd Qtr	3rd Qtr	4th Qtr	Total
1987	---	---	---	---	---
1988	---	---	---	---	---
1989	---	---	---	---	---
1990	---	---	---	---	---
1991	---	---	---	---	---
1992	---	---	---	---	---
1993	---	---	11.63	15.66	38.28 *
1994	-20.72	-4.73	19.47	-7.43	-16.47

Bear Market Performance

Decile Rank (5-year period)

Worst | Best

	Worst 3 Mo Period 1985-89	Worst 3 Mo Period 1990-94
Fidelity New Markets Income	---	---
+/- LB Aggregate	---	---
+/- Best Fit Index :	---	---

Trailing Returns

	Total Return %	+/- LB Aggregate	+/- SB World	% Rank All	% Rank Obj	Growth of $10,000
3 Mo	-7.43	-7.81	-8.00	96	90	9,257
6 Mo	10.59	9.60	8.36	4	1	11,059
1 Yr	-16.47	-13.55	-23.17	99	90	8,353
3 Yr Avg	---	---	---	---	---	---
5 Yr Avg	---	---	---	---	---	---
10 Yr Avg	---	---	---	---	---	---
15 Yr Avg	---	---	---	---	---	---

Risk Analysis

Time Period	Load-Adj Return %	Risk % Rank All	Risk % Rank Obj	Morningstar[2] Return	Morningstar Risk	Morningstar Risk-Adj Rating
1 Yr	-16.47					
3 Yr	---	---	---	---	---	---
5 Yr	---	---	---	---	---	---
10 Yr	---	---	---	---	---	---

Average Historical Rating ---

[1] 1 = low, 100 = high   [2] 1.00 = Hybrid Avg   [3] 1.00 = 90-day T-bill return

Other Measures

			Standard LB Agg	Best Fit
Standard Deviation	---	Alpha	---	---
Mean	---	Beta	---	---
Sharpe Ratio	---	R-Squared	---	---

Investment Style

Interest-Rate Stance
Avg Effective Maturity   9.5 Yrs

Quality
Avg Credit Quality   NA
Avg Weighted Coupon   6.38%

Not Available

Diversification Value for Portfolio Types

Large Cap: Small Cap: Bond: Balanced: Diversified:

Portfolio 06-30-94

Amount 000	Date of Maturity	Total Stocks: 10 / Total Fixed-Income: 26	Value $000	% Net Assets
166	08-15-99	Siderurgica Brasileiras 6%	20139	12.26
25690	09-01-02	Republic of Argentina 3.1875%	15497	9.44
29500	01-05-10	Central Bank of Nigeria FRN	8080	4.92
19000	04-15-14	Republic of Brazil 8%	7671	4.67
10250	04-15-12	Republic of Brazil 5.25%	4920	3.00
206		YPF CI D	4900	2.98
7106	04-01-01	Republic of Argentina 3.25%	4865	2.96
4881	03-15-98	Alpargatas 9%	4442	2.70
115		Telebras	4328	2.64
7030	12-23-23	Kingdom of Jordan 4%	3304	2.01
133	07-01-05	Telebras 17.5%	2914	1.77
3000	12-01-11	Tribasa Toll Trust 10.5%	2670	1.63
2713	01-28-95	Province of Cordoba 10%	2648	1.61
2000	02-19-00	Intl Container Term Svcs 6%	2600	1.58
2750	10-15-00	Indorayon Yankee 9.125%	2365	1.44
2500	05-02-06	Indorayon 7%	2325	1.42
2000	09-15-96	First Mexican Accept 10.75%	2046	1.25
76200		Siderurgica Nacional	1967	1.20
16500	12-31-19	United Mexican States 6.63%	1849	1.13
1500	06-01-00	Bancomer 9%	1474	0.90
2000	01-03-09	Govt of Morocco 4.5%	1435	0.87
1580		Alpargatas (Reg)	1172	0.71
322		Fondo Opcion CI B	837	0.51
1500	03-31-23	Republic of Argentina 4%	741	0.45
1000		Kingdom of Jordan 0%	715	0.44

Composition % 11-30-94

Cash	7.5	Preferreds	0.0
Stocks	0.0	Convertibles	0.0
Bonds	92.5	Other	0.0

Tax Analysis

	Tax-Adj Historical Return %	% Pretax Return
3 Yr Avg	---	---
5 Yr Avg	---	---
10 Yr Avg	---	---

Potential Capital Gain Exposure (% of assets)   -18%

Most Similar Funds in MF500
Fund lacks three-year record

Country Exposure 11-30-94

	% of Bonds
Brazil	20
Argentina	19
Ecuador	12
Bulgaria	10
Panama	9

Currency Exposure 07-31-94

	% of Net Assets
U.S.	69%
Mexico	18%
Brazil	11%
Switzerland	1%
France	1%

Operations

Address and Telephone	82 Devonshire Street, Boston, MA 02109, 800-544-8888
Advisor	Fidelity Management & Research
Subadvisor	FMR (UK)/FMR (Far East)/Fidelity Intl
Distributor	Fidelity Distributors
States Available	All
Report Grade	A-
Income Distrib	Paid Monthly
* Date of Inception	05-04-93
Fiscal Year End	December

Min Initial Purchase	$2500 (Addt'l: $250)
Min IRA Purchase	$500 (Addt'l: $250)
Min Auto Invest Plan	$2500 (Systematic Inv: $100)

Expenses & Fees
Sales Fees	0.00% front
	0.00% deferred
	0.00% 12b-1
Management Fee	0.55% flat fee+0.37%G
3-,5-,10-yr Expense Projections	$38, N/A, N/A

Fidelity New Millennium

Ticker	Load	NAV	Yield	SEC Yield	Assets	Objective
FMILX	3.00%	12.11	0.0%	N/A	319.7	Growth

Fidelity New Millennium Fund seeks capital appreciation.

The fund invests in all types of foreign and domestic equity securities, including common and preferred stock and securities that are convertible into common or preferred stock. It seeks undervalued stocks that may benefit from social and economic trends. The fund may also invest in indexed securities, illiquid investments, restricted securities, repurchase agreements, securities loans, and interfund loans. Although the fund may purchase lower-rated, higher-yielding bonds, it intends to limit such investments to 5% of assets.

Manager's Investment Style

This fund stands out from other Fidelity offerings because it uses a top-down approach rather than bottom-up stockpicking. Management buys stocks it feels are in the best position to capitalize on macroeconomic changes or social trends. Typically, manager Neal Miller buys smaller-cap stocks with high growth rates and above-market prices, and will make bets on foreign markets.

Fund Manager(s)

Neal P. Miller, since 12-92. Birthdate: 11-42.
BA, Carleton C. 1965 MBA, U. of Michigan 1967

Manager Experience

	Dates Managed	Invest Obj	Std Dev	+/- Index
Not available.				

Historical Profile

Return ---
Risk ---
Rating   Not Rated

Investment Style History
Equity

Average % Stocks Held in Portfolio 93% ... 94%

Growth of $10,000
IIII Value of Fund ($000)
— Value of Index ($000)
S&P 500
▼ Manager Change
▽ Partial Manager Change
► Mgr Unknown After
◄ Mgr Unknown Before

Performance Quartile (Within Objective)

	1983	1984	1985	1986	1987	1988	1989	1990	1991	1992	1993	1994	History
NAV	---	---	---	---	---	---	---	---	---	10.08	12.30	12.11	
Total Return %	---	---	---	---	---	---	---	---	---	0.80 *	24.67	0.83	
+/- S&P 500	---	---	---	---	---	---	---	---	---	1.38 *	14.62	-0.49	
+/- Wilshire 5000	---	---	---	---	---	---	---	---	---	---	13.39	0.90	
Income Return %	---	---	---	---	---	---	---	---	---	0.00	0.08	0.00	
Capital Return %	---	---	---	---	---	---	---	---	---	0.80	24.59	0.83	
Total Rtn % Rank All	---	---	---	---	---	---	---	---	---	---	11	15	
Total Rtn % Rank Obj	---	---	---	---	---	---	---	---	---	---	6	25	
Income $	---	---	---	---	---	---	---	---	---	0.00	0.01	0.00	
Capital Gains $	---	---	---	---	---	---	---	---	---	0.00	0.25	0.28	
Expense Ratio %	---	---	---	---	---	---	---	---	---	---	1.32	1.32	
Income Ratio %	---	---	---	---	---	---	---	---	---	---	-0.10	0.00	
Turnover Rate %	---	---	---	---	---	---	---	---	---	---	204	185	
Net Assets ($mil)	---	---	---	---	---	---	---	---	---	1.8	276.0	319.7	

Performance 12-31-94

	1st Qtr	2nd Qtr	3rd Qtr	4th Qtr	Total
1987	---	---	---	---	---
1988	---	---	---	---	---
1989	---	---	---	---	---
1990	---	---	---	---	---
1991	---	---	---	---	---
1992	---	---	---	---	0.80 *
1993	6.75	5.76	7.73	2.50	24.67
1994	-4.16	-3.40	9.60	-0.63	0.83

Bear Market Performance

Decile Rank (5-year period)

Worst _____ Best

	Worst 3 Mo Period 1985-89	Worst 3 Mo Period 1990-94
Fidelity New Millennium	---	---
+/- S&P 500	---	---
+/- Best Fit Index :	---	---

Trailing Returns

	Total Return %	+/- S&P 500	+/- Wil 5000	% Rank All	% Rank Obj	Growth of $10,000
3 Mo	-0.63	-0.61	0.14	37	35	9,937
6 Mo	8.91	4.05	4.29	5	11	10,891
1 Yr	0.83	-0.49	0.90	15	25	10,083
3 Yr Avg	---	---	---	---	---	---
5 Yr Avg	---	---	---	---	---	---
10 Yr Avg	---	---	---	---	---	---
15 Yr Avg	---	---	---	---	---	---

Operations

Address and Telephone	82 Devonshire Street, Boston, MA 02109, 800-544-8888
Advisor	Fidelity Management & Research
Subadvisor	FMR (U.K.)/FMR (Far East)
Distributor	Fidelity Distributors
States Available	All
Report Grade	A
Income Distrib	Paid Annually
Date of Inception	12-28-92
Fiscal Year End	November

Min Initial Purchase	$2500 (Addt'l: $250)
Min IRA Purchase	$500 (Addt'l: $250)
Min Auto Invest Plan	$2500 (Systematic Inv: $100)

Expenses & Fees

Sales Fees	3.00% front, 0.00% deferred, 0.00% 12b-1
Management Fee	0.35% flat fee+0.52%G+(-)0.20%P
3-,5-,10-yr Expense Projections	$71, $100, $184
Annual Brokerage Cost	0.53%

Risk Analysis

Time Period	Load-Adj Return %	Risk % Rank All	Risk % Rank Obj	Morningstar Return	Morningstar Risk	Morningstar Risk-Adj Rating
1 Yr	-2.20	---	---	---	---	---
3 Yr	---	---	---	---	---	---
5 Yr	---	---	---	---	---	---
10 Yr	---	---	---	---	---	---

Average Historical Rating ---

1 = low, 100 = high   2 1.00 = Equity Avg   3 1.00 = 90-day T-bill return

Other Measures

			Standard S&P 500	Best Fit
Standard Deviation	---	Alpha	---	---
Mean	---	Beta	---	---
Sharpe Ratio	---	R-Squared	---	---

Investment Style

	Stock Portfolio Avg	Relative S&P 500
Price/Earnings Ratio	25.3	1.37
Price/Book Ratio	5.0	1.47
5 Yr Earnings Gr %	10.5#	1.89
Return on Assets %	10.5	1.40
Debt % Total Cap	24.3	0.86
Med Mkt Cap ($mil)	952	0.07

figure is based on 50% or less of stocks

Diversification Value for Portfolio Types

Large Cap: Small Cap: Bond: Balanced: Diversified:

Portfolio 11-30-94

Total Stocks: 219
Total Fixed-Income: 1

Share Chg (05-94) 000	Amount 000		Value $000	% Net Assets
-15	464	Herman Miller	11645	3.73
53	202	Oracle Systems	8316	2.66
114	312	Bowater	7925	2.54
73	312	EMC	7016	2.25
168	195	Promus	5403	1.73
2	251	La Quinta Inns	5341	1.71
-41	119	Diebold	4985	1.60
249	249	Bolt Beranek & Newman	4955	1.59
272	272	Acuson	4563	1.46
11	89	Becton Dickinson	4182	1.34
-25	10	Schlumberger	4133	1.32
132	132	Times Mirror Cl A	4088	1.31
-70	95	Dell Computer	4087	1.31
72	72	StrataCom	4039	1.29
25	131	Silicon Graphics	4025	1.29
55	55	IBM	3856	1.24
158	158	Amphenol Cl A	3767	1.21
126	147	Wellman	3728	1.19
0	109	Butler Manufacturing	3716	1.19
29	50	Intuit	3481	1.11
21	267	Abitibi-Price	3450	1.10
76	102	Adobe Systems	3366	1.08
185	354	Weatherford International	3275	1.05
61	162	Novell	3218	1.03
2	48	PeopleSoft	3005	0.96

Composition % 12-31-94

Cash	6.1	Preferreds	0.0
Stocks	93.9	Convertibles	0.0
Bonds	0.0	Other	0.0

Tax Analysis

	Tax-Adj Historical Return %	% Pretax Return
3 Yr Avg	---	---
5 Yr Avg	---	---
10 Yr Avg	---	---
Potential Capital Gain Exposure (% of assets)		9%

Most Similar Funds in MF500

Fund lacks three-year record

Index Allocation

	% of Stocks
S&P 500	24.4
S&P MidCap 400	27.0
U.S. Small Cap	44.3
Foreign	4.3

Sector Weightings

	% of Stocks	Relative S&P 500
Utilities	0.6	0.04
Energy	6.8	0.67
Financials	1.2	0.11
Industrial Cyclicals	15.3	0.93
Consumer Durables	9.2	1.48
Consumer Staples	1.9	0.15
Services	16.2	2.00
Retail	2.7	0.47
Health	12.6	1.45
Technology	33.5	3.66

Fidelity OTC

	Ticker	Load	NAV	Yield	SEC Yield	Assets	Objective
	FOCPX	3.00%	23.27	0.9%	N/A	1381.3	Growth

Fidelity OTC Portfolio seeks capital appreciation.

The fund invests at least 65% of its assets in securities traded on the over-the-counter (OTC) market. These companies are smaller or newer than those listed on major exchanges; their shares may have limited marketability and greater price fluctuation, but greater capital-appreciation potential. It may continue to hold, for up to six months, securities purchased on the OTC market but currently listed on the NYSE or AMEX, or a foreign exchange. The fund may invest up to 5% of its assets in lower-quality debt; up to 30% may be invested in foreign securities.

Manager's Investment Style

Management hunts out stocks with improving earnings and that are selling at low prices relative to their projected growth rates. A management change in 1994, however, brought a new look to this one-time small-company fund. When Abigail Johnson took over from Alan Radlo, she picked up some larger-cap stocks, and now plans to fashion the portfolio to reflect the Nasdaq index, which has more of a mid-cap than a small-cap bias. She also takes a less-concentrated approach than her predecessor, and has thus doubled the number of names in the portfolio.

Fund Manager(s)

Abigail Johnson, since 04-94. BA, Hobart C. 1984 MBA, Harvard 1988

Manager Experience

	Dates Managed	Invest Obj	Std Dev	+/- Index
Abigail Johnson				
Fidelity Sel Indstl Equip	12/88 - 09/91	ST	20.65	-10.36
Fidelity Sel Dev Commun	06/91 - 03/93	ST	15.59	16.89

Historical Profile

Return	Above Average
Risk	Average
Rating	★★★★ Above Average

Investment Style History Equity

Average % Stocks Held in Portfolio

93% 92% 84% 76% 81% 80% 76% 81%

Growth of $10,000

- |||| Value of Fund ($000)
- — Value of Index ($000) Wil 4500
- ▼ Manager Change
- ▽ Partial Manager Change
- ► Mgr Unknown After
- ◄ Mgr Unknown Before

Performance Quartile (Within Objective)

1983	1984	1985	1986	1987	1988	1989	1990	1991	1992	1993	1994	History
---	9.77	15.93	16.47	14.64	17.68	20.14	18.54	24.78	25.65	24.14	23.27	NAV
---	---	68.64	11.40	1.60	22.85	30.39	-4.75	49.16	14.94	8.33	-2.70	Total Return %
---	---	36.90	-7.28	-3.66	6.24	-1.29	-1.63	18.68	7.32	-1.72	-4.01	+/- S&P 500
---	---	36.08	-4.70	-0.77	4.91	1.22	1.43	14.95	5.97	-2.95	-2.63	+/- Wilshire 5000
---	---	0.08	0.12	0.15	2.09	2.59	0.27	0.53	1.04	0.43	0.91	Income Return %
---	---	68.56	11.28	1.45	20.77	27.81	-5.02	48.63	13.90	7.91	-3.60	Capital Return %
---	---	1	77	46	9	13	70	8	10	77	40	Total Rtn % Rank All
---	---	1	76	58	13	34	53	15	16	66	57	Total Rtn % Rank Obj
---	0.00	0.01	0.02	0.02	0.30	0.51	0.05	0.12	0.25	0.10	0.21	Income $
---	0.00	0.45	1.27	1.93	0.00	2.41	0.58	2.51	2.24	3.42	0.00	Capital Gains $
---	---	1.50	1.31	1.36	1.42	1.32	1.35	1.29	1.17	1.08	0.88	Expense Ratio %
---	---	0.51	0.57	0.12	0.90	2.02	2.30	1.00	0.59	0.53	0.48	Income Ratio %
---	---	122	132	191	193	118	212	198	245	213	222	Turnover Rate %
---	---	162.6	630.7	764.5	720.1	750.3	618.7	1070.2	1243.6	1343.0	1381.3	Net Assets ($mil)

Performance 12-31-94

	1st Qtr	2nd Qtr	3rd Qtr	4th Qtr	Total
1987	24.04	1.76	9.04	-26.19	1.60
1988	12.98	8.89	1.00	-1.12	22.85
1989	10.80	9.34	9.68	-1.87	30.39
1990	-0.89	3.66	-14.78	8.79	-4.75
1991	22.76	-0.35	11.71	9.15	49.16
1992	1.17	-3.71	2.66	14.93	14.94
1993	0.08	-0.19	5.80	2.52	8.33
1994	-2.44	-6.84	7.57	-0.47	-2.70

Bear Market Performance

Decile Rank (5-year period)

Worst _____ Best

	Worst 3 Mo Period 1985-89	Best 3 Mo Period 1990-94
Fidelity OTC	-34.77	-15.47
+/- S&P 500	-5.18	-1.63
+/- Best Fit Index : Wil 4500	-4.63	3.93

Trailing Returns

	Total Return %	+/- S&P 500	+/- Wil 5000	% Rank All	% Rank Obj	Growth of $10,000
3 Mo	-0.47	-0.45	0.30	34	31	9,953
6 Mo	7.06	2.20	2.44	7	19	10,706
1 Yr	-2.70	-4.01	-2.63	40	57	9,730
3 Yr Avg	6.61	0.34	0.00	29	43	12,116
5 Yr Avg	11.47	2.78	2.66	11	15	17,214
10 Yr Avg	18.07	3.68	4.21	3	3	52,629
15 Yr Avg	---	---	---	---	---	---

Operations

Address and Telephone	82 Devonshire Street
	Boston, MA 02109
	800-544-8888
Advisor	Fidelity Management & Research
Subadvisor	FMR (U.K.)/FMR (Far East)
Distributor	Fidelity Distributors
States Available	All
Report Grade	A
Income Distrib	Paid Annually
* Date of Inception	12-31-84
Fiscal Year End	July

Risk Analysis

Time Period	Load-Adj Return %	Risk % Rank [1] All	Obj	Morningstar [2] Return	Morningstar Risk	Morningstar Risk-Adj Rating
1 Yr	-5.61					
3 Yr	5.53	79	56	0.57 [3]	0.93	★★★
5 Yr	10.80	77	54	1.58 [3]	0.93	★★★★
10 Yr	17.71	74	54	2.18	0.96	★★★★★
Average Historical Rating (85 months)					3.9	★s

[1] 1 = low, 100 = high [2] 1.00 = Equity Avg [3] 1.00 = 90-day T-bill return

Other Measures

			Standard S&P 500	Best Fit Wil 4500
Standard Deviation	10.01	Alpha	1.3	-0.7
Mean	6.91	Beta	0.74	0.94
Sharpe Ratio	0.34	R-Squared	35	84

Investment Style

	Stock Portfolio Avg	Relative S&P 500	Style
Price/Earnings Ratio	21.7	1.17	Value Blend Growth
Price/Book Ratio	4.4	1.29	
5 Yr Earnings Gr %	23.8#	4.29	
Return on Assets %	11.9	1.59	
Debt % Total Cap	23.9	0.84	
Med Mkt Cap ($mil)	1080	0.08	

figure is based on 50% or less of stocks

Diversification Value for Portfolio Types

Large Cap: Medium | Small Cap: None | Bond: High | Balanced: Medium | Diversified: Medium

Expenses & Fees

Sales Fees	3.00% front
	0.00% deferred
	0.00% 12b-1
Management Fee	0.35% flat fee+0.52%G+(-)0.20%P
3-,5-,10-yr Expense Projections	$58, $79, $138
Annual Brokerage Cost	0.19%

Min Initial Purchase $2500 (Addt'l: $250)
Min IRA Purchase $500 (Addt'l: $250)
Min Auto Invest Plan $2500 (Systematic Inv: $100)

Portfolio 07-31-94

Share Chg (01-94) 000	Amount 000	Total Stocks: 291 Total Fixed-Income: 0	Value $000	% Net Assets
309	838	Intel	49646	4.04
357	653	Microsoft	33640	2.74
139	700	US Healthcare	26501	2.16
638	638	Oracle Systems	24400	1.99
-136	864	Tele-Communications CI A	20133	1.64
-19	290	Fifth Third Bancorp	15023	1.22
-40	279	Amgen	13870	1.13
-225	337	State Street Boston	12917	1.05
85	291	Wisconsin Central Transport	11406	0.93
210	210	Motorola	11130	0.91
217	217	Willamette Industries	10791	0.88
200	200	McCaw Cellular Comm CI A	10625	0.86
359	359	Arctco	10588	0.86
191	191	LM Ericsson Telephone (ADR)	10388	0.85
59	208	Glenayre Technologies	10316	0.84
75	75	Lin Broadcasting	9375	0.76
234	234	Linear Technology	9372	0.76
282	282	BanPonce	9087	0.74
148	148	General Instrument	8997	0.73
198	198	Applied Materials	8852	0.72
-8	373	Schuler Homes	8574	0.70
162	324	Schnitzer Steel Industries	8508	0.69
156	156	Cellular Communications CI A	8152	0.66
146	146	SAFECO	8101	0.66
161	324	Parametric Technology	8011	0.65

Composition % 11-30-94

Cash	9.0	Preferreds	0.0
Stocks	90.8	Convertibles	0.0
Bonds	0.2	Other	0.0

Tax Analysis

	Tax-Adj Historical Return %	% Pretax Return
3 Yr Avg	4.25	62.9
5 Yr Avg	9.14	76.1
10 Yr Avg	15.62	76.7
Potential Capital Gain Exposure (% of assets)		6%

Most Similar Funds in MF500

Fidelity Growth Company	Fair Fit
Founders Frontier	Fair Fit
Harbor Capital Appreciation	Fair Fit

Index Allocation

	% of Stocks
S&P 500	27.5
S&P MidCap 400	18.3
U.S. Small Cap	52.1
Foreign	2.2

Sector Weightings

	% of Stocks	Relative S&P 500
Utilities	0.8	0.06
Energy	0.6	0.05
Financials	16.7	1.58
Industrial Cyclicals	11.6	0.71
Consumer Durables	8.3	1.33
Consumer Staples	3.4	0.27
Services	11.8	1.45
Retail	2.7	0.46
Health	10.2	1.17
Technology	34.0	3.71

MORNINGSTAR 1995 Mutual Fund 500

Fidelity Puritan

	Ticker	Load	NAV	Yield	SEC Yield	Assets	Objective
	FPURX	2.00%	14.81	3.5%	4.04%	11769.4	Balanced

Fidelity Puritan Fund seeks income consistent with preservation of capital.

The fund invests in a diversified array of high-yielding securities such as common stocks, preferred stocks, and bonds. The relative holdings vary in response to changing market conditions. The bonds may have any quality rating or maturity; up to 35% of the fund's assets may be invested in lower-quality, higher-yielding assets. The fund may purchase foreign securities, zero-coupon bonds, and indexed securities. It may also engage in futures contracts, short sales, and swap agreements.

Manager's Investment Style

Management sticks with a bottom-up strategy, focusing on low prices and strong fundamentals. It often stands apart from the balanced-fund norm in its willingness to explore uncommon combinations of holdings, as long as they meet the strict value criteria. This approach often results in an unusual collection of contrarian, often beaten down, stocks and bonds.

Fund Manager(s)

Richard B. Fentin, since 04-87. Birthdate: 06-55. BA, Emory U. 1976 MBA, Harvard 1980

Manager Experience

	Dates Managed	Invest Obj	Std Dev	+/- Index
Richard B. Fentin				
Fidelity Value	07/92 - 12/92	G	8.42	1.39

Historical Profile

Return	Above Average
Risk	Below Average
Rating	★★★★★ Highest

| | 56% | 60% | 60% | 55% | 58% | 51% | 49% | 59% |

Investment Style History
Equity
Average % Stocks Held in Portfolio

Growth of $10,000

|||| Value of Fund ($000)
— Value of Index ($000)
S&P 500
▼ Manager Change
▽ Partial Manager Change
► Mgr Unknown After
◄ Mgr Unknown Before

Performance Quartile (Within Objective)

1983	1984	1985	1986	1987	1988	1989	1990	1991	1992	1993	1994	History
12.24	11.57	12.52	13.34	11.53	12.76	13.70	12.05	14.14	14.74	15.75	14.81	NAV
25.85	10.62	28.71	20.75	-1.79	18.89	19.60	-6.35	24.46	15.43	21.45	1.78	Total Return %
3.38	4.36	-3.03	2.08	-7.05	2.28	-12.09	-3.23	-6.03	7.81	11.39	0.47	+/- S&P 500
17.47	-4.53	6.58	5.51	-4.55	11.01	5.06	-15.30	8.46	8.18	11.70	4.70	+/- LB Aggregate
8.91	8.95	8.93	7.69	7.05	8.22	7.82	5.69	7.11	5.98	4.83	3.47	Income Return %
16.94	1.67	19.77	13.06	-8.84	10.67	11.78	-12.04	17.34	9.45	16.61	-1.68	Capital Return %
21	22	30	17	73	16	36	75	37	9	15	10	Total Rtn % Rank All
1	32	42	15	77	8	47	92	49	2	2	5	Total Rtn % Rank Obj
1.00	0.97	0.97	0.92	0.94	0.91	0.99	0.80	0.80	0.82	0.72	0.54	Income $
1.37	0.82	1.16	0.76	0.77	0.00	0.54	0.00	0.00	0.69	1.36	0.71	Capital Gains $
0.63	0.60	0.61	0.63	0.70	0.72	0.64	0.65	0.66	0.64	0.74	0.79	Expense Ratio %
8.21	8.05	8.40	7.50	6.40	6.58	7.41	6.30	5.94	6.23	4.89	4.00	Income Ratio %
90	74	133	85	63	88	77	58	108	102	76	74	Turnover Rate %
823.1	870.4	1297.7	2965.0	3959.1	4295.5	4861.5	4356.7	5108.9	5911.8	8988.2	11769.4	Net Assets ($mil)

Performance 12-31-94

	1st Qtr	2nd Qtr	3rd Qtr	4th Qtr	Total
1987	9.99	1.84	2.75	-14.67	-1.79
1988	7.27	6.86	2.04	1.64	18.89
1989	5.89	7.58	5.06	-0.07	19.60
1990	-3.07	2.43	-11.22	6.24	-6.35
1991	11.27	2.08	5.36	3.99	24.46
1992	3.17	3.88	3.28	4.28	15.43
1993	9.10	3.97	3.69	3.26	21.45
1994	-0.54	0.95	3.26	-1.82	1.78

Bear Market Performance

Decile Rank (5-year period)

Worst ———————————— Best

	Worst 3 Mo Period 1985-89	Worst 3 Mo Period 1990-94
Fidelity Puritan	-19.51	-11.96
+/- S&P 500	10.07	1.88
+/- Best Fit Index : S&P 500	10.07	1.88

Trailing Returns

	Total Return %	+/- S&P 500	+/- LB Aggregate	% Rank All	% Rank Obj	Growth of $10,000
3 Mo	-1.82	-1.81	-2.20	65	77	9,818
6 Mo	1.38	-3.49	0.38	32	52	10,138
1 Yr	1.78	0.47	4.70	10	5	10,178
3 Yr Avg	12.58	6.31	8.03	7	1	14,268
5 Yr Avg	10.71	2.02	3.08	14	4	16,630
10 Yr Avg	13.70	-0.69	3.75	20	10	36,092
15 Yr Avg	15.46	0.98	4.65	9	1	86,420

Operations

Address and Telephone	82 Devonshire Street
	Boston, MA 02109
	800-544-8888
Advisor	Fidelity Management & Research
Subadvisor	None
Distributor	Fidelity Distributors
States Available	All
Report Grade	A
Income Distrib	Paid Quarterly
Date of Inception	04-16-47
Fiscal Year End	July

Min Initial Purchase	$2500 (Addt'l: $250)
Min IRA Purchase	$500 (Addt'l: $250)
Min Auto Invest Plan	$2500 (Systematic Inv: $100)

Expenses & Fees

Sales Fees	2.00% front
	0.00% deferred
	0.00% 12b-1
Management Fee	0.20% flat fee+0.52%G
3-,5-,10-yr Expense Projections	$25, $44, $98
Annual Brokerage Cost	0.12%

Risk Analysis

Time Period	Load-Adj Return %	Risk % Rank [1] All	Obj	Morningstar [2] Return	Risk	Morningstar Risk-Adj Rating
1 Yr	-0.25					
3 Yr	11.82	36	10	2.58[3]	0.60	★★★★★
5 Yr	10.26	54	61	1.43[3]	0.80	★★★★
10 Yr	13.47	41	35	1.39	0.67	★★★★★
Average Historical Rating (109 months)				4.6 ★s		

[1] 1 = low, 100 = high [2] 1.00 = Hybrid Avg [3] 1.00 = 90-day T-bill return

Other Measures

				Standard S&P 500	Best Fit S&P 500
Standard Deviation	6.75	Alpha		6.7	6.7
Mean	12.13	Beta		0.71	0.71
Sharpe Ratio	1.28	R-Squared		70	70

Investment Style

Stocks

	Port Avg	Rel S&P 500
Price/Earnings Ratio	23.4	1.27
Price/Book Ratio	2.2	0.65
5 Yr Earnings Gr %	0.0	0.01
Med Mkt Cap ($mil)	4161	0.32

Style V B G / Size L M S

Bonds

Avg Effective Duration	4.5 Yrs
Avg Effective Maturity	11.0 Yrs
Avg Credit Quality	A
Avg Weighted Coupon	8.73%

Maturity S I L / Quality H M L

Diversification Value for Portfolio Types

Large Cap: Low	Small Cap: Medium	Bond: Medium	Balanced: Low	Diversified: Low

Portfolio 07-31-94

Share Chg (01-94)000	Amount 000	Total Stocks: 308 Total Fixed-Income: 410	Date of Maturity	Value $000	% Net Assets
	240650	US Treasury Bond 8.125%	08-15-19	257683	2.36
1940	4023	Schlumberger		237375	2.18
228	2184	British Petroleum (ADR)		165954	1.52
567	1702	Loews		150228	1.38
-205	3278	WR Grace		136044	1.25
786	2327	Philip Morris		128007	1.17
	91260	US Treasury Bond 10.75%	08-15-05	115501	1.06
-50	1369	Dayton Hudson		112943	1.04
	161259	Republic of Argentina FRN	04-01-01	107658	0.99
0	2029	Amerada Hess		105518	0.97
2723	3042	Travelers		100774	0.92
2968	2968	Nalco Chemical		96831	0.89
2409	4903	The Limited		96824	0.89
165	1278	AMP		95553	0.88
1108	3804	Alcan Aluminium		93292	0.86
1824	2056	Betz Laboratories		90473	0.83
	71300	US Treasury Bond 9.875%	11-15-15	89381	0.82
1498	1498	Great Lakes Chemical		89155	0.82
	94110	US Treasury Note 6.25%	02-15-03	89140	0.82
	63745	US Treasury Bond 12%	08-15-23	88925	0.82

Index Allocation

	% of Stocks
S&P 500	51.3
S&P MidCap 400	9.0
U.S. Small Cap	11.4
Foreign	31.1

Composition % 11-30-94

Cash	10.2	Preferreds	0.0
Stocks	63.4	Convertibles	3.1
Bonds	23.3	Other	0.0

Tax Analysis

	Tax-Adj Historical Return %	% Pretax Return
3 Yr Avg	9.07	69.7
5 Yr Avg	7.80	68.7
10 Yr Avg	9.96	60.8
Potential Capital Gain Exposure (% of assets)		1%

Most Similar Funds in MF500

Fidelity Equity-Income II	Strong Fit
Fidelity Equity-Income	Strong Fit
T. Rowe Price Equity-Income	Fair Fit

Bond Credit Analysis 08-31-94
% of Bonds

US Govt	9	BB	19
AAA	37	B	0
AA	4	Below B	0
A	8	NR/NA	1
BBB	22		

Stock Sector Weightings

	% of Stocks	Relative S&P 500
Utilities	5.2	0.42
Energy	14.7	1.45
Financials	12.6	1.19
Industrial Cyclicals	23.1	1.41
Consumer Durables	10.3	1.66
Consumer Staples	8.5	0.67
Services	6.4	0.79
Retail	7.7	1.32
Health	5.8	0.66
Technology	5.9	0.64

Fidelity Real Estate Investment

	Ticker	Load	NAV	Yield	SEC Yield	Assets	Objective
	FRESX	None	13.20	4.8%	N/A	555.7	Specialty

Fidelity Real Estate Investment Portfolio seeks above-average income and long-term capital growth consistent with reasonable risk.

The fund normally invests at least 65% of its assets in equity securities of companies in the real-estate industry. These include REITs, mortgage REITs, real-estate developers or brokers, and companies with substantial real-estate holdings. The rest may be invested outside the industry; some investments may be related to the real-estate industry. The fund may invest up to 35% of assets in investment-grade debt; up to 20% may be invested in lower-quality debt.

Manager's Investment Style

Management takes a conservative approach to the real-estate market. The portfolio is well-diversified by region and by sector, and it has also, at times, diversified beyond REITs and into real-estate-related stocks, such as homebuilders and realtors.

Fund Manager(s)

Barry Greenfield, since 11-86. BA, Bates C. 1956 MBA, Columbia U. 1958

Manager Experience

	Dates Managed	Invest Obj	Std Dev	+/- Index
Barry Greenfield				
Fidelity	03/82 - 08/93	GI	15.24	-0.88

Historical Profile

Return	Above Average
Risk	Below Average
Rating	★★★★
	Above Average

87% 92% 90% 90% 89% 86% 93% 92%

Investment Style History
Equity
Average % Stocks Held in Portfolio

Growth of $10,000
|||| Value of Fund ($000)
— Value of Index ($000) Wil REIT
▼ Manager Change
▽ Partial Manager Change
► Mgr Unknown After
◄ Mgr Unknown Before

Performance Quartile (Within Objective)

	1983	1984	1985	1986	1987	1988	1989	1990	1991	1992	1993	1994	History
	---	---	---	9.94	8.62	8.92	9.59	8.26	10.94	12.60	13.57	13.20	NAV
	---	---	---	-0.60 *	-7.68	10.36	13.77	-8.70	39.19	19.51	12.51	2.04	Total Return %
	---	---	---	-0.73 *	-12.94	-6.25	-17.91	-5.58	8.70	11.89	2.46	0.72	+/- S&P 500
	---	---	---	---	-10.04	-7.58	-15.40	-2.51	4.98	10.54	1.23	2.11	+/- Wilshire 5000
	---	---	---	0.00	5.60	6.88	6.26	5.17	6.74	4.34	4.81	4.76	Income Return %
	---	---	---	-0.60	-13.28	3.48	7.51	-13.87	32.45	15.17	7.70	-2.73	Capital Return %
	---	---	---	---	93	59	51	81	15	5	46	10	Total Rtn % Rank All
	---	---	---	---	61	85	71	38	23	27	68	24	Total Rtn % Rank Obj
	---	---	---	0.00	0.60	0.59	0.54	0.51	0.49	0.43	0.60	0.63	Income $
	---	---	---	0.00	0.00	0.00	0.00	0.00	0.00	0.00	0.00	0.00	Capital Gains $
	---	---	---	---	1.50	1.50	1.28	1.39	1.47	1.24	1.16	1.13	Expense Ratio %
	---	---	---	---	7.17	6.26	6.87	7.11	8.45	5.84	5.81	4.34	Income Ratio %
	---	---	---	---	6	89	42	70	49	84	82	110	Turnover Rate %
	---	---	---	21.1	67.9	64.0	53.2	39.7	62.6	146.9	424.4	555.7	Net Assets ($mil)

Performance 12-31-94

	1st Qtr	2nd Qtr	3rd Qtr	4th Qtr	Total
1987	8.15	-1.86	-4.67	-8.76	-7.68
1988	9.03	0.99	0.99	-0.75	10.36
1989	2.12	8.16	5.23	-2.11	13.77
1990	-2.29	-0.21	-11.15	5.40	-8.70
1991	20.17	1.82	5.61	7.71	39.19
1992	3.11	0.36	7.57	7.37	19.51
1993	15.20	-3.24	6.96	-5.64	12.51
1994	1.97	0.48	-1.84	1.46	2.04

Bear Market Performance

Decile Rank (5-year period)

Worst ———————————— Best

	Worst 3 Mo Period 1985-89	Worst 3 Mo Period 1990-94
Fidelity Real Estate Investment	---	-14.28
+/- S&P 500	---	-0.43
+/- Best Fit Index : Wil REIT	---	5.78

Trailing Returns

	Total Return %	+/- S&P 500	+/- Wil 5000	% Rank All	Obj	Growth of $10,000
3 Mo	1.46	1.48	2.23	5	20	10,146
6 Mo	-0.40	-5.27	-5.03	63	58	9,960
1 Yr	2.04	0.72	2.11	10	24	10,204
3 Yr Avg	11.12	4.85	4.51	10	40	13,720
5 Yr Avg	11.76	3.07	2.94	10	38	17,436
10 Yr Avg	---	---	---	---	---	---
15 Yr Avg	---	---	---	---	---	---

Operations

Address and Telephone	82 Devonshire Street Boston, MA 02109 800-544-8888
Advisor	Fidelity Management & Research
Subadvisor	FMR (U.K.)/FMR (Far East)
Distributor	Fidelity Distributors
States Available	All
Report Grade	A
Income Distrib	Paid Quarterly
* Date of Inception	11-17-86
Fiscal Year End	January

Risk Analysis

Time Period	Load-Adj Return %	Risk % Rank [1] All	Obj	Morningstar [2] Return	Risk	Morningstar Risk-Adj Rating
1 Yr	2.04					
3 Yr	11.12	78	40	2.34 [3]	0.92	★★★★
5 Yr	11.76	65	5	1.87 [3]	0.78	★★★★
10 Yr	---	---	---	---	---	---

Average Historical Rating (62 months)   3.4 ★s

[1] 1 = low, 100 = high   [2] 1.00 = Equity Avg   [3] 1.00 = 90-day T-bill return

Other Measures

			Standard S&P 500	Best Fit Wil REIT
Standard Deviation	11.85	Alpha	6.8	1.3
Mean	11.28	Beta	0.40	0.92
Sharpe Ratio	0.65	R-Squared	7	87

Investment Style

	Stock Portfolio Avg	Relative S&P 500
Price/Earnings Ratio	23.6	1.28
Price/Book Ratio	2.7	0.81
5 Yr Earnings Gr %	---	---
Return on Assets %	4.8	0.65
Debt % Total Cap	45.7	1.62
Med Mkt Cap ($mil)	462	0.04

Style
Value Blend Growth
Size Large Med Small

Diversification Value for Portfolio Types

Large Cap: High	Small Cap: Medium	Bond: High	Balanced: High	Diversified: High

Expenses & Fees

Sales Fees	0.00% front
	0.00% deferred
	0.00% 12b-1
Management Fee	0.30% flat fee+0.52%G
3-,5-,10-yr Expense Projections	$36, $62, $137
Annual Brokerage Cost	0.36%

Min Initial Purchase	$2500 (Addt'l: $250)
Min IRA Purchase	$500 (Addt'l: $250)
Min Auto Invest Plan	$2500 (Systematic Inv: $100)

Portfolio 07-31-94

Share Chg (01-94) 000	Amount 000	Total Stocks: 84 Total Fixed-Income: 3	Value $000	% Net Assets
259	1014	Equity Residential Ppty Tr	33205	6.22
124	1045	Developers Diversified Rlty	32009	6.00
-3	962	Simon Property Group	25611	4.80
125	654	Kimco Realty	24198	4.53
71	853	Federal Realty Invstmt Trust	21211	3.97
257	567	Oasis Residential	13879	2.60
958	958	Debartolo Realty	13657	2.56
165	347	Weingarten Realty	13020	2.44
231	431	Duke Realty Investments	11632	2.18
-152	641	Property Trust America	11618	2.18
-12	312	Vornado Realty Trust	11448	2.15
31	552	Manufactured Home Community	11320	2.12
78	345	Post Properties	10692	2.00
50	1242	Bradley Real Estate Trust	10556	1.98
325	478	Avalon Properties	10102	1.89
77	327	Chelsea GCA Realty	9156	1.72
323	323	TriNet Corporate Realty Tr	9052	1.70
147	377	Colonial Properties Trust	8429	1.58
-27	401	Merry Land & Investment	8265	1.55
343	448	RFS Hotel Investors	7730	1.45
360	360	Spieker Properties	7650	1.43
311	311	Horizon Outlet Centers	7498	1.41
96	421	Alexander Haagen Properties	7362	1.38
262	262	Storage USA	6930	1.30
255	255	Smith Residential Realty	6407	1.20

Composition % 11-30-94

Cash	9.4	Preferreds	0.0
Stocks	90.6	Convertibles	0.0
Bonds	0.0	Other	0.0

Index Allocation

	% of Stocks
S&P 500	0.0
S&P MidCap 400	0.0
U.S. Small Cap	100.0
Foreign	0.0

Tax Analysis

	Tax-Adj Historical Return %	% Pretax Return
3 Yr Avg	9.43	83.4
5 Yr Avg	10.00	82.1
10 Yr Avg	---	---
Potential Capital Gain Exposure (% of assets)		0%

Most Similar Funds in MF500

CGM Mutual	Weak Fit
Ariel Growth	Weak Fit
Dreyfus New Leaders	Weak Fit

Sector Weightings

	% of Stocks	Relative S&P 500
Utilities	0.0	0.00
Energy	0.0	0.00
Financials	97.9	9.26
Industrial Cyclicals	0.1	0.01
Consumer Durables	0.0	0.00
Consumer Staples	0.0	0.00
Services	2.0	0.24
Retail	0.0	0.00
Health	0.0	0.00
Technology	0.0	0.00

MORNINGSTAR 1995 Mutual Fund 500

Fidelity Select Health Care

	Ticker	Load	NAV	Yield	SEC Yield	Assets	Objective
	FSPHX	3.00%	70.80	0.8%	N/A	796.1	Sp.-Health

Fidelity Select Health Care Portfolio seeks capital appreciation.

The fund invests at least 80% of its assets in the equities of companies in the health-care industry. This may include companies engaged in the design, manufacture, or sale of products or services used for or in connection with health care or medicine. Up to 25% of the fund's assets may be invested in one issuer; up to 5% may be invested in lower-quality bonds.

The fund waives sales charges on shares purchased through personal advisory services.

Historical Profile

Return	Above Average
Risk	Above Average
Rating	★★★★ Above Average

Investment Style History
Equity
Average % Stocks Held in Portfolio

| 96% | 96% | 91% | --- | 97% | 86% | 88% | 89% |

Growth of $10,000
|||| Value of Fund ($000)
— Value of Index ($000) SPMid400
▼ Manager Change
▽ Partial Manager Change
◄ Mgr Unknown After
◀ Mgr Unknown Before

Performance Quartile (Within Objective)

Manager's Investment Style

Manager Charles Mangum gives priority to health-care stocks that are selling below their earnings-growth rates. Portfolio turnover is very high, but Mangum has shown a willingness to stick with more-established firms that he expects to continue posting strong earnings growth.

Fund Manager(s)

Charles Mangum, since 03-92. Birthdate: 08-64.
BA, Southern Methodist U. 1986 MBA, U. of Chicago 1990

Manager Experience

	Dates Managed	Invest Obj	Std Dev	+/- Index
Charles Mangum				
Fidelity Sel Med Delivry	02/91 - 03/93	SH	26.85	-13.28

1983	1984	1985	1986	1987	1988	1989	1990	1991	1992	1993	1994	History
17.40	17.06	27.15	32.78	31.62	34.13	47.58	52.98	85.95	62.19	63.62	70.80	NAV
14.11	-1.07	59.44	21.98	-0.64	8.83	42.49	24.32	83.69	-17.43	2.42	21.43	Total Return %
-8.35	-7.33	27.70	3.30	-5.90	-7.78	10.81	27.43	53.21	-25.05	-7.64	20.11	+/- S&P 500
---	---	---	---	---	-3.71	-3.15	6.87	29.68	-1.14	10.82	8.31	+/- S&P Health
0.00	0.37	0.29	0.00	0.00	0.89	0.31	0.40	0.52	0.25	0.12	0.93	Income Return %
14.11	-1.43	59.14	21.98	-0.64	7.94	42.17	23.92	83.17	-17.69	2.30	20.50	Capital Return %
62	69	1	14	65	69	3	1	1	100	97	1	Total Rtn % Rank All
1	1	1	14	50	50	44	20	20	72	46	1	Total Rtn % Rank Obj
0.00	0.06	0.05	0.00	0.00	0.28	0.13	0.40	0.34	0.16	0.07	0.62	Income $
0.06	0.09	0.00	0.36	0.92	0.00	0.84	5.67	8.81	8.51	0.00	5.74	Capital Gains $
1.50	1.21	1.26	1.29	1.39	1.64	1.41	1.74	1.53	1.44	1.46	1.55	Expense Ratio %
0.80	0.54	0.56	0.53	-0.01	0.06	0.95	1.61	1.28	-0.02	0.24	0.26	Income Ratio %
32	139	159	217	213	122	114	126	159	154	112	213	Turnover Rate %
81.8	60.8	194.9	229.3	231.6	181.1	222.5	373.2	1169.8	753.9	573.0	796.1	Net Assets ($mil)

Performance 12-31-94

	1st Qtr	2nd Qtr	3rd Qtr	4th Qtr	Total
1987	31.18	0.93	4.88	-28.45	-0.64
1988	7.91	0.76	0.41	-0.31	8.83
1989	10.55	6.30	15.94	4.59	42.49
1990	-3.01	17.64	-6.08	16.01	24.32
1991	34.45	-1.08	16.59	18.46	83.69
1992	-13.15	-7.43	-3.98	6.96	-17.43
1993	-13.14	3.59	3.32	10.16	2.42
1994	-6.98	8.14	16.22	3.86	21.43

Bear Market Performance

Decile Rank (5-year period)

Worst — Best

	Worst 3 Mo Period 1985-89	Worst 3 Mo Period 1990-94
Fidelity Select Health Care	-34.77	-16.84
+/- S&P 500	-5.19	-20.30
+/- Best Fit Index : SPMid400	-5.96	-20.02

Trailing Returns

	Total Return %	+/- S&P 500	+/- S&P Health	% Rank All	% Rank Obj	Growth of $10,000
3 Mo	3.86	3.88	0.67	2	6	10,386
6 Mo	20.71	15.85	1.81	1	1	12,071
1 Yr	21.43	20.11	8.31	1	1	12,143
3 Yr Avg	0.89	-5.38	5.52	95	45	10,268
5 Yr Avg	18.58	9.89	9.16	2	1	23,448
10 Yr Avg	21.53	7.14	---	1	1	70,261
15 Yr Avg	---	---	---	---	---	---

Operations

Address and Telephone	82 Devonshire Street	
	Boston, MA 02109	
	800-544-8888	
Advisor	Fidelity Management & Research	
Subadvisor	FMR (U.K.)/FMR (Far East)	
Distributor	Fidelity Distributors	
States Available	All	
Report Grade	A	
Income Distrib	Paid Semiannually	
Date of Inception	07-14-81	
Fiscal Year End	February	

Min Initial Purchase	$2500 (Addt'l: $250)
Min IRA Purchase	$500 (Addt'l: $250)
Min Auto Invest Plan	$2500 (Systematic Inv: $100)

Expenses & Fees
Sales Fees	3.00% front
	0.00% deferred
	0.00% 12b-1
Management Fee	0.30% flat fee+0.52%G
3-,5-,10-yr Expense Projections	$77, $112, $209
Annual Brokerage Cost	0.34%

Risk Analysis

Time Period	Load-Adj Return %	Risk % Rank [1] All	Obj	Morningstar [2] Return	Morningstar Risk	Morningstar Risk-Adj Rating
1 Yr	17.78					
3 Yr	-0.13	97	27	-1.04 [3]	1.63	★
5 Yr	17.86	88	30	3.91 [3]	1.11	★★★★★
10 Yr	21.16	88	40	3.29	1.13	★★★★★

Average Historical Rating (109 months)   4.1 ★s

[1] 1 = low, 100 = high   [2] 1.00 = Equity Avg   [3] 1.00 = 90-day T-bill return

Other Measures

				Standard S&P 500	Best Fit SPMid400
Standard Deviation	16.33	Alpha		-4.0	-4.7
Mean	2.21	Beta		0.95	0.89
Sharpe Ratio	-0.08	R-Squared		22	30

Investment Style

	Stock Portfolio Avg	Relative S&P 500
Price/Earnings Ratio	21.5	1.17
Price/Book Ratio	4.6	1.36
5 Yr Earnings Gr %	8.3	1.49
Return on Assets %	13.3	1.78
Debt % Total Cap	17.9	0.63
Med Mkt Cap ($mil)	10325	0.80

Diversification Value for Portfolio Types

Large Cap:	Small Cap:	Bond:	Balanced:	Diversified:
High	High	High	High	High

Portfolio 08-31-94

Total Stocks: 82
Total Fixed-Income: 3

Share Chg (02-94) 000	Amount 000		Value $000	% Net Assets
255	928	Pfizer	63302	9.66
-84	701	Warner-Lambert	58621	8.95
16	693	Schering-Plough	48395	7.39
600	600	American Home Products	35625	5.44
581	581	Bristol-Myers Squibb	33413	5.10
20	663	Johnson & Johnson	33238	5.07
35	259	American Cyanamid	25022	3.82
31	913	Allergan	24985	3.81
520	680	Saint Jude Medical	23474	3.58
-98	200	McKesson	20500	3.13
160	553	Elan (ADR)	19913	3.04
288	450	Becton Dickinson	19272	2.94
53	363	Amgen	19138	2.92
248	248	Chiron	17270	2.64
452	554	Baxter International	15714	2.40
-73	771	Bergen Brunswig Cl A	11558	1.76
-16	224	Forest Laboratories	10537	1.61
415	415	Alza Cl A	9757	1.49
-75	90	Medtronic	8897	1.36
297	406	Boston Scientific	6741	1.03
	222	US Surgical Cv Pfd $2.20	6466	0.99
-14	218	Lincare Holdings	5385	0.82
321	321	Pharmacia Cl A Free	5346	0.82
213	290	Abbey Healthcare Group	5285	0.81
200	200	Humana	4250	0.65

Composition % 08-31-94

Cash	12.2	Preferreds	0.0
Stocks	86.5	Convertibles	0.9
Bonds	0.4	Other	0.0

Index Allocation

	% of Stocks
S&P 500	67.1
S&P MidCap 400	10.3
U.S. Small Cap	18.1
Foreign	4.5

Tax Analysis

	Tax-Adj Historical Return %	% Pretax Return
3 Yr Avg	-1.14	---
5 Yr Avg	15.71	79.9
10 Yr Avg	19.80	84.5
Potential Capital Gain Exposure (% of assets)		7%

Most Similar Funds in MF500

Vanguard Spec Health Care	Weak Fit
General Amer Inv	Weak Fit
AIM Weingarten	Weak Fit

Sector Weightings

	% of Stocks	Relative S&P 500
Utilities	0.4	0.03
Energy	0.0	0.00
Financials	0.0	0.00
Industrial Cyclicals	0.2	0.01
Consumer Durables	0.2	0.04
Consumer Staples	5.6	0.45
Services	1.2	0.15
Retail	0.0	0.00
Health	91.6	10.55
Technology	0.8	0.08

Fidelity Short-Term Bond

	Ticker	Load	NAV	Yield	SEC Yield	Assets	Objective
	FSHBX	None	8.60	6.6%	7.09%	1514.8	Corp General

Fidelity Short-Term Bond Portfolio seeks current income consistent with preservation of capital.

The fund invests primarily in a broad range of investment-grade fixed-income securities. It may also invest a portion of its assets in lower-rated securities. The portfolio's dollar-weighted average maturity may not exceed three years. The fund may buy and sell futures contracts and options with respect to 25% of its assets.

Historical Profile
Return	Average
Risk	Below Average
Rating	★★★★ Above Average

Investment Style History
Fixed Income
Income Rtn % Rank Obj

64 60 56 40 25 18 24 39

Growth of $10,000
|||| Value of Fund ($000)
— Value of Index ($000) LB Int
▼ Manager Change
▽ Partial Manager Change
► Mgr Unknown After
◄ Mgr Unknown Before

Performance Quartile (Within Objective)

Manager's Investment Style
Management has employed an atypical strategy relative to the short-term bond group. While keeping maturity within a prescribed limit of three years or less, management has parlayed its foreign and lower-quality bonds into a performance that resembles that of an intermediate- or long-term fund in terms of return and yield. Recently, though it has not abandoned this strategy, management has pulled back from its emerging-markets and foreign exposure, due to the effects of the U.S. reversal in interest rates. Compared to others the short-term group, however, management is still adventurous.

Fund Manager(s)
Donald G. Taylor, since 09-89. Birthdate: 05-54.
BS, U. of Pennsylvania 1976

Manager Experience
	Dates Managed	Invest Obj	Std Dev	+/- Index
Donald G. Taylor				
Fidelity Adv Short F/I A	09/89 - 12/94	CG	2.63	-1.29
Fidelity Spartan S-T Inc	10/92 - 12/94	CG	3.39	-1.38

1983	1984	1985	1986	1987	1988	1989	1990	1991	1992	1993	1994	History
---	---	---	9.96	9.50	9.21	9.34	9.05	9.45	9.38	9.55	8.60	NAV
---	---	---	0.81 *	3.97	5.71	10.52	5.78	14.03	7.38	9.13	-4.09	Total Return %
---	---	---		1.21	-2.17	-4.02	-3.16	-1.98	0.14	-0.63	-1.17	+/- LB Aggregate
---	---	---		1.41	-3.51	-3.46	-1.37	-4.48	-1.32	-3.04	-0.17	+/- LB Corporate
---	---	---	1.21	8.59	8.77	9.10	8.89	9.49	8.12	7.31	5.86	Income Return %
---	---	---	-0.40	-4.62	-3.05	1.41	-3.10	4.54	-0.74	1.81	-9.95	Capital Return %
---	---	---		28	90	68	37	62	53	73	54	Total Rtn % Rank All
---	---	---		26	94	62	71	75	47	65	60	Total Rtn % Rank Obj
---	---	---	0.12	0.83	0.82	0.80	0.81	0.81	0.75	0.66	0.57	Income $
---	---	---	0.00	0.00	0.00	0.00	0.00	0.01	0.00	0.00	0.00	Capital Gains $
---	---	---		0.90	0.88	0.89	0.83	0.83	0.86	0.77	0.80	Expense Ratio %
---	---	---		8.40	8.77	8.77	8.28	8.65	8.23	7.68	6.70	Income Ratio %
---	---	---		149	251	171	148	164	87	63	73	Turnover Rate %
---	---	---	51.7	246.6	287.6	203.5	224.3	568.8	1659.4	2469.5	1514.8	Net Assets ($mil)

Performance 12-31-94
	1st Qtr	2nd Qtr	3rd Qtr	4th Qtr	Total
1987	1.04	-0.01	-0.10	3.01	3.97
1988	2.54	0.87	1.19	1.00	5.71
1989	1.35	4.54	1.39	2.87	10.52
1990	0.63	2.62	1.18	1.24	5.78
1991	2.98	2.77	3.55	4.05	14.03
1992	1.98	2.46	2.92	-0.15	7.38
1993	3.42	1.76	2.06	1.60	9.13
1994	-2.12	-1.14	1.33	-2.18	-4.09

Bear Market Performance
Decile Rank (5-year period)

Worst ———————————— Best

	Worst 3 Mo Period 1985-89	Worst 3 Mo Period 1990-94
Fidelity Short-Term Bond	---	-3.50
+/- LB Aggregate	---	1.43
+/- Best Fit Index : LB Int	---	0.72

Trailing Returns
	Total Return %	+/- LB Aggregate	+/- LB Corp	% Rank All	% Rank Obj	Growth of $10,000
3 Mo	-2.18	-2.56	-2.62	72	95	9,782
6 Mo	-0.88	-1.87	-2.06	71	92	9,912
1 Yr	-4.09	-1.17	-0.17	54	60	9,591
3 Yr Avg	3.97	-0.58	-1.44	70	68	11,238
5 Yr Avg	6.27	-1.35	-1.99	69	84	13,556
10 Yr Avg	---	---	---	---	---	---
15 Yr Avg	---	---	---	---	---	---

Operations
Address and Telephone	82 Devonshire Street
	Boston, MA 02109
	800-544-8888
Advisor	Fidelity Management & Research
Subadvisor	FMR (U.K.)/FMR (Far East)
Distributor	Fidelity Distributors
States Available	All
Report Grade	A
Income Distrib	Paid Monthly
* Date of Inception	09-15-86
Fiscal Year End	April

Risk Analysis
Time Period	Load-Adj Return %	Risk % Rank All	Risk % Rank Obj	Morningstar Return	Morningstar Risk	Morningstar Risk-Adj Rating
1 Yr	-4.09					
3 Yr	3.97	6	11	0.11[3]	0.66	★★★★
5 Yr	6.27	5	14	0.37[3]	0.63	★★★★
10 Yr	---	---	---	---	---	

Average Historical Rating (64 months) 4.4 ★s

[1] = low, 100 = high [2] 1.00 = Taxable Avg [3] 1.00 = 90-day T-bill return

Other Measures
			Standard LB Agg	Best Fit LB Int
Standard Deviation	2.85	Alpha	-0.1	0.1
Mean	3.94	Beta	0.49	0.61
Sharpe Ratio	0.15	R-Squared	46	52

Investment Style
Interest-Rate Stance
Avg Effective Duration	1.1 Yrs
Avg Effective Maturity	2.4 Yrs

Quality
Avg Credit Quality	AA
Avg Weighted Coupon	6.06%
Avg Weighted Price	92.49% of Par

Maturity Short Intm Long
Quality High Med Low

Diversification Value for Portfolio Types
Large Cap: High	Small Cap: High	Bond: Medium	Balanced: High	Diversified: High

Min Initial Purchase
Min Initial Purchase	$2500 (Addt'l: $250)
Min IRA Purchase	$500 (Addt'l: $250)
Min Auto Invest Plan	$2500 (Systematic Inv: $100)

Expenses & Fees
Sales Fees	
	0.00% front
	0.00% deferred
	0.00% 12b-1
Management Fee	0.30% flat fee+0.37%G
3-,5-,10-yr Expense Projections	$26, $44, $99

Portfolio 10-31-94
Total Stocks: 0
Total Fixed-Income: 192

Amount 000	Date of Maturity		Value $000	% Net Assets
363947	11-01-94	Repurchase Agreement 4.78%	363899	21.19
115950	04-06-95	FNMA Debenture 0%	113159	6.59
54130	08-15-98	US Treasury Note 9.25%	57513	3.35
59605	04-15-04	Govt of New Zealand 8%	34363	2.00
34495	02-02-95	Ridgefield Investments 0%	32463	1.89
65312	09-01-02	Republic of Argentina 6.25%	27563	1.60
26000	05-01-95	RJR Nabisco 9.25%	26273	1.53
26000	07-01-95	Time Warner 6.05%	25843	1.50
25000	03-31-98	US Treasury Note 5.125%	23418	1.36
83470	10-11-95	United Mexican States 0%	21385	1.24
19567	03-01-97	Marine Midland Banks 8.625%	19935	1.16
35973	04-01-01	Republic of Argentina 3.25%	18886	1.10
19890	02-15-03	US Treasury Note 6.25%	18091	1.05
17750	09-27-96	Marine Midland Banks FRN	17683	1.03
16850	06-01-95	McDermott 10.25%	17190	1.00
16900	02-16-95	GMAC 5.55%	16873	0.98
16000	02-15-95	Household Finance 9.25%	16146	0.94
16350	08-26-98	Bank of Boston 5.05%	16135	0.94
15500	07-15-97	Manufacturers Hanover FRN	15461	0.90
15350	04-06-98	CIT Group Holdings FRN LIBOR	15276	0.89
14791	04-15-19	FHLMC CMO Z 9.3%	14928	0.87
59133	12-07-95	United Mexican States 0%	14846	0.86
15000	04-15-96	Chrysler Financial 6%	14808	0.86
15150	08-01-97	Mattel 6.875%	14756	0.86
71814	04-25-03	Govt of France 8.5%	14370	0.84

Composition % 11-30-94
Cash	11.2	Preferreds	0.0
Stocks	0.0	Convertibles	0.0
Bonds	88.8	Other	0.0

Tax Analysis
	Tax-Adj Historical Return %	% Pretax Return
3 Yr Avg	1.35	33.2
5 Yr Avg	3.53	53.2
10 Yr Avg	---	---

Potential Capital Gain Exposure (% of assets) -13%

Most Similar Funds in MF500
Scudder Short-Term Bond	Fair Fit
Putnam Diversified Income A	Weak Fit
Strong Short-Term Bond	Weak Fit

Coupon Range
	% of Bonds	Rel Obj
0%	7.5	3.42
0% to 8.5%	45.2	0.71
8.5% to 9.5%	17.2	1.06
9.5% to 11%	15.7	1.70
More than 11%	3.8	0.99
Not applicable	10.6	2.12

Credit Analysis 11-30-94
% of Bonds
US Govt	0	BB	1
AAA	33	B	0
AA	3	Below B	0
A	11	NR/NA	25
BBB	27		

M⚬RNINGSTAR **1995 Mutual Fund 500**

Fidelity Small Cap Stock

Ticker	Load	NAV	Yield	SEC Yield	Assets	Objective
FDSCX	3.00%	10.45	0.1%	N/A	664.8	Small Company

Fidelity Small Cap Stock Fund seeks capital appreciation.
The fund normally invests at least 65% of its assets in common and preferred stock issued by companies with less than $750 million in market capitalization. The fund may also invest a portion of its assets in larger, more-established companies. To select securities, the fund relies on a computer-aided quantitative analysis supported by fundamental research. This model examines historical earnings, dividend yield, earnings per share, payout ratio, financial leverage, and other factors.

Manager's Investment Style

As he does at this fund's siblings, Fidelity Disciplined Equity and Fidelity Stock Selector, manager Brad Lewis uses neural networks that identify price patterns in the market. He chooses stocks with very high growth rates selling at near-market prices. With this fund, he does so in the small-cap realm. Lewis will also raise cash on the basis of his model's predictions.

Fund Manager(s)

Brad Lewis CFA(1978), since 06-93. Birthdate: 01-55. BS, Naval Academy 1977 MBA, Wharton 1985

Manager Experience

	Dates Managed	Invest Obj	Std Dev	+/- Index
Brad Lewis				
Fidelity Disciplined Eq	12/88 - 12/94	G	13.23	3.85
Fidelity Stock Selector	09/90 - 12/94	G	12.92	6.44

Historical Profile

Return	---
Risk	---
Rating	Not Rated

Investment Style History
Equity
Average % Stocks Held in Portfolio
80% 84%

Growth of $10,000
IIII Value of Fund ($000)
— Value of Index ($000)
   S&P 500
▼ Manager Change
▽ Partial Manager Change
► Mgr Unknown After
◄ Mgr Unknown Before

Performance Quartile (Within Objective)

1983	1984	1985	1986	1987	1988	1989	1990	1991	1992	1993	1994	History
---	---	---	---	---	---	---	---	---	---	10.82	10.45	NAV
---	---	---	---	---	---	---	---	---	---	8.82 *	-3.32	Total Return %
---	---	---	---	---	---	---	---	---	---	3.95 *	-4.64	+/- S&P 500
---	---	---	---	---	---	---	---	---	---	---	-0.67	+/- Wilshire 4500
---	---	---	---	---	---	---	---	---	---	0.20	0.10	Income Return %
---	---	---	---	---	---	---	---	---	---	8.62	-3.42	Capital Return %
---	---	---	---	---	---	---	---	---	---	---	46	Total Rtn % Rank All
---	---	---	---	---	---	---	---	---	---	---	68	Total Rtn % Rank Obj
---	---	---	---	---	---	---	---	---	---	0.02	0.01	Income $
---	---	---	---	---	---	---	---	---	---	0.04	0.00	Capital Gains $
---	---	---	---	---	---	---	---	---	---	---	1.18	Expense Ratio %
---	---	---	---	---	---	---	---	---	---	---	0.03	Income Ratio %
---	---	---	---	---	---	---	---	---	---	---	210	Turnover Rate %
---	---	---	---	---	---	---	---	---	---	666.3	664.8	Net Assets ($mil)

Performance 12-31-94

	1st Qtr	2nd Qtr	3rd Qtr	4th Qtr	Total
1987	---	---	---	---	---
1988	---	---	---	---	---
1989	---	---	---	---	---
1990	---	---	---	---	---
1991	---	---	---	---	---
1992	---	---	---	---	---
1993	---	---	6.60	2.08	8.82 *
1994	-3.51	-5.94	7.33	-0.76	-3.32

Bear Market Performance

Decile Rank (5-year period)

Worst   Best

	Worst 3 Mo Period 1985-89	Worst 3 Mo Period 1990-94
Fidelity Small Cap Stock	---	---
+/- S&P 500	---	---
+/- Best Fit Index :	---	---

Trailing Returns

	Total Return %	+/- S&P 500	+/- Wil 4500	% Rank All	% Rank Obj	Growth of $10,000
3 Mo	-0.76	-0.74	1.75	39	46	9,924
6 Mo	6.52	1.66	2.33	8	46	10,652
1 Yr	-3.32	-4.64	-0.67	46	68	9,668
3 Yr Avg	---	---	---	---	---	---
5 Yr Avg	---	---	---	---	---	---
10 Yr Avg	---	---	---	---	---	---
15 Yr Avg	---	---	---	---	---	---

Operations

Address and Telephone	82 Devonshire Street
	Boston, MA 02109
	800-544-8888
Advisor	Fidelity Management & Research
Subadvisor	FMR (Far East)/FMR (U.K.)
Distributor	Fidelity Distributors
States Available	All
Report Grade	A
Income Distrib	Paid Semiannually
* Date of Inception	06-28-93
Fiscal Year End	April

Risk Analysis

Time Period	Load-Adj Return %	Risk % Rank[1] All	Obj	Morningstar[2] Return	Morningstar Risk	Morningstar Risk-Adj Rating
1 Yr	-6.22					
3 Yr	---	---	---	---	---	---
5 Yr	---	---	---	---	---	---
10 Yr	---	---	---	---	---	---
Average Historical Rating ---						---

[1] 1 = low, 100 = high   [2] 1.00 = Equity Avg   [3] 1.00 = 90-day T-bill return

Other Measures

			Standard S&P 500	Best Fit
Standard Deviation	---	Alpha	---	---
Mean	---	Beta	---	---
Sharpe Ratio	---	R-Squared	---	---

Investment Style

	Stock Portfolio Avg	Relative S&P 500
Price/Earnings Ratio	20.3	1.10
Price/Book Ratio	2.9	0.86
5 Yr Earnings Gr %	13.6#	2.45
Return on Assets %	8.6	1.16
Debt % Total Cap	25.4	0.90
Med Mkt Cap ($mil)	402	0.03

figure is based on 50% or less of stocks

Style
Value Blend Growth
Size Large Med Small

Diversification Value for Portfolio Types

Large Cap: Small Cap: Bond: Balanced: Diversified:

Expenses & Fees

Sales Fees	3.00% front
	0.00% deferred
	0.00% 12b-1
Management Fee	0.35% flat fee+0.52%G+(-)0.20%P
3-,5-,10-yr Expense Projections	$66, $93, $169
Annual Brokerage Cost	0.27%

Min Initial Purchase	$2500 (Addt'l: $250)
Min IRA Purchase	$500 (Addt'l: $250)
Min Auto Invest Plan	$2500 (Systematic Inv: $100)

Portfolio 10-31-94

Share Chg (04-94)000	Amount 000	Total Stocks: 389 Total Fixed-Income: 0	Value $000	% Net Assets
0	418	Novellus Systems	22781	3.31
212	637	Williams-Sonoma	21978	3.20
-433	433	Atmel	15974	2.32
202	272	KLA Instruments	14353	2.09
640	640	Cadence Design Systems	12800	1.86
0	420	Integrated Device Technology	11915	1.73
52	211	Integrated Health Services	8598	1.25
712	836	Dime Bancorp	7315	1.06
0	281	FileNet	7160	1.04
228	228	ANTEC	6498	0.94
163	295	Cypress Semiconductor	6158	0.90
275	336	Waban	5957	0.87
285	338	Smith International	5665	0.82
105	254	Exabyte	5584	0.81
0	354	PennCorp Financial Group	5576	0.81
-65	247	Input/Output	5315	0.77
154	186	Kennametal	5243	0.76
43	181	CMAC Investment	4986	0.73
0	163	Saint John Knits	4972	0.72
328	328	WHX	4920	0.72
399	399	Sterling Chemicals	4833	0.70
27	87	United HealthCare	4607	0.67
258	258	Alaska Air Group	4515	0.66
117	117	Duracraft	4373	0.64
-7	175	Fremont General	4303	0.63

Composition % 11-30-94

Cash	13.0	Preferreds	0.0
Stocks	87.0	Convertibles	0.0
Bonds	0.0	Other	0.0

Tax Analysis

	Tax-Adj Historical Return %	% Pretax Return
3 Yr Avg	---	---
5 Yr Avg	---	---
10 Yr Avg	---	---
Potential Capital Gain Exposure (% of assets)		1%

Most Similar Funds in MF500

Fund lacks three-year record

Index Allocation

	% of Stocks
S&P 500	4.5
S&P MidCap 400	21.4
U.S. Small Cap	74.0
Foreign	0.1

Sector Weightings

	% of Stocks	Relative S&P 500
Utilities	2.2	0.17
Energy	2.9	0.29
Financials	15.2	1.44
Industrial Cyclicals	15.1	0.92
Consumer Durables	7.8	1.25
Consumer Staples	2.4	0.19
Services	8.6	1.06
Retail	11.1	1.90
Health	6.4	0.74
Technology	28.4	3.10

Fidelity Spartan Ginnie Mae

	Ticker	Load	NAV	Yield	SEC Yield	Assets	Objective
	SGNMX	None	9.32	6.7%	7.79%	347.8	Gvt Mortgage

Fidelity Spartan Ginnie Mae Fund seeks current income.
The fund invests at least 65% of its assets in Government National Mortgage Association mortgage-backed pass-through certificates (GNMAs). It focuses on securities with high yields, including Ginnie Maes that may be trading at a premium to their par value, but this emphasis does not preclude investment for capital gains. The balance of the fund's assets may be invested in any high-quality U.S. or foreign debt or other income-producing investments, including other types of mortgage securities, government securities, asset-backed securities, and corporate debt.

Historical Profile

Return	Average
Risk	Below Average
Rating	★★★
	Neutral

Investment Style History
Fixed Income
Income Rtn % Rank Obj

| | | | | | | 50 | 38 | 88 | 45 |

Growth of $10,000
|||| Value of Fund ($000)
— Value of Index ($000)
LB Mtg
▼ Manager Change
▽ Partial Manager Change
► Mgr Unknown After
◄ Mgr Unknown Before

Performance Quartile
(Within Objective)

Manager's Investment Style

Manager Bob Ives says he works hard to keep the portfolio's duration in line with its benchmark, the Lehman Brothers Mortgage-Backed Securities Index. He also emphasizes seasoned mortgages, which offer relatively predictible prepayment patterns and so won't likely show a sudden drop off in prepayment rates which extends duration. Though Ives recently cleaned up the portfolio, under prior management the strategy did include use of asset-backed securities and mortgage derivatives. In general, however, management prefers plain-vanilla GNMA pass-throughs.

Fund Manager(s)

Robert C. Ives, since 02-93. Birthdate: 1962.
MS, Stanford U. 1985 MBA, U. of Chicago 1991

Manager Experience	Dates Managed	Invest Obj	Std Dev	+/- Index
Robert C. Ives				
Fidelity Mortgage Secs	01/93 - 07/93	GM	1.07	-1.04

1983	1984	1985	1986	1987	1988	1989	1990	1991	1992	1993	1994	History
---	---	---	---	---	---	---	10.01	10.46	10.11	10.10	9.32	NAV
---	---	---	---	---	---	---	0.10 *	13.79	5.91	6.43	-1.51	Total Return %
---	---	---	---	---	---	---		-2.22	-1.34	-3.32	1.41	+/- LB Aggregate
---	---	---	---	---	---	---		-1.93	-1.05	-0.41	0.10	+/- LB Mortgage
---	---	---	---	---	---	---	0.00	9.08	7.75	5.83	6.21	Income Return %
---	---	---	---	---	---	---	0.10	4.71	-1.85	0.59	-7.72	Capital Return %
---	---	---	---	---	---	---		63	70	86	30	Total Rtn % Rank All
---	---	---	---	---	---	---		66	72	57	25	Total Rtn % Rank Obj
---	---	---	---	---	---	---	0.00	0.85	0.78	0.58	0.63	Income $
---	---	---	---	---	---	---	0.00	0.02	0.16	0.07	0.00	Capital Gains $
---	---	---	---	---	---	---		0.25	0.17	0.41	0.65	Expense Ratio %
---	---	---	---	---	---	---		8.69	8.09	7.63	7.36	Income Ratio %
---	---	---	---	---	---	---		41	168	241	285	Turnover Rate %
---	---	---	---	---	---	---	1.0	702.0	761.6	579.4	347.8	Net Assets ($mil)

Performance 12-31-94

	1st Qtr	2nd Qtr	3rd Qtr	4th Qtr	Total
1987	---	---	---	---	---
1988	---	---	---	---	---
1989	---	---	---	---	---
1990	---	---	---	---	0.10 *
1991	2.40	1.38	5.03	4.37	13.79
1992	-0.05	3.83	1.47	0.57	5.91
1993	3.01	2.02	0.65	0.62	6.43
1994	-2.09	-0.99	0.95	0.64	-1.51

Bear Market Performance

Decile Rank (5-year period)

Worst ———————————————— Best

	Worst 3 Mo Period 1985-89	Worst 3 Mo Period 1990-94
Fidelity Spartan Ginnie Mae	---	---
+/- LB Aggregate	---	---
+/- Best Fit Index :	---	---

Trailing Returns

	Total Return %	+/- LB Aggregate	+/- LB Mortgage	% Rank All	% Rank Obj	Growth of $10,000
3 Mo	0.64	0.26	0.21	9	11	10,064
6 Mo	1.60	0.60	0.29	30	4	10,160
1 Yr	-1.51	1.41	0.10	30	25	9,849
3 Yr Avg	3.54	-1.00	-0.44	78	37	11,102
5 Yr Avg	---	---	---	---	---	---
10 Yr Avg	---	---	---	---	---	---
15 Yr Avg	---	---	---	---	---	---

Operations

Address and Telephone	82 Devonshire Street
	Boston, MA 02109
	800-544-8888
Advisor	Fidelity Management & Research
Subadvisor	None
Distributor	Fidelity Distributors
States Available	All
Report Grade	A
Income Distrib	Paid Monthly
* Date of Inception	12-27-90
Fiscal Year End	August

Risk Analysis

Time Period	Load-Adj Return %	Risk % Rank¹ All	Risk % Rank¹ Obj	Morningstar² Return	Morningstar Risk	Morningstar Risk-Adj Rating
1 Yr	-1.51					
3 Yr	3.55	14	40	-0.01³	0.86	★★★
5 Yr	---	---	---	---	---	
10 Yr	---	---	---	---	---	

Average Historical Rating (13 months)   3.7 ★ s

¹ 1 = low, 100 = high   ² 1.00 = Taxable Avg   ³ 1.00 = 90-day T-bill return

Other Measures

		Standard LB Agg	Best Fit LB Mtg
Standard Deviation	3.27	Alpha	-0.7	-0.4
Mean	3.54	Beta	0.71	0.97
Sharpe Ratio	0.01	R-Squared	76	92

Investment Style

Interest-Rate Stance
Avg Effective Duration   5.4 Yrs
Avg Effective Maturity   9.2 Yrs

Quality
Avg Credit Quality   AAA
Avg Weighted Coupon   8.27%
Avg Weighted Price 100.08% of Par

Maturity
Short Intm Long

Diversification Value for Portfolio Types

Large Cap: High	Small Cap: High	Bond: Low	Balanced: Medium	Diversified: Medium

Min Initial Purchase	$10000 (Addt'l: $1000)
Min IRA Purchase	$10000 (Addt'l: $1000)
Min Auto Invest Plan	$10000 (Systematic Inv: $500)

Expenses & Fees

Sales Fees	0.00% front
	0.00% deferred
	0.00% 12b-1
Management Fee	0.65% flat fee
3-,5-,10-yr Expense Projections	$26, $41, $86

Portfolio 08-31-94

Amount 000	Date of Maturity	Total Stocks: 0 Total Fixed-Income: 33	Value $000	% Net Assets
85395	01-15-24	GNMA 7%	80710	20.13
73803	08-15-24	GNMA 7.5%	71244	17.77
64301	08-15-24	GNMA 8%	63881	15.93
53518	03-15-10	GNMA 9%	56225	14.02
29852	01-15-23	GNMA 9.5%	31794	7.93
20915	04-15-24	GNMA 6.5%	18828	4.70
15832	08-15-24	GNMA 8.5%	16140	4.02
10633	09-15-19	GNMA 10%	11456	2.86
8145	11-01-20	FHLMC 10%	8616	2.15
9000	09-15-24	GNMA Forward 6.5%	8106	2.02
7198	07-01-21	FHLMC 9%	7560	1.89
4763	01-15-16	GNMA 11%	5309	1.32
3998	10-15-15	GNMA 12.5%	4596	1.15
2493	11-01-05	FNMA 10.5%	2677	0.67
2192	05-01-21	FNMA 12.5%	2483	0.62
1665	05-01-15	FHLMC 12.5%	1900	0.47
1523	11-01-16	FHLMC 10.25%	1612	0.40
1377	10-01-17	FNMA 12%	1546	0.39
972	02-01-17	FHLMC 12%	1069	0.27
964	08-01-10	FNMA 11%	1063	0.27
836	05-15-14	GNMA 12%	953	0.24
735	09-01-11	FNMA 13.25%	839	0.21
764	04-01-13	FHLMC 9.75%	803	0.20
670	01-15-15	GNMA 13%	778	0.19
676	06-01-19	FHLMC 11.5%	742	0.19

Composition % 11-30-94

Cash	2.8	Preferreds	0.0
Stocks	0.0	Convertibles	0.0
Bonds	97.2	Other	0.0

Tax Analysis

	Tax-Adj Historical Return %	% Pretax Return
3 Yr Avg	0.91	24.9
5 Yr Avg	---	---
10 Yr Avg	---	---

Potential Capital Gain Exposure
(% of assets)   -12%

Most Similar Funds in MF500

Franklin U.S. Government Sec	Strong Fit
T. Rowe Price GNMA	Strong Fit
Benham GNMA Income	Strong Fit

Coupon Range

	% of Bonds	Rel Obj
0%	0.0	0.00
0% to 8%	60.2	1.09
8% to 9%	19.8	0.91
9% to 10%	13.2	1.54
More than 10%	6.8	1.04
Not applicable	0.0	0.00

Sector Analysis 08-31-94

% of Bonds

US Treas	0	CMOs	0
GNMA mtgs	92	ARMs	0
FNMA mtgs	2	Other	0
FHLMC mtgs	6		

MORNINGSTAR   1995 Mutual Fund 500

Fidelity Spartan Lim Mat Govt

	Ticker	Load	NAV	Yield	SEC Yield	Assets	Objective
	FSTGX	None	9.35	5.9%	7.12%	830.6	Gvt General

Fidelity Spartan Limited Maturity Government Fund seeks income consistent with capital preservation.

The fund normally invests at least 65% of its assets in U.S. government obligations and related repurchase agreements. Its portfolio's average weighted maturity may not exceed 10 years. The fund attempts to maintain an overall sensitivity to interest rates in a range similar to the average for short- to intermediate-term government bonds with maturities of one to four years.

Prior to June 14, 1990, the fund was named Fidelity Short-Term Government Fund.

Manager's Investment Style

The fund has always had one of the highest turnover rates in the government-general group. Annual turnover topped 800% in 1989, and it has remained around 300% ever since. Manager Curtis Hollingsworth actively trades among various government-bond sectors based on which one has the best yield after adjusting for expected prepayment levels. He keeps the portfolio's interest-rate sensitivity in a narrow range, which enables the fund to hold up fairly well when interest rates rise.

Fund Manager(s)

Curtis Hollingsworth, since 05-88. Birthdate: 05-57. BA, Boston U. 1983

Manager Experience	Dates Managed	Invest Obj	Std Dev	+/- Index
Curtis Hollingsworth				
Fidelity Instl Sh-Int Gov	01/87 - 12/94	GG	2.32	-0.84
Fidelity Government Secs	02/90 - 12/94	GG	4.85	0.25

Historical Profile
Return	Average
Risk	Low
Rating	★★★★★ Highest

History	1983	1984	1985	1986	1987	1988	1989	1990	1991	1992	1993	1994
						72	50	34	78	58	46	
NAV	---	---	---	---	---	9.80	9.96	9.99	10.25	10.17	10.00	9.35
Total Return %	---	---	---	---	---	3.49 *	10.35	9.13	11.91	5.77	6.42	-0.95
+/- LB Aggregate	---	---	---	---	---		-4.19	0.19	-4.09	-1.48	-3.33	1.97
+/- LB Government	---	---	---	---	---		-3.87	0.42	-3.40	-1.46	-4.24	2.42
Income Return %	---	---	---	---	---	5.49	8.72	8.63	8.69	6.06	5.84	5.55
Capital Return %	---	---	---	---	---	-2.00	1.63	0.50	3.23	-0.30	0.58	-6.50
Total Rtn % Rank All	---	---	---	---	---		70	8	76	72	86	26
Total Rtn % Rank Obj	---	---	---	---	---		83	35	83	60	73	15
Income $	---	---	---	---	---	0.54	0.82	0.82	0.82	0.60	0.58	0.56
Capital Gains $	---	---	---	---	---	0.00	0.00	0.02	0.06	0.05	0.23	0.00
Expense Ratio %	---	---	---	---	---	0.21	0.68	0.83	0.50	0.61	0.65	0.65
Income Ratio %	---	---	---	---	---	8.70	8.20	8.28	8.63	8.24	8.05	7.37
Turnover Rate %	---	---	---	---	---	471	806	270	288	330	324	391
Net Assets ($mil)	---	---	---	---	---	107.5	134.3	161.7	2085.2	1618.6	1356.6	830.6

Investment Style History
Fixed Income
Income Rtn % Rank Obj

Growth of $10,000
- |||| Value of Fund ($000)
- — Value of Index ($000) LB Agg
- ▼ Manager Change
- ▽ Partial Manager Change
- ► Mgr Unknown After
- ◄ Mgr Unknown Before

Performance Quartile (Within Objective)

Performance 12-31-94

	1st Qtr	2nd Qtr	3rd Qtr	4th Qtr	Total
1987	---	---	---	---	---
1988	---	---	1.33	1.32	3.49 *
1989	1.36	4.58	1.14	2.93	10.35
1990	0.66	2.62	2.41	3.15	9.13
1991	2.74	1.78	3.44	3.45	11.91
1992	-0.02	2.54	2.19	0.95	5.77
1993	2.50	2.04	1.44	0.30	6.42
1994	-1.19	-0.62	1.09	-0.21	-0.95

Bear Market Performance

Decile Rank (5-year period)

Worst ──────────────── Best

	Worst 3 Mo Period 1985-89	Worst 3 Mo Period 1990-94
Fidelity Spartan Lim Mat Govt	---	-2.69
+/- LB Aggregate	---	2.25
+/- Best Fit Index : LB Agg	---	2.25

Trailing Returns

	Total Return %	+/- LB Aggregate	+/- LB Govt	% Rank All	% Rank Obj	Growth of $10,000
3 Mo	-0.21	-0.59	-0.57	28	70	9,979
6 Mo	0.88	-0.12	0.09	40	21	10,088
1 Yr	-0.95	1.97	2.42	26	15	9,905
3 Yr Avg	3.69	-0.86	-0.97	76	39	11,148
5 Yr Avg	6.37	-1.26	-1.16	67	54	13,616
10 Yr Avg	---	---	---	---	---	---
15 Yr Avg	---	---	---	---	---	---

Operations

Address and Telephone: 82 Devonshire Street, Boston, MA 02109, 800-544-8888
Advisor: Fidelity Management & Research
Subadvisor: FMR (U.K.)/FMR (Far East)
Distributor: Fidelity Distributors
States Available: All
Report Grade: A
Income Distrib: Paid Monthly
* Date of Inception: 05-02-88
Fiscal Year End: July

Risk Analysis

Time Period	Load-Adj Return %	Risk % Rank¹ All	Obj	Morningstar² Return	Morningstar Risk	Morningstar Risk-Adj Rating
1 Yr	-0.95					
3 Yr	3.69	5	7	0.03³	0.57	★★★★
5 Yr	6.37	3	5	0.39³	0.47	★★★★★
10 Yr	---					

Average Historical Rating (44 months) 4.7 ★s

¹ 1 = low, 100 = high ² 1.00 = Taxable Avg ³ 1.00 = 90-day T-bill return

Other Measures

				Standard LB Agg	Best Fit LB Agg
Standard Deviation	2.11	Alpha		-0.4	-0.4
Mean	3.65	Beta		0.48	0.48
Sharpe Ratio	0.06	R-Squared		81	81

Investment Style

Interest-Rate Stance
		Maturity
Avg Effective Duration	4.2 Yrs**	Short Intm Long
Avg Effective Maturity	4.7 Yrs	

Quality
Avg Credit Quality AAA
Avg Weighted Coupon 8.76%
Avg Weighted Price 104.76% of Par
**figure provided by fund

Diversification Value for Portfolio Types

Large Cap: High | Small Cap: High | Bond: Low | Balanced: Medium | Diversified: Medium

Portfolio 07-31-94

Total Stocks: 0
Total Fixed-Income: 74

Amount 000	Date of Maturity		Value $000	% Net Assets
144700	03-31-98	US Treasury Note 5.125%	138325	13.62
103711	04-15-19	GNMA 12.5%	118876	11.70
113000	02-15-96	US Treasury Note 7.875%	116443	11.46
89700	11-15-96	US Treasury Note 7.25%	91858	9.04
50990	09-15-23	GNMA 8%	50992	5.02
42385	09-15-17	GNMA 9%	44525	4.38
41500	05-15-96	US Treasury Note 7.375%	42518	4.19
34350	08-15-98	US Treasury Note 9.25%	37565	3.70
33455	08-15-24	GNMA 9.5%	35577	3.50
28818	08-01-19	GNMA 11.5%	32218	3.17
19623	08-01-07	FNMA 9%	20474	2.02
17859	11-15-17	GNMA 10%	19240	1.89
18905	02-15-99	Aid to Israel 6%	18261	1.80
17209	07-01-22	FNMA 8%	17481	1.72
15462	06-01-21	FHLMC 9.5%	16215	1.60
14080	11-15-01	Govt Trust Certificate 9.25%	15365	1.51
13457	03-01-17	FNMA 12%	15187	1.50
11751	12-01-22	FNMA 8.5%	12102	1.19
9507	11-01-05	FNMA 10.5%	10170	1.00
8876	05-01-21	FNMA 12.5%	10118	1.00
6482	12-01-15	GNMA 12%	7226	0.71
6750	03-15-00	Aid to Israel 5.75%	6356	0.63
5314	07-15-17	GNMA 10.5%	5808	0.57
5504	07-01-21	FHLMC 9%	5783	0.57
4695	09-01-15	FNMA 11%	5218	0.51

Composition % 12-22-94

Cash	1.1	Preferreds	0.0
Stocks	0.0	Convertibles	0.0
Bonds	98.9	Other	0.0

Tax Analysis

	Tax-Adj Historical Return %	% Pretax Return
3 Yr Avg	1.27	33.7
5 Yr Avg	3.78	56.4
10 Yr Avg	---	---

Potential Capital Gain Exposure (% of assets) -10%

Most Similar Funds in MF500

Prudential Struct Maturity A	Fair Fit
Vanguard F/I Short-Trm US Tr	Fair Fit
T. Rowe Price Short-Trm Bond	Fair Fit

Coupon Range

	% of Bonds	Rel Obj
0%	0.0	0.00
0% to 8%	51.4	0.82
8% to 9%	8.9	0.58
9% to 10%	13.5	1.68
More than 10%	25.7	4.11
Not applicable	0.4	0.07

Sector Analysis 07-31-94

% of Bonds

US Treas	44	CMOs	1
GNMA mtgs	35	ARMs	0
FNMA mtgs	13	Other	5
FHLMC mtgs	4		

Min Initial Purchase
Min Initial Purchase $10000 (Addt'l: $1000)
Min IRA Purchase $10000 (Addt'l: $1000)
Min Auto Invest Plan $10000 (Systematic Inv: $500)

Expenses & Fees
Sales Fees: 0.00% front / 0.00% deferred / 0.00% 12b-1
Management Fee: 0.65% flat fee
3-,5-,10-yr Expense Projections $26, $41, $86

Fidelity Spartan Sh-Interm Muni

Ticker	Load	NAV	Yield	SEC Yield	Assets	Objective
FSTFX	None	9.66	4.5%	4.84%	913.1	Muni Nat

Fidelity Spartan Short-Intermediate Municipal Fund seeks current income exempt from federal income tax, consistent with preservation of capital.

The fund normally invests in high-quality short-term municipal obligations with maturities of five years or less; the portfolio's dollar-weighted average maturity is limited to four years or less. Eighty percent or more of assets are exempt from federal income tax.

The fund was named Fidelity Short-Term Tax-Free Portfolio prior to Oct. 1, 1990.

Manager's Investment Style

Manager David Murphy prioritizes income with this portfolio. As such, he keeps the fund's duration on the long side of the short-intermediate spectrum, and invests some assets in less-popular or little-understood states and sectors. He has also shown a willingness to invest in short-term Treasuries when they appear more attractive than comparable municipal bonds.

Fund Manager(s)

David L. Murphy CFA, since 12-89. Birthdate: 01-48. MA, Columbia U. 1976 MBA, Columbia U. 1981

Manager Experience	Dates Managed	Invest Obj	Std Dev	+/- Index
David L. Murphy				
Fidelity NY T-F Insured	09/92 - 03/94	MY	5.72	2.17

Historical Profile

Return	Below Average
Risk	Low
Rating	★★★★★ Highest

Investment Style History
Fixed Income
Income Rtn % Rank Obj

Growth of $10,000
- IIII Value of Fund ($000)
- — Value of Index ($000) LB Muni
- ▼ Manager Change
- ▽ Partial Manager Change
- ► Mgr Unknown After
- ◄ Mgr Unknown Before

Performance Quartile (Within Objective)

	1983	1984	1985	1986	1987	1988	1989	1990	1991	1992	1993	1994	History
	---	---	---	10.00	9.51	9.45	9.49	9.52	9.78	9.88	10.11	9.66	NAV
	---	---	---	0.00 *	-0.54	4.89	6.30	6.42	8.86	6.38	7.29	-0.08	Total Return %
	---	---	---		-3.29	-2.99	-8.24	-2.53	-7.15	-0.87	-2.46	2.83	+/- LB Aggregate
	---	---	---		-2.04	-5.27	-4.48	-0.88	-3.29	-2.44	-4.99	5.52	+/- LB Muni
	---	---	---	0.00	4.36	5.52	5.88	6.10	6.12	5.35	4.86	4.37	Income Return %
	---	---	---	0.00	-4.90	-0.63	0.42	0.32	2.73	1.02	2.43	-4.45	Capital Return %
	---	---	---		64	93	94	29	94	65	82	20	Total Rtn % Rank All
	---	---	---		60	100	98	45	93	93	92	5	Total Rtn % Rank Obj
	---	---	---	0.00	0.43	0.52	0.54	0.56	0.56	0.51	0.47	0.44	Income $
	---	---	---	0.00	0.00	0.00	0.00	0.00	0.00	0.00	0.01	0.00	Capital Gains $
	---	---	---	0.60	0.60	0.35	0.58	0.60	0.55	0.55	0.55	0.47	Expense Ratio %
	---	---	---	4.00	4.58	5.48	5.69	5.90	5.68	4.95	4.55	4.45	Income Ratio %
	---	---	---	0	180	96	82	75	59	28	56	44	Turnover Rate %
	---	---	---	1.2	59.1	76.0	57.4	58.7	242.3	655.8	1188.2	913.1	Net Assets ($mil)

Performance 12-31-94

	1st Qtr	2nd Qtr	3rd Qtr	4th Qtr	Total
1987	0.00	-1.24	-1.28	2.01	-0.54
1988	1.54	1.06	1.11	1.10	4.89
1989	0.07	2.51	1.40	2.21	6.30
1990	1.25	1.26	1.57	2.19	6.42
1991	1.95	1.83	2.29	2.50	8.86
1992	0.87	2.04	1.63	1.69	6.38
1993	2.63	1.54	1.83	1.11	7.29
1994	-2.09	1.14	1.00	-0.10	-0.08

Bear Market Performance

Decile Rank (5-year period)

	Worst 3 Mo Period 1985-89	Worst 3 Mo Period 1990-94
Fidelity Spartan Sh-Interm Mun	---	-2.37
+/- LB Aggregate	---	2.56
+/- Best Fit Index : LB Muni	---	3.39

Trailing Returns

	Total Return %	+/- LB Aggregate	+/- LB Muni	% Rank All	% Rank Obj	Growth of $10,000
3 Mo	-0.10	-0.48	1.33	25	6	9,990
6 Mo	0.90	-0.09	2.15	39	5	10,090
1 Yr	-0.08	2.83	5.52	20	5	9,992
3 Yr Avg	4.47	-0.07	-0.39	59	54	11,403
5 Yr Avg	5.73	-1.90	-1.05	81	75	13,210
10 Yr Avg	---	---	---	---	---	---
15 Yr Avg	---	---	---	---	---	---

Operations

Address and Telephone	82 Devonshire Street
	Boston, MA 02109
	800-544-8888
Advisor	Fidelity Management & Research
Subadvisor	None
Distributor	Fidelity Distributors
States Available	All
Report Grade	A
Income Distrib	Paid Monthly
* Date of Inception	12-24-86
Fiscal Year End	August

Risk Analysis

Time Period	Load-Adj Return %	Risk % Rank [1] All	Obj	Morningstar [2] Return	Morningstar Risk	Morningstar Risk-Adj Rating
1 Yr	-0.08					
3 Yr	4.47	2	5	0.98	0.31	★★★★★
5 Yr	5.73	2	5	0.80	0.29	★★★★★
10 Yr	---					

Average Historical Rating (61 months) 3.9 ★s

[1] 1 = low, 100 = high [2] 1.00 = Muni Avg [3] 1.00 = 90-day T-bill return

Other Measures

			Standard LB Agg	Best Fit LB Muni
Standard Deviation	2.34	Alpha	0.4	0.3
Mean	4.41	Beta	0.44	0.42
Sharpe Ratio	0.38	R-Squared	55	94

Investment Style

Interest-Rate Stance
Avg Effective Maturity 3.5 Yrs

Quality
Avg Credit Quality A
Avg Weighted Coupon 5.73%
Avg Weighted Price 102.08% of Par

Diversification Value for Portfolio Types

Large Cap: Medium	Small Cap: High	Bond: Low	Balanced: Low	Diversified: Medium

Portfolio 08-31-94

Total Stocks: 0
Total Fixed-Income: 246

Amount 000	Date of Maturity		Value $000	% Net Assets
28015	06-30-97	AK North Slope GO 7.5%	29941	2.77
25400	07-01-99	MA New England Ed Loan Mktg Ser E 5%	25083	2.32
21000	12-01-99	MA New England Educ Loan Mktg 4.75%	20580	1.90
17535	05-01-99	LA State GO Ins 8%	19326	1.78
17175	07-01-15	WA Hlth Care Fac Franciscan Sys 9.25%	18227	1.68
17790	05-15-96	FL COP Const Equip Fin Prog 5.9%	17946	1.66
12950	12-01-97	CA First Custodial Pooled Receipts RIB	17062	1.58
13960	10-01-08	NH Higher Educ/Hlth Fac Frisbie 9.5%	16089	1.49
17400	08-15-97	TX Dallas GO ISD Cap Apprec 0%	15508	1.43
15500	09-01-98	MS Higher Educ Assist Student Loan 4.8%	15209	1.40
15000	12-01-25	CO Denver Arpt Sys 4.25%	14888	1.38
17600	01-01-01	KY Owensboro Elec Lt/Pwr Sys 0%	14333	1.32
14000	12-01-97	RI Student Loan 6%	14315	1.32
12820	11-15-98	NY State GO Crossover Rfdg 7.8%	14262	1.32
12505	11-15-96	TX Austin Combined Util Sys 11%	13943	1.29
13250	06-01-99	TX Brazos Higher Educ Student Loan 5.15%	13150	1.21
12420	12-01-99	MT Higher Educ Student Loan 4.9%	12327	1.14
11500	09-01-98	MA New England Ed Loan Mktg Ser A 6%	11816	1.09
11700	06-01-98	TX Brazos Higher Educ Student Loan 4.95%	11597	1.07
11600	06-01-97	TX Brazos Higher Educ Student Loan 4.75%	11528	1.06

Credit Analysis % of Bonds 10-31-94

US Govt	0	BB	0
AAA	34	B	0
AA	8	Below B	0
A	29	NR/NA	30
BBB	0		

Composition % of Assets 10-31-94

Cash	14.6	Preferreds	0.0
Stocks	0.0	Convertibles	0.0
Bonds	85.4	Other	0.0

Tax Analysis

	Tax-Adj Historical Return %	% Pretax Return
3 Yr Avg	4.47	99.8
5 Yr Avg	5.72	99.9
10 Yr Avg	---	---
Potential Capital Gain Exposure (% of assets)		-3%

Most Similar Funds in MF500

Thornburg Ltd-Term Natl A	Strong Fit
Vanguard Muni Limited-Term	Strong Fit
T. Rowe Price Tax-Fr Sh-Intm	Strong Fit

Coupon Range

	% Bonds	Rel Obj
0%	10.3	4.11
0% to 6.8%	48.6	0.80
6.8% to 7.5%	8.6	0.55
7.5% to 8.3%	10.5	1.18
More than 8.3%	12.6	1.43
Not applicable	9.4	2.42

Sector Weightings

	% Bonds	Rel Obj
General Obl	22.44	1.07
Utilities	11.74	0.94
Health	6.53	0.50
Water/Waste	0.89	0.14
Housing	0.94	0.13
Education	28.59	4.47
Transportation	6.97	0.68
COP/Lease	5.19	1.63
Private	5.94	0.51
Misc Revenue	4.33	0.87
Demand	6.45	2.62

Top 5 States % of Bonds

MA	11.27	CA	8.03
TX	9.80	WA	5.32
LA	8.87		

Min Initial Purchase / Expenses

Min Initial Purchase	$10000 (Addt'l: $1000)
Min IRA Purchase	N/A
Min Auto Invest Plan	$10000 (Systematic Inv: $500)

Expenses & Fees

Sales Fees	
	0.00% front
	0.00% deferred
	0.00% 12b-1
Management Fee	0.55% flat fee
3-,5-,10-yr Expense Projections	$23, $36, $74

MORNINGSTAR 1995 Mutual Fund 500

Fidelity Stock Selector

	Ticker	Load	NAV	Yield	SEC Yield	Assets	Objective
	FDSSX	None	17.91	0.8%	N/A	786.7	Growth

Fidelity Stock Selector Fund seeks capital growth.
The fund normally invests at least 65% of its assets in common stocks. It is actively managed and covers a broad range of foreign and domestic companies. The fund's stocks are selected according to both fundamental and technical valuation factors, such as historical earnings, dividend yield, market price relative to book value, earnings per share, payout ratio, financial leverage, and other evaluation criteria.

Historical Profile

Return	Above Average
Risk	Average
Rating	★★★★
	Above Average

Investment Style History
Equity

Average % Stocks Held in Portfolio

| | | | --- | 94% | 92% | 84% | 86% |

Growth of $10,000

‖‖‖ Value of Fund ($000)
— Value of Index ($000)
 SPMid400
▼ Manager Change
▽ Partial Manager Change
► Mgr Unknown After
◄ Mgr Unknown Before

Performance Quartile
(Within Objective)

1983	1984	1985	1986	1987	1988	1989	1990	1991	1992	1993	1994	History
---	---	---	---	---	---	---	11.12	15.63	17.61	18.75	17.91	NAV
---	---	---	---	---	---	---	11.51 *	45.95	15.42	13.97	0.78	Total Return %
---	---	---	---	---	---	---	2.55 *	15.46	7.81	3.92	-0.54	+/- S&P 500
---	---	---	---	---	---	---		11.74	6.45	2.69	0.85	+/- Wilshire 5000
---	---	---	---	---	---	---	0.31	0.59	0.60	1.32	0.85	Income Return %
---	---	---	---	---	---	---	11.20	45.35	14.82	12.66	-0.08	Capital Return %
---	---	---	---	---	---	---		10	9	33	15	Total Rtn % Rank All
---	---	---	---	---	---	---		20	15	38	26	Total Rtn % Rank Obj
---	---	---	---	---	---	---	0.03	0.08	0.10	0.24	0.15	Income $
---	---	---	---	---	---	---	0.00	0.47	0.32	1.06	0.81	Capital Gains $
---	---	---	---	---	---	---	2.50	1.43	1.22	1.10	1.09	Expense Ratio %
---	---	---	---	---	---	---	2.27	1.20	1.43	1.52	1.01	Income Ratio %
---	---	---	---	---	---	---		207	317	268	192	187	Turnover Rate %
---	---	---	---	---	---	---	59.9	126.6	350.0	624.7	786.7	Net Assets ($mil)

Manager's Investment Style

When picking stocks, management performs quantitative analysis using several sophisticated proprietary models. One program details how the market is pricing stocks; a second assigns the stocks an attractiveness rating based on fundamental factors such as earnings growth, price-to-earnings multiples, and debt levels; and a third, the portfolio optimizer, combines this data and produces a list of investments. The models are adjusted regularly to expand their scope. Management has recently expanded the models to include international markets, and plans to keep foreign exposure around 20% of assets.

Fund Manager(s)

Brad Lewis CFA(1978), since 09-90. Birthdate: 01-55. BS, Naval Academy 1977 MBA, Wharton 1985

Manager Experience

	Dates Managed	Invest Obj	Std Dev	+/- Index
Brad Lewis				
Fidelity Disciplined Eq	12/88 - 12/94	G	13.23	3.85
Fidelity Small Cap Stock	06/93 - 12/94	SC	11.81	-0.74

Performance 12-31-94

	1st Qtr	2nd Qtr	3rd Qtr	4th Qtr	Total
1987	---	---	---	---	---
1988	---	---	---	---	---
1989	---	---	---	---	---
1990	---	---	---	11.51	11.51 *
1991	25.09	0.29	6.31	9.43	45.95
1992	4.86	-2.01	2.43	9.67	15.42
1993	6.25	1.60	7.05	-1.37	13.97
1994	-0.32	-1.18	3.30	-0.97	0.78

Bear Market Performance

Decile Rank (5-year period)

Worst ————————————— Best

	Worst 3 Mo Period 1985-89	Worst 3 Mo Period 1990-94
Fidelity Stock Selector	---	---
+/- S&P 500	---	---
+/- Best Fit Index :	---	---

Trailing Returns

	Total Return %	+/- S&P 500	+/- Wil 5000	% Rank All	% Rank Obj	Growth of $10,000
3 Mo	-0.97	-0.95	-0.20	43	43	9,903
6 Mo	2.30	-2.56	-2.32	24	68	10,230
1 Yr	0.78	-0.54	0.85	15	26	10,078
3 Yr Avg	9.85	3.59	3.24	14	19	13,257
5 Yr Avg	---	---	---	---	---	---
10 Yr Avg	---	---	---	---	---	---
15 Yr Avg	---	---	---	---	---	---

Operations

Address and Telephone	82 Devonshire Street
	Boston, MA 02109
	800-544-8888
Advisor	Fidelity Management & Research
Subadvisor	None
Distributor	Fidelity Distributors
States Available	All
Report Grade	A
Income Distrib	Paid Annually
* Date of Inception	09-28-90
Fiscal Year End	October

Min Initial Purchase	$2500 (Addt'l: $250)
Min IRA Purchase	$500 (Addt'l: $250)
Min Auto Invest Plan	$2500 (Systematic Inv: $100)

Expenses & Fees

Sales Fees	0.00% front
	0.00% deferred
	0.00% 12b-1
Management Fee	0.30% flat fee+0.52%G+(-)0.20%P
3-,5-,10-yr Expense Projections	$35, $61, $134
Annual Brokerage Cost	0.27%

Risk Analysis

Time Period	Load-Adj Return %	Risk % Rank[1] All	Obj	Morningstar[2] Return	Risk	Morningstar Risk-Adj Rating
1 Yr	0.77					
3 Yr	9.85	75	44	1.92[3]	0.85	★★★★
5 Yr	---	---	---	---	---	
10 Yr	---	---	---	---	---	

Average Historical Rating (16 months) 4.2 ★s

[1] 1 = low, 100 = high [2] 1.00 = Equity Avg [3] 1.00 = 90-day T-bill return

Other Measures

			Standard S&P 500	Best Fit SPMid400
Standard Deviation	9.89	Alpha	3.7	2.9
Mean	9.92	Beta	0.97	0.91
Sharpe Ratio	0.65	R-Squared	61	83

Investment Style

	Stock Portfolio Avg	Relative S&P 500
Price/Earnings Ratio	18.2	0.98
Price/Book Ratio	2.8	0.82
5 Yr Earnings Gr %	-2.1	-0.37
Return on Assets %	7.6	1.01
Debt % Total Cap	29.5	1.04
Med Mkt Cap ($mil)	5711	0.44

Style Value Blend Growth
Size Large/Med/Small

Diversification Value for Portfolio Types

Large Cap: Low	Small Cap: Low	Bond: High	Balanced: Low	Diversified: Low

Portfolio 10-31-94

Total Stocks: 223
Total Fixed-Income: 0

Share Chg (04-94)000	Amount 000		Value $000	% Net Assets
450	450	Philip Morris	27550	3.31
106	346	IBM	25747	3.10
309	309	EI DuPont de Nemours	18418	2.22
0	450	Micron Technology	17821	2.14
335	335	Citicorp	15996	1.92
215	215	Pfizer	15937	1.92
71	383	General Motors	15142	1.82
233	233	Procter & Gamble	14563	1.75
32	414	Sprint	13500	1.62
199	362	Chase Manhattan	13028	1.57
146	152	Capital Cities/ABC	12635	1.52
258	258	Eastman Kodak	12416	1.49
-3	158	Deere	11337	1.36
-58	216	JC Penney	10935	1.32
148	148	Georgia-Pacific	10934	1.32
316	316	Union Carbide	10458	1.26
149	363	Archer-Daniels-Midland	10391	1.25
147	147	Scott Paper	9720	1.17
110	265	Breed Technologies	9367	1.13
83	381	Humana	9284	1.12
177	177	Tellabs	8604	1.04
120	120	CIGNA	7925	0.95
0	759	Hitachi	7911	0.95
50	50	Nokia Free	7531	0.91
0	132	KLA Instruments	6968	0.84

Composition % 11-30-94

Cash	15.0	Preferreds	0.0
Stocks	85.0	Convertibles	0.0
Bonds	0.0	Other	0.0

Tax Analysis

	Tax-Adj Historical Return %	% Pretax Return
3 Yr Avg	8.34	83.4
5 Yr Avg	---	---
10 Yr Avg	---	---
Potential Capital Gain Exposure (% of assets)		1%

Most Similar Funds in MF500

Fidelity Disciplined Equity	Strong Fit
Vanguard Index Extended Mkt	Strong Fit
Vista Capital Growth A	Fair Fit

Index Allocation % of Stocks

S&P 500	58.3
S&P MidCap 400	6.9
U.S. Small Cap	14.2
Foreign	20.6

Sector Weightings

	% of Stocks	Relative S&P 500
Utilities	4.4	0.36
Energy	1.8	0.18
Financials	16.7	1.58
Industrial Cyclicals	23.4	1.43
Consumer Durables	8.2	1.32
Consumer Staples	11.3	0.91
Services	6.8	0.83
Retail	5.3	0.91
Health	5.6	0.65
Technology	16.6	1.81

 **1995 Mutual Fund 500**

Fidelity Utilities

	Ticker	Load	NAV	Yield	SEC Yield	Assets	Objective
	FIUIX	None	13.06	3.9%	5.08%	1079.6	Sp.-Util

Fidelity Utilities Fund seeks current income and capital appreciation.

The fund normally invests at least 65% of its assets in public utilities; these companies include providers of electricity, natural gas, water, sanitary services, telephone or telegraph service, or other communication services.

On Oct. 1, 1991, Fidelity Qualified Dividend Fund merged into this fund. On Dec. 31, 1991, Fidelity Corporate Trust Adjustable-Rate Preferred merged into this fund. Prior to Sept. 8, 1994, the fund was named Fidelity Utilities Income Fund.

Manager's Investment Style

Unlike many peers, management takes a total-return approach. That focus allows it to remain more fully invested than many rivals, and leads management to invest in utility-related stocks with greater growth prospects than more-typical electric utilities, such as telephone stocks and natural-gas issues.

Fund Manager(s)

John Muresianu, since 12-92. Birthdate: 1953.
BA, Harvard 1974 PhD, Harvard 1982

Manager Experience

	Dates Managed	Invest Obj	Std Dev	+/- Index
John Muresianu				
Fidelity Sel Natural Gas	04/93 - 02/94	SN	16.87	-10.09

Historical Profile
Return	Average
Risk	Low
Rating	★★★★ Above Average

Average % Stocks Held: --- 89% 93% 84% 90% 87% 92% 84%

Investment Style History Equity
Average % Stocks Held in Portfolio

Growth of $10,000
IIII Value of Fund ($000)
— Value of Index ($000) LB L-T
▼ Manager Change
▽ Partial Manager Change
► Mgr Unknown After
◄ Mgr Unknown Before

Performance Quartile (Within Objective)

	1983	1984	1985	1986	1987	1988	1989	1990	1991	1992	1993	1994	History
	---	---	---	---	10.02	10.93	12.60	11.79	13.38	13.79	15.18	13.06	NAV
	---	---	---	---	0.60 *	14.77	25.92	1.85	21.18	10.90	15.61	-5.29	Total Return %
	---	---	---	---	-2.85 *	-1.85	-5.76	4.96	-9.30	3.28	5.55	-6.60	+/- S&P 500
	---	---	---	---		-3.28	-21.30	4.41	6.56	2.81	1.17	2.66	+/- S&P Util
	---	---	---	---	0.40	5.36	7.42	5.95	5.89	4.79	3.77	3.79	Income Return %
	---	---	---	---	0.20	9.41	18.51	-4.10	15.29	6.11	11.84	-9.08	Capital Return %
	---	---	---	---		29	21	50	43	18	26	66	Total Rtn % Rank All
	---	---	---	---		50	58	21	50	14	32	16	Total Rtn % Rank Obj
	---	---	---	---	0.04	0.52	0.76	0.69	0.63	0.60	0.52	0.54	Income $
	---	---	---	---	0.00	0.03	0.31	0.30	0.18	0.38	0.22	0.80	Capital Gains $
	---	---	---	---		2.00	1.47	1.02	0.94	0.95	0.87	0.86	Expense Ratio %
	---	---	---	---		5.36	6.14	6.19	5.93	5.11	4.57	3.39	Income Ratio %
	---	---	---	---			10	61	43	39	73	47	Turnover Rate %
	---	---	---	---	8.8	129.7	165.7	215.0	620.4	960.8	1456.0	1079.6	Net Assets ($mil)

Performance 12-31-94

	1st Qtr	2nd Qtr	3rd Qtr	4th Qtr	Total
1987	---	---	---	---	0.60 *
1988	4.38	5.59	1.88	2.21	14.77
1989	0.75	10.22	4.67	8.34	25.92
1990	-4.93	1.03	-3.54	9.92	1.85
1991	4.36	-0.75	9.02	7.32	21.18
1992	-4.78	6.41	5.86	3.40	10.90
1993	9.32	4.00	5.94	-4.02	15.61
1994	-3.72	-0.09	1.13	-2.64	-5.29

Bear Market Performance
Decile Rank (5-year period)

Worst ——————————————— Best

	Worst 3 Mo Period 1985-89	Worst 3 Mo Period 1990-94
Fidelity Utilities	---	-5.84
+/- S&P 500	---	-1.96
+/- Best Fit Index : LB L-T	---	-2.92

Trailing Returns

	Total Return %	+/- S&P 500	+/- S&P Util	% Rank All	Obj	Growth of $10,000
3 Mo	-2.64	-2.62	-2.53	79	71	9,736
6 Mo	-1.54	-6.40	-1.90	82	94	9,846
1 Yr	-5.29	-6.60	2.66	66	16	9,471
3 Yr Avg	6.69	0.42	2.26	29	17	12,143
5 Yr Avg	8.43	-0.26	3.50	29	10	14,987
10 Yr Avg	---	---	---	---	---	---
15 Yr Avg	---	---	---	---	---	---

Operations

Address and Telephone	82 Devonshire Street
	Boston, MA 02109
	800-544-8888
Advisor	Fidelity Management & Research
Subadvisor	FMR (U.K.)/FMR (Far East)
Distributor	Fidelity Distributors
States Available	All
Report Grade	A
Income Distrib	Paid Quarterly
* Date of Inception	11-27-87
Fiscal Year End	January

Risk Analysis

Time Period	Load-Adj Return %	Risk % Rank [1] All	Obj	Morningstar [2] Return	Morningstar Risk	Morningstar Risk-Adj Rating
1 Yr	-5.29					
3 Yr	6.69	67	39	0.92 [3]	0.74	★★★
5 Yr	8.43	54	42	0.92 [3]	0.59	★★★★
10 Yr	---					

Average Historical Rating (50 months) 4.3 ★s

[1] 1 = low, 100 = high [2] 1.00 = Equity Avg [3] 1.00 = 90-day T-bill return

Other Measures

		Standard S&P 500	Best Fit LB L-T
Standard Deviation	8.97	Alpha	1.1	1.5
Mean	6.89	Beta	0.80	0.96
Sharpe Ratio	0.38	R-Squared	49	68

Investment Style

	Stock Portfolio Avg	Relative S&P 500
Price/Earnings Ratio	17.7	0.96
Price/Book Ratio	2.1	0.61
5 Yr Earnings Gr %	2.5	0.44
Return on Assets %	4.5	0.60
Debt % Total Cap	41.7	1.48
Med Mkt Cap ($mil)	3769	0.29

Style Value Blend Growth — Size Large/Med/Small

Diversification Value for Portfolio Types

Large Cap: Medium	Small Cap: High	Bond: Low	Balanced: Low	Diversified: Medium

Expenses & Fees

Min Initial Purchase	$2500 (Addt'l: $250)
Min IRA Purchase	$500 (Addt'l: $250)
Min Auto Invest Plan	$2500 (Systematic Inv: $100)

Sales Fees	0.00% front
	0.00% deferred
	0.00% 12b-1
Management Fee	0.20% flat fee+0.52%G+(-)0.15%P
3-,5-,10-yr Expense Projections	$27, $48, $106
Annual Brokerage Cost	0.13%

Portfolio 07-31-94

Share Chg (01-94) 000	Amount 000	Total Stocks: 241 Total Fixed-Income: 29	Value $000	% Net Assets
	70	US Treasury Bond 8.125%	74954	5.99
252	1223	Ameritech	50155	4.01
1097	1097	Southwestern Bell	46053	3.68
-22	635	BellSouth	39700	3.17
70	928	NYNEX	35713	2.85
-28	1092	GTE	34665	2.77
-16	857	US West	34491	2.75
-6	944	Williams	30798	2.46
-310	450	Bell Atlantic	25470	2.03
111	1476	ENSERCH	23253	1.86
45	67	Veba	21828	1.74
202	988	Pacific Enterprises	20252	1.62
-105	562	Pacific Telesis Group	18399	1.47
-421	525	Sonat	17374	1.39
201	548	NIPSCO Industries	16035	1.28
322	682	Illinova	14237	1.14
-40	826	Westcoast Energy (Canada)	13408	1.07
-60	376	Questar	12499	1.00
-592	480	Entergy	12244	0.98
288	364	Coastal	11427	0.91
407	407	AirTouch Communications	10577	0.84
150	555	Pinnacle West Capital	9789	0.78
233	365	Detroit Edison	9632	0.77
18	342	Columbia Gas System	9570	0.76
	10	Georgia Power 6.875%	9496	0.76

Composition % 11-30-94

Cash	12.4	Preferreds	0.0
Stocks	85.8	Convertibles	0.0
Bonds	1.8	Other	0.0

Tax Analysis

	Tax-Adj Historical Return %	% Pretax Return
3 Yr Avg	4.24	61.9
5 Yr Avg	5.99	67.6
10 Yr Avg	---	---
Potential Capital Gain Exposure (% of assets)		0%

Most Similar Funds in MF500

Prudential Utility B	Strong Fit
Flag Inv Telephone Income A	Fair Fit
Fortress Utility	Fair Fit

Index Allocation

	% of Stocks
S&P 500	56.4
S&P MidCap 400	14.3
U.S. Small Cap	15.4
Foreign	13.8

Sector Weightings

	% of Stocks	Relative S&P 500
Utilities	80.6	6.51
Energy	4.9	0.48
Financials	6.4	0.60
Industrial Cyclicals	2.2	0.13
Consumer Durables	0.6	0.09
Consumer Staples	0.5	0.04
Services	2.5	0.31
Retail	0.2	0.05
Health	0.0	0.00
Technology	2.1	0.23

190

Fidelity Value

	Ticker	Load	NAV	Yield	SEC Yield	Assets	Objective
	FDVLX	None	40.81	0.4%	N/A	3720.4	Growth

Fidelity Value Fund seeks capital appreciation.

The fund invests in the securities of companies with valuable fixed assets. It also seeks securities that are undervalued in relation to the issuer's assets, earnings, or growth potential. Such companies generally have plants and equipment with high replacement costs; real estate with a current value substantially in excess of book value; large reserves of exploitable natural resources; or valuable consumer or commercial franchises, such as well-recognized trademarks or product names.

Prior to July 1986, the fund was called Fidelity Discoverer Fund.

Manager's Investment Style

Management takes a somewhat less conventional approach to value investing by emphasizing companies that are cheap relative to their free cash flows. This price-to-cash-flow approach has often led the portfolio to include down-and-out growth names. Because many of the fund's stocks feature depressed earnings, the portfolio's overall price/earnings mutliple seems steep relative to most value funds, oftentimes driving the fund into the blend column of the style box.

Fund Manager(s)

Jeffrey Ubben, since 12-92. Birthdate: 1961. BA, Duke U. 1983 MBA, Northwestern U. 1987

Manager Experience

Manager Experience	Dates Managed	Invest Obj	Std Dev	+/- Index
Jeffrey Ubben				
Fidelity Sel Def & Aero	01/90 - 04/92	S	16.11	-1.91
Fidelity Sel Utilities Gr	04/91 - 12/92	SU	7.14	2.06

Historical Profile

Return	Above Average
Risk	Below Average
Rating ★★★★	
	Above Average

94% 94% 98% 86% 86% 83% 88% 91%

Growth of $10,000

- |||| Value of Fund ($000)
- — Value of Index ($000) S&P 500
- ▼ Manager Change
- ▽ Partial Manager Change
- ◄— Mgr Unknown After
- —► Mgr Unknown Before

Performance Quartile (Within Objective)

	1983	1984	1985	1986	1987	1988	1989	1990	1991	1992	1993	1994	History
	20.43	18.17	21.76	23.06	20.63	26.14	28.99	24.10	29.50	35.35	40.23	40.81	NAV
	32.27	-8.59	22.10	14.74	-8.58	29.05	22.95	-12.82	26.20	21.15	22.94	7.63	Total Return %
	9.81	-14.85	-9.64	-3.94	-13.84	12.44	-8.74	-9.71	-4.29	13.53	12.88	6.31	+/- S&P 500
	8.81	-11.64	-10.47	-1.36	-10.94	11.11	-6.23	-6.64	-8.01	12.18	11.66	7.70	+/- Wilshire 5000
	1.36	2.47	2.34	0.00	0.61	2.34	1.04	4.05	3.79	0.75	0.88	0.42	Income Return %
	30.91	-11.06	19.76	14.74	-9.19	26.71	21.90	-16.87	22.41	20.40	22.06	7.21	Capital Return %
	8	88	60	56	95	3	29	89	34	4	13	3	Total Rtn % Rank All
	9	86	86	48	94	5	69	89	80	5	9	4	Total Rtn % Rank Obj
	0.27	0.49	0.42	0.00	0.15	0.48	0.30	1.17	0.85	0.23	0.34	0.17	Income $
	3.63	0.00	0.00	1.99	0.37	0.00	2.85	0.00	0.00	0.15	2.80	2.28	Capital Gains $
	0.88	1.26	1.13	1.07	1.07	1.11	1.13	1.06	0.98	1.00	1.11	0.77	Expense Ratio %
	2.87	4.84	3.43	2.20	1.02	4.74	1.45	4.55	2.93	2.01	1.43	0.92	Income Ratio %
	353	389	246	281	442	480	386	165	137	81	117	112	Turnover Rate %
	108.3	107.2	113.2	121.4	85.2	124.8	152.0	97.9	123.4	667.5	1716.1	3720.4	Net Assets ($mil)

Investment Style History Equity
Average % Stocks Held in Portfolio

Performance 12-31-94

	1st Qtr	2nd Qtr	3rd Qtr	4th Qtr	Total
1987	11.98	4.16	6.69	-26.53	-8.58
1988	12.65	3.74	6.51	3.67	29.05
1989	5.89	12.03	7.68	-3.75	22.95
1990	-6.49	2.36	-12.97	4.65	-12.82
1991	13.86	2.00	6.61	1.92	26.20
1992	6.37	3.38	2.56	7.42	21.15
1993	8.35	2.64	5.65	4.64	22.94
1994	0.15	3.70	5.22	-1.50	7.63

Bear Market Performance

Decile Rank (5-year period)

Worst ——————— Best

	Worst 3 Mo Period 1985-89	Worst 3 Mo Period 1990-94
Fidelity Value	-30.46	-14.11
+/- S&P 500	-0.88	-0.27
+/- Best Fit Index : S&P 500	-0.88	-0.27

Trailing Returns

	Total Return %	+/- S&P 500	+/- Wil 5000	% Rank All	% Rank Obj	Growth of $10,000
3 Mo	-1.50	-1.49	-0.73	57	54	9,850
6 Mo	3.64	-1.23	-0.99	17	54	10,364
1 Yr	7.63	6.31	7.70	3	4	10,763
3 Yr Avg	17.03	10.77	10.42	2	2	16,030
5 Yr Avg	12.02	3.32	3.20	9	14	17,635
10 Yr Avg	13.61	-0.77	-0.25	21	35	35,834
15 Yr Avg	14.93	0.44	0.95	13	27	80,595

Operations

Address and Telephone	82 Devonshire Street
	Boston, MA 02109
	800-544-8888
Advisor	Fidelity Management & Research
Subadvisor	FMR (U.K.)/FMR (Far East)
Distributor	Fidelity Distributors
States Available	All
Report Grade	A
Income Distrib	Paid Annually
Date of Inception	12-01-78
Fiscal Year End	October

Risk Analysis

Time Period	Load-Adj Return %	Risk % Rank[1] All	Risk % Rank[1] Obj	Morningstar[2] Return	Morningstar Risk	Morningstar Risk-Adj Rating
1 Yr	7.63					
3 Yr	17.03	44	4	4.42[3]	0.50	★★★★★
5 Yr	12.02	62	13	1.94[3]	0.74	★★★★
10 Yr	13.61	63	27	1.19	0.87	★★★★

Average Historical Rating (109 months)   3.3 ★s

[1] 1 = low, 100 = high   [2] 1.00 = Equity Avg   [3] 1.00 = 90-day T-bill return

Other Measures

			Standard S&P 500	Best Fit S&P 500
Standard Deviation	8.38	Alpha	10.7	10.7
Mean	16.18	Beta	0.86	0.86
Sharpe Ratio	1.51	R-Squared	66	66

Investment Style

	Stock Portfolio Avg	Relative S&P 500
Price/Earnings Ratio	22.9	1.24
Price/Book Ratio	2.3	0.67
5 Yr Earnings Gr %	1.0	0.17
Return on Assets %	6.0	0.80
Debt % Total Cap	25.3	0.90
Med Mkt Cap ($mil)	4070	0.31

Style: Value Blend Growth / Size Large Med Small

Diversification Value for Portfolio Types

Large Cap: Low	Small Cap: Low	Bond: High	Balanced: Low	Diversified: Low

Expenses & Fees

Sales Fees	0.00% front
	0.00% deferred
	0.00% 12b-1
Management Fee	0.30% flat fee+0.52%G+(-)0.20%P
3-,5-,10-yr Expense Projections	$32, $56, $125
Annual Brokerage Cost	0.34%

Portfolio 10-31-94

Total Stocks: 263
Total Fixed-Income: 14

Share Chg (09-94) 000	Amount 000		Value $000	% Net Assets
0	1682	Schlumberger	98835	2.66
0	2570	American Express	79038	2.13
0	2906	Alcan Aluminium	77830	2.10
0	827	British Petroleum (ADR)	70319	1.89
0	1983	Seagram	61003	1.64
0	937	United Technologies	59057	1.59
0	790	IBM	58840	1.58
0	8504	RJR Nabisco	58462	1.57
0	884	Philip Morris	54114	1.46
0	160	Veba	53626	1.44
0	1814	Unifi	46948	1.26
0	985	Western Atlas	45301	1.22
0	1189	Halliburton	43997	1.18
0	486	ALCOA	41432	1.12
0	848	Tyco International	40913	1.10
0	600	Exxon	37725	1.02
0	608	Roadway Services	34831	0.94
0	1183	WMX Technologies	34741	0.94
0	2070	Matsushita Electric Indl	34392	0.93
0	684	Amerada Hess	34014	0.92
0	2114	Canadian Pacific	33773	0.91
0	678	Martin Marietta	31117	0.84
0	472	American Home Products	29953	0.81
0	2815	Hitachi	29340	0.79
0	884	TOTAL CI B (ADR)	29174	0.79

Composition % 11-30-94

Cash	5.3	Preferreds	0.0
Stocks	93.1	Convertibles	0.0
Bonds	1.6	Other	0.0

Tax Analysis

	Tax-Adj Historical Return %	% Pretax Return
3 Yr Avg	15.45	89.3
5 Yr Avg	10.57	85.4
10 Yr Avg	12.07	82.2
Potential Capital Gain Exposure (% of assets)		2%

Most Similar Funds in MF500

Fidelity Equity-Income II	Strong Fit
Fidelity Adv Growth Opport A	Fair Fit
Fidelity Puritan	Fair Fit

Index Allocation

	% of Stocks
S&P 500	51.2
S&P MidCap 400	13.1
U.S. Small Cap	10.7
Foreign	29.9

Sector Weightings

	% of Stocks	Relative S&P 500
Utilities	1.8	0.14
Energy	14.5	1.43
Financials	8.1	0.76
Industrial Cyclicals	22.5	1.38
Consumer Durables	12.3	1.98
Consumer Staples	8.3	0.66
Services	15.7	1.92
Retail	6.6	1.14
Health	4.4	0.50
Technology	6.0	0.65

Min Initial Purchase / Min IRA Purchase / Min Auto Invest Plan

Min Initial Purchase	$2500 (Addt'l: $250)
Min IRA Purchase	$500 (Addt'l: $250)
Min Auto Invest Plan	$2500 (Systematic Inv: $100)

First Financial

	Ticker	NAV	Mkt Price	Prem/Disc	Yield	Objective
	FF	$14.31	$12.75	-10.9%	0.3%	Domestic Eq

First Financial Fund seeks long-term capital appreciation; its secondary objective is current income.

Normally, at least 65% of assets are in securities of small- to medium-sized savings and banking institutions (those with total assets of $2 billion or less) and in holding companies whose principal revenues are derived from subsidiary savings and banking institutions. At least 75% of assets will be in equities and up to 25% may be in debt securities.

The fund is leveraged through a credit agreement with an unaffiliated lender.

In June 1993, the fund began distributing its gains annually instead of quarterly.

As of Jan. 31, 1994, Tiger Management, a private investment manager operated by Julian Robertson, owned 18.8% of the fund's outstanding shares.

Manager's Investment Style

As the fund's tiny median-market cap suggests, management buys some of the smallest banks and thrifts around. It is willing to shift in and out of subsectors--such as mortgage banks or California thrifts--as opportunities present themselves; turnover is thus relatively high. The fund has been known for its aggressive tendencies: Management has used bank borrowing to leverage the portfolio. Additionally, management has in the past hedged against adverse market conditions by purchasing S&P index puts.

Fund Manager(s)

Nicholas Adams. Since 5-86.

Historical Profile

Return	High
Risk	Average
Rating	★★★★★ Highest

| | | | | -3.2 | -14.7 | -14.4 | -4.2 | 1.8 | 7.1 | -3.6 | -2.6 | 4.4 | Highest Prem/Disc |
| | | | | -20.6 | -25.4 | -21.9 | -17.8 | -11.4 | -13.5 | -14.4 | -12.7 | -12.3 | Lowest Prem/Disc |

Growth of $10,000
— at NAV ($000)
— at Market Price ($000)

Premium Discount %

1983	1984	1985	1986	1987	1988	1989	1990	1991	1992	1993	1994	History
---	---	---	8.38	7.31	8.73	8.35	4.96	9.23	13.75	19.69	14.31	NAV
---	---	---	-8.94*	-6.85	22.36	9.29	-38.14	89.41	74.50	43.20	13.79	NAV Total Return %
---	---	---	-14.29*	-12.11	5.75	-22.40	-35.03	58.93	66.88	33.14	12.47	+/- S&P 500
---	---	---	---	-3.77	-0.03	-8.83	-18.75	40.41	45.26	29.08	15.75	+/- Wil Small Value
---	---	---	0.95*	2.28	2.94	2.98	2.46	3.32	0.43	0.00	0.42	Income Return %
---	---	---	-9.89*	-9.13	19.43	6.31	-40.60	86.09	74.06	43.20	13.37	Capital Return %
---	---	---	---	84	17	68	98	2	1	10	3	Total Rtn % Rank All
---	---	---	---	77	23	85	96	3	3	1	1	Total Rtn % Rank Obj
---	---	---	-29.26*	-12.28	24.73	30.59	-39.80	78.81	83.81	39.22	12.46	Market Total Rtn %
---	---	---	-14.1	-18.4	-18.6	-11.7	-6.6	-6.6	-10.1	-9.5	-4.8	Avg Prem/Disc %
---	---	---	0.08	0.16	0.18	0.25	0.22	0.13	0.05	0.00	0.05	Income $
---	---	---	0.00	0.33	0.00	0.86	0.00	0.00	2.02	0.00	6.63	Capital Gains $
---	---	---	1.37	1.46	1.45	1.59	2.14	1.65	1.21	1.36	1.51	Expense Ratio %
---	---	---	1.95	1.73	2.30	2.40	3.06	1.33	0.62	0.25	0.09	Income Ratio %
---	---	---	51	69	41	58	42	89	105	139	---	Turnover Rate %
---	---	---	---	76.5	78.1	74.5	47.1	87.0	120.9	174.6	161.2	Net Assets ($mil)
---	---	---	---	0.0	0.0	0.0	2.8	7.0	0.0	15.0	11.0	Pfd/Debt Leverage ($mil)

Manager Experience

	Dates Managed	Invest Obj	Std Dev	+/- Index
Not available.				

NAV Performance % 12-30-94

	1st Qtr	2nd Qtr	3rd Qtr	4th Qtr	Total
1987	26.50	-9.86	2.12	-20.01	-6.85
1988	18.60	2.61	3.44	-2.79	22.36
1989	7.31	15.80	11.31	-20.99	9.29
1990	-13.59	-6.51	-25.51	2.78	-38.14
1991	28.98	10.52	23.60	7.50	89.41
1992	14.21	14.65	10.29	20.83	74.50
1993	20.15	-0.73	16.40	3.14	43.20
1994	1.30	17.90	7.46	-11.34	13.79

Bear Market Performance

Decile Rank (5-year period)

Worst | Best

	Worst 3 Mo Period 1985-89	Worst 3 Mo Period 1990-94
First Financial	---	-28.49
+/- S&P 500		-14.65

Trailing Returns

	NAV Total Return %	+/- S&P 500	+/- Wil Sm Value	% Rank All	% Rank Obj	Mkt Total Return %
3 Mo	-11.34	-11.32	-9.49	95	92	-17.74
6 Mo	-4.73	-9.59	-6.02	92	86	-10.53
1 Yr	13.79	12.47	15.75	3	1	12.46
3 Yr Avg	41.67	35.40	28.59	1	1	42.24
5 Yr Avg	27.21	18.52	15.54	1	1	25.38
Incept Avg	16.57*	---	---	---	---	14.07*

Operations

Address and Telephone	One Seaport Plaza New York, NY 10292 212-214-3332 / 800-451-6788
Advisor	Wellington Management Co.
Subadvisor	N/A
Administrator	Prudential Mutual Fund Mgmt., Inc.
Transfer Agent	State Street Bank and Trust Co.
Custodian	State Street Bank and Trust Co.
Auditor	Deloitte & Touche
Legal Counsel	Kirkpatrick & Lockhart

Income Distrib Schedule	Paid Annually
Management Fee	0.75%
Reinvestment Plan	Yes
Direct Purchase Plan	No
Shares Outstanding	12,769,605
Exchange	NYSE
*Date of Inception	05-01-86
Shareholder Report	A

Risk Analysis

	Risk % Rank[1] All	Obj	Morningstar[2] Return	Risk	Morningstar Risk-Adj Rating
3 Yr	69	37	6.90	0.50	★★★★★
5 Yr	85	72	6.01	0.88	★★★★★
10 Yr					

Average Historical Rating (68 months)   3.1 ★s

[1] 1 = Low, 100 = High   [2] 1.00 = Equity Avg   [3] 1.00 = 90-day T-bill Return

Other Measures

			S&P 500
Standard Deviation	15.71	Alpha	34.64
Mean	36.55	Beta	1.01
Sharpe Ratio	2.10	R-Squared	26

Investment Style

	Stock Portfolio Avg	Relative S&P 500	Style Value Blend Growth
Price/Earnings Ratio	9.8#	0.53	
Price/Cash Flow Ratio	---	---	
Price/Book Ratio	1.2#	0.35	
5 Yr Earnings Gr %	---	---	
Return on Assets %	2.5#	0.33	
Debt % Total Cap	4.3#	0.15	
Med Mkt Cap ($mil)	187#	0.01	

figure is based on less than 50% of stocks

Size: Large/Med/Small

Index Allocation

	% of Stocks
Dow 30	0.0
S&P 500	1.4
S&P Mid-Cap 400	0.0
US Small-Cap	98.6
Foreign	0.0

Diversification Value for Portfolio Types

Large Cap: Medium	Small Cap: Medium	Bond: High	Balanced: Medium	Diversified: High

Portfolio 09-30-94

Share Chg (06-94)	Amount	Total Equity: 72 Total Fixed-Income: 3	Value $000	% Total Invest
-522800	714000	GP Financial	16958	8.49
6000	1000000	Long Island Bancorp	15625	7.82
121630	436630	EquiCredit	12826	6.42
493018	518018	MLF Bancorp	8094	4.05
-10000	167000	Queens County Bancorp	7223	3.62
4000	508000	Bay Ridge Bancorp	7176	3.59
8000	127000	Security Capital	5842	2.92
147000	196000	Standard Federal Bank (MI)	5341	2.67
224000	485000	River Bank America New York	5335	2.67
301300	301300	Anchor Bancorp	4858	2.43
104500	358000	First Financial Caribbean	4833	2.42
154400	252400	FirstFed Financial	3912	1.96
0	30000	Tempest Reinsurance	3900	1.95
109000	193000	CENFED Financial	3812	1.91
0	315000	Imperial Credit Industries	3623	1.81
-20000	285600	Redfed Bancorp	3570	1.79
-15000	237000	Main Street Cmnty Bancorp	3555	1.78
0	295800	CTL Credit	3328	1.67
195600	195600	Prime Residential	3105	1.55
70000	70000	Republic New York	3045	1.52
-6000	156000	Fleet Mortgage Group	3042	1.52
0	174600	Perpetual Federal Svgs Bank	2554	1.28
---	94000	River Bank America NY Pfd	2538	1.27
11828	248393	Resource Bancshares Mtg Grp	2484	1.24
---	100000	Comnty Bank Huntington Pk Pfd	2450	1.23

Composition % 12-31-94

Cash	5.4	Preferreds	2.7
Stocks	91.9	Convertibles	0.0
Bonds	0.0	Other	0.0

Leverage factor: 1.07

Tax Analysis

	Tax-Adj Historical Return %	% Pretax Return
3 Yr Avg	34.80	78.7
5 Yr Avg	22.83	77.0
10 Yr Avg	---	---

Potential Capital Gain Exposure (% of assets)   32

Most Similar Funds in MF500

Hancock Regional Bank B	Weak Fit
Evergreen Foundation	Weak Fit
Fidelity Equity-Income	Weak Fit

Sector Weightings

	% of Stocks	Relative S&P 500
Utilities	0.0	0.00
Energy	0.0	0.00
Financials	96.0	9.08
Industrial Cyclicals	3.7	0.22
Consumer Durables	0.0	0.00
Consumer Staples	0.0	0.00
Services	0.4	0.05
Retail	0.0	0.00
Health	0.0	0.00
Technology	0.0	0.00

First Investors Insured Tax-Ex A

	Ticker	Load	NAV	Yield	SEC Yield	Assets	Objective
	FITAX	6.25%	9.42	5.4%	5.79%	1297.4	Muni Nat

First Investors Insured Tax-Exempt Fund seeks interest income exempt from federal income tax and the Alternative Minimum Tax.

The fund invests at least 80% of its assets in municipal bonds. Although the fund generally invests in bonds rated BBB or higher, it may invest up to 5% of its assets in lower- or unrated municipal bonds. It may not invest in municipal bonds unless they are insured either by the issuer or by the fund's own insurance.

Prior to Aug. 25, 1988, the fund was named First Investors Tax-Exempt Fund.

Manager's Investment Style

Manager Clark Wagner has imbued this fund with a highly competitive yield by holding onto older, premium high-coupon debt and by buying bonds in higher-yielding states and sectors. He also keeps about one quarter of the portfolio in bonds that are not themselves insured, but for which he purchases low-cost insurance.

Fund Manager(s)

Clark D. Wagner, since 07-91. Birthdate: 02-59.
BA, Williams C. 1981 MA, Columbia U. 1985

Manager Experience

Manager Experience	Dates Managed	Invest Obj	Std Dev	+/- Index
Clark D. Wagner				
Executive Invstrs Ins T/E	07/91 - 12/94	MN	6.55	-1.65
First Invest M/S Ins VA A	07/91 - 12/94	MS	5.99	-0.28

Historical Profile

Return	Below Average
Risk	Below Average
Rating	★★ Below Average

Investment Style History
Fixed Income
Income Rtn % Rank Obj

Growth of $10,000
IIII Value of Fund ($000)
— Value of Index ($000)
LB Muni
▼ Manager Change
▽ Partial Manager Change
◄— Mgr Unknown After
—► Mgr Unknown Before

Performance Quartile (Within Objective)

1983	1984	1985	1986	1987	1988	1989	1990	1991	1992	1993	1994	History
8.76	8.70	9.48	10.14	9.64	9.91	10.04	9.92	10.22	10.32	10.56	9.42	NAV
13.55	8.42	18.50	15.38	2.21	10.64	9.34	6.02	10.26	8.05	9.89	-6.07	Total Return %
5.17	-6.73	-3.62	0.13	-0.55	2.76	-5.21	-2.93	-5.74	0.81	0.13	-3.15	+/- LB Aggregate
5.50	-2.13	-1.52	-3.94	0.70	0.48	-1.45	-1.28	-1.89	-0.77	-2.39	-0.47	+/- LB Muni
9.51	9.10	9.54	8.41	7.14	7.84	8.02	7.21	7.23	6.61	6.04	4.72	Income Return %
4.04	-0.68	8.97	6.96	-4.93	2.80	1.31	-1.20	3.02	1.44	3.84	-10.80	Capital Return %
64	35	81	52	41	56	81	34	89	45	68	72	Total Rtn % Rank All
8	68	64	73	18	55	53	64	78	62	76	60	Total Rtn % Rank Obj
0.77	0.76	0.78	0.76	0.72	0.72	0.77	0.70	0.69	0.65	0.61	0.51	Income $
0.00	0.00	0.00	0.00	0.00	0.00	0.00	0.00	0.00	0.05	0.15	0.00	Capital Gains $
1.22	1.21	1.11	1.02	1.13	1.04	1.01	1.14	1.13	1.16	1.15	1.21	Expense Ratio %
8.96	9.17	8.62	7.75	7.39	7.33	7.16	7.03	6.82	6.32	5.69	5.53	Income Ratio %
39	46	24	16	18	43	26	28	34	52	58	---	Turnover Rate %
241.5	354.8	507.5	730.1	848.9	966.7	1080.0	1132.6	1208.3	1352.3	1484.0	1297.4	Net Assets ($mil)

Performance 12-31-94

	1st Qtr	2nd Qtr	3rd Qtr	4th Qtr	Total
1987	3.49	-4.13	-2.37	5.51	2.21
1988	2.55	2.34	2.53	2.82	10.64
1989	0.34	5.31	0.58	2.87	9.34
1990	0.35	1.77	0.24	3.55	6.02
1991	2.17	1.76	3.27	2.68	10.26
1992	0.93	3.32	1.69	1.89	8.05
1993	3.26	2.51	2.85	0.93	9.89
1994	-5.43	0.41	0.47	-1.55	-6.07

Bear Market Performance

Decile Rank (5-year period)

Worst — Best

	Worst 3 Mo Period 1985-89	Worst 3 Mo Period 1990-94
First Investors Insured Tax-Ex A	-4.13	-6.03
+/- LB Aggregate	-2.35	-1.10
+/- Best Fit Index : LB Muni	-1.41	-0.27

Trailing Returns

	Total Return %	+/- LB Aggregate	+/- LB Muni	% Rank All	% Rank Obj	Growth of $10,000
3 Mo	-1.55	-1.92	-0.11	58	61	9,846
6 Mo	-1.08	-2.07	0.16	75	56	9,892
1 Yr	-6.07	-3.15	-0.47	72	60	9,393
3 Yr Avg	3.70	-0.84	-1.17	75	88	11,152
5 Yr Avg	5.45	-2.18	-1.33	85	88	13,036
10 Yr Avg	8.22	-1.72	-1.21	84	69	22,036
15 Yr Avg	7.91	-2.90	-0.56	93	51	31,322

Operations

Address and Telephone	95 Wall Street 23rd Floor
	New York, NY 10005-4297
	800-423-4026 / 212-858-8000
Advisor	First Investors Management
Subadvisor	None
Distributor	First Investors
States Available	All plus PR
Report Grade	C
Income Distrib	Paid Monthly
Date of Inception	08-03-77
Fiscal Year End	December

Min Initial Purchase	$1000 (Addt'l: None)
Min IRA Purchase	N/A
Min Auto Invest Plan	$50 (Systematic Inv: $50)

Expenses & Fees

Sales Fees	6.25% front
	0.00% deferred
	0.30% 12b-1
Management Fee	0.60% flat fee
3-,5-,10-yr Expense Projections	$97, $122, $194

Risk Analysis

Time Period	Load-Adj Return %	Risk % Rank[1] All	Risk % Rank[1] Obj	Morningstar[2] Return	Morningstar[2] Risk	Morningstar Risk-Adj Rating
1 Yr	-11.94					
3 Yr	1.49	21	38	0.32	0.90	★
5 Yr	4.09	14	34	0.58	0.87	★★
10 Yr	7.53	6	21	0.83	0.81	★★★

Average Historical Rating (109 months) 3.6 ★s

[1] 1 = low, 100 = high [2] 1.00 = Muni Avg [3] 1.00 = 90-day T-bill return

Other Measures

	Standard LB Agg	Best Fit LB Muni
Standard Deviation	4.99	
Mean	3.77	
Sharpe Ratio	0.05	
Alpha	-0.7	-1.0
Beta	0.93	0.90
R-Squared	56	98

Investment Style

Interest-Rate Stance

Avg Effective Maturity 20.0 Yrs

Maturity Short Intm Long
Quality High Med Low

Quality

Avg Credit Quality AAA
Avg Weighted Coupon 6.91%
Avg Weighted Price 97.62% of Par

Diversification Value for Portfolio Types

Large Cap: Medium	Small Cap: High	Bond: Low	Balanced: Medium	Diversified: Medium

Portfolio 12-29-94

Amount 000	Date of Maturity	Total Stocks: 0 / Total Fixed-Income: 251	Value $000	% Net Assets
33935	05-01-11	LA State GO 6%	31651	2.44
26745	08-15-17	TX Harris Toll Rd 6.5%	27002	2.08
23550	08-01-09	MA State GO 6%	22678	1.75
23400	11-15-22	TX Coastal Bend Hlth Fac Dev IFRN	21353	1.65
22130	06-01-11	DC GO 6%	20481	1.58
20600	07-01-11	GA Atlanta Metro Rapid Transit Tax 6.25%	20162	1.55
17015	06-01-11	MO Hlth/Educ Fac 6.75%	17279	1.33
16750	11-01-28	IL Dev Fin Poll Cntrl Pwr 6.75%	16666	1.28
17165	12-15-13	TX Houston COP Wtr Convynce Sys 6.25%	16342	1.26
14615	01-01-19	SC Piedmont Muni Pwr 9.25%	15638	1.21
17000	01-01-20	IL Chicago GO Brd Educ 6%	15321	1.18
14840	09-01-17	WI Hsg/Econ Dev Homeownshp 7.75%	15137	1.17
14000	01-01-17	GA Muni Elec Spcl Obl 8.125%	15050	1.16
15470	01-01-10	NC Muni Pwr #1 Catawba Elec 6%	14598	1.13
15500	01-01-09	IL Chicago O'Hare Intl Arpt 5.75%	14279	1.10
12520	06-30-13	ND Mercer Poll Cntrl Basin Elec 10.5%	12783	0.99
59875	05-15-24	TX Austin Combined Util Sys 0%	11832	0.91
11300	07-01-01	NY Dorm Dept Hlth 7.375%	11794	0.91
10500	02-15-29	NY Med Care Fac Fin St Luke Hosp 7.45%	11484	0.89
10530	06-01-05	DC GO 8%	11478	0.88

Credit Analysis % of Bonds 12-31-94

US Govt	0	BB	0
AAA	87	B	0
AA	6	Below B	0
A	4	NR/NA	3
BBB	0		

Composition % of Assets 12-31-94

Cash	0.0	Preferreds	0.0
Stocks	0.0	Convertibles	0.0
Bonds	100.0	Other	0.0

Tax Analysis

	Tax-Adj Historical Return %	% Pretax Return
3 Yr Avg	3.52	95.0
5 Yr Avg	5.34	97.8
10 Yr Avg	8.16	99.0
Potential Capital Gain Exposure (% of assets)	-1%	

Most Similar Funds in MF500

IDS High-Yield Tax-Exempt	Strong Fit
Dreyfus Intermediate Muni	Strong Fit
Smith Barney Tax-Ex Inc B	Strong Fit

Coupon Range

	% Bonds	Rel Obj
0%	0.7	0.26
0% to 6.8%	48.0	0.79
6.8% to 7.5%	9.1	0.59
7.5% to 8.3%	20.1	2.27
More than 8.3%	19.0	2.15
Not applicable	3.1	0.81

Sector Weightings

	% Bonds	Rel Obj
General Obl	17.38	0.83
Utilities	17.72	1.42
Health	22.25	1.69
Water/Waste	6.91	1.08
Housing	7.58	1.03
Education	1.87	0.29
Transportation	8.78	0.86
COP/Lease	5.59	1.75
Private	7.25	0.62
Misc Revenue	2.93	0.59
Demand	1.73	0.70

Top 5 States % of Bonds

TX	14.51	CA	5.82
IL	9.02	LA	5.14
NY	8.25		

First Philippine

	Ticker	NAV	Mkt Price	Prem/Disc	Yield	Objective
	FPF	$23.61	$19.38	-17.9%	0.0%	Pacific/Asia

First Philippine Fund seeks long-term capital appreciation.
The fund invests at least 80% of its assets in equities of Philippine-incorporated companies that generate at least 50% of their revenues from operations within the Philippines. The fund can invest up to 15% of its assets in nonpublicly traded securities. The fund uses a trust arrangement between it and Philippine National Bank to invest in stocks that have nationality restrictions on their sale to foreigners.

25.6	18.5	-13.0	-11.4	-7.7	-10.4	Highest Prem/Disc
24.7	-32.9	-28.0	-29.5	-26.4	-25.8	Lowest Prem/Disc

Historical Profile
Return High
Risk Average
Rating ★★★★★
Highest

Growth of $10,000
■■ at NAV ($000)
— at Market Price ($000)

Premium Discount %

History

	1983	1984	1985	1986	1987	1988	1989	1990	1991	1992	1993	1994	
	---	---	---	---	---	---	11.03	9.15	11.27	13.12	25.76	23.61	NAV
	---	---	---	---	---	---	-0.59*	-9.37	26.14	23.49	104.14	2.65	NAV Total Return %
	---	---	---	---	---	---	-5.02*	-6.25	-4.34	15.88	94.09	1.34	+/- S&P 500
	---	---	---	---	---	---	---	14.08	14.01	35.67	71.58	-5.13	+/- MSCI EAFE
	---	---	---	---	---	---	---	38.30	-57.31	-13.60	-17.29	10.92	+/- MSCI Philippines
	---	---	---	---	---	---	0.58*	7.68	2.97	2.86	0.00	0.00	Income Return %
	---	---	---	---	---	---	-1.17*	-17.04	23.17	20.64	104.14	2.65	Capital Return %
	---	---	---	---	---	---	---	78	30	5	2	9	Total Rtn % Rank All
	---	---	---	---	---	---	---	30	20	13	10	28	Total Rtn % Rank Obj
	---	---	---	---	---	---	15.25*	-48.35	35.89	26.07	135.84	-6.67	Market Total Rtn %
	---	---	---	---	---	---	---	-15.0	-21.8	-21.7	-15.3	-17.7	Avg Prem/Disc %
	---	---	---	---	---	---	0.08	0.59	0.19	0.25	0.00	0.00	Income $
	---	---	---	---	---	---	0.00	0.00	0.00	0.32	0.76	2.10	Capital Gains $
	---	---	---	---	---	---	---	2.00	1.90	1.79	1.72	1.79	Expense Ratio %
	---	---	---	---	---	---	---	5.78	3.92	0.42	-0.45	-1.08	Income Ratio %
	---	---	---	---	---	---	---	---	1	22	37	39	Turnover Rate %
	---	---	---	---	---	---	---	98.5	102.7	117.8	231.3	212.0	Net Assets ($mil)

Manager's Investment Style

Management minimizes the fund's market risk by underweighting the handful of blue-chip companies that dominate the Philippine market. Management instead seeks out lesser-known small companies to round out the portfolio's holdings. This strategy has allowed the fund to outperform the index during bear markets.

Fund Manager(s)

Roberto Ticzon. Since 4-94.

Manager Experience

	Dates Managed	Invest Obj	Std Dev	+/- Index
Not available.				

NAV Performance % 12-30-94

	1st Qtr	2nd Qtr	3rd Qtr	4th Qtr	Total
1987	---	---	---	---	---
1988	---	---	---	---	---
1989	---	---	---	-0.59*	-0.59*
1990	1.54	-2.05	-11.67	3.17	-9.37
1991	12.46	0.58	-3.77	15.88	26.14
1992	4.26	24.00	-0.69	-3.82	23.49
1993	11.28	1.85	9.75	64.12	104.14
1994	-13.74	4.05	10.47	3.54	2.65

Bear Market Performance

Decile Rank (5-year period)

Worst ▬▬ Best

	Worst 3 Mo Period 1985-89	Worst 3 Mo Period 1990-94
First Philippine	---	-13.74
+/- S&P 500	---	-9.96

Trailing Returns

	NAV Total Return %	+/- S&P 500	+/- MSCI Philippine	% Rank All	% Rank Obj	Mkt Total Return %
3 Mo	3.54	3.55	1.79	3	2	0.35
6 Mo	14.37	9.51	8.97	2	6	18.90
1 Yr	2.65	1.34	10.92	9	28	-6.67
3 Yr Avg	37.29	31.03	-3.40	1	1	40.52
5 Yr Avg	24.23	15.54	2.49	2	1	14.26
Incept Avg	23.42*	---	---	---	---	17.09*

Operations

Address and Telephone	152 West 57th Street New York, NY 10019 212-765-0700 / 800-524-4458
Advisor	Clemente Capital Inc.
Subadvisor	N/A
Administrator	Provident Financial Process. Corp.
Transfer Agent	Bank of New York
Custodian	Brown Brothers Harriman & Co.
Auditor	Price Waterhouse LLP
Legal Counsel	Fulbright & Jaworski

Income Distrib Schedule	Paid Annually
Management Fee	1.00%, 0.10%A
Reinvestment Plan	Yes
Direct Purchase Plan	Yes
Shares Outstanding	8,980,000
Exchange	NYSE
*Date of Inception	11-15-89
Shareholder Report	B

Risk Analysis

	Risk % Rank[1] All	Risk % Rank[1] Obj	Morningstar[2] Return	Morningstar[2] Risk	Morningstar Risk-Adj Rating
3 Yr	81	6	5.88	0.84	★★★★★
5 Yr	81	1	4.93	0.73	★★★★★
10 Yr	---	---	---	---	---
Average Historical Rating (26 months)				4.4	★s

[1] 1 = Low, 100 = High   [2] 1.00 = Equity Avg   [3] 1.00 = 90-day T-bill Return

Other Measures

			S&P 500
Standard Deviation	26.45	Alpha	34.08
Mean	35.29	Beta	0.72
Sharpe Ratio	1.20	R-Squared	5

Investment Style

	Stock Portfolio Avg	Rel WS Philipp	Rel WS Foreign
Price/Earnings Ratio	35.3	0.83	0.72
Price/Cash Flow Ratio	18.8	0.91	1.29
Price/Book Ratio	5.5	0.86	1.82
5 Yr Earnings Gr %	---	---	---
Return on Assets %	11.2	1.22	2.43
Debt % Total Cap	21.1	1.21	0.65
Med Mkt Cap ($mil)	3341	0.91	0.53

figure is based on less than 50% of stocks

Country Exposure (top five) 12-31-94

	Securities %		Currency %
Philippines	100	Philippines	100

Diversification Value for Portfolio Types

Large Cap: High	Small Cap: High	Bond: High	Balanced: High	Diversified: High

Portfolio 09-30-94

Total Equity: 49
Total Fixed-Income: 4

Share Chg (06-94)	Amount		Value $000	% Total Invest
-800000	11091162	San Miguel Cl A	41699	18.22
-110000	2708308	Manila Electric Cl A	28080	12.27
-31000	500020	Philippine Long Distance Tel	28001	12.23
254538	507226	Metro Bank & Trust	15728	6.87
-1200000	9339121	Ayala Cl A	11583	5.06
0	8148250	Ayala Land Cl B	10738	4.69
108500	325500	Far East Bank & Trust	10093	4.41
22200	1918000	First Philippine Hldgs Cl A	6096	2.66
0	485215	Philippine Comm Intl Bank	4589	2.00
0	10800000	Filinvest Land	3809	1.66
0	346239	Bacnotan Consolidated	3758	1.64
0	3764000	Universal Robina	3501	1.53
---	2500000	Intl Container Terminal Svc 6%	3500	1.53
0	367.500M	Manila Mining Cl A	3490	1.52
-1	3318398	Globe Telecom	3473	1.52
0	5681500	Grand Plaza Hotel	3083	1.35
94800	2002850	Republic Flour Mills	2678	1.17
6895333	17238333	Metro Pacific Cl A	2606	1.14
---	3000000	JG Summit Cv 3.5%	2513	1.10
0	4800.00M	United Paragon Mining	2419	1.06
0	4841691	Keppel (Philippines)	2252	0.98
0	5370000	JG Summit	2238	0.98
2400000	2400000	Petron	2047	0.89
0	4413996	Matsushita Elec Philippines	1989	0.87
0	703462	Sime Darby Pilipinas	1909	0.83

Composition % 12-31-94

Cash	0.0	Preferreds	0.0
Stocks	96.0	Convertibles	0.0
Bonds	4.0	Other	0.0

Tax Analysis

	Tax-Adj Historical Return %	% Pretax Return
3 Yr Avg	34.73	90.6
5 Yr Avg	21.90	86.2
10 Yr Avg	---	---

Potential Capital Gain Exposure (% of assets) 49

Most Similar Funds in MF500

Thai Fund	Weak Fit
Newport Tiger	Weak Fit
Asia Pacific	Weak Fit

Sector Weightings

	% of Stocks
Utilities	30.6
Energy	0.7
Financials	30.3
Industrial Cyclicals	10.0
Consumer Durables	1.1
Consumer Staples	24.0
Services	1.7
Retail	0.0
Health	0.4
Technology	1.1

MORNINGSTAR 1995 Mutual Fund 500

Flag Investors Telephone Inc A

	Ticker	Load	NAV	Yield	SEC Yield	Assets	Objective
	TISHX	4.50%	12.30	3.1%	3.00%	436.2	Sp.-Util

Flag Investors Telephone Income Trust - Class A seeks current income; capital growth is a secondary objective.

The fund normally invests at least 65% of its assets in income-producing common stocks, convertible securities, and debt obligations of companies in the telephone industry. These companies are well capitalized and have demonstrated stable growth; they may be affected by technological and regulatory changes. The fund may purchase American Depositary Receipts.

Class A shares have front loads and lower 12b-1 fees; Class B shares have low front loads and a 1% redemption fee within four years.

Historical Profile
Return	Average
Risk	Below Average
Rating	★★★★ Above Average

Manager's Investment Style

Management maintains a two-sided strategy. It starts with a core of Baby Bell stocks to provide high dividends and steady performance. It then supplements these holdings with a stake in small, growth-oriented telecommunications and related technology stocks. To compensate for the income lost by owning these smaller issues, the fund has recently held a modest stake in high-yielding real-estate investment trusts.

Investment Style History
Equity
Average % Stocks Held in Portfolio: 80% 86% 83% 79% 83% 82% 78% 82%

Growth of $10,000
|||| Value of Fund ($000)
— Value of Index ($000) S&P 500
▼ Manager Change
▽ Partial Manager Change
► Mgr Unknown After
◄ Mgr Unknown Before

Performance Quartile (Within Objective)

Fund Manager(s)

Bruce E. Behrens CFA, since 01-84. Birthdate: 1944. BA, Denison U. 1966 MBA, U. of Michigan 1968
Hobart C. Buppert, since 01-84. Birthdate: 1946. BS, Loyola C. 1970 MBA, Loyola C. 1975

Manager Experience	Dates Managed	Invest Obj	Std Dev	+/- Index
Hobart C. Buppert				
Flag Inv Value Builder A	06/92 - 12/94	B	6.48	-0.51

	1983	1984	1985	1986	1987	1988	1989	1990	1991	1992	1993	1994	History
	---	6.99	8.02	7.84	7.50	8.24	10.98	9.57	11.28	12.20	13.70	12.30	NAV
	---	14.95 *	29.94	24.76	1.51	19.87	49.67	-7.57	23.38	12.33	18.22	-6.33	Total Return %
	---	10.35 *	-1.80	6.08	-3.75	3.26	17.98	-4.45	-7.10	4.72	8.16	-7.64	+/- S&P 500
	---	---	---	-3.68	4.41	1.83	2.45	-5.01	8.76	4.24	3.78	1.62	+/- S&P Util
	---	6.99	9.39	6.66	5.18	6.70	6.53	4.25	5.30	4.08	3.41	2.86	Income Return %
	---	7.96	20.55	18.10	-3.67	13.17	43.14	-11.82	18.08	8.25	14.80	-9.19	Capital Return %
	---	---	25	9	46	14	1	79	39	14	20	74	Total Rtn % Rank All
	---	---	37	11	20	16	11	84	29	7	25	19	Total Rtn % Rank Obj
	---	0.41	0.59	0.54	0.42	0.49	0.56	0.46	0.46	0.42	0.42	0.39	Income $
	---	0.00	0.32	1.55	0.05	0.23	0.71	0.13	0.02	0.01	0.28	0.15	Capital Gains $
	---	1.06	0.95	0.87	0.88	0.92	0.93	0.92	0.92	0.92	0.92	0.92	Expense Ratio %
	---	7.57	6.93	5.58	5.37	5.35	4.41	4.54	4.38	3.81	3.12	3.12	Income Ratio %
	---		36	26	30	4	11	27	2	7	6	14	---	Turnover Rate %
	---	71.3	85.9	99.6	94.7	102.8	162.2	177.9	238.6	307.6	468.9	436.2	Net Assets ($mil)

Performance 12-31-94

	1st Qtr	2nd Qtr	3rd Qtr	4th Qtr	Total
1987	4.01	1.35	11.00	-13.25	1.51
1988	5.71	7.85	3.06	2.02	19.87
1989	9.18	13.19	11.65	8.47	49.67
1990	-6.26	0.34	-6.36	4.94	-7.57
1991	7.43	-0.74	5.87	9.29	23.38
1992	-4.71	2.00	6.64	8.37	12.33
1993	10.52	2.08	6.99	-2.06	18.22
1994	-5.71	-0.83	4.16	-3.82	-6.33

Bear Market Performance
Decile Rank (5-year period)

Worst — Best

	Worst 3 Mo Period 1985-89	Worst 3 Mo Period 1990-94
Flag Investors Telephone Inc A	-13.25	-11.04
+/- S&P 500	9.28	-1.09
+/- Best Fit Index : S&P 500	9.28	-1.09

Trailing Returns
	Total Return %	+/- S&P 500	+/- S&P Util	% Rank All	% Rank Obj	Growth of $10,000
3 Mo	-3.82	-3.81	-3.72	88	87	9,618
6 Mo	0.18	-4.68	-0.19	53	60	10,018
1 Yr	-6.33	-7.64	1.62	74	19	9,367
3 Yr Avg	7.55	1.28	3.12	23	7	12,440
5 Yr Avg	7.24	-1.45	2.32	44	36	14,186
10 Yr Avg	15.40	1.02	---	9	1	41,881
15 Yr Avg	---	---	---	---	---	---

Operations

Address and Telephone	135 E. Baltimore Street
	Baltimore, MD 21202
	800-767-3524
Advisor	Investment Capital
Subadvisor	Alex. Brown Investment Management
Distributor	Alex. Brown & Sons
States Available	All
Report Grade	B+
Income Distrib	Paid Monthly
* Date of Inception	01-18-84
Fiscal Year End	December

Risk Analysis

Time Period	Load-Adj Return %	Risk % Rank [1] All	Risk % Rank [1] Obj	Morningstar [2] Return	Morningstar [2] Risk	Morningstar Risk-Adj Rating
1 Yr	-10.54					
3 Yr	5.91	77	82	0.69 [3]	0.90	★★★
5 Yr	6.26	67	78	0.37 [3]	0.80	★★★
10 Yr	14.87	51	62	1.46	0.74	★★★★
Average Historical Rating (96 months)					4.5	★s

[1] 1 = low, 100 = high [2] 1.00 = Equity Avg [3] 1.00 = 90-day T-bill return

Other Measures
			Standard S&P 500	Best Fit S&P 500
Standard Deviation	10.01	Alpha	1.2	1.2
Mean	7.80	Beta	1.06	1.06
Sharpe Ratio	0.43	R-Squared	70	70

Investment Style
	Stock Portfolio Avg	Relative S&P 500
Price/Earnings Ratio	18.8	1.02
Price/Book Ratio	2.8	0.83
5 Yr Earnings Gr %	3.2	0.57
Return on Assets %	5.3	0.71
Debt % Total Cap	33.1	1.17
Med Mkt Cap ($mil)	16039	1.24

Style Value Blend Growth
Size Large Med Small

Diversification Value for Portfolio Types
Large Cap: Low	Small Cap: High	Bond: Medium	Balanced: Low	Diversified: Low

Expenses & Fees
Sales Fees	4.50% front
	0.00% deferred
	0.25% 12b-1
Management Fee	0.65% max./0.45% min.
3-,5-,10-yr Expense Projections	$73, $95, $158
Annual Brokerage Cost	0.06%

Portfolio 09-30-94

Share Chg (06-94)	Amount 000	Total Stocks: 46 Total Fixed-Income: 20	Value $000	% Net Assets
-2	508	AT & T	27413	5.85
-1	429	Telefonos de Mexico L (ADR)	26817	5.72
-2	615	Southwestern Bell	26129	5.57
-3	758	GTE	23016	4.91
-3	867	MCI Communications	22229	4.74
92	523	US West	20256	4.32
-2	481	Pacific Telesis Group	14783	3.15
-1	320	Conseco	14356	3.06
-1	373	BCE	13385	2.86
-1	244	Bell Atlantic	12953	2.76
-1	318	NYNEX	12232	2.61
148	245	British Telecom (ADR)	12190	2.60
-1	187	Philip Morris	11403	2.43
	229	American Express Cv Pfd 6.25%	10211	2.18
-1	187	Eastman Kodak	9654	2.06
0	65	Wells Fargo	9476	2.02
-1	388	Rochester Telephone	8541	1.82
-1	326	QUALCOMM	8264	1.76
-1	192	Ameritech	7734	1.65
-1	187	Nationwide Health Properties	7182	1.53
0	63	Xerox	6731	1.44
-1	356	Alexander Haagen Properties	6057	1.29
-1	206	AirTouch Communications	5885	1.26
	2798	Mobile Telecomm Tech Cv 6.75%	5831	1.24
0	140	Telefonica de Espana (ADR)	5667	1.21

Composition % 09-30-94
Cash	2.2	Preferreds	0.0
Stocks	83.0	Convertibles	6.1
Bonds	8.7	Other	0.0

Tax Analysis
	Tax-Adj Historical Return %	% Pretax Return
3 Yr Avg	5.98	78.1
5 Yr Avg	5.63	75.2
10 Yr Avg	12.33	68.9
Potential Capital Gain Exposure (% of assets)		18%

Most Similar Funds in MF500
New York Venture A	Fair Fit
Prudential Utility B	Weak Fit
Fidelity Utilities	Weak Fit

Index Allocation
	% of Stocks
S&P 500	59.8
S&P MidCap 400	4.6
U.S. Small Cap	17.9
Foreign	17.8

Sector Weightings
	% of Stocks	Relative S&P 500
Utilities	57.2	4.62
Energy	0.0	0.00
Financials	13.2	1.25
Industrial Cyclicals	4.2	0.26
Consumer Durables	3.5	0.57
Consumer Staples	3.0	0.24
Services	9.4	1.15
Retail	0.0	0.00
Health	0.8	0.09
Technology	8.7	0.95

Flagship All-American Tax-Ex A

	Ticker	Load	NAV	Yield	SEC Yield	Assets	Objective
	FLAAX	4.20%	10.03	6.3%	5.89%	168.0	Muni Nat

Flagship All-American Tax-Exempt Fund - Class A seeks current after-tax income consistent with liquidity and preservation of capital.

The fund invests in a nationally diversified portfolio of investment-grade municipal securities with an average weighted maturity of 15 to 25 years. Municipal bonds must be rated BBB; municipal notes must be rated SP-1 through SP-2; tax-exempt commercial paper must be rated A-1+ through A-2. No more than 20% of the fund's assets are typically invested in securities subject to the Alternative Minimum Tax.

Class A shares have front loads; Class C shares have level loads.

Manager's Investment Style

Management sets the fund's duration at a slightly long seven to nine years, and tries to keep it there. Management also invests in higher-paying sectors, and is comfortable shifting in and out of sectors based on macroeconomic changes. When buying bonds in riskier sectors, management prefers to focus on high-quality bonds.

Historical Profile

Return	Above Average
Risk	Above Average
Rating	★★★
	Neutral

Investment Style History
Fixed Income
Income Rtn % Rank Obj

Growth of $10,000

- |||| Value of Fund ($000)
- — Value of Index ($000) LB Muni
- ▼ Manager Change
- ▽ Partial Manager Change
- ► Mgr Unknown After
- ◄ Mgr Unknown Before

Performance Quartile (Within Objective)

	1983	1984	1985	1986	1987	1988	1989	1990	1991	1992	1993	1994	History
NAV	---	---	---	---	---	9.57	9.90	9.72	10.36	10.65	11.32	10.03	NAV
	---	---	---	---	---	1.22 *	11.62	5.76	14.45	10.66	14.29	-5.89	Total Return %
	---	---	---	---	---	---	-2.92	-3.19	-1.55	3.41	4.54	-2.97	+/- LB Aggregate
	---	---	---	---	---	---	0.84	-1.54	2.31	1.84	2.02	-0.29	+/- LB Muni
	---	---	---	---	---	1.32	8.04	7.58	7.85	6.95	6.45	5.50	Income Return %
	---	---	---	---	---	-0.10	3.58	-1.82	6.60	3.70	7.84	-11.40	Capital Return %
	---	---	---	---	---	---	61	38	60	19	31	71	Total Rtn % Rank All
	---	---	---	---	---	---	3	76	3	4	8	57	Total Rtn % Rank Obj
	---	---	---	---	---	0.13	0.73	0.72	0.71	0.69	0.66	0.64	Income $
	---	---	---	---	---	0.00	0.01	0.00	0.00	0.09	0.16	0.00	Capital Gains $
	---	---	---	---	---	---	0.00	0.42	0.42	0.56	0.65	0.62	Expense Ratio %
	---	---	---	---	---	---	7.27	7.29	7.33	6.81	6.24	5.77	Income Ratio %
	---	---	---	---	---	---	---	132	94	86	72	81	Turnover Rate %
	---	---	---	---	---	6.8	37.7	60.4	113.8	147.0	189.8	168.0	Net Assets ($mil)

Investment Style History numbers: 7 10 10 13 11 15

Fund Manager(s)

Robert M. Ashbaugh, since 10-88. Birthdate: 10-43. BS, Indiana U. 1965 MBA, Ohio U. 1967

Manager Experience	Dates Managed	Invest Obj	Std Dev	+/- Index
Robert M. Ashbaugh				
Flagship KY Triple T-E A	11/87 - 09/93	MS	4.88	-0.18
Flagship CT Double T-E A	11/87 - 03/92	MS	4.54	-1.88

Performance 12-31-94

	1st Qtr	2nd Qtr	3rd Qtr	4th Qtr	Total
1987	---	---	---	---	---
1988	---	---	---	---	1.22 *
1989	1.19	6.06	0.12	3.87	11.62
1990	-0.01	2.61	-0.71	3.82	5.76
1991	2.26	3.29	4.47	3.73	14.45
1992	0.21	5.12	2.68	2.30	10.66
1993	4.38	4.27	3.81	1.16	14.29
1994	-5.54	1.12	0.36	-1.83	-5.89

Bear Market Performance

Decile Rank (5-year period)

Worst .... Best

	Worst 3 Mo Period 1985-89	Worst 3 Mo Period 1990-94
Flagship All-American Tax-Ex A	---	-6.52
+/- LB Aggregate	---	-1.59
+/- Best Fit Index : LB Muni	---	-0.76

Trailing Returns

	Total Return %	+/- LB Aggregate	+/- LB Muni	% Rank All	% Rank Obj	Growth of $10,000
3 Mo	-1.83	-2.21	-0.39	65	75	9,817
6 Mo	-1.48	-2.47	-0.23	82	76	9,852
1 Yr	-5.89	-2.97	-0.29	71	57	9,411
3 Yr Avg	5.98	1.43	1.11	34	6	11,902
5 Yr Avg	7.58	-0.05	0.80	39	3	14,406
10 Yr Avg	---	---	---	---	---	---
15 Yr Avg	---	---	---	---	---	---

Operations

Address and Telephone	One First National Plaza Ste 910
	Dayton, OH 45402-1506
	800-227-4648
Advisor	Flagship Financial
Subadvisor	None
Distributor	Flagship Funds
States Available	All
Report Grade	A-
Income Distrib	Paid Monthly
* Date of Inception	10-03-88
Fiscal Year End	May

Risk Analysis

Time Period	Load-Adj Return %	Risk % Rank [1] All	Risk % Rank [1] Obj	Morningstar [2] Return	Morningstar [2] Risk	Morningstar Risk-Adj Rating
1 Yr	-9.84					
3 Yr	4.47	34	55	1.21	1.07	★★★
5 Yr	6.66	30	62	1.20	1.14	★★★
10 Yr	---					

Average Historical Rating (39 months)   3.2 ★s

[1] 1 = low, 100 = high   [2] 1.00 = Muni Avg   [3] 1.00 = 90-day T-bill return

Other Measures

			Standard LB Agg	Best Fit LB Muni
Standard Deviation	6.28	Alpha	1.3	0.9
Mean	6.02	Beta	1.21	1.13
Sharpe Ratio	0.40	R-Squared	60	97

Investment Style

Interest-Rate Stance

Avg Effective Maturity   21.5 Yrs

Maturity: Short Intm Long

Quality

Avg Credit Quality   AA

Avg Weighted Coupon   7.01%
Avg Weighted Price 103.05% of Par

Diversification Value for Portfolio Types

Large Cap: Medium	Small Cap: High	Bond: Low	Balanced: Medium	Diversified: Medium

Portfolio 05-31-94

Total Stocks: 0
Total Fixed-Income: 154

Amount 000	Date of Maturity		Value $000	% Net Assets
3999	07-01-16	PR Elec Pwr 6%	3880	2.43
3200	01-01-20	GA Muni Elec Pwr 6%	3110	1.95
3200	06-01-23	NM Farmington Poll Cntrl Edison 5.875%	3032	1.90
2800	09-01-18	OH Shelby Wilson Meml Hosp 7.7%	3004	1.88
2536	12-01-20	OH Air Qlty Dev Poll Cntrl Pwr 6.25%	2410	1.51
2400	10-01-16	FL Orange Tourist Dev Tax 6%	2358	1.48
2400	01-01-24	IL Chicago Midway Arpt 6.25%	2340	1.46
1908	08-01-19	TN Shelby Hlth Educ/Hsg Fac Brd 9.75%	2205	1.38
2308	12-01-17	OH Wtr Dev Pure/Impr 5.5%	2126	1.33
2000	10-01-20	DC Howard Univ 7.25%	2125	1.33
1892	12-01-08	FL Broward Resource Rec North 7.95%	2063	1.29
2000	10-01-25	NJ Hsg/Mtg Fin Home Buyer 6.2%	1959	1.23
1880	11-15-15	OH Garfield Heights Marymount Hosp 6.7%	1905	1.19
1680	12-15-16	OH Mahoning Vlly San Dist 7.9%	1843	1.15
1600	06-01-08	MA GO Consumer Loan 7.625%	1840	1.15
1600	07-01-10	WA Pub Pwr Sply Sys Proj #2 7.625%	1833	1.15
2000	11-01-21	WY Lincoln Poll Cntrl Pacificorp 5.625%	1812	1.13
1600	12-01-08	LA Regl Transit 8%	1810	1.13
1588	01-01-23	FL Nassau Amelia Island Ppty 9.75%	1792	1.12
1760	04-01-15	NY Local Govt Assist 6.5%	1789	1.12

Credit Analysis % of Bonds 12-31-94

US Govt	0	BB	0
AAA	40	B	0
AA	11	Below B	0
A	23	NR/NA	8
BBB	18		

Composition % of Assets 12-31-94

Cash	0.9	Preferreds	0.0
Stocks	0.0	Convertibles	0.0
Bonds	99.1	Other	0.0

Tax Analysis

	Tax-Adj Historical Return %	% Pretax Return
3 Yr Avg	5.76	96.2
5 Yr Avg	7.44	98.0
10 Yr Avg	---	---
Potential Capital Gain Exposure (% of assets)		-2%

Most Similar Funds in MF500

Vista Tax-Free Income A	Strong Fit
Dreyfus Muni Bond	Strong Fit
USAA Tax-Exempt Long-Term	Strong Fit

Min / Expenses

Min Initial Purchase	$3000 (Addt'l: $50)
Min IRA Purchase	N/A
Min Auto Invest Plan	$3000 (Systematic Inv: $50)

Expenses & Fees

Sales Fees	4.20% front
	0.00% deferred
	0.40% 12b-1
Management Fee	0.50% flat fee
3-,5-,10-yr Expense Projections	$69, $90, $148

Coupon Range

	% Bonds	Rel Obj
0%	1.4	0.57
0% to 6.8%	45.5	0.75
6.8% to 7.5%	16.4	1.06
7.5% to 8.3%	28.6	3.22
More than 8.3%	8.2	0.92
Not applicable	0.0	0.00

Sector Weightings

	% Bonds	Rel Obj
General Obl	11.12	0.53
Utilities	17.53	1.40
Health	16.05	1.22
Water/Waste	4.45	0.70
Housing	7.06	0.96
Education	7.76	1.21
Transportation	9.91	0.97
COP/Lease	1.86	0.58
Private	20.04	1.72
Misc Revenue	4.22	0.85
Demand	0.00	0.00

Top 5 States % of Bonds

OH	15.83	PA	5.98
NY	12.39	IN	4.80
FL	9.37		

196

MORNINGSTAR 1995 Mutual Fund 500

Flex-funds Muirfield

	Ticker	Load	NAV	Yield	SEC Yield	Assets	Objective
	FLMFX	None	5.34	2.6%	N/A	81.8	Asset Alloc.

Flex-funds Muirfield Fund seeks growth of capital.

The fund normally invests in a diversified array of mutual funds that invest primarily in common stocks or securities convertible into or exchangeable for common stocks, and those that seek long-term growth or appreciation. It does not invest in other funds in the Flex-funds family. The fund generally purchases no-load mutual funds, although it may also occasionally purchase mutual funds subject to a sales charge. The fund may at times purchase index funds.

Manager's Investment Style

Management uses market timing in a fund-of-funds structure. A variety of technical factors contribute to asset allocation decisions. Management evaluates the current interest-rate environment, examines the price trends of the Dow Jones Industrial Index versus those of broader market indexes, and looks at the advance/decline ratio. Management then uses fundamental analysis (the market's price/earning and price/book ratios, etc.) as confirmation of its outlook for stocks and bonds. In picking funds for the portfolio, management focuses on the sectors and styles it expects to outperform, and then chooses funds with records of recent success.

Fund Manager(s)

Robert S. Meeder, Jr., since 08-88. Birthdate: 03-61. BS, U. of Florida 1983

Manager Experience

	Dates Managed	Invest Obj	Std Dev	+/- Index
Robert S. Meeder, Jr.				
Flex-funds Growth	02/92 - 12/94	AA	6.48	-4.27

Historical Profile
Return	Above Average
Risk	Low
Rating	★★★★ Above Average

| | 63% | 44% | 71% | 69% | 82% | 0% | Investment Style History Equity / Average % Stocks Held in Portfolio |

Growth of $10,000
Value of Fund ($000)
— Value of Index ($000) Wil 4500
▼ Manager Change
▽ Partial Manager Change
► Mgr Unknown After
◄ Mgr Unknown Before

Performance Quartile (Within Objective)

	1983	1984	1985	1986	1987	1988	1989	1990	1991	1992	1993	1994	History
NAV	---	---	---	---	---	5.31	5.81	5.19	6.39	6.25	5.36	5.34	NAV
Total Return %	---	---	---	---	---	6.20 *	13.37	2.26	29.75	7.61	8.13	2.70	Total Return %
+/- S&P 500	---	---	---	---	---	-1.63 *	-18.32	5.38	-0.74	-0.01	-1.93	1.39	+/- S&P 500
+/- LB Aggregate	---	---	---	---	---	-1.17	-6.68	13.75	0.36	-1.62	5.62	+/- LB Aggregate
Income Return %	---	---	---	---	---	0.00	1.62	2.00	6.62	1.04	0.40	2.62	Income Return %
Capital Return %	---	---	---	---	---	6.20	11.75	0.26	23.12	6.56	7.72	0.08	Capital Return %
Total Rtn % Rank All	---	---	---	---	---		52	49	27	50	78	8	Total Rtn % Rank All
Total Rtn % Rank Obj	---	---	---	---	---		69	27	8	31	86	5	Total Rtn % Rank Obj
Income $	---	---	---	---	---	0.00	0.08	0.10	0.27	0.06	0.02	0.14	Income $
Capital Gains $	---	---	---	---	---	0.00	0.11	0.64	0.00	0.52	1.31	0.02	Capital Gains $
Expense Ratio %	---	---	---	---	---	1.42	1.53	1.52	1.50	1.40	1.26	1.25	Expense Ratio %
Income Ratio %	---	---	---	---	---	5.02	1.65	4.46	1.25	1.05	-0.13	2.05	Income Ratio %
Turnover Rate %	---	---	---	---	---	---	202	649	107	324	280	---	Turnover Rate %
Net Assets ($mil)	---	---	---	---	---	24.6	26.0	29.4	43.3	62.2	64.8	81.8	Net Assets ($mil)

Performance 12-31-94

	1st Qtr	2nd Qtr	3rd Qtr	4th Qtr	Total
1987	---	---	---	---	---
1988	---	---	---	1.92	6.20 *
1989	0.69	6.40	9.65	-3.49	13.37
1990	1.08	3.90	-6.19	3.80	2.26
1991	16.92	0.15	2.42	8.19	29.75
1992	-0.33	-0.34	1.40	6.84	7.61
1993	1.32	1.42	5.26	-0.04	8.13
1994	0.00	0.66	0.89	1.12	2.70

Bear Market Performance

Decile Rank (5-year period)

Worst ———————————— Best

	Worst 3 Mo Period 1985-89	Worst 3 Mo Period 1990-94
Flex-funds Muirfield	---	-6.19
+/- S&P 500	---	7.56
+/- Best Fit Index : Wil 4500	---	12.04

Trailing Returns

	Total Return %	+/- S&P 500	+/- LB Aggregate	% Rank All	% Rank Obj	Growth of $10,000
3 Mo	1.12	1.14	0.75	6	3	10,112
6 Mo	2.02	-2.84	1.03	26	38	10,202
1 Yr	2.70	1.39	5.62	8	5	10,270
3 Yr Avg	6.12	-0.15	1.57	32	36	11,949
5 Yr Avg	9.66	0.96	2.03	19	16	15,855
10 Yr Avg	---	---	---	---	---	---
15 Yr Avg	---	---	---	---	---	---

Operations

Address and Telephone	6000 Memorial Drive
	Dublin, OH 43017
	800-325-3539 / 614-766-7000
Advisor	R. Meeder & Associates
Subadvisor	None
Distributor	Flex-funds
States Available	Selected states
Report Grade	C+
Income Distrib	Paid Quarterly
* Date of Inception	08-10-88
Fiscal Year End	December

Risk Analysis

Time Period	Load-Adj Return %	Risk % Rank [1] All	Risk % Rank [1] Obj	Morningstar [2] Return	Morningstar Risk	Morningstar Risk-Adj Rating
1 Yr	2.70					
3 Yr	6.12	20	9	0.75 [3]	0.48	★★★★
5 Yr	9.66	43	10	1.26 [3]	0.52	★★★★
10 Yr						

Average Historical Rating (41 months) 3.9 ★s

[1] = low, 100 = high [2] 1.00 = Hybrid Avg [3] 1.00 = 90-day T-bill return

Other Measures

	Standard S&P 500	Best Fit Wil 4500
Standard Deviation	5.51	Alpha 1.4 / 0.8
Mean	6.10	Beta 0.42 / 0.42
Sharpe Ratio	0.47	R-Squared 36 / 56

Investment Style

Stocks

	Port Avg	Rel S&P 500
Price/Earnings Ratio	22.5#	1.22
Price/Book Ratio	2.8#	0.81
5 Yr Earnings Gr %	---	---
Med Mkt Cap ($mil)	3407#	0.26

figure is based on 50% or less of stocks

Bonds

Avg Effective Duration	0.1 Yrs
Avg Effective Maturity	0.4 Yrs
Avg Credit Quality	---
Avg Weighted Coupon	4.85%

Not Available

Diversification Value for Portfolio Types

Large Cap: Medium	Small Cap: Medium	Bond: High	Balanced: Medium	Diversified: Medium

Portfolio 10-31-94

Share Chg (06-94)000	Amount 000	Total Stocks: 5 / Total Fixed-Income: 4	Date of Maturity	Value $000	% Net Assets
	20500	US Treasury Bill 4.76%	12-15-94	20391	23.68
	20000	US Treasury Bill 4.94%	02-09-95	19714	22.89
	550	Waste Management 5.3%	03-07-95	540	0.63
	24	US Treasury Bill 3.35%	01-12-95	23	0.03
0	0	Weingarten Equity Fund		6	0.01
0	0	Mutual Shares Fund		3	0.00
0	0	T. Rowe Price New Era Fund		2	0.00
0	0	Constellation Fund		1	0.00
0	0	Acorn International Fund		1	0.00

Index Allocation

	% of Stocks
S&P 500	45.5
S&P MidCap 400	8.1
U.S. Small Cap	24.5
Foreign	26.5

Composition % 12-31-94

Cash	100.0	Preferreds	0.0
Stocks	0.0	Convertibles	0.0
Bonds	0.0	Other	0.0

Tax Analysis

	Tax-Adj Historical Return %	% Pretax Return
3 Yr Avg	2.74	43.4
5 Yr Avg	6.38	61.9
10 Yr Avg	---	---
Potential Capital Gain Exposure (% of assets)		0%

Most Similar Funds in MF500

Nicholas	Weak Fit
Quantitative Grth & Inc Ord	Weak Fit
Adams Express	Weak Fit

Bond Credit Analysis --/--/--
% of Bonds

US Govt	0	BB	0
AAA	0	B	0
AA	0	Below B	0
A	0	NR/NA	0
BBB	0		

Stock Sector Weightings

	% of Stocks	Relative S&P 500
Utilities	2.9	0.23
Energy	17.7	1.75
Financials	18.2	1.72
Industrial Cyclicals	18.1	1.10
Consumer Durables	8.1	1.30
Consumer Staples	4.9	0.39
Services	13.7	1.69
Retail	6.1	1.05
Health	6.3	0.72
Technology	4.1	0.44

Min Initial Purchase	$2500 (Addt'l: $100)
Min IRA Purchase	$500 (Addt'l: $100)
Min Auto Invest Plan	$2500 (Systematic Inv: $100)

Expenses & Fees

Sales Fees	0.00% front
	0.00% deferred
	0.20% 12b-1
Management Fee	1.00% max./0.60% min.
3-,5-,10-yr Expense Projections	$40, $69, $152
Annual Brokerage Cost	---

Fortis Advantage Asset Alloc A

	Ticker	Load	NAV	Yield	SEC Yield	Assets	Objective
	FAAAX	4.50%	14.03	2.8%	N/A	116.3	Asset Alloc.

Fortis Advantage Asset Allocation Portfolio - Class A seeks total return.

The fund follows a flexible allocation strategy; it maintains no relative percentage requirements. It may invest in domestic and foreign equity and debt, although no more than 20% of its assets may be invested in foreign securities.

On June 22, 1990, Morison Asset Allocation merged into this fund. On June 6, 1992, Carnegie-Cappiello Trust Total Return Series merged into this fund. Prior to Jan. 31, 1992, this fund was named AMEV Advantage Asset Allocation Portfolio.

Manager's Investment Style

The management team is known for opportunistic buying on the bond side and a growth emphasis in stocks. Contrary to many in the asset-allocation group, it often divides assets fairly evenly between bonds and stocks. Fixed-income manager Dennis Ott invests across the bond spectrum, often using market downturns as a chance to pick up bonds on the cheap. His choices run the gamut from Treasuries to non-investment-grade issues. Equity manager Stephen Poling delves into high-multiple growth sectors such as technology and health care, alongside selected growth-oriented issues in value sectors such as financials.

Fund Manager(s)

Management Team

Manager Experience

	Dates Managed	Invest Obj	Std Dev	+/- Index
David G. Carroll				
Fortis Advant Hi-Yld A	01/88 - 12/94	CY	9.39	0.40
Keith R. Thomson				
Fortis Advant Cap Appr A	01/88 - 12/94	SC	20.92	2.49

Performance 12-31-94

	1st Qtr	2nd Qtr	3rd Qtr	4th Qtr	Total
1987	---	---	---	---	---
1988	0.30	1.69	0.88	0.20	3.11
1989	3.45	9.31	8.34	0.12	22.67
1990	-3.42	6.68	-8.95	5.48	-1.05
1991	9.71	0.90	6.82	9.38	29.34
1992	-2.31	1.11	4.89	2.59	6.29
1993	2.90	1.67	4.67	1.62	11.27
1994	-3.51	-3.29	5.76	0.48	-0.83

Bear Market Performance

Decile Rank (5-year period)

	Worst 3 Mo Period 1985-89	Worst 3 Mo Period 1990-94
Fortis Advantage Asset Alloc A	---	-8.95
+/- S&P 500	---	4.79
+/- Best Fit Index : SPMid400	---	8.83

Trailing Returns

	Total Return %	+/- S&P 500	+/- LB Aggregate	% Rank All	% Rank Obj	Growth of $10,000
3 Mo	0.48	0.50	0.10	12	10	10,048
6 Mo	6.27	1.41	5.28	8	2	10,627
1 Yr	-0.83	-2.14	2.09	25	21	9,917
3 Yr Avg	5.46	-0.80	0.92	39	51	11,730
5 Yr Avg	8.46	-0.23	0.84	28	37	15,012
10 Yr Avg	---	---	---	---	---	---
15 Yr Avg	---	---	---	---	---	---

Operations

Address and Telephone	P.O. Box 64284
	St. Paul, MN 55164
	800-800-2638 / 612-738-4000
Advisor	Fortis Advisers
Subadvisor	None
Distributor	Fortis Investors
States Available	All
Report Grade	B-
Income Distrib	Paid Quarterly
* Date of Inception	01-04-88
Fiscal Year End	October

Historical Profile

Return	Average
Risk	Below Average
Rating	★★★
	Neutral

27% 48% 33% 38% 35% 46% 46%

Performance Quartile (Within Objective)

	1983	1984	1985	1986	1987	1988	1989	1990	1991	1992	1993	1994	History
NAV	---	---	---	---	10.00	9.86	11.68	11.12	13.87	14.17	14.64	14.03	NAV
Total Return %	---	---	---	---	---	3.21 *	22.67	-1.05	29.34	6.29	11.27	-0.83	Total Return %
+/- S&P 500	---	---	---	---	---	-9.36 *	-9.02	2.07	-1.14	-1.32	1.22	-2.14	+/- S&P 500
+/- LB Aggregate	---	---	---	---	---	---	8.13	-10.00	13.34	-0.95	1.52	2.09	+/- LB Aggregate
Income Return %	---	---	---	---	---	4.51	4.21	3.74	4.61	4.13	2.67	2.74	Income Return %
Capital Return %	---	---	---	---	---	-1.30	18.46	-4.79	24.73	2.16	8.60	-3.57	Capital Return %
Total Rtn % Rank All	---	---	---	---	---	---	29	58	28	65	57	25	Total Rtn % Rank All
Total Rtn % Rank Obj	---	---	---	---	---	---	11	62	10	56	63	21	Total Rtn % Rank Obj
Income $	---	---	---	---	---	0.45	0.41	0.45	0.49	0.55	0.38	0.40	Income $
Capital Gains $	---	---	---	---	---	0.00	0.00	0.00	0.00	0.00	0.72	0.09	Capital Gains $
Expense Ratio %	---	---	---	---	---	1.95	1.95	1.98	1.83	1.58	1.58	1.53	Expense Ratio %
Income Ratio %	---	---	---	---	---	5.55	4.62	3.89	4.11	4.05	2.90	2.15	Income Ratio %
Turnover Rate %	---	---	---	---	---	---	67	112	64	45	103	---	Turnover Rate %
Net Assets ($mil)	---	---	---	---	---	6.9	9.7	22.6	29.8	92.4	110.7	116.3	Net Assets ($mil)

Investment Style History

Equity

Average % Stocks Held in Portfolio

Growth of $10,000

‖‖‖ Value of Fund ($000)
— Value of Index ($000) SPMid400
▼ Manager Change
▽ Partial Manager Change
► Mgr Unknown After
◄ Mgr Unknown Before

Risk Analysis

Time Period	Load-Adj Return %	Risk % Rank [1] All	Risk % Rank [1] Obj	Morningstar [2] Return	Morningstar [2] Risk	Morningstar Risk-Adj Rating
1 Yr	-5.29					
3 Yr	3.86	62	75	0.08 [3]	0.89	★★★
5 Yr	7.47	53	60	0.67 [3]	0.78	★★★
10 Yr	---	---	---	---	---	---

Average Historical Rating (49 months) 3.4 ★s

[1] = low, 100 = high [2] 1.00 = Hybrid Avg [3] 1.00 = 90-day T-bill return

Other Measures

	Standard S&P 500		Best Fit SPMid400
Standard Deviation	7.11	Alpha	0.0	-0.3
Mean	5.58	Beta	0.72	0.62
Sharpe Ratio	0.29	R-Squared	64	74

Investment Style

Stocks

	Port Avg	Rel S&P 500
Price/Earnings Ratio	24.5	1.33
Price/Book Ratio	5.2	1.54
5 Yr Earnings Gr %	27.4#	4.94
Med Mkt Cap ($mil)	3543	0.27

figure is based on 50% or less of stocks

Bonds

Avg Effective Duration	6.1 Yrs
Avg Effective Maturity	9.5 Yrs
Avg Credit Quality	A
Avg Weighted Coupon	8.03%

Diversification Value for Portfolio Types

Large Cap: Low	Small Cap: Low	Bond: Medium	Balanced: Low	Diversified: Low

Portfolio 09-30-94

Share Chg (06-94)000	Amount 000	Total Stocks: 50 / Total Fixed-Income: 51	Date of Maturity	Value $000	% Net Assets
	7000	Federal Home Loan Bnk 6.125%	08-05-96	6946	5.82
	5000	FNMA 7.4%	07-01-04	4838	4.05
	4993	FNMA 6.5%	04-01-24	4444	3.72
	4000	Mortgage Oblig Struct Tr 6.85%	10-25-18	3837	3.21
	3500	US Treasury Note 7.5%	11-15-01	3503	2.93
	3055	GNMA 7.5%	09-15-23	2870	2.40
	3042	FNMA 7%	04-01-24	2796	2.34
	3000	Green Tree Financial 7.65%	04-15-19	2744	2.30
	2500	Federal Home Loan Bank 7.31%	06-16-04	2411	2.02
0	56	Oracle Systems		2408	2.02
30	60	3Com		2243	1.88
	2000	US Treasury Note 9%	05-15-98	2121	1.78
0	56	Franklin Resources		2097	1.76
	2000	US Treasury Bond 8.125%	05-15-21	2029	1.70
	1958	Vanderbilt Mortgage 7%	07-10-19	1956	1.64
	2000	Hydro-Quebec 8%	02-01-13	1840	1.54
60	60	Blockbuster Entertainment		1721	1.44
0	66	Silicon Graphics		1700	1.42
0	30	First Data		1528	1.28
0	69	LDDS Communications Cl A		1511	1.27

Index Allocation

	% of Stocks
S&P 500	44.2
S&P MidCap 400	26.1
U.S. Small Cap	21.9
Foreign	7.8

Composition % 09-30-94

Cash	1.1	Preferreds	0.0
Stocks	47.0	Convertibles	0.0
Bonds	51.9	Other	0.0

Tax Analysis

	Tax-Adj Historical Return %	% Pretax Return
3 Yr Avg	3.81	68.7
5 Yr Avg	6.94	79.5
10 Yr Avg	---	---
Potential Capital Gain Exposure (% of assets)		10%

Most Similar Funds in MF500

American Cap Harbor A	Fair Fit
MIMLIC Asset Allocation A	Fair Fit
IAI Regional	Fair Fit

Bond Credit Analysis 09-30-94

% of Bonds

US Govt	42	BB	5
AAA	6	B	15
AA	3	Below B	1
A	4	NR/NA	18
BBB	6		

Stock Sector Weightings

	% of Stocks	Relative S&P 500
Utilities	3.7	0.30
Energy	0.0	0.00
Financials	7.5	0.70
Industrial Cyclicals	2.4	0.15
Consumer Durables	9.1	1.46
Consumer Staples	0.0	0.00
Services	14.9	1.82
Retail	13.1	2.25
Health	9.0	1.04
Technology	40.4	4.41

Expenses & Fees

Sales Fees	4.50% front
	0.00% deferred
	0.45% 12b-1
Management Fee	1.00% max./0.70% min.
3-,5-,10-yr Expense Projections	$93, $127, $224
Annual Brokerage Cost	0.11%

Min Initial Purchase	$500 (Addt'l: $50)
Min IRA Purchase	$500 (Addt'l: $50)
Min Auto Invest Plan	$25 (Systematic Inv: $25)

MORNINGSTAR 1995 Mutual Fund 500

Fortress Municipal Income

Ticker	Load	NAV	Yield	SEC Yield	Assets	Objective
FHTFX	1.00%	10.02	6.0%	6.63%	413.7	Muni Nat

Fortress Municipal Income Fund seeks current income exempt from federal income tax.

The fund invests at least 80% of its assets in federally tax-exempt, investment-grade municipal bonds. It may invest without limitation in bonds subject to the Alternative Minimum Tax. For liquidity or temporary defensive purposes, the fund may make taxable short-term investments.

Prior to Aug. 1, 1988, the fund was named Fortress High-Yield Tax-Free Fund. From that date until Aug. 13, 1990, the fund was named Fortress High-Yield Municipal Fund. Under these names, the fund invested the majority of assets in long-term lower-rated municipal securities.

Manager's Investment Style

Management has a yield focus. It emphasizes high-yielding sectors, lower-quality bonds, and premium bonds. It typically keeps large portions of assets in nonrated issues and private-activity bonds, which are subject to the alternative minimum tax. It also searches for yield in unpopular or downtrodden areas.

Fund Manager(s)

Jonathan C. Conley CFA(1983), since 04-87.
Birthdate: 10-53. BA, Harvard 1975 MBA, U. of Virginia 1979

Manager Experience	Dates Managed	Invest Obj	Std Dev	+/- Index
Jonathan C. Conley				
Ohio Intermediate Muni	01/94 - 10/94	MS	6.44	-1.86
Pennsylvania Interm Muni	01/94 - 10/94	MS	6.34	-1.45

Historical Profile
Return	Average
Risk	Average
Rating	★★★
	Neutral

Investment Style History
Fixed Income
Income Rtn % Rank Obj

--- | 30 | 12 | 18 | 28 | 38 | 28 | 22

Growth of $10,000
|||| Value of Fund ($000)
— Value of Index ($000)
LB Muni
▼ Manager Change
▽ Partial Manager Change
► Mgr Unknown After
◄ Mgr Unknown Before

Performance Quartile (Within Objective)

	1983	1984	1985	1986	1987	1988	1989	1990	1991	1992	1993	1994	History
	---	---	---	---	9.55	9.96	10.25	10.17	10.55	10.72	11.26	10.02	NAV
	---	---	---	---	0.89 *	12.20	10.77	6.57	10.94	7.97	11.08	-5.75	Total Return %
	---	---	---	---	---	4.32	-3.77	-2.38	-5.06	0.72	1.33	-2.83	+/- LB Aggregate
	---	---	---	---	---	2.04	-0.01	-0.73	-1.20	-0.85	-1.20	-0.14	+/- LB Muni
	---	---	---	---	5.39	7.91	7.86	7.35	7.20	6.36	6.04	5.26	Income Return %
	---	---	---	---	-4.50	4.29	2.91	-0.78	3.74	1.61	5.04	-11.01	Capital Return %
	---	---	---	---	---	44	66	27	85	46	59	70	Total Rtn % Rank All
	---	---	---	---	---	31	15	37	67	64	62	54	Total Rtn % Rank Obj
	---	---	---	---	0.54	0.72	0.75	0.72	0.69	0.64	0.62	0.60	Income $
	---	---	---	---	0.00	0.00	0.00	0.00	0.00	0.00	0.00	0.00	Capital Gains $
	---	---	---	---	0.86	1.02	0.90	1.01	1.02	1.05	1.09	1.09	Expense Ratio %
	---	---	---	---	7.14	8.03	7.27	7.07	6.86	6.18	5.65	5.56	Income Ratio %
	---	---	---	---	---	34	24	24	18	14	7	27	Turnover Rate %
	---	---	---	---	22.8	24.9	65.6	110.1	181.0	277.4	504.5	413.7	Net Assets ($mil)

Performance 12-31-94

	1st Qtr	2nd Qtr	3rd Qtr	4th Qtr	Total
1987	---	---	-1.37	0.18	0.89 *
1988	3.27	2.42	3.52	2.49	12.20
1989	1.83	4.85	0.83	2.90	10.77
1990	0.10	1.91	0.69	3.75	6.57
1991	1.95	2.32	3.36	2.89	10.94
1992	0.50	3.79	2.45	1.03	7.97
1993	2.99	3.76	3.11	0.82	11.08
1994	-5.39	0.96	0.08	-1.40	-5.75

Bear Market Performance

Decile Rank (5-year period)

Worst | | Best

	Worst 3 Mo Period 1985-89	Worst 3 Mo Period 1990-94
Fortress Municipal Income	---	-6.03
+/- LB Aggregate	---	-1.09
+/- Best Fit Index : LB Muni	---	-0.26

Trailing Returns

	Total Return %	+/- LB Aggregate	+/- LB Muni	% Rank All	% Rank Obj	Growth of $10,000
3 Mo	-1.40	-1.78	0.03	54	53	9,860
6 Mo	-1.32	-2.31	-0.08	79	67	9,868
1 Yr	-5.75	-2.83	-0.14	70	54	9,425
3 Yr Avg	4.17	-0.38	-0.70	66	70	11,303
5 Yr Avg	5.97	-1.66	-0.80	76	61	13,364
10 Yr Avg	---	---	---	---	---	---
15 Yr Avg	---	---	---	---	---	---

Operations

Address and Telephone	Federated Investors Tower
	Pittsburgh, PA 15222-3779
	800-245-5051 / 412-288-1900
Advisor	Federated Advisers
Subadvisor	None
Distributor	Federated Securities
States Available	All plus PR
Report Grade	C
Income Distrib	Paid Monthly
* Date of Inception	04-10-87
Fiscal Year End	August

Min Initial Purchase	$1500 (Addt'l: $100)
Min IRA Purchase	$50 (Addt'l: $50)
Min Auto Invest Plan	$1500 (Systematic Inv: $100)

Expenses & Fees
Sales Fees	1.00% front
	0.00% deferred
	0.25% 12b-1
Management Fee	0.60% flat fee, 0.15%A
3-,5-,10-yr Expense Projections	$55, $69, $142

Risk Analysis

Time Period	Load-Adj Return %	Risk % Rank [1] All	Obj	Morningstar [2] Return	Morningstar Risk	Morningstar Risk-Adj Rating
1 Yr	-7.69					
3 Yr	3.47	30	48	0.87	1.01	★★★
5 Yr	5.76	17	43	0.95	0.94	★★★
10 Yr	---					

Average Historical Rating (57 months) 4.2 ★s

[1] 1 = low, 100 = high [2] 1.00 = Muni Avg [3] 1.00 = 90-day T-bill return

Other Measures
			Standard LB Agg	Best Fit LB Muni
Standard Deviation	5.54	Alpha	-0.3	-0.7
Mean	4.25	Beta	1.06	0.99
Sharpe Ratio	0.13	R-Squared	59	96

Investment Style

Interest-Rate Stance
Avg Effective Maturity   24.9 Yrs

Maturity
Short Intm Long
Quality High Med Low

Quality
Avg Credit Quality   A
Avg Weighted Coupon   7.26%
Avg Weighted Price 100.26% of Par

Diversification Value for Portfolio Types

Large Cap: Medium	Small Cap: High	Bond: Low	Balanced: Low	Diversified: Medium

Portfolio 08-31-94

Total Stocks: 0
Total Fixed-Income: 142

Amount 000	Date of Maturity		Value $000	% Net Assets
21000	07-01-16	MA Indl Fin Waste Disp 9%	21102	4.47
17000	11-01-17	MN St Paul Hsg/Redev Healtheast 6.625%	16294	3.45
10300	08-15-22	LA Lake Charles Harbor/Term 7.75%	11141	2.36
11915	05-01-22	TX Sabine Rvr Poll Cntrl Util Elec 5.85%	10784	2.28
10750	05-01-10	ME Bucksport Solid Waste Disp 6.25%	10422	2.21
10000	07-01-24	IL Hlth Fac Edgewater Hosp/M/C 9.25%	10077	2.13
9500		TX Houston Hlth fac Dev Methodist DMD	9500	2.01
9780	12-01-12	TX Richardson Hosp Impr M/C 6.5%	9410	1.99
10000	10-01-23	NH Higher Educ/Hlth Fac Nashua Hosp 6%	9207	1.95
9400	07-01-14	TN Memphis/Shelby Arpt Spcl Fac 6.2%	8871	1.88
8000	12-01-24	CA Poll Cntrl Fin South Edison 6.4%	7957	1.68
7800	04-01-24	TN Springfield Hlth/Educ Fac 8.5%	7558	1.60
7075	07-01-15	NH Hsg Fin Sngl Fam Mtg 7.25%	7273	1.54
7630	12-01-23	TX Richardson Hosp Impr M/C 6.75%	7257	1.54
7000	06-01-22	PA Allegheny Hosp Dev Rehab Inst 7%	7056	1.49
7320	11-01-26	TX Dallas/Ft Worth Intl Arpt Impr 7.125%	6878	1.46
6400	07-01-22	CT Hlth/Educ Fac Univ Hartford 6.8%	6449	1.37
6200	12-01-30	OK Tulsa Muni Arpt Trust American 7.6%	6224	1.32
6000	05-01-22	SC Richland Solid Waste Disp Fac 6.75%	6210	1.32
6000	04-01-24	PA Hsg Fin Sngl Fam Mtg 7%	6189	1.31

Credit Analysis % of Bonds 06-30-94
US Govt	0	BB	5
AAA	6	B	0
AA	27	Below B	0
A	13	NR/NA	8
BBB	42		

Composition % of Assets 09-30-94
Cash	2.0	Preferreds	0.0
Stocks	0.0	Convertibles	0.0
Bonds	98.0	Other	0.0

Tax Analysis
	Tax-Adj Historical Return %	% Pretax Return
3 Yr Avg	4.17	100.0
5 Yr Avg	5.97	100.0
10 Yr Avg	---	---
Potential Capital Gain Exposure (% of assets)		-7%

Most Similar Funds in MF500
Smith Barney Tax-Ex IncB	Strong Fit
Colonial Tax-Exempt A	Strong Fit
Dreyfus Muni Bond	Strong Fit

Coupon Range
	% Bonds	Rel Obj
0%	0.0	0.00
0% to 6.8%	39.5	0.65
6.8% to 7.5%	21.0	1.35
7.5% to 8.3%	22.0	2.49
More than 8.3%	13.7	1.56
Not applicable	3.7	0.96

Sector Weightings
	% Bonds	Rel Obj
General Obl	0.94	0.04
Utilities	0.77	0.06
Health	27.13	2.06
Water/Waste	0.35	0.05
Housing	21.82	2.98
Education	6.13	0.96
Transportation	11.80	1.16
COP/Lease	0.00	0.00
Private	27.35	2.35
Misc Revenue	0.00	0.00
Demand	3.72	1.51

Top 5 States % of Bonds
TX	15.09	MA	6.20
PA	13.25	LA	6.01
TN	6.49		

Fortress Utility

Fortress Utility Fund seeks current income and moderate capital appreciation.

The fund invests primarily in the common stocks of utility companies. It may invest in preferred stocks, corporate bonds, notes, and warrants of these companies, and in cash, U.S. government securities, and money-market instruments in proportions determined by its advisor.

Prior to June 15, 1990, the fund was named Federated Utility Trust. On June 14, 1990, Federated Corporated Cash Trust merged into the fund.

	Ticker	Load	NAV	Yield	SEC Yield	Assets	Objective
	FEUTX	1.00%	11.72	5.4%	5.08%	768.2	Sp.-Util

Historical Profile
Return	Average
Risk	Low
Rating	★★★
	Neutral

Investment Style History
Equity

Average % Stocks Held in Portfolio

--- 65% 91% 68% 63% 63% 62% 64%

Growth of $10,000
|||| Value of Fund ($000)
— Value of Index ($000)
LB L-T
▼ Manager Change
▽ Partial Manager Change
► Mgr Unknown After
◄ Mgr Unknown Before

Performance Quartile (Within Objective)

Manager's Investment Style

Although management centers this portfolio on high-yielding electric utilities, it attempts to diversify away interest-rate risk by sinking more than one fourth of assets into nonutility issues and another fourth of assets into higher-yielding convertibles. Currently, it places more than 50% of this latter position in other hybrid securities, such as PRIDES and PEPS. The fund's growth edge comes from the nonutilities and foreign holdings, particularly foreign utilities in emerging markets.

Fund Manager(s)

Christopher H. Wiles CFA(1987), since 05-90.
Birthdate: 11-59. BS, Youngstown State U. 1982 MBA, Cleveland State U. 1984
Linda Duessel, since 12-94.

Manager Experience	Dates Managed	Invest Obj	Std Dev	+/- Index
Christopher H. Wiles				
Liberty Utility A	05/90 - 12/94	SU	8.11	1.16
Liberty Equity-Income A	07/91 - 12/94	EI	7.21	2.05

History	1983	1984	1985	1986	1987	1988	1989	1990	1991	1992	1993	1994
NAV	---	---	---	---	8.56	9.13	10.85	10.09	11.93	12.22	13.40	11.72
Total Return %	---	---	---	---	-9.74 *	13.75	26.14	0.91	25.93	8.88	15.17	-7.95
+/- S&P 500	---	---	---	---	-2.51 *	-2.87	-5.55	4.03	-4.55	1.27	5.11	-9.26
+/- S&P Util	---	---	---	---	---	-4.30	-21.08	3.47	11.31	0.79	0.73	0.00
Income Return %	---	---	---	---	4.91	7.09	7.30	7.20	7.70	6.03	5.40	4.59
Capital Return %	---	---	---	---	-14.66	6.66	18.84	-6.28	18.24	2.86	9.76	-12.54
Total Rtn % Rank All	---	---	---	---	---	33	21	53	34	35	28	85
Total Rtn % Rank Obj	---	---	---	---	---	75	52	26	8	57	37	39
Income $	---	---	---	---	0.52	0.58	0.59	0.73	0.68	0.67	0.63	0.63
Capital Gains $	---	---	---	---	0.00	0.00	0.00	0.08	0.00	0.05	0.01	0.00
Expense Ratio %	---	---	---	---	0.53	1.04	1.08	1.05	1.03	1.10	1.07	1.11
Income Ratio %	---	---	---	---	7.95	7.18	6.92	6.77	7.12	6.01	5.45	4.92
Turnover Rate %	---	---	---	---	---	23	17	49	53	26	27	28
Net Assets ($mil)	---	---	---	---	8.0	12.9	22.7	46.7	167.1	465.1	1016.7	768.2

Performance 12-31-94

	1st Qtr	2nd Qtr	3rd Qtr	4th Qtr	Total
1987	---	-3.35	-0.86	-3.86	-9.74 *
1988	3.48	4.23	2.15	3.24	13.75
1989	0.23	10.55	4.85	8.57	26.14
1990	-4.83	2.94	-5.50	9.00	0.91
1991	6.89	0.66	8.01	8.37	25.93
1992	-3.24	3.49	5.80	2.78	8.88
1993	8.02	1.94	4.86	-0.26	15.17
1994	-7.19	-2.01	3.64	-2.33	-7.95

Bear Market Performance

Decile Rank (5-year period)

Worst ────────────────────── Best

	Worst 3 Mo Period 1985-89	Worst 3 Mo Period 1990-94
Fortress Utility	---	-7.19
+/- S&P 500	---	-3.40
+/- Best Fit Index : LB L-T	---	-1.08

Trailing Returns

	Total Return %	+/- S&P 500	+/- S&P Util	% Rank All	% Rank Obj	Growth of $10,000
3 Mo	-2.33	-2.32	-2.23	74	64	9,767
6 Mo	1.22	-3.64	0.85	34	32	10,122
1 Yr	-7.95	-9.26	0.00	85	39	9,205
3 Yr Avg	4.90	-1.36	0.47	50	50	11,543
5 Yr Avg	7.97	-0.73	3.04	33	21	14,670
10 Yr Avg	---	---	---	---	---	---
15 Yr Avg	---	---	---	---	---	---

Operations

Address and Telephone	Federated Investors Tower
	Pittsburgh, PA 15222-3779
	800-245-5051 / 412-288-1900
Advisor	Federated Management
Subadvisor	None
Distributor	Federated Securities
States Available	All plus PR
Report Grade	B-
Income Distrib	Paid Monthly
* Date of Inception	01-30-87
Fiscal Year End	May

Risk Analysis

Time Period	Load-Adj Return %	Risk % Rank [1] All	Risk % Rank [1] Obj	Morningstar [2] Return	Morningstar Risk	Morningstar Risk-Adj Rating
1 Yr	-9.87					
3 Yr	4.20	63	14	0.18 [3]	0.69	★★★
5 Yr	7.75	52	26	0.74 [3]	0.56	★★★
10 Yr	---					
Average Historical Rating (60 months)				4.2		★ s

[1] = low, 100 = high   [2] 1.00 = Equity Avg   [3] 1.00 = 90-day T-bill return

Other Measures
				Standard S&P 500	Best Fit LB L-T
Standard Deviation	7.50	Alpha		-0.5	0.1
Mean	5.08	Beta		0.73	0.75
Sharpe Ratio	0.21	R-Squared		59	59

Investment Style
	Stock Portfolio Avg	Relative S&P 500
Price/Earnings Ratio	15.8	0.85
Price/Book Ratio	2.1	0.61
5 Yr Earnings Gr %	2.2	0.40
Return on Assets %	4.0	0.54
Debt % Total Cap	45.8	1.62
Med Mkt Cap ($mil)	3246	0.25

Style   Value Blend Growth
Size Large Med Small

Diversification Value for Portfolio Types

Large Cap: Low	Small Cap: High	Bond: Low	Balanced: Low	Diversified: Low

Expenses & Fees
Sales Fees	1.00% front
	0.00% deferred
	0.00% 12b-1
Management Fee	0.75% flat fee
3-,5-,10-yr Expense Projections	$56, $71, $144
Annual Brokerage Cost	0.05%

Min Initial Purchase etc.
Min Initial Purchase	$1500 (Addt'l: $100)
Min IRA Purchase	$50 (Addt'l: $50)
Min Auto Invest Plan	$1500 (Systematic Inv: $100)

Portfolio 09-30-94

Share Chg (05-94) 000	Amount 000	Total Stocks: 40 / Total Fixed-Income: 23	Value $000	% Net Assets
-25	600	British Telecom (ADR)	34350	4.13
	1627	Westinghouse Elec Cv Pfd 9%	24812	2.98
	451	Occidental Petro Cv Pfd 7.75%	23744	2.85
0	750	Sonat	23531	2.83
	350	Nacional Fin Cv Pfd 11.25%	22794	2.74
	118	National Power Cv 6.25%	20936	2.52
0	300	Texaco	18000	2.16
-200	500	BCE	17938	2.16
0	800	Pacific Enterprises	17000	2.04
0	1000	PacifiCorp	16875	2.03
397	397	Southwestern Bell	16851	2.03
0	500	Southern New England Telecom	16813	2.02
	300	Sears Roebuck Cv Pfd $3.75	16800	2.02
	2397	RJR Nabisco Hldg Cv Pfd 6.375%	16776	2.02
	170	Enserch ARP	16448	1.98
-14	486	Meditrust	15539	1.87
-150	400	NYNEX	15400	1.85
0	500	GTE	15188	1.83
-66	550	UtiliCorp United	14988	1.80
	761	Citicorp Cv Pfd 8.25%	14840	1.78
0	500	DQE	14500	1.74
	200	Telefonica Argentina Cv Pfd 7%	13839	1.66
450	450	Enron	13613	1.64
250	250	AT & T	13500	1.62
350	350	Sprint	13344	1.60

Composition % 09-30-94
Cash	4.6	Preferreds	23.1
Stocks	63.7	Convertibles	1.3
Bonds	2.5	Other	4.8

Tax Analysis
	Tax-Adj Historical Return %	% Pretax Return
3 Yr Avg	2.92	58.4
5 Yr Avg	5.82	70.1
10 Yr Avg	---	---
Potential Capital Gain Exposure (% of assets)		-5%

Most Similar Funds in MF500
Prudential Utility B	Strong Fit
Fidelity Utilities	Fair Fit
Evergreen Total Return	Fair Fit

Index Allocation
	% of Stocks
S&P 500	50.1
S&P MidCap 400	16.5
U.S. Small Cap	19.4
Foreign	14.0

Sector Weightings
	% of Stocks	Relative S&P 500
Utilities	64.9	5.24
Energy	6.0	0.59
Financials	14.3	1.35
Industrial Cyclicals	2.4	0.15
Consumer Durables	0.0	0.00
Consumer Staples	0.0	0.00
Services	9.9	1.22
Retail	0.0	0.00
Health	0.0	0.00
Technology	2.5	0.28

MORNINGSTAR **1995 Mutual Fund 500**

Founders Balanced

	Ticker	Load	NAV	Yield	SEC Yield	Assets	Objective
	FRINX	None	8.56	2.3%	3.21%	96.0	Balanced

Founders Balanced Fund seeks current income and capital appreciation.

The fund normally invests at least 65% of its assets in dividend-yielding common stocks of established companies, convertible corporate obligations, and preferred stocks. It may also purchase U.S. and foreign government obligations, and high-quality corporate bonds. Up to 30% of fund assets may be invested in income-producing foreign securities. There is no limit on the amount of straight debt securities in which it may invest.

Prior to June 30, 1986, the fund was named Founders Income Fund. From then until Nov. 12, 1993, it was named Founders Equity-Income Fund.

Manager's Investment Style

Manager Patrick Adams looks for dividend-paying issues with capital-appreciation potential. He also makes judicious use of cash when the market appears rocky. Income is the primary objective for the fund's bond portfolio. Management uses duration adjustments to stay in step with the steeper parts of the yield curve. A stake in convertibles allows management to gain access to companies that don't offer dividend-paying stocks.

Fund Manager(s)

Patrick S. Adams, since 03-93. Birthdate: 10-60 BS, Ohio State U. 1983 MBA, Xavier U. 1985
Bjorn E. Borgen, since 1969. Birthday: 09-37 BS, U. of Wisconsin 1962 MBA, Harvard 1966

Manager Experience	Dates Managed	Invest Obj	Std Dev	+/- Index
Bjorn E. Borgen				
Founders Special	01/85 - 12/94	AG	19.57	0.40
Founders Frontier	01/87 - 12/94	SC	19.26	7.64

Historical Profile

Return	Average	
Risk	Below Average	
Rating	★★★★	
	Above Average	

	1983	1984	1985	1986	1987	1988	1989	1990	1991	1992	1993	1994	History
	7.08	7.07	7.38	7.65	6.55	6.89	7.97	7.22	8.19	8.30	8.93	8.56	NAV
	15.35	11.63	12.71	14.59	1.96	11.09	25.27	-4.99	22.86	6.02	21.85	-1.94	Total Return %
	-7.12	5.37	-19.03	-4.09	-3.30	-5.52	-6.42	-1.87	-7.62	-1.59	11.79	-3.25	+/- S&P 500
	6.97	-3.52	-9.42	-0.66	-0.80	3.21	10.73	-13.94	6.86	-1.22	12.10	0.98	+/- LB Aggregate
	6.21	6.96	6.06	4.63	5.20	5.90	4.65	4.42	4.42	3.54	2.41	2.21	Income Return %
	9.13	4.67	6.65	9.96	-3.25	5.19	20.62	-9.41	18.44	2.49	19.44	-4.14	Capital Return %
	57	19	95	57	43	52	23	70	40	69	14	34	Total Rtn % Rank All
	50	25	96	57	47	56	10	87	59	65	1	38	Total Rtn % Rank Obj
	0.41	0.46	0.41	0.33	0.41	0.38	0.33	0.35	0.32	0.28	0.21	0.20	Income $
	0.25	0.32	0.15	0.44	0.87	0.00	0.31	0.00	0.33	0.09	0.96	0.00	Capital Gains $
	1.50	1.50	1.50	1.59	1.84	1.64	1.52	1.65	1.73	1.88	1.34	1.33	Expense Ratio %
	6.14	6.67	5.88	4.44	4.16	5.39	4.19	4.63	4.01	3.57	2.30	2.04	Income Ratio %
	159	145	126	178	141	182	85	103	133	96	251	283	Turnover Rate %
	7.3	7.3	10.0	13.4	13.2	12.6	15.1	13.7	18.6	31.4	72.6	96.0	Net Assets ($mil)

Investment Style History
Equity
Average % Stocks Held in Portfolio

58% 43% 72% 49% 40% 33% 50% 56%

Growth of $10,000
|||| Value of Fund ($000)
— Value of Index ($000) S&P 500
▼ Manager Change
▽ Partial Manager Change
► Mgr Unknown After
◄ Mgr Unknown Before

Performance Quartile (Within Objective)

Performance 12-31-94

	1st Qtr	2nd Qtr	3rd Qtr	4th Qtr	Total
1987	10.60	2.47	4.41	-13.84	1.96
1988	5.43	1.11	2.42	1.75	11.09
1989	5.31	9.38	9.21	-0.41	25.27
1990	-3.45	2.17	-7.20	3.79	-4.99
1991	7.01	0.59	7.94	5.75	22.86
1992	-2.51	0.57	5.77	2.23	6.02
1993	5.73	3.85	7.40	3.33	21.85
1994	-1.02	-0.45	1.49	-1.94	-1.94

Bear Market Performance

Decile Rank (5-year period)

Worst — Best

	Worst 3 Mo Period 1985-89	Worst 3 Mo Period 1990-94
Founders Balanced	-14.15	-7.20
+/- S&P 500	15.43	6.54
+/- Best Fit Index : S&P 500	15.43	6.54

Trailing Returns

	Total Return %	+/- S&P 500	+/- LB Aggregate	% Rank All	% Rank Obj	Growth of $10,000
3 Mo	-1.94	-1.93	-2.32	67	82	9,806
6 Mo	-0.48	-5.34	-1.47	65	94	9,952
1 Yr	-1.94	-3.25	0.98	34	38	9,806
3 Yr Avg	8.20	1.94	3.66	20	8	12,669
5 Yr Avg	8.14	-0.55	0.51	32	36	14,788
10 Yr Avg	10.48	-3.90	0.54	53	67	27,099
15 Yr Avg	12.08	-2.40	1.27	53	64	55,320

Operations

Address and Telephone	2930 E. Third Avenue Denver, CO 80206 800-525-2440 / 303-394-4404
Advisor	Founders Asset Management
Subadvisor	None
Distributor	Founders Asset Management
States Available	All
Report Grade	C+
Income Distrib	Paid Quarterly
Date of Inception	02-19-63
Fiscal Year End	December

Min Initial Purchase	$1000 (Addt'l: $100)
Min IRA Purchase	$500 (Addt'l: $100)
Min Auto Invest Plan	$50 (Systematic Inv: $50)

Expenses & Fees

Sales Fees	0.00% front
	0.00% deferred
	0.25% 12b-1
Management Fee	0.65% flat fee
3-,5-,10-yr Expense Projections	$43, $74, $162
Annual Brokerage Cost	---

Risk Analysis

Time Period	Load-Adj Return %	Risk % Rank [1] All	Obj	Morningstar [2] Return	Risk	Morningstar Risk-Adj Rating
1 Yr	-1.94					
3 Yr	8.20	46	40	1.40 [3]	0.68	★★★★
5 Yr	8.14	51	31	0.85 [3]	0.70	★★★★
10 Yr	10.48	39	10	0.75	0.63	★★★
Average Historical Rating (109 months)				3.6 ★s		

[1] 1 = low, 100 = high [2] 1.00 = Hybrid Avg [3] 1.00 = 90-day T-bill return

Other Measures

		Standard S&P 500	Best Fit S&P 500
Standard Deviation	6.42	Alpha	2.8	2.8
Mean	8.12	Beta	0.64	0.64
Sharpe Ratio	0.72	R-Squared	60	60

Investment Style

Stocks

	Port Avg	Rel S&P 500
Price/Earnings Ratio	14.6	0.79
Price/Book Ratio	2.6	0.76
5 Yr Earnings Gr %	9.8	1.76
Med Mkt Cap ($mil)	6032	0.46

Bonds

Avg Effective Duration	3.1 Yrs
Avg Effective Maturity	3.0 Yrs
Avg Credit Quality	A
Avg Weighted Coupon	5.98%

Diversification Value for Portfolio Types

Large Cap: Low	Small Cap: Medium	Bond: Medium	Balanced: Low	Diversified: Low

Portfolio 06-30-94

Share Chg (12-93)000	Amount 000		Date of Maturity	Value $000	% Net Assets
		Total Stocks: 51 Total Fixed-Income: 17			
	4000	Compaq Computer 6.5%	03-15-99	3822	3.87
	4000	Ford Motor Credit 5.625%	01-15-99	3723	3.77
	3000	US Treasury Note 4.25%	12-31-95	2931	2.97
	3000	GMAC 6.2%	01-16-01	2740	2.77
22	57	Gap		2415	2.45
110	110	Liberty Properties		2200	2.23
73	82	MGIC Investment		2173	2.20
44	44	Chrysler		2074	2.10
	45	AMR Cl A Cv Pfd $3.00		2025	2.05
	2000	Sholodge Cv 7.5%	05-01-04	1985	2.01
80	80	Teledenmark		1970	1.99
39	79	Wal-Mart Stores		1916	1.94
20	35	JC Penney		1899	1.92
60	60	Vastar Resources		1763	1.78
5	21	Texas Instruments		1670	1.69
	1400	Home Depot Cv 4.5%	02-15-97	1638	1.66
65	65	Phillips-Van Heusen		1633	1.65
9	23	Deere		1555	1.57
	1500	US Treasury Note 6.75%	06-30-99	1486	1.50
8	24	Intel		1404	1.42

Index Allocation

	% of Stocks
S&P 500	64.8
S&P MidCap 400	9.6
U.S. Small Cap	11.1
Foreign	14.5

Composition % 12-31-94

Cash	13.0	Preferreds	1.9
Stocks	57.9	Convertibles	4.9
Bonds	22.4	Other	0.0

Tax Analysis

	Tax-Adj Historical Return %	% Pretax Return
3 Yr Avg	6.13	73.2
5 Yr Avg	6.08	71.7
10 Yr Avg	7.71	64.4
Potential Capital Gain Exposure (% of assets)		-1%

Most Similar Funds in MF500

Fortis Advant Asset Alloc A	Weak Fit
SteinRoe Total Return	Weak Fit
Salomon Bros Opportunity	Weak Fit

Bond Credit Analysis 12-31-94

% of Bonds

US Govt	10	BB	18
AAA	9	B	9
AA	9	Below B	9
A	9	NR/NA	0
BBB	36		

Stock Sector Weightings

	% of Stocks	Relative S&P 500
Utilities	10.8	0.87
Energy	3.0	0.30
Financials	14.4	1.36
Industrial Cyclicals	7.4	0.45
Consumer Durables	19.8	3.19
Consumer Staples	3.8	0.30
Services	14.6	1.79
Retail	16.6	2.85
Health	0.0	0.00
Technology	9.7	1.06

Founders Blue Chip

	Ticker	Load	NAV	Yield	SEC Yield	Assets	Objective
	FRMUX	None	6.16	0.9%	N/A	312.2	Growth/Inc.

Founders Blue Chip Fund seeks long-term growth of both capital and income.

The fund invests primarily in common stocks of large companies with proven records of earnings and dividends that management feels are in sound financial condition. Investments in foreign securities are limited to 30% of the fund's assets.

Prior to Nov. 30, 1987, the fund was named Founders Mutual Fund. Prior to Dec. 1, 1983, the fund operated as a unit investment trust and invested in a fixed list of common stocks.

Historical Profile
Return Average
Risk   Below Average
Rating ★★★★
        Above Average

92%	86%	96%	83%	85%	83%	84%	75%	

Investment Style History
Equity
Average % Stocks Held
in Portfolio

Growth of $10,000
|||| Value of Fund ($000)
— Value of Index ($000)
S&P 500
▼ Manager Change
▽ Partial Manager Change
► Mgr Unknown After
◄ Mgr Unknown Before

Performance Quartile
(Within Objective)

Manager's Investment Style

Management focuses more on the growth side than the income side of the growth-and-income equation. Although management insists on buying stocks with dividends, it looks for high current and potential earnings growth, as well. The portfolio thus features more growth names than the typical utilities and energy names that populate most growth-and-income portfolios. Since new management hopped aboard in 1993, trading activity has picked up; as such, the fund hasn't been all that tax efficient.

Fund Manager(s)

Patrick S. Adams, since 03-93. Birthdate: 10-60 BS, Ohio State U. 1983 MBA, Xavier U. 1985

Michael K. Haines, since 12-89. Birthday: 08-61 BA, Colorado C. 1983 MBA, U. of Denver 1985

Manager Experience	Dates Managed	Invest Obj	Std Dev	+/- Index
Michael K. Haines				
Founders Special	01/85 - 12/94	AG	19.57	0.40
Founders Growth	01/85 - 12/94	G	17.81	1.11

	1983	1984	1985	1986	1987	1988	1989	1990	1991	1992	1993	1994	History
	10.72	9.38	9.75	7.87	6.14	6.31	7.32	6.67	7.67	6.91	6.49	6.16	NAV
	25.14	1.92	31.94	17.33	1.91	10.07	35.59	0.44	28.34	-0.26	14.49	0.52	Total Return %
	2.67	-4.35	0.21	-1.35	-3.35	-6.54	3.90	3.56	-2.14	-7.87	4.43	-0.79	+/- S&P 500
	1.67	-1.13	-0.62	1.24	-0.45	-7.87	6.41	6.62	-5.87	-9.23	3.21	0.59	+/- Wilshire 5000
	4.00	3.33	4.15	2.91	2.78	3.12	2.24	2.41	1.62	1.18	0.57	0.93	Income Return %
	21.14	-1.42	27.79	14.42	-0.87	6.95	33.35	-1.97	26.72	-1.43	13.92	-0.41	Capital Return %
	23	60	19	37	43	61	6	54	29	90	31	16	Total Rtn % Rank All
	28	63	20	43	49	79	4	14	50	97	24	33	Total Rtn % Rank Obj
	0.39	0.32	0.38	0.28	0.24	0.19	0.16	0.17	0.12	0.08	0.04	0.06	Income $
	0.71	1.17	1.85	3.22	1.71	0.25	1.04	0.51	0.74	0.66	1.38	0.31	Capital Gains $
	0.42	0.74	0.70	0.74	0.98	1.00	0.98	1.07	1.10	1.23	1.22	1.24	Expense Ratio %
	3.91	3.90	3.69	2.64	2.41	2.81	2.03	2.35	1.52	1.13	0.57	0.61	Income Ratio %
	0	16	18	42	31	58	64	82	95	103	212	242	Turnover Rate %
	143.6	134.9	138.8	178.9	174.6	173.5	231.3	233.6	290.3	290.4	307.4	312.2	Net Assets ($mil)

Performance 12-31-94

	1st Qtr	2nd Qtr	3rd Qtr	4th Qtr	Total
1987	18.12	3.70	5.64	-21.24	1.91
1988	2.20	2.41	1.43	3.68	10.07
1989	8.33	10.79	12.15	0.74	35.59
1990	-3.76	10.14	-11.26	6.78	0.44
1991	12.68	-1.94	5.84	9.74	28.34
1992	-6.59	-1.26	2.20	5.80	-0.26
1993	3.19	1.83	6.35	2.45	14.49
1994	-0.70	-2.80	5.27	-1.07	0.53

Bear Market Performance

Decile Rank (5-year period)

Worst | Best

	Worst 3 Mo Period 1985-89	Worst 3 Mo Period 1990-94
Founders Blue Chip	-27.87	-11.26
+/- S&P 500	1.71	2.48
+/- Best Fit Index : S&P 500	1.71	2.48

Trailing Returns

	Total Return %	+/- S&P 500	+/- Wil 5000	% Rank All	% Rank Obj	Growth of $10,000
3 Mo	-1.07	-1.06	-0.31	46	43	9,893
6 Mo	4.14	-0.72	-0.48	15	28	10,414
1 Yr	0.52	-0.79	0.59	16	33	10,052
3 Yr Avg	4.71	-1.56	-1.91	54	67	11,479
5 Yr Avg	8.15	-0.54	-0.66	31	45	14,798
10 Yr Avg	13.30	-1.09	-0.56	23	27	34,844
15 Yr Avg	13.32	-1.16	-0.65	34	42	65,277

Operations

Address and Telephone	2930 E. Third Avenue
	Denver, CO 80206
	800-525-2440 / 303-394-4404
Advisor	Founders Asset Management
Subadvisor	None
Distributor	Founders Asset Management
States Available	All
Report Grade	C+
Income Distrib	Paid Annually
Date of Inception	07-05-38
Fiscal Year End	December

Risk Analysis

Time Period	Load-Adj Return %	Risk % Rank[1] All	Obj	Morningstar[2] Return	Morningstar Risk	Morningstar Risk-Adj Rating
1 Yr	0.52					
3 Yr	4.71	72	75	0.33[3]	0.82	★★★
5 Yr	8.15	64	43	0.85[3]	0.77	★★★
10 Yr	13.30	61	62	1.13	0.85	★★★★
Average Historical Rating (109 months)				3.6 ★s		

[1] 1 = low, 100 = high [2] 1.00 = Equity Avg [3] 1.00 = 90-day T-bill return

Other Measures

				Standard S&P 500	Best Fit S&P 500
Standard Deviation	8.51	Alpha		-1.2	-1.2
Mean	4.97	Beta		0.92	0.92
Sharpe Ratio	0.17	R-Squared		73	73

Investment Style

	Stock Portfolio Avg	Relative S&P 500
Price/Earnings Ratio	17.8	0.97
Price/Book Ratio	4.2	1.22
5 Yr Earnings Gr %	15.4	2.78
Return on Assets %	11.2	1.49
Debt % Total Cap	27.0	0.96
Med Mkt Cap ($mil)	4612	0.36

Style Value Blend Growth
Size Large Med Small

Diversification Value for Portfolio Types

Large Cap: Low	Small Cap: Medium	Bond: High	Balanced: Low	Diversified: Low

Expenses & Fees

Sales Fees	0.00% front
	0.00% deferred
	0.25% 12b-1
Management Fee	0.64% flat fee
3-,5-,10-yr Expense Projections	$39, $67, $148
Annual Brokerage Cost	---

Min Initial Purchase	$1000 (Addt'l: $100)
Min IRA Purchase	$500 (Addt'l: $100)
Min Auto Invest Plan	$50 (Systematic Inv: $50)

Portfolio 06-30-94

Share Chg (12-93) 000	Amount 000	Total Stocks: 69 / Total Fixed-Income: 8	Value $000	% Net Assets
40	195	Gap	8336	2.77
140	265	MGIC Investment	7023	2.33
80	145	Chrysler	6833	2.27
	150	AMR Cl A Cv Pfd $3.00	6752	2.24
70	275	Wal-Mart Stores	6669	2.21
101	156	Computer Associates Intl	6240	2.07
180	180	Newbridge Networks	6188	2.05
-20	110	JC Penney	5968	1.98
-83	70	FNMA	5812	1.93
175	175	Promus	5184	1.72
26	71	Deere	4801	1.59
-6	60	Texas Instruments	4770	1.58
	4676	Sholodge Cv 7.5%	4641	1.54
56	176	Nine West Group	4586	1.52
3	103	Home Depot	4354	1.45
100	100	BMC Software	4325	1.44
40	90	General Electric	4196	1.39
180	185	Circus Circus Enterprises	3978	1.32
-65	120	Toys 'R' Us	3930	1.31
195	195	Liberty Properties	3900	1.30
1	66	Intel	3861	1.28
-130	197	Wheelabrator Technologies	3667	1.22
0	90	Coca-Cola	3656	1.21
200	200	USG	3625	1.20
90	90	Magna International Cl A	3600	1.20

Composition % 12-31-94

				% of Stocks
Cash	22.2	Preferreds	3.2	
Stocks	72.7	Convertibles	1.9	
Bonds	0.0	Other	0.0	

Tax Analysis

	Tax-Adj Historical Return %	% Pretax Return
3 Yr Avg	1.37	28.1
5 Yr Avg	4.79	55.0
10 Yr Avg	8.56	51.3
Potential Capital Gain Exposure (% of assets)		5%

Most Similar Funds in MF500

Liberty All-Star	Strong Fit
Gabelli Growth	Strong Fit
IDS New Dimensions	Fair Fit

Index Allocation

	% of Stocks
S&P 500	54.7
S&P MidCap 400	15.2
U.S. Small Cap	17.1
Foreign	13.0

Sector Weightings

	% of Stocks	Relative S&P 500
Utilities	2.4	0.19
Energy	1.4	0.14
Financials	8.6	0.81
Industrial Cyclicals	8.5	0.52
Consumer Durables	11.4	1.84
Consumer Staples	5.3	0.42
Services	21.3	2.62
Retail	21.7	3.72
Health	0.0	0.00
Technology	19.4	2.12

MORNINGSTAR 1995 Mutual Fund 500

Founders Frontier

	Ticker	Load	NAV	Yield	SEC Yield	Assets	Objective
	FOUNX	None	26.50	0.0%	N/A	249.2	Small Company

Founders Frontier Fund seeks capital appreciation.

The fund typically invests at least 65% of its assets in small and medium-sized companies. These companies ordinarily are traded on the over-the-counter market and have market capitalizations or revenues of $200 million to $750 million; the fund may also invest in larger companies with growth potential. The fund normally invests at least 50% of its assets in securities of U.S. issuers, but it may invest fully in foreign securities depending on available investment opportunities. No more than 25% of the fund's assets may be invested in any one foreign country.

Manager's Investment Style

In addition to searching for high growth rates, and paying high prices for them, manager Michael Haines follows a productivity theme: He prioritizes cost-conscious companies, or firms that develop more-efficient technological systems for other companies, in the fund's portfolio. He also at times maintains rather high cash positions.

Fund Manager(s)

Michael K. Haines, since 1990. Birthdate: 08-61 BA, Colorado C. 1983 MBA, U. of Denver 1985

Bjorn E. Borgen, since 01-87. Birthday: 09-37 BS, U. of Wisconsin 1962 MBA, Harvard 1966

Manager Experience	Dates Managed	Invest Obj	Std Dev	+/- Index
Bjorn E. Borgen				
Founders Balanced	01/69 - 12/94	B	9.39	-1.31
Founders Special	01/85 - 12/94	AG	19.57	0.40

Historical Profile
Return	Above Average
Risk	Above Average
Rating	★★★★ Above Average

Stocks Held in Portfolio: 74% 83% 95% 66% 76% 77% 83% 71%

Investment Style History Equity
Average % Stocks Held in Portfolio

Growth of $10,000
|||| Value of Fund ($000)
— Value of Index ($000) Wil 4500
▼ Manager Change
▽ Partial Manager Change
► Mgr Unknown After
◄ Mgr Unknown Before

Performance Quartile (Within Objective)

	1983	1984	1985	1986	1987	1988	1989	1990	1991	1992	1993	1994	History
NAV	---	---	---	---	11.03	13.45	18.49	16.87	24.21	25.03	27.94	26.50	NAV
	---	---	---	---	16.10 *	29.20	44.31	-7.46	49.33	8.94	16.54	-2.81	Total Return %
	---	---	---	---	23.04 *	12.59	12.63	-4.34	18.85	1.32	6.48	-4.13	+/- S&P 500
	---	---	---	---	---	8.67	20.37	6.10	5.88	-2.82	2.00	-0.16	+/- Wilshire 4500
	---	---	---	---	0.00	0.00	0.30	0.89	0.03	0.00	0.00	0.00	Income Return %
	---	---	---	---	16.10	29.20	44.01	-8.35	49.31	8.93	16.54	-2.81	Capital Return %
	---	---	---	---	---	3	2	78	8	34	24	41	Total Rtn % Rank All
	---	---	---	---	---	10	8	35	49	74	51	64	Total Rtn % Rank Obj
	---	---	---	---	0.00	0.00	0.05	0.16	0.01	0.00	0.00	0.00	Income $
	---	---	---	---	0.58	0.78	0.84	0.08	0.93	1.31	1.20	0.65	Capital Gains $
	---	---	---	---	2.25	1.89	1.46	1.71	1.68	1.83	1.66	1.63	Expense Ratio %
	---	---	---	---	-0.74	-0.43	0.38	0.78	0.05	-0.58	-0.75	-0.58	Income Ratio %
	---	---	---	---	---	312	198	207	158	155	109	105	Turnover Rate %
	---	---	---	---	3.3	8.8	49.4	39.4	102.5	145.7	253.0	249.2	Net Assets ($mil)

Performance 12-31-94

	1st Qtr	2nd Qtr	3rd Qtr	4th Qtr	Total
1987	---	2.04	13.03	-17.89	16.10 *
1988	14.69	11.46	-1.21	2.30	29.20
1989	17.32	10.90	20.23	-7.75	44.31
1990	-4.38	8.99	-17.80	8.02	-7.46
1991	26.32	-2.96	13.97	6.88	49.33
1992	-1.69	-5.88	1.21	16.33	8.94
1993	0.36	2.63	12.61	0.48	16.54
1994	-5.87	-7.07	9.66	1.32	-2.81

Bear Market Performance

Decile Rank (5-year period)

Worst | Best

	Worst 3 Mo Period 1985-89	Worst 3 Mo Period 1990-94
Founders Frontier	---	-18.07
+/- S&P 500	---	-4.22
+/- Best Fit Index : Wil 4500	---	1.34

Trailing Returns

	Total Return %	+/- S&P 500	+/- Wil 4500	% Rank All	% Rank Obj	Growth of $10,000
3 Mo	1.32	1.34	3.82	5	24	10,132
6 Mo	11.10	6.24	6.91	4	28	11,110
1 Yr	-2.81	-4.13	-0.16	41	64	9,719
3 Yr Avg	7.25	0.99	-0.35	25	65	12,338
5 Yr Avg	11.26	2.57	2.17	11	54	17,050
10 Yr Avg	---	---	---	---	---	---
15 Yr Avg	---	---	---	---	---	---

Operations

Address and Telephone	2930 E. Third Avenue
	Denver, CO 80206
	800-525-2440 / 303-394-4404
Advisor	Founders Asset Management
Subadvisor	None
Distributor	Founders Asset Management
States Available	All
Report Grade	C+
Income Distrib	Paid Annually
* Date of Inception	01-22-87
Fiscal Year End	December

Min Initial Purchase	$1000 (Addt'l: $100)
Min IRA Purchase	$500 (Addt'l: $100)
Min Auto Invest Plan	$50 (Systematic Inv: $50)

Expenses & Fees
Sales Fees	0.00% front
	0.00% deferred
	0.25% 12b-1
Management Fee	1.00% flat fee
3-,5-,10-yr Expense Projections	$53, $91, $198
Annual Brokerage Cost	---

Risk Analysis

Time Period	Load-Adj Return %	Risk % Rank [1] All	Obj	Morningstar [2] Return	Morningstar Risk	Morningstar Risk-Adj Rating
1 Yr	-2.81					
3 Yr	7.25	91	63	1.10 [3]	1.22	★★★
5 Yr	11.26	92	66	1.72 [3]	1.21	★★★★
10 Yr	---	---	---	---	---	

Average Historical Rating (60 months) 4.5 ★s

[1] 1 = low, 100 = high [2] 1.00 = Equity Avg [3] 1.00 = 90-day T-bill return

Other Measures
			Standard S&P 500	Best Fit Wil 4500
Standard Deviation	13.55	Alpha	1.1	-1.2
Mean	7.94	Beta	1.16	1.30
Sharpe Ratio	0.33	R-Squared	46	88

Investment Style
	Stock Portfolio Avg	Relative S&P 500
Price/Earnings Ratio	23.0	1.24
Price/Book Ratio	3.9	1.14
5 Yr Earnings Gr %	27.6#	4.96
Return on Assets %	10.9	1.46
Debt % Total Cap	22.4	0.79
Med Mkt Cap ($mil)	835	0.06

figure is based on 50% or less of stocks

Style Value Blend Growth / Size Large Med Small

Diversification Value for Portfolio Types
Large Cap: Medium	Small Cap: Low	Bond: High	Balanced: Low	Diversified: Low

Portfolio 06-30-94

Share Chg (12-93) 000	Amount 000	Total Stocks: 74 / Total Fixed-Income: 0	Value $000	% Net Assets
70	100	Maxim Integrated Products	5175	2.33
10	160	Midlantic	4620	2.08
-20	150	ALC Communications	4613	2.08
130	130	Cyrix	4128	1.86
58	121	Frontier Insurance Group	3764	1.70
5	140	Teradyne	3710	1.67
110	110	NWNL	3658	1.65
25	140	Oakwood Homes	3290	1.48
61	110	Healthsource	3135	1.41
90	180	Sanmina	3015	1.36
-35	115	LSI Logic	2875	1.30
90	150	Pyxis	2850	1.29
-19	70	CHIPCOM	2748	1.24
0	83	RP Scherer	2723	1.23
0	75	Coventry	2719	1.23
0	144	Mirage Resorts	2695	1.22
100	100	Rouge Steel	2688	1.21
0	80	Michaels Stores	2680	1.21
34	150	Watson Pharmaceuticals	2663	1.20
10	60	Intergroup Healthcare	2640	1.19
0	65	ADC Telecommunications	2616	1.18
-23	80	LCI International	2560	1.15
0	90	Jones Apparel Group	2543	1.15
67	147	LDDS Communications Cl A	2540	1.15
50	100	HBO	2525	1.14

Composition % 12-31-94
Cash	31.1	Preferreds	0.0
Stocks	67.2	Convertibles	1.7
Bonds	0.0	Other	0.0

Tax Analysis
	Tax-Adj Historical Return %	% Pretax Return
3 Yr Avg	6.11	83.2
5 Yr Avg	10.21	88.8
10 Yr Avg	---	---
Potential Capital Gain Exposure (% of assets)		13%

Most Similar Funds in MF500
Berger 100	Strong Fit
MainStay Capital Apprec B	Strong Fit
T. Rowe Price New America G	Strong Fit

Index Allocation
	% of Stocks
S&P 500	3.5
S&P MidCap 400	11.8
U.S. Small Cap	73.5
Foreign	11.2

Sector Weightings
	% of Stocks	Relative S&P 500
Utilities	2.2	0.18
Energy	0.0	0.00
Financials	16.1	1.52
Industrial Cyclicals	5.3	0.32
Consumer Durables	6.2	1.00
Consumer Staples	1.5	0.12
Services	14.8	1.82
Retail	7.0	1.20
Health	10.5	1.21
Technology	36.4	3.98

Founders Special

Founders Special Fund seeks capital appreciation.

The fund typically invests at least 65% of its assets in common stocks of medium-size companies; however, it does not maintain strict limitations on market capitalization. To a lesser extent, the fund invests in stocks of larger companies whose earning power has been depressed but is expected to improve. The fund may engage in aggressive techniques, such as leveraging and short-term trading. It may also invest up to 30% of its assets in foreign securities.

Prior to June 10, 1992, the fund emphasized investments in smaller companies.

Manager's Investment Style

Management follows the Founders principle of seeking firms that are cutting costs and boosting productivity, or are making it easier for other companies to do so through technology. Management also follows other growth-oriented themes, and strongly emphasizes high growth rates. Management keeps price targets for its favored stocks, often selling and rebuying as stocks move through the targets. This results in high turnover.

Fund Manager(s)

Charles W. Hooper, Jr., since 01-92 Birthdate: 07-45
BFT, Thunderbird School of Int'l Mgmt. 1968
Michael K. Haines, since 1985 Birthdate: 08-61 BA, Colorado C. 1983 MBA U. of Denver 1985

Manager Experience	Dates Managed	Invest Obj	Std Dev	+/- Index
Michael K. Haines				
Founders Growth	01/85 - 12/94	G	17.81	1.11
Founders Government Secs	03/88 - 12/94	GG	4.92	-2.22

Ticker	Load	NAV	Yield	SEC Yield	Assets	Objective
FRSPX	None	7.01	0.0%	N/A	300.9	Aggr. Growth

Historical Profile

Return	Above Average
Risk	Above Average
Rating	★★★★
	Above Average

91% 87% 96% 70% 77% 82% 91% 86%

Investment Style History
Equity
Average % Stocks Held
in Portfolio

Growth of $10,000

|||| Value of Fund ($000)
— Value of Index ($000)
SPMid400
▼ Manager Change
▽ Partial Manager Change
► Mgr Unknown After
◄ Mgr Unknown Before

Performance Quartile
(Within Objective)

	1983	1984	1985	1986	1987	1988	1989	1990	1991	1992	1993	1994	History
	5.46	4.68	5.34	5.60	5.14	5.47	6.64	5.03	7.59	7.76	7.67	7.01	NAV
	22.75	-12.19	15.27	18.76	5.25	13.19	39.21	-10.41	63.66	8.30	16.02	-4.90	Total Return %
	0.28	-18.45	-16.67	-0.01	-3.42	7.52	-7.29	33.17	0.68	5.97	-6.22	+/- S&P 500
	---	-10.47	-16.75	7.00	8.76	-7.34	15.26	3.15	20.20	-3.46	1.49	-2.25	+/- Wilshire 4500
	0.92	2.10	1.16	1.07	0.58	0.62	2.24	1.89	0.63	0.00	0.00	0.00	Income Return %
	21.83	-14.29	14.10	17.69	4.67	12.58	36.96	-12.30	63.03	8.30	16.02	-4.90	Capital Return %
	30	92	92	28	22	36	4	85	4	42	25	63	Total Rtn % Rank All
	36	33	92	25	26	50	9	67	38	51	67	64	Total Rtn % Rank Obj
	0.05	0.11	0.05	0.06	0.03	0.03	0.14	0.10	0.04	0.00	0.00	0.00	Income $
	0.61	0.00	0.00	0.69	0.72	0.31	0.81	0.81	0.57	0.46	1.33	0.28	Capital Gains $
	1.20	1.11	1.02	1.06	1.14	1.12	1.06	1.20	1.15	1.23	1.33	1.35	Expense Ratio %
	0.90	2.20	0.85	0.73	0.45	0.59	1.95	1.54	0.76	-0.05	-0.14	-0.48	Income Ratio %
	141	191	192	138	210	160	151	146	102	223	285	296	Turnover Rate %
	94.5	81.3	95.4	70.3	66.9	63.1	91.3	58.0	224.4	455.4	432.9	300.9	Net Assets ($mil)

Performance 12-31-94

	1st Qtr	2nd Qtr	3rd Qtr	4th Qtr	Total
1987	20.11	4.39	9.34	-23.23	5.25
1988	4.86	5.38	-1.41	3.89	13.19
1989	13.71	9.49	16.01	-3.61	39.21
1990	-6.93	5.50	-18.25	11.61	-10.41
1991	28.83	0.31	11.08	14.02	63.66
1992	0.92	-7.31	1.69	13.85	8.30
1993	1.68	2.79	6.41	4.33	16.02
1994	-3.39	-8.64	9.60	-1.70	-4.90

Bear Market Performance

Decile Rank (5-year period)

Worst _____ Best

	Worst 3 Mo Period 1985-89	Worst 3 Mo Period 1990-94
Founders Special	-31.79	-18.25
+/- S&P 500	-2.21	-4.50
+/- Best Fit Index : SPMid400	-2.98	-0.47

Trailing Returns

	Total Return %	+/- S&P 500	+/- Wil 4500	% Rank All	% Rank Obj	Growth of $10,000
3 Mo	-1.70	-1.68	0.80	62	70	9,830
6 Mo	7.74	2.88	3.54	6	53	10,774
1 Yr	-4.90	-6.22	-2.25	63	64	9,510
3 Yr Avg	6.11	-0.15	-1.49	32	51	11,949
5 Yr Avg	11.87	3.18	2.78	9	41	17,519
10 Yr Avg	14.80	0.42	2.17	12	40	39,770
15 Yr Avg	14.30	-0.18	---	21	26	74,280

Operations

Address and Telephone	2930 E. Third Avenue
	Denver, CO 80206
	800-525-2440 / 303-394-4404
Advisor	Founders Asset Management
Subadvisor	None
Distributor	Founders Asset Management
States Available	All
Report Grade	C+
Income Distrib	Paid Annually
Date of Inception	09-07-61
Fiscal Year End	December

Min Initial Purchase	$1000 (Addt'l: $100)
Min IRA Purchase	$500 (Addt'l: $100)
Min Auto Invest Plan	$50 (Systematic Inv: $50)

Expenses & Fees

Sales Fees	0.00% front
	0.00% deferred
	0.25% 12b-1
Management Fee	0.75% flat fee
3-,5-,10-yr Expense Projections	$42, $73, $161
Annual Brokerage Cost	---

Risk Analysis

Time Period	Load-Adj Return %	Risk % Rank [1] All	Obj	Morningstar [2] Return	Morningstar Risk	Morningstar Risk-Adj Rating
1 Yr	-4.90					
3 Yr	6.11	94	63	0.75 [3]	1.33	★★★
5 Yr	11.87	92	44	1.90 [3]	1.20	★★★★
10 Yr	14.80	89	22	1.44	1.17	★★★★
Average Historical Rating (109 months)				3.4		★s

[1] 1 = low, 100 = high [2] 1.00 = Equity Avg [3] 1.00 = 90-day T-bill return

Other Measures

			Standard S&P 500	Best Fit SPMid400
Standard Deviation	13.78	Alpha	-0.3	-1.6
Mean	6.90	Beta	1.28	1.29
Sharpe Ratio	0.24	R-Squared	55	86

Investment Style

	Stock Portfolio Avg	Relative S&P 500
Price/Earnings Ratio	20.2	1.09
Price/Book Ratio	3.6	1.06
5 Yr Earnings Gr %	25.0	4.50
Return on Assets %	12.3	1.64
Debt % Total Cap	19.8	0.70
Med Mkt Cap ($mil)	2297	0.18

Style Value Blend Growth
Size Large Med Small

Diversification Value for Portfolio Types

Large Cap: Low   Small Cap: Low   Bond: High   Balanced: Low   Diversified: Medium

Portfolio 06-30-94

Share Chg (12-93)000	Amount 000	Total Stocks: 61 / Total Fixed-Income: 0	Value $000	% Net Assets
-80	120	Texas Instruments	9540	3.26
450	525	LDDS Communications Cl A	9058	3.10
200	200	BMC Software	8650	2.96
300	300	Williams	8596	2.94
250	250	Newbridge Networks	8594	2.94
80	190	Lotus Development	6935	2.37
-145	160	Applied Materials	6800	2.32
60	170	Chipcom	6673	2.28
-40	200	Storage Technology	6525	2.23
200	400	Informix	6200	2.12
300	300	Pyxis	5700	1.95
250	250	Parametric Technology	5625	1.92
500	500	Tandem Computers	5625	1.92
-30	120	Carnival Cl A	5310	1.81
140	140	Franklin Resources	5198	1.78
-40	100	Anadarko Petroleum	5113	1.75
0	150	Compaq Computer	4838	1.65
175	175	Heilig-Meyers	4747	1.62
-75	100	Chrysler	4713	1.61
-15	110	Gap	4703	1.61
5	125	Dean Witter Discover	4688	1.60
50	175	CUC International	4681	1.60
100	100	Newell	4625	1.58
190	200	Quilmes Industrial	4465	1.53
-25	100	Motorola	4450	1.52

Composition % 12-31-94

Cash	5.4	Preferreds	0.4
Stocks	94.3	Convertibles	0.0
Bonds	0.0	Other	0.0

Tax Analysis

	Tax-Adj Historical Return %	% Pretax Return
3 Yr Avg	3.71	59.3
5 Yr Avg	8.75	69.2
10 Yr Avg	11.72	68.2
Potential Capital Gain Exposure (% of assets)		6%

Most Similar Funds in MF500

Berger 100	Strong Fit
T. Rowe Price New Amer Gr	Strong Fit
Hancock Emerging Growth B	Fair Fit

Index Allocation

	% of Stocks
S&P 500	37.0
S&P MidCap 400	36.7
U.S. Small Cap	17.1
Foreign	9.2

Sector Weightings

	% of Stocks	Relative S&P 500
Utilities	3.4	0.27
Energy	3.7	0.36
Financials	3.9	0.37
Industrial Cyclicals	6.4	0.39
Consumer Durables	9.2	1.48
Consumer Staples	4.2	0.34
Services	12.8	1.57
Retail	7.9	1.35
Health	1.3	0.15
Technology	47.3	5.16

MORNINGSTAR 1995 Mutual Fund 500

FPA Capital

	Ticker	Load	NAV	Yield	SEC Yield	Assets	Objective
	FPPTX	6.50%	20.61	0.2%	N/A	191.8	Small Company

FPA Capital Fund seeks long-term growth of capital. Current income is secondary.

The fund invests in common stocks, preferred stocks, and convertible securities of small- and medium-size companies perceived by the average investor to be unpopular or unfamiliar. The fund identifies undervalued companies by book value, low P/E ratios, replacement cost of assets, and other relevant factors. Foreign issues may comprise 10% of assets.

First Pacific Advisors has managed the fund since July 1984.

Manager's Investment Style

Robert Rodriguez looks for underfollowed or neglected stocks selling at extremely cheap prices. The fund's price/earnings and price/book ratios are among the smallest of its peers. Rodriguez requires strong management, below-average debt, and increasing profitability. He keeps the fund's holdings at around 30 stocks, because of the time needed for intensive research. The fund's turnover ratio rarely surpasses 20%.

Historical Profile
Return	High
Risk	Above Average
Rating	★★★★★ Highest

Investment Style History
Equity
Average % Stocks Held in Portfolio

| 97% | 93% | 95% | 96% | 96% | 96% | 93% | 92% |

Growth of $10,000
|||| Value of Fund ($000)
— Value of Index ($000)
Russ 2000
▼ Manager Change
▽ Partial Manager Change
► Mgr Unknown After
◄ Mgr Unknown Before

Performance Quartile (Within Objective)

1983	1984	1985	1986	1987	1988	1989	1990	1991	1992	1993	1994	History
11.74	9.17	11.41	11.08	11.74	12.46	13.89	10.91	16.96	18.89	20.06	20.61	NAV
18.37	-7.90	28.96	12.57	10.97	18.11	25.25	-13.80	64.51	21.57	16.74	10.37	Total Return %
-4.09	-14.16	-2.78	-6.11	5.71	1.50	-6.43	-10.68	34.03	13.95	6.68	9.06	+/- S&P 500
---	-6.18	-3.06	0.81	14.48	-2.42	1.31	-0.24	21.06	9.81	2.20	13.03	+/- Wilshire 4500
6.24	3.73	4.53	3.07	2.39	2.23	1.85	1.53	1.47	0.44	0.28	0.21	Income Return %
12.13	-11.63	24.43	9.49	8.57	15.89	23.40	-15.33	63.04	21.13	16.46	10.16	Capital Return %
46	87	29	70	9	18	23	91	3	3	23	2	Total Rtn % Rank All
70	61	35	38	6	59	38	69	16	16	50	6	Total Rtn % Rank Obj
0.61	0.35	0.35	0.37	0.30	0.26	0.22	0.21	0.15	0.07	0.05	0.04	Income $
0.00	1.25	0.00	1.47	0.31	1.03	1.21	1.06	0.58	1.34	1.70	1.34	Capital Gains $
0.90	0.92	0.99	0.95	0.89	0.89	0.92	1.17	1.21	1.08	1.06	1.03	Expense Ratio %
5.95	3.00	3.90	3.38	2.55	1.66	1.77	1.37	1.32	0.55	0.29	0.20	Income Ratio %
38	130	76	34	44	31	22	21	12	13	19	16	Turnover Rate %
41.1	38.5	39.8	47.9	51.1	62.4	76.0	66.1	98.9	125.1	153.7	191.8	Net Assets ($mil)

Fund Manager(s)

Robert L. Rodriguez CFA(1980), since 07-84.
Birthdate: 12-48. BS, U. of Southern California 1971 MBA, U. of Southern California 1975

Manager Experience

	Dates Managed	Invest Obj	Std Dev	+/- Index
Robert L. Rodriguez				
FPA New Income	07/84 - 12/94	CG	4.50	1.00

Performance 12-31-94

	1st Qtr	2nd Qtr	3rd Qtr	4th Qtr	Total
1987	23.65	3.20	14.30	-23.91	10.97
1988	14.55	14.53	-3.32	-6.88	18.11
1989	8.88	11.39	11.38	-7.28	25.25
1990	3.21	5.65	-31.24	14.96	-13.80
1991	36.98	-1.23	13.63	7.00	64.51
1992	11.43	-11.68	0.84	22.50	21.57
1993	4.69	0.26	7.72	3.24	16.74
1994	1.45	-2.28	6.41	4.62	10.37

Bear Market Performance

Decile Rank (5-year period)

Worst | Best

	Worst 3 Mo Period 1985-89	Worst 3 Mo Period 1990-94
FPA Capital	-30.01	-32.19
+/- S&P 500	-0.42	-18.34
+/- Best Fit Index : Russ 2000	5.54	-6.29

Trailing Returns

	Total Return %	+/- S&P 500	+/- Wil 4500	% Rank All	% Rank Obj	Growth of $10,000
3 Mo	4.62	4.64	7.12	2	10	10,462
6 Mo	11.33	6.47	7.14	4	26	11,133
1 Yr	10.37	9.06	13.03	2	6	11,037
3 Yr Avg	16.14	9.87	8.53	3	10	15,665
5 Yr Avg	17.31	8.62	8.22	2	12	22,215
10 Yr Avg	18.13	3.75	5.50	3	2	52,940
15 Yr Avg	15.41	0.92	---	10	5	85,778

Operations

Address and Telephone	11400 W. Olympic Blvd Ste 1200
	Los Angeles, CA 90064
	800-982-4372 / 310-473-0225
Advisor	First Pacific Advisors
Subadvisor	None
Distributor	FPA Fund Distributors
States Available	All
Report Grade	B+
Income Distrib	Paid Semiannually
Date of Inception	02-01-68
Fiscal Year End	March

Risk Analysis

Time Period	Load-Adj Return %	Risk % Rank [1] All	Risk % Rank [1] Obj	Morningstar [2] Return	Morningstar Risk	Morningstar Risk-Adj Rating
1 Yr	3.20					
3 Yr	13.57	86	51	3.17 [3]	1.08	★★★★★
5 Yr	15.74	95	77	3.15 [3]	1.35	★★★★★
10 Yr	17.34	92	69	2.08	1.27	★★★★
Average Historical Rating (109 months)				3.0 ★s		

[1] 1 = low, 100 = high [2] 1.00 = Equity Avg [3] 1.00 = 90-day T-bill return

Other Measures

			Standard S&P 500	Best Fit Russ 2000
Standard Deviation	15.05	Alpha	9.9	3.6
Mean	16.17	Beta	1.09	1.14
Sharpe Ratio	0.84	R-Squared	33	80

Investment Style

	Stock Portfolio Avg	Relative S&P 500
Price/Earnings Ratio	12.5	0.68
Price/Book Ratio	1.6	0.48
5 Yr Earnings Gr %	14.6	2.62
Return on Assets %	7.5	1.00
Debt % Total Cap	16.4#	0.58
Med Mkt Cap ($mil)	386	0.03

figure is based on 50% or less of stocks

Style Value Blend Growth
Size Large Med Small

Diversification Value for Portfolio Types

Large Cap: Medium	Small Cap: Low	Bond: High	Balanced: Medium	Diversified: Medium

Expenses & Fees

Sales Fees	6.50% front
	0.00% deferred
	0.00% 12b-1
Management Fee	0.75% max./0.65% min.
3-5-,10-yr Expense Projections	$96, $118, $183
Annual Brokerage Cost	0.07%

Min Initial Purchase	$1500 (Addt'l: $100)
Min IRA Purchase	$100 (Addt'l: $100)
Min Auto Invest Plan	$1500 (Systematic Inv: $100)

Portfolio 09-30-94

Share Chg (03-94)000	Amount 000	Total Stocks: 34 / Total Fixed-Income: 4	Value $000	% Net Assets
270	620	Green Tree Financial	16663	9.66
0	400	Seagate Technology	9600	5.56
-5	145	NIKE Cl B	8537	4.95
30	260	Anthem Electronics	8385	4.86
0	300	Komag	7950	4.61
20	260	Rouge Steel Cl A	7638	4.43
10	290	Marshall Industries	7286	4.22
0	275	Quick & Reilly Group	7116	4.12
25	245	Storage Technology	7044	4.08
0	438	Puritan-Bennett	6899	4.00
0	260	Fleetwood Enterprises	6533	3.79
0	306	Comdisco	6339	3.67
-10	250	Photronics	5313	3.08
3	190	Angelica	5273	3.06
0	230	Thor Industries	5118	2.97
	5000	US Treasury Note 4.25%	4834	2.80
180	310	Countrywide Credit Industry	4379	2.54
0	160	Intl Aluminum	4320	2.50
-10	290	Coherent	3988	2.31
0	150	Bay View Capital	3750	2.17
0	255	Ross Stores	3729	2.16
0	347	Westcorp	3337	1.93
0	220	Coachmen Industries	3080	1.79
50	250	Good Guys	3063	1.78
200	200	Rawlings Sporting Goods	2400	1.39

Composition % 12-31-94

Cash	5.2	Preferreds	0.0
Stocks	90.4	Convertibles	0.7
Bonds	3.6	Other	0.0

Tax Analysis

	Tax-Adj Historical Return %	% Pretax Return
3 Yr Avg	13.79	83.6
5 Yr Avg	14.77	81.2
10 Yr Avg	15.30	73.4
Potential Capital Gain Exposure (% of assets)		35%

Most Similar Funds in MF500

Invesco Strat Technology	Weak Fit
Hancock Special Equities A	Weak Fit
Columbia Special	Weak Fit

Index Allocation

	% of Stocks
S&P 500	10.1
S&P MidCap 400	18.9
U.S. Small Cap	70.9
Foreign	0.1

Sector Weightings

	% of Stocks	Relative S&P 500
Utilities	0.0	0.00
Energy	0.0	0.00
Financials	13.9	1.32
Industrial Cyclicals	2.9	0.18
Consumer Durables	20.4	3.29
Consumer Staples	0.0	0.00
Services	12.2	1.50
Retail	4.6	0.79
Health	7.4	0.86
Technology	38.6	4.21

FPA New Income

	Ticker	Load	NAV	Yield	SEC Yield	Assets	Objective
	FPNIX	4.50%	10.40	6.7%	N/A	129.9	Corp General

FPA New Income seeks current income consistent with preservation of capital.

The fund invests at least 75% of its assets in U.S. government securities, nonconvertible debt securities rated at least AA, U.S.-dollar-denominated Canadian government debt, repurchase agreements, and cash. The balance of assets may be rated below AA and be convertible.

Prior to January 1982 the fund purchased mainly equities. In July 1984, First Pacific Advisors became the fund's investment advisor and the fund changed its name from Transamerica New Income.

Manager's Investment Style

Manager Bob Rodriguez is a contrarian investor. He invests in a broad array of income producing securities, and is known for making his bets during times of market troubles. For example, he scooped up high-yield issues during 1990 when that market blew up. In 1994, he extended the fund's duration when most others were shortening. This contrarian, and often conservative, bent has served the fund well through both market rallies and fallouts.

Fund Manager(s)

Robert L. Rodriguez CFA(1980), since 07-84.
Birthdate: 12-48. BS, U. of Southern California 1971 MBA, U. of Southern California 1975

Manager Experience

	Dates Managed	Invest Obj	Std Dev	+/- Index
Robert L. Rodriguez				
FPA Capital	07/84 - 12/94	SC	21.69	3.30

Historical Profile
- **Return** High
- **Risk** Below Average
- **Rating** ★★★★★ Highest

Investment Style History Fixed Income
Income Rtn % Rank Obj

35	99	79	64	19	52	40	16

Growth of $10,000
||| Value of Fund ($000)
— Value of Index ($000) LB Agg
▼ Manager Change
▽ Partial Manager Change
► Mgr Unknown After
◄ Mgr Unknown Before

Performance Quartile (Within Objective)

1983	1984	1985	1986	1987	1988	1989	1990	1991	1992	1993	1994	History
8.16	8.50	9.37	9.50	9.37	9.61	9.92	9.84	10.72	10.92	11.23	10.40	NAV
6.17	16.43	21.31	11.11	7.87	8.55	12.23	8.38	18.80	11.12	10.17	1.46	Total Return %
-2.20	1.28	-0.81	-4.14	5.12	0.67	-2.31	-0.57	2.80	3.88	0.42	4.38	+/- LB Aggregate
-3.10	-0.19	-2.75	-5.42	5.32	-0.67	-1.75	1.23	0.29	2.43	-2.00	5.39	+/- LB Corporate
10.95	12.26	11.08	9.39	9.24	5.88	8.44	8.47	9.74	7.24	6.64	6.64	Income Return %
-4.78	4.17	10.24	1.72	-1.37	2.67	3.79	-0.09	9.07	3.89	3.53	-5.17	Capital Return %
96	3	64	79	14	70	57	13	46	17	65	11	Total Rtn % Rank All
83	8	54	75	2	51	42	20	17	5	49	3	Total Rtn % Rank Obj
0.92	0.90	0.84	0.84	0.84	0.54	0.76	0.78	0.86	0.72	0.69	0.71	Income $
0.00	0.00	0.00	0.03	0.00	0.01	0.05	0.07	0.01	0.20	0.07	0.27	Capital Gains $
1.52	1.54	1.53	1.52	1.52	1.52	1.10	0.94	0.87	0.78	0.73	0.74	Expense Ratio %
10.62	11.12	9.39	9.22	8.28	7.76	8.16	8.48	8.46	7.17	6.48	6.41	Income Ratio %
30	24	132	73	103	55	18	29	26	22	41	39	Turnover Rate %
4.6	4.6	5.3	6.1	7.3	15.4	25.2	38.3	54.9	87.7	114.8	129.9	Net Assets ($mil)

Performance 12-31-94

	1st Qtr	2nd Qtr	3rd Qtr	4th Qtr	Total
1987	2.98	0.32	-1.11	5.59	7.87
1988	6.01	1.24	0.62	0.52	8.55
1989	2.24	6.91	0.61	2.06	12.23
1990	-0.42	3.29	-0.84	6.25	8.38
1991	5.40	2.62	5.02	4.59	18.80
1992	1.16	3.88	3.81	1.86	11.12
1993	4.21	2.65	2.26	0.72	10.17
1994	0.28	-0.65	1.25	0.58	1.46

Bear Market Performance

Decile Rank (5-year period)

	Worst 3 Mo Period 1985-89	Worst 3 Mo Period 1990-94
FPA New Income	-2.13	-1.65
+/- LB Aggregate	0.00	-2.39
+/- Best Fit Index : LB Agg	0.00	-2.39

Trailing Returns

	Total Return %	+/- LB Aggregate	+/- LB Corp	% Rank All	% Rank Obj	Growth of $10,000
3 Mo	0.58	0.20	0.14	10	13	10,058
6 Mo	1.84	0.85	0.66	28	4	10,184
1 Yr	1.46	4.38	5.39	11	3	10,146
3 Yr Avg	7.49	2.95	2.08	23	4	12,421
5 Yr Avg	9.85	2.22	1.58	18	3	15,993
10 Yr Avg	10.97	1.03	0.35	47	4	28,330
15 Yr Avg	10.97	0.16	-0.35	66	14	47,666

Operations

Address and Telephone	11400 W. Olympic Blvd Ste 1200	
	Los Angeles, CA 90064	
	800-982-4372 / 310-473-0225	
Advisor	First Pacific Advisors	
Subadvisor	None	
Distributor	FPA Fund Distributors	
States Available	All	
Report Grade	A-	
Income Distrib	Paid Quarterly	
Date of Inception	04-01-69	
Fiscal Year End	September	

Risk Analysis

Time Period	Load-Adj Return %	Risk % Rank [1] All	Risk % Rank [1] Obj	Morningstar [2] Return	Morningstar Risk	Morningstar Risk-Adj Rating
1 Yr	-3.10					
3 Yr	5.86	2	3	0.67 [3]	0.38	★★★★★
5 Yr	8.84	5	11	1.03 [3]	0.62	★★★★★
10 Yr	10.46	6	6	1.27 [3]	0.76	★★★★★

Average Historical Rating (109 months) 3.9 ★s

[1] 1 = low, 100 = high [2] 1.00 = Taxable Avg [3] 1.00 = 90-day T-bill return

Other Measures

		Standard LB Agg	Best Fit LB Agg
Standard Deviation	2.43	Alpha	3.2	3.2
Mean	7.28	Beta	0.56	0.56
Sharpe Ratio	1.54	R-Squared	81	81

Investment Style

Interest-Rate Stance
Avg Effective Duration	4.1 Yrs
Avg Effective Maturity	8.6 Yrs

Quality
Avg Credit Quality	AA
Avg Weighted Coupon	6.40%
Avg Weighted Price	84.63% of Par

Diversification Value for Portfolio Types

Large Cap: High	Small Cap: High	Bond: Low	Balanced: Medium	Diversified: High

Tax Analysis

	Tax-Adj Historical Return %	% Pretax Return
3 Yr Avg	4.57	59.2
5 Yr Avg	6.94	66.5
10 Yr Avg	7.71	60.2

Potential Capital Gain Exposure (% of assets) 0%

Most Similar Funds in MF500

Prudential Struct Maturity A	Fair Fit
Vanguard F/I Short-Trm Corp	Weak Fit
Vanguard F/I Short-Trm US Tr	Weak Fit

Expenses & Fees

Sales Fees	4.50% front
	0.00% deferred
	0.00% 12b-1
Management Fee	0.50% flat fee
3-,5-,10-yr Expense Projections	$67, $84, $132

Min Purchases

Min Initial Purchase	$1500 (Addt'l: $100)
Min IRA Purchase	$100 (Addt'l: $100)
Min Auto Invest Plan	$1500 (Systematic Inv: $100)

Portfolio 12-30-94

Total Stocks: 1
Total Fixed-Income: 60

Amount 000	Date of Maturity		Value $000	% Net Assets
41000	08-15-09	US Treasury Bond 0%	12945	9.96
9600	04-30-97	US Treasury Note 6.875%	9325	7.18
7424	09-15-12	GNMA Mobile Home 9.75%	7656	5.89
7000	05-15-96	US Treasury Note 4.25%	6709	5.16
6060	11-15-20	FHLMC CMO PAC 7%	5659	4.35
5000	12-31-99	US Treasury Note 7.75%	4983	3.83
4149	11-15-11	GNMA Mobile Home 8.75%	4171	3.21
4100	04-15-12	MLMI 8.3%	4028	3.10
3400	10-01-99	Tennessee Valley Auth 8.375%	3447	2.65
3205	10-15-11	GNMA Mobile Home 9%	3261	2.51
3000	11-30-96	US Treasury Note 7.25%	2977	2.29
3000	08-15-04	US Treasury Note 7.25%	2879	2.22
3631	03-01-02	Fabri-Centers America Cv 6.25%	2760	2.12
8000	02-15-20	FHLMC CMO PAC I/O 7%	2640	2.03
3000	05-01-12	Seagate Technology Cv 6.75%	2490	1.92
2600	07-15-03	FHLMC CMO REMIC 7%	2412	1.86
2500	04-01-02	Quantum Cv 6.375%	2400	1.85
2500	01-15-00	RJR Nabisco 8%	2359	1.82
9915	04-25-17	FNMA CMO REMIC PAC I/O 7%	2277	1.75
3000	11-15-98	Govt Trust Cert Turkey 0%	2220	1.71
2785	11-15-98	Govt Trust Cert Israel 0%	2061	1.59
2600	11-01-02	Dr Pepper/Seven-Up Step 0%	2054	1.58
30		Storage Technology Cv Pfd	1980	1.52
1800	05-15-05	US Treasury Bond 8.25%	1816	1.40
1700	08-01-98	Diagnostic Rtrvl Sys Cv 8.5%	1649	1.27

Composition % 12-31-94

Cash	2.5	Preferreds	0.0
Stocks	0.0	Convertibles	12.2
Bonds	85.3	Other	0.0

Coupon Range

	% of Bonds	Rel Obj
0%	13.3	6.09
0% to 8.5%	59.7	0.94
8.5% to 9.5%	10.8	0.67
9.5% to 11%	12.4	1.34
More than 11%	1.8	0.45
Not applicable	2.1	0.41

Credit Analysis 12-31-94
% of Bonds

US Govt	73	BB	0
AAA	4	B	9
AA	4	Below B	1
A	0	NR/NA	5
BBB	3		

MORNINGSTAR 1995 Mutual Fund 500

FPA Paramount

	Ticker	Load	NAV	Yield	SEC Yield	Assets	Objective
	FPRAX	6.50%	14.41	1.6%	N/A	489.6	Growth/Inc.

FPA Paramount Fund seeks capital appreciation and income. The fund normally invests in common stocks. It may also invest in fixed-income and convertible securities. The fund generally holds a portion of its assets in high-quality short-term debt securities to provide liquidity. Such investments may be increased when management considers the expected total return to be more attractive than that offered by common stocks. The fund may invest up to 25% of its assets in foreign securities, provided that no more than 10% are in securities not represented by ADRs.

Historical Profile

Return	Above Average
Risk	Low
Rating	★★★★ Above Average

Investment Style History
Equity
Average % Stocks Held in Portfolio

82% 67% 58% 49% 56% 55% 61% 69%

Growth of $10,000
||| Value of Fund ($000)
— Value of Index ($000) S&P 500
▼ Manager Change
▽ Partial Manager Change
► Mgr Unknown After
◄ Mgr Unknown Before

Performance Quartile (Within Objective)

Manager's Investment Style

Preferring out-of-favor or rarely followed stocks, management strictly seeks extremely undervalued issues. It applies this strategy to small- and mid-cap arena, and is willing to hold large cash stakes when it cannot find suitable values.

Fund Manager(s)

William M. Sams, since 1981. Accounting/Finance, Southern Methodist U. 1960

Manager Experience	Dates Managed	Invest Obj	Std Dev	+/- Index
William M. Sams				
American Cap Pace A	01/76 - 01/81	G	20.82	19.41

	1983	1984	1985	1986	1987	1988	1989	1990	1991	1992	1993	1994	History
	13.04	13.07	13.18	12.44	14.39	13.91	14.73	12.63	14.20	13.60	14.93	14.41	NAV
	31.31	10.07	18.84	5.34	21.91	19.78	22.63	1.60	24.31	9.90	20.53	9.40	Total Return %
	8.85	3.81	-12.89	-13.34	16.65	3.17	-9.06	4.72	-6.17	2.28	10.48	8.09	+/- S&P 500
	7.85	7.02	-13.72	-10.76	19.55	1.84	-6.55	7.78	-9.89	0.93	9.25	9.47	+/- Wilshire 5000
	2.02	5.01	5.89	4.03	2.67	2.68	3.62	4.31	4.19	2.84	1.96	1.88	Income Return %
	29.30	5.07	12.95	1.31	19.24	17.09	19.00	-2.71	20.12	7.06	18.57	7.52	Capital Return %
	8	26	79	95	4	14	29	51	37	23	16	2	Total Rtn % Rank All
	6	20	95	95	1	24	56	9	73	30	5	1	Total Rtn % Rank Obj
	0.26	0.61	0.79	0.53	0.34	0.34	0.45	0.56	0.48	0.36	0.25	0.25	Income $
	1.36	0.62	1.54	0.93	0.35	2.55	1.47	1.76	0.75	1.49	0.98	1.52	Capital Gains $
	1.11	1.10	1.04	1.02	1.01	1.01	0.95	0.95	0.93	0.92	0.89	0.90	Expense Ratio %
	3.33	5.25	5.48	4.90	2.21	2.10	3.60	4.30	3.08	2.33	1.83	1.69	Income Ratio %
	130	156	158	137	98	103	132	94	101	146	98	76	Turnover Rate %
	88.5	118.8	135.6	105.7	117.4	134.3	217.4	206.7	256.1	292.8	335.1	489.6	Net Assets ($mil)

Performance 12-31-94

	1st Qtr	2nd Qtr	3rd Qtr	4th Qtr	Total
1987	27.22	4.42	9.31	-16.04	21.91
1988	14.59	6.78	-0.99	-1.14	19.78
1989	8.24	6.75	5.98	0.14	22.63
1990	-1.51	5.53	-6.82	4.90	1.60
1991	16.47	0.96	4.67	1.00	24.31
1992	4.73	-1.07	2.09	3.90	9.90
1993	10.05	1.24	-0.58	8.82	20.53
1994	-0.97	2.35	10.33	-2.17	9.40

Bear Market Performance

Decile Rank (5-year period)

Worst   Best

	Worst 3 Mo Period 1985-89	Worst 3 Mo Period 1990-94
FPA Paramount	-22.09	-8.67
+/- S&P 500	7.50	5.17
+/- Best Fit Index : S&P 500	7.50	5.17

Trailing Returns

	Total Return %	+/- S&P 500	+/- Wil 5000	% Rank All	% Rank Obj	Growth of $10,000
3 Mo	-2.17	-2.16	-1.40	72	70	9,783
6 Mo	7.93	3.07	3.31	6	1	10,793
1 Yr	9.40	8.09	9.47	2	1	10,940
3 Yr Avg	13.16	6.90	6.55	6	4	14,492
5 Yr Avg	12.85	4.16	4.03	7	3	18,304
10 Yr Avg	15.16	0.78	1.30	10	3	41,029
15 Yr Avg	16.23	1.75	2.25	5	1	95,454

Operations

Address and Telephone	11400 W. Olympic Blvd Ste 1200 Los Angeles, CA 90064 800-982-4372 / 310-473-0225		
Advisor	First Pacific Advisors		
Subadvisor	None		
Distributor	FPA Fund Distributors		
States Available	All		
Report Grade	B		
Income Distrib	Paid Semiannually		
Date of Inception	09-08-58		
Fiscal Year End	September		

Min Initial Purchase	Closed (Addt'l: $100)
Min IRA Purchase	$100 (Addt'l: $100)
Min Auto Invest Plan	$1500 (Systematic Inv: $100)

Expenses & Fees

Sales Fees	6.50% front
	0.00% deferred
	0.00% 12b-1
Management Fee	0.75% max./0.65% min.
3-,5-,10-yr Expense Projections	$92, $111, $167
Annual Brokerage Cost	0.32%

Risk Analysis

Time Period	Load-Adj Return %	Risk % Rank All [1]	Obj	Morningstar [2] Return	Morningstar Risk	Morningstar Risk-Adj Rating
1 Yr	2.29					
3 Yr	10.66	62	34	2.19 [3]	0.68	★★★★
5 Yr	11.34	56	12	1.74 [3]	0.63	★★★★
10 Yr	14.39	45	10	1.35	0.65	★★★★
Average Historical Rating (109 months)				4.3 ★s		

[1] = low, 100 = high   [2] 1.00 = Equity Avg   [3] 1.00 = 90-day T-bill return

Other Measures

				Standard S&P 500	Best Fit S&P 500
Standard Deviation	9.82	Alpha		7.0	7.0
Mean	12.91	Beta		0.90	0.90
Sharpe Ratio	0.96	R-Squared		54	54

Investment Style

	Stock Portfolio Avg	Relative S&P 500	Style Value Blend Growth
Price/Earnings Ratio	24.4	1.32	
Price/Book Ratio	2.2	0.65	
5 Yr Earnings Gr %	-4.9#	-0.88	
Return on Assets %	4.2	0.56	
Debt % Total Cap	36.0	1.28	
Med Mkt Cap ($mil)	1312	0.10	

Size: Large Med Small

figure is based on 50% or less of stocks

Diversification Value for Portfolio Types

Large Cap: Low	Small Cap: Medium	Bond: High	Balanced: Low	Diversified: Low

Portfolio 12-30-94

Total Stocks: 26
Total Fixed-Income: 1

Share Chg (09-94) 000	Amount 000		Value $000	% Net Assets
1250	1300	TIG Holdings	24375	4.98
200	1300	Woolworth	19500	3.98
636	886	Life Partners	19383	3.96
0	1000	Occidental Petroleum	19250	3.93
225	700	Coastal	18025	3.68
0	2400	Guinness	16800	3.43
0	2800	Western Mining	16212	3.31
800	800	Baker Hughes	14600	2.98
2500	2500	Noble Drilling	14375	2.94
0	500	Inco	14313	2.92
0	800	Magma Copper	13400	2.74
1034	1034	Energy Service	12667	2.59
0	650	Freeport-McMoRan	11538	2.36
0	250	Leucadia National	11125	2.27
0	930	Oryx Energy	11044	2.26
300	640	California Energy	10000	2.04
0	250	EXEL	9875	2.02
0	700	ENSERCH	9188	1.88
-100	400	Caraustar Industries	8900	1.82
0	340	Quanex	7778	1.59
0	700	Kaiser Aluminum	7613	1.55
8	319	Freeport-McMoRan Cop/Gold A	6787	1.39
0	200	Unifi	5100	1.04
200	300	Town & Country Trust	4275	0.87
-275	150	Bowater	3994	0.82

Composition % 12-31-94

Cash	34.9	Preferreds	0.0
Stocks	64.6	Convertibles	0.5
Bonds	0.0	Other	0.0

Tax Analysis

	Tax-Adj Historical Return %	% Pretax Return
3 Yr Avg	9.77	71.9
5 Yr Avg	9.12	65.9
10 Yr Avg	11.09	60.0
Potential Capital Gain Exposure (% of assets)		10%

Most Similar Funds in MF500

Templeton Smaller Comp Grth	Weak Fit
United Income	Weak Fit
UMB Stock	Weak Fit

Index Allocation

	% of Stocks
S&P 500	36.3
S&P MidCap 400	6.9
U.S. Small Cap	42.5
Foreign	19.1

Sector Weightings

	% of Stocks	Relative S&P 500
Utilities	12.4	1.00
Energy	24.0	2.37
Financials	19.7	1.87
Industrial Cyclicals	25.7	1.57
Consumer Durables	2.7	0.43
Consumer Staples	5.6	0.45
Services	3.3	0.41
Retail	6.5	1.12
Health	0.0	0.00
Technology	0.0	0.00

FPA Perennial

	Ticker	Load	NAV	Yield	SEC Yield	Assets	Objective
	FPPFX	6.50%	21.97	2.0%	N/A	52.0	Growth/Inc.

FPA Perennial Fund seeks long-term growth of capital; current income is a secondary concern.

The fund invests in common stocks chosen for their attractive value, growth prospects, and quality of management. It generally favors companies with consistently high returns on invested capital and substantial reinvestment in the business. The fund may invest up to 25% of its assets in foreign securities; it may not invest more than 10% of assets in foreign issues that are not ADRs.

The fund serves primarily as an investment vehicle for individual, partnership, and corporate retirement plans.

Manager's Investment Style

Management buys an elite set of large-cap stocks with excellent business fundamentals and industry-leading positions. They avoid firms with high levels of business debt, and only buy their favored stocks at modest, below-market multiples. When management cannot find stocks it likes, it will hold sometimes-large levels of cash.

Fund Manager(s)

Christopher Linden, since 04-84. Birthdate: 05-50. BS, U. of Southern California 1971 MBA, U. of California-Los Angeles 1972

Manager Experience

	Dates Managed	Invest Obj	Std Dev	+/- Index
Not available.				

Historical Profile

Return	Below Average
Risk	Low
Rating	★★★ Neutral

Investment Style History Equity
Average % Stocks Held in Portfolio

65% 65% 65% 64% 63% 71% 70% 78%

Growth of $10,000

|||| Value of Fund ($000)
— Value of Index ($000) S&P 500
▼ Manager Change
▽ Partial Manager Change
► Mgr Unknown After
◄ Mgr Unknown Before

Performance Quartile (Within Objective)

	1983	1984	1985	1986	1987	1988	1989	1990	1991	1992	1993	1994	History
	---	16.09	18.84	18.47	17.16	19.28	22.60	19.82	22.40	23.94	23.76	21.97	NAV
	---	17.19 *	20.39	10.21	-1.06	19.92	25.79	0.96	21.69	13.07	4.64	-0.03	Total Return %
	---	7.48 *	-11.34	-8.47	-6.32	3.31	-5.90	4.08	-8.79	5.45	-5.42	-1.35	+/- S&P 500
	---	---	-12.17	-5.88	-3.42	1.98	-3.39	7.15	-12.51	4.10	-6.64	0.04	+/- Wilshire 5000
	---	0.00	1.28	2.87	3.26	4.27	4.40	5.59	4.07	2.73	2.08	2.10	Income Return %
	---	17.19	19.11	7.34	-4.32	15.65	21.39	-4.62	17.62	10.34	2.56	-2.13	Capital Return %
	---	---	71	84	68	14	22	52	42	13	92	20	Total Rtn % Rank All
	---	---	92	88	79	22	39	12	86	15	88	40	Total Rtn % Rank Obj
	---	0.00	0.20	0.51	0.63	0.63	0.72	1.15	0.73	0.57	0.47	0.46	Income $
	---	0.00	0.27	1.70	0.58	0.45	0.59	1.85	0.71	0.67	0.76	1.31	Capital Gains $
	---	1.50	1.21	1.14	1.11	1.17	1.12	1.14	1.10	1.08	1.02	1.17	Expense Ratio %
	---	4.48	4.23	3.71	2.98	3.62	3.45	3.78	3.11	2.37	2.03	1.83	Income Ratio %
	---	---	83	59	84	75	29	27	29	33	30	43	37	Turnover Rate %
	---	---	14.2	48.4	62.0	48.5	51.6	56.0	51.5	62.4	76.3	88.3	52.0	Net Assets ($mil)

Performance 12-31-94

	1st Qtr	2nd Qtr	3rd Qtr	4th Qtr	Total
1987	11.45	1.19	4.60	-16.13	-1.06
1988	12.65	4.53	-0.32	2.17	19.92
1989	7.20	8.00	8.22	0.40	25.79
1990	-0.71	5.10	-10.72	8.37	0.96
1991	10.79	0.43	2.82	6.36	21.69
1992	4.21	0.76	3.63	3.91	13.07
1993	0.93	-0.65	1.58	2.72	4.64
1994	-3.62	0.42	2.68	0.60	-0.04

Bear Market Performance

Decile Rank (5-year period)

Worst _____ Best

	Worst 3 Mo Period 1985-89	Worst 3 Mo Period 1990-94
FPA Perennial	-20.68	-11.63
+/- S&P 500	8.90	2.21
+/- Best Fit Index : S&P 500	8.90	2.21

Trailing Returns

	Total Return %	+/- S&P 500	+/- Wil 5000	% Rank All	Obj	Growth of $10,000
3 Mo	0.60	0.61	1.37	10	6	10,060
6 Mo	3.29	-1.57	-1.33	19	39	10,329
1 Yr	-0.03	-1.35	0.04	20	40	9,997
3 Yr Avg	5.75	-0.51	-0.86	36	56	11,827
5 Yr Avg	7.76	-0.93	-1.06	36	55	14,532
10 Yr Avg	11.15	-3.23	-2.71	46	73	28,779
15 Yr Avg	---	---	---	---	---	---

Operations

Address and Telephone	11400 W. Olympic Blvd Ste 1200
	Los Angeles, CA 90064
	800-982-4372 / 310-473-0225
Advisor	First Pacific Advisors
Subadvisor	None
Distributor	FPA Fund Distributors
States Available	All
Report Grade	C
Income Distrib	Paid Semiannually
* Date of Inception	04-02-84
Fiscal Year End	December

Risk Analysis

Time Period	Load-Adj Return %	Risk % Rank [1] All	Obj	Morningstar [2] Return	Risk	Morningstar Risk-Adj Rating
1 Yr	-6.53					
3 Yr	3.41	51	9	-0.05 [3]	0.55	★★★
5 Yr	6.32	53	6	0.38 [3]	0.57	★★★
10 Yr	10.40	42	6	0.61	0.57	★★★

Average Historical Rating (93 months) 3.2 ★s

[1] = low, 100 = high   [2] 1.00 = Equity Avg   [3] 1.00 = 90-day T-bill return

Other Measures

			Standard S&P 500	Best Fit S&P 500
Standard Deviation	6.09	Alpha	0.5	0.5
Mean	5.79	Beta	0.63	0.63
Sharpe Ratio	0.37	R-Squared	67	67

Investment Style

	Stock Portfolio Avg	Relative S&P 500
Price/Earnings Ratio	15.1	0.82
Price/Book Ratio	3.4	1.01
5 Yr Earnings Gr %	8.9	1.59
Return on Assets %	11.0	1.47
Debt % Total Cap	16.0	0.57
Med Mkt Cap ($mil)	2162	0.17

Style: Value Blend Growth / Size Large Med Small

Diversification Value for Portfolio Types

Large Cap: Low	Small Cap: Medium	Bond: High	Balanced: Low	Diversified: Medium

Expenses & Fees

Sales Fees	6.50% front
	0.00% deferred
	0.00% 12b-1
Management Fee	0.75% max./0.65% min.
3-,5-,10-yr Expense Projections	$95, $118, $182
Annual Brokerage Cost	0.07%

Min Initial Purchase $1500 (Addt'l: $100)
Min IRA Purchase $100 (Addt'l: $100)
Min Auto Invest Plan $1500 (Systematic Inv: $100)

Portfolio 12-30-94

Total Stocks: 40
Total Fixed-Income: 3

Share Chg (06-94) 000	Amount 000		Value $000	% Net Assets
0	41	Bandag Cl A	2215	4.26
0	27	Marsh & McLennan	2156	4.15
-13	33	Johnson & Johnson	1812	3.49
0	100	Washington Fed S & L (WA)	1730	3.33
0	51	Lubrizol	1711	3.29
-7	31	Minnesota Mining & Mfg	1671	3.21
0	27	Emerson Electric	1669	3.21
-12	35	Loctite	1641	3.16
0	29	VF	1425	2.74
19	31	Walgreen	1374	2.64
0	1	First National Bk Anchorage	1305	2.51
-9	35	Golden West Financial	1241	2.39
-7	16	Pfizer	1221	2.35
0	41	Cedar Fair	1212	2.33
0	39	Hasbro	1150	2.21
-8	35	Abbott Laboratories	1132	2.18
25	43	Bancorp Hawaii	1078	2.08
0	38	Allergan	1065	2.05
0	27	EXEL	1051	2.02
-45	51	Mercantile Bankshares (MD)	1002	1.93
0	34	McDonald's	992	1.91
0	48	Arbor Drugs	970	1.87
-7	27	Nalco Chemical	901	1.73
30	30	John Alden Financial	851	1.64
1	30	Kelly Services Cl A	820	1.58

Composition % 12-31-94

Cash	14.7	Preferreds	0.0
Stocks	81.7	Convertibles	2.1
Bonds	1.5	Other	0.0

Tax Analysis

	Tax-Adj Historical Return %	% Pretax Return
3 Yr Avg	3.85	65.7
5 Yr Avg	5.26	64.5
10 Yr Avg	8.80	70.5

Potential Capital Gain Exposure (% of assets) 25%

Most Similar Funds in MF500

Source Capital	Strong Fit
Vanguard Index 500	Fair Fit
Wayne Hummer Growth	Fair Fit

Index Allocation

	% of Stocks
S&P 500	49.0
S&P MidCap 400	20.1
U.S. Small Cap	26.5
Foreign	4.4

Sector Weightings

	% of Stocks	Relative S&P 500
Utilities	0.0	0.00
Energy	1.5	0.15
Financials	16.1	1.52
Industrial Cyclicals	19.8	1.21
Consumer Durables	18.2	2.92
Consumer Staples	8.0	0.64
Services	17.5	2.15
Retail	7.5	1.29
Health	10.2	1.18
Technology	1.3	0.14

MORNINGSTAR 1995 Mutual Fund 500

France Growth

	Ticker	NAV	Mkt Price	Prem/Disc	Yield	Objective
	FRF	$10.97	$9.13	-16.8%	0.3%	Europe Stock

France Growth Fund seeks capital appreciation.

Normally, the fund will invest at least 65% of its assets in French equities. The fund may invest up to 20% in unlisted French securities, both equity and debt; up to 35% in investment-grade French debt; and up to 10% in non-French Western European securities denominated in currencies other than the franc. The fund may also engage in various hedging strategies involving futures and options.

Board members serve staggered terms to discourage possible takeover attempts.

As of Feb.18, 1994, Stichting Akzo-Pensioenfonds held 704,000 shares of this fund, representing 6.1% of outstanding shares.

The fund held a fully subscribed rights offering in March 1994 that raised $38.8 million.

| | | | | | | | | | 9.4 | -12.5 | -6.3 | 13.5 | 8.3 | Highest Prem/Disc |
| | | | | | | | | | -26.7 | -21.9 | -21.1 | -12.2 | -18.6 | Lowest Prem/Disc |

Historical Profile
Return Below Average
Risk Average
Rating ★★★
Neutral

Growth of $10,000
■ at NAV ($000)
— at Market Price ($000)

Premium Discount %

1983	1984	1985	1986	1987	1988	1989	1990	1991	1992	1993	1994	History
---	---	---	---	---	---	---	10.35	10.75	10.53	12.94	10.97	NAV
---	---	---	---	---	---	---	-1.67*	6.77	-1.60	22.89	-5.79	NAV Total Return %
---	---	---	---	---	---	---	2.78*	-23.72	-9.22	12.83	-7.10	+/- S&P 500
---	---	---	---	---	---	---	---	-5.36	10.57	-9.67	-13.56	+/- MSCI EAFE
---	---	---	---	---	---	---	---	-11.06	-4.41	1.97	-0.60	+/- MSCI France
---	---	---	---	---	---	---	3.86*	2.90	0.44	0.00	0.33	Income Return %
---	---	---	---	---	---	---	-5.53*	3.87	-2.05	22.89	-6.11	Capital Return %
---	---	---	---	---	---	---	---	91	87	21	45	Total Rtn % Rank All
---	---	---	---	---	---	---	---	26	15	94	84	Total Rtn % Rank Obj
---	---	---	---	---	---	---	-23.79*	5.78	4.70	47.30	-25.57	Market Total Rtn %
---	---	---	---	---	---	---	-13.5	-17.5	-16.0	-1.3	-12.8	Avg Prem/Disc %
---	---	---	---	---	---	---	0.35	0.24	0.04	0.00	0.03	Income $
---	---	---	---	---	---	---	0.17	0.00	0.00	0.00	0.55	Capital Gains $
---	---	---	---	---	---	---	2.18	2.14	1.76	1.71	1.64	Expense Ratio %
---	---	---	---	---	---	---	5.17	1.46	0.23	0.23	0.81	Income Ratio %
---	---	---	---	---	---	---	---	75	40	57	---	Turnover Rate %
---	---	---	---	---	---	---	118.9	123.8	121.2	148.9	168.4	Net Assets ($mil)

Manager's Investment Style

When picking stocks, management tries to play market cycles. For example, the fund has in the past overweighted commodity and cyclical stocks to take advantage of a recovering European economy, and has underweighted financials to guard against rising interest rates.

Fund Manager(s)

Jean-Luc Buchalet. Since 5-90.
Didier LeConte. Since 2-93.

Manager Experience

	Dates Managed	Invest Obj	Std Dev	+/- Index
Not available.				

NAV Performance % 12-30-94

	1st Qtr	2nd Qtr	3rd Qtr	4th Qtr	Total
1987	---	---	---	---	---
1988	---	---	---	---	---
1989	---	---	---	---	---
1990	---	-0.72*	-6.14	5.52	-1.67*
1991	1.35	-7.36	12.29	1.26	6.77
1992	2.79	8.42	-2.25	-9.67	-1.60
1993	12.35	-4.56	9.12	5.03	22.89
1994	2.23	-9.08	3.13	-1.71	-5.79

Bear Market Performance

Decile Rank (5-year period)

Worst			Best
		Worst 3 Mo Period 1985-89	Worst 3 Mo Period 1990-94
France Growth		---	---
+/- S&P 500		---	---

Trailing Returns

	NAV Total Return %	+/- S&P 500	+/- MSCI France	% Rank All	% Rank Obj	Mkt Total Return %
3 Mo	-1.71	-1.69	-0.64	47	45	-1.72
6 Mo	1.37	-3.50	-0.51	25	36	-2.95
1 Yr	-5.79	-7.10	-0.60	45	84	-25.57
3 Yr Avg	4.44	-1.83	-1.19	73	47	4.70
5 Yr Avg	---	---	---	---	---	---
Incept Avg	3.95*	---	---	---	---	-1.67*

Risk Analysis

	Risk % Rank[1] All	Obj	Morningstar[2] Return	Risk	Morningstar Risk-Adj Rating
3 Yr	84	42	0.11	0.88	★★★
5 Yr	---	---	---	---	---
10 Yr	---	---	---	---	---

Average Historical Rating (20 months) 2.8 ★s

[1]1 = Low, 100 = High [2]1.00 = Equity Avg [3]1.00 = 90-day T-bill Return

Other Measures

			S&P 500
Standard Deviation	14.71	Alpha	0.03
Mean	5.42	Beta	0.65
Sharpe Ratio	0.13	R-Squared	12

Investment Style

	Stock Portfolio Avg	Rel WS France	Rel WS Foreign
Price/Earnings Ratio	28.1	1.17	0.57
Price/Cash Flow Ratio	8.8	0.96	0.60
Price/Book Ratio	1.8	1.01	0.60
5 Yr Earnings Gr %	-5.3	NMF	NMF
Return on Assets %	4.1	0.99	0.89
Debt % Total Cap	35.2	1.05	1.09
Med Mkt Cap ($mil)	6860	2.00	1.09

figure is based on less than 50% of stocks

Country Exposure (top five) 12-31-94

	Securities %		Currency %
France	100	France	100

Diversification Value for Portfolio Types

● Large Cap: High　● Small Cap: High　◨ Bond: Medium　● Balanced: High　● Diversified: High

Portfolio 06-30-94

Share Chg (12-93)	Amount	Total Equity: 62 Total Fixed-Income: 0	Value $000	% Total Invest
83390	143390	Nationale Elf Aquitaine	10014	5.77
27000	77724	Alcatel Alsthom Genl d'Elec	8451	4.87
25500	143922	Total	8304	4.79
15768	56287	Danone	8129	4.69
38100	42100	LVMH Moet-Henn Louis Vuitton	6483	3.74
107000	140000	Banque Nationale de Paris	6027	3.47
47090	92931	Financiere de Paribas	5902	3.40
11898	47078	Saint Gobain	5509	3.18
2400	12796	Generale des Eaux	5167	2.98
16800	48369	Societe Generale	4974	2.87
8250	34750	Peugeot	4936	2.85
100924	117405	AXA	4843	2.79
200	23200	L'Oreal (Cert)	4567	2.63
4000	29535	L'Air Liquide	3999	2.31
5000	12000	Carrefour	3980	2.29
19800	27800	Ecco	3836	2.21
108000	168000	Rhone-Poulenc	3833	2.21
15400	37400	Lyonnaise des Eaux-Dumez	3427	1.98
15200	20900	Pinault-Printemps	3268	1.88
38000	108000	CSF Holdings CI B	3064	1.77
2000	39050	Lafarge-Coppee	2924	1.69
2432	13432	Cetelem	2837	1.64
4800	23885	Accor	2698	1.56
1500	11500	BIC (France)	2423	1.40
20600	20600	Euro RSCG Worldwide	2403	1.39

Composition % 12-31-94

Cash	0.3	Preferreds	0.0
Stocks	99.8	Convertibles	0.0
Bonds	0.0	Other	0.0

Tax Analysis

	Tax-Adj Historical Return %	% Pretax Return
3 Yr Avg	4.49	73.9
5 Yr Avg	---	---
10 Yr Avg	---	---
Potential Capital Gain Exposure (% of assets)		1

Most Similar Funds in MF500

Invesco European	Weak Fit
GT Greater Europe	Weak Fit
New Germany	Weak Fit

Sector Weightings

	% of Stocks
Utilities	0.9
Energy	6.7
Financials	22.5
Industrial Cyclicals	20.7
Consumer Durables	5.0
Consumer Staples	13.6
Services	15.6
Retail	5.4
Health	4.1
Technology	5.6

Operations

Address and Telephone	1285 Avenue of the Americas New York, NY 10019 212-713-2421 / 212-713-2848	Income Distrib Schedule	Paid Irregularly
Advisor	Indosuez Intl. Investment Services	Management Fee	0.90%, 0.20%A
Subadvisor	N/A	Reinvestment Plan	Yes
Administrator	Mitchell Hutchins Asset Management	Direct Purchase Plan	No
Transfer Agent	Provident National Bank	Shares Outstanding	15,345,333
Custodian	Brown Brothers Harriman & Co.	Exchange	NYSE
Auditor	Price Waterhouse LLP	*Date of Inception	05-18-90
Legal Counsel	Donovan Leisure Newton & Irvine	Shareholder Report	B-

Franklin AGE High-Income

	Ticker	Load	NAV	Yield	SEC Yield	Assets	Objective
	AGEFX	4.25%	2.60	10.2%	9.97%	1719.6	Corp Hi Yld

Franklin AGE High-Income Fund seeks high current income. Capital appreciation is secondary.

The fund invests in both fixed-income debt securities and dividend-paying common or preferred stocks. It seeks the highest-yielding security currently offered without excessive risk. The fund may invest in securities of any rating.

Prior to 1981, the fund was named AGE Fund. On June 30, 1992, Franklin Pennsylvania Investors Fund High-Income Portfolio merged into this fund.

Manager's Investment Style

Wary of an aging bull market, this fund's management has gradually retreated into the high-yield market's upper rungs over the past few years. In mid-1990, 40% of its portfolio was devoted to issues rated below B; such issues have since dwindled to a much smaller percentage of bond holdings. Credits rated B now take up the lion's share of assets. These moves are in keeping with management's stated goal of maximizing total return, as opposed to emphasizing income only. Should management again see opportunity in the lower credit tiers, it will likely go there.

Fund Manager(s)

R. Martin Wiskemann, since 01-72. Birthdate: 01-27. Business Admin., Handelsschule of Zurich
Christopher J. Molumphy CFA, since 01-91. BA, Stanford U. MBA, U. of Chicago

Manager Experience

Manager Experience	Dates Managed	Invest Obj	Std Dev	+/- Index
R. Martin Wiskemann				
Franklin Premier Return	01/72 - 12/94	GI	14.17	-1.28
Franklin Gold	01/72 - 12/94	SP	32.70	-0.09

Historical Profile
Return Average
Risk Low
Rating ★★★★ Above Average

	29	15	18	9	5	69	45	21

Investment Style History
Fixed Income
Income Rtn % Rank Obj

Growth of $10,000
|||| Value of Fund ($000)
— Value of Index ($000)
LB Agg
▼ Manager Change
▽ Partial Manager Change
► Mgr Unknown After
◄ Mgr Unknown Before

Performance Quartile (Within Objective)

	1983	1984	1985	1986	1987	1988	1989	1990	1991	1992	1993	1994	History
	3.77	3.56	3.70	3.67	3.29	3.30	2.77	2.01	2.58	2.72	2.91	2.60	NAV
	18.07	8.82	18.97	12.97	1.23	14.10	-3.63	-14.45	48.28	16.61	17.64	-1.55	Total Return %
	9.70	-6.34	-3.16	-2.28	-1.52	6.22	-18.17	-23.39	32.27	9.36	7.89	1.37	+/- LB Aggregate
	---	---	---	-2.67	-5.29	2.66	-4.01	-8.07	4.52	-0.06	-1.26	-0.57	+/- FB High-Yield
	13.93	14.39	15.04	13.78	11.59	13.79	12.44	12.99	19.92	11.18	10.65	9.10	Income Return %
	4.14	-5.57	3.93	-0.81	-10.35	0.30	-16.06	-27.44	28.36	5.43	6.99	-10.65	Capital Return %
	47	32	78	68	48	31	99	91	8	8	21	30	Total Rtn % Rank All
	20	46	93	58	59	28	73	72	10	62	63	19	Total Rtn % Rank Obj
	0.48	0.51	0.49	0.49	0.43	0.43	0.43	0.40	0.34	0.27	0.27	0.26	Income $
	0.00	0.00	0.00	0.00	0.00	0.00	0.00	0.00	0.00	0.00	0.00	0.00	Capital Gains $
	0.97	0.85	0.80	0.67	0.59	0.57	0.56	0.56	0.59	0.58	0.56	0.59	Expense Ratio %
	12.86	13.00	13.33	11.66	11.46	12.72	13.06	14.47	14.87	12.18	10.78	9.61	Income Ratio %
	20	23	26	22	23	24	29	18	29	44	38	42	Turnover Rate %
	61.7	70.0	159.1	1433.7	1600.0	2070.5	1938.7	1253.6	1753.0	1829.5	2600.0	1719.6	Net Assets ($mil)

Performance 12-31-94

	1st Qtr	2nd Qtr	3rd Qtr	4th Qtr	Total
1987	6.84	-2.95	-2.08	-0.29	1.23
1988	6.39	2.95	1.44	2.69	14.10
1989	1.76	1.84	-1.37	-5.72	-3.63
1990	-4.82	5.14	-10.68	-4.28	-14.45
1991	20.38	8.58	7.91	5.13	48.28
1992	7.64	2.86	4.72	0.57	16.61
1993	5.45	4.22	1.99	4.96	17.64
1994	-3.33	-0.13	1.74	0.23	-1.55

Bear Market Performance

Decile Rank (5-year period)

Worst   Best

	Worst 3 Mo Period 1985-89	Worst 3 Mo Period 1990-94
Franklin AGE High-Income	-6.99	-19.19
+/- LB Aggregate	-7.81	-19.93
+/- Best Fit Index : FB HY	---	-5.08

Trailing Returns

	Total Return %	+/- LB Aggregate	+/- FB High-Yield	% Rank All	% Rank Obj	Growth of $10,000
3 Mo	0.23	-0.14	0.28	16	10	10,023
6 Mo	1.98	0.99	0.42	27	4	10,198
1 Yr	-1.55	1.37	-0.57	30	19	9,845
3 Yr Avg	10.53	5.99	-0.63	12	45	13,505
5 Yr Avg	11.37	3.74	-1.71	11	32	17,132
10 Yr Avg	9.87	-0.08	---	59	54	25,629
15 Yr Avg	10.69	-0.12	---	69	59	45,865

Operations

Address and Telephone	777 Mariners Island Boulevard
	San Mateo, CA 94403-7777
	800-342-5236 / 415-312-2000
Advisor	Franklin Advisers
Subadvisor	None
Distributor	Franklin/Templeton Distributors
States Available	All
Report Grade	B-
Income Distrib	Paid Monthly
Date of Inception	12-31-69
Fiscal Year End	May

Risk Analysis

Time Period	Load-Adj Return %	Risk % Rank All	Risk % Rank Obj	Morningstar[2] Return	Morningstar Risk	Morningstar Risk-Adj Rating
1 Yr	-5.73					
3 Yr	8.95	6	20	1.63[3]	0.33	★★★★
5 Yr	10.40	48	77	1.47[3]	0.64	★★★★
10 Yr	9.39	37	80	0.55	0.55	★★★
Average Historical Rating (109 months)				2.9	★ s	

[1] = low, 100 = high   [2] 1.00 = Hybrid Avg   [3] 1.00 = 90-day T-bill return

Other Measures

	Standard LB Agg	Best Fit FB HY
Standard Deviation	4.78	Alpha	6.1	-0.6
Mean	10.17	Beta	0.67	1.01
Sharpe Ratio	1.39	R-Squared	32	85

Investment Style

Interest-Rate Stance
Avg Effective Duration	4.6 Yrs
Avg Effective Maturity	8.7 Yrs

Maturity Short Intm Long
Quality High Med Low

Quality
Avg Credit Quality	B
Avg Weighted Coupon	9.97%
Avg Weighted Price	90.92% of Par

Diversification Value for Portfolio Types

Large Cap: High   Small Cap: High   Bond: Medium   Balanced: Medium   Diversified: High

Portfolio 10-31-94

Total Stocks: 10
Total Fixed-Income: 143

Amount 000	Date of Maturity		Value $000	% Net Assets
43550	11-01-02	Dr Pepper/Seven-Up 11.5%	35058	2.02
25500	12-01-03	Owens-Illinois 11%	26839	1.55
27729	09-01-02	Del Monte PIK 12.25%	26343	1.52
23000	05-15-04	American Standard 11.375%	24553	1.41
28000	12-31-19	United Mexican States FRN	23977	1.38
25500	02-01-06	Fort Howard 9%	21548	1.24
20000	04-15-04	Huntsman 11%	20650	1.19
11400	11-26-05	American Medical Intl 15%	20577	1.18
21000	07-15-02	Ralphs Grocery 10.25%	20475	1.18
199		First Nationwide PFD	20398	1.17
20000	04-01-04	Cablevision Systems 10.75%	20300	1.17
20000	02-01-12	TCI Communications 9.8%	20260	1.17
19000	09-01-03	Joy Technologies 10.25%	20093	1.16
20000	04-01-04	AK Steel 10.75%	19975	1.15
19075	03-15-02	Infinity Broadcasting 10.375%	19743	1.14
19900	10-01-04	Aztar 13.75%	19701	1.13
18000	05-01-02	Healthtrust 10.75%	19575	1.13
18900	08-01-01	Tjiwi Kimia Intl 13.25%	19562	1.13
108800	06-01-08	Escom 11%	18927	1.09
20000	08-15-13	RJR Nabisco 9.25%	18300	1.05
17500	04-15-02	Embassy Suites 10.875%	18288	1.05
18000	04-01-02	Coltec Industries 10.25%	18000	1.04
2550		RJR Nabisco Percs	17850	1.03
20000	02-15-04	John Q Hammons Hotels 8.875%	17825	1.03
19000	08-15-01	Specialty Foods 10.25%	17765	1.02

Composition % 10-31-94

Cash	5.0	Preferreds	1.0
Stocks	3.0	Convertibles	0.5
Bonds	90.5	Other	0.0

Coupon Range

	% of Bonds	Rel Obj
0%, PIK	7.8	1.05
0% to 11%	67.9	1.38
11% to 13%	14.7	0.44
13% to 14.5%	5.5	1.02
More than 14.5%	1.4	0.86
Not applicable	2.7	0.87

Tax Analysis

	Tax-Adj Historical Return %	% Pretax Return
3 Yr Avg	6.77	62.0
5 Yr Avg	6.93	55.8
10 Yr Avg	4.83	38.6
Potential Capital Gain Exposure (% of assets)		-40%

Credit Analysis 09-30-94

% of Bonds

US Govt	0	BB	17
AAA	1	B	68
AA	0	Below B	5
A	0	NR/NA	4
BBB	5		

Most Similar Funds in MF500

Vanguard F/I High-Yield Corp	Strong Fit
Liberty High-Income Bond A	Strong Fit
MFS High-Income A	Strong Fit

Min Initial Purchase	$100 (Addt'l: $25)
Min IRA Purchase	None (Addt'l: None)
Min Auto Invest Plan	$25 (Systematic Inv: $25)

Expenses & Fees
Sales Fees	4.25% front
	0.00% deferred
	0.15% 12b-1
Management Fee	0.63% max./0.45% min.
3-,5-,10-yr Expense Projections	$65, $81, $129

MORNINGSTAR **1995 Mutual Fund 500**

Franklin Federal Tax-Free Inc

	Ticker	Load	NAV	Yield	SEC Yield	Assets	Objective
	FKTIX	4.25%	11.29	6.9%	5.98%	6561.4	Muni Nat

Franklin Federal Tax-Free Income Fund seeks interest income exempt from federal income taxes, consistent with capital preservation.

The fund normally invests at least 80% of its assets in investment-grade securities that generate income exempt from federal taxes. It may invest up to 20% of its assets in taxable or AMT-subject bonds. The fund typically maintains an average weighted maturity ranging from 20 to 25 years; it places no restrictions on the maturity of individual securities it purchases.

Prior to Oct. 7, 1983, the fund was a money-market fund and was named Franklin Cash Management Fund.

Manager's Investment Style

Like other Franklin muni funds, this fund's emphasis is on yield. Management has achieved its aim by holding onto older bonds (many from the mid to late 1980s) that carried high yields. Management supplements these issues by buying (and holding on to) the highest-paying bonds it can find in the current market. These payouts usually come from the lower-credit-quality regions of the market, or from private-activity bonds (subject to the alternative minimum tax).

Fund Manager(s)

Andrew Jennings, Sr. et al. Villanova U.

Manager Experience

	Dates Managed	Invest Obj	Std Dev	+/- Index
Andrew R. Johnson				
Franklin CA Tax-Free Inc	03/77 - 12/94	MC	7.59	-3.70
Franklin MN Ins T/F Inc	04/85 - 12/94	MS	5.92	-1.75

Historical Profile

Return	Above Average
Risk	Below Average
Rating	★★★★
	Above Average

Investment Style History
Fixed Income
Income Rtn % Rank Obj

	11	3	8	8	5	4	4	3

Growth of $10,000

|||| Value of Fund ($000)
— Value of Index ($000)
LB Muni
▼ Manager Change
▽ Partial Manager Change
► Mgr Unknown After
◄ Mgr Unknown Before

Performance Quartile (Within Objective)

1983	1984	1985	1986	1987	1988	1989	1990	1991	1992	1993	1994	History
10.03	10.09	11.08	12.06	10.81	11.32	11.44	11.19	11.76	12.01	12.53	11.29	NAV
0.40 *	10.97	20.73	18.94	-2.66	13.89	9.06	5.53	13.23	9.56	11.25	-3.73	Total Return %
---	-4.19	-1.40	3.69	-5.42	6.01	-5.49	-3.42	-2.77	2.31	1.50	-0.81	+/- LB Aggregate
---	0.42	0.71	-0.38	-4.17	3.73	-1.73	-1.78	1.09	0.74	-1.02	1.87	+/- LB Muni
0.00	10.37	10.92	9.88	7.70	9.09	7.99	7.71	8.14	7.43	6.92	6.16	Income Return %
0.40	0.60	9.81	9.06	-10.36	4.80	1.06	-2.19	5.09	2.13	4.33	-9.90	Capital Return %
---	21	68	26	79	32	84	39	67	26	57	51	Total Rtn % Rank All
---	7	38	35	86	6	61	80	11	17	58	29	Total Rtn % Rank Obj
0.00	0.97	1.00	1.01	0.92	0.92	0.86	0.85	0.85	0.83	0.79	0.78	Income $
0.00	0.00	0.00	0.02	0.00	0.01	0.00	0.00	0.00	0.00	0.00	0.00	Capital Gains $
1.40	0.70	0.85	0.64	0.54	0.52	0.51	0.50	0.50	0.51	0.51	0.52	Expense Ratio %
7.80	5.70	8.60	7.72	7.14	7.83	7.59	7.39	7.34	7.07	6.68	6.27	Income Ratio %
---	24	99	74	20	19	16	18	29	15	13	25	Turnover Rate %
0.1	31.6	275.5	2171.4	2600.0	3458.1	3890.0	4086.1	4986.5	5959.5	7060.4	6561.4	Net Assets ($mil)

Performance 12-31-94

	1st Qtr	2nd Qtr	3rd Qtr	4th Qtr	Total
1987	2.08	-6.63	-3.23	5.54	-2.66
1988	4.06	2.78	3.49	2.89	13.89
1989	0.66	5.00	-0.07	3.25	9.06
1990	0.21	2.46	-0.43	3.22	5.53
1991	2.64	2.71	4.12	3.15	13.23
1992	0.75	3.89	2.08	2.53	9.56
1993	3.34	3.05	2.85	1.58	11.25
1994	-3.93	0.56	0.81	-1.15	-3.73

Bear Market Performance

Decile Rank (5-year period)

Worst ▬ Best

	Worst 3 Mo Period 1985-89	Worst 3 Mo Period 1990-94
Franklin Federal Tax-Free Inc	-9.17	-4.52
+/- LB Aggregate	-5.61	0.41
+/- Best Fit Index : LB Muni	-2.68	1.24

Trailing Returns

	Total Return %	+/- LB Aggregate	+/- LB Muni	% Rank All	% Rank Obj	Growth of $10,000
3 Mo	-1.15	-1.53	0.29	48	38	9,885
6 Mo	-0.35	-1.34	0.89	63	28	9,965
1 Yr	-3.73	-0.81	1.87	51	29	9,627
3 Yr Avg	5.47	0.93	0.61	39	12	11,734
5 Yr Avg	6.99	-0.63	0.22	50	14	14,020
10 Yr Avg	9.30	-0.64	-0.13	68	27	24,339
15 Yr Avg	---	---	---	---	---	---

Operations

Address and Telephone	777 Mariners Island Boulevard
	San Mateo, CA 94403-7777
	800-342-5236 / 415-312-2000
Advisor	Franklin Advisers
Subadvisor	None
Distributor	Franklin/Templeton Distributors
States Available	All plus PR
Report Grade	B-
Income Distrib	Paid Monthly
* Date of Inception	10-07-83
Fiscal Year End	April

Min Initial Purchase	$100 (Addt'l: $25)
Min IRA Purchase	None (Addt'l: None)
Min Auto Invest Plan	$25 (Systematic Inv: $25)

Expenses & Fees
Sales Fees	4.25% front
	0.00% deferred
	0.10% 12b-1
Management Fee	0.63% max./0.45% min.
3-,5-,10-yr Expense Projections	$62, $76, $117

Risk Analysis

Time Period	Load-Adj Return %	Risk % Rank [1] All	Obj	Morningstar [2] Return	Morningstar Risk	Morningstar Risk-Adj Rating
1 Yr	-7.82					
3 Yr	3.96	11	20	1.16	0.72	★★★★
5 Yr	6.07	9	26	1.12	0.79	★★★★
10 Yr	8.83	9	32	1.19	0.94	★★★★
Average Historical Rating (99 months)					3.4	★ s

[1] = low, 100 = high [2] 1.00 = Muni Avg [3] 1.00 = 90-day T-bill return

Other Measures

			Standard LB Agg	Best Fit LB Muni
Standard Deviation	4.70	Alpha	1.1	0.8
Mean	5.45	Beta	0.86	0.83
Sharpe Ratio	0.41	R-Squared	54	93

Investment Style

Interest-Rate Stance
Avg Effective Maturity   23.2 Yrs

Quality
Avg Credit Quality   A
Avg Weighted Coupon   7.38%
Avg Weighted Price 100.74% of Par

Diversification Value for Portfolio Types

Large Cap: Medium	Small Cap: High	Bond: Low	Balanced: Medium	Diversified: Medium

Portfolio 10-31-94

Total Stocks: 0
Total Fixed-Income: 746

Amount 000	Date of Maturity		Value $000	% Net Assets
105000	07-01-24	GA Burke Dev Poll Cntrl Pwr 6.6%	02194	1.54
99000	11-01-24	TX Dallas/Ft Worth Intl Arpt Fac 8%	01573	1.53
79945	11-15-23	CO Denver Arpt Sys 8.5%	81426	1.22
60480	01-01-15	NC East Muni Pwr Sys 7.75%	64377	0.97
58800	08-15-21	NY New York City GO Ser A 8%	64024	0.96
58225	12-13-08	MI Detroit Resource Rec 9.25%	61366	0.92
54265	09-01-21	MD Takoma Park Washington Hosp 8.25%	57964	0.87
58120	09-01-32	NV Clark Indl Dev SW Gas 7.5%	56618	0.85
50000	01-01-18	GA Muni Elec Pwr 7.75%	53771	0.81
45875	12-01-08	FL Broward Resource Rec North 7.95%	49389	0.74
43010	04-01-05	TX Harris Hosp Dist 8.5%	46014	0.69
43225	09-01-21	MD Gaithersberg Hosp Fac 8.25%	45509	0.68
40000	06-15-20	NY New York City Muni Wtr Fin Swr 7.75%	45344	0.68
41800	02-01-09	MN Bloomington Port Tax 8.55%	44553	0.67
41300	12-01-13	PA Delaware Indl Dev Resource Rec 8.1%	43758	0.66
40975	02-01-19	TX Matagorda Navig Dist #1 Lt/Pwr 7.7%	43134	0.65
37585	03-01-21	MA GO Bay Transp Genl 7.875%	42715	0.64
41250	05-01-21	NH Indl Dev Poll Cntrl Pub Svc 7.5%	41648	0.63
38705	01-01-15	NM Los Alamos Util Sys 7.75%	41541	0.62
47800	10-01-32	CO Denver Spcl Fac Arpt Proj 6.875%	41069	0.62

Credit Analysis % of Bonds 09-30-94

US Govt	0	BB	2
AAA	27	B	0
AA	16	Below B	0
A	24	NR/NA	11
BBB	21		

Composition % of Assets 09-30-94

Cash	1.1	Preferreds	0.0
Stocks	0.0	Convertibles	0.0
Bonds	98.9	Other	0.0

Tax Analysis

	Tax-Adj Historical Return %	% Pretax Return
3 Yr Avg	5.47	100.0
5 Yr Avg	6.99	100.0
10 Yr Avg	9.30	99.9
Potential Capital Gain Exposure (% of assets)		-2%

Most Similar Funds in MF500

Franklin Insured T/F Income	Strong Fit
American Cap Muni Bond A	Strong Fit
T. Rowe Price Tax-Fr Hi-Yld	Strong Fit

Coupon Range

	% Bonds	Rel Obj
0%	1.3	0.50
0% to 6.8%	30.4	0.50
6.8% to 7.5%	19.2	1.24
7.5% to 8.3%	32.1	3.62
More than 8.3%	16.8	1.91
Not applicable	0.3	0.07

Sector Weightings

	% Bonds	Rel Obj
General Obl	13.21	0.63
Utilities	15.28	1.22
Health	12.01	0.91
Water/Waste	5.06	0.79
Housing	13.56	1.85
Education	3.24	0.51
Transportation	10.71	1.05
COP/Lease	2.83	0.89
Private	20.96	1.80
Misc Revenue	2.89	0.58
Demand	0.26	0.11

Top 5 States % of Bonds

NY	11.35	IL	5.19
TX	8.32	PA	5.08
WA	6.31		

Franklin Global Health Care

	Ticker	Load	NAV	Yield	SEC Yield	Assets	Objective
	FKGHX	4.50%	10.99	0.5%	N/A	11.0	Sp.-Health

Franklin Global Health Care Fund seeks capital appreciation.
The fund normally invests at least 70% of its assets in equity securities of companies which derive at least one half of their earnings from healthcare products or services. These companies must demonstrate a potential for above average growth in revenues and/or earnings. The fund is diversified globally; 70% of its assets are invested in three or more countries at all times, and not more than 40% of its assets may be concentrated in any one country. It may also invest up to 30% of its assets in foreign or domestic debt, rated B or above.

Historical Profile
Return ---
Risk ---
Rating
Not Rated

Investment Style History
Equity
Average % Stocks Held in Portfolio

	1992	1993	1994
	94%	91%	89%

Growth of $10,000
IIII Value of Fund ($000)
— Value of Index ($000)
  S&P 500
▼ Manager Change
▽ Partial Manager Change
► Mgr Unknown After
◄ Mgr Unknown Before

Performance Quartile (Within Objective)

Manager's Investment Style
Despite the global moniker, management has heavily emphasized domestic health-care firms thus far. Management has split its attention between more-mature health firms and lesser-known entities, generally keeping a concentrated portfolio of small issues with visible growth or high return on assets, and selling at above-market prices. Management has also positioned the fund to take advantage of mergers and acquisitions in the health-care field.

Fund Manager(s)
Rupert H. Johnson, Jr., since 02-92. Birthdate: 08-40. BA, Washington & Lee U. 1962

Manager Experience	Dates Managed	Invest Obj	Std Dev	+/- Index
Rupert H. Johnson, Jr.				
Franklin DynaTech	01/68 - 12/94	ST	19.92	0.68

History	1983	1984	1985	1986	1987	1988	1989	1990	1991	1992	1993	1994
NAV	---	---	---	---	---	---	---	---	---	9.96	10.19	10.99
Total Return %	---	---	---	---	---	---	---	---	---	0.54 *	6.21	14.20
+/- S&P 500	---	---	---	---	---	---	---	---	---	-8.14 *	-3.85	12.88
+/- S&P Health	---	---	---	---	---	---	---	---	---	---	14.61	1.08
Income Return %										0.94	0.82	0.58
Capital Return %										-0.40	5.39	13.62
Total Rtn % Rank All	---	---	---	---	---	---	---	---	---	---	87	1
Total Rtn % Rank Obj											15	26
Income $	---	---	---	---	---	---	---	---	---	0.09	0.08	0.06
Capital Gains $										0.00	0.30	0.56
Expense Ratio %	---	---	---	---	---	---	---	---	---	0.00	0.00	0.10
Income Ratio %										1.68	1.13	0.68
Turnover Rate %										---	63	111
Net Assets ($mil)	---	---	---	---	---	---	---	---	---	2.9	4.9	11.0

Performance 12-31-94

	1st Qtr	2nd Qtr	3rd Qtr	4th Qtr	Total
1987	---	---	---	---	---
1988	---	---	---	---	---
1989	---	---	---	---	---
1990	---	---	---	---	---
1991	---	---	---	---	---
1992	---	-8.20	0.81	14.24	0.54 *
1993	-12.35	10.42	-1.25	11.13	6.21
1994	3.43	-4.35	16.63	-1.03	14.20

Bear Market Performance
Decile Rank (5-year period)

Worst | Best

	Worst 3 Mo Period 1985-89	Worst 3 Mo Period 1990-94
Franklin Global Health Care	---	---
+/- S&P 500	---	---
+/- Best Fit Index :	---	---

Trailing Returns

	Total Return %	+/- S&P 500	+/- S&P Health	% Rank All	Obj	Growth of $10,000
3 Mo	-1.03	-1.01	-4.23	45	50	9,897
6 Mo	15.43	10.57	-3.46	2	37	11,543
1 Yr	14.20	12.88	1.08	1	26	11,420
3 Yr Avg	---	---	---	---	---	---
5 Yr Avg	---	---	---	---	---	---
10 Yr Avg	---	---	---	---	---	---
15 Yr Avg	---	---	---	---	---	---

Risk Analysis

Time Period	Load-Adj Return %	Risk % Rank [1] All	Obj	Morningstar [2] Return	Morningstar Risk	Morningstar Risk-Adj Rating
1 Yr	9.06					
3 Yr	---	---	---	---	---	---
5 Yr	---	---	---	---	---	---
10 Yr	---	---	---	---	---	---

Average Historical Rating --- | ---

[1] 1 = low, 100 = high [2] 1.00 = Equity Avg [3] 1.00 = 90-day T-bill return

Other Measures

			Standard S&P 500	Best Fit
Standard Deviation	---	Alpha	---	---
Mean	---	Beta	---	---
Sharpe Ratio	---	R-Squared	---	---

Investment Style

	Stock Portfolio Avg	Relative S&P 500
Price/Earnings Ratio	24.1	1.30
Price/Book Ratio	4.1	1.21
5 Yr Earnings Gr %	26.2#	4.73
Return on Assets %	13.1	1.75
Debt % Total Cap	20.3#	0.72
Med Mkt Cap ($mil)	664	0.05

figure is based on 50% or less of stocks

Diversification Value for Portfolio Types

Large Cap: | Small Cap: | Bond: | Balanced: | Diversified:

Operations

Address and Telephone	777 Mariners Island Boulevard San Mateo, CA 94403-7777 800-342-5236 / 415-312-2000
Advisor	Franklin Advisers
Subadvisor	None
Distributor	Franklin/Templeton Distributors
States Available	All plus PR
Report Grade	N/A
Income Distrib	Paid Semiannually
* Date of Inception	02-14-92
Fiscal Year End	April

Min Initial Purchase	$100 (Addt'l: $25)
Min IRA Purchase	None (Addt'l: None)
Min Auto Invest Plan	$25 (Systematic Inv: $25)

Expenses & Fees
Sales Fees	4.50% front
	0.00% deferred
	0.25% 12b-1
Management Fee	0.63% max./0.40% min.
3-,5-,10-yr Expense Projections	$110, $156, $283
Annual Brokerage Cost	0.29%

Portfolio 10-31-94

Share Chg (05-94) 000	Amount 000	Total Stocks: 52 / Total Fixed-Income: 0	Value $000	% Net Assets
25	35	Noven Pharmaceuticals	534	5.82
34	55	Penederm	454	4.94
0	20	Matrix Pharmaceuticals	288	3.13
5	14	Pyxis	270	2.94
7	10	Astra Cl B Free	267	2.91
0	6	Columbia/HCA Healthcare	262	2.86
0	8	Sierra Health Services	260	2.83
2	5	US Healthcare	213	2.32
-2	4	United HealthCare	211	2.30
3	6	Healthtrust	210	2.29
9	9	Mariner Health Group	204	2.22
25	40	Abaxis	200	2.18
7	7	Allergan	185	2.01
10	10	Laboratorio Chile (ADR)	184	2.00
0	5	Homedco Group	181	1.97
7	7	Hunsfos Fabrikker	171	1.86
0	4	Cerner	163	1.78
0	2	Schering-Plough	157	1.71
2	3	Medtronic	156	1.70
10	10	Circa Pharmaceuticals	149	1.62
0	2	Pfizer	148	1.62
20	20	K-V Pharmaceutical Cl B	148	1.61
6	6	CR Bard	147	1.60
-2	2	PacifiCare Health Sys Cl B	146	1.59
3	3	Sanofi	146	1.59

Composition % 09-30-94
Cash	14.5	Preferreds	0.0
Stocks	85.5	Convertibles	0.0
Bonds	0.0	Other	0.0

Tax Analysis
	Tax-Adj Historical Return %	% Pretax Return
3 Yr Avg	---	---
5 Yr Avg	---	---
10 Yr Avg	---	---
Potential Capital Gain Exposure (% of assets)		8%

Most Similar Funds in MF500
Fund lacks three-year record

Index Allocation
	% of Stocks
S&P 500	21.4
S&P MidCap 400	9.3
U.S. Small Cap	55.8
Foreign	13.5

Sector Weightings
	% of Stocks	Relative S&P 500
Utilities	0.0	0.00
Energy	0.0	0.00
Financials	0.0	0.00
Industrial Cyclicals	5.0	0.30
Consumer Durables	0.0	0.00
Consumer Staples	7.2	0.57
Services	1.6	0.19
Retail	0.0	0.00
Health	76.1	8.77
Technology	10.1	1.11

MORNINGSTAR 1995 Mutual Fund 500

Franklin Growth

	Ticker	Load	NAV	Yield	SEC Yield	Assets	Objective
	FKGRX	4.50%	15.00	0.9%	N/A	538.0	Growth

Franklin Growth Series seeks capital appreciation. Current income is a secondary consideration.

The fund invests primarily in common stocks and convertible securities. It may invest in any shares traded on any national securities exchange. The fund may also write covered call options.

Historical Profile

Return	Average
Risk	Below Average
Rating	★★★
	Neutral

Investment Style History
Equity

Average % Stocks Held in Portfolio

| 71% | 96% | 93% | 83% | 62% | 71% | 87% | 98% |

Growth of $10,000

IIII Value of Fund ($000)
— Value of Index ($000)
   S&P 500
▼ Manager Change
▽ Partial Manager Change
► Mgr Unknown After
◄ Mgr Unknown Before

Performance Quartile
(Within Objective)

Manager's Investment Style

Management favors large-cap companies with steady growth potential, but that sell at a discount to their future earnings power. Once management finds a stock fitting its criteria, it holds on for the long term: Annual turnover hasn't cracked 10% since 1983. The portfolio isn't stuffed with typical growth stocks, though: Because management buys issues based on future earnings, the portfolio has often included such nontraditional fare as airline stocks.

Fund Manager(s)

V. Jerry Palmieri, since 1965. BA, Williams C.

Manager Experience

	Dates Managed	Invest Obj	Std Dev	+/- Index

Not available.

1983	1984	1985	1986	1987	1988	1989	1990	1991	1992	1993	1994	History
5.95	5.83	7.20	7.98	9.02	9.62	11.49	11.46	13.98	14.13	14.75	15.00	NAV
17.89	0.79	26.43	14.71	20.02	9.14	23.79	2.07	26.71	2.96	7.13	2.93	Total Return %
-4.57	-5.48	-5.31	-3.97	14.76	-7.47	-7.89	5.19	-3.78	-4.66	-2.93	1.61	+/- S&P 500
-5.57	-2.26	-6.14	-1.39	17.65	-8.80	-5.38	8.26	-7.50	-6.01	-4.15	3.00	+/- Wilshire 5000
1.44	1.73	2.64	2.00	4.34	2.45	2.00	2.34	3.17	1.36	2.13	0.94	Income Return %
16.45	-0.94	23.79	12.72	15.67	6.69	21.79	-0.26	23.54	1.60	5.00	1.99	Capital Return %
48	63	41	56	4	67	26	50	32	84	83	8	Total Rtn % Rank All
64	34	69	49	2	77	66	13	78	81	71	14	Total Rtn % Rank Obj
0.06	0.10	0.13	0.13	0.35	0.22	0.21	0.27	0.35	0.19	0.30	0.14	Income $
0.00	0.06	0.01	0.12	0.19	0.01	0.20	0.00	0.15	0.07	0.08	0.04	Capital Gains $
1.01	0.85	0.87	0.87	0.81	0.77	0.76	0.73	0.70	0.66	0.64	0.77	Expense Ratio %
1.78	2.34	2.13	2.12	2.34	2.27	1.94	2.74	2.58	2.06	1.64	1.23	Income Ratio %
10	2	4	1	9	0	2	0	8	1	2	7	Turnover Rate %
16.6	20.1	24.1	48.2	100.5	105.9	144.0	195.9	407.8	589.9	566.9	538.0	Net Assets ($mil)

Performance 12-31-94

	1st Qtr	2nd Qtr	3rd Qtr	4th Qtr	Total
1987	18.86	5.69	5.48	-9.42	20.02
1988	4.77	4.60	-2.48	2.12	9.14
1989	5.04	6.34	11.45	-0.56	23.79
1990	-0.04	6.66	-12.73	9.71	2.07
1991	14.09	-0.23	3.10	7.96	26.71
1992	-1.75	-2.19	2.01	5.03	2.96
1993	-0.92	0.64	1.14	6.23	7.13
1994	-6.51	3.05	5.28	1.48	2.93

Bear Market Performance

Decile Rank (5-year period)

Worst ————————————————— Best

	Worst 3 Mo Period 1985-89	Worst 3 Mo Period 1990-94
Franklin Growth	-17.16	-12.73
+/- S&P 500	12.42	1.01
+/- Best Fit Index : S&P 500	12.42	1.01

Trailing Returns

	Total Return %	+/- S&P 500	+/- Wil 5000	% Rank All	% Rank Obj	Growth of $10,000
3 Mo	1.48	1.50	2.25	5	8	10,148
6 Mo	6.84	1.98	2.22	7	21	10,684
1 Yr	2.93	1.61	3.00	8	14	10,293
3 Yr Avg	4.32	-1.94	-2.29	62	63	11,354
5 Yr Avg	7.99	-0.70	-0.83	33	63	14,685
10 Yr Avg	13.19	-1.19	-0.67	25	43	34,533
15 Yr Avg	13.31	-1.17	-0.67	34	52	65,153

Operations

Address and Telephone	777 Mariners Island Boulevard	
	San Mateo, CA 94403-7777	
	800-342-5236 / 415-312-2000	
Advisor	Franklin Advisers	
Subadvisor	None	
Distributor	Franklin/Templeton Distributors	
States Available	All plus PR	
Report Grade	B	
Income Distrib	Paid Annually	
Date of Inception	03-31-48	
Fiscal Year End	September	

Min Initial Purchase	$100 (Addt'l: $25)
Min IRA Purchase	None (Addt'l: None)
Min Auto Invest Plan	$25 (Systematic Inv: $25)

Expenses & Fees

Sales Fees	4.50% front
	0.00% deferred
	0.25% 12b-1
Management Fee	0.63% max./0.40% min.
3-,5-,10-yr Expense Projections	$72, $92, $150
Annual Brokerage Cost	0.03%

Risk Analysis

Time Period	Load-Adj Return %	Risk % Rank [1] All	Obj	Morningstar [2] Return	Morningstar Risk	Morningstar Risk-Adj Rating
1 Yr	-1.70					
3 Yr	2.73	70	33	-0.24[3]	0.78	★★
5 Yr	7.00	62	12	0.55[3]	0.74	★★★
10 Yr	12.67	52	9	1.00	0.75	★★★
Average Historical Rating (109 months)					3.6	★ s

[1] 1 = low, 100 = high   [2] 1.00 = Equity Avg   [3] 1.00 = 90-day T-bill return

Other Measures

				Standard S&P 500	Best Fit S&P 500
Standard Deviation	7.80	Alpha		-1.4	-1.4
Mean	4.54	Beta		0.84	0.84
Sharpe Ratio	0.13	R-Squared		74	74

Investment Style

	Stock Portfolio Avg	Relative S&P 500	Style
Price/Earnings Ratio	21.8	1.18	Value Blend Growth
Price/Book Ratio	3.5	1.04	
5 Yr Earnings Gr %	6.9	1.24	
Return on Assets %	9.7	1.29	
Debt % Total Cap	20.9	0.74	
Med Mkt Cap ($mil)	7530	0.58	

Size Large Med Small

Diversification Value for Portfolio Types

Large Cap: Low	Small Cap: Medium	Bond: High	Balanced: Low	Diversified: Low

Portfolio 10-31-94

Share Chg (09-94) 000	Amount 000	Total Stocks: 89 Total Fixed-Income: 0	Value $000	% Net Assets
0	450	Computer Sciences	20925	3.90
0	310	AMR	17089	3.18
0	225	Schering-Plough	16031	2.98
0	280	Minnesota Mining & Mfg	15505	2.89
0	200	AMP	15125	2.82
0	244	Dun & Bradstreet	14305	2.66
0	221	Raytheon	14089	2.62
0	250	Delta Air Lines	13031	2.43
0	160	Pfizer	11860	2.21
0	200	Automatic Data Processing	11675	2.17
0	225	Cabletron Systems	11306	2.10
0	200	Johnson & Johnson	10925	2.03
0	300	Time Warner	10650	1.98
0	140	IBM	10430	1.94
0	200	Millipore	10275	1.91
0	90	Atlantic Richfield	9754	1.82
0	200	Air Products & Chemicals	9550	1.78
0	150	American Home Products	9525	1.77
0	160	Bristol-Myers Squibb	9340	1.74
0	90	Hewlett-Packard	8798	1.64
0	200	Boeing	8775	1.63
0	300	Coastal	8550	1.59
0	100	Capital Cities/ABC	8313	1.55
0	88	UAL	8269	1.54
0	300	American Greetings Cl A	8213	1.53

Composition % 09-30-94

Cash	3.6	Preferreds	0.0
Stocks	96.4	Convertibles	0.0
Bonds	0.0	Other	0.0

Tax Analysis

	Tax-Adj Historical Return %	% Pretax Return
3 Yr Avg	3.66	84.2
5 Yr Avg	7.19	88.6
10 Yr Avg	12.11	87.1
Potential Capital Gain Exposure (% of assets)		25%

Most Similar Funds in MF500

Dreyfus Appreciation	Fair Fit
Liberty All-Star	Fair Fit
Gabelli Growth	Fair Fit

Index Allocation

	% of Stocks
S&P 500	78.4
S&P MidCap 400	13.1
U.S. Small Cap	7.5
Foreign	2.5

Sector Weightings

	% of Stocks	Relative S&P 500
Utilities	1.6	0.13
Energy	4.1	0.41
Financials	0.0	0.00
Industrial Cyclicals	17.1	1.04
Consumer Durables	4.0	0.65
Consumer Staples	3.3	0.26
Services	24.6	3.03
Retail	0.3	0.05
Health	20.7	2.39
Technology	24.2	2.64

Franklin High-Yield T/F Income

	Ticker	Load	NAV	Yield	SEC Yield	Assets	Objective
	FRHIX	4.25%	10.35	7.2%	6.85%	3124.5	Muni Nat

Franklin High-Yield Tax-Free Income Fund seeks a high current yield exempt from federal income taxes.

The fund generally invests in municipal securities rated from CC to BB. It expects to generally hold longer-term securities. Under normal circumstances, at least 80% of the fund's securities will be exempt from the Alternative Minimum Tax. The fund generally keeps about 10% of its assets in bonds subject to the Alternative Minimum Tax.

Historical Profile

Return	Above Average
Risk	Low
Rating	★★★★★ Highest

Investment Style History
Fixed Income

Income Rtn % Rank Obj

| 1 | 1 | 1 | 3 | 2 | 1 | 2 | 2 |

Growth of $10,000

|||| Value of Fund ($000)
— Value of Index ($000)
   LB Muni
▼ Manager Change
▽ Partial Manager Change
► Mgr Unknown After
◄ Mgr Unknown Before

Performance Quartile
(Within Objective)

Manager's Investment Style

This is a high-yield fund in a family that emphasizes income. Following the Franklin philosophy, management finds the best-yielding current issues and holds them for the long term. Management has found the highest yields in nonrated bonds, which take up a very large portion of the portfolio, and in lower-quality and private-activity bonds.

Fund Manager(s)

Sheila Amoroso. BS, San Francisco State U.
Andrew R. Johnson. BA, U. of Virginia 1952 BS,
U. of Virginia 1954 JD, U. of Virginia 1970

Manager Experience	Dates Managed	Invest Obj	Std Dev	+/- Index
Andrew R. Johnson				
Franklin CA Tax-Free Inc	03/77 - 12/94	MC	7.59	-3.70
Franklin Fed Tax-Free Inc	10/83 - 12/94	MN	5.89	-1.03

	1983	1984	1985	1986	1987	1988	1989	1990	1991	1992	1993	1994	History
	---	---	---	10.62	10.13	10.51	10.60	10.28	10.66	10.77	11.38	10.35	NAV
	---	---	---	6.20 *	4.49	13.85	9.79	5.12	12.40	9.06	13.27	-2.58	Total Return %
	---	---	---		1.73	5.97	-4.75	-3.83	-3.61	1.81	3.52	0.34	+/- LB Aggregate
	---	---	---		2.98	3.68	-1.00	-2.19	0.25	0.24	0.99	3.02	+/- LB Muni
	---	---	---	0.00	9.10	10.09	8.93	8.13	8.70	7.93	7.60	6.47	Income Return %
	---	---	---	6.20	-4.61	3.75	0.86	-3.02	3.70	1.12	5.66	-9.05	Capital Return %
	---	---	---		25	32	76	42	72	32	38	39	Total Rtn % Rank All
	---	---	---		2	8	38	89	23	28	20	18	Total Rtn % Rank Obj
	---	---	---	0.00	0.93	0.96	0.90	0.84	0.84	0.81	0.78	0.75	Income $
	---	---	---	0.00	0.00	0.00	0.00	0.00	0.00	0.01	0.00	0.00	Capital Gains $
	---	---	---	0.00	0.65	0.61	0.54	0.52	0.53	0.53	0.54	0.53	Expense Ratio %
	---	---	---	7.10	7.79	7.68	7.52	7.90	7.73	7.45	6.79	Income Ratio %
	---	---	---		---	27	2	23	71	103	33	16	Turnover Rate %
	---	---	---	2.0	68.2	582.4	1525.7	1683.4	2044.1	2568.2	3327.3	3124.5	Net Assets ($mil)

Performance 12-31-94

	1st Qtr	2nd Qtr	3rd Qtr	4th Qtr	Total
1987	1.53	-1.30	-0.33	4.61	4.49
1988	2.87	3.89	3.62	2.80	13.85
1989	1.48	5.16	0.04	2.82	9.79
1990	0.67	2.52	-0.49	2.36	5.12
1991	2.15	2.74	3.90	3.07	12.40
1992	0.10	4.09	2.01	2.60	9.06
1993	3.96	3.07	3.38	2.24	13.27
1994	-3.02	0.89	0.88	-1.30	-2.58

Bear Market Performance

Decile Rank (5-year period)

Worst   Best

	Worst 3 Mo Period 1985-89	Worst 3 Mo Period 1990-94
Franklin High-Yield T/F Income	---	-3.96
+/- LB Aggregate	---	0.97
+/- Best Fit Index : LB Muni	---	1.80

Trailing Returns

	Total Return %	+/- LB Aggregate	+/- LB Muni	% Rank All	% Rank Obj	Growth of $10,000
3 Mo	-1.30	-1.67	0.14	52	47	9,870
6 Mo	-0.43	-1.42	0.82	64	30	9,957
1 Yr	-2.58	0.34	3.02	39	18	9,742
3 Yr Avg	6.36	1.82	1.50	31	2	12,034
5 Yr Avg	7.29	-0.34	0.52	44	7	14,217
10 Yr Avg	---	---	---	---	---	---
15 Yr Avg	---	---	---	---	---	---

Operations

Address and Telephone	777 Mariners Island Boulevard
	San Mateo, CA 94403-7777
	800-342-5236 / 415-312-2000
Advisor	Franklin Advisers
Subadvisor	None
Distributor	Franklin/Templeton Distributors
States Available	All plus PR
Report Grade	C+
Income Distrib	Paid Monthly
* Date of Inception	03-01-86
Fiscal Year End	February

Risk Analysis

Time Period	Load-Adj Return %	Risk % Rank [1] All	Obj	Morningstar [2] Return	Morningstar Risk	Morningstar Risk-Adj Rating
1 Yr	-6.72					
3 Yr	4.84	7	13	1.48	0.60	★★★★★
5 Yr	6.36	6	17	1.26	0.68	★★★★★
10 Yr	---	---	---	---	---	

Average Historical Rating (70 months)   4.9 ★s

[1] = low, 100 = high   [2] 1.00 = Muni Avg   [3] 1.00 = 90-day T-bill return

Other Measures

			Standard LB Agg	Best Fit LB Muni
Standard Deviation	4.57	Alpha	1.9	1.7
Mean	6.29	Beta	0.84	0.78
Sharpe Ratio	0.61	R-Squared	54	87

Investment Style

Interest-Rate Stance

Avg Effective Maturity	21.4 Yrs

Quality

Avg Credit Quality	BBB
Avg Weighted Coupon	7.80%
Avg Weighted Price	99.75% of Par

Maturity: Short Intm Long
Quality: High Med Low

Diversification Value for Portfolio Types

Large Cap: Medium	Small Cap: High	Bond: Low	Balanced: Medium	Diversified: High

Min Initial Purchase	$100 (Addt'l: $25)
Min IRA Purchase	None (Addt'l: None)
Min Auto Invest Plan	$25 (Systematic Inv: $25)

Expenses & Fees

Sales Fees	4.25% front
	0.00% deferred
	0.10% 12b-1
Management Fee	0.63% max./0.45% min.
3-,5-,10-yr Expense Projections	$62, $76, $118

Portfolio 10-31-94

Amount 000	Date of Maturity	Total Stocks: 0 / Total Fixed-Income: 526	Value $000	% Net Assets
480100	01-01-27	CA San Joaquin Hills Transp Toll Rd 0%	58313	1.80
56995	08-01-13	NV Henderson GO Local Impt Dist 8.5%	53299	1.65
41200	08-01-09	CO Eagle Sports Fac 8%	42717	1.32
35000	08-15-22	LA Lake Charles Harbor/Term 7.75%	36313	1.12
35910	02-01-22	NY New York City GO 7%	35209	1.09
32405	04-01-18	NY Local Govt Assist 7.25%	34829	1.08
29500	11-15-16	PA Philadelphia Muni Lease 8.625%	34433	1.06
30655	04-01-16	MS Claiborne Poll Cntrl Engy 9.5%	33476	1.03
35000	12-31-19	MT Brd Invest Resource Yellowstone 7%	32216	1.00
37350	08-15-23	NM Farmington Poll Cntrl 6.4%	32098	0.99
30765	05-01-21	NH Indl Dev Poll Cntrl Pub Svc 7.65%	30918	0.96
30600	09-01-01	CA Los Angeles Comnty Fac Dist #4 9.25%	30501	0.94
27650	12-01-15	NY Port of NY/NJ Consolid 9.125%	29934	0.93
28500	07-01-07	RI Depositors Econ Protection Obl 10%	28388	0.88
30950	11-15-25	CO Denver Arpt Sys 7.25%	28368	0.88
25500	06-01-14	LA St Charles Poll Cntrl Pwr 8.25%	27618	0.85
25500	07-01-18	OH Montgomery Hlth Sys 8.1%	26912	0.83
24785	02-01-22	NY New York City GO 7.5%	25500	0.79
24360	11-15-23	CO Denver Arpt Sys 8.5%	24811	0.77
23400	02-01-15	NY New York City GO 7.625%	24186	0.75

Credit Analysis % of Bonds 09-30-94

US Govt	0	BB	7
AAA	8	B	1
AA	4	Below B	1
A	11	NR/NA	48
BBB	20		

Composition % of Assets 09-30-94

Cash	2.0	Preferreds	0.0
Stocks	0.0	Convertibles	0.0
Bonds	98.0	Other	0.0

Tax Analysis

	Tax-Adj Historical Return %	% Pretax Return
3 Yr Avg	6.36	99.9
5 Yr Avg	7.29	99.9
10 Yr Avg	---	---
Potential Capital Gain Exposure (% of assets)		-2%

Most Similar Funds in MF500

Franklin Fed Tax-Free Income	Strong Fit
United Municipal High-Inc	Strong Fit
Franklin Insured T/F Income	Strong Fit

Coupon Range

	% Bonds	Rel Obj
0%	2.1	0.82
0% to 6.8%	16.4	0.27
6.8% to 7.5%	19.0	1.22
7.5% to 8.3%	26.8	3.03
More than 8.3%	35.3	4.00
Not applicable	0.4	0.11

Sector Weightings

	% Bonds	Rel Obj
General Obl	12.99	0.62
Utilities	2.91	0.23
Health	17.69	1.34
Water/Waste	2.91	0.46
Housing	4.03	0.55
Education	1.53	0.24
Transportation	14.48	1.42
COP/Lease	6.57	2.06
Private	22.12	1.90
Misc Revenue	14.34	2.89
Demand	0.44	0.18

Top 5 States % of Bonds

CA	14.53	FL	7.81
NY	10.21	CO	5.24
PA	8.01		

MORNINGSTAR **1995 Mutual Fund 500**

Franklin Income

Franklin Income Series seeks income while maintaining prospects for capital appreciation.

The fund invests in a diversified portfolio of income-producing securities; there are no restrictions as to the proportion of any particular type of security. These securities are traded on any national securities exchange or issued by an entity with assets in excess of $1 million. The fund may also invest in securities of any rating or unrated securities, but does not intend to purchase securities rated below CCC.

	Ticker	Load	NAV	Yield	SEC Yield	Assets	Objective
	FKINX	4.25%	2.10	8.5%	8.12%	4789.3	Income

Manager's Investment Style

Management's formula is a diversified combination of Treasuries, junk bonds, equity-like and busted convertibles, high-dividend stocks, and gold-related securities; the bond and equity stakes both include foreign holdings. The goal of this extreme diversification is to dilute some of the risks involved in a high-paying fund. As income is a key pursuit, management has specific income targets for each sector and it sells when prices rise. Management is also known for its calm approach: It does not panic over short-term losses, and it will not abandon its strategy in order to ride short-term market waves.

Fund Manager(s)

Charles B. Johnson, since 01-57. Birthdate: 01-33. BA, Yale 1954

Matthew F. Avery, since 01-89. Birthdate: 01-60. BS, Stanford U. 1982. MBA, U. of California-Los Angeles 1987

Manager Experience	Dates Managed	Invest Obj	Std Dev	+/- Index
Charles B. Johnson				
Franklin Utilities	01/57 - 12/94	SU	11.54	-1.20
Franklin Global Utilities	07/92 - 12/94	SU	10.08	3.38

Performance 12-31-94

	1st Qtr	2nd Qtr	3rd Qtr	4th Qtr	Total
1987	10.16	-2.29	-1.15	-1.44	4.87
1988	4.98	2.16	0.70	0.76	8.81
1989	3.16	5.67	1.64	1.71	12.69
1990	-2.20	3.40	-8.58	-1.32	-8.77
1991	16.67	6.11	9.06	4.55	41.15
1992	6.69	5.07	1.76	1.04	15.26
1993	8.02	4.54	4.42	3.07	21.54
1994	-5.17	-1.54	2.51	-2.16	-6.37

Bear Market Performance

Decile Rank (5-year period)

	Worst 3 Mo Period 1985-89	Worst 3 Mo Period 1990-94
Franklin Income	-6.78	-14.97
+/- S&P 500	13.62	-1.13
+/- Best Fit Index : FB HY	---	-0.86

Trailing Returns

	Total Return %	+/- S&P 500	+/- LB Aggregate	% Rank All	% Rank Obj	Growth of $10,000
3 Mo	-2.16	-2.15	-2.54	71	71	9,784
6 Mo	0.29	-4.57	-0.70	51	43	10,029
1 Yr	-6.37	-7.68	-3.45	75	85	9,363
3 Yr Avg	9.46	3.20	4.92	15	7	13,117
5 Yr Avg	11.05	2.36	3.43	12	5	16,890
10 Yr Avg	11.90	-2.48	1.96	39	7	30,781
15 Yr Avg	13.58	-0.90	2.77	30	16	67,544

Operations

Address and Telephone	777 Mariners Island Boulevard
	San Mateo, CA 94403-7777
	800-342-5236 / 415-312-2000
Advisor	Franklin Advisers
Subadvisor	None
Distributor	Franklin/Templeton Distributors
States Available	All plus PR
Report Grade	B-
Income Distrib	Paid Monthly
Date of Inception	08-31-48
Fiscal Year End	September

Historical Profile

Return	Above Average
Risk	Low
Rating	★★★★
	Above Average

19 7 10 23 2 13 16 20

Investment Style History
Fixed Income
Income Rtn % Rank Obj

Growth of $10,000

||| Value of Fund ($000)
— Value of Index ($000) S&P 500
▼ Manager Change
▽ Partial Manager Change
► Mgr Unknown After
◄ Mgr Unknown Before

Performance Quartile (Within Objective)

	1983	1984	1985	1986	1987	1988	1989	1990	1991	1992	1993	1994	History
NAV	1.99	2.02	2.09	2.24	2.11	2.06	2.07	1.68	2.11	2.21	2.46	2.10	NAV
Total Return %	15.42	15.52	18.45	19.65	4.87	8.81	12.69	-8.77	41.15	15.26	21.54	-6.37	Total Return %
+/- S&P 500	-7.04	9.25	-13.29	0.97	-0.39	-7.80	-18.99	-5.66	10.67	7.65	11.48	-7.68	+/- S&P 500
+/- LB Aggregate	7.05	0.36	-3.68	4.40	2.11	0.93	-1.85	-17.72	25.15	8.02	11.79	-3.45	+/- LB Aggregate
Income Return %	12.23	12.43	11.78	11.44	9.73	10.67	11.29	10.07	14.91	9.92	8.75	7.29	Income Return %
Capital Return %	3.20	3.09	6.66	8.21	-4.86	-1.86	1.40	-18.84	26.24	5.35	12.78	-13.66	Capital Return %
Total Rtn % Rank All	57	4	81	22	23	69	55	82	13	10	15	75	Total Rtn % Rank All
Total Rtn % Rank Obj	50	7	64	12	9	80	44	91	2	13	1	85	Total Rtn % Rank Obj
Income $	0.23	0.22	0.22	0.22	0.22	0.22	0.22	0.22	0.22	0.20	0.18	0.18	Income $
Capital Gains $	0.04	0.03	0.06	0.02	0.02	0.01	0.02	0.00	0.01	0.01	0.03	0.03	Capital Gains $
Expense Ratio %	0.83	0.77	0.76	0.71	0.64	0.61	0.57	0.55	0.56	0.55	0.54	0.64	Expense Ratio %
Income Ratio %	10.33	10.90	10.14	9.76	9.20	10.50	10.46	10.73	10.17	9.11	7.84	7.37	Income Ratio %
Turnover Rate %	8	12	24	31	18	10	12	12	34	23	25	23	Turnover Rate %
Net Assets ($mil)	62.5	74.1	105.3	226.8	501.0	883.4	1317.2	1252.9	1796.4	2739.8	4327.8	4789.3	Net Assets ($mil)

Risk Analysis

Time Period	Load-Adj Return %	Risk % Rank All	Risk % Rank Obj	Morningstar Return	Morningstar Risk	Morningstar Risk-Adj Rating
1 Yr	-10.35					
3 Yr	7.89	26	50	1.30[3]	0.53	★★★★
5 Yr	10.09	48	73	1.38[3]	0.63	★★★★
10 Yr	11.41	36	42	0.93	0.53	★★★★
Average Historical Rating (109 months)					4.1	★s

[1] 1 = low, 100 = high   [2] 1.00 = Hybrid Avg   [3] 1.00 = 90-day T-bill return

Other Measures

		Standard S&P 500	Best Fit FB HY
Standard Deviation	5.51	Alpha	4.8	-1.4
Mean	9.23	Beta	0.35	0.99
Sharpe Ratio	1.04	R-Squared	24	60

Investment Style

Stocks	Port Avg	Rel S&P 500
Price/Earnings Ratio	14.4	0.78
Price/Book Ratio	2.1	0.63
5 Yr Earnings Gr %	-1.8	-0.33
Med Mkt Cap ($mil)	6538	0.50

Bonds	
Avg Effective Duration	4.5 Yrs
Avg Effective Maturity	7.5 Yrs
Avg Credit Quality	BB
Avg Weighted Coupon	8.75%

Diversification Value for Portfolio Types

Large Cap: High	Small Cap: High	Bond: Medium	Balanced: Medium	Diversified: Medium

Portfolio 10-31-94

Share Chg (05-94)000	Amount 000	Total Stocks: 45 / Total Fixed-Income: 151	Date of Maturity	Value $000	% Net Assets
	188000	Govt of Canada 8%	06-01-23	120927	2.45
	120000	US Treasury Note 7.5%	11-15-01	119137	2.41
	110000	US Treasury Note 6.375%	08-15-02	101613	2.06
	100000	US Treasury Bond 8.125%	08-15-21	100406	2.03
	100000	US Treasury Bond 7.875%	02-15-21	97594	1.98
	1000	Chemical Bank Cv Pfd $5.00		72500	1.47
	385838	Escom 11%	06-01-08	67122	1.36
150	1125	Bristol-Myers Squibb		65695	1.33
25	850	American Home Products		53975	1.09
600	2350	Pacific Gas & Electric		52875	1.07
0	1600	Texas Utilities		52200	1.06
0	850	Philip Morris		52063	1.05
215	1565	American Electric Power		50083	1.01
	100000	Republic of Argentina 4%	03-31-23	46875	0.95
0	1580	Florida Progress		46212	0.94
0	2325	Southern		45919	0.93
	350	Citicorp Cv ARP		45894	0.93
	50000	US Treasury Bond 7.25%	08-15-22	45547	0.92
0	1358	FPL Group		44994	0.91
	1020	McDermott Intl C Cv Pfd $2.875		44128	0.89

Index Allocation

	% of Stocks
S&P 500	65.4
S&P MidCap 400	11.5
U.S. Small Cap	6.7
Foreign	16.5

Composition % 09-30-94

Cash	16.1	Preferreds	0.5
Stocks	22.0	Convertibles	20.7
Bonds	40.7	Other	0.0

Tax Analysis

	Tax-Adj Historical Return %	% Pretax Return
3 Yr Avg	6.02	61.5
5 Yr Avg	7.37	62.0
10 Yr Avg	7.68	52.7
Potential Capital Gain Exposure (% of assets)		-5%

Most Similar Funds in MF500

Seligman Income A	Fair Fit
Fidelity Asset Manager	Fair Fit
Phoenix High-Yield A	Fair Fit

Bond Credit Analysis 09-30-94

% of Bonds			
US Govt	0	BB	6
AAA	25	B	33
AA	0	Below B	8
A	0	NR/NA	25
BBB	4		

Stock Sector Weightings

	% of Stocks	Relative S&P 500
Utilities	57.9	4.67
Energy	0.6	0.06
Financials	1.5	0.14
Industrial Cyclicals	11.3	0.69
Consumer Durables	0.0	0.00
Consumer Staples	4.9	0.39
Services	3.5	0.43
Retail	0.0	0.00
Health	17.7	2.04
Technology	2.7	0.29

Min Initial Purchase / Expenses

Min Initial Purchase	$100 (Addt'l: $25)
Min IRA Purchase	None (Addt'l: None)
Min Auto Invest Plan	$25 (Systematic Inv: $25)

Expenses & Fees

Sales Fees	4.25% front
	0.00% deferred
	0.15% 12b-1
Management Fee	0.63% max./0.40% min.
3-,5-,10-yr Expense Projections	$64, $79, $125
Annual Brokerage Cost	0.03%

Franklin Insured Tax-Free Inc

	Ticker	Load	NAV	Yield	SEC Yield	Assets	Objective
	FTFIX	4.25%	11.54	6.2%	5.54%	1621.4	Muni Nat

Franklin Insured Tax-Free Income Fund seeks current income exempt from federal income taxes, consistent with preservation of capital.

The fund invests at least 80% of its net assets in securities that generate interest exempt from federal income taxes. It may not invest more than 25% of its assets in the municipal securities of a single state or territory. The fund's municipal securities are insured by the issuer or by an independent insurance agency.

Manager's Investment Style

Manager Don Duerson not only buys insured bonds, but also attempts to further mitigate volatility by only buying the most-liquid bonds, because the muni market can often be highly illiquid. He has kept the fund's yield competitive despite the fund's conservatism by holding onto older bonds from the late 1980s which currently offer premium income streams.

Fund Manager(s)

Donald S. Duerson et al. BS, U. of Arizona 1956
Andrew R. Johnson. BA, U. of Virginia 1952 BS, U. of Virginia 1954 JD, U. of Virginia 1970

Manager Experience	Dates Managed	Invest Obj	Std Dev	+/- Index
Andrew R. Johnson				
Franklin CA Tax-Free Inc	03/77 - 12/94	MC	7.59	-3.70
Franklin Fed Tax-Free Inc	10/83 - 12/94	MN	5.89	-1.03

Historical Profile

Return	Average
Risk	Below Average
Rating ★★★★	Above Average

Investment Style History
Fixed Income

Income Rtn % Rank Obj

| 32 | 8 | 23 | 22 | 30 | 20 | 15 | 12 |

Growth of $10,000

|||| Value of Fund ($000)
— Value of Index ($000)
LB Muni
▼ Manager Change
▽ Partial Manager Change
► Mgr Unknown After
◄ Mgr Unknown Before

Performance Quartile (Within Objective)

	1983	1984	1985	1986	1987	1988	1989	1990	1991	1992	1993	1994	History
NAV	---	---	10.79	11.87	10.64	11.10	11.36	11.28	11.75	12.04	12.70	11.54	NAV
	---	---	10.74 *	19.27	-3.08	12.80	9.99	6.57	11.35	9.20	11.84	-3.58	Total Return %
	---	---		4.03	-5.84	4.92	-4.56	-2.38	-4.65	1.95	2.09	-0.66	+/- LB Aggregate
	---	---		-0.04	-4.58	2.64	-0.80	-0.74	-0.80	0.38	-0.44	2.02	+/- LB Muni
	---	---	2.95	8.43	7.27	8.48	7.64	7.27	7.18	6.73	6.36	5.55	Income Return %
	---	---	7.79	10.85	-10.35	4.32	2.34	-0.70	4.17	2.47	5.48	-9.13	Capital Return %
	---	---		24	81	39	74	27	81	30	52	49	Total Rtn % Rank All
	---	---		30	90	20	35	38	55	25	46	29	Total Rtn % Rank Obj
	---	---	0.28	0.85	0.85	0.85	0.81	0.79	0.77	0.76	0.73	0.71	Income $
	---	---	0.00	0.08	0.00	0.00	0.00	0.00	0.00	0.00	0.00	0.00	Capital Gains $
	---	---		0.24	0.72	0.62	0.58	0.54	0.53	0.53	0.53	0.52	Expense Ratio %
	---	---		6.29	6.14	7.03	7.01	6.92	6.95	6.55	6.22	5.79	Income Ratio %
	---	---		98	19	6	13	12	10	6	8	7	Turnover Rate %
	---	---	18.8	141.0	285.6	489.2	696.4	819.1	1072.2	1432.5	1807.3	1621.4	Net Assets ($mil)

Performance 12-31-94

	1st Qtr	2nd Qtr	3rd Qtr	4th Qtr	Total
1987	1.10	-5.96	-4.47	6.71	-3.08
1988	3.03	2.86	3.39	2.96	12.80
1989	1.07	5.68	-0.18	3.15	9.99
1990	0.28	2.27	-0.02	3.94	6.57
1991	2.69	2.05	3.54	2.62	11.35
1992	0.79	3.64	2.41	2.08	9.20
1993	3.63	2.82	3.32	1.59	11.84
1994	-4.22	0.75	0.90	-0.97	-3.58

Bear Market Performance

Decile Rank (5-year period)

Worst   Best

	Worst 3 Mo Period 1985-89	Worst 3 Mo Period 1990-94
Franklin Insured Tax-Free Inc	---	-4.73
+/- LB Aggregate	---	0.21
+/- Best Fit Index : LB Muni	---	1.03

Trailing Returns

	Total Return %	+/- LB Aggregate	+/- LB Muni	% Rank All	% Rank Obj	Growth of $10,000
3 Mo	-0.97	-1.35	0.47	43	28	9,903
6 Mo	-0.08	-1.07	1.17	58	18	9,992
1 Yr	-3.58	-0.66	2.02	49	29	9,642
3 Yr Avg	5.60	1.05	0.73	38	10	11,775
5 Yr Avg	6.92	-0.71	0.14	52	15	13,972
10 Yr Avg	---	---	---	---	---	---
15 Yr Avg	---	---	---	---	---	---

Operations

Address and Telephone	777 Mariners Island Boulevard
	San Mateo, CA 94403-7777
	800-342-5236 / 415-312-2000
Advisor	Franklin Advisers
Subadvisor	None
Distributor	Franklin/Templeton Distributors
States Available	All plus PR
Report Grade	C+
Income Distrib	Paid Monthly
* Date of Inception	04-03-85
Fiscal Year End	February

Risk Analysis

Time Period	Load-Adj Return %	Risk % Rank All	Risk % Rank Obj	Morningstar Return	Morningstar Risk	Morningstar Risk-Adj Rating
1 Yr	-7.68					
3 Yr	4.08	13	22	1.08	0.77	★★★★
5 Yr	5.99	12	32	1.02	0.84	★★★★
10 Yr	---	---	---	---	---	

Average Historical Rating (81 months)   2.4 ★s

[1] 1 = low, 100 = high   [2] 1.00 = Muni Avg   [3] 1.00 = 90-day T-bill return

Other Measures

			Standard LB Agg	Best Fit LB Muni
Standard Deviation	4.94	Alpha	1.1	0.8
Mean	5.58	Beta	0.91	0.87
Sharpe Ratio	0.42	R-Squared	55	94

Investment Style

Interest-Rate Stance

Avg Effective Maturity   21.3 Yrs

Quality

Avg Credit Quality   AAA

Avg Weighted Coupon   7.05%
Avg Weighted Price 102.74% of Par

Diversification Value for Portfolio Types

| Large Cap: Medium | Small Cap: High | Bond: Low | Balanced: Medium | Diversified: Medium |

Min Initial Purchase	$100 (Addt'l: $25)
Min IRA Purchase	None (Addt'l: None)
Min Auto Invest Plan	$25 (Systematic Inv: $25)

Expenses & Fees

Sales Fees	4.25% front
	0.00% deferred
	0.10% 12b-1
Management Fee	0.63% max./0.45% min.
3-,5-,10-yr Expense Projections	$62, $76, $117

Portfolio 10-31-94

Amount 000	Date of Maturity	Total Stocks: 0 Total Fixed-Income: 649	Value $000	% Net Assets
15000	09-01-20	CA Corona COP Comnty Hosp 7%	19188	1.16
18500	07-01-20	AK Engy Util 6.75%	18654	1.13
15950	01-01-19	WA Snohomish PUD #1 Elec 7.375%	17015	1.03
15560	07-01-21	AK Engy Bradley Lake Hydro Proj 7.25%	16518	1.00
14000	01-01-11	WA Spokane Regl Solid Waste Mgmt 7.625	15395	0.93
12720	04-01-14	OH Montgomery Hosp Fac 7.5%	13587	0.82
12555	06-01-20	MA Hlth/Educ Fac Fallon Care Sys 6.75%	12611	0.76
11300	11-15-18	PA Philadelphia Muni Lease 7.125%	12477	0.75
14000	07-01-13	OK Comanche Meml Hosp 5.5%	12144	0.73
13000	06-15-21	NY New York City Muni Wtr Fin Swr 6.2%	12136	0.73
10965	07-01-21	TX Tarrant Hsg Fin Sngl Fam Mtg 8%	11623	0.70
12230	01-01-17	TX Coastal Bend Hlth Fac Dev 6.3%	11560	0.70
11560	08-01-24	WV Harrison Solid Waste Disp 6.75%	11255	0.68
10000	08-15-20	IN Hlth Fac Fin 7.75%	11245	0.68
10000	11-15-11	PA Philadelphia Muni Justice Lease 7.1%	11027	0.67
10000	07-01-18	IN Indianapolis Arpt 8.3%	10897	0.66
9900	02-01-16	TX San Antonio Elec/Gas Sys 8%	10888	0.66
10000	08-01-05	AZ COP Muni Fin Prog Ser 26 7.7%	10772	0.65
10650	07-01-25	MA Hlth/Educ Fac New England M/C 6.625	10437	0.63
10000	11-01-09	IA Polk Catholic Hlth Mercy Ctr 7.1%	10396	0.63

Credit Analysis % of Bonds 09-30-94

US Govt	0	BB	0
AAA	100	B	0
AA	0	Below B	0
A	0	NR/NA	0
BBB	0		

Composition % of Assets 09-30-94

Cash	2.0	Preferreds	0.0
Stocks	0.0	Convertibles	0.0
Bonds	98.0	Other	0.0

Tax Analysis

	Tax-Adj Historical Return %	% Pretax Return
3 Yr Avg	5.60	100.0
5 Yr Avg	6.92	100.0
10 Yr Avg	---	---
Potential Capital Gain Exposure (% of assets)		1%

Most Similar Funds in MF500

Franklin Fed Tax-Free Income	Strong Fit
American Cap Muni Bond A	Strong Fit
Dreyfus Intermediate Muni	Strong Fit

Coupon Range

	% Bonds	Rel Obj
0%	0.0	0.00
0% to 6.8%	42.7	0.71
6.8% to 7.5%	28.9	1.87
7.5% to 8.3%	23.7	2.67
More than 8.3%	4.5	0.51
Not applicable	0.2	0.06

Sector Weightings

	% Bonds	Rel Obj
General Obl	10.95	0.52
Utilities	15.00	1.20
Health	23.30	1.77
Water/Waste	12.50	1.96
Housing	6.10	0.83
Education	6.13	0.96
Transportation	4.07	0.40
COP/Lease	10.12	3.17
Private	8.46	0.73
Misc Revenue	3.36	0.68
Demand	0.02	0.01

Top 5 States % of Bonds

WA	10.21	NY	5.52
TX	9.99	MA	5.48
IL	6.40		

MORNINGSTAR   1995 Mutual Fund 500

Franklin Rising Dividends

	Ticker	Load	NAV	Yield	SEC Yield	Assets	Objective
	FRDPX	4.50%	14.29	1.9%	2.10%	239.7	Growth/Inc.

Franklin Rising Dividends Fund seeks capital appreciation. Preservation of capital is also a consideration.

The fund invests at least 65% of its assets in common stocks and convertible securities. To be considered for selection, companies must have most or all of the following characteristics: consistent and substantial dividend increases, reinvested earnings, strong balance sheets, and attractive prices. The fund's managers also consider factors such as return on equity, price/earnings ratios, and earnings growth.

Prior to June 28, 1988, the fund was named LF Rothschild Managed Trust Rising Dividends.

Manager's Investment Style

Management chooses stocks based on five specific screens. The company must have raised its dividend in at least eight of the past 10 years, and never cut the dividend in that time. The total for these dividend increases over 10 years must have been at least 100%. The firm must have high reinvested earnings and a strong balance sheet. Finally, the stock must be selling in the lower half of its 10-year price/earnings range. These criteria ensure that the fund will own large and midsized dividend-paying companies that have suffered recent setbacks.

Fund Manager(s)

William J. Lippman, since 1987. Birthdate: 02-25. BBA, City C. of New York MBA, New York U.
Bruce C. Baughman, since 1987. Birthdate: 03-48. BA, Stanford U. 1970 MS, New York U. 1979

Manager Experience	Dates Managed	Invest Obj	Std Dev	+/- Index
William J. Lippman				
Franklin Bal Sheet Invmt	04/90 - 12/94	G	12.02	3.20
Bruce C. Baughman				
Franklin Bal Sheet Invmt	04/90 - 12/94	G	12.02	3.20

Historical Profile
Return	Below Average
Risk	Below Average
Rating ★★	Below Average

Investment Style History Equity
Average % Stocks Held in Portfolio

Growth of $10,000
|||| Value of Fund ($000)
— Value of Index ($000) S&P 500
▼ Manager Change
▽ Partial Manager Change
► Mgr Unknown After
◄ Mgr Unknown Before

Performance Quartile (Within Objective)

	1983	1984	1985	1986	1987	1988	1989	1990	1991	1992	1993	1994	History
	---	---	---	---	8.70	10.01	11.58	11.21	14.91	16.18	15.36	14.29	NAV
	---	---	---	---	-11.52 *	18.94	19.60	0.26	35.95	10.38	-3.50	-5.17	Total Return %
	---	---	---	---	-8.58 *	2.33	-12.09	3.38	5.46	2.76	-13.55	-6.48	+/- S&P 500
	---	---	---	---		0.99	-9.58	6.44	1.74	1.41	-14.78	-5.10	+/- Wilshire 5000
	---	---	---	---	1.65	3.88	3.91	3.46	2.94	1.86	1.57	1.80	Income Return %
	---	---	---	---	-13.17	15.06	15.68	-3.20	33.01	8.52	-5.07	-6.97	Capital Return %
	---	---	---	---		16	36	55	18	20	100	65	Total Rtn % Rank All
	---	---	---	---		27	73	17	13	26	99	88	Total Rtn % Rank Obj
	---	---	---	---	0.19	0.32	0.36	0.39	0.30	0.26	0.26	0.28	Income $
	---	---	---	---	0.00	0.00	0.00	0.00	0.00	0.00	0.00	0.00	Capital Gains $
	---	---	---	---	1.79	1.62	1.70	1.60	1.53	1.46	1.40	1.43	Expense Ratio %
	---	---	---	---	3.06	3.44	3.28	2.99	2.16	1.67	1.73	1.81	Income Ratio %
	---	---	---	---		18	27	29	17	13	11	26	Turnover Rate %
	---	---	---	---	37.5	31.0	40.5	39.9	71.4	197.8	341.9	239.7	Net Assets ($mil)

Average % Stocks Held: 74% | 86% | 80% | 91% | 78% | 82% | 77% | 88%

Performance 12-31-94

	1st Qtr	2nd Qtr	3rd Qtr	4th Qtr	Total
1987	---	0.60	3.01	-14.71	-11.52 *
1988	12.16	4.90	1.70	-0.61	18.94
1989	5.34	7.33	5.16	0.59	19.60
1990	-1.92	3.05	-12.72	13.66	0.26
1991	17.36	3.09	5.92	6.08	35.95
1992	-1.04	1.05	4.57	5.56	10.38
1993	-1.70	-3.45	1.74	-0.06	-3.50
1994	-7.12	1.27	2.78	-1.91	-5.17

Bear Market Performance

Decile Rank (5-year period)

Worst — Best

	Worst 3 Mo Period 1985-89	Worst 3 Mo Period 1990-94
Franklin Rising Dividends	---	-13.64
+/- S&P 500	---	0.20
+/- Best Fit Index : S&P 500	---	0.20

Trailing Returns

	Total Return %	+/- S&P 500	+/- Wil 5000	% Rank All	% Rank Obj	Growth of $10,000
3 Mo	-1.91	-1.89	-1.14	67	60	9,809
6 Mo	0.82	-4.04	-3.80	41	79	10,082
1 Yr	-5.17	-6.48	-5.10	65	88	9,483
3 Yr Avg	0.34	-5.93	-6.27	96	95	10,102
5 Yr Avg	6.61	-2.09	-2.21	60	79	13,769
10 Yr Avg	---	---	---	---	---	---
15 Yr Avg	---	---	---	---	---	---

Operations

Address and Telephone	777 Mariners Island Boulevard
	San Mateo, CA 94404-7777
	800-342-5236 / 415-312-2000
Advisor	Franklin Advisers
Subadvisor	None
Distributor	Franklin/Templeton Distributors
States Available	All except NH
Report Grade	B
Income Distrib	Paid Quarterly
* Date of Inception	01-14-87
Fiscal Year End	September

Risk Analysis

Time Period	Load-Adj Return %	Risk % Rank [1] All	Risk % Rank [1] Obj	Morningstar [2] Return	Morningstar [2] Risk	Morningstar Risk-Adj Rating
1 Yr	-9.44					
3 Yr	-1.19	69	64	-1.32 [3]	0.78	★
5 Yr	5.63	59	22	0.21 [3]	0.70	★★★
10 Yr	---					

Average Historical Rating (60 months)   3.6 ★s

[1] = low, 100 = high [2] 1.00 = Equity Avg   [3] 1.00 = 90-day T-bill return

Other Measures

				Standard S&P 500	Best Fit S&P 500
Standard Deviation	6.99	Alpha		-4.9	-4.9
Mean	0.58	Beta		0.73	0.73
Sharpe Ratio	-0.42	R-Squared		69	69

Investment Style

	Stock Portfolio Avg	Relative S&P 500
Price/Earnings Ratio	15.0	0.81
Price/Book Ratio	3.0	0.88
5 Yr Earnings Gr %	8.7	1.56
Return on Assets %	8.9	1.19
Debt % Total Cap	18.3	0.65
Med Mkt Cap ($mil)	3413	0.26

Style Value Blend Growth Size Large Med Small

Diversification Value for Portfolio Types

Large Cap: Low	Small Cap: Low	Bond: High	Balanced: Low	Diversified: Low

Expenses & Fees

Sales Fees	4.50% front
	0.00% deferred
	0.50% 12b-1
Management Fee	0.75% max./0.50% min.
3-,5-,10-yr Expense Projections	$83, $114, $201
Annual Brokerage Cost	0.09%

Min Initial Purchase	$100 (Addt'l: $25)
Min IRA Purchase	None (Addt'l: None)
Min Auto Invest Plan	$25 (Systematic Inv: $25)

Portfolio 10-31-94

Total Stocks: 49
Total Fixed-Income: 0

Share Chg (05-94) 000	Amount 000		Value $000	% Net Assets
-10	142	Philip Morris	8698	2.78
0	376	Dibrell Brothers	8178	2.61
-50	332	Arnold Industries	7728	2.47
-97	255	Mercury General	7650	2.44
-20	387	TrustCo Bank New York	7643	2.44
-50	283	UST (Inc)	7500	2.39
-110	292	Rite Aid	7015	2.24
-10	181	Merck	6471	2.06
-15	85	Schering-Plough	6056	1.93
0	86	Chubb	6009	1.92
-7	234	Wilmington Trust	5850	1.87
-8	100	Bristol-Myers Squibb	5838	1.86
-25	313	Hanson (ADR)	5833	1.86
7	140	Walgreen	5827	1.86
-5	75	Monsanto	5709	1.82
0	152	Torchmark	5605	1.79
-20	260	Mercantile Bankshares (MD)	5460	1.74
20	210	Selective Insurance Group	5303	1.69
126	252	Newell	5292	1.69
-87	226	National Commerce Bancorp	5212	1.66
32	68	FNMA	5168	1.65
5	178	Banc One	5131	1.64
-60	369	Stride Rite	5117	1.63
-15	150	Melville	5006	1.60
0	67	Pfizer	4966	1.58

Composition % 09-30-94

Cash	11.0	Preferreds	0.0
Stocks	89.0	Convertibles	0.0
Bonds	0.0	Other	0.0

Tax Analysis

	Tax-Adj Historical Return %	% Pretax Return
3 Yr Avg	-0.30	---
5 Yr Avg	5.83	86.9
10 Yr Avg	---	---
Potential Capital Gain Exposure (% of assets)		-4%

Most Similar Funds in MF500

Dreyfus	Fair Fit
Vanguard U.S. Growth	Weak Fit
Nicholas	Weak Fit

Index Allocation

	% of Stocks
S&P 500	56.0
S&P MidCap 400	17.9
U.S. Small Cap	23.6
Foreign	4.5

Sector Weightings

	% of Stocks	Relative S&P 500
Utilities	0.0	0.00
Energy	2.0	0.20
Financials	39.9	3.77
Industrial Cyclicals	6.9	0.42
Consumer Durables	7.4	1.19
Consumer Staples	14.3	1.14
Services	7.0	0.86
Retail	11.2	1.92
Health	10.1	1.16
Technology	1.4	0.15

Franklin U.S. Government

	Ticker	Load	NAV	Yield	SEC Yield	Assets	Objective
	FKUSX	4.25%	6.42	7.8%	7.27%	10984.6	Gvt Mortgage

Franklin U.S. Government Securities Series seeks income.
The fund invests in U.S. government obligations such as U.S. Treasury obligations and securities issued by instrumentalities of the U.S. government, especially obligations of the Government National Mortgage Association (GNMA).

On Sept. 9, 1993, Franklin Pennsylvania Investors U.S. Government Securities Fund merged into this fund.

Manager's Investment Style

Despite its U.S. government moniker, this fund has been fashioned into a pure GNMA play. With all new monies, management buys current-coupon GNMAs; it doesn't attempt to play the direction of interest rates. As the portfolio's modest turnover indicates, management has held on to a number of older, seasoned mortgage-backeds that tout fat yields.

Fund Manager(s)

Jack Lemein, since 03-84.
David Capurro, since 1988.
Tony Coffey CFA(1992), since 09-93.

Manager Experience

	Dates Managed	Invest Obj	Std Dev	+/- Index
Jack Lemein				
Franklin Short-Interm Gov	04/87 - 12/94	GT	2.91	-1.17
Franklin Tax-Adv U.S. Gov	05/87 - 12/94	GM	4.12	-0.51

Historical Profile

Return	Average
Risk	Below Average
Rating	★★★★
	Above Average

Numbers along top: 14 6 4 2 10 17 12 10

Growth of $10,000

	Value of Fund ($000)
—	Value of Index ($000) LB Mtg
▼	Manager Change
▽	Partial Manager Change
►	Mgr Unknown After
◄	Mgr Unknown Before

Investment Style History
Fixed Income
Income Rtn % Rank Obj

Performance Quartile (Within Objective)

	1983	1984	1985	1986	1987	1988	1989	1990	1991	1992	1993	1994	History
	7.17	7.10	7.52	7.42	7.01	6.82	6.97	6.99	7.25	7.18	7.11	6.42	NAV
	9.14	12.88	19.97	10.74	4.32	7.45	13.11	10.78	13.71	7.41	6.91	-2.68	Total Return %
	0.77	-2.27	-2.15	-4.51	1.56	-0.43	-1.44	1.83	-2.29	0.16	-2.84	0.24	+/- LB Aggregate
	-0.99	-1.44	-5.24	-1.27	0.03	-1.27	-2.24	0.06	-2.01	0.45	0.08	-1.07	+/- LB Mortgage
	13.03	13.86	14.06	11.88	9.85	10.16	10.91	10.49	9.99	8.37	7.89	7.02	Income Return %
	-3.89	-0.98	5.92	-1.14	-5.53	-2.71	2.20	0.29	3.72	-0.97	-0.97	-9.70	Capital Return %
	84	13	73	81	26	77	53	3	64	53	84	40	Total Rtn % Rank All
	25	55	22	68	7	55	47	4	69	13	45	52	Total Rtn % Rank Obj
	0.94	0.90	0.90	0.84	0.71	0.70	0.70	0.68	0.65	0.58	0.55	0.50	Income $
	0.00	0.00	0.00	0.01	0.00	0.00	0.00	0.00	0.00	0.00	0.00	0.00	Capital Gains $
	0.73	0.60	0.57	0.54	0.52	0.53	0.52	0.52	0.52	0.53	0.52	0.55	Expense Ratio %
	8.28	11.70	11.06	9.93	9.49	9.85	9.99	9.72	9.26	8.46	7.71	7.37	Income Ratio %
	60	6	9	36	53	34	26	18	22	39	43	18	Turnover Rate %
	339.2	2116.9	6516.0	14400.0	12700.0	11649.9	11376.0	11388.2	13028.3	13631.9	13857.1	10984.6	Net Assets ($mil)

Performance 12-31-94

	1st Qtr	2nd Qtr	3rd Qtr	4th Qtr	Total
1987	2.45	-1.18	-1.52	4.63	4.32
1988	3.80	1.94	1.36	0.19	7.45
1989	1.09	6.72	1.21	3.59	13.11
1990	0.36	3.32	2.32	4.41	10.78
1991	2.72	2.34	4.23	3.78	13.71
1992	-0.23	3.51	3.12	0.86	7.41
1993	2.97	2.11	1.09	0.59	6.91
1994	-2.84	-1.06	0.75	0.48	-2.68

Bear Market Performance

Decile Rank (5-year period)

Worst ———————————— Best

	Worst 3 Mo Period 1985-89	Worst 3 Mo Period 1990-94
Franklin U.S. Government	-2.59	-4.36
+/- LB Aggregate	0.97	0.58
+/- Best Fit Index : LB Mtg	0.69	-0.36

Trailing Returns

	Total Return %	+/- LB Aggregate	+/- LB Mortgage	% Rank All	% Rank Obj	Growth of $10,000
3 Mo	0.48	0.10	0.05	12	17	10,048
6 Mo	1.24	0.24	-0.07	34	16	10,124
1 Yr	-2.68	0.24	-1.07	40	52	9,732
3 Yr Avg	3.77	-0.77	-0.21	74	28	11,175
5 Yr Avg	7.08	-0.55	-0.50	48	28	14,077
10 Yr Avg	9.02	-0.93	-1.33	72	27	23,710
15 Yr Avg	8.95	-1.85	-2.25	87	50	36,192

Operations

Address and Telephone	777 Mariners Island Boulevard
	San Mateo, CA 94403-7777
	800-342-5236 / 415-312-2000
Advisor	Franklin Advisers
Subadvisor	None
Distributor	Franklin/Templeton Distributors
States Available	All plus PR
Report Grade	B-
Income Distrib	Paid Monthly
Date of Inception	05-30-70
Fiscal Year End	September

Min Initial Purchase	$100 (Addt'l: $25)
Min IRA Purchase	None (Addt'l: None)
Min Auto Invest Plan	$25 (Systematic Inv: $25)

Expenses & Fees

Sales Fees	
	4.25% front
	0.00% deferred
	0.15% 12b-1
Management Fee	0.63% max./0.40% min.
3-,5-,10-yr Expense Projections	$63, $78, $122

Risk Analysis

Time Period	Load-Adj Return %	Risk % Rank [1] All	Risk % Rank [1] Obj	Morningstar [2] Return	Morningstar Risk	Morningstar Risk-Adj Rating
1 Yr	-6.82					
3 Yr	2.28	11	19	-0.37 [3]	0.79	★★★
5 Yr	6.15	6	17	0.34 [3]	0.66	★★★★
10 Yr	8.54	5	13	0.69 [3]	0.70	★★★★

Average Historical Rating (109 months) 3.3 ★ s

[1] 1 = low, 100 = high [2] 1.00 = Taxable Avg [3] 1.00 = 90-day T-bill return

Other Measures

		Standard LB Agg	Best Fit LB Mtg
Standard Deviation	3.17	Alpha	-0.5	-0.2
Mean	3.76	Beta	0.74	0.96
Sharpe Ratio	0.07	R-Squared	87	96

Investment Style

Interest-Rate Stance

Avg Effective Duration	5.1 Yrs
Avg Effective Maturity	9.0 Yrs

Quality

Avg Credit Quality	AAA
Avg Weighted Coupon	8.32%
Avg Weighted Price	96.67% of Par

Diversification Value for Portfolio Types

Large Cap: Medium	Small Cap: High	Bond: None	Balanced: Medium	Diversified: Medium

Portfolio 10-31-94

Total Stocks: 0
Total Fixed-Income: 36

Amount 000	Date of Maturity		Value $000	% Net Assets
2342574	12-15-22	GNMA 7%	2099532	18.45
2104498	12-15-22	GNMA 7.5%	1953951	17.17
1694892	12-15-22	GNMA 8%	1625200	14.28
1525107	12-15-22	GNMA 6.5%	1317311	11.57
666689	12-15-22	GNMA 9%	678805	5.96
573101	12-15-22	GNMA 10%	613430	5.39
545694	12-15-22	GNMA 8.5%	538903	4.73
371915	12-15-22	GNMA 10.5%	403379	3.54
380030	12-15-22	GNMA 9.5%	397283	3.49
289151	12-15-22	GNMA 12%	327032	2.87
250572	12-15-22	GNMA 12.5%	286214	2.51
219906	12-15-22	GNMA 13%	251868	2.21
196501	12-15-22	GNMA 11%	216618	1.90
64408	12-15-22	GNMA 11.5%	71979	0.63
35895	01-15-28	GNMA Project Loan 7.375%	32247	0.28
36738	12-15-22	GNMA Project Loan 6.75%	31503	0.28
32664	12-15-22	GNMA Project Loan 6.5%	27478	0.24
23057	12-15-24	GNMA GPM 11%	24959	0.22
25145	12-15-22	GNMA Project Loan 8.25%	23923	0.21
24749	12-15-22	GNMA Project Loan 8%	23186	0.20
24509	12-15-22	GNMA 6%	20312	0.18
21465	12-15-22	GNMA Project Loan 7.425%	19389	0.17
16829	12-15-22	GNMA Project Loan 9.25%	16829	0.15
12135	12-15-22	GNMA GPM 11.25%	13220	0.12
11542	12-15-22	GNMA GPM 10.25%	12161	0.11

Composition % 09-30-94

Cash	3.2	Preferreds	0.0
Stocks	0.0	Convertibles	0.0
Bonds	96.8	Other	0.0

Tax Analysis

	Tax-Adj Historical Return %	% Pretax Return
3 Yr Avg	0.90	23.2
5 Yr Avg	4.08	54.3
10 Yr Avg	5.20	48.2

Potential Capital Gain Exposure (% of assets) -13%

Most Similar Funds in MF500

Dreyfus GNMA	Strong Fit
T. Rowe Price GNMA	Strong Fit
Benham GNMA Income	Strong Fit

Coupon Range

	% of Bonds	Rel Obj
0%	0.0	0.00
0% to 8%	64.7	1.18
8% to 9%	11.3	0.52
9% to 10%	9.4	1.09
More than 10%	14.6	2.23
Not applicable	0.0	0.00

Sector Analysis 10-31-94

% of Bonds

US Treas	0	CMOs	0
GNMA mtgs	100	ARMs	0
FNMA mtgs	0	Other	0
FHLMC mtgs	0		

MORNINGSTAR 1995 Mutual Fund 500

Franklin Utilities

Ticker	Load	NAV	Yield	SEC Yield	Assets	Objective
FKUTX	4.25%	8.47	6.2%	6.04%	2543.3	Sp.-Util

Franklin Utilities Series seeks capital appreciation and current income.

The fund primarily invests in dividend-paying common stocks in the public-utilities industry. This industry includes companies engaged in the manufacture, production, transmission, and sale of gas and electric energy, as well as those engaged in communications activities, including the telephone, telegraph, satellite, and microwave areas, but excluding public broadcasting.

Manager's Investment Style

Management places a heavy emphasis on electric-utilities stocks, but will also hold utilities bonds. Management allocates assets based on the yield spread between electric-utilities stocks and the 30-year Treasury, and chooses exposure to utilities subsectors using relative-valuation models. Management seeks stocks with reliable earnings, good regulatory relationships, and ability to succeed in a competitive environment.

Fund Manager(s)

Charles B. Johnson, since 01-57.
Greg Johnson, since 01-87.
Sally Edwards Haff CFA(1992), since 01-90.

Manager Experience	Dates Managed	Invest Obj	Std Dev	+/- Index
Charles B. Johnson				
Franklin Income	01/57 - 12/94	I	10.05	0.81
Franklin Global Utilities	07/92 - 12/94	SU	10.08	3.38

Historical Profile

Return	Below Average
Risk	Below Average
Rating ★★	
	Below Average

Average % Stocks Held in Portfolio: 88% 94% 95% 81% 77% 75% 77% 83%

Investment Style History
Equity
Average % Stocks Held in Portfolio

Growth of $10,000
- ‖‖‖ Value of Fund ($000)
- — Value of Index ($000) LB L-T
- ▼ Manager Change
- ▽ Partial Manager Change
- ► Mgr Unknown After
- ◄ Mgr Unknown Before

Performance Quartile (Within Objective)

	1983	1984	1985	1986	1987	1988	1989	1990	1991	1992	1993	1994	History
	5.64	6.24	7.09	8.18	7.19	7.44	8.69	8.11	9.40	9.66	10.19	8.47	NAV
	15.75	21.43	22.85	23.77	-5.49	11.64	25.83	0.38	24.18	9.08	11.47	-11.66	Total Return %
	-6.72	15.16	-8.88	5.09	-10.75	-4.97	-5.85	3.50	-6.31	1.47	1.41	-12.98	+/- S&P 500
	---	---	---	-4.68	-2.59	-6.41	-21.39	2.94	9.56	0.99	-2.97	-3.72	+/- S&P Util
	9.73	10.79	9.18	8.22	6.61	8.16	8.81	7.06	8.27	6.32	5.54	5.16	Income Return %
	6.02	10.64	13.68	15.54	-12.10	3.48	17.02	-6.67	15.91	2.77	5.93	-16.82	Capital Return %
	55	1	55	10	90	48	21	54	37	32	55	96	Total Rtn % Rank All
	20	28	62	33	60	83	64	36	20	46	65	88	Total Rtn % Rank Obj
	0.50	0.52	0.53	0.56	0.57	0.57	0.58	0.59	0.59	0.55	0.54	0.52	Income $
	0.00	0.00	0.00	0.01	0.00	0.00	0.01	0.01	0.00	0.00	0.04	0.01	Capital Gains $
	0.92	0.84	0.81	0.74	0.65	0.64	0.62	0.60	0.59	0.57	0.55	0.64	Expense Ratio %
	8.77	9.14	8.13	5.95	6.55	7.36	7.10	6.50	6.44	5.90	5.30	5.76	Income Ratio %
	0	2	7	3	0	2	4	2	1	1	8	6	Turnover Rate %
	24.1	28.9	59.6	461.3	587.4	608.3	748.4	865.0	1483.5	2440.3	3487.4	2543.3	Net Assets ($mil)

Performance 12-31-94

	1st Qtr	2nd Qtr	3rd Qtr	4th Qtr	Total
1987	2.53	-2.27	-0.76	-4.95	-5.49
1988	3.84	4.93	0.76	1.69	11.64
1989	-0.34	10.25	4.77	9.31	25.83
1990	-4.90	1.05	-5.41	10.44	0.38
1991	4.18	-0.29	10.28	8.41	24.18
1992	-4.69	6.46	5.61	1.79	9.08
1993	8.17	2.33	4.76	-3.86	11.47
1994	-9.94	-7.33	2.41	3.36	-11.66

Bear Market Performance

Decile Rank (5-year period)

Worst ———————————————— Best

	Worst 3 Mo Period 1985-89	Worst 3 Mo Period 1990-94
Franklin Utilities	-7.94	-9.94
+/- S&P 500	-13.94	-6.15
+/- Best Fit Index : LB L-T	-2.60	-3.83

Trailing Returns

	Total Return %	+/- S&P 500	+/- S&P Util	% Rank All	% Rank Obj	Growth of $10,000
3 Mo	3.36	3.37	3.46	2	2	10,336
6 Mo	5.85	0.99	5.48	9	3	10,585
1 Yr	-11.66	-12.98	-3.72	96	88	8,834
3 Yr Avg	2.41	-3.85	-2.01	89	82	10,742
5 Yr Avg	6.01	-2.68	1.09	76	63	13,390
10 Yr Avg	10.46	-3.93	---	54	50	27,031
15 Yr Avg	13.19	-1.29	---	36	1	64,175

Operations

Address and Telephone	777 Mariners Island Boulevard San Mateo, CA 94403-7777 800-342-5236 / 415-312-2000
Advisor	Franklin Advisers
Subadvisor	None
Distributor	Franklin/Templeton Distributors
States Available	All plus PR
Report Grade	B-
Income Distrib	Paid Quarterly
Date of Inception	09-30-48
Fiscal Year End	September

Risk Analysis

Time Period	Load-Adj Return %	Risk % Rank [1] All	Obj	Morningstar [2] Return	Morningstar Risk	Morningstar Risk-Adj Rating
1 Yr	-15.42					
3 Yr	0.94	77	78	-0.74 [3]	0.89	★★
5 Yr	5.10	58	57	0.09 [3]	0.68	★★
10 Yr	9.98	50	50	0.54 [3]	0.72	★★

Average Historical Rating (109 months): 3.6 ★s

[1] 1 = low, 100 = high [2] 1.00 = Equity Avg [3] 1.00 = 90-day T-bill return

Other Measures

	Standard S&P 500	Best Fit LB L-T
Standard Deviation	9.25	
Mean	2.82	
Sharpe Ratio	-0.08	
Alpha	-2.3	-2.6
Beta	0.58	0.95
R-Squared	25	63

Investment Style

	Stock Portfolio Avg	Relative S&P 500
Price/Earnings Ratio	14.7	0.80
Price/Book Ratio	1.5	0.45
5 Yr Earnings Gr %	-1.7	-0.30
Return on Assets %	3.6	0.49
Debt % Total Cap	43.5	1.54
Med Mkt Cap ($mil)	4417	0.34

Style Value Blend Growth / Size Large Med Small

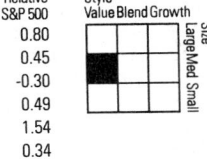

Diversification Value for Portfolio Types

Large Cap: High	Small Cap: High	Bond: Low	Balanced: Medium	Diversified: High

Portfolio 10-31-94

Share Chg (09-94)000	Amount 000	Total Stocks: 48 / Total Fixed-Income: 26	Value $000	% Net Assets
0	5857	Southern	115676	4.46
0	2823	Duke Power	111857	4.31
0	2854	Dominion Resources	105953	4.09
0	3205	Texas Utilities	104548	4.03
0	2886	American Electric Power	92355	3.56
0	3562	General Public Utilities	91722	3.54
0	2751	FPL Group	91127	3.51
0	3878	Central & Southwest	87255	3.36
	80000	US Treasury Bond 8%	79325	3.06
0	1834	SCANA	79109	3.05
0	3427	Pacific Gas & Electric	77104	2.97
-702	3709	Allegheny Power System	76960	2.97
0	3922	TECO Energy	75997	2.93
0	5285	SCEcorp	73334	2.83
0	3134	Entergy	73257	2.82
0	2364	GTE	72696	2.80
0	3676	Pennsylvania Power & Light	72142	2.78
0	2369	NIPSCO Industries	66047	2.55
0	2220	Florida Progress	64940	2.50
0	2063	New England Electric System	64725	2.50
0	3126	San Diego Gas & Electric	62512	2.41
0	2788	New York State Electric/Gas	52973	2.04
0	2158	CINergy	49899	1.92
0	1337	Pacific Telesis Group	42279	1.63
0	1337	AirTouch Communications	39940	1.54

Composition % 09-30-94

Cash	2.1	Preferreds	0.0
Stocks	85.5	Convertibles	0.0
Bonds	12.4	Other	0.0

Tax Analysis

	Tax-Adj Historical Return %	% Pretax Return
3 Yr Avg	0.29	11.8
5 Yr Avg	3.82	60.8
10 Yr Avg	7.73	64.9
Potential Capital Gain Exposure (% of assets)		-7%

Most Similar Funds in MF500

Stratton Monthly Dividend	Fair Fit
Fortress Utility	Weak Fit
Prudential Utility B	Weak Fit

Index Allocation

	% of Stocks
S&P 500	56.2
S&P MidCap 400	29.9
U.S. Small Cap	13.9
Foreign	0.0

Sector Weightings

	% of Stocks	Relative S&P 500
Utilities	93.3	7.53
Energy	0.0	0.00
Financials	0.0	0.00
Industrial Cyclicals	0.0	0.00
Consumer Durables	0.0	0.00
Consumer Staples	0.0	0.00
Services	4.8	0.59
Retail	0.0	0.00
Health	0.0	0.00
Technology	1.9	0.20

Expenses & Fees

Min Initial Purchase	$100 (Addt'l: $25)
Min IRA Purchase	None (Addt'l: None)
Min Auto Invest Plan	$25 (Systematic Inv: $25)

Sales Fees	
	4.25% front
	0.00% deferred
	0.15% 12b-1
Management Fee	0.63% max./0.40% min.
3-,5-,10-yr Expense Projections	$64, $80, $126
Annual Brokerage Cost	0.06%

MORNINGSTAR 1995 Mutual Fund 500

Fundamental Investors

	Ticker	Load	NAV	Yield	SEC Yield	Assets	Objective
	ANCFX	5.75%	17.50	2.5%	2.31%	2611.1	Growth/Inc.

Fundamental Investors seeks growth of capital and income return.

The fund invests primarily in common stocks. It may also invest in preferred stocks, corporate or government bonds, and similar securities with fixed-income characteristics. Straight debt securities are generally rated A or better, but the fund may invest up to 5% of its assets in lower-rated debt securities. In anticipation of generally declining markets, the fund may increase its investments in U.S. government securities and short-term money-market instruments or retain cash.

Historical Profile
Return Above Average
Risk Average
Rating ★★★★ Above Average

Investment Style History
Equity
Average % Stocks Held in Portfolio

Manager's Investment Style

Management targets undervalued large-cap stocks that boast strong earnings growth. Although the fund's charter allows it to invest in a number of different asset classes, management has done little more than dabble in nonstock areas: Allowed to invest up to 10% in high-yield bonds, management has remained well below that target. This is one of four growth-and-income funds offered by Capital Research and Management, and it is the most growth-oriented--and thus lowest yielding--of the lot.

Growth of $10,000
IIII Value of Fund ($000)
— Value of Index ($000) S&P 500
▼ Manager Change
▽ Partial Manager Change
► Mgr Unknown After
◄ Mgr Unknown Before

Performance Quartile (Within Objective)

1983	1984	1985	1986	1987	1988	1989	1990	1991	1992	1993	1994	History
12.17	11.94	14.36	14.21	13.45	14.60	16.43	14.32	17.47	17.52	18.15	17.50	NAV
26.22	5.84	30.21	22.13	3.77	15.95	28.56	-6.24	30.34	10.19	18.16	1.33	Total Return %
3.76	-0.43	-1.53	3.45	-1.49	-0.66	-3.12	-3.12	-0.14	2.57	8.10	0.01	+/- S&P 500
2.76	2.79	-2.35	6.03	1.41	-1.99	-0.61	-0.05	-3.87	1.22	6.87	1.40	+/- Wilshire 5000
4.77	3.73	3.51	2.81	2.54	3.61	3.97	3.16	2.71	2.47	2.43	2.46	Income Return %
21.46	2.11	26.70	19.32	1.23	12.35	24.59	-9.39	27.63	7.72	15.72	-1.14	Capital Return %
20	48	25	13	29	25	16	74	26	21	21	12	Total Rtn % Rank All
21	41	34	10	34	48	25	70	35	27	11	17	Total Rtn % Rank Obj
0.44	0.40	0.40	0.40	0.40	0.47	0.62	0.49	0.40	0.42	0.43	0.44	Income $
0.00	0.43	0.59	2.75	0.95	0.46	1.66	0.58	0.68	1.24	2.03	0.45	Capital Gains $
0.64	0.71	0.65	0.62	0.63	0.68	0.67	0.70	0.69	0.65	0.65	---	Expense Ratio %
3.48	3.46	3.22	2.53	2.42	2.97	3.40	3.15	2.50	2.56	2.43	---	Income Ratio %
21	16	20	19	12	8	19	12	17	24	29	---	Turnover Rate %
408.1	386.4	460.0	502.4	609.7	632.3	757.9	823.5	1155.6	1439.7	1979.3	2611.1	Net Assets ($mil)

Fund Manager(s)

James E. Drasdo, since 08-78.
Gordon Crawford, since 08-91.
Dina N. Perry, since 1993.

Manager Experience	Dates Managed	Invest Obj	Std Dev	+/- Index
James E. Drasdo				
Amcap	01/85 - 12/94	G	15.76	-1.41
Growth Fund of America	01/86 - 12/94	G	16.84	0.56

Performance 12-31-94

	1st Qtr	2nd Qtr	3rd Qtr	4th Qtr	Total
1987	20.92	4.92	5.06	-22.15	3.77
1988	4.92	9.35	-0.97	2.05	15.95
1989	7.75	8.08	12.42	-1.81	28.56
1990	0.22	4.53	-17.24	8.16	-6.24
1991	14.53	0.42	4.90	8.04	30.34
1992	0.20	0.57	2.20	6.99	10.19
1993	6.37	2.33	4.86	3.52	18.16
1994	-2.57	0.28	4.35	-0.61	1.33

Bear Market Performance

Decile Rank (5-year period)

Worst ——— Best

	Worst 3 Mo Period 1985-89	Worst 3 Mo Period 1990-94
Fundamental Investors	-29.37	-17.24
+/- S&P 500	0.22	-3.50
+/- Best Fit Index : S&P 500	0.22	-3.50

Trailing Returns

	Total Return %	+/- S&P 500	+/- Wil 5000	% Rank All	% Rank Obj	Growth of $10,000
3 Mo	-0.61	-0.59	0.16	36	35	9,939
6 Mo	3.72	-1.14	-0.91	17	33	10,372
1 Yr	1.33	0.01	1.40	12	17	10,133
3 Yr Avg	9.68	3.41	3.06	14	12	13,193
5 Yr Avg	10.02	1.33	1.21	17	14	16,123
10 Yr Avg	14.77	0.39	0.91	13	7	39,661
15 Yr Avg	15.34	0.85	1.36	10	7	85,023

Operations

Address and Telephone	4 Embarcadero Cntr P.O. Box 7650 San Francisco, CA 94120 800-421-4120 / 415-421-9360
Advisor	Capital Research & Management
Subadvisor	None
Distributor	American Funds Distributors
States Available	All plus GU,PR,VI
Report Grade	A
Income Distrib	Paid Quarterly
Date of Inception	01-01-33
Fiscal Year End	December

Risk Analysis

Time Period	Load-Adj Return %	Risk % Rank [1] All	Obj	Morningstar [2] Return	Morningstar Risk	Morningstar Risk-Adj Rating
1 Yr	-4.50					
3 Yr	7.53	59	26	1.19 [3]	0.65	★★★★
5 Yr	8.73	67	54	1.00 [3]	0.80	★★★
10 Yr	14.09	63	68	1.29	0.88	★★★★
Average Historical Rating (109 months)					4.0 ★s	

[1] 1 = low, 100 = high   [2] 1.00 = Equity Avg   [3] 1.00 = 90-day T-bill return

Other Measures

			Standard S&P 500	Best Fit S&P 500
Standard Deviation	8.00	Alpha	3.3	3.3
Mean	9.59	Beta	0.96	0.96
Sharpe Ratio	0.76	R-Squared	91	91

Investment Style

	Stock Portfolio Avg	Relative S&P 500
Price/Earnings Ratio	17.8	0.96
Price/Book Ratio	3.0	0.90
5 Yr Earnings Gr %	4.0	0.72
Return on Assets %	5.9	0.78
Debt % Total Cap	32.5	1.15
Med Mkt Cap ($mil)	8934	0.69

Diversification Value for Portfolio Types

Large Cap: None
Small Cap: Low
Bond: Medium
Balanced: None
Diversified: Low

Expenses & Fees

Sales Fees: 5.75% front / 0.00% deferred / 0.25% 12b-1
Management Fee: 0.39% max./0.28% min.
3-,5-,10-yr Expense Projections: $77, $92, $134
Annual Brokerage Cost: 0.17%

Min Initial Purchase $250 (Addt'l: $50)
Min IRA Purchase $250 (Addt'l: $50)
Min Auto Invest Plan $50 (Systematic Inv: $50)

Portfolio 09-30-94

Share Chg (06-94) 000	Amount 000	Total Stocks: 113 Total Fixed-Income: 14	Value $000	% Net Assets
0	1824	Time Warner	64068	2.58
200	805	IBM	55948	2.25
0	1100	News (ADR)	55688	2.24
25	1540	Phillips Petroleum	52745	2.12
0	600	Capital Cities/ABC	49200	1.98
0	825	Amoco	48881	1.97
400	800	Caterpillar	43300	1.74
200	675	Intel	41513	1.67
0	650	Federal Express	40219	1.62
0	400	American Cyanamid	39800	1.60
0	430	First Interstate Bancorp	34884	1.40
0	975	Houston Industries	34369	1.38
0	790	Citicorp	33575	1.35
200	575	Dun & Bradstreet	33063	1.33
0	600	Eastman Chemical	32625	1.31
0	516	Phelps Dodge	32050	1.29
50	360	ALCOA	30510	1.23
0	525	Textron	26709	1.07
40	475	Tribune	25650	1.03
-250	610	Parker-Hannifin	24324	0.98
100	800	Seagram	24200	0.97
26	75	CBS	24084	0.97
0	425	AT & T	22950	0.92
853	1004	Tele-Communications Cl A	22214	0.89
1000	7000	Citic Pacific	21652	0.87

Composition % 12-31-94

Cash	5.7	Preferreds	0.0
Stocks	87.0	Convertibles	2.9
Bonds	4.5	Other	0.0

Tax Analysis

	Tax-Adj Historical Return %	% Pretax Return
3 Yr Avg	6.82	68.5
5 Yr Avg	7.41	70.2
10 Yr Avg	11.60	67.3
Potential Capital Gain Exposure (% of assets)		12%

Most Similar Funds in MF500

Fidelity	Strong Fit
United Income	Strong Fit
Neuberger&Berman Guardian	Strong Fit

Index Allocation

	% of Stocks
S&P 500	85.4
S&P MidCap 400	3.0
U.S. Small Cap	6.4
Foreign	8.1

Sector Weightings

	% of Stocks	Relative S&P 500
Utilities	8.9	0.72
Energy	9.0	0.89
Financials	11.3	1.07
Industrial Cyclicals	19.4	1.18
Consumer Durables	5.1	0.83
Consumer Staples	5.9	0.47
Services	23.2	2.85
Retail	1.8	0.31
Health	5.8	0.66
Technology	9.6	1.05

G.T. Global Government Income A

	Ticker	Load	NAV	Yield	SEC Yield	Assets	Objective
	GGINX	4.75%	8.31	7.5%	6.70%	458.8	World Bond

G.T. Global Government Income Fund - Class A seeks current income; protection of value and capital appreciation are secondary objectives.

The fund normally invests at least 65% of its assets in high-quality debt obligations issued or guaranteed by the U.S. or foreign governments, including Japan, Canada, the Western European nations, New Zealand, and Australia, as well as in multi-national currency. It intends to protect capital by actively managing its maturity structure and currency exposure.

Class A shares have a front-end load; Class B shares carry a deferred load and a higher 12b-1 fee.

Manager's Investment Style

Manager Robert Allen alters the portfolio according to his outlook for interest rates worldwide. After the fund's early years as a moderate-duration player, management took interest-rate exposure out as far as possible, to get in on declining rates around the globe. More recently, as the fund suffered an interest-rate backlash, management has been pulling in duration. Meanwhile, country exposure is typically widespread, though management tended to hedge currency exposure back into the dollar. In the recent about-face, however, management has moderated country exposure and added non-dollar currencies, in the wake of a falling Greenback.

Fund Manager(s)

Robert Allen et al.

Manager Experience	Dates Managed	Invest Obj	Std Dev	+/- Index
Gary H. Kreps				
Putnam Global Govtl Inc A	01/89 - 01/92	WB	6.69	-0.01

Historical Profile
Return	Below Average
Risk	Below Average
Rating	★★★
	Neutral

Investment Style History
Fixed Income

Income Rtn % Rank Obj

Growth of $10,000
- |||| Value of Fund ($000)
- — Value of Index ($000) LB L-T
- ▼ Manager Change
- ▽ Partial Manager Change
- ► Mgr Unknown After
- ◄ Mgr Unknown Before

Performance Quartile (Within Objective)

	1983	1984	1985	1986	1987	1988	1989	1990	1991	1992	1993	1994	History
	---	---	---	---	---	10.70	10.61	10.31	10.47	9.72	10.40	8.31	NAV
	---	---	---	---	---	1.12 *	11.24	8.67	13.67	1.95	25.52	-14.39	Total Return %
	---	---	---	---	---	---	-3.30	-0.27	-2.33	-5.30	15.77	-11.47	+/- LB Aggregate
	---	---	---	---	---	---	14.67	-6.62	-2.57	-2.83	10.41	-21.09	+/- SB World Govt
	---	---	---	---	---	6.51	7.11	11.50	12.12	9.11	14.20	5.71	Income Return %
	---	---	---	---	---	-5.39	4.13	-2.83	1.55	-7.16	11.33	-20.10	Capital Return %
	---	---	---	---	---	---	63	11	64	87	11	98	Total Rtn % Rank All
	---	---	---	---	---	---	8	81	51	52	8	86	Total Rtn % Rank Obj
	---	---	---	---	---	0.72	0.70	1.15	1.16	0.94	1.31	0.63	Income $
	---	---	---	---	---	0.12	0.50	0.00	0.00	0.00	0.39	0.00	Capital Gains $
	---	---	---	---	---	---	1.74	1.75	1.59	1.57	1.40	1.29	Expense Ratio %
	---	---	---	---	---	---	10.74	11.43	9.52	9.03	7.10	6.30	Income Ratio %
	---	---	---	---	---	---	413	334	326	351	495	652	Turnover Rate %
	---	---	---	---	---	66.4	146.2	287.1	433.2	605.6	719.6	458.8	Net Assets ($mil)

Performance 12-31-94

	1st Qtr	2nd Qtr	3rd Qtr	4th Qtr	Total
1987	---	---	---	---	---
1988	---	-2.46	0.95	2.70	1.12 *
1989	-1.70	5.16	2.12	5.37	11.24
1990	-2.94	4.67	2.94	3.91	8.67
1991	1.92	0.08	5.41	5.72	13.67
1992	-1.73	2.41	0.27	1.02	1.95
1993	6.83	5.77	5.73	5.07	25.52
1994	-8.76	-3.99	-1.20	-1.09	-14.39

Bear Market Performance

Decile Rank (5-year period)

Worst — Best

	Worst 3 Mo Period 1985-89	Worst 3 Mo Period 1990-94
G.T. Global Government Income	---	-10.91
+/- LB Aggregate	---	-5.97
+/- Best Fit Index : LB L-T	---	-1.52

Trailing Returns

	Total Return %	+/- LB Aggregate	+/- SB World	% Rank All	% Rank Obj	Growth of $10,000
3 Mo	-1.09	-1.47	-1.66	46	71	9,891
6 Mo	-2.28	-3.27	-4.51	90	92	9,772
1 Yr	-14.39	-11.47	-21.09	98	86	8,561
3 Yr Avg	3.09	-1.46	-5.68	84	64	10,955
5 Yr Avg	6.24	-1.39	-5.28	70	75	13,533
10 Yr Avg	---	---	---	---	---	---
15 Yr Avg	---	---	---	---	---	---

Operations

Address and Telephone	50 California Street 27th Floor San Francisco, CA 94111 800-824-1580 / 415-392-6181	
Advisor	G.T. Capital Management	
Subadvisor	None	
Distributor	G.T. Global Financial Services	
States Available	All	
Report Grade	B+	
Income Distrib	Paid Monthly	
* Date of Inception	03-29-88	
Fiscal Year End	October	

Risk Analysis

Time Period	Load-Adj Return %	Risk % Rank [1] All	Obj	Morningstar [2] Return	Morningstar Risk	Morningstar Risk-Adj Rating
1 Yr	-18.46					
3 Yr	1.43	64	80	-0.61 [3]	0.95	★★
5 Yr	5.21	49	66	0.11 [3]	0.65	★★★
10 Yr	---					

Average Historical Rating (46 months) 3.2 ★ s

[1] 1 = low, 100 = high [2] 1.00 = Hybrid Avg [3] 1.00 = 90-day T-bill return

Other Measures

				Standard LB Agg	Best Fit LB L-T
Standard Deviation	7.80	Alpha		-1.4	-1.5
Mean	3.35	Beta		1.19	0.66
Sharpe Ratio	-0.02	R-Squared		38	43

Investment Style

Interest-Rate Stance
Avg Effective Maturity 6.3 Yrs

Not Available

Quality
Avg Credit Quality ---

Avg Weighted Coupon 7.21%

Diversification Value for Portfolio Types

Large Cap: High	Small Cap: High	Bond: Medium	Balanced: High	Diversified: High

Expenses & Fees
Min Initial Purchase	$500 (Addt'l: $100)
Min IRA Purchase	$100 (Addt'l: $25)
Min Auto Invest Plan	$100 (Systematic Inv: $100)

Sales Fees	4.75% front
	0.00% deferred
	0.35% 12b-1
Management Fee	0.73% max./0.65% min.
3-,5-,10-yr Expense Projections	$90, $121, $207

Portfolio 12-31-94

Total Stocks: 0
Total Fixed-Income: 15

Amount 000	Date of Maturity		Value $000	% Net Assets
51413	07-15-03	Govt of Netherlands 6.5%	30831	6.72
41830	04-15-00	Govt of Australia 7%	28483	6.21
19008	08-10-99	United Kingdom Treasury 6%	26808	5.84
18838	04-01-99	Republic of Ireland 6.25%	26438	5.76
42124756	01-01-99	Republic of Italy 8.5%	23354	5.09
2322094	03-20-03	Intl Bank Reconstr/Dev 4.5%	23268	5.07
20539	05-06-99	Intl Bank Reconstr/Dev 6%	22986	5.01
138672	11-15-00	Kingdom of Denmark 9%	22879	4.99
36369	07-15-98	Govt of New Zealand 8%	22547	4.91
99425	01-15-99	Republic of Finland 11%	22091	4.82
32051	09-01-99	Govt of Canada 7.75%	21794	4.75
3176364	12-15-98	Kingdom of Spain 8.3%	21692	4.73
131803	04-25-04	Govt of France 5.5%	20355	4.44
20801	01-21-02	Republic of Germany 8%	13667	2.98
817639	09-20-01	Japan Dev Bank 6.5%	9152	1.99

Composition % 12-31-94
Cash	12.0	Preferreds	0.0
Stocks	0.0	Convertibles	0.0
Bonds	88.0	Other	0.0

Tax Analysis
	Tax-Adj Historical Return %	% Pretax Return
3 Yr Avg	-0.75	---
5 Yr Avg	2.45	36.3
10 Yr Avg	---	---

Potential Capital Gain Exposure (% of assets) -27%

Most Similar Funds in MF500
Fidelity Global Bond	Weak Fit
MFS World Governments A	Weak Fit
PaineWebber Global Income E	Weak Fit

Country Exposure 12-31-94
	% of Bonds
U.S.	13
Germany	11
Australia	9
Japan	8
United Kingdom	7

Currency Exposure 09-30-94
	% of Net Assets
U.S.	31
Germany	20
Japan	15
Australia	10
Mexico	9

G.T. Global Telecommunications A

	Ticker	Load	NAV	Yield	SEC Yield	Assets	Objective
	GTTCX	4.75%	15.58	0.0%	N/A	1481.0	Sp.-Util

G.T. Global Telecommunications Fund - Class A seeks long-term growth of capital.

The fund normally invests at least 65% of its assets in equities issued by companies involved in the development, manufacture, or sale of telecommunication services or equipment. It looks for characteristics such as above-average per share earnings growth, high return, and overall financial strength. The fund typically invests in at least three countries including the United States; investments in any one country may not exceed 40% of assets.

Class A shares have front loads and lower 12b-1 fees; Class B shares have deferred loads.

Manager's Investment Style

Management emphasizes four themes: increasing infrastructure needs in emerging markets, privatization, deregulation, and the development of new technologies. Although the bulk of assets are held overseas in both developed and emerging markets, management does seek opportunities in the U.S., and attempts to reduce risk through issue diversification.

Fund Manager(s)

Michael J. Mahoney, since 1993. Birthdate: 07-60.
BA, Whitman C. 1982 MBA, Stanford U. 1991

Manager Experience

	Dates Managed	Invest Obj	Std Dev	+/- Index
Michael J. Mahoney				
G.T. Global Infrastr A	05/94 - 12/94	WW	9.49	0.77

Historical Profile
Return ---
Risk ---
Rating
Not Rated

											77%	89%	93%	Investment Style History Equity

Average % Stocks Held in Portfolio

Growth of $10,000
IIII Value of Fund ($000)
— Value of Index ($000) S&P 500
▼ Manager Change
▽ Partial Manager Change
▶ Mgr Unknown After
◀ Mgr Unknown Before

Performance Quartile (Within Objective)

	1983	1984	1985	1986	1987	1988	1989	1990	1991	1992	1993	1994	History
	---	---	---	---	---	---	---	---	---	11.83	17.17	15.58	NAV
	---	---	---	---	---	---	---	---	---	-0.13 *	47.66	-4.40	Total Return %
	---	---	---	---	---	---	---	---	---	-8.29 *	37.60	-5.72	+/- S&P 500
	---	---	---	---	---	---	---	---	---	---	33.21	3.54	+/- S&P Util
	---	---	---	---	---	---	---	---	---	1.29	0.00	0.00	Income Return %
	---	---	---	---	---	---	---	---	---	-1.42	47.65	-4.40	Capital Return %
	---	---	---	---	---	---	---	---	---	---	3	57	Total Rtn % Rank All
	---	---	---	---	---	---	---	---	---	---	1	13	Total Rtn % Rank Obj
	---	---	---	---	---	---	---	---	---	0.15	0.00	0.00	Income $
	---	---	---	---	---	---	---	---	---	0.00	0.28	0.86	Capital Gains $
	---	---	---	---	---	---	---	---	---	2.29	2.00	1.83	Expense Ratio %
	---	---	---	---	---	---	---	---	---	2.05	0.80	-0.74	Income Ratio %
	---	---	---	---	---	---	---	---	---	4	41	57	Turnover Rate %
	---	---	---	---	---	---	---	---	---	489.4	1386.9	1481.0	Net Assets ($mil)

Performance 12-31-94

	1st Qtr	2nd Qtr	3rd Qtr	4th Qtr	Total
1987	---	---	---	---	---
1988	---	---	---	---	---
1989	---	---	---	---	---
1990	---	---	---	---	---
1991	---	---	---	---	---
1992	---	-2.01	-3.12	10.35	---
1993	7.10	10.58	14.85	8.56	47.66
1994	-4.89	-1.47	7.77	-5.34	-4.40

Bear Market Performance
Decile Rank (5-year period)

Worst   Best

	Worst 3 Mo Period 1985-89	Worst 3 Mo Period 1990-94
G.T. Global Telecommunication	---	---
+/- S&P 500	---	---
+/- Best Fit Index :	---	---

Trailing Returns

	Total Return %	+/- S&P Util	+/- S&P 500	% Rank All	% Rank Obj	Growth of $10,000
3 Mo	-5.34	-5.32	-5.24	92	94	9,466
6 Mo	2.01	-2.85	1.65	26	19	10,201
1 Yr	-4.40	-5.72	3.54	57	13	9,560
3 Yr Avg	---	---	---	---	---	---
5 Yr Avg	---	---	---	---	---	---
10 Yr Avg	---	---	---	---	---	---
15 Yr Avg	---	---	---	---	---	---

Risk Analysis

Time Period	Load-Adj Return %	Risk % Rank [1] All	Risk % Rank [1] Obj	Morningstar [2] Return	Morningstar Risk	Morningstar Risk-Adj Rating
1 Yr	-8.95					
3 Yr	---	---	---	---	---	---
5 Yr	---	---	---	---	---	---
10 Yr	---	---	---	---	---	---
Average Historical Rating	---			---		

[1] 1 = low, 100 = high   [2] 1.00 = Equity Avg   [3] 1.00 = 90-day T-bill return

Other Measures

			Standard S&P 500	Best Fit
Standard Deviation	---	Alpha	---	---
Mean	---	Beta	---	---
Sharpe Ratio	---	R-Squared	---	---

Investment Style

	Stock Portfolio Avg	Relative S&P 500
Price/Earnings Ratio	28.8	1.56
Price/Book Ratio	3.8	1.12
5 Yr Earnings Gr %	7.1#	1.28
Return on Assets %	8.1	1.08
Debt % Total Cap	25.8	0.91
Med Mkt Cap ($mil)	9669	0.74

figure is based on 50% or less of stocks

Style: Value Blend Growth — Size Large/Med/Small

Diversification Value for Portfolio Types

Large Cap: Small Cap: Bond: Balanced: Diversified:

Portfolio 12-31-94

Share Chg (09-94) 000	Amount 000	Total Stocks: 116 Total Fixed-Income: 2	Value $000	% Net Assets
-10	457	Nokia Cl K	67414	4.55
	1016965	Telebras Pfd	45559	3.08
0	5	DDI	41493	2.80
690	690	Motorola	39958	2.70
-282	894	cisco Systems	31411	2.12
420	1408	Tele-Communications Cl A	30620	2.07
-2087	4682	British Telecommunications	27677	1.87
373	781	Time Warner	27437	1.85
-16	812	MFS Communications	26601	1.80
11	1667	Comcast Special Cl A	26158	1.77
21	92	Mannesmann (Germany)	25027	1.69
-7	333	Kyocera	24747	1.67
-9	428	Sony	24299	1.64
-6	280	Alcatel Alsthom Genl D'Elec	23953	1.62
543	1705	Advanced Information Svcs	23637	1.60
-19	874	Kyushu Matsushita Electric	21421	1.45
251	2331	IDB Communications Group	21414	1.45
-465	1781	Telefonica de Espana	21053	1.42
-216	9838	Telefonos de Mexico Cl L	20772	1.40
1274	8380	STET (Risp)	19873	1.34
-55	2478	Grupo Carso Cl A1	18649	1.26
-7	322	Glenayre Technologies	18576	1.25
725	1305	ECI Telecommunications	17774	1.20
-57	219	Telefonos de Chile (ADR)	17285	1.17
-95	343	Bell Atlantic	17039	1.15

Composition % 12-31-94

Cash	11.2	Preferreds	0.0
Stocks	88.4	Convertibles	0.0
Bonds	0.4	Other	0.0

Tax Analysis

	Tax-Adj Historical Return %	% Pretax Return
3 Yr Avg	---	---
5 Yr Avg	---	---
10 Yr Avg	---	---
Potential Capital Gain Exposure (% of assets)	5%	

Most Similar Funds in MF500
Fund lacks three-year record

Index Allocation

	% of Stocks
S&P 500	18.7
S&P MidCap 400	2.6
U.S. Small Cap	13.7
Foreign	65.0

Sector Weightings

	% of Stocks	Relative S&P 500
Utilities	25.9	2.09
Energy	0.1	0.01
Financials	1.7	0.16
Industrial Cyclicals	6.5	0.39
Consumer Durables	16.6	2.67
Consumer Staples	1.6	0.13
Services	20.3	2.49
Retail	0.3	0.05
Health	0.0	0.00
Technology	27.1	2.96

Operations

Address and Telephone	50 California Street 27th Floor San Francisco, CA 94111 800-824-1580 / 415-392-6181
Advisor	G.T. Capital Management
Subadvisor	None
Distributor	G.T. Global Financial Services
States Available	All
Report Grade	A
Income Distrib	Paid Annually
* Date of Inception	01-27-92
Fiscal Year End	October

Min Initial Purchase	$500 (Addt'l: $100)
Min IRA Purchase	$100 (Addt'l: $25)
Min Auto Invest Plan	$100 (Systematic Inv: $100)

Expenses & Fees

Sales Fees	4.75% front
	0.00% deferred
	0.50% 12b-1
Management Fee	0.98% max./0.90% min.
3-,5-,10-yr Expense Projections	$107, $149, $266
Annual Brokerage Cost	0.22%

MORNINGSTAR **1995 Mutual Fund 500**

G.T. Global Worldwide Growth A

	Ticker	Load	NAV	Yield	SEC Yield	Assets	Objective
	GTWGX	4.75%	15.53	0.0%	N/A	182.2	World Stock

G.T. Worldwide Growth Fund - Class A seeks long-term capital growth.

The fund normally invests at least 80% of its assets in equities issued in at least three countries. It typically allocates 20% to 60% of its assets to the U.S. market. The fund attempts to identify countries and industries likely to experience above-average growth rates. Up to 20% of assets may be invested in convertible bonds and investment-grade debt. The fund may invest in ADRs.

Class A shares have front loads; Class B shares have deferred loads and higher 12b-1 fees.

Manager's Investment Style

Management prioritizes its investment process: macroeconomic research occurs first, and then it searches for individual securities within the chosen markets that sell at discounts to their cash flows. Management's top-down approach has often led to rapid shifts among countries and sectors in order to capitalize on global trends. Active currency hedging has also characterized this fund's approach to international investing.

Fund Manager(s)

Christian Wignall et al. MA, Cambridge U.

Manager Experience

	Dates Managed	Invest Obj	Std Dev	+/- Index
Christian Wignall				
G.T. Global New Pac Gr A	01/87 - 12/94	WP	18.98	0.93
G.T. Global Intl Growth A	01/87 - 12/94	WF	16.84	-1.52

Performance 12-31-94

	1st Qtr	2nd Qtr	3rd Qtr	4th Qtr	Total
1987	---	---	11.85	-23.86	-11.60 *
1988	7.92	3.46	-4.15	8.69	16.31
1989	9.43	4.58	12.10	7.25	37.59
1990	-3.74	6.71	-17.21	2.86	-12.53
1991	12.26	-0.68	6.52	1.26	20.26
1992	0.92	1.83	-5.81	6.68	3.27
1993	7.88	3.27	8.06	5.96	27.57
1994	-4.81	-0.60	5.08	-6.11	-6.65

Bear Market Performance

Decile Rank (5-year period)

	Worst 3 Mo Period 1985-89	Worst 3 Mo Period 1990-94
G.T. Global Worldwide Growth	---	-17.21
+/- S&P 500	---	-3.47
+/- Best Fit Index : MSAIICtry	---	1.75

Trailing Returns

	Total Return %	+/- S&P 500	+/- MSCI World	% Rank All	% Rank Obj	Growth of $10,000
3 Mo	-6.11	-6.10	-5.38	94	76	9,389
6 Mo	-1.34	-6.20	-2.74	79	68	9,866
1 Yr	-6.65	-7.97	-11.73	77	81	9,335
3 Yr Avg	7.14	0.87	0.29	26	62	12,297
5 Yr Avg	5.28	-3.41	1.61	87	45	12,935
10 Yr Avg	---	---	---	---	---	---
15 Yr Avg	---	---	---	---	---	---

Operations

Address and Telephone	50 California Street 27th Floor San Francisco, CA 94111 800-824-1580 / 415-392-6181
Advisor	G.T. Capital Management
Subadvisor	None
Distributor	G.T. Global Financial Services
States Available	All
Report Grade	A-
Income Distrib	Paid Annually
* Date of Inception	06-09-87
Fiscal Year End	December

Historical Profile

Return	Below Average
Risk	Average
Rating	★★ Below Average

	1983	1984	1985	1986	1987	1988	1989	1990	1991	1992	1993	1994	History
	---	---	---	---	8.84	10.18	13.63	11.83	14.07	14.47	17.47	15.53	NAV
	---	---	---	---	-11.60 *	16.31	37.59	-12.53	20.26	3.27	27.57	-6.65	Total Return %
	---	---	---	---	3.74 *	-0.30	5.91	-9.42	-10.23	-4.35	17.51	-7.97	+/- S&P 500
	---	---	---	---	---	-6.97	20.98	4.48	1.97	8.50	5.06	-11.73	+/- MSCI World
	---	---	---	---	0.00	0.00	0.24	0.67	1.32	0.43	0.00	0.00	Income Return %
	---	---	---	---	-11.60	16.31	37.35	-13.21	18.93	2.84	27.56	-6.65	Capital Return %
	---	---	---	---	---	23	5	89	44	83	10	77	Total Rtn % Rank All
	---	---	---	---	---	27	2	65	33	25	63	81	Total Rtn % Rank Obj
	---	---	---	---	0.00	0.00	0.03	0.09	0.15	0.06	0.00	0.00	Income $
	---	---	---	---	0.00	0.10	0.33	0.00	0.00	0.00	0.96	0.78	Capital Gains $
	---	---	---	---	2.80	2.00	2.00	2.10	2.01	2.10	1.90	1.78	Expense Ratio %
	---	---	---	---	-1.40	0.20	-0.10	0.70	0.80	0.50	0.90	0.25	Income Ratio %
	---	---	---	---	271	181	91	107	122	95	92	89	Turnover Rate %
	---	---	---	---	6.7	11.6	38.1	85.9	128.1	141.2	193.8	182.2	Net Assets ($mil)

Investment Style History Equity

Average % Stocks Held in Portfolio: 95% 92% 84% 91% 88% 99% 88%

Growth of $10,000

‖‖‖ Value of Fund ($000)
— Value of Index ($000) S&P 500
▼ Manager Change
▽ Partial Manager Change
► Mgr Unknown After
◄ Mgr Unknown Before

Performance Quartile (Within Objective)

Risk Analysis

Time Period	Load-Adj Return %	Risk % Rank [1] All	Risk % Rank [1] Obj	Morningstar [2] Return	Morningstar [2] Risk	Morningstar Risk-Adj Rating
1 Yr	-11.09					
3 Yr	5.41	82	64	0.54 [3]	1.00	★★★
5 Yr	4.26	79	34	-0.11 [3]	0.96	★★
10 Yr						

Average Historical Rating (55 months) 3.0 ★s

[1] 1 = low, 100 = high [2] 1.00 = Equity Avg [3] 1.00 = 90-day T-bill return

Other Measures

	Standard S&P 500		Best Fit MSAIICtry
Standard Deviation	11.17	Alpha	1.2	1.8
Mean	7.53	Beta	0.96	0.89
Sharpe Ratio	0.36	R-Squared	47	70

Investment Style

	Stock Portfolio Avg	Rel MSCI EAFE	Rel Obj	Style
Price/Earnings Ratio	29.1	0.79	1.18	
Price/Cash Flow	14.6	0.94	1.08	
Price/Book Ratio	2.9	1.11	0.99	
5 Yr Earnings Gr %	-0.2	---	-0.04	
Return on Assets %	5.9	1.30	0.86	
Debt % Total Cap	26.2	0.77	0.91	
Med Mkt Cap ($mil)	4812	0.40	0.96	

Diversification Value for Portfolio Types

Large Cap: Medium	Small Cap: Medium	Bond: High	Balanced: Low	Diversified: Low

Tax Analysis

	Tax-Adj Historical Return %	% Pretax Return
3 Yr Avg	6.09	84.5
5 Yr Avg	4.54	84.7
10 Yr Avg	---	---
Potential Capital Gain Exposure (% of assets)		7%

Most Similar Funds in MF500

Putnam Global Growth A	Weak Fit
T. Rowe Price Intl Stock	Weak Fit
Strong Discovery	Weak Fit

Portfolio 12-31-94

Share Chg (09-94) 000	Amount 000	Total Stocks: 99 Total Fixed-Income: 5	Value $000	% Net Assets
-3	142	Fuji Machine Manufacturing	4681	2.57
-1	54	Kyocera	4034	2.21
-1	54	IBM	3960	2.17
-4	233	Canon	3953	2.17
-1	78	Shimamura	3899	2.14
-2	124	Tokyo Electron	3868	2.12
0	12	Volkswagen	3416	1.87
-23	1226	SIP	3194	1.75
-1	26	Autobacs Seven	3155	1.73
5	5	Swiss Reinsurance (Reg)	3042	1.67
-4	194	Bridgestone	3041	1.67
233	233	Takeda Chemical Industries	2831	1.55
163	163	Forsakringsbola Skandia Free	2820	1.55
-1	46	Siam Cement (For)	2745	1.51
-21	1126	British Steel	2714	1.49
183	183	Lehman Brothers Holdings	2692	1.48
-15	776	Tomkins	2656	1.46
-7	363	Toshiba	2633	1.44
-1	49	Futaba	2623	1.44
-1	52	Tandy	2595	1.42

Regional Exposure 12-31-94

% of Stocks

Europe	35	Pacific Rim	14
Japan	22	U.S.	20
Latin Amer	7	Other	3

Composition % 12-31-94

Cash	7.2	Preferreds	0.0
Stocks	92.8	Convertibles	0.0
Bonds	0.0	Other	0.0

Top 5 Countries 12-31-94

	% of Stocks
Japan	22
U.S.	20
United Kingdom	18
Thailand	4
South Korea	4

Total Number of Countries: 23
Hedging Policy: Active

Sector Weightings

	% of Stocks	Relative S&P 500
Utilities	8.9	1.07
Energy	2.8	0.58
Financials	20.4	1.24
Industrial Cyclicals	18.0	0.78
Consumer Durables	10.6	1.03
Consumer Staples	4.3	0.84
Services	10.2	0.87
Retail	6.0	1.04
Health	3.3	0.62
Technology	15.4	1.74

Expenses & Fees

Min Initial Purchase	$500 (Addt'l: $100)
Min IRA Purchase	$100 (Addt'l: $25)
Min Auto Invest Plan	$100 (Systematic Inv: $100)
Sales Fees	4.75% front 0.00% deferred 0.35% 12b-1
Management Fee	0.98% max./0.90% min.
3-,5-,10-yr Expense Projections	$104, $144, $256
Annual Brokerage Cost	0.39%

Gabelli Asset

	Ticker	Load	NAV	Yield	SEC Yield	Assets	Objective
	GABAX	None	22.21	4.7%	N/A	981.8	Growth

Gabelli Asset Fund seeks capital growth. Current income, while considered important, is secondary.

The fund invests primarily in a diversified portfolio of readily marketable equity securities. At least 80% of the portfolio's holdings are listed on a nationally recognized securities exchange or included in the NASDAQ National Market System. The fund seeks securities that have favorable value-to-price characteristics. It may invest in preferred stocks and may place up to 25% of its assets in convertible securities.

Historical Profile

Return	Above Average
Risk	Low
Rating	★★★★
	Above Average

Investment Style History
Equity

Average % Stocks Held in Portfolio

73% 72% 56% 53% 76% 84% 84% 78%

Growth of $10,000

||| Value of Fund ($000)
— Value of Index ($000)
Wil 4500
▼ Manager Change
▽ Partial Manager Change
► Mgr Unknown After
◄ Mgr Unknown Before

Performance Quartile (Within Objective)

Manager's Investment Style

Manager Mario Gabelli chooses stocks that are cheap relative to their free cash flow, defined as earnings before depreciation, interest, and taxes. He stresses particular themes and sectors, such as his signature interactive-couch-potato theme, which gives attention to telecom, entertainment, and media stocks. He distinguishes this fund from others in the Gabelli family by holding a very diversified portfolio of 270 stocks, and by consistently holding a healthy cash cushion.

1983	1984	1985	1986	1987	1988	1989	1990	1991	1992	1993	1994	History
---	---	---	11.29	12.61	14.69	17.41	15.63	17.96	19.88	23.30	22.21	NAV
---	---	---	8.14 *	16.20	31.12	27.22	-5.80	18.14	14.89	21.84	-0.17	Total Return %
---	---	---	-2.39 *	10.94	14.51	-4.47	-2.68	-12.35	7.28	11.78	-1.49	+/- S&P 500
---	---	---	---	13.84	13.17	-1.96	0.38	-16.07	5.92	10.55	-0.10	+/- Wilshire 5000
---	---	---	0.00	0.73	2.92	3.46	4.42	2.39	1.32	0.73	4.51	Income Return %
---	---	---	8.14	15.47	28.20	23.75	-10.22	15.75	13.57	21.11	-4.68	Capital Return %
---	---	---	---	5	2	18	73	48	10	14	21	Total Rtn % Rank All
---	---	---	---	4	3	49	60	96	16	11	35	Total Rtn % Rank Obj
---	---	---	0.00	0.09	0.38	0.56	0.77	0.39	0.25	0.17	1.05	Income $
---	---	---	0.00	0.42	1.23	0.72	0.00	0.12	0.50	0.76	0.00	Capital Gains $
---	---	---	1.67	1.26	1.31	1.26	1.20	1.30	1.31	1.31	1.33	Expense Ratio %
---	---	---	1.87	1.19	2.04	4.17	4.51	2.34	1.42	0.82	0.94	Income Ratio %
---	---	---	---	90	47	49	56	20	14	16	---	Turnover Rate %
---	---	---	48.9	76.8	143.0	361.6	342.7	485.4	631.8	948.0	981.8	Net Assets ($mil)

Fund Manager(s)

Mario J. Gabelli CFA, since 03-86. Birthdate: 06-42. BS, Fordham U. 1965 MBA, Columbia U. 1967

Manager Experience

	Dates Managed	Invest Obj	Std Dev	+/- Index
Mario J. Gabelli				
Gabelli Equity	08/86 - 12/94	DE	13.51	1.96
Gabelli Convertible Secs	07/89 - 12/94	CV	3.29	0.99

Performance 12-31-94

	1st Qtr	2nd Qtr	3rd Qtr	4th Qtr	Total
1987	19.52	7.40	5.24	-13.98	16.20
1988	14.37	8.38	2.19	3.51	31.12
1989	12.25	9.82	3.92	-0.70	27.22
1990	-5.34	2.00	-9.52	7.82	-5.80
1991	11.07	0.00	3.11	3.16	18.14
1992	6.01	-0.68	0.58	8.49	14.89
1993	6.14	4.74	6.92	2.50	21.84
1994	-2.88	-1.19	5.37	-1.27	-0.17

Bear Market Performance

Decile Rank (5-year period)

Worst —————————— Best

	Worst 3 Mo Period 1985-89	Worst 3 Mo Period 1990-94
Gabelli Asset	---	-9.52
+/- S&P 500	---	4.23
+/- Best Fit Index : Wil 4500	---	8.71

Trailing Returns

	Total Return %	+/- S&P 500	+/- Wil 5000	% Rank All	% Rank Obj	Growth of $10,000
3 Mo	-1.27	-1.26	-0.50	51	50	9,873
6 Mo	4.03	-0.84	-0.60	15	48	10,403
1 Yr	-0.17	-1.49	-0.10	21	35	9,983
3 Yr Avg	11.80	5.54	5.19	8	11	13,974
5 Yr Avg	9.23	0.54	0.42	22	41	15,551
10 Yr Avg	---	---	---	---	---	---
15 Yr Avg	---	---	---	---	---	---

Operations

Address and Telephone	One Corporate Center Rye, NY 10580-1434 800-422-3554 / 914-921-5100
Advisor	Gabelli Funds
Subadvisor	None
Distributor	Gabelli & Company
States Available	All plus GU,PR,VI
Report Grade	A
Income Distrib	Paid Irregularly
* Date of Inception	03-03-86
Fiscal Year End	December

Risk Analysis

Time Period	Load-Adj Return %	Risk % Rank [1] All	Risk % Rank [1] Obj	Morningstar [2] Return	Morningstar Risk	Morningstar Risk-Adj Rating
1 Yr	-0.17					
3 Yr	11.80	53	6	2.57 [3]	0.57	★★★★★
5 Yr	9.23	56	5	1.14 [3]	0.63	★★★★
10 Yr	---	---	---	---	---	

Average Historical Rating (70 months) 4.4 ★s

[1] = low, 100 = high [2] 1.00 = Equity Avg [3] 1.00 = 90-day T-bill return

Other Measures

	Standard S&P 500	Best Fit Wil 4500
Standard Deviation	7.69	Alpha	5.9	5.1
Mean	11.50	Beta	0.77	0.70
Sharpe Ratio	1.04	R-Squared	63	78

Investment Style

	Stock Portfolio Avg	Relative S&P 500
Price/Earnings Ratio	19.7	1.06
Price/Book Ratio	4.3	1.26
5 Yr Earnings Gr %	4.9	0.88
Return on Assets %	6.7	0.89
Debt % Total Cap	35.6	1.26
Med Mkt Cap ($mil)	3139	0.24

Style Value Blend Growth
Size Large Med Small

Diversification Value for Portfolio Types

Large Cap: Low	Small Cap: Low	Bond: High	Balanced: Low	Diversified: Low

Portfolio 09-30-94

Share Chg (06-94) 000	Amount 000	Total Stocks: 282 Total Fixed-Income: 11	Value $000	% Net Assets
450	450	American Cyanamid	44775	4.40
	31731	Time Warner Cv 8.75%	31652	3.11
252	380	AT & T	20520	2.02
0	1010	Pet	19948	1.96
40	640	American Express	19440	1.91
0	365	General Motors	17109	1.68
-15	425	Sprint	16203	1.59
2	440	Time Warner	15455	1.52
70	420	American Brands	15225	1.50
0	374	Chris-Craft Industries	15023	1.48
0	106	LIN Broadcasting	14747	1.45
-12	370	Varity	13829	1.36
0	375	Harcourt General	12891	1.27
141	261	General Electric	12561	1.23
5	390	Media General Cl A	11603	1.14
0	275	IDEX	11138	1.09
55	185	Procter & Gamble	11031	1.08
0	214	Johnson & Johnson	11022	1.08
173	275	Viacom Cl B	10931	1.07
50	330	PepsiCo	10931	1.07
0	153	Deere	10465	1.03
0	340	Echlin	10328	1.01
14	239	Ralston-Purina Group	9889	0.97
-286	32	GTE	9659	0.95
50	270	Genuine Parts	9484	0.93

Composition % 09-30-94

Cash	16.0	Preferreds	0.0
Stocks	79.0	Convertibles	4.0
Bonds	1.0	Other	0.0

Tax Analysis

	Tax-Adj Historical Return %	% Pretax Return
3 Yr Avg	10.31	86.1
5 Yr Avg	7.84	82.6
10 Yr Avg	---	---
Potential Capital Gain Exposure (% of assets)		18%

Most Similar Funds in MF500

Gabelli Small Cap Growth	Strong Fit
Fidelity Contrafund	Fair Fit
Lindner	Fair Fit

Index Allocation

	% of Stocks
S&P 500	53.2
S&P MidCap 400	15.9
U.S. Small Cap	25.3
Foreign	7.8

Sector Weightings

	% of Stocks	Relative S&P 500
Utilities	7.8	0.63
Energy	3.0	0.30
Financials	4.9	0.46
Industrial Cyclicals	16.2	0.99
Consumer Durables	13.1	2.11
Consumer Staples	15.4	1.23
Services	22.8	2.79
Retail	1.9	0.32
Health	7.3	0.84
Technology	7.7	0.84

Expenses & Fees

Sales Fees	0.00% front
	0.00% deferred
	0.25% 12b-1
Management Fee	1.00% flat fee
3-,5-,10-yr Expense Projections	$42, $72, $158
Annual Brokerage Cost	---

Min Initial Purchase	$1000 (Addt'l: None)
Min IRA Purchase	$1000 (Addt'l: None)
Min Auto Invest Plan	$100 (Systematic Inv: $100)

MORNINGSTAR 1995 Mutual Fund 500

Gabelli Convertible Securities

	Ticker	Load	NAV	Yield	SEC Yield	Assets	Objective
	GACSX	Clsd	10.60	5.2%	N/A	112.1	Convrt. Bond

Gabelli Convertible Securities Fund seeks total return.
　　The fund normally invests at least 65% of its assets in securities convertible into common stock or other equity securities. It is anticipated that not more than 50% of the fund's portfolio consists of securities rated CCC or lower. Up to 35% of the fund's assets may be invested in common stocks, nonconvertible preferred stocks, nonconvertible corporate debt obligations, options on debt or equity securities, and money-market securities.
　　This fund is offered on a no-load basis for tax-free accounts.

Manager's Investment Style

　　Manager Mario Gabelli looks for rising free cash flows, which he believes foreshadow net earnings increases. Gabelli also insists on low equity valuations and some kind of industry or company-specific catalyst that could change an issue's prospects. In adhering to this strict value orientation, management often has trouble finding enough convertibles that it likes; since inception, the fund has never been fully invested. The convertibles it does hold, however, are generally those with strong yields but decent participation in the underlying stock, or busted convertibles if the underlying stocks appear poised for rebound.

Fund Manager(s)

　　Mario J. Gabelli CFA, since 07-89. Birthdate: 06-42. BS, Fordham U. 1965 MBA, Columbia U. 1967

Manager Experience	Dates Managed	Invest Obj	Std Dev	+/- Index
Mario J. Gabelli				
Gabelli Asset	03/86 - 12/94	G	11.85	3.17
Gabelli Equity	08/86 - 12/94	DE	13.51	1.96

Historical Profile
Return	Above Average
Risk	Low
Rating	★★★★
	Closed

Income Rtn % Rank Obj

Growth of $10,000
|||| Value of Fund ($000)
— Value of Index ($000)
Russ 2000
▼ Manager Change
▽ Partial Manager Change
► Mgr Unknown After
◄ Mgr Unknown Before

Performance Quartile (Within Objective)

	1983	1984	1985	1986	1987	1988	1989	1990	1991	1992	1993	1994	History
	---	---	---	---	---	---	14	43	29	20	7		Income Rtn % Rank Obj
	---	---	---	---	---	---	10.51	10.47	10.91	11.45	11.52	10.60	NAV
	---	---	---	---	---	---	6.25 *	6.26	12.46	12.98	13.06	-0.17	Total Return %
	---	---	---	---	---	---	---	-2.68	-3.54	5.74	3.31	2.75	+/- LB Aggregate
	---	---	---	---	---	---	3.55 *	9.38	-18.02	5.36	3.00	-1.49	+/- S&P 500
	---	---	---	---	---	---	1.15	6.64	6.69	5.92	4.88	5.13	Income Return %
	---	---	---	---	---	---	5.10	-0.38	5.77	7.06	8.18	-5.30	Capital Return %
	---	---	---	---	---	---	---	31	71	13	40	21	Total Rtn % Rank All
	---	---	---	---	---	---	---	1	91	41	64	3	Total Rtn % Rank Obj
	---	---	---	---	---	---	0.12	0.69	0.71	0.65	0.56	0.57	Income $
	---	---	---	---	---	---	0.00	0.00	0.16	0.22	0.86	0.33	Capital Gains $
	---	---	---	---	---	---	2.50	1.52	1.45	1.40	1.38	1.36	Expense Ratio %
	---	---	---	---	---	---	5.74	6.85	5.50	5.53	4.58	4.69	Income Ratio %
	---	---	---	---	---	---	---	282	51	32	45	---	Turnover Rate %
	---	---	---	---	---	---	49.8	81.9	92.6	92.2	108.6	112.1	Net Assets ($mil)

Performance 12-31-94

	1st Qtr	2nd Qtr	3rd Qtr	4th Qtr	Total
1987	---	---	---	---	---
1988	---	---	---	---	---
1989	---	---	---	0.81	6.25 *
1990	1.43	2.09	-1.12	3.79	6.26
1991	5.64	1.90	2.66	1.77	12.46
1992	3.48	2.04	3.30	3.58	12.98
1993	5.41	2.40	3.16	1.53	13.06
1994	0.17	-1.30	1.84	-0.86	-0.17

Bear Market Performance

Decile Rank (5-year period)

Worst —————————————————— Best

	Worst 3 Mo Period 1985-89	Worst 3 Mo Period 1990-94
Gabelli Convertible Securities	---	-2.66
+/- LB Aggregate	---	0.60
+/- Best Fit Index : Russ 2000	---	3.12

Trailing Returns

	Total Return %	+/- LB Aggregate	+/- S&P 500	% Rank All	% Rank Obj	Growth of $10,000
3 Mo	-0.86	-1.24	-0.85	41	3	9,914
6 Mo	0.97	-0.03	-3.90	38	32	10,097
1 Yr	-0.17	2.75	-1.49	21	3	9,983
3 Yr Avg	8.44	3.89	2.17	19	25	12,751
5 Yr Avg	8.79	1.16	0.10	25	57	15,238
10 Yr Avg	---	---	---	---	---	---
15 Yr Avg	---	---	---	---	---	---

Operations

Address and Telephone	One Corporate Center Rye, NY 10580-1434 800-422-3554 / 914-921-5100
Advisor	Gabelli Funds
Subadvisor	None
Distributor	Gabelli & Company
States Available	All plus GU,PR,VI
Report Grade	A
Income Distrib	Paid Annually
* Date of Inception	07-03-89
Fiscal Year End	December

Min Initial Purchase	Closed (Addt'l: None)
Min IRA Purchase	$1000 (Addt'l: None)
Min Auto Invest Plan	$100 (Systematic Inv: $100)

Expenses & Fees
Sales Fees	0.00% front
	0.00% deferred
	0.00% 12b-1
Management Fee	1.00% flat fee, 0.10%A
3-,5-,10-yr Expense Projections	$44, $76, $166

Risk Analysis

Time Period	Load-Adj Return %	Risk % Rank All	Risk % Rank Obj	Morningstar[2] Return	Morningstar[2] Risk	Morningstar Risk-Adj Rating
1 Yr	-0.17					
3 Yr	8.44	5	1	1.47[3]	0.29	★★★★
5 Yr	8.79	7	1	1.02[3]	0.25	★★★★
10 Yr	---	---	---	---	---	

Average Historical Rating (30 months)　　4.0 ★s

[1] 1 = low, 100 = high　[2] 1.00 = Hybrid Avg　[3] 1.00 = 90-day T-bill return

Other Measures

			Standard LB Agg	Best Fit Russ 2000
Standard Deviation	3.47	Alpha	4.3	3.0
Mean	8.19	Beta	0.42	0.21
Sharpe Ratio	1.35	R-Squared	23	49

Investment Style

Interest-Rate Stance
Avg Effective Maturity　　---

Quality
Avg Credit Quality　　---

Not Applicable

Avg Weighted Coupon　　7.41%
Avg Weighted Price　91.11% of Par

Diversification Value for Portfolio Types

Large Cap: Medium	Small Cap: Low	Bond: High	Balanced: Medium	Diversified: Medium

Portfolio 12-31-94

Amount 000	Date of Maturity	Total Stocks: 7 / Total Fixed-Income: 96	Value $000	% Net Assets
14000	01-10-15	Time Warner Cv 8.75%	13230	11.80
85		QVC	3581	3.19
2800	03-15-12	Fieldcrest Cannon Cv 6%	2100	1.87
36		Navistar Intl Cl G Cv Pfd $6	1854	1.65
1250	03-15-11	Park Communications Cv 6.875%	1797	1.60
1759	11-15-03	Ketema Cv 8%	1790	1.60
25		Caesars World	1669	1.49
2200	02-15-02	General Host Cv 8%	1661	1.48
14		ITT Cl N Cv Pfd $2.25	1547	1.38
6		Atlantic Richfield Cv Pfd $2.8	1513	1.35
35		Tenneco	1485	1.32
880	02-15-07	Mark IV Industries Cv 6.25%	1168	1.04
1195	05-15-06	M/A-Communications Cv 9.25%	1108	0.99
20		GATX Cv Pfd $3.875	1080	0.96
1150	08-01-02	GenCorp Cv 8%	1049	0.94
1200	05-01-09	Kollmorgen Cv 8.75%	1030	0.92
1300	03-31-06	UNC Cv 7.5%	1003	0.89
930	10-15-08	Ingles Markets Cv 10%	986	0.88
1050	09-15-06	Chock Full O'Nuts Cv 8%	961	0.86
17		Sequa Cv Pfd $5.00	955	0.85
1300	11-01-14	Flagstar Cv 10%	917	0.82
1005	04-01-12	Chock Full O'Nuts Cv 7%	814	0.73
13		Magma Copper Cv Pfd 5.625%	803	0.72
1100	01-15-08	Moran Energy 8.75%	772	0.69
700	06-15-03	Pacific Scientific Cv 7.75%	770	0.69

Composition % 09-30-94
Cash	26.0	Preferreds	0.0
Stocks	15.0	Convertibles	59.0
Bonds	0.0	Other	0.0

Tax Analysis
	Tax-Adj Historical Return %	% Pretax Return
3 Yr Avg	5.36	61.7
5 Yr Avg	6.00	64.6
10 Yr Avg	---	---
Potential Capital Gain Exposure (% of assets)		-4%

Most Similar Funds in MF500
Lord Abbett Bond-Debenture	Fair Fit
Lindner Dividend	Weak Fit
Merrill Lynch Global Alloc B	Weak Fit

Coupon Range
	% of Bonds	Rel Obj
0%	2.3	0.27
0% to 6%	12.5	0.37
6% to 7%	16.2	1.09
7% to 8.5%	17.5	1.49
More than 8.5%	29.9	5.47
Not applicable	21.6	0.84

Credit Analysis 12-31-93
% of Bonds
US Govt	0	BB	29
AAA	0	B	33
AA	0	Below B	5
A	8	NR/NA	9
BBB	17		

M○**RNINGSTAR**　1995 Mutual Fund 500　　225

Gabelli Equity-Income

	Ticker	Load	NAV	Yield	SEC Yield	Assets	Objective
	GABEX	4.50%	10.72	2.8%	N/A	48.4	Equity-Inc.

Gabelli Equity-Income Fund seeks total return with an emphasis on income.

The fund invests at least 65% of its assets in income-producing equity securities, looking for issues with a higher yield than the S&P 500 average and capital gains potential. It may invest up to 35% of its assets in fixed-income securities rated lower than BBB or unrated. The fund may also invest up to 35% of its assets in foreign securities. For temporary defensive purposes, it may also invest without limit in money-market instruments. To achieve higher returns the fund may use various special investment techniques.

Manager's Investment Style

Manager Mario Gabelli applies his value strategy to income-generating stocks. His low-turnover, bottom-up approach focuses on firms selling at a discount to cash flow, earnings trends, or underlying assets. A number of portfolio holdings represent one of Gabelli's favorite long-term themes, such as interactive media or energy. When considering yield, Gabelli targets firms whose yields surpass that of the S&P 500.

Fund Manager(s)

Mario J. Gabelli CFA, since 01-92. Birthdate: 06-42. BS, Fordham U. 1965 MBA, Columbia U. 1967

Manager Experience

Manager Experience	Dates Managed	Invest Obj	Std Dev	+/- Index
Mario J. Gabelli				
Gabelli Asset	03/86 - 12/94	G	11.85	3.17
Gabelli Equity	08/86 - 12/94	DE	13.51	1.96

Historical Profile

Return ---
Risk ---
Rating
Not Rated

51%	71%	76%

Investment Style History
Equity
Average % Stocks Held in Portfolio

Growth of $10,000

|||| Value of Fund ($000)
— Value of Index ($000) S&P 500
▼ Manager Change
▽ Partial Manager Change
► Mgr Unknown After
◄ Mgr Unknown Before

Performance Quartile (Within Objective)

	1983	1984	1985	1986	1987	1988	1989	1990	1991	1992	1993	1994	History
	---	---	---	---	---	---	---	---	---	10.64	11.57	10.72	NAV
	---	---	---	---	---	---	---	---	---	8.60 *	17.88	1.08	Total Return %
	---	---	---	---	---	---	---	---	---	1.02 *	7.82	-0.23	+/- S&P 500
	---	---	---	---	---	---	---	---	---	---	6.60	1.15	+/- Wilshire 5000
	---	---	---	---	---	---	---	---	---	2.73	2.52	2.82	Income Return %
	---	---	---	---	---	---	---	---	---	5.86	15.36	-1.74	Capital Return %
	---	---	---	---	---	---	---	---	---	---	21	13	Total Rtn % Rank All
	---	---	---	---	---	---	---	---	---	---	18	16	Total Rtn % Rank Obj
	---	---	---	---	---	---	---	---	---	0.27	0.28	0.31	Income $
	---	---	---	---	---	---	---	---	---	0.06	0.68	0.66	Capital Gains $
	---	---	---	---	---	---	---	---	---	1.93	1.78	1.81	Expense Ratio %
	---	---	---	---	---	---	---	---	---	2.65	2.62	2.58	Income Ratio %
	---	---	---	---	---	---	---	---	---	---	76	20	Turnover Rate %
	---	---	---	---	---	---	---	---	---	48.9	54.4	48.4	Net Assets ($mil)

Performance 12-31-94

	1st Qtr	2nd Qtr	3rd Qtr	4th Qtr	Total
1987	---	---	---	---	---
1988	---	---	---	---	---
1989	---	---	---	---	---
1990	---	---	---	---	---
1991	---	---	---	---	---
1992	1.29	2.26	1.06	3.75	8.60
1993	7.42	3.79	4.18	1.48	17.88
1994	-2.16	-0.80	4.87	-0.69	1.08

Bear Market Performance

Decile Rank (5-year period)

Worst — Best

	Worst 3 Mo Period 1985-89	Worst 3 Mo Period 1990-94
Gabelli Equity-Income	---	---
+/- S&P 500	---	---
+/- Best Fit Index :	---	---

Trailing Returns

	Total Return %	+/- S&P 500	+/- Wil 5000	% Rank All	% Rank Obj	Growth of $10,000
3 Mo	-0.69	-0.68	0.08	38	15	9,931
6 Mo	4.15	-0.72	-0.48	15	5	10,415
1 Yr	1.08	-0.23	1.15	13	16	10,108
3 Yr Avg	---	---	---	---	---	---
5 Yr Avg	---	---	---	---	---	---
10 Yr Avg	---	---	---	---	---	---
15 Yr Avg	---	---	---	---	---	---

Operations

Address and Telephone	One Corporate Center Rye, NY 10580-1434 800-422-3554 / 914-921-5100
Advisor	Gabelli Funds
Subadvisor	None
Distributor	Gabelli & Company
States Available	All plus GU,PR,VI
Report Grade	A-
Income Distrib	Paid Quarterly
* Date of Inception	01-02-92
Fiscal Year End	September

Risk Analysis

Time Period	Load-Adj Return %	Risk % Rank All	Risk % Rank Obj	Morningstar Return	Morningstar Risk	Morningstar Risk-Adj Rating
1 Yr	-3.47					
3 Yr	---	---	---	---	---	
5 Yr	---	---	---	---	---	
10 Yr	---	---	---	---	---	

Average Historical Rating ---

¹1 = low, 100 = high ²1.00 = Equity Avg ³1.00 = 90-day T-bill return

Other Measures

			Standard S&P 500	Best Fit
Standard Deviation	---	Alpha	---	---
Mean	---	Beta	---	---
Sharpe Ratio	---	R-Squared	---	---

Investment Style

	Stock Portfolio Avg	Relative S&P 500
Price/Earnings Ratio	20.3	1.10
Price/Book Ratio	2.6	0.77
5 Yr Earnings Gr %	0.0	0.01
Return on Assets %	5.1	0.69
Debt % Total Cap	31.3	1.11
Med Mkt Cap ($mil)	13173	1.01

Style: Value Blend Growth — Large Med Small

Diversification Value for Portfolio Types

Large Cap: Small Cap: Bond: Balanced: Diversified:

Expenses & Fees

Sales Fees	
	4.50% front
	0.00% deferred
	0.25% 12b-1
Management Fee	1.00% flat fee
3-,5-,10-yr Expense Projections	$99, $137, $245
Annual Brokerage Cost	0.15%

Min Initial Purchase	$1000 (Addt'l: None)
Min IRA Purchase	$1000 (Addt'l: None)
Min Auto Invest Plan	$100 (Systematic Inv: $100)

Portfolio 09-30-94

Share Chg (06-94) 000	Amount 000	Total Stocks: 70 Total Fixed-Income: 30	Value $000	% Net Assets
	2300	Time Warner Cv 8.75%	2294	4.57
0	63	American Express	1898	3.78
0	70	Eastern Enterprises	1838	3.66
6	30	Exxon	1729	3.44
0	30	Minnesota Mining & Mfg	1658	3.30
0	20	British Petroleum (ADR)	1515	3.02
0	14	Atlantic Richfield	1412	2.81
0	40	Southern New England Telecom	1345	2.68
-4	37	American Brands	1323	2.64
0	30	Chevron	1249	2.49
0	30	BCE	1076	2.14
	9	ITT Cl M Cv Pfd $2.25	996	1.99
0	55	Southwest Gas	969	1.93
1	26	Burlington Resources	956	1.91
0	15	JP Morgan	911	1.82
0	15	Texaco	900	1.79
0	12	IBM	834	1.66
-7	12	Deere	789	1.57
0	2	Deutsche Bank (ADR)	696	1.39
0	40	PacifiCorp	675	1.34
0	14	General Electric	674	1.34
-2	14	General Motors	656	1.31
0	32	Freeport-McMoRan	620	1.24
0	10	Procter & Gamble	596	1.19
	14	Tenneco Cl A Cv Pfd $2.80	571	1.14

Composition % 09-30-94

Cash	8.0	Preferreds	0.0
Stocks	75.0	Convertibles	17.0
Bonds	0.0	Other	0.0

Tax Analysis

	Tax-Adj Historical Return %	% Pretax Return
3 Yr Avg	---	---
5 Yr Avg	---	---
10 Yr Avg	---	---
Potential Capital Gain Exposure (% of assets)		5%

Most Similar Funds in MF500

Fund lacks three-year record

Index Allocation

	% of Stocks
S&P 500	66.9
S&P MidCap 400	7.1
U.S. Small Cap	10.8
Foreign	15.3

Sector Weightings

	% of Stocks	Relative S&P 500
Utilities	15.8	1.27
Energy	22.4	2.21
Financials	17.7	1.67
Industrial Cyclicals	15.3	0.93
Consumer Durables	5.6	0.90
Consumer Staples	11.7	0.93
Services	5.9	0.72
Retail	1.0	0.17
Health	2.0	0.24
Technology	2.7	0.29

MORNINGSTAR 1995 Mutual Fund 500

Gabelli Gold

	Ticker	Load	NAV	Yield	SEC Yield	Assets	Objective
	GOLDX	None	11.07	N/A	N/A	17.5	Sp.-Metals

Gabelli Gold Fund seeks long-term capital appreciation.

The fund typically invests at least 65% of its assets in equity securities of companies principally engaged in gold-related activities. These may include exploration, mining, fabrication, processing, distribution, or trading of gold, as well as financing, managing, controlling, or operating gold companies. A substantial portion of the fund's assets may be invested in foreign securities issued in both developed and emerging markets. Up to 10% of the fund's assets may be invested in bullion of gold and other precious metals.

Manager's Investment Style

The fund's manager, Caesar Bryan, seeks gold-producing companies from all over the world. In North America, Bryan buys small- to mid-cap companies with growth potential and aggressive management. He is also inclined to purchase larger producers that have been unfairly beat up by the market. Management sees opportunities for price growth in South Africa, and is willing to pay a premium to get on board. Bryan's horizons are not limited to these two areas, though. Purchases in Australia, Ireland, and Peru make this an internationally diverse fund.

Fund Manager(s)

Caesar M. P. Bryan, since 07-94. Birthdate: 12-54. LLB, U. of Southampton 1976

Manager Experience

Manager Experience	Dates Managed	Invest Obj	Std Dev	+/- Index
Caesar M. P. Bryan				
Lexington Goldfund	12/86 - 05/94	SP	27.12	-6.75
Lexington Global	03/87 - 05/94	WW	15.59	-0.78

Historical Profile

Return ---
Risk ---
Rating Not Rated

Historical Profile box notes (right legend):

Investment Style History
Equity

Average % Stocks Held in Portfolio — 86%

Growth of $10,000

||| Value of Fund ($000)
— Value of Index ($000) S&P 500
▼ Manager Change
▽ Partial Manager Change
► Mgr Unknown After
◄ Mgr Unknown Before

Performance Quartile (Within Objective)

History

	1983	1984	1985	1986	1987	1988	1989	1990	1991	1992	1993	1994	History
	---	---	---	---	---	---	---	---	---	---	---	11.07	NAV
	---	---	---	---	---	---	---	---	---	---	---	10.70 *	Total Return %
	---	---	---	---	---	---	---	---	---	---	---	6.73 *	+/- S&P 500
	---	---	---	---	---	---	---	---	---	---	---	---	+/- S&P Metals
	---	---	---	---	---	---	---	---	---	---	---	0.00	Income Return %
	---	---	---	---	---	---	---	---	---	---	---	10.70	Capital Return %
	---	---	---	---	---	---	---	---	---	---	---	---	Total Rtn % Rank All
	---	---	---	---	---	---	---	---	---	---	---	---	Total Rtn % Rank Obj
	---	---	---	---	---	---	---	---	---	---	---	0.00	Income $
	---	---	---	---	---	---	---	---	---	---	---	0.00	Capital Gains $
	---	---	---	---	---	---	---	---	---	---	---	---	Expense Ratio %
	---	---	---	---	---	---	---	---	---	---	---	---	Income Ratio %
	---	---	---	---	---	---	---	---	---	---	---	---	Turnover Rate %
	---	---	---	---	---	---	---	---	---	---	---	17.5	Net Assets ($mil)

Performance 12-31-94

	1st Qtr	2nd Qtr	3rd Qtr	4th Qtr	Total
1987	---	---	---	---	---
1988	---	---	---	---	---
1989	---	---	---	---	---
1990	---	---	---	---	---
1991	---	---	---	---	---
1992	---	---	---	---	---
1993	---	---	---	---	---
1994	---	---	---	-10.51	10.70 *

Bear Market Performance

Decile Rank (5-year period)

Worst — Best

	Worst 3 Mo Period 1985-89	Worst 3 Mo Period 1990-94
Gabelli Gold	---	---
+/- S&P 500	---	---
+/- Best Fit Index :	---	---

Trailing Returns

	Total Return %	+/- S&P 500	+/- S&P Metals	% Rank All	% Rank Obj	Growth of $10,000
3 Mo	-10.51	-10.49	-4.16	98	5	8,949
6 Mo	---	---	---	---	---	---
1 Yr	---	---	---	---	---	---
3 Yr Avg	---	---	---	---	---	---
5 Yr Avg	---	---	---	---	---	---
10 Yr Avg	---	---	---	---	---	---
15 Yr Avg	---	---	---	---	---	---

Operations

Address and Telephone	One Corporate Center Rye, NY 10580-1434 800-422-3554 / 914-921-5100	
Advisor	Gabelli Funds	
Subadvisor	None	
Distributor	Gabelli & Company	
States Available	N/A	
Report Grade	N/A	
Income Distrib	Paid Annually	
* Date of Inception	07-11-94	
Fiscal Year End	December	

Min Initial Purchase	$1000 (Addt'l: None)
Min IRA Purchase	$1000 (Addt'l: None)
Min Auto Invest Plan	$1000 (Systematic Inv: None)

Expenses & Fees

Sales Fees	0.00% front
	0.00% deferred
	0.25% 12b-1
Management Fee	1.00% flat fee
3-,5-,10-yr Expense Projections	$55, N/A, N/A
Annual Brokerage Cost	---

Risk Analysis

Time Period	Load-Adj Return %	Risk % Rank [1] All	Risk % Rank [1] Obj	Morningstar [2] Return	Morningstar [2] Risk	Morningstar Risk-Adj Rating
1 Yr	---					
3 Yr	---	---	---	---	---	
5 Yr	---	---	---	---	---	
10 Yr	---	---	---	---	---	

Average Historical Rating ---

[1] 1 = low, 100 = high [2] 1.00 = Equity Avg [3] 1.00 = 90-day T-bill return

Other Measures

			Standard S&P 500	Best Fit
Standard Deviation	---	Alpha	---	---
Mean	---	Beta	---	---
Sharpe Ratio	---	R-Squared	---	---

Investment Style

	Stock Portfolio Avg	Relative S&P 500
Price/Earnings Ratio	32.0#	1.73
Price/Book Ratio	3.4#	1.01
5 Yr Earnings Gr %	5.9#	1.07
Return on Assets %	11.7#	1.57
Debt % Total Cap	---	---
Med Mkt Cap ($mil)	1029#	0.08

figure is based on 50% or less of stocks

Diversification Value for Portfolio Types

Large Cap: Small Cap: Bond: Balanced: Diversified:

Portfolio 12-31-94

Total Stocks: 57
Total Fixed-Income: 2

Share Chg (09-94)000	Amount 000		Value $000	% Net Assets
16	71	Stillwater Mining	914	5.21
12	17	Newmont Mining	612	3.49
14	21	Placer Dome	550	3.14
55	79	TVX Gold	535	3.05
48	108	Randgold & Exploration	535	3.05
18	33	Kloof Gold Mining	491	2.80
35	40	Pegasus Gold	460	2.62
17	20	American Barrick Resources	443	2.53
16	19	Pioneer Group	422	2.41
23	33	Cambior	407	2.32
160	305	Lebowa Platinum	387	2.21
7	14	Rustenburg Platinum	385	2.19
20	40	Saint Helena Gold Mines	380	2.17
28	51	North American Palladium	376	2.14
18	29	Santa Fe Pacific Gold	373	2.13
11	15	Impala Platinum	368	2.10
70	70	Kinross Gold	362	2.06
14	32	Harmony Gold Mining (ADR)	344	1.96
50	80	Miramar Mining	342	1.95
41	60	Goldcorp Cl A	333	1.90
5	7	Franco-Nevada Mining	332	1.89
15	15	Ashanti Goldfields (ADR)	324	1.85
50	180	Deelkrall Gold Mining (ADR)	294	1.67
9	13	Euro-Nevada Mining	269	1.53
136	150	Zapopan	266	1.52

Composition % 09-30-94

Cash	10.0	Preferreds	0.0
Stocks	86.0	Convertibles	4.0
Bonds	0.0	Other	0.0

Tax Analysis

	Tax-Adj Historical Return %	% Pretax Return
3 Yr Avg	---	---
5 Yr Avg	---	---
10 Yr Avg	---	---
Potential Capital Gain Exposure (% of assets)	---	

Most Similar Funds in MF500

Fund lacks three-year record

Index Allocation

	% of Stocks
S&P 500	17.9
S&P MidCap 400	0.0
U.S. Small Cap	3.8
Foreign	87.3

Regional Exposure 09-30-94

	% of Stocks
N. America	45
S. Africa	35
Australia	15
Other	5
Bullion	0

Morningstar   1995 Mutual Fund 500

Gabelli Growth

Ticker	Load	NAV	Yield	SEC Yield	Assets	Objective
GABGX	None	19.68	0.4%	N/A	483.6	Growth

Gabelli Growth Fund seeks capital appreciation. Current income is a secondary objective.

The fund invests in a diversified portfolio of readily marketable common stocks and convertibles. It seeks undervalued securities that have favorable prospects for earnings growth and anticipates that investments may be made largely in companies expected to have above-average or expanding market shares, profit margins, and returns on equity. When the fund's investments lose their perceived value relative to other similar or alternative investments, they are sold. The fund may invest up to 25% of its assets in foreign securities.

Manager's Investment Style

Given that the manager of this fund was only appointed at the start of 1995, the strategy going forward is not yet known. Prior to this, Mario Gabelli stood in as manager while he searched for a successor to Elizabeth Bramwell. The fund's history shows a combination of top-down and bottom-up strategies guiding the selection of stocks. Management emphasized strong earnings along with an expanding market share. High profit margins and return on equity were also priorities. This methodology produced a high-growth portfolio filled with pricy issues.

Fund Manager(s)

Howard F. Ward CFA, since 01-95. Birthdate: 02-56. BA, Northwestern U. 1978.

Manager Experience

	Dates Managed	Invest Obj	Std Dev	+/- Index
Not available.				

Historical Profile
Return: Average
Risk: Average
Rating: ★★★ Neutral

Investment Style History
Equity
Average % Stocks Held in Portfolio

Growth of $10,000
|||| Value of Fund ($000)
— Value of Index ($000) SPMid400
▼ Manager Change
▽ Partial Manager Change
► Mgr Unknown After
◄ Mgr Unknown Before

Performance Quartile (Within Objective)

	1983	1984	1985	1986	1987	1988	1989	1990	1991	1992	1993	1994	History
	---	---	---	---	9.51	12.65	17.07	16.27	21.28	21.59	23.26	19.68	NAV
	---	---	---	---	-5.47 *	39.16	40.11	-1.99	34.32	4.49	11.26	-3.40	Total Return %
	---	---	---	---	8.03 *	22.55	8.43	1.13	3.83	-3.13	1.20	-4.71	+/- S&P 500
	---	---	---	---	---	21.21	10.94	4.19	0.11	-4.48	-0.03	-3.33	+/- Wilshire 5000
	---	---	---	---	0.00	2.24	1.09	2.30	0.78	0.40	0.39	0.43	Income Return %
	---	---	---	---	-5.47	36.92	39.02	-4.29	33.53	4.09	10.86	-3.83	Capital Return %
	---	---	---	---	---	1	4	62	21	79	57	47	Total Rtn % Rank All
	---	---	---	---	---	1	7	35	52	74	52	64	Total Rtn % Rank Obj
	---	---	---	---	0.00	0.20	0.39	0.39	0.15	0.09	0.09	0.09	Income $
	---	---	---	---	0.00	0.33	0.48	0.07	0.42	0.56	0.67	2.70	Capital Gains $
	---	---	---	---	2.00	2.30	1.85	1.50	1.45	1.41	1.41	1.41	Expense Ratio %
	---	---	---	---	2.94	0.72	2.24	2.67	0.97	0.46	0.22	0.17	Income Ratio %
	---	---	---	---	---	82	48	75	50	46	81	---	Turnover Rate %
	---	---	---	---	3.5	12.0	110.7	203.0	420.9	624.4	695.9	483.6	Net Assets ($mil)

Performance 12-31-94

	1st Qtr	2nd Qtr	3rd Qtr	4th Qtr	Total
1987	---	---	4.06	-15.69	-5.47 *
1988	16.11	14.08	2.50	2.49	39.16
1989	10.59	12.44	11.00	1.51	40.11
1990	-1.99	6.40	-11.52	6.22	-1.99
1991	11.74	-0.88	8.27	12.01	34.32
1992	-4.75	-2.71	3.96	8.47	4.49
1993	0.56	0.60	7.28	2.52	11.26
1994	-5.85	-3.06	6.36	-0.49	-3.40

Bear Market Performance

Decile Rank (5-year period)

Worst —————————————— Best

	Worst 3 Mo Period 1985-89	Worst 3 Mo Period 1990-94
Gabelli Growth	---	-11.52
+/- S&P 500	---	2.23
+/- Best Fit Index : SPMid400	---	6.26

Trailing Returns

	Total Return %	+/- S&P 500	+/- Wil 5000	% Rank All	% Rank Obj	Growth of $10,000
3 Mo	-0.49	-0.47	0.28	34	32	9,951
6 Mo	5.84	0.98	1.22	9	26	10,584
1 Yr	-3.40	-4.71	-3.33	47	64	9,660
3 Yr Avg	3.94	-2.32	-2.67	71	66	11,230
5 Yr Avg	8.13	-0.56	-0.68	32	60	14,784
10 Yr Avg	---	---	---	---	---	---
15 Yr Avg	---	---	---	---	---	---

Operations

Address and Telephone	One Corporate Center Rye, NY 10580-1434 800-422-3554 / 914-921-5100
Advisor	Gabelli Funds
Subadvisor	None
Distributor	Gabelli & Company
States Available	All plus GU,PR,VI
Report Grade	A-
Income Distrib	Paid Irregularly
* Date of Inception	04-10-87
Fiscal Year End	December

Min Initial Purchase	$1000 (Addt'l: None)
Min IRA Purchase	$1000 (Addt'l: None)
Min Auto Invest Plan	$100 (Systematic Inv: $100)

Expenses & Fees
Sales Fees	0.00% front
	0.00% deferred
	0.25% 12b-1
Management Fee	1.00% flat fee
3-,5-,10-yr Expense Projections	$45, $77, $170
Annual Brokerage Cost	---

Risk Analysis

Time Period	Load-Adj Return %	Risk % Rank [1] All	Risk % Rank [1] Obj	Morningstar [2] Return	Morningstar Risk	Morningstar Risk-Adj Rating
1 Yr	-3.40					
3 Yr	3.94	78	53	0.11 [3]	0.91	★★★
5 Yr	8.13	71	29	0.84 [3]	0.84	★★★
10 Yr	---	---	---	---	---	---

Average Historical Rating (57 months)   4.4 ★s

[1] 1 = low, 100 = high   [2] 1.00 = Equity Avg   [3] 1.00 = 90-day T-bill return

Other Measures
	Standard S&P 500	Best Fit SPMid400
Standard Deviation	9.27	
Mean	4.30	
Sharpe Ratio	0.08	
Alpha	-2.0	-2.5
Beta	0.97	0.86
R-Squared	69	84

Investment Style

	Stock Portfolio Avg	Relative S&P 500
Price/Earnings Ratio	22.2	1.20
Price/Book Ratio	3.8	1.11
5 Yr Earnings Gr %	10.7	1.93
Return on Assets %	8.2	1.10
Debt % Total Cap	26.6	0.94
Med Mkt Cap ($mil)	4489	0.35

Style: Value Blend Growth / Size Large Med Small

Diversification Value for Portfolio Types

Large Cap: Low	Small Cap: Low	Bond: High	Balanced: Low	Diversified: Low

Portfolio 09-30-94

Total Stocks: 145
Total Fixed-Income: 5

Share Chg (06-94) 000	Amount 000		Value $000	% Net Assets
-36	344	Genentech	18060	3.46
0	235	JP Morgan	14276	2.74
100	280	General Electric	13475	2.58
530	600	Tele-Communications Cl A	13313	2.55
80	240	AT & T	12960	2.48
0	245	CPC International	12403	2.38
0	175	Gillette	12381	2.37
-38	382	ALLTEL	10314	1.98
100	100	American Cyanamid	9950	1.91
0	220	Illinois Tool Works	9405	1.80
-4	157	Emerson Electric	9361	1.79
-10	290	Lubrizol	9026	1.73
35	160	Minnesota Mining & Mfg	8840	1.69
-25	170	Johnson & Johnson	8776	1.68
0	150	Colgate-Palmolive	8700	1.67
10	175	Hershey Foods	7875	1.51
5	100	AMP	7738	1.48
-10	260	Minerals Technologies	7703	1.48
-2	162	Nestle (Reg) (ADR)	7338	1.41
-55	225	Hospitality Franchise System	7059	1.35
-75	295	LDDS Communications Cl A	6508	1.25
-2	134	Coca-Cola	6491	1.24
-30	170	Walgreen	6396	1.23
0	200	American Express	6075	1.16
0	100	Hilton Hotels	5988	1.15

Composition % 09-30-94

				% of Stocks
Cash	2.0	Preferreds	0.0	
Stocks	97.0	Convertibles	1.0	
Bonds	0.0	Other	0.0	

Index Allocation

	% of Stocks
S&P 500	54.4
S&P MidCap 400	13.9
U.S. Small Cap	25.8
Foreign	7.1

Tax Analysis

	Tax-Adj Historical Return %	% Pretax Return
3 Yr Avg	2.11	52.5
5 Yr Avg	6.63	79.1
10 Yr Avg	---	---
Potential Capital Gain Exposure (% of assets)		11%

Most Similar Funds in MF500

IDS New Dimensions	Strong Fit
Liberty All-Star	Fair Fit
Warburg Pincus Cap Appr Con	Fair Fit

Sector Weightings

	% of Stocks	Relative S&P 500
Utilities	5.0	0.40
Energy	0.2	0.02
Financials	8.7	0.83
Industrial Cyclicals	18.7	1.14
Consumer Durables	4.0	0.64
Consumer Staples	17.1	1.37
Services	16.2	1.98
Retail	6.9	1.18
Health	10.1	1.17
Technology	13.2	1.44

MORNINGSTAR 1995 Mutual Fund 500

Gabelli Small Cap Growth

	Ticker	Load	NAV	Yield	SEC Yield	Assets	Objective
	GABSX	4.50%	15.84	0.0%	N/A	196.2	Small Company

Gabelli Small Cap Growth Fund seeks high capital appreciation. The fund normally invests at least 65% of its assets in the equity securities of smaller companies (those with market capitalizations of less than $500 million) that are likely to have rapid growth in revenue and/or earnings and above-average capital appreciation. The balance of its assets may be invested in nonconvertible debt securities of any credit rating. Up to 35% of fund assets may be invested in foreign securities.

Historical Profile

Return	Above Average
Risk	Below Average
Rating	★★★★
	Above Average

Investment Style History
Equity
Average % Stocks Held in Portfolio

46% 78% 82% 96%

Growth of $10,000
- |||| Value of Fund ($000)
- — Value of Index ($000)
  Russ 2000
- ▼ Manager Change
- ▽ Partial Manager Change
- ▶ Mgr Unknown After
- ◀ Mgr Unknown Before

Performance Quartile
(Within Objective)

Manager's Investment Style

Manager Mario Gabelli takes his value-driven strategy to the small-cap-stock arena. Gabelli picks stocks by hunting out issues with plenty of free cash flow, hearty earnings and revenue growth, and low prices relative to their private market values. Gabelli also typically plays a few themes in his portfolios; interactive media stocks have been long-time Gabelli favorites. He doesn't actively shift among sectors, though: Turnover in most Gabelli offerings is moderate.

Fund Manager(s)

Mario J. Gabelli CFA, since 10-91. Birthdate: 06-42. BS, Fordham U. 1965 MBA, Columbia U. 1967

Manager Experience	Dates Managed	Invest Obj	Std Dev	+/- Index
Mario J. Gabelli				
Gabelli Asset	03/86 - 12/94	G	11.85	3.17
Gabelli Equity	08/86 - 12/94	DE	13.51	1.96

	1983	1984	1985	1986	1987	1988	1989	1990	1991	1992	1993	1994	History
	---	---	---	---	---	---	---	---	12.21	14.50	17.38	15.84	NAV
	---	---	---	---	---	---	---	---	22.78 *	20.27	22.76	-2.93	Total Return %
	---	---	---	---	---	---	---	---	14.39 *	12.65	12.70	-4.25	+/- S&P 500
	---	---	---	---	---	---	---	---		8.51	8.22	-0.28	+/- Wilshire 4500
	---	---	---	---	---	---	---	---	0.12	0.18	0.00	0.00	Income Return %
	---	---	---	---	---	---	---	---	22.66	20.09	22.76	-2.93	Capital Return %
	---	---	---	---	---	---	---	---		4	13	43	Total Rtn % Rank All
	---	---	---	---	---	---	---	---		22	24	65	Total Rtn % Rank Obj
	---	---	---	---	---	---	---	---	0.01	0.03	0.00	0.00	Income $
	---	---	---	---	---	---	---	---	0.07	0.16	0.42	1.03	Capital Gains $
	---	---	---	---	---	---	---	---		1.97	1.64	1.54	Expense Ratio %
	---	---	---	---	---	---	---	---		0.32	0.03	-0.28	Income Ratio %
	---	---	---	---	---	---	---	---		---	14	19	Turnover Rate %
	---	---	---	---	---	---	---	---	25.7	123.9	215.0	196.2	Net Assets ($mil)

Performance 12-31-94

	1st Qtr	2nd Qtr	3rd Qtr	4th Qtr	Total
1987	---	---	---	---	---
1988	---	---	---	---	---
1989	---	---	---	---	---
1990	---	---	---	---	---
1991	---	---	---	---	22.78 *
1992	9.91	-0.07	-2.31	12.10	20.27
1993	6.62	1.81	7.37	5.33	22.76
1994	-3.57	-2.57	5.57	-2.15	-2.93

Bear Market Performance

Decile Rank (5-year period)

Worst ———————————————— Best

	Worst 3 Mo Period 1985-89	Worst 3 Mo Period 1990-94
Gabelli Small Cap Growth	---	---
+/- S&P 500	---	---
+/- Best Fit Index :	---	---

Trailing Returns

	Total Return %	+/- S&P 500	+/- Wil 4500	% Rank All	% Rank Obj	Growth of $10,000
3 Mo	-2.15	-2.13	0.36	71	70	9,785
6 Mo	3.31	-1.55	-0.89	19	71	10,331
1 Yr	-2.93	-4.25	-0.28	43	65	9,707
3 Yr Avg	12.74	6.48	5.14	7	25	14,331
5 Yr Avg	---	---	---	---	---	---
10 Yr Avg	---	---	---	---	---	---
15 Yr Avg	---	---	---	---	---	---

Operations

Address and Telephone	One Corporate Center	Min Initial Purchase
	Rye, NY 10580-1434	Min IRA Purchase
	800-422-3554 / 914-921-5100	Min Auto Invest Plan
Advisor	Gabelli Funds	
Subadvisor	None	**Expenses & Fees**
Distributor	Gabelli & Company	Sales Fees
States Available	All plus GU,PR,VI	
Report Grade	A-	
Income Distrib	Paid Annually	Management Fee
* Date of Inception	10-22-91	3-,5-,10-yr Expense Projections
Fiscal Year End	September	Annual Brokerage Cost

Min Initial Purchase	$1000 (Addt'l: None)
Min IRA Purchase	$1000 (Addt'l: None)
Min Auto Invest Plan	$100 (Systematic Inv: $100)

Sales Fees	4.50% front
	0.00% deferred
	0.25% 12b-1
Management Fee	1.00% flat fee
3-,5-,10-yr Expense Projections	$94, $130, $231
Annual Brokerage Cost	0.18%

Risk Analysis

Time Period	Load-Adj Return %	Risk % Rank [1] All	Obj	Morningstar [2] Return	Morningstar Risk	Morningstar Risk-Adj Rating
1 Yr	-7.30					
3 Yr	11.03	60	11	2.31 [3]	0.66	★★★★
5 Yr	---			---	---	
10 Yr	---			---	---	

Average Historical Rating (3 months) 4.0 ★s

[1] 1 = low, 100 = high [2] 1.00 = Equity Avg [3] 1.00 = 90-day T-bill return

Other Measures

			Standard S&P 500	Best Fit Russ 2000
Standard Deviation	9.27	Alpha	6.9	3.5
Mean	12.48	Beta	0.77	0.69
Sharpe Ratio	0.97	R-Squared	44	76

Investment Style

	Stock Portfolio Avg	Relative S&P 500
Price/Earnings Ratio	22.2	1.20
Price/Book Ratio	3.1	0.93
5 Yr Earnings Gr %	1.8#	0.32
Return on Assets %	6.6	0.88
Debt % Total Cap	33.2	1.17
Med Mkt Cap ($mil)	236	0.02

figure is based on 50% or less of stocks

Style: Value Blend Growth / Size: Large Med Small

Diversification Value for Portfolio Types

Large Cap: Medium	Small Cap: Low	Bond: High	Balanced: Low	Diversified: Medium

Portfolio 09-30-94

Total Stocks: 278
Total Fixed-Income: 8

Share Chg (06-94) 000	Amount 000		Value $000	% Net Assets
-9	188	Liberty	5006	2.43
-28	139	Pittway Cl A	5004	2.43
0	223	CLARCOR	4506	2.19
20	220	AMETEK	3905	1.90
0	205	Tredegar Industries	3793	1.84
0	70	United Television	3763	1.83
0	200	Eskimo Pie	3450	1.68
10	230	Neiman-Marcus Group	3421	1.66
0	470	Lamson & Sessions	3290	1.60
-25	120	AptarGroup	3240	1.58
0	103	Media General Cl A	3064	1.49
0	152	Dynamics of America	3002	1.46
0	410	Aztar	2871	1.40
1	66	Greif Brothers Cl A	2854	1.39
0	58	Pioneer Group	2703	1.31
16	596	Tyler	2680	1.30
0	170	Intl Family Entertainment B	2465	1.20
0	150	BET Holdings Cl A	2419	1.18
0	10	Brau & Brunnen	2373	1.15
0	310	M/A-Communications	2364	1.15
0	100	Contel Cellular Cl A	2363	1.15
-15	110	Allen Group	2269	1.10
-2	98	Church & Dwight	2254	1.10
-5	100	CalMat	2113	1.03
0	50	IDEX	2025	0.98

Composition % 09-30-94

Cash	1.0	Preferreds	0.0
Stocks	98.0	Convertibles	1.0
Bonds	0.0	Other	0.0

Tax Analysis

	Tax-Adj Historical Return %	% Pretax Return
3 Yr Avg	11.72	91.0
5 Yr Avg	---	---
10 Yr Avg	---	---
Potential Capital Gain Exposure (% of assets)		14%

Most Similar Funds in MF500

MainStay Value B	Fair Fit
Columbia Special	Fair Fit
Neuberger&Berman Partners	Fair Fit

Index Allocation

	% of Stocks
S&P 500	5.4
S&P MidCap 400	11.8
U.S. Small Cap	76.2
Foreign	7.6

Sector Weightings

	% of Stocks	Relative S&P 500
Utilities	1.2	0.09
Energy	0.9	0.09
Financials	9.1	0.86
Industrial Cyclicals	29.6	1.81
Consumer Durables	13.5	2.18
Consumer Staples	6.3	0.50
Services	19.8	2.44
Retail	4.4	0.76
Health	0.2	0.02
Technology	15.0	1.64

GAM International

GAM International Fund seeks long-term capital appreciation. The fund normally invests at least 65% of its assets in securities issued in at least three foreign countries. It invests primarily in equity securities, although it may invest a substantial portion of its assets in debt securities. The fund may invest in Canada, the United Kingdom, Continental Europe, and the Pacific Basin. No more than 5% of the fund's assets may be invested in debt securities rated below investment grade. In addition to direct foreign investment, the fund may purchase American Depositary Receipts and European Depositary Receipts.

Manager's Investment Style

Manager John Horseman has taken an unusual approach to international investing. Unlike many of his peers, he maintains consistent stakes in bonds (especially European issues) and cash, and regularly underweights Japan. Although he emphasizes larger, well-known names in the markets he invests in, he is willing to move quickly in and out of positions and to concentrate assets in favored positions.

Fund Manager(s)

John Horseman, since 04-90. Birthdate: 10-58.
Economics, U. of Birmingham 1980

Manager Experience

	Dates Managed	Invest Obj	Std Dev	+/- Index
John Horseman				
GAM Global	04/90 - 12/94	WW	17.04	-2.22

Ticker	Load	NAV	Yield	SEC Yield	Assets	Objective
GAMNX	5.00%	172.06	3.1%	N/A	159.4	Foreign Stock

Historical Profile

Return	Above Average
Risk	Average
Rating	★★★★
	Above Average

Investment Style History
Equity

Average % Stocks Held in Portfolio

--- | --- | --- | 96% | 50% | 60% | 42% | 72% | 44%

Growth of $10,000

- IIII Value of Fund ($000)
- — Value of Index ($000) MSEASEA
- ▼ Manager Change
- ▽ Partial Manager Change
- ► Mgr Unknown After
- ◄ Mgr Unknown Before

Performance Quartile (Within Objective)

	1983	1984	1985	1986	1987	1988	1989	1990	1991	1992	1993	1994	History
NAV	---	---	159.26	219.12	132.91	148.08	170.23	128.74	148.63	145.64	239.03	172.06	NAV
Total Return %	---	---	57.95 *	47.51	12.05	21.51	22.46	-7.30	15.56	3.08	79.97	-10.22	Total Return %
+/- S&P 500	---	---	26.21 *	28.83	6.79	4.90	-9.22	-4.19	-14.92	-4.54	69.91	-11.54	+/- S&P 500
+/- MSCI EAFE	---	---	---	-21.93	-12.58	-6.76	11.92	16.15	3.43	15.25	47.40	-18.00	+/- MSCI EAFE
Income Return %	---	---	0.00	0.02	1.49	0.39	0.16	0.00	0.00	3.02	2.97	3.58	Income Return %
Capital Return %	---	---	57.95	47.48	10.56	21.12	22.30	-7.30	15.50	0.06	76.99	-13.80	Capital Return %
Total Rtn % Rank All	---	---	---	3	8	11	30	78	55	84	1	94	Total Rtn % Rank All
Total Rtn % Rank Obj	---	---	---	60	23	14	48	20	33	5	2	87	Total Rtn % Rank Obj
Income $	---	---	0.00	0.04	2.34	0.56	0.26	0.00	0.08	4.31	3.39	6.59	Income $
Capital Gains $	---	---	0.00	12.36	108.7	11.83	9.98	29.06	0.05	3.02	9.48	37.94	Capital Gains $
Expense Ratio %	---	---	2.00	1.81	2.23	2.76	2.74	2.30	2.11	2.03	1.99	1.58	Expense Ratio %
Income Ratio %	---	---	0.12	0.66	0.38	0.27	0.19	1.32	3.25	4.85	2.28	2.05	Income Ratio %
Turnover Rate %	---	---	---	82	80	23	33	254	161	109	98	---	Turnover Rate %
Net Assets ($mil)	---	---	10.0	25.0	21.0	19.6	20.8	23.4	40.4	41.0	80.7	159.4	Net Assets ($mil)

Performance 12-31-94

	1st Qtr	2nd Qtr	3rd Qtr	4th Qtr	Total
1987	22.48	3.90	4.48	-15.72	12.05
1988	2.66	-0.65	3.24	15.40	21.51
1989	-2.94	2.61	11.81	9.97	22.46
1990	-2.84	8.31	-9.06	-3.13	-7.30
1991	3.71	-3.23	6.63	7.98	15.56
1992	-3.18	11.67	5.20	-9.37	3.08
1993	12.42	5.61	18.26	28.19	79.97
1994	-10.58	0.97	0.91	-1.47	-10.22

Bear Market Performance

Decile Rank (5-year period)

Worst |||||||||||| Best

	Worst 3 Mo Period 1985-89	Worst 3 Mo Period 1990-94
GAM International	---	-12.97
+/- S&P 500	---	-17.95
+/- Best Fit Index : MSEASEA	---	-5.42

Trailing Returns

	Total Return %	+/- S&P 500	+/- MSCI EAFE	% Rank All	% Rank Obj	Growth of $10,000
3 Mo	-1.47	-1.45	-0.45	56	7	9,853
6 Mo	-0.57	-5.43	0.35	66	39	9,943
1 Yr	-10.22	-11.54	-18.00	94	87	8,978
3 Yr Avg	18.53	12.27	10.67	2	1	16,654
5 Yr Avg	12.27	3.58	10.78	8	1	17,840
10 Yr Avg	---	---	---	---	---	---
15 Yr Avg	---	---	---	---	---	---

Operations

Address and Telephone	135 East 57th Street 25th Floor New York, NY 10022 800-426-4685 / 212-407-4600	
Advisor	GAM International Management	
Subadvisor	None	
Distributor	GAM Services	
States Available	Selected states	
Report Grade	B-	
Income Distrib	Paid Annually	
* Date of Inception	01-01-85	
Fiscal Year End	December	

Risk Analysis

Time Period	Load-Adj Return %	Risk % Rank [1] All	Obj	Morningstar [2] Return	Morningstar Risk	Morningstar Risk-Adj Rating
1 Yr	-14.71					
3 Yr	16.52	83	26	4.23 [3]	1.02	★★★★★
5 Yr	11.13	76	6	1.68 [3]	0.91	★★★★
10 Yr	---	---	---	---	---	---

Average Historical Rating (84 months)   4.0 ★s

[1] = low, 100 = high   [2] 1.00 = Equity Avg   [3] 1.00 = 90-day T-bill return

Other Measures

			Standard S&P 500	Best Fit MSEASEA
Standard Deviation	16.98	Alpha	14.3	9.8
Mean	18.49	Beta	0.52	0.88
Sharpe Ratio	0.88	R-Squared	6	48

Investment Style

	Stock Portfolio Avg	Rel MSCI EAFE	Rel Obj
Price/Earnings Ratio	39.9	1.08	1.42
Price/Cash Flow	20.1	1.29	1.50
Price/Book Ratio	2.6	1.01	0.89
5 Yr Earnings Gr %	-8.7#	---	-2.28
Return on Assets %	4.8#	1.05	0.66
Debt % Total Cap	57.8	1.70	2.09
Med Mkt Cap ($mil)	9935	0.83	1.93

figure is based on 50% or less of stocks

Style: V B G / Size L M S

Diversification Value for Portfolio Types

Large Cap: High	Small Cap: High	Bond: High	Balanced: High	Diversified: High

Expenses & Fees

Sales Fees	5.00% front
	0.00% deferred
	0.00% 12b-1
Management Fee	1.00% flat fee
3-,5-,10-yr Expense Projections	$109, $152, $270
Annual Brokerage Cost	0.88%

Min Initial Purchase	$10000 (Addt'l: $1000)
Min IRA Purchase	$10000 (Addt'l: $1000)
Min Auto Invest Plan	N/A

Portfolio 12-31-94

Share Chg (06-94)000	Amount 000	Total Stocks: 31 / Total Fixed-Income: 10	Value $000	% Net Assets
	51300	Republic of Germany 6.25%	26748	16.78
	32000	Govt of Netherlands 7.5%	17338	10.87
8300	8300	Mitsubishi	8300	5.21
8227	8300	Industrial Bank of Japan	8300	5.21
8300	8300	Credit Suisse	8300	5.21
	12500	United Kingdom Treasury 3.5%	8087	5.07
	570000	Govt of France 6%	7705	4.83
68	68	AMEV	2869	1.80
-22	308	North West Water	2611	1.64
	1400	ASDA Cv 10.75%	2322	1.46
200	200	United Overseas Bank (For)	2113	1.33
	55	ABN AMRO Holding Cv Pfd 6%	1846	1.16
	1005	Thames Water Cv	1832	1.15
	1055	Land Securities Cv	1783	1.12
53	53	Koninklijke Ptt	1780	1.12
1007	1007	Bicc Group	1741	1.09
950	950	Hong Kong & China Gas	1535	0.96
	9	Lyonnaise des Eaux Cv 6.5%	1475	0.93
0	20	Accor	1443	0.91
0	20	Credit Local de France	1430	0.90

Regional Exposure 09-30-94

% of Stocks

Europe	29	Pacific Rim	18
Japan	24	Other	0
Latin Amer	15		

Composition % 09-30-94

Cash	17.9	Preferreds	0.0
Stocks	42.2	Convertibles	7.3
Bonds	31.2	Other	1.4

Tax Analysis

	Tax-Adj Historical Return %	% Pretax Return
3 Yr Avg	14.73	76.7
5 Yr Avg	8.71	66.1
10 Yr Avg	---	---

Potential Capital Gain Exposure
(% of assets)   -6%

Most Similar Funds in MF500

Scudder International	Weak Fit
Vanguard Intl Growth	Weak Fit
T. Rowe Price Intl Stock	Weak Fit

Country Exposure 09-30-94

% of Stocks

United Kingdom	29
Germany	24
Netherlands	15
France	10
Singapore	8

Total Number of Countries: 11
Hedging Policy: Occasional

Sector Weightings

	% of Stocks	Relative S&P 500
Utilities	8.0	0.90
Energy	4.8	1.18
Financials	50.2	2.66
Industrial Cyclicals	11.0	0.44
Consumer Durables	2.6	0.24
Consumer Staples	0.0	0.00
Services	7.2	0.66
Retail	15.1	2.59
Health	0.0	0.00
Technology	1.1	0.21

MORNINGSTAR   1995 Mutual Fund 500

Gateway Index Plus

Ticker	Load	NAV	Yield	SEC Yield	Assets	Objective
GATEX	None	15.48	1.6%	1.80%	164.7	Growth/Inc.

Gateway Index Plus Fund seeks current return consistent with low risk.

The fund purchases securities of the same type and in virtually the same proportion as are found in the S&P 100 Index. It then writes options on that index rather than on individual stocks in its portfolio. The fund is designed for conservative investors who wish to maximize their total rate of return over a complete market cycle.

The fund was named Gateway Option Income Fund prior to Feb. 4, 1988. From that date until April 2, 1990, the fund was known as Gateway Option Index Fund.

Manager's Investment Style

Manager Peter Thayer buys a market-cap-weighted index of the S&P 100, then sells call options on the index which limit the fund's potential for losses. The premiums from these options also provide income for distribution, but the strategy does restricts the fund's ability to participate fully in a stock rally.

Fund Manager(s)

Peter W. Thayer CFA(1978), since 12-77.
Birthdate: 09-48. BBA, U. of Wisconsin 1971 MBA, Harvard 1973

Manager Experience	Dates Managed	Invest Obj	Std Dev	+/- Index
Peter W. Thayer				
Gateway Mid-Cap Index	09/92 - 12/94	G	7.72	-7.05
Gateway Small Cap Index	06/93 - 12/94	SC	9.04	-4.76

Historical Profile

Return	Average
Risk	Low
Rating	★★★★ Above Average

Investment Style History
Equity

Average % Stocks Held in Portfolio

| 100% | 100% | 100% | 98% | 99% | 97% | 99% | 100% |

Performance Quartile (Within Objective)

1983	1984	1985	1986	1987	1988	1989	1990	1991	1992	1993	1994	History
14.91	14.23	14.69	14.63	11.60	13.67	15.49	13.64	15.24	15.51	15.85	15.48	NAV
14.80	4.04	15.89	12.69	-5.65	19.76	19.45	10.32	17.80	5.15	7.40	5.57	Total Return %
-7.67	-2.23	-15.84	-5.99	-10.91	3.15	-12.24	-12.69	-2.47	-2.65	4.25	+/- S&P 500
-8.67	0.99	-16.67	-3.41	-8.02	1.82	-9.73	16.50	-16.41	-3.83	-3.88	5.64	+/- Wilshire 5000
3.83	4.21	3.34	2.43	2.33	1.91	2.72	2.78	2.14	1.85	1.87	1.75	Income Return %
10.96	-0.18	12.55	10.26	-7.98	17.84	16.73	7.54	15.65	3.30	5.53	3.82	Capital Return %
58	54	90	69	90	14	36	4	49	76	82	4	Total Rtn % Rank All
81	48	98	73	94	25	74	1	95	78	79	3	Total Rtn % Rank Obj
0.55	0.57	0.46	0.34	0.34	0.21	0.37	0.41	0.30	0.28	0.29	0.27	Income $
1.31	0.65	1.22	1.46	1.91	0.00	0.43	3.00	0.51	0.23	0.51	0.97	Capital Gains $
1.41	1.45	1.50	1.49	1.48	2.08	1.40	1.34	1.22	1.11	1.11	---	Expense Ratio %
3.50	3.84	2.81	2.23	1.83	1.75	2.21	2.59	2.17	1.96	1.58	---	Income Ratio %
170	103	96	85	175	10	30	79	31	15	17	---	Turnover Rate %
26.9	21.6	28.4	45.3	27.3	27.3	31.5	38.0	81.4	212.3	207.2	164.7	Net Assets ($mil)

Growth of $10,000

- IIII Value of Fund ($000)
- — Value of Index ($000) S&P 500
- ▼ Manager Change
- ▽ Partial Manager Change
- ► Mgr Unknown After
- ◄ Mgr Unknown Before

Performance 12-31-94

	1st Qtr	2nd Qtr	3rd Qtr	4th Qtr	Total
1987	4.81	5.68	1.91	-16.42	-5.65
1988	6.12	5.55	3.73	3.08	19.76
1989	3.08	3.93	5.53	5.66	19.45
1990	2.00	4.01	-4.61	9.01	10.32
1991	6.38	1.66	4.38	4.35	17.80
1992	0.92	1.83	1.35	0.95	5.15
1993	1.55	1.79	1.51	2.37	7.40
1994	-2.59	1.37	4.58	2.23	5.57

Bear Market Performance

Decile Rank (5-year period)

Worst ———————————————————— Best

	Worst 3 Mo Period 1985-89	Worst 3 Mo Period 1990-94
Gateway Index Plus	-19.96	-4.84
+/- S&P 500	9.62	9.01
+/- Best Fit Index : S&P 500	9.62	9.01

Trailing Returns

	Total Return %	+/- S&P 500	+/- Wil 5000	% Rank All	% Rank Obj	Growth of $10,000
3 Mo	2.23	2.25	3.00	3	1	10,223
6 Mo	6.91	2.05	2.29	7	3	10,691
1 Yr	5.57	4.25	5.64	4	3	10,557
3 Yr Avg	6.03	-0.23	-0.58	33	48	11,922
5 Yr Avg	9.15	0.46	0.33	22	20	15,492
10 Yr Avg	10.57	-3.81	-3.29	52	83	27,307
15 Yr Avg	10.30	-4.19	-3.68	73	90	43,494

Operations

Address and Telephone	400 TechneCenter Drive Suite 220
	Milford, OH 45150
	800-354-6339 / 513-248-2700
Advisor	Gateway Investment Advisers
Subadvisor	None
Distributor	Gateway Trust
States Available	All
Report Grade	B+
Income Distrib	Paid Quarterly
Date of Inception	12-07-77
Fiscal Year End	December

Min Initial Purchase	$1000 (Addt'l: $100)
Min IRA Purchase	$1000 (Addt'l: $100)
Min Auto Invest Plan	$1000 (Systematic Inv: $100)

Expenses & Fees

Sales Fees	0.00% front
	0.00% deferred
	0.00% 12b-1
Management Fee	0.90% max./0.60% min.
3-,5-,10-yr Expense Projections	$37, $64, $141
Annual Brokerage Cost	0.15%

Risk Analysis

Time Period	Load-Adj Return %	Risk % Rank All	Risk % Rank Obj	Morningstar Return	Morningstar Risk	Morningstar Risk-Adj Rating
1 Yr	5.57					
3 Yr	6.03	10	1	0.73[3]	0.29	★★★
5 Yr	9.15	31	1	1.12[3]	0.30	★★★★
10 Yr	10.57	32	1	0.64	0.36	★★★★
Average Historical Rating (109 months)					3.3	★s

[1] = low, 100 = high   [2] 1.00 = Equity Avg   [3] 1.00 = 90-day T-bill return

Other Measures

			Standard S&P 500	Best Fit S&P 500
Standard Deviation	4.05	Alpha	1.3	1.3
Mean	5.96	Beta	0.40	0.40
Sharpe Ratio	0.60	R-Squared	63	63

Investment Style

	Stock Portfolio Avg	Relative S&P 500
Price/Earnings Ratio	17.1	0.93
Price/Book Ratio	3.3	0.97
5 Yr Earnings Gr %	4.3	0.77
Return on Assets %	6.9	0.92
Debt % Total Cap	27.6	0.98
Med Mkt Cap ($mil)	26570	2.05

Style: Value Blend Growth — Size Large/Med/Small

Diversification Value for Portfolio Types

| Large Cap: Low | Small Cap: High | Bond: High | Balanced: Low | Diversified: Medium |

Portfolio 06-30-94

Share Chg (03-94) 000	Amount 000		Value $000	% Net Assets
		Total Stocks: 100		
		Total Fixed-Income: 0		
110	222	General Electric	10351	5.99
-1	176	AT & T	9570	5.54
-1	162	Exxon	9151	5.30
-1	299	Wal-Mart Stores	7256	4.20
-11	169	Coca-Cola	6866	3.97
0	89	El duPont de Nemours	5172	2.99
-1	167	Merck	4965	2.87
0	93	General Motors	4668	2.70
0	75	IBM	4424	2.56
0	52	Mobil	4261	2.47
0	65	Ford Motor	3835	2.22
-1	65	Amoco	3688	2.13
-8	84	Johnson & Johnson	3606	2.09
-1	67	Bristol-Myers Squibb	3582	2.07
-1	41	American International Group	3578	2.07
0	57	Bell Atlantic	3192	1.85
-4	54	Intel	3183	1.84
0	104	PepsiCo	3176	1.84
0	70	Walt Disney	2930	1.70
-1	56	Minnesota Mining & Mfg	2782	1.61
0	72	Ameritech	2739	1.59
44	92	McDonald's	2651	1.53
-1	33	Hewlett-Packard	2480	1.44
0	36	Dow Chemical	2347	1.36
0	46	Sears Roebuck	2203	1.28

Composition % 12-31-94

Cash	2.3	Preferreds	0.0
Stocks	98.8	Convertibles	0.0
Bonds	0.0	Other	-1.1

Tax Analysis

	Tax-Adj Historical Return %	% Pretax Return
3 Yr Avg	4.33	70.6
5 Yr Avg	6.29	64.9
10 Yr Avg	7.67	63.2
Potential Capital Gain Exposure (% of assets)		6%

Most Similar Funds in MF500

Analytic Optioned Equity	Weak Fit
Vanguard STAR	Weak Fit
George Putnam of Boston A	Weak Fit

Index Allocation

	% of Stocks
S&P 500	99.8
S&P MidCap 400	0.0
U.S. Small Cap	0.3
Foreign	0.5

Sector Weightings

	% of Stocks	Relative S&P 500
Utilities	12.4	1.00
Energy	13.2	1.30
Financials	7.7	0.73
Industrial Cyclicals	21.1	1.29
Consumer Durables	6.9	1.11
Consumer Staples	9.7	0.77
Services	6.0	0.74
Retail	8.0	1.38
Health	6.1	0.70
Technology	9.0	0.98

Gemini II Capital

	Ticker	NAV	Mkt Price	Prem/Disc	Yield	Objective
	GMI	$19.64	$17.63	-10.3%	0.0%	Domestic Eq

Gemini II seeks long-term capital appreciation and current income with long-term growth potential.

The fund will pursue its objective primarily through investment in dividend-paying stocks that meet a minimum income-rate objective of 110% of the S&P 500's yield.

Capital shares are entitled to any capital appreciation from the fund's assets, and they will own all the remaining assets once the fund redeems the income shares on Jan. 1, 1997. Capital shareholders will receive no income as long as income shares are outstanding. Any realized capital gains needed to pay the income shares' minimum cumulative dividends will reduce the return to capital shareholders.

On Jan. 31, 1997, capital shareholders will vote on open-ending or liquidating the fund.

| 20.4 | -9.5 | -8.1 | -22.3 | -10.4 | -11.4 | -13.3 | -16.5 | -9.7 | -9.2 | Highest Prem/Disc |
| -4.1 | -21.4 | -18.1 | -29.7 | -22.4 | -19.2 | -24.1 | -24.2 | -21.1 | -17.9 | Lowest Prem/Disc |

Historical Profile

Return Average
Risk Above Average
Rating ★★ Below Average

Growth of $10,000
— at NAV ($000)
— at Market Price ($000)

Premium Discount %

	1983	1984	1985	1986	1987	1988	1989	1990	1991	1992	1993	1994	History
	---	---	11.47	14.61	12.98	16.56	17.44	11.51	16.28	18.71	22.10	19.64	NAV
	---	---	24.01*	35.15	-1.95	32.68	8.85	-32.61	49.45	18.40	23.71	-8.06	NAV Total Return %
	---	---	3.11*	16.47	-7.21	16.07	-22.84	-29.50	18.96	10.79	13.65	-9.37	+/- S&P 500
	---	---	---	11.97	3.92	9.66	-12.67	-16.25	0.92	-4.22	10.87	-5.32	+/- Wil Mid Value
	---	---	0.00*	0.00	0.00	0.00	0.00	0.00	0.00	0.00	0.00	0.00	Income Return %
	---	---	24.01*	35.15	-1.95	32.68	8.85	-32.61	49.45	18.40	23.71	-8.06	Capital Return %
	---	---	---	9	76	7	72	96	8	10	20	58	Total Rtn % Rank All
	---	---	---	7	68	7	88	89	19	18	14	83	Total Rtn % Rank Obj
	---	---	10.60*	16.96	-3.29	25.98	25.40	-37.92	41.79	12.87	33.61	-8.25	Market Total Rtn %
	---	---	4.8	-15.2	-14.1	-25.6	-16.4	-15.9	-19.4	-20.6	-14.5	-12.8	Avg Prem/Disc %
	---	---	0.00	0.00	0.00	0.00	0.00	0.00	0.00	0.00	0.00	0.00	Income $
	---	---	0.06	0.74	1.11	0.51	0.52	0.20	0.75	0.45	0.94	0.61	Capital Gains $
	---	---	0.00	0.00	0.00	0.00	0.00	0.00	0.00	0.00	0.00	0.00	Expense Ratio %
	---	---	---	---	---	---	---	---	---	---	---	---	Income Ratio %
	---	---	---	---	---	---	---	---	---	---	---	---	Turnover Rate %
	---	---	125.3	151.5	141.7	237.7	190.4	125.6	186.0	205.5	241.3	207.8	Net Assets ($mil)

Manager's Investment Style

Manager John Neff seeks stocks with high dividend yields--a sign of an underpriced security. Unfortunately for this fund, all of the dividends from its investments are collected by its sibling, Gemini II Income. Therefore, this fund only receives the capital gains and losses from the portfolio. Further, the income shares leverage the capital shares, so when stock prices are weak this fund endures enhanced capital losses. The fund has kept its head above water, though, and hopes to push up capital returns with a heavy stake in modest-P/E financials.

Fund Manager(s)

John B. Neff. Since 2-85. BBA U. of Toledo; MBA Case Western Reserve U.

Manager Experience

	Dates Managed	Invest Obj	Std Dev	+/- Index
John B. Neff				
Vanguard/Windsor	06/64 - 12/94	GI	14.79	3.20
Gemini II Inc	02/85 - 12/94	I	2.88	-0.63

NAV Performance % 12-30-94

	1st Qtr	2nd Qtr	3rd Qtr	4th Qtr	Total
1987	21.20	9.34	-1.61	-24.80	-1.95
1988	11.86	17.70	1.64	-0.85	32.68
1989	5.31	10.32	8.58	-13.72	8.85
1990	-9.06	1.01	-33.83	10.87	-32.61
1991	34.93	-1.22	6.19	5.60	49.45
1992	2.83	5.50	-2.32	11.75	18.40
1993	11.28	2.55	9.13	-0.66	23.71
1994	-5.38	4.11	-0.87	-5.84	-8.06

Bear Market Performance

Decile Rank (5-year period)

Worst ————————————— Best

	Worst 3 Mo Period 1985-89	Worst 3 Mo Period 1990-94
Gemini II Cap	---	-38.97
+/- S&P 500	---	-25.13

Trailing Returns

	NAV Total Return %	+/- S&P 500	+/- Wil Mid Value	% Rank All	% Rank Obj	Mkt Total Return %
3 Mo	-5.84	-5.82	-2.93	86	77	-5.88
6 Mo	-6.66	-11.52	-6.73	97	92	-4.65
1 Yr	-8.06	-9.37	-5.32	58	83	-8.25
3 Yr Avg	10.43	4.17	0.02	20	21	14.09
5 Yr Avg	6.28	-2.41	-4.54	77	68	6.32
Incept Avg	12.56*	---	---	---	---	10.52*

Operations

Address and Telephone	Vanguard Financial Center Valley Forge, PA 19482 215-669-1000 / 800-662-7447
Advisor	Wellington Management Co.
Subadvisor	N/A
Administrator	Vanguard Group
Transfer Agent	First Bank of Boston
Custodian	State Street Bank and Trust Co.
Auditor	Price Waterhouse LLP
Legal Counsel	Internally Counselled

Income Distrib Schedule	Paid Irregularly
Management Fee	0.00%
Reinvestment Plan	No
Direct Purchase Plan	No
Shares Outstanding	10,920,550
Exchange	NYSE
*Date of Inception	02-15-85
Shareholder Report	B+

Risk Analysis

	Risk % Rank[1]		Morningstar[2]		Morningstar
	All	Obj	Return	Risk	Risk-Adj Rating
3 Yr	79	65	0.94	0.77	★★★
5 Yr	91	89	0.28	1.22	★★
10 Yr	---	---			

Average Historical Rating (83 months) 2.8 ★s

[1] = Low, 100 = High [2] 1.00 = Equity Avg [3] 1.00 = 90-day T-bill Return

Other Measures

				S&P 500
Standard Deviation	14.13	Alpha		3.32
Mean	10.97	Beta		1.45
Sharpe Ratio	0.53	R-Squared		66

Investment Style

	Stock Portfolio Avg	Relative S&P 500
Price/Earnings Ratio	16.6	0.90
Price/Cash Flow Ratio	5.5	0.47
Price/Book Ratio	1.2	0.37
5 Yr Earnings Gr %	-9.5	---
Return on Assets %	0.5	0.07
Debt % Total Cap	28.0	0.99
Med Mkt Cap ($mil)	5114	0.39

figure is based on less than 50% of stocks

Index Allocation

	% of Stocks
Dow 30	0.0
S&P 500	97.2
S&P Mid-Cap 400	0.4
US Small-Cap	0.0
Foreign	2.4

Diversification Value for Portfolio Types

Large Cap: Low	Small Cap: Medium	Bond: Medium	Balanced: Low	Diversified: Low

Portfolio 09-30-94

Total Equity: 18
Total Fixed-Income: 24

Share Chg (06-94)	Amount		Value $000	% Total Invest
0	188500	Atlantic Richfield	19015	5.58
0	584189	KeyCorp	17818	5.23
0	287100	CIGNA	17693	5.19
0	404000	First Union	17473	5.13
0	254592	Bankers Trust New York	16994	4.99
0	342260	Aetna Life & Casualty	15872	4.66
0	867100	USX-Marathon Group	15391	4.52
19000	776875	Great Western Financial	14955	4.39
0	703100	HF Ahmanson	14677	4.31
658937	658937	Unicom	14661	4.30
293900	396400	Chemical Banking	13874	4.07
---	12000000	Chrysler 10.4%	12990	3.81
654800	654800	K Mart	11705	3.44
---	1376000	Kaiser Aluminum Cv Pfd $1.00	11352	3.33
---	250000	Delta Air Lines Cv Pfd $3.50	11188	3.28
---	171000	Advanced Micro Devices Cv Pfd $3	10175	2.99
---	11000000	Seagate Technology Cv 6.75%	9212	2.70
0	185500	Pennzoil	8695	2.55
---	73000	Citicorp Cv Pfd 10.75%	8650	2.54
---	7000000	Geneva Steel 11.125%	7035	2.07
---	124400	Reynolds Metals Cv Pfd $3.31	6686	1.96
---	124400	Sea Containers Cv Pfd $4.00	5505	1.62
0	203400	Ultramar	5187	1.52
---	93600	Bethlehem Steel Cv Pfd $5.00	4937	1.45
0	100000	NationsBank	4900	1.44

Composition % 12-31-94

Cash	0.3	Preferreds	0.0
Stocks	60.3	Convertibles	34.9
Bonds	4.5	Other	0.0

Tax Analysis

	Tax-Adj Historical Return %	% Pretax Return
3 Yr Avg	9.32	88.4
5 Yr Avg	5.19	80.5
10 Yr Avg	---	---

Potential Capital Gain Exposure (% of assets)	1

Most Similar Funds in MF500

Vanguard/Windsor	Fair Fit
American Leaders A	Weak Fit
Smith Barney Income & Grth	Weak Fit

Sector Weightings

	% of Stocks	Relative S&P 500
Utilities	6.8	0.55
Energy	22.3	2.20
Financials	65.6	6.20
Industrial Cyclicals	0.0	0.00
Consumer Durables	0.0	0.00
Consumer Staples	0.0	0.00
Services	0.0	0.00
Retail	5.4	0.93
Health	0.0	0.00
Technology	0.0	0.00

Gemini II Income

	Ticker	NAV	Mkt Price	Prem/Disc	Yield	Objective
	GMIpr	$9.34	$10.50	12.4%	16.5%	Income

Gemini II seeks long-term capital appreciation and current and long-term growth of income.

The fund seeks to achieve its objective primarily through investment in dividend-paying stocks that meet a minimum income rate objective of 110% of the S&P's yield.

Income shares are entitled to any net income earned from fund holdings. The income shares are not entitled to any capital gains from fund holdings except as necessary to meet a minimum annual distribution of $0.80 per share.

The fund will redeem the income shares on Jan. 31, 1997, for $9.30 per share plus unpaid dividends.

Historical Profile

Return	High
Risk	Low
Rating	★★★★★ Highest

Highest Prem/Disc: 25.1 46.9 51.6 38.0 38.7 36.3 43.2 47.9 35.8 26.3
Lowest Prem/Disc: 14.6 20.1 20.1 28.7 27.7 14.2 21.8 22.7 17.6 5.2

Growth of $10,000
■ at NAV ($000)
— at Market Price ($000)

Premium Discount %

History	1983	1984	1985	1986	1987	1988	1989	1990	1991	1992	1993	1994
NAV	---	---	9.83	9.73	9.39	9.38	9.37	9.34	9.34	9.33	9.33	9.34
NAV Total Return %	---	---	11.54*	9.79	9.94	11.50	12.82	14.28	13.29	13.67	14.41	16.76
+/- S&P 500	---	---	-9.35*	-8.89	4.68	-5.11	-18.87	17.40	-17.20	6.06	4.36	15.45
+/- LB Aggregate	---	---	---	-5.46	7.18	3.62	-1.73	5.34	-2.71	6.43	4.66	19.68
Income Return %	---	---	5.84*	10.80	13.44	11.61	12.92	14.60	13.29	13.78	14.41	16.66
Capital Return %	---	---	5.70*	-1.02	-3.49	-0.11	-0.11	-0.32	0.00	-0.11	0.00	0.11
Total Rtn % Rank All	---	---	---	85	17	59	41	5	71	20	59	3
Total Rtn % Rank Obj	---	---	---	50	50	50	33	1	66	10	50	1
Market Total Rtn %	---	---	22.73*	29.94	-0.71	17.49	17.45	-0.78	34.69	2.10	12.03	4.23
Avg Prem/Disc %	---	---	19.2	39.9	37.0	32.6	32.3	28.0	35.3	35.2	29.9	18.3
Income $	---	---	0.60	1.33	1.72	1.42	1.59	1.66	1.65	1.67	1.66	1.73
Capital Gains $	---	---	0.00	0.00	0.00	0.00	0.00	0.00	0.00	0.00	0.00	0.00
Expense Ratio %	---	---	---	---	---	---	---	---	---	---	---	---
Income Ratio %	---	---	---	---	---	---	---	---	---	---	---	---
Turnover Rate %	---	---	---	---	---	---	---	---	---	---	---	---
Net Assets ($mil)	---	---	107.0	106.3	102.6	102.0	102.3	102.0	109.1	102.0	101.9	102.0

Manager's Investment Style

Manager John Neff seeks to deliver a high payout while also maintaining a stable NAV. Common-stock dividends are the primary ingredient in the fund's payout, with a recent emphasis on the financials sector. Management also employs junk bonds, convertibles, and preferreds in the portfolio and is known for its value bent. Neff will retire at the end of 1995.

Fund Manager(s)

John B. Neff. Since 2-85. BBA U. of Toledo; MBA Case Western Reserve U.

Manager Experience

	Dates Managed	Invest Obj	Std Dev	+/- Index
John B. Neff				
Vanguard/Windsor	06/64 - 12/94	GI	14.79	3.20
Gemini II Cap	02/85 - 12/94	DE	23.63	-1.01

NAV Performance % 12-30-94

	1st Qtr	2nd Qtr	3rd Qtr	4th Qtr	Total
1987	0.88	2.90	3.46	2.37	9.94
1988	2.78	3.35	3.15	1.76	11.50
1989	3.32	3.30	4.32	1.33	12.82
1990	3.98	3.37	3.54	2.69	14.28
1991	3.43	3.40	3.78	2.06	13.29
1992	3.67	3.69	3.75	1.92	13.67
1993	3.60	3.49	3.80	2.81	14.41
1994	4.04	3.76	4.37	3.63	16.76

Bear Market Performance

Decile Rank (5-year period)

Worst | | | | | | | | | | Best

	Worst 3 Mo Period 1985-89	Worst 3 Mo Period 1990-94
Gemini II Inc	---	1.75
+/- S&P 500	---	-1.71

Trailing Returns

	NAV Total Return %	+/- S&P 500	+/- LB Agg	% Rank All	% Rank Obj	Mkt Total Return %
3 Mo	3.63	3.65	3.26	3	1	-0.85
6 Mo	8.16	3.30	7.17	5	1	3.33
1 Yr	16.76	15.45	19.68	3	1	4.23
3 Yr Avg	14.94	8.68	10.40	9	1	6.03
5 Yr Avg	14.48	5.79	6.85	6	1	9.76
Incept Avg	12.95*	---	---	---	---	13.46*

Risk Analysis

	Risk % Rank[1] All	Obj	Morningstar[2] Return	Morningstar Risk	Morningstar Risk-Adj Rating
3 Yr	4	20	2.45	0.17	★★★★★
5 Yr	3	25	2.33	0.13	★★★★★
10 Yr					

Average Historical Rating (83 months) 4.5 ★s

[1] = Low, 100 = High [2] 1.00 = Hybrid Avg [3] 1.00 = 90-day T-bill Return

Other Measures

				S&P 500
Standard Deviation	4.34	Alpha		10.69
Mean	14.10	Beta		0.13
Sharpe Ratio	2.43	R-Squared		6

Investment Style

	Stock Portfolio Avg	Relative S&P 500
Price/Earnings Ratio	16.6	0.90
Price/Cash Flow Ratio	5.5	0.47
Price/Book Ratio	1.2	0.37
5 Yr Earnings Gr %	-9.5	---
Return on Assets %	0.5	0.07
Debt % Total Cap	28.0	0.99
Med Mkt Cap ($mil)	5114	0.39

figure is based on less than 50% of stocks

Index Allocation

	% of Stocks
Dow 30	0.0
S&P 500	97.2
S&P Mid-Cap 400	0.4
US Small-Cap	0.0
Foreign	2.4

Diversification Value for Portfolio Types

Large Cap: High	Small Cap: High	Bond: High	Balanced: High	Diversified: High

Portfolio 09-30-94

Share Chg (06-94)	Amount	Total Equity: 18 / Total Fixed-Income: 24	Value $000	% Total Invest
0	188500	Atlantic Richfield	19015	5.58
0	584189	KeyCorp	17818	5.23
0	287100	CIGNA	17693	5.19
0	404000	First Union	17473	5.13
0	254592	Bankers Trust New York	16994	4.99
0	342260	Aetna Life & Casualty	15872	4.66
0	867100	USX-Marathon Group	15391	4.52
19000	776875	Great Western Financial	14955	4.39
0	703100	HF Ahmanson	14677	4.31
658937	658937	Unicom	14661	4.30
293900	396400	Chemical Banking	13874	4.07
---	12000000	Chrysler 10.4%	12990	3.81
654800	654800	K Mart	11705	3.44
---	1376000	Kaiser Aluminum Cv Pfd $1.00	11352	3.33
---	250000	Delta Air Lines Cv Pfd $3.50	11188	3.28
---	171000	Advanced Micro Devices Cv Pfd $3	10175	2.99
---	11000000	Seagate Technology Cv 6.75%	9212	2.70
0	185500	Pennzoil	8695	2.55
---	73000	Citicorp Cv Pfd 10.75%	8650	2.54
---	7000000	Geneva Steel 11.125%	7035	2.07
---	124400	Reynolds Metals Cv Pfd $3.31	6686	1.96
---	124400	Sea Containers Cv Pfd $4.00	5505	1.62
0	203400	Ultramar	5187	1.52
---	93600	Bethlehem Steel Cv Pfd $5.00	4937	1.45
0	100000	NationsBank	4900	1.44

Composition % 12-31-94

Cash	0.3	Preferred	0.0
Stocks	60.3	Convertibles	34.9
Bonds	4.5	Other	0.0

Tax Analysis

	Tax-Adj Historical Return %	% Pretax Return
3 Yr Avg	9.24	58.5
5 Yr Avg	9.21	57.3
10 Yr Avg	---	---
Potential Capital Gain Exposure (% of assets)		0

Most Similar Funds in MF500

Gabelli Equity-Income	Weak Fit
Sequoia	Weak Fit
Lexington Corporate Leaders	Weak Fit

Sector Weightings

	% of Stocks	Relative S&P 500
Utilities	6.8	0.55
Energy	22.3	2.20
Financials	65.6	6.20
Industrial Cyclicals	0.0	0.00
Consumer Durables	0.0	0.00
Consumer Staples	0.0	0.00
Services	0.0	0.00
Retail	5.4	0.93
Health	0.0	0.00
Technology	0.0	0.00

Operations

Address and Telephone	Vanguard Financial Center, Valley Forge, PA 19482, 215-669-1000 / 800-662-7447
Advisor	Wellington Management Co.
Subadvisor	N/A
Administrator	N/A
Transfer Agent	First Bank of Boston
Custodian	State Street Bank and Trust Co.
Auditor	Price Waterhouse LLP
Legal Counsel	Internally Counselled
Income Distrib Schedule	Paid Quarterly
Management Fee	0.35%, 0.10%P
Reinvestment Plan	No
Direct Purchase Plan	No
Shares Outstanding	10,920,550
Exchange	NYSE
*Date of Inception	02-15-85
Shareholder Report	B+

General American Investors

	Ticker	NAV	Mkt Price	Prem/Disc	Yield	Objective
	GAM	$22.31	$19.00	-14.8%	0.3%	Domestic Eq

General American Investors seeks long-term capital appreciation. Current income is secondary.

The fund invests principally in common stocks believed by management to have better-than-average growth potential. Investment is permitted, however, in all forms of securities without limiting the portion of assets that may be invested in any one type.

The fund is permitted to use leverage and to underwrite securities. It may issue debt and senior equity securities. The fund has not employed any such financing methods for several years, however, and does not intend to leverage itself in the foreseeable future.

| 1.0 | 9.2 | -1.4 | -6.7 | -8.7 | -14.9 | -15.0 | -14.3 | -3.0 | 5.3 | 7.8 | -8.6 | Highest Prem/Disc |
| -12.4 | -1.5 | -6.7 | -13.5 | -23.7 | -21.5 | -18.9 | -18.2 | -18.1 | -8.3 | -10.5 | -15.3 | Lowest Prem/Disc |

Historical Profile

Return Above Average
Risk Average
Rating ★★★★ Above Average

Growth of $10,000
- ▬ at NAV ($000)
- — at Market Price ($000)

Premium Discount %

Manager's Investment Style

Management takes a bottom-up approach to growth investing, emphasizing companies with strong earnings-growth potential and solid management. Once management dedicates assets to a stock, it holds on for the long-term: Turnover at the fund is modest. The fund doesn't play market trends by shifting in and out of sectors. The fund sells stocks based on changes in fundamentals or in management, not based on its sector's prospects.

Fund Manager(s)

William J. Gedale. Since 3-89. MBA'67 New York U.; JD'71 Fordham U.

1983	1984	1985	1986	1987	1988	1989	1990	1991	1992	1993	1994	History
21.41	16.72	20.63	19.29	16.70	17.03	21.41	20.60	30.60	28.56	24.75	22.31	NAV
23.01	-7.09	35.00	11.17	2.53	17.78	37.84	6.68	61.10	3.59	-1.75	-2.75	NAV Total Return %
0.55	-13.36	3.26	-7.51	-2.73	1.17	6.16	9.79	30.61	-4.03	-11.81	-4.07	+/- S&P 500
5.61	-10.06	2.05	-4.29	-2.21	2.57	2.63	6.34	14.47	-2.34	-1.21	-5.73	+/- Wil Large Growth
2.03	3.97	1.68	2.57	4.65	3.35	1.63	1.77	0.75	0.11	0.27	0.31	Income Return %
20.98	-11.06	33.32	8.60	-2.13	14.43	36.21	4.91	60.35	3.48	-2.02	-3.06	Capital Return %
19	84	2	70	44	21	9	29	5	77	98	27	Total Rtn % Rank All
36	69	7	71	45	34	11	6	9	62	82	70	Total Rtn % Rank Obj
16.31	-7.16	24.81	11.17	-16.11	21.16	48.58	3.99	85.00	14.82	-15.92	-7.88	Market Total Rtn %
-4.0	2.6	-3.9	-9.4	-14.4	-17.9	-17.0	-16.2	-11.8	0.7	-4.4	-12.0	Avg Prem/Disc %
0.36	0.67	0.28	0.47	0.70	0.46	0.27	0.31	0.16	0.03	0.06	0.06	Income $
1.15	2.38	1.35	2.84	1.71	1.69	1.46	1.60	1.99	3.06	2.98	1.49	Capital Gains $
1.25	1.49	1.29	1.09	1.19	1.14	1.04	1.07	1.02	1.16	1.16	1.13•	Expense Ratio %
1.71	1.64	1.84	1.86	1.69	1.60	0.96	0.84	0.37	0.00	0.14	0.27•	Income Ratio %
42	38	26	31	30	19	27	19	21	14	20	---	Turnover Rate %
262.7	227.2	296.1	306.6	287.2	301.8	381.9	382.2	587.2	586.5	553.9	519.7	Net Assets ($mil)

• ratio annualized by Morningstar

Manager Experience

	Dates Managed	Invest Obj	Std Dev	+/- Index

Not available.

NAV Performance % 12-30-94

	1st Qtr	2nd Qtr	3rd Qtr	4th Qtr	Total
1987	22.37	5.23	3.76	-23.27	2.53
1988	9.71	6.37	-1.15	2.09	17.78
1989	7.41	8.61	15.61	2.20	37.84
1990	1.05	16.51	-18.84	11.64	6.68
1991	23.39	2.88	10.86	14.47	61.10
1992	-6.96	-2.73	7.57	6.42	3.59
1993	-6.10	-2.82	1.75	5.82	-1.75
1994	-4.47	-3.04	6.50	-1.42	-2.75

Bear Market Performance

Decile Rank (5-year period)

Worst ▬ Best

	Worst 3 Mo Period 1985-89	Worst 3 Mo Period 1990-94
General Amer Inv	-31.17	-18.84
+/- S&P 500	-1.59	-5.10

Trailing Returns

	NAV Total Return %	+/- S&P 500	+/- Wil Lg Grow	% Rank All	% Rank Obj	Mkt Total Return %
3 Mo	-1.42	-1.40	-3.03	41	52	-4.30
6 Mo	4.99	0.13	-3.42	9	18	1.72
1 Yr	-2.75	-4.07	-5.73	27	70	-7.88
3 Yr Avg	-0.34	-6.61	-3.10	94	81	-3.83
5 Yr Avg	11.21	2.52	1.40	18	27	11.34
10 Yr Avg	15.56	1.18	0.70	11	15	13.62

Risk Analysis

	Risk % Rank[1]		Morningstar[2]		Morningstar
	All	Obj	Return	Risk	Risk-Adj Rating
3 Yr	80	68	-0.48	0.78	★★
5 Yr	82	65	1.28	0.75	★★★★
10 Yr	77	61	1.11	0.80	★★★★

Average Historical Rating (145 months) 3.0 ★s

[1] = Low, 100 = High [2]1.00 = Equity Avg [3]1.00 = 90-day T-bill Return

Other Measures

			S&P 500
Standard Deviation	10.59	Alpha	-6.02
Mean	0.21	Beta	1.00
Sharpe Ratio	-0.31	R-Squared	56

Investment Style

	Stock Portfolio Avg	Relative S&P 500
Price/Earnings Ratio	22.9	1.24
Price/Cash Flow Ratio	18.9	1.64
Price/Book Ratio	4.0	1.19
5 Yr Earnings Gr %	23.0	4.14
Return on Assets %	9.1	1.21
Debt % Total Cap	15.9	0.56
Med Mkt Cap ($mil)	4406	0.34

Style: Value Blend Growth — Size Large/Med/Small

figure is based on less than 50% of stocks

Index Allocation

	% of Stocks
Dow 30	3.1
S&P 500	44.1
S&P Mid-Cap 400	21.5
US Small-Cap	17.5
Foreign	16.9

Diversification Value for Portfolio Types

Large Cap: Low	Small Cap: Medium	Bond: High	Balanced: Low	Diversified: Medium

Portfolio 09-30-94

Share Chg (06-94)	Amount	Total Equity: 73 / Total Fixed-Income: 7	Value $000	% Total Invest
0	1018500	Home Depot	42777	7.94
0	1101000	Wal-Mart Stores	25736	4.78
0	466500	US Healthcare	21722	4.03
0	538000	Luxottica Group (ADR)	18225	3.38
0	1119000	Buffets	17624	3.27
159000	318000	Medtronic	16814	3.12
0	415500	Walt Disney	16101	2.99
0	278000	United HealthCare	14734	2.73
0	381000	Toys 'R' Us	13573	2.52
0	196000	Pfizer	13549	2.51
0	150500	American International Group	13376	2.48
0	552000	Brinker International	13248	2.46
483000	483000	Manpower	13222	2.45
0	289000	Reuters Holdings (ADR)	13005	2.41
0	357000	Sensormatic Electronics	12227	2.27
-23000	153500	AMP	11877	2.20
200000	570000	Glaxo Holdings (ADR)	10403	1.93
0	206500	Transatlantic Holdings	10402	1.93
7000	172000	Biogen	9374	1.74
0	571500	Boston Scientific	9073	1.68
127000	127000	Wolters Kluwer	9017	1.67
0	84500	General Re	8946	1.66
0	267000	PepsiCo	8844	1.64
0	56500	First Empire State	8560	1.59
9500	122500	Chiron	8146	1.51

Composition % 12-31-94

Cash	3.7	Preferreds	0.0
Stocks	96.3	Convertibles	0.0
Bonds	0.0	Other	0.0

Tax Analysis

	Tax-Adj Historical Return %	% Pretax Return
3 Yr Avg	-3.11	NMF
5 Yr Avg	8.14	68.4
10 Yr Avg	11.83	63.4

Potential Capital Gain Exposure (% of assets) 24

Sector Weightings

	% of Stocks	Relative S&P 500
Utilities	0.0	0.00
Energy	1.0	0.10
Financials	14.2	1.34
Industrial Cyclicals	1.8	0.11
Consumer Durables	2.9	0.46
Consumer Staples	2.2	0.18
Services	23.5	2.89
Retail	18.8	3.23
Health	31.9	3.67
Technology	3.7	0.40

Most Similar Funds in MF500

20th Century Growth Inv	Fair Fit
Pasadena Growth A	Fair Fit
AIM Weingarten	Fair Fit

Operations

Address and Telephone	450 Lexington Ave., Ste. 3300 New York, NY 10017 212-916-8400 / 800-436-8401
Advisor	General American Investors Co. Inc.
Subadvisor	N/A
Administrator	Internally Administered
Transfer Agent	State Street Bank and Trust Co.
Custodian	Bankers Trust Company
Auditor	Ernst & Young LLP
Legal Counsel	Sullivan & Cromwell

Income Distrib Schedule	Paid Irregularly
Management Fee	0.54%
Reinvestment Plan	Yes
Direct Purchase Plan	No
Shares Outstanding	23,291,771
Exchange	NYSE
Date of Inception	01-30-27
Shareholder Report	B

MORNINGSTAR 1995 Mutual Fund 500

General Municipal Bond

	Ticker	Load	NAV	Yield	SEC Yield	Assets	Objective
	GMBDX	None	13.72	6.2%	6.26%	829.1	Muni Nat

General Municipal Bond Fund seeks current income exempt from federal income tax, consistent with capital preservation.

The fund invests at least 80% of its assets in tax-exempt municipal obligations (except when maintaining a temporary defensive posture). It also maintains at least 65% of its assets in bonds and debentures; also, at least 65% of the debt obligations must be investment grade. The fund may invest without limitation in private-activity bonds subject to the Alternative Minimum Tax.

Prior to Sept. 30, 1990, the fund was named General Tax-Exempt Bond Fund.

Manager's Investment Style

Manager A. Paul Disdier maintains a relatively long duration with this portfolio. He emphasizes medium-quality bonds as well as private-activity bonds (which are subject to the alternative minimum tax) for their yield, and will at times hold issues that are highly unpopular. He has also placed a small amount of assets in municipal-bonds derivatives, primarily inverse floating-rate bonds.

Fund Manager(s)

A. Paul Disdier, since 05-88. Birthdate: 08-55.
BS, Villanova U. 1977   MBA, Drexel U. 1980

Manager Experience

	Dates Managed	Invest Obj	Std Dev	+/- Index
A. Paul Disdier				
Premier State Mun Bd MN	05/88 - 05/94	MS	4.50	-0.64
Premier State Mun Bd MI	05/88 - 05/94	MS	4.78	-0.13

Performance 12-31-94

	1st Qtr	2nd Qtr	3rd Qtr	4th Qtr	Total
1987	1.92	-7.37	-3.64	3.85	-5.52
1988	3.55	2.29	3.10	3.10	12.60
1989	1.16	7.75	-1.07	3.38	11.48
1990	1.09	2.57	-0.09	3.90	7.64
1991	2.65	3.15	4.56	3.58	14.68
1992	0.72	4.87	2.43	1.52	9.84
1993	3.68	4.46	3.67	0.94	13.32
1994	-6.14	0.24	0.03	-1.52	-7.32

Bear Market Performance

Decile Rank (5-year period)

Worst   Best

	Worst 3 Mo Period 1985-89	Worst 3 Mo Period 1990-94
General Municipal Bond	-9.63	-7.04
+/- LB Aggregate	-6.08	-2.11
+/- Best Fit Index : LB Muni	-3.14	-1.28

Trailing Returns

	Total Return %	+/- LB Aggregate	+/- LB Muni	% Rank All	% Rank Obj	Growth of $10,000
3 Mo	-1.52	-1.90	-0.09	57	60	9,848
6 Mo	-1.49	-2.48	-0.25	82	77	9,851
1 Yr	-7.32	-4.40	-1.71	82	76	9,268
3 Yr Avg	4.88	0.33	0.01	50	34	11,536
5 Yr Avg	7.32	-0.30	0.55	43	6	14,240
10 Yr Avg	9.12	-0.82	-0.30	70	33	23,945
15 Yr Avg	---	---	---	---	---	---

Operations

Address and Telephone	One Exchange Place
	Boston, MA 02109
	800-645-6561 / 718-895-1206
Advisor	Dreyfus
Subadvisor	None
Distributor	Premier Mutual Fund Services
States Available	All plus PR
Report Grade	B+
Income Distrib	Paid Monthly
* Date of Inception	03-21-84
Fiscal Year End	February

Min Initial Purchase	$2500 (Addt'l: $100)
Min IRA Purchase	N/A
Min Auto Invest Plan	$2500 (Systematic Inv: $100)

Expenses & Fees

Sales Fees	0.00% front
	0.00% deferred
	0.20% 12b-1
Management Fee	0.55% flat fee
3-,5-,10-yr Expense Projections	$27, $47, $105

Historical Profile

Return	Above Average
Risk	Above Average
Rating	★★★ Neutral

61	35	13	3	4	10	18	16

Investment Style History
Fixed Income
Income Rtn % Rank Obj

Growth of $10,000
‖‖ Value of Fund ($000)
— Value of Index ($000)
   LB Muni
▼ Manager Change
▽ Partial Manager Change
► Mgr Unknown After
◄ Mgr Unknown Before

Performance Quartile
(Within Objective)

	1983	1984	1985	1986	1987	1988	1989	1990	1991	1992	1993	1994	History
	---	12.37	13.69	14.89	12.87	13.48	13.97	13.90	14.76	15.02	15.84	13.72	NAV
	---	6.76 *	21.08	17.11	-5.52	12.60	11.48	7.64	14.68	9.84	13.32	-7.32	Total Return %
	---	---	-1.04	1.86	-8.28	4.72	-3.06	-1.30	-1.32	2.59	3.57	-4.40	+/- LB Aggregate
	---	---	1.06	-2.21	-7.03	2.44	0.69	0.34	2.54	1.02	1.04	-1.71	+/- LB Muni
	---	7.80	10.41	8.34	6.77	7.86	7.85	8.14	8.18	7.03	6.28	5.44	Income Return %
	---	-1.04	10.67	8.77	-12.29	4.74	3.64	-0.50	6.50	2.80	7.04	-12.75	Capital Return %
	---	---	66	39	90	41	61	16	59	24	38	82	Total Rtn % Rank All
	---	---	32	61	97	23	5	3	2	12	18	76	Total Rtn % Rank Obj
	---	0.93	1.17	1.07	0.98	0.96	1.01	1.09	1.06	0.99	0.91	0.86	Income $
	---	0.00	0.00	0.00	0.25	0.00	0.00	0.04	0.15	0.23	0.12	Capital Gains $	
	---	---	0.00	0.41	0.77	0.80	0.80	0.28	0.00	0.01	0.41	0.82	Expense Ratio %
	---	---	9.57	8.66	7.22	7.30	7.27	7.58	7.83	7.30	6.46	5.71	Income Ratio %
	---	---	72	88	105	67	218	110	50	38	65	59	Turnover Rate %
	---	3.3	30.8	55.1	33.1	34.8	77.4	270.2	683.1	1101.3	1260.5	829.1	Net Assets ($mil)

Risk Analysis

Time Period	Load-Adj Return %	Risk % Rank All	Risk % Rank Obj	Morningstar Return	Morningstar Risk	Morningstar Risk-Adj Rating
1 Yr	-7.32					
3 Yr	4.88	43	73	1.32	1.20	★★★
5 Yr	7.32	28	60	1.38	1.12	★★★★
10 Yr	9.12	24	72	1.18	1.17	★★★

Average Historical Rating (94 months)   3.2 ★ s

[1] = low, 100 = high   [2] 1.00 = Muni Avg   [3] 1.00 = 90-day T-bill return

Other Measures

			Standard LB Agg	Best Fit LB Muni
Standard Deviation	6.62	Alpha	0.2	-0.2
Mean	4.99	Beta	1.26	1.18
Sharpe Ratio	0.22	R-Squared	58	96

Investment Style

Interest-Rate Stance

Avg Effective Maturity   22.4 Yrs

Quality

Avg Credit Quality   A

Avg Weighted Coupon   6.77%
Avg Weighted Price   98.35% of Par

Diversification Value for Portfolio Types

Large Cap: Medium	Small Cap: High	Bond: Low	Balanced: Medium	Diversified: High

Portfolio 08-31-94

Total Stocks: 0
Total Fixed-Income: 175

Amount 000	Date of Maturity		Value $000	% Net Assets
23000	01-01-03	AZ Salt Rvr Agri Impr/Pwr Dist 5.05%	19972	1.93
20000	07-01-23	MI Detroit Swr Disp Sys 5.7%	18612	1.80
16535	11-15-12	CO Denver Arpt Sys 7.25%	16017	1.55
15000	05-01-26	TX Gulf Coast Waste Disp Champion 7.45%	15735	1.52
18400	01-01-18	SC Pub Svc 5%	15167	1.47
13800	02-01-12	KY Kenton Arpt Brd 7.5%	13863	1.34
13900	12-01-11	TX Alliance Arpt Spcl Fac American 7%	13674	1.32
14000	12-01-13	MI Strategic Fund Ltd Obl WMX Tech 6%	13534	1.31
14400	04-01-29	VA Fairfax Wtr 5.75%	13403	1.30
16000	04-01-23	NY Local Govt Assist 5%	13222	1.28
13000	11-28-14	LA Pub Fac Our Lady Lake Regl M/C VAR	12886	1.25
12700	01-01-23	OK McGee Creek Wtr 6%	12550	1.21
12500	06-01-13	NE Higher Educ Loan Prog 6.4%	12512	1.21
12885	08-01-11	RI Depositors Econ Protection Obl 5.875%	12249	1.18
12000	12-01-30	OK Tulsa Muni Arpt Trust American 7.6%	12047	1.16
11000	04-01-20	NY Urban Dev Crtnl Fac 7.5%	11948	1.15
9750	11-15-14	TX Austin Conv Ctr 8.25%	11249	1.09
10000	07-01-22	MI Detroit Wtr Sply Sys VAR	11228	1.09
10150	01-01-15	FL Polk Indl Dev Imc Fertilizer 7.525%	10429	1.01
10000	07-02-24	TX Dept Hsg/Comnty Affairs Mtg VAR	10400	1.01

Credit Analysis % of Bonds 09-30-94

US Govt	0	BB	5
AAA	15	B	0
AA	18	Below B	1
A	20	NR/NA	10
BBB	32		

Composition % of Assets 09-30-94

Cash	2.8	Preferreds	0.0
Stocks	0.0	Convertibles	0.0
Bonds	97.2	Other	0.0

Tax Analysis

	Tax-Adj Historical Return %	% Pretax Return
3 Yr Avg	4.56	93.3
5 Yr Avg	7.11	96.7
10 Yr Avg	8.96	97.5
Potential Capital Gain Exposure (% of assets)		-4%

Most Similar Funds in MF500

Van Kampen Ins T/F Income A	Strong Fit
Scudder High-Yield Tax-Free	Strong Fit
Dreyfus Muni Bond	Strong Fit

Coupon Range % Bonds / Rel Obj

	% Bonds	Rel Obj
0%	3.1	1.23
0% to 6.8%	33.8	0.56
6.8% to 7.5%	28.6	1.85
7.5% to 8.3%	18.7	2.11
More than 8.3%	9.1	1.03
Not applicable	6.7	1.71

Sector Weightings % Bonds / Rel Obj

	% Bonds	Rel Obj
General Obl	5.87	0.28
Utilities	10.73	0.86
Health	10.95	0.83
Water/Waste	6.93	1.09
Housing	7.62	1.04
Education	4.43	0.69
Transportation	15.55	1.53
COP/Lease	3.57	1.12
Private	24.35	2.09
Misc Revenue	7.36	1.48
Demand	2.65	1.08

Top 5 States % of Bonds

TX	10.68	PA	6.10
NY	10.41	CO	6.00
MI	6.44		

Global Health Sciences

	Ticker	NAV	Mkt Price	Prem/Disc	Yield	Objective
	GHS	$12.46	$9.88	-20.7%	0.0%	Domestic Eq

Global Health Sciences Fund seeks capital appreciation.

Normally, the fund invests at least 80% of assets in health-sciences companies, principally in pharmaceuticals, biotechnology, medical equipment or supplies, and health-care delivery. The fund may also invest in industries related to health science, animal or plant study, or health-science technology. It invests at least 65% of assets in at least three countries, one of which is the United States. The fund may invest the remainder of assets in companies that are related to, but not principally engaged in, the health-care industry, or in debt securities of health-care companies. It may invest up to 25% of assets in private placements or venture-capital projects.

To discourage takeovers, board members serve staggered terms and supermajority voting rules are in effect.

8.3	-1.5	-9.8	Highest Prem/Disc
-14.3	-14.9	-20.9	Lowest Prem/Disc

Historical Profile
Return Not Rated
Risk Not Rated
Rating

Growth of $10,000
■ at NAV ($000)
— at Market Price ($000)

Premium Discount %

Manager's Investment Style

The now-infamous John Kaweske first guided this fund; upon his firing, Barry Kurokawa took his place. Kurokawa shuns the small biotech concerns that Kaweske embraced. Instead, he has stuffed the portfolio with large- and mid-cap names. Kurokawa is willing to shift among subsectors in the industry: When being defensive, he has favored more-staid health-care delivery firms over big-name pharmaceuticals, for example. Despite the fund's name, Kurokawa hasn't done much foreign investing. About 20% of assets are in private placements giving the portfolio a racy edge.

Fund Manager(s)
Barry Kurokawa. Since 1-94. BS California State U.; MBA Loyola Marymount U.

	1983	1984	1985	1986	1987	1988	1989	1990	1991	1992	1993	1994	History
	---	---	---	---	---	---	---	---	---	13.12	12.19	12.46	NAV
	---	---	---	---	---	---	---	---	---	-5.32*	-5.43	2.21	NAV Total Return %
	---	---	---	---	---	---	---	---	---	-13.13*	-15.48	0.90	+/- S&P 500
	---	---	---	---	---	---	---	---	---	---	-23.41	1.67	+/- Wil Small Growth
	---	---	---	---	---	---	---	---	---	0.63*	1.66	0.00	Income Return %
	---	---	---	---	---	---	---	---	---	-5.95*	-7.09	2.22	Capital Return %
	---	---	---	---	---	---	---	---	---	---	100	9	Total Rtn % Rank All
	---	---	---	---	---	---	---	---	---	---	97	21	Total Rtn % Rank Obj
	---	---	---	---	---	---	---	---	---	-24.50*	-1.60	-9.20	Market Total Rtn %
	---	---	---	---	---	---	---	---	---	-3.7	-9.3	-16.2	Avg Prem/Disc %
	---	---	---	---	---	---	---	---	---	0.08	0.20	0.00	Income $
	---	---	---	---	---	---	---	---	---	0.00	0.00	0.00	Capital Gains $
	---	---	---	---	---	---	---	---	---	1.35	1.39	1.41	Expense Ratio %
	---	---	---	---	---	---	---	---	---	0.72	1.74	-0.70	Income Ratio %
	---	---	---	---	---	---	---	---	---	---	226	121	Turnover Rate %
	---	---	---	---	---	---	---	---	---	264.4	250.1	255.5	Net Assets ($mil)

Manager Experience

	Dates Managed	Invest Obj	Std Dev	+/- Index
Barry Kurokawa				
Invesco Strat Hlth Sci	05/92 - 12/94	SH	17.60	-8.60

NAV Performance % 12-30-94

	1st Qtr	2nd Qtr	3rd Qtr	4th Qtr	Total
1987	---	---	---	---	---
1988	---	---	---	---	---
1989	---	---	---	---	---
1990	---	---	---	---	---
1991	---	---	---	---	---
1992	-5.45*	-6.82	0.33	5.24	-5.32*
1993	-14.56	0.71	4.25	5.42	-5.43
1994	-0.74	-6.53	9.20	0.89	2.22

Bear Market Performance

Decile Rank (5-year period)

Worst ——————————————— Best

	Worst 3 Mo Period 1985-89	Worst 3 Mo Period 1990-94
Global Health Sci	---	---
+/- S&P 500	---	---

Trailing Returns

	NAV Total Return %	+/- S&P 500	+/- Wil Sm Grow	% Rank All	% Rank Obj	Mkt Total Return %
3 Mo	0.89	0.91	0.07	11	12	-3.66
6 Mo	10.17	5.31	-2.75	3	7	1.28
1 Yr	2.21	0.90	1.67	9	21	-9.20
3 Yr Avg	---	---	---	---	---	---
5 Yr Avg	---	---	---	---	---	---
Incept Avg	-2.96*	---	---	---	---	-12.51*

Operations

Address and Telephone	7800 E. Union Ave., Suite 800
	Denver, CO 80237
	303-930-6300 / 800-528-8765
Advisor	INVESCO Trust Company
Subadvisor	N/A
Administrator	Mitchell Hutchins Asset Management
Transfer Agent	State Street Bank and Trust Co.
Custodian	State Street Bank and Trust Co.
Auditor	Price Waterhouse LLP
Legal Counsel	Kirkpatrick & Lockhart

Income Distrib Schedule	Paid Annually
Management Fee	1.00%, 0.20%A
Reinvestment Plan	Yes
Direct Purchase Plan	No
Shares Outstanding	20,507,200
Exchange	NYSE
*Date of Inception	01-20-92
Shareholder Report	B+

Risk Analysis

	Risk % Rank[1]		Morningstar[2]		Morningstar
	All	Obj	Return	Risk	Risk-Adj Rating
3 Yr	---	---	---	---	---
5 Yr	---	---	---	---	---
10 Yr	---	---	---	---	---

[1] = Low, 100 = High   [2] 1.00 = Equity Avg   [3] 1.00 = 90-day T-bill Return

Other Measures
				S&P 500
Standard Deviation	---	Alpha		---
Mean	---	Beta		---
Sharpe Ratio	---	R-Squared		---

Investment Style

	Stock Portfolio Avg	Relative S&P 500
Price/Earnings Ratio	25.1	1.36
Price/Cash Flow Ratio	20.7	1.79
Price/Book Ratio	4.2	1.23
5 Yr Earnings Gr %	22.0#	3.96
Return on Assets %	9.5	1.27
Debt % Total Cap	17.2	0.61
Med Mkt Cap ($mil)	1007	0.08

figure is based on less than 50% of stocks

Style Value Blend Growth — Size Large/Med/Small

Index Allocation
	% of Stocks
Dow 30	0.0
S&P 500	26.7
S&P Mid-Cap 400	15.2
US Small-Cap	53.6
Foreign	4.6

Diversification Value for Portfolio Types

Large Cap: Small Cap: Bond: Balanced: Diversified:

Portfolio 10-31-94

Share Chg (04-94)	Amount	Total Equity: 73 Total Fixed-Income: 30	Value $000	% Total Invest
78000	78000	American Cyanamid	7703	3.04
95000	203000	HBO	6598	2.60
230000	230000	Mylan Laboratories	6440	2.54
0	350000	AL Pharma Cl A	6256	2.47
0	274000	Salick Health Care	6234	2.46
0	140000	Columbia/HCA Healthcare	5828	2.30
245000	245000	Sun Healthcare Group	5635	2.22
116000	116000	US Healthcare	5481	2.16
114000	114000	SciMed Life Systems	5444	2.15
0	200000	Astra Cl B Free	5406	2.13
39000	150000	Healthtrust	5250	2.07
41000	166000	Nellcor	5146	2.03
72000	72000	Schering-Plough	5130	2.02
165000	165000	Abbott Laboratories	5115	2.02
96000	96000	United HealthCare	5064	2.00
225000	225000	Hillhaven	5006	1.98
90000	90000	Johnson & Johnson	4916	1.94
200000	200000	Humana	4875	1.92
63000	63000	Warner-Lambert	4804	1.90
285850	285850	Coram Healthcare	4717	1.86
140000	140000	Upjohn	4620	1.82
300000	300000	Beverly Enterprises	4538	1.79
0	110000	Olsten	3946	1.56
-82200	317800	ICN Pharmaceuticals	3694	1.46
89200	89200	Cerner	3635	1.43

Composition % 12-31-94
Cash	1.4	Preferreds	9.2
Stocks	83.3	Convertibles	6.0
Bonds	0.1	Other	0.1

Tax Analysis
	Tax-Adj Historical Return %	% Pretax Return
3 Yr Avg	---	---
5 Yr Avg	---	---
10 Yr Avg	---	---

Potential Capital Gain Exposure (% of assets)   -11

Most Similar Funds in MF500
Fund lacks 3-year record

Sector Weightings
	% of Stocks	Relative S&P 500
Utilities	2.7	0.21
Energy	0.0	0.00
Financials	0.0	0.00
Industrial Cyclicals	0.4	0.02
Consumer Durables	0.0	0.00
Consumer Staples	3.7	0.29
Services	5.2	0.64
Retail	0.0	0.00
Health	80.7	9.30
Technology	7.4	0.80

M○RNINGSTAR 1995 Mutual Fund 500

Global Income Plus

	Ticker	NAV	Mkt Price	Prem/Disc	Yield	Objective
	GLI	$8.62	$8.00	-7.2%	8.3%	Intl Bond

Global Income Plus Fund seeks high current income. Capital appreciation is secondary.

The fund invests at least 65% of assets in debt securities rated AA and above. Securities can be denominated in foreign currencies or in U.S. dollars. The fund may invest up to 35% in issues rated below AA.

Commencing Nov. 1, 1993, and each November 1 thereafter, if the fund's shares have traded at an average discount of more than 10% during the preceding 16 weeks, a proposal to open-end the fund will be submitted to shareholders.

9.0	0.7	0.3	4.4	7.9	2.9	0.6	Highest Prem/Disc
3.5	-10.9	-12.5	-3.7	-6.6	-5.9	-16.8	Lowest Prem/Disc

Historical Profile
Return Above Average
Risk Average
Rating ★★★
Neutral

Growth of $10,000
■ at NAV ($000)
— at Market Price ($000)

Premium Discount %

	1983	1984	1985	1986	1987	1988	1989	1990	1991	1992	1993	1994	History
	---	---	---	---	---	9.40	9.23	9.60	9.86	9.18	9.69	8.62	NAV
	---	---	---	---	---	4.71*	8.46	18.19	13.58	1.71	16.49	-3.64	NAV Total Return %
	---	---	---	---	---	---	-6.09	9.25	-2.42	-5.54	6.74	-0.72	+/- LB Aggregate
	---	---	---	---	---	---	11.88	2.90	-2.66	-3.07	1.37	-10.34	+/- SB World Govt
	---	---	---	---	---	3.64*	7.49	14.18	10.87	8.14	9.16	7.40	Income Return %
	---	---	---	---	---	1.08*	0.97	4.01	2.71	-6.43	7.33	-11.04	Capital Return %
	---	---	---	---	---	---	74	2	70	83	48	30	Total Rtn % Rank All
	---	---	---	---	---	---	1	14	50	1	64	22	Total Rtn % Rank Obj
	---	---	---	---	---	6.19*	-8.41	28.68	17.77	-6.75	15.30	-5.03	Market Total Rtn %
	---	---	---	---	---	---	-4.1	-6.1	0.9	1.5	-1.4	-7.3	Avg Prem/Disc %
	---	---	---	---	---	0.36	0.64	1.18	0.97	0.82	0.81	0.67	Income $
	---	---	---	---	---	0.00	0.24	0.00	0.00	0.05	0.15	0.00	Capital Gains $
	---	---	---	---	---	1.40	1.17	1.27	1.13	1.12	1.50	1.11	Expense Ratio %
	---	---	---	---	---	7.53	10.30	10.61	9.50	8.60	7.75	6.79	Income Ratio %
	---	---	---	---	---	---	180	128	54	86	101	---	Turnover Rate %
	---	---	---	---	---	227.1	227.7	237.2	250.7	239.7	252.9	224.9	Net Assets ($mil)

Manager's Investment Style

Although the recent loss of one of the fund's managers creates a slight uncertainty for the future, the remaining current management has been a part of the team since the fund's inception. Until this point, management has favored a contrarian strategy with active hedging a key component, as well. A value bent has succeeded in keeping price risk at bay. The fund's days as a closed-end offering could be numbered, though: Shareholders vote in 1995 to open-end the fund.

Fund Manager(s)

Stuart Waugh, CFA. Since 9-88. BA U. of Rhode Island; MBA Tulane U.

Manager Experience

	Dates Managed	Invest Obj	Std Dev	+/- Index
Stuart Waugh				
PaineWebber Glob Inc B	03/87 - 12/94	WB	6.06	1.16
Strat Global Inc	02/92 - 12/94	IB	7.24	-0.38

NAV Performance % 12-30-94

	1st Qtr	2nd Qtr	3rd Qtr	4th Qtr	Total
1987	---	---	---	---	---
1988	---	---	-0.22*	4.94	4.71*
1989	-0.43	-0.24	4.19	4.79	8.46
1990	1.08	6.33	5.29	4.43	18.19
1991	-0.10	-0.65	7.53	6.43	13.58
1992	-1.32	4.39	-0.91	-0.37	1.71
1993	5.56	2.49	2.85	4.69	16.49
1994	-4.02	-2.11	1.49	1.07	-3.64

Bear Market Performance

Decile Rank (5-year period)

Worst — Best

	Worst 3 Mo Period 1985-89	Worst 3 Mo Period 1990-94
Global Income Plus	---	-6.24
+/- LB Aggregate		-1.31

Trailing Returns

	NAV Total Return %	+/- LB Agg	+/- SB Wld Govt	% Rank All	Obj	Mkt Total Return %
3 Mo	1.07	0.69	0.50	10	18	8.99
6 Mo	2.57	1.58	0.34	16	37	2.81
1 Yr	-3.64	-0.72	-10.34	30	22	-5.03
3 Yr Avg	4.51	-0.03	-4.26	72	22	0.64
5 Yr Avg	8.91	1.29	-2.60	34	28	9.08
Incept Avg	9.15*	---	---	---	---	6.64*

Operations

Address and Telephone	1285 Avenue of the Americas New York, NY 10019 212-713-2000 / 800-647-1568
Advisor	Mitchell Hutchins Asset Management
Subadvisor	N/A
Administrator	Mitchell Hutchins Asset Management
Transfer Agent	PFPC, Inc.
Custodian	Brown Brothers Harriman & Co.
Auditor	Price Waterhouse LLP
Legal Counsel	Kirkpatrick & Lockhart

Income Distrib Schedule	Paid Quarterly
Management Fee	0.85%
Reinvestment Plan	Yes
Direct Purchase Plan	No
Shares Outstanding	26,096,317
Exchange	NYSE
*Date of Inception	09-01-88
Shareholder Report	B+

Risk Analysis

	Risk % Rank[1] All	Obj	Morningstar[2] Return	Risk	Morningstar Risk-Adj Rating
3 Yr	34	1	0.27[3]	0.82	★★★
5 Yr	32	1	1.05[3]	0.80	★★★
10 Yr	---	---	---	---	

Average Historical Rating (40 months)   3.3 ★s

[1] = Low, 100 = High   [2] 1.00 = Fixed-Inc Avg   [3] 1.00 = 90-day T-bill Return

Other Measures | | | | LB Aggregate |
|---|---|---|---|
| Standard Deviation | 4.63 | Alpha | 0.18 |
| Mean | 4.53 | Beta | 0.82 |
| Sharpe Ratio | 0.22 | R-Squared | 50 |

Investment Style

Interest-Rate Stance

	Fund	Relative Objective
Avg Effective Maturity	11.6 Yrs	0.99
Avg Weighted Coupon	9.26%	1.07
Avg Weighted Price	NMF	---

Quality

Avg Credit Quality	AA

Country Exposure (top five) 08-31-94

	Securities %		Currency %
Germany	15	US	69
US	11	Germany	15
Spain	11	Canada	7
Australia	9	Australia	4
Canada	7	Denmark	3

Diversification Value for Portfolio Types

Large Cap: High	Small Cap: High	Bond: Low	Balanced: Medium	Diversified: Medium

Portfolio 04-30-94

Amount 000	Total Equity: 0 Total Fixed-Income: 35	Maturity	Value $000	% Total Invest
3023860	Govt of Spain 10.9-13.45%	08-30-03	24646	11.36
9508	United Kingdom Treasury 8-13.25%	06-10-03	15670	7.22
66450	Govt of France 8.25-8.5%	10-25-19	13016	6.00
13778	New So Wales Treas 11.5-12.1%	12-01-01	11381	5.24
80400	Kingdom of Sweden 11.5%	09-01-95	10957	5.05
63130	Kingdom of Denmark 9%	11-15-96	10253	4.72
10240	Govt of New Zealand 8-10%	04-15-04	6701	3.09
7813	Govt of Canada 9.75-10.25%	06-01-21	6392	2.94
7200	Queensland Treasury 10.5-12%	05-15-03	6020	2.77
3600	Republic of Ireland 9%	07-15-01	5636	2.60
5000	Grupo Televisa 10%	11-09-19	5113	2.36
6000	Petroleos Mexicanos 8.625%	12-01-23	4988	2.30
5000	Penn Traffic 9.625%	04-15-05	4750	2.19
7000	United Mexican States 6.25%	12-31-19	4480	2.06
6155	Ontario Hydro 8.625%	02-06-02	4435	2.04
4000	Sealed Air 12.625%	07-01-99	4218	1.94
4000	Owens-Illinois 10.25%	04-01-99	4020	1.85
4313	Republic of Venezuela 4.313%	12-18-07	3360	1.55
5000	Republic Philippines 5.25%	12-01-17	3175	1.46
3000	Banco Nacl Desenvel 9.25%	05-14-95	3000	1.38
14000	Republic of Finland 11%	01-15-99	2910	1.34
3000	Embassy Suites 8.75%	03-15-00	2888	1.33
3000	Republic of Venezuela 9-9.125%	05-27-96	2888	1.33
2500	K-III Communications 10.625%	05-01-02	2600	1.20
2500	Reeves Industries 11%	07-15-02	2575	1.19

Composition % 12-31-94

Cash	18.5	Preferreds	0.0
Stocks	0.0	Convertibles	0.0
Bonds	81.5	Other	0.0

Coupon Range

	% of Bonds	Relative Objective
0%	1.7	0.5
0% to 8%	21.5	1.1
8% to 10%	36.4	1.9
10% to 12%	38.1	1.9
More than 12%	2.3	0.2
Not applicable	0.0	0.0

1.0 = Objective Average

Tax Analysis

	Tax-Adj Historical Return %	% Pretax Return
3 Yr Avg	1.24	26.6
5 Yr Avg	5.31	55.5
10 Yr Avg	---	---

Potential Capital Gain Exposure (% of assets)   -7

Most Similar Funds in MF500

PaineWebber Global Inc	Strong Fit
Oppenheimer Strat Income	Fair Fit
Templeton Income	Weak Fit

Govett Emerging Markets

	Ticker	Load	NAV	Yield	SEC Yield	Assets	Objective
	GIEMX	4.95%	13.29	0.0%	N/A	76.7	Foreign Stock

Govett Emerging Markets Fund seeks long-term capital appreciation.

The fund normally invests at least 80% of its assets in equity securities of companies located in emerging-market nations. It defines emerging markets as those with low- to middle-range per capita income, consistent with World Bank classification. The fund invests at least 65% of its assets in no less than three countries, and no more than 25% of its assets in any single country.

Prior to April 1, 1993, the fund was named Govett International Emerging Markets Fund.

Manager's Investment Style

The fund is heavily weighted, yet well diversified, in the Pacific Rim. The portfolio also holds many companies in Mexico, Brazil, and Argentina. The fund has been hurt by the political climate in Latin America, but has chosen to ride out the storm. Management has trimmed its holdings in the Pacific Rim to avoid losses from profit takers.

Fund Manager(s)

Rachael Maunder, since 01-92. BA, Bath U. 1984

Manager Experience

	Dates Managed	Invest Obj	Std Dev	+/- Index

Not available.

Historical Profile

Return	---
Risk	---
Rating	
	Not Rated

Investment Style History
Equity

Average % Stocks Held in Portfolio

90% 96% 83%

Growth of $10,000

- |||| Value of Fund ($000)
- — Value of Index ($000) S&P 500
- ▼ Manager Change
- ▽ Partial Manager Change
- ► Mgr Unknown After
- ◄ Mgr Unknown Before

Performance Quartile (Within Objective)

	1983	1984	1985	1986	1987	1988	1989	1990	1991	1992	1993	1994	History
	---	---	---	---	---	---	---	---	---	10.72	17.70	13.29	NAV
	---	---	---	---	---	---	---	---	---	7.20 *	79.73	-12.70	Total Return %
	---	---	---	---	---	---	---	---	---	-0.34 *	69.68	-14.01	+/- S&P 500
	---	---	---	---	---	---	---	---	---	---	14.23	-10.28	+/- MSCI Emerging
	---	---	---	---	---	---	---	---	---	0.00	0.00	0.00	Income Return %
	---	---	---	---	---	---	---	---	---	7.20	79.73	-12.70	Capital Return %
	---	---	---	---	---	---	---	---	---	---	1	97	Total Rtn % Rank All
	---	---	---	---	---	---	---	---	---	---	3	93	Total Rtn % Rank Obj
	---	---	---	---	---	---	---	---	---	0.00	0.00	0.00	Income $
	---	---	---	---	---	---	---	---	---	0.00	1.33	2.36	Capital Gains $
	---	---	---	---	---	---	---	---	---	2.50	2.50	2.18	Expense Ratio %
	---	---	---	---	---	---	---	---	---	-0.49	-0.88	-0.33	Income Ratio %
	---	---	---	---	---	---	---	---	---	---	143	---	Turnover Rate %
	---	---	---	---	---	---	---	---	---	5.6	70.7	76.7	Net Assets ($mil)

Performance 12-31-94

	1st Qtr	2nd Qtr	3rd Qtr	4th Qtr	Total
1987	---	---	---	---	---
1988	---	---	---	---	---
1989	---	---	---	---	---
1990	---	---	---	---	---
1991	---	---	---	---	---
1992	---	-0.54	-5.71	3.08	7.20 *
1993	9.98	10.94	11.54	32.06	79.73
1994	-8.98	-4.22	19.91	-16.48	-12.70

Bear Market Performance

Decile Rank (5-year period)

Worst ――――――――――――――――― Best

	Worst 3 Mo Period 1985-89	Worst 3 Mo Period 1990-94
Govett Emerging Markets	---	---
+/- S&P 500	---	---
+/- Best Fit Index :	---	---

Trailing Returns

	Total Return %	+/- S&P 500	+/- MSCI Emerging	% Rank All	% Rank Obj	Growth of $10,000
3 Mo	-16.48	-16.47	-4.37	100	93	8,352
6 Mo	0.14	-4.72	-5.88	54	31	10,014
1 Yr	-12.70	-14.01	-10.28	97	93	8,730
3 Yr Avg	---	---	---	---	---	---
5 Yr Avg	---	---	---	---	---	---
10 Yr Avg	---	---	---	---	---	---
15 Yr Avg	---	---	---	---	---	---

Operations

Address and Telephone	P.O. Box 168021
	Sacramento, CA 95816-8021
	800-634-6838 / 415-391-7494
Advisor	John Govett & Co
Subadvisor	None
Distributor	Govett Financial Services
States Available	All except IA
Report Grade	C+
Income Distrib	Paid Annually
* Date of Inception	01-07-92
Fiscal Year End	December

Risk Analysis

Time Period	Load-Adj Return %	Risk % Rank [1] All	Risk % Rank [1] Obj	Morningstar [2] Return	Morningstar [2] Risk	Morningstar Risk-Adj Rating
1 Yr	-17.02					
3 Yr	---	---	---	---	---	---
5 Yr	---	---	---	---	---	---
10 Yr	---	---	---	---	---	---
Average Historical Rating ---				---		

[1] 1 = low, 100 = high   [2] 1.00 = Equity Avg   [3] 1.00 = 90-day T-bill return

Other Measures

			Standard S&P 500	Best Fit
Standard Deviation	---	Alpha	---	---
Mean	---	Beta	---	---
Sharpe Ratio	---	R-Squared	---	

Investment Style

	Stock Portfolio Avg	Rel MSCI EAFE	Rel Obj	
Price/Earnings Ratio	22.4#	0.61	0.80	Not Available
Price/Cash Flow	---	---	---	
Price/Book Ratio	3.5#	1.33	1.17	
5 Yr Earnings Gr %	---	---	---	
Return on Assets %	---	---	---	
Debt % Total Cap	---	---	---	
Med Mkt Cap ($mil)	1425#	0.12	0.28	

figure is based on 50% or less of stocks

Diversification Value for Portfolio Types

Large Cap: Small Cap: Bond: Balanced: Diversified:

Expenses & Fees

Sales Fees	4.95% front
	0.00% deferred
	0.50% 12b-1
Management Fee	1.00% flat fee
3-,5-,10-yr Expense Projections	$124, $176, $319
Annual Brokerage Cost	---

Portfolio 06-30-94

Share Chg (12-93)000	Amount 000	Total Stocks: 97 / Total Fixed-Income: 24	Value $000	% Net Assets
86	600	Telefonos de Mexico CI L	1684	2.35
56	56	Taiwan Fund	1505	2.10
18	38	Korea Electric Power	1265	1.76
510	510	Panca Wiratama Sakti	1233	1.72
	30087	Telebras Pfd	1191	1.66
530	738	Guney Biracilik	1099	1.53
3	17	Telefonica De Argentina ADR	1035	1.44
8	17	Samsung Electronics (Gds)	999	1.39
	810	Far East Textile Cv 4%	932	1.30
	48532	Banco do Brasil Pfd	874	1.22
300	520	Panin Bank	863	1.20
	8633	Petroleo Brasileiro Pfd	862	1.20
	1000	Pacific Construct Cv 2.125%	849	1.18
	480	Acer 4%	845	1.18
	39614	Banco Nacional Pfd	804	1.12
46	46	Creative Technology	799	1.11
275	275	Migros	783	1.09
44	124	Mavesa (ADR)	776	1.08
60	161	Perez	767	1.07
10	150	Singapore Land	737	1.03

Regional Exposure 09-30-94
% of Stocks

Europe	15	Pacific Rim	44
Japan	14	Other	13
Latin Amer	10		

Country Exposure 09-30-94
% of Stocks

Brazil	15
Mexico	14
Argentina	10
South Korea	9
Hong Kong	8

Total Number of Countries: 18
Hedging Policy: Never

Composition % 09-30-94

Cash	3.1	Preferreds	6.7
Stocks	82.2	Convertibles	5.7
Bonds	0.0	Other	2.3

Tax Analysis

	Tax-Adj Historical Return %	% Pretax Return
3 Yr Avg	---	---
5 Yr Avg	---	---
10 Yr Avg	---	---
Potential Capital Gain Exposure (% of assets)		-8%

Most Similar Funds in MF500

Fund lacks three-year record

Sector Weightings

	% of Stocks	Relative S&P 500
Utilities	15.9	1.78
Energy	1.6	0.39
Financials	22.8	1.21
Industrial Cyclicals	23.5	0.94
Consumer Durables	9.6	0.89
Consumer Staples	8.7	1.26
Services	8.2	0.75
Retail	4.4	0.75
Health	0.0	0.00
Technology	5.4	1.06

Min Initial Purchase / IRA / Auto Invest

Min Initial Purchase	$500 (Addt'l: $100)
Min IRA Purchase	$500 (Addt'l: $100)
Min Auto Invest Plan	$100 (Systematic Inv: $100)

MORNINGSTAR   1995 Mutual Fund 500

Gradison-McDonald Govt Inc

	Ticker	Load	NAV	Yield	SEC Yield	Assets	Objective
	GGIFX	2.00%	12.02	6.2%	6.74%	184.0	Gvt General

Gradison-McDonald Government Income Fund seeks current income.

The fund normally invests at least 65% of its assets in securities issued by the U.S. government or its agencies or instrumentalities, with nominal maturities generally in the range of eight to 30 years. It may also hold a portion of its assets in cash and repurchase agreements. The fund may invest a substantial portion of its assets in GNMA certificates, primarily of the modified pass-through type. It may also write covered call options.

Prior to April 23, 1992, the fund was named Gradison Government Income Fund.

Manager's Investment Style

Management doesn't do a lot of fancy footwork with this fund. Instead, it keeps duration neutral relative to that of the broad market. Forty percent of assets are dedicated to each GNMAs and Treasuries, and management will shift the remaining 20% of assets to the more attractive of these two sectors. Management does, however, write covered calls when it thinks the market is overpriced.

Fund Manager(s)

Michael J. Link, since 09-87. Birthdate: 04-36.
BS, Manhattan C. 1957 MS, Lehigh U. 1958

Manager Experience

	Dates Managed	Invest Obj	Std Dev	+/- Index
Not available.				

Historical Profile
Return Average
Risk   Average
Rating ★★★
        Neutral

	75	68	63	70	61	62	41

Investment Style History
Fixed Income
Income Rtn % Rank Obj

Growth of $10,000
|||| Value of Fund ($000)
— Value of Index ($000)
   LB Mtg
▼ Manager Change
▽ Partial Manager Change
◄- Mgr Unknown After
-► Mgr Unknown Before

Performance Quartile
(Within Objective)

	1983	1984	1985	1986	1987	1988	1989	1990	1991	1992	1993	1994	History
	---	---	---	---	12.95	12.65	13.03	12.93	13.55	13.33	13.37	12.02	NAV
	---	---	---	---	4.99 *	7.12	12.75	8.79	14.08	6.29	7.53	-3.69	Total Return %
	---	---	---	---	---	-0.76	-1.79	-0.15	-1.92	-0.96	-2.22	-0.77	+/- LB Aggregate
	---	---	---	---	---	0.09	-1.48	0.08	-1.24	-0.94	-3.13	-0.32	+/- LB Government
	---	---	---	---	1.45	7.92	8.79	8.45	7.88	6.63	5.67	5.67	Income Return %
	---	---	---	---	3.55	-0.80	3.96	0.34	6.20	-0.34	1.85	-9.36	Capital Return %
	---	---	---	---	---	80	55	10	62	66	81	50	Total Rtn % Rank All
	---	---	---	---	---	29	30	51	53	42	55	56	Total Rtn % Rank Obj
	---	---	---	---	0.18	0.99	1.05	1.03	0.95	0.86	0.74	0.75	Income $
	---	---	---	---	0.01	0.20	0.12	0.14	0.17	0.17	0.20	0.11	Capital Gains $
	---	---	---	---	1.25	1.25	1.22	1.08	0.99	0.94	0.90	0.89	Expense Ratio %
	---	---	---	---	7.74	8.12	8.27	8.13	7.33	6.39	5.48	2.85	Income Ratio %
	---	---	---	---	---	90	174	71	108	83	134	---	Turnover Rate %
	---	---	---	---	6.7	25.3	40.3	78.0	151.8	210.9	266.0	184.0	Net Assets ($mil)

Performance 12-31-94

	1st Qtr	2nd Qtr	3rd Qtr	4th Qtr	Total
1987	---	---	---	5.41	4.99 *
1988	2.90	1.00	2.00	1.05	7.12
1989	1.41	5.57	1.88	3.37	12.75
1990	-0.74	3.32	0.81	5.24	8.79
1991	2.27	1.47	5.05	4.64	14.08
1992	-1.68	3.92	3.74	0.27	6.29
1993	3.29	2.18	1.46	0.42	7.53
1994	-3.05	-1.04	0.22	0.17	-3.69

Bear Market Performance

Decile Rank (5-year period)

Worst | | | | | | | | | Best

	Worst 3 Mo Period 1985-89	Worst 3 Mo Period 1990-94
Gradison-McDonald Govt Inc	---	-4.80
+/- LB Aggregate	---	0.13
+/- Best Fit Index : LB Mtg	---	-0.80

Trailing Returns

	Total Return %	+/- LB Aggregate	+/- LB Govt	% Rank All	% Rank Obj	Growth of $10,000
3 Mo	0.17	-0.21	-0.19	18	39	10,017
6 Mo	0.38	-0.61	-0.40	49	50	10,038
1 Yr	-3.69	-0.77	-0.32	50	56	9,631
3 Yr Avg	3.25	-1.29	-1.41	83	57	11,007
5 Yr Avg	6.44	-1.19	-1.09	65	50	13,661
10 Yr Avg	---	---	---	---	---	---
15 Yr Avg	---	---	---	---	---	---

Operations

Address and Telephone	580 Walnut Street	Min Initial Purchase	$1000 (Addt'l: $50)
	Cincinnati, OH 45202	Min IRA Purchase	$1000 (Addt'l: $50)
	800-869-5999 / 513-579-5700	Min Auto Invest Plan	$1000 (Systematic Inv: $50)
Advisor	Gradison Division of McDonald	**Expenses & Fees**	
Subadvisor	None	Sales Fees	2.00% front
Distributor	Gradison Division of McDonald		0.00% deferred
States Available	All		0.25% 12b-1
Report Grade	C	Management Fee	0.50% flat fee
Income Distrib	Paid Monthly	3-,5-,10-yr Expense Projections	$48, $69, $129
* Date of Inception	09-16-87		
Fiscal Year End	December		

Risk Analysis

Time Period	Load-Adj Return %	Risk % Rank [1] All	Risk % Rank [1] Obj	Morningstar [2] Return	Morningstar Risk	Morningstar Risk-Adj Rating
1 Yr	-5.61					
3 Yr	2.56	23	48	-0.29 [3]	1.01	★★★
5 Yr	6.01	21	48	0.31 [3]	0.97	★★★
10 Yr	---	---	---	---	---	---
Average Historical Rating (52 months)				3.1 ★ s		

[1] 1 = low, 100 = high [2] 1.00 = Taxable Avg [3] 1.00 = 90-day T-bill return

Other Measures

	Standard LB Agg	Best Fit LB Mtg
Standard Deviation	3.78	
Mean	3.28	
Sharpe Ratio	-0.07	
Alpha	-1.2	-0.7
Beta	0.91	1.14
R-Squared	93	94

Investment Style

Interest-Rate Stance
Avg Effective Duration	5.4 Yrs
Avg Effective Maturity	7.0 Yrs

Quality
Avg Credit Quality	AAA
Avg Weighted Coupon	7.21%
Avg Weighted Price	93.27% of Par

Diversification Value for Portfolio Types

Large Cap: Medium	Small Cap: High	Bond: None	Balanced: Medium	Diversified: Medium

Portfolio 11-30-94

Total Stocks: 0
Total Fixed-Income: 14

Amount 000	Date of Maturity		Value $000	% Net Assets
30551	01-15-24	GNMA 7%	27133	13.98
30000	08-15-03	US Treasury Note 5.75%	25969	13.38
25823	03-15-24	GNMA 7.5%	23749	12.23
21330	04-15-23	GNMA 8%	20583	10.60
21066	12-15-08	GNMA 6.5%	19229	9.91
20000	02-15-03	US Treasury Note 6.25%	18019	9.28
12327	11-15-22	GNMA 8.5%	12046	6.21
10000	11-15-08	US Treasury Bond 8.75%	10403	5.36
10000	08-15-00	US Treasury Bond 8.375%	10078	5.19
10000	01-15-00	US Treasury Note 6.375%	9400	4.84
10000	04-15-00	US Treasury Note 5.5%	9003	4.64
4933	06-15-21	GNMA 10%	5212	2.68
4823	06-15-21	GNMA 9.5%	4977	2.56
3162	05-15-21	GNMA 9%	3174	1.63

Composition % 12-31-94

Cash	0.0	Preferreds	0.0
Stocks	0.0	Convertibles	0.0
Bonds	100.0	Other	0.0

Tax Analysis

	Tax-Adj Historical Return %	% Pretax Return
3 Yr Avg	0.70	20.9
5 Yr Avg	3.74	55.1
10 Yr Avg	---	---
Potential Capital Gain Exposure (% of assets)		-12%

Most Similar Funds in MF500

Scudder GNMA	Strong Fit
American Cap Govt Secs A	Strong Fit
Lexington GNMA Income	Strong Fit

Coupon Range

	% of Bonds	Rel Obj
0%	0.0	0.00
0% to 8%	78.9	1.25
8% to 9%	16.1	1.05
9% to 10%	5.0	0.62
More than 10%	0.0	0.00
Not applicable	0.0	0.00

Sector Analysis 11-30-94

% of Bonds

US Treas	42	CMOs	0
GNMA mtgs	58	ARMs	0
FNMA mtgs	0	Other	0
FHLMC mtgs	0		

Greater China

	Ticker	NAV	Mkt Price	Prem/Disc	Yield	Objective
	GCH	$14.29	$12.13	-15.2%	0.8%	Pacific/Asia

Greater China Fund seeks long-term capital appreciation.

Normally the fund invests at least 65% of assets in equity securities of China-related companies that are listed on stock exchanges in China or Hong Kong. It may also invest in China-related companies listed on other exchanges. The fund may invest in preferred stock, convertibles, rights, and warrants. It may invest up to 15% of assets in unlisted equities of China-related companies for which there is no public trading market. The fund may invest up to 20% of assets in debt obligations of China-related companies.

Of its 10-million-share offering, the fund offered eight million shares in the United States and two million outside the U.S.

To discourage takeovers, board members serve staggered terms and supermajority voting is required to merge, sell, or liquidate the fund.

In June 1994, the fund completed an oversubscribed rights offering that raised $42 million.

Historical Profile

Return   Not Rated
Risk   Not Rated
Rating

2.1	15.3	18.9	Highest Prem/Disc
-10.9	-10.1	-15.2	Lowest Prem/Disc

Growth of $10,000
— at NAV ($000)
— at Market Price ($000)

Premium Discount %

Manager's Investment Style

Management takes an aggressive approach to investing in China. Instead of sticking with more-liquid Hong Kong blue chips, it has upped its exposure to China B shares and H shares (that are trading in Hong Kong), and it typically has more-direct exposure to these stocks than any of its China-focused rivals. The fund also invests fewer of its assets in the surrounding China region than many of its rivals.

Fund Manager(s)

Tom Walker. Since 10-93.

History	1983	1984	1985	1986	1987	1988	1989	1990	1991	1992	1993	1994	
	---	---	---	---	---	---	---	---	---	13.40	23.79	14.29	NAV
	---	---	---	---	---	---	---	---	---	-3.94*	82.34	-36.54	NAV Total Return %
	---	---	---	---	---	---	---	---	---	-9.96*	72.29	-37.86	+/- S&P 500
	---	---	---	---	---	---	---	---	---	---	49.78	-44.32	+/- MSCI EAFE
	---	---	---	---	---	---	---	---	---	---	-34.35	-7.64	+/- MSCI Hong Kong
	---	---	---	---	---	---	---	---	---	0.00*	0.04	0.77	Income Return %
	---	---	---	---	---	---	---	---	---	-3.94*	82.30	-37.31	Capital Return %
	---	---	---	---	---	---	---	---	---	---	3	99	Total Rtn % Rank All
	---	---	---	---	---	---	---	---	---	---	25	92	Total Rtn % Rank Obj
	---	---	---	---	---	---	---	---	---	-17.50*	122.01	-52.07	Market Total Rtn %
	---	---	---	---	---	---	---	---	---	-3.8	1.3	4.4	Avg Prem/Disc %
	---	---	---	---	---	---	---	---	---	0.00	0.01	0.10	Income $
	---	---	---	---	---	---	---	---	---	0.00	0.62	0.05	Capital Gains $
	---	---	---	---	---	---	---	---	---	2.43	2.22	2.09	Expense Ratio %
	---	---	---	---	---	---	---	---	---	-0.04	0.11	0.99	Income Ratio %
	---	---	---	---	---	---	---	---	---	---	31	---	Turnover Rate %
	---	---	---	---	---	---	---	---	---	90.6	160.8	137.0	Net Assets ($mil)

Manager Experience

	Dates Managed	Invest Obj	Std Dev	+/- Index
Tom Walker				
Pacific European Growth	04/90 - 01/94	WF	15.80	-2.77

NAV Performance % 12-30-94

	1st Qtr	2nd Qtr	3rd Qtr	4th Qtr	Total
1987	---	---	---	---	---
1988	---	---	---	---	---
1989	---	---	---	---	---
1990	---	---	---	---	---
1991	---	---	---	---	---
1992	---	---	-4.44*	0.53	-3.94*
1993	10.45	3.18	5.11	52.24	82.34
1994	-28.29	0.51	7.50	-18.10	-36.54

Bear Market Performance

Decile Rank (5-year period)

Worst   Best

	Worst 3 Mo Period 1985-89	Worst 3 Mo Period 1990-94
Greater China	---	---
+/- S&P 500	---	---

Trailing Returns

	NAV Total Return %	+/- S&P 500	+/- MSCI HK	% Rank All	% Rank Obj	Mkt Total Return %
3 Mo	-18.10	-18.09	-3.89	99	97	-30.15
6 Mo	-11.96	-16.82	-5.68	99	86	-25.71
1 Yr	-36.54	-37.86	-7.64	99	92	-52.07
3 Yr Avg	---	---	---	---	---	---
5 Yr Avg	---	---	---	---	---	---
Incept Avg	4.39*	---	---	---	---	-5.15*

Risk Analysis

	Risk % Rank[1]		Morningstar[2]		Morningstar
	All	Obj	Return	Risk	Risk-Adj Rating
3 Yr	---	---	---	---	---
5 Yr	---	---	---	---	---
10 Yr	---	---	---	---	---

[1] = Low, 100 = High   [2]1.00 = Equity Avg   [3]1.00 = 90-day T-bill Return

Other Measures

				S&P 500
Standard Deviation	---	Alpha		---
Mean	---	Beta		---
Sharpe Ratio	---	R-Squared		---

Investment Style

	Stock Portfolio Avg	Rel WS Hong Kong	Rel WS Foreign
Price/Earnings Ratio	14.4#	1.07	0.29
Price/Cash Flow Ratio	23.2#	1.21	1.59
Price/Book Ratio	3.0#	1.22	1.00
5 Yr Earnings Gr %	17.6#	0.71	NMF
Return on Assets %	17.1#	1.30	3.71
Debt % Total Cap	14.7#	0.97	0.45
Med Mkt Cap ($mil)	4253#	0.43	0.68

\# figure is based on less than 50% of stocks

Country Exposure (top five) 12-31-94

Securities %		Currency %	
Hong Kong	75	Hong Kong	75
China	20	China	20
South Korea	2	South Korea	2
Taiwan	2	Taiwan	2

Diversification Value for Portfolio Types

Large Cap: Small Cap: Bond: Balanced: Diversified:

Portfolio 06-30-94

Share Chg (12-93)	Amount	Total Equity: 63 Total Fixed-Income: 0	Value $000	% Total Invest
0	1700000	Hutchison Whampoa	7038	5.38
0	6353800	Shanghai Dazhong Taxi Cl B	6875	5.26
0	1900000	New World Development	5285	4.04
-1000000	6000000	Hopewell Holdings	4890	3.74
0	1200000	Television Broadcasts	4735	3.62
0	1200000	Wharf Holdings	4440	3.40
0	770000	Sun Hung Kai Properties	4433	3.39
-700000	1500000	Citic Pacific	4036	3.09
-380000	700000	China Light & Power	3577	2.74
0	6168000	Guangdong Investments	3551	2.72
0	4000000	Shanghai Jinqiao Cl B	3320	2.54
624734	5622609	Ka Wah Bank	3055	2.34
0	1500000	Hong Kong Telecommunications	2814	2.15
0	200000	New World China Investments	2050	1.57
1000000	3000000	Shanghai Outer Gaoqiao Cl B	2034	1.56
1081000	3081000	Shanghai Jin Jiang Tower B	2009	1.54
0	7000000	CP Pokphand	1992	1.52
0	8600000	Tem Fat Hing Fung	1869	1.43
397200	1721200	China Southern Glass Cl B	1848	1.41
0	1500000	Kumagai-Gumi	1805	1.38
0	6000000	China Travel International	1708	1.31
490200	2532200	Li & Fung	1671	1.28
0	47320	Dong Kuk Steel Mill	1669	1.28
0	1780000	Shanghai Diesel Engine Cl B	1620	1.24
0	57000	Taiwan Fund	1532	1.17

Composition % 12-31-94

Cash	1.3	Preferreds	0.0
Stocks	98.7	Convertibles	0.0
Bonds	0.0	Other	0.0

Tax Analysis

	Tax-Adj Historical Return %	% Pretax Return
3 Yr Avg	---	---
5 Yr Avg	---	---
10 Yr Avg	---	---
Potential Capital Gain Exposure (% of assets)		-1

Most Similar Funds in MF500

Fund lacks 3-year record

Sector Weightings

	% of Stocks
Utilities	7.9
Energy	0.0
Financials	39.5
Industrial Cyclicals	12.6
Consumer Durables	19.5
Consumer Staples	2.5
Services	18.1
Retail	0.0
Health	0.0
Technology	0.0

Operations

Address and Telephone	1285 Avenue of the Americas New York, NY 10019 212-713-2000
Advisor	Baring International Investment
Subadvisor	N/A
Administrator	Mitchell Hutchins Asset Management
Transfer Agent	PNC Bank N.A.
Custodian	Brown Brothers Harriman & Co.
Auditor	Price Waterhouse LLP
Legal Counsel	White & Case

Income Distrib Schedule	Paid Irregularly
Management Fee	1.25%, 0.22%A
Reinvestment Plan	Yes
Direct Purchase Plan	No
Shares Outstanding	9,584,377
Exchange	NYSE
*Date of Inception	07-15-92
Shareholder Report	B

MORNINGSTAR 1995 Mutual Fund 500

Greenspring

	Ticker	Load	NAV	Yield	SEC Yield	Assets	Objective
	GRSPX	None	13.39	3.7%	N/A	50.3	Growth

Greenspring Fund seeks long-term capital appreciation. Income is a secondary objective.

The fund invests primarily in common stocks, preferred stocks, and convertible securities selected on the basis of fundamental investment value. It seeks out-of-favor companies that may be facing changes due to management changes, industry developments, new products, or improved financial structures. The fund may also invest in high-yield, high-risk debt securities rated as low as C, and from time to time in reorganizations or liquidations. It may also write covered or uncovered call options, write put options, and purchase call or put options.

Manager's Investment Style

In choosing stocks, manager Chip Carlson prefers issues that have been sharply beaten down by the market, especially if they therefore offer high yields. Although Carlson seeks price appreciation from these issues, he has given much emphasis to income returns. He has on several occasions purchased high-yielding convertibles, straight bonds, and real-estate investment trusts, and has at times held large levels of cash.

Fund Manager(s)

Charles vK. Carlson CFA(1986), since 01-87.
Birthdate: 11-59. BA, Johns Hopkins U. 1982

Manager Experience	Dates Managed	Invest Obj	Std Dev	+/- Index
Not available.				

Historical Profile
Return	Average
Risk	Low
Rating	★★★★ Above Average

Investment Style History
Equity
Average % Stocks Held in Portfolio

41%	48%	46%	45%	43%	43%

Growth of $10,000

|||| Value of Fund ($000)
— Value of Index ($000) S&P 500
▼ Manager Change
▽ Partial Manager Change
►■ Mgr Unknown After
◄■ Mgr Unknown Before

Performance Quartile (Within Objective)

1983	1984	1985	1986	1987	1988	1989	1990	1991	1992	1993	1994	History
11.22	12.66	13.85	13.61	11.89	12.50	12.83	11.32	12.91	13.78	13.96	13.39	NAV
13.55 *	13.12	20.03	16.01	9.19	16.08	10.55	-6.48	19.28	16.52	14.69	2.88	Total Return %
13.81 *	6.85	-11.71	-2.67	3.93	-0.53	-21.14	-3.36	-11.20	8.90	4.63	1.56	+/- S&P 500
---	10.07	-12.53	-0.09	6.83	-1.87	-18.63	-0.30	-14.92	7.55	3.41	2.95	+/- Wilshire 5000
0.00	0.28	10.27	6.09	13.37	10.55	6.40	5.29	4.58	3.91	2.86	3.75	Income Return %
13.55	12.83	9.76	9.92	-4.18	5.52	4.15	-11.77	14.71	12.60	11.83	-0.87	Capital Return %
---	12	73	48	11	24	68	75	45	8	30	8	Total Rtn % Rank All
---	1	90	41	15	45	96	65	94	12	34	15	Total Rtn % Rank Obj
0.00	0.03	1.13	0.74	1.65	1.25	0.79	0.68	0.52	0.51	0.40	0.51	Income $
0.00	0.00	0.04	1.47	1.26	0.04	0.18	0.00	0.07	0.72	1.41	0.45	Capital Gains $
---	1.50	1.49	1.46	1.36	1.29	1.27	1.31	1.33	1.48	1.31	1.35	Expense Ratio %
---	3.74	5.96	5.55	8.57	11.13	6.23	4.82	3.79	3.68	2.78	3.62	Income Ratio %
---	353	350	502	929	199	71	90	70	100	122	---	Turnover Rate %
2.3	7.7	13.0	14.0	18.4	21.2	22.1	20.0	18.9	20.0	29.9	50.3	Net Assets ($mil)

Performance 12-31-94

	1st Qtr	2nd Qtr	3rd Qtr	4th Qtr	Total
1987	9.58	3.82	3.46	-7.23	9.19
1988	5.64	7.01	2.01	0.67	16.08
1989	3.62	4.10	2.97	-0.48	10.55
1990	3.74	-1.09	-6.71	-2.30	-6.48
1991	9.98	3.61	1.47	3.15	19.28
1992	3.25	1.20	5.85	5.34	16.52
1993	8.13	1.07	4.45	0.48	14.69
1994	2.15	0.07	1.93	-1.26	2.88

Bear Market Performance

Decile Rank (5-year period)

Worst | Best

	Worst 3 Mo Period 1985-89	Worst 3 Mo Period 1990-94
Greenspring	-9.39	-10.80
+/- S&P 500	20.19	3.04
+/- Best Fit Index : Wil 4500	20.75	8.60

Trailing Returns

	Total Return %	+/- S&P 500	+/- Wil 5000	% Rank All	% Rank Obj	Growth of $10,000
3 Mo	-1.26	-1.24	-0.49	51	50	9,874
6 Mo	0.64	-4.22	-3.98	44	84	10,064
1 Yr	2.88	1.56	2.95	8	15	10,288
3 Yr Avg	11.19	4.93	4.58	10	13	15,336
5 Yr Avg	8.93	0.24	0.11	24	46	15,336
10 Yr Avg	11.58	-2.80	-2.28	42	71	29,923
15 Yr Avg	---	---	---	---	---	---

Operations

Address and Telephone	2330 W. Joppa Road Suite 110
	Lutherville, MD 21093-4641
	800-366-3863 / 410-823-5353
Advisor	Key Equity Management
Subadvisor	None
Distributor	Greenspring Fund
States Available	All except ID,MT,SD,WY
Report Grade	B+
Income Distrib	Paid Annually
* Date of Inception	07-01-83
Fiscal Year End	December

Risk Analysis

Time Period	Load-Adj Return %	Risk % Rank [1] All	Obj	Morningstar [2] Return	Morningstar Risk	Morningstar Risk-Adj Rating
1 Yr	2.88					
3 Yr	11.19	8	1	2.37 [3]	0.28	★★★★★
5 Yr	8.93	45	2	1.06 [3]	0.41	★★★★
10 Yr	11.58	30	1	0.81	0.34	★★★★

Average Historical Rating (102 months)   4.0 ★s

[1] 1 = low, 100 = high   [2] 1.00 = Equity Avg   [3] 1.00 = 90-day T-bill return

Other Measures

			Standard S&P 500	Best Fit Wil 4500
Standard Deviation	4.99	Alpha	6.3	6.0
Mean	10.78	Beta	0.39	0.33
Sharpe Ratio	1.45	R-Squared	37	41

Investment Style

	Stock Portfolio Avg	Relative S&P 500
Price/Earnings Ratio	17.7	0.96
Price/Book Ratio	1.8	0.52
5 Yr Earnings Gr %	1.5#	0.28
Return on Assets %	5.6	0.75
Debt % Total Cap	30.7#	1.09
Med Mkt Cap ($mil)	217	0.02

figure is based on 50% or less of stocks

Style
Value Blend Growth
Size Large Med Small

Diversification Value for Portfolio Types

Large Cap: Medium	Small Cap: Medium	Bond: High	Balanced: Medium	Diversified: Medium

Expenses & Fees

Sales Fees	0.00% front
	0.00% deferred
	0.00% 12b-1
Management Fee	0.75% flat fee
3-,5-,10-yr Expense Projections	$42, $72, $158
Annual Brokerage Cost	0.31%

Min Initial Purchase	$1000 (Addt'l: $100)
Min IRA Purchase	$1000 (Addt'l: $100)
Min Auto Invest Plan	N/A

Portfolio 06-30-94

Share Chg (03-94) 000	Amount 000	Total Stocks: 28 / Total Fixed-Income: 17	Value $000	% Net Assets
27	110	Town & Country Trust	2000	5.06
7	103	USLICO	1909	4.83
0	73	Loyola Capital	1624	4.11
	1500	MBO Properties 10%	1502	3.80
	1450	American Capital Bond Cv 8.5%	1461	3.70
-2	64	Carr Realty	1380	3.49
0	68	PartnerRe Holdings	1367	3.46
-23	89	Mark Centers Trust	1283	3.25
0	31	Pioneer Group	1139	2.88
	1000	Civic Center Holdings 13.5%	1029	2.60
	42	Manville Cl B Pfd	988	2.50
	975	Transco Energy 9.125%	985	2.49
	1000	Medical Care Intl Cv 7%	978	2.47
	35	Royal Bank Scotland Pfd 11.25%	932	2.36
36	88	Alliance Global Enviro Fund	828	2.09
	800	Flagstar 11.25%	714	1.81
	700	Pacific Gulf Prop Cv 8.375%	681	1.72
0	18	First Brands	670	1.70
12	115	UNR Industries	631	1.60
	600	Zapata 10.25%	615	1.56
	15	Illinois Power Cl A Pfd	602	1.52
0	50	AFC Cable Systems	566	1.43
	21	Westpac Banking Pfd 12%	557	1.41
	500	Liberty Properties Cv 8%	507	1.28
0	37	Reading Cl A	378	0.96

Composition % 12-31-94

Cash	26.7	Preferreds	3.8
Stocks	38.0	Convertibles	11.4
Bonds	20.2	Other	0.0

Tax Analysis

	Tax-Adj Historical Return %	% Pretax Return
3 Yr Avg	8.12	70.4
5 Yr Avg	6.42	68.4
10 Yr Avg	8.01	58.2
Potential Capital Gain Exposure (% of assets)		-1%

Most Similar Funds in MF500

Royce Equity-Income	Weak Fit
Gabelli Asset	Weak Fit
Evergreen Foundation	Weak Fit

Index Allocation

	% of Stocks
S&P 500	4.2
S&P MidCap 400	5.2
U.S. Small Cap	77.1
Foreign	13.6

Sector Weightings

	% of Stocks	Relative S&P 500
Utilities	0.0	0.00
Energy	1.3	0.13
Financials	68.3	6.46
Industrial Cyclicals	16.0	0.97
Consumer Durables	4.1	0.66
Consumer Staples	0.0	0.00
Services	10.3	1.27
Retail	0.0	0.00
Health	0.0	0.00
Technology	0.0	0.00

Growth Fund of America

	Ticker	Load	NAV	Yield	SEC Yield	Assets	Objective
	AGTHX	5.75%	25.53	0.6%	0.93%	5274.2	Growth

Growth Fund of America seeks growth of capital. Current income is not a consideration.

The fund invests primarily in common stocks, but convertible securities that meet the fund's objective may also be purchased. It may invest in a wide range of companies, including growing and profitable companies, turnaround situations, and unseasoned companies.

Historical Profile
Return	Above Average
Risk	Average
Rating ★★★★	Above Average

Investment Style History
Equity

Average % Stocks Held in Portfolio

84% 86% 76% 78% 80% 85% 84% 82%

Growth of $10,000
|||| Value of Fund ($000)
— Value of Index ($000) SPMid400
▼ Manager Change
▽ Partial Manager Change
► Mgr Unknown After
◄ Mgr Unknown Before

Performance Quartile (Within Objective)

Manager's Investment Style
Despite working separately to fill individual portions of the portfolio, the members of the management team all follow the same investing style. Assets are typically invested in value plays and left to appreciate over the long term. While bulking up in sectors such as technology, the fund has avoided large losses by staying away from more-volatile stocks, and by keeping large percentages of assets in cash. Management is also assisted in their choices by their advisor, Capital Research and Management.

Fund Manager(s)
Management Team

	1983	1984	1985	1986	1987	1988	1989	1990	1991	1992	1993	1994	History
	13.58	12.41	14.51	15.76	15.56	17.51	20.17	18.02	22.93	24.34	26.75	25.53	NAV
	27.11	-5.58	27.22	16.26	7.29	18.46	30.41	-4.12	35.79	7.40	14.50	0.02	Total Return %
	4.64	-11.84	-4.52	-2.42	2.03	1.85	-1.28	-1.01	5.31	-0.22	4.44	-1.29	+/- S&P 500
	3.64	-8.63	-5.34	0.17	4.93	0.52	1.23	2.06	1.59	-1.57	3.21	0.09	+/- Wilshire 5000
	3.43	2.26	1.84	1.89	1.48	1.89	3.22	2.59	1.77	0.83	0.47	0.67	Income Return %
	23.67	-7.84	25.38	14.38	5.82	16.57	27.19	-6.72	34.02	6.57	14.03	-0.65	Capital Return %
	17	81	37	46	15	18	13	68	18	53	31	19	Total Rtn % Rank All
	22	68	65	38	23	34	33	46	45	55	35	33	Total Rtn % Rank Obj
	0.40	0.29	0.22	0.28	0.29	0.31	0.61	0.48	0.35	0.19	0.12	0.17	Income $
	0.27	0.11	0.87	0.79	1.10	0.59	1.99	0.82	1.07	0.09	0.97	1.04	Capital Gains $
	0.68	0.68	0.69	0.66	0.66	0.71	0.78	0.79	0.83	0.79	0.77	0.78	Expense Ratio %
	3.85	2.57	1.66	1.84	1.50	1.56	2.82	2.67	2.13	1.11	0.56	0.49	Income Ratio %
	26	23	24	24	20	18	30	18	19	11	25	25	Turnover Rate %
	383.0	507.9	603.0	791.9	957.9	1121.4	1806.9	2060.6	3457.7	4332.9	5062.5	5274.2	Net Assets ($mil)

Manager Experience
	Dates Managed	Invest Obj	Std Dev	+/- Index
William C. Newton				
Amcap	05/67 - 12/76	G	19.09	1.38
R. Michael Shanahan				
American Mutual	01/86 - 12/94	GI	10.91	-1.56

Performance 12-31-94
	1st Qtr	2nd Qtr	3rd Qtr	4th Qtr	Total
1987	21.76	3.02	5.91	-19.25	7.29
1988	10.60	7.32	-1.57	1.39	18.46
1989	9.77	10.67	10.01	-2.42	30.41
1990	-1.34	6.28	-17.64	11.01	-4.12
1991	19.37	-3.16	7.11	9.68	35.79
1992	-1.44	-2.88	2.00	9.99	7.40
1993	0.90	2.97	7.59	2.42	14.50
1994	-2.50	-2.57	5.82	-0.50	0.02

Bear Market Performance
Decile Rank (5-year period)

Worst ————————————— Best

	Worst 3 Mo Period 1985-89	Worst 3 Mo Period 1990-94
Growth Fund of America	-28.38	-17.64
+/- S&P 500	1.20	-3.89
+/- Best Fit Index : SPMid400	0.43	0.14

Trailing Returns
	Total Return %	+/- S&P 500	+/- Wil 5000	% Rank All	% Rank Obj	Growth of $10,000
3 Mo	-0.50	-0.48	0.27	34	32	9,950
6 Mo	5.30	0.44	0.67	10	32	10,530
1 Yr	0.02	-1.29	0.09	19	33	10,002
3 Yr Avg	7.14	0.88	0.53	26	38	12,300
5 Yr Avg	9.87	1.18	1.06	18	31	16,014
10 Yr Avg	14.65	0.27	0.79	13	18	39,256
15 Yr Avg	15.15	0.67	1.17	12	23	82,983

Operations
Address and Telephone	4 Embarcadero Cntr P.O. Box 7650
	San Francisco, CA 94120
	800-421-4120 / 415-421-9360
Advisor	Capital Research & Management
Subadvisor	None
Distributor	American Funds Distributors
States Available	All plus GU,PR,VI
Report Grade	A+
Income Distrib	Paid Annually
Date of Inception	01-01-59
Fiscal Year End	August

Min Initial Purchase	$1000 (Addt'l: $50)
Min IRA Purchase	$250 (Addt'l: $50)
Min Auto Invest Plan	$50 (Systematic Inv: $50)

Expenses & Fees
Sales Fees	5.75% front
	0.00% deferred
	0.25% 12b-1
Management Fee	0.50% flat fee
3-,5-,10-yr Expense Projections	$81, $98, $149
Annual Brokerage Cost	0.11%

Risk Analysis
Time Period	Load-Adj Return %	Risk % Rank[1] All	Obj	Morningstar[2] Return	Morningstar Risk	Morningstar Risk-Adj Rating
1 Yr	-5.73					
3 Yr	5.05	74	42	0.43[3]	0.84	★★★
5 Yr	8.58	77	53	0.96[3]	0.93	★★★
10 Yr	13.98	74	52	1.26	0.95	★★★★
Average Historical Rating (109 months)					3.7	★ s

[1] 1 = low, 100 = high [2] 1.00 = Equity Avg [3] 1.00 = 90-day T-bill return

Other Measures
			Standard S&P 500	Best Fit SPMid400
Standard Deviation	9.76	Alpha	0.9	0.4
Mean	7.39	Beta	1.04	0.90
Sharpe Ratio	0.40	R-Squared	71	82

Investment Style
	Stock Portfolio Avg	Relative S&P 500	Style
Price/Earnings Ratio	21.6	1.17	
Price/Book Ratio	4.3	1.27	
5 Yr Earnings Gr %	21.2#	3.82	
Return on Assets %	9.6	1.28	
Debt % Total Cap	29.9	1.06	
Med Mkt Cap ($mil)	6797	0.52	

figure is based on 50% or less of stocks

Diversification Value for Portfolio Types
Large Cap: Low	Small Cap: Low	Bond: High	Balanced: Low	Diversified: Low

Portfolio 09-30-94
Total Stocks: 113
Total Fixed-Income: 1

Share Chg (08-94) 000	Amount 000		Value $000	% Net Assets
0	5252	Time Warner	184477	3.51
0	8039	Tele-Communications Cl A	177870	3.39
0	2225	FNMA	175219	3.34
100	4570	Advanced Micro Devices	135958	2.59
0	2675	News (ADR)	135422	2.58
180	1955	Intel	120233	2.29
375	2575	Walt Disney	100103	1.91
0	2253	Columbia/HCA Healthcare	97984	1.87
	1755	Cellular Communications Cv Pfd	93015	1.77
150	1355	Texas Instruments	92648	1.76
0	3440	Silicon Graphics	88580	1.69
-4	621	LIN Broadcasting	86945	1.66
0	5498	National Semiconductor	85905	1.64
0	1600	United HealthCare	84800	1.61
0	3275	MCI Communications	83103	1.58
0	2550	Vodafone Group (ADR)	80006	1.52
0	2938	Mattel	79680	1.52
0	950	Capital Cities/ABC	77900	1.48
0	4195	Comcast Special Cl A	63449	1.21
0	1110	Microsoft	62299	1.19
25	2975	Turner Broadcasting Cl B	59500	1.13
0	930	Federal Express	57544	1.10
0	1725	Adobe Systems	56063	1.07
0	985	AMR	50728	0.97
0	720	IBM	50040	0.95

Composition % 12-31-94
Cash	18.2	Preferreds	0.0
Stocks	81.8	Convertibles	0.0
Bonds	0.0	Other	0.0

Tax Analysis
	Tax-Adj Historical Return %	% Pretax Return
3 Yr Avg	6.13	85.0
5 Yr Avg	8.40	82.6
10 Yr Avg	12.55	77.4
Potential Capital Gain Exposure (% of assets)		23%

Most Similar Funds in MF500
IDS New Dimensions	Strong Fit
Fidelity Growth Company	Strong Fit
Columbia Growth	Strong Fit

Index Allocation
	% of Stocks
S&P 500	64.8
S&P MidCap 400	15.5
U.S. Small Cap	11.5
Foreign	8.2

Sector Weightings
	% of Stocks	Relative S&P 500
Utilities	3.3	0.26
Energy	0.8	0.08
Financials	8.6	0.81
Industrial Cyclicals	3.2	0.20
Consumer Durables	2.7	0.43
Consumer Staples	1.9	0.15
Services	36.3	4.46
Retail	1.0	0.17
Health	8.3	0.96
Technology	33.9	3.70

MORNINGSTAR 1995 Mutual Fund 500

Growth Fund of Spain

	Ticker	NAV	Mkt Price	Prem/Disc	Yield	Objective
	GSP	$11.37	$9.50	-16.4%	4.7%	Europe Stock

Growth Fund of Spain seeks long-term capital appreciation.

Normally, the fund invests at least 65% of its assets in equity securities of Spanish companies. The fund may invest up to 25% in unlisted debt or equity securities and up to 35% in investment-grade fixed-income instruments. It may also engage in hedging strategies involving futures and options.

Directors serve staggered terms as a takeover defense. Beginning Dec. 1, 1994, the fund will propose to open-end if its shares are trading at an average discount of more than 10% during the 12 weeks preceding December 31 of each year, and if at least 10% of outstanding shares request in writing that such a proposal be submitted.

Options on the fund are traded on the Chicago Board Options Exchange.

Historical Profile

Return	Below Average
Risk	Average
Rating	★★ Below Average

	4.4	-5.0	-8.7	-1.9	-5.2	Highest Prem/Disc
	-28.1	-22.4	-18.6	-15.7	-20.4	Lowest Prem/Disc

Growth of $10,000
- at NAV ($000)
- at Market Price ($000)

Premium Discount %

	1983	1984	1985	1986	1987	1988	1989	1990	1991	1992	1993	1994	History
	---	---	---	---	---	---	---	10.25	11.71	8.96	11.54	11.37	NAV
	---	---	---	---	---	---	---	-4.10*	16.08	-23.48	28.80	3.19	NAV Total Return %
	---	---	---	---	---	---	.	-7.03*	-14.40	-31.10	18.74	1.88	+/- S&P 500
	---	---	---	---	---	---	---	---	3.95	-11.31	-3.77	-4.58	+/- MSCI EAFE
	---	---	---	---	---	---	---	---	0.45	-1.62	-0.99	8.00	+/- MSCI Spain
	---	---	---	---	---	---	---	4.06*	1.84	0.00	0.00	4.67	Income Return %
	---	---	---	---	---	---	---	-8.15*	14.24	-23.48	28.80	-1.47	Capital Return %
	---	---	---	---	---	---	---	---	57	98	15	8	Total Rtn % Rank All
	---	---	---	---	---	---	---	---	5	78	57	36	Total Rtn % Rank Obj
	---	---	---	---	---	---	---	-29.30*	17.24	-18.67	34.43	-2.93	Market Total Rtn %
	---	---	---	---	---	---	---	-16.1	-12.3	-14.2	-8.8	-16.3	Avg Prem/Disc %
	---	---	---	---	---	---	---	0.36	0.15	0.00	0.00	0.45	Income $
	---	---	---	---	---	---	---	0.00	0.00	0.00	0.00	0.00	Capital Gains $
	---	---	---	---	---	---	---	1.26	1.23	1.22	1.22	1.23	Expense Ratio %
	---	---	---	---	---	---	---	3.46	3.32	4.98	3.97	2.49	Income Ratio %
	---	---	---	---	---	---	---	19	104	72	50	---	Turnover Rate %
	---	---	---	---	---	---	---	178.7	203.9	155.4	200.0	196.3	Net Assets ($mil)

Manager's Investment Style

Management takes a bottom-up approach to the Spanish market. It often invests in lesser-known securities, and is willing to move into sectors based on market trends. Overall, though, the strategy is a conservative one that doesn't dramatically overweight particular sectors. Additionally, management is willing to hold cash, and it occasionally hedges the portfolio's currency exposure into the U.S. dollar.

Fund Manager(s)

Gonzalo Milans. Since 10-90. Instituto de Empresa; BA U. Autonoma de Madrid.

Eduardo Suarez. Since 2-90. '77 Deusto U.; '78 ICADE.

Dennis Ferro. Since 7-94. BA'67 Villanova U.; MBA'74 St. John's U.

Manager Experience	Dates Managed	Invest Obj	Std Dev	+/- Index
Dennis Ferro				
Kemper International A	04/94 - 12/94	WF	10.29	-6.62

NAV Performance % 12-30-94

	1st Qtr	2nd Qtr	3rd Qtr	4th Qtr	Total
1987	---	---	---	---	---
1988	---	---	---	---	---
1989	---	---	---	---	---
1990	-2.96*	17.54	-23.57	10.00	-4.10*
1991	12.29	-6.34	9.55	0.75	16.08
1992	-0.34	-5.06	-21.84	3.46	-23.48
1993	9.71	-1.63	10.86	7.65	28.80
1994	6.76	-1.87	2.56	-3.96	3.19

Bear Market Performance

Decile Rank (5-year period)

Worst ———— Best

	Worst 3 Mo Period 1985-89	Worst 3 Mo Period 1990-94
Growth Fund Spain	---	---
+/- S&P 500	---	---

Trailing Returns

	NAV Total Return %	+/- S&P 500	+/- MSCI Spain	% Rank All	Obj	Mkt Total Return %
3 Mo	-3.96	-3.95	1.21	80	70	-5.24
6 Mo	-1.50	-6.36	1.99	60	68	3.38
1 Yr	3.19	1.88	8.00	8	36	-2.93
3 Yr Avg	0.56	-5.70	1.73	93	78	2.00
5 Yr Avg	---	---	---	---	---	---
Incept Avg	2.58*	---	---	---	---	-2.59*

Operations

Address and Telephone	120 S. LaSalle Street
	Chicago, IL 60603
	312-781-1121 / 800-621-1148
Advisor	Kemper Financial Services Inc.
Subadvisor	BSN Gestion de Patrimonios, S.A.
Administrator	N/A
Transfer Agent	Investors Fiduciary Trust Co.
Custodian	Investors Fiduciary Trust Co.
Auditor	Ernst & Young LLP
Legal Counsel	Vedder, Price, Kaufman & Kammholz

Income Distrib Schedule	Paid Irregularly
Management Fee	1.00%
Reinvestment Plan	Yes
Direct Purchase Plan	No
Shares Outstanding	17,288,293
Exchange	NYSE/CHX
*Date of Inception	02-14-90
Shareholder Report	B-

Risk Analysis

	Risk % Rank[1] All	Obj	Morningstar[2] Return	Risk	Morningstar Risk-Adj Rating
3 Yr	91	68	-0.38	1.17	★★
5 Yr	---	---	---	---	
10 Yr	---	---	---	---	
Average Historical Rating (23 months)				2.0 ★s	

[1] 1 = Low, 100 = High [2] 1.00 = Equity Avg [3] 1.00 = 90-day T-bill Return

Other Measures

				S&P 500
Standard Deviation	18.81	Alpha		-3.61
Mean	2.33	Beta		0.86
Sharpe Ratio	-0.06	R-Squared		13

Investment Style

	Stock Portfolio Avg	Rel WS Spain	Rel WS Foreign
Price/Earnings Ratio	13.7	0.94	0.28
Price/Cash Flow Ratio	7.5	1.08	0.51
Price/Book Ratio	1.9	1.18	0.63
5 Yr Earnings Gr %	1.4	2.83	NMF
Return on Assets %	5.9	1.27	1.28
Debt % Total Cap	23.9	0.83	0.74
Med Mkt Cap ($mil)	1577	0.38	0.25

figure is based on less than 50% of stocks

Country Exposure (top five) 01-10-95

	Securities %		Currency %
Spain	98	Spain	98
		US	2

Diversification Value for Portfolio Types

Large Cap: High	Small Cap: High	Bond: High	Balanced: High	Diversified: Medium

Portfolio 05-31-94

Total Equity: 36 Total Fixed-Income: 1

Share Chg (11-93)	Amount		Value $000	% Total Invest
55000	440000	Repsol	13890	6.73
52925	113600	Banco Popular Espanol (Reg)	12795	6.20
-270000	800000	Telefonica de Espana	10857	5.26
120000	450000	Banco Bilbao Vizcaya (Reg)	10605	5.14
-850	210000	Empresa Nacional Electricid	10145	4.91
25500	115000	Bankinter	10136	4.91
145275	229275	Argentaria	9724	4.71
-64500	290357	Cantabrico	9166	4.44
-13250	351750	Viscofan Indl Navarra Envolt	8691	4.21
-19641	69000	Zardoya Otis	8586	4.16
18325	83325	Acerinox	8482	4.11
-88700	1089426	Iberdrola	8011	3.88
-699200	753439	Fecsa	5552	2.69
89850	296000	Dragados & Construcciones	5000	2.42
-353350	527290	Acesa	4901	2.37
5425	36935	Banco de Andalucia (Reg)	4076	1.97
-26000	81000	Gas & Electricidad	4009	1.94
---	500.000M	Bono del Estado 10.55%	3837	1.86
24225	39725	Cubiertas & Mzov	3499	1.69
111550	311450	Autopistas Del Mare Nost	3377	1.64
-204800	629504	Union Electrica Fenosa	3078	1.49
35800	35800	Gas Natural (Reg)	3005	1.46
51775	51775	Cristaleria Espanola	2944	1.43
200000	200000	Pryca	2906	1.41
-101000	249000	Ebro Azucares Y Alimentacion	2893	1.40

Composition % 01-10-95

Cash	10.0	Preferreds	0.0
Stocks	88.0	Convertibles	0.0
Bonds	10.0	Other	0.0

Tax Analysis

	Tax-Adj Historical Return %	% Pretax Return
3 Yr Avg	0.09	15.9
5 Yr Avg	---	---
10 Yr Avg	---	---
Potential Capital Gain Exposure (% of assets)		1

Most Similar Funds in MF500

G.T. Global Worldwide Grth	Weak Fit
GT Greater Europe	Weak Fit
Invesco European	Weak Fit

Sector Weightings

	% of Stocks
Utilities	30.0
Energy	11.0
Financials	21.6
Industrial Cyclicals	27.1
Consumer Durables	0.0
Consumer Staples	2.7
Services	5.6
Retail	2.0
Health	0.0
Technology	0.0

G.T. Greater Europe

	Ticker	NAV	Mkt Price	Prem/Disc	Yield	Objective
	GTF	$14.10	$11.88	-15.8%	0.2%	Europe Stock

G.T. Greater Europe Fund seeks long-term capital appreciation. The fund will invest at least 65% of its total assets in the securities of European issuers in established and emerging markets. It will invest the balance in the securities of issuers in countries that are linked to Europe by tradition, economic markets, cultural similarities, or geography, or in securities of issuers in other countries that stand to benefit from conditions or developments in Europe.

If the fund is trading at a discount to NAV during the second quarter of 1995, the board may decide to repurchase shares. If the board does not repurchase shares, it must submit a proposal to open-end the fund to shareholders no later than Jan. 31, 1996. The fund may open-end prior to this date only by a 75% shareholder approval.

	7.3	-3.0	-6.5	5.5	0.8	Highest Prem/Disc
	-19.2	-19.9	-17.4	-16.0	-16.9	Lowest Prem/Disc

Historical Profile
Return Average
Risk Below Average
Rating ★★★
Neutral

Growth of $10,000
■ at NAV ($000)
— at Market Price ($000)

Premium Discount %

	1983	1984	1985	1986	1987	1988	1989	1990	1991	1992	1993	1994	History
	---	---	---	---	---	---	---	11.29	11.32	10.57	14.52	14.10	NAV
	---	---	---	---	---	---	---	-18.58*	1.28	-6.63	39.67	-0.50	NAV Total Return %
	---	---	---	---	---	---	---	-18.43*	-29.20	-14.24	29.61	-1.81	+/- S&P 500
	---	---	---	---	---	---	---	---	-10.85	5.55	7.11	-8.27	+/- MSCI EAFE
	---	---	---	---	---	---	---	---	-8.47	0.99	13.10	-0.63	+/- MSCI Europe
	---	---	---	---	---	---	---	1.29*	1.02	0.00	2.30	0.16	Income Return %
	---	---	---	---	---	---	---	-19.87*	0.27	-6.63	37.37	-0.65	Capital Return %
	---	---	---	---	---	---	---	---	94	91	10	14	Total Rtn % Rank All
	---	---	---	---	---	---	---	---	47	21	21	63	Total Rtn % Rank Obj
	---	---	---	---	---	---	---	-38.14*	5.17	-6.58	66.12	-16.08	Market Total Rtn %
	---	---	---	---	---	---	---	-8.0	-14.0	-14.2	-5.6	-10.0	Avg Prem/Disc %
	---	---	---	---	---	---	---	0.15	0.11	0.00	0.24	0.02	Income $
	---	---	---	---	---	---	---	0.01	0.00	0.00	0.00	0.33	Capital Gains $
	---	---	---	---	---	---	---	1.78	1.87	1.92	1.88	1.82	Expense Ratio %
	---	---	---	---	---	---	---	1.82	0.21	1.20	1.04	-0.10	Income Ratio %
	---	---	---	---	---	---	---	---	41	47	109	87	---	Turnover Rate %
	---	---	---	---	---	---	---	246.4	181.2	166.4	232.4	226.2	Net Assets ($mil)

Manager's Investment Style
Management takes a bottom-up approach to markets in Europe, but it is also willing to place some sector bets. For example, management began cutting back in interest-rate-sensitive financials in 1994 and moving into cyclicals. The fund actively hedges its currency. Although management at this fund has changed four times in three years, the overall strategy has remained intact.

Fund Manager(s)
James Dickson. Since 3-94.
John R. Legat. Since 3-94.

Manager Experience

	Dates Managed	Invest Obj	Std Dev	+/- Index
John R. Legat				
G.T. Global Europe Growth	07/85 - 04/94	WE	18.39	0.15

NAV Performance % 12-30-94

	1st Qtr	2nd Qtr	3rd Qtr	4th Qtr	Total
1987	---	---	---	---	---
1988	---	---	---	---	---
1989	---	---	---	---	---
1990	0.00*	2.41	-22.71	2.88	-18.58*
1991	3.81	-4.01	0.00	1.64	1.28
1992	-1.50	2.42	-3.15	-4.43	-6.63
1993	7.47	6.60	10.90	9.93	39.67
1994	3.10	-2.67	4.05	-4.70	-0.50

Bear Market Performance
Decile Rank (5-year period)

Worst _____ Best

	Worst 3 Mo Period 1985-89	Worst 3 Mo Period 1990-94
GT Greater Europe	---	---
+/- S&P 500	---	---

Trailing Returns

	NAV Total Return %	+/- S&P 500	+/- MSCI Europe	% Rank All	% Rank Obj	Mkt Total Return %
3 Mo	-4.70	-4.68	-5.06	83	75	-5.49
6 Mo	-0.84	-5.70	-4.95	51	63	-3.62
1 Yr	-0.50	-1.81	-0.63	14	63	-16.08
3 Yr Avg	9.07	2.81	3.67	25	31	9.20
5 Yr Avg	---	---	---	---	---	---
Incept Avg	1.44*	---	---	---	---	-3.42*

Operations

Address and Telephone	50 California St., 27th Floor
	San Francisco, CA 94111
	415-392-6181 / 800-824-1580
Advisor	G.T. Capital
Subadvisor	N/A
Administrator	Princeton Administrators, Inc.
Transfer Agent	State Street Bank and Trust Co.
Custodian	State Street Bank and Trust Co.
Auditor	Coopers & Lybrand
Legal Counsel	Gaston & Snow

Income Distrib Schedule	Paid Irregularly
Management Fee	1.25%, 0.25%A
Reinvestment Plan	Yes
Direct Purchase Plan	No
Shares Outstanding	16,045,345
Exchange	NYSE
*Date of Inception	03-29-90
Shareholder Report	A-

Risk Analysis

	Risk % Rank[1] All	Risk % Rank[1] Obj	Morningstar[2] Return	Morningstar[2] Risk	Morningstar Risk-Adj Rating
3 Yr	76	5	0.74	0.70	★★★
5 Yr	---	---	---	---	
10 Yr	---	---	---	---	

Average Historical Rating (22 months) 2.8 ★s
[1] = Low, 100 = High [2]1.00 = Equity Avg [3]1.00 = 90-day T-bill Return

Other Measures

				S&P 500
Standard Deviation	13.02	Alpha		3.64
Mean	9.55	Beta		0.85
Sharpe Ratio	0.46	R-Squared		27

Investment Style

	Stock Portfolio Avg	Rel WS Europe	Rel WS Foreign
Price/Earnings Ratio	19.3	0.81	0.39
Price/Cash Flow Ratio	8.3	0.96	0.57
Price/Book Ratio	2.4	0.94	0.80
5 Yr Earnings Gr %	-3.5	NMF	NMF
Return on Assets %	5.6	1.14	1.21
Debt % Total Cap	31.3	1.08	0.97
Med Mkt Cap ($mil)	1648	0.31	0.26
figure is based on less than 50% of stocks

Country Exposure (top five) 12-31-94

Securities %		Currency %	
UK	30	UK	30
Germany	11	Germany	11
Sweden	11	Sweden	11
Spain	9	Spain	9
Netherlands	7	Netherlands	7

Diversification Value for Portfolio Types

Large Cap: Medium Small Cap: High Bond: Medium Balanced: Medium Diversified: Low

Portfolio 06-30-94

Share Chg (10-93)	Amount	Total Equity: 85 / Total Fixed-Income: 1	Value $000	% Total Invest
6800	16800	Volkswagen	4891	2.13
-102000	700000	National Westminster Bank	4749	2.07
0	687500	Provident Financial	4516	1.97
2140	2700	Interdiscount Holding (Br)	4356	1.90
1907500	1907500	Crockfords	4334	1.89
0	2000	SAP	4254	1.85
-1600000	1600000	SIP	4221	1.84
-335000	665000	Skandinaviska Enskild A Free	4110	1.79
-150000	850000	Edison	4095	1.78
-100000	200000	IHC Caland	4083	1.78
191800	191800	Marieberg Tidn Cl A	3934	1.71
-80666	1586000	Unitas Bank Cl A	3897	1.70
345000	345000	Allgon Cl B	3846	1.68
156900	156900	Sparbanken Norway	3822	1.67
0	900000	Fotex	3797	1.65
74279	74279	Tele Danmark	3761	1.64
2000	12000	Veba	3750	1.63
280000	280000	Telefonica de Espana	3732	1.63
0	349000	SG Warburg Group	3708	1.62
0	60000	Pick Szeged	3630	1.58
30000	30000	Euro Rscg Worldwide	3390	1.48
5000	20000	Berliner Bank	3370	1.47
62500	384500	Great Universal Stores Cl A	3313	1.44
-2000000	1000000	STET	3260	1.42
-25000	25000	Sita	3077	1.34

Composition % 12-31-94

Cash	2.5	Preferreds	0.0
Stocks	97.5	Convertibles	0.0
Bonds	0.0	Other	0.0

Tax Analysis

	Tax-Adj Historical Return %	% Pretax Return
3 Yr Avg	8.59	94.2
5 Yr Avg	---	---
10 Yr Avg	---	---
Potential Capital Gain Exposure (% of assets)		-8

Most Similar Funds in MF500

Invesco European	Weak Fit
T. Rowe Price Intl Stock	Weak Fit
Scudder International	Weak Fit

Sector Weightings

	% of Stocks
Utilities	11.9
Energy	0.0
Financials	21.8
Industrial Cyclicals	24.5
Consumer Durables	9.2
Consumer Staples	2.6
Services	19.0
Retail	7.8
Health	0.0
Technology	3.3

Guardian Park Avenue

	Ticker	Load	NAV	Yield	SEC Yield	Assets	Objective
	GPAFX	4.50%	26.89	1.1%	N/A	640.7	Growth

Guardian Park Avenue Fund seeks long-term growth of capital. Current income is incidental.

The fund invests at least 80% of its assets in common stocks and convertible securities. It selects individual securities by analyzing a company's business fundamentals to determine whether the current stock price represents good relative value in the marketplace. The fund uses numerous other quantitative methodologies to identify securities with prospects for superior relative price performance.

Historical Profile
Return	Above Average
Risk	Average
Rating	★★★★ Above Average

Investment Style History
Equity
Average % Stocks Held in Portfolio

78% 78% 75% 79% 85% 89% 89% 91%

Growth of $10,000
|||| Value of Fund ($000)
— Value of Index ($000) S&P 500
▼ Manager Change
▽ Partial Manager Change
► Mgr Unknown After
◄ Mgr Unknown Before

Performance Quartile (Within Objective)

1983	1984	1985	1986	1987	1988	1989	1990	1991	1992	1993	1994	History
19.20	18.17	21.20	20.74	18.63	20.47	21.59	18.26	22.23	25.17	28.63	26.89	NAV
28.57	12.53	33.04	18.38	2.96	20.78	23.83	-12.33	35.16	20.48	20.28	-1.44	Total Return %
6.10	6.26	1.30	-0.30	-2.30	4.17	-7.85	-9.22	4.68	12.86	10.22	-2.75	+/- S&P 500
5.11	9.48	0.48	2.28	0.60	2.84	-5.34	-6.15	0.95	11.51	9.00	-1.37	+/- Wilshire 5000
3.41	3.57	2.90	1.61	2.82	2.76	4.62	3.09	3.28	1.96	1.14	1.13	Income Return %
25.16	8.96	30.14	16.77	0.14	18.02	19.22	-15.42	31.88	18.52	19.14	-2.57	Capital Return %
13	15	16	30	36	12	26	88	19	4	17	29	Total Rtn % Rank All
15	3	29	26	50	22	65	88	47	6	15	46	Total Rtn % Rank Obj
0.54	0.60	0.49	0.33	0.60	0.55	0.98	0.71	0.66	0.44	0.31	0.31	Income $
0.48	2.36	2.04	3.81	2.18	1.46	2.72	0.00	1.73	1.12	1.30	1.02	Capital Gains $
0.71	0.78	0.70	0.71	0.68	0.69	0.70	0.69	0.67	0.68	0.81	0.84	Expense Ratio %
2.71	3.75	2.48	1.79	2.08	2.82	4.01	3.51	2.96	1.94	1.89	1.14	Income Ratio %
66	95	80	48	50	58	47	47	57	64	46	---	Turnover Rate %
51.2	58.1	89.6	131.2	157.0	175.8	227.9	216.5	270.1	335.7	560.0	640.7	Net Assets ($mil)

Manager's Investment Style

Management uses a number of screens to choose from a universe of about 1,000 stocks. Historical price/earnings and price/book ratios are compared against the current multiples to make sure that the stocks aren't too expensive. Management also focuses on growth, with price and earnings momentum, as well as changes in dividend policy, stressed in finding growing issues. Management also watches for other indicators such as insider trading and seasonal patterns. This model is used to pick a balanced portfolio of about 270 stocks, with no one issue taking up more than 2% of holdings.

Fund Manager(s)

Charles E. Albers CFA, since 06-72. Birthdate: 11-40. BA, Kenyon C. 1962 MBA, Columbia U. 1967

Manager Experience	Dates Managed	Invest Obj	Std Dev	+/- Index
Charles E. Albers				
Guardian Asset Allocation	02/93 - 12/94	AA	8.18	-0.38

Performance 12-31-94

	1st Qtr	2nd Qtr	3rd Qtr	4th Qtr	Total
1987	23.77	-2.13	7.05	-20.60	2.96
1988	12.83	6.95	-1.36	1.47	20.78
1989	9.33	5.83	9.05	-1.86	23.83
1990	-1.39	0.64	-15.65	4.74	-12.33
1991	18.73	-1.15	9.06	5.60	35.16
1992	2.83	-1.61	4.75	13.67	20.48
1993	9.69	3.54	8.66	-2.54	20.28
1994	-2.86	-1.19	3.87	-1.14	-1.44

Bear Market Performance

Decile Rank (5-year period)

Worst ————————————— Best

	Worst 3 Mo Period 1985-89	Worst 3 Mo Period 1990-94
Guardian Park Avenue	-28.57	-17.52
+/- S&P 500	1.01	-3.67
+/- Best Fit Index : Wil 4500	1.57	1.89

Trailing Returns

	Total Return %	+/- S&P 500	+/- Wil 5000	% Rank All	% Rank Obj	Growth of $10,000
3 Mo	-1.14	-1.12	-0.37	47	47	9,886
6 Mo	2.69	-2.17	-1.93	22	65	10,269
1 Yr	-1.44	-2.75	-1.37	29	46	9,856
3 Yr Avg	12.62	6.35	6.00	7	8	14,283
5 Yr Avg	11.10	2.41	2.28	12	19	16,924
10 Yr Avg	15.17	0.78	1.31	10	14	41,045
15 Yr Avg	16.22	1.74	2.25	6	14	95,357

Operations

Address and Telephone	201 Park Avenue South New York, NY 10003 800-221-3253
Advisor	Guardian Investor Services
Subadvisor	None
Distributor	Guardian Investor Services
States Available	All plus PR
Report Grade	C+
Income Distrib	Paid Semiannually
Date of Inception	06-01-72
Fiscal Year End	December

Risk Analysis

Time Period	Load-Adj Return %	Risk % Rank [1] All	Risk % Rank [1] Obj	Morningstar [2] Return	Morningstar Risk	Morningstar Risk-Adj Rating
1 Yr	-5.87					
3 Yr	10.90	65	25	2.27 [3]	0.73	★★★★
5 Yr	10.08	72	34	1.38 [3]	0.86	★★★★
10 Yr	14.64	69	40	1.41	0.91	★★★★
Average Historical Rating (109 months)				4.3		★s

[1] 1 = low, 100 = high [2] 1.00 = Equity Avg [3] 1.00 = 90-day T-bill return

Other Measures

		Standard S&P 500	Best Fit Wil 4500
Standard Deviation	9.61	Alpha	6.3	5.2
Mean	12.40	Beta	0.94	0.89
Sharpe Ratio	0.92	R-Squared	60	82

Investment Style

	Stock Portfolio Avg	Relative S&P 500
Price/Earnings Ratio	16.3	0.88
Price/Book Ratio	2.7	0.80
5 Yr Earnings Gr %	9.5	1.72
Return on Assets %	8.0	1.07
Debt % Total Cap	25.8	0.91
Med Mkt Cap ($mil)	1719	0.13

Style: Value Blend Growth — Large/Med/Small

Diversification Value for Portfolio Types

Large Cap: Low	Small Cap: Low	Bond: High	Balanced: Low	Diversified: Low

Expenses & Fees

Sales Fees	4.50% front / 0.00% deferred / 0.25% 12b-1
Management Fee	0.50% flat fee
3-,5-,10-yr Expense Projections	$70, $88, $141
Annual Brokerage Cost	0.16%

Min Initial Purchase $1000 (Addt'l: $100)
Min IRA Purchase $250 (Addt'l: $50)
Min Auto Invest Plan $50 (Systematic Inv: $100)

Portfolio 12-31-94

Total Stocks: 293
Total Fixed-Income: 4

Share Chg (11-94) 000	Amount 000		Value $000	% Net Assets
0	224	IBM	16442	2.57
0	258	Computer Associates Intl	12513	1.95
0	77	McDonnell Douglas	10934	1.71
0	238	US Healthcare	9834	1.53
0	73	Hercules	8376	1.31
0	288	Ford Motor	8064	1.26
0	140	El DuPont de Nemours	7858	1.23
0	92	Capital Cities/ABC	7843	1.22
0	95	Texas Instruments	7076	1.10
0	150	Micron Technology	6608	1.03
0	100	Eli Lilly	6563	1.02
0	159	Paychex	6444	1.01
3	134	Cummins Engine	6051	0.94
0	114	Andrew	5972	0.93
225	600	Host Marriott	5773	0.90
0	113	Eastman Chemical	5691	0.89
300	435	Santa Fe Pacific Gold	5601	0.87
35	183	Rayonier	5582	0.87
0	155	Rockwell International	5541	0.86
0	145	PPG Industries	5383	0.84
25	155	Briggs & Stratton	5076	0.79
-205	97	Coca-Cola	4996	0.78
61	149	First USA	4905	0.77
0	112	General Dynamics	4889	0.76
0	161	Echlin	4830	0.75

Composition % 12-31-94

Cash	6.0	Preferreds	0.0
Stocks	91.5	Convertibles	0.8
Bonds	1.7	Other	0.0

Tax Analysis

	Tax-Adj Historical Return %	% Pretax Return
3 Yr Avg	10.82	84.3
5 Yr Avg	9.13	79.1
10 Yr Avg	12.00	67.8
Potential Capital Gain Exposure (% of assets)		12%

Most Similar Funds in MF500

Vista Capital Growth A	Fair Fit
Fidelity Stock Selector	Fair Fit
Neuberger&Berman Partners	Fair Fit

Index Allocation

	% of Stocks
S&P 500	49.9
S&P MidCap 400	14.1
U.S. Small Cap	34.2
Foreign	1.8

Sector Weightings

	% of Stocks	Relative S&P 500
Utilities	0.3	0.03
Energy	8.8	0.87
Financials	15.4	1.46
Industrial Cyclicals	21.8	1.33
Consumer Durables	9.7	1.56
Consumer Staples	4.4	0.35
Services	10.0	1.23
Retail	4.4	0.76
Health	5.7	0.66
Technology	19.5	2.12

Hancock Emerging Growth B

	Ticker	Load	NAV	Yield	SEC Yield	Assets	Objective
	TSEGX	5.00%d	25.16	0.0%	N/A	289.0	Small Company

John Hancock Emerging Growth Fund - Class B seeks long-term growth of capital.

The fund normally invests at least 80% of its assets in common stocks of companies with market capitalizations under $1 billion. It may invest a significant portion of its assets in foreign equity securities.

Class A shares have front loads; Class B shares have deferred loads, higher 12b-1 fees, and conversion features. In August and September 1991, Transamerica Special Global Growth and Transamerica Sunbelt Growth merged into this fund. Prior to May 22, 1994, the fund was named Transamerica Special Emerging Growth Fund - Class A. From that date until Dec. 22, 1994, it was named Transamerica Emerging Growth Fund - Class B.

Manager's Investment Style

Following a strategy of picking stocks in rapidly growing small to mid-size companies, management looks for sales and earnings numbers that exceed industry averages, and tends to invest in stocks with earnings growth rates that exceed price to equity ratios. This methodology keeps the fund invested heavily in the health and technology sectors, while avoiding more-mature companies.

Historical Profile
Return	Above Average
Risk	Above Average
Rating	★★★★ Above Average

Investment Style History
Equity

Average % Stocks Held in Portfolio

| | | | 82% | 90% | 92% | 95% | 92% | 96% |

Growth of $10,000
- IIII Value of Fund ($000)
- — Value of Index ($000) Russ 2000
- ▼ Manager Change
- ▽ Partial Manager Change
- ► Mgr Unknown After
- ◄ Mgr Unknown Before

Performance Quartile (Within Objective)

	1983	1984	1985	1986	1987	1988	1989	1990	1991	1992	1993	1994	History
	---	---	---	---	8.88	10.28	13.02	12.87	20.37	22.84	25.54	25.16	NAV
	---	---	---	---	12.55 *	17.40	28.85	-1.15	58.82	12.13	11.82	-1.49	Total Return %
	---	---	---	---	3.03 *	0.79	-2.84	1.97	28.34	4.51	1.76	-2.80	+/- S&P 500
	---	---	---	---	---	-3.14	4.91	12.41	15.37	0.37	-2.72	1.17	+/- Wilshire 4500
	---	---	---	---	0.00	0.41	0.00	0.00	0.00	0.00	0.00	0.00	Income Return %
	---	---	---	---	12.55	16.99	28.85	-1.15	58.82	12.13	11.82	-1.49	Capital Return %
	---	---	---	---	---	20	15	59	5	15	52	30	Total Rtn % Rank All
	---	---	---	---	---	63	28	21	25	59	74	53	Total Rtn % Rank Obj
	---	---	---	---	0.00	0.04	0.00	0.00	0.00	0.00	0.00	0.00	Income $
	---	---	---	---	0.00	0.10	0.22	0.00	0.06	0.00	0.00	0.00	Capital Gains $
	---	---	---	---	---	3.05	3.48	3.11	2.85	2.64	2.28	---	Expense Ratio %
	---	---	---	---	---	0.81	-0.67	-1.64	-1.83	-1.99	-1.58	---	Income Ratio %
	---	---	---	---	---	252	90	82	66	48	29	---	Turnover Rate %
	---	---	---	---	0.4	3.1	8.1	18.2	65.9	107.0	243.1	289.0	Net Assets ($mil)

Fund Manager(s)

Edgar M. Larsen CFA, since 10-87. Birthdate: 05-40. BA, Stanford U. 1962 MBA, U. of Chicago 1967

Manager Experience

	Dates Managed	Invest Obj	Std Dev	+/- Index
Edgar M. Larsen				
Hancock Growth & Income	01/90 - 01/93	GI	13.79	0.64

Performance 12-31-94

	1st Qtr	2nd Qtr	3rd Qtr	4th Qtr	Total
1987	---	---	---	---	12.55 *
1988	11.71	8.37	-1.02	-2.02	17.40
1989	5.64	7.64	13.26	0.04	28.85
1990	1.54	11.72	-23.09	13.29	-1.15
1991	30.85	-3.80	14.32	10.37	58.82
1992	1.62	-13.72	6.94	19.58	12.13
1993	-1.09	1.15	9.72	1.87	11.82
1994	-3.72	-7.12	10.99	-0.75	-1.49

Bear Market Performance

Decile Rank (5-year period)

Worst   Best

	Worst 3 Mo Period 1985-89	Worst 3 Mo Period 1990-94
Hancock Emerging Growth B	---	-23.09
+/- S&P 500	---	-9.34
+/- Best Fit Index : Russ 2000	---	1.45

Trailing Returns

	Total Return %	+/- S&P 500	+/- Wil 4500	% Rank All	% Rank Obj	Growth of $10,000
3 Mo	-0.75	-0.73	1.75	39	45	9,925
6 Mo	10.16	5.30	5.96	4	32	11,016
1 Yr	-1.49	-2.80	1.17	30	53	9,851
3 Yr Avg	7.29	1.03	-0.31	25	64	12,351
5 Yr Avg	14.16	5.47	5.07	5	26	19,391
10 Yr Avg	---	---	---	---	---	---
15 Yr Avg	---	---	---	---	---	---

Operations

Address and Telephone	101 Huntington Avenue Boston, MA 02199-7603 800-225-5291
Advisor	Transamerica Fund Management
Subadvisor	None
Distributor	John Hancock Funds
States Available	All plus PR
Report Grade	B+
Income Distrib	Paid Annually
* Date of Inception	10-26-87
Fiscal Year End	October

Risk Analysis

Time Period	Load-Adj Return %	Risk % Rank All	Obj	Morningstar[2] Return	Morningstar Risk	Morningstar Risk-Adj Rating
1 Yr	-5.43					
3 Yr	6.42	95	75	0.84[3]	1.39	★★★
5 Yr	14.04	95	76	2.58[3]	1.33	★★★★
10 Yr	---	---	---	---	---	---

Average Historical Rating (51 months)   4.3 ★s

[1] = low, 100 = high   [2] 1.00 = Equity Avg   [3] 1.00 = 90-day T-bill return

Other Measures

				Standard S&P 500	Best Fit Russ 2000
Standard Deviation	15.58	Alpha		1.5	-5.0
Mean	8.27	Beta		1.12	1.24
Sharpe Ratio	0.30	R-Squared		32	87

Investment Style

	Stock Portfolio Avg	Relative S&P 500
Price/Earnings Ratio	22.3	1.21
Price/Book Ratio	3.4	1.01
5 Yr Earnings Gr %	30.0#	5.40
Return on Assets %	11.2	1.50
Debt % Total Cap	22.1	0.78
Med Mkt Cap ($mil)	475	0.04

figure is based on 50% or less of stocks

Style: Value Blend Growth / Size: Large Med Small

Diversification Value for Portfolio Types

| Large Cap: Medium | Small Cap: None | Bond: High | Balanced: Medium | Diversified: Medium |

Portfolio 04-30-94

Share Chg (10-93)000	Amount 000	Total Stocks: 545 / Total Fixed-Income: 0	Value $000	% Net Assets
-9	51	3Com	3010	1.18
-2	84	Electroglas	2854	1.12
29	61	Best Buy	2221	0.87
11	34	Tellabs	2186	0.86
18	68	US Robotics	2167	0.85
-5	72	IHOP	2141	0.84
6	46	Michaels Stores	2054	0.81
-2	27	WellFleet Communications	1971	0.77
29	72	Outback Steakhouse	1935	0.76
18	38	Sybase	1911	0.75
18	65	Sterling Software	1896	0.75
-12	68	Hayes Wheels International	1877	0.74
42	51	Micron Technology	1875	0.74
3	55	Lam Research	1652	0.65
9	75	Alliance Capital Management	1614	0.63
34	96	Redman Industries	1588	0.62
14	42	Novellus Systems	1539	0.60
12	105	Brookstone	1503	0.59
32	63	Teradyne	1483	0.58
0	48	Noble Affiliates	1391	0.55
-5	68	Credence Systems	1391	0.55
34	41	Zilog	1372	0.54
-5	73	Tencor Instruments	1369	0.54
7	109	IEC Electronics	1365	0.54
-4	58	Horizon Healthcare	1356	0.53

Composition % 09-30-94

Cash	3.0	Preferreds	0.0
Stocks	97.0	Convertibles	0.0
Bonds	0.0	Other	0.0

Tax Analysis

	Tax-Adj Historical Return %	% Pretax Return
3 Yr Avg	7.29	100.0
5 Yr Avg	14.14	99.8
10 Yr Avg	---	---

Potential Capital Gain Exposure (% of assets)   18%

Most Similar Funds in MF500

Oppenheimer Discovery A	Strong Fit
T. Rowe Price New America G	Strong Fit
MainStay Capital Apprec B	Strong Fit

Index Allocation

	% of Stocks
S&P 500	4.1
S&P MidCap 400	16.8
U.S. Small Cap	75.4
Foreign	3.7

Sector Weightings

	% of Stocks	Relative S&P 500
Utilities	0.0	0.00
Energy	6.5	0.64
Financials	12.0	1.14
Industrial Cyclicals	5.4	0.33
Consumer Durables	5.4	0.87
Consumer Staples	1.4	0.12
Services	17.0	2.08
Retail	11.6	1.99
Health	10.3	1.19
Technology	30.4	3.31

Expenses & Fees

Sales Fees	
	0.00% front
	5.00% deferred
	1.00% 12b-1
Management Fee	0.75% flat fee
3-,5-,10-yr Expense Projections	$97, $135, $229
Annual Brokerage Cost	0.15%

Min Initial Purchase	$1000 (Addt'l: $50)
Min IRA Purchase	$250 (Addt'l: $25)
Min Auto Invest Plan	$25 (Systematic Inv: $25)

MORNINGSTAR 1995 Mutual Fund 500

Hancock Regional Bank B

	Ticker	Load	NAV	Yield	SEC Yield	Assets	Objective
	FRBFX	5.00%d	19.62	1.2%	N/A	477.2	Sp.-Financ'l

John Hancock Regional Bank Fund - Class B seeks capital appreciation; income is secondary.

The fund normally invests at least 65% of its assets in equity securities of regional banks. It may also invest in financial-services companies, companies with significant lending operations, or money-center banks with international connections. The fund seeks regional banks that may benefit from changes in the banking industry.

Class A shares have front loads; Class B shares have deferred loads and 12b-1 fees. Prior to Oct. 1, 1992, the fund was named Freedom Regional Bank Fund. From that date until Jan. 1, 1995, it was named John Hancock Freedom Regional Bank Fund B.

Manager's Investment Style

Management maintains a highly diversified portfolio that includes many large national banks, but focuses on tiny and underfollowed regional banks with modest prices and significant growth potential. Management has also successfully taken advantage of merger-and-acquisition activity by targeting companies it believes make good takeover targets.

Fund Manager(s)

James K. Schmidt CFA, since 10-85. Birthdate: 08-50. SB, Brown U. 1972 SM, MIT 1974

Manager Experience	Dates Managed	Invest Obj	Std Dev	+/- Index
James K. Schmidt				
Hancock Sovereign Achvr	01/90 - 07/92	G	16.21	-5.13

Historical Profile

Return	High
Risk	Below Average
Rating	★★★★★ Highest

Investment Style History
Equity

Average % Stocks Held in Portfolio

| 95% | 90% | 89% | 88% | 90% | 92% | 88% | 86% |

Growth of $10,000

|||| Value of Fund ($000)
— Value of Index ($000) Wil REIT
▼ Manager Change
▽ Partial Manager Change
► Mgr Unknown After
◄ Mgr Unknown Before

Performance Quartile (Within Objective)

1983	1984	1985	1986	1987	1988	1989	1990	1991	1992	1993	1994	History
---	---	10.53	10.92	9.14	10.78	11.62	8.90	13.42	17.82	20.24	19.62	NAV
---	---	5.30 *	20.24	-0.29	29.98	17.34	-20.57	63.78	47.37	20.54	-0.20	Total Return %
---	---	-11.17 *	1.57	-5.55	13.37	-14.34	-17.45	33.30	39.75	10.48	-1.51	+/- S&P 500
---	---	---	12.24	16.47	11.62	-15.31	0.87	13.04	24.00	9.44	3.34	+/- S&P Financial
---	---	0.00	2.50	1.18	1.45	1.37	2.84	2.68	1.27	0.83	1.19	Income Return %
---	---	5.30	17.75	-1.47	28.52	15.97	-23.41	61.10	46.10	19.71	-1.39	Capital Return %
---	---		19	62	2	41	97	3	1	16	21	Total Rtn % Rank All
---	---		14	1	1	70	60	50	16	23	30	Total Rtn % Rank Obj
---	---	0.00	0.29	0.13	0.15	0.16	0.34	0.28	0.20	0.17	0.25	Income $
---	---	0.00	1.48	1.68	0.94	0.90	0.00	0.78	1.69	1.06	0.34	Capital Gains $
---	---		1.33	2.47	2.17	1.99	1.99	2.04	1.96	1.88	2.01	Expense Ratio %
---	---		3.13	0.73	1.50	1.67	2.51	2.65	1.21	0.76	1.02	Income Ratio %
---	---		86	58	87	85	56	75	53	35	---	Turnover Rate %
---	---	34.1	47.0	37.1	49.0	73.0	42.2	50.0	70.7	175.5	477.2	Net Assets ($mil)

Performance 12-31-94

	1st Qtr	2nd Qtr	3rd Qtr	4th Qtr	Total
1987	16.82	0.56	3.10	-17.67	-0.29
1988	17.42	5.67	4.66	0.10	29.98
1989	6.32	7.31	11.73	-7.94	17.34
1990	-3.70	0.00	-20.90	4.28	-20.57
1991	19.45	12.56	12.24	8.53	63.78
1992	12.45	9.11	4.04	15.45	47.37
1993	13.58	-0.97	9.57	-2.20	20.54
1994	0.89	8.05	0.89	-9.26	-0.20

Bear Market Performance

Decile Rank (5-year period)

	Worst 3 Mo Period 1985-89	Worst 3 Mo Period 1990-94
Hancock Regional Bank B	---	-22.94
+/- S&P 500	---	-9.09
+/- Best Fit Index : Wil REIT	---	-2.88

Trailing Returns

	Total Return %	+/- S&P 500	+/- S&P Financial	% Rank All	Obj	Growth of $10,000
3 Mo	-9.26	-9.24	-6.15	97	86	9,074
6 Mo	-8.45	-13.31	-3.72	99	80	9,155
1 Yr	-0.20	-1.51	3.34	21	30	9,981
3 Yr Avg	21.03	14.77	11.27	1	8	17,729
5 Yr Avg	18.19	9.50	8.81	2	10	23,065
10 Yr Avg	---	---	---	---	---	---
15 Yr Avg	---	---	---	---	---	---

Operations

Address and Telephone	101 Huntington Avenue
	Boston, MA 02199-7603
	800-225-5291
Advisor	John Hancock Advisers
Subadvisor	None
Distributor	John Hancock Funds
States Available	All plus PR
Report Grade	A-
Income Distrib	Paid Quarterly
* Date of Inception	10-04-85
Fiscal Year End	October

Risk Analysis

Time Period	Load-Adj Return %	Risk % Rank [1] All	Obj	Morningstar [2] Return	Morningstar Risk	Morningstar Risk-Adj Rating
1 Yr	-4.07					
3 Yr	20.34	60	1	5.67 [3]	0.65	★★★★★
5 Yr	18.09	70	1	4.00 [3]	0.83	★★★★★
10 Yr	---	---	---	---	---	

Average Historical Rating (75 months)   4.2 ★s

[1] 1 = low, 100 = high   [2] 1.00 = Equity Avg   [3] 1.00 = 90-day T-bill return

Other Measures

			Standard S&P 500	Best Fit Wil REIT
Standard Deviation	10.44	Alpha	15.2	13.1
Mean	19.78	Beta	0.70	0.55
Sharpe Ratio	1.56	R-Squared	28	40

Investment Style

	Stock Portfolio Avg	Relative S&P 500
Price/Earnings Ratio	9.8	0.53
Price/Book Ratio	1.3	0.37
5 Yr Earnings Gr %	9.1	1.65
Return on Assets %	1.1	0.15
Debt % Total Cap	19.2	0.68
Med Mkt Cap ($mil)	1108	0.09

Diversification Value for Portfolio Types

| Large Cap: Medium | Small Cap: Medium | Bond: High | Balanced: Medium | Diversified: High |

Portfolio 12-31-94

Total Stocks: 258
Total Fixed-Income: 6

Share Chg (04-94)000	Amount 000		Value $000	% Net Assets
391	391	Bancorp Hawaii	9928	2.08
243	318	First of America Bank	9546	2.00
349	447	Union Planters	9321	1.95
153	224	Integra Financial	9215	1.93
300	300	Brooklyn Bancorp	9064	1.90
120	133	First Interstate Bancorp	8972	1.88
162	224	Barnett Banks	8599	1.80
264	296	Bank of Boston	7662	1.61
444	460	Shawmut National	7533	1.58
198	286	AmSouth Bancorp	7369	1.54
70	230	Mercantile Bancorp	7177	1.50
336	336	GP Financial	6925	1.45
201	307	Compass Bancshares	6753	1.42
208	294	US Bancorp (OR)	6644	1.39
309	338	SouthTrust	6089	1.28
124	244	Comerica	5944	1.25
194	269	First Commerce	5914	1.24
176	224	Astoria Financial	5882	1.23
324	356	Roosevelt Financial Group	5792	1.21
112	127	Republic New York	5762	1.21
155	238	UJB Financial	5749	1.20
91	210	Meridian Bancorp	5597	1.17
172	201	First American (TN)	5401	1.13
156	210	Banc One	5330	1.12
-70	19	Chase Manhattan	5086	1.07

Composition % 12-31-94

Cash	5.9	Preferreds	1.2
Stocks	92.4	Convertibles	0.2
Bonds	0.3	Other	0.0

Tax Analysis

	Tax-Adj Historical Return %	% Pretax Return
3 Yr Avg	18.85	87.8
5 Yr Avg	16.12	85.1
10 Yr Avg	---	---

Potential Capital Gain Exposure (% of assets)   2%

Most Similar Funds in MF500

Guardian Park Avenue	Weak Fit
Schafer Value	Weak Fit
Evergreen Foundation	Weak Fit

Expenses & Fees

Sales Fees	0.00% front
	5.00% deferred
	1.00% 12b-1
Management Fee	0.80% max./0.75% min.
3-,5-,10-yr Expense Projections	$98, $137, $233
Annual Brokerage Cost	0.09%

Min Initial Purchase	$1000 (Addt'l: None)
Min IRA Purchase	$500 (Addt'l: None)
Min Auto Invest Plan	$25 (Systematic Inv: $25)

Index Allocation

	% of Stocks
S&P 500	21.1
S&P MidCap 400	17.8
U.S. Small Cap	61.1
Foreign	0.0

Sector Weightings

	% of Stocks	Relative S&P 500
Utilities	0.0	0.00
Energy	0.0	0.00
Financials	100.0	9.46
Industrial Cyclicals	0.0	0.00
Consumer Durables	0.0	0.00
Consumer Staples	0.0	0.00
Services	0.0	0.00
Retail	0.0	0.00
Health	0.0	0.00
Technology	0.0	0.00

Hancock Sovereign Investors A

	Ticker	Load	NAV	Yield	SEC Yield	Assets	Objective
	SOVIX	5.00%	14.24	3.2%	3.20%	1090.2	Growth/Inc.

John Hancock Sovereign Investors Fund - Class A seeks long-term growth of capital and income without assuming undue risk.

The fund invests primarily in common stocks that have increased their dividend payouts in each of the preceding 10 years. It may also hold preferred stocks, bonds, and cash. The fund may not invest more than 5% of assets in non-investment-grade bonds.

Class A shares have front loads; Class B shares have deferred loads, higher 12b-1 fees, and conversion features; Class C shares are designed for institutional investors. Prior to Oct. 24, 1991, the fund was named Sovereign Investors.

Manager's Investment Style

Management focuses on dividends. It invests in firms that have shown 10 years of increasing dividends, but that are nonetheless selling at attractive price multiples. To find these securities, management looks to established firms that have come under pressure, despite good fundamentals, and so are offering high dividends.

Fund Manager(s)

John F. Snyder III, since 01-84.
Thomas M. Weary CFA(1993), since 01-92.
Jere E. Estes CFA(1978), since 07-92.
James T. Moorhead, since 07-92.

Manager Experience	Dates Managed	Invest Obj	Std Dev	+/- Index
John F. Snyder III				
Hancock Sovergn Achvr A	07/92 - 12/94	G	9.32	-1.58
Hancock Sovereign Bal A	10/92 - 12/94	B	5.37	-2.97

Historical Profile
Return	Average
Risk	Low
Rating	★★★
	Neutral

Percent stocks held: 73% 63% 62% 62% 63% 70% 70% 71%

Average % Stocks Held in Portfolio

Growth of $10,000
- ‖‖‖ Value of Fund ($000)
- — Value of Index ($000) S&P 500
- ▼ Manager Change
- ▽ Partial Manager Change
- ► Mgr Unknown After
- ◄ Mgr Unknown Before

Performance Quartile (Within Objective)

	1983	1984	1985	1986	1987	1988	1989	1990	1991	1992	1993	1994	History
NAV	9.22	9.45	11.31	12.37	10.96	11.19	12.60	11.94	14.31	14.78	15.10	14.24	NAV
	19.61	11.18	30.54	21.80	0.20	11.23	23.76	4.38	30.49	7.23	5.71	-1.85	Total Return %
	-2.86	4.91	-1.20	3.13	-5.06	-5.38	-7.93	7.50	0.00	-0.39	-4.34	-3.17	+/- S&P 500
	-3.86	8.13	-2.02	5.71	-2.16	-6.72	-5.42	10.56	-3.72	-1.74	-5.57	-1.78	+/- Wilshire 5000
	5.95	5.95	5.76	4.55	4.45	5.54	5.50	4.89	4.29	3.29	2.93	3.14	Income Return %
	13.65	5.23	24.78	17.26	-4.25	5.69	18.26	-0.51	26.19	3.94	2.78	-4.99	Capital Return %
	40	21	23	14	58	52	27	45	26	55	89	33	Total Rtn % Rank All
	60	15	31	14	67	73	50	2	33	54	86	61	Total Rtn % Rank Obj
	0.49	0.51	0.53	0.55	0.58	0.60	0.61	0.59	0.52	0.45	0.42	0.46	Income $
	0.24	0.25	0.44	0.87	0.90	0.38	0.58	0.60	0.68	0.09	0.09	0.11	Capital Gains $
	0.92	0.97	0.86	0.70	0.85	0.86	1.07	1.14	1.18	1.13	1.10	1.17	Expense Ratio %
	5.48	5.54	5.23	4.28	3.96	4.97	4.80	4.77	4.01	3.32	2.94	3.04	Income Ratio %
	17	37	31	34	59	35	40	55	67	30	46	---	Turnover Rate %
	13.2	15.7	23.8	34.6	40.5	45.9	66.4	83.5	194.1	872.9	1256.6	1090.2	Net Assets ($mil)

Performance 12-31-94

	1st Qtr	2nd Qtr	3rd Qtr	4th Qtr	Total
1987	13.09	0.43	2.99	-14.34	0.20
1988	5.80	1.76	1.84	1.45	11.23
1989	4.11	6.78	7.43	3.63	23.76
1990	-0.95	5.77	-9.03	9.51	4.38
1991	.11.32	1.04	7.61	7.80	30.49
1992	-2.03	1.58	4.21	3.39	7.23
1993	2.03	-1.00	1.77	2.84	5.71
1994	-4.11	-0.90	3.23	0.04	-1.85

Bear Market Performance

Decile Rank (5-year period)

Worst — Best

	Worst 3 Mo Period 1985-89	Worst 3 Mo Period 1990-94
Hancock Sovereign Investors A	-20.11	-9.83
+/- S&P 500	9.47	4.01
+/- Best Fit Index : S&P 500	9.47	4.01

Trailing Returns

	Total Return %	+/- S&P 500	+/- Wil 5000	% Rank All	% Rank Obj	Growth of $10,000
3 Mo	0.04	0.06	0.81	21	13	10,004
6 Mo	3.27	-1.59	-1.35	19	39	10,327
1 Yr	-1.85	-3.17	-1.78	33	61	9,815
3 Yr Avg	3.62	-2.65	-2.99	77	80	11,125
5 Yr Avg	8.67	-0.02	-0.15	27	32	15,153
10 Yr Avg	12.76	-1.62	-1.10	30	39	33,230
15 Yr Avg	13.82	-0.66	-0.15	26	33	69,725

Operations

Address and Telephone	101 Huntington Avenue Boston, MA 02199-7603 800-225-5291
Advisor	John Hancock Advisers
Subadvisor	None
Distributor	John Hancock Funds
States Available	All plus PR
Report Grade	A
Income Distrib	Paid Quarterly
Date of Inception	05-01-36
Fiscal Year End	December

Min Initial Purchase	$1000 (Addt'l: None)
Min IRA Purchase	$500 (Addt'l: None)
Min Auto Invest Plan	$25 (Systematic Inv: $25)

Expenses & Fees
Sales Fees	5.00% front
	0.00% deferred
	0.30% 12b-1
Management Fee	0.60% flat fee
3-,5-,10-yr Expense Projections	$85, $110, $183
Annual Brokerage Cost	0.13%

Risk Analysis

Time Period	Load-Adj Return %	Risk % Rank[1] All	Obj	Morningstar[2] Return	Risk	Morningstar Risk-Adj Rating
1 Yr	-6.76					
3 Yr	1.86	56	16	-0.49[3]	0.60	★★
5 Yr	7.56	52	5	0.69[3]	0.56	★★★
10 Yr	12.18	46	15	0.91	0.66	★★★
Average Historical Rating (109 months)				3.8	★s	

[1] 1 = low, 100 = high [2] 1.00 = Equity Avg [3] 1.00 = 90-day T-bill return

Other Measures
			Standard S&P 500	Best Fit S&P 500
Standard Deviation	6.30	Alpha	-1.9	-1.9
Mean	3.76	Beta	0.74	0.74
Sharpe Ratio	0.04	R-Squared	88	88

Investment Style

	Stock Portfolio Avg	Relative S&P 500
Price/Earnings Ratio	17.3	0.94
Price/Book Ratio	3.3	0.96
5 Yr Earnings Gr %	6.3	1.13
Return on Assets %	7.7	1.03
Debt % Total Cap	27.7	0.98
Med Mkt Cap ($mil)	8503	0.65

Style: Value Blend Growth / Size Large Med Small

Diversification Value for Portfolio Types

Large Cap: None	Small Cap: Medium	Bond: Medium	Balanced: None	Diversified: Low

Portfolio 12-31-94

Total Stocks: 56
Total Fixed-Income: 39

Share Chg (10-94)000	Amount 000		Value $000	% Net Assets
28	796	General Electric	36594	3.36
44	486	Procter & Gamble	30384	2.79
-101	826	PepsiCo	29236	2.68
125	579	Air Products & Chemicals	25691	2.36
34	789	Abbott Laboratories	25160	2.31
-6	453	Johnson & Johnson	24202	2.22
48	522	NationsBank	23402	2.15
-6	463	Gannett	21930	2.01
59	619	Leggett & Platt	21888	2.01
	22098	US Treasury Note 7.25%	21086	1.93
93	742	ALLTEL	20882	1.92
85	354	Emerson Electric	20860	1.91
-5	344	Philip Morris	20544	1.88
167	884	Wal-Mart Stores	20440	1.87
-8	566	PPG Industries	20365	1.87
-14	1044	Hanson (ADR)	19051	1.75
-7	518	May Department Stores	18773	1.72
304	683	WMX Technologies	17594	1.61
103	354	VF	17148	1.57
-9	629	Witco	16511	1.51
-9	641	Sysco	16501	1.51
-4	265	Exxon	16010	1.47
	367	American Express Cv DECS 6.25%	15865	1.46
-5	362	Campbell Soup	15583	1.43
81	632	Sara Lee	15405	1.41

Composition % 12-31-94
Cash	3.6	Preferreds	2.1
Stocks	74.9	Convertibles	0.4
Bonds	19.0	Other	0.0

Tax Analysis
	Tax-Adj Historical Return %	% Pretax Return
3 Yr Avg	2.31	63.0
5 Yr Avg	6.67	74.0
10 Yr Avg	9.94	68.0
Potential Capital Gain Exposure (% of assets)		0%

Most Similar Funds in MF500
Smith Barney Appreciation A	Strong Fit
Dean Witter Dividend Growth	Fair Fit
Investment Comp of America	Fair Fit

Index Allocation
	% of Stocks
S&P 500	79.2
S&P MidCap 400	14.1
U.S. Small Cap	4.3
Foreign	2.5

Sector Weightings
	% of Stocks	Relative S&P 500
Utilities	6.0	0.48
Energy	3.2	0.32
Financials	16.3	1.54
Industrial Cyclicals	23.0	1.40
Consumer Durables	6.1	0.99
Consumer Staples	21.6	1.72
Services	8.7	1.07
Retail	5.2	0.89
Health	5.0	0.57
Technology	5.0	0.54

MORNINGSTAR 1995 Mutual Fund 500

Hancock Special Equities A

	Ticker	Load	NAV	Yield	SEC Yield	Assets	Objective
	JHNSX	Clsd	16.15	0.0%	N/A	310.9	Small Company

John Hancock Special Equities Fund - Class A seeks growth; current income is not a factor.

The fund invests at least 65% of its assets in emerging-growth and special-situations companies. It favors emerging-growth firms with sustained increases in earnings over a six-month period. It may also invest in equities of established companies with growth potential and investment-grade corporate debt.

Class A shares have a front-end load; Class B shares have a deferred sales charge and a higher 12b-1 fee. Prior to March 1, 1991, the fund was named John Hancock Special Equities Trust.

Manager's Investment Style

Manager Michael DiCarlo runs this as a highly aggressive fund, prone to large swings in performance. He chooses very small-cap stocks that have annual earnings or revenue growth of at least 25% and dominant market share, and that sell at extremely high price multiples. He has long favored popular issues in the technology and health fields.

Fund Manager(s)

Michael P. DiCarlo, since 01-88. Birthdate: 03-56. BA, U. of Massachusetts 1980

Manager Experience

	Dates Managed	Invest Obj	Std Dev	+/- Index
Michael P. DiCarlo				
Hancock Global A	08/92 - 04/93	WW	10.25	-5.70

Historical Profile

Return	High
Risk	Above Average
Rating	★★★★★
	Closed

Average % Stocks Held in Portfolio: 85% 80% 81% 88% 95% 96% 94% 93%

Investment Style History: Equity

Growth of $10,000

IIII Value of Fund ($000)
— Value of Index ($000) Wil 4500
▼ Manager Change
▽ Partial Manager Change
► Mgr Unknown After
◄ Mgr Unknown Before

Performance Quartile (Within Objective)

	1983	1984	1985	1986	1987	1988	1989	1990	1991	1992	1993	1994	History
	---	---	6.05	5.71	4.23	5.05	6.44	5.88	10.21	13.22	15.83	16.15	NAV
	---	---	21.00 *	-4.28	-18.34	20.63	27.87	-8.70	84.49	30.41	19.74	2.02	Total Return %
	---	---	-0.73 *	-22.96	-23.60	4.02	-3.81	-5.58	54.00	22.80	9.69	0.71	+/- S&P 500
	---	---	---	-16.04	-14.83	0.09	3.93	4.86	41.04	18.66	5.21	4.68	+/- Wilshire 4500
	---	---	0.00	0.45	0.00	1.24	0.35	0.00	0.00	0.00	0.00	0.00	Income Return %
	---	---	21.00	-4.73	-18.34	19.39	27.52	-8.70	84.49	30.41	19.74	2.02	Capital Return %
	---	---	---	99	99	12	17	81	1	1	17	10	Total Rtn % Rank All
	---	---	---	95	94	46	30	41	6	4	36	28	Total Rtn % Rank Obj
	---	---	0.00	0.03	0.00	0.05	0.02	0.00	0.00	0.00	0.00	0.00	Income $
	---	---	0.00	0.06	0.44	0.00	0.00	0.00	0.67	0.09	0.00	0.00	Capital Gains $
	---	---	1.50	1.50	1.50	1.50	1.50	2.63	2.75	2.24	1.84	1.63	Expense Ratio %
	---	---	1.42	-0.57	-0.57	0.82	0.47	-1.58	-2.12	-1.91	-1.49	-1.45	Income Ratio %
	---	---	---	64	93	91	115	113	163	114	33	---	Turnover Rate %
	---	---	2.5	13.4	10.6	11.7	12.1	9.4	23.1	69.7	287.8	310.9	Net Assets ($mil)

Performance 12-31-94

	1st Qtr	2nd Qtr	3rd Qtr	4th Qtr	Total
1987	25.92	-3.34	-0.29	-32.72	-18.34
1988	13.48	9.79	-5.31	2.25	20.63
1989	7.13	10.91	11.00	-3.04	27.87
1990	-3.26	10.75	-25.94	15.07	-8.70
1991	32.31	0.26	19.74	16.14	84.49
1992	2.45	-11.28	8.73	31.97	30.41
1993	-1.89	9.48	10.99	0.44	19.74
1994	-7.26	-8.24	13.36	5.76	2.02

Bear Market Performance

Decile Rank (5-year period)

Worst ▬▬▬▬▬▬▬ Best

	Worst 3 Mo Period 1985-89	Worst 3 Mo Period 1990-94
Hancock Special Equities A	---	-25.94
+/- S&P 500	---	-12.20
+/- Best Fit Index : Wil 4500	---	-7.71

Trailing Returns

	Total Return %	+/- S&P 500	+/- Wil 4500	% Rank All	% Rank Obj	Growth of $10,000
3 Mo	5.76	5.78	8.26	1	8	10,576
6 Mo	19.90	15.03	15.70	1	9	11,990
1 Yr	2.02	0.71	4.68	10	28	10,202
3 Yr Avg	16.79	10.53	9.19	2	8	15,932
5 Yr Avg	21.83	13.14	12.74	1	3	26,837
10 Yr Avg	---	---	---	---	---	---
15 Yr Avg	---	---	---	---	---	---

Operations

Address and Telephone	101 Huntington Avenue
	Boston, MA 02199-7603
	800-225-5291
Advisor	John Hancock Advisers
Subadvisor	None
Distributor	John Hancock Funds
States Available	All plus PR
Report Grade	A-
Income Distrib	Paid Annually
* Date of Inception	02-04-85
Fiscal Year End	October

Risk Analysis

Time Period	Load-Adj Return %	Risk % Rank[1] All	Obj	Morningstar[2] Return	Morningstar Risk	Morningstar Risk-Adj Rating
1 Yr	-3.08					
3 Yr	14.81	97	86	3.61[3]	1.54	★★★★★
5 Yr	20.58	96	79	4.97[3]	1.36	★★★★★
10 Yr						

Average Historical Rating (83 months) 2.9 ★s

[1] = low, 100 = high [2] 1.00 = Equity Avg [3] 1.00 = 90-day T-bill return

Other Measures

			Standard S&P 500	Best Fit Wil 4500
Standard Deviation	19.07	Alpha	10.3	6.6
Mean	17.42	Beta	1.40	1.73
Sharpe Ratio	0.73	R-Squared	34	79

Investment Style

	Stock Portfolio Avg	Relative S&P 500
Price/Earnings Ratio	32.8	1.77
Price/Book Ratio	6.0	1.77
5 Yr Earnings Gr %	42.2#	7.60
Return on Assets %	15.5	2.07
Debt % Total Cap	18.2	0.64
Med Mkt Cap ($mil)	749	0.06

figure is based on 50% or less of stocks

Style Value Blend Growth / Size Large Med Small

Diversification Value for Portfolio Types

Large Cap: Medium	Small Cap: Low	Bond: High	Balanced: Medium	Diversified: Medium

Expenses & Fees

Sales Fees	
	0.00% front
	0.00% deferred
	0.30% 12b-1
Management Fee	0.85% max./0.80% min.
3-,5-,10-yr Expense Projections	$102, $140, $246
Annual Brokerage Cost	0.00%

Min Initial Purchase	Closed (Addt'l: None)
Min IRA Purchase	$500 (Addt'l: None)
Min Auto Invest Plan	$25 (Systematic Inv: $25)

Portfolio 12-31-94

Total Stocks: 55
Total Fixed-Income: 0

Share Chg (10-94)000	Amount 000		Value $000	% Net Assets
304	426	America Online	17772	5.72
176	389	Cobra Golf	13914	4.48
-1	426	Viking Office Products	12132	3.90
-1	365	Mid-Atlantic Medical Svcs	8438	2.71
0	232	Healthsource	8316	2.68
-1	365	Adaptec	7981	2.57
-1	258	Infinity Broadcasting Cl A	7624	2.45
-1	319	Office Depot	7582	2.44
0	219	ALC Communications	7443	2.39
0	172	Sunglass Hut International	7413	2.38
-1	281	AutoZone	7199	2.32
-1	353	LDDS Communications Cl A	7051	2.27
0	182	AnnTaylor Stores	6841	2.20
-1	243	Starbucks	6476	2.08
60	243	CIDCO	6446	2.07
-1	243	Coventry	6081	1.96
0	182	Gymboree	5564	1.79
0	182	Williams-Sonoma	5473	1.76
122	122	BMC Software	5351	1.72
0	140	Electroglas	5210	1.68
255	255	Softkey International	5108	1.64
0	170	PETsMART	5066	1.63
24	167	Digidesign	5017	1.61
0	144	Franklin Quest	4744	1.53
0	91	Novellus Systems	4743	1.53

Composition % 12-31-94

Cash	10.1	Preferreds	0.0
Stocks	89.9	Convertibles	0.0
Bonds	0.0	Other	0.0

Tax Analysis

	Tax-Adj Historical Return %	% Pretax Return
3 Yr Avg	16.72	99.5
5 Yr Avg	21.36	97.0
10 Yr Avg	---	---
Potential Capital Gain Exposure (% of assets)		19%

Most Similar Funds in MF500

Kaufmann	Fair Fit
Invesco Strat Technology	Fair Fit
AIM Constellation	Fair Fit

Index Allocation

	% of Stocks
S&P 500	0.0
S&P MidCap 400	21.7
U.S. Small Cap	78.3
Foreign	0.0

Sector Weightings

	% of Stocks	Relative S&P 500
Utilities	0.0	0.00
Energy	0.0	0.00
Financials	5.0	0.48
Industrial Cyclicals	4.0	0.25
Consumer Durables	8.2	1.32
Consumer Staples	2.5	0.20
Services	5.6	0.69
Retail	20.6	3.54
Health	12.7	1.47
Technology	41.3	4.51

Hancock Strategic Income A

	Ticker	Load	NAV	Yield	SEC Yield	Assets	Objective
	JHFIX	4.50%	6.81	9.5%	8.84%	317.9	Income

John Hancock Strategic Income Fund - Class A seeks current income.

The fund invests primarily in the following assets types: foreign government and corporate debt, U.S. government securities, and debt securities of U.S. issuers rated as low as CC. There is no fixed allocation among the types of securities. The portfolio may be completely invested in any one sector. The fund may invest up to 10% of its assets in equities.

Prior to Aug. 1, 1991, the fund was named John Hancock High-Income Trust Fixed-Income Portfolio. Class A shares have front loads; Class B shares have deferred loads and higher 12b-1 fees.

Manager's Investment Style

Management focuses primarily on income. In this pursuit, it follows the typical strategic-income strategy of splitting assets between U.S. Treasuries, foreign bonds, and junk bonds. Due to management's belief that U.S. government bonds have not offered enough yield advantage over foreign debt or junk to make them worthwhile, governments are typically underweighted. Management has long favored higher-yielding noninvestment-grade and foreign bonds, indeed, this fund started out as a junk-bond offering, and its exposure to this sector has yet to sink below 40%.

Fund Manager(s)

Frederick L. Cavanaugh, Jr., since 08-86.
Birthdate: 06-44. BS, Salem State C. 1969 MBA, Suffolk U. 1973

Manager Experience

	Dates Managed	Invest Obj	Std Dev	+/- Index
Not available.				

Historical Profile

Return	Average
Risk	Low
Rating	★★★
	Neutral

Investment Style History
Fixed Income

Income Rtn % Rank Obj

Growth of $10,000

‖‖ Value of Fund ($000)
— Value of Index ($000)
FB HY
▼ Manager Change
▽ Partial Manager Change
► Mgr Unknown After
◄ Mgr Unknown Before

Performance Quartile
(Within Objective)

	1983	1984	1985	1986	1987	1988	1989	1990	1991	1992	1993	1994	History
	---	---	---	9.80	9.13	9.22	8.08	6.37	7.56	7.38	7.69	6.81	NAV
	---	---	---	1.05 *	4.86	13.79	-1.38	-9.77	33.55	7.54	13.74	-3.05	Total Return %
	---	---	---	1.76 *	-0.40	-2.82	-33.06	-6.65	3.06	-0.08	3.68	-4.37	+/- S&P 500
	---	---	---	---	2.10	5.91	-15.92	-18.71	17.55	0.30	3.98	-0.13	+/- LB Aggregate
	---	---	---	3.05	11.69	12.81	10.99	11.39	14.87	9.92	9.53	8.39	Income Return %
	---	---	---	-2.00	-6.84	0.99	-12.36	-21.16	18.68	-2.38	4.20	-11.44	Capital Return %
	---	---	---	---	23	33	99	84	22	51	35	44	Total Rtn % Rank All
	---	---	---	---	14	34	96	94	5	65	54	27	Total Rtn % Rank Obj
	---	---	---	0.30	1.14	1.11	1.06	0.96	0.86	0.74	0.67	0.65	Income $
	---	---	---	0.00	0.00	0.00	0.00	0.00	0.00	0.00	0.00	0.00	Capital Gains $
	---	---	---	1.00	1.09	1.33	1.53	1.75	1.69	1.58	1.32		Expense Ratio %
	---	---	---	10.87	12.07	12.28	12.60	13.46	10.64	9.63	8.71		Income Ratio %
	---	---	---	---	67	125	81	60	80	97	91		Turnover Rate %
	---	---	---	8.0	47.6	83.9	92.9	67.5	114.5	219.7	339.4	317.9	Net Assets ($mil)

Performance 12-31-94

	1st Qtr	2nd Qtr	3rd Qtr	4th Qtr	Total
1987	6.03	-0.88	-1.08	0.86	4.86
1988	4.64	2.75	2.25	3.51	13.79
1989	0.59	3.58	-0.45	-4.91	-1.38
1990	-6.20	2.87	-6.71	0.23	-9.77
1991	14.15	6.15	6.92	3.09	33.55
1992	4.06	2.35	0.29	0.69	7.54
1993	4.09	3.46	2.13	3.41	13.74
1994	-3.00	-1.39	0.40	0.95	-3.05

Bear Market Performance

Decile Rank (5-year period)

Worst _____ Best

	Worst 3 Mo Period 1985-89	Worst 3 Mo Period 1990-94
Hancock Strategic Income A	---	-12.08
+/- S&P 500	---	1.76
+/- Best Fit Index : FB HY	---	2.03

Trailing Returns

	Total Return %	+/- S&P 500	+/- LB Aggregate	% Rank All	% Rank Obj	Growth of $10,000
3 Mo	0.95	0.97	0.57	7	2	10,095
6 Mo	1.36	-3.51	0.36	32	14	10,136
1 Yr	-3.05	-4.37	-0.13	44	27	9,695
3 Yr Avg	5.84	-0.42	1.30	36	44	11,858
5 Yr Avg	7.40	-1.29	-0.23	42	67	14,289
10 Yr Avg	---	---	---	---	---	---
15 Yr Avg	---	---	---	---	---	---

Operations

Address and Telephone	101 Huntington Avenue
	Boston, MA 02199-7603
	800-225-5291
Advisor	John Hancock Advisers
Subadvisor	None
Distributor	John Hancock Funds
States Available	All plus PR
Report Grade	A
Income Distrib	Paid Monthly
* Date of Inception	08-18-86
Fiscal Year End	May

Risk Analysis

Time Period	Load-Adj Return %	Risk % Rank All	Risk % Rank Obj	Morningstar[2] Return	Morningstar[2] Risk	Morningstar Risk-Adj Rating
1 Yr	-7.41					
3 Yr	4.23	10	10	0.19[3]	0.39	★★★
5 Yr	6.41	45	58	0.41[3]	0.56	★★★
10 Yr	---	---	---	---	---	---

Average Historical Rating (64 months) 2.6 ★s

[1] 1 = low, 100 = high [2] 1.00 = Hybrid Avg [3] 1.00 = 90-day T-bill return

Other Measures

				Standard S&P 500	Best Fit FB HY
Standard Deviation	3.74	Alpha		1.5	-2.8
Mean	5.76	Beta		0.25	0.70
Sharpe Ratio	0.60	R-Squared		27	66

Investment Style

Stocks

	Port Avg	Rel S&P 500
Price/Earnings Ratio	---	---
Price/Book Ratio	---	---
5 Yr Earnings Gr %	---	---
Med Mkt Cap ($mil)	1086	0.08

Not Available

Bonds

		Maturity S I L
Avg Effective Duration	4.8 Yrs	
Avg Effective Maturity	8.1 Yrs	Quality H M L
Avg Credit Quality	BBB	
Avg Weighted Coupon	10.16%	

Diversification Value for Portfolio Types

Large Cap: Medium	Small Cap: High	Bond: Medium	Balanced: Medium	Diversified: Medium

Portfolio 12-31-94

Share Chg (10-94)000	Amount 000	Total Stocks: 24 — Total Fixed-Income: 137	Date of Maturity	Value $000	% Net Assets
	14075	US Treasury Note 8%	05-15-01	14203	4.47
	8149	US Treasury Bond 9.25%	02-15-16	9076	2.85
	296318	Kingdom of Spain 13.45%	04-15-96	8283	2.61
	44448	Kingdom of Denmark 7%	12-15-04	6453	2.03
-4	207	UAL		5523	1.74
	2963	United Kingdom Treasury 9.75%	08-27-02	4930	1.55
	7408	Govt of New Zealand 8%	07-15-98	4521	1.42
	7408	Govt of New Zealand 8%	04-15-04	4394	1.38
	4074	US Treasury Bond 8.125%	08-15-19	4076	1.28
	25928	Norgeskreditt 10.75%	06-19-96	3988	1.25
	3704	NWA 8.625%	08-01-96	3648	1.15
	2222	United Kingdom Treasury 9%	10-13-08	3631	1.14
	5408	Victoria Pub Auth Fin 8.25%	10-15-03	3510	1.10
	2222	United Kingdom Treasury 7%	11-06-01	3212	1.01
	18520	Kingdom of Denmark 9%	11-15-96	3094	0.97
	2963	Kaiser Aluminium/Chem 12.75%	02-01-03	2993	0.94
	2963	Thrifty Payless 12.25%	04-15-04	2756	0.87
	2593	Weirton Steel 10.875%	10-15-99	2541	0.80
-3	148	Northwest Airlines Cl A		2463	0.77
	2963	Computervision 11.375%	08-15-99	2430	0.76

Index Allocation

	% of Stocks
S&P 500	4.8
S&P MidCap 400	0.8
U.S. Small Cap	75.8
Foreign	18.7

Composition % 12-31-94

Cash	5.8	Preferreds	4.2
Stocks	1.4	Convertibles	0.6
Bonds	88.0	Other	0.0

Tax Analysis

	Tax-Adj Historical Return %	% Pretax Return
3 Yr Avg	2.39	39.5
5 Yr Avg	3.59	45.0
10 Yr Avg	---	---
Potential Capital Gain Exposure (% of assets)		-16%

Most Similar Funds in MF500

Colonial Strategic Income A	Fair Fit
Merrill Lynch World Income A	Fair Fit
Oppenheimer Strat Income A	Fair Fit

Bond Credit Analysis 12-31-94

% of Bonds

US Govt	15	BB	8
AAA	14	B	44
AA	10	Below B	1
A	6	NR/NA	0
BBB	2		

Stock Sector Weightings

	% of Stocks	Relative S&P 500
Utilities	0.0	0.00
Energy	11.3	1.11
Financials	27.9	2.64
Industrial Cyclicals	0.8	0.05
Consumer Durables	0.0	0.00
Consumer Staples	14.0	1.12
Services	45.6	5.61
Retail	0.0	0.00
Health	0.4	0.04
Technology	0.0	0.00

Min Initial Purchase / Expenses & Fees

Min Initial Purchase	$1000 (Addt'l: None)
Min IRA Purchase	$500 (Addt'l: None)
Min Auto Invest Plan	$25 (Systematic Inv: $25)

Expenses & Fees

Sales Fees	4.50% front
	0.00% deferred
	0.30% 12b-1
Management Fee	0.60% max./0.30% min.
3-,5-,10-yr Expense Projections	$80, $106, $180
Annual Brokerage Cost	0.00%

MORNINGSTAR 1995 Mutual Fund 500

Harbor Bond

	Ticker	Load	NAV	Yield	SEC Yield	Assets	Objective
	HABDX	None	10.28	5.9%	7.17%	167.0	Corp General

Harbor Bond Fund seeks total return consistent with preservation of capital.

The fund invests at least 65% of its assets in high-quality domestic or foreign obligations, including those issued by governments, supranational organizations, and corporations, as well as mortgage-related and other asset-backed securities. Normally, at least 60% of fund assets are invested in domestic issues and at least 80% of assets are denominated in U.S. dollars. The fund's portfolio normally consists of securities with varying maturities; the fund intends to maintain a portfolio duration of three to six years.

Manager's Investment Style

Manager Bill Gross makes interest-rate calls, lengthening or shortening the portfolio's duration depending on its rate outlook. He will also focus on particular areas of the yield curve--such as the intermediate portion--that it thinks have been oversold. Gross has also initiated large positions in non-corporate fare, such as foreign debt, straight mortgage-backeds, and mortgage-backed derivatives--at times, moving in and out of these market sectors at a rapid pace.

Fund Manager(s)

William H. Gross CFA(1977), since 12-87.
Birthdate: 04-44. BA, Duke U. 1966 MS, U. of California-Los Angeles 1971

Manager Experience

	Dates Managed	Invest Obj	Std Dev	+/- Index
William H. Gross				
PIMCo Total Return Instl	05/87 - 12/94	CG	4.71	0.89
PIMCo Low Duration Instl	05/87 - 12/94	CG	2.77	-0.28

Historical Profile

Return	High
Risk	Average
Rating	★★★★★
	Highest

Investment Style History
Fixed Income
Income Rtn % Rank Obj

Growth of $10,000
|||| Value of Fund ($000)
— Value of Index ($000)
  LB Govt
▼ Manager Change
▽ Partial Manager Change
► Mgr Unknown After
◄ Mgr Unknown Before

Performance Quartile (Within Objective)

	1983	1984	1985	1986	1987	1988	1989	1990	1991	1992	1993	1994	History
	---	---	---	---	10.00	9.96	10.36	10.29	11.11	11.10	11.31	10.28	NAV
	---	---	---	---	0.00 *	7.17	13.68	7.94	19.65	9.11	12.41	-3.76	Total Return %
	---	---	---	---		-0.71	-0.86	-1.01	3.65	1.86	2.66	-0.84	+/- LB Aggregate
	---	---	---	---		-2.05	-0.30	0.79	1.15	0.41	0.25	0.17	+/- LB Corporate
	---	---	---	---	0.00	6.83	8.70	8.62	8.98	6.93	5.88	5.35	Income Return %
	---	---	---	---	0.00	0.34	4.98	-0.68	10.68	2.18	6.53	-9.11	Capital Return %
	---	---	---	---		79	51	15	45	31	47	51	Total Rtn % Rank All
	---	---	---	---		78	16	30	10	15	22	51	Total Rtn % Rank Obj
	---	---	---	---	0.00	0.67	0.83	0.85	0.86	0.74	0.65	0.61	Income $
	---	---	---	---	0.00	0.07	0.09	0.00	0.26	0.25	0.50	0.00	Capital Gains $
	---	---	---	---		1.55	1.21	1.22	0.86	0.77	0.72	0.77	Expense Ratio %
	---	---	---	---		7.42	8.20	8.30	8.12	7.30	6.19	6.29	Income Ratio %
	---	---	---	---		---	91	91	58	53	120	151	Turnover Rate %
	---	---	---	---		15.1	21.4	26.0	41.1	76.6	171.8	167.0	Net Assets ($mil)

Performance 12-31-94

	1st Qtr	2nd Qtr	3rd Qtr	4th Qtr	Total
1987	---	---	---	---	0.00 *
1988	2.01	1.79	2.10	1.09	7.17
1989	1.45	7.11	0.82	3.76	13.68
1990	-1.15	3.33	0.03	5.65	7.94
1991	2.66	1.69	8.49	5.65	19.65
1992	-0.89	4.40	4.62	0.79	9.11
1993	4.64	3.36	3.03	0.88	12.41
1994	-3.13	-1.43	1.16	-0.36	-3.76

Bear Market Performance

Decile Rank (5-year period)

Worst ←――――――――→ Best

	Worst 3 Mo Period 1985-89	Worst 3 Mo Period 1990-94
Harbor Bond	---	-4.53
+/- LB Aggregate	---	0.41
+/- Best Fit Index : LB Govt	---	0.55

Trailing Returns

	Total Return %	+/- LB Aggregate	+/- LB Corp	% Rank All	% Rank Obj	Growth of $10,000
3 Mo	-0.36	-0.74	-0.80	31	75	9,964
6 Mo	0.80	-0.20	-0.38	41	30	10,080
1 Yr	-3.76	-0.84	0.17	51	51	9,624
3 Yr Avg	5.69	1.14	0.27	37	16	11,804
5 Yr Avg	8.80	1.17	0.54	25	7	15,246
10 Yr Avg	---	---	---	---	---	---
15 Yr Avg	---	---	---	---	---	---

Operations

Address and Telephone	One SeaGate
	Toledo, OH 43666
	800-422-1050 / 419-247-2477
Advisor	Harbor Capital Advisors
Subadvisor	Pacific Investment Management
Distributor	HCA Securities
States Available	All plus PR
Report Grade	C+
Income Distrib	Paid Annually
* Date of Inception	12-29-87
Fiscal Year End	October

Min Initial Purchase	$2000 (Addt'l: $500)
Min IRA Purchase	$500 (Addt'l: $100)
Min Auto Invest Plan	$500 (Systematic Inv: $100)

Expenses & Fees

Sales Fees	0.00% front
	0.00% deferred
	0.00% 12b-1
Management Fee	0.70% flat fee
3-,5-,10-yr Expense Projections	$23, $41, $93

Risk Analysis

Time Period	Load-Adj Return %	Risk % Rank All	Risk % Rank Obj	Morningstar Return	Morningstar Risk	Morningstar Risk-Adj Rating
1 Yr	-3.76					
3 Yr	5.69	18	32	0.62[3]	0.93	★★★★★
5 Yr	8.80	21	38	1.02[3]	0.97	★★★★★
10 Yr						
Average Historical Rating (49 months)				4.5 ★s		

[1] = low, 100 = high [2] 1.00 = Taxable Avg [3] 1.00 = 90-day T-bill return

Other Measures

			Standard LB Agg	Best Fit LB Govt
Standard Deviation	4.12	Alpha	1.1	1.1
Mean	5.63	Beta	0.99	0.91
Sharpe Ratio	0.51	R-Squared	91	92

Investment Style

Interest-Rate Stance

Avg Effective Duration	3.0 Yrs**
Avg Effective Maturity	7.6 Yrs

Quality

Avg Credit Quality	AA
Avg Weighted Coupon	8.50%
Avg Weighted Price	95.91% of Par

**figure provided by fund

Diversification Value for Portfolio Types

Large Cap: High	Small Cap: High	Bond: None	Balanced: Medium	Diversified: Medium

Portfolio 11-30-94

Amount 000	Date of Maturity	Total Stocks: 0 / Total Fixed-Income: 71	Value $000	% Net Assets
10172	09-20-24	GNMA ARM	10019	6.28
7541	03-25-20	FNMA CMO REMIC Z 9%	7461	4.68
7000	01-15-19	FHLMC CMO PAC 8.5%	7075	4.44
6577	04-01-17	Drexel Burnham Lamb CMO Z 8.5%	6145	3.85
5000	11-04-96	Premier Auto Trust 5.75%	4963	3.11
4948	08-01-24	FHLMC ARM	4948	3.10
5000	02-15-20	FHLMC CMO PAC 8.7%	4947	3.10
4797	04-25-24	Prudential Hm Mtg CMO 7.425%	4443	2.79
4400	12-01-97	Cleveland Elec Illum 9.45%	4359	2.73
4231	12-15-20	FHLMC CMO Z 9%	4132	2.59
4000	07-07-98	Bancomer 8%	3790	2.38
4000	12-01-97	United Air Lines 6.75%	3734	2.34
3470	11-01-09	FNMA 9%	3504	2.20
3000	03-18-96	Lehman Brothers Hldgs FRN	3008	1.89
3000	07-25-22	Ryland Mortgage CMO FRN	2989	1.87
3000	11-02-98	AMR 8.73%	2937	1.84
3000	07-28-02	Banesto 8.25%	2933	1.84
3000	08-25-21	Resolution Tr CMO REMIC FRN	2930	1.84
3000	06-11-96	Salomon 5.72%	2899	1.82
3000	08-15-02	Time Warner FRN	2831	1.78
3000	10-15-03	Unicom 8%	2796	1.75
3000	10-01-98	Banco Nacional Obra 6.875%	2776	1.74
3000	06-17-15	United Air Lines 9.06%	2519	1.58
2000	03-07-01	AMR 10%	2048	1.28
2000	04-25-03	Banesto Finance FRN	2012	1.26

Composition % 12-31-94

Cash	0.1	Preferreds	0.0
Stocks	0.0	Convertibles	0.0
Bonds	99.9	Other	0.0

Tax Analysis

	Tax-Adj Historical Return %	% Pretax Return
3 Yr Avg	2.83	48.5
5 Yr Avg	5.85	62.7
10 Yr Avg	---	---
Potential Capital Gain Exposure (% of assets)	-9%	

Most Similar Funds in MF500

Babson Bond L	Strong Fit
Strong Government Securities	Strong Fit
Portico Bond Immdex Ret	Strong Fit

Coupon Range

	% of Bonds	Rel Obj
0%	2.1	0.96
0% to 8.5%	40.4	0.64
8.5% to 9.5%	27.0	1.66
9.5% to 11%	6.6	0.71
More than 11%	7.5	1.94
Not applicable	16.4	3.28

Credit Analysis 12-31-94

% of Bonds

US Govt	0	BB	10
AAA	57	B	0
AA	7	Below B	0
A	13	NR/NA	0
BBB	13		

Harbor Capital Appreciation

	Ticker	Load	NAV	Yield	SEC Yield	Assets	Objective
	HACAX	None	16.71	0.2%	N/A	239.1	Growth

Harbor Capital Appreciation Fund seeks long-term growth of capital; dividend income is incidental.

The fund invests primarily in equity securities of established companies, typically those with market capitalizations of at least $1 billion. Under most conditions, the fund intends to stay fully invested. Securities are chosen on the basis of fundamental analysis; this research emphasizes a company's sales, earnings, prospects for increasing dividends, and other factors.

Prior to May 1, 1990, the fund was named Harbor U.S. Equities Fund.

Historical Profile
Return High
Risk Above Average
Rating ★★★★ Above Average

Objective: Growth

Investment Style History
Equity
Average % Stocks Held in Portfolio

Growth of $10,000
|||| Value of Fund ($000)
— Value of Index ($000) SPMid400
▼ Manager Change
▽ Partial Manager Change
► Mgr Unknown After
◄ Mgr Unknown Before

Performance Quartile (Within Objective)

Manager's Investment Style

Manager Spiros Segalas takes a bottom-up approach to growth, demanding a top-line growth rate twice that of the S&P 500. Mid- to large-cap stocks with stable earnings dominate the portfolio. Segalas also invests in global companies and he likes domestic stocks that derive sales and growth from solid overseas divisions.

Fund Manager(s)

Spiros Segalas, since 05-90. Birthdate: 07-33. BA, Princeton U. 1955

Manager Experience

	Dates Managed	Invest Obj	Std Dev	+/- Index

Not available.

1983	1984	1985	1986	1987	1988	1989	1990	1991	1992	1993	1994	History
---	---	---	---	10.07	11.05	12.31	11.09	16.11	15.65	16.37	16.71	NAV
---	---	---	---	0.70 *	15.37	24.21	-1.81	54.79	9.98	12.12	3.37	Total Return %
---	---	---	---	-0.62 *	-1.24	-7.48	1.31	24.30	2.36	2.06	2.06	+/- S&P 500
---	---	---	---		-2.57	-4.97	4.37	20.58	1.01	0.84	3.44	+/- Wilshire 5000
---	---	---	---	0.00	1.69	1.74	1.25	0.28	0.13	0.21	0.23	Income Return %
---	---	---	---	0.70	13.69	22.46	-3.06	54.50	9.85	11.91	3.14	Capital Return %
---	---	---	---		27	25	61	6	22	50	7	Total Rtn % Rank All
---	---	---	---		51	63	33	11	37	47	12	Total Rtn % Rank Obj
---	---	---	---	0.00	0.18	0.21	0.14	0.04	0.02	0.03	0.04	Income $
---	---	---	---	0.00	0.38	1.18	0.86	0.98	2.04	1.13	0.17	Capital Gains $
---	---	---	---		0.99	0.92	0.88	0.89	0.91	0.86	0.81	Expense Ratio %
---	---	---	---		1.48	1.77	1.18	0.47	0.12	0.24	0.24	Income Ratio %
---	---	---	---		---	75	162	90	69	93	73	Turnover Rate %
---	---	---	---		46.2	61.8	62.1	90.9	105.0	149.9	239.1	Net Assets ($mil)

Performance 12-31-94

	1st Qtr	2nd Qtr	3rd Qtr	4th Qtr	Total
1987	---	---	---	---	0.70 *
1988	7.75	7.19	-1.81	1.73	15.37
1989	6.24	7.24	11.76	-2.45	24.21
1990	-1.62	11.89	-20.59	12.33	-1.81
1991	23.53	-5.40	11.73	18.55	54.79
1992	-2.23	-5.08	4.21	13.72	9.98
1993	0.19	1.02	5.56	4.95	12.12
1994	-2.87	-4.78	9.58	2.00	3.37

Bear Market Performance

Decile Rank (5-year period)

Worst ▬ Best

	Worst 3 Mo Period 1985-89	Worst 3 Mo Period 1990-94
Harbor Capital Appreciation	---	-20.59
+/- S&P 500	---	-6.84
+/- Best Fit Index : SPMid400	---	-2.81

Trailing Returns

	Total Return %	+/- S&P 500	+/- Wil 5000	% Rank All	Obj	Growth of $10,000
3 Mo	2.00	2.02	2.77	3	5	10,200
6 Mo	11.77	6.91	7.15	3	6	11,177
1 Yr	3.37	2.06	3.44	7	12	10,337
3 Yr Avg	8.43	2.16	1.81	19	27	12,747
5 Yr Avg	14.14	5.45	5.32	5	7	19,373
10 Yr Avg	---	---	---	---	---	---
15 Yr Avg	---	---	---	---	---	---

Operations

Address and Telephone	One SeaGate	Min Initial Purchase	$2000 (Addt'l: $500)
	Toledo, OH 43666	Min IRA Purchase	$500 (Addt'l: $100)
	800-422-1050 / 419-247-2477	Min Auto Invest Plan	$500 (Systematic Inv: $100)
Advisor	Harbor Capital Advisors		
Subadvisor	Jennison Associates Capital	**Expenses & Fees**	
Distributor	HCA Securities	Sales Fees	0.00% front
States Available	All plus PR		0.00% deferred
Report Grade	C+		0.00% 12b-1
Income Distrib	Paid Annually	Management Fee	0.60% flat fee
* Date of Inception	12-29-87	3-,5-,10-yr Expense Projections	$28, $49, $111
Fiscal Year End	October	Annual Brokerage Cost	0.26%

Risk Analysis

Time Period	Load-Adj Return %	Risk % Rank [1] All	Obj	Morningstar [2] Return	Morningstar Risk	Morningstar Risk-Adj Rating
1 Yr	3.37					
3 Yr	8.43	87	77	1.47 [3]	1.11	★★★
5 Yr	14.14	87	84	2.61 [3]	1.09	★★★★★
10 Yr	---					
Average Historical Rating (49 months)				4.1 ★ s		

[1] 1 = low, 100 = high [2] 1.00 = Equity Avg [3] 1.00 = 90-day T-bill return

Other Measures

			Standard S&P 500	Best Fit SPMid400
Standard Deviation	12.17	Alpha	2.0	1.1
Mean	8.86	Beta	1.16	1.10
Sharpe Ratio	0.44	R-Squared	57	80

Investment Style

	Stock Portfolio Avg	Relative S&P 500
Price/Earnings Ratio	24.5	1.32
Price/Book Ratio	5.3	1.56
5 Yr Earnings Gr %	12.2#	2.21
Return on Assets %	12.1	1.62
Debt % Total Cap	18.2	0.64
Med Mkt Cap ($mil)	7602	0.59

figure is based on 50% or less of stocks

Diversification Value for Portfolio Types

Large Cap: Low | Small Cap: Low | Bond: High | Balanced: Low | Diversified: Low

Portfolio 11-30-94

Share Chg (06-94) 000	Amount 000	Total Stocks: 60 Total Fixed-Income: 0	Value $000	% Net Assets
15	92	Hewlett-Packard	8996	3.97
19	148	Motorola	8327	3.67
53	123	Intel	7783	3.43
11	115	Microsoft	7249	3.20
10	116	Coca-Cola	5910	2.61
99	219	Astra CI A Free	5891	2.60
12	127	Reuters Holdings (ADR)	5812	2.56
39	147	Compaq Computer	5736	2.53
70	70	Pfizer	5424	2.39
-21	112	United HealthCare	5334	2.35
111	157	Vodafone Group (ADR)	5096	2.25
22	106	Computer Associates Intl	4841	2.13
15	104	Home Depot	4821	2.12
46	142	cisco Systems	4583	2.02
8	97	Duracell International	4383	1.93
11	95	Walt Disney	4131	1.82
44	83	Sybase	4056	1.79
65	107	Autodesk	4022	1.77
20	77	Omnicom Group	4003	1.76
-15	74	Telefonos de Mexico L (ADR)	3933	1.73
28	121	Ascend Communications	3859	1.70
8	134	McDonald's	3811	1.68
72	205	Cemex CI B (ADR)	3790	1.67
12	97	PhyCor	3755	1.66
9	159	YPF (ADR)	3600	1.59

Composition % 12-31-94

Cash	3.6	Preferreds	0.0
Stocks	96.4	Convertibles	0.0
Bonds	0.0	Other	0.0

Tax Analysis

	Tax-Adj Historical Return %	% Pretax Return
3 Yr Avg	6.43	74.8
5 Yr Avg	11.87	80.3
10 Yr Avg	---	---
Potential Capital Gain Exposure (% of assets)		16%

Most Similar Funds in MF500

Fidelity Growth Company	Strong Fit
Putnam Voyager A	Strong Fit
Fidelity Emerging Growth	Strong Fit

Index Allocation

	% of Stocks
S&P 500	55.9
S&P MidCap 400	13.6
U.S. Small Cap	14.9
Foreign	15.6

Sector Weightings

	% of Stocks	Relative S&P 500
Utilities	1.9	0.15
Energy	3.7	0.37
Financials	2.9	0.28
Industrial Cyclicals	5.0	0.30
Consumer Durables	4.7	0.76
Consumer Staples	2.8	0.22
Services	14.3	1.75
Retail	8.8	1.51
Health	13.9	1.60
Technology	42.0	4.59

MORNINGSTAR 1995 Mutual Fund 500

Harbor International

Ticker	Load	NAV	Yield	SEC Yield	Assets	Objective
HAINX	Clsd	24.45	1.0%	N/A	2953.1	Foreign Stock

Harbor International Fund seeks growth of capital. Current income is a secondary consideration.

The fund invests in common stocks or comparable equity securities of issuers who do business primarily outside of the United States. It will be invested in a minimum of three countries exclusive of the United States, emphasizing Europe, the Pacific Basin, and the more industrialized emerging markets. The fund may invest in non-equities or U.S.-issued securities, purchase options on foreign currencies, or otherwise hedge for temporary defensive purposes.

Historical Profile

Return	Above Average
Risk	Average
Rating	★★★★
	Closed

Manager's Investment Style

Management restricts this fund generally to larger-sized stocks in developed markets, or the more-sophisticated emerging markets. He prefers solid firms with a strong committment to shareholders and few governmental ties. The fund's stand-out success derives from management's ability to concentrate assets in countries it believes have the best chance for near-term success, although it is willing to wait for the long-term for a preferred country to live up to expectations.

Fund Manager(s)

Hakan Castegren, since 12-87. Birthdate: 1934. MBA, Stockholm School of Econ. 1957

Manager Experience

	Dates Managed	Invest Obj	Std Dev	+/- Index
Hakan Castegren				
Ivy International I	10/93 - 12/94	WF	15.62	7.09

Investment Style History
Equity
Average % Stocks Held in Portfolio

					89%	91%	95%	90%	93%	95%

Growth of $10,000
- |||| Value of Fund ($000)
- — Value of Index ($000) MSEASEA
- ▼ Manager Change
- ▽ Partial Manager Change
- ► Mgr Unknown After
- ◄ Mgr Unknown Before

Performance Quartile (Within Objective)

1983	1984	1985	1986	1987	1988	1989	1990	1991	1992	1993	1994	History
---	---	---	---	10.00	12.90	16.74	14.42	17.30	16.87	24.32	24.45	NAV
---	---	---	---	0.00 *	37.71	36.86	-9.76	21.46	-0.20	45.42	5.43	Total Return %
---	---	---	---	-1.32 *	21.10	5.17	-6.64	-9.02	-7.82	35.36	4.11	+/- S&P 500
---	---	---	---	---	9.44	26.32	13.69	9.33	11.97	12.86	-2.35	+/- MSCI EAFE
---	---	---	---	0.00	0.83	1.09	2.20	1.49	1.27	1.26	1.02	Income Return %
---	---	---	---	0.00	36.87	35.76	-11.96	19.97	-1.47	44.16	4.41	Capital Return %
---	---	---	---	1	6	84	42	90	3	4		Total Rtn % Rank All
---	---	---	---	1	4	42	7	23	29	10		Total Rtn % Rank Obj
---	---	---	---	0.00	0.10	0.17	0.34	0.21	0.22	0.21	0.25	Income $
---	---	---	---	0.00	0.00	0.76	0.72	0.34	0.00	0.18	0.00	0.94	Capital Gains $
---	---	---	---		1.78	1.15	1.40	1.35	1.28	1.20	1.10	Expense Ratio %
---	---	---	---		0.87	1.56	2.82	1.76	1.98	1.28	1.09	Income Ratio %
---	---	---	---		---	21	28	19	25	16	29	Turnover Rate %
---	---	---	---	11.2	35.1	61.6	220.8	761.9	2537.9	2953.1	Net Assets ($mil)

Performance 12-31-94

	1st Qtr	2nd Qtr	3rd Qtr	4th Qtr	Total
1987	---	---	---	---	0.00 *
1988	13.90	2.19	2.49	15.43	37.71
1989	11.01	3.56	14.63	3.85	36.86
1990	-2.39	9.67	-17.13	1.73	-9.76
1991	15.40	-0.54	6.53	-0.65	21.46
1992	3.18	4.15	-4.14	-3.11	-0.20
1993	9.84	6.37	9.23	13.94	45.42
1994	-3.21	0.64	10.34	-1.91	5.43

Bear Market Performance

Decile Rank (5-year period)

Worst | | | | | | | | | Best

	Worst 3 Mo Period 1985-89	Worst 3 Mo Period 1990-94
Harbor International	---	-17.13
+/- S&P 500	---	-3.39
+/- Best Fit Index : MSEASEA	---	-0.51

Trailing Returns

	Total Return %	+/- S&P 500	+/- MSCI EAFE	% Rank All	% Rank Obj	Growth of $10,000
3 Mo	-1.91	-1.89	-0.89	67	12	9,809
6 Mo	8.23	3.37	9.16	6	3	10,823
1 Yr	5.43	4.11	-2.35	4	10	10,543
3 Yr Avg	15.23	8.97	7.37	3	5	15,301
5 Yr Avg	10.89	2.20	9.40	13	6	16,771
10 Yr Avg	---	---	---	---	---	---
15 Yr Avg	---	---	---	---	---	---

Operations

Address and Telephone	One SeaGate
	Toledo, OH 43666
	800-422-1050 / 419-247-2477
Advisor	Harbor Capital Advisors
Subadvisor	Northern Cross Investments
Distributor	HCA Securities
States Available	All plus PR
Report Grade	C+
Income Distrib	Paid Annually
* Date of Inception	12-29-87
Fiscal Year End	October

Min Initial Purchase	Closed (Addt'l: $500)
Min IRA Purchase	$500 (Addt'l: $100)
Min Auto Invest Plan	$500 (Systematic Inv:$100)

Expenses & Fees

Sales Fees	0.00% front
	0.00% deferred
	0.00% 12b-1
Management Fee	0.85% flat fee
3-,5-,10-yr Expense Projections	$38, $68, $155
Annual Brokerage Cost	0.23%

Risk Analysis

Time Period	Load-Adj Return %	Risk % Rank [1] All	Risk % Rank [1] Obj	Morningstar [2] Return	Morningstar [2] Risk	Morningstar Risk-Adj Rating
1 Yr	5.43					
3 Yr	15.23	83	24	3.76 [3]	1.01	★★★★★
5 Yr	10.90	80	18	1.61 [3]	0.98	★★★★
10 Yr	---					
Average Historical Rating (49 months)					3.7	★s

[1] 1 = low, 100 = high [2] 1.00 = Equity Avg [3] 1.00 = 90-day T-bill return

Other Measures

	Standard S&P 500	Best Fit MSEASEA
Standard Deviation	13.86	Alpha	9.0	5.6
Mean	15.21	Beta	1.07	0.98
Sharpe Ratio	0.84	R-Squared	37	88

Investment Style

	Stock Portfolio Avg	Rel MSCI EAFE	Rel Obj
Price/Earnings Ratio	23.6	0.64	0.84
Price/Cash Flow	10.4	0.67	0.77
Price/Book Ratio	2.1	0.80	0.70
5 Yr Earnings Gr %	3.3	---	0.87
Return on Assets %	5.9	1.29	0.81
Debt % Total Cap	29.9	0.88	1.08
Med Mkt Cap ($mil)	7574	0.63	1.47

Diversification Value for Portfolio Types

Large Cap: Medium	Small Cap: High	Bond: High	Balanced: Medium	Diversified: Low

Portfolio 11-30-94

Total Stocks: 88
Total Fixed-Income: 3

Share Chg (10-94) 000	Amount 000		Value $000	% Net Assets
0	26250	Gencor (ADR)	92248	3.09
0	1260	Anglo American of SA (ADR)	69458	2.33
1500	3500	Canon	60487	2.03
0	6600	Keppel (Singapore)	53649	1.80
0	11000	British Gas	53201	1.78
2331	2331	Fuji Photo Film	51828	1.74
0	2625	Volvo Cl B	50504	1.69
0	1600	Kinnevik Cl B	49890	1.67
0	450	Royal Dutch Petroleum (Reg)	48881	1.64
0	1800	Astra Cl A	48484	1.63
0	3312	Trelleborg Cl B Free	48344	1.62
35	35	SGS Holdings (Br)	47687	1.60
0	2000	South African Breweries ADR	47180	1.58
0	7182	Malayan Banking	46636	1.56
0	624	Financiere de Paribas	44147	1.48
0	5165	National Westminster Bank	42117	1.41
72	72	Schweizer Ruckvers (Reg)	41927	1.41
0	865000	Telebras Pfd	41433	1.39
0	5750	Guinness	41130	1.38
0	6034	British Petroleum	40090	1.34

Regional Exposure 12-31-94

% of Stocks

Europe	16	Pacific Rim	27
Japan	9	Other	9
Latin Amer	9		

Composition % 12-31-94

Cash	5.1	Preferreds	0.0
Stocks	94.9	Convertibles	0.0
Bonds	0.0	Other	0.0

Tax Analysis

	Tax-Adj Historical Return %	% Pretax Return
3 Yr Avg	14.30	93.0
5 Yr Avg	9.94	89.5
10 Yr Avg	---	---
Potential Capital Gain Exposure (% of assets)		17%

Most Similar Funds in MF500

Templeton Foreign	Fair Fit
20th Century Intl Equity	Fair Fit
T. Rowe Price Intl Stock	Fair Fit

Country Exposure 12-31-94

% of Stocks

United Kingdom	16
Switzerland	9
South Africa	9
Japan	9

Total Number of Countries: 17
Hedging Policy: Occasional

Sector Weightings

	% of Stocks	Relative S&P 500
Utilities	11.8	1.32
Energy	8.8	2.17
Financials	23.2	1.23
Industrial Cyclicals	25.8	1.03
Consumer Durables	11.8	1.10
Consumer Staples	6.1	0.89
Services	3.1	0.28
Retail	1.4	0.24
Health	8.1	2.26
Technology	0.0	0.00

High Yield Plus

	Ticker	NAV	Mkt Price	Prem/Disc	Yield	Objective
	HYP	$7.70	$7.25	-5.8%	11.9%	Corp Hi Yld

High Yield Plus Fund seeks a high level of current income; capital appreciation is a secondary objective.

The fund normally invests at least 65% of its assets in publicly traded or privately offered high-yield debt securities rated BB or lower, or in nonrated securities of comparable quality. No more than 25% of assets will be invested in privately offered or otherwise restricted securities. The fund will invest no more than 20% of assets in foreign debt or equity.

The fund is leveraged through a borrowing agreement with The First National Bank of Boston.

Board members serve staggered terms to thwart takeover attempts; additionally, supermajority voting is necessary to amend the fund's articles of incorporation.

| | | | | | 7.6 | 0.8 | 0.1 | 1.2 | 5.1 | 4.7 | 4.7 | Highest Prem/Disc |
| | | | | | -4.8 | -5.2 | -19.0 | -12.8 | -8.0 | -5.6 | -5.8 | Lowest Prem/Disc |

Historical Profile

Return	Above Average
Risk	Below Average
Rating	★★★★ Above Average

Growth of $10,000
— at NAV ($000)
— at Market Price ($000)

Premium Discount %

1983	1984	1985	1986	1987	1988	1989	1990	1991	1992	1993	1994	History
---	---	---	---	---	9.06	7.75	6.04	7.58	8.08	9.01	7.70	NAV
---	---	---	---	---	5.85*	-2.14	-7.13	42.73	18.46	22.72	-5.04	NAV Total Return %
---	---	---	---	---	---	-16.68	-16.08	26.73	11.21	12.97	-2.12	+/- LB Aggregate
---	---	---	---	---	---	-2.53	-0.75	-1.02	1.80	3.82	-4.07	+/- FB High Yield
---	---	---	---	---	8.33*	12.32	14.93	17.24	11.86	11.21	9.50	Income Return %
---	---	---	---	---	-2.48*	-14.46	-22.07	25.50	6.60	11.51	-14.54	Capital Return %
---	---	---	---	---	---	92	74	14	10	22	40	Total Rtn % Rank All
---	---	---	---	---	---	16	6	60	53	46	41	Total Rtn % Rank Obj
---	---	---	---	---	-6.29*	-0.52	-16.59	51.65	27.00	22.09	-9.23	Market Total Rtn %
---	---	---	---	---	0.9	-2.8	-7.4	-5.1	-0.4	1.1	-0.6	Avg Prem/Disc %
---	---	---	---	---	0.75	1.14	1.13	0.89	0.84	0.84	0.86	Income $
---	---	---	---	---	0.01	0.00	0.00	0.00	0.00	0.00	0.00	Capital Gains $
---	---	---	---	---	1.44	2.57	2.21	2.26	2.03	2.01	2.76	Expense Ratio %
---	---	---	---	---	10.89	13.68	15.23	11.69	10.94	10.15	10.34	Income Ratio %
---	---	---	---	---	33	32	38	46	82	100		Turnover Rate %
---	---	---	---	---	98.3	91.0	65.6	82.1	88.0	98.7	84.7	Net Assets ($mil)
---	---	---	---	---	0.0	9.0	5.0	12.0	16.0	16.0	19.8	Pfd/Debt Leverage ($mil)

Manager's Investment Style

Management steers clear of the junkiest junk bonds, instead preferring higher-quality and solid B fare. Management compensates for the lower coupons associated with better-quality fare by leveraging the portfolio. Wide diversification across sectors, however, has limited the fund's vulnerability to sector-specific troubles. Although interest-rate hikes don't lead management to change its longer-duration course, it has unwound some of the portfolio's leverage when rates rise.

Fund Manager(s)

Catherine A. Smith, CFA. Since 4-88. BA'83 Harvard.

Manager Experience

	Dates Managed	Invest Obj	Std Dev	+/- Index
Catherine A. Smith				
New Amer High Inc	02/92 - 12/94	CY	10.18	10.20
Global Utility A	11/93 - 12/94	SU	9.01	-6.01

NAV Performance % 12-30-94

	1st Qtr	2nd Qtr	3rd Qtr	4th Qtr	Total
1987	---	---	---	---	---
1988	---	1.23*	1.09	3.44	5.85*
1989	1.45	3.41	-2.16	-4.65	-2.14
1990	-3.08	5.69	-11.66	2.63	-7.13
1991	16.71	8.49	7.00	5.36	42.73
1992	7.26	3.42	4.96	1.74	18.46
1993	7.53	6.01	2.17	5.37	22.72
1994	-4.68	0.35	0.34	-1.06	-5.04

Bear Market Performance

Decile Rank (5-year period)

Worst ◼ Best

	Worst 3 Mo Period 1985-89	Worst 3 Mo Period 1990-94
High Yield Plus	---	-16.43
+/- LB Aggregate	---	-17.18

Trailing Returns

	NAV Total Return %	+/- LB Agg	+/- FB High Yld	% Rank All	% Rank Obj	Mkt Total Return %
3 Mo	-1.06	-1.44	-1.01	34	44	-6.84
6 Mo	-0.72	-1.71	-2.28	49	32	-5.78
1 Yr	-5.04	-2.12	-4.07	40	41	-9.23
3 Yr Avg	11.34	6.80	0.18	16	60	12.07
5 Yr Avg	12.84	5.22	-0.23	10	6	12.23
Incept Avg	10.02*	---	---	---	---	7.86*

Operations

Address and Telephone	One Seaport Plaza New York, NY 10292 212-214-3332 / 800-451-6788	
Advisor	Wellington Management Co.	
Subadvisor	N/A	
Administrator	Prudential Mutual Fund Mgmt., Inc.	
Transfer Agent	State Street Bank and Trust Co.	
Custodian	State Street Bank and Trust Co.	
Auditor	Deloitte & Touche	
Legal Counsel	Kirkpatrick & Lockhart	

Risk Analysis

	Risk % Rank[1] All	Risk % Rank[1] Obj	Morningstar[2] Return	Morningstar[2] Risk	Morningstar Risk-Adj Rating
3 Yr	36	53	1.62	0.46	★★★★
5 Yr	56	20	1.88	0.67	★★★★
10 Yr	---	---	---	---	

Average Historical Rating (45 months) 3.4 ★s

[1] 1 = Low, 100 = High [2] 1.00 = Hybrid Avg [3] 1.00 = 90-day T-bill Return

Other Measures

				LB Aggregate
Standard Deviation	7.04	Alpha		6.70
Mean	11.05	Beta		1.01
Sharpe Ratio	1.07	R-Squared		33

Investment Style

Interest-Rate Stance

	Fund	Relative Objective
Avg Eff Duration	5.7 Yrs**	1.25
Avg Eff Maturity	8.7 Yrs	1.02
Avg Wtd Coupon	9.32%	0.92
Avg Wtd Price	92.2% Par	1.00

Duration Short Intm Long

Quality
Avg Cred Quality B
** figure provided by fund

Credit Analysis 12-31-94

	% of Bonds		% of Bonds
US Govt	0	BB	17
AAA	0	B	80
AA	0	Below B	2
A	0	NR/NA	2
BBB	0		

Diversification Value for Portfolio Types

Large Cap: High	Small Cap: High	Bond: Medium	Balanced: Medium	Diversified: High

Portfolio 09-30-94

Amount 000	Total Equity: 3 Total Fixed-Income: 132	Maturity	Value $000	% Total Invest
4000	Bethlehem Steel 10.375%	09-01-03	3985	3.61
3500	Westpoint Stevens 8.75%	12-15-01	3238	2.93
2750	Sweetheart Cup 10.5%	09-01-03	2613	2.37
2500	PMI 10.25%	09-01-03	2481	2.25
3750	American Standard 0%	06-01-05	2447	2.22
2000	Magma Copper 12%	12-15-01	2170	1.96
2000	Burlington Motor 11.5%	11-01-03	1940	1.76
2000	Fort Howard 9.25%	03-15-01	1920	1.74
2000	Armco 9.375%	11-01-00	1850	1.68
2250	Spanish Broadcasting Sys 7.5%	06-15-02	1834	1.66
1750	Arcadian Partner 10.75%	05-01-01	1733	1.57
1500	Domtar 11.75%	03-15-99	1601	1.45
1500	Rogers Cantel Mobile 11.125%	07-15-02	1545	1.40
1500	Weirton Steel 10.875%	10-15-99	1521	1.38
1650	K & F Industries 13.75%	08-01-01	1518	1.37
1500	Hillhaven 10.125%	09-01-01	1515	1.37
1500	AK Steel 10.75%	04-01-04	1515	1.37
1500	Texas-New Mexico Power 10.75%	09-15-03	1500	1.36
1500	Stone Container 11%	08-15-99	1478	1.34
2500	Family Restaurants 0%	02-01-04	1475	1.34
1500	Container of America 9.75%	04-01-03	1448	1.31
1500	Stone Container 9.875%	02-01-01	1410	1.28
2750	Pathmark Stores 0%	11-01-03	1361	1.23
1250	Rohr 11.625%	05-15-03	1275	1.15
1250	Santa Fe Energy Resources 11%	05-15-04	1263	1.14

Composition % 12-31-94

Cash	0.7	Preferreds	0.5
Stocks	0.0	Convertibles	0.0
Bonds	98.8	Other	0.0

Leverage factor: 1.23

Tax Analysis

	Tax-Adj Historical Return %	% Pretax Return
3 Yr Avg	7.26	61.5
5 Yr Avg	8.22	58.3
10 Yr Avg		

Potential Capital Gain Exposure (% of assets) -20

Most Similar Funds in MF500

Invesco High-Yield	Fair Fit
American High-Income	Fair Fit
Vanguard F/I High-Yield	Fair Fit

Coupon Range

	% of Bonds	Relative Objective
0%, PIK	8.4	1.3
0% to 11%	69.6	1.5
11% to 13%	19.0	0.5
13% to 14.5%	1.4	0.3
More than 14.5%	0.0	0.0
Not applicable	1.6	0.5

1.0 = Objective Average

Income Distrib Schedule	Paid Monthly
Management Fee	0.50%, 0.20%A
Reinvestment Plan	Yes
Direct Purchase Plan	No
Shares Outstanding	10,787,710
Exchange	NYSE
*Date of Inception	04-22-88
Shareholder Report	C+

MORNINGSTAR 1995 Mutual Fund 500

Wayne Hummer Growth

	Ticker	Load	NAV	Yield	SEC Yield	Assets	Objective
	WHGRX	None	21.34	1.4%	N/A	87.7	Growth

Wayne Hummer Growth Fund seeks long-term capital growth. Current income is secondary.

The fund invests primarily in common stocks of domestic corporations, such as cyclical companies at a low point. Limited investments may be made in investment-grade preferred stocks, bonds, or convertible debentures when such securities are believed to offer good opportunities for capital growth. For defensive purposes, the fund may invest in fixed-income securities or retain cash. It usually intends to hold securities at least six months.

Manager's Investment Style

Management likes to maintain a steady course. Low turnover and mid-cap focus is characteristic of this strategy. Management looks for companies with substantial insider ownership, low debt, projected earnings growth rates of 15% or more, and growing dividends. Most recently, management has made a few modest changes, slightly turning up its trading volume and moving toward a lower median market cap and a portfolio of fewer names.

Fund Manager(s)

Alan W. Bird CFA(1971), since 12-83. Birthdate: 08-39. BBA, U. of Iowa 1962 MBA, Northwestern U. 1968
Thomas J. Rowland CFA(1979), since 03-87. Birthdate: 11-45. MBA, Northwestern U. 1972

Manager Experience	Dates Managed	Invest Obj	Std Dev	+/- Index
Not available.				

Historical Profile
Return	Average
Risk	Below Average
Rating	★★★ Neutral

Stocks Held %: 85% 92% 92% 77% 73% 77% 84% 94%

Growth of $10,000
- |||| Value of Fund ($000)
- — Value of Index ($000) S&P 500
- ▼ Manager Change
- ▽ Partial Manager Change
- ► Mgr Unknown After
- ◄ Mgr Unknown Before

Performance Quartile (Within Objective)

	1983	1984	1985	1986	1987	1988	1989	1990	1991	1992	1993	1994	History
NAV	10.00	10.17	12.25	13.33	13.22	13.74	16.41	16.00	20.02	21.64	22.06	21.34	NAV
	0.00 *	4.15	24.36	13.71	9.70	7.18	24.04	5.01	28.86	10.36	3.26	-0.90	Total Return %
	0.00 *	-2.12	-7.38	-4.97	4.44	-9.43	-7.65	8.12	-1.63	2.74	-6.80	-2.22	+/- S&P 500
	---	1.10	-8.20	-2.38	7.33	-10.76	-5.14	11.19	-5.35	1.39	-8.02	-0.83	+/- Wilshire 5000
	0.00	2.45	3.83	1.95	2.11	1.81	1.63	2.83	2.45	1.49	1.01	1.42	Income Return %
	0.00	1.70	20.53	11.76	7.59	5.37	22.40	2.18	26.41	8.87	2.25	-2.32	Capital Return %
	---	54	48	63	10	79	26	43	29	20	96	26	Total Rtn % Rank All
	---	26	77	61	84	84	65	5	70	34	85	42	Total Rtn % Rank Obj
	0.00	0.23	0.34	0.24	0.31	0.24	0.24	0.44	0.39	0.29	0.21	0.31	Income $
	0.00	0.00	0.01	0.35	1.16	0.18	0.37	0.75	0.17	0.14	0.07	0.21	Capital Gains $
	---	1.50	1.50	1.50	1.50	1.50	1.50	1.50	1.36	1.23	1.12	1.07	Expense Ratio %
	---	5.09	4.12	2.44	1.64	1.73	1.83	1.91	2.87	2.01	1.41	1.33	Income Ratio %
	---	---	26	27	28	10	12	13	3	1	2	Turnover Rate %
	---	1.7	4.3	13.5	18.6	20.8	24.7	26.4	50.3	79.2	99.0	87.7	Net Assets ($mil)

Investment Style History
Equity
Average % Stocks Held in Portfolio

Performance 12-31-94

	1st Qtr	2nd Qtr	3rd Qtr	4th Qtr	Total
1987	21.56	3.27	7.27	-18.54	9.70
1988	4.62	3.38	-1.76	0.87	7.18
1989	5.17	6.05	8.53	2.48	24.04
1990	0.79	5.68	-12.02	12.05	5.01
1991	12.75	1.71	3.87	8.17	28.86
1992	0.75	-0.72	6.02	4.07	10.36
1993	0.37	-1.29	0.43	3.78	3.26
1994	-3.76	-1.20	4.55	-0.32	-0.90

Bear Market Performance

Decile Rank (5-year period)

	Worst 3 Mo Period 1985-89	Worst 3 Mo Period 1990-94
Wayne Hummer Growth	-25.26	-12.02
+/- S&P 500	4.32	1.73
+/- Best Fit Index : S&P 500	4.32	1.73

Trailing Returns

	Total Return %	+/- S&P 500	+/- Wil 5000	% Rank All	Obj	Growth of $10,000
3 Mo	-0.32	-0.30	0.45	30	27	9,968
6 Mo	4.22	-0.64	-0.40	15	46	10,422
1 Yr	-0.90	-2.22	-0.83	26	42	9,910
3 Yr Avg	4.14	-2.13	-2.48	67	65	11,293
5 Yr Avg	8.85	0.16	0.03	25	48	15,280
10 Yr Avg	12.16	-2.22	-1.70	36	64	31,513
15 Yr Avg	---	---	---	---	---	---

Risk Analysis

Time Period	Load-Adj Return %	Risk % Rank[1] All	Obj	Morningstar[2] Return	Morningstar Risk	Morningstar Risk-Adj Rating
1 Yr	-0.90					
3 Yr	4.14	58	13	0.16[3]	0.64	★★★
5 Yr	8.85	57	5	1.04[3]	0.64	★★★★
10 Yr	12.16	57	18	0.91	0.82	★★★
Average Historical Rating (97 months)				3.4 ★s		

[1] 1 = low, 100 = high [2] 1.00 = Equity Avg [3] 1.00 = 90-day T-bill return

Other Measures

			Standard S&P 500	Best Fit S&P 500
Standard Deviation	6.99	Alpha	-1.4	-1.4
Mean	4.30	Beta	0.75	0.75
Sharpe Ratio	0.11	R-Squared	74	74

Investment Style

	Stock Portfolio Avg	Relative S&P 500
Price/Earnings Ratio	19.3	1.05
Price/Book Ratio	2.8	0.83
5 Yr Earnings Gr %	7.6	1.36
Return on Assets %	7.7	1.03
Debt % Total Cap	20.9	0.74
Med Mkt Cap ($mil)	1999	0.15

Style: Value Blend Growth / Size Large Med Small

Diversification Value for Portfolio Types

Large Cap: Low	Small Cap: Medium	Bond: High	Balanced: Low	Diversified: Low

Portfolio 09-30-94

Total Stocks: 50
Total Fixed-Income: 0

Share Chg (06-94) 000	Amount 000		Value $000	% Net Assets
0	100	Avery Dennison	3438	3.78
80	120	Morton International	3300	3.63
0	55	Emerson Electric	3279	3.61
0	110	A Schulman	2970	3.27
0	70	RP Scherer	2914	3.20
0	55	Consolidated Papers	2846	3.13
0	65	Illinois Tool Works	2779	3.06
0	60	H & R Block	2753	3.03
0	75	First of America Bank	2644	2.91
0	75	Interpublic Group	2475	2.72
0	94	Kelly Services Cl A	2467	2.71
0	80	Dean Foods	2420	2.66
0	45	Cincinnati Financial	2351	2.59
0	60	Burlington Resources	2250	2.47
15	60	Northern Trust	2231	2.45
0	80	Rubbermaid	2130	2.34
0	120	Pall	2070	2.28
0	100	McCormick	1988	2.19
0	85	Sonoco Products	1982	2.18
0	25	AMP	1934	2.13
0	45	Intl Flavors & Fragrances	1873	2.06
0	80	Sara Lee	1800	1.98
0	100	Albany International Cl A	1763	1.94
0	80	JM Smucker Cl B	1730	1.90
0	35	Gannett	1680	1.85

Composition % 12-31-94

Cash	4.1	Preferreds	0.0
Stocks	95.9	Convertibles	0.0
Bonds	0.0	Other	0.0

Tax Analysis

	Tax-Adj Historical Return %	% Pretax Return
3 Yr Avg	3.49	83.7
5 Yr Avg	7.75	85.7
10 Yr Avg	10.69	81.9
Potential Capital Gain Exposure (% of assets)		19%

Most Similar Funds in MF500

Franklin Growth	Fair Fit
Liberty All-Star	Fair Fit
Hancock Sovereign Investor A	Fair Fit

Index Allocation

	% of Stocks
S&P 500	52.3
S&P MidCap 400	28.5
U.S. Small Cap	19.3
Foreign	0.0

Sector Weightings

	% of Stocks	Relative S&P 500
Utilities	0.0	0.00
Energy	3.8	0.37
Financials	14.2	1.34
Industrial Cyclicals	39.2	2.39
Consumer Durables	8.8	1.41
Consumer Staples	11.1	0.88
Services	13.3	1.64
Retail	1.7	0.30
Health	4.1	0.48
Technology	3.8	0.41

Operations

Address and Telephone	300 S. Wacker Drive 14th Floor Chicago, IL 60606 800-621-4477 / 312-431-1700
Advisor	Wayne Hummer Management
Subadvisor	None
Distributor	Wayne Hummer & Company
States Available	All
Report Grade	B
Income Distrib	Paid Quarterly
* Date of Inception	12-30-83
Fiscal Year End	March

Expenses & Fees

Sales Fees	0.00% front
	0.00% deferred
	0.00% 12b-1
Management Fee	0.80% max./0.50% min.
3-,5-,10-yr Expense Projections	$34, $59, $130
Annual Brokerage Cost	0.03%

Min Initial Purchase	$1000 (Addt'l: $500)
Min IRA Purchase	$500 (Addt'l: $200)
Min Auto Invest Plan	$1000 (Systematic Inv: $100)

IAI Midcap Growth

IAI Midcap Growth Fund seeks long-term capital appreciation. The fund normally invests in equity securities of U.S. companies with market capitalizations between $1 billion and $3 billion that have above-average prospects for growth. It focuses on companies with superior performance records, solid market positions, and strong balance sheets. As a short-term defensive measure, the fund may invest substantially in high-quality fixed-income securities.

	Ticker	Load	NAV	Yield	SEC Yield	Assets	Objective
	IAMCX	None	14.05	0.0%	N/A	84.8	Growth

Historical Profile
Return ---
Risk ---
Rating
Not Rated

Investment Style History
Equity

Average % Stocks Held in Portfolio
75% 89% 91%

Growth of $10,000
|||| Value of Fund ($000)
— Value of Index ($000)
   S&P 500
▼ Manager Change
▽ Partial Manager Change
► Mgr Unknown After
◄ Mgr Unknown Before

Performance Quartile
(Within Objective)

Manager's Investment Style

Management takes a research-driven, bottom-up approach to the market. It favors firms touting solid management, growth rates of at least 12%, and a competitive edge within their given industries. She isn't willing to pay sky-high multiple for these stocks, though.

Fund Manager(s)

Suzanne Zak CFA(1986), since 07-93. Birthdate: 12-59. BA, Princeton U. 1982 MBA, Rutgers U. 1983

Manager Experience

	Dates Managed	Invest Obj	Std Dev	+/- Index
Suzanne Zak				
Seligman Growth A	01/89 - 08/92	G	17.56	0.31

	1983	1984	1985	1986	1987	1988	1989	1990	1991	1992	1993	1994	History
	---	---	---	---	---	---	---	---	---	11.47	13.93	14.05	NAV
	---	---	---	---	---	---	---	---	---	14.98 *	22.85	5.65	Total Return %
	---	---	---	---	---	---	---	---	---	5.09 *	12.79	4.34	+/- S&P 500
	---	---	---	---	---	---	---	---	---	---	11.57	5.72	+/- Wilshire 5000
	---	---	---	---	---	---	---	---	---	0.28	0.00	0.00	Income Return %
	---	---	---	---	---	---	---	---	---	14.70	22.85	5.65	Capital Return %
	---	---	---	---	---	---	---	---	---	---	13	3	Total Rtn % Rank All
	---	---	---	---	---	---	---	---	---	---	9	6	Total Rtn % Rank Obj
	---	---	---	---	---	---	---	---	---	0.03	0.00	0.00	Income $
	---	---	---	---	---	---	---	---	---	0.00	0.16	0.63	Capital Gains $
	---	---	---	---	---	---	---	---	---	---	1.25	1.25	Expense Ratio %
	---	---	---	---	---	---	---	---	---	---	0.24	-0.45	Income Ratio %
	---	---	---	---	---	---	---	---	---	---	---	50	Turnover Rate %
	---	---	---	---	---	---	---	---	---	13.2	43.9	84.8	Net Assets ($mil)

Performance 12-31-94

	1st Qtr	2nd Qtr	3rd Qtr	4th Qtr	Total
1987	---	---	---	---	---
1988	---	---	---	---	---
1989	---	---	---	---	---
1990	---	---	---	---	---
1991	---	---	---	---	---
1992	---	---	5.08	11.09	14.98 *
1993	3.57	0.25	11.59	6.03	22.85
1994	-1.87	-2.58	7.59	2.72	5.65

Bear Market Performance

Decile Rank (5-year period)

Worst ——————————————— Best

	Worst 3 Mo Period 1985-89	Worst 3 Mo Period 1990-94
IAI Midcap Growth	---	---
+/- S&P 500	---	---
+/- Best Fit Index :	---	---

Trailing Returns

	Total Return %	+/- S&P 500	+/- Wil 5000	% Rank All	% Rank Obj	Growth of $10,000
3 Mo	2.72	2.74	3.49	3	4	10,272
6 Mo	10.52	5.66	5.90	4	7	11,052
1 Yr	5.65	4.34	5.72	3	6	10,565
3 Yr Avg	---	---	---	---	---	---
5 Yr Avg	---	---	---	---	---	---
10 Yr Avg	---	---	---	---	---	---
15 Yr Avg	---	---	---	---	---	---

Operations

Address and Telephone	3700 First Bank Pl P.O. Box 357 Minneapolis, MN 55440-0357 800-945-3863 / 612-376-2600
Advisor	Investment Advisers
Subadvisor	None
Distributor	IAI Securities
States Available	All
Report Grade	A-
Income Distrib	Paid Semiannually
* Date of Inception	04-06-92
Fiscal Year End	March

Risk Analysis

Time Period	Load-Adj Return %	Risk % Rank [1] All	Risk % Rank [1] Obj	Morningstar [2] Return	Morningstar [2] Risk	Morningstar Risk-Adj Rating
1 Yr	5.65					
3 Yr	---	---	---	---	---	---
5 Yr	---	---	---	---	---	---
10 Yr	---	---	---	---	---	---

Average Historical Rating ---

[1] 1 = low, 100 = high   [2] 1.00 = Equity Avg   [3] 1.00 = 90-day T-bill return

Other Measures

			Standard S&P 500	Best Fit
Standard Deviation	---	Alpha	---	---
Mean	---	Beta	---	---
Sharpe Ratio	---	R-Squared	---	---

Investment Style

	Stock Portfolio Avg	Relative S&P 500
Price/Earnings Ratio	23.4	1.27
Price/Book Ratio	3.4	1.00
5 Yr Earnings Gr %	19.2#	3.46
Return on Assets %	9.1	1.22
Debt % Total Cap	26.9	0.95
Med Mkt Cap ($mil)	1589	0.12

Style Value Blend Growth / Large Med Small

figure is based on 50% or less of stocks

Diversification Value for Portfolio Types

Large Cap: Small Cap: Bond: Balanced: Diversified:

Portfolio 12-30-94

Total Stocks: 48
Total Fixed-Income: 5

Share Chg (09-94) 000	Amount 000		Value $000	% Net Assets
22	58	Alco Standard	3608	4.26
29	109	Minerals Technologies	3179	3.75
14	81	Harcourt General	2841	3.35
5	79	Barnes & Noble	2456	2.90
112	112	Danka Business Systems	2400	2.83
4	79	Century Telephone Enterprise	2342	2.76
0	56	Reebok International	2216	2.61
14	80	Hospitality Franchise System	2128	2.51
16	98	Flserv	2103	2.48
4	82	Unifi	2086	2.46
11	62	MGIC Investment	2060	2.43
4	40	Scholastic	2035	2.40
6	74	Jones Apparel Group	1916	2.26
5	53	Sensormatic Electronics	1899	2.24
6	40	Tyco International	1876	2.21
58	86	Carnival Cl A	1819	2.15
7	39	RP Scherer	1783	2.10
42	88	TriMas	1756	2.07
3	51	CUC International	1702	2.01
11	63	American Greetings Cl A	1682	1.99
7	62	LCI International	1667	1.97
-15	54	ALC Communications	1665	1.96
5	88	Camco International	1652	1.95
3	68	Cooper Tire & Rubber	1597	1.88
-14	1	Circus Circus Enterprises	1597	1.88

Composition % 12-31-94

Cash	8.3	Preferreds	1.9
Stocks	89.8	Convertibles	0.0
Bonds	0.0	Other	0.0

Tax Analysis

	Tax-Adj Historical Return %	% Pretax Return
3 Yr Avg	---	---
5 Yr Avg	---	---
10 Yr Avg	---	---

Potential Capital Gain Exposure (% of assets) — 9%

Most Similar Funds in MF500

Fund lacks three-year record

Index Allocation

	% of Stocks
S&P 500	28.2
S&P MidCap 400	21.1
U.S. Small Cap	43.7
Foreign	6.9

Sector Weightings

	% of Stocks	Relative S&P 500
Utilities	3.0	0.24
Energy	4.1	0.41
Financials	4.3	0.41
Industrial Cyclicals	24.2	1.48
Consumer Durables	14.8	2.38
Consumer Staples	1.4	0.11
Services	27.8	3.41
Retail	6.6	1.13
Health	2.2	0.25
Technology	11.7	1.28

Purchase / Expenses

Min Initial Purchase	$5000 (Addt'l: $100)
Min IRA Purchase	$2000 (Addt'l: $100)
Min Auto Invest Plan	$5000 (Systematic Inv: $100)

Expenses & Fees

Sales Fees	0.00% front
	0.00% deferred
	0.25% 12b-1
Management Fee	0.75% max./0.65% min., 0.20%A
3-,5-,10-yr Expense Projections	$40, $69, $151
Annual Brokerage Cost	0.33%

IAI Regional

	Ticker	Load	NAV	Yield	SEC Yield	Assets	Objective
	IARGX	None	20.15	0.9%	N/A	514.0	Growth

IAI Regional Fund seeks capital appreciation. The fund may not provide significant current income.

The fund makes at least 80% of its equity investments in companies headquartered in Minnesota, Wisconsin, Illinois, Iowa, Nebraska, Montana, North Dakota, or South Dakota. The balance of assets may be invested outside the eight-state region. The fund invests in both large and small companies and may invest up to 10% of its total assets in venture capital limited partnerships, leveraged buyouts, or restricted securities.

In 1987, the fund changed its name from North Star Regional Fund.

Manager's Investment Style

Management can and will invest in any type of company within its realm of eight states. Despite this latitude, the fund does give itself reasonable guidelines. Growth at a good price is the basic rule. Low leverage, high profitability, and strong growth are all also strong considerations. Management is also committed to being hands-on, visiting most companies before investing in their stock.

Fund Manager(s)

Julian P. Carlin CFA, since 05-80. Birthdate: 05-35. BS, U. of Notre Dame 1957
Mark C. Hoonsbeen CFA(1989), since 07-94. Birthdate: 06-61. MBA, U. of Illinois 1986

Manager Experience	Dates Managed	Invest Obj	Std Dev	+/- Index
Julian P. Carlin				
IAI Growth & Income	01/91 - 11/93	GI	10.46	-3.01

Historical Profile

Return	Above Average
Risk	Below Average
Rating	★★★★ Above Average

81% 84% 73% 65% --- 77% 75% 76%

Investment Style History
Equity
Average % Stocks Held in Portfolio

Growth of $10,000
‖‖‖ Value of Fund ($000)
— Value of Index ($000) S&P 500
▼ Manager Change
▽ Partial Manager Change
► Mgr Unknown After
◄ Mgr Unknown Before

Performance Quartile (Within Objective)

1983	1984	1985	1986	1987	1988	1989	1990	1991	1992	1993	1994	History
17.61	15.51	20.53	18.42	15.86	17.99	18.98	17.79	21.62	21.58	21.45	20.15	NAV
13.22	-2.44	38.84	24.63	5.14	18.80	31.37	-0.33	35.38	3.54	8.96	0.69	Total Return %
-9.25	-8.70	7.10	5.95	-0.12	2.19	-0.31	2.79	4.89	-4.08	-1.10	-0.63	+/- S&P 500
-10.25	-5.49	6.28	8.53	2.78	0.86	2.20	5.85	1.17	-5.43	-2.32	0.76	+/- Wilshire 5000
2.32	3.11	2.87	2.11	2.29	1.62	2.73	1.85	1.21	1.09	0.85	1.00	Income Return %
10.89	-5.55	35.97	22.52	2.85	17.19	28.65	-2.18	34.17	2.45	8.11	-0.31	Capital Return %
66	73	7	9	22	17	11	56	19	82	74	15	Total Rtn % Rank All
88	53	6	4	35	32	29	24	46	80	64	26	Total Rtn % Rank Obj
0.40	0.48	0.43	0.42	0.40	0.27	0.51	0.33	0.24	0.23	0.18	0.20	Income $
1.19	1.11	0.40	6.45	3.21	0.57	3.97	0.82	2.08	0.52	1.83	1.19	Capital Gains $
1.00	0.90	0.80	0.80	0.80	0.80	1.00	0.99	1.01	1.25	1.25	1.25	Expense Ratio %
3.10	2.60	3.00	2.10	1.80	1.60	2.00	2.31	2.27	1.20	1.09	0.94	Income Ratio %
116	77	80	112	133	85	94	116	169	141	140	163	Turnover Rate %
38.4	44.9	56.5	89.4	81.9	92.4	121.1	210.9	454.2	628.6	650.8	514.0	Net Assets ($mil)

Performance 12-31-94

	1st Qtr	2nd Qtr	3rd Qtr	4th Qtr	Total
1987	15.04	4.89	3.93	-16.16	5.14
1988	7.88	7.05	0.11	2.76	18.80
1989	7.73	6.48	13.48	0.92	31.37
1990	-0.16	8.31	-14.25	7.49	-0.33
1991	18.21	-0.65	6.92	7.81	35.38
1992	-1.53	-2.67	1.29	6.65	3.54
1993	3.01	0.07	6.58	-0.83	8.96
1994	-2.38	-2.71	5.72	0.27	0.69

Bear Market Performance

Decile Rank (5-year period)

Worst ———————————— Best

	Worst 3 Mo Period 1985-89	Worst 3 Mo Period 1990-94
IAI Regional	-24.30	-14.25
+/- S&P 500	5.28	-0.50
+/- Best Fit Index : Wil 4500	5.84	3.98

Trailing Returns

	Total Return %	+/- S&P 500	+/- Wil 5000	% Rank All	% Rank Obj	Growth of $10,000
3 Mo	0.27	0.29	1.04	15	17	10,027
6 Mo	6.01	1.15	1.39	9	25	10,601
1 Yr	0.69	-0.63	0.76	15	26	10,069
3 Yr Avg	4.34	-1.93	-2.27	62	62	11,359
5 Yr Avg	8.92	0.22	0.10	24	47	15,327
10 Yr Avg	15.84	1.46	1.98	7	8	43,522
15 Yr Avg	---	---	---	---	---	---

Operations

Address and Telephone	3700 First Bank Pl P.O. Box 357 Minneapolis, MN 55440-0357 800-945-3863 / 612-376-2600
Advisor	Investment Advisers
Subadvisor	None
Distributor	IAI Securities
States Available	All
Report Grade	A
Income Distrib	Paid Semiannually
Date of Inception	05-20-80
Fiscal Year End	March

Risk Analysis

Time Period	Load-Adj Return %	Risk % Rank¹ All	Obj	Morningstar² Return	Risk	Morningstar Risk-Adj Rating
1 Yr	0.68					
3 Yr	4.34	73	38	0.22³	0.82	★★★
5 Yr	8.92	67	21	1.05³	0.80	★★★★
10 Yr	15.84	56	17	1.69	0.81	★★★★★
Average Historical Rating (109 months)					4.5	★ s

¹ 1 = low, 100 = high ² 1.00 = Equity Avg ³ 1.00 = 90-day T-bill return

Other Measures

			Standard S&P 500	Best Fit Wil 4500
Standard Deviation	8.24	Alpha	-1.3	-2.3
Mean	4.59	Beta	0.81	0.78
Sharpe Ratio	0.13	R-Squared	61	85

Investment Style

	Stock Portfolio Avg	Relative S&P 500
Price/Earnings Ratio	20.6	1.11
Price/Book Ratio	3.0	0.90
5 Yr Earnings Gr %	11.9	2.14
Return on Assets %	8.1	1.08
Debt % Total Cap	24.8	0.88
Med Mkt Cap ($mil)	1928	0.15

Style Value Blend Growth — Size Large Med Small

Diversification Value for Portfolio Types

Large Cap: Low	Small Cap: Low	Bond: High	Balanced: Low	Diversified: Low

Portfolio 12-30-94

Total Stocks: 111
Total Fixed-Income: 17

Share Chg (09-94)000	Amount 000		Value $000	% Net Assets
55	550	McDonald's	16088	3.13
182	326	Sears Roebuck	14996	2.92
160	250	Illinois Tool Works	10938	2.13
190	190	Minnesota Mining & Mfg	10141	1.97
-39	196	ADC Telecommunications	9692	1.89
141	291	Honeywell	9167	1.78
162	320	Harley-Davidson	8960	1.74
0	300	NWNL	8700	1.69
293	293	RR Donnelley & Sons	8646	1.68
125	275	Green Tree Financial	8353	1.62
-93	160	SciMed Life Systems	8080	1.57
-219	516	Casey's General Stores	7680	1.49
0	480	BMC Industries	7497	1.46
130	130	Philip Morris	7475	1.45
-89	223	MGIC Investment	7387	1.44
0	0	Berkshire Hathaway	7140	1.39
210	210	Nalco Chemical	7035	1.37
79	239	AptarGroup	6871	1.34
115	115	Amoco	6799	1.32
0	200	Valspar	6700	1.30
145	145	Saint Paul	6489	1.26
240	240	Fruit of the Loom Cl A	6480	1.26
35	160	Department 56	6360	1.24
25	140	United HealthCare	6318	1.23
270	270	Norwest	6311	1.23

Composition % 12-31-94

Cash	20.2	Preferreds	0.0
Stocks	79.6	Convertibles	0.0
Bonds	0.2	Other	0.0

Tax Analysis

	Tax-Adj Historical Return %	% Pretax Return
3 Yr Avg	2.45	55.3
5 Yr Avg	6.68	71.6
10 Yr Avg	12.15	64.1
Potential Capital Gain Exposure (% of assets)		3%

Most Similar Funds in MF500

Gabelli Growth	Strong Fit
MainStay Total Return B	Strong Fit
Liberty All-Star	Fair Fit

Index Allocation

	% of Stocks
S&P 500	45.5
S&P MidCap 400	18.5
U.S. Small Cap	36.0
Foreign	0.0

Sector Weightings

	% of Stocks	Relative S&P 500
Utilities	3.9	0.32
Energy	1.7	0.17
Financials	12.0	1.13
Industrial Cyclicals	20.0	1.22
Consumer Durables	12.9	2.08
Consumer Staples	6.1	0.49
Services	15.5	1.91
Retail	7.6	1.31
Health	10.1	1.17
Technology	10.2	1.11

Expenses & Fees

Sales Fees	0.00% front
	0.00% deferred
	0.25% 12b-1
Management Fee	0.75% max./0.65% min., 0.20%A
3-,5-,10-yr Expense Projections	$40, $69, $151
Annual Brokerage Cost	0.44%

Min Initial Purchase $5000 (Addt'l: $100)
Min IRA Purchase $2000 (Addt'l: $100)
Min Auto Invest Plan $5000 (Systematic Inv: $100)

IDS Extra Income

IDS Extra Income Fund seeks high current income. Capital appreciation is secondary.

The fund ordinarily invests in domestic and foreign long-term high-yielding corporate fixed-income securities in the lower rating categories of recognized rating agencies. It may invest up to 40% of its assets in electric utilities that, while more highly rated, may offer similarly high yields. Normally, the fund's holdings are rated BBB, BB, or B, but both higher- and lower-rated, as well as unrated, securities may be held.

	Ticker	Load	NAV	Yield	SEC Yield	Assets	Objective
	INEAX	5.00%	3.78	11.6%	8.91%	1526.0	Corp Hi Yld

Historical Profile
Return: Average
Risk: Low
Rating: ★★★★ Above Average

Investment Style History
Fixed Income
Income Rtn % Rank Obj

86 75 87 92 70 40 63 19

Growth of $10,000
|||| Value of Fund ($000)
— Value of Index ($000) LB Agg
▼ Manager Change
▽ Partial Manager Change
► Mgr Unknown After
◄ Mgr Unknown Before

Performance Quartile (Within Objective)

1983	1984	1985	1986	1987	1988	1989	1990	1991	1992	1993	1994	History
5.00	4.74	5.06	5.16	4.58	4.63	3.95	3.12	3.85	4.14	4.54	3.78	NAV
0.00 *	8.84	20.84	16.48	0.57	13.07	-3.85	-10.63	38.50	19.55	19.84	-7.57	Total Return %
---	-6.31	-1.29	1.23	-2.19	5.19	-18.39	-19.57	22.50	12.30	10.09	-4.65	+/- LB Aggregate
---	---	---	0.84	-5.96	1.64	-4.24	-4.25	-5.25	2.89	0.94	-6.60	+/- FB High-Yield
0.00	14.04	14.08	11.50	10.17	11.98	10.84	10.38	15.10	12.01	10.18	9.17	Income Return %
0.00	-5.20	6.75	4.98	-9.60	1.09	-14.69	-21.01	23.40	7.53	9.66	-16.74	Capital Return %
---	32	68	45	55	37	100	86	16	5	17	83	Total Rtn % Rank All
---	42	77	14	65	51	76	51	38	27	34	85	Total Rtn % Rank Obj
0.00	0.67	0.61	0.55	0.53	0.53	0.53	0.43	0.42	0.44	0.39	0.44	Income $
0.00	0.00	0.00	0.15	0.10	0.00	0.00	0.00	0.00	0.00	0.00	0.00	Capital Gains $
---	0.80	0.91	0.84	0.82	0.81	0.82	0.84	0.88	0.83	0.81	0.79	Expense Ratio %
---	14.50	13.15	11.14	10.34	11.38	11.67	12.28	12.45	11.13	10.03	9.87	Income Ratio %
---	---	89	117	87	105	102	88	88	89	70	---	Turnover Rate %
---	167.6	499.2	960.7	1061.6	1251.8	1139.5	792.1	1058.6	1270.9	1664.8	1526.0	Net Assets ($mil)

Manager's Investment Style

In most ways, this fund has a conservative strategy, and looks like the average offering of the high-yield group. Its maturity tends to stick close to the objective's average. In its credit selection, this fund rarely rides too low in the saddle, putting few of its assets in issues rated below B, and keeping a healthy-sized share in BB rated paper. Management's deviations from the norm have been few in recent years. It has kept a larger-than-average stake in zero-coupon bonds (which lengthens duration), for example, and, on occasion, its sector weightings have been atypical.

Fund Manager(s)

Jack Utter CFA, since 12-83. Birthdate: 10-39.
Business Admin., Macalester C. 1961

Manager Experience

	Dates Managed	Invest Obj	Std Dev	+/- Index
Jack Utter				
IDS Selective	01/83 - 07/85	CQ	8.31	-0.56

Performance 12-31-94

	1st Qtr	2nd Qtr	3rd Qtr	4th Qtr	Total
1987	6.03	-2.09	-2.37	-0.77	0.57
1988	6.18	2.12	2.30	1.93	13.07
1989	1.65	3.34	-2.88	-5.75	-3.85
1990	-6.48	4.38	-7.65	-0.86	-10.63
1991	12.93	8.79	6.85	5.51	38.50
1992	10.40	3.79	3.58	0.72	19.55
1993	8.24	4.24	1.43	4.72	19.84
1994	-0.63	-2.73	-2.11	-2.32	-7.57

Bear Market Performance

Decile Rank (5-year period)

Worst — Best

	Worst 3 Mo Period 1985-89	Worst 3 Mo Period 1990-94
IDS Extra Income	-6.16	-12.06
+/- LB Aggregate	-6.97	-12.80
+/- Best Fit Index : FB HY	---	2.05

Trailing Returns

	Total Return %	+/- LB Aggregate	+/- FB High-Yield	% Rank All	% Rank Obj	Growth of $10,000
3 Mo	-2.32	-2.70	-2.28	74	75	9,768
6 Mo	-4.38	-5.37	-5.93	97	88	9,562
1 Yr	-7.57	-4.65	-6.60	83	85	9,243
3 Yr Avg	9.81	5.27	-1.35	14	61	13,242
5 Yr Avg	10.39	2.76	-2.69	15	49	16,391
10 Yr Avg	9.69	-0.25	---	61	61	25,225
15 Yr Avg	---	---	---	---	---	---

Operations

Address and Telephone	IDS Tower 10 Minneapolis, MN 55440-0010 800-328-8300 / 612-671-3733
Advisor	IDS Financial
Subadvisor	None
Distributor	IDS Financial Services
States Available	All plus GU,PR,VI
Report Grade	B-
Income Distrib	Paid Monthly
* Date of Inception	12-08-83
Fiscal Year End	August

Risk Analysis

Time Period	Load-Adj Return %	Risk % Rank [1] All	Obj	Morningstar [2] Return	Morningstar Risk	Morningstar Risk-Adj Rating
1 Yr	-12.19					
3 Yr	7.95	26	85	1.32 [3]	0.53	★★★★
5 Yr	9.26	47	66	1.15 [3]	0.61	★★★★
10 Yr	9.13	36	74	0.50	0.53	★★★
Average Historical Rating (97 months)					3.0	★s

[1] 1 = low, 100 = high [2] 1.00 = Hybrid Avg [3] 1.00 = 90-day T-bill return

Other Measures

	Standard LB Agg	Best Fit FB HY
Standard Deviation	5.85	
Mean	9.57	
Sharpe Ratio	1.03	
Alpha	5.5	-3.0
Beta	0.64	1.27
R-Squared	19	88

Investment Style

Interest-Rate Stance
Avg Effective Duration: 4.6 Yrs
Avg Effective Maturity: 8.2 Yrs

Quality
Avg Credit Quality: B
Avg Weighted Coupon: 9.97%
Avg Weighted Price: 85.22% of Par

Maturity: Short Intm Long
Quality: High Med Low

Diversification Value for Portfolio Types

Large Cap: High	Small Cap: High	Bond: High	Balanced: High	Diversified: High

Portfolio 12-31-94

Total Stocks: 14
Total Fixed-Income: 179

Amount 000	Date of Maturity		Value $000	% Net Assets
28000	05-15-05	Gaylord Container 12.75%	24850	1.63
33000	03-05-00	Comcast Cellular 0%	22358	1.47
20000	06-16-02	Inda Kiat Intl 11.875%	19550	1.28
20000	04-01-97	Robin Media Group 11.125%	18825	1.23
30000	10-01-98	G-I Holdings 0%	18488	1.21
26558	11-15-99	Trump Taj Mahal Funding 11.35%	17661	1.16
20000	04-15-05	Penn Traffic 9.625%	17400	1.14
20000	12-15-03	Bally's Grand 10.375%	17400	1.14
20000	12-15-03	Silgan Holdings 13.25%	16800	1.10
18000	12-15-05	Westpoint Stevens 9.375%	16245	1.06
15000	04-15-04	Huntsman 11%	15638	1.02
16203	07-15-05	Amerisource 0%	15393	1.01
14000	05-01-02	MGM Grand Hotel Finance 12%	15260	1.00
15000	08-01-01	Tjiwi Kimia 13.25%	14963	0.98
16500	03-15-04	Doman Industries 8.75%	14520	0.95
15000	09-01-00	TransTexas Gas 10.5%	14438	0.95
16900	01-15-04	GB Property Funding 10.875%	13774	0.90
14000	04-01-02	Super Rite Foods 10.625%	13773	0.90
21500	06-01-05	American Standard 0%	13760	0.90
22000	08-01-03	PanAmSat Capital 11.375%	13750	0.90
16000	08-15-03	Specialty Foods 11.25%	13700	0.90
15000	05-01-03	Kloster Cruise 13%	13463	0.88
26000	11-01-03	Pathmark Stores 0%	13163	0.86
14000	08-15-03	Associated Materials 11.5%	13125	0.86
13000	11-01-04	Fort Howard 14.125%	13114	0.86

Composition % 11-30-94

Cash	2.0	Preferreds	5.0
Stocks	2.0	Convertibles	1.0
Bonds	90.0	Other	0.0

Tax Analysis

	Tax-Adj Historical Return %	% Pretax Return
3 Yr Avg	5.89	57.8
5 Yr Avg	6.39	56.8
10 Yr Avg	5.13	42.7
Potential Capital Gain Exposure (% of assets)		-28%

Most Similar Funds in MF500

Putnam High Yield Adv A	Strong Fit
Delaware Delchester A	Fair Fit
Phoenix High-Yield A	Fair Fit

Coupon Range

	% of Bonds	Rel Obj
0%, PIK	12.7	1.71
0% to 11%	43.2	0.88
11% to 13%	33.9	1.02
13% to 14.5%	4.9	0.90
More than 14.5%	1.2	0.72
Not applicable	4.2	1.37

Credit Analysis 11-30-94

% of Bonds

US Govt	0	BB	23
AAA	0	B	63
AA	0	Below B	7
A	0	NR/NA	6
BBB	1		

Expenses & Fees

Sales Fees	
	5.00% front
	0.00% deferred
	0.00% 12b-1
Management Fee	0.21% flat fee+0.46%G
3-,5-,10-yr Expense Projections	$75, $93, $145

Min Initial Purchase	$2000 (Addt'l: $100)
Min IRA Purchase	None (Addt'l: None)
Min Auto Invest Plan	$100 (Systematic Inv: $100)

MORNINGSTAR 1995 Mutual Fund 500

IDS High-Yield Tax-Exempt

	Ticker	Load	NAV	Yield	SEC Yield	Assets	Objective
	INHYX	5.00%	4.25	6.9%	6.17%	5604.9	Muni Nat

IDS High-Yield Tax-Exempt Fund seeks income exempt from federal income taxes.

The fund normally invests at least 80% of its assets in municipal bonds and notes, including industrial revenue bonds. It may also purchase taxable short-term securities. Normally, at least 75% of the fund's bonds and notes are rated A, BBB, or BB; the other 25% may be invested in unrated issues believed to be of comparable quality. The fund may invest up to 20% of its assets in bonds subject to the Alternative Minimum Tax. It may also invest in interest-rate futures contracts, buy options on such contracts, purchase put and call options, and write covered calls options.

Manager's Investment Style

Manager Kurt Larson looks for high yields in the usual places, including lower-quality credits and private-activity bonds (subject to the alternative minimum tax). Unlike many peers, however, he also provides some safety by holding a large stake in essential-services bonds and keeping nearly a third of assets in AAA-rated bonds, some of which are insured or prefunded. He keeps yield up by holding on to older issues with higher payouts, and by buying bonds that are selling cheaply compared with other issues with similar credit and duration characteristics.

Fund Manager(s)

Kurt Larson CFA(1975), since 05-79. Birthdate: 10-39. BS, Concordia C. 1961

Manager Experience	Dates Managed	Invest Obj	Std Dev	+/- Index
Kurt Larson				
IDS Tax-Exempt Bond	11/76 - 09/86	MN	11.22	-4.38
IDS MN Tax-Exempt	08/86 - 07/93	MS	5.20	-2.22

Historical Profile
Return **Average**
Risk **Below Average**
Rating **★★★★** Above Average

| | 21 | 22 | 8 | 9 | 12 | 7 | 8 | 5 | |

Investment Style History
Fixed Income
Income Rtn % Rank Obj

Growth of $10,000
|||| Value of Fund ($000)
— Value of Index ($000) LB Muni
▼ Manager Change
▽ Partial Manager Change
► Mgr Unknown After
◄ Mgr Unknown Before

Performance Quartile (Within Objective)

1983	1984	1985	1986	1987	1988	1989	1990	1991	1992	1993	1994	History
3.92	3.93	4.30	4.69	4.34	4.42	4.57	4.44	4.61	4.66	4.78	4.25	NAV
12.95	10.46	20.64	20.38	0.23	9.89	11.39	5.20	11.99	8.70	9.69	-5.05	Total Return %
4.57	-4.70	-1.49	5.13	-2.53	2.02	-3.15	-3.75	-4.01	1.46	-0.07	-2.13	+/- LB Aggregate
4.90	-0.10	0.62	1.06	-1.28	-0.27	0.61	-2.10	-0.15	-0.12	-2.59	0.56	+/- LB Muni
10.06	10.20	10.49	8.82	7.41	8.05	8.00	7.69	7.72	7.15	6.64	6.04	Income Return %
2.89	0.26	10.15	11.56	-7.18	1.84	3.39	-2.49	4.27	1.56	3.05	-11.09	Capital Return %
67	24	69	18	58	63	62	42	76	37	69	64	Total Rtn % Rank All
12	18	39	15	66	66	6	87	36	45	79	45	Total Rtn % Rank Obj
0.37	0.37	0.38	0.36	0.34	0.34	0.34	0.34	0.32	0.32	0.30	0.29	Income $
0.00	0.00	0.03	0.10	0.01	0.00	0.00	0.00	0.02	0.02	0.02	0.00	Capital Gains $
0.65	0.65	0.62	0.60	0.60	0.59	0.60	0.60	0.60	0.62	0.61	0.59	Expense Ratio %
9.43	9.73	9.22	7.84	7.80	7.66	7.50	7.62	7.26	6.86	6.32	6.37	Income Ratio %
13	14	21	12	15	13	7	22	10	12	10	---	Turnover Rate %
1286.7	1681.5	2553.4	3729.6	3739.7	4069.9	4593.7	4749.9	5435.8	6116.3	6845.7	5604.9	Net Assets ($mil)

Performance 12-31-94

	1st Qtr	2nd Qtr	3rd Qtr	4th Qtr	Total
1987	2.72	-5.05	-2.38	5.26	0.23
1988	2.41	2.40	2.64	2.10	9.89
1989	1.01	6.29	-0.14	3.89	11.39
1990	-0.84	2.36	-0.59	4.26	5.20
1991	2.00	2.28	3.89	3.33	11.99
1992	0.23	4.20	1.86	2.18	8.70
1993	3.07	2.45	2.82	1.02	9.69
1994	-5.05	0.79	0.50	-1.27	-5.05

Bear Market Performance

Decile Rank (5-year period)

Worst ——————————————— Best

	Worst 3 Mo Period 1985-89	Worst 3 Mo Period 1990-94
IDS High-Yield Tax-Exempt	-7.65	-5.78
+/- LB Aggregate	-4.10	-0.84
+/- Best Fit Index : LB Muni	-1.16	-0.01

Trailing Returns

	Total Return %	+/- LB Aggregate	+/- LB Muni	% Rank All	Obj	Growth of $10,000
3 Mo	-1.27	-1.65	0.16	51	46	9,873
6 Mo	-0.78	-1.77	0.47	70	45	9,922
1 Yr	-5.05	-2.13	0.56	64	45	9,495
3 Yr Avg	4.22	-0.32	-0.64	65	66	11,322
5 Yr Avg	5.93	-1.70	-0.84	77	63	13,338
10 Yr Avg	9.04	-0.90	-0.39	72	39	23,764
15 Yr Avg	8.45	-2.36	-0.02	89	24	33,772

Operations

Address and Telephone	IDS Tower 10
	Minneapolis, MN 55440-0010
	800-328-8300 / 612-671-3733
Advisor	IDS Financial
Subadvisor	None
Distributor	IDS Financial Services
States Available	All plus GU,PR,VI
Report Grade	B-
Income Distrib	Paid Monthly
Date of Inception	05-07-79
Fiscal Year End	November

Min Initial Purchase	$2000 (Addt'l: $100)
Min IRA Purchase	N/A
Min Auto Invest Plan	$100 (Systematic Inv: $100)

Expenses & Fees
Sales Fees	5.00% front
	0.00% deferred
	0.00% 12b-1
Management Fee	0.11% flat fee+0.46%G
3-,5-,10-yr Expense Projections	$69, $82, $123

Risk Analysis

Time Period	Load-Adj Return %	Risk % Rank [1] All	Obj	Morningstar [2] Return	Risk	Morningstar Risk-Adj Rating
1 Yr	-9.79					
3 Yr	2.46	19	33	0.71	0.86	★★★
5 Yr	4.85	15	38	0.83	0.91	★★★
10 Yr	8.48	9	28	1.07	0.93	★★★★
Average Historical Rating (109 months)					4.0	★s

[1] 1 = low, 100 = high   [2] 1.00 = Muni Avg   [3] 1.00 = 90-day T-bill return

Other Measures

		Standard LB Agg	Best Fit LB Muni
Standard Deviation	5.07	Alpha	-0.2	-0.5
Mean	4.27	Beta	0.97	0.91
Sharpe Ratio	0.15	R-Squared	59	96

Investment Style

Interest-Rate Stance
Avg Effective Maturity   20.5 Yrs

Quality
Avg Credit Quality   A

Avg Weighted Coupon   7.43%
Avg Weighted Price   96.38% of Par

Diversification Value for Portfolio Types
Large Cap: Medium Small Cap: High Bond: Low Balanced: Medium Diversified: Medium

Tax Analysis
	Tax-Adj Historical Return %	% Pretax Return
3 Yr Avg	4.14	97.8
5 Yr Avg	5.83	98.1
10 Yr Avg	8.92	98.1
Potential Capital Gain Exposure (% of assets)		-1%

Most Similar Funds in MF500
First Invest Insured T/E A	Strong Fit
Fortress Municipal Income	Strong Fit
Smith Barney Tax-Ex IncB	Strong Fit

Portfolio 12-30-94

Total Stocks: 0
Total Fixed-Income: 573

Amount 000	Date of Maturity		Value $000	% Net Assets
66945	07-01-17	WA Pub Pwr Sply Sys Proj #1 6%	58817	1.05
55500	06-15-21	NY New York City Muni Wtr Fin Swr 6.25%	51200	0.91
55000	01-01-19	NC East Muni Pwr Sys 5.75%	45519	0.81
42040	12-01-08	FL Broward Resource Rec South 7.95%	45321	0.81
40250	12-01-19	MI Monroe Poll Cntrl Edison 7.75%	41982	0.75
49635	07-01-09	CA North Pwr Geotherm Proj #3 5%	41077	0.73
39975	07-01-25	NY Engy Rsrch/Dev Elec Fac Edison 7.5%	40446	0.72
47200	11-15-15	CA Sacramento MUD Elec IFRN	38379	0.68
36060	02-01-19	TX Matagorda Navig Dist #1 Poll 7.875%	37399	0.67
40000	07-01-10	PR Elec Pwr Ser N 6%	37289	0.67
37400	12-01-29	TX Alliance Arpt Spcl Fac American 7.5%	35293	0.63
35735	05-01-21	NH Indl Dev Poll Cntrl Pub Svc 7.5%	35125	0.63
35000	12-01-14	MI Strategic Fund Ltd Obl 10.25%	35089	0.63
34650	09-01-24	PA Beaver Indl Dev Poll Cntrl 7.75%	34823	0.62
39465	07-01-16	NY Dorm City Univ 6%	34714	0.62
32250	01-01-17	IL Chicago O'Hare Intl Arpt 7.5%	33328	0.59
30500	07-23-09	MI Midland Poll Cntrl Cogen Proj 9.5%	32126	0.57
30500	02-01-20	TX Sabine Rvr Poll Cntrl Util 8.125%	31921	0.57
37800	01-01-11	NC East Muni Pwr Sys 5.5%	31911	0.57
34490	01-01-25	GA Muni Elec Pwr Ser S5 6%	31592	0.56

Credit Analysis % of Bonds 10-21-94
US Govt	0	BB	13
AAA	27	B	3
AA	7	Below B	0
A	23	NR/NA	1
BBB	26		

Composition % of Assets 10-21-94
Cash	4.0	Preferreds	0.0
Stocks	0.0	Convertibles	0.0
Bonds	96.0	Other	0.0

Coupon Range
	% Bonds	Rel Obj
0%	0.4	0.15
0% to 6.8%	34.9	0.58
6.8% to 7.5%	17.5	1.13
7.5% to 8.3%	18.7	2.11
More than 8.3%	24.3	2.75
Not applicable	4.2	1.09

Sector Weightings
	% Bonds	Rel Obj
General Obl	6.80	0.32
Utilities	24.58	1.96
Health	12.09	0.92
Water/Waste	4.40	0.69
Housing	1.71	0.23
Education	2.91	0.45
Transportation	10.26	1.01
COP/Lease	2.38	0.75
Private	31.68	2.72
Misc Revenue	3.19	0.64
Demand	0.00	0.00

Top 5 States % of Bonds
TX	10.52	CA	5.37
IL	8.81	PA	5.17
NY	7.51		

IDS Mutual

	Ticker	Load	NAV	Yield	SEC Yield	Assets	Objective
	INMUX	5.00%	11.02	4.9%	N/A	2924.8	Balanced

IDS Mutual Fund seeks a reasonable return on investment, conservation of capital, and long-term appreciation.

The fund balances its investments between common stocks and senior securities (bonds and preferred stocks). It may not invest more than 65% of its assets in common stocks, and must invest at least 35% in preferred stocks, bonds, convertible senior securities, and short-term investments. The fund may also use put and call options, interest-rate futures, stock-index futures, and options on stock-index futures.

Historical Profile
Return	Average
Risk	Below Average
Rating	★★★★ Above Average

Investment Style History
Equity
Average % Stocks Held in Portfolio

63% 62% 59% 58% 61% 61% 63% 58%

Growth of $10,000
- ‖‖ Value of Fund ($000)
- — Value of Index ($000) S&P 500
- ▼ Manager Change
- ▽ Partial Manager Change
- ► Mgr Unknown After
- ◄ Mgr Unknown Before

Performance Quartile (Within Objective)

Manager's Investment Style
Management takes an aggressive stance for the balanced-fund category. The fund's typically long-duration bond portfolio sets it apart from its balanced peers; in 1993, its duration stretched to 7.5 years. Its equity portfolio also hasn't been the tamest in the bunch. The fund has, at times, invested up to 25% of its assets overseas--among the highest percentages in the balanced objective. Management is, however, willing to be flexible and pare down its boldness as necessary by reining in duration or holding cash, for example.

Fund Manager(s)
Thomas W. Medcalf CFA, since 03-83. Birthdate: 06-47. BS, U. of Minnesota 1969 MBA, U. of Minnesota 1970
Edward Labenski, Jr. CFA, since 08-84. Birthdate: 11-36. BA, Dartmouth C. 1959

Manager Experience	Dates Managed	Invest Obj	Std Dev	+/- Index
Thomas W. Medcalf				
IDS Strategy Equity	07/89 - 12/94	GI	11.60	-0.70

1983	1984	1985	1986	1987	1988	1989	1990	1991	1992	1993	1994	History
10.98	11.01	11.74	12.27	11.22	11.56	12.18	10.70	12.22	11.98	12.46	11.02	NAV
15.60	13.72	21.36	21.93	7.39	12.66	18.60	-3.03	23.65	10.44	14.36	-2.97	Total Return %
-6.87	7.45	-10.38	3.25	2.14	-3.95	-13.09	0.09	-6.83	2.82	4.31	-4.28	+/- S&P 500
7.23	-1.44	-0.77	6.68	4.64	4.78	4.06	-11.97	7.65	3.20	4.61	-0.05	+/- LB Aggregate
8.22	9.30	9.02	6.86	6.19	6.91	6.46	6.18	6.21	5.08	4.48	4.74	Income Return %
7.38	4.42	12.34	15.07	1.21	5.74	12.14	-9.21	17.44	5.36	9.89	-7.71	Capital Return %
56	11	63	14	15	40	38	64	38	20	31	43	Total Rtn % Rank All
46	17	89	12	8	41	56	76	53	16	19	55	Total Rtn % Rank Obj
0.85	0.92	0.93	0.81	0.78	0.76	0.75	0.71	0.63	0.60	0.54	0.57	Income $
0.54	0.42	0.54	1.14	1.33	0.29	0.74	0.39	0.30	0.88	0.68	0.51	Capital Gains $
0.59	0.60	0.61	0.59	0.63	0.63	0.67	0.69	0.71	0.78	0.79	0.79	Expense Ratio %
8.45	8.05	8.29	6.91	5.78	6.49	5.94	6.04	5.81	4.99	4.41	4.45	Income Ratio %
81	54	83	91	52	60	46	37	47	50	48	---	Turnover Rate %
1132.7	1043.8	1069.7	1289.6	1366.3	1449.4	1689.7	1595.1	1989.9	2307.1	2891.2	2924.8	Net Assets ($mil)

Performance 12-31-94
	1st Qtr	2nd Qtr	3rd Qtr	4th Qtr	Total
1987	12.33	2.41	2.76	-9.16	7.39
1988	5.28	4.12	1.24	1.51	12.66
1989	4.97	7.01	5.70	-0.12	18.60
1990	-4.03	2.35	-9.06	8.56	-3.03
1991	8.95	1.56	5.61	5.81	23.65
1992	-0.61	3.50	4.10	3.14	10.44
1993	5.36	2.62	4.65	1.07	14.36
1994	-3.78	0.82	1.84	-1.79	-2.97

Bear Market Performance
Decile Rank (5-year period)

Worst — Best

	Worst 3 Mo Period 1985-89	Worst 3 Mo Period 1990-94
IDS Mutual	-15.03	-9.68
+/- S&P 500	14.55	4.16
+/- Best Fit Index : S&P 500	14.55	4.16

Trailing Returns
	Total Return %	+/- S&P 500	+/- LB Aggregate	% Rank All	% Rank Obj	Growth of $10,000
3 Mo	-1.79	-1.77	-2.17	64	76	9,821
6 Mo	0.02	-4.84	-0.97	57	85	10,002
1 Yr	-2.97	-4.28	-0.05	43	55	9,703
3 Yr Avg	7.02	0.75	2.47	27	24	12,256
5 Yr Avg	8.00	-0.69	0.38	33	39	14,695
10 Yr Avg	12.05	-2.33	2.11	37	39	31,200
15 Yr Avg	12.96	-1.52	2.15	40	40	62,227

Operations

Address and Telephone	IDS Tower 10 Minneapolis, MN 55440-0010 800-328-8300 / 612-671-3733	Min Initial Purchase	$2000 (Addt'l: $100)
		Min IRA Purchase	$50 (Addt'l: None)
Advisor	IDS Financial	Min Auto Invest Plan	$100 (Systematic Inv: $100)
Subadvisor	None		
Distributor	IDS Financial Services	**Expenses & Fees**	
States Available	All plus GU,PR,VI	Sales Fees	5.00% front
Report Grade	C+		0.00% deferred
Income Distrib	Paid Quarterly		0.00% 12b-1
Date of Inception	06-01-40	Management Fee	0.14% flat fee+0.46%G
Fiscal Year End	September	3-,5-,10-yr Expense Projections	$74, $92, $143
		Annual Brokerage Cost	0.15%

Risk Analysis
Time Period	Load-Adj Return %	Risk % Rank [1] All	Obj	Morningstar [2] Return	Risk	Morningstar Risk-Adj Rating
1 Yr	-7.82					
3 Yr	5.20	49	49	0.48 [3]	0.70	★★★
5 Yr	6.90	53	51	0.53 [3]	0.76	★★★
10 Yr	11.48	42	46	0.95	0.70	★★★★
Average Historical Rating (109 months)				4.0	★s	

[1] 1 = low, 100 = high   [2] 1.00 = Hybrid Avg   [3] 1.00 = 90-day T-bill return

Other Measures
				Standard S&P 500	Best Fit S&P 500
Standard Deviation	6.34	Alpha		1.4	1.4
Mean	7.00	Beta		0.71	0.71
Sharpe Ratio	0.55	R-Squared		78	78

Investment Style
Stocks
	Port Avg	Rel S&P 500	Style
Price/Earnings Ratio	16.0	0.87	V B G
Price/Book Ratio	2.3	0.68	
5 Yr Earnings Gr %	-1.5	-0.27	
Med Mkt Cap ($mil)	4499	0.35	

Bonds
		Maturity
Avg Effective Duration	7.2 Yrs **	S I L
Avg Effective Maturity	10.5 Yrs	
Avg Credit Quality	AA	
Avg Weighted Coupon	7.44%	

**figure provided by fund

Diversification Value for Portfolio Types
Large Cap: Low	Small Cap: Medium	Bond: Low	Balanced: None	Diversified: Low

Portfolio 12-31-94
Total Stocks: 95
Total Fixed-Income: 96

Share Chg (09-94)000	Amount 000		Date of Maturity	Value $000	% Net Assets
	40000	US Treasury Bond 10.375%	11-15-12	47682	1.63
	40000	US Treasury Note 6.375%	06-30-97	38766	1.33
	45356	FNMA CMO 7%	10-25-22	35037	1.20
	33750	FNMA 7.4%	07-01-04	32355	1.11
0	525	General Electric		26775	0.92
0	450	Philip Morris		25875	0.88
25	425	Exxon		25819	0.88
0	250	Atlantic Richfield		25438	0.87
-50	900	American General		25425	0.87
111	750	Lubrizol		25406	0.87
0	575	ARCO Chemical		25300	0.87
75	300	Mobil		25275	0.86
50	375	Dow Chemical		25219	0.86
0	400	American Home Products		25100	0.86
100	900	UST (Inc)		24975	0.85
0	550	Saint Paul		24613	0.84
	25000	Federal Home Ln Bank 5.625%	09-03-96	24348	0.83
	25000	US Treasury Note 7.125%	09-30-99	24308	0.83
0	375	Raytheon		23953	0.82
0	475	Textron		23928	0.82

Index Allocation
	% of Stocks
S&P 500	72.8
S&P MidCap 400	7.3
U.S. Small Cap	10.1
Foreign	12.7

Composition % 11-16-94
Cash	13.0	Preferreds	0.0
Stocks	58.0	Convertibles	2.0
Bonds	27.0	Other	0.0

Tax Analysis
	Tax-Adj Historical Return %	% Pretax Return
3 Yr Avg	3.65	50.4
5 Yr Avg	4.81	56.4
10 Yr Avg	8.05	55.1
Potential Capital Gain Exposure (% of assets)		-3%

Most Similar Funds in MF500
Vanguard/Wellington	Strong Fit
American Mutual	Strong Fit
George Putnam of Boston A	Strong Fit

Bond Credit Analysis 11-16-94
% of Bonds
US Govt	30	BB	0
AAA	35	B	1
AA	6	Below B	0
A	14	NR/NA	0
BBB	14		

Stock Sector Weightings
	% of Stocks	Relative S&P 500
Utilities	5.8	0.47
Energy	7.7	0.76
Financials	24.2	2.29
Industrial Cyclicals	24.7	1.51
Consumer Durables	8.7	1.40
Consumer Staples	6.0	0.48
Services	8.6	1.05
Retail	6.6	1.13
Health	5.1	0.58
Technology	2.7	0.29

IDS New Dimensions

IDS New Dimensions Fund seeks long-term capital appreciation. The fund invests primarily in common stocks of American companies. These companies usually operate in areas where dynamic economic and technological changes are occurring. They may also exhibit excellence in technology, marketing, or management. Up to 30% of the fund's assets may be invested in foreign securities. The fund may engage in a variety of futures and options activities.

Ticker	**Load**	**NAV**	**Yield**	**SEC Yield**	**Assets**	**Objective**
INNDX	5.00%	13.29	0.9%	N/A	4458.4	Growth

Historical Profile

Return	Above Average
Risk	Average
Rating ★★★★	
	Above Average

Investment Style History
Equity
Average % Stocks Held in Portfolio

80% 84% 81% 83% 81% 86% 87% 86%

Growth of $10,000

- |||| Value of Fund ($000)
- — Value of Index ($000) SPMid400
- ▼ Manager Change
- ▽ Partial Manager Change
- ► Mgr Unknown After
- ◄ Mgr Unknown Before

Performance Quartile (Within Objective)

Manager's Investment Style

Management picks the largest, best-known stocks for its portfolio. While not adverse to paying hefty sums for these issues, management does require that the stock have promise. This strategy fares better than average in a down market, but misses the gains that a small-cap fund would reap on the upside. The fund does receive a kick, though, from foreign holdings. As much as 20% of assets has been invested abroad in the past.

Fund Manager(s)

Gordon Fines, since 04-91. Northwestern U.

Manager Experience	Dates Managed	Invest Obj	Std Dev	+/- Index
Gordon Fines				
IDS Managed Retirement	01/85 - 04/91	GI	17.18	1.09
IDS Growth	01/90 - 04/92	G	18.78	9.99

	1983	1984	1985	1986	1987	1988	1989	1990	1991	1992	1993	1994	History
	8.97	7.46	9.23	8.52	7.71	8.06	9.88	9.23	13.28	13.21	14.34	13.29	NAV
	20.03	-4.51	36.08	19.08	15.34	8.09	31.73	5.40	50.67	5.27	14.03	-2.98	Total Return %
	-2.44	-10.77	4.34	0.40	10.09	-8.53	0.05	8.52	20.19	-2.35	3.97	-4.29	+/- S&P 500
	-3.43	-7.56	3.52	2.98	12.98	-9.86	2.56	11.59	16.47	-3.70	2.75	-2.91	+/- Wilshire 5000
	1.15	2.67	2.17	2.14	2.09	1.59	2.05	2.37	1.18	0.30	0.50	0.88	Income Return %
	18.88	-7.18	33.91	16.94	13.25	6.49	29.68	3.04	49.50	4.97	13.53	-3.85	Capital Return %
	39	79	10	25	6	73	11	40	7	75	33	43	Total Rtn % Rank All
	55	63	13	22	6	81	27	3	14	69	37	60	Total Rtn % Rank Obj
	0.11	0.21	0.17	0.18	0.20	0.12	0.19	0.22	0.14	0.04	0.07	0.12	Income $
	1.25	0.92	0.64	2.19	2.16	0.15	0.54	0.96	0.49	0.73	0.65	0.51	Capital Gains $
	0.83	0.81	0.74	0.63	0.79	0.87	0.82	0.88	0.90	0.95	0.92	0.90	Expense Ratio %
	1.18	2.43	2.04	1.68	1.60	1.65	1.70	2.43	1.65	0.57	0.51	0.75	Income Ratio %
	88	88	105	128	113	119	67	91	81	75	60	48	Turnover Rate %
	375.9	352.1	403.6	528.9	638.5	620.0	769.7	929.2	1948.1	2668.5	3739.8	4458.4	Net Assets ($mil)

Performance 12-31-94

	1st Qtr	2nd Qtr	3rd Qtr	4th Qtr	Total
1987	26.64	2.32	4.22	-14.59	15.34
1988	1.30	7.17	-2.41	2.02	8.09
1989	6.20	7.59	13.46	1.60	31.73
1990	-0.71	11.62	-13.70	10.20	5.40
1991	19.83	-1.45	10.18	15.80	50.67
1992	-4.07	-4.16	2.95	11.22	5.27
1993	2.95	2.21	6.98	1.30	14.03
1994	-3.28	-3.03	4.54	-1.05	-2.98

Bear Market Performance

Decile Rank (5-year period)

Worst ▬ Best

	Worst 3 Mo Period 1985-89	Worst 3 Mo Period 1990-94
IDS New Dimensions	-24.58	-13.70
+/- S&P 500	5.01	0.05
+/- Best Fit Index : SPMid400	4.23	4.08

Trailing Returns

	Total Return %	+/- S&P 500	+/- Wil 5000	% Rank All	% Rank Obj	Growth of $10,000
3 Mo	-1.05	-1.03	-0.28	45	45	9,895
6 Mo	3.44	-1.42	-1.18	18	56	10,344
1 Yr	-2.98	-4.29	-2.91	43	60	9,702
3 Yr Avg	5.21	-1.05	-1.40	44	54	11,646
5 Yr Avg	13.09	4.40	4.27	6	11	18,496
10 Yr Avg	17.28	2.90	3.42	4	5	49,220
15 Yr Avg	17.87	3.38	3.89	1	3	117,720

Operations

Address and Telephone	IDS Tower 10 Minneapolis, MN 55440-0010 800-328-8300 / 612-671-3733
Advisor	IDS Financial
Subadvisor	None
Distributor	IDS Financial Services
States Available	All plus GU,PR,VI
Report Grade	B-
Income Distrib	Paid Annually
Date of Inception	07-30-68
Fiscal Year End	September

Risk Analysis

Time Period	Load-Adj Return %	Risk % Rank [1] All	Obj	Morningstar [2] Return	Morningstar Risk	Morningstar Risk-Adj Rating
1 Yr	-7.83					
3 Yr	3.43	84	70	-0.04 [3]	1.04	★★
5 Yr	11.93	74	40	1.92 [3]	0.88	★★★★
10 Yr	16.68	69	40	1.90	0.91	★★★★★
Average Historical Rating (109 months)					4.5	★s

[1] 1 = low, 100 = high [2] 1.00 = Equity Avg [3] 1.00 = 90-day T-bill return

Other Measures

				Standard S&P 500	Best Fit SPMid400
Standard Deviation	10.39	Alpha		-1.1	-1.7
Mean	5.63	Beta		1.12	0.98
Sharpe Ratio	0.20	R-Squared		73	87

Investment Style

	Stock Portfolio Avg	Relative S&P 500
Price/Earnings Ratio	21.5	1.17
Price/Book Ratio	4.3	1.28
5 Yr Earnings Gr %	12.3	2.21
Return on Assets	9.9	1.32
Debt % Total Cap	25.0	0.88
Med Mkt Cap ($mil)	10189	0.78

Style
Value Blend Growth
Size Large Med Small

Diversification Value for Portfolio Types

Large Cap: Low	Small Cap: Low	Bond: High	Balanced: Low	Diversified: Low

Portfolio 12-30-94

Share Chg (09-94) 000	Amount 000	Total Stocks: 125 Total Fixed-Income: 1	Value $000	% Net Assets
0	2600	Motorola	150475	3.38
0	3000	Citicorp	124125	2.78
200	1600	Dow Chemical	107600	2.41
300	1600	Intel	102200	2.29
0	2700	cisco Systems	94838	2.13
1200	1200	Pfizer	92700	2.08
200	1600	Caterpillar	88200	1.98
120	820	American International Group	80360	1.80
40	740	Royal Dutch Petroleum	79550	1.78
0	1600	Computer Associates Intl	77600	1.74
150	1300	Amoco	76863	1.72
0	1000	Gillette	74750	1.68
200	1400	General Electric	71400	1.60
0	1800	Compaq Computer	71100	1.59
0	1600	Oracle Systems	70600	1.58
400	2400	McDonald's	70200	1.57
0	1000	CSX	69625	1.56
80	700	Xerox	69300	1.55
200	2200	AirTouch Communications	64075	1.44
0	1300	First Chicago	62075	1.39
110	2000	Enron	61000	1.37
100	1100	Coca-Cola	56650	1.27
200	900	Microsoft	55013	1.23
250	500	Hewlett-Packard	49938	1.12
0	800	First Financial Management	49300	1.11

Composition % 09-30-94

Cash	12.2	Preferreds	0.1
Stocks	87.7	Convertibles	0.0
Bonds	0.0	Other	0.0

Tax Analysis

	Tax-Adj Historical Return %	% Pretax Return
3 Yr Avg	3.70	70.0
5 Yr Avg	10.97	80.4
10 Yr Avg	14.11	70.0
Potential Capital Gain Exposure (% of assets)		11%

Most Similar Funds in MF500

PIMCo Adv Growth C	Strong Fit
Fidelity Growth Company	Strong Fit
Liberty All-Star	Strong Fit

Index Allocation

	% of Stocks
S&P 500	78.1
S&P MidCap 400	12.6
U.S. Small Cap	4.9
Foreign	7.0

Sector Weightings

	% of Stocks	Relative S&P 500
Utilities	1.1	0.09
Energy	7.4	0.73
Financials	10.9	1.03
Industrial Cyclicals	13.1	0.80
Consumer Durables	8.2	1.32
Consumer Staples	4.4	0.35
Services	14.5	1.79
Retail	3.0	0.51
Health	9.0	1.04
Technology	28.3	3.09

Expenses & Fees

Sales Fees	5.00% front 0.00% deferred 0.00% 12b-1
Management Fee	0.23% flat fee+0.46%G
3-,5-,10-yr Expense Projections	$77, $97, $156
Annual Brokerage Cost	0.14%

Min Initial Purchase	$2000 (Addt'l: $100)
Min IRA Purchase	None (Addt'l: None)
Min Auto Invest Plan	$100 (Systematic Inv: $100)

Income Fund of America

	Ticker	Load	NAV	Yield	SEC Yield	Assets	Objective
	AMECX	5.75%	13.14	6.3%	6.34%	10502.7	Income

Income Fund of America seeks current income; capital appreciation is a secondary objective.

The fund allocates its assets between common and preferred stocks, straight debt securities, convertibles, and cash equivalents. The relative percentages vary according to market conditions. The fund may invest in dollar-denominated foreign fixed-income securities. Straight debt securities purchased by the fund may be rated as low as CC, although no more than 20% of the fund's assets may be invested in securities rated below BBB.

Manager's Investment Style

The fund's assets are divvied up among six managers; each portion is run separately. In general, however, management emphasizes equities (relative to its income-fund peers). It typically grants at least half of assets to value-priced, dividend-paying stocks. (Because equity payout cannot compete with that of bonds, the fund's total return record is superior to the objective, while its income, understandably, has lagged the group.) On the bond side, Treasuries have often outnumbered corporates, though management has long held a position in broadcast communications and telecom bonds, and will hold below-investment-grade issues.

Fund Manager(s)

Management Team

Manager Experience	Dates Managed	Invest Obj	Std Dev	+/- Index
Abner D. Goldstine				
Bond Fund of America	05/74 - 12/94	CG	6.62	0.65
Bond Port for Endowments	01/75 - 12/94	CG	6.65	0.13

Historical Profile

Return	Average
Risk	Low
Rating	★★★★ Above Average

Investment Style History
Fixed Income

Income Rtn % Rank Obj

| 28 | 61 | 79 | 76 | 68 | 68 | 64 | 62 |

Growth of $10,000

||||| Value of Fund ($000)
— Value of Index ($000) LB L-T
▼ Manager Change
▽ Partial Manager Change
►■ Mgr Unknown After
◄■ Mgr Unknown Before

Performance Quartile (Within Objective)

History	1983	1984	1985	1986	1987	1988	1989	1990	1991	1992	1993	1994
NAV	10.49	10.70	11.78	12.03	10.72	11.48	12.80	11.46	13.19	13.68	14.39	13.14
Total Return %	17.23	14.42	27.79	15.34	0.80	14.79	22.94	-2.95	23.78	12.03	14.00	-2.50
+/- S&P 500	-5.23	8.16	-3.95	-3.34	-4.46	-1.82	-8.74	0.17	-6.71	4.41	3.94	-3.82
+/- LB Aggregate	8.86	-0.73	5.67	0.09	-1.96	6.92	8.40	-11.90	7.78	4.79	4.25	0.41
Income Return %	8.59	8.97	8.75	7.85	8.88	7.70	7.89	7.03	7.89	6.58	6.14	5.80
Capital Return %	8.64	5.45	19.04	7.49	-8.08	7.09	15.05	-9.98	15.89	5.45	7.86	-8.31
Total Rtn % Rank All	50	8	34	52	53	28	29	64	38	15	33	38
Total Rtn % Rank Obj	33	23	14	43	38	23	3	67	42	21	47	20
Income $	0.82	0.85	0.88	0.88	1.08	0.80	0.88	0.88	0.85	0.84	0.83	0.83
Capital Gains $	0.33	0.34	0.80	0.59	0.38	0.00	0.37	0.07	0.08	0.22	0.35	0.06
Expense Ratio %	0.66	0.66	0.60	0.55	0.54	0.55	0.69	0.67	0.73	0.66	0.62	0.63
Income Ratio %	8.33	8.31	7.84	7.32	6.55	7.14	7.45	7.36	7.23	6.40	6.05	5.92
Turnover Rate %	64	45	51	42	39	43	34	19	23	23	29	26
Net Assets ($mil)	273.2	268.9	359.4	705.3	838.0	956.7	1625.1	2171.2	3525.3	6501.5	10338.9	10502.7

Performance 12-31-94

	1st Qtr	2nd Qtr	3rd Qtr	4th Qtr	Total
1987	7.60	1.52	-0.16	-7.57	0.80
1988	6.81	3.74	1.75	1.82	14.79
1989	4.88	9.36	5.57	1.54	22.94
1990	-3.20	2.22	-8.16	6.79	-2.95
1991	9.53	1.36	5.85	5.33	23.78
1992	1.59	4.40	4.05	1.51	12.03
1993	6.29	2.38	3.31	1.41	14.00
1994	-4.48	0.66	2.61	-1.18	-2.50

Bear Market Performance

Decile Rank (5-year period)

Worst _____■__ Best

	Worst 3 Mo Period 1985-89	Worst 3 Mo Period 1990-94
Income Fund of America	-11.78	-8.16
+/- S&P 500	17.81	5.59
+/- Best Fit Index : LB L-T	-14.36	-5.96

Trailing Returns

	Total Return %	+/- S&P 500	+/- LB Aggregate	% Rank All	% Rank Obj	Growth of $10,000
3 Mo	-1.18	-1.16	-1.56	49	46	9,882
6 Mo	1.40	-3.46	0.41	32	13	10,140
1 Yr	-2.50	-3.82	0.41	38	20	9,750
3 Yr Avg	7.58	1.32	3.04	23	18	12,452
5 Yr Avg	8.39	-0.31	0.76	29	38	14,958
10 Yr Avg	12.11	-2.27	2.17	36	1	31,365
15 Yr Avg	13.87	-0.61	3.06	25	8	70,157

Operations

Address and Telephone	4 Embarcadero Cntr P.O. Box 7650
	San Francisco, CA 94120
	800-421-4120 / 415-421-9360
Advisor	Capital Research & Management
Subadvisor	None
Distributor	American Funds Distributors
States Available	All plus GU,PR,VI
Report Grade	A
Income Distrib	Paid Quarterly
Date of Inception	01-01-71
Fiscal Year End	July

Risk Analysis

Time Period	Load-Adj Return %	Risk % Rank [1] All	Obj	Morningstar [2] Return	Morningstar Risk	Morningstar Risk-Adj Rating
1 Yr	-8.11					
3 Yr	5.48	25	44	0.56 [3]	0.52	★★★★
5 Yr	7.11	47	67	0.58 [3]	0.61	★★★
10 Yr	11.45	38	50	0.94	0.57	★★★★
Average Historical Rating (109 months)				4.0 ★s		

[1] 1 = low, 100 = high   [2] 1.00 = Hybrid Avg   [3] 1.00 = 90-day T-bill return

Other Measures

				Standard S&P 500	Best Fit LB L-T
Standard Deviation	5.23	Alpha		2.6	3.0
Mean	7.47	Beta		0.47	0.49
Sharpe Ratio	0.75	R-Squared		51	53

Investment Style

Stocks	Port Avg	Rel S&P 500	Style
Price/Earnings Ratio	16.8	0.91	V B G
Price/Book Ratio	2.6	0.76	
5 Yr Earnings Gr %	-0.7	-0.13	
Med Mkt Cap ($mil)	6941	0.53	

Bonds		
Avg Effective Duration	4.8 Yrs	
Avg Effective Maturity	---	
Avg Credit Quality	A	Not Available
Avg Weighted Coupon	8.39%	

Diversification Value for Portfolio Types

Large Cap: Low	Small Cap: High	Bond: Low	Balanced: Low	Diversified: Medium

Min Initial Purchase	$1000 (Addt'l: $50)
Min IRA Purchase	$250 (Addt'l: $50)
Min Auto Invest Plan	$50 (Systematic Inv: $50)

Expenses & Fees

Sales Fees	5.75% front
	0.00% deferred
	0.25% 12b-1
Management Fee	0.24% max./0.15% min.+3.00%I
3-,5-,10-yr Expense Projections	$77, $91, $132
Annual Brokerage Cost	0.29%

Portfolio 07-31-94

Share Chg (01-94)000	Amount 000	Total Stocks: 107 / Total Fixed-Income: 437	Date of Maturity	Value $000	% Net Assets
	172000	US Treasury Bond 7.125%	02-15-23	166033	1.58
560	3150	Eli Lilly		153169	1.45
185	2815	Bristol-Myers Squibb		148139	1.41
250	2500	Philip Morris		137500	1.30
	90000	US Treasury Bond 11.625%	11-15-04	118927	1.13
0	3370	American Brands		115001	1.09
0	1930	American Home Products		110734	1.05
	100000	US Treasury Note 8%	01-15-97	104125	0.99
0	3300	Upjohn		99000	0.94
750	3720	American Express		98580	0.94
	100000	US Treasury Note 5.75%	10-31-97	98078	0.93
	100000	US Treasury Note 5.625%	08-31-97	97969	0.93
30	1510	Texaco		95885	0.91
660	2540	Lincoln National		95568	0.91
1425	3675	Entergy		93713	0.89
400	3350	Baxter International		88356	0.84
640	2650	Phillips Petroleum		86787	0.82
	65000	US Treasury Bond 11.75%	02-15-10	85952	0.82
	75000	US Treasury Note 8.625%	08-15-97	79629	0.76
0	1275	Phelps Dodge		78731	0.75

Index Allocation

	% of Stocks
S&P 500	88.7
S&P MidCap 400	5.0
U.S. Small Cap	6.3
Foreign	0.0

Composition % 12-31-94

Cash	3.8	Preferreds	0.2
Stocks	44.6	Convertibles	7.4
Bonds	44.0	Other	0.0

Tax Analysis

	Tax-Adj Historical Return %	% Pretax Return
3 Yr Avg	4.87	62.5
5 Yr Avg	5.73	64.8
10 Yr Avg	8.65	60.5
Potential Capital Gain Exposure (% of assets)		-2%

Most Similar Funds in MF500

MFS Total Return A	Strong Fit
George Putnam of Boston A	Fair Fit
IDS Mutual	Fair Fit

Bond Credit Analysis 12-31-94

% of Bonds

US Govt	46	BB	12
AAA	1	B	20
AA	1	Below B	2
A	4	NR/NA	0
BBB	15		

Stock Sector Weightings

	% of Stocks	Relative S&P 500
Utilities	17.9	1.44
Energy	14.1	1.39
Financials	25.1	2.37
Industrial Cyclicals	10.0	0.61
Consumer Durables	3.0	0.48
Consumer Staples	8.9	0.71
Services	2.8	0.34
Retail	1.8	0.31
Health	15.8	1.82
Technology	0.6	0.07

MORNINGSTAR 1995 Mutual Fund 500

India Growth

	Ticker	NAV	Mkt Price	Prem/Disc	Yield	Objective
	IGF	$20.92	$19.25	-8.0%	0.0%	Pacific/Asia

India Growth Fund seeks long-term capital appreciation.

Normally, the fund invests at least 80% of its net assets in equity securities of Indian companies that derive at least 65% of their revenues from operations within India. The fund invests the balance in debt securities of India's government, corporations, or banks, or in dollar- denominated debt securities of U.S. issuers. As market regulation and availability permit, the fund may engage in various hedging activities. To discourage takeovers, the fund's directors serve staggered terms, and supermajority voter approval is required to remove a director from office.

As of August 1993, the following groups held 5% or more of outstanding shares: United Nations Joint Staff Pension Fund, 10.08% and Fiduciary Trust Company International, 10.08%.

In March and April 1994, a 78% subscribed rights offering raised $38 million.

Manager's Investment Style

New management could bring changes to the fund. Previous management generally invested in larger-cap Indian stocks. In 1993, however, it made an agressive push into more mid- to small-cap names that have been undervalued and underfollowed. Management had also overweighted certain sectors; in 1994, those were domestically competitive industries such as textiles and agriculture. Management's didn't move swiftly in and out of these sectors, however: Turnover is low.

Fund Manager(s)

S.S. Nayak. Since 1-95.

Manager Experience

	Dates Managed	Invest Obj	Std Dev	+/- Index
Not available.				

Historical Profile

Return	Above Average
Risk	High
Rating	★★★ Neutral

					1983	1984	1985	1986	1987	1988	1989	1990	1991	1992	1993	1994	History
				-7.2	31.8	32.4	4.6	13.6	53.5	54.3							Highest Prem/Disc
				-28.9	-26.4	-25.5	-23.2	-23.3	-3.7	-9.7							Lowest Prem/Disc
						---	---	---	12.18	14.79	13.91	16.60	15.96	18.84	20.92	NAV
						---	---	---	12.68*	28.28	-4.58	27.88	-3.86	34.16	23.26	NAV Total Return %
						---	---	---	4.16*	-3.41	-1.46	-2.61	-11.47	24.11	21.94	+/- S&P 500
						---	---	---	---	17.74	18.87	15.75	8.32	1.60	15.48	+/- MSCI EAFE
						---	---	---	---	11.41	-39.21	-54.22	-40.87	1.65	9.80	+/- BSE Sensitive
						---	---	---	1.70*	2.03	0.00	1.25	0.00	0.00	0.00	Income Return %
						---	---	---	10.98*	26.24	-4.58	26.63	-3.86	34.16	23.26	Capital Return %
						---	---	---	---	17	72	27	89	12	2	Total Rtn % Rank All
						---	---	---	---	75	10	6	60	75	12	Total Rtn % Rank Obj
						---	---	---	-20.42*	122.70	-42.77	30.29	14.95	110.62	-21.30	Market Total Rtn %
						---	---	---	---	-2.0	5.1	-12.2	-5.5	23.1	3.5	Avg Prem/Disc %
						---	---	---	0.15	0.37	0.00	0.16	0.00	0.00	0.00	Income $
						---	---	---	0.15	0.73	0.16	0.77	0.00	1.81	0.92	Capital Gains $
						---	---	---	---	3.27	3.00	2.30	2.79	2.22	Expense Ratio %
						---	---	---	---	0.01	0.01	0.11	-0.34	-0.51	Income Ratio %
						---	---	---	---	19	14	27	19	19	Turnover Rate %
						---	---	---	153.4	74.1	69.7	83.3	80.2	94.9	146.8	Net Assets ($mil)

Risk Analysis

	Risk % Rank[1] All	Obj	Morningstar[2] Return	Risk	Morningstar Risk-Adj Rating
3 Yr	99	93	1.91	2.15	★★★
5 Yr	98	90	1.98	1.74	★★★
10 Yr					
Average Historical Rating (41 months)				3.0 ★s	

[1] 1 = Low, 100 = High [2] 1.00 = Equity Avg [3] 1.00 = 90-day T-bill Return

Other Measures

			S&P 500
Standard Deviation	49.36	Alpha	24.36
Mean	26.24	Beta	0.25
Sharpe Ratio	0.46	R-Squared	0

Investment Style

	Stock Portfolio Avg	Rel WS India	Rel WS Foreign
Price/Earnings Ratio	---	---	---
Price/Cash Flow Ratio	---	---	---
Price/Book Ratio	---	---	---
5 Yr Earnings Gr %	---	---	---
Return on Assets %	---	---	---
Debt % Total Cap	---	---	---
Med Mkt Cap ($mil)	---	---	---

figure is based on less than 50% of stocks

Country Exposure (top five) 06-30-94

	Securities %		Currency %
India	100	India	100

Diversification Value for Portfolio Types

Large Cap: High	Small Cap: High	Bond: High	Balanced: High	Diversified: High

NAV Performance % 12-30-94

	1st Qtr	2nd Qtr	3rd Qtr	4th Qtr	Total
1987	---	---	---	---	---
1988	---	---	1.97*	10.50	12.68*
1989	6.81	7.84	0.21	11.13	28.28
1990	-16.97	2.12	49.76	-24.85	-4.58
1991	2.52	-0.63	13.48	10.62	27.88
1992	80.96	-34.85	0.56	-18.90	-3.86
1993	-11.85	-0.08	22.92	23.92	34.16
1994	21.73	1.06	7.50	-6.80	23.26

Bear Market Performance

Decile Rank (5-year period)

		Worst 3 Mo Period 1985-89	Worst 3 Mo Period 1990-94
India Growth		---	-34.85
+/- S&P 500		---	-36.76

Trailing Returns

	NAV Total Return %	+/- S&P 500	+/- BSE Sensitive	% Rank All	Obj	Mkt Total Return %
3 Mo	-6.80	-6.78	1.35	88	50	-11.86
6 Mo	0.19	-4.67	3.97	37	46	-5.12
1 Yr	23.26	21.94	9.80	2	12	-21.30
3 Yr Avg	16.71	10.45	-10.52	7	40	23.99
5 Yr Avg	14.17	5.48	-24.07	7	20	7.28
Incept Avg	17.58*	---	---	---	---	15.62*

Operations

Address and Telephone	1285 Avenue of the Americas New York, NY 10019 212-713-2000 / 800-852-4750
Advisor	Unit Trust of India Investment
Subadvisor	N/A
Administrator	Mitchell Hutchins Asset Management
Transfer Agent	Boston Safe Deposit & Trust Co.
Custodian	Brown Brothers Harriman & Co.
Auditor	Price Waterhouse LLP
Legal Counsel	Rogers & Wells

Income Distrib Schedule	Paid Irregularly
Management Fee	0.75%, 0.35%A
Reinvestment Plan	Yes
Direct Purchase Plan	Yes
Shares Outstanding	7,016,021
Exchange	NYSE
*Date of Inception	08-19-88
Shareholder Report	A-

Portfolio 06-30-94

Share Chg (12-93)	Amount	Total Equity: 195 / Total Fixed-Income: 9	Value $000	% Total Invest
-5800	358320	ITC (Ltd)	8995	5.33
220000	507700	Reliance Industries	6003	3.55
16196	437156	Colgate Palmolive (India)	5921	3.51
-1075	19211	Century Textiles	5267	3.12
-147931	323820	ITC Bhadrachalam Paper	4622	2.74
209590	594969	Arvind Mills	4003	2.37
64000	365060	Tata Iron & Steel	3404	2.02
55000	218350	Tata Engineering	3393	2.01
50000	290900	Usha Beltron	3385	2.00
294642	1312215	Great Eastern Shipping	3297	1.95
30000	304000	Larsen & Toubro	2883	1.71
26500	121104	Grasim Industries	2857	1.69
81612	228736	Mahindra & Mahindra	2750	1.63
35000	165905	Brooke Bond	2525	1.50
91400	234300	Indalco	2465	1.46
78600	117200	Bajaj Auto	2391	1.42
137800	342800	Videocon International	2349	1.39
73100	117400	Finolex Cables	2320	1.37
-2500	112273	Hindustan Lever	2264	1.34
0	99750	Tata Tea	2226	1.32
16200	17450	Associated Cement	2186	1.29
-10850	130938	Tata Chemicals	1933	1.14
-5525	164487	Nicholas Piramal	1914	1.13
0	47979	Indian Hotels	1874	1.11
80100	151800	East India Hotels	1863	1.10

Composition % 06-30-94

Cash	0.0	Preferreds	0.0
Stocks	102.1	Convertibles	0.4
Bonds	0.3	Other	-2.7

Tax Analysis

	Tax-Adj Historical Return %	% Pretax Return
3 Yr Avg	17.29	79.8
5 Yr Avg	13.90	79.1
10 Yr Avg	---	---
Potential Capital Gain Exposure (% of assets)		45

Most Similar Funds in MF500

Monetta	Weak Fit
General Amer Inv	Weak Fit
Pasadena Balanced Return	Weak Fit

Sector Weightings

	% of Stocks
Utilities	4.5
Energy	5.3
Financials	0.4
Industrial Cyclicals	31.3
Consumer Durables	30.7
Consumer Staples	10.9
Services	7.9
Retail	0.0
Health	3.6
Technology	5.6

Growth of $10,000

— at NAV ($000)
— at Market Price ($000)

Premium Discount %

Invesco European

Invesco European Fund seeks capital appreciation.

The fund, under normal circumstances, invests at least 80% of its assets in the equity securities of companies domiciled in Europe, including England, France, Germany, Belgium, Italy, the Netherlands, Switzerland, Denmark, Sweden, Norway, Finland, and Spain. The securities chosen by the fund will generally be listed on the principal stock exchanges of these countries. There is no limitation on the percentage of the fund's assets that may be invested in any one country.

Prior to July 1, 1993, the fund was named Financial European Fund.

Manager's Investment Style

Manager Steven Chamberlain rarely strays too far from the MSCI Europe Index, unless top-down economic analysis indicates a country included in the index will underperform. Roughly 70% of the fund's assets--and most of its largest holdings--are devoted to a core portfolio of established mid- to large-cap companies. Chamberlain funnels the other 30% of the fund's assets into little-known and less-liquid issues for a performance boost.

Fund Manager(s)

Steven Chamberlain et al. BS, Kingston Polytechnic

Manager Experience

	Dates Managed	Invest Obj	Std Dev	+/- Index
Not available.				

	Ticker	Load	NAV	Yield	SEC Yield	Assets	Objective
	FEURX	None	12.29	1.3%	N/A	245.5	Europe Stock

Historical Profile

Return	Below Average
Risk	Above Average
Rating ★★	
	Below Average

85% 83% 90% 88% 94% 93% 92% 96%

Investment Style History
Equity
Average % Stocks Held in Portfolio

Growth of $10,000

IIII Value of Fund ($000)
— Value of Index ($000) MSCI Eur
▼ Manager Change
▽ Partial Manager Change
► Mgr Unknown After
◄ Mgr Unknown Before

Performance Quartile (Within Objective)

	1983	1984	1985	1986	1987	1988	1989	1990	1991	1992	1993	1994	History
	---	---	---	8.77	8.31	9.11	11.17	10.99	11.49	10.41	12.83	12.29	NAV
	---	---	---	6.50 *	-4.55	10.60	24.25	0.71	8.01	-7.63	24.59	-3.05	Total Return %
	---	---	---	5.68 *	-9.81	-6.01	-7.44	3.83	-22.48	-15.25	14.53	-4.36	+/- S&P 500
	---	---	---	---	-8.21	-5.21	-4.26	4.56	-5.11	-2.92	-4.69	-5.33	+/- MSCI Europe
	---	---	---	0.06	0.60	0.97	1.64	2.32	3.45	1.77	1.34	1.16	Income Return %
	---	---	---	6.43	-5.15	9.63	22.61	-1.61	4.55	-9.40	23.25	-4.21	Capital Return %
	---	---	---	---	87	56	25	53	95	97	11	44	Total Rtn % Rank All
	---	---	---	---	60	25	50	18	38	54	64	68	Total Rtn % Rank Obj
	---	---	---	0.01	0.05	0.08	0.14	0.26	0.37	0.20	0.13	0.16	Income $
	---	---	---	0.00	0.01	0.00	0.00	0.00	0.00	0.00	0.00	0.00	Capital Gains $
	---	---	---	1.50	1.50	1.88	1.78	1.29	1.43	1.29	1.28	1.20	Expense Ratio %
	---	---	---	1.44	1.08	1.57	3.38	1.83	2.23	1.76	1.28	Income Ratio %
	---	---	---	---	131	75	118	20	61	87	44	70	Turnover Rate %
	---	---	---	1.8	8.4	7.0	21.1	72.5	79.1	124.8	307.2	245.5	Net Assets ($mil)

Performance 12-31-94

	1st Qtr	2nd Qtr	3rd Qtr	4th Qtr	Total
1987	10.72	3.91	4.16	-20.36	-4.55
1988	0.60	1.08	0.47	8.25	10.60
1989	3.84	4.76	11.20	2.71	24.25
1990	1.07	8.41	-15.11	8.27	0.71
1991	1.00	-5.77	11.28	1.97	8.01
1992	-2.61	7.15	-6.76	-5.07	-7.63
1993	2.40	3.00	7.56	9.82	24.59
1994	-0.47	-3.52	3.98	-2.90	-3.05

Bear Market Performance

Decile Rank (5-year period)

Worst .... Best

	Worst 3 Mo Period 1985-89	Worst 3 Mo Period 1990-94
Invesco European	---	-15.11
+/- S&P 500	---	-1.37
+/- Best Fit Index : MSCI Eur	---	2.06

Trailing Returns

	Total Return %	+/- S&P 500	+/- MSCI Europe	% Rank All	Rank Obj	Growth of $10,000
3 Mo	-2.90	-2.88	-3.83	82	75	9,710
6 Mo	0.97	-3.90	-4.28	38	60	10,097
1 Yr	-3.05	-4.36	-5.33	44	68	9,695
3 Yr Avg	3.72	-2.55	-4.29	75	62	11,158
5 Yr Avg	3.95	-4.74	-2.56	93	45	12,137
10 Yr Avg	---	---	---	---	---	---
15 Yr Avg	---	---	---	---	---	---

Operations

Address and Telephone	P.O. Box 173706
	Denver, CO 80217-3706
	800-525-8085 / 303-930-6300
Advisor	Invesco Funds Group
Subadvisor	MIM International
Distributor	Invesco Funds Group
States Available	All plus GU,PR,VI
Report Grade	B-
Income Distrib	Paid Annually
* Date of Inception	06-02-86
Fiscal Year End	October

Risk Analysis

Time Period	Load-Adj Return %	Risk % Rank All	Obj	Morningstar[2] Return	Risk	Morningstar Risk-Adj Rating
1 Yr	-3.05					
3 Yr	3.72	93	70	0.04[3]	1.30	★★
5 Yr	3.95	89	45	-0.18[3]	1.12	★★
10 Yr	---	---	---	---	---	

Average Historical Rating (67 months) 2.4 ★s

[1] 1 = low, 100 = high [2] 1.00 = Equity Avg [3] 1.00 = 90-day T-bill return

Other Measures

	Standard S&P 500	Best Fit MSCI Eur
Standard Deviation	13.39	
Mean	4.55	
Sharpe Ratio	0.08	
Alpha	-1.7	-3.9
Beta	0.95	0.99
R-Squared	32	90

Investment Style

	Stock Portfolio Avg	Rel MSCI EAFE	Rel Obj
Price/Earnings Ratio	21.4	0.58	1.05
Price/Cash Flow	10.9	0.70	1.15
Price/Book Ratio	2.3	0.90	1.03
5 Yr Earnings Gr %	-1.7	---	0.98
Return on Assets %	5.9	1.30	0.97
Debt % Total Cap	27.7	0.81	0.92
Med Mkt Cap ($mil)	7655	0.64	1.71

Style
V B G / L M S (Size)

Diversification Value for Portfolio Types

Large Cap: Medium	Small Cap: High	Bond: High	Balanced: Medium	Diversified: Low

Portfolio 12-30-94

Share Chg (09-94) 000	Amount 000	Total Stocks: 136 Total Fixed-Income: 7	Value $000	% Net Assets
0	250	Glaxo Holdings (ADR)	5094	2.07
0	758	British Telecommunications	4477	1.82
3	19	Bayer	4451	1.81
0	100	Fortis	4247	1.73
0	12	Veba	4182	1.70
0	34	Banco Popular Espanol	4040	1.65
-25	80	British Gas (ADR)	3900	1.59
0	120	Philips Electronics	3554	1.45
0	748	BTR	3435	1.40
0	252	B-A-T Industries (ADR)	3395	1.38
0	428	Commercial Union Assurance	3395	1.38
0	48	Nationale Elf Aquitaine	3379	1.38
3	7	Deutsche Bank	3290	1.34
12	12	Mannesmann (Germany)	3268	1.33
0	1100	STET	3244	1.32
0	4	Publicitas Holding (Reg)	3162	1.29
1	1	Roche Holding (Gen)	3145	1.28
0	2	Allianz Holding (Reg)	3085	1.26
110	440	Legal & General Group	2974	1.21
0	60	Banque Nationale de Paris	2759	1.12

Index Allocation

	% of Stocks
S&P 500	1.3
S&P MidCap 400	1.0
U.S. Small Cap	0.0
Foreign	98.0

Composition % 12-31-94

Cash	2.8	Preferreds	3.3
Stocks	93.2	Convertibles	0.0
Bonds	0.0	Other	0.7

Tax Analysis

	Tax-Adj Historical Return %	% Pretax Return
3 Yr Avg	3.21	85.8
5 Yr Avg	3.28	82.0
10 Yr Avg	---	---
Potential Capital Gain Exposure (% of assets)		3%

Most Similar Funds in MF500

France Growth	Weak Fit
Irish Investment	Weak Fit
GT Greater Europe	Weak Fit

Country Exposure 12-31-94

	% of Stocks
United Kingdom	38
France	8
Switzerland	8
Netherlands	7
Italy	6

Total Number of Countries: 10
Hedging Policy: Occasional

Sector Weightings

	% of Stocks	Relative S&P 500
Utilities	9.6	1.22
Energy	8.0	1.65
Financials	17.6	0.91
Industrial Cyclicals	21.7	0.92
Consumer Durables	7.8	0.66
Consumer Staples	6.6	0.88
Services	11.2	0.97
Retail	6.1	1.05
Health	8.7	1.59
Technology	2.8	1.26

Expenses & Fees

Sales Fees	
	0.00% front
	0.00% deferred
	0.00% 12b-1
Management Fee	0.75% max./0.55% min., 0.02%A
3-,5-,10-yr Expense Projections	$41, $71, $155
Annual Brokerage Cost	0.06%

Min Initial Purchase	$1000 (Addt'l: $50)
Min IRA Purchase	$250 (Addt'l: $50)
Min Auto Invest Plan	$50 (Systematic Inv: $50)

MORNINGSTAR 1995 Mutual Fund 500

Invesco High-Yield

	Ticker	Load	NAV	Yield	SEC Yield	Assets	Objective
	FHYPX	None	6.38	10.2%	10.80%	210.8	Corp Hi Yld

Invesco High-Yield Fund seeks high current income. Capital appreciation is a secondary objective.

The fund invests virtually all of its assets in debt securities and preferred stocks. The fund primarily purchases medium- and lower-rated securities, but may also purchase unrated securities. In addition, the fund may invest in U.S. government securities or bank certificates of deposit to preserve liquidity or capital.

Prior to July 1, 1993, the fund was named Financial Bond Shares High-Yield Portfolio.

Manager's Investment Style

Since taking over in May 1994, manager Jerry Paul has repositioned the fund lower on the credit scale. He has strengthened the fund's focus on B issues, while cutting its BB stake severely and eliminating BBB credits entirely. In their place, he has some positions in nonrated and below-B debt. He buys bonds he believes will profit in one of two ways. First, he looks for companies with improving fundamentals. Second, he looks for special situations, where a company has upgrade or merger potential. Even if that never happens, he expects his insistence on sound balance sheets to come up with winners.

Fund Manager(s)

Jerry Paul CFA(1980), since 05-94. BBA, U. of Iowa MBA, U. of Northern Iowa

Manager Experience	Dates Managed	Invest Obj	Std Dev	+/- Index
Jerry Paul				
SteinRoe Income	01/87 - 01/90	CG	4.95	-0.77

Historical Profile
Return Average
Risk Low
Rating ★★★★ Above Average

| | 56 | 53 | 37 | 62 | 89 | 89 | 89 | 33 |

Investment Style History
Fixed Income
Income Rtn % Rank Obj

Growth of $10,000
||| Value of Fund ($000)
— Value of Index ($000) LB Agg
▼ Manager Change
▽ Partial Manager Change
► Mgr Unknown After
◄ Mgr Unknown Before

Performance Quartile (Within Objective)

1983	1984	1985	1986	1987	1988	1989	1990	1991	1992	1993	1994	History
---	7.51	8.37	8.38	7.75	7.82	7.16	6.00	6.66	6.97	7.43	6.38	NAV
---	11.65 *	26.45	14.64	3.61	13.44	3.69	-4.55	23.52	14.62	15.76	-4.98	Total Return %
---	---	4.32	-0.61	0.85	5.56	-10.85	-13.50	7.51	7.38	6.01	-2.07	+/- LB Aggregate
---	---	---	-0.99	-2.92	2.01	3.30	1.83	-20.24	-2.04	-3.14	-4.01	+/- FB High-Yield
---	11.55	15.02	12.36	11.13	12.53	12.13	11.65	12.51	9.97	9.16	8.78	Income Return %
---	0.11	11.43	2.28	-7.52	0.90	-8.44	-16.20	11.00	4.65	6.60	-13.76	Capital Return %
---	---	41	57	31	35	96	69	39	11	26	63	Total Rtn % Rank All
---	---	3	44	22	42	19	19	92	81	92	72	Total Rtn % Rank Obj
---	0.81	1.03	1.01	0.94	0.93	0.95	0.85	0.68	0.63	0.60	0.66	Income $
---	0.00	0.00	0.17	0.00	0.00	0.00	0.00	0.00	0.00	0.00	0.00	Capital Gains $
---	---	0.93	0.76	0.86	0.82	0.83	0.94	1.05	1.00	0.97	0.97	Expense Ratio %
---	---	12.97	11.35	11.22	11.72	12.27	12.57	10.57	9.29	8.28	8.70	Income Ratio %
---	---	96	134	89	42	53	28	64	120	68	195	Turnover Rate %
---	8.1	18.3	46.6	37.5	60.5	49.0	40.4	99.1	212.2	306.1	210.8	Net Assets ($mil)

Performance 12-31-94

	1st Qtr	2nd Qtr	3rd Qtr	4th Qtr	Total
1987	6.86	-1.24	-1.83	0.01	3.61
1988	5.58	3.89	1.94	1.46	13.44
1989	1.84	3.79	1.03	-2.90	3.69
1990	-3.44	4.01	-5.02	0.06	-4.55
1991	7.91	4.15	4.96	4.71	23.52
1992	4.13	2.98	4.61	2.18	14.62
1993	5.92	3.80	1.46	3.77	15.76
1994	-3.37	-1.22	1.09	-1.53	-4.99

Bear Market Performance
Decile Rank (5-year period)

Worst — Best

	Worst 3 Mo Period 1985-89	Worst 3 Mo Period 1990-94
Invesco High-Yield	-6.29	-8.96
+/- LB Aggregate	-7.11	-9.71
+/- Best Fit Index : FB HY	---	5.14

Trailing Returns
	Total Return %	+/- LB Aggregate	+/- FB High-Yield	% Rank All	% Rank Obj	Growth of $10,000
3 Mo	-1.53	-1.91	-1.49	57	59	9,847
6 Mo	-0.46	-1.45	-2.01	64	37	9,954
1 Yr	-4.98	-2.07	-4.01	63	72	9,502
3 Yr Avg	8.03	3.48	-3.13	21	91	12,607
5 Yr Avg	8.25	0.62	-4.83	30	92	14,863
10 Yr Avg	10.13	0.19	---	56	48	26,256
15 Yr Avg	---	---	---			

Operations

Address and Telephone	P.O. Box 173706 Denver, CO 80217-3706 800-525-8085 / 303-930-6300
Advisor	Invesco Funds Group
Subadvisor	Invesco Trust
Distributor	Invesco Funds Group
States Available	All plus GU,PR,VI
Report Grade	B-
Income Distrib	Paid Monthly
* Date of Inception	03-01-84
Fiscal Year End	August

Risk Analysis

Time Period	Load-Adj Return %	Risk % Rank [1] All	Obj	Morningstar [2] Return	Risk	Morningstar Risk-Adj Rating
1 Yr	-4.98					
3 Yr	8.03	11	64	1.34 [3]	0.40	★★★★
5 Yr	8.25	38	16	0.87 [3]	0.45	★★★★
10 Yr	10.13	21	6	0.68	0.38	★★★★
Average Historical Rating (94 months)					3.8	★s

[1] 1 = low, 100 = high [2] 1.00 = Hybrid Avg [3] 1.00 = 90-day T-bill return

Other Measures
	Standard LB Agg	Best Fit FB HY
Standard Deviation	4.75	
Mean	7.86	
Sharpe Ratio	0.91	
Alpha	3.7	-2.6
Beta	0.73	0.97
R-Squared	38	78

Investment Style
Interest-Rate Stance
Avg Effective Duration 5.2 Yrs
Avg Effective Maturity 9.2 Yrs

Maturity Short Intm Long
Quality High Med Low

Quality
Avg Credit Quality B
Avg Weighted Coupon 9.24%
Avg Weighted Price 87.00% of Par

Diversification Value for Portfolio Types
Large Cap: High | Small Cap: High | Bond: Medium | Balanced: Medium | Diversified: High

Portfolio 12-30-94

Total Stocks: 0
Total Fixed-Income: 68

Amount 000	Date of Maturity		Value $000	% Net Assets
8000	07-07-06	Viacom International 8%	6860	3.25
8500	02-01-04	Calpine 9.25%	6800	3.23
6900	02-01-06	Petroleum Heat & Power 9.375%	5865	2.78
5500	03-01-04	Jones Intercable 10.5%	5404	2.56
6930	06-30-00	Resorts International 0%	5254	2.49
5600	12-15-03	Act III Broadcasting 9.625%	5138	2.44
4923	11-01-00	Anacomp 15%	4972	2.36
5500	04-01-08	Cablevision Industries 9.25%	4923	2.34
5700	02-01-07	USA Mobile Communications 9.5%	4617	2.19
5000	12-15-08	Anchor Glass Container 9.875%	4338	2.06
4500	07-15-04	Moran Transportation 11.75%	4264	2.02
4300	11-01-03	Burlington Motor Hldgs 11.5%	4021	1.91
4000	11-15-19	NorAm Energy 10%	3999	1.90
4000	06-01-02	Petro PSC Properties 12.5%	3810	1.81
4000	06-15-04	Chattem 12.75%	3765	1.79
4000	05-15-04	JB Poindexter 12.5%	3720	1.76
4000	06-15-04	Plitt Theaters 10.875%	3700	1.76
7000	08-01-04	Marcus Cable 0%	3675	1.74
4500	04-01-03	Envirotest Systems 9.625%	3544	1.68
6500	02-01-04	Family Restaurants 0%	3510	1.67
4000	07-01-01	Presley 12.5%	3500	1.66
4000	12-15-03	Bally's Grand 10.375%	3460	1.64
3500	07-23-06	Midland Funding 13.25%	3431	1.63
4321	12-15-03	Sola Group 6%	3327	1.58
3395	05-15-01	Buckeye Cellulose 10.25%	3157	1.50

Composition % 12-31-94
Cash	10.5	Preferreds	0.0
Stocks	0.0	Convertibles	0.0
Bonds	89.5	Other	0.0

Tax Analysis
	Tax-Adj Historical Return %	% Pretax Return
3 Yr Avg	4.53	54.5
5 Yr Avg	4.55	51.3
10 Yr Avg	5.63	44.9
Potential Capital Gain Exposure (% of assets)		-12%

Most Similar Funds in MF500
American High-Income	Strong Fit
Vanguard F/I High-Yield Corp	Strong Fit
Phoenix High-Yield A	Strong Fit

Coupon Range
	% of Bonds	Rel Obj
0%, PIK	11.5	1.56
0% to 11%	58.4	1.19
11% to 13%	25.3	0.76
13% to 14.5%	2.3	0.43
More than 14.5%	2.4	1.52
Not applicable	0.0	0.00

Credit Analysis 12-31-94
% of Bonds
US Govt	0	BB	14
AAA	0	B	71
AA	0	Below B	12
A	0	NR/NA	3
BBB	0		

Expenses & Fees
Sales Fees	0.00% front, 0.00% deferred, 0.25% 12b-1
Management Fee	0.50% max./0.30% min., 0.02%A
3-,5-,10-yr Expense Projections	$31, $54, $119

Min Initial Purchase / etc.
Min Initial Purchase $1000 (Addt'l: $50)
Min IRA Purchase $250 (Addt'l: $50)
Min Auto Invest Plan $50 (Systematic Inv: $50)

Invesco Industrial Income

	Ticker	Load	NAV	Yield	SEC Yield	Assets	Objective
	FIIIX	None	10.52	3.7%	3.94%	3695.4	Equity-Inc.

Invesco Industrial Income Fund seeks current income; capital appreciation is a secondary consideration.

The fund normally invests between 60% and 75% of its assets in dividend-paying common stocks of domestic industrial issuers. It may also invest in convertible bonds, preferred stocks, and straight debt securities.

On Sept. 25, 1992, Commonwealth Balanced Fund merged into this fund. Prior to July 1, 1993, the fund was named Financial Industrial Income Fund.

Historical Profile

Return	Above Average
Risk	Below Average
Rating	★★★★
	Above Average

Investment Style History
Equity
Average % Stocks Held in Portfolio

72% 69% 69% 75% 75% 72% 70% 66%

Growth of $10,000
IIII Value of Fund ($000)
— Value of Index ($000)
S&P 500
▼ Manager Change
▽ Partial Manager Change
► Mgr Unknown After
◄ Mgr Unknown Before

Performance Quartile (Within Objective)

1983	1984	1985	1986	1987	1988	1989	1990	1991	1992	1993	1994	History
8.98	8.16	9.37	8.00	7.24	7.98	9.32	8.62	11.70	11.10	11.93	10.52	NAV
23.49	9.76	30.77	14.13	4.94	15.35	31.89	7.32	46.28	0.99	16.68	-3.88	Total Return %
1.03	3.50	-0.97	-4.55	-0.32	-1.27	0.21	10.43	15.79	-6.63	6.62	-5.20	+/- S&P 500
0.03	6.71	-1.79	-1.97	2.58	-2.60	2.72	13.50	12.07	-7.98	5.40	-3.81	+/- Wilshire 5000
5.87	6.97	6.21	4.75	4.24	5.12	5.05	4.37	3.46	2.75	3.87	3.61	Income Return %
17.62	2.79	24.56	9.38	0.70	10.22	26.84	2.95	42.81	-1.76	12.80	-7.49	Capital Return %
29	28	22	60	22	27	11	19	9	88	24	52	Total Rtn % Rank All
46	40	18	78	8	54	1	1	2	97	24	70	Total Rtn % Rank Obj
0.48	0.54	0.48	0.42	0.36	0.36	0.42	0.38	0.31	0.30	0.43	0.41	Income $
0.56	0.96	0.66	2.41	0.90	0.00	0.73	1.01	0.47	0.38	0.55	0.54	Capital Gains $
0.63	0.64	0.68	0.71	0.74	0.78	0.78	0.76	0.94	0.98	0.96	0.92	Expense Ratio %
5.48	5.92	5.72	4.85	3.96	4.29	5.08	4.14	3.92	2.75	2.94	3.11	Income Ratio %
57	54	54	160	195	148	124	132	104	119	121	56	Turnover Rate %
222.6	182.6	249.3	328.1	357.3	372.7	448.1	549.7	1596.7	2751.3	3905.8	3695.4	Net Assets ($mil)

Manager's Investment Style

A series of manager changes (including the firing of now-infamous John Kaweske) has left this fund's strategy slightly blurred. Currently, management generates yield through the bond portion (which may dip into noninvestment-grade issues) of the portfolio, while choosing growth-oriented, large-cap, capital-goods firms in the equity portion.

Fund Manager(s)

Charles P. Mayer, since 03-93. Birthdate: 06-48. BA, St. Peter's C. MS, St. John's U.

Jerry Paul CFA(1980), since 05-94. BBA, U. of Iowa MBA, U. of Northern Iowa

Manager Experience	Dates Managed	Invest Obj	Std Dev	+/- Index
Jerry Paul				
SteinRoe Income	01/87 - 01/90	CG	4.95	-0.77

Performance 12-31-94

	1st Qtr	2nd Qtr	3rd Qtr	4th Qtr	Total
1987	17.63	1.77	5.54	-16.94	4.94
1988	6.91	5.49	0.38	1.89	15.35
1989	6.27	8.96	11.94	1.76	31.89
1990	-3.33	14.45	-12.26	10.55	7.32
1991	16.82	2.00	11.91	9.70	46.28
1992	-4.02	-0.69	-0.94	6.95	0.99
1993	9.02	0.10	3.50	3.31	16.68
1994	-2.11	-1.37	1.21	-1.63	-3.88

Bear Market Performance

Decile Rank (5-year period)

Worst _____ Best

	Worst 3 Mo Period 1985-89	Worst 3 Mo Period 1990-94
Invesco Industrial Income	-23.39	-12.51
+/- S&P 500	6.19	1.34
+/- Best Fit Index : Wil 4500	6.75	6.90

Trailing Returns

	Total Return %	+/- S&P 500	+/- Wil 5000	% Rank All	% Rank Obj	Growth of $10,000
3 Mo	-1.63	-1.61	-0.86	60	27	9,837
6 Mo	-0.44	-5.30	-5.06	64	84	9,956
1 Yr	-3.88	-5.20	-3.81	52	70	9,612
3 Yr Avg	4.24	-2.03	-2.38	64	80	11,325
5 Yr Avg	12.20	3.51	3.38	8	1	17,778
10 Yr Avg	15.53	1.15	1.67	8	1	42,362
15 Yr Avg	15.41	0.93	1.43	10	15	85,815

Operations

Address and Telephone	P.O. Box 173706
	Denver, CO 80217-3706
	800-525-8085 / 303-930-6300
Advisor	Invesco Funds Group
Subadvisor	Invesco Trust
Distributor	Invesco Funds Group
States Available	All plus GU,PR,VI
Report Grade	B+
Income Distrib	Paid Quarterly
Date of Inception	02-01-60
Fiscal Year End	June

Risk Analysis

Time Period	Load-Adj Return %	Risk % Rank¹ All	Obj	Morningstar² Return	Morningstar Risk	Morningstar Risk-Adj Rating
1 Yr	-3.88					
3 Yr	4.24	64	78	0.19³	0.72	★★★
5 Yr	12.20	59	46	2.00³	0.69	★★★★
10 Yr	15.53	50	37	1.61	0.72	★★★★★

Average Historical Rating (109 months) 4.5 ★s

¹ 1 = low, 100 = high ² 1.00 = Equity Avg ³ 1.00 = 90-day T-bill return

Other Measures

	Standard S&P 500		Best Fit Wil 4500
Standard Deviation	7.32	Alpha	-1.2	-1.7
Mean	4.42	Beta	0.74	0.62
Sharpe Ratio	0.12	R-Squared	63	67

Investment Style

	Stock Portfolio Avg	Relative S&P 500
Price/Earnings Ratio	17.3	0.94
Price/Book Ratio	2.7	0.80
5 Yr Earnings Gr %	4.0	0.72
Return on Assets %	6.0	0.81
Debt % Total Cap	32.7	1.16
Med Mkt Cap ($mil)	8192	0.63

Style: Value Blend Growth / Size Large Med Small

Diversification Value for Portfolio Types

Large Cap:	Small Cap:	Bond:	Balanced:	Diversified:
Low	Low	Medium	Low	Low

Min Purchase

Min Initial Purchase	$1000 (Addt'l: $50)
Min IRA Purchase	$250 (Addt'l: $50)
Min Auto Invest Plan	$50 (Systematic Inv: $50)

Expenses & Fees

Sales Fees	0.00% front
	0.00% deferred
	0.25% 12b-1
Management Fee	0.60% max./0.50% min., 0.02%A
3-,5-,10-yr Expense Projections	$31, $53, $118
Annual Brokerage Cost	0.00%

Portfolio 12-30-94

Share Chg (09-94) 000	Amount 000	Total Stocks: 103 / Total Fixed-Income: 116	Value $000	% Net Assets
0	2400	Bank of New York	69600	1.98
	75000	US Treasury Note 5.875%	65414	1.86
-200	2000	El Paso Natural Gas	61000	1.73
100	700	IBM	51450	1.46
100	1000	AT & T	50250	1.43
0	1100	Cummins Engine	49775	1.41
0	1000	Chrysler	49000	1.39
25	725	Hilton Hotels	48847	1.39
100	800	Exxon	48600	1.38
0	800	El duPont de Nemours	45000	1.28
-100	300	McDonnell Douglas	42600	1.21
50	400	Atlantic Richfield	40700	1.16
	44348	FNMA 6.5%	40545	1.15
0	600	Deere	39750	1.13
0	800	Eaton	39600	1.12
-400	1400	Ford Motor	39200	1.11
0	1257	Kansas City Southern Inds	38810	1.10
0	800	Imperial Chemical Inds (ADR)	37200	1.06
0	300	General Re	37125	1.05
	37250	SLMA 5.8%	36993	1.05
0	800	Sears Roebuck	36800	1.04
	39554	FHLMC Gold 6.5%	35972	1.02
0	800	JC Penney	35700	1.01
0	1000	US West	35625	1.01
0	600	Amoco	35475	1.01

Composition % 12-31-94

Cash	4.0	Preferreds	0.0
Stocks	67.5	Convertibles	0.4
Bonds	28.1	Other	0.0

Tax Analysis

	Tax-Adj Historical Return %	% Pretax Return
3 Yr Avg	1.77	40.8
5 Yr Avg	9.11	70.3
10 Yr Avg	11.55	61.3
Potential Capital Gain Exposure (% of assets)		-1%

Most Similar Funds in MF500

Alliance Growth & Income A	Fair Fit
Janus	Fair Fit
CGM Mutual	Fair Fit

Index Allocation

	% of Stocks
S&P 500	79.8
S&P MidCap 400	9.3
U.S. Small Cap	6.3
Foreign	7.1

Sector Weightings

	% of Stocks	Relative S&P 500
Utilities	8.2	0.66
Energy	14.4	1.42
Financials	11.5	1.09
Industrial Cyclicals	20.4	1.24
Consumer Durables	8.8	1.41
Consumer Staples	6.6	0.52
Services	12.9	1.58
Retail	5.3	0.90
Health	4.9	0.56
Technology	7.3	0.80

Invesco Strategic Leisure

	Ticker	Load	NAV	Yield	SEC Yield	Assets	Objective
	FLISX	None	21.21	0.0%	N/A	262.8	Specialty

Invesco Strategic Portfolios Leisure seeks capital appreciation.

The fund normally invests at least 80% of its assets in the equity securities of companies engaged in providing and promoting leisure goods and activities. These companies may be involved in sporting goods, toys, photographic equipment, musical instruments, recordings, motion pictures, broadcasting, transportation, lodging, sports arenas, restaurants, or a variety of other businesses.

Prior to July 1, 1993, the fund was named Financial Strategic Portfolios Leisure Portfolio.

Manager's Investment Style

Management attempts to diversify this fund as much as possible under the leisure rubric, investing in everything from entertainment to restaurants to travel to food and beverages. Management prefers smaller companies and is willing to pay up for the high-growth rates its favored stocks carry. Recently the fund has been focused on multimedia stocks.

Fund Manager(s)

Timothy J. Miller CFA, since 02-92. BS, St. Louis U. MBA, U. of Missouri-St. Louis

Manager Experience

	Dates Managed	Invest Obj	Std Dev	+/- Index
Timothy J. Miller				
Invesco Strat Energy	10/92 - 05/94	SN	15.45	2.52

Performance 12-31-94

	1st Qtr	2nd Qtr	3rd Qtr	4th Qtr	Total
1987	21.70	0.38	7.73	-23.47	0.72
1988	14.10	8.58	3.04	0.67	28.53
1989	13.99	11.02	14.36	-4.46	38.27
1990	-5.23	9.55	-25.04	14.40	-10.97
1991	23.97	-0.07	9.54	12.53	52.71
1992	5.40	-4.46	4.42	17.38	23.41
1993	9.00	1.43	19.80	2.46	35.71
1994	-5.58	-5.37	7.79	-1.33	-4.98

Bear Market Performance

Decile Rank (5-year period)

	Worst 3 Mo Period 1985-89	Worst 3 Mo Period 1990-94
Invesco Strategic Leisure	-32.12	-25.04
+/- S&P 500	-2.54	-11.29
+/- Best Fit Index : Wil 4500	-1.98	-6.81

Trailing Returns

	Total Return %	+/- S&P 500	+/- Wil 5000	% Rank All	% Rank Obj	Growth of $10,000
3 Mo	-1.33	-1.32	-0.56	52	50	9,867
6 Mo	6.35	1.49	1.73	8	8	10,635
1 Yr	-4.98	-6.29	-4.91	63	40	9,502
3 Yr Avg	16.75	10.49	10.14	2	13	15,915
5 Yr Avg	16.69	8.00	7.88	3	1	21,637
10 Yr Avg	19.88	5.49	6.02	1	1	61,284
15 Yr Avg	---	---	---	---	---	---

Operations

Address and Telephone	P.O. Box 173706
	Denver, CO 80217-3706
	800-525-8085 / 303-930-6300
Advisor	Invesco Funds Group
Subadvisor	Invesco Trust
Distributor	Invesco Funds Group
States Available	All plus GU,PR,VI
Report Grade	B
Income Distrib	Paid Annually
* Date of Inception	01-19-84
Fiscal Year End	October

Historical Profile
Return	High
Risk	Average
Rating	★★★★★ Highest

Investment Style History
Equity
Average % Stocks Held in Portfolio

90% 80% 89% 83% 82% 87% 85% 80%

Growth of $10,000
|||| Value of Fund ($000)
— Value of Index ($000) Wil 4500
▼ Manager Change
▽ Partial Manager Change
► Mgr Unknown After
◄ Mgr Unknown Before

Performance Quartile (Within Objective)

	1983	1984	1985	1986	1987	1988	1989	1990	1991	1992	1993	1994	History
	---	8.43	11.18	10.69	9.29	11.94	14.34	11.93	15.94	18.55	23.28	21.21	NAV
	---	6.12 *	33.15	18.84	0.72	28.53	38.27	-10.97	52.71	23.41	35.71	-4.98	Total Return %
	---	1.20 *	1.41	0.16	-4.54	11.92	6.58	-7.85	22.22	15.80	25.65	-6.29	+/- S&P 500
	---	---	0.59	2.74	-1.64	10.58	9.09	-4.79	18.50	14.44	24.43	-4.91	+/- Wilshire 5000
	---	0.75	0.53	0.00	0.00	0.00	1.46	0.32	0.00	0.00	0.00	0.00	Income Return %
	---	5.38	32.62	18.84	0.72	28.53	36.81	-11.29	52.71	23.41	35.71	-4.98	Capital Return %
	---	---	16	27	54	4	5	86	7	2	5	63	Total Rtn % Rank All
	---	---	25	37	38	28	7	50	14	9	13	40	Total Rtn % Rank Obj
	---	0.06	0.04	0.00	0.00	0.00	0.21	0.03	0.00	0.00	0.00	0.00	Income $
	---	0.00	0.00	2.76	1.43	0.00	1.99	0.68	2.12	0.99	1.89	0.91	Capital Gains $
	---	1.50	1.50	1.50	1.50	1.89	1.38	1.84	1.86	1.51	1.14	---	Expense Ratio %
	---	---	0.57	-0.11	-0.37	0.16	1.44	0.10	-0.24	-0.33	-0.11	---	Income Ratio %
	---	---	160	458	376	136	119	89	122	148	116	---	Turnover Rate %
	---	0.4	1.2	2.3	2.4	4.1	8.6	7.1	17.9	79.3	304.5	262.8	Net Assets ($mil)

Risk Analysis

Time Period	Load-Adj Return %	Risk % Rank [1] All	Risk % Rank [1] Obj	Morningstar [2] Return	Morningstar Risk	Morningstar Risk-Adj Rating
1 Yr	-4.98					
3 Yr	16.75	68	18	4.31 [3]	0.76	★★★★★
5 Yr	16.69	81	44	3.49 [3]	0.98	★★★★★
10 Yr	19.88	82	25	2.84	1.05	★★★★★
Average Historical Rating (96 months)				4.4	★s	

[1] 1 = low, 100 = high [2] 1.00 = Equity Avg [3] 1.00 = 90-day T-bill return

Other Measures

	Standard S&P 500	Best Fit Wil 4500
Standard Deviation	12.13	Alpha 10.9 8.8
Mean	16.30	Beta 0.82 1.01
Sharpe Ratio	1.05	R-Squared 29 65

Investment Style

	Stock Portfolio Avg	Relative S&P 500
Price/Earnings Ratio	25.6	1.38
Price/Book Ratio	4.4	1.31
5 Yr Earnings Gr %	6.6#	1.19
Return on Assets %	6.4	0.86
Debt % Total Cap	39.7	1.41
Med Mkt Cap ($mil)	1965	0.15

Style
Value Blend Growth
Size: Large Med Small

figure is based on 50% or less of stocks

Diversification Value for Portfolio Types

Large Cap: Medium	Small Cap: Low	Bond: High	Balanced: Medium	Diversified: Medium

Min Initial Purchase / Fees

Min Initial Purchase	$1000 (Addt'l: $50)
Min IRA Purchase	$250 (Addt'l: $50)
Min Auto Invest Plan	$50 (Systematic Inv: $50)

Expenses & Fees

Sales Fees	0.00% front
	0.00% deferred
	0.00% 12b-1
Management Fee	0.75% max./0.55% min., 0.02%A
3-,5-,10-yr Expense Projections	$39, $68, $150
Annual Brokerage Cost	---

Portfolio 12-31-94

Share Chg (09-94) 000	Amount 000	Total Stocks: 64 / Total Fixed-Income: 0	Value $000	% Net Assets
0	186	Pulitzer Publishing	7463	2.84
0	194	Sierra On-Line	6631	2.53
0	200	Seagram	5900	2.25
0	250	Tele-Communications Cl A	5438	2.07
0	200	Heritage Media Cl A	5375	2.05
95	195	Starbucks	5363	2.04
0	156	AnnTaylor Stores	5352	2.04
0	144	Harcourt General	5076	1.93
0	75	McGraw-Hill	5016	1.91
0	140	Time Warner	4918	1.87
110	220	Carnival Cl A	4675	1.78
0	45	Verenigde Nederland Uitgever	4672	1.78
0	175	Hospitality Franchise System	4638	1.77
110	110	Nordstrom	4620	1.76
0	184	Mattel	4617	1.76
150	150	General Instrument	4500	1.71
0	80	LM Ericsson Telephone (ADR)	4410	1.68
0	65	Hilton Hotels	4379	1.67
0	191	Gaylord Entertainment Cl A	4338	1.65
163	163	Officemax	4306	1.64
50	50	Capital Cities/ABC	4263	1.62
0	175	Office Depot	4200	1.60
0	90	Walt Disney	4151	1.58
-3	193	La Quinta Inns	4115	1.57
-45	148	Renaissance Communications	4093	1.56

Composition % 12-31-94

Cash	21.4	Preferreds	0.0
Stocks	78.5	Convertibles	0.0
Bonds	0.0	Other	0.1

Tax Analysis

	Tax-Adj Historical Return %	% Pretax Return
3 Yr Avg	14.94	87.6
5 Yr Avg	14.41	82.5
10 Yr Avg	17.20	75.8
Potential Capital Gain Exposure (% of assets)		5%

Most Similar Funds in MF500

Acorn	Weak Fit
PIMCo Adv Opportunity C	Weak Fit
Oppenheimer Main St I&G A	Weak Fit

Index Allocation

	% of Stocks
S&P 500	37.1
S&P MidCap 400	7.0
U.S. Small Cap	41.4
Foreign	17.8

Sector Weightings

	% of Stocks	Relative S&P 500
Utilities	1.5	0.12
Energy	0.0	0.00
Financials	0.0	0.00
Industrial Cyclicals	2.3	0.14
Consumer Durables	7.1	1.15
Consumer Staples	6.3	0.50
Services	57.7	7.08
Retail	11.4	1.95
Health	0.0	0.00
Technology	13.7	1.50

Invesco Strategic Technology

	Ticker	Load	NAV	Yield	SEC Yield	Assets	Objective
	FTCHX	None	24.04	0.0%	N/A	310.1	Sp.-Tech

Invesco Strategic Portfolios Technology seeks capital appreciation.

The fund normally invests at least 80% of its assets in the equity securities of companies engaged in technology-related fields. These related areas may include computers, communications, video, electronics, oceanography, office and factory automation, and robotics. The fund will not invest more than 25% of its assets in any one technology-related industry.

Prior to July 1, 1993, the fund was named Financial Strategic Portfolios Technology Portfolio.

Manager's Investment Style

Manager Daniel Leonard looks at small- and mid-cap companies with rapid earnings acceleration. The fund's portfolio is usually loaded with tech stocks, but management will also hold stakes in firms indirectly linked to the technology industry.

Historical Profile

Return	High
Risk	High
Rating	★★★★★
	Highest

Investment Style History
Equity

Average % Stocks Held in Portfolio

Average % Stocks: 92% 94% 92% 93% 91% 94% 92% 95%

Growth of $10,000
- IIII Value of Fund ($000)
- — Value of Index ($000)
  Wil 4500
- ▼ Manager Change
- ▽ Partial Manager Change
- ► Mgr Unknown After
- ◄ Mgr Unknown Before

Performance Quartile (Within Objective)

	1983	1984	1985	1986	1987	1988	1989	1990	1991	1992	1993	1994	History
	---	6.93	8.85	9.67	9.15	10.45	12.69	13.78	19.62	23.31	23.59	24.04	NAV
	---	-13.13 *	27.71	21.82	-5.30	14.21	21.44	8.59	76.88	18.81	15.04	5.27	Total Return %
	---	-18.05 *	-4.03	3.14	-10.55	-2.40	-10.25	11.71	46.40	11.19	4.98	3.95	+/- S&P 500
	---	---	---	---	-12.67	12.55	22.81	6.47	62.80	14.68	-7.98	-11.28	+/- S&P Tech
	---	0.24	0.00	0.00	0.00	0.00	0.00	0.00	0.00	0.00	0.00	0.00	Income Return %
	---	-13.38	27.71	21.82	-5.29	14.21	21.44	8.59	76.88	18.81	15.03	5.27	Capital Return %
	---	---	34	14	89	30	32	11	1	6	28	4	Total Rtn % Rank All
	---	---	9	1	53	12	50	12	1	23	75	63	Total Rtn % Rank Obj
	---	0.02	0.00	0.00	0.00	0.00	0.00	0.00	0.00	0.00	0.00	0.00	Income $
	---	0.00	0.00	1.07	0.01	0.00	0.00	0.00	4.39	0.00	3.22	0.79	Capital Gains $
	---	1.50	1.50	1.50	1.47	1.72	1.59	1.25	1.19	1.12	1.13	---	Expense Ratio %
	---	---	0.03	-0.71	-0.68	-0.90	-0.62	-0.06	-0.53	-0.45	-0.69	---	Income Ratio %
	---	---	175	368	556	356	259	345	307	169	184	---	Turnover Rate %
	---	0.9	2.5	4.0	14.4	14.5	10.1	27.0	106.7	256.5	251.6	310.1	Net Assets ($mil)

Fund Manager(s)

Daniel B. Leonard, since 01-85. Birthdate: 05-36.
BA, Washington & Lee U. 1960 Business, New York U.

Manager Experience	Dates Managed	Invest Obj	Std Dev	+/- Index
Daniel B. Leonard				
Invesco Strat Envrnmt Svc	01/91 - 06/93	S	16.28	-25.58
Invesco Dynamics	01/88 - 10/89	AG	13.96	-2.67

Performance 12-31-94

	1st Qtr	2nd Qtr	3rd Qtr	4th Qtr	Total
1987	33.92	-0.39	3.95	-31.71	-5.30
1988	9.73	12.45	-8.06	0.67	14.21
1989	5.26	2.82	16.53	-3.72	21.44
1990	10.56	16.61	-28.55	17.88	8.59
1991	34.76	-7.92	23.51	15.41	76.88
1992	1.48	-9.84	5.07	23.60	18.81
1993	-6.65	10.62	11.92	-0.47	15.04
1994	-4.37	-4.17	10.64	3.82	5.27

Bear Market Performance

Decile Rank (5-year period)

Worst ____ Best

	Worst 3 Mo Period 1985-89	Worst 3 Mo Period 1990-94
Invesco Strategic Technology	-41.39	-28.55
+/- S&P 500	-11.81	-14.80
+/- Best Fit Index : Wil 4500	-11.25	-10.32

Trailing Returns

	Total Return %	+/- S&P 500	+/- S&P Tech	% Rank All	% Rank Obj	Growth of $10,000
3 Mo	3.82	3.83	-3.43	2	44	10,382
6 Mo	14.86	10.00	-2.61	3	60	11,486
1 Yr	5.27	3.95	-11.28	4	63	10,527
3 Yr Avg	12.89	6.62	-1.40	6	64	14,387
5 Yr Avg	22.54	13.85	10.84	1	18	27,633
10 Yr Avg	18.90	4.52	---	2	9	56,465
15 Yr Avg	---	---	---	---	---	---

Operations

Address and Telephone	P.O. Box 173706
	Denver, CO 80217-3706
	800-525-8085 / 303-930-6300
Advisor	Invesco Funds Group
Subadvisor	Invesco Trust
Distributor	Invesco Funds Group
States Available	All plus GU,PR,VI
Report Grade	B
Income Distrib	Paid Annually
* Date of Inception	01-19-84
Fiscal Year End	October

Risk Analysis

Time Period	Load-Adj Return %	Risk % Rank All [1]	Risk % Rank Obj [1]	Morningstar Return [2]	Morningstar Risk	Morningstar Risk-Adj Rating
1 Yr	5.27					
3 Yr	12.89	95	76	2.94 [3]	1.40	★★★★
5 Yr	22.54	94	50	5.80 [3]	1.29	★★★★★
10 Yr	18.90	96	63	2.53	1.42	★★★★★
Average Historical Rating (96 months)					3.4	★s

[1] 1 = low, 100 = high [2] 1.00 = Equity Avg [3] 1.00 = 90-day T-bill return

Other Measures

	Standard S&P 500		Best Fit Wil 4500
Standard Deviation	17.31	Alpha	6.9	3.5
Mean	13.68	Beta	1.19	1.57
Sharpe Ratio	0.59	R-Squared	30	79

Investment Style

	Stock Portfolio Avg	Relative S&P 500
Price/Earnings Ratio	23.7	1.28
Price/Book Ratio	4.0	1.17
5 Yr Earnings Gr %	11.3#	2.03
Return on Assets %	12.4	1.65
Debt % Total Cap	19.0	0.67
Med Mkt Cap ($mil)	2187	0.17

figure is based on 50% or less of stocks

Style: Value Blend Growth / Size Large Med Small

Diversification Value for Portfolio Types

Large Cap:	Small Cap:	Bond:	Balanced:	Diversified:
Medium	Low	High	Medium	Medium

Expenses & Fees

Min Initial Purchase	$1000 (Addt'l: $50)
Min IRA Purchase	$250 (Addt'l: $50)
Min Auto Invest Plan	$50 (Systematic Inv: $50)

Sales Fees: 0.00% front / 0.00% deferred / 0.00% 12b-1

Management Fee	0.75% max./0.55% min., 0.02%A
3-,5-,10-yr Expense Projections	$39, $68, $150
Annual Brokerage Cost	---

Portfolio 12-30-94

Share Chg (09-94) 000	Amount 000	Total Stocks: 85 / Total Fixed-Income: 5	Value $000	% Net Assets
175	373	Micron Technology	16437	5.30
100	200	IBM	14700	4.74
0	302	General Instrument	9060	2.92
250	250	Digital Equipment	8313	2.68
100	200	General Motors Cl E	7700	2.48
0	150	Computer Sciences	7650	2.47
-173	427	ICN Pharmaceuticals	7367	2.38
0	200	Sensormatic Electronics	7200	2.32
0	150	First Data	7106	2.29
13	263	National Data	6762	2.18
0	10	SAP	6615	2.13
100	100	First Financial Management	6163	1.99
50	150	Compaq Computer	5925	1.91
100	100	Amgen	5900	1.90
0	200	Ceridian	5375	1.73
150	150	Cisco Systems	5269	1.70
0	150	Analog Devices	5269	1.70
0	200	Komag	5225	1.68
150	150	Sierra On-Line	5138	1.66
100	100	Vishay Intertechnology	4900	1.58
23	123	Kent Electronics	4878	1.57
0	100	Computer Associates Intl	4850	1.56
0	198	Keane	4699	1.52
0	250	Read-Rite	4641	1.50
0	200	EMC	4325	1.39

Composition % 12-31-94

Cash	6.0	Preferreds	2.1
Stocks	91.8	Convertibles	0.0
Bonds	0.0	Other	0.0

Tax Analysis

	Tax-Adj Historical Return %	% Pretax Return
3 Yr Avg	11.27	86.1
5 Yr Avg	20.24	85.8
10 Yr Avg	17.54	86.8
Potential Capital Gain Exposure (% of assets)		12%

Most Similar Funds in MF500

AIM Constellation	Fair Fit
Hancock Special Equities A	Fair Fit
MFS Emerging Growth B	Fair Fit

Index Allocation

	% of Stocks
S&P 500	34.8
S&P MidCap 400	16.9
U.S. Small Cap	45.5
Foreign	2.7

Sector Weightings

	% of Stocks	Relative S&P 500
Utilities	0.0	0.00
Energy	0.0	0.00
Financials	0.4	0.04
Industrial Cyclicals	5.0	0.30
Consumer Durables	5.9	0.96
Consumer Staples	0.0	0.00
Services	3.7	0.46
Retail	0.0	0.00
Health	5.4	0.63
Technology	79.5	8.68

MORNINGSTAR 1995 Mutual Fund 500

Investment Company of America

	Ticker	Load	NAV	Yield	SEC Yield	Assets	Objective
	AIVSX	5.75%	17.67	2.6%	2.48%	19279.6	Growth/Inc.

Investment Company of America seeks long-term growth of capital and income.

The fund invests primarily in common stocks, but it may also invest in high-quality convertibles and debt securities. When choosing securities, management gives the possibility of appreciation and potential dividends more weight than current yield. Stocks are chosen from a list prepared by the fund's directors. The fund may invest in foreign issues.

Historical Profile
Return	Above Average
Risk	Below Average
Rating	★★★★ Above Average

Investment Style History
Equity
Average % Stocks Held in Portfolio

81% 79% 78% 75% 80% 78% 73% 76%

Growth of $10,000

|||| Value of Fund ($000)
— Value of Index ($000) S&P 500
▼ Manager Change
▽ Partial Manager Change
►◄ Mgr Unknown After
◄■ Mgr Unknown Before

Performance Quartile (Within Objective)

Manager's Investment Style

Management divides assets between several managers and one team of analysts; each portion is invested independently of the others. All of the managers operate under a growth-at-a-reasonable price discipline which, lately, has led to a low-turnover, blue-chip focus. In addition, management boosts income by overweighting bonds relative to the fund's objective.

1983	1984	1985	1986	1987	1988	1989	1990	1991	1992	1993	1994	History
11.26	11.00	13.51	13.19	12.61	12.94	15.24	14.52	17.48	17.89	18.72	17.67	NAV
20.18	6.79	33.31	21.81	5.51	13.34	29.41	0.68	26.54	6.99	11.62	0.15	Total Return %
-2.28	0.52	1.57	3.13	0.25	-3.27	-2.28	3.80	-3.94	-0.63	1.56	-1.16	+/- S&P 500
-3.28	3.74	0.75	5.71	3.15	-4.61	0.23	6.86	-7.66	-1.98	0.34	0.22	+/- Wilshire 5000
4.35	4.33	4.19	3.36	3.77	4.46	4.38	3.99	3.05	2.77	2.63	2.60	Income Return %
15.83	2.45	29.12	18.45	1.74	8.87	25.02	-3.31	23.49	4.22	8.99	-2.45	Capital Return %
39	44	15	14	20	36	14	53	33	58	54	18	Total Rtn % Rank All
57	33	12	13	22	66	21	13	63	58	42	38	Total Rtn % Rank Obj
0.44	0.44	0.44	0.44	0.52	0.56	0.59	0.59	0.44	0.47	0.47	0.48	Income $
0.45	0.51	0.49	2.45	0.75	0.76	0.85	0.22	0.38	0.42	0.75	0.60	Capital Gains $
0.44	0.47	0.43	0.41	0.42	0.48	0.52	0.55	0.59	0.58	0.59	---	Expense Ratio %
4.03	3.98	3.80	3.47	3.14	3.78	4.11	3.95	3.29	3.06	3.03	---	Income Ratio %
18	20	18	11	12	16	18	11	6	10	18	---	Turnover Rate %
2359.9	2402.4	3073.0	3730.0	3888.5	4119.0	5376.2	5922.8	10525.9	15428.4	19005.0	19279.6	Net Assets ($mil)

Fund Manager(s)
Management Team

Manager Experience
	Dates Managed	Invest Obj	Std Dev	+/- Index
Jon B. Lovelace, Jr.				
New Perspective	03/73 - 12/94	WW	14.55	3.08
American Mutual	12/83 - 12/94	GI	11.19	-1.26

Performance 12-31-94
	1st Qtr	2nd Qtr	3rd Qtr	4th Qtr	Total
1987	16.76	3.70	7.07	-18.62	5.51
1988	3.52	6.46	0.90	1.92	13.34
1989	6.90	8.85	10.24	0.89	29.41
1990	-2.02	5.67	-10.84	9.07	0.68
1991	12.12	-0.70	6.19	7.04	26.54
1992	-2.00	1.82	4.01	3.09	6.99
1993	3.47	1.14	3.30	3.24	11.62
1994	-3.71	1.15	3.93	-1.07	0.15

Bear Market Performance
Decile Rank (5-year period)

Worst _____ Best

	Worst 3 Mo Period 1985-89	Worst 3 Mo Period 1990-94
Investment Company of Americ	-24.68	-10.84
+/- S&P 500	4.90	2.91
+/- Best Fit Index : S&P 500	4.90	2.91

Trailing Returns
	Total Return %	+/- S&P 500	+/- Wil 5000	% Rank All	% Rank Obj	Growth of $10,000
3 Mo	-1.07	-1.05	-0.30	46	43	9,894
6 Mo	2.82	-2.04	-1.80	22	46	10,282
1 Yr	0.15	-1.16	0.22	18	38	10,015
3 Yr Avg	6.15	-0.12	-0.47	32	45	11,960
5 Yr Avg	8.79	0.10	-0.03	25	28	15,237
10 Yr Avg	14.37	-0.01	0.51	15	10	38,288
15 Yr Avg	14.90	0.42	0.92	14	8	80,294

Operations
Address and Telephone	333 S. Hope Street
	Los Angeles, CA 90071
	800-421-4120 / 213-486-9200
Advisor	Capital Research & Management
Subadvisor	None
Distributor	American Funds Distributors
States Available	All plus GU,PR,VI
Report Grade	A-
Income Distrib	Paid Quarterly
Date of Inception	01-01-34
Fiscal Year End	December

Risk Analysis
Time Period	Load-Adj Return %	Risk % Rank [1] All	Obj	Morningstar [2] Return	Morningstar Risk	Morningstar Risk-Adj Rating
1 Yr	-5.61					
3 Yr	4.07	63	38	0.14 [3]	0.70	★★★
5 Yr	7.51	59	22	0.68 [3]	0.69	★★★
10 Yr	13.69	49	25	1.21	0.71	★★★★
Average Historical Rating (109 months):					4.2	★ s

[1] 1 = low, 100 = high [2] 1.00 = Equity Avg [3] 1.00 = 90-day T-bill return

Other Measures
				Standard S&P 500	Best Fit S&P 500
Standard Deviation	7.43	Alpha		0.1	0.1
Mean	6.26	Beta		0.91	0.91
Sharpe Ratio	0.37	R-Squared		95	95

Investment Style
	Stock Portfolio Avg	Relative S&P 500	Style Value Blend Growth
Price/Earnings Ratio	17.7	0.96	
Price/Book Ratio	3.4	1.01	
5 Yr Earnings Gr %	3.8	0.68	
Return on Assets %	6.2	0.83	
Debt % Total Cap	31.5	1.11	
Med Mkt Cap ($mil)	10862	0.84	

Diversification Value for Portfolio Types
Large Cap: None	Small Cap: Medium	Bond: Medium	Balanced: None	Diversified: Low

Expenses & Fees
Sales Fees	5.75% front
	0.00% deferred
	0.25% 12b-1
Management Fee	0.39% max./0.24% min.
3-,5-,10-yr Expense Projections	$75, $89, $127
Annual Brokerage Cost	0.06%

Portfolio 09-30-94
Share Chg (06-94) 000	Amount 000	Total Stocks: 168 / Total Fixed-Income: 8	Value $000	% Net Assets
0	5635	FNMA	443756	2.28
0	3890	Royal Dutch Petroleum	417689	2.15
0	6700	Philip Morris	409538	2.11
2990	5980	Caterpillar	323668	1.66
0	4645	IBM	322828	1.66
0	9081	Time Warner	318970	1.64
1680	12141	Tele-Communications Cl A	268617	1.38
-875	4500	El duPont de Nemours	261000	1.34
0	5600	BankAmerica	247100	1.27
-1166	8925	MCI Communications	226472	1.16
-400	7550	WMX Technologies	218006	1.12
0	3895	AT & T	210330	1.08
875	7025	Banc One	209872	1.08
388	5900	Merck	209450	1.08
-150	3225	Telefonos de Mexico L (ADR)	201563	1.04
60	1410	LIN Broadcasting	195934	1.01
-100	6400	GTE	194400	1.00
-475	1900	American Cyanamid	189050	0.97
0	3250	Schlumberger	176719	0.91
0	2175	First Interstate Bancorp	176447	0.91
0	5124	Phillips Petroleum	175487	0.90
0	2955	Amoco	175084	0.90
3648	5472	Vodafone Group (ADR)	171684	0.88
0	5250	Compaq Computer	171281	0.88
-100	1570	Xerox	167598	0.86

Composition % 12-31-94
Cash	10.3	Preferreds	0.0	
Stocks	75.9	Convertibles	1.4	
Bonds	12.5	Other	0.0	

Tax Analysis
	Tax-Adj Historical Return %	% Pretax Return
3 Yr Avg	4.30	68.7
5 Yr Avg	6.97	76.5
10 Yr Avg	11.58	70.4
Potential Capital Gain Exposure (% of assets)		16%

Most Similar Funds in MF500
Vanguard Index 500	Strong Fit
Massachusetts Inv A	Strong Fit
Dean Witter Dividend Growth	Strong Fit

Index Allocation
	% of Stocks
S&P 500	86.2
S&P MidCap 400	1.1
U.S. Small Cap	5.2
Foreign	10.8

Sector Weightings
	% of Stocks	Relative S&P 500
Utilities	10.6	0.86
Energy	9.7	0.96
Financials	19.6	1.86
Industrial Cyclicals	16.3	0.99
Consumer Durables	3.0	0.48
Consumer Staples	6.1	0.49
Services	15.5	1.90
Retail	1.5	0.25
Health	7.9	0.91
Technology	9.9	1.08

Min Purchase
Min Initial Purchase	$250 (Addt'l: $50)
Min IRA Purchase	$250 (Addt'l: $50)
Min Auto Invest Plan	$50 (Systematic Inv: $50)

Irish Investment

	Ticker	NAV	Mkt Price	Prem/Disc	Yield	Objective
	IRL	$10.27	$8.63	-16.0%	0.0%	Europe Stock

					Highest Prem/Disc
-14.4	-14.8	-9.9	-2.8	-2.4	Highest Prem/Disc
-30.3	-25.9	-22.8	-18.6	-16.0	Lowest Prem/Disc

Irish Investment Fund seeks long-term capital appreciation.

Normally, the fund invests at least 65% of total assets in equity securities of Irish companies. It can invest the balance of assets in fixed-income securities or equity securities of companies domiciled outside Ireland that are likely to be affected by Ireland's international economic relations.

Board members serve staggered terms to discourage takeover attempts; additionally, the fund has supermajority voting requirements for open-ending, merging, or dissolving.

Historical Profile
Return Below Average
Risk Average
Rating ★★ Below Average

Growth of $10,000
■ at NAV ($000)
— at Market Price ($000)

Premium Discount %

	1983	1984	1985	1986	1987	1988	1989	1990	1991	1992	1993	1994	History
	---	---	---	---	---	---	---	9.12	9.74	7.84	9.86	10.27	NAV
	---	---	---	---	---	---	---	-15.24*	11.28	-17.15	26.79	5.43	NAV Total Return %
	---	---	---	---	---	---	---	-15.13*	-19.21	-24.76	16.73	4.11	+/- S&P 500
	---	---	---	---	---	---	---	---	-0.85	-4.97	-5.78	-2.35	+/- MSCI EAFE
	---	---	---	---	---	---	---	---	1.67	6.22	-12.13	-6.48	+/- MSCI Ireland
	---	---	---	---	---	---	---	3.04*	4.48	2.36	1.02	0.00	Income Return %
	---	---	---	---	---	---	---	-18.28*	6.80	-19.51	25.77	5.43	Capital Return %
	---	---	---	---	---	---	---	---	80	97	18	6	Total Rtn % Rank All
	---	---	---	---	---	---	---	---	10	63	73	21	Total Rtn % Rank Obj
	---	---	---	---	---	---	---	-37.34*	9.59	-10.57	40.76	-5.62	Market Total Rtn %
	---	---	---	---	---	---	---	-21.2	-19.9	-16.8	-9.8	-10.3	Avg Prem/Disc %
	---	---	---	---	---	---	---	0.33	0.42	0.23	0.07	0.00	Income $
	---	---	---	---	---	---	---	0.00	0.00	0.00	0.00	0.11	Capital Gains $
	---	---	---	---	---	---	---	1.70	2.03	1.80	1.88	1.87	Expense Ratio %
	---	---	---	---	---	---	---	4.28	1.55	1.62	1.39	0.93	Income Ratio %
	---	---	---	---	---	---	---	6	28	7	15	13	Turnover Rate %
	---	---	---	---	---	---	---	45.7	48.8	39.3	49.4	51.4	Net Assets ($mil)

Manager's Investment Style
Management tries to fairly represent the Irish market. As such, it doesn't make wily sector shifts; it's primarily a buy-and-hold investor, in part because of illiquidity in the Irish market. Management has been willing, however, to nip and tuck the portfolio, depending on market conditions. To take advantage of a growing economy, for instance, management will add to its cyclical positions and trim back in its food stocks. The fund cannot invest in Bank of Ireland, because it is the advisor's parent.

Fund Manager(s)
Jane Neill. Since 6-94.

Manager Experience
	Dates Managed	Invest Obj	Std Dev	+/- Index
Not available.

NAV Performance % 12-30-94
	1st Qtr	2nd Qtr	3rd Qtr	4th Qtr	Total
1987	---	---	---	---	---
1988	---	---	---	---	---
1989	---	---	---	---	---
1990	---	---	-16.91	2.37	-15.24*
1991	6.69	-8.84	12.40	1.79	11.28
1992	-5.44	3.91	-7.11	-9.22	-17.15
1993	10.46	2.66	4.61	6.88	26.79
1994	3.75	-4.30	10.21	-3.66	5.43

Bear Market Performance
Decile Rank (5-year period)

Worst — Best

	Worst 3 Mo Period 1985-89	Worst 3 Mo Period 1990-94
Irish Investment	---	---
+/- S&P 500	---	---

Trailing Returns
	NAV Total Return %	+/- S&P 500	+/- MSCI Ireland	% Rank All	% Rank Obj	Mkt Total Return %
3 Mo	-3.66	-3.64	-3.74	77	65	-15.86
6 Mo	6.18	1.32	-6.25	8	26	4.24
1 Yr	5.43	4.11	-6.48	6	21	-5.62
3 Yr Avg	3.46	-2.80	-2.55	83	57	5.91
5 Yr Avg	---	---	---	---	---	---
Incept Avg	0.92*	---	---	---	---	-4.19*

Operations
Address and Telephone	Exchange Place-EX04B, Boston, MA 02109, 800-468-6475
Advisor	Bank of Ireland Asset Mgmt. Ltd.
Subadvisor	Salomon Brothers Asset Mgmt.
Administrator	Boston Company Advisors, Inc.
Transfer Agent	American Stock Transfer & Trust
Custodian	Bank of Ireland
Auditor	Price Waterhouse LLP
Legal Counsel	Sullivan & Cromwell

Income Distrib Schedule	Paid Annually
Management Fee	1.00%, 0.08%A
Reinvestment Plan	Yes
Direct Purchase Plan	Yes
Shares Outstanding	5,009,000
Exchange	NYSE
*Date of Inception	03-30-90
Shareholder Report	C+

Risk Analysis
	Risk % Rank¹ All	Obj	Morningstar² Return	Risk	Morningstar Risk-Adj Rating
3 Yr	88	52	-0.02	1.02	★★
5 Yr	---	---	---	---	---
10 Yr	---	---	---	---	---

Average Historical Rating (21 months) 2.0 ★s

¹1 = Low, 100 = High ²1.00 = Equity Avg ³1.00 = 90-day T-bill Return

Other Measures
			S&P 500
Standard Deviation	17.23	Alpha	-1.61
Mean	4.85	Beta	1.02
Sharpe Ratio	0.08	R-Squared	22

Investment Style
	Stock Portfolio Avg	Rel WS Ireland	Rel WS Foreign
Price/Earnings Ratio	12.8	0.85	0.26
Price/Cash Flow Ratio	10.9	0.89	0.75
Price/Book Ratio	2.2	0.93	0.73
5 Yr Earnings Gr %	-1.0	NMF	NMF
Return on Assets %	5.8	1.78	1.26
Debt % Total Cap	32.3	0.92	1.00
Med Mkt Cap ($mil)	890	0.46	0.14

figure is based on less than 50% of stocks

Country Exposure (top five) 12-31-94
	Securities %		Currency %
Ireland	96	Ireland	96
UK	2	UK	2
US	2	US	2

Diversification Value for Portfolio Types
Large Cap: High Small Cap: High Bond: High Balanced: High Diversified: Medium

Portfolio 10-31-94
Total Equity: 31
Total Fixed-Income: 2

Share Chg (07-94)	Amount		Value $000	% Total Invest
150000	1885333	Allied Irish Banks	7678	14.06
100000	1207200	Jefferson Smurfit Group	7287	13.35
250000	1048036	CRH (Ireland)	5854	10.72
-20000	655000	Independent Newspapers (Ire)	3057	5.60
-150000	465000	Kerry Group Cl A	2582	4.73
0	800000	Irish Life Assurance	2447	4.48
0	1135000	Fyffes	1863	3.41
0	344943	Irish Wire Products Intl A	1804	3.30
0	347625	James Crean	1483	2.72
0	300000	Unidare	1400	2.56
0	557356	Jury's Hotel Group	1391	2.55
-100000	218168	Greencore	1352	2.48
0	298850	Clondalkin Group	1323	2.42
0	525000	Green Property Group	1310	2.40
0	500000	Kingspan Group	1086	1.99
0	1000356	Barlo Group	1079	1.98
0	732156	Waterford Foods Cl A	1061	1.94
0	234000	Boxmore Intl (Ireland)	1040	1.90
0	495000	Abbey	1036	1.90
0	214571	CBT Group	966	1.77
0	1000000	Anglo Irish Bank	885	1.62
0	130000	Grand Metropolitan	882	1.62
0	105000	Inishtech Capital Fund	693	1.27
0	260000	FBD Holdings	670	1.23
0	200000	Hibernian Group	612	1.12

Composition % 12-31-94
Cash	0.0	Preferreds	0.0
Stocks	100.0	Convertibles	0.0
Bonds	0.0	Other	0.0

Tax Analysis
	Tax-Adj Historical Return %	% Pretax Return
3 Yr Avg	2.95	84.9
5 Yr Avg	---	---
10 Yr Avg	---	---

Potential Capital Gain Exposure (% of assets) -8

Most Similar Funds in MF500
Invesco European	Weak Fit
Growth Fund Spain	Weak Fit
GT Greater Europe	Weak Fit

Sector Weightings
	% of Stocks
Utilities	0.0
Energy	0.9
Financials	28.5
Industrial Cyclicals	34.6
Consumer Durables	2.0
Consumer Staples	21.5
Services	11.3
Retail	0.4
Health	0.9
Technology	0.0

Jakarta Growth

	Ticker	NAV	Mkt Price	Prem/Disc	Yield	Objective
	JGF	$8.62	$9.00	4.4%	0.3%	Pacific/Asia

Jakarta Growth Fund seeks long-term capital appreciation. Current income is incidental.

Under normal conditions, the fund will invest at least 65% of its assets in companies listed on the Jakarta Stock Exchange. The fund will invest the balance of assets in rupiah-denominated or U.S.-dollar-denominated fixed-income securities.

The fund has supermajority voting requirements designed to discourage a third party from attempting to assume control: A 75% vote of outstanding shares is necessary to remove directors, authorize a merger or liquidation, or convert to an open-end fund.

26.5	8.9	23.2	34.9	24.9	Highest Prem/Disc
-30.3	-19.9	-7.9	-2.4	-1.2	Lowest Prem/Disc

Historical Profile
Return Above Average
Risk Average
Rating ★★★
Neutral

Growth of $10,000
— at NAV ($000)
— at Market Price ($000)

Premium Discount %

	1983	1984	1985	1986	1987	1988	1989	1990	1991	1992	1993	1994	History
	---	---	---	---	---	---	---	8.79	6.19	6.28	10.19	8.62	NAV
	---	---	---	---	---	---	---	-19.77*	-27.86	2.65	62.97	-15.11	NAV Total Return %
	---	---	---	---	---	---	---	-20.20*	-58.35	-4.97	52.92	-16.43	+/- S&P 500
	---	---	---	---	---	---	---	---	-39.99	14.83	30.41	-22.89	+/- MSCI EAFE
	---	---	---	---	---	---	---	---	18.57	4.77	-39.21	11.87	+/- MSCI Indonesia
	---	---	---	---	---	---	---	1.47*	1.40	1.20	0.41	0.29	Income Return %
	---	---	---	---	---	---	---	-21.24*	-29.26	1.45	62.56	-15.41	Capital Return %
	---	---	---	---	---	---	---	---	100	81	5	83	Total Rtn % Rank All
	---	---	---	---	---	---	---	---	93	40	50	60	Total Rtn % Rank Obj
	---	---	---	---	---	---	---	-40.58*	-15.75	25.38	94.10	-34.32	Market Total Rtn %
	---	---	---	---	---	---	---	-5.9	-3.7	8.5	13.0	9.2	Avg Prem/Disc %
	---	---	---	---	---	---	---	0.14	0.12	0.08	0.04	0.03	Income $
	---	---	---	---	---	---	---	0.00	0.05	0.00	0.02	0.00	Capital Gains $
	---	---	---	---	---	---	---	1.83	2.15	2.06	1.88	1.84	Expense Ratio %
	---	---	---	---	---	---	---	2.30	0.63	1.06	0.36	1.36	Income Ratio %
	---	---	---	---	---	---	---	---	24	35	42	---	Turnover Rate %
	---	---	---	---	---	---	---	44.0	31.0	31.4	51.1	43.2	Net Assets ($mil)

Manager's Investment Style

A new year brought new management to this fund. Previously, management underweighted or overweighted sectors based on Indonesia's economic outlook. For example, the fund has carried a below-market weighting in textiles, which have suffered in the past as competition has heated up, and has instead favored cyclicals to play robust domestic growth. Management favored Indonesian securities and did not foray into other markets.

Fund Manager(s)

Iwao Komatsu. Since 1-95. BA'61 Tokoyo U.

Manager Experience

	Dates Managed	Invest Obj	Std Dev	+/- Index
Not available.				

NAV Performance % 12-30-94

	1st Qtr	2nd Qtr	3rd Qtr	4th Qtr	Total
1987	---	---	---	---	---
1988	---	---	---	---	---
1989	---	---	---	---	---
1990	---	-2.15*	-12.91	-5.85	-19.77*
1991	-3.19	-4.99	-19.22	-2.91	-27.86
1992	4.68	10.96	-3.34	-8.57	2.65
1993	14.81	7.63	6.57	23.76	62.97
1994	-8.83	-7.53	10.59	-8.95	-15.11

Bear Market Performance

Decile Rank (5-year period)

Worst — Best

	Worst 3 Mo Period 1985-89	Worst 3 Mo Period 1990-94
Jakarta Growth	---	---
+/- S&P 500	---	---

Trailing Returns

	NAV Total Return %	+/- S&P 500	+/- MSCI Indonesia	% Rank All	% Rank Obj	Mkt Total Return %
3 Mo	-8.95	-8.93	3.48	92	61	-18.82
6 Mo	0.70	-4.16	7.11	31	40	6.25
1 Yr	-15.11	-16.43	11.87	83	60	-34.32
3 Yr Avg	12.40	6.14	-0.65	12	66	16.87
5 Yr Avg	---	---	---	---	---	---
Incept Avg	-4.08*	---	---	---	---	-4.68*

Risk Analysis

	Risk % Rank[1] All	Obj	Morningstar[2] Return	Risk	Morningstar Risk-Adj Rating
3 Yr	90	26	1.23	1.08	★★★
5 Yr	---	---	---	---	
10 Yr	---	---	---	---	

Average Historical Rating (21 months)   2.0 ★s

[1] 1 = Low, 100 = High   [2] 1.00 = Equity Avg   [3] 1.00 = 90-day T-bill Return

Other Measures

				S&P 500
Standard Deviation	19.24	Alpha		7.07
Mean	13.59	Beta		1.12
Sharpe Ratio	0.52	R-Squared		21

Investment Style

	Stock Portfolio Avg	Rel WS Indonesia	Rel WS Foreign
Price/Earnings Ratio	23.3#	0.69	0.47
Price/Cash Flow Ratio	12.0#	0.88	0.82
Price/Book Ratio	3.2#	0.81	1.06
5 Yr Earnings Gr %	---	---	---
Return on Assets %	---	---	---
Debt % Total Cap	21.8#	0.95	0.67
Med Mkt Cap ($mil)	292#	0.30	0.05

figure is based on less than 50% of stocks

Country Exposure (top five) 12-31-94

	Securities %		Currency %
Indonesia	92	Indonesia	100

Diversification Value for Portfolio Types

Large Cap: High	Small Cap: High	Bond: High	Balanced: High	Diversified: High

Operations

Address and Telephone	180 Maiden Lane
	New York, NY 10038
	212-509-8181
Advisor	Nomura Investment Mgmt.
Subadvisor	N/A
Administrator	N/A
Transfer Agent	State Street Bank and Trust Co.
Custodian	Brown Brothers Harriman & Co.
Auditor	Price Waterhouse LLP
Legal Counsel	Brown & Wood

Income Distrib Schedule	Paid Annually
Management Fee	1.10%
Reinvestment Plan	Yes
Direct Purchase Plan	No
Shares Outstanding	5,012,819
Exchange	NYSE
*Date of Inception	04-19-90
Shareholder Report	B+

Portfolio 09-30-94

Share Chg (06-94)	Amount	Total Equity: 40 Total Fixed-Income: 0	Value $000	% Total Invest
375000	875000	HM Sampoerna	3719	7.86
740000	1000000	Astra International	2206	4.66
-138000	906000	Dynaplast	2082	4.40
240000	540000	Semen Cibinong	2035	4.30
0	352500	Gudang Garam	1928	4.07
-139500	1060500	Gadjah Tunggal	1815	3.84
-163000	800000	Trias Sentosa	1691	3.57
0	388000	Indorama Synthetics	1569	3.32
-233000	350200	Kalbe Farma	1368	2.89
-9000	160000	Multi-Bintang	1323	2.80
-72104	250296	Mayora Indah	1323	2.80
0	336500	Petrosea	1299	2.74
0	700000	Panin Bank	1279	2.70
0	300000	Tigarausa Satria	1241	2.62
0	500000	Tjiwi Kimia	1218	2.57
-111000	400000	Bank Bali	1094	2.31
-60000	300000	Bank International Indonesia	1089	2.30
0	250000	Charoen Pokphand Indonesia	1080	2.28
-200000	316000	Intl Nickel Indonesia	944	1.99
0	360000	United Tractor	914	1.93
150500	619500	Barito Pacific Timber	904	1.91
0	150000	Semen Gresik (For)	844	1.78
-78000	300000	Intl Indorayon Utama	772	1.63
0	560000	Berlian Laju Tanker	721	1.52
0	684500	Metrodata Electronics	716	1.51

Composition % 12-31-94

Cash	8.0	Preferreds	0.0
Stocks	92.0	Convertibles	0.0
Bonds	0.0	Other	0.0

Tax Analysis

	Tax-Adj Historical Return %	% Pretax Return
3 Yr Avg	12.16	97.8
5 Yr Avg	---	---
10 Yr Avg	---	---
Potential Capital Gain Exposure (% of assets)		-18

Sector Weightings

	% of Stocks
Utilities	3.7
Energy	0.0
Financials	7.0
Industrial Cyclicals	32.4
Consumer Durables	12.4
Consumer Staples	21.8
Services	7.0
Retail	6.2
Health	7.5
Technology	2.0

Most Similar Funds in MF500

Mexico Fund	Weak Fit
Fidelity Global Bond	Weak Fit
Templeton Real Estate Secs	Weak Fit

Janus Enterprise

Janus Enterprise Fund seeks growth of capital consistent with preservation of capital. Income is incidental.

The fund invests primarily in common stocks of companies with market capitalizations between $1 billion and $5 billion, although it may also invest in larger or smaller companies. It may also, to a lesser degree, invest in preferred stock, ADRs, convertibles, corporate and government debt securities, and cash equivalents. The fund may invest in special situations from time to time. It may invest without limit in foreign securities.

Manager's Investment Style

Management has fashioned a concentrated portfolio of lesser-known companies that it considers to have superior earnings-growth potential and pricing power. It also searches for a catalyst--such as expanding market share--that will drive the growth. The fund's concentrated holdings--the top-10 holds have, at times, consumed nearly half of the fund's assets--make it a volatile holding.

Fund Manager(s)

James P. Goff CFA, since 09-92. Birthdate: 03-64.
BA, Yale 1986

Manager Experience	Dates Managed	Invest Obj	Std Dev	+/- Index
James P. Goff				
Sierra Emerging Growth A	09/93 - 12/94	SC	13.72	2.62
Janus Venture	12/93 - 12/94	SC	11.09	4.15

Performance 12-31-94

	1st Qtr	2nd Qtr	3rd Qtr	4th Qtr	Total
1987	---	---	---	---	---
1988	---	---	---	---	---
1989	---	---	---	---	---
1990	---	---	---	---	---
1991	---	---	---	---	---
1992	---	---	---	24.58	29.73 *
1993	3.24	-1.00	7.85	4.93	15.67
1994	-4.24	-2.48	11.77	4.35	8.92

Bear Market Performance

Decile Rank (5-year period)

Worst ——————————————— Best

	Worst 3 Mo Period 1985-89	Worst 3 Mo Period 1990-94
Janus Enterprise	---	---
+/- S&P 500	---	---
+/- Best Fit Index :	---	---

Trailing Returns

	Total Return %	+/- S&P 500	+/- Wil 5000	% Rank All	% Rank Obj	Growth of $10,000
3 Mo	4.35	4.37	5.12	2	2	10,435
6 Mo	16.63	11.77	12.01	2	2	11,663
1 Yr	8.92	7.60	8.99	2	3	10,892
3 Yr Avg	---	---	---	---	---	---
5 Yr Avg	---	---	---	---	---	---
10 Yr Avg	---	---	---	---	---	---
15 Yr Avg	---	---	---	---	---	---

Operations

Address and Telephone	100 Fillmore Street Suite 300
	Denver, CO 80206-4923
	800-525-8983
Advisor	Janus Capital
Subadvisor	None
Distributor	Janus Distributors
States Available	All plus PR,GU,VI
Report Grade	B-
Income Distrib	Paid Annually
* Date of Inception	09-01-92
Fiscal Year End	October

Ticker	Load	NAV	Yield	SEC Yield	Assets	Objective
JAENX	None	22.98	2.2%	N/A	354.1	Growth

Historical Profile
Return ---
Risk ---
Rating
Not Rated

86% 89% 79%

Investment Style History
Equity
Average % Stocks Held in Portfolio

Growth of $10,000
|||| Value of Fund ($000)
— Value of Index ($000)
S&P 500
▼ Manager Change
▽ Partial Manager Change
► Mgr Unknown After
◄ Mgr Unknown Before

Performance Quartile
(Within Objective)

1983	1984	1985	1986	1987	1988	1989	1990	1991	1992	1993	1994	History
---	---	---	---	---	---	---	---	---	19.44	21.92	22.98	NAV
---	---	---	---	---	---	---	---	---	29.73 *	15.67	8.92	Total Return %
---	---	---	---	---	---	---	---	---	23.98 *	5.62	7.60	+/- S&P 500
---	---	---	---	---	---	---	---	---		4.39	8.99	+/- Wilshire 5000
---	---	---	---	---	---	---	---	---	0.13	0.08	2.32	Income Return %
---	---	---	---	---	---	---	---	---	29.60	15.59	6.60	Capital Return %
---	---	---	---	---	---	---	---	---		26	2	Total Rtn % Rank All
---	---	---	---	---	---	---	---	---		30	3	Total Rtn % Rank Obj
---	---	---	---	---	---	---	---	---	0.02	0.02	0.52	Income $
---	---	---	---	---	---	---	---	---	0.00	0.55	0.38	Capital Gains $
---	---	---	---	---	---	---	---	---	2.50	1.36	1.25	Expense Ratio %
---	---	---	---	---	---	---	---	---	-0.81	0.14	-0.32	Income Ratio %
---	---	---	---	---	---	---	---	---	53	201	193	Turnover Rate %
---	---	---	---	---	---	---	---	---	98.9	258.6	354.1	Net Assets ($mil)

Risk Analysis

Time Period	Load-Adj Return %	Risk % Rank[1] All	Risk % Rank[1] Obj	Morningstar[2] Return	Morningstar[2] Risk	Morningstar Risk-Adj Rating
1 Yr	8.92					
3 Yr	---	---	---	---	---	---
5 Yr	---	---	---	---	---	---
10 Yr	---	---	---	---	---	---

Average Historical Rating ---

[1] = low, 100 = high [2] 1.00 = Equity Avg [3] 1.00 = 90-day T-bill return

Other Measures

		Standard S&P 500	Best Fit
Standard Deviation	---	Alpha	---	---
Mean	---	Beta	---	---
Sharpe Ratio	---	R-Squared	---	---

Investment Style

	Stock Portfolio Avg	Relative S&P 500
Price/Earnings Ratio	28.0	1.52
Price/Book Ratio	4.6	1.36
5 Yr Earnings Gr %	---	---
Return on Assets %	6.9	0.92
Debt % Total Cap	48.0	1.70
Med Mkt Cap ($mil)	982	0.08

Style
Value Blend Growth
Size Large Med Small

Diversification Value for Portfolio Types

Large Cap: Small Cap: Bond: Balanced: Diversified:

Portfolio 12-31-94

Share Chg (07-94)000	Amount 000	Total Stocks: 21 / Total Fixed-Income: 1	Value $000	% Net Assets
417	946	Exide	53235	15.03
266	550	RP Scherer	24956	7.05
83	877	APS Holding Cl A	24777	7.00
-24	819	Insignia Financial Group	16482	4.65
246	558	Minerals Technologies	16309	4.61
-60	350	Paging Network	11900	3.36
565	565	Trigen Energy	11092	3.13
223	552	Credit Acceptance	9803	2.77
-151	264	Progressive	9237	2.61
250	250	Kinnevik Cl B	8266	2.33
-358	350	Lone Star Steakhouse/Saloon	7000	1.98
74	757	Therapeutic Technology	7000	1.98
11	83	Safra Republic Holdings	6892	1.95
	43	Nokia Pfd	6271	1.77
-30	200	Papa John's International	5750	1.62
-195	700	JD Wetherspoon	4911	1.39
-170	200	World Acceptance	4700	1.33
-435	255	Mercury Finance	3315	0.94
-137	93	Littletou	2706	0.76
-402	998	Grupo Financiero Imbursa C	2608	0.74
-298	800	Catalytica	2300	0.65
70	70	Heilig-Meyers	1778	0.50

Expenses & Fees

Sales Fees	0.00% front
	0.00% deferred
	0.00% 12b-1
Management Fee	1.00% max./0.65% min.
3-,5-,10-yr Expense Projections	$43, $74, $164
Annual Brokerage Cost	0.56%

Min Initial Purchase	$1000 (Addt'l: $50)
Min IRA Purchase	$250 (Addt'l: $50)
Min Auto Invest Plan	$50 (Systematic Inv: $50)

Composition % 12-31-94

Cash	30.1	Preferreds	1.8
Stocks	66.3	Convertibles	0.0
Bonds	0.0	Other	1.9

Tax Analysis

	Tax-Adj Historical Return %	% Pretax Return
3 Yr Avg	---	---
5 Yr Avg	---	---
10 Yr Avg	---	---

Potential Capital Gain Exposure (% of assets) 12%

Most Similar Funds in MF500

Fund lacks three-year record

Index Allocation

	% of Stocks
S&P 500	0.0
S&P MidCap 400	5.4
U.S. Small Cap	84.8
Foreign	9.8

Sector Weightings

	% of Stocks	Relative S&P 500
Utilities	0.0	0.00
Energy	0.0	0.00
Financials	14.3	1.35
Industrial Cyclicals	49.8	3.04
Consumer Durables	13.1	2.10
Consumer Staples	2.6	0.21
Services	6.7	0.83
Retail	0.9	0.16
Health	3.7	0.43
Technology	8.9	0.97

MORNINGSTAR 1995 Mutual Fund 500

Janus Flexible Income

	Ticker	Load	NAV	Yield	SEC Yield	Assets	Objective
	JAFIX	None	8.75	8.2%	8.76%	353.9	Income

Janus Flexible Income Fund seeks total return consistent with capital preservation. Income is usually the primary component of total return.

The fund ordinarily invests at least 80% of its assets in income-producing securities. It may purchase domestic and foreign corporate or government securities of any rating and may deliberately vary the overall quality of its portfolio from time to time. Investments may also include mortgage- and asset-backed securities, preferred stocks, and income-producing common stocks. The fund may invest without limit in foreign securities.

Manager's Investment Style

After a recent change in the fund's charter, manager Ron Speaker can further execute his flexible strategy. In 1994 the fund adopted a floating as opposed to a fixed dividend policy, which allows management to hold more cash. Mainly, though management buys a mix of domestic or foreign corporate or government bonds, as well as non-investment grade issues. Recent strategy has included a prescient move to short interest-rate futures at the end of 1993, and into 1994. Speker also reduced the fund's effective maturity by selling off some longer paper, and picking up higher-yield cushion bonds that are trading on a yield-to-call basis.

Fund Manager(s)

Ronald V. Speaker CFA(1991), since 12-91.
Birthdate: 10-64. BS, U. of Colorado 1986

Manager Experience

	Dates Managed	Invest Obj	Std Dev	+/- Index
Ronald V. Speaker				
Idex II Flexible Income A	11/90 - 12/94	I	4.30	-1.30
Janus Intermed Govt Secs	07/91 - 12/94	GG	3.29	-2.59

Historical Profile
Return	Above Average
Risk	Low
Rating	★★★★ Above Average

Investment Style History
Fixed Income
Income Rtn % Rank Obj

	23	37	26	20	26	22	22

Growth of $10,000

|||| Value of Fund ($000)
— Value of Index ($000)
FB HY
▼ Manager Change
▽ Partial Manager Change
► Mgr Unknown After
◄ Mgr Unknown Before

Performance Quartile
(Within Objective)

1983	1984	1985	1986	1987	1988	1989	1990	1991	1992	1993	1994	History
---	---	---	---	9.92	9.99	9.35	8.00	9.09	9.31	9.74	8.75	NAV
---	---	---	---	3.40 *	10.70	3.30	-4.72	25.97	11.85	15.70	-2.92	Total Return %
---	---	---	---	21.26 *	-5.91	-28.38	-1.60	-4.51	4.24	5.64	-4.24	+/- S&P 500
---	---	---	---	---	2.83	-11.24	-13.66	9.97	4.61	5.95	0.00	+/- LB Aggregate
---	---	---	---	4.20	10.00	9.71	9.72	12.35	9.17	8.49	7.24	Income Return %
---	---	---	---	-0.80	0.71	-6.41	-14.44	13.63	2.69	7.21	-10.16	Capital Return %
---	---	---	---	---	55	97	70	34	16	26	42	Total Rtn % Rank All
---	---	---	---	---	61	89	73	25	23	18	23	Total Rtn % Rank Obj
---	---	---	---	0.41	0.94	0.97	0.90	0.90	0.80	0.76	0.72	Income $
---	---	---	---	0.00	0.00	0.00	0.00	0.00	0.02	0.23	0.00	Capital Gains $
---	---	---	---	1.00	1.00	1.00	1.00	1.00	1.00	1.00	0.93	Expense Ratio %
---	---	---	---	8.52	9.32	10.00	11.24	9.38	8.98	7.96	7.75	Income Ratio %
---	---	---	---	---	130	76	75	96	88	210	201	137	Turnover Rate %
---	---	---	---	---	6.0	9.6	18.1	13.4	71.4	207.5	469.6	353.9	Net Assets ($mil)

Performance 12-31-94

	1st Qtr	2nd Qtr	3rd Qtr	4th Qtr	Total
1987	---	---	---	7.44	3.40 *
1988	2.48	0.52	3.13	4.20	10.70
1989	2.48	2.22	0.08	-1.47	3.30
1990	-8.47	4.39	-5.28	5.28	-4.72
1991	8.17	3.97	6.32	5.35	25.97
1992	3.13	3.09	4.52	0.66	11.85
1993	5.32	3.83	3.99	1.75	15.70
1994	-1.17	-1.42	0.87	-1.22	-2.92

Bear Market Performance

Decile Rank (5-year period)

Worst ———————————————— Best

	Worst 3 Mo Period 1985-89	Worst 3 Mo Period 1990-94
Janus Flexible Income		-8.47
+/- S&P 500	---	-5.47
+/- Best Fit Index : FB HY	---	-5.90

Trailing Returns

	Total Return %	+/- S&P 500	+/- LB Aggregate	% Rank All	% Rank Obj	Growth of $10,000
3 Mo	-1.22	-1.20	-1.60	50	49	9,878
6 Mo	-0.36	-5.22	-1.35	63	55	9,964
1 Yr	-2.92	-4.24	0.00	42	23	9,708
3 Yr Avg	7.90	1.64	3.36	22	13	12,563
5 Yr Avg	8.56	-0.13	0.94	28	32	15,079
10 Yr Avg	---	---	---	---	---	---
15 Yr Avg	---	---	---	---	---	---

Operations

Address and Telephone	100 Fillmore Street Suite 300
	Denver, CO 80206-4923
	800-525-8983
Advisor	Janus Capital
Subadvisor	None
Distributor	Janus Distributors
States Available	All plus PR,GU,VI
Report Grade	B-
Income Distrib	Paid Monthly
* Date of Inception	07-02-87
Fiscal Year End	October

Risk Analysis

Time Period	Load-Adj Return %	Risk % Rank [1] All	Obj	Morningstar [2] Return	Morningstar Risk	Morningstar Risk-Adj Rating
1 Yr	-2.92					
3 Yr	7.90	9	2	1.30 [3]	0.38	★★★★
5 Yr	8.56	42	50	0.96 [3]	0.50	★★★★
10 Yr	---					

Average Historical Rating (54 months)   3.4 ★s

[1] = low, 100 = high   [2] 1.00 = Hybrid Avg   [3] 1.00 = 90-day T-bill return

Other Measures

			Standard S&P 500	Best Fit FB HY
Standard Deviation	4.06	Alpha	3.5	-1.3
Mean	7.71	Beta	0.24	0.76
Sharpe Ratio	1.03	R-Squared	22	65

Investment Style

Stocks

	Port Avg	Rel S&P 500
Price/Earnings Ratio	9.6#	0.52
Price/Book Ratio	1.4#	0.41
5 Yr Earnings Gr %	-16.5#	-2.97
Med Mkt Cap ($mil)	1538#	0.12

figure is based on 50% or less of stocks

Bonds

Avg Effective Duration	5.7 Yrs
Avg Effective Maturity	10.0 Yrs
Avg Credit Quality	BB
Avg Weighted Coupon	10.01%

Diversification Value for Portfolio Types

Large Cap: High	Small Cap: High	Bond: Low	Balanced: Medium	Diversified: Medium

Min Initial Purchase	$1000 (Addt'l: $50)
Min IRA Purchase	$250 (Addt'l: $50)
Min Auto Invest Plan	$50 (Systematic Inv: $50)

Expenses & Fees

Sales Fees	0.00% front
	0.00% deferred
	0.00% 12b-1
Management Fee	0.65% max./0.55% min.
3-,5-,10-yr Expense Projections	$32, $55, $122
Annual Brokerage Cost	0.01%

Portfolio 12-31-94

Share Chg (06-90)000	Amount 000	Total Stocks: 0 / Total Fixed-Income: 52	Date of Maturity	Value $000	% Net Assets
	25000	US Treasury Note 7.25%	11-30-96	24817	7.01
	18700	Dr Pepper/Seven-Up 11.5%	11-01-02	14820	4.19
	15000	Ford Motor Credit 7.75%	10-01-99	14644	4.14
	10000	Leucadia National 10.375%	06-15-02	10475	2.96
	11000	Delphi Financial Group 8%	10-01-03	9378	2.65
	8550	Life Partners Group 12.75%	07-15-02	9352	2.64
	300	Chevy Chase Savings Pfd 13%		8400	2.37
	8338	Orion Capital 9.125%	09-01-02	8380	2.37
	7670	Texas Eastern Transmsn 10%	10-01-11	8101	2.29
	8250	Super Rite Foods 10.625%	04-01-02	8095	2.29
	8000	Western National 7.125%	02-15-04	7090	2.00
	7166	Great Dane Holdings 14.5%	01-01-06	7050	1.99
	6857	Southeastern Pub Svc 11.875%	02-01-98	6797	1.92
	6250	KENETECH 12.75%	12-15-02	6586	1.86
	6750	Williamhouse Regency 11.5%	06-15-05	6303	1.78
	6000	News Amer Holdings 10.125%	10-15-12	6165	1.74
	7000	American Pres Lines 8%	01-15-24	5968	1.69
	6150	Pilgrim's Pride 10.875%	08-01-03	5919	1.67
	6000	Westinghouse Electric 8.625%	08-01-12	5520	1.56
	248	Conagra Capital Pfd		5387	1.52

Index Allocation

	% of Stocks
S&P 500	60.7
S&P MidCap 400	0.0
U.S. Small Cap	0.0
Foreign	39.4

Composition % 12-31-94

Cash	20.0	Preferreds	4.5
Stocks	0.0	Convertibles	0.0
Bonds	75.4	Other	0.1

Tax Analysis

	Tax-Adj Historical Return %	% Pretax Return
3 Yr Avg	4.58	56.1
5 Yr Avg	5.17	56.5
10 Yr Avg	---	---
Potential Capital Gain Exposure (% of assets)		-9%

Most Similar Funds in MF500

Allmerica Sec Trust	Strong Fit
Invesco High-Yield	Fair Fit
American High-Income	Fair Fit

Bond Credit Analysis 12-31-94
% of Bonds

US Govt	0	BB	10
AAA	3	B	26
AA	1	Below B	7
A	6	NR/NA	25
BBB	22		

Stock Sector Weightings

	% of Stocks	Relative S&P 500
Utilities	0.0	0.00
Energy	0.0	0.00
Financials	39.4	3.72
Industrial Cyclicals	0.0	0.00
Consumer Durables	0.0	0.00
Consumer Staples	0.0	0.00
Services	0.0	0.00
Retail	0.0	0.00
Health	0.0	0.00
Technology	60.7	6.62

Janus

Janus Fund seeks capital appreciation consistent with preservation of capital.

The fund invests primarily in common stocks of companies and industries that experience increasing demand for their products and services, or operate in a favorable regulatory climate. It invests in a large number of issuers of any size. The fund may invest without limit in foreign securities. The fund may also invest in preferred stocks, warrants, government securities, and corporate debt.

	Ticker	Load	NAV	Yield	SEC Yield	Assets	Objective
	JANSX	None	18.78	0.0%	N/A	9400.6	Growth

Historical Profile
Return	Above Average
Risk	Below Average
Rating	★★★★
	Above Average

Investment Style History
Equity
Average % Stocks Held in Portfolio

65% 68% 91% 60% 77% 69% 75% 71%

Growth of $10,000
- ||| Value of Fund ($000)
- — Value of Index ($000) S&P 500
- ▼ Manager Change
- ▽ Partial Manager Change
- ► Mgr Unknown After
- ◄ Mgr Unknown Before

Performance Quartile (Within Objective)

Manager's Investment Style

Reasoning that there exists limited upside potential in the market, management has decided to increase its number of stocks from 75 to over 100. Making this task easier is the reduction of its minimum stock position to $25 million, from $100 million. This has afforded the fund the opportunity to pick up many small- and mid-cap issues and to lower its median market capitalization by $2 billion. This is not a complete departure from management's strategy, because it continues to stay invested in mostly large, high-quality companies.

Fund Manager(s)

James P. Craig, since 06-86. Birthdate: 07-56.
Business, U. of Alabama 1978 MBA, Wharton 1981

1983	1984	1985	1986	1987	1988	1989	1990	1991	1992	1993	1994	History
13.34	11.61	13.19	12.47	10.39	11.55	14.21	13.79	18.60	18.68	19.39	18.78	NAV
26.09	-0.14	24.55	11.22	4.20	16.58	46.32	-0.74	42.80	6.87	10.92	-1.10	Total Return %
3.62	-6.41	-7.19	-7.46	-1.06	-0.03	14.64	2.37	12.32	-0.75	0.86	-2.42	+/- S&P 500
2.62	-3.19	-8.02	-4.88	1.84	-1.36	17.15	5.44	8.59	-2.11	-0.36	-1.03	+/- Wilshire 5000
0.00	10.47	4.33	0.00	8.49	5.41	1.36	2.18	1.06	1.57	2.03	0.04	Income Return %
26.09	-10.61	20.22	11.22	-4.29	11.16	44.96	-2.92	41.74	5.30	8.89	-1.15	Capital Return %
21	66	47	79	26	23	2	57	12	59	60	27	Total Rtn % Rank All
29	39	76	78	43	43	2	26	24	59	53	44	Total Rtn % Rank Obj
0.00	1.30	0.54	0.00	0.99	0.56	0.19	0.31	0.19	0.29	0.39	0.01	Income $
0.00	0.35	0.73	2.20	1.61	0.00	2.50	0.01	0.91	0.90	0.94	0.39	Capital Gains $
1.11	1.06	1.03	1.00	1.01	0.98	0.92	1.02	0.98	0.97	0.92	0.91	Expense Ratio %
2.07	4.26	4.01	2.82	1.55	4.99	1.68	2.11	1.77	1.54	1.55	1.12	Income Ratio %
94	162	163	254	214	175	205	307	132	153	127	139	Turnover Rate %
264.7	319.1	410.7	460.3	377.1	377.7	705.0	1156.1	2993.0	5831.9	9199.6	9400.6	Net Assets ($mil)

Manager Experience

	Dates Managed	Invest Obj	Std Dev	+/- Index
James P. Craig				
Janus Venture	04/85 - 12/93	SC	15.21	4.08
Janus Worldwide	05/91 - 10/92	WW	10.50	5.68

Performance 12-31-94

	1st Qtr	2nd Qtr	3rd Qtr	4th Qtr	Total
1987	13.31	2.39	7.37	-16.35	4.20
1988	4.04	4.90	5.20	1.53	16.58
1989	11.86	14.63	17.02	-2.48	46.32
1990	-3.73	12.43	-13.91	6.53	-0.74
1991	19.07	-1.64	10.22	10.63	42.80
1992	-2.69	0.39	0.44	8.91	6.87
1993	5.25	-0.15	3.36	2.12	10.92
1994	-2.63	-1.17	2.63	0.14	-1.10

Bear Market Performance

Decile Rank (5-year period)

Worst ——————————— Best

	Worst 3 Mo Period 1985-89	Worst 3 Mo Period 1990-94
Janus	-18.59	-13.91
+/- S&P 500	11.00	-0.17
+/- Best Fit Index : S&P 500	11.00	-0.17

Trailing Returns

	Total Return %	+/- S&P 500	+/- Wil 5000	% Rank All	% Rank Obj	Growth of $10,000
3 Mo	0.14	0.15	0.91	18	18	10,014
6 Mo	2.76	-2.10	-1.86	22	64	10,276
1 Yr	-1.10	-2.42	-1.03	27	44	9,890
3 Yr Avg	5.44	-0.83	-1.17	40	52	11,722
5 Yr Avg	10.69	2.00	1.87	14	24	16,615
10 Yr Avg	15.13	0.75	1.27	10	15	40,908
15 Yr Avg	17.29	2.81	3.31	2	5	109,369

Risk Analysis

Time Period	Load-Adj Return %	Risk % Rank [1] All	Risk % Rank [1] Obj	Morningstar [2] Return	Morningstar Risk	Morningstar Risk-Adj Rating
1 Yr	-1.10					
3 Yr	5.44	64	22	0.55 [3]	0.72	★★★
5 Yr	10.69	64	16	1.55 [3]	0.77	★★★★
10 Yr	15.13	51	8	1.52	0.74	★★★★
Average Historical Rating (109 months)					4.5	★s

[1] 1 = low, 100 = high [2] 1.00 = Equity Avg [3] 1.00 = 90-day T-bill return

Other Measures

		Standard S&P 500	Best Fit S&P 500
Standard Deviation	7.46	Alpha	-0.4	-0.4
Mean	5.59	Beta	0.85	0.85
Sharpe Ratio	0.28	R-Squared	81	81

Investment Style

	Stock Portfolio Avg	Relative S&P 500
Price/Earnings Ratio	19.8	1.07
Price/Book Ratio	5.1	1.50
5 Yr Earnings Gr %	12.9	2.33
Return on Assets %	8.5	1.14
Debt % Total Cap	23.6	0.83
Med Mkt Cap ($mil)	6253	0.48

Style
Value Blend Growth
Size Large Med Small

Diversification Value for Portfolio Types

Large Cap: Low	Small Cap: Medium	Bond: High	Balanced: Low	Diversified: Low

Portfolio 12-31-94

Total Stocks: 107
Total Fixed-Income: 3

Share Chg (07-94) 000	Amount 000		Value $000	% Net Assets
2783	7193	Citicorp	297623	3.17
0	3758	Wolters Kluwer (Netherlands)	278199	2.96
9335	10252	Astra CI A Free	264966	2.82
4926	6813	General Motors CI E	262313	2.79
1162	4849	First Data	229721	2.44
2949	2949	Pfizer	227826	2.42
-419	1603	Hercules	184989	1.97
243	6055	Bank of New York	175598	1.87
875	4172	UNUM	157505	1.68
38	1069	McDonnell Douglas	151734	1.61
486	1162	General Re	143785	1.53
874	1074	LIN Broadcasting	143402	1.53
-295	5674	Mattel	142554	1.52
-33	2168	First Financial Management	133631	1.42
-1100	1521	CSX	105894	1.13
1043	1765	Amgen	104113	1.11
2450	2450	Merck	93403	0.99
7996	8867	Elsevier (Netherlands)	92538	0.98
-268	5234	Santa Fe Pacific	91601	0.97
1968	2605	Lowe's	90506	0.96
-1971	1193	Gillette	89164	0.95
-3412	2918	Philips Electronics	86472	0.92
1125	1408	Automatic Data Processing	82368	0.88
1218	1602	Conrail	80876	0.86
283	1129	Alco Standard	70815	0.75

Composition % 12-31-94
Cash	40.0	Preferreds	0.6
Stocks	58.4	Convertibles	0.0
Bonds	1.1	Other	0.0

Tax Analysis
	Tax-Adj Historical Return %	% Pretax Return
3 Yr Avg	3.92	70.9
5 Yr Avg	9.22	83.7
10 Yr Avg	12.12	69.2
Potential Capital Gain Exposure (% of assets)		6%

Most Similar Funds in MF500
Massachusetts Inv A	Strong Fit
Vanguard Index 500	Fair Fit
Alliance Growth & Income A	Fair Fit

Index Allocation
	% of Stocks
S&P 500	62.5
S&P MidCap 400	13.5
U.S. Small Cap	7.1
Foreign	17.0

Sector Weightings
	% of Stocks	Relative S&P 500
Utilities	0.6	0.04
Energy	0.0	0.00
Financials	23.6	2.23
Industrial Cyclicals	5.9	0.36
Consumer Durables	7.8	1.26
Consumer Staples	6.3	0.50
Services	17.4	2.14
Retail	3.1	0.52
Health	17.1	1.97
Technology	18.3	2.00

Operations

Address and Telephone	100 Fillmore Street Suite 300
	Denver, CO 80206-4923
	800-525-8983
Advisor	Janus Capital
Subadvisor	None
Distributor	Janus Distributors
States Available	All plus PR,GU,VI
Report Grade	B-
Income Distrib	Paid Annually
Date of Inception	02-27-70
Fiscal Year End	October

Min Initial Purchase	$1000 (Addt'l: $50)
Min IRA Purchase	$250 (Addt'l: $50)
Min Auto Invest Plan	$50 (Systematic Inv: $50)

Expenses & Fees
Sales Fees	0.00% front
	0.00% deferred
	0.00% 12b-1
Management Fee	1.00% max./0.65% min.
3-,5-,10-yr Expense Projections	$29, $51, $113
Annual Brokerage Cost	0.21%

MORNINGSTAR 1995 Mutual Fund 500

Janus Growth & Income

Janus Growth and Income Fund seeks long-term growth of capital and current income.

The fund invests in any combination of equity and fixed-income securities, provided that at least 25% of its assets are invested in securities selected for their growth potential, and at least 25% of its assets are invested in securities selected for current income. The fixed-income portion consists primarily of investment-grade debt securities. The fund may invest without limit in foreign securities. It may engage in options and futures strategies.

Manager's Investment Style

Management is more concerned with growth than income. This is illustrated in the fund's higher than average P/E ratio and earnings-growth rate. While this attention is given to growth, income is virtually ignored. Yield is much lower than the catagory average, and is supported mostly by a 5% holding in five-year Treasuries. Despite some past pitfalls, management plans to continue this focused approach toward growth by investing in high-priced sectors such as consumer durables and technology.

Fund Manager(s)

Thomas F. Marsico, since 05-91. Birthdate: 08-55.
Biology, U. of Colorado 1977 Finance, U. of Denver 1979

Manager Experience	Dates Managed	Invest Obj	Std Dev	+/- Index
Thomas F. Marsico				
Janus Flexible Income	10/90 - 12/91	I	2.77	0.09
Idex II Flexible Income A	11/90 - 12/91	I	2.91	3.14

Performance 12-31-94

	1st Qtr	2nd Qtr	3rd Qtr	4th Qtr	Total
1987	---	---	---	---	---
1988	---	---	---	---	---
1989	---	---	---	---	---
1990	---	---	---	---	---
1991	---	---	16.86	15.05	37.14 *
1992	-6.55	-1.41	2.48	11.59	5.35
1993	0.56	2.66	3.62	-0.26	6.70
1994	-2.79	-3.79	4.08	-2.28	-4.87

Bear Market Performance

Decile Rank (5-year period)

	Worst			Best

	Worst 3 Mo Period 1985-89	Worst 3 Mo Period 1990-94
Janus Growth & Income	---	---
+/- S&P 500	---	---
+/- Best Fit Index :	---	---

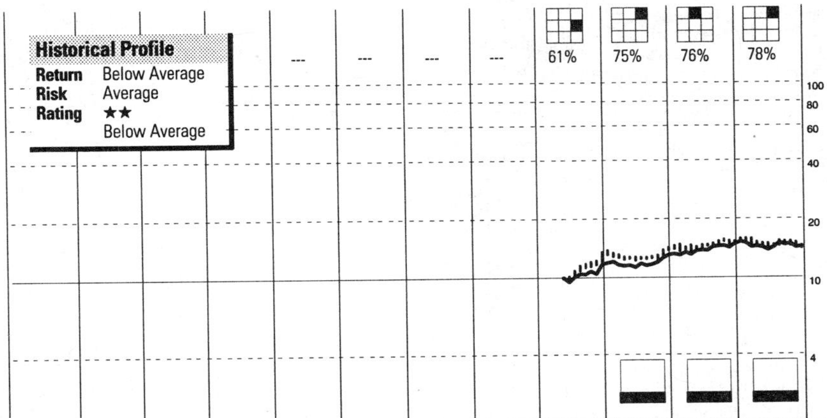

Trailing Returns

	Total Return %	+/- S&P 500	+/- Wil 5000	% Rank All	% Rank Obj	Growth of $10,000
3 Mo	-2.28	-2.27	-1.51	73	72	9,772
6 Mo	1.71	-3.15	-2.92	29	63	10,171
1 Yr	-4.87	-6.19	-4.80	62	87	9,513
3 Yr Avg	2.26	-4.01	-4.35	90	87	10,693
5 Yr Avg	---	---	---	---	---	---
10 Yr Avg	---	---	---	---	---	---
15 Yr Avg	---	---	---	---	---	---

Operations

Address and Telephone	100 Fillmore Street Suite 300 Denver, CO 80206-4923 800-525-8983
Advisor	Janus Capital
Subadvisor	None
Distributor	Janus Distributors
States Available	All plus PR,GU,VI
Report Grade	B-
Income Distrib	Paid Quarterly
* Date of Inception	05-15-91
Fiscal Year End	October

	Ticker	Load	NAV	Yield	SEC Yield	Assets	Objective
	JAGIX	None	13.88	0.7%	N/A	456.5	Growth/Inc.

Historical Profile
Return	Below Average
Risk	Average
Rating ★★	Below Average

Investment Style History
Equity

Average % Stocks Held in Portfolio

61%	75%	76%	78%

Growth of $10,000
- IIII Value of Fund ($000)
- — Value of Index ($000) SPMid400
- ▼ Manager Change
- ▽ Partial Manager Change
- ► Mgr Unknown After
- ◄ Mgr Unknown Before

Performance Quartile (Within Objective)

	1983	1984	1985	1986	1987	1988	1989	1990	1991	1992	1993	1994	History
NAV	---	---	---	---	---	---	---	---	13.68	14.24	14.69	13.88	
Total Return %	---	---	---	---	---	---	---	---	37.14 *	5.35	6.70	-4.87	
+/- S&P 500	---	---	---	---	---	---	---	---	21.39 *	-2.27	-3.36	-6.19	
+/- Wilshire 5000	---	---	---	---	---	---	---	---	---	-3.62	-4.58	-4.80	
Income Return %	---	---	---	---	---	---	---	---	0.34	1.26	1.15	0.64	
Capital Return %	---	---	---	---	---	---	---	---	36.80	4.09	5.55	-5.51	
Total Rtn % Rank All	---	---	---	---	---	---	---	---	---	74	85	62	
Total Rtn % Rank Obj	---	---	---	---	---	---	---	---	---	77	81	87	
Income $	---	---	---	---	---	---	---	---	0.03	0.15	0.17	0.09	
Capital Gains $	---	---	---	---	---	---	---	---	0.00	0.00	0.33	0.00	
Expense Ratio %	---	---	---	---	---	---	---	---	2.33	1.52	1.28	1.22	
Income Ratio %	---	---	---	---	---	---	---	---	0.76	1.61	1.13	1.26	
Turnover Rate %	---	---	---	---	---	---	---	---	---	120	138	123	
Net Assets ($mil)	---	---	---	---	---	---	---	---	93.3	311.0	513.8	456.5	

Risk Analysis

Time Period	Load-Adj Return %	Risk % Rank [1] All	Risk % Rank [1] Obj	Morningstar [2] Return	Morningstar Risk	Morningstar Risk-Adj Rating
1 Yr	-4.87					
3 Yr	2.26	85	97	-0.38 [3]	1.05	★★
5 Yr	---	---	---	---	---	
10 Yr	---	---	---	---	---	

Average Historical Rating (8 months)   3.0 ★s

[1] 1 = low, 100 = high   [2] 1.00 = Equity Avg   [3] 1.00 = 90-day T-bill return

Other Measures

				Standard S&P 500	Best Fit SPMid400
Standard Deviation	9.89	Alpha		-3.6	-4.1
Mean	2.72	Beta		0.99	0.87
Sharpe Ratio	-0.08	R-Squared		63	75

Investment Style

	Stock Portfolio Avg	Relative S&P 500
Price/Earnings Ratio	20.8	1.12
Price/Book Ratio	4.3	1.26
5 Yr Earnings Gr %	12.8#	2.31
Return on Assets %	8.8	1.17
Debt % Total Cap	21.5	0.76
Med Mkt Cap ($mil)	13820	1.06

figure is based on 50% or less of stocks

Style
Value Blend Growth
Size Large/Med/Small

Diversification Value for Portfolio Types

Large Cap: Low	Small Cap: Low	Bond: High	Balanced: Low	Diversified: Low

Portfolio 12-31-94

Total Stocks: 33
Total Fixed-Income: 6

Share Chg (10-94) 000	Amount 000		Value $000	% Net Assets
	590	American Express Cv DECS 6.25%	25149	5.51
	25000	US Treasury Note 7.25%	24817	5.44
0	564	Lowe's	19612	4.30
0	405	First Data	19187	4.20
0	219	Pfizer	16908	3.70
179	290	Motorola	16798	3.68
0	313	Home Depot	14417	3.16
0	283	FHLMC	14283	3.13
0	273	Coca-Cola	14052	3.08
-8	190	FNMA	13879	3.04
60	135	Hewlett-Packard	13483	2.95
-35	324	Citicorp	13402	2.94
0	449	Philips Electronics (ADR)	13195	2.89
0	258	United HealthCare	11620	2.55
0	317	Merrill Lynch	11338	2.48
0	330	First Bank System	10987	2.41
0	375	AirTouch Communications	10922	2.39
0	321	Vodafone Group (ADR)	10805	2.37
0	250	Digital Equipment	8313	1.82
	143	Sears Roebuck A Cv Pfd $3.75	7951	1.74
43	127	Microsoft	7766	1.70
100	100	Nokia (ADR)	7500	1.64
287	287	Astra CI A Free	7410	1.62
0	144	Conrail	7285	1.60
-54	183	Compaq Computer	7223	1.58

Composition % 12-31-94

Cash	19.5	Preferreds	10.3
Stocks	63.1	Convertibles	1.4
Bonds	5.7	Other	0.0

Tax Analysis

	Tax-Adj Historical Return %	% Pretax Return
3 Yr Avg	1.69	74.5
5 Yr Avg	---	---
10 Yr Avg	---	---
Potential Capital Gain Exposure (% of assets)		5%

Most Similar Funds in MF500

Janus Twenty	Strong Fit
Enterprise Capital Apprec	Fair Fit
AIM Weingarten	Fair Fit

Investment Style History
Equity

History column (right side)

Index Allocation
	% of Stocks
S&P 500	80.1
S&P MidCap 400	5.5
U.S. Small Cap	3.0
Foreign	11.4

Sector Weightings
	% of Stocks	Relative S&P 500
Utilities	0.0	0.00
Energy	2.0	0.20
Financials	23.8	2.25
Industrial Cyclicals	1.9	0.12
Consumer Durables	8.9	1.43
Consumer Staples	5.3	0.42
Services	4.3	0.53
Retail	12.1	2.08
Health	13.4	4.05
Technology	28.4	3.10

Expenses & Fees

Sales Fees	
	0.00% front
	0.00% deferred
	0.00% 12b-1
Management Fee	1.00% max./0.65% min.
3-,5-,10-yr Expense Projections	$41, $70, $155
Annual Brokerage Cost	0.21%

Min Purchases

Min Initial Purchase	$1000 (Addt'l: $50)
Min IRA Purchase	$250 (Addt'l: $50)
Min Auto Invest Plan	$50 (Systematic Inv: $50)

Janus Mercury

	Ticker	Load	NAV	Yield	SEC Yield	Assets	Objective
	JAMRX	None	13.61	1.2%	N/A	690.1	Growth

Janus Mercury Fund seeks long-term growth of capital.

The fund invests virtually all of its assets in common stocks. Stocks acquired by the fund are typically issued by companies that appear to be experiencing favorable demand for their products and services and operating in a favorable competitive and regulatory climate. The fund may invest up to 35% of its assets in debt securities rated below investment grade. It may invest without limit in foreign securities.

Historical Profile

Return ---
Risk ---
Rating
Not Rated

Investment Style History
Equity

Average % Stocks Held
in Portfolio 79% 66%

Growth of $10,000

IIII Value of Fund ($000)
— Value of Index ($000)
  S&P 500
▼ Manager Change
▽ Partial Manager Change
► Mgr Unknown After
◄ Mgr Unknown Before

Performance Quartile
(Within Objective)

Manager's Investment Style

As with most Janus funds, management favors stocks with considerable earnings growth that have some sort of catalyst to drive that growth. Management has, at different times, found opportunities among all different market caps and in international markets, as well. He sells issues once their price multiples exceed their earnings growth rates--which has resulted in a high turnover ratio.

Fund Manager(s)

Warren B. Lammert CFA(1987), since 05-93.
Birthdate: 01-62. BA, Yale 1984 MS, London School of Economics 1989

Manager Experience

	Dates Managed	Invest Obj	Std Dev	+/- Index
Warren B. Lammert				
Janus Balanced	09/92 - 12/93	B	6.30	5.27

	1983	1984	1985	1986	1987	1988	1989	1990	1991	1992	1993	1994	History
	---	---	---	---	---	---	---	---	---	---	11.98	13.61	NAV
	---	---	---	---	---	---	---	---	---	---	19.80 *	15.86	Total Return %
	---	---	---	---	---	---	---	---	---	---	12.29 *	14.54	+/- S&P 500
	---	---	---	---	---	---	---	---	---	---	---	15.93	+/- Wilshire 5000
	---	---	---	---	---	---	---	---	---	---	0.00	1.31	Income Return %
	---	---	---	---	---	---	---	---	---	---	19.80	14.55	Capital Return %
	---	---	---	---	---	---	---	---	---	---	---	1	Total Rtn % Rank All
	---	---	---	---	---	---	---	---	---	---	---	1	Total Rtn % Rank Obj
	---	---	---	---	---	---	---	---	---	---	0.00	0.16	Income $
	---	---	---	---	---	---	---	---	---	---	0.00	0.11	Capital Gains $
	---	---	---	---	---	---	---	---	---	---	1.75	1.33	Expense Ratio %
	---	---	---	---	---	---	---	---	---	---	-0.40	0.25	Income Ratio %
	---	---	---	---	---	---	---	---	---	---	151	283	Turnover Rate %
	---	---	---	---	---	---	---	---	---	---	126.9	690.1	Net Assets ($mil)

Performance 12-31-94

	1st Qtr	2nd Qtr	3rd Qtr	4th Qtr	Total
1987	---	---	---	---	---
1988	---	---	---	---	---
1989	---	---	---	---	---
1990	---	---	---	---	---
1991	---	---	---	---	---
1992	---	---	---	---	---
1993	---	---	5.29	5.55	19.80 *
1994	5.68	-6.56	14.54	2.43	15.86

Bear Market Performance

Decile Rank (5-year period)

Worst | Best

	Worst 3 Mo Period 1985-89	Worst 3 Mo Period 1990-94
Janus Mercury	---	---
+/- S&P 500	---	---
+/- Best Fit Index :	---	---

Trailing Returns

	Total Return %	+/- S&P 500	+/- Wil 5000	% Rank All	% Rank Obj	Growth of $10,000
3 Mo	2.43	2.45	3.20	3	4	10,243
6 Mo	17.33	12.46	12.70	2	1	11,733
1 Yr	15.86	14.54	15.93	1	1	11,586
3 Yr Avg	---	---	---	---	---	---
5 Yr Avg	---	---	---	---	---	---
10 Yr Avg	---	---	---	---	---	---
15 Yr Avg	---	---	---	---	---	---

Risk Analysis

Time Period	Load-Adj Return %	Risk % Rank[1] All	Obj	Morningstar[2] Return	Morningstar Risk	Morningstar Risk-Adj Rating
1 Yr	15.86					
3 Yr	---	---	---	---	---	---
5 Yr	---	---	---	---	---	---
10 Yr	---	---	---	---	---	---

Average Historical Rating ---

[1] 1 = low, 100 = high [2] 1.00 = Equity Avg [3] 1.00 = 90-day T-bill return

Other Measures

			Standard S&P 500	Best Fit
Standard Deviation	---	Alpha	---	---
Mean	---	Beta	---	---
Sharpe Ratio	---	R-Squared	---	---

Investment Style

	Stock Portfolio Avg	Relative S&P 500
Price/Earnings Ratio	21.2	1.15
Price/Book Ratio	4.7	1.37
5 Yr Earnings Gr %	10.6#	1.91
Return on Assets %	10.5	1.40
Debt % Total Cap	31.6#	1.12
Med Mkt Cap ($mil)	2413	0.19

figure is based on 50% or less of stocks

Diversification Value for Portfolio Types

Large Cap: | Small Cap: | Bond: | Balanced: | Diversified:

Portfolio 12-31-94

Share Chg (07-94) 000	Amount 000	Total Stocks: 97 / Total Fixed-Income: 4	Value $000	% Net Assets
	235	Nokia Pfd	34663	5.02
	58	SAP Pfd	32655	4.73
984	984	Kinnevik Cl B	32571	4.72
1025	1220	Astra Cl A	31530	4.57
572	675	LSI Logic	27255	3.95
324	324	Citicorp	13403	1.94
353	353	Sun Healthcare Group	8961	1.30
116	116	Intel	7398	1.07
156	156	First Data	7367	1.07
117	121	Motorola	6988	1.01
156	340	Itron	6876	1.00
203	203	CUC International	6795	0.98
0	200	Vodafone Group (ADR)	6708	0.97
328	328	National Semiconductor	6403	0.93
43	43	Nokia Cl K	6287	0.91
364	364	Coram Healthcare	6010	0.87
171	171	AK Steel Holding	5273	0.76
-26	1981	Grupo Financiero Imbursa C	5175	0.75
339	339	Valassis Communications	5078	0.74
186	186	Cultor Cl 2	5036	0.73
35	35	McDonnell Douglas	5023	0.73
63	63	Pfizer	4888	0.71
27	130	Paging Network	4416	0.64
310	310	Central European Media Entpr	4341	0.63
0	149	APS Holding Cl A	4218	0.61

Composition % 12-31-94

Cash	38.6	Preferreds	5.2
Stocks	56.0	Convertibles	0.2
Bonds	0.0	Other	0.0

Tax Analysis

	Tax-Adj Historical Return %	% Pretax Return
3 Yr Avg	---	---
5 Yr Avg	---	---
10 Yr Avg	---	---
Potential Capital Gain Exposure (% of assets)		6%

Most Similar Funds in MF500

Fund lacks three-year record

Index Allocation

	% of Stocks
S&P 500	21.6
S&P MidCap 400	17.2
U.S. Small Cap	27.1
Foreign	34.1

Sector Weightings

	% of Stocks	Relative S&P 500
Utilities	3.2	0.26
Energy	0.4	0.04
Financials	7.9	0.74
Industrial Cyclicals	4.7	0.29
Consumer Durables	8.8	1.41
Consumer Staples	3.5	0.29
Services	9.1	1.11
Retail	2.8	0.48
Health	22.8	2.62
Technology	36.9	4.03

Operations

Address and Telephone	100 Fillmore Street Suite 300 Denver, CO 80206-4923 800-525-8983
Advisor	Janus Capital
Subadvisor	None
Distributor	Janus Distributors
States Available	All plus PR,GU,VI
Report Grade	B-
Income Distrib	Paid Annually
* Date of Inception	05-03-93
Fiscal Year End	October

Min Initial Purchase	$1000 (Addt'l: $50)
Min IRA Purchase	$250 (Addt'l: $50)
Min Auto Invest Plan	$50 (Systematic Inv: $50)

Expenses & Fees

Sales Fees	0.00% front
	0.00% deferred
	0.00% 12b-1
Management Fee	1.00% max./0.65% min.
3-,5-,10-yr Expense Projections	$43, N/A, N/A
Annual Brokerage Cost	---

MORNINGSTAR **1995 Mutual Fund 500**

Janus Twenty

	Ticker	Load	NAV	Yield	SEC Yield	Assets	Objective
	JAVLX	Clsd	22.71	0.3%	N/A	2504.3	Growth

Janus Twenty Fund seeks capital appreciation.

The fund invests primarily in a concentrated portfolio of common stocks. Investments are selected by evaluating factors such as improving profit margins and improvement in earnings and unit growth; these factors indicate the fundamental investment value of the security. The fund intends to purchase stocks with strong current financial positions and potential for future growth. It may invest without limit in foreign securities.

Prior to May 22, 1989, the fund was named Janus Value Fund.

Manager's Investment Style

Management has an unswerving preference for steady-growing, large-cap growth stocks. It particularly likes such firms when it can buy them at discounts to their future growth potential. It has recently exercised its ability to invest in foreign firms by purchasing large-cap growth issues in Europe and the occasional emerging-market stock.

Fund Manager(s)

Thomas F. Marsico, since 03-88. Birthdate: 08-55.
Biology, U. of Colorado 1977 Finance, U. of Denver 1979

Manager Experience	Dates Managed	Invest Obj	Std Dev	+/- Index
Thomas F. Marsico				
Janus Flexible Income	10/90 - 12/91	I	2.77	0.09
Idex II Flexible Income A	11/90 - 12/91	I	2.91	3.14

Performance 12-31-94

	1st Qtr	2nd Qtr	3rd Qtr	4th Qtr	Total
1987	14.08	2.40	-2.77	-22.22	-11.65
1988	4.85	4.94	3.40	4.65	19.05
1989	9.79	14.83	27.10	-5.86	50.85
1990	-4.09	17.64	-17.71	8.35	0.59
1991	23.01	1.06	15.75	17.60	69.21
1992	-8.10	-2.43	3.04	10.37	1.97
1993	0.33	2.30	3.61	-2.73	3.43
1994	-3.73	-6.42	5.64	-1.99	-6.73

Bear Market Performance

Decile Rank (5-year period)

	Worst 3 Mo Period 1985-89	Worst 3 Mo Period 1990-94
Janus Twenty	---	-17.71
+/- S&P 500	---	-3.97
+/- Best Fit Index : SPMid400	---	0.06

Trailing Returns

	Total Return %	+/- S&P 500	+/- Wil 5000	% Rank All	% Rank Obj	Growth of $10,000
3 Mo	-1.99	-1.97	-1.22	68	64	9,801
6 Mo	3.53	-1.33	-1.09	18	55	10,353
1 Yr	-6.73	-8.04	-6.66	78	84	9,327
3 Yr Avg	-0.54	-6.81	-7.16	97	91	9,838
5 Yr Avg	10.86	2.17	2.04	13	21	16,745
10 Yr Avg	---	---	---	---	---	---
15 Yr Avg	---	---	---	---	---	---

Operations

Address and Telephone	100 Fillmore Street Suite 300	
	Denver, CO 80206-4923	
	800-525-8983	
Advisor	Janus Capital	
Subadvisor	None	
Distributor	Janus Distributors	
States Available	All plus PR,GU,VI	
Report Grade	B-	
Income Distrib	Paid Annually	
* Date of Inception	04-26-85	
Fiscal Year End	October	

Min Initial Purchase	Closed (Addt'l: $50)
Min IRA Purchase	$250 (Addt'l: $50)
Min Auto Invest Plan	$50 (Systematic Inv: $50)

Expenses & Fees

Sales Fees	0.00% front
	0.00% deferred
	0.00% 12b-1
Management Fee	1.00% max./0.65% min.
3-,5-,10-yr Expense Projections	$33, $58, $128
Annual Brokerage Cost	0.14%

Historical Profile

Return	Average
Risk	Above Average
Rating	★★★
	Closed

	1983	1984	1985	1986	1987	1988	1989	1990	1991	1992	1993	1994	History
			55%	68%	89%	70%	82%	75%	85%	88%			
	---	---	12.16	12.07	9.08	10.01	14.66	14.56	24.19	24.29	24.42	22.71	NAV
	---	---	13.70 *	12.43	-11.65	19.05	50.85	0.59	69.21	1.97	3.43	-6.73	Total Return %
	---	---	-5.94 *	-6.25	-16.91	2.44	19.17	3.71	38.73	-5.65	-6.62	-8.04	+/- S&P 500
	---	---		-3.67	-14.01	1.11	21.68	6.77	35.01	-7.00	-7.85	-6.66	+/- Wilshire 5000
	---	---	4.20	6.53	4.20	8.81	0.10	1.27	0.10	0.75	1.04	0.28	Income Return %
	---	---	9.50	5.90	-15.85	10.24	50.75	-0.68	69.11	1.22	2.40	-7.00	Capital Return %
	---	---	---	71	98	16	1	54	2	87	95	78	Total Rtn % Rank All
	---	---	---	70	99	31	1	20	2	86	85	84	Total Rtn % Rank Obj
	---	---	0.44	0.80	0.41	0.80	0.02	0.19	0.02	0.18	0.25	0.07	Income $
	---	---	0.09	0.82	1.18	0.00	0.43	0.00	0.42	0.19	0.45	0.00	Capital Gains $
	---	---	1.99	2.00	1.79	1.70	1.88	1.32	1.07	1.12	1.05	1.02	Expense Ratio %
	---	---	5.68	3.55	2.98	3.35	0.68	1.28	1.30	1.27	0.87	0.57	Income Ratio %
	---	---	68	152	202	317	220	228	163	79	99	102	Turnover Rate %
	---	---	2.5	17.0	13.5	7.1	67.8	243.9	1348.4	3137.2	3515.9	2504.3	Net Assets ($mil)

Investment Style History Equity

Average % Stocks Held in Portfolio

Growth of $10,000

- |||| Value of Fund ($000)
- — Value of Index ($000) SPMid400
- ▼ Manager Change
- ▽ Partial Manager Change
- ► Mgr Unknown After
- ◄ Mgr Unknown Before

Performance Quartile (Within Objective)

Risk Analysis

Time Period	Load-Adj Return %	Risk % Rank [1] All	Obj	Morningstar [2] Return	Morningstar Risk	Morningstar Risk-Adj Rating
1 Yr	-6.73					
3 Yr	-0.54	94	93	-1.15 [3]	1.34	★
5 Yr	10.86	89	87	1.60 [3]	1.12	★★★★
10 Yr	---					
Average Historical Rating (81 months)					4.0	★ s

[1] 1 = low, 100 = high   [2] 1.00 = Equity Avg   [3] 1.00 = 90-day T-bill return

Other Measures

	Standard S&P 500	Best Fit SPMid400
Standard Deviation	11.25	Alpha	-6.5	-7.1
Mean	0.09	Beta	1.13	1.00
Sharpe Ratio	-0.31	R-Squared	63	78

Investment Style

	Stock Portfolio Avg	Relative S&P 500
Price/Earnings Ratio	22.1	1.20
Price/Book Ratio	4.7	1.37
5 Yr Earnings Gr %	15.5	2.79
Return on Assets %	10.5	1.41
Debt % Total Cap	22.5	0.80
Med Mkt Cap ($mil)	9840	0.76

Style: Value Blend Growth / Size Large Med Small

Diversification Value for Portfolio Types

Large Cap:	Small Cap:	Bond:	Balanced:	Diversified:
Low	Low	High	Low	Low

Portfolio 12-31-94

Share Chg (07-94)000	Amount 000	Total Stocks: 32 / Total Fixed-Income: 2	Value $000	% Net Assets
531	3986	Lowe's	138511	5.53
-248	2452	Coca-Cola	126259	5.04
-56	2634	First Data	124773	4.98
1393	2042	Motorola	118175	4.72
188	2271	FHLMC	114680	4.58
0	3785	Philips Electronics	111182	4.44
50	2497	Citicorp	103313	4.13
-62	1335	FNMA	97310	3.89
-648	1984	Home Depot	91247	3.64
-1570	2503	Merrill Lynch	89478	3.57
1082	1082	Pfizer	83608	3.34
1014	1348	Amgen	79545	3.18
7	1557	United HealthCare	70281	2.81
2067	2067	Digital Equipment	68730	2.74
670	1121	Microsoft	68497	2.74
-169	2275	AirTouch Communications	66246	2.65
659	1187	Conrail	59941	2.39
547	547	Hewlett-Packard	54677	2.18
-182	2638	Lone Star Steakhouse/Saloon	52763	2.11
-91	1440	Columbia/HCA Healthcare	52571	2.10
-540	1171	Oracle Systems	51672	2.06
-958	1719	Browning-Ferris Industries	48776	1.95
-375	1100	Compaq Computer	43454	1.74
370	830	General Motors Cl E	31972	1.28
236	487	Intel	31115	1.24

Composition % 12-31-94

Cash	13.9	Preferreds	6.6
Stocks	78.9	Convertibles	0.0
Bonds	0.7	Other	0.0

Tax Analysis

	Tax-Adj Historical Return %	% Pretax Return
3 Yr Avg	-1.03	NMF
5 Yr Avg	10.33	94.1
10 Yr Avg	---	---
Potential Capital Gain Exposure (% of assets)		9%

Most Similar Funds in MF500

AIM Weingarten	Strong Fit
Janus Growth & Income	Strong Fit
20th Century Growth Investor	Strong Fit

Index Allocation

	% of Stocks
S&P 500	86.4
S&P MidCap 400	2.5
U.S. Small Cap	4.9
Foreign	6.3

Sector Weightings

	% of Stocks	Relative S&P 500
Utilities	0.0	0.00
Energy	0.0	0.00
Financials	20.3	1.92
Industrial Cyclicals	1.2	0.08
Consumer Durables	13.6	2.19
Consumer Staples	6.5	0.52
Services	7.7	0.95
Retail	11.0	1.89
Health	13.7	1.58
Technology	25.9	2.83

Janus Venture

Janus Venture Fund seeks only capital appreciation.
The fund emphasizes investments in common stocks of small companies listed on a national securities exchange or NASDAQ. It expects that the majority of issuers will be companies with less than $250 million in annual revenues. The fund may also invest in large or well-known companies with potential for capital appreciation. Investments may include both domestic and foreign companies.

Ticker JAVTX	**Load** Clsd	**NAV** 48.68	**Yield** 0.1%	**SEC Yield** N/A	**Assets** 1496.1

Objective
Small Company

Manager's Investment Style

Management takes a typical Janus approach in pursuing stocks that have high earnings-growth rates and that sell at a discount to those rates. When price multiples exceed those growth rates, the stock is a sell candidate. With this fund, management attempts to combine fast-growing stocks in both mature and emerging domestic industries, concentrating its portfolio on those favored industries. The fund maintains a small position in foreign stocks and has often held large cash stakes.

Historical Profile
Return	Above Average
Risk	Below Average
Rating	★★★★
	Closed

67% 71% 87% 62% 68% 71% 74% 82%

Investment Style History
Equity
Average % Stocks Held
in Portfolio

Growth of $10,000
‖‖ Value of Fund ($000)
— Value of Index ($000)
SPMid400
▼ Manager Change
▽ Partial Manager Change
► Mgr Unknown After
◄ Mgr Unknown Before

Performance Quartile
(Within Objective)

Fund Manager(s)

Warren B. Lammert CFA(1987), since 12-93.
Birthdate: 01-62. BA, Yale 1984 MS, London School of Economics 1989
James P. Goff CFA, since 12-93. Birthdate: 03-64.

Manager Experience	Dates Managed	Invest Obj	Std Dev	+/- Index
Warren B. Lammert				
Janus Balanced	09/92 - 12/93	B	6.30	5.27
James P. Goff				
Janus Enterprise	09/92 - 12/94	G	13.34	14.91

	1983	1984	1985	1986	1987	1988	1989	1990	1991	1992	1993	1994	History
	---	---	24.88	27.45	24.55	27.85	35.85	34.71	47.63	49.30	48.88	48.68	NAV
	---	---	13.91 *	20.42	5.16	19.63	38.74	-0.40	47.82	7.44	9.08	5.46	Total Return %
	---	---	-5.74 *	1.74	-0.10	3.02	7.06	2.72	17.34	-0.18	-0.98	4.15	+/- S&P 500
	---	---	---	8.66	8.67	-0.90	14.80	13.16	4.37	-4.32	-5.46	8.12	+/- Wilshire 4500
	---	---	3.17	5.70	0.59	6.19	1.28	0.30	0.53	2.41	1.08	0.06	Income Return %
	---	---	10.74	14.72	4.57	13.44	37.46	-0.70	47.29	5.03	8.00	5.40	Capital Return %
	---	---	18	22	15	4	57	8	52	73	4		Total Rtn % Rank All
	---	---	6	16	55	9	20	52	78	82	11		Total Rtn % Rank Obj
	---	---	0.68	1.48	0.15	1.52	0.44	0.11	0.25	1.16	0.53	0.03	Income $
	---	---	0.70	1.04	4.17	0.00	2.35	0.89	3.43	0.71	4.37	2.84	Capital Gains $
	---	---	2.00	1.90	1.44	1.41	1.28	1.16	1.04	1.07	0.97	0.96	Expense Ratio %
	---	---	2.03	1.47	0.40	5.11	1.10	1.24	2.10	1.32	1.29	0.27	Income Ratio %
	---	---	293	248	250	299	219	184	167	124	139	114	Turnover Rate %
	---	---	7.8	31.3	30.4	34.7	104.7	276.9	1464.1	1706.4	1778.7	1496.1	Net Assets ($mil)

Performance 12-31-94

	1st Qtr	2nd Qtr	3rd Qtr	4th Qtr	Total
1987	16.25	4.42	4.23	-16.89	5.16
1988	7.90	7.06	3.77	-0.20	19.63
1989	6.61	14.89	13.87	-0.52	38.74
1990	-2.04	9.57	-14.81	8.93	-0.40
1991	22.27	-1.34	11.37	10.03	47.82
1992	-1.76	-3.61	2.39	10.81	7.44
1993	6.21	-1.30	1.70	2.32	9.08
1994	-3.05	-2.79	9.96	1.76	5.46

Bear Market Performance
Decile Rank (5-year period)

Worst ▬ Best

	Worst 3 Mo Period 1985-89	Worst 3 Mo Period 1990-94
Janus Venture	---	-14.81
+/- S&P 500	---	-1.07
+/- Best Fit Index : SPMid400	---	2.97

Trailing Returns

	Total Return %	+/- S&P 500	+/- Wil 4500	% Rank All	% Rank Obj	Growth of $10,000
3 Mo	1.76	1.77	4.26	4	22	10,176
6 Mo	11.89	7.03	7.70	3	23	11,189
1 Yr	5.46	4.15	8.12	4	11	10,546
3 Yr Avg	7.32	1.05	-0.29	25	63	12,360
5 Yr Avg	12.72	4.03	3.63	7	40	18,197
10 Yr Avg	---	---	---	---	---	---
15 Yr Avg	---	---	---	---	---	---

Operations

Address and Telephone	100 Fillmore Street Suite 300 Denver, CO 80206-4923 800-525-8983
Advisor	Janus Capital
Subadvisor	None
Distributor	Janus Distributors
States Available	All plus PR,GU,VI
Report Grade	B-
Income Distrib	Paid Annually
* Date of Inception	04-26-85
Fiscal Year End	October

Risk Analysis

Time Period	Load-Adj Return %	Risk % Rank [1] All	Risk % Rank [1] Obj	Morningstar [2] Return	Morningstar Risk	Morningstar Risk-Adj Rating
1 Yr	5.46					
3 Yr	7.32	67	21	1.12 [3]	0.75	★★★
5 Yr	12.72	62	8	2.16 [3]	0.74	★★★★★
10 Yr	---					

Average Historical Rating (81 months) 4.8 ★s

[1] 1 = low, 100 = high [2] 1.00 = Equity Avg [3] 1.00 = 90-day T-bill return

Other Measures

			Standard S&P 500	Best Fit SPMid400
Standard Deviation	8.88	Alpha	1.6	1.0
Mean	7.48	Beta	0.83	0.78
Sharpe Ratio	0.45	R-Squared	56	75

Investment Style

	Stock Portfolio Avg	Relative S&P 500
Price/Earnings Ratio	22.7	1.23
Price/Book Ratio	4.5	1.34
5 Yr Earnings Gr %	---	---
Return on Assets %	7.1	0.94
Debt % Total Cap	40.5	1.43
Med Mkt Cap ($mil)	717	0.06

Style
Value Blend Growth / Size LargeMedSmall

Diversification Value for Portfolio Types

Large Cap: Low	Small Cap: Low	Bond: High	Balanced: Low	Diversified: Low

Portfolio 12-31-94

Share Chg (07-94)000	Amount 000	Total Stocks: 97 Total Fixed-Income: 1	Value $000	% Net Assets
281	1191	Exide	66989	4.48
468	1432	RP Scherer	64972	4.34
	413	Nokia Pfd	60907	4.07
-288	1256	Wisconsin Central Transport	51812	3.46
155	1354	Paging Network	46048	3.08
233	1563	Minerals Technologies	45706	3.06
0	1334	APS Holding Cl A	37697	2.52
-5	1000	GFC Financial	31750	2.12
0	224	First Empire State	30464	2.04
150	780	AK Steel Holding	23985	1.60
-153	722	Illinois Central	22210	1.48
-77	800	Heritage Media Cl A	21500	1.44
0	937	Fiserv	20138	1.35
250	450	LSI Logic	18169	1.21
498	1019	Credit Acceptance	18095	1.21
463	463	Wabash National	18038	1.21
29	29	SAP Pfd	16328	1.09
261	786	TriMas	15718	1.05
93	528	Littelfuse	15438	1.03
0	173	Safra Republic Holdings	14419	0.96
-50	1101	Mercury Finance	14312	0.96
131	699	US Can	13284	0.89
0	285	Cardinal Health	13217	0.88
-50	372	Progressive	13015	0.87
-6	550	World Acceptance	12916	0.86

Composition % 12-31-94

Cash	27.4	Preferreds	4.1
Stocks	68.4	Convertibles	0.0
Bonds	0.0	Other	0.2

Tax Analysis

	Tax-Adj Historical Return %	% Pretax Return
3 Yr Avg	5.41	72.6
5 Yr Avg	10.85	82.2
10 Yr Avg	---	---
Potential Capital Gain Exposure (% of assets)		15%

Most Similar Funds in MF500

Fidelity Growth Company	Fair Fit
Columbia Growth	Fair Fit
Fidelity OTC	Fair Fit

Index Allocation

	% of Stocks
S&P 500	2.3
S&P MidCap 400	14.9
U.S. Small Cap	78.8
Foreign	4.0

Sector Weightings

	% of Stocks	Relative S&P 500
Utilities	1.2	0.09
Energy	1.5	0.15
Financials	15.1	1.43
Industrial Cyclicals	32.6	1.99
Consumer Durables	8.9	1.44
Consumer Staples	0.4	0.03
Services	20.4	2.50
Retail	1.9	0.32
Health	2.3	0.26
Technology	15.7	1.72

Expenses & Fees

Min Initial Purchase	Closed (Addt'l: $50)
Min IRA Purchase	$250 (Addt'l: $50)
Min Auto Invest Plan	$50 (Systematic Inv: $50)

Sales Fees	0.00% front
	0.00% deferred
	0.00% 12b-1
Management Fee	1.00% max./0.65% min.
3-,5-,10-yr Expense Projections	$31, $54, $119
Annual Brokerage Cost	0.21%

MORNINGSTAR 1995 Mutual Fund 500

Janus Worldwide

Ticker	Load	NAV	Yield	SEC Yield	Assets	Objective
JAWWX	None	24.39	2.1%	N/A	1542.6	World Stock

Janus Worldwide Fund seeks long-term growth of capital consistent with preservation of capital.

The fund normally invests nearly all of its assets in the common stocks of foreign and domestic issuers. Its portfolio is usually spread across at least five different countries, although it may at times invest in fewer than five countries. Common stock investments are selected from companies and industries that are experiencing favorable demand for their products or services and that operate in a favorable competitive environment. The fund may engage in futures and options strategies.

Manager's Investment Style

Management has moved its strategy abroad. After years of sticking to the stability of the U.S. market, the fund has finally moved assets overseas. Tempted by the low-valuation and cost-cutting policies of electronic companies, management now owns a small stake in the Japanese market. The fund also holds a large portion of assets in classic European growth stocks.

Fund Manager(s)

Helen Young Hayes CFA(1987), since 10-92. BA, Yale 1984

Manager Experience

	Dates Managed	Invest Obj	Std Dev	+/- Index
Helen Young Hayes				
Idex II Global A	10/92 - 12/94	WW	13.09	11.02
Janus Overseas	05/94 - 12/94	WF	6.65	-1.39

Historical Profile

Return	High
Risk	Average
Rating	★★★★★
	Highest

Investment Style History
Equity
Average % Stocks Held in Portfolio

								66%	69%	83%	76%

Growth of $10,000
|||| Value of Fund ($000)
— Value of Index ($000) MSAllCtry
▼ Manager Change
▽ Partial Manager Change
► Mgr Unknown After
◄ Mgr Unknown Before

Performance Quartile (Within Objective)

	1983	1984	1985	1986	1987	1988	1989	1990	1991	1992	1993	1994	History
NAV	---	---	---	---	---	---	---	---	18.55	20.00	25.03	24.39	NAV
	---	---	---	---	---	---	---	---	24.00 *	9.01	28.41	3.61	Total Return %
	---	---	---	---	---	---	---	---	8.25 *	1.39	18.35	2.30	+/- S&P 500
	---	---	---	---	---	---	---	---	---	14.23	5.91	-1.46	+/- MSCI World
	---	---	---	---	---	---	---	---	0.01	1.19	1.22	2.18	Income Return %
	---	---	---	---	---	---	---	---	23.99	7.82	27.19	1.43	Capital Return %
	---	---	---	---	---	---	---	---	---	33	9	6	Total Rtn % Rank All
	---	---	---	---	---	---	---	---	---	2	61	6	Total Rtn % Rank Obj
	---	---	---	---	---	---	---	---	0.00	0.22	0.28	0.54	Income $
	---	---	---	---	---	---	---	---	0.05	0.00	0.38	1.01	Capital Gains $
	---	---	---	---	---	---	---	---	2.50	1.73	1.32	1.12	Expense Ratio %
	---	---	---	---	---	---	---	---	0.02	1.74	0.92	0.42	Income Ratio %
	---	---	---	---	---	---	---	---	---	147	124	158	Turnover Rate %
	---	---	---	---	---	---	---	---	29.1	208.3	935.2	1542.6	Net Assets ($mil)

Performance 12-31-94

	1st Qtr	2nd Qtr	3rd Qtr	4th Qtr	Total
1987	---	---	---	---	---
1988	---	---	---	---	---
1989	---	---	---	---	---
1990	---	---	---	---	---
1991	---	---	12.47	9.67	24.00 *
1992	-0.05	2.05	-4.07	11.41	9.01
1993	6.25	0.56	6.64	12.69	28.41
1994	-0.88	-1.09	6.23	-0.52	3.61

Bear Market Performance

Decile Rank (5-year period)

Worst _____ Best

	Worst 3 Mo Period 1985-89	Worst 3 Mo Period 1990-94
Janus Worldwide	---	---
+/- S&P 500	---	---
+/- Best Fit Index :	---	---

Trailing Returns

	Total Return %	+/- S&P 500	+/- MSCI World	% Rank All	% Rank Obj	Growth of $10,000
3 Mo	-0.52	-0.51	0.21	35	6	9,948
6 Mo	5.68	0.82	4.28	9	4	10,568
1 Yr	3.61	2.30	-1.46	6	6	10,361
3 Yr Avg	13.19	6.93	6.34	6	9	14,503
5 Yr Avg	---	---	---	---	---	---
10 Yr Avg	---	---	---	---	---	---
15 Yr Avg	---	---	---	---	---	---

Operations

Address and Telephone	100 Fillmore Street Suite 300 Denver, CO 80206-4923 800-525-8983	Min Initial Purchase	$1000 (Addt'l: $50)	
		Min IRA Purchase	$250 (Addt'l: $50)	
		Min Auto Invest Plan	$50 (Systematic Inv: $50)	
Advisor	Janus Capital			
Subadvisor	None	**Expenses & Fees**		
Distributor	Janus Distributors	Sales Fees	0.00% front	
States Available	All plus PR,GU,VI		0.00% deferred	
Report Grade	B		0.00% 12b-1	
Income Distrib	Paid Annually	Management Fee	1.00% max./0.65% min.	
* Date of Inception	05-15-91	3-,5-,10-yr Expense Projections	$42, $72, $159	
Fiscal Year End	October	Annual Brokerage Cost	0.22%	

Risk Analysis

Time Period	Load-Adj Return %	Risk % Rank[1] All	Obj	Morningstar[2] Return	Morningstar Risk	Morningstar Risk-Adj Rating
1 Yr	3.61					
3 Yr	13.19	70	20	3.04[3]	0.78	★★★★★
5 Yr	---	---	---	---	---	---
10 Yr	---	---	---	---	---	---
Average Historical Rating (8 months)				5.0	★s	

[1] 1 = low, 100 = high [2] 1.00 = Equity Avg [3] 1.00 = 90-day T-bill return

Other Measures

				Standard S&P 500	Best Fit MSAllCtry
Standard Deviation	10.52	Alpha		7.0	7.8
Mean	13.00	Beta		0.93	0.75
Sharpe Ratio	0.90	R-Squared		49	57

Investment Style

	Stock Portfolio Avg	Rel MSCI EAFE	Rel Obj	Style
Price/Earnings Ratio	27.8	0.75	1.13	
Price/Cash Flow	15.8	1.02	1.17	
Price/Book Ratio	4.3	1.66	1.48	
5 Yr Earnings Gr %	3.0#	---	0.63	
Return on Assets %	6.4#	1.40	0.92	
Debt % Total Cap	23.6#	0.69	0.82	
Med Mkt Cap ($mil)	10887	0.91	2.16	

figure is based on 50% or less of stocks

Diversification Value for Portfolio Types

Large Cap: Medium	Small Cap: Medium	Bond: High	Balanced: Medium	Diversified: Low

Portfolio 12-31-94

Share Chg (07-94)000	Amount 000	Total Stocks: 82 Total Fixed-Income: 2	Value $000	% Net Assets
3338	3338	Kinnevik Cl B	110525	7.17
2385	3310	Astra Cl A Free	85551	5.55
1070	1070	Citicorp	44275	2.87
194	692	Sony	39233	2.54
19	525	Wolters Kluwer (Netherlands)	38888	2.52
3261	3575	Elsevier (Netherlands)	37312	2.42
-39	10548	Grupo Financiero Imbursa	27555	1.79
	179	Nokia Pfd	26377	1.71
-1469	948	Teledenmark Cl B (ADR)	24174	1.57
217	879	Securitas Cl B Free	23658	1.53
67	457	RP Scherer	20733	1.34
-1328	603	Philips Electronics	17859	1.16
863	1769	Hitachi	17548	1.14
329	2167	Mitsubishi Heavy Industries	16519	1.07
280	280	Motorola	16204	1.05
137	137	Accor	14940	0.97
-11	17	BBC Brown Boveri (Br)	14728	0.95
34	34	Carrefour	14248	0.92
-261	804	Matsushita Electric Indl	13225	0.86
1110	1110	Trygg-Hansa Spp Cl B Free	11953	0.77

Regional Exposure 10-01-94

% of Stocks			
Europe	49	Pacific Rim	0
Japan	15	U.S.	17
Latin Amer	13	Other	0

Composition % 12-31-94

Cash	41.7	Preferreds	2.7
Stocks	55.7	Convertibles	0.0
Bonds	0.0	Other	0.0

Tax Analysis

	Tax-Adj Historical Return %	% Pretax Return
3 Yr Avg	12.03	90.2
5 Yr Avg	---	---
10 Yr Avg	---	---
Potential Capital Gain Exposure (% of assets)		5%

Most Similar Funds in MF500

New Perspective	Weak Fit
G.T. Global Worldwide Grth A	Weak Fit
Putnam Global Growth A	Weak Fit

Top 5 Countries 10-01-94

	% of Stocks
U.S.	17
Germany	17
Japan	15
Netherlands	13
Sweden	12

Total Number of Countries: 19
Hedging Policy: Occasional

Sector Weightings

	% of Stocks	Relative S&P 500
Utilities	3.2	0.39
Energy	0.0	0.00
Financials	22.1	1.34
Industrial Cyclicals	6.7	0.29
Consumer Durables	19.6	1.90
Consumer Staples	2.2	0.42
Services	14.1	1.19
Retail	7.4	1.28
Health	14.6	2.78
Technology	10.2	1.15

Japan

	Ticker	Load	NAV	Yield	SEC Yield	Assets	Objective
	SJPNX	None	10.51	0.0%	N/A	586.0	Pacific Stock

Japan Fund seeks capital appreciation. Current income is of secondary importance.

The fund will invest at least 80% of its assets in Japanese securities (i.e., securities issued by entities organized under the laws of Japan that have either 50% or more of their assets in Japan or derive 50% of their revenues from Japan). The fund may also invest in other securities issued by Japanese entities, such as warrants and corporate debt securities, including convertible debentures.

Prior to Aug. 14, 1987, Japan Fund operated as a closed-end investment company.

Manager's Investment Style

Though value can be hard to come by in Japan's expensive market, the fund's managers have a commitment to bargains. Their value approach, low-turnover, and willingness to use convertibles or cash have yielded high returns and low risk relative to the pure-Japan group.

Fund Manager(s)

Seung Kwak CFA(1988), since 1989. Birthdate: 06-61. BA, Middlebury C. 1983 MA, Yale 1985

Elizabeth J. Allan, since 1990. MA, Princeton U. 1982 MBA, New York U. 1988

Manager Experience

	Dates Managed	Invest Obj	Std Dev	+/- Index
Elizabeth J. Allan				
Scudder New Asia	02/94 - 12/94	WP	13.72	-7.20
Scudder Pacific Opport	02/94 - 12/94	WP	18.29	-8.62

Performance 12-31-94

	1st Qtr	2nd Qtr	3rd Qtr	4th Qtr	Total
1987	8.31	14.67	7.53	-0.47	32.93
1988	16.42	-8.74	0.28	12.12	19.47
1989	-2.26	-6.05	16.53	4.45	11.76
1990	-16.10	16.26	-22.44	10.55	-16.36
1991	8.35	0.44	0.43	-5.66	3.11
1992	-15.15	-0.66	0.22	-1.44	-16.75
1993	15.28	12.88	10.89	-14.32	23.64
1994	16.84	5.30	-5.19	-5.67	10.03

Bear Market Performance

Decile Rank (5-year period)

Worst | Best

	Worst 3 Mo Period 1985-89	Worst 3 Mo Period 1990-94
Japan	-8.74	-22.44
+/- S&P 500	-15.41	-8.70
+/- Best Fit Index : MSCI Pac	-2.83	1.86

Trailing Returns

	Total Return %	+/- S&P 500	+/- MSCI Japan	% Rank All	Obj	Growth of $10,000
3 Mo	-5.67	-5.66	-4.36	93	33	9,433
6 Mo	-10.57	-15.43	-4.00	100	96	8,943
1 Yr	10.03	8.72	-11.40	2	10	11,003
3 Yr Avg	4.24	-2.03	-1.94	64	81	11,327
5 Yr Avg	-0.47	-9.16	3.12	99	69	9,768
10 Yr Avg	15.64	1.26	-1.05	8	50	42,754
15 Yr Avg	15.61	1.12	---	9	33	88,035

Operations

Address and Telephone	Two International Place
	Boston, MA 02110
	800-535-2726 / 617-439-4640
Advisor	Asia Management
Subadvisor	Nikko International Capital Manager
Distributor	Scudder Investor Services
States Available	All
Report Grade	A+
Income Distrib	Paid Annually
Date of Inception	04-01-62
Fiscal Year End	December

Historical Profile
Return Average
Risk High
Rating ★★★ Neutral

88% | 86% | 87% | 83% | 90% | 83% | 91% | 99%

Growth of $10,000
‖‖‖ Value of Fund ($000)
— Value of Index ($000) MSCI Pac
▼ Manager Change
▽ Partial Manager Change
► Mgr Unknown After
◄ Mgr Unknown Before

Performance Quartile (Within Objective)

1983	1984	1985	1986	1987	1988	1989	1990	1991	1992	1993	1994	History
13.90	12.60	15.53	20.28	16.96	16.24	14.27	10.76	10.69	8.90	10.33	10.51	NAV
29.04	-1.78	38.89	77.55	32.93	19.47	11.76	-16.36	3.11	-16.75	23.64	10.03	Total Return %
6.57	-8.04	7.15	58.87	27.67	2.86	-19.92	-13.24	-27.37	-24.36	13.58	8.72	+/- S&P 500
4.51	-18.63	-4.18	-21.86	-10.10	-15.92	10.05	19.74	-5.81	4.71	-1.84	-11.40	+/- MSCI Japan
1.25	0.79	0.63	0.15	1.14	0.13	0.70	1.73	0.00	0.00	2.91	0.00	Income Return %
27.79	-2.56	38.26	77.39	31.79	19.35	11.06	-18.09	3.11	-16.74	20.73	10.03	Capital Return %
12	71	7	1	2	15	59	94	98	100	12	2	Total Rtn % Rank All
66	33	25	1	37	70	81	46	83	77	87	10	Total Rtn % Rank Obj
0.13	0.10	0.07	0.02	0.20	0.02	0.10	0.20	0.00	0.00	0.28	0.00	Income $
1.00	1.05	1.36	4.67	9.08	3.88	3.59	0.99	0.41	0.00	0.39	0.85	Capital Gains $
0.69	0.66	0.64	0.70	0.90	1.01	1.02	1.05	1.26	1.42	1.25	1.12	Expense Ratio %
1.59	0.73	0.63	0.51	0.41	0.28	0.34	0.72	-0.15	-0.31	-0.47	-0.34	Income Ratio %
33	27	24	38	34	39	60	53	46	47	82	76	Turnover Rate %
282.9	269.8	360.0	584.3	311.8	403.9	400.8	313.5	334.9	409.1	471.1	586.0	Net Assets ($mil)

Risk Analysis

Time Period	Load-Adj Return %	Risk % Rank [1] All	Obj	Morningstar [2] Return	Morningstar Risk	Morningstar Risk-Adj Rating
1 Yr	10.03					
3 Yr	4.24	99	81	0.19 [3]	1.94	★★
5 Yr	-0.47	99	76	-1.09 [3]	1.92	★
10 Yr	15.64	95	75	1.64	1.35	★★★★
Average Historical Rating (109 months)					3.9	★s

[1] 1 = low, 100 = high [2] 1.00 = Equity Avg [3] 1.00 = 90-day T-bill return

Other Measures

	Standard S&P 500		Best Fit MSCI Pac
Standard Deviation	21.72	Alpha	2.5	-2.4
Mean	6.47	Beta	0.17	0.77
Sharpe Ratio	0.14	R-Squared	0	75

Investment Style

	Stock Portfolio Avg	Rel MSCI EAFE	Rel Obj
Price/Earnings Ratio	50.2	1.36	1.58
Price/Cash Flow	18.8#	1.21	0.98
Price/Book Ratio	2.4	0.93	0.83
5 Yr Earnings Gr %	-2.5	---	-0.22
Return on Assets %	3.7	0.80	0.45
Debt % Total Cap	25.7	0.76	1.07
Med Mkt Cap ($mil)	4378	0.37	1.06

Style V B G Size L M S

figure is based on 50% or less of stocks

Diversification Value for Portfolio Types

Large Cap: High	Small Cap: High	Bond: High	Balanced: High	Diversified: Medium

Expenses & Fees

Sales Fees	0.00% front
	0.00% deferred
	0.00% 12b-1
Management Fee	0.85% max./0.65% min.
3-,5-,10-yr Expense Projections	$38, $66, $145
Annual Brokerage Cost	0.43%

Min Initial Purchase	$1000 (Addt'l: $100)
Min IRA Purchase	$500 (Addt'l: None)
Min Auto Invest Plan	$50 (Systematic Inv: $50)

Portfolio 06-30-94

Total Stocks: 66
Total Fixed-Income: 0

Share Chg (12-93)000	Amount 000		Value $000	% Net Assets
94	407	Nichiei	36171	4.92
89	376	Kyocera	28135	3.83
323	1472	Canon	25855	3.52
159	2751	Toshiba	22568	3.07
30	304	Secom	21142	2.88
38	336	Sony (ADR)	20436	2.78
18	147	Autobacs Seven	20322	2.77
113	348	Ito-Yokado	19256	2.62
1699	1699	Hitachi	17767	2.42
57	148	Keyence	17707	2.41
1502	1502	Fujitsu	17232	2.34
850	850	Takuma	16397	2.23
-325	1224	Suzuki Motor	16279	2.22
225	512	Ten Allied	15959	2.17
0	0	DDI	15465	2.10
719	2019	Itochu	15210	2.07
506	1437	Nippon Shokubai	14590	1.99
11	225	Sony Music Entertainment	14547	1.98
453	453	Komori	14488	1.97
761	761	Matsushita Electric Indl	13985	1.90

Index Allocation

	% of Stocks
S&P 500	0.0
S&P MidCap 400	0.0
U.S. Small Cap	0.0
Foreign	100.0

Composition % 12-31-94

Cash	-4.3	Preferreds	0.0
Stocks	104.3	Convertibles	0.0
Bonds	0.0	Other	0.0

Tax Analysis

	Tax-Adj Historical Return %	% Pretax Return
3 Yr Avg	2.81	65.4
5 Yr Avg	-2.17	NMF
10 Yr Avg	11.20	57.7

Potential Capital Gain Exposure (% of assets) 4%

Most Similar Funds in MF500

Japan OTC Equity	Fair Fit
Growth Fund Spain	Weak Fit
Scudder International	Weak Fit

Country Exposure 12-31-94

	% of Stocks
Japan	97
U.S.	3

Total Number of Countries: 2
Hedging Policy: Active

Sector Weightings

	% of Stocks	Relative S&P 500
Utilities	1.3	0.21
Energy	0.0	0.00
Financials	2.0	0.08
Industrial Cyclicals	39.8	1.79
Consumer Durables	18.6	1.35
Consumer Staples	0.5	0.19
Services	13.1	1.02
Retail	7.0	1.31
Health	2.1	1.20
Technology	15.6	1.95

Japan OTC Equity

	Ticker	NAV	Mkt Price	Prem/Disc	Yield	Objective
	JOF	$10.13	$9.75	-3.8%	0.0%	Pacific/Asia

Japan OTC Equity Fund seeks long-term capital appreciation.
The fund intends to maintain at least 65% of its assets in equity securities (including convertibles) traded in the Japanese OTC market. The fund may invest the balance in small-cap growth stocks traded on Japanese exchanges (such as the Second Section of the Tokyo Stock Exchange) and in yen-denominated or U.S.-dollar-denominated fixed-income securities.

Supermajority voting requirements are in place to discourage takeover attempts.

The fund conducted a secondary public offering in 1994's second quarter. An additional 2,875,000 shares were offered, raising $32,661,406.

Historical Profile
Return	Below Average
Risk	High
Rating	★ Lowest

	Highest Prem/Disc	Lowest Prem/Disc
	42.4 / -26.2	27.1 / -16.7 ...

(Highest Prem/Disc: 42.4 27.1 41.8 23.0 33.3)
(Lowest Prem/Disc: -26.2 -16.7 -0.2 -9.0 -9.3)

Growth of $10,000
- ■ at NAV ($000)
- — at Market Price ($000)

Premium / Discount %

Manager's Investment Style
An early 1995 management change leaves this fund facing a new future. Before the switch, management had restricted itself to Japan's over-the-counter market and had avoided the larger-cap stocks of Japan's First Section. This focus had limited management ability to shift assets among sectors, because the OTC market is domestically oriented and consumer driven. As such, banks and export-driven industries are underrepresented in the market--and thus in this portfolio. Management had fashioned a concentrated portfolio, which enhanced risk.

Fund Manager(s)
Iwao Komatsu. Since 1-95. BA'61 Tokoyo U.

	1983	1984	1985	1986	1987	1988	1989	1990	1991	1992	1993	1994	History
	---	---	---	---	---	---	---	8.91	10.14	6.92	8.95	10.13	NAV
	---	---	---	---	---	---	---	-13.77*	15.97	-31.76	29.34	13.18	NAV Total Return %
	---	---	---	---	---	---	---	-14.78*	-14.52	-39.37	19.28	11.87	+/- S&P 500
	---	---	---	---	---	---	---	---	3.84	-19.58	-3.23	5.41	+/- MSCI EAFE
	---	---	---	---	---	---	---	---	7.04	-10.30	3.85	-8.25	+/- MSCI Japan
	---	---	---	---	---	---	---	2.55*	2.16	0.00	0.00	0.00	Income Return %
	---	---	---	---	---	---	---	-16.33*	13.81	-31.76	29.34	13.18	Capital Return %
	---	---	---	---	---	---	---	---	59	100	15	3	Total Rtn % Rank All
	---	---	---	---	---	---	---	---	46	93	80	24	Total Rtn % Rank Obj
	---	---	---	---	---	---	---	-24.63*	26.24	-26.51	29.51	-1.27	Market Total Rtn %
	---	---	---	---	---	---	---	1.0	-0.4	15.8	3.9	8.9	Avg Prem/Disc %
	---	---	---	---	---	---	---	0.24	0.19	0.00	0.00	0.00	Income $
	---	---	---	---	---	---	---	0.46	0.00	0.00	0.00	0.00	Capital Gains $
	---	---	---	---	---	---	---	---	1.43	1.57	1.55	1.39	Expense Ratio %
	---	---	---	---	---	---	---	---	2.19	-0.89	-0.98	-0.71	Income Ratio %
	---	---	---	---	---	---	---	---	32	36	36	---	Turnover Rate %
	---	---	---	---	---	---	---	---	86.3	58.9	76.2	115.4	Net Assets ($mil)

Manager Experience
	Dates Managed	Invest Obj	Std Dev	+/- Index
Not available.				

NAV Performance % 12-30-94
	1st Qtr	2nd Qtr	3rd Qtr	4th Qtr	Total
1987	---	---	---	---	---
1988	---	---	---	---	---
1989	---	---	---	---	---
1990	-0.72*	14.62	-24.96	0.97	-13.77*
1991	23.01	15.05	-4.84	-13.89	15.97
1992	-14.69	-7.98	-3.14	-10.25	-31.76
1993	16.33	17.27	17.48	-19.30	29.34
1994	23.02	10.26	-8.73	-8.57	13.18

Bear Market Performance
Decile Rank (5-year period)

Worst ————————————— Best

	Worst 3 Mo Period 1985-89	Worst 3 Mo Period 1990-94
Japan OTC Equity	---	---
+/- S&P 500	---	---

Trailing Returns
	NAV Total Return %	+/- S&P 500	+/- MSCI Japan	% Rank All	% Rank Obj	Mkt Total Return %
3 Mo	-8.57	-8.56	-7.27	91	58	-15.22
6 Mo	-16.56	-21.42	-9.99	99	93	-21.21
1 Yr	13.18	11.87	-8.25	3	24	-1.27
3 Yr Avg	-0.03	-6.30	-6.21	93	93	-2.05
5 Yr Avg	---	---	---	---	---	---
Incept Avg	-0.02*	---	---	---	---	-2.30*

Risk Analysis
	Risk % Rank[1] All	Obj	Morningstar[2] Return	Morningstar[2] Risk	Morningstar Risk-Adj Rating
3 Yr	99	86	-0.45	1.82	★
5 Yr	---	---	---	---	
10 Yr	---	---	---	---	
Average Historical Rating (22 months)				1.2 ★s	

[1]1 = Low, 100 = High [2]1.00 = Equity Avg [3]1.00 = 90-day T-bill Return

Other Measures
				S&P 500
Standard Deviation	27.08	Alpha		0.36
Mean	3.59	Beta		-0.10
Sharpe Ratio	0.00	R-Squared		0

Investment Style
	Stock Portfolio Avg	Rel WS Japan	Rel WS Foreign
Price/Earnings Ratio	---	---	---
Price/Cash Flow Ratio	---	---	---
Price/Book Ratio	---	---	---
5 Yr Earnings Gr %	---	---	---
Return on Assets %	---	---	---
Debt % Total Cap	---	---	---
Med Mkt Cap ($mil)	---	---	---

figure is based on less than 50% of stocks

Country Exposure (top five) 12-31-94
	Securities %		Currency %
Japan	92	Japan	92
		US	8

Diversification Value for Portfolio Types
Large Cap: High	Small Cap: High	Bond: High	Balanced: High	Diversified: High

Portfolio 08-31-94
Total Equity: 44 Total Fixed-Income: 0

Share Chg (05-94)	Amount		Value $000	% Total Invest
0	96000	Nippon Kanzai	5082	3.90
-28000	177000	Ishiguro Homa	4985	3.83
137000	137000	Joyo Bank	3763	2.89
0	169000	Well Mart	3595	2.76
150000	150000	Daikin Manufacturing	3566	2.74
0	81000	Ariake Japan	3551	2.73
0	247000	Canon Copier Sales	3528	2.71
0	70000	Shinmei Electric	3482	2.67
0	110000	USC	3472	2.67
0	170000	Paltac	3396	2.61
15000	30000	Sanyo Shinpan Finance	3146	2.42
0	254000	Nihon Plast	3120	2.40
110000	110000	Techono Ryowa	3109	2.39
0	90000	Kyoritsu Air Tech	3101	2.38
12000	90000	Maezawa Industries	3074	2.36
83000	83000	Beltechno	3059	2.35
30000	180000	Daika	3020	2.32
19000	120000	ArcLand Sakamoto	2996	2.30
19600	61000	Seikagaku	2991	2.30
0	188000	Daiichi Kyoken	2985	2.29
9000	26000	Tsutsumi Jewelry	2947	2.26
26000	50000	Getz Brothers	2926	2.25
30000	107000	Sumida Electric	2848	2.19
12000	100000	Cox	2797	2.15
0	221000	Sekiwa Real Estate	2781	2.14

Composition % 12-31-94
Cash	7.9	Preferreds	0.0
Stocks	92.1	Convertibles	0.0
Bonds	0.0	Other	0.0

Tax Analysis
	Tax-Adj Historical Return %	% Pretax Return
3 Yr Avg	-0.03	NMF
5 Yr Avg	---	---
10 Yr Avg	---	---
Potential Capital Gain Exposure (% of assets)		-9

Most Similar Funds in MF500
Japan	Weak Fit
Growth Fund Spain	Weak Fit
Scudder International	Weak Fit

Sector Weightings
	% of Stocks
Utilities	0.0
Energy	0.0
Financials	5.7
Industrial Cyclicals	8.1
Consumer Durables	14.5
Consumer Staples	10.5
Services	22.2
Retail	21.6
Health	8.9
Technology	8.6

Operations
Address and Telephone	180 Maiden Lane, New York, NY 10038, 212-509-7583
Advisor	Nomura Investment Mgmt.
Subadvisor	N/A
Administrator	N/A
Transfer Agent	State Street Bank and Trust Co.
Custodian	State Street Bank and Trust Co.
Auditor	Price Waterhouse LLP
Legal Counsel	Brown & Wood

Income Distrib Schedule	Paid Irregularly
Management Fee	1.10%
Reinvestment Plan	Yes
Direct Purchase Plan	No
Shares Outstanding	11,384,000
Exchange	NYSE
*Date of Inception	03-14-90
Shareholder Report	B+

John Hancock Income Securities

	Ticker	NAV	Mkt Price	Prem/Disc	Yield	Objective
	JHS	$15.11	$13.75	-9.0%	9.2%	Corp General

John Hancock Income Securities Trust seeks a high level of current income consistent with prudent investment risk. The fund invests virtually all of its assets in fixed-income instruments. It may invest up to 20% in income-producing preferred and common stocks.

-5.0	-6.3	-2.7	4.0	4.7	0.3	-0.7	0.1	5.8	7.7	4.7	1.1	Highest Prem/Disc
-11.4	-10.7	-7.3	-3.3	-7.7	-5.0	-5.5	-9.2	-3.2	0.2	-2.8	-11.2	Lowest Prem/Disc

Historical Profile

Return	Above Average
Risk	Below Average
Rating	★★★★ Above Average

Growth of $10,000
- ■ at NAV ($000)
- — at Market Price ($000)

Premium Discount %

	1983	1984	1985	1986	1987	1988	1989	1990	1991	1992	1993	1994	History
	14.18	14.60	16.19	16.90	15.30	15.24	15.61	15.20	16.25	16.31	16.97	15.11	NAV
	9.89	16.42	24.36	14.86	2.48	9.71	12.81	7.59	17.15	9.16	13.25	-2.63	NAV Total Return %
	1.52	1.27	2.24	-0.39	-0.28	1.83	-1.74	-1.36	1.15	1.91	3.50	0.29	+/- LB Aggregate
	0.62	-0.20	0.30	-1.68	-0.08	0.48	-1.18	0.43	-1.35	0.46	1.09	1.30	+/- LB Corp
	11.83	13.46	13.47	10.47	11.94	10.10	10.38	10.21	10.25	8.79	8.34	7.94	Income Return %
	-1.94	2.96	10.89	4.39	-9.47	-0.39	2.43	-2.63	6.91	0.37	4.91	-10.56	Capital Return %
	64	9	51	41	47	74	42	19	53	51	67	25	Total Rtn % Rank All
	46	13	37	35	45	57	32	8	80	50	51	35	Total Rtn % Rank Obj
	9.93	16.37	33.31	17.89	-5.25	13.06	17.73	6.93	24.20	7.16	7.22	-8.87	Market Total Rtn %
	-8.9	-8.5	-5.3	0.8	-1.5	-3.0	-3.4	-3.8	3.0	3.5	0.2	-5.5	Avg Prem/Disc %
	1.55	1.58	1.63	1.57	1.90	1.47	1.47	1.47	1.46	1.38	1.32	1.28	Income $
	0.00	0.00	0.00	0.00	0.00	0.00	0.00	0.00	0.00	0.00	0.13	0.08	Capital Gains $
	---	0.72	0.70	0.66	0.68	0.71	0.71	0.70	0.74	0.81	0.84	0.86	Expense Ratio %
	---	11.63	10.80	9.49	9.18	9.39	9.55	9.64	9.28	8.46	7.67	7.96	Income Ratio %
	---	24	34	49	36	24	66	85	92	111	95	---	Turnover Rate %
	---	132.2	147.0	155.0	142.7	143.7	149.2	147.3	160.0	162.0	170.4	153.7	Net Assets ($mil)

Manager's Investment Style

Management employs a dual-barbell strategy, balancing long-term high-quality Treasuries with lower-quality and shorter-term high-yield corporate bonds. The fund also invests regularly in mortgage-backed securities. Management alters the portfolio's duration to reflect its interest-rate outlook, but doesn't stray much from the four- to six-year range.

Fund Manager(s)

Barry Evans, CFA. Since 5-88. BBA'83 U. of Georgia; MBA'86 Northeastern U.

Manager Experience

	Dates Managed	Invest Obj	Std Dev	+/- Index
Barry Evans				
J Hancock Inv	05/88 - 12/94	CB	4.33	0.55
Hancock Sovereign Bal A	10/92 - 12/94	B	5.37	-2.97

NAV Performance % 12-30-94

	1st Qtr	2nd Qtr	3rd Qtr	4th Qtr	Total
1987	2.31	-2.27	-3.69	6.41	2.48
1988	4.10	1.33	2.71	1.26	9.71
1989	1.21	7.34	1.24	2.56	12.81
1990	-0.76	3.69	-0.11	4.66	7.59
1991	3.27	2.33	5.40	5.18	17.15
1992	-0.32	3.90	4.67	0.70	9.16
1993	5.24	3.57	3.45	0.44	13.25
1994	-2.79	-1.30	0.81	0.67	-2.63

Bear Market Performance

Decile Rank (5-year period)

Worst — Best

	Worst 3 Mo Period 1985-89	Worst 3 Mo Period 1990-94
J Hancock Inc	-4.06	-5.21
+/- LB Aggregate	-0.51	-0.28

Trailing Returns

	NAV Total Return %	+/- LB Agg	+/- LB Corp	% Rank All	% Rank Obj	Mkt Total Return %
3 Mo	0.67	0.29	0.23	14	50	-3.15
6 Mo	1.48	0.49	0.31	23	35	-1.03
1 Yr	-2.63	0.29	1.30	25	35	-8.87
3 Yr Avg	6.38	1.83	0.96	42	34	1.55
5 Yr Avg	8.70	1.07	0.43	39	40	6.82
10 Yr Avg	10.64	0.69	0.01	42	25	10.67

Operations

Address and Telephone	101 Huntington Avenue, Boston, MA 02199, 617-375-1500 / 800-843-0090
Advisor	John Hancock Advisers, Inc.
Subadvisor	N/A
Administrator	John Hancock Advisers, Inc.
Transfer Agent	Bank of Boston
Custodian	Investors Bank & Trust Co.
Auditor	Ernst & Young LLP
Legal Counsel	Hale & Dorr

Risk Analysis

	Risk % Rank[1] All	Risk % Rank[1] Obj	Morningstar[2] Return	Morningstar[2] Risk	Morningstar Risk-Adj Rating
3 Yr	23	38	0.83[3]	0.67	★★★★
5 Yr	19	8	0.99[3]	0.64	★★★★
10 Yr	14	31	1.08	0.89	★★★★
Average Historical Rating (144 months)				3.8 ★s	

[1] 1 = Low, 100 = High [2] 1.00 = Fixed-Inc Avg [3] 1.00 = 90-day T-bill Return

Other Measures

			LB Aggregate
Standard Deviation	4.29	Alpha	1.72
Mean	6.29	Beta	1.05
Sharpe Ratio	0.64	R-Squared	95

Investment Style

Interest-Rate Stance

	Fund	Relative Objective
Avg Eff Duration	5.0 Yrs**	0.78
Avg Eff Maturity	15.3 Yrs	0.97
Avg Wtd Coupon	9.81%	1.10
Avg Wtd Price	103.8% Par 1.05	

Duration Short Intm Long

Quality
Avg Cred Quality A
** figure provided by fund

Credit Analysis 12-31-94

	% of Bonds		% of Bonds
US Govt	41	BB	13
AAA	0	B	9
AA	9	Below B	0
A	15	NR/NA	0
BBB	13		

Diversification Value for Portfolio Types

Large Cap: Medium	Small Cap: High	Bond: None	Balanced: Medium	Diversified: Medium

Portfolio 09-30-94

Amount 000	Total Equity: 1 Total Fixed-Income: 111	Maturity	Value $000	% Total Invest
8425	US Treasury Bond 10.75%	08-15-05	10294	6.79
5210	US Treasury Bond 8.875%	08-15-17	5669	3.74
4000	Intl Bank Reconstr/Dev 9.25%	07-15-17	4384	2.89
4134	GNMA 8.5%	04-15-23	4127	2.72
4000	CTC Mansfield Funding 11.125%	09-30-16	3815	2.52
3000	US Treasury Note 7.25%	11-15-96	3035	2.00
2589	RJR Nabisco 10.5%	04-15-98	2741	1.81
2250	US Treasury Bond 9.125%	05-15-18	2510	1.66
2000	FICO 9.8%	04-06-18	2316	1.53
2000	FICO 9.4%	02-08-18	2232	1.47
1910	Kroger 12.95%	02-01-09	2203	1.45
2254	GNMA 8%	05-15-23	2186	1.44
2265	NWA 8.625%	08-01-96	2186	1.44
2000	Unisys 13.5%	07-01-97	2165	1.43
2000	American Airlines 14.375%	01-06-05	2151	1.42
2000	TKR Cable I 10.5%	10-30-07	2127	1.40
2000	Scotland Intl Finance 8.8%	01-27-04	2044	1.35
2000	Chugach Electric Assn 9.14%	03-15-22	2034	1.34
2000	Iberdrola 7.5%	10-01-02	1907	1.26
1750	Magma Copper 12%	12-15-01	1899	1.25
1821	RailCar Trust 7.75%	06-01-04	1818	1.20
1500	Midland American Cap 12.75%	11-15-03	1755	1.16
1690	US Treasury Note 8%	05-15-01	1741	1.15
1913	GNMA 7%	10-15-23	1733	1.14
1500	Security Pacific 10.5%	04-26-01	1702	1.12

Composition % 12-31-94

Cash	3.3	Preferreds	0.1
Stocks	0.0	Convertibles	0.0
Bonds	96.6	Other	0.0

Tax Analysis

	Tax-Adj Historical Return %	% Pretax Return
3 Yr Avg	3.13	47.6
5 Yr Avg	5.41	58.2
10 Yr Avg	6.63	51.5

Potential Capital Gain Exposure (% of assets) -7

Coupon Range

	% of Bonds	Relative Objective
0%, PIK	0.0	0.0
0% to 8.5%	23.6	0.7
8.5% to 9.5%	25.4	1.0
9.5% to 11%	29.7	1.3
More than 11%	21.3	2.5
Not applicable	0.0	0.0

1.0 = Objective Average

Most Similar Funds in MF500

Strong Government Sec	Strong Fit
Putnam Income A	Strong Fit
Portico Bond Immdex Ret	Strong Fit

Income Distrib Schedule	Paid Quarterly
Management Fee	0.50%
Reinvestment Plan	Yes
Direct Purchase Plan	No
Shares Outstanding	10,172,686
Exchange	NYSE
Date of Inception	02-14-73
Shareholder Report	B+

Kaufmann

Kaufmann Fund seeks long-term capital appreciation. Income is incidental.

The fund invests primarily in common stocks of small and medium companies; however, the fund may also purchase convertibles. In portfolio selection, it examines a company's growth prospects, the economic outlook for its industry, new-product development, management, security value, and financial characteristics. The fund may invest up to 10% of its assets in options and may leverage up to one third of its holdings.

The fund was reorganized and adopted its current investment strategy in 1986.

Manager's Investment Style

The fund's managers seek fast-growing firms with dominance in niche markets. When the fund began, a small asset base allowed management to hold as few as 10 issues in the portfolio. Inflows of investor capital have required the fund to expand its list. Now, the fund holds a larger, more-diversified portfolio, which has actually helped tone down risk. Management also shorts stocks it believes have weak earnings.

Fund Manager(s)

Lawrence Auriana, since 02-86. BS, Fordham U. 1965 New York U.

Hans Utsch, since 02-86. Birthdate: 07-36. BA, Amherst C. 1958 MBA, Columbia U. 1960

Manager Experience	Dates Managed	Invest Obj	Std Dev	+/- Index

Not available.

	Ticker	Load	NAV	Yield	SEC Yield	Assets	Objective
	KAUFX	None	3.76	0.0%	N/A	1590.6	Aggr. Growth

Historical Profile
Return High
Risk Above Average
Rating ★★★★
 Highest

Investment Style History
Equity
Average % Stocks Held in Portfolio

71% 74% 86% 89% 82% 91% 86% 94%

Growth of $10,000
|||| Value of Fund ($000)
— Value of Index ($000) Wil 4500
▼ Manager Change
▽ Partial Manager Change
► Mgr Unknown After
◄ Mgr Unknown Before

Performance Quartile (Within Objective)

1983	1984	1985	1986	1987	1988	1989	1990	1991	1992	1993	1994	History
---	---	---	1.13	0.70	1.11	1.63	1.53	2.65	2.95	3.45	3.76	NAV
---	---	---	1.80 *	-37.16	58.57	46.85	-6.14	79.43	11.32	18.18	8.99	Total Return %
---	---	---	-9.47 *	-42.41	41.96	15.16	-3.02	48.95	3.70	8.13	7.67	+/- S&P 500
---	---	---	---	-33.64	38.04	22.91	7.42	35.98	-0.44	3.65	11.64	+/- Wilshire 4500
---	---	---	0.00	0.90	0.00	0.00	0.00	0.00	0.00	1.23	0.00	Income Return %
---	---	---	1.80	-38.05	58.57	46.85	-6.13	79.43	11.32	16.95	8.99	Capital Return %
---	---	---	100	1	2	74	1	17	21	2		Total Rtn % Rank All
---	---	---	94	1	2	46	4	36	53	2		Total Rtn % Rank Obj
---	---	---	0.00	0.01	0.00	0.00	0.00	0.00	0.00	0.04	0.00	Income $
---	---	---	0.00	0.00	0.00	0.00	0.00	0.08	0.00	0.00	0.00	Capital Gains $
---	---	---	1.48	2.00	2.00	2.36	3.45	3.64	2.94	2.53	2.48	Expense Ratio %
---	---	---	1.67	0.92	-0.23	-1.41	-2.56	-1.96	-1.74	-1.34	-1.81	Income Ratio %
---	---	---	125	228	343	202	195	128	51	55		Turnover Rate %
---	---	---	1.9	1.9	5.7	36.0	39.5	140.1	313.2	965.4	1590.6	Net Assets ($mil)

Performance 12-31-94

	1st Qtr	2nd Qtr	3rd Qtr	4th Qtr	Total
1987	9.73	-4.03	-8.40	-34.85	-37.16
1988	15.71	25.93	18.63	-8.26	58.57
1989	18.92	7.58	19.01	-3.55	46.85
1990	0.61	12.20	-28.26	15.91	-6.14
1991	28.76	1.52	16.50	17.82	79.43
1992	-1.89	-12.31	5.70	22.41	11.32
1993	0.34	2.70	9.87	4.38	18.18
1994	-1.45	-5.88	12.50	4.44	8.99

Bear Market Performance

Decile Rank (5-year period)

Worst ▬▬▬▬▬ Best

	Worst 3 Mo Period 1985-89	Worst 3 Mo Period 1990-94
Kaufmann	---	-28.26
+/- S&P 500	---	-14.51
+/- Best Fit Index : Wil 4500	---	-10.03

Trailing Returns

	Total Return %	+/- S&P 500	+/- Wil 4500	% Rank All	% Rank Obj	Growth of $10,000
3 Mo	4.44	4.46	6.95	2	9	10,444
6 Mo	17.50	12.64	13.31	2	12	11,750
1 Yr	8.99	7.67	11.64	2	2	10,899
3 Yr Avg	12.76	6.50	5.15	7	10	14,338
5 Yr Avg	19.28	10.59	10.19	1	6	24,149
10 Yr Avg	---	---	---	---	---	---
15 Yr Avg	---	---	---	---	---	---

Operations

Address and Telephone	140 E. 45th Street 43rd Floor
	New York, NY 10017
	800-237-0132 / 212-922-0123
Advisor	Edgemont Asset Management
Subadvisor	None
Distributor	Kaufmann Fund
States Available	All except NE
Report Grade	B-
Income Distrib	Paid Annually
* Date of Inception	02-21-86
Fiscal Year End	December

Risk Analysis

Time Period	Load-Adj Return %	Risk % Rank [1] All	Obj	Morningstar [2] Return	Morningstar Risk	Morningstar Risk-Adj Rating
1 Yr	8.77					
3 Yr	12.69	90	38	2.87 [3]	1.21	★★★★
5 Yr	19.24	91	41	4.44 [3]	1.17	★★★★★
10 Yr	---	---	---	---	---	---

Average Historical Rating (71 months) 4.4 ★s

[1] = low, 100 = high [2] 1.00 = Equity Avg [3] 1.00 = 90-day T-bill return

Other Measures

				Standard S&P 500	Best Fit Wil 4500
Standard Deviation	15.41	Alpha		6.8	3.9
Mean	13.24	Beta		1.10	1.38
Sharpe Ratio	0.63	R-Squared		32	77

Investment Style

	Stock Portfolio Avg	Relative S&P 500
Price/Earnings Ratio	25.1	1.36
Price/Book Ratio	4.1	1.22
5 Yr Earnings Gr %	---	---
Return on Assets %	11.9	1.59
Debt % Total Cap	25.8	0.91
Med Mkt Cap ($mil)	451	0.03

Style Value Blend Growth
Size Large Med Small

Diversification Value for Portfolio Types

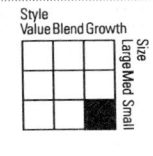

Large Cap: Medium Small Cap: Low Bond: High Balanced: Medium Diversified: Medium

Portfolio 06-30-94

Total Stocks: 298
Total Fixed-Income: 12

Share Chg (12-93) 000	Amount 000		Value $000	% Net Assets
595	1095	Microchip	38599	3.27
870	1570	Hospitality Franchise System	38465	3.26
275	800	Compuware	33100	2.81
679	1400	Life Partners	24500	2.08
226	566	Danka Business Systems (ADR)	22569	1.91
358	768	Altera	21682	1.84
27	777	Breed Technologies	21562	1.83
253	465	Exide	21404	1.81
448	840	Viking Office Products	21000	1.78
501	1001	Manufactured Home Cmntys	20771	1.76
772	1050	Lincare Holdings	20344	1.72
151	553	Department 56	17627	1.49
170	900	Nu-Kote Holdings Cl A	15525	1.32
528	828	Sun Healthcare Group	15422	1.31
0	430	Amway Asia Pacific	14943	1.27
300	700	Wolverine World Wide	14875	1.26
30	555	Advantage Health	12349	1.05
285	600	Health Management Assoc Cl A	12300	1.04
205	460	O'Reilly Automotive	12018	1.02
160	250	Kohl's	11750	1.00
2	702	Isomedix	11627	0.99
260	460	Primadonna Resorts	11155	0.95
0	450	Horizon Healthcare	10294	0.87
430	430	Blyth Industries	9738	0.83
400	400	Infosoft International	9200	0.78

Composition % 12-31-94

Cash	3.1	Preferreds	0.0
Stocks	93.4	Convertibles	0.4
Bonds	0.0	Other	3.1

Tax Analysis

	Tax-Adj Historical Return %	% Pretax Return
3 Yr Avg	12.61	98.7
5 Yr Avg	18.98	97.9
10 Yr Avg	---	---
Potential Capital Gain Exposure (% of assets)		22%

Most Similar Funds in MF500

Invesco Strat Technology	Strong Fit
AIM Constellation	Strong Fit
Hancock Special Equities A	Fair Fit

Index Allocation

	% of Stocks
S&P 500	0.6
S&P MidCap 400	5.2
U.S. Small Cap	86.6
Foreign	7.5

Sector Weightings

	% of Stocks	Relative S&P 500
Utilities	0.0	0.00
Energy	1.8	0.18
Financials	6.4	0.61
Industrial Cyclicals	9.7	0.59
Consumer Durables	6.6	1.07
Consumer Staples	0.8	0.07
Services	18.8	2.31
Retail	11.3	1.94
Health	17.0	1.96
Technology	27.5	3.00

Min Initial Purchase	$1500 (Addt'l: $100)
Min IRA Purchase	$500 (Addt'l: None)
Min Auto Invest Plan	$500 (Systematic Inv: $50)

Expenses & Fees

Sales Fees	0.00% front
	0.00% deferred
	1.00% 12b-1
Management Fee	1.50% flat fee
3-,5-,10-yr Expense Projections	$81, $137, $290
Annual Brokerage Cost	0.49%

Kemper Growth A

Ticker	Load	NAV	Yield	SEC Yield	Assets	Objective
KGRAX	5.75%	12.68	0.0%	N/A	1531.6	Growth

Kemper Growth Fund - Class A seeks growth of capital; current income is incidental.

The fund invests primarily in common stocks and convertible securities. Factors considered in investment selection include patterns of increasing growth in sales and earnings, development of new products or services, and favorable outlook for growth in the industry. The fund may invest up to 25% of its assets directly in foreign securities; it may invest without limit in American Depositary Receipts.

Class A shares have front loads; Class B shares have deferred loads, higher 12b-1 fees, and conversion features; Class C shares have level loads. Kemper Invstmnt Portfolios Growth Initial and Premier Shares merged into this fund on May 31, 1994.

Manager's Investment Style

Under previous management, the fund used an aggressive, earnings-momentum style that led to returns that either soared or severely flopped. Further, these managers often made concentrated sector bets on growth favorites technology or health care. The fund's current manager, C. Beth Cotner, favors diversification across sectors, with each stock limited to a 1.5% to 2% position in the portfolio. She is also willing to hold some less-expensive, more-defensive growth stocks.

Fund Manager(s)

C. Beth Cotner CFA, since 04-94. Birthdate: 12-52. BA, Ohio State U. 1974 MBA, George Washington U. 1976

Manager Experience

	Dates Managed	Invest Obj	Std Dev	+/- Index
C. Beth Cotner				
Kemper Small Cap Equity A	01/87 - 09/94	SC	20.44	0.25

Historical Profile
Return	Average
Risk	Above Average
Rating ★★★	Neutral

	92%	75%	82%	91%	94%	96%	99%	96%

Investment Style History
Equity
Average % Stocks Held in Portfolio

Growth of $10,000
IIII Value of Fund ($000)
— Value of Index ($000)
SPMid400
▼ Manager Change
▽ Partial Manager Change
► Mgr Unknown After
◄ Mgr Unknown Before

Performance Quartile (Within Objective)

1983	1984	1985	1986	1987	1988	1989	1990	1991	1992	1993	1994	History
13.63	11.22	12.21	10.06	6.99	7.47	9.58	9.36	14.74	14.45	13.67	12.68	NAV
25.10	-7.15	26.92	13.41	5.73	10.82	30.76	3.86	66.85	-1.56	1.63	-5.91	Total Return %
2.63	-13.41	-4.82	-5.27	0.47	-5.79	-0.93	6.98	36.37	-9.18	-8.43	-7.23	+/- S&P 500
1.63	-10.20	-5.65	-2.69	3.37	-7.12	1.58	10.04	32.65	-10.53	-9.65	-5.84	+/- Wilshire 5000
2.01	2.69	3.22	0.73	2.42	3.95	2.51	1.95	0.39	0.21	0.00	0.00	Income Return %
23.09	-9.84	23.69	12.68	3.31	6.87	28.25	1.91	66.46	-1.76	1.63	-5.91	Capital Return %
23	85	38	65	20	55	12	46	3	91	98	71	Total Rtn % Rank All
34	78	67	63	29	69	32	8	5	93	90	80	Total Rtn % Rank Obj
0.27	0.32	0.35	0.10	0.21	0.26	0.18	0.18	0.05	0.03	0.00	0.00	Income $
1.74	1.10	1.44	3.57	3.31	0.00	0.00	0.38	0.74	0.03	1.00	0.18	Capital Gains $
0.66	0.75	0.79	0.78	0.80	0.82	0.83	0.89	1.04	1.03	1.00	1.09	Expense Ratio %
1.91	3.26	2.73	1.96	1.67	3.38	2.11	1.84	0.59	0.32	0.06	0.24	Income Ratio %
73	94	97	181	247	61	160	194	143	83	139	115	Turnover Rate %
248.6	235.7	246.5	272.9	275.0	273.7	327.3	348.4	984.6	1660.4	1662.2	1531.6	Net Assets ($mil)

Performance 12-31-94

	1st Qtr	2nd Qtr	3rd Qtr	4th Qtr	Total
1987	22.17	4.98	7.27	-23.14	5.73
1988	4.86	6.80	-1.42	0.38	10.82
1989	6.02	10.85	12.40	-1.02	30.76
1990	-1.04	12.59	-15.09	9.79	3.86
1991	27.24	-2.94	13.67	18.85	66.85
1992	-6.85	-7.65	3.23	10.85	-1.56
1993	0.69	-1.58	7.05	-4.20	1.63
1994	-3.44	-7.35	5.72	-0.53	-5.91

Bear Market Performance

Decile Rank (5-year period)

Worst — Best

	Worst 3 Mo Period 1985-89	Worst 3 Mo Period 1990-94
Kemper Growth A	-30.41	-15.09
+/- S&P 500	-0.83	-1.35
+/- Best Fit Index : SPMid400	-1.60	2.68

Trailing Returns

	Total Return %	+/- S&P 500	+/- Wil 5000	% Rank All	% Rank Obj	Growth of $10,000
3 Mo	-0.53	-0.51	0.24	35	33	9,947
6 Mo	5.17	0.30	0.54	10	33	10,517
1 Yr	-5.91	-7.23	-5.84	71	80	9,409
3 Yr Avg	-2.00	-8.26	-8.61	99	96	9,413
5 Yr Avg	10.28	1.59	1.47	15	27	16,313
10 Yr Avg	13.66	-0.73	-0.20	20	34	35,972
15 Yr Avg	13.71	-0.77	-0.26	28	44	68,731

Operations

Address and Telephone	120 S. LaSalle Street
	Chicago, IL 60603
	800-621-1048 / 312-781-1121
Advisor	Kemper Financial Services
Subadvisor	None
Distributor	Kemper Financial Services
States Available	All plus PR
Report Grade	B+
Income Distrib	Paid Annually
Date of Inception	04-04-66
Fiscal Year End	September

Risk Analysis

Time Period	Load-Adj Return %	Risk % Rank [1] All	Risk % Rank [1] Obj	Morningstar [2] Return	Morningstar [2] Risk	Morningstar Risk-Adj Rating
1 Yr	-11.32					
3 Yr	-3.91	95	94	-2.01 [3]	1.38	★
5 Yr	8.98	86	81	1.07 [3]	1.07	★★★
10 Yr	12.99	80	70	1.06 [3]	1.03	★★★

Average Historical Rating (109 months) 3.4 ★s

[1] 1 = low, 100 = high   [2] 1.00 = Equity Avg   [3] 1.00 = 90-day T-bill return

Other Measures

				Standard S&P 500	Best Fit SPMid400
Standard Deviation	11.61	Alpha		-7.9	-8.6
Mean	-1.34	Beta		1.14	1.06
Sharpe Ratio	-0.42	R-Squared		61	81

Investment Style

	Stock Portfolio Avg	Relative S&P 500
Price/Earnings Ratio	23.6	1.28
Price/Book Ratio	4.6	1.35
5 Yr Earnings Gr %	15.3	2.76
Return on Assets %	9.8	1.31
Debt % Total Cap	23.6	0.83
Med Mkt Cap ($mil)	7171	0.55

Style: Value Blend Growth / Size Large Med Small

Diversification Value for Portfolio Types

Large Cap: Low	Small Cap: Low	Bond: High	Balanced: Low	Diversified: Low

Min Initial Purchase	$1000 (Addt'l: $100)
Min IRA Purchase	$250 (Addt'l: $50)
Min Auto Invest Plan	$50 (Systematic Inv: $50)

Expenses & Fees

Sales Fees	5.75% front
	0.00% deferred
	0.00% 12b-1
Management Fee	0.58% max./0.42% min., 0.25%A
3-,5-,10-yr Expense Projections	$89, $112, $178
Annual Brokerage Cost	0.48%

Portfolio 12-30-94

Total Stocks: 145
Total Fixed-Income: 2

Share Chg (09-94)	Amount 000		Value $000	% Net Assets
-1	691	Home Depot	31776	2.07
83	502	Procter & Gamble	31114	2.03
212	606	AT & T	30432	1.99
166	585	Coca-Cola	30152	1.97
49	559	General Electric	28494	1.86
374	1319	Wal-Mart Stores	28033	1.83
69	413	Philip Morris	23762	1.55
383	383	First Financial Management	23624	1.54
-2	836	Manpower	23523	1.54
292	481	Walt Disney	22183	1.45
-1	424	3Com	21879	1.43
-90	294	Schering-Plough	21786	1.42
0	176	General Re	21762	1.42
-1	650	MGIC Investment	21529	1.41
13	376	Medtronic	20936	1.37
-2	885	MBNA	20693	1.35
93	467	Campbell Soup	20606	1.35
-2	941	Newell	19760	1.29
-1	316	Emerson Electric	19742	1.29
-281	632	Silicon Graphics	19527	1.27
-1	362	CPC International	19300	1.26
27	307	Alco Standard	19244	1.26
-1	629	Enron	19183	1.25
0	230	Warner-Lambert	17737	1.16
-1	237	Gillette	17714	1.16

Composition % 09-30-94

Cash	2.3	Preferreds	0.0
Stocks	97.3	Convertibles	0.4
Bonds	0.0	Other	0.0

Tax Analysis

	Tax-Adj Historical Return %	% Pretax Return
3 Yr Avg	-2.79	NMF
5 Yr Avg	9.02	85.5
10 Yr Avg	10.67	67.7
Potential Capital Gain Exposure (% of assets)		6%

Most Similar Funds in MF500

20th Century Growth Investor	Strong Fit
Janus Twenty	Fair Fit
AIM Weingarten	Fair Fit

Index Allocation

	% of Stocks
S&P 500	64.1
S&P MidCap 400	14.1
U.S. Small Cap	17.4
Foreign	5.3

Sector Weightings

	% of Stocks	Relative S&P 500
Utilities	2.4	0.19
Energy	2.1	0.21
Financials	10.5	1.00
Industrial Cyclicals	12.8	0.78
Consumer Durables	3.5	0.57
Consumer Staples	13.7	1.10
Services	13.4	1.65
Retail	7.5	1.29
Health	14.9	1.72
Technology	19.1	2.08

MORNINGSTAR 1995 Mutual Fund 500

Kemper High-Yield A

	Ticker	Load	NAV	Yield	SEC Yield	Assets	Objective
	KHYAX	4.50%	7.56	10.1%	10.46%	2249.5	Corp Hi Yld

Kemper High-Yield Fund - Class A seeks high current income.
The fund normally invests at least 90% of its assets in fixed-income securities. It may invest without limit in high-yield, low-quality debt securities; it may also invest without limit in money market instruments. Foreign securities may constitute a portion of the fund's investments.
Class A shares have front loads and no 12b-1 fees; Class B shares have deferred loads and conversion features; Class C shares have level loads. Kemper Investment Portfolios High-Yield Fund - merged into this fund on May 31, 1994.

Historical Profile
Return	Above Average
Risk	Low
Rating	★★★★ Above Average

Investment Style History
Fixed Income
Income Rtn % Rank Obj

18	28	47	21	17	62	35	27	

Growth of $10,000
- |||| Value of Fund ($000)
- — Value of Index ($000) LB Agg
- ▼ Manager Change
- ▽ Partial Manager Change
- ► Mgr Unknown After
- ◄ Mgr Unknown Before

Performance Quartile (Within Objective)

	1983	1984	1985	1986	1987	1988	1989	1990	1991	1992	1993	1994	History
	8.44	8.16	8.87	9.38	8.77	8.87	7.71	5.74	7.33	7.75	8.47	7.56	NAV
	17.67	10.16	23.08	18.26	9.02	14.43	-1.15	-12.98	46.83	17.09	20.29	-1.72	Total Return %
	9.29	-4.99	0.96	3.01	6.27	6.55	-15.69	-21.92	30.83	9.84	10.53	1.20	+/- LB Aggregate
	---	---	---	2.62	2.50	3.00	-1.54	-6.60	3.08	0.43	1.39	-0.75	+/- FB High-Yield
	13.62	13.47	14.45	12.54	11.71	13.30	11.97	12.52	19.17	11.38	10.99	8.98	Income Return %
	4.04	-3.30	8.64	5.72	-2.68	1.13	-13.11	-25.50	27.67	5.70	9.30	-10.70	Capital Return %
	49	25	54	31	11	29	98	89	9	7	17	32	Total Rtn % Rank All
	25	26	32	2	1	26	54	66	13	51	31	24	Total Rtn % Rank Obj
	1.05	1.06	1.06	1.03	1.06	1.11	1.10	1.06	0.96	0.80	0.78	0.76	Income $
	0.00	0.00	0.00	0.00	0.36	0.00	0.00	0.00	0.00	0.00	0.00	0.00	Capital Gains $
	0.74	0.74	0.72	0.68	0.72	0.72	0.67	0.73	0.85	0.82	0.80	0.86	Expense Ratio %
	12.89	13.09	13.27	11.90	11.42	12.59	12.40	14.46	14.02	11.00	10.22	9.22	Income Ratio %
	108	78	87	95	118	76	45	37	31	69	101	93	Turnover Rate %
	183.5	190.7	228.1	384.1	500.4	1149.1	1406.3	1104.4	1658.3	1912.0	2299.5	2249.5	Net Assets ($mil)

Manager's Investment Style

Management hasn't entirely tamed its wild streak. Known for a massive stake in zero-coupon bonds, PIKs, and non-rated issues, the team has nonetheless scaled down this exposure over the past few years. It still relies in part, however, on these deferred-interest bonds to keep the fund's yield above its average peers'. (While deferred-interest bonds behave as zeros for the first few years, if they have a high yield to maturity, management can distribute most of this as current income.) The team is also willing to hold on to defaulted issues when it knows coupon payments are forthcoming.

Fund Manager(s)

Michael A. McNamara, since 1990. Birthdate: 12-44. BS, U. of Missouri 1971 MBA, Loyola U. 1979
Harry Resis, since 1992. Birthdate: 11-45. BA, Michigan State U. 1967

Manager Experience	Dates Managed	Invest Obj	Std Dev	+/- Index
Michael A. McNamara				
Kemper High-Income	01/89 - 12/94	CY	10.63	-0.23
Kemper Diversified Inc A	01/89 - 12/94	I	9.91	0.06

Performance 12-31-94

	1st Qtr	2nd Qtr	3rd Qtr	4th Qtr	Total
1987	8.07	-0.60	-0.59	2.10	9.02
1988	7.27	2.75	1.50	2.28	14.43
1989	1.91	3.20	-1.53	-4.55	-1.15
1990	-3.88	6.44	-11.77	-3.60	-12.98
1991	23.40	6.47	8.03	3.45	46.83
1992	10.18	2.65	2.52	0.98	17.09
1993	6.19	4.97	1.19	6.63	20.29
1994	-2.08	-0.56	0.78	0.14	-1.72

Bear Market Performance
Decile Rank (5-year period)

Worst ——————— Best

	Worst 3 Mo Period 1985-89	Worst 3 Mo Period 1990-94
Kemper High-Yield A	-4.91	-18.58
+/- LB Aggregate	-8.87	-19.32
+/- Best Fit Index : FB HY	---	-4.47

Trailing Returns
	Total Return %	+/- LB Aggregate	+/- FB High-Yield	% Rank All	% Rank Obj	Growth of $10,000
3 Mo	0.14	-0.23	0.19	18	12	10,014
6 Mo	0.93	-0.06	-0.63	39	13	10,093
1 Yr	-1.72	1.20	-0.75	32	24	9,828
3 Yr Avg	11.44	6.90	0.28	9	23	13,841
5 Yr Avg	12.08	4.45	-1.00	9	19	17,685
10 Yr Avg	12.25	2.30	---	35	1	31,745
15 Yr Avg	12.91	2.10	---	40	1	61,805

Operations

Address and Telephone	120 S. LaSalle Street Chicago, IL 60603 800-621-1048 / 312-781-1121	Min Initial Purchase	$1000 (Addt'l: $100)
		Min IRA Purchase	$250 (Addt'l: $50)
		Min Auto Invest Plan	$50 (Systematic Inv: $50)
Advisor	Kemper Financial Services		
Subadvisor	None	**Expenses & Fees**	
Distributor	Kemper Financial Services	Sales Fees	4.50% front
States Available	All plus PR		0.00% deferred
Report Grade	C+		0.00% 12b-1
Income Distrib	Paid Monthly	Management Fee	0.58% max./0.42% min., 0.25%A
Date of Inception	01-26-78	3-,5-,10-yr Expense Projections	$71, $90, $144
Fiscal Year End	September		

Risk Analysis

Time Period	Load-Adj Return %	Risk % Rank All	Risk % Rank Obj	Morningstar Return [2]	Morningstar Risk	Morningstar Risk-Adj Rating
1 Yr	-6.15					
3 Yr	9.75	9	53	1.89 [3]	0.38	★★★★★
5 Yr	11.05	49	82	1.66 [3]	0.66	★★★★
10 Yr	11.73	35	54	1.00	0.49	★★★★
Average Historical Rating (109 months)					3.9	★s

[1] 1 = low, 100 = high [2] 1.00 = Hybrid Avg [3] 1.00 = 90-day T-bill return

Other Measures
		Standard LB Agg	Best Fit FB HY
Standard Deviation	5.54	Alpha	7.3	-1.0
Mean	11.04	Beta	0.48	1.19
Sharpe Ratio	1.36	R-Squared	12	87

Investment Style

Interest-Rate Stance
Avg Effective Duration	4.3 Yrs
Avg Effective Maturity	7.8 Yrs

Quality
Avg Credit Quality	B
Avg Weighted Coupon	10.76%
Avg Weighted Price	90.34% of Par

Diversification Value for Portfolio Types
Large Cap: High	Small Cap: High	Bond: High	Balanced: High	Diversified: High

Portfolio 12-30-94

Total Stocks: 10
Total Fixed-Income: 181

Amount 000	Date of Maturity		Value $000	% Net Assets
48559	08-01-01	K & F Industries 13.75%	44431	1.98
58373	11-15-99	Trump Taj Mahal Funding 11.35%	38891	1.73
50996	12-15-03	Southland 5%	34422	1.53
32448	08-01-13	Continental Cablevision 9.5%	29689	1.32
27848	02-15-97	Amstar 11.375%	27430	1.22
28039	08-15-04	Owens-Illinois 9.75%	26497	1.18
28978	01-15-08	Comcast 9.5%	26225	1.17
28500	03-15-04	Bally's Park Place Fdg 9.25%	24367	1.08
46796	06-01-04	Echostar Communications Cv 12%	24217	1.08
23891	01-30-02	Cablevision Industries 10.75%	23771	1.06
23736	03-15-03	Pamida 11.75%	22905	1.02
22475	08-01-05	Great Dane Holding 12.75%	22250	0.99
22427	12-01-01	Beatrice Foods 12%	22090	0.98
23468	05-15-02	Adelphia Communications 12.5%	21943	0.98
20400	05-15-02	OrNda HealthCorp 12.25%	21828	0.97
22582	10-01-04	Foamex LP/Foamex Cap 11.875%	21565	0.96
22265	05-01-01	Arcadian Partner 10.75%	21152	0.94
20525	07-15-02	Rogers Cantel Mobile 11.125%	20935	0.93
20942	10-01-02	Stone Container 10.75%	20864	0.93
24749	10-15-01	Fairchild 12%	20789	0.92
31969	07-15-03	Eagle Industries 10.5%	20780	0.92
23935	06-30-98	Mesa Capital 0%	20704	0.92
22856	12-15-01	ColorTile 10.75%	19999	0.89
19844	04-15-04	Charter Medical 11.25%	19894	0.88
22979	07-07-06	Viacom International 8%	19705	0.88

Composition % 11-30-94
Cash	4.0	Preferreds	0.0
Stocks	3.0	Convertibles	0.0
Bonds	93.0	Other	0.0

Tax Analysis
	Tax-Adj Historical Return %	% Pretax Return
3 Yr Avg	7.63	64.2
5 Yr Avg	7.68	58.2
10 Yr Avg	7.30	47.1
Potential Capital Gain Exposure (% of assets)		-11%

Most Similar Funds in MF500
Putnam High Yield Adv A	Strong Fit
Liberty High-Income Bond A	Strong Fit
IDS Extra Income	Fair Fit

Coupon Range
	% of Bonds	Rel Obj
0%, PIK	0.2	0.03
0% to 11%	48.3	0.98
11% to 13%	44.3	1.33
13% to 14.5%	7.1	1.30
More than 14.5%	0.0	0.00
Not applicable	0.1	0.03

Credit Analysis 11-30-94
% of Bonds
US Govt	0	BB	18
AAA	0	B	71
AA	0	Below B	7
A	1	NR/NA	3
BBB	0		

Keystone Amer Omega A

	Ticker	Load	NAV	Yield	SEC Yield	Assets	Objective
	OMGAX	5.75%	15.54	0.0%	N/A	99.6	Aggr. Growth

Keystone America Omega Fund - Class A seeks capital appreciation.

The fund normally invests primarily in common stocks. The fund's fully-managed investment technique entails review of both individual securities and general economic conditions. It may employ leverage and may also engage in short-term trading.

Class A shares have front loads; Class B shares have deferred loads and higher 12b-1 fees; Class C shares are only available through certain dealers. Prior to April 19, 1989, the fund was named Omega Fund and had a different advisor. On Aug. 28, 1992, Keystone America Fund of Growth Stocks was merged into this fund.

Manager's Investment Style

Taking both a top-down and bottom-up approach, manager Maureen Cullinane looks at economic indicators to determine which sectors or market segments will outperform in the coming 18 to 24 months. The top-down portion of the strategy involves capitalizing in trends that are already in motion, which means not getting in too early or too late.

Fund Manager(s)

Maureen E. Cullinane CFA(1984), since 08-89. MA, Emmanuel C. 1970 MBA, Boston U. 1981

Manager Experience

	Dates Managed	Invest Obj	Std Dev	+/- Index
Not available.				

Historical Profile

Return	Above Average
Risk	Above Average
Rating	★★★★
	Above Average

Average % Stocks Held in Portfolio: 96% 90% 90% 92% 95% 93% 93% 85%

Investment Style History Equity

Growth of $10,000
- IIII Value of Fund ($000)
- — Value of Index ($000) S&P 500
- ▼ Manager Change
- ▽ Partial Manager Change
- ► Mgr Unknown After
- ◄ Mgr Unknown Before

Performance Quartile (Within Objective)

	1983	1984	1985	1986	1987	1988	1989	1990	1991	1992	1993	1994	History
	12.69	10.78	14.12	13.44	12.08	13.66	16.03	13.37	17.68	15.84	17.11	15.54	NAV
	21.97	0.24	32.28	12.08	8.27	14.05	33.03	-2.37	54.49	4.00	19.33	-5.66	Total Return %
	-0.50	-6.02	0.54	-6.60	8.27	-2.56	1.34	0.75	24.01	-3.61	9.27	-6.98	+/- S&P 500
	---	1.96	0.26	0.32	11.78	-6.49	9.09	11.19	11.04	-7.75	4.79	-3.01	+/- Wilshire 4500
	1.68	0.97	1.29	1.96	1.58	0.97	1.29	1.87	0.46	0.00	0.00	0.00	Income Return %
	20.28	-0.73	30.98	10.11	6.69	13.08	31.73	-4.24	54.03	4.00	19.33	-5.66	Capital Return %
	32	64	18	73	13	31	9	63	6	81	18	70	Total Rtn % Rank All
	42	4	25	42	14	42	30	25	53	65	46	65	Total Rtn % Rank Obj
	0.16	0.10	0.12	0.28	0.24	0.12	0.20	0.29	0.07	0.00	0.00	0.00	Income $
	0.00	1.66	0.00	2.12	2.25	0.00	1.90	2.09	2.50	2.23	1.73	0.61	Capital Gains $
	1.81	1.78	1.65	1.47	1.99	1.78	1.84	1.73	1.57	1.52	1.51	1.46	Expense Ratio %
	0.68	1.21	2.26	1.60	0.13	2.22	1.03	0.70	-0.31	-0.01	-0.48	-0.28	Income Ratio %
	242	164	188	178	106	84	77	108	115	176	162	---	Turnover Rate %
	28.6	25.3	31.0	31.8	30.3	34.0	39.7	38.5	58.7	73.2	90.4	99.6	Net Assets ($mil)

Performance 12-31-94

	1st Qtr	2nd Qtr	3rd Qtr	4th Qtr	Total
1987	26.91	2.01	3.77	-19.40	8.27
1988	8.03	4.90	-1.97	2.66	14.05
1989	6.52	8.11	13.41	1.86	33.03
1990	-0.62	9.23	-14.81	5.58	-2.37
1991	26.03	-2.61	12.68	11.71	54.49
1992	-0.91	-5.25	0.90	9.79	4.00
1993	5.37	2.76	12.38	-1.93	19.33
1994	-4.15	-5.61	5.68	-1.33	-5.66

Bear Market Performance

Decile Rank (5-year period)

Worst — Best

	Worst 3 Mo Period 1985-89	Worst 3 Mo Period 1990-94
Keystone Amer Omega A	-31.13	-16.17
+/- S&P 500	-1.54	-2.32
+/- Best Fit Index : Wil 4500	-0.99	3.24

Trailing Returns

	Total Return %	+/- S&P 500	+/- Wil 4500	% Rank All	% Rank Obj	Growth of $10,000
3 Mo	-1.33	-1.32	1.17	53	61	9,867
6 Mo	4.27	-0.59	0.08	14	71	10,427
1 Yr	-5.66	-6.98	-3.01	70	65	9,434
3 Yr Avg	5.40	-0.87	-2.21	40	59	11,708
5 Yr Avg	12.05	3.35	2.95	9	39	17,660
10 Yr Avg	15.71	1.32	3.07	7	29	43,005
15 Yr Avg	12.78	-1.70	---	43	53	60,754

Operations

Address and Telephone	200 Berkeley Street Boston, MA 02116-5034 800-343-2898 / 617-338-3400
Advisor	Keystone Management
Subadvisor	Keystone
Distributor	Keystone Distributors
States Available	All plus PR,GU,VI
Report Grade	B+
Income Distrib	Paid Annually
Date of Inception	04-01-68
Fiscal Year End	December

Risk Analysis

Time Period	Load-Adj Return %	Risk % Rank [1] All	Risk % Rank [1] Obj	Morningstar [2] Return	Morningstar Risk	Morningstar Risk-Adj Rating
1 Yr	-11.09					
3 Yr	3.34	87	26	-0.07 [3]	1.12	★★
5 Yr	10.73	87	25	1.56 [3]	1.08	★★★★
10 Yr	15.02	83	7	1.49	1.07	★★★★
Average Historical Rating (109 months)					3.0	★s

[1] 1 = low, 100 = high [2] 1.00 = Equity Avg [3] 1.00 = 90-day T-bill return

Other Measures

			Standard S&P 500	Best Fit Wil 4500
Standard Deviation	12.01	Alpha	-0.5	-2.4
Mean	5.99	Beta	1.02	1.13
Sharpe Ratio	0.21	R-Squared	45	84

Investment Style

	Stock Portfolio Avg	Relative S&P 500
Price/Earnings Ratio	24.9	1.35
Price/Book Ratio	4.2	1.23
5 Yr Earnings Gr %	12.8	2.31
Return on Assets %	9.8	1.30
Debt % Total Cap	29.7	1.05
Med Mkt Cap ($mil)	3058	0.24

Style: Value Blend Growth — Size Large/Med/Small

Diversification Value for Portfolio Types

Large Cap: Medium	Small Cap: Low	Bond: High	Balanced: Low	Diversified: Low

Tax Analysis

	Tax-Adj Historical Return %	% Pretax Return
3 Yr Avg	2.90	52.4
5 Yr Avg	8.48	65.6
10 Yr Avg	12.32	66.5
Potential Capital Gain Exposure (% of assets)		5%

Most Similar Funds in MF500

Founders Frontier	Fair Fit
T. Rowe Price New America G	Fair Fit
20th Century Ultra Investors	Fair Fit

Min Initial Purchase	$1000 (Addt'l: None)
Min IRA Purchase	None (Addt'l: None)
Min Auto Invest Plan	$100 (Systematic Inv: $100)

Expenses & Fees

Sales Fees	5.75% front
	0.00% deferred
	0.25% 12b-1
Management Fee	0.75% max./0.50% min.
3-,5-,10-yr Expense Projections	$102, $135, $227
Annual Brokerage Cost	---

Portfolio 12-31-94

Total Stocks: 53
Total Fixed-Income: 1

Share Chg (09-94) 000	Amount 000		Value $000	% Net Assets
-5	141	EMC	3054	3.07
56	100	AGCO	3041	3.05
-2	49	Caterpillar	2711	2.72
-2	53	General Electric	2687	2.70
-2	56	Department 56	2234	2.24
2	49	Oracle Systems	2176	2.19
8	44	KLA Instruments	2174	2.18
-13	60	DSC Communications	2153	2.16
-13	60	Analog Devices	2097	2.11
34	70	Union Carbide	2064	2.07
53	53	Merck	2009	2.02
49	49	Viacom Cl B	1998	2.01
70	70	OfficeMax	1862	1.87
6	25	Gillette	1838	1.85
-1	21	Mobil	1776	1.78
22	72	Staples	1765	1.77
20	46	Lam Research	1695	1.70
-24	49	Teradyne	1666	1.67
-1	28	Amoco	1661	1.67
	71	US Surgical Cv Pfd	1642	1.65
-1	35	Forest Laboratories	1638	1.64
16	28	Exide	1600	1.61
-2	56	Unocal	1531	1.54
70	70	Mariner Health Group	1528	1.53
-27	44	Parametric Technology	1497	1.50

Composition % 12-31-94

Cash	17.6	Preferreds	0.0
Stocks	82.4	Convertibles	0.0
Bonds	0.0	Other	0.0

Index Allocation

	% of Stocks
S&P 500	47.3
S&P MidCap 400	23.5
U.S. Small Cap	29.2
Foreign	0.0

Sector Weightings

	% of Stocks	Relative S&P 500
Utilities	0.0	0.00
Energy	13.6	1.34
Financials	2.9	0.27
Industrial Cyclicals	20.6	1.26
Consumer Durables	4.4	0.71
Consumer Staples	0.0	0.00
Services	9.0	1.10
Retail	3.2	0.54
Health	10.6	1.22
Technology	35.9	3.91

MORNINGSTAR **1995 Mutual Fund 500**

Keystone Custodian K-1

	Ticker	Load	NAV	Yield	SEC Yield	Assets	Objective
	KKONX	4.00%d	8.99	4.0%	3.37%	1286.3	Balanced

Keystone Custodian K-1 Fund seeks to provide current income. The fund may invest in both equity and debt securities. It emphasizes securities that have a liberal current yield, are consistent with investment quality, and have reasonably secure dividend or interest payments.

Historical Profile

Return	Average
Risk	Average
Rating	★★★
	Neutral

59% 52% 56% 49% 58% 34% 54% 58%

Investment Style History
Equity

Average % Stocks Held
in Portfolio

Growth of $10,000

|||| Value of Fund ($000)
— Value of Index ($000)
S&P 500
▼ Manager Change
▽ Partial Manager Change
► Mgr Unknown After
◄ Mgr Unknown Before

Performance Quartile
(Within Objective)

Manager's Investment Style

Management generally keeps between 50% and 60% of its assets in stocks (mostly S&P 500 companies), with the remainder in bonds. In order to keep the yield 15% ahead of the S&P 500's, management only buys dividend-paying stocks. On the bond side, management avoids the lower-credit rungs, while using long bonds to keep yield competitive.

	1983	1984	1985	1986	1987	1988	1989	1990	1991	1992	1993	1994	History
	8.95	8.08	9.01	8.67	8.00	8.37	9.27	8.52	10.03	9.70	9.91	8.99	NAV
	18.80	5.23	22.44	19.86	3.70	11.54	19.84	-1.78	24.00	3.50	10.33	-4.68	Total Return %
	-3.66	-1.04	-9.30	1.18	-1.56	-5.07	-11.85	1.34	-6.49	-4.12	0.27	-6.00	+/- S&P 500
	10.43	-9.93	0.32	4.61	0.95	3.66	5.30	-10.73	8.00	-3.75	0.58	-1.76	+/- LB Aggregate
	9.52	9.81	6.34	6.40	7.17	6.92	6.75	5.99	6.27	4.36	4.11	3.63	Income Return %
	9.28	-4.59	16.10	13.46	-3.46	4.63	13.08	-7.78	17.72	-0.86	6.21	-8.31	Capital Return %
	44	50	57	21	30	49	35	61	37	82	64	60	Total Rtn % Rank All
	28	64	85	21	25	50	41	62	52	82	59	78	Total Rtn % Rank Obj
	0.74	0.80	0.49	0.56	0.63	0.53	0.54	0.54	0.48	0.39	0.39	0.36	Income $
	0.00	0.45	0.34	1.49	0.42	0.00	0.18	0.03	0.00	0.24	0.38	0.11	Capital Gains $
	0.87	1.18	0.87	0.86	1.93	1.91	1.96	1.99	1.88	1.97	1.93	1.71	Expense Ratio %
	8.48	8.22	6.73	5.82	4.47	5.34	5.48	4.94	4.56	3.25	3.07	2.81	Income Ratio %
	51	78	109	92	79	64	49	35	60	52	74	88	Turnover Rate %
	67.5	63.5	319.5	509.5	656.2	655.2	773.6	823.2	1069.7	1335.8	1529.0	1286.3	Net Assets ($mil)

Fund Manager(s)

Walter T. McCormick CFA(1976), since 06-84.
Birthdate: 07-46. BA, Providence C. 1968 MBA, Rutgers U. 1970

Manager Experience	Dates Managed	Invest Obj	Std Dev	+/- Index
Walter T. McCormick				
Keystone Amer Fund T/R A	04/87 - 12/94	EI	11.54	-1.72
Keystone Custodian K-2	04/89 - 12/94	G	15.03	0.05

Performance 12-31-94

	1st Qtr	2nd Qtr	3rd Qtr	4th Qtr	Total
1987	13.46	1.79	1.72	-11.72	3.70
1988	4.27	3.21	1.22	2.40	11.54
1989	4.78	6.87	5.95	1.01	19.84
1990	-2.67	3.68	-7.03	4.69	-1.78
1991	9.36	0.98	5.70	6.23	24.00
1992	-2.29	1.96	1.73	2.12	3.50
1993	4.77	1.41	2.70	1.10	10.33
1994	-4.39	-0.44	1.62	-1.47	-4.68

Bear Market Performance

Decile Rank (5-year period)

Worst — ███ — Best

	Worst 3 Mo Period 1985-89	Worst 3 Mo Period 1990-94
Keystone Custodian K-1	-17.39	-8.61
+/- S&P 500	12.20	5.23
+/- Best Fit Index : S&P 500	12.20	5.23

Trailing Returns

	Total Return %	+/- S&P 500	+/- LB Aggregate	% Rank All	% Rank Obj	Growth of $10,000
3 Mo	-1.47	-1.45	-1.85	56	68	9,853
6 Mo	0.13	-4.73	-0.86	55	82	10,013
1 Yr	-4.68	-6.00	-1.76	60	78	9,532
3 Yr Avg	2.86	-3.40	-1.68	87	77	10,884
5 Yr Avg	2.89	-2.89	-1.83	80	87	13,255
10 Yr Avg	10.43	-3.95	0.48	54	71	26,963
15 Yr Avg	11.53	-2.95	0.72	60	84	51,406

Operations

Address and Telephone	200 Berkeley Street
	Boston, MA 02116-5034
	800-343-2898 / 617-338-3400
Advisor	Keystone Management
Subadvisor	None
Distributor	Keystone Distributors
States Available	All plus PR,GU,VI
Report Grade	A
Income Distrib	Paid Quarterly
Date of Inception	02-01-36
Fiscal Year End	June

Risk Analysis

Time Period	Load-Adj Return %	Risk % Rank [1] All	Obj	Morningstar [2] Return	Morningstar Risk	Morningstar Risk-Adj Rating
1 Yr	-7.40					
3 Yr	2.58	56	61	-0.29 [3]	0.79	★★
5 Yr	5.80	54	66	0.25 [3]	0.80	★★★
10 Yr	10.43	43	60	0.74	0.82	★★★

Average Historical Rating (109 months)   3.5 ★s

[1] = low, 100 = high   [2] 1.00 = Hybrid Avg   [3] 1.00 = 90-day T-bill return

Other Measures

			Standard S&P 500	Best Fit S&P 500
Standard Deviation	6.00	Alpha	-2.5	-2.5
Mean	3.01	Beta	0.70	0.70
Sharpe Ratio	-0.09	R-Squared	86	86

Investment Style

Stocks

	Port Avg	Rel S&P 500
Price/Earnings Ratio	18.6	1.01
Price/Book Ratio	3.0	0.89
5 Yr Earnings Gr %	0.4	0.08
Med Mkt Cap ($mil)	15132	1.17

Bonds

Avg Effective Duration	5.7 Yrs **
Avg Effective Maturity	9.2 Yrs
Avg Credit Quality	AAA
Avg Weighted Coupon	7.75%

**figure provided by fund

Diversification Value for Portfolio Types

Large Cap: None	Small Cap: Medium	Bond: Low	Balanced: None	Diversified: Low

Expenses & Fees

Sales Fees	
	0.00% front
	4.00% deferred
	1.00% 12b-1
Management Fee	0.60% flat fee+1.50%l
3-,5-,10-yr Expense Projections	$74, $93, $202
Annual Brokerage Cost	0.03%

Min Initial Purchase	$1000 (Addt'l: None)
Min IRA Purchase	None (Addt'l: None)
Min Auto Invest Plan	$100 (Systematic Inv: $100)

Portfolio 12-31-94

Share Chg (09-94)000	Amount 000	Total Stocks: 164 / Total Fixed-Income: 63	Date of Maturity	Value $000	% Net Assets
	59150	US Treasury Bond 7.875%	02-15-21	58411	4.54
	48850	US Treasury Bond 9.375%	02-15-06	54178	4.21
	47300	US Treasury Note 8%	10-15-96	47551	3.70
0	796	General Electric		40596	3.16
	31591	FHLMC 9%	07-01-21	31606	2.46
	26500	US Treasury Note 8.5%	04-15-97	26898	2.09
	26011	FHLMC 5.659%	08-01-22	25995	2.02
0	431	El DuPont de Nemours		24244	1.88
-50	405	Johnson & Johnson		22185	1.72
	23508	FNMA CMO REMIC 6%	11-25-08	20988	1.63
0	464	Chevron		20688	1.61
	22714	FNMA CMO REMIC 0%	11-25-23	19981	1.55
0	380	Bell Atlantic		18905	1.47
0	456	PPG Industries		16929	1.32
0	330	Conrail		16665	1.30
0	233	Monsanto		16455	1.28
	16340	FHLMC 5.688%	02-01-23	16243	1.26
	17499	GNMA 7.5%	04-15-24	16236	1.26
0	530	Union Carbide		15569	1.21
0	200	Gillette		14950	1.16

Index Allocation

	% of Stocks
S&P 500	96.3
S&P MidCap 400	1.7
U.S. Small Cap	1.8
Foreign	1.3

Composition % 12-31-94

Cash	2.2	Preferreds	0.0
Stocks	55.8	Convertibles	1.6
Bonds	40.3	Other	0.0

Tax Analysis

	Tax-Adj Historical Return %	% Pretax Return
3 Yr Avg	0.71	24.2
5 Yr Avg	3.72	61.5
10 Yr Avg	7.39	61.4
Potential Capital Gain Exposure (% of assets)		6%

Most Similar Funds in MF500

Dean Witter Dividend Growth	Strong Fit
Oppenheimer Equity-Inc A	Strong Fit
Vanguard/Wellington	Strong Fit

Bond Credit Analysis 12-31-94

% of Bonds

US Govt	62	BB	0
AAA	22	B	1
AA	1	Below B	3
A	6	NR/NA	0
BBB	4		

Stock Sector Weightings

	% of Stocks	Relative S&P 500
Utilities	10.8	0.87
Energy	13.6	1.34
Financials	12.8	1.21
Industrial Cyclicals	28.4	1.74
Consumer Durables	3.2	0.52
Consumer Staples	9.9	0.79
Services	8.4	1.04
Retail	1.6	0.27
Health	8.6	0.99
Technology	2.7	0.29

Korea Fund

	Ticker	NAV	Mkt Price	Prem/Disc	Yield	Objective
	KF	$20.65	$22.75	10.2%	0.0%	Pacific/Asia

Korea Fund seeks capital appreciation.

The fund intends to invest at least 80% of its assets in securities listed on the Korean Stock Exchange. Investments are principally in securities of established companies, although investments may be made in securities of new or little-known companies.

Following an initial public offering of five million shares in August 1984, the fund offered an additional 1,240,310 shares in May 1986. On Oct. 11, 1988, the fund paid a 200% stock dividend, resulting in a three-for-one stock split. In November 1993, the fund raised an additional $115 million in a secondary public offering of 6,865,671 shares.

| 29.6 | 39.2 | 69.2 | 156.8 | 108.2 | 119.7 | 73.7 | 54.9 | 44.6 | 44.2 | 37.0 | Highest Prem/Disc |
| 17.6 | 9.2 | 18.9 | 42.3 | 47.8 | 59.4 | 11.4 | 15.6 | -6.3 | 10.3 | -2.7 | Lowest Prem/Disc |

Historical Profile

Return Above Average
Risk Above Average
Rating ★★★
Neutral

Growth of $10,000
■ at NAV ($000)
— at Market Price ($000)

Premium Discount %

	1983	1984	1985	1986	1987	1988	1989	1990	1991	1992	1993	1994	History
	---	3.82	4.47	8.16	11.28	15.93	18.55	11.10	10.55	10.62	16.64	20.65	NAV
	---	2.61*	22.78	85.24	47.97	65.83	28.80	-28.36	-2.05	2.71	56.77	24.84	NAV Total Return %
	---	0.57*	-8.96	66.56	42.71	49.22	-2.89	-25.24	-32.53	-4.91	46.71	23.52	+/- S&P 500
	---	---	-33.38	15.80	23.34	37.56	18.26	-4.91	-14.18	14.88	24.20	17.06	+/- MSCI EAFE
	---	N/A	N/A	N/A	N/A	-28.17	28.37	0.11	15.00	2.70	27.68	2.71	+/- MSCI Korea
	---	0.00*	5.60	1.77	2.95	2.20	0.46	0.00	0.36	0.35	0.00	0.00	Income Return %
	---	2.61*	17.19	83.47	45.02	63.63	28.34	-28.36	-2.41	2.36	56.77	24.84	Capital Return %
	---	---	62	2	2	2	16	94	97	80	7	1	Total Rtn % Rank All
	---	---	NMF	1	33	1	62	70	80	33	55	1	Total Rtn % Rank Obj
	---	18.75*	29.59	95.80	73.62	67.75	44.84	-56.46	4.09	13.14	71.52	-4.65	Market Total Rtn %
	---	---	25.9	46.0	96.3	75.1	92.5	37.4	33.9	15.0	29.8	15.4	Avg Prem/Disc %
	---	0.02	0.18	0.11	0.29	0.52	0.08	0.00	0.05	0.04	0.00	0.00	Income $
	---	0.00	0.00	0.03	0.68	3.14	1.88	2.20	0.35	0.20	0.01	0.15	Capital Gains $
	---	---	2.00	1.88	1.47	1.53	1.54	1.44	1.47	1.52	1.42	1.37	Expense Ratio %
	---	---	5.63	2.37	3.25	0.92	0.24	0.21	0.83	0.70	-0.59	-0.18	Income Ratio %
	---	---	0	7	4	20	15	18	19	18	4	---	Turnover Rate %
	---	---	57.6	140.9	210.2	549.9	386.5	242.2	235.9	240.0	490.4	610.0	Net Assets ($mil)

Manager's Investment Style

Early in the fund's history, management bought several Korean blue-chip stocks, and it has held on: Turnover hasn't cracked 20% in the fund's history. Because of a government-imposed cap on foreign ownership of Korean stocks, newer Korea funds are typically forced to buy stocks at premiums in the secondary market. This fund, because of its age and willingness to hold onto its original positions, thus has an advantage over its Korea-focused competition.

Fund Manager(s)

John J. Lee. Since 12-92. '80 Yonsei U. (Korea); BS'85 New York U.

Nicholas Bratt. Since 1985. BA Oxford U.; MBA Columbia U.

Manager Experience

	Dates Managed	Invest Obj	Std Dev	+/- Index
Nicholas Bratt				
Scudder International	01/76 - 12/94	WF	15.38	0.54
Brazil Fund	01/89 - 12/94	WL	57.09	11.54

NAV Performance % 12-30-94

	1st Qtr	2nd Qtr	3rd Qtr	4th Qtr	Total
1987	36.71	-0.36	1.62	6.89	47.97
1988	14.72	7.96	1.43	32.00	65.83
1989	18.46	-10.76	23.68	-1.49	28.80
1990	-6.42	-16.76	-14.49	7.55	-28.36
1991	-2.52	-5.08	6.14	-0.26	-2.05
1992	20.09	-15.15	-6.80	8.15	2.71
1993	0.75	6.54	0.44	45.40	56.77
1994	2.64	9.25	15.58	-3.68	24.84

Bear Market Performance

Decile Rank (5-year period)

Worst — Best

	Worst 3 Mo Period 1985-89	Worst 3 Mo Period 1990-94
Korea Fund	-10.76	-23.52
+/- S&P 500	-19.58	-24.90

Trailing Returns

	NAV Total Return %	+/- S&P 500	+/- MSCI Korea	% Rank All	% Rank Obj	Mkt Total Return %
3 Mo	-3.68	-3.67	6.27	77	23	-12.88
6 Mo	11.32	6.46	2.22	3	13	4.02
1 Yr	24.84	23.52	2.71	1	4	-4.65
3 Yr Avg	26.20	19.94	9.81	3	20	22.77
5 Yr Avg	7.12	-1.57	8.45	62	60	-3.46
10 Yr Avg	26.07	11.68	N/A	2	1	24.54

Operations

Address and Telephone	345 Park Avenue New York, NY 10154 212-326-6200 / 800-349-4281
Advisor	Scudder, Stevens & Clark
Subadvisor	Daewoo Capital Management
Administrator	N/A
Transfer Agent	State Street Bank and Trust Co.
Custodian	Brown Brothers Harriman & Co.
Auditor	Coopers & Lybrand
Legal Counsel	Debevoise & Plimpton

Income Distrib Schedule	Paid Irregularly
Management Fee	1.10%
Reinvestment Plan	Yes
Direct Purchase Plan	Yes
Shares Outstanding	29,540,356
Exchange	NYSE/OSE
*Date of Inception	08-29-84
Shareholder Report	A-

Risk Analysis

	Risk % Rank[1]		Morningstar[2]		Morningstar
	All	Obj	Return	Risk	Risk-Adj Rating
3 Yr	94	73	3.58	1.41	★★★★
5 Yr	96	70	0.44	1.45	★★
10 Yr	85	1	3.72	1.14	★★★★

Average Historical Rating (89 months) 3.6 ★s

[1] = Low, 100 = High [2]1.00 = Equity Avg [3]1.00 = 90-day T-bill Return

Other Measures

			S&P 500
Standard Deviation	29.05	Alpha	27.25
Mean	27.54	Beta	-0.11
Sharpe Ratio	0.83	R-Squared	0

Investment Style

	Stock Portfolio Avg	Rel WS Korea	Rel WS Foreign
Price/Earnings Ratio	33.2#	1.17	0.67
Price/Cash Flow Ratio	---	---	---
Price/Book Ratio	2.6#	1.43	0.86
5 Yr Earnings Gr %	3.6#	0.33	NMF
Return on Assets %	4.9#	1.01	1.06
Debt % Total Cap	50.6#	1.04	1.56
Med Mkt Cap ($mil)	6974#	2.50	1.11

figure is based on less than 50% of stocks

Country Exposure (top five) 12-31-94

	Securities %			Currency %
South Korea	97	South Korea		99
		US		1

Diversification Value for Portfolio Types

Large Cap: High	Small Cap: High	Bond: High	Balanced: High	Diversified: High

Portfolio 09-30-94

Share Chg (06-94)	Amount	Total Equity: 80 Total Fixed-Income: 32	Value $000	% Total Invest
21652	513307	Samsung Electronics	97933	15.50
0	100702	Korea Mobile Telecom	94115	14.90
0	67867	Samsung Fire & Marine Ins	23868	3.78
0	302347	Keum Kang	22957	3.63
0	637421	Korea Long-Term Credit	18618	2.95
0	332545	Hyundai Motor Services	18024	2.85
0	169216	Han Kook Tire Manufacturing	16733	2.65
35349	320239	Samsung Heavy Industries	15874	2.51
0	282098	Cheil Food & Chemical	15113	2.39
0	114577	Shinsegae	10871	1.72
0	250042	Samsung	9838	1.56
33274	210712	Hansol Paper Manufacturing	9231	1.46
0	165730	Hwa Sung Industries	8817	1.40
0	61000	Pohang Iron & Steel	8669	1.37
0	167073	Samsung ElectroMechanics	8211	1.30
0	160499	Yukong	8071	1.28
0	165000	Inchon Iron & Steel	7724	1.22
0	197307	Ssangyong Cement Industrial	7409	1.17
0	137548	Yuhan	7403	1.17
0	78471	Samsung Electron Devices	7386	1.17
---	3000.00M	Korean Green Cross Cv 1%	7174	1.14
12797	229853	Lucky	7020	1.11
0	113341	Mando Machinery	6952	1.10
0	116209	Hyundai Motor	6735	1.07
-30000	130900	Korea Electric Power	6062	0.96

Composition % 12-31-94

Cash	0.5	Preferreds	2.7
Stocks	90.1	Convertibles	6.8
Bonds	0.0	Other	0.0

Tax Analysis

	Tax-Adj Historical Return %	% Pretax Return
3 Yr Avg	25.89	98.5
5 Yr Avg	5.56	75.7
10 Yr Avg	23.51	79.4
Potential Capital Gain Exposure (% of assets)		52

Most Similar Funds in MF500

Mexico Fund	Weak Fit
Dreyfus Global Growth	Weak Fit
Irish Investment	Weak Fit

Sector Weightings

	% of Stocks
Utilities	20.1
Energy	3.2
Financials	8.6
Industrial Cyclicals	21.5
Consumer Durables	31.3
Consumer Staples	1.9
Services	2.9
Retail	4.7
Health	2.4
Technology	3.4

Latin American Discovery

	Ticker	NAV	Mkt Price	Prem/Disc	Yield	Objective
	LDF	$17.16	$18.25	6.4%	0.0%	Latin America

Latin American Discovery Fund seeks long-term capital appreciation.

Normally, the fund invests at least 80% of assets in Latin American equity securities, including depository receipts and sovereign debt. By policy, the fund invests at least 55% of assets in Argentine, Brazilian, Chilean, and Mexican equities.

Of its initial 3.3-million-share offering, the fund offered 1.2 million shares in Latin America and 2.1 million shares outside Latin America.

The fund's Latin American subadvisors include Roberts Management (for Argentina), Unibanco Consultoria de Investimentos (for Brazil), Bice Chileconsult Finanzas y Servicios (for Chile), and Impulsora del Fondo Mexico (for Mexico).

To discourage takeovers, the fund's board members serve staggered terms, and supermajority voting rules are in effect.

The fund held a rights offering in the fourth quarter of 1993 that raised $33,883,500.

Manager's Investment Style

Management takes a contrarian approach, attempting to allocate its assets to countries that are suffering fallouts, and away from countries enjoying rallies. Within countries, the fund mostly owns large, well-known firms. Management attempts to maintain a diversified, fully invested portfolio.

Fund Manager(s)

Robert Meyer. Since 6-92. BA Yale; JD Harvard.

Historical Profile

Return — Not Rated
Risk — Not Rated
Rating

										4.2	16.4	14.1	Highest Prem/Disc
										-15.7	-13.8	-13.5	Lowest Prem/Disc

Growth of $10,000
— at NAV ($000)
— at Market Price ($000)

Premium Discount %

1983	1984	1985	1986	1987	1988	1989	1990	1991	1992	1993	1994	History
---	---	---	---	---	---	---	---	---	15.23	23.31	17.16	NAV
---	---	---	---	---	---	---	---	---	8.01*	61.94	0.81	NAV Total Return %
---	---	---	---	---	---	---	---	---	-0.55*	51.88	-0.51	+/- S&P 500
---	---	---	---	---	---	---	---	---	---	29.38	-6.97	+/- MSCI EAFE
---	---	---	---	---	---	---	---	---	---	12.87	9.11	+/- MSCI Latin Am
---	---	---	---	---	---	---	---	---	0.00*	0.00	0.01	Income Return %
---	---	---	---	---	---	---	---	---	8.01*	61.94	0.80	Capital Return %
---	---	---	---	---	---	---	---	---	---	6	11	Total Rtn % Rank All
---	---	---	---	---	---	---	---	---	---	10	50	Total Rtn % Rank Obj
---	---	---	---	---	---	---	---	---	-11.67*	121.19	-7.87	Market Total Rtn %
---	---	---	---	---	---	---	---	---	-7.9	-2.5	-1.9	Avg Prem/Disc %
---	---	---	---	---	---	---	---	---	0.00	0.00	0.00	Income $
---	---	---	---	---	---	---	---	---	0.00	0.00	5.74	Capital Gains $
---	---	---	---	---	---	---	---	---	2.73	2.23	2.12	Expense Ratio %
---	---	---	---	---	---	---	---	---	-1.02	0.22	-0.22	Income Ratio %
---	---	---	---	---	---	---	---	---	---	56	---	Turnover Rate %
---	---	---	---	---	---	---	---	---	87.7	180.3	135.3	Net Assets ($mil)

Manager Experience

	Dates Managed	Invest Obj	Std Dev	+/- Index
Robert Meyer				
American Cap Emerg Grow	04/86 - 04/89	SC	21.30	-9.84
Common Sense Growth	04/88 - 05/89	G	13.41	-6.79

Risk Analysis

	Risk % Rank[1]		Morningstar[2]		Morningstar
	All	Obj	Return	Risk	Risk-Adj Rating
3 Yr	---	---	---	---	
5 Yr	---	---	---	---	
10 Yr	---	---	---	---	

[1] 1 = Low, 100 = High [2] 1.00 = Equity Avg [3] 1.00 = 90-day T-bill Return

Other Measures — S&P 500

Standard Deviation	---	Alpha	---
Mean	---	Beta	---
Sharpe Ratio	---	R-Squared	---

Investment Style

	Stock Portfolio Avg	Rel WS Latin	Rel WS Foreign
Price/Earnings Ratio	61.1#	1.19	1.24
Price/Cash Flow Ratio	---	---	---
Price/Book Ratio	---	---	---
5 Yr Earnings Gr %	---	---	---
Return on Assets %	---	---	---
Debt % Total Cap	---	---	---
Med Mkt Cap ($mil)	2125#	0.42	0.34

figure is based on less than 50% of stocks

NAV Performance % 12-30-94

	1st Qtr	2nd Qtr	3rd Qtr	4th Qtr	Total
1987	---	---	---	---	---
1988	---	---	---	---	---
1989	---	---	---	---	---
1990	---	---	---	---	---
1991	---	---	---	---	---
1992	---	-1.21*	-1.22	10.68	8.01*
1993	7.29	9.98	9.57	25.26	61.94
1994	10.07	-15.32	36.34	-20.67	0.81

Bear Market Performance

Decile Rank (5-year period)

Worst — Best

	Worst 3 Mo Period 1985-89	Worst 3 Mo Period 1990-94
Latin Amer Discover	---	---
+/- S&P 500	---	---

Trailing Returns

	NAV Total Return %	+/- S&P 500	+/- MSCI Latin Am	% Rank All	% Rank Obj	Mkt Total Return %
3 Mo	-20.67	-20.65	1.10	100	60	-11.07
6 Mo	8.16	3.30	10.34	5	50	15.12
1 Yr	0.81	-0.51	9.11	11	50	-7.87
3 Yr Avg	---	---	---	---	---	---
5 Yr Avg	---	---	---	---	---	---
Incept Avg	25.02*	---	---	---	---	26.04*

Portfolio 09-30-94

Share Chg (06-94)	Amount	Total Equity: 109 Total Fixed-Income: 1	Value $000	% Total Invest
108900	238880	Telefonos de Mexico L (ADR)	14930	6.78
-2000000	43886999	Petrobras	8700	3.95
0	1253500	Banacci Cl B	7752	3.52
-49.882M	123.058M	Telebras PN	7679	3.49
-1	346612	Cemex Cl B (ADR)	6367	2.89
-108000	1319000	Grupo Sidek Cl B	6301	2.86
-20.000M	127.899M	Telebras	6301	2.86
20636	247636	Austral de Inversiones	6191	2.81
-11.141M	10970000	Eletrobras PN	4723	2.14
-48500	205900	Grupo Carso (144A)	4633	2.10
1932000	7129600	Telecom de Sao Paolo PN	4092	1.86
9500	172300	Quilmes Industrial	4028	1.83
---	3700000	Banco de Colombia Cv 5.2%	3978	1.81
16000000	48360000	Paulista de Forca E Luz	3971	1.80
-670000	11499000	Banco Itau	3912	1.78
-420000	9525100	Brasmotor	3799	1.72
0	57433.1M	Banco de Colombia	3542	1.61
0	229200	Tolmex Cl B	3476	1.58
110000	7810000	Eletrobras	3390	1.54
13500000	76124000	Siderurgica Nacional	3349	1.52
-25000	175000	Capex (ADR)	3325	1.51
125990	125990	Cementos Paz Del Rio (ADR)	3244	1.47
9786212	325.119M	Banco Bradesco PN	3204	1.45
-16000	216222	Renault Argentina	3168	1.44
110850	110850	Energetics Minas Gerais (ADR)	3048	1.38

Composition % 12-31-94

Cash	5.2	Preferreds	0.0
Stocks	94.8	Convertibles	0.0
Bonds	0.0	Other	0.0

Country Exposure (top five) 12-31-94

Securities %		Currency %	
Brazil	48	Brazil	48
Mexico	22	Mexico	22
Argentina	9	Argentina	9
Chile	6	Chile	6
Peru	5	Peru	5

Diversification Value for Portfolio Types

Large Cap: Small Cap: Bond: Balanced: Diversified:

Tax Analysis

	Tax-Adj Historical Return %	% Pretax Return
3 Yr Avg	---	---
5 Yr Avg	---	---
10 Yr Avg	---	---
Potential Capital Gain Exposure (% of assets)		-8

Most Similar Funds in MF500

Fund lacks 3-year record

Sector Weightings

	% of Stocks
Utilities	33.1
Energy	8.9
Financials	15.0
Industrial Cyclicals	19.4
Consumer Durables	3.5
Consumer Staples	10.8
Services	6.0
Retail	2.4
Health	0.9
Technology	0.0

Operations

Address and Telephone	1221 Avenue of the Americas, New York, NY 10020, 212-296-7200
Advisor	Morgan Stanley Asset Management (see criteria)
Subadvisor	
Administrator	United States Trust Co. New York
Transfer Agent	First National Bank of Boston
Custodian	Morgan Guaranty Trust Co. of New York
Auditor	Price Waterhouse LLP
Legal Counsel	Rogers & Wells
Income Distrib Schedule	Paid Irregularly
Management Fee	1.25%, 0.46%A
Reinvestment Plan	Yes
Direct Purchase Plan	Yes
Shares Outstanding	7,885,082
Exchange	NYSE
*Date of Inception	06-16-92
Shareholder Report	B

Legg Mason Special Invmnt

Ticker	**Load**	**NAV**	**Yield**	**SEC Yield**	**Assets**	**Objective**
LMASX	None	19.03	0.0%	N/A	605.7	Small Company

Legg Mason Special Investment Trust seeks capital appreciation. Current income is not a consideration.

The fund invests primarily in equity securities of companies with market capitalizations of less than $1 billion, emphasizing securities that appear to be undervalued in relation to their long-term earning power or asset values. The fund also seeks firms involved in special situations that may prompt a price increase in their securities. The fund may invest up to 20% of its assets in companies involved in actual or anticipated reorganizations or restructurings. Up to 35% of assets may be invested in debt rated below BBB.

Manager's Investment Style

Management's bargain-hunting philosophy drives the fund toward companies that have been unfairly or temporarily beaten down. As long as the firm's management and cash flows remain strong, they will be considered for purchase. The fund's portfolio tends to be heavy in financials, which management chooses to buy while rising interest rates drive the market to sell. Casino and Mexico stocks have also been areas in which management has used market instability to profit.

Fund Manager(s)

William H. Miller III CFA(1985), since 12-85.
Birthdate: 01-50. Economics, Washington & Lee U. 1972 PhD, Johns Hopkins U.

Manager Experience

	Dates Managed	Invest Obj	Std Dev	+/- Index
William H. Miller III				
Legg Mason Total Return	11/90 - 12/94	GI	10.39	2.96

Performance 12-31-94

	1st Qtr	2nd Qtr	3rd Qtr	4th Qtr	Total
1987	21.88	-1.48	3.52	-27.34	-9.68
1988	16.71	8.09	-3.01	-2.17	19.70
1989	14.07	11.40	15.00	-9.62	32.08
1990	-0.37	7.14	-12.53	7.66	0.52
1991	20.38	0.96	9.88	4.42	39.44
1992	3.99	-5.91	0.20	17.67	15.36
1993	-0.39	7.05	10.92	4.95	24.13
1994	-2.62	-7.40	5.02	-8.20	-13.07

Bear Market Performance

Decile Rank (5-year period)

Worst — Best

	Worst 3 Mo Period 1985-89	Worst 3 Mo Period 1990-94
Legg Mason Special Invmnt	---	-16.25
+/- S&P 500	---	-2.41
+/- Best Fit Index : Wil 4500	---	3.15

Trailing Returns

	Total Return %	+/- S&P 500	+/- Wil 4500	% Rank All	% Rank Obj	Growth of $10,000
3 Mo	-8.20	-8.18	-5.70	96	99	9,180
6 Mo	-3.60	-8.46	-7.79	96	99	9,640
1 Yr	-13.07	-14.39	-10.42	97	98	8,693
3 Yr Avg	7.57	1.31	-0.04	23	59	12,448
5 Yr Avg	11.78	3.08	2.68	10	46	17,448
10 Yr Avg	---	---	---	---	---	---
15 Yr Avg	---	---	---	---	---	---

Operations

Address and Telephone	111 S. Calvert St P.O. Box 1476 Baltimore, MD 21203-1476 800-822-5544 / 410-539-0000
Advisor	Legg Mason Fund Adviser
Subadvisor	None
Distributor	Legg Mason Wood Walker
States Available	All except AK,MO plus PR
Report Grade	A-
Income Distrib	Paid Annually
* Date of Inception	12-30-85
Fiscal Year End	March

Historical Profile

Return	Above Average
Risk	Average
Rating	★★★★ Above Average

Performance Quartile (Within Objective)

	1983	1984	1985	1986	1987	1988	1989	1990	1991	1992	1993	1994	History
	---	---	10.00	10.51	8.68	10.38	13.63	12.12	16.78	17.98	22.14	19.03	NAV
	---	---	0.00 *	7.35	-9.68	19.70	32.08	0.52	39.44	15.36	24.13	-13.07	Total Return %
	---	---	-0.60 *	-11.33	-14.94	3.09	0.39	3.64	8.96	7.74	14.07	-14.39	+/- S&P 500
	---	---	---	-4.41	-6.17	-0.84	8.14	14.08	-4.01	3.61	9.59	-10.42	+/- Wilshire 4500
	---	---	0.00	0.18	0.84	0.11	0.77	2.06	0.22	0.68	0.17	0.00	Income Return %
	---	---	0.00	7.17	-10.52	19.59	31.31	-1.54	39.23	14.68	23.95	-13.07	Capital Return %
	---	---	---	92	96	15	10	54	15	10	12	97	Total Rtn % Rank All
	---	---	---	61	84	52	18	16	77	44	16	98	Total Rtn % Rank Obj
	---	---	0.00	0.02	0.08	0.01	0.08	0.27	0.03	0.11	0.03	0.00	Income $
	---	---	0.00	0.22	0.97	0.00	0.00	1.32	0.08	1.10	0.14	0.23	Capital Gains $
	---	---	---	2.50	2.50	2.50	2.50	2.30	2.30	2.10	2.00	1.94	Expense Ratio %
	---	---	---	1.20	0.00	1.00	0.70	1.00	1.40	0.80	0.20	0.00	Income Ratio %
	---	---	---	41	77	159	122	116	76	57	33	17	Turnover Rate %
	---	---	---	45.2	41.1	40.5	63.7	76.2	163.6	287.4	510.0	605.7	Net Assets ($mil)

Investment Style History
Equity

Average % Stocks Held in Portfolio
(74% | 78% | 84% | 73% | 66% | 82% | 91% | 91%)

Growth of $10,000

- |||| Value of Fund ($000)
- — Value of Index ($000) Wil 4500
- ▼ Manager Change
- ▽ Partial Manager Change
- ► Mgr Unknown After
- ◄ Mgr Unknown Before

Risk Analysis

Time Period	Load-Adj Return %	Risk % Rank [1] All	Obj	Morningstar [2] Return	Risk	Morningstar Risk-Adj Rating
1 Yr	-13.07					
3 Yr	7.57	91	64	1.20 [3]	1.23	★★★
5 Yr	11.78	84	43	1.87 [3]	1.02	★★★★
10 Yr	---	---	---	---	---	---

Average Historical Rating (73 months)   3.7 ★s

[1] 1 = low, 100 = high   [2] 1.00 = Equity Avg   [3] 1.00 = 90-day T-bill return

Other Measures

			Standard S&P 500	Best Fit Wil 4500
Standard Deviation	13.42	Alpha	1.4	-0.5
Mean	8.22	Beta	1.16	1.21
Sharpe Ratio	0.35	R-Squared	47	77

Investment Style

	Stock Portfolio Avg	Relative S&P 500
Price/Earnings Ratio	21.9	1.19
Price/Book Ratio	2.7	0.80
5 Yr Earnings Gr %	10.3#	1.85
Return on Assets %	6.4	0.85
Debt % Total Cap	24.4	0.86
Med Mkt Cap ($mil)	724	0.06

figure is based on 50% or less of stocks

Style
Value Blend Growth
Size: Large / Med / Small

Diversification Value for Portfolio Types

Large Cap: Medium   Small Cap: Low   Bond: High   Balanced: Low   Diversified: Medium

Expenses & Fees

Sales Fees	0.00% front
	0.00% deferred
	1.00% 12b-1
Management Fee	1.00% max./0.75% min.
3-,5-,10-yr Expense Projections	$61, $105, $226
Annual Brokerage Cost	0.09%

Min Initial Purchase	$1000 (Addt'l: $100)
Min IRA Purchase	$1000 (Addt'l: $100)
Min Auto Invest Plan	$50 (Systematic Inv: $50)

Portfolio 12-30-94

Total Stocks: 65
Total Fixed-Income: 3

Share Chg (09-94) 000	Amount 000		Value $000	% Net Assets
0	699	Caesars World	46645	7.70
525	2225	Home Shopping Network	22250	3.67
644	794	Circus Circus Enterprises	18461	3.05
375	1125	Diagnostek	17859	2.95
0	10200	WPP Group	17474	2.89
377	908	SafeCard Services	17146	2.83
375	750	Pioneer Group	16500	2.72
0	650	Standard Federal Bank (MI)	15519	2.56
99	399	United Asset Management	14709	2.43
0	490	CMAC Investment	14149	2.34
149	475	John Alden Financial	13656	2.25
869	1207	Hollywood Park	13277	2.19
50	600	Charter Medical	12900	2.13
225	225	America Online	12600	2.08
150	750	Shawmut National	12281	2.03
0	304	BankAmerica	11997	1.98
210	700	Washington Mutual	11813	1.95
-56	350	ALC Communications	10894	1.80
0	670	Boomtown	10553	1.74
125	500	Physician of America	10250	1.69
275	900	California Federal Bank Cl A	9788	1.62
0	225	Lotus Development	9225	1.52
0	955	Chic by HIS	9076	1.50
-175	450	MacFrugals Bargains	9000	1.49
0	425	Mirage Resorts	8707	1.44

Composition % 09-30-94

Cash	8.3	Preferreds	0.8
Stocks	90.1	Convertibles	0.2
Bonds	0.0	Other	0.7

Tax Analysis

	Tax-Adj Historical Return %	% Pretax Return
3 Yr Avg	6.72	88.0
5 Yr Avg	10.32	85.1
10 Yr Avg	---	---
Potential Capital Gain Exposure (% of assets)		8%

Most Similar Funds in MF500

MainStay Capital Apprec B	Fair Fit
T. Rowe Price New America G	Fair Fit
Founders Special	Fair Fit

Index Allocation

	% of Stocks
S&P 500	7.2
S&P MidCap 400	29.0
U.S. Small Cap	57.5
Foreign	6.4

Sector Weightings

	% of Stocks	Relative S&P 500
Utilities	1.3	0.10
Energy	0.0	0.00
Financials	34.7	3.28
Industrial Cyclicals	2.9	0.18
Consumer Durables	4.6	0.73
Consumer Staples	3.1	0.25
Services	25.0	3.07
Retail	9.8	1.68
Health	7.4	0.86
Technology	11.2	1.22

MORNINGSTAR 1995 Mutual Fund 500

Legg Mason Total Return

	Ticker	Load	NAV	Yield	SEC Yield	Assets	Objective
	LMTRX	None	12.15	2.3%	N/A	193.3	Growth/Inc.

Legg Mason Total Return Trust seeks capital appreciation and current income consistent with reasonable risk.

The fund invests in dividend-paying common stocks. It may also hold non-dividend-paying issues and various debt securities. The fund normally limits its investment in intermediate-term and long-term debt securities to 50%; it may hold no more than 25% of assets in lower-quality debt obligations. The fund may write put and call options, and it may invest up to 25% of its assets in foreign securities. The fund may also engage in various futures transactions.

Historical Profile
Return Average
Risk Average
Rating ★★★
Neutral

Investment Style History
Equity
Average % Stocks Held in Portfolio

78% 92% 88% 80% 66% 65% 68% 82%

Growth of $10,000
|||| Value of Fund ($000)
— Value of Index ($000) S&P 500
▼ Manager Change
▽ Partial Manager Change
► Mgr Unknown After
◄ Mgr Unknown Before

Performance Quartile (Within Objective)

Manager's Investment Style

Management has a flexible and unique approach toward stock selection. Instead of restricting themselves to stocks that are cheap based on their P/E ratios, management buys issues that are inexpensive relative to their future market value. Plays in the Mexican market have also added to the portfolio's variety. Setbacks in the market have not swayed management away from its path. In an attempt to focus its research efforts, management has trimmed its holdings from 60 to 40.

Fund Manager(s)

William H. Miller III CFA(1985), since 11-90.
Birthdate: 01-50. Economics, Washington & Lee U. 1972 PhD, Johns Hopkins U.
Nancy T. Dennin CFA(1988), since 01-92.

Manager Experience	Dates Managed	Invest Obj	Std Dev	+/- Index
William H. Miller III				
Legg Mason Spec Inv	12/85 - 12/94	SC	18.26	-1.05

1983	1984	1985	1986	1987	1988	1989	1990	1991	1992	1993	1994	History
---	---	10.09	10.04	7.83	9.40	10.54	8.43	11.64	12.98	14.00	12.15	NAV
---	---	0.90 *	1.40	-7.24	21.76	16.37	-16.82	40.49	14.32	14.08	-7.12	Total Return %
---	---	-4.68 *	-17.28	-12.50	5.15	-15.31	-13.71	10.00	6.70	4.02	-8.43	+/- S&P 500
---	---	---	-14.70	-9.60	3.82	-12.80	-10.64	6.28	5.35	2.80	-7.05	+/- Wilshire 5000
---	---	0.00	1.53	3.12	1.71	2.14	2.75	2.41	2.81	3.30	2.18	Income Return %
---	---	0.90	-0.13	-10.35	20.05	14.23	-19.57	38.08	11.51	10.78	-9.30	Capital Return %
---	---	---	98	92	10	43	95	14	11	33	80	Total Rtn % Rank All
---	---	---	98	96	18	84	98	7	11	28	94	Total Rtn % Rank Obj
---	---	0.00	0.16	0.29	0.13	0.21	0.29	0.18	0.30	0.41	0.29	Income $
---	---	0.00	0.04	1.39	0.00	0.18	0.07	0.00	0.00	0.34	0.60	Capital Gains $
---	---	---	2.20	2.40	2.30	2.40	2.40	2.50	2.34	1.95	1.94	Expense Ratio %
---	---	---	3.80	1.70	1.90	1.60	2.00	3.10	3.10	3.10	2.70	Income Ratio %
---	---	---	40	83	50	26	39	62	38	41	47	Turnover Rate %
---	---	0.1	43.0	36.7	30.1	29.7	18.6	40.1	110.9	175.1	193.3	Net Assets ($mil)

Performance 12-31-94

	1st Qtr	2nd Qtr	3rd Qtr	4th Qtr	Total
1987	16.16	0.08	4.33	-23.52	-7.24
1988	13.15	6.00	-0.63	2.16	21.76
1989	7.02	5.08	10.81	-6.61	16.37
1990	-4.84	0.70	-18.90	7.02	-16.82
1991	14.35	3.22	10.84	7.39	40.49
1992	0.61	4.46	2.49	6.14	14.32
1993	5.50	-0.09	4.33	3.73	14.08
1994	-3.29	0.02	5.00	-8.56	-7.12

Bear Market Performance

Decile Rank (5-year period)

Worst — Best

	Worst 3 Mo Period 1985-89	Worst 3 Mo Period 1990-94
Legg Mason Total Return	---	-18.97
+/- S&P 500	---	-5.13
+/- Best Fit Index : S&P 500	---	-5.13

Trailing Returns

	Total Return %	+/- S&P 500	+/- Wil 5000	% Rank All	% Rank Obj	Growth of $10,000
3 Mo	-8.56	-8.54	-7.79	97	99	9,144
6 Mo	-3.99	-8.85	-8.61	96	99	9,601
1 Yr	-7.12	-8.43	-7.05	80	94	9,288
3 Yr Avg	6.60	0.33	-0.01	29	36	12,113
5 Yr Avg	7.20	-1.50	-1.62	45	69	14,155
10 Yr Avg	---	---	---	---	---	---
15 Yr Avg	---	---	---	---	---	---

Operations

Address and Telephone	111 S. Calvert St P.O. Box 1476
	Baltimore, MD 21203-1476
	800-822-5544 / 410-539-0000
Advisor	Legg Mason Fund Adviser
Subadvisor	None
Distributor	Legg Mason Wood Walker
States Available	All except AK
Report Grade	A-
Income Distrib	Paid Quarterly
* Date of Inception	11-21-85
Fiscal Year End	March

Risk Analysis

Time Period	Load-Adj Return %	Risk % Rank [1] All	Obj	Morningstar [2] Return	Morningstar Risk	Morningstar Risk-Adj Rating
1 Yr	-7.12					
3 Yr	6.60	72	72	0.90 [3]	0.81	★★★
5 Yr	7.20	72	78	0.60 [3]	0.86	★★★
10 Yr	---	---	---	---	---	---

Average Historical Rating (73 months) 2.6 ★ s

[1] 1 = low, 100 = high [2] 1.00 = Equity Avg [3] 1.00 = 90-day T-bill return

Other Measures

			Standard S&P 500	Best Fit S&P 500
Standard Deviation	8.92	Alpha	0.6	0.6
Mean	6.80	Beta	0.94	0.94
Sharpe Ratio	0.37	R-Squared	69	69

Investment Style

	Stock Portfolio Avg	Relative S&P 500
Price/Earnings Ratio	13.1	0.71
Price/Book Ratio	2.1	0.61
5 Yr Earnings Gr %	9.7	1.74
Return on Assets %	4.8	0.64
Debt % Total Cap	34.2	1.21
Med Mkt Cap ($mil)	3471	0.27

Style: Value Blend Growth / Size Large Med Small

Diversification Value for Portfolio Types

Large Cap: Low | Small Cap: Medium | Bond: High | Balanced: Low | Diversified: Low

Expenses & Fees

Sales Fees	
	0.00% front
	0.00% deferred
	1.00% 12b-1
Management Fee	0.75% flat fee
3-,5-,10-yr Expense Projections	$61, $105, $226
Annual Brokerage Cost	0.19%

Min Purchase

Min Initial Purchase	$1000 (Addt'l: $100)
Min IRA Purchase	$250 (Addt'l: $100)
Min Auto Invest Plan	$50 (Systematic Inv: $50)

Portfolio 12-30-94

Total Stocks: 39
Total Fixed-Income: 3

Share Chg (09-94) 000	Amount 000		Value $000	% Net Assets
	9000	US Treasury Bond 7.25%	8322	4.31
157	344	National Golf Properties	7604	3.93
0	167	BankAmerica	6593	3.41
15	88	FNMA	6413	3.32
0	731	Lloyds Bank	6317	3.27
-16	85	IBM	6248	3.23
127	127	Chrysler	6223	3.22
59	403	Bear Stearns	6195	3.21
0	265	MBNA	6194	3.21
-8	82	Schering-Plough	6068	3.14
-35	165	PepsiCo	5981	3.10
18	108	Bankers Trust New York	5981	3.09
20	250	Standard Federal Bank (MI)	5969	3.09
-12	100	Philip Morris	5750	2.98
20	165	Chase Manhattan	5672	2.93
28	138	Telefonos de Mexico L (ADR)	5658	2.93
	915	RJR Nabisco Cl C Pfd	5490	2.84
118	301	Washington Fed S & L (WA)	5221	2.70
0	149	Torchmark	5210	2.70
3	283	Enhance Financial Services	4848	2.51
170	170	Williams	4271	2.21
	3925	Harrahs Jazz 14.25%	4121	2.13
0	130	Baxter International	3673	1.90
80	180	Summit Properties Trust	3465	1.79
0	100	Post Properties	3150	1.63

Composition % 09-30-94

Cash	8.4	Preferreds	0.0
Stocks	79.9	Convertibles	8.3
Bonds	3.4	Other	0.0

Tax Analysis

	Tax-Adj Historical Return %	% Pretax Return
3 Yr Avg	4.93	73.4
5 Yr Avg	5.79	78.2
10 Yr Avg	---	---
Potential Capital Gain Exposure (% of assets)		-3%

Most Similar Funds in MF500

Warburg Pincus Cap Appr Con	Fair Fit
Liberty All-Star	Weak Fit
Massachusetts Inv A	Weak Fit

Index Allocation

	% of Stocks
S&P 500	52.0
S&P MidCap 400	3.9
U.S. Small Cap	34.8
Foreign	9.4

Sector Weightings

	% of Stocks	Relative S&P 500
Utilities	6.4	0.52
Energy	1.9	0.19
Financials	64.4	6.09
Industrial Cyclicals	0.0	0.00
Consumer Durables	4.3	0.69
Consumer Staples	7.6	0.61
Services	0.0	0.00
Retail	3.3	0.56
Health	8.0	0.93
Technology	4.1	0.44

MORNINGSTAR 1995 Mutual Fund 500

Lexington Corporate Leaders

	Ticker	Load	NAV	Yield	SEC Yield	Assets	Objective
	LEXCX	None	10.51	3.7%	N/A	156.4	Growth/Inc.

Lexington Corporate Leaders Trust Fund seeks long-term growth of capital and income.

The fund was established as a Grantor Trust in 1935. The stocks of 30 then-major U.S. companies were selected on the basis of being leaders in their respective industries. The fund's portfolio is share-weighted; it holds the same number of shares in each company in which it invests. Since the fund's inception, seven of its original 30 companies have been eliminated because they no longer meet its investment criteria, and one spinoff name was added.

The fund will cease operations on Nov. 30, 2100.

Manager's Investment Style

This fund holds a static list of high-profile, large-cap stocks that were considered the leading companies in 1935, the date of this fund's inception. It intends to hold these firms until its planned termination date in 2100. The portfolio is heavily weighted in utilities, energy, and industrial cyclicals.

Historical Profile

Return	Above Average
Risk	Below Average
Rating ★★★★	Above Average

Investment Style History
Equity

Average % Stocks Held in Portfolio

Growth of $10,000
- |||| Value of Fund ($000)
- — Value of Index ($000) S&P 500
- ▼ Manager Change
- ▽ Partial Manager Change
- ► Mgr Unknown After
- ◄ Mgr Unknown Before

Performance Quartile (Within Objective)

	1983	1984	1985	1986	1987	1988	1989	1990	1991	1992	1993	1994	History
	12.78	11.52	13.27	13.82	11.75	11.84	13.68	10.53	11.62	11.62	12.78	10.51	NAV
	23.24	4.61	35.90	25.11	2.69	15.31	35.63	-4.20	19.41	9.63	17.58	-0.77	Total Return %
	0.77	-1.66	4.16	6.44	-2.57	-1.30	3.95	-1.09	-11.07	2.01	7.53	-2.08	+/- S&P 500
	-0.23	1.56	3.34	9.02	0.32	-2.64	6.46	1.98	-14.79	0.66	6.30	-0.70	+/- Wilshire 5000
	5.51	5.78	5.20	4.72	4.36	5.61	5.15	3.76	3.71	3.19	2.69	4.20	Income Return %
	17.72	-1.17	30.70	20.40	-1.67	9.70	30.48	-7.96	15.70	6.44	14.90	-4.97	Capital Return %
	29	52	10	9	37	27	6	68	45	25	21	25	Total Rtn % Rank All
	37	46	4	2	44	52	4	54	91	31	12	52	Total Rtn % Rank Obj
	0.68	0.64	0.63	0.65	0.55	0.65	0.63	0.43	0.40	0.35	0.32	0.44	Income $
	1.40	1.04	1.63	2.10	1.99	1.03	1.63	2.24	0.63	0.60	0.54	1.67	Capital Gains $
	0.11	0.11	0.10	0.08	0.08	0.26	0.72	0.67	0.67	0.60	0.57	0.62	Expense Ratio %
	5.03	5.40	4.85	4.47	4.01	5.88	3.34	3.57	3.46	3.16	2.78	2.78	Income Ratio %
	---	---	---	---	---	---	---	---	---	---	---	---	Turnover Rate %
	55.1	52.6	63.4	78.7	70.4	78.1	85.6	85.7	98.2	105.7	142.8	156.4	Net Assets ($mil)

Fund Manager(s)

Management Team

Manager Experience

	Dates Managed	Invest Obj	Std Dev	+/- Index
Alan H. Wapnick				
Security Global A	10/93 - 12/94	WW	12.23	2.69
Lexington Growth & Inc	07/94 - 12/94	GI	10.50	-4.35

Performance 12-31-94

	1st Qtr	2nd Qtr	3rd Qtr	4th Qtr	Total
1987	18.74	4.69	6.07	-22.12	2.69
1988	7.16	4.91	1.44	1.11	15.31
1989	9.74	8.57	9.32	4.13	35.63
1990	-3.00	3.31	-9.69	5.85	-4.20
1991	9.40	-1.79	5.97	4.88	19.41
1992	-0.69	2.28	5.12	2.68	9.63
1993	9.81	2.41	5.28	-0.69	17.58
1994	-5.09	1.16	4.02	-0.64	-0.77

Bear Market Performance

Decile Rank (5-year period)

Worst ———————— Best

	Worst 3 Mo Period 1985-89	Worst 3 Mo Period 1990-94
Lexington Corporate Leaders	-26.06	-11.52
+/- S&P 500	3.52	2.32
+/- Best Fit Index : S&P 500	3.52	2.32

Trailing Returns

	Total Return %	+/- S&P 500	+/- Wil 5000	% Rank All	% Rank Obj	Growth of $10,000
3 Mo	-0.64	-0.63	0.13	37	36	9,936
6 Mo	3.35	-1.51	-1.27	18	38	10,335
1 Yr	-0.77	-2.08	-0.70	25	52	9,923
3 Yr Avg	8.55	2.29	1.94	19	17	12,791
5 Yr Avg	7.91	-0.78	-0.91	34	51	14,632
10 Yr Avg	14.86	0.47	1.00	12	6	39,953
15 Yr Avg	14.76	0.28	0.79	16	13	78,896

Operations

Address and Telephone	P.O. Box 1515 Park 80 W. Plz Two Saddle Brook, NJ 07662 800-526-0057 / 201-845-7300
Advisor	Lexington Management
Subadvisor	None
Distributor	Lexington Funds Distributor
States Available	Selected states
Report Grade	C+
Income Distrib	Paid Semiannually
Date of Inception	11-18-35
Fiscal Year End	December

Min Initial Purchase	$1000 (Addt'l: $50)
Min IRA Purchase	$250 (Addt'l: $50)
Min Auto Invest Plan	$500 (Systematic Inv: $50)

Expenses & Fees

Sales Fees	0.00% front
	0.00% deferred
	0.00% 12b-1
Management Fee	0.35% flat fee
3-,5-,10-yr Expense Projections	N/A, N/A, N/A
Annual Brokerage Cost	---

Risk Analysis

Time Period	Load-Adj Return %	Risk % Rank [1] All	Obj	Morningstar [2] Return	Morningstar Risk	Morningstar Risk-Adj Rating
1 Yr	-0.77					
3 Yr	8.55	69	64	1.51 [3]	0.78	★★★★
5 Yr	7.91	64	44	0.79 [3]	0.77	★★★
10 Yr	14.86	55	42	1.46	0.80	★★★★

Average Historical Rating (109 months)   4.2 ★s

[1] 1 = low, 100 = high   [2] 1.00 = Equity Avg   [3] 1.00 = 90-day T-bill return

Other Measures

			Standard S&P 500	Best Fit S&P 500
Standard Deviation	9.21	Alpha	2.2	2.2
Mean	8.66	Beta	1.03	1.03
Sharpe Ratio	0.56	R-Squared	78	78

Investment Style

	Stock Portfolio Avg	Relative S&P 500
Price/Earnings Ratio	15.6	0.84
Price/Book Ratio	2.8	0.81
5 Yr Earnings Gr %	1.2	0.22
Return on Assets %	4.7	0.62
Debt % Total Cap	31.1	1.10
Med Mkt Cap ($mil)	15824	1.22

Style: Value Blend Growth / Size Large Med Small

Diversification Value for Portfolio Types

Large Cap: Low	Small Cap: High	Bond: Medium	Balanced: Low	Diversified: Low

Portfolio 12-31-94

Total Stocks: 24
Total Fixed-Income: 0

Share Chg (11-94)000	Amount 000		Value $000	% Net Assets
1	173	Mobil	14533	9.29
1	173	Procter & Gamble	10695	6.84
1	173	Exxon	10479	6.70
1	173	El duPont de Nemours	9703	6.20
1	173	General Electric	8798	5.63
1	173	AT & T	8668	5.54
1	173	Eastman Kodak	8237	5.27
1	173	Sears Roebuck	7935	5.07
1	173	Union Pacific	7870	5.03
1	173	Chevron	7698	4.92
1	173	American Brands	6469	4.14
1	173	Union Electric	6102	3.90
1	173	AlliedSignal	5865	3.75
1	173	Travelers	5606	3.58
1	173	Union Carbide	5067	3.24
1	173	Consolidated Edison	4442	2.84
1	173	Pacific Gas & Electric	4205	2.69
1	173	Columbia Gas System	4054	2.59
1	173	Praxair	3536	2.26
1	173	Santa Fe Pacific	3019	1.93
1	173	USX-Marathon Group	2825	1.81
1	173	Woolworth	2588	1.65
1	173	Borden	2135	1.36
1	173	Westinghouse Electric	2113	1.35

Composition % 12-31-94

Cash	2.4	Preferreds	0.0
Stocks	97.6	Convertibles	0.0
Bonds	0.0	Other	0.0

Tax Analysis

	Tax-Adj Historical Return %	% Pretax Return
3 Yr Avg	5.09	57.6
5 Yr Avg	3.80	44.3
10 Yr Avg	9.97	53.0
Potential Capital Gain Exposure (% of assets)		35%

Most Similar Funds in MF500

Flag Inv Telephone Income A	Fair Fit
Vanguard Equity-Income	Fair Fit
Washington Mutual Investors	Fair Fit

Index Allocation

	% of Stocks
S&P 500	100.0
S&P MidCap 400	0.0
U.S. Small Cap	0.0
Foreign	0.0

Sector Weightings

	% of Stocks	Relative S&P 500
Utilities	18.0	1.45
Energy	23.3	2.30
Financials	3.7	0.35
Industrial Cyclicals	24.5	1.50
Consumer Durables	3.8	0.62
Consumer Staples	12.6	1.01
Services	7.1	0.88
Retail	6.9	1.18
Health	0.0	0.00
Technology	0.0	0.00

MORNINGSTAR 1995 Mutual Fund 500

Lexington GNMA Income

	Ticker	Load	NAV	Yield	SEC Yield	Assets	Objective
	LEXNX	None	7.60	7.2%	7.65%	132.4	Gvt Mortgage

Lexington GNMA Income Fund seeks current income consistent with liquidity and safety of principal.

The fund normally invests at least 80% of its assets in Government National Mortgage Association (GNMA) certificates. The balance of assets may be invested in other securities issued or guaranteed by the U.S. government, including U.S. Treasury bills, notes, and bonds. The fund may also invest in repurchase agreements secured by such U.S. government securities or GNMA certificates.

Prior to Dec. 29, 1980, the fund was named Lexington Income Fund and followed different investment criteria.

Historical Profile

Return	Average
Risk	Average
Rating	★★★
	Neutral

Investment Style History
Fixed Income
Income Rtn % Rank Obj

46 79 52 64 64 63 36 30

Growth of $10,000
|||| Value of Fund ($000)
— Value of Index ($000) LB Mtg
▼ Manager Change
▽ Partial Manager Change
► Mgr Unknown After
◄ Mgr Unknown Before

Manager's Investment Style

Management sticks to GNMAs and an occasional stake in U.S. Treasuries. Management's tendency toward longer-than-average duration makes this an aggressive player among the mortgage funds. Recently, management has maintained above-average yield by holding project-loan mortgages, which tend to have slower prepayment rates that single-family GNMAs.

Performance Quartile (Within Objective)

1983	1984	1985	1986	1987	1988	1989	1990	1991	1992	1993	1994	History
7.72	7.74	8.06	8.22	7.58	7.45	7.88	7.90	8.45	8.26	8.32	7.60	NAV
7.62	11.86	17.36	11.98	1.56	6.94	15.60	9.23	15.75	5.19	8.06	-2.07	Total Return %
-0.75	-3.30	-4.77	-3.27	-1.20	-0.94	1.06	0.28	-0.25	-2.06	-1.69	0.84	+/- LB Aggregate
-2.51	-3.94	-7.85	-1.45	-2.74	-1.78	0.25	-1.49	0.03	-1.77	1.23	-0.47	+/- LB Mortgage
10.52	11.60	13.22	10.00	9.03	8.65	9.82	8.98	8.79	7.43	7.34	6.58	Income Return %
-2.89	0.26	4.13	1.99	-7.48	-1.72	5.77	0.25	6.96	-2.25	0.73	-8.65	Capital Return %
89	18	85	74	46	81	45	8	54	75	79	35	Total Rtn % Rank All
62	88	72	18	65	71	1	75	20	85	26	43	Total Rtn % Rank Obj
0.80	0.82	0.93	0.75	0.73	0.64	0.68	0.66	0.64	0.61	0.59	0.55	Income $
0.00	0.00	0.00	0.00	0.03	0.00	0.00	0.00	0.00	0.00	0.00	0.00	Capital Gains $
1.47	1.22	1.01	0.86	0.98	1.07	1.03	1.04	1.02	1.01	1.02	0.97	Expense Ratio %
10.77	11.89	11.06	9.30	8.49	8.31	8.88	8.43	7.97	7.31	6.96	6.69	Income Ratio %
207	133	168	300	89	233	103	113	139	180	52	39	Turnover Rate %
22.4	25.4	87.3	141.3	106.9	97.4	96.4	97.9	122.2	132.0	150.0	132.4	Net Assets ($mil)

Fund Manager(s)

Denis P. Jamison CFA, since 07-81. Birthdate: 09-47. BA, City C. of New York 1969

Manager Experience

	Dates Managed	Invest Obj	Std Dev	+/- Index
Denis P. Jamison				
Lexington Remirez Glb Inc	07/86 - 12/94	WB	5.37	-1.76

Performance 12-31-94

	1st Qtr	2nd Qtr	3rd Qtr	4th Qtr	Total
1987	2.31	-1.75	-4.81	6.15	1.56
1988	3.03	1.56	2.21	-0.01	6.94
1989	0.70	8.88	1.19	4.18	15.60
1990	-1.01	3.58	0.68	5.81	9.23
1991	2.60	1.36	5.85	5.15	15.75
1992	-2.04	4.22	3.62	-0.57	5.19
1993	3.19	2.27	1.00	1.38	8.06
1994	-2.42	-0.84	0.65	0.55	-2.08

Bear Market Performance

Decile Rank (5-year period)

Worst ▮ Best

	Worst 3 Mo Period 1985-89	Worst 3 Mo Period 1990-94
Lexington GNMA Income	-4.81	-4.01
+/- LB Aggregate	-2.09	0.93
+/- Best Fit Index : LB Mtg	-2.74	-0.01

Trailing Returns

	Total Return %	+/- LB Aggregate	+/- LB Mortgage	% Rank All	% Rank Obj	Growth of $10,000
3 Mo	0.55	0.17	0.12	11	14	10,055
6 Mo	1.20	0.21	-0.11	34	19	10,120
1 Yr	-2.07	0.84	-0.47	35	43	9,793
3 Yr Avg	3.64	-0.91	-0.35	77	32	11,131
5 Yr Avg	7.07	-0.55	-0.50	48	34	14,073
10 Yr Avg	8.79	-1.16	-1.56	76	36	23,218
15 Yr Avg	8.90	-1.91	-2.31	87	75	35,906

Operations

Address and Telephone	P.O. Box 1515 Park 80 W. Plz Two Saddle Brook, NJ 07662 800-526-0057 / 201-845-7300
Advisor	Lexington Management
Subadvisor	None
Distributor	Lexington Funds Distributor
States Available	All plus GU,PR,VI
Report Grade	C+
Income Distrib	Paid Monthly
Date of Inception	10-10-73
Fiscal Year End	December

Risk Analysis

Time Period	Load-Adj Return %	Risk % Rank [1] All	Obj	Morningstar [2] Return	Morningstar Risk	Morningstar Risk-Adj Rating
1 Yr	-2.07					
3 Yr	3.64	20	60	0.02 [3]	0.96	★★★
5 Yr	7.07	23	77	0.57 [3]	0.99	★★★
10 Yr	8.79	22	72	0.76 [3]	1.04	★★★

Average Historical Rating (109 months) 2.5 ★s

[1] = low, 100 = high [2] 1.00 = Taxable Avg [3] 1.00 = 90-day T-bill return

Other Measures

			Standard LB Agg	Best Fit LB Mtg
Standard Deviation	3.77	Alpha	-0.7	-0.4
Mean	3.65	Beta	0.85	1.12
Sharpe Ratio	0.03	R-Squared	82	92

Investment Style

Interest-Rate Stance
Avg Effective Duration	3.5 Yrs**
Avg Effective Maturity	10.7 Yrs

Maturity: Short Intm Long

Quality
Avg Credit Quality	AAA
Avg Weighted Coupon	8.59%
Avg Weighted Price	101.66% of Par

**figure provided by fund

Diversification Value for Portfolio Types

Large Cap: Medium	Small Cap: High	Bond: None	Balanced: Medium	Diversified: Medium

Expenses & Fees

Sales Fees	0.00% front
	0.00% deferred
	0.00% 12b-1
Management Fee	0.60% flat fee
3-,5-,10-yr Expense Projections	$32, $56, $125

Portfolio 06-30-94

Amount 000	Date of Maturity	Total Stocks: 0 Total Fixed-Income: 35	Value $000	% Net Assets
15000	11-15-12	US Treasury Bond 10.375%	18387	12.14
15000	05-15-16	US Treasury Bond 7.25%	14235	9.40
12837	2036	GNMA 8%	12425	8.20
10410	2029	GNMA 8.75%	10394	6.86
9600		US Treasury Bill N/A	9553	6.31
8843	2030	GNMA 9.75%	9183	6.06
9365	2015	GNMA 8.15%	9099	6.01
9013	2028	GNMA 8.5%	9099	6.01
8999	2017	GNMA 8.2%	8777	5.79
7880	2022	GNMA 8.25%	7688	5.08
6909	2022	GNMA 9%	7077	4.67
6755	2019	GNMA 8.08%	6542	4.32
6049	2029	GNMA 9.25%	6168	4.07
5047	2029	GNMA 8.63%	5119	3.38
3800	05-31-96	US Treasury Note 5.875%	3779	2.49
3112	2013	GNMA 7.5%	2930	1.93
2039	2023	GNMA 9.5%	2098	1.38
2035	2012	GNMA 8.1%	1973	1.30
1470	2014	GNMA 6.65%	1296	0.86
1129	2025	GNMA 10%	1183	0.78
1023	2029	GNMA 10.25%	1082	0.71
966	2022	GNMA 7.75%	920	0.61
865	2016	GNMA 10.05%	908	0.60
888	2013	GNMA 7.7%	844	0.56
886	2029	GNMA 7.63%	838	0.55

Composition % 12-31-94

Cash	16.5	Preferreds	0.0
Stocks	0.0	Convertibles	0.0
Bonds	83.5	Other	0.0

Tax Analysis

	Tax-Adj Historical Return %	% Pretax Return
3 Yr Avg	1.00	26.7
5 Yr Avg	4.39	58.8
10 Yr Avg	5.38	52.1
Potential Capital Gain Exposure (% of assets)		-9%

Most Similar Funds in MF500

Gradison-McDonald Govt Inc	Strong Fit
Scudder GNMA	Strong Fit
Dreyfus GNMA	Strong Fit

Coupon Range

	% of Bonds	Rel Obj
0%	0.0	0.00
0% to 8%	25.0	0.45
8% to 9%	42.6	1.95
9% to 10%	12.5	1.45
More than 10%	13.8	2.10
Not applicable	6.2	0.85

Sector Analysis 06-30-94
% of Bonds

US Treas	30	CMOs	0
GNMA mtgs	70	ARMs	0
FNMA mtgs	0	Other	0
FHLMC mtgs	0		

Liberty All-Star Equity

	Ticker	NAV	Mkt Price	Prem/Disc	Yield	Objective
	USA	$9.27	$8.38	-9.7%	5.4%	Domestic Eq

Liberty All-Star Equity Fund seeks total return.

Normally, the fund will invest at least 65% of its assets in equity securities. The fund allocates its assets equally among five independent investment managers. Three of the managers follow value strategies, and the other two are growth investors.

To discourage takeovers, directors serve staggered terms, and supermajority voting is in effect to merge, liquidate, or open-end the fund.

The fund had a rights offering in the first quarter of 1992, which raised $54.6 million. A rights offering in 1993's third quarter added approximately $44 million to the fund's coffers. In 1994's third quarter, the fund staged a rights offering that raised $43 million.

The fund has an annual 10% payout policy.

The fund may, on occasion, retain capital gains and pay taxes on them.

Manager's Investment Style

This fund relies on a multimanagement strategy. Assets are evenly divided among five managers; three employ value styles and two are growth-oriented. Because it balances two opposing styles, the fund limits its downside when either growth or value investing fall out of favor. This balancing act keeps risk modest and returns in the middle of the road.

Fund Manager(s)

Multiple Managers.

	7.5	-5.4	-12.5	-13.9	-11.7	-0.6	5.4	7.6	8.4	Highest Prem/Disc
	5.7	-24.1	-21.7	-19.7	-17.2	-15.1	-5.5	-0.7	-9.7	Lowest Prem/Disc

Historical Profile

Return Average
Risk Below Average
Rating ★★★★ Above Average

Growth of $10,000
— at NAV ($000)
— at Market Price ($000)

Premium Discount %

	1983	1984	1985	1986	1987	1988	1989	1990	1991	1992	1993	1994	History
	---	---	---	9.11	7.90	8.29	9.58	8.92	11.20	10.78	10.40	9.27	NAV
	---	---	---	-8.90*	-1.05	14.64	29.96	4.20	39.27	7.11	8.54	-1.32	NAV Total Return %
	---	---	---	-11.40*	-6.30	-1.97	-1.72	7.31	8.79	-0.51	-1.51	-2.64	+/- S&P 500
	---	---	---	0.00*	3.73	2.31	2.68	2.65	1.66	1.69	1.13	4.76	Income Return %
	---	---	---	-8.90*	-4.77	12.32	27.29	1.55	37.61	5.43	7.41	-6.08	Capital Return %
	---	---	---		75	34	14	49	17	66	88	17	Total Rtn % Rank All
	---	---	---		63	57	29	13	38	43	58	51	Total Rtn % Rank Obj
	---	---	---	-3.75*	-28.87	32.00	27.97	5.12	53.86	15.39	12.63	-16.66	Market Total Rtn %
	---	---	---		-17.0	-17.5	-17.2	-14.1	-7.3	0.8	3.6	0.9	Avg Prem/Disc %
	---	---	---	0.00	0.30	0.16	0.20	0.20	0.15	0.18	0.12	0.48	Income $
	---	---	---	0.00	0.88	0.48	0.75	0.70	0.87	0.89	1.14	0.52	Capital Gains $
	---	---	---	2.77	1.92	1.33	1.25	1.23	1.16	1.08	1.08	1.08	Expense Ratio %
	---	---	---	1.81	0.80	1.96	2.07	1.98	1.66	1.44	1.08	1.15	Income Ratio %
	---	---	---	---	72	73	70	68	72	57	72	---	Turnover Rate %
	---	---	---	552.8	424.1	669.2	514.2	478.7	601.3	664.7	713.7	698.0	Net Assets ($mil)

Manager Experience

	Dates Managed	Invest Obj	Std Dev	+/- Index
Jeffrey J. Miller				
Managers Special Equity	06/84 - 10/94	SC	17.63	-0.14
Irwin F. Smith				
PIMCo Adv Growth C	01/86 - 01/93	G	17.63	1.49

NAV Performance % 12-30-94

	1st Qtr	2nd Qtr	3rd Qtr	4th Qtr	Total
1987	21.70	2.15	5.44	-24.51	-1.05
1988	5.55	4.58	0.98	2.85	14.64
1989	6.82	8.69	11.53	0.37	29.96
1990	-1.97	9.48	-12.76	11.29	4.20
1991	17.20	-0.50	7.43	11.17	39.27
1992	-2.64	-0.54	4.61	5.73	7.11
1993	2.26	0.68	4.93	0.48	8.54
1994	-2.92	-1.34	4.86	-1.75	-1.32

Bear Market Performance

Decile Rank (5-year period)

Worst ──────── Best

	Worst 3 Mo Period 1985-89	Worst 3 Mo Period 1990-94
Liberty All-Star	---	-12.76
+/- S&P 500	---	0.99

Trailing Returns

	NAV Total Return %	+/- S&P 500	% Rank All	% Rank Obj	Mkt Total Return %
3 Mo	-1.75	-1.73	48	57	-11.78
6 Mo	3.03	-1.83	14	36	-11.76
1 Yr	-1.32	-2.64	17	51	-16.66
3 Yr Avg	4.69	-1.58	69	53	2.71
5 Yr Avg	10.73	2.04	21	34	11.87
Incept Avg	10.33*	---	---	---	9.01*

Operations

Address and Telephone	One Financial Center, 23rd Floor
	Boston, MA 02111
	617-772-7380 / 800-542-3863
Advisor	Liberty Asset Management Co.
Subadvisor	N/A
Administrator	Liberty Asset Management Co.
Transfer Agent	State Street Bank and Trust Co.
Custodian	State Street Bank and Trust Co.
Auditor	KPMG Peat Marwick
Legal Counsel	Bingham, Dana & Gould

Risk Analysis

	Risk % Rank[1]		Morningstar[2]		Morningstar
	All	Obj	Return	Risk	Risk-Adj Rating
3 Yr	72	50	0.14	0.57	★★★
5 Yr	73	27	1.18	0.60	★★★★
10 Yr	---	---	---	---	

Average Historical Rating (63 months)   3.7 ★s

[1] 1 = Low, 100 = High   [2] 1.00 = Equity Avg   [3] 1.00 = 90-day T-bill Return

Other Measures

				S&P 500
Standard Deviation	8.84	Alpha		-1.55
Mean	4.98	Beta		1.05
Sharpe Ratio	0.16	R-Squared		88

Investment Style

	Stock Portfolio Avg	Relative S&P 500
Price/Earnings Ratio	19.6	1.06
Price/Cash Flow Ratio	13.9	1.20
Price/Book Ratio	3.8	1.11
5 Yr Earnings Gr %	10.4	1.87
Return on Assets %	8.0	1.07
Debt % Total Cap	23.2	0.82
Med Mkt Cap ($mil)	6656	0.51

figure is based on less than 50% of stocks

Style
Value Blend Growth
Size Large Med Small

Index Allocation

	% of Stocks
Dow 30	11.5
S&P 500	75.9
S&P Mid-Cap 400	10.4
US Small-Cap	7.4
Foreign	8.0

Diversification Value for Portfolio Types

Large Cap: None
Small Cap: Low
Bond: High
Balanced: None
Diversified: Low

Portfolio 09-30-94

Share Chg (06-94)	Amount	Total Equity: 180 Total Fixed-Income: 0	Value $000	% Total Invest
9400	251000	Motorola	13240	1.87
-2000	106100	Royal Dutch Petroleum	11392	1.61
0	232475	US Healthcare	10825	1.53
-98600	215800	General Electric	10385	1.47
9100	179600	United HealthCare	9519	1.34
39700	220400	Boeing	9505	1.34
2000	160700	Microsoft	9019	1.27
12200	128400	IBM	8924	1.26
0	125000	Schering-Plough	8875	1.25
14000	220000	May Department Stores	8663	1.22
-7400	101100	Monsanto	8126	1.15
4000	96000	Capital Cities/ABC	7872	1.11
0	125000	Avon Products	7469	1.06
-19100	62900	Unilever (Netherlands)	7131	1.01
0	80000	American International Group	7110	1.00
21000	165200	Oracle Systems	7104	1.00
18000	128000	FHLMC	6832	0.97
-72000	88000	AMP	6809	0.96
57200	257200	YPF (ADR)	6494	0.92
0	147100	Columbia/HCA Healthcare	6399	0.90
0	135100	Applied Materials	6316	0.89
24400	116200	AT & T	6275	0.89
0	80000	Marsh & McLennan	6250	0.88
73900	183100	Compaq Computer	5974	0.84
-76200	171300	Avery Dennison	5888	0.83

Composition % 12-31-94

Cash	5.0	Preferreds	0.0
Stocks	95.0	Convertibles	0.0
Bonds	0.0	Other	0.0

Tax Analysis

	Tax-Adj Historical Return %	% Pretax Return
3 Yr Avg	1.62	30.6
5 Yr Avg	7.35	62.1
10 Yr Avg	---	---

Potential Capital Gain Exposure
(% of assets)   15

Most Similar Funds in MF500

IDS New Dimensions	Strong Fit
Gabelli Growth	Strong Fit
Alliance Growth & Income A	Strong Fit

Sector Weightings

	% of Stocks	Relative S&P 500
Utilities	4.1	0.33
Energy	8.1	0.79
Financials	15.4	1.46
Industrial Cyclicals	17.5	1.07
Consumer Durables	7.6	1.22
Consumer Staples	6.9	0.55
Services	10.6	1.30
Retail	5.1	0.87
Health	10.8	1.24
Technology	14.0	1.53

Income Distrib Schedule	Paid Irregularly
Management Fee	0.80%, 0.20%A
Reinvestment Plan	Yes
Direct Purchase Plan	No
Shares Outstanding	75,278,882
Exchange	NYSE
*Date of Inception	10-24-86
Shareholder Report	A

Liberty High-Income Bond A

	Ticker	Load	NAV	Yield	SEC Yield	Assets	Objective
	FHIIX	4.50%	10.23	10.0%	10.53%	421.2	Corp Hi Yld

Liberty High-Income Bond Fund - Class A seeks high current income. Capital growth is considered when consistent with the primary objective.

The fund invests primarily in lower-rated fixed-income securities, including preferred stocks, bonds, debentures, notes, equipment-lease certificates, and equipment-trust certificates. It may also invest temporarily in short-term cash and cash items for defensive purposes.

Prior to Oct. 18, 1990, the fund was named Federated High-Income Securities.

Historical Profile

Return	Above Average
Risk	Low
Rating	★★★★ Above Average

Investment Style History
Fixed Income
Income Rtn % Rank Obj

| 38 | 17 | 38 | 41 | 4 | 34 | 44 | 31 |

Growth of $10,000

- |||| Value of Fund ($000)
- — Value of Index ($000) LB Agg
- ▼ Manager Change
- ▽ Partial Manager Change
- ► Mgr Unknown After
- ◄ Mgr Unknown Before

Performance Quartile (Within Objective)

	1983	1984	1985	1986	1987	1988	1989	1990	1991	1992	1993	1994	History
	11.93	11.56	12.35	12.32	10.91	11.06	9.68	7.28	10.22	10.72	11.44	10.23	NAV
	14.45	10.81	21.74	12.52	0.00	15.15	-0.36	-12.80	60.34	17.17	17.42	-1.68	Total Return %
	6.08	-4.34	-0.38	-2.73	-2.76	7.27	-14.90	-21.74	44.34	9.92	7.67	1.24	+/- LB Aggregate
	---	---	---	-3.12	-6.53	3.72	-0.75	-6.42	16.59	0.51	-1.48	-0.71	+/- FB High-Yield
	13.61	13.92	14.91	12.76	11.44	13.77	12.11	12.00	19.95	12.27	10.70	8.89	Income Return %
	0.85	-3.10	6.83	-0.24	-11.44	1.37	-12.48	-24.79	40.38	4.89	6.72	-10.58	Capital Return %
	61	22	61	71	60	27	98	89	4	7	22	31	Total Rtn % Rank All
	66	11	58	64	77	22	45	64	2	50	69	21	Total Rtn % Rank Obj
	1.54	1.54	1.56	1.51	1.44	1.42	1.39	1.27	1.20	1.19	1.07	1.03	Income $
	0.00	0.00	0.00	0.00	0.00	0.00	0.00	0.00	0.00	0.00	0.00	0.00	Capital Gains $
	1.11	1.11	1.14	1.06	1.02	1.05	1.00	1.02	1.03	1.02	1.08	1.18	Expense Ratio %
	12.68	13.26	13.27	12.41	11.72	12.37	12.55	13.01	14.62	12.40	10.44	9.27	Income Ratio %
	19	21	26	27	25	52	43	40	32	37	49	76	Turnover Rate %
	112.7	156.2	251.4	372.0	342.6	373.8	318.6	207.0	307.3	382.8	462.0	421.2	Net Assets ($mil)

Manager's Investment Style

Management traditionaly sticks with the upper credit range of the high-yield market by favoring B paper. It will, however, go into more-adventurous territory through PIKs or zeros, for example. Management takes a bottom-up approach when chosing individual credits and sectors.

Fund Manager(s)

Mark E. Durbiano CFA(1985), since 01-87.
Birthdate: 09-59. BA, Dickinson U. 1981 MBA, U. of Pittsburgh 1982

Manager Experience

	Dates Managed	Invest Obj	Std Dev	+/- Index
Mark E. Durbiano				
Federated S-T Inc Instl	07/86 - 09/91	CQ	2.70	-1.21
Liberty Equity-Income A	12/86 - 07/91	EI	12.57	-4.86

Performance 12-31-94

	1st Qtr	2nd Qtr	3rd Qtr	4th Qtr	Total
1987	4.75	-0.61	-3.81	-0.15	0.00
1988	6.31	2.77	3.38	1.94	15.15
1989	2.52	3.53	-1.54	-4.66	-0.36
1990	-4.12	6.21	-8.70	-6.21	-12.80
1991	25.55	10.17	9.10	6.24	60.34
1992	8.60	2.77	3.68	1.25	17.17
1993	6.96	3.70	0.40	5.43	17.42
1994	-1.78	0.23	0.73	-0.86	-1.68

Bear Market Performance

Decile Rank (5-year period)

Worst ———————————— Best

	Worst 3 Mo Period 1985-89	Worst 3 Mo Period 1990-94
Liberty High-Income Bond A	-6.97	-17.76
+/- LB Aggregate	-7.79	-18.50
+/- Best Fit Index : FB HY	---	-3.65

Trailing Returns

	Total Return %	+/- LB Aggregate	+/- FB High-Yield	% Rank All	% Rank Obj	Growth of $10,000
3 Mo	-0.86	-1.24	-0.81	41	42	9,914
6 Mo	-0.13	-1.12	-1.68	59	29	9,987
1 Yr	-1.68	1.24	-0.71	31	21	9,832
3 Yr Avg	10.59	6.05	-0.57	11	40	13,526
5 Yr Avg	13.59	5.97	0.52	5	2	18,912
10 Yr Avg	11.51	1.56	---	42	12	29,721
15 Yr Avg	11.81	1.00	---	57	31	53,333

Operations

Address and Telephone	Liberty Cntr Federated Inv. Twr Pittsburgh, PA 15222-3779 800-245-5051 / 412-288-1900
Advisor	Federated Advisers
Subadvisor	None
Distributor	Federated Securities
States Available	All plus PR
Report Grade	B+
Income Distrib	Paid Monthly
Date of Inception	11-30-77
Fiscal Year End	March

Min Initial Purchase	$500 (Addt'l: $100)
Min IRA Purchase	$50 (Addt'l: $50)
Min Auto Invest Plan	$500 (Systematic Inv: $100)

Expenses & Fees

Sales Fees	4.50% front
	0.00% deferred
	0.00% 12b-1
Management Fee	0.75% flat fee
3-,5-,10-yr Expense Projections	$81, $108, $184

Risk Analysis

Time Period	Load-Adj Return %	Risk % Rank[1] All	Obj	Morningstar[2] Return	Risk	Morningstar Risk-Adj Rating
1 Yr	-6.11					
3 Yr	8.91	9	51	1.62[3]	0.38	★★★★
5 Yr	12.55	47	67	2.11[3]	0.61	★★★★★
10 Yr	11.00	36	58	0.85	0.51	★★★★
Average Historical Rating (109 months)					3.5	★ s

[1] 1 = low, 100 = high [2] 1.00 = Hybrid Avg [3] 1.00 = 90-day T-bill return

Other Measures

			Standard LB Agg	Best Fit FB HY
Standard Deviation	5.27	Alpha	6.4	-1.4
Mean	10.25	Beta	0.52	1.14
Sharpe Ratio	1.28	R-Squared	16	87

Investment Style

Interest-Rate Stance

Avg Effective Duration	5.2 Yrs
Avg Effective Maturity	7.6 Yrs

Quality

Avg Credit Quality	B
Avg Weighted Coupon	10.47%
Avg Weighted Price	89.21% of Par

Maturity Short Intm Long / Quality High Med Low

Diversification Value for Portfolio Types

Large Cap: High	Small Cap: High	Bond: High	Balanced: High	Diversified: High

Portfolio 10-31-94

Total Stocks: 12
Total Fixed-Income: 119

Amount 000	Date of Maturity		Value $000	% Net Assets
20000	03-15-98	Revlon Worldwide Step 12%	11100	2.34
13000	06-01-05	American Standard 0%	8775	1.85
9375	12-15-05	WestPoint Stevens 9.375%	8461	1.79
8850	02-01-01	Stone Container 9.875%	8352	1.76
19000	08-15-05	Specialty Foods Step 13%	8265	1.75
13000	10-01-98	G-I Holdings 0%	7930	1.67
7300	06-30-05	SCI Television 11%	7410	1.56
7500	05-01-05	Arcadian Partner 10.75%	7369	1.56
10500	07-15-02	Grand Union 12.25%	7350	1.55
69		K-III Comm Pfd Pik 11.625%	6734	1.42
7050	12-01-02	Flagstar 10.875%	6645	1.40
6116	07-15-05	AmeriSource PIK 11.25%	6146	1.30
6000	10-01-04	Foamex LP/Foamex Cap 11.875%	6030	1.27
6000	10-01-03	Ackerley Communications 10.75%	5775	1.22
7000	12-15-02	Silgan Holdings 13.25%	5653	1.19
5500	09-01-03	Carbide/Graphite 11.5%	5555	1.17
7750	01-15-04	California Energy Step 10.25%	5512	1.16
5500	07-15-02	Polymer Group 12.75%	5500	1.16
6000	08-01-13	Continental Cablevision 9.5%	5430	1.15
5250	02-15-03	Mid-American Waste Sys 12.25%	5171	1.09
5000	08-15-04	Allbritton Comm 11.5%	5100	1.08
7250	08-01-03	PanAmSat Capital 11.375%	4912	1.04
5000	12-15-00	TRISM 10.75%	4900	1.03
7000	02-15-03	Dr Pepper Bottling 11.625%	4795	1.01
4250	01-15-02	US Can 13.5%	4739	1.00

Composition % 11-30-94

Cash	5.0	Preferreds	0.0
Stocks	0.0	Convertibles	0.0
Bonds	93.0	Other	2.0

Tax Analysis

	Tax-Adj Historical Return %	% Pretax Return
3 Yr Avg	6.71	61.1
5 Yr Avg	9.22	62.2
10 Yr Avg	6.60	45.4
Potential Capital Gain Exposure (% of assets)		-19%

Most Similar Funds in MF500

AIM High-Yield A	Strong Fit
Putnam High Yield Adv A	Strong Fit
Kemper High-Yield A	Strong Fit

Coupon Range

	% of Bonds	Rel Obj
0%, PIK	15.5	2.09
0% to 11%	39.7	0.81
11% to 13%	39.8	1.19
13% to 14.5%	2.9	0.54
More than 14.5%	2.1	1.27
Not applicable	0.0	0.00

Credit Analysis 11-30-94

% of Bonds

US Govt	0	BB	12
AAA	0	B	76
AA	0	Below B	8
A	0	NR/NA	4
BBB	0		

Lincoln National Convertible Securities

	Ticker	NAV	Mkt Price	Prem/Disc	Yield	Objective
	LNV	$17.10	$15.38	-10.1%	6.1%	Convertible

Lincoln National Convertible Securities Fund seeks a high level of total return on its assets through a combination of capital appreciation and current income.

The fund will invest at least 65% of its assets in convertibles. The remainder may include preferred and common stock and debt instruments.

The fund intends to retain and reinvest all long-term capital gains. Therefore, the fund is required to pay tax on such gains at the prevailing corporate rate.

The fund may leverage by borrowing up to 33% of its net assets, but has not done so.

A total of 629,300 shares, or approximately 9% of the outstanding capitalization, has been retired since the inception of the repurchase program in July 1988.

Historical Profile
Return High
Risk Average
Rating ★★★★★
Highest

16.5	-0.2	-7.7	-12.1	-7.2	-9.1	-4.4	2.2	3.8	Highest Prem/Disc
8.6	-18.3	-16.8	-16.6	-15.8	-15.4	-14.8	-9.2	-12.7	Lowest Prem/Disc

Growth of $10,000
— at NAV ($000)
— at Market Price ($000)

Premium Discount %

	1983	1984	1985	1986	1987	1988	1989	1990	1991	1992	1993	1994	History
	---	---	---	14.38	12.62	13.41	15.21	13.59	18.04	17.62	18.84	17.10	NAV
	---	---	---	4.41*	-4.71	15.28	27.20	-2.93	42.27	10.19	27.97	-1.45	NAV Total Return %
	---	---	---	---	-7.47	7.40	12.66	-11.87	26.27	2.95	18.22	1.47	+/- LB Aggregate
	---	---	---	---	-9.97	-1.33	-4.49	0.19	11.78	2.57	17.91	-2.77	+/- S&P 500
	---	---	---	1.33*	7.53	9.02	9.07	7.73	9.52	5.86	5.71	5.54	Income Return %
	---	---	---	3.08*	-12.24	6.26	18.12	-10.65	32.75	4.34	22.26	-6.99	Capital Return %
	---	---	---	---	80	31	18	68	15	44	16	17	Total Rtn % Rank All
	---	---	---	---	50	12	1	22	1	88	1	22	Total Rtn % Rank Obj
	---	---	---	6.36*	-19.00	8.49	27.65	-6.58	44.45	20.10	39.63	-13.28	Market Total Rtn %
	---	---	---	11.0	-11.4	-14.0	-14.3	-12.0	-13.4	-8.2	-4.4	-5.3	Avg Prem/Disc %
	---	---	---	0.20	1.13	0.95	1.07	1.02	1.02	0.97	1.05	0.96	Income $
	---	---	---	0.00	0.00	0.00	0.50	0.00	0.00	1.17	2.55	0.41	Capital Gains $
	---	---	---	---	0.88	0.96	0.94	0.97	0.89	0.83	1.02	1.11●	Expense Ratio %
	---	---	---	---	6.43	6.90	6.64	7.21	5.96	5.49	4.58	4.97●	Income Ratio %
	---	---	---	---	73	111	147	135	133	166	220	---	Turnover Rate %
	---	---	---	---	99.5	87.3	91.6	92.0	85.4	113.4	110.7	118.6	108.8	Net Assets ($mil)

● ratio annualized by Morningstar

Manager's Investment Style

Management emphasizes thin-premium convertibles of growth-oriented firms. As such, the fund is one of the more equity-like convertible offerings around, and is thus more sensitive to stock-market movements than most convertible funds. As the portfolio's high turnover indicates, management moves in and out of individual issues and sectors to take advantage of developing trends and themes.

Fund Manager(s)

Robert D. Schwartz. Since 7-93.

Manager Experience

	Dates Managed	Invest Obj	Std Dev	+/- Index

Not available.

NAV Performance % 12-30-94

	1st Qtr	2nd Qtr	3rd Qtr	4th Qtr	Total
1987	5.22	0.34	1.14	-10.76	-4.71
1988	8.08	5.45	0.90	0.25	15.28
1989	7.46	8.82	8.02	0.69	27.20
1990	-2.50	4.58	-10.91	6.87	-2.93
1991	15.97	3.34	9.62	8.29	42.27
1992	3.55	-0.34	2.27	4.40	10.19
1993	6.36	7.64	6.75	4.71	27.97
1994	-3.03	-4.82	9.11	-2.14	-1.45

Bear Market Performance

Decile Rank (5-year period)

Worst ← → Best

	Worst 3 Mo Period 1985-89	Worst 3 Mo Period 1990-94
Lincoln Natl Convert	---	-11.27
+/- LB Aggregate	---	-12.01

Trailing Returns

	NAV Total Return %	+/- LB Agg	+/- S&P 500	% Rank All	% Rank Obj	Mkt Total Return %
3 Mo	-2.14	-2.52	-2.13	54	55	0.73
6 Mo	6.78	5.78	1.91	7	1	-2.43
1 Yr	-1.45	1.47	-2.77	17	22	-13.28
3 Yr Avg	11.59	7.05	5.33	16	11	13.30
5 Yr Avg	13.93	6.30	5.23	8	11	14.43
Incept Avg	12.52*	---	---	---	---	10.24*

Operations

Address and Telephone	1300 S. Clinton St., P.O. Box 1110 Fort Wayne, IN 46801 219-455-2210	Income Distrib Schedule	Paid Quarterly
		Management Fee	0.88%
		Reinvestment Plan	Yes
Advisor	Lincoln National Inv. Mgmt.	Direct Purchase Plan	No
Subadvisor	Lynch & Mayer, Inc.	Shares Outstanding	6,363,695
Administrator	N/A	Exchange	NYSE
Transfer Agent	First National Bank of Boston	*Date of Inception	04-10-86
Custodian	Bankers Trust Company	Shareholder Report	B-
Auditor	Coopers & Lybrand		
Legal Counsel	Gardner, Carton & Douglas		

Risk Analysis

	Risk % Rank[1] All	Obj	Morningstar[2] Return	Risk	Morningstar Risk-Adj Rating
3 Yr	50	55	1.67	0.60	★★★★
5 Yr	60	55	2.17	0.75	★★★★★
10 Yr					

Average Historical Rating (67 months) 4.3 ★s

[1] = Low, 100 = High [2]1.00 = Hybrid Avg [3]1.00 = 90-day T-bill Return

Other Measures

				LB Aggregate
Standard Deviation	8.26	Alpha		6.95
Mean	11.36	Beta		1.08
Sharpe Ratio	0.95	R-Squared		28

Investment Style

Interest-Rate Stance

	Fund	Relative Objective
Avg Effective Maturity	9.3 Yrs	0.86
Avg Weighted Coupon	6.78%	1.05
Avg Weighted Price	97.6% Par	1.00

Quality

Avg Credit Quality	B

Credit Analysis 09-30-94

	% of Bonds		% of Bonds
US Govt	0	BB	10
AAA	0	B	46
AA	0	Below B	0
A	3	NR/NA	29
BBB	12		

Diversification Value for Portfolio Types

Large Cap: Low	Small Cap: Low	Bond: Medium	Balanced: Low	Diversified: Low

Portfolio 06-30-94

Amount 000	Total Equity: 0 Total Fixed-Income: 63	Maturity	Value $000	% Total Invest
68	AGCO Cv Pfd $1.625		3364	3.13
2600	Integrated Health Svc Cv 5.75%	01-01-01	2782	2.59
2435	Riverwood Intl Cv 6.75%	09-15-03	2679	2.49
60	Offshore Pipeline Cv Pfd $2.25		2640	2.46
2130	Mediplex Cv 6.5%	08-01-03	2513	2.34
2510	Seacor Holdings Cv 6%	07-01-03	2510	2.33
57	AMR Cv Pfd $3.00		2510	2.33
3135	Hechinger Cv 5.5%	04-01-12	2500	2.33
2725	EMC Cv 6.25%	04-01-02	2466	2.29
62	American Express Cv Pfd 6.25%		2441	2.27
40	Telefonica Argentina Cv Pfd 7%		2375	2.21
37	Roosevelt Fin Cv Pfd $3.25		2319	2.16
1750	Summit Health Cv 7.5%	04-01-03	2297	2.14
1800	Lam Research Cv 6%	05-01-03	2268	2.11
90	LCI Intl Cv Pfd $1.25		2211	2.06
3370	US Home Cv 4.875%	11-01-05	2191	2.04
38	Newmont Mining Cv Pfd $2.75		2190	2.04
2685	Conner Peripherals Cv 6.5%	03-01-02	2188	2.04
1745	J Baker Cv 7%	06-01-02	2185	2.03
2000	ITI Acquisition 13.5%	05-11-02	2000	1.86
15	Chrysler Cv Pfd $4.625		1976	1.84
5300	Fidelity National Finance 0%	02-15-09	1948	1.81
96	Kenetech Cv Pfd 8.25%		1940	1.80
2000	Healthsouth Rehab 9.5%	04-01-01	1920	1.79
2015	Medusa Cv 6%	11-15-03	1919	1.78

Composition % 12-31-94

Cash	4.1	Preferreds	0.0
Stocks	0.0	Convertibles	93.9
Bonds	1.1	Other	0.9

Coupon Range

	% of Bonds	Relative Objective
0%	1.9	0.4
0% to 6%	30.5	1.2
6% to 7%	19.4	1.1
7% to 8.5%	10.1	0.6
More than 8.5%	10.3	1.0
Not applicable	27.8	1.2

1.0 = Objective Average

Tax Analysis

	Tax-Adj Historical Return %	% Pretax Return
3 Yr Avg	7.25	59.9
5 Yr Avg	10.12	67.4
10 Yr Avg	---	---

Potential Capital Gain Exposure (% of assets) 10

Most Similar Funds in MF500

SteinRoe Special	Fair Fit
Neuberger&Berman Part	Weak Fit
Fidelity Magellan	Weak Fit

MORNINGSTAR 1995 Mutual Fund 500

Lindner Bulwark

	Ticker	Load	NAV	Yield	SEC Yield	Assets	Objective
	LDNBX	None	7.45	N/A	N/A	83.2	Asset Alloc.

Lindner Bulwark Fund seeks capital appreciation.

The fund invests primarily in undervalued equities and precious-metal investments that can maintain value during inflationary periods. Investments may also include securities of real estate investment trusts (REITs); U.S. government obligations; gold, silver, and platinum bullion; options and futures; and short sales of securities. Any time the S&P 500 Index declines more than 10% from its 12-month high point, the fund concentrates more than 25% of its assets in securities of companies in the precious-metals industry and other natural resources. The fund may invest up to 35% of its assets in foreign securities.

Manager's Investment Style

Management's strategy revolves around preserving capital during times of distress--such as a high-inflation climate. To do so, management places at least 25% of assets in precious metals and other natural resources when the S&P 500 Index drops a specific amount, as it did in 1994. Other bearish techniques have included stashing assets in puts and engaging in short sales, as well as holding cash.

Fund Manager(s)

Larry Callahan, since 02-94. Birthdate: 05-61.
BSBA, U. of Missouri-Columbia 1983
Eric E. Ryback, since 02-94. Birthdate: 03-52.
BS, Idaho State U. 1975

Manager Experience	Dates Managed	Invest Obj	Std Dev	+/- Index
Larry Callahan				
Lindner	01/93 - 12/94	G	7.48	2.21
Eric E. Ryback				
Lindner Dividend	03/82 - 12/94	I	7.21	-0.19

Historical Profile
Return ---
Risk ---
Rating
Not Rated

Investment Style History
Equity
Average % Stocks Held in Portfolio
51%

Growth of $10,000
|||| Value of Fund ($000)
— Value of Index ($000) S&P 500
▼ Manager Change
▽ Partial Manager Change
► Mgr Unknown After
◄ Mgr Unknown Before

Performance Quartile (Within Objective)

	1983	1984	1985	1986	1987	1988	1989	1990	1991	1992	1993	1994	History
	---	---	---	---	---	---	---	---	---	---	---	7.45	NAV
	---	---	---	---	---	---	---	---	---	---	---	7.18 *	Total Return %
	---	---	---	---	---	---	---	---	---	---	---	6.81 *	+/- S&P 500
	---	---	---	---	---	---	---	---	---	---	---	---	+/- LB Aggregate
	---	---	---	---	---	---	---	---	---	---	---	0.75	Income Return %
	---	---	---	---	---	---	---	---	---	---	---	6.43	Capital Return %
	---	---	---	---	---	---	---	---	---	---	---	---	Total Rtn % Rank All
	---	---	---	---	---	---	---	---	---	---	---	---	Total Rtn % Rank Obj
	---	---	---	---	---	---	---	---	---	---	---	0.05	Income $
	---	---	---	---	---	---	---	---	---	---	---	0.00	Capital Gains $
	---	---	---	---	---	---	---	---	---	---	---	0.66	Expense Ratio %
	---	---	---	---	---	---	---	---	---	---	---	0.26	Income Ratio %
	---	---	---	---	---	---	---	---	---	---	---	---	Turnover Rate %
	---	---	---	---	---	---	---	---	---	---	---	83.2	Net Assets ($mil)

Performance 12-31-94

	1st Qtr	2nd Qtr	3rd Qtr	4th Qtr	Total
1987	---	---	---	---	---
1988	---	---	---	---	---
1989	---	---	---	---	---
1990	---	---	---	---	---
1991	---	---	---	---	---
1992	---	---	---	---	---
1993	---	---	---	---	---
1994	---	1.70	0.22	4.42	7.18 *

Bear Market Performance

Decile Rank (5-year period)

Worst | Best

	Worst 3 Mo Period 1985-89	Worst 3 Mo Period 1990-94
Lindner Bulwark	---	---
+/- S&P 500	---	---
+/- Best Fit Index :	---	---

Trailing Returns

	Total Return %	+/- S&P 500	+/- LB Aggregate	% Rank All	% Rank Obj	Growth of $10,000
3 Mo	4.42	4.43	4.04	2	1	10,442
6 Mo	4.64	-0.22	3.65	13	3	10,464
1 Yr	---	---	---	---	---	---
3 Yr Avg	---	---	---	---	---	---
5 Yr Avg	---	---	---	---	---	---
10 Yr Avg	---	---	---	---	---	---
15 Yr Avg	---	---	---	---	---	---

Operations

Address and Telephone	7711 Carondelet P.O. Box 11208 St. Louis, MO 63105 314-727-5305	
Advisor	Ryback Management	
Subadvisor	None	
Distributor	Ryback Management	
States Available	All except AR,NE,OH	
Report Grade	B-	
Income Distrib	Paid Annually	
* Date of Inception	02-11-94	
Fiscal Year End	June	

Risk Analysis

Time Period	Load-Adj Return %	Risk % Rank[1] All		Obj	Morningstar[2] Return	Morningstar Risk	Morningstar Risk-Adj Rating
1 Yr	---	---		---	---	---	---
3 Yr	---	---		---	---	---	---
5 Yr	---	---		---	---	---	---
10 Yr	---	---		---	---	---	---

Average Historical Rating ---
[1] 1 = low, 100 = high [2] 1.00 = Hybrid Avg [3] 1.00 = 90-day T-bill return

Other Measures
		Standard S&P 500	Best Fit
Standard Deviation	---	Alpha	---	---
Mean	---	Beta	---	---
Sharpe Ratio	---	R-Squared	---	---

Investment Style

Stocks
	Port Avg	Rel S&P 500
Price/Earnings Ratio	27.2	1.47
Price/Book Ratio	2.4	0.70
5 Yr Earnings Gr %	-1.6#	-0.28
Med Mkt Cap ($mil)	198	0.02

figure is based on 50% or less of stocks

Bonds
Avg Effective Duration	5.0 Yrs **
Avg Effective Maturity	8.0 Yrs
Avg Credit Quality	B
Avg Weighted Coupon	6.50%

**figure provided by fund

Diversification Value for Portfolio Types

Large Cap: | Small Cap: | Bond: | Balanced: | Diversified:

Portfolio 06-30-94

Total Stocks: 30
Total Fixed-Income: 1

Share Chg (05-94)000	Amount 000		Date of Maturity	Value $000	% Net Assets
60	99	Metricom		1564	4.98
21	40	Helmerich & Payne		1060	3.37
191	191	Parallan Computer		860	2.73
28	201	Micronics Computers		853	2.71
50	164	Peruana De Telefonos Cl B		839	2.67
0	30	Tidewater		698	2.22
0	50	Zale		463	1.47
0	70	North Flinders Mines		432	1.38
0	20	Placer Dome		430	1.37
116	126	AutoInfo		424	1.35
55	96	Diasonics Ultrasound		384	1.22
0	73	Providential		374	1.19
0	54	Greenman Brothers		358	1.14
36	36	Norex America		322	1.03
58	58	Maynard Oil		305	0.97
0	68	RPS Realty Trust		288	0.92
-100	92	Dayton Mining		272	0.87
0	40	Varco International		270	0.86
	10	Reading & Bates Cv Pfd 6.5%		260	0.83
0	50	MedChem Products		229	0.73

Index Allocation
	% of Stocks
S&P 500	13.0
S&P MidCap 400	8.5
U.S. Small Cap	59.4
Foreign	22.9

Composition % 12-31-94
Cash	44.4	Preferreds	2.4
Stocks	54.3	Convertibles	7.2
Bonds	5.3	Other	-13.5

Tax Analysis
	Tax-Adj Historical Return %	% Pretax Return
3 Yr Avg	---	---
5 Yr Avg	---	---
10 Yr Avg	---	---
Potential Capital Gain Exposure (% of assets)		3%

Most Similar Funds in MF500
Fund lacks three-year record

Bond Credit Analysis 11-06-94
% of Bonds
US Govt	0	BB	0
AAA	0	B	100
AA	0	Below B	0
A	0	NR/NA	0
BBB	0		

Stock Sector Weightings
	% of Stocks	Relative S&P 500
Utilities	7.5	0.60
Energy	16.3	1.61
Financials	10.7	1.01
Industrial Cyclicals	13.7	0.84
Consumer Durables	17.1	2.75
Consumer Staples	0.0	0.00
Services	6.2	0.76
Retail	4.1	0.71
Health	5.5	0.63
Technology	19.0	2.07

Expenses & Fees

Min Initial Purchase	$3000 (Addt'l: $100)	
Min IRA Purchase	$250 (Addt'l: $100)	
Min Auto Invest Plan	N/A	

Sales Fees
0.00% front
0.00% deferred
0.00% 12b-1
Management Fee 0.70% flat fee
3-,5-,10-yr Expense Projections $21, $37, $82
Annual Brokerage Cost ---

Lindner Dividend

	Ticker	Load	NAV	Yield	SEC Yield	Assets	Objective
	LDDVX	None	23.97	7.7%	N/A	1605.2	Income

Lindner Dividend Fund seeks current income. Capital appreciation is secondary.

The fund invests in the following securities, in order of preference: common stocks, preferred stock convertible or not convertible into common stock, corporate bonds, and debt securities issued or guaranteed by the U.S. government or its agencies. It may invest up to 40% of its assets in electric and gas utilities. The fund does not generally invest more than 35% of its assets in high-yield debt securities, but it reserves the right to do so.

The fund reopenend on Nov. 8, 1993 to new investors.

Investment Style History
Fixed Income

Income Rtn % Rank Obj

42	26	34	64	37	34	54	27

Historical Profile

Return	Above Average
Risk	Low
Rating	★★★★ Above Average

Growth of $10,000
- ‖‖ Value of Fund ($000)
- — Value of Index ($000) S&P 500
- ▼ Manager Change
- ▽ Partial Manager Change
- ► Mgr Unknown After
- ◄ Mgr Unknown Before

Performance Quartile (Within Objective)

Manager's Investment Style

Management mutes interest-rate sensitivity by holding bonds from the lower rungs of the credit ladder. As allowed by the fund's prospectus, management will occasionally further boost yield through private placements (144a securities) and REITs. Foreign bonds and convertibles are also likely to show up. On the stock end, management favors small-to-mid cap value plays.

1983	1984	1985	1986	1987	1988	1989	1990	1991	1992	1993	1994	History
21.62	22.52	24.42	23.74	19.87	22.67	23.11	19.77	23.06	25.84	27.32	23.97	NAV
43.92	15.28	17.12	20.76	-4.08	24.23	11.88	-6.51	27.36	21.10	14.92	-3.31	Total Return %
21.45	9.02	-14.62	2.09	-9.34	7.62	-19.80	-3.39	-3.13	13.49	4.86	-4.62	+/- S&P 500
35.54	0.13	-5.01	5.52	-6.83	16.35	-2.66	-15.45	11.35	13.86	5.17	-0.39	+/- LB Aggregate
4.99	6.54	8.66	9.53	7.74	9.78	9.94	7.87	10.71	8.57	6.81	7.16	Income Return %
38.92	8.74	8.46	11.23	-11.82	14.45	1.94	-14.37	16.64	12.53	8.10	-10.47	Capital Return %
1	5	86	17	85	7	59	76	31	4	29	46	Total Rtn % Rank All
1	15	78	6	66	1	48	79	20	2	35	29	Total Rtn % Rank Obj
1.12	1.27	1.77	2.17	1.87	1.76	2.20	1.86	1.99	1.86	1.74	1.90	Income $
5.24	0.86	0.00	3.26	1.16	0.06	0.00	0.02	0.00	0.10	0.58	0.57	Capital Gains $
0.94	---	1.14	0.95	1.00	1.04	0.97	0.87	0.87	0.80	0.74	0.64	Expense Ratio %
6.23	---	8.40	8.08	7.43	7.43	7.57	8.90	8.98	9.75	7.10	7.01	Income Ratio %
14	---	11	26	56	17	2	5	3	24	14	43	Turnover Rate %
1.3	1.2	51.5	64.1	46.0	83.8	136.1	149.6	234.5	711.6	1374.5	1605.2	Net Assets ($mil)

Fund Manager(s)

Eric E. Ryback, since 03-82. Birthdate: 03-52.
BS, Idaho State U. 1975

Manager Experience

	Dates Managed	Invest Obj	Std Dev	+/- Index
Eric E. Ryback				
Lindner	03/82 - 12/94	G	10.08	-1.34
Lindner Utility	10/93 - 12/94	SU	11.85	-2.87

Performance 12-31-94

	1st Qtr	2nd Qtr	3rd Qtr	4th Qtr	Total
1987	5.14	-1.90	-0.01	-7.00	-4.08
1988	11.53	3.65	4.05	3.28	24.23
1989	3.57	4.66	3.26	-0.04	11.88
1990	-0.04	-1.53	-2.60	-2.47	-6.51
1991	10.88	3.40	6.07	4.73	27.36
1992	6.46	4.53	4.65	3.98	21.10
1993	6.93	3.10	3.43	0.78	14.92
1994	-1.94	-0.71	2.02	-2.66	-3.31

Bear Market Performance

Decile Rank (5-year period)

	Worst 3 Mo Period 1985-89	Worst 3 Mo Period 1990-94
Lindner Dividend	-9.61	-6.13
+/- S&P 500	10.79	7.71
+/- Best Fit Index : FB HY	---	7.97

Trailing Returns

	Total Return %	+/- S&P 500	+/- LB Aggregate	% Rank All	% Rank Obj	Growth of $10,000
3 Mo	-2.66	-2.64	-3.03	79	85	9,734
6 Mo	-0.69	-5.55	-1.68	68	61	9,931
1 Yr	-3.31	-4.62	-0.39	46	29	9,669
3 Yr Avg	10.40	4.14	5.86	12	5	13,457
5 Yr Avg	9.89	1.20	2.26	18	11	16,023
10 Yr Avg	11.69	-2.69	1.75	41	21	30,214
15 Yr Avg	16.96	2.48	6.15	2	1	104,859

Operations

Address and Telephone	7711 Carondelet P.O. Box 11208 St. Louis, MO 63105 314-727-5305
Advisor	Ryback Management
Subadvisor	None
Distributor	Ryback Management
States Available	All except NE,GU,PR
Report Grade	B
Income Distrib	Paid Quarterly
Date of Inception	06-22-76
Fiscal Year End	February

Risk Analysis

Time Period	Load-Adj Return %	Risk % Rank All	Risk % Rank Obj	Morningstar Return	Morningstar Risk	Morningstar Risk-Adj Rating
1 Yr	-3.31					
3 Yr	10.40	13	23	2.10[3]	0.42	★★★★★
5 Yr	9.89	40	35	1.32[3]	0.47	★★★★
10 Yr	11.69	29	14	0.99	0.42	★★★★
Average Historical Rating (109 months)					4.9	★s

[1] = low, 100 = high   [2] 1.00 = Hybrid Avg   [3] 1.00 = 90-day T-bill return

Other Measures

	Standard S&P 500	Best Fit FB HY
Standard Deviation	4.85	Alpha 5.6	0.1
Mean	10.06	Beta 0.38	0.90
Sharpe Ratio	1.35	R-Squared 38	64

Investment Style

Stocks

	Port Avg	Rel S&P 500
Price/Earnings Ratio	20.8	1.12
Price/Book Ratio	2.2	0.63
5 Yr Earnings Gr %	-9.5	-1.71
Med Mkt Cap ($mil)	3938	0.30

Bonds

Avg Effective Duration	3.9 Yrs
Avg Effective Maturity	7.2 Yrs
Avg Credit Quality	BB
Avg Weighted Coupon	8.76%

Diversification Value for Portfolio Types

Large Cap: Medium	Small Cap: Medium	Bond: Medium	Balanced: Low	Diversified: Medium

Portfolio 08-31-94

Share Chg (05-94)000	Amount 000	Total Stocks: 27 Total Fixed-Income: 118	Date of Maturity	Value $000	% Net Assets
0	915	Glendale Fed Bk E Cv Pfd 8.75%		32015	1.89
	500	Telefonos de Mexico L (ADR)		31375	1.85
	1088	AMC Entertainment Cv Pfd 7%		27472	1.62
0	250	Atlantic Richfield		26781	1.58
	700	Unisys Cl A Cv Pfd 3.75%		26250	1.55
0	1000	Minorco (ADR)		25797	1.52
26	426	Bristol-Myers Squibb		24489	1.44
	26100	Transport Maritima Mex 9.25%	2003	24012	1.41
	25500	Kaiser Aluminum & Chem 9.875[	2002	23779	1.40
	400	Occidental Petro Cv Pfd $3.875		22200	1.31
	29672	Greyhound Lines 10%	07-31-01	20770	1.22
	639	Mobile Telecom Cv Pfd $2.25		20595	1.21
	1023	Flagstar Cl A Cv Pfd 2.25%		20332	1.20
	750	Riggs National Cl B Cv Pfd 10.75%		19500	1.15
0	600	GTE		19050	1.12
	305	Tosco Cl F Cv Pfd $4.375		18948	1.12
	331	Federal Paper Bd Cv Pfd $2.875		18530	1.09
	362	Transco Energy Cv Pfd $4.75		18347	1.08
	20000	Fresh Del Monte Produce 10%	05-01-03	18325	1.08
	17000	First Nationwide Hldgs 12.25%	2001	17850	1.05

Index Allocation

	% of Stocks
S&P 500	34.2
S&P MidCap 400	23.6
U.S. Small Cap	13.3
Foreign	28.9

Composition % 12-31-94

Cash	4.9	Preferreds	8.6
Stocks	23.1	Convertibles	34.0
Bonds	29.3	Other	0.0

Tax Analysis

	Tax-Adj Historical Return %	% Pretax Return
3 Yr Avg	7.18	66.9
5 Yr Avg	6.75	64.1
10 Yr Avg	7.86	55.9
Potential Capital Gain Exposure (% of assets)		-9%

Most Similar Funds in MF500

Loomis Sayles Bond	Fair Fit
Putnam Convert Income Gr A	Fair Fit
Franklin Income	Fair Fit

Bond Credit Analysis 06-30-94

% of Bonds

US Govt	0	BB	24
AAA	0	B	30
AA	0	Below B	1
A	0	NR/NA	43
BBB	3		

Stock Sector Weightings

	% of Stocks	Relative S&P 500
Utilities	51.6	4.16
Energy	13.8	1.36
Financials	0.9	0.09
Industrial Cyclicals	17.6	1.08
Consumer Durables	8.5	1.37
Consumer Staples	0.0	0.00
Services	0.0	0.00
Retail	0.0	0.00
Health	7.6	0.88
Technology	0.0	0.00

Operations (continued)

Min Initial Purchase	$2000 (Addt'l: $100)
Min IRA Purchase	$250 (Addt'l: $100)
Min Auto Invest Plan	N/A

Expenses & Fees

Sales Fees	0.00% front 0.00% deferred 0.00% 12b-1
Management Fee	0.70% max./0.50% min.
3-,5-,10-yr Expense Projections	$20, $36, $80
Annual Brokerage Cost	0.08%

M❂RNINGSTAR 1995 Mutual Fund 500

Lindner

	Ticker	Load	NAV	Yield	SEC Yield	Assets	Objective
	LDNRX	None	20.89	1.5%	N/A	1503.0	Growth

Lindner Fund seeks long-term capital appreciation; income is secondary.

The fund invests substantially all of its assets in common stocks or convertible securities. To a limited degree, preferred stocks and debt securities may be held; the fund may invest up to 10% of its assets in lower-rated debt. It invests in both listed and unlisted securities. The fund may also borrow money equivalent to 12.5% of total assets in order to make additional investments. The fund may invest up to 25% of its net assets in securities issued and primarily traded in foreign countries. Derivative securities may not be purchased by the fund, but may be retained if received as distributions.

Manager's Investment Style

Management takes a standard approach to value investing: It seeks out companies that sell at a discount to what the team determines is their intrinsic worth. The team also seeks similar stocks outside the United States. To minimize currency risk, management tends to stick to established European markets, which generally show less economic and political instability. The team often shows a preference for financials, industrial cyclicals, and cheap technology stocks---both in the U.S. and abroad---usually picking up smaller-cap issues. Management, however, will also delve into growth stocks, if the price is right.

Fund Manager(s)

Robert A. Lange, since 07-77.
Eric E. Ryback, since 03-82.
Larry Callahan, since 01-93.

Manager Experience

	Dates Managed	Invest Obj	Std Dev	+/- Index
Eric E. Ryback				
Lindner Dividend	03/82 - 12/94	I	7.21	-0.19
Lindner Utility	10/93 - 12/94	SU	11.85	-2.87

Historical Profile

Return	Average
Risk	Low
Rating	★★★★ Above Average

Investment Style History
Equity

Average % Stocks Held in Portfolio: 69% 86% 75% 72% 81% 86% 84% 87%

Growth of $10,000

|||| Value of Fund ($000)
— Value of Index ($000) Russ 2000
▼ Manager Change
▽ Partial Manager Change
► Mgr Unknown After
◄ Mgr Unknown Before

Performance Quartile (Within Objective)

1983	1984	1985	1986	1987	1988	1989	1990	1991	1992	1993	1994	History
18.60	18.34	19.16	16.12	15.12	17.31	19.21	15.58	18.55	20.22	23.22	20.89	NAV
24.66	12.80	19.51	14.06	8.83	20.36	21.21	-11.32	23.42	12.76	19.85	-0.66	Total Return %
2.19	6.54	-12.23	-4.62	3.57	3.75	-10.47	-8.20	-7.07	5.14	9.79	-1.98	+/- S&P 500
1.19	9.75	-13.05	-2.04	6.47	2.42	-7.96	-5.14	-10.79	3.79	8.56	-0.59	+/- Wilshire 5000
3.93	5.02	9.72	8.63	5.78	4.70	6.24	4.72	4.36	2.86	2.17	1.60	Income Return %
20.73	7.78	9.79	5.42	3.05	15.66	14.98	-16.04	19.06	9.90	17.68	-2.26	Capital Return %
24	14	76	60	12	13	33	87	39	14	17	24	Total Rtn % Rank All
35	2	92	57	16	25	77	85	87	24	16	40	Total Rtn % Rank Obj
0.66	0.89	1.71	1.49	1.02	0.71	1.10	0.86	0.66	0.53	0.46	0.34	Income $
0.57	1.58	0.87	4.09	1.57	0.16	0.65	0.71	0.00	0.15	0.53	1.84	Capital Gains $
0.78	0.89	0.65	0.58	0.89	1.07	0.92	0.74	0.83	0.80	0.80	0.65	Expense Ratio %
6.13	6.22	7.44	5.83	4.56	3.76	4.93	4.84	4.64	3.05	2.52	1.69	Income Ratio %
15	40	46	33	39	21	18	19	13	11	19	38	Turnover Rate %
270.8	339.7	397.9	355.6	350.1	425.2	595.2	650.8	836.3	1073.8	1469.4	1503.0	Net Assets ($mil)

Performance 12-31-94

	1st Qtr	2nd Qtr	3rd Qtr	4th Qtr	Total
1987	15.26	3.01	9.54	-16.32	8.83
1988	11.90	4.85	-1.38	4.02	20.36
1989	9.24	3.97	6.51	0.20	21.21
1990	-0.94	2.05	-11.31	-1.09	-11.32
1991	15.92	-1.88	6.79	1.62	23.42
1992	7.28	1.01	-0.70	4.80	12.76
1993	8.80	1.45	5.49	2.92	19.85
1994	-1.25	-2.22	5.44	-2.43	-0.66

Bear Market Performance

Decile Rank (5-year period)

Worst — Best

	Worst 3 Mo Period 1985-89	Worst 3 Mo Period 1990-94
Lindner	-17.00	-15.22
+/- S&P 500	12.58	-1.38
+/- Best Fit Index : Russ 2000	18.55	10.67

Trailing Returns

	Total Return %	+/- S&P 500	+/- Wil 5000	% Rank All	% Rank Obj	Growth of $10,000
3 Mo	-2.43	-2.41	-1.66	76	72	9,757
6 Mo	2.88	-1.98	-1.74	21	63	10,288
1 Yr	-0.66	-1.98	-0.59	24	40	9,934
3 Yr Avg	10.31	4.05	3.70	12	17	13,424
5 Yr Avg	8.00	-0.69	-0.82	33	62	14,692
10 Yr Avg	12.26	-2.12	-1.60	35	62	31,798
15 Yr Avg	16.72	2.24	2.75	4	8	101,699

Operations

Address and Telephone	7711 Carondelet P.O. Box 11208 St. Louis, MO 63105 314-727-5305
Advisor	Ryback Management
Subadvisor	None
Distributor	Ryback Management
States Available	All except NE,GU,PR
Report Grade	B-
Income Distrib	Paid Annually
Date of Inception	05-24-73
Fiscal Year End	June

Risk Analysis

Time Period	Load-Adj Return %	Risk % Rank [1] All	Risk % Rank [1] Obj	Morningstar [2] Return	Morningstar Risk	Morningstar Risk-Adj Rating
1 Yr	-0.66					
3 Yr	10.31	54	8	2.08 [3]	0.58	★★★★
5 Yr	8.00	57	6	0.81 [3]	0.65	★★★
10 Yr	12.26	42	2	0.93	0.57	★★★★
Average Historical Rating (109 months)					4.5	★s

[1] = low, 100 = high   [2] 1.00 = Equity Avg   [3] 1.00 = 90-day T-bill return

Other Measures

			Standard S&P 500	Best Fit Russ 2000
Standard Deviation	7.64	Alpha	4.7	2.3
Mean	10.15	Beta	0.69	0.54
Sharpe Ratio	0.87	R-Squared	51	69

Investment Style

	Stock Portfolio Avg	Relative S&P 500
Price/Earnings Ratio	22.2	1.20
Price/Book Ratio	2.0	0.59
5 Yr Earnings Gr %	-2.6#	-0.48
Return on Assets %	4.6	0.61
Debt % Total Cap	31.3#	1.11
Med Mkt Cap ($mil)	424	0.03

figure is based on 50% or less of stocks

Style Value Blend Growth
Size Large Med Small

Diversification Value for Portfolio Types

Large Cap: Low	Small Cap: Low	Bond: High	Balanced: Low	Diversified: Low

Min Initial Purchase / Expenses & Fees

Min Initial Purchase	$2000 (Addt'l: $100)
Min IRA Purchase	$250 (Addt'l: $100)
Min Auto Invest Plan	N/A

Expenses & Fees

Sales Fees	0.00% front
	0.00% deferred
	0.00% 12b-1
Management Fee	0.70% max./0.50% min.+(-)0.20%P
3-,5-,10-yr Expense Projections	$21, $36, $81
Annual Brokerage Cost	0.24%

Portfolio 09-30-94

Total Stocks: 178
Total Fixed-Income: 21

Share Chg (06-94) 000	Amount 000		Value $000	% Net Assets
0	1360	Minorco (ADR)	35530	2.23
72	1196	Acordia	32586	2.05
0	3857	LASMO (ADR)	27482	1.73
0	722	Norsk Hydro (ADR)	26632	1.67
0	1000	Digital Equipment	26500	1.66
0	1100	Tidewater	23650	1.49
0	700	Alliant Techsystems	21788	1.37
0	600	Phillips Petroleum	20550	1.29
0	420	General Motors	19688	1.24
31	1700	Hemlo Gold Mines	19550	1.23
0	902	Old Republic International	18829	1.18
235	1537	Zale	18641	1.17
0	530	Brooklyn Bancorp	18285	1.15
155	1155	Metricom	18191	1.14
195	2732	Noram Energy	17760	1.12
0	1000	USX-Marathon Group	17750	1.12
0	1707	Wharf Resources	17066	1.07
-1085	1495	VLSI Technology	16445	1.03
10	752	Overseas Shipholding Group	16363	1.03
8515	10811	Peruana de Telefonos Cl B	16359	1.03
0	35	Solvay Cl A	15844	1.00
0	130	Akzo	15269	0.96
10	61	Mannesmann (Germany)	15221	0.96
0	600	Placer Dome	15075	0.95
0	531	Birmingham Steel	14590	0.92

Composition % 12-31-94

Cash	7.1	Preferreds	0.0
Stocks	86.1	Convertibles	2.8
Bonds	4.0	Other	0.0

Tax Analysis

	Tax-Adj Historical Return %	% Pretax Return
3 Yr Avg	8.38	79.8
5 Yr Avg	5.96	71.6
10 Yr Avg	8.76	60.4
Potential Capital Gain Exposure (% of assets)		9%

Most Similar Funds in MF500

Fidelity	Fair Fit
Fidelity Contrafund	Fair Fit
Fidelity Adv Growth Opport A	Fair Fit

Index Allocation

	% of Stocks
S&P 500	14.9
S&P MidCap 400	9.3
U.S. Small Cap	45.5
Foreign	31.7

Sector Weightings

	% of Stocks	Relative S&P 500
Utilities	6.4	0.51
Energy	10.7	1.05
Financials	12.8	1.21
Industrial Cyclicals	25.1	1.53
Consumer Durables	10.0	1.61
Consumer Staples	1.4	0.11
Services	17.0	2.09
Retail	3.5	0.60
Health	2.1	0.09
Technology	11.1	1.21

Lindner Utility

	Ticker	Load	NAV	Yield	SEC Yield	Assets	Objective
	LDUTX	None	10.27	1.4%	N/A	43.4	Sp.-Util

Lindner Utility Fund seeks current income. Capital appreciation is a secondary objective.

The fund normally invests at least 65% of its assets in securities issued by public utility companies. These companies may be involved in gas, electricity, television, telecommunications, cable, water, and energy. The fund may purchase equities and debt securities. Up to 35% of assets may be invested in debt securities rated below investment grade. Also, the fund may invest up to 35% of its assets in foreign securities. Some equities may currently not be paying a dividend, however, these securities are expected to yield dividend payments in the foreseeable future.

Manager's Investment Style

Manager Eric Ryback holds a nontraditional view of the utilities industry. He not only focuses his attention on traditional water, gas, and electric utilities, but he also looks at those companies that provide goods or services to those utilities. Because of deregulation in the United States, and privatization in other countries, he believes the sector is very different now from the way it was several years ago. Communication companies and foreign stocks, in particular, offer the best growth opportunities according to Ryback.

Fund Manager(s)

Eric E. Ryback, since 10-93. Birthdate: 03-52.
BS, Idaho State U. 1975

Manager Experience

	Dates Managed	Invest Obj	Std Dev	+/- Index
Eric E. Ryback				
Lindner Dividend	03/82 - 12/94	I	7.21	-0.19
Lindner	03/82 - 12/94	G	10.08	-1.34

Performance 12-31-94

	1st Qtr	2nd Qtr	3rd Qtr	4th Qtr	Total
1987	---	---	---	---	---
1988	---	---	---	---	---
1989	---	---	---	---	---
1990	---	---	---	---	---
1991	---	---	---	---	---
1992	---	---	---	---	---
1993	---	---	---	---	0.57 *
1994	-1.51	-3.93	7.21	-2.36	-0.95

Bear Market Performance

Decile Rank (5-year period)

Worst — Best

	Worst 3 Mo Period 1985-89	Worst 3 Mo Period 1990-94
Lindner Utility	---	---
+/- S&P 500	---	---
+/- Best Fit Index :	---	---

Trailing Returns

	Total Return %	+/- S&P 500	+/- S&P Util	% Rank All	% Rank Obj	Growth of $10,000
3 Mo	-2.36	-2.34	-2.26	75	67	9,764
6 Mo	4.68	-0.18	4.31	12	4	10,468
1 Yr	-0.95	-2.27	6.99	26	2	9,905
3 Yr Avg	---	---	---	---	---	---
5 Yr Avg	---	---	---	---	---	---
10 Yr Avg	---	---	---	---	---	---
15 Yr Avg	---	---	---	---	---	---

Operations

Address and Telephone	7711 Carondelet P.O. Box 11208 St. Louis, MO 63105 314-727-5305
Advisor	Ryback Management
Subadvisor	None
Distributor	Ryback Management
States Available	All except NE
Report Grade	B-
Income Distrib	Paid Annually
* Date of Inception	10-04-93
Fiscal Year End	June

Historical Profile

Return ---
Risk ---
Rating Not Rated

											70%	73%

1983	1984	1985	1986	1987	1988	1989	1990	1991	1992	1993	1994	History
---	---	---	---	---	---	---	---	---	---	10.61	10.27	NAV
---	---	---	---	---	---	---	---	---	---	0.57 *	-0.95	Total Return %
---	---	---	---	---	---	---	---	---	---	-1.21 *	-2.27	+/- S&P 500
---	---	---	---	---	---	---	---	---	---	---	6.99	+/- S&P Util
---	---	---	---	---	---	---	---	---	---	0.00	1.44	Income Return %
---	---	---	---	---	---	---	---	---	---	0.57	-2.39	Capital Return %
---	---	---	---	---	---	---	---	---	---	---	26	Total Rtn % Rank All
---	---	---	---	---	---	---	---	---	---	---	2	Total Rtn % Rank Obj
---	---	---	---	---	---	---	---	---	---	0.00	0.15	Income $
---	---	---	---	---	---	---	---	---	---	0.00	0.09	Capital Gains $
---	---	---	---	---	---	---	---	---	---	---	1.30	Expense Ratio %
---	---	---	---	---	---	---	---	---	---	---	0.76	Income Ratio %
---	---	---	---	---	---	---	---	---	---	---	---	Turnover Rate %
---	---	---	---	---	---	---	---	---	---	6.6	43.4	Net Assets ($mil)

Risk Analysis

Time Period	Load-Adj Return %	Risk % Rank [1] All	Risk % Rank [1] Obj	Morningstar [2] Return	Morningstar [2] Risk	Morningstar Risk-Adj Rating
1 Yr	-0.95					
3 Yr	---	---	---	---	---	---
5 Yr	---	---	---	---	---	---
10 Yr	---	---	---	---	---	---

Average Historical Rating ---

[1] 1 = low, 100 = high [2] 1.00 = Equity Avg [3] 1.00 = 90-day T-bill return

Other Measures

			Standard S&P 500	Best Fit
Standard Deviation	---	Alpha	---	---
Mean	---	Beta	---	---
Sharpe Ratio	---	R-Squared	---	

Investment Style

	Stock Portfolio Avg	Relative S&P 500
Price/Earnings Ratio	19.2	1.04
Price/Book Ratio	2.7	0.80
5 Yr Earnings Gr %	-0.6#	-0.11
Return on Assets %	4.9#	0.66
Debt % Total Cap	38.6#	1.37
Med Mkt Cap ($mil)	1589	0.12

figure is based on 50% or less of stocks

Diversification Value for Portfolio Types

Large Cap: Small Cap: Bond: Balanced: Diversified:

Min Initial Purchase	$3000 (Addt'l: $100)
Min IRA Purchase	$250 (Addt'l: $100)
Min Auto Invest Plan	N/A

Expenses & Fees

Sales Fees	0.00% front
	0.00% deferred
	0.00% 12b-1
Management Fee	0.70% flat fee
3-,5-,10-yr Expense Projections	$41, $71, $157
Annual Brokerage Cost	---

Portfolio 06-30-94

Share Chg (05-94) 000	Amount 000	Total Stocks: 38 Total Fixed-Income: 9	Value $000	% Net Assets
0	25	Energetics Minas Gerais ADR	452	4.07
0	81	Peruana De Telefonos Cl B	427	3.85
0	11	GTE	347	3.13
	2	RWE Aktienesellschaft Cv Pfd	343	3.09
0	4	Telefonos de Chile (ADR)	342	3.08
0	17	Comcast Special Cl A	306	2.76
0	19	Metricom	299	2.70
0	45	LASMO (ADR)	288	2.60
	300	Gascart 9%	288	2.60
10	10	Koninklijke Ptt	281	2.53
0	17	General DataComm Industries	272	2.45
0	22	Vertex Communications	264	2.38
	6	Valero Energy Cv Pfd 6.25%	258	2.33
0	5	Telefonos de Mexico L (ADR)	257	2.32
	12	Santa Fe Energy Cv Pfd 7%	240	2.16
0	16	Westcoast Energy	236	2.13
0	15	Gilbert Associates Cl A	233	2.10
	5	Tejas Gas Cv Pfd 5.25%	229	2.06
0	22	Able Telecom Holding	225	2.03
0	5	Southwestern Bell	218	1.96
0	3	BellSouth	208	1.88
0	6	Consolidated Natural Gas	208	1.87
1	7	Norsk Hydro (ADR)	206	1.85
	7	Mobile Telecomm Cv Pfd $2.25	205	1.85
0	13	Hungarian Telephone & Cable	203	1.83

Composition % 12-31-94

Cash	7.2	Preferreds	3.6
Stocks	77.8	Convertibles	9.5
Bonds	2.0	Other	0.0

Tax Analysis

	Tax-Adj Historical Return %	% Pretax Return
3 Yr Avg	---	---
5 Yr Avg	---	---
10 Yr Avg	---	---
Potential Capital Gain Exposure (% of assets)		0%

Most Similar Funds in MF500

Fund lacks three-year record

Index Allocation

	% of Stocks
S&P 500	23.3
S&P MidCap 400	9.2
U.S. Small Cap	23.0
Foreign	44.6

Sector Weightings

	% of Stocks	Relative S&P 500
Utilities	69.1	5.57
Energy	2.7	0.27
Financials	0.0	0.00
Industrial Cyclicals	3.1	0.19
Consumer Durables	10.7	1.73
Consumer Staples	0.0	0.00
Services	8.1	0.99
Retail	0.0	0.00
Health	0.0	0.00
Technology	6.4	0.69

Investment Style History

Equity

Average % Stocks Held in Portfolio

Growth of $10,000

|||| Value of Fund ($000)
— Value of Index ($000) S&P 500
▼ Manager Change
▽ Partial Manager Change
► Mgr Unknown After
◄ Mgr Unknown Before

Performance Quartile (Within Objective)

MORNINGSTAR 1995 Mutual Fund 500

Longleaf Partners

Ticker	Load	NAV	Yield	SEC Yield	Assets	Objective
LLPFX	None	17.13	0.9%	N/A	753.5	Growth

Longleaf Partners Fund seeks long-term capital growth.

The fund normally invests at least 75% of its assets in common stocks of companies with capitalizations greater than $500 million. It seeks companies that have unrecognized intrinsic value. A company has intrinsic value if its equity securities 1) sell at a substantial discount from the company's liquidating value; 2) sell at a relatively low multiple of the company's free cash flow; or 3) sell at a substantial discount from the price at which securities of comparable businesses have sold.

Prior to July 22, 1994, the fund was named Southeastern Asset Management Value Trust.

Manager's Investment Style

Management seeks small- and mid-sized stocks (above $500 million in market cap) that are selling at deep discounts to their liquidation value or are cheap compared with free cash flow. Management likes to use the sales of comparable businesses to determine the value of individual holdings. The fund's criteria often lead it to potential merger and acquisition targets. The portfolio is often highly concentrated on just a few issues.

Fund Manager(s)

O. Mason Hawkins CFA(1979), since 04-87.
Birthdate: 03-48. BBA, U. of Florida 1970 MBA, U. of Georgia 1971
G. Staley Cates CFA(1989), since 04-94.

Manager Experience	Dates Managed	Invest Obj	Std Dev	+/- Index
O. Mason Hawkins				
Longleaf Partners Sml-Cap	03/91 - 12/94	SC	9.63	0.83
G. Staley Cates				
Longleaf Partners Sml-Cap	04/94 - 12/94	SC	10.70	0.12

Performance 12-31-94

	1st Qtr	2nd Qtr	3rd Qtr	4th Qtr	Total
1987			4.80	-20.33	-13.35 *
1988	15.89	5.01	5.53	5.33	35.27
1989	6.03	9.27	11.39	-4.48	23.28
1990	-5.59	1.69	-17.76	5.66	-16.58
1991	23.80	2.45	3.09	6.44	39.17
1992	6.67	-0.84	2.34	11.32	20.50
1993	8.23	0.94	4.92	6.63	22.23
1994	3.61	4.96	5.38	-4.92	8.97

Bear Market Performance

Decile Rank (5-year period)

Worst | Best

	Worst 3 Mo Period 1985-89	Worst 3 Mo Period 1990-94
Longleaf Partners	---	-20.56
+/- S&P 500	---	-6.71
+/- Best Fit Index : SPMid400	---	-2.14

Trailing Returns

	Total Return %	+/- S&P 500	+/- Wil 5000	% Rank All	% Rank Obj	Growth of $10,000
3 Mo	-4.92	-4.90	-4.15	91	93	9,508
6 Mo	0.20	-4.66	-4.42	53	87	10,020
1 Yr	8.96	7.65	9.03	2	3	10,896
3 Yr Avg	17.08	10.81	10.47	2	2	16,048
5 Yr Avg	13.25	4.56	4.44	6	9	18,632
10 Yr Avg	---	---	---	---	---	---
15 Yr Avg	---	---	---	---	---	---

Operations

Address and Telephone	6075 Poplar Avenue Suite 900
	Memphis, TN 38119
	800-445-9469 / 901-761-2474
Advisor	Southeastern Asset Management
Subadvisor	None
Distributor	Southeastern Asset Management
States Available	Selected states
Report Grade	B-
Income Distrib	Paid Annually
* Date of Inception	04-08-87
Fiscal Year End	December

Historical Profile
Return	Above Average
Risk	Below Average
Rating	★★★★★
	Highest

51% | 88% | 92% | 95% | 95% | 93% | 95% | 95%

Growth of $10,000
|||| Value of Fund ($000)
— Value of Index ($000) SPMid400
▼ Manager Change
▽ Partial Manager Change
► Mgr Unknown After
◄ Mgr Unknown Before

Investment Style History
Equity
Average % Stocks Held in Portfolio

Performance Quartile (Within Objective)

History	1983	1984	1985	1986	1987	1988	1989	1990	1991	1992	1993	1994
NAV	---	---	---	---	8.62	11.60	12.62	10.21	13.34	14.70	16.92	17.13
Total Return %	---	---	---	---	-13.35 *	35.27	23.28	-16.58	39.17	20.50	22.23	8.96
+/- S&P 500	---	---	---	---	1.54 *	18.66	-8.41	-13.46	8.69	12.88	12.17	7.65
+/- Wilshire 5000	---	---	---	---	---	17.33	-5.90	-10.40	4.97	11.53	10.94	9.03
Income Return %	---	---	---	---	0.80	0.70	1.14	1.24	0.44	0.49	0.56	0.94
Capital Return %	---	---	---	---	-14.14	34.57	22.14	-17.82	38.74	20.01	21.66	8.02
Total Rtn % Rank All	---	---	---	---	---	---	1	28	94	15	4	14	2
Total Rtn % Rank Obj	---	---	---	---	---	2	68	95	35	6	10	3
Income $	---	---	---	---	0.08	0.06	0.15	0.15	0.06	0.07	0.09	0.16
Capital Gains $	---	---	---	---	0.00	0.00	1.53	0.20	0.79	1.29	0.95	1.14
Expense Ratio %	---	---	---	---	1.50	1.50	1.31	1.32	1.30	1.29	1.26	1.21
Income Ratio %	---	---	---	---	1.61	1.40	1.73	1.13	0.42	0.50	0.63	1.08
Turnover Rate %	---	---	---	---	---	93	7	52	45	29	19	---
Net Assets ($mil)	---	---	---	---	25.8	74.6	148.7	129.6	177.9	243.7	397.3	753.5

Risk Analysis

Time Period	Load-Adj Return %	Risk % Rank [1] All	Risk % Rank [1] Obj	Morningstar [2] Return	Morningstar Risk	Morningstar Risk-Adj Rating
1 Yr	8.96					
3 Yr	17.08	31	2	4.43 [3]	0.43	★★★★★
5 Yr	13.25	63	15	2.33 [3]	0.76	★★★★★
10 Yr	---					

Average Historical Rating (57 months)   4.0 ★s

[1] 1 = low, 100 = high   [2] 1.00 = Equity Avg   [3] 1.00 = 90-day T-bill return

Other Measures

				Standard S&P 500	Best Fit SPMid400
Standard Deviation	7.81	Alpha		11.2	11.0
Mean	16.18	Beta		0.68	0.56
Sharpe Ratio	1.62	R-Squared		48	50

Investment Style

	Stock Portfolio Avg	Relative S&P 500
Price/Earnings Ratio	14.7	0.80
Price/Book Ratio	4.0	1.19
5 Yr Earnings Gr %	10.6	1.91
Return on Assets %	6.9	0.92
Debt % Total Cap	36.1	1.28
Med Mkt Cap ($mil)	2301	0.18

Style: Value Blend Growth / Size Large Med Small

Diversification Value for Portfolio Types

Large Cap: Medium	Small Cap: Medium	Bond: High	Balanced: Medium	Diversified: Medium

Expenses & Fees

Sales Fees	0.00% front
	0.00% deferred
	0.00% 12b-1
Management Fee	1.00% max./0.75% min., 0.10%A
3-,5-,10-yr Expense Projections	$40, $69, $152
Annual Brokerage Cost	0.14%

Min Initial Purchase $10000 (Addt'l: None)
Min IRA Purchase $10000 (Addt'l: None)
Min Auto Invest Plan $10000 (Systematic Inv: $100)

Portfolio 12-31-94

Share Chg (09-94) 000	Amount 000	Total Stocks: 31 / Total Fixed-Income: 0	Value $000	% Net Assets
0	840	Knight-Ridder	42420	5.63
951	1286	Quaker Oats	39545	5.25
594	1450	WMX Technologies	38063	5.05
0	847	Ralston-Purina Group	37775	5.01
16	154	Washington Post Cl B	37345	4.96
712	2900	Horsham	36975	4.91
503	1033	Franklin Resources	36811	4.89
79	606	Federal Express	36493	4.84
570	1170	Mellon Bank	35831	4.76
208	2363	PaineWebber Group	35450	4.70
195	1565	Alexander & Baldwin	34821	4.62
710	1201	Multimedia	34234	4.54
300	2500	John Labatt	34118	4.53
195	1447	Alexander & Alexander Svcs	26761	3.55
0	1520	Whitman	26220	3.48
765	765	McKesson	24958	3.31
1325	1325	Coca-Cola	23679	3.14
37	765	Hasbro	22376	2.97
0	500	Kemper	18938	2.51
389	778	Pioneer Group	17116	2.27
0	106	Alleghany	16161	2.14
0	490	American Express	14455	1.92
0	520	American Stores	13975	1.85
0	788	Cousins Properties	13692	1.82
0	600	Ecolab	12600	1.67

Composition % 12-31-94

Cash	1.6	Preferreds	0.0
Stocks	98.5	Convertibles	0.0
Bonds	0.0	Other	0.0

Tax Analysis

	Tax-Adj Historical Return %	% Pretax Return
3 Yr Avg	14.68	84.0
5 Yr Avg	11.23	81.4
10 Yr Avg	---	---
Potential Capital Gain Exposure (% of assets)		8%

Most Similar Funds in MF500

Third Avenue Value	Weak Fit
Gabelli Asset	Weak Fit
Strong Common Stock	Weak Fit

Index Allocation

	% of Stocks
S&P 500	51.6
S&P MidCap 400	23.3
U.S. Small Cap	15.5
Foreign	9.7

Sector Weightings

	% of Stocks	Relative S&P 500
Utilities	0.0	0.00
Energy	0.0	0.00
Financials	29.4	2.78
Industrial Cyclicals	5.1	0.31
Consumer Durables	3.1	0.49
Consumer Staples	23.8	1.90
Services	33.2	4.07
Retail	2.2	0.37
Health	3.4	0.39
Technology	0.0	0.00

Loomis Sayles Bond

	Ticker	Load	NAV	Yield	SEC Yield	Assets	Objective
	LSBDX	None	10.05	8.6%	9.83%	82.5	Corp General

Loomis Sayles Bond Fund seeks total return through a combination of current income and capital appreciation.

The fund normally invests at least 65% of its assets in investment-grade debt securities (including convertibles), although up to 20% of its assets may be invested in preferred stocks. It may invest up to 10% of its assets in foreign securities and up to 35% in securities rated below investment grade.

Historical Profile

Return	High
Risk	Average
Rating	★★★★★
	Highest

Investment Style History
Fixed Income
Income Rtn % Rank Obj

Growth of $10,000

|||| Value of Fund ($000)
— Value of Index ($000)
LB Corp
▼ Manager Change
▽ Partial Manager Change
► Mgr Unknown After
◄ Mgr Unknown Before

Performance Quartile
(Within Objective)

Manager's Investment Style

Management takes an iconoclast's approach to the corporate-general arena, targeting issues that show adverse price correlations with the U.S. bond market. In particular, it favors discount-priced bonds, convertible holdings, and foreign debt. Management also keeps risk at bay by minimizing rate sensitivity and call risk. Credit risk, however, is a byproduct of the strategy.

Fund Manager(s)

Daniel J. Fuss CFA(1967), since 05-91. Birthdate: 09-33. BS, Marquette U. 1955 MBA, Marquette U. 1965

Manager Experience	Dates Managed	Invest Obj	Std Dev	+/- Index
Daniel J. Fuss				
Managers Bond	06/84 - 12/94	CG	5.47	-0.44

	1983	1984	1985	1986	1987	1988	1989	1990	1991	1992	1993	1994	History
	---	---	---	---	---	---	---	---	10.23	10.36	11.37	10.05	NAV
	---	---	---	---	---	---	---	---	8.83 *	14.29	22.22	-4.07	Total Return %
	---	---	---	---	---	---	---	---	---	7.04	12.47	-1.15	+/- LB Aggregate
	---	---	---	---	---	---	---	---	---	5.59	10.05	-0.15	+/- LB Corporate
	---	---	---	---	---	---	---	---	5.25	7.57	7.76	7.54	Income Return %
	---	---	---	---	---	---	---	---	3.58	6.72	14.46	-11.61	Capital Return %
	---	---	---	---	---	---	---	---	---	11	14	54	Total Rtn % Rank All
	---	---	---	---	---	---	---	---	---	1	1	59	Total Rtn % Rank Obj
	---	---	---	---	---	---	---	---	0.52	0.76	0.81	0.86	Income $
	---	---	---	---	---	---	---	---	0.12	0.54	0.46	0.00	Capital Gains $
	---	---	---	---	---	---	---	---	1.00	1.00	0.94	0.88	Expense Ratio %
	---	---	---	---	---	---	---	---	8.97	7.50	8.26	7.33	Income Ratio %
	---	---	---	---	---	---	---	---	---	101	170	78	Turnover Rate %
	---	---	---	---	---	---	---	---	9.7	18.4	64.2	82.5	Net Assets ($mil)

Performance 12-31-94

	1st Qtr	2nd Qtr	3rd Qtr	4th Qtr	Total
1987	---	---	---	---	---
1988	---	---	---	---	---
1989	---	---	---	---	---
1990	---	---	---	---	---
1991	---	---	6.83	3.85	8.83 *
1992	3.32	4.81	4.75	0.76	14.29
1993	7.63	5.34	4.45	3.20	22.22
1994	-1.50	-2.88	1.81	-1.51	-4.07

Bear Market Performance

Decile Rank (5-year period)

Worst ———————————— Best

	Worst 3 Mo Period 1985-89	Worst 3 Mo Period 1990-94
Loomis Sayles Bond	---	---
+/- LB Aggregate	---	---
+/- Best Fit Index :	---	---

Trailing Returns

	Total Return %	+/- LB Aggregate	+/- LB Corp	% Rank All	% Rank Obj	Growth of $10,000
3 Mo	-1.51	-1.89	-1.95	57	93	9,849
6 Mo	0.27	-0.72	-0.90	51	66	10,027
1 Yr	-4.07	-1.15	-0.15	54	59	9,593
3 Yr Avg	10.25	5.70	4.83	13	1	13,399
5 Yr Avg	---	---	---	---	---	---
10 Yr Avg	---	---	---	---	---	---
15 Yr Avg	---	---	---	---	---	---

Operations

Address and Telephone	One Financial Center
	Boston, MA 02111
	800-633-3330 / 617-482-2450
Advisor	Loomis Sayles
Subadvisor	None
Distributor	Loomis Sayles
States Available	All
Report Grade	C
Income Distrib	Paid Quarterly
* Date of Inception	05-16-91
Fiscal Year End	December

Risk Analysis

Time Period	Load-Adj Return %	Risk % Rank [1] All	Risk % Rank [1] Obj	Morningstar [2] Return	Morningstar [2] Risk	Morningstar Risk-Adj Rating
1 Yr	-4.07	---	---	---	---	---
3 Yr	10.25	24	53	2.05 [3]	1.02	★★★★★
5 Yr	---	---	---	---	---	---
10 Yr	---	---	---	---	---	---

Average Historical Rating (8 months)   5.0 ★s

[1] 1 = low, 100 = high [2] 1.00 = Taxable Avg [3] 1.00 = 90-day T-bill return

Other Measures

			Standard LB Agg	Best Fit LB Corp
Standard Deviation	5.71	Alpha	5.4	4.8
Mean	9.96	Beta	1.11	0.91
Sharpe Ratio	1.13	R-Squared	60	63

Investment Style

Interest-Rate Stance

Avg Effective Duration	8.1 Yrs
Avg Effective Maturity	19.0 Yrs

Quality

Avg Credit Quality   BBB

Avg Weighted Coupon   7.12%
Avg Weighted Price   74.94% of Par

Diversification Value for Portfolio Types

Large Cap: Medium	Small Cap: High	Bond: Low	Balanced: Low	Diversified: Medium

Expenses & Fees

Sales Fees	0.00% front
	0.00% deferred
	0.00% 12b-1
Management Fee	0.60% flat fee
3-,5-,10-yr Expense Projections	$30, $52, $115

Min Initial Purchase	$2500 (Addt'l: $50)
Min IRA Purchase	$250 (Addt'l: $50)
Min Auto Invest Plan	$1000 (Systematic Inv: $50)

Portfolio 09-30-94

Amount 000	Date of Maturity	Total Stocks: 0 / Total Fixed-Income: 87	Value $000	% Net Assets
6750	01-16-23	Province of Quebec 9.375%	4765	4.98
5500	09-01-23	Westinghouse Electric 7.875%	4567	4.77
6500	08-18-22	Ontario Hydro 8.9%	4521	4.72
4350	09-15-03	RJR Nabisco 7.625%	3613	3.78
8100	12-31-00	Rockefeller Center Cv 0%	3402	3.55
3700	03-15-23	Time Warner Entertnmnt 8.375%	3214	3.36
25000	04-20-09	Kingdom of Sweden 9%	2767	2.89
2875	07-15-23	USX 8.125%	2480	2.59
21600	08-15-23	US Treasury Note 0%	2343	2.45
4500	03-31-23	Republic of Argentina FRN	2236	2.34
1500	08-18-15	Republic of Ireland 8.25%	2196	2.29
2500	03-15-22	Delta Air Lines 9.25%	2186	2.28
28	03-31-23	Citicorp ARP	2162	2.26
2600	03-01-17	Rohr Industries 9.25%	2080	2.17
2500	02-01-24	News America Holdings 7.75%	2034	2.13
2100	07-23-02	Rouse Cv 5.75%	1869	1.95
2000	08-01-12	AMR 9%	1777	1.86
30		Bethlehem Steel Cv Pfd 3.5%	1740	1.82
1800	01-15-12	United Air Lines 9.125%	1577	1.65
2110	08-04-02	Fuqua Industries Cv 6.5%	1477	1.54
18	03-31-23	BankAmerica ARP	1395	1.46
1500	08-15-21	United Air Lines 9.75%	1366	1.43
1813	10-01-12	Rohr Industries Cv 7%	1333	1.39
1750	04-01-23	Digital Equipment 7.75%	1290	1.35
1000	10-04-05	Lasmo USA Cv 7.75%	1277	1.33

Composition % 09-30-94

Cash	0.3	Preferreds	6.5
Stocks	0.0	Convertibles	26.0
Bonds	67.2	Other	0.0

Tax Analysis

	Tax-Adj Historical Return %	% Pretax Return
3 Yr Avg	6.46	60.8
5 Yr Avg	---	---
10 Yr Avg	---	---

Potential Capital Gain Exposure
(% of assets)   -13%

Most Similar Funds in MF500

High Yield Plus	Weak Fit
Janus Flexible Income	Weak Fit
Phoenix High-Yield A	Weak Fit

Coupon Range

	% of Bonds	Rel Obj
0%	6.5	2.99
0% to 8.5%	55.3	0.87
8.5% to 9.5%	28.3	1.75
9.5% to 11%	4.2	0.46
More than 11%	0.0	0.00
Not applicable	5.5	1.11

Credit Analysis 11-11-94

% of Bonds

US Govt	2	BB	15
AAA	5	B	19
AA	8	Below B	2
A	8	NR/NA	0
BBB	40		

MORNINGSTAR 1995 Mutual Fund 500

Loomis Sayles Small Cap

	Ticker	Load	NAV	Yield	SEC Yield	Assets	Objective
	LSSCX	None	12.85	0.0%	N/A	74.1	Small Company

Loomis Sayles Small Cap Fund seeks long-term capital appreciation. Current income is not a consideration.

The fund normally invests at least 65% of its assets in companies with market capitalizations of less than $500 million, and emphasizes undervalued securities of companies with significant potential for growth. It may invest a limited portion of its assets in foreign issues.

Historical Profile

Return	Above Average
Risk	Above Average
Rating	★★★ Neutral

Investment Style History
Equity
Average % Stocks Held in Portfolio

99% 92% 89% 93%

Growth of $10,000

|||| Value of Fund ($000)
— Value of Index ($000)
Russ 2000
▼ Manager Change
▽ Partial Manager Change
◄■ Mgr Unknown After
◄ Mgr Unknown Before

Performance Quartile (Within Objective)

Manager's Investment Style

The fund divides assets between two managers. Barbara Friedman uses a high-growth style, targeting companies with projected growth rates of 20% to 30%, and buying at prices of up to two thirds projected earnings. Jeffrey Petherick picks stocks with growth rates from 10% to 15% and priced at 10 times earnings. The end result is a portfolio that hovers between a blend and a growth style.

Fund Manager(s)

Barbara C. Friedman CFA(1991), since 05-91.
Birthdate: 11-46. BA, Smith C. 1968 MA, New York U. 1971
Jeffrey C. Petherick CFA(1991), since 07-93.
Birthdate: 02-63. BA, Albion C. 1985 MBA, U. of Michigan

Manager Experience	Dates Managed	Invest Obj	Std Dev	+/- Index
Barbara C. Friedman				
New England Star Adv A	07/94 - 12/94	G	9.56	3.59

	1983	1984	1985	1986	1987	1988	1989	1990	1991	1992	1993	1994	History
	—	—	—	—	—	—	—	—	12.49	12.88	14.13	12.85	NAV
	—	—	—	—	—	—	—	—	30.48 *	13.12	24.68	-8.31	Total Return %
	—	—	—	—	—	—	—	—	17.24 *	5.50	14.62	-9.62	+/- S&P 500
	—	—	—	—	—	—	—	—	—	1.36	10.14	-5.65	+/- Wilshire 4500
	—	—	—	—	—	—	—	—	0.00	0.00	0.00	0.00	Income Return %
	—	—	—	—	—	—	—	—	30.48	13.12	24.68	-8.31	Capital Return %
	—	—	—	—	—	—	—	—	—	13	11	87	Total Rtn % Rank All
	—	—	—	—	—	—	—	—	—	53	13	91	Total Rtn % Rank Obj
	—	—	—	—	—	—	—	—	0.00	0.00	0.00	0.00	Income $
	—	—	—	—	—	—	—	—	0.53	1.22	1.90	0.11	Capital Gains $
	—	—	—	—	—	—	—	—	1.50	1.50	1.35	1.29	Expense Ratio %
	—	—	—	—	—	—	—	—	-0.19	-0.79	-0.38	-0.31	Income Ratio %
	—	—	—	—	—	—	—	—	—	109	106	59	Turnover Rate %
	—	—	—	—	—	—	—	—	14.4	39.3	67.8	74.1	Net Assets ($mil)

Performance 12-31-94

	1st Qtr	2nd Qtr	3rd Qtr	4th Qtr	Total
1987	—	—	—	—	—
1988	—	—	—	—	—
1989	—	—	—	—	—
1990	—	—	—	—	—
1991	—	—	16.23	13.85	30.48 *
1992	10.09	-13.24	0.50	17.83	13.12
1993	6.44	2.12	12.86	1.64	24.68
1994	-5.24	-4.93	5.18	-3.24	-8.31

Bear Market Performance

Decile Rank (5-year period)

Worst ———————————— Best

	Worst 3 Mo Period 1985-89	Worst 3 Mo Period 1990-94
Loomis Sayles Small Cap	—	—
+/- S&P 500	—	—
+/- Best Fit Index :	—	—

Trailing Returns

	Total Return %	+/- S&P 500	+/- Wil 4500	% Rank All	% Rank Obj	Growth of $10,000
3 Mo	-3.24	-3.22	-0.74	85	85	9,676
6 Mo	1.78	-3.08	-2.42	28	84	10,178
1 Yr	-8.31	-9.62	-5.65	87	91	9,169
3 Yr Avg	8.95	2.68	1.34	17	51	12,932
5 Yr Avg	—	—	—	—	—	—
10 Yr Avg	—	—	—	—	—	—
15 Yr Avg	—	—	—	—	—	—

Risk Analysis

Time Period	Load-Adj Return %	Risk % Rank All [1]	Risk % Rank Obj [1]	Morningstar [2] Return	Morningstar Risk	Morningstar Risk-Adj Rating
1 Yr	-8.31					
3 Yr	8.95	91	64	1.63 [3]	1.23	★★★
5 Yr	—	—	—	—	—	
10 Yr	—	—	—	—	—	

Average Historical Rating (8 months)   4.1 ★s

[1] 1 = low, 100 = high   [2] 1.00 = Equity Avg   [3] 1.00 = 90-day T-bill return

Other Measures

			Standard S&P 500	Best Fit Russ 2000
Standard Deviation	14.37	Alpha	3.6	-3.3
Mean	9.63	Beta	0.90	1.18
Sharpe Ratio	0.42	R-Squared	25	93

Investment Style

	Stock Portfolio Avg	Relative S&P 500
Price/Earnings Ratio	20.1	1.09
Price/Book Ratio	2.5	0.75
5 Yr Earnings Gr %	22.3#	4.02
Return on Assets %	8.2	1.10
Debt % Total Cap	28.5	1.01
Med Mkt Cap ($mil)	233	0.02

figure is based on 50% or less of stocks

Style
Value Blend Growth
Size: Large Med Small

Diversification Value for Portfolio Types

Large Cap: High	Small Cap: None	Bond: High	Balanced: Medium	Diversified: Medium

Portfolio 12-31-94

Share Chg (09-94)000	Amount 000	Total Stocks: 125 Total Fixed-Income: 0	Value $000	% Net Assets
-5	32	Harman International	1180	1.59
-5	34	Genesis Health Ventures	1078	1.46
-6	37	Intl CableTel	1035	1.40
46	46	Huntco	1001	1.35
47	47	Hillhaven	991	1.34
18	70	InterVoice	957	1.29
40	40	Credence Systems	947	1.28
-6	38	Elsag Bailey Process Auto	941	1.27
13	28	Atmel	931	1.26
-9	60	Monaco Coach	913	1.23
-11	70	Davel Communications Group	898	1.21
-5	34	Horizon Outlet Centers	883	1.19
-25	33	FSI International	878	1.18
-10	68	Thermedics	863	1.16
56	56	CasTech Aluminum Group	848	1.14
0	23	Lam Research	846	1.14
-8	52	Thermo Fibertek	827	1.12
-4	56	Maxxim Medical	809	1.09
30	49	Johnstown America	809	1.09
-14	29	Capital Re	802	1.08
25	60	Intelcom Group	800	1.08
-5	34	Abbey Healthcare Group	792	1.07
-2	36	Chateau Properties	788	1.06
19	45	NCI Building Systems	780	1.05
-2	25	Zilog	743	1.00

Composition % 09-30-94

Cash	7.4	Preferreds	0.0
Stocks	92.6	Convertibles	0.0
Bonds	0.0	Other	0.0

Tax Analysis

	Tax-Adj Historical Return %	% Pretax Return
3 Yr Avg	6.77	74.1
5 Yr Avg	—	—
10 Yr Avg	—	—
Potential Capital Gain Exposure (% of assets)		-2%

Most Similar Funds in MF500

Hancock Emerging Growth B	Fair Fit
Delaware Trend A	Fair Fit
MainStay Capital Apprec B	Fair Fit

Index Allocation

	% of Stocks
S&P 500	0.0
S&P MidCap 400	2.4
U.S. Small Cap	94.9
Foreign	2.7

Sector Weightings

	% of Stocks	Relative S&P 500
Utilities	0.0	0.00
Energy	8.0	0.79
Financials	11.5	1.09
Industrial Cyclicals	23.6	1.44
Consumer Durables	8.4	1.35
Consumer Staples	1.6	0.13
Services	2.7	0.33
Retail	4.2	0.72
Health	15.2	1.75
Technology	24.8	2.71

Operations

Address and Telephone	One Financial Center Boston, MA 02111 800-633-3330 / 617-482-2450
Advisor	Loomis Sayles
Subadvisor	None
Distributor	Loomis Sayles
States Available	All
Report Grade	C
Income Distrib	Paid Annually
* Date of Inception	05-13-91
Fiscal Year End	December

Min Initial Purchase	$2500 (Addt'l: $50)
Min IRA Purchase	$250 (Addt'l: $50)
Min Auto Invest Plan	$1000 (Systematic Inv: $50)

Expenses & Fees

Sales Fees	0.00% front 0.00% deferred 0.00% 12b-1
Management Fee	1.00% flat fee
3-,5-,10-yr Expense Projections	$43, $74, $162
Annual Brokerage Cost	0.28%

Lord Abbett Bond-Debenture

	Ticker	Load	NAV	Yield	SEC Yield	Assets	Objective
	LBNDX	4.75%	8.71	10.1%	9.01%	987.6	Corp Hi Yld

Lord Abbett Bond-Debenture Fund seeks total return.

The fund normally invests at least 65% of its assets in bonds and debentures. At least 20% of the fund's assets must be maintained in investment-grade debt securities, U.S. government obligations, and/or cash and short-term instruments. The balance of assets may be invested in securities rated below investment grade. No more than 10% of the fund's assets may be invested in debt securities that are in default. The fund may invest up to 10% of its assets in foreign debt securities.

Trust shares have level loads; Fund shares have front loads and lower 12b-1 fees.

Manager's Investment Style

Management's strategy is unusual relative to the high-yield group. With at least 20% of assets earmarked by prospectus for investment-grade securities, the remaining portion of the portfolio may be invested at any credit level---even as low as C or credits in default. Management also employs straight bonds, convertible debentures, convertible preferreds, mortgage-backeds, and common stock.

Fund Manager(s)

Morais A. Taylor, since 06-92. Birthdate: 1952.
MS, MIT 1977   MBA, Wharton 1980

Manager Experience

	Dates Managed	Invest Obj	Std Dev	+/- Index
Morais A. Taylor				
Lord Abbett Bd-DebntureTr	01/94 - 12/94	CY	3.50	0.15

Historical Profile

Return	Average
Risk	Low
Rating	★★★★
	Above Average

	79	81	83	82	63	58	50	42

Investment Style History
Fixed Income
Income Rtn % Rank Obj

Growth of $10,000

|||| Value of Fund ($000)
— Value of Index ($000) LB Agg
▼ Manager Change
▽ Partial Manager Change
► Mgr Unknown After
◄ Mgr Unknown Before

Performance Quartile (Within Objective)

	1983	1984	1985	1986	1987	1988	1989	1990	1991	1992	1993	1994	History
NAV	10.68	9.82	10.56	10.28	9.39	9.59	9.03	7.36	9.02	9.43	9.95	8.71	NAV
	16.90	4.96	21.01	10.50	1.98	13.82	5.06	-7.57	38.34	16.00	15.99	-3.86	Total Return %
	8.53	-10.19	-1.11	-4.75	-0.78	5.94	-9.48	-16.52	22.34	8.75	6.24	-0.94	+/- LB Aggregate
	---	---	---	-5.13	-4.55	2.39	4.67	-1.19	-5.41	-0.66	-2.91	-2.89	+/- FB High-Yield
	11.37	11.79	13.48	11.83	10.64	11.69	10.90	10.92	15.79	11.45	10.48	8.60	Income Return %
	5.53	-6.83	7.54	-1.33	-8.66	2.13	-5.84	-18.49	22.55	4.55	5.51	-12.46	Capital Return %
	51	51	67	82	43	33	95	79	16	8	25	52	Total Rtn % Rank All
	33	84	74	82	45	33	7	37	41	67	90	57	Total Rtn % Rank Obj
	1.10	1.18	1.20	1.19	1.12	1.04	1.04	1.04	0.98	0.96	0.92	0.88	Income $
	0.00	0.15	0.00	0.14	0.00	0.00	0.00	0.00	0.00	0.00	0.00	0.00	Capital Gains $
	0.69	0.71	0.68	0.61	0.65	0.64	0.59	0.80	0.85	0.84	0.88	---	Expense Ratio %
	10.40	12.07	11.69	11.09	10.49	11.29	10.97	12.48	11.96	10.18	9.17	---	Income Ratio %
	89	64	82	137	176	140	124	145	208	188	160	---	Turnover Rate %
	203.4	203.1	299.2	700.6	733.2	717.8	644.0	480.8	594.0	734.0	969.7	987.6	Net Assets ($mil)

Performance 12-31-94

	1st Qtr	2nd Qtr	3rd Qtr	4th Qtr	Total
1987	7.72	-0.63	0.06	-4.80	1.98
1988	6.72	3.47	1.36	1.69	13.82
1989	3.16	3.50	0.42	-2.01	5.06
1990	-1.14	3.24	-8.24	-1.31	-7.57
1991	13.83	6.14	8.09	5.94	38.34
1992	5.52	3.30	4.58	1.76	16.00
1993	6.04	3.45	2.17	3.49	15.99
1994	-0.86	-1.68	0.53	-1.90	-3.86

Bear Market Performance

Decile Rank (5-year period)

Worst ——————————— Best

	Worst 3 Mo Period 1985-89	Worst 3 Mo Period 1990-94
Lord Abbett Bond-Debenture	-8.36	-13.76
+/- LB Aggregate	-10.53	-14.51
+/- Best Fit Index : FB HY	---	0.34

Trailing Returns

	Total Return %	+/- LB Aggregate	+/- FB High-Yield	% Rank All	% Rank Obj	Growth of $10,000
3 Mo	-1.90	-2.28	-1.86	66	69	9,810
6 Mo	-1.37	-2.37	-2.93	80	54	9,863
1 Yr	-3.86	-0.94	-2.89	52	57	9,614
3 Yr Avg	8.96	4.41	-2.20	17	81	12,935
5 Yr Avg	10.59	2.96	-2.49	14	46	16,540
10 Yr Avg	10.43	0.49	---	54	41	26,970
15 Yr Avg	11.08	0.28	---	64	50	48,391

Operations

Address and Telephone	General Motors Bld. 767 Fifth Ave New York, NY 10153-0203 800-874-3733 / 212-848-1800
Advisor	Lord Abbett
Subadvisor	None
Distributor	Lord Abbett
States Available	All
Report Grade	B
Income Distrib	Paid Monthly
Date of Inception	04-01-71
Fiscal Year End	December

Risk Analysis

Time Period	Load-Adj Return %	Risk % Rank All	Risk % Rank Obj [1]	Morningstar Return [2]	Morningstar Risk	Morningstar Risk-Adj Rating
1 Yr	-8.43					
3 Yr	7.20	10	54	1.08 [3]	0.38	★★★★
5 Yr	9.52	44	39	1.22 [3]	0.53	★★★★
10 Yr	9.89	33	41	0.64	0.46	★★★
Average Historical Rating (109 months)					3.3	★s

[1] = low, 100 = high   [2] 1.00 = Hybrid Avg   [3] 1.00 = 90-day T-bill return

Other Measures

				Standard LB Agg	Best Fit FB HY
Standard Deviation	4.46	Alpha		4.6	-1.5
Mean	8.71	Beta		0.70	0.93
Sharpe Ratio	1.16	R-Squared		38	81

Investment Style

Interest-Rate Stance

Avg Effective Duration	3.7 Yrs
Avg Effective Maturity	8.0 Yrs

Maturity: Short Intm Long

Quality

Avg Credit Quality	BB
Avg Weighted Coupon	8.41%
Avg Weighted Price	90.16% of Par

Quality: High Med Low

Diversification Value for Portfolio Types

Large Cap: Medium	Small Cap: Medium	Bond: Medium	Balanced: Medium	Diversified: Medium

Portfolio 06-30-94

Total Stocks: 7
Total Fixed-Income: 238

Amount 000	Date of Maturity		Value $000	% Net Assets
10000	06-15-00	General Instrument Cv 5%	13075	1.30
10000	04-15-04	Huntsman 11%	10250	1.02
17000	2004	Videotron Holdings 0%	9913	0.98
10000	2004	Heilman Acquisition 9.625%	9350	0.93
10000	2004	Essex Group 0%	8775	0.87
15000	2004	MFS Communications 0%	8625	0.86
14000	06-01-05	American Standard 0%	8575	0.85
13000	1998	Dal-Tile International 0%	8060	0.80
8000	08-01-03	Big Flower Press 10.75%	7620	0.76
7500	04-01-04	AK Steel 10.75%	7538	0.75
75		Ford Motor Cl A Cv Pfd	7275	0.72
10000	11-30-09	Stelco 10.4%	6942	0.69
7000	07-15-02	Grand Union 12.25%	6913	0.69
8500	2001	Harris Chemical 0%	6906	0.69
10000	12-15-03	Southland 5%	6650	0.66
6800	2000	Scotsman Group 9.5%	6460	0.64
7000	07-31-03	US Leather 10.25%	6440	0.64
6000	10-15-99	Weirton Steel 10.875%	6180	0.61
8500	12-15-04	Food 4 Less Holdings 0%	6099	0.61
6000	2000	TRISM 10.75%	6060	0.60
10000	03-05-00	Comcast Cellular 0%	6050	0.60
6000	07-01-03	Continental Broadcstng 10.625%	6045	0.60
5959	1996	Sahara Finance 12.125%	5959	0.59
10000	02-15-00	Clark R & M Holdings 0%	5650	0.56
200		Greater NY Svgs Cl B Pfd $3.00	5600	0.56

Composition % 12-31-94

Cash	12.4	Preferreds	2.1
Stocks	0.2	Convertibles	18.0
Bonds	67.3	Other	0.0

Tax Analysis

	Tax-Adj Historical Return %	% Pretax Return
3 Yr Avg	5.25	56.6
5 Yr Avg	6.69	58.4
10 Yr Avg	6.04	47.0
Potential Capital Gain Exposure (% of assets)		-19%

Most Similar Funds in MF500

American High-Income	Strong Fit
Vanguard F/I High-Yield Corp	Strong Fit
Invesco High-Yield	Strong Fit

Coupon Range

	% of Bonds	Rel Obj
0%, PIK	15.0	2.03
0% to 11%	45.6	0.93
11% to 13%	24.5	0.73
13% to 14.5%	3.6	0.66
More than 14.5%	1.3	0.82
Not applicable	9.8	3.24

Credit Analysis 12-31-94

% of Bonds

US Govt	0	BB	8
AAA	21	B	54
AA	0	Below B	7
A	3	NR/NA	3
BBB	4		

Min Initial Purchase

Min Initial Purchase	$1000 (Addt'l: None)
Min IRA Purchase	$250 (Addt'l: None)
Min Auto Invest Plan	$250 (Systematic Inv: $50)

Expenses & Fees

Sales Fees	4.75% front
	0.00% deferred
	0.25% 12b-1
Management Fee	0.50% max./0.45% min.
3-,5-,10-yr Expense Projections	$74, $94, $151

MORNINGSTAR   1995 Mutual Fund 500

Lord Abbett Tax-Fr Inc Ntl

	Ticker	Load	NAV	Yield	SEC Yield	Assets	Objective
	LANSX	4.75%	10.22	6.8%	5.53%	614.6	Muni Nat

Lord Abbett Tax-Free Income Fund National Series seeks interest income exempt from federal income tax, consistent with preservation of capital.

The fund normally invests at least 80% of its assets in investment-grade municipal bonds. It intends to purchase primarily intermediate-term (five to 10 years) to long-term (over 10 years) bonds. The fund may invest up to 20% of its net assets in securities that are subject to the Alternative Minimum Tax.

Historical Profile

Return	Average
Risk	Above Average
Rating	★★ Below Average

Investment Style History
Fixed Income
Income Rtn % Rank Obj

11 45 32 34 40 33 13 8

Growth of $10,000

- IIII Value of Fund ($000)
- — Value of Index ($000) LB Muni
- ▼ Manager Change
- ▽ Partial Manager Change
- ► Mgr Unknown After
- ◄ Mgr Unknown Before

Performance Quartile (Within Objective)

Manager's Investment Style

Management carefully chooses the risks it will take. Although up to 20% of the fund's assets may be kept in noninvestment-grade credits, management currently favors only the highest-quality bonds. Sector choices, as well, reflect caution, as management largely avoids riskier COP/leases and health-care bonds, while overweighting safer revenue-backed areas such as utilities, water, and waste bonds. Management is, however, aggressive on interest-rate risk. The portfolio is typically on the long to intermediate end. The fund has owned municipal derivatives.

Fund Manager(s)

Robert S. Dow et al. Birthdate: 03-45 MSC, New York U. 1971 MBA, Columbia U. 1973

History	1983	1984	1985	1986	1987	1988	1989	1990	1991	1992	1993	1994
NAV	---	9.41	10.18	11.23	10.29	10.79	11.01	10.99	11.51	11.49	11.83	10.22
Total Return %	---	7.83 *	19.66	20.11	0.57	12.58	9.52	7.25	12.51	8.74	13.32	-7.94
+/- LB Aggregate	---	---	-2.47	4.86	-2.19	4.70	-5.02	-1.69	-3.49	1.50	3.56	-5.02
+/- LB Muni	---	---	-0.37	0.79	-0.94	2.42	-1.27	-0.05	0.37	-0.08	1.04	-2.33
Income Return %	---	7.19	9.90	9.01	7.71	7.72	7.48	7.09	6.97	6.46	6.40	5.67
Capital Return %	---	0.64	9.76	11.09	-7.14	4.86	2.04	0.16	5.54	2.28	6.91	-13.61
Total Rtn % Rank All	---	---	75	19	55	41	79	19	71	36	38	85
Total Rtn % Rank Obj	---	---	53	18	37	24	48	8	20	42	19	85
Income $	---	0.64	0.86	0.85	0.83	0.76	0.78	0.75	0.72	0.72	0.72	0.69
Capital Gains $	---	0.00	0.13	0.07	0.16	0.00	0.00	0.04	0.08	0.28	0.44	0.00
Expense Ratio %	---	---	0.59	0.66	0.60	0.62	0.66	0.61	0.75	0.83	0.87	0.86
Income Ratio %	---	---	8.96	8.20	7.10	7.51	7.26	7.00	6.79	6.00	5.79	5.76
Turnover Rate %	---	---	292	124	47	93	81	43	58	88	138	184
Net Assets ($mil)	---	23.6	71.0	226.6	258.2	284.6	315.5	331.4	440.1	573.1	715.9	614.6

Manager Experience

	Dates Managed	Invest Obj	Std Dev	+/- Index
Philip Fang				
Lord Abbett T/F Inc WA	06/93 - 12/94	MS	7.76	-2.10
Lord Abbett Natl T/F Inc Tr	12/93 - 12/94	MN	9.21	-6.21

Performance 12-31-94

	1st Qtr	2nd Qtr	3rd Qtr	4th Qtr	Total
1987	2.62	-5.07	-3.09	6.51	0.57
1988	3.18	2.40	3.16	3.30	12.58
1989	0.17	5.81	-0.25	3.59	9.52
1990	-0.03	2.36	0.07	4.74	7.25
1991	2.19	2.00	3.92	3.87	12.51
1992	0.25	4.17	2.14	1.94	8.74
1993	4.86	3.30	3.67	0.91	13.32
1994	-6.37	-0.27	0.47	-1.86	-7.94

Bear Market Performance

Decile Rank (5-year period)

Worst | Best

	Worst 3 Mo Period 1985-89	Worst 3 Mo Period 1990-94
Lord Abbett Tax-Fr Inc Ntl	-7.61	-7.48
+/- LB Aggregate	-4.05	-2.55
+/- Best Fit Index : LB Muni	-1.11	-1.72

Trailing Returns

	Total Return %	+/- LB Aggregate	+/- LB Muni	% Rank All	% Rank Obj	Growth of $10,000
3 Mo	-1.86	-2.24	-0.43	66	76	9,814
6 Mo	-1.40	-2.40	-0.16	80	71	9,860
1 Yr	-7.94	-5.02	-2.33	85	85	9,206
3 Yr Avg	4.29	-0.25	-0.57	63	63	11,344
5 Yr Avg	6.48	-1.14	-0.29	64	33	13,689
10 Yr Avg	9.33	-0.62	-0.10	67	26	24,392
15 Yr Avg	---	---	---	---	---	---

Operations

Address and Telephone	General Motors Bld. 767 Fifth Ave
	New York, NY 10153-0203
	800-874-3733 / 212-848-1800
Advisor	Lord Abbett
Subadvisor	None
Distributor	Lord Abbett
States Available	All
Report Grade	C
Income Distrib	Paid Monthly
* Date of Inception	04-02-84
Fiscal Year End	September

Min Initial Purchase	$1000 (Addt'l: None)
Min IRA Purchase	N/A
Min Auto Invest Plan	$250 (Systematic Inv: $50)

Expenses & Fees

Sales Fees	4.75% front
	0.00% deferred
	0.25% 12b-1
Management Fee	0.50% flat fee
3-,5-,10-yr Expense Projections	$74, $93, $150

Risk Analysis

Time Period	Load-Adj Return %	Risk % Rank[1] All	Risk % Rank[1] Obj	Morningstar[2] Return	Morningstar[2] Risk	Morningstar Risk-Adj Rating
1 Yr	-12.31					
3 Yr	2.62	47	84	0.69	1.25	★
5 Yr	5.45	35	76	0.89	1.23	★★
10 Yr	8.80	23	69	1.09	1.16	★★★
Average Historical Rating (93 months)					2.9	◄ s

[1] 1 = low, 100 = high [2] 1.00 = Muni Avg [3] 1.00 = 90-day T-bill return

Other Measures

				Standard LB Agg	Best Fit LB Muni
Standard Deviation	6.82	Alpha		-0.4	-0.8
Mean	4.44	Beta		1.28	1.22
Sharpe Ratio	0.14	R-Squared		57	97

Investment Style

Interest-Rate Stance	
Avg Effective Maturity	18.8 Yrs

Quality	
Avg Credit Quality	AA
Avg Weighted Coupon	7.32%
Avg Weighted Price	102.11% of Par

Maturity Short Intm Long
Quality High Med Low

Diversification Value for Portfolio Types

Large Cap: Medium	Small Cap: High	Bond: Low	Balanced: Medium	Diversified: Medium

Portfolio 09-30-94

Amount 000	Date of Maturity	Total Stocks: 0 / Total Fixed-Income: 214	Value $000	% Net Assets
27000	10-01-21	DC Metro Washington Transp 5.75%	24334	3.67
25000	01-07-22	TN Nashville Metro Wtr/Swr RIB	22656	3.42
20000	05-01-15	NY Battery Park City 7.7%	22400	3.38
25000	06-15-13	NY New York City Muni Wtr Fin Swr RIB	19969	3.01
14000	07-01-14	VA Capital Region Arpt Com 10.125%	16188	2.44
15025	10-01-27	NY Port of NY/NJ Consolid 7.35%	16114	2.43
11255	12-01-17	NJ Camden Muni Util Swr 8.25%	12493	1.89
10500	02-01-17	NE Omaha Pub Pwr Dist Elec Sys 6.5%	11235	1.70
10000	02-01-24	NY Engy Rsrch/Dev Gas Fac Bklyn 6.75%	10288	1.55
10000	11-15-09	MN Rochester Hlth Care Fac Mayo IFRN	9350	1.41
8000	01-01-17	IL Chicago O'Hare Intl Arpt 7.5%	8850	1.34
10000	07-01-20	WI Pub Pwr Sply Sys 5.3%	8825	1.33
7500	02-01-22	GA Effingham Dev Poll Cntrl 6.75%	7781	1.17
7000	12-01-23	PR Indl Med Educ/Envir Poll Cntrl 7.5%	7639	1.15
7350	07-01-21	MO St Louis Redev Land Clearance 7.75%	7626	1.15
8000	08-15-14	IL Hlth Fac Univ Chicago Hosp RIB	7470	1.13
8700	08-23-27	VA Henrico Indl Dev RIB	7308	1.10
6000	07-01-18	WA Pub Pwr Sply Sys Proj #1 7.5%	6735	1.02
6000	07-01-04	NY New York City Muni Assist 7.6%	6675	1.01
5845	07-01-10	FL Palm Beach Solid Waste 8.75%	6510	0.98

Credit Analysis % of Bonds 12-31-94

US Govt	0	BB	0
AAA	63	B	0
AA	24	Below B	0
A	7	NR/NA	0
BBB	6		

Composition % of Assets 12-31-94

Cash	0.6	Preferreds	0.0
Stocks	0.0	Convertibles	0.0
Bonds	99.4	Other	0.0

Tax Analysis

	Tax-Adj Historical Return %	% Pretax Return
3 Yr Avg	3.72	86.2
5 Yr Avg	6.07	92.8
10 Yr Avg	9.03	95.5
Potential Capital Gain Exposure (% of assets)		-9%

Most Similar Funds in MF500

Fidelity Insured Tax-Free	Strong Fit
Fidelity Municipal Bond	Strong Fit
Safeco Municipal Bond	Strong Fit

Coupon Range

	% Bonds	Rel Obj
0%	0.0	0.00
0% to 6.8%	36.6	0.61
6.8% to 7.5%	22.0	1.42
7.5% to 8.3%	19.2	2.17
More than 8.3%	7.2	0.82
Not applicable	14.9	3.84

Sector Weightings

	% Bonds	Rel Obj
General Obl	10.82	0.51
Utilities	13.74	1.10
Health	12.32	0.93
Water/Waste	9.88	1.55
Housing	6.88	0.94
Education	5.29	0.83
Transportation	16.58	1.63
COP/Lease	1.93	0.61
Private	14.33	1.23
Misc Revenue	5.19	1.04
Demand	3.05	1.24

Top 5 States % of Bonds

NY	16.50	TN	4.74
TX	6.07	DC	4.65
VA	4.82		

MainStay Capital Appreciation B

Ticker	Load	NAV	Yield	SEC Yield	Assets	Objective
MCSCX	5.00%d	19.11	0.0%	N/A	501.1	Growth

MainStay Capital Appreciation Fund seeks long-term growth of capital. Dividend income is incidental.

The fund has a flexible approach toward investing. Generally, it seeks securities with participation in expanding markets, increasing unit-sales volume, growth in revenues, and earnings per share superior to stock-market indexes. Exceptions to these guidelines are made when the fund sees special developments that may increase a company's growth in earnings. The fund may purchase securities that demonstrate above-average risk.

Manager's Investment Style

The fund's managers look for rapid-fire earnings growth and momentum, and are willing to pay a high price (as necessary) for these traits. Small- to mid-cap technology, health-care, and retail stocks are typical holdings. For defensiveness, the team has been known to hold some cash and larger-cap issues when its preferred picks are out of favor.

Fund Manager(s)

Edmund C. Spelman, since 02-91. Birthdate: 04-52. BA, U. of Pennsylvania 1979 MS, U. of Pennsylvania 1979
Rudy Carryl, since 08-92. Birthdate: 08-51. BS, U. of London 1975

Manager Experience	Dates Managed	Invest Obj	Std Dev	+/- Index
Edmund C. Spelman				
MainStay Inst Gr Eq Inst	02/91 - 12/94	G	18.78	3.63
MainStay Total Return B	02/91 - 12/94	B	10.46	0.02

Historical Profile

Return	Above Average
Risk	Above Average
Rating	★★★★ Above Average

Investment Style History
Equity

Average % Stocks Held in Portfolio: 85% 95% 89% 82% 94% 91% 87% 87%

Growth of $10,000
|||| Value of Fund ($000)
— Value of Index ($000) Wil 4500
▼ Manager Change
▽ Partial Manager Change
► Mgr Unknown After
◄ Mgr Unknown Before

Performance Quartile (Within Objective)

	1983	1984	1985	1986	1987	1988	1989	1990	1991	1992	1993	1994	History
NAV	---	---	---	9.63	9.42	9.66	11.47	11.51	16.08	17.65	19.55	19.11	NAV
	---	---	---	-3.56 *	-2.18	2.55	26.06	4.12	68.36	11.00	14.01	-1.52	Total Return %
	---	---	---	-8.92 *	-7.44	-14.06	-5.63	7.23	37.88	3.38	3.96	-2.84	+/- S&P 500
	---	---	---	---	-4.54	-15.39	-3.12	10.30	34.16	2.03	2.73	-1.45	+/- Wilshire 5000
	---	---	---	0.14	0.00	0.00	0.18	0.00	0.00	0.00	0.00	0.00	Income Return %
	---	---	---	-3.70	-2.18	2.55	25.88	4.12	68.36	11.00	14.01	-1.52	Capital Return %
	---	---	---	---	76	96	21	46	2	17	33	30	Total Rtn % Rank All
	---	---	---	---	79	95	56	7	2	30	38	47	Total Rtn % Rank Obj
	---	---	---	0.02	0.00	0.00	0.02	0.00	0.00	0.00	0.00	0.00	Income $
	---	---	---	0.00	0.00	0.00	0.69	0.42	2.93	0.19	0.55	0.14	Capital Gains $
	---	---	---	2.90	2.90	2.70	2.80	2.50	2.50	2.00	1.80	1.80	Expense Ratio %
	---	---	---	-0.10	-1.50	-1.30	-0.80	-0.20	-1.00	-1.20	-0.70	-0.60	Income Ratio %
	---	---	---	---	16	60	256	259	327	157	73	31	Turnover Rate %
	---	---	---	16.5	29.6	28.1	34.5	38.4	92.6	185.6	343.5	501.1	Net Assets ($mil)

Performance 12-31-94

	1st Qtr	2nd Qtr	3rd Qtr	4th Qtr	Total
1987	26.17	0.41	4.92	-26.41	-2.18
1988	6.79	0.89	-3.94	-0.92	2.55
1989	6.73	10.28	11.35	-3.81	26.06
1990	-0.61	10.26	-12.49	8.56	4.12
1991	19.46	-3.85	26.10	16.25	68.36
1992	-0.37	-11.36	1.97	23.26	11.00
1993	2.49	2.93	8.16	-0.08	14.01
1994	-1.38	-6.17	8.84	-2.22	-1.52

Bear Market Performance

Decile Rank (5-year period)

Worst [bar] Best

	Worst 3 Mo Period 1985-89	Worst 3 Mo Period 1990-94
MainStay Capital Appreciation	---	-12.49
+/- S&P 500	---	1.26
+/- Best Fit Index : Wil 4500	---	5.74

Trailing Returns

	Total Return %	+/- S&P 500	+/- Wil 5000	% Rank All	% Rank Obj	Growth of $10,000
3 Mo	-2.22	-2.21	-1.45	72	68	9,778
6 Mo	6.42	1.56	1.80	8	23	10,642
1 Yr	-1.52	-2.84	-1.45	30	47	9,848
3 Yr Avg	7.61	1.35	1.00	23	34	12,463
5 Yr Avg	16.92	8.22	8.10	3	3	21,846
10 Yr Avg	---	---	---	---	---	---
15 Yr Avg	---	---	---	---	---	---

Operations

Address and Telephone	51 Madison Avenue New York, NY 10010 800-522-4202
Advisor	MacKay-Shields Financial
Subadvisor	None
Distributor	NYLife Distributors
States Available	All
Report Grade	C
Income Distrib	Paid Quarterly
* Date of Inception	05-01-86
Fiscal Year End	August

Risk Analysis

Time Period	Load-Adj Return %	Risk % Rank[1] All	Risk % Rank[1] Obj	Morningstar[2] Return	Morningstar Risk	Morningstar Risk-Adj Rating
1 Yr	-5.43					
3 Yr	7.04	95	95	1.03[3]	1.39	★★★
5 Yr	16.81	91	90	3.53[3]	1.17	★★★★★
10 Yr	---	---	---	---	---	---

Average Historical Rating (68 months) 3.5 ★s

[1] 1 = low, 100 = high [2] 1.00 = Equity Avg [3] 1.00 = 90-day T-bill return

Other Measures

			Standard S&P 500	Best Fit Wil 4500
Standard Deviation	15.40	Alpha	1.8	-1.3
Mean	8.54	Beta	1.13	1.47
Sharpe Ratio	0.33	R-Squared	34	87

Investment Style

	Stock Portfolio Avg	Relative S&P 500
Price/Earnings Ratio	18.8	1.02
Price/Book Ratio	3.9	1.16
5 Yr Earnings Gr %	29.2	5.25
Return on Assets %	11.0	1.47
Debt % Total Cap	22.4	0.79
Med Mkt Cap ($mil)	3226	0.25

Style: Value Blend Growth / Large Med Small (Size)

Diversification Value for Portfolio Types

Large Cap: Medium	Small Cap: None	Bond: High	Balanced: Medium	Diversified: Medium

Expenses & Fees

Sales Fees	0.00% front 5.00% deferred 1.00% 12b-1
Management Fee	0.36% flat fee, 0.36%A
3-,5-,10-yr Expense Projections	$88, $120, $216
Annual Brokerage Cost	0.17%

Min Initial Purchase	$500 (Addt'l: $50)
Min IRA Purchase	$500 (Addt'l: $50)
Min Auto Invest Plan	$100 (Systematic Inv: $50)

Portfolio 08-31-94

Total Stocks: 80
Total Fixed-Income: 0

Share Chg (02-94) 000	Amount 000		Value $000	% Net Assets
15	205	3Com	13722	2.90
53	158	Telefonos de Mexico L (ADR)	9915	2.10
179	285	Green Tree Financial	9531	2.02
57	143	Intel	9402	1.99
119	177	United HealthCare	9248	1.96
52	97	American International Group	9090	1.92
130	208	US Healthcare	8996	1.90
46	112	First Interstate Bancorp	8978	1.90
70	197	SunAmerica	8744	1.85
165	242	Lowe's	8742	1.85
58	218	Computer Associates Intl	8727	1.85
93	322	Blockbuster Entertainment	8332	1.76
75	147	News (ADR)	7964	1.69
80	150	Amgen	7886	1.67
34	100	Texas Instruments	7764	1.64
77	169	Columbia/HCA Healthcare	7187	1.52
283	283	Dollar General	7149	1.51
10	72	Medtronic	7110	1.50
156	391	EMC	7029	1.49
11	101	PacifiCare Health Sys Cl B	6958	1.47
11	126	Cordis	6930	1.47
106	106	Alco Standard	6917	1.46
42	121	Harley-Davidson	6820	1.44
56	183	Elan (ADR)	6595	1.40
38	178	First USA	6519	1.38

Composition % 09-30-94

Cash	7.5	Preferreds	0.0
Stocks	92.5	Convertibles	0.0
Bonds	0.0	Other	0.0

Tax Analysis

	Tax-Adj Historical Return %	% Pretax Return
3 Yr Avg	7.16	93.6
5 Yr Avg	15.34	87.9
10 Yr Avg	---	---

Potential Capital Gain Exposure (% of assets) 12%

Most Similar Funds in MF500

Hancock Emerging Growth B	Strong Fit
Oppenheimer Discovery A	Strong Fit
20th Century Ultra Investors	Strong Fit

Index Allocation

	% of Stocks
S&P 500	42.4
S&P MidCap 400	19.7
U.S. Small Cap	30.2
Foreign	7.7

Sector Weightings

	% of Stocks	Relative S&P 500
Utilities	2.3	0.18
Energy	0.5	0.05
Financials	17.3	1.63
Industrial Cyclicals	6.4	0.39
Consumer Durables	2.9	0.47
Consumer Staples	0.0	0.00
Services	14.4	1.76
Retail	11.7	2.01
Health	20.1	2.32
Technology	24.5	2.67

MORNINGSTAR **1995 Mutual Fund 500**

MainStay Convertible B

	Ticker	Load	NAV	Yield	SEC Yield	Assets	Objective
	MCSVX	5.00%d	11.67	4.0%	N/A	180.2	Convrt. Bond

MainStay Convertible Fund - Class B seeks capital appreciation and current income.

The fund normally invests at least 65% of its assets in bonds, debentures, corporate notes, preferred stocks, or other securities that are convertible into common stock and that are rated at least BBB. The balance may be invested in nonconvertible debt, equity securities, or U.S. government securities, or may be held in cash or cash equivalents.

Historical Profile

Return	High
Risk	Below Average
Rating	★★★★★ Highest

Income Rtn % Rank Obj: 81 85 75 95 78 79 64 50

Growth of $10,000

IIII Value of Fund ($000)
— Value of Index ($000) Wil 4500
▼ Manager Change
▽ Partial Manager Change
► Mgr Unknown After
◄ Mgr Unknown Before

Performance Quartile (Within Objective)

Manager's Investment Style

Management takes a two-pronged approach. Comanager Denis Laplaige handles value-oriented stock picking, while Neil Feinberg chooses the fund's convertibles. The result is a portfolio that can hold a greater-than-average stake in equities. Management moves in and out of holdings if they appear overvalued. Above all, management employs a flexibility of strategy.

Fund Manager(s)

Denis Laplaige, since 04-91. Birthdate: 08-51.
BBA, Baruch C. 1977 MBA, New York U. 1980
Neil Feinberg, since 02-92. Birthdate: 11-62.
BA, Rutgers U. 1984 MBA, New York U. 1989

Manager Experience	Dates Managed	Invest Obj	Std Dev	+/- Index
Denis Laplaige				
MainStay Total Return B	01/90 - 01/92	B	13.34	6.18

1983	1984	1985	1986	1987	1988	1989	1990	1991	1992	1993	1994	History
---	---	---	9.86	8.55	8.77	8.82	7.90	11.43	12.06	12.69	11.67	NAV
---	---	---	1.01 *	-8.58	7.13	6.74	-6.70	48.47	13.11	24.47	-1.34	Total Return %
---	---	---		-11.34	-0.75	-7.80	-15.64	32.47	5.86	14.72	1.58	+/- LB Aggregate
---	---	---	-7.46 *	-13.84	-9.48	-24.94	-3.58	17.99	5.49	14.41	-2.65	+/- S&P 500
---	---	---		2.41	3.99	4.56	6.17	3.73	3.79	3.10	3.81	3.87	Income Return %
---	---	---		-1.40	-12.57	2.57	0.57	-10.43	44.68	10.00	20.66	-5.21	Capital Return %
---	---	---		94	80	94	77	8	13	12	29	Total Rtn % Rank All
---	---	---		63	78	90	57	1	37	1	11	Total Rtn % Rank Obj
---	---	---	0.24	0.42	0.39	0.53	0.34	0.25	0.34	0.47	0.48	Income $
---	---	---	0.00	0.08	0.00	0.00	0.00	0.00	0.49	1.79	0.38	Capital Gains $
---	---	---	2.80	2.70	2.60	2.60	2.50	2.70	2.30	1.90	1.90	Expense Ratio %
---	---	---	3.70	4.10	4.40	5.60	4.70	2.80	2.90	3.40	3.50	Income Ratio %
---	---	---		147	182	308	204	283	291	370	269	Turnover Rate %
---	---	---	22.1	31.2	28.1	22.8	16.9	23.3	35.3	77.4	180.2	Net Assets ($mil)

Performance 12-31-94

	1st Qtr	2nd Qtr	3rd Qtr	4th Qtr	Total
1987	6.44	-1.86	-0.25	-12.26	-8.58
1988	5.32	3.92	-0.50	-1.63	7.13
1989	1.81	3.63	2.53	-1.31	6.74
1990	-4.87	5.29	-10.11	3.62	-6.70
1991	15.76	2.74	10.45	13.02	48.47
1992	1.12	-0.47	2.73	9.40	13.11
1993	7.37	4.51	6.62	4.04	24.47
1994	1.41	-3.10	3.79	-3.26	-1.34

Bear Market Performance

Decile Rank (5-year period)

Worst — Best

	Worst 3 Mo Period 1985-89	Worst 3 Mo Period 1990-94
MainStay Convertible B	---	-10.30
+/- LB Aggregate	---	-11.04
+/- Best Fit Index : Wil 4500	---	9.10

Trailing Returns

	Total Return %	+/- LB Aggregate	+/- S&P 500	% Rank All	% Rank Obj	Growth of $10,000
3 Mo	-3.26	-3.64	-3.24	85	65	9,674
6 Mo	0.40	-0.59	-4.46	49	39	10,040
1 Yr	-1.34	1.58	-2.65	29	11	9,866
3 Yr Avg	11.57	7.03	5.31	9	16	13,889
5 Yr Avg	13.98	6.36	5.29	5	1	19,240
10 Yr Avg	---	---	---	---	---	---
15 Yr Avg	---	---	---	---	---	---

Operations

Address and Telephone	51 Madison Avenue New York, NY 10010 800-522-4202
Advisor	MacKay-Shields Financial
Subadvisor	None
Distributor	NYLife Distributors
States Available	All
Report Grade	C
Income Distrib	Paid Quarterly
* Date of Inception	05-01-86
Fiscal Year End	August

Risk Analysis

Time Period	Load-Adj Return %	Risk % Rank [1] All	Risk % Rank [1] Obj	Morningstar [2] Return	Morningstar Risk	Morningstar Risk-Adj Rating
1 Yr	-5.02					
3 Yr	11.04	48	45	2.31 [3]	0.69	★★★★★
5 Yr	13.86	53	38	2.52 [3]	0.76	★★★★★
10 Yr						

Average Historical Rating (68 months)   3.1 ★s

[1] 1 = low, 100 = high   [2] 1.00 = Hybrid Avg   [3] 1.00 = 90-day T-bill return

Other Measures

			Standard LB Agg	Best Fit Wil 4500
Standard Deviation	7.25	Alpha	7.3	5.1
Mean	11.26	Beta	0.68	0.63
Sharpe Ratio	1.07	R-Squared	14	72

Investment Style

Interest-Rate Stance

Avg Effective Maturity   12.0 Yrs

Not Applicable

Quality

Avg Credit Quality	BB
Avg Weighted Coupon	5.66%
Avg Weighted Price	85.73% of Par

Diversification Value for Portfolio Types

Large Cap: Medium	Small Cap: Low	Bond: High	Balanced: Low	Diversified: Low

Expenses & Fees

Sales Fees	0.00% front 5.00% deferred 1.00% 12b-1
Management Fee	0.36% flat fee, 0.36%A
3-,5-,10-yr Expense Projections	$89, $121, $220

Min Initial Purchase	$500 (Addt'l: $50)
Min IRA Purchase	$500 (Addt'l: $50)
Min Auto Invest Plan	$100 (Systematic Inv: $50)

Portfolio 08-31-94

Total Stocks: 49
Total Fixed-Income: 92

Amount 000	Date of Maturity		Value $000	% Net Assets
7200	01-10-15	Time Warner Cv 8.75%	7227	4.51
85		Occidental Petro Cv Pfd $3.875	4590	2.86
101		AMR Cl A Cv Pfd $3.00	4573	2.85
11300	10-12-13	Fremont General Cv 0%	3899	2.43
3350	01-15-03	Pennzoil Cv 6.5%	3717	2.32
4500	03-01-01	Hanson America Cv 2.39%	3358	2.09
8525	02-15-09	Fidelity National Finl Cv 0%	3176	1.98
63		Corning Delaware Cv Pfd 6%	3087	1.92
3700	06-15-02	Spanish Broadcasting 7.5%	2960	1.85
2650	05-15-98	Chubb Cv 6%	2716	1.69
3435	01-15-03	CML Group Cv 5.5%	2601	1.62
2450	04-15-11	Kroger Cv 8.25%	2585	1.61
2600	06-01-03	Food Lion Cv 5%	2464	1.54
52		Alexander & Alex Cv Pfd $3.625	2262	1.41
41		Parker & Parsley Cv Pfd 6.25%	2163	1.35
2150	09-15-13	Interface Cv 8%	2123	1.32
6500	10-20-07	Valhi Cv 0%	2096	1.31
2000	08-15-01	Airborne Freight Cv 6.75%	2080	1.30
43		Delta Air Lines Cv Pfd $3.50	2075	1.29
2850	11-01-05	US Home Cv 4.875%	2031	1.27
41		Chiquita Brands Cv Pfd $2.875	1994	1.24
1858	08-01-02	GenCorp Cv 8%	1979	1.23
2300	09-15-03	United Gaming Cv 7.5%	1926	1.20
2000	08-01-00	Re Capital Cv 5.5%	1850	1.15
19		Washington Mutual Cv Pfd $6.00	1791	1.12

Composition % 09-30-94

Cash	8.6	Preferreds	0.0
Stocks	10.6	Convertibles	78.7
Bonds	2.1	Other	0.0

Tax Analysis

	Tax-Adj Historical Return %	% Pretax Return
3 Yr Avg	8.23	68.8
5 Yr Avg	11.46	78.0
10 Yr Avg	---	---

Potential Capital Gain Exposure (% of assets)   -7%

Most Similar Funds in MF500

Pacific Horizon Capital Inc	Fair Fit
Fidelity Contrafund	Fair Fit
Fidelity Convertible Secs	Fair Fit

Coupon Range

	% of Bonds	Rel Obj
0%	9.2	1.08
0% to 6%	28.5	0.85
6% to 7%	15.6	1.05
7% to 8.5%	15.1	1.29
More than 8.5%	6.0	1.10
Not applicable	25.6	0.99

Credit Analysis 09-30-94

% of Bonds

US Govt	0	BB	25
AAA	0	B	40
AA	3	Below B	0
A	12	NR/NA	6
BBB	14		

MainStay Hi-Yield Corp Bond B

Ticker	Load	NAV	Yield	SEC Yield	Assets	Objective
MKHCX	5.00%d	7.44	9.0%	8.92%	1122.1	Corp Hi Yld

MainStay High-Yield Corporate Bond Fund - Class B seeks current income; capital appreciation is a secondary consideration.

The fund invests in a diversified portfolio of domestic and foreign high-yield debt securities rated from BBB to B, or in ones unrated but of comparable quality. Up to 15% of its assets may be invested in securities rated lower than B or of comparable quality. Normally, at least 75% of the fund's assets are invested in corporate debt securities. The fund may invest more than 25% of its assets in U.S. government securities for temporary defensive purposes.

Historical Profile

Return	High
Risk	Low
Rating	★★★★★ Highest

Investment Style History
Fixed Income

Income Rtn % Rank Obj

75 1 90 7 41 39 28 53

Growth of $10,000
- |||| Value of Fund ($000)
- — Value of Index ($000) FB HY
- ▼ Manager Change
- ▽ Partial Manager Change
- ► Mgr Unknown After
- ◄ Mgr Unknown Before

Performance Quartile (Within Objective)

Manager's Investment Style

Management emphasizes free and improving cash flow, on the belief that a high-debt concern needs to maintain suitable cash reserves to pay its debt. The team also demands good prices, and a yield that compensates investors for the level of risk involved. They will hold cash if nothing suits their criteria. Management will overweight slightly what it views as promising sectors.

Fund Manager(s)

Denis Laplaige, since 1991. Birthdate: 08-51.
BBA, Baruch C. 1977 MBA, New York U. 1980
Steven Tananbaum, since 01-90. Birthdate: 06-65.
BA, Vassar C. 1987

Manager Experience	Dates Managed	Invest Obj	Std Dev	+/- Index
Denis Laplaige				
MainStay Total Return B	01/90 - 01/92	B	13.34	6.18

	1983	1984	1985	1986	1987	1988	1989	1990	1991	1992	1993	1994	History
	---	---	---	9.80	8.76	8.79	7.41	5.86	6.75	7.40	7.99	7.44	NAV
	---	---	---	4.99 *	0.20	16.89	-5.04	-7.85	32.27	21.65	21.65	1.50	Total Return %
	---	---	---		-2.56	9.01	-19.58	-16.79	16.27	14.40	11.90	4.41	+/- LB Aggregate
	---	---	---		-6.33	5.46	-5.43	-1.47	-11.48	4.99	2.75	2.47	+/- FB High-Yield
	---	---	---	6.99	10.81	16.55	10.66	13.07	17.08	12.02	11.16	8.38	Income Return %
	---	---	---	-2.00	-10.61	0.34	-15.70	-20.92	15.19	9.63	10.50	-6.88	Capital Return %
	---	---	---		58	21	100	79	23	3	15	11	Total Rtn % Rank All
	---	---	---		72	8	82	39	68	13	19	5	Total Rtn % Rank Obj
	---	---	---	0.69	1.08	1.38	1.00	1.01	0.88	0.75	0.76	0.67	Income $
	---	---	---	0.00	0.00	0.00	0.00	0.00	0.00	0.00	0.17	0.00	Capital Gains $
	---	---	---	1.00	2.10	2.20	2.10	2.10	2.10	1.90	1.70	1.60	Expense Ratio %
	---	---	---	12.00	11.20	12.10	15.30	14.30	14.40	11.00	9.90	8.70	Income Ratio %
	---	---	---		48	437	403	305	214	226	207	190	Turnover Rate %
---	---	---	---	40.7	87.9	129.4	177.3	184.7	296.4	507.7	935.5	1122.1	Net Assets ($mil)

Performance 12-31-94

	1st Qtr	2nd Qtr	3rd Qtr	4th Qtr	Total
1987	4.28	-1.67	-2.52	0.24	0.20
1988	5.75	3.45	3.74	2.99	16.89
1989	1.33	2.72	-2.86	-6.09	-5.04
1990	-2.53	2.75	-6.36	-1.75	-7.85
1991	12.84	3.68	8.95	3.77	32.27
1992	10.31	3.72	4.02	2.20	21.65
1993	6.86	5.01	2.89	5.37	21.65
1994	2.08	-0.90	1.27	-0.94	1.50

Bear Market Performance

Decile Rank (5-year period)

Worst ———————————————— Best

	Worst 3 Mo Period 1985-89	Worst 3 Mo Period 1990-94
MainStay Hi-Yield Corp Bond B	---	-11.40
+/- LB Aggregate	---	-12.14
+/- Best Fit Index : FB HY	---	2.71

Trailing Returns

	Total Return %	+/- LB Aggregate	+/- FB High-Yield	% Rank All	% Rank Obj	Growth of $10,000
3 Mo	-0.94	-1.32	-0.90	43	46	9,906
6 Mo	0.32	-0.67	-1.23	50	24	10,032
1 Yr	1.50	4.41	2.47	11	5	10,150
3 Yr Avg	14.52	9.98	3.36	4	5	15,020
5 Yr Avg	12.86	5.23	-0.22	7	9	18,308
10 Yr Avg	---	---	---	---	---	---
15 Yr Avg	---	---	---	---	---	---

Operations

Address and Telephone	51 Madison Avenue New York, NY 10010 800-522-4202
Advisor	MacKay-Shields Financial
Subadvisor	None
Distributor	NYLife Distributors
States Available	All
Report Grade	C
Income Distrib	Paid Monthly
* Date of Inception	05-01-86
Fiscal Year End	August

Risk Analysis

Time Period	Load-Adj Return %	Risk % Rank [1] All	Obj	Morningstar [2] Return	Morningstar Risk	Morningstar Risk-Adj Rating
1 Yr	-2.23					
3 Yr	14.01	3	2	3.33 [3]	0.23	★★★★★
5 Yr	12.73	41	19	2.16 [3]	0.48	★★★★★
10 Yr						

Average Historical Rating (68 months) 3.2 ★s

[1] 1 = low, 100 = high [2] 1.00 = Hybrid Avg [3] 1.00 = 90-day T-bill return

Other Measures

			Standard LB Agg	Best Fit FB HY
Standard Deviation	4.67	Alpha	10.3	3.0
Mean	13.74	Beta	0.38	1.01
Sharpe Ratio	2.19	R-Squared	11	86

Investment Style

Interest-Rate Stance
Avg Effective Duration	3.9 Yrs
Avg Effective Maturity	7.0 Yrs

Maturity
Short Intm Long

Quality
Avg Credit Quality	B
Avg Weighted Coupon	10.29%
Avg Weighted Price	89.03% of Par

Diversification Value for Portfolio Types

Large Cap: High	Small Cap: Medium	Bond: High	Balanced: High	Diversified: High

Min Initial Purchase	$500 (Addt'l: $50)
Min IRA Purchase	$500 (Addt'l: $50)
Min Auto Invest Plan	$100 (Systematic Inv: $50)

Expenses & Fees

Sales Fees	0.00% front 5.00% deferred 1.00% 12b-1
Management Fee	0.30% flat fee, 0.30%A
3-,5-,10-yr Expense Projections	$83, $111, $199

Portfolio 08-31-94

Amount 000	Date of Maturity	Total Stocks: 34 Total Fixed-Income: 134	Value $000	% Net Assets
40300	06-15-02	Spanish Broadcasting Sys 7.5%	32240	2.96
27000	11-01-04	Flagstar 11.25%	23490	2.15
20625	10-15-03	Affinity Group 11.5%	20625	1.89
18000	11-01-02	Bankers Life Holding 13%	20520	1.88
36250	02-01-01	Marcus Cable 0%	19213	1.76
10969	11-26-05	American Medical Intl 15%	18647	1.71
22500	01-15-04	Greate Bay Funding 10.875%	17100	1.57
29000	07-15-03	Consolidated Hydro 0%	16820	1.54
20660	02-01-02	Claridge Hotel & Casino 11.75%	14462	1.33
28000	07-01-06	Affiliated Newspaper 0%	14280	1.31
14000	08-01-09	Showboat 13%	13790	1.26
14500	03-01-04	Greystone Homes 10.75%	13123	1.20
13500	09-15-01	President Riverboat Casino 13%	12353	1.13
11500	06-15-02	Nuevo Energy 12.5%	12248	1.12
18450	02-01-99	Liggett Group 11.5%	12177	1.12
11250	11-15-02	Newflo 13.25%	11700	1.07
12000	04-01-02	BF Saul REIT 11.625%	11280	1.03
17255	10-01-01	SpectraVision 11.5%	11129	1.02
11625	12-31-00	General Media 10.625%	10986	1.01
9930	12-01-99	Container of America 13.5%	10811	0.99
12000	11-01-03	Boomtown 11.5%	10800	0.99
10053	07-15-04	Jones Intercable 11.5%	10581	0.97
10000	04-15-04	Charter Medical 11.25%	10300	0.94
11	06-01-02	Petro PSC Properties 12.5%	10290	0.94
11000	08-15-97	Computervision 10.875%	10230	0.94

Composition % 11-30-94

Cash	8.0	Preferreds	0.0
Stocks	8.5	Convertibles	3.0
Bonds	80.5	Other	0.0

Tax Analysis

	Tax-Adj Historical Return %	% Pretax Return
3 Yr Avg	10.51	69.7
5 Yr Avg	8.45	60.2
10 Yr Avg	---	---
Potential Capital Gain Exposure (% of assets)		-5%

Most Similar Funds in MF500

Seligman High-Yield Bond A	Strong Fit
Merrill Lynch Corp Hi-Inc A	Strong Fit
Fidelity Adv High-Yield A	Fair Fit

Coupon Range

	% of Bonds	Rel Obj
0%, PIK	11.0	1.48
0% to 11%	22.8	0.46
11% to 13%	51.2	1.53
13% to 14.5%	7.8	1.43
More than 14.5%	2.9	1.79
Not applicable	4.3	1.42

Credit Analysis 10-31-94

% of Bonds

US Govt	0	BB	10
AAA	0	B	78
AA	0	Below B	9
A	1	NR/NA	0
BBB	2		

Morningstar 1995 Mutual Fund 500

MainStay Total Return B

	Ticker	Load	NAV	Yield	SEC Yield	Assets	Objective
	MKTRX	5.00%d	14.76	2.4%	N/A	648.6	Balanced

MainStay Total Return Fund - Class B seeks current income consistent with reasonable opportunity for future growth of capital and income.

The fund may invest in common stocks, convertibles, warrants, and fixed-income securities such as bonds, preferred stocks, money-market instruments, and other debt obligations. Normally, a minimum of 30% of the fund's assets is invested in equities. A minimum of 30% of assets is also invested in high-quality debt securities.

Prior to Nov. 27, 1989, the fund was named MacKay-Shields MainStay Total Return Fund.

Manager's Investment Style

Management has a split personality. On the equity side, management takes an aggressive tack and looks for solid companies that feature above-average and increasing earnings growth, and a stock price with above-average relative strength. Although the team doesn't like P/E ratios that are higher than the companies' growth rates, it will pay up for growth. On the bond side, high-quality corporates and government securities are favored, with interest-rate risk kept to a minimum.

Fund Manager(s)

Ravi Akhoury, since 12-87.
Edmund C. Spelman, since 02-91.
Rudy Carryl, since 08-92.

Manager Experience	Dates Managed	Invest Obj	Std Dev	+/- Index
Ravi Akhoury				
MainStay Hi-Yld Corp Bd B	05/86 - 01/91	CY	6.27	-7.77
Edmund C. Spelman				
MainStay Inst Gr Eq Inst	02/91 - 12/94	G	18.78	3.63

Performance 12-31-94

	1st Qtr	2nd Qtr	3rd Qtr	4th Qtr	Total
1987	---	---	---	---	0.50 *
1988	3.11	1.73	0.72	1.90	7.65
1989	2.33	6.71	6.31	-0.95	14.98
1990	-0.98	8.28	-7.43	5.85	5.06
1991	13.30	-1.80	12.99	8.85	36.84
1992	-2.34	-4.93	2.09	9.33	3.62
1993	2.19	2.17	5.54	0.27	10.50
1994	-1.89	-4.16	5.22	-1.36	-2.41

Bear Market Performance

Decile Rank (5-year period)

Worst — Best

	Worst 3 Mo Period 1985-89	Worst 3 Mo Period 1990-94
MainStay Total Return B	---	-7.43
+/- S&P 500	---	6.31
+/- Best Fit Index : Wil 4500	---	10.80

Trailing Returns

	Total Return %	+/- S&P 500	+/- LB Aggregate	% Rank All	% Rank Obj	Growth of $10,000
3 Mo	-1.36	-1.34	-1.73	53	65	9,864
6 Mo	3.79	-1.07	2.80	16	8	10,379
1 Yr	-2.41	-3.72	0.51	38	47	9,759
3 Yr Avg	3.77	-2.50	-0.78	74	70	11,174
5 Yr Avg	9.94	1.25	2.32	17	11	16,064
10 Yr Avg	---	---	---	---	---	---
15 Yr Avg	---	---	---	---	---	---

Operations

Address and Telephone	51 Madison Avenue
	New York, NY 10010
	800-522-4202
Advisor	MacKay-Shields Financial
Subadvisor	None
Distributor	NYLife Distributors
States Available	All
Report Grade	C
Income Distrib	Paid Quarterly
* Date of Inception	12-29-87
Fiscal Year End	August

Historical Profile

Return	Average
Risk	Average
Rating	★★★ Neutral

Investment Style History
Equity
Average % Stocks Held in Portfolio

Growth of $10,000
|||| Value of Fund ($000)
— Value of Index ($000) Wil 4500
▼ Manager Change
▽ Partial Manager Change
◄ Mgr Unknown After
◄ Mgr Unknown Before

Performance Quartile (Within Objective)

Portfolio % Held: 34% 47% 43% 57% 47% 48% 59%

	1983	1984	1985	1986	1987	1988	1989	1990	1991	1992	1993	1994	History
	---	---	---	---	10.05	10.42	11.13	11.39	14.44	14.50	15.49	14.76	NAV
	---	---	---	---	0.50 *	7.65	14.98	5.06	36.84	3.62	10.50	-2.41	Total Return %
	---	---	---	---	-0.82 *	-8.96	-16.70	8.18	6.35	-4.00	0.44	-3.72	+/- S&P 500
	---	---	---	---	-0.23	0.44	-3.89	20.84	-3.62	0.75	0.51	+/- LB Aggregate
	---	---	---	---	0.00	3.04	3.71	2.72	1.68	1.58	2.68	2.31	Income Return %
	---	---	---	---	0.50	4.60	11.28	2.34	35.16	2.04	7.82	-4.71	Capital Return %
	---	---	---	---		76	47	43	17	82	63	38	Total Rtn % Rank All
	---	---	---	---		86	75	11	17	81	56	47	Total Rtn % Rank Obj
	---	---	---	---	0.00	0.30	0.39	0.30	0.21	0.22	0.38	0.36	Income $
	---	---	---	---	0.00	0.09	0.45	0.00	0.83	0.23	0.13	0.00	Capital Gains $
	---	---	---	---		3.40	2.80	2.40	2.40	2.00	1.80	1.70	Expense Ratio %
	---	---	---	---		3.00	3.60	2.80	2.10	1.70	2.40	2.50	Income Ratio %
	---	---	---	---			271	171	213	316	340	273	Turnover Rate %
	---	---	---	---	5.0	12.7	28.2	57.0	164.9	367.3	554.0	648.6	Net Assets ($mil)

Risk Analysis

Time Period	Load-Adj Return %	Risk % Rank [1] All	Obj	Morningstar [2] Return	Morningstar Risk	Morningstar Risk-Adj Rating
1 Yr	-6.22					
3 Yr	3.15	74	91	-0.13 [3]	1.12	★★
5 Yr	9.81	60	87	1.30 [3]	0.97	★★★★
10 Yr	---	---	---	---	---	---

Average Historical Rating (49 months)   3.8 ★s

[1] 1 = low, 100 = high   [2] 1.00 = Hybrid Avg   [3] 1.00 = 90-day T-bill return

Other Measures

		Standard S&P 500	Best Fit Wil 4500
Standard Deviation	8.30	Alpha	-1.6	-2.9
Mean	4.05	Beta	0.74	0.81
Sharpe Ratio	0.06	R-Squared	51	90

Investment Style

Stocks	Port Avg	Rel S&P 500
Price/Earnings Ratio	18.8	1.02
Price/Book Ratio	3.9	1.16
5 Yr Earnings Gr %	29.5	5.32
Med Mkt Cap ($mil)	3226	0.25

Bonds	
Avg Effective Duration	5.1 Yrs
Avg Effective Maturity	10.7 Yrs
Avg Credit Quality	AAA
Avg Weighted Coupon	7.21%

Diversification Value for Portfolio Types

Large Cap: Low	Small Cap: Low	Bond: High	Balanced: Low	Diversified: Low

Portfolio 08-31-94

Total Stocks: 78
Total Fixed-Income: 47

Share Chg (03-94)000	Amount 000		Date of Maturity	Value $000	% Net Assets
	29160	US Treasury Bond 6.25%	08-15-23	24741	3.87
	22800	US Treasury Note 4.25%	12-31-95	22369	3.50
	20555	US Treasury Note 8%	01-15-97	21332	3.34
	17945	US Treasury Note 6.25%	02-15-03	16944	2.65
	15675	GNMA TBA 8.5%		15900	2.49
	15100	US Treasury Note 8.125%	02-15-98	15820	2.47
2	170	3Com		11379	1.78
	7775	US Treasury Bond 12%	08-15-13	10762	1.68
	10385	FNMA 8%	10-01-99	10622	1.66
	10187	FHLMC 7%	07-01-24	9634	1.51
	8460	GNMA TBA 6.5%		8037	1.26
28	124	Telefonos de Mexico L (ADR)		7776	1.22
122	232	Green Tree Financial		7772	1.22
34	112	Intel		7364	1.15
34	140	United HealthCare		7315	1.14
22	76	American International Group		7144	1.12
99	197	Lowe's		7117	1.11
54	163	US Healthcare		7054	1.10
0	88	First Interstate Bancorp		6989	1.09
23	173	Computer Associates Intl		6942	1.09

Index Allocation

	% of Stocks
S&P 500	42.0
S&P MidCap 400	19.9
U.S. Small Cap	31.0
Foreign	7.1

Composition % 11-14-94

Cash	5.0	Preferreds	0.0
Stocks	52.0	Convertibles	0.0
Bonds	43.0	Other	0.0

Tax Analysis

	Tax-Adj Historical Return %	% Pretax Return
3 Yr Avg	2.73	71.6
5 Yr Avg	8.67	85.0
10 Yr Avg	---	---

Potential Capital Gain Exposure
(% of assets)   5%

Most Similar Funds in MF500

Gabelli Growth	Strong Fit
IDS New Dimensions	Fair Fit
PIMCo Adv Growth C	Fair Fit

Bond Credit Analysis 09-30-94
% of Bonds

US Govt	81	BB	0
AAA	13	B	0
AA	3	Below B	0
A	3	NR/NA	0
BBB	0		

Stock Sector Weightings

	% of Stocks	Relative S&P 500
Utilities	2.2	0.18
Energy	0.0	0.00
Financials	16.9	1.60
Industrial Cyclicals	6.5	0.39
Consumer Durables	3.0	0.48
Consumer Staples	0.3	0.02
Services	14.5	1.78
Retail	11.4	1.96
Health	20.2	2.33
Technology	25.1	2.74

Min Initial Purchase / Expenses & Fees

Min Initial Purchase	$500 (Addt'l: $50)
Min IRA Purchase	$500 (Addt'l: $50)
Min Auto Invest Plan	$100 (Systematic Inv: $50)

Expenses & Fees

Sales Fees	0.00% front
	5.00% deferred
	1.00% 12b-1
Management Fee	0.32% flat fee, 0.32%A
3-,5-,10-yr Expense Projections	$87, $118, $212
Annual Brokerage Cost	0.10%

MainStay Value B

	Ticker	Load	NAV	Yield	SEC Yield	Assets	Objective
	MKVAX	5.00%d	14.66	0.6%	N/A	472.0	Growth/Inc.

MainStay Value Fund - Class B seeks long-term total return from capital growth and income.

The fund follows a flexible investment policy emphasizing common stocks that are undervalued at the time of purchase. It may also invest in other equity securities, U.S. government securities, and cash equivalents. To select issues, management considers price/book ratios, estimated liquidating value, and projected cash flow in assessing relative value. Growth rates and earnings forecasts are of lesser significance. The fund liquidates securities that management believes are fully valued.

Prior to Nov. 27, 1989, the fund was named MacKay-Shields MainStay Value Fund.

Manager's Investment Style

Management looks at the 20% of firms that are selling the cheapest compared with earnings or cash flow, then focuses specifically on companies with high and reliable free cash flow. It then looks for two of six catalysts that might propel the stock to gains. These catalysts include stock prices that are at 50% discounts to free market value, restructuring events, share repurchases, management ownership, exceptionally high free cash flow, and improved earnings estimates.

Fund Manager(s)

Denis Laplaige, since 01-88.
Thomas Kolefas CFA(1991), since 01-91.
Jeff Simon, since 12-93.

Manager Experience	Dates Managed	Invest Obj	Std Dev	+/- Index
Denis Laplaige				
MainStay Total Return B	01/90 - 01/92	B	13.34	6.18
Thomas Kolefas				
MainStay Inst Val Eq Inst	01/91 - 12/94	GI	11.36	6.26

Performance 12-31-94

	1st Qtr	2nd Qtr	3rd Qtr	4th Qtr	Total
1987	18.49	0.84	4.17	-21.73	-2.57
1988	7.06	1.91	3.97	2.36	16.11
1989	10.82	4.16	8.65	-3.20	21.41
1990	-1.69	2.95	-11.17	4.50	-6.05
1991	17.98	2.17	8.73	7.78	41.26
1992	7.76	-1.14	0.69	11.42	19.52
1993	6.03	0.95	5.36	0.69	13.55
1994	-0.06	0.14	4.22	-4.33	-0.22

Bear Market Performance

Decile Rank (5-year period)

	Worst 3 Mo Period 1985-89	Worst 3 Mo Period 1990-94
MainStay Value B	---	-11.70
+/- S&P 500	---	2.14
+/- Best Fit Index : Russ 2000	---	14.19

Trailing Returns

	Total Return %	+/- S&P 500	+/- Wil 5000	% Rank All	% Rank Obj	Growth of $10,000
3 Mo	-4.33	-4.31	-3.56	90	94	9,567
6 Mo	-0.29	-5.15	-4.91	62	91	9,971
1 Yr	-0.22	-1.53	-0.15	21	44	9,978
3 Yr Avg	10.64	4.37	4.02	11	10	13,542
5 Yr Avg	12.44	3.75	3.62	8	4	17,972
10 Yr Avg	---	---	---	---	---	---
15 Yr Avg	---	---	---	---	---	---

Operations

Address and Telephone	51 Madison Avenue
	New York, NY 10010
	800-522-4202
Advisor	MacKay-Shields Financial
Subadvisor	None
Distributor	NYLife Distributors
States Available	All
Report Grade	C
Income Distrib	Paid Quarterly
*Date of Inception	05-01-86
Fiscal Year End	August

Historical Profile

Return	Above Average
Risk	Below Average
Rating	★★★★
	Above Average

92% 88% 83% 76% 91% 81% 86% 90%

Performance Quartile (Within Objective)

	1983	1984	1985	1986	1987	1988	1989	1990	1991	1992	1993	1994	History
	---	---	---	9.03	8.75	9.99	11.25	10.26	13.02	14.19	15.40	14.66	NAV
	---	---	---	-9.51 *	-2.57	16.11	21.41	-6.05	41.26	19.52	13.55	-0.22	Total Return %
	---	---	---	-14.86 *	-7.83	-0.50	-10.28	-2.93	10.77	11.90	3.49	-1.53	+/- S&P 500
	---	---	---		-4.93	-1.83	-7.77	0.14	7.05	10.55	2.27	-0.15	+/- Wilshire 5000
	---	---	---	0.19	0.00	1.94	1.27	1.31	1.83	0.38	0.41	0.55	Income Return %
	---	---	---	-9.70	-2.57	14.17	20.13	-7.35	39.43	19.14	13.14	-0.77	Capital Return %
	---	---	---		78	24	33	74	13	5	36	21	Total Rtn % Rank All
	---	---	---		83	46	67	69	6	4	31	44	Total Rtn % Rank Obj
	---	---	---	0.02	0.00	0.16	0.14	0.15	0.21	0.05	0.06	0.09	Income $
	---	---	---	0.00	0.05	0.00	0.73	0.16	1.12	1.29	0.64	0.62	Capital Gains $
	---	---	---	2.90	3.30	2.90	2.80	2.60	2.40	1.90	1.90	1.90	Expense Ratio %
	---	---	---	0.10	-1.10	0.90	1.70	2.20	1.20	0.80	0.50	0.50	Income Ratio %
	---	---	---		41	88	107	117	150	145	77	53	Turnover Rate %
	---	---	---	10.5	16.8	18.1	28.5	32.0	50.3	102.3	310.2	472.0	Net Assets ($mil)

Investment Style History Equity

Average % Stocks Held in Portfolio

Growth of $10,000

- IIII Value of Fund ($000)
- — Value of Index ($000) Russ 2000
- ▼ Manager Change
- ▽ Partial Manager Change
- ► Mgr Unknown After
- ◄ Mgr Unknown Before

Risk Analysis

Time Period	Load-Adj Return %	Risk % Rank [1] All	Obj	Morningstar [2] Return	Risk	Morningstar Risk-Adj Rating
1 Yr	-4.03					
3 Yr	10.09	57	19	2.00 [3]	0.62	★★★★
5 Yr	12.31	59	24	2.03 [3]	0.71	★★★★
10 Yr	---					

Average Historical Rating (68 months)   3.6 ★s

[1] 1 = low, 100 = high   [2] 1.00 = Equity Avg   [3] 1.00 = 90-day T-bill return

Other Measures

	Standard S&P 500	Best Fit Russ 2000
Standard Deviation	8.52	
Mean	10.51	
Sharpe Ratio	0.82	
Alpha	4.9	1.9
Beta	0.74	0.64
R-Squared	48	78

Investment Style

	Stock Portfolio Avg	Relative S&P 500
Price/Earnings Ratio	16.4	0.89
Price/Book Ratio	2.3	0.67
5 Yr Earnings Gr %	5.6	1.00
Return on Assets %	4.8	0.64
Debt % Total Cap	38.4	1.36
Med Mkt Cap ($mil)	3113	0.24

Style Value Blend Growth / Size Large Med Small

Diversification Value for Portfolio Types

Large Cap: Medium	Small Cap: Low	Bond: High	Balanced: Low	Diversified: Medium

Portfolio 08-31-94

Total Stocks: 91
Total Fixed-Income: 1

Share Chg (02-94)000	Amount 000		Value $000	% Net Assets
210	430	Occidental Petroleum	9568	2.13
236	236	IMC Global	9486	2.11
28	141	FMC	8243	1.83
21	98	Warner-Lambert	8195	1.82
35	131	Philip Morris	7991	1.78
75	165	Weyerhaeuser	7569	1.68
30	62	McDonnell Douglas	7332	1.63
35	203	American Brands	7297	1.62
17	151	Sears Roebuck	7154	1.59
0	219	Seagram	7101	1.58
138	138	Martin Marietta	7021	1.56
87	87	Lockheed	6851	1.52
22	119	MAPCO	6813	1.51
43	90	Chubb	6593	1.47
0	347	MacFrugals Bargains	6544	1.45
97	290	Chicago & North West Transp	6384	1.42
24	115	SAFECO	6282	1.40
142	274	Tidewater	6199	1.38
74	183	Providian	6140	1.37
30	152	SLMA	5860	1.30
172	172	Chesapeake	5709	1.27
121	242	Dial	5687	1.26
0	104	Anheuser-Busch	5684	1.26
170	170	Rayonier	5661	1.26
8	68	First Interstate Bancorp	5432	1.21

Composition % 12-31-94

Cash	5.0	Preferreds	0.3
Stocks	94.7	Convertibles	0.0
Bonds	0.0	Other	0.0

Tax Analysis

	Tax-Adj Historical Return %	% Pretax Return
3 Yr Avg	8.77	81.0
5 Yr Avg	10.49	81.1
10 Yr Avg	---	---
Potential Capital Gain Exposure (% of assets)		-1%

Most Similar Funds in MF500

Neuberger&Berman Partners	Fair Fit
Fidelity Stock Selector	Fair Fit
Vanguard Index Extended Mkt	Fair Fit

Index Allocation

	% of Stocks
S&P 500	60.6
S&P MidCap 400	19.4
U.S. Small Cap	16.8
Foreign	5.0

Sector Weightings

	% of Stocks	Relative S&P 500
Utilities	1.9	0.15
Energy	15.7	1.55
Financials	13.4	1.27
Industrial Cyclicals	23.7	1.44
Consumer Durables	4.4	0.71
Consumer Staples	11.1	0.88
Services	9.4	1.16
Retail	12.6	2.16
Health	4.4	0.51
Technology	3.5	0.38

Expenses & Fees

Sales Fees	0.00% front
	5.00% deferred
	1.00% 12b-1
Management Fee	0.36% max./0.25% min., 0.36%A
3-,5-,10-yr Expense Projections	$89, $121, $220
Annual Brokerage Cost	0.41%

Min Purchases

Min Initial Purchase	$500 (Addt'l: $50)
Min IRA Purchase	$500 (Addt'l: $50)
Min Auto Invest Plan	$100 (Systematic Inv: $50)

MORNINGSTAR 1995 Mutual Fund 500

Malaysia Fund

	Ticker	NAV	Mkt Price	Prem/Disc	Yield	Objective
	MF	$18.61	$17.38	-6.6%	0.0%	Pacific/Asia

Malaysia Fund seeks long-term capital appreciation.

The fund invests at least 80% of assets in Malaysian equities. The balance may be in Malaysian debt securities and/or money-market instruments.

The fund has been granted concessions by the Malaysian government that allow an exemption from tax on income derived from Malaysia (an exemption not generally available to foreign investors). The exemption expires Nov. 1, 1995.

The board will consider measures to narrow the fund's discount, such as repurchasing shares or open-ending the fund, if the fund trades at a substantial discount for any fiscal quarter.

In October 1993, the fund raised approximately $43 million in an oversubscribed rights offering.

Manager's Investment Style

Management takes a sector-based approach to the market, moving in and out of industries that hold promise. In the past, for example, management has beefed up its real-estate holdings to play the increased wealth among Malaysians, and has focused on cyclicals to profit from a booming economy. If the market seems headed for a correction, management is also willing to raise cash as a cushion.

Fund Manager(s)

Joseph Tern. Since 2-92. BA National U. of Singapore.

Manager Experience

	Dates Managed	Invest Obj	Std Dev	+/- Index
Not available.

NAV Performance % 12-30-94

	1st Qtr	2nd Qtr	3rd Qtr	4th Qtr	Total
1987	---	-0.81*	-3.70	-29.01	-32.20*
1988	4.85	22.37	-7.88	4.34	23.32
1989	10.36	11.71	10.75	13.22	54.58
1990	1.89	1.64	-18.72	9.15	-8.13
1991	12.14	5.73	-15.66	9.54	9.54
1992	10.41	1.67	2.96	3.90	20.07
1993	3.30	18.30	22.49	38.67	107.57
1994	-28.88	6.38	18.29	-14.74	-23.70

Bear Market Performance

Decile Rank (5-year period)

	Worst 3 Mo Period 1985-89	Worst 3 Mo Period 1990-94
Malaysia Fund	---	-28.88
+/- S&P 500	---	-25.10

Trailing Returns

	NAV Total Return %	+/- S&P 500	+/- MSCI Malaysia	% Rank All	% Rank Obj	Mkt Total Return %
3 Mo	-14.74	-14.72	-1.18	98	85	-19.33
6 Mo	0.85	-4.01	2.80	29	36	-4.48
1 Yr	-23.70	-25.01	-2.97	96	76	-30.49
3 Yr Avg	23.89	17.63	0.02	4	26	26.98
5 Yr Avg	13.86	5.17	1.82	8	30	5.59
Incept Avg	12.55*	---	---	---	---	10.49*

Operations

Address and Telephone	126 High St.
	Boston, MA 02110
	617-557-8000 / 212-296-7200
Advisor	Morgan Stanley Asset Management
Subadvisor	Arab-Malaysian Consultant Sdn Bhd
Administrator	United States Trust Co. New York
Transfer Agent	First National Bank of Boston
Custodian	Citibank N.A.
Auditor	Price Waterhouse LLP
Legal Counsel	Sullivan & Cromwell

Income Distrib Schedule	Paid Irregularly
Management Fee	0.90%, 0.20%A
Reinvestment Plan	Yes
Direct Purchase Plan	Yes
Shares Outstanding	7,262,922
Exchange	NYSE
*Date of Inception	05-04-87
Shareholder Report	B

Historical Profile

Return Above Average
Risk Above Average
Rating ★★★★ Above Average

40.8	-5.3	36.2	66.9	12.3	-0.1	15.0	17.4	Highest Prem/Disc
-30.9	-23.0	-25.6	-8.6	-17.1	-16.9	-8.7	-9.7	Lowest Prem/Disc

Growth of $10,000
■ at NAV ($000)
— at Market Price ($000)

Premium Discount %

1983	1984	1985	1986	1987	1988	1989	1990	1991	1992	1993	1994	History
---	---	---	---	7.42	8.98	13.77	12.44	13.55	16.27	27.32	18.61	NAV
---	---	---	---	-32.20*	23.32	54.58	-8.13	9.54	20.07	107.57	-23.70	NAV Total Return %
---	---	---	---	-19.41*	6.71	22.89	-5.01	-20.95	12.46	97.51	-25.01	+/- S&P 500
---	---	---	---	---	-4.95	44.04	15.32	-2.59	32.25	75.01	-31.47	+/- MSCI EAFE
---	---	---	---	---	-0.54	1.97	1.74	6.46	4.40	0.31	-2.97	+/- MSCI Malaysia
---	---	---	---	1.32*	2.29	1.24	1.53	0.62	0.00	1.16	0.00	Income Return %
---	---	---	---	-33.51*	21.02	53.34	-9.66	8.92	20.07	106.41	-23.70	Capital Return %
---	---	---	---	---	13	5	76	86	6	1	96	Total Rtn % Rank All
---	---	---	---	---	50	37	20	73	20	1	76	Total Rtn % Rank Obj
---	---	---	---	-49.01*	27.37	152.02	-38.31	3.88	38.30	113.00	-30.49	Market Total Rtn %
---	---	---	---	7.4	-14.4	-2.2	10.5	-4.1	-9.7	1.3	0.4	Avg Prem/Disc %
---	---	---	---	0.15	0.17	0.11	0.21	0.07	0.00	0.18	0.00	Income $
---	---	---	---	0.00	0.00	0.00	0.00	0.00	0.00	2.83	1.91	Capital Gains $
---	---	---	---	1.80	2.29	1.95	1.93	1.70	1.72	1.60	1.29	Expense Ratio %
---	---	---	---	2.43	2.30	0.88	1.07	0.77	0.86	0.14	0.33	Income Ratio %
---	---	---	---	5	14	30	18	15	38	43	---	Turnover Rate %
---	---	---	---	53.9	201.0	99.9	90.4	98.3	118.2	265.4	180.9	Net Assets ($mil)

Risk Analysis

	Risk % Rank[1] All	Risk % Rank[1] Obj	Morningstar[2] Return	Morningstar[2] Risk	Morningstar Risk-Adj Rating
3 Yr	91	40	3.15	1.21	★★★★
5 Yr	92	40	1.90	1.23	★★★★
10 Yr					

Average Historical Rating (56 months) 3.5 ★s

[1] 1 = Low, 100 = High [2] 1.00 = Equity Avg [3] 1.00 = 90-day T-bill Return

Other Measures

			S&P 500
Standard Deviation	28.72	Alpha	22.27
Mean	25.72	Beta	0.67
Sharpe Ratio	0.77	R-Squared	3

Investment Style

	Stock Portfolio Avg	Rel WS Malaysia	Rel WS Foreign
Price/Earnings Ratio	51.4	1.22	1.04
Price/Cash Flow Ratio	23.3	1.13	1.60
Price/Book Ratio	5.8	1.18	1.92
5 Yr Earnings Gr %	32.9	1.29	NMF
Return on Assets %	12.2	1.09	2.64
Debt % Total Cap	8.6	0.86	0.27
Med Mkt Cap ($mil)	2525	1.39	0.40

figure is based on less than 50% of stocks

Country Exposure (top five) 12-31-94

	Securities %		Currency %
Malaysia	92	Malaysia	100

Diversification Value for Portfolio Types

Large Cap: High	Small Cap: High	Bond: High	Balanced: High	Diversified: High

Portfolio 09-30-94

Total Equity: 49
Total Fixed-Income: 0

Share Chg (06-94)	Amount		Value $000	% Total Invest
658000	1974000	Genting	17711	7.53
0	2354100	Malayan Banking	15703	6.67
0	1798000	Telekom Malaysia	14098	5.99
0	2418000	United Engineers (Malaysia)	13583	5.77
0	2106666	Resorts World	13313	5.66
0	2111000	Tenaga Nasional	11117	4.73
0	2126000	Tanjong	9455	4.02
-152131	1365199	Hong Leong Credit	8627	3.67
400000	1985000	Technology Resources	8131	3.46
50000	2712000	Sime Darby (Malaysia)	7829	3.33
770000	5120000	Renong	7749	3.29
0	5900000	Promet	7411	3.15
0	2091000	Time Engineering	6852	2.91
250000	2790000	Malaysian Resources	6421	2.73
0	925000	Rothmans Pall Mall Malaysia	6134	2.61
0	2688333	Public Bank (For)	6082	2.59
658000	1732000	Uniphone Telecommunications	4797	2.04
0	1700000	Development & Commercial Bank	4576	1.94
333000	1332000	Malaysian Intl Shipping	4443	1.89
1368328	1368328	Lingui Developments	4243	1.80
410000	906000	Land & General	4170	1.77
401000	902000	Ekran	4152	1.76
100000	1200000	Diversified Resources	4096	1.74
0	916500	TH Loy Industries	3718	1.58
420400	420400	Aokam Perdana Cl A	3313	1.41

Composition % 12-31-94

Cash	7.8	Preferreds	0.0
Stocks	92.1	Convertibles	0.0
Bonds	0.0	Other	0.1

Tax Analysis

	Tax-Adj Historical Return %	% Pretax Return
3 Yr Avg	22.11	80.0
5 Yr Avg	12.71	78.8
10 Yr Avg	---	---

Potential Capital Gain Exposure (% of assets) 28

Most Similar Funds in MF500

T. Rowe Price New Asia	Weak Fit
Asia Pacific	Weak Fit
Newport Tiger	Weak Fit

Sector Weightings

	% of Stocks
Utilities	17.1
Energy	0.5
Financials	25.1
Industrial Cyclicals	14.8
Consumer Durables	7.7
Consumer Staples	2.9
Services	32.0
Retail	0.0
Health	0.0
Technology	0.0

Massachusetts Investors A

	Ticker	Load	NAV	Yield	SEC Yield	Assets	Objective
	MITTX	5.75%	10.07	2.2%	1.84%	1535.2	Growth/Inc.

Massachusetts Investors Trust - Class A seeks current income and long-term growth of capital and income.

The fund invests primarily in common stocks and convertible securities, emphasizing securities that management considers to be of high or improving quality. The fund may invest up to 35% of its assets in foreign securities; this limit does not apply to American Depositary Receipts. A portion of the fund's assets may be held in debt securities and cash equivalents.

Class A shares have front loads and lower 12b-1 fees; Class B shares have deferred loads and conversion features.

Manager's Investment Style

Management divides the fund's assets among three portfolio-manager-team members, who each invest seperately. Each manager is required to invest in stocks above $2 billion in market cap and with a minimum of 10% annual dividend growth. Typically, management focuses on large-cap issues with a mild growth bent.

Fund Manager(s)

John D. Laupheimer, Jr. CFA(1984), since 01-92.
Kevin R. Parke, since 12-91.
Mitchell D. Dynan CFA, since 01-95.

Manager Experience	Dates Managed	Invest Obj	Std Dev	+/- Index
Kevin R. Parke				
MFS Capital Growth B	03/88 - 12/94	G	11.88	-1.83

Historical Profile

Return	Average
Risk	Below Average
Rating	★★★
	Neutral

95% 87% 90% 86% 89% 87% 89% 91%

Investment Style History
Equity
Average % Stocks Held in Portfolio

Growth of $10,000
- Value of Fund ($000)
- Value of Index ($000) S&P 500
- ▼ Manager Change
- ▽ Partial Manager Change
- ► Mgr Unknown After
- ◄ Mgr Unknown Before

Performance Quartile
(Within Objective)

1983	1984	1985	1986	1987	1988	1989	1990	1991	1992	1993	1994	History
11.61	11.02	12.12	12.09	11.26	11.22	13.55	12.28	13.87	12.31	11.50	10.07	NAV
20.88	2.94	24.56	17.21	7.47	10.38	36.12	-0.10	27.67	7.38	10.03	-1.02	Total Return %
-1.58	-3.33	-7.18	-1.47	2.21	-6.23	4.44	3.02	-2.82	-0.23	-0.03	-2.33	+/- S&P 500
-2.58	-0.11	-8.00	1.11	5.10	-7.56	6.95	6.08	-6.54	-1.59	-1.25	-0.95	+/- Wilshire 5000
3.89	4.21	4.21	3.07	2.83	3.45	3.71	3.29	2.99	2.60	3.19	2.24	Income Return %
17.00	-1.27	20.35	14.13	4.64	6.93	32.41	-3.39	24.67	4.79	6.84	-3.26	Capital Return %
37	57	47	38	15	59	6	56	31	53	66	27	Total Rtn % Rank All
51	53	74	44	15	76	2	19	55	50	51	54	Total Rtn % Rank Obj
0.47	0.46	0.46	0.40	0.40	0.39	0.45	0.43	0.39	0.34	0.39	0.25	Income $
1.26	0.45	1.08	1.75	1.39	0.81	1.23	0.82	1.35	2.23	1.67	1.07	Capital Gains $
0.53	0.56	0.55	0.49	0.45	0.55	0.50	0.47	0.62	0.62	0.68	0.69	Expense Ratio %
3.69	4.18	3.91	2.99	2.63	3.39	3.40	3.28	2.73	2.30	3.04	2.18	Income Ratio %
25	21	33	26	23	19	20	26	44	46	41	---	Turnover Rate %
1123.9	1049.4	1155.4	1187.2	1081.3	1083.7	1421.9	1265.7	1530.3	1546.4	1626.1	1535.2	Net Assets ($mil)

Performance 12-31-94

	1st Qtr	2nd Qtr	3rd Qtr	4th Qtr	Total
1987	21.96	5.46	8.66	-23.11	7.47
1988	2.35	5.64	0.42	1.66	10.38
1989	7.49	9.19	13.07	2.58	36.12
1990	-2.73	8.68	-12.23	7.67	-0.10
1991	11.85	-0.46	5.55	8.64	27.67
1992	-3.98	1.87	4.46	5.10	7.38
1993	4.78	-0.39	3.77	1.58	10.03
1994	-1.83	-0.53	2.72	-1.31	-1.02

Bear Market Performance

Decile Rank (5-year period)

Worst ——————————————— Best

	Worst 3 Mo Period 1985-89	Worst 3 Mo Period 1990-94
Massachusetts Investors A	-29.18	-12.23
+/- S&P 500	0.40	1.52
+/- Best Fit Index : S&P 500	0.40	1.52

Trailing Returns

	Total Return %	+/- S&P 500	+/- Wil 5000	% Rank All	% Rank Obj	Growth of $10,000
3 Mo	-1.31	-1.29	-0.54	52	46	9,869
6 Mo	1.37	-3.49	-3.25	32	69	10,137
1 Yr	-1.02	-2.33	-0.95	27	54	9,898
3 Yr Avg	5.36	-0.91	-1.26	41	60	11,695
5 Yr Avg	8.33	-0.37	-0.49	30	40	14,916
10 Yr Avg	13.40	-0.98	-0.46	22	26	35,163
15 Yr Avg	13.24	-1.24	-0.74	36	46	64,550

Operations

Address and Telephone	500 Boylston Street	Min Initial Purchase	$1000 (Addt'l: $50)
	Boston, MA 02116	Min IRA Purchase	$250 (Addt'l: $50)
	800-637-2929 / 617-954-5000	Min Auto Invest Plan	$50 (Systematic Inv: $50)
Advisor	Massachusetts Financial Services		
Subadvisor	None	**Expenses & Fees**	
Distributor	MFS Financial Services	Sales Fees	5.75% front
States Available	All		0.00% deferred
Report Grade	B		0.50% 12b-1
Income Distrib	Paid Quarterly	Management Fee	0.30% max./0.12% min.+6.67%I
Date of Inception	07-15-24	3-,5-,10-yr Expense Projections	$78, $93, $137
Fiscal Year End	December	Annual Brokerage Cost	0.13%

Risk Analysis

Time Period	Load-Adj Return %	Risk % Rank [1] All	Obj	Morningstar [2] Return	Morningstar Risk	Morningstar Risk-Adj Rating
1 Yr	-6.71					
3 Yr	3.30	70	65	-0.08 [3]	0.78	★★
5 Yr	7.05	64	41	0.56 [3]	0.77	★★★
10 Yr	12.73	58	51	1.01	0.83	★★★
Average Historical Rating (109 months)					3.4	★s

[1] 1 = low, 100 = high   [2] 1.00 = Equity Avg   [3] 1.00 = 90-day T-bill return

Other Measures

				Standard S&P 500	Best Fit S&P 500
Standard Deviation	8.27	Alpha		-0.8	-0.8
Mean	5.57	Beta		1.00	1.00
Sharpe Ratio	0.25	R-Squared		92	92

Investment Style

	Stock Portfolio Avg	Relative S&P 500	Style Value Blend Growth
Price/Earnings Ratio	17.5	0.94	
Price/Book Ratio	3.1	0.91	
5 Yr Earnings Gr %	6.9	1.24	
Return on Assets %	6.3	0.84	
Debt % Total Cap	31.7	1.12	
Med Mkt Cap ($mil)	8789	0.68	

Diversification Value for Portfolio Types

Large Cap: None	Small Cap: Medium	Bond: Medium	Balanced: None	Diversified: Low

Portfolio 06-30-94

Share Chg (12-93) 000	Amount 000	Total Stocks: 146 Total Fixed-Income: 15	Value $000	% Net Assets
264	739	General Electric	34477	2.19
462	739	Chevron	30965	1.97
-21	1148	Norwest	29994	1.90
90	735	May Department Stores	28833	1.83
250	559	Microsoft	28812	1.83
17	423	Deere	28621	1.82
-233	450	Intel	26353	1.67
-9	467	JC Penney	25336	1.61
121	433	EI duPont de Nemours	25297	1.61
-150	350	Gillette	22811	1.45
-6	302	CSX	22772	1.45
-6	336	Warner-Lambert	22154	1.41
-218	263	Mobil	21443	1.36
146	394	Procter & Gamble	21032	1.34
502	551	Columbia/HCA Healthcare	20669	1.31
-66	355	Exxon	20109	1.28
-32	414	Sears Roebuck	19848	1.26
506	506	Banc One	17328	1.10
547	547	ConAgra	16678	1.06
-4	195	FNMA	16248	1.03
103	311	Colgate-Palmolive	16190	1.03
219	467	AlliedSignal	16171	1.03
119	268	NIKE Cl B	15987	1.01
-5	253	FHLMC	15305	0.97
710	710	Sara Lee	15093	0.96

Composition % 12-31-94

Cash	4.5	Preferreds	0.0
Stocks	92.5	Convertibles	3.0
Bonds	0.0	Other	0.0

Tax Analysis

	Tax-Adj Historical Return %	% Pretax Return
3 Yr Avg	0.73	13.0
5 Yr Avg	4.09	45.2
10 Yr Avg	9.09	55.1
Potential Capital Gain Exposure (% of assets)		12%

Most Similar Funds in MF500

Liberty All-Star	Strong Fit
Vanguard Index 500	Strong Fit
Sentinel Common Stock	Strong Fit

Index Allocation

	% of Stocks
S&P 500	84.2
S&P MidCap 400	4.2
U.S. Small Cap	3.9
Foreign	8.7

Sector Weightings

	% of Stocks	Relative S&P 500
Utilities	9.6	0.78
Energy	9.1	0.90
Financials	18.3	1.73
Industrial Cyclicals	13.4	0.82
Consumer Durables	9.3	1.49
Consumer Staples	8.5	0.68
Services	10.1	1.23
Retail	7.6	1.31
Health	8.0	0.92
Technology	6.2	0.68

Merger

	Ticker	Load	NAV	Yield	SEC Yield	Assets	Objective
	MERFX	None	13.17	0.0%	N/A	171.2	Growth

Merger Fund seeks capital appreciation.

The fund normally invests at least 65% of its assets in the equity securities of companies that are the object of a publicly announced acquisition or other reorganization proposals. The fund may, for temporary defensive purposes, invest all or a portion of its assets in cash or cash equivalents.

Prior to Jan. 1989, the fund was known as The Risk Portfolio of the Ayco Fund, and operated under a different charter. Ayco Corporation was the fund's advisor, and Westchester Capital Management and two other subadvisors managed portions of the portfolio.

Historical Profile
Return: Above Average
Risk: Low
Rating: ★★★★ Above Average

Investment Style History
Equity

Average % Stocks Held in Portfolio: 68% 59% 80% 92% 92%

Manager's Investment Style
Management plays the M & A game by focusing on stocks of companies involved in mergers and acquisitions. Management seeks only to earn the difference between the current stock price of a soon-to-be-acquired firm and the per-share price at which the firm is to be bought. Management hedges market risk by shorting the stock of the acquiring firm (many acquirers suffer stock losses). Management particularly likes takeover deals with unusual twists, because they tend to discourage other investors and increase arbitrage spreads. Finally, management prefers stock-swap arrangements, where companies merge for strategic purposes.

Fund Manager(s)
Frederick W. Green, since 01-89. Birthdate: 11-46. BA, Princeton U. 1969

Bonnie L. Smith, since 01-89. Birthdate: 01-48. BA, U. of Rochester 1969

Manager Experience

	Dates Managed	Invest Obj	Std Dev	+/- Index

Not available.

Growth of $10,000
|||| Value of Fund ($000)
— Value of Index ($000) LB L-T
▼ Manager Change
▽ Partial Manager Change
► Mgr Unknown After
◄ Mgr Unknown Before

Performance Quartile (Within Objective)

1983	1984	1985	1986	1987	1988	1989	1990	1991	1992	1993	1994	History
---	---	---	---	---	---	11.49	10.83	11.95	11.95	12.96	13.17	NAV
---	---	---	---	---	---	6.82 *	1.10	16.84	5.34	17.69	7.13	Total Return %
---	---	---	---	---	---	-15.89 *	4.21	-13.65	-2.28	7.63	5.82	+/- S&P 500
---	---	---	---	---	---	---	7.28	-17.37	-3.63	6.41	7.20	+/- Wilshire 5000
---	---	---	---	---	---	9.69	0.47	0.25	0.00	0.00	0.00	Income Return %
---	---	---	---	---	---	-2.87	0.62	16.58	5.34	17.69	7.13	Capital Return %
---	---	---	---	---	---	---	52	51	75	21	3	Total Rtn % Rank All
---	---	---	---	---	---	---	16	97	69	22	5	Total Rtn % Rank Obj
---	---	---	---	---	---	1.13	0.05	0.03	0.00	0.00	0.00	Income $
---	---	---	---	---	---	0.00	0.73	0.68	0.64	1.10	0.71	Capital Gains $
---	---	---	---	---	---	2.80	3.26	3.05	2.75	2.19	1.76	Expense Ratio %
---	---	---	---	---	---	-0.17	-1.20	0.21	-1.42	-0.57	0.11	Income Ratio %
---	---	---	---	---	---	430	357	312	231	186	---	Turnover Rate %
---	---	---	---	---	---	10.5	9.6	10.4	11.6	27.2	171.2	Net Assets ($mil)

Performance 12-31-94

	1st Qtr	2nd Qtr	3rd Qtr	4th Qtr	Total
1987	---	---	---	---	---
1988	---	---	---	---	---
1989	---	2.69	-0.48	0.53	6.82 *
1990	-1.01	3.80	-10.04	9.38	1.10
1991	3.69	4.99	2.63	4.57	16.84
1992	2.26	-1.23	5.05	-0.72	5.34
1993	2.26	5.48	3.82	5.09	17.69
1994	1.00	2.67	3.27	0.03	7.13

Bear Market Performance

Decile Rank (5-year period)

Worst | | | | | | | | Best

	Worst 3 Mo Period 1985-89	Worst 3 Mo Period 1990-94
Merger	---	-10.04
+/- S&P 500	---	3.70
+/- Best Fit Index : LB L-T	---	-7.85

Trailing Returns

	Total Return %	+/- S&P 500	+/- Wil 5000	% Rank All	% Rank Obj	Growth of $10,000
3 Mo	0.03	0.05	0.80	21	21	10,003
6 Mo	3.31	-1.55	-1.32	19	58	10,331
1 Yr	7.13	5.82	7.20	3	5	10,713
3 Yr Avg	9.92	3.66	3.31	13	18	13,282
5 Yr Avg	9.42	0.73	0.61	20	37	15,687
10 Yr Avg	---	---	---	---	---	---
15 Yr Avg	---	---	---	---	---	---

Operations

Address and Telephone	100 Summit Lake Drive Valhalla, NY 10595 800-343-8959 / 914-741-5600	
Advisor	Westchester Capital Management	
Subadvisor	None	
Distributor	Mercer Allied	
States Available	All	
Report Grade	B+	
Income Distrib	Paid Annually	
* Date of Inception	01-31-89	
Fiscal Year End	November	

Risk Analysis

Time Period	Load-Adj Return %	Risk % Rank [1] All	Obj	Morningstar [2] Return	Risk	Morningstar Risk-Adj Rating
1 Yr	7.13					
3 Yr	9.92	5	1	1.95 [3]	0.22	★★★★
5 Yr	9.42	36	1	1.19 [3]	0.32	★★★★
10 Yr	---					
Average Historical Rating (36 months)				3.4 ★s		

[1] 1 = low, 100 = high [2] 1.00 = Equity Avg [3] 1.00 = 90-day T-bill return

Other Measures

	Standard S&P 500		Best Fit LB L-T
Standard Deviation	4.08	Alpha	6.0 5.9
Mean	9.58	Beta	0.06 0.15
Sharpe Ratio	1.48	R-Squared	1 9

Investment Style

	Stock Portfolio Avg	Relative S&P 500	Style Value Blend Growth
Price/Earnings Ratio	19.0#	1.03	
Price/Book Ratio	1.7#	0.50	
5 Yr Earnings Gr %	---	---	
Return on Assets %	3.9#	0.52	
Debt % Total Cap	---	---	
Med Mkt Cap ($mil)	505#	0.04	

figure is based on 50% or less of stocks

Diversification Value for Portfolio Types

Large Cap: High	Small Cap: High	Bond: High	Balanced: High	Diversified: High

Expenses & Fees

Sales Fees	0.00% front
	0.00% deferred
	0.25% 12b-1
Management Fee	1.00% flat fee
3-,5-,10-yr Expense Projections	$69, $119, $254
Annual Brokerage Cost	0.86%

Portfolio 08-31-94

Share Chg (07-94) 000	Amount 000	Total Stocks: 45 Total Fixed-Income: 2	Value $000	% Net Assets
85	85	American Cyanamid	8231	5.93
9	138	McCaw Cellular Comm Cl A	7491	5.40
10	104	Kemper	6423	4.63
20	98	Germantown Savings Bank	6002	4.33
95	241	Syntex	5784	4.17
2	139	Adia Services	5001	3.60
10	48	McKesson	4910	3.54
34	169	Fidelity New York	4573	3.30
0	141	Medical Care America	4165	3.00
44	153	OneComm	4066	2.93
62	62	Intergroup Healthcare	3898	2.81
31	171	PSI Resources	3835	2.76
20	189	Baltimore Bancorp	3802	2.74
110	110	Adobe Systems	3483	2.51
10	141	Metropolitan Financial	3329	2.40
77	103	Central Jersey Bancorp	3283	2.37
41	250	US Facilities	3141	2.26
0	225	Nichols Institute Cl C	2949	2.13
0	53	Kendall International	2893	2.09
0	159	Premier Bancorp (LA)	2709	1.95
60	269	Northeast Federal	2692	1.94
68	68	Arrow Electronics	2592	1.87
251	251	North Canadian Oils	2386	1.72
47	47	BankAmerica	2317	1.67
166	211	LAC Minerals	2316	1.67

Composition % 12-31-94

Cash	5.2	Preferreds	0.0
Stocks	93.8	Convertibles	1.0
Bonds	0.0	Other	0.0

Tax Analysis

	Tax-Adj Historical Return %	% Pretax Return
3 Yr Avg	8.08	80.0
5 Yr Avg	7.49	76.5
10 Yr Avg	---	---
Potential Capital Gain Exposure (% of assets)		0%

Most Similar Funds in MF500

SBSF	Weak Fit
GT Greater Europe	Weak Fit
Templeton Developing Mkts	Weak Fit

Index Allocation

	% of Stocks
S&P 500	1.9
S&P MidCap 400	10.1
U.S. Small Cap	84.2
Foreign	3.8

Sector Weightings

	% of Stocks	Relative S&P 500
Utilities	3.2	0.26
Energy	2.4	0.24
Financials	39.4	3.73
Industrial Cyclicals	4.7	0.29
Consumer Durables	0.0	0.00
Consumer Staples	0.5	0.04
Services	7.4	0.90
Retail	0.0	0.00
Health	27.6	3.18
Technology	14.8	1.61

Min Initial Purchase / Min IRA Purchase / Min Auto Invest Plan

Min Initial Purchase	$2000 (Addt'l: None)
Min IRA Purchase	$2000 (Addt'l: None)
Min Auto Invest Plan	N/A

Meridian

	Ticker	Load	NAV	Yield	SEC Yield	Assets	Objective
	MERDX	None	25.12	0.7%	N/A	256.6	Small Company

Meridian Fund seeks long-term growth of capital. Current income is incidental.

The fund invests primarily in industries and companies experiencing above-average growth in revenues and earnings that operate in a favorable competitive and regulatory climate. It examines economic and political conditions when making a purchase; stock-market cycles are also analyzed. The fund may invest in high-quality corporate debt, preferred stock, or cash vehicles. Up to 25% of assets may be invested in companies with less than three years of operating history.

Manager's Investment Style

Manager Richard Aster blends a growth-oriented, small-cap style with some conservatism: When the market looks shaky, he will hold cash. Sector overweightings may include technology, and healthcare. He also looks for niche-dominating firms in growth industries with high return on equity and sound management. While the overall portfolio shows high price multiples, Aster will not go too far afield in paying for growth.

Fund Manager(s)

Richard F. Aster, Jr., since 08-84. Birthdate: 05-40. BA, U. of California-Santa Barbara 1963 MA, U. of California-Santa Barbara 1965

Manager Experience

	Dates Managed	Invest Obj	Std Dev	+/- Index
Richard F. Aster, Jr.				
Meridian Value	02/94 - 12/94	G	3.67	-4.71

Historical Profile

Return	Above Average
Risk	Above Average
Rating ★★★★	
	Above Average

Historical Profile chart header values: 89% --- 81% 66% 78% 80% 70% 72%

Investment Style History Equity
Average % Stocks Held in Portfolio

Growth of $10,000
- |||| Value of Fund ($000)
- — Value of Index ($000) Wil 4500
- ▼ Manager Change
- ▽ Partial Manager Change
- ► Mgr Unknown After
- ◄ Mgr Unknown Before

Performance Quartile (Within Objective)

	1983	1984	1985	1986	1987	1988	1989	1990	1991	1992	1993	1994	History
	---	10.33	13.01	13.57	11.51	13.59	15.09	14.44	20.75	23.29	25.87	25.12	NAV
	---	3.30 *	27.06	13.12	-7.84	18.07	19.57	3.83	58.02	15.52	13.05	0.55	Total Return %
	---	-7.36 *	-4.68	-5.56	-13.10	1.46	-12.12	6.95	27.53	7.90	3.00	-0.76	+/- S&P 500
	---	---	---	-4.96	1.36	-4.33	-2.47	-4.38	17.39	14.56	3.76	-1.48	3.21	+/- Wilshire 4500
	---	0.00	1.12	8.82	7.34	0.00	3.42	2.54	0.51	0.17	1.27	0.71	Income Return %
	---	3.30	25.94	4.30	-15.18	18.07	16.14	1.29	57.50	15.35	11.78	-0.15	Capital Return %
	---	---	38	67	93	18	36	47	5	9	40	16	Total Rtn % Rank All
	---	---	48	31	74	60	61	7	27	42	67	36	Total Rtn % Rank Obj
	---	0.00	0.10	1.23	1.24	0.00	0.48	0.35	0.09	0.03	0.30	0.17	Income $
	---	0.00	0.00	0.00	0.00	0.00	0.64	0.81	1.70	0.56	0.15	0.70	Capital Gains $
	---	---	2.00	1.91	1.72	1.85	2.01	2.08	1.68	1.75	1.47	1.22	Expense Ratio %
	---	---	2.58	0.80	0.15	-0.59	2.83	0.14	0.98	0.24	-0.01	0.38	Income Ratio %
	---	---	156	75	88	58	62	66	85	61	61	43	Turnover Rate %
	---	1.7	8.1	16.4	11.9	8.8	9.2	9.6	16.9	34.2	160.3	256.6	Net Assets ($mil)

Performance 12-31-94

	1st Qtr	2nd Qtr	3rd Qtr	4th Qtr	Total
1987	15.92	-2.80	9.39	-25.23	-7.84
1988	10.43	7.40	-4.25	3.98	18.07
1989	7.28	9.26	6.65	-4.36	19.57
1990	-0.07	17.51	-17.92	7.73	3.83
1991	21.68	-1.88	11.77	18.41	58.02
1992	-0.48	-8.14	6.82	18.28	15.52
1993	0.30	2.18	10.92	-0.56	13.05
1994	-3.87	-2.41	6.05	1.07	0.55

Bear Market Performance

Decile Rank (5-year period)

Worst — Best

	Worst 3 Mo Period 1985-89	Worst 3 Mo Period 1990-94
Meridian	-36.77	-17.92
+/- S&P 500	-7.19	-4.18
+/- Best Fit Index : Wil 4500	-6.63	0.30

Trailing Returns

	Total Return %	+/- S&P 500	+/- Wil 4500	% Rank All	% Rank Obj	Growth of $10,000
3 Mo	1.07	1.08	3.57	6	25	10,107
6 Mo	7.18	2.32	2.99	7	41	10,718
1 Yr	0.55	-0.76	3.21	16	36	10,055
3 Yr Avg	9.51	3.24	1.90	15	44	13,131
5 Yr Avg	16.59	7.90	7.50	3	17	21,544
10 Yr Avg	14.95	0.57	2.32	11	23	40,288
15 Yr Avg	---	---	---	---	---	---

Operations

Address and Telephone	60 E. Sir Francis Drake Bvd #306 Larkspur, CA 94939 800-446-6662
Advisor	Aster Capital Management
Subadvisor	None
Distributor	Meridian Fund
States Available	Selected states
Report Grade	C
Income Distrib	Paid Annually
* Date of Inception	08-01-84
Fiscal Year End	June

Min Initial Purchase	$1000 (Addt'l: $50)
Min IRA Purchase	$1000 (Addt'l: $50)
Min Auto Invest Plan	$1000 (Systematic Inv: $50)

Expenses & Fees

Sales Fees	0.00% front
	0.00% deferred
	0.00% 12b-1
Management Fee	1.00% max./0.75% min.
3-,5-,10-yr Expense Projections	$39, $67, $148
Annual Brokerage Cost	0.00%

Risk Analysis

Time Period	Load-Adj Return %	Risk % Rank All	Risk % Rank Obj	Morningstar[2] Return	Morningstar Risk	Morningstar Risk-Adj Rating
1 Yr	0.55					
3 Yr	9.51	83	48	1.81[3]	1.01	★★★★
5 Yr	16.59	77	24	3.45[3]	0.93	★★★★★
10 Yr	14.95	87	48	1.48	1.11	★★★★
Average Historical Rating (89 months)					3.3	★s

[1] 1 = low, 100 = high [2] 1.00 = Equity Avg [3] 1.00 = 90-day T-bill return

Other Measures

			Standard S&P 500	Best Fit Wil 4500
Standard Deviation	11.74	Alpha	3.8	1.7
Mean	9.80	Beta	0.89	1.08
Sharpe Ratio	0.53	R-Squared	36	80

Investment Style

	Stock Portfolio Avg	Relative S&P 500
Price/Earnings Ratio	25.8	1.40
Price/Book Ratio	5.1	1.51
5 Yr Earnings Gr %	19.4#	3.50
Return on Assets %	8.4	1.12
Debt % Total Cap	32.6	1.16
Med Mkt Cap ($mil)	551	0.04

figure is based on 50% or less of stocks

Style Value Blend Growth — Size Large/Med/Small

Diversification Value for Portfolio Types

Large Cap: Medium	Small Cap: Low	Bond: High	Balanced: Medium	Diversified: Medium

Portfolio 09-30-94

Share Chg (06-94) 000	Amount 000	Total Stocks: 40 Total Fixed-Income: 0	Value $000	% Net Assets
94	282	Vanguard Cellular Systems A	7403	3.13
18	267	Vivra	7287	3.08
226	250	AirTouch Communications	7156	3.03
26	267	Service International	6875	2.91
19	137	H & R Block	6285	2.66
61	389	Town & Country Trust	6119	2.59
12	240	Watson Pharmaceuticals	6060	2.56
0	114	Cellular Communications Cl A	6026	2.55
6	204	Paging Network	5891	2.49
14	140	Paychex	5285	2.23
0	114	Vishay Intertechnology	5150	2.18
20	290	Systems & Computer Tech	5148	2.18
10	244	Kemet	5124	2.17
24	331	Beverly Enterprises	5089	2.15
0	35	LIN Broadcasting	4869	2.06
46	206	Fingerhut	4736	2.00
36	166	WellPoint Health Networks A	4690	1.98
15	189	Stewart Enterprises Cl A	4678	1.98
15	245	Quorum Health Group	4655	1.97
80	580	Pier 1 Imports	4640	1.96
54	183	Tanger Factory Outlet Center	4575	1.93
58	257	Snyder Oil	4562	1.93
43	353	Sotheby's Holdings Cl A	4546	1.92
0	128	Fritz	4533	1.92
27	185	Factory Stores of America	4533	1.92

Composition % 12-31-94

Cash	29.0	Preferreds	0.0
Stocks	70.6	Convertibles	0.0
Bonds	0.4	Other	0.0

Tax Analysis

	Tax-Adj Historical Return %	% Pretax Return
3 Yr Avg	8.65	90.2
5 Yr Avg	14.94	87.2
10 Yr Avg	12.90	78.1
Potential Capital Gain Exposure (% of assets)		5%

Most Similar Funds in MF500

Warburg Pincus Emerg Gr	Strong Fit
Fidelity Emerging Growth	Fair Fit
Founders Frontier	Fair Fit

Index Allocation

	% of Stocks
S&P 500	15.1
S&P MidCap 400	17.4
U.S. Small Cap	67.4
Foreign	0.0

Sector Weightings

	% of Stocks	Relative S&P 500
Utilities	0.0	0.00
Energy	4.1	0.40
Financials	11.7	1.11
Industrial Cyclicals	0.0	0.00
Consumer Durables	2.9	0.46
Consumer Staples	0.0	0.00
Services	26.8	3.29
Retail	11.6	1.99
Health	15.4	1.78
Technology	27.5	3.00

MORNINGSTAR 1995 Mutual Fund 500

Merrill Lynch Capital A

	Ticker	Load	NAV	Yield	SEC Yield	Assets	Objective
	MACPX	5.25%	25.70	4.2%	N/A	2296.1	Growth/Inc.

Merrill Lynch Capital Fund - Class A seeks total return consistent with prudent risk.

The fund allocates its assets among equities issued by high-quality large-cap companies, debt instruments, and money markets.

Class A shares have front loads and no 12b-1 fees and are designed for institutions and fund employees; Class B shares have deferred loads and conversion features; Class C shares have level loads; Class D shares have front loads and lower 12b-1 fees. Prior to June 1, 1976, the fund was named Lionel D. Edie Capital.

Manager's Investment Style

Management likes value, and in addition tends to hold large stakes in bonds. Its value criteria attends to measures of price and yields of at least 3%. It also looks at quality of management and handling of debt in the companies it evaluates. Management not only uses these screens for its equities, but it also picks out bonds with underlying issuers that pass these tests.

Fund Manager(s)

Ernest S. Watts CFA, since 04-83. Birthdate: 11-32. BS, U. of Maryland 1954

Manager Experience	Dates Managed	Invest Obj	Std Dev	+/- Index
Not available.				

Historical Profile

Return	Average
Risk	Low
Rating	★★★★ Above Average

Average % Stocks Held in Portfolio: 67% 60% 59% 67% 63% 74% 64% 59%

Investment Style History
Equity

Growth of $10,000

||| Value of Fund ($000)
— Value of Index ($000) S&P 500
▼ Manager Change
▽ Partial Manager Change
► Mgr Unknown After
◄ Mgr Unknown Before

Performance Quartile (Within Objective)

1983	1984	1985	1986	1987	1988	1989	1990	1991	1992	1993	1994	History
20.63	19.33	22.57	24.40	19.79	21.39	24.43	22.92	26.92	26.33	27.97	25.70	NAV
23.13	8.66	29.88	19.89	4.60	17.04	22.98	0.69	25.18	5.03	13.71	0.91	Total Return %
0.66	2.39	-1.86	1.21	-0.66	0.43	-8.71	3.80	-5.31	-2.59	3.65	-0.40	+/- S&P 500
-0.34	5.61	-2.69	3.79	2.24	-0.90	-6.20	6.87	-9.03	-3.94	2.43	0.98	+/- Wilshire 5000
3.75	3.81	3.38	1.90	0.95	3.55	5.07	5.33	4.61	3.58	3.65	4.27	Income Return %
19.38	4.84	26.49	17.99	3.66	13.49	17.91	-4.65	20.57	1.44	10.06	-3.36	Capital Return %
30	33	26	20	24	21	29	53	35	76	35	14	Total Rtn % Rank All
38	22	36	23	27	36	54	13	71	81	30	27	Total Rtn % Rank Obj
0.69	0.67	0.66	0.44	0.22	0.73	1.10	1.29	1.02	0.92	0.95	1.13	Income $
0.60	1.99	1.60	2.10	5.76	1.02	0.72	0.39	0.60	0.95	0.95	1.36	Capital Gains $
0.81	0.75	0.69	0.64	0.62	0.60	0.64	0.60	0.58	0.56	0.55	0.53	Expense Ratio %
6.27	4.32	5.05	3.81	3.52	3.57	4.79	4.80	5.13	4.21	3.56	3.52	Income Ratio %
40	101	154	87	109	85	63	85	86	59	55	86	Turnover Rate %
201.0	268.5	366.7	580.4	626.4	645.8	858.0	958.1	1420.1	1869.5	2227.9	2296.1	Net Assets ($mil)

Performance 12-31-94

	1st Qtr	2nd Qtr	3rd Qtr	4th Qtr	Total
1987	14.71	3.05	5.27	-15.94	4.60
1988	7.73	4.97	0.56	2.92	17.04
1989	4.39	7.57	6.38	2.94	22.98
1990	-3.19	5.71	-8.34	7.34	0.69
1991	10.73	-0.20	6.89	5.97	25.18
1992	-0.07	0.19	1.07	3.80	5.03
1993	5.92	0.82	4.25	2.13	13.71
1994	-1.82	1.31	3.36	-1.84	0.91

Bear Market Performance

Decile Rank (5-year period)

Worst — Best

	Worst 3 Mo Period 1985-89	Worst 3 Mo Period 1990-94
Merrill Lynch Capital A	-20.97	-9.27
+/- S&P 500	8.61	4.57
+/- Best Fit Index : S&P 500	8.61	4.57

Trailing Returns

	Total Return %	+/- S&P 500	+/- Wil 5000	% Rank All	% Rank Obj	Growth of $10,000
3 Mo	-1.84	-1.83	-1.07	65	58	9,816
6 Mo	1.46	-3.40	-3.17	31	67	10,146
1 Yr	0.91	-0.40	0.98	14	27	10,091
3 Yr Avg	6.42	0.15	-0.19	30	40	12,052
5 Yr Avg	8.72	0.03	-0.10	26	31	15,190
10 Yr Avg	13.54	-0.84	-0.32	21	23	35,609
15 Yr Avg	14.78	0.30	0.81	15	12	79,102

Operations

Address and Telephone	Box 9011
	Princeton, NJ 08543-9011
	800-637-3863 / 609-282-2800
Advisor	Merrill Lynch Asset Management
Subadvisor	None
Distributor	Merrill Lynch Funds Distributor
States Available	All plus PR
Report Grade	A
Income Distrib	Paid Semiannually
Date of Inception	12-10-73
Fiscal Year End	March

Min Initial Purchase	$1000 (Addt'l: $50)
Min IRA Purchase	$100 (Addt'l: $1)
Min Auto Invest Plan	$1000 (Systematic Inv: $50)

Expenses & Fees

Sales Fees	5.25% front
	0.00% deferred
	0.00% 12b-1
Management Fee	0.50% max./0.40% min.
3-,5-,10-yr Expense Projections	$69, $81, $116
Annual Brokerage Cost	0.17%

Risk Analysis

Time Period	Load-Adj Return %	Risk % Rank¹ All	Obj	Morningstar² Return	Risk	Morningstar Risk-Adj Rating
1 Yr	-4.38					
3 Yr	4.52	53	12	0.27³	0.57	★★★
5 Yr	7.55	54	8	0.69³	0.58	★★★
10 Yr	12.93	43	8	1.05	0.59	★★★★
Average Historical Rating (109 months)					4.0	★s

¹1 = low, 100 = high ²1.00 = Equity Avg ³1.00 = 90-day T-bill return

Other Measures

			Standard S&P 500	Best Fit S&P 500
Standard Deviation	6.51	Alpha	0.8	0.8
Mean	6.45	Beta	0.75	0.75
Sharpe Ratio	0.45	R-Squared	84	84

Investment Style

	Stock Portfolio Avg	Relative S&P 500
Price/Earnings Ratio	15.9	0.86
Price/Book Ratio	2.1	0.61
5 Yr Earnings Gr %	1.3	0.24
Return on Assets %	4.3	0.58
Debt % Total Cap	30.8	1.09
Med Mkt Cap ($mil)	5083	0.39

Style Value Blend Growth
Size Large Med Small

Diversification Value for Portfolio Types

Large Cap: None
Small Cap: Low
Bond: Medium
Balanced: None
Diversified: Low

Portfolio 09-30-94

Share Chg (03-94) 000	Amount 000	Total Stocks: 105 Total Fixed-Income: 141	Value $000	% Net Assets
550	1358	Goodyear Tire & Rubber	45318	1.91
-98	1162	HJ Heinz	42573	1.79
330	1214	Chemical Banking	42484	1.79
-78	848	NationsBank	41533	1.75
-95	848	Sears Roebuck	40686	1.71
	41147	US Treasury Note 4.25%	40227	1.69
	41147	US Treasury Note 4.25%	39790	1.67
	41147	US Treasury Note 4.375%	39321	1.65
-167	442	Warner-Lambert	35497	1.49
-80	391	American International Group	34741	1.46
	32917	US Treasury Note 4%	31991	1.35
402	597	General Electric	28713	1.21
114	691	WR Grace	28670	1.21
186	438	United Technologies	27417	1.15
362	1350	SouthTrust	26655	1.12
-61	808	Federal Paper Board	25456	1.07
430	704	Merck	24978	1.05
-16	687	PHH	24909	1.05
-452	1162	Occidental Petroleum	24410	1.03
720	720	Travel Ports of America	23672	1.00
-132	1341	National Medical Enterprises	22971	0.97
-114	658	Union Carbide	22384	0.94
	22631	Hanson Overseas BV 5.5%	22305	0.94
156	451	Conrail	22303	0.94
714	714	GTE	21685	0.91

Composition % 09-30-94

Cash	1.9	Preferreds	0.9
Stocks	54.3	Convertibles	1.0
Bonds	42.0	Other	0.0

Tax Analysis

	Tax-Adj Historical Return %	% Pretax Return
3 Yr Avg	3.87	58.8
5 Yr Avg	6.29	68.7
10 Yr Avg	10.34	65.4
Potential Capital Gain Exposure (% of assets)		-1%

Most Similar Funds in MF500

Oppenheimer Equity-Income	Strong Fit
Smith Barney Income & Grth	Strong Fit
Investment Comp of America	Strong Fit

Index Allocation

	% of Stocks
S&P 500	66.3
S&P MidCap 400	13.4
U.S. Small Cap	7.9
Foreign	12.4

Sector Weightings

	% of Stocks	Relative S&P 500
Utilities	4.4	0.35
Energy	5.9	0.58
Financials	23.7	2.24
Industrial Cyclicals	22.5	1.37
Consumer Durables	7.8	1.26
Consumer Staples	5.6	0.44
Services	10.5	1.29
Retail	5.7	0.98
Health	13.1	1.50
Technology	0.9	0.10

Merrill Lynch Corp High-Income A

	Ticker	Load	NAV	Yield	SEC Yield	Assets	Objective
	MAHIX	4.00%	7.31	9.6%	N/A	811.2	Corp Hi Yld

Merrill Lynch Corporate Bond Fund High-Income Portfolio - Class A seeks high current income.

The fund generally invests at least 65% of its assets in corporate debt rated as low as CCC. To select securities, the fund examines factors such as the company's responsiveness to business conditions, cash flow, borrowing requirements, and strength of management.

Class A shares have front loads and no 12b-1 fees and are designed for institutions and fund employees; Class B shares have deferred loads and conversion features; Class C shares have level loads; Class D shares have front loads and lower 12b-1 fees.

Manager's Investment Style

Management plays the high-yield market cautiously and seeks overlooked values. It will move into very low-quality fare if the rewards justify the risk; however, it will not take on unworthy paper simply to boost yield. Overall, management prefers recession-resistant areas within the junk category.

Fund Manager(s)

Vincent T. Lathbury III CFA(1978), since 10-82. Birthdate: 10-40. BA, Washington & Lee U. 1962 MBA, Temple U. 1976

Manager Experience	Dates Managed	Invest Obj	Std Dev	+/- Index
Vincent T. Lathbury III				
Merrill Lynch World Inc B	11/91 - 12/94	I	4.19	-5.11
Corp High Yield	06/93 - 12/94	CY	7.00	0.13

Historical Profile

Return	Above Average
Risk	Low
Rating	★★★★ Above Average

43 51 21 4 39 20 58 64

Growth of $10,000

- |||| Value of Fund ($000)
- — Value of Index ($000) LB Agg
- ▼ Manager Change
- ▽ Partial Manager Change
- ► Mgr Unknown After
- ◄ Mgr Unknown Before

Performance Quartile (Within Objective)

Investment Style History Fixed Income

Income Rtn % Rank Obj

1983	1984	1985	1986	1987	1988	1989	1990	1991	1992	1993	1994	History
8.10	7.72	8.29	8.34	7.80	7.80	7.17	5.88	7.21	7.78	8.32	7.31	NAV
18.33	8.67	21.61	12.95	4.95	12.71	4.34	-4.61	39.76	20.65	17.28	-3.98	Total Return %
9.96	-6.49	-0.52	-2.30	2.19	4.83	-10.20	-13.55	23.75	13.40	7.53	-1.06	+/- LB Aggregate
---	---	---	-2.69	-1.58	1.28	3.95	1.77	-4.00	3.99	-1.62	-3.00	+/- FB High-Yield
13.68	13.36	14.23	12.34	11.42	12.71	12.42	13.38	17.14	12.74	10.34	8.16	Income Return %
4.65	-4.69	7.38	0.60	-6.47	0.00	-8.08	-17.99	22.62	7.91	6.94	-12.14	Capital Return %
46	33	62	68	22	40	96	69	14	4	22	53	Total Rtn % Rank All
16	53	61	61	11	53	11	21	33	18	73	58	Total Rtn % Rank Obj
1.01	1.02	1.01	0.98	0.95	0.95	0.97	1.00	0.90	0.86	0.75	0.86	Income $
0.00	0.00	0.00	0.00	0.00	0.00	0.00	0.00	0.00	0.00	0.00	0.04	Capital Gains $
0.86	0.84	0.86	0.71	0.65	0.64	0.66	0.68	0.66	0.59	0.55	0.52	Expense Ratio %
12.56	12.97	12.87	11.68	11.31	12.33	12.30	14.22	14.13	11.44	9.78	8.98	Income Ratio %
136	94	82	33	57	39	56	48	40	41	35	---	Turnover Rate %
247.2	235.3	299.0	686.0	744.2	707.2	574.1	429.2	543.0	710.1	923.1	811.2	Net Assets ($mil)

Performance 12-31-94

	1st Qtr	2nd Qtr	3rd Qtr	4th Qtr	Total
1987	6.25	0.22	-1.79	0.35	4.95
1988	5.08	3.25	2.16	1.68	12.71
1989	2.24	3.09	0.49	-1.48	4.34
1990	-1.48	6.78	-5.39	-4.15	-4.61
1991	15.94	7.80	5.57	5.92	39.76
1992	9.75	3.28	4.31	2.04	20.65
1993	6.12	3.93	1.51	4.76	17.28
1994	-0.71	-1.63	0.82	-2.48	-3.98

Bear Market Performance

Decile Rank (5-year period)

Worst — Best

	Worst 3 Mo Period 1985-89	Worst 3 Mo Period 1990-94
Merrill Lynch Corp High-Income	-6.34	-13.53
+/- LB Aggregate	-7.16	-14.28
+/- Best Fit Index : FB HY	---	0.57

Trailing Returns

	Total Return %	+/- LB Aggregate	+/- FB High-Yield	% Rank All	% Rank Obj	Growth of $10,000
3 Mo	-2.48	-2.86	-2.44	77	76	9,752
6 Mo	-1.69	-2.68	-3.24	84	57	9,831
1 Yr	-3.98	-1.06	-3.00	53	58	9,602
3 Yr Avg	10.76	6.21	-0.40	11	37	13,587
5 Yr Avg	12.62	4.99	-0.46	7	12	18,114
10 Yr Avg	11.87	1.93	---	39	9	30,706
15 Yr Avg	11.81	1.00	---	57	27	53,333

Operations

Address and Telephone	Box 9011
	Princeton, NJ 08543-9011
	800-637-3863 / 609-282-2800
Advisor	Fund Asset Management
Subadvisor	None
Distributor	Merrill Lynch Funds Distributor
States Available	All
Report Grade	B-
Income Distrib	Paid Monthly
Date of Inception	11-10-78
Fiscal Year End	September

Min Initial Purchase	$1000 (Addt'l: $50)
Min IRA Purchase	$100 (Addt'l: $1)
Min Auto Invest Plan	$1000 (Systematic Inv: $50)

Expenses & Fees

Sales Fees	4.00% front
	0.00% deferred
	0.00% 12b-1
Management Fee	0.55% max./0.40% min.
3-,5-,10-yr Expense Projections	$57, $70, $106

Risk Analysis

Time Period	Load-Adj Return %	Risk % Rank All	Risk % Rank Obj	Morningstar Return	Morningstar Risk	Morningstar Risk-Adj Rating
1 Yr	-7.82					
3 Yr	9.26	9	43	1.73[3]	0.37	★★★★
5 Yr	11.70	42	29	1.85[3]	0.50	★★★★★
10 Yr	11.42	25	12	0.93	0.40	★★★★

Average Historical Rating (109 months) 3.9 ★s

[1] = low, 100 = high [2] 1.00 = Hybrid Avg [3] 1.00 = 90-day T-bill return

Other Measures

				Standard LB Agg	Best Fit FB HY
Standard Deviation	5.07	Alpha		6.5	-1.1
Mean	10.39	Beta		0.51	1.11
Sharpe Ratio	1.35	R-Squared		16	90

Investment Style

Interest-Rate Stance

Avg Effective Duration	4.8 Yrs
Avg Effective Maturity	8.2 Yrs

Maturity Short Intm Long

Quality

Avg Credit Quality	B
Avg Weighted Coupon	10.59%
Avg Weighted Price	91.26% of Par

Diversification Value for Portfolio Types

Large Cap: High	Small Cap: Medium	Bond: High	Balanced: High	Diversified: High

Portfolio 06-30-94

Amount 000	Date of Maturity	Total Stocks: 14 Total Fixed-Income: 233	Value $000	% Net Assets
13790	04-15-98	Marvel 11.475%	8550	0.96
9653	06-01-17	Beaver Valley II Fdg 9%	8012	0.90
8136	07-15-02	Grand Union 12.25%	7912	0.89
8274	09-15-03	Flagstar 11.375%	7571	0.85
7722	04-30-16	Delta Air Lines 10.5%	7539	0.85
8274	12-15-05	Westpoint Stevens 9.375%	7519	0.84
13652	02-15-00	Clark R & M Holdings 11%	7509	0.84
7378	02-01-03	Kaiser Aluminium/Chem 12.75%	7488	0.84
8999	12-15-02	Silgan Holdings 13.25%	7289	0.82
11733	10-01-98	G-I Holdings 0%	7245	0.81
6895	05-15-01	Gaylord Container 11.5%	7205	0.81
8619	06-15-01	Trump Plaza Funding 10.875%	7154	0.80
11351	08-01-03	MAXXAM Group 12.25%	6981	0.78
6619	06-15-02	Riverwood International 11.25%	6884	0.77
8021	03-01-17	US Gypsum 8.75%	6818	0.77
6895	04-01-03	Sherritt 9.75%	6809	0.76
6619	04-15-03	Thrifty Payless 11.75%	6785	0.76
12877	06-01-04	Echostar Communication 13.01%	6760	0.76
10825	10-01-01	SpectraVision 11.5%	6603	0.74
6826	03-15-03	GNS Finance 9.25%	6553	0.74
6895	04-15-05	Penn Traffic 9.625%	6516	0.73
7298	12-01-01	Envirodyne Industries 10.25%	6496	0.73
6895	08-01-03	ADT Operations 9.25%	6464	0.73
6895	08-01-05	Seagull Energy 8.625%	6378	0.72
6343	09-01-00	Trans Texas Gas 10.5%	6359	0.71

Composition % 09-30-94

Cash	7.8	Preferreds	1.6
Stocks	0.5	Convertibles	1.2
Bonds	88.7	Other	0.2

Tax Analysis

	Tax-Adj Historical Return %	% Pretax Return
3 Yr Avg	6.97	62.4
5 Yr Avg	8.32	60.6
10 Yr Avg	7.10	47.6
Potential Capital Gain Exposure (% of assets)		-10%

Most Similar Funds in MF500

AIM High-Yield A	Strong Fit
Kemper High-Yield A	Strong Fit
MFS High-Income A	Strong Fit

Coupon Range

	% of Bonds	Rel Obj
0%, PIK	1.2	0.17
0% to 11%	61.5	1.25
11% to 13%	30.9	0.93
13% to 14.5%	4.8	0.89
More than 14.5%	0.1	0.07
Not applicable	1.4	0.44

Credit Analysis 10-31-94

% of Bonds

US Govt	0	BB	30
AAA	0	B	62
AA	0	Below B	6
A	0	NR/NA	0
BBB	2		

MORNINGSTAR 1995 Mutual Fund 500

Merrill Lynch Dragon B

	Ticker	Load	NAV	Yield	SEC Yield	Assets	Objective
	MBDRX	4.00%d	15.03	0.8%	N/A	917.4	Pacific Stock

Merrill Lynch Dragon Fund - Class B seeks long-term capital appreciation.

The fund normally invests at least 65% of its assets in equity and debt securities issued in the Asia-Pacific region. The fund intends to invest in a number of countries. The fund does not intend to capitalize on short-term currency fluctuations. The fund may hold debt of any credit quality; 5% of assets may be in default.

Class A shares have front loads and no 12b-1 fees and are designed for institutions and fund employees; Class B shares have deferred loads and conversion features; Class C shares have level loads; Class D shares have front loads and lower 12b-1 fees.

Manager's Investment Style

Mangagement is willing to make reasonably large bets in just a couple of emerging markets. At one time, for example, 60% of assets were held in Hong Kong and Malaysia combined. Macroeconomic considerations drive stock selection, as management looks to play specific themes in particular markets. Infrastructure, for example, has been a large part of stock selection in Malaysia.

Fund Manager(s)

Kara Tan Bhala, since 05-92. BS, City U. of London 1982

Manager Experience

	Dates Managed	Invest Obj	Std Dev	+/- Index
Kara Tan Bhala				
FT International Equity A	01/91 - 05/92	WF	11.81	-13.00

Historical Profile

Return	---	
Risk	---	
Rating	---	Not Rated

Investment Style History Equity

Average % Stocks Held in Portfolio

66%	82%	90%

Growth of $10,000

‖‖‖ Value of Fund ($000)
— Value of Index ($000)
    S&P 500
▮ Manager Change
▽ Partial Manager Change
► Mgr Unknown After
◄ Mgr Unknown Before

Performance Quartile (Within Objective)

	1983	1984	1985	1986	1987	1988	1989	1990	1991	1992	1993	1994	History
	---	---	---	---	---	---	---	---	---	10.13	18.70	15.03	NAV
	---	---	---	---	---	---	---	---	---	1.56 *	87.03	-16.98	Total Return %
	---	---	---	---	---	---	---	---	---	-5.17 *	76.97	-18.30	+/- S&P 500
	---	---	---	---	---	---	---	---	---	---	1.01	-8.08	+/- MSCI FE ex Jpn
	---	---	---	---	---	---	---	---	---	0.20	1.04	0.82	Income Return %
	---	---	---	---	---	---	---	---	---	1.36	85.99	-17.81	Capital Return %
	---	---	---	---	---	---	---	---	---	---	1	99	Total Rtn % Rank All
	---	---	---	---	---	---	---	---	---	---	12	62	Total Rtn % Rank Obj
	---	---	---	---	---	---	---	---	---	0.02	0.12	0.13	Income $
	---	---	---	---	---	---	---	---	---	0.01	0.11	0.36	Capital Gains $
	---	---	---	---	---	---	---	---	---	---	2.35	2.35	Expense Ratio %
	---	---	---	---	---	---	---	---	---	---	-0.15	-0.38	Income Ratio %
	---	---	---	---	---	---	---	---	---	---	---	---	Turnover Rate %
	---	---	---	---	---	---	---	---	---	266.7	988.9	917.4	Net Assets ($mil)

Performance 12-31-94

	1st Qtr	2nd Qtr	3rd Qtr	4th Qtr	Total
1987	---	---	---	---	---
1988	---	---	---	---	---
1989	---	---	---	---	---
1990	---	---	---	---	---
1991	---	---	---	---	---
1992	---	---	-0.60	1.36	1.56 *
1993	10.27	7.61	11.31	41.60	87.03
1994	-19.63	2.46	11.49	-9.59	-16.98

Bear Market Performance

Decile Rank (5-year period)

Worst ⟷ Best

	Worst 3 Mo Period 1985-89	Worst 3 Mo Period 1990-94
Merrill Lynch Dragon B	---	---
+/- S&P 500	---	---
+/- Best Fit Index :	---	---

Trailing Returns

	Total Return %	+/- S&P 500	+/- MSCI FE ex Jpn	% Rank All	% Rank Obj	Growth of $10,000
3 Mo	-9.59	-9.57	-1.33	98	57	9,041
6 Mo	0.81	-4.06	-4.55	41	21	10,081
1 Yr	-16.98	-18.30	-8.08	99	62	8,302
3 Yr Avg	---	---	---	---	---	---
5 Yr Avg	---	---	---	---	---	---
10 Yr Avg	---	---	---	---	---	---
15 Yr Avg	---	---	---	---	---	---

Operations

Address and Telephone	Box 9011	
	Princeton, NJ 08543-9011	
	800-637-3863 / 609-282-2800	
Advisor	Merrill Lynch Asset Management	
Subadvisor	None	
Distributor	Merrill Lynch Funds Distributor	
States Available	All	
Report Grade	A-	
Income Distrib	Paid Annually	
* Date of Inception	05-29-92	
Fiscal Year End	December	

Risk Analysis

Time Period	Load-Adj Return %	Risk % Rank¹ All	Risk % Rank¹ Obj	Morningstar² Return	Morningstar Risk	Morningstar Risk-Adj Rating
1 Yr	-19.40					
3 Yr	---	---	---	---	---	---
5 Yr	---	---	---	---	---	---
10 Yr	---	---	---	---	---	---
Average Historical Rating ---					---	

¹ 1 = low, 100 = high   ² 1.00 = Equity Avg   ³ 1.00 = 90-day T-bill return

Other Measures

		Standard S&P 500	Best Fit
Standard Deviation	---	Alpha	---	---
Mean	---	Beta	---	---
Sharpe Ratio	---	R-Squared	---	---

Investment Style

	Stock Portfolio Avg	Rel MSCI EAFE	Rel Obj	Style V B G
Price/Earnings Ratio	25.1	0.68	0.79	
Price/Cash Flow	20.9	1.35	1.09	
Price/Book Ratio	4.1	1.57	1.40	
5 Yr Earnings Gr %	27.3#	---	2.45	
Return on Assets %	13.2#	2.89	1.64	
Debt % Total Cap	17.2#	0.51	0.72	
Med Mkt Cap ($mil)	3138	0.26	0.76	

Size L M S

figure is based on 50% or less of stocks

Diversification Value for Portfolio Types

Large Cap:	Small Cap:	Bond:	Balanced:	Diversified:

Portfolio 06-30-94

Share Chg (12-93)000	Amount 000	Total Stocks: 116 / Total Fixed-Income: 3	Value $000	% Net Assets
1917	3706	San Miguel CI B	18671	2.27
-5679	1678	HSBC Holdings	18342	2.23
36	2604	Leader Universal Holdings	13902	1.69
105	1519	Arab-Malaysian Merchant Bank	13537	1.65
-5887	1872	Swire Pacific CI A	13444	1.64
1070	3072	Guoco Group	13115	1.60
23	1674	Hanjaya Mandala Sampoerna	12730	1.55
23	1666	Bangkok Bank	12648	1.54
3379	3379	Wharf Holdings	12459	1.52
-106	2199	Malayan Banking	12330	1.50
149	2126	Resorts World	12250	1.49
10	683	Land & House	12015	1.46
119	1952	Sun Hung Kai Properties	11237	1.37
190	2699	Hutchison Whampoa	11088	1.35
1405	18860	Guangdong Investments	10858	1.32
233	3042	Land & General	10168	1.24
710	11062	IPC	10165	1.24
97	588	Singapore Press Holdings	9839	1.20
344	779	Manila Electric CI B	9805	1.19
280	980	Development Bank Singapore	9389	1.14

Index Allocation

	% of Stocks
S&P 500	0.0
S&P MidCap 400	0.0
U.S. Small Cap	0.0
Foreign	100.0

Composition % 09-30-94

Cash	8.2	Preferreds	0.0
Stocks	90.1	Convertibles	0.0
Bonds	1.0	Other	0.7

Tax Analysis

	Tax-Adj Historical Return %	% Pretax Return
3 Yr Avg	---	---
5 Yr Avg	---	---
10 Yr Avg	---	---
Potential Capital Gain Exposure (% of assets)		19%

Most Similar Funds in MF500

Fund lacks three-year record

Country Exposure 09-23-94

	% of Stocks
Hong Kong	28
Malaysia	24
Singapore	12
Thailand	9
Philippines	6

Total Number of Countries: 10
Hedging Policy: Occasional

Sector Weightings

	% of Stocks	Relative S&P 500
Utilities	8.0	1.29
Energy	1.2	0.71
Financials	39.6	1.55
Industrial Cyclicals	10.9	0.49
Consumer Durables	5.3	0.38
Consumer Staples	5.8	2.14
Services	19.6	1.53
Retail	2.8	0.52
Health	0.6	0.33
Technology	6.2	0.78

Min Initial Purchase $1000 (Addt'l: $50)
Min IRA Purchase $100 (Addt'l: $1)
Min Auto Invest Plan $1000 (Systematic Inv: $50)

Expenses & Fees

Sales Fees	0.00% front
	4.00% deferred
	1.00% 12b-1
Management Fee	1.00% flat fee
3-,5-,10-yr Expense Projections	$93, $126, $250
Annual Brokerage Cost	0.44%

Merrill Lynch Global Alloc B

	Ticker	Load	NAV	Yield	SEC Yield	Assets	Objective
	MBLOX	4.00%d	12.12	2.5%	N/A	6155.3	Asset Alloc.

Merrill Lynch Global Allocation Fund - Class B seeks total return consistent with prudent risk.

The fund invests in domestic and foreign equities, debt, and money-markets issued in at least three countries. The fund does not prescribe limits on allocation of securities or markets. Equity purchases are made in stocks with below average P/E and P/B ratios. Up to 35% of assets may be in debt rated below BBB.

Class A shares have front loads and no 12b-1 fees and are designed for institutions and fund employees; Class B shares have deferred loads and conversion features; Class C shares have level loads; Class D shares have front loads and lower 12b-1 fees.

Manager's Investment Style

Management combines a value discipline with a penchant for badly beaten-up securities. It pays attention to relative valuations when allocating assets. Further, it moves out of asset classes that have already turned in high returns, in order to pick up on securities that have fallen on hard times. Stocks are usually 30% to 55% of assets, a large portion of which are often foreign. Bonds generally take up the remaining significant portion of assets. Here, management is willing to move down the credit ladder, out on the yield curve, or into foreign debt.

Fund Manager(s)

Bryan N. Ison CFA(1984), since 02-89. SB, MIT MBA, U. of Chicago

Manager Experience

	Dates Managed	Invest Obj	Std Dev	+/- Index

Not available.

Historical Profile

Return	Above Average
Risk	Below Average
Rating	★★★★
	Above Average

Investment Style History
Equity
Average % Stocks Held in Portfolio

| | | | | | | | | | | 36% | 47% | 55% | 42% | 35% | 36% |

Growth of $10,000

||||Value of Fund ($000)
— Value of Index ($000) S&P 500
▼ Manager Change
▽ Partial Manager Change
► Mgr Unknown After
◄ Mgr Unknown Before

Performance Quartile (Within Objective)

1983	1984	1985	1986	1987	1988	1989	1990	1991	1992	1993	1994	History
---	---	---	---	---	---	10.75	9.88	11.03	11.47	13.11	12.12	NAV
---	---	---	---	---	---	13.58 *	0.84	27.47	11.06	20.02	-2.89	Total Return %
---	---	---	---	---	---	-9.33 *	3.96	-3.01	3.44	9.96	-4.21	+/- S&P 500
---	---	---	---	---	---	---	-8.10	11.47	3.81	10.27	0.03	+/- LB Aggregate
---	---	---	---	---	---	3.96	4.04	9.08	5.95	3.52	2.42	Income Return %
---	---	---	---	---	---	9.62	-3.20	18.39	5.11	16.50	-5.31	Capital Return %
---	---	---	---	---	---	---	53	31	17	17	42	Total Rtn % Rank All
---	---	---	---	---	---	---	43	22	11	20	56	Total Rtn % Rank Obj
---	---	---	---	---	---	0.39	0.43	0.89	0.65	0.41	0.31	Income $
---	---	---	---	---	---	0.20	0.55	0.60	0.12	0.23	0.30	Capital Gains $
---	---	---	---	---	---	2.40	2.31	2.31	2.09	1.95	1.86	Expense Ratio %
---	---	---	---	---	---	4.29	3.35	7.98	11.95	2.87	3.08	Income Ratio %
---	---	---	---	---	---	---	130	81	60	50	---	Turnover Rate %
---	---	---	---	---	---	123.0	115.1	176.4	1117.4	4874.2	6155.3	Net Assets ($mil)

Performance 12-31-94

	1st Qtr	2nd Qtr	3rd Qtr	4th Qtr	Total
1987	---	---	---	---	---
1988	---	---	---	---	---
1989	---	3.22	6.74	3.81	13.58 *
1990	-2.14	5.99	-8.32	6.05	0.84
1991	12.04	1.63	8.17	3.50	27.47
1992	2.81	3.53	0.93	3.38	11.06
1993	7.06	3.91	3.73	4.01	20.02
1994	-0.15	-0.31	0.58	-3.01	-2.89

Bear Market Performance

Decile Rank (5-year period)

Worst — Best

	Worst 3 Mo Period 1985-89	Worst 3 Mo Period 1990-94
Merrill Lynch Global Alloc B	---	-8.32
+/- S&P 500	---	5.43
+/- Best Fit Index : MSAllCtry	---	10.64

Trailing Returns

	Total Return %	+/- S&P 500	+/- LB Aggregate	% Rank All	% Rank Obj	Growth of $10,000
3 Mo	-3.01	-2.99	-3.39	83	79	9,699
6 Mo	-2.44	-7.31	-3.44	91	94	9,756
1 Yr	-2.89	-4.21	0.03	42	56	9,711
3 Yr Avg	8.98	2.72	4.44	17	12	12,944
5 Yr Avg	10.72	2.03	3.09	14	6	16,638
10 Yr Avg	---	---	---	---	---	---
15 Yr Avg	---	---	---	---	---	---

Operations

Address and Telephone	Box 9011
	Princeton, NJ 08543-9011
	800-637-3863 / 609-282-2800
Advisor	Merrill Lynch Asset Management
Subadvisor	Merrill Lynch Asset Management (U.K.)
Distributor	Merrill Lynch Funds Distributor
States Available	All plus PR
Report Grade	A-
Income Distrib	Paid Annually
* Date of Inception	02-03-89
Fiscal Year End	October

Risk Analysis

Time Period	Load-Adj Return %	Risk % Rank[1] All	Risk % Rank[1] Obj	Morningstar[2] Return	Morningstar Risk	Morningstar Risk-Adj Rating
1 Yr	-5.66					
3 Yr	8.70	24	12	1.55[3]	0.51	★★★★
5 Yr	10.72	46	25	1.56[3]	0.58	★★★★
10 Yr	---					

Average Historical Rating (35 months) 4.7 ★s

[1] 1 = low, 100 = high [2] 1.00 = Hybrid Avg [3] 1.00 = 90-day T-bill return

Other Measures

			Standard S&P 500	Best Fit MSAllCtry
Standard Deviation	5.29	Alpha	4.1	4.3
Mean	8.77	Beta	0.42	0.40
Sharpe Ratio	0.99	R-Squared	39	62

Investment Style

Stocks	Port Avg	Rel S&P 500	Style
Price/Earnings Ratio	20.1	1.09	
Price/Book Ratio	1.9	0.57	
5 Yr Earnings Gr %	2.2	0.40	
Med Mkt Cap ($mil)	5114	0.39	

Bonds		
Avg Effective Duration	4.1 Yrs	
Avg Effective Maturity	---	Not Available
Avg Credit Quality	---	
Avg Weighted Coupon	8.38%	

Diversification Value for Portfolio Types

Large Cap: Medium	Small Cap: Medium	Bond: Medium	Balanced: Low	Diversified: Low

Expenses & Fees

Sales Fees	
	0.00% front
	4.00% deferred
	1.00% 12b-1
Management Fee	0.75% flat fee
3-,5-,10-yr Expense Projections	$81, $105, $208
Annual Brokerage Cost	0.12%

Min Initial Purchase

Min Initial Purchase	$1000 (Addt'l: $50)
Min IRA Purchase	$100 (Addt'l: $1)
Min Auto Invest Plan	$1000 (Systematic Inv: $50)

Portfolio 07-31-94

Share Chg (04-94)000	Amount 000	Total Stocks: 307 / Total Fixed-Income: 255	Date of Maturity	Value $000	% Net Assets
	109536	Govt of France 8.25%	04-25-22	131507	2.08
	103336	US Treasury Note 7.5%	11-15-01	106517	1.68
	165338	Republic of Germany 6.75%	04-22-03	102880	1.62
	144671	Treuhandanstalt 6.875%	06-11-03	90613	1.43
	103336	Banco Nacional 7.25%	02-02-04	85252	1.35
	413344	Govt of France 8.5%	04-25-23	82020	1.30
	132270	Republic of Germany 6.5%	07-15-03	81162	1.28
	135577	Land Hessen 6%	11-29-13	78852	1.25
	152524	Republic of Argentina 4.25%	03-31-23	78169	1.23
	82669	United Mexican States FRN	12-31-19	69649	1.10
	93416	Republic of Argentina Euro FRN	03-31-23	65391	1.03
	90936	Mecklenberg Vorpmmrn 6.15%	06-16-23	52745	0.83
	6406839	Kingdom of Spain 10.9%	08-30-03	50032	0.79
	80602	Nordrhein-Westfalen 6.125%	12-21-18	48148	0.76
0	1251	Chemical Banking		48015	0.76
	49601	Banco Rio de la Plata 8.5%	07-15-98	46873	0.74
	5786822	Kingdom of Spain 11.3%	01-15-02	46162	0.73
	31001	United Kingdom Treasury 8%	06-10-03	46026	0.73
	5621484	Kingdom of Spain 10.3%	06-15-02	42646	0.67
	55388	Sherritt 11%	03-31-04	38678	0.61

Index Allocation

	% of Stocks
S&P 500	31.4
S&P MidCap 400	9.3
U.S. Small Cap	15.5
Foreign	44.1

Composition % 09-30-94

Cash	3.0	Preferred	1.0
Stocks	38.1	Convertibles	4.4
Bonds	53.5	Other	0.0

Tax Analysis

	Tax-Adj Historical Return %	% Pretax Return
3 Yr Avg	7.07	77.3
5 Yr Avg	8.09	71.6
10 Yr Avg	---	---
Potential Capital Gain Exposure (% of assets)		-4%

Most Similar Funds in MF500

Fidelity Asset Manager	Fair Fit
Fidelity Balanced	Weak Fit
Lindner	Weak Fit

Bond Credit Analysis 04-30-94

% of Bonds			
US Govt	10	BB	63
AAA	0	B	0
AA	27	Below B	0
A	0	NR/NA	0
BBB	0		

Stock Sector Weightings

	% of Stocks	Relative S&P 500
Utilities	11.3	0.91
Energy	4.3	0.42
Financials	37.1	3.51
Industrial Cyclicals	14.7	0.90
Consumer Durables	6.1	0.98
Consumer Staples	5.8	0.46
Services	5.1	0.63
Retail	3.7	0.64
Health	9.2	1.06
Technology	2.7	0.29

MORNINGSTAR 1995 Mutual Fund 500

Merrill Lynch Muni Ltd Mat A

	Ticker	Load	NAV	Yield	SEC Yield	Assets	Objective
	MALMX	1.00%	9.77	3.7%	N/A	638.5	Muni Nat

Merrill Lynch Municipal Bond Fund Limited Maturity Portfolio - Class A seeks income exempt from federal income taxes.

The fund normally invests at least 80% of its assets in short-term investment-grade municipal securities; these include municipal bonds with remaining maturities of less than four years as well as short-term municipal notes. The balance of assets may be invested in taxable securities.

Class A shares have front loads and no 12b-1 fees and are designed for institutions and fund employees; Class B shares have deferred loads and conversion features; Class C shares have level loads; Class D shares have front loads and lower 12b-1 fees.

Manager's Investment Style

By charter, management is limited to bonds with maturities of four or fewer years. In practice, management generally keeps maturity to two or fewer years. Management is also limited to high-quality bonds, with an 80% exposure to investment-grade issues mandated by charter. As a result of its charter, as well as management's bent, the fund is extremely conservative, even relative to other short-term muni offerings.

Fund Manager(s)

Vincent R. Giordano, since 11-79. BS, Fordham U.
Peter Hayes, since 01-90. BA, Holy Cross C. 1981

Manager Experience	Dates Managed	Invest Obj	Std Dev	+/- Index
Vincent R. Giordano				
Merrill Lynch Muni Natl A	11/79 - 12/94	MN	7.48	-1.62
Merrill Lynch CA Muni B	09/85 - 12/94	MC	6.51	-1.74

Historical Profile

Return	Low
Risk	Low
Rating	★★★★ Above Average

Investment Style History
Fixed Income
Income Rtn % Rank Obj

Growth of $10,000
- |||| Value of Fund ($000)
- — Value of Index ($000) LB Muni
- ▼ Manager Change
- ▽ Partial Manager Change
- ► Mgr Unknown After
- ◄ Mgr Unknown Before

Performance Quartile (Within Objective)

	1983	1984	1985	1986	1987	1988	1989	1990	1991	1992	1993	1994	History
	9.76	9.74	9.75	9.90	9.68	9.68	9.74	9.72	9.88	9.97	10.01	9.77	NAV
	5.57	6.91	6.70	7.47	3.18	5.90	6.93	6.11	7.39	5.62	4.60	1.27	Total Return %
	-2.80	-8.25	-15.42	-7.78	0.42	-1.98	-7.61	-2.83	-8.61	-1.62	-5.15	4.19	+/- LB Aggregate
	-2.48	-3.64	-13.32	-11.85	1.68	-4.27	-3.86	-1.19	-4.75	-3.19	-7.68	6.87	+/- LB Muni
	6.89	7.11	6.60	5.93	5.29	5.90	6.31	6.32	5.74	4.71	4.20	3.67	Income Return %
	-1.31	-0.20	0.10	1.54	-2.11	0.00	0.62	-0.21	1.65	0.91	0.40	-2.40	Capital Return %
	97	42	98	92	34	89	93	33	96	73	92	12	Total Rtn % Rank All
	91	83	98	99	8	93	94	58	97	96	98	2	Total Rtn % Rank Obj
	0.67	0.67	0.63	0.56	0.52	0.56	0.59	0.60	0.54	0.45	0.41	0.37	Income $
	0.00	0.00	0.00	0.00	0.01	0.00	0.00	0.00	0.00	0.00	0.00	0.00	Capital Gains $
	0.49	0.43	0.43	0.42	0.40	0.40	0.41	0.40	0.40	0.40	0.41	0.40	Expense Ratio %
	7.15	6.67	6.83	6.04	5.27	5.42	6.00	6.21	5.88	5.02	4.13	3.68	Income Ratio %
	43	86	81	8	20	146	229	106	93	96	65	46	Turnover Rate %
	460.3	423.2	428.7	623.9	630.7	472.4	358.6	332.1	465.3	706.4	885.0	638.5	Net Assets ($mil)

Performance 12-31-94

	1st Qtr	2nd Qtr	3rd Qtr	4th Qtr	Total
1987	1.18	0.69	-0.24	1.52	3.18
1988	2.42	1.06	1.12	1.18	5.90
1989	0.95	2.59	1.33	1.89	6.93
1990	1.13	1.67	1.31	1.87	6.11
1991	1.73	1.39	1.81	2.27	7.39
1992	0.58	2.11	1.63	1.19	5.62
1993	1.33	1.14	0.84	1.21	4.60
1994	-0.20	0.50	0.82	0.14	1.27

Bear Market Performance

Decile Rank (5-year period)

Worst ———————————— Best

	Worst 3 Mo Period 1985-89	Worst 3 Mo Period 1990-94
Merrill Lynch Muni Ltd Mat A	-0.56	-0.40
+/- LB Aggregate	-1.37	4.53
+/- Best Fit Index : LB Muni	2.57	5.36

Trailing Returns

	Total Return %	+/- LB Aggregate	+/- LB Muni	% Rank All	% Rank Obj	Growth of $10,000
3 Mo	0.14	-0.24	1.58	18	3	10,014
6 Mo	0.96	-0.03	2.21	38	4	10,096
1 Yr	1.27	4.19	6.87	12	2	10,127
3 Yr Avg	3.81	-0.73	-1.06	74	84	11,188
5 Yr Avg	4.98	-2.65	-1.80	90	95	12,749
10 Yr Avg	5.50	-4.44	-3.93	98	96	17,082
15 Yr Avg	6.05	-4.75	-2.42	98	94	24,152

Operations

Address and Telephone	Box 9011
	Princeton, NJ 08543-9011
	800-637-3863 / 609-282-2800
Advisor	Fund Asset Management
Subadvisor	None
Distributor	Merrill Lynch Funds Distributor
States Available	All
Report Grade	B-
Income Distrib	Paid Monthly
Date of Inception	11-02-79
Fiscal Year End	June

Risk Analysis

Time Period	Load-Adj Return %	Risk % Rank [1] All	Obj	Morningstar [2] Return	Risk	Morningstar Risk-Adj Rating
1 Yr	0.26					
3 Yr	3.47	1	1	0.60	0.12	★★★★
5 Yr	4.77	1	2	0.55	0.11	★★★★★
10 Yr	5.39	1	4	0.34	0.15	★★★★
Average Historical Rating (109 months)					3.9	★ s

[1] 1 = low, 100 = high [2] 1.00 = Muni Avg [3] 1.00 = 90-day T-bill return

Other Measures

		Standard LB Agg	Best Fit LB Muni
Standard Deviation	1.16	Alpha	0.0	0.0
Mean	3.75	Beta	0.19	0.17
Sharpe Ratio	0.20	R-Squared	40	60

Investment Style

Interest-Rate Stance
Avg Effective Maturity   2.7 Yrs

Maturity: Short Intm Long
Quality: High Med Low

Quality
Avg Credit Quality   A
Avg Weighted Coupon   4.84%
Avg Weighted Price 100.47% of Par

Diversification Value for Portfolio Types

Large Cap: High   Small Cap: High   Bond: Medium   Balanced: Medium   Diversified: High

Portfolio 06-30-94

Total Stocks: 0
Total Fixed-Income: 197

Amount 000	Date of Maturity		Value $000	% Net Assets
21112	12-15-97	NJ Transp Trust Fund Sys 5%	21244	2.69
20472	05-01-97	UT Carbon Solid Waste Disp 6.04%	20433	2.59
19000	10-31-95	IL Chicago DMD	19039	2.41
12667	11-15-94	FL COP Const Equip Fin Prog 5.55%	12759	1.61
12245	11-15-14	MO Envir Impr/Engy Resource Poll 3.9%	12046	1.52
10978	09-01-96	KY Ppty/Bldg Com 3.6%	10756	1.36
9880	08-15-20	WY Uinta Hosp Fac Poll Cntrl DMD	9880	1.25
8656	11-01-12	OH Trumbull Meml Hosp 9.625%	9434	1.19
9289	06-01-95	DC Genl Rec Fund 5.5%	9390	1.19
8787	02-01-95	NY New York City GO Ins 6.4%	8909	1.13
8867	08-01-96	OH Air Qlty Dev Poll Cntrl 4.25%	8805	1.11
8445	01-01-96	MS Higher Educ Assist Student Loan 5.4%	8551	1.08
8445	07-01-95	FL Brd Fin Genl Svc Dept Resource 6.1%	8538	1.08
8445	09-01-95	CO Denver Arpt Sys 4.25%	8478	1.07
8445	10-01-95	CA GO Various Purp 4%	8470	1.07
8445	10-01-94	IL Chicago GO Park District 3.25%	8433	1.07
8445	06-01-97	OH Cleveland GO Sch Dist Impr 4.35%	8325	1.05
8022	12-01-95	TX Houston Wtr/Swr Sys 5.55%	8189	1.04
8014	01-01-97	NC Muni Pwr #1 Catawba Elec 4.6%	7997	1.01
7600	02-01-06	TX San Antonio Elec/Gas Sys 5.8%	7692	0.97

Credit Analysis % of Bonds 09-30-94

US Govt	0	BB	0
AAA	28	B	0
AA	22	Below B	0
A	35	NR/NA	14
BBB	2		

Composition % of Assets 09-30-94

Cash	15.9	Preferreds	0.0
Stocks	0.0	Convertibles	0.0
Bonds	84.1	Other	0.0

Tax Analysis

	Tax-Adj Historical Return %	% Pretax Return
3 Yr Avg	3.81	100.0
5 Yr Avg	4.98	100.0
10 Yr Avg	5.50	99.9
Potential Capital Gain Exposure (% of assets)		-2%

Most Similar Funds in MF500

Vanguard Muni Short-Term	Fair Fit
USAA Tax-Exempt Short-Term	Weak Fit
Dreyfus Short-Intrm Muni Bd	Weak Fit

Expenses & Fees

Sales Fees	
	1.00% front
	0.00% deferred
	0.00% 12b-1
Management Fee	0.40% max./0.33% min.
3-,5-,10-yr Expense Projections	$23, $32, $60

Min Initial Purchase	$1000 (Addt'l: $100)
Min IRA Purchase	N/A
Min Auto Invest Plan	$1000 (Systematic Inv: $50)

Coupon Range

	% Bonds	Rel Obj
0%	0.0	0.00
0% to 6.8%	85.1	1.41
6.8% to 7.5%	2.3	0.15
7.5% to 8.3%	0.2	0.03
More than 8.3%	2.4	0.27
Not applicable	9.9	2.56

Sector Weightings

	% Bonds	Rel Obj
General Obl	20.74	0.99
Utilities	10.04	0.80
Health	3.39	0.26
Water/Waste	5.65	0.89
Housing	6.18	0.84
Education	7.95	1.24
Transportation	11.78	1.16
COP/Lease	4.18	1.31
Private	11.73	1.01
Misc Revenue	8.91	1.79
Demand	9.45	3.84

Top 5 States % of Bonds

OH	11.67	IL	7.25
TX	9.53	FL	4.82
NJ	7.86		

Merrill Lynch World Income A

	Ticker	Load	NAV	Yield	SEC Yield	Assets	Objective
	MAWIX	4.00%	8.20	8.5%	N/A	311.2	Income

Merrill Lynch World Income Fund - Class A seeks current income.

The fund normally invests at least 90% of its assets in debt obligations issued by U.S. and foreign governments and corporations. The fund allocates its assets among different types of fixed-income investments based upon analysis of yield, maturity, and currency considerations.

Class A shares have front loads and no 12b-1 fees and are designed for institutions and fund employees; Class B shares have deferred loads and conversion features; Class C shares have level loads; Class D shares have front loads and lower 12b-1 fees.

Manager's Investment Style

Management relies on bargain hunting around the world. It does, however, tend to keep the larger portion of its assets in U.S. dollar-denominated bonds, most of which are domestic high-yield bonds. It further divides assets between U.S. government paper and foreign debt. The fund's penchant for bargains dovetails with its emphasis on yield.

Historical Profile

Return	Above Average
Risk	Low
Rating	★★★★
	Above Average

Investment Style History
Fixed Income
Income Rtn % Rank Obj

Growth of $10,000

||| Value of Fund ($000)
— Value of Index ($000) FB HY
▼ Manager Change
▽ Partial Manager Change
► Mgr Unknown After
◄ Mgr Unknown Before

Performance Quartile (Within Objective)

	1983	1984	1985	1986	1987	1988	1989	1990	1991	1992	1993	1994	History
	---	---	---	---	---	9.68	9.13	8.51	9.30	8.85	9.28	8.20	NAV
	---	---	---	---	---	---	6.83	9.67	23.34	6.16	14.06	-4.25	Total Return %
	---	---	---	---	---	---	-24.85	12.79	-7.15	-1.46	4.00	-5.57	+/- S&P 500
	---	---	---	---	---	---	-7.71	0.72	7.34	-1.09	4.30	-1.33	+/- LB Aggregate
	---	---	---	---	---	---	12.07	16.46	14.05	10.20	8.86	7.39	Income Return %
	---	---	---	---	---	---	-5.24	-6.79	9.28	-4.05	5.19	-11.64	Capital Return %
	---	---	---	---	---	---	94	6	39	67	33	56	Total Rtn % Rank All
	---	---	---	---	---	---	72	1	48	71	43	43	Total Rtn % Rank Obj
	---	---	---	---	---	0.28	1.12	1.46	1.11	0.93	0.75	0.71	Income $
	---	---	---	---	---	0.00	0.05	0.00	0.00	0.08	0.03	0.00	Capital Gains $
	---	---	---	---	---	---	0.81	0.86	0.85	0.88	0.78	0.75	Expense Ratio %
	---	---	---	---	---	---	10.87	16.27	12.38	11.16	8.22	7.75	Income Ratio %
	---	---	---	---	---	---	158	100	64	76	183	---	Turnover Rate %
	---	---	---	---	---	302.0	288.4	271.9	298.7	455.7	467.6	311.2	Net Assets ($mil)

Fund Manager(s)

Vincent T. Lathbury III CFA(1978), since 09-88.
Birthdate: 10-40. BA, Washington & Lee U. 1962 MBA, Temple U. 1976
Robert Parrish CFA, since 01-93.

Manager Experience	Dates Managed	Invest Obj	Std Dev	+/- Index
Robert Parrish				
Merrill Lynch Glb Bd B	03/93 - 12/94	WB	4.54	-0.69

Performance 12-31-94

	1st Qtr	2nd Qtr	3rd Qtr	4th Qtr	Total
1987	---	---	---	---	---
1988	---	---	---	---	---
1989	-0.49	0.48	3.74	3.00	6.83
1990	0.70	6.66	1.95	0.15	9.67
1991	6.16	3.00	7.53	4.90	23.34
1992	2.85	3.54	-2.01	1.72	6.16
1993	4.86	2.66	2.31	3.55	14.06
1994	-2.99	-1.89	1.22	-0.61	-4.25

Bear Market Performance

Decile Rank (5-year period)

Worst			Best

	Worst 3 Mo Period 1985-89	Worst 3 Mo Period 1990-94
Merrill Lynch World Income A	---	-5.32
+/- S&P 500	---	0.44
+/- Best Fit Index : FB HY	---	-1.22

Trailing Returns

	Total Return %	+/- S&P 500	+/- LB Aggregate	% Rank All	% Rank Obj	Growth of $10,000
3 Mo	-0.61	-0.60	-0.99	36	28	9,939
6 Mo	0.60	-4.27	-0.40	45	34	10,060
1 Yr	-4.25	-5.57	-1.33	56	43	9,575
3 Yr Avg	5.05	-1.22	0.50	47	57	11,593
5 Yr Avg	9.41	0.72	1.79	21	20	15,680
10 Yr Avg	---	---	---	---	---	---
15 Yr Avg	---	---	---	---	---	---

Operations

Address and Telephone	Box 9011
	Princeton, NJ 08543-9011
	800-637-3863 / 609-282-2800
Advisor	Fund Asset Management
Subadvisor	None
Distributor	Merrill Lynch Funds Distributor
States Available	All plus GU,PR,VI
Report Grade	A
Income Distrib	Paid Monthly
* Date of Inception	09-29-88
Fiscal Year End	December

Risk Analysis

Time Period	Load-Adj Return %	Risk % Rank All	Risk % Rank Obj	Morningstar Return	Morningstar Risk	Morningstar Risk-Adj Rating
1 Yr	-8.08					
3 Yr	3.63	15	28	0.01[3]	0.44	★★★
5 Yr	8.52	27	14	0.95[3]	0.38	★★★★
10 Yr	---	---	---	---	---	

Average Historical Rating (39 months) 4.1 ★s

[1] 1 = low, 100 = high [2] 1.00 = Hybrid Avg [3] 1.00 = 90-day T-bill return

Other Measures

			Standard S&P 500	Best Fit FB HY
Standard Deviation	4.10	Alpha	0.8	-2.9
Mean	5.02	Beta	0.23	0.62
Sharpe Ratio	0.37	R-Squared	20	43

Investment Style

Stocks

	Port Avg	Rel S&P 500	Style
Price/Earnings Ratio	22.5#	1.22	
Price/Book Ratio	1.1	0.31	
5 Yr Earnings Gr %	19.1#	3.45	
Med Mkt Cap ($mil)	464	0.04	

figure is based on 50% or less of stocks

Bonds

Avg Effective Duration	4.7 Yrs
Avg Effective Maturity	8.9 Yrs
Avg Credit Quality	---
Avg Weighted Coupon	9.14%

Not Available

Diversification Value for Portfolio Types

●	●	▨	▨	▨
Large Cap: High	Small Cap: High	Bond: Medium	Balanced: Medium	Diversified: Medium

Expenses & Fees

Sales Fees	4.00% front
	0.00% deferred
	0.00% 12b-1
Management Fee	0.60% flat fee
3-,5-,10-yr Expense Projections	$64, $82, $133
Annual Brokerage Cost	0.00%

Min Initial Purchase $1000 (Addt'l: $50)
Min IRA Purchase $100 (Addt'l: $1)
Min Auto Invest Plan $1000 (Systematic Inv: $50)

Portfolio 06-30-94

Share Chg (12-93)000	Amount 000	Total Stocks: 14 / Total Fixed-Income: 179	Date of Maturity	Value $000	% Net Assets
	10768	United Kingdom Treasury 8.5%	07-16-07	16454	4.32
	1736766	Kingdom of Spain 9%	02-28-97	12997	3.41
	2143170	Republic of Italy 9%	10-01-98	12917	3.39
	87533	Kingdom of Sweden 11%	01-21-99	11927	3.13
	7989	United Kingdom Treasury 7%	11-06-01	11237	2.95
	74073	Kingdom of Denmark 7%	12-15-04	10762	2.82
	17107	Govt of Canada 6.5%	06-01-04	10218	2.68
	1024692	Kingdom of Spain 8.3%	12-15-98	7194	1.89
	9135	Commonwealth Australia 9.5%	08-15-03	6619	1.74
	9552	Govt of Canada 6.5%	09-01-98	6338	1.66
	47935	Kingdom of Sweden 10.25%	05-05-03	6332	1.66
	7989	Commonwealth Australia 7%	08-15-98	5468	1.44
	7208	Queensland Treasury 8%	05-14-03	4737	1.24
	4342	Grand Union 11.25%	07-15-00	4255	1.12
	4689	US Treasury Bond 6.25%	08-15-23	3943	1.04
	3474	Owens-Illinois 11%	12-01-03	3682	0.97
	5881	G-I Holdings Cv 12.07%	10-01-98	3573	0.94
	3474	Coltec Industries 10.25%	04-01-02	3508	0.92
	3474	Heileman Acquisition 9.625%	01-31-04	3170	0.83
	3474	Fresh Del Monte Produce 10%	05-01-03	3161	0.83

Index Allocation

	% of Stocks
S&P 500	28.7
S&P MidCap 400	0.0
U.S. Small Cap	71.3
Foreign	0.0

Composition % 09-30-94

Cash	8.6	Preferreds	0.0
Stocks	0.1	Convertibles	4.5
Bonds	87.4	Other	-0.6

Tax Analysis

	Tax-Adj Historical Return %	% Pretax Return
3 Yr Avg	1.68	32.1
5 Yr Avg	5.41	53.1
10 Yr Avg	---	---
Potential Capital Gain Exposure (% of assets)		-14%

Most Similar Funds in MF500

Global Income Plus	Fair Fit
Capital World Bond	Weak Fit
Oppenheimer Strat Income A	Weak Fit

Bond Credit Analysis 05-27-94

% of Bonds			
US Govt	6	BB	38
AAA	22	B	0
AA	2	Below B	1
A	3	NR/NA	1
BBB	27		

Stock Sector Weightings

	% of Stocks	Relative S&P 500
Utilities	6.8	0.55
Energy	6.6	0.65
Financials	26.5	2.51
Industrial Cyclicals	18.2	1.11
Consumer Durables	10.5	1.70
Consumer Staples	11.9	0.95
Services	0.0	0.00
Retail	0.0	0.00
Health	0.0	0.00
Technology	19.6	2.14

MORNINGSTAR 1995 Mutual Fund 500

Mexico Fund

	Ticker	NAV	Mkt Price	Prem/Disc	Yield	Objective
	MXF	$20.53	$22.63	10.2%	1.0%	Latin America

Mexico Fund seeks long-term capital appreciation.

The fund invests in securities, primarily equities, listed on the Bolsa Mexicana de Valores, S.A. de C.V. (the Mexican Stock Exchange).

The fund had a rights offering in December 1983 that raised $28 million. An offering in March 1992 raised $131.5 million; one in September 1993 raised $188 million.

| 134.7 | 7.7 | -12.8 | -9.8 | -7.3 | -11.4 | -4.6 | 11.1 | 7.7 | -2.0 | 8.7 | 14.5 | Highest Prem/Disc |
| 17.6 | -19.1 | -39.1 | -45.9 | -38.6 | -35.5 | -28.7 | -16.1 | -18.2 | -23.5 | -20.6 | -10.5 | Lowest Prem/Disc |

Historical Profile

Return High
Risk Above Average
Rating ★★★★ Above Average

Growth of $10,000
■ at NAV ($000)
— at Market Price ($000)

Premium Discount %

	1983	1984	1985	1986	1987	1988	1989	1990	1991	1992	1993	1994	History
	2.63	3.26	3.49	5.30	4.72	7.86	12.55	15.64	25.32	25.31	36.60	20.53	NAV
	-0.42	31.62	21.67	64.01	-7.23	77.85	69.98	27.91	72.63	26.87	58.47	-43.33	NAV Total Return %
	-22.88	25.35	-10.07	45.33	-12.49	61.24	38.30	31.02	42.15	19.26	48.41	-44.65	+/- S&P 500
	-24.11	24.24	-34.50	-5.43	-31.87	49.58	59.45	51.36	60.50	39.05	51.11	-51.11	+/- MSCI EAFE
	N/A	N/A	N/A	N/A	N/A	17.35	-10.72	-18.11	-47.33	-2.95	14.45	1.02	+/- MSCI Mexico
	22.23	7.66	14.61	12.15	3.71	11.33	10.31	3.29	1.90	2.88	2.25	0.50	Income Return %
	-22.65	23.95	7.06	51.86	-10.94	66.53	59.67	24.62	70.73	24.00	56.21	-43.84	Capital Return %
	93	1	71	4	86	1	2	1	3	4	6	100	Total Rtn % Rank All
	NMF	NMF	NMF	NMF	NMF	NMF	1	33	66	1	30	90	Total Rtn % Rank Obj
	28.74	-13.48	-12.18	84.24	25.72	34.27	120.18	18.43	80.77	32.63	83.82	-41.39	Market Total Rtn %
	81.4	-7.2	-22.1	-31.0	-30.4	-25.7	-15.4	-4.9	-9.0	-10.6	-6.5	-3.3	Avg Prem/Disc %
	0.97	0.17	0.29	0.29	0.29	0.34	0.62	0.40	0.35	0.62	0.55	0.23	Income $
	0.00	0.00	0.00	0.00	0.00	0.00	0.00	0.00	1.02	2.34	0.15	0.07	Capital Gains $
	---	---	2.26	1.99	1.74	1.74	1.77	1.60	1.25	1.08	1.08	0.92	Expense Ratio %
	---	---	8.19	9.03	4.77	4.44	7.81	4.21	-0.23	1.89	2.27	0.63	Income Ratio %
	---	---	43	33	35	20	11	9	3	16	5	4	Turnover Rate %
	---	---	64.8	104.7	93.1	155.0	246.6	287.7	495.7	665.6	1363.7	1248.1	Net Assets ($mil)

Manager's Investment Style

As the fund's low turnover ratio suggests, management takes a buy-and-hold approach to the Mexican market. Management doesn't merely index the market, though: Instead, it buys businesses, not just stocks. As such, the fund doesn't play sectors or particular stories. It typically keeps a small cash position on hand so it can add to its favorite stocks on weakness.

Fund Manager(s)

Jose Luis Gomez-Pimienta. Since 6-81. BA Universidad Iberoamericana.

Manager Experience

	Dates Managed	Invest Obj	Std Dev	+/- Index
Not available.				

NAV Performance % 12-30-94

	1st Qtr	2nd Qtr	3rd Qtr	4th Qtr	Total
1987	62.64	21.55	67.07	-71.91	-7.23
1988	46.61	6.21	4.87	8.91	77.85
1989	9.54	34.62	15.39	-0.11	69.98
1990	4.86	14.86	-10.25	18.32	27.91
1991	18.41	27.16	3.64	10.62	72.63
1992	48.28	-22.32	-17.75	33.91	26.87
1993	2.53	-1.21	11.97	39.72	58.47
1994	-12.51	-7.30	21.47	-42.48	-43.33

Bear Market Performance

Decile Rank (5-year period)

Worst ——————— Best

	Worst 3 Mo Period 1985-89	Worst 3 Mo Period 1990-94
Mexico Fund	-71.91	-42.48
+/- S&P 500	-49.39	-42.46

Trailing Returns

	NAV Total Return %	+/- S&P 500	+/- MSCI Mexico	% Rank All	% Rank Obj	Mkt Total Return %
3 Mo	-42.48	-42.46	-2.25	100	90	-31.76
6 Mo	-30.13	-34.99	-0.34	100	90	-18.96
1 Yr	-43.33	-44.65	1.02	100	90	-41.39
3 Yr Avg	4.44	-1.82	3.12	73	75	12.63
5 Yr Avg	20.26	11.57	-7.03	3	33	25.06
10 Yr Avg	30.27	15.89	N/A	1	NMF	33.80

Operations

Address and Telephone	342 Madison Avenue, Suite 909 New York, NY 10173 212-936-5100 / 800-224-4134
Advisor	Impulsora del Fondo Mexico
Subadvisor	N/A
Administrator	Impulsora del Fondo Mexico
Transfer Agent	American Stock Transfer & Trust
Custodian	S.D. Indeval S.A. de C.V.
Auditor	Arthur Andersen & Co.
Legal Counsel	Dechert Price & Rhoads

Income Distrib Schedule	Paid Irregularly
Management Fee	0.85%, 0.25%A
Reinvestment Plan	Yes
Direct Purchase Plan	No
Shares Outstanding	37,282,359
Exchange	NYSE
Date of Inception	06-11-81
Shareholder Report	B-

Risk Analysis

	Risk % Rank[1] All	Obj	Morningstar[2] Return	Risk	Morningstar Risk-Adj Rating
3 Yr	100	87	0.11	2.28	★
5 Yr	97	33	3.65	1.48	★★★★
10 Yr	91	NMF	5.47	1.65	★★★★★

Average Historical Rating (127 months) 4.1 ★s

[1] 1 = Low, 100 = High [2] 1.00 = Equity Avg [3] 1.00 = 90-day T-bill Return

Other Measures

			S&P 500
Standard Deviation	38.25	Alpha	6.57
Mean	12.48	Beta	0.89
Sharpe Ratio	0.23	R-Squared	3

Investment Style

	Stock Portfolio Avg	Rel WS Mexico	Rel WS Foreign
Price/Earnings Ratio	22.7	1.14	0.46
Price/Cash Flow Ratio	19.1	1.12	1.31
Price/Book Ratio	3.1	1.03	1.03
5 Yr Earnings Gr %	26.1#	1.22	NMF
Return on Assets %	11.9#	0.79	2.58
Debt % Total Cap	19.9	1.13	0.62
Med Mkt Cap ($mil)	4395	0.79	0.70

figure is based on less than 50% of stocks

Country Exposure (top five) 12-31-94

	Securities %		Currency %
Mexico	93	Mexico	100

Diversification Value for Portfolio Types

● Large Cap: High ● Small Cap: High ● Bond: High ● Balanced: High ● Diversified: High

Portfolio 10-31-94

Share Chg (07-94)	Amount	Total Equity: 51 Total Fixed-Income: 0	Value $000	% Total Invest
0	43698422	Cifra Cl B	124424	9.94
0	11621958	Cemex Cl A	104045	8.31
0	4258400	Kimberly-Clark de Mexico A	84553	6.76
0	6975994	Grupo Carso Cl A1	74232	5.93
0	7650043	Apasco Cl A	71271	5.69
0	6958474	Grupo Industrial Bimbo Cl A	56522	4.52
0	3582500	Tolmex Cl B2	52150	4.17
0	6968450	Grupo Fin Banamex Accival C	47879	3.83
0	17085328	Telefonos de Mexico Cl L	47653	3.81
0	16232807	Cifra Cl C	43763	3.50
0	18960000	Controladora Com Mexicana B	34555	2.76
0	19736000	Grupo Industrial Maseca Cl B	32177	2.57
0	11390218	Telefonos de Mexico Cl A	31569	2.52
0	6380834	Grupo Sidek Cl A	27308	2.18
0	6093000	Fomento Economico Mexicana B	26786	2.14
0	1950000	Alfa (Mexico)	26683	2.13
250000	6152232	Grupo Sidek Cl B	26330	2.10
0	880332	Empresa ICA	26271	2.10
210000	1137200	Grupo Televisa (Mexico)	25162	2.01
0	3331861	Vitro Cl A	23329	1.86
0	4372941	Grupo Financiero Serfin Cl B	18842	1.51
0	16482501	Grupo Financiero Bancomer B	15836	1.27
0	863298	Grupo Tribasa	13623	1.09
0	1789190	Desc Soc de Fomento Ind Cl B	13231	1.06
0	1789190	Desc Soc de Fomento Ind Cl A	12762	1.02

Composition % 12-31-94

Cash	7.0	Preferreds	0.0
Stocks	93.0	Convertibles	0.0
Bonds	0.0	Other	0.0

Tax Analysis

	Tax-Adj Historical Return %	% Pretax Return
3 Yr Avg	5.93	50.5
5 Yr Avg	20.57	76.1
10 Yr Avg	27.98	67.9

Potential Capital Gain Exposure (% of assets) 9

Most Similar Funds in MF500

American Heritage	Weak Fit
Growth Fund Spain	Weak Fit
Fidelity Global Bond	Weak Fit

Sector Weightings

	% of Stocks
Utilities	8.1
Energy	0.0
Financials	9.9
Industrial Cyclicals	34.2
Consumer Durables	3.9
Consumer Staples	18.1
Services	5.2
Retail	20.6
Health	0.0
Technology	0.0

MFS Bond A

	Ticker	Load	NAV	Yield	SEC Yield	Assets	Objective
	MFBFX	4.75%	12.13	7.4%	7.48%	434.6	Corp General

MFS Bond Fund - Class A seeks current income.
The fund invests at least 80% of its assets in investment-grade debt securities and unrated securities of comparable quality. Up to 20% of its assets may be invested in lower-rated securities, convertible securities, or preferred stocks. Up to 10% of assets may be held in common stocks acquired through conversion of other securities.
Class A shares have front loads and lower 12b-1 fees; Class B shares have deferred loads and conversion features; Class C shares have level loads. Prior to Aug. 3, 1992, the fund was named Massachusetts Financial Bond Fund.

Historical Profile
Return	Above Average
Risk	Above Average
Rating	★★★
	Neutral

Investment Style History
Fixed Income
Income Rtn % Rank Obj

| 61 | 39 | 39 | 67 | 10 | 20 | 3 | 19 |

Growth of $10,000
- ‖‖ Value of Fund ($000)
- — Value of Index ($000)
  LB Corp
- ▼ Manager Change
- ▽ Partial Manager Change
- ► Mgr Unknown After
- ◄ Mgr Unknown Before

Performance Quartile
(Within Objective)

	1983	1984	1985	1986	1987	1988	1989	1990	1991	1992	1993	1994	History
	12.67	12.74	14.31	14.66	12.87	12.75	13.24	13.05	14.05	13.80	13.63	12.13	NAV
	9.94	12.58	25.24	15.97	-1.03	8.33	13.33	6.99	18.13	6.28	13.86	-4.46	Total Return %
	1.56	-2.57	3.11	0.72	-3.78	0.45	-1.21	-1.95	2.13	-0.97	4.11	-1.54	+/- LB Aggregate
	0.66	-4.04	1.18	-0.56	-3.58	-0.89	-0.65	-0.16	-0.38	-2.42	1.69	-0.54	+/- LB Corporate
	11.57	12.03	12.92	10.59	8.63	9.26	9.49	8.43	10.47	8.06	8.82	6.54	Income Return %
	-1.63	0.55	12.32	5.38	-9.66	-0.93	3.84	-1.44	7.66	-1.78	5.04	-11.01	Capital Return %
	79	14	45	49	67	72	52	22	48	66	34	58	Total Rtn % Rank All
	29	48	12	27	88	56	23	48	26	71	13	67	Total Rtn % Rank Obj
	1.43	1.40	1.44	1.47	1.27	1.17	1.17	1.08	1.24	1.10	1.19	0.90	Income $
	0.00	0.00	0.00	0.40	0.43	0.00	0.00	0.00	0.00	0.00	0.85	0.00	Capital Gains $
	0.84	0.81	0.84	0.79	0.68	0.76	0.83	0.75	0.79	0.91	0.88	0.96	Expense Ratio %
	11.92	11.11	11.53	10.29	8.44	8.85	8.93	9.10	8.82	8.39	7.82	7.17	Income Ratio %
	238	216	262	218	334	287	160	186	189	243	330	410	Turnover Rate %
	270.4	235.5	246.4	309.0	302.2	305.1	315.7	305.6	499.5	463.5	494.5	434.6	Net Assets ($mil)

Manager's Investment Style
Management delves into a broad array of securities, including not only corporates and Treasuries, but also foreign debt and occasionally high-yield and municipal bonds. Management shifts among these categories frequently, swinging from an aggressive to defensive stance.

Fund Manager(s)
Geoffrey L. Kurinsky, since 1989. Birthdate: 07-53. BBA, U. of Massachusetts 1976 MBA, Boston U. 1984

Manager Experience

	Dates Managed	Invest Obj	Std Dev	+/- Index
Geoffrey L. Kurinsky				
MFS Limited Maturity A	02/92 - 12/94	CG	2.36	-0.95
MFS Municipal Ltd Mat B	09/93 - 12/94	MN	2.77	1.27

Performance 12-31-94

	1st Qtr	2nd Qtr	3rd Qtr	4th Qtr	Total
1987	2.21	-4.71	-3.72	5.54	-1.03
1988	4.90	1.12	1.12	1.00	8.33
1989	0.87	7.03	1.77	3.15	13.33
1990	-1.34	3.85	-0.60	5.05	6.99
1991	3.17	1.73	6.38	5.80	18.13
1992	-1.15	4.67	3.66	-0.91	6.28
1993	5.39	3.46	4.08	0.33	13.86
1994	-3.58	-2.27	0.64	0.75	-4.46

Bear Market Performance
Decile Rank (5-year period)

Worst ▬▬ Best

	Worst 3 Mo Period 1985-89	Worst 3 Mo Period 1990-94
MFS Bond A	-6.12	-6.59
+/- LB Aggregate	-2.57	-1.66
+/- Best Fit Index : LB Corp	-2.01	-0.33

Trailing Returns

	Total Return %	+/- LB Aggregate	+/- LB Corp	% Rank All	% Rank Obj	Growth of $10,000
3 Mo	0.75	0.37	0.31	8	10	10,075
6 Mo	1.39	0.40	0.22	32	10	10,139
1 Yr	-4.46	-1.54	-0.54	58	67	9,554
3 Yr Avg	4.95	0.41	-0.46	49	34	11,561
5 Yr Avg	7.88	0.25	-0.39	35	25	14,611
10 Yr Avg	9.94	-0.01	-0.69	58	24	25,785
15 Yr Avg	10.55	-0.25	-0.77	71	28	45,038

Operations

Address and Telephone	500 Boylston Street
	Boston, MA 02116
	800-637-2929 / 617-954-5000
Advisor	Massachusetts Financial Services
Subadvisor	None
Distributor	MFS Financial Services
States Available	All
Report Grade	C+
Income Distrib	Paid Monthly
Date of Inception	05-08-74
Fiscal Year End	April

Min Initial Purchase	$1000 (Addt'l: $50)
Min IRA Purchase	$250 (Addt'l: $50)
Min Auto Invest Plan	$50 (Systematic Inv: $50)

Expenses & Fees
Sales Fees	4.75% front
	0.00% deferred
	0.35% 12b-1
Management Fee	0.23% max./0.19% min.+2.75%l
3-,5-,10-yr Expense Projections	$76, $98, $159

Risk Analysis

Time Period	Load-Adj Return %	Risk % Rank All	Risk % Rank Obj	Morningstar[2] Return	Morningstar Risk	Morningstar Risk-Adj Rating
1 Yr	-9.00					
3 Yr	3.26	33	73	-0.09[3]	1.15	★★★
5 Yr	6.83	32	67	0.51[3]	1.13	★★★
10 Yr	9.40	25	51	0.94[3]	1.12	★★★

Average Historical Rating (109 months)   3.0 ★s

[1] 1 = low, 100 = high [2] 1.00 = Taxable Avg [3] 1.00 = 90-day T-bill return

Other Measures

			Standard LB Agg	Best Fit LB Corp
Standard Deviation	4.90	Alpha	0.3	-0.3
Mean	4.96	Beta	1.15	0.93
Sharpe Ratio	0.29	R-Squared	89	91

Investment Style

Interest-Rate Stance
Avg Effective Duration	5.6 Yrs
Avg Effective Maturity	11.8 Yrs

Quality
Avg Credit Quality	A
Avg Weighted Coupon	7.67%
Avg Weighted Price	86.76% of Par

Diversification Value for Portfolio Types

Large Cap: Medium	Small Cap: High	Bond: None	Balanced: Medium	Diversified: Medium

Portfolio 10-31-94

Amount 000	Date of Maturity	Total Stocks: 0 Total Fixed-Income: 149	Value $000	% Net Assets
40025	11-15-24	US Treasury Bond 7.5%	37892	8.60
76314	2009	US Treasury Bond 0%	22431	5.09
13342	1998	GMAC 7.125%	13018	2.95
15630	08-15-23	US Treasury Bond 6.25%	12509	2.84
7560	2004	American Express Cred 7.85%	7315	1.66
8005	08-10-18	News America Holdings 8.25%	6934	1.57
7204	2013	USX-Marathon Group 9.125%	6886	1.56
8005	12-01-03	Korea Electric Power 6.375%	6791	1.54
8272	10-15-05	Unicom 6.4%	6595	1.50
6226	1997	ADVANTA 7.04%	6105	1.38
6448	01-15-16	First PV Funding 10.15%	5884	1.33
6537	2017	Federal Express 7.96%	5685	1.29
5684	1999	United Companies Finl 9.35%	5684	1.29
5434	07-15-98	US Treasury Note 8.25%	5595	1.27
6137	2011	GG1B Funding 7.43%	5251	1.19
5025	06-01-02	Owens-Corning Fiberglas 8.875%	5066	1.15
4892	1998	Westinghouse Credit 9%	4962	1.13
4447	10-01-10	Coastal 10.75%	4938	1.12
4536	05-15-22	Georgia-Pacific 9.5%	4513	1.02
4447	1997	GMAC 7.875%	4473	1.01
4759	01-15-13	Time Warner 9.125%	4329	0.98
4447	2001	Stone Container 9.875%	4169	0.95
4269	07-15-24	News America Holdings 9.5%	4168	0.95
4447	06-30-03	Qantas Airways 7.5%	4051	0.92
4127	12-01-97	AMR 7.75%	4043	0.92

Composition % 12-31-94

Cash	3.5	Preferreds	0.0
Stocks	0.1	Convertibles	0.0
Bonds	96.4	Other	0.0

Tax Analysis

	Tax-Adj Historical Return %	% Pretax Return
3 Yr Avg	1.48	28.8
5 Yr Avg	4.61	54.8
10 Yr Avg	6.08	50.9
Potential Capital Gain Exposure (% of assets)		-12%

Most Similar Funds in MF500

Scudder Income	Strong Fit
Fidelity Government Secs	Strong Fit
PaineWebber Invmt Grade Inc	Strong Fit

Coupon Range

	% of Bonds	Rel Obj
0%	5.4	2.48
0% to 8.5%	35.8	0.56
8.5% to 9.5%	23.4	1.44
9.5% to 11%	19.3	2.08
More than 11%	16.1	4.14
Not applicable	0.0	0.00

Credit Analysis 11-30-94
% of Bonds

US Govt	36	BB	19
AAA	3	B	0
AA	3	Below B	0
A	4	NR/NA	0
BBB	35		

MORNINGSTAR 1995 Mutual Fund 500

MFS Emerging Growth B

	Ticker	Load	NAV	Yield	SEC Yield	Assets	Objective
	MEGBX	4.00%d	18.89	0.0%	N/A	801.4	Small Company

MFS Emerging Growth Fund - Class B seeks long-term growth of capital; income is incidental.

The fund normally invests at least 80% of its assets in common stocks of small- and medium-size companies. These companies have just begun their life cycles but have the potential to become major enterprises. The fund may also invest in established companies whose earnings growth is expected to accelerate. It may invest up to 25% of its assets in foreign securities. The fund may also invest in investment-grade debt obligations.

Prior to Sept. 3, 1993, the fund was named MFS Lifetime Emerging Growth Fund.

Manager's Investment Style

Manager John Ballen seeks fast-growing, emerging companies that have the potential to become established firms, focusing specifically on the technology, health, and services sectors. Although he considers valuations, he is willing to pay up for growth. He is willing to hold his stock choices for the long term, even through short-term periods of market disfavor.

Fund Manager(s)

John W. Ballen, since 12-86. MA, U. of New South Wales 1982 MBA, Sranford U. 1984

Manager Experience

	Dates Managed	Invest Obj	Std Dev	+/- Index
John W. Ballen				
MFS Research A	09/91 - 09/93	G	14.17	6.18

Historical Profile

Return	High
Risk	High
Rating	★★★★★
	Highest

Investment Style History
Equity

Average % Stocks Held in Portfolio

Stocks Held: 88% 96% 94% 92% 94% 96% 99% 97%

Growth of $10,000

||||| Value of Fund ($000)
— Value of Index ($000)
Russ 2000
▼ Manager Change
▽ Partial Manager Change
► Mgr Unknown After
◄ Mgr Unknown Before

Performance Quartile (Within Objective)

1983	1984	1985	1986	1987	1988	1989	1990	1991	1992	1993	1994	History
---	---	---	5.49	5.75	6.21	7.88	7.68	13.79	15.25	18.40	18.89	NAV
---	---	---	-0.18 *	4.74	8.00	26.89	-2.54	87.62	11.72	24.02	4.00	Total Return %
---	---	---	-0.52 *	-0.52	-8.61	-4.79	0.58	57.13	4.10	13.97	2.69	+/- S&P 500
---	---	---	---	8.25	-12.54	2.95	11.02	44.16	-0.04	9.49	6.66	+/- Wilshire 4500
---	---	---	0.00	0.00	0.00	0.00	0.00	0.00	0.00	0.00	0.00	Income Return %
---	---	---	-0.18	4.74	8.00	26.89	-2.54	87.61	11.71	24.02	4.00	Capital Return %
---	---	---	24	73	19	63	1	16	12	5		Total Rtn % Rank All
---	---	---	19	88	31	26	3	61	17	17		Total Rtn % Rank Obj
---	---	---	0.00	0.00	0.00	0.00	0.00	0.00	0.00	0.00	0.00	Income $
---	---	---	0.00	0.00	0.00	0.00	0.00	0.59	0.15	0.50	0.25	Capital Gains $
---	---	---	2.40	2.30	2.81	2.75	2.50	2.33	2.19	2.23		Expense Ratio %
---	---	---	-1.50	-1.65	-1.91	-1.86	-1.98	-2.00	-1.61	-1.95		Income Ratio %
---	---	---	---	57	95	86	112	59	58	---		Turnover Rate %
---	---	---	---	57.6	68.1	84.9	76.3	189.4	385.5	678.1	801.4	Net Assets ($mil)

Performance 12-31-94

	1st Qtr	2nd Qtr	3rd Qtr	4th Qtr	Total
1987	46.63	-0.75	-0.25	-27.85	4.74
1988	13.04	5.38	-10.22	0.98	8.00
1989	3.54	9.80	11.61	0.00	26.89
1990	1.02	15.33	-30.83	20.94	-2.54
1991	33.59	-2.14	18.13	21.49	87.62
1992	1.31	-11.24	2.82	20.83	11.72
1993	-4.39	14.13	6.07	7.16	24.02
1994	0.16	-9.22	16.02	-1.41	4.00

Bear Market Performance

Decile Rank (5-year period)

Worst | Best

	Worst 3 Mo Period 1985-89	Worst 3 Mo Period 1990-94
MFS Emerging Growth B	---	-30.83
+/- S&P 500	---	-17.08
+/- Best Fit Index : Russ 2000	---	-6.29

Trailing Returns

	Total Return %	+/- S&P 500	+/- Wil 4500	% Rank All	Obj	Growth of $10,000
3 Mo	-1.41	-1.39	1.09	54	57	9,859
6 Mo	14.39	9.52	10.19	3	19	11,439
1 Yr	4.00	2.69	6.66	5	17	10,400
3 Yr Avg	12.95	6.69	5.34	6	23	14,410
5 Yr Avg	21.38	12.69	12.29	1	4	26,349
10 Yr Avg	---	---	---	---	---	---
15 Yr Avg	---	---	---	---	---	---

Operations

Address and Telephone	500 Boylston Street
	Boston, MA 02116
	800-637-2929 / 617-954-5000
Advisor	Massachusetts Financial Services
Subadvisor	None
Distributor	MFS Financial Services
States Available	All
Report Grade	B
Income Distrib	Paid Annually
* Date of Inception	12-29-86
Fiscal Year End	November

Min Initial Purchase	$1000 (Addt'l: $50)
Min IRA Purchase	$250 (Addt'l: $50)
Min Auto Invest Plan	$50 (Systematic Inv: $50)

Expenses & Fees

Sales Fees	0.00% front
	4.00% deferred
	1.00% 12b-1
Management Fee	0.75% flat fee
3-,5-,10-yr Expense Projections	$99, $138, $233
Annual Brokerage Cost	0.16%

Risk Analysis

Time Period	Load-Adj Return %	Risk % Rank [1] All	Obj	Morningstar [2] Return	Morningstar Risk	Morningstar Risk-Adj Rating
1 Yr	0.00					
3 Yr	12.16	96	84	2.69 [3]	1.50	★★★★
5 Yr	21.29	97	85	5.26 [3]	1.45	★★★★★
10 Yr	---	---	---	---	---	

Average Historical Rating (61 months) 3.8 ★s

[1] 1 = low, 100 = high [2] 1.00 = Equity Avg [3] 1.00 = 90-day T-bill return

Other Measures

			Standard S&P 500	Best Fit Russ 2000
Standard Deviation	18.96	Alpha	7.3	-0.3
Mean	14.01	Beta	1.17	1.34
Sharpe Ratio	0.55	R-Squared	24	70

Investment Style

	Stock Portfolio Avg	Relative S&P 500
Price/Earnings Ratio	26.3	1.43
Price/Book Ratio	5.1	1.50
5 Yr Earnings Gr %	40.7#	7.32
Return on Assets %	12.2	1.63
Debt % Total Cap	23.0	0.81
Med Mkt Cap ($mil)	980	0.08

figure is based on 50% or less of stocks

Style Value Blend Growth / Size Large Med Small

Diversification Value for Portfolio Types

Large Cap: High	Small Cap: Low	Bond: High	Balanced: Medium	Diversified: High

Portfolio 05-31-94

Total Stocks: 275
Total Fixed-Income: 3

Share Chg (11-93)000	Amount 000		Value $000	% Net Assets
19	1356	Oracle Systems	46436	6.32
770	1519	Hospitality Franchise System	41202	5.61
10	734	Mid-Atlantic Medical Svcs	35526	4.84
13	942	Office Depot	35189	4.79
12	865	CUC International	25300	3.44
56	444	Autodesk	22867	3.11
75	297	PacifiCare Health Sys Cl B	16983	2.31
507	623	Micro Warehouse	15738	2.14
28	265	Grupo Televisa (ADR)	15326	2.09
8	973	System Software Associates	14590	1.99
-185	942	Cadence Design Systems	14005	1.91
362	362	Promus	13820	1.88
403	965	Applebee's International	13748	1.87
153	276	United HealthCare	13297	1.81
-2	427	Integrated Health Services	12477	1.70
539	783	IDB Communications Group	11360	1.55
-4	367	Medical Care America	10053	1.37
-9	211	Compuware	8950	1.22
179	544	Informix	8743	1.19
-21	721	T2 Medical	8656	1.18
472	517	Hometown Buffet	8265	1.13
200	550	Consolidated Stores	7904	1.08
12	433	Grand Casinos	7524	1.02
542	757	President Riverboat Casinos	7191	0.98
115	251	Nine West Group	6873	0.94

Composition % 12-31-94

Cash	0.9	Preferreds	0.0
Stocks	98.5	Convertibles	0.6
Bonds	0.0	Other	0.0

Index Allocation

	% of Stocks
S&P 500	15.1
S&P MidCap 400	16.5
U.S. Small Cap	66.3
Foreign	2.1

Tax Analysis

	Tax-Adj Historical Return %	% Pretax Return
3 Yr Avg	12.43	95.5
5 Yr Avg	20.77	96.0
10 Yr Avg	---	---
Potential Capital Gain Exposure (% of assets)		31%

Most Similar Funds in MF500

Berger 100	Weak Fit
AIM Constellation	Weak Fit
Hancock Emerging Growth B	Weak Fit

Sector Weightings

	% of Stocks	Relative S&P 500
Utilities	0.2	0.02
Energy	0.0	0.00
Financials	7.8	0.74
Industrial Cyclicals	6.6	0.40
Consumer Durables	1.7	0.27
Consumer Staples	0.1	0.01
Services	28.0	3.44
Retail	9.5	1.63
Health	16.6	1.91
Technology	29.6	3.23

MFS High-Income A

	Ticker	Load	NAV	Yield	SEC Yield	Assets	Objective
	MHITX	4.75%	4.82	9.2%	10.02%	501.7	Corp Hi Yld

MFS High-Income Fund - Class A seeks high income.

The fund invests primarily in fixed-income securities rated BBB or lower. No more than 25% of the fund's assets may be invested in equity securities, including common stocks, warrants, and rights. The fund may invest up to 50% of its assets in foreign securities.

Class A shares have front loads; Class B shares have deferred loads, higher 12b-1 fees, and conversion features; Class C shares have level loads. Prior to Aug. 3, 1992, the fund was named Massachusetts Financial High-Income Trust Series I. On Sept. 27, 1993, MFS Lifetime High-Income Fund merged into this fund.

Manager's Investment Style

A recent management change makes long-term categorization of the strategy unavailable. To date, however, management has maintained the relatively higher credit portfolio adopted by the fund in 1992. It is likely, though, that the change in manager will bring some exploration of lower-credit paper, as current manager Robert Manning's background is in distressed issues. The overall criteria remains the same, nonetheless. Management looks for management ownership, strong cash flows, tangible assets, appealing capital structures, and favorable industry positioning. It also buys cheap high-yield paper.

Fund Manager(s)

Robert J. Manning, since 06-94. BS, U. of Lowell 1984 MS, Boston C. 1987

Manager Experience

	Dates Managed	Invest Obj	Std Dev	+/- Index
Robert J. Manning				
MFS Special Value	06/92 - 12/94	DE	8.49	0.64

Historical Profile
Return	Average
Risk	Low
Rating	★★★★
	Above Average

Investment Style History
Fixed Income

Income Rtn % Rank Obj

Growth of $10,000
- |||| Value of Fund ($000)
- — Value of Index ($000) LB Agg
- ▼ Manager Change
- ▽ Partial Manager Change
- ► Mgr Unknown After
- ◄ Mgr Unknown Before

Performance Quartile
(Within Objective)

1983	1984	1985	1986	1987	1988	1989	1990	1991	1992	1993	1994	History
7.68	6.70	7.22	6.92	6.02	5.93	5.09	3.60	4.69	4.93	5.40	4.82	NAV
26.50	6.15	23.48	10.32	-0.42	12.35	-1.98	-16.73	48.90	17.04	19.41	-2.61	Total Return %
18.12	-9.00	1.35	-4.93	-3.18	4.47	-16.52	-25.68	32.90	9.80	9.66	0.31	+/- LB Aggregate
---	---	---	-5.32	-6.95	0.92	-2.37	-10.35	5.15	0.38	0.51	-1.63	+/- FB High-Yield
14.22	13.44	15.71	13.14	12.45	13.05	12.18	12.54	18.62	11.93	9.87	8.13	Income Return %
12.28	-7.29	7.76	-2.83	-12.87	-0.70	-14.17	-29.27	30.28	5.12	9.53	-10.74	Capital Return %
19	47	52	83	63	43	99	94	8	7	18	40	Total Rtn % Rank All
1	76	22	85	81	62	64	87	9	53	38	37	Total Rtn % Rank Obj
0.91	0.91	0.94	0.94	0.94	0.75	0.76	0.71	0.59	0.53	0.46	0.44	Income $
0.00	0.49	0.00	0.10	0.01	0.05	0.00	0.00	0.00	0.00	0.00	0.00	Capital Gains $
1.03	0.83	0.87	0.80	0.71	0.75	0.87	0.87	1.05	1.10	1.03	1.00	Expense Ratio %
16.07	13.19	14.36	12.47	12.49	11.49	12.44	12.17	14.97	11.59	10.21	8.22	Income Ratio %
162	101	79	49	46	28	34	25	24	28	75	68	Turnover Rate %
239.6	358.0	407.6	581.1	982.1	863.7	628.6	375.3	531.5	567.4	628.7	501.7	Net Assets ($mil)

Performance 12-31-94

	1st Qtr	2nd Qtr	3rd Qtr	4th Qtr	Total
1987	6.60	-1.31	-1.95	-3.46	-0.42
1988	5.39	1.88	3.21	1.38	12.35
1989	2.29	3.61	-2.10	-5.53	-1.98
1990	-5.55	3.29	-9.21	-5.98	-16.73
1991	20.69	9.95	7.89	3.99	48.90
1992	8.19	2.77	3.97	1.25	17.04
1993	7.55	4.58	1.78	4.30	19.41
1994	-1.25	-2.27	1.57	-0.65	-2.61

Bear Market Performance

Decile Rank (5-year period)

Worst ———————————— Best

	Worst 3 Mo Period 1985-89	Worst 3 Mo Period 1990-94
MFS High-Income A	-8.02	-15.95
+/- LB Aggregate	-8.83	-16.69
+/- Best Fit Index : FB HY	---	-1.84

Trailing Returns

	Total Return %	+/- LB Aggregate	+/- FB High-Yield	% Rank All	% Rank Obj	Growth of $10,000
3 Mo	-0.65	-1.02	-0.60	37	31	9,935
6 Mo	0.92	-0.07	-0.64	39	14	10,092
1 Yr	-2.61	0.31	-1.63	40	37	9,739
3 Yr Avg	10.82	6.28	-0.34	11	35	13,611
5 Yr Avg	11.03	3.41	-2.04	12	36	16,876
10 Yr Avg	9.69	-0.26	---	62	64	25,208
15 Yr Avg	11.54	0.74	---	60	40	51,480

Operations

Address and Telephone	500 Boylston Street Boston, MA 02116 800-637-2929 / 617-954-5000
Advisor	Massachusetts Financial Services
Subadvisor	None
Distributor	MFS Financial Services
States Available	All
Report Grade	B
Income Distrib	Paid Monthly
Date of Inception	02-17-78
Fiscal Year End	January

Risk Analysis

Time Period	Load-Adj Return %	Risk % Rank [1] All	Obj	Morningstar [2] Return	Risk	Morningstar Risk-Adj Rating
1 Yr	-7.24					
3 Yr	9.04	9	42	1.66 [3]	0.37	★★★★
5 Yr	9.96	49	81	1.34 [3]	0.65	★★★★
10 Yr	9.15	37	77	0.51	0.53	★★★

Average Historical Rating (101 months)   3.2 ★s

[1] 1 = low, 100 = high   [2] 1.00 = Hybrid Avg   [3] 1.00 = 90-day T-bill return

Other Measures

			Standard LB Agg	Best Fit FB HY
Standard Deviation	5.19	Alpha	6.4	-1.3
Mean	10.46	Beta	0.68	1.15
Sharpe Ratio	1.33	R-Squared	28	92

Investment Style

Interest-Rate Stance
Avg Effective Duration	4.8 Yrs
Avg Effective Maturity	8.3 Yrs

Quality
Avg Credit Quality	B
Avg Weighted Coupon	9.47%
Avg Weighted Price	91.75% of Par

Diversification Value for Portfolio Types

Large Cap: High	Small Cap: Medium	Bond: Medium	Balanced: High	Diversified: High

Portfolio 07-31-94

Total Stocks: 29
Total Fixed-Income: 187

Amount 000	Date of Maturity		Value $000	% Net Assets
10168	03-01-03	Pacific Lumber 10.5%	9457	1.82
9981	2004	American Financial 9.75%	9307	1.79
9848	2001	Stone Container 9.875%	9183	1.77
365		Supermarkets Genl Pfd $3.52	9128	1.75
13120	2003	Eagle Industries 0%	8265	1.59
8565	02-15-03	Revlon Consumer Prods 10.5%	6852	1.32
588		Mayflower Group	6317	1.21
6672	03-01-02	Interlake 12.125%	6272	1.21
5870	06-15-02	Riverwood International 11.25%	6127	1.18
6060	09-15-03	Falcon Holdings Group 11%	5696	1.09
5710	01-30-02	Cablevision Industries 10.75%	5653	1.09
6095	2004	Geneva Steel 9.5%	5577	1.07
5998	2005	Westpoint Stevens 9.375%	5429	1.04
4809	2002	Gillett Holdings 12.25%	5242	1.01
8260	06-01-05	American Standard 0%	5183	1.00
5196	07-23-05	Midland Funding 11.75%	5164	0.99
5164	09-01-12	Rogers Cablesystems 10.125%	5087	0.98
4876	08-15-04	Allbritton Comm 11.5%	5071	0.97
8661	2004	MFS Communications 0%	4893	0.94
4683	03-15-07	Safeway 9.875%	4871	0.94
4491	12-15-02	KENETECH 12.75%	4850	0.93
4555	10-15-03	NL Industries 11.75%	4692	0.90
12157	03-15-98	Revlon Worldwide 0%	4681	0.90
5132	08-15-01	Specialty Foods 10.25%	4645	0.89
4362	12-01-03	Owens-Illinois 11%	4624	0.89

Composition % 12-31-94

Cash	8.4	Preferreds	2.1
Stocks	3.2	Convertibles	0.2
Bonds	86.1	Other	0.0

Tax Analysis

	Tax-Adj Historical Return %	% Pretax Return
3 Yr Avg	7.20	64.2
5 Yr Avg	6.73	56.0
10 Yr Avg	4.60	37.4

Potential Capital Gain Exposure (% of assets)   -40%

Most Similar Funds in MF500

Putnam High Yield Adv A	Strong Fit
Kemper High-Yield A	Strong Fit
Liberty High-Income Bond A	Strong Fit

Expenses & Fees

Min Initial Purchase	$1000 (Addt'l: $50)
Min IRA Purchase	$250 (Addt'l: $50)
Min Auto Invest Plan	$50 (Systematic Inv: $50)
Sales Fees	4.75% front
	0.00% deferred
	0.25% 12b-1
Management Fee	0.22% max./0.19% min.+3.00%l
3-,5-,10-yr Expense Projections	$78, $100, $164

Coupon Range

	% of Bonds	Rel Obj
0%, PIK	10.2	1.38
0% to 11%	59.3	1.21
11% to 13%	24.7	0.74
13% to 14.5%	2.6	0.47
More than 14.5%	0.4	0.23
Not applicable	2.9	0.96

Credit Analysis 12-31-94
% of Bonds

US Govt	0	BB	16
AAA	0	B	64
AA	0	Below B	9
A	0	NR/NA	11
BBB	0		

M☉RNINGSTAR   **1995 Mutual Fund 500**

MFS Municipal Bond A

	Ticker	Load	NAV	Yield	SEC Yield	Assets	Objective
	MMBFX	4.75%	10.17	5.4%	5.67%	1886.6	Muni Nat

MFS Municipal Bond Fund - Class A seeks high current income exempt from federal taxes, consistent with prudent investing and protection of capital.

The fund intends to invest at least 80% of its assets in U.S. government securities and municipal securities rated A or better. Not more than 20% of the fund's assets may be invested in issues rated below A or in unrated securities. The fund may engage in options and futures transactions for non-hedging purposes. It may also invest in AMT-subject bonds.

Class A shares have front loads; Class B shares have deferred loads and 12b-1 fees. Prior to Aug. 3, 1992, the fund was named MFS Managed Municipal Bond Trust.

Manager's Investment Style

Management prefers long, interest-rate-sensitive bonds, as well as bonds at the upper end of the credit tier. Further, management emphasizes liquidity in the portfolio. Management has also been known to use inverse floaters and short positions to boost yield and hedge risks. While sticking to high-quality issues in general, management will buy on relative value, and thus has been known to show a slightly contrarian bent.

Fund Manager(s)

Robert A. Dennis CFA, since 01-84. Birthdate: 12-48. BS, MIT 1970 MS, MIT 1971

Manager Experience	Dates Managed	Invest Obj	Std Dev	+/- Index
Robert A. Dennis MFS Municipal Income B	12/86 - 04/93	MN	5.27	-2.81

Historical Profile
Return Average
Risk Above Average
Rating ★★ Below Average

52	49	48	50	41	33	9	48

Investment Style History
Fixed Income
Income Rtn % Rank Obj

Growth of $10,000
‖‖‖ Value of Fund ($000)
— Value of Index ($000)
LB Muni
▼ Manager Change
▽ Partial Manager Change
► Mgr Unknown After
◄ Mgr Unknown Before

Performance Quartile (Within Objective)

1983	1984	1985	1986	1987	1988	1989	1990	1991	1992	1993	1994	History
9.19	9.30	10.03	10.63	10.09	10.41	10.39	10.33	10.77	10.93	11.51	10.17	NAV
12.79	10.57	20.61	18.22	1.78	11.66	9.71	6.29	12.85	9.38	13.70	-6.94	Total Return %
4.42	-4.59	-1.51	2.98	-0.98	3.78	-4.83	-2.66	-3.15	2.14	3.95	-4.02	+/- LB Aggregate
4.74	0.02	0.59	-1.09	0.27	1.50	-1.08	-1.01	0.71	0.56	1.42	-1.33	+/- LB Muni
9.29	9.37	9.35	8.11	6.86	7.66	7.18	6.87	6.94	6.44	6.56	4.71	Income Return %
3.50	1.20	11.27	10.11	-5.08	4.00	2.52	-0.58	5.91	2.94	7.14	-11.64	Capital Return %
67	23	70	31	44	48	77	30	69	28	35	79	Total Rtn % Rank All
14	13	41	48	21	34	41	49	14	21	12	71	Total Rtn % Rank Obj
0.79	0.80	0.80	0.78	0.72	0.73	0.72	0.68	0.67	0.66	0.69	0.55	Income $
0.02	0.00	0.29	0.39	0.00	0.00	0.28	0.00	0.16	0.15	0.19	0.00	Capital Gains $
0.80	0.75	0.69	0.64	0.61	0.65	0.64	0.60	0.59	0.57	0.59	0.59	Expense Ratio %
8.67	8.70	8.50	7.45	6.96	7.16	6.87	6.69	6.47	6.12	5.63	5.49	Income Ratio %
316	348	225	164	218	190	199	160	98	87	56	74	Turnover Rate %
138.4	234.7	318.0	844.6	934.0	1004.0	1287.4	1460.6	1766.4	1956.6	2199.6	1886.6	Net Assets ($mil)

Performance 12-31-94

	1st Qtr	2nd Qtr	3rd Qtr	4th Qtr	Total
1987	3.35	-3.61	-3.09	5.42	1.78
1988	2.79	2.61	3.08	2.70	11.66
1989	0.29	6.59	-0.98	3.64	9.71
1990	-0.37	2.49	-0.90	5.04	6.29
1991	1.93	2.02	4.92	3.43	12.85
1992	-0.22	4.63	2.43	2.29	9.38
1993	4.99	3.06	3.49	1.53	13.70
1994	-6.28	0.37	0.65	-1.70	-6.94

Bear Market Performance

Decile Rank (5-year period)

Worst ▬ Best

	Worst 3 Mo Period 1985-89	Worst 3 Mo Period 1990-94
MFS Municipal Bond A	-6.27	-6.89
+/- LB Aggregate	-2.71	-1.95
+/- Best Fit Index : LB Muni	0.22	-1.13

Trailing Returns

	Total Return %	+/- LB Aggregate	+/- LB Muni	% Rank All	% Rank Obj	Growth of $10,000
3 Mo	-1.70	-2.08	-0.27	62	70	9,830
6 Mo	-1.06	-2.06	0.18	75	56	9,894
1 Yr	-6.94	-4.02	-1.33	79	71	9,306
3 Yr Avg	4.99	0.45	0.12	48	29	11,573
5 Yr Avg	6.78	-0.85	0.01	56	20	13,882
10 Yr Avg	9.45	-0.49	0.03	65	18	24,679
15 Yr Avg	10.08	-0.73	1.61	76	9	42,245

Operations

Address and Telephone	500 Boylston Street Boston, MA 02116 800-637-2929 / 617-954-5000
Advisor	Massachusetts Financial Services
Subadvisor	None
Distributor	MFS Financial Services
States Available	All
Report Grade	C+
Income Distrib	Paid Monthly
Date of Inception	12-16-76
Fiscal Year End	August

Risk Analysis

Time Period	Load-Adj Return %	Risk % Rank[1] All	Obj	Morningstar[2] Return	Morningstar Risk	Morningstar Risk-Adj Rating
1 Yr	-11.36					
3 Yr	3.30	44	75	0.82	1.20	★★
5 Yr	5.75	39	89	0.92	1.32	★
10 Yr	8.92	23	67	1.07	1.15	★★★

Average Historical Rating (109 months) 3.4 ★s

[1] = low, 100 = high [2] 1.00 = Muni Avg [3] 1.00 = 90-day T-bill return

Other Measures

			Standard LB Agg	Best Fit LB Muni
Standard Deviation	6.62	Alpha	0.4	-0.1
Mean	5.10	Beta	1.21	1.18
Sharpe Ratio	0.24	R-Squared	54	95

Investment Style

Interest-Rate Stance
Avg Effective Maturity 18.7 Yrs

Maturity Short Intm Long
Quality High Med Low

Quality
Avg Credit Quality AA
Avg Weighted Coupon 6.50%
Avg Weighted Price 101.87% of Par

Diversification Value for Portfolio Types

Large Cap: Medium | Small Cap: High | Bond: Low | Balanced: Medium | Diversified: Medium

Min Initial Purchase	$1000 (Addt'l: $50)	
Min IRA Purchase	$250 (Addt'l: $50)	
Min Auto Invest Plan	$50 (Systematic Inv: $50)	

Expenses & Fees
Sales Fees	4.75% front 0.00% deferred 0.00% 12b-1
Management Fee	0.22% max./0.17% min.+4.12%l
3-,5-,10-yr Expense Projections	$66, $79, $118

Portfolio 08-31-94

Total Stocks: 0
Total Fixed-Income: 226

Amount 000	Date of Maturity		Value $000	% Net Assets
52470	2020	CA State GO 5.5%	48089	2.37
55537	2015	PA State COP 5%	47440	2.34
42070	2008	NY New York City GO 7.5%	46042	2.27
41747	2014	NY Envir Fac Wtr Poll Cntrl Fund 5.875%	40340	1.99
32399	2000	CA Alameda COP 7.25%	36920	1.82
28221	2000	WA Pub Pwr Sply Sys Proj #2 7.375%	31911	1.57
32775	2017	WA State GO 5.75%	31208	1.54
29351	2014	TX Harris Toll Rd 6.75%	30854	1.52
27340	2002	PA GO Conv Ctr 6.7%	29105	1.43
29053	2015	IL Chicago GO Brd Educ Lease 6.25%	28946	1.43
29327	2017	CA State GO 5.125%	25191	1.24
22755	2009	MA GO Consolid Loan 7%	24863	1.22
22409	2010	NY Triborough Bridge/Tunnel Conv 7.25%	24825	1.22
21054	2003	MO Regl Conv Sports Complex Lease 6.9%	23586	1.16
24997	2014	NY GO Med Care Fac Fin Mental 5.375%	22299	1.10
24899	2014	TX State GO 5%	21931	1.08
19567	2000	WA Pub Pwr Sply Sys Proj #3 7.25%	21850	1.08
18188	2000	MI Hosp Fin Oakwood Hosp 7.2%	20530	1.01
20937	2013	CA San Joaquin COP Genl Hosp Proj 6.25%	20252	1.00
22136	2011	PA State COP 5.25%	19929	0.98

Credit Analysis % of Bonds 12-31-94

US Govt	0	BB	0
AAA	48	B	0
AA	20	Below B	0
A	18	NR/NA	5
BBB	9		

Composition % of Assets 12-31-94

Cash	3.2	Preferreds	0.0
Stocks	0.0	Convertibles	0.0
Bonds	96.8	Other	0.0

Tax Analysis

	Tax-Adj Historical Return %	% Pretax Return
3 Yr Avg	4.70	93.9
5 Yr Avg	6.52	95.6
10 Yr Avg	9.06	94.1
Potential Capital Gain Exposure (% of assets)		0%

Most Similar Funds in MF500

Scudder High-Yield Tax-Free	Strong Fit
Vanguard Muni Insured L/T	Strong Fit
General Municipal Bond	Strong Fit

Coupon Range

	% Bonds	Rel Obj
0%	1.3	0.50
0% to 6.8%	52.2	0.86
6.8% to 7.5%	33.0	2.13
7.5% to 8.3%	7.2	0.81
More than 8.3%	3.6	0.41
Not applicable	2.8	0.72

Sector Weightings

	% Bonds	Rel Obj
General Obl	32.20	1.53
Utilities	8.75	0.70
Health	12.58	0.95
Water/Waste	4.84	0.76
Housing	0.21	0.03
Education	4.84	0.76
Transportation	5.47	0.54
COP/Lease	15.81	4.96
Private	7.88	0.68
Misc Revenue	6.15	1.24
Demand	1.28	0.52

Top 5 States % of Bonds

CA	19.88	PA	8.56
NY	19.62	MA	7.87
WA	8.77		

MFS Total Return A

	Ticker	Load	NAV	Yield	SEC Yield	Assets	Objective
	MSFRX	4.75%	12.44	4.3%	4.62%	1825.1	Balanced

MFS Total Return Fund - Class A seeks income; growth of capital and income is secondary.

The fund generally maintains at least 40% of its assets in equities. The balance of assets is typically invested in debt securities, including up to 20% of assets in high-yield debt. The fund may invest in foreign securities.

Class A shares have front loads; Class B shares have deferred loads, higher 12b-1 fees, and conversion features; Class C shares have level loads. Prior to March 31, 1986, the fund was named Massachusetts Income Development. Prior to Aug. 3, 1992, it was named Massachusetts Financial Total Return Trust.

Manager's Investment Style

Management considers 65% in equities to be neutral, though it will travel well below this amount on bearish indicators. The remaining assets are typically overweighted in convertibles (which offer bond-like payouts combined with the ability to participate in the stock market's upturn). In bonds, primarily corporates, management displays a willingness to take on an aggressive slant through a relatively long average maturity and stakes in lower-rated and unrated bonds.

Fund Manager(s)

Richard E. Dahlberg CFA, since 06-85. Birthdate: 10-39. BS, Northeastern U. 1964 Finance, Wharton 1966

Manager Experience

	Dates Managed	Invest Obj	Std Dev	+/- Index
Richard E. Dahlberg				
MFS Research A	10/71 - 01/79	G	15.62	4.68
Massachusetts Inv A	01/80 - 01/85	GI	14.96	-2.49

Historical Profile

Return	Above Average
Risk	Below Average
Rating	★★★★ Above Average

	55%	55%	56%	48%	50%	50%	47%	43%

Growth of $10,000

IIII Value of Fund ($000)
— Value of Index ($000) S&P 500
▼ Manager Change
▽ Partial Manager Change
► Mgr Unknown After
◄ Mgr Unknown Before

Performance Quartile (Within Objective)

	1983	1984	1985	1986	1987	1988	1989	1990	1991	1992	1993	1994	History
	8.82	8.53	9.78	10.19	9.63	10.23	11.57	10.62	12.06	12.28	13.34	12.44	NAV
	19.09	6.96	30.21	19.50	3.44	14.91	23.06	-2.33	21.62	10.06	15.15	-2.69	Total Return %
	-3.37	0.69	-1.53	0.82	-1.82	-1.70	-8.63	0.79	-8.87	2.44	5.09	-4.00	+/- S&P 500
	10.72	-8.20	8.09	4.25	0.68	7.03	8.52	-11.27	5.62	2.81	5.40	0.23	+/- LB Aggregate
	7.58	7.65	7.51	5.52	5.10	6.49	6.64	5.79	5.91	5.10	4.70	3.99	Income Return %
	11.51	-0.69	22.70	13.98	-1.67	8.42	16.42	-8.11	15.71	4.96	10.45	-6.68	Capital Return %
	44	42	25	23	32	28	28	63	42	22	28	40	Total Rtn % Rank All
	25	46	25	24	36	26	26	67	68	20	15	51	Total Rtn % Rank Obj
	0.64	0.62	0.62	0.58	0.57	0.62	0.64	0.67	0.60	0.60	0.57	0.54	Income $
	0.65	0.23	0.56	0.88	0.45	0.20	0.31	0.01	0.20	0.37	0.21	0.01	Capital Gains $
	0.80	0.82	0.78	0.67	0.63	0.71	0.72	0.85	0.87	0.84	0.84	0.79	Expense Ratio %
	7.18	7.17	6.73	5.67	5.05	6.06	5.97	5.71	5.89	5.40	4.51	4.76	Income Ratio %
	121	82	71	94	58	52	53	50	74	84	95	---	Turnover Rate %
	209.2	199.3	216.1	343.1	464.2	515.3	663.1	745.5	998.7	1269.1	1735.2	1825.1	Net Assets ($mil)

Investment Style History
Equity
Average % Stocks Held in Portfolio

Performance 12-31-94

	1st Qtr	2nd Qtr	3rd Qtr	4th Qtr	Total
1987	13.60	2.11	1.79	-12.40	3.44
1988	6.13	4.43	1.13	2.52	14.91
1989	5.03	7.46	7.15	1.75	23.06
1990	-2.16	3.43	-8.31	5.27	-2.33
1991	9.51	0.77	5.24	4.73	21.62
1992	0.50	3.55	3.00	2.67	10.06
1993	6.92	3.12	4.51	-0.07	15.15
1994	-2.79	-0.28	2.13	-1.71	-2.69

Bear Market Performance

Decile Rank (5-year period)

Worst —————— Best

	Worst 3 Mo Period 1985-89	Worst 3 Mo Period 1990-94
MFS Total Return A	-18.99	-8.31
+/- S&P 500	10.59	5.43
+/- Best Fit Index : S&P 500	10.59	5.43

Trailing Returns

	Total Return %	+/- S&P 500	+/- LB Aggregate	% Rank All	% Rank Obj	Growth of $10,000
3 Mo	-1.71	-1.69	-2.09	62	74	9,829
6 Mo	0.38	-4.48	-0.61	49	77	10,038
1 Yr	-2.69	-4.00	0.23	40	51	9,731
3 Yr Avg	7.24	0.97	2.69	25	21	12,332
5 Yr Avg	7.94	-0.76	0.31	34	46	14,649
10 Yr Avg	12.80	-1.59	2.85	30	14	33,339
15 Yr Avg	13.59	-0.89	2.79	29	24	67,668

Risk Analysis

Time Period	Load-Adj Return %	Risk % Rank [1] All	Risk % Rank [1] Obj	Morningstar [2] Return	Morningstar Risk	Morningstar Risk-Adj Rating
1 Yr	-7.31					
3 Yr	5.51	42	24	0.57 [3]	0.64	★★★
5 Yr	6.89	51	36	0.52 [3]	0.71	★★★
10 Yr	12.25	42	50	1.11	0.70	★★★★
Average Historical Rating (109 months)				4.0 ★ s		

[1] 1 = low, 100 = high [2] 1.00 = Hybrid Avg [3] 1.00 = 90-day T-bill return

Other Measures

		Standard S&P 500	Best Fit S&P 500
Standard Deviation	5.96	Alpha	1.8	1.8
Mean	7.19	Beta	0.65	0.65
Sharpe Ratio	0.61	R-Squared	73	73

Investment Style

Stocks

	Port Avg	Rel S&P 500
Price/Earnings Ratio	16.9	0.91
Price/Book Ratio	2.4	0.70
5 Yr Earnings Gr %	1.1	0.19
Med Mkt Cap ($mil)	7762	0.60

Style V B G / Size L M S

Bonds

Avg Effective Duration	6.4 Yrs **	
Avg Effective Maturity	9.2 Yrs	
Avg Credit Quality	AA	
Avg Weighted Coupon	7.01%	
**figure provided by fund		

Maturity S I L / Quality H M L

Diversification Value for Portfolio Types

Large Cap: Low	Small Cap: Medium	Bond: Low	Balanced: None	Diversified: Low

Portfolio 09-30-94

Total Stocks: 138
Total Fixed-Income: 212

Share Chg (03-94) 000	Amount 000		Date of Maturity	Value $000	% Net Assets
	51568	US Treasury Note 6.75%	1999	50515	2.72
	44604	US Treasury Bond 6.25%	08-15-23	36199	1.95
-7	179	Royal Dutch Petroleum		19195	1.03
62	241	Dow Chemical		18831	1.01
159	398	General Motors		18638	1.00
	18565	US Treasury Note 7.25%	2004	18115	0.98
128	390	Aetna Life & Casualty		18067	0.97
61	272	Philip Morris		16618	0.89
-21	550	YPF (ADR)		13889	0.75
-14	350	May Department Stores		13801	0.74
34	223	CIGNA		13762	0.74
-4	426	Williams		12789	0.69
-6	152	PowerGen (ADR)		12618	0.68
	186	Cointel Cv Pfd 7%		12522	0.67
	412	Atlantic Richfield Cv Pfd 9%		12363	0.67
206	206	Colgate-Palmolive		11964	0.64
-7	191	United Technologies		11946	0.64
	22346	Roche Holding Cv 0%	09-23-08	11788	0.63
-6	168	Deere		11527	0.62
-15	399	National City		11216	0.60

Index Allocation

	% of Stocks
S&P 500	79.9
S&P MidCap 400	5.4
U.S. Small Cap	6.4
Foreign	10.8

Composition % 12-31-94

Cash	17.4	Preferreds	0.9
Stocks	41.0	Convertibles	11.9
Bonds	28.8	Other	0.0

Tax Analysis

	Tax-Adj Historical Return %	% Pretax Return
3 Yr Avg	5.10	69.0
5 Yr Avg	5.79	70.0
10 Yr Avg	9.80	66.3
Potential Capital Gain Exposure (% of assets)		8%

Most Similar Funds in MF500

IDS Mutual	Strong Fit
Oppenheimer Equity-Inc A	Strong Fit
Safeco Income	Strong Fit

Bond Credit Analysis 11-30-94
% of Bonds

US Govt	57	BB	17
AAA	2	B	0
AA	1	Below B	0
A	2	NR/NA	0
BBB	21		

Stock Sector Weightings

	% of Stocks	Relative S&P 500
Utilities	16.7	1.35
Energy	15.9	1.57
Financials	21.1	1.99
Industrial Cyclicals	18.2	1.11
Consumer Durables	5.4	0.87
Consumer Staples	7.1	0.56
Services	2.6	0.32
Retail	3.9	0.67
Health	3.6	0.41
Technology	5.7	0.62

Operations

Address and Telephone	500 Boylston Street Boston, MA 02116 800-637-2929 / 617-954-5000
Advisor	Massachusetts Financial Services
Subadvisor	None
Distributor	MFS Financial Services
States Available	All
Report Grade	C
Income Distrib	Paid Monthly
Date of Inception	10-06-70
Fiscal Year End	September

Min Initial Purchase	$1000 (Addt'l: $50)
Min IRA Purchase	$250 (Addt'l: $50)
Min Auto Invest Plan	$50 (Systematic Inv: $50)

Expenses & Fees

Sales Fees	4.75% front
	0.00% deferred
	0.35% 12b-1
Management Fee	0.25% max./0.21% min.+3.57%l
3-,5-,10-yr Expense Projections	$73, $92, $146
Annual Brokerage Cost	0.02%

M⊙RNINGSTAR 1995 Mutual Fund 500

MFS World Governments A

	Ticker	Load	NAV	Yield	SEC Yield	Assets	Objective
	MWGTX	4.75%	10.91	1.4%	6.46%	358.8	World Bond

MFS World Governments Fund - Class A seeks growth of capital and current income.

The fund normally invests at least 80% of its assets in foreign and domestic debt securities. It may invest up to 20% of its assets in equities.

Class A shares have front loads and lower 12b-1 fees; Class B shares have deferred loads and conversion features; Class C shares have level loads. Prior to Nov. 1, 1990, the fund was called Massachusetts Financial International Trust Bond Portfolio. From that date until Aug. 3, 1992, it was named MFS Worldwide Governments Trust. Then until Sept. 7, 1993, it was named MFS Worldwide Governments Fund.

Manager's Investment Style

Management relies on savvy country picks, allocating assets over a variety of world and domestic fixed-income markets. Currency hedging is also used as part of the strategy. Management generates a high turnover rate as it moves in and out of holdings to manage its duration, currency risk, and yield profile.

Fund Manager(s)

Leslie J. Nanberg CFA, since 01-84. MA, Northwestern U. 1968 MBA, Northwestern U. 1970

Manager Experience	Dates Managed	Invest Obj	Std Dev	+/- Index
Leslie J. Nanberg				
MFS Intermediate Income	08/88 - 01/92	I	3.78	-9.98

Historical Profile
Return	Average
Risk	Below Average
Rating	★★★★ Above Average

History

1983	1984	1985	1986	1987	1988	1989	1990	1991	1992	1993	1994	History
9.94	9.36	10.70	11.46	11.86	11.10	11.45	12.00	12.63	11.50	12.33	10.91	NAV
1.55	2.34	29.91	30.05	24.42	4.39	7.37	17.90	13.42	1.35	18.39	-6.57	Total Return %
-6.83	-12.82	7.78	14.80	21.66	-3.49	-7.17	8.96	-2.58	-5.90	8.64	-3.65	+/- LB Aggregate
---	---	-5.10	-1.30	-10.73	2.03	10.80	2.62	-2.83	-3.43	3.27	-13.27	+/- SB World Govt
7.51	8.17	8.02	7.40	19.29	9.76	4.22	8.16	6.18	6.39	8.54	1.36	Income Return %
-5.96	-5.84	21.88	22.65	5.13	-5.38	3.15	9.75	7.24	-5.04	9.84	-7.93	Capital Return %
100	59	26	7	3	93	92	1	66	88	20	77	Total Rtn % Rank All
1	50	1	1	10	40	33	18	54	54	23	59	Total Rtn % Rank Obj
0.79	0.79	0.74	0.83	2.17	1.15	0.47	0.95	0.75	0.78	1.00	0.16	Income $
0.00	0.00	0.65	1.60	0.18	0.13	0.00	0.55	0.23	0.52	0.29	0.45	Capital Gains $
1.35	1.40	1.43	1.17	1.13	1.12	1.42	1.44	1.61	1.53	1.54	1.58	Expense Ratio %
7.41	7.98	7.45	6.57	7.54	7.91	8.42	8.06	7.75	6.78	5.66	4.85	Income Ratio %
192	135	307	371	378	232	282	220	208	163	179	---	Turnover Rate %
39.8	35.5	69.6	118.0	159.9	175.7	121.0	131.1	270.7	316.2	443.9	358.8	Net Assets ($mil)

Investment Style History
Fixed Income
Income Rtn % Rank Obj

Growth of $10,000
||| Value of Fund ($000)
— Value of Index ($000) LB Agg
▼ Manager Change
▽ Partial Manager Change
► Mgr Unknown After
◄ Mgr Unknown Before

Performance Quartile (Within Objective)

Performance 12-31-94

	1st Qtr	2nd Qtr	3rd Qtr	4th Qtr	Total
1987	9.25	2.24	-5.32	17.65	24.42
1988	1.43	-3.41	0.95	5.54	4.39
1989	-0.81	0.00	2.18	5.94	7.37
1990	0.70	4.34	5.82	6.05	17.90
1991	-3.00	-0.43	7.08	9.67	13.42
1992	-3.40	6.23	1.16	-2.36	1.35
1993	4.17	4.92	4.69	3.46	18.39
1994	-6.89	-1.70	0.27	1.81	-6.57

Bear Market Performance

Decile Rank (5-year period)

Worst ⟷ Best

	Worst 3 Mo Period 1985-89	Worst 3 Mo Period 1990-94
MFS World Governments A	-5.32	-6.89
+/- LB Aggregate	-2.59	-4.02
+/- Best Fit Index : SB World	-1.49	-8.83

Trailing Returns

	Total Return %	+/- LB Aggregate	+/- SB World	% Rank All	% Rank Obj	Growth of $10,000
3 Mo	1.81	1.43	1.24	4	7	10,181
6 Mo	2.08	1.09	-0.15	26	23	10,208
1 Yr	-6.57	-3.65	-13.27	77	59	9,343
3 Yr Avg	3.88	-0.66	-4.89	72	48	11,210
5 Yr Avg	8.43	0.81	-3.08	28	21	14,990
10 Yr Avg	13.45	3.50	-1.67	22	1	35,315
15 Yr Avg	---	---	---	---	---	---

Operations

Address and Telephone	500 Boylston Street Boston, MA 02116 800-637-2929 / 617-954-5000	
Advisor	Massachusetts Financial Services	
Subadvisor	None	
Distributor	MFS Financial Services	
States Available	All	
Report Grade	B-	
Income Distrib	Paid Annually	
Date of Inception	02-25-81	
Fiscal Year End	November	

Risk Analysis

Time Period	Load-Adj Return %	Risk % Rank[1] All	Obj	Morningstar[2] Return	Risk	Morningstar Risk-Adj Rating
1 Yr	-11.01					
3 Yr	2.21	55	56	-0.39[3]	0.78	★★
5 Yr	7.38	45	51	0.65[3]	0.57	★★★
10 Yr	12.90	38	50	1.26	0.60	★★★★★
Average Historical Rating (109 months)					4.0 ★s	

[1] 1 = low, 100 = high [2] 1.00 = Hybrid Avg [3] 1.00 = 90-day T-bill return

Other Measures

				Standard LB Agg	Best Fit SB World
Standard Deviation	6.29	Alpha		-0.4	-2.2
Mean	4.01	Beta		0.87	0.53
Sharpe Ratio	0.08	R-Squared		31	32

Investment Style

Interest-Rate Stance

Avg Effective Maturity	5.0 Yrs

Not Available

Quality

Avg Credit Quality	NA
Avg Weighted Coupon	7.93%

Diversification Value for Portfolio Types

Large Cap: High	Small Cap: High	Bond: Medium	Balanced: High	Diversified: High

Min Initial Purchase	$1000 (Addt'l: $50)
Min IRA Purchase	$250 (Addt'l: $50)
Min Auto Invest Plan	$50 (Systematic Inv: $50)

Expenses & Fees

Sales Fees	4.75% front
	0.00% deferred
	0.35% 12b-1
Management Fee	0.90% max./0.70% min.
3-,5-,10-yr Expense Projections	$94, $127, $222

Portfolio 05-31-94

Total Stocks: 0
Total Fixed-Income: 32

Amount 000	Date of Maturity		Value $000	% Net Assets
48	2002	Republic of Germany 7.25%	29493	7.42
43	1999	Govt of Netherlands 7%	23988	6.03
140	1999	Kingdom of Sweden 11%	19238	4.84
24	2000	Commonwealth Australia 7%	16416	4.13
10	2002	United Kingdom Treasury 9.75%	15090	3.80
1872	1998	Kingdom of Spain 8.3%	13308	3.35
8	2001	Republic of Ireland 9%	13021	3.28
59	2001	Govt of France 9.5%	11878	2.99
71	11-15-00	Kingdom of Denmark 9%	11558	2.91
48	2004	Republic of Finland 9.5%	9080	2.28
1187	1998	Kingdom of Spain 10.25%	9034	2.27
13	2000	New So Wales Treasury 7%	8902	2.24
77	2000	Govt of France 0%	8869	2.23
15	2007	Govt of Netherlands 8.25%	8656	2.18
11	1999	Western Australia Treasury 9%	8423	2.12
49	02-15-17	US Treasury Bond 0%	8357	2.10
42	1998	Govt of France 5.75%	7291	1.83
49	2026	Kingdom of Denmark 6%	5974	1.50
8478	1998	Republic of Italy 11.5%	5573	1.40
4	2004	Republic of Ireland 6.25%	5293	1.33
721	1999	Kingdom of Spain 7.4%	4864	1.22
7207	1998	Republic of Italy 10%	4569	1.15
6	2003	Queensland Treasury 8%	4226	1.06
40	2005	Kingdom of Sweden 6%	3946	0.99
3	2003	Republic of Ireland 9.25%	3916	0.99

Composition % 12-31-94

Cash	10.3	Preferreds	0.0
Stocks	0.0	Convertibles	0.0
Bonds	91.2	Other	-1.5

Tax Analysis

	Tax-Adj Historical Return %	% Pretax Return
3 Yr Avg	1.05	26.2
5 Yr Avg	5.39	60.1
10 Yr Avg	9.50	58.4
Potential Capital Gain Exposure (% of assets)		-12%

Most Similar Funds in MF500

G.T. Global Govt Income A	Weak Fit
Templeton Income	Weak Fit
Capital World Bond	Weak Fit

Country Exposure 12-31-94

	% of Bonds
U.S.	48
Japan	12
United Kingdom	10
Italy	5
Netherlands	3

Currency Exposure 12-31-94

	% of Net Assets
U.S.	48
Japan	12
New Zealand	11
United Kingdom	10
Italy	5

MIMLIC Asset Allocation A

	Ticker	Load	NAV	Yield	SEC Yield	Assets	Objective
	MIAAX	5.00%	12.78	2.6%	3.55%	53.9	Asset Alloc.

MIMLIC Asset Allocation Fund - Class A seeks total return consistent with capital preservation.

The fund invests in equities, debt securities, and money-market instruments; the percentage in each asset type varies according to prevailing economic conditions. The fund may engage in derivative hedging techniques.

Class A shares have front loads; Class B shares have deferred loads and higher 12b-1 fees. Prior to July 1, 1987, the fund operated under a different investment objective as MIMLIC Investors Fund II. The fund was not offered for sale to the public prior to Nov. 16, 1987.

Manager's Investment Style

Management favors steady-growth blue chips, often heavily weighted toward traditional growth sectors such as health, technology, retail, and services. Bonds tend to be from the higher credit tiers.

Fund Manager(s)

Thomas Gunderson CFA(1987), since 01-89.
Birthdate: 05-60. BA, St. Olaf C. 1982 MBA, U. of Michigan 1984

Manager Experience

	Dates Managed	Invest Obj	Std Dev	+/- Index
Thomas Gunderson				
MIMLIC Fixed-Inc Secs A	01/90 - 05/91	CG	3.19	-1.34

Performance 12-31-94

	1st Qtr	2nd Qtr	3rd Qtr	4th Qtr	Total
1987	1.01	1.10	1.19	1.05	0.46 *
1988	4.38	3.57	0.45	1.50	10.21
1989	3.15	7.92	4.28	2.81	19.35
1990	-2.16	5.73	-6.17	6.56	3.44
1991	10.17	-0.40	6.55	9.57	28.10
1992	-3.43	1.37	4.77	3.62	6.28
1993	2.12	0.91	1.79	0.59	5.51
1994	-3.37	-2.65	4.10	-0.07	-2.14

Bear Market Performance

Decile Rank (5-year period)

Worst _____ Best

	Worst 3 Mo Period 1985-89	Worst 3 Mo Period 1990-94
MIMLIC Asset Allocation A	---	-6.57
+/- S&P 500	---	-0.82
+/- Best Fit Index : S&P 500	---	-0.82

Trailing Returns

	Total Return %	+/- S&P 500	+/- LB Aggregate	% Rank All	% Rank Obj	Growth of $10,000
3 Mo	-0.07	-0.05	-0.45	24	20	9,993
6 Mo	4.02	-0.84	3.03	15	7	10,402
1 Yr	-2.14	-3.46	0.78	35	44	9,786
3 Yr Avg	3.14	-3.12	-1.40	84	85	10,973
5 Yr Avg	7.77	-0.92	0.15	36	47	14,540
10 Yr Avg	---	---	---	---	---	---
15 Yr Avg	---	---	---	---	---	---

Operations

Address and Telephone	400 N. Robert Street
	St. Paul, MN 55101
	800-443-3677 / 612-298-7833
Advisor	MIMLIC Asset Management
Subadvisor	None
Distributor	MIMLIC Sales
States Available	All
Report Grade	B+
Income Distrib	Paid Quarterly
* Date of Inception	11-16-87
Fiscal Year End	September

Min Initial Purchase	$250 (Addt'l: $25)	
Min IRA Purchase	$250 (Addt'l: $25)	
Min Auto Invest Plan	$25 (Systematic Inv: $25)	

Expenses & Fees

Sales Fees	5.00% front
	0.00% deferred
	0.35% 12b-1
Management Fee	0.60% flat fee
3-,5-,10-yr Expense Projections	$87, $114, $190
Annual Brokerage Cost	0.19%

Historical Profile

Return	Average
Risk	Below Average
Rating	★★★ Neutral

	47%	39%	44%	54%	58%	67%	55%

Investment Style History Equity
Average % Stocks Held in Portfolio

Growth of $10,000

- |||| Value of Fund ($000)
- — Value of Index ($000) S&P 500
- ▼ Manager Change
- ▽ Partial Manager Change
- ► Mgr Unknown After
- ◄ Mgr Unknown Before

Performance Quartile (Within Objective)

	1983	1984	1985	1986	1987	1988	1989	1990	1991	1992	1993	1994	History
	---	---	---	---	10.05	10.48	11.61	11.35	13.51	13.43	13.80	12.78	NAV
	---	---	---	---	0.46 *	10.21	19.35	3.44	28.10	6.28	5.51	-2.14	Total Return %
	---	---	---	---	-0.30 *	-6.40	-12.34	6.56	-2.39	-1.34	-4.55	-3.46	+/- S&P 500
	---	---	---	---	---	2.33	4.81	-5.51	12.10	-0.97	-4.24	0.78	+/- LB Aggregate
	---	---	---	---	2.70	5.93	7.10	5.06	4.70	2.79	2.15	2.56	Income Return %
	---	---	---	---	-2.24	4.28	12.25	-1.62	23.40	3.49	3.36	-4.71	Capital Return %
	---	---	---	---	---	60	36	48	30	66	90	35	Total Rtn % Rank All
	---	---	---	---	---	40	30	16	20	58	98	44	Total Rtn % Rank Obj
	---	---	---	---	0.28	0.59	0.72	0.57	0.52	0.36	0.29	0.34	Income $
	---	---	---	---	0.00	0.00	0.14	0.07	0.43	0.55	0.08	0.38	Capital Gains $
	---	---	---	---	---	1.09	1.33	1.35	1.35	1.35	1.22	1.27	Expense Ratio %
	---	---	---	---	---	5.06	5.36	4.98	4.07	3.02	2.16	2.24	Income Ratio %
	---	---	---	---	---	---	111	66	56	123	92	124	Turnover Rate %
	---	---	---	---	2.2	6.5	8.5	10.7	22.0	42.5	58.1	53.9	Net Assets ($mil)

Risk Analysis

Time Period	Load-Adj Return %	Risk % Rank[1] All	Risk % Rank[1] Obj	Morningstar[2] Return	Morningstar Risk	Morningstar Risk-Adj Rating
1 Yr	-7.04					
3 Yr	1.40	62	77	-0.62[3]	0.90	★★
5 Yr	6.67	52	56	0.47[3]	0.75	★★★
10 Yr	---	---	---	---	---	---

Average Historical Rating (50 months)   3.6 ★s

[1] 1 = low, 100 = high   [2] 1.00 = Hybrid Avg   [3] 1.00 = 90-day T-bill return

Other Measures

			Standard S&P 500	Best Fit S&P 500
Standard Deviation	6.76	Alpha	-2.4	-2.4
Mean	3.33	Beta	0.76	0.76
Sharpe Ratio	-0.03	R-Squared	79	79

Investment Style

Stocks

	Port Avg	Rel S&P 500
Price/Earnings Ratio	20.1	1.09
Price/Book Ratio	4.1	1.21
5 Yr Earnings Gr %	17.4	3.13
Med Mkt Cap ($mil)	5146	0.40

Bonds

Avg Effective Duration	4.4 Yrs
Avg Effective Maturity	---
Avg Credit Quality	---
Avg Weighted Coupon	7.77%

Not Available

Diversification Value for Portfolio Types

Large Cap: Low	Small Cap: Medium	Bond: Medium	Balanced: None	Diversified: Low

Portfolio 12-31-94

Total Stocks: 59
Total Fixed-Income: 35

Share Chg (03-94)000	Amount 000		Date of Maturity	Value $000	% Net Assets
	2430	US Treasury Bond 8.125%	08-15-19	2461	4.56
	2381	US Treasury Note 8.5%	04-15-97	2416	4.48
	2232	US Treasury Note 6.25%	02-15-03	2018	3.74
	1240	US Treasury Note 8.875%	11-15-98	1282	2.38
	1240	Federal Home Loan Bank 7.27%	10-17-97	1211	2.25
	1091	US Treasury Note 7.875%	04-15-98	1092	2.03
	992	Consolidated Nat Gas 8.75%	06-01-99	1009	1.87
	992	GMAC 8.625%	06-15-99	995	1.84
6	19	General Electric		962	1.78
	992	United Dominion Realty Tr 8.8%	09-15-24	959	1.78
	992	Ford Motor Credit 5.625%	12-15-98	901	1.67
	893	Associates North Amer 6.75%	10-15-99	831	1.54
-7	22	Columbia/HCA Healthcare		805	1.49
	794	US Treasury Note 8%	01-15-97	798	1.48
	843	American Home Products 6.5%	10-15-02	748	1.39
	744	Occidental Petroleum 8.5%	09-15-04	723	1.34
	744	Tennessee Valley Auth 6.87%	09-19-97	720	1.34
-6	21	MGIC Investment		710	1.32
	742	GNMA 8%	08-15-24	709	1.31
8	19	DSC Communications		696	1.29

Index Allocation

	% of Stocks
S&P 500	56.9
S&P MidCap 400	16.5
U.S. Small Cap	19.6
Foreign	8.4

Composition % 06-30-94

Cash	4.0	Preferreds	0.0
Stocks	51.0	Convertibles	0.0
Bonds	45.0	Other	0.0

Tax Analysis

	Tax-Adj Historical Return %	% Pretax Return
3 Yr Avg	1.54	48.2
5 Yr Avg	5.95	73.8
10 Yr Avg	---	---
Potential Capital Gain Exposure (% of assets)		1%

Most Similar Funds in MF500

Alliance Growth & Income A	Fair Fit
Dreyfus	Fair Fit
Fortis Advant Asset Alloc A	Fair Fit

Bond Credit Analysis 06-30-94

% of Bonds

US Govt	45	BB	0
AAA	7	B	0
AA	19	Below B	0
A	19	NR/NA	0
BBB	10		

Stock Sector Weightings

	% of Stocks	Relative S&P 500
Utilities	6.7	0.54
Energy	5.9	0.58
Financials	13.4	1.26
Industrial Cyclicals	19.5	1.19
Consumer Durables	6.1	0.98
Consumer Staples	2.5	0.20
Services	6.9	0.85
Retail	5.7	0.98
Health	10.0	1.16
Technology	23.4	2.55

MORNINGSTAR 1995 Mutual Fund 500

Monetta

Monetta Fund seeks capital appreciation. Income is secondary.
The fund normally invests at least 70% of its assets in equity securities with growth potential. The balance may be invested in high-quality long-term debt securities. It may not engage in selling securities short, purchasing securities on margin, or writing put and call options. The fund also may not invest more than 5% of its total assets in the securities of any one issuer, or more than 25% of total assets in the securities of companies in one single industry.

Manager's Investment Style

Manager Rob Bacarella starts by looking at firms with the highest concensus earnings estimates, then adjusts the estimates based on his own interviews and research. He uses this information, combined with a proprietary measure of market sentiment, to set a price from which he thinks a stock will appreciate 30% in a year. He buys the stock at this price, then immediately sells once it appreciates 30%, and won't buy it back for at least 30 days.

Fund Manager(s)

Robert S. Bacarella, since 05-86. Birthdate: 05-49. Finance, St. Joseph's C. 1971 MBA, Roosevelt U. 1982

Manager Experience	Dates Managed	Invest Obj	Std Dev	+/- Index
Not available.				

	Ticker	Load	NAV	Yield	SEC Yield	Assets	Objective
	MONTX	Clsd	14.52	0.0%	N/A	364.9	Small Company

Historical Profile
Return Average
Risk Average
Rating ★★★
Closed

Investment Style History
Equity
Average % Stocks Held in Portfolio

Growth of $10,000
|||| Value of Fund ($000)
— Value of Index ($000) Wil 4500
▼ Manager Change
▽ Partial Manager Change
► Mgr Unknown After
◄ Mgr Unknown Before

Performance Quartile (Within Objective)

	1983	1984	1985	1986	1987	1988	1989	1990	1991	1992	1993	1994	History
	---	---	---	9.67	9.68	9.93	10.44	10.96	15.73	15.99	15.54	14.52	NAV
	---	---	---	-2.20 *	1.54	23.07	15.23	11.38	55.90	5.49	0.49	-6.20	Total Return %
	---	---	---	-6.63 *	-3.72	6.46	-16.46	14.49	25.41	-2.13	-9.57	-7.51	+/- S&P 500
	---	---	---	5.05	2.53	-8.72	24.93	12.44	-6.27	-14.05	-3.54	+/- Wilshire 4500
	---	---	---	1.10	1.43	0.74	2.12	0.95	0.34	0.30	0.00	0.00	Income Return %
	---	---	---	-3.30	0.10	22.33	13.11	10.42	55.56	5.19	0.49	-6.19	Capital Return %
	---	---	---	46	8	46	3	6	74	98	73	Total Rtn % Rank All
	---	---	---	29	33	81	2	34	85	97	84	Total Rtn % Rank Obj
	---	---	---	0.11	0.15	0.07	0.22	0.10	0.05	0.05	0.00	0.00	Income $
	---	---	---	0.00	0.00	1.91	0.77	0.58	1.30	0.55	0.53	0.06	Capital Gains $
	---	---	---	1.27	2.31	1.50	1.57	1.50	1.42	1.45	1.38	1.36	Expense Ratio %
	---	---	---	2.45	1.33	0.96	2.18	1.09	0.93	0.16	-0.19	-0.35	Income Ratio %
	---	---	---	---	333	170	258	207	154	127	227	---	Turnover Rate %
	---	---	---	1.9	2.0	2.6	3.9	6.1	57.1	408.0	524.3	364.9	Net Assets ($mil)

Investment Style History: 66% | 66% | 81% | 85%

Performance 12-31-94

	1st Qtr	2nd Qtr	3rd Qtr	4th Qtr	Total
1987	15.10	0.71	-3.24	-9.47	1.54
1988	6.20	12.65	2.33	0.53	23.07
1989	3.12	7.99	4.74	-1.21	15.23
1990	5.36	11.83	-19.29	17.11	11.38
1991	18.52	3.00	13.53	12.48	55.90
1992	0.64	-6.38	2.98	8.73	5.49
1993	-6.63	0.74	7.78	-0.87	0.49
1994	-2.64	-5.42	7.06	-4.85	-6.20

Bear Market Performance

Decile Rank (5-year period)

Worst [ ] Best

	Worst 3 Mo Period 1985-89	Worst 3 Mo Period 1990-94
Monetta	---	-20.43
+/- S&P 500	---	-6.58
+/- Best Fit Index : Wil 4500	---	-1.02

Trailing Returns

	Total Return %	+/- S&P 500	+/- Wil 4500	% Rank All	% Rank Obj	Growth of $10,000
3 Mo	-4.85	-4.83	-2.35	91	91	9,515
6 Mo	1.87	-2.99	-2.33	27	83	10,187
1 Yr	-6.20	-7.51	-3.54	73	84	9,381
3 Yr Avg	-0.19	-6.45	-7.80	97	98	9,944
5 Yr Avg	11.54	2.85	2.45	11	52	17,266
10 Yr Avg	---	---	---	---	---	---
15 Yr Avg	---	---	---	---	---	---

Operations

Address and Telephone	1776-A S. Naperville Road Wheaton, IL 60187 800-666-3882 / 708-462-9800
Advisor	Monetta Financial Services
Subadvisor	None
Distributor	Monetta Funds
States Available	All except VT
Report Grade	B
Income Distrib	Paid Annually
* Date of Inception	05-06-86
Fiscal Year End	December

Min Initial Purchase	Closed (Addt'l: $50)
Min IRA Purchase	$100 (Addt'l: $50)
Min Auto Invest Plan	$100 (Systematic Inv: $50)

Expenses & Fees
Sales Fees	0.00% front
	0.00% deferred
	0.00% 12b-1
Management Fee	1.00% flat fee
3-,5-,10-yr Expense Projections	$45, $78, $170
Annual Brokerage Cost	0.41%

Risk Analysis

Time Period	Load-Adj Return %	Risk % Rank [1] All	Risk % Rank [1] Obj	Morningstar [2] Return	Morningstar Risk	Morningstar Risk-Adj Rating
1 Yr	-6.19					
3 Yr	-0.19	91	62	-1.05 [3]	1.21	★
5 Yr	11.54	82	37	1.80 [3]	1.00	★★★★
10 Yr	---					
Average Historical Rating (68 months)				4.3 ★s		

[1] 1 = low, 100 = high [2] 1.00 = Equity Avg [3] 1.00 = 90-day T-bill return

Other Measures

				Standard S&P 500	Best Fit Wil 4500
Standard Deviation	10.72	Alpha		-5.4	-7.1
Mean	0.39	Beta		0.82	0.98
Sharpe Ratio	-0.29	R-Squared		36	80

Investment Style

	Stock Portfolio Avg	Relative S&P 500
Price/Earnings Ratio	23.5	1.27
Price/Book Ratio	3.3	0.97
5 Yr Earnings Gr %	12.5#	2.25
Return on Assets %	6.3	0.85
Debt % Total Cap	24.2	0.86
Med Mkt Cap ($mil)	1023	0.08

Style Value Blend Growth — Size Large Med Small

figure is based on 50% or less of stocks

Diversification Value for Portfolio Types

| Large Cap: Medium | Small Cap: Low | Bond: High | Balanced: Medium | Diversified: Medium |

Portfolio 12-31-94

Total Stocks: 83
Total Fixed-Income: 0

Share Chg (09-94) 000	Amount 000		Value $000	% Net Assets
200	300	Kemper	11363	3.11
0	140	Andrew	7315	2.00
0	200	Louisiana Land & Exploration	7275	1.99
0	250	Nine West Group	7094	1.94
202	402	ICN Pharmaceuticals	6943	1.90
0	250	McDermott International	6188	1.70
155	155	Kohl's	6161	1.69
25	125	KLA Instruments	6125	1.68
0	330	Jacobs Engineering Group	6105	1.67
75	225	PhyCor	6019	1.65
-50	400	Roosevelt Financial Group	6000	1.64
0	140	Lotus Development	5740	1.57
27	87	Florida East Coast Inds	5716	1.57
400	800	CKE Restaurants	5500	1.51
0	300	Baker Hughes	5475	1.50
50	140	Tiffany	5460	1.50
165	165	Tekelec	5424	1.49
19	200	CR Bard	5400	1.48
145	175	IBP	5294	1.45
0	150	Charles Schwab	5231	1.43
329	700	Interdigital Communications	5163	1.41
118	118	Biogen	4927	1.35
-18	153	Roberts Pharmaceutical	4842	1.33
-25	200	MGM Grand	4825	1.32
45	175	Firstar	4703	1.29

Composition % 12-31-94

Cash	19.4	Preferreds	0.0
Stocks	80.6	Convertibles	0.0
Bonds	0.0	Other	0.0

Tax Analysis

	Tax-Adj Historical Return %	% Pretax Return
3 Yr Avg	-0.88	NMF
5 Yr Avg	10.14	85.4
10 Yr Avg	---	---
Potential Capital Gain Exposure (% of assets)		-6%

Most Similar Funds in MF500

20th Century Growth Investor	Fair Fit
Enterprise Capital Apprec	Fair Fit
Sit Growth	Fair Fit

Index Allocation

	% of Stocks
S&P 500	17.2
S&P MidCap 400	36.2
U.S. Small Cap	46.3
Foreign	0.2

Sector Weightings

	% of Stocks	Relative S&P 500
Utilities	0.6	0.05
Energy	12.3	1.22
Financials	16.8	1.59
Industrial Cyclicals	5.3	0.32
Consumer Durables	6.4	1.04
Consumer Staples	1.8	0.15
Services	17.0	2.09
Retail	9.4	1.61
Health	16.2	1.86
Technology	14.1	1.54

Montgomery Emerging Mkts

	Ticker	Load	NAV	Yield	SEC Yield	Assets	Objective
	MNEMX	None	13.65	0.0%	N/A	878.0	Foreign Stock

Montgomery Emerging Markets Fund seeks capital appreciation.
The fund invests at least 65% of its assets in equity securities issued in emerging markets, as designated by the World Bank or the United Nations. Optimal market allocations are identified by a proprietary, quantitative asset-allocation model. To select individual securities, fundamental analysis is employed. No more than 35% of assets may be invested in one country; the portfolio represents at least six emerging-market countries. Up to 20% of assets may be invested in equities listed on the EAFE Index.

Manager's Investment Style
Management takes a diversified approach to emerging-markets investing, at times holding positions in more than 25 separate markets. This vast diversification allows management to dabble in some more-obscure markets, including Russia, Ghana, and Vietnam. It determines these country allocations by using six quantitative models and by selecting markets with low correlations to one another. Within each market, they set out to play the most promising sectors. Large-cap, blue-chip stocks aren't the only issues on the roster, though: Management dedicates 40% of assets to small, undiscovered stocks with market caps between $25 million and $60 million.

Fund Manager(s)
Josephine S. Jimenez CFA(1989), since 03-92. BS, New York U. 1979 MS, MIT 1981
Bryan Sudweeks CFA(1992), since 03-92. PhD, George Washington U. MBA, Brigham Young U.

Manager Experience	Dates Managed	Invest Obj	Std Dev	+/- Index
Bryan Sudweeks				
Montgomery Instl Emrg Mk	12/93 - 12/94	WF	17.94	-10.57
Josephine S. Jimenez				
Montgomery Instl Emrg Mk	12/93 - 12/94	WF	17.94	-10.57

Historical Profile
Return ---
Risk ---
Rating
Not Rated

Investment Style History
Equity
Average % Stocks Held in Portfolio

Growth of $10,000
|||| Value of Fund ($000)
— Value of Index ($000) S&P 500
▼ Manager Change
▽ Partial Manager Change
► Mgr Unknown After
◄ Mgr Unknown Before

Performance Quartile (Within Objective)

	1983	1984	1985	1986	1987	1988	1989	1990	1991	1992	1993	1994	History
	---	---	---	---	---	---	---	---	---	10.02	15.58	13.65	NAV
	---	---	---	---	---	---	---	---	---	0.31 *	58.59	-7.72	Total Return %
	---	---	---	---	---	---	---	---	---	-7.94 *	48.54	-9.04	+/- S&P 500
	---	---	---	---	---	---	---	---	---	---	-6.91	-5.30	+/- MSCI Emerging
	---	---	---	---	---	---	---	---	---	0.10	0.14	0.00	Income Return %
	---	---	---	---	---	---	---	---	---	0.21	58.45	-7.72	Capital Return %
	---	---	---	---	---	---	---	---	---	---	2	84	Total Rtn % Rank All
	---	---	---	---	---	---	---	---	---	---	10	75	Total Rtn % Rank Obj
	---	---	---	---	---	---	---	---	---	0.01	0.02	0.00	Income $
	---	---	---	---	---	---	---	---	---	0.00	0.25	0.79	Capital Gains $
	---	---	---	---	---	---	---	---	---	1.90	1.90	1.85	Expense Ratio %
	---	---	---	---	---	---	---	---	---	1.70	0.66	-0.14	Income Ratio %
	---	---	---	---	---	---	---	---	---	---	21	64	Turnover Rate %
	---	---	---	---	---	---	---	---	---	97.1	610.2	878.0	Net Assets ($mil)

Performance 12-31-94

	1st Qtr	2nd Qtr	3rd Qtr	4th Qtr	Total
1987	---	---	---	---	---
1988	---	---	---	---	---
1989	---	---	---	---	---
1990	---	---	---	---	---
1991	---	---	---	---	---
1992	---	-0.10	-3.92	4.82	0.31 *
1993	4.49	5.73	11.20	29.09	58.59
1994	-9.24	-3.25	17.62	-10.65	-7.72

Bear Market Performance
Decile Rank (5-year period)

Worst | Best

	Worst 3 Mo Period 1985-89	Worst 3 Mo Period 1990-94
Montgomery Emerging Mkts	---	---
+/- S&P 500	---	---
+/- Best Fit Index :	---	---

Trailing Returns

	Total Return %	+/- S&P 500	+/- MSCI Emerging	% Rank All	% Rank Obj	Growth of $10,000
3 Mo	-10.65	-10.63	1.47	98	83	8,935
6 Mo	5.10	0.23	-0.93	11	6	10,510
1 Yr	-7.72	-9.04	-5.30	84	75	9,228
3 Yr Avg	---	---	---	---	---	---
5 Yr Avg	---	---	---	---	---	---
10 Yr Avg	---	---	---	---	---	---
15 Yr Avg	---	---	---	---	---	---

Operations

Address and Telephone	600 Montgomery Street	
	San Francisco, CA 94111	
	800-572-3863 / 415-627-2400	
Advisor	Montgomery Asset Management	
Subadvisor	None	
Distributor	Montgomery Securities	
States Available	All	
Report Grade	C+	
Income Distrib	Paid Annually	
* Date of Inception	03-01-92	
Fiscal Year End	June	

Risk Analysis

Time Period	Load-Adj Return %	Risk % Rank All	Risk % Rank Obj	Morningstar Return	Morningstar Risk	Morningstar Risk-Adj Rating
1 Yr	-7.72					
3 Yr	---	---	---	---	---	---
5 Yr	---	---	---			
10 Yr	---	---	---			

Average Historical Rating ---

[1] 1 = low, 100 = high [2] 1.00 = Equity Avg [3] 1.00 = 90-day T-bill return

Other Measures

			Standard S&P 500	Best Fit
Standard Deviation	---	Alpha	---	---
Mean	---	Beta	---	---
Sharpe Ratio	---	R-Squared	---	

Investment Style

	Stock Portfolio Avg	Rel MSCI EAFE	Rel Obj
Price/Earnings Ratio	29.8#	0.81	1.06
Price/Cash Flow	21.4#	1.37	1.59
Price/Book Ratio	4.4#	1.69	1.49
5 Yr Earnings Gr %	---		
Return on Assets %	---		
Debt % Total Cap	22.8#	0.67	0.82
Med Mkt Cap ($mil)	2309#	0.19	0.45

figure is based on 50% or less of stocks

Diversification Value for Portfolio Types

Large Cap: | Small Cap: | Bond: | Balanced: | Diversified:

Expenses & Fees
Sales Fees
0.00% front
0.00% deferred
0.00% 12b-1
Management Fee 1.25% max./1.00% min., 0.07%A
3-,5-,10-yr Expense Projections $58, $100, $217
Annual Brokerage Cost 0.00%

Min Initial Purchase	$1000 (Addt'l: $100)
Min IRA Purchase	$1000 (Addt'l: $100)
Min Auto Invest Plan	$1000 (Systematic Inv: $100)

Portfolio 06-30-94

Share Chg (12-93)000	Amount 000	Total Stocks: 231 / Total Fixed-Income: 28	Value $000	% Net Assets
120	256	Korea Electric Power	9134	1.39
1573	3156	DBS Land	9107	1.39
	8466395	Usiminas PN Pfd	8682	1.33
489	1084	United Overseas Bank (For)	8673	1.32
563	904	Development Bk Singapore For	8658	1.32
-238	6216	Ayala Cl B	8518	1.30
64	76	Pohang Iron & Steel	8188	1.25
79	184	Chile Fund	7909	1.21
579	1070	Sembawang Shipyards	7719	1.18
2312	2312	Central Costanera	7368	1.12
567	653	CIADEA	7194	1.10
291	807	Jurong Shipyard	7145	1.09
78	361	China Steel (ADR)	7086	1.08
-127	248	Taiwan Fund	6654	1.02
818	999	Galicia Y Buenos Aires	6606	1.01
454	1114	Resorts World	6417	0.98
942	1860	IJM Engineering	6214	0.95
	1120392	Bradesco Pfd	6070	0.93
	157325	Telebras Pfd	5921	0.90
1103	1103	Hong Leong Credit	5716	0.87

Regional Exposure 09-30-94
% of Stocks

Europe	15	Pacific Rim	60
Japan	14	Other	3
Latin Amer	7		

Composition % 12-31-94

Cash	1.9	Preferreds	21.8
Stocks	73.6	Convertibles	2.7
Bonds	0.0	Other	0.0

Tax Analysis

	Tax-Adj Historical Return %	% Pretax Return
3 Yr Avg	---	---
5 Yr Avg	---	---
10 Yr Avg	---	---
Potential Capital Gain Exposure (% of assets)		7%

Most Similar Funds in MF500
Fund lacks three-year record

Country Exposure 09-28-94

	% of Stocks
Brazil	15
U.S.	14
Malaysia	7
South Korea	7
Thailand	7

Total Number of Countries: 26
Hedging Policy: Never

Sector Weightings

	% of Stocks	Relative S&P 500
Utilities	9.3	1.04
Energy	2.0	0.50
Financials	38.4	2.04
Industrial Cyclicals	21.4	0.85
Consumer Durables	6.0	0.55
Consumer Staples	5.0	0.73
Services	12.0	1.09
Retail	1.4	0.24
Health	0.6	0.17
Technology	4.1	0.79

 **1995 Mutual Fund 500**

Montgomery Growth

	Ticker	Load	NAV	Yield	SEC Yield	Assets	Objective
	MNGFX	None	16.93	0.4%	N/A	592.7	Growth

Montgomery Growth Fund seeks capital appreciation.

The fund normally invests at least 65% of its assets in equities issued by domestic companies; it emphasizes companies that have market capitalizations of $500 million or more. It may invest the balance of assets in high-quality debt securities. In selecting equity securities, the fund targets rapidly growing companies that are reasonably valued, then narrows down its choices based on analysis of balance sheets and income statements, company visits and discussions with management, and contact with industry analysts. The fund may invest in American Depositary Receipts.

Manager's Investment Style

Roger Honour's stock-picking process is broken down into three stages. First, he takes a quantitative approach, using a computer model to identify firms experiencing positive changes in earnings, revenues, or margins. He then examines a company's fundamentals to determine if the earnings change is sustainable for at least four to six quarters. He ends the process by looking at valuations, and buying only when a stock's P/E is at a discount to both the firm's growth rate and to the growth rates of its competitors. If the valuations aren't low enough, Honour won't buy; he's willing to wait things out and hold cash.

Fund Manager(s)

Roger W. Honour, since 09-93. Birthdate: 06-54. BS, U. of Louisville 1977

Manager Experience

	Dates Managed	Invest Obj	Std Dev	+/- Index
Roger W. Honour				
Alliance Technology A	04/90 - 04/92	ST	31.45	3.56

Historical Profile

Return ---
Risk ---
Rating ---
Not Rated

Investment Style History
Equity

Average % Stocks Held in Portfolio

77% 61%

Growth of $10,000

|||| Value of Fund ($000)
— Value of Index ($000)
S&P 500
▼ Manager Change
▽ Partial Manager Change
► Mgr Unknown After
◄ Mgr Unknown Before

Performance Quartile (Within Objective)

1983	1984	1985	1986	1987	1988	1989	1990	1991	1992	1993	1994	History
---	---	---	---	---	---	---	---	---	---	14.12	16.93	NAV
---	---	---	---	---	---	---	---	---	---	18.34 *	20.91	Total Return %
---	---	---	---	---	---	---	---	---	---	16.02 *	19.60	+/- S&P 500
---	---	---	---	---	---	---	---	---	---	---	20.98	+/- Wilshire 5000
---	---	---	---	---	---	---	---	---	---	0.07	0.46	Income Return %
---	---	---	---	---	---	---	---	---	---	18.27	20.45	Capital Return %
---	---	---	---	---	---	---	---	---	---	---	1	Total Rtn % Rank All
---	---	---	---	---	---	---	---	---	---	---	1	Total Rtn % Rank Obj
---	---	---	---	---	---	---	---	---	---	0.01	0.07	Income $
---	---	---	---	---	---	---	---	---	---	0.07	0.07	Capital Gains $
---	---	---	---	---	---	---	---	---	---	---	1.49	Expense Ratio %
---	---	---	---	---	---	---	---	---	---	---	1.09	Income Ratio %
---	---	---	---	---	---	---	---	---	---	---	---	Turnover Rate %
---	---	---	---	---	---	---	---	---	---	3.8	592.7	Net Assets ($mil)

Performance 12-31-94

	1st Qtr	2nd Qtr	3rd Qtr	4th Qtr	Total
1987	---	---	---	---	---
1988	---	---	---	---	---
1989	---	---	---	---	---
1990	---	---	---	---	---
1991	---	---	---	---	---
1992	---	---	---	---	---
1993	---	---	---	18.34	18.34 *
1994	5.88	2.14	8.19	3.34	20.91

Bear Market Performance

Decile Rank (5-year period)

Worst ———————————————— Best

	Worst 3 Mo Period 1985-89	Worst 3 Mo Period 1990-94
Montgomery Growth	---	---
+/- S&P 500	---	---
+/- Best Fit Index :	---	---

Trailing Returns

	Total Return %	+/- S&P 500	+/- Wil 5000	% Rank All	Obj	Growth of $10,000
3 Mo	3.34	3.36	4.11	2	3	10,334
6 Mo	11.80	6.94	7.18	3	6	11,180
1 Yr	20.91	19.60	20.98	1	1	12,091
3 Yr Avg	---	---	---	---	---	---
5 Yr Avg	---	---	---	---	---	---
10 Yr Avg	---	---	---	---	---	---
15 Yr Avg	---	---	---	---	---	---

Operations

Address and Telephone	600 Montgomery Street San Francisco, CA 94111 800-572-3863		Min Initial Purchase	$1000 (Addt'l: $100)
			Min IRA Purchase	$1000 (Addt'l: $100)
			Min Auto Invest Plan	$1000 (Systematic Inv: $100)
Advisor	Montgomery Asset Management			
Subadvisor	None		Expenses & Fees	
Distributor	Montgomery Securities		Sales Fees	0.00% front
States Available	All			0.00% deferred
Report Grade	C			0.00% 12b-1
Income Distrib	Paid Annually		Management Fee	1.00% flat fee, 0.07%A
* Date of Inception	09-30-93		3-,5-,10-yr Expense Projections	$47, N/A, N/A
Fiscal Year End	June		Annual Brokerage Cost	---

Risk Analysis

Time Period	Load-Adj Return %	Risk % Rank [1] All	Obj	Morningstar [2] Return	Risk	Morningstar Risk-Adj Rating
1 Yr	20.91					
3 Yr	---	---	---	---	---	
5 Yr	---	---	---	---	---	
10 Yr	---	---	---	---	---	
Average Historical Rating ---					---	

[1] 1 = low, 100 = high   [2] 1.00 = Equity Avg   [3] 1.00 = 90-day T-bill return

Other Measures

				Standard S&P 500	Best Fit
Standard Deviation	---	Alpha		---	---
Mean	---	Beta		---	---
Sharpe Ratio	---	R-Squared		---	---

Investment Style

	Stock Portfolio Avg	Relative S&P 500	Style Value Blend Growth
Price/Earnings Ratio	25.3	1.37	
Price/Book Ratio	4.4	1.28	
5 Yr Earnings Gr %	6.0#	1.08	
Return on Assets %	9.5	1.27	
Debt % Total Cap	26.7	0.94	
Med Mkt Cap ($mil)	2995	0.23	

figure is based on 50% or less of stocks

Diversification Value for Portfolio Types

Large Cap: Small Cap: Bond: Balanced: Diversified:

Portfolio 06-30-94

Share Chg (12-93) 000	Amount 000	Total Stocks: 37 Total Fixed-Income: 1	Value $000	% Net Assets
64	65	Xerox	6354	4.26
105	105	Nordstrom	4463	2.99
175	175	Mattel	4441	2.98
128	128	TRINOVA	4432	2.97
63	63	Nucor	4316	2.89
130	130	FORE Systems	3803	2.55
48	50	Federal Express	3731	2.50
70	70	Hilton Hotels	3710	2.49
81	81	Broderbund Software	3665	2.46
195	195	VMARK Software	3461	2.32
235	235	Dialogic	3408	2.29
115	115	Abbott Laboratories	3335	2.24
100	100	Owens-Corning	3113	2.09
50	50	FHLMC	3025	2.03
165	165	Corel	2939	1.97
100	100	Vastar Resources	2938	1.97
50	50	Amoco	2850	1.91
185	185	Price/Costco	2763	1.85
85	86	Compaq Computer	2757	1.85
185	185	Electronic Arts	2590	1.74
112	112	Security Connecticut	2557	1.71
54	55	Willamette Industries	2351	1.58
130	130	Expeditors Intl Washington	2243	1.50
39	40	AT & T	2175	1.46
49	49	ADC Telecommunications	1952	1.31

Composition % 12-31-94

Cash	23.0	Preferreds	0.0
Stocks	77.0	Convertibles	0.0
Bonds	0.0	Other	0.0

Tax Analysis

	Tax-Adj Historical Return %	% Pretax Return
3 Yr Avg	---	---
5 Yr Avg	---	---
10 Yr Avg	---	---
Potential Capital Gain Exposure (% of assets)		6%

Most Similar Funds in MF500

Fund lacks three-year record

Index Allocation

	% of Stocks
S&P 500	59.3
S&P MidCap 400	6.2
U.S. Small Cap	27.2
Foreign	7.3

Sector Weightings

	% of Stocks	Relative S&P 500
Utilities	2.5	0.20
Energy	3.2	0.32
Financials	5.1	0.48
Industrial Cyclicals	30.2	1.84
Consumer Durables	6.4	1.03
Consumer Staples	1.8	0.14
Services	13.1	1.61
Retail	8.2	1.41
Health	3.8	0.44
Technology	25.8	2.81

MORNINGSTAR 1995 Mutual Fund 500

Morgan Stanley Africa Investment

	Ticker	NAV	Mkt Price	Prem/Disc	Yield	Objective
	AFF	$14.37	$11.38	-20.8%	NMF	World Stock

Morgan Stanley Africa Investment Fund seeks long-term capital appreciation.

The fund will eventually invest at least 80% of its assets in equity securities (1) of companies organized in Africa, (2) denominated in African currencies, (3) or of companies that derive at least 50% of their revenues from business activities in Africa. The fund may also invest in African sovereign debt. It may use American Depositary Receipts (ADRs) and Global Depositary Receipts (GDRs) to invest in African issuers. Initially, the fund expects to invest primarily in Morocco and South Africa; it expects to invest in other African markets when they meet the requirements of the 1940 Act. The fund may engage in hedging activities.

To discourage takeover attempts, board members serve staggered terms and supermajority voter approval is required to open-end, liquidate, or merge the fund.

Manager's Investment Style
Management doesn't restrict its stock and bond picks to South Africa; rather, it invests in markets around the region. Past debt exposure, for example, has included issues from Morocco, Nigeria, and Algeria. Management intends to keep diversifying into the bonds of these countries until their stock markets develop. In South Africa, management seeks smaller firms that benefit from political and economic programs in the country, such as the reconstruction program. Given the research required to find small firms, however, management will hold its conglomerates until they find the issues that fit the bill.

Fund Manager(s)
Marianne Hay. Since 2-94. BS U. of Edinburgh.

Historical Profile

Return Not Rated
Risk Not Rated
Rating

	12.0 Highest Prem/Disc
	-23.3 Lowest Prem/Disc

Growth of $10,000
■ at NAV ($000)
— at Market Price ($000)

Premium Discount %

	1983	1984	1985	1986	1987	1988	1989	1990	1991	1992	1993	1994	History
	---	---	---	---	---	---	---	---	---	---	---	14.37	NAV
	---	---	---	---	---	---	---	---	---	---	---	6.86*	NAV Total Return %
	---	---	---	---	---	---	---	---	---	---	---	6.46*	+/- S&P 500
	---	---	---	---	---	---	---	---	---	---	---	---	+/- MSCI EAFE
	---	---	---	---	---	---	---	---	---	---	---	---	+/- MSCI Emerging
	---	---	---	---	---	---	---	---	---	---	---	4.94*	Income Return %
	---	---	---	---	---	---	---	---	---	---	---	1.92*	Capital Return %
	---	---	---	---	---	---	---	---	---	---	---	---	Total Rtn % Rank All
	---	---	---	---	---	---	---	---	---	---	---	---	Total Rtn % Rank Obj
	---	---	---	---	---	---	---	---	---	---	-20.49*		Market Total Rtn %
	---	---	---	---	---	---	---	---	---	---	-13.5		Avg Prem/Disc %
	---	---	---	---	---	---	---	---	---	---	---	0.54	Income $
	---	---	---	---	---	---	---	---	---	---	---	0.00	Capital Gains $
	---	---	---	---	---	---	---	---	---	---	---	2.16	Expense Ratio %
	---	---	---	---	---	---	---	---	---	---	---	5.44	Income Ratio %
	---	---	---	---	---	---	---	---	---	---	---	---	Turnover Rate %
	---	---	---	---	---	---	---	---	---	---	---	222.0	Net Assets ($mil)

Manager Experience

	Dates Managed	Invest Obj	Std Dev	+/- Index
Marianne Hay				
Morgan Stanley Instl Emg	06/93 - 12/94	WF	23.35	20.14
Turkish Investment	03/94 - 12/94	WE	38.87	-7.56

NAV Performance % 12-30-94

	1st Qtr	2nd Qtr	3rd Qtr	4th Qtr	Total
1987	---	---	---	---	---
1988	---	---	---	---	---
1989	---	---	---	---	---
1990	---	---	---	---	---
1991	---	---	---	---	---
1992	---	---	---	---	---
1993	---	---	---	---	---
1994	-14.04*	5.69	11.32	5.66	6.86*

Bear Market Performance

Decile Rank (5-year period)

Worst — Best

	Worst 3 Mo Period 1985-89	Worst 3 Mo Period 1990-94
Morgan Stan Africa	---	---
+/- S&P 500	---	---

Trailing Returns

	NAV Total Return %	+/- S&P 500	+/- MSCI Emerging	% Rank All	% Rank Obj	Mkt Total Return %
3 Mo	5.66	5.67	17.77	2	11	6.01
6 Mo	17.62	12.75	11.59	2	11	8.42
1 Yr	---	---	---	---	---	---
3 Yr Avg	---	---	---	---	---	---
5 Yr Avg	---	---	---	---	---	---
Inception	6.86*	---	---	---	---	-20.49*

Operations

Address and Telephone	1221 Avenue of the Americas, New York, NY 10020, 212-296-7200 / 800-221-6726
Advisor	Morgan Stanley Asset Management
Subadvisor	Standard New York, Inc.
Administrator	United States Trust Co. New York
Transfer Agent	American Stock Transfer & Trust
Custodian	Morgan Stanley Trust Co.
Auditor	Price Waterhouse LLP
Legal Counsel	Rogers & Wells
Income Distrib Schedule	Paid Irregularly
Management Fee	1.20%, 0.06%A
Reinvestment Plan	Yes
Direct Purchase Plan	Yes
Shares Outstanding	15,448,477
Exchange	NYSE
*Date of Inception	02-04-94
Shareholder Report	B-

Risk Analysis

	Risk % Rank[1] All	Obj	Morningstar[2] Return	Risk	Morningstar Risk-Adj Rating
3 Yr	---	---	---	---	
5 Yr	---	---	---	---	
10 Yr	---	---	---	---	

[1] 1 = Low, 100 = High [2] 1.00 = Equity Avg [3] 1.00 = 90-day T-bill Return

Other Measures

			S&P 500
Standard Deviation	---	Alpha	---
Mean	---	Beta	---
Sharpe Ratio	---	R-Squared	---

Investment Style

	Stock Portfolio Avg	Rel WS S Africa	Rel WS World
Price/Earnings Ratio	18.4	0.75	0.45
Price/Cash Flow Ratio	17.0	1.09	1.21
Price/Book Ratio	3.8	1.07	1.21
5 Yr Earnings Gr %	0.7	1.30	NMF
Return on Assets	11.8	0.94	2.10
Debt % Total Cap	9.9	0.93	0.31
Med Mkt Cap ($mil)	3614	1.36	0.47

figure is based on less than 50% of stocks

Country Exposure (top five) 12-31-94

Securities %		Currency %	
South Africa	68	South Africa	67
Morocco	13	US	24
Nigeria	6	Morocco	4
Ivory Coast	2	France	2
UK	2	UK	2

Diversification Value for Portfolio Types

Large Cap: Small Cap: Bond: Balanced: Diversified:

Tax Analysis

	Tax-Adj Historical Return %	% Pretax Return
3 Yr Avg	---	---
5 Yr Avg	---	---
10 Yr Avg	---	---
Potential Capital Gain Exposure (% of assets)	1	

Most Similar Funds in MF500
Fund lacks 3-year record

Portfolio 09-30-94

Share Chg (06-94)	Amount	Total Equity: 45 / Total Fixed-Income: 13	Value $000	% Total Invest
---	30000000	Kingdom of Morocco Loan A FRN	21919	9.68
0	212600	Anglo American of So Africa	11963	5.28
---	63000000	Republic of South Africa 12%	11377	5.03
0	80500	Anglo American Gold Invest	9116	4.03
---	30000000	Central Bk Nigeria Annuity 8%	8662	3.83
493000	2200300	Gencor	7609	3.36
---	32000000	Transnet 15%	7594	3.35
0	669000	Financiere Richemont	6274	2.77
---	15000000	Central Bank Nigeria 5.5%	6248	2.76
---	168.857M	Ivory Coast Syndicated Loan	6137	2.71
127000	665600	Sasol	5610	2.48
3500	277700	South African Breweries	5469	2.42
---	10000000	Algeria Refinanced Loan A FRN	4700	2.08
0	187300	Johannesburg Consolidated	4655	2.06
---	20000000	Republic of South Africa 14%	4508	1.99
---	20000000	Transnet 12.5%	4404	1.95
0	35000	Vaal Reefs Exploration/Mines	3923	1.73
---	20000000	Republic of South Africa 11.5%	3839	1.70
-178300	137900	Minorco (South Africa)	3621	1.60
---	12500000	Corporate Africa Pfd	3517	1.55
25000	1675000	Lonrho	3468	1.53
0	494500	Barlow	3333	1.47
738200	1322400	Amalgamated Bank	3163	1.40
-6500	365700	Potgieterstrust Platinum	3130	1.38
0	444300	Nedcor	3125	1.38

Composition % 12-31-94

Cash	5.6	Preferreds	0.0
Stocks	59.8	Convertibles	0.0
Bonds	34.6	Other	0.0

Sector Weightings

	% of Stocks
Utilities	0.0
Energy	0.0
Financials	54.4
Industrial Cyclicals	17.0
Consumer Durables	4.6
Consumer Staples	3.0
Services	14.4
Retail	6.3
Health	0.4
Technology	0.0

MORNINGSTAR 1995 Mutual Fund 500

Morgan Stanley Asian Growth A

	Ticker	Load	NAV	Yield	SEC Yield	Assets	Objective
	MSAAX	4.75%	15.26	0.0%	N/A	158.5	Pacific Stock

Morgan Stanley Asian Growth Fund - Class A seeks capital appreciation. Current income is incidental.

The fund normally invests at least 65% of its assets in at least three Asian countries, excluding Japan. There is no set allocation of assets among the various countries. The fund emphasizes individual stock selection and follows a value-oriented style. These securities are usually issued by larger companies and are undervalued in relation to the issuer's assets, cash flow, earnings, and future value. The fund does not normally trade for short-term profits.

Class A shares have front loads and lower 12b-1 fees; Class B shares have deferred loads.

Manager's Investment Style

Management uses a multitiered investment strategy that generally considers country allocation first, followed by stock selection. Such factors as economic forecasts, political developments, and market valuations are considered along with individual stock screens for dividends and more-subjective criteria on the companies' prospects. The net is generally a portfolio of high-growth stocks. Turnover usually is low.

Fund Manager(s)

Ean Wah Chin, since 06-93. U. of Singapore

Manager Experience	Dates Managed	Invest Obj	Std Dev	+/- Index
Ean Wah Chin				
Morgan Stanley Inst Asia	07/91 - 12/94	WP	22.24	18.22

Historical Profile

Return	---
Risk	---
Rating	Not Rated

Investment Style History
Equity

Average % Stocks Held in Portfolio
88% / 91%

Growth of $10,000
- ||| Value of Fund ($000)
- — Value of Index ($000) S&P 500
- ▼ Manager Change
- ▽ Partial Manager Change
- ► Mgr Unknown After
- ◄ Mgr Unknown Before

Performance Quartile (Within Objective)

	1983	1984	1985	1986	1987	1988	1989	1990	1991	1992	1993	1994	History
	---	---	---	---	---	---	---	---	---	---	18.38	15.26	NAV
	---	---	---	---	---	---	---	---	---	---	53.17 *	-14.18	Total Return %
	---	---	---	---	---	---	---	---	---	---	46.25 *	-15.49	+/- S&P 500
	---	---	---	---	---	---	---	---	---	---	---	-27.01	+/- MSCI Pacific
	---	---	---	---	---	---	---	---	---	---	0.00	0.00	Income Return %
	---	---	---	---	---	---	---	---	---	---	53.17	-14.18	Capital Return %
	---	---	---	---	---	---	---	---	---	---	---	98	Total Rtn % Rank All
	---	---	---	---	---	---	---	---	---	---	---	52	Total Rtn % Rank Obj
	---	---	---	---	---	---	---	---	---	---	0.00	0.00	Income $
	---	---	---	---	---	---	---	---	---	---	0.00	0.51	Capital Gains $
	---	---	---	---	---	---	---	---	---	---	1.90	1.90	Expense Ratio %
	---	---	---	---	---	---	---	---	---	---	-0.81	-0.39	Income Ratio %
	---	---	---	---	---	---	---	---	---	---	0	---	Turnover Rate %
	---	---	---	---	---	---	---	---	---	---	129.6	158.5	Net Assets ($mil)

Performance 12-31-94

	1st Qtr	2nd Qtr	3rd Qtr	4th Qtr	Total
1987	---	---	---	---	---
1988	---	---	---	---	---
1989	---	---	---	---	---
1990	---	---	---	---	---
1991	---	---	---	---	---
1992	---	---	---	---	---
1993	---	---	6.58	43.71	53.17 *
1994	-18.61	3.61	13.94	-10.68	-14.18

Bear Market Performance

Decile Rank (5-year period)

Worst | Best

	Worst 3 Mo Period 1985-89	Worst 3 Mo Period 1990-94
Morgan Stanley Asian Growth	---	---
+/- S&P 500	---	---
+/- Best Fit Index :	---	---

Trailing Returns

	Total Return %	+/- S&P 500	+/- MSCI Pacific	% Rank All	% Rank Obj	Growth of $10,000
3 Mo	-10.68	-10.66	-8.14	98	77	8,932
6 Mo	1.77	-3.09	7.17	28	12	10,177
1 Yr	-14.18	-15.49	-27.01	98	52	8,582
3 Yr Avg	---	---	---	---	---	---
5 Yr Avg	---	---	---	---	---	---
10 Yr Avg	---	---	---	---	---	---
15 Yr Avg	---	---	---	---	---	---

Operations

Address and Telephone	P.O. Box 2798
	Boston, MA 02208-2798
	800-282-4404
Advisor	Morgan Stanley Asset Management
Subadvisor	None
Distributor	Morgan Stanley
States Available	All
Report Grade	B+
Income Distrib	Paid Annually
* Date of Inception	06-23-93
Fiscal Year End	June

Risk Analysis

Time Period	Load-Adj Return %	Risk % Rank [1] All	Obj	Morningstar [2] Return	Morningstar Risk	Morningstar Risk-Adj Rating
1 Yr	-18.25	---	---	---	---	---
3 Yr	---	---	---	---	---	---
5 Yr	---	---	---	---	---	---
10 Yr	---	---	---	---	---	---

Average Historical Rating ---

[1] 1 = low, 100 = high   [2] 1.00 = Equity Avg   [3] 1.00 = 90-day T-bill return

Other Measures

			Standard S&P 500	Best Fit
Standard Deviation	---	Alpha	---	---
Mean	---	Beta	---	---
Sharpe Ratio	---	R-Squared	---	---

Investment Style

	Stock Portfolio Avg	Rel MSCI EAFE	Rel Obj
Price/Earnings Ratio	29.3	0.79	0.92
Price/Cash Flow	21.0	1.35	1.09
Price/Book Ratio	4.4	1.67	1.49
5 Yr Earnings Gr %	26.6#	---	2.39
Return on Assets %	11.9#	2.62	1.48
Debt % Total Cap	18.7#	0.55	0.78
Med Mkt Cap ($mil)	6502	0.54	1.58

figure is based on 50% or less of stocks

Style: V B G / Size L M S

Diversification Value for Portfolio Types

Large Cap: Small Cap: Bond: Balanced: Diversified:

Expenses & Fees

Sales Fees	4.75% front
	0.00% deferred
	0.25% 12b-1
Management Fee	1.00% flat fee, 0.25%A
3-,5-,10-yr Expense Projections	$104, N/A, N/A
Annual Brokerage Cost	---

Min Initial Purchase $1000 (Addt'l: $100)
Min IRA Purchase $250 (Addt'l: $50)
Min Auto Invest Plan $1000 (Systematic Inv: $100)

Portfolio 12-31-94

Share Chg (12-93) 000	Amount 000	Total Stocks: 143 / Total Fixed-Income: 1	Value $000	% Net Assets
2557	3032	Hong Kong Telecommunications	5780	3.65
774	910	Malayan Banking	5489	3.46
565	647	Telekom Malaysia	4380	2.76
591	1065	Hutchison Whampoa	4306	2.72
720	1057	Cheung Kong Holdings	4305	2.72
229	385	Overseas Chinese Banking	3959	2.50
448	448	Bangkok Bank (For)	3675	2.32
531	531	Thai Farmers Bank (For)	3662	2.31
354	426	Genting	3656	2.31
338	338	Hong Kong & Shanghai Banking	3649	2.30
224	402	Keppel (Singapore)	3420	2.16
421	558	Resorts World	3276	2.07
222	313	Development Bank Singapore	3219	2.03
4073	5768	Guangdong Investments	2851	1.80
618	714	Tenaga National	2826	1.78
331	468	City Developments	2614	1.65
407	521	United Engineers (Malaysia)	2572	1.62
517	1014	Citic Pacific	2445	1.54
78	153	Finance One (For)	2370	1.50
515	825	New World Development	2203	1.39

Index Allocation

	% of Stocks
S&P 500	0.0
S&P MidCap 400	0.0
U.S. Small Cap	1.3
Foreign	98.7

Composition % 10-31-94

Cash	5.1	Preferreds	0.0
Stocks	91.5	Convertibles	0.5
Bonds	0.0	Other	2.9

Tax Analysis

	Tax-Adj Historical Return %	% Pretax Return
3 Yr Avg	---	---
5 Yr Avg	---	---
10 Yr Avg	---	---

Potential Capital Gain Exposure (% of assets) 2%

Most Similar Funds in MF500

Fund lacks three-year record

Country Exposure 10-31-94

	% of Stocks
Hong Kong	22
Malaysia	21
Singapore	16
Thailand	14
Indonesia	7

Total Number of Countries: 10
Hedging Policy: ---

Sector Weightings

	% of Stocks	Relative S&P 500
Utilities	14.8	2.41
Energy	0.1	0.06
Financials	42.6	1.67
Industrial Cyclicals	12.8	0.58
Consumer Durables	6.7	0.48
Consumer Staples	2.5	0.93
Services	16.5	1.28
Retail	0.0	0.00
Health	1.1	0.66
Technology	2.9	0.36

Morgan Stanley Emerging Markets

	Ticker	NAV	Mkt Price	Prem/Disc	Yield	Objective
	MSF	$20.02	$21.50	7.4%	0.0%	World Stock

Morgan Stanley Emerging Markets Fund seeks long-term capital appreciation.

Under normal conditions, the fund invests at least 65% of its assets in the equity securities of emerging countries. The fund may invest up to 25% of its assets in unlisted securities. It may engage in options and futures transactions for hedging purposes.

Board members serve staggered terms, and a 75% majority of stockholders is required to merge, liquidate, or open-end the fund.

In June 1993, the fund held a fully subscribed rights offering that raised $55.2 million. In March 1994, the fund raised an additional $23.6 million through a secondary offering of 900,000 shares.

14.9	12.3	18.0	15.9	Highest Prem/Disc
-2.2	-5.9	-4.3	-6.0	Lowest Prem/Disc

Historical Profile
- **Return** High
- **Risk** Average
- **Rating** ★★★★★ Highest

Growth of $10,000
— at NAV ($000)
— at Market Price ($000)

Premium Discount %

History

	1983	1984	1985	1986	1987	1988	1989	1990	1991	1992	1993	1994	History
	---	---	---	---	---	---	---	---	14.72	16.74	28.20	20.02	NAV
	---	---	---	---	---	---	---	---	4.69*	13.86	97.05	-6.84	NAV Total Return %
	---	---	---	---	---	---	---	---	-4.73*	6.25	87.00	-8.16	+/- S&P 500
	---	---	---	---	---	---	---	---	---	26.04	64.49	-14.62	+/- MSCI EAFE
	---	---	---	---	---	---	---	---	---	11.26	31.55	-4.43	+/- MSCI Emerging
	---	---	---	---	---	---	---	---	0.29*	0.06	0.00	0.00	Income Return %
	---	---	---	---	---	---	---	---	4.40*	13.80	97.05	-6.84	Capital Return %
	---	---	---	---	---	---	---	---	---	19	2	53	Total Rtn % Rank All
	---	---	---	---	---	---	---	---	---	1	1	58	Total Rtn % Rank Obj
	---	---	---	---	---	---	---	---	-3.07*	25.15	104.20	-10.79	Market Total Rtn %
	---	---	---	---	---	---	---	---	---	3.6	10.7	5.4	Avg Prem/Disc %
	---	---	---	---	---	---	---	---	0.04	0.01	0.00	0.00	Income $
	---	---	---	---	---	---	---	---	0.00	0.01	1.49	6.50	Capital Gains $
	---	---	---	---	---	---	---	---	2.25	2.02	1.85	1.74	Expense Ratio %
	---	---	---	---	---	---	---	---	2.32	0.14	-0.03	-0.22	Income Ratio %
	---	---	---	---	---	---	---	---	---	60	68	---	Turnover Rate %
	---	---	---	---	---	---	---	---	371.6	176.9	412.0	317.3	Net Assets ($mil)

Manager's Investment Style

Management takes a top-down, macroeconomic approach to emerging-markets investing. It's willing to move in and out of markets based, in part, on valuation levels. In late 1993, for example, management reduced its exposure to frothy Malaysia and Turkey, and upped its ante in undervalued India. The fund is willing, on occasion, to buy individual companies based on their strong earnings potential or fundamentals, even if the top-down situation is poor.

Fund Manager(s)

Madhav Dhar. Since 10-91. BS St. Stephens C. Delhi U.-India; MBA Carnegie Mellon U.

Manager Experience

	Dates Managed	Invest Obj	Std Dev	+/- Index
Madhav Dhar				
Blanchard Global Growth	02/92 - 07/93	AA	5.96	-0.14

NAV Performance % 12-30-94

	1st Qtr	2nd Qtr	3rd Qtr	4th Qtr	Total
1987	---	---	---	---	---
1988	---	---	---	---	---
1989	---	---	---	---	---
1990	---	---	---	---	---
1991	---	---	---	4.69*	4.69*
1992	15.29	2.12	-3.00	-0.30	13.86
1993	9.35	15.09	14.21	37.09	97.05
1994	-4.11	-5.18	20.77	-15.16	-6.84

Bear Market Performance

Decile Rank (5-year period)

Worst ──────────────── Best

	Worst 3 Mo Period 1985-89	Worst 3 Mo Period 1990-94
Morgan Stan Em Mkts	---	---
+/- S&P 500	---	---

Trailing Returns

	NAV Total Return %	+/- S&P 500	+/- MSCI Emerging	% Rank All	% Rank Obj	Mkt Total Return %
3 Mo	-15.16	-15.15	-3.05	98	94	-12.17
6 Mo	2.45	-2.41	-3.57	17	66	0.69
1 Yr	-6.84	-8.16	-4.43	53	58	-10.79
3 Yr Avg	27.86	21.59	9.52	3	1	31.61
5 Yr Avg	---	---	---	---	---	---
Incept Avg	27.88*	---	---	---	---	28.28*

Risk Analysis

	Risk % Rank[1] All	Obj	Morningstar[2] Return	Risk	Morningstar Risk-Adj Rating
3 Yr	79	37	3.90	0.77	★★★★★
5 Yr	---	---	---	---	
10 Yr	---	---	---	---	

Average Historical Rating (3 months)   5.0 ★s
[1] = Low, 100 = High   [2]1.00 = Equity Avg   [3]1.00 = 90-day T-bill Return

Other Measures

			S&P 500
Standard Deviation	18.63	Alpha	22.67
Mean	26.53	Beta	0.83
Sharpe Ratio	1.24	R-Squared	13

Investment Style

	Stock Portfolio Avg	Rel WS Foreign	Rel WS World
Price/Earnings Ratio	47.7#	0.97	1.16
Price/Cash Flow Ratio	---	---	---
Price/Book Ratio	9.1#	3.02	2.91
5 Yr Earnings Gr %	---	---	---
Return on Assets %	---	---	---
Debt % Total Cap	---	---	---
Med Mkt Cap ($mil)	2668#	0.42	0.35

figure is based on less than 50% of stocks

Country Exposure (top five) 12-31-94

Securities %		Currency %	
India	19	India	19
Brazil	15	Brazil	15
Mexico	9	Mexico	9
Thailand	7	Thailand	7
Hong Kong	6	Hong Kong	6

Diversification Value for Portfolio Types

● Large Cap: High ● Small Cap: High ● Bond: High ● Balanced: High ● Diversified: High

Portfolio 09-30-94

Share Chg (06-94)	Amount	Total Equity: 234 Total Fixed-Income: 14	Value $000	% Total Invest
0	3125000	Bharat Heavy Electricals	16690	3.67
-98.879M	183.809M	Telebras PN	11471	2.52
---	25807000	Bank Foreign Econ Affairs FRN	9871	2.17
-10.400M	21714138	Electrobras CI B	9348	2.06
-10.850M	45669999	Petrobras	9053	1.99
0	1299600	Banacci CI B	8038	1.77
125900	125900	Telefonos de Mexico L (ADR)	7869	1.73
0	925000	Bangkok Bank	7630	1.68
1047000	1047000	Taiwan Semiconductor	6848	1.51
0	3656.50M	Usinas Siderurgicas de Minas	6005	1.32
0	329800	Finance One	5995	1.32
295200	1033200	Hocheng Group	5571	1.22
0	828710	Thai Farmers Bank	5442	1.20
24000	36000	Bank of Rajasthan	4821	1.06
0	22290000	Vale do Rio Doce	4654	1.02
-512950	2003050	Nan Ya Plastic	4519	0.99
0	1469000	EGE Biracilik	4507	0.99
-154583	875086	United Microelectronics	4417	0.97
0	45880	Housing Development Finance	4403	0.97
---	5795000	Polish People's Repub 0%	4331	0.95
-67.585M	2615000	Banco de Colombia	4243	0.93
0	187316	Grupo Carso (ADR)	4215	0.93
0	111852	Grupo Tribasa (ADR)	4111	0.90
12199255	414.261M	Banco Bradesco PN	4082	0.90
0	11621000	Banco Itau	3953	0.87

Composition % 12-31-94

Cash	1.6	Preferreds	0.0
Stocks	93.2	Convertibles	0.0
Bonds	5.2	Other	0.0

Tax Analysis

	Tax-Adj Historical Return %	% Pretax Return
3 Yr Avg	25.18	77.3
5 Yr Avg	---	---
10 Yr Avg	---	---

Potential Capital Gain Exposure (% of assets)   16

Most Similar Funds in MF500

Templtn Em Mkts	Weak Fit
Templeton Developing M	Weak Fit
Asia Pacific	Weak Fit

Sector Weightings

	% of Stocks
Utilities	13.9
Energy	6.3
Financials	28.3
Industrial Cyclicals	22.5
Consumer Durables	8.8
Consumer Staples	8.2
Services	3.4
Retail	0.8
Health	2.6
Technology	5.2

Operations

Address and Telephone	1221 Avenue of the Americas
	New York, NY 10020
	212-296-7200 / 800-221-6726
Advisor	Morgan Stanley Asset Management
Subadvisor	N/A
Administrator	United States Trust Co. New York
Transfer Agent	First National Bank of Boston
Custodian	Morgan Guaranty Trust Co. of New York
Auditor	Price Waterhouse LLP
Legal Counsel	Rogers & Wells

Income Distrib Schedule	Paid Irregularly
Management Fee	1.25%
Reinvestment Plan	Yes
Direct Purchase Plan	Yes
Shares Outstanding	15,846,436
Exchange	NYSE
*Date of Inception	10-25-91
Shareholder Report	B+

MORNINGSTAR 1995 Mutual Fund 500

Mutual Beacon

	Ticker	Load	NAV	Yield	SEC Yield	Assets	Objective
	BEGRX	None	31.03	3.3%	N/A	2056.4	Growth/Inc.

Mutual Beacon Fund seeks capital appreciation. Income is secondary.

The fund invests in common and preferred stocks and corporate debt securities of any credit quality. These securities are trading at prices below their intrinsic value, according to factors such as price/book ratio, price/earnings ratio, and cash flow. The fund may invest up to 50% of assets in securities of companies involved in mergers, consolidations, liquidations, and reorganizations. It invests from time to time in foreign securities, and in securities of other investment companies.

Heine Securities became the advisor in 1985.

Manager's Investment Style

Management's value bent leads it to look for companies that are cheap relative to their assets, resulting in a very low price/book ratio. Further, it often favors mergers-and-acquisitions and bankruptcy candidates. Foreign holdings also have a place in the portfolio, as do bonds. If nothing meets its criteria, management will hold cash.

Historical Profile
Return Above Average
Risk Low
Rating ★★★★★ Highest

Investment Style History
Equity

Average % Stocks Held in Portfolio

	1983	1984	1985	1986	1987	1988	1989	1990	1991	1992	1993	1994	History
					61%	63%	64%	55%	70%	76%	70%	72%	
	14.47	14.19	17.24	18.64	19.47	22.85	24.09	20.80	23.36	27.10	31.09	31.03	NAV
	14.02	-1.94	23.31	15.47	12.73	28.92	17.46	-8.17	17.60	22.92	22.93	5.61	Total Return %
	-8.45	-8.20	-8.43	-3.21	7.47	12.31	-14.22	-5.05	-12.88	15.31	12.88	4.30	+/- S&P 500
	-9.44	-4.98	-9.25	-0.63	10.36	10.98	-11.71	-1.99	-16.61	13.95	11.65	5.68	+/- Wilshire 5000
	1.94	0.00	1.82	1.72	2.64	3.78	5.01	4.56	3.54	1.81	1.24	3.39	Income Return %
	12.08	-1.94	21.49	13.75	10.08	25.14	12.45	-12.73	14.06	21.11	21.69	2.22	Capital Return %
	62	72	53	51	7	3	41	80	49	3	13	4	Total Rtn % Rank All
	84	83	83	56	3	2	82	78	95	1	2	3	Total Rtn % Rank Obj
	0.25	0.00	0.25	0.31	0.51	0.80	1.17	1.08	0.74	0.46	0.37	1.05	Income $
	0.00	0.00	0.00	0.94	1.04	1.41	1.55	0.26	0.33	1.10	1.82	0.75	Capital Gains $
	1.30	1.60	1.39	1.16	0.87	0.59	0.67	0.85	0.85	0.81	0.73	0.72	Expense Ratio %
	2.30	1.70	1.99	2.86	2.86	3.64	4.98	4.59	3.07	1.90	1.53	2.07	Income Ratio %
	10	10	72	113	73	87	67	58	57	58	53	---	Turnover Rate %
	6.8	5.9	9.4	65.0	131.9	213.7	408.2	387.5	399.0	533.2	1060.8	2056.4	Net Assets ($mil)

Growth of $10,000
|||| Value of Fund ($000)
— Value of Index ($000) S&P 500
▼ Manager Change
▽ Partial Manager Change
► Mgr Unknown After
◄ Mgr Unknown Before

Performance Quartile (Within Objective)

Fund Manager(s)

Michael F. Price, since 01-85. Finance, U. of Oklahoma 1973

Manager Experience	Dates Managed	Invest Obj	Std Dev	+/- Index
Michael F. Price				
Mutual Shares	01/75 - 12/94	GI	12.19	5.63
Mutual Qualified	09/80 - 12/94	GI	10.29	3.53

Performance 12-31-94

	1st Qtr	2nd Qtr	3rd Qtr	4th Qtr	Total
1987	19.10	5.50	6.96	-16.12	12.73
1988	14.38	7.52	2.35	2.42	28.92
1989	7.88	5.47	5.08	-1.75	17.46
1990	-1.91	2.83	-9.81	0.95	-8.17
1991	10.87	1.69	3.50	0.78	17.60
1992	5.52	4.87	3.80	7.02	22.92
1993	9.19	1.96	6.32	3.86	22.93
1994	0.84	1.98	5.19	-2.36	5.62

Bear Market Performance

Decile Rank (5-year period)

Worst ———————————— Best

	Worst 3 Mo Period 1985-89	Worst 3 Mo Period 1990-94
Mutual Beacon	-19.09	-12.80
+/- S&P 500	10.49	1.04
+/- Best Fit Index : Wil 4500	11.05	6.60

Trailing Returns

	Total Return %	+/- S&P 500	+/- Wil 5000	% Rank All	% Rank Obj	Growth of $10,000
3 Mo	-2.36	-2.34	-1.59	75	75	9,764
6 Mo	2.71	-2.15	-1.92	22	48	10,271
1 Yr	5.61	4.30	5.68	4	3	10,561
3 Yr Avg	16.86	10.60	10.25	2	1	15,960
5 Yr Avg	11.50	2.81	2.69	11	8	17,235
10 Yr Avg	15.40	1.02	1.54	9	2	41,892
15 Yr Avg	13.34	-1.14	-0.63	33	39	65,464

Operations

Address and Telephone	51 John F. Kennedy Parkway Short Hills, NJ 07078 800-553-3014 / 201-912-2100
Advisor	Heine Securities
Subadvisor	None
Distributor	Heine Securities
States Available	All
Report Grade	B+
Income Distrib	Paid Annually
Date of Inception	08-01-61
Fiscal Year End	December

Risk Analysis

Time Period	Load-Adj Return %	Risk % Rank [1] All	Risk % Rank [1] Obj	Morningstar [2] Return	Morningstar Risk	Morningstar Risk-Adj Rating
1 Yr	5.61					
3 Yr	16.86	20	1	4.35 [3]	0.37	★★★★★
5 Yr	11.50	51	3	1.79 [3]	0.52	★★★★
10 Yr	15.40	39	1	1.58	0.49	★★★★★
Average Historical Rating (109 months)					3.8	★ s

[1] 1 = low, 100 = high   [2] 1.00 = Equity Avg   [3] 1.00 = 90-day T-bill return

Other Measures

				Standard S&P 500	Best Fit Wil 4500
Standard Deviation	6.53	Alpha		11.1	10.5
Mean	15.90	Beta		0.62	0.55
Sharpe Ratio	1.90	R-Squared		57	68

Investment Style

	Stock Portfolio Avg	Relative S&P 500
Price/Earnings Ratio	16.2	0.88
Price/Book Ratio	2.1	0.63
5 Yr Earnings Gr %	10.2	1.84
Return on Assets %	5.1	0.68
Debt % Total Cap	30.3	1.07
Med Mkt Cap ($mil)	1895	0.15

Style
Value Blend Growth
Size Large/Med/Small

Diversification Value for Portfolio Types

Large Cap: Low	Small Cap: Low	Bond: Medium	Balanced: Low	Diversified: Low

Portfolio 06-30-94

Total Stocks: 239
Total Fixed-Income: 25

Share Chg (12-93)000	Amount 000		Value $000	% Net Assets
0	5334	Sunbeam-Oster	32845	2.15
758	758	US West	31720	2.08
471	594	Sears Roebuck	28512	1.87
332	692	Litton Industries	23269	1.52
801	801	American Express	20626	1.35
	20000	US Treasury Note 5.125%	19700	1.29
213	353	Philip Morris	18180	1.19
436	436	Dean Witter Discover	16346	1.07
	1070	Algoma Steel Cl A Pfd 5.5%	16243	1.06
333	333	Nutricia	16020	1.05
224	224	Elf Aquitaine (ADR)	15660	1.02
65	65	Dresdner Bank	15236	1.00
428	428	Brooklyn Bancorp	14963	0.98
7	300	Dreyfus	14550	0.95
12	903	National Medical Enterprises	14111	0.92
14	193	Michigan National	13896	0.91
2171	2171	Service Merchandise	13838	0.91
221	221	Schering-Plough	13542	0.89
0	1335	Dime Bancorp	13179	0.86
356	356	Telephone & Data Systems	13168	0.86
139	484	Columbia Gas System	13073	0.86
360	6610	Semi-Tech Global	12058	0.79
796	796	Lehman Brothers Holdings	12046	0.79
614	751	PaineWebber Group	11727	0.77
0	54	Bayer	11630	0.76

Composition % 12-31-94

Cash	20.8	Preferreds	1.2
Stocks	68.5	Convertibles	0.0
Bonds	9.5	Other	0.0

Tax Analysis

	Tax-Adj Historical Return %	% Pretax Return
3 Yr Avg	14.72	85.6
5 Yr Avg	9.53	79.7
10 Yr Avg	13.10	76.0
Potential Capital Gain Exposure (% of assets)		6%

Most Similar Funds in MF500

Mutual Qualified	Strong Fit
Mutual Shares	Strong Fit
Fidelity Value	Fair Fit

Expenses & Fees

Sales Fees	0.00% front
	0.00% deferred
	0.00% 12b-1
Management Fee	0.60% flat fee
3-,5-,10-yr Expense Projections	$24, $42, $93
Annual Brokerage Cost	0.22%

Min Initial Purchase	$5000 (Addt'l: $100)
Min IRA Purchase	$2000 (Addt'l: $100)
Min Auto Invest Plan	$5000 (Systematic Inv: $100)

Index Allocation

	% of Stocks
S&P 500	31.1
S&P MidCap 400	12.6
U.S. Small Cap	39.5
Foreign	17.3

Sector Weightings

	% of Stocks	Relative S&P 500
Utilities	5.4	0.43
Energy	5.0	0.49
Financials	33.3	3.15
Industrial Cyclicals	4.8	0.29
Consumer Durables	6.5	1.05
Consumer Staples	9.9	0.79
Services	13.5	1.65
Retail	7.8	1.34
Health	9.0	1.04
Technology	5.0	0.54

Mutual Benefit

	Ticker	Load	NAV	Yield	SEC Yield	Assets	Objective
	MUBFX	4.75%	16.67	2.0%	N/A	43.9	Growth

Mutual Benefit Fund seeks long-term appreciation of capital. Current income is secondary.

The fund invests primarily in equity securities. In selecting specific securities, the fund emphasizes well-managed companies that possess substantial growth potential. The fund also seeks opportunities for capital appreciation in undervalued securities. It may also hold fixed-income securities.

Markston Investment Management has managed the fund since April 1981. Prior to that time, the fund was managed by a different group following different investment strategies.

Manager's Investment Style

Management divides the fund's assets into three stakes of varying sizes, with one portion for each manager. Overall, the strategy is one of cost-consciousness, devotion to consumer-related stocks, and a willingness to hold cash. Manager John Stone is known for favoring moderately priced firms with niche dominance or brand-name recognition. Manager Michael Mullarkey tends toward small-cap value stocks. The third-manager, Roger Lob, handles the smallest portion of the fund's assets.

Fund Manager(s)

John R. Stone, since 04-81.
Michael J. Mullarkey, since 04-81.
Roger M. Lob, since 01-86.

Manager Experience

	Dates Managed	Invest Obj	Std Dev	+/- Index

Not available.

Historical Profile
Return	Above Average
Risk	Low
Rating	★★★★ Above Average

90% 89% 87% 83% 84% 87% 68% 79%

Investment Style History
Equity
Average % Stocks Held in Portfolio

Growth of $10,000

|||| Value of Fund ($000)
— Value of Index ($000) S&P 500
▼ Manager Change
▽ Partial Manager Change
► Mgr Unknown After
◄ Mgr Unknown Before

Performance Quartile (Within Objective)

1983	1984	1985	1986	1987	1988	1989	1990	1991	1992	1993	1994	History
13.93	11.07	12.89	13.66	11.65	14.28	17.46	15.84	19.66	20.00	18.13	16.67	NAV
26.58	0.31	31.61	22.02	-4.53	29.92	28.23	-5.09	27.69	10.50	8.74	2.80	Total Return %
4.11	-5.96	-0.13	3.34	-9.79	13.31	-3.45	-1.98	-2.80	2.88	-1.32	1.49	+/- S&P 500
3.11	-2.74	-0.95	5.92	-6.90	11.98	-0.94	1.09	-6.52	1.53	-2.54	2.87	+/- Wilshire 5000
3.23	3.48	3.69	2.37	3.32	2.40	2.59	3.18	3.19	1.56	1.91	2.12	Income Return %
23.35	-3.17	27.92	19.65	-7.85	27.52	25.64	-8.27	24.49	8.94	6.83	0.68	Capital Return %
18	64	20	13	87	2	16	71	31	19	75	8	Total Rtn % Rank All
25	36	35	9	86	3	43	55	74	34	65	15	Total Rtn % Rank Obj
0.37	0.39	0.38	0.32	0.48	0.31	0.41	0.54	0.49	0.31	0.36	0.37	Income $
0.28	2.51	1.01	1.66	1.03	0.52	0.44	0.19	0.05	1.40	3.21	1.59	Capital Gains $
1.50	1.34	1.30	1.32	1.34	1.52	1.45	1.01	0.85	1.01	1.04	---	Expense Ratio %
3.35	3.30	2.93	2.25	2.29	2.57	2.47	3.32	2.69	2.01	1.76	---	Income Ratio %
34	54	32	48	21	17	14	6	9	18	20	---	Turnover Rate %
10.3	10.1	11.9	15.6	14.3	20.0	35.9	37.1	45.6	48.6	49.4	43.9	Net Assets ($mil)

Performance 12-31-94

	1st Qtr	2nd Qtr	3rd Qtr	4th Qtr	Total
1987	15.19	2.75	2.19	-21.06	-4.53
1988	16.01	5.68	2.34	3.55	29.92
1989	9.31	10.63	7.32	-1.20	28.23
1990	-3.55	4.99	-14.53	9.66	-5.09
1991	13.26	-0.11	4.38	8.13	27.69
1992	1.27	1.21	4.29	3.38	10.50
1993	5.45	-1.00	2.27	1.85	8.74
1994	-0.83	-0.50	4.48	-0.29	2.80

Bear Market Performance

Decile Rank (5-year period)

| Worst | | | | | | | | | | Best |

	Worst 3 Mo Period 1985-89	Worst 3 Mo Period 1990-94
Mutual Benefit	-26.44	-14.53
+/- S&P 500	3.14	-0.78
+/- Best Fit Index : S&P 500	3.14	-0.78

Trailing Returns

	Total Return %	+/- S&P 500	+/- Wil 5000	% Rank All	% Rank Obj	Growth of $10,000
3 Mo	-0.29	-0.27	0.48	30	27	9,971
6 Mo	4.18	-0.68	-0.44	15	46	10,418
1 Yr	2.80	1.49	2.87	8	15	10,280
3 Yr Avg	7.30	1.03	0.68	25	37	12,353
5 Yr Avg	8.40	-0.29	-0.41	29	55	14,970
10 Yr Avg	14.35	-0.03	0.49	15	22	38,232
15 Yr Avg	14.85	0.36	0.87	14	28	79,756

Operations

Address and Telephone	520 Broad Street
	Newark, NJ 07102-3111
	800-559-5535 / 201-268-4549
Advisor	Markston Investment Management
Subadvisor	None
Distributor	First Priority Investment
States Available	All
Report Grade	B
Income Distrib	Paid Semiannually
Date of Inception	01-21-71
Fiscal Year End	December

Risk Analysis

Time Period	Load-Adj Return %	Risk % Rank [1] All	Obj	Morningstar [2] Return	Morningstar Risk	Morningstar Risk-Adj Rating
1 Yr	-2.08					
3 Yr	5.57	29	2	0.59 [3]	0.42	★★★
5 Yr	7.35	55	4	0.64 [3]	0.61	★★★
10 Yr	13.80	47	6	1.23	0.68	★★★★
Average Historical Rating (109 months)					3.8	★s

[1] 1 = low, 100 = high   [2] 1.00 = Equity Avg   [3] 1.00 = 90-day T-bill return

Other Measures

			Standard S&P 500	Best Fit S&P 500
Standard Deviation	5.65	Alpha	2.1	2.1
Mean	7.22	Beta	0.56	0.56
Sharpe Ratio	0.65	R-Squared	62	62

Investment Style

	Stock Portfolio Avg	Relative S&P 500
Price/Earnings Ratio	20.8	1.12
Price/Book Ratio	3.0	0.88
5 Yr Earnings Gr %	-0.4	-0.06
Return on Assets %	6.2	0.83
Debt % Total Cap	28.6	1.01
Med Mkt Cap ($mil)	1429	0.11

Style: Value Blend Growth / Size Large Med Small

Diversification Value for Portfolio Types

Large Cap: Low	Small Cap: Medium	Bond: High	Balanced: Low	Diversified: Medium

Expenses & Fees

Sales Fees	4.75% front
	0.00% deferred
	0.00% 12b-1
Management Fee	0.50% max./0.35% min.+(-)0.30%P
3-,5-,10-yr Expense Projections	$79, $102, $169
Annual Brokerage Cost	0.06%

Min Initial Purchase	$250 (Addt'l: $50)
Min IRA Purchase	N/A
Min Auto Invest Plan	$25 (Systematic Inv: $25)

Portfolio 11-30-94

Share Chg (06-94) 000	Amount 000	Total Stocks: 84 / Total Fixed-Income: 3	Value $000	% Net Assets
80	101	Rite Aid	2294	4.79
45	89	Panhandle Eastern	1875	3.91
52	70	National Service Industries	1782	3.72
48	94	Commerce Clearing House Cl A	1509	3.15
-3	23	Clorox	1346	2.81
-3	27	Meredith	1299	2.71
11	43	Caldor	1258	2.63
0	38	Stanhome	1258	2.63
-2	17	Gillette	1253	2.62
0	11	Royal Dutch Petroleum	1227	2.56
-5	44	ALLTEL	1224	2.56
-1	21	Kellogg	1206	2.52
0	42	McDonald's	1192	2.49
-7	29	Pentair	1146	2.39
14	32	First Brands	1103	2.30
0	25	National Presto Industries	1044	2.18
-6	34	GTE	1029	2.15
-14	33	Archer-Daniels-Midland	905	1.89
-2	30	BanPonce	898	1.87
-9	17	CPC International	876	1.83
52	55	National Computer Systems	843	1.76
-1	16	Coca-Cola	823	1.72
-2	14	Minnesota Mining & Mfg	728	1.52
-3	36	Edison Brothers Stores	694	1.45
3	27	Revco Drug Stores	609	1.27

Composition % 12-31-94

Cash	3.5	Preferreds	0.4
Stocks	95.5	Convertibles	0.5
Bonds	0.0	Other	0.0

Tax Analysis

	Tax-Adj Historical Return %	% Pretax Return
3 Yr Avg	3.55	46.9
5 Yr Avg	5.63	63.4
10 Yr Avg	11.39	68.7
Potential Capital Gain Exposure (% of assets)		16%

Most Similar Funds in MF500

SteinRoe Prime Equities	Weak Fit
Source Capital	Weak Fit
Colonial A	Weak Fit

Index Allocation

	% of Stocks
S&P 500	53.6
S&P MidCap 400	19.3
U.S. Small Cap	26.9
Foreign	3.3

Sector Weightings

	% of Stocks	Relative S&P 500
Utilities	8.8	0.71
Energy	6.2	0.61
Financials	9.2	0.87
Industrial Cyclicals	9.1	0.55
Consumer Durables	11.0	1.77
Consumer Staples	15.8	1.26
Services	13.7	1.68
Retail	14.3	2.46
Health	4.0	0.47
Technology	8.0	0.87

MORNINGSTAR 1995 Mutual Fund 500

Mutual Discovery

	Ticker	Load	NAV	Yield	SEC Yield	Assets	Objective
	MDISX	Clsd	12.55	5.1%	N/A	725.8	Small Company

Mutual Discovery Fund seeks long-term capital appreciation. The fund invests primarily in companies with small market capitalizations. It may purchase common and preferred stocks, convertibles, and bonds of any quality. The fund seeks undervalued securities based on price/book ratios, cash flow, and earnings multiples. It may invest up to 50% of its assets in companies involved in mergers, consolidations, liquidations, and reorganizations. The fund may invest up to 50% of its assets in foreign issues.

Historical Profile
Return ---
Risk ---
Rating
Closed

Investment Style History
Equity
Average % Stocks Held in Portfolio
73% 84%

Growth of $10,000
|||| Value of Fund ($000)
— Value of Index ($000) S&P 500
▼ Manager Change
▽ Partial Manager Change
► Mgr Unknown After
◄ Mgr Unknown Before

Performance Quartile
(Within Objective)

Manager's Investment Style
Manager Michael Price looks for small- to mid-cap stocks (although he is willing to buy large caps) that are trading at a discount to their underlying assets. He especially likes turnaround candidates or firms that may be subject to mergers and acquisitions, and has a large stake in overseas stocks.

	1983	1984	1985	1986	1987	1988	1989	1990	1991	1992	1993	1994	History
	---	---	---	---	---	---	---	---	---	10.00	13.05	12.55	NAV
	---	---	---	---	---	---	---	---	---	---	35.85 *	3.62	Total Return %
	---	---	---	---	---	---	---	---	---	---	25.71 *	2.31	+/- S&P 500
	---	---	---	---	---	---	---	---	---	---	---	6.28	+/- Wilshire 4500
	---	---	---	---	---	---	---	---	---	---	0.73	5.10	Income Return %
	---	---	---	---	---	---	---	---	---	---	35.12	-1.48	Capital Return %
	---	---	---	---	---	---	---	---	---	---	---	6	Total Rtn % Rank All
	---	---	---	---	---	---	---	---	---	---	---	20	Total Rtn % Rank Obj
	---	---	---	---	---	---	---	---	---	---	0.09	0.65	Income $
	---	---	---	---	---	---	---	---	---	---	0.44	0.32	Capital Gains $
	---	---	---	---	---	---	---	---	---	---	1.07	0.99	Expense Ratio %
	---	---	---	---	---	---	---	---	---	---	1.17	2.35	Income Ratio %
	---	---	---	---	---	---	---	---	---	---	90	---	Turnover Rate %
	---	---	---	---	---	---	---	---	---	---	546.8	725.8	Net Assets ($mil)

Fund Manager(s)
Michael F. Price, since 01-93. Finance, U. of Oklahoma 1973

Manager Experience	Dates Managed	Invest Obj	Std Dev	+/- Index
Michael F. Price				
Mutual Shares	01/75 - 12/94	GI	12.19	5.63
Mutual Qualified	09/80 - 12/94	GI	10.29	3.53

Performance 12-31-94

	1st Qtr	2nd Qtr	3rd Qtr	4th Qtr	Total
1987	---	---	---	---	---
1988	---	---	---	---	---
1989	---	---	---	---	---
1990	---	---	---	---	---
1991	---	---	---	---	---
1992	---	---	---	---	---
1993	12.30	2.58	6.25	10.99	35.85
1994	3.14	0.22	3.61	-3.25	3.62

Bear Market Performance
Decile Rank (5-year period)

Worst — Best

	Worst 3 Mo Period 1985-89	Worst 3 Mo Period 1990-94
Mutual Discovery	---	---
+/- S&P 500	---	---
+/- Best Fit Index :	---	---

Trailing Returns

	Total Return %	+/- S&P 500	+/- Wil 4500	% Rank All	% Rank Obj	Growth of $10,000
3 Mo	-3.25	-3.24	-0.75	85	86	9,675
6 Mo	0.24	-4.62	-3.95	52	91	10,024
1 Yr	3.62	2.31	6.28	6	20	10,362
3 Yr Avg	---	---	---	---	---	---
5 Yr Avg	---	---	---	---	---	---
10 Yr Avg	---	---	---	---	---	---
15 Yr Avg	---	---	---	---	---	---

Operations

Address and Telephone	51 John F. Kennedy Parkway Short Hills, NJ 07078 800-553-3014 / 201-912-2100	Min Initial Purchase	Closed (Addt'l: $50)
		Min IRA Purchase	$1000 (Addt'l: $50)
		Min Auto Invest Plan	$1000 (Systematic Inv: $50)
Advisor	Heine Securities		
Subadvisor	None	**Expenses & Fees**	
Distributor	Heine Securities	Sales Fees	0.00% front
States Available	All		0.00% deferred
Report Grade	B-		0.00% 12b-1
Income Distrib	Paid Annually	Management Fee	0.80% flat fee
Date of Inception	01-04-93	3-,5-,10-yr Expense Projections	$35, $61, $134
Fiscal Year End	December	Annual Brokerage Cost	0.56%

Risk Analysis

Time Period	Load-Adj Return %	Risk % Rank [1] All	Obj	Morningstar [2] Return	Morningstar Risk	Morningstar Risk-Adj Rating
1 Yr	3.62					
3 Yr	---	---	---	---	---	---
5 Yr	---	---	---	---	---	---
10 Yr	---	---	---	---	---	---

Average Historical Rating --- ---

[1] 1 = low, 100 = high [2] 1.00 = Equity Avg [3] 1.00 = 90-day T-bill return

Other Measures

		Standard S&P 500	Best Fit
Standard Deviation	---	Alpha	---	---
Mean	---	Beta	---	---
Sharpe Ratio	---	R-Squared	---	---

Investment Style

	Stock Portfolio Avg	Relative S&P 500
Price/Earnings Ratio	14.0	0.76
Price/Book Ratio	2.0	0.59
5 Yr Earnings Gr %	10.1#	1.81
Return on Assets %	5.9	0.79
Debt % Total Cap	30.3#	1.07
Med Mkt Cap ($mil)	935	0.07

figure is based on 50% or less of stocks

Diversification Value for Portfolio Types

Large Cap: Small Cap: Bond: Balanced: Diversified:

Portfolio 06-30-94

Total Stocks: 164
Total Fixed-Income: 16

Share Chg (12-93)000	Amount 000		Value $000	% Net Assets
	1390	Algoma Steel Cl A Pfd 5.5%	21104	2.97
251	313	Sears Roebuck	15010	2.11
313	313	Dean Witter Discover	11749	1.65
0	700	National Medical Enterprises	10938	1.54
-2	12	Nestle (Reg)	10482	1.47
194	295	Litton Industries	9903	1.39
381	381	American Express	9811	1.38
3	153	Van Melle	9470	1.33
	103	Wang Laboratories Pfd 11%	9287	1.31
3096	5063	Semi-Tech Global	9235	1.30
933	933	Dime Bancorp	9217	1.30
1405	1405	Service Merchandise	8957	1.26
182	182	Nutricia	8724	1.23
108	168	Philip Morris	8673	1.22
0	39	Bayer	8369	1.18
9	11	Bucher Holding (Br)	7872	1.11
23	23	Hills Stores	7763	1.09
0	332	Independent Bancorp (AZ)	7628	1.07
3	6	Swiss Industrial (Br)	7582	1.07
1263	1263	Transocean Drilling	7478	1.05
-212	784	Algoma Steel	7368	1.04
47	53	Rieter Holding (Reg)	7313	1.03
2982	4826	Shaw Brothers (Hong Kong)	7118	1.00
195	240	Multimedia	6954	0.98
73	73	Telegraaf Holdings	6792	0.96

Composition % 12-31-94

Cash	3.3	Preferreds	1.4
Stocks	87.7	Convertibles	0.0
Bonds	7.6	Other	0.0

Tax Analysis

	Tax-Adj Historical Return %	% Pretax Return
3 Yr Avg	---	---
5 Yr Avg	---	---
10 Yr Avg	---	---
Potential Capital Gain Exposure (% of assets)		3%

Most Similar Funds in MF500
Fund lacks three-year record

Index Allocation

	% of Stocks
S&P 500	22.6
S&P MidCap 400	8.5
U.S. Small Cap	40.0
Foreign	29.4

Sector Weightings

	% of Stocks	Relative S&P 500
Utilities	2.5	0.20
Energy	3.6	0.36
Financials	32.2	3.05
Industrial Cyclicals	9.8	0.60
Consumer Durables	6.3	1.02
Consumer Staples	13.3	1.06
Services	8.0	0.99
Retail	10.3	1.77
Health	8.8	1.02
Technology	5.0	0.55

Mutual Qualified

	Ticker	Load	NAV	Yield	SEC Yield	Assets	Objective
	MQIFX	None	26.67	2.8%	N/A	1788.8	Growth/Inc.

Mutual Qualified Fund seeks capital appreciation; income is secondary.

The fund invests primarily in undervalued common stocks, preferred stocks, and debt securities. Debt securities may have any rating, or may be unrated. The fund also invests in the securities of companies involved in prospective mergers, consolidations, liquidations, or other special situations; these investments may not compose more than 50% of the fund's assets.

Historical Profile

Return	Above Average
Risk	Low
Rating	★★★★★ Highest

61% 58% 61% 59% 68% 76% 71% 78%

Investment Style History
Equity

Average % Stocks Held in Portfolio

Growth of $10,000

|||| Value of Fund ($000)
— Value of Index ($000) S&P 500
▼ Manager Change
▽ Partial Manager Change
► Mgr Unknown After
◄ Mgr Unknown Before

Performance Quartile (Within Objective)

Manager's Investment Style

Management prefers bargain shopping. As is the case with the two other Mutual growth-and-income offerings managed by Michael Price, this fund shows a bias toward holdings that are cheap relative to assets---often found in unusual spots. Merger candidates, bankruptcies, foreign issues, and other relatively illiquid holdings pepper the portfolio. When management can't find what it likes, it holds cash. It also holds bonds.

Fund Manager(s)

Michael F. Price, since 09-80. Finance, U. of Oklahoma 1973

Manager Experience

	Dates Managed	Invest Obj	Std Dev	+/- Index
Michael F. Price				
Mutual Shares	01/75 - 12/94	GI	12.19	5.63
Mutual Beacon	01/85 - 12/94	GI	10.53	1.10

	1983	1984	1985	1986	1987	1988	1989	1990	1991	1992	1993	1994	History
	15.91	16.75	19.22	20.04	19.34	22.71	22.21	18.37	21.18	24.43	27.00	26.67	NAV
	34.54	14.71	25.62	16.97	7.66	30.36	14.45	-10.12	21.13	22.70	22.71	5.73	Total Return %
	12.08	8.44	-6.12	-1.71	2.40	13.75	-17.24	-7.00	-9.35	15.08	12.65	4.41	+/- S&P 500
	11.08	11.66	-6.94	0.87	5.30	12.41	-14.73	-3.94	-13.07	13.73	11.42	5.80	+/- Wilshire 5000
	2.55	2.14	3.43	4.36	4.17	3.94	6.11	5.76	3.59	2.15	1.40	2.90	Income Return %
	31.99	12.57	22.19	12.61	3.49	26.42	8.33	-15.88	17.54	20.55	21.30	2.83	Capital Return %
	6	7	44	41	14	2	48	85	43	3	13	3	Total Rtn % Rank All
	4	9	67	50	14	2	89	86	89	1	3	2	Total Rtn % Rank Obj
	0.39	0.35	0.61	0.85	0.88	0.83	1.36	1.23	0.67	0.49	0.37	0.77	Income $
	1.33	1.13	1.17	1.56	1.44	1.62	2.39	0.38	0.37	1.02	2.56	1.09	Capital Gains $
	1.11	0.81	0.70	0.68	0.71	0.62	0.70	0.89	0.87	0.82	0.78	0.76	Expense Ratio %
	2.83	3.58	4.27	4.55	3.43	3.96	5.61	5.40	3.09	2.10	1.65	1.77	Income Ratio %
	79	107	96	124	74	85	73	46	52	47	56	---	Turnover Rate %
	59.3	178.0	432.5	561.5	688.4	1091.7	1470.1	1074.8	1111.4	1251.9	1539.8	1788.8	Net Assets ($mil)

Performance 12-31-94

	1st Qtr	2nd Qtr	3rd Qtr	4th Qtr	Total
1987	15.57	4.79	6.21	-16.30	7.66
1988	14.48	6.96	3.72	2.65	30.36
1989	6.83	4.69	5.48	-2.98	14.45
1990	-3.65	2.19	-11.42	3.06	-10.12
1991	11.76	2.29	4.78	1.13	21.13
1992	5.19	4.94	3.42	7.48	22.70
1993	8.06	1.36	7.52	4.19	22.71
1994	-1.56	1.88	7.02	-1.50	5.73

Bear Market Performance

Decile Rank (5-year period)

Worst _____ Best

	Worst 3 Mo Period 1985-89	Worst 3 Mo Period 1990-94
Mutual Qualified	-19.60	-14.02
+/- S&P 500	9.98	-0.18
+/- Best Fit Index : Wil 4500	10.54	5.38

Trailing Returns

	Total Return %	+/- S&P 500	+/- Wil 5000	% Rank All	% Rank Obj	Growth of $10,000
3 Mo	-1.50	-1.48	-0.73	57	52	9,850
6 Mo	5.41	0.55	0.79	10	7	10,541
1 Yr	5.73	4.41	5.80	3	2	10,573
3 Yr Avg	16.76	10.50	10.15	2	2	15,918
5 Yr Avg	11.62	2.93	2.81	10	8	17,330
10 Yr Avg	15.13	0.74	1.27	11	4	40,898
15 Yr Avg	---	---	---	---	---	---

Operations

Address and Telephone	51 John F. Kennedy Parkway
	Short Hills, NJ 07078
	800-553-3014 / 201-912-2100
Advisor	Heine Securities
Subadvisor	None
Distributor	Heine Securities
States Available	All
Report Grade	B+
Income Distrib	Paid Annually
Date of Inception	09-16-80
Fiscal Year End	December

Risk Analysis

Time Period	Load-Adj Return %	Risk % Rank [1] All	Obj	Morningstar [2] Return	Morningstar Risk	Morningstar Risk-Adj Rating
1 Yr	5.73					
3 Yr	16.76	28	2	4.31 [3]	0.42	★★★★★
5 Yr	11.62	53	6	1.83 [3]	0.57	★★★★
10 Yr	15.13	40	3	1.52	0.51	★★★★★
Average Historical Rating (109 months)					4.8	★s

[1] 1 = low, 100 = high [2] 1.00 = Equity Avg [3] 1.00 = 90-day T-bill return

Other Measures

			Standard S&P 500	Best Fit Wil 4500
Standard Deviation	6.96	Alpha	10.8	10.3
Mean	15.84	Beta	0.69	0.58
Sharpe Ratio	1.77	R-Squared	61	66

Investment Style

	Stock Portfolio Avg	Relative S&P 500
Price/Earnings Ratio	16.0	0.87
Price/Book Ratio	2.3	0.69
5 Yr Earnings Gr %	8.5	1.54
Return on Assets %	5.4	0.72
Debt % Total Cap	29.1	1.03
Med Mkt Cap ($mil)	1895	0.15

Style Value Blend Growth — Size Large Med Small

Diversification Value for Portfolio Types

Large Cap: Low	Small Cap: Low	Bond: Medium	Balanced: Low	Diversified: Low

Portfolio 06-30-94

Total Stocks: 206
Total Fixed-Income: 23

Share Chg (12-93) 000	Amount 000		Value $000	% Net Assets
0	17294	Sunbeam-Oster	106492	6.84
15	1841	National Medical Enterprises	28761	1.85
273	588	Sears Roebuck	28224	1.81
251	820	Litton Industries	27569	1.77
9	444	Van Melle	27462	1.76
147	470	Philip Morris	24205	1.55
936	936	American Express	24102	1.55
-4	28	Nestle (Reg)	23222	1.49
10	451	Dreyfus	21874	1.40
472	472	US West	19761	1.27
200	584	GFC Financial	19491	1.25
352	352	Nutricia	16894	1.08
442	442	Dean Witter Discover	16560	1.06
34	414	Chemical Banking	15939	1.02
	12	Zenith Laboratories Cv Pfd 10%	15731	1.01
4	217	Fund American Enterpr Hldg	15304	0.98
36	526	Multimedia	15263	0.98
996	996	Lehman Brothers Holdings	15068	0.97
0	373	Unitrin	14912	0.96
942	1005	Daily Mail & General Trust A	14583	0.94
630	630	Syntex	14479	0.93
10	201	Michigan National	14472	0.93
705	889	PaineWebber Group	13888	0.89
343	606	American President	13561	0.87
216	216	Schering-Plough	13230	0.85

Composition % 12-31-94

Cash	19.3	Preferreds	2.6
Stocks	72.1	Convertibles	0.0
Bonds	6.0	Other	0.0

Tax Analysis

	Tax-Adj Historical Return %	% Pretax Return
3 Yr Avg	14.13	82.2
5 Yr Avg	9.20	75.4
10 Yr Avg	11.84	66.8
Potential Capital Gain Exposure (% of assets)		16%

Most Similar Funds in MF500

Mutual Shares	Strong Fit
Mutual Beacon	Strong Fit
Fidelity Value	Fair Fit

Index Allocation

	% of Stocks
S&P 500	32.3
S&P MidCap 400	12.3
U.S. Small Cap	43.8
Foreign	12.8

Sector Weightings

	% of Stocks	Relative S&P 500
Utilities	3.6	0.29
Energy	4.2	0.42
Financials	32.4	3.06
Industrial Cyclicals	3.9	0.24
Consumer Durables	10.8	1.74
Consumer Staples	10.6	0.85
Services	15.6	1.92
Retail	6.0	1.03
Health	9.6	1.11
Technology	3.4	0.37

Expenses & Fees

Min Initial Purchase	$1000 (Addt'l: $50)
Min IRA Purchase	$1000 (Addt'l: $50)
Min Auto Invest Plan	$1000 (Systematic Inv: $50)

Sales Fees	0.00% front
	0.00% deferred
	0.00% 12b-1
Management Fee	0.60% flat fee
3-,5-,10-yr Expense Projections	$26, $45, $99
Annual Brokerage Cost	0.15%

MORNINGSTAR 1995 Mutual Fund 500

Mutual Shares

	Ticker	Load	NAV	Yield	SEC Yield	Assets	Objective
	MUTHX	None	78.69	3.0%	N/A	3745.3	Growth/Inc.

Mutual Shares Fund seeks capital appreciation. Income is secondary.

The fund invests in common and preferred stocks and corporate debt securities of any credit quality. These securities are trading at prices below their intrinsic value, according to factors such as price/book ratio, price/earnings ratio, and cash flow. The fund may invest up to 50% of assets in securities of companies involved in mergers, consolidations, liquidations, and reorganizations. It invests from time to time in foreign securities, and in securities of other investment companies.

Manager's Investment Style

Renowned value manager Michael Price seeks firms that are cheap relative to their assets. He also specializes in mergers and bankruptcies. This fund was closed to new investment between 1989 and early 1994; Price reopened the fund to new investment to take advantage of escalating merger activity and a first-half stock-market correction. This fund and its siblings, Mutual Qualified and Mutual Beacon, are all near-clones of one another.

Fund Manager(s)

Michael F. Price, since 01-75. Finance, U. of Oklahoma 1973

Manager Experience

	Dates Managed	Invest Obj	Std Dev	+/- Index
Michael F. Price				
Mutual Qualified	09/80 - 12/94	GI	10.29	3.53
Mutual Beacon	01/85 - 12/94	GI	10.53	1.10

Historical Profile

Return	Above Average
Risk	Low
Rating	★★★★★ Highest

Investment Style History Equity

Average % Stocks Held in Portfolio: 61% 59% 61% 63% 67% 73% 69% 79%

Growth of $10,000

|||| Value of Fund ($000)
— Value of Index ($000) S&P 500
▼ Manager Change
▽ Partial Manager Change
◄■ Mgr Unknown After
◄ Mgr Unknown Before

Performance Quartile (Within Objective)

	1983	1984	1985	1986	1987	1988	1989	1990	1991	1992	1993	1994	History
NAV	49.49	50.30	57.54	60.39	57.73	67.77	67.16	56.39	64.49	73.36	80.97	78.69	NAV
	37.74	14.47	26.66	16.98	6.22	30.92	14.93	-9.82	20.99	21.33	21.00	4.53	Total Return %
	15.27	8.21	-5.08	-1.70	0.96	14.31	-16.76	-6.71	-9.50	13.71	10.95	3.22	+/- S&P 500
	14.27	11.42	-5.90	0.88	3.86	12.98	-14.25	-3.64	-13.22	12.36	9.72	4.60	+/- Wilshire 5000
	2.92	2.87	3.56	3.93	4.06	4.17	6.14	5.12	3.45	2.30	1.76	3.10	Income Return %
	34.82	11.61	23.10	13.04	2.17	26.75	8.78	-14.94	17.53	19.02	19.25	1.43	Capital Return %
	4	8	39	40	18	2	47	84	43	3	16	5	Total Rtn % Rank All
	2	11	59	49	19	1	88	85	90	2	5	4	Total Rtn % Rank Obj
	1.37	1.42	1.88	2.34	2.52	2.63	4.09	3.34	2.00	1.59	1.38	2.45	Income $
	4.63	4.83	4.12	4.52	4.09	5.05	6.55	0.89	1.63	3.16	6.31	3.45	Capital Gains $
	0.83	0.73	0.67	0.70	0.69	0.67	0.65	0.85	0.82	0.78	0.74	0.73	Expense Ratio %
	3.20	3.42	4.08	4.07	3.32	4.16	5.57	4.88	3.08	2.18	1.90	1.81	Income Ratio %
	70	102	91	122	78	90	72	43	48	41	49	---	Turnover Rate %
	241.1	496.0	1076.1	1402.4	1682.2	2544.7	3401.8	2514.1	2642.9	2915.3	3527.1	3745.3	Net Assets ($mil)

Performance 12-31-94

	1st Qtr	2nd Qtr	3rd Qtr	4th Qtr	Total
1987	14.65	4.30	6.11	-16.29	6.22
1988	14.72	7.31	3.86	2.39	30.92
1989	6.64	5.09	5.76	-3.04	14.93
1990	-3.62	2.51	-11.68	3.34	-9.82
1991	11.35	2.48	5.07	0.90	20.99
1992	4.61	4.68	3.02	7.55	21.33
1993	7.99	1.19	7.06	3.44	21.00
1994	-2.84	2.17	6.95	-1.54	4.53

Bear Market Performance

Decile Rank (5-year period)

Worst | Best

	Worst 3 Mo Period 1985-89	Worst 3 Mo Period 1990-94
Mutual Shares	-19.28	-14.24
+/- S&P 500	10.30	-0.39
+/- Best Fit Index : Wil 4500	10.86	5.17

Trailing Returns

	Total Return %	+/- S&P 500	+/- Wil 5000	% Rank All	% Rank Obj	Growth of $10,000
3 Mo	-1.54	-1.52	-0.77	58	53	9,846
6 Mo	5.30	0.44	0.68	10	7	10,530
1 Yr	4.53	3.22	4.60	5	4	10,453
3 Yr Avg	15.35	9.08	8.73	3	3	15,347
5 Yr Avg	10.86	2.17	2.04	13	9	16,743
10 Yr Avg	14.77	0.39	0.91	13	8	39,647
15 Yr Avg	15.86	1.38	1.89	7	3	91,025

Operations

Address and Telephone	51 John F. Kennedy Parkway
	Short Hills, NJ 07078
	800-553-3014 / 201-912-2100
Advisor	Heine Securities
Subadvisor	None
Distributor	Heine Securities
States Available	All
Report Grade	B+
Income Distrib	Paid Annually
Date of Inception	07-01-49
Fiscal Year End	December

Min Initial Purchase	$5000 (Addt'l: $100)
Min IRA Purchase	$2000 (Addt'l: $100)
Min Auto Invest Plan	$5000 (Systematic Inv: $100)

Expenses & Fees

Sales Fees	0.00% front
	0.00% deferred
	0.00% 12b-1
Management Fee	0.60% flat fee
3-,5-,10-yr Expense Projections	$24, $42, $94
Annual Brokerage Cost	0.11%

Risk Analysis

Time Period	Load-Adj Return %	Risk % Rank [1] All	Obj	Morningstar [2] Return	Risk	Morningstar Risk-Adj Rating
1 Yr	4.53					
3 Yr	15.35	36	4	3.80 [3]	0.46	★★★★★
5 Yr	10.86	54	8	1.60 [3]	0.59	★★★★
10 Yr	14.77	40	4	1.44	0.52	★★★★★
Average Historical Rating (109 months)					4.7	★s

[1] 1 = low, 100 = high [2] 1.00 = Equity Avg [3] 1.00 = 90-day T-bill return

Other Measures

	Standard S&P 500	Best Fit Wil 4500
Standard Deviation	7.12	
Mean	14.61	
Sharpe Ratio	1.56	
Alpha	9.4	8.9
Beta	0.72	0.58
R-Squared	63	64

Investment Style

	Stock Portfolio Avg	Relative S&P 500
Price/Earnings Ratio	17.2	0.93
Price/Book Ratio	2.4	0.71
5 Yr Earnings Gr %	9.8	1.77
Return on Assets %	5.2	0.70
Debt % Total Cap	29.3	1.04
Med Mkt Cap ($mil)	1988	0.15

Style: Value Blend Growth / Size Large Med Small

Diversification Value for Portfolio Types

Large Cap: Low	Small Cap: Low	Bond: Medium	Balanced: Low	Diversified: Low

Portfolio 06-30-94

Total Stocks: 193
Total Fixed-Income: 24

Share Chg (12-93) 000	Amount 000		Value $000	% Net Assets
0	40563	Sunbeam-Oster	249785	7.11
809	1584	Sears Roebuck	76008	2.16
899	2251	Litton Industries	75690	2.15
33	4191	National Medical Enterprises	65489	1.86
447	1251	Philip Morris	64447	1.83
2255	2255	American Express	58053	1.65
17	889	Van Melle	55049	1.57
10	1063	Dreyfus	51551	1.47
-9	57	Nestle (Reg)	47928	1.36
480	1407	GFC Financial	46969	1.34
85	1216	Chemical Banking	46824	1.33
-847	955	Salomon	45587	1.30
6	639	Fund American Enterpr Hldg	45076	1.28
1065	1065	US West	44597	1.27
1177	1177	Dean Witter Discover	44149	1.26
947	1671	American President	37389	1.06
	28	Zenith Laboratories Cv Pfd 10%	37243	1.06
78	1220	Multimedia	35389	1.01
2312	2312	Lehman Brothers Holdings	34972	1.00
	35700	Wachovia Bank 4.625%	34843	0.99
559	559	Schering-Plough	34227	0.97
1750	2190	PaineWebber Group	34225	0.97
0	845	Unitrin	33808	0.96
1442	1442	Syntex	33169	0.94
-41	769	AH Belo	33159	0.94

Composition % 12-31-94

Cash	17.1	Preferreds	1.1
Stocks	76.2	Convertibles	0.0
Bonds	5.6	Other	0.0

Tax Analysis

	Tax-Adj Historical Return %	% Pretax Return
3 Yr Avg	12.77	81.2
5 Yr Avg	8.50	74.7
10 Yr Avg	11.56	67.0
Potential Capital Gain Exposure (% of assets)		18%

Most Similar Funds in MF500

Mutual Qualified	Strong Fit
Fidelity Equity-Income II	Fair Fit
Fidelity Equity-Income	Fair Fit

Index Allocation

	% of Stocks
S&P 500	39.0
S&P MidCap 400	12.4
U.S. Small Cap	41.8
Foreign	8.1

Sector Weightings

	% of Stocks	Relative S&P 500
Utilities	3.7	0.30
Energy	6.2	0.61
Financials	33.3	3.15
Industrial Cyclicals	3.7	0.23
Consumer Durables	10.9	1.76
Consumer Staples	7.8	0.62
Services	16.1	1.97
Retail	4.8	0.83
Health	9.0	1.04
Technology	4.5	0.49

Neuberger & Berman Guardian

	Ticker	Load	NAV	Yield	SEC Yield	Assets	Objective
	NGUAX	None	18.23	2.2%	N/A	2423.8	Growth/Inc.

Neuberger & Berman Guardian Fund seeks capital appreciation; current income is a secondary objective.

The fund invests principally in common stocks of well-established companies. Management selects securities based on low P/E ratios, strong balance sheets, solid management, and consistent earnings. The fund may invest up to 10% of its assets directly in foreign securities; it may also invest in ADRs.

Fund shares are designed for individual investors; Trust shares are available through pension plans and certain financial service providers. Prior to April 1, 1989, the fund was named Guardian Mutual Fund.

Manager's Investment Style

Management seeks large-cap stocks, especially in out-of-market sectors, with above-market earnings and cash flow, and that are selling at below-market multiples. The fund's criteria often lead management to overweight financials.

Historical Profile

Return	Above Average
Risk	Average
Rating	★★★★ Above Average

93% 93% 89% 88% 89% 91% 84% 92%

Investment Style History
Equity
Average % Stocks Held in Portfolio

Growth of $10,000
‖‖‖ Value of Fund ($000)
— Value of Index ($000) S&P 500
▼ Manager Change
▽ Partial Manager Change
► Mgr Unknown After
◄ Mgr Unknown Before

Performance Quartile
(Within Objective)

	1983	1984	1985	1986	1987	1988	1989	1990	1991	1992	1993	1994	History
	12.76	12.81	13.10	12.71	10.74	12.17	13.22	12.08	14.97	16.87	18.60	18.23	NAV
	25.27	7.29	25.05	11.91	-1.01	28.08	21.52	-4.71	34.36	18.99	14.47	1.42	Total Return %
	2.81	1.02	-6.69	-6.77	-6.27	11.47	-10.16	-1.59	3.87	11.37	4.41	0.10	+/- S&P 500
	1.81	4.24	-7.51	-4.18	-3.38	10.14	-7.65	1.47	0.15	10.02	3.19	1.49	+/- Wilshire 5000
	4.16	3.91	4.66	3.78	3.91	3.04	2.73	2.77	2.40	1.68	1.74	2.18	Income Return %
	21.11	3.38	20.39	8.14	-4.92	25.04	18.79	-7.48	31.95	17.30	12.73	-0.76	Capital Return %
	23	40	46	74	67	4	32	70	20	6	31	12	Total Rtn % Rank All
	27	28	72	79	77	4	65	58	17	5	24	16	Total Rtn % Rank Obj
	0.48	0.48	0.59	0.50	0.50	0.36	0.36	0.35	0.32	0.26	0.30	0.40	Income $
	0.79	0.37	2.15	1.50	1.40	1.23	1.19	0.17	0.91	0.66	0.40	0.23	Capital Gains $
	0.67	0.77	0.76	0.73	0.74	0.84	0.84	0.86	0.84	0.82	0.81	0.80	Expense Ratio %
	3.92	3.81	4.58	3.59	2.72	2.80	2.59	2.89	2.46	1.90	2.01	1.36	Income Ratio %
	50	32	57	70	91	73	52	58	59	41	27	24	Turnover Rate %
	309.2	365.2	499.1	505.7	442.4	529.7	571.3	519.9	685.2	1038.5	2000.9	2423.8	Net Assets ($mil)

Fund Manager(s)

Kent Simons CFA, since 01-81. Birthdate: 05-35.
BA, Princeton U. 1957
Lawrence Marx III, since 01-88. Birthdate: 03-46.
BA, Stanford U. 1968

Manager Experience

	Dates Managed	Invest Obj	Std Dev	+/- Index
Kent Simons				
Neuberger&Berman Focus	01/88 - 12/94	G	12.47	1.38
Lawrence Marx III				
Neuberger&Berman Focus	01/88 - 12/94	G	12.47	1.38

Performance 12-31-94

	1st Qtr	2nd Qtr	3rd Qtr	4th Qtr	Total
1987	21.12	1.38	5.10	-23.29	-1.01
1988	14.99	8.13	2.33	0.67	28.08
1989	7.42	5.79	10.91	-3.59	21.52
1990	-3.38	4.94	-15.76	11.57	-4.71
1991	17.42	-1.66	7.57	8.17	34.36
1992	2.58	0.54	4.78	10.10	18.99
1993	4.68	0.91	4.35	3.85	14.47
1994	-2.74	1.28	2.96	0.00	1.42

Bear Market Performance

Decile Rank (5-year period)

Worst ▬ Best

	Worst 3 Mo Period 1985-89	Worst 3 Mo Period 1990-94
Neuberger & Berman Guardian	-30.80	-17.40
+/- S&P 500	-1.21	-3.56
+/- Best Fit Index : S&P 500	-1.21	-3.56

Trailing Returns

	Total Return %	+/- S&P 500	+/- Wil 5000	% Rank All	% Rank Obj	Growth of $10,000
3 Mo	0.00	0.02	0.77	22	15	10,000
6 Mo	2.96	-1.90	-1.66	21	44	10,296
1 Yr	1.42	0.10	1.49	12	16	10,142
3 Yr Avg	11.37	5.10	4.76	9	6	13,813
5 Yr Avg	12.08	3.39	3.26	9	5	17,685
10 Yr Avg	14.32	-0.06	0.46	15	11	38,134
15 Yr Avg	14.89	0.41	0.92	14	10	80,247

Operations

Address and Telephone	605 Third Avenue 2nd Floor
	New York, NY 10158-0006
	800-877-9700 / 212-476-8800
Advisor	Neuberger & Berman Management
Subadvisor	Neuberger & Berman
Distributor	Neuberger & Berman Management
States Available	All plus PR
Report Grade	B-
Income Distrib	Paid Quarterly
Date of Inception	06-01-50
Fiscal Year End	August

Risk Analysis

Time Period	Load-Adj Return %	Risk % Rank [1] All	Obj	Morningstar [2] Return	Risk	Morningstar Risk-Adj Rating
1 Yr	1.42					
3 Yr	11.37	59	23	2.42 [3]	0.64	★★★★
5 Yr	12.08	72	75	1.96 [3]	0.85	★★★★
10 Yr	14.32	67	76	1.34	0.90	★★★★
Average Historical Rating (109 months)				3.9 ★s		

[1] 1 = low, 100 = high [2] 1.00 = Equity Avg [3] 1.00 = 90-day T-bill return

Other Measures

		Standard S&P 500	Best Fit S&P 500
Standard Deviation	8.53	Alpha	4.9	4.9
Mean	11.18	Beta	0.99	0.99
Sharpe Ratio	0.90	R-Squared	85	85

Investment Style

	Stock Portfolio Avg	Relative S&P 500
Price/Earnings Ratio	15.9	0.86
Price/Book Ratio	2.6	0.77
5 Yr Earnings Gr %	8.8	1.58
Return on Assets %	7.0	0.93
Debt % Total Cap	29.5	1.04
Med Mkt Cap ($mil)	5083	0.39

Style Value Blend Growth
Size Large Med Small

Diversification Value for Portfolio Types

○ Large Cap: None | ◌ Small Cap: Low | ● Bond: High | ○ Balanced: None | ◌ Diversified: Low

Tax Analysis

	Tax-Adj Historical Return %	% Pretax Return
3 Yr Avg	9.92	86.1
5 Yr Avg	10.40	83.3
10 Yr Avg	11.11	66.3
Potential Capital Gain Exposure (% of assets)		15%

Most Similar Funds in MF500

Fundamental Investors	Strong Fit
Neuberger&Berman Partners	Strong Fit
Evergreen Growth & Income Y	Strong Fit

Portfolio 12-31-94

Total Stocks: 120
Total Fixed-Income: 6

Share Chg (11-94) 000	Amount 000		Value $000	% Net Assets
-3	709	Texas Instruments	53073	2.19
-3	693	FNMA	50537	2.09
-5	1031	Chrysler	50524	2.08
24	985	AT & T	49499	2.04
67	1151	Citicorp	47623	1.96
-2	480	Capital Cities/ABC	40884	1.69
4	269	Wells Fargo	38942	1.61
-4	863	Micron Technology	38091	1.57
148	1218	Foundation Health	37762	1.56
63	837	Tenneco	35571	1.47
-4	767	General Motors	32420	1.34
26	633	FHLMC	31969	1.32
-2	326	American International Group	31959	1.32
-3	705	NationsBank	31813	1.31
-10	1957	Comcast Special Cl A	30696	1.27
-1	200	Alleghany	30337	1.25
-2	456	Intel	29102	1.20
-2	369	Chubb	28573	1.18
-1	230	General Re	28487	1.18
-4	825	Travelers	26809	1.11
-4	743	Time Warner	26110	1.08
174	793	First USA	26055	1.08
-3	539	Willamette Industries	25582	1.06
-3	671	Stratus Computer	25514	1.05
-4	719	Harcourt General	25358	1.05

Composition % 12-31-94

Cash	1.8	Preferreds	0.0
Stocks	96.1	Convertibles	1.5
Bonds	0.6	Other	0.0

Index Allocation

	% of Stocks
S&P 500	65.1
S&P MidCap 400	15.6
U.S. Small Cap	12.5
Foreign	7.0

Sector Weightings

	% of Stocks	Relative S&P 500
Utilities	6.7	0.54
Energy	4.1	0.40
Financials	26.6	2.51
Industrial Cyclicals	15.3	0.94
Consumer Durables	8.9	1.43
Consumer Staples	2.1	0.17
Services	16.7	2.06
Retail	1.6	0.27
Health	5.7	0.65
Technology	12.3	1.35

Expenses & Fees

Min Initial Purchase	$1000 (Addt'l: $100)
Min IRA Purchase	$250 (Addt'l: None)
Min Auto Invest Plan	$50 (Systematic Inv: $50)
Sales Fees	0.00% front
	0.00% deferred
	0.00% 12b-1
Management Fee	0.55% max./0.43% min., 0.15%A
3-,5-,10-yr Expense Projections	$26, $45, $100
Annual Brokerage Cost	0.13%

MORNINGSTAR 1995 Mutual Fund 500

Neuberger & Berman Partners

	Ticker	Load	NAV	Yield	SEC Yield	Assets	Objective
	NPRTX	None	18.52	0.5%	N/A	1246.6	Growth

Neuberger & Berman Partners Trust seeks capital growth.

The fund invests primarily in common stocks of established companies. It focuses on securities judged to be undervalued based on low P/E ratios, consistent cash flow, and support from asset values. On occasion the fund may invest in preferred stocks, convertible securities, and debt securities. The fund may invest up to 10% of its assets directly in foreign securities; it may also invest in ADRs.

Fund shares are for individual investors; Trust shares are offered to institutions only. Prior to April 10, 1989, the fund was named Partners Fund.

Historical Profile

Return	Above Average
Risk	Below Average
Rating	★★★★ Above Average

67% 68% 74% 71% 81% 90% 94% 95%

Investment Style History
Equity
Average % Stocks Held in Portfolio

Growth of $10,000
|||| Value of Fund ($000)
— Value of Index ($000)
S&P 500
▼ Manager Change
▽ Partial Manager Change
▶ Mgr Unknown After
◀ Mgr Unknown Before

Manager's Investment Style

As in other Neuberger & Berman funds, management seeks issues selling cheaply compared with earnings or free cash flow. In this fund, management applies these principles to the mid-cap arena. Financials are a fund favorite, although management will concentrate assets in other sectors as well.

Performance Quartile
(Within Objective)

1983	1984	1985	1986	1987	1988	1989	1990	1991	1992	1993	1994	History
14.76	14.85	17.16	17.37	15.06	16.72	18.06	16.02	18.44	19.69	20.62	18.52	NAV
19.17	8.04	29.94	14.89	4.32	15.46	22.78	-5.11	22.36	17.52	16.46	-1.89	Total Return %
-3.30	1.77	-1.79	-3.79	-0.94	-1.15	-8.91	-1.99	9.90	6.40	-3.21	-1.89	+/- S&P 500
-4.29	4.99	-2.62	-1.20	1.95	-2.48	-6.40	1.07	-11.84	8.55	5.17	-1.82	+/- Wilshire 5000
6.00	5.39	4.44	2.21	4.02	4.44	4.32	4.41	1.99	0.97	0.53	0.59	Income Return %
13.17	2.64	25.51	12.68	0.29	11.02	18.46	-9.52	20.37	16.55	15.92	-2.48	Capital Return %
43	37	25	55	26	26	29	71	41	7	24	33	Total Rtn % Rank All
61	13	46	47	40	50	70	55	91	10	27	51	Total Rtn % Rank Obj
0.84	0.72	0.65	0.44	0.70	0.65	0.76	0.74	0.34	0.19	0.11	0.11	Income $
1.96	0.27	1.27	2.25	2.79	0.00	1.68	0.34	0.78	1.79	2.20	1.60	Capital Gains $
0.97	0.91	0.93	0.89	0.86	0.95	0.97	0.91	0.88	0.86	0.86	0.81	Expense Ratio %
6.29	5.44	4.80	3.23	2.93	3.28	3.96	4.53	2.84	1.23	0.83	0.48	Income Ratio %
232	227	146	181	169	210	157	136	161	97	82	75	Turnover Rate %
148.1	168.7	282.4	515.2	637.4	683.6	764.9	727.2	889.0	974.6	1127.7	1246.6	Net Assets ($mil)

Fund Manager(s)

Robert I. Gendelman, since 10-94. Birthdate: 03-58. JD, U. of Chicago 1984 MBA, U. of Chicago 1984
Michael Kassen, since 06-90. BA, Princeton U. 1976 MBA, Harvard 1978

Manager Experience

	Dates Managed	Invest Obj	Std Dev	+/- Index
Not available.				

Performance 12-31-94

	1st Qtr	2nd Qtr	3rd Qtr	4th Qtr	Total
1987	15.95	3.43	5.78	-17.77	4.32
1988	6.31	5.18	0.90	2.34	15.46
1989	5.38	8.06	8.20	-0.36	22.78
1990	-3.32	3.72	-9.61	4.69	-5.11
1991	12.30	-1.06	5.00	4.88	22.36
1992	4.23	-1.35	3.53	10.39	17.52
1993	4.98	1.50	7.58	1.60	16.46
1994	-4.41	-0.96	6.81	-2.97	-1.89

Bear Market Performance

Decile Rank (5-year period)

Worst ————————— Best

	Worst 3 Mo Period 1985-89	Worst 3 Mo Period 1990-94
Neuberger & Berman Partners	-23.85	-13.68
+/- S&P 500	5.73	0.16
+/- Best Fit Index : Wil 4500	6.29	5.72

Trailing Returns

	Total Return %	+/- S&P 500	+/- Wil 5000	% Rank All	% Rank Obj	Growth of $10,000
3 Mo	-2.97	-2.96	-2.20	83	79	9,703
6 Mo	3.64	-1.22	-0.99	17	54	10,364
1 Yr	-1.89	-3.21	-1.82	33	51	9,811
3 Yr Avg	10.32	4.05	3.71	12	16	13,427
5 Yr Avg	9.29	0.60	0.47	21	40	15,590
10 Yr Avg	13.16	-1.23	-0.70	25	44	34,419
15 Yr Avg	14.83	0.35	0.85	14	29	79,594

Operations

Address and Telephone	605 Third Avenue 2nd Floor New York, NY 10158-0006 800-877-9700 / 212-476-8800
Advisor	Neuberger & Berman Management
Subadvisor	Neuberger & Berman
Distributor	Neuberger & Berman Management
States Available	All plus PR
Report Grade	B-
Income Distrib	Paid Annually
Date of Inception	07-16-68
Fiscal Year End	August

Risk Analysis

Time Period	Load-Adj Return %	Risk % Rank [1] All	Obj	Morningstar [2] Return	Morningstar Risk	Morningstar Risk-Adj Rating
1 Yr	-1.89					
3 Yr	10.32	69	32	2.08 [3]	0.76	★★★★
5 Yr	9.29	68	23	1.15 [3]	0.81	★★★★
10 Yr	13.16	57	18	1.10	0.82	★★★★
Average Historical Rating (109 months)				4.4 ★s		

[1] 1 = low, 100 = high [2] 1.00 = Equity Avg [3] 1.00 = 90-day T-bill return

Other Measures

				Standard S&P 500	Best Fit Wil 4500
Standard Deviation	9.84	Alpha		3.8	2.9
Mean	10.35	Beta		1.08	0.92
Sharpe Ratio	0.69	R-Squared		76	84

Investment Style

	Stock Portfolio Avg	Relative S&P 500
Price/Earnings Ratio	16.4	0.89
Price/Book Ratio	3.6	1.06
5 Yr Earnings Gr %	16.3	2.94
Return on Assets %	6.8	0.91
Debt % Total Cap	33.6	1.19
Med Mkt Cap ($mil)	2022	0.16

Style Value Blend Growth / Size Large Med Small

Diversification Value for Portfolio Types

Large Cap: Low	Small Cap: Low	Bond: High	Balanced: None	Diversified: Low

Expenses & Fees

Sales Fees	0.00% front
	0.00% deferred
	0.00% 12b-1
Management Fee	0.55% max./0.43% min., 0.15%A
3-,5-,10-yr Expense Projections	$27, $47, $104
Annual Brokerage Cost	0.25%

Min Initial Purchase	$1000 (Addt'l: $100)
Min IRA Purchase	$250 (Addt'l: $100)
Min Auto Invest Plan	$50 (Systematic Inv: $50)

Portfolio 12-31-94

Share Chg (11-94) 000	Amount 000	Total Stocks: 70 Total Fixed-Income: 3	Value $000	% Net Assets
24	1037	Progressive	36280	2.91
0	888	EXEL	35095	2.82
0	938	Time Warner	32942	2.64
0	494	Intel	31529	2.53
-1	1974	Comcast Special Cl A	30973	2.48
0	395	Texas Instruments	29567	2.37
-25	395	Georgia-Pacific	28234	2.26
-223	1185	Revco Drug Stores	27987	2.25
0	98	Mannesmann (ADR)	26771	2.15
0	1638	LTV	26622	2.14
-25	543	Chrysler	26605	2.13
0	1283	Mirage Resorts	26309	2.11
24	938	Fruit of the Loom Cl A	25322	2.03
123	1357	MCI Communications	24942	2.00
0	569	Biogen	23740	1.90
0	691	Triton Energy	23495	1.88
0	1283	Equitable	23261	1.87
197	1728	Price/Costco	22243	1.78
0	642	King World Productions	22138	1.78
0	617	Orion Capital	21745	1.74
0	691	Toys 'R' Us	21077	1.69
0	1037	USG	20213	1.62
0	592	Goodyear Tire & Rubber	19917	1.60
0	415	Tejas Gas	19746	1.58
77	279	Monsanto	19703	1.58

Composition % 12-31-94

Cash	4.4	Preferreds	0.0
Stocks	93.8	Convertibles	1.8
Bonds	0.0	Other	0.0

Tax Analysis

	Tax-Adj Historical Return %	% Pretax Return
3 Yr Avg	7.42	69.9
5 Yr Avg	6.74	68.9
10 Yr Avg	9.82	63.6
Potential Capital Gain Exposure (% of assets)		2%

Most Similar Funds in MF500

Columbia Growth	Strong Fit
Vanguard Index Extended Mkt	Strong Fit
Growth Fund of America	Fair Fit

Index Allocation

	% of Stocks
S&P 500	40.9
S&P MidCap 400	17.8
U.S. Small Cap	32.1
Foreign	9.3

Sector Weightings

	% of Stocks	Relative S&P 500
Utilities	2.2	0.18
Energy	7.5	0.74
Financials	16.0	1.51
Industrial Cyclicals	16.8	1.02
Consumer Durables	8.0	1.28
Consumer Staples	3.6	0.28
Services	20.5	2.51
Retail	10.5	1.80
Health	6.9	0.80
Technology	8.1	0.89

Neuberger & Berman Ultra Sh

Ticker	Load	NAV	Yield	SEC Yield	Assets	Objective
NBMMX	None	9.45	3.9%	5.45%	90.7	Corp Hi Qlty

Neuberger & Berman Ultra Short Bond Fund seeks current income consistent with low risk to principal and liquidity.

The fund invests in U.S. government obligations and related repurchase agreements, high-quality debt securities issued by corporations or financial institutions, mortgage- and asset-backed securities, money-market instruments, and U.S. dollar-denominated securities of foreign issuers. It maintains an average weighted maturity of two years or less.

Fund shares are for individual investors; Trust shares are offered to institutions only. Prior to March 1, 1991, the fund was named Neuberger & Berman Money-Market Plus Fund.

Manager's Investment Style

Management keeps a tight rein on maturity, tending to keep it well below the two-year limit set forth in the fund's charter. Management typically keeps most of the fund's assets in government or AAA debt, with occasional dabbles in AA rated paper. In general, though, management keeps the fund a small step above a money-market vehicle.

Historical Profile
Return: Below Average
Risk: Low
Rating: ★★★★ Above Average

Fund Manager(s)

Theresa A. Havell, since 11-86. Birthdate: 09-46.
BA, Manhattanville C. 1968 MA, New York U. 1971
Josephine Mahaney, since 07-93. Birthdate: 04-42.
BA, CUNY 1976

Manager Experience

	Dates Managed	Invest Obj	Std Dev	+/- Index
Theresa A. Havell				
Neuberger&Berman Lim	6/86 - 12/94	CQ	2.36	-1.30
Neuberger&Berman Muni	07/87 - 12/94	MN	3.50	-2.50

History	1983	1984	1985	1986	1987	1988	1989	1990	1991	1992	1993	1994
NAV	---	---	---	9.98	9.88	9.83	9.80	9.82	9.86	9.69	9.61	9.45
Total Return %	---	---	---	0.71*	5.56	6.85	9.40	8.39	7.42	3.64	3.22	2.23
+/- LB Aggregate	---	---	---		2.80	-1.03	-5.14	-0.55	-8.58	-3.60	-6.54	5.15
+/- LB Corporate	---	---	---		3.00	-2.37	-4.58	1.24	-11.08	-5.06	-8.95	6.16
Income Return %	---	---	---	0.91	6.56	7.35	9.70	8.19	7.02	5.37	4.04	3.90
Capital Return %	---	---	---	-0.20	-1.00	-0.51	-0.31	0.20	0.41	-1.72	-0.83	-1.66
Total Rtn % Rank All	---	---	---		20	82	80	12	96	82	96	9
Total Rtn % Rank Obj	---	---	---		8	60	84	33	94	95	94	11
Income $	---	---	---	0.09	0.64	0.71	0.92	0.77	0.67	0.52	0.39	0.37
Capital Gains $	---	---	---	0.00	0.00	0.00	0.00	0.00	0.00	0.00	0.00	0.00
Expense Ratio %	---	---	---		0.50	0.63	0.65	0.65	0.65	0.65	0.65	0.65
Income Ratio %	---	---	---		6.03	7.01	9.06	8.14	6.97	5.70	4.09	3.50
Turnover Rate %	---	---	---		39	121	85	120	89	66	115	---
Net Assets ($mil)	---	---	---		66.0	123.1	96.4	105.7	85.1	94.2	103.0	105.9	90.7

Performance 12-31-94

	1st Qtr	2nd Qtr	3rd Qtr	4th Qtr	Total
1987	1.13	0.97	1.26	2.08	5.56
1988	2.13	1.30	1.63	1.62	6.85
1989	1.80	3.16	1.92	2.21	9.40
1990	1.64	2.08	2.03	2.38	8.39
1991	1.75	1.44	2.01	2.02	7.42
1992	0.72	1.24	1.18	0.45	3.64
1993	1.02	0.71	1.08	0.37	3.22
1994	0.01	0.38	0.90	0.93	2.23

Risk Analysis

Time Period	Load-Adj Return %	Risk % Rank All	Obj	Morningstar Return	Morningstar Risk	Morningstar Risk-Adj Rating
1 Yr	2.23					
3 Yr	3.03	1	7	-0.16[3]	0.23	★★★★★
5 Yr	4.95	1	9	0.05[3]	0.18	★★★★
10 Yr	---					

Average Historical Rating (62 months) 4.5 ★s

[1] = low, 100 = high [2] 1.00 = Taxable Avg [3] 1.00 = 90-day T-bill return

Other Measures

		Standard LB Agg	Best Fit LB Int
Standard Deviation	0.70	Alpha	-0.7	-0.6
Mean	2.99	Beta	0.14	0.18
Sharpe Ratio	-0.76	R-Squared	67	75

Investment Style

Interest-Rate Stance
Avg Effective Duration 0.9 Yrs**
Avg Effective Maturity 0.4 Yrs

Quality
Avg Credit Quality AAA
Avg Weighted Coupon 5.32%
Avg Weighted Price 99.17% of Par

**figure provided by fund

Bear Market Performance

Decile Rank (5-year period)

	Worst 3 Mo Period 1985-89	Worst 3 Mo Period 1990-94
Neuberger & Berman Ultra Sh	---	-0.51
+/- LB Aggregate	---	4.42
+/- Best Fit Index : LB Int	---	3.71

Trailing Returns

	Total Return %	+/- LB Aggregate	+/- LB Corporate	% Rank All	Obj	Growth of $10,000
3 Mo	0.93	0.56	0.50	7	9	10,093
6 Mo	1.84	0.85	0.67	28	8	10,184
1 Yr	2.23	5.15	6.16	9	11	10,223
3 Yr Avg	3.03	-1.52	-2.39	85	91	10,936
5 Yr Avg	4.95	-2.67	-3.31	90	95	12,734
10 Yr Avg	---	---	---	---	---	---
15 Yr Avg	---	---	---	---	---	---

Diversification Value for Portfolio Types
Large Cap: High Small Cap: High Bond: Low Balanced: High Diversified: High

Portfolio 12-31-94

Total Stocks: 0
Total Fixed-Income: 42

Amount 000	Date of Maturity		Value $000	% Net Assets
5916	03-03-95	FHLMC Note 0%	5855	6.45
4930	01-11-95	FCC National Bank FRN	4930	5.43
4930	02-22-95	Northern Trust FRN LIBOR Qtrly	4887	5.39
4930	07-27-95	Banc One 5.4%	4882	5.38
3944	07-01-96	SLMA FRN	3928	4.33
3944	03-04-96	USAA Capital 4.7%	3834	4.23
3550	06-13-97	Toyota Motor Credit 6.6%	3555	3.92
2958	06-30-96	US Treasury Note 7.875%	2973	3.28
2958	05-05-95	Old Kent Bank 6.1125%	2958	3.26
2958	01-13-95	Commerzbank 5.46%	2958	3.26
2958	01-19-95	General Electric Cap 5.42%	2952	3.25
2958	01-19-95	Lubirzol 5.85%	2949	3.25
2958	01-18-95	Sara Lee 5.45%	2949	3.25
2958	01-23-95	Ford Motor Credit 5.4%	2947	3.25
2958	01-27-95	Hitachi 5.5%	2945	3.25
2958	02-21-95	Asset Securitization 5.77%	2932	3.23
2958	05-16-95	Swedish Export Credit 6.27%	2886	3.18
2801	01-03-95	Societe Generale 4.95%	2801	3.09
1972	01-24-95	Metlife Capital 5.41%	1964	2.16
1972	01-27-95	Merrill Lynch 5.45%	1963	2.16
1972	03-21-95	Republic New York 5.82%	1944	2.14
2008	04-15-19	Green Tree Financial 5.6%	1931	2.13
1972	09-25-00	World Omni 6.45%	1930	2.13
1685	05-25-04	Citicorp Mortgage Secs 6.5%	1652	1.82
1248	03-25-09	FNMA CMO REMIC 8.5%	1252	1.38

Composition % 12-31-94

Cash	70.5	Preferreds	0.0
Stocks	0.0	Convertibles	0.0
Bonds	29.5	Other	0.0

Coupon Range

	% of Bonds	Rel Obj
0%	0.0	0.00
0% to 8.5%	77.0	1.10
8.5% to 9.5%	0.0	0.00
9.5% to 11%	0.2	0.04
More than 11%	0.1	0.05
Not applicable	22.7	2.98

Tax Analysis

	Tax-Adj Historical Return %	% Pretax Return
3 Yr Avg	1.42	46.1
5 Yr Avg	3.02	58.7
10 Yr Avg	---	---

Potential Capital Gain Exposure (% of assets) -6%

Credit Analysis 12-31-94
% of Bonds

US Govt	42	BB	0
AAA	51	B	0
AA	7	Below B	0
A	0	NR/NA	0
BBB	0		

Most Similar Funds in MF500
Strong Advantage	Weak Fit
Overland Exp Var Rate Govt A	Weak Fit
Scudder Short-Term GlobalInc	Weak Fit

Operations

Address and Telephone	605 Third Avenue 2nd Floor New York, NY 10158-0006 800-877-9700 / 212-476-8800
Advisor	Neuberger & Berman Management
Subadvisor	Neuberger & Berman
Distributor	Neuberger & Berman Management
States Available	All plus PR
Report Grade	C
Income Distrib	Paid Monthly
*Date of Inception	11-07-86
Fiscal Year End	October

Min Initial Purchase	$2000 (Addt'l: $100)
Min IRA Purchase	$250 (Addt'l: $50)
Min Auto Invest Plan	$50 (Systematic Inv: $50)

Expenses & Fees
Sales Fees	0.00% front
	0.00% deferred
	0.00% 12b-1
Management Fee	0.25% max./0.15% min.
3-,5-,10-yr Expense Projections	$21, $36, $81

MORNINGSTAR 1995 Mutual Fund 500

New England Bond Income A

	Ticker	Load	NAV	Yield	SEC Yield	Assets	Objective
	NEFRX	4.50%	10.95	6.6%	7.50%	155.8	Corp General

New England Bond Income Fund - Class A seeks current income consistent with reasonable risk.

The fund normally invests at least 80% of its assets in investment-grade corporate bonds and U.S. government securities. The balance may be invested in unrated or lower-rated bonds. The average weighted maturity of the fund's portfolio usually ranges between five and 15 years. The fund may invest up to 10% of its assets in foreign securities.

Prior to Jan. 9, 1987, the fund was named NEL Income Fund. From that date until April 1, 1992, the fund was named New England Bond Income Fund. From then until April 18, 1994, it was named TNE Bond Income Fund - Class A.

Manager's Investment Style

Management is moderate. To limit interest rate risk, it typically keeps duration between three and 6.5 years. Similarly, management is cautious on credit quality. It often holds large amounts of Treasuries, while its stake in high-yield issues is generally lower than average. Further, management does not deviate far from its chosen path.

Fund Manager(s)

Catherine L. Bunting, since 01-89. Birthdate: 03-58. BA, Dickinson C. 1980

Manager Experience

	Dates Managed	Invest Obj	Std Dev	+/- Index

Not available.

Historical Profile
Return	Average
Risk	Average
Rating	★★★ Neutral

85	80	70	66	44	45	44	38

Investment Style History
Fixed Income
Income Rtn % Rank Obj

Growth of $10,000
IIII Value of Fund ($000)
— Value of Index ($000) LB Govt
▼ Manager Change
▽ Partial Manager Change
► Mgr Unknown After
◄ Mgr Unknown Before

Performance Quartile
(Within Objective)

	1983	1984	1985	1986	1987	1988	1989	1990	1991	1992	1993	1994	History
	10.37	10.45	11.01	11.65	10.98	10.89	11.23	11.12	12.14	12.12	12.18	10.95	NAV
	5.35	11.93	18.51	14.62	2.11	7.36	11.89	7.48	18.13	7.44	11.98	-4.24	Total Return %
	-3.02	-3.22	-3.62	-0.63	-0.65	-0.52	-2.65	-1.47	2.13	0.20	2.23	-1.32	+/- LB Aggregate
	-3.92	-4.69	-5.55	-1.92	-0.45	-1.87	-2.09	0.33	-0.38	-1.25	-0.18	-0.31	+/- LB Corporate
	10.04	11.16	13.15	8.80	7.86	8.18	8.77	8.46	8.96	7.43	6.48	5.86	Income Return %
	-4.69	0.77	5.36	5.81	-5.75	-0.82	3.12	-0.98	9.17	0.02	5.50	-10.10	Capital Return %
	98	18	80	57	41	78	59	17	48	52	51	56	Total Rtn % Rank All
	91	60	75	40	40	75	49	38	25	44	26	62	Total Rtn % Rank Obj
	1.07	1.06	1.25	0.92	0.90	0.88	0.91	0.90	0.90	0.86	0.77	0.72	Income $
	0.00	0.00	0.00	0.00	0.00	0.00	0.00	0.00	0.00	0.02	0.59	0.00	Capital Gains $
	0.86	0.82	0.85	1.02	1.31	1.20	1.18	1.18	1.15	1.08	1.04	1.08	Expense Ratio %
	10.31	10.44	10.63	8.29	8.03	7.68	8.27	8.05	7.69	7.08	6.10	5.97	Income Ratio %
	289	382	217	352	307	88	77	126	218	89	202	79	Turnover Rate %
	34.9	33.7	37.4	46.0	60.1	67.6	76.7	85.4	113.8	145.2	179.3	155.8	Net Assets ($mil)

Performance 12-31-94

	1st Qtr	2nd Qtr	3rd Qtr	4th Qtr	Total
1987	2.74	-2.62	-2.18	4.33	2.11
1988	3.76	1.19	1.93	0.31	7.36
1989	1.15	6.43	0.93	2.97	11.89
1990	-0.76	3.02	0.88	4.21	7.48
1991	3.04	1.57	6.28	6.21	18.13
1992	-1.56	3.94	5.75	-0.70	7.44
1993	5.14	3.10	3.14	0.16	11.98
1994	-3.32	-2.16	1.33	-0.09	-4.24

Bear Market Performance

Decile Rank (5-year period)

Worst _____ Best

	Worst 3 Mo Period 1985-89	Worst 3 Mo Period 1990-94
New England Bond Income A	-3.99	-5.79
+/- LB Aggregate	-0.43	-0.86
+/- Best Fit Index : LB Govt	-0.53	-0.71

Trailing Returns

	Total Return %	+/- LB Aggregate	+/- LB Corp	% Rank All	% Rank Obj	Growth of $10,000
3 Mo	-0.09	-0.47	-0.53	24	58	9,991
6 Mo	1.24	0.25	0.07	34	14	10,124
1 Yr	-4.24	-1.32	-0.31	56	62	9,576
3 Yr Avg	4.84	0.29	-0.58	51	35	11,522
5 Yr Avg	7.91	0.28	-0.36	34	23	14,629
10 Yr Avg	9.32	-0.63	-1.31	67	63	24,373
15 Yr Avg	9.50	-1.31	-1.83	83	90	39,001

Operations

Address and Telephone	399 Boylston Street
	Boston, MA 02116
	800-225-7670 / 617-578-1400
Advisor	Back Bay Advisors
Subadvisor	None
Distributor	New England Funds
States Available	All
Report Grade	B-
Income Distrib	Paid Monthly
Date of Inception	11-07-73
Fiscal Year End	December

Min Initial Purchase	$2500 (Addt'l: $50)
Min IRA Purchase	$250 (Addt'l: $50)
Min Auto Invest Plan	$50 (Systematic Inv: $50)

Expenses & Fees
Sales Fees	4.50% front
	0.00% deferred
	0.25% 12b-1
Management Fee	0.50% max./0.38% min.
3-,5-,10-yr Expense Projections	$77, $100, $166

Risk Analysis

Time Period	Load-Adj Return %	Risk % Rank [1] All	Obj	Morningstar [2] Return	Risk	Morningstar Risk-Adj Rating
1 Yr	-8.55					
3 Yr	3.24	32	70	-0.10 [3]	1.15	★★★
5 Yr	6.92	28	54	0.53 [3]	1.06	★★★
10 Yr	8.82	17	33	0.77 [3]	1.00	★★★

Average Historical Rating (109 months) 2.6 ★s

[1] 1 = low, 100 = high [2] 1.00 = Taxable Avg [3] 1.00 = 90-day T-bill return

Other Measures
			Standard LB Agg	Best Fit LB Govt
Standard Deviation	4.88	Alpha	0.1	0.1
Mean	4.85	Beta	1.19	1.10
Sharpe Ratio	0.27	R-Squared	95	97

Investment Style

Interest-Rate Stance
Avg Effective Duration	4.9 Yrs
Avg Effective Maturity	9.0 Yrs

Quality
Avg Credit Quality	A
Avg Weighted Coupon	8.10%
Avg Weighted Price	98.46% of Par

Diversification Value for Portfolio Types

Large Cap: Medium	Small Cap: High	Bond: None	Balanced: Medium	Diversified: High

Portfolio 06-30-94

Total Stocks: 0
Total Fixed-Income: 57

Amount 000	Date of Maturity		Value $000	% Net Assets
8797	06-15-23	GNMA 7.5%	8407	5.11
7802	02-15-24	GNMA 7%	7200	4.38
6237	05-01-98	Transco Energy 9.125%	6206	3.78
5554	10-15-09	Dow Chemical 8.55%	5890	3.58
6237	07-15-99	Long Island Lighting 7.3%	5724	3.48
5276	2023	GNMA 8.5%	5340	3.25
4774	10-15-09	American General Fin 8.45%	5087	3.09
7197	04-01-02	Govt of Canada 8.5%	4990	3.04
4798	07-01-98	Gulf States Utilities 9.72%	4977	3.03
3838	10-15-02	Intl Bank Reconstr/Dev 12.375%	4945	3.01
4798	07-15-99	US Treasury Note 6.375%	4682	2.85
4606	04-30-99	GMAC 7.15%	4499	2.74
3838	10-01-01	Victorian Pub Auth Fin 8.45%	3999	2.43
3838	02-01-02	Province of Manitoba 7.75%	3857	2.35
3838	05-15-97	US Treasury Note 6.5%	3840	2.34
3838	03-25-99	US WEST Communications 5.64%	3838	2.33
3838	06-04-02	Province of Ontario 7.75%	3824	2.33
3598	07-15-09	Associates North Amer 8.55%	3821	2.32
3838	02-15-99	Ford Motor Credit 5.710%	3809	2.32
4798	10-15-05	Commonwealth Edison 6.4%	3807	2.32
3838	04-01-08	General Electric Cap 5.8%	3723	2.26
3838	09-15-02	Western Publishing Group 7.65%	3291	2.00
2879	05-15-20	Arizona Public Service 10.25%	3262	1.98
4798	06-16-23	Province Brit Columbia 7.75%	3091	1.88
2600	10-01-00	Coastal 10.375%	2861	1.74

Composition % 11-30-94
Cash	5.0	Preferreds	0.0
Stocks	0.0	Convertibles	0.0
Bonds	95.0	Other	0.0

Tax Analysis
	Tax-Adj Historical Return %	% Pretax Return
3 Yr Avg	1.94	38.9
5 Yr Avg	5.09	60.8
10 Yr Avg	6.01	55.1
Potential Capital Gain Exposure (% of assets)		-8%

Most Similar Funds in MF500
Vanguard F/I Interm-Term US	Strong Fit
Scudder Income	Strong Fit
Fidelity Government Secs	Strong Fit

Coupon Range
	% of Bonds	Rel Obj
0%	0.0	0.00
0% to 8.5%	64.9	1.02
8.5% to 9.5%	15.5	0.96
9.5% to 11%	15.1	1.63
More than 11%	4.4	1.14
Not applicable	0.0	0.00

Credit Analysis 11-30-94
% of Bonds
US Govt	8	BB	18
AAA	27	B	0
AA	9	Below B	0
A	20	NR/NA	0
BBB	18		

New Germany

New Germany Fund seeks capital appreciation.
The fund invests at least 65% of its total assets in medium- and smaller-size German companies. The fund may invest up to 20% of assets in securities outside Germany, with no more than 10% in any single country outside Germany. By charter, the fund may engage in currency-hedging transactions, but in practice, it does not.
Board members serve staggered terms to discourage takeover attempts.
The fund completed a fully subscribed rights offering in May 1994. The offering raised $64,725,290, net of approximately $3 million in fees and expenses.

	Ticker	NAV	Mkt Price	Prem/Disc	Yield	Objective
	GF	$14.54	$11.50	-20.9%	1.4%	Europe Stock

64.2	-1.6	0.3	-0.8	-8.7	Highest Prem/Disc
-19.6	-21.7	-17.7	-14.7	-21.5	Lowest Prem/Disc

Historical Profile
Return Average
Risk Average
Rating ★★★
Neutral

Growth of $10,000
■ at NAV ($000)
— at Market Price ($000)

Premium Discount %

	1983	1984	1985	1986	1987	1988	1989	1990	1991	1992	1993	1994	History
	---	---	---	---	---	---	---	12.76	12.63	11.00	14.25	14.54	NAV
	---	---	---	---	---	---	---	-6.64*	-0.35	-11.43	30.49	3.85	NAV Total Return %
	---	---	---	---	---	---	---	-12.65*	-30.84	-19.05	20.43	2.54	+/- S&P 500
	---	---	---	---	---	---	---	---	-12.48	0.74	-2.07	-3.93	+/- MSCI EAFE
	---	---	---	---	---	---	---	---	-8.51	-1.16	-5.15	-0.81	+/- MSCI Germany
	---	---	---	---	---	---	---	1.55*	0.00	1.19	0.94	1.37	Income Return %
	---	---	---	---	---	---	---	-8.19*	-0.35	-12.62	29.55	2.48	Capital Return %
	---	---	---	---	---	---	---	---	96	95	13	7	Total Rtn % Rank All
	---	---	---	---	---	---	---	---	68	47	47	31	Total Rtn % Rank Obj
	---	---	---	---	---	---	---	-23.45*	-3.80	-10.13	41.82	-12.49	Market Total Rtn %
	---	---	---	---	---	---	---	-1.1	-13.2	-13.7	-9.1	-17.0	Avg Prem/Disc %
	---	---	---	---	---	---	---	0.21	0.00	0.14	0.09	0.16	Income $
	---	---	---	---	---	---	---	0.05	0.07	0.04	0.00	0.00	Capital Gains $
	---	---	---	---	---	---	---	1.21	1.13	1.28	1.07	1.06 •	Expense Ratio %
	---	---	---	---	---	---	---	1.65	1.02	1.14	0.93	0.85 •	Income Ratio %
	---	---	---	---	---	---	---	---	49	42	48		Turnover Rate %
	---	---	---	---	---	---	---	358.5	349.7	298.1	386.6	472.6	Net Assets ($mil)

• ratio annualized by Morningstar

Manager's Investment Style
Management differentiates this fund by focusing on the small- and medium-sized stocks of the German market. The fund is therefore prone to the problems of high volatility and low liquidity. Although the fund's prospectus allows management to invest outside of Germany to take advantage of possible developments in Eastern Europe, the fund has so far kept nearly all of its modest non-Germany stakes in Western-European exchanges.

Fund Manager(s)
John Abbink. Since 1-90. BA'76 Michigan State U.; PhD'81 Yale.

Manager Experience

	Dates Managed	Invest Obj	Std Dev	+/- Index
John Abbink				
Germany Fund	02/90 - 12/94	WE	19.30	-5.98
Future Germany	03/90 - 12/94	WE	19.05	-7.61

NAV Performance % 12-30-94

	1st Qtr	2nd Qtr	3rd Qtr	4th Qtr	Total
1987	---	---	---	---	---
1988	---	---	---	---	---
1989	---	---	---	---	---
1990	6.67*	-0.47	-19.85	9.72	-6.64*
1991	-9.25	-1.12	8.24	2.60	-0.35
1992	4.12	4.56	-9.75	-9.86	-11.43
1993	10.45	-4.69	15.40	7.41	30.49
1994	3.23	-2.44	3.15	-0.03	3.85

Bear Market Performance
Decile Rank (5-year period)

Worst   Best

	Worst 3 Mo Period 1985-89	Worst 3 Mo Period 1990-94
New Germany	---	---
+/- S&P 500	---	---

Trailing Returns

	NAV Total Return %	+/- S&P 500	+/- MSCI Germany	% Rank All	Obj	Mkt Total Return %
3 Mo	-0.03	-0.01	-3.66	20	35	-3.88
6 Mo	3.12	-1.74	-2.91	13	31	0.26
1 Yr	3.85	2.54	-0.81	7	31	-12.49
3 Yr Avg	6.27	0.01	-2.13	43	42	3.71
5 Yr Avg	---	---	---	---	---	---
Incept Avg	2.27*	---	---	---	---	-3.92*

Risk Analysis

	Risk % Rank[1]		Morningstar[2]		Morningstar
	All	Obj	Return	Risk	Risk-Adj Rating
3 Yr	82	31	0.35	0.85	★★★
5 Yr	---	---	---	---	---
10 Yr	---	---	---	---	

Average Historical Rating (24 months)   2.4 ★s

[1] 1 = Low, 100 = High   [2] 1.00 = Equity Avg   [3] 1.00 = 90-day T-bill Return

Other Measures

				S&P 500
Standard Deviation	13.56	Alpha		1.93
Mean	7.01	Beta		0.55
Sharpe Ratio	0.26	R-Squared		10

Investment Style

	Stock Portfolio Avg	Rel WS Germany	Rel WS Foreign
Price/Earnings Ratio	32.3	0.92	0.66
Price/Cash Flow Ratio	10.2	1.40	0.70
Price/Book Ratio	2.7	0.69	0.90
5 Yr Earnings Gr %	1.0	0.25	NMF
Return on Assets %	3.5	1.25	0.76
Debt % Total Cap	29.6	1.12	0.91
Med Mkt Cap ($mil)	4422	0.49	0.70

figure is based on less than 50% of stocks

Country Exposure (top five) 12-31-94

Securities %		Currency %	
Germany	83	Germany	83
France	8	France	8
Netherlands	6	Netherlands	6
Denmark	1	Denmark	1
Norway	1	Norway	1

Diversification Value for Portfolio Types

Large Cap: High	Small Cap: High	Bond: High	Balanced: High	Diversified: High

Portfolio 09-30-94

Share Chg (06-94)	Amount	Total Equity: 60 Total Fixed-Income: 10	Value $000	% Total Invest
0	70000	Mannesmann (Germany)	17606	3.38
0	25800	Schering	15869	3.04
0	53000	Volkswagen	14580	2.80
0	29800	Deutsche Pfandbrief-Hypothek	14432	2.77
0	46500	Preussag	13293	2.55
6500	16000	Heidelberger Zement	13132	2.52
0	38700	Veba	12865	2.47
0	24000	Daimler-Benz	11468	2.20
0	56000	Thyssen	10198	1.96
0	47000	Hoechst	10055	1.93
0	17100	Linde	9607	1.84
0	27350	Gehe	9131	1.75
0	15031	Bilfinger & Berger	8299	1.59
4550	50050	LVMH Moet-Henn Louis Vuitton	8257	1.58
0	70000	Akzo	8236	1.58
---	14628	Sto Pfd	8218	1.58
0	74000	VNU	8029	1.54
0	47000	Fag Kugelfischer Schafer	7375	1.41
2917	30000	Berliner Hand-und Frank Bk	7323	1.40
---	20000	Henkel Pfd	7303	1.40
8350	12850	Asko Deutsche Kaufhaus	7136	1.37
0	48000	Peugeot	7120	1.37
0	20100	Vossloh	7113	1.36
0	23000	Degussa	7070	1.36
---	20000	Suedzucker Pfd	7064	1.35

Composition % 12-31-94

Cash	0.6	Preferreds	0.0
Stocks	98.5	Convertibles	0.0
Bonds	0.0	Other	1.0

Tax Analysis

	Tax-Adj Historical Return %	% Pretax Return
3 Yr Avg	5.87	90.9
5 Yr Avg	---	---
10 Yr Avg	---	---
Potential Capital Gain Exposure (% of assets)		6

Most Similar Funds in MF500

Invesco European	Weak Fit
France Growth	Weak Fit
Growth Fund Spain	Weak Fit

Sector Weightings

	% of Stocks
Utilities	1.9
Energy	1.1
Financials	17.8
Industrial Cyclicals	34.7
Consumer Durables	13.6
Consumer Staples	2.3
Services	8.9
Retail	3.1
Health	14.7
Technology	1.9

Operations

Address and Telephone	31 W. 52nd Street
	New York, NY 10019
	212-474-7000 / 800-437-6269
Advisor	Deutsche Asset Management
Subadvisor	N/A
Administrator	Deutsche Bank Securities Corp.
Transfer Agent	Investors Bank & Trust Co.
Custodian	Investors Bank & Trust Co.
Auditor	Price Waterhouse LLP
Legal Counsel	Sullivan & Cromwell

Income Distrib Schedule	Paid Irregularly
Management Fee	0.65%
Reinvestment Plan	Yes
Direct Purchase Plan	No
Shares Outstanding	32,501,483
Exchange	NYSE
*Date of Inception	01-30-90
Shareholder Report	B+

New Perspective

	Ticker	Load	NAV	Yield	SEC Yield	Assets	Objective
	ANWPX	5.75%	14.37	1.5%	1.91%	6540.2	World Stock

New Perspective Fund's primary objective is long-term growth of capital; potential dividend income is a secondary objective.

The fund invests in common stocks of both foreign and domestic companies. It looks for worldwide changes in international trade patterns and economic and political relationships. The fund then searches for companies that may benefit from the new opportunities created by such changes. The advisor attempts to closely follow securities, industries, governments, and currency-exchange markets worldwide.

Manager's Investment Style

Management prefers larger-cap stocks in developed international markets, especially multinational corporations. The fund holds issues with low valuations, and typically keeps large stakes in cash. Turnover is low.

Fund Manager(s)

Management Team

Historical Profile

Return	Above Average	
Risk	Below Average	
Rating	★★★★★	
	Highest	

Investment Style History
Equity
Average % Stocks Held in Portfolio

79% 79% 80% 77% 83% 82% 83% 79%

Growth of $10,000

|||| Value of Fund ($000)
— Value of Index ($000) MSEASEA
▼ Manager Change
▽ Partial Manager Change
► Mgr Unknown After
◄ Mgr Unknown Before

Performance Quartile (Within Objective)

1983	1984	1985	1986	1987	1988	1989	1990	1991	1992	1993	1994	History
8.47	7.56	9.10	9.99	9.89	9.95	11.18	10.24	12.07	12.30	15.01	14.37	NAV
23.57	0.13	34.29	26.83	13.50	10.39	26.09	-2.08	22.64	3.98	26.98	2.97	Total Return %
1.11	-6.14	2.55	8.15	8.24	-6.22	-5.59	1.04	-7.85	-3.64	16.92	1.65	+/- S&P 500
1.64	-4.59	-6.28	-15.06	-2.67	-12.90	9.49	14.94	4.36	9.20	4.47	-2.11	+/- MSCI World
3.44	3.10	2.89	2.34	2.38	3.25	2.83	2.69	2.52	1.65	1.63	1.59	Income Return %
20.14	-2.97	31.40	24.50	11.11	7.14	23.27	-4.77	20.12	2.33	25.34	1.37	Capital Return %
28	65	14	8	7	58	21	62	40	81	10	7	Total Rtn % Rank All
70	41	62	64	9	58	20	11	27	22	66	9	Total Rtn % Rank Obj
0.27	0.24	0.21	0.22	0.24	0.32	0.29	0.30	0.26	0.20	0.21	0.23	Income $
0.60	0.65	0.68	1.25	1.14	0.63	1.01	0.43	0.20	0.05	0.37	0.84	Capital Gains $
0.77	0.76	0.73	0.66	0.64	0.69	0.76	0.82	0.86	0.85	0.87	0.84	Expense Ratio %
3.47	2.90	2.46	2.40	2.06	2.47	2.69	2.55	2.80	1.82	1.40	1.48	Income Ratio %
50	37	27	17	17	21	29	14	8	6	15	25	Turnover Rate %
592.5	609.7	673.1	899.0	975.1	998.8	1276.0	1569.7	2457.8	3320.4	5086.0	6540.2	Net Assets ($mil)

Manager Experience

	Dates Managed	Invest Obj	Std Dev	+/- Index
William C. Newton Amcap	05/67 - 12/76	G	19.09	1.38
Jon B. Lovelace, Jr. Investment Comp of Amer	04/58 - 12/94	GI	13.86	1.41

Performance 12-31-94

	1st Qtr	2nd Qtr	3rd Qtr	4th Qtr	Total
1987	17.82	6.67	10.19	-18.04	13.50
1988	3.94	2.92	-2.19	5.50	10.39
1989	4.02	4.83	11.26	3.94	26.09
1990	-0.72	7.39	-14.04	6.84	-2.08
1991	10.55	-2.70	7.78	5.79	22.64
1992	0.41	3.37	-1.61	1.81	3.98
1993	4.31	2.02	9.22	9.24	26.98
1994	-1.73	-0.62	5.55	-0.11	2.97

Bear Market Performance

Decile Rank (5-year period)

Worst ◄――――――► Best

	Worst 3 Mo Period 1985-89	Worst 3 Mo Period 1990-94
New Perspective	-23.24	-14.04
+/- S&P 500	6.34	-0.30
+/- Best Fit Index : MSEASEA	1.08	2.58

Trailing Returns

	Total Return %	+/- S&P 500	+/- MSCI World	% Rank All	% Rank Obj	Growth of $10,000
3 Mo	-0.11	-0.09	0.62	25	4	9,989
6 Mo	5.44	0.58	4.04	10	5	10,544
1 Yr	2.97	1.65	-2.11	7	9	10,297
3 Yr Avg	10.78	4.51	3.93	11	22	13,594
5 Yr Avg	10.30	1.61	6.63	15	8	16,325
10 Yr Avg	15.95	1.57	1.11	6	12	43,925
15 Yr Avg	15.30	0.82	---	11	1	84,618

Operations

Address and Telephone	333 S. Hope Street Los Angeles, CA 90071 800-421-4120 / 213-486-9200
Advisor	Capital Research & Management
Subadvisor	None
Distributor	American Funds Distributors
States Available	All plus GU,PR,VI
Report Grade	A+
Income Distrib	Paid Semiannually
Date of Inception	03-13-73
Fiscal Year End	September

Risk Analysis

Time Period	Load-Adj Return %	Risk % Rank All	Risk % Rank Obj [1]	Morningstar [2] Return	Morningstar Risk	Morningstar Risk-Adj Rating
1 Yr	-2.95					
3 Yr	8.61	69	18	1.53 [3]	0.77	★★★★
5 Yr	9.00	66	11	1.08 [3]	0.79	★★★★
10 Yr	15.27	50	1	1.55	0.73	★★★★★
Average Historical Rating (109 months)				4.1	★ s	

[1] = low, 100 = high [2] 1.00 = Equity Avg [3] 1.00 = 90-day T-bill return

Other Measures

			Standard S&P 500	Best Fit MSEASEA
Standard Deviation	9.83	Alpha	4.6	2.9
Mean	10.76	Beta	0.93	0.68
Sharpe Ratio	0.74	R-Squared	57	85

Investment Style

	Stock Portfolio Avg	Rel MSCI EAFE	Rel Obj
Price/Earnings Ratio	22.0	0.59	0.89
Price/Cash Flow	14.8	0.95	1.10
Price/Book Ratio	2.9	1.11	0.99
5 Yr Earnings Gr %	4.8	---	0.99
Return on Assets %	7.5	1.66	1.09
Debt % Total Cap	27.2	0.80	0.95
Med Mkt Cap ($mil)	10207	0.86	2.03

Style: V B G / L M S — Size L M S

Diversification Value for Portfolio Types

Large Cap: Low | Small Cap: Medium | Bond: High | Balanced: Low | Diversified: Low

Min / Expenses

Min Initial Purchase	$250 (Addt'l: $50)
Min IRA Purchase	$250 (Addt'l: $50)
Min Auto Invest Plan	$50 (Systematic Inv: $50)

Expenses & Fees

Sales Fees	5.75% front
	0.00% deferred
	0.25% 12b-1
Management Fee	0.60% max./0.40% min.
3-,5-,10-yr Expense Projections	$84, $103, $159
Annual Brokerage Cost	0.11%

Portfolio 09-30-94

Total Stocks: 210
Total Fixed-Income: 13

Share Chg (06-94) 000	Amount 000		Value $000	% Net Assets
35	1850	Telefonos de Mexico L (ADR)	115596	1.84
0	1996	News (ADR)	101037	1.61
930	1860	Caterpillar	100673	1.60
91171	91262	Nestle (Reg)	82895	1.32
42	327	Mannesmann (Germany)	82213	1.31
0	1285	Philip Morris	78546	1.25
0	939	IBM	65260	1.04
75	1035	Intel	63652	1.01
0	1772	Time Warner	62242	0.99
1320	1980	Vodafone Group (ADR)	62123	0.99
13964	13964	Eurotunnel (Paris)	57934	0.92
0	17400	Telecom New Zealand (144A)	55202	0.88
0	30	Munchener Ruckvers (Reg)	54765	0.87
0	970	Microsoft	54441	0.87
9050	10000	Schlumberger	54375	0.87
0	760	Asea CI B	53744	0.86
0	463	Royal Dutch Petroleum (Reg)	49715	0.79
0	1110	Polygram (Netherlands)	48138	0.77
49	1112	Intl Nederlander Groep	48018	0.76
0	1075	BankAmerica	47434	0.76

Regional Exposure 12-31-94

% of Stocks

Europe	43	Pacific Rim	10
Japan	4	U.S.	35
Latin Amer	3	Other	5

Composition % 12-31-94

Cash	21.6	Preferreds	0.0
Stocks	78.0	Convertibles	0.1
Bonds	0.3	Other	0.0

Tax Analysis

	Tax-Adj Historical Return %	% Pretax Return
3 Yr Avg	9.32	85.3
5 Yr Avg	8.70	81.8
10 Yr Avg	13.30	73.2
Potential Capital Gain Exposure (% of assets)		17%

Most Similar Funds in MF500

EuroPacific Growth	Strong Fit
Putnam Global Growth A	Strong Fit
Templeton Growth	Strong Fit

Top 5 Countries 12-31-94

	% of Stocks
U.S.	35
United Kingdom	10
Germany	8
Netherlands	7
France	6

Total Number of Countries: 19
Hedging Policy: Occasional

Sector Weightings

	% of Stocks	Relative S&P 500
Utilities	7.7	0.93
Energy	4.8	0.99
Financials	12.5	0.76
Industrial Cyclicals	19.4	0.83
Consumer Durables	10.0	0.97
Consumer Staples	8.8	1.72
Services	15.5	1.31
Retail	1.8	0.30
Health	5.9	1.13
Technology	13.7	1.54

New York Venture A

	Ticker	Load	NAV	Yield	SEC Yield	Assets	Objective
	NYVTX	4.75%	11.16	1.0%	N/A	1090.5	Growth

New York Venture Fund - Class A seeks growth of capital.

The fund invests predominantly in equity securities of companies with market capitalizations of at least $250 million, but it may also hold issues with smaller capitalizations. The fund may invest up to 10% of its assets in securities of foreign issuers and up to 10% of its assets in restricted securities. It may also lend securities and write covered call options.

Class A shares have front loads; Class B shares have deferred loads, higher 12b-1 fees, and conversion features; Class C shares have level loads.

Manager's Investment Style

Fund manager Shelby Davis seeks long-term holdings in good companies selling at below-market prices. He looks for strong earnings and cash flow, market dominance, and good management. In recent years, the fund has been heavily weighted in financials.

Fund Manager(s)

Shelby M. C. Davis, since 02-69. Birthdate: 03-37. BA, Princeton U. 1958

Manager Experience

	Dates Managed	Invest Obj	Std Dev	+/- Index
Shelby M. C. Davis				
Retirement Plan Growth B	05/84 - 01/87	G	11.33	-8.93
Selected Special	05/93 - 11/94	SC	9.35	-1.60

Historical Profile

Return	Above Average
Risk	Average
Rating	★★★★ Above Average

88% | 86% | 92% | 93% | 95% | 98% | 97% | 96%

Growth of $10,000

- |||| Value of Fund ($000)
- — Value of Index ($000) S&P 500
- ▼ Manager Change
- ▽ Partial Manager Change
- ► Mgr Unknown After
- ◄ Mgr Unknown Before

Investment Style History Equity
Average % Stocks Held in Portfolio

Performance Quartile (Within Objective)

	1983	1984	1985	1986	1987	1988	1989	1990	1991	1992	1993	1994	History
	7.86	7.33	9.04	9.20	6.98	7.64	9.15	8.16	10.51	11.06	11.97	11.16	NAV
	23.03	4.75	37.54	22.00	-1.49	21.38	34.71	-2.90	40.55	12.04	16.09	-1.93	Total Return %
	0.57	-1.52	5.80	3.32	-6.75	4.77	3.03	0.22	10.07	4.42	6.03	-3.24	+/- S&P 500
	-0.43	1.70	4.98	5.90	-3.85	3.44	5.54	3.28	6.34	3.07	4.81	-1.86	+/- Wilshire 5000
	2.04	2.23	2.42	1.01	2.63	3.15	4.98	2.02	2.22	1.55	2.32	1.08	Income Return %
	20.99	2.51	35.12	20.99	-4.12	18.22	29.73	-4.93	38.33	10.49	13.77	-3.00	Capital Return %
	30	52	8	13	71	11	7	64	14	15	25	33	Total Rtn % Rank All
	43	23	7	10	76	19	18	40	32	26	28	51	Total Rtn % Rank Obj
	0.16	0.16	0.18	0.10	0.22	0.22	0.40	0.17	0.19	0.17	0.26	0.12	Income $
	1.64	0.70	0.72	1.68	2.14	0.56	0.70	0.54	0.65	0.53	0.58	0.45	Capital Gains $
	1.05	1.15	1.05	0.99	0.93	1.01	0.97	0.97	0.97	0.91	0.89	0.87	Expense Ratio %
	2.47	2.25	2.33	1.56	1.48	2.42	2.45	3.78	1.84	1.36	0.85	1.19	Income Ratio %
	97	102	75	98	55	38	58	47	52	26	24	13	Turnover Rate %
	86.1	71.2	122.9	146.8	159.2	239.3	308.2	341.9	459.0	547.9	937.7	1090.5	Net Assets ($mil)

Performance 12-31-94

	1st Qtr	2nd Qtr	3rd Qtr	4th Qtr	Total
1987	15.65	0.38	3.98	-18.39	-1.49
1988	6.57	9.26	2.26	1.93	21.38
1989	9.86	9.29	12.03	0.15	34.71
1990	-2.39	5.87	-12.15	6.96	-2.90
1991	15.33	-1.18	10.20	11.91	40.55
1992	-5.76	2.14	9.07	6.71	12.04
1993	8.89	-0.17	10.40	-3.27	16.09
1994	-3.43	1.30	1.88	-1.60	-1.93

Bear Market Performance

Decile Rank (5-year period)

	Worst 3 Mo Period 1985-89	Worst 3 Mo Period 1990-94
New York Venture A	-26.11	-15.12
+/- S&P 500	3.47	-1.28
+/- Best Fit Index : S&P 500	3.47	-1.28

Trailing Returns

	Total Return %	+/- S&P 500	+/- Wil 5000	% Rank All	% Rank Obj	Growth of $10,000
3 Mo	-1.60	-1.58	-0.83	59	56	9,840
6 Mo	0.25	-4.61	-4.37	51	87	10,025
1 Yr	-1.93	-3.24	-1.86	33	51	9,807
3 Yr Avg	8.45	2.19	1.84	18	27	12,756
5 Yr Avg	11.72	3.03	2.91	9	14	17,408
10 Yr Avg	16.75	2.37	2.89	5	6	47,050
15 Yr Avg	17.39	2.90	3.41	2	4	110,735

Operations

Address and Telephone	124 E. Marcy Street
	Santa Fe, NM 87501
	800-279-0279 / 505-983-4335
Advisor	Selected/Venture Advisers
Subadvisor	None
Distributor	Selected/Venture Advisers
States Available	All
Report Grade	B-
Income Distrib	Paid Semiannually
Date of Inception	02-17-69
Fiscal Year End	July

Risk Analysis

Time Period	Load-Adj Return %	Risk % Rank [1] All	Risk % Rank [1] Obj	Morningstar [2] Return	Morningstar Risk	Morningstar Risk-Adj Rating
1 Yr	-6.59					
3 Yr	6.71	84	70	0.93 [3]	1.04	★★★
5 Yr	10.64	80	64	1.54 [3]	0.98	★★★★
10 Yr	16.18	65	34	1.77	0.89	★★★★★
Average Historical Rating (109 months)					4.8	★s

[1] 1 = low, 100 = high [2] 1.00 = Equity Avg [3] 1.00 = 90-day T-bill return

Other Measures

			Standard S&P 500	Best Fit S&P 500
Standard Deviation	11.39	Alpha	1.7	1.7
Mean	8.79	Beta	1.23	1.23
Sharpe Ratio	0.46	R-Squared	74	74

Investment Style

	Stock Portfolio Avg	Relative S&P 500
Price/Earnings Ratio	16.6	0.90
Price/Book Ratio	2.7	0.80
5 Yr Earnings Gr %	12.0	2.16
Return on Assets %	5.5	0.74
Debt % Total Cap	25.7	0.91
Med Mkt Cap ($mil)	6623	0.51

Style Value Blend Growth — Size Large/Med/Small

Diversification Value for Portfolio Types

Large Cap: Low	Small Cap: Medium	Bond: Medium	Balanced: None	Diversified: Low

Expenses & Fees

Sales Fees	4.75% front
	0.00% deferred
	0.25% 12b-1
Management Fee	0.75% max./0.55% min.
3-,5-,10-yr Expense Projections	$75, $94, $152
Annual Brokerage Cost	0.08%

Min Purchase

Min Initial Purchase	$1000 (Addt'l: $25)
Min IRA Purchase	$250 (Addt'l: $25)
Min Auto Invest Plan	$1000 (Systematic Inv: $25)

Portfolio 12-30-94

Total Stocks: 108
Total Fixed-Income: 3

Share Chg (07-94) 000	Amount 000		Value $000	% Net Assets
79	444	Chubb	34390	3.15
190	277	General Re	34299	3.15
79	529	Intel	33746	3.09
-1	654	Coca-Cola	33692	3.09
0	228	Wells Fargo	33020	3.03
556	1525	Archer-Daniels-Midland	31463	2.89
16	513	Morgan Stanley Group	30295	2.78
99	899	Travelers	29223	2.68
-1	799	SunAmerica	28968	2.66
-1	850	First Bank System	28278	2.59
0	275	Hewlett-Packard	27432	2.52
	233	Citicorp Cv Pfd	26870	2.46
-1	469	JP Morgan	26288	2.41
0	300	Pfizer	23147	2.12
0	226	American International Group	22146	2.03
29	600	Burlington Resources	21006	1.93
-50	400	FHLMC	20175	1.85
-1	564	Golden West Financial	19867	1.82
-1	1074	Equitable	19459	1.78
49	674	State Street Boston	19256	1.77
-16	391	Nestle (Reg) (ADR)	18606	1.71
44	494	WR Berkley	18355	1.68
-1	564	SLMA	18340	1.68
34	534	NAC Re	18034	1.65
-1	499	Telefonica de Espana (ADR)	17541	1.61

Composition % 12-31-94

Cash	0.4	Preferreds	0.0
Stocks	92.7	Convertibles	3.0
Bonds	3.9	Other	0.0

Tax Analysis

	Tax-Adj Historical Return %	% Pretax Return
3 Yr Avg	6.54	76.0
5 Yr Avg	9.48	77.3
10 Yr Avg	13.16	65.9
Potential Capital Gain Exposure (% of assets)		16%

Most Similar Funds in MF500

Massachusetts Inv A	Fair Fit
Warburg Pincus Cap Appr	Fair Fit
Liberty All-Star	Weak Fit

Index Allocation

	% of Stocks
S&P 500	63.6
S&P MidCap 400	11.3
U.S. Small Cap	20.9
Foreign	4.2

Sector Weightings

	% of Stocks	Relative S&P 500
Utilities	4.0	0.33
Energy	5.3	0.53
Financials	50.7	4.79
Industrial Cyclicals	2.3	0.14
Consumer Durables	1.5	0.24
Consumer Staples	9.6	0.76
Services	5.5	0.67
Retail	5.0	0.87
Health	5.5	0.64
Technology	10.6	1.16

MORNINGSTAR 1995 Mutual Fund 500

Newport Tiger

	Ticker	Load	NAV	Yield	SEC Yield	Assets	Objective
	NWTRX	5.00%	10.80	0.3%	N/A	455.9	Pacific Stock

Newport Tiger Fund seeks capital appreciation.

The fund invests primarily in equity securities of Hong Kong, Singapore, South Korea, Taiwan, and other nations of Southeast Asia. Securities of companies of any size may be purchased; the portfolio may not represent all economic sectors. Companies that adapt to changing markets and technologies are particularly attractive.

Prior to July 6, 1990, the fund was named Tyndall-Newport Tiger Fund. From this date until March 7, 1991, its name was Tyndall Tiger Fund. On Dec. 28, 1990, Tyndall Far East Fund was merged into this fund.

Manager's Investment Style

Manager John Mussey takes a conservative approach to investing in the Pacific Rim: He favors large-cap companies with 15% to 20% earnings growth and low price multiples relative to Pacific-Rim specialty funds. His approach has led the fund to impressive performances in both bull and bear markets.

Historical Profile

Return	High
Risk	Above Average
Rating	★★★★ Above Average

Investment Style History
Equity
Average % Stocks Held in Portfolio

Average % Stocks Held: 84% 93% 94% 92% 92%

Growth of $10,000
|||| Value of Fund ($000)
— Value of Index ($000) MSPacxJp
▼ Manager Change
▽ Partial Manager Change
► Mgr Unknown After
◄ Mgr Unknown Before

Performance Quartile (Within Objective)

Fund Manager(s)

John M. Mussey CFA, since 05-89. Birthdate: 09-41. BA, U. of Redlands 1963 MBA, U. of California-Berkeley 1965

Manager Experience

	Dates Managed	Invest Obj	Std Dev	+/- Index

Not available.

	1983	1984	1985	1986	1987	1988	1989	1990	1991	1992	1993	1994	History
	---	---	---	---	---	---	5.54	4.65	5.86	7.13	12.44	10.80	NAV
	---	---	---	---	---	---	10.80 *	-15.14	26.02	22.10	75.24	-11.99	Total Return %
	---	---	---	---	---	---	-2.66 *	-12.02	-4.46	14.48	65.19	-13.31	+/- S&P 500
	---	---	---	---	---	---	---	16.45	12.91	15.91	-10.77	-3.09	+/- MSCI FE ex Jpn
	---	---	---	---	---	---	0.00	0.93	0.00	0.43	0.56	0.32	Income Return %
	---	---	---	---	---	---	10.80	-16.06	26.02	21.67	74.68	-12.32	Capital Return %
	---	---	---	---	---	---	---	92	34	3	1	97	Total Rtn % Rank All
	---	---	---	---	---	---	---	30	5	4	25	47	Total Rtn % Rank Obj
	---	---	---	---	---	---	0.00	0.06	0.00	0.03	0.04	0.04	Income $
	---	---	---	---	---	---	0.00	0.00	0.00	0.00	0.01	0.11	Capital Gains $
	---	---	---	---	---	---	3.30	2.88	2.49	1.85	1.56	1.56	Expense Ratio %
	---	---	---	---	---	---	2.01	0.05	-0.40	0.36	0.59	0.78	Income Ratio %
	---	---	---	---	---	---	---	58	59	17	11	---	Turnover Rate %
	---	---	---	---	---	---	4.1	14.5	26.3	98.7	396.2	455.9	Net Assets ($mil)

Performance 12-31-94

	1st Qtr	2nd Qtr	3rd Qtr	4th Qtr	Total
1987	---	---	---	---	---
1988	---	---	---	---	---
1989	---	---	3.72	7.47	10.80 *
1990	0.90	5.92	-23.90	4.34	-15.14
1991	16.99	4.04	-3.89	7.72	26.02
1992	6.48	12.98	-5.11	6.95	22.10
1993	9.40	8.21	8.06	37.00	75.24
1994	-18.65	6.03	10.72	-7.84	-11.99

Bear Market Performance

Decile Rank (5-year period)

Worst ————————————— Best

	Worst 3 Mo Period 1985-89	Worst 3 Mo Period 1990-94
Newport Tiger	---	-23.90
+/- S&P 500	---	-10.15
+/- Best Fit Index : MSPacxJp	---	-12.12

Trailing Returns

	Total Return %	+/- S&P 500	+/- MSCI FE ex Jpn	% Rank All	% Rank Obj	Growth of $10,000
3 Mo	-7.84	-7.83	0.42	96	47	9,216
6 Mo	2.03	-2.83	-3.32	26	7	10,203
1 Yr	-11.99	-13.31	-3.09	97	47	8,801
3 Yr Avg	23.49	17.22	1.86	1	1	18,831
5 Yr Avg	15.03	6.34	8.19	4	1	20,139
10 Yr Avg	---	---	---	---	---	---
15 Yr Avg	---	---	---	---	---	---

Operations

Address and Telephone	1500 Forest Avenue Suite 223 Richmond, VA 23229 800-776-5455
Advisor	Newport Fund Management
Subadvisor	None
Distributor	Newport Distributors
States Available	All
Report Grade	C
Income Distrib	Paid Annually
* Date of Inception	05-30-89
Fiscal Year End	December

Risk Analysis

Time Period	Load-Adj Return %	Risk % Rank [1] All	Risk % Rank [1] Obj	Morningstar [2] Return	Morningstar Risk	Morningstar Risk-Adj Rating
1 Yr	-16.39					
3 Yr	21.39	93	36	6.08 [3]	1.30	★★★★★
5 Yr	13.85	92	23	2.52 [3]	1.21	★★★★
10 Yr	---	---	---	---	---	

Average Historical Rating (32 months)   3.8 ★s

[1] = low, 100 = high [2] 1.00 = Equity Avg [3] 1.00 = 90-day T-bill return

Other Measures

			Standard S&P 500	Best Fit MSPacxJp
Standard Deviation	21.10	Alpha	18.1	5.4
Mean	23.42	Beta	1.09	0.96
Sharpe Ratio	0.94	R-Squared	17	89

Investment Style

	Stock Portfolio Avg	Rel MSCI EAFE	Rel Obj	Style V B G
Price/Earnings Ratio	21.7	0.59	0.68	
Price/Cash Flow	21.6	1.38	1.12	
Price/Book Ratio	3.4	1.32	1.18	
5 Yr Earnings Gr %	25.2	---	2.26	
Return on Assets %	14.4#	3.17	1.80	
Debt % Total Cap	15.8	0.46	0.66	
Med Mkt Cap ($mil)	6002	0.50	1.46	

figure is based on 50% or less of stocks

Diversification Value for Portfolio Types

Large Cap: High	Small Cap: High	Bond: High	Balanced: High	Diversified: High

Expenses & Fees

Sales Fees	5.00% front 0.00% deferred 0.00% 12b-1
Management Fee	1.00% max./0.75% min.
3-,5-,10-yr Expense Projections	$97, $131, $226
Annual Brokerage Cost	0.49%

Min Initial Purchase	$1000 (Addt'l: $100)
Min IRA Purchase	$1000 (Addt'l: $100)
Min Auto Invest Plan	$100 (Systematic Inv: $100)

Portfolio 12-31-94

Share Chg (09-94) 000	Amount 000	Total Stocks: 42 Total Fixed-Income: 1	Value $000	% Net Assets
2500	12000	Hong Kong & China Gas	19386	4.25
400	2500	Hang Seng Bank	17851	3.92
1000	9000	Hong Kong Telecommunications	17099	3.75
0	2000	Keppel (Singapore)	17015	3.73
400	2700	Swire Pacific Cl A	16854	3.70
100	1600	Development Bk Singapore For	16467	3.61
100	1901	Genting	16300	3.58
100	1964	Thai Farmers Bank (For)	15960	3.50
0	258	Siam Cement (For)	15456	3.39
0	800	Singapore Press Hldgs (For)	14545	3.19
0	3500	Cheung Kong Holdings	14249	3.13
100	1300	Hong Kong & Shanghai Banking	14029	3.08
1000	6000	Sime Darby (Malaysia)	13746	3.02
100	2300	Sun Hung Kai Properties	13733	3.01
400	2000	Telecom Malaysia	13550	2.97
200	1291	Overseas Chinese Bkg (For)	13286	2.91
500	5500	Citic Pacific	13257	2.91
1200	2200	City Developments	12302	2.70
500	4500	Hong Kong Electric	12300	2.70
500	2500	Guoco Group	10695	2.35

Index Allocation

	% of Stocks
S&P 500	0.0
S&P MidCap 400	0.0
U.S. Small Cap	1.4
Foreign	98.6

Composition % 12-31-94

Cash	2.0	Preferreds	0.0
Stocks	92.0	Convertibles	0.0
Bonds	6.0	Other	0.0

Tax Analysis

	Tax-Adj Historical Return %	% Pretax Return
3 Yr Avg	23.21	98.6
5 Yr Avg	14.79	97.9
10 Yr Avg	---	---
Potential Capital Gain Exposure (% of assets)		20%

Most Similar Funds in MF500

T. Rowe Price New Asia	Fair Fit
Asia Pacific	Weak Fit
Malaysia Fund	Weak Fit

Country Exposure 12-31-94

	% of Stocks
Hong Kong	42
Singapore	19
Malaysia	15
Thailand	9
Indonesia	4
Total Number of Countries: 8	
Hedging Policy: Occasional	

Sector Weightings

	% of Stocks	Relative S&P 500
Utilities	10.7	1.73
Energy	5.2	3.01
Financials	41.4	1.62
Industrial Cyclicals	11.5	0.52
Consumer Durables	9.1	0.66
Consumer Staples	0.0	0.00
Services	17.9	1.39
Retail	1.7	0.32
Health	1.4	0.81
Technology	1.2	0.15

Nicholas

	Ticker	Load	NAV	Yield	SEC Yield	Assets	Objective
	NICSX	None	48.03	1.4%	N/A	2820.2	Growth

Nicholas Fund seeks long-term capital appreciation. Current income is secondary.

The fund invests substantially in common stocks, issued primarily by small- and mid-cap companies, that are expected to increase in value. However, the fund does not maintain strict limitations on the percentage of assets it may hold in various asset classes. It may invest up to 5% of assets in regulated investment companies and companies with less than three years of operating history. It may invest up to 10% of fund assets in securities of real estate investment trusts. The fund may not sell short, leverage, or participate in a joint trading account.

Manager's Investment Style

Manager Albert Nicholas favors midsize firms with high and steady growth rates that are selling at below-market multiples, either due to market neglect or to short-term corrections. He then keeps turnover low to recognize the full value of these stocks. Nicholas particularly favors financials.

Fund Manager(s)

Albert O. Nicholas CFA(1967), since 07-69.
Birthdate: 01-31. BS, U. of Wisconsin 1952 MBA, U. of Wisconsin 1955

Manager Experience	Dates Managed	Invest Obj	Std Dev	+/- Index
Albert O. Nicholas				
Nicholas II	10/83 - 04/93	SC	14.58	-0.24
Nicholas Limited Edition	05/87 - 04/93	SC	15.69	3.68

Historical Profile

Return	Average
Risk	Below Average
Rating	★★★★ Above Average

Investment Style History
Equity
Average % Stocks Held in Portfolio

	69%	85%	89%	90%	91%	90%	92%	91%

Growth of $10,000

|||| Value of Fund ($000)
— Value of Index ($000) SPMid400
▼ Manager Change
▽ Partial Manager Change
◄ Mgr Unknown After
► Mgr Unknown Before

Performance Quartile (Within Objective)

	1983	1984	1985	1986	1987	1988	1989	1990	1991	1992	1993	1994	History
NAV	25.84	25.84	32.18	34.87	28.94	32.63	38.61	35.76	49.17	52.47	53.64	48.03	NAV
	24.12	10.87	29.65	11.68	-0.75	18.00	24.53	-4.81	41.98	12.63	5.90	-2.84	Total Return %
	1.66	4.61	-2.09	-7.00	-6.01	1.39	-7.15	-1.70	11.50	5.01	-4.16	-4.16	+/- S&P 500
	0.66	7.82	-2.91	-4.41	-3.12	0.06	-4.64	1.37	7.77	3.66	-5.39	-2.77	+/- Wilshire 5000
	2.77	2.89	2.23	2.71	5.76	3.52	2.67	2.05	1.72	1.46	1.59	1.46	Income Return %
	21.35	7.99	27.42	8.98	-6.52	14.48	21.86	-6.86	40.26	11.17	4.31	-4.30	Capital Return %
	27	21	27	75	65	18	25	70	12	14	89	42	Total Rtn % Rank All
	37	6	49	74	73	36	61	53	27	25	76	59	Total Rtn % Rank Obj
	0.64	0.64	0.58	0.88	1.84	1.03	0.92	0.79	0.68	0.68	0.82	0.71	Income $
	1.07	1.58	0.61	0.19	4.03	0.45	1.05	0.23	0.82	2.04	1.05	3.32	Capital Gains $
	0.95	0.87	0.82	0.86	0.86	0.86	0.86	0.82	0.81	0.78	0.76	0.78	Expense Ratio %
	4.05	2.69	3.24	4.11	3.13	3.04	2.84	2.56	2.17	1.60	1.53	1.40	Income Ratio %
	31	22	14	14	27	32	24	21	22	15	10	33	Turnover Rate %
	126.1	153.4	557.1	1181.0	1029.0	1100.0	1386.0	1379.7	2103.1	2668.2	3179.1	2820.2	Net Assets ($mil)

Performance 12-31-94

	1st Qtr	2nd Qtr	3rd Qtr	4th Qtr	Total
1987	14.60	0.80	3.14	-16.70	-0.75
1988	11.09	5.82	0.81	-0.43	18.00
1989	8.09	8.14	7.72	-1.10	24.53
1990	-2.31	7.45	-17.70	10.18	-4.81
1991	20.22	2.57	5.31	9.33	41.98
1992	1.04	-1.86	3.06	10.21	12.63
1993	0.84	-0.01	2.41	2.55	5.90
1994	-4.74	0.79	3.42	-2.16	-2.84

Bear Market Performance

Decile Rank (5-year period)

Worst — Best

	Worst 3 Mo Period 1985-89	Worst 3 Mo Period 1990-94
Nicholas	-21.96	-19.13
+/- S&P 500	7.62	-5.29
+/- Best Fit Index : SPMid400	6.84	-0.71

Trailing Returns

	Total Return %	+/- S&P 500	+/- Wil 5000	% Rank All	% Rank Obj	Growth of $10,000
3 Mo	-2.16	-2.14	-1.39	71	67	9,784
6 Mo	1.19	-3.67	-3.43	34	79	10,119
1 Yr	-2.84	-4.16	-2.77	42	59	9,716
3 Yr Avg	5.04	-1.23	-1.58	47	55	11,588
5 Yr Avg	9.39	0.69	0.57	21	38	15,661
10 Yr Avg	12.71	-1.68	-1.15	31	55	33,070
15 Yr Avg	15.85	1.36	1.87	7	16	90,829

Operations

Address and Telephone	700 N. Water Street Suite 1010	Min Initial Purchase	$500 (Addt'l: $100)
	Milwaukee, WI 53202	Min IRA Purchase	$500 (Addt'l: $100)
	414-272-6133	Min Auto Invest Plan	$500 (Systematic Inv: $50)
Advisor	Nicholas		
Subadvisor	None	**Expenses & Fees**	
Distributor	Nicholas	Sales Fees	0.00% front
States Available	All plus GU,PR,VI		0.00% deferred
Report Grade	C		0.00% 12b-1
Income Distrib	Paid Semiannually	Management Fee	0.75% max./0.65% min.
Date of Inception	07-14-69	3-,5-,10-yr Expense Projections	$25, $43, $97
Fiscal Year End	March	Annual Brokerage Cost	0.09%

Risk Analysis

Time Period	Load-Adj Return %	Risk % Rank [1] All	Obj	Morningstar [2] Return	Morningstar Risk	Morningstar Risk-Adj Rating
1 Yr	-2.84					
3 Yr	5.04	67	27	0.43 [3]	0.74	★★★
5 Yr	9.39	71	32	1.18 [3]	0.85	★★★★
10 Yr	12.71	52	10	1.01	0.76	★★★★

Average Historical Rating (109 months) 4.5 ★s

[1] = low, 100 = high [2] 1.00 = Equity Avg [3] 1.00 = 90-day T-bill return

Other Measures

			Standard S&P 500	Best Fit SPMid400
Standard Deviation	7.94	Alpha	-0.6	-1.2
Mean	5.24	Beta	0.81	0.76
Sharpe Ratio	0.22	R-Squared	65	90

Investment Style

	Stock Portfolio Avg	Relative S&P 500
Price/Earnings Ratio	16.7	0.90
Price/Book Ratio	3.2	0.95
5 Yr Earnings Gr %	16.5	2.97
Return on Assets %	8.4	1.12
Debt % Total Cap	20.0	0.71
Med Mkt Cap ($mil)	2132	0.16

Diversification Value for Portfolio Types

Large Cap: Low	Small Cap: Low	Bond: High	Balanced: Low	Diversified: Low

Portfolio 12-31-94

Share Chg (09-94) 000	Amount 000	Total Stocks: 126 Total Fixed-Income: 0	Value $000	% Net Assets
50	1100	FNMA	80163	2.84
0	1505	FHLMC	76018	2.70
0	950	Pfizer	73388	2.60
0	2430	Mercury General	69863	2.48
0	2026	MGIC Investment	67098	2.38
127	2500	Circuit City Stores	55625	1.97
0	2067	Unifi	52699	1.87
0	350	Wells Fargo	50750	1.80
0	668	Schering-Plough	49439	1.75
0	1039	Tyco International	49329	1.75
0	1819	Heilig-Meyers	45929	1.63
-86	930	Protective Life	45241	1.60
-150	975	Cardinal Health	45216	1.60
0	1402	Aon	44861	1.59
0	1510	A Schulman	41525	1.47
0	898	Walt Disney	41439	1.47
0	2154	Marshall & Ilsley	40926	1.45
0	1148	Torchmark	40033	1.42
0	1857	Watts Industries Cl A	39229	1.39
0	700	Coca-Cola	36050	1.28
0	1090	Abbott Laboratories	35561	1.26
0	732	Fifth Third Bancorp	35112	1.25
0	602	WW Grainger	34777	1.23
0	600	Bristol-Myers Squibb	34725	1.23
248	910	Columbia/HCA Healthcare	33215	1.18

Composition % 12-31-94

Cash	6.8	Preferreds	0.0
Stocks	93.2	Convertibles	0.0
Bonds	0.0	Other	0.0

Tax Analysis

	Tax-Adj Historical Return %	% Pretax Return
3 Yr Avg	3.31	64.6
5 Yr Avg	7.92	81.9
10 Yr Avg	10.68	76.3
Potential Capital Gain Exposure (% of assets)		23%

Most Similar Funds in MF500

Evergreen	Strong Fit
Liberty All-Star	Strong Fit
Gabelli Growth	Fair Fit

Index Allocation

	% of Stocks
S&P 500	46.7
S&P MidCap 400	25.6
U.S. Small Cap	25.3
Foreign	2.4

Sector Weightings

	% of Stocks	Relative S&P 500
Utilities	0.8	0.06
Energy	0.0	0.00
Financials	36.3	3.44
Industrial Cyclicals	9.7	0.59
Consumer Durables	6.4	1.02
Consumer Staples	3.3	0.26
Services	11.7	1.44
Retail	8.6	1.47
Health	21.0	2.42
Technology	2.4	0.26

MORNINGSTAR 1995 Mutual Fund 500

Nicholas II

	Ticker	Load	NAV	Yield	SEC Yield	Assets	Objective
	NCTWX	None	24.46	0.8%	N/A	603.9	Small Company

Nicholas II seeks long-term growth; current income is secondary.

The fund invests primarily in common stocks of companies with potential for consistent growth in earnings and sales. These stocks are frequently small- or mid-cap issues with newer, more-innovative products. Up to 5% of the fund's assets may be invested in companies with less than three years of operating history. Although common stocks make up the bulk of assets, the fund does not maintain minimums or maximums of relative holdings; debt and preferred stocks may also be purchased.

Manager's Investment Style

Manager David Nicholas looks for established firms, stable earnings, and the right price in his equity selections. He won't pay too much for growth nor buy weak firms just because they are cheap. Sector corrections often offer opportunities for Nicholas to load up on firms that post dependable earnings, despite a sector's overall troubles. Turnover is especially low.

Fund Manager(s)

David O. Nicholas CFA, since 04-93. Birthdate: 1961. BBA, U. of Wisconsin 1983 MS, U. of Wisconsin 1987

Manager Experience

	Dates Managed	Invest Obj	Std Dev	+/- Index
David O. Nicholas				
Nicholas Limited Edition	04/93 - 12/94	SC	6.44	-0.20

Historical Profile

Return	Average
Risk	Below Average
Rating	★★★★ Above Average

Investment Style History Equity
Average % Stocks Held in Portfolio

84% 91% 91% 93% 91% 89% 93% 93%

Growth of $10,000

IIII Value of Fund ($000)
— Value of Index ($000) S&P 500
▼ Manager Change
▽ Partial Manager Change
► Mgr Unknown After
◄ Mgr Unknown Before

Performance Quartile (Within Objective)

	1983	1984	1985	1986	1987	1988	1989	1990	1991	1992	1993	1994	History
	10.33	11.79	15.54	16.22	15.69	17.98	20.16	18.42	25.02	26.32	26.32	24.46	NAV
	3.30 *	16.92	33.85	10.35	7.76	17.30	17.66	-6.21	39.56	9.38	6.67	1.03	Total Return %
	5.49 *	10.66	2.11	-8.33	2.50	0.69	-14.02	-3.09	9.08	1.76	-3.39	-0.28	+/- S&P 500
		18.64	1.83	-1.41	11.27	-3.24	-6.28	7.35	-3.89	-2.38	-7.87	3.69	+/- Wilshire 4500
	0.00	0.85	1.39	2.63	2.32	2.13	1.63	1.76	1.18	0.91	1.03	0.85	Income Return %
	3.30	16.07	32.46	7.72	5.44	15.17	16.03	-7.96	38.39	8.47	5.63	0.18	Capital Return %
	---	2	15	83	14	20	41	74	15	28	85	13	Total Rtn % Rank All
	---	1	25	51	11	64	68	30	76	72	90	32	Total Rtn % Rank Obj
	0.00	0.09	0.16	0.42	0.34	0.34	0.31	0.34	0.24	0.24	0.20	0.21	Income $
	0.00	0.19	0.06	0.51	1.30	0.08	0.67	0.14	0.40	0.80	1.47	1.89	Capital Gains $
	---	1.85	1.11	0.79	0.74	0.77	0.74	0.71	0.70	0.66	0.67	0.67	Expense Ratio %
	---	1.98	3.29	2.70	1.37	1.97	1.43	1.78	1.24	1.01	0.79	0.72	Income Ratio %
	---	29	10	15	26	18	8	19	12	11	27	17	Turnover Rate %
	2.6	11.4	140.1	299.0	339.9	361.1	404.4	355.4	557.4	742.3	703.7	603.9	Net Assets ($mil)

Performance 12-31-94

	1st Qtr	2nd Qtr	3rd Qtr	4th Qtr	Total
1987	22.56	2.87	2.74	-16.81	7.76
1988	12.11	5.00	0.60	-0.95	17.30
1989	5.90	6.93	6.88	-2.78	17.66
1990	-3.12	7.58	-17.23	8.73	-6.21
1991	20.79	4.27	2.89	7.70	39.56
1992	0.24	-4.19	2.08	11.56	9.38
1993	-0.30	0.23	2.43	4.21	6.67
1994	-2.93	-0.35	4.91	-0.44	1.03

Bear Market Performance

Decile Rank (5-year period)

Worst — Best

	Worst 3 Mo Period 1985-89	Worst 3 Mo Period 1990-94
Nicholas II	-24.32	-19.54
+/- S&P 500	5.27	-5.70
+/- Best Fit Index : Wil 4500	5.82	-0.14

Trailing Returns

	Total Return %	+/- S&P 500	+/- Wil 4500	% Rank All	% Rank Obj	Growth of $10,000
3 Mo	-0.44	-0.43	2.06	33	41	9,956
6 Mo	4.44	-0.42	0.25	13	58	10,444
1 Yr	1.03	-0.28	3.69	13	32	10,103
3 Yr Avg	5.64	-0.63	-1.97	37	78	11,788
5 Yr Avg	9.06	0.37	-0.03	23	72	15,430
10 Yr Avg	12.98	-1.40	0.35	28	48	33,897
15 Yr Avg	---	---	---	---	---	---

Operations

Address and Telephone	700 N. Water Street Suite 1010
	Milwaukee, WI 53202
	414-272-6133
Advisor	Nicholas
Subadvisor	None
Distributor	Nicholas
States Available	All plus GU,PR,VI
Report Grade	D
Income Distrib	Paid Annually
* Date of Inception	10-17-83
Fiscal Year End	September

Risk Analysis

Time Period	Load-Adj Return %	Risk % Rank All	Risk % Rank Obj	Morningstar Return	Morningstar Risk	Morningstar Risk-Adj Rating
1 Yr	1.03					
3 Yr	5.64	65	20	0.61[3]	0.73	★★★
5 Yr	9.06	69	12	1.09[3]	0.82	★★★★
10 Yr	12.98	56	5	1.06	0.81	★★★★

Average Historical Rating (99 months) 3.8 ★s

[1] 1 = low, 100 = high [2] 1.00 = Equity Avg [3] 1.00 = 90-day T-bill return

Other Measures

	Standard S&P 500	Best Fit Wil 4500
Standard Deviation	8.45	
Mean	5.85	
Sharpe Ratio	0.28	
Alpha	0.5	-1.0
Beta	0.64	0.77
R-Squared	36	80

Investment Style

	Stock Portfolio Avg	Relative S&P 500
Price/Earnings Ratio	19.2	1.04
Price/Book Ratio	2.6	0.76
5 Yr Earnings Gr %	19.1	3.45
Return on Assets %	7.9	1.06
Debt % Total Cap	19.1	0.68
Med Mkt Cap ($mil)	799	0.06

Style
Value Blend Growth
Size Large Med Small

Diversification Value for Portfolio Types

Large Cap: Medium	Small Cap: Low	Bond: High	Balanced: Medium	Diversified: Medium

Expenses & Fees

Sales Fees	0.00% front
	0.00% deferred
	0.00% 12b-1
Management Fee	0.75% max./0.50% min.
3-,5-,10-yr Expense Projections	$21, $37, $83
Annual Brokerage Cost	0.06%

Min Initial Purchase $1000 (Addt'l: $100)
Min IRA Purchase $1000 (Addt'l: $100)
Min Auto Invest Plan $1000 (Systematic Inv: $50)

Portfolio 12-31-94

Share Chg (09-94) 000	Amount 000	Total Stocks: 73 Total Fixed-Income: 0	Value $000	% Net Assets
0	1033	Health Management Assoc Cl A	25824	4.28
0	964	Keane	22887	3.79
0	763	Vivra	21354	3.54
0	390	Vishay Intertechnology	19115	3.17
0	369	Cardinal Health	17101	2.83
0	599	Firstar	16087	2.66
0	611	Unifi	15581	2.58
0	515	A Schulman	14169	2.35
0	633	Fiserv	13599	2.25
0	216	Tootsie Roll Industries	13304	2.20
0	388	MGIC Investment	12836	2.13
0	347	Teleflex	12317	2.04
-3	251	Protective Life	12205	2.02
0	464	Mutual Risk Management	12191	2.02
0	304	Block Drug Cl A	11535	1.91
-190	593	Marshall & Ilsley	11265	1.87
0	7	First National Bk Anchorage	11105	1.84
0	494	Expeditors Intl Washington	10745	1.78
0	495	Watts Industries Cl A	10457	1.73
0	220	Forest Laboratories	10258	1.70
0	543	Consolidated Stores	10104	1.67
0	275	United Wisconsin Services	9848	1.63
0	435	Circuit City Stores	9679	1.60
0	694	First Financial (WI)	9537	1.58
0	441	Newell	9258	1.53

Composition % 12-31-94

Cash	4.7	Preferred	0.0
Stocks	95.3	Convertibles	0.0
Bonds	0.0	Other	0.0

Tax Analysis

	Tax-Adj Historical Return %	% Pretax Return
3 Yr Avg	3.79	66.1
5 Yr Avg	7.57	81.1
10 Yr Avg	11.36	80.9
Potential Capital Gain Exposure (% of assets)		31%

Most Similar Funds in MF500

Evergreen	Fair Fit
Vanguard Index Extended Mkt	Fair Fit
Nicholas	Fair Fit

Index Allocation

	% of Stocks
S&P 500	6.8
S&P MidCap 400	26.5
U.S. Small Cap	61.2
Foreign	5.5

Sector Weightings

	% of Stocks	Relative S&P 500
Utilities	0.0	0.00
Energy	0.0	0.00
Financials	20.1	1.91
Industrial Cyclicals	12.4	0.76
Consumer Durables	7.2	1.15
Consumer Staples	3.6	0.28
Services	8.2	1.19
Retail	11.1	1.91
Health	26.5	3.05
Technology	10.9	1.19

Nicholas Income

	Ticker	Load	NAV	Yield	SEC Yield	Assets	Objective
	NCINX	None	3.21	9.4%	N/A	140.9	Corp Hi Yld

Nicholas Income Fund seeks current income, consistent with preservation of capital. It also looks for improvement in income flow.

The fund may invest in senior or fixed-income securities such as bonds, debentures, and preferred stocks; senior securities convertible into common stocks; and common stocks. It may invest in debt securities rated as low as B and in unrated securities. At least 10%, but not more than 50%, of the fund's assets are invested in securities of electric-utility companies and systems.

Nicholas Company has been the fund's advisor since November 1977.

Manager's Investment Style

By charter, management tends toward safety. It cannot venture into the lowest-rated high-yield debt. It is allowed to buy nonrated issues, though it cannot dip below B credits. By choice, management passes up more-volatile instruments such as zeros and PIKs, in order to keep the fund's interest-rate risk low. As far as sectors are concerned, management favors recession-resistant areas, with at least 10% of the assets allocated to electric utilities, by charter.

Fund Manager(s)

Albert O. Nicholas CFA(1967), since 11-77.
Birthdate: 01-31. BS, U. of Wisconsin 1952 MBA, U. of Wisconsin 1955

Manager Experience

	Dates Managed	Invest Obj	Std Dev	+/- Index
Albert O. Nicholas				
Nicholas II	10/83 – 04/93	SC	14.58	-0.24
Nicholas Limited Edition	05/87 – 04/93	SC	15.69	3.68

Performance 12-31-94

	1st Qtr	2nd Qtr	3rd Qtr	4th Qtr	Total
1987	4.32	-1.41	-1.47	1.17	2.53
1988	5.22	2.38	2.19	1.33	11.55
1989	1.90	2.30	-0.09	-0.21	3.94
1990	0.58	1.75	-3.68	0.41	-1.03
1991	8.64	5.29	3.65	3.79	23.05
1992	2.40	2.80	3.24	1.52	10.33
1993	5.03	2.64	2.27	2.46	12.95
1994	-1.99	0.40	1.32	0.12	-0.17

Bear Market Performance

Decile Rank (5-year period)

	Worst 3 Mo Period 1985-89	Worst 3 Mo Period 1990-94
Nicholas Income	-2.72	-7.12
+/- LB Aggregate	-3.54	-7.86
+/- Best Fit Index : FB HY	---	6.99

Trailing Returns

	Total Return %	+/- LB Aggregate	+/- FB High-Yield	% Rank All	% Rank Obj	Growth of $10,000
3 Mo	0.12	-0.26	0.16	18	13	10,012
6 Mo	1.44	0.45	-0.11	31	8	10,144
1 Yr	-0.17	2.75	0.80	21	9	9,983
3 Yr Avg	7.55	3.00	-3.61	23	94	12,440
5 Yr Avg	8.66	1.04	-4.41	27	89	15,151
10 Yr Avg	9.30	-0.64	---	68	67	24,342
15 Yr Avg	10.06	-0.75	---	77	77	42,128

Operations

Address and Telephone	700 N. Water Street Suite 1010		
	Milwaukee, WI 53202		
	414-272-6133		
Advisor	Nicholas		
Subadvisor	None		
Distributor	Nicholas		
States Available	All plus GU,PR,VI		
Report Grade	D		
Income Distrib	Paid Quarterly		
Date of Inception	05-01-30		
Fiscal Year End	December		

Min Initial Purchase	$500 (Addt'l: $100)	
Min IRA Purchase	$500 (Addt'l: $100)	
Min Auto Invest Plan	$500 (Systematic Inv: $50)	

Expenses & Fees

Sales Fees	0.00% front	
	0.00% deferred	
	0.00% 12b-1	
Management Fee	0.50% max./0.30% min.	
3-,5-,10-yr Expense Projections	$20, $35, $77	

Historical Profile

Return	Average	
Risk	Low	
Rating	★★★★	
	Above Average	

| 15 | 97 | 97 | 67 | 92 | 97 | 93 | 41 |

Growth of $10,000

	Value of Fund ($000)
	Value of Index ($000) LB Agg
▼	Manager Change
▽	Partial Manager Change
►	Mgr Unknown After
◄	Mgr Unknown Before

Performance Quartile (Within Objective)

1983	1984	1985	1986	1987	1988	1989	1990	1991	1992	1993	1994	History
3.67	3.65	3.96	4.01	3.64	3.68	3.44	3.01	3.34	3.38	3.52	3.21	NAV
12.33	12.70	21.29	11.43	2.53	11.55	3.94	-1.03	23.05	10.33	12.95	-0.17	Total Return %
3.96	-2.45	-0.83	-3.82	-0.22	3.67	-10.61	-9.97	7.05	3.08	3.20	2.75	+/- LB Aggregate
---	---	---	-4.21	-3.99	-3.99	0.12	3.55	5.35	-20.70	-6.33	-5.95	0.80	+/- FB High-Yield
12.60	13.25	12.80	10.17	11.76	10.45	10.46	11.47	12.09	9.13	8.81	8.63	Income Return %
-0.27	-0.54	8.49	1.26	-9.23	1.10	-6.52	-12.50	10.96	1.20	4.14	-8.81	Capital Return %
68	14	64	77	38	49	96	58	40	20	42	21	Total Rtn % Rank All
87	7	64	70	38	77	14	9	96	99	98	9	Total Rtn % Rank Obj
0.44	0.44	0.42	0.38	0.47	0.37	0.38	0.40	0.35	0.30	0.29	0.30	Income $
0.00	0.00	0.00	0.00	0.00	0.00	0.00	0.00	0.00	0.00	0.00	0.00	Capital Gains $
1.00	1.00	1.00	0.96	0.86	0.83	0.81	0.77	0.76	0.69	0.62	0.59	Expense Ratio %
12.09	12.82	12.57	10.22	9.79	10.03	10.46	11.74	10.70	9.23	8.42	8.68	Income Ratio %
19	14	12	20	48	12	40	40	28	56	39	36	Turnover Rate %
14.6	16.9	34.8	48.0	69.6	78.2	75.4	60.6	79.9	119.1	158.3	140.9	Net Assets ($mil)

Investment Style History
Fixed Income
Income Rtn % Rank Obj

Risk Analysis

Time Period	Load-Adj Return %	Risk % Rank [1] All	Obj	Morningstar [2] Return	Risk	Morningstar Risk-Adj Rating
1 Yr	-0.17					
3 Yr	7.55	3	4	1.19[3]	0.23	★★★★
5 Yr	8.66	15	4	0.99[3]	0.32	★★★★
10 Yr	9.30	7	1	0.53	0.29	★★★★
Average Historical Rating (109 months)				3.4	★s	

[1] 1 = low, 100 = high [2] 1.00 = Hybrid Avg [3] 1.00 = 90-day T-bill return

Other Measures

		Standard LB Agg	Best Fit FB HY
Standard Deviation	3.19	Alpha	3.3	-0.6
Mean	7.35	Beta	0.57	0.62
Sharpe Ratio	1.20	R-Squared	51	69

Investment Style

Interest-Rate Stance

Avg Effective Duration	4.1 Yrs
Avg Effective Maturity	7.0 Yrs

Maturity Short Intm Long

Quality

Avg Credit Quality	B
Avg Weighted Coupon	9.63%
Avg Weighted Price	93.28% of Par

Diversification Value for Portfolio Types

Large Cap: Medium	Small Cap: High	Bond: Low	Balanced: Medium	Diversified: Medium

Portfolio 12-31-94

Total Stocks: 0
Total Fixed-Income: 53

Amount 000	Date of Maturity		Value $000	% Net Assets
5000	01-30-02	Cablevision Industries 10.75%	4975	3.53
5000	12-15-03	Canandaigua Wine 8.75%	4550	3.23
4000	05-15-00	Delta Air Lines 9.875%	3979	2.82
4250	03-15-01	Fort Howard 9.25%	3963	2.81
4500	11-15-03	Coca-Cola Bottling 9%	3938	2.79
4220	03-01-01	Stater Brothers Hldgs 11%	3798	2.70
4550	12-01-96	Southwestern Life 11.25%	3777	2.68
4000	12-01-02	Flagstar 10.875%	3735	2.65
4000	10-01-00	Best Buy 8.625%	3585	2.54
4150	12-15-01	Sequa 8.75%	3579	2.54
3860	12-31-03	Beverly Enterprises 8.75%	3542	2.51
3500	06-01-01	Chiquita Brands Intl 11.5%	3430	2.43
3500	04-15-00	Food 4 Less Supermkts 10.45%	3413	2.42
3250	12-01-01	Rowan 11.875%	3380	2.40
4000	03-15-03	Long Island Lighting 7.05%	3266	2.32
3750	05-01-03	Borg-Warner Security 9.125%	3178	2.26
3250	06-01-01	American Standard 9.875%	3161	2.24
3000	09-15-96	Unisys 9.75%	3020	2.14
3000	04-15-04	Charter Medical 11.25%	3000	2.13
3000	04-01-99	Owens-Illinois 10.25%	2985	2.12
3100	08-15-01	American Annuity Group 9.5%	2930	2.08
3000	06-01-03	ARA Group 8.5%	2805	1.99
3000	08-01-00	Royal Crown 9.75%	2670	1.89
2800	03-15-01	Outboard Marine 8.625%	2630	1.87
3000	08-01-02	Cleveland Elec Illum 7.625%	2605	1.85

Composition % 12-31-94

Cash	3.7	Preferreds	0.0
Stocks	10.4	Convertibles	0.4
Bonds	85.4	Other	0.0

Tax Analysis

	Tax-Adj Historical Return %	% Pretax Return
3 Yr Avg	4.26	54.7
5 Yr Avg	5.14	55.3
10 Yr Avg	5.29	47.0
Potential Capital Gain Exposure (% of assets)		-16%

Most Similar Funds in MF500

Janus Flexible Income	Fair Fit
Putnam Diversified Income A	Fair Fit
Lord Abbett Bond-Debenture	Fair Fit

Coupon Range

	% of Bonds	Rel Obj
0%, PIK	0.0	0.00
0% to 11%	88.5	1.80
11% to 13%	11.5	0.35
13% to 14.5%	0.0	0.00
More than 14.5%	0.0	0.00
Not applicable	0.0	0.00

Credit Analysis 12-31-94
% of Bonds

US Govt	0	BB	31
AAA	0	B	58
AA	0	Below B	0
A	0	NR/NA	5
BBB	6		

MORNINGSTAR 1995 Mutual Fund 500

Nicholas Limited Edition

	Ticker	Load	NAV	Yield	SEC Yield	Assets	Objective
	NCLEX	Clsd	17.09	0.6%	N/A	142.6	Small Company

Nicholas Limited Edition seeks long-term growth. Current income is a small consideration.

The fund invests primarily in common stocks, including those of smaller companies, companies with limited operating histories, and companies that are out of favor. The fund may also invest in lower-quality debt securities. The fund maintains no minimum or maximum percentage on relative holdings of equity and debt issues.

After 10 million shares were issued and outstanding (not counting those acquired through reinvestment), the fund was closed to additional purchases on Nov. 25, 1991.

Manager's Investment Style

Manager David Nicholas tries to buy industry-leading stocks with aggressive and sustainable earnings growth at prices at or below market multiples. As long as growth rates remain stable, he will hold the stock through rough periods.

Fund Manager(s)

David O. Nicholas CFA, since 04-93. Birthdate: 1961. BBA, U. of Wisconsin 1983 MS, U. of Wisconsin 1987

Manager Experience	Dates Managed	Invest Obj	Std Dev	+/- Index
David O. Nicholas				
Nicholas II	04/93 - 12/94	SC	7.45	1.40

Historical Profile

Return	Above Average
Risk	Below Average
Rating	★★★★
	Closed

Investment Style History
Equity

Average % Stocks Held in Portfolio: 78% 91% 87% 90% 85% 95% 94% 93%

Growth of $10,000

- |||| Value of Fund ($000)
- — Value of Index ($000) Russ 2000
- ▼ Manager Change
- ▽ Partial Manager Change
- ► Mgr Unknown After
- ◄ Mgr Unknown Before

Performance Quartile (Within Objective)

	1983	1984	1985	1986	1987	1988	1989	1990	1991	1992	1993	1994	History
	---	---	---	---	9.15	11.29	12.49	12.03	16.86	18.77	18.68	17.09	NAV
	---	---	---	---	-7.58 *	27.26	17.36	-1.73	43.22	16.78	9.03	-3.04	Total Return %
	---	---	---	---	4.38 *	10.65	14.32	1.39	12.74	9.17	-1.03	-4.36	+/- S&P 500
	---	---	---	---		6.72	-6.58	11.83	-0.23	5.03	-5.51	-0.39	+/- Wilshire 4500
	---	---	---	---	0.92	0.93	1.19	0.99	0.84	0.44	0.47	0.61	Income Return %
	---	---	---	---	-8.50	26.33	16.18	-2.72	42.38	16.34	8.56	-3.65	Capital Return %
	---	---	---	---	---	4	41	61	11	8	74	44	Total Rtn % Rank All
	---	---	---	---	---	14	70	24	67	33	83	65	Total Rtn % Rank Obj
	---	---	---	---	0.09	0.10	0.15	0.12	0.12	0.08	0.09	0.10	Income $
	---	---	---	---	0.00	0.25	0.62	0.12	0.24	0.83	1.68	0.91	Capital Gains $
	---	---	---	---	1.48	1.32	1.12	1.07	0.94	0.92	0.88	0.88	Expense Ratio %
	---	---	---	---	2.21	1.03	1.37	1.10	1.05	0.45	0.42	0.50	Income Ratio %
	---	---	---	---	0	31	31	15	13	24	24	14	Turnover Rate %
	---	---	---	---	19.3	33.0	54.2	70.9	175.3	190.2	180.8	142.6	Net Assets ($mil)

Performance 12-31-94

	1st Qtr	2nd Qtr	3rd Qtr	4th Qtr	Total
1987	---	---	4.63	-12.97	-7.58 *
1988	14.97	6.94	-0.27	3.78	27.26
1989	5.49	3.95	7.11	-0.07	17.36
1990	-1.20	8.02	-18.45	12.92	-1.73
1991	21.86	2.32	6.53	7.82	43.22
1992	3.44	-6.71	5.59	14.61	16.78
1993	0.96	-0.32	4.55	3.62	9.03
1994	-2.19	-3.45	2.89	-0.21	-3.04

Bear Market Performance

Decile Rank (5-year period)

Worst ———— Best

	Worst 3 Mo Period 1985-89	Worst 3 Mo Period 1990-94
Nicholas Limited Edition	---	-20.48
+/- S&P 500		-6.64
+/- Best Fit Index : Russ 2000		5.41

Trailing Returns

	Total Return %	+/- S&P 500	+/- Wil 4500	% Rank All	% Rank Obj	Growth of $10,000
3 Mo	-0.21	-0.19	2.29	28	40	9,979
6 Mo	2.67	-2.19	-1.52	22	76	10,267
1 Yr	-3.04	-4.36	-0.39	44	65	9,696
3 Yr Avg	7.27	1.01	-0.33	25	64	12,345
5 Yr Avg	11.68	2.99	2.59	10	49	17,376
10 Yr Avg	---	---	---	---	---	---
15 Yr Avg	---	---	---	---	---	---

Risk Analysis

Time Period	Load-Adj Return %	Risk % Rank [1] All	Obj	Morningstar [2] Return	Morningstar Risk	Morningstar Risk-Adj Rating
1 Yr	-3.04					
3 Yr	7.27	64	14	1.11 [3]	0.71	★★★
5 Yr	11.68	67	11	1.84 [3]	0.80	★★★★
10 Yr	---	---	---	---		

Average Historical Rating (56 months) 4.3 ★s

[1] 1 = low, 100 = high [2] 1.00 = Equity Avg [3] 1.00 = 90-day T-bill return

Other Measures

			Standard S&P 500	Best Fit Russ 2000
Standard Deviation	8.96	Alpha	2.2	-1.3
Mean	7.44	Beta	0.61	0.65
Sharpe Ratio	0.44	R-Squared	29	73

Investment Style

	Stock Portfolio Avg	Relative S&P 500
Price/Earnings Ratio	18.4	1.00
Price/Book Ratio	2.9	0.84
5 Yr Earnings Gr %	19.4	3.50
Return on Assets %	9.9	1.32
Debt % Total Cap	21.3	0.75
Med Mkt Cap ($mil)	359	0.03

Style Value Blend Growth — Size Large Med Small

Diversification Value for Portfolio Types

Large Cap: Medium	Small Cap: Low	Bond: High	Balanced: Medium	Diversified: Medium

Portfolio 12-31-94

Total Stocks: 61
Total Fixed-Income: 0

Share Chg (09-94) 000	Amount 000		Value $000	% Net Assets
0	369	Keane	8769	6.15
0	225	Heartland Express	6758	4.74
0	241	Analysts International	4946	3.47
0	173	Vivra	4830	3.39
-20	241	Juno Lighting	4278	3.00
0	83	Vishay Intertechnology	4089	2.87
0	88	Cardinal Health	4058	2.85
0	224	Brandon Systems	4008	2.81
0	38	Intl Speedway	3845	2.70
0	141	Firstar	3784	2.65
0	250	Treadco	3750	2.63
0	177	Arnold Industries	3664	2.57
0	99	United Wisconsin Services	3535	2.48
-60	125	A Schulman	3442	2.41
0	366	Jason	3290	2.31
0	119	National Health Investors	3109	2.18
0	138	Poe & Brown	3002	2.10
0	91	River Forest Bancorp	2988	2.10
71	180	Mercury Finance	2342	1.64
0	50	Forest Laboratories	2331	1.63
-38	169	First Financial (WI)	2320	1.63
0	128	Lunar	2304	1.62
0	80	Marcus	2240	1.57
0	245	AutoFinance Group	2144	1.50
0	85	Respironics	2019	1.42

Composition % 12-31-94

Cash	7.3	Preferreds	0.0
Stocks	92.7	Convertibles	0.0
Bonds	0.0	Other	0.0

Tax Analysis

	Tax-Adj Historical Return %	% Pretax Return
3 Yr Avg	5.34	72.1
5 Yr Avg	10.19	84.7
10 Yr Avg	---	---
Potential Capital Gain Exposure (% of assets)		31%

Most Similar Funds in MF500

Nicholas II	Fair Fit
20th Century Heritage Invest	Fair Fit
Columbia Growth	Fair Fit

Index Allocation

	% of Stocks
S&P 500	
S&P MidCap 400	15.5
U.S. Small Cap	83.9
Foreign	0.6

Sector Weightings

	% of Stocks	Relative S&P 500
Utilities	0.0	0.00
Energy	0.0	0.00
Financials	23.9	2.26
Industrial Cyclicals	5.5	0.34
Consumer Durables	9.8	1.57
Consumer Staples	0.0	0.00
Services	23.7	2.91
Retail	2.9	0.49
Health	18.6	2.14
Technology	15.7	1.71

Operations

Address and Telephone	700 N. Water Street Suite 1010 Milwaukee, WI 53202 414-272-6133
Advisor	Nicholas
Subadvisor	None
Distributor	Nicholas
States Available	All plus GU,PR,VI
Report Grade	C+
Income Distrib	Paid Annually
* Date of Inception	05-18-87
Fiscal Year End	December

Min Initial Purchase	Closed (Addt'l: $100)
Min IRA Purchase	$2000 (Addt'l: $100)
Min Auto Invest Plan	$2000 (Systematic Inv: $50)

Expenses & Fees

Sales Fees	0.00% front
	0.00% deferred
	0.00% 12b-1
Management Fee	0.75% flat fee
3-,5-,10-yr Expense Projections	$28, $49, $108
Annual Brokerage Cost	0.08%

Northeast Investors

	Ticker	Load	NAV	Yield	SEC Yield	Assets	Objective
	NTHEX	None	9.55	10.3%	8.98%	554.6	Corp Hi Yld

Northeast Investors Trust seeks income. Capital appreciation is secondary.

The fund invests primarily in securities of established companies, including bonds, preferred stocks, dividend-paying common stocks, convertibles, and warrants. Because the fund does not impose any particular ratings standards, its portfolio has generally included debt securities rated below investment grade. Many holdings are unrated. The fund may borrow money (up to 25% of its assets) in order to make additional investment purchases.

Historical Profile
Return	Above Average
Risk	Low
Rating	★★★★
	Highest

Investment Style History
Fixed Income

Income Rtn % Rank Obj

| | 77 | 22 | 32 | 14 | 33 | 13 | 14 | 9 |

Growth of $10,000
- ||| Value of Fund ($000)
- — Value of Index ($000) LB Agg
- ▼ Manager Change
- ▽ Partial Manager Change
- ► Mgr Unknown After
- ◄ Mgr Unknown Before

Performance Quartile (Within Objective)

Manager's Investment Style
Management dabbles in both equities and fixed-income securities. On the equity side, it targets large, established, low-multiple stocks, while the fixed-income holdings tend to be lower credit quality or nonrated.

Fund Manager(s)
Ernest E. Monrad, since 06-60. Birthdate: 05-30. BA, Harvard 1951 LLB, U. of Virginia 1956

Bruce H. Monrad CFA(1992), since 01-93. Birthdate: 02-62. BA, Harvard 1984 MBA, Harvard 1989

Manager Experience	Dates Managed	Invest Obj	Std Dev	+/- Index
Not available.				

	1983	1984	1985	1986	1987	1988	1989	1990	1991	1992	1993	1994	History
	11.49	11.39	12.68	13.70	11.83	11.89	10.43	8.14	8.83	9.21	10.29	9.55	NAV
	11.25	13.07	25.64	20.36	0.14	14.05	0.02	-9.17	26.38	17.49	23.60	2.20	Total Return %
	2.88	-2.09	3.51	5.11	-2.62	6.17	-14.52	-18.12	10.38	10.24	13.85	5.12	+/- LB Aggregate
	---	---	---	4.73	-6.39	2.62	-0.37	-2.79	-17.37	0.83	4.70	3.18	+/- FB High-Yield
	12.63	13.94	14.31	12.32	10.72	13.54	12.30	12.78	17.90	13.18	11.87	9.39	Income Return %
	-1.37	-0.87	11.33	8.04	-10.59	0.51	-12.28	-21.96	8.48	4.30	11.73	-7.19	Capital Return %
	73	13	44	19	59	31	98	82	33	7	12	9	Total Rtn % Rank All
	95	3	6	1	75	30	44	46	86	43	8	3	Total Rtn % Rank Obj
	1.45	1.46	1.46	1.46	1.46	1.54	1.49	1.40	1.30	1.11	1.00	0.98	Income $
	0.00	0.00	0.00	0.00	0.46	0.00	0.00	0.00	0.00	0.00	0.00	0.00	Capital Gains $
	1.60	1.34	1.34	1.24	1.47	1.41	1.33	1.47	1.89	1.44	1.21	1.06	Expense Ratio %
	12.42	12.92	12.70	11.53	11.59	13.16	12.68	14.35	15.38	12.36	10.53	9.37	Income Ratio %
	30	14	22	43	52	17	34	21	34	59	76	73	Turnover Rate %
	169.9	168.3	218.1	342.8	337.0	408.1	339.2	243.2	304.6	399.1	548.6	554.6	Net Assets ($mil)

Performance 12-31-94
	1st Qtr	2nd Qtr	3rd Qtr	4th Qtr	Total
1987	5.12	-1.01	-2.05	-1.75	0.14
1988	6.43	2.49	3.09	1.42	14.05
1989	1.01	2.02	0.34	-3.26	0.02
1990	-5.39	2.92	-3.16	-3.68	-9.17
1991	3.09	9.31	8.37	3.49	26.38
1992	8.04	4.59	4.19	-0.22	17.49
1993	8.44	5.02	2.30	6.09	23.60
1994	2.94	0.40	1.21	-2.29	2.20

Bear Market Performance
Decile Rank (5-year period)

Worst — Best

	Worst 3 Mo Period 1985-89	Worst 3 Mo Period 1990-94
Northeast Investors	-7.06	-7.51
+/- LB Aggregate	-7.88	-8.26
+/- Best Fit Index : FB HY	---	6.59

Trailing Returns
	Total Return %	+/- LB Aggregate	+/- FB High-Yield	% Rank All	% Rank Obj	Growth of $10,000
3 Mo	-2.29	-2.67	-2.25	74	73	9,771
6 Mo	-1.11	-2.10	-2.66	75	50	9,889
1 Yr	2.20	5.12	3.18	9	3	10,220
3 Yr Avg	14.07	9.52	2.91	5	7	14,841
5 Yr Avg	11.24	3.62	-1.83	11	34	17,035
10 Yr Avg	11.40	1.45	---	44	19	29,425
15 Yr Avg	11.83	1.02	---	56	22	53,487

Risk Analysis
Time Period	Load-Adj Return %	Risk % Rank [1] All	Risk % Rank [1] Obj	Morningstar [2] Return	Morningstar Risk	Morningstar Risk-Adj Rating
1 Yr	2.20					
3 Yr	14.07	7	26	3.35 [3]	0.34	★★★★★
5 Yr	11.24	43	36	1.71 [3]	0.52	★★★★★
10 Yr	11.40	23	9	0.93	0.39	★★★★
Average Historical Rating (109 months)					3.7	★ s

[1] 1 = low, 100 = high [2] 1.00 = Hybrid Avg [3] 1.00 = 90-day T-bill return

Other Measures
			Standard LB Agg	Best Fit FB HY
Standard Deviation	5.63	Alpha	9.6	2.3
Mean	13.39	Beta	0.65	1.05
Sharpe Ratio	1.75	R-Squared	21	65

Investment Style

Interest-Rate Stance
		Maturity
Avg Effective Duration	4.1 Yrs	Short Intm Long
Avg Effective Maturity	7.1 Yrs	

Quality
Avg Credit Quality B

Avg Weighted Coupon 10.54%
Avg Weighted Price 86.88% of Par

Diversification Value for Portfolio Types
| Large Cap: High | Small Cap: High | Bond: High | Balanced: High | Diversified: High |

Portfolio 09-30-94
Total Stocks: 34
Total Fixed-Income: 90

Amount 000	Date of Maturity		Value $000	% Net Assets
26636	06-30-98	Mesa Capital 0%	23506	4.04
300		Bankers Trust New York	20025	3.44
300		JP Morgan	18225	3.13
18000	07-15-01	Genmar Holdings 13.5%	17910	3.08
250		Chubb	17781	3.05
20395	12-01-01	Envirodyne Industries 10.25%	16520	2.84
30000	08-01-03	MAXXAM Group 12.25%	15900	2.73
15000	10-01-04	Aztar 13.75%	14850	2.55
14000	10-01-07	Acadia Partners 13%	14298	2.46
16000	05-15-05	Gaylord Container 12.75%	13440	2.31
13500	07-31-03	US Leather 10.25%	12015	2.06
12195	03-15-99	Darling-Delaware 14%	11707	2.01
15700	11-01-02	Tiphook Finance 10.75%	11618	2.00
16000	06-15-01	Trump Plaza Funding 10.875%	11440	1.97
12994	06-30-03	Natl Convenience Stores 9.5%	11305	1.94
12871	03-01-17	JP Stevens 9%	11166	1.92
12000	12-01-03	Plastic Specialties 11.25%	11040	1.90
14592	06-01-99	JPS Textile Group 10.85%	10944	1.88
600		Vons	10800	1.86
11049	10-20-99	American Financial 10%	10676	1.83
17000	12-31-95	Olympia & York 10.375%	10200	1.75
10130	02-01-03	Kaiser Aluminium/Chem 12.75%	9877	1.70
9639	11-15-99	Rexene 9%	9639	1.66
9293	09-15-01	Southwest Forest Inds 12.125%	9386	1.61
15869	12-01-03	Indspec Chemical 11.5%	9363	1.61

Composition % 12-31-94
Cash	-10.7	Preferreds	0.0
Stocks	21.2	Convertibles	87.2
Bonds	0.0	Other	2.2

Tax Analysis
	Tax-Adj Historical Return %	% Pretax Return
3 Yr Avg	9.92	67.7
5 Yr Avg	6.74	54.8
10 Yr Avg	6.48	45.0

Potential Capital Gain Exposure (% of assets) -21%

Most Similar Funds in MF500
IDS Extra Income	Weak Fit
Putnam High Yield Adv A	Weak Fit
Liberty High-Income Bond A	Weak Fit

Coupon Range
	% of Bonds	Rel Obj
0%, PIK	9.7	1.31
0% to 11%	43.9	0.90
11% to 13%	32.3	0.97
13% to 14.5%	13.7	2.52
More than 14.5%	0.0	0.00
Not applicable	0.4	0.12

Credit Analysis 12-31-94
% of Bonds
US Govt	0	BB	12
AAA	0	B	32
AA	0	Below B	24
A	0	NR/NA	31
BBB	2		

Operations
Address and Telephone	50 Congress Street Boston, MA 02109 800-225-6704 / 617-523-3588
Advisor	Northeast Investors Trustees
Subadvisor	None
Distributor	Northeast Investors Trust
States Available	All
Report Grade	C
Income Distrib	Paid Quarterly
Date of Inception	08-01-50
Fiscal Year End	September

Min Initial Purchase	$1000 (Addt'l: None)
Min IRA Purchase	$500 (Addt'l: None)
Min Auto Invest Plan	$1000 (Systematic Inv: None)

Expenses & Fees
Sales Fees	0.00% front
	0.00% deferred
	0.00% 12b-1
Management Fee	0.50% flat fee
3-,5-,10-yr Expense Projections	$23, $42, $92

MORNINGSTAR 1995 Mutual Fund 500

Nuveen Municipal Bond

	Ticker	Load	NAV	Yield	SEC Yield	Assets	Objective
	NUVBX	4.75%	8.65	5.8%	5.62%	2590.8	Muni Nat

Nuveen Municipal Bond Fund seeks current income exempt from federal taxes, consistent with capital preservation.

The fund normally invests at least 80% of its assets in investment-grade municipal bonds. Up to 10% of the fund's assets may be invested in unrated securities deemed to be of comparable quality. The fund intends to maintain an average weighted maturity of 20 to 30 years; the average maturity may be shortened from time to time depending on market conditions. It may invest up to 20% of its assets in bonds subject to the Alternative Minimum Tax, but has no present intention of doing so.

Manager's Investment Style

Management typically favors a premium-coupon strategy that yields a competitive payout. Its yield-curve posture is, however, conservative relative to the fund's peer group. Aside from building a portfolio with short duration, management takes a value tack and emphasizes sectors and states that are suffering from supply and demand imbalances and narrowing yield spreads. Management does generally allocate approximately 10% of assets to Illinois bonds, because the fund is headquartered in Chicago.

Fund Manager(s)

Thomas C. Spalding CFA(1979), since 07-78.
Birthdate: 07-51. BA, U. of Michigan 1973 MBA, U. of Michigan 1975

Manager Experience

	Dates Managed	Invest Obj	Std Dev	+/- Index
Thomas C. Spalding				
Nuv Muni Value	06/87 - 12/94	MN	4.36	-0.49
Nuv Prem Muni Inc	01/92 - 12/94	MN	7.38	1.84

Historical Profile

Return	Average
Risk	Below Average
Rating	★★★★
	Above Average

	45	55	43	82	75	41	41	16

Growth of $10,000

|||| Value of Fund ($000)
— Value of Index ($000) LB Muni
▼ Manager Change
▽ Partial Manager Change
►◄ Mgr Unknown After
◄■ Mgr Unknown Before

Investment Style History
Fixed Income
Income Rtn % Rank Obj

Performance Quartile (Within Objective)

	1983	1984	1985	1986	1987	1988	1989	1990	1991	1992	1993	1994	History
	7.28	7.31	8.24	8.96	8.38	8.59	8.87	8.77	9.11	9.25	9.41	8.65	NAV
	9.90	8.75	21.41	19.19	2.10	10.40	10.88	5.69	10.72	8.49	8.60	-1.85	Total Return %
	1.53	-6.41	-0.72	3.94	-0.66	2.52	-3.66	-3.25	-5.28	1.25	-1.16	1.07	+/- LB Aggregate
	1.85	-1.81	1.38	-0.13	0.59	0.24	0.09	-1.61	-1.42	-0.33	-3.68	3.76	+/- LB Muni
	8.08	8.33	8.68	7.63	6.97	7.45	7.26	6.39	6.37	6.33	5.79	5.48	Income Return %
	1.82	0.41	12.72	11.56	-4.87	2.95	3.62	-0.70	4.35	2.16	2.81	-7.33	Capital Return %
	80	33	63	25	42	58	65	38	87	39	76	33	Total Rtn % Rank All
	43	57	21	31	18	60	13	77	72	50	88	13	Total Rtn % Rank Obj
	0.57	0.58	0.58	0.60	0.60	0.60	0.60	0.55	0.53	0.55	0.52	0.51	Income $
	0.00	0.00	0.00	0.21	0.15	0.04	0.03	0.04	0.04	0.05	0.10	0.08	Capital Gains $
	0.75	0.74	0.73	0.71	0.68	0.65	0.64	0.62	0.60	0.62	0.61	0.62	Expense Ratio %
	7.81	7.91	7.68	6.95	6.85	7.11	6.85	6.78	6.48	6.24	5.95	5.49	Income Ratio %
	78	44	28	39	16	8	12	8	10	15	14	15	Turnover Rate %
	272.2	337.6	459.5	668.1	764.0	993.4	1183.5	1399.5	1754.0	2216.4	2683.0	2590.8	Net Assets ($mil)

Performance 12-31-94

	1st Qtr	2nd Qtr	3rd Qtr	4th Qtr	Total
1987	2.25	-3.88	-0.54	4.44	2.10
1988	2.24	2.39	2.81	2.58	10.40
1989	1.04	5.99	0.21	3.33	10.88
1990	-0.35	2.30	0.09	3.58	5.69
1991	1.81	2.34	3.35	2.83	10.72
1992	0.92	3.46	2.15	1.72	8.49
1993	2.73	2.35	2.12	1.14	8.60
1994	-3.15	1.18	0.54	-0.37	-1.85

Bear Market Performance

Decile Rank (5-year period)

Worst   Best

	Worst 3 Mo Period 1985-89	Worst 3 Mo Period 1990-94
Nuveen Municipal Bond	-6.64	-3.44
+/- LB Aggregate	-3.09	1.49
+/- Best Fit Index : LB Muni	-0.15	2.32

Trailing Returns

	Total Return %	+/- LB Aggregate	+/- LB Muni	% Rank All	% Rank Obj	Growth of $10,000
3 Mo	-0.37	-0.75	1.06	32	10	9,963
6 Mo	0.16	-0.83	1.41	54	13	10,016
1 Yr	-1.85	1.07	3.76	33	13	9,815
3 Yr Avg	4.96	0.42	0.09	49	30	11,564
5 Yr Avg	6.24	-1.39	-0.54	70	50	13,533
10 Yr Avg	9.36	-0.58	-0.06	66	23	24,473
15 Yr Avg	8.01	-2.79	-0.46	92	45	31,784

Operations

Address and Telephone	333 W. Wacker Drive
	Chicago, IL 60606
	800-351-4100 / 312-917-7844
Advisor	Nuveen Advisory
Subadvisor	None
Distributor	John Nuveen & Company
States Available	All
Report Grade	B-
Income Distrib	Paid Monthly
Date of Inception	11-29-76
Fiscal Year End	February

Min Initial Purchase	$1000 (Addt'l: $100)
Min IRA Purchase	N/A
Min Auto Invest Plan	$1000 (Systematic Inv: $25)

Expenses & Fees

Sales Fees	4.75% front
	0.00% deferred
	0.00% 12b-1
Management Fee	0.50% max./0.43% min.
3-,5-,10-yr Expense Projections	$66, $80, $121

Risk Analysis

Time Period	Load-Adj Return %	Risk % Rank All	Risk % Rank Obj	Morningstar Return	Morningstar Risk	Morningstar Risk-Adj Rating
1 Yr	-6.51					
3 Yr	3.27	6	13	0.81	0.58	★★★★
5 Yr	5.21	6	15	0.78	0.67	★★★
10 Yr	8.83	5	19	1.02	0.78	★★★★
Average Historical Rating (109 months)					3.5	★s

[1] 1 = low, 100 = high   [2] 1.00 = Muni Avg   [3] 1.00 = 90-day T-bill return

Other Measures

			Standard LB Agg	Best Fit LB Muni
Standard Deviation	3.77	Alpha	0.7	0.5
Mean	4.92	Beta	0.69	0.67
Sharpe Ratio	0.37	R-Squared	53	96

Investment Style

Interest-Rate Stance

Avg Effective Maturity	19.0 Yrs

Quality

Avg Credit Quality	AA
Avg Weighted Coupon	6.83%
Avg Weighted Price	96.80% of Par

Diversification Value for Portfolio Types

Large Cap: Medium	Small Cap: High	Bond: Low	Balanced: Medium	Diversified: Medium

Portfolio 12-31-94

Total Stocks: 0
Total Fixed-Income: 210

Amount 000	Date of Maturity		Value $000	% Net Assets
51290	03-01-11	IL Du Page GO Wtr Com 7.875%	53814	2.08
54980	06-15-27	IL Metro Pier/Expo McCormick Expsn 6.5%	51471	1.99
50000	01-01-33	VA Hsg Dev Sngl Fam Mtg 7.15%	50263	1.94
53810	01-01-12	NC East Muni Pwr Sys 6.25%	48794	1.88
41500	10-01-16	MI Hosp Fin Harper Grace/Huron Vlly 10%	43809	1.69
51070	07-01-15	WA Pub Pwr Sply Sys Proj #3 5.375%	42107	1.63
40595	01-01-03	NE Consumers Pub Pwr Dist 5.1%	40463	1.56
49000	08-15-23	MI Hosp Fin 5.5%	38272	1.48
34500	09-15-16	KY Carroll Poll Cntrl Util Proj 7.45%	35945	1.39
33700	10-01-09	FL Orlando Util Com Wtr/Elec 8.5%	35244	1.36
31000	05-01-22	FL Hillsborough Indl Dev Poll Cntrl 8%	33931	1.31
32080	07-01-14	UT Intermountain Pwr Spcl Obl 7.875%	33612	1.30
33576	07-01-13	WA Chelan PUD #1 5%	33019	1.27
30945	11-01-31	CO Hsg Fin Sngl Fam Mtg 7.25%	31302	1.21
27600	03-01-15	CA Hlth Fac Fin O'Connor Hosp 9.25%	29285	1.13
26950	01-01-14	FL North Broward Hosp Dist M/C 8%	28465	1.10
27250	12-01-23	AK Hsg Fin Genl Purp 6.6%	28450	1.10
28075	07-01-14	PA Philadelphia Hosp/Higher Educ 7.25%	28101	1.08
33620	11-15-25	IL Hlth Fac 5.5%	27599	1.07
29670	08-01-02	MA State GO 4.7%	27126	1.05

Credit Analysis % of Bonds 12-31-94

US Govt	0	BB	0
AAA	33	B	0
AA	38	Below B	0
A	25	NR/NA	1
BBB	3		

Composition % of Assets 12-31-94

Cash	0.4	Preferreds	0.0
Stocks	0.0	Convertibles	0.0
Bonds	99.6	Other	0.0

Tax Analysis

	Tax-Adj Historical Return %	% Pretax Return
3 Yr Avg	4.72	94.9
5 Yr Avg	6.04	96.4
10 Yr Avg	9.13	96.5
Potential Capital Gain Exposure (% of assets)		-1%

Most Similar Funds in MF500

Nuv Muni Value	Strong Fit
Sit Tax-Free Income	Strong Fit
Franklin Fed Tax-Free Income	Strong Fit

Coupon Range

	% Bonds	Rel Obj
0%	0.8	0.33
0% to 6.8%	44.4	0.74
6.8% to 7.5%	19.1	1.23
7.5% to 8.3%	18.4	2.08
More than 8.3%	16.0	1.81
Not applicable	1.3	0.33

Sector Weightings

	% Bonds	Rel Obj
General Obl	10.49	0.50
Utilities	24.64	1.97
Health	16.18	1.23
Water/Waste	8.15	1.28
Housing	15.47	2.11
Education	1.67	0.26
Transportation	8.43	0.83
COP/Lease	3.10	0.97
Private	7.13	0.61
Misc Revenue	4.74	0.95
Demand	0.00	0.00

Top 5 States % of Bonds

IL	16.09	NY	7.08
CA	12.08	FL	5.26
WA	7.64		

Nuveen Municipal Value

	Ticker	NAV	Mkt Price	Prem/Disc	Yield	Objective
	NUV	$9.79	$9.38	-4.2%	7.0%	Muni National

Nuveen Municipal Value Fund seeks current income exempt from regular federal income tax. Enhancing portfolio value is a secondary consideration.

Normally, the fund invests 80% of assets in tax-exempt municipal obligations rated BBB or better. It may invest half of the remaining 20% of assets in comparably valued nonrated obligations and the other half in obligations rated no lower than BB. The fund emphasizes investments in municipal securities that are, in the opinion of the advisor, undervalued. The fund emphasizes long maturities, although in defensive periods it may make high-quality short-term investments.

To discourage takeover attempts, board members serve staggered terms, and supermajority voting requirements govern takeovers, liquidations, and mergers.

The fund completed a rights offering in January 1994. The offering was 47% subscribed, raising $255,645,000.

Historical Profile

Return	Below Average
Risk	Below Average
Rating ★★★	
	Neutral

| | | | | 7.0 | 1.4 | 1.1 | 2.3 | 5.8 | 8.9 | 9.5 | 3.3 | Highest Prem/Disc |
| | | | | -13.3 | -4.9 | -2.5 | -1.6 | 0.4 | 3.7 | -5.1 | -7.9 | Lowest Prem/Disc |

Growth of $10,000
■ at NAV ($000)
— at Market Price ($000)

Premium Discount %

1983	1984	1985	1986	1987	1988	1989	1990	1991	1992	1993	1994	History
---	---	---	---	9.52	9.85	10.19	10.11	10.48	10.69	10.84	9.79	NAV
---	---	---	---	3.47*	11.59	11.45	6.67	11.56	8.73	8.33	-1.62	NAV Total Return %
---	---	---	---	---	3.71	-3.09	-2.27	-4.44	1.49	-1.42	1.30	+/- LB Aggregate
---	---	---	---	---	1.43	0.67	-0.63	-0.58	-0.08	-3.94	3.99	+/- LB Muni
---	---	---	---	1.65*	7.86	7.68	7.32	7.39	6.64	6.33	6.37	Income Return %
---	---	---	---	1.82*	3.73	3.78	-0.65	4.17	2.09	2.01	-7.99	Capital Return %
---	---	---	---	---	55	50	30	79	55	89	18	Total Rtn % Rank All
---	---	---	---	---	60	13	36	62	65	90	10	Total Rtn % Rank Obj
---	---	---	---	-16.16*	27.46	11.88	8.85	15.50	10,23	-2.56	-1.57	Market Total Rtn %
---	---	---	---	-0.8	-1.9	-0.3	0.4	3.5	5.6	5.1	-0.7	Avg Prem/Disc %
---	---	---	---	0.15	0.70	0.72	0.71	0.71	0.71	0.69	0.66	Income $
---	---	---	---	0.00	0.02	0.03	0.01	0.05	0.01	0.06	0.03	Capital Gains $
---	---	---	---	0.80	0.94	0.89	0.88	0.83	0.79	0.74	0.70	Expense Ratio %
---	---	---	---	4.99	7.12	7.13	7.15	6.98	6.84	6.45	6.31	Income Ratio %
---	---	---	---	---	42	7	5	7	4	8	7	Turnover Rate %
---	---	---	---	1445.1	1559.1	1624.0	1620.3	1701.7	1759.4	1807.2	1919.0	Net Assets ($mil)

Manager's Investment Style

As the fund's minuscule turnover ratio suggests, management takes a buy-and-hold approach to the municipal-bond market. The portfolio therefore features older, less-interest-rate-sensitive higher-coupon bonds. In typical Nuveen style, the fund buys undervalued munis and holds on for the long term. Attention to quality is key: Management rarely dabbles in below-investment-grade and nonrated fare.

Fund Manager(s)

Thomas C. Spalding, CFA. Since 6-87. BA'73 U. of Michigan; MBA'75 U. of Michigan.

Manager Experience

	Dates Managed	Invest Obj	Std Dev	+/- Index
Thomas C. Spalding				
Nuveen Municipal Bond	07/78 - 12/94	MN	7.31	-2.66
Nuv Prem Muni Inc	01/92 - 12/94	MN	7.38	1.84

NAV Performance % 12-30-94

	1st Qtr	2nd Qtr	3rd Qtr	4th Qtr	Total
1987	---	0.00*	-3.10	6.78	3.47*
1988	1.92	2.62	3.56	3.02	11.59
1989	0.99	6.94	-0.30	3.51	11.45
1990	0.09	2.41	0.18	3.89	6.67
1991	1.87	2.57	3.85	2.81	11.56
1992	0.73	3.67	2.33	1.76	8.73
1993	2.54	2.18	1.96	1.41	8.33
1994	-2.63	0.53	0.73	-0.21	-1.62

Bear Market Performance

Decile Rank (5-year period)

Worst ━━━ Best

	Worst 3 Mo Period 1985-89	Worst 3 Mo Period 1990-94
Nuv Muni Value	---	-3.33
+/- LB Aggregate	---	1.60

Trailing Returns

	NAV Total Return %	+/- LB Agg	+/- LB Muni	% Rank All	% Rank Obj	Mkt Total Return %
3 Mo	-0.21	-0.59	1.22	22	5	-4.35
6 Mo	0.51	-0.48	1.76	33	12	-5.16
1 Yr	-1.62	1.30	3.99	18	10	-1.57
3 Yr Avg	5.04	0.49	0.17	66	71	1.87
5 Yr Avg	6.64	-0.99	-0.13	71	53	5.86
Incept Avg	7.90*	---	---	---	---	6.33*

Operations

Address and Telephone	333 W. Wacker Drive
	Chicago, IL 60606
	312-917-7700 / 800-257-8787
Advisor	Nuveen Advisory Corporation
Subadvisor	N/A
Administrator	N/A
Transfer Agent	United States Trust Co. New York
Custodian	United States Trust Co. New York
Auditor	Ernst & Young LLP
Legal Counsel	Schiff Hardin & Waite

Income Distrib Schedule	Paid Monthly
Management Fee	0.40%, 4.25%l
Reinvestment Plan	Yes
Direct Purchase Plan	Yes
Shares Outstanding	194,516,213
Exchange	NYSE
*Date of Inception	06-17-87
Shareholder Report	B-

Risk Analysis

	Risk % Rank[1] All	Risk % Rank[1] Obj	Morningstar[2] Return	Morningstar[2] Risk	Morningstar Risk-Adj Rating
3 Yr	6	18	0.78	0.47	★★★★
5 Yr	9	30	0.87	0.69	★★★
10 Yr					
Average Historical Rating (55 months)				2.5 ★s	

[1] = Low, 100 = High   [2] 1.00 = Muni Avg   [3] 1.00 = 90-day T-bill Return

Other Measures

				LB Muni
Standard Deviation	3.56	Alpha		0.60
Mean	4.99	Beta		0.63
Sharpe Ratio	0.41	R-Squared		93

Investment Style

Interest-Rate Stance

	Fund	Relative Objective
Avg Effective Maturity	22.1 Yrs	1.01
Avg Weighted Coupon	7.68%	1.01
Avg Weighted Price	99.2% Par	0.98

Quality

Avg Credit Quality	AA

Credit Analysis 12-31-94

	% of Bonds		% of Bonds
AAA	42	BB	0
AA	16	B	1
A	22	Below B	0
BBB	16	NR/NA	4

Diversification Value for Portfolio Types

Large Cap: Medium	Small Cap: High	Bond: Low	Balanced: Medium	Diversified: High

Portfolio 12-31-94

Amount 000	Total Equity: 0 Total Fixed-Income: 206	Maturity	Value $000	% Total Invest
51930	SC Piedmont Muni Pwr Elec 7.25%	01-01-22	52600	2.80
45015	UT Intermountain Pwr Spcl Obl 7.875%	07-01-14	47164	2.51
24265	TX Austin Combined Util Sys 12.5%	11-15-07	38001	2.02
37625	NC East Muni Pwr Sys 7.25%	01-01-21	37883	2.01
28900	MA Muni Whlse Elec Pwr Sply Sys 8.75%	07-01-18	31656	1.68
31240	CO Denver Arpt Sys 8.5%	11-15-23	31555	1.68
28845	TX Houston Wtr/Swr Sys 8.125%	12-01-17	31522	1.68
29750	UT Intermountain Pwr Sply 7%	07-01-23	30118	1.60
28105	GA Burke Dev Poll Cntrl Pwr 10.5%	11-01-15	29899	1.59
28070	MA Hsg Fin Multi-Fam 8.8%	08-01-21	29661	1.58
26815	NC Muni Pwr #1 Catawba Elec 8.5%	01-01-17	28196	1.50
25710	TX Muni Pwr 8%	09-01-12	27346	1.45
31025	CO Denver Arpt Sys 6.75%	11-15-22	26687	1.42
29205	CO Denver Arpt Sys 7%	11-15-25	25844	1.37
22865	LA Pub Fac South Baptist Hosp 8%	05-15-12	25609	1.36
23610	NC East Muni Pwr Sys 7.75%	01-01-15	24926	1.32
22755	UT Intermountain Pwr Sply 7.75%	07-01-17	24013	1.28
22390	KY Dev Fin Good Samaritan Hosp 10.25%	12-01-11	23861	1.27
21850	FL Jacksonville Elec St John Rvr 7.5%	10-01-14	22575	1.20
20730	NC East Muni Pwr Sys 7.5%	01-01-15	21950	1.17

Composition % 12-31-94

Cash	0.0	Preferreds	0.0
Stocks	0.0	Convertibles	0.0
Bonds	100.0	Other	0.0

Tax Analysis

	Tax-Adj Historical Return %	% Pretax Return
3 Yr Avg	5.21	92.0
5 Yr Avg	6.71	95.2
10 Yr Avg	---	---
Potential Capital Gain Exposure (% of assets)		3

Most Similar Funds in MF500

Nuveen Municipal Bond	Strong Fit
Sit Tax-Free Income	Strong Fit
Franklin High-Yld T/F Inc	Strong Fit

Top Five States

	% of Bonds
Texas	16.70
Utah	12.14
Colorado	8.36
North Carolina	7.48
Massachusetts	7.32

Coupon Range

	% of Bonds	Relative Objective
0%	0.8	0.4
0% to 6%	20.0	1.7
6% to 7.5%	24.6	0.7
7.5% to 8.5%	26.4	1.2
More than 8.5%	27.7	1.0
Not applicable	0.3	0.1

1.0 = Objective Average

Sector Weightings

	% of Bonds	Rel Muni Avg
General Obligation	1.62	0.18
Utilities	40.77	4.14
Health	19.23	0.91
Water/Sewer	5.90	1.10
Housing	5.79	0.49
Education	2.19	0.55
Transportation	10.77	1.10
COP/Lease	3.30	0.59
Private	8.09	0.50
Demand	0.02	0.02
Miscellaneous	2.33	0.38
AMT	13.16	
Prerefunded	35.52	

M❍RNINGSTAR 1995 Mutual Fund 500

Oak Hall Equity

	Ticker	Load	NAV	Yield	SEC Yield	Assets	Objective
	OHEFX	None	11.38	0.0%	N/A	20.3	Small Company

Oak Hall Equity Fund seeks capital appreciation.

The fund normally invests at least 65% of its assets in common stock and securities convertible into common stock rated B or higher. These issuers have above-average growth potential or attractive valuations. To select securities, the fund employs a company-by-company analysis. It emphasizes industries that may be experiencing an upswing in the economic cycle and seeks a minimum of downside risk. The fund may invest up to 15% of its assets in high-risk corporate debt and up to 30% of its assets in foreign issues. These issues may be denominated in foreign currency or may be ADRs.

Manager's Investment Style

Management defies easy categorization. During the fund's two-year life, though, it has tended toward a value-oriented contrarian style, which is nonetheless unusual. Most recently the portfolio shows a large chunk of gold-mining and natural-resources stocks intended as inflation hedges. Management has placed the rest of its assets on a range of market castaways that show rebound potential, as indicated by strong management incentives, changing industry circumstances, or interest from other investors.

Fund Manager(s)

John C. Hathaway CFA, since 07-92. Birthdate: 07-41. BA, Harvard 1963 MBA, U. of Virginia 1967

Manager Experience

	Dates Managed	Invest Obj	Std Dev	+/- Index
John C. Hathaway				
Target Small Cap Value	01/93 - 12/94	SC	12.71	3.55

Historical Profile

Return ---
Risk ---
Rating
Not Rated

Investment Style History
Equity
Average % Stocks Held in Portfolio

Growth of $10,000
|||| Value of Fund ($000)
— Value of Index ($000)
S&P 500
▼ Manager Change
▽ Partial Manager Change
► Mgr Unknown After
◄ Mgr Unknown Before

Performance Quartile (Within Objective)

	1983	1984	1985	1986	1987	1988	1989	1990	1991	1992	1993	1994	History
	---	---	---	---	---	---	---	---	---	10.75	14.11	11.38	NAV
	---	---	---	---	---	---	---	---	---	7.60 *	41.87	-11.62	Total Return %
	---	---	---	---	---	---	---	---	---	1.02 *	31.82	-12.94	+/- S&P 500
	---	---	---	---	---	---	---	---	---	---	27.34	-8.97	+/- Wilshire 4500
	---	---	---	---	---	---	---	---	---	0.10	0.00	0.00	Income Return %
	---	---	---	---	---	---	---	---	---	7.50	41.87	-11.62	Capital Return %
	---	---	---	---	---	---	---	---	---	---	4	96	Total Rtn % Rank All
	---	---	---	---	---	---	---	---	---	---	2	97	Total Rtn % Rank Obj
	---	---	---	---	---	---	---	---	---	0.01	0.00	0.00	Income $
	---	---	---	---	---	---	---	---	---	0.00	1.14	1.09	Capital Gains $
	---	---	---	---	---	---	---	---	---	---	1.23	2.01	Expense Ratio %
	---	---	---	---	---	---	---	---	---	---	-0.07	-0.96	Income Ratio %
	---	---	---	---	---	---	---	---	---	---	---	169	Turnover Rate %
	---	---	---	---	---	---	---	---	---	3.8	26.7	20.3	Net Assets ($mil)

Performance 12-31-94

	1st Qtr	2nd Qtr	3rd Qtr	4th Qtr	Total
1987	---	---	---	---	---
1988	---	---	---	---	---
1989	---	---	---	---	---
1990	---	---	---	---	---
1991	---	---	---	---	---
1992	---	---	---	8.36	7.60 *
1993	12.00	18.77	-3.50	10.52	41.87
1994	-3.05	-8.26	6.77	-6.94	-11.62

Bear Market Performance

Decile Rank (5-year period)

	Worst			Best
		Worst 3 Mo Period 1985-89		Worst 3 Mo Period 1990-94
Oak Hall Equity		---		---
+/- S&P 500		---		---
+/- Best Fit Index :		---		---

Trailing Returns

	Total Return %	+/- S&P 500	+/- Wil 4500	% Rank All	% Rank Obj	Growth of $10,000
3 Mo	-6.94	-6.92	-4.44	95	97	9,306
6 Mo	-0.64	-5.50	-4.83	67	95	9,936
1 Yr	-11.62	-12.94	-8.97	96	97	8,838
3 Yr Avg	---	---	---	---	---	---
5 Yr Avg	---	---	---	---	---	---
10 Yr Avg	---	---	---	---	---	---
15 Yr Avg	---	---	---	---	---	---

Operations

Address and Telephone	P.O. Box 446
	Portland, ME 04112
	800-625-4255 / 207-879-0001
Advisor	Oak Hall Capital Advisors
Subadvisor	None
Distributor	Forum Financial Services
States Available	All
Report Grade	C
Income Distrib	Paid Annually
* Date of Inception	07-13-92
Fiscal Year End	June

Risk Analysis

Time Period	Load-Adj Return %	Risk % Rank [1] All	Obj	Morningstar [2] Return	Morningstar Risk	Morningstar Risk-Adj Rating
1 Yr	-11.62					
3 Yr	---	---	---	---	---	---
5 Yr	---	---	---	---	---	---
10 Yr	---	---	---	---	---	---

Average Historical Rating ---

[1] 1 = low, 100 = high   [2] 1.00 = Equity Avg   [3] 1.00 = 90-day T-bill return

Other Measures

	Standard S&P 500	Best Fit
Standard Deviation	---	Alpha	---	---
Mean	---	Beta	---	---
Sharpe Ratio	---	R-Squared	---	---

Investment Style

	Stock Portfolio Avg	Relative S&P 500
Price/Earnings Ratio	27.1#	1.46
Price/Book Ratio	2.4	0.72
5 Yr Earnings Gr %	---	---
Return on Assets %	6.3#	0.84
Debt % Total Cap	33.5#	1.18
Med Mkt Cap ($mil)	340	0.03

figure is based on 50% or less of stocks

Diversification Value for Portfolio Types

Large Cap: Small Cap: Bond: Balanced: Diversified:

Expenses & Fees

Sales Fees	0.00% front
	0.00% deferred
	0.20% 12b-1
Management Fee	0.75% flat fee, 0.25%A
3-,5-,10-yr Expense Projections	$63, $108, $233
Annual Brokerage Cost	1.50%

Min Initial Purchase	$10000 (Addt'l: $5000)
Min IRA Purchase	$2000 (Addt'l: $250)
Min Auto Invest Plan	N/A

Portfolio 06-30-94

Share Chg (12-93) 000	Amount 000	Total Stocks: 79 / Total Fixed-Income: 11	Value $000	% Net Assets
73	159	Amax Gold	1254	3.54
65	88	Cambior	1140	3.21
10	44	Homestake Mining	827	2.33
20	36	Charter Medical	815	2.30
25	50	Addington Resources	814	2.30
33	46	Allied Capital Commercial	778	2.19
48	62	Agnico-Eagle Mines	744	2.10
48	63	Echo Bay Mines	677	1.91
205	205	Intl Gold Resources	668	1.88
0	0	Bank Intl Zahlungsausgleich	628	1.77
13	32	WMS Industries	615	1.73
43	72	LAC Minerals	608	1.71
63	63	Santa Fe Energy Resources	591	1.67
16	41	USX-Delhi Group	583	1.64
18	58	Saint Helena Gold Mines ADR	573	1.61
42	79	Global Natural Resources	569	1.60
-5	96	TVX Gold	561	1.58
25	25	Advantage Health	556	1.57
50	121	Forest Oil	516	1.45
125	350	Saint Barbara Mines	511	1.44
62	91	UNC	502	1.41
-30	44	Kloof Gold Mining (ADR)	497	1.40
0	45	Dravo	489	1.38
20	23	Diagnostek	489	1.38
-6	17	Champion Enterprises	478	1.35

Composition % 12-31-94

Cash	14.2	Preferreds	0.0
Stocks	74.0	Convertibles	5.0
Bonds	6.0	Other	0.8

Tax Analysis

	Tax-Adj Historical Return %	% Pretax Return
3 Yr Avg	---	---
5 Yr Avg	---	---
10 Yr Avg	---	---
Potential Capital Gain Exposure (% of assets)		-26%

Most Similar Funds in MF500

Fund lacks three-year record

Index Allocation

	% of Stocks
S&P 500	8.5
S&P MidCap 400	2.0
U.S. Small Cap	62.2
Foreign	30.1

Sector Weightings

	% of Stocks	Relative S&P 500
Utilities	0.0	0.00
Energy	15.4	1.52
Financials	10.5	0.99
Industrial Cyclicals	47.1	2.87
Consumer Durables	3.0	0.48
Consumer Staples	1.3	0.10
Services	7.6	0.93
Retail	3.2	0.54
Health	7.4	0.85
Technology	4.5	0.49

Oakmark

	Ticker	Load	NAV	Yield	SEC Yield	Assets	Objective
	OAKMX	None	22.97	0.9%	N/A	1626.9	Growth

Oakmark Fund seeks long-term capital appreciation; income is a consideration.

The fund invests primarily in common stocks and convertibles. To select individual securities, the fund uses several qualitative and quantitative methods to determine economic value. The primary determinant of value is a company's ability to generate cash; other key factors include the quality of management and amount of management stock ownership. The fund especially seeks securities that are priced significantly below their long-term value. The fund may invest up to 25% of its assets in foreign equity or debt securities; it may invest up to 5% in emerging markets.

Manager's Investment Style

Value manager Robert Sanborn buys firms at a discount to their cash flows, defined as earnings before interest, taxes, depreciation, and amortization. Sanborn has a special interest in cash-rich cable stocks. His value bent leads him to gravitate towards companies that are prime merger targets.

Fund Manager(s)

Robert J. Sanborn CFA(1986), since 08-91.
Birthdate: 03-58. BA, Dartmouth C. 1980 MBA, U. of Chicago 1983

Manager Experience

	Dates Managed	Invest Obj	Std Dev	+/- Index
Not available.				

Historical Profile

Return	High
Risk	Low
Rating	★★★★★
	Highest

Investment Style History
Equity

Average % Stocks Held in Portfolio: 82% 91% 91% 93%

Growth of $10,000

- |||| Value of Fund ($000)
- — Value of Index ($000)
  - Russ 2000
- ▼ Manager Change
- ▽ Partial Manager Change
- ► Mgr Unknown After
- ◄ Mgr Unknown Before

Performance Quartile (Within Objective)

	1983	1984	1985	1986	1987	1988	1989	1990	1991	1992	1993	1994	History
	---	---	---	---	---	---	---	---	13.02	19.13	23.93	22.97	NAV
	---	---	---	---	---	---	---	---	30.20 *	48.90	30.50	3.31	Total Return %
	---	---	---	---	---	---	---	---	20.32 *	41.28	20.45	2.00	+/- S&P 500
	---	---	---	---	---	---	---	---	---	39.93	19.22	3.38	+/- Wilshire 5000
	---	---	---	---	---	---	---	---	0.00	0.23	1.05	1.03	Income Return %
	---	---	---	---	---	---	---	---	30.20	48.67	29.45	2.28	Capital Return %
	---	---	---	---	---	---	---	---	---	1	8	7	Total Rtn % Rank All
	---	---	---	---	---	---	---	---	---	1	2	13	Total Rtn % Rank Obj
	---	---	---	---	---	---	---	---	0.00	0.04	0.23	0.23	Income $
	---	---	---	---	---	---	---	---	0.00	0.21	0.77	1.47	Capital Gains $
	---	---	---	---	---	---	---	---	2.50	1.70	1.32	1.25	Expense Ratio %
	---	---	---	---	---	---	---	---	-0.66	-0.24	0.94	1.51	Income Ratio %
	---	---	---	---	---	---	---	---	---	---	34	18	Turnover Rate %
	---	---	---	---	---	---	---	---	8.3	328.8	1214.1	1626.9	Net Assets ($mil)

Performance 12-31-94

	1st Qtr	2nd Qtr	3rd Qtr	4th Qtr	Total
1987	---	---	---	---	---
1988	---	---	---	---	---
1989	---	---	---	---	---
1990	---	---	---	---	---
1991	---	---	---	17.83	30.20 *
1992	12.83	3.68	10.31	15.39	48.90
1993	7.95	2.71	7.45	9.54	30.50
1994	-4.18	2.92	6.86	-1.97	3.32

Bear Market Performance

Decile Rank (5-year period)

Worst ———————————— Best

	Worst 3 Mo Period 1985-89	Worst 3 Mo Period 1990-94
Oakmark	---	---
+/- S&P 500	---	---
+/- Best Fit Index :	---	---

Trailing Returns

	Total Return %	+/- S&P 500	+/- Wil 5000	% Rank All	% Rank Obj	Growth of $10,000
3 Mo	-1.97	-1.95	-1.20	68	63	9,803
6 Mo	4.76	-0.10	0.14	12	38	10,476
1 Yr	3.31	2.00	3.38	7	13	10,331
3 Yr Avg	26.15	19.89	19.54	1	1	20,075
5 Yr Avg	---	---	---	---	---	---
10 Yr Avg	---	---	---	---	---	---
15 Yr Avg	---	---	---	---	---	---

Operations

Address and Telephone	Two N. LaSalle Street Chicago, IL 60602-3790 800-625-6275
Advisor	Harris Associates
Subadvisor	None
Distributor	Oakmark Fund
States Available	All States
Report Grade	B
Income Distrib	Paid Annually
* Date of Inception	08-05-91
Fiscal Year End	October

Risk Analysis

Time Period	Load-Adj Return %	Risk % Rank [1] All	Obj	Morningstar [2] Return	Morningstar Risk	Morningstar Risk-Adj Rating
1 Yr	3.31					
3 Yr	26.15	34	2	8.05 [3]	0.44	★★★★★
5 Yr	---	---	---	---	---	
10 Yr	---	---	---	---	---	

Average Historical Rating (5 months) 5.0 ★s

[1] 1 = low, 100 = high   [2] 1.00 = Equity Avg   [3] 1.00 = 90-day T-bill return

Other Measures

			Standard S&P 500	Best Fit Russ 2000
Standard Deviation	10.05	Alpha	19.6	15.8
Mean	23.95	Beta	0.83	0.71
Sharpe Ratio	2.03	R-Squared	43	69

Investment Style

	Stock Portfolio Avg	Relative S&P 500
Price/Earnings Ratio	18.0	0.97
Price/Book Ratio	2.7	0.80
5 Yr Earnings Gr %	9.5#	1.72
Return on Assets %	6.6	0.88
Debt % Total Cap	32.5	1.15
Med Mkt Cap ($mil)	1988	0.15

Style: Value Blend Growth — Size Large/Med/Small

figure is based on 50% or less of stocks

Diversification Value for Portfolio Types

 Large Cap: Medium   Small Cap: Low   Bond: High   Balanced: Low   Diversified: Medium

Expenses & Fees

Sales Fees	0.00% front
	0.00% deferred
	0.00% 12b-1
Management Fee	1.00% flat fee
3-,5-,10-yr Expense Projections	$42, $72, $159
Annual Brokerage Cost	0.19%

Min Initial Purchase	$2500 (Addt'l: $100)
Min IRA Purchase	$1000 (Addt'l: $100)
Min Auto Invest Plan	$1000 (Systematic Inv: $100)

Portfolio 12-31-94

Share Chg (07-94) 000	Amount 000	Total Stocks: 88 / Total Fixed-Income: 0	Value $000	% Net Assets
50	1557	Philip Morris	89499	5.50
330	1526	Anheuser-Busch	77635	4.77
523	2279	First USA	74935	4.61
470	1810	AMBAC	67419	4.14
1489	2067	Mellon Bank	63288	3.89
-70	845	Lockheed	61368	3.77
2049	2734	Tele-Communications CI A	59468	3.66
150	915	American Home Products	57416	3.53
0	2325	DeBeers Consolid Mines (ADR)	54347	3.34
-20	814	Eli Lilly	53399	3.28
0	1152	Saint Jude Medical	45792	2.81
939	939	Tyco International	44600	2.74
50	974	Martin Marietta	43239	2.66
-75	1265	Harnischfeger Industries	35570	2.19
300	1120	Quaker Oats	34440	2.12
50	780	Unitrin	33531	2.06
1275	1695	Federated Department Stores	32629	2.01
-50	528	Great Lakes Chemical	30096	1.85
478	478	Clorox	28125	1.73
100	1280	YPF (ADR)	27360	1.68
960	960	Geon	26272	1.61
521	985	American Prem Underwriters	25479	1.57
15	649	Sybron International	22387	1.38
476	476	EVC	21078	1.30
700	928	Old Republic International	19724	1.21

Composition % 12-31-94

Cash	6.0	Preferreds	0.0
Stocks	94.0	Convertibles	0.0
Bonds	0.0	Other	0.0

Tax Analysis

	Tax-Adj Historical Return %	% Pretax Return
3 Yr Avg	24.62	92.8
5 Yr Avg	---	---
10 Yr Avg	---	---
Potential Capital Gain Exposure (% of assets)		8%

Most Similar Funds in MF500

Mutual Shares	Weak Fit
Skyline Special Equities	Weak Fit
Mutual Qualified	Weak Fit

Index Allocation

	% of Stocks
S&P 500	51.7
S&P MidCap 400	5.1
U.S. Small Cap	36.9
Foreign	6.3

Sector Weightings

	% of Stocks	Relative S&P 500
Utilities	0.0	0.00
Energy	2.7	0.26
Financials	21.3	2.01
Industrial Cyclicals	19.7	1.20
Consumer Durables	3.7	0.59
Consumer Staples	19.0	1.52
Services	10.7	1.31
Retail	5.0	0.86
Health	13.1	1.50
Technology	5.0	0.54

MORNINGSTAR **1995 Mutual Fund 500**

Oakmark International

	Ticker	Load	NAV	Yield	SEC Yield	Assets	Objective
	OAKIX	None	12.41	0.0%	N/A	1079.7	Foreign Stock

Oakmark International Fund seeks long-term capital appreciation.

The fund normally invests at least 65% of its assets in foreign securities. These securities are undervalued relative to their underlying economic value, as determined by the fund. The fund assigns long-term value primarily on the basis of the company's ability to generate cash flow. Quality of management, market share, and degree of pricing power provide other parameters of value. The fund may invest up to 10% of assets in low-quality debt.

The unusually large income ratio for 1992 reflects a large income distribution made after one month of operation, and then annualized.

Manager's Investment Style

Management adheres to a value discipline that emphasizes low prices and strong management. It looks for companies that are selling at a discount to the present value of their future cash flows, or those that appear cheap relative to their normalized earnings or underlying assets. Unlike many in the foreign-stock-fund group, management does not allocate assets based on top-down analysis of countries and regions.

Fund Manager(s)

David G. Herro CFA(1989), since 09-92. Birthdate: 12-60. Business/Economics, U. of Wisconsin-Platteville 1983 Economics, U. of Wisconsin-Milwaukee 1985

Manager Experience	Dates Managed	Invest Obj	Std Dev	+/- Index
David G. Herro				
Princor World A	08/88 - 03/89	WF	7.69	-4.09

Historical Profile

Return ---
Risk ---
Rating
Not Rated

Investment Style History
Equity

Average % Stocks Held in Portfolio

	92%	93%	95%

Growth of $10,000

IIII Value of Fund ($000)
— Value of Index ($000)
S&P 500
▼ Manager Change
▽ Partial Manager Change
► Mgr Unknown After
◄ Mgr Unknown Before

Performance Quartile (Within Objective)

	1983	1984	1985	1986	1987	1988	1989	1990	1991	1992	1993	1994	History
NAV	---	---	---	---	---	---	---	---	---	9.79	14.79	12.41	NAV
Total Return %	---	---	---	---	---	---	---	---	---	0.43 *	53.58	-9.06	Total Return %
+/- S&P 500	---	---	---	---	---	---	---	---	---	-4.60 *	43.52	-10.38	+/- S&P 500
+/- MSCI EAFE	---	---	---	---	---	---	---	---	---	---	21.02	-16.84	+/- MSCI EAFE
Income Return %	---	---	---	---	---	---	---	---	---	2.53	0.68	0.00	Income Return %
Capital Return %	---	---	---	---	---	---	---	---	---	-2.10	52.90	-9.06	Capital Return %
Total Rtn % Rank All	---	---	---	---	---	---	---	---	---	---	2	91	Total Rtn % Rank All
Total Rtn % Rank Obj	---	---	---	---	---	---	---	---	---	---	12	84	Total Rtn % Rank Obj
Income $	---	---	---	---	---	---	---	---	---	0.25	0.08	0.00	Income $
Capital Gains $	---	---	---	---	---	---	---	---	---	0.00	0.15	1.06	Capital Gains $
Expense Ratio %	---	---	---	---	---	---	---	---	---	2.04	1.26	1.37	Expense Ratio %
Income Ratio %	---	---	---	---	---	---	---	---	---	37.02	1.55	1.44	Income Ratio %
Turnover Rate %	---	---	---	---	---	---	---	---	---	---	21	55	Turnover Rate %
Net Assets ($mil)	---	---	---	---	---	---	---	---	---	30.8	1108.4	1079.7	Net Assets ($mil)

Performance 12-31-94

	1st Qtr	2nd Qtr	3rd Qtr	4th Qtr	Total
1987	---	---	---	---	---
1988	---	---	---	---	---
1989	---	---	---	---	---
1990	---	---	---	---	---
1991	---	---	---	---	---
1992	---	---	---	0.43	0.43 *
1993	18.39	3.45	8.84	15.21	53.58
1994	-1.08	-5.95	6.47	-8.19	-9.06

Bear Market Performance

Decile Rank (5-year period)

Worst — Best

	Worst 3 Mo Period 1985-89	Worst 3 Mo Period 1990-94
Oakmark International	---	---
+/- S&P 500	---	---
+/- Best Fit Index :	---	---

Trailing Returns

	Total Return %	+/- S&P 500	+/- MSCI EAFE	% Rank All	% Rank Obj	Growth of $10,000
3 Mo	-8.19	-8.18	-7.17	96	74	9,181
6 Mo	-2.26	-7.12	-1.33	90	67	9,774
1 Yr	-9.06	-10.38	-16.84	91	84	9,094
3 Yr Avg	---	---	---	---	---	---
5 Yr Avg	---	---	---	---	---	---
10 Yr Avg	---	---	---	---	---	---
15 Yr Avg	---	---	---	---	---	---

Operations

Address and Telephone	Two N. LaSalle Street Chicago, IL 60602-3790 800-625-6275	Min Initial Purchase	$2500 (Addt'l: $100)
		Min IRA Purchase	$1000 (Addt'l: $100)
		Min Auto Invest Plan	$1000 (Systematic Inv: $100)
Advisor	Harris Associates		
Subadvisor	None	**Expenses & Fees**	
Distributor	Oakmark International Fund	Sales Fees	0.00% front
States Available	All		0.00% deferred
Report Grade	B+		0.00% 12b-1
Income Distrib	Paid Annually	Management Fee	1.00% flat fee
* Date of Inception	09-30-92	3-,5-,10-yr Expense Projections	$40, $69, $152
Fiscal Year End	October	Annual Brokerage Cost	0.93%

Risk Analysis

Time Period	Load-Adj Return %	Risk % Rank [1] All	Risk % Rank [1] Obj	Morningstar [2] Return	Morningstar [2] Risk	Morningstar Risk-Adj Rating
1 Yr	-9.06					
3 Yr	---					
5 Yr	---					
10 Yr	---					

Average Historical Rating ---

[1] 1 = low, 100 = high   [2] 1.00 = Equity Avg   [3] 1.00 = 90-day T-bill return

Other Measures

		Standard S&P 500	Best Fit
Standard Deviation	Alpha	---	---
Mean	Beta	---	---
Sharpe Ratio	R-Squared	---	---

Investment Style

	Stock Portfolio Avg	Rel MSCI EAFE	Rel Obj
Price/Earnings Ratio	20.1	0.54	0.71
Price/Cash Flow	10.0	0.64	0.74
Price/Book Ratio	1.9	0.73	0.64
5 Yr Earnings Gr %	1.9#	---	0.50
Return on Assets %	7.1#	1.57	0.99
Debt % Total Cap	33.1	0.97	1.19
Med Mkt Cap ($mil)	1208	0.10	0.24

figure is based on 50% or less of stocks

Style
V B G
Size L M S

Diversification Value for Portfolio Types

Large Cap: Small Cap: Bond: Balanced: Diversified:

Portfolio 12-31-94

Total Stocks: 49
Total Fixed-Income: 0

Share Chg (10-94) 000	Amount 000		Value $000	% Net Assets
-1559	21820	Pioneer International	54144	5.01
-1075	20894	Saatchi & Saatchi	48713	4.51
-189	1013	Kvaerner	45838	4.25
-188	2262	Banco Espirito Santo & Com	43807	4.06
-109	353	Banco Popular Espanol (Reg)	42008	3.89
-770	9988	Union Electrica Fenosa	41584	3.85
-1258	6126	British Aerospace	40975	3.79
-1003	4377	Reckitt & Colman	40203	3.72
-595	3630	Wellcome	39816	3.69
-87	2753	Svenska Handelsbanken	36314	3.36
900	18649	Lion Nathan	35577	3.29
-273	14348	Burns Philp	33934	3.14
-75	1950	Scitex	32410	3.00
0	1715	Volvo	32312	2.99
15	697	Telefonos de Mexico	28565	2.65
0	47236	Giordano Holdings	27319	2.53
-1279	9511	Rolls-Royce	26712	2.47
-1085	2754	Canadian Tire	24536	2.27
-1	158	Hollandsche Beton Groep	24456	2.27
74	456	MO Och Domsjo Cl A	21215	1.96

Regional Exposure 09-30-94

% of Stocks

Europe	19	Pacific Rim	19
Japan	9	Other	17
Latin Amer	8		

Composition % 12-31-94

Cash	6.0	Preferreds	0.0
Stocks	94.0	Convertibles	0.0
Bonds	0.0	Other	0.0

Tax Analysis

	Tax-Adj Historical Return %	% Pretax Return
3 Yr Avg	---	---
5 Yr Avg	---	---
10 Yr Avg	---	---
Potential Capital Gain Exposure (% of assets)		-10%

Most Similar Funds in MF500

Fund lacks three-year record

Country Exposure 12-31-94

% of Stocks

United Kingdom	19
Spain	9
Australia	8
Mexico	7
France	7

Total Number of Countries: 16
Hedging Policy: Occasional

Sector Weightings

	% of Stocks	Relative S&P 500
Utilities	5.0	0.57
Energy	8.2	2.02
Financials	16.6	0.88
Industrial Cyclicals	13.6	0.54
Consumer Durables	10.5	0.97
Consumer Staples	17.8	2.58
Services	7.7	0.70
Retail	5.2	0.89
Health	4.8	1.35
Technology	10.6	2.07

Oppenheimer Discovery A

	Ticker	Load	NAV	Yield	SEC Yield	Assets	Objective
	OPOCX	5.75%	33.37	0.0%	N/A	605.5	Small Company

Oppenheimer Discovery Fund - Class A seeks capital appreciation.

The fund invests primarily in common stocks; over-the-counter securities usually constitute a substantial portion of the fund's investments. The fund may invest up to 20% of its assets in companies with less than three years of operating history. It may invest without limit in ADRs and other dollar-denominated foreign securities.

Class A shares have front loads; Class B shares have deferred loads, higher 12b-1 fees, and conversion features; Class Y shares are sold to institutional investors. Prior to Feb. 1, 1990, the fund was named Oppenheimer OTC Fund.

Manager's Investment Style

In spite of several management changes over the past few years, manager Jay Tracey consistently follows a strict growth discipline, with a preference for rapid-fire earnings growth. He has maintained a penchant for companies with market caps under $500 million that show potential for 20% earnings increases each year. Valuation takes second place to earnings.

Fund Manager(s)

Jay W. Tracey III CFA(1982), since 09-94. BS, U. of Redlands

Historical Profile

Return	Above Average
Risk	Above Average
Rating	★★★ Neutral

	81%	84%	83%	77%	86%	85%	91%	79%		Investment Style History

Average % Stocks Held in Portfolio

Growth of $10,000

- IIII Value of Fund ($000)
- — Value of Index ($000) Russ 2000
- ▼ Manager Change
- ▽ Partial Manager Change
- ► Mgr Unknown After
- ◄ Mgr Unknown Before

Performance Quartile (Within Objective)

	1983	1984	1985	1986	1987	1988	1989	1990	1991	1992	1993	1994	History
	---	---	---	15.08	15.11	17.94	22.13	17.93	29.46	34.36	39.46	33.37	NAV
	---	---	---	5.53 *	13.70	19.69	34.16	-15.05	72.19	16.63	17.84	-11.18	Total Return %
	---	---	---	1.37 *	8.45	3.08	2.47	-11.93	41.70	9.02	7.78	-12.49	+/- S&P 500
	---	---	---	---	17.22	-0.85	10.22	-1.49	28.74	4.88	3.30	-8.53	+/- Wilshire 4500
	---	---	---	0.00	0.45	0.96	1.47	1.02	0.00	0.00	0.00	0.00	Income Return %
	---	---	---	5.53	13.25	18.73	32.69	-16.07	72.19	16.63	17.84	-11.18	Capital Return %
	---	---	---	---	6	15	8	92	2	8	21	96	Total Rtn % Rank All
	---	---	---	---	1	53	11	73	9	34	46	97	Total Rtn % Rank Obj
	---	---	---	0.00	0.07	0.14	0.30	0.19	0.00	0.00	0.00	0.00	Income $
	---	---	---	0.00	1.98	0.00	1.56	0.68	1.29	0.00	1.00	1.62	Capital Gains $
	---	---	---	1.50	1.74	1.52	1.46	1.53	1.42	1.52	1.27	1.20	Expense Ratio %
	---	---	---	3.55	0.19	0.80	1.52	0.83	0.22	-0.62	-0.54	-0.43	Income Ratio %
	---	---	---	0	145	169	132	235	158	68	85	---	Turnover Rate %
	---	---	---	1.4	30.0	32.7	55.5	54.2	166.7	427.1	622.2	605.5	Net Assets ($mil)

Manager Experience	Dates Managed	Invest Obj	Std Dev	+/- Index
Jay W. Tracey III				
Oppenheimer Time	11/91 - 03/94	G	14.76	1.66

Performance 12-31-94

	1st Qtr	2nd Qtr	3rd Qtr	4th Qtr	Total
1987	30.53	1.02	8.21	-20.31	13.70
1988	8.60	7.50	-0.11	2.64	19.69
1989	10.70	11.53	10.65	-1.80	34.16
1990	-7.00	5.35	-17.11	4.62	-15.05
1991	25.93	-2.08	17.73	18.61	72.19
1992	0.51	-11.38	5.26	24.40	16.63
1993	-2.18	4.61	13.48	1.48	17.84
1994	-7.88	-9.88	9.31	-2.13	-11.18

Bear Market Performance

Decile Rank (5-year period)

Worst _____ Best

	Worst 3 Mo Period 1985-89	Worst 3 Mo Period 1990-94
Oppenheimer Discovery A	---	-17.11
+/- S&P 500	---	-3.37
+/- Best Fit Index : Russ 2000	---	7.43

Trailing Returns

	Total Return %	+/- S&P 500	+/- Wil 4500	% Rank All	% Rank Obj	Growth of $10,000
3 Mo	-2.13	-2.11	0.37	71	69	9,787
6 Mo	6.99	2.12	2.79	7	43	10,699
1 Yr	-11.18	-12.49	-8.53	96	97	8,882
3 Yr Avg	6.88	0.61	-0.73	27	68	12,208
5 Yr Avg	12.30	3.60	3.20	8	42	17,857
10 Yr Avg	---	---	---	---	---	---
15 Yr Avg	---	---	---	---	---	---

Operations

Address and Telephone	P.O. Box 5270
	Denver, CO 80217-5270
	800-525-7048 / 303-671-3200
Advisor	Oppenheimer Management
Subadvisor	None
Distributor	Oppenheimer Funds Distributor
States Available	All plus PR
Report Grade	B
Income Distrib	Paid Annually
* Date of Inception	09-11-86
Fiscal Year End	September

Min Initial Purchase	$1000 (Addt'l: $25)
Min IRA Purchase	$250 (Addt'l: $25)
Min Auto Invest Plan	$25 (Systematic Inv: $25)

Expenses & Fees

Sales Fees	5.75% front
	0.00% deferred
	0.25% 12b-1
Management Fee	0.75% max./0.60% min.
3-,5-,10-yr Expense Projections	$95, $123, $202
Annual Brokerage Cost	1.25%

Risk Analysis

Time Period	Load-Adj Return %	Risk % Rank[1] All	Risk % Rank[1] Obj	Morningstar[2] Return	Morningstar Risk	Morningstar Risk-Adj Rating
1 Yr	-16.29					
3 Yr	4.79	96	85	0.35[3]	1.52	★★
5 Yr	10.97	94	73	1.63[3]	1.31	★★★★
10 Yr	---	---	---	---	---	

Average Historical Rating (64 months) 4.0 ★s

[1] 1 = low, 100 = high [2] 1.00 = Equity Avg [3] 1.00 = 90-day T-bill return

Other Measures

			Standard S&P 500	Best Fit Russ 2000
Standard Deviation	16.54	Alpha	1.4	-5.6
Mean	8.03	Beta	1.07	1.28
Sharpe Ratio	0.27	R-Squared	26	84

Investment Style

	Stock Portfolio Avg	Relative S&P 500
Price/Earnings Ratio	26.4	1.43
Price/Book Ratio	4.7	1.37
5 Yr Earnings Gr %	31.8#	5.72
Return on Assets %	10.8	1.45
Debt % Total Cap	25.3	0.89
Med Mkt Cap ($mil)	413	0.03

figure is based on 50% or less of stocks

Diversification Value for Portfolio Types

Large Cap: Medium	Small Cap: None	Bond: High	Balanced: Medium	Diversified: Medium

Portfolio 12-30-94

Total Stocks: 129
Total Fixed-Income: 11

Share Chg (03-94) 000	Amount 000		Value $000	% Net Assets
-87	493	EMC	10657	1.76
354	474	Mariner Health Group	10247	1.69
21	220	Tommy Hilfiger	9947	1.64
87	329	Horizon Healthcare	9216	1.52
252	328	LCI International	8540	1.41
-14	246	HBO	8501	1.40
303	303	Softkey International	7733	1.28
31	161	Fritz	7572	1.25
-64	246	Nautica Enterprises	7454	1.23
235	235	Symbol Technologies	7245	1.20
223	223	FTP Software	7043	1.16
265	265	Hudson Foods Cl A	6667	1.10
261	261	Sun Healthcare Group	6613	1.09
251	251	Watson Pharmaceuticals	6593	1.09
260	351	Recoton	6575	1.09
148	498	Apple South	6530	1.08
256	256	United Waste Systems	6397	1.06
-51	219	General Nutrition	6360	1.05
275	275	Medisense	6356	1.05
	3791	Medaphis Cv 6.5%	6340	1.05
49	109	Glenayre Technologies	6294	1.04
	10709	Solectron Cv 0%	6118	1.01
58	408	Foothill Group Cl A	6113	1.01
223	223	IHOP	6069	1.00
474	474	OrNda Healthcorp	5923	0.98

Composition % 12-31-94

Cash	13.4	Preferreds	0.4
Stocks	81.5	Convertibles	4.7
Bonds	0.0	Other	0.0

Tax Analysis

	Tax-Adj Historical Return %	% Pretax Return
3 Yr Avg	6.17	89.1
5 Yr Avg	11.24	89.6
10 Yr Avg	---	---
Potential Capital Gain Exposure (% of assets)	8%	

Most Similar Funds in MF500

Hancock Emerging Growth B	Strong Fit
Berger 100	Fair Fit
20th Century Ultra Investors	Fair Fit

Index Allocation % of Stocks

S&P 500	3.1
S&P MidCap 400	6.4
U.S. Small Cap	87.3
Foreign	3.3

Sector Weightings

	% of Stocks	Relative S&P 500
Utilities	0.0	0.00
Energy	4.5	0.44
Financials	5.4	0.51
Industrial Cyclicals	7.3	0.45
Consumer Durables	11.7	1.89
Consumer Staples	1.7	0.14
Services	16.4	2.02
Retail	6.6	1.13
Health	20.1	2.31
Technology	26.3	2.87

MORNINGSTAR **1995 Mutual Fund 500**

Oppenheimer Equity-Income A

	Ticker	Load	NAV	Yield	SEC Yield	Assets	Objective
	OPPEX	5.75%	9.14	5.2%	N/A	1713.6	Equity-Inc.

Oppenheimer Equity-Income Fund - Class A seeks current income. Conservation of principal and capital appreciation are secondary.

The fund normally invests at least 65% of its assets in income-producing equity securities. It may also purchase bonds, debentures, and notes. Although the fund may invest in debt securities of any rating, it does not expect to invest more than 10% of its assets in those rated below BBB.

Class A shares have front loads; Class B shares have deferred loads and higher 12b-1 fees.

On Oct. 18, 1991, Advance America Funds Equity-Income Fund merged into this fund.

Manager's Investment Style

Management doesn't cling to the typical equity-income approach. Instead of filling the portfolio with utilities stocks for their high yields--as most funds in the objective do--management instead favors bonds and convertibles to pump up yield. The portfolio's stock position is therefore typically lower than that of the average equity-income fund, and is more akin to a balanced fund. Stocks that do make the cut are bought on a value basis.

Fund Manager(s)

John P. Doney CFA, since 06-92. Birthdate: 02-30.
BS, U. of Notre Dame 1951 MA, Trinity C. 1959

Manager Experience	Dates Managed	Invest Obj	Std Dev	+/- Index
John P. Doney				
American National Growth	01/68 - 12/80	G	17.81	9.34
Phoenix Inc & Growth A	01/87 - 07/92	B	8.76	-0.45

Historical Profile

Return	Below Average
Risk	Low
Rating	★★★ Neutral

Average % Stocks Held in Portfolio: 52% 54% 58% 58% 57% 52% 45% 42%

Investment Style History: Equity

Growth of $10,000
||| Value of Fund ($000)
— Value of Index ($000) S&P 500
▼ Manager Change
▽ Partial Manager Change
► Mgr Unknown After
◄ Mgr Unknown Before

Performance Quartile (Within Objective)

1983	1984	1985	1986	1987	1988	1989	1990	1991	1992	1993	1994	History
7.72	6.87	8.30	8.46	7.85	8.44	9.24	8.49	9.32	9.33	10.02	9.14	NAV
33.33	3.25	30.98	15.08	9.44	14.02	18.56	-1.37	17.26	6.83	14.57	-2.79	Total Return %
10.87	-3.01	-0.76	-3.60	4.18	-2.59	-13.13	1.75	-13.22	-0.79	4.51	-4.10	+/- S&P 500
9.87	0.21	-1.59	-1.01	7.07	-3.92	-10.62	4.82	-16.94	-2.14	3.29	-2.72	+/- Wilshire 5000
6.03	8.96	7.44	5.91	6.94	6.30	6.00	5.27	5.95	5.15	5.21	4.81	Income Return %
27.31	-5.70	23.54	9.18	2.49	7.72	12.56	-6.64	11.31	1.68	9.35	-7.60	Capital Return %
7	56	22	54	11	31	38	59	50	59	30	41	Total Rtn % Rank All
1	80	12	73	1	64	68	18	89	75	40	61	Total Rtn % Rank Obj
0.45	0.61	0.45	0.47	0.60	0.48	0.50	0.48	0.49	0.46	0.48	0.48	Income $
1.99	0.39	0.15	0.61	0.88	0.02	0.24	0.15	0.12	0.15	0.17	0.13	Capital Gains $
1.00	1.04	1.11	1.03	0.91	0.83	0.85	0.79	0.79	0.82	0.79	0.90	Expense Ratio %
4.38	6.61	7.01	6.00	5.08	5.48	5.89	5.10	5.31	5.33	5.12	4.72	Income Ratio %
287	183	123	105	95	124	91	122	64	37	59	30	Turnover Rate %
64.1	66.3	134.8	483.5	695.0	855.4	1192.7	1266.4	1587.9	1647.7	1860.9	1713.6	Net Assets ($mil)

Performance 12-31-94

	1st Qtr	2nd Qtr	3rd Qtr	4th Qtr	Total
1987	15.87	3.12	4.72	-12.53	9.44
1988	5.99	5.25	-0.47	2.70	14.02
1989	5.11	5.46	7.03	-0.07	18.56
1990	-0.11	2.08	-6.09	3.01	-1.37
1991	8.38	-1.10	5.42	3.78	17.26
1992	-1.51	2.33	2.41	3.51	6.83
1993	6.86	2.86	3.60	0.61	14.57
1994	-3.73	0.31	4.24	-3.42	-2.79

Bear Market Performance

Decile Rank (5-year period)

	Worst									Best

	Worst 3 Mo Period 1985-89	Worst 3 Mo Period 1990-94
Oppenheimer Equity-Income A	-18.85	-8.71
+/- S&P 500	10.73	5.13
+/- Best Fit Index : S&P 500	10.73	5.13

Trailing Returns

	Total Return %	+/- S&P 500	+/- Wil 5000	% Rank All	% Rank Obj	Growth of $10,000
3 Mo	-3.42	-3.41	-2.65	86	72	9,658
6 Mo	0.67	-4.19	-3.95	43	65	10,067
1 Yr	-2.79	-4.10	-2.72	41	61	9,721
3 Yr Avg	5.96	-0.30	-0.65	34	63	11,898
5 Yr Avg	6.59	-2.10	-2.22	60	62	13,761
10 Yr Avg	11.87	-2.52	-1.99	39	31	30,687
15 Yr Avg	13.92	-0.56	-0.06	25	23	70,624

Operations

Address and Telephone	P.O. Box 5270
	Denver, CO 80217-5270
	800-525-7048 / 303-671-3200
Advisor	Oppenheimer Management
Subadvisor	None
Distributor	Oppenheimer Funds Distributor
States Available	All plus PR
Report Grade	A-
Income Distrib	Paid Quarterly
Date of Inception	12-01-70
Fiscal Year End	June

Risk Analysis

Time Period	Load-Adj Return %	Risk % Rank [1] All	Risk % Rank [1] Obj	Morningstar [2] Return	Morningstar Risk	Morningstar Risk-Adj Rating
1 Yr	-8.38					
3 Yr	3.89	54	41	0.09 [3]	0.58	★★★
5 Yr	5.34	54	6	0.14 [3]	0.58	★★★
10 Yr	11.20	43	12	0.74	0.59	★★★

Average Historical Rating (109 months) 3.9 s

[1] = low, 100 = high   [2] 1.00 = Equity Avg   [3] 1.00 = 90-day T-bill return

Other Measures

				Standard S&P 500	Best Fit S&P 500
Standard Deviation	6.50	Alpha		0.4	0.4
Mean	6.02	Beta		0.74	0.74
Sharpe Ratio	0.38	R-Squared		80	80

Investment Style

	Stock Portfolio Avg	Relative S&P 500
Price/Earnings Ratio	14.8	0.80
Price/Book Ratio	1.9	0.57
5 Yr Earnings Gr %	1.6	0.29
Return on Assets %	3.5	0.46
Debt % Total Cap	33.6	1.19
Med Mkt Cap ($mil)	6546	0.50

Style Value Blend Growth — Size Large Med Small

Diversification Value for Portfolio Types

Large Cap: Low
Small Cap: Medium
Bond: Low
Balanced: None
Diversified: Low

Expenses & Fees

Sales Fees	5.75% front
	0.00% deferred
	0.25% 12b-1
Management Fee	0.75% max./0.50% min.
3-,5-,10-yr Expense Projections	$85, $104, $162
Annual Brokerage Cost	0.06%

Min Initial Purchase	$1000 (Addt'l: $25)
Min IRA Purchase	$250 (Addt'l: $25)
Min Auto Invest Plan	$25 (Systematic Inv: $25)

Portfolio 12-30-94

Share Chg (06-94) 000	Amount 000	Total Stocks: 61 / Total Fixed-Income: 56	Value $000	% Net Assets
-10	562	Philip Morris	32299	1.88
-12	655	Chemical Banking	23510	1.37
-12	655	Chase Manhattan	22527	1.31
	521	American Express Cv DECS 6.25%	22227	1.30
85	562	BankAmerica	22188	1.29
	187	Citicorp Cv Pfd 10.75%	21626	1.26
-3	189	Royal Dutch Petroleum	20279	1.18
-8	468	Tenneco	19894	1.16
-12	655	American Express	19332	1.13
-7	421	First Fidelity Bancorp (NJ)	18905	1.10
-68	445	General Motors	18788	1.10
	374	Occidental Petro Cv Pfd 7.75%	18256	1.07
	2916	RJR Nabisco Cv PERCS 9.25%	17497	1.02
-12	655	National City	16957	0.99
369	655	Banc One	16629	0.97
-8	472	Texas Utilities	15099	0.88
158	492	Mellon Bank	15052	0.88
-10	565	Public Service Enterprise	14985	0.87
	257	Sears Roebuck Cv PERCS $3.75	14321	0.84
-4	235	Texaco	14098	0.82
-8	425	American Electric Power	13973	0.82
-3	165	Mobil	13921	0.81
	1030	Westinghouse C Cv Pfd $12.125	13774	0.80
-3	187	AMP	13622	0.79
	164	UAL Cl A Cv Pfd 6.25%	13608	0.79

Composition % 12-31-94

Cash	2.9	Preferreds	0.4
Stocks	41.6	Convertibles	9.5
Bonds	45.6	Other	0.0

Tax Analysis

	Tax-Adj Historical Return %	% Pretax Return
3 Yr Avg	3.66	60.0
5 Yr Avg	4.31	62.4
10 Yr Avg	8.80	64.0
Potential Capital Gain Exposure (% of assets)		4%

Most Similar Funds in MF500

Smith Barney Inc & Grth A	Strong Fit
Dean Witter Dividend Growth	Strong Fit
Investment Comp of America	Strong Fit

Index Allocation

	% of Stocks
S&P 500	89.0
S&P MidCap 400	5.7
U.S. Small Cap	5.3
Foreign	4.6

Sector Weightings

	% of Stocks	Relative S&P 500
Utilities	11.5	0.93
Energy	10.3	1.02
Financials	40.4	3.82
Industrial Cyclicals	11.8	0.72
Consumer Durables	3.4	0.55
Consumer Staples	8.2	0.65
Services	7.7	0.94
Retail	3.0	0.52
Health	0.0	0.00
Technology	3.7	0.41

Oppenheimer High-Yield A

	Ticker	Load	NAV	Yield	SEC Yield	Assets	Objective
	OPPHX	4.75%	12.83	10.5%	9.63%	958.3	Corp Hi Yld

Oppenheimer High-Yield Fund - Class A seeks high current income. As a secondary objective, the fund may seek capital growth.

The fund invests primarily in unrated or lower-rated fixed-income securities (BBB or lower). It may invest in securities rated as low as CC if the fund perceives that the financial condition of the issuer is stronger than the rating suggests. Normally, at least 80% of the fund's assets are invested in fixed-income securities. The balance may be held in equity securities or cash equivalents.

Class A shares have front loads and lower 12b-1 fees; Class B shares have deferred loads and conversion features.

Manager's Investment Style

Management typically takes a cautious approach to the high-yield market, favoring higher-quality securities and underweighting riskier PIKs and zeros. Unlike some high-yield fund managers who don't pay much attention to interest-rate movements, management here does keep a watchful eye on rates, and is willing to pull in duration when interest rates are poised to rise. Management is nevertheless willing to make hefty sector plays, such as overweighting cyclicals in late 1992. The fund has also dabbled in Brady bonds.

Fund Manager(s)

Ralph W. Stellmacher, since 11-87. Birthdate: 01-59. BS, Cornell U. 1982 MBA, Pace U. 1990

Manager Experience

	Dates Managed	Invest Obj	Std Dev	+/- Index
Ralph W. Stellmacher				
Oppenheim Multi-Govt	11/88 - 01/93	MB	3.19	-7.34

Historical Profile
Return	Average
Risk	Low
Rating ★★★★	Above Average

Investment Style History
Fixed Income
Income Rtn % Rank Obj

Style boxes: 2, 30, 30, 6, 36, 21, 5, 17

Growth of $10,000
- |||| Value of Fund ($000)
- — Value of Index ($000) LB Agg
- ▼ Manager Change
- ▽ Partial Manager Change
- ► Mgr Unknown After
- ◄ Mgr Unknown Before

Performance Quartile (Within Objective)

1983	1984	1985	1986	1987	1988	1989	1990	1991	1992	1993	1994	History
18.64	16.81	17.37	16.73	15.77	15.56	14.25	11.92	13.24	13.39	14.50	12.83	NAV
14.66	3.54	18.84	9.76	7.20	11.94	3.89	-3.21	28.60	13.85	20.57	-2.33	Total Return %
6.29	-11.61	-3.29	-5.49	4.44	4.07	-10.65	-12.16	12.60	6.61	10.82	0.58	+/- LB Aggregate
---	---	---	-5.87	0.67	0.51	3.51	3.17	-15.15	-2.81	1.67	-1.36	+/- FB High-Yield
14.14	13.36	15.51	13.45	12.94	13.28	12.31	13.14	17.53	12.72	12.28	9.18	Income Return %
0.52	-9.82	3.33	-3.68	-5.74	-1.33	-8.42	-16.35	11.07	1.13	8.29	-11.52	Capital Return %
59	55	79	85	15	46	96	65	29	12	16	37	Total Rtn % Rank All
62	92	96	88	2	70	16	12	83	88	29	31	Total Rtn % Rank Obj
2.56	2.40	2.40	2.24	2.16	2.00	1.92	1.92	1.91	1.62	1.51	1.35	Income $
0.24	0.00	0.00	0.00	0.00	0.00	0.00	0.00	0.00	0.00	0.00	0.00	Capital Gains $
0.97	0.97	0.93	0.89	0.88	0.89	0.88	0.93	0.96	0.92	0.97	0.96	Expense Ratio %
12.91	13.13	14.13	13.24	12.79	12.72	12.88	13.00	14.94	13.15	11.59	10.10	Income Ratio %
201	85	113	91	46	41	57	63	90	64	87	97	Turnover Rate %
412.6	388.7	474.9	627.0	763.9	858.6	718.1	544.9	731.4	942.3	1150.4	958.3	Net Assets ($mil)

Performance 12-31-94

	1st Qtr	2nd Qtr	3rd Qtr	4th Qtr	Total
1987	7.19	1.49	0.93	-2.36	7.20
1988	3.84	4.31	1.72	1.60	11.94
1989	2.47	2.90	1.04	-2.48	3.89
1990	-0.90	3.28	-4.08	-1.42	-3.21
1991	12.94	4.78	4.94	3.56	28.60
1992	7.52	2.76	2.79	0.25	13.85
1993	6.74	4.83	2.06	5.58	20.57
1994	-1.30	-0.07	0.81	-1.77	-2.33

Bear Market Performance

Decile Rank (5-year period)

Worst ———— Best

	Worst 3 Mo Period 1985-89	Worst 3 Mo Period 1990-94
Oppenheimer High-Yield A	-4.51	-6.66
+/- LB Aggregate	-5.33	-7.40
+/- Best Fit Index : FB HY	---	7.45

Trailing Returns

	Total Return %	+/- LB Aggregate	+/- FB High-Yield	% Rank All	% Rank Obj	Growth of $10,000
3 Mo	-1.77	-2.15	-1.73	63	65	9,823
6 Mo	-0.97	-1.96	-2.53	73	49	9,903
1 Yr	-2.33	0.58	-1.36	37	31	9,767
3 Yr Avg	10.27	5.72	-0.89	12	53	13,407
5 Yr Avg	10.78	3.16	-2.29	13	41	16,687
10 Yr Avg	10.50	0.55	---	53	38	27,139
15 Yr Avg	10.47	-0.33	---	72	63	44,556

Operations

Address and Telephone	P.O. Box 5270
	Denver, CO 80217-5270
	800-525-7048 / 303-671-3200
Advisor	Oppenheimer Management
Subadvisor	None
Distributor	Oppenheimer Fund Management
States Available	All plus PR
Report Grade	C+
Income Distrib	Paid Monthly
Date of Inception	07-28-78
Fiscal Year End	June

Risk Analysis

Time Period	Load-Adj Return %	Risk % Rank All	Risk % Rank Obj	Morningstar[2] Return	Morningstar[2] Risk	Morningstar Risk-Adj Rating
1 Yr	-6.97					
3 Yr	8.49	8	40	1.49[3]	0.37	★★★★
5 Yr	9.71	26	9	1.27[3]	0.38	★★★★
10 Yr	9.96	13	3	0.65	0.34	★★★★
Average Historical Rating (109 months)					3.3	★s

[1] 1 = low, 100 = high [2] 1.00 = Hybrid Avg [3] 1.00 = 90-day T-bill return

Other Measures

		Standard LB Agg	Best Fit FB HY
Standard Deviation	4.80	Alpha	6.0	-1.0
Mean	9.93	Beta	0.56	1.02
Sharpe Ratio	1.33	R-Squared	21	85

Investment Style

Interest-Rate Stance
Avg Effective Duration	4.1 Yrs
Avg Effective Maturity	9.4 Yrs

Quality
Avg Credit Quality	BB
Avg Weighted Coupon	9.92%
Avg Weighted Price	89.00% of Par

Maturity: Short Intm Long
Quality: High Med Low

Diversification Value for Portfolio Types

Large Cap: High	Small Cap: High	Bond: High	Balanced: High	Diversified: High

Min Initial Purchase	$1000 (Addt'l: $25)
Min IRA Purchase	$250 (Addt'l: $25)
Min Auto Invest Plan	$25 (Systematic Inv: $25)

Expenses & Fees
Sales Fees	
	4.75% front
	0.00% deferred
	0.25% 12b-1
Management Fee	0.75% max./0.50% min.
3-,5-,10-yr Expense Projections	$77, $97, $161

Portfolio 12-30-94

Amount 000	Date of Maturity	Total Stocks: 18 / Total Fixed-Income: 151	Value $000	% Net Assets
23858	09-01-01	Armco 8.5%	21353	2.24
46562	09-25-23	FNMA CMO 7%	17366	1.82
12201	01-15-00	Revco Drug Stores 9.125%	12231	1.28
13328	12-15-05	Westpoint Stevens 9.375%	12129	1.27
25329	04-01-04	Republic of Argentina FRN	12095	1.27
12024	04-15-03	Thrifty Payless 11.75%	11874	1.24
11494	12-15-02	USG 10.25%	11752	1.23
10402	07-15-02	OPI International 12.875%	11598	1.22
10609	08-01-02	Harman Intl Industries 12%	11511	1.21
11299	05-15-04	Santa Fe Energy Resources 11%	11384	1.19
10676	06-30-02	Gillett Holdings 12.25%	11343	1.19
10234	05-01-02	Healthtrust 10.75%	10873	1.14
10543	08-01-02	Wainoco Oil 12%	10807	1.13
10698	08-01-01	Ferrellgas 10%	10591	1.11
15472	05-27-98	Coleman Holdings 0%	10521	1.10
21219	03-01-05	Bell & Howell 0%	10503	1.10
10212	04-15-00	Georgia Gulf 15%	10467	1.10
11052	02-15-03	Di Giorgio 12%	10388	1.09
9770	05-15-01	Gaylord Container 11.5%	10087	1.06
11096	08-01-00	Royal Crown 9.75%	9931	1.04
10123	10-01-01	Cole National 11.25%	9794	1.03
10609	12-01-02	Synthetic Industries 12.75%	9389	0.98
10477	07-15-00	Grand Union 11.25%	9324	0.98
8819	10-01-03	Card Establishment Svc 10%	9216	0.97
8709	06-15-02	Riverwood Intl 11.25%	9013	0.94

Composition % 12-31-94

Cash	12.5	Preferreds	1.4
Stocks	1.3	Convertibles	0.0
Bonds	84.0	Other	0.8

Tax Analysis

	Tax-Adj Historical Return %	% Pretax Return
3 Yr Avg	6.09	56.9
5 Yr Avg	6.26	53.1
10 Yr Avg	5.40	40.4
Potential Capital Gain Exposure (% of assets)	-24%	

Most Similar Funds in MF500

Liberty High-Income Bond A	Strong Fit
AIM High-Yield A	Strong Fit
Putnam High Yield Adv A	Strong Fit

Coupon Range

	% of Bonds	Rel Obj
0%, PIK	10.8	1.46
0% to 11%	47.2	0.96
11% to 13%	34.9	1.05
13% to 14.5%	2.3	0.42
More than 14.5%	0.2	0.12
Not applicable	4.6	1.52

Credit Analysis 12-31-94
% of Bonds

US Govt	4	BB	12
AAA	12	B	51
AA	0	Below B	5
A	0	NR/NA	14
BBB	2		

MORNINGSTAR 1995 Mutual Fund 500

Oppenheimer Main St Inc & Grth A

	Ticker	Load	NAV	Yield	SEC Yield	Assets	Objective
	MSIGX	5.75%	20.98	2.1%	N/A	1268.8	Growth/Inc.

Oppenheimer Main Street Income & Growth Fund - Class A seeks total return.

The fund invests in income-producing common stocks, preferred stocks, convertible securities, bonds, debentures, and notes. The fund may invest without limit in foreign equity and debt securities. It may invest up to 10% of its assets in convertible securities rated below investment grade.

Class A shares have front loads and lower 12b-1 fees; Class C shares have level loads. Main Street Asset Allocation Fund was merged into this fund on Oct. 1, 1992. Prior to Nov. 1, 1993, the fund was named Main Street Income and Growth Fund.

Manager's Investment Style

Management surrounds a core of stable dividend-paying stocks (including utilities and high-dividend large-cap growth issues) with bonds on the one hand and small-cap earnings-growth issues on the other. The fund's turnover is quite high.

Historical Profile
Return High
Risk Average
Rating ★★★★★ Highest

Investment Style History
Equity
Average % Stocks Held in Portfolio

72% 54% 81% 85% 86% 73%

Growth of $10,000
|||| Value of Fund ($000)
— Value of Index ($000)
  Russ 2000
▼ Manager Change
▽ Partial Manager Change
► Mgr Unknown After
◄ Mgr Unknown Before

Performance Quartile (Within Objective)

	1983	1984	1985	1986	1987	1988	1989	1990	1991	1992	1993	1994	History
	---	---	---	---	---	10.11	12.29	11.14	15.52	17.85	21.76	20.98	NAV
	---	---	---	---	---	8.04 *	25.18	-6.15	66.37	31.08	35.39	-1.53	Total Return %
	---	---	---	---	---	-6.02 *	-6.51	-3.03	35.89	23.46	25.33	-2.85	+/- S&P 500
	---	---	---	---	---	---	-4.00	0.03	32.16	22.11	24.10	-1.46	+/- Wilshire 5000
	---	---	---	---	---	1.29	1.94	3.21	1.65	1.23	1.40	2.04	Income Return %
	---	---	---	---	---	6.75	23.24	-9.36	64.72	29.85	33.99	-3.57	Capital Return %
	---	---	---	---	---	---	23	74	3	1	6	30	Total Rtn % Rank All
	---	---	---	---	---	---	44	69	1	1	1	58	Total Rtn % Rank Obj
	---	---	---	---	---	0.13	0.20	0.40	0.22	0.19	0.28	0.44	Income $
	---	---	---	---	---	0.13	0.15	0.00	2.51	2.20	1.99	0.00	Capital Gains $
	---	---	---	---	---	0.00	2.12	2.21	1.84	1.66	1.46	1.28	Expense Ratio %
	---	---	---	---	---	2.86	2.67	2.33	3.15	1.63	1.02	2.46	Income Ratio %
	---	---	---	---	---	---	137	214	209	290	283	199	Turnover Rate %
	---	---	---	---	---	0.8	7.6	13.9	23.7	38.9	164.4	1268.8	Net Assets ($mil)

Fund Manager(s)

John L. Wallace, since 01-91. Birthdate: 04-54.
BA, U. of Idaho 1978   MBA, Pace U. 1987

Manager Experience

	Dates Managed	Invest Obj	Std Dev	+/- Index

Not available.

Performance 12-31-94

	1st Qtr	2nd Qtr	3rd Qtr	4th Qtr	Total
1987	---	---	---	---	---
1988	---	2.73	-0.59	2.59	8.04 *
1989	7.62	8.21	7.63	-0.13	25.18
1990	-0.90	2.39	-9.95	2.71	-6.15
1991	19.04	0.45	20.35	15.61	66.37
1992	7.09	-6.39	2.91	27.05	31.08
1993	8.18	3.38	14.41	5.81	35.39
1994	-0.25	-5.22	5.84	-1.60	-1.53

Bear Market Performance

Decile Rank (5-year period)

Worst ——————— Best

	Worst 3 Mo Period 1985-89	Worst 3 Mo Period 1990-94
Oppenheimer Main St Inc & Grt	---	-13.03
+/- S&P 500	---	0.81
+/- Best Fit Index : Russ 2000	---	12.87

Trailing Returns

	Total Return %	+/- S&P 500	+/- Wil 5000	% Rank All	% Rank Obj	Growth of $10,000
3 Mo	-1.60	-1.58	-0.83	59	54	9,840
6 Mo	4.15	-0.71	-0.48	15	27	10,415
1 Yr	-1.53	-2.85	-1.46	30	58	9,847
3 Yr Avg	20.45	14.18	13.84	1	1	17,474
5 Yr Avg	22.23	13.54	13.41	1	1	27,284
10 Yr Avg	---	---	---	---	---	---
15 Yr Avg	---	---	---	---	---	---

Operations

Address and Telephone	P.O. Box 5270	
	Denver, CO 80217-5270	
	800-525-7048	
Advisor	Oppenheimer Management	
Subadvisor	None	
Distributor	Oppenheimer Funds Distributor	
States Available	All plus PR	
Report Grade	B-	
Income Distrib	Paid Quarterly	
* Date of Inception	02-03-88	
Fiscal Year End	June	

Min Initial Purchase	$1000 (Addt'l: $25)
Min IRA Purchase	$250 (Addt'l: $25)
Min Auto Invest Plan	$25 (Systematic Inv: $25)

Expenses & Fees
Sales Fees	5.75% front
	0.00% deferred
	0.25% 12b-1
Management Fee	0.65% flat fee
3-,5-,10-yr Expense Projections	$96, $124, $203
Annual Brokerage Cost	1.94%

Risk Analysis

Time Period	Load-Adj Return %	Risk % Rank [1] All	Obj	Morningstar [2] Return	Morningstar Risk	Morningstar Risk-Adj Rating
1 Yr	-7.19					
3 Yr	18.09	78	90	4.81 [3]	0.92	★★★★★
5 Yr	20.79	70	68	5.06 [3]	0.83	★★★★★
10 Yr						

Average Historical Rating (47 months)   4.7 ★ s

[1] 1 = low, 100 = high   [2] 1.00 = Equity Avg   [3] 1.00 = 90-day T-bill return

Other Measures

			Standard S&P 500	Best Fit Russ 2000
Standard Deviation	14.07	Alpha	13.9	7.7
Mean	19.72	Beta	1.09	1.10
Sharpe Ratio	1.15	R-Squared	38	84

Investment Style

	Stock Portfolio Avg	Relative S&P 500
Price/Earnings Ratio	20.9	1.13
Price/Book Ratio	3.4	1.01
5 Yr Earnings Gr %	13.3	2.39
Return on Assets %	9.4	1.26
Debt % Total Cap	30.9	1.09
Med Mkt Cap ($mil)	2889	0.22

Style
Value Blend Growth
Size Large/Med/Small

Diversification Value for Portfolio Types

Large Cap: Medium	Small Cap: None	Bond: High	Balanced: Medium	Diversified: Medium

Portfolio 12-30-94

Total Stocks: 206
Total Fixed-Income: 22

Share Chg (06-94)000	Amount 000		Value $000	% Net Assets
535	535	Compuware	19253	1.52
98	280	Philip Morris	16128	1.27
241	404	H & R Block	14995	1.18
317	561	Public Service Enterprise	14866	1.17
188	411	Houston Industries	14656	1.16
	14960	Time Warner Cv 8.75%	14099	1.11
358	561	Pacific Gas & Electric	13674	1.08
246	449	GTE	13632	1.07
168	168	Texas Instruments	12601	0.99
210	393	Texas Utilities	12566	0.99
26	168	NIKE Cl B	12559	0.99
296	296	Cyrk	12240	0.96
337	337	cisco Systems	11823	0.93
146	243	First Chicago	11608	0.91
214	385	Millicom	11584	0.91
449	449	Unifi	11444	0.90
224	224	AT & T	11276	0.89
97	479	Rite Aid	11207	0.88
378	378	Bay Networks	11143	0.88
269	269	Lotus Development	11040	0.87
243	243	Genentech	11030	0.87
269	411	CoreStates Financial	10696	0.84
524	524	Occidental Petroleum	10079	0.79
168	168	Amgen	9929	0.78
109	150	Eli Lilly	9817	0.77

Composition % 09-30-94

Cash	10.6	Preferreds	5.0
Stocks	74.8	Convertibles	0.0
Bonds	9.6	Other	0.0

Tax Analysis

	Tax-Adj Historical Return %	% Pretax Return
3 Yr Avg	17.65	84.1
5 Yr Avg	19.21	81.4
10 Yr Avg	---	---
Potential Capital Gain Exposure (% of assets)		-1%

Most Similar Funds in MF500

Acorn	Fair Fit
T. Rowe Price Science & Tech	Fair Fit
FPA Capital	Fair Fit

Index Allocation

	% of Stocks
S&P 500	53.2
S&P MidCap 400	15.1
U.S. Small Cap	27.2
Foreign	5.1

Sector Weightings

	% of Stocks	Relative S&P 500
Utilities	16.5	1.33
Energy	4.6	0.46
Financials	9.7	0.92
Industrial Cyclicals	6.4	0.39
Consumer Durables	5.5	0.89
Consumer Staples	5.3	0.42
Services	14.9	1.83
Retail	3.4	0.58
Health	10.4	1.19
Technology	23.3	2.55

Oppenheimer Strategic Income A

	Ticker	Load	NAV	Yield	SEC Yield	Assets		Objective
	OPSIX	4.75%	4.55	9.2%	9.65%	2986.9		Income

Oppenheimer Strategic Income Fund - Class A seeks current income.

The fund intends to invest primarily in the following: 1) foreign government and corporate debt securities; 2) U.S. government securities; and 3) lower-rated, high-yield domestic bonds. It also writes covered call options on these securities.

Class A shares have front loads; Class B shares have deferred loads and higher 12b-1 fees.

On Oct. 18, 1991, Advance Americas Funds Strategic Income Fund merged into this fund.

Manager's Investment Style

Unlike some other strategic fund managers, who rely heavily on asset allocation, this fund's management changes its sector choices gradually, and rarely goes to extremes in any single market. Within each sector, however, management has been known to be aggressive, investing heavily in long Treasuries, low-quality cyclicals, and emerging-market debt.

Fund Manager(s)

Arthur P. Steinmetz, since 10-89. Birthdate: 10-58. BA, Denison U. 1980 MBA, Columbia U. 1983
David P. Negri, since 10-89. Birthdate: 04-54. PhD, Harvard MBA, Wharton

Manager Experience

	Dates Managed	Invest Obj	Std Dev	+/- Index
Arthur P. Steinmetz				
Oppenheimer U.S. Govt A	01/87 - 01/94	GG	3.78	-1.24
Oppenheimer Mortg Inc A	09/86 - 04/92	GM	3.95	-0.89

Historical Profile

Return	Above Average
Risk	Low
Rating	★★★★
	Above Average

Income Rtn % Rank Obj	5	11	18	2	8

Investment Style History
Fixed Income

Growth of $10,000

- |||| Value of Fund ($000)
- — Value of Index ($000) LB L-T
- ▼ Manager Change
- ▽ Partial Manager Change
- ► Mgr Unknown After
- ◄ Mgr Unknown Before

Performance Quartile (Within Objective)

	1983	1984	1985	1986	1987	1988	1989	1990	1991	1992	1993	1994	History
	---	---	---	---	---	---	5.00	4.75	5.06	4.89	5.22	4.55	NAV
	---	---	---	---	---	---	1.52 *	8.44	20.26	7.74	19.51	-4.70	Total Return %
	---	---	---	---	---	---	-2.42 *	11.55	-10.23	0.12	9.46	-6.02	+/- S&P 500
	---	---	---	---	---	---	---	-0.51	4.26	0.50	9.76	-1.78	+/- LB Aggregate
	---	---	---	---	---	---	1.12	12.39	12.77	9.36	10.48	7.93	Income Return %
	---	---	---	---	---	---	0.40	-3.96	7.49	-1.62	9.03	-12.63	Capital Return %
	---	---	---	---	---	---	---	12	44	49	18	61	Total Rtn % Rank All
	---	---	---	---	---	---	---	5	71	60	4	53	Total Rtn % Rank Obj
	---	---	---	---	---	---	0.06	0.60	0.56	0.46	0.48	0.43	Income $
	---	---	---	---	---	---	0.02	0.06	0.04	0.09	0.10	0.01	Capital Gains $
	---	---	---	---	---	---	---	1.36	1.27	1.16	1.09	0.99	Expense Ratio %
	---	---	---	---	---	---	---	12.79	11.82	9.39	9.78	8.53	Income Ratio %
	---	---	---	---	---	---	---	425	195	208	149	---	Turnover Rate %
	---	---	---	---	---	---	217.9	763.4	1917.3	3016.4	2986.9		Net Assets ($mil)

Performance 12-31-94

	1st Qtr	2nd Qtr	3rd Qtr	4th Qtr	Total
1987	---	---	---	---	---
1988	---	---	---	---	---
1989	---	---	---	---	1.52 *
1990	0.79	5.84	0.57	1.07	8.44
1991	6.65	2.36	5.93	3.99	20.26
1992	1.13	4.57	2.32	-0.43	7.74
1993	6.22	4.16	3.10	4.77	19.51
1994	-3.58	-0.43	1.42	-2.12	-4.70

Bear Market Performance

Decile Rank (5-year period)

Worst ▮ Best

	Worst 3 Mo Period 1985-89	Worst 3 Mo Period 1990-94
Oppenheimer Strategic Income	---	-6.20
+/- S&P 500	---	-0.45
+/- Best Fit Index : LB L-T	---	3.19

Trailing Returns

	Total Return %	+/- S&P 500	+/- LB Aggregate	% Rank All	% Rank Obj	Growth of $10,000
3 Mo	-2.12	-2.10	-2.50	71	70	9,788
6 Mo	-0.73	-5.60	-1.73	69	63	9,927
1 Yr	-4.70	-6.02	-1.78	61	53	9,530
3 Yr Avg	7.06	0.80	2.52	26	26	12,271
5 Yr Avg	9.86	1.17	2.23	18	14	16,002
10 Yr Avg	---	---	---	---	---	---
15 Yr Avg	---	---	---	---	---	---

Operations

Address and Telephone	P.O. Box 5270
	Denver, CO 80217-5270
	800-525-7048 / 303-671-3200
Advisor	Oppenheimer Management
Subadvisor	None
Distributor	Oppenheimer Fund Management
States Available	All plus PR
Report Grade	B
Income Distrib	Paid Monthly
* Date of Inception	10-16-89
Fiscal Year End	September

Risk Analysis

Time Period	Load-Adj Return %	Risk % Rank [1] All	Obj	Morningstar [2] Return	Risk	Morningstar Risk-Adj Rating
1 Yr	-9.23					
3 Yr	5.34	24	36	0.52 [3]	0.51	★★★
5 Yr	8.79	23	8	1.02 [3]	0.36	★★★★
10 Yr	---	---	---	---	---	---

Average Historical Rating (27 months)   4.0 ★s

[1] = low, 100 = high   [2] 1.00 = Hybrid Avg   [3] 1.00 = 90-day T-bill return

Other Measures

			Standard S&P 500	Best Fit LB L-T
Standard Deviation	4.87	Alpha	2.7	2.6
Mean	6.96	Beta	0.28	0.45
Sharpe Ratio	0.71	R-Squared	20	50

Investment Style

Stocks

	Port Avg	Rel S&P 500
Price/Earnings Ratio	---	---
Price/Book Ratio	---	---
5 Yr Earnings Gr %	---	---
Med Mkt Cap ($mil)	---	---

Not Available

Bonds

Avg Effective Duration	5.1 Yrs **
Avg Effective Maturity	---
Avg Credit Quality	BBB
Avg Weighted Coupon	9.05%

**figure provided by fund

Not Available

Diversification Value for Portfolio Types

Large Cap: High	Small Cap: High	Bond: Low	Balanced: Medium	Diversified: Medium

Expenses & Fees

Sales Fees	4.75% front
	0.00% deferred
	0.25% 12b-1
Management Fee	0.75% max./0.50% min.
3-,5-,10-yr Expense Projections	$81, $105, $174
Annual Brokerage Cost	---

Min Initial Purchase	$1000 (Addt'l: $25)
Min IRA Purchase	$250 (Addt'l: $25)
Min Auto Invest Plan	$25 (Systematic Inv: $25)

Portfolio 12-30-94

Share Chg (03-94)000	Amount 000		Date of Maturity	Value $000	% Net Assets
		Total Stocks: 10 Total Fixed-Income: 348			
	162296	US Treasury Note 8.75%	08-15-00	169092	5.66
	128988	US Treasury Bond 7.875%	02-15-21	127295	4.26
	84067	US Treasury Note 8.875%	11-15-97	86352	2.89
	10424173	Kingdom of Spain 12.25%	03-25-00	80321	2.69
	65310	US Treasury Bond 8.125%	08-15-21	66351	2.22
	65310	US Treasury Bond 7.125%	02-15-23	59412	1.99
	28569	United Kingdom Treasury 10%	11-20-98	49354	1.65
	67558	Republic of Argentina 5.625%	04-01-01	43276	1.45
	61412	Govt of New Zealand 10%	07-15-97	39948	1.34
	100765	FNMA CMO I/O 7%	09-25-23	37582	1.26
	56820	Republic of Argentina 6.5%	03-31-05	36329	1.22
	50462	Commonwealth Australia 8%	08-14-01	34793	1.16
	32655	GNMA TBA 7.5%	03-01-25	32604	1.09
	46338	Kingdom of Morocco FRN	01-01-09	30757	1.03
	42661	Govt of New Zealand 12.5%	07-25-97	29261	0.98
	25079	FNMA CMO REMIC PAC 10.5%	11-25-20	27674	0.93
	68790	FNMA CMO I/O 8%	07-25-24	27517	0.92
	3569859	Kingdom of Spain 10.25%	11-30-98	25941	0.87
	57108	FNMA CMO I/O 7.5%	11-30-23	21763	0.73
	55407	FNMA CMO I/O 7.5%	05-25-23	20760	0.70

Index Allocation

	% of Stocks
S&P 500	0.0
S&P MidCap 400	0.0
U.S. Small Cap	93.0
Foreign	7.0

Composition % 12-31-94

Cash	2.4	Preferreds	1.0
Stocks	0.2	Convertibles	0.0
Bonds	94.4	Other	2.0

Tax Analysis

	Tax-Adj Historical Return %	% Pretax Return
3 Yr Avg	3.23	44.0
5 Yr Avg	5.82	54.5
10 Yr Avg	---	---

Potential Capital Gain Exposure (% of assets)   -12%

Most Similar Funds in MF500

Global Income Plus	Fair Fit
Colonial Strategic Income A	Weak Fit
Phoenix Multi-Sector F/I A	Weak Fit

Bond Credit Analysis 12-31-94

% of Bonds

US Govt	32	BB	6
AAA	5	B	17
AA	0	Below B	4
A	1	NR/NA	34
BBB	2		

Stock Sector Weightings

	% of Stocks	Relative S&P 500
Utilities	0.0	0.00
Energy	0.0	0.00
Financials	7.4	0.70
Industrial Cyclicals	0.0	0.00
Consumer Durables	0.0	0.00
Consumer Staples	0.0	0.00
Services	26.2	3.22
Retail	66.4	11.40
Health	0.0	0.00
Technology	0.0	0.00

362

Oppenheimer Tax-Free Bond A

	Ticker	Load	NAV	Yield	SEC Yield	Assets	Objective
	OPTAX	4.75%	8.93	6.2%	5.66%	541.2	Muni Nat

Oppenheimer Tax-Free Bond Fund - Class A seeks current income exempt from federal income taxes, consistent with capital preservation.

The fund normally invests at least 80% of its assets in investment-grade tax-exempt securities. It may invest up to 20% of its assets in AMT-subject bonds, and up to 25% in bonds rated BBB; no bonds rated below BBB may be purchased.

Class A shares have front loads; Class B shares have deferred loads and higher 12b-1 fees. MassMutual Tax-Exempt Bond Fund merged into the fund in March 1991, Advance America Funds Tax-Free Income Fund in Oct. 1991, and Main Street Tax-Free Income Fund in Oct. 1992.

Manager's Investment Style

Management historically has shown a reluctance to move quickly, as illustrated by the portfolio's low turnover rate. Inverse floaters balanced by prefunded issues and high-coupon yield-to-call paper are also part of the strategy, while management is restricted by charter to BBB or better credits.

Fund Manager(s)

Robert E. Patterson, since 11-85. Birthdate: 1943. BA, Rutgers U. 1965

Manager Experience	Dates Managed	Invest Obj	Std Dev	+/- Index
Robert E. Patterson				
Oppenheim Multi-Sect	03/88 - 01/93	MB	3.91	-5.77

Historical Profile
Return — Below Average
Risk — Above Average
Rating ★★ Below Average

	40	31	30	32	22	30	21	26

Income Rtn % Rank Obj

Investment Style History
Fixed Income

Growth of $10,000
|||| Value of Fund ($000)
— Value of Index ($000) LB Muni
▼ Manager Change
▽ Partial Manager Change
► Mgr Unknown After
◄ Mgr Unknown Before

Performance Quartile (Within Objective)

	1983	1984	1985	1986	1987	1988	1989	1990	1991	1992	1993	1994	History
NAV	7.77	7.87	8.80	9.81	9.12	9.27	9.45	9.33	9.77	9.94	10.44	8.93	NAV
	16.92	10.60	21.38	19.75	0.00	9.51	9.46	5.87	12.14	9.50	13.48	-9.30	Total Return %
	8.55	-4.55	-0.75	4.50	-2.76	1.64	-5.08	-3.08	-3.86	2.26	3.73	-6.38	+/- LB Aggregate
	8.87	0.05	1.35	0.44	-1.51	-0.65	-1.32	-1.43	0.00	0.68	1.20	-3.70	+/- LB Muni
	9.45	9.32	9.56	8.27	7.03	7.87	7.52	7.14	7.42	6.52	6.22	5.13	Income Return %
	7.47	1.29	11.82	11.48	-7.03	1.64	1.94	-1.27	4.72	2.98	7.26	-14.43	Capital Return %
	51	23	63	21	60	65	80	36	75	27	37	91	Total Rtn % Rank All
	2	9	23	21	51	68	51	72	31	19	14	96	Total Rtn % Rank Obj
	0.64	0.68	0.68	0.67	0.68	0.69	0.67	0.65	0.65	0.61	0.60	0.55	Income $
	0.00	0.00	0.00	0.00	0.00	0.00	0.00	0.00	0.00	0.12	0.21	0.00	Capital Gains $
	0.85	0.86	0.82	0.78	0.78	0.72	0.82	0.89	0.89	0.94	0.88	0.88	Expense Ratio %
	8.21	8.91	8.36	7.33	7.41	7.48	7.18	7.08	6.70	6.34	5.71	5.82	Income Ratio %
	608	386	211	28	29	23	57	29	24	34	30	---	Turnover Rate %
	62.7	79.4	89.3	126.9	133.5	172.0	224.2	256.6	393.6	496.4	608.1	541.2	Net Assets ($mil)

Performance 12-31-94

	1st Qtr	2nd Qtr	3rd Qtr	4th Qtr	Total
1987	2.53	-4.65	-2.25	4.64	0.00
1988	2.76	2.30	2.52	1.62	9.51
1989	0.96	5.12	-0.10	3.24	9.46
1990	0.43	1.96	-0.42	3.83	5.87
1991	2.59	1.82	4.07	3.15	12.14
1992	0.23	4.34	2.16	2.50	9.50
1993	3.67	3.46	4.54	1.22	13.48
1994	-6.59	-0.66	0.20	-2.46	-9.30

Bear Market Performance

Decile Rank (5-year period)

Worst ————————— Best

	Worst 3 Mo Period 1985-89	Worst 3 Mo Period 1990-94
Oppenheimer Tax-Free Bond A	-7.26	-8.30
+/- LB Aggregate	-3.70	-3.37
+/- Best Fit Index : LB Muni	-0.76	-2.54

Trailing Returns

	Total Return %	+/- LB Aggregate	+/- LB Muni	% Rank All	% Rank Obj	Growth of $10,000
3 Mo	-2.46	-2.84	-1.02	76	94	9,754
6 Mo	-2.26	-3.25	-1.02	90	92	9,774
1 Yr	-9.30	-6.38	-3.70	91	96	9,070
3 Yr Avg	4.07	-0.48	-0.80	68	73	11,270
5 Yr Avg	6.00	-1.63	-0.78	76	60	13,379
10 Yr Avg	8.83	-1.11	-0.60	75	47	23,312
15 Yr Avg	8.39	-2.42	-0.08	90	27	33,478

Operations

Address and Telephone	P.O. Box 5270
	Denver, CO 80217-5270
	800-525-7048 / 303-671-3200
Advisor	Oppenheimer Management
Subadvisor	None
Distributor	Oppenheimer Funds Distributor
States Available	All plus PR
Report Grade	B-
Income Distrib	Paid Monthly
Date of Inception	10-27-76
Fiscal Year End	December

Min Initial Purchase	$1000 (Addt'l: $25)
Min IRA Purchase	$250 (Addt'l: $25)
Min Auto Invest Plan	$25 (Systematic Inv: $25)

Expenses & Fees
Sales Fees	4.75% front
	0.00% deferred
	0.25% 12b-1
Management Fee	0.60% max./0.35% min.
3-,5-,10-yr Expense Projections	$74, $94, $151

Risk Analysis

Time Period	Load-Adj Return %	Risk % Rank All	Risk % Rank Obj	Morningstar Return	Morningstar Risk	Morningstar Risk-Adj Rating
1 Yr	-13.61					
3 Yr	2.39	49	89	0.59	1.28	★
5 Yr	4.97	34	73	0.78	1.22	★
10 Yr	8.30	18	51	0.97	1.09	★★
Average Historical Rating (109 months)				3.4 ★s		

[1] 1 = low, 100 = high [2] 1.00 = Muni Avg [3] 1.00 = 90-day T-bill return

Other Measures

				Standard LB Agg	Best Fit LB Muni
Standard Deviation	6.80	Alpha		-0.6	-1.0
Mean	4.22	Beta		1.28	1.20
Sharpe Ratio	0.10	R-Squared		57	94

Investment Style

Interest-Rate Stance
Avg Effective Maturity 20.5 Yrs

Quality
Avg Credit Quality AA
Avg Weighted Coupon 6.21%
Avg Weighted Price 91.04% of Par

Diversification Value for Portfolio Types

Large Cap: Medium | Small Cap: High | Bond: Low | Balanced: Low | Diversified: Medium

Portfolio 12-30-94

Total Stocks: 0
Total Fixed-Income: 107

Amount 000	Date of Maturity		Value $000	% Net Assets
18204	02-01-11	MA State GO 5.5%	16270	3.01
16839	02-01-20	TX San Antonio Elec/Gas Sys 6%	15820	2.92
61429	09-01-16	TX Muni Pwr Cap Apprec 0%	15118	2.79
16784	01-01-16	DE Transp Sys 5.5%	14439	2.67
15928	03-01-12	KS Dept Transp Hwy 5.375%	14037	2.59
13789	01-01-16	NJ Tpk 6.5%	13789	2.55
15928	03-01-22	PA Higher Educ Assist Student Loan RIB	12202	2.25
11377	07-01-18	PR Hwy/Transp 6.625%	11693	2.16
10012	08-01-15	NY New York City GO 8%	11375	2.10
42734	02-15-16	TX Cypress/Fairbanks GO ISD 0%	11207	2.07
11377	12-01-29	TX Alliance Arpt Spcl Fac American 7.5%	10724	1.98
11127	07-15-19	MA Wtr Resource 6.5%	10718	1.98
11377	02-01-17	WA State GO 5.75%	10140	1.87
11969	02-01-14	TX San Antonio Elec/Gas Sys 5%	9696	1.79
11559	01-01-32	CA San Joaquin Hills Transp Toll 6.75%	9620	1.78
10922	03-01-12	MA GO Bay Transp Genl Sys 5.5%	9586	1.77
9102	07-01-24	SC Pub Svc Santee Cooper 6.5%	9535	1.76
9785	01-01-17	GA Muni Elec Spcl Obl 6.5%	9506	1.76
8488	07-01-20	NY Dorm City Univ Sys 7.625%	9427	1.74
9102	01-15-17	IN Indianapolis Arpt 7.1%	8750	1.62

Credit Analysis % of Bonds 12-31-94

US Govt	0	BB	4
AAA	36	B	0
AA	25	Below B	0
A	23	NR/NA	6
BBB	7		

Composition % of Assets 12-31-94

Cash	1.5	Preferreds	0.0
Stocks	0.0	Convertibles	0.0
Bonds	98.5	Other	0.0

Tax Analysis

	Tax-Adj Historical Return %	% Pretax Return
3 Yr Avg	3.76	92.1
5 Yr Avg	5.81	96.5
10 Yr Avg	8.74	98.4
Potential Capital Gain Exposure (% of assets)		-7%

Most Similar Funds in MF500

Lord Abbett T/F Income Natl	Strong Fit
Fidelity Municipal Bond	Strong Fit
Safeco Municipal Bond	Strong Fit

Coupon Range

	% Bonds	Rel Obj
0%	4.7	1.88
0% to 6.8%	60.9	1.01
6.8% to 7.5%	11.1	0.71
7.5% to 8.3%	9.8	1.11
More than 8.3%	1.8	0.21
Not applicable	11.7	3.01

Sector Weightings

	% Bonds	Rel Obj
General Obl	18.81	0.89
Utilities	17.75	1.42
Health	9.62	0.73
Water/Waste	7.81	1.23
Housing	5.17	0.71
Education	7.03	1.10
Transportation	22.98	2.26
COP/Lease	2.52	0.79
Private	6.13	0.53
Misc Revenue	2.17	0.44
Demand	0.00	0.00

Top 5 States % of Bonds

TX	17.65	MA	8.70
NY	14.63	MI	5.55
CA	9.39		

Overland Express Asset Alloc A

Ticker	Load	NAV	Yield	SEC Yield	Assets	Objective
OEAAX	4.50%	10.67	2.7%	N/A	40.3	Asset Alloc.

Overland Express Asset Allocation Fund - Class A seeks long-term total return consistent with reasonable risk.

The fund may invest in three asset classes: common stocks in the S&P 500 Index, U.S. Treasury bonds with maturities generally between 20 and 30 years, and high-quality money-market instruments. It seeks to maximize its long-term investment results by shifting its investments periodically among the various asset classes according to prevailing market conditions.

Class A shares have front loads; Class D shares have level loads.

Historical Profile
Return	Average
Risk	Below Average
Rating ★★★★	Above Average

Manager's Investment Style

Management relies on a quantitative asset-allocation model that recommends stock and bond weightings according to such factors as bond yields and equity valuations. At times, this approach has put the fund wholly into equities, for example. Both the stock and bond strategies are relatively staid, with the equity stake indexing the S&P 500, and the bonds stake following the Lehman Brothers Long-Term Government Bond Index.

Fund Manager(s)
Management Team

Investment Style History
Equity

Average % Stocks Held in Portfolio

---	---	16%	33%	49%	82%	72%

Growth of $10,000
- |||| Value of Fund ($000)
- — Value of Index ($000) S&P 500
- ▼ Manager Change
- ▽ Partial Manager Change
- ► Mgr Unknown After
- ◄ Mgr Unknown Before

Performance Quartile (Within Objective)

Manager Experience

	Dates Managed	Invest Obj	Std Dev	+/- Index
Janice L. Deringer				
Stagecoach Asset Alloc A	11/86 - 12/94	AA	7.27	-1.73
Stagecoach U.S. Gvt All A	03/87 - 12/94	GT	5.96	-0.33

	1983	1984	1985	1986	1987	1988	1989	1990	1991	1992	1993	1994	History
NAV	---	---	---	---	---	10.32	10.58	10.65	11.95	11.45	11.90	10.67	NAV
Total Return %	---	---	---	---	---	4.60 *	10.23	7.08	20.65	7.44	12.54	-0.68	Total Return %
+/- S&P 500	---	---	---	---	---	-2.71 *	-21.45	10.20	-9.84	-0.18	2.48	-2.00	+/- S&P 500
+/- LB Aggregate	---	---	---	---	---	---	-4.31	-1.87	4.65	0.19	2.79	2.23	+/- LB Aggregate
Income Return %	---	---	---	---	---	1.40	6.39	5.93	6.18	5.59	2.61	2.74	Income Return %
Capital Return %	---	---	---	---	---	3.20	3.84	1.15	14.47	1.85	9.93	-3.42	Capital Return %
Total Rtn % Rank All	---	---	---	---	---	---	71	21	44	52	46	25	Total Rtn % Rank All
Total Rtn % Rank Obj	---	---	---	---	---	---	85	4	56	38	57	19	Total Rtn % Rank Obj
Income $	---	---	---	---	---	0.14	0.62	0.59	0.59	0.63	0.30	0.31	Income $
Capital Gains $	---	---	---	---	---	0.00	0.13	0.05	0.19	0.71	0.67	0.84	Capital Gains $
Expense Ratio %	---	---	---	---	---	1.76	1.76	1.59	1.38	1.25	1.36	1.31	Expense Ratio %
Income Ratio %	---	---	---	---	---	4.69	6.44	6.01	5.23	4.08	2.64	3.36	Income Ratio %
Turnover Rate %	---	---	---	---	---	---	62	94	18	38	53	---	Turnover Rate %
Net Assets ($mil)	---	---	---	---	---	13.2	24.3	28.6	38.7	41.2	50.3	40.3	Net Assets ($mil)

Performance 12-31-94

	1st Qtr	2nd Qtr	3rd Qtr	4th Qtr	Total
1987	---	---	---	---	---
1988	---	---	0.35	1.79	4.60 *
1989	2.14	2.36	3.54	1.83	10.23
1990	0.40	2.86	-1.46	5.22	7.08
1991	5.18	-0.22	7.09	7.34	20.65
1992	-4.62	4.07	4.84	3.24	7.44
1993	5.84	1.45	2.86	1.91	12.54
1994	-3.62	-0.63	3.25	0.44	-0.68

Bear Market Performance
Decile Rank (5-year period)

Worst ——————————————— Best

	Worst 3 Mo Period 1985-89	Worst 3 Mo Period 1990-94
Overland Express Asset Alloc A	---	-6.03
+/- S&P 500	---	-0.28
+/- Best Fit Index : S&P 500	---	-0.28

Trailing Returns

	Total Return %	+/- S&P 500	+/- LB Aggregate	% Rank All	Obj	Growth of $10,000
3 Mo	0.44	0.46	0.06	13	11	10,044
6 Mo	3.71	-1.16	2.71	17	11	10,371
1 Yr	-0.68	-2.00	2.23	25	19	9,932
3 Yr Avg	6.29	0.02	1.74	31	29	12,008
5 Yr Avg	9.18	0.49	1.55	22	27	15,513
10 Yr Avg	---	---	---	---	---	---
15 Yr Avg	---	---	---	---	---	---

Operations

Address and Telephone	111 Center Street
	Little Rock, AR 72201
	800-552-9612 / 501-377-2569
Advisor	Wells Fargo Bank
Subadvisor	None
Distributor	Stephens
States Available	All
Report Grade	C
Income Distrib	Paid Quarterly
* Date of Inception	04-07-88
Fiscal Year End	December

Risk Analysis

Time Period	Load-Adj Return %	Risk % Rank [1] All	Obj	Morningstar [2] Return	Morningstar Risk	Morningstar Risk-Adj Rating
1 Yr	-5.15					
3 Yr	4.67	58	68	0.32 [3]	0.84	★★★
5 Yr	8.18	46	18	0.86 [3]	0.58	★★★★
10 Yr						
Average Historical Rating (45 months)				3.8 ★s		

[1] 1 = low, 100 = high [2] 1.00 = Hybrid Avg [3] 1.00 = 90-day T-bill return

Other Measures

		Standard S&P 500	Best Fit S&P 500
Standard Deviation	7.05	Alpha	0.4	0.4
Mean	6.36	Beta	0.83	0.83
Sharpe Ratio	0.40	R-Squared	88	88

Investment Style

Stocks
	Port Avg	Rel S&P 500
Price/Earnings Ratio	18.1	0.98
Price/Book Ratio	3.3	0.97
5 Yr Earnings Gr %	5.2	0.94
Med Mkt Cap ($mil)	12641	0.97

Style V B G

Bonds
Avg Effective Duration	NMF
Avg Effective Maturity	25 Yrs
Avg Credit Quality	AAA
Avg Weighted Coupon	8.36%

Maturity S I L

Diversification Value for Portfolio Types

Large Cap: None	Small Cap: High	Bond: Low	Balanced: None	Diversified: Low

Expenses & Fees

Sales Fees	
	4.50% front
	0.00% deferred
	0.25% 12b-1
Management Fee	0.70% max./0.60% min., 0.10%A
3-,5-,10-yr Expense Projections	$86, $116, $201
Annual Brokerage Cost	0.02%

Min Initial Purchase	$1000 (Addt'l: $100)
Min IRA Purchase	$250 (Addt'l: $100)
Min Auto Invest Plan	$1000 (Systematic Inv: $100)

Portfolio 06-30-94

Share Chg (12-93)000	Amount 000	Total Stocks: 500 Total Fixed-Income: 9	Date of Maturity	Value $000	% Net Assets
	1778	US Treasury Bond 8.75%	05-15-17	1967	4.05
	1374	US Treasury Bond 8%	11-15-21	1419	2.92
	1131	US Treasury Bond 8.5%	02-15-20	1225	2.52
	1051	US Treasury Bond 8.125%	08-15-19	1093	2.25
7	21	General Electric		960	1.98
	970	US Treasury Bond 7.25%	05-15-16	921	1.90
	889	US Treasury Bond 7.875%	02-15-21	902	1.86
-5	16	AT & T		888	1.83
	1051	US Treasury Bond 6.25%	08-15-23	882	1.82
-5	15	Exxon		845	1.74
-2	6	Royal Dutch Petroleum		675	1.39
-9	28	Wal-Mart Stores		670	1.38
-5	16	Coca-Cola		631	1.30
-3	11	Philip Morris		544	1.12
-3	8	El DuPont de Nemours		477	0.98
	323	US Treasury Bond 12.5%	08-15-14	462	0.95
-2	9	General Motors		455	0.94
-5	15	Merck		453	0.93
	323	US Treasury Bond 11.25%	02-15-15	440	0.91
-3	8	Procter & Gamble		439	0.90

Index Allocation
	% of Stocks
S&P 500	98.8
S&P MidCap 400	0.0
U.S. Small Cap	1.2
Foreign	3.6

Composition % 09-30-94
Cash	1.0	Preferreds	0.0
Stocks	59.2	Convertibles	0.0
Bonds	39.8	Other	0.0

Tax Analysis
	Tax-Adj Historical Return %	% Pretax Return
3 Yr Avg	3.22	49.6
5 Yr Avg	6.45	66.6
10 Yr Avg	---	---
Potential Capital Gain Exposure (% of assets)		-4%

Most Similar Funds in MF500
Vanguard Asset Allocation	Strong Fit
Stagecoach Asset Alloc A	Strong Fit
Investment Comp of America	Strong Fit

Bond Credit Analysis 09-30-94
% of Bonds
US Govt	100	BB	0
AAA	0	B	0
AA	0	Below B	0
A	0	NR/NA	0
BBB	0		

Stock Sector Weightings
	% of Stocks	Relative S&P 500
Utilities	12.9	1.04
Energy	10.4	1.03
Financials	11.6	1.10
Industrial Cyclicals	16.4	1.00
Consumer Durables	6.4	1.02
Consumer Staples	11.6	0.92
Services	8.3	1.02
Retail	6.4	1.10
Health	7.9	0.91
Technology	8.1	0.88

 **1995 Mutual Fund 500**

Overland Express Var Rate Govt A

	Ticker	Load	NAV	Yield	SEC Yield	Assets	Objective
	OEVGX	3.00%	9.19	4.7%	4.84%	1215.5	Adj Mortgage

Overland Express Variable Rate Government Fund - Class A seeks current income while reducing principal volatility.

The fund normally invests at least 65% of its assets in adjustable-rate mortgage securities issued or guaranteed by the U.S. government. Ordinarily, the average weighted maturity of the fund's portfolio is expected to be between 20 and 30 years.

Class A shares have front loads; Class D shares have deferred loads and higher 12b-1 fees.

Manager's Investment Style

Management blends aggressiveness and conservatism. It has a larger-than-average stake of its variable- and floating-rate assets tied to the COFI index. On the other hand, the absence of nonagency issues helps minimize credit and liquidity risk. Furthermore, management avoids derivatives.

Fund Manager(s)

Richard L. Glessmann CFA, since 09-92. BS, U. of Pennsylvania 1983
Paul Single, since 11-90. BS, Springfield C. 1980

Manager Experience	Dates Managed	Invest Obj	Std Dev	+/- Index
Paul Single				
Benham Treasury Note	01/83 - 02/88	GT	8.35	-2.40
Overland Exp S-T US Govt	05/92 - 12/92	GG	1.00	-2.48

Historical Profile
Return Low
Risk Below Average
Rating ★★ Below Average

	1983	1984	1985	1986	1987	1988	1989	1990	1991	1992	1993	1994	History
												50	32	55	54	Income Rtn % Rank Obj
	---	---	---	---	---	---	---	10.12	10.13	9.95	9.99	9.19	NAV
	---	---	---	---	---	---	---	2.55 *	8.60	4.23	4.87	-3.81	Total Return %
	---	---	---	---	---	---	---	---	-7.40	-3.02	-4.88	-0.89	+/- LB Aggregate
	---	---	---	---	---	---	---	---	---	---	-1.11	-3.23	+/- LB ARM
	---	---	---	---	---	---	---	1.55	8.50	6.01	4.47	4.20	Income Return %
	---	---	---	---	---	---	---	1.00	0.10	-1.78	0.40	-8.01	Capital Return %
	---	---	---	---	---	---	---	---	94	80	92	52	Total Rtn % Rank All
	---	---	---	---	---	---	---	---	66	45	23	84	Total Rtn % Rank Obj
	---	---	---	---	---	---	---	0.15	0.83	0.60	0.44	0.43	Income $
	---	---	---	---	---	---	---	0.00	0.00	0.00	0.00	0.00	Capital Gains $
	---	---	---	---	---	---	---	0.00	0.50	0.75	0.76	0.79	Expense Ratio %
	---	---	---	---	---	---	---	4.93	7.36	5.62	4.37	4.11	Income Ratio %
	---	---	---	---	---	---	---	---	250	197	201	---	Turnover Rate %
	---	---	---	---	---	---	---	6.9	566.8	2559.3	1949.0	1215.5	Net Assets ($mil)

Investment Style History
Fixed Income

Growth of $10,000
‖‖‖ Value of Fund ($000)
— Value of Index ($000)
FB HY
▼ Manager Change
▽ Partial Manager Change
► Mgr Unknown After
◄ Mgr Unknown Before

Performance Quartile
(Within Objective)

Performance 12-31-94

	1st Qtr	2nd Qtr	3rd Qtr	4th Qtr	Total
1987	---	---	---	---	---
1988	---	---	---	---	---
1989	---	---	---	---	---
1990	---	---	---	---	2.55 *
1991	2.54	1.72	2.16	1.93	8.60
1992	1.01	1.78	1.31	0.08	4.23
1993	1.63	1.41	1.40	0.35	4.87
1994	-0.29	-1.23	-0.25	-2.09	-3.81

Bear Market Performance

Decile Rank (5-year period)

Worst — Best

	Worst 3 Mo Period 1985-89	Worst 3 Mo Period 1990-94
Overland Express Var Rate Govt	---	---
+/- LB Aggregate	---	---
+/- Best Fit Index :	---	---

Trailing Returns

	Total Return %	+/- LB Aggregate	+/- LB ARM	% Rank All	% Rank Obj	Growth of $10,000
3 Mo	-2.09	-2.47	-2.25	70	87	9,791
6 Mo	-2.33	-3.33	-2.79	91	85	9,767
1 Yr	-3.81	-0.89	-3.23	52	84	9,619
3 Yr Avg	1.68	-2.86	---	93	61	10,514
5 Yr Avg	---	---	---	---	---	---
10 Yr Avg	---	---	---	---	---	---
15 Yr Avg	---	---	---	---	---	---

Risk Analysis

Time Period	Load-Adj Return %	Risk % Rank [1] All	Obj	Morningstar [2] Return	Morningstar Risk	Morningstar Risk-Adj Rating
1 Yr	-6.70					
3 Yr	0.66	5	74	-0.82 [3]	0.60	★★
5 Yr	---	---	---	---	---	---
10 Yr	---	---	---	---	---	---

Average Historical Rating (14 months) 2.4 ★ s

[1] 1 = low, 100 = high   [2] 1.00 = Taxable Avg   [3] 1.00 = 90-day T-bill return

Other Measures

			Standard LB Agg	Best Fit FB HY
Standard Deviation	1.65	Alpha	-2.1	-3.7
Mean	1.69	Beta	0.27	0.27
Sharpe Ratio	-1.11	R-Squared	38	44

Investment Style

Interest-Rate Stance
Avg Effective Duration
Avg Reset Interval ---

Maturity Short Intm Long
Quality High Med Low

Quality
Avg Credit Quality AAA

Avg Weighted Coupon ---
Avg Weighted Price 99.22% of Par

Diversification Value for Portfolio Types

Large Cap: High	Small Cap: High	Bond: Medium	Balanced: High	Diversified: High

Portfolio 06-30-94

Total Stocks: 0
Total Fixed-Income: 8

Amount 000	Date of Maturity		Value $000	% Net Assets
457454	03-01-33	FNMA ARM CMT	463670	27.40
428042	09-01-30	FHLMC ARM COF	432436	25.55
318301	01-15-24	FHLMC CMO REMIC FRN	309778	18.30
262630	04-20-24	GNMA ARM CMT	252762	14.94
143995	03-25-24	FNMA CMO REMIC FRN	139158	8.22
48730	03-25-24	FNMA CMO REMIC PAC FRN	48144	2.84
23173	10-15-08	FHLMC CMO REMIC TAC FRN	22418	1.32
1005	04-25-23	FNMA CMO REMIC P/O 0%	1029	0.06

Composition % 12-31-94

Cash	15.0	Preferreds	0.0
Stocks	0.0	Convertibles	0.0
Bonds	85.0	Other	0.0

Tax Analysis

	Tax-Adj Historical Return %	% Pretax Return
3 Yr Avg	-0.11	---
5 Yr Avg	---	---
10 Yr Avg	---	---

Potential Capital Gain Exposure
(% of assets) -14%

Most Similar Funds in MF500

T. Rowe Price Short-Trm Bond	Weak Fit
Strong Short-Term Bond	Weak Fit
Scudder Short-Term Bond	Weak Fit

Indexes 12-31-94

	% of ARMs/ Floaters	Rel Obj
11th District COFI	3.5	0.56
1 Yr CMT	90.6	1.14
6 Month LIBOR	5.9	0.98
6 Month T-bill	0.0	0.00
Other	0.0	0.00

Sector Analysis 12-31-94
% of Bonds

Agency ARM	88	Fixed CMO	0
Private ARM	0	Inv Floater	0
Fixed Mtg	0	IO	0
Floating CMO	12	Other	0

Operations

Address and Telephone	111 Center Street Little Rock, AR 72201 800-552-9612 / 501-377-2569
Advisor	Wells Fargo Bank
Subadvisor	None
Distributor	Stephens
States Available	All
Report Grade	C
Income Distrib	Paid Quarterly
* Date of Inception	11-01-90
Fiscal Year End	December

Min Initial Purchase	$1000 (Addt'l: $100)
Min IRA Purchase	$250 (Addt'l: $100)
Min Auto Invest Plan	$1000 (Systematic Inv: $100)

Expenses & Fees

Sales Fees	3.00% front
	0.00% deferred
	0.25% 12b-1
Management Fee	0.50% flat fee, 0.15%A
3-,5-,10-yr Expense Projections	$54, $72, $121

M︎ORNINGSTAR **1995 Mutual Fund 500**

Pacific American Income

	Ticker	NAV	Mkt Price	Prem/Disc	Yield	Objective
	PAI	$14.35	$13.13	-8.5%	9.1%	Corp General

Pacific American Income Shares seeks a high level of current income consistent with prudent investment risk. Capital appreciation is secondary.

The fund invests at least 75% of assets in investment-grade securities. It may hold up to 25% of assets in other fixed-income securities, convertibles, and preferreds. No more than 25% of assets may be in restricted securities.

On Oct. 20, 1983, the fund issued $18.5 million of 12.20% five-year convertible notes, due Oct. 15, 1988, which were extendable to Oct. 15, 1993. The annual interest rate was adjusted to 9.25% on Oct. 15, 1988, and $13.5 million of the notes were converted into common stock at the conversion price of $13.73 per share. The remaining $5 million of notes were converted to common stock on May 20, 1993, at the conversion price (adjusted for the 1992 rights offering) of $13.33 per share.

A rights offering in the fourth quarter of 1992 raised $32 million.

Manager's Investment Style

Management blends a variety of fixed-income securities--including high-quality corporate bonds, lower-quality junk, Treasuries, and mortgage-backeds. It is willing to tinker with the portfolio's sector allocation in an effort to fashion the portfolio around its expectations. In 1994's third quarter, for example, management moved about 40% of assets into mortgage-backeds, because it expected rates to stabilize.

Fund Manager(s)

Kent S. Engel. Since 3-73. BA'72 California State U.-Los Angeles.

Manager Experience

	Dates Managed	Invest Obj	Std Dev	+/- Index

Not available.

NAV Performance % 12-30-94

	1st Qtr	2nd Qtr	3rd Qtr	4th Qtr	Total
1987	3.78	-2.78	0.52	1.13	2.57
1988	6.00	2.20	2.53	0.08	11.17
1989	0.91	5.96	1.66	2.09	10.97
1990	-0.67	3.85	-1.03	3.69	5.87
1991	5.81	2.62	5.58	5.40	20.84
1992	2.25	3.55	3.51	0.68	10.34
1993	5.30	3.09	5.32	-0.07	14.25
1994	-3.07	-2.24	0.35	1.17	-3.80

Bear Market Performance

Decile Rank (5-year period)

Worst ——————— Best

	Worst 3 Mo Period 1985-89	Worst 3 Mo Period 1990-94
Pacific American Inc	---	-5.24
+/- LB Aggregate	---	-0.30

Trailing Returns

	NAV Total Return %	+/- LB Agg	+/- LB Corp	% Rank All	% Rank Obj	Mkt Total Return %
3 Mo	1.17	0.79	0.73	8	23	-8.42
6 Mo	1.52	0.53	0.35	21	26	-6.58
1 Yr	-3.80	-0.88	0.13	30	47	-12.57
3 Yr Avg	6.64	2.09	1.23	38	26	4.23
5 Yr Avg	9.18	1.55	0.91	31	12	7.09
10 Yr Avg	---	---	---	---	---	11.47

Operations

Address and Telephone	P.O. Box 983, 117 E. Colorado Blvd. Pasadena, CA 91105 818-584-4300
Advisor	Western Asset Management Co.
Subadvisor	N/A
Administrator	N/A
Transfer Agent	First Interstate Bank California
Custodian	Manufacturers Hanover Trust Co.
Auditor	Price Waterhouse LLP
Legal Counsel	Gibson, Dunn & Crutcher

Income Distrib Schedule	Paid Quarterly
Management Fee	0.70%
Reinvestment Plan	Yes
Direct Purchase Plan	No
Shares Outstanding	9,319,423
Exchange	NYSE
Date of Inception	03-22-73
Shareholder Report	B+

Historical Profile

Return	Above Average
Risk	Below Average
Rating ★★★★	Above Average

0.0	-1.1	2.2	1.4	4.3	5.0	3.3	1.4	Highest Prem/Disc
-6.8	-5.3	-4.4	-13.0	-8.3	-5.0	-4.3	-10.2	Lowest Prem/Disc

Growth of $10,000
- at NAV ($000)
- at Market Price ($000)

Premium Discount %

	1983	1984	1985	1986	1987	1988	1989	1990	1991	1992	1993	1994	History
	13.67	13.92	16.04	16.62	15.09	15.16	15.24	14.62	16.06	15.84	16.25	14.35	NAV
	---	---	---	---	2.57	11.17	10.97	5.87	20.84	10.34	14.25	-3.80	NAV Total Return %
	---	---	---	---	-0.19	3.30	-3.57	-3.08	4.84	3.09	4.50	-0.88	+/- LB Aggregate
	---	---	---	---	0.01	1.95	-3.01	-1.29	2.33	1.64	2.08	0.13	+/- LB Corp
	12.52	13.50	13.47	10.22	11.77	10.71	10.44	9.94	10.99	9.16	8.29	7.44	Income Return %
	-0.73	1.83	15.23	3.62	-9.21	0.46	0.53	-4.07	9.85	1.18	5.96	-11.24	Capital Return %
	---	---	---	---	42	63	54	41	41	43	61	30	Total Rtn % Rank All
	---	---	---	---	40	33	56	44	28	30	37	47	Total Rtn % Rank Obj
	13.78	15.59	31.99	23.01	2.62	11.59	13.15	-1.31	26.00	10.98	16.71	-12.57	Market Total Rtn %
	---	---	---	---	-2.3	-2.9	-1.5	-4.9	-1.7	-1.2	-0.3	-3.3	Avg Prem/Disc %
	1.48	1.50	1.54	1.54	1.91	1.54	1.53	1.46	1.46	1.40	1.28	1.20	Income $
	0.00	0.00	0.00	0.00	0.00	0.00	0.00	0.00	0.00	0.00	0.52	0.08	Capital Gains $
	0.90	0.97	0.91	0.91	0.91	0.94	0.88	0.89	0.84	0.79	0.72	---	Expense Ratio %
	10.52	11.37	10.37	9.24	9.44	9.79	10.04	10.02	9.60	8.31	7.71	---	Income Ratio %
	67	59	52	76	75	36	60	48	42	86	130	---	Turnover Rate %
	78.2	79.7	91.8	96.9	88.1	101.7	102.2	98.1	107.7	142.3	151.4	133.7	Net Assets ($mil)

Risk Analysis

	Risk % Rank[1] All	Obj	Morningstar[2] Return	Risk	Morningstar Risk-Adj Rating
3 Yr	23	42	0.91[3]	0.67	★★★★
5 Yr	26	28	1.13[3]	0.72	★★★★
10 Yr					

Average Historical Rating (61 months)　3.8 ★s

[1] 1 = Low, 100 = High　[2] 1.00 = Fixed-Inc Avg　[3] 1.00 = 90-day T-bill Return

Other Measures

			LB Aggregate
Standard Deviation	4.39	Alpha	2.24
Mean	6.54	Beta	0.79
Sharpe Ratio	0.69	R-Squared	52

Investment Style

Interest-Rate Stance

	Fund	Relative Objective
Avg Eff Duration	7.0 Yrs	1.10
Avg Eff Maturity	15.8 Yrs	1.00
Avg Wtd Coupon	8.86%	0.99
Avg Wtd Price	96.4% Par	0.98

Quality

Avg Cred Quality　A

Credit Analysis 12-31-94

	% of Bonds		% of Bonds
US Govt	32	BB	23
AAA	0	B	5
AA	1	Below B	0
A	8	NR/NA	0
BBB	32		

Diversification Value for Portfolio Types

Large Cap: High	Small Cap: High	Bond: Low	Balanced: Medium	Diversified: High

Portfolio 06-30-94

Amount 000	Total Equity: 0 Total Fixed-Income: 59	Maturity	Value $000	% Total Invest
9370	US Treasury Bond 7.125%	02-15-23	8776	6.08
5400	FHLMC 7%	04-15-24	5048	3.50
5400	GNMA 6.5%	05-15-24	4799	3.33
5000	Western Financial Svgs Bk 8.5%	07-15-03	4563	3.16
4747	AMR 9%	08-01-12	4367	3.03
4500	Resolution Trust 8.5%	03-25-25	4319	2.99
4000	Dow Corning 9.375%	02-01-08	4231	2.93
4890	Republic of China 6.5%	02-17-04	4218	2.92
3900	McDonnell Douglas 9.75%	04-01-12	4202	2.91
5000	Long Island Lighting 7.05%	03-15-03	4162	2.88
4000	Resolution Trust 9.4%	05-25-24	4045	2.80
3850	System Energy Resources 14%	11-15-94	3936	2.73
4000	Sithe Independent Funding 9%	12-30-13	3932	2.72
3585	FHLMC CMO REMIC 8.5%	03-15-97	3628	2.51
3175	Resolution Funding 8.875%	04-15-30	3604	2.50
3000	Coastal 11.75%	06-15-06	3294	2.28
3500	First PV Funding 10.15%	01-15-16	3194	2.21
3100	Unisys 10.625%	10-01-99	3133	2.17
3000	FNMA 8%	04-25-06	2982	2.07
3180	Time Warner 9.125%	01-15-13	2957	2.05
3500	US Treasury Bond 6.25%	08-15-23	2942	2.04
3000	Transco Energy 9.625%	06-15-00	2905	2.01
2094	Auburn Hills Trust 12.375%	05-01-20	2837	1.97
2500	Litton Industries 12.625%	07-01-05	2731	1.89
3600	Republic of Argentina 7.9%	03-31-98	2615	1.81

Composition % 12-31-94

Cash	1.7	Preferreds	0.0
Stocks	0.0	Convertibles	0.0
Bonds	98.3	Other	0.0

Coupon Range

	% of Bonds	Relative Objective
0%, PIK	0.0	0.0
0% to 8.5%	48.7	1.4
8.5% to 9.5%	25.7	1.0
9.5% to 11%	11.9	0.5
More than 11%	13.7	1.6
Not applicable	0.0	0.0

1.0 = Objective Average

Tax Analysis

	Tax-Adj Historical Return %	% Pretax Return
3 Yr Avg	3.58	45.7
5 Yr Avg	5.97	56.9
10 Yr Avg	7.12	50.8

Potential Capital Gain Exposure (% of assets)　-6

Most Similar Funds in MF500

Transamerica Income	Fair Fit
MFS Bond A	Weak Fit
Vanguard F/I L/T Corp Bond	Weak Fit

M⚈RNINGSTAR 1995 Mutual Fund 500

Pacific Horizon Capital Income

Ticker	Load	NAV	Yield	SEC Yield	Assets	Objective
PACIX	4.50%	13.28	4.4%	4.92%	200.6	Convrt. Bond

Pacific Horizon Capital Income Fund seeks total return consistent with prudent risk.

The fund normally invests at least 65% of its assets in convertible securities. The balance may be invested in nonconvertible bonds, dividend-paying equities, U.S. government securities, options and futures.

Prior to Jan. 1, 1989, the fund was named Horizon Capital Total Return Fund. From that date until Oct. 7, 1991, the fund was named Pacific Horizon Convertible Securities Fund.

Historical Profile
Return	High
Risk	Average
Rating ★★★★★	Highest

Manager's Investment Style

As this fund's above-average turnover ratio suggests, management is willing to move in and out of sectors rather quickly to take advantage of earnings momentum. At different times during the past few years, for example, health-care concerns, technology names, and cyclically oriented firms have been overweighted. Some of the portfolio's securities are lower-quality than those found in most convertible-bond portfolios; nevertheless, because management focuses on earnings growth and company fundamentals instead of yield, the fund usually pays out less income than some of its more-yield-oriented rivals.

Fund Manager(s)

Ed Cassens CFA(1976), since 11-94. Birthdate: 1940. BA, Washington State U. 1965 MBA, Gonzaga U. 1980

Manager Experience

	Dates Managed	Invest Obj	Std Dev	+/- Index

Not available.

Income Rtn % Rank Obj

Growth of $10,000
- IIII Value of Fund ($000)
- — Value of Index ($000)
  Wil 4500
- ▼ Manager Change
- ▽ Partial Manager Change
- ► Mgr Unknown After
- ◄ Mgr Unknown Before

Performance Quartile
(Within Objective)

	1983	1984	1985	1986	1987	1988	1989	1990	1991	1992	1993	1994	History
	---	---	---	---	8.26	8.96	10.19	8.99	11.56	12.90	15.04	13.28	NAV
	---	---	---	---	-11.98 *	15.26	27.08	-4.31	38.24	21.33	22.70	-5.85	Total Return %
	---	---	---	---	---	7.38	12.54	-13.25	22.24	14.09	12.95	-2.93	+/- LB Aggregate
	---	---	---	---	-17.80 *	-1.35	-4.61	-1.19	7.76	13.72	12.64	-7.17	+/- S&P 500
	---	---	---	---	1.52	6.78	5.20	5.60	6.22	5.49	3.75	4.06	Income Return %
	---	---	---	---	-13.51	8.47	21.88	-9.91	32.02	15.84	18.95	-9.92	Capital Return %
	---	---	---	---	---	27	19	68	16	3	13	71	Total Rtn % Rank All
	---	---	---	---	---	28	1	38	17	8	4	65	Total Rtn % Rank Obj
	---	---	---	---	0.14	0.54	0.48	0.56	0.55	0.60	0.48	0.60	Income $
	---	---	---	---	0.00	0.00	0.67	0.23	0.26	0.44	0.28	0.30	Capital Gains $
	---	---	---	---	---	0.35	0.00	0.00	0.00	0.00	0.07	0.46	Expense Ratio %
	---	---	---	---	---	7.14	6.26	5.87	6.32	5.63	5.00	4.19	Income Ratio %
	---	---	---	---	---	---	253	153	236	278	216	103	Turnover Rate %
	---	---	---	---	---	0.3	0.9	1.2	4.7	12.4	154.2	200.6	Net Assets ($mil)

Performance 12-31-94

	1st Qtr	2nd Qtr	3rd Qtr	4th Qtr	Total
1987	---	---	---	-11.98	-11.98 *
1988	8.20	4.69	0.50	1.25	15.26
1989	6.61	11.73	5.90	0.74	27.08
1990	1.21	6.05	-12.28	1.63	-4.31
1991	17.59	4.56	6.26	5.81	38.24
1992	2.29	2.30	6.06	9.32	21.33
1993	6.73	5.08	4.27	4.92	22.70
1994	-2.63	-3.04	4.71	-4.77	-5.85

Bear Market Performance

Decile Rank (5-year period)

Worst ——————————— Best

	Worst 3 Mo Period 1985-89	Worst 3 Mo Period 1990-94
Pacific Horizon Capital Income	---	-15.30
+/- LB Aggregate	---	-16.05
+/- Best Fit Index : Wil 4500	---	4.10

Trailing Returns

	Total Return %	+/- LB Aggregate	+/- S&P 500	% Rank All	% Rank Obj	Growth of $10,000
3 Mo	-4.77	-5.14	-4.75	91	75	9,523
6 Mo	-0.28	-1.27	-5.14	62	57	9,972
1 Yr	-5.85	-2.93	-7.17	71	65	9,415
3 Yr Avg	11.91	7.37	5.65	8	8	14,016
5 Yr Avg	13.14	5.52	4.45	6	9	18,542
10 Yr Avg	---	---	---	---	---	---
15 Yr Avg	---	---	---	---	---	---

Operations

Address and Telephone	125 W. 55th Street 11th Floor
	New York, NY 10019
	800-332-3863
Advisor	Bank of America Natl Trust & Savings
Subadvisor	None
Distributor	Concord Financial Group
States Available	All
Report Grade	B
Income Distrib	Paid Quarterly
* Date of Inception	09-25-87
Fiscal Year End	February

Min Initial Purchase	$1000 (Addt'l: $100)
Min IRA Purchase	$750 (Addt'l: None)
Min Auto Invest Plan	$100 (Systematic Inv: $100)

Expenses & Fees
Sales Fees	4.50% front
	0.00% deferred
	0.00% 12b-1
Management Fee	0.45% flat fee, 0.20%A
3-,5-,10-yr Expense Projections	$81, $107, $181

Risk Analysis

Time Period	Load-Adj Return %	Risk % Rank [1] All	Obj	Morningstar [2] Return	Morningstar Risk	Morningstar Risk-Adj Rating
1 Yr	-10.09					
3 Yr	10.21	51	54	2.04 [3]	0.73	★★★★
5 Yr	12.11	56	71	1.97 [3]	0.86	★★★★★
10 Yr	---	---	---			

Average Historical Rating (52 months)   4.6 ★s

[1] 1 = low, 100 = high   [2] 1.00 = Hybrid Avg   [3] 1.00 = 90-day T-bill return

Other Measures
			Standard LB Agg	Best Fit Wil 4500
Standard Deviation	7.65	Alpha	7.2	5.3
Mean	11.60	Beta	1.11	0.67
Sharpe Ratio	1.06	R-Squared	34	72

Investment Style

Interest-Rate Stance
Avg Effective Maturity	8.8 Yrs

Quality
Avg Credit Quality	BB
Avg Weighted Coupon	5.59%
Avg Weighted Price	100.44% of Par

Not Applicable

Diversification Value for Portfolio Types

Large Cap: Low	Small Cap: Low	Bond: Medium	Balanced: Low	Diversified: Low

Portfolio 08-31-94

Total Stocks: 15
Total Fixed-Income: 114

Amount 000	Date of Maturity		Value $000	% Net Assets
10000	10-15-99	US Treasury Note 6%	9663	4.33
9000	02-15-03	US Treasury Note 6.25%	8505	3.81
40		Atlantic Richfield	4285	1.92
50		ALCOA	4200	1.88
58		Bethlehem Steel Cv Pfd $3.50	3589	1.61
60		Unocal Cv Pfd $3.50	3293	1.48
2300	03-15-01	LSI Logic Cv 5.5%	3266	1.46
80		Fleet Financial Group	3170	1.42
3000	01-10-15	Time Warner Cv 8.75%	3019	1.35
46		Phelps Dodge	2921	1.31
50		General Motors E Cv Pfd $3.25	2869	1.29
42		CIGNA	2814	1.26
3000	11-01-03	Noble Affiliates Cv 4.25%	2749	1.23
60		AMR Cv Pfd $3.00	2745	1.23
65		USX-US Steel Group	2649	1.19
2400	03-15-04	Empresas ICA Cv 5%	2520	1.09
75		Cyprus Amax Mineral	2438	1.09
45		USX Cv Pfd $3.25	2419	1.08
35		IBM	2402	1.08
45		Reynolds Metals Cv Pfd $2.00	2396	1.07
2000	02-01-03	Sterling Software Cv 5.75%	2365	1.06
2000	07-01-02	Outboard Marine Cv 7%	2360	1.06
1500	05-01-03	Lam Research Cv 6%	2321	1.04
2000	09-15-03	Riverwood Intl Cv 6.75%	2260	1.01
60		Unisys Cv Pfd $3.75	2250	1.01

Composition % 12-31-94
Cash	1.2	Preferreds	0.0
Stocks	14.1	Convertibles	28.1
Bonds	56.6	Other	0.0

Tax Analysis
	Tax-Adj Historical Return %	% Pretax Return
3 Yr Avg	9.56	78.5
5 Yr Avg	10.64	77.0
10 Yr Avg	---	---
Potential Capital Gain Exposure (% of assets)		-10%

Most Similar Funds in MF500
Fidelity Asset Manager: Grth	Strong Fit
MainStay Convertible B	Fair Fit
Fidelity Convertible Secs	Fair Fit

Coupon Range
	% of Bonds	Rel Obj
0%	2.9	0.34
0% to 6%	34.8	1.03
6% to 7%	18.5	1.24
7% to 8.5%	4.9	0.42
More than 8.5%	1.8	0.33
Not applicable	37.0	1.44

Credit Analysis 12-31-94
% of Bonds
US Govt	22	BB	0
AAA	0	B	0
AA	0	Below B	0
A	0	NR/NA	78
BBB	0		

PaineWebber Global Income B

Ticker	Load	NAV	Yield	SEC Yield	Assets	Objective
PGBBX	5.00%d	9.87	5.7%	N/A	660.3	World Bond

PaineWebber Global Income Fund - Class B seeks income; capital appreciation is secondary.

The fund normally invests at least 65% of its assets in AA-rated debt issued in at least three countries, including the United States. It may invest up to 35% of its assets in debt rated A or BBB and up to 20% in debt rated BB.

Class A shares have front loads and lower 12b-1 fees; Class B shares have deferred loads and conversion features; Class D shares have level loads. Prior to July 1, 1991, the fund was named PaineWebber Master Global Income Fund. On Nov 3, 1993, PaineWebber Short-Term Global Income Fund B merged into this fund.

Manager's Investment Style

Management typically targets high-quality issues, shunning emerging-market debt. The fund is also willing to raise cash as a defensive measure. Management generally hedges most of the portfolio's currency exposure, but during the past few years has abandoned the practice of cross-hedging. The portfolio typically lands in the intermediate-term range of the style box.

Historical Profile
Return: Average
Risk: Low
Rating: ★★★★ Above Average

Investment Style History
Fixed Income
Income Rtn % Rank Obj

Growth of $10,000
|||| Value of Fund ($000)
— Value of Index ($000) LB Agg
▼ Manager Change
▽ Partial Manager Change
► Mgr Unknown After
◄ Mgr Unknown Before

Performance Quartile (Within Objective)

Fund Manager(s)

Stuart Waugh CFA, since 03-87. BA, U. of Rhode Island MBA, Tulane U.

Manager Experience

	Dates Managed	Invest Obj	Std Dev	+/- Index
Stuart Waugh				
Global Income Plus	09/88 - 12/94	IB	5.96	0.80
Strat Global Inc	02/92 - 12/94	IB	7.24	-0.38

	1983	1984	1985	1986	1987	1988	1989	1990	1991	1992	1993	1994	History
	---	---	---	---	10.86	10.64	10.25	10.87	11.05	10.41	10.96	9.87	NAV
	---	---	---	---	17.22 *	12.15	5.44	17.72	10.75	0.38	13.37	-4.74	Total Return %
	---	---	---	---	---	4.27	-9.10	8.77	-5.25	-6.87	3.61	-1.82	+/- LB Aggregate
	---	---	---	---	---	9.80	8.87	2.43	-5.49	-4.40	-1.75	-11.44	+/- SB World Govt
	---	---	---	---	6.98	9.99	8.88	10.21	8.42	4.81	6.61	5.20	Income Return %
	---	---	---	---	10.25	2.17	-3.44	7.51	2.33	-4.44	6.76	-9.95	Capital Return %
	---	---	---	---	---	45	95	1	87	89	37	61	Total Rtn % Rank All
	---	---	---	---	---	13	66	21	75	72	61	45	Total Rtn % Rank Obj
	---	---	---	---	0.66	1.04	0.90	0.99	0.85	0.52	0.67	0.57	Income $
	---	---	---	---	0.18	0.45	0.03	0.14	0.07	0.16	0.14	0.00	Capital Gains $
	---	---	---	---	2.08	2.05	1.95	1.90	1.94	1.98	2.11	1.96	Expense Ratio %
	---	---	---	---	8.39	9.13	9.73	9.88	8.09	7.11	5.97	5.58	Income Ratio %
	---	---	---	---	---	120	124	126	53	92	90	---	Turnover Rate %
	---	---	---	---	---	789.2	1158.7	1087.6	1384.3	1667.9	1449.8	1175.6	660.3	Net Assets ($mil)

Performance 12-31-94

	1st Qtr	2nd Qtr	3rd Qtr	4th Qtr	Total
1987	---	2.78	2.07	11.74	17.22 *
1988	4.14	0.93	0.28	6.41	12.15
1989	-2.16	-1.73	4.58	4.86	5.44
1990	0.88	6.61	5.28	3.97	17.72
1991	-1.29	-0.90	7.17	5.63	10.75
1992	-2.17	4.31	-0.34	-1.30	0.38
1993	5.00	1.66	2.85	3.26	13.37
1994	-3.92	-2.50	0.70	0.98	-4.74

Bear Market Performance

Decile Rank (5-year period)

Worst ———————— Best

	Worst 3 Mo Period 1985-89	Worst 3 Mo Period 1990-94
PaineWebber Global Income B	---	-6.13
+/- LB Aggregate	---	-1.20
+/- Best Fit Index : LB Agg	---	-1.20

Trailing Returns

	Total Return %	+/- LB Aggregate	+/- SB World	% Rank All	% Rank Obj	Growth of $10,000
3 Mo	0.98	0.60	0.41	6	25	10,098
6 Mo	1.69	0.70	-0.54	29	28	10,169
1 Yr	-4.74	-1.82	-11.44	61	45	9,526
3 Yr Avg	2.72	-1.82	-6.05	87	70	10,840
5 Yr Avg	7.16	-0.46	-4.35	46	57	14,132
10 Yr Avg	---	---	---	---	---	---
15 Yr Avg	---	---	---	---	---	---

Operations

Address and Telephone	1285 Avenue of the Americas New York, NY 10019 800-647-1568 / 201-902-7341
Advisor	Mitchell Hutchins Asset Management
Subadvisor	None
Distributor	Mitchell Hutchins Asset Management
States Available	All
Report Grade	C+
Income Distrib	Paid Quarterly
* Date of Inception	03-20-87
Fiscal Year End	October

Risk Analysis

Time Period	Load-Adj Return %	Risk % Rank All	Risk % Rank Obj [1]	Morningstar [2] Return	Morningstar Risk	Morningstar Risk-Adj Rating
1 Yr	-8.34	---	---	---	---	---
3 Yr	2.16	38	20	-0.41 [3]	0.61	★★★
5 Yr	7.02	35	3	0.56 [3]	0.43	★★★★
10 Yr	---	---	---	---	---	---

Average Historical Rating (58 months)   3.8 ★s

[1] 1 = low, 100 = high   [2] 1.00 = Hybrid Avg   [3] 1.00 = 90-day T-bill return

Other Measures

			Standard LB Agg	Best Fit LB Agg
Standard Deviation	4.36	Alpha	-1.6	-1.6
Mean	2.79	Beta	0.82	0.82
Sharpe Ratio	-0.17	R-Squared	57	57

Investment Style

Interest-Rate Stance
Avg Effective Maturity   4.9 Yrs

Quality
Avg Credit Quality   NA
Avg Weighted Coupon   10.53%

Not Available

Diversification Value for Portfolio Types

Large Cap: High	Small Cap: High	Bond: Low	Balanced: Medium	Diversified: Medium

Portfolio 10-31-94

Total Stocks: 0
Total Fixed-Income: 32

Amount 000	Date of Maturity		Value $000	% Net Assets
9648	08-30-03	Govt of Spain 13.45%	78833	10.87
79	01-04-24	Republic of Germany 8.875%	51426	7.09
284	11-15-00	Govt of Denmark 9%	48639	6.70
157	10-25-99	Govt of France 8.5%	30463	4.20
33	12-01-01	New South Wales Treasury 12%	26543	3.66
25	07-15-96	GMAC 8.625%	25576	3.52
13	07-14-00	United Kingdom Treasury 13%	24514	3.38
14	05-15-96	United Kingdom Treasury 13.25%	24482	3.37
31	08-15-01	Queensland Treasury 12%	23749	3.27
141	06-15-01	Kingdom of Sweden 13%	21677	2.99
12	07-15-01	Republic of Ireland 11.5%	19987	2.75
17	11-30-96	US Treasury Bond 7.5%	17049	2.35
19	11-01-03	National Bank of Hungary 7.95%	15083	2.08
18	06-01-21	Govt of Canada 10%	14193	1.96
20	07-15-97	Govt of New Zealand 10%	12461	1.72
17	02-06-02	Ontario Hydro 8.625%	12392	1.71
45	03-15-02	Republic of Finland 10.75%	10093	1.39
9	12-01-97	Chase Manhattan 7.5%	9024	1.24
8	07-15-01	Clorox 8.8%	8337	1.15
9	08-06-97	Republic of Turkey 8.125%	8057	1.11
8	07-01-01	Ford Motor Credit 9.5%	8006	1.10
5	06-30-03	Bank of Greece 9.75%	7384	1.02
36	04-11-11	Ontario Hydro 10.551%	6922	0.95
8	01-21-02	Republic of Germany 8%	5120	0.71
5	02-23-96	Govt of Philippines 7.875%	5066	0.70

Composition % 09-30-94

Cash	27.5	Preferreds	0.0
Stocks	0.0	Convertibles	0.0
Bonds	72.5	Other	0.0

Tax Analysis

	Tax-Adj Historical Return %	% Pretax Return
3 Yr Avg	0.40	14.5
5 Yr Avg	4.50	59.6
10 Yr Avg	---	---
Potential Capital Gain Exposure (% of assets)		-6%

Most Similar Funds in MF500

Global Income Plus	Strong Fit
Capital World Bond	Fair Fit
Templeton Income	Fair Fit

Country Exposure 08-31-94

	% of Bonds
Germany	16
U.S.	16
Spain	10
United Kingdom	7
Denmark	5

Currency Exposure 08-31-94

	% of Net Assets
U.S.	62
Germany	16
Canada	8
Denmark	3
Australia	3

Expenses & Fees

Min Initial Purchase	$1000 (Addt'l: $100)
Min IRA Purchase	None (Addt'l: None)
Min Auto Invest Plan	$50 (Systematic Inv: $50)

Sales Fees
0.00% front
5.00% deferred
1.00% 12b-1

Management Fee   0.75% max./0.65% min.
3-,5-,10-yr Expense Projections $96, $133, $205

MORNINGSTAR 1995 Mutual Fund 500

PaineWebber Invmt Grd Inc A

	Ticker	Load	NAV	Yield	SEC Yield	Assets	Objective
	PIGAX	4.00%	9.70	7.9%	N/A	265.0	Corp General

PaineWebber Investment Grade Income Fund - Class A seeks current income.

The fund normally invests at least 65% of its assets in investment-grade corporate bonds and U.S. government securities. The balance of assets may be invested in lower-rated bonds, preferred stocks, or convertibles.

Class A shares have front loads and lower 12b-1 fees; Class B shares have deferred loads and conversion features; Class D shares have level loads. Prior to April 1, 1991, the fund was named PaineWebber Investment Grade Bond Portfolio. Or April 29, 1994, PaineWebber Income Fund - Class A merged into this fund.

Manager's Investment Style

Since current management came aboard in 1991, the strategy has shown its aggressive side. A long-maturity stance coupled with an above-average stake in lower- and below-investment-grade holdings was key over the past three years. More recently, management has shortened duration and has become pickier about taking on credit risk. Further, the strategy no longer includes its small stake in unpredictable CMOs.

Fund Manager(s)

Mary B. King, since 02-91. BS, Montclair State C.

Manager Experience

	Dates Managed	Invest Obj	Std Dev	+/- Index

Not available.

Historical Profile

Return	Above Average
Risk	Above Average
Rating	★★★ Neutral

Investment Style History
Fixed Income
Income Rtn % Rank Obj

28	62	51	45	32	19	15	10

Growth of $10,000
IIII Value of Fund ($000)
— Value of Index ($000) LB Corp
▼ Manager Change
▽ Partial Manager Change
► Mgr Unknown After
◄ Mgr Unknown Before

Performance Quartile (Within Objective)

	1983	1984	1985	1986	1987	1988	1989	1990	1991	1992	1993	1994	History
	---	9.77	10.52	10.75	9.55	9.51	9.77	9.54	10.42	10.50	11.08	9.70	NAV
	---	5.88 *	22.76	14.47	-1.51	8.88	11.97	6.47	18.45	8.87	13.35	-5.60	Total Return %
	---	---	0.64	-0.78	-4.26	1.00	-2.57	-2.47	2.45	1.63	3.60	-2.68	+/- LB Aggregate
	---	---	-1.30	-2.07	-4.06	-0.35	-2.01	-0.68	-0.06	0.17	1.18	-1.68	+/- LB Corporate
	---	3.79	15.09	12.16	9.46	8.76	9.24	8.83	9.22	8.10	7.82	6.85	Income Return %
	---	2.09	7.68	2.31	-10.96	0.12	2.73	-2.35	9.22	0.77	5.52	-12.45	Capital Return %
	---	---	55	58	71	68	59	28	47	35	38	69	Total Rtn % Rank All
	---	---	36	45	90	43	47	56	22	18	16	84	Total Rtn % Rank Obj
	---	0.35	1.31	1.21	1.01	0.81	0.84	0.83	0.82	0.81	0.79	0.77	Income $
	---	0.00	0.00	0.01	0.03	0.05	0.00	0.00	0.00	0.00	0.00	0.00	Capital Gains $
	---	0.64	0.78	0.68	0.72	0.70	0.65	0.66	0.91	1.01	0.96	1.09	Expense Ratio %
	---	12.26	10.55	9.27	8.67	8.83	8.96	8.76	8.32	7.81	7.24	7.15	Income Ratio %
	---	---	166	81	88	35	47	31	46	44	17	---	Turnover Rate %
	---	8.8	213.9	474.4	536.8	321.0	265.5	225.2	220.2	200.3	205.7	265.0	Net Assets ($mil)

Performance 12-31-94

	1st Qtr	2nd Qtr	3rd Qtr	4th Qtr	Total
1987	2.18	-4.14	-5.80	6.74	-1.51
1988	4.24	0.67	1.95	1.77	8.88
1989	0.44	6.42	1.15	3.57	11.97
1990	-0.62	3.04	-0.11	4.09	6.47
1991	3.98	2.46	5.67	5.23	18.45
1992	-0.37	3.77	4.94	0.35	8.87
1993	5.45	3.02	4.04	0.29	13.35
1994	-4.27	-3.18	0.35	1.50	-5.60

Bear Market Performance

Decile Rank (5-year period)

Worst _____ Best

	Worst 3 Mo Period 1985-89	Worst 3 Mo Period 1990-94
PaineWebber Invmt Grd Inc A	-5.80	-7.02
+/- LB Aggregate	-3.08	-2.09
+/- Best Fit Index : LB Corp	-2.17	-0.75

Trailing Returns

	Total Return %	+/- LB Aggregate	+/- LB Corp	% Rank All	% Rank Obj	Growth of $10,000
3 Mo	1.50	1.12	1.06	5	3	10,150
6 Mo	1.85	0.86	0.67	28	4	10,185
1 Yr	-5.60	-2.68	-1.68	69	84	9,440
3 Yr Avg	5.22	0.67	-0.19	44	28	11,649
5 Yr Avg	8.00	0.37	-0.27	33	19	14,691
10 Yr Avg	9.50	-0.44	-1.12	64	57	24,788
15 Yr Avg	---	---	---	---	---	---

Operations

Address and Telephone	1285 Avenue of the Americas
	New York, NY 10019
	800-647-1568 / 201-902-7341
Advisor	Mitchell Hutchins Asset Management
Subadvisor	None
Distributor	Mitchell Hutchins Asset Management
States Available	All
Report Grade	B-
Income Distrib	Paid Monthly
* Date of Inception	08-31-84
Fiscal Year End	November

Min Initial Purchase	$1000 (Addt'l: $100)
Min IRA Purchase	N/A
Min Auto Invest Plan	$50 (Systematic Inv: $50)

Expenses & Fees

Sales Fees	4.00% front
	0.00% deferred
	0.25% 12b-1
Management Fee	0.50% flat fee
3-,5-,10-yr Expense Projections	$69, $91, $153

Risk Analysis

Time Period	Load-Adj Return %	Risk % Rank [1] All	Obj	Morningstar [2] Return	Morningstar Risk	Morningstar Risk-Adj Rating
1 Yr	-9.38					
3 Yr	3.80	35	78	0.06 [3]	1.19	★★★
5 Yr	7.12	29	59	0.58 [3]	1.07	★★★
10 Yr	9.06	28	72	0.84 [3]	1.16	★★★
Average Historical Rating (89 months)					2.6	★s

[1] 1 = low, 100 = high [2] 1.00 = Taxable Avg [3] 1.00 = 90-day T-bill return

Other Measures

			Standard LB Agg	Best Fit LB Corp
Standard Deviation	5.18	Alpha	0.5	-0.2
Mean	5.23	Beta	1.23	1.00
Sharpe Ratio	0.33	R-Squared	90	93

Investment Style

Interest-Rate Stance

Avg Effective Duration	5.7 Yrs
Avg Effective Maturity	13.2 Yrs

Quality

Avg Credit Quality	BBB
Avg Weighted Coupon	9.83%
Avg Weighted Price	101.33% of Par

Diversification Value for Portfolio Types

Large Cap: Medium	Small Cap: High	Bond: None	Balanced: Medium	Diversified: Medium

Portfolio 12-31-94

Total Stocks: 1
Total Fixed-Income: 58

Amount 000	Date of Maturity		Value $000	% Net Assets
13303	10-15-12	News America Holdings 10.125%	14131	5.33
9102	05-01-20	Auburn Hills Trust 15.375%	11838	4.47
10502	11-01-04	Citicorp 8.625%	10531	3.97
10047	11-01-21	Georgia-Pacific 9.875%	10409	3.93
8227	04-30-16	Delta Air Lines 10.5%	8190	3.09
7702	01-15-23	TCI Communications 9.25%	7299	2.75
7002	06-01-01	Bear Stearns 9.375%	7079	2.67
7002	07-28-97	Columbia/HCA Healthcare 5.15%	6984	2.64
6301	02-01-03	BankAmerica 10%	6713	2.53
5601	08-15-31	Pacific Bell 8.5%	5383	2.03
5426	03-01-21	Duke Power 8.75%	5274	1.99
5003	05-01-21	Texas Utilities Elec 9.75%	5191	1.96
4901	03-15-19	Cooperative Utils Tr 9.52%	5144	1.94
5601	02-01-23	Time Warner 9.15%	5013	1.89
4901	05-01-04	United Air Lines 10.67%	4992	1.88
4201	06-15-20	Unicom 9.875%	4257	1.61
4376	12-01-22	Dayton Hudson 8.5%	4189	1.58
4201	12-01-97	Ford Motor Credit 8%	4160	1.57
4201	05-28-99	GMAC 7.375%	4008	1.51
3851	04-15-01	Huntsman 10.625%	3937	1.49
4201	08-01-04	Chase Manhattan 7.875%	3913	1.48
4201	07-01-24	Long Island Lighting 9.625%	3887	1.47
3501	05-01-02	Healthtrust 10.75%	3720	1.40
3571	03-01-21	ALLTEL 9.5%	3685	1.39
3501	09-01-03	Joy Technologies 10.25%	3658	1.38

Composition % 11-30-94

Cash	10.0	Preferreds	0.0
Stocks	0.0	Convertibles	1.0
Bonds	89.0	Other	0.0

Tax Analysis

	Tax-Adj Historical Return %	% Pretax Return
3 Yr Avg	2.41	44.9
5 Yr Avg	5.17	61.1
10 Yr Avg	5.81	51.3
Potential Capital Gain Exposure (% of assets)		-20%

Most Similar Funds in MF500

Scudder Income	Strong Fit
Fidelity Government Secs	Strong Fit
Vanguard F/I L/T Corp Bond	Strong Fit

Coupon Range

	% of Bonds	Rel Obj
0%	0.0	0.00
0% to 8.5%	22.5	0.36
8.5% to 9.5%	23.6	1.45
9.5% to 11%	45.9	4.95
More than 11%	8.0	2.06
Not applicable	0.0	0.00

Credit Analysis 11-30-94

% of Bonds

US Govt	0	BB	10
AAA	11	B	9
AA	5	Below B	0
A	31	NR/NA	0
BBB	34		

Papp America-Abroad

Papp America-Abroad Fund seeks long-term capital growth. The fund invests at least 70% of its common stock assets in stocks of U.S.-domiciled companies that have substantial international activities. The balance (a maximum of 30%) may be invested in common stocks of foreign companies that are traded publicly, either directly or by ADRs, in United States securities markets. The fund seeks companies that it regards as having excellent prospects for capital appreciation at a price that it believes to be undervalued by the market. It intends to hold such securities as long as the advisor believes appreciation prospects continue to be favorable.

	Ticker	Load	NAV	Yield	SEC Yield	Assets	Objective
	N/A	None	12.24	0.8%	N/A	11.6	Growth

Historical Profile

Return	Average
Risk	Average
Rating	★★★
	Neutral

Investment Style History
Equity

Average % Stocks Held
in Portfolio

	99%	99%	98%

Growth of $10,000

- IIII Value of Fund ($000)
- — Value of Index ($000)
  S&P 500
- ▼ Manager Change
- ▽ Partial Manager Change
- ► Mgr Unknown After
- ◄ Mgr Unknown Before

Performance Quartile
(Within Objective)

Manager's Investment Style

Management maintains a concentrated portfolio in very-large-cap firms that have, and derive significant earnings from, overseas operations. It prefers firms known for steady earnings growth, especially when much of that growth comes from emerging markets. It has thus far taken advantage of its freedom to invest on foreign-based multinational corporations.

1983	1984	1985	1986	1987	1988	1989	1990	1991	1992	1993	1994	History
---	---	---	---	---	---	---	---	10.98	11.67	11.45	12.24	NAV
---	---	---	---	---	---	---	---	9.97 *	7.05	-0.01	7.78	Total Return %
---	---	---	---	---	---	---	---	-0.33 *	-0.57	-10.07	6.46	+/- S&P 500
---	---	---	---	---	---	---	---	---	-1.92	-11.29	7.85	+/- Wilshire 5000
---	---	---	---	---	---	---	---	0.17	0.55	0.88	0.88	Income Return %
---	---	---	---	---	---	---	---	9.80	6.50	-0.89	6.90	Capital Return %
---	---	---	---	---	---	---	---	---	57	99	3	Total Rtn % Rank All
---	---	---	---	---	---	---	---	---	57	95	4	Total Rtn % Rank Obj
---	---	---	---	---	---	---	---	0.02	0.06	0.10	0.09	Income $
---	---	---	---	---	---	---	---	0.00	0.02	0.12	0.00	Capital Gains $
---	---	---	---	---	---	---	---	1.25	1.25	1.25	1.25	Expense Ratio %
---	---	---	---	---	---	---	---	4.51	2.28	2.28	2.15	Income Ratio %
---	---	---	---	---	---	---	---	---	16	8	---	Turnover Rate %
---	---	---	---	---	---	---	---	1.0	5.0	10.9	11.6	Net Assets ($mil)

Fund Manager(s)

L. Roy Papp, since 12-91. Birthdate: 03-27. BA, Brown U. MBA, Wharton
Rosellen C. Papp CFA(1984), since 12-91. Birthdate: 12-54. BBA, U. of Michigan 1977 MM, Northwestern

Manager Experience

	Dates Managed	Invest Obj	Std Dev	+/- Index
Rosellen C. Papp				
L. Roy Papp Stock	11/89 - 12/94	G	13.48	0.98
L. Roy Papp				
L. Roy Papp Stock	11/89 - 12/94	G	13.48	0.98

Performance 12-31-94

	1st Qtr	2nd Qtr	3rd Qtr	4th Qtr	Total
1987	---	---	---	---	---
1988	---	---	---	---	---
1989	---	---	---	---	---
1990	---	---	---	---	---
1991	---	---	---	---	9.97 *
1992	-5.56	1.30	6.67	4.89	7.05
1993	-4.03	-5.21	3.41	6.29	-0.01
1994	-3.23	-0.71	8.49	3.39	7.78

Bear Market Performance

Decile Rank (5-year period)

Worst ——————— Best

	Worst 3 Mo Period 1985-89	Worst 3 Mo Period 1990-94
Papp America-Abroad	---	---
+/- S&P 500	---	---
+/- Best Fit Index :	---	---

Trailing Returns

	Total Return %	+/- S&P 500	+/- Wil 5000	% Rank All	% Rank Obj	Growth of $10,000
3 Mo	3.39	3.41	4.16	2	2	10,339
6 Mo	12.17	7.31	7.55	3	5	11,217
1 Yr	7.78	6.46	7.85	3	4	10,778
3 Yr Avg	4.88	-1.39	-1.73	50	58	11,536
5 Yr Avg	---	---	---	---	---	---
10 Yr Avg	---	---	---	---	---	---
15 Yr Avg	---	---	---	---	---	---

Operations

Address and Telephone	4400 N. 32nd Street Suite 280 Phoenix, AZ 85018 800-421-4004 / 602-956-0980
Advisor	L. Roy Papp & Associates
Subadvisor	None
Distributor	L. Roy Papp & Associates
States Available	AZ,CA,IL,TX
Report Grade	C+
Income Distrib	Paid Annually
* Date of Inception	12-06-91
Fiscal Year End	December

Risk Analysis

Time Period	Load-Adj Return %	Risk % Rank [1] All	Obj	Morningstar [2] Return	Risk	Morningstar Risk-Adj Rating
1 Yr	7.78					
3 Yr	4.88	80	58	0.38 [3]	0.95	★★★
5 Yr	---	---	---	---	---	---
10 Yr	---	---	---	---	---	---

Average Historical Rating (1 month)   3.0 ★s

[1] 1 = low, 100 = high   [2] 1.00 = Equity Avg   [3] 1.00 = 90-day T-bill return

Other Measures

		Standard S&P 500	Best Fit S&P 500
Standard Deviation	10.05	Alpha	-1.0	-1.0
Mean	5.27	Beta	0.97	0.97
Sharpe Ratio	0.17	R-Squared	59	59

Investment Style

	Stock Portfolio Avg	Relative S&P 500
Price/Earnings Ratio	24.5	1.33
Price/Book Ratio	5.0	1.48
5 Yr Earnings Gr %	13.2	2.38
Return on Assets %	10.6	1.42
Debt % Total Cap	19.6	0.69
Med Mkt Cap ($mil)	16267	1.25

Style: Value Blend Growth / Size Large Med Small

Diversification Value for Portfolio Types

Large Cap: Low	Small Cap: High	Bond: High	Balanced: Medium	Diversified: Medium

Composition % 12-31-94

Cash	1.5	Preferreds	0.0
Stocks	98.5	Convertibles	0.0
Bonds	0.0	Other	0.0

Tax Analysis

	Tax-Adj Historical Return %	% Pretax Return
3 Yr Avg	4.49	91.6
5 Yr Avg	---	---
10 Yr Avg	---	---

Potential Capital Gain Exposure (% of assets)   12%

Most Similar Funds in MF500

Dreyfus Appreciation	Fair Fit
L. Roy Papp Stock	Weak Fit
Vanguard U.S. Growth	Weak Fit

Portfolio 01-01-95

Share Chg (06-94) 000	Amount 000	Total Stocks: 23 Total Fixed-Income: 0	Value $000	% Net Assets
0	15	Motorola	880	7.60
0	10	Gillette	748	6.46
0	20	Interpublic Group	643	5.55
7	31	Air Express International	627	5.42
1	13	Reader's Digest Assn Cl B	624	5.39
0	12	Coca-Cola	608	5.25
0	23	Sara Lee	581	5.02
0	12	Intl Flavors & Fragrances	569	4.92
0	19	McDonald's	567	4.90
4	19	State Street Boston	544	4.70
-2	10	CPC International	533	4.60
0	12	Reuters Holdings (ADR)	527	4.55
0	8	Procter & Gamble	477	4.13
0	12	Merck	469	4.05
0	5	Marsh & McLennan	396	3.42
6	6	Intel	383	3.31
2	7	Johnson & Johnson	383	3.31
-3	19	Hong Kong Telecom (ADR)	370	3.20
6	6	Microsoft	367	3.17
18	18	Advance Ross	360	3.11
0	7	Bandag Cl A	352	3.04
-2	10	Bausch & Lomb	339	2.93
0	6	MacNeal-Schwendler	57	0.49

Index Allocation

	% of Stocks
S&P 500	69.7
S&P MidCap 400	4.8
U.S. Small Cap	17.7
Foreign	7.9

Sector Weightings

	% of Stocks	Relative S&P 500
Utilities	3.3	0.26
Energy	0.0	0.00
Financials	7.9	0.75
Industrial Cyclicals	5.0	0.30
Consumer Durables	10.8	1.74
Consumer Staples	22.6	1.81
Services	29.7	3.65
Retail	0.0	0.00
Health	13.6	1.57
Technology	7.1	0.77

Expenses & Fees

Sales Fees	0.00% front
	0.00% deferred
	0.00% 12b-1
Management Fee	1.00% flat fee
3-,5-,10-yr Expense Projections	$41, $71, $155
Annual Brokerage Cost	0.08%

Min Initial Purchase	$10000 (Addt'l: $2000)
Min IRA Purchase	$2000 (Addt'l: $2000)
Min Auto Invest Plan	N/A

MORNINGSTAR **1995 Mutual Fund 500**

L. Roy Papp Stock

	Ticker	Load	NAV	Yield	SEC Yield	Assets	Objective
	LRPSX	None	14.63	0.9%	N/A	36.6	Growth

L. Roy Papp Stock Fund seeks long-term capital growth.
The fund normally invests virtually all of its assets in common stocks. It may also invest up to 5% of its assets in securities convertible into common stocks. Portfolio securities include only issues traded in the United States on stock exchanges or on the NASDAQ National Market System. The fund seeks to purchase the shares of companies regarded as having excellent prospects for capital appreciation at a price, relative to the market as a whole, that does not fully reflect the superiority of a particular company.

Historical Profile

Return	Above Average
Risk	Below Average
Rating	★★★★
	Above Average

Investment Style History
Equity
Average % Stocks Held in Portfolio

						100%	100%	99%	99%

Growth of $10,000

‖‖‖ Value of Fund ($000)
— Value of Index ($000)
     S&P 500
▼ Manager Change
▽ Partial Manager Change
► Mgr Unknown After
◄ Mgr Unknown Before

Performance Quartile
(Within Objective)

Manager's Investment Style

Management seeks companies with a long-term history, preferably longer than 10 years, of sales and earnings growth. Management is particularly smitten with services stocks, which includes any firm that provides a valuable service to other firms or individuals.

Fund Manager(s)

L. Roy Papp, since 11-89. Birthdate: 03-27. BA, Brown U. MBA, Wharton
Rosellen C. Papp CFA(1984), since 11-89. Birthdate: 12-54. BBA, U. of Michigan 1977 MM, Northwestern

Manager Experience	Dates Managed	Invest Obj	Std Dev	+/- Index
Rosellen C. Papp				
Papp America-Abroad	12/91 - 12/94	G	10.05	-1.39
L. Roy Papp				
Papp America-Abroad	12/91 - 12/94	G	10.05	-1.39

	1983	1984	1985	1986	1987	1988	1989	1990	1991	1992	1993	1994	History
	---	---	---	---	---	---	10.38	10.42	13.45	14.96	14.98	14.63	NAV
	---	---	---	---	---	---	3.98 *	2.56	33.65	13.51	1.66	-1.45	Total Return %
	---	---	---	---	---	---	0.48 *	5.68	3.17	5.89	-8.40	-2.76	+/- S&P 500
	---	---	---	---	---	---		8.74	-0.56	4.54	-9.62	-1.38	+/- Wilshire 5000
	---	---	---	---	---	---	0.18	1.14	1.16	0.99	0.90	0.89	Income Return %
	---	---	---	---	---	---	3.80	1.42	32.49	12.52	0.76	-2.34	Capital Return %
	---	---	---	---	---	---	---	49	21	12	98	29	Total Rtn % Rank All
	---	---	---	---	---	---	---	11	55	21	90	46	Total Rtn % Rank Obj
	---	---	---	---	---	---	0.02	0.12	0.14	0.13	0.13	0.13	Income $
	---	---	---	---	---	---	0.00	0.11	0.32	0.17	0.09	0.00	Capital Gains $
	---	---	---	---	---	---	1.25	1.25	1.25	1.25	1.25	1.25	Expense Ratio %
	---	---	---	---	---	---	2.23	2.82	2.46	2.28	2.22	2.17	Income Ratio %
	---	---	---	---	---	---	---	28	11	11	15	---	Turnover Rate %
	---	---	---	---	---	---	1.3	6.0	13.4	22.9	39.5	36.6	Net Assets ($mil)

Performance 12-31-94

	1st Qtr	2nd Qtr	3rd Qtr	4th Qtr	Total
1987	---	---	---	---	---
1988	---	---	---	---	---
1989	---	---	---	---	3.98 *
1990	-1.83	10.69	-16.74	13.36	2.56
1991	20.73	-1.56	5.19	6.90	33.65
1992	0.30	-1.07	5.20	8.75	13.51
1993	0.20	-2.97	1.73	2.79	1.66
1994	-2.20	-3.22	3.54	0.56	-1.45

Bear Market Performance

Decile Rank (5-year period)

Worst					Best

	Worst 3 Mo Period 1985-89	Worst 3 Mo Period 1990-94
L. Roy Papp Stock	---	-16.74
+/- S&P 500	---	-2.99
+/- Best Fit Index : S&P 500	---	-2.99

Trailing Returns

	Total Return %	+/- S&P 500	+/- Wil 5000	% Rank All	Obj	Growth of $10,000
3 Mo	0.56	0.58	1.33	10	13	10,056
6 Mo	4.13	-0.73	-0.50	15	47	10,413
1 Yr	-1.45	-2.76	-1.38	29	46	9,855
3 Yr Avg	4.38	-1.89	-2.23	61	61	11,372
5 Yr Avg	9.28	0.59	0.47	21	40	15,588
10 Yr Avg	---	---	---	---	---	---
15 Yr Avg	---	---	---	---	---	---

Operations

Address and Telephone	4400 N. 32nd Street Suite 280
	Phoenix, AZ 85018
	800-421-4004 / 602-956-1115
Advisor	L. Roy Papp & Associates
Subadvisor	None
Distributor	L. Roy Papp & Associates
States Available	All
Report Grade	B+
Income Distrib	Paid Annually
* Date of Inception	11-29-89
Fiscal Year End	December

Risk Analysis

Time Period	Load-Adj Return %	Risk % Rank [1] All	Obj	Morningstar [2] Return	Morningstar Risk	Morningstar Risk-Adj Rating
1 Yr	-1.45					
3 Yr	4.38	66	26	0.23 [3]	0.74	★★★
5 Yr	9.28	68	23	1.15 [3]	0.81	★★★★
10 Yr	---	---	---	---	---	
Average Historical Rating (26 months)				3.5 ★s		

[1] 1 = low, 100 = high [2] 1.00 = Equity Avg [3] 1.00 = 90-day T-bill return

Other Measures

			Standard S&P 500	Best Fit S&P 500
Standard Deviation	8.35	Alpha	-1.3	-1.3
Mean	4.64	Beta	0.85	0.85
Sharpe Ratio	0.13	R-Squared	65	65

Investment Style

	Stock Portfolio Avg	Relative S&P 500	Style Value Blend Growth
Price/Earnings Ratio	19.0	1.03	
Price/Book Ratio	3.3	0.97	
5 Yr Earnings Gr %	13.6	2.46	
Return on Assets %	9.1	1.22	
Debt % Total Cap	19.6	0.69	
Med Mkt Cap ($mil)	3096	0.24	

Diversification Value for Portfolio Types

Large Cap: Low	Small Cap: Medium	Bond: High	Balanced: Low	Diversified: Medium

Portfolio 12-31-94

Total Stocks: 27
Total Fixed-Income: 0

Share Chg (11-94) 000	Amount 000		Value $000	% Net Assets
0	131	Marshall Industries	3504	9.58
0	46	Motorola	2662	7.28
0	86	Service International	2387	6.52
-2	68	Interpublic Group	2197	6.01
0	49	Merck	1868	5.11
0	69	Sara Lee	1747	4.78
0	30	Clorox	1743	4.76
0	50	Northern Trust	1733	4.74
0	50	Pitney Bowes	1591	4.35
0	53	State Street Boston	1506	4.12
0	42	May Department Stores	1418	3.88
0	46	Albertson's	1328	3.63
0	48	Dillard Department Stores A	1289	3.52
0	75	G & K Services Cl A	1247	3.41
0	35	Bausch & Lomb	1186	3.24
2	16	Microsoft	978	2.67
0	42	Rollins	949	2.60
0	20	Intl Flavors & Fragrances	925	2.53
0	30	McDonald's	878	2.40
0	17	Reader's Digest Assn Cl A	835	2.28
0	14	WW Grainger	820	2.24
0	21	H & R Block	761	2.08
0	12	American Home Products	753	2.06
0	12	Bandag Cl A	647	1.77
0	12	Walgreen	525	1.44

Composition % 12-31-94

Cash	0.8	Preferreds	0.0
Stocks	99.2	Convertibles	0.0
Bonds	0.0	Other	0.0

Tax Analysis

	Tax-Adj Historical Return %	% Pretax Return
3 Yr Avg	3.88	88.1
5 Yr Avg	8.61	91.4
10 Yr Avg	---	---
Potential Capital Gain Exposure (% of assets)		12%

Most Similar Funds in MF500

Papp America-Abroad	Fair Fit
Dreyfus	Fair Fit
Gabelli Growth	Fair Fit

Index Allocation

	% of Stocks
S&P 500	70.5
S&P MidCap 400	11.5
U.S. Small Cap	18.0
Foreign	

Sector Weightings

	% of Stocks	Relative S&P 500
Utilities	0.0	0.00
Energy	0.0	0.00
Financials	8.9	0.84
Industrial Cyclicals	4.8	0.29
Consumer Durables	12.6	2.02
Consumer Staples	9.6	0.77
Services	26.5	3.25
Retail	12.6	2.16
Health	10.5	1.21
Technology	14.6	1.59

Expenses & Fees

Sales Fees	0.00% front
	0.00% deferred
	0.00% 12b-1
Management Fee	1.00% flat fee
3-,5-,10-yr Expense Projections	$41, $81, $155
Annual Brokerage Cost	0.10%

Min Initial Purchase	$10000 (Addt'l: $2000)
Min IRA Purchase	$2000 (Addt'l: None)
Min Auto Invest Plan	N/A

Pasadena Balanced Return A

	Ticker	Load	NAV	Yield	SEC Yield	Assets	Objective
	PABRX	5.50%	20.54	2.2%	N/A	53.0	Balanced

Pasadena Balanced Return Fund - Class A Shares seeks total return.

The fund allocates assets among high- quality growth stocks and U.S. government securities; actual allocation is based on financial trends and changes in economic conditions. At least 25% of assets are invested in U.S. government obligations. Up to 35% of assets may be invested in foreign securities, special situations, and unseasoned companies.

Prior to Jan. 1, 1992, the fund was named Pasadena Fundamental Value Fund. Class A shares have front loads and lower 12b-1 fees; Class B shares have deferred loads and conversion features; Class C shares have level loads.

Manager's Investment Style

Management goes to extremes and stays there. On the fixed-income end, management has been known to rack up one of the objective's longest average-maturity figures. On the stock side, concentrated sector weightings and a large-cap, growth focus is typical. Turnover is minimal for this buy-and-hold approach.

Historical Profile

Return	Below Average
Risk	Above Average
Rating	★★
	Below Average

Investment Style History
Equity

Average % Stocks Held in Portfolio

84%	65%	59%	62%	65%	58%

Growth of $10,000

IIII	Value of Fund ($000)
—	Value of Index ($000) S&P 500
▼	Manager Change
▽	Partial Manager Change
►	Mgr Unknown After
◄	Mgr Unknown Before

Performance Quartile (Within Objective)

	1983	1984	1985	1986	1987	1988	1989	1990	1991	1992	1993	1994	History
	---	---	---	---	11.50	12.51	15.90	15.30	20.94	21.76	21.97	20.54	NAV
	---	---	---	---	15.00 *	13.42	32.98	-0.39	38.82	4.54	2.44	-4.43	Total Return %
	---	---	---	---	30.18 *	-3.19	1.29	2.72	8.34	-3.08	-7.62	-5.75	+/- S&P 500
	---	---	---	---	---	5.54	18.44	-9.34	22.82	-2.71	-7.31	-1.51	+/- LB Aggregate
	---	---	---	---	0.00	4.64	1.28	1.23	0.94	0.60	1.47	2.08	Income Return %
	---	---	---	---	15.00	8.78	31.69	-1.63	37.88	3.94	0.97	-6.51	Capital Return %
	---	---	---	---	---	35	9	57	15	79	97	58	Total Rtn % Rank All
	---	---	---	---	---	36	1	46	14	76	96	75	Total Rtn % Rank Obj
	---	---	---	---	0.00	0.50	0.19	0.19	0.16	0.13	0.32	0.46	Income $
	---	---	---	---	0.00	0.00	0.54	0.35	0.13	0.00	0.00	0.00	Capital Gains $
	---	---	---	---	0.00	2.00	2.10	2.50	2.50	2.30	2.10	2.00	Expense Ratio %
	---	---	---	---	5.30	1.70	1.50	1.00	1.30	1.20	1.50	1.70	Income Ratio %
	---	---	---	---	---	31	24	36	6	6	5	---	Turnover Rate %
	---	---	---	---	0.7	1.9	3.7	5.0	15.6	75.1	84.7	53.0	Net Assets ($mil)

Fund Manager(s)

Roger Engemann, since 6-87. Birthdate: 10-40 BA, U. of Oregon 1964 MA, U. of California-Los Angeles 1966
John S. Tilson, since 6-87. Birthdate: 3-44 BS, U. of Southern Cal 1966 MBA, U. of Southern Cal. 1969

Manager Experience	Dates Managed	Invest Obj	Std Dev	+/- Index
John S. Tilson				
Pasadena Growth A	06/86 - 12/94	G	21.41	-1.92
Pasadena Nifty Fifty A	12/90 - 12/94	G	13.96	3.11

Performance 12-31-94

	1st Qtr	2nd Qtr	3rd Qtr	4th Qtr	Total
1987	---	---	11.75	2.50	15.00 *
1988	4.77	3.57	3.36	1.13	13.42
1989	4.72	13.13	10.32	1.74	32.98
1990	-4.15	12.07	-16.28	10.75	-0.39
1991	15.95	0.56	10.20	8.03 *	38.82
1992	-3.30	0.59	3.49	3.84	4.54
1993	-0.51	-1.52	1.69	2.82	2.44
1994	-6.10	-1.31	2.26	0.85	-4.43

Bear Market Performance

Decile Rank (5-year period)

Worst — Best

	Worst 3 Mo Period 1985-89	Worst 3 Mo Period 1990-94
Pasadena Balanced Return A	---	-16.28
+/- S&P 500	---	-2.53
+/- Best Fit Index : S&P 500	---	-2.53

Trailing Returns

	Total Return %	+/- S&P 500	+/- LB Aggregate	% Rank All	% Rank Obj	Growth of $10,000
3 Mo	0.85	0.86	0.47	7	3	10,085
6 Mo	3.13	-1.74	2.13	20	16	10,313
1 Yr	-4.43	-5.75	-1.51	58	75	9,557
3 Yr Avg	0.77	-5.49	-3.77	95	93	10,234
5 Yr Avg	7.19	-1.50	-0.43	45	67	14,151
10 Yr Avg	---	---	---	---	---	---
15 Yr Avg	---	---	---	---	---	---

Operations

Address and Telephone	600 N. Rosemead Boulevard Pasadena, CA 91107-2101 800-882-2855 / 818-351-4276
Advisor	Roger Engemann Management
Subadvisor	None
Distributor	Pasadena Fund Services
States Available	All plus GU,PR
Report Grade	A
Income Distrib	Paid Annually
* Date of Inception	06-08-87
Fiscal Year End	December

Risk Analysis

Time Period	Load-Adj Return %	Risk % Rank [1] All	Obj	Morningstar [2] Return	Risk	Morningstar Risk-Adj Rating
1 Yr	-9.69					
3 Yr	-1.11	69	86	-1.30 [3]	1.01	★
5 Yr	5.99	68	96	0.30 [3]	1.09	★★
10 Yr	---	---	---	---	---	

Average Historical Rating (55 months) 3.7 ★s

[1] 1 = low, 100 = high [2] 1.00 = Hybrid Avg [3] 1.00 = 90-day T-bill return

Other Measures

			Standard S&P 500	Best Fit S&P 500
Standard Deviation	7.22	Alpha	-4.7	-4.7
Mean	1.03	Beta	0.79	0.79
Sharpe Ratio	-0.34	R-Squared	76	76

Investment Style

Stocks

	Port Avg	Rel S&P 500
Price/Earnings Ratio	20.9	1.13
Price/Book Ratio	5.3	1.57
5 Yr Earnings Gr %	14.7	2.64
Med Mkt Cap ($mil)	12983	1.00

Style V B G / Size L M S

Bonds

Avg Effective Duration	10.4 Yrs
Avg Effective Maturity	21.1 Yrs
Avg Credit Quality	AAA
Avg Weighted Coupon	8.22%

Maturity S I L / Quality H M L

Diversification Value for Portfolio Types

Large Cap: Low	Small Cap: Medium	Bond: Medium	Balanced: Low	Diversified: Medium

Portfolio 11-30-94

Share Chg (06-94)000	Amount 000	Total Stocks: 44 Total Fixed-Income: 4	Date of Maturity	Value $000	% Net Assets
	10532	US Treasury Bond 7.875%	02-15-21	10252	18.78
	6386	US Treasury Bond 8.875%	08-15-17	6873	12.59
-3	23	Gillette		1689	3.09
-9	69	Wal-Mart Stores		1594	2.92
-3	15	Pfizer		1185	2.17
-2	23	Coca-Cola		1175	2.15
	1053	US Treasury Bond 8.75%	05-15-17	1120	2.05
-3	23	Reuters Holdings (ADR)		1054	1.93
-2	29	Toys 'R' Us		1052	1.93
-2	16	Procter & Gamble		1017	1.86
-2	16	Philip Morris		973	1.78
-2	15	Colgate-Palmolive		919	1.68
-2	18	FHLMC		907	1.66
-9	24	Merck		892	1.63
-1	12	FNMA		872	1.60
-2	19	Walt Disney		835	1.53
-3	19	Carnival Cl A		828	1.52
-3	23	PepsiCo		813	1.49
6	15	Medtronic		812	1.49
-4	28	Albertson's		798	1.46

Index Allocation

	% of Stocks
S&P 500	86.2
S&P MidCap 400	2.8
U.S. Small Cap	7.8
Foreign	3.3

Composition % 12-31-94

Cash	3.3	Preferreds	0.0
Stocks	60.7	Convertibles	0.0
Bonds	36.0	Other	0.0

Tax Analysis

	Tax-Adj Historical Return %	% Pretax Return
3 Yr Avg	0.23	29.1
5 Yr Avg	6.51	89.4
10 Yr Avg	---	---
Potential Capital Gain Exposure (% of assets)		3%

Most Similar Funds in MF500

Dreyfus	Fair Fit
Vanguard U.S. Growth	Fair Fit
Dreyfus Appreciation	Fair Fit

Bond Credit Analysis 12-31-94

% of Bonds

US Govt	100	BB	0
AAA	0	B	0
AA	0	Below B	0
A	0	NR/NA	0
BBB	0		

Stock Sector Weightings

	% of Stocks	Relative S&P 500
Utilities	0.0	0.00
Energy	0.0	0.00
Financials	11.1	1.05
Industrial Cyclicals	2.3	0.14
Consumer Durables	5.4	0.86
Consumer Staples	24.1	1.92
Services	17.9	2.20
Retail	17.9	3.07
Health	15.8	1.82
Technology	5.6	0.61

Expenses & Fees

Sales Fees	5.50% front
	0.00% deferred
	0.25% 12b-1
Management Fee	1.00% max./0.40% min., 1.05%A
3-,5-,10-yr Expense Projections	$117, $161, $280
Annual Brokerage Cost	0.03%

Min Initial Purchase	$1000 (Addt'l: $50)
Min IRA Purchase	$500 (Addt'l: $50)
Min Auto Invest Plan	$500 (Systematic Inv: $50)

MORNINGSTAR 1995 Mutual Fund 500

Pasadena Growth A

	Ticker	Load	NAV	Yield	SEC Yield	Assets	Objective
	PASGX	5.50%	15.40	0.0%	N/A	391.8	Growth

Pasadena Growth Fund - Class A seeks long-term capital appreciation.

The fund invests primarily in equities issued by seasoned or unseasoned companies with rapidly growing earnings per share. Up to 30% of assets may be invested in special situations: liquidations, reorganizations, mergers, or new management. The fund may also invest in undervalued companies. It may invest a small portion of assets in investment-grade debt and may invest 15% of assets in foreign issues.

Class A shares have front loads and lower 12b-1 fees; Class B shares have deferred loads and conversion features; Class C shares have level loads.

Manager's Investment Style

Management sticks to a large-cap growth strategy, no matter what the market tides. This caused the fund to lag its more-flexible growth-oriented peers as cyclicals came to the fore in 1992 and 1993. Management also targets firms with at least a 15% annual growth rate, strong management, and franchise value. These criteria have led to heavy weightings in the consumer-staples, services, and health-care sectors. Because management takes a long-term approach, turnover is modest.

Fund Manager(s)

Roger Engemann, since 6-86. Birthdate: 10-40 BA, U. of Oregon 1964 MA, U. of California-Los Angeles 1966
John S. Tilson, since 6-86. Birthdate: 3-44 BS, U. of Southern Cal. 1966 MBA, U. of Southern Cal. 1969

Manager Experience	Dates Managed	Invest Obj	Std Dev	+/- Index
John S. Tilson				
Pasadena Balanced Ret A	06/87 - 12/94	B	12.33	3.54
Pasadena Nifty Fifty A	12/90 - 12/94	G	13.96	3.11

Historical Profile

Return	Below Average
Risk	Above Average
Rating ★★	Below Average

	92%	95%	99%	99%	99%	99%	98%	95%

Investment Style History
Equity
Average % Stocks Held in Portfolio

Growth of $10,000

|||| Value of Fund ($000)
— Value of Index ($000)
SPMid400
▼ Manager Change
▽ Partial Manager Change
► Mgr Unknown After
◄ Mgr Unknown Before

Performance Quartile (Within Objective)

	1983	1984	1985	1986	1987	1988	1989	1990	1991	1992	1993	1994	History
NAV	---	---	---	6.99	6.19	8.41	10.53	10.04	16.80	17.00	16.00	15.40	NAV
	---	---	---	-9.27 *	-11.45	35.78	31.67	-4.55	67.83	2.24	-5.87	-3.75	Total Return %
	---	---	---	-9.28 *	-16.70	19.17	-0.01	-1.43	37.35	-5.38	-15.93	-5.06	+/- S&P 500
	---	---	---	---	-13.81	17.84	2.50	1.64	33.63	-6.73	-17.15	-3.68	+/- Wilshire 5000
	---	---	---	0.00	0.00	0.00	0.57	0.00	0.00	0.00	0.00	0.00	Income Return %
	---	---	---	-9.27	-11.44	35.78	31.10	-4.55	67.83	2.24	-5.87	-3.75	Capital Return %
	---	---	---	---	97	1	11	69	2	86	100	51	Total Rtn % Rank All
	---	---	---	---	98	1	27	51	3	84	99	66	Total Rtn % Rank Obj
	---	---	---	0.00	0.00	0.00	0.06	0.00	0.00	0.00	0.00	0.00	Income $
	---	---	---	0.03	0.00	0.00	0.47	0.01	0.05	0.18	0.00	0.00	Capital Gains $
	---	---	---	2.00	2.00	1.80	1.80	2.20	1.80	1.60	1.60	1.60	Expense Ratio %
	---	---	---	-0.60	-0.90	0.00	-0.50	-0.90	-0.60	-0.30	0.00	0.00	Income Ratio %
	---	---	---	---	115	99	94	32	24	25	23	---	Turnover Rate %
	---	---	---	0.5	10.9	18.9	36.7	80.6	323.5	625.6	534.0	391.8	Net Assets ($mil)

Performance 12-31-94

	1st Qtr	2nd Qtr	3rd Qtr	4th Qtr	Total
1987	27.04	-8.15	-0.96	-23.37	-11.45
1988	18.42	7.71	3.48	2.88	35.78
1989	11.78	12.45	14.62	-8.61	31.67
1990	-2.66	14.15	-24.96	14.48	-4.55
1991	31.23	-2.43	14.35	14.63	67.83
1992	-0.95	-6.49	2.31	7.89	2.24
1993	-5.59	-5.36	1.32	3.98	-5.87
1994	-6.00	-2.79	7.66	-2.16	-3.75

Bear Market Performance

Decile Rank (5-year period)

Worst | Best

	Worst 3 Mo Period 1985-89	Worst 3 Mo Period 1990-94
Pasadena Growth A	---	-24.96
+/- S&P 500	---	-11.21
+/- Best Fit Index : SPMid400	---	-7.18

Trailing Returns

	Total Return %	+/- S&P 500	+/- Wil 5000	% Rank All	% Rank Obj	Growth of $10,000
3 Mo	-2.16	-2.14	-1.39	71	66	9,784
6 Mo	5.34	0.47	0.71	10	31	10,534
1 Yr	-3.75	-5.06	-3.68	51	66	9,625
3 Yr Avg	-2.52	-8.78	-9.13	99	97	9,263
5 Yr Avg	8.21	-0.48	-0.60	31	58	14,840
10 Yr Avg	---	---	---	---	---	---
15 Yr Avg	---	---	---	---	---	---

Operations

Address and Telephone	600 N. Rosemead Boulevard Pasadena, CA 91107-2101 800-882-2855 / 818-351-4276
Advisor	Roger Engemann Management
Subadvisor	None
Distributor	Pasadena Fund Services
States Available	All plus GU,PR
Report Grade	A
Income Distrib	Paid Annually
* Date of Inception	06-24-86
Fiscal Year End	December

Risk Analysis

Time Period	Load-Adj Return %	Risk % Rank All	Obj	Morningstar Return	Morningstar Risk	Morningstar Risk-Adj Rating
1 Yr	-9.04					
3 Yr	-4.34	93	90	-2.12[3]	1.29	★
5 Yr	7.00	93	94	0.55[3]	1.26	★★
10 Yr	---	---	---	---	---	---
Average Historical Rating (67 months)				3.8	★s	

[1] = low, 100 = high [2] 1.00 = Equity Avg [3] 1.00 = 90-day T-bill return

Other Measures

			Standard S&P 500	Best Fit SPMid400
Standard Deviation	11.44	Alpha	-8.2	-8.8
Mean	-1.89	Beta	1.08	0.98
Sharpe Ratio	-0.47	R-Squared	56	72

Investment Style

	Stock Portfolio Avg	Relative S&P 500
Price/Earnings Ratio	21.9	1.19
Price/Book Ratio	4.8	1.42
5 Yr Earnings Gr %	17.6	3.16
Return on Assets %	10.8	1.44
Debt % Total Cap	24.7	0.87
Med Mkt Cap ($mil)	7607	0.59

Style: Large, Growth

Diversification Value for Portfolio Types

Large Cap: Low	Small Cap: Low	Bond: High	Balanced: Low	Diversified: Medium

Expenses & Fees

Sales Fees	5.50% front 0.00% deferred 0.25% 12b-1
Management Fee	1.00% max./0.40% min., 1.05%A
3-,5-,10-yr Expense Projections	$102, $137, $233
Annual Brokerage Cost	0.17%

Min Initial Purchase	$1000 (Addt'l: $50)
Min IRA Purchase	$500 (Addt'l: $50)
Min Auto Invest Plan	$500 (Systematic Inv: $50)

Portfolio 11-30-94

Total Stocks: 105
Total Fixed-Income: 1

Share Chg (06-94)000	Amount 000		Value $000	% Net Assets
-113	624	Wal-Mart Stores	14439	3.59
-63	183	Gillette	13415	3.34
-60	255	Coca-Cola	13015	3.24
-55	240	Toys 'R' Us	8796	2.19
-27	110	Pfizer	8548	2.13
46	144	Motorola	8123	2.02
-53	173	Home Depot	7997	1.99
-28	168	Reuters Holdings (ADR)	7712	1.92
-26	53	Wells Fargo	7635	1.90
-38	168	Carnival Cl A	7271	1.81
-17	120	Colgate-Palmolive	7205	1.79
46	134	Medtronic	7128	1.77
-59	137	FHLMC	6851	1.70
-23	125	Johnson & Johnson	6666	1.66
-32	91	FNMA	6491	1.61
-61	106	Philip Morris	6314	1.57
-52	144	Walt Disney	6286	1.56
-20	216	McDonald's	6133	1.52
-7	91	Microsoft	5738	1.43
-48	149	Merck	5546	1.38
-2	96	Automatic Data Processing	5368	1.33
46	144	Gap	5079	1.26
-4	192	WMX Technologies	4947	1.23
94	192	AutoZone	4923	1.22
-59	137	CDW Computer Centers	4671	1.16

Composition % 12-31-94

Cash	1.2	Preferreds	0.0
Stocks	98.8	Convertibles	0.0
Bonds	0.0	Other	0.0

Tax Analysis

	Tax-Adj Historical Return %	% Pretax Return
3 Yr Avg	-2.61	NMF
5 Yr Avg	8.13	98.7
10 Yr Avg	---	---
Potential Capital Gain Exposure (% of assets)		9%

Most Similar Funds in MF500

General Amer Inv	Fair Fit
20th Century Growth Investor	Weak Fit
Kemper Growth A	Weak Fit

Index Allocation

	% of Stocks
S&P 500	60.8
S&P MidCap 400	9.4
U.S. Small Cap	25.7
Foreign	4.1

Sector Weightings

	% of Stocks	Relative S&P 500
Utilities	0.0	0.00
Energy	0.0	0.00
Financials	9.4	0.89
Industrial Cyclicals	1.9	0.11
Consumer Durables	5.5	0.89
Consumer Staples	14.1	1.12
Services	22.6	2.78
Retail	22.9	3.93
Health	14.4	1.65
Technology	9.2	1.00

Pax World

Pax World Fund primarily seeks income and capital preservation; long-term growth of capital is secondary.

The fund normally invests about 70% of its assets in common and preferred stocks; the balance may be invested in debt. It seeks companies producing life-supportive goods and services. Companies engaged in manufacturing defense or weapons-related products or those engaged in the liquor, tobacco, and gambling industries are excluded from the portfolio. The fund also avoids U.S. Treasuries, because these monies could be used to finance defense.

	Ticker	Load	NAV	Yield	SEC Yield	Assets	Objective
	PAXWX	None	13.39	3.7%	N/A	388.3	Balanced

Manager's Investment Style

A combined dividend preference and socially responsible orientation keeps management's choices largely concentrated in a few sectors such as consumer staples and pharmaceuticals. The fund invests only in life-supportive industries, while also avoiding environmental offenders. These two criteria generally eliminate industrial cyclicals, while the fund's requirement of a dividend-paying stock largely eliminates technology, a sector oft-favored by the socially responsible set. The bond portfolio is largely government mortgages.

Fund Manager(s)

Anthony S. Brown, since 11-71. Birthdate: 12-34.
BS, U. of Pennsylvania 1956 MBA, Boston U.

Manager Experience

	Dates Managed	Invest Obj	Std Dev	+/- Index
Not available.				

Historical Profile
Return	Average
Risk	Below Average
Rating	★★★ Neutral

Investment Style History Equity
Average % Stocks Held in Portfolio

66% 54% 55% 60% 42% 67% 61% 66%

Growth of $10,000
- |||| Value of Fund ($000)
- — Value of Index ($000) S&P 500
- ▼ Manager Change
- ▽ Partial Manager Change
- ► Mgr Unknown After
- ◄ Mgr Unknown Before

Performance Quartile (Within Objective)

	1983	1984	1985	1986	1987	1988	1989	1990	1991	1992	1993	1994	History
	11.97	11.47	13.34	13.19	11.57	11.93	13.98	13.98	14.99	14.27	13.55	13.39	NAV
	24.17	7.39	25.79	8.45	2.49	11.70	24.81	10.53	20.60	0.63	-1.06	2.65	Total Return %
	1.71	1.13	-5.94	-10.23	-2.77	-4.91	-6.87	13.65	-9.89	-6.99	-11.11	1.33	+/- S&P 500
	15.80	-7.76	3.67	-6.80	-0.27	3.82	10.27	1.59	4.59	-6.62	-10.81	5.57	+/- LB Aggregate
	5.16	4.88	5.10	3.87	5.92	5.27	5.31	4.41	5.50	4.60	3.52	3.83	Income Return %
	19.01	2.52	20.69	4.58	-3.44	6.43	19.50	6.12	15.09	-3.97	-4.58	-1.18	Capital Return %
	26	40	43	89	39	48	24	3	44	89	99	8	Total Rtn % Rank All
	7	42	64	93	41	47	15	1	80	93	100	3	Total Rtn % Rank Obj
	0.49	0.51	0.52	0.50	0.75	0.61	0.63	0.61	0.77	0.67	0.50	0.50	Income $
	0.28	0.77	0.37	0.71	1.24	0.37	0.25	0.84	1.04	0.13	0.07	0.00	Capital Gains $
	1.40	1.50	1.40	1.20	1.10	1.10	1.10	1.20	1.20	1.00	0.94	0.99	Expense Ratio %
	4.30	6.50	4.30	3.20	4.10	5.00	5.80	5.40	5.10	3.70	3.63	3.81	Income Ratio %
	29	34	48	57	124	58	37	39	26	17	22	---	Turnover Rate %
	12.2	16.9	32.8	53.8	65.7	73.7	93.0	119.9	270.5	468.6	464.4	388.3	Net Assets ($mil)

Performance 12-31-94

	1st Qtr	2nd Qtr	3rd Qtr	4th Qtr	Total
1987	12.44	2.05	3.29	-13.52	2.49
1988	5.70	2.62	1.81	1.15	11.70
1989	3.27	8.85	5.17	5.57	24.81
1990	-1.50	7.33	-5.47	10.59	10.53
1991	7.30	2.33	6.66	2.97	20.60
1992	-1.80	-0.95	2.19	1.24	0.63
1993	0.42	-1.19	-1.86	1.61	-1.06
1994	-3.69	0.61	6.27	-0.32	2.65

Bear Market Performance

Decile Rank (5-year period)

Worst ← → Best

	Worst 3 Mo Period 1985-89	Worst 3 Mo Period 1990-94
Pax World	-17.68	-5.47
+/- S&P 500	11.91	8.28
+/- Best Fit Index : S&P 500	11.91	8.28

Trailing Returns

	Total Return %	+/- S&P 500	+/- LB Aggregate	% Rank All	Obj	Growth of $10,000
3 Mo	-0.32	-0.31	-0.70	30	26	9,968
6 Mo	5.93	1.07	4.94	9	3	10,593
1 Yr	2.65	1.33	5.57	8	3	10,265
3 Yr Avg	0.73	-5.54	-3.82	95	94	10,220
5 Yr Avg	6.38	-2.31	-1.25	67	82	13,623
10 Yr Avg	10.26	-4.12	0.31	55	82	26,553
15 Yr Avg	11.28	-3.20	0.47	62	88	49,679

Operations

Address and Telephone	224 State Street
	Portsmouth, NH 03801
	800-767-1729 / 603-431-8022
Advisor	Pax World Management
Subadvisor	None
Distributor	Pax World Fund
States Available	All plus GU,PR,VI
Report Grade	B
Income Distrib	Paid Annually
Date of Inception	11-30-71
Fiscal Year End	December

Risk Analysis

Time Period	Load-Adj Return %	Risk % Rank All [1]	Obj	Morningstar [2] Return	Risk	Morningstar Risk-Adj Rating
1 Yr	2.65					
3 Yr	0.73	58	70	-0.80 [3]	0.83	★★
5 Yr	6.38	49	24	0.40 [3]	0.66	★★★
10 Yr	10.26	43	57	0.71	0.71	★★★
Average Historical Rating (109 months)				3.4 ★s		

[1] = low, 100 = high [2] 1.00 = Hybrid Avg [3] 1.00 = 90-day T-bill return

Other Measures

			Standard S&P 500	Best Fit S&P 500
Standard Deviation	5.62	Alpha	-4.0	-4.0
Mean	0.88	Beta	0.51	0.51
Sharpe Ratio	-0.47	R-Squared	52	52

Investment Style

Stocks
	Port Avg	Rel S&P 500
Price/Earnings Ratio	15.6	0.84
Price/Book Ratio	3.1	0.92
5 Yr Earnings Gr %	4.5	0.80
Med Mkt Cap ($mil)	4612	0.36

Style V B G — Size L M S

Bonds
Avg Effective Duration	1.4 Yrs
Avg Effective Maturity	1.8 Yrs
Avg Credit Quality	AAA
Avg Weighted Coupon	7.32%

Maturity S I L — Quality H M L

Diversification Value for Portfolio Types

Large Cap: Low	Small Cap: Medium	Bond: High	Balanced: Medium	Diversified: Medium

Expenses & Fees

Sales Fees	0.00% front
	0.00% deferred
	0.25% 12b-1
Management Fee	0.75% max./0.50% min.
3-,5-,10-yr Expense Projections	$29, $51, $113
Annual Brokerage Cost	0.08%

Min Initial Purchase / Min IRA Purchase / Min Auto Invest Plan
Min Initial Purchase	$250 (Addt'l: $50)
Min IRA Purchase	$250 (Addt'l: $50)
Min Auto Invest Plan	$250 (Systematic Inv: $50)

Portfolio 12-31-94

Total Stocks: 35
Total Fixed-Income: 11

Share Chg (11-94)000	Amount 000		Date of Maturity	Value $000	% Net Assets
0	700	Merck		26688	6.87
0	675	HJ Heinz		24806	6.39
	15000	Federal Home Loan Bank 8.25%	09-25-96	15113	3.89
-1	749	Pet		14795	3.81
0	552	Peoples Energy		14418	3.71
-49	566	Bay State Gas		13584	3.50
	14000	FNMA Debenture 6.05%	11-10-97	13325	3.43
-185	588	Brooklyn Union Gas		13074	3.37
0	659	Sierra Pacific Resources		12431	3.20
0	200	Bristol-Myers Squibb		11575	2.98
0	200	General Mills		11400	2.94
0	700	Acuson		11375	2.93
-50	150	Nike Cl B		11194	2.88
0	300	NYNEX		11025	2.84
	10000	Federal Farm Credit Bk 7.75%	12-09-97	9963	2.57
	10000	FNMA Debenture 7.6%	01-10-97	9934	2.56
	10000	FNMA 7.51%	11-01-97	9888	2.55
	10000	Fed Home Loan Bank 6.995%	11-08-96	9860	2.54
	10000	World Bank Global 5.875%	07-16-97	9694	2.50
	9000	Federal Home Loan Bank 8.1%	03-25-96	9048	2.33

Index Allocation
	% of Stocks
S&P 500	73.9
S&P MidCap 400	10.1
U.S. Small Cap	16.1
Foreign	0.0

Composition % 12-31-94
Cash	9.9	Preferreds	0.0
Stocks	63.1	Convertibles	0.0
Bonds	27.0	Other	0.0

Bond Credit Analysis 12-31-94
% of Bonds			
US Govt	100	BB	0
AAA	0	B	0
AA	0	Below B	0
A	0	NR/NA	0
BBB	0		

Tax Analysis
	Tax-Adj Historical Return %	% Pretax Return
3 Yr Avg	-0.83	---
5 Yr Avg	4.04	60.5
10 Yr Avg	7.44	63.4
Potential Capital Gain Exposure (% of assets)		-8%

Most Similar Funds in MF500
Franklin Rising Dividends	Weak Fit
Vanguard U.S. Growth	Weak Fit
Pasadena Balanced Return A	Weak Fit

Stock Sector Weightings
	% of Stocks	Relative S&P 500
Utilities	27.9	2.25
Energy	0.6	0.06
Financials	0.6	0.06
Industrial Cyclicals	0.9	0.06
Consumer Durables	7.0	1.13
Consumer Staples	23.7	1.89
Services	1.9	0.24
Retail	13.5	2.32
Health	23.7	2.73
Technology	0.0	0.00

MORNINGSTAR 1995 Mutual Fund 500

PBHG Emerging Growth

	Ticker	Load	NAV	Yield	SEC Yield	Assets	Objective
	PBEGX	None	15.10	0.0%	0.00%	177.7	Small Company

PBHG Emerging Growth Fund seeks long-term growth of capital.
The fund normally invests at least 65% of its assets in common stocks of U.S. companies with capitalizations ranging from $10 million to $250 million. These companies have historically exhibited strong growth characteristics and have higher-than-average expected earnings trends. The fund reserves the right to invest up to 30% of its assets in restricted securities and securities of foreign issuers traded outside the United States and Canada. It may also invest in ADRs.

Prior to May 31, 1994, the fund was named Pilgrim Baxter Emerging Growth Fund.

Manager's Investment Style

Management follows an earnings-momentum strategy that uses bottom-up research to choose from stocks that have earnings-growth rates of more than 20%. This initial screen nets 250 to 300 companies, which are then ranked with preference to earnings-estimate revisions and earnings surprises. Management buys among the top 35% of stocks on this list.

Fund Manager(s)

Gary L. Pilgrim CFA(1974), since 06-93.
Birthdate: 11-40. BS, U. of Tulsa 1967 MBA, Drexel U. 1971
Christine M. Baxter CFA(1994), since 06-93.
Birthdate: 05-69. BA, U. of Pennsylvania 1991

Manager Experience	Dates Managed	Invest Obj	Std Dev	+/- Index
Gary L. Pilgrim				
PBHG Growth	12/85 - 12/94	SC	24.91	7.47
Managers Special Equity	10/94 - 12/94	SC	12.68	0.91

Historical Profile

Return ---
Risk ---
Rating
Not Rated

	90%	83%	Investment Style History Equity

Average % Stocks Held in Portfolio

Growth of $10,000
||| Value of Fund ($000)
— Value of Index ($000) S&P 500
▼ Manager Change
▽ Partial Manager Change
► Mgr Unknown After
◄ Mgr Unknown Before

Performance Quartile (Within Objective)

	1983	1984	1985	1986	1987	1988	1989	1990	1991	1992	1993	1994	History
	---	---	---	---	---	---	---	---	---	---	12.23	15.10	NAV
	---	---	---	---	---	---	---	---	---	---	32.58 *	23.78	Total Return %
	---	---	---	---	---	---	---	---	---	---	26.39 *	22.47	+/- S&P 500
	---	---	---	---	---	---	---	---	---	---	---	26.44	+/- Wilshire 4500
	---	---	---	---	---	---	---	---	---	---	0.00	0.00	Income Return %
	---	---	---	---	---	---	---	---	---	---	32.58	23.78	Capital Return %
	---	---	---	---	---	---	---	---	---	---	---	1	Total Rtn % Rank All
	---	---	---	---	---	---	---	---	---	---	---	1	Total Rtn % Rank Obj
	---	---	---	---	---	---	---	---	---	---	0.00	0.00	Income $
	---	---	---	---	---	---	---	---	---	---	0.98	0.04	Capital Gains $
	---	---	---	---	---	---	---	---	---	---	1.50	1.41	Expense Ratio %
	---	---	---	---	---	---	---	---	---	---	-0.72	-0.48	Income Ratio %
	---	---	---	---	---	---	---	---	---	---	---	---	Turnover Rate %
	---	---	---	---	---	---	---	---	---	---	39.7	177.7	Net Assets ($mil)

Performance 12-31-94

	1st Qtr	2nd Qtr	3rd Qtr	4th Qtr	Total
1987	---	---	---	---	---
1988	---	---	---	---	---
1989	---	---	---	---	---
1990	---	---	---	---	---
1991	---	---	---	---	---
1992	---	---	---	---	---
1993	---	---	25.00	4.80	32.58 *
1994	0.00	-8.34	21.77	10.91	23.78

Bear Market Performance

Decile Rank (5-year period)

Worst — Best

	Worst 3 Mo Period 1985-89	Worst 3 Mo Period 1990-94
PBHG Emerging Growth	---	---
+/- S&P 500	---	---
+/- Best Fit Index :	---	---

Trailing Returns

	Total Return %	+/- S&P 500	+/- Wil 4500	% Rank All	% Rank Obj	Growth of $10,000
3 Mo	10.91	10.92	13.41	1	2	11,091
6 Mo	35.05	30.18	30.85	1	1	13,505
1 Yr	23.78	22.47	26.44	1	1	12,378
3 Yr Avg	---	---	---	---	---	---
5 Yr Avg	---	---	---	---	---	---
10 Yr Avg	---	---	---	---	---	---
15 Yr Avg	---	---	---	---	---	---

Operations

Address and Telephone	680 E. Swedesford Road
	Wayne, PA 19087-1658
	800-433-0051
Advisor	Pilgrim Baxter & Associates
Subadvisor	None
Distributor	SEI Financial Services
States Available	All plus PR
Report Grade	C
Income Distrib	Paid Annually
* Date of Inception	06-15-93
Fiscal Year End	October

Min Initial Purchase	$1000 (Addt'l: None)
Min IRA Purchase	$1000 (Addt'l: None)
Min Auto Invest Plan	$1000 (Systematic Inv: $25)

Expenses & Fees

Sales Fees	0.00% front
	0.00% deferred
	0.00% 12b-1
Management Fee	0.85% flat fee, 0.20%A
3-,5-,10-yr Expense Projections	$44, N/A, N/A
Annual Brokerage Cost	---

Risk Analysis

Time Period	Load-Adj Return %	Risk % Rank[1] All	Risk % Rank[1] Obj	Morningstar[2] Return	Morningstar Risk	Morningstar Risk-Adj Rating
1 Yr	23.78					
3 Yr	---	---	---	---	---	---
5 Yr	---	---	---	---	---	---
10 Yr	---	---	---	---	---	---

Average Historical Rating ---

[1] 1 = low, 100 = high [2] 1.00 = Equity Avg [3] 1.00 = 90-day T-bill return

Other Measures

			Standard S&P 500	Best Fit
Standard Deviation	---	Alpha	---	---
Mean	---	Beta	---	---
Sharpe Ratio	---	R-Squared	---	---

Investment Style

	Stock Portfolio Avg	Relative S&P 500
Price/Earnings Ratio	30.0	1.62
Price/Book Ratio	5.0	1.46
5 Yr Earnings Gr %	39.1#	7.05
Return on Assets %	15.9	2.12
Debt % Total Cap	12.6#	0.45
Med Mkt Cap ($mil)	258	0.02

figure is based on 50% or less of stocks

Style Value Blend Growth — Size Large Med Small

Diversification Value for Portfolio Types

Large Cap: Small Cap: Bond: Balanced: Diversified:

Portfolio 09-30-94

Total Stocks: 75
Total Fixed-Income: 0

Share Chg (04-94) 000	Amount 000		Value $000	% Net Assets
18	28	Cobra Golf	1539	1.97
11	40	IMRS	1504	1.93
45	55	Infosoft International	1498	1.92
21	47	Level One Communications	1491	1.91
34	34	Microtouch Systems	1410	1.81
30	57	Fossil	1382	1.77
36	46	Gulf South Medical Supply	1380	1.77
38	61	Xpedite Systems	1338	1.71
21	46	Integrated Silicon Systems	1334	1.71
8	33	Omnicare	1324	1.70
10	43	Cyrk	1320	1.69
30	52	Landry's Seafood Restaurants	1313	1.68
16	29	Three-Five Systems	1287	1.65
47	84	Cambridge Tech Partners	1242	1.59
34	34	Ultratech Stepper	1238	1.59
66	88	Books-A-Million	1210	1.55
48	48	Intl Imaging Materials	1183	1.52
15	33	Fair Isaac	1174	1.51
24	42	Safety 1st	1166	1.49
30	55	Cornerstone Imaging	1147	1.47
56	56	Day Runner	1138	1.46
43	58	Lund International	1124	1.44
40	40	Urban Outfitters	1102	1.41
31	52	Active Voice	1094	1.40
0	40	CIDCO	1058	1.36

Composition % 12-31-94

Cash	16.4	Preferreds	0.0
Stocks	83.6	Convertibles	0.0
Bonds	0.0	Other	0.0

Tax Analysis

	Tax-Adj Historical Return %	% Pretax Return
3 Yr Avg	---	---
5 Yr Avg	---	---
10 Yr Avg	---	---
Potential Capital Gain Exposure (% of assets)		15%

Most Similar Funds in MF500

Fund lacks three-year record

Index Allocation

	% of Stocks
S&P 500	0.0
S&P MidCap 400	0.0
U.S. Small Cap	100.0
Foreign	0.0

Sector Weightings

	% of Stocks	Relative S&P 500
Utilities	0.0	0.00
Energy	0.0	0.00
Financials	1.4	0.13
Industrial Cyclicals	4.1	0.25
Consumer Durables	17.0	2.74
Consumer Staples	0.0	0.00
Services	15.3	1.88
Retail	8.6	1.48
Health	9.1	1.05
Technology	44.5	4.86

PBHG Growth

	Ticker	Load	NAV	Yield	SEC Yield	Assets	Objective
	PBHGX	None	15.91	0.0%	0.00%	745.8	Small Company

PBHG Growth Fund seeks capital appreciation.

The fund invests primarily in common stocks of companies with the potential for significant capital appreciation and a strong growth in earnings. Generally, at least 50% of the fund's assets are invested in over-the-counter securities. Companies in this fund typically have superior profitability characteristics while having a less-diversified business mix than the average company included in the S&P 500 Index. The fund may also invest in convertible securities and short-term debt. Up to 15% of the fund's assets may be invested in foreign securities.

Manager's Investment Style

Management's aggressive bottom-up growth strategy targets small firms that are increasing their earnings by more than 20% per year. Management ranks the stocks that qualify using a quantitative system, and buys from the companies that make the top 30%. The fund is also known for dabbling in IPOs. Management sells if it expects a company to underperform earnings targets, or if a position grows to more than 3% of the portfolio. The fund has generated sizable capital gains.

Fund Manager(s)

Gary L. Pilgrim CFA(1974), since 12-85.
Birthdate: 11-40. BS, U. of Tulsa 1967 MBA, Drexel U. 1971

Manager Experience

	Dates Managed	Invest Obj	Std Dev	+/- Index
Gary L. Pilgrim				
PBHG Emerging Growth	06/93 - 12/94	SC	19.12	33.85
Managers Special Equity	10/94 - 12/94	SC	12.68	0.91

Performance 12-31-94

	1st Qtr	2nd Qtr	3rd Qtr	4th Qtr	Total
1987	36.12	-1.79	6.16	-21.08	11.99
1988	5.98	6.99	-5.99	0.24	6.85
1989	3.14	11.54	17.01	-3.77	29.54
1990	1.31	12.63	-29.05	11.51	-9.73
1991	31.24	-8.81	11.66	13.46	51.63
1992	-1.52	-8.68	0.42	42.29	28.51
1993	2.38	15.61	18.89	4.16	46.57
1994	-3.49	-12.61	17.94	5.30	4.75

Bear Market Performance

Decile Rank (5-year period)

Worst   Best

	Worst 3 Mo Period 1985-89	Worst 3 Mo Period 1990-94
PBHG Growth	---	-29.05
+/- S&P 500	---	-15.30
+/- Best Fit Index : Wil 4500	---	-10.82

Trailing Returns

	Total Return %	+/- S&P 500	+/- Wil 4500	% Rank All	% Rank Obj	Growth of $10,000
3 Mo	5.30	5.32	7.81	1	8	10,530
6 Mo	24.20	19.34	20.00	1	2	12,420
1 Yr	4.75	3.44	7.40	4	15	10,475
3 Yr Avg	25.42	19.16	17.82	1	1	19,731
5 Yr Avg	21.98	13.29	12.89	1	2	27,006
10 Yr Avg	---	---	---	---	---	---
15 Yr Avg	---	---	---	---	---	---

Operations

Address and Telephone	680 E. Swedesford Road
	Wayne, PA 19087-1658
	800-433-0051
Advisor	Pilgrim Baxter & Associates
Subadvisor	None
Distributor	SEI Financial Services
States Available	All plus PR
Report Grade	C
Income Distrib	Paid Annually
* Date of Inception	12-19-85
Fiscal Year End	March

Historical Profile

Return	High
Risk	High
Rating	★★★★★ Highest

95%   94%   91%   89%   84%   90%   82%   85%

Growth of $10,000

- |||| Value of Fund ($000)
- — Value of Index ($000) Wil 4500
- ▼ Manager Change
- ▽ Partial Manager Change
- ► Mgr Unknown After
- ◄ Mgr Unknown Before

Performance Quartile (Within Objective)

	1983	1984	1985	1986	1987	1988	1989	1990	1991	1992	1993	1994	History
	---	---	10.00	12.32	9.86	10.51	10.71	8.74	10.53	10.51	15.20	15.91	NAV
	---	---	0.00 *	23.94	11.99	6.85	29.54	-9.73	51.63	28.51	46.57	4.75	Total Return %
	---	---	-0.92 *	5.26	6.73	-9.76	-2.15	-6.61	21.14	20.89	36.51	3.44	+/- S&P 500
	---	---		12.18	15.50	-13.69	5.59	3.83	8.17	16.75	32.03	7.40	+/- Wilshire 4500
	---	---	0.00	0.74	0.00	0.00	0.34	0.00	0.00	0.00	0.00	0.00	Income Return %
	---	---	0.00	23.20	11.99	6.85	29.19	-9.73	51.63	28.51	46.57	4.75	Capital Return %
	---	---		10	8	82	14	84	7	1	3	4	Total Rtn % Rank All
	---	---		4	2	91	23	46	42	6	1	15	Total Rtn % Rank Obj
	---	---	0.00	0.07	0.00	0.00	0.04	0.00	0.00	0.00	0.00	0.00	Income $
	---	---	0.00	0.00	4.24	0.03	2.81	0.79	2.43	2.45	0.19	0.01	Capital Gains $
	---	---		1.52	1.31	1.21	1.19	1.32	1.50	1.52	2.39	1.55	Expense Ratio %
	---	---		0.82	0.36	0.02	0.20	-0.35	-0.09	-0.55	-1.69	-0.78	Income Ratio %
	---	---		---	214	208	175	219	228	115	209	94	Turnover Rate %
	---	---		20.5	27.0	24.3	22.0	12.1	8.4	3.0	183.7	745.8	Net Assets ($mil)

Risk Analysis

Time Period	Load-Adj Return %	Risk % Rank [1] All	Risk % Rank [1] Obj	Morningstar [2] Return	Morningstar Risk	Morningstar Risk-Adj Rating
1 Yr	4.75					
3 Yr	25.42	95	78	7.74 [3]	1.41	★★★★★
5 Yr	21.98	97	87	5.56 [3]	1.46	★★★★★
10 Yr	---	---	---	---	---	

Average Historical Rating (73 months)   3.6 ★ s

[1] 1 = low, 100 = high   [2] = Equity Avg   [3] 1.00 = 90-day T-bill return

Other Measures

	Standard S&P 500	Best Fit Wil 4500
Standard Deviation	21.67	
Mean	25.13	
Sharpe Ratio	1.00	
Alpha	19.3	14.9
Beta	1.34	1.78
R-Squared	24	65

Investment Style

	Stock Portfolio Avg	Relative S&P 500
Price/Earnings Ratio	31.5	1.71
Price/Book Ratio	5.7	1.69
5 Yr Earnings Gr %	41.3#	7.44
Return on Assets %	14.8	1.97
Debt % Total Cap	17.0	0.60
Med Mkt Cap ($mil)	637	0.05

figure is based on 50% or less of stocks

Style: Value Blend Growth — Size Large Med Small

Diversification Value for Portfolio Types

Large Cap: High	Small Cap: Low	Bond: High	Balanced: Medium	Diversified: Medium

Portfolio 09-30-94

Total Stocks: 81
Total Fixed-Income: 0

Share Chg (03-94) 000	Amount 000		Value $000	% Net Assets
170	225	America Online	15371	2.46
347	404	Micro Warehouse	12821	2.05
201	268	Three-Five Systems	11870	1.90
295	370	Gymboree	11008	1.76
202	324	Level One Communications	10358	1.66
101	192	Clear Channel Communications	9860	1.58
102	225	Quantum Health Resources	9492	1.52
249	249	Tencor Instruments	9268	1.48
295	393	Coventry	9243	1.48
165	227	Lam Research	9133	1.46
251	251	AnnTaylor Stores	9032	1.45
159	159	Cobra Golf	8782	1.41
193	223	Microchip	8747	1.40
126	257	Avid Technology	8684	1.39
303	303	Mid-Atlantic Medical Svcs	8525	1.37
330	462	Apple South	8194	1.31
179	179	Cyrix	8118	1.30
100	202	Omnicare	8089	1.30
84	194	Michaels Stores	8018	1.28
154	192	Fastenal	7944	1.27
205	205	StrataCom	7629	1.22
93	140	Chipcom	7490	1.20
81	158	Novellus Systems	7447	1.19
360	360	Exabyte	7378	1.18
85	202	Healthsource	7182	1.15

Composition % 12-31-94

			% of Stocks
Cash	11.1	Preferreds	0.0
Stocks	88.9	Convertibles	0.0
Bonds	0.0	Other	0.0

Tax Analysis

	Tax-Adj Historical Return %	% Pretax Return
3 Yr Avg	23.11	89.0
5 Yr Avg	18.71	79.8
10 Yr Avg	---	---

Potential Capital Gain Exposure (% of assets)   8%

Most Similar Funds in MF500

Hancock Special Equities A	Weak Fit
PIMCo Adv Opportunity C	Weak Fit
Brandywine	Weak Fit

Investment Style History

Equity

Average % Stocks Held in Portfolio

Min Initial / Purchase

Min Initial Purchase	$1000 (Addt'l: None)
Min IRA Purchase	$1000 (Addt'l: None)
Min Auto Invest Plan	$1000 (Systematic Inv: $25)

Expenses & Fees

Sales Fees	0.00% front
	0.00% deferred
	0.00% 12b-1
Management Fee	0.85% flat fee, 0.20%A
3-,5-,10-yr Expense Projections	$41, $71, $157
Annual Brokerage Cost	0.20%

Index Allocation

	% of Stocks
S&P 500	0.0
S&P MidCap 400	8.5
U.S. Small Cap	90.3
Foreign	1.2

Sector Weightings

	% of Stocks	Relative S&P 500
Utilities	0.0	0.00
Energy	0.0	0.00
Financials	3.6	0.34
Industrial Cyclicals	2.8	0.17
Consumer Durables	10.4	1.67
Consumer Staples	0.0	0.00
Services	8.4	1.03
Retail	12.9	2.22
Health	19.3	2.22
Technology	42.7	4.66

MORNINGSTAR   1995 Mutual Fund 500

Pennsylvania Mutual

	Ticker	Load	NAV	Yield	SEC Yield	Assets	**Objective**
	PENNX	None	7.41	1.4%	N/A	771.4	Small Company

Pennsylvania Mutual Fund seeks long-term growth of capital; income is incidental.

The fund generally invests at least 65% of its assets in common stocks and convertible securities of small- and medium-size companies that are selected on a value basis. In its value approach, the fund analyzes each company's balance sheet, cash flow, and the relationships of these factors to the price of a prospective security. The fund may invest in fixed-income securities, including up to 35% of its assets in securities rated BBB and up to 10% in securities rated BB or lower. The fund may invest up to 10% of its assets in foreign securities.

Manager's Investment Style

Manager Charles Royce is regarded as one of the best value investors around. He and his team attempt to buy firms at 50% of their underlying value. In this fund, they typically target three types of companies: those that have consistently shown superior earnings growth, but are still inexpensive; those that may boast less-sterling fundamentals, but are selling at dirt-cheap levels; and those that are trading at a discount to their asset values. These biases have often led the fund to favor more-cyclical industries.

Fund Manager(s)

Charles M. Royce et al. Birthdate: 09-39 BA, Brown U. 1961 MBA, Columbia U. 1963

Manager Experience

	Dates Managed	Invest Obj	Std Dev	+/- Index
Charles M. Royce				
Royce Value	12/82 - 12/94	SC	12.51	-2.12
Royce Value	11/86 - 12/94	DE	12.85	-0.75

Performance 12-31-94

	1st Qtr	2nd Qtr	3rd Qtr	4th Qtr	Total
1987	14.54	1.29	4.71	-16.55	1.38
1988	14.44	6.55	1.35	0.81	24.58
1989	7.02	5.83	4.27	-1.19	16.69
1990	-0.88	3.24	-16.55	3.59	-11.53
1991	20.24	1.01	3.99	4.38	31.83
1992	7.54	-2.55	2.36	8.31	16.19
1993	5.13	-1.07	3.97	3.35	11.75
1994	-1.08	-2.19	3.73	-1.08	-0.72

Bear Market Performance

Decile Rank (5-year period)

Worst — Best

	Worst 3 Mo Period 1985-89	Worst 3 Mo Period 1990-94
Pennsylvania Mutual	-21.45	-19.80
+/- S&P 500	8.14	-5.96
+/- Best Fit Index : Russ 2000	14.10	6.10

Trailing Returns

	Total Return %	+/- S&P 500	+/- Wil 4500	% Rank All	% Rank Obj	Growth of $10,000
3 Mo	-1.08	-1.06	1.42	46	50	9,892
6 Mo	2.61	-2.25	-1.58	23	77	10,261
1 Yr	-0.72	-2.04	1.93	25	46	9,928
3 Yr Avg	8.83	2.57	1.22	18	53	12,890
5 Yr Avg	8.50	-0.20	-0.60	28	78	15,034
10 Yr Avg	12.06	-2.32	-0.57	36	56	31,228
15 Yr Avg	14.44	-0.04	---	20	29	75,664

Operations

Address and Telephone	1414 Avenue of the Americas New York, NY 10019 800-221-4268 / 212-355-7311
Advisor	Quest Advisory
Subadvisor	None
Distributor	Pennsylvania Mutual Fund
States Available	All plus GU,PR,VI
Report Grade	A-
Income Distrib	Paid Annually
Date of Inception	12-12-62
Fiscal Year End	December

Historical Profile

Return	Average
Risk	Low
Rating	★★★★ Above Average

79%	76%	71%	88%	89%	78%	78%	89%

Growth of $10,000

||| Value of Fund ($000)
— Value of Index ($000) Russ 2000
▼ Manager Change
▽ Partial Manager Change
► Mgr Unknown After
◄ Mgr Unknown Before

Performance Quartile (Within Objective)

1983	1984	1985	1986	1987	1988	1989	1990	1991	1992	1993	1994	History
6.55	6.09	7.43	6.98	5.47	6.41	6.85	5.78	7.29	8.00	8.31	7.41	NAV
40.50	3.14	26.77	11.18	1.38	24.58	16.69	-11.53	31.83	16.19	11.75	-0.72	Total Return %
18.04	-3.12	-4.97	-7.50	-3.88	7.97	-14.99	-8.42	1.35	8.57	1.69	-2.04	+/- S&P 500
---	4.86	-5.25	-0.59	4.90	4.04	-7.25	2.03	-11.62	4.43	-2.79	1.93	+/- Wilshire 4500
0.63	1.22	1.52	1.84	5.23	1.99	3.29	2.52	1.80	1.28	1.33	1.46	Income Return %
39.87	1.92	25.25	9.34	-3.84	22.59	13.40	-14.05	30.03	14.91	10.42	-2.19	Capital Return %
2	56	39	79	47	6	42	87	24	8	53	25	Total Rtn % Rank All
8	11	56	46	31	26	72	56	90	36	75	46	Total Rtn % Rank Obj
0.03	0.07	0.09	0.13	0.33	0.12	0.22	0.16	0.12	0.10	0.11	0.11	Income $
0.60	0.55	0.16	1.11	1.30	0.28	0.41	0.12	0.21	0.37	0.52	0.73	Capital Gains $
1.29	1.18	1.03	0.98	0.99	1.01	0.97	0.96	0.95	0.91	0.98	0.97	Expense Ratio %
1.73	2.44	2.17	1.85	2.02	2.35	2.93	2.62	1.73	1.48	1.23	1.22	Income Ratio %
35	15	15	19	23	24	23	15	29	22	24	---	Turnover Rate %
108.6	226.7	354.3	333.0	274.8	436.1	550.2	548.4	789.1	1100.2	1022.2	771.4	Net Assets ($mil)

Risk Analysis

Time Period	Load-Adj Return %	Risk % Rank All	Risk % Rank Obj	Morningstar Return	Morningstar Risk	Morningstar Risk-Adj Rating
1 Yr	-1.72					
3 Yr	8.83	44	4	1.60[3]	0.50	★★★★
5 Yr	8.50	58	4	0.94[3]	0.67	★★★★
10 Yr	12.06	45	1	0.89	0.64	★★★

Average Historical Rating (109 months)   4.0 ★s

[1] = low, 100 = high   [2] 1.00 = Equity Avg   [3] 1.00 = 90-day T-bill return

Other Measures

			Standard S&P 500	Best Fit Russ 2000
Standard Deviation	6.57	Alpha	3.7	1.1
Mean	8.71	Beta	0.52	0.51
Sharpe Ratio	0.79	R-Squared	40	84

Investment Style

	Stock Portfolio Avg	Relative S&P 500
Price/Earnings Ratio	18.8	1.02
Price/Book Ratio	1.9	0.55
5 Yr Earnings Gr %	5.5	0.99
Return on Assets %	6.6	0.88
Debt % Total Cap	20.8	0.74
Med Mkt Cap ($mil)	282	0.02

Style Value Blend Growth / Size Large Med Small

Diversification Value for Portfolio Types

Large Cap: Medium	Small Cap: None	Bond: High	Balanced: Low	Diversified: Medium

Portfolio 09-30-94

Total Stocks: 486
Total Fixed-Income: 7

Share Chg (06-94) 000	Amount 000		Value $000	% Net Assets
0	63	Farmer Brothers	7982	0.96
0	51	Alleghany	7384	0.89
0	119	US Trust	6253	0.75
0	130	Pioneer Group	6101	0.73
0	185	Allied Group	5596	0.67
0	90	NCH	5533	0.67
0	195	Air Express International	5376	0.65
0	327	Baldwin & Lyons Cl B	5070	0.61
0	243	Comdisco	5034	0.61
-5	222	Scitex	4986	0.60
0	211	Kimball International Cl B	4959	0.60
0	100	Tecumseh Products Cl A	4946	0.59
0	133	WR Berkley	4771	0.57
0	105	Mine Safety Appliances	4747	0.57
0	148	Fab Industries	4583	0.55
-2	142	Anthem Electronics	4576	0.55
0	65	Florida East Coast Inds	4550	0.55
0	166	Manitowoc	4479	0.54
0	136	Puerto Rican Cement	4438	0.53
0	230	Arnold Industries	4364	0.52
15	144	Orion Capital	4332	0.52
0	75	Saint Joe Paper	4269	0.51
0	166	Marshall Industries	4163	0.50
0	9	Conbraco Industries	4154	0.50
23	115	Leucadia National	4132	0.50

Composition % 12-31-94

Cash	5.6	Preferreds	0.3
Stocks	94.1	Convertibles	0.0
Bonds	0.0	Other	0.0

Tax Analysis

	Tax-Adj Historical Return %	% Pretax Return
3 Yr Avg	6.39	70.7
5 Yr Avg	6.43	72.7
10 Yr Avg	9.14	65.8
Potential Capital Gain Exposure (% of assets)		21%

Most Similar Funds in MF500

Royce Value	Strong Fit
Delaware Value A	Fair Fit
Lindner	Fair Fit

Index Allocation

	% of Stocks
S&P 500	5.3
S&P MidCap 400	17.8
U.S. Small Cap	74.7
Foreign	2.2

Sector Weightings

	% of Stocks	Relative S&P 500
Utilities	1.5	0.12
Energy	4.4	0.43
Financials	19.9	1.88
Industrial Cyclicals	22.2	1.35
Consumer Durables	11.4	1.84
Consumer Staples	5.5	0.44
Services	17.8	2.19
Retail	5.8	0.99
Health	3.6	0.41
Technology	8.1	0.89

Expenses & Fees

Sales Fees	0.00% front
	0.00% deferred
	0.00% 12b-1
Management Fee	1.00% max./0.75% min.
3-,5-,10-yr Expense Projections	$31, $54, $120
Annual Brokerage Cost	---

Min Initial Purchase / IRA / Auto

Min Initial Purchase	$2000 (Addt'l: $50)
Min IRA Purchase	$500 (Addt'l: $50)
Min Auto Invest Plan	$500 (Systematic Inv: $50)

Investment Style History Equity
Average % Stocks Held in Portfolio

Phoenix Balanced A

	Ticker	Load	NAV	Yield	SEC Yield	Assets	Objective
	PHBLX	4.75%	14.83	3.2%	3.67%	2415.7	Balanced

Phoenix Balanced Fund Series - Class A seeks reasonable income, long-term growth of capital, and conservation of capital.

The fund may invest in both stocks and debt securities; it maintains at least 25% of its assets in fixed-income senior securities. No more than 35% of assets may be invested in securities rated below investment grade.

Class A shares have front loads; Class B shares have deferred loads, higher 12b-1 fees, and conversion features. Prior to Oct. 12, 1982, the fund was named Phoenix-Chase Balanced Fund Series. At inception, the fund acquired most of the assets of the Shareholder's Trust of Boston and the Phoenix Fund.

Manager's Investment Style

A conservative management keeps 10% to 20% of its assets in cash. The majority of its stocks are large, S&P 500 names with a slight growth bias. On the bond side, management generally keeps duration moderate. It favors Treasuries, mortgage-backed securities, and, on occasion, Brady bonds.

Historical Profile
Return	Average
Risk	Below Average
Rating	★★★
	Neutral

Investment Style History
Equity
Average % Stocks Held in Portfolio

Growth of $10,000
- |||| Value of Fund ($000)
- — Value of Index ($000) S&P 500
- ▼ Manager Change
- ▽ Partial Manager Change
- ► Mgr Unknown After
- ◄ Mgr Unknown Before

Performance Quartile (Within Objective)

	1983	1984	1985	1986	1987	1988	1989	1990	1991	1992	1993	1994	History
NAV	10.45	10.95	12.98	12.75	12.25	11.99	14.15	13.85	15.72	15.89	16.03	14.83	NAV
	18.05	13.98	29.89	19.95	9.72	2.89	24.93	7.31	25.94	6.74	6.41	-4.55	Total Return %
	-4.42	7.71	-1.84	1.27	4.46	-13.72	-6.76	10.43	-4.55	-0.88	-3.65	-5.87	+/- S&P 500
	9.68	-1.18	7.77	4.70	6.96	-4.99	10.39	-1.64	9.94	-0.50	-3.34	-1.63	+/- LB Aggregate
	7.15	9.19	8.45	5.24	4.43	5.01	6.59	4.94	4.10	3.36	3.04	2.94	Income Return %
	10.90	4.78	21.44	14.71	5.29	-2.12	18.34	2.37	21.83	3.38	3.37	-7.49	Capital Return %
	48	10	26	20	10	95	23	19	34	61	86	59	Total Rtn % Rank All
	32	7	28	18	2	97	13	6	37	59	85	76	Total Rtn % Rank Obj
	0.78	0.87	0.83	0.69	0.59	0.61	0.73	0.68	0.58	0.51	0.48	0.48	Income $
	1.69	0.00	0.24	2.07	1.18	0.00	0.03	0.63	1.03	0.36	0.39	0.00	Capital Gains $
	0.81	0.83	0.80	0.75	0.72	0.80	0.93	0.85	0.98	0.98	0.95	0.96	Expense Ratio %
	6.89	8.21	7.06	5.04	4.28	4.87	5.28	4.91	4.22	3.55	2.88	3.03	Income Ratio %
	178	126	154	129	171	226	172	181	196	136	130	159	Turnover Rate %
	68.4	69.2	85.7	164.9	373.1	415.4	460.4	509.8	1108.0	2349.2	3089.5	2415.7	Net Assets ($mil)

Style grid stock held percentages: 54% | 45% | 46% | 46% | 45% | 40% | 37% | 39%

Fund Manager(s)

Patricia A. Bannan CFA(1987), since 01-85.
Birthdate: 12-61. BS, U. of New Hampshire 1982

Manager Experience

	Dates Managed	Invest Obj	Std Dev	+/- Index
Not available.				

Performance 12-31-94

	1st Qtr	2nd Qtr	3rd Qtr	4th Qtr	Total
1987	14.04	1.44	4.00	-8.79	9.72
1988	0.14	0.83	1.09	0.80	2.89
1989	4.31	7.69	7.95	3.03	24.93
1990	-1.35	6.24	-4.28	6.97	7.31
1991	13.44	-1.68	4.42	8.13	25.94
1992	-1.79	1.84	3.24	3.38	6.74
1993	3.78	-0.54	2.23	0.85	6.41
1994	-3.70	-1.31	1.60	-1.15	-4.55

Bear Market Performance

Decile Rank (5-year period)

	Worst 3 Mo Period 1985-89	Worst 3 Mo Period 1990-94
Phoenix Balanced A	-14.69	-5.15
+/- S&P 500	14.89	0.61
+/- Best Fit Index : S&P 500	14.89	0.61

Trailing Returns

	Total Return %	+/- S&P 500	+/- LB Aggregate	% Rank All	% Rank Obj	Growth of $10,000
3 Mo	-1.15	-1.13	-1.53	48	57	9,885
6 Mo	0.43	-4.43	-0.56	48	75	10,043
1 Yr	-4.55	-5.87	-1.63	59	76	9,545
3 Yr Avg	2.73	-3.54	-1.82	87	81	10,841
5 Yr Avg	7.94	-0.75	0.31	34	45	14,651
10 Yr Avg	12.40	-1.98	2.46	33	32	32,195
15 Yr Avg	---	---	---	---	---	---

Operations

Address and Telephone	100 Bright Meadow Bvd PO Box 2200
	Enfield, CT 06083-2200
	800-243-4361 / 203-253-1000
Advisor	Phoenix Investment Counsel
Subadvisor	None
Distributor	Phoenix Equity Planning
States Available	All plus PR
Report Grade	C
Income Distrib	Paid Quarterly
Date of Inception	01-30-81
Fiscal Year End	October

Risk Analysis

Time Period	Load-Adj Return %	Risk % Rank [1] All	Risk % Rank [1] Obj	Morningstar [2] Return	Morningstar Risk	Morningstar Risk-Adj Rating
1 Yr	-9.08					
3 Yr	1.08	44	33	-0.71 [3]	0.66	★★
5 Yr	6.89	47	14	0.52 [3]	0.62	★★★
10 Yr	11.86	39	14	1.03	0.63	★★★★
Average Historical Rating (109 months)					4.5	★s

[1] 1 = low, 100 = high   [2] 1.00 = Hybrid Avg   [3] 1.00 = 90-day T-bill return

Other Measures

			Standard S&P 500	Best Fit S&P 500
Standard Deviation	4.69	Alpha	-2.2	-2.2
Mean	2.81	Beta	0.53	0.53
Sharpe Ratio	-0.15	R-Squared	79	79

Investment Style

Stocks
	Port Avg	Rel S&P 500
Price/Earnings Ratio	21.6	1.17
Price/Book Ratio	4.0	1.17
5 Yr Earnings Gr %	11.6	2.09
Med Mkt Cap ($mil)	12845	0.99

Style: V B G / L M S (Size)

Bonds
Avg Effective Duration	3.3 Yrs
Avg Effective Maturity	3.6 Yrs
Avg Credit Quality	AAA
Avg Weighted Coupon	6.01%

Maturity: S I L / H M L (Quality)

Diversification Value for Portfolio Types

Large Cap: Low	Small Cap: Medium	Bond: Medium	Balanced: None	Diversified: Low

Portfolio 10-31-94

Share Chg (06-94)000	Amount 000	Total Stocks: 48 / Total Fixed-Income: 28	Date of Maturity	Value $000	% Net Assets
	106311	US Treasury Note 5.75%	08-15-03	92856	3.57
	74767	US Treasury Note 7%	04-15-99	73597	2.83
	68877	US Treasury Note 6%	10-15-99	64727	2.49
298	1098	Home Depot		49961	1.92
	44920	US Treasury Note 4.625%	02-15-96	43887	1.69
	44920	US Treasury Note 4.75%	08-31-98	41061	1.58
249	799	Computer Associates Intl		39629	1.52
	41925	US Treasury Note 5.125%	03-31-98	39244	1.51
	36934	US Treasury Note 6.875%	03-31-97	36846	1.42
	36934	US Treasury Note 6.375%	07-15-99	35430	1.36
199	449	Dayton Hudson		34813	1.34
	34938	Time Warner Cv 8.75%	01-10-15	34632	1.33
-101	399	Mobil		34339	1.32
307	807	Columbia/HCA Healthcare		33573	1.29
324	324	Xerox		33253	1.28
	33940	US Treasury Note 4.75%	02-15-97	32374	1.24
629	629	General Electric		30737	1.18
	31943	US Treasury Note 5.825%	03-31-99	30125	1.16
-246	499	EI DuPont de Nemours		29760	1.14
	29947	US Treasury Note 5.125%	11-15-95	29606	1.14

Index Allocation

	% of Stocks
S&P 500	95.3
S&P MidCap 400	3.3
U.S. Small Cap	0.0
Foreign	3.6

Composition % 12-31-94

Cash	25.5	Preferreds	0.0
Stocks	38.3	Convertibles	3.3
Bonds	32.9	Other	0.0

Tax Analysis

	Tax-Adj Historical Return %	% Pretax Return
3 Yr Avg	1.15	41.6
5 Yr Avg	5.72	68.9
10 Yr Avg	9.44	66.0
Potential Capital Gain Exposure (% of assets)		-3%

Most Similar Funds in MF500

Calvert Social Inv Managed A	Strong Fit
Sentinel Balanced	Fair Fit
Keystone Custodian K-1	Fair Fit

Bond Credit Analysis 11-17-94

% of Bonds			
US Govt	100	BB	0
AAA	0	B	0
AA	0	Below B	0
A	0	NR/NA	0
BBB	0		

Stock Sector Weightings

	% of Stocks	Relative S&P 500
Utilities	3.9	0.32
Energy	11.3	1.11
Financials	3.8	0.36
Industrial Cyclicals	14.3	0.87
Consumer Durables	6.3	1.01
Consumer Staples	7.5	0.60
Services	11.0	1.35
Retail	11.8	2.02
Health	15.2	1.75
Technology	15.1	1.65

Expenses & Fees

Sales Fees	4.75% front
	0.00% deferred
	0.25% 12b-1
Management Fee	0.55% max./0.45% min.
3-,5-,10-yr Expense Projections	$76, $97, $157
Annual Brokerage Cost	0.16% (aggregate)

(Operations - Purchase)

Min Initial Purchase	$500 (Addt'l: $25)
Min IRA Purchase	$500 (Addt'l: $25)
Min Auto Invest Plan	$25 (Systematic Inv: $25)

Phoenix Convertible A

	Ticker	Load	NAV	Yield	SEC Yield	Assets	Objective
	PHCVX	4.75%	16.55	4.8%	4.44%	211.7	Convrt. Bond

Phoenix Convertible Fund Series - Class A seeks income and capital appreciation.

The fund typically invests at least 65% of its assets in debt securities and preferred stocks that are convertible into common stocks. The balance of assets may be invested in common stocks, warrants, and nonconvertible debt securities. The convertible securities acquired by the fund are not subject to any credit quality limitations.

Class A shares have front loads; Class B shares have deferred loads, higher 12b-1 fees, and conversion features. Prior to Oct. 12, 1982, this fund operated as a closed-end fund named Chase Convertible Fund of Boston.

Manager's Investment Style

Management is conservative, favoring large-cap, high-quality convertibles. It has also been willing to raise cash as a defensive measure. Management generally takes a top-down approach to the convertibles market, playing certain macroeconomic themes. The fund also owns one of the largest positions in defensive zero-coupon convertibles among all convertible-bond funds; these zeros come with a put option that allows the holder to sell the bond at a predetermined price.

Fund Manager(s)

John Hamlin, since 08-92. BS, U. of Notre Dame MBA, U. of Connecticut

Manager Experience	Dates Managed	Invest Obj	Std Dev	+/- Index
John Hamlin				
Phoenix Income & Growth I	07/93 - 12/94	B	6.10	-7.27

Performance 12-31-94

	1st Qtr	2nd Qtr	3rd Qtr	4th Qtr	Total
1987	12.84	3.31	3.30	-8.25	10.48
1988	1.26	2.44	-0.57	1.33	4.52
1989	3.22	5.66	5.51	4.36	20.09
1990	-0.81	4.66	-4.76	5.32	4.14
1991	7.95	-1.70	2.45	3.74	12.78
1992	2.85	2.30	4.54	2.67	12.93
1993	3.96	1.35	3.50	0.80	9.92
1994	-2.38	0.00	1.09	-2.52	-3.81

Bear Market Performance

Decile Rank (5-year period)

Worst ▬ Best

	Worst 3 Mo Period 1985-89	Worst 3 Mo Period 1990-94
Phoenix Convertible A	-15.69	-5.78
+/- LB Aggregate	-17.85	-6.52
+/- Best Fit Index : Wil 4500	14.45	13.62

Trailing Returns

	Total Return %	+/- LB Aggregate	+/- S&P 500	% Rank All	% Rank Obj	Growth of $10,000
3 Mo	-2.52	-2.90	-2.50	77	34	9,748
6 Mo	-1.46	-2.45	-6.32	81	75	9,854
1 Yr	-3.81	-0.89	-5.12	51	42	9,619
3 Yr Avg	6.09	1.55	-0.17	33	66	11,941
5 Yr Avg	7.00	-0.63	-1.69	50	66	14,023
10 Yr Avg	10.80	0.85	-3.58	49	33	27,881
15 Yr Avg	13.83	3.02	-0.66	26	1	69,765

Operations

Address and Telephone	100 Bright Meadow Bvd PO Box 2200
	Enfield, CT 06083-2200
	800-243-4361 / 203-253-1000
Advisor	Phoenix Investment Counsel
Subadvisor	None
Distributor	Phoenix Equity Planning
States Available	All plus PR
Report Grade	C
Income Distrib	Paid Quarterly
Date of Inception	03-19-72
Fiscal Year End	October

Historical Profile
Return	Average
Risk	Low
Rating	★★★ Neutral

	9	64	70	52	69	66	56	26	Income Rtn % Rank Obj

Growth of $10,000

IIII Value of Fund ($000)
— Value of Index ($000) LB Agg
▼ Manager Change
▽ Partial Manager Change
► Mgr Unknown After
◄ Mgr Unknown Before

Performance Quartile (Within Objective)

	1983	1984	1985	1986	1987	1988	1989	1990	1991	1992	1993	1994	History
	20.49	16.36	17.80	17.44	15.63	15.43	17.53	17.24	17.50	17.98	18.22	16.55	NAV
	26.18	5.03	22.29	17.25	10.48	4.52	20.09	4.14	12.78	12.93	9.92	-3.81	Total Return %
	17.81	-10.13	0.16	2.00	7.72	-3.36	5.55	-4.81	-3.23	5.68	0.17	-0.89	+/- LB Aggregate
	3.71	-1.24	-9.45	-1.43	5.22	-12.09	-11.60	7.25	-17.71	5.31	-0.14	-5.12	+/- S&P 500
	7.60	7.53	7.06	5.18	6.33	5.80	6.48	5.79	4.54	4.30	3.98	4.40	Income Return %
	18.58	-2.50	15.23	12.06	4.15	-1.28	13.61	-1.65	8.23	8.63	5.94	-8.20	Capital Return %
	20	50	58	38	10	93	35	45	69	13	67	51	Total Rtn % Rank All
	33	33	66	1	1	92	20	4	86	45	92	42	Total Rtn % Rank Obj
	1.19	1.18	1.02	0.89	1.13	0.90	0.93	1.00	0.78	0.75	0.71	0.80	Income $
	0.00	3.76	0.84	2.38	2.56	0.00	0.00	0.00	1.09	1.00	0.81	0.19	Capital Gains $
	0.96	0.90	0.88	0.80	0.73	0.83	1.03	0.99	1.14	1.20	1.15	1.14	Expense Ratio %
	6.33	6.96	6.20	4.99	5.12	5.51	5.71	5.17	4.84	4.28	3.70	4.27	Income Ratio %
	171	108	170	187	299	213	214	194	284	200	94	91	Turnover Rate %
	64.2	62.3	72.0	111.4	157.3	156.1	159.2	150.2	173.3	209.0	247.3	211.7	Net Assets ($mil)

Risk Analysis

Time Period	Load-Adj Return %	Risk % Rank [1] All	Obj	Morningstar [2] Return	Morningstar Risk	Morningstar Risk-Adj Rating
1 Yr	-8.37					
3 Yr	4.38	13	4	0.23 [3]	0.42	★★★
5 Yr	5.96	42	4	0.29 [3]	0.51	★★★
10 Yr	10.26	37	1	0.71	0.55	★★★

Average Historical Rating (109 months) 3.9 ★s

[1] 1 = low, 100 = high [2] 1.00 = Hybrid Avg [3] 1.00 = 90-day T-bill return

Other Measures

			Standard LB Agg	Best Fit Wil 4500
Standard Deviation	4.07	Alpha	1.9	1.1
Mean	6.01	Beta	0.61	0.32
Sharpe Ratio	0.61	R-Squared	35	56

Investment Style

Interest-Rate Stance
Avg Effective Maturity ---

Quality
Avg Credit Quality BBB
Avg Weighted Coupon 3.46%
Avg Weighted Price 74.42% of Par

Not Applicable

Diversification Value for Portfolio Types

Large Cap: Low	Small Cap: Medium	Bond: Medium	Balanced: Low	Diversified: Medium

Portfolio 10-31-94

Amount 000	Date of Maturity	Total Stocks: 14 Total Fixed-Income: 44	Value $000	% Net Assets
25404	07-24-06	Rite Aid Cv 0%	11559	5.11
34868	06-25-11	US West Cv 0%	10766	4.76
25404	08-16-10	Chemical Waste Mgmt Cv 0%	9876	4.36
9918	01-10-15	Time Warner Cv 8.75%	9832	4.34
17434	03-13-06	Halliburton Cv 0%	8717	3.85
7970	05-15-98	Chubb Capital Cv 6%	7950	3.51
7472	11-01-03	Noble Affiliates Cv 4.25%	7257	3.21
6226	12-15-15	Consolidated Nat Gas Cv 7.25%	6234	2.75
125		Eastman Kodak	5993	2.65
299		Citicorp Cv Pfd	5865	2.59
7771	2001	Hanson America Cv 2.39%	5711	2.52
12652	04-15-07	Comcast Cv 1.125%	5330	2.36
5479	03-01-01	Price/Costco Cv 6.75%	5233	2.31
11457	08-09-05	USX Cv 0%	5041	2.23
4184	01-15-03	Pennzoil Cv 6.5%	4791	2.12
11257	03-11-13	News America Holdings Cv 0%	4404	1.95
3238	09-01-13	Amoco Canada Petro A Cv 7.375%	3982	1.76
9464	02-20-12	Automatic Data Process Cv 0%	3939	1.74
4732	01-15-00	NovaCare Cv 5.5%	3857	1.70
2491	09-01-01	Medco Containment Svcs Cv 6%	3499	1.55
3487	01-15-01	Freeport-McMoRan Cv 6.55%	3173	1.40
55		Occidental Petro Cv Pfd $3.875	2904	1.28
4234	12-31-19	United Mexican States 6.25%	2667	1.18
2989	09-09-05	Comcast Cv 3.375%	2581	1.14
90		Apache	2522	1.11

Composition % 12-31-94

Cash	16.1	Preferreds	0.0
Stocks	9.5	Convertibles	74.4
Bonds	0.0	Other	0.0

Tax Analysis

	Tax-Adj Historical Return %	% Pretax Return
3 Yr Avg	3.47	55.6
5 Yr Avg	4.40	59.7
10 Yr Avg	7.44	58.7

Potential Capital Gain Exposure (% of assets) -6%

Most Similar Funds in MF500

Seligman Income A	Fair Fit
Vanguard STAR	Fair Fit
SBSF Convertible Securities	Weak Fit

Coupon Range

	% of Bonds	Rel Obj
0%	37.2	4.37
0% to 6%	27.5	0.82
6% to 7%	13.6	0.92
7% to 8.5%	6.9	0.59
More than 8.5%	6.5	1.18
Not applicable	8.3	0.32

Credit Analysis 09-30-94
% of Bonds

US Govt	0	BB	22
AAA	2	B	5
AA	10	Below B	0
A	29	NR/NA	16
BBB	16		

Expenses & Fees

Sales Fees	4.75% front
	0.00% deferred
	0.25% 12b-1
Management Fee	0.65% max./0.55% min.
3-,5-,10-yr Expense Projections	$82, $107, $178

Min Initial Purchase	$500 (Addt'l: $25)
Min IRA Purchase	$500 (Addt'l: $25)
Min Auto Invest Plan	$25 (Systematic Inv: $25)

MORNINGSTAR 1995 Mutual Fund 500

Phoenix Growth A

Phoenix Growth Fund Series - Class A seeks long-term appreciation of capital.

The fund invests primarily in common stocks. It may also invest in preferred stocks, investment-grade bonds, and convertible securities that offer potential for appreciation. The fund may invest up to 25% of its assets in foreign securities.

Class A shares have front loads; Class B shares have deferred loads, higher 12b-1 fees, and conversion features. Prior to July 28, 1980, the fund was named Chase Fund of Boston. Between that date and Oct. 12, 1982, the fund was named Phoenix-Chase Growth Fund Series.

Manager's Investment Style

Highly regarded comanager Robert Chesek left the fund in October 1993, leaving current manager Catherine Dudley behind as sole captain. This rapid-turnover fund has been known to raise cash in uncertain markets--oftentimes raising cash levels to more than 50%. The fund targets large-cap growth stocks selling at moderate prices, but sells a stock when it gets pricey, produces disappointing earnings, or underperforms the broad market or its group.

Fund Manager(s)

Catherine Dudley CFA(1991), since 11-90. BA, U. of Connecticut 1983

Manager Experience

	Dates Managed	Invest Obj	Std Dev	+/- Index
Catherine Dudley				
Phoenix Capital Apprec A	11/89 - 12/94	G	13.16	6.63
Cambridge Capital Grwth B	04/92 - 12/94	G	7.03	-5.06

Performance 12-31-94

	1st Qtr	2nd Qtr	3rd Qtr	4th Qtr	Total
1987	17.93	2.84	5.41	-13.04	11.18
1988	1.84	2.66	1.08	1.20	6.95
1989	4.99	6.38	9.12	4.59	27.47
1990	-1.72	7.98	-7.44	7.97	6.05
1991	15.69	-1.84	5.69	6.65	28.01
1992	-1.40	-1.17	2.59	4.31	4.29
1993	1.58	-1.50	2.50	1.74	4.35
1994	-3.09	-1.03	3.53	-0.91	-1.60

Bear Market Performance

Decile Rank (5-year period)

Worst   Best

	Worst 3 Mo Period 1985-89	Worst 3 Mo Period 1990-94
Phoenix Growth A	-23.10	-8.93
+/- S&P 500	6.48	4.91
+/- Best Fit Index : S&P 500	6.48	4.91

Trailing Returns

	Total Return %	+/- S&P 500	+/- Wil 5000	% Rank All	% Rank Obj	Growth of $10,000
3 Mo	-0.91	-0.89	-0.14	42	41	9,909
6 Mo	2.60	-2.27	-2.03	23	66	10,260
1 Yr	-1.60	-2.92	-1.53	30	48	9,840
3 Yr Avg	2.31	-3.96	-4.31	90	78	10,708
5 Yr Avg	7.77	-0.92	-1.05	36	64	14,537
10 Yr Avg	13.27	-1.11	-0.59	24	41	34,764
15 Yr Avg	16.92	2.44	2.94	3	7	104,321

Operations

Address and Telephone	100 Bright Meadow Blvd PO Box 2200 Enfield, CT 06083-2200 800-243-4361 / 203-253-1000
Advisor	Phoenix Investment Counsel
Subadvisor	None
Distributor	Phoenix Equity Planning
States Available	All plus PR
Report Grade	C
Income Distrib	Paid Semiannually
Date of Inception	09-01-58
Fiscal Year End	October

Ticker	Load	NAV	Yield	SEC Yield	Assets	Objective
PHGRX	4.75%	19.60	1.4%	1.50%	2019.4	Growth

Historical Profile

Return   Average
Risk   Below Average
Rating   ★★★
        Neutral

78%   76%   67%   75%   70%   63%   56%   77%

Investment Style History
Equity
Average % Stocks Held in Portfolio

Growth of $10,000
|||| Value of Fund ($000)
— Value of Index ($000) S&P 500
▼ Manager Change
▽ Partial Manager Change
► Mgr Unknown After
◄ Mgr Unknown Before

Performance Quartile (Within Objective)

1983	1984	1985	1986	1987	1988	1989	1990	1991	1992	1993	1994	History
12.43	13.21	16.43	16.40	15.18	15.82	19.15	18.86	20.76	20.93	21.04	19.60	NAV
28.41	10.15	32.32	19.24	11.18	6.95	27.47	6.05	28.01	4.29	4.35	-1.60	Total Return %
5.95	3.89	0.59	0.56	5.92	-9.66	-4.22	9.17	-2.47	-3.33	-5.71	-2.92	+/- S&P 500
4.95	7.10	-0.24	3.14	8.81	-10.99	-1.71	12.23	-6.19	-4.68	-6.93	-1.53	+/- Wilshire 5000
3.92	3.88	4.88	1.87	3.35	2.74	4.37	3.54	2.24	1.64	1.53	1.44	Income Return %
24.49	6.28	27.45	17.37	7.83	4.22	23.09	2.51	25.77	2.65	2.82	-3.04	Capital Return %
14	26	18	24	9	81	18	34	30	80	93	30	Total Rtn % Rank All
16	7	32	21	11	86	47	2	72	75	81	48	Total Rtn % Rank Obj
0.49	0.42	0.62	0.34	0.57	0.41	0.67	0.68	0.44	0.33	0.32	0.29	Income $
2.86	0.00	0.32	2.91	2.56	0.00	0.28	0.77	2.72	0.38	0.48	0.81	Capital Gains $
0.90	0.88	0.82	0.78	0.71	0.85	1.06	1.01	1.15	1.17	1.18	1.19	Expense Ratio %
3.80	4.83	3.87	2.68	2.64	2.48	3.79	3.37	2.49	1.86	1.55	1.22	Income Ratio %
208	150	151	170	185	221	180	203	227	192	176	118	Turnover Rate %
66.1	76.2	112.3	271.9	523.4	587.2	715.8	743.5	1451.8	2385.8	2491.3	2019.4	Net Assets ($mil)

Risk Analysis

Time Period	Load-Adj Return %	Risk % Rank¹ All	Obj	Morningstar² Return	Morningstar Risk	Morningstar Risk-Adj Rating
1 Yr	-6.28					
3 Yr	0.66	59	13	-0.82³	0.64	★★
5 Yr	6.73	57	5	0.48³	0.64	★★★
10 Yr	12.72	49	7	1.01	0.71	★★★★
Average Historical Rating (109 months)				4.4 ★s		

¹ 1 = low, 100 = high   ² 1.00 = Equity Avg   ³ 1.00 = 90-day T-bill return

Other Measures

			Standard S&P 500	Best Fit S&P 500
Standard Deviation	6.21	Alpha	-3.1	-3.1
Mean	2.48	Beta	0.74	0.74
Sharpe Ratio	-0.17	R-Squared	88	88

Investment Style

	Stock Portfolio Avg	Relative S&P 500
Price/Earnings Ratio	19.1	1.03
Price/Book Ratio	3.4	0.99
5 Yr Earnings Gr %	10.7	1.92
Return on Assets %	8.8	1.17
Debt % Total Cap	23.6	0.83
Med Mkt Cap ($mil)	9514	0.73

Style Value Blend Growth / Size Large Med Small

Diversification Value for Portfolio Types

Large Cap: None   Small Cap: Medium   Bond: High   Balanced: None   Diversified: Low

Portfolio 10-31-94

Share Chg (06-94) 000	Amount 000	Total Stocks: 60 Total Fixed-Income: 1	Value $000	% Net Assets
	75	US Treasury Note 6%	74171	3.47
249	999	Computer Associates Intl	49556	2.32
248	1248	Toys 'R' Us	48058	2.25
-1	499	American International Group	46748	2.18
199	999	Home Depot	45437	2.12
699	699	Philip Morris	42816	2.00
248	1248	Philips Electronics	40881	1.91
-2	1248	Abbott Laboratories	38696	1.81
-1	599	Raytheon	38197	1.78
-1	449	British Petroleum (ADR)	38197	1.78
-1	499	FNMA	37947	1.77
-21	379	Hewlett-Packard	37094	1.73
49	424	Mobil	36499	1.71
199	799	Chevron	35950	1.68
-1	999	Merck	35701	1.67
249	949	May Department Stores	35694	1.67
-1	499	Schering-Plough	35576	1.66
474	474	IBM	35339	1.65
249	849	Columbia/HCA Healthcare	35332	1.65
-1	399	ITT	35251	1.65
0	300	Royal Dutch Petroleum	34902	1.63
74	574	El DuPont de Nemours	34237	1.60
149	749	Carnival Cl A	34078	1.59
-1	399	Capital Cities/ABC	33204	1.55
999	999	Sprint	32580	1.52

Composition % 12-31-94

Cash	17.0	Preferreds	0.0
Stocks	83.0	Convertibles	0.0
Bonds	0.0	Other	0.0

Tax Analysis

	Tax-Adj Historical Return %	% Pretax Return
3 Yr Avg	1.00	43.0
5 Yr Avg	5.62	69.3
10 Yr Avg	10.58	70.0

Potential Capital Gain Exposure (% of assets)   1%

Most Similar Funds in MF500

Dreyfus	Strong Fit
Smith Barney Appreciation A	Strong Fit
AIM Charter	Strong Fit

Index Allocation

	% of Stocks
S&P 500	78.8
S&P MidCap 400	4.7
U.S. Small Cap	3.9
Foreign	14.8

Sector Weightings

	% of Stocks	Relative S&P 500
Utilities	3.1	0.25
Energy	12.1	1.20
Financials	5.1	0.48
Industrial Cyclicals	13.6	0.83
Consumer Durables	6.2	1.00
Consumer Staples	3.6	0.29
Services	12.0	1.47
Retail	11.2	1.92
Health	15.2	1.75
Technology	17.9	1.95

Min Initial Purchase / Expenses & Fees

Min Initial Purchase	$500 (Addt'l: $25)
Min IRA Purchase	$500 (Addt'l: $25)
Min Auto Invest Plan	$25 (Systematic Inv: $25)

Expenses & Fees

Sales Fees	4.75% front
	0.00% deferred
	0.25% 12b-1
Management Fee	0.70% max./0.60% min.
3-,5-,10-yr Expense Projections	$83, $109, $183
Annual Brokerage Cost	0.16% (aggregate)

MORNINGSTAR 1995 Mutual Fund 500

Phoenix High-Yield A

Ticker	Load	NAV	Yield	SEC Yield	Assets	Objective
PHCHX	4.75%	7.73	10.1%	9.82%	504.2	Corp Hi Yld

Phoenix High-Yield Fund Series - Class A seeks high current income.

The fund normally invests at least 65% of its assets in high-yielding fixed-income securities rated BBB or lower. These may include preferred stocks, convertibles, debt obligations, certificates of deposit, commercial paper, and bankers' acceptances.

Class A shares have front loads and lower 12b-1 fees; Class B shares have deferred loads and convert to Class A shares after eight years. Prior to Oct. 12, 1982, the fund was named Phoenix-Chase High-Yield Fund Series. On Dec. 10, 1993, National Bond Fund merged into this fund.

Manager's Investment Style

Management takes a nonconformist approach to the high-yield market, at times holding large positions in emerging-market debt and nonagency mortgage-backed bonds (including asset-backeds). The fund has also purchased out-of-favor issues, such as supermarket and utilities debt in 1990. In its domestic portfolio, the fund keeps the bulk of assets in B rated debt, and buys few domestic nonrateds; the fund's nonrated portion is primarily foreign debt.

Fund Manager(s)

Curtiss O. Barrows, since 03-85. Birthdate: 05-51. BA, U. of Vermont 1973 MBA, Fairleigh Dickinson U. 1980

Manager Experience	Dates Managed	Invest Obj	Std Dev	+/- Index
Not available.				

Historical Profile

Return	Average
Risk	Low
Rating	★★★★ Above Average

Investment Style History
Fixed Income
Income Rtn % Rank Obj

	27	61	76	97	94	81	72	70

Growth of $10,000

- ‖‖‖ Value of Fund ($000)
- — Value of Index ($000) LB Agg
- ▼ Manager Change
- ▽ Partial Manager Change
- ▶ Mgr Unknown After
- ◀ Mgr Unknown Before

Performance Quartile (Within Objective)

	1983	1984	1985	1986	1987	1988	1989	1990	1991	1992	1993	1994	History
NAV	9.29	8.79	9.40	9.64	8.68	8.80	7.74	6.87	7.74	8.25	9.21	7.73	
Total Return %	13.38	7.86	21.06	15.91	1.65	13.58	-0.95	-1.08	24.67	16.96	21.48	-7.97	
+/- LB Aggregate	5.00	-7.30	-1.07	0.66	-1.11	5.71	-15.49	-10.02	8.67	9.71	11.73	-5.05	
+/- FB High-Yield	---	---	---	0.27	-4.88	2.15	-1.34	5.30	-19.08	0.30	2.58	-7.00	
Income Return %	13.12	13.24	14.12	13.36	11.60	12.20	11.10	10.16	12.01	10.37	9.84	8.10	
Capital Return %	0.25	-5.38	6.94	2.55	-9.96	1.38	-12.05	-11.24	12.66	6.59	11.64	-16.07	
Total Rtn % Rank All	65	38	66	49	45	34	98	58	36	7	15	85	
Total Rtn % Rank Obj	75	61	70	26	52	35	51	11	89	56	21	87	
Income $	1.23	1.17	1.14	1.20	1.13	1.01	1.00	0.78	0.75	0.76	0.75	0.78	
Capital Gains $	0.39	0.00	0.00	0.00	0.00	0.00	0.00	0.00	0.00	0.00	0.00	0.00	
Expense Ratio %	0.97	0.91	0.88	0.79	0.72	0.76	0.85	0.89	1.08	1.08	1.04	1.19	
Income Ratio %	12.34	13.37	12.93	12.01	11.42	11.45	11.81	11.02	10.12	9.51	8.46	9.01	
Turnover Rate %	104	99	75	91	97	217	285	321	326	205	157	222	
Net Assets ($mil)	39.1	50.1	66.0	126.5	145.2	156.4	130.9	77.8	95.6	128.7	714.3	504.2	

Performance 12-31-94

	1st Qtr	2nd Qtr	3rd Qtr	4th Qtr	Total
1987	6.48	-2.61	-1.64	-0.35	1.65
1988	4.59	3.19	2.32	2.85	13.58
1989	1.46	2.40	-1.79	-2.92	-0.95
1990	-3.43	3.34	-4.03	3.29	-1.08
1991	7.70	4.00	5.92	5.09	24.67
1992	6.63	3.75	4.86	0.82	16.96
1993	6.95	4.46	2.89	5.68	21.48
1994	-2.51	-2.80	1.03	-3.87	-7.97

Bear Market Performance

Decile Rank (5-year period)

Worst — Best

	Worst 3 Mo Period 1985-89	Worst 3 Mo Period 1990-94
Phoenix High-Yield A	-7.14	-6.95
+/- LB Aggregate	-7.96	-2.02
+/- Best Fit Index : FB HY	---	-2.86

Trailing Returns

	Total Return %	+/- LB Aggregate	+/- FB High-Yield	% Rank All	% Rank Obj	Growth of $10,000
3 Mo	-3.87	-4.25	-3.83	88	91	9,613
6 Mo	-2.88	-3.87	-4.44	94	72	9,712
1 Yr	-7.97	-5.05	-7.00	85	87	9,203
3 Yr Avg	9.35	4.80	-1.81	16	74	13,075
5 Yr Avg	10.03	2.40	-3.05	17	61	16,126
10 Yr Avg	9.97	0.03	---	58	51	25,875
15 Yr Avg	---	---	---	---	---	---

Operations

Address and Telephone	100 Bright Meadow Bvd PO Box 2200 Enfield, CT 06083-2200 800-243-4361 / 203-253-1000
Advisor	Phoenix Investment Counsel
Subadvisor	None
Distributor	Phoenix Equity Planning
States Available	All plus PR
Report Grade	C
Income Distrib	Paid Monthly
Date of Inception	07-28-80
Fiscal Year End	October

Risk Analysis

Time Period	Load-Adj Return %	Risk % Rank [1] All	Risk % Rank [1] Obj	Morningstar [2] Return	Morningstar Risk	Morningstar Risk-Adj Rating
1 Yr	-12.34					
3 Yr	7.59	26	88	1.20 [3]	0.53	★★★★
5 Yr	8.96	41	24	1.07 [3]	0.49	★★★★
10 Yr	9.44	30	29	0.56	0.43	★★★
Average Historical Rating (109 months)					3.4	★ s

[1] 1 = low, 100 = high   [2] 1.00 = Hybrid Avg   [3] 1.00 = 90-day T-bill return

Other Measures

				Standard LB Agg	Best Fit FB HY
Standard Deviation	5.68	Alpha		4.8	-2.9
Mean	9.13	Beta		0.89	1.19
Sharpe Ratio	0.99	R-Squared		39	81

Investment Style

Interest-Rate Stance

		Maturity Short Intm Long
Avg Effective Duration	4.9 Yrs	
Avg Effective Maturity	7.9 Yrs	

Quality
High Med Low

Avg Credit Quality	B
Avg Weighted Coupon	9.55%
Avg Weighted Price	83.35% of Par

Diversification Value for Portfolio Types

Large Cap: High	Small Cap: High	Bond: Medium	Balanced: Medium	Diversified: High

Expenses & Fees

Sales Fees	4.75% front
	0.00% deferred
	0.25% 12b-1
Management Fee	0.65% max./0.55% min.
3-,5-,10-yr Expense Projections	$83, $109, $183

Min Initial Purchase $500 (Addt'l: $25)
Min IRA Purchase $500 (Addt'l: $25)
Min Auto Invest Plan $25 (Systematic Inv: $25)

Portfolio 12-31-94

Amount 000	Date of Maturity	Total Stocks: 3 Total Fixed-Income: 81	Value $000	% Net Assets
26633	07-23-05	Midland Funding 11.75%	25667	5.09
20961	12-15-02	Federated Dept Store 11.25%	21118	4.19
20715	02-01-06	Paging Network 8.875%	16416	3.26
15585	06-30-05	SCI Television 11%	15780	3.13
34524	06-01-04	Echostar Communicatns 12.875%	15536	3.08
18248	12-15-98	GPA Delaware 8.75%	14051	2.79
14796	09-15-01	USG 9.25%	14038	2.78
14796	05-01-03	Borg-Warner Security 9.125%	12669	2.51
14303	07-01-13	Turner Broadcasting Sys 8.375%	11550	2.29
11344	12-01-10	Centra Gas 10.65%	10805	2.14
11837	03-15-01	Ispat Mexicana 10.375%	10061	2.00
9864	10-31-96	US Treasury Note 6.875%	9724	1.93
9469	11-30-03	Community Health Sys 10.25%	9446	1.87
9864	11-18-99	Bridas 12.5%	9420	1.87
14204	08-01-03	PanAmSat Capital Step 11.375%	8842	1.75
8730	07-15-02	Polymer Group 12.25%	8533	1.69
15782	11-28-04	Call-Net 9%	8286	1.64
9864	12-23-98	Transport de Gas Sur 7.75%	8187	1.62
8878	01-31-02	Aracruz Celulose 10.375%	8145	1.62
11344	01-15-04	California Energy 0%	8111	1.61
7891	02-01-05	Curtice Burns Foods 12.25%	8000	1.59
9805	04-01-03	Envirotest Systems 9.625%	7942	1.58
11344	04-15-06	Republic of Brazil FRN	7607	1.51
7891	06-15-00	AES 9.75%	7566	1.50
20715	08-15-04	NEXTEL Communications 0%	7354	1.46

Composition % 12-31-94

Cash	1.7	Preferreds	1.9
Stocks	0.0	Convertibles	0.0
Bonds	96.0	Other	0.4

Tax Analysis

	Tax-Adj Historical Return %	% Pretax Return
3 Yr Avg	5.85	60.5
5 Yr Avg	6.52	60.6
10 Yr Avg	5.60	45.7
Potential Capital Gain Exposure (% of assets)		-81%

Most Similar Funds in MF500

T. Rowe Price High-Yield	Strong Fit
IDS Extra Income	Fair Fit
American High-Income	Fair Fit

Coupon Range

	% of Bonds	Rel Obj
0%, PIK	13.0	1.75
0% to 11%	54.5	1.11
11% to 13%	21.2	0.64
13% to 14.5%	3.8	0.70
More than 14.5%	0.0	0.00
Not applicable	7.6	2.49

Credit Analysis 12-31-94

% of Bonds

US Govt	3	BB	21
AAA	0	B	39
AA	2	Below B	5
A	0	NR/NA	30
BBB	0		

Phoenix Multi-Sector Fixed-Inc A

	Ticker	Load	NAV	Yield	SEC Yield	Assets	Objective
	NAMFX	4.75%	11.53	8.2%	7.95%	162.5	Income

Phoenix Multi-Sector Fixed-Income Fund - Class A seeks current income consistent with the preservation of capital.

The fund invests in U.S. government and foreign government obligations, investment-grade corporate debt, and high-yield bonds. It may invest up to 35% of its assets in high-yield debt; however, there are no limitations on other types of investments.

Class A shares have front loads; Class B shares have deferred loads and higher 12b-1 fees. On Nov. 17, 1993, Phoenix High-Quality Bond Fund merged into this fund. Prior to Dec. 31, 1993, this fund was named National Multi-Sector Fixed-Income Fund.

Historical Profile

Return	Above Average
Risk	Low
Rating	★★★★
	Above Average

Investment Style History
Fixed Income

Income Rtn % Rank Obj
| | | | | | 17 | 22 | 15 | 18 | 34 |

Growth of $10,000
- |||| Value of Fund ($000)
- — Value of Index ($000) LB L-T
- ▼ Manager Change
- ▽ Partial Manager Change
- ► Mgr Unknown After
- ◄ Mgr Unknown Before

Performance Quartile (Within Objective)

Manager's Investment Style

Management is known for its value-driven sector-rotation approach--which can often lead the fund into securities not usually found in multimarket funds, including mezzanine mortgage-backed bonds and emerging-market debt. Management sidesteps interest-rate bets by pegging the portfolio's duration to that of the Lehman Brothers Aggregate Index.

Fund Manager(s)

Michael Haylon, since 07-93. Birthdate: 12-57. BA, Bowdoin C. 1979 MBA, U. of Connecticut 1990
David Albrycht CFA(1991), since 07-93. Birthdate: 07-61. BA, Central Connecticut State C.

Manager Experience	Dates Managed	Invest Obj	Std Dev	+/- Index
David Albrycht				
Phoenix Asset Reserve B	07/93 - 12/94	CG	2.74	1.02

History

	1983	1984	1985	1986	1987	1988	1989	1990	1991	1992	1993	1994	
	---	---	---	---	---	---	11.87	11.26	13.03	13.14	13.34	11.53	NAV
	---	---	---	---	---	---	-0.21 *	5.29	28.25	12.06	15.19	-6.77	Total Return %
	---	---	---	---	---	---	-3.30 *	8.40	-2.24	4.45	5.13	-8.08	+/- S&P 500
	---	---	---	---	---	---	---	-3.66	12.25	4.82	5.44	-3.85	+/- LB Aggregate
	---	---	---	---	---	---	0.12	10.43	12.06	9.87	8.74	6.80	Income Return %
	---	---	---	---	---	---	-0.34	-5.14	16.18	2.20	6.44	-13.57	Capital Return %
	---	---	---	---	---	---	---	41	29	15	28	78	Total Rtn % Rank All
	---	---	---	---	---	---	---	20	14	18	27	90	Total Rtn % Rank Obj
	---	---	---	---	---	---	0.01	1.20	1.23	1.23	1.12	0.95	Income $
	---	---	---	---	---	---	0.00	0.00	0.05	0.17	0.63	0.00	Capital Gains $
	---	---	---	---	---	---	---	1.20	1.50	1.48	1.29	1.06	Expense Ratio %
	---	---	---	---	---	---	---	9.59	10.13	9.42	8.27	6.55	Income Ratio %
	---	---	---	---	---	---	---	---	180	116	207	149	Turnover Rate %
	---	---	---	---	---	---	4.2	12.1	89.4	148.6	232.0	162.5	Net Assets ($mil)

Performance 12-31-94

	1st Qtr	2nd Qtr	3rd Qtr	4th Qtr	Total
1987	---	---	---	---	---
1988	---	---	---	---	---
1989	---	---	---	---	-0.21 *
1990	-0.67	3.52	-0.74	3.15	5.29
1991	9.51	5.57	5.18	5.47	28.25
1992	2.04	5.39	5.37	-1.10	12.06
1993	6.66	4.57	2.29	0.96	15.19
1994	-3.00	-2.01	1.28	-3.16	-6.77

Bear Market Performance

Decile Rank (5-year period)

	Worst 3 Mo Period 1985-89	Worst 3 Mo Period 1990-94
Phoenix Multi-Sector Fixed-Inc	---	-5.77
+/- S&P 500	---	-0.02
+/- Best Fit Index : LB L-T	---	3.62

Trailing Returns

	Total Return %	+/- S&P 500	+/- LB Aggregate	% Rank All	% Rank Obj	Growth of $10,000
3 Mo	-3.16	-3.14	-3.54	84	93	9,684
6 Mo	-1.92	-6.78	-2.91	87	91	9,808
1 Yr	-6.77	-8.08	-3.85	78	90	9,323
3 Yr Avg	6.37	0.10	1.82	31	34	12,035
5 Yr Avg	10.20	1.51	2.57	16	8	16,250
10 Yr Avg	---	---	---	---	---	---
15 Yr Avg	---	---	---	---	---	---

Operations

Address and Telephone	100 Bright Meadow Bvd PO Box 2200
	Enfield, CT 06083-2200
	800-243-4361 / 203-253-1000
Advisor	National Securities & Research
Subadvisor	None
Distributor	Phoenix Equity Planning
States Available	All plus PR
Report Grade	C
Income Distrib	Paid Monthly
* Date of Inception	12-18-89
Fiscal Year End	October

Risk Analysis

Time Period	Load-Adj Return %	Risk % Rank [1] All	Obj	Morningstar [2] Return	Morningstar Risk	Morningstar Risk-Adj Rating
1 Yr	-11.20					
3 Yr	4.66	30	55	0.31 [3]	0.56	★★★
5 Yr	9.13	31	23	1.11 [3]	0.40	★★★★
10 Yr	---					
Average Historical Rating (25 months)					4.3 ★s	

[1] 1 = low, 100 = high   [2] 1.00 = Hybrid Avg   [3] 1.00 = 90-day T-bill return

Other Measures

		Standard S&P 500	Best Fit LB L-T
Standard Deviation	4.97	Alpha	1.9	1.9
Mean	6.31	Beta	0.30	0.47
Sharpe Ratio	0.56	R-Squared	23	53

Investment Style

Stocks

	Port Avg	Rel S&P 500
Price/Earnings Ratio	---	---
Price/Book Ratio	---	---
5 Yr Earnings Gr %	---	---
Med Mkt Cap ($mil)	---	---

Not Available

Bonds

		Maturity
Avg Effective Duration	5.2 Yrs **	S I L
Avg Effective Maturity	9.8 Yrs	
Avg Credit Quality	BBB	
Avg Weighted Coupon	8.29%	
**figure provided by fund

Diversification Value for Portfolio Types

Large Cap: High	Small Cap: High	Bond: Low	Balanced: Medium	Diversified: Medium

Expenses & Fees

Sales Fees	
	4.75% front
	0.00% deferred
	0.30% 12b-1
Management Fee	0.55% max./0.45% min.
3-,5-,10-yr Expense Projections	$81, $105, $174
Annual Brokerage Cost	---

Min Initial Purchase	$500 (Addt'l: $25)
Min IRA Purchase	$25 (Addt'l: $25)
Min Auto Invest Plan	$25 (Systematic Inv: $25)

Portfolio 12-31-94

Share Chg -000	Amount 000	Total Stocks: 0 Total Fixed-Income: 91	Date of Maturity	Value $000	% Net Assets
	6580	Kingdom of Spain 13.45%	04-15-96	5176	3.19
	6316	Govt of Canada 6.5%	08-01-96	4370	2.69
	4211	US Treasury Note 6.5%	05-15-97	4096	2.52
	4547	Prudential Hm Mtg Sec 6.759%	09-28-08	3911	2.41
	4724	Turner Broadcstng Sys 8.375%	07-01-13	3815	2.35
	4456	Countrywide Funding 6.5%	10-25-08	3782	2.33
	4211	Banco Rio de la Plata 8.5%	07-15-98	3642	2.24
	5079	Republic of Argentina 8.375%	12-20-03	3619	2.23
	3500	DLJ Mortgage Acceptance 10%	12-22-02	3514	2.16
	3685	FDIC CMO REMIC 8.7%	09-25-25	3486	2.15
	4051	Residential Funding 6.5%	10-25-08	3414	2.10
	3158	Federated Dept Stores 11.29%	06-30-02	3182	1.96
	3145	Videotron 10.25%	10-15-02	3090	1.90
	3685	Residential Funding 6.97%	08-28-23	2975	1.83
	5264	United Mexican States 6.25%	12-31-19	2869	1.77
	3127	Resolution Trust 8%	06-25-26	2786	1.71
	2895	US Treasury Bond 7.5%	11-15-24	2768	1.70
	3290	National Power 7.625%	11-15-00	2755	1.70
	842	Middletown Trust 11.75%	07-15-10	2611	1.61
	6448	Republic of Brazil 6%	04-15-24	2579	1.59

Index Allocation

	% of Stocks
S&P 500	---
S&P MidCap 400	---
U.S. Small Cap	---
Foreign	---

Composition % 12-31-94

Cash	2.9	Preferreds	0.5
Stocks	0.0	Convertibles	34.9
Bonds	61.8	Other	0.0

Tax Analysis

	Tax-Adj Historical Return %	% Pretax Return
3 Yr Avg	2.65	40.1
5 Yr Avg	6.52	59.4
10 Yr Avg	---	---
Potential Capital Gain Exposure (% of assets)		-15%

Most Similar Funds in MF500

Bond Fund of America	Fair Fit
SteinRoe Income	Fair Fit
PaineWebber Invmt Grade Inc	Weak Fit

Bond Credit Analysis 12-31-94

% of Bonds				
US Govt	9	BB	23
AAA	9	B	2
AA	14	Below B	1
A	5	NR/NA	12
BBB	24		

Stock Sector Weightings

	% of Stocks	Relative S&P 500
Utilities	---	---
Energy	---	---
Financials	---	---
Industrial Cyclicals	---	---
Consumer Durables	---	---
Consumer Staples	---	---
Services	---	---
Retail	---	---
Health	---	---
Technology	---	---

MORNINGSTAR 1995 Mutual Fund 500

Phoenix Total Return A

	Ticker	Load	NAV	Yield	SEC Yield	Assets	Objective
	PTRFX	4.75%	14.82	2.1%	2.75%	335.2	Asset Alloc.

Phoenix Total Return Fund - Class A seeks total return consistent with reasonable risk.

The fund invests in stocks, bonds, and money-market instruments; the relative holdings are adjusted to achieve an optimal return. Equity securities may be selected for current income or capital appreciation Selected debt securities are either government issues or investment-grade corporate debt.

Class A shares have front loads; Class B shares have deferred loads and higher 12b-1 fees. Prior to July 2, 1986, the fund was named P-C Capital Fund. On Dec. 10, 1993, National Total Return Fund merged into this fund.

Historical Profile
Return — Above Average
Risk — Below Average
Rating ★★★★ Above Average

Manager's Investment Style

Management shifts its assets based on stock and bond market climates. It has been known to move drastically, at times holding the largest cash position among all asset-allocation funds. Among its stock picks, management seeks strong earnings at a good price. During the past few years, bonds haven't played much of a role in this portfolio compared with the average asset-allocation fund.

Investment Style History
Equity
Average % Stocks Held in Portfolio

83% 46% 61% 41% 64% 41% 46% 39%

Growth of $10,000
IIII Value of Fund ($000)
— Value of Index ($000) SPMid400
▼ Manager Change
▽ Partial Manager Change
► Mgr Unknown After
◄ Mgr Unknown Before

Performance Quartile (Within Objective)

Fund Manager(s)

Robert Milnamow, since 11-89. Birthdate: 10-50.
BA, Pennsylvania State U. 1972 MBA, New York U. 1980

	1983	1984	1985	1986	1987	1988	1989	1990	1991	1992	1993	1994	History
	---	---	---	12.38	12.58	12.55	13.90	13.43	15.22	14.89	15.48	14.82	NAV
	---	---	---	-4.85 *	11.02	3.35	18.42	4.45	28.63	10.32	10.49	-2.26	Total Return %
	---	---	---	-2.34 *	5.76	-13.26	-13.27	7.57	-1.86	2.70	0.44	-3.57	+/- S&P 500
	---	---	---		8.26	-4.53	3.88	-4.50	12.62	3.08	0.74	0.66	+/- LB Aggregate
	---	---	---	3.11	1.81	3.59	4.39	5.17	2.59	1.68	0.79	2.00	Income Return %
	---	---	---	-7.96	9.21	-0.24	14.03	-0.72	26.04	8.64	9.71	-4.26	Capital Return %
	---	---	---		9	95	39	44	29	20	63	36	Total Rtn % Rank All
	---	---	---		29	77	40	10	16	16	68	45	Total Rtn % Rank Obj
	---	---	---	0.43	0.24	0.45	0.55	0.71	0.37	0.25	0.12	0.31	Income $
	---	---	---	0.00	1.00	0.00	0.38	0.38	1.65	1.64	0.84	0.00	Capital Gains $
	---	---	---	1.33	1.54	1.52	1.45	1.58	1.58	1.36	1.29	1.17	Expense Ratio %
	---	---	---	2.15	2.52	3.72	3.79	4.23	2.51	2.06	1.26	1.88	Income Ratio %
	---	---	---	378	323	317	315	279	249	322	246	218	Turnover Rate %
	---	---	---	5.2	29.3	34.9	32.4	29.9	35.2	58.0	370.4	335.2	Net Assets ($mil)

Manager Experience

	Dates Managed	Invest Obj	Std Dev	+/- Index
Robert Milnamow				
Phoenix Equity Opport A	07/93 - 09/94	G	8.28	-5.61

Performance 12-31-94

	1st Qtr	2nd Qtr	3rd Qtr	4th Qtr	Total
1987	17.85	1.30	5.44	-11.81	11.02
1988	1.51	1.36	-0.23	0.68	3.35
1989	1.75	7.50	8.34	-0.08	18.42
1990	-1.37	5.57	-5.01	5.60	4.45
1991	12.81	-0.10	5.45	8.23	28.63
1992	0.20	1.12	3.92	4.77	10.32
1993	4.77	0.26	3.66	1.47	10.49
1994	-2.45	-0.73	1.62	-0.67	-2.26

Bear Market Performance

Decile Rank (5-year period)

Worst — Best

	Worst 3 Mo Period 1985-89	Worst 3 Mo Period 1990-94
Phoenix Total Return A	---	-5.01
+/- S&P 500	---	8.74
+/- Best Fit Index : SPMid400	---	12.77

Trailing Returns

	Total Return %	+/- S&P 500	+/- LB Aggregate	% Rank All	% Rank Obj	Growth of $10,000
3 Mo	-0.67	-0.65	-1.05	38	44	9,933
6 Mo	0.94	-3.92	-0.05	38	55	10,094
1 Yr	-2.26	-3.57	0.66	36	45	9,774
3 Yr Avg	6.01	-0.25	1.47	34	43	11,914
5 Yr Avg	9.87	1.17	2.24	18	12	16,007
10 Yr Avg	---	---	---	---	---	---
15 Yr Avg	---	---	---	---	---	---

Operations

Address and Telephone	100 Bright Meadow Bvd PO Box 2200 Enfield, CT 06083-2200 800-243-4361 / 203-253-1000	
Advisor	Phoenix Investment Counsel	
Subadvisor	None	
Distributor	Phoenix Equity Planning	
States Available	All plus PR	
Report Grade	C	
Income Distrib	Paid Annually	
• Date of Inception	07-02-86	
Fiscal Year End	December	

Risk Analysis

Time Period	Load-Adj Return %	Risk % Rank All	Obj	Morningstar Return	Risk	Morningstar Risk-Adj Rating
1 Yr	-6.90					
3 Yr	4.31	29	17	0.21 [3]	0.55	★★★
5 Yr	8.80	46	20	1.02 [3]	0.58	★★★★
10 Yr	---	---	---	---	---	

Average Historical Rating (66 months)   3.4 ★s

[1] 1 = low, 100 = high [2] 1.00 = Hybrid Avg [3] 1.00 = 90-day T-bill return

Other Measures

		Standard S&P 500	Best Fit SPMid400
Standard Deviation	4.96	Alpha	0.9	0.8
Mean	5.98	Beta	0.52	0.43
Sharpe Ratio	0.49	R-Squared	69	71

Investment Style

Stocks	Port Avg	Rel S&P 500
Price/Earnings Ratio	21.2	1.15
Price/Book Ratio	3.6	1.07
5 Yr Earnings Gr %	0.0	0.00
Med Mkt Cap ($mil)	8934	0.69

Bonds

Avg Effective Duration	3.8 Yrs **
Avg Effective Maturity	7.3 Yrs
Avg Credit Quality	AAA
Avg Weighted Coupon	7.23%

**figure provided by fund

Diversification Value for Portfolio Types

Large Cap: Low   Small Cap: Low   Bond: High   Balanced: Low   Diversified: Low

Portfolio 06-30-94

Total Stocks: 50
Total Fixed-Income: 4

Share Chg (12-93)000	Amount 000		Date of Maturity	Value $000	% Net Assets
	17500	US Treasury Note 6.5%	04-30-99	17182	5.06
	8000	US Treasury Note 5.875%	02-15-04	7190	2.12
92	148	Eastman Kodak		7123	2.10
90	90	Eli Lilly		5119	1.51
	5000	Eastman Kodak 9.625%	11-15-99	5063	1.49
67	67	McGraw-Hill		4475	1.32
-10	90	Omnicom Group		4343	1.28
95	95	Johnson & Johnson		4073	1.20
55	55	CIGNA		4022	1.19
40	194	Tele-Communications Cl A		3953	1.17
70	70	Kellogg		3817	1.13
80	80	Western Atlas		3810	1.12
-16	189	Federated Department Stores		3788	1.12
-5	70	Tribune		3728	1.10
	3500	Kroger 10%	05-01-99	3623	1.07
-50	105	Campbell Soup		3596	1.06
0	119	Times Mirror Cl A		3585	1.06
80	80	Motorola		3560	1.05
90	90	May Department Stores		3533	1.04
-83	132	Marriott International		3520	1.04

Index Allocation

	% of Stocks
S&P 500	82.5
S&P MidCap 400	7.8
U.S. Small Cap	4.3
Foreign	5.4

Composition % 12-31-94

Cash	44.6	Preferreds	0.0
Stocks	35.7	Convertibles	0.0
Bonds	19.7	Other	0.0

Tax Analysis

	Tax-Adj Historical Return %	% Pretax Return
3 Yr Avg	3.97	64.7
5 Yr Avg	7.30	70.3
10 Yr Avg	---	---
Potential Capital Gain Exposure (% of assets)		-1%

Most Similar Funds in MF500

Delaware A	Fair Fit
Prudential Alloc Cons Mgd B	Fair Fit
T. Rowe Price Balanced	Fair Fit

Bond Credit Analysis 11-17-94
% of Bonds

US Govt	100	BB	0
AAA	0	B	0
AA	0	Below B	0
A	0	NR/NA	0
BBB	0		

Stock Sector Weightings

	% of Stocks	Relative S&P 500
Utilities	0.0	0.00
Energy	4.9	0.48
Financials	7.3	0.69
Industrial Cyclicals	20.3	1.24
Consumer Durables	6.3	1.01
Consumer Staples	9.2	0.73
Services	29.3	3.60
Retail	9.0	1.54
Health	7.2	0.83
Technology	6.5	0.71

Expenses & Fees

Sales Fees	4.75% front
	0.00% deferred
	0.25% 12b-1
Management Fee	0.65% max./0.55% min.
3-,5-,10-yr Expense Projections	$91, $122, $211
Annual Brokerage Cost	0.29%

Min Initial Purchase $500 (Addt'l: $25)
Min IRA Purchase $25 (Addt'l: $25)
Min Auto Invest Plan $25 (Systematic Inv: $25)

PIMCo Adv Growth C

Ticker	Load	NAV	Yield	SEC Yield	Assets	Objective
PGWCX	1.00%d	20.01	0.0%	N/A	1054.0	Growth

PIMCo Advisors Growth Fund - Class C seeks long-term growth of capital.

The fund normally invests at least 65% of its assets in equities, but it may also invest in convertible securities, preferred stocks, and money-market instruments. It may invest without limit in foreign securities traded in domestic markets, and may invest up to 10% of its assets in foreign securities traded principally outside the United States.

Class A shares have front loads and lower 12b-1 fees; Class C shares have deferred loads. Prior to Nov. 14, 1994, the fund was named Thomson Growth Fund B and Thomson McKinnon Growth Fund.

Manager's Investment Style

Management looks for large companies with strong earnings momentum and a history of exceeding earnings expectations. Management also looks behind the earnings to ferret out surprises by examining macroeconomic data, secular patterns, industry trends, and company-specific events. While management is willing to pay high multiples for that growth, it is also quick to sell losers.

Fund Manager(s)

Management Team

Manager Experience

	Dates Managed	Invest Obj	Std Dev	+/- Index
Management Team				
SteinRoe Total Return	08/49 - 01/81	EI	13.51	-2.34
SteinRoe Stock	07/58 - 01/89	G	19.99	-2.42

Historical Profile
Return	Above Average
Risk	Average
Rating ★★★★	
	Above Average

Investment Style History Equity
Average % Stocks Held in Portfolio

83% 88% 87% 86% 88% 91% 92% 93%

Growth of $10,000
|||| Value of Fund ($000)
— Value of Index ($000) SPMid400
▼ Manager Change
▽ Partial Manager Change
► Mgr Unknown After
◄ Mgr Unknown Before

Performance Quartile (Within Objective)

1983	1984	1985	1986	1987	1988	1989	1990	1991	1992	1993	1994	History
---	10.76	12.65	13.28	12.89	14.03	18.04	16.21	21.56	21.49	21.36	20.01	NAV
---	11.99 *	30.67	23.11	7.62	9.37	37.46	0.30	41.88	2.08	10.36	-0.74	Total Return %
---	1.12 *	-1.07	4.43	2.36	-7.24	5.77	3.41	11.39	-5.54	0.31	-2.06	+/- S&P 500
---	---	-1.89	7.01	5.26	-8.57	8.28	6.48	7.67	-6.89	-0.92	-0.67	+/- Wilshire 5000
---	2.33	3.45	2.65	1.24	0.53	0.80	1.28	0.33	0.00	0.99	0.00	Income Return %
---	9.66	27.22	20.46	6.39	8.84	36.65	-0.98	41.55	2.08	9.37	-0.74	Capital Return %
---	---	23	12	14	66	5	55	12	86	64	25	Total Rtn % Rank All
---	---	41	7	21	76	12	21	27	85	55	40	Total Rtn % Rank Obj
---	0.23	0.37	0.35	0.18	0.07	0.14	0.22	0.06	0.00	0.22	0.00	Income $
---	0.20	0.88	1.92	1.13	0.00	1.13	1.66	1.25	0.52	2.09	1.19	Capital Gains $
---	2.50	1.90	1.70	1.60	1.80	1.70	1.70	1.80	1.90	1.90	1.90	Expense Ratio %
---	4.00	3.20	2.40	0.80	0.60	0.70	1.00	0.60	-0.10	-0.30	-0.20	Income Ratio %
---	---	198	169	128	104	83	89	95	92	110	115	Turnover Rate %
---	35.9	76.1	214.7	360.9	317.1	347.9	343.2	669.9	942.1	1068.9	1054.0	Net Assets ($mil)

Performance 12-31-94

	1st Qtr	2nd Qtr	3rd Qtr	4th Qtr	Total
1987	23.02	4.98	5.86	-21.28	7.62
1988	3.49	7.65	-2.78	0.98	9.37
1989	8.91	13.60	13.93	-2.48	37.46
1990	-2.77	11.70	-13.14	6.32	0.30
1991	15.73	-0.86	10.73	11.67	41.88
1992	-3.99	-2.32	2.08	6.63	2.08
1993	2.51	1.18	6.66	-0.24	10.36
1994	-1.97	-2.29	5.18	-1.48	-0.75

Bear Market Performance

Decile Rank (5-year period)

Worst — Best

	Worst 3 Mo Period 1985-89	Worst 3 Mo Period 1990-94
PIMCo Adv Growth C	-28.41	-13.14
+/- S&P 500	1.17	0.61
+/- Best Fit Index : SPMid400	0.40	4.64

Trailing Returns

	Total Return %	+/- S&P 500	+/- Wil 5000	% Rank All	% Rank Obj	Growth of $10,000
3 Mo	-1.48	-1.47	-0.71	56	54	9,852
6 Mo	3.62	-1.24	-1.00	17	54	10,362
1 Yr	-0.74	-2.06	-0.67	25	40	9,926
3 Yr Avg	3.79	-2.47	-2.82	74	68	11,182
5 Yr Avg	9.73	1.04	0.92	18	33	15,911
10 Yr Avg	15.27	0.89	1.41	10	13	41,414
15 Yr Avg	---	---	---	---	---	---

Operations

Address and Telephone	One Station Place
	Stamford, CT 06902
	800-426-0107 / 203-352-4900
Advisor	PIMCo Advisors
Subadvisor	Columbus Circle Investors
Distributor	PIMCo Advisors Distribution
States Available	All plus PR
Report Grade	B-
Income Distrib	Paid Annually
* Date of Inception	02-24-84
Fiscal Year End	September

Risk Analysis

Time Period	Load-Adj Return %	Risk % Rank [1] All	Risk % Rank [1] Obj	Morningstar [2] Return	Morningstar Risk	Morningstar Risk-Adj Rating
1 Yr	-0.75					
3 Yr	3.79	83	66	0.06 [3]	1.02	★★
5 Yr	9.73	76	50	1.28 [3]	0.91	★★★★
10 Yr	15.27	66	36	1.55	0.89	★★★★
Average Historical Rating (94 months)					4.4	★s

[1] = low, 100 = high [2] 1.00 = Equity Avg [3] 1.00 = 90-day T-bill return

Other Measures

	Standard S&P 500	Best Fit SPMid400
Standard Deviation	9.88	Alpha -2.3 / -2.6
Mean	4.22	Beta 1.03 / 0.86
Sharpe Ratio	0.07	R-Squared 69 / 73

Investment Style

	Stock Portfolio Avg	Relative S&P 500
Price/Earnings Ratio	20.0	1.08
Price/Book Ratio	4.1	1.22
5 Yr Earnings Gr %	13.2	2.38
Return on Assets %	10.0	1.33
Debt % Total Cap	25.5	0.90
Med Mkt Cap ($mil)	10815	0.83

Style: Value Blend Growth / Size Large Med Small

Diversification Value for Portfolio Types

Large Cap: Low	Small Cap: Low	Bond: High	Balanced: Low	Diversified: Low

Min Initial Purchase / Expenses

Min Initial Purchase	$1000 (Addt'l: $100)
Min IRA Purchase	$25 (Addt'l: $25)
Min Auto Invest Plan	$50 (Systematic Inv: $50)

Expenses & Fees

Sales Fees	0.00% front
	1.00% deferred
	1.00% 12b-1
Management Fee	0.70% max./0.65% min.
3-,5-,10-yr Expense Projections	$58, $100, $217
Annual Brokerage Cost	0.30%

Portfolio 09-30-94

Share Chg (03-94)000	Amount 000	Total Stocks: 46 / Total Fixed-Income: 0	Value $000	% Net Assets
280	601	IBM	41745	3.85
361	774	Motorola	40805	3.76
160	774	Columbia/HCA Healthcare	33650	3.10
146	742	Computer Associates Intl	33006	3.04
-69	755	Citicorp	32102	2.96
665	937	Compaq Computer	30581	2.82
105	710	Oracle Systems	30523	2.81
18	751	Loral	29563	2.72
-210	623	US Healthcare	29027	2.67
-13	546	United HealthCare	28940	2.67
345	546	Medtronic	28872	2.66
253	473	Caterpillar	25614	2.36
79	578	Boeing	24921	2.30
473	473	Johnson & Johnson	24431	2.25
423	423	Microsoft	23751	2.19
-241	373	Intel	22947	2.11
162	382	Amoco	22647	2.09
-1	211	Xerox	22539	2.08
296	296	British Petroleum (ADR)	22405	2.06
455	455	Coca-Cola	22126	2.04
400	400	AT & T	21574	1.99
205	205	Atlantic Richfield	20656	1.90
239	546	Fleet Financial Group	20545	1.89
152	354	El duPont de Nemours	20533	1.89
85	250	Dayton Hudson	19145	1.76

Composition % 12-31-94

Cash	6.0	Preferreds	0.0
Stocks	94.0	Convertibles	0.0
Bonds	0.0	Other	0.0

Tax Analysis

	Tax-Adj Historical Return %	% Pretax Return
3 Yr Avg	2.02	52.2
5 Yr Avg	7.49	73.6
10 Yr Avg	12.78	74.2
Potential Capital Gain Exposure (% of assets)		9%

Most Similar Funds in MF500

IDS New Dimensions	Strong Fit
Enterprise Capital Apprec	Fair Fit
Liberty All-Star	Fair Fit

Index Allocation

	% of Stocks
S&P 500	93.9
S&P MidCap 400	0.0
U.S. Small Cap	2.0
Foreign	4.1

Sector Weightings

	% of Stocks	Relative S&P 500
Utilities	2.2	0.18
Energy	8.4	0.83
Financials	7.1	0.67
Industrial Cyclicals	15.7	0.96
Consumer Durables	12.8	2.05
Consumer Staples	6.5	0.52
Services	2.5	0.30
Retail	1.9	0.33
Health	14.7	1.70
Technology	28.3	3.09

MORNINGSTAR 1995 Mutual Fund 500

PIMCo Adv Opportunity C

Ticker	Load	NAV	Yield	SEC Yield	Assets	Objective
POPCX	Clsd	27.48	0.0%	N/A	551.0	Aggr. Growth

PIMCo Advisors Opportunity Fund - Class C seeks capital appreciation.

The fund invests primarily in common stocks, although it may also purchase convertible securities. A substantial portion of its assets may be invested in companies with relatively low market capitalizations, including those with limited operating histories. The fund may invest without limit in foreign securities traded on U.S. markets.

Class A shares have front loads; Class C shares have deferred loads and higher 12b-1 fees. Prior to Nov. 14, 1994, the fund was named Thomson Opportunity Fund - Class B.

Manager's Investment Style

Management invests in companies that it thinks will post better-than-expected results. To find them, the fund's advisor, Thompson Advisory Group, tracks a broad array of stocks for balance-sheet data and industry-specific information. Buy decisions are skewed in favor of stocks that carry especially low expectations.

Fund Manager(s)

Management Team

Manager Experience

	Dates Managed	Invest Obj	Std Dev	+/- Index

Not available.

Historical Profile

Return	High
Risk	Above Average
Rating	★★★★★
	Closed

Investment Style History
Equity
Average % Stocks Held in Portfolio

Growth of $10,000

|||| Value of Fund ($000)
— Value of Index ($000)
Wil 4500
▼ Manager Change
▽ Partial Manager Change
► Mgr Unknown After
◄ Mgr Unknown Before

Performance Quartile (Within Objective)

	1983	1984	1985	1986	1987	1988	1989	1990	1991	1992	1993	1994	History
	---	10.82	13.14	12.41	10.27	11.71	13.58	12.21	18.64	23.68	29.79	27.48	NAV
	---	11.86 *	29.85	4.50	6.40	14.02	30.66	-7.34	68.08	28.46	36.16	-4.73	Total Return %
	---	0.99 *	-1.88	-14.18	1.15	-2.59	-1.03	-4.23	37.60	20.84	26.10	-6.05	+/- S&P 500
	---	---	-2.16	-7.26	9.92	-6.52	6.71	6.21	24.63	16.70	21.62	-2.08	+/- Wilshire 4500
	---	1.13	0.00	0.16	0.26	0.00	0.00	0.00	0.00	0.00	0.00	0.00	Income Return %
	---	10.74	29.85	4.34	6.14	14.02	30.65	-7.34	68.08	28.46	36.16	-4.73	Capital Return %
	---	---	26	96	18	31	12	78	2	1	5	61	Total Rtn % Rank All
	---	---	33	89	23	45	45	62	25	2	4	62	Total Rtn % Rank Obj
	---	0.12	0.00	0.03	0.03	0.00	0.00	0.00	0.00	0.00	0.00	0.00	Income $
	---	0.25	0.80	1.27	2.55	0.00	1.71	0.37	1.68	0.26	2.37	0.87	Capital Gains $
	---	2.50	2.00	1.80	1.70	2.00	1.90	1.90	2.00	2.00	2.00	1.90	Expense Ratio %
	---	1.50	0.20	-0.30	0.10	0.30	-0.20	-0.10	-0.80	-1.00	-1.30	-1.40	Income Ratio %
	---	---	66	109	189	125	153	106	145	94	105	78	Turnover Rate %
	---	15.4	33.8	50.1	54.0	45.8	45.9	38.9	79.7	354.6	614.5	551.0	Net Assets ($mil)

Investment Style History (top bars): 78% 82% 89% 91% 94% 85% 88% 88%

Performance 12-31-94

	1st Qtr	2nd Qtr	3rd Qtr	4th Qtr	Total
1987	26.67	-2.04	8.64	-21.07	6.40
1988	11.20	8.32	-4.28	-1.10	14.02
1989	8.54	10.62	12.23	-3.04	30.66
1990	-2.43	9.06	-17.44	5.47	-7.34
1991	28.67	-2.80	17.03	14.85	68.08
1992	7.46	-7.04	5.26	22.17	28.46
1993	7.69	10.51	16.29	-1.61	36.16
1994	-6.61	-13.55	16.59	1.21	-4.73

Bear Market Performance

Decile Rank (5-year period)

Worst | Best

	Worst 3 Mo Period 1985-89	Worst 3 Mo Period 1990-94
PIMCo Adv Opportunity C	-30.96	-19.55
+/- S&P 500	-1.37	-5.71
+/- Best Fit Index : Wil 4500	-0.82	-0.15

Trailing Returns

	Total Return %	+/- S&P 500	+/- Wil 4500	% Rank All	% Rank Obj	Growth of $10,000
3 Mo	1.21	1.23	3.71	5	25	10,121
6 Mo	18.00	13.14	13.81	2	11	11,800
1 Yr	-4.73	-6.05	-2.08	61	62	9,527
3 Yr Avg	18.56	12.29	10.95	2	4	16,663
5 Yr Avg	21.01	12.32	11.92	1	2	25,951
10 Yr Avg	18.76	4.38	6.13	2	7	55,820
15 Yr Avg	---	---	---	---	---	---

Operations

Address and Telephone	One Station Place
	Stamford, CT 06902
	800-426-0107 / 203-352-4900
Advisor	PIMCo Advisors
Subadvisor	Columbus Circle Investors
Distributor	PIMCo Advisors Distribution
States Available	All plus PR
Report Grade	B
Income Distrib	Paid Annually
* Date of Inception	02-24-84
Fiscal Year End	September

Risk Analysis

Time Period	Load-Adj Return %	Risk % Rank [1] All	Obj	Morningstar [2] Return	Morningstar Risk	Morningstar Risk-Adj Rating
1 Yr	-4.73					
3 Yr	18.55	96	75	4.98 [3]	1.49	★★★★★
5 Yr	21.01	95	62	5.15 [3]	1.34	★★★★★
10 Yr	18.76	93	37	2.49	1.30	★★★★★
Average Historical Rating (95 months)				3.7	★s	

[1] 1 = low, 100 = high [2] 1.00 = Equity Avg [3] 1.00 = 90-day T-bill return

Other Measures

			Standard S&P 500	Best Fit Wil 4500
Standard Deviation	17.82	Alpha	12.1	8.4
Mean	18.73	Beta	1.31	1.66
Sharpe Ratio	0.85	R-Squared	34	83

Investment Style

	Stock Portfolio Avg	Relative S&P 500
Price/Earnings Ratio	28.4	1.54
Price/Book Ratio	6.2	1.84
5 Yr Earnings Gr %	19.8#	3.56
Return on Assets %	14.0	1.87
Debt % Total Cap	24.3	0.86
Med Mkt Cap ($mil)	749	0.06

figure is based on 50% or less of stocks

Style: Value Blend Growth / Size Large Med Small

Diversification Value for Portfolio Types

Large Cap: Medium	Small Cap: Low	Bond: High	Balanced: Medium	Diversified: Medium

Portfolio 10-31-94

Share Chg (03-94) 000	Amount 000	Total Stocks: 46 / Total Fixed-Income: 0	Value $000	% Net Assets
1	2134	EMC	45888	7.89
413	925	Atmel	34113	5.87
-43	512	Lam Research	23051	3.97
0	277	Oxford Health Plans	22752	3.91
235	576	Williams-Sonoma	19881	3.42
-41	348	KLA Instruments	18338	3.15
256	512	Gymboree	16648	2.86
85	341	Tommy Hilfiger	15068	2.59
255	255	StrataCom	14459	2.49
427	427	Symbol Technologies	14407	2.48
-85	427	HBO	13873	2.39
21	384	Harman International	13734	2.36
384	384	Wabash National	13352	2.30
156	427	Intl CableTel	13233	2.28
43	299	Altera	11784	2.03
39	295	Callaway Golf	11286	1.94
512	512	First Alert	10885	1.87
188	188	BayBanks	10847	1.87
64	427	Oakwood Homes	10138	1.74
0	341	Airgas	9903	1.70
461	461	Comcast Cable Partners	9220	1.59
-87	233	ALC Communications	8834	1.52
341	341	Harnischfeger Industries	8537	1.47
324	324	Electronics For Imaging	8516	1.46
131	131	Broderbund Software	8387	1.44

Composition % 09-30-94

Cash	14.0	Preferreds	0.0
Stocks	86.0	Convertibles	0.0
Bonds	0.0	Other	0.0

Tax Analysis

	Tax-Adj Historical Return %	% Pretax Return
3 Yr Avg	17.28	92.0
5 Yr Avg	19.44	89.7
10 Yr Avg	16.52	78.8
Potential Capital Gain Exposure (% of assets)		26%

Most Similar Funds in MF500

Hancock Special Equities A	Strong Fit
Brandywine	Fair Fit
AIM Constellation	Fair Fit

Index Allocation

	% of Stocks
S&P 500	1.8
S&P MidCap 400	31.7
U.S. Small Cap	62.9
Foreign	3.7

Sector Weightings

	% of Stocks	Relative S&P 500
Utilities	0.2	0.02
Energy	6.0	0.60
Financials	9.4	0.89
Industrial Cyclicals	6.5	0.40
Consumer Durables	15.4	2.48
Consumer Staples	0.0	0.00
Services	0.0	0.00
Retail	10.5	1.81
Health	0.0	
Technology	51.9	5.67

Min Purchases / Expenses

Min Initial Purchase	Closed (Addt'l: $100)
Min IRA Purchase	$25 (Addt'l: $25)
Min Auto Invest Plan	$50 (Systematic Inv: $50)

Expenses & Fees

Sales Fees	0.00% front
	1.00% deferred
	1.00% 12b-1
Management Fee	0.75% max./0.70% min.
3-,5-,10-yr Expense Projections	$60, $103, $222
Annual Brokerage Cost	0.23%

PIMCo Adv Target A

Ticker	Load	NAV	Yield	SEC Yield	Assets	Objective
PTAAX	5.50%	12.89	0.0%	N/A	94.8	Growth

PIMCo Advisors Target Fund - Class A seeks capital appreciation.

The fund normally invests at least 65% of its assets in equity securities of medium-size companies with capitalizations between $800 million and $5 billion. A portion of fund assets may be invested in foreign equities. The fund may also invest in U.S. government securities. It may engage in options and futures transactions to generate current income.

Class A shares have front loads; Class C shares have deferred loads and higher 12b-1 fees. Prior to Nov. 14, 1994, the fund was named Thomson Target Fund - Class A.

Manager's Investment Style

Management takes a momentum approach to investing. It favors small- and medium-size companies that boast strong earnings driven by recent secular or industry trends, positive events, changes within the company, or a combination thereof. Management is willing to pay hefty multiples for earnings.

Fund Manager(s)

Management Team

Manager Experience

	Dates Managed	Invest Obj	Std Dev	+/- Index
Management Team				
SteinRoe Total Return	08/49 - 01/81	EI	13.51	-2.34
SteinRoe Stock	07/58 - 01/89	G	19.99	-2.42

Historical Profile

Return	---
Risk	---
Rating	Not Rated

Investment Style History
Equity

Average % Stocks Held in Portfolio: 87% 93%

Growth of $10,000
- ‖‖‖ Value of Fund ($000)
- — Value of Index ($000) S&P 500
- ▼ Manager Change
- ▽ Partial Manager Change
- ► Mgr Unknown After
- ◄ Mgr Unknown Before

Performance Quartile (Within Objective)

	1983	1984	1985	1986	1987	1988	1989	1990	1991	1992	1993	1994	History
	---	---	---	---	---	---	---	---	---	10.11	12.57	12.89	NAV
	---	---	---	---	---	---	---	---	---	1.10 *	25.51	3.86	Total Return %
	---	---	---	---	---	---	---	---	---	0.82 *	15.45	2.55	+/- S&P 500
	---	---	---	---	---	---	---	---	---	---	14.23	3.93	+/- Wilshire 5000
	---	---	---	---	---	---	---	---	---	0.00	0.00	0.00	Income Return %
	---	---	---	---	---	---	---	---	---	1.10	25.51	3.86	Capital Return %
	---	---	---	---	---	---	---	---	---	---	11	6	Total Rtn % Rank All
	---	---	---	---	---	---	---	---	---	---	6	10	Total Rtn % Rank Obj
	---	---	---	---	---	---	---	---	---	0.00	0.00	0.00	Income $
	---	---	---	---	---	---	---	---	---	0.00	0.12	0.16	Capital Gains $
	---	---	---	---	---	---	---	---	---	---	1.30	1.20	Expense Ratio %
	---	---	---	---	---	---	---	---	---	---	-0.30	-0.30	Income Ratio %
	---	---	---	---	---	---	---	---	---	---	---	104	Turnover Rate %
	---	---	---	---	---	---	---	---	---	---	63.4	94.8	Net Assets ($mil)

Performance 12-31-94

	1st Qtr	2nd Qtr	3rd Qtr	4th Qtr	Total
1987	---	---	---	---	---
1988	---	---	---	---	---
1989	---	---	---	---	---
1990	---	---	---	---	---
1991	---	---	---	---	---
1992	---	---	---	---	1.10 *
1993	5.64	6.93	11.38	-0.24	25.51
1994	-2.47	-3.34	10.80	-0.57	3.86

Bear Market Performance

Decile Rank (5-year period)

Worst ─────────────── Best

	Worst 3 Mo Period 1985-89	Worst 3 Mo Period 1990-94
PIMCo Adv Target A	---	---
+/- S&P 500	---	---
+/- Best Fit Index :	---	---

Trailing Returns

	Total Return %	+/- S&P 500	+/- Wil 5000	% Rank All	% Rank Obj	Growth of $10,000
3 Mo	-0.57	-0.55	0.20	36	34	9,943
6 Mo	10.17	5.31	5.55	4	8	11,017
1 Yr	3.86	2.55	3.93	6	10	10,386
3 Yr Avg	---	---	---	---	---	---
5 Yr Avg	---	---	---	---	---	---
10 Yr Avg	---	---	---	---	---	---
15 Yr Avg	---	---	---	---	---	---

Operations

Address and Telephone	One Station Place
	Stamford, CT 06902
	800-426-0107 / 203-352-4900
Advisor	PIMCo Advisors
Subadvisor	Columbus Circle Investors
Distributor	PIMCo Advisors Distribution
States Available	All
Report Grade	B-
Income Distrib	Paid Annually
* Date of Inception	12-17-92
Fiscal Year End	September

Risk Analysis

Time Period	Load-Adj Return %	Risk % Rank [1] All	Obj	Morningstar [2] Return	Morningstar Risk	Morningstar Risk-Adj Rating
1 Yr	-1.85					
3 Yr	---	---	---	---		---
5 Yr	---	---	---	---		
10 Yr	---	---	---	---		

Average Historical Rating ---

[1] 1 = low, 100 = high [2] 1.00 = Equity Avg [3] 1.00 = 90-day T-bill return

Other Measures

		Standard S&P 500	Best Fit
Standard Deviation	---	Alpha	---	---
Mean	---	Beta	---	---
Sharpe Ratio	---	R-Squared	---	---

Investment Style

	Stock Portfolio Avg	Relative S&P 500
Price/Earnings Ratio	22.5	1.22
Price/Book Ratio	3.9	1.16
5 Yr Earnings Gr %	8.1#	1.46
Return on Assets %	9.5	1.27
Debt % Total Cap	24.6	0.87
Med Mkt Cap ($mil)	1621	0.12

figure is based on 50% or less of stocks

Diversification Value for Portfolio Types

Large Cap: Small Cap: Bond: Balanced: Diversified:

Portfolio 09-30-94

Share Chg (03-94) 000	Amount 000	Total Stocks: 48 / Total Fixed-Income: 0	Value $000	% Net Assets
93	137	DSC Communications	3898	4.31
61	93	LSI Logic	3492	3.86
11	75	Diebold	3066	3.39
83	95	Hospitality Franchise System	2982	3.29
28	48	Scott Paper	2924	3.23
-9	116	Humana	2735	3.02
21	57	Compuware	2705	2.99
74	74	Wellman	2528	2.79
65	91	Harley-Davidson	2518	2.78
39	100	Ceridian	2455	2.71
78	118	Revco Drug Stores	2454	2.71
75	75	Teradyne	2201	2.43
16	42	Willamette Industries	2161	2.39
34	94	Amphenol Cl A	2087	2.30
71	71	Storage Technology	2028	2.24
79	79	Mylan Laboratories	2012	2.22
6	42	Value Health	2002	2.21
33	58	Micron Technology	2001	2.21
52	52	Tektronix	2001	2.21
10	41	Applied Materials	1922	2.12
67	67	Tosco	1896	2.09
30	70	Green Tree Financial	1874	2.07
-1	65	Pittston Services Group	1851	2.04
22	55	Healthtrust	1807	2.00
83	83	Jefferson Smurfit Group	1660	1.83

Composition % 09-30-94

Cash	4.3	Preferreds	0.0
Stocks	95.7	Convertibles	0.0
Bonds	0.0	Other	0.0

Tax Analysis

	Tax-Adj Historical Return %	% Pretax Return
3 Yr Avg	---	---
5 Yr Avg	---	---
10 Yr Avg	---	---
Potential Capital Gain Exposure (% of assets)		9%

Most Similar Funds in MF500

Fund lacks three-year record

Index Allocation

	% of Stocks
S&P 500	29.8
S&P MidCap 400	37.2
U.S. Small Cap	28.4
Foreign	4.6

Sector Weightings

	% of Stocks	Relative S&P 500
Utilities	1.8	0.14
Energy	4.8	0.47
Financials	0.0	0.00
Industrial Cyclicals	21.9	1.34
Consumer Durables	5.2	0.83
Consumer Staples	0.0	0.00
Services	11.1	1.36
Retail	6.6	1.13
Health	13.6	1.57
Technology	35.1	3.83

Min Initial Purchase / Expenses & Fees

Min Initial Purchase	$1000 (Addt'l: $100)
Min IRA Purchase	$25 (Addt'l: $25)
Min Auto Invest Plan	$50 (Systematic Inv: $50)

Expenses & Fees

Sales Fees	5.50% front
	0.00% deferred
	0.25% 12b-1
Management Fee	0.75% max./0.70% min.
3-,5-,10-yr Expense Projections	$92, $120, $198
Annual Brokerage Cost	0.41%

M⊙RNINGSTAR 1995 Mutual Fund 500

PIMCo Commercial Mortgage Securities

	Ticker	NAV	Mkt Price	Prem/Disc	Yield	Objective
	PCM	$12.68	$11.13	-12.3%	10.1%	Corp General

PIMCo Commercial Mortgage Securities Trust seeks high current income.

The fund invests at least 65% of its total assets in investment-grade or equivalent commercial mortgage-backed securities. It may invest the remaining portion, up to 35%, in the following: commercial mortgage-backed securities rated below investment grade; securities issued or guaranteed by the U.S. government, or one of its agencies or instrumentalities; residential mortgage-backed securities; municipal securities; and corporate debt. The fund may use financial futures, options, and interest-rate transactions in an effort to increase returns and hedge portfolio positions.

The fund is leveraged with reverse-repurchase agreements.

To discourage takeover attempts, board members serve staggered terms and supermajority voting is required for open-ending, applying for REIT conversion, or liquidation. The board will submit a proposal to liquidate the fund in 2004.

Manager's Investment Style

While the fund has only been in existence a short time, management has heretofore demonstrated defensiveness that has limited rate sensitivity. This stems from management's preference for securities backed by commercial mortgages, as well as its penchant for lower-credit issues. The fund's low-credit holdings, however, as well as the portfolio's leverage, add risk to the offering.

Fund Manager(s)

Benjamin Trosky, CFA. Since 9-93. BBA'82 Drexel U.
William C. Powers. Since 9-93.

Historical Profile

Return	Not Rated
Risk	Not Rated
Rating	

	8.7	-0.8	Highest Prem/Disc
	-6.3	-14.2	Lowest Prem/Disc

Growth of $10,000
— at NAV ($000)
— at Market Price ($000)

Premium Discount %

	1983	1984	1985	1986	1987	1988	1989	1990	1991	1992	1993	1994	History
	---	---	---	---	---	---	---	---	---	---	13.75	12.68	NAV
	---	---	---	---	---	---	---	---	---	---	0.38*	1.20	NAV Total Return %
	---	---	---	---	---	---	---	---	---	---	---	4.12	+/- LB Aggregate
	---	---	---	---	---	---	---	---	---	---	---	5.13	+/- LB Corp
	---	---	---	---	---	---	---	---	---	---	---	2.81	+/- LB Mortgage
	---	---	---	---	---	---	---	---	---	---	1.81*	8.98	Income Return %
	---	---	---	---	---	---	---	---	---	---	-1.43*	-7.78	Capital Return %
	---	---	---	---	---	---	---	---	---	---	---	10	Total Rtn % Rank All
	---	---	---	---	---	---	---	---	---	---	---	5	Total Rtn % Rank Obj
	---	---	---	---	---	---	---	---	---	---	-7.50*	-10.48	Market Total Rtn %
	---	---	---	---	---	---	---	---	---	---	---	-6.2	Avg Prem/Disc %
	---	---	---	---	---	---	---	---	---	---	0.25	1.13	Income $
	---	---	---	---	---	---	---	---	---	---	0.00	0.00	Capital Gains $
	---	---	---	---	---	---	---	---	---	---	1.11	1.94	Expense Ratio %
	---	---	---	---	---	---	---	---	---	---	5.59	8.52	Income Ratio %
	---	---	---	---	---	---	---	---	---	---	---	---	Turnover Rate %
	---	---	---	---	---	---	---	---	---	---	151.4	136.6	Net Assets ($mil)
	---	---	---	---	---	---	---	---	---	---	36.7	59.7	Pfd/Debt Leverage ($mil)

Manager Experience

Manager Experience	Dates Managed	Invest Obj	Std Dev	+/- Index
Benjamin Trosky				
PIMCo High-Yield Instl	12/92 - 12/94	CY	4.16	7.04
PIMCo Adv High-Income C	11/94 - 12/94	CG	0.00	0.02

NAV Performance % 12-30-94

	1st Qtr	2nd Qtr	3rd Qtr	4th Qtr	Total
1987	---	---	---	---	---
1988	---	---	---	---	---
1989	---	---	---	---	---
1990	---	---	---	---	---
1991	---	---	---	---	---
1992	---	---	---	---	---
1993	---	---	-0.07*	0.45	0.38*
1994	-1.18	-0.91	1.36	1.97	1.20

Bear Market Performance

Decile Rank (5-year period)

Worst   Best

	Worst 3 Mo Period 1985-89	Worst 3 Mo Period 1990-94
PIMCo Commrcial Mtg	---	---
+/- LB Aggregate	---	---

Trailing Returns

	NAV Total Return %	+/- LB Agg	+/- LB Mortgage	% Rank All	% Rank Obj	Mkt Total Return %
3 Mo	1.97	1.59	1.54	5	8	-7.83
6 Mo	3.35	2.36	2.05	13	5	-2.75
1 Yr	1.20	4.12	2.81	10	5	-10.48
3 Yr Avg	---	---	---	---	---	---
5 Yr Avg	---	---	---	---	---	---
Incept Avg	1.19*	---	---	---	---	-13.20*

Operations

Address and Telephone	840 Newport Center Drive Newport Beach, CA 92660 800-213-3606	Income Distrib Schedule	Paid Quarterly
		Management Fee	0.73%, 0.10%A
		Reinvestment Plan	Yes
Advisor	PIMCO	Direct Purchase Plan	No
Subadvisor	N/A	Shares Outstanding	11,007,169
Administrator	Pacific Investment Adm. Svcs. Co.	Exchange	NYSE
Transfer Agent	Investors Fiduciary Trust Co.	*Date of Inception	09-02-93
Custodian	Investors Fiduciary Trust Co.	Shareholder Report	A
Auditor	Ernst & Young LLP		
Legal Counsel	Dechert Price & Rhoads		

Risk Analysis

	Risk % Rank[1]		Morningstar[2]	Morningstar	
	All	Obj	Return	Risk	Risk-Adj Rating
3 Yr	---	---	---	---	---
5 Yr	---	---	---	---	---
10 Yr	---	---	---	---	---

[1] 1 = Low, 100 = High [2] 1.00 = Fixed-Inc Avg [3] 1.00 = 90-day T-bill Return

Other Measures

				LB Aggregate
Standard Deviation	---	Alpha		---
Mean	---	Beta		---
Sharpe Ratio	---	R-Squared		---

Investment Style

Interest-Rate Stance

		Relative Objective	Duration Short Intm Long
Avg Eff Duration	3.9 Yrs**	0.61	
Avg Eff Maturity	6.0 Yrs	0.38	
Avg Wtd Coupon	8.37%	0.94	
Avg Wtd Price	95.0% Par	0.96	

Quality: High Med Low

Quality

Avg Cred Quality A
** figure provided by fund

Credit Analysis 12-31-94

	% of Bonds		% of Bonds
US Govt	7	BB	14
AAA	28	B	15
AA	15	Below B	0
A	5	NR/NA	1
BBB	15		

Diversification Value for Portfolio Types

Large Cap:	Small Cap:	Bond:	Balanced:	Diversified:

Portfolio 06-30-94

Amount 000	Total Equity: 0 / Total Fixed-Income: 39	Maturity	Value $000	% Total Invest
17266	Resolution Trust 8.25%	07-15-20	15851	7.76
10041	Resolution Trust 9%	03-25-17	10028	4.91
10242	Resolution Trust 8.25%	12-25-20	9996	4.89
12100	Holiday 6.68%	12-15-01	9674	4.73
9826	Cooper Hotel 7.5%	07-15-13	9086	4.45
8785	Resolution Trust 8.835%	12-25-23	8437	4.13
9800	Lehman Brothers ARM	02-25-24	7277	3.56
6687	Resolution Trust 8%	07-25-24	6486	3.17
6633	Lennar Var	06-15-14	5944	2.91
6122	FHA 8.569%	03-29-23	5944	2.91
6000	Resolution Trust 7.875%	01-15-04	5833	2.85
6000	Donaldson Lufkin Jen 7.35%	12-18-05	5562	2.72
5136	FHA 7.43%	07-01-21	4985	2.44
4987	Kidder Peabody Mortgage 8.88%	08-01-03	4962	2.43
5000	SKW Realty 10.75%	04-15-04	4925	2.41
4842	Resolution Trust 9.45%	05-25-24	4887	2.39
4694	Conseco Commercial Mtg 9.7%	07-15-04	4856	2.38
5000	Merrill Lynch Mortgage 8.227%	04-25-23	4833	2.37
4578	FNMA 9.375%	04-01-16	4780	2.34
4366	GNMA 9.5%	09-15-30	4625	2.26
5000	SC Commercial 7.8%	11-28-13	4470	2.19
5000	SC Commercial 7.05%	11-28-13	4420	2.16
4188	Resolution Trust 8.5%	03-25-25	4119	2.02
3889	JHM Acceptance CMO 8.96%	04-01-19	3978	1.95
3942	Resolution Trust 7.7%	07-25-24	3862	1.89

Composition % 12-31-94

Cash	1.1	Preferreds	0.0
Stocks	0.0	Convertibles	0.0
Bonds	98.9	Other	0.0
Leverage factor: 1.44			

Tax Analysis

	Tax-Adj Historical Return %	% Pretax Return
3 Yr Avg	---	---
5 Yr Avg	---	---
10 Yr Avg	---	---

Potential Capital Gain Exposure (% of assets) -10

Most Similar Funds in MF500

Fund lacks 3-year record

Coupon Range

	% of Bonds	Relative Objective
0%, PIK	0.0	0.0
0% to 8.5%	55.1	1.6
8.5% to 9.5%	27.8	1.1
9.5% to 11%	8.7	0.4
More than 11%	0.0	0.0
Not applicable	8.4	1.1

1.0 = Objective Average

Pioneer Income

Ticker	Load	NAV	Yield	SEC Yield	Assets	Objective
MOMIX	4.50%	9.11	7.4%	6.94%	259.9	Income

Pioneer Income Fund seeks current income consistent with preservation of capital. Growth of capital is secondary.

The fund invests in dividend-paying common stocks, together with preferred stocks, bonds, and debentures that may be convertible into common stocks. It seeks companies with above-average earnings potential that are well-situated in industries that may reap the greatest benefit from predicted economic environments. It may also invest in lower-rated or unrated debt securities.

Prior to Dec. 1, 1993, the fund was named Mutual of Omaha Income Fund.

Historical Profile
Return	Below Average
Risk	Low
Rating	★★★ Neutral

Investment Style History
Fixed Income
Income Rtn % Rank Obj

33 38 51 67 71 63 58 46

Growth of $10,000
||| Value of Fund ($000)
— Value of Index ($000) LB L-T
▼ Manager Change
▽ Partial Manager Change
► Mgr Unknown After
◄ Mgr Unknown Before

Performance Quartile (Within Objective)

Manager's Investment Style

This income fund welcomed new managers in 1994. The new conservative management shoots for a 75/25 split between bonds and stocks. To thwart credit risk, the bond portion of the portfolio favors high-quality credits, but does play cross-over bonds--debt securities with S&P and Moody's ratings that differ along the investment-grade/non-investment-grade border--for their upgrade potential. Stock picking is value focused, driven by yield.

1983	1984	1985	1986	1987	1988	1989	1990	1991	1992	1993	1994	History
8.23	8.28	9.17	8.94	8.67	8.92	9.53	9.14	10.14	10.13	10.21	9.11	NAV
7.37	12.38	23.84	9.29	6.78	12.10	15.90	3.59	18.62	7.59	10.24	-4.31	Total Return %
-15.09	6.11	-7.89	-9.39	1.52	-4.51	-15.79	6.70	-11.86	-0.03	0.18	-5.62	+/- S&P 500
-1.00	-2.78	1.72	-5.96	4.03	4.22	1.36	-5.36	2.62	0.34	0.49	-1.39	+/- LB Aggregate
10.43	11.77	10.43	8.86	8.40	9.07	9.06	7.68	7.68	6.75	6.43	6.47	Income Return %
-3.06	0.61	13.41	0.43	-1.62	3.03	6.84	-4.09	10.94	0.84	3.81	-10.77	Capital Return %
91	16	50	87	16	45	44	47	47	51	65	57	Total Rtn % Rank All
83	38	42	62	1	53	34	35	85	63	77	44	Total Rtn % Rank Obj
0.87	0.90	0.80	0.80	0.77	0.78	0.76	0.71	0.65	0.66	0.64	0.67	Income $
0.00	0.00	0.20	0.27	0.13	0.01	0.00	0.00	0.00	0.09	0.30	0.00	Capital Gains $
0.90	0.85	0.80	0.77	0.79	0.80	0.78	0.94	1.04	0.99	1.06	1.07	Expense Ratio %
10.20	10.85	9.05	8.46	8.29	8.55	7.98	7.67	6.73	6.47	6.52	6.51	Income Ratio %
164	165	136	76	115	87	69	44	43	54	69	44	Turnover Rate %
45.7	51.4	75.7	119.1	149.7	159.2	169.6	166.2	197.2	250.0	296.8	259.9	Net Assets ($mil)

Fund Manager(s)

Sherman B. Russ, since 12-93. Birthdate: 07-37.
BA, Middlebury C. 1960   MBA, Columbia U. 1962
John A. Carey CFA(1982), since 12-93. Birthdate: 05-49. AM, Harvard 1972   PhD, Harvard 1979

Manager Experience	Dates Managed	Invest Obj	Std Dev	+/- Index
Sherman B. Russ				
Pioneer Bond A	01/87 - 12/94	CQ	4.09	-0.48
Pioneer Int Shares	12/93 - 12/94	CB	4.23	-0.93

Performance 12-31-94

	1st Qtr	2nd Qtr	3rd Qtr	4th Qtr	Total
1987	7.48	1.91	1.02	-3.50	6.78
1988	5.17	2.51	1.68	2.26	12.10
1989	2.26	6.74	2.89	3.20	15.90
1990	-1.15	3.58	-4.59	6.04	3.59
1991	5.82	0.95	6.58	4.18	18.62
1992	-1.28	2.54	4.43	1.77	7.59
1993	3.45	3.01	3.35	0.09	10.24
1994	-2.97	-1.56	0.73	-0.54	-4.31

Bear Market Performance

Decile Rank (5-year period)

Worst ——————————— Best

	Worst 3 Mo Period 1985-89	Worst 3 Mo Period 1990-94
Pioneer Income	-7.69	-5.70
+/- S&P 500	12.71	8.14
+/- Best Fit Index : LB L-T	-8.56	-4.80

Trailing Returns

	Total Return %	+/- S&P 500	+/- LB Aggregate	% Rank All	Obj	Growth of $10,000
3 Mo	-0.54	-0.52	-0.92	35	27	9,946
6 Mo	0.19	-4.67	-0.80	53	49	10,019
1 Yr	-4.31	-5.62	-1.39	57	44	9,569
3 Yr Avg	4.31	-1.96	-0.24	63	73	11,349
5 Yr Avg	6.88	-1.81	-0.75	53	82	13,945
10 Yr Avg	10.10	-4.28	0.16	57	57	26,185
15 Yr Avg	10.37	-4.12	-0.44	72	83	43,909

Operations

Address and Telephone	60 State Street
	Boston, MA 02109-1820
	800-225-6292 / 617-742-7825
Advisor	Pioneering Management
Subadvisor	None
Distributor	Pioneer Funds Distributor
States Available	All plus PR,GU,VI
Report Grade	B-
Income Distrib	Paid Annually
Date of Inception	05-08-68
Fiscal Year End	December

Risk Analysis

Time Period	Load-Adj Return %	Risk % Rank [1] All	Obj	Morningstar [2] Return	Morningstar Risk	Morningstar Risk-Adj Rating
1 Yr	-8.61					
3 Yr	2.72	35	63	-0.25[3]	0.60	★★★
5 Yr	5.90	44	55	0.28[3]	0.54	★★★
10 Yr	9.60	34	21	0.59	0.48	★★★

Average Historical Rating (109 months)   3.3 ★s

[1] = low, 100 = high   [2] 1.00 = Hybrid Avg   [3] 1.00 = 90-day T-bill return

Other Measures

			Standard S&P 500	Best Fit LB L-T
Standard Deviation	4.62	Alpha	-0.4	-0.3
Mean	4.33	Beta	0.44	0.53
Sharpe Ratio	0.18	R-Squared	55	79

Investment Style

Stocks	Port Avg	Rel S&P 500	Style
Price/Earnings Ratio	19.3	1.05	
Price/Book Ratio	2.5	0.73	
5 Yr Earnings Gr %	-2.6	-0.46	
Med Mkt Cap ($mil)	9125	0.70	

Bonds		Maturity
Avg Effective Duration	6.6 Yrs **	
Avg Effective Maturity	13.0 Yrs	
Avg Credit Quality	A	
Avg Weighted Coupon	9.14%	

**figure provided by fund

Diversification Value for Portfolio Types

Large Cap: Low	Small Cap: High	Bond: Low	Balanced: Low	Diversified: Low

Portfolio 09-30-94

Share Chg (06-94)000	Amount 000	Total Stocks: 31 / Total Fixed-Income: 49	Date of Maturity	Value $000	% Net Assets
	11000	Rural Electric Co-Op 9.7%	09-30-17	12128	4.48
	10000	Rural Electric Co-Op 9.73%	12-15-17	11013	4.06
	102	United Water Res B Pfd 7.625%		10175	3.75
	8000	USX 9.375%	02-15-12	7794	2.88
	6000	Texas Utilities Elec 10.625%	09-01-20	6570	2.42
	5400	US Treasury Note 8.5%	05-15-97	5615	2.07
	5000	BP America 10%	07-01-18	5444	2.01
	5000	General Motors 9.4%	07-15-21	5267	1.94
	5000	General Electric Cap 8.85%	04-01-05	5255	1.94
	4850	Hydro-Quebec 9.75%	01-15-18	5248	1.94
	5000	NorAm Energy 10%	11-15-19	5125	1.89
	5000	Commonwealth Edison 9.75%	02-15-20	5099	1.88
0	50	Atlantic Richfield		5044	1.86
	5000	Bowater 9%	08-01-09	4940	1.82
	4922	Mexico City-Toluca Toll Rd 11%	06-16-02	4844	1.79
	5000	BellSouth Telecomm 8.625%	09-01-26	4836	1.78
	4950	AMR 9.875%	06-15-20	4672	1.72
	5000	Banco Nacl de Comercio 7.5%	07-01-00	4606	1.70
	5000	Old Dominion Electric 7.48%	12-01-13	4552	1.68
	5000	Delta Air Lines 9.2%	09-23-14	4340	1.60

Index Allocation
	% of Stocks
S&P 500	57.2
S&P MidCap 400	15.7
U.S. Small Cap	27.1
Foreign	0.0

Composition % 12-31-94
Cash	0.0	Preferreds	0.0
Stocks	26.5	Convertibles	7.8
Bonds	65.7	Other	0.0

Tax Analysis
	Tax-Adj Historical Return %	% Pretax Return
3 Yr Avg	1.51	34.0
5 Yr Avg	4.22	58.2
10 Yr Avg	6.75	57.0
Potential Capital Gain Exposure (% of assets)		-4%

Most Similar Funds in MF500
Scudder Income	Strong Fit
USAA Mutual Income	Strong Fit
Fidelity Government Secs	Strong Fit

Bond Credit Analysis 12-31-94
% of Bonds
US Govt	12	BB	11
AAA	22	B	3
AA	3	Below B	0
A	7	NR/NA	3
BBB	39		

Stock Sector Weightings
	% of Stocks	Relative S&P 500
Utilities	34.8	2.81
Energy	11.6	1.15
Financials	26.6	2.51
Industrial Cyclicals	3.4	0.21
Consumer Durables	3.9	0.63
Consumer Staples	14.9	1.19
Services	2.1	0.26
Retail	2.6	0.45
Health	0.0	0.00
Technology	0.0	0.00

Min Initial Purchase / Expenses & Fees
Min Initial Purchase	$1000 (Addt'l: $50)
Min IRA Purchase	$1000 (Addt'l: $50)
Min Auto Invest Plan	$50 (Systematic Inv: $50)

Expenses & Fees	
Sales Fees	4.50% front
	0.00% deferred
	0.25% 12b-1
Management Fee	0.50% max./0.45% min.
3-,5-,10-yr Expense Projections	$78, $103, $173
Annual Brokerage Cost	0.02%

MORNINGSTAR   **1995 Mutual Fund 500**

Portico Bond Immdex Ret

	Ticker	Load	NAV	Yield	SEC Yield	Assets	Objective
	POBIX	2.00%	25.29	6.5%	7.86%	249.5	Corp Hi Qlty

Portico Bond Immdex Fund - Retail Shares seeks a total return that replicates the Lehman Brothers Government/Corporate Bond Index.

The fund normally invests at least 65% of its assets in investment-grade fixed-income securities. It uses quantitative investment techniques, including an index immunization model designed to define and measure the overall price sensitivity of the index. Normally, the majority of the securities held by the fund are included in the index. The fund attempts to maintain a dollar-weighted average portfolio maturity of more than five years and a correlation between its own performance and that of the index within +/- 0.5%.

Manager's Investment Style

Management stays in step with the Lehman Brothers Government Corporate Index by pegging duration to this benchmark, with a goal of beating the index over the long run via methods other than interest-rate plays. Sector selection, for example, is a key component of the team's efforts through over- or underweighting certain sectors. Further, the team aims to add value through yield-curve plays that depart from the index.

Historical Profile
Return: High
Risk: Average
Rating: ★★★★ Above Average

Investment Style History
Fixed Income
Income Rtn % Rank Obj

Growth of $10,000
|||| Value of Fund ($000)
— Value of Index ($000) LB Govt
▼ Manager Change
▽ Partial Manager Change
► Mgr Unknown After
◄ Mgr Unknown Before

Performance Quartile (Within Objective)

Fund Manager(s)

Mary Ellen Stanek CFA, since 12-89. Birthdate: 04-56. BA, Marquette U. 1978 MBA, U. of Wisconsin-Milwaukee 1984

Teresa Westman CFA(1990), since 01-92.

Manager Experience	Dates Managed	Invest Obj	Std Dev	+/- Index
Mary Ellen Stanek				
Portico Shrt-Trm Bond Ret	12/89 - 12/94	CG	2.36	-0.61
Portico Int Bond Mkt Ret	01/93 - 12/94	CG	2.91	0.04

	1983	1984	1985	1986	1987	1988	1989	1990	1991	1992	1993	1994	History
	---	---	---	---	---	---	25.00	25.05	27.03	27.04	27.82	25.29	NAV
	---	---	---	---	---	---	0.00 *	8.22	16.59	7.56	10.96	-3.06	Total Return %
	---	---	---	---	---	---	---	-0.73	0.58	0.31	1.21	-0.14	+/- LB Aggregate
	---	---	---	---	---	---	---	1.07	-1.92	-1.14	-1.21	0.87	+/- LB Corporate
	---	---	---	---	---	---	0.00	8.02	8.10	6.74	6.17	5.90	Income Return %
	---	---	---	---	---	---	0.00	0.20	8.49	0.82	4.79	-8.96	Capital Return %
	---	---	---	---	---	---	---	13	52	51	60	44	Total Rtn % Rank All
	---	---	---	---	---	---	---	42	20	15	21	55	Total Rtn % Rank Obj
	---	---	---	---	---	---	0.00	1.90	1.89	1.77	1.65	1.64	Income $
	---	---	---	---	---	---	0.00	0.00	0.14	0.21	0.50	0.04	Capital Gains $
	---	---	---	---	---	---	---	0.50	0.50	0.50	0.50	0.49	Expense Ratio %
	---	---	---	---	---	---	---	8.10	7.85	6.92	6.10	5.96	Income Ratio %
	---	---	---	---	---	---	---	---	132	38	81	---	Turnover Rate %
	---	---	---	---	---	---	---	61.6	100.7	189.4	255.0	249.5	Net Assets ($mil)

Performance 12-31-94

	1st Qtr	2nd Qtr	3rd Qtr	4th Qtr	Total
1987	---	---	---	---	---
1988	---	---	---	---	---
1989	---	---	---	---	0.00 *
1990	-1.03	3.12	0.83	5.17	8.22
1991	2.39	1.91	6.02	5.38	16.59
1992	-1.35	3.70	4.98	0.14	7.56
1993	4.57	3.12	3.19	-0.29	10.96
1994	-2.90	-1.02	0.64	0.22	-3.06

Bear Market Performance

Decile Rank (5-year period)
Worst — Best

	Worst 3 Mo Period 1985-89	Worst 3 Mo Period 1990-94
Portico Bond Immdex Ret	---	-5.30
+/- LB Aggregate	---	-0.37
+/- Best Fit Index : LB Govt	---	-0.22

Trailing Returns

	Total Return %	+/- LB Aggregate	+/- LB Corporate	% Rank All	% Rank Obj	Growth of $10,000
3 Mo	0.22	-0.16	-0.22	16	42	10,022
6 Mo	0.86	-0.13	-0.31	40	35	10,086
1 Yr	-3.06	-0.14	0.87	44	55	9,694
3 Yr Avg	4.98	0.43	-0.43	49	11	11,569
5 Yr Avg	7.86	0.23	-0.41	35	6	14,597
10 Yr Avg	---	---	---	---	---	---
15 Yr Avg	---	---	---	---	---	---

Operations

Address and Telephone	207 E. Buffalo Street
	Milwaukee, WI 53202
	800-228-1024 / 414-287-3808
Advisor	Firstar Investment Research & Managem
Subadvisor	None
Distributor	Sunstone Financial Group
States Available	All
Report Grade	B-
Income Distrib	Paid Quarterly
* Date of Inception	12-29-89
Fiscal Year End	October

Risk Analysis

Time Period	Load-Adj Return %	Risk % Rank All	Risk % Rank Obj	Morningstar Return	Morningstar Risk	Morningstar Risk-Adj Rating
1 Yr	-3.06					
3 Yr	4.98	21	54	0.41 [3]	0.98	★★★★
5 Yr	7.86	20	55	0.77 [3]	0.95	★★★★
10 Yr	---	---	---			

Average Historical Rating (25 months) 4.8 ★ s

[1] 1 = low, 100 = high [2] 1.00 = Taxable Avg [3] 1.00 = 90-day T-bill return

Other Measures

			Standard LB Agg	Best Fit LB Govt
Standard Deviation	4.36	Alpha	0.4	0.3
Mean	4.96	Beta	1.08	1.00
Sharpe Ratio	0.33	R-Squared	97	99

Investment Style

Interest-Rate Stance
Avg Effective Duration 5.7 Yrs
Avg Effective Maturity 6.9 Yrs

Quality
Avg Credit Quality AA
Avg Weighted Coupon 8.33%
Avg Weighted Price 102.80% of Par

Diversification Value for Portfolio Types

Large Cap: Medium
Small Cap: High
Bond: None
Balanced: Medium
Diversified: Medium

Portfolio 12-31-94

Total Stocks: 0
Total Fixed-Income: 53

Amount 000	Date of Maturity		Value $000	%.Net Assets
62000	02-15-16	US Treasury Bond 9.25%	69692	27.94
19000	01-31-98	US Treasury Note 5.625%	17866	7.16
12000	05-15-99	Discover Card Master Tr 5.4%	10908	4.37
8890	03-15-98	Heller Financial 9.375%	9112	3.65
9400	09-15-00	MBNA CC Master Trust 5.4%	8559	3.43
8750	08-15-00	Sears Master Trust 7%	8356	3.35
8600	09-15-99	Goldman Sachs 6.875%	7980	3.20
8575	01-07-99	Standard CC Master Tr 5.5%	7774	3.12
5753	10-15-99	Chrysler Financial 13.25%	6772	2.71
6060	05-15-99	Lehman Brothers Hldgs 10%	6181	2.48
6300	02-26-98	Ford Motor Credit 6.25%	5921	2.37
5050	04-07-97	Mony Funding 8.125%	4981	2.00
4280	06-15-99	Chase Manhattan 10%	4482	1.80
3900	11-10-20	FNMA Note 9.5%	4098	1.64
3925	06-15-99	Chemical Banking 9.75%	4076	1.63
3500	12-15-98	Intl Lease Finance 9.82%	3698	1.48
3250	02-01-03	BankAmerica 10%	3463	1.39
2479	11-15-03	Midland American Cap 12.75%	2823	1.13
2600	09-20-03	Household Finance CC Tr 7.8%	2572	1.03
2600	12-15-00	Banc One CC Master Trust 7.8%	2571	1.03
2800	01-30-98	Salomon 5.5%	2548	1.02
2365	06-15-96	Household Finance 10.125%	2434	0.98
2300	07-15-00	Household Finance 9.625%	2398	0.96
2400	11-01-98	Lehman Brothers Hldgs 8.875%	2351	0.94
2300	06-01-98	Lehman Brothers Hldgs 6.375%	2096	0.84

Composition % 12-31-94

Cash	6.6	Preferreds	0.0
Stocks	0.0	Convertibles	0.0
Bonds	93.5	Other	0.0

Tax Analysis

	Tax-Adj Historical Return %	% Pretax Return
3 Yr Avg	2.40	47.1
5 Yr Avg	5.28	63.8
10 Yr Avg	---	---
Potential Capital Gain Exposure (% of assets)		-6%

Most Similar Funds in MF500

Columbia Fixed-Income Secs	Strong Fit
U.S. Government Securities	Strong Fit
American Cap Corp Bond A	Strong Fit

Coupon Range

	% of Bonds	Rel Obj
0%	0.0	0.00
0% to 8.5%	27.7	0.40
8.5% to 9.5%	46.4	3.55
9.5% to 11%	16.3	3.54
More than 11%	8.9	3.83
Not applicable	0.7	0.10

Credit Analysis 12-31-94

% of Bonds
US Govt	42	BB	0
AAA	17	B	0
AA	1	Below B	0
A	37	NR/NA	0
BBB	3		

Expenses & Fees

Sales Fees	2.00% front
	0.00% deferred
	0.00% 12b-1
Management Fee	0.30% flat fee+0.40%l, 0.13%A
3-,5-,10-yr Expense Projections	$19, $31, $67

Min Initial Purchase	$1000 (Addt'l: $100)
Min IRA Purchase	$100 (Addt'l: $100)
Min Auto Invest Plan	$50 (Systematic Inv: $50)

T. Rowe Price Balanced

	Ticker	Load	NAV	Yield	SEC Yield	Assets	Objective
	RPBAX	None	11.14	3.8%	N/A	392.0	Balanced

T. Rowe Price Balanced Fund seeks capital appreciation and current income consistent with preservation of capital.

The fund normally invests approximately 60% of its assets in common stocks and maintains at least 25% of assets in senior fixed-income securities. The fund may invest up to 15% of its assets in foreign securities, and up to 20% in mortgage-backed securities. It may also invest up to 10% of its assets in debt securities rated below investment grade.

Prior to Aug. 31, 1992, this fund was named USF&G Axe-Houghton Fund - Class B. On Aug. 31, 1992, the original T. Rowe Price Balanced Fund merged into this fund.

Manager's Investment Style

Management's strategy blends a fixed-income stake with domestic equities, and throws in a foreign-stock kicker for good measure. The bond and foreign positions are managed from the top down, while domestic stock picks shadow the S&P 500. This fund provides high diversification.

Historical Profile

Return	Above Average
Risk	Below Average
Rating	★★★★ Above Average

Investment Style History Equity

Average % Stocks Held in Portfolio

| 58% | 44% | 33% | 34% | 50% | 56% | 60% | 57% |

Growth of $10,000

- |||| Value of Fund ($000)
- — Value of Index ($000) S&P 500
- ▼ Manager Change
- ▽ Partial Manager Change
- ► Mgr Unknown After
- ◄ Mgr Unknown Before

Performance Quartile (Within Objective)

	1983	1984	1985	1986	1987	1988	1989	1990	1991	1992	1993	1994	History
	11.25	11.08	13.81	12.81	8.85	9.15	10.33	10.37	11.42	11.07	12.02	11.14	NAV
	10.98	6.37	33.01	23.12	-3.38	8.99	20.69	7.14	21.99	7.27	13.35	-2.05	Total Return %
	-11.48	0.11	1.27	4.44	-8.64	-7.62	-11.00	10.26	-8.49	-0.35	3.29	-3.37	+/- S&P 500
	2.61	-8.78	10.88	7.87	-6.13	1.12	6.15	-1.80	5.99	0.02	3.60	0.86	+/- LB Aggregate
	6.29	6.56	8.32	5.56	6.79	5.58	7.79	6.75	6.05	4.34	3.66	3.68	Income Return %
	4.69	-0.19	24.69	17.56	-10.17	3.41	12.90	0.39	15.94	2.93	9.69	-5.73	Capital Return %
	75	45	17	11	82	68	34	20	41	54	38	34	Total Rtn % Rank All
	92	57	14	6	83	76	39	7	64	51	27	39	Total Rtn % Rank Obj
	0.68	0.68	0.76	0.76	0.78	0.48	0.68	0.66	0.61	0.47	0.39	0.43	Income $
	0.15	0.15	0.00	3.21	2.84	0.00	0.00	0.00	0.57	0.67	0.11	0.20	Capital Gains $
	0.73	0.76	0.74	0.98	1.18	1.25	1.15	0.94	1.10	1.00	1.00	1.00	Expense Ratio %
	6.89	6.60	6.93	5.76	3.81	5.19	6.27	6.82	5.61	3.85	3.45	3.67	Income Ratio %
	64	88	97	239	324	251	219	127	240	58	9	46	Turnover Rate %
	147.7	141.2	152.6	180.7	169.6	158.8	163.9	162.4	174.0	250.0	340.8	392.0	Net Assets ($mil)

Fund Manager(s)

Richard T. Whitney CFA(1988), since 03-91.
Birthdate: 05-58. MS, Rice U. 1981 MBA, U. of Chicago 1985
Edmund Notzon III, since 03-91.

Manager Experience

	Dates Managed	Invest Obj	Std Dev	+/- Index
Richard T. Whitney				
T. Rowe Price Equity Idx	03/90 - 12/94	GI	11.92	-0.42
Advance Capital I Bal	12/93 - 12/94	B	8.24	-4.03

Performance 12-31-94

	1st Qtr	2nd Qtr	3rd Qtr	4th Qtr	Total
1987	16.54	-2.53	4.22	-18.38	-3.38
1988	3.75	2.37	0.82	1.78	8.99
1989	3.50	7.68	5.82	2.34	20.69
1990	-1.45	2.79	-2.28	8.24	7.14
1991	6.27	1.47	3.93	8.86	21.99
1992	-3.43	3.38	3.34	3.96	7.27
1993	4.34	1.06	4.30	3.06	13.35
1994	-3.92	-1.14	3.74	-0.61	-2.05

Bear Market Performance

Decile Rank (5-year period)

Worst ———————————— Best

	Worst 3 Mo Period 1985-89	Worst 3 Mo Period 1990-94
T. Rowe Price Balanced	-24.03	-4.99
+/- S&P 500	5.56	0.76
+/- Best Fit Index : S&P 500	5.56	0.76

Trailing Returns

	Total Return %	+/- S&P 500	+/- LB Aggregate	% Rank All	% Rank Obj	Growth of $10,000
3 Mo	-0.61	-0.59	-0.99	36	38	9,939
6 Mo	3.11	-1.75	2.12	20	16	10,311
1 Yr	-2.05	-3.37	0.86	34	39	9,795
3 Yr Avg	6.00	-0.27	1.45	34	38	11,909
5 Yr Avg	9.25	0.56	1.63	22	19	15,565
10 Yr Avg	12.47	-1.91	2.53	32	21	32,397
15 Yr Avg	12.45	-2.03	1.65	49	60	58,159

Operations

Address and Telephone	100 E. Pratt Street
	Baltimore, MD 21202
	800-638-5660 / 410-547-2308
Advisor	T. Rowe Price Associates
Subadvisor	None
Distributor	T. Rowe Price Investment Services
States Available	All
Report Grade	A+
Income Distrib	Paid Quarterly
Date of Inception	05-01-38
Fiscal Year End	December

Risk Analysis

Time Period	Load-Adj Return %	Risk % Rank [1] All	Risk % Rank [1] Obj	Morningstar [2] Return	Morningstar Risk	Morningstar Risk-Adj Rating
1 Yr	-2.05					
3 Yr	6.00	50	51	0.71 [3]	0.71	★★★
5 Yr	9.25	46	9	1.15 [3]	0.58	★★★★
10 Yr	12.47	42	42	1.16	0.69	★★★★

Average Historical Rating (109 months) 3.6 ★s

[1] 1 = low, 100 = high   [2] 1.00 = Hybrid Avg   [3] 1.00 = 90-day T-bill return

Other Measures

		Standard S&P 500	Best Fit S&P 500
Standard Deviation	6.21	Alpha	0.5	0.5
Mean	6.03	Beta	0.70	0.70
Sharpe Ratio	0.40	R-Squared	80	80

Investment Style

Stocks

	Port Avg	Rel S&P 500
Price/Earnings Ratio	20.0	1.08
Price/Book Ratio	3.5	1.02
5 Yr Earnings Gr %	7.6	1.37
Med Mkt Cap ($mil)	7762	0.60

Style: V B G / Size L M S

Bonds

Avg Effective Duration	5.0 Yrs
Avg Effective Maturity	9.7 Yrs
Avg Credit Quality	AA
Avg Weighted Coupon	8.69%

Maturity: S I L / Quality H M L

Diversification Value for Portfolio Types

Large Cap: Low	Small Cap: Medium	Bond: Medium	Balanced: None	Diversified: Low

Portfolio 12-31-94

Total Stocks: 346
Total Fixed-Income: 144

Share Chg (06-94)000	Amount 000		Date of Maturity	Value $000	% Net Assets
	6317	GNMA 8.5%	01-15-27	6224	1.59
	6289	GNMA 7.5%	12-15-23	5840	1.49
	5616	GNMA 8%	08-15-23	5391	1.38
	5200	US Treasury Note 7%	04-15-99	5039	1.29
	4000	US Treasury Note 8%	05-15-01	4031	1.03
0	75	General Electric		3845	0.98
	4000	US Treasury Note 6.375%	01-15-00	3761	0.96
	4074	GNMA 7%	01-15-24	3660	0.93
	3600	US Treasury Note 6.375%	06-30-97	3489	0.89
0	35	American International Group		3469	0.88
	3408	GNMA 9%	08-20-22	3446	0.88
	4000	FNMA Debenture 5.8%	12-10-03	3410	0.87
	3218	GNMA 9.5%	09-15-21	3327	0.85
0	39	Mobil		3277	0.84
	2800	US Treasury Note 8.25%	07-15-98	2835	0.72
0	30	ALCOA		2599	0.66
	2125	British Col Hydro Pwr 15.5%	11-15-11	2508	0.64
	2500	US Treasury Note 7.75%	02-15-01	2490	0.64
0	41	Exxon		2466	0.63
0	46	Coca-Cola		2384	0.61

Index Allocation

	% of Stocks
S&P 500	61.1
S&P MidCap 400	10.3
U.S. Small Cap	10.6
Foreign	18.6

Composition % 12-31-94

Cash	9.1	Preferreds	0.0
Stocks	54.1	Convertibles	0.3
Bonds	36.6	Other	0.0

Tax Analysis

	Tax-Adj Historical Return %	% Pretax Return
3 Yr Avg	3.79	61.8
5 Yr Avg	6.83	70.3
10 Yr Avg	8.65	57.7

Potential Capital Gain Exposure (% of assets) 3%

Most Similar Funds in MF500

Overland Exp Asset Alloc A	Strong Fit
Vanguard Asset Allocation	Strong Fit
Investment Comp of America	Strong Fit

Min Initial Purchase / Expenses & Fees

Min Initial Purchase	$2500 (Addt'l: $100)
Min IRA Purchase	$1000 (Addt'l: $50)
Min Auto Invest Plan	$50 (Systematic Inv: $50)

Expenses & Fees

Sales Fees	0.00% front
	0.00% deferred
	0.00% 12b-1
Management Fee	0.15% flat fee+0.48%G
3-,5-,10-yr Expense Projections	$32, $55, $122
Annual Brokerage Cost	0.03%

Bond Credit Analysis 12-31-94
% of Bonds

US Govt	19	BB	7
AAA	36	B	10
AA	7	Below B	0
A	12	NR/NA	0
BBB	9		

Stock Sector Weightings

	% of Stocks	Relative S&P 500
Utilities	10.9	0.88
Energy	8.2	0.80
Financials	14.8	1.40
Industrial Cyclicals	17.8	1.09
Consumer Durables	7.6	1.23
Consumer Staples	10.0	0.79
Services	10.8	1.33
Retail	4.7	0.81
Health	6.6	0.76
Technology	8.7	0.95

T. Rowe Price Capital Apprec

	Ticker	Load	NAV	Yield	SEC Yield	Assets	Objective
	PRWCX	None	12.10	2.7%	N/A	655.0	Growth

T. Rowe Price Capital Appreciation Fund seeks capital appreciation consistent with low volatility.

The fund invests primarily in common stocks that are undervalued relative to a company's assets, earnings and growth potential, replacement cost of plants or equipment, and/or consumer or commercial franchise value. Securities that are temporarily out of favor are also prime candidates for portfolio selection. The fund may invest up to 35% of its assets in debt obligations; up to 5% of the debt may be rated below investment grade. The fund may also invest up to 10% of its assets in foreign issues.

Manager's Investment Style

Management practices an extreme value approach, and uses a stock's price/book ratio as the measurement. If there aren't good stock values available, management will look elsewhere. This approach has led the portfolio to appear a lot different than most growth-fund portfolios: It includes securities from every asset class, and typically features at least a 20% cash position. The fund thus looks more like an asset-allocation vehicle than a growth offering.

Fund Manager(s)

Richard P. Howard CFA(1976), since 01-89.
Birthdate: 09-46. BS, Millikin U. 1969 MBA, Harvard 1971

Manager Experience

	Dates Managed	Invest Obj	Std Dev	+/- Index

Not available.

Historical Profile

Return	Above Average
Risk	Low
Rating	★★★★ Above Average

Investment Style History
Equity
Average % Stocks Held in Portfolio

Average % Stocks Held: 61% 80% 56% 57% 55% 54% 52% 51%

Growth of $10,000

- |||| Value of Fund ($000)
- — Value of Index ($000) S&P 500
- ▼ Manager Change
- ▽ Partial Manager Change
- ► Mgr Unknown After
- ◄ Mgr Unknown Before

Performance Quartile (Within Objective)

	1983	1984	1985	1986	1987	1988	1989	1990	1991	1992	1993	1994	History
NAV	---	---	---	10.85	9.15	10.42	10.82	9.98	11.02	11.39	12.66	12.10	
Total Return %	---	---	---	8.50 *	5.74	21.21	21.42	-1.25	21.59	9.36	15.66	3.80	
+/- S&P 500	---	---	---	10.28 *	0.48	4.60	-10.26	1.87	-8.90	1.74	5.60	2.48	
+/- Wilshire 5000	---	---	---		3.38	3.27	-7.75	4.93	-12.62	0.39	4.38	3.87	
Income Return %	---	---	---	0.00	4.88	2.90	4.25	3.77	4.23	4.51	1.49	2.85	
Capital Return %	---	---	---	8.50	0.86	18.30	17.17	-5.01	17.35	4.85	14.17	0.95	
Total Rtn % Rank All	---	---	---		20	11	33	59	42	28	26	6	
Total Rtn % Rank Obj	---	---	---		29	19	76	28	92	41	30	10	
Income $	---	---	---	0.00	0.48	0.28	0.45	0.39	0.43	0.50	0.18	0.35	
Capital Gains $	---	---	---	0.00	1.85	0.37	1.36	0.31	0.64	0.16	0.33	0.69	
Expense Ratio %	---	---	---	1.20	1.20	1.50	1.50	1.25	1.20	1.08	1.09	1.11	
Income Ratio %	---	---	---	2.16	3.03	2.76	3.85	3.44	3.90	4.28	2.37	2.63	
Turnover Rate %	---	---	---		291	166	99	50	51	30	39	50	
Net Assets ($mil)	---	---	---	69.0	63.9	101.3	133.2	141.9	215.7	359.3	535.7	655.0	

Performance 12-31-94

	1st Qtr	2nd Qtr	3rd Qtr	4th Qtr	Total
1987	9.85	2.28	4.38	-9.83	5.74
1988	7.92	8.37	0.47	3.16	21.21
1989	6.81	6.65	6.99	-0.38	21.42
1990	-0.37	2.13	-9.90	7.71	-1.25
1991	12.22	1.70	2.81	3.63	21.59
1992	1.27	2.15	3.60	2.05	9.36
1993	4.48	2.77	2.62	4.97	15.66
1994	-0.79	0.24	5.64	-1.20	3.80

Bear Market Performance

Decile Rank (5-year period)

Worst ————————————— Best

	Worst 3 Mo Period 1985-89	Worst 3 Mo Period 1990-94
T. Rowe Price Capital Apprec	---	-12.79
+/- S&P 500	---	1.06
+/- Best Fit Index : S&P 500	---	1.06

Trailing Returns

	Total Return %	+/- S&P 500	+/- Wil 5000	% Rank All	% Rank Obj	Growth of $10,000
3 Mo	-1.20	-1.18	-0.43	49	49	9,880
6 Mo	4.38	-0.49	-0.25	14	43	10,438
1 Yr	3.80	2.48	3.87	6	10	10,380
3 Yr Avg	9.50	3.23	2.89	15	21	13,129
5 Yr Avg	9.53	0.84	0.71	20	35	15,764
10 Yr Avg	---	---	---	---	---	---
15 Yr Avg	---	---	---	---	---	---

Operations

Address and Telephone	100 E. Pratt Street
	Baltimore, MD 21202
	800-638-5660 / 410-547-2308
Advisor	T. Rowe Price Associates
Subadvisor	None
Distributor	T. Rowe Price Investment Services
States Available	All plus GU,PR,VI
Report Grade	A-
Income Distrib	Paid Annually
* Date of Inception	06-30-86
Fiscal Year End	December

Risk Analysis

Time Period	Load-Adj Return %	Risk % Rank [1] All	Obj	Morningstar [2] Return	Risk	Morningstar Risk-Adj Rating
1 Yr	3.80					
3 Yr	9.50	12	1	1.81 [3]	0.31	★★★★
5 Yr	9.53	48	3	1.22 [3]	0.47	★★★★
10 Yr	---	---	---	---	---	

Average Historical Rating (67 months)   4.4 ★s

[1] 1 = low, 100 = high [2] 1.00 = Equity Avg [3] 1.00 = 90-day T-bill return

Other Measures

		Standard S&P 500	Best Fit S&P 500
Standard Deviation	5.02	Alpha	4.2	4.2
Mean	9.23	Beta	0.54	0.54
Sharpe Ratio	1.14	R-Squared	71	71

Investment Style

	Stock Portfolio Avg	Relative S&P 500
Price/Earnings Ratio	20.8	1.13
Price/Book Ratio	2.0	0.60
5 Yr Earnings Gr %	3.4	0.61
Return on Assets %	4.2	0.56
Debt % Total Cap	38.0	1.35
Med Mkt Cap ($mil)	2301	0.18

Style Value Blend Growth / Size Large Med Small

Diversification Value for Portfolio Types

Large Cap: Low	Small Cap: Medium	Bond: High	Balanced: Low	Diversified: Low

Expenses & Fees

Sales Fees	0.00% front
	0.00% deferred
	0.00% 12b-1
Management Fee	0.30% flat fee+0.48%G+(-)0.30%P
3-,5-,10-yr Expense Projections	$35, $60, $133
Annual Brokerage Cost	0.25%

Portfolio 12-31-94

Total Stocks: 56
Total Fixed-Income: 31

Share Chg (06-94) 000	Amount 000		Value $000	% Net Assets
	70000	Automatic Data Process Cv 0%	28788	4.40
538	1090	Petrie Stores	24384	3.72
	17950	Rockefeller Center Euro Cv 8%	16604	2.53
465	700	Entergy	15313	2.34
25	175	Loews	15203	2.32
-75	250	Philip Morris	14375	2.19
440	440	SLMA	14300	2.18
	550	Manville Cl B Pfd $2.70	12788	1.95
	18000	Delta Air Lines Cv 3.23%	12735	1.94
35	200	Texaco	11975	1.83
2	48	Washington Post Cl B	11640	1.78
-30	160	Eli Lilly	10500	1.60
0	100	Atlantic Richfield	10175	1.55
130	280	PHH	9730	1.49
	232	Tandy Cl C PERCS $2.14	8758	1.34
50	220	Weyerhaeuser	8250	1.26
	7500	Champion International Cv 6.5%	8152	1.24
	8500	Federated Department Stores 6%	8128	1.24
	8000	CIGNA Cv 8.2%	8125	1.24
9	250	Polaroid	8125	1.24
600	900	Centerior Energy	7988	1.22
20	600	Public Service New Mexico	7800	1.19
20	260	American Express	7670	1.17
15	175	Unitrin	7525	1.15
70	820	Manville	7380	1.13

Composition % 12-31-94

Cash	19.1	Preferreds	4.5
Stocks	50.4	Convertibles	21.5
Bonds	4.6	Other	0.0

Tax Analysis

	Tax-Adj Historical Return %	% Pretax Return
3 Yr Avg	7.52	77.6
5 Yr Avg	7.30	73.3
10 Yr Avg	---	---
Potential Capital Gain Exposure (% of assets)		4%

Most Similar Funds in MF500

T. Rowe Price Equity-Income	Fair Fit
Dodge & Cox Balanced	Fair Fit
Crabbe Huson Asset Alloc	Fair Fit

Index Allocation

	% of Stocks
S&P 500	51.4
S&P MidCap 400	17.5
U.S. Small Cap	30.4
Foreign	0.8

Sector Weightings

	% of Stocks	Relative S&P 500
Utilities	12.5	1.01
Energy	19.0	1.88
Financials	13.6	1.28
Industrial Cyclicals	11.4	0.69
Consumer Durables	2.2	0.35
Consumer Staples	7.2	0.57
Services	18.4	2.26
Retail	9.2	1.57
Health	5.0	0.57
Technology	1.7	0.19

Min Purchase

Min Initial Purchase	$2500 (Addt'l: $100)
Min IRA Purchase	$1000 (Addt'l: $50)
Min Auto Invest Plan	$50 (Systematic Inv: $50)

T. Rowe Price Dividend Growth

	Ticker	Load	NAV	Yield	SEC Yield	Assets	Objective
	PRDGX	None	11.04	3.0%	N/A	53.6	Growth/Inc.

T. Rowe Price Dividend Growth Fund seeks income and capital appreciation.

The fund normally invests at least 65% of its assets in dividend-paying common stocks that demonstrate increasing dividend payments and long-term capital growth. It intends to diversify; no more than 25% of its assets may be invested in any one industry sector. Up to 25% of the fund's assets may be invested in convertible securities, preferred stocks, and corporate or government debt; these securities are primarily investment-grade. Up to 25% of its assets may be invested in foreign securities.

Manager's Investment Style

Management combines a dividend-growth-rate approach with a value bent. It limits stock picks to those common stocks with histories of rising dividends, or those with the future probability of accelerating income. Further, it avoids overweighting any one individual sector, and it will hold cash when appropriate.

Historical Profile
Return ---
Risk ---
Rating
Not Rated

Investment Style History
Equity
Average % Stocks Held in Portfolio
72% 76%

Growth of $10,000
‖‖‖ Value of Fund ($000)
— Value of Index ($000)
S&P 500
▼ Manager Change
▽ Partial Manager Change
► Mgr Unknown After
◄ Mgr Unknown Before

Performance Quartile
(Within Objective)

Fund Manager(s)

William J. Stromberg CFA(1990), since 12-92.
Birthdate: 03-60. BA, Johns Hopkins U. 1982 MBA, Dartmouth C. 1987

Manager Experience

	Dates Managed	Invest Obj	Std Dev	+/- Index
Not available.				

	1983	1984	1985	1986	1987	1988	1989	1990	1991	1992	1993	1994	History
	---	---	---	---	---	---	---	---	---	10.00	11.48	11.04	NAV
	---	---	---	---	---	---	---	---	---	---	19.41	2.16	Total Return %
	---	---	---	---	---	---	---	---	---	---	9.35	0.85	+/- S&P 500
	---	---	---	---	---	---	---	---	---	---	8.12	2.23	+/- Wilshire 5000
	---	---	---	---	---	---	---	---	---	---	2.95	3.05	Income Return %
	---	---	---	---	---	---	---	---	---	---	16.46	-0.89	Capital Return %
	---	---	---	---	---	---	---	---	---	---	18	10	Total Rtn % Rank All
	---	---	---	---	---	---	---	---	---	---	7	12	Total Rtn % Rank Obj
	---	---	---	---	---	---	---	---	---	0.00	0.29	0.34	Income $
	---	---	---	---	---	---	---	---	---	0.00	0.15	0.34	Capital Gains $
	---	---	---	---	---	---	---	---	---	---	1.00	1.00	Expense Ratio %
	---	---	---	---	---	---	---	---	---	---	2.60	2.85	Income Ratio %
	---	---	---	---	---	---	---	---	---	---	51	79	Turnover Rate %
	---	---	---	---	---	---	---	---	---	---	40.7	53.6	Net Assets ($mil)

Performance 12-31-94

	1st Qtr	2nd Qtr	3rd Qtr	4th Qtr	Total
1987	---	---	---	---	---
1988	---	---	---	---	---
1989	---	---	---	---	---
1990	---	---	---	---	---
1991	---	---	---	---	---
1992	---	---	---	---	---
1993	8.90	1.02	3.32	5.05	19.41
1994	-2.97	0.81	3.89	0.53	2.16

Bear Market Performance

Decile Rank (5-year period)

Worst — Best

	Worst 3 Mo Period 1985-89	Worst 3 Mo Period 1990-94
T. Rowe Price Dividend Growth	---	---
+/- S&P 500	---	---
+/- Best Fit Index :	---	---

Trailing Returns

	Total Return %	+/- S&P 500	+/- Wil 5000	% Rank All	% Rank Obj	Growth of $10,000
3 Mo	0.53	0.55	1.30	11	7	10,053
6 Mo	4.44	-0.42	-0.18	13	23	10,444
1 Yr	2.16	0.85	2.23	10	12	10,216
3 Yr Avg	---	---	---	---	---	---
5 Yr Avg	---	---	---	---	---	---
10 Yr Avg	---	---	---	---	---	---
15 Yr Avg	---	---	---	---	---	---

Risk Analysis

Time Period	Load-Adj Return %	Risk % Rank All	Obj	Morningstar Return	Morningstar Risk	Morningstar Risk-Adj Rating
1 Yr	2.16					
3 Yr	---	---	---	---	---	---
5 Yr	---	---	---	---	---	---
10 Yr	---	---	---	---	---	---

Average Historical Rating ---

[1] 1 = low, 100 = high [2] 1.00 = Equity Avg [3] 1.00 = 90-day T-bill return

Other Measures

		Standard S&P 500	Best Fit
Standard Deviation	---	Alpha	---	---
Mean	---	Beta	---	---
Sharpe Ratio	---	R-Squared	---	---

Investment Style

	Stock Portfolio Avg	Relative S&P 500
Price/Earnings Ratio	18.1	0.98
Price/Book Ratio	3.3	0.99
5 Yr Earnings Gr %	5.5	0.99
Return on Assets %	7.7	1.03
Debt % Total Cap	26.6	0.94
Med Mkt Cap ($mil)	8087	0.62

Style
Value Blend Growth
Size: Large Med Small

Diversification Value for Portfolio Types

Large Cap: Small Cap: Bond: Balanced: Diversified:

Portfolio 12-31-94

Total Stocks: 89
Total Fixed-Income: 18

Share Chg (06-94) 000	Amount 000		Value $000	% Net Assets
3	24	Hubbell Cl B	1278	2.38
1	13	FNMA	947	1.77
-1	15	Alco Standard	941	1.76
-2	16	Philip Morris	920	1.72
-4	18	General Electric	918	1.71
1	11	Pfizer	811	1.51
0	32	Selective Insurance Group	808	1.51
0	8	Royal Dutch Petroleum	806	1.50
6	14	Great Lakes Chemical	798	1.49
14	26	Mellon Bank	781	1.46
2	22	AlliedSignal	748	1.40
5	21	SmithKline Beecham (Unit)ADR	719	1.34
2	13	Dun & Bradstreet	715	1.33
0	11	Colgate-Palmolive	697	1.30
0	11	Exxon	668	1.25
17	25	Sbarro	650	1.21
3	31	Analysts International	636	1.19
11	21	ALLTEL	633	1.18
23	26	Norwest	608	1.13
5	12	Kimberly-Clark	606	1.13
0	7	Mobil	590	1.10
-3	18	Abbott Laboratories	587	1.10
9	10	Automatic Data Processing	585	1.09
1	13	Reader's Digest Assn Cl B	582	1.09
3	16	PepsiCo	580	1.08

Composition % 12-31-94

Cash	13.2	Preferreds	1.6
Stocks	78.1	Convertibles	2.2
Bonds	3.7	Other	1.3

Tax Analysis

	Tax-Adj Historical Return %	% Pretax Return
3 Yr Avg	---	---
5 Yr Avg	---	---
10 Yr Avg	---	---
Potential Capital Gain Exposure (% of assets)		1%

Most Similar Funds in MF500

Fund lacks three-year record

Index Allocation

	% of Stocks
S&P 500	66.6
S&P MidCap 400	7.8
U.S. Small Cap	18.9
Foreign	8.8

Sector Weightings

	% of Stocks	Relative S&P 500
Utilities	6.2	0.50
Energy	10.0	0.99
Financials	18.0	1.70
Industrial Cyclicals	15.4	0.94
Consumer Durables	3.5	0.56
Consumer Staples	10.5	0.83
Services	10.4	1.28
Retail	2.9	0.49
Health	10.4	1.20
Technology	12.6	1.38

Operations

Address and Telephone	100 E. Pratt Street, Baltimore, MD 21202, 800-638-5660 / 410-547-2308
Advisor	T. Rowe Price Associates
Subadvisor	None
Distributor	T. Rowe Price Investment Services
States Available	All
Report Grade	A
Income Distrib	Paid Quarterly
* Date of Inception	12-31-92
Fiscal Year End	December

Min Initial Purchase	$2500 (Addt'l: $100)
Min IRA Purchase	$1000 (Addt'l: $50)
Min Auto Invest Plan	$50 (Systematic Inv: $50)

Expenses & Fees

Sales Fees	0.00% front
	0.00% deferred
	0.00% 12b-1
Management Fee	0.20% flat fee+0.48%G
3-,5-,10-yr Expense Projections	$32, $55, $122
Annual Brokerage Cost	0.88%

MORNINGSTAR 1995 Mutual Fund 500

T. Rowe Price Equity-Income

	Ticker	Load	NAV	Yield	SEC Yield	Assets	Objective
	PRFDX	None	15.98	3.5%	N/A	3203.9	Equity-Inc.

T. Rowe Price Equity-Income Fund seeks dividend income. Potential for capital appreciation is also considered.

The fund invests at least 65% of its assets in income-producing common stocks. In evaluating a security, the fund considers the yield and prospects for earnings and dividend growth, the relative valuation of the security, and the overall competitive and financial strength of the company. Fixed-income securities may be held for enhancement of income.

On Feb. 7, 1992, Bell Atlantic Equity Portfolio merged into this fund.

Historical Profile

Return	Above Average
Risk	Low
Rating	★★★★ Above Average

Investment Style History
Equity

Average % Stocks Held in Portfolio

60% 65% 66% 71% 72% 73% 72% 79%

Growth of $10,000

- IIII Value of Fund ($000)
- — Value of Index ($000) S&P 500
- ▼ Manager Change
- ▽ Partial Manager Change
- ► Mgr Unknown After
- ◄ Mgr Unknown Before

Performance Quartile (Within Objective)

Manager's Investment Style

Management's bottom-up, value-driven approach emphasizes companies with dividends at least 25% higher than the S&P 500's average. As such, the portfolio typically features stocks with depressed prices. The portfolio also usually includes a 10% to 20% cash position, and modest bond exposure.

Fund Manager(s)

Brian C. Rogers CFA, since 10-85. Birthdate: 06-55. BA, Harvard 1977 MBA, Harvard 1982

Manager Experience

	Dates Managed	Invest Obj	Std Dev	+/- Index

Not available.

	1983	1984	1985	1986	1987	1988	1989	1990	1991	1992	1993	1994	History
	---	---	11.00	12.96	11.29	13.38	14.06	12.27	14.62	15.63	16.65	15.98	NAV
	---	---	10.00 *	26.78	3.54	27.69	13.74	-6.79	25.28	14.13	14.84	4.53	Total Return %
	---	---	-2.03 *	8.10	-1.72	11.08	-17.95	-3.67	-5.20	6.51	4.79	3.21	+/- S&P 500
	---	---	---	10.69	1.18	9.75	-15.44	-0.61	-8.93	5.16	3.56	4.60	+/- Wilshire 5000
	---	---	0.00	6.32	6.22	5.43	5.58	4.73	5.16	4.41	3.45	3.67	Income Return %
	---	---	10.00	20.46	-2.68	22.26	8.16	-11.52	20.12	9.72	11.39	0.86	Capital Return %
	---	---	---	9	31	4	51	77	35	11	29	5	Total Rtn % Rank All
	---	---	---	1	21	3	87	54	63	13	35	4	Total Rtn % Rank Obj
	---	---	0.00	0.65	0.82	0.63	0.76	0.65	0.61	0.63	0.54	0.59	Income $
	---	---	0.00	0.26	1.35	0.38	0.39	0.19	0.10	0.39	0.72	0.81	Capital Gains $
	---	---	1.00	1.00	1.10	1.30	1.11	1.13	1.05	0.97	0.91	0.91	Expense Ratio %
	---	---	7.62	5.16	4.58	4.83	5.31	5.09	4.44	3.95	3.23	3.49	Income Ratio %
	---	---	37	73	80	36	34	24	34	30	31	39	Turnover Rate %
	---	---	16.6	94.0	185.1	500.9	968.4	862.1	1335.4	2091.5	2848.5	3203.9	Net Assets ($mil)

Performance 12-31-94

	1st Qtr	2nd Qtr	3rd Qtr	4th Qtr	Total
1987	13.45	1.90	3.99	-13.87	3.54
1988	12.75	6.16	4.32	2.26	27.69
1989	5.31	6.16	4.98	-3.08	13.74
1990	-2.20	1.33	-13.46	8.69	-6.79
1991	14.76	1.72	3.28	3.92	25.28
1992	3.49	3.96	2.60	3.40	14.13
1993	6.15	1.59	3.29	3.11	14.84
1994	-2.78	1.95	5.53	-0.06	4.53

Bear Market Performance

Decile Rank (5-year period)

Worst ─────────────── Best

	Worst 3 Mo Period 1985-89	Worst 3 Mo Period 1990-94
T. Rowe Price Equity-Income	---	-14.05
+/- S&P 500	---	-0.20
+/- Best Fit Index : S&P 500	---	-0.20

Trailing Returns

	Total Return %	+/- S&P 500	+/- Wil 5000	% Rank All	% Rank Obj	Growth of $10,000
3 Mo	-0.06	-0.04	0.71	23	9	9,994
6 Mo	5.47	0.61	0.85	10	4	10,547
1 Yr	4.53	3.21	4.60	5	4	10,453
3 Yr Avg	11.07	4.80	4.45	10	8	13,701
5 Yr Avg	9.85	1.16	1.04	18	11	15,999
10 Yr Avg	---	---	---	---	---	---
15 Yr Avg	---	---	---	---	---	---

Operations

Address and Telephone	100 E. Pratt Street Baltimore, MD 21202 800-638-5660 / 410-547-2308
Advisor	T. Rowe Price Associates
Subadvisor	None
Distributor	T. Rowe Price Investment Services
States Available	All plus GU,PR,VI
Report Grade	A
Income Distrib	Paid Quarterly
* Date of Inception	10-31-85
Fiscal Year End	December

Risk Analysis

Time Period	Load-Adj Return %	Risk % Rank [1] All	Obj	Morningstar[2] Return	Risk	Morningstar Risk-Adj Rating
1 Yr	4.53					
3 Yr	11.07	38	4	2.32 [3]	0.47	★★★★
5 Yr	9.85	56	23	1.31 [3]	0.62	★★★★
10 Yr	---	---	---			

Average Historical Rating (75 months)   3.9 ★ s

[1] 1 = low, 100 = high [2] 1.00 = Equity Avg [3] 1.00 = 90-day T-bill return

Other Measures

				Standard S&P 500	Best Fit S&P 500
Standard Deviation	6.76	Alpha		5.1	5.1
Mean	10.77	Beta		0.78	0.78
Sharpe Ratio	1.07	R-Squared		84	84

Investment Style

	Stock Portfolio Avg	Relative S&P 500
Price/Earnings Ratio	17.4	0.94
Price/Book Ratio	2.9	0.85
5 Yr Earnings Gr %	0.0	0.00
Return on Assets %	5.9	0.79
Debt % Total Cap	31.9	1.13
Med Mkt Cap ($mil)	8353	0.64

Style Value Blend Growth — Size Large/Med/Small

Diversification Value for Portfolio Types

Large Cap: None	Small Cap: Medium	Bond: High	Balanced: Low	Diversified: Low

Portfolio 12-31-94

Total Stocks: 121
Total Fixed-Income: 40

Share Chg (10-94) 000	Amount 000		Value $000	% Net Assets
100	1000	Exxon	60750	1.90
0	1700	SmithKline Beecham (Unit)ADR	58225	1.82
0	950	Philip Morris	54625	1.70
0	500	Atlantic Richfield	50875	1.59
0	1600	Upjohn	49200	1.54
0	1305	American Brands	48938	1.53
0	800	Texaco	47900	1.50
-50	700	Eli Lilly	45938	1.43
100	900	General Electric	45900	1.43
0	425	Royal Dutch Petroleum	45688	1.43
300	1400	Honeywell	44100	1.38
0	1400	GTE	42525	1.33
150	750	JP Morgan	42000	1.31
0	1400	American Express	41300	1.29
0	650	American Home Products	40788	1.27
0	500	British Petroleum (ADR)	39938	1.25
525	1300	Mellon Bank	39813	1.24
50	650	Dun & Bradstreet	35750	1.12
0	1600	Entergy	35000	1.09
0	600	General Mills	34200	1.07
0	400	Mobil	33700	1.05
0	675	Eastman Kodak	32231	1.01
0	1750	PacifiCorp	31719	0.99
0	800	Tambrands	30900	0.96
0	400	Warner-Lambert	30800	0.96

Composition % 12-31-94

Cash	9.1	Preferreds	0.3
Stocks	79.2	Convertibles	3.8
Bonds	7.6	Other	0.0

Tax Analysis

	Tax-Adj Historical Return %	% Pretax Return
3 Yr Avg	8.50	74.9
5 Yr Avg	7.54	73.0
10 Yr Avg	---	---
Potential Capital Gain Exposure (% of assets)		6%

Most Similar Funds in MF500

Putnam Fund for Grth & Inc A	Strong Fit
Fidelity Equity-Income	Strong Fit
Affiliated	Strong Fit

Index Allocation

	% of Stocks
S&P 500	80.9
S&P MidCap 400	5.5
U.S. Small Cap	9.6
Foreign	5.8

Sector Weightings

	% of Stocks	Relative S&P 500
Utilities	14.9	1.20
Energy	14.6	1.44
Financials	18.3	1.73
Industrial Cyclicals	11.3	0.69
Consumer Durables	3.5	0.56
Consumer Staples	13.7	1.09
Services	7.4	0.91
Retail	3.4	0.58
Health	13.0	1.50
Technology	0.0	0.00

Min Initial Purchase / Expenses & Fees

Min Initial Purchase	$2500 (Addt'l: $100)
Min IRA Purchase	$1000 (Addt'l: $50)
Min Auto Invest Plan	$50 (Systematic Inv: $50)

Expenses & Fees

Sales Fees	0.00% front
	0.00% deferred
	0.00% 12b-1
Management Fee	0.25% flat fee+0.48%G
3-,5-,10-yr Expense Projections	$29, $50, $112
Annual Brokerage Cost	0.18%

T. Rowe Price GNMA

	Ticker	Load	NAV	Yield	SEC Yield	Assets	Objective
	PRGMX	None	8.88	7.6%	7.13%	752.2	Gvt Mortgage

T. Rowe Price GNMA Fund seeks current income consistent with capital preservation and maximum credit protection.

The fund invests exclusively in securities guaranteed by the U.S. government, primarily in Government National Mortgage Association (GNMA) mortgage-backed securities. At least 65% of the fund's assets are always invested in modified pass-through GNMA certificates. It may not hold government agency securities unless these issues are backed by the full faith and credit of the U.S. Treasury.

The fund may also engage in various futures and options strategies.

Historical Profile
Return	Above Average
Risk	Below Average
Rating	★★★★ Above Average

Investment Style History
Fixed Income
Income Rtn % Rank Obj

Growth of $10,000
- |||| Value of Fund ($000)
- — Value of Index ($000) LB Mtg
- ▼ Manager Change
- ▽ Partial Manager Change
- ► Mgr Unknown After
- ◄ Mgr Unknown Before

Performance Quartile (Within Objective)

Manager's Investment Style

Management invests almost entirely in GNMAs, with only an occasional Treasury in the mix. Mortgage-derivative products are also absent from the portfolio. Management uses coupon structure and duration adjustments to keep yield solid. GNMA project loans and graduated-payment mortgages are also favored for their income-boosting properties.

Fund Manager(s)

Peter Van Dyke, since 10-87. Birthdate: 11-38.
BS, Webb Inst. of Naval Architecture 1960 PhD, Harvard 1964

Manager Experience
	Dates Managed	Invest Obj	Std Dev	+/- Index
Peter Van Dyke				
Liberty Financial U.S.Gov	06/87 - 06/89	GM	3.71	-2.07

1983	1984	1985	1986	1987	1988	1989	1990	1991	1992	1993	1994	History
---	---	10.09	10.23	9.38	9.01	9.37	9.42	9.97	9.82	9.72	8.88	NAV
---	---	1.39 *	10.90	0.86	5.91	14.02	10.01	15.04	6.46	6.13	-1.64	Total Return %
---	---		-4.35	-1.90	-1.97	-0.52	1.07	-0.96	-0.79	-3.62	1.28	+/- LB Aggregate
---	---		-2.54	-3.43	-2.81	-1.33	-0.71	-0.68	-0.50	-0.70	-0.03	+/- LB Mortgage
---	---	0.99	9.51	9.01	9.85	10.03	9.48	9.20	7.96	7.15	7.01	Income Return %
---	---	0.40	1.39	-8.15	-3.94	4.00	0.53	5.84	-1.50	-1.02	-8.64	Capital Return %
---	---		80	52	89	50	5	58	64	87	31	Total Rtn % Rank All
---	---		59	82	91	21	42	45	43	68	29	Total Rtn % Rank Obj
---	---	0.10	0.91	0.91	0.91	0.85	0.83	0.80	0.77	0.69	0.68	Income $
---	---	0.00	0.00	0.02	0.00	0.00	0.00	0.00	0.00	0.00	0.00	Capital Gains $
---	---		1.00	1.00	0.99	0.94	0.90	0.85	0.86	0.79	0.77	Expense Ratio %
---	---		10.06	8.82	9.56	9.75	9.19	8.94	8.25	7.65	6.93	Income Ratio %
---	---		51	226	193	135	171	92	66	94	93	Turnover Rate %
---	---	33.9	209.0	332.0	360.1	387.8	452.1	734.5	863.6	916.6	752.2	Net Assets ($mil)

Performance 12-31-94

	1st Qtr	2nd Qtr	3rd Qtr	4th Qtr	Total
1987	1.51	-2.22	-1.78	3.45	0.86
1988	3.32	1.31	1.42	-0.23	5.91
1989	0.83	7.73	1.30	3.62	14.02
1990	-0.53	3.54	1.47	5.27	10.01
1991	2.47	1.59	5.37	4.89	15.04
1992	-0.87	3.65	2.94	0.65	6.46
1993	2.71	1.82	1.23	0.25	6.13
1994	-2.40	-1.14	1.04	0.90	-1.64

Bear Market Performance

Decile Rank (5-year period)

Worst ———————————— Best

	Worst 3 Mo Period 1985-89	Worst 3 Mo Period 1990-94
T. Rowe Price GNMA	---	-3.81
+/- LB Aggregate	---	1.12
+/- Best Fit Index : LB Mtg	---	0.19

Trailing Returns

	Total Return %	+/- LB Aggregate	+/- LB Mortgage	% Rank All	Obj	Growth of $10,000
3 Mo	0.90	0.52	0.47	7	1	10,090
6 Mo	1.95	0.96	0.64	27	1	10,195
1 Yr	-1.64	1.28	-0.03	31	29	9,836
3 Yr Avg	3.58	-0.96	-0.40	77	35	11,114
5 Yr Avg	7.06	-0.57	-0.51	49	31	14,065
10 Yr Avg	---	---	---	---	---	---
15 Yr Avg	---	---	---	---	---	---

Operations

Address and Telephone	100 E. Pratt Street
	Baltimore, MD 21202
	800-638-5660 / 410-547-2308
Advisor	T. Rowe Price Associates
Subadvisor	None
Distributor	T. Rowe Price Investment Services
States Available	All plus PR
Report Grade	A
Income Distrib	Paid Monthly
* Date of Inception	11-26-85
Fiscal Year End	February

Min Initial Purchase $2500 (Addt'l: $100)
Min IRA Purchase $1000 (Addt'l: $50)
Min Auto Invest Plan $50 (Systematic Inv: $50)

Expenses & Fees
Sales Fees	
	0.00% front
	0.00% deferred
	0.00% 12b-1
Management Fee	0.15% flat fee+0.48%G
3-,5-,10-yr Expense Projections	$25, $43, $95

Risk Analysis

Time Period	Load-Adj Return %	Risk % Rank [1] All	Obj	Morningstar [2] Return	Morningstar Risk	Morningstar Risk-Adj Rating
1 Yr	-1.64					
3 Yr	3.58	12	32	0.00 [3]	0.82	★★★★
5 Yr	7.06	12	39	0.57 [3]	0.80	★★★★
10 Yr	---	---	---	---	---	---

Average Historical Rating (74 months)   3.9 ★s

[1] 1 = low, 100 = high   [2] 1.00 = Taxable Avg   [3] 1.00 = 90-day T-bill return

Other Measures
				Standard LB Agg	Best Fit LB Mtg
Standard Deviation	3.19	Alpha		-0.7	-0.4
Mean	3.58	Beta		0.76	0.96
Sharpe Ratio	0.02	R-Squared		91	94

Investment Style

Interest-Rate Stance
Avg Effective Duration	5.1 Yrs
Avg Effective Maturity	9.0 Yrs

Quality
Avg Credit Quality	AAA
Avg Weighted Coupon	8.00%
Avg Weighted Price	96.09% of Par

Diversification Value for Portfolio Types

Large Cap: Medium	Small Cap: High	Bond: None	Balanced: Medium	Diversified: Medium

Portfolio 11-30-94

Amount 000	Date of Maturity	Total Stocks: 0 / Total Fixed-Income: 35	Value $000	% Net Assets
148879	10-20-24	GNMA 8%	144603	19.08
141497	08-15-24	GNMA 7%	126024	16.63
124861	09-15-24	GNMA 7.5%	115630	15.26
86162	09-15-24	GNMA 9%	87487	11.54
78770	02-20-23	GNMA 8.5%	77817	10.27
65625	08-15-95	US Treasury Note 4.625%	64712	8.54
61183	12-15-24	GNMA 9.5%	63704	8.41
47991	06-15-24	GNMA 6.5%	41156	5.43
20000	11-15-24	US Treasury Bond 7.5%	18772	2.48
17269	07-15-24	GNMA 10%	18383	2.43
14361	10-15-15	GNMA 12%	16228	2.14
14189	09-15-21	GNMA GPM 9.75%	14503	1.91
45800	08-15-10	US Treasury Bond 0%	12933	1.71
10922	02-15-30	GNMA Project Loan 10%	11459	1.51
10289	08-15-21	GNMA GPM 9.25%	10241	1.35
9948	10-15-23	GNMA Project Loan 9.25%	10012	1.32
7600	11-15-21	GNMA 10.5%	8226	1.09
6175	03-15-26	GNMA Project Loan 10.75%	6616	0.87
5495	07-20-20	GNMA 11.5%	6060	0.80
4869	09-20-20	GNMA 11%	5289	0.70
4990	10-01-32	FHA 9.95%	5077	0.67
3942	01-20-16	GNMA 12.5%	4485	0.59
18890	06-16-23	GNMA CMO I/O 8%	4061	0.54
3565	11-15-09	GNMA GPM 9.5%	3645	0.48
3076	09-20-15	GNMA 13%	3503	0.46

Composition % 12-31-94
Cash	-9.0	Preferreds	0.0
Stocks	0.0	Convertibles	0.0
Bonds	109.0	Other	0.0

Tax Analysis
	Tax-Adj Historical Return %	% Pretax Return
3 Yr Avg	0.85	23.0
5 Yr Avg	4.26	57.0
10 Yr Avg	---	---
Potential Capital Gain Exposure (% of assets)		-10%

Most Similar Funds in MF500
Dreyfus GNMA	Strong Fit
Vanguard F/I GNMA	Strong Fit
Franklin U.S. Government Sec	Strong Fit

Coupon Range
	% of Bonds	Rel Obj
0%	1.4	1.91
0% to 8%	57.6	1.05
8% to 9%	18.8	0.86
9% to 10%	15.3	1.78
More than 10%	6.8	1.04
Not applicable	0.0	0.00

Sector Analysis 11-30-94
% of Bonds
US Treas	11	CMOs	0
GNMA mtgs	88	ARMs	0
FNMA mtgs	0	Other	1
FHLMC mtgs	0		

MORNINGSTAR 1995 Mutual Fund 500

T. Rowe Price High-Yield

	Ticker	Load	NAV	Yield	SEC Yield	Assets	Objective
	PRHYX	None	7.75	9.7%	10.34%	1040.4	Corp Hi Yld

T. Rowe Price High-Yield Fund seeks high current income; growth of capital is secondary.

The fund normally invests at least 80% of its assets in high-yielding, income-producing debt and preferred stocks. The portfolio may include asset-backed debt, bank obligations, and corporate debt. Up to 20% of the fund's assets may be invested in both foreign securities and common stocks. Average portfolio maturity is expected to be about 10 years.

Pacific Horizon High-Yield Bond and Security Income Fund High-Yield merged into this fund in March and December 1991, respectively.

Manager's Investment Style

Catherine Bray took over as manager of this fund--replacing Dick Swingle--in late 1993, so it's tough to gauge what direction this fund will take. Former management invested in higher-quality high-yield bonds. The fund is also known for making sector plays, including moving into gaming stocks in 1993, and dabbling in emerging-markets debt. The fund hasn't stuck with the most-liquid developing markets, though: Issues from Morocco, Russia, and Poland have peppered the portfolio.

Fund Manager(s)

Catherine H. Bray, since 09-94. BA, Smith MBA, Columbia

Manager Experience

	Dates Managed	Invest Obj	Std Dev	+/- Index
Not available.				

Historical Profile

Return	Average
Risk	Below Average
Rating	★★★★ Above Average

25 24 51 56 76 74 48 73

Investment Style History
Fixed Income
Income Rtn % Rank Obj

Growth of $10,000

IIII Value of Fund ($000)
— Value of Index ($000) LB Agg
▼ Manager Change
▽ Partial Manager Change
◄— Mgr Unknown After
—◄ Mgr Unknown Before

Performance Quartile (Within Objective)

	1983	1984	1985	1986	1987	1988	1989	1990	1991	1992	1993	1994	History
	---	10.00	10.75	10.87	9.82	10.25	8.88	6.86	7.98	8.29	9.22	7.75	NAV
	---	---	22.48	15.08	3.05	17.91	-1.46	-10.96	30.90	14.73	21.82	-8.00	Total Return %
	---	---	0.35	-0.17	0.29	10.03	-16.00	-19.91	14.89	7.49	12.07	-5.08	+/- LB Aggregate
	---	---	---	-0.55	-3.48	6.48	-1.85	-4.58	-12.86	-1.93	2.92	-7.02	+/- FB High-Yield
	---	---	14.98	12.74	11.67	13.53	11.90	11.79	14.57	10.85	10.60	7.94	Income Return %
	---	---	7.50	2.35	-8.62	4.38	-13.37	-22.75	16.33	3.88	11.22	-15.94	Capital Return %
	---	---	57	54	35	19	99	86	25	10	14	86	Total Rtn % Rank All
	---	---	38	32	34	2	57	54	73	80	16	88	Total Rtn % Rank Obj
	---	0.00	1.36	1.30	1.26	1.25	1.27	1.11	0.90	0.82	0.75		Income $
	---	0.00	0.00	0.13	0.14	0.00	0.00	0.00	0.00	0.00	0.00		Capital Gains $
	---	---	1.00	1.00	0.99	0.99	0.95	1.02	1.03	0.97	0.89	0.85	Expense Ratio %
	---	---	16.69	13.01	11.57	12.10	12.32	13.01	14.02	11.22	9.85	8.99	Income Ratio %
	---	---	164	166	138	80	66	83	59	104	107		Turnover Rate %
	---	---	22.5	765.3	703.2	1129.6	774.0	478.1	968.7	1204.6	1622.2	1040.4	Net Assets ($mil)

Performance 12-31-94

	1st Qtr	2nd Qtr	3rd Qtr	4th Qtr	Total
1987	7.10	-1.24	-1.00	-1.59	3.05
1988	6.94	4.48	2.73	2.72	17.91
1989	2.02	2.80	-1.36	-4.75	-1.46
1990	-5.09	3.95	-6.22	-3.76	-10.96
1991	10.47	7.65	5.39	4.45	30.90
1992	6.16	2.77	3.46	1.64	14.73
1993	8.05	5.78	1.69	4.81	21.82
1994	-4.12	-3.53	2.54	-3.00	-8.00

Bear Market Performance

Decile Rank (5-year period)

Worst | | Best

	Worst 3 Mo Period 1985-89	Worst 3 Mo Period 1990-94
T. Rowe Price High-Yield	-5.98	-11.90
+/- LB Aggregate	-6.79	-12.65
+/- Best Fit Index : FB HY	---	2.20

Trailing Returns

	Total Return %	+/- LB Aggregate	+/- FB High-Yield	% Rank All	% Rank Obj	Growth of $10,000
3 Mo	-3.00	-3.38	-2.96	83	80	9,700
6 Mo	-0.54	-1.53	-2.09	66	39	9,946
1 Yr	-8.00	-5.08	-7.02	86	88	9,210
3 Yr Avg	8.74	4.20	-2.42	18	86	12,859
5 Yr Avg	8.43	0.80	-4.65	29	91	14,987
10 Yr Avg	9.72	-0.22	---	61	58	25,290
15 Yr Avg	---	---	---	---	---	---

Operations

Address and Telephone	100 E. Pratt Street Baltimore, MD 21202 800-638-5660 / 410-547-2308	
Advisor	T. Rowe Price Associates	
Subadvisor	None	
Distributor	T. Rowe Price Investment Services	
States Available	All plus GU,PR,VI	
Report Grade	A-	
Income Distrib	Paid Monthly	
∗ Date of Inception	12-31-84	
Fiscal Year End	May	

Risk Analysis

Time Period	Load-Adj Return %	Risk % Rank [1] All	Obj	Morningstar [2] Return	Risk	Morningstar Risk-Adj Rating
1 Yr	-9.00					
3 Yr	8.74	27	89	1.57 [3]	0.54	★★★★
5 Yr	8.43	47	62	0.92 [3]	0.61	★★★★
10 Yr	9.72	34	51	0.61	0.48	★★★
Average Historical Rating (85 months)					3.6	★ s

[1] 1 = low, 100 = high [2] 1.00 = Hybrid Avg [3] 1.00 = 90-day T-bill return

Other Measures

		Standard LB Agg		Best Fit FB HY
Standard Deviation	5.77	Alpha	4.3	-3.7
Mean	8.58	Beta	0.81	1.23
Sharpe Ratio	0.88	R-Squared	32	85

Investment Style

Interest-Rate Stance

Avg Effective Duration	4.0 Yrs
Avg Effective Maturity	7.2 Yrs

Quality

Avg Credit Quality	B
Avg Weighted Coupon	10.87%
Avg Weighted Price	89.86% of Par

Maturity: Short Intm Long
Quality: High Med Low

Diversification Value for Portfolio Types

Large Cap: High	Small Cap: Medium	Bond: Medium	Balanced: Medium	Diversified: Medium

Expenses & Fees

Sales Fees	0.00% front
	0.00% deferred
	0.00% 12b-1
Management Fee	0.30% flat fee+0.48%G
3-,5-,10-yr Expense Projections	$27, $47, $105

Minimum Purchase

Min Initial Purchase	$2500 (Addt'l: $100)
Min IRA Purchase	$1000 (Addt'l: $50)
Min Auto Invest Plan	$50 (Systematic Inv: $50)

Portfolio 11-30-94

Amount 000	Date of Maturity	Total Stocks: 29 Total Fixed-Income: 104	Value $000	% Net Assets
22720	11-01-01	Delaval Imo Industries 12%	23146	2.12
21450	09-30-03	Agricultural Min/Chem 10.75%	21503	1.97
24225	09-15-01	President Rvrbt Casinos 13%	20107	1.84
19350	05-01-04	Container of America 11.25%	19543	1.79
755		Berg Electronics Cl E Pfd PIK	19453	1.78
1000	12-01-04	Sea Containers 12.5%	19062	1.75
18750	07-15-01	Solon Automated Svcs 12.75%	18000	1.65
18725	12-01-02	Synthetic Industries 12.75%	17976	1.65
17138	03-15-01	Tesoro Petroleum 12.75%	17309	1.59
16750	06-15-03	IMC Fertilizer Group 10.75%	17085	1.57
16490	12-01-03	Owens-Illinois 11%	16902	1.55
17750	04-01-02	Stone Container 10.75%	16552	1.52
15675	04-15-05	Summit Comm Group 10.5%	16459	1.51
15750	05-15-04	American Standard 11.375%	16222	1.49
17500	11-01-03	Maxus Energy 9.375%	15225	1.40
15300	10-01-02	Heritage Media Services 11%	14994	1.37
15000	04-01-02	Coltec Industries 10.25%	14700	1.35
13625	12-15-02	Quorum Health Group 11.875%	14579	1.34
1638		Gaylord Container Cl A	14332	1.31
14100	07-01-00	Wright Medical Tech 10.75%	13818	1.27
16600	05-01-08	Showboat 9.25%	13612	1.25
13250	12-15-02	Exide 10.75%	13383	1.23
15000	08-15-02	Continental Med Sys 10.875%	13275	1.22
13130	02-15-00	Dial Page 12.25%	12867	1.18
17850	02-15-03	Dr Pepper Bottling 11.625%	12316	1.13

Composition % 12-31-94

Cash	8.7	Preferreds	1.9
Stocks	6.8	Convertibles	1.6
Bonds	81.1	Other	0.0

Tax Analysis

	Tax-Adj Historical Return %	% Pretax Return
3 Yr Avg	5.14	56.8
5 Yr Avg	4.49	49.2
10 Yr Avg	5.00	41.1
Potential Capital Gain Exposure (% of assets)		-28%

Most Similar Funds in MF500

Phoenix High-Yield A	Fair Fit
High Yield Plus	Fair Fit
American High-Income	Fair Fit

Coupon Range

	% of Bonds	Rel Obj
0%, PIK	1.7	0.24
0% to 11%	45.7	0.93
11% to 13%	43.5	1.30
13% to 14.5%	3.2	0.59
More than 14.5%	0.4	0.26
Not applicable	5.4	1.77

Credit Analysis 12-31-94
% of Bonds

US Govt	0	BB	16
AAA	0	B	63
AA	0	Below B	5
A	0	NR/NA	15
BBB	0		

T. Rowe Price Intl Stock

	Ticker	Load	NAV	Yield	SEC Yield	Assets	Objective
	PRITX	None	11.32	1.0%	N/A	5786.9	Foreign Stock

T. Rowe Price International Stock Fund seeks total return on its assets from long-term growth of capital and income. The fund ordinarily invests at least 65% of its assets in common stocks of established non-U.S. issuers. The balance of assets may be invested in preferred stocks, warrants, convertible securities, and/or debt securities. The fund typically maintains investments in at least three foreign countries; it may invest in both industrialized and developing countries.

Prior to Sept. 10, 1986, the fund was named T. Rowe Price International Fund.

Manager's Investment Style

Under lead manager Martin Wade, this fund splits its management among nine different individuals, each of whom invests in a specific type of stock or region. Management generally employs a low-turnover strategy, picking countries and stocks with promising long-term potential. Although the fund is willing to dabble in emerging markets, it keeps overall volatility down, and often outperforms during weak global markets, by focusing on large companies and employing high diversification.

Fund Manager(s)

Martin G. Wade et al. Birthdate: 02-43 MA, Cambridge U. 1965

Manager Experience

	Dates Managed	Invest Obj	Std Dev	+/- Index
Martin G. Wade				
T. Rowe Price Intl Dscvry	12/88 - 12/94	WF	17.25	-2.63
T. Rowe Price Euro Stock	02/90 - 12/94	WE	14.51	-4.72

Historical Profile

Return	Above Average
Risk	Average
Rating	★★★★ Above Average

Investment Style History
Equity
Average % Stocks Held in Portfolio

93% 87% 89% 87% 90% 89% 92% 92%

Growth of $10,000

IIII	Value of Fund ($000)	
—	Value of Index ($000) MSEASEA	
▼	Manager Change	
▽	Partial Manager Change	
►	Mgr Unknown After	
◄	Mgr Unknown Before	

Performance Quartile (Within Objective)

1983	1984	1985	1986	1987	1988	1989	1990	1991	1992	1993	1994	History
7.16	6.59	9.04	12.89	8.54	8.97	10.24	8.81	9.54	8.89	12.16	11.32	NAV
28.62	-5.88	45.29	61.29	7.99	17.94	23.71	-8.89	15.87	-3.47	40.11	-0.76	Total Return %
6.15	-12.14	13.55	42.61	2.73	1.33	-7.97	-5.78	-14.62	-11.09	30.06	-2.07	+/- S&P 500
4.93	-13.26	-10.87	-8.15	-16.64	-10.33	13.17	14.56	3.74	8.70	7.55	-8.54	+/- MSCI EAFE
2.43	1.02	2.72	1.33	2.32	1.82	1.63	1.74	1.67	1.73	0.84	1.06	Income Return %
26.19	-6.90	42.57	59.96	5.66	16.13	22.08	-10.63	14.20	-5.20	39.27	-1.82	Capital Return %
13	83	4	1	13	19	27	82	54	94	4	25	Total Rtn % Rank All
45	58	43	5	50	42	41	26	30	49	38	48	Total Rtn % Rank Obj
0.11	0.08	0.15	0.11	0.24	0.16	0.16	0.16	0.15	0.16	0.16	0.12	Income $
0.00	0.08	0.23	1.38	4.98	0.93	0.67	0.36	0.49	0.16	0.20	0.62	Capital Gains $
1.14	1.11	1.11	1.10	1.14	1.16	1.10	1.09	1.10	1.05	1.01	0.96	Expense Ratio %
1.24	2.29	1.54	0.89	0.93	1.78	1.63	2.16	1.51	1.49	1.52	1.11	Income Ratio %
69	38	62	56	77	42	48	47	45	38	30	23	Turnover Rate %
130.0	180.6	376.9	790.0	642.5	630.1	970.5	1030.8	1476.3	1949.6	4290.0	5786.9	Net Assets ($mil)

Performance 12-31-94

	1st Qtr	2nd Qtr	3rd Qtr	4th Qtr	Total
1987	10.71	10.20	6.96	-17.24	7.99
1988	6.32	1.76	-1.19	10.32	17.94
1989	5.26	-1.81	14.89	4.19	23.71
1990	-3.03	8.26	-18.70	6.74	-8.89
1991	7.26	-2.33	8.13	2.28	15.87
1992	-2.41	5.16	-4.19	-1.83	-3.47
1993	7.54	5.02	10.66	12.12	40.11
1994	-2.38	0.84	5.26	-4.22	-0.76

Bear Market Performance

Decile Rank (5-year period)

Worst _____ Best

	Worst 3 Mo Period 1985-89	Worst 3 Mo Period 1990-94
T. Rowe Price Intl Stock	-24.46	-18.70
+/- S&P 500	5.12	-4.95
+/- Best Fit Index : MSEASEA	-0.14	-2.08

Trailing Returns

	Total Return %	+/- S&P 500	+/- MSCI EAFE	% Rank All	% Rank Obj	Growth of $10,000
3 Mo	-4.22	-4.21	-3.20	89	41	9,578
6 Mo	0.82	-4.04	1.74	41	22	10,082
1 Yr	-0.76	-2.07	-8.54	25	48	9,924
3 Yr Avg	10.31	4.04	2.45	12	35	13,422
5 Yr Avg	7.22	-1.47	5.72	45	30	14,169
10 Yr Avg	18.00	3.61	0.45	3	6	52,318
15 Yr Avg	---	---	---	---	---	---

Operations

Address and Telephone	100 E. Pratt Street	Min Initial Purchase	$2500 (Addt'l: $100)
	Baltimore, MD 21202	Min IRA Purchase	$1000 (Addt'l: $50)
	800-638-5660 / 410-547-2308	Min Auto Invest Plan	$50 (Systematic Inv: $50)
Advisor	Rowe Price-Fleming International		
Subadvisor	None	**Expenses & Fees**	
Distributor	T. Rowe Price Investment Services	Sales Fees	0.00% front
States Available	All plus GU,PR,VI		0.00% deferred
Report Grade	A		0.00% 12b-1
Income Distrib	Paid Annually	Management Fee	0.35% flat fee+0.48%G
Date of Inception	05-09-80	3-,5-,10-yr Expense Projections	$32, $56, $124
Fiscal Year End	October	Annual Brokerage Cost	0.19%

Risk Analysis

Time Period	Load-Adj Return %	Risk % Rank[1] All	Obj	Morningstar[2] Return	Morningstar Risk	Morningstar Risk-Adj Rating
1 Yr	-0.76					
3 Yr	10.31	84	33	2.07[3]	1.04	★★★★
5 Yr	7.22	85	38	0.61[3]	1.05	★★★
10 Yr	18.00	68	31	2.26	0.90	★★★★★

Average Historical Rating (109 months) 4.4 ★s

[1] = low, 100 = high [2] 1.00 = Equity Avg [3] 1.00 = 90-day T-bill return

Other Measures

			Standard S&P 500	Best Fit MSEASEA
Standard Deviation	12.76	Alpha	4.9	1.5
Mean	10.65	Beta	0.81	0.90
Sharpe Ratio	0.56	R-Squared	25	86

Investment Style

	Stock Portfolio Avg	Rel MSCI EAFE	Rel Obj	Style
Price/Earnings Ratio	29.5	0.80	1.05	
Price/Cash Flow	14.6	0.94	1.09	
Price/Book Ratio	2.9	1.12	0.98	
5 Yr Earnings Gr %	1.3	---	0.35	
Return on Assets %	6.5	1.44	0.91	
Debt % Total Cap	26.4	0.78	0.95	
Med Mkt Cap ($mil)	6839	0.57	1.33	

Style V B G / Size L M S

Diversification Value for Portfolio Types

Large Cap: High	Small Cap: High	Bond: High	Balanced: Medium	Diversified: Low

Portfolio 10-31-94

Share Chg (04-94) 000	Amount 000	Total Stocks: 340 / Total Fixed-Income: 9	Value $000	% Net Assets
329	1536	Wolters Kluwer (Netherlands)	111	1.79
8678	9488	Elsevier (Netherlands)	97	1.56
103	652	Royal Dutch Petroleum (Neth)	76	1.22
-1823	9638	Swire Pacific Cl A	74	1.19
-14	1293	TMX	72	1.16
124	842	Kyocera	64	1.03
598	7029	National Westminster Bank	58	0.93
2019	14030	Technology Resources	55	0.88
5342	12922	Nippon Steel	53	0.86
2129	13192	Wharf Holdings	52	0.84
454	566	Generale Des Eaux	52	0.84
2716	18487	Fletcher Challenge	50	0.80
21	57	BBC Brown Boveri (Reg)	49	0.79
328	2245	Nippondenso	48	0.77
833	5864	Mitsubishi Heavy Industries	48	0.77
465	3180	Sumitomo Electric Industries	48	0.77
503	6730	Cable & Wireless	46	0.75
357	2433	Sharp	45	0.73
662	806	Valeo (France)	44	0.71
3	46	Nestle (Reg)	43	0.70

Regional Exposure 12-31-94
% of Stocks

Europe	25	Pacific Rim	17
Japan	15	Other	0
Latin Amer	9		

Composition % 12-31-94

Cash	6.7	Preferreds	1.7
Stocks	91.1	Convertibles	0.2
Bonds	0.0	Other	0.3

Tax Analysis

	Tax-Adj Historical Return %	% Pretax Return
3 Yr Avg	8.99	86.1
5 Yr Avg	5.67	76.1
10 Yr Avg	14.59	68.6

Potential Capital Gain Exposure (% of assets) 6%

Most Similar Funds in MF500

Vanguard Intl Growth	Strong Fit
Scudder International	Strong Fit
Putnam Global Growth A	Strong Fit

Country Exposure 12-31-94
% of Stocks

Japan	25
United Kingdom	15
Netherlands	9
France	7
Germany	4

Total Number of Countries: 29
Hedging Policy: Occasional

Sector Weightings

	% of Stocks	Relative S&P 500
Utilities	7.5	0.84
Energy	4.0	0.98
Financials	16.2	0.86
Industrial Cyclicals	28.0	1.12
Consumer Durables	8.8	0.82
Consumer Staples	5.8	0.84
Services	13.2	1.21
Retail	6.7	1.15
Health	4.9	1.38
Technology	4.9	0.95

MORNINGSTAR 1995 Mutual Fund 500

T. Rowe Price Mid-Cap Growth

	Ticker	Load	NAV	Yield	SEC Yield	Assets	Objective
	RPMGX	None	14.85	0.0%	N/A	100.5	Growth

T. Rowe Price Mid-Cap Growth Fund seeks long-term growth of capital.

The fund normally invests at least 65% of its assets in mid-cap common stocks with above-average growth potential. A mid-cap company is defined as one with a market capitalization that falls within the capitalization range of companies included in the S&P MidCap 400 Index. The fund seeks companies which 1) offer proven products or services; 2) have an above-average historical record of earnings growth; 3) have the potential for sustaining growth; 4) operate in industries experiencing increasing demand; and/or 5) are reasonably valued. The fund may invest up to 25% of its assets in foreign securities.

Manager's Investment Style

Management plays the middle ground. Not wishing to outpace its peers in bull or bear markets, the fund rather seeks out get-rich-slow companies. These firms should hold their value well in market downturns, and have growth rates of at least 15%. Management favors mid-cap issues, seeking market capitalizations between 500 and 1,500 million. Strong cash flows and good valuations are among management's other criteria. While not a requirement for selection, the fund likes companies that have a dominant market share.

Fund Manager(s)

Brian W. H. Berghuis CFA(1987), since 06-92.
Birthdate: 10-58. BA, Princeton U. 1981 MBA, Harvard 1985

Manager Experience

	Dates Managed	Invest Obj	Std Dev	+/- Index
Brian W. H. Berghuis				
T. Rowe Price New America	01/92 - 12/94	G	14.20	-2.02

Historical Profile

Return	---
Risk	---
Rating	

Not Rated

Investment Style History
Equity
Average % Stocks Held in Portfolio
90% 90% 90%

Growth of $10,000

- |||| Value of Fund ($000)
- — Value of Index ($000) S&P 500
- ▼ Manager Change
- ▽ Partial Manager Change
- ► Mgr Unknown After
- ◄ Mgr Unknown Before

Performance Quartile
(Within Objective)

	1983	1984	1985	1986	1987	1988	1989	1990	1991	1992	1993	1994	History
	---	---	---	---	---	---	---	---	---	12.27	15.18	14.85	NAV
	---	---	---	---	---	---	---	---	---	24.54 *	26.24	0.29	Total Return %
	---	---	---	---	---	---	---	---	---	16.20 *	16.18	-1.02	+/- S&P 500
	---	---	---	---	---	---	---	---	---	---	14.96	0.36	+/- Wilshire 5000
	---	---	---	---	---	---	---	---	---	0.00	0.00	0.00	Income Return %
	---	---	---	---	---	---	---	---	---	24.54	26.24	0.29	Capital Return %
	---	---	---	---	---	---	---	---	---	---	10	17	Total Rtn % Rank All
	---	---	---	---	---	---	---	---	---	---	5	29	Total Rtn % Rank Obj
	---	---	---	---	---	---	---	---	---	0.00	0.00	0.00	Income $
	---	---	---	---	---	---	---	---	---	0.18	0.30	0.37	Capital Gains $
	---	---	---	---	---	---	---	---	---	1.25	1.25	1.25	Expense Ratio %
	---	---	---	---	---	---	---	---	---	0.16	-0.12	-0.07	Income Ratio %
	---	---	---	---	---	---	---	---	---	52	62	40	Turnover Rate %
	---	---	---	---	---	---	---	---	---	27.6	64.5	100.5	Net Assets ($mil)

Performance 12-31-94

	1st Qtr	2nd Qtr	3rd Qtr	4th Qtr	Total
1987	---	---	---	---	---
1988	---	---	---	---	---
1989	---	---	---	---	---
1990	---	---	---	---	---
1991	---	---	---	---	---
1992	---	---	6.70	16.72	24.54 *
1993	4.40	5.31	8.08	6.24	26.24
1994	-4.22	-1.65	7.06	-0.56	0.29

Bear Market Performance

Decile Rank (5-year period)

Worst — Best

	Worst 3 Mo Period 1985-89	Worst 3 Mo Period 1990-94
T. Rowe Price Mid-Cap Growth	---	---
+/- S&P 500	---	---
+/- Best Fit Index :	---	---

Trailing Returns

	Total Return %	+/- S&P 500	+/- Wil 5000	% Rank All	% Rank Obj	Growth of $10,000
3 Mo	-0.56	-0.54	0.21	35	34	9,944
6 Mo	6.46	1.60	1.84	8	22	10,646
1 Yr	0.29	-1.02	0.36	17	29	10,029
3 Yr Avg	---	---	---	---	---	---
5 Yr Avg	---	---	---	---	---	---
10 Yr Avg	---	---	---	---	---	---
15 Yr Avg	---	---	---	---	---	---

Operations

Address and Telephone	100 E. Pratt Street
	Baltimore, MD 21202
	800-638-5660 / 410-547-2308
Advisor	T. Rowe Price Associates
Subadvisor	None
Distributor	T. Rowe Price Investment Services
States Available	All plus GU,PR,VI
Report Grade	A-
Income Distrib	Paid Annually
* Date of Inception	06-30-92
Fiscal Year End	December

Risk Analysis

Time Period	Load-Adj Return %	Risk % Rank[1] All	Obj	Morningstar[2] Return	Risk	Morningstar Risk-Adj Rating
1 Yr	0.29	---	---	---	---	---
3 Yr	---	---	---	---	---	---
5 Yr	---	---	---	---	---	---
10 Yr	---	---	---	---	---	---

Average Historical Rating ---

[1] 1 = low, 100 = high   [2] 1.00 = Equity Avg   [3] 1.00 = 90-day T-bill return

Other Measures

			Standard S&P 500	Best Fit
Standard Deviation	---	Alpha	---	---
Mean	---	Beta	---	---
Sharpe Ratio	---	R-Squared	---	---

Investment Style

	Stock Portfolio Avg	Relative S&P 500	Style
Price/Earnings Ratio	24.9	1.35	
Price/Book Ratio	3.3	0.97	
5 Yr Earnings Gr %	14.9#	2.68	
Return on Assets %	8.7	1.16	
Debt % Total Cap	23.3	0.82	
Med Mkt Cap ($mil)	735	0.06	

figure is based on 50% or less of stocks

Diversification Value for Portfolio Types

Large Cap: Small Cap: Bond: Balanced: Diversified:

Expenses & Fees

Sales Fees	0.00% front
	0.00% deferred
	0.00% 12b-1
Management Fee	0.35% flat fee+0.48%G
3-,5-,10-yr Expense Projections	$40, $69, $151
Annual Brokerage Cost	1.07%

Min Initial Purchase	$2500 (Addt'l: $100)
Min IRA Purchase	$1000 (Addt'l: $50)
Min Auto Invest Plan	$50 (Systematic Inv: $50)

Portfolio 06-30-94

Share Chg (12-93) 000	Amount 000	Total Stocks: 70 / Total Fixed-Income: 0	Value $000	% Net Assets
29	179	Smith International	2734	3.14
35	65	Sbarro	2421	2.78
15	40	Alco Standard	2285	2.62
30	60	SunGard Data Systems	2175	2.50
5	45	Danaher	1879	2.16
25	70	Pittston Services Group	1872	2.15
28	53	Mercantile Bancorp	1844	2.12
11	33	First Financial Management	1831	2.10
15	50	Fred Meyer	1819	2.09
40	90	Duff & Phelps	1789	2.05
25	60	Minerals Technologies	1740	2.00
35	95	SEI	1734	1.99
24	40	Catalina Marketing	1680	1.93
15	35	Integra Financial	1636	1.88
20	90	Reliance Electric Cl A	1631	1.87
40	100	Addington Resources	1625	1.86
0	70	TriMas	1610	1.85
15	85	Albany International Cl A	1605	1.84
21	60	CUC International	1605	1.84
32	57	Sealed Air	1582	1.82
20	70	Placer Dome	1505	1.73
50	50	Jones Apparel Group	1412	1.62
50	100	Oceaneering International	1400	1.61
10	60	Freeport-McMoRan Cop/Gold A	1335	1.53
0	40	Teleflex	1305	1.50

Composition % 12-31-94

Cash	8.8	Preferreds	0.0
Stocks	91.2	Convertibles	0.0
Bonds	0.0	Other	0.0

Tax Analysis

	Tax-Adj Historical Return %	% Pretax Return
3 Yr Avg	---	---
5 Yr Avg	---	---
10 Yr Avg	---	---
Potential Capital Gain Exposure (% of assets)		10%

Most Similar Funds in MF500

Fund lacks three-year record

Index Allocation

	% of Stocks
S&P 500	13.4
S&P MidCap 400	32.5
U.S. Small Cap	51.4
Foreign	4.7

Sector Weightings

	% of Stocks	Relative S&P 500
Utilities	0.0	0.00
Energy	7.8	0.77
Financials	11.8	1.11
Industrial Cyclicals	25.6	1.56
Consumer Durables	7.4	1.18
Consumer Staples	0.0	0.00
Services	18.1	2.22
Retail	6.3	1.07
Health	7.1	0.82
Technology	16.0	1.75

T. Rowe Price New America Gr

	Ticker	Load	NAV	Yield	SEC Yield	Assets	Objective
	PRWAX	None	25.42	0.0%	N/A	646.1	Growth

T. Rowe Price New America Growth Fund seeks long-term growth of capital.

The fund invests primarily in common stocks of U.S. companies that operate in the service sector of the economy. It seeks companies that are above-average performers in their field, without regard to the company's size. The fund stresses long-term earnings-growth potential, high and stable unit growth in services delivered, proprietary industry position, superior management, and above-average profitability.

On Aug. 31, 1992, USF&G Axe-Houghton Growth Fund was merged into this fund.

Historical Profile
Return	Above Average
Risk	Above Average
Rating	★★★★ Above Average

Investment Style History
Equity
Average % Stocks Held in Portfolio

94% 95% 96% 90% 89% 92% 94% 96%

Growth of $10,000
IIII Value of Fund ($000)
— Value of Index ($000) Wil 4500
▼ Manager Change
▽ Partial Manager Change
► Mgr Unknown After
◄ Mgr Unknown Before

Manager's Investment Style

Management focuses on service-oriented issues that have strong cash flow and three- and five-year earnings-growth rates above 15%. Although the prospectus doesn't place a limitation on the size of the companies in which the fund invests, management typically favors small- to mid-cap firms.

Performance Quartile (Within Objective)

	1983	1984	1985	1986	1987	1988	1989	1990	1991	1992	1993	1994	History
	---	---	11.85	13.14	10.45	12.38	16.90	14.66	22.79	24.86	28.04	25.42	NAV
	---	---	18.50 *	14.37	-9.40	18.47	38.41	-12.24	61.95	9.89	17.44	-7.43	Total Return %
	---	---	1.28 *	-4.31	-14.66	1.86	6.73	-9.13	31.47	2.27	7.38	-8.75	+/- S&P 500
	---	---	---	-1.73	-11.76	0.53	9.24	-6.06	27.74	0.92	6.16	-7.36	+/- Wilshire 5000
	---	---	0.00	0.90	0.42	0.00	0.00	1.01	0.00	0.00	0.00	0.00	Income Return %
	---	---	18.50	13.47	-9.82	18.47	38.41	-13.25	61.95	9.89	17.44	-7.43	Capital Return %
	---	---	---	58	96	17	4	88	4	23	22	82	Total Rtn % Rank All
	---	---	---	53	96	33	10	87	7	38	23	86	Total Rtn % Rank Obj
	---	---	0.00	0.10	0.00	0.00	0.00	0.17	0.00	0.00	0.00	0.00	Income $
	---	---	0.00	0.30	1.39	0.00	0.23	0.00	0.87	0.18	1.13	0.53	Capital Gains $
	---	---	1.00	1.00	1.23	1.50	1.50	1.25	1.25	1.25	1.23	1.19	Expense Ratio %
	---	---	3.40	0.38	-0.08	-0.36	-0.02	0.81	-0.12	-0.44	-0.39	-0.37	Income Ratio %
	---	---	---	49	81	72	45	40	42	42	26	44	35	Turnover Rate %
	---	---	30.5	83.3	62.4	66.4	134.1	95.7	231.7	480.2	618.6	646.1	Net Assets ($mil)

Fund Manager(s)

John H. Laporte CFA, since 09-85. Birthdate: 07-45. BA, Princeton U. 1967 MBA, Harvard 1969
Brian W. H. Berghuis CFA(1987), since 1992. Birthdate: 10-58. BA, Princeton U. 1981 MBA, Harvard 1985

Manager Experience	Dates Managed	Invest Obj	Std Dev	+/- Index
John H. Laporte				
T. Rowe Price New Horizon	09/87 - 12/94	SC	21.58	1.40
Brian W. H. Berghuis				
T. Rowe Price Mid-Cap Gr	06/92 - 12/94	G	11.64	12.12

Performance 12-31-94

	1st Qtr	2nd Qtr	3rd Qtr	4th Qtr	Total
1987	18.07	-3.96	5.57	-24.31	-9.40
1988	12.82	6.53	0.00	-1.43	18.47
1989	13.33	12.62	12.59	-3.68	38.41
1990	-3.61	8.59	-25.21	12.10	-12.24
1991	25.92	0.60	15.94	10.27	61.95
1992	-0.35	-9.73	5.17	16.16	9.89
1993	-0.20	3.75	10.10	3.02	17.44
1994	-5.53	-4.68	6.69	-3.65	-7.43

Bear Market Performance

Decile Rank (5-year period)

Worst ——————— Best

	Worst 3 Mo Period 1985-89	Worst 3 Mo Period 1990-94
T. Rowe Price New America Gr	---	-25.21
+/- S&P 500	---	-11.47
+/- Best Fit Index : Wil 4500	---	-6.98

Trailing Returns

	Total Return %	+/- S&P 500	+/- Wil 5000	% Rank All	% Rank Obj	Growth of $10,000
3 Mo	-3.65	-3.63	-2.88	87	85	9,635
6 Mo	2.80	-2.06	-1.83	22	64	10,280
1 Yr	-7.43	-8.75	-7.36	82	86	9,257
3 Yr Avg	6.11	-0.16	-0.50	33	48	11,947
5 Yr Avg	11.17	2.48	2.35	12	18	16,979
10 Yr Avg	---	---	---	---	---	---
15 Yr Avg	---	---	---	---	---	---

Operations

Address and Telephone	100 E. Pratt Street	
	Baltimore, MD 21202	
	800-638-5660 / 410-547-2308	
Advisor	T. Rowe Price Associates	
Subadvisor	None	
Distributor	T. Rowe Price Investment Services	
States Available	All plus GU,PR,VI	
Report Grade	A-	
Income Distrib	Paid Annually	
* Date of Inception	09-30-85	
Fiscal Year End	December	

Risk Analysis

Time Period	Load-Adj Return %	Risk % Rank [1] All	Risk % Rank [1] Obj	Morningstar [2] Return	Morningstar Risk	Morningstar Risk-Adj Rating
1 Yr	-7.43					
3 Yr	6.11	91	86	0.75 [3]	1.22	★★★
5 Yr	11.17	91	91	1.69 [3]	1.19	★★★★
10 Yr	---	---	---	---	---	---
Average Historical Rating (76 months)					3.4	★s

[1] 1 = low, 100 = high [2] 1.00 = Equity Avg [3] 1.00 = 90-day T-bill return

Other Measures

			Standard S&P 500	Best Fit Wil 4500
Standard Deviation	14.10	Alpha	0.1	-2.3
Mean	6.92	Beta	1.15	1.34
Sharpe Ratio	0.24	R-Squared	42	86

Investment Style

	Stock Portfolio Avg	Relative S&P 500
Price/Earnings Ratio	25.1	1.36
Price/Book Ratio	4.1	1.22
5 Yr Earnings Gr %	24.1#	4.33
Return on Assets %	9.8	1.30
Debt % Total Cap	23.6	0.83
Med Mkt Cap ($mil)	1200	0.09

figure is based on 50% or less of stocks

Style
Value Blend Growth
Size Large Med Small

Diversification Value for Portfolio Types

Large Cap: Medium	Small Cap: None	Bond: High	Balanced: Medium	Diversified: Medium

Expenses & Fees

Sales Fees
	0.00% front
	0.00% deferred
	0.00% 12b-1
Management Fee	0.35% flat fee+0.48%G
3-,5-,10-yr Expense Projections	$37, $65, $143
Annual Brokerage Cost	0.44%

Min Initial Purchase	$2500 (Addt'l: $100)
Min IRA Purchase	$1000 (Addt'l: $50)
Min Auto Invest Plan	$50 (Systematic Inv: $50)

Portfolio 12-31-94

Total Stocks: 91
Total Fixed-Income: 0

Share Chg (06-94) 000	Amount 000		Value $000	% Net Assets
50	892	CUC International	29866	4.62
0	400	United HealthCare	18050	2.79
25	275	First Financial Management	16947	2.62
42	292	Catalina Marketing	16231	2.51
25	250	Alco Standard	15688	2.43
0	500	Foundation Health	15500	2.40
364	364	Viacom Cl B	14775	2.29
209	542	Sbarro	14099	2.18
12	363	SunGard Data Systems	13976	2.16
0	338	Paychex	13669	2.12
81	350	Columbia/HCA Healthcare	12775	1.98
265	375	Vodafone Group (ADR)	12609	1.95
25	350	Franklin Resources	12469	1.93
0	375	MGIC Investment	12422	1.92
188	650	Brinker International	11781	1.82
199	459	Sanifill	11473	1.78
25	650	ADVO	11213	1.74
134	234	Cardinal Health	10866	1.68
0	500	Wal-Mart Stores	10625	1.64
-54	493	Fiserv	10597	1.64
325	475	Danka Business Systems (ADR)	10272	1.59
244	244	Nordstrom	10248	1.59
50	422	Office Depot	10128	1.57
0	350	State Street Boston	10019	1.55
-63	337	General Nutrition	9767	1.51

Composition % 12-31-94

Cash	3.9	Preferreds	0.0
Stocks	96.1	Convertibles	0.0
Bonds	0.0	Other	0.0

Tax Analysis

	Tax-Adj Historical Return %	% Pretax Return
3 Yr Avg	5.45	88.7
5 Yr Avg	10.44	92.2
10 Yr Avg	---	---
Potential Capital Gain Exposure (% of assets)		19%

Most Similar Funds in MF500

Hancock Emerging Growth B	Strong Fit
MainStay Capital Apprec B	Strong Fit
Oppenheimer Discovery A	Strong Fit

Index Allocation

	% of Stocks
S&P 500	23.0
S&P MidCap 400	34.2
U.S. Small Cap	38.8
Foreign	4.0

Sector Weightings

	% of Stocks	Relative S&P 500
Utilities	0.0	0.00
Energy	3.2	0.31
Financials	12.7	1.20
Industrial Cyclicals	6.7	0.41
Consumer Durables	3.0	0.48
Consumer Staples	0.0	0.00
Services	28.8	3.53
Retail	13.7	2.36
Health	13.0	1.50
Technology	18.9	2.06

MORNINGSTAR 1995 Mutual Fund 500

T. Rowe Price New Asia

	Ticker	Load	NAV	Yield	SEC Yield	Assets	Objective
	PRASX	None	8.01	0.8%	N/A	1987.6	Pacific Stock

T. Rowe Price New Asia Fund seeks capital appreciation.

The fund invests primarily in the common stocks of large- and small-capitalization companies domiciled, or with primary operations, in Asia and the Pacific Basin (excluding Japan). At least 65% of its assets will be invested in the equity securities of Asian companies, excluding Japan. The fund may invest in countries such as China, Sri Lanka, Laos, Vietnam, or Cambodia, as their markets become more accessible. The fund may purchase up to 35% of its assets in non-U.S.-dollar-denominated high-grade debt securities.

Manager's Investment Style

Management takes a well-diversified approach to the Pacific Basin, spreading the fund's assets among hundreds of stocks.

Fund Manager(s)

Martin G. Wade, since 09-90. Birthdate: 02-43. MA, Cambridge U. 1965

Manager Experience

	Dates Managed	Invest Obj	Std Dev	+/- Index
Martin G. Wade				
T. Rowe Price Intl Stock	05/80 - 12/94	WF	16.07	0.56
T. Rowe Price Intl Dscvry	12/88 - 12/94	WF	17.25	-2.63

Historical Profile

Return	High
Risk	Above Average
Rating	★★★★★ Highest

Investment Style History Equity — Average % Stocks Held in Portfolio

							92%	93%	89%	92%

Growth of $10,000

||||| Value of Fund ($000)
— Value of Index ($000) MSPacxJp
▼ Manager Change
▽ Partial Manager Change
► Mgr Unknown After
◄ Mgr Unknown Before

Performance Quartile (Within Objective)

	1983	1984	1985	1986	1987	1988	1989	1990	1991	1992	1993	1994	History
	---	---	---	---	---	---	---	5.04	5.91	6.34	11.10	8.01	NAV
	---	---	---	---	---	---	---	1.60 *	19.32	11.24	78.76	-19.15	Total Return %
	---	---	---	---	---	---	---	-7.36 *	-11.17	3.62	68.70	-20.47	+/- S&P 500
	---	---	---	---	---	---	---	---	6.21	5.05	-7.26	-10.25	+/- MSCI FE ex Jpn
	---	---	---	---	---	---	---	0.80	2.05	1.66	0.37	0.86	Income Return %
	---	---	---	---	---	---	---	0.80	17.26	9.58	78.39	-20.01	Capital Return %
	---	---	---	---	---	---	---	---	45	17	1	99	Total Rtn % Rank All
	---	---	---	---	---	---	---	---	16	13	22	77	Total Rtn % Rank Obj
	---	---	---	---	---	---	---	0.04	0.10	0.10	0.04	0.07	Income $
	---	---	---	---	---	---	---	0.00	0.00	0.13	0.19	0.89	Capital Gains $
	---	---	---	---	---	---	---	1.75	1.75	1.51	1.29	1.22	Expense Ratio %
	---	---	---	---	---	---	---	2.10	1.75	1.64	1.02	0.85	Income Ratio %
	---	---	---	---	---	---	---	---	49	36	40	63	Turnover Rate %
	---	---	---	---	---	---	---	80.0	102.9	314.5	2234.4	1987.6	Net Assets ($mil)

Performance 12-31-94

	1st Qtr	2nd Qtr	3rd Qtr	4th Qtr	Total
1987	---	---	---	---	---
1988	---	---	---	---	---
1989	---	---	---	---	---
1990	---	---	---	1.60	1.60 *
1991	19.05	-2.08	-1.96	4.40	19.32
1992	3.55	10.95	-6.19	3.20	11.24
1993	7.49	7.78	15.25	33.88	78.76
1994	-20.14	0.79	13.33	-11.36	-19.15

Bear Market Performance

Decile Rank (5-year period)

Worst — Best

	Worst 3 Mo Period 1985-89	Worst 3 Mo Period 1990-94
T. Rowe Price New Asia	---	---
+/- S&P 500	---	---
+/- Best Fit Index :	---	---

Trailing Returns

	Total Return %	+/- S&P 500	+/- MSCI FE ex Jpn	% Rank All	% Rank Obj	Growth of $10,000
3 Mo	-11.36	-11.35	-3.10	99	84	8,864
6 Mo	0.45	-4.41	-4.90	48	25	10,045
1 Yr	-19.15	-20.47	-10.25	99	77	8,085
3 Yr Avg	17.15	10.88	-4.48	2	22	16,076
5 Yr Avg	---	---	---	---	---	---
10 Yr Avg	---	---	---	---	---	---
15 Yr Avg	---	---	---	---	---	---

Risk Analysis

Time Period	Load-Adj Return %	Risk % Rank [1] All	Risk % Rank [1] Obj	Morningstar [2] Return	Morningstar Risk	Morningstar Risk-Adj Rating
1 Yr	-19.15					
3 Yr	17.15	95	54	4.46 [3]	1.41	★★★★★
5 Yr	---	---	---	---	---	
10 Yr	---	---	---	---	---	

Average Historical Rating (16 months) 4.7 ★s

[1] 1 = low, 100 = high [2] 1.00 = Equity Avg [3] 1.00 = 90-day T-bill return

Other Measures

			Standard S&P 500	Best Fit MSPacxJp
Standard Deviation	20.63	Alpha	11.8	0.0
Mean	18.01	Beta	1.12	0.96
Sharpe Ratio	0.70	R-Squared	19	92

Investment Style

	Stock Portfolio Avg	Rel MSCI EAFE	Rel Obj
Price/Earnings Ratio	25.1	0.68	0.79
Price/Cash Flow	21.5	1.38	1.12
Price/Book Ratio	2.8	1.07	0.96
5 Yr Earnings Gr %	18.2#	---	1.64
Return on Assets %	8.7#	1.92	1.09
Debt % Total Cap	24.2	0.71	1.01
Med Mkt Cap ($mil)	2045	0.17	0.50

figure is based on 50% or less of stocks

Style: V B G / Size L M S

Diversification Value for Portfolio Types

Large Cap: High	Small Cap: High	Bond: High	Balanced: High	Diversified: Medium

Portfolio 10-31-94

Share Chg (04-94) 000	Amount 000	Total Stocks: 153 / Total Fixed-Income: 8	Value $000	% Net Assets
532	5614	United Overseas Bank	62	2.67
905	5146	Bangkok Bank	56	2.42
1928	6683	Swire Pacific CI A	51	2.22
15092	30000	Renong	47	2.04
3139	11000	Technology Resources	43	1.86
11769	11769	Telecom New Zealand	41	1.78
628	7574	United Engineers	41	1.78
1173	4562	Thai Farmers Bank	40	1.75
2201	8650	Hutchison Whampoa	40	1.74
701	6020	Western Mining	38	1.63
2351	7659	Guoco Group	36	1.57
3827	7411	Golden Plus Holdings	36	1.56
1220	14661	Carter Holt Harvey	36	1.54
954	4104	Aokam Perdana	34	1.47
6432	12707	Hysan Development	34	1.47
980	4613	Westmont	33	1.42
908	11992	Fletcher Challenge (NZ)	32	1.40
8610	31248	Hopewell Holdings	32	1.40
-88	556	Siam Cement	32	1.39
4877	4877	Singapore Land	31	1.36

Index Allocation

	% of Stocks
S&P 500	0.9
S&P MidCap 400	0.0
U.S. Small Cap	0.9
Foreign	98.2

Composition % 12-31-94

Cash	4.9	Preferreds	0.3
Stocks	92.9	Convertibles	1.1
Bonds	0.0	Other	0.8

Country Exposure 12-31-94

	% of Stocks
Malaysia	21
Hong Kong	20
Singapore	15
Australia	12
Thailand	11

Total Number of Countries: 12
Hedging Policy: Occasional

Tax Analysis

	Tax-Adj Historical Return %	% Pretax Return
3 Yr Avg	15.30	87.7
5 Yr Avg	---	---
10 Yr Avg	---	---
Potential Capital Gain Exposure (% of assets)		-6%

Most Similar Funds in MF500

Asia Pacific	Fair Fit
Newport Tiger	Fair Fit
Malaysia Fund	Weak Fit

Sector Weightings

	% of Stocks	Relative S&P 500
Utilities	2.0	0.32
Energy	1.1	0.61
Financials	41.1	1.61
Industrial Cyclicals	27.6	1.24
Consumer Durables	6.1	0.44
Consumer Staples	0.7	0.26
Services	17.0	1.32
Retail	1.6	0.29
Health	0.0	0.01
Technology	2.9	0.37

Operations

Address and Telephone	100 E. Pratt Street
	Baltimore, MD 21202
	800-638-5660 / 410-547-2308
Advisor	Rowe Price-Fleming International
Subadvisor	None
Distributor	T. Rowe Price Investment Services
States Available	All plus GU,PR,VI
Report Grade	A+
Income Distrib	Paid Annually
* Date of Inception	09-28-90
Fiscal Year End	October

Min Initial Purchase	$2500 (Addt'l: $100)
Min IRA Purchase	$1000 (Addt'l: $50)
Min Auto Invest Plan	$50 (Systematic Inv: $50)

Expenses & Fees

Sales Fees	0.00% front
	0.00% deferred
	0.00% 12b-1
Management Fee	0.50% flat fee+0.48%G
3-,5-,10-yr Expense Projections	$41, $71, $156
Annual Brokerage Cost	0.75%

T. Rowe Price New Era

	Ticker	Load	NAV	Yield	SEC Yield	Assets	Objective
	PRNEX	None	20.15	1.8%	N/A	979.5	Sp.-Nat. Res.

T. Rowe Price New Era Fund seeks long-term growth of capital; current income is not a consideration.

The fund invests primarily in the common stocks of companies whose earnings or value is expected to grow faster than the rate of inflation over the long term. Usually, it invests in companies that own or develop natural resources, or demonstrate the flexibility to adjust prices or the ability to control operating costs.

Historical Profile
Return — Average
Risk — Below Average
Rating — ★★★ Neutral

Investment Style History
Equity
Average % Stocks Held in Portfolio

84% 89% 91% 86% 87% 93% 89% 86%

Growth of $10,000
||| Value of Fund ($000)
— Value of Index ($000) S&P 500
▼ Manager Change
▽ Partial Manager Change
► Mgr Unknown After
◄ Mgr Unknown Before

Manager's Investment Style

Diversification is a key component to manager George Roche's investment style. Roche has dampened the fund's risk by investing one fourth of the fund's assets outside of the natural-resources sector, by owning a broad array of energy-related stocks (including energy, metal, chemical, and paper firms), and by holding a substantial portion of assets outside the U.S..

Performance Quartile
(Within Objective)

	1983	1984	1985	1986	1987	1988	1989	1990	1991	1992	1993	1994	History
	18.44	17.13	18.67	17.76	18.08	18.79	21.73	18.48	19.86	18.88	20.35	20.15	NAV
	25.47	3.35	23.42	15.99	17.84	10.32	24.29	-8.76	14.74	2.08	15.33	5.17	Total Return %
	3.00	-2.92	-8.32	-2.69	12.58	-6.29	-7.39	-5.64	-15.75	-5.54	5.28	3.86	+/- S&P 500
	---	---	---	---	7.97	-8.39	-15.41	-11.91	7.21	0.04	-0.39	1.34	+/- S&P Energy
	6.10	3.53	4.43	2.85	5.60	2.91	2.74	3.16	3.00	2.35	1.93	1.88	Income Return %
	19.37	-0.18	18.98	13.14	12.23	7.41	21.55	-11.92	11.74	-0.27	13.41	3.29	Capital Return %
	22	55	52	49	5	59	25	81	59	86	27	4	Total Rtn % Rank All
	25	1	1	22	18	56	64	50	10	60	82	7	Total Rtn % Rank Obj
	0.81	0.61	0.68	0.50	0.98	0.53	0.56	0.62	0.55	0.45	0.38	0.38	Income $
	0.07	1.29	1.41	3.25	1.77	1.05	1.05	0.71	0.73	0.94	1.03	0.87	Capital Gains $
	0.68	0.68	0.69	0.73	0.82	0.89	0.83	0.83	0.85	0.81	0.80	0.82	Expense Ratio %
	3.45	3.96	2.76	1.98	3.11	2.41	2.52	2.81	2.56	2.22	1.92	1.74	Income Ratio %
	37	39	37	32	30	16	19	9	9	17	25	21	Turnover Rate %
	485.1	472.1	529.5	496.2	756.5	726.5	826.6	707.5	756.8	699.6	752.6	979.5	Net Assets ($mil)

Fund Manager(s)

George A. Roche, since 1979. Birthdate: 07-41.
BA, Georgetown U. 1963   MBA, Harvard 1966

Manager Experience

	Dates Managed	Invest Obj	Std Dev	+/- Index
Not available.				

Performance 12-31-94

	1st Qtr	2nd Qtr	3rd Qtr	4th Qtr	Total
1987	26.83	2.14	13.26	-19.69	17.84
1988	5.03	7.11	-4.77	2.97	10.32
1989	6.76	3.89	8.45	3.34	24.29
1990	-1.52	-0.61	-6.54	-0.27	-8.76
1991	7.47	1.96	3.31	1.36	14.74
1992	-5.59	4.75	3.21	0.01	2.08
1993	5.99	1.90	1.08	5.65	15.33
1994	-1.38	1.94	7.28	-2.49	5.17

Bear Market Performance

Decile Rank (5-year period)

Worst ———————————————— Best

	Worst 3 Mo Period 1985-89	Worst 3 Mo Period 1990-94
T. Rowe Price New Era	-24.99	-14.51
+/- S&P 500	4.59	-0.67
+/- Best Fit Index : S&P 500	4.59	-0.67

Trailing Returns

	Total Return %	+/- S&P 500	+/- S&P Energy	% Rank All	% Rank Obj	Growth of $10,000
3 Mo	-2.49	-2.48	-4.38	77	3	9,751
6 Mo	4.61	-0.26	1.09	13	3	10,461
1 Yr	5.17	3.86	1.34	4	7	10,517
3 Yr Avg	7.38	1.11	0.35	24	45	12,381
5 Yr Avg	5.33	-3.37	-1.02	86	22	12,962
10 Yr Avg	11.61	-2.78	---	41	14	29,980
15 Yr Avg	11.67	-2.82	---	58	1	52,340

Operations

Address and Telephone	100 E. Pratt Street	
	Baltimore, MD 21202	
	800-638-5660 / 410-547-2308	
Advisor	T. Rowe Price Associates	
Subadvisor	None	
Distributor	T. Rowe Price Investment Services	
States Available	All plus GU,PR,VI	
Report Grade	A	
Income Distrib	Paid Annually	
Date of Inception	01-20-69	
Fiscal Year End	December	

Risk Analysis

Time Period	Load-Adj Return %	Risk % Rank All	Obj	Morningstar Return	Morningstar Risk	Morningstar Risk-Adj Rating
1 Yr	5.17					
3 Yr	7.38	59	1	1.14[3]	0.64	★★★★
5 Yr	5.33	64	1	0.14[3]	0.77	★★
10 Yr	11.61	59	1	0.81	0.83	★★★
Average Historical Rating (109 months)					3.2	★s

[1] = low, 100 = high   [2] 1.00 = Equity Avg   [3] 1.00 = 90-day T-bill return

Other Measures

				Standard S&P 500	Best Fit S&P 500
Standard Deviation	7.81	Alpha		1.7	1.7
Mean	7.45	Beta		0.78	0.78
Sharpe Ratio	0.50	R-Squared		63	63

Investment Style

	Stock Portfolio Avg	Relative S&P 500	Style Value Blend Growth
Price/Earnings Ratio	27.9	1.51	
Price/Book Ratio	2.8	0.82	
5 Yr Earnings Gr %	1.8	0.32	
Return on Assets %	5.6	0.74	
Debt % Total Cap	31.2	1.10	
Med Mkt Cap ($mil)	6166	0.47	

Size: Large Med Small

Diversification Value for Portfolio Types

Large Cap: Low	Small Cap: High	Bond: High	Balanced: Low	Diversified: Low

Expenses & Fees

Sales Fees
0.00% front
0.00% deferred
0.00% 12b-1

Management Fee   0.25% flat fee+0.48%G
3-,5-,10-yr Expense Projections $26, $44, $98
Annual Brokerage Cost   0.24%

Min Initial Purchase $2500 (Addt'l: $100)
Min IRA Purchase $1000 (Addt'l: $50)
Min Auto Invest Plan $50 (Systematic Inv: $50)

Portfolio 12-31-94

Total Stocks: 76
Total Fixed-Income: 2

Share Chg (06-94) 000	Amount 000		Value $000	% Net Assets
0	2053	Wal-Mart Stores	43619	4.45
0	440	Mobil	37070	3.78
50	358	Atlantic Richfield	36457	3.72
0	559	El DuPont de Nemours	31444	3.21
114	800	Newmont Mining	28800	2.94
90	260	Royal Dutch Petroleum	27907	2.85
180	500	Schlumberger	25188	2.57
121	1121	American Barrick Resources	24934	2.55
10000	10000	Lonrho	23780	2.43
450	3450	TVX Gold	23288	2.38
920	920	Ashanti Goldfields	19780	2.02
0	430	Union Pacific	19619	2.00
1000	1000	USX-Marathon Group	16375	1.67
200	700	Placer Dome	15225	1.55
-150	790	Rouse	15010	1.53
100	320	Amerada Hess	14600	1.49
0	340	Murphy Oil	14450	1.48
0	430	Northern Telecom	14351	1.47
50	280	Kimberly-Clark	14140	1.44
200	200	CSX	13925	1.42
75	400	Halliburton	13250	1.35
0	200	Bristol-Myers Squibb	11575	1.18
0	190	Texaco	11376	1.16
-100	600	Camco International	11325	1.16
0	170	Eli Lilly	11156	1.14

Composition % 12-31-94

Cash	12.1	Preferreds	0.0
Stocks	87.1	Convertibles	0.8
Bonds	0.0	Other	0.0

Tax Analysis

	Tax-Adj Historical Return %	% Pretax Return
3 Yr Avg	5.29	70.2
5 Yr Avg	3.26	58.7
10 Yr Avg	8.75	65.7
Potential Capital Gain Exposure (% of assets)		19

Most Similar Funds in MF500

Dean Witter Dividend Growth	Weak Fit
Vanguard Index 500	Weak Fit
Lexington Corporate Leaders	Weak Fit

Index Allocation

	% of Stocks
S&P 500	70.8
S&P MidCap 400	6.2
U.S. Small Cap	12.6
Foreign	20.8

Sector Weightings

	% of Stocks	Relative S&P 500
Utilities	1.1	0.09
Energy	36.7	3.63
Financials	1.5	0.14
Industrial Cyclicals	35.8	2.18
Consumer Durables	4.0	0.64
Consumer Staples	0.0	0.00
Services	7.9	0.97
Retail	6.8	1.16
Health	2.9	0.34
Technology	3.4	0.37

MORNINGSTAR 1995 Mutual Fund 500

T. Rowe Price New Income

	Ticker	Load	NAV	Yield	SEC Yield	Assets	Objective
	PRCIX	None	8.39	6.8%	7.28%	1367.8	Corp Hi Qlty

T. Rowe Price New Income Fund seeks income over the long term consistent with capital preservation.

The fund normally invests at least 80% of its assets in investment-grade, income-producing securities. It may hold corporate debt, U.S. government obligations, cash equivalents, foreign securities, private placements, futures contracts, convertibles, and preferred and common stocks. The fund may write covered call options and purchase covered put options.

On Feb. 7, 1992, Bell Atlantic Bond Portfolio merged into this fund. On Aug. 31, 1992, USF&G Axe-Houghton Income Fund merged into this fund.

Manager's Investment Style

Management doesn't deviate far from the norm; performance that closely resembles the Lehman Brothers Aggregate Bond Index comes from several factors. Maturity, for example, is generally close to that of the index. Management also follows an index-like asset allocation, with a 30% mortgage position being neutral. Management has also favored a barbelled maturity strategy, while cushioning risk with a cash position.

Fund Manager(s)

Charles P. Smith, since 03-86. Birthdate: 12-43.
BS, Boston C. 1966   MBA, Loyola C. 1973

Manager Experience

	Dates Managed	Invest Obj	Std Dev	+/- Index
Charles P. Smith				
T. Rowe Price US Tres Int	09/89 - 12/94	GT	3.50	-0.69

Historical Profile

Return	Above Average
Risk	Average
Rating ★★★	Neutral

	1983	1984	1985	1986	1987	1988	1989	1990	1991	1992	1993	1994	History
	8.27	8.26	8.73	9.13	8.55	8.37	8.59	8.58	9.16	9.00	9.24	8.39	NAV
	9.74	11.85	17.64	13.85	2.04	7.59	12.22	8.76	15.52	4.96	9.07	-2.21	Total Return %
	1.37	-3.31	-4.49	-1.40	-0.71	-0.29	-2.32	-0.18	-0.49	-2.28	-0.68	0.71	+/- LB Aggregate
	0.47	-4.78	-6.42	-2.68	-0.51	-1.63	-1.76	1.61	-2.99	-3.74	-3.09	1.71	+/- LB Corporate
	11.99	11.97	11.95	9.27	8.40	9.70	9.60	8.78	8.56	6.71	5.61	6.33	Income Return %
	-2.25	-0.12	5.69	4.58	-6.35	-2.11	2.63	-0.01	6.95	-1.75	3.46	-8.54	Capital Return %
	80	18	84	62	42	76	57	10	55	77	73	36	Total Rtn % Rank All
	15	78	70	46	47	30	39	18	36	85	42	43	Total Rtn % Rank Obj
	0.98	0.93	0.90	0.77	0.75	0.81	0.76	0.71	0.67	0.60	0.49	0.58	Income $
	0.00	0.00	0.00	0.00	0.00	0.00	0.00	0.01	0.02	0.00	0.07	0.07	Capital Gains $
	0.57	0.62	0.64	0.66	0.65	0.80	0.91	0.86	0.88	0.87	0.84	0.82	Expense Ratio %
	12.10	11.13	11.53	10.39	8.22	8.77	9.50	8.85	8.33	7.64	6.36	5.77	Income Ratio %
	67	84	155	185	125	158	92	51	21	50	86	58	Turnover Rate %
	640.3	695.5	707.8	933.0	789.8	859.8	1043.6	1093.0	1400.7	1461.3	1558.1	1367.8	Net Assets ($mil)

Investment Style History
Fixed Income
Income Rtn % Rank Obj

Growth of $10,000
- |||| Value of Fund ($000)
- — Value of Index ($000) LB Govt
- ▼ Manager Change
- ▽ Partial Manager Change
- ► Mgr Unknown After
- ◄ Mgr Unknown Before

Performance Quartile (Within Objective)

Performance 12-31-94

	1st Qtr	2nd Qtr	3rd Qtr	4th Qtr	Total
1987	0.89	-2.37	-1.94	5.65	2.04
1988	3.59	0.90	1.69	1.22	7.59
1989	0.61	6.63	1.13	3.43	12.22
1990	-1.18	3.37	1.26	5.15	8.76
1991	2.09	1.52	5.65	5.51	15.52
1992	-2.00	3.63	3.73	-0.37	4.96
1993	3.82	2.59	2.96	-0.54	9.07
1994	-2.19	-1.15	0.58	0.56	-2.21

Bear Market Performance

Decile Rank (5-year period)

Worst .... Best

	Worst 3 Mo Period 1985-89	Worst 3 Mo Period 1990-94
T. Rowe Price New Income	-4.14	-3.97
+/- LB Aggregate	-0.59	0.97
+/- Best Fit Index : LB Govt	-0.68	1.11

Trailing Returns

	Total Return %	+/- LB Aggregate	+/- LB Corporate	% Rank All	% Rank Obj	Growth of $10,000
3 Mo	0.56	0.18	0.13	10	24	10,056
6 Mo	1.14	0.15	-0.03	35	22	10,114
1 Yr	-2.21	0.71	1.71	36	43	9,779
3 Yr Avg	3.84	-0.71	-1.58	73	62	11,195
5 Yr Avg	7.06	-0.56	-1.20	49	34	14,066
10 Yr Avg	8.79	-1.16	-1.84	76	59	23,212
15 Yr Avg	9.47	-1.34	-1.85	83	78	38,867

Operations

Address and Telephone	100 E. Pratt Street
	Baltimore, MD 21202
	800-638-5660 / 410-547-2308
Advisor	T. Rowe Price Associates
Subadvisor	None
Distributor	T. Rowe Price Investment Services
States Available	All plus PR
Report Grade	A-
Income Distrib	Paid Monthly
Date of Inception	10-15-73
Fiscal Year End	February

Min Initial Purchase	$2500 (Addt'l: $100)
Min IRA Purchase	$1000 (Addt'l: $50)
Min Auto Invest Plan	$50 (Systematic Inv: $50)

Expenses & Fees

Sales Fees	0.00% front
	0.00% deferred
	0.00% 12b-1
Management Fee	0.15% flat fee+0.48%G
3-,5-,10-yr Expense Projections	$26, $46, $101

Risk Analysis

Time Period	Load-Adj Return %	Risk % Rank All	Risk % Rank Obj	Morningstar Return	Morningstar Risk	Morningstar Risk-Adj Rating
1 Yr	-2.21					
3 Yr	3.84	20	52	0.07[3]	0.97	★★★
5 Yr	7.06	19	53	0.57[3]	0.95	★★★
10 Yr	8.79	11	29	0.76[3]	0.92	★★★

Average Historical Rating (109 months) 4.2 ★s

[1] 1 = low, 100 = high   [2] 1.00 = Taxable Avg   [3] 1.00 = 90-day T-bill return

Other Measures

			Standard LB Agg	Best Fit LB Govt
Standard Deviation	3.73	Alpha	-0.6	-0.6
Mean	3.84	Beta	0.92	0.85
Sharpe Ratio	0.08	R-Squared	96	97

Investment Style

Interest-Rate Stance

Avg Effective Duration	4.9 Yrs
Avg Effective Maturity	10.1 Yrs

Maturity Short Intm Long

Quality

Avg Credit Quality	AA
Avg Weighted Coupon	7.86%
Avg Weighted Price	98.26% of Par

Diversification Value for Portfolio Types

Large Cap: Medium	Small Cap: High	Bond: None	Balanced: Medium	Diversified: Medium

Portfolio 11-30-94

Amount 000	Date of Maturity	Total Stocks: 0 / Total Fixed-Income: 124	Value $000	% Net Assets
135850	08-15-04	US Treasury Note 7.25%	130193	9.50
101027	03-15-23	GNMA 9.5%	104705	7.64
81938	08-15-24	GNMA 7.5%	75804	5.53
53678	11-15-24	GNMA 8%	52119	3.80
42160	11-15-21	US Treasury Bond 8%	41739	3.05
45889	08-15-24	GNMA 7%	40824	2.98
39120	11-15-24	GNMA 9%	39350	2.87
33972	01-15-21	GNMA 11%	37487	2.74
35000	02-15-21	US Treasury Bond 7.875%	34103	2.49
32140	05-15-21	US Treasury Bond 8.125%	32200	2.35
31000	08-01-95	IBM Credit 4.7%	30538	2.23
30152	11-15-24	GNMA 8.5%	29633	2.16
25750		US Treasury Note 6.875%	25080	1.83
14150	11-15-11	British Col Hydro Pwr 15.5%	16823	1.23
16015	11-15-04	US Treasury Note 7.875%	15972	1.17
15000	01-30-95	GMAC 6%	14987	1.09
15000	02-12-96	Citicorp 5.7%	14710	1.07
15000	08-07-95	Central Fidelity Banks 4.38%	14583	1.06
13000	06-16-95	Southern California Gas 4.69%	12867	0.94
1150	08-15-21	Capital Cities/ABC 8.75%	11496	0.84
12727	06-01-24	FHLMC 6.5%	11180	0.82
11000	06-20-95	Coca-Cola Enterprises 8.35%	11094	0.81
9000	03-15-12	Province of Ontario 15.75%	10848	0.79
10600	02-01-03	Weyerhaeuser 9.05%	10819	0.79
13295	08-15-23	US Treasury Bond 6.25%	10642	0.78

Composition % 12-31-94

Cash	7.0	Preferreds	0.0
Stocks	0.0	Convertibles	0.0
Bonds	93.0	Other	0.0

Tax Analysis

	Tax-Adj Historical Return %	% Pretax Return
3 Yr Avg	1.39	35.3
5 Yr Avg	4.50	60.6
10 Yr Avg	5.53	54.0

Potential Capital Gain Exposure
(% of assets) -4%

Most Similar Funds in MF500

Vanguard Bond Indx Total Bd	Strong Fit
American Cap Govt Secs A	Strong Fit
U.S. Government Securities	Strong Fit

Coupon Range

	% of Bonds	Rel Obj
0%	1.0	0.42
0% to 8.5%	66.3	0.95
8.5% to 9.5%	18.0	1.37
9.5% to 11%	12.1	2.63
More than 11%	2.7	1.16
Not applicable	0.0	0.00

Credit Analysis 12-31-94
% of Bonds

US Govt	65	BB	0
AAA	4	B	0
AA	9	Below B	0
A	12	NR/NA	6
BBB	4		

Investment Style box (bottom-right of Quality): Quality High/Med/Low

T. Rowe Price Science & Tech

	Ticker	Load	NAV	Yield	SEC Yield	Assets	Objective
	PRSCX	None	21.64	0.0%	N/A	915.1	Sp.-Tech

T. Rowe Price Science and Technology Fund seeks long-term growth of capital; current income is not an important factor.

The fund normally invests at least 65% of its assets in companies, both foreign and domestic, that seek to develop or use scientific and technological advances. Industries include computers and peripherals, software, electronics, pharmaceuticals and medical devices, telecommunications, biotechnology, waste management, chemicals, synthetic materials, defense, and aerospace. These holdings may include both new and established companies.

Historical Profile
Return	High
Risk	High
Rating	★★★★★ Highest

Average % Stocks Held in Portfolio

Investment Style History
Equity

| --- | 90% | 89% | 78% | 85% | 96% | 93% | 91% |

Manager's Investment Style

Management mixes stocks from a variety of science and technology fields to thwart sector risk. Sector shifts haven't been perfectly timed, though: In 1993, management pared back in semiconductors and towards communications-related areas, but in early 1994, interactive-media stocks tumbled while semiconductors held up. The fund has often invested in pricier stocks than some of its competitors.

Growth of $10,000
- |||| Value of Fund ($000)
- — Value of Index ($000) Wil 4500
- ▼ Manager Change
- ▽ Partial Manager Change
- ► Mgr Unknown After
- ◄ Mgr Unknown Before

Performance Quartile (Within Objective)

Fund Manager(s)
Charles A. Morris CFA, since 08-91. Birthdate: 01-63. BS, Indiana U. 1985 MBA, Stanford U. 1987

	1983	1984	1985	1986	1987	1988	1989	1990	1991	1992	1993	1994	History
	---	---	---	---	8.02	8.57	10.53	10.05	15.57	17.33	18.95	21.64	NAV
	---	---	---	---	-19.39 *	13.27	40.67	-1.33	60.17	18.76	24.25	15.79	Total Return %
	---	---	---	---	3.13 *	-3.34	8.99	1.79	29.68	11.14	14.19	14.47	+/- S&P 500
	---	---	---	---	---	11.61	42.04	-3.45	46.08	14.63	1.24	-0.76	+/- S&P Tech
	---	---	---	---	0.41	0.83	0.61	0.90	0.00	0.00	0.00	0.00	Income Return %
	---	---	---	---	-19.80	12.44	40.06	-2.23	60.17	18.76	24.25	15.79	Capital Return %
	---	---	---	---	---	36	3	59	4	6	12	1	Total Rtn % Rank All
	---	---	---	---	---	18	1	43	11	29	50	36	Total Rtn % Rank Obj
	---	---	---	---	0.04	0.07	0.06	0.09	0.00	0.00	0.00	0.00	Income $
	---	---	---	---	0.00	0.44	1.39	0.24	0.48	1.12	2.51	0.30	Capital Gains $
	---	---	---	---	1.20	1.20	1.20	1.25	1.25	1.25	1.25	1.21	Expense Ratio %
	---	---	---	---	2.09	0.68	0.50	0.91	-0.07	-0.81	-0.68	-0.76	Income Ratio %
	---	---	---	---	---	92	203	183	148	144	163	118	Turnover Rate %
	---	---	---	---	9.6	12.4	23.8	61.5	166.0	281.0	500.3	915.1	Net Assets ($mil)

Manager Experience
	Dates Managed	Invest Obj	Std Dev	+/- Index
Not available.

Performance 12-31-94
	1st Qtr	2nd Qtr	3rd Qtr	4th Qtr	Total
1987	---	---	---	-19.39	-19.39 *
1988	8.23	8.30	-3.30	-0.06	13.27
1989	6.07	13.75	13.73	2.51	40.67
1990	4.59	14.98	-29.53	16.43	-1.33
1991	43.58	-12.61	11.82	14.16	60.17
1992	-0.32	-7.54	5.64	21.97	18.76
1993	-1.27	10.05	11.21	2.83	24.25
1994	-1.85	-7.85	17.68	8.78	15.79

Bear Market Performance
Decile Rank (5-year period)

Worst — Best

	Worst 3 Mo Period 1985-89	Worst 3 Mo Period 1990-94
T. Rowe Price Science & Tech	---	-29.53
+/- S&P 500	---	-15.78
+/- Best Fit Index : Wil 4500	---	-11.30

Trailing Returns
	Total Return %	+/- S&P 500	+/- S&P Tech	% Rank All	Obj	Growth of $10,000
3 Mo	8.78	8.80	1.54	1	24	10,878
6 Mo	28.01	23.15	10.54	1	28	12,801
1 Yr	15.79	14.47	-0.76	1	36	11,579
3 Yr Avg	19.55	13.28	5.26	1	35	17,085
5 Yr Avg	21.98	13.28	10.27	1	31	26,999
10 Yr Avg	---	---	---	---	---	---
15 Yr Avg	---	---	---	---	---	---

Risk Analysis
Time Period	Load-Adj Return %	Risk % Rank[1] All	Obj	Morningstar[2] Return	Morningstar Risk	Morningstar Risk-Adj Rating
1 Yr	15.79					
3 Yr	19.55	93	52	5.36[3]	1.31	★★★★★
5 Yr	21.97	96	68	5.55[3]	1.41	★★★★★
10 Yr	---					

Average Historical Rating (52 months) 4.9 ★s

[1] = low, 100 = high [2] 1.00 = Equity Avg [3] 1.00 = 90-day T-bill return

Other Measures
			Standard S&P 500	Best Fit Wil 4500
Standard Deviation	17.59	Alpha	13.0	9.6
Mean	19.51	Beta	1.29	1.57
Sharpe Ratio	0.91	R-Squared	34	76

Investment Style
	Stock Portfolio Avg	Relative S&P 500
Price/Earnings Ratio	31.9	1.73
Price/Book Ratio	5.5	1.61
5 Yr Earnings Gr %	25.6#	4.61
Return on Assets %	13.6	1.82
Debt % Total Cap	7.9	0.28
Med Mkt Cap ($mil)	2502	0.19

figure is based on 50% or less of stocks

Style: Value Blend Growth / Size Large Med Small

Diversification Value for Portfolio Types
| Large Cap: Medium | Small Cap: Low | Bond: High | Balanced: Medium | Diversified: Medium |

Portfolio 12-31-94
Share Chg (06-94) 000	Amount 000	Total Stocks: 40 Total Fixed-Income: 0	Value $000	% Net Assets
550	1000	Xilinx	59250	6.48
350	850	First Financial Management	52381	5.72
600	600	Nokia (ADR)	45000	4.92
1165	1300	Vodafone Group (ADR)	43713	4.78
500	500	Chiron	40188	4.39
400	1000	Autodesk	39625	4.33
550	550	Amgen	32450	3.55
-75	700	Synopsys	30625	3.35
100	500	Sybase	26000	2.84
600	600	Biogen	25050	2.74
800	800	AirTouch Communications	23300	2.55
750	750	Adobe Systems	22313	2.44
625	625	Sun Microsystems	22188	2.42
100	600	Silicon Graphics	18525	2.02
-200	400	Oracle Systems	17650	1.93
200	500	Maxim Integrated Products	17500	1.91
-150	250	Intuit	16688	1.82
300	300	LM Ericsson Telephone (ADR)	16538	1.81
800	800	Silicon Valley Group	16500	1.80
-350	400	DSC Communications	14350	1.57
0	400	CUC International	13400	1.46
0	325	SunGard Data Systems	12513	1.37
0	700	United International Hldgs	12250	1.34
500	500	QUALCOMM	12000	1.31
25	200	Motorola	11575	1.26

Composition % 12-31-94
Cash	11.7	Preferreds	1.2
Stocks	87.1	Convertibles	0.0
Bonds	0.0	Other	0.0

Tax Analysis
	Tax-Adj Historical Return %	% Pretax Return
3 Yr Avg	17.41	87.3
5 Yr Avg	20.20	88.8
10 Yr Avg		
Potential Capital Gain Exposure (% of assets)		21%

Most Similar Funds in MF500
Hancock Special Equities A	Fair Fit
Invesco Strat Technology	Fair Fit
PIMCo Adv Opportunity C	Fair Fit

Index Allocation
	% of Stocks
S&P 500	23.4
S&P MidCap 400	33.0
U.S. Small Cap	27.9
Foreign	15.7

Sector Weightings
	% of Stocks	Relative S&P 500
Utilities	0.0	0.00
Energy	0.0	0.00
Financials	0.0	0.00
Industrial Cyclicals	0.0	0.00
Consumer Durables	5.2	0.83
Consumer Staples	0.0	0.00
Services	3.2	0.40
Retail	0.0	0.00
Health	14.3	1.65
Technology	77.3	8.44

Operations
Address and Telephone	100 E. Pratt Street, Baltimore, MD 21202, 800-638-5660 / 410-547-2308
Advisor	T. Rowe Price Associates
Subadvisor	None
Distributor	T. Rowe Price Investment Services
States Available	All plus GU,PR,VI
Report Grade	A
Income Distrib	Paid Annually
* Date of Inception	09-30-87
Fiscal Year End	December

Min Initial Purchase	$2500 (Addt'l: $100)
Min IRA Purchase	$1000 (Addt'l: $50)
Min Auto Invest Plan	$50 (Systematic Inv: $50)

Expenses & Fees
Sales Fees	0.00% front, 0.00% deferred, 0.00% 12b-1
Management Fee	0.35% flat fee+0.48%G
3-,5-,10-yr Expense Projections	$47, $65, $143
Annual Brokerage Cost	0.59%

MORNINGSTAR 1995 Mutual Fund 500

T. Rowe Price Short-Term Bond

Ticker	Load	NAV	Yield	SEC Yield	Assets	Objective
PRWBX	None	4.63	6.0%	7.06%	474.9	Corp Hi Qlty

T. Rowe Price Short-Term Bond Fund seeks income consistent with minimum fluctuation in principal value and liquidity.

The fund invests primarily in a diversified portfolio of short- and intermediate-term debt securities. These securities are rated A or better or, if not rated, are deemed by the fund's advisor to be of comparable quality. The fund's average weighted maturity may not exceed three years. It may invest in a wide variety of debt securities, and may write covered call options and purchase covered put options (limited to 25% of the fund's assets).

Historical Profile

Return	Below Average
Risk	Below Average
Rating	★★★ Neutral

Manager's Investment Style

Management looks in out-of-favor places to find yield. As such, management has regularly included short- and intermediate-term Treasuries and mortgage-backeds in the portfolio; when such issues are out of favor, they have taken up more than a third of the portfolio. In an effort to enhance yield on this short-term fund, management has also used derivatives; the portfolio has, in the past, included inverse floaters, structured notes, floating-rate securities, interest-only strips, and principal-only strips. After the fallout with derivatives in 1994, management vowed to tone down exposure to such securities in the future.

Fund Manager(s)

Edward Weiss, since 01-95.

Manager Experience

	Dates Managed	Invest Obj	Std Dev	+/- Index

Not available.

Investment Style History
Fixed Income
Income Rtn % Rank Obj

Growth of $10,000

|||| Value of Fund ($000)
— Value of Index ($000) LB Int
▼ Manager Change
▽ Partial Manager Change
► Mgr Unknown After
◄ Mgr Unknown Before

Performance Quartile (Within Objective)

	1983	1984	1985	1986	1987	1988	1989	1990	1991	1992	1993	1994	History
	---	5.02	5.16	5.19	5.06	4.92	4.97	4.95	5.13	5.04	5.05	4.63	NAV
	---	9.89 *	12.79	8.95	5.23	5.51	9.91	8.63	11.22	5.01	6.60	-2.92	Total Return %
	---	---	-9.34	-6.30	2.48	-2.37	-4.63	-0.32	-4.79	-2.23	-3.16	0.00	+/- LB Aggregate
	---	---	-11.27	-7.59	2.68	-3.72	-4.07	1.47	-7.29	-3.68	-5.57	1.00	+/- LB Corporate
	---	9.49	10.00	8.36	7.74	8.27	8.89	8.34	7.58	6.77	6.40	5.39	Income Return %
	---	0.40	2.79	0.58	-2.50	-2.77	1.02	0.28	3.64	-1.75	0.20	-8.32	Capital Return %
	---	---	95	88	22	91	75	11	83	77	85	42	Total Rtn % Rank All
	---	---	88	85	14	91	76	26	82	84	70	53	Total Rtn % Rank Obj
	---	0.45	0.47	0.42	0.39	0.41	0.42	0.40	0.35	0.34	0.32	0.28	Income $
	---	0.00	0.00	0.00	0.00	0.00	0.00	0.03	0.00	0.00	0.00	0.00	Capital Gains $
	---	---	0.90	1.31	0.94	0.91	0.94	0.95	0.93	0.88	0.76	0.74	Expense Ratio %
	---	---	10.73	9.12	7.58	7.85	8.27	8.43	7.90	7.07	6.59	6.00	Income Ratio %
	---	---	73	21	7	203	309	161	980	381	68	91	Turnover Rate %
	---	16.8	42.0	126.0	234.4	264.0	216.1	215.4	401.4	543.8	681.0	474.9	Net Assets ($mil)

Performance 12-31-94

	1st Qtr	2nd Qtr	3rd Qtr	4th Qtr	Total
1987	1.54	-0.32	0.15	3.81	5.23
1988	2.02	0.95	1.13	1.30	5.51
1989	1.31	3.89	1.49	2.89	9.91
1990	0.36	2.65	2.42	2.95	8.63
1991	1.55	1.03	4.19	4.04	11.22
1992	-0.84	3.11	2.85	-0.13	5.01
1993	2.63	1.84	1.52	0.47	6.60
1994	-0.98	-0.72	0.21	-1.46	-2.92

Bear Market Performance

Decile Rank (5-year period)

Worst — Best

	Worst 3 Mo Period 1985-89	Worst 3 Mo Period 1990-94
T. Rowe Price Short-Term Bond	-0.95	-2.39
+/- LB Aggregate	2.61	2.55
+/- Best Fit Index : LB Int	1.19	1.84

Trailing Returns

	Total Return %	+/- LB Aggregate	+/- LB Corporate	% Rank All	% Rank Obj	Growth of $10,000
3 Mo	-1.46	-1.84	-1.90	56	96	9,854
6 Mo	-1.25	-2.24	-2.42	78	98	9,875
1 Yr	-2.92	0.00	1.00	42	53	9,708
3 Yr Avg	2.81	-1.74	-2.60	87	95	10,867
5 Yr Avg	5.59	-2.03	-2.67	83	87	13,128
10 Yr Avg	7.01	-2.94	-3.62	94	92	19,686
15 Yr Avg	---	---	---	---	---	---

Operations

Address and Telephone	100 E. Pratt Street
	Baltimore, MD 21202
	800-638-5660 / 410-547-2308
Advisor	T. Rowe Price Associates
Subadvisor	None
Distributor	T. Rowe Price Investment Services
States Available	All plus PR
Report Grade	A
Income Distrib	Paid Monthly
* Date of Inception	03-02-84
Fiscal Year End	February

Risk Analysis

Time Period	Load-Adj Return %	Risk % Rank¹ All	Risk % Rank¹ Obj	Morningstar² Return	Morningstar Risk	Morningstar Risk-Adj Rating
1 Yr	-2.92					
3 Yr	2.81	8	30	-0.22³	0.71	★★★
5 Yr	5.59	5	27	0.21³	0.61	★★★
10 Yr	7.01	3	11	0.29³	0.52	★★★

Average Historical Rating (94 months)   4.1 ★s

¹ 1 = low, 100 = high   ² 1.00 = Taxable Avg   ³ 1.00 = 90-day T-bill return

Other Measures

			Standard LB Agg	Best Fit LB Int
Standard Deviation	2.24	Alpha	-1.2	-1.1
Mean	2.80	Beta	0.51	0.61
Sharpe Ratio	-0.32	R-Squared	77	83

Investment Style

Interest-Rate Stance

Avg Effective Duration	1.9 Yrs
Avg Effective Maturity	2.2 Yrs

Quality

Avg Credit Quality	AA
Avg Weighted Coupon	7.88%
Avg Weighted Price	96.56% of Par

Diversification Value for Portfolio Types

Large Cap: High	Small Cap: High	Bond: Low	Balanced: Medium	Diversified: High

Expenses & Fees

Sales Fees	
	0.00% front
	0.00% deferred
	0.00% 12b-1
Management Fee	0.10% flat fee+0.48%G
3-,5-,10-yr Expense Projections	$24, $41, $92

Min Initial Purchase	$2500 (Addt'l: $100)
Min IRA Purchase	$1000 (Addt'l: $50)
Min Auto Invest Plan	$50 (Systematic Inv: $50)

Portfolio 11-30-94

Total Stocks: 0
Total Fixed-Income: 126

Amount 000	Date of Maturity		Value $000	% Net Assets
94000	04-15-96	US Treasury Note 9.375%	96570	19.70
14316	08-15-18	GNMA 11%	15797	3.22
11500	10-15-96	US Treasury Note 8%	11622	2.37
10445	10-01-21	FNMA ARM	10355	2.11
10340	01-01-20	FHLMC ARM	10117	2.06
10000	03-15-01	MBNA CC Master Trust FRN	9938	2.03
10000	03-30-97	Goldman Sachs Group 4.8%	9934	2.03
10000	04-15-95	MAS Capital 0%	9725	1.98
10343	12-20-23	GNMA ARM	9566	1.95
296363	01-25-22	American Housing CMO I/O N/A	7688	1.57
7000	04-01-97	American General Fin 5.8%	6675	1.36
36986	08-25-13	FNMA CMO I/O 6.5%	6195	1.26
5000	04-08-96	Ford Capital 9.125%	5106	1.04
5000	06-06-96	First Chicago 9%	5105	1.04
5000	03-13-96	Philip Morris 8.5%	5062	1.03
5000	10-15-97	Sears Credit Account Tr 9.35%	5061	1.03
5000	05-01-98	IBM 9%	5043	1.03
5000	08-15-96	Grand Metro Investment 8.125%	5032	1.03
5000	06-13-96	Northern Telecom 8.25%	5028	1.03
5000	10-15-96	Morgan Stanley Group 8%	5006	1.02
5000	12-13-96	Toyota Motor Credit 7.25%	4976	1.02
5000	05-29-98	Citicorp Euro FRN	4973	1.01
5000	11-15-96	Avco Financial Svcs 7.5%	4970	1.01
5000	08-01-95	Mellon Financial 5.375%	4947	1.01
5000	12-01-95	NationsBank 5.375%	4906	1.00

Composition % 12-31-94

Cash	2.7	Preferreds	0.0
Stocks	0.0	Convertibles	0.0
Bonds	97.3	Other	0.0

Tax Analysis

	Tax-Adj Historical Return %	% Pretax Return
3 Yr Avg	0.52	18.0
5 Yr Avg	3.17	54.0
10 Yr Avg	4.03	50.0
Potential Capital Gain Exposure (% of assets)		-11%

Most Similar Funds in MF500

Prudential Struct Maturity A	Strong Fit
Vanguard F/I Short-Trm Fed	Strong Fit
Vanguard F/I Short-Trm Corp	Fair Fit

Coupon Range

	% of Bonds	Rel Obj
0%	2.2	0.94
0% to 8.5%	61.3	0.87
8.5% to 9.5%	10.2	0.78
9.5% to 11%	2.3	0.49
More than 11%	2.0	0.85
Not applicable	22.2	2.91

Credit Analysis 12-31-94

% of Bonds

US Govt	44	BB	2
AAA	8	B	0
AA	2	Below B	0
A	27	NR/NA	1
BBB	16		

T. Rowe Price Small-Cap Value

	Ticker	Load	NAV	Yield	SEC Yield	Assets	Objective
	PRSVX	Clsd	13.40	1.0%	N/A	408.4	Small Company

T. Rowe Price Small-Cap Value Fund seeks long-term capital growth.

The fund invests primarily in small companies (capitalizations of $500 million or less), using a value-oriented approach. These undervalued securities are identified by analyzing assets, earnings, cash flow, and business franchises. The fund may invest up to 20% of its assets in foreign issues; 5% of its assets may be invested in debt.

Prior to June 30, 1988, the fund, then known as PEMCO, operated as a limited partnership with a different investment objective and was open only to partners of Peat, Marwick, & Mitchell.

Manager's Investment Style

Manager Preston Athey takes a value-oriented approach to small-cap stocks, favoring those that have been overlooked or have suffered excessive price losses but that are poised for a turnaround. He seeks to avoid stocks that deserve their low prices by emphasizing strong potential earnings and franchise growth.

Fund Manager(s)

Preston Athey CFA, since 06-88. Birthdate: 07-49.
BA, Yale 1971 MBA, Stanford U. 1978

Manager Experience

	Dates Managed	Invest Obj	Std Dev	+/- Index
Not available.				

Historical Profile

Return	Above Average
Risk	Below Average
Rating	★★★★
	Closed

Investment Style History
Equity
Average % Stocks Held in Portfolio

| --- | 89% | 86% | 82% | 80% | 79% | 83% | 92% |

Growth of $10,000

|||| Value of Fund ($000)
— Value of Index ($000)
Russ 2000
▼ Manager Change
▽ Partial Manager Change
► Mgr Unknown After
◄ Mgr Unknown Before

Performance Quartile (Within Objective)

	1983	1984	1985	1986	1987	1988	1989	1990	1991	1992	1993	1994	History
NAV	---	---	---	---	---	8.98	9.53	8.09	10.37	12.28	14.68	13.40	NAV
	---	---	---	---	---	-3.82 *	18.08	-11.27	34.18	20.87	23.30	-1.38	Total Return %
	---	---	---	---	---	-7.24 *	-13.60	-8.15	3.69	13.25	13.24	-2.69	+/- S&P 500
	---	---	---	---	---		-5.86	2.29	-9.28	9.11	8.76	1.28	+/- Wilshire 4500
	---	---	---	---	---	0.91	1.53	2.71	1.31	0.89	0.73	1.05	Income Return %
	---	---	---	---	---	-4.73	16.55	-13.98	32.87	19.98	22.57	-2.43	Capital Return %
	---	---	---	---	---		39	87	21	4	13	29	Total Rtn % Rank All
	---	---	---	---	---		66	55	87	18	21	51	Total Rtn % Rank Obj
	---	---	---	---	---	0.08	0.14	0.24	0.12	0.10	0.10	0.14	Income $
	---	---	---	---	---	0.55	0.90	0.12	0.34	0.15	0.35	0.92	Capital Gains $
	---	---	---	---	---	1.25	1.25	1.25	1.25	1.25	1.05	0.98	Expense Ratio %
	---	---	---	---	---	1.81	1.42	2.57	1.31	0.98	0.91	1.00	Income Ratio %
	---	---	---	---	---		43	33	31	12	12	18	Turnover Rate %
	---	---	---	---	---	25.6	32.8	26.4	53.2	264.0	453.8	408.4	Net Assets ($mil)

Performance 12-31-94

	1st Qtr	2nd Qtr	3rd Qtr	4th Qtr	Total
1987	---	---	---	---	---
1988	---	---	-4.26	0.46	-3.82 *
1989	7.91	3.82	8.15	-2.54	18.08
1990	-3.15	7.91	-19.18	5.04	-11.27
1991	17.68	4.31	1.91	7.26	34.18
1992	11.09	-4.69	2.82	11.02	20.87
1993	8.71	2.77	4.59	5.51	23.30
1994	-0.68	-1.37	3.96	-3.16	-1.38

Bear Market Performance

Decile Rank (5-year period)

Worst ___ Best

	Worst 3 Mo Period 1985-89	Worst 3 Mo Period 1990-94
T. Rowe Price Small-Cap Value	---	-20.88
+/- S&P 500	---	-7.04
+/- Best Fit Index : Russ 2000	---	5.01

Trailing Returns

	Total Return %	+/- S&P 500	+/- Wil 4500	% Rank All	% Rank Obj	Growth of $10,000
3 Mo	-3.16	-3.14	-0.66	84	85	9,684
6 Mo	0.68	-4.18	-3.51	43	89	10,068
1 Yr	-1.38	-2.69	1.28	29	51	9,862
3 Yr Avg	13.70	7.43	6.09	5	22	14,698
5 Yr Avg	11.84	3.15	2.75	9	45	17,498
10 Yr Avg	---	---	---	---	---	---
15 Yr Avg	---	---	---	---	---	---

Operations

Address and Telephone	100 E. Pratt Street
	Baltimore, MD 21202
	800-638-5660 / 410-547-2308
Advisor	T. Rowe Price Associates
Subadvisor	None
Distributor	T. Rowe Price Investment Services
States Available	All plus GU,PR,VI
Report Grade	A-
Income Distrib	Paid Annually
* Date of Inception	06-30-88
Fiscal Year End	December

Risk Analysis

Time Period	Load-Adj Return %	Risk % Rank [1] All	Obj	Morningstar [2] Return	Morningstar Risk	Morningstar Risk-Adj Rating
1 Yr	-1.38					
3 Yr	13.70	46	6	3.22 [3]	0.51	★★★★★
5 Yr	11.84	59	5	1.89 [3]	0.68	★★★★
10 Yr	---					
Average Historical Rating (43 months)				3.7 ★ s		

[1] 1 = low, 100 = high   [2] 1.00 = Equity Avg   [3] 1.00 = 90-day T-bill return

Other Measures

			Standard S&P 500	Best Fit Russ 2000
Standard Deviation	8.37	Alpha	8.5	4.9
Mean	13.25	Beta	0.53	0.61
Sharpe Ratio	1.16	R-Squared	25	74

Investment Style

	Stock Portfolio Avg	Relative S&P 500
Price/Earnings Ratio	17.5	0.95
Price/Book Ratio	2.0	0.59
5 Yr Earnings Gr %	9.5	1.71
Return on Assets %	7.5	1.01
Debt % Total Cap	25.7	0.91
Med Mkt Cap ($mil)	137	0.01

Style
Value Blend Growth
Size: Large Med Small

Diversification Value for Portfolio Types

● Large Cap: High
◌ Small Cap: Low
● Bond: High
◍ Balanced: Medium
◍ Diversified: Medium

Min Initial Purchase / Fees

Min Initial Purchase	Closed (Addt'l: $100)
Min IRA Purchase	$1000 (Addt'l: $50)
Min Auto Invest Plan	$50 (Systematic Inv: $50)

Expenses & Fees

Sales Fees	
	0.00% front
	0.00% deferred
	0.00% 12b-1
Management Fee	0.35% flat fee+0.48%G
3-,5-,10-yr Expense Projections	$32, $55, $122
Annual Brokerage Cost	0.25%

Portfolio 12-31-94

Share Chg (06-94) 000	Amount 000	Total Stocks: 153 / Total Fixed-Income: 9	Value $000	% Net Assets
0	575	Electro Rent	9479	2.32
0	470	Seattle Film Works	8108	1.99
0	52	Grey Advertising	7832	1.92
-50	450	CSS Industries	7763	1.90
-10	280	DH Technology	6720	1.65
0	380	McGrath RentCorp	6460	1.58
-8	442	Owens & Minor	6296	1.54
110	330	Unitog	6105	1.49
12	233	Mutual Assurance	6047	1.48
-253	258	La Quinta Inns	5504	1.35
-30	160	United Insurance	5440	1.33
20	381	Silicon Valley Bancshares	5137	1.26
0	362	Intertrans	4700	1.15
0	200	CMG Information Services	4650	1.14
0	176	National Health Investors	4598	1.13
160	410	Builders Transport	4459	1.09
6	186	Keane	4422	1.08
78	478	Hancock Fabrics	4246	1.04
-21	200	Commercial Federal (NE)	4225	1.03
0	300	Aceto	4200	1.03
0	251	Allied Capital Commercial	4177	1.02
-10	230	Lunar	4140	1.01
0	146	Puerto Rican Cement	4111	1.01
0	321	First Financial Fund	4092	1.00
0	90	Mine Safety Appliances	4050	0.99

Composition % 12-31-94

Cash	2.1	Preferreds	0.0
Stocks	94.0	Convertibles	3.6
Bonds	0.3	Other	0.0

Tax Analysis

	Tax-Adj Historical Return %	% Pretax Return
3 Yr Avg	12.31	88.7
5 Yr Avg	10.43	85.7
10 Yr Avg	---	---
Potential Capital Gain Exposure (% of assets)		13%

Most Similar Funds in MF500

Babson Enterprise	Strong Fit
Strong Common Stock	Fair Fit
Pennsylvania Mutual	Fair Fit

Index Allocation

	% of Stocks
S&P 500	0.0
S&P MidCap 400	2.1
U.S. Small Cap	96.2
Foreign	1.7

Sector Weightings

	% of Stocks	Relative S&P 500
Utilities	0.6	0.04
Energy	2.4	0.24
Financials	20.4	1.93
Industrial Cyclicals	13.0	0.79
Consumer Durables	11.3	1.82
Consumer Staples	1.9	0.15
Services	29.3	3.60
Retail	4.2	0.73
Health	6.5	0.75
Technology	10.3	1.12

MORNINGSTAR **1995 Mutual Fund 500**

T. Rowe Price Spectrum Income

Ticker	Load	NAV	Yield	SEC Yield	Assets	Objective
RPSIX	None	10.11	6.7%	7.02%	624.9	Income

T. Rowe Price Spectrum Income Fund seeks current income and preservation of capital.

The fund invests in a diversified group of T. Rowe Price mutual funds that invest primarily in fixed-income securities. These include T. Rowe Price Equity-Income Fund, which invests in dividend-paying common stocks, and T. Rowe Price International Bond Fund, which invests in non-U.S. fixed-income securities. The fund may also invest in T. Rowe Price's GNMA Fund, High-Yield Fund, New Income Fund, Prime Reserve Fund, and Short-Term Bond Fund.

The fund's management fee is based on the aggregate fees of the underlying funds.

Investment Style History
Fixed Income
Income Rtn % Rank Obj

| | | | | | | 60 | 50 | 56 | 51 |

Historical Profile
Return Average
Risk   Low
Rating ★★★★
        Above Average

Growth of $10,000
|||| Value of Fund ($000)
— Value of Index ($000)
LB L-T
▼ Manager Change
▽ Partial Manager Change
◄ Mgr Unknown After
◄ Mgr Unknown Before

Performance Quartile
(Within Objective)

Manager's Investment Style

The management committee that works on this fund of T. Rowe Price funds reviews the portfolio and the asset allocation on a monthly basis. Allocation decisions are based on the interest-rate scenario and other macroeconomic factors. Two funds in the mix, Prime Reserve and New Income, are allowed a larger maximum allocation (30% each) than the others. The fund is also willing to raise cash for defensive purposes.

1983	1984	1985	1986	1987	1988	1989	1990	1991	1992	1993	1994	History
---	---	---	---	---	---	---	9.77	10.73	10.70	11.11	10.11	NAV
---	---	---	---	---	---	---	2.66 *	19.64	7.84	12.37	-1.93	Total Return %
---	---	---	---	---	---	---	8.68 *	-10.84	0.23	2.31	-3.25	+/- S&P 500
---	---	---	---	---	---	---	---	3.64	0.60	2.62	0.99	+/- LB Aggregate
---	---	---	---	---	---	---	4.47	9.15	7.37	6.69	6.24	Income Return %
---	---	---	---	---	---	---	-1.81	10.50	0.47	5.68	-8.17	Capital Return %
---	---	---	---	---	---	---	---	45	48	48	34	Total Rtn % Rank All
---	---	---	---	---	---	---	---	74	57	68	13	Total Rtn % Rank Obj
---	---	---	---	---	---	---	0.44	0.83	0.76	0.69	0.69	Income $
---	---	---	---	---	---	---	0.05	0.06	0.08	0.19	0.10	Capital Gains $
---	---	---	---	---	---	---	0.00	0.00	0.00	0.00	0.00	Expense Ratio %
---	---	---	---	---	---	---	9.58	8.03	7.10	6.19	6.24	Income Ratio %
---	---	---	---	---	---	---	---	19	14	14	17	Turnover Rate %
---	---	---	---	---	---	---	40.1	147.9	376.4	583.8	624.9	Net Assets ($mil)

Fund Manager(s)

Peter Van Dyke et al. Birthdate: 11-38 BS, Webb Inst. of Naval Architecture 1960 PhD, Harvard 1964

Manager Experience

	Dates Managed	Invest Obj	Std Dev	+/- Index
Peter Van Dyke				
Liberty Financial U.S.Gov	06/87 - 06/89	GM	3.71	-2.07

Performance 12-31-94

	1st Qtr	2nd Qtr	3rd Qtr	4th Qtr	Total
1987	---	---	---	---	---
1988	---	---	---	---	---
1989	---	---	---	---	---
1990	---	---	-1.50	4.22	2.66 *
1991	5.21	2.54	5.53	5.09	19.64
1992	0.25	3.83	3.16	0.43	7.84
1993	4.62	2.87	2.63	1.73	12.37
1994	-2.63	-0.82	1.98	-0.43	-1.93

Bear Market Performance

Decile Rank (5-year period)

Worst ———————————————— Best

	Worst 3 Mo Period 1985-89	Worst 3 Mo Period 1990-94
T. Rowe Price Spectrum Inc	---	---
+/- S&P 500	---	---
+/- Best Fit Index :	---	---

Trailing Returns

	Total Return %	+/- S&P 500	+/- LB Aggregate	% Rank All	% Rank Obj	Growth of $10,000
3 Mo	-0.43	-0.41	-0.81	33	22	9,957
6 Mo	1.55	-3.31	0.56	30	11	10,155
1 Yr	-1.93	-3.25	0.99	34	13	9,807
3 Yr Avg	5.92	-0.34	1.38	35	42	11,884
5 Yr Avg	---	---	---	---	---	---
10 Yr Avg	---	---	---	---	---	---
15 Yr Avg	---	---	---	---	---	---

Operations

Address and Telephone	100 E. Pratt Street
	Baltimore, MD 21202
	800-638-5660 / 410-547-2308
Advisor	T. Rowe Price Associates
Subadvisor	None
Distributor	T. Rowe Price Investment Services
States Available	All plus PR
Report Grade	A-
Income Distrib	Paid Monthly
* Date of Inception	06-29-90
Fiscal Year End	December

Risk Analysis

Time Period	Load-Adj Return %	Risk % Rank All	Risk % Rank Obj	Morningstar[2] Return	Morningstar Risk	Morningstar Risk-Adj Rating
1 Yr	-1.93					
3 Yr	5.92	9	5	0.69[3]	0.38	★★★★
5 Yr	---					
10 Yr	---					

Average Historical Rating (19 months)   4.0 ★s

[1] 1 = low, 100 = high   [2] 1.00 = Hybrid Avg   [3] 1.00 = 90-day T-bill return

Other Measures

			Standard S&P 500	Best Fit LB L-T
Standard Deviation	3.51	Alpha	1.4	1.6
Mean	5.83	Beta	0.31	0.37
Sharpe Ratio	0.66	R-Squared	47	66

Investment Style

Stocks

	Port Avg	Rel S&P 500
Price/Earnings Ratio	---	---
Price/Book Ratio	---	---
5 Yr Earnings Gr %	---	---
Med Mkt Cap ($mil)	3745#	0.29

figure is based on 50% or less of stocks

Not Available

Bonds

Avg Effective Duration	3.8 Yrs **
Avg Effective Maturity	7.9 Yrs
Avg Credit Quality	---
Avg Weighted Coupon	---

**figure provided by fund

Not Available

Diversification Value for Portfolio Types

Large Cap: Medium	Small Cap: High	Bond: Low	Balanced: Low	Diversified: Low

Portfolio 06-30-94

Share Chg (12-93)000	Amount 000	Total Stocks: 7 Total Fixed-Income: 0	Date of Maturity	Value $000	% Net Assets
16533	16533	T Rowe Price High-Yield Fund		135078	21.77
13241	13241	T Rowe Price New Income Fund		113743	18.33
11492	11492	T Rowe Price Intl Bond Fund		112510	18.14
6092	6092	T Rowe Price Eqty Income Fd		98020	15.80
10250	10250	T Rowe Price GNMA Fund		92760	14.95
7766	7766	T Rowe Price Short-Term Bond		37508	6.05
31342	31342	T Rowe Price Prime Reserve		31342	5.05

Index Allocation

	% of Stocks
S&P 500	43.7
S&P MidCap 400	2.3
U.S. Small Cap	46.8
Foreign	8.0

Composition % 12-31-94

Cash	12.0	Preferreds	0.0
Stocks	13.0	Convertibles	1.0
Bonds	74.0	Other	0.0

Tax Analysis

	Tax-Adj Historical Return %	% Pretax Return
3 Yr Avg	3.11	51.0
5 Yr Avg	---	---
10 Yr Avg	---	---
Potential Capital Gain Exposure (% of assets)		-6%

Most Similar Funds in MF500

Putnam Income A	Strong Fit
Colonial Strategic Income A	Strong Fit
Putnam Diversified Income A	Strong Fit

Bond Credit Analysis 12-31-94
% of Bonds

US Govt	0	BB	0
AAA	0	B	0
AA	0	Below B	0
A	0	NR/NA	100
BBB	0		

Stock Sector Weightings

	% of Stocks	Relative S&P 500
Utilities	6.3	0.51
Energy	6.2	0.61
Financials	9.3	0.88
Industrial Cyclicals	36.0	2.19
Consumer Durables	7.9	1.27
Consumer Staples	12.6	1.01
Services	6.0	0.74
Retail	2.7	0.47
Health	5.5	0.63
Technology	7.7	0.84

Min Initial Purchase / Expenses & Fees

Min Initial Purchase	$2500 (Addt'l: $100)
Min IRA Purchase	$1000 (Addt'l: $50)
Min Auto Invest Plan	$50 (Systematic Inv: $50)

Expenses & Fees

Sales Fees	0.00% front
	0.00% deferred
	0.00% 12b-1
Management Fee	Provided at cost.
3-,5-,10-yr Expense Projections	$27, $47, $104
Annual Brokerage Cost	---

T. Rowe Price Tax-Fr High-Yield

	Ticker	Load	NAV	Yield	SEC Yield	Assets	Objective
	PRFHX	None	11.16	6.5%	6.53%	802.2	Muni Nat

T. Rowe Price Tax-Free High-Yield Fund seeks high current income exempt from federal income tax.

The fund invests primarily in medium- to low-quality municipal bonds. It has no strict maturity restrictions; however, at least 80% of its bonds have maturities longer than 15 years. The fund may also purchase bonds that are in default if the securities demonstrate significant capital appreciation potential--such purchases are not expected to exceed 10% of assets. For temporary, defensive purposes, the fund may invest in higher-quality bonds.

Manager's Investment Style

Though only recently arrived, current management intends to continue its predecessor's approach, whereby the portfolio is viewed as two parts. High-yield, low-quality bonds make up the core portfolio. Other, more-current-coupon issues form the tradable part of the portfolio.

Fund Manager(s)

C. Stephen Wolfe, since 03-94. Birthdate: 04-59.
BA, West Virginia U. 1981 MPA, Syracuse U. 1982

Manager Experience

	Dates Managed	Invest Obj	Std Dev	+/- Index
Not available.				

Historical Profile

Return	High
Risk	Below Average
Rating	★★★★★ Highest

Investment Style History Fixed Income
Income Rtn % Rank Obj

27	27	14	10	17	9	10	7

Growth of $10,000

|||| Value of Fund ($000)
— Value of Index ($000) LB Muni
▼ Manager Change
▽ Partial Manager Change
► Mgr Unknown After
◄ Mgr Unknown Before

Performance Quartile (Within Objective)

	1983	1984	1985	1986	1987	1988	1989	1990	1991	1992	1993	1994	History
	---	---	10.68	11.92	10.86	11.21	11.45	11.37	11.74	11.93	12.46	11.16	NAV
	---	---	14.53 *	20.40	0.23	11.17	10.51	7.11	11.74	9.56	12.98	-4.38	Total Return %
	---	---	---	5.15	-2.53	3.29	-4.03	-1.83	-4.26	2.32	3.23	-1.46	+/- LB Aggregate
	---	---	---	1.09	-1.28	1.00	-0.27	-0.19	-0.40	0.74	0.70	1.23	+/- LB Muni
	---	---	7.73	8.79	7.33	7.94	7.82	7.55	7.56	7.06	6.50	5.78	Income Return %
	---	---	6.80	11.61	-7.11	3.22	2.69	-0.44	4.18	2.50	6.48	-10.16	Capital Return %
	---	---	---	18	58	52	68	21	78	26	41	57	Total Rtn % Rank All
	---	---	---	14	45	45	22	13	44	16	25	36	Total Rtn % Rank Obj
	---	---	---	0.72	0.88	0.84	0.83	0.84	0.83	0.81	0.79	0.75	0.72	Income $
	---	---	---	0.00	0.00	0.25	0.00	0.06	0.03	0.10	0.10	0.23	0.04	Capital Gains $
	---	---	---	1.00	0.98	0.96	0.92	0.88	0.85	0.83	0.81	0.79	Expense Ratio %
	---	---	---	8.47	7.45	7.49	7.45	7.38	7.30	7.01	6.58	5.95	Income Ratio %
	---	---	---	---	111	128	62	72	51	51	35	59	Turnover Rate %
	---	---	129.9	274.3	250.0	312.4	431.2	490.8	622.9	761.5	953.5	802.2	Net Assets ($mil)

Performance 12-31-94

	1st Qtr	2nd Qtr	3rd Qtr	4th Qtr	Total
1987	3.20	-4.22	-1.09	2.51	0.23
1988	3.43	2.35	2.81	2.14	11.17
1989	1.71	5.04	0.42	3.00	10.51
1990	0.78	2.31	0.65	3.21	7.11
1991	1.79	2.85	3.46	3.17	11.74
1992	0.85	3.89	2.39	2.13	9.56
1993	3.74	3.88	3.37	1.42	12.98
1994	-4.28	0.71	0.39	-1.20	-4.38

Bear Market Performance

Decile Rank (5-year period)

Worst ———————————————————— Best

	Worst 3 Mo Period 1985-89	Worst 3 Mo Period 1990-94
T. Rowe Price Tax-Fr High-Yield	---	-5.18
+/- LB Aggregate	---	-0.24
+/- Best Fit Index : LB Muni	---	0.59

Trailing Returns

	Total Return %	+/- LB Aggregate	+/- LB Muni	% Rank All	% Rank Obj	Growth of $10,000
3 Mo	-1.20	-1.58	0.24	49	40	9,880
6 Mo	-0.82	-1.81	0.43	70	46	9,562
1 Yr	-4.38	-1.46	1.23	57	36	9,562
3 Yr Avg	5.78	1.23	0.91	36	8	11,836
5 Yr Avg	7.21	-0.41	0.44	45	9	14,166
10 Yr Avg	---	---	---	---	---	---
15 Yr Avg	---	---	---	---	---	---

Operations

Address and Telephone	100 E. Pratt Street
	Baltimore, MD 21202
	800-638-5660 / 410-547-2308
Advisor	T. Rowe Price Associates
Subadvisor	None
Distributor	T. Rowe Price Investment Services
States Available	All plus PR
Report Grade	A-
Income Distrib	Paid Monthly
* Date of Inception	03-01-85
Fiscal Year End	February

Risk Analysis

Time Period	Load-Adj Return %	Risk % Rank All	Risk % Rank Obj	Morningstar Return	Morningstar Risk	Morningstar Risk-Adj Rating
1 Yr	-4.38					
3 Yr	5.78	14	27	1.62	0.79	★★★★★
5 Yr	7.21	8	22	1.34	0.76	★★★★★
10 Yr	---	---	---	---	---	---

Average Historical Rating (82 months) 5.0 ★s

¹1 = low, 100 = high ²1.00 = Muni Avg ³1.00 = 90-day T-bill return

Other Measures

			Standard LB Agg	Best Fit LB Muni
Standard Deviation	4.98	Alpha	1.3	1.0
Mean	5.76	Beta	0.97	0.90
Sharpe Ratio	0.45	R-Squared	61	97

Investment Style

Interest-Rate Stance

Avg Effective Maturity 19.6 Yrs

Maturity Short Intm Long
Quality High Med Low

Quality

Avg Credit Quality	A
Avg Weighted Coupon	7.49%
Avg Weighted Price	101.83% of Par

Diversification Value for Portfolio Types

Large Cap: Medium	Small Cap: High	Bond: Low	Balanced: Low	Diversified: Medium

Expenses & Fees

Sales Fees	0.00% front
	0.00% deferred
	0.00% 12b-1
Management Fee	0.30% flat fee+0.48%G
3-,5-,10-yr Expense Projections	$25, $44, $98

Portfolio 08-31-94

Total Stocks: 0
Total Fixed-Income: 287

Amount 000	Date of Maturity		Value $000	% Net Assets
12000	09-15-22	OH Cleveland Parking Fac 8.1%	13016	1.44
11000	12-01-14	MS Claiborne Poll Cntrl Engy 9.875%	12729	1.41
12500	06-01-31	NJ Salem Poll Cntrl Fin 6.25%	12498	1.39
58700	01-28	CA San Joaquin Hills Transp Toll Rd 0%	9830	1.09
10000	12-31-19	MT Brd Invest Resource Yellowstone 7%	9722	1.08
10000	01-01-32	CA San Joaquin Hills Transp Toll 6.75%	9682	1.07
9500	05-01-22	IL Hlth Fac Meml Hosp 7.25%	9643	1.07
9500	02-01-12	KY Kenton Arpt Brd 7.5%	9531	1.06
8930	01-01-08	NC East Muni Pwr 7%	9520	1.06
9000	01-01-27	VA Hsg Dev Sngl Fam Mtg 7.1%	9322	1.03
8500	09-01-10	LA Offshore Term Deepwtr Port 7.6%	9260	1.03
7635	12-01-07	PR Indl Med Educ/Envir Poll 9.375%	8842	0.98
10000	07-01-26	TX Tomball Regl Hosp 6.125%	8765	0.97
9000	06-01-23	WY Comnty Dev Sngl Fam Mtg 6%	8340	0.92
8000	02-01-18	NY New York City GO 7%	8318	0.92
6750	10-01-13	AL Marshall Hosp B.d Arab M/C 10.25%	8134	0.90
8000	09-01-13	GA Fulco Hosp Baptist M/C 6.25%	7592	0.84
8500	02-01-05	MI Hosp Fin Pontiac Osteo 6%	7342	0.81
7500	01-01-10	PA Schuylkill Indl Dev Resource Rec 6.5%	7103	0.79
7000	10-01-23	OH Wtr Dev Poll Cntrl Toledo Edison 7.4%	7078	0.78

Credit Analysis % of Bonds 10-18-94

US Govt	0	BB	7
AAA	16	B	0
AA	15	Below B	0
A	12	NR/NA	25
BBB	25		

Composition % of Assets 09-30-94

Cash	6.7	Preferreds	0.0
Stocks	0.0	Convertibles	0.0
Bonds	93.3	Other	0.0

Tax Analysis

	Tax-Adj Historical Return %	% Pretax Return
3 Yr Avg	5.49	94.7
5 Yr Avg	6.97	96.1
10 Yr Avg	---	---

Potential Capital Gain Exposure (% of assets) -3%

Most Similar Funds in MF500

Dreyfus Intermediate Muni	Strong Fit
Franklin Insured T/F Income	Strong Fit
American Cap Muni Bond A	Strong Fit

Coupon Range

	% Bonds	Rel Obj
0%	1.9	0.77
0% to 6.8%	26.4	0.44
6.8% to 7.5%	23.8	1.53
7.5% to 8.3%	16.8	1.89
More than 8.3%	26.2	2.97
Not applicable	4.9	1.27

Sector Weightings

	% Bonds	Rel Obj
General Obl	5.65	0.27
Utilities	3.74	0.30
Health	36.14	2.74
Water/Waste	0.70	0.11
Housing	14.30	1.95
Education	2.67	0.42
Transportation	9.08	0.89
COP/Lease	1.21	0.38
Private	20.47	1.76
Misc Revenue	2.67	0.54
Demand	3.36	1.37

Top 5 States % of Bonds

NY	6.86	CA	5.30
TX	6.63	MI	4.65
IL	6.13		

Min Initial/Purchase

Min Initial Purchase	$2500 (Addt'l: $100)
Min IRA Purchase	N/A
Min Auto Invest Plan	$50 (Systematic Inv: $50)

MORNINGSTAR 1995 Mutual Fund 500

T. Rowe Price Tax-Fr Short-Intrm

Ticker	Load	NAV	Yield	SEC Yield	Assets	Objective
PRFSX	None	5.18	4.2%	4.69%	451.1	Muni Nat

T. Rowe Price Tax-Free Short-Intermediate Fund seeks higher yields than money markets with moderate price volatility.

The fund invests primarily in short- and intermediate-term, high- and upper-medium quality municipal securities, the interest on which is exempt from federal income tax. It may only purchase a security whose maturity or tender date, measured from the date of settlement, does not exceed seven years. Average portfolio maturity may not exceed five years.

Manager's Investment Style

Restricted to a short-maturity stance, management keeps a high-quality focus and parks a significant chunk of assets in both insured bonds and prerefundeds. The liquidity and reduced interest-rate sensitivity of this portfolio give the fund a bear-market advantage. Management favors states that levy no income tax, such as Texas, whose muni bonds thus offer higher yields.

Fund Manager(s)

Mary J. Miller CFA, since 02-89. Birthdate: 07-55. BA, Cornell U. 1977 MA, U. of North Carolina-Chapel Hill 1980

Manager Experience

	Dates Managed	Invest Obj	Std Dev	+/- Index
Mary J. Miller				
T. Rowe Price CA T/F Bond	02/90 - 12/94	MC	5.37	-1.37
T. Rowe Price MD Tax-Free	02/90 - 12/94	MS	5.09	-1.36

Historical Profile
Return Low
Risk Low
Rating ★★★★ Above Average

Investment Style History
Fixed Income
Income Rtn % Rank Obj

	96	97	91	96	94	96	90	82

Growth of $10,000
|||| Value of Fund ($000)
— Value of Index ($000)
   LB Muni
▼ Manager Change
▽ Partial Manager Change
► Mgr Unknown After
◄ Mgr Unknown Before

Performance Quartile (Within Objective)

	1983	1984	1985	1986	1987	1988	1989	1990	1991	1992	1993	1994	History
NAV	4.97	4.98	5.09	5.27	5.09	5.06	5.10	5.11	5.22	5.28	5.38	5.18	NAV
	-0.42 *	6.81	8.86	9.70	2.21	4.95	6.89	6.04	7.88	6.02	6.32	0.33	Total Return %
	---	-8.35	-13.27	-5.55	-0.55	-2.93	-7.65	-2.90	-8.13	-1.22	-3.43	3.25	+/- LB Aggregate
	---	-3.74	-11.17	-9.62	0.70	-5.21	-3.90	-1.26	-4.27	-2.80	-5.95	5.93	+/- LB Muni
	0.18	6.61	6.65	6.16	5.27	5.54	6.10	5.85	5.72	4.87	4.43	4.05	Income Return %
	-0.60	0.20	2.21	3.54	-3.06	-0.59	0.79	0.20	2.15	1.15	1.89	-3.72	Capital Return %
	---	43	97	86	41	92	93	34	95	69	86	17	Total Rtn % Rank All
	---	88	89	92	17	99	95	61	96	95	95	3	Total Rtn % Rank Obj
	0.01	0.32	0.32	0.30	0.27	0.28	0.30	0.29	0.28	0.25	0.23	0.22	Income $
	0.00	0.00	0.00	0.00	0.02	0.00	0.00	0.00	0.00	0.00	0.00	0.00	Capital Gains $
	---	0.90	0.90	0.90	0.73	0.74	0.74	0.75	0.74	0.67	0.63	0.60	Expense Ratio %
	---	7.11	6.51	6.26	5.60	5.29	5.46	5.93	5.67	5.34	4.61	4.18	Income Ratio %
	---	111	301	129	120	225	53	191	190	81	39	51	Turnover Rate %
	0.5	55.0	131.3	306.9	275.3	267.2	220.7	227.3	307.0	424.6	534.4	451.1	Net Assets ($mil)

Performance 12-31-94

	1st Qtr	2nd Qtr	3rd Qtr	4th Qtr	Total
1987	1.47	-1.15	-0.31	2.21	2.21
1988	1.98	0.90	0.98	1.01	4.95
1989	0.62	2.72	0.89	2.51	6.89
1990	0.84	1.64	1.40	2.04	6.04
1991	1.78	1.60	1.95	2.32	7.88
1992	0.63	2.19	1.73	1.34	6.02
1993	1.85	1.66	1.63	1.04	6.32
1994	-1.25	0.59	1.06	-0.06	0.33

Bear Market Performance

Decile Rank (5-year period)

Worst									Best

	Worst 3 Mo Period 1985-89	Worst 3 Mo Period 1990-94
T. Rowe Price Tax-Fr Short-Int	-2.93	-1.61
+/- LB Aggregate	-0.42	3.32
+/- Best Fit Index : LB Muni	2.63	4.15

Trailing Returns

	Total Return %	+/- LB Aggregate	+/- LB Muni	% Rank All	Obj	Growth of $10,000
3 Mo	-0.06	-0.44	1.37	24	6	9,994
6 Mo	1.00	0.01	2.24	37	4	10,100
1 Yr	0.33	3.25	5.93	17	3	10,033
3 Yr Avg	4.19	-0.36	-0.68	65	68	11,309
5 Yr Avg	5.29	-2.34	-1.49	87	92	12,937
10 Yr Avg	5.88	-4.06	-3.54	97	92	17,714
15 Yr Avg	---	---	---	---	---	---

Operations

Address and Telephone	100 E. Pratt Street	Min Initial Purchase	$2500 (Addt'l: $100)
	Baltimore, MD 21202	Min IRA Purchase	N/A
	800-638-5660 / 410-547-2308	Min Auto Invest Plan	$50 (Systematic Inv: $50)
Advisor	T. Rowe Price Associates		
Subadvisor	None	**Expenses & Fees**	
Distributor	T. Rowe Price Investment Services	Sales Fees	0.00% front
States Available	All plus PR		0.00% deferred
Report Grade	A-		0.00% 12b-1
Income Distrib	Paid Monthly	Management Fee	0.10% flat fee+0.48%G
* Date of Inception	12-23-83	3-,5-,10-yr Expense Projections	$19, $33, $75
Fiscal Year End	February		

Risk Analysis

Time Period	Load-Adj Return %	Risk % Rank [1] All	Obj	Morningstar [2] Return	Morningstar Risk	Morningstar Risk-Adj Rating
1 Yr	0.33					
3 Yr	4.19	2	4	0.84	0.28	★★★★★
5 Yr	5.29	1	5	0.67	0.28	★★★★
10 Yr	5.88	2	9	0.41	0.36	★★★
Average Historical Rating (97 months)					3.2	★ s

[1] 1 = low, 100 = high   [2] 1.00 = Muni Avg   [3] 1.00 = 90-day T-bill return

Other Measures

			Standard LB Agg	Best Fit LB Muni
Standard Deviation	2.01	Alpha	0.2	0.1
Mean	4.13	Beta	0.36	0.34
Sharpe Ratio	0.30	R-Squared	51	85

Investment Style

Interest-Rate Stance
Avg Effective Maturity 2.8 Yrs

Quality
Avg Credit Quality AA
Avg Weighted Coupon 5.92%
Avg Weighted Price 103.06% of Par

Diversification Value for Portfolio Types

Large Cap: Medium	Small Cap: High	Bond: Low	Balanced: Medium	Diversified: High

Portfolio 08-31-94

Total Stocks: 0
Total Fixed-Income: 172

Amount 000	Date of Maturity		Value $000	% Net Assets
10000	01-01-14	MD Hlth/Higher Educ Fac Univ Med 9.5%	11104	2.24
9980	03-01-00	MA GO Bay Transp Genl Sys 6%	10440	2.11
9400	05-01-17	GA Fulton GO Sch Dist 7.625%	10352	2.09
9545	01-01-15	NC East Muni Pwr Sys 7.75%	10241	2.07
9375	09-29-95	CA San Diego GO 4.5%	9366	1.89
7315	12-01-04	MD Baltimore Indl Dev Days Inn 12.625%	9061	1.83
7575	07-01-99	PA Indl Dev 6%	7891	1.59
7500		IL Dev Fin Palos Comnty Hosp DMD	7500	1.52
5800	07-01-98	AZ Mesa GO 6.75%	6202	1.25
5890	09-01-95	LA Offshore Term Deepwtr Port 4.6%	5917	1.20
5615	07-01-97	UT Intermountain Pwr Sply 5%	5672	1.15
5500	03-01-96	GA State GO 5.8%	5631	1.14
5200	01-01-14	NY Triborough Bridge/Tunnel Genl 7.625%	5534	1.12
5500	08-01-96	WA State GO 3.7%	5449	1.10
5000	10-01-19	FL Jacksonville Elec St John Rvr 6.9%	5347	1.08
4900	01-01-21	NY Urban Dev Crtnl Cap Fac Tax 6.5%	5300	1.07
5000	06-15-98	PA Intergovt Coop Spcl Tax 5.6%	5137	1.04
5000	05-15-98	TX San Antonio Wtr Sys 5.6%	5127	1.04
5000	01-01-01	MS Higher Educ Assist Student Loan 6.1%	5081	1.03
5000	07-01-00	MS Higher Educ Assist Student Loan 6%	5076	1.03

Credit Analysis % of Bonds 12-31-94

US Govt	0	BB	0
AAA	46	B	0
AA	18	Below B	0
A	12	NR/NA	24
BBB	0		

Composition % of Assets 12-31-94

Cash	18.8	Preferreds	0.0
Stocks	0.0	Convertibles	0.0
Bonds	81.2	Other	0.0

Tax Analysis

	Tax-Adj Historical Return %	% Pretax Return
3 Yr Avg	4.19	100.0
5 Yr Avg	5.29	100.0
10 Yr Avg	5.87	99.8
Potential Capital Gain Exposure (% of assets)		-1%

Most Similar Funds in MF500

Vanguard Muni Limited-Term	Strong Fit
Fidelity Spartan Sh-Int Muni	Strong Fit
USAA Tax-Exempt Short-Term	Strong Fit

Coupon Range

	% Bonds	Rel Obj
0%	6.3	2.51
0% to 6.8%	59.6	0.99
6.8% to 7.5%	7.1	0.46
7.5% to 8.3%	9.9	1.12
More than 8.3%	11.7	1.32
Not applicable	5.4	1.39

Sector Weightings

	% Bonds	Rel Obj
General Obl	31.45	1.49
Utilities	14.51	1.16
Health	9.11	0.69
Water/Waste	2.53	0.40
Housing	6.89	0.94
Education	9.37	1.46
Transportation	7.07	0.69
COP/Lease	0.75	0.24
Private	6.62	0.57
Misc Revenue	6.65	1.34
Demand	5.05	2.05

Top 5 States % of Bonds

TX	9.43	PA	5.88
AZ	6.05	WA	5.49
MD	5.96		

Prudential Allocation Conserv B

Ticker	Load	NAV	Yield	SEC Yield	Assets	Objective
PRFCX	5.00%d	10.63	2.3%	2.50%	427.6	Asset Alloc.

Prudential Allocation Conservatively Managed Portfolio - Class B seeks total return consistent with moderate risk.

The fund invests in equities, debt obligations, and money market instruments. The equity portion consists chiefly of common stocks of major, established companies. No more than 10% of the fund's assets may be invested in high-yield debt securities. The fund may invest up to 30% of its assets in foreign securities.

Class A shares have front loads; Class B shares have deferred loads, higher 12b-1 fees, and conversion features; Class C shares have level loads. Prior to Aug. 2, 1994, the fund was named Prudential FlexiFund Conservatively Managed Portfolio - Class B.

Manager's Investment Style

To allocate its assets, management uses a quantitative relative-valuation model that considers such factors as interest rates and expected returns. Nevertheless, the fund rarely strays from its neutral 45/45/10 allocation among stocks, bonds, and cash. Stock picking focuses on value-priced established names with reasonable earnings and attractive dividends. Bonds tend to be investment grade, typically split between Treasuries and corporates.

Fund Manager(s)

Mark Stumpp, since 11-94.
Tony Rodriguez, since 01-93.
Roger Ford, since 12-91.

Manager Experience	Dates Managed	Invest Obj	Std Dev	+/- Index
Tony Rodriguez				
Prudential Instl Balanced	07/94 - 12/94	B	5.44	-2.53

Historical Profile

Return	Average	
Risk	Below Average	
Rating	★★★★ Above Average	

Investment Style History
Equity
Average % Stocks Held in Portfolio

	26%	33%	41%	58%	44%	51%	46%

Growth of $10,000

|||| Value of Fund ($000)
— Value of Index ($000)
S&P 500
▼ Manager Change
▽ Partial Manager Change
► Mgr Unknown After
◄ Mgr Unknown Before

Performance Quartile
(Within Objective)

	1983	1984	1985	1986	1987	1988	1989	1990	1991	1992	1993	1994	History
	---	---	---	---	9.16	9.35	10.13	9.80	10.93	10.83	11.49	10.63	NAV
	---	---	---	---	-7.77 *	7.03	15.51	2.88	21.44	6.60	13.84	-3.59	Total Return %
	---	---	---	---	13.58 *	-9.58	-16.18	6.00	-9.04	-1.02	3.78	-4.90	+/- S&P 500
	---	---	---	---	---	-0.85	0.97	-6.07	5.44	-0.64	4.09	-0.67	+/- LB Aggregate
	---	---	---	---	0.46	4.95	6.01	3.94	3.81	3.13	2.53	2.23	Income Return %
	---	---	---	---	-8.23	2.07	9.50	-1.06	17.64	3.47	11.31	-5.81	Capital Return %
	---	---	---	---	---	80	45	48	43	62	34	49	Total Rtn % Rank All
	---	---	---	---	---	62	64	20	51	48	50	66	Total Rtn % Rank Obj
	---	---	---	---	0.05	0.45	0.54	0.39	0.37	0.33	0.28	0.25	Income $
	---	---	---	---	0.02	0.10	0.23	0.54	0.47	0.54	0.54	0.20	Capital Gains $
	---	---	---	---	---	2.08	2.09	2.07	2.16	2.09	1.97	2.00	Expense Ratio %
	---	---	---	---	---	4.22	5.47	4.42	3.55	3.25	3.04	2.08	Income Ratio %
	---	---	---	---	---	---	137	106	137	105	83	108	Turnover Rate %
	---	---	---	---	108.9	141.5	143.5	144.8	185.1	256.2	381.7	427.6	Net Assets ($mil)

Performance 12-31-94

	1st Qtr	2nd Qtr	3rd Qtr	4th Qtr	Total
1987	---	---	---	-8.23	-7.77 *
1988	3.46	2.35	0.00	1.07	7.03
1989	2.68	5.16	4.06	2.80	15.51
1990	-1.68	4.17	-5.02	5.76	2.88
1991	7.67	1.14	4.49	6.73	21.44
1992	-1.56	1.41	2.66	4.02	6.60
1993	6.19	2.68	4.24	0.16	13.84
1994	-3.94	-0.10	2.16	-1.66	-3.59

Bear Market Performance

Decile Rank (5-year period)

Worst ——————————————————— Best

	Worst 3 Mo Period 1985-89	Worst 3 Mo Period 1990-94
Prudential Allocation Conserv B	---	-5.68
+/- S&P 500	---	8.16
+/- Best Fit Index : S&P 500	---	8.16

Trailing Returns

	Total Return %	+/- S&P 500	+/- LB Aggregate	% Rank All	% Rank Obj	Growth of $10,000
3 Mo	-1.66	-1.65	-2.04	61	58	9,834
6 Mo	0.46	-4.40	-0.53	48	66	10,046
1 Yr	-3.59	-4.90	-0.67	49	66	9,641
3 Yr Avg	5.37	-0.89	0.83	41	53	11,700
5 Yr Avg	7.89	-0.80	0.26	35	45	14,618
10 Yr Avg	---	---	---	---	---	---
15 Yr Avg	---	---	---	---	---	---

Operations

Address and Telephone	One Seaport Plaza New York, NY 10292 800-225-1852
Advisor	Prudential Mutual Fund Management
Subadvisor	Prudential Investment
Distributor	Prudential Securities
States Available	All plus PR
Report Grade	B-
Income Distrib	Paid Quarterly
* Date of Inception	09-15-87
Fiscal Year End	July

Risk Analysis

Time Period	Load-Adj Return %	Risk % Rank [1] All	Obj	Morningstar [2] Return	Risk	Morningstar Risk-Adj Rating
1 Yr	-7.29					
3 Yr	4.79	47	38	0.35 [3]	0.68	★★★
5 Yr	7.74	48	35	0.74 [3]	0.63	★★★★
10 Yr						

Average Historical Rating (52 months)   3.8 ★s

[1] 1 = low, 100 = high   [2] 1.00 = Hybrid Avg   [3] 1.00 = 90-day T-bill return

Other Measures

		Standard S&P 500	Best Fit S&P 500
Standard Deviation	5.65	Alpha	0.1	0.1
Mean	5.40	Beta	0.63	0.63
Sharpe Ratio	0.33	R-Squared	78	78

Investment Style

Stocks	Port Avg	Rel S&P 500	Style
Price/Earnings Ratio	17.9	0.97	V B G
Price/Book Ratio	2.8	0.82	
5 Yr Earnings Gr %	11.8	2.13	
Med Mkt Cap ($mil)	1695	0.13	

Bonds		Maturity S I L
Avg Effective Duration	6.1 Yrs**	
Avg Effective Maturity	9.5 Yrs	
Avg Credit Quality	AA	
Avg Weighted Coupon	8.63%	

**figure provided by fund

Diversification Value for Portfolio Types

Large Cap: Low	Small Cap: Medium	Bond: Medium	Balanced: None	Diversified: Low

Expenses & Fees

Sales Fees	
	0.00% front
	5.00% deferred
	1.00% 12b-1
Management Fee	0.65% flat fee
3-,5-,10-yr Expense Projections	$92, $116, $201
Annual Brokerage Cost	0.12%

Min Initial Purchase	$1000 (Addt'l: $100)
Min IRA Purchase	None (Addt'l: None)
Min Auto Invest Plan	$50 (Systematic Inv: $50)

Portfolio 07-31-94

Share Chg (01-94)000	Amount 000	Total Stocks: 119 Total Fixed-Income: 64	Date of Maturity	Value $000	% Net Assets
	29008	US Treasury Bond 11.25%	02-15-15	40439	9.08
	15127	US Treasury Note 6%	11-30-97	14935	3.35
	11529	US Treasury Note 5.125%	03-31-98	11021	2.47
	6733	US Treasury Bond 10.375%	11-15-12	8394	1.88
27	120	Dean Witter Discover		4826	1.08
47	184	Norwest		4819	1.08
42	144	KeyCorp		4696	1.05
	3182	US Treasury Bond 12%	08-15-13	4439	1.00
	3689	Standard CC Master Tr 8%	10-07-97	3800	0.85
-1	109	Zeneca Group		3734	0.84
-1	97	Time Warner		3609	0.81
-3	81	Mead		3606	0.81
40	91	Nationale Elf Aquitaine		3500	0.79
22	148	Tele-Communications Cl A		3440	0.77
19	72	Diebold		3246	0.73
-11	63	Imperial Chemical Inds (ADR)		3233	0.73
22	59	Motorola		3119	0.70
0	49	Schering-Plough		3117	0.70
27	92	Owens-Corning		3067	0.69
	3044	Chrysler Financial 5.25%	11-15-96	3049	0.68

Index Allocation

	% of Stocks
S&P 500	40.7
S&P MidCap 400	23.9
U.S. Small Cap	29.0
Foreign	6.8

Composition % 10-31-94

Cash	15.1	Preferreds	0.0
Stocks	46.7	Convertibles	0.0
Bonds	38.2	Other	0.0

Tax Analysis

	Tax-Adj Historical Return %	% Pretax Return
3 Yr Avg	3.40	62.1
5 Yr Avg	5.76	70.0
10 Yr Avg	---	---

Potential Capital Gain Exposure (% of assets)   0%

Most Similar Funds in MF500

SteinRoe Total Return	Strong Fit
Oppenheimer Equity-Inc A	Strong Fit
MFS Total Return A	Strong Fit

Bond Credit Analysis 10-31-94

% of Bonds			
US Govt	48	BB	5
AAA	12	B	1
AA	1	Below B	0
A	7	NR/NA	9
BBB	16		

Stock Sector Weightings

	% of Stocks	Relative S&P 500
Utilities	4.0	0.32
Energy	7.2	0.69
Financials	17.8	1.69
Industrial Cyclicals	20.6	1.26
Consumer Durables	12.2	1.96
Consumer Staples	1.9	0.15
Services	13.9	1.71
Retail	2.0	0.34
Health	10.3	1.18
Technology	10.1	1.10

MORNINGSTAR   **1995 Mutual Fund 500**

Prudential Structured Mat A

	Ticker	Load	NAV	Yield	SEC Yield	Assets	Objective
	PBSMX	3.25%	10.97	5.9%	6.76%	91.8	Corp General

Prudential Structured Maturity Fund - Class A seeks income.

The fund invests primarily in investment-grade corporate debt securities and U.S. government securities with maturities of six years or less. These securities are allocated by maturity among six annual maturity categories with each category representing approximately one sixth of assets.

Class A shares have front loads; Class B shares have deferred loads, higher 12b-1 fees, and conversion features; Class C shares have level loads. Prior to March 21, 1991, the fund was named Prudential-Bache Structured Maturity Fund - Class A.

Manager's Investment Style

The fund's laddering mandate forces management to buy bonds with maturities of up to six years and then allocate them into six maturity rungs of roughly equal weight. Management is willing to dip a toe into the lower tiers of the investment-grade-bond universe for yield pickup: The fund has three times as much exposure to BBB rated bonds as its average rival. In August 1994, the fund loosened its credit-quality restrictions; shareholders cast their votes, allowing the fund to invest up to 10% of assets in non-investment-grade issues. The fund also invests in Treasuries, and has dabbled in the mortgage-backed market.

Fund Manager(s)

Annamarie Carlucci, since 04-92. BS, Mercy C. 1960 MBA, Iona C. 1963

Manager Experience

	Dates Managed	Invest Obj	Std Dev	+/- Index
Annamarie Carlucci				
Prudential GNMA B	01/91 - 09/91	GM	1.80	-2.07

Historical Profile
Return	Average
Risk	Below Average
Rating	★★★★ Above Average

	1983	1984	1985	1986	1987	1988	1989	1990	1991	1992	1993	1994	History
	---	---	---	---	---	---	11.63	11.67	12.13	11.79	11.78	10.97	NAV
	---	---	---	---	---	---	3.35 *	9.41	13.14	6.67	7.02	-1.39	Total Return %
	---	---	---	---	---	---	---	0.46	-2.86	-0.58	-2.73	1.53	+/- LB Aggregate
	---	---	---	---	---	---	---	2.25	-5.37	-2.03	-5.14	2.54	+/- LB Corporate
	---	---	---	---	---	---	3.06	9.06	8.31	7.34	5.96	5.49	Income Return %
	---	---	---	---	---	---	0.29	0.34	4.84	-0.68	1.07	-6.88	Capital Return %
	---	---	---	---	---	---	---	7	68	62	83	29	Total Rtn % Rank All
	---	---	---	---	---	---	---	5	72	40	63	37	Total Rtn % Rank Obj
	---	---	---	---	---	---	0.35	1.00	0.91	0.86	0.69	0.65	Income $
	---	---	---	---	---	---	0.01	0.00	0.10	0.26	0.14	0.00	Capital Gains $
	---	---	---	---	---	---	0.00	0.13	0.37	0.70	0.80	0.81	Expense Ratio %
	---	---	---	---	---	---	8.41	8.67	7.89	7.15	5.92	5.92	Income Ratio %
	---	---	---	---	---	---	---	46	117	91	137	---	Turnover Rate %
	---	---	---	---	---	---	---	113.2	110.0	109.8	119.4	91.8	Net Assets ($mil)

Investment Style History Fixed Income
Income Rtn % Rank Obj
23 42 29 52 47

Growth of $10,000

Performance 12-31-94

	1st Qtr	2nd Qtr	3rd Qtr	4th Qtr	Total
1987	---	---	---	---	---
1988	---	---	---	---	---
1989	---	---	---	3.57	3.35 *
1990	0.47	2.89	2.28	3.48	9.41
1991	2.13	2.10	4.23	4.09	13.14
1992	-0.52	3.62	3.93	-0.45	6.67
1993	3.19	1.64	1.89	0.15	7.02
1994	-1.37	-0.47	0.83	-0.37	-1.39

Bear Market Performance

Decile Rank (5-year period)

	Worst 3 Mo Period 1985-89	Worst 3 Mo Period 1990-94
Prudential Structured Mat A	---	-2.68
+/- LB Aggregate	---	2.26
+/- Best Fit Index : LB Int	---	1.55

Trailing Returns

	Total Return %	+/- LB Aggregate	+/- LB Corp	% Rank All	% Rank Obj	Growth of $10,000
3 Mo	-0.37	-0.75	-0.81	32	85	9,963
6 Mo	0.46	-0.54	-0.72	48	57	10,046
1 Yr	-1.39	1.53	2.54	29	37	9,861
3 Yr Avg	4.03	-0.52	-1.39	69	52	11,257
5 Yr Avg	6.86	-0.77	-1.40	53	45	13,934
10 Yr Avg	---	---	---	---	---	---
15 Yr Avg	---	---	---	---	---	---

Operations

Address and Telephone	One Seaport Plaza, New York, NY 10292, 800-225-1852
Advisor	Prudential Mutual Fund Management
Subadvisor	Prudential Investment
Distributor	Prudential Mutual Fund Distributors
States Available	All plus PR
Report Grade	B
Income Distrib	Paid Monthly
* Date of Inception	09-01-89
Fiscal Year End	December

Risk Analysis

Time Period	Load-Adj Return %	Risk % Rank All	Risk % Rank Obj	Morningstar[2] Return	Morningstar Risk	Morningstar Risk-Adj Rating
1 Yr	-4.59					
3 Yr	2.89	7	28	-0.20[3]	0.69	★★★
5 Yr	6.16	4	24	0.34[3]	0.57	★★★★
10 Yr	---	---	---	---	---	---

Average Historical Rating (28 months)   3.4 ★s

[1] 1 = low, 100 = high   [2] 1.00 = Taxable Avg   [3] 1.00 = 90-day T-bill return

Other Measures

			Standard LB Agg	Best Fit LB Int
Standard Deviation	2.65	Alpha	-0.2	0.0
Mean	3.99	Beta	0.63	0.76
Sharpe Ratio	0.18	R-Squared	90	97

Investment Style

Interest-Rate Stance
Avg Effective Duration	2.1 Yrs
Avg Effective Maturity	3.0 Yrs

Quality
Avg Credit Quality	A
Avg Weighted Coupon	6.97%
Avg Weighted Price	98.90% of Par

Diversification Value for Portfolio Types

Large Cap: High	Small Cap: High	Bond: None	Balanced: Medium	Diversified: High

Min Initial Purchase	$1000 (Addt'l: $100)
Min IRA Purchase	None (Addt'l: None)
Min Auto Invest Plan	$50 (Systematic Inv: $50)

Expenses & Fees
Sales Fees	3.25% front
	0.00% deferred
	0.30% 12b-1
Management Fee	0.40% flat fee
3-,5-,10-yr Expense Projections	$57, $75, $128

Portfolio 06-30-94

Total Stocks: 0
Total Fixed-Income: 89

Amount 000	Date of Maturity		Value $000	% Net Assets
17471	10-15-99	US Treasury Note 6%	16720	15.70
10621	11-30-98	US Treasury Note 5.125%	9918	9.31
2601	05-15-97	US Treasury Note 8.5%	2736	2.57
2124	06-01-01	FHLMC 7.5%	2132	2.00
1832	07-10-97	ITT Financial 8.85%	1930	1.81
1864	09-25-96	Govt of New Zealand 8.25%	1916	1.80
1734	05-01-96	Centex 9.05%	1790	1.68
1734	06-03-96	Westinghouse Credit 8.75%	1776	1.67
1734	06-15-99	MBNA Master Card Trust 7.25%	1748	1.64
1734	05-15-19	Green Tree Financial 7.35%	1714	1.61
1626	09-11-95	Occidental Petroleum 5.37%	1606	1.51
1392	11-01-00	FNMA 11%	1550	1.46
1517	12-12-96	Bausch & Lomb 6.8%	1520	1.43
1517	04-28-97	Potomac Capital Invstmt 6.19%	1472	1.38
1517	10-29-96	Associates North Amer 4.56%	1446	1.36
1301	05-01-95	PaineWebber Group 9.625%	1335	1.25
1301	08-03-98	Countrywide Funding 6.88%	1278	1.20
1301	06-15-99	Crane 7.25%	1271	1.19
1301	04-01-98	Texas Utilities Elec 5.875%	1239	1.16
1171	07-01-95	WMX Technologies 4.875%	1159	1.09
1084	11-01-95	Norwest Financial 7.25%	1098	1.03
1084	05-15-95	Unicom 6.125%	1080	1.01
1084	09-08-94	Petroleos Mexicanos FRN	1068	1.00
1084	02-01-96	Oryx Energy 6.05%	1048	0.98
1084	03-15-98	Carnival 5.75%	1031	0.97

Composition % 09-30-94
Cash	14.3	Preferreds	0.0
Stocks	0.0	Convertibles	0.0
Bonds	85.7	Other	0.0

Tax Analysis
	Tax-Adj Historical Return %	% Pretax Return
3 Yr Avg	1.42	34.3
5 Yr Avg	4.15	57.3
10 Yr Avg	---	---
Potential Capital Gain Exposure (% of assets)		-8%

Most Similar Funds in MF500
Vanguard F/I Short-Trm Fed	Strong Fit
Vanguard F/I Short-Trm US Tr	Strong Fit
Vanguard F/I Short-Trm Corp	Strong Fit

Coupon Range
	% of Bonds	Rel Obj
0%	0.0	0.00
0% to 8.5%	74.9	1.18
8.5% to 9.5%	14.7	0.91
9.5% to 11%	8.7	0.94
More than 11%	0.0	0.00
Not applicable	1.7	0.35

Credit Analysis 09-30-94
% of Bonds

US Govt	25	BB	7
AAA	9	B	0
AA	4	Below B	0
A	30	NR/NA	3
BBB	23		

Prudential Utility B

	Ticker	Load	NAV	Yield	SEC Yield	Assets	Objective
	PRUTX	5.00%d	8.26	2.8%	2.49%	3530.4	Sp.-Util

Prudential Utility Fund - Class B seeks current income and moderate capital appreciation.

The fund normally invests at least 80% of its assets in equity and debt securities of utility companies, including electric, gas, telephone, and cable companies. These investments consist chiefly of common stocks, but preferred stocks, money-market instruments, and debt securities may also be held.

Class A shares have front loads; Class B shares have deferred loads, higher 12b-1 fees, and conversion features; Class C shares have level loads. Prior to March 21, 1991, the fund was named Prudential-Bache Utility Fund - Class B.

Manager's Investment Style

Management looks for utilities with strong earnings prospects that can, in turn, increase their dividends. A focus on earnings-growth potential gives this fund a slightly different profile than others in the specialty-utility group. For one, management's total-return focus has resulted in a below-average yield. The fund hasn't been shy about investing internationally, either: Foreign exposure has risen above 25%.

Fund Manager(s)

Warren E. Spitz, since 01-88. BS, Allegheny C. 1977. MBA, Wharton 1984.

Manager Experience

	Dates Managed	Invest Obj	Std Dev	+/- Index
Warren E. Spitz				
Prudential Equity-Inc B	01/87 - 12/94	EI	12.92	-1.31

Historical Profile

Return	Average
Risk	Below Average
Rating ★★★	Neutral

Investment Style History Equity

Average % Stocks Held in Portfolio

		93%	94%	92%	97%	78%	82%	80%	93%

Growth of $10,000

- ‖‖‖ Value of Fund ($000)
- — Value of Index ($000) LB L-T
- ▼ Manager Change
- ▽ Partial Manager Change
- ► Mgr Unknown After
- ◄ Mgr Unknown Before

Performance Quartile (Within Objective)

	1983	1984	1985	1986	1987	1988	1989	1990	1991	1992	1993	1994	History
	5.04	5.62	6.44	7.39	6.29	7.31	9.17	7.63	8.71	8.96	9.69	8.26	NAV
	12.07	38.72	33.30	32.64	-8.72	23.22	37.17	-6.48	19.01	9.02	15.34	-8.51	Total Return %
	-10.40	32.45	1.57	13.96	-13.98	6.61	5.49	-3.37	-11.47	1.41	5.28	-9.82	+/- S&P 500
	---	---	---	4.19	-5.82	5.17	-10.05	-3.92	4.39	0.93	0.90	-0.56	+/- S&P Util
	0.00	17.61	8.33	4.26	4.22	6.99	4.86	4.24	4.86	4.09	2.39	2.63	Income Return %
	12.07	21.11	24.97	28.38	-12.94	16.23	32.31	-10.72	14.15	4.93	12.95	-11.14	Capital Return %
	70	1	16	6	95	8	6	75	46	33	27	88	Total Rtn % Rank All
	40	1	1	1	80	4	23	78	62	50	35	48	Total Rtn % Rank Obj
	0.00	0.82	0.43	0.29	0.33	0.38	0.36	0.34	0.34	0.34	0.23	0.24	Income $
	0.00	0.41	0.44	0.77	0.17	0.00	0.44	0.60	0.00	0.18	0.41	0.38	Capital Gains $
	5.20	2.50	1.13	1.42	1.53	1.56	1.46	1.73	1.67	1.61	1.60	1.59	Expense Ratio %
	8.91	13.35	6.70	4.41	4.69	4.44	4.19	3.94	3.89	3.34	2.36	2.62	Income Ratio %
	93	122	39	49	65	66	75	53	38	24	24	---	Turnover Rate %
	180.6	97.9	338.1	1520.6	1390.8	1583.8	2306.3	2394.7	2839.1	3437.5	4756.4	3530.4	Net Assets ($mil)

Performance 12-31-94

	1st Qtr	2nd Qtr	3rd Qtr	4th Qtr	Total
1987	2.54	-2.55	2.33	-10.73	-8.72
1988	6.36	7.80	4.05	3.29	23.22
1989	4.80	13.92	7.78	6.60	37.17
1990	-5.60	0.31	-7.56	6.83	-6.48
1991	6.37	-1.31	7.42	5.55	19.01
1992	-3.31	4.34	5.55	2.39	9.02
1993	9.89	3.39	5.09	-3.41	15.34
1994	-4.98	-3.24	4.06	-4.37	-8.51

Bear Market Performance

Decile Rank (5-year period)

Worst ———————————————————— Best

	Worst 3 Mo Period 1985-89	Worst 3 Mo Period 1990-94
Prudential Utility B	-12.82	-7.56
+/- S&P 500	16.76	6.19
+/- Best Fit Index : LB L-T	-15.41	-5.36

Trailing Returns

	Total Return %	+/- S&P 500	+/- S&P Util	% Rank All	% Rank Obj	Growth of $10,000
3 Mo	-4.37	-4.35	-4.26	90	91	9,563
6 Mo	-0.48	-5.34	-0.85	65	80	9,952
1 Yr	-8.51	-9.82	-0.56	88	48	9,149
3 Yr Avg	4.78	-1.48	0.36	53	57	11,505
5 Yr Avg	5.07	-3.62	0.14	89	78	12,804
10 Yr Avg	13.32	-1.06	---	23	25	34,929
15 Yr Avg	---	---	---	---	---	---

Operations

Address and Telephone	One Seaport Plaza	
	New York, NY 10292	
	800-225-1852	
Advisor	Prudential Mutual Fund Management	
Subadvisor	Prudential Investment	
Distributor	Prudential Securities	
States Available	All plus PR	
Report Grade	A	
Income Distrib	Paid Quarterly	
Date of Inception	08-10-81	
Fiscal Year End	December	

Risk Analysis

Time Period	Load-Adj Return %	Risk % Rank [1] All	Obj	Morningstar [2] Return	Risk	Morningstar Risk-Adj Rating
1 Yr	-11.92					
3 Yr	4.20	73	71	0.18 [3]	0.83	★★★
5 Yr	4.92	59	63	0.05 [3]	0.68	★★
10 Yr	13.32	49	37	1.13	0.72	★★★★

Average Historical Rating (109 months)   4.5 ★s

[1] 1 = low, 100 = high   [2] 1.00 = Equity Avg   [3] 1.00 = 90-day T-bill return

Other Measures

		Standard S&P 500	Best Fit LB L-T
Standard Deviation	8.91	Alpha	-0.9	-0.2
Mean	5.08	Beta	0.84	0.90
Sharpe Ratio	0.17	R-Squared	55	61

Investment Style

	Stock Portfolio Avg	Relative S&P 500
Price/Earnings Ratio	15.2	0.82
Price/Book Ratio	1.7	0.50
5 Yr Earnings Gr %	4.5	0.80
Return on Assets %	3.9	0.52
Debt % Total Cap	44.4	1.57
Med Mkt Cap ($mil)	2699	0.21

Style: Value Blend Growth / Size Large Med Small

Diversification Value for Portfolio Types

 Large Cap: Low   Small Cap: High   Bond: Low   Balanced: Low   Diversified: Low

Portfolio 06-30-94

Total Stocks: 97
Total Fixed-Income: 26

Share Chg (12-93)000	Amount 000		Value $000	% Net Assets
-97023	2343	Telefonos de Mexico L (ADR)	130941	3.28
1	3521	Sprint	122801	3.08
547	2901	British Gas (ADR)	120398	3.02
1	4107	Williams	117564	2.95
31	3357	Sonat	103220	2.59
-127	3574	Coastal	96509	2.42
1	2382	Telefonica de Espana (ADR)	95881	2.40
2406	3865	Entergy	95664	2.40
16	4505	Panhandle Eastern	88980	2.23
2	7193	TransCanada Pipelines	85183	2.14
342	2245	NYNEX	85033	2.13
1	2540	Southern New England Telecom	77476	1.94
1	3456	CMS Energy	72153	1.81
1797	3593	Southern	67362	1.69
0	1601	US West	67037	1.68
-279	2533	Peco Energy	66818	1.68
1	3311	Pacific Enterprises	65806	1.65
3300	9184	Iberdrola	64613	1.62
1	2335	Columbia Gas System	63056	1.58
1	2620	Commonwealth Edison	59604	1.49
1	3131	Illinova	58707	1.47
-526	2218	General Public Utilities	58210	1.46
1	1757	Questar	56870	1.43
5004	18216	STET	56214	1.41
0	1166	Empresa Nacl De Elec (ADR)	52305	1.31

Composition % 10-18-94

Cash	4.0	Preferreds	0.0
Stocks	96.0	Convertibles	0.0
Bonds	0.0	Other	0.0

Tax Analysis

	Tax-Adj Historical Return %	% Pretax Return
3 Yr Avg	2.70	55.4
5 Yr Avg	2.78	52.3
10 Yr Avg	10.39	67.7
Potential Capital Gain Exposure (% of assets)		3%

Most Similar Funds in MF500

Fidelity Utilities	Strong Fit
Fortress Utility	Fair Fit
Flag Inv Telephone Income A	Fair Fit

Min Initial Purchase / Expenses & Fees

Min Initial Purchase	$1000 (Addt'l: $100)
Min IRA Purchase	None (Addt'l: None)
Min Auto Invest Plan	$50 (Systematic Inv: $50)

Expenses & Fees

Sales Fees	0.00% front
	5.00% deferred
	1.00% 12b-1
Management Fee	0.60% max./0.03% min.
3-,5-,10-yr Expense Projections	$80, $97, $160
Annual Brokerage Cost	0.10%

Index Allocation

	% of Stocks
S&P 500	44.0
S&P MidCap 400	16.8
U.S. Small Cap	12.3
Foreign	26.9

Sector Weightings

	% of Stocks	Relative S&P 500
Utilities	80.4	6.49
Energy	9.8	0.97
Financials	2.8	0.27
Industrial Cyclicals	0.0	0.00
Consumer Durables	0.0	0.00
Consumer Staples	0.0	0.00
Services	2.2	0.28
Retail	0.0	0.00
Health	0.0	0.00
Technology	4.8	0.52

 **1995 Mutual Fund 500**

Putnam Convertible Income Grth A

	Ticker	Load	NAV	Yield	SEC Yield	Assets	Objective
	PCONX	5.75%	17.13	5.2%	5.61%	667.0	Convrt. Bond

Putnam Convertible Income Growth Trust - Class A seeks current income and capital appreciation.

The fund normally invests at least 65% of its assets in convertible securities. The remainder may be invested in nonconvertible equity or debt securities rated at least CCC. The fund may invest up to 10% of its assets in foreign securities. It may also invest up to 10% of assets in securities rated as low as C.

Class A shares have front loads; Class B shares have deferred loads and higher 12b-1 fees. Prior to Aug. 13, 1982, the fund was named Putnam Convertible Fund.

Manager's Investment Style

Management takes a value-driven approach to the convertible-bond market. It targets blue-chip names, smaller-cap concerns, and high-yielding (or busted) bonds. They determine the allocation among these three subgroups according to valuations, moving out of overvalued securities and into undervalued ones. The fund holds common stocks to round out industry diversification, selecting these equities for income, as well as growth potential.

Fund Manager(s)

Charles G. Pohl, since 11-92. BA, Bowdoin C.
Hugh Mullin, since 11-92. BA, U. of Massachusetts

Manager Experience	Dates Managed	Invest Obj	Std Dev	+/- Index
Charles G. Pohl				
Putnam H/I Conv	01/91 - 12/94	CV	7.24	13.78

Historical Profile

Return	Above Average
Risk	Below Average
Rating ★★★★	Above Average

| 36 | 35 | 30 | 19 | 21 | 12 | 12 | 15 | Income Rtn % Rank Obj |

Growth of $10,000

|||| Value of Fund ($000)
— Value of Index ($000)
LB Agg
▼ Manager Change
▽ Partial Manager Change
► Mgr Unknown After
◄ Mgr Unknown Before

Performance Quartile (Within Objective)

	1983	1984	1985	1986	1987	1988	1989	1990	1991	1992	1993	1994	History
	14.90	13.01	15.30	16.24	13.61	14.28	15.65	13.09	15.90	18.22	19.62	17.13	NAV
	13.90	5.54	27.08	15.84	-5.51	12.14	16.51	-10.02	29.40	21.09	17.03	-1.92	Total Return %
	5.53	-9.61	4.95	0.59	-8.27	4.26	1.97	-18.96	13.40	13.85	7.28	1.00	+/- LB Aggregate
	-8.56	-0.73	-4.66	-2.84	-10.77	-4.47	-15.18	-6.90	-1.09	13.47	6.98	-3.24	+/- S&P 500
	7.09	7.05	7.64	6.45	5.67	7.21	6.91	6.34	7.93	6.50	5.35	5.06	Income Return %
	6.82	-1.51	19.44	9.39	-11.18	4.92	9.59	-16.36	21.47	14.59	11.68	-6.98	Capital Return %
	63	49	37	50	90	45	43	84	28	4	23	33	Total Rtn % Rank All
	66	1	1	42	45	50	30	85	34	12	32	26	Total Rtn % Rank Obj
	1.00	0.88	0.91	0.96	0.96	0.96	0.96	1.04	0.96	0.96	0.96	0.96	Income $
	0.74	1.60	0.19	0.44	0.88	0.00	0.00	0.00	0.00	0.00	0.68	1.16	Capital Gains $
	1.08	1.01	0.88	0.83	0.84	0.92	0.93	1.12	1.15	1.11	0.96	0.99	Expense Ratio %
	6.62	7.13	6.21	5.54	4.91	6.12	6.32	6.37	6.07	5.32	4.55	3.69	Income Ratio %
	69	76	120	78	87	116	49	60	79	60	67	---	Turnover Rate %
	41.0	55.4	225.3	917.7	1036.1	904.9	812.3	556.1	568.6	628.8	704.1	667.0	Net Assets ($mil)

Performance 12-31-94

	1st Qtr	2nd Qtr	3rd Qtr	4th Qtr	Total
1987	12.08	1.44	3.04	-19.34	-5.51
1988	7.33	3.14	-0.46	1.77	12.14
1989	5.89	5.83	5.41	-1.37	16.51
1990	-2.04	2.24	-12.74	2.97	-10.02
1991	14.90	2.30	5.10	4.75	29.40
1992	6.92	2.21	4.91	5.62	21.09
1993	6.54	2.62	4.02	2.91	17.03
1994	-1.98	-1.02	4.25	-3.03	-1.92

Bear Market Performance

Decile Rank (5-year period)

Worst   Best

	Worst 3 Mo Period 1985-89	Worst 3 Mo Period 1990-94
Putnam Convertible Income Grt	-25.79	-18.21
+/- LB Aggregate	-27.95	-18.95
+/- Best Fit Index : Wil 4500	4.35	1.19

Trailing Returns

	Total Return %	+/- LB Aggregate	+/- S&P 500	% Rank All	% Rank Obj	Growth of $10,000
3 Mo	-3.03	-3.41	-3.02	83	51	9,697
6 Mo	1.09	0.10	-3.77	36	21	10,109
1 Yr	-1.92	1.00	-3.24	33	26	9,808
3 Yr Avg	11.60	7.05	5.33	9	12	13,899
5 Yr Avg	10.11	2.48	1.42	16	33	16,183
10 Yr Avg	11.39	1.45	-2.99	44	1	29,408
15 Yr Avg	13.72	2.91	-0.76	28	33	68,791

Operations

Address and Telephone	One Post Office Square
	Boston, MA 02109
	800-225-1581 / 617-292-1000
Advisor	Putnam Investment Management
Subadvisor	None
Distributor	Putnam Mutual Funds
States Available	All
Report Grade	B+
Income Distrib	Paid Quarterly
Date of Inception	06-29-72
Fiscal Year End	October

Min Initial Purchase	$500 (Addt'l: $50)
Min IRA Purchase	$250 (Addt'l: $50)
Min Auto Invest Plan	$25 (Systematic Inv: $25)

Expenses & Fees

Sales Fees	5.75% front
	0.00% deferred
	0.25% 12b-1
Management Fee	0.70% max./0.43% min.
3-,5-,10-yr Expense Projections	$89, $113, $179

Risk Analysis

Time Period	Load-Adj Return %	Risk % Rank [1] All	Obj	Morningstar [2] Return	Morningstar Risk	Morningstar Risk-Adj Rating
1 Yr	-7.56					
3 Yr	9.42	22	8	1.78 [3]	0.50	★★★★
5 Yr	8.81	55	52	1.02 [3]	0.82	★★★★
10 Yr	10.73	46	66	0.80	0.82	★★★
Average Historical Rating (109 months)					3.2	★s

[1] 1 = low, 100 = high   [2] 1.00 = Hybrid Avg   [3] 1.00 = 90-day T-bill return

Other Measures

				Standard LB Agg	Best Fit Wil 4500
Standard Deviation	5.98	Alpha		7.2	5.6
Mean	11.20	Beta		0.74	0.52
Sharpe Ratio	1.28	R-Squared		24	70

Investment Style

Interest-Rate Stance

Avg Effective Maturity   ---

Quality

Avg Credit Quality   BB

Avg Weighted Coupon   5.22%
Avg Weighted Price   85.88% of Par

Not Applicable

Diversification Value for Portfolio Types

Large Cap: Low	Small Cap: Low	Bond: High	Balanced: Low	Diversified: Low

Tax Analysis

	Tax-Adj Historical Return %	% Pretax Return
3 Yr Avg	8.59	71.9
5 Yr Avg	7.37	69.1
10 Yr Avg	8.37	63.6
Potential Capital Gain Exposure (% of assets)		-2%

Most Similar Funds in MF500

Fidelity Equity-Income II	Fair Fit
Royce Equity-Income	Fair Fit
Seligman Income A	Fair Fit

Portfolio 12-30-94

Total Stocks: 129
Total Fixed-Income: 174

Amount 000	Date of Maturity		Value $000	% Net Assets
8562	08-15-10	SFP Pipeline Holdings Cv FRN	10103	1.51
7833	01-10-15	Time Warner Cv 8.75%	7402	1.11
9037	07-27-99	Cellular Communications Cv 0%	7377	1.11
281		Arco/Lyondell Cv Pfd $2.23	7349	1.10
219		Unisys Cv Pfd $3.75	6947	1.04
142		Eastman Kodak	6757	1.01
119		Freeport-McMoran Cv Pfd $4.375	5648	0.85
425		Westinghouse Elec Cv Pfd $1.30	5634	0.84
5708	07-01-01	Liberty Property Tr 8%	5537	0.83
102		Burlington Nrthn Cv Pfd $3.125	5446	0.82
6659	12-15-99	Banamex Cv 7%	5227	0.78
383		Chrysler Cv Pfd $4.625	5217	0.78
57		Ford Motor Cv Pfd $4.20	5207	0.78
9989	11-26-05	Rogers Communications Cv 2%	5194	0.78
121		Tenneco	5125	0.78
12843	04-15-07	Comcast Cv 1.125%	5121	0.77
14270	04-13-12	WMX Technologies Cv 0%	5101	0.76
5708	06-01-01	Data General Cv 7.75%	4966	0.74
4804	05-15-98	Chubb Cv 6%	4852	0.73
100		First Chicago Cv Pfd $2.875	4720	0.71
90		Service Intl Cv Pfd $6.25	4675	0.70
7083	03-31-07	Standard Commercial Cv 7.25%	4674	0.70
4043	09-01-13	Amoco Canada Petro A Cv 7.375%	4650	0.70
4757	08-15-02	Old Republic Intl Cv 5.75%	4578	0.69
76		Beverly Enterp Cv Pfd $2.75	4490	0.70

Composition % 12-31-94

Cash	3.8	Preferred	0.0
Stocks	26.4	Convertibles	69.5
Bonds	0.3	Other	0.0

Coupon Range

	% of Bonds	Rel Obj
0%	11.4	1.35
0% to 6%	19.7	0.58
6% to 7%	9.6	0.65
7% to 8.5%	14.3	1.22
More than 8.5%	4.0	0.72
Not applicable	41.0	1.59

Credit Analysis 11-30-94

% of Bonds

US Govt	0	BB	20
AAA	0	B	28
AA	4	Below B	4
A	10	NR/NA	13
BBB	23		

Putnam Diversified Income A

	Ticker	Load	NAV	Yield	SEC Yield	Assets	Objective
	PDINX	4.75%	11.23	8.8%	9.98%	1439.3	Income

Putnam Diversified Income Trust - Class A seeks income consistent with preservation of capital.

The fund allocates its investments among three types of fixed-income securities: U.S. government debt obligations and related options, futures and repurchase agreements; high-yielding, lower-rated U.S. corporate fixed-income securities; and debt obligations of foreign governments.

Class A shares have front loads; Class B shares have deferred loads and higher 12b-1 fees.

Putnam Diversified Premium Income Trust, a closed-end fund, merged into this fund on Jan. 17, 1992.

Historical Profile
Return	Above Average
Risk	Low
Rating	★★★★
	Above Average

Manager's Investment Style

Management seeks out income in three distinct markets--high-yield corporate bonds, foreign debt, and U.S. government securities. In the corporate-bond arena, management has pumped up yields by exposing the fund to the lower end of the credit-quality spectrum. The foreign bonds in the fund's portfolio are fully hedged in the dollar, but still represent a risk if U.S. currency falls. Finally, the fund's government portion leans toward intermediate to long mortgages.

Investment Style History
Fixed Income
Income Rtn % Rank Obj

Growth of $10,000
- ‖‖‖ Value of Fund ($000)
- — Value of Index ($000) LB L-T
- ▼ Manager Change
- ▽ Partial Manager Change
- ► Mgr Unknown After
- ◄ Mgr Unknown Before

Performance Quartile (Within Objective)

Fund Manager(s)
Jennifer Leichter CFA(1987), since 09-89.
Neil Powers CFA, since 1994.
D. William Kohli, since 1994.

Manager Experience
	Dates Managed	Invest Obj	Std Dev	+/- Index
Jennifer Leichter				
Putnam Master Int	09/89 - 12/94	MB	4.50	0.43
Putnam H/I Conv	01/93 - 12/94	CV	4.75	5.99

1983	1984	1985	1986	1987	1988	1989	1990	1991	1992	1993	1994	History
							41	20	31	28	41	13	
---	---	---	---	---	12.53	11.80	10.99	12.22	12.20	12.98	11.23	NAV
---	---	---	---	---	2.05 *	5.13	5.02	23.62	12.27	15.86	-5.59	Total Return %
---	---	---	---	---	-1.24 *	-26.56	8.13	-6.87	4.65	5.80	-6.91	+/- S&P 500
---	---	---	---	---		-9.41	-3.93	7.62	5.02	6.11	-2.68	+/- LB Aggregate
---	---	---	---	---	1.81	9.55	10.07	10.80	9.02	7.30	7.54	Income Return %
---	---	---	---	---	0.24	-4.42	-5.05	12.82	3.24	8.56	-13.14	Capital Return %
---	---	---	---	---		95	43	38	14	26	69	Total Rtn % Rank All
---	---	---	---	---		79	23	45	15	16	72	Total Rtn % Rank Obj
---	---	---	---	---	0.22	1.16	1.12	1.07	1.04	0.84	0.99	Income $
---	---	---	---	---	0.00	0.19	0.23	0.15	0.40	0.24	0.06	Capital Gains $
---	---	---	---	---		1.25	1.25	1.47	1.36	1.21	1.01	Expense Ratio %
---	---	---	---	---		9.63	9.98	9.18	8.27	6.80	7.96	Income Ratio %
---	---	---	---	---		164	264	481	221	244	202	Turnover Rate %
---	---	---	---	---	40.0	117.5	137.4	185.3	411.8	1196.8	1439.3	Net Assets ($mil)

Performance 12-31-94
	1st Qtr	2nd Qtr	3rd Qtr	4th Qtr	Total
1987	---	---	---	---	---
1988	---	---	---	---	2.05 *
1989	1.17	2.52	0.45	0.91	5.13
1990	-2.08	4.70	-1.41	3.90	5.02
1991	7.05	2.66	6.39	5.74	23.62
1992	1.99	3.92	5.18	0.71	12.27
1993	4.97	3.63	3.01	3.39	15.86
1994	-2.61	-2.12	0.51	-1.47	-5.60

Bear Market Performance
Decile Rank (5-year period)

	Worst 3 Mo Period 1985-89	Worst 3 Mo Period 1990-94
Putnam Diversified Income A	---	-5.33
+/- S&P 500	---	0.43
+/- Best Fit Index : LB L-T	---	4.07

Trailing Returns
	Total Return %	+/- S&P 500	+/- LB Aggregate	% Rank All	% Rank Obj	Growth of $10,000
3 Mo	-1.47	-1.46	-1.85	56	52	9,853
6 Mo	-0.97	-5.83	-1.96	73	71	9,903
1 Yr	-5.59	-6.91	-2.68	69	72	9,441
3 Yr Avg	7.08	0.82	2.54	26	23	12,279
5 Yr Avg	9.77	1.08	2.15	18	17	15,940
10 Yr Avg	---	---	---	---	---	---
15 Yr Avg	---	---	---	---	---	---

Risk Analysis
Time Period	Load-Adj Return %	Risk % Rank All	Risk % Rank Obj	Morningstar[2] Return	Morningstar Risk	Morningstar Risk-Adj Rating
1 Yr	-10.08					
3 Yr	5.36	11	13	0.52[3]	0.40	★★★★
5 Yr	8.71	25	11	1.00[3]	0.37	★★★★
10 Yr	---	---	---	---	---	

Average Historical Rating (39 months)   4.1 ★s

[1] = low, 100 = high   [2] 1.00 = Hybrid Avg   [3] 1.00 = 90-day T-bill return

Other Measures
			Standard S&P 500	Best Fit LB L-T
Standard Deviation	3.90	Alpha	2.7	2.7
Mean	6.94	Beta	0.25	0.39
Sharpe Ratio	0.88	R-Squared	25	56

Investment Style
Stocks
	Port Avg	Rel S&P 500
Price/Earnings Ratio	9.9#	0.54
Price/Book Ratio	1.5#	0.45
5 Yr Earnings Gr %	---	---
Med Mkt Cap ($mil)	332#	0.03

figure is based on 50% or less of stocks

Bonds
Avg Effective Duration	5.3 Yrs
Avg Effective Maturity	8.8 Yrs
Avg Credit Quality	---
Avg Weighted Coupon	8.53%

Diversification Value for Portfolio Types
Large Cap: High	Small Cap: High	Bond: Low	Balanced: Medium	Diversified: Medium

Portfolio 09-30-94
Total Stocks: 18
Total Fixed-Income: 337

Share Chg (03-94)000	Amount 000		Date of Maturity	Value $000	% Net Assets
	66415	GNMA TBA 8%	10-14-24	64423	4.19
	89448	Govt of Canada 5.75%	1999	60490	3.93
	61256	GNMA 7.5%	06-15-24	57542	3.74
	61171	FNMA 7%	06-01-24	56182	3.65
	48639	GNMA 7%	06-15-24	44079	2.86
	29704	US Treasury Note 7.5%	11-15-01	29741	1.93
	180676	Govt of France 5.5%	2004	28344	1.84
	40454724	Republic of Italy 12%	01-01-03	26068	1.69
	46686	Commonwealth Australia 6.75%	11-15-06	25823	1.68
	24169	US Treasury Note 8.875%	2005	25612	1.66
	17823	United Kingdom Treasury 6.75%	2004	24250	1.58
	24909	US Treasury Note 5.75%	10-31-97	24099	1.57
	21752	US Treasury Note 9.25%	08-15-98	23282	1.51
	11990	United Kingdom Treasury 9.75%	1998	19514	1.27
	30530772	Republic of Italy 8.5%	2004	16334	1.06
	14502	US Treasury Note 8.75%	10-15-97	15209	0.99
	15507	US Treasury Note 5.25%	07-31-98	14548	0.95
	13876	US Treasury Note 6%	11-30-97	13503	0.88
	13994	Viacom International 8%	2006	12175	0.79
	12157	Fresh Del Monte Produce 10%	05-01-03	10698	0.70

Index Allocation
	% of Stocks
S&P 500	0.0
S&P MidCap 400	0.0
U.S. Small Cap	100.0
Foreign	0.0

Composition % 12-31-94
Cash	5.8	Preferreds	0.0
Stocks	0.0	Convertibles	0.0
Bonds	94.2	Other	0.0

Bond Credit Analysis 12-31-94
% of Bonds
US Govt	0	BB	7
AAA	56	B	22
AA	0	Below B	2
A	0	NR/NA	12
BBB	1		

Tax Analysis
	Tax-Adj Historical Return %	% Pretax Return
3 Yr Avg	3.60	49.1
5 Yr Avg	6.16	58.6
10 Yr Avg	---	---

Potential Capital Gain Exposure (% of assets)   -10%

Stock Sector Weightings
	% of Stocks	Relative S&P 500
Utilities	0.0	0.00
Energy	0.0	0.00
Financials	0.0	0.00
Industrial Cyclicals	58.9	3.60
Consumer Durables	0.0	0.00
Consumer Staples	0.0	0.00
Services	20.1	2.47
Retail	8.6	1.48
Health	0.0	0.00
Technology	12.3	1.34

Most Similar Funds in MF500
Colonial Strategic Income A	Strong Fit
Putnam Income A	Fair Fit
Bond Fund of America	Fair Fit

Operations
Address and Telephone	One Post Office Square
	Boston, MA 02109
	800-225-1581 / 617-292-1000
Advisor	Putnam Investment Management
Subadvisor	None
Distributor	Putnam Mutual Funds
States Available	All
Report Grade	B
Income Distrib	Paid Monthly
* Date of Inception	10-03-88
Fiscal Year End	September

Min Initial Purchase	$500 (Addt'l: $50)
Min IRA Purchase	$250 (Addt'l: $50)
Min Auto Invest Plan	$25 (Systematic Inv: $25)

Expenses & Fees
Sales Fees	4.75% front
	0.00% deferred
	0.25% 12b-1
Management Fee	0.85% max./0.50% min.
3-,5-,10-yr Expense Projections	$85, $112, $189
Annual Brokerage Cost	---

MORNINGSTAR 1995 Mutual Fund 500

Putnam Fund for Gr & Inc A

	Ticker	Load	NAV	Yield	SEC Yield	Assets	Objective
	PGRWX	5.75%	12.72	3.0%	3.59%	5848.1	Growth/Inc.

Putnam Fund for Growth and Income - Class A seeks capital growth and current income.

The fund invests primarily in common stocks. These equities, issued by well-established companies with a steady history of profits, have attractive price/earnings ratios. The fund may also purchase preferred stocks, convertible securities, and corporate bonds, notes, and debentures of any credit quality. It may invest up to 20% of its assets in foreign securities. The fund may write covered calls on to 25% of its assets.

Class A shares have front loads; Class B shares have deferred loads and higher 12b-1 fees.

Manager's Investment Style

Management looks for issues with sustainable dividends that are selling cheaply relative to their long-term earnings power. This gives the fund a mild value bent, but it shouldn't be branded as an extreme value player, because it prefers issues with visible earnings, as opposed to deep cyclicals. Current management, which took over the fund in 1993, has focused on equities more than bonds and cash, keeping at least 80% of assets in stocks.

Fund Manager(s)

Anthony I. Kreisel CFA, since 01-93. BA, Franklin & Marshall C. 1966 MBA, Columbia U. 1968
David L. King CFA, since 01-93. BS, U. of New Hampshire 1978 MBA, Harvard 1983

Manager Experience	Dates Managed	Invest Obj	Std Dev	+/- Index
Anthony I. Kreisel				
Putnam Convert Inc Gr A	03/89 - 11/92	CV	11.22	-0.73
David L. King				
Putnam Convert Inc Gr A	11/90 - 11/92	CV	8.11	13.16

Historical Profile

Return	Average
Risk	Low
Rating	★★★★ Above Average

Performance Quartile (Within Objective)

1983	1984	1985	1986	1987	1988	1989	1990	1991	1992	1993	1994	History
13.10	10.91	12.82	13.69	9.99	11.21	12.12	11.35	12.38	12.84	13.60	12.72	NAV
21.91	5.39	28.47	22.85	2.43	20.72	20.70	2.39	19.18	11.78	14.45	-0.28	Total Return %
-0.56	-0.88	-3.27	4.17	-2.83	4.11	-10.98	5.51	-11.30	4.16	4.39	-1.59	+/- S&P 500
-1.55	2.34	-4.09	6.75	0.07	2.78	-8.47	8.57	-15.03	2.81	3.17	-0.21	+/- Wilshire 5000
4.24	4.85	6.30	5.39	5.78	6.19	5.49	5.26	5.29	4.28	4.08	2.98	Income Return %
17.67	0.53	22.17	17.46	-3.34	14.53	15.21	-2.87	13.89	7.50	10.37	-3.26	Capital Return %
33	49	31	12	39	12	34	49	46	16	31	21	Total Rtn % Rank All
42	43	43	7	45	20	7	93	20	25	45		Total Rtn % Rank Obj
0.48	0.51	0.62	0.65	0.73	0.60	0.62	0.62	0.60	0.52	0.52	0.40	Income $
0.56	2.17	0.39	1.13	3.41	0.21	0.75	0.43	0.49	0.45	0.54	0.44	Capital Gains $
0.62	0.63	0.55	0.53	0.64	0.72	0.72	0.89	0.95	1.07	0.93	0.95	Expense Ratio %
3.72	4.79	5.65	5.10	4.12	3.99	6.00	5.01	4.45	3.72	3.18	3.18	Income Ratio %
197	139	243	176	143	86	103	81	77	67	64	49	Turnover Rate %
783.1	777.8	876.2	1261.5	1492.8	1647.7	1956.1	2117.8	2799.8	3791.3	5327.0	5848.1	Net Assets ($mil)

Growth of $10,000

IIII Value of Fund ($000)
— Value of Index ($000) S&P 500
▼ Manager Change
▽ Partial Manager Change
► Mgr Unknown After
◄ Mgr Unknown Before

Investment Style History Equity
Average % Stocks Held in Portfolio

| 71% | 77% | 63% | 68% | 61% | 57% | 73% | 87% |

Performance 12-31-94

	1st Qtr	2nd Qtr	3rd Qtr	4th Qtr	Total
1987	15.81	3.32	6.67	-19.75	2.43
1988	7.67	6.16	0.83	4.75	20.72
1989	5.36	5.32	6.98	1.68	20.70
1990	0.01	3.49	-9.37	9.16	2.39
1991	10.03	-0.45	5.19	3.44	19.18
1992	1.94	3.68	3.05	2.63	11.78
1993	6.02	1.87	3.60	2.29	14.45
1994	-4.00	1.76	4.34	-2.16	-0.28

Bear Market Performance

Decile Rank (5-year period)

Worst — Best

	Worst 3 Mo Period 1985-89	Worst 3 Mo Period 1990-94
Putnam Fund for Gr & Inc A	-25.55	-11.21
+/- S&P 500	4.03	2.63
+/- Best Fit Index : S&P 500	4.03	2.63

Trailing Returns

	Total Return %	+/- S&P 500	+/- Wil 5000	% Rank All	% Rank Obj	Growth of $10,000
3 Mo	-2.16	-2.15	-1.39	71	69	9,784
6 Mo	2.09	-2.78	-2.54	26	57	10,209
1 Yr	-0.28	-1.59	-0.21	21	45	9,972
3 Yr Avg	8.45	2.19	1.84	19	18	12,757
5 Yr Avg	9.26	0.56	0.44	22	19	15,567
10 Yr Avg	13.88	-0.51	0.02	18	18	36,669
15 Yr Avg	14.57	0.08	0.59	18	19	76,894

Risk Analysis

Time Period	Load-Adj Return %	Risk % Rank [1] All	Obj	Morningstar [2] Return	Morningstar Risk	Morningstar Risk-Adj Rating
1 Yr	-6.01					
3 Yr	6.33	54	13	0.82 [3]	0.58	★★★
5 Yr	7.97	55	11	0.80 [3]	0.61	★★★
10 Yr	13.20	46	13	1.11	0.66	★★★★
Average Historical Rating (109 months)				4.0	★ s	

[1] 1 = low, 100 = high   [2] 1.00 = Equity Avg   [3] 1.00 = 90-day T-bill return

Other Measures

				Standard S&P 500	Best Fit S&P 500
Standard Deviation	7.12	Alpha		2.5	2.5
Mean	8.40	Beta		0.84	0.84
Sharpe Ratio	0.68	R-Squared		87	87

Investment Style

	Stock Portfolio Avg	Relative S&P 500
Price/Earnings Ratio	16.4	0.89
Price/Book Ratio	3.1	0.91
5 Yr Earnings Gr %	0.2	0.04
Return on Assets %	5.0	0.67
Debt % Total Cap	33.7	1.19
Med Mkt Cap ($mil)	8789	0.68

Style: Value Blend Growth / Size Large Med Small

Diversification Value for Portfolio Types

Large Cap: None	Small Cap: Medium	Bond: Medium	Balanced: None	Diversified: Low

Portfolio 12-30-94

Total Stocks: 169
Total Fixed-Income: 40

Share Chg (10-94) 000	Amount 000		Value $000	% Net Assets
	208	US Treasury Bond 8.125%	210242	3.60
-17	2598	Philip Morris	149368	2.55
15	1243	Xerox	123102	2.11
-101	1965	Avon Products	117422	2.01
481	2433	Eastman Kodak	116182	1.99
-45	1862	Exxon	113090	1.93
248	2023	Dun & Bradstreet	111247	1.90
-3	1465	TRW	96704	1.65
-157	1888	General Electric	96285	1.65
-6	964	ITT	85411	1.46
-9	1158	IBM	85122	1.46
110	1274	American Home Products	79951	1.37
-82	2627	American Express	77499	1.33
75	719	Royal Dutch Petroleum	77267	1.32
-9	1821	General Motors	76923	1.32
-149	1282	Bristol-Myers Squibb	74205	1.27
-75	1127	Eli Lilly	73946	1.26
-105	1906	American Brands	71485	1.22
-8	1262	JP Morgan	70654	1.21
54	1467	Sears Roebuck	67497	1.15
197	1887	US West	67219	1.15
131	1717	Beneficial	66960	1.14
259	1726	WR Grace	66657	1.14
-46	1765	NYNEX	64857	1.11
-10	1515	Tenneco	64403	1.10

Composition % 12-31-94

Cash	2.1	Preferreds	0.0
Stocks	87.2	Convertibles	5.2
Bonds	5.5	Other	0.0

Tax Analysis

	Tax-Adj Historical Return %	% Pretax Return
3 Yr Avg	6.03	69.6
5 Yr Avg	6.63	68.0
10 Yr Avg	9.98	59.6
Potential Capital Gain Exposure (% of assets)		-1%

Most Similar Funds in MF500

Scudder Growth & Income	Strong Fit
Vanguard/Windsor II	Strong Fit
Smith Barney Inc & Grth A	Strong Fit

Index Allocation

	% of Stocks
S&P 500	89.6
S&P MidCap 400	5.3
U.S. Small Cap	3.0
Foreign	3.9

Sector Weightings

	% of Stocks	Relative S&P 500
Utilities	12.9	1.04
Energy	11.6	1.55
Financials	18.9	1.79
Industrial Cyclicals	19.1	1.17
Consumer Durables	4.6	0.74
Consumer Staples	8.9	0.71
Services	7.1	0.88
Retail	4.4	0.75
Health	9.4	1.08
Technology	3.0	0.33

Operations

Address and Telephone	One Post Office Square Boston, MA 02109 800-225-1581 / 617-292-1000
Advisor	Putnam Investment Management
Subadvisor	None
Distributor	Putnam Mutual Funds
States Available	All
Report Grade	B
Income Distrib	Paid Quarterly
Date of Inception	11-06-57
Fiscal Year End	October

Min Initial Purchase	$500 (Addt'l: $50)
Min IRA Purchase	$250 (Addt'l: $50)
Min Auto Invest Plan	$25 (Systematic Inv: $25)

Expenses & Fees

Sales Fees	5.75% front
	0.00% deferred
	0.25% 12b-1
Management Fee	0.65% max./0.45% min.
3-,5-,10-yr Expense Projections	$85, $106, $165
Annual Brokerage Cost	0.20%

George Putnam Fund of Boston A

	Ticker	Load	NAV	Yield	SEC Yield	Assets	Objective
	PGEOX	5.75%	12.91	4.3%	5.06%	911.5	Balanced

George Putnam Fund of Boston - Class A seeks capital appreciation and current income.

The fund may invest in any type of security; ordinarily, no more than 75% of its assets are invested in common stocks and convertibles. The balance may be invested in debt obligations or money-market instruments. The debt portion may not contain securities rated lower than B. The fund may invest up to 20% of its assets in foreign securities; Eurodollar certificates are not subject to this percentage limitation.

Class A shares carry a front-end load; Class B shares have a deferred sales charge.

Manager's Investment Style

Stock management focuses on out-of-favor companies with strong balance sheets as well as mature companies in slow-growth industries, and typically buys dividend-paying issues. Similarly, bond management emphasizes underappreciated bonds that provide above-average yields. The fund has dabbled in international bonds.

Fund Manager(s)

Kenneth J. Taubes, since 10-93. BS, Syracuse U. MBA, Suffolk U.
Edward P. Bousa, since 11-93. BA, Williams C. MBA, Harvard

Manager Experience	Dates Managed	Invest Obj	Std Dev	+/- Index
Kenneth J. Taubes				
Putnam American Gvt I A	03/92 - 03/94	GG	3.46	-3.22
Edward P. Bousa				
Putnam Managed Inc A	12/92 - 12/94	I	5.47	-0.23

Historical Profile
Return: Average
Risk: Below Average
Rating: ★★★★ Above Average

Investment Style History
Equity
Average % Stocks Held in Portfolio

	67%	63%	64%	65%	65%	66%	65%	58%

Growth of $10,000
|||| Value of Fund ($000)
— Value of Index ($000) S&P 500
▼ Manager Change
▽ Partial Manager Change
► Mgr Unknown After
◄ Mgr Unknown Before

Performance Quartile (Within Objective)

1983	1984	1985	1986	1987	1988	1989	1990	1991	1992	1993	1994	History
14.63	10.95	13.13	14.66	11.91	12.32	13.46	12.10	13.75	13.64	13.86	12.91	NAV
14.96	-2.22	29.84	18.84	3.70	12.10	23.60	-0.92	22.80	7.96	10.90	-0.38	Total Return %
-7.51	-8.49	-1.90	0.16	-1.56	-4.51	-8.08	2.20	-7.69	0.34	0.84	-1.69	+/- S&P 500
6.59	-17.38	7.71	3.59	0.94	4.22	9.06	-9.86	6.80	0.71	1.15	2.54	+/- LB Aggregate
7.54	8.86	9.93	6.21	5.90	6.19	6.62	5.34	5.80	5.12	4.72	4.22	Income Return %
7.42	-11.08	19.91	12.63	-2.20	5.91	16.98	-6.26	17.00	2.83	6.17	-4.59	Capital Return %
58	73	27	27	30	45	27	58	40	46	60	22	Total Rtn % Rank All
53	92	32	36	27	43	23	56	61	38	51	17	Total Rtn % Rank Obj
1.00	0.96	0.96	0.80	0.80	0.72	0.81	0.68	0.68	0.68	0.63	0.57	Income $
0.00	2.24	0.00	0.11	2.63	0.28	0.88	0.52	0.36	0.48	0.60	0.32	Capital Gains $
0.59	0.63	0.62	0.58	0.71	0.73	0.48	0.84	0.94	1.06	0.90	0.95	Expense Ratio %
7.12	6.61	6.84	5.66	4.86	5.82	3.41	5.52	5.42	4.62	4.34	4.15	Income Ratio %
162	223	187	143	130	139	53	71	65	79	89	101	Turnover Rate %
328.9	276.1	324.1	371.9	384.1	387.4	430.2	417.9	530.0	657.3	833.0	911.5	Net Assets ($mil)

Performance 12-31-94

	1st Qtr	2nd Qtr	3rd Qtr	4th Qtr	Total
1987	13.93	1.95	3.36	-13.62	3.70
1988	4.07	5.36	0.91	1.31	12.10
1989	4.81	6.91	7.35	2.76	23.60
1990	-2.21	3.38	-9.02	7.71	-0.92
1991	10.69	1.06	3.95	5.60	22.80
1992	-0.44	3.18	3.27	1.77	7.96
1993	4.87	1.65	2.77	1.23	10.90
1994	-3.65	1.22	3.56	-1.35	-0.38

Bear Market Performance

Decile Rank (5-year period)

Worst — Best

	Worst 3 Mo Period 1985-89	Worst 3 Mo Period 1990-94
George Putnam Fund of Boston	-19.66	-9.98
+/- S&P 500	9.92	3.86
+/- Best Fit Index : S&P 500	9.92	3.86

Trailing Returns

	Total Return %	+/- S&P 500	+/- LB Aggregate	% Rank All	% Rank Obj	Growth of $10,000
3 Mo	-1.35	-1.34	-1.73	53	65	9,865
6 Mo	2.16	-2.70	1.17	25	35	10,216
1 Yr	-0.38	-1.69	2.54	22	17	9,962
3 Yr Avg	6.05	-0.22	1.50	33	36	11,927
5 Yr Avg	7.73	-0.96	0.11	37	58	14,511
10 Yr Avg	12.40	-1.99	2.45	33	35	32,173
15 Yr Avg	12.84	-1.64	2.03	42	48	61,233

Risk Analysis

Time Period	Load-Adj Return %	Risk % Rank[1] All	Obj	Morningstar[2] Return	Morningstar Risk	Morningstar Risk-Adj Rating
1 Yr	-6.11					
3 Yr	3.98	46	41	0.11[3]	0.68	★★★
5 Yr	6.46	52	44	0.42[3]	0.76	★★★
10 Yr	11.73	44	64	1.00	0.75	★★★★

Average Historical Rating (109 months) 3.2 ★s

[1] = low, 100 = high [2] 1.00 = Hybrid Avg [3] 1.00 = 90-day T-bill return

Other Measures

		Standard S&P 500	Best Fit S&P 500
Standard Deviation	5.82	Alpha	0.6	0.6
Mean	6.06	Beta	0.68	0.68
Sharpe Ratio	0.44	R-Squared	87	87

Investment Style

Stocks	Port Avg	Rel S&P 500
Price/Earnings Ratio	16.2	0.88
Price/Book Ratio	2.8	0.82
5 Yr Earnings Gr %	-1.3	-0.24
Med Mkt Cap ($mil)	8270	0.64

Style: V B G / L M S (Size)

Bonds	
Avg Effective Duration	5.0 Yrs
Avg Effective Maturity	10.6 Yrs
Avg Credit Quality	---
Avg Weighted Coupon	7.77%

Not Available

Diversification Value for Portfolio Types

Large Cap: None	Small Cap: High	Bond: Medium	Balanced: None	Diversified: Low

Portfolio 07-31-94

Share Chg (01-94)000	Amount 000	Total Stocks: 127 / Total Fixed-Income: 147	Date of Maturity	Value $000	% Net Assets
	35934	US Treasury Note 5%	01-31-99	33643	3.68
	16295	GNMA TBA 6.5%	02-15-24	14762	1.62
	14991	US Treasury Note 5.125%	12-31-98	14134	1.55
98	215	JP Morgan		13571	1.49
-9	226	Exxon		13420	1.47
	13045	GNMA TBA 7.5%	09-15-23	12670	1.39
	9995	US Treasury Bond 11.125%	08-15-03	12641	1.38
106	323	NYNEX		12440	1.36
	11924	US Treasury Note 4.25%	11-30-95	11719	1.28
	10916	US Treasury Bond 8.125%	08-15-19	11687	1.28
-2	111	Xerox		11350	1.24
-1	181	Philip Morris		11273	1.23
	11161	US Treasury Note 3.875%	10-31-95	10934	1.20
165	322	Ford Motor		10208	1.12
29	177	American Home Products		10146	1.11
	9384	US Treasury Note 8.875%	11-15-97	10056	1.10
23	110	Mobil		9209	1.01
56	135	Bankers Trust New York		9040	0.99
26	165	AT & T		9001	0.99
73	177	General Electric		8908	0.98

Index Allocation

	% of Stocks
S&P 500	87.7
S&P MidCap 400	6.6
U.S. Small Cap	4.5
Foreign	3.4

Composition % 12-31-94

Cash	4.2	Preferreds	0.0
Stocks	55.6	Convertibles	3.3
Bonds	36.9	Other	0.0

Tax Analysis

	Tax-Adj Historical Return %	% Pretax Return
3 Yr Avg	3.38	54.4
5 Yr Avg	4.98	61.0
10 Yr Avg	8.71	58.8
Potential Capital Gain Exposure (% of assets)		-1%

Most Similar Funds in MF500

IDS Mutual	Strong Fit
Vanguard/Wellington	Strong Fit
American Mutual	Strong Fit

Bond Credit Analysis 03-31-94
% of Bonds

US Govt	10	BB	18
AAA	27	B	0
AA	4	Below B	1
A	13	NR/NA	0
BBB	27		

Stock Sector Weightings

	% of Stocks	Relative S&P 500
Utilities	16.2	1.31
Energy	11.9	1.17
Financials	19.3	1.82
Industrial Cyclicals	19.6	1.20
Consumer Durables	3.7	0.60
Consumer Staples	10.1	0.81
Services	8.0	0.99
Retail	2.0	0.35
Health	7.7	0.89
Technology	1.4	0.15

Operations

Address and Telephone	One Post Office Square
	Boston, MA 02109
	800-225-1581 / 617-292-1000
Advisor	Putnam Investment Management
Subadvisor	None
Distributor	Putnam Mutual Funds
States Available	All
Report Grade	B+
Income Distrib	Paid Quarterly
Date of Inception	11-05-37
Fiscal Year End	July

Min Initial Purchase	$500 (Addt'l: $50)
Min IRA Purchase	$250 (Addt'l: $50)
Min Auto Invest Plan	$25 (Systematic Inv: $25)

Expenses & Fees

Sales Fees	5.75% front
	0.00% deferred
	0.25% 12b-1
Management Fee	0.60% max./0.30% min.
3-,5-,10-yr Expense Projections	$85, $105, $164
Annual Brokerage Cost	0.19%

 **1995 Mutual Fund 500**

Putnam Global Govt Inc A

	Ticker	Load	NAV	Yield	SEC Yield	Assets	Objective
	PGGIX	4.75%	12.92	7.0%	8.61%	428.7	World Bond

Putnam Global Governmental Income Trust - Class A seeks current income and long-term total return consistent with preservation of capital.

The fund normally invests at least 80% of its assets in high-quality foreign debt securities and investment-grade domestic debt securities. At least 65% of assets are invested in debt securities of governmental issuers located in at least three countries. The fund may invest up to 15% of its assets in securities rated as low as CCC, and up to 5% in securities rated lower than CCC.

Class A shares have front loads and lower 12b-1 fees; Class B shares have deferred loads and conversion features.

Historical Profile

Return	Below Average
Risk	Below Average
Rating	★★★ Neutral

Investment Style History
Fixed Income
Income Rtn % Rank Obj

| | 1 | 16 | 9 | 48 | 4 | 58 | 49 |

Growth of $10,000

|||| Value of Fund ($000)
— Value of Index ($000) LB Govt
▼ Manager Change
▽ Partial Manager Change
► Mgr Unknown After
◄ Mgr Unknown Before

Performance Quartile (Within Objective)

Manager's Investment Style

A manager change in early 1994 could add some life to this traditionally lackluster offering. Mark Turner, who guided Scudder International Bond through some tough times, joined the management team of this fund in April, 1994. He and his team have thus far practiced a strategy of shifting out of lower-yielding, in-favor markets and into higher-yielding, out-of-favor markets in an attempt to capture higher real yields. They have also actively hedged the portfolio's currency exposure.

Fund Manager(s)

F. Mark Turner, since 04-94.
Jonathan H. Francis, since 04-94.
D. William Kohli, since 07-94.

Manager Experience	Dates Managed	Invest Obj	Std Dev	+/- Index
F. Mark Turner				
Scudder International Bd	01/89 - 10/92	WB	8.52	4.10
Scudder S-T Global Inc	03/91 - 11/92	SW	2.81	-2.56

	1983	1984	1985	1986	1987	1988	1989	1990	1991	1992	1993	1994	History
	---	---	---	---	15.55	15.89	15.43	15.63	16.37	14.52	15.32	12.92	NAV
	---	---	---	---	16.18 *	14.89	7.65	16.33	15.15	4.41	13.65	-9.98	Total Return %
	---	---	---	---	---	7.01	-6.89	7.39	-0.85	-2.83	3.90	-7.06	+/- LB Aggregate
	---	---	---	---	---	12.54	11.07	1.04	-1.09	-0.36	-1.47	-16.67	+/- SB World Govt
	---	---	---	---	6.05	12.61	10.54	13.40	8.81	10.90	7.05	5.69	Income Return %
	---	---	---	---	10.13	2.29	-2.89	2.93	6.34	-6.49	6.60	-15.67	Capital Return %
	---	---	---	---	---	28	91	1	57	79	36	94	Total Rtn % Rank All
	---	---	---	---	---	1	29	30	32	20	58	81	Total Rtn % Rank Obj
	---	---	---	---	0.78	1.86	1.56	1.90	1.25	1.68	0.98	0.90	Income $
	---	---	---	---	0.00	0.02	0.00	0.24	0.23	0.85	0.15	0.00	Capital Gains $
	---	---	---	---	---	1.66	1.62	1.58	1.48	1.46	1.27	1.29	Expense Ratio %
	---	---	---	---	---	10.04	9.35	8.50	7.97	6.77	6.12	6.11	Income Ratio %
	---	---	---	---	---	---	249	387	498	314	407	444	Turnover Rate %
	---	---	---	---	---	76.3	153.1	187.2	238.9	376.7	418.3	578.2	428.7	Net Assets ($mil)

Performance 12-31-94

	1st Qtr	2nd Qtr	3rd Qtr	4th Qtr	Total
1987	---	---	3.95	11.76	16.18 *
1988	5.57	2.44	-0.01	6.25	14.89
1989	-1.72	-0.13	2.58	6.92	7.65
1990	-1.50	4.27	5.62	7.24	16.33
1991	0.35	0.39	6.63	7.21	15.15
1992	-4.90	4.39	5.48	-0.28	4.41
1993	4.43	2.59	2.98	3.02	13.65
1994	-5.37	-4.05	0.49	-1.33	-9.98

Bear Market Performance

Decile Rank (5-year period)

Worst ———————————————— Best

	Worst 3 Mo Period 1985-89	Worst 3 Mo Period 1990-94
Putnam Global Govt Inc A	---	-7.40
+/- LB Aggregate	---	-2.46
+/- Best Fit Index : LB Govt	---	-2.32

Trailing Returns

	Total Return %	+/- LB Aggregate	+/- SB World	% Rank All	% Rank Obj	Growth of $10,000
3 Mo	-1.33	-1.71	-1.90	53	73	9,867
6 Mo	-0.85	-1.84	-3.08	71	80	9,915
1 Yr	-9.98	-7.06	-16.67	94	81	9,002
3 Yr Avg	2.22	-2.32	-6.55	91	74	10,682
5 Yr Avg	7.43	-0.20	-4.09	41	48	14,309
10 Yr Avg	---	---	---	---	---	---
15 Yr Avg	---	---	---	---	---	---

Operations

Address and Telephone	One Post Office Square
	Boston, MA 02109
	800-225-1581 / 617-292-1000
Advisor	Putnam Investment Management
Subadvisor	None
Distributor	Putnam Mutual Funds
States Available	All
Report Grade	B
Income Distrib	Paid Monthly
* Date of Inception	06-01-87
Fiscal Year End	October

Min Initial Purchase	$500 (Addt'l: $50)
Min IRA Purchase	N/A
Min Auto Invest Plan	$25 (Systematic Inv: $25)

Expenses & Fees

Sales Fees	4.75% front
	0.00% deferred
	0.25% 12b-1
Management Fee	0.80% max./0.60% min.
3-,5-,10-yr Expense Projections	$86, $114, $194

Risk Analysis

Time Period	Load-Adj Return %	Risk % Rank All	Risk % Rank Obj	Morningstar Return	Morningstar Risk	Morningstar Risk-Adj Rating
1 Yr	-14.25					
3 Yr	0.58	58	64	-0.84[3]	0.84	★★
5 Yr	6.39	45	45	0.40[3]	0.55	★★★
10 Yr	---	---	---	---	---	
Average Historical Rating (55 months)				3.8 ★s		

[1] = low, 100 = high [2] 1.00 = Hybrid Avg [3] 1.00 = 90-day T-bill return

Other Measures

				Standard LB Agg	Best Fit LB Govt
Standard Deviation	6.00	Alpha		-2.2	-2.3
Mean	2.38	Beta		1.11	1.03
Sharpe Ratio	-0.19	R-Squared		55	55

Investment Style

Interest-Rate Stance

Avg Effective Maturity 11.8 Yrs

Quality

Avg Credit Quality ---

Avg Weighted Coupon 8.48%

Not Available

Diversification Value for Portfolio Types

● Large Cap: High ● Small Cap: High ◐ Bond: Low ◐ Balanced: Medium ◐ Diversified: Medium

Portfolio 10-31-94

Amount 000	Date of Maturity	Total Stocks: 0 — Total Fixed-Income: 85	Value $000	% Net Assets
28159	1999	United Kingdom Treasury 10.25%	48170	10.44
51330	2004	Govt of Canada 6.5%	31760	6.88
48383045	2004	Republic of Italy 8.5%	26218	5.68
41454	11-15-06	Commonwealth Australia 6.75%	22696	4.92
17453	03-07-11	Republic of Italy 9.25%	21239	4.60
1047	03-30-98	United Kingdom Treasury 7.25%	16493	3.57
27734653	1999	Republic of Italy 8.5%	16173	3.50
8107	1999	European Investment Bk 10.5%	13878	3.01
100619	2003	Kingdom of Sweden 10.25%	13646	2.96
73915	2003	Kingdom of Denmark 8%	11826	2.56
15813	2022	Province of Ontario 9.5%	11336	2.46
15260	2004	Govt of Canada 9%	11197	2.43
46733	03-15-02	Republic of Finland 10.75%	10573	2.29
18364	2000	Govt of New Zealand 6.5%	10146	2.20
63900	2001	Govt of Sweden 13%	9865	2.14
13529	1999	Govt of Canada 5.75%	9030	1.96
10172	08-15-03	Commonwealth Australia 9.5%	7120	1.54
4988	2004	United Kingdom Treasury 6.75%	7089	1.54
9638	07-01-97	Govt of Canada 7.5%	7035	1.52
9537	1999	Queensland Treasury 8%	6503	1.41
44826	1999	Statens Bostads 11%	6248	1.35
3729	2000	United Kingdom Treasury 9%	6167	1.34
7716	2003	Victoria Treasury 8.25%	4919	1.07
6199	2023	Petro Mexico 8.625%	4901	1.06
8197	01-15-23	Govt of Netherlands 7.5%	4591	0.99

Composition % 12-31-94

Cash	6.8	Preferreds	0.0
Stocks	0.0	Convertibles	0.0
Bonds	93.2	Other	0.0

Tax Analysis

	Tax-Adj Historical Return %	% Pretax Return
3 Yr Avg	-1.20	---
5 Yr Avg	3.81	47.7
10 Yr Avg	---	---
Potential Capital Gain Exposure (% of assets)		-18%

Most Similar Funds in MF500

Scudder International Bond	Weak Fit
Franklin Utilities	Weak Fit
Fidelity Global Bond	Weak Fit

Country Exposure 08-31-94

	% of Bonds
United Kingdom	22
Canada	20
Italy	10
Australia	8
Sweden	5

Currency Exposure 08-31-94

	% of Net Assets
U.S.	65
Canada	20
United Kingdom	15

Putnam Global Growth A

	Ticker	Load	NAV	Yield	SEC Yield	Assets	Objective
	PEQUX	5.75%	9.22	0.0%	0.0%	1477.5	World Stock

Putnam Global Growth Fund - Class A seeks capital appreciation.

The fund invests in domestic and foreign securities; it may invest up to 100% of its assets in securities principally traded in foreign markets or in any one country. The fund may invest in large or small companies with earnings showing strong growth trends or in undervalued nongrowth companies.

Class A shares carry a front-end load; Class B shares have a deferred sales charge.

Prior to Aug. 1, 1990, the fund was named Putnam International Equities Fund.

Manager's Investment Style

The fund's management team seeks stock of firms with above-average earnings or unit growth selling at below-average prices. Management also tries to help the fund benefit from economic or industrial shifts within countries. Although management does invest modestly in emerging markets, it prefers the better-known names in these markets. The team targets reasonable and consistent performance, and has achieved this goal.

Fund Manager(s)

Anthony W. Regan, since 1988.
Gerald S. Zukowski CFA, since 1993. BS, Miami U.
MBA, Harvard

Manager Experience

	Dates Managed	Invest Obj	Std Dev	+/- Index
Gerald S. Zukowski				
Putnam Vista A	01/89 - 12/91	G	14.27	-0.90
Putnam Fund for G & I A	12/91 - 01/93	GI	5.40	4.16

Historical Profile

Return	Above Average
Risk	Average
Rating	★★★★ Above Average

Value of Fund ($000)
— Value of Index ($000) MSEASEA
▼ Manager Change
▽ Partial Manager Change
► Mgr Unknown After
◄ Mgr Unknown Before

Investment Style History Equity
Average % Stocks Held in Portfolio

	91%	91%	94%	88%	91%	92%		94%	92%

Growth of $10,000

Performance Quartile (Within Objective)

1983	1984	1985	1986	1987	1988	1989	1990	1991	1992	1993	1994	History
4.93	3.94	5.88	7.60	6.07	6.50	7.88	6.59	7.49	7.43	9.62	9.22	NAV
27.93	0.74	65.04	37.69	7.23	9.00	24.58	-9.20	17.97	0.24	31.84	-0.85	Total Return %
5.46	-5.52	33.30	19.01	1.98	-7.61	-7.10	-6.08	-12.52	-7.38	21.79	-2.17	+/- S&P 500
6.00	-3.98	24.48	-4.20	-8.93	-14.28	7.97	7.82	-0.32	5.46	9.34	-5.93	+/- MSCI World
2.12	0.57	1.65	0.53	2.15	1.78	2.05	2.13	1.71	0.92	0.00	0.00	Income Return %
25.81	0.17	63.39	37.16	5.08	7.22	22.53	-11.33	16.26	-0.68	31.84	-0.85	Capital Return %
16	63	1	5	15	68	24	83	48	89	7	26	Total Rtn % Rank All
40	25	6	47	28	72	26	42	39	44	46	34	Total Rtn % Rank Obj
0.07	0.02	0.06	0.03	0.13	0.11	0.14	0.15	0.12	0.07	0.00	0.00	Income $
0.00	0.99	0.34	0.38	1.91	0.00	0.08	0.42	0.16	0.01	0.17	0.31	Capital Gains $
1.46	1.28	1.32	1.07	1.39	1.40	1.06	1.44	1.47	1.56	1.39	1.31	Expense Ratio %
0.62	1.52	1.04	0.85	1.03	1.34	1.52	1.56	1.60	1.28	0.85	0.58	Income Ratio %
132	167	134	176	113	103	67	95	71	62	50	---	Turnover Rate %
44.7	47.2	90.4	411.4	524.2	479.0	534.3	561.9	660.4	657.2	1057.3	1477.5	Net Assets ($mil)

Performance 12-31-94

	1st Qtr	2nd Qtr	3rd Qtr	4th Qtr	Total
1987	15.23	7.19	7.06	-18.91	7.23
1988	3.87	-0.11	-2.38	7.62	9.00
1989	3.52	2.60	12.20	4.54	24.58
1990	-4.57	9.44	-17.62	5.53	-9.20
1991	11.23	-1.77	5.97	1.89	17.97
1992	-2.00	4.63	-3.78	1.59	0.24
1993	7.27	4.27	7.94	9.21	31.84
1994	-3.01	0.43	3.95	-2.08	-0.85

Bear Market Performance

Decile Rank (5-year period)

Worst 3 Mo Period 1985-89	Worst 3 Mo Period 1990-94

	Worst 3 Mo Period 1985-89	Worst 3 Mo Period 1990-94
Putnam Global Growth A	-26.39	-17.62
+/- S&P 500	3.19	-3.87
+/- Best Fit Index : MSEASEA	-2.07	-1.00

Trailing Returns

	Total Return %	+/- S&P 500	+/- MSCI World	% Rank All	% Rank Obj	Growth of $10,000
3 Mo	-2.08	-2.06	-1.34	70	18	9,792
6 Mo	1.79	-3.07	0.39	28	29	10,179
1 Yr	-0.85	-2.17	-5.93	26	34	9,915
3 Yr Avg	9.43	3.16	2.57	15	34	13,103
5 Yr Avg	7.01	-1.68	3.35	50	25	14,035
10 Yr Avg	16.60	2.22	1.76	5	6	46,444
15 Yr Avg	15.06	0.57	---	12	12	81,979

Operations

Address and Telephone	One Post Office Square Boston, MA 02109 800-225-1581 / 617-292-1000		
Advisor	Putnam Investment Management		
Subadvisor	None		
Distributor	Putnam Mutual Funds		
States Available	All		
Report Grade	B+		
Income Distrib	Paid Annually		
Date of Inception	09-01-67		
Fiscal Year End	October		

Risk Analysis

Time Period	Load-Adj Return %	Risk % Rank All	Obj	Morningstar [2] Return	Risk	Morningstar Risk-Adj Rating
1 Yr	-6.56					
3 Yr	7.29	75	36	1.11 [3]	0.86	★★★
5 Yr	5.75	74	22	0.24 [3]	0.89	★★
10 Yr	15.91	55	25	1.70	0.80	★★★★★

Average Historical Rating (109 months)   4.2 ★s

[1] = low, 100 = high   [2] 1.00 = Equity Avg   [3] 1.00 = 90-day T-bill return

Other Measures

	Standard S&P 500	Best Fit MSEASEA
Standard Deviation	10.46	
Mean	9.58	
Sharpe Ratio	0.58	
Alpha	3.7	1.4
Beta	0.84	0.73
R-Squared	40	86

Investment Style

	Stock Portfolio Avg	Rel MSCI EAFE	Rel Obj	Style
Price/Earnings Ratio	30.3	0.82	1.23	
Price/Cash Flow	13.3	0.85	0.98	
Price/Book Ratio	2.9	1.11	0.99	
5 Yr Earnings Gr %	1.3	---	0.27	
Return on Assets %	5.6	1.23	0.81	
Debt % Total Cap	26.9	0.79	0.93	
Med Mkt Cap ($mil)	4812	0.40	0.96	

Diversification Value for Portfolio Types

Large Cap: Medium   Small Cap: High   Bond: High   Balanced: Medium   Diversified: Low

Portfolio 10-31-94

Share Chg (04-94) 000	Amount 000	Total Stocks: 360 Total Fixed-Income: 4	Value $000	% Net Assets
59	261	Sony	15892	1.05
185	869	Matsushita Electric Indl	14431	0.96
31	784	Omron	14314	0.95
4	928	Daiwa Securities	13493	0.90
-56	1176	Fujitsu	13465	0.89
-30	627	Nippondenso	13392	0.89
747	2548	Nisshin Steel	13378	0.89
40	40	Veba	13350	0.89
130	719	Dai Nippon Printing	13344	0.89
-4	461	Teledenmark (ADR)	13267	0.88
84	323	Murata Manufacturing	13210	0.88
171	719	Marui	13121	0.87
69	237	Ito-Yokado	12941	0.86
114	1633	Toray Industries	12889	0.86
761	1796	Tate & Lyle	12508	0.83
-28	594	Repola	12477	0.83
82	171	Wolters Kluwer (Netherlands)	12368	0.82
-40	2923	Allied Irish Banks	11907	0.79
109	725	Svenska Cellulosa CI A Free	11848	0.79
1320	1320	Mitsui	11843	0.79

Regional Exposure 12-31-94
% of Stocks

Japan	23	U.S.	24
Latin Amer	18	Other	22
Pacific Rim	11		

Composition % 12-31-94

Cash	7.6	Preferreds	0.0
Stocks	92.4	Convertibles	0.0
Bonds	0.0	Other	0.0

Tax Analysis

	Tax-Adj Historical Return %	% Pretax Return
3 Yr Avg	8.79	92.7
5 Yr Avg	5.87	81.8
10 Yr Avg	14.58	79.6
Potential Capital Gain Exposure (% of assets)		9%

Most Similar Funds in MF500

Scudder International	Strong Fit
T. Rowe Price Intl Stock	Strong Fit
Vanguard Intl Growth	Strong Fit

Country Exposure 09-30-94
% of Stocks

Japan	23
U.S.	18
United Kingdom	11
France	7
Switzerland	4

Total Number of Countries: 25
Hedging Policy: Occasional

Sector Weightings

	% of Stocks	Relative S&P 500
Utilities	5.4	0.66
Energy	2.7	0.56
Financials	18.9	1.14
Industrial Cyclicals	28.1	1.21
Consumer Durables	11.9	1.16
Consumer Staples	4.5	0.89
Services	13.7	1.16
Retail	5.2	0.89
Health	2.5	0.47
Technology	7.1	0.81

Expenses & Fees

Sales Fees	5.75% front
	0.00% deferred
	0.25% 12b-1
Management Fee	0.80% max./0.60% min.
3-,5-,10-yr Expense Projections	$99, $130, $216
Annual Brokerage Cost	0.38%

Min Initial Purchase / IRA / Auto Invest

Min Initial Purchase	$500 (Addt'l: $50)
Min IRA Purchase	$250 (Addt'l: $50)
Min Auto Invest Plan	$25 (Systematic Inv: $25)

Putnam High Yield Advantage A

	Ticker	Load	NAV	Yield	SEC Yield	Assets	Objective
	PHYIX	4.75%	9.00	11.3%	10.20%	666.4	Corp Hi Yld

Putnam High Yield Advantage Fund - Class A seeks high current income; capital growth is a secondary objective.

The fund normally invests at least 80% of its assets in high-yielding, lower-rated fixed-income securities, constituting a diversified portfolio that does not involve undue risk to income or principal. Generally, these higher yields are found in securities rated BBB or lower. The fund does not invest in securities rated lower than CCC. Normally, at least 80% of the fund's assets are invested in fixed-income securities.

Prior to April 1, 1992, the fund was named Putnam High-Yield Trust II.

Historical Profile

Return	Above Average
Risk	Low
Rating	★★★★★ Highest

Manager's Investment Style

The fund attempts to deliver high yield while achieving capital return by investing in the junk-bond market. The fund does take on some additional credit risk by purchasing low-rated bonds, yet has not often been punished for the chances it takes. While management's main goal is yield, they do seek out sectors that they think will deliver capital returns as well. Investments in telecommunications and cable companies have helped management reach its goals.

Fund Manager(s)

Jin W. Ho, since 10-89. BA, Claremont C. 1982
Edward D'Alelio, since 03-86.

Manager Experience	Dates Managed	Invest Obj	Std Dev	+/- Index
Edward D'Alelio				
Putnam High Yield A	03/85 - 12/94	CY	6.55	0.76
Putnam Mgd H/Y	06/93 - 12/94	CY	5.16	2.21

Investment Style History
Fixed Income
Income Rtn % Rank Obj

34	19	40	16	13	7	2	10

Growth of $10,000

|||| Value of Fund ($000)
— Value of Index ($000)
FB HY
▼ Manager Change
▽ Partial Manager Change
►◄ Mgr Unknown After
◄► Mgr Unknown Before

Performance Quartile (Within Objective)

	1983	1984	1985	1986	1987	1988	1989	1990	1991	1992	1993	1994	History
	---	---	---	11.62	10.99	11.14	9.26	7.33	9.26	9.71	10.53	9.00	NAV
	---	---	---	4.34 *	6.09	15.06	-4.35	-8.09	45.71	18.61	21.04	-5.15	Total Return %
	---	---	---		3.33	7.19	-18.89	-17.04	29.71	11.37	11.29	-2.23	+/- LB Aggregate
	---	---	---		-0.44	3.63	-4.74	-1.71	1.96	1.95	2.14	-4.17	+/- FB High-Yield
	---	---	---	7.51	11.51	13.70	12.04	12.75	19.38	13.75	12.59	9.38	Income Return %
	---	---	---	-3.17	-5.42	1.36	-16.38	-20.84	26.33	4.86	8.44	-14.53	Capital Return %
	---	---	---		18	28	100	80	10	6	16	65	Total Rtn % Rank All
	---	---	---		9	24	78	41	17	34	27	77	Total Rtn % Rank Obj
	---	---	---	0.88	1.32	1.43	1.41	1.23	1.22	1.22	1.12	1.02	Income $
	---	---	---	0.00	0.00	0.00	0.07	0.00	0.00	0.00	0.00	0.00	Capital Gains $
	---	---	---		1.12	1.07	1.23	1.37	1.33	1.14	0.96	0.96	Expense Ratio %
	---	---	---		11.65	12.04	12.55	13.92	13.38	12.40	11.04	10.95	Income Ratio %
	---	---	---		121	97	77	63	74	68	51	---	Turnover Rate %
	---	---	---	215.5	308.7	423.9	330.4	247.9	351.6	493.8	759.7	666.4	Net Assets ($mil)

Performance 12-31-94

	1st Qtr	2nd Qtr	3rd Qtr	4th Qtr	Total
1987	6.69	-1.48	-0.56	1.49	6.09
1988	5.70	3.70	2.23	2.68	15.06
1989	2.35	2.86	-2.40	-6.91	-4.35
1990	-5.87	6.33	-6.51	-1.78	-8.09
1991	17.90	7.33	7.89	6.73	45.71
1992	10.80	3.78	2.21	0.92	18.61
1993	7.34	4.57	1.71	6.01	21.04
1994	-0.97	-1.33	-1.38	-1.56	-5.15

Bear Market Performance

Decile Rank (5-year period)

Worst _____ Best

	Worst 3 Mo Period 1985-89	Worst 3 Mo Period 1990-94
Putnam High Yield Advantage	---	-10.86
+/- LB Aggregate	---	-11.60
+/- Best Fit Index : FB HY	---	3.25

Trailing Returns

	Total Return %	+/- LB Aggregate	+/- FB High-Yield	% Rank All	% Rank Obj	Growth of $10,000
3 Mo	-1.56	-1.94	-1.52	58	60	9,844
6 Mo	-2.92	-3.91	-4.48	94	73	9,708
1 Yr	-5.15	-2.23	-4.17	65	77	9,485
3 Yr Avg	10.84	6.30	-0.32	11	34	13,618
5 Yr Avg	12.77	5.14	-0.31	7	11	18,237
10 Yr Avg	---	---	---	---	---	---
15 Yr Avg	---	---	---	---	---	---

Operations

Address and Telephone	One Post Office Square
	Boston, MA 02109
	800-225-1581 / 617-292-1000
Advisor	Putnam Investment Management
Subadvisor	None
Distributor	Putnam Mutual Funds
States Available	All
Report Grade	A-
Income Distrib	Paid Monthly
* Date of Inception	03-25-86
Fiscal Year End	November

Risk Analysis

Time Period	Load-Adj Return %	Risk % Rank All	Obj	Morningstar Return	Morningstar Risk	Morningstar Risk-Adj Rating
1 Yr	-9.65					
3 Yr	9.06	13	77	1.67 [3]	0.43	★★★★
5 Yr	11.68	45	49	1.84 [3]	0.55	★★★★★
10 Yr	---	---	---			

Average Historical Rating (70 months)   3.4 ★s

[1] 1 = low, 100 = high   [2] 1.00 = Hybrid Avg   [3] 1.00 = 90-day T-bill return

Other Measures

			Standard LB Agg	Best Fit FB HY
Standard Deviation	5.76	Alpha	6.6	-2.0
Mean	10.50	Beta	0.54	1.25
Sharpe Ratio	1.21	R-Squared	14	88

Investment Style

Interest-Rate Stance
Avg Effective Duration	4.6 Yrs
Avg Effective Maturity	8.4 Yrs

Maturity Short Intm Long
Quality High Med Low

Quality
Avg Credit Quality	B
Avg Weighted Coupon	10.58%
Avg Weighted Price	91.63% of Par

Diversification Value for Portfolio Types

Large Cap: High	Small Cap: High	Bond: High	Balanced: High	Diversified: High
●	●	●	●	●

Expenses & Fees

Sales Fees	4.75% front
	0.00% deferred
	0.25% 12b-1
Management Fee	0.70% max./0.43% min.
3-,5-,10-yr Expense Projections	$81, $105, $175

Min Initial Purchase $500 (Addt'l: $50)
Min IRA Purchase $250 (Addt'l: $50)
Min Auto Invest Plan $25 (Systematic Inv: $25)

Portfolio 05-31-94

Amount 000	Date of Maturity	Total Stocks: 13 Total Fixed-Income: 135	Value $000	% Net Assets
28435	05-15-05	Gaylord Container 12.75%	23601	3.34
21451	05-15-02	Adelphia Communications 12.5%	22094	3.12
16063	02-01-03	Kaiser Aluminium/Chem 12.75%	16384	2.32
23945	04-15-98	Marvel 0%	14607	2.06
11973	2004	PSF Finance 12.25%	11973	1.69
18458	08-01-03	PanAmSat Capital 11.375%	11674	1.65
11723	08-15-99	Haynes International 13.5%	11489	1.62
12968	11-15-99	Trump Taj Mahal Funding 11.35%	11347	1.60
12372	11-01-01	Centennial Cellular 8.875%	11320	1.60
10027	12-15-02	Amphenol 12.75%	11130	1.57
11612	09-15-03	Falcon Holdings Group 11%	11032	1.56
21950	08-15-03	Intl Semi-Tech 11.5%	10975	1.55
10775	06-01-99	Horsehead Industries 14%	10398	1.47
9478	09-01-00	TransTexas Gas 10.5%	9478	1.34
9728	08-01-03	Jordan Industries 10.375%	9339	1.32
10013	11-01-04	Flagstar 11.25%	9262	1.31
8685	12-15-02	Ivex Packaging 12.5%	9141	1.29
14966	2004	NEXTEL Communications 0%	8755	1.24
13469	09-01-03	NEXTEL Communications 0%	8553	1.21
7982	01-15-99	Texas-New Mexico Power 12.5%	8540	1.21
7483	10-15-05	Southdown 14%	8418	1.19
7483	04-15-02	Blue Bird Body 11.75%	7782	1.10
6485	11-01-02	Bankers Life Holding 13%	7393	1.05
8131	12-15-03	Playtex Family Products 9%	7257	1.03
6984	06-15-02	Riverwood Intl 11.25%	7237	1.02

Composition % 12-31-94

Cash	10.3	Preferreds	1.9
Stocks	0.0	Convertibles	0.0
Bonds	87.8	Other	0.0

Tax Analysis

	Tax-Adj Historical Return %	% Pretax Return
3 Yr Avg	6.46	57.1
5 Yr Avg	8.09	57.7
10 Yr Avg	---	---

Potential Capital Gain Exposure (% of assets)   -20%

Most Similar Funds in MF500

IDS Extra Income	Strong Fit
Liberty High-Income Bond A	Fair Fit
Delaware Delchester A	Fair Fit

Coupon Range

	% of Bonds	Rel Obj
0%, PIK	8.5	1.14
0% to 11%	32.3	0.66
11% to 13%	47.9	1.43
13% to 14.5%	9.3	1.70
More than 14.5%	0.3	0.21
Not applicable	1.8	0.58

Credit Analysis 09-30-94

% of Bonds

US Govt	0	BB	11
AAA	0	B	73
AA	0	Below B	16
A	0	NR/NA	0
BBB	1		

Putnam High Yield Municipal

	Ticker	NAV	Mkt Price	Prem/Disc	Yield	Objective
	PYM	$8.63	$8.63	-0.1%	8.7%	Muni National

8.4	6.0	10.8	14.4	16.1	11.6	Highest Prem/Disc
-2.5	-7.7	-7.8	5.1	3.6	-1.7	Lowest Prem/Disc

Putnam High Yield Municipal Trust seeks high current income exempt from federal income tax.

The fund invests at least 80% of assets in tax-exempt municipal securities; it invests a substantial portion of assets in tax-exempt municipal securities rated BB or lower, although not lower than B-. There is no limit on the portion of the fund's assets that may be invested in any one ranking category. The fund may write options and futures as a hedging strategy. For defensive purposes, the fund may invest in high-quality obligations.

The fund is leveraged by a class of remarketed preferred shares.

Conversion to open-end status before fiscal 1994 required a supermajority vote of shareholders; currently, only a majority is required.

Historical Profile
Return Average
Risk Average
Rating ★★★★
Above Average

Growth of $10,000
— at NAV ($000)
— at Market Price ($000)

Premium Discount %

History

	1983	1984	1985	1986	1987	1988	1989	1990	1991	1992	1993	1994	History
	---	---	---	---	---	---	9.36	8.94	9.04	9.33	9.78	8.63	NAV
	---	---	---	---	---	---	4.89*	4.30	10.55	12.24	13.05	-4.32	NAV Total Return %
	---	---	---	---	---	---	---	-4.65	-5.45	4.99	3.30	-1.40	+/- LB Aggregate
	---	---	---	---	---	---	---	-3.00	-1.59	3.42	0.78	1.28	+/- LB Muni
	---	---	---	---	---	---	4.25*	8.79	9.43	9.03	8.23	7.44	Income Return %
	---	---	---	---	---	---	0.65*	-4.49	1.12	3.21	4.82	-11.76	Capital Return %
	---	---	---	---	---	---	---	48	84	27	69	34	Total Rtn % Rank All
	---	---	---	---	---	---	---	90	74	12	62	22	Total Rtn % Rank Obj
	---	---	---	---	---	---	-4.90*	-1.27	29.21	14.33	10.48	-10.94	Market Total Rtn %
	---	---	---	---	---	---	4.8	-0.3	5.4	10.2	9.8	6.3	Avg Prem/Disc %
	---	---	---	---	---	---	0.39	0.80	0.81	0.81	0.77	0.75	Income $
	---	---	---	---	---	---	0.00	0.00	0.00	0.00	0.00	0.00	Capital Gains $
	---	---	---	---	---	---	0.82	0.90	1.13	1.17	1.17	0.59	Expense Ratio %
	---	---	---	---	---	---	8.34	8.55	8.77	8.58	7.97	4.10	Income Ratio %
	---	---	---	---	---	---	---	20	62	54	29	---	Turnover Rate %
	---	---	---	---	---	---	187.9	186.5	184.2	192.3	203.9	189.7	Net Assets ($mil)
	---	---	---	---	---	---	0.0	0.0	45.0	45.0	45.0	45.0	Pfd/Debt Leverage ($mil)

Manager's Investment Style

Management's quest for yield often leads it to lower-rated and less-liquid issues. More than a third of the portfolio usually features nonrated credits, most of which management deems to be of below-investment-grade quality. Although management doesn't aggressively turn over the portfolio, it is willing now and then to change the portfolio to take advantage of certain themes. In 1994, for example, it emphasized cyclical issues to take advantage of the growing economy.

Fund Manager(s)

Triet M. Nguyen. Since 5-89. BA'77 U. of Chicago; MBA'79 U. of Chicago.

Manager Experience

	Dates Managed	Invest Obj	Std Dev	+/- Index
Triet M. Nguyen				
Putnam NJ Tax Exempt Inc	02/90 - 06/93	MS	4.19	-1.55

NAV Performance % 12-30-94

	1st Qtr	2nd Qtr	3rd Qtr	4th Qtr	Total
1987	---	---	---	---	---
1988	---	---	---	---	---
1989	---	0.86*	1.21	2.76	4.89*
1990	1.24	1.06	0.37	1.57	4.30
1991	1.27	2.73	2.82	3.36	10.55
1992	1.57	3.94	3.86	2.36	12.24
1993	3.75	3.62	3.87	1.24	13.05
1994	-3.76	-0.08	1.01	-1.49	-4.32

Bear Market Performance

Decile Rank (5-year period)

Worst ————————————— Best

	Worst 3 Mo Period 1985-89	Worst 3 Mo Period 1990-94
Putnam H/Y Muni	---	-5.14
+/- LB Aggregate	---	-0.21

Trailing Returns

	NAV Total Return %	+/- LB Agg	+/- LB Muni	% Rank All	% Rank Obj	Mkt Total Return %
3 Mo	-1.49	-1.87	-0.06	43	44	-7.25
6 Mo	-0.50	-1.49	0.74	45	28	-8.97
1 Yr	-4.32	-1.40	1.28	34	22	-10.94
3 Yr Avg	6.68	2.13	1.81	39	18	4.00
5 Yr Avg	6.96	-0.67	0.18	66	36	7.49
Incept Avg	7.10*	---	---	---	---	5.71*

Operations

Address and Telephone	One Post Office Square
	Boston, MA 02109
	617-292-1000 / 800-634-1587
Advisor	Putnam Management Co.
Subadvisor	N/A
Administrator	N/A
Transfer Agent	Putnam Investor Services
Custodian	Putnam Fiduciary Trust Co.
Auditor	Price Waterhouse LLP
Legal Counsel	Ropes & Gray

Income Distrib Schedule	Paid Monthly
Management Fee	0.70%
Reinvestment Plan	Yes
Direct Purchase Plan	No
Shares Outstanding	21,126,796
Exchange	NYSE
*Date of Inception	05-25-89
Shareholder Report	B+

Risk Analysis

	Risk % Rank[1] All	Obj	Morningstar[2] Return	Morningstar Risk	Morningstar Risk-Adj Rating
3 Yr	15	28	1.19	0.67	★★★★★
5 Yr	11	40	1.08	0.76	★★★★
10 Yr					

Average Historical Rating (32 months)   4.4 ★s

[1] = Low, 100 = High   [2]1.00 = Muni Avg   [3]1.00 = 90-day T-bill Return

Other Measures

				LB Muni
Standard Deviation	5.18	Alpha		1.86
Mean	6.62	Beta		0.90
Sharpe Ratio	0.60	R-Squared		90

Investment Style

Interest-Rate Stance

	Fund	Relative Objective
Avg Effective Maturity	10.4 Yrs	0.47
Avg Weighted Coupon	8.99%	1.18
Avg Weighted Price	102.9% Par	1.02

Quality

Avg Credit Quality   BBB

Credit Analysis 09-30-94

	% of Bonds		% of Bonds
AAA	17	BB	7
AA	1	B	4
A	4	Below B	0
BBB	25	NR/NA	42

Diversification Value for Portfolio Types

Large Cap: Medium	Small Cap: High	Bond: Low	Balanced: Medium	Diversified: High

Portfolio 09-30-94

Total Equity: 0
Total Fixed-Income: 89

Amount 000		Maturity	Value $000	% Total Invest
6235	AZ Gila Indl Dev Poll Cntrl Asarco 8.9%	07-01-06	6890	3.00
6500	IA Fin Sisters Mercy Hlth 9.95%	07-01-19	6500	2.84
5800	MA Port Spcl Proj Harborside Hyatt 10%	03-01-26	6242	2.72
5500	TX Corpus Christi Indl Dev Port 10.625%	06-01-08	6194	2.70
5821	IN Hammond COP Port 9.65%	06-01-14	5974	2.61
5000	MO Kansas City Indl Dev Hlth Fac 8.75%	01-01-15	5400	2.36
4550	OH Dayton Spcl Fac Emery Air 12.5%	10-01-09	5295	2.31
5000	CO Denver Arpt Sys 8.75%	11-15-23	5275	2.30
4480	TX Corpus Christi Indl Dev Port 10.25%	06-01-17	5001	2.18
5000	NJ Camden Hsg Dev Impr 8.75%	12-15-16	4475	1.95
4030	CA Hlth Fac Vlly Presbyterian Hosp 9%	05-01-17	4070	1.78
3845	IL Chicago O'Hare Intl Arpt 8.2%	05-01-18	4056	1.77
3500	NH Indl Dev Poll Cntrl Illum 10.75%	10-01-12	4034	1.76
5700	CA COP Cmnty Dev Motion Picture/TV IFRN	01-01-22	3940	1.72
4200	CO Denver Arpt Sys 7.25%	11-15-23	3938	1.72
3500	MA Indl Fin Resource Rec Semass 9%	07-01-15	3876	1.69
3965	FL Levy Indl Dev Natl Med Assn 10%	07-01-19	3747	1.63
3500	PA Beaver Indl Dev Poll Cntrl Elec 10.5%	09-01-15	3697	1.61
3440	LA St James Solid Waste Disp 7.75%	08-01-22	3530	1.54
3350	CO Denver Arpt Sys 8.5%	11-15-23	3471	1.51

Composition % 12-31-94

Cash	2.0	Preferreds	0.0
Stocks	0.0	Convertibles	0.0
Bonds	98.0	Other	0.0
Leverage factor: 1.24			

Tax Analysis

	Tax-Adj Historical Return %	% Pretax Return
3 Yr Avg	6.68	100.0
5 Yr Avg	6.96	100.0
10 Yr Avg	---	---
Potential Capital Gain Exposure (% of assets)		-5

Most Similar Funds in MF500

T. Rowe Price Tax-Fr Hi-Yld	Strong Fit
Franklin Insured T/F Income	Strong Fit
Fidelity Aggressive Tax-Free	Strong Fit

Top Five States

	% of Bonds
California	9.83
Massachusetts	9.18
Texas	8.33
Illinois	7.93
Pennsylvania	7.87

Coupon Range

	% of Bonds	Relative Objective
0%	0.0	0.0
0% to 6%	5.2	0.4
6% to 7.5%	9.8	0.3
7.5% to 8.5%	12.7	0.6
More than 8.5%	61.5	2.2
Not applicable	10.7	3.4

1.0 = Objective Average

Sector Weightings

	% of Bonds	Rel Muni Avg
General Obligation	2.67	0.30
Utilities	0.40	0.04
Health	21.02	0.99
Water/Sewer	0.00	0.00
Housing	4.56	0.38
Education	1.08	0.27
Transportation	19.08	1.95
COP/Lease	9.31	1.66
Private	29.78	1.84
Demand	1.66	1.46
Miscellaneous	10.44	1.69
AMT	25.55	
Prerefunded	2.74	

MORNINGSTAR 1995 Mutual Fund 500

Putnam Income A

	Ticker	Load	NAV	Yield	SEC Yield	Assets	Objective
	PINCX	4.75%	6.47	8.0%	7.90%	764.4	Corp General

Putnam Income Fund - Class A seeks high current income consistent with prudent risk.

The fund invests corporate debt securities, government obligations, preferred stocks, and dividend-paying common stocks. The debt may be rated as low as B at the time of purchase. The fund minimizes risk associated with lower-rated securities through diversification and careful analysis. The fund may invest up to 20% of its assets in foreign securities. The fund may pay a premium for securities bearing coupon rates higher than prevailing market conditions.

Class A shares have front loads and lower 12b-1 fees; Class B shares have deferred loads.

Manager's Investment Style

Management emphasizes yield, and thus keeps about 20% or more of the fund's assets in non-investment-grade issues. It will move in and out of segments of the bond market in search of yield, swapping out of Treasuries, for example, for higher-paying mortgage-backeds. Management also moves between industries to improve overall performance; in 1994, for example, management rotated out of overvalued banks and into lower-priced--and higher-yielding--energy issues.

Fund Manager(s)

Kenneth J. Taubes et al. BS, Syracuse U. MBA, Suffolk U.

Manager Experience

Manager Experience	Dates Managed	Invest Obj	Std Dev	+/- Index
Kenneth J. Taubes				
Putnam Amercn Gvt Inc A	03/92 - 03/94	GG	3.46	-3.22

Historical Profile

Return	Above Average
Risk	Average
Rating	★★★ Neutral

	7	6	6	6	5	4	6	7

Growth of $10,000

- IIII Value of Fund ($000)
- — Value of Index ($000) LB Corp
- ▼ Manager Change
- ▽ Partial Manager Change
- ► Mgr Unknown After
- ◄ Mgr Unknown Before

Performance Quartile (Within Objective)

Investment Style History Fixed Income
Income Rtn % Rank Obj

	1983	1984	1985	1986	1987	1988	1989	1990	1991	1992	1993	1994	History
NAV	6.71	6.81	7.33	7.42	6.75	6.74	6.84	6.44	6.93	6.98	7.22	6.47	NAV
	11.47	14.57	20.48	12.69	1.86	10.35	12.17	4.35	18.35	9.79	11.95	-3.29	Total Return %
	3.09	-0.59	-1.64	-2.56	-0.90	2.47	-2.37	-4.59	2.35	2.55	2.20	-0.38	+/- LB Aggregate
	2.19	-2.05	-3.58	-3.85	-0.70	1.12	-1.81	-2.80	-0.16	1.10	-0.22	0.63	+/- LB Corporate
	12.20	13.08	12.85	11.46	10.89	10.49	10.51	10.20	10.74	9.07	8.44	7.09	Income Return %
	-0.74	1.49	7.64	1.23	-9.03	-0.15	1.66	-5.85	7.61	0.72	3.51	-10.39	Capital Return %
	72	7	70	69	43	59	47	45	47	24	51	46	Total Rtn % Rank All
	8	28	66	64	50	17	43	82	23	8	26	44	Total Rtn % Rank Obj
	0.79	0.79	0.79	0.79	0.79	0.68	0.67	0.67	0.63	0.60	0.57	0.52	Income $
	0.00	0.00	0.00	0.00	0.00	0.00	0.01	0.00	0.00	0.00	0.01	0.00	Capital Gains $
	0.83	0.79	0.73	0.73	0.78	0.76	0.80	0.80	0.91	0.97	0.77	0.79	Expense Ratio %
	11.46	12.33	11.72	10.06	8.72	9.86	9.67	9.87	9.66	8.62	7.71	6.82	Income Ratio %
	207	265	312	202	203	201	97	68	84	147	130	---	Turnover Rate %
	152.1	149.3	168.6	189.0	334.7	348.3	431.5	444.7	526.4	667.6	810.5	764.4	Net Assets ($mil)

Performance 12-31-94

	1st Qtr	2nd Qtr	3rd Qtr	4th Qtr	Total
1987	3.22	-3.79	-2.82	5.55	1.86
1988	4.45	2.04	1.91	1.60	10.35
1989	1.46	6.50	1.13	2.64	12.17
1990	0.00	0.91	-0.05	3.46	4.35
1991	4.62	2.39	5.17	5.04	18.35
1992	1.12	3.84	4.44	0.12	9.79
1993	5.02	3.30	3.16	0.03	11.95
1994	-2.62	-1.62	0.73	0.20	-3.30

Bear Market Performance

Decile Rank (5-year period)

Worst — Best

	Worst 3 Mo Period 1985-89	Worst 3 Mo Period 1990-94
Putnam Income A	-5.42	-5.22
+/- LB Aggregate	-1.87	-0.29
+/- Best Fit Index : LB Corp	-1.31	1.04

Trailing Returns

	Total Return %	+/- LB Aggregate	+/- LB Corp	% Rank All	% Rank Obj	Growth of $10,000
3 Mo	0.20	-0.18	-0.23	17	34	10,020
6 Mo	0.94	-0.05	-0.24	38	24	10,094
1 Yr	-3.29	-0.38	0.63	46	44	9,671
3 Yr Avg	5.93	1.38	0.52	34	10	11,886
5 Yr Avg	7.98	0.35	-0.28	33	20	14,680
10 Yr Avg	9.65	-0.29	-0.98	62	45	25,127
15 Yr Avg	10.88	0.07	-0.44	67	19	47,089

Operations

Address and Telephone	One Post Office Square Boston, MA 02109 800-225-1581 / 617-292-1000
Advisor	Putnam Investment Management
Subadvisor	None
Distributor	Putnam Mutual Funds
States Available	All
Report Grade	B-
Income Distrib	Paid Monthly
Date of Inception	11-01-54
Fiscal Year End	October

Risk Analysis

Time Period	Load-Adj Return %	Risk % Rank [1] All	Obj	Morningstar [2] Return	Morningstar Risk	Morningstar Risk-Adj Rating
1 Yr	-7.89					
3 Yr	4.22	13	20	0.19 [3]	0.85	★★★★
5 Yr	6.93	25	45	0.54 [3]	1.00	★★★
10 Yr	9.12	17	30	0.86 [3]	0.99	★★★

Average Historical Rating (109 months) 3.2 ★ s

[1] 1 = low, 100 = high [2] 1.00 = Taxable Avg [3] 1.00 = 90-day T-bill return

Other Measures

			Standard LB Agg	Best Fit LB Corp
Standard Deviation	4.03	Alpha	1.4	0.9
Mean	5.85	Beta	0.96	0.78
Sharpe Ratio	0.58	R-Squared	91	94

Investment Style

Interest-Rate Stance

Avg Effective Duration	4.9 Yrs
Avg Effective Maturity	8.8 Yrs

Quality

Avg Credit Quality	A
Avg Weighted Coupon	8.16%
Avg Weighted Price	94.95% of Par

Diversification Value for Portfolio Types

Large Cap: Medium | Small Cap: High | Bond: None | Balanced: Medium | Diversified: Medium

Portfolio 12-30-94

Total Stocks: 0
Total Fixed-Income: 178

Amount 000	Date of Maturity		Value $000	% Net Assets
101649	02-29-96	US Treasury Note 4.625%	98536	12.89
73266	11-15-24	US Treasury Bond 7.5%	70083	9.17
39888	01-31-96	US Treasury Note 4%	38517	5.04
35210	12-15-24	GNMA 8%	33659	4.40
20632	07-15-24	GNMA 7.5%	19147	2.50
18825	12-15-24	GNMA 8.5%	18498	2.42
16898	02-15-23	US Treasury Bond 7.125%	15377	2.01
14827	04-15-08	GNMA 15yr 8%	14498	1.90
10117	10-15-21	Petro-Canada 9.25%	10382	1.36
10845	06-15-98	Great Western Financial 6.125%	10100	1.32
9162	08-01-17	Chrysler 10.95%	10061	1.32
9995	09-29-14	American Airlines 9.73%	9383	1.23
10926	02-01-04	ANZ Bank 6.25%	9349	1.22
7284	04-15-11	British Col Hydro Pwr 15%	8231	1.08
6960	10-01-13	Province of Quebec 13%	8222	1.08
8296	11-13-12	United Air Lines 10.36%	7954	1.04
9712	11-01-05	PaineWebber Group 6.5%	7897	1.03
8093	02-15-05	News America Holdings 8.5%	7754	1.01
8741	01-01-15	Texas Utilities Elec 7.46%	7626	1.00
7325	07-01-01	USX 9.8%	7503	0.98
6879	03-15-11	Occidental Petroleum 11.75%	7447	0.97
8231	01-15-13	Time Warner 9.125%	7418	0.97
6216	07-01-00	Public Svc New Hamp 15.23%	7311	0.96
8154	06-01-03	LASMO USA 7.125%	7257	0.95
7284	11-15-04	Crestar Financial 8.75%	7257	0.95

Composition % 12-31-94

Cash	0.2	Preferreds	0.0
Stocks	0.0	Convertibles	0.0
Bonds	99.8	Other	0.0

Coupon Range

	% of Bonds	Rel Bonds
0%	0.7	0.30
0% to 8.5%	45.8	0.72
8.5% to 9.5%	20.9	1.29
9.5% to 11%	21.4	2.31
More than 11%	11.3	2.90
Not applicable	0.1	0.01

Tax Analysis

	Tax-Adj Historical Return %	% Pretax Return
3 Yr Avg	2.90	47.5
5 Yr Avg	4.84	57.0
10 Yr Avg	5.79	49.9
Potential Capital Gain Exposure (% of assets)		-8%

Credit Analysis 12-31-94

% of Bonds

US Govt	0	BB	7
AAA	47	B	5
AA	7	Below B	8
A	7	NR/NA	15
BBB	4		

Most Similar Funds in MF500

J Hancock Inc	Strong Fit
Bond Fund of America	Strong Fit
Strong Government Securities	Strong Fit

Expenses & Fees

Sales Fees	4.75% front
	0.00% deferred
	0.25% 12b-1
Management Fee	0.65% max./0.45% min.
3-,5-,10-yr Expense Projections	$78, $101, $165

Min Initial Purchase $500 (Addt'l: $50)
Min IRA Purchase $250 (Addt'l: $50)
Min Auto Invest Plan $25 (Systematic Inv: $25)

Putnam Managed Municipal Income

	Ticker	NAV	Mkt Price	Prem/Disc	Yield	Objective
	PMM	$9.32	$9.50	1.9%	8.0%	Muni National

Putnam Managed Municipal Income Trust seeks to provide a high level of current income exempt from federal income tax.

The fund invests in a diversified portfolio of tax-exempt municipal securities. It may invest up to 50% of its assets in municipal securities rated BB or lower, although not lower than B-. The fund may use options and futures for hedging purposes.

The fund is leveraged by three classes of remarketed preferred shares.

The fund may be open-ended if a majority of shareholders approve.

7.5	4.8	7.4	8.2	8.4	8.8
1.9	-0.7	0.6	-2.0	0.9	-4.6

Highest Prem/Disc
Lowest Prem/Disc

Historical Profile
Return Above Average
Risk Average
Rating ★★★
Neutral

Growth of $10,000
■ at NAV ($000)
— at Market Price ($000)

Premium
Discount %

Manager's Investment Style

Although management typically holds the majority of assets in investment grade's lower tiers, it has also invested a portion of assets in nonrated municipal issues. For extra income, the fund has dabbled in derivative securities, including inverse floaters. Management has, in the past, overweighted particular sectors or states that it considered undervalued.

Fund Manager(s)

Howard Manning. Since 2-94. MA'77 U. of Michigan; PhD'82 U. of Michigan.

	1983	1984	1985	1986	1987	1988	1989	1990	1991	1992	1993	1994	History
	---	---	---	---	---	---	9.32	9.05	9.61	10.00	10.77	9.32	NAV
	---	---	---	---	---	---	7.01*	5.51	15.21	13.22	16.68	-6.55	NAV Total Return %
	---	---	---	---	---	---	---	-3.44	-0.79	5.97	6.93	-3.63	+/- LB Aggregate
	---	---	---	---	---	---	---	-1.80	3.07	4.40	4.40	-0.95	+/- LB Muni
	---	---	---	---	---	---	6.57*	8.40	9.02	8.30	8.00	6.91	Income Return %
	---	---	---	---	---	---	0.43*	-2.90	6.19	4.91	8.68	-13.46	Capital Return %
	---	---	---	---	---	---	---	44	62	23	46	50	Total Rtn % Rank All
	---	---	---	---	---	---	---	86	25	6	34	43	Total Rtn % Rank Obj
	---	---	---	---	---	---	1.44*	4.36	20.39	14.17	13.44	-7.79	Market Total Rtn %
	---	---	---	---	---	---	4.4	1.7	5.1	5.1	4.8	3.1	Avg Prem/Disc %
	---	---	---	---	---	---	0.60	0.76	0.76	0.76	0.76	0.76	Income $
	---	---	---	---	---	---	0.02	0.00	0.00	0.08	0.09	0.00	Capital Gains $
	---	---	---	---	---	---	0.91	1.29	1.33	1.24	1.22	1.23	Expense Ratio %
	---	---	---	---	---	---	8.72	8.39	8.92	8.94	8.44	9.20	Income Ratio %
	---	---	---	---	---	---	---	41	50	68	35	48	Turnover Rate %
	---	---	---	---	---	---	393.6	385.9	413.6	434.6	474.0	434.2	Net Assets ($mil)
	---	---	---	---	---	---	175.1	175.1	175.1	175.1	175.1	175.3	Pfd/Debt Leverage ($mil)

Manager Experience

	Dates Managed	Invest Obj	Std Dev	+/- Index
Howard Manning				
Putnam H/Y Muni	05/89 - 01/92	MN	2.11	-5.01

NAV Performance % 12-30-94

	1st Qtr	2nd Qtr	3rd Qtr	4th Qtr	Total
1987	---	---	---	---	---
1988	---	---	---	---	---
1989	-0.43*	4.43	0.17	2.73	7.01*
1990	-0.13	2.20	0.10	3.26	5.51
1991	2.44	2.98	5.16	3.86	15.21
1992	1.22	5.69	3.64	2.11	13.22
1993	5.01	4.01	5.07	1.68	16.68
1994	-5.25	0.29	1.03	-2.66	-6.55

Bear Market Performance

Decile Rank (5-year period)

Worst — Best

	Worst 3 Mo Period 1985-89	Worst 3 Mo Period 1990-94
Putnam Mgd Muni Inc	---	-6.65
+/- LB Aggregate	---	-4.88

Trailing Returns

	NAV Total Return %	+/- LB Agg	+/- LB Muni	% Rank All	Obj	Mkt Total Return %
3 Mo	-2.66	-3.04	-1.23	63	76	0.71
6 Mo	-1.66	-2.65	-0.41	62	58	-6.97
1 Yr	-6.55	-3.63	-0.95	50	43	-7.79
3 Yr Avg	7.27	2.73	2.40	31	6	6.10
5 Yr Avg	8.45	0.83	1.68	42	3	8.45
Incept Avg	8.40*	---	---	---	---	7.42*

Operations

Address and Telephone	One Post Office Square
	Boston, MA 02109
	617-292-1000 / 800-634-1587
Advisor	Putnam Management Co.
Subadvisor	N/A
Administrator	N/A
Transfer Agent	Putnam Investor Services
Custodian	Putnam Fiduciary Trust Co.
Auditor	Coopers & Lybrand
Legal Counsel	Ropes & Gray

Income Distrib Schedule	Paid Monthly
Management Fee	0.70%
Reinvestment Plan	Yes
Direct Purchase Plan	No
Shares Outstanding	44,516,726
Exchange	NYSE
*Date of Inception	02-16-89
Shareholder Report	B+

Risk Analysis

	Risk % Rank[1]		Morningstar[2]		Morningstar
	All	Obj	Return	Risk	Risk-Adj Rating
3 Yr	32	48	1.23	0.94	★★★★
5 Yr	24	63	1.28	1.19	★★★
10 Yr	---	---	---	---	---
Average Historical Rating (35 months)				3.9	★s

[1] = Low, 100 = High [2] 1.00 = Muni Avg [3] 1.00 = 90-day T-bill Return

Other Measures

				LB Muni
Standard Deviation	6.42	Alpha		2.23
Mean	7.25	Beta		1.09
Sharpe Ratio	0.58	R-Squared		87

Investment Style

Interest-Rate Stance

	Fund	Relative Objective
Avg Effective Maturity	13.3 Yrs	0.61
Avg Weighted Coupon	7.95%	1.04
Avg Weighted Price	99.9% Par	0.99

Quality

Avg Credit Quality	BBB

Credit Analysis 12-31-94

	% of Bonds		% of Bonds
AAA	1	BB	8
AA	6	B	12
A	11	Below B	0
BBB	33	NR/NA	28

Diversification Value for Portfolio Types

Large Cap: Medium	Small Cap: High	Bond: Low	Balanced: Low	Diversified: Medium

Portfolio 10-31-94

Amount 000	Total Equity: 0	Maturity	Value $000	% Total Invest
	Total Fixed-Income: 129			
22800	CA Metro Wtr Dist South Wtrwks 6.75%	07-01-18	24624	4.20
20000	OH Air Qlty Dev Poll Cntrl 8%	12-01-13	22450	3.83
16350	FL Tampa Cap Impr Prog 8.375%	10-01-18	17249	2.94
15000	CA Univ USCD M/C 7.9%	12-01-19	15581	2.66
14470	CO Denver Arpt Fac United Proj 6.875%	10-01-32	12426	2.12
12605	CA Pub Wks Brd Comnty Clg Lease 5.625%	12-01-13	10714	1.83
9685	WA Pub Pwr Sply Sys Proj #1 7.5%	07-01-15	10641	1.82
12000	CO Denver Arpt Sys 7%	11-15-25	10530	1.80
10500	NC East Muni Pwr 6%	01-01-22	9161	1.56
8840	TN Nashville/Davidson Metro Govt 10.5%	12-01-14	9050	1.54
10685	NY Urban Dev Crtnl Fac 5.5%	01-01-15	8975	1.53
9900	AZ Salt Rvr Agri Impr/Pwr Dist 5.25%	01-01-19	8093	1.38
8400	KS Wichita Hosp Var	10-01-17	8001	1.37
7000	NY New York City GO 8.25%	11-15-10	7761	1.32
7500	KS Burlington Poll Cntrl Var	06-01-31	7753	1.32
7250	TX Brazos Rvr Poll Cntrl Util 7.875%	03-01-21	7622	1.30
7000	MI Strategic Fund Ltd Obl Rsrch 8.125%	10-01-14	7420	1.27
7070	NE Invest Fin Sngl Fam Mtg RIB	08-15-38	7344	1.25
7900	FL Lee Hosp Brd Var	03-26-20	7179	1.23
7000	CO Denver Arpt Sys 8.5%	11-15-23	7131	1.22

Composition % 12-31-94

Cash	5.9	Preferreds	0.0
Stocks	0.0	Convertibles	0.0
Bonds	94.1	Other	0.0
Leverage factor: 1.40			

Tax Analysis

	Tax-Adj Historical Return %	% Pretax Return
3 Yr Avg	7.11	97.6
5 Yr Avg	8.36	98.7
10 Yr Avg	---	---

Potential Capital Gain Exposure (% of assets) -4

Most Similar Funds in MF500

Strong Municipal Bond	Strong Fit
Vista Tax-Free Income A	Strong Fit
Flagship All-American T/E A	Strong Fit

Top Five States

	% of Bonds
California	16.27
Michigan	9.92
Texas	7.48
Colorado	6.75
Florida	6.73

Coupon Range

	% of Bonds	Relative Objective
0%	0.0	0.0
0% to 6%	16.2	1.3
6% to 7.5%	21.5	0.6
7.5% to 8.5%	26.3	1.2
More than 8.5%	27.4	1.0
Not applicable	8.5	2.7

1.0 = Objective Average

Sector Weightings

	% of Bonds	Rel Muni Avg
General Obligation	2.99	0.34
Utilities	7.99	0.81
Health	30.27	1.43
Water/Sewer	5.52	1.03
Housing	5.05	0.42
Education	3.42	0.87
Transportation	12.25	1.25
COP/Lease	3.03	0.54
Private	19.82	1.23
Demand	0.50	0.44
Miscellaneous	9.18	1.49
AMT	22.07	
Prerefunded	7.36	

Putnam Municipal Income A

	Ticker	Load	NAV	Yield	SEC Yield	Assets	Objective
	PTFHX	4.75%	8.25	6.5%	6.73%	784.3	Muni Nat

Putnam Municipal Income Fund - Class A seeks current income exempt from federal income tax, consistent with preservation of capital.

The fund normally invests at least 65% of its assets in investment-grade tax-exempt securities. It may actively trade its investments in order to seek short-term profits, which may result in taxable capital gains. It may also buy and sell futures contracts and options.

Class A shares have front loads; Class B shares have deferred loads and higher 12b-1 fees. Prior to May 11, 1992, the fund was named Putnam Tax-Free High-Income Fund and invested primarily in lower-rated municipal securities.

Manager's Investment Style

Management is known for a willingness to take on greater-than-average credit risk. It also pays attention, however, to other factors such as interest rates. Most recently, management has used short positions that reduce rate sensitivity. Despite some duration tinkering, though, credit plays largely determine the fund's behavior. In addition to generally using low-quality bonds, management is willing to overweight situations that seem underpriced.

Fund Manager(s)

Richard P. Wyke CFA, since 07-93. Birthdate: 1956. BS, Indiana U. 1978 MBA, Indiana U. 1981

Manager Experience

	Dates Managed	Invest Obj	Std Dev	+/- Index
Richard P. Wyke				
Putnam Tax Free Insured B	11/88 - 12/94	MN	5.23	-2.32
Putnam FL Tax Ex IncB	01/93 - 12/94	MS	6.86	-1.47

Historical Profile
Return: Average
Risk: Below Average
Rating: ★★★★ Above Average

	1983	1984	1985	1986	1987	1988	1989	1990	1991	1992	1993	1994	History
	---	---	---	---	---	---	8.53	8.39	8.69	8.94	9.37	8.25	NAV
	---	---	---	---	---	---	4.37 *	6.69	12.35	11.31	11.99	-6.40	Total Return %
	---	---	---	---	---	---	---	-2.26	-3.66	4.07	2.24	-3.48	+/- LB Aggregate
	---	---	---	---	---	---	---	-0.61	0.20	2.50	-0.29	-0.79	+/- LB Muni
	---	---	---	---	---	---	4.02	8.33	8.66	7.83	6.51	5.55	Income Return %
	---	---	---	---	---	---	0.35	-1.64	3.69	3.48	5.48	-11.95	Capital Return %
	---	---	---	---	---	---	---	25	72	17	51	75	Total Rtn % Rank All
	---	---	---	---	---	---	---	30	24	2	44	65	Total Rtn % Rank Obj
	---	---	---	---	---	---	0.33	0.69	0.68	0.65	0.56	0.53	Income $
	---	---	---	---	---	---	0.00	0.00	0.01	0.05	0.06	0.00	Capital Gains $
	---	---	---	---	---	---	---	---	0.95	0.91	1.05	0.97	Expense Ratio %
	---	---	---	---	---	---	---	---	8.08	7.80	6.83	5.73	Income Ratio %
	---	---	---	---	---	---	---	---	50	44	31	47	Turnover Rate %
	---	---	---	---	---	---	162.7	229.8	303.2	483.6	882.4	784.3	Net Assets ($mil)

Investment Style History
Fixed Income
Income Rtn % Rank Obj

Growth of $10,000
|||| Value of Fund ($000)
— Value of Index ($000) LB Muni
▼ Manager Change
▽ Partial Manager Change
▶ Mgr Unknown After
◀ Mgr Unknown Before

Performance Quartile (Within Objective)

Performance 12-31-94

	1st Qtr	2nd Qtr	3rd Qtr	4th Qtr	Total
1987	---	---	---	---	---
1988	---	---	---	---	---
1989	---	---	1.41	3.05	4.37 *
1990	1.23	1.99	0.63	2.69	6.69
1991	1.70	2.89	4.19	3.05	12.35
1992	1.48	4.04	3.15	2.20	11.31
1993	3.69	3.31	3.33	1.18	11.99
1994	-5.49	0.94	0.39	-2.27	-6.40

Bear Market Performance

Decile Rank (5-year period)

Worst ─────────── Best

	Worst 3 Mo Period 1985-89	Worst 3 Mo Period 1990-94
Putnam Municipal Income A	---	-6.06
+/- LB Aggregate	---	-1.13
+/- Best Fit Index : LB Muni	---	-0.30

Trailing Returns

	Total Return %	+/- LB Aggregate	+/- LB Muni	% Rank All	Obj	Growth of $10,000
3 Mo	-2.27	-2.64	-0.83	73	89	9,773
6 Mo	-1.88	-2.88	-0.64	86	86	9,812
1 Yr	-6.40	-3.48	-0.79	75	65	9,360
3 Yr Avg	5.28	0.73	0.41	42	17	11,668
5 Yr Avg	6.94	-0.69	0.17	52	14	13,986
10 Yr Avg	---	---	---	---	---	---
15 Yr Avg	---	---	---	---	---	---

Operations

Address and Telephone	One Post Office Square
	Boston, MA 02109
	800-225-1581 / 617-292-1000
Advisor	Putnam Investment Management
Subadvisor	None
Distributor	Putnam Mutual Funds
States Available	All
Report Grade	B+
Income Distrib	Paid Monthly
* Date of Inception	05-22-89
Fiscal Year End	March

Risk Analysis

Time Period	Load-Adj Return %	Risk % Rank [1] All	Obj	Morningstar [2] Return	Morningstar Risk	Morningstar Risk-Adj Rating
1 Yr	-10.84					
3 Yr	3.58	25	41	1.01	0.95	★★★
5 Yr	5.90	12	31	1.10	0.84	★★★★
10 Yr	---	---	---	---	---	

Average Historical Rating (32 months)   4.7 ★s

[1] 1 = low, 100 = high   [2] 1.00 = Muni Avg   ▲ 1.00 = 90-day T-bill return

Other Measures

				Standard LB Agg	Best Fit LB Muni
Standard Deviation	5.58	Alpha		0.7	0.4
Mean	5.31	Beta		1.03	1.01
Sharpe Ratio	0.32	R-Squared		55	98

Investment Style

Interest-Rate Stance
Avg Effective Maturity   21.6 Yrs

Quality
Avg Credit Quality   A
Avg Weighted Coupon   7.16%
Avg Weighted Price   96.81% of Par

Maturity Short Intm Long
Quality High Med Low

Diversification Value for Portfolio Types

Large Cap: Medium	Small Cap: High	Bond: Low	Balanced: Medium	Diversified: High

Expenses & Fees

Sales Fees	4.75% front
	0.00% deferred
	0.25% 12b-1
Management Fee	0.65% max./0.45% min.
3-,5-,10-yr Expense Projections	$77, $99, $161

Min Initial Purchase	$500 (Addt'l: $50)
Min IRA Purchase	N/A
Min Auto Invest Plan	$25 (Systematic Inv: $25)

Portfolio 09-30-94

Amount 000	Date of Maturity	Total Stocks: 0 / Total Fixed-Income: 287	Value $000	% Net Assets
14863	12-01-14	FL Hernando Indl Dev Crushed Stone 8.5%	15383	1.83
14375	08-15-22	LA Lake Charles Harbor/Term Dist 7.75%	15075	1.79
11483	01-01-21	NY Urban Dev Crtnl Cap Fac Tax 6.5%	11483	1.36
12216	04-01-12	CA State GO Ins 5.5%	11183	1.33
10180	04-25-96	CA State GO 5.75%	10314	1.22
10520	11-15-23	CO Denver Arpt Sys 7.25%	9862	1.17
8823	07-01-15	MA Indl Fin Resource Rec Semass 9%	9771	1.16
10180	03-01-20	CA State GO 5.5%	8819	1.05
8619	10-01-32	CO Denver Spcl Fac Arpt Proj 6.875%	7671	0.91
6787	07-01-10	PR GO Linked Pub Offering RIB	7253	0.86
8144	06-01-21	CA Pub Wks Brd Univ Regents Lease 5.5%	6851	0.81
6787	01-01-16	GA Rockdale Visay Paper 7.4%	6626	0.79
6787	01-01-21	MI Strategic Fund Solid Waste Disp 7.5%	6609	0.78
5738	12-01-14	MS Claiborne Poll Cntrl Engy 9.875%	6599	0.78
6787	08-01-19	IL State GO 5.875%	6286	0.75
5769	07-15-10	AZ Pima Indl Dev Tucson Elec 7.25%	6129	0.73
6108	06-01-17	WA State GO 6.4%	6123	0.73
6719	11-15-25	CO Denver Arpt Sys 7%	6097	0.72
4751	01-01-97	IL Cook COP Comnty Clg Dist RIB	6051	0.72
5986	04-01-14	HI Honolulu GO 6.25%	6016	0.71

Credit Analysis % of Bonds 12-31-94

US Govt	0	BB	11
AAA	27	B	14
AA	11	Below B	1
A	9	NR/NA	0
BBB	28		

Composition % of Assets 12-31-94

Cash	1.5	Preferreds	0.0
Stocks	0.0	Convertibles	0.0
Bonds	98.5	Other	0.0

Tax Analysis

	Tax-Adj Historical Return %	% Pretax Return
3 Yr Avg	5.16	97.7
5 Yr Avg	6.86	98.8
10 Yr Avg	---	---
Potential Capital Gain Exposure (% of assets)		-9%

Most Similar Funds in MF500

Fidelity Aggressive Tax-Free	Strong Fit
Smith Barney Tax-Ex IncB	Strong Fit
Fortress Municipal Income	Strong Fit

Coupon Range

	% Bonds	Rel Obj
0%	2.1	0.84
0% to 6.8%	34.5	0.57
6.8% to 7.5%	17.6	1.13
7.5% to 8.3%	12.6	1.43
More than 8.3%	22.3	2.52
Not applicable	10.9	2.82

Sector Weightings

	% Bonds	Rel Obj
General Obl	10.43	0.50
Utilities	8.67	0.69
Health	17.05	1.29
Water/Waste	1.32	0.21
Housing	4.28	0.58
Education	4.99	0.78
Transportation	14.21	1.39
COP/Lease	6.26	1.96
Private	23.32	2.00
Misc Revenue	5.32	1.07
Demand	4.14	1.68

Top 5 States % of Bonds

CA	13.57	LA	5.93
NY	6.88	PA	5.62
MI	6.21		

Putnam Voyager A

	Ticker	Load	NAV	Yield	SEC Yield	Assets	Objective
	PVOYX	5.75%	11.52	0.0%	N/A	3469.0	Aggr. Growth

Putnam Voyager Fund - Class A seeks capital appreciation. Current income is not a consideration.

The fund invests primarily in common stocks. Preferred stocks, debt securities, and convertible issues may also be held. The fund generally invests largely in the securities of smaller and less-seasoned companies. It may employ leverage by borrowing money to purchase additonal securities. The fund may also purchase stock-index futures contracts and related options and trade for short-term profits.

Class A shares have front loads; Class B shares have deferred loads and a higher 12b-1 fee.

Historical Profile
Return	Above Average
Risk	Above Average
Rating	★★★★ Above Average

Investment Style History
Equity
Average % Stocks Held in Portfolio

95% 93% 93% 94% 93% 91% 93% 94%

Growth of $10,000
- |||| Value of Fund ($000)
- — Value of Index ($000) S&P 500
- ▼ Manager Change
- ▽ Partial Manager Change
- ► Mgr Unknown After
- ◄ Mgr Unknown Before

Performance Quartile (Within Objective)

	1983	1984	1985	1986	1987	1988	1989	1990	1991	1992	1993	1994	History
	5.62	4.90	6.30	6.53	6.07	6.63	8.00	7.07	10.07	10.52	11.99	11.52	NAV
	14.91	-5.73	37.44	20.06	10.79	11.69	35.11	-2.80	50.31	9.72	18.40	0.44	Total Return %
	-7.55	-11.99	5.70	1.38	5.53	-4.92	3.43	0.32	19.83	2.10	8.35	-0.87	+/- S&P 500
	---	-4.01	5.42	8.30	14.30	-8.85	11.17	10.76	6.86	-2.04	3.87	3.10	+/- Wilshire 4500
	0.56	1.10	0.94	0.82	0.49	0.31	1.56	0.99	0.29	0.01	0.00	0.00	Income Return %
	14.35	-6.82	36.50	19.23	10.30	11.38	33.55	-3.79	50.02	9.71	18.40	0.44	Capital Return %
	58	82	8	20	9	48	7	64	7	25	20	16	Total Rtn % Rank All
	57	14	22	21	8	61	23	30	63	42	51	26	Total Rtn % Rank Obj
	0.03	0.06	0.05	0.05	0.03	0.02	0.11	0.07	0.03	0.00	0.00	0.00	Income $
	0.36	0.36	0.32	0.91	1.31	0.13	0.80	0.63	0.48	0.52	0.46	0.51	Capital Gains $
	1.06	1.04	1.02	0.89	1.20	1.05	1.00	0.97	1.10	1.20	1.12	1.10	Expense Ratio %
	0.74	1.37	0.99	0.72	0.41	0.68	1.04	1.10	0.29	0.27	-0.14	-0.18	Income Ratio %
	65	136	60	76	79	66	71	62	49	44	65	58	Turnover Rate %
	217.6	191.9	282.9	389.7	529.6	545.1	731.4	751.7	1320.0	1932.4	2884.4	3469.0	Net Assets ($mil)

Manager's Investment Style

Management takes a two-pronged approach: It invests two thirds of the portfolio in traditional high-priced aggressive-growth fare--including media and technology--for their long-term growth prospects, and one third in short-term, low-priced turnaround plays. In 1994, worldwide economic improvement led management to add energy stocks to the portfolio as turnaround opportunities. The turnaround plays add gains if they return to favor; if not, their low valuations cushion the fund when growth stocks are out of fashion.

Fund Manager(s)

Matthew A. Weatherbie CFA, since 10-83. Birthdate: 04-45. BA, U. of Toronto 1971 MBA, Harvard 1973
Charles H. Swanberg CFA, since 02-94. MA, Middlebury C. MBA, Boston C.

Manager Experience

	Dates Managed	Invest Obj	Std Dev	+/- Index
Not available.				

Performance 12-31-94

	1st Qtr	2nd Qtr	3rd Qtr	4th Qtr	Total
1987	24.24	2.92	8.61	-20.22	10.79
1988	7.57	3.93	-3.14	3.13	11.69
1989	9.61	11.17	11.29	-0.36	35.11
1990	-5.00	8.16	-19.59	17.64	-2.80
1991	21.64	-2.79	11.60	13.90	50.31
1992	-3.67	-3.61	3.85	13.79	9.72
1993	-0.19	3.43	9.21	5.03	18.40
1994	-6.26	-3.38	10.41	0.44	0.44

Bear Market Performance

Decile Rank (5-year period)

Worst | Best

	Worst 3 Mo Period 1985-89	Worst 3 Mo Period 1990-94
Putnam Voyager A	-30.66	-19.59
+/- S&P 500	-1.07	-5.84
+/- Best Fit Index : Wil 4500	-0.52	-1.36

Trailing Returns

	Total Return %	+/- S&P 500	+/- Wil 4500	% Rank All	% Rank Obj	Growth of $10,000
3 Mo	0.44	0.46	2.94	12	31	10,044
6 Mo	10.89	6.03	6.70	4	29	11,089
1 Yr	0.44	-0.87	3.10	16	26	10,044
3 Yr Avg	9.27	3.01	1.67	16	38	13,048
5 Yr Avg	13.77	5.08	4.68	5	27	19,064
10 Yr Avg	18.06	3.67	5.42	3	11	52,592
15 Yr Avg	16.79	2.30	---	3	6	102,542

Operations

Address and Telephone	One Post Office Square Boston, MA 02109 800-225-1581 / 617-292-1000
Advisor	Putnam Investment Management
Subadvisor	None
Distributor	Putnam Mutual Funds
States Available	All
Report Grade	B+
Income Distrib	Paid Annually
Date of Inception	06-01-69
Fiscal Year End	July

Risk Analysis

Time Period	Load-Adj Return %	Risk % Rank [1] All	Obj	Morningstar [2] Return	Risk	Morningstar Risk-Adj Rating
1 Yr	-5.33					
3 Yr	7.14	84	20	1.06 [3]	1.04	★★★
5 Yr	12.43	87	27	2.07 [3]	1.08	★★★★
10 Yr	17.36	84	11	2.08	1.08	★★★★★

Average Historical Rating (109 months)   3.8 ★s

[1] 1 = low, 100 = high   [2] 1.00 = Equity Avg   [3] 1.00 = 90-day T-bill return

Other Measures

		Standard S&P 500	Best Fit Wil 4500
Standard Deviation	12.60	Alpha	2.6	1.0
Mean	9.69	Beta	1.26	1.19
Sharpe Ratio	0.49	R-Squared	63	86

Investment Style

	Stock Portfolio Avg	Relative S&P 500
Price/Earnings Ratio	26.5	1.43
Price/Book Ratio	5.7	1.69
5 Yr Earnings Gr %	19.4#	3.50
Return on Assets %	11.0	1.47
Debt % Total Cap	27.8	0.98
Med Mkt Cap ($mil)	1777	0.14

Style: Value Blend Growth / Size Large Med Small

figure is based on 50% or less of stocks

Diversification Value for Portfolio Types

Large Cap: Low	Small Cap: Low	Bond: High	Balanced: Low	Diversified: Low

Min Initial Purchase / Expenses & Fees

Min Initial Purchase	$500 (Addt'l: $50)
Min IRA Purchase	$250 (Addt'l: $50)
Min Auto Invest Plan	$25 (Systematic Inv: $25)

Expenses & Fees

Sales Fees	5.75% front
	0.00% deferred
	0.25% 12b-1
Management Fee	0.70% max./0.50% min.
3-,5-,10-yr Expense Projections	$90, $115, $184
Annual Brokerage Cost	0.12%

Portfolio 07-31-94

Total Stocks: 218
Total Fixed-Income: 3

Share Chg (01-94) 000	Amount 000		Value $000	% Net Assets
518	631	LIN Broadcasting	78874	2.58
2681	3303	Liberty Media Cl A	73900	2.42
1486	1780	H & R Block	69406	2.27
1303	1451	FlightSafety International	52586	1.72
1033	1252	Telephone & Data Systems	51004	1.67
1453	1841	Century Telephone Enterprise	47873	1.57
2160	2505	Comcast Special Cl A	41653	1.36
1065	1538	Tele-Communications Cl A	35860	1.18
	665	Cellular Comm Cv Pfd $0.01	34643	1.14
1168	1291	Hospitality Franchise System	34534	1.13
316	376	Medtronic	33539	1.10
600	733	First Data	32824	1.08
665	727	Danka Business Systems (ADR)	31152	1.02
934	1023	Bed Bath & Beyond	30948	1.01
1001	1156	Paging Network	30790	1.01
879	1064	Infinity Broadcasting Cl A	30711	1.01
1240	1399	Office Depot	29564	0.97
755	890	Interpublic Group	28819	0.94
498	588	Maxim Integrated Products	28371	0.93
590	668	Home Depot	27379	0.90
552	691	Sybase	27199	0.89
807	907	Kelly Services Cl A	26752	0.88
726	851	CUC International	25632	0.84
1224	1441	Buffets	24588	0.81
808	861	HBO	24549	0.80

Composition % 12-31-94

Cash	5.3	Preferreds	0.0
Stocks	93.4	Convertibles	1.2
Bonds	0.1	Other	0.0

Tax Analysis

	Tax-Adj Historical Return %	% Pretax Return
3 Yr Avg	7.99	85.1
5 Yr Avg	11.99	84.0
10 Yr Avg	15.52	75.9
Potential Capital Gain Exposure (% of assets)		18%

Most Similar Funds in MF500

Harbor Capital Appreciation	Strong Fit
Fidelity Emerging Growth	Strong Fit
Founders Frontier	Strong Fit

Index Allocation

	% of Stocks
S&P 500	32.7
S&P MidCap 400	18.5
U.S. Small Cap	40.8
Foreign	8.8

Sector Weightings

	% of Stocks	Relative S&P 500
Utilities	3.2	0.26
Energy	1.9	0.19
Financials	9.9	0.93
Industrial Cyclicals	6.1	0.37
Consumer Durables	1.7	0.28
Consumer Staples	1.9	0.15
Services	34.2	4.20
Retail	9.0	1.54
Health	13.4	1.54
Technology	18.8	2.06

422

Quantitative Growth & Inc Ord

	Ticker	Load	NAV	Yield	SEC Yield	Assets	Objective
	USBOX	1.00%d	12.62	1.2%	N/A	34.5	Growth/Inc.

Quantitative Group Growth and Income Series - Ordinary Shares seeks growth of capital and income.

The fund invests primarily in dividend-paying common stocks; it may also invest in convertibles and investment-grade fixed-income securities.

Ordinary shares have redemption fees and 12b-1 fees; Institutional shares have higher minimum initial investments. Prior to July 19, 1993, the fund was named U.S. Boston Investment Company Boston Growth and Income Series. From that date until Aug. 1, 1994, it was named Quantitative Group Boston Growth and Income Series - Ordinary Shares.

Manager's Investment Style

Management buys stocks with low prices relative to earnings growth and increasing earnings momentum. The fund is structured such that no stock or industry sector can vary from the S&P 500's weighting by more than 2.5 percentage points. Management will hold up to 10% of assets in exchange-listed ADRs or exchange-listed foreign stocks.

Historical Profile

Return	Average
Risk	Below Average
Rating	★★★ Neutral

99% 98% 98% 98% 98% 96% 98% 98% 99%

Investment Style History
Equity
Average % Stocks Held in Portfolio

Growth of $10,000

|||| Value of Fund ($000)
— Value of Index ($000) S&P 500
▼ Manager Change
▽ Partial Manager Change
► Mgr Unknown After
◄ Mgr Unknown Before

Performance Quartile (Within Objective)

	1983	1984	1985	1986	1987	1988	1989	1990	1991	1992	1993	1994	History
	---	---	11.19	13.24	10.27	11.87	14.79	13.96	16.27	16.36	14.47	12.62	NAV
	---	---	11.90 *	19.41	1.49	16.97	37.17	-1.13	27.98	6.32	11.88	-0.66	Total Return %
	---	---	-7.47 *	0.74	-3.77	0.36	5.49	1.99	-2.50	-1.30	1.82	-1.98	+/- S&P 500
	---	---		3.32	-0.87	-0.97	8.00	5.06	-6.23	-2.65	0.60	-0.59	+/- Wilshire 5000
	---	---	0.00	1.07	3.49	1.39	1.12	1.70	1.47	1.11	1.12	1.31	Income Return %
	---	---	11.90	18.34	-2.00	15.58	36.05	-2.83	26.51	5.21	10.76	-1.97	Capital Return %
	---	---		23	47	21	46	58	30	65	52	24	Total Rtn % Rank All
	---	---		29	53	37	2	25	53	66	40	50	Total Rtn % Rank Obj
	---	---	0.00	0.12	0.35	0.14	0.16	0.24	0.21	0.18	0.16	0.16	Income $
	---	---	0.00	0.00	2.66	0.00	1.32	0.42	1.23	0.75	3.64	1.56	Capital Gains $
	---	---	---	1.92	1.83	2.00	1.85	1.80	1.84	1.84	1.72		Expense Ratio %
	---	---	---	1.25	1.44	1.51	1.12	1.64	1.16	0.98	1.02		Income Ratio %
	---	---	---	99	124	102	92	96	60	78	110		Turnover Rate %
	---	---	9.0	15.3	26.4	25.2	35.5	34.1	44.4	42.0	39.3	34.5	Net Assets ($mil)

Fund Manager(s)

Steven M. Esielonis, since 01-93. Birthdate: 09-56. BA, St. Anselm C. 1978
Peter Stonberg CFA(1981), since 05-85. Birthdate: 11-43. BA, Carleton C. 1965 MBA, Columbia U. 1971

Manager Experience	Dates Managed	Invest Obj	Std Dev	+/- Index
Peter Stonberg				
Colonial U.S. Fund GrthB	07/92 - 12/94	G	7.86	0.43

Performance 12-31-94

	1st Qtr	2nd Qtr	3rd Qtr	4th Qtr	Total
1987	18.13	3.58	6.30	-21.97	1.49
1988	10.03	5.13	-0.93	2.06	16.97
1989	9.52	8.69	15.22	0.01	37.17
1990	-3.52	7.50	-12.91	9.46	-1.13
1991	14.97	-1.99	5.09	8.08	27.98
1992	-1.35	-1.12	2.90	5.93	6.32
1993	5.56	1.04	3.32	1.51	11.88
1994	-4.22	-0.51	5.08	-0.80	-0.66

Bear Market Performance

Decile Rank (5-year period)

Worst   Best

	Worst 3 Mo Period 1985-89	Worst 3 Mo Period 1990-94
Quantitative Growth & Inc Ord	---	-13.60
+/- S&P 500	---	0.24
+/- Best Fit Index : S&P 500	---	0.24

Trailing Returns

	Total Return %	+/- S&P 500	+/- Wil 5000	% Rank All	% Rank Obj	Growth of $10,000
3 Mo	-0.80	-0.78	-0.03	40	38	9,920
6 Mo	4.24	-0.63	-0.39	14	26	10,424
1 Yr	-0.66	-1.98	-0.59	24	50	9,934
3 Yr Avg	5.72	-0.55	-0.89	37	56	11,816
5 Yr Avg	8.38	-0.31	-0.44	29	37	14,952
10 Yr Avg	---	---	---	---	---	---
15 Yr Avg	---	---	---	---	---	---

Operations

Address and Telephone	Lincoln North Lincoln, MA 01773 800-331-1244 / 617-259-1144
Advisor	Quantitative Advisors
Subadvisor	State Street Global Advisors
Distributor	U.S. Boston Capital
States Available	Selected states
Report Grade	C
Income Distrib	Paid Annually
* Date of Inception	05-09-85
Fiscal Year End	March

Risk Analysis

Time Period	Load-Adj Return %	Risk % Rank [1] All	Obj	Morningstar [2] Return	Risk	Morningstar Risk-Adj Rating
1 Yr	-1.53					
3 Yr	5.49	65	43	0.56 [3]	0.72	★★★
5 Yr	8.25	66	49	0.88 [3]	0.79	★★★
10 Yr	---	---	---	---	---	---

Average Historical Rating (80 months)   4.0 ★s

[1] 1 = low, 100 = high [2] 1.00 = Equity Avg [3] 1.00 = 90-day T-bill return

Other Measures

	Standard S&P 500	Best Fit S&P 500
Standard Deviation 8.12	Alpha	-0.4	-0.4
Mean 5.90	Beta	0.95	0.95
Sharpe Ratio 0.29	R-Squared	86	86

Investment Style

	Stock Portfolio Avg	Relative S&P 500
Price/Earnings Ratio	16.1	0.87
Price/Book Ratio	3.3	0.97
5 Yr Earnings Gr %	11.5	2.06
Return on Assets %	10.2	1.36
Debt % Total Cap	25.8	0.91
Med Mkt Cap ($mil)	5744	0.44

Style Value Blend Growth — Size Large Med Small

Diversification Value for Portfolio Types

○ Large Cap: None
◔ Small Cap: Medium
● Bond: High
○ Balanced: None
◔ Diversified: Low

Expenses & Fees

Sales Fees	0.00% front
	1.00% deferred
	0.50% 12b-1
Management Fee	0.75% flat fee
3-,5-,10-yr Expense Projections	$65, $105, $217
Annual Brokerage Cost	0.23%

Min Initial Purchase	$5000 (Addt'l: None)
Min IRA Purchase	None (Addt'l: None)
Min Auto Invest Plan	$100 (Systematic Inv: $100)

Portfolio 09-30-94

Share Chg (03-94) 000	Amount 000	Total Stocks: 91 Total Fixed-Income: 0	Value $000	% Net Assets
19	19	Philip Morris	1151	3.31
8	32	Merck	1149	3.30
17	21	Johnson & Johnson	1075	3.09
1	14	Intel	859	2.47
-1	11	Mobil	856	2.46
-2	19	Southwestern Bell	816	2.35
12	16	Cabletron Systems	762	2.19
8	13	Amoco	753	2.17
-3	19	Ameritech	747	2.15
17	17	First Union	741	2.13
8	23	Wachovia	732	2.11
-3	19	Sprint	728	2.10
19	19	Franklin Resources	697	2.01
-5	22	Abbott Laboratories	679	1.95
19	19	Leggett & Platt	673	1.93
15	15	General Dynamics	666	1.92
0	13	JC Penney	661	1.90
1	18	Genuine Parts	639	1.84
8	8	British Petroleum	608	1.75
0	12	Clorox	606	1.74
0	13	US Healthcare	604	1.74
11	11	Medtronic	581	1.67
3	14	Walgreen	515	1.48
-3	19	ALLTEL	513	1.48
8	19	American General	513	1.48

Composition % 12-31-94

Cash	1.0	Preferreds	0.0
Stocks	99.0	Convertibles	0.0
Bonds	0.0	Other	0.0

Tax Analysis

	Tax-Adj Historical Return %	% Pretax Return
3 Yr Avg	1.85	31.1
5 Yr Avg	5.17	57.9
10 Yr Avg	---	---
Potential Capital Gain Exposure (% of assets)		2%

Most Similar Funds in MF500

Liberty All-Star	Strong Fit
Massachusetts Inv A	Strong Fit
Vanguard Index 500	Strong Fit

Index Allocation

	% of Stocks
S&P 500	77.5
S&P MidCap 400	14.8
U.S. Small Cap	5.5
Foreign	3.1

Sector Weightings

	% of Stocks	Relative S&P 500
Utilities	9.3	0.75
Energy	8.5	0.84
Financials	11.3	1.07
Industrial Cyclicals	12.3	0.75
Consumer Durables	9.3	1.49
Consumer Staples	15.5	1.24
Services	6.4	0.79
Retail	7.8	1.34
Health	8.8	1.01
Technology	10.9	1.19

Quantitative Numeric Ord

	Ticker	Load	NAV	Yield	SEC Yield	Assets	Objective
	USBNX	1.00%d	14.92	0.0%	N/A	47.8	Small Company

Quantitative Group Numeric Fund - Ordinary Shares seeks long-term capital appreciation.

The fund invests primarily in common stocks of companies that have market capitalizations of less than $800 million or have substantial equity capital and above-average expected earnings-growth rates.

Ordinary shares have redemption fees and 12b-1 fees; Institutional shares have higher minimum initial investments. Prior to July 19, 1993, the fund was named U.S. Boston Investment Boston Numeric Series - Ordinary Shares. From that date until Aug. 1, 1994, it was named Quantitative Group Boston Numeric Series - Ordinary Shares.

Manager's Investment Style

Management bases stock selection on a two-part quantitative model. One component identifies companies that are experiencing upward revisions of analysts' earnings expectations, while the other component evaluates stock prices relative to the company's fundamental value. The portfolio consists of stocks that represent the best trade-offs between these two models. Management notes that the model can lead to solid weightings in retail and technology, which often offer stocks that represent a good blend of the two criteria.

Fund Manager(s)

John C. Bogle, Jr. CFA(1990), since 08-92.
Birthdate: 11-59. BS, Vanderbilt U. 1982 MBA, Vanderbilt U. 1983

Manager Experience

	Dates Managed	Invest Obj	Std Dev	+/- Index
Not available.				

Historical Profile

Return	---
Risk	---
Rating	Not Rated

Investment Style History
Equity
Average % Stocks Held in Portfolio

94% 91% 94%

Growth of $10,000

IIII Value of Fund ($000)
— Value of Index ($000) S&P 500
▼ Manager Change
▽ Partial Manager Change
► Mgr Unknown After
◄ Mgr Unknown Before

Performance Quartile (Within Objective)

1983	1984	1985	1986	1987	1988	1989	1990	1991	1992	1993	1994	History
---	---	---	---	---	---	---	---	---	12.87	15.29	14.92	NAV
---	---	---	---	---	---	---	---	---	28.70 *	28.89	4.31	Total Return %
---	---	---	---	---	---	---	---	---	24.62 *	18.83	2.99	+/- S&P 500
---	---	---	---	---	---	---	---	---		14.35	6.96	+/- Wilshire 4500
---	---	---	---	---	---	---	---	---	0.00	0.00	0.00	Income Return %
---	---	---	---	---	---	---	---	---	28.70	28.89	4.31	Capital Return %
---	---	---	---	---	---	---	---	---		9	5	Total Rtn % Rank All
---	---	---	---	---	---	---	---	---		9	17	Total Rtn % Rank Obj
---	---	---	---	---	---	---	---	---	0.00	0.00	0.00	Income $
---	---	---	---	---	---	---	---	---	0.00	1.27	0.99	Capital Gains $
---	---	---	---	---	---	---	---	---	---	2.07	1.83	Expense Ratio %
---	---	---	---	---	---	---	---	---	---	-1.41	-1.30	Income Ratio %
---	---	---	---	---	---	---	---	---	---	---	389	Turnover Rate %
---	---	---	---	---	---	---	---	---	7.6	34.3	47.8	Net Assets ($mil)

Performance 12-31-94

	1st Qtr	2nd Qtr	3rd Qtr	4th Qtr	Total
1987	---	---	---	---	---
1988	---	---	---	---	---
1989	---	---	---	---	---
1990	---	---	---	---	---
1991	---	---	---	---	---
1992	---	---	---	25.93	28.70 *
1993	9.71	5.17	13.06	-1.21	28.89
1994	0.26	-8.02	12.48	0.56	4.31

Bear Market Performance

Decile Rank (5-year period)

Worst | Best

	Worst 3 Mo Period 1985-89	Worst 3 Mo Period 1990-94
Quantitative Numeric Ord		
+/- S&P 500	---	---
+/- Best Fit Index :	---	---

Trailing Returns

	Total Return %	+/- S&P 500	+/- Wil 4500	% Rank All	% Rank Obj	Growth of $10,000
3 Mo	0.56	0.57	3.06	11	30	10,056
6 Mo	13.11	8.25	8.92	3	21	11,311
1 Yr	4.31	2.99	6.96	5	17	10,431
3 Yr Avg	---	---	---	---	---	---
5 Yr Avg	---	---	---	---	---	---
10 Yr Avg	---	---	---	---	---	---
15 Yr Avg	---	---	---	---	---	---

Risk Analysis

Time Period	Load-Adj Return %	Risk % Rank All	Risk % Rank Obj	Morningstar Return	Morningstar Risk	Morningstar Risk-Adj Rating
1 Yr	3.33					
3 Yr	---	---	---	---	---	---
5 Yr	---	---	---	---	---	---
10 Yr	---	---	---	---	---	---

Average Historical Rating ---

[1] 1 = low, 100 = high   [2] 1.00 = Equity Avg   [3] 1.00 = 90-day T-bill return

Other Measures

	Standard S&P 500	Best Fit
Standard Deviation	---	Alpha	---	---
Mean	---	Beta	---	---
Sharpe Ratio	---	R-Squared	---	---

Investment Style

	Stock Portfolio Avg	Relative S&P 500
Price/Earnings Ratio	21.8	1.18
Price/Book Ratio	4.5	1.32
5 Yr Earnings Gr %	12.3#	2.21
Return on Assets %	12.5	1.68
Debt % Total Cap	25.5	0.90
Med Mkt Cap ($mil)	900	0.07

figure is based on 50% or less of stocks

Style: Value Blend Growth / Size Large Med Small

Diversification Value for Portfolio Types

Large Cap: Small Cap: Bond: Balanced: Diversified:

Portfolio 09-30-94

Share Chg (03-94)000	Amount 000	Total Stocks: 77 Total Fixed-Income: 0	Value $000	% Net Assets
23	31	Micro Warehouse	972	2.09
28	28	Wellman	950	2.05
15	20	US Healthcare	935	2.01
23	23	HEALTHSOUTH Rehabilitation	914	1.97
-2	46	Waban	909	1.96
27	27	HBO	907	1.95
24	24	Varity	901	1.94
34	34	Circuit City Stores	871	1.87
16	16	Cobra Golf	860	1.85
18	18	Novellus Systems	853	1.84
32	34	Fleetwood Enterprises	845	1.82
20	20	Premark International	838	1.81
25	25	ALC Communications	823	1.77
35	35	Humana	822	1.77
6	29	Pittston Services Group	821	1.77
12	12	Briggs & Stratton	820	1.77
24	24	AFLAC	807	1.74
20	20	Tommy Hilfiger	792	1.70
16	16	Electroglas	784	1.69
15	27	General Instrument	784	1.69
25	25	Symbol Technologies	775	1.67
21	21	Tencor Instruments	774	1.67
21	21	Dean Witter Discover	773	1.66
17	17	Cyrix	747	1.61
20	20	Sunglass Hut International	738	1.59

Composition % 12-31-94

Cash	7.9	Preferreds	0.0
Stocks	92.1	Convertibles	0.0
Bonds	0.0	Other	0.0

Tax Analysis

	Tax-Adj Historical Return %	% Pretax Return
3 Yr Avg	---	---
5 Yr Avg	---	---
10 Yr Avg	---	---
Potential Capital Gain Exposure (% of assets)		1%

Most Similar Funds in MF500

Fund lacks three-year record

Index Allocation

	% of Stocks
S&P 500	24.4
S&P MidCap 400	23.9
U.S. Small Cap	49.7
Foreign	4.1

Sector Weightings

	% of Stocks	Relative S&P 500
Utilities	0.0	0.00
Energy	0.0	0.00
Financials	9.6	0.91
Industrial Cyclicals	12.8	0.78
Consumer Durables	16.1	2.58
Consumer Staples	0.0	0.00
Services	5.4	0.66
Retail	13.0	2.23
Health	12.2	1.40
Technology	31.0	3.39

Operations

Address and Telephone	Lincoln North Lincoln, MA 01773 800-331-1244 / 617-259-1144	Min Initial Purchase	$5000 (Addt'l: None)
		Min IRA Purchase	None (Addt'l: None)
Advisor	Quantitative Advisors	Min Auto Invest Plan	$100 (Systematic Inv: $100)
Subadvisor	Numeric Investors	**Expenses & Fees**	
Distributor	U.S. Boston Capital	Sales Fees	0.00% front
States Available	Selected states		1.00% deferred
Report Grade	C		0.50% 12b-1
Income Distrib	Paid Annually	Management Fee	1.00% flat fee
* Date of Inception	08-01-92	3-,5-,10-yr Expense Projections	$69, $111, $228
Fiscal Year End	March	Annual Brokerage Cost	0.39%

Quest For Value Dual Purpose Capital

	Ticker	NAV	Mkt Price	Prem/Disc	Yield	Objective
	KFV	$25.79	$23.00	-10.8%	0.0%	Domestic Eq

7.2	-20.7	-20.9	-19.3	-22.0	-10.6	-6.5	-9.9	Highest Prem/Disc
-37.6	-29.0	-31.0	-32.2	-31.5	-26.0	-15.8	-17.7	Lowest Prem/Disc

Quest For Value Dual Purpose Fund seeks long-term capital appreciation, current income, and long-term growth of income.

The fund invests at least 65% of assets in dividend-paying common stocks and interest-bearing securities with potential for capital appreciation. It may invest the remainder in preferred stocks, bonds, cash equivalents, options, or futures.

The fund's capital shares are entitled to the fund's capital appreciation but not to any income derived from its holdings. In addition, some capital gains may be paid to the income shares to meet those shares' required annual return. For more information concerning the fund's income shares, see Quest For Value Income Shares.

The fund's income shares will be redeemed on Jan. 31, 1997, after which capital shareholders are entitled to the full value of the fund and may vote to liquidate or open-end the fund.

Historical Profile
Return Above Average
Risk Below Average
Rating ★★★★ Above Average

Growth of $10,000
— at NAV ($000)
— at Market Price ($000)

Premium Discount %

Manager's Investment Style
Management takes a bottom-up approach to the market. The fund typically targets undervalued growth-oriented stocks. To guard against market weakness, the fund has actively hedged the portfolio by selling S&P 500 Index futures. The fund doesn't stick with common stocks, though. To meet the needs of its income shares, management has dedicated a portion of assets to high-yield bonds, preferred stocks, and convertible bonds.

Fund Manager(s)
George A. Long, CFA. Since 5-91. BA'63 Georgetown U.; MBA'65 Wharton.

	1983	1984	1985	1986	1987	1988	1989	1990	1991	1992	1993	1994	History
	---	---	---	---	8.70	11.93	18.05	16.43	22.59	26.29	27.09	25.79	NAV
	---	---	---	---	-16.97*	37.13	53.92	-5.00	41.27	27.26	9.98	-0.80	NAV Total Return %
	---	---	---	---	-7.87*	20.52	22.24	-1.88	10.79	19.64	-0.08	-2.12	+/- S&P 500
	---	---	---	---	---	14.10	32.41	11.36	-7.26	4.63	-2.86	1.93	+/- Wil Mid Value
	---	---	---	---	0.00*	0.00	0.00	0.00	0.00	0.00	0.00	0.00	Income Return %
	---	---	---	---	-16.97*	37.13	53.92	-5.00	41.27	27.26	9.98	-0.80	Capital Return %
	---	---	---	---		4	6	72	16	3	83	15	Total Rtn % Rank All
	---	---	---	---		1	3	48	35	12	44	43	Total Rtn % Rank Obj
	---	---	---	---	-43.39*	35.29	66.61	-11.33	50.91	42.70	11.37	-0.14	Market Total Rtn %
	---	---	---	---	-17.2	-25.7	-26.1	-26.0	-28.3	-17.9	-10.2	-14.5	Avg Prem/Disc %
	---	---	---	---	0.00	0.00	0.00	0.00	0.00	0.00	0.00	0.00	Income $
	---	---	---	---	0.92	0.00	0.31	0.71	0.62	2.39	1.60	0.95	Capital Gains $
	---	---	---	---	0.00	0.00	0.00	0.00	0.00	0.00	0.00	0.00	Expense Ratio %
	---	---	---	---	0.00	0.00	0.00	0.00	0.00	0.00	0.00	0.00	Income Ratio %
	---	---	---	---	137	155	76	78	62	45	51	---	Turnover Rate %
	---	---	---	---	156.6	508.9	324.9	295.8	406.8	473.3	487.7	464.4	Net Assets ($mil)

Manager Experience

	Dates Managed	Invest Obj	Std Dev	+/- Index
George A. Long Quest For Val Inc	05/91 - 12/94	I	1.70	3.03

NAV Performance % 12-30-94

	1st Qtr	2nd Qtr	3rd Qtr	4th Qtr	Total
1987	-0.69*	1.82	7.31	-23.48	-16.97*
1988	16.44	4.64	6.13	6.04	37.13
1989	16.76	11.92	11.48	5.66	53.92
1990	-5.82	6.94	-14.85	10.77	-5.00
1991	19.15	-1.58	8.16	11.39	41.27
1992	7.08	5.58	7.64	4.58	27.26
1993	5.59	1.84	0.81	1.45	9.98
1994	-1.52	1.73	2.11	-3.03	-0.80

Bear Market Performance
Decile Rank (5-year period)

Worst — Best

	Worst 3 Mo Period 1985-89	Worst 3 Mo Period 1990-94
Quest For Val Cap	---	-19.23
+/- S&P 500	---	-5.39

Trailing Returns

	NAV Total Return %	+/- S&P 500	+/- Wil Mid Value	% Rank All	% Rank Obj	Mkt Total Return %
3 Mo	-3.03	-3.01	-0.12	70	65	-1.46
6 Mo	-0.99	-5.85	-1.05	54	73	0.08
1 Yr	-0.80	-2.12	1.93	15	43	-0.14
3 Yr Avg	11.56	5.29	1.15	16	18	16.64
5 Yr Avg	13.25	4.56	2.43	10	17	16.25
Incept Avg	16.20*	---	---	---	---	13.48*

Risk Analysis

	Risk % Rank[1] All	Risk % Rank[1] Obj	Morningstar[2] Return	Morningstar Risk	Morningstar Risk-Adj Rating
3 Yr	69	40	1.10	0.50	★★★★
5 Yr	75	34	1.75	0.62	★★★★
10 Yr	---	---	---	---	---

Average Historical Rating (59 months) 4.3 ★s
[1] 1 = Low, 100 = High [2] 1.00 = Equity Avg [3] 1.00 = 90-day T-bill Return

Other Measures

				S&P 500
Standard Deviation	9.87	Alpha		5.50
Mean	11.47	Beta		0.90
Sharpe Ratio	0.81	R-Squared		52

Investment Style

	Portfolio Avg	Stock Relative S&P 500
Price/Earnings Ratio	16.1	0.87
Price/Cash Flow Ratio	10.5	0.91
Price/Book Ratio	3.6	1.05
5 Yr Earnings Gr %	10.1	1.83
Return on Assets %	4.3	0.57
Debt % Total Cap	28.3	1.00
Med Mkt Cap ($mil)	4812	0.37

figure is based on less than 50% of stocks

Style
Value Blend Growth
Size Large Med Small

Index Allocation

	% of Stocks
Dow 30	10.3
S&P 500	72.0
S&P Mid-Cap 400	19.5
US Small-Cap	5.1
Foreign	3.4

Diversification Value for Portfolio Types

Large Cap: Low Small Cap: Medium Bond: High Balanced: Low Diversified: Medium

Portfolio 09-30-94

Total Equity: 27
Total Fixed-Income: 18

Share Chg (06-94)	Amount		Value $000	% Total Invest
-50000	650000	FHLMC	34694	4.93
-50000	650000	Transamerica	32663	4.64
-122500	427500	Philip Morris	26131	3.71
0	245200	Hercules	25225	3.58
---	1210000	Flagstar Cv Pfd $2.28	24503	3.48
25000	200000	McDonnell Douglas	23100	3.28
-50000	600000	Sprint	22875	3.25
2012	24346	Security Capital Realty	22257	3.16
-80600	369400	Avon Products	22072	3.14
182723	382723	Mellon Bank	21528	3.06
0	700000	American Express	21263	3.02
500000	500000	Citicorp	21250	3.02
-50000	250000	Monsanto	20094	2.86
0	250000	Warner-Lambert	20063	2.85
---	56380000	ALZA Cv 0%	19663	2.79
0	1000000	Freeport-McMoRan	19375	2.75
0	500000	Arrow Electronics	18750	2.66
0	720300	Fruit of the Loom Cl A	18458	2.62
0	200000	American International Group	17775	2.53
---	18442151	Security Capital Realty Cv 12%	16118	2.29
0	328000	Becton Dickinson	15826	2.25
-200000	400000	EXEL	15550	2.21
0	454500	AFLAC	15510	2.20
0	475000	Triton Energy	15438	2.19
-20000	551600	Dole Food	15307	2.18

Composition % 12-31-94

Cash	1.0	Preferreds	2.0
Stocks	69.0	Convertibles	16.0
Bonds	12.0	Other	0.0

Tax Analysis

	Tax-Adj Historical Return %	% Pretax Return
3 Yr Avg	9.57	81.2
5 Yr Avg	11.56	84.3
10 Yr Avg	---	---

Potential Capital Gain Exposure (% of assets) 18

Sector Weightings

	% of Stocks	Relative S&P 500
Utilities	0.0	0.00
Energy	3.3	0.33
Financials	39.6	3.75
Industrial Cyclicals	17.7	1.08
Consumer Durables	4.0	0.64
Consumer Staples	19.2	1.54
Services	3.4	0.41
Retail	0.0	0.00
Health	7.8	0.90
Technology	5.0	0.54

Most Similar Funds in MF500

Quest for Value A	Weak Fit
Gemini II Cap	Weak Fit
Neuberger&Berman Par	Weak Fit

Operations

Address and Telephone	One World Financial Center New York, NY 10281 212-667-7561 / 800-232-3863
Advisor	Quest for Value Advisors
Subadvisor	N/A
Administrator	Oppenheimer Capital
Transfer Agent	State Street Bank and Trust Co.
Custodian	State Street Bank and Trust Co.
Auditor	Price Waterhouse LLP
Legal Counsel	Gordon, Altman, Butowsky, Weitzen, Shalov & Wein

Income Distrib Schedule	Paid Irregularly
Management Fee	0.00%
Reinvestment Plan	Yes
Direct Purchase Plan	No
Shares Outstanding	18,004,302
Exchange	NYSE
*Date of Inception	02-13-87
Shareholder Report	B-

Quest for Value A

	Ticker	Load	NAV	Yield	SEC Yield	Assets	Objective
	QFVFX	5.50%	11.20	0.7%	N/A	222.6	Growth

Quest for Value Fund - Class A seeks capital appreciation.
The fund invests primarily in equity securities issued by companies that are undervalued relative to assets, earnings, growth potential, and cash flow. The fund may invest without limit in foreign securities. It may also invest a portion of its assets in debt securities.

Class A shares have front loads and lower 12b-1 fees; Class B shares have deferred loads and conversion features; Class C shares have level loads. On Nov. 1, 1991, AMA Classic Growth Fund merged into this fund. On Dec. 31, 1992, Unified Growth Fund merged into this fund.

Historical Profile

Return	Average
Risk	Below Average
Rating	★★★
	Neutral

Investment Style %: 80% 83% 86% 86% 90% 88% 79% 87%

Investment Style History
Equity
Average % Stocks Held in Portfolio

Growth of $10,000

|||| Value of Fund ($000)
— Value of Index ($000)
SPMid400
▼ Manager Change
▽ Partial Manager Change
◄■ Mgr Unknown After
◄ Mgr Unknown Before

Manager's Investment Style

Management rummages for stocks with sound fundamentals that have P/E ratios well below the market's, even if the stock carries a slightly higher-than-average price-book ratio. It usually scoops up cheap stocks in industries the market neglects or scorns. It also focuses on companies led by management teams willing to reinvest cash flows for the long-term benefit of their shareholders.

Performance Quartile
(Within Objective)

	1983	1984	1985	1986	1987	1988	1989	1990	1991	1992	1993	1994	History
	7.91	6.74	8.23	8.50	7.55	8.41	9.28	8.48	10.49	11.77	12.02	11.20	NAV
	39.01	4.51	27.54	14.26	-2.14	17.66	19.98	-6.86	32.82	17.91	6.57	0.85	Total Return %
	16.54	-1.76	-4.20	-4.42	-7.40	1.05	-11.70	-3.74	2.34	10.29	-3.49	-0.46	+/- S&P 500
	15.55	1.46	-5.03	-1.84	-4.50	-0.28	-9.19	-0.68	-1.38	8.94	-4.71	0.92	+/- Wilshire 5000
	2.38	1.82	1.31	0.73	1.63	1.24	2.88	1.76	0.72	0.41	0.34	0.74	Income Return %
	36.63	2.69	26.22	13.53	-3.77	16.42	17.10	-8.62	32.10	17.50	6.23	0.11	Capital Return %
	3	53	35	59	76	19	35	77	22	6	85	14	Total Rtn % Rank All
	3	24	63	54	78	39	80	69	58	9	73	25	Total Rtn % Rank Obj
	0.17	0.11	0.09	0.07	0.14	0.10	0.26	0.16	0.07	0.05	0.04	0.08	Income $
	1.61	1.27	0.24	0.86	0.68	0.37	0.55	0.00	0.64	0.55	0.47	0.83	Capital Gains $
	2.48	2.29	2.34	2.18	2.24	2.21	1.81	1.82	1.83	1.75	1.75	1.73	Expense Ratio %
	2.56	1.68	1.90	1.18	0.76	0.94	2.31	1.71	1.06	0.53	0.40	0.53	Income Ratio %
	93	74	42	68	21	15	30	51	48	41	27	---	Turnover Rate %
	8.9	13.4	33.3	75.0	87.3	79.1	77.7	55.3	111.9	168.3	243.9	222.6	Net Assets ($mil)

Fund Manager(s)

Eileen P. Rominger, since 01-89. BA, Fairfield U. 1976 MBA, Wharton 1981

Manager Experience

	Dates Managed	Invest Obj	Std Dev	+/- Index
Not available.				

Performance 12-31-94

	1st Qtr	2nd Qtr	3rd Qtr	4th Qtr	Total
1987	12.59	2.54	7.37	-21.05	-2.14
1988	11.26	5.32	0.86	-0.45	17.66
1989	6.93	2.97	8.32	0.60	19.98
1990	-4.20	6.71	-16.72	9.41	-6.86
1991	15.57	1.26	4.03	9.10	32.82
1992	3.81	-0.55	6.37	7.37	17.91
1993	2.55	1.49	2.20	0.19	6.57
1994	-2.50	1.54	4.37	-2.40	0.85

Bear Market Performance

Decile Rank (5-year period)

Worst — Best

	Worst 3 Mo Period 1985-89	Worst 3 Mo Period 1990-94
Quest for Value A	-25.74	-16.72
+/- S&P 500	3.84	-2.98
+/- Best Fit Index : SPMid400	3.07	1.05

Trailing Returns

	Total Return %	+/- S&P 500	+/- Wil 5000	% Rank All	% Rank Obj	Growth of $10,000
3 Mo	-2.40	-2.38	-1.63	75	72	9,760
6 Mo	1.87	-2.99	-2.76	27	73	10,187
1 Yr	0.85	-0.46	0.92	14	25	10,085
3 Yr Avg	8.22	1.95	1.60	20	29	12,673
5 Yr Avg	9.41	0.72	0.59	21	37	15,677
10 Yr Avg	12.18	-2.20	-1.68	36	63	31,561
15 Yr Avg	---	---	---	---	---	---

Operations

| Address and Telephone | One World Financial Center
New York, NY 10281
800-232-3863 / 212-667-7587 |
|---|---|
| Advisor | Quest for Value Advisors |
| Subadvisor | None |
| Distributor | Quest for Value Distributors |
| States Available | All plus PR |
| Report Grade | B- |
| Income Distrib | Paid Annually |
| Date of Inception | 05-01-80 |
| Fiscal Year End | October |

Risk Analysis

Time Period	Load-Adj Return %	Risk % Rank [1] All	Obj	Morningstar [2] Return	Morningstar Risk	Morningstar Risk-Adj Rating
1 Yr	-4.70					
3 Yr	6.19	65	24	0.77 [3]	0.73	★★★
5 Yr	8.18	67	20	0.86 [3]	0.80	★★★
10 Yr	11.55	54	12	0.80	0.78	★★★

Average Historical Rating (109 months)   3.7 ★s

[1] 1 = low, 100 = high   [2] 1.00 = Equity Avg   [3] 1.00 = 90-day T-bill return

Other Measures

	Standard S&P 500	Best Fit SPMid400
Standard Deviation	8.41	Alpha 2.2 / 1.9
Mean	8.27	Beta 0.88 / 0.75
Sharpe Ratio	0.56	R-Squared 69 / 76

Investment Style

	Stock Portfolio Avg	Relative S&P 500
Price/Earnings Ratio	16.6	0.90
Price/Book Ratio	3.5	1.03
5 Yr Earnings Gr %	11.4	2.06
Return on Assets %	6.5	0.87
Debt % Total Cap	28.3	1.00
Med Mkt Cap ($mil)	4699	0.36

Style: Value Blend Growth / Size Large Med Small

Diversification Value for Portfolio Types

Large Cap: Low	Small Cap: Low	Bond: High	Balanced: Low	Diversified: Low

Portfolio 04-30-94

Total Stocks: 48
Total Fixed-Income: 1

Share Chg (12-93) 000	Amount 000		Value $000	% Net Assets
48	284	EXEL	12475	5.27
12	146	FHLMC	8226	3.48
-4	199	Becton Dickinson	7696	3.25
-2	89	First Interstate Bancorp	7104	3.00
12	79	American International Group	6696	2.83
-16	110	Avon Products	6541	2.76
-10	89	Warner-Lambert	6046	2.56
201	201	American Express	5959	2.52
5	47	McDonnell Douglas	5515	2.33
-1	48	Unilever	5316	2.25
48	155	Hasbro	5276	2.23
-3	139	Sprint	5111	2.16
-1	61	Monsanto	5042	2.13
-2	105	Sundstrand	5005	2.11
-2	97	Transamerica	4874	2.06
-4	172	UST (Inc)	4806	2.03
34	50	General Electric	4793	2.03
34	122	Arrow Electronics	4592	1.94
-3	134	Warnaco Group Cl A	4552	1.92
7	41	General Re	4539	1.92
47	105	Johnson & Johnson	4360	1.84
42	87	UNUM	4304	1.82
22	95	Martin Marietta	4220	1.78
-2	77	Philip Morris	4176	1.76
20	217	Freeport-McMoRan	4159	1.76

Composition % 12-31-94

Cash	10.0	Preferreds	0.0
Stocks	89.0	Convertibles	1.0
Bonds	0.0	Other	0.0

Tax Analysis

	Tax-Adj Historical Return %	% Pretax Return
3 Yr Avg	6.51	77.9
5 Yr Avg	7.84	80.8
10 Yr Avg	10.17	75.8

Potential Capital Gain Exposure (% of assets)   9%

Most Similar Funds in MF500

Neuberger&Berman Partners	Fair Fit
Fidelity Stock Selector	Fair Fit
Vanguard Index Extended Mkt	Fair Fit

Expenses & Fees

Sales Fees	5.50% front
	0.00% deferred
	0.50% 12b-1
Management Fee	1.00% flat fee
3-,5-,10-yr Expense Projections	$107, $145, $250
Annual Brokerage Cost	---

Min Initial Purchase	$1000 (Addt'l: $250)
Min IRA Purchase	$250 (Addt'l: $50)
Min Auto Invest Plan	$50 (Systematic Inv: $50)

Index Allocation

	% of Stocks
S&P 500	64.8
S&P MidCap 400	17.1
U.S. Small Cap	10.2
Foreign	10.6

Sector Weightings

	% of Stocks	Relative S&P 500
Utilities	0.0	0.00
Energy	3.3	0.33
Financials	30.4	2.88
Industrial Cyclicals	14.5	0.89
Consumer Durables	7.5	1.21
Consumer Staples	18.6	1.48
Services	7.5	0.92
Retail	3.7	0.63
Health	9.8	1.13
Technology	4.7	0.51

MORNINGSTAR 1995 Mutual Fund 500

Quest for Value Opportunity A

	Ticker	Load	NAV	Yield	SEC Yield	Assets	Objective
	QVOPX	5.50%	18.30	0.6%	N/A	166.5	Asset Alloc.

Quest for Value Opportunity Fund - Class A seeks growth of capital.

The fund allocates its assets among stocks, bonds, and cash equivalents. Although common stocks and convertible securities normally constitute the majority of the fund's investments, more than 50% of the fund's assets may be invested in bonds and other fixed-income obligations. The fund may invest without limit in foreign securities.

Class A shares have front loads and lower 12b-1 fees; Class B shares have deferred loads and conversion features; Class C shares have level loads. Prior to Sept. 3, 1991, the fund was named Quest for Value Asset Allocation Fund.

Manager's Investment Style

Although the fund has the flexibility to shift among various asset classes, management has historically emphasized stocks. Management takes a bottom-up approach to stock investing, targeting undervalued companies with solid fundamentals. In particular, it looks for firms with strong niche positions, considerable cash reserves, and high return on capital. This approach has often led the portfolio to be concentrated in just a few sectors.

Fund Manager(s)

Richard Glasebrook II CFA(1976), since 03-91. BA, Kenyon C. 1970 MBA, Harvard 1972

Manager Experience	Dates Managed	Invest Obj	Std Dev	+/- Index
Richard Glasebrook II				
Quest for Value Gbl Eq A	09/91 - 12/94	WW	9.73	1.80
Enterprise Managed	10/94 - 12/94	AA	5.13	-1.11

Historical Profile
Return	Above Average
Risk	Average
Rating	★★★★ Above Average

Investment Style History
Equity

Average % Stocks Held in Portfolio

	56%	79%	65%	75%	82%

Growth of $10,000
- |||| Value of Fund ($000)
- — Value of Index ($000) S&P 500
- ▼ Manager Change
- ▽ Partial Manager Change
- ► Mgr Unknown After
- ◄ Mgr Unknown Before

Performance Quartile (Within Objective)

1983	1984	1985	1986	1987	1988	1989	1990	1991	1992	1993	1994	History
---	---	---	---	---	---	11.80	10.32	14.97	17.27	18.14	18.30	NAV
---	---	---	---	---	---	22.65 *	-10.29	51.46	17.97	8.21	4.92	Total Return %
---	---	---	---	---	---	-9.03 *	-7.17	20.97	10.35	-1.85	3.61	+/- S&P 500
---	---	---	---	---	---	---	-19.23	35.46	10.73	-1.55	7.84	+/- LB Aggregate
---	---	---	---	---	---	2.07	2.03	0.48	0.41	1.87	0.64	Income Return %
---	---	---	---	---	---	20.58	-12.32	50.98	17.56	6.34	4.28	Capital Return %
---	---	---	---	---	---	---	85	7	6	78	4	Total Rtn % Rank All
---	---	---	---	---	---	---	91	1	2	84	2	Total Rtn % Rank Obj
---	---	---	---	---	---	0.22	0.23	0.07	0.07	0.33	0.12	Income $
---	---	---	---	---	---	0.24	0.03	0.55	0.32	0.22	0.61	Capital Gains $
---	---	---	---	---	---	1.84	2.00	2.35	2.27	1.83	1.78	Expense Ratio %
---	---	---	---	---	---	3.75	2.30	0.30	0.72	2.69	0.96	Income Ratio %
---	---	---	---	---	---	---	206	88	32	24	---	Turnover Rate %
						1.0	5.1	10.1	55.1	126.1	166.5	Net Assets ($mil)

Performance 12-31-94

	1st Qtr	2nd Qtr	3rd Qtr	4th Qtr	Total
1987	---	---	---	---	---
1988	---	---	---	---	---
1989	6.50	3.57	6.35	4.56	22.65
1990	-5.93	7.48	-15.00	4.40	-10.29
1991	21.90	4.93	7.88	9.76	51.46
1992	5.61	1.33	4.49	5.50	17.97
1993	2.61	2.82	3.24	-0.65	8.21
1994	-0.72	3.66	2.52	-0.56	4.92

Bear Market Performance

Decile Rank (5-year period)

Worst ———— Best

	Worst 3 Mo Period 1985-89	Worst 3 Mo Period 1990-94
Quest for Value Opportunity A	---	-16.75
+/- S&P 500	---	-2.91
+/- Best Fit Index : S&P 500	---	-2.91

Trailing Returns

	Total Return %	+/- S&P 500	+/- LB Aggregate	% Rank All	% Rank Obj	Growth of $10,000
3 Mo	-0.56	-0.54	-0.94	36	40	9,944
6 Mo	1.94	-2.92	0.95	27	40	10,194
1 Yr	4.92	3.61	7.84	4	2	10,492
3 Yr Avg	10.23	3.96	5.68	13	4	13,393
5 Yr Avg	12.72	4.03	5.10	7	1	18,199
10 Yr Avg	---	---	---	---	---	---
15 Yr Avg	---	---	---	---	---	---

Operations

Address and Telephone	One World Financial Center New York, NY 10281 800-232-3863 / 212-667-7587
Advisor	Quest for Value Advisors
Subadvisor	None
Distributor	Quest for Value Distributors
States Available	All plus PR
Report Grade	B-
Income Distrib	Paid Annually
* Date of Inception	01-01-89
Fiscal Year End	October

Min Initial Purchase	$1000 (Addt'l: $250)
Min IRA Purchase	$1000 (Addt'l: $250)
Min Auto Invest Plan	$50 (Systematic Inv: $50)

Expenses & Fees
Sales Fees	5.50% front
	0.00% deferred
	0.50% 12b-1
Management Fee	1.00% flat fee
3-,5-,10-yr Expense Projections	$109, $149, $258
Annual Brokerage Cost	

Risk Analysis

Time Period	Load-Adj Return %	Risk % Rank [1] All / Obj	Morningstar [2] Return / Risk	Morningstar Risk-Adj Rating
1 Yr	-0.85			
3 Yr	8.17	53 / 51	1.39[3] / 0.75	★★★★
5 Yr	11.45	59 / 81	1.77[3] / 0.95	★★★★
10 Yr	---	--- / ---	--- / ---	
Average Historical Rating (37 months)				4.6 ★s

[1] 1 = low, 100 = high [2] 1.00 = Hybrid Avg [3] 1.00 = 90-day T-bill return

Other Measures
			Standard S&P 500	Best Fit S&P 500
Standard Deviation	7.52	Alpha	4.4	4.4
Mean	10.06	Beta	0.78	0.78
Sharpe Ratio	0.87	R-Squared	68	68

Investment Style

Stocks	Port Avg	Rel S&P 500	Style
Price/Earnings Ratio	15.2	0.82	V B G
Price/Book Ratio	3.3	0.97	
5 Yr Earnings Gr %	9.1	1.65	
Med Mkt Cap ($mil)	4812	0.37	

Bonds		
Avg Effective Duration	NMF	
Avg Effective Maturity	---	
Avg Credit Quality	AAA	Not Available
Avg Weighted Coupon	7.64%	

Diversification Value for Portfolio Types

Large Cap: Low	Small Cap: Medium	Bond: High	Balanced: Low	Diversified: Low

Portfolio 04-30-94

Share Chg (12-93)000	Amount 000	Total Stocks: 31 Total Fixed-Income: 5	Date of Maturity	Value $000	% Net Assets
9	72	McDonnell Douglas		8475	6.47
-5	137	FHLMC		7743	5.92
2	86	First Interstate Bancorp		6831	5.22
31	140	Exel		6149	4.70
4	108	Mellon Bank		6032	4.61
19	189	American Express		5609	4.29
5	81	Warner-Lambert		5508	4.21
38	38	Wells Fargo		5491	4.19
84	108	Dreyfus		5220	3.99
-8	72	MAPCO		4652	3.55
392	392	National Health Lab Hldgs		4559	3.48
7	50	FNMA		4128	3.15
61	108	Sprint		3976	3.04
-5	99	Becton Dickinson		3831	2.93
1	25	First Empire State		3509	2.68
41	81	General Dynamics		3286	2.51
-20	54	Avon Products		3212	2.45
30	50	Morgan Stanley Group		3056	2.33
-3	54	Transamerica		2725	2.08
-5	90	Triton Energy		2649	2.02

Index Allocation
	% of Stocks
S&P 500	69.4
S&P MidCap 400	13.0
U.S. Small Cap	12.3
Foreign	5.4

Composition % 11-17-94
Cash	21.0	Preferreds	0.0
Stocks	78.0	Convertibles	0.0
Bonds	1.0	Other	0.0

Tax Analysis
	Tax-Adj Historical Return %	% Pretax Return
3 Yr Avg	9.19	89.0
5 Yr Avg	11.65	89.6
10 Yr Avg	---	---
Potential Capital Gain Exposure (% of assets)		5%

Most Similar Funds in MF500
Quest for Value A	Fair Fit
Neuberger&Berman Guardian	Fair Fit
Fidelity Disciplined Equity	Fair Fit

Bond Credit Analysis 11-17-94
% of Bonds
US Govt	100	BB	0
AAA	0	B	0
AA	0	Below B	0
A	0	NR/NA	0
BBB	0		

Stock Sector Weightings
	% of Stocks	Relative S&P 500
Utilities	0.0	0.00
Energy	6.4	0.63
Financials	44.2	4.18
Industrial Cyclicals	18.0	1.10
Consumer Durables	4.9	0.78
Consumer Staples	2.8	0.22
Services	9.4	1.15
Retail	0.0	0.00
Health	8.2	0.94
Technology	6.2	0.68

Reich & Tang Equity

	Ticker	Load	NAV	Yield	SEC Yield	Assets	Objective
	RCHTX	None	15.39	1.4%	N/A	91.6	Growth

Reich and Tang Equity Fund seeks growth of capital. Current income is secondary.

The fund normally invests at least 65% of its assets in undervalued equity securities; the relative valuation is determined by fundamental analysis. It may invest up to 35% of its assets in debt securities and preferred stocks that may offer significant opportunities for price appreciation. The fund may invest in both listed and unlisted securities, and it may invest up to 15% of its assets in foreign securities.

Manager's Investment Style

This fund's management team seeks companies with good franchises, free cash flow, a clean balance sheet, and motivated management. Stocks' prices must also be depressed for management to buy. The team spends a lot of time on research, and so is content to hold securities for the long term.

Fund Manager(s)

Robert F. Hoerle, since 01-85. Birthdate: 03-33.
BS, Yale 1956 MBA, Harvard 1962
Steven M. Wilson CFA(1984), since 01-86.
Birthdate: 01-60. BS, U. of Pennsylvania 1981

Manager Experience

	Dates Managed	Invest Obj	Std Dev	+/- Index
Not available.				

Historical Profile

Return	Above Average
Risk	Below Average
Rating	★★★★
	Above Average

Investment Style History
Equity

Average % Stocks Held in Portfolio

Growth of $10,000

- |||| Value of Fund ($000)
- — Value of Index ($000) SPMid400
- ▼ Manager Change
- ▽ Partial Manager Change
- ► Mgr Unknown After
- ◄ Mgr Unknown Before

Performance Quartile (Within Objective)

	1983	1984	1985	1986	1987	1988	1989	1990	1991	1992	1993	1994	History
	---	---	13.44	14.50	13.11	14.11	14.24	13.05	15.64	16.92	17.61	15.39	NAV
	---	---	24.81 *	14.67	5.29	22.86	18.00	-5.83	23.05	16.96	13.83	1.69	Total Return %
	---	---	-9.80 *	-4.01	0.03	6.25	-13.69	-2.72	-7.43	9.34	3.77	0.38	+/- S&P 500
	---	---	---	-1.43	2.93	4.92	-11.18	0.35	-11.15	7.99	2.55	1.76	+/- Wilshire 5000
	---	---	2.96	1.94	2.53	3.16	3.01	2.52	2.94	1.95	1.17	1.42	Income Return %
	---	---	21.85	12.72	2.76	19.70	14.99	-8.36	20.12	15.01	12.66	0.27	Capital Return %
	---	---	---	56	21	8	40	73	40	7	34	11	Total Rtn % Rank All
	---	---	---	51	34	13	85	61	89	11	38	20	Total Rtn % Rank Obj
	---	---	0.30	0.28	0.40	0.45	0.45	0.36	0.37	0.31	0.21	0.24	Income $
	---	---	0.00	0.63	1.78	1.53	1.93	0.00	0.03	1.04	1.43	2.28	Capital Gains $
	---	---	0.99	1.21	1.11	1.11	1.10	1.12	1.14	1.15	1.15	---	Expense Ratio %
	---	---	3.70	2.51	2.07	2.87	2.68	2.56	2.33	1.35	1.15	---	Income Ratio %
	---	---	20	35	43	27	48	27	43	27	27	---	Turnover Rate %
	---	---	54.2	106.8	90.0	102.4	121.9	97.1	83.2	92.7	105.2	91.6	Net Assets ($mil)

Performance 12-31-94

	1st Qtr	2nd Qtr	3rd Qtr	4th Qtr	Total
1987	16.25	3.04	6.90	-17.77	5.29
1988	10.14	6.42	2.44	2.33	22.86
1989	5.53	9.18	5.43	-2.85	18.00
1990	-2.11	2.16	-15.83	11.86	-5.83
1991	12.49	0.48	-0.41	9.32	23.05
1992	1.03	2.43	5.93	6.70	16.96
1993	4.26	2.10	4.58	2.26	13.83
1994	-1.77	-0.29	6.30	-2.33	1.69

Bear Market Performance

Decile Rank (5-year period)

	Worst 3 Mo Period 1985-89	Worst 3 Mo Period 1990-94
Reich & Tang Equity	---	-15.83
+/- S&P 500	---	-2.08
+/- Best Fit Index : SPMid400	---	1.95

Trailing Returns

	Total Return %	+/- S&P 500	+/- Wil 5000	% Rank All	% Rank Obj	Growth of $10,000
3 Mo	-2.33	-2.32	-1.56	74	71	9,767
6 Mo	3.82	-1.04	-0.80	16	51	10,382
1 Yr	1.69	0.38	1.76	11	20	10,169
3 Yr Avg	10.63	4.36	4.01	11	15	13,539
5 Yr Avg	9.42	0.73	0.61	20	36	15,688
10 Yr Avg	---	---	---	---	---	---
15 Yr Avg	---	---	---	---	---	---

Operations

Address and Telephone	600 Fifth Avenue New York, NY 10020 800-676-6779 / 212-830-5220
Advisor	New England Investment
Subadvisor	None
Distributor	Reich & Tang Distributors
States Available	Selected states
Report Grade	A
Income Distrib	Paid Semiannually
Date of Inception	01-04-85
Fiscal Year End	December

Risk Analysis

Time Period	Load-Adj Return %	Risk % Rank[1] All	Obj	Morningstar[2] Return	Risk	Morningstar Risk-Adj Rating
1 Yr	1.69					
3 Yr	10.63	38	3	2.18[3]	0.47	★★★★
5 Yr	9.42	60	10	1.19[3]	0.72	★★★★
10 Yr	---	---	---	---	---	---
Average Historical Rating (84 months)				3.5 ★s		

[1] 1 = low, 100 = high [2] 1.00 = Equity Avg [3] 1.00 = 90-day T-bill return

Other Measures

			Standard S&P 500	Best Fit SPMid400
Standard Deviation	7.66	Alpha	4.7	4.4
Mean	10.43	Beta	0.78	0.68
Sharpe Ratio	0.90	R-Squared	66	77

Investment Style

	Stock Portfolio Avg	Relative S&P 500
Price/Earnings Ratio	17.4	0.94
Price/Book Ratio	2.9	0.86
5 Yr Earnings Gr %	7.4	1.33
Return on Assets %	7.3	0.97
Debt % Total Cap	24.5	0.87
Med Mkt Cap ($mil)	1855	0.14

Style: Value Blend Growth / Size Large Med Small

Diversification Value for Portfolio Types

Large Cap: Low	Small Cap: Low	Bond: High	Balanced: Low	Diversified: Low

Expenses & Fees

Sales Fees	0.00% front
	0.00% deferred
	0.05% 12b-1
Management Fee	0.80% flat fee, 0.20%A
3-,5-,10-yr Expense Projections	$37, $63, $140
Annual Brokerage Cost	0.04%

Min Initial Purchase	$5000 (Addt'l: None)
Min IRA Purchase	$250 (Addt'l: None)
Min Auto Invest Plan	N/A

Tax Analysis

	Tax-Adj Historical Return %	% Pretax Return
3 Yr Avg	7.38	67.3
5 Yr Avg	7.13	72.3
10 Yr Avg	---	---
Potential Capital Gain Exposure (% of assets)		14%

Most Similar Funds in MF500

Evergreen Growth & Income	Fair Fit
SteinRoe Special	Fair Fit
Fidelity Disciplined Equity	Fair Fit

Portfolio 09-30-94

Total Stocks: 47
Total Fixed-Income: 0

Share Chg (06-94)000	Amount 000		Value $000	% Net Assets
0	100	Becton Dickinson	4801	5.01
0	190	Sonoco Products	4429	4.62
-52	42	American Cyanamid	4129	4.31
0	70	Kerr-McGee	3404	3.55
23	96	Universal Foods	2844	2.97
0	95	Hasbro	2810	2.93
0	61	UNUM	2801	2.92
0	93	Equitable Resources	2790	2.91
0	160	Woolworth	2780	2.90
0	70	Snap-On	2468	2.57
0	69	Lee Enterprises	2381	2.48
0	57	Harsco	2366	2.47
8	75	Pioneer Hi-Bred Intl	2347	2.45
0	39	Avon Products	2318	2.42
-8	105	US Shoe	2310	2.41
0	77	Equifax	2281	2.38
0	119	Albany International Cl A	2092	2.18
8	67	Lubrizol	2070	2.16
49	74	Morton International	2021	2.11
0	59	Corning	1910	1.99
64	64	Deluxe	1880	1.96
0	51	AMBAC	1869	1.95
0	18	Hercules	1852	1.93
-11	49	Varian Associates	1770	1.85
0	75	Dexter	1734	1.81

Composition % 12-31-94

Cash	-6.9	Preferreds	0.0
Stocks	106.9	Convertibles	0.0
Bonds	0.0	Other	0.0

Index Allocation

	% of Stocks
S&P 500	45.1
S&P MidCap 400	37.5
U.S. Small Cap	17.4
Foreign	0.0

Sector Weightings

	% of Stocks	Relative S&P 500
Utilities	3.2	0.26
Energy	4.9	0.48
Financials	10.0	0.95
Industrial Cyclicals	24.4	1.49
Consumer Durables	13.7	2.21
Consumer Staples	12.9	1.03
Services	4.8	0.59
Retail	7.9	1.36
Health	12.6	1.45
Technology	5.7	0.62

MORNINGSTAR 1995 Mutual Fund 500

Robertson Stephens Contrarian

	Ticker	Load	NAV	Yield	SEC Yield	Assets	Objective
	RSCOX	None	10.53	0.0%	N/A	485.7	Asset Alloc.

Robertson Stephens Contrarian Fund seeks long-term capital appreciation.

The fund normally invests at least 65% of its assets in equities. In selecting securities, the fund seeks domestic, multinational, and foreign companies that are undiscovered or temporarily out of favor. It may purchase domestic and foreign equities issued by companies of all sizes, industries, and geographical markets. The balance of assets may be invested in foreign or domestic debt, including lower-rated, high-yielding securities. The fund may not invest more than 35% of its assets in one foreign country or currency.

Manager's Investment Style

As its name implies, the fund takes a defensive stance. Management shows a willingness to explore unconventional stocks and themes, including gold stocks, base metals, and oil and gas. Management also uses options to go short on selected stocks, as well as the S&P 500. Although the fund's charter outlines few limitations, current management has a stated preference for value prices.

Fund Manager(s)

Paul H. Stephens, since 06-93. Birthdate: 02-45.
BS, U. of California-Berkeley 1967 MBA, U. of California-Berkeley 1969

Manager Experience

	Dates Managed	Invest Obj	Std Dev	+/- Index

Not available.

Historical Profile
Return ---
Risk ---
Rating
Not Rated

Investment Style History
Equity

Average % Stocks Held in Portfolio

65% 62%

Growth of $10,000
IIII Value of Fund ($000)
— Value of Index ($000) S&P 500
▼ Manager Change
▽ Partial Manager Change
► Mgr Unknown After
◄ Mgr Unknown Before

Performance Quartile (Within Objective)

	1983	1984	1985	1986	1987	1988	1989	1990	1991	1992	1993	1994	History
											11.41	10.53	NAV
	---	---	---	---	---	---	---	---	---	---	11.86 *	-5.53	Total Return %
	---	---	---	---	---	---	---	---	---	---	6.91 *	-6.84	+/- S&P 500
	---	---	---	---	---	---	---	---	---	---	---	-2.61	+/- LB Aggregate
											0.00	0.00	Income Return %
											11.86	-5.53	Capital Return %
	---	---	---	---	---	---	---	---	---	---	---	68	Total Rtn % Rank All
											---	79	Total Rtn % Rank Obj
											0.00	0.00	Income $
											0.00	0.25	Capital Gains $
	---	---	---	---	---	---	---	---	---	---	---	2.22	Expense Ratio %
	---	---	---	---	---	---	---	---	---	---	---	-0.77	Income Ratio %
	---	---	---	---	---	---	---	---	---	---	---	---	Turnover Rate %
	---	---	---	---	---	---	---	---	---	---	161.4	485.7	Net Assets ($mil)

Performance 12-31-94

	1st Qtr	2nd Qtr	3rd Qtr	4th Qtr	Total
1987	---	---	---	---	---
1988	---	---	---	---	---
1989	---	---	---	---	---
1990	---	---	---	---	---
1991	---	---	---	---	---
1992	---	---	---	---	---
1993	---	---	-4.41	17.03	11.86 *
1994	8.59	-4.36	-4.64	-4.61	-5.53

Bear Market Performance

Decile Rank (5-year period)

Worst |——————————————————| Best

	Worst 3 Mo Period 1985-89	Worst 3 Mo Period 1990-94
Robertson Stephens Contrarian	---	---
+/- S&P 500	---	---
+/- Best Fit Index :	---	---

Trailing Returns

	Total Return %	+/- S&P 500	+/- LB Aggregate	% Rank All	% Rank Obj	Growth of $10,000
3 Mo	-4.61	-4.59	-4.98	90	93	9,539
6 Mo	-9.03	-13.90	-10.03	99	100	9,097
1 Yr	-5.53	-6.84	-2.61	68	79	9,447
3 Yr Avg	---	---	---	---	---	---
5 Yr Avg	---	---	---	---	---	---
10 Yr Avg	---	---	---	---	---	---
15 Yr Avg	---	---	---	---	---	---

Operations

Address and Telephone	555 California Street Suite 2600 San Francisco, CA 94104 800-766-3863 / 415-781-9700	
Advisor	Robertson Stephens Investment	
Subadvisor	None	
Distributor	Robertson Stephens	
States Available	All except AK,MO,OH,WI	
Report Grade	B	
Income Distrib	Paid Annually	
* Date of Inception	06-30-93	
Fiscal Year End	March	

Risk Analysis

Time Period	Load-Adj Return %	Risk % Rank [1] All	Obj	Morningstar [2] Return	Morningstar Risk	Morningstar Risk-Adj Rating
1 Yr	-5.53	---	---	---	---	---
3 Yr	---	---	---	---	---	---
5 Yr	---	---	---	---	---	---
10 Yr	---	---	---	---	---	---

Average Historical Rating ---

[1] 1 = low, 100 = high   [2] 1.00 = Hybrid Avg   [3] 1.00 = 90-day T-bill return

Other Measures

			Standard S&P 500	Best Fit
Standard Deviation	---	Alpha	---	---
Mean	---	Beta	---	---
Sharpe Ratio	---	R-Squared	---	---

Investment Style

Stocks	Port Avg	Rel S&P 500	Style
Price/Earnings Ratio	33.5	1.81	V B G
Price/Book Ratio	2.3	0.68	
5 Yr Earnings Gr %	11.0#	1.98	
Med Mkt Cap ($mil)	563	0.04	

figure is based on 50% or less of stocks

Bonds		
Avg Effective Duration	NMF	
Avg Effective Maturity	---	
Avg Credit Quality	---	Not Available
Avg Weighted Coupon	6.61%	

Diversification Value for Portfolio Types

Large Cap:	Small Cap:	Bond:	Balanced:	Diversified:

Expenses & Fees

Sales Fees	0.00% front
	0.00% deferred
	0.75% 12b-1
Management Fee	1.50% flat fee
3-,5-,10-yr Expense Projections	$75, $128, $274
Annual Brokerage Cost	

Min Initial Purchase $5000 (Addt'l: $100)
Min IRA Purchase $1000 (Addt'l: $1)
Min Auto Invest Plan N/A

Portfolio 09-30-94

Share Chg (03-94)000	Amount 000	Total Stocks: 52 Total Fixed-Income: 2	Date of Maturity	Value $000	% Net Assets
728	1828	Cambior		28631	4.95
163	1259	Santa Fe Pacific		28489	4.92
1005	1005	Ashanti Goldfields		19899	3.44
795	1421	Golden Star Resources		19079	3.30
285	721	Freeport-McMoRan Cop/Gold A		18032	3.12
381	381	Anadarko Petroleum		17045	2.94
364	364	Newmont Mining		16367	2.83
765	2053	Dundee Bancorp Cl B		16266	2.81
191	438	MAXXAM		14016	2.42
100	987	Rayrock Yellowknife		12333	2.13
-53	561	Freeport-McMoRan		10871	1.88
243	243	Louisiana Land & Exploration		10644	1.84
220	571	Conwest Exploration Cl A		10641	1.84
610	610	American Buildings		10446	1.80
562	562	Santa Fe Pacific Gold		9761	1.69
-91	300	Alumax		9638	1.67
34	268	Avatar		9634	1.66
343	535	Intertape Polymer Group		8495	1.47
240	240	Phillips Petroleum		8234	1.42
806	2184	Vengold		7331	1.27

Index Allocation

	% of Stocks
S&P 500	25.8
S&P MidCap 400	16.9
U.S. Small Cap	20.3
Foreign	37.1

Composition % 12-31-94

Cash	4.4	Preferreds	0.2
Stocks	66.1	Convertibles	0.8
Bonds	0.0	Other	28.5

Tax Analysis

	Tax-Adj Historical Return %	% Pretax Return
3 Yr Avg	---	---
5 Yr Avg	---	---
10 Yr Avg	---	---

Potential Capital Gain Exposure (% of assets) -12%

Most Similar Funds in MF500

Fund lacks three-year record

Bond Credit Analysis --/--/--

% of Bonds			
US Govt	0	BB	0
AAA	0	B	0
AA	0	Below B	0
A	0	NR/NA	0
BBB	0		

Stock Sector Weightings

	% of Stocks	Relative S&P 500
Utilities	2.5	0.21
Energy	21.1	2.08
Financials	17.6	1.66
Industrial Cyclicals	44.8	2.73
Consumer Durables	2.2	0.36
Consumer Staples	0.0	0.00
Services	11.6	1.43
Retail	0.2	0.03
Health	0.0	0.00
Technology	0.0	0.00

Robertson Stephens Value + Grth

	Ticker	Load	NAV	Yield	SEC Yield	Assets	Objective
	RSVPX	None	15.88	0.0%	N/A	132.5	Small Company

Robertson Stephens Value + Growth Fund seeks capital appreciation.

The fund typically invests at least 65% of its assets in equity securities, focusing on common stocks of small companies with favorable growth prospects and modest valuations. Market capitalizations of these companies range from less than $250 million to approximately $1 billion. The fund may also purchase preferred stocks, convertibles, and American Depositary Receipts. Up to 35% of the fund's assets may be invested in U.S. government obligations.

Prior to Oct. 14, 1994, the fund was named Robertson Stephens Value Plus Fund.

Manager's Investment Style

Management targets industries that will benefit from long-term trends (such as changing consumer needs), while also showing short-term gains potential. In addition, management looks for growth at reasonable prices; when holdings hit prices of 20 times projected next-year earnings, it sells. The fund's turnover rate should remain virile, as management works to capitalize on short-term price movement. Sector overweightings in health and technology, however, are likely to continue for the time being.

Fund Manager(s)

Ronald E. Elijah, since 05-92. Birthdate: 11-52.
MA, Humboldt State U. 1976   MBA, Golden Gate U. 1980

Manager Experience

	Dates Managed	Invest Obj	Std Dev	+/- Index
Not available.				

Historical Profile

Return ---
Risk ---
Rating ---
Not Rated

Investment Style History
Equity
Average % Stocks Held in Portfolio

61% 86% 97%

Growth of $10,000

|||| Value of Fund ($000)
— Value of Index ($000) S&P 500
▼ Manager Change
▽ Partial Manager Change
► Mgr Unknown After
◄ Mgr Unknown Before

Performance Quartile (Within Objective)

	1983	1984	1985	1986	1987	1988	1989	1990	1991	1992	1993	1994	History
	---	---	---	---	---	---	---	---	---	11.01	13.06	15.88	NAV
	---	---	---	---	---	---	---	---	---	10.04 *	18.62	23.12	Total Return %
	---	---	---	---	---	---	---	---	---	3.14 *	8.56	21.80	+/- S&P 500
	---	---	---	---	---	---	---	---	---	---	4.08	25.77	+/- Wilshire 4500
	---	---	---	---	---	---	---	---	---	0.60	0.00	0.00	Income Return %
	---	---	---	---	---	---	---	---	---	9.44	18.62	23.12	Capital Return %
	---	---	---	---	---	---	---	---	---	---	19	1	Total Rtn % Rank All
	---	---	---	---	---	---	---	---	---	---	41	1	Total Rtn % Rank Obj
	---	---	---	---	---	---	---	---	---	0.06	0.00	0.00	Income $
	---	---	---	---	---	---	---	---	---	0.00	0.00	0.20	Capital Gains $
	---	---	---	---	---	---	---	---	---	---	1.33	1.55	Expense Ratio %
	---	---	---	---	---	---	---	---	---	---	1.26	-0.51	Income Ratio %
	---	---	---	---	---	---	---	---	---	---	---	250	Turnover Rate %
	---	---	---	---	---	---	---	---	---	9.0	23.1	132.5	Net Assets ($mil)

Performance 12-31-94

	1st Qtr	2nd Qtr	3rd Qtr	4th Qtr	Total
1987	---	---	---	---	---
1988	---	---	---	---	---
1989	---	---	---	---	---
1990	---	---	---	---	---
1991	---	---	---	---	---
1992	---	---	3.04	8.96	10.04 *
1993	8.45	0.08	7.53	1.63	18.62
1994	3.75	-4.35	17.21	5.85	23.12

Bear Market Performance

Decile Rank (5-year period)

Worst | Best

	Worst 3 Mo Period 1985-89	Worst 3 Mo Period 1990-94
Robertson Stephens Value + Gr	---	---
+/- S&P 500	---	---
+/- Best Fit Index :	---	---

Trailing Returns

	Total Return %	+/- S&P 500	+/- Wil 4500	% Rank All	Rank Obj	Growth of $10,000
3 Mo	5.85	5.87	8.36	1	1	10,585
6 Mo	24.07	19.21	19.88	1	5	12,407
1 Yr	23.12	21.80	25.77	1	1	12,312
3 Yr Avg	---	---	---	---	---	---
5 Yr Avg	---	---	---	---	---	---
10 Yr Avg	---	---	---	---	---	---
15 Yr Avg	---	---	---	---	---	---

Operations

Address and Telephone	555 California Street Suite 2600 San Francisco, CA 94104 800-766-3863 / 415-781-9700
Advisor	Robertson Stephens Investment
Subadvisor	None
Distributor	Robertson Stephens
States Available	All except AK,MO,OH,WI
Report Grade	B
Income Distrib	Paid Annually
* Date of Inception	05-12-92
Fiscal Year End	September

Risk Analysis

Time Period	Load-Adj Return %	Risk % Rank All	Obj	Morningstar Return	Morningstar Risk	Morningstar Risk-Adj Rating
1 Yr	23.12	---	---	---	---	---
3 Yr	---	---	---	---	---	---
5 Yr	---	---	---	---	---	---
10 Yr	---	---	---	---	---	---

Average Historical Rating ---

[1] 1 = low, 100 = high   [2] 1.00 = Equity Avg   [3] 1.00 = 90-day T-bill return

Other Measures

			Standard S&P 500	Best Fit
Standard Deviation	---	Alpha	---	---
Mean	---	Beta	---	---
Sharpe Ratio	---	R-Squared	---	---

Investment Style

	Stock Portfolio Avg	Relative S&P 500
Price/Earnings Ratio	21.5	1.16
Price/Book Ratio	4.7	1.37
5 Yr Earnings Gr %	32.7	5.89
Return on Assets %	15.5	2.07
Debt % Total Cap	18.3	0.65
Med Mkt Cap ($mil)	1700	0.13

Style: Value Blend Growth — Size Large/Med/Small

Diversification Value for Portfolio Types

Large Cap: Small Cap: Bond: Balanced: Diversified:

Portfolio 09-30-94

Total Stocks: 47
Total Fixed-Income: 0

Share Chg (03-94) 000	Amount 000		Value $000	% Net Assets
70	70	3Com	2616	5.11
75	75	Compaq Computer	2447	4.77
40	40	Electroglas	1990	3.88
40	40	Cabletron Systems	1905	3.72
38	58	Atmel	1804	3.52
20	35	US Healthcare	1630	3.18
-45	35	Vencor	1593	3.11
30	30	United HealthCare	1590	3.10
45	45	Micron Technology	1553	3.03
-25	20	PacifiCare Health Sys Cl B	1500	2.93
-40	40	LSI Logic	1495	2.92
24	24	Intel	1476	2.88
30	30	Novellus Systems	1418	2.77
15	25	Microsoft	1403	2.74
30	30	Applied Materials	1403	2.74
37	37	Tencor Instruments	1378	2.69
75	75	Cadence Design Systems	1359	2.65
35	35	IMRS	1313	2.56
-5	35	Integrated Health Services	1243	2.42
45	45	cisco Systems	1232	2.40
30	30	Lam Research	1208	2.36
47	47	Marshall Industries	1191	2.32
40	40	Charles Schwab	1185	2.31
30	30	Best Buy	1174	2.29
40	40	Informix	1110	2.17

Composition % 12-31-94

Cash	1.9	Preferreds	0.0
Stocks	98.1	Convertibles	0.0
Bonds	0.0	Other	0.0

Tax Analysis

	Tax-Adj Historical Return %	% Pretax Return
3 Yr Avg	---	---
5 Yr Avg	---	---
10 Yr Avg	---	---

Potential Capital Gain Exposure (% of assets)   12%

Most Similar Funds in MF500

Fund lacks three-year record

Index Allocation

	% of Stocks
S&P 500	28.7
S&P MidCap 400	24.9
U.S. Small Cap	46.4
Foreign	0.0

Sector Weightings

	% of Stocks	Relative S&P 500
Utilities	0.0	0.00
Energy	0.0	0.00
Financials	6.5	0.61
Industrial Cyclicals	0.0	0.00
Consumer Durables	0.0	0.00
Consumer Staples	0.0	0.00
Services	0.3	0.03
Retail	5.3	0.92
Health	20.2	2.33
Technology	67.7	7.39

Expenses & Fees

Min Initial Purchase	$5000 (Addt'l: $100)
Min IRA Purchase	$1000 (Addt'l: $1)
Min Auto Invest Plan	N/A

Sales Fees: 0.00% front / 0.00% deferred / 0.00% 12b-1
Management Fee: 1.25% flat fee
3-,5-,10-yr Expense Projections: $55, $95, $206
Annual Brokerage Cost: 1.18%

MORNINGSTAR 1995 Mutual Fund 500

Royce Equity-Income

	Ticker	Load	NAV	Yield	SEC Yield	Assets	Objective
	RYEQX	None	5.12	3.5%	N/A	77.1	Equity-Inc.

Royce Fund Equity-Income Series seeks income. Potential for capital appreciation is considered.

The fund normally invests at least 90% of its assets in dividend-paying common stocks and securities convertible into common stocks. It primarily invests in securities of small and medium-size companies with market capitalizations ranging from $15 million to $1 billion. These securities are selected on a value basis, with primary emphasis on balance-sheet and cash-flow analysis.

On June 28, 1991, Royce Fund Total Return and Royce Fund Income merged into this fund.

Manager's Investment Style

The fund is unique among its objective, choosing to invest in small-cap offerings in spite of the objective's usual preference for mid- to large-cap companies. Management screens for high payouts from small, undiscovered companies with strong fundamentals. Manager Charles Royce's focus on this type of equity has generally led to an underweighting in utilities, which are generally popular equity-income stocks. He also holds convertible bonds for their yield and stability.

Fund Manager(s)

Charles M. Royce et al. Birthdate: 09-39 BA, Brown U. 1961 MBA, Columbia U. 1963

Manager Experience

	Dates Managed	Invest Obj	Std Dev	+/- Index
Charles M. Royce				
Pennsylvania Mutual	05/73 - 12/94	SC	17.74	4.22
Royce Value	12/82 - 12/94	SC	12.51	-2.12

Historical Profile

Return	Average
Risk	Low
Rating	★★★
	Neutral

Investment Style History
Equity

Average % Stocks Held in Portfolio

Growth of $10,000

||| Value of Fund ($000)
— Value of Index ($000) Russ 2000
▼ Manager Change
▽ Partial Manager Change
► Mgr Unknown After
◄ Mgr Unknown Before

Performance Quartile (Within Objective)

	1983	1984	1985	1986	1987	1988	1989	1990	1991	1992	1993	1994	History
								71%	69%	63%	76%		
	---	---	---	---	---	---	---	4.03	4.93	5.49	5.58	5.12	NAV
	---	---	---	---	---	---	---	-15.35 *	30.30	19.39	13.07	-3.26	Total Return %
	---	---	---	---	---	---	---	-10.54 *	-0.18	11.77	3.01	-4.57	+/- S&P 500
	---	---	---	---	---	---	---	---	-3.90	10.42	1.78	-3.19	+/- Wilshire 5000
	---	---	---	---	---	---	---	4.05	5.42	4.55	3.78	3.30	Income Return %
	---	---	---	---	---	---	---	-19.40	24.88	14.84	9.29	-6.56	Capital Return %
	---	---	---	---	---	---	---		26	5	40	46	Total Rtn % Rank All
	---	---	---	---	---	---	---		22	2	43	63	Total Rtn % Rank Obj
	---	---	---	---	---	---	---	0.22	0.22	0.22	0.21	0.18	Income $
	---	---	---	---	---	---	---	0.00	0.09	0.16	0.41	0.10	Capital Gains $
	---	---	---	---	---	---	---	1.00	0.99	0.99	1.00	1.28	Expense Ratio %
	---	---	---	---	---	---	---	4.74	4.58	4.31	3.79	3.12	Income Ratio %
	---	---	---	---	---	---	---		28	72	59	100	---	Turnover Rate %
	---	---	---	---	---	---	---	19.5	41.1	54.1	84.7	77.1	Net Assets ($mil)

Performance 12-31-94

	1st Qtr	2nd Qtr	3rd Qtr	4th Qtr	Total
1987	---	---	---	---	---
1988	---	---	---	---	---
1989	---	---	---	---	---
1990	-0.80	0.41	-16.06	1.24	-15.35
1991	20.37	0.83	3.55	3.67	30.30
1992	7.91	-0.95	4.46	6.93	19.39
1993	7.83	0.35	1.72	2.72	13.07
1994	-1.45	-1.65	2.63	-2.75	-3.26

Bear Market Performance

Decile Rank (5-year period)

Worst — Best

	Worst 3 Mo Period 1985-89	Worst 3 Mo Period 1990-94
Royce Equity-Income	---	-18.66
+/- S&P 500	---	-4.82
+/- Best Fit Index : Russ 2000	---	7.23

Trailing Returns

	Total Return %	+/- S&P 500	+/- Wil 5000	% Rank All	% Rank Obj	Growth of $10,000
3 Mo	-2.75	-2.73	-1.98	80	55	9,725
6 Mo	-0.19	-5.05	-4.81	60	80	9,981
1 Yr	-3.26	-4.57	-3.19	46	63	9,674
3 Yr Avg	9.30	3.04	2.69	16	17	13,059
5 Yr Avg	7.57	-1.12	-1.25	39	39	14,404
10 Yr Avg	---	---	---	---	---	---
15 Yr Avg	---	---	---	---	---	---

Operations

Address and Telephone	1414 Avenue of the Americas New York, NY 10019 800-221-4268 / 212-355-7311	Min Initial Purchase	$2000 (Addt'l: $50)
		Min IRA Purchase	$500 (Addt'l: $50)
		Min Auto Invest Plan	$500 (Systematic Inv: $50)
Advisor	Quest Advisory		
Subadvisor	None	**Expenses & Fees**	
Distributor	Quest Distributors	Sales Fees	0.00% front
States Available	All plus GU,PR,VI		0.00% deferred
Report Grade	A-		0.00% 12b-1
Income Distrib	Paid Quarterly	Management Fee	1.00% flat fee
* Date of Inception	01-02-90	3-,5-,10-yr Expense Projections	$32, $55, $122
Fiscal Year End	December	Annual Brokerage Cost	0.33%

Risk Analysis

Time Period	Load-Adj Return %	Risk % Rank [1] All	Obj	Morningstar [2] Return	Risk	Morningstar Risk-Adj Rating
1 Yr	-4.26					
3 Yr	9.30	22	1	1.75 [3]	0.38	★★★★
5 Yr	7.57	54	13	0.70 [3]	0.59	★★★
10 Yr	---					
Average Historical Rating (25 months)				4.0 ★s		

[1] 1 = low, 100 = high   [2] 1.00 = Equity Avg   [3] 1.00 = 90-day T-bill return

Other Measures

			Standard S&P 500	Best Fit Russ 2000
Standard Deviation	5.83	Alpha	4.4	2.4
Mean	9.10	Beta	0.42	0.39
Sharpe Ratio	0.96	R-Squared	32	62

Investment Style

	Stock Portfolio Avg	Relative S&P 500
Price/Earnings Ratio	16.7	0.90
Price/Book Ratio	1.7	0.50
5 Yr Earnings Gr %	-0.8	-0.15
Return on Assets %	5.7	0.77
Debt % Total Cap	19.6	0.69
Med Mkt Cap ($mil)	383	0.03

Style Value Blend Growth / Size Large Med Small

Diversification Value for Portfolio Types

| Large Cap: Medium | Small Cap: Low | Bond: High | Balanced: Medium | Diversified: Medium |

Portfolio 09-30-94

Total Stocks: 101
Total Fixed-Income: 28

Share Chg (06-94) 000	Amount 000		Value $000	% Net Assets
0	42	Argonaut Group	1235	1.40
9	45	Manitowoc	1218	1.38
0	22	US Trust	1171	1.33
0	31	CB Bancshares	1096	1.24
	1422	Waterhouse Investors Svc Cv 6%	1077	1.22
19	19	Mellon Bank	1059	1.20
0	76	Lawter International	988	1.12
	37	Cliffs Drilling Cv Pfd $2.3125	987	1.12
	1000	Waban Cv 6.5%	980	1.11
0	50	Standard Register	980	1.11
0	23	National Presto Industries	978	1.11
0	16	NCH	969	1.10
12	56	Flowers Industries	959	1.09
-17	42	Scitex	952	1.08
4	40	Kimball International Cl B	949	1.07
52	83	Family Dollar Stores	938	1.06
28	28	SLMA	930	1.05
	1091	Seagate Technology Cv 6.75%	927	1.05
	28	Glendale Fed Bk E Cv Pfd 8.75%	914	1.03
0	50	Guaranty National	906	1.03
0	53	PH Glatfelter	906	1.03
0	41	Mercantile Bankshares (MD)	900	1.02
0	48	Lance	895	1.01
0	1	Central Steel & Wire	894	1.01
0	26	Longs Drug Stores	890	1.01

Composition % 12-31-94

Cash	3.0	Preferreds	4.5
Stocks	74.0	Convertibles	18.5
Bonds	0.0	Other	0.0

Tax Analysis

	Tax-Adj Historical Return %	% Pretax Return
3 Yr Avg	6.72	70.4
5 Yr Avg	5.28	66.6
10 Yr Avg	---	---
Potential Capital Gain Exposure (% of assets)		-5%

Most Similar Funds in MF500

Pennsylvania Mutual	Strong Fit
Royce Value	Fair Fit
Putnam Convert Inc Grth A	Fair Fit

Index Allocation

	% of Stocks
S&P 500	13.9
S&P MidCap 400	27.5
U.S. Small Cap	56.5
Foreign	2.1

Sector Weightings

	% of Stocks	Relative S&P 500
Utilities	2.8	0.23
Energy	3.3	0.32
Financials	25.1	2.37
Industrial Cyclicals	21.5	1.31
Consumer Durables	15.3	2.46
Consumer Staples	7.5	0.60
Services	12.0	1.48
Retail	7.4	1.27
Health	1.1	0.13
Technology	4.1	0.44

Royce Premier

		Ticker	Load	NAV	Yield	SEC Yield	Assets	Objective
		RYPRX	None	6.48	0.8%	N/A	202.4	Small Company

Royce Fund Premier Series seeks long-term growth; current income is secondary.

The fund normally invests at least 80% of its assets in common stocks and convertibles; at least 65% of the securities may be income producing and/or issued by companies with stock-market capitalizations under $1 billion. The balance of assets may be invested in securities with higher stock-market capitalizations, non-dividend-paying common or preferred stock, and nonconvertible bonds. Up to 5% of assets may be invested in high-yield bonds. The portfolio usually contains a limited number of issues.

Historical Profile

Return	Above Average
Risk	Low
Rating	★★★★★ Highest

Investment Style History
Equity
Average % Stocks Held in Portfolio

66%	73%	79%

Growth of $10,000

- |||| Value of Fund ($000)
- — Value of Index ($000) SPMid400
- ▼ Manager Change
- ▽ Partial Manager Change
- ► Mgr Unknown After
- ◄ Mgr Unknown Before

Performance Quartile (Within Objective)

Manager's Investment Style

Management follows the typical Royce value-oriented strategy by looking for firms selling below their intrinsic value. Unlike other Royce funds, however, management avoids cheap turnaround plays or undervalued sector bets with this fund; instead, it sticks strictly to high-quality firms with strong growth records and with earnings that haven't been recognized by the market. The portfolio is limited to 50 to 60 names--as such, it's a more-aggressive play than more-diversified Royce funds.

Fund Manager(s)

Charles M. Royce et al. Birthdate: 09-39 BA, Brown U. 1961 MBA, Columbia U. 1963

Manager Experience	Dates Managed	Invest Obj	Std Dev	+/- Index
Charles M. Royce				
Pennsylvania Mutual	05/73 - 12/94	SC	17.74	4.22
Royce Value	12/82 - 12/94	SC	12.51	-2.12

	1983	1984	1985	1986	1987	1988	1989	1990	1991	1992	1993	1994	History
NAV	---	---	---	---	---	---	---	---	5.00	5.52	6.41	6.48	NAV
Total Return %	---	---	---	---	---	---	---	---	---	15.80	19.02	3.28	Total Return %
+/- S&P 500	---	---	---	---	---	---	---	---	---	8.18	8.97	1.96	+/- S&P 500
+/- Wilshire 4500	---	---	---	---	---	---	---	---	---	4.04	4.49	5.93	+/- Wilshire 4500
Income Return %	---	---	---	---	---	---	---	---	---	0.37	0.32	0.77	Income Return %
Capital Return %	---	---	---	---	---	---	---	---	---	15.43	18.70	2.50	Capital Return %
Total Rtn % Rank All	---	---	---	---	---	---	---	---	---	9	19	7	Total Rtn % Rank All
Total Rtn % Rank Obj	---	---	---	---	---	---	---	---	---	40	36	22	Total Rtn % Rank Obj
Income $	---	---	---	---	---	---	---	0.00	0.00	0.02	0.02	0.05	Income $
Capital Gains $	---	---	---	---	---	---	---	0.00	0.00	0.25	0.14	0.09	Capital Gains $
Expense Ratio %	---	---	---	---	---	---	---	---	---	1.77	1.50	1.46	Expense Ratio %
Income Ratio %	---	---	---	---	---	---	---	---	---	0.53	0.68	0.88	Income Ratio %
Turnover Rate %	---	---	---	---	---	---	---	---	---	116	85	---	Turnover Rate %
Net Assets ($mil)	---	---	---	---	---	---	---	---	---	2.3	36.0	202.4	Net Assets ($mil)

Performance 12-31-94

	1st Qtr	2nd Qtr	3rd Qtr	4th Qtr	Total
1987	---	---	---	---	---
1988	---	---	---	---	---
1989	---	---	---	---	---
1990	---	---	---	---	---
1991	---	---	---	---	---
1992	1.60	-0.20	2.96	10.92	15.80
1993	4.71	3.98	2.50	6.66	19.02
1994	0.78	-1.08	3.76	-0.15	3.28

Bear Market Performance

Decile Rank (5-year period)

Worst   Best

	Worst 3 Mo Period 1985-89	Worst 3 Mo Period 1990-94
Royce Premier	---	---
+/- S&P 500	---	---
+/- Best Fit Index :	---	---

Trailing Returns

	Total Return %	+/- S&P 500	+/- Wil 4500	% Rank All	% Rank Obj	Growth of $10,000
3 Mo	-0.15	-0.13	2.35	26	39	9,985
6 Mo	3.60	-1.26	-0.59	17	67	10,360
1 Yr	3.28	1.96	5.93	7	22	10,328
3 Yr Avg	12.49	6.22	4.88	7	27	14,234
5 Yr Avg	---	---	---	---	---	---
10 Yr Avg	---	---	---	---	---	---
15 Yr Avg	---	---	---	---	---	---

Operations

Address and Telephone	1414 Avenue of the Americas New York, NY 10019 800-221-4268 / 212-355-7311
Advisor	Quest Advisory
Subadvisor	None
Distributor	Quest Distributors
States Available	All
Report Grade	A-
Income Distrib	Paid Annually
* Date of Inception	12-31-91
Fiscal Year End	December

Risk Analysis

Time Period	Load-Adj Return %	Risk % Rank [1] All	Obj	Morningstar [2] Return	Morningstar Risk	Morningstar Risk-Adj Rating
1 Yr	2.24					
3 Yr	12.49	6	1	2.80 [3]	0.25	★★★★★
5 Yr	---	---	---	---	---	---
10 Yr	---	---	---	---	---	---

Average Historical Rating (1 month)   5.0 ★s

[1] 1 = low, 100 = high   [2] 1.00 = Equity Avg   [3] 1.00 = 90-day T-bill return

Other Measures

				Standard S&P 500	Best Fit SPMid400
Standard Deviation	5.12	Alpha		7.4	7.0
Mean	11.96	Beta		0.43	0.43
Sharpe Ratio	1.65	R-Squared		43	66

Investment Style

	Stock Portfolio Avg	Relative S&P 500
Price/Earnings Ratio	19.7	1.06
Price/Book Ratio	2.0	0.58
5 Yr Earnings Gr %	9.7	1.75
Return on Assets %	7.9	1.05
Debt % Total Cap	18.9	0.67
Med Mkt Cap ($mil)	450	0.03

Style
Value Blend Growth
Size Large Med Small

Diversification Value for Portfolio Types

Large Cap: Medium	Small Cap: Low	Bond: High	Balanced: Low	Diversified: Medium

Expenses & Fees

Sales Fees	0.00% front
	0.00% deferred
	0.00% 12b-1
Management Fee	1.00% flat fee
3-,5-,10-yr Expense Projections	$47, $82, $179
Annual Brokerage Cost	0.49%

Portfolio 09-30-94

Share Chg (06-94) 000	Amount 000	Total Stocks: 65 Total Fixed-Income: 0	Value $000	% Net Assets
30	334	Claire's Stores	3673	2.02
-28	162	Scitex	3654	2.01
65	368	Dress Barn	3629	1.99
0	54	NCH	3322	1.82
25	166	Standard Register	3273	1.80
2	28	Wesco Financial	3271	1.80
5	141	EW Blanch Holdings	3225	1.77
15	195	Consolidated Stores	3193	1.75
19	86	WR Berkley	3089	1.70
146	146	Comdisco	3023	1.66
1	36	Woodward Governor	3022	1.66
-5	82	Saint Jude Medical	2922	1.60
19	175	Mikasa	2871	1.58
5	79	Leucadia National	2834	1.56
90	90	Orion Capital	2706	1.49
35	94	Sturm Ruger	2635	1.45
0	60	Louisiana Land & Exploration	2625	1.44
3	16	Grey Advertising	2599	1.43
13	78	Blessings	2587	1.42
3	82	Fab Industries	2554	1.40
-2	68	Franklin Resources	2527	1.39
30	131	Camco International	2505	1.38
5	117	CalMat	2472	1.36
-67	77	Anthem Electronics	2467	1.35
19	186	Sotheby's Holdings Cl A	2397	1.32

Composition % 12-31-94

Cash	17.3	Preferreds	0.0
Stocks	82.7	Convertibles	0.0
Bonds	0.0	Other	0.0

Tax Analysis

	Tax-Adj Historical Return %	% Pretax Return
3 Yr Avg	11.47	91.0
5 Yr Avg	---	---
10 Yr Avg	---	---
Potential Capital Gain Exposure (% of assets)		1%

Most Similar Funds in MF500

Royce Value	Weak Fit
Pennsylvania Mutual	Weak Fit
MainStay Convertible B	Weak Fit

Index Allocation

	% of Stocks
S&P 500	9.4
S&P MidCap 400	27.2
U.S. Small Cap	59.6
Foreign	3.8

Sector Weightings

	% of Stocks	Relative S&P 500
Utilities	0.0	0.00
Energy	5.2	0.51
Financials	17.0	1.61
Industrial Cyclicals	15.1	0.92
Consumer Durables	10.5	1.69
Consumer Staples	0.0	0.00
Services	19.5	2.40
Retail	12.3	2.12
Health	6.5	0.75
Technology	14.0	1.53

Min Initial Purchase / etc.

Min Initial Purchase	$2000 (Addt'l: $50)
Min IRA Purchase	$500 (Addt'l: $50)
Min Auto Invest Plan	$500 (Systematic Inv: $50)

MORNINGSTAR   1995 Mutual Fund 500

Royce Value

	Ticker	NAV	Mkt Price	Prem/Disc	Yield	Objective
	RVT	$12.34	$11.00	-10.9%	0.1%	Domestic Eq

Royce Value Trust seeks long-term capital appreciation. Current income is secondary.

The fund invests primarily in equities, including convertibles, that have market capitalizations ranging from $100 million to $1 billion. The advisor uses a value approach in its selection, emphasizing balance-sheet and cash-flow analysis in the belief that securities of small- and medium-sized companies may sell at a discount to their "business worth."

The fund has held five rights offerings: one in the third quarter of 1989 that raised $4.36 million; one in the third quarter of 1990 that raised $4.84 million; one in the third quarter of 1991 that raised $6.52 million; one in the third quarter of 1992 that raised $8.4 million; and one in the third quarter of 1993 that raised $16.95 million.

As of March 21, 1994, Yale University owned 1.57 million, about 8%, of the fund's outstanding shares.

The fund is leveraged with 5.75%-coupon Investment Company Convertible Notes (ICONS) due June 30, 2004.

Manager's Investment Style

Manager Chuck Royce and his team take a value-oriented, bottom-up approach to the small-cap market. As they do with many of their open-end offerings, the group looks for firms selling below their private worth by scouring balance sheets and practicing cash-flow analysis. The fund may become racier than its open-end siblings, though, because it became leveraged in mid-1994.

Fund Manager(s)

Charles M. Royce et al. Since 11-86. BA'61 Brown U.; MBA'63 Columbia U.

Historical Profile

Return	Average
Risk	Low
Rating	★★★★ Above Average

| | 7.8 | 10.8 | -9.7 | -8.2 | -5.3 | 1.4 | 0.4 | 0.7 | -3.7 | Highest Prem/Disc |
| | 6.4 | -15.6 | -15.8 | -13.9 | -12.3 | -12.2 | -9.7 | -7.1 | -15.5 | Lowest Prem/Disc |

Growth of $10,000
— at NAV ($000)
— at Market Price ($000)

Premium Discount %

	1983	1984	1985	1986	1987	1988	1989	1990	1991	1992	1993	1994	History
	---	---	---	9.28	7.98	9.25	10.35	8.58	11.23	12.50	13.47	12.34	NAV
	---	---	---	-0.22*	-7.55	22.77	18.27	-13.79	38.58	19.34	17.48	0.62	NAV Total Return %
	---	---	---	1.89*	-12.81	6.16	-13.42	-10.67	8.10	11.72	7.42	-0.69	+/- S&P 500
	---	---	---	---	-4.47	0.38	0.15	5.60	-10.42	-9.89	3.36	2.59	+/- Wil Small Value
	---	---	---	0.00*	4.69	0.71	1.94	1.93	1.78	1.22	0.68	0.09	Income Return %
	---	---	---	-0.22*	-12.25	22.06	16.33	-15.72	36.80	18.12	16.79	0.53	Capital Return %
	---	---	---		88	14	26	83	18	8	43	12	Total Rtn % Rank All
	---	---	---		81	15	70	75	41	15	20	35	Total Rtn % Rank Obj
	---	---	---	-1.25*	-26.52	27.49	24.20	-10.35	35.47	26.59	14.52	-6.16	Market Total Rtn %
	---	---	---		-9.1	-12.2	-11.8	-9.7	-6.3	-4.9	-2.4	-8.1	Avg Prem/Disc %
	---	---	---	0.00	0.36	0.06	0.17	0.17	0.17	0.15	0.09	0.01	Income $
	---	---	---	0.00	0.16	0.45	0.35	0.15	0.44	0.75	1.06	1.04	Capital Gains $
	---	---	---	1.79	0.40	1.09	0.95	0.94	0.79	0.81	1.33	1.52	Expense Ratio %
	---	---	---	3.45	2.92	1.42	1.48	1.78	1.52	1.31	0.74	0.44	Income Ratio %
	---	---	---	13	66	29	36	28	34	40	33	---	Turnover Rate %
	---	---	---	100.4	90.3	107.3	140.8	118.3	166.5	202.5	246.6	269.0	Net Assets ($mil)
	---	---	---	0.0	0.0	0.0	0.0	0.0	0.0	0.0	0.0	40.0	Pfd/Debt Leverage ($mil)

Manager Experience

	Dates Managed	Invest Obj	Std Dev	+/- Index
Charles M. Royce				
Pennsylvania Mutual	05/73 - 12/94	SC	17.74	4.22
Royce Value	12/82 - 12/94	SC	12.51	-2.12

NAV Performance % 12-30-94

	1st Qtr	2nd Qtr	3rd Qtr	4th Qtr	Total
1987	9.38	1.18	3.80	-19.52	-7.55
1988	14.91	4.25	2.82	-0.34	22.77
1989	7.14	7.77	4.59	-2.06	18.27
1990	-0.87	4.19	-18.43	2.33	-13.79
1991	22.96	1.42	4.49	6.35	38.58
1992	8.37	-2.79	2.47	10.56	19.34
1993	6.56	1.05	4.93	3.97	17.48
1994	-1.19	-1.13	4.46	-1.40	0.62

Bear Market Performance

Decile Rank (5-year period)

Worst ─────────────── Best

	Worst 3 Mo Period 1985-89	Worst 3 Mo Period 1990-94
Royce Value	---	-20.42
+/- S&P 500	---	-6.58

Trailing Returns

	NAV Total Return %	+/- S&P 500	+/- Wil Sm Value	% Rank All	Obj	Mkt Total Return %
3 Mo	-1.40	-1.38	0.45	41	50	0.42
6 Mo	2.99	-1.87	1.70	15	39	-1.37
1 Yr	0.62	-0.69	2.59	12	35	-6.16
3 Yr Avg	12.15	5.89	-0.92	13	12	10.81
5 Yr Avg	11.01	2.31	-0.66	20	31	10.56
Incept Avg	10.58*	---	---	---	---	8.24*

Operations

Address and Telephone	1414 Avenue of the Americas, New York, NY 10019, 212-355-7311 / 800-221-4268
Advisor	Quest Advisory Corp.
Subadvisor	N/A
Administrator	N/A
Transfer Agent	State Street Bank and Trust Co.
Custodian	State Street Bank and Trust Co.
Auditor	Coopers & Lybrand
Legal Counsel	Howard J. Kashner, Esq.

Risk Analysis

	Risk % Rank[1]		Morningstar[2]		Morningstar Risk-Adj Rating
	All	Obj	Return	Risk	
3 Yr	31	3	1.19	0.27	★★★★
5 Yr	66	17	1.24	0.49	★★★★
10 Yr	---	---	---	---	

Average Historical Rating (62 months)   3.1 ★s

[1] = Low, 100 = High [2] 1.00 = Equity Avg [3] 1.00 = 90-day T-bill Return

Other Measures

			S&P 500
Standard Deviation	6.69	Alpha	7.07
Mean	11.75	Beta	0.48
Sharpe Ratio	1.23	R-Squared	32

Investment Style

	Stock Portfolio Avg	Relative S&P 500
Price/Earnings Ratio	17.7	0.96
Price/Cash Flow Ratio	13.8	1.19
Price/Book Ratio	1.9	0.55
5 Yr Earnings Gr %	8.0	1.44
Return on Assets %	6.5	0.87
Debt % Total Cap	12.8	0.45
Med Mkt Cap ($mil)	201	0.02

figure is based on less than 50% of stocks

Style: Value Blend Growth; Size: Large Med Small

Index Allocation

	% of Stocks
Dow 30	0.0
S&P 500	2.0
S&P Mid-Cap 400	10.9
US Small-Cap	83.4
Foreign	3.7

Diversification Value for Portfolio Types

Large Cap: Medium	Small Cap: Low	Bond: High	Balanced: Medium	Diversified: Medium

Portfolio 12-31-94

Total Equity: 313
Total Fixed-Income: 10

Share Chg (09-94)	Amount		Value $000	% Total Invest
65900	178200	Comdisco	4121	1.40
0	50700	Velcro Industries	3460	1.18
125400	145400	Transnational Re	3417	1.16
3700	124600	Florida Rock Industries	3411	1.16
0	228900	Baldwin & Lyons Cl B	3376	1.15
0	20438	Alleghany	3107	1.06
23722	260942	Lifetime Hoan	3066	1.04
0	283200	Dress Barn	3044	1.03
80900	226300	Offshore Logistics	2942	1.00
20000	110000	Diagnostic Products	2888	0.98
0	38759	Ash Grove Cement Cl B	2636	0.90
59200	118400	Pioneer Group	2605	0.89
-1000	38400	NCH	2568	0.87
42637	127912	Air Express International	2558	0.87
0	49770	National Bancorp of Alaska	2538	0.86
34350	103050	Exar	2525	0.86
34400	95800	Kimball International Cl B	2491	0.85
3000	155400	Thomaston Mills Cl A	2448	0.83
0	86300	Puerto Rican Cement	2427	0.82
0	64400	WR Berkley	2415	0.82
0	200800	Claire's Stores	2410	0.82
0	20900	Wesco Financial	2406	0.82
8300	67887	Orion Capital	2393	0.81
4000	144600	Mikasa	2368	0.80
0	74900	Fab Industries	2331	0.79

Composition % 12-31-94

Cash	3.2	Preferreds	0.0
Stocks	94.9	Convertibles	1.8
Bonds	0.0	Other	0.0

Leverage factor: 1.15

Tax Analysis

	Tax-Adj Historical Return %	% Pretax Return
3 Yr Avg	9.79	76.9
5 Yr Avg	9.11	76.5
10 Yr Avg	---	---

Potential Capital Gain Exposure (% of assets)   16

Most Similar Funds in MF500

Pennsylvania Mutual	Strong Fit
T. Rowe Price Small-Cap V	Strong Fit
Gabelli Asset	Fair Fit

Sector Weightings

	% of Stocks	Relative S&P 500
Utilities	0.1	0.01
Energy	3.3	0.33
Financials	21.3	2.01
Industrial Cyclicals	18.7	1.14
Consumer Durables	13.2	2.12
Consumer Staples	2.6	0.21
Services	19.1	2.34
Retail	7.0	1.20
Health	3.2	0.37
Technology	11.5	1.25

Income Distrib Schedule	Paid Annually
Management Fee	1.00%, 0.50%P
Reinvestment Plan	Yes
Direct Purchase Plan	No
Shares Outstanding	21,806,505
Exchange	NYSE
*Date of Inception	11-26-86
Shareholder Report	A-

Rydex Nova

RYDEX Series Trust Nova Fund seeks capital appreciation. Income is not a consideration.

The fund invests in stocks, and engages in transactions in options on securities and stock indices and futures on stock indices. It also uses leverage and market-timing investment techniques. The fund's stock holdings are listed on the NYSE, AMEX, or in the national over-the-counter market. In selecting the securities, the fund relies more heavily on technical factors than on fundamental analysis. These factors include historical price trends, trading volume, short interest, over-bought/over-sold indicators, and more.

Manager's Investment Style

Management attempts to exaggerate the performance of the S&P 500 by using Spiders (S&P depositary receipts), index futures, and options. This is in direct opposition to the fund's sibling, Rydex Ursa, which employs a similar strategy in reverse to achieve performance that contrasts to the S&P.

Fund Manager(s)

Thomas G. Michael, since 04-94. Birthdate: 06-52. BA, Colgate U. 1974

Manager Experience

	Dates Managed	Invest Obj	Std Dev	+/- Index
Not available.				

Ticker	Load	NAV	Yield	SEC Yield	Assets	Objective
RYNVX	None	9.99	0.0%	N/A	58.4	Aggr. Growth

Historical Profile
Return ---
Risk ---
Rating
Not Rated

	1983	1984	1985	1986	1987	1988	1989	1990	1991	1992	1993	1994	History
											23%	2%	Investment Style History Equity. Average % Stocks Held in Portfolio
NAV	---	---	---	---	---	---	---	---	---	---	10.71	9.99	NAV
	---	---	---	---	---	---	---	---	---	---	6.99 *	-6.72	Total Return %
	---	---	---	---	---	---	---	---	---	---	1.68 *	-8.04	+/- S&P 500
	---	---	---	---	---	---	---	---	---	---	---	-4.07	+/- Wilshire 4500
	---	---	---	---	---	---	---	---	---	---	0.00	0.00	Income Return %
	---	---	---	---	---	---	---	---	---	---	6.99	-6.72	Capital Return %
	---	---	---	---	---	---	---	---	---	---	---	78	Total Rtn % Rank All
	---	---	---	---	---	---	---	---	---	---	---	74	Total Rtn % Rank Obj
	---	---	---	---	---	---	---	---	---	---	0.00	0.00	Income $
	---	---	---	---	---	---	---	---	---	---	0.00	0.00	Capital Gains $
	---	---	---	---	---	---	---	---	---	---	---	1.73	Expense Ratio %
	---	---	---	---	---	---	---	---	---	---	---	1.05	Income Ratio %
	---	---	---	---	---	---	---	---	---	---	---	---	Turnover Rate %
	---	---	---	---	---	---	---	---	---	---	---	58.4	Net Assets ($mil)

Growth of $10,000
|||| Value of Fund ($000)
— Value of Index ($000) S&P 500
▼ Manager Change
▽ Partial Manager Change
► Mgr Unknown After
◄ Mgr Unknown Before

Performance Quartile (Within Objective)

Performance 12-31-94

	1st Qtr	2nd Qtr	3rd Qtr	4th Qtr	Total
1987	---	---	---	---	---
1988	---	---	---	---	---
1989	---	---	---	---	---
1990	---	---	---	---	---
1991	---	---	---	---	---
1992	---	---	---	---	---
1993	---	---	---	2.98	6.99 *
1994	-8.31	-0.51	5.73	-3.29	-6.72

Bear Market Performance

Decile Rank (5-year period)

Worst | Best

	Worst 3 Mo Period 1985-89	Worst 3 Mo Period 1990-94
Rydex Nova	---	---
+/- S&P 500	---	---
+/- Best Fit Index :	---	---

Trailing Returns

	Total Return %	+/- S&P 500	+/- Wil 4500	% Rank All	% Rank Obj	Growth of $10,000
3 Mo	-3.29	-3.27	-0.79	85	87	9,671
6 Mo	2.25	-2.61	-1.94	25	84	10,225
1 Yr	-6.72	-8.04	-4.07	78	74	9,328
3 Yr Avg	---	---	---	---	---	---
5 Yr Avg	---	---	---	---	---	---
10 Yr Avg	---	---	---	---	---	---
15 Yr Avg	---	---	---	---	---	---

Operations

Address and Telephone	4641 Montgomery Avenue Suite 400
	Bethesda, MD 20814
	800-820-0888 / 301-652-4402
Advisor	PADCO Advisors
Subadvisor	None
Distributor	Rydex Series Trust
States Available	Selected states
Report Grade	N/A
Income Distrib	Paid Annually
* Date of Inception	07-12-93
Fiscal Year End	June

Risk Analysis

Time Period	Load-Adj Return %	Risk % Rank[1] All	Obj	Morningstar[2] Return	Morningstar Risk	Morningstar Risk-Adj Rating
1 Yr	-6.72					
3 Yr	---	---	---	---	---	---
5 Yr	---	---	---	---	---	---
10 Yr	---	---	---	---	---	---

Average Historical Rating ---   ---

[1] 1 = low, 100 = high   [2] 1.00 = Equity Avg   [3] 1.00 = 90-day T-bill return

Other Measures

	Standard S&P 500	Best Fit
Standard Deviation	---	
Mean	---	
Sharpe Ratio	---	
Alpha	---	---
Beta	---	---
R-Squared	---	---

Investment Style

	Stock Portfolio Avg	Relative S&P 500
Price/Earnings Ratio	---	---
Price/Book Ratio	---	---
5 Yr Earnings Gr %	---	---
Return on Assets %	---	---
Debt % Total Cap	---	---
Med Mkt Cap ($mil)	---	---

Not Available

Diversification Value for Portfolio Types

Large Cap: Small Cap: Bond: Balanced: Diversified:

Min Purchase

Min Initial Purchase	$5000 (Addt'l: None)
Min IRA Purchase	$1000 (Addt'l: None)
Min Auto Invest Plan	N/A

Expenses & Fees

Sales Fees	0.00% front
	0.00% deferred
	0.00% 12b-1
Management Fee	0.75% flat fee, 0.25%A
3-,5-,10-yr Expense Projections	$47, N/A, N/A
Annual Brokerage Cost	---

Portfolio 06-30-94

Share Chg --- 000	Amount 000	Total Stocks: 0 Total Fixed-Income: 2	Value $000	% Net Assets
		US Treasury Bill	57825	74.22
		US Treasury Bill	14387	18.47

Composition % 12-31-94

Cash	0.0	Preferreds	0.0
Stocks	0.3	Convertibles	0.0
Bonds	0.0	Other	99.7

Tax Analysis

	Tax-Adj Historical Return %	% Pretax Return
3 Yr Avg	---	---
5 Yr Avg	---	---
10 Yr Avg	---	---
Potential Capital Gain Exposure (% of assets)		-5%

Most Similar Funds in MF500

Fund lacks three-year record

Index Allocation

	% of Stocks
S&P 500	---
S&P MidCap 400	---
U.S. Small Cap	---
Foreign	---

Sector Weightings

	% of Stocks	Relative S&P 500
Utilities	---	---
Energy	---	---
Financials	---	---
Industrial Cyclicals	---	---
Consumer Durables	---	---
Consumer Staples	---	---
Services	---	---
Retail	---	---
Health	---	---
Technology	---	---

MORNINGSTAR **1995 Mutual Fund 500**

Safeco Equity

	Ticker	Load	NAV	Yield	SEC Yield	Assets	Objective
	SAFQX	None	13.68	1.9%	N/A	449.1	Growth/Inc.

Safeco Equity Fund seeks long-term growth of capital and current income.

The fund invests primarily in common stocks. Some equity investments are made for capital appreciation, other investments are made for current income. Up to 35% of assets may be invested in convertibles and debt securities that are linked to specific equities or equity indexes; these securities may be rated as low as CC. The fund does not usually engage in trading for short-term profits. It may invest up to 10% of its assets in REITs and may purchase American depositary receipts.

Manager's Investment Style

An early 1995 manager change raises some questions about this fine long-term performer's future. Previous manager Douglas Johnson held a concentrated portfolio of growth and value stocks, choosing downtrodden stocks across the board. He also picked up large- and small-cap issues, with small caps often providing growth and the larger-cap holdings providing dividend income. Overall, this strategy delivered more capital than income.

Fund Manager(s)

Richard Meagley CFA(1986), since 01-95.
Birthdate: 12-55. BA, Wake Forest U. 1977 MBA, U. of Washington 1982

Manager Experience

	Dates Managed	Invest Obj	Std Dev	+/- Index

Not available.

Historical Profile
Return	High
Risk	Average
Rating	★★★★
	Highest

Performance Quartile (Within Objective)

Investment Style History
Equity
Average % Stocks Held in Portfolio

Growth of $10,000
- |||| Value of Fund ($000)
- — Value of Index ($000) S&P 500
- ▼ Manager Change
- ▽ Partial Manager Change
- ► Mgr Unknown After
- ◄ Mgr Unknown Before

Stocks held: 95% 98% 96% 98% 98% 98% 93% 97%

	1983	1984	1985	1986	1987	1988	1989	1990	1991	1992	1993	1994	History
NAV	10.15	9.22	10.50	9.54	7.09	8.55	10.48	8.97	10.59	10.87	13.18	13.68	NAV
	21.44	2.63	33.27	12.71	-4.81	25.30	35.79	-8.57	27.91	9.26	30.91	9.93	Total Return %
	-1.02	-3.64	1.53	-5.97	-10.06	8.69	4.11	-5.45	-2.57	1.64	20.85	8.62	+/- S&P 500
	-2.02	-0.42	0.71	-3.39	-7.17	7.35	6.62	-2.39	-6.30	0.29	19.63	10.00	+/- Wilshire 5000
	5.12	4.81	4.21	2.73	2.63	2.71	4.74	2.07	1.79	1.32	1.51	2.01	Income Return %
	16.32	-2.19	29.06	9.98	-7.44	22.58	31.05	-10.64	26.12	7.95	29.40	7.93	Capital Return %
	34	58	16	69	88	6	6	30	30	8	2		Total Rtn % Rank All
	46	59	13	72	91	6	3	81	53	35	1		Total Rtn % Rank Obj
	0.47	0.45	0.40	0.29	0.25	0.20	0.40	0.20	0.18	0.13	0.18	0.26	Income $
	0.58	0.72	1.22	2.03	1.79	0.13	0.64	0.39	0.68	0.49	0.81	0.54	Capital Gains $
	0.65	0.64	0.68	0.88	0.97	1.00	0.96	0.97	0.98	0.96	0.94	0.85	Expense Ratio %
	4.78	4.66	3.97	2.55	1.92	2.16	4.13	2.19	1.70	1.34	1.50	1.72	Income Ratio %
	16	20	56	86	85	88	64	51	45	40	38	33	Turnover Rate %
	34.5	31.4	34.9	44.9	41.1	43.9	59.6	55.6	75.8	84.5	194.0	449.1	Net Assets ($mil)

Performance 12-31-94

	1st Qtr	2nd Qtr	3rd Qtr	4th Qtr	Total
1987	22.83	2.01	3.77	-26.78	-4.81
1988	16.70	3.00	2.35	1.84	25.30
1989	6.91	10.06	10.26	4.67	35.79
1990	-4.01	6.32	-16.44	7.21	-8.57
1991	14.52	-0.66	6.91	5.17	27.91
1992	2.90	-7.30	0.09	14.45	9.26
1993	8.96	6.19	7.06	5.68	30.91
1994	-0.63	2.38	8.37	-0.29	9.94

Bear Market Performance

Decile Rank (5-year period)

Worst		Best

	Worst 3 Mo Period 1985-89	Worst 3 Mo Period 1990-94
Safeco Equity	-33.61	-16.73
+/- S&P 500	-4.03	-2.89
+/- Best Fit Index : Wil 4500	-3.47	2.67

Trailing Returns

	Total Return %	+/- S&P 500	+/- Wil 5000	% Rank All	% Rank Obj	Growth of $10,000
3 Mo	-0.29	-0.27	0.48	30	27	9,971
6 Mo	8.06	3.19	3.43	6	1	10,806
1 Yr	9.93	8.62	10.00	2	1	10,993
3 Yr Avg	16.29	10.02	9.67	3	2	15,724
5 Yr Avg	12.96	4.27	4.14	7	2	18,390
10 Yr Avg	16.16	1.78	2.30	6	1	44,740
15 Yr Avg	14.40	-0.08	0.42	21	20	75,227

Operations

Address and Telephone	P.O. Box 34890
	Seattle, WA 98124-1890
	800-426-6730 / 206-545-5530
Advisor	Safeco Asset Management
Subadvisor	None
Distributor	Safeco Securities
States Available	All
Report Grade	A-
Income Distrib	Paid Quarterly
Date of Inception	03-01-32
Fiscal Year End	September

Min Initial Purchase	$1000 (Addt'l: $100)
Min IRA Purchase	$250 (Addt'l: $100)
Min Auto Invest Plan	$100 (Systematic Inv: $100)

Expenses & Fees
Sales Fees	0.00% front
	0.00% deferred
	0.00% 12b-1
Management Fee	0.75% flat fee
3-,5-,10-yr Expense Projections	$30, $52, $115
Annual Brokerage Cost	0.22%

Risk Analysis

Time Period	Load-Adj Return %	Risk % Rank [1] All	Obj	Morningstar [2] Return	Morningstar Risk	Morningstar Risk-Adj Rating
1 Yr	9.93					
3 Yr	16.29	75	84	4.14 [3]	0.86	★★★★★
5 Yr	12.96	79	92	2.23 [3]	0.97	★★★★
10 Yr	16.16	74	88	1.77	0.95	★★★★★
Average Historical Rating (109 months)					3.4	★s

[1] 1 = low, 100 = high [2] 1.00 = Equity Avg [3] 1.00 = 90-day T-bill return

Other Measures
			Standard S&P 500	Best Fit Wil 4500
Standard Deviation	12.41	Alpha	9.5	8.0
Mean	15.95	Beta	1.15	1.09
Sharpe Ratio	1.00	R-Squared	54	74

Investment Style
	Stock Portfolio Avg	Relative S&P 500
Price/Earnings Ratio	17.9	0.97
Price/Book Ratio	2.7	0.80
5 Yr Earnings Gr %	6.1	1.10
Return on Assets %	7.8	1.04
Debt % Total Cap	28.5	1.01
Med Mkt Cap ($mil)	664	0.05

Style: Value Blend Growth / Large Med Small (Size)

Diversification Value for Portfolio Types

Large Cap: Low / Small Cap: Low / Bond: High / Balanced: Low / Diversified: Medium

Portfolio 12-31-94

Total Stocks: 86
Total Fixed-Income: 1

Share Chg (09-94) 000	Amount 000		Value $000	% Net Assets
0	130	Warner-Lambert	9972	2.22
0	651	Mentor Graphics	9928	2.21
102	701	Information Resources	9639	2.15
0	296	Century Telephone Enterprise	8738	1.95
7	226	Block Drug Cl A	8603	1.92
30	134	Texaco	8023	1.79
219	219	Arrow Electronics	7854	1.75
0	383	Glaxo Holdings (ADR)	7804	1.74
109	434	Maybelline	7803	1.74
160	245	Grupo Televisa	7779	1.73
133	133	JP Morgan	7431	1.65
-31	519	Smart & Final	7262	1.62
80	396	Equitable	7178	1.60
0	117	Microsoft	7152	1.59
187	535	Evans & Sutherland Computer	7089	1.58
0	383	Landauer	6359	1.42
0	141	WD-40	6217	1.38
20	195	Genzyme	6143	1.37
1	528	GTE	6050	1.35
407	407	Giddings & Lewis	6003	1.34
0	58	American International Group	5684	1.27
216	216	Horizon Outlet Centers	5630	1.25
280	580	Ethyl	5583	1.24
0	287	Dresser Industries	5417	1.21
59	300	Knight-Ridder	5135	1.14

Composition % 12-31-94
Cash	3.6	Preferreds	0.0
Stocks	96.3	Convertibles	0.1
Bonds	0.0	Other	0.0

Tax Analysis
	Tax-Adj Historical Return %	% Pretax Return
3 Yr Avg	14.17	85.3
5 Yr Avg	10.77	79.6
10 Yr Avg	12.77	67.0
Potential Capital Gain Exposure (% of assets)		10%

Most Similar Funds in MF500
FPA Capital	Fair Fit
Columbia Special	Weak Fit
Neuberger&Berman Partners	Weak Fit

Index Allocation
	% of Stocks
S&P 500	27.6
S&P MidCap 400	24.9
U.S. Small Cap	41.1
Foreign	6.4

Sector Weightings
	% of Stocks	Relative S&P 500
Utilities	6.7	0.54
Energy	4.1	0.40
Financials	23.3	2.20
Industrial Cyclicals	14.8	0.91
Consumer Durables	2.4	0.39
Consumer Staples	8.9	0.71
Services	7.9	0.97
Retail	0.0	0.00
Health	13.3	1.53
Technology	18.7	2.04

Safeco Income

	Ticker	Load	NAV	Yield	SEC Yield	Assets	Objective
	SAFIX	None	16.54	4.8%	N/A	180.7	Equity-Inc.

Safeco Income Fund seeks current income. Long-term growth of capital may be sought when consistent with the primary objective.

The fund invests primarily in common stock, convertible corporate bonds, and convertible preferred stock. Up to 35% of assets may be invested in convertibles and debt securities that are linked to specific equities or equity indices; these securities may be rated as low as CC. Up to 1% of assets may be in default. The fund does not usually engage in trading for short-term profits.

Historical Profile

Return	Average
Risk	Below Average
Rating	★★★ Neutral

Investment Style History
Equity
Average % Stocks Held in Portfolio

63% 69% 70% 64% 62% 57% 56% 56%

Growth of $10,000

|||| Value of Fund ($000)
— Value of Index ($000) S&P 500
▼ Manager Change
▽ Partial Manager Change
► Mgr Unknown After
◄ Mgr Unknown Before

Manager's Investment Style

Management takes the income side of the equity-income equation to heart. It targets income-generating stocks yielding at least 4%. Owing to these criteria, the fund is typically heavy in the utilities, energy, and financials sectors. Convertibles have also been a staple in this portfolio.

Performance Quartile (Within Objective)

	1983	1984	1985	1986	1987	1988	1989	1990	1991	1992	1993	1994	History
	12.65	11.76	14.03	15.28	12.64	14.23	16.03	13.37	15.58	16.50	17.77	16.54	NAV
	28.57	9.97	31.73	20.08	-5.97	18.98	19.22	-10.75	23.25	11.47	12.55	-1.09	Total Return %
	6.11	3.71	-0.01	1.41	-11.23	2.37	-12.47	-7.64	-7.23	3.85	2.49	-2.41	+/- S&P 500
	5.11	6.92	-0.84	3.99	-8.33	1.04	-9.96	-4.57	-10.95	2.50	1.27	-1.02	+/- Wilshire 5000
	7.51	7.53	6.76	5.64	6.37	6.40	5.92	5.34	6.28	5.28	4.85	4.62	Income Return %
	21.06	2.44	24.97	14.44	-12.34	12.58	13.29	-16.09	16.97	6.19	7.70	-5.71	Capital Return %
	13	26	19	19	91	16	37	86	39	16	46	27	Total Rtn % Rank All
	30	33	6	31	69	41	60	75	77	24	53	37	Total Rtn % Rank Obj
	0.83	0.87	0.75	0.78	0.99	0.79	0.81	0.86	0.80	0.78	0.78	0.81	Income $
	0.87	1.17	0.56	0.73	0.84	0.00	0.08	0.09	0.05	0.04	0.00	0.24	Capital Gains $
	0.63	0.63	0.73	0.95	0.94	0.97	0.92	0.92	0.93	0.90	0.90	0.86	Expense Ratio %
	6.85	7.02	6.41	5.08	4.53	5.58	5.28	5.59	5.58	5.06	4.55	4.59	Income Ratio %
	32	34	29	29	33	34	16	19	22	20	21	19	Turnover Rate %
	21.5	19.8	31.5	144.1	219.1	219.4	226.8	174.6	181.6	185.7	200.9	180.7	Net Assets ($mil)

Fund Manager(s)

Arley N. Hudson CFA(1968), since 12-78.
Birthdate: 02-34. BA, U. of Washington 1956

Manager Experience	Dates Managed	Invest Obj	Std Dev	+/- Index
Arley N. Hudson				
Safeco Equity	07/84 - 06/86	GI	12.30	2.67

Performance 12-31-94

	1st Qtr	2nd Qtr	3rd Qtr	4th Qtr	Total
1987	13.09	0.21	2.74	-19.24	-5.97
1988	10.00	5.92	1.37	0.74	18.98
1989	4.95	7.04	6.92	-0.75	19.22
1990	-3.89	0.91	-12.80	5.53	-10.75
1991	11.54	1.52	5.80	2.88	23.25
1992	0.12	4.27	4.06	2.62	11.47
1993	7.65	0.46	3.04	1.01	12.55
1994	-2.57	-0.26	4.91	-2.99	-1.09

Bear Market Performance

Decile Rank (5-year period)

Worst ▬ Best

	Worst 3 Mo Period 1985-89	Worst 3 Mo Period 1990-94
Safeco Income	-24.99	-13.35
+/- S&P 500		4.59	0.49
+/- Best Fit Index : S&P 500	4.59	0.49

Trailing Returns

	Total Return %	+/- S&P 500	+/- Wil 5000	% Rank All	% Rank Obj	Growth of $10,000
3 Mo	-2.99	-2.97	-2.22	83	63	9,701
6 Mo	1.77	-3.09	-2.85	28	42	10,177
1 Yr	-1.09	-2.41	-1.02	27	37	9,891
3 Yr Avg	7.46	1.19	0.85	24	43	12,409
5 Yr Avg	6.42	-2.27	-2.40	66	67	13,650
10 Yr Avg	11.16	-3.23	-2.70	46	50	28,799
15 Yr Avg	13.29	-1.19	-0.69	35	38	64,974

Operations

Address and Telephone	P.O. Box 34890
	Seattle, WA 98124-1890
	800-426-6730 / 206-545-5530
Advisor	Safeco Asset Management
Subadvisor	None
Distributor	Safeco Securities
States Available	All
Report Grade	A-
Income Distrib	Paid Quarterly
Date of Inception	10-16-69
Fiscal Year End	September

Min Initial Purchase	$1000 (Addt'l: $100)
Min IRA Purchase	$250 (Addt'l: $100)
Min Auto Invest Plan	$100 (Systematic Inv: $100)

Expenses & Fees

Sales Fees	
	0.00% front
	0.00% deferred
	0.00% 12b-1
Management Fee	0.75% flat fee
3-,5-,10-yr Expense Projections	$29, $50, $111
Annual Brokerage Cost	0.06%

Risk Analysis

Time Period	Load-Adj Return %	Risk % Rank [1] All	Obj	Morningstar [2] Return	Risk	Morningstar Risk-Adj Rating
1 Yr	-1.09					
3 Yr	7.46	49	21	1.16 [3]	0.53	★★★★
5 Yr	6.42	58	41	0.41 [3]	0.67	★★★
10 Yr	11.16	48	31	0.73	0.70	★★★

Average Historical Rating (109 months) 4.0 ★s

[1] = low, 100 = high [2] 1.00 = Equity Avg [3] 1.00 = 90-day T-bill return

Other Measures

			Standard S&P 500	Best Fit S&P 500
Standard Deviation	6.63	Alpha	1.8	1.8
Mean	7.44	Beta	0.74	0.74
Sharpe Ratio	0.59	R-Squared	78	78

Investment Style

	Stock Portfolio Avg	Relative S&P 500	Style
Price/Earnings Ratio	16.9	0.91	
Price/Book Ratio	2.6	0.75	
5 Yr Earnings Gr %	0.5	0.08	
Return on Assets %	7.2	0.96	
Debt % Total Cap	32.0	1.13	
Med Mkt Cap ($mil)	7762	0.60	

Diversification Value for Portfolio Types

  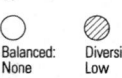

Large Cap: Low	Small Cap: Medium	Bond: Medium	Balanced: None	Diversified: Low

Portfolio 12-31-94

Share Chg (09-94) 000	Amount 000	Total Stocks: 42 / Total Fixed-Income: 30	Value $000	% Net Assets
0	250	GTE	7594	4.20
	90	Gatx Cv Pfd $3.875	4860	2.69
0	80	Texaco	4790	2.65
	50	Ford Motor Cl A Cv Pfd 8.4%	4600	2.55
	4000	Amoco Canada Petro A Cv 7.375%	4600	2.55
-5	40	Royal Dutch Petroleum	4300	2.38
	120	Conagra Cl E Cv Pfd $1.6875	3930	2.18
0	60	American Home Products	3765	2.08
0	100	Weyerhaeuser	3750	2.08
79	149	Omega Healthcare Investors	3585	1.98
91	92	Merck	3498	1.94
	160	Cooper Industries Cv Pfd $1.60	3280	1.82
10	60	Minnesota Mining & Mfg	3203	1.77
	65	BankAmerica Cl G Cv Pfd 6.5%	3201	1.77
	40	Washington Mutual C Cv Pfd 6%	3170	1.75
0	50	Exxon	3038	1.68
0	80	American Brands	3000	1.66
	50	AGCO Cv Pfd $25	3000	1.66
	32	Salomon Pfd (ELK)	2976	1.65
0	100	Sturm Ruger	2838	1.57
	2982	Time Warner Cv 8.75%	2818	1.56
	2500	Pennzoil Cv 6.5%	2794	1.55
	50	Sears Roebuck PERCS	2781	1.54
0	70	WR Grace	2704	1.50
	120	Consolidated Freightways PERCS	2685	1.49

Composition % 12-31-94

Cash	1.5	Preferreds	0.0
Stocks	58.3	Convertibles	40.2
Bonds	0.0	Other	0.0

Tax Analysis

	Tax-Adj Historical Return %	% Pretax Return
3 Yr Avg	5.51	72.5
5 Yr Avg	4.44	66.4
10 Yr Avg	8.51	67.2
Potential Capital Gain Exposure (% of assets)		7%

Most Similar Funds in MF500

Putnam Fund for Grth & Inc A	Strong Fit
George Putnam of Boston A	Strong Fit
Colonial A	Strong Fit

Index Allocation

	% of Stocks
S&P 500	72.3
S&P MidCap 400	4.4
U.S. Small Cap	21.0
Foreign	6.6

Sector Weightings

	% of Stocks	Relative S&P 500
Utilities	20.2	1.63
Energy	14.3	1.41
Financials	21.2	2.00
Industrial Cyclicals	14.6	0.89
Consumer Durables	2.8	0.45
Consumer Staples	2.9	0.23
Services	9.5	1.17
Retail	3.0	0.51
Health	9.8	1.13
Technology	1.7	0.19

MORNINGSTAR 1995 Mutual Fund 500

Safeco Municipal Bond

	Ticker	Load	NAV	Yield	SEC Yield	Assets	Objective
	SFCOX	None	12.46	6.2%	6.11%	434.4	Muni Nat

Safeco Municipal Bond Fund seeks current income exempt from federal income tax, consistent with relative stability of capital.

The fund normally invests at least 80% of its assets in investment-grade municipal obligations, provided that bonds rated BBB take up no more than 33% of assets. Up to 20% of assets may be invested in unrated bonds deemed to be of comparable quality to securities rated A or above. The fund may not purchase AMT-subject private-activity bonds.

Historical Profile

Return	Above Average
Risk	High
Rating	★★★
	Neutral

Income Rtn % Rank Obj: 31 29 47 37 36 40 28 22

Investment Style History
Fixed Income
Income Rtn % Rank Obj

Growth of $10,000
|||| Value of Fund ($000)
— Value of Index ($000) LB Muni
▼ Manager Change
▽ Partial Manager Change
► Mgr Unknown After
◄ Mgr Unknown Before

Manager's Investment Style

Management employs a far-sighted strategy that has one central component: buying bonds with high tax-free yields and holding them. Management always stays fully invested in long bonds, refusing to bet one way or another on interest rates. It prefers to balance premium-coupon bonds with discount coupons.

Performance Quartile (Within Objective)

1983	1984	1985	1986	1987	1988	1989	1990	1991	1992	1993	1994	History
11.45	11.46	12.76	13.97	12.60	13.05	12.97	12.88	13.68	13.82	14.43	12.46	NAV
10.53	10.10	21.62	19.78	0.17	13.88	10.08	6.65	13.78	8.75	12.79	-8.25	Total Return %
2.15	-5.06	-0.51	4.53	-2.59	6.00	-4.46	-2.29	-2.22	1.51	3.04	-5.33	+/- LB Aggregate
2.48	-0.46	1.59	0.47	-1.33	3.71	-0.71	-0.65	1.64	-0.07	0.51	-2.64	+/- LB Muni
9.43	10.01	10.04	8.47	7.28	7.91	7.19	7.02	7.05	6.33	6.03	5.23	Income Return %
1.10	0.09	11.57	11.31	-7.11	5.96	2.89	-0.37	6.73	2.42	6.76	-13.48	Capital Return %
77	26	62	21	59	32	72	26	64	36	43	87	Total Rtn % Rank All
37	23	17	20	47	7	31	33	6	42	27	88	Total Rtn % Rank Obj
1.04	1.07	1.06	1.01	0.97	0.95	0.89	0.87	0.85	0.82	0.80	0.77	Income $
0.00	0.00	0.02	0.21	0.40	0.29	0.44	0.04	0.06	0.18	0.31	0.03	Capital Gains $
0.72	0.64	0.63	0.63	0.59	0.61	0.60	0.57	0.54	0.54	0.53	0.52	Expense Ratio %
9.28	9.17	9.43	8.29	7.20	7.42	7.23	6.76	6.68	6.37	5.91	5.49	Income Ratio %
40	92	47	21	23	72	136	66	39	25	32	22	Turnover Rate %
45.3	74.8	137.4	195.9	174.6	222.1	282.0	311.9	422.1	512.2	572.9	434.4	Net Assets ($mil)

Fund Manager(s)

Stephen C. Bauer, since 11-81. Birthdate: 01-45.
BS, U. of Washington 1967 MBA, U. of Washington 1971

Manager Experience

	Dates Managed	Invest Obj	Std Dev	+/- Index
Stephen C. Bauer				
Safeco CA Tax-Free Inc	10/83 - 12/94	MC	7.76	-1.60
Safeco WA State Muni Bd	03/93 - 12/94	MS	8.11	-1.77

Performance 12-31-94

	1st Qtr	2nd Qtr	3rd Qtr	4th Qtr	Total
1987	3.08	-4.23	-3.37	5.01	0.17
1988	3.86	2.50	3.29	3.57	13.88
1989	0.77	5.58	0.05	3.41	10.08
1990	-0.17	2.52	-0.93	5.18	6.65
1991	2.15	2.35	4.78	3.87	13.78
1992	-0.74	4.86	1.92	2.51	8.75
1993	3.69	4.05	3.52	0.99	12.79
1994	-6.77	0.18	-0.15	-1.61	-8.25

Bear Market Performance

Decile Rank (5-year period)

Worst _____ Best

	Worst 3 Mo Period 1985-89	Worst 3 Mo Period 1990-94
Safeco Municipal Bond	-7.10	-7.80
+/- LB Aggregate	-3.54	-2.87
+/- Best Fit Index : LB Muni	-0.60	-2.04

Trailing Returns

	Total Return %	+/- LB Aggregate	+/- LB Muni	% Rank All	% Rank Obj	Growth of $10,000
3 Mo	-1.61	-1.99	-0.17	60	65	9,839
6 Mo	-1.76	-2.75	-0.51	85	82	9,824
1 Yr	-8.25	-5.33	-2.64	87	88	9,175
3 Yr Avg	4.02	-0.53	-0.85	69	75	11,254
5 Yr Avg	6.43	-1.19	-0.34	65	38	13,657
10 Yr Avg	9.59	-0.36	0.16	63	14	24,981
15 Yr Avg	---	---	---	---	---	---

Operations

Address and Telephone	P.O. Box 34890
	Seattle, WA 98124-1890
	800-426-6730 / 206-545-5530
Advisor	Safeco Asset Management
Subadvisor	None
Distributor	Safeco Securities
States Available	All
Report Grade	B+
Income Distrib	Paid Monthly
Date of Inception	11-18-81
Fiscal Year End	March

Risk Analysis

Time Period	Load-Adj Return %	Risk % Rank [1] All	Obj	Morningstar [2] Return	Risk	Morningstar Risk-Adj Rating
1 Yr	-8.25					
3 Yr	4.02	54	96	1.03	1.38	★★
5 Yr	6.43	42	96	1.08	1.42	★★
10 Yr	9.59	27	83	1.23	1.22	★★★

Average Historical Rating (109 months)   3.5 ★ s

[1] 1 = low, 100 = high   [2] 1.00 = Muni Avg   [3] 1.00 = 90-day T-bill return

Other Measures

				Standard LB Agg	Best Fit LB Muni
Standard Deviation	7.06	Alpha		-0.7	-1.1
Mean	4.19	Beta		1.36	1.26
Sharpe Ratio	0.09	R-Squared		60	96

Investment Style

Interest-Rate Stance
Avg Effective Maturity   21.2 Yrs

Maturity: Short Intm Long

Quality
Avg Credit Quality   AA

Avg Weighted Coupon   6.36%
Avg Weighted Price   89.45% of Par

Diversification Value for Portfolio Types

Large Cap: Medium	Small Cap: High	Bond: Low	Balanced: Medium	Diversified: Medium

Portfolio 12-31-94

Total Stocks: 0
Total Fixed-Income: 116

Amount 000	Date of Maturity		Value $000	% Net Assets
10000	11-15-07	TX Austin Combined Util Sys 12.5%	15619	3.60
25000	01-01-33	CA San Joaquin Hills Transp Toll Rd 5%	15509	3.57
17500	12-01-25	IL Educ Fac Univ Chicago 5.7%	14810	3.41
11000	11-15-16	IN East Chicago GO Elem Sch Bldg 7%	11055	2.54
13000	11-15-26	CA Los Angeles Dept Wtr/Pwr Elec 5.25%	10058	2.32
8805	11-01-14	KY Local Crtnl Fac Const Impr 7%	9350	2.15
11000	01-01-22	NC East Muni Pwr 6%	9267	2.13
12225	01-01-22	AZ Salt Rvr Agri Impr/Pwr Dist 5%	9184	2.11
7255	09-01-18	WA Douglas PUD #1 Wells Proj 8.75%	8673	2.00
10250	10-01-22	SC Charleston Hosp Fac Impr 5%	7805	1.80
10000	01-01-32	SC Pub Svc Santee Cooper 5.125%	7552	1.74
8500	07-01-17	WA Pub Pwr Sply Sys Proj #1 6%	7492	1.72
7415	08-01-18	PA Philadelphia Wtr/Swr 7%	7364	1.70
7715	07-10-15	IN Hammond GO Multi Sch Bldg 6.2%	7174	1.65
9800	07-01-23	AZ Phoenix Civic Impr Wastewtr 4.75%	7121	1.64
7735	06-15-20	IL Sales Tax 5.5%	6436	1.48
6350	01-01-21	WA Hlth Care Fac Yakima Vlly Meml 7.25%	6392	1.47
6000	06-15-22	PA Intergovt Coop Spcl Tax 6.8%	6366	1.47
4350	11-15-01	TX Austin Wtr Swr/Elec 14%	6069	1.40
5500	06-01-18	WA Yakima/Tieton Irr Dist 8.4%	5994	1.38

Credit Analysis % of Bonds 09-30-94

US Govt	0	BB	0
AAA	39	B	1
AA	20	Below B	0
A	26	NR/NA	8
BBB	6		

Composition % of Assets 12-31-94

Cash	0.3	Preferreds	0.0
Stocks	0.0	Convertibles	0.0
Bonds	99.7	Other	0.0

Tax Analysis

	Tax-Adj Historical Return %	% Pretax Return
3 Yr Avg	3.67	91.2
5 Yr Avg	6.17	95.5
10 Yr Avg	9.14	93.3
Potential Capital Gain Exposure (% of assets)		-2%

Most Similar Funds in MF500

Value Line Tax-Exempt Hi-Yld	Strong Fit
Fidelity Municipal Bond	Strong Fit
Lord Abbett T/F Income Natl	Strong Fit

Coupon Range

	% Bonds	Rel Obj
0%	0.0	0.00
0% to 6.8%	72.2	1.19
6.8% to 7.5%	14.1	0.91
7.5% to 8.3%	4.4	0.49
More than 8.3%	9.4	1.06
Not applicable	0.0	0.00

Sector Weightings

	% Bonds	Rel Obj
General Obl	9.47	0.45
Utilities	30.41	2.43
Health	8.25	0.63
Water/Waste	19.10	3.00
Housing	2.24	0.31
Education	7.89	1.23
Transportation	9.00	0.88
COP/Lease	2.43	0.76
Private	3.09	0.27
Misc Revenue	8.13	1.64
Demand	0.00	0.00

Top 5 States % of Bonds

CA	17.45	NY	6.80
WA	12.20	TX	6.72
IL	9.42		

Min Purchase / Expenses

Min Initial Purchase	$1000 (Addt'l: $100)
Min IRA Purchase	N/A
Min Auto Invest Plan	$100 (Systematic Inv: $100)

Expenses & Fees

Sales Fees	0.00% front
	0.00% deferred
	0.00% 12b-1
Management Fee	0.55% max./0.25% min.
3-,5-,10-yr Expense Projections	$17, $29, $65

Salomon Bros Opportunity

	Ticker	Load	NAV	Yield	SEC Yield	Assets	Objective
	SAOPX	None	28.39	1.2%	N/A	108.8	Growth

Salomon Brothers Opportunity Fund seeks long-term capital appreciation. Current income is secondary. The fund invests primarily in common stocks or convertible securities of companies with share prices that are believed to be inadequate reflections of the underlying value of the companies' assets or potential earnings power. It may invest in both established and emerging companies. The fund may also borrow money for either investment or temporary purposes.

Prior to April 30, 1990, the fund was named Lehman Opportunity Fund.

Manager's Investment Style

Manager Irving Brilliant is a value stalwart who is not afraid of heavy sector bets, as illustrated by the hefty stake in financials he has held since the early 1980s. He is also willing to concentrate assets heavily in individual stocks. He looks for equities that sell at a discount to their asset values or cash flows.

Fund Manager(s)

Irving Brilliant, since 02-79. Birthdate: 11-11. LLB, Harvard

Manager Experience

	Dates Managed	Invest Obj	Std Dev	+/- Index

Not available.

Historical Profile

Return	Average
Risk	Below Average
Rating	★★★
	Neutral

89% 89% 89% 84% 83% 90% 88% 90%

Growth of $10,000

IIII Value of Fund ($000)
— Value of Index ($000) S&P 500
▼ Manager Change
▽ Partial Manager Change
► Mgr Unknown After
◄ Mgr Unknown Before

Investment Style History
Equity
Average % Stocks Held in Portfolio

Performance Quartile (Within Objective)

1983	1984	1985	1986	1987	1988	1989	1990	1991	1992	1993	1994	History
19.45	19.75	24.29	22.60	19.91	22.40	25.35	20.65	26.24	28.70	30.01	28.39	NAV
39.14	10.96	32.90	6.48	4.36	23.29	20.99	-15.99	30.60	13.87	12.82	0.81	Total Return %
16.67	4.70	1.16	-12.20	-0.90	6.68	-10.69	-12.88	0.11	6.25	2.76	-0.50	+/- S&P 500
15.67	7.91	0.34	-9.62	1.99	5.35	-8.18	-9.81	-3.61	4.90	1.54	0.88	+/- Wilshire 5000
2.41	2.14	2.17	2.48	3.67	2.52	3.52	2.50	2.49	1.27	2.19	1.30	Income Return %
36.72	8.82	30.73	4.00	0.68	20.77	17.47	-18.49	28.11	12.60	10.63	-0.48	Capital Return %
3	21	17	93	26	7	33	94	26	12	43	15	Total Rtn % Rank All
2	5	30	93	40	11	77	94	66	20	44	25	Total Rtn % Rank Obj
0.43	0.41	0.48	0.59	0.76	0.54	0.82	0.63	0.50	0.35	0.64	0.37	Income $
1.39	1.37	1.40	2.79	2.95	1.58	0.89	0.02	0.17	0.81	1.70	1.48	Capital Gains $
1.30	1.23	1.23	1.16	1.16	1.20	1.19	1.26	1.30	1.25	1.23	1.22	Expense Ratio %
2.88	2.44	2.71	2.44	1.92	2.29	3.20	2.38	2.31	1.28	1.86	1.29	Income Ratio %
46	32	24	28	25	29	15	13	11	11	10	13	Turnover Rate %
38.7	48.5	71.2	95.0	86.8	96.0	114.7	87.8	104.9	107.0	116.4	108.8	Net Assets ($mil)

Performance 12-31-94

	1st Qtr	2nd Qtr	3rd Qtr	4th Qtr	Total
1987	16.24	3.39	7.84	-19.48	4.36
1988	12.66	5.17	2.80	1.23	23.29
1989	9.55	7.62	6.55	-3.69	20.99
1990	-6.23	0.63	-18.19	8.82	-15.99
1991	17.53	-0.21	4.67	6.38	30.60
1992	1.14	2.64	5.58	3.89	13.87
1993	7.77	0.23	3.61	0.80	12.82
1994	-1.70	1.36	1.57	-0.38	0.82

Bear Market Performance

Decile Rank (5-year period)

Worst ▬▬ Best

	Worst 3 Mo Period 1985-89	Worst 3 Mo Period 1990-94
Salomon Bros Opportunity	-23.10	-19.19
+/- S&P 500	6.49	-5.34
+/- Best Fit Index : S&P 500	6.49	-5.34

Trailing Returns

	Total Return %	+/- S&P 500	+/- Wil 5000	% Rank All	% Rank Obj	Growth of $10,000
3 Mo	-0.38	-0.36	0.39	32	29	9,962
6 Mo	1.19	-3.68	-3.44	34	79	10,119
1 Yr	0.81	-0.50	0.88	15	25	10,081
3 Yr Avg	9.00	2.74	2.39	17	24	12,951
5 Yr Avg	7.28	-1.41	-1.54	44	72	14,209
10 Yr Avg	12.09	-2.30	-1.77	36	65	31,299
15 Yr Avg	14.76	0.28	0.79	15	31	78,907

Operations

Address and Telephone	7 World Trade Center New York, NY 10048 800-725-6666 / 212-783-1301
Advisor	Salomon Brothers Asset Management
Subadvisor	None
Distributor	Salomon Brothers
States Available	All
Report Grade	C+
Income Distrib	Paid Annually
Date of Inception	02-28-79
Fiscal Year End	August

Risk Analysis

Time Period	Load-Adj Return %	Risk % Rank [1] All	Obj	Morningstar [2] Return	Morningstar Risk	Morningstar Risk-Adj Rating
1 Yr	0.81					
3 Yr	9.00	61	17	1.65 [3]	0.68	★★★★
5 Yr	7.28	76	50	0.62 [3]	0.91	★★★
10 Yr	12.09	60	23	0.90	0.84	★★★

Average Historical Rating (109 months) 4.0 ★s

[1] 1 = low, 100 = high   [2] 1.00 = Equity Avg   [3] 1.00 = 90-day T-bill return

Other Measures

	Standard S&P 500	Best Fit S&P 500
Standard Deviation	8.15	
Mean	8.98	
Sharpe Ratio	0.67	
Alpha	2.9	2.9
Beta	0.89	0.89
R-Squared	75	75

Investment Style

	Stock Portfolio Avg	Relative S&P 500
Price/Earnings Ratio	15.7	0.85
Price/Book Ratio	2.0	0.58
5 Yr Earnings Gr %	5.2	0.94
Return on Assets %	3.8	0.51
Debt % Total Cap	25.8	0.91
Med Mkt Cap ($mil)	4351	0.34

Style
Value Blend Growth
Large Med Small Size

Diversification Value for Portfolio Types

Large Cap: Low	Small Cap: Medium	Bond: Medium	Balanced: None	Diversified: Low

Expenses & Fees

Sales Fees	0.00% front
	0.00% deferred
	0.00% 12b-1
Management Fee	1.00% flat fee, 0.08%A
3-,5-,10-yr Expense Projections	$39, $68, $149
Annual Brokerage Cost	0.04%

Min Initial Purchase	$1000 (Addt'l: $100)
Min IRA Purchase	$250 (Addt'l: $100)
Min Auto Invest Plan	N/A

Portfolio 08-31-94

Share Chg (05-94) 000	Amount 000	Total Stocks: 101 Total Fixed-Income: 2	Value $000	% Net Assets
0	164	Chubb	12013	10.12
0	246	Bank of New York	8003	6.74
0	67	Royal Dutch Petroleum	7546	6.35
0	59	Loews	5369	4.52
-4	110	Orion Capital	3587	3.02
0	103	Philips	3353	2.82
0	116	American President	3060	2.58
0	40	AMR	2386	2.01
0	35	IBM	2368	1.99
0	45	First Chicago	2340	1.97
0	46	Tecumseh Products Cl A	2274	1.91
0	36	FHLMC	2237	1.88
-2	7	CBS	2098	1.77
0	40	UNUM	1965	1.65
-3	54	USLIFE	1926	1.62
0	42	General Dynamics	1895	1.60
0	1872	Time Warner Reset 0%	1750	1.47
0	26	CNA Financial	1610	1.36
0	40	Forest City Enterprises Cl A	1434	1.21
0	17	Monsanto	1413	1.19
-4	36	Foundation Health	1364	1.15
0	28	Murphy Oil	1327	1.12
-7	40	KeyCorp	1315	1.11
0	35	Leucadia National	1300	1.09
0	40	Airborne Freight	1220	1.03

Composition % 12-31-94

Cash	9.9	Preferreds	0.0
Stocks	87.9	Convertibles	0.5
Bonds	1.7	Other	0.0

Tax Analysis

	Tax-Adj Historical Return %	% Pretax Return
3 Yr Avg	7.10	77.5
5 Yr Avg	5.78	77.1
10 Yr Avg	9.63	70.8
Potential Capital Gain Exposure (% of assets)		42%

Most Similar Funds in MF500

Vanguard/Windsor II	Fair Fit
American Leaders A	Fair Fit
Fidelity Stock Selector	Fair Fit

Index Allocation

	% of Stocks
S&P 500	47.5
S&P MidCap 400	22.4
U.S. Small Cap	28.3
Foreign	9.3

Sector Weightings

	% of Stocks	Relative S&P 500
Utilities	0.0	0.00
Energy	8.8	0.87
Financials	52.6	4.98
Industrial Cyclicals	10.4	0.63
Consumer Durables	0.5	0.09
Consumer Staples	1.7	0.13
Services	12.2	1.50
Retail	0.6	0.11
Health	7.4	0.85
Technology	5.7	0.63

MORNINGSTAR **1995 Mutual Fund 500**

SBSF Convertible Securities

	Ticker	Load	NAV	Yield	SEC Yield	Assets	Objective
	SBFCX	None	10.41	5.5%	5.70%	57.9	Convrt. Bond

SBSF Funds Convertible Securities Fund seeks current income as well as long-term capital appreciation.

The fund invests at least 65% of its assets in convertible securities, although it is not required to sell securities in order to maintain this percentage. These securities are generally rated from BBB to CCC. The balance of assets may be invested in preferred stocks, dividend- and non-dividend-paying common stocks, U.S. government securities, corporate bonds, and money-market instruments of various kinds. The fund may also invest in synthetic convertibles.

Historical Profile

Return	Above Average
Risk	Below Average
Rating	★★★★ Above Average

Income Rtn % Rank Obj: --- 1 1 13 8 8 11

Growth of $10,000

|||| Value of Fund ($000)
— Value of Index ($000) FB HY
▼ Manager Change
▽ Partial Manager Change
► Mgr Unknown After
◄ Mgr Unknown Before

Performance Quartile (Within Objective)

Manager's Investment Style

Management invests in many convertibles with B ratings or lower. This has helped to beef up the fund's yield while protecting it from interest-rate-related losses that more-liquid, highly rated issues have experienced. The fund, as of yet, has not been hurt by its low-rated bonds, because these securities are often inconsistently priced. Management prefers to buy bonds issued by mid- and large-cap companies and stays away from pure yield vehicles, as capital appreciation is also a priority.

Fund Manager(s)

Louis R. Benzak, since 04-88. Birthdate: 08-39.
BA, Pennsylvania State U. 1961

Manager Experience

	Dates Managed	Invest Obj	Std Dev	+/- Index
Louis R. Benzak				
SBSF	10/83 - 12/94	GI	11.33	-2.24

1983	1984	1985	1986	1987	1988	1989	1990	1991	1992	1993	1994	History
---	---	---	---	---	9.73	10.52	9.06	10.67	10.93	12.21	10.41	NAV
---	---	---	---	---	1.81 *	18.91	-5.06	28.47	11.29	20.09	-6.45	Total Return %
---	---	---	---	---		4.37	-14.01	12.47	4.05	10.34	-3.54	+/- LB Aggregate
---	---	---	---	---	-2.73 *	-12.77	-1.94	-2.02	3.67	10.03	-7.77	+/- S&P 500
---	---	---	---	---	4.51	8.69	8.55	8.62	6.63	5.98	5.07	Income Return %
---	---	---	---	---	-2.70	10.22	-13.61	19.84	4.66	14.11	-11.52	Capital Return %
---	---	---	---	---		37	71	29	17	17	76	Total Rtn % Rank All
---	---	---	---	---		25	42	47	58	16	73	Total Rtn % Rank Obj
---	---	---	---	---	0.45	0.82	0.90	0.74	0.68	0.64	0.60	Income $
---	---	---	---	---	0.00	0.19	0.03	0.16	0.23	0.24	0.43	Capital Gains $
---	---	---	---	---	0.84	1.15	1.52	1.37	1.32	1.24	1.32	Expense Ratio %
---	---	---	---	---	7.90	8.72	9.12	7.13	5.46	4.75	5.02	Income Ratio %
---	---	---	---	---		76	32	53	42	30	---	Turnover Rate %
---	---	---	---	---	5.0	12.6	15.2	29.6	49.3	62.5	57.9	Net Assets ($mil)

Performance 12-31-94

	1st Qtr	2nd Qtr	3rd Qtr	4th Qtr	Total
1987	---	---	---	---	---
1988	---	---	0.01	-0.98	1.81 *
1989	5.26	9.10	4.31	-0.72	18.91
1990	-1.71	0.89	-6.69	2.60	-5.06
1991	9.38	4.32	8.86	3.42	28.47
1992	1.69	2.34	4.84	2.00	11.29
1993	7.14	4.33	5.30	2.03	20.09
1994	-2.54	-1.88	2.91	-4.94	-6.45

Bear Market Performance

Decile Rank (5-year period)

Worst ——————————————— Best

	Worst 3 Mo Period 1985-89	Worst 3 Mo Period 1990-94
SBSF Convertible Securities	---	-10.47
+/- LB Aggregate	---	-11.21
+/- Best Fit Index : FB HY	---	3.64

Trailing Returns

	Total Return %	+/- LB Aggregate	+/- S&P 500	% Rank All	% Rank Obj	Growth of $10,000
3 Mo	-4.94	-5.32	-4.93	91	86	9,506
6 Mo	-2.18	-3.17	-7.04	89	89	9,782
1 Yr	-6.45	-3.54	-7.77	76	73	9,355
3 Yr Avg	7.73	3.18	1.46	22	37	12,502
5 Yr Avg	8.80	1.18	0.11	25	52	15,248
10 Yr Avg	---	---	---	---	---	---
15 Yr Avg	---	---	---	---	---	---

Operations

Address and Telephone	45 Rockefeller Plaza New York, NY 10111 800-422-7273 / 212-903-1200	
Advisor	Spears Benzak Salomon & Farrell	
Subadvisor	None	
Distributor	SBSF Funds	
States Available	All except ID,MO,NM,ND,SD	
Report Grade	D	
Income Distrib	Paid Quarterly	
Fiscal Year End	November	

Risk Analysis

Time Period	Load-Adj Return %	Risk % Rank [1] All	Risk % Rank [1] Obj	Morningstar [2] Return	Morningstar Risk	Morningstar Risk-Adj Rating
1 Yr	-6.45					
3 Yr	7.73	33	33	1.25 [3]	0.58	★★★★
5 Yr	8.80	48	9	1.02 [3]	0.64	★★★★
10 Yr	---	---	---	---	---	---

Average Historical Rating (45 months)   3.9 ★s

[1] = low, 100 = high   [2] 1.00 = Hybrid Avg   [3] 1.00 = 90-day T-bill return

Other Measures

			Standard LB Agg	Best Fit FB HY
Standard Deviation	5.45	Alpha	3.3	-1.8
Mean	7.61	Beta	0.86	0.82
Sharpe Ratio	0.75	R-Squared	39	42

Investment Style

Interest-Rate Stance

Avg Effective Maturity   7.4 Yrs

Not Applicable

Quality

Avg Credit Quality   BBB

Avg Weighted Coupon   7.45%

Avg Weighted Price   96.92% of Par

Diversification Value for Portfolio Types

Large Cap: Medium	Small Cap: Medium	Bond: Medium	Balanced: Medium	Diversified: Medium

Expenses & Fees

Sales Fees	0.00% front
	0.00% deferred
	0.00% 12b-1
Management Fee	0.75% flat fee, 0.25%A
3-,5-,10-yr Expense Projections	$41, $70, $154

Min Initial Purchase $5000 (Addt'l: $100)
Min IRA Purchase $500 (Addt'l: $100)
Min Auto Invest Plan $100 (Systematic Inv: $100)

Portfolio 12-31-94

Amount 000	Date of Maturity	Total Stocks: 11 Total Fixed-Income: 54	Value $000	% Net Assets
6000	11-30-96	US Treasury Note 7.25%	5955	10.28
50		Unocal Cv Pfd $3.50	2450	4.23
125		Santa Fe Energy Cv Pfd	2016	3.48
40		Amax Gold Cl B Cv Pfd	1940	3.35
35		Newmont Mining Cv Pfd $5.50	1873	3.23
25		First Bank Sys Cv Pfd $7.125	1494	2.58
1500	12-15-15	Consolidated Nat Gas Cv 7.25%	1448	2.50
75		USX-Marathon Group	1228	2.12
1461	04-15-11	Recognition Intl Cv 7.25%	1198	2.07
20		General Motors Cl C Cv Pfd	1148	1.98
35		ConAgra Cl E Cv Pfd	1146	1.98
1200	07-01-10	Midlantic Banks Cv 8.25%	1143	1.97
45		Riggs National B Cv Pfd 10.75%	1114	1.92
20		Diamond Shamrock Cv Pfd $2.50	1088	1.88
600	01-15-01	CommNet Cellular Cv 8.75%	1080	1.86
50		Noble Drilling Cv Pfd	1050	1.81
1070	01-10-15	Time Warner Cv 8.75%	1011	1.75
1000	08-01-00	Unisys Cv 8.25%	1004	1.73
30		Echo Bay Mines Finl A Cv Pfd	986	1.70
1000	06-23-00	Homestake Mining Cv 5.5%	963	1.66
45		Commerce Bancorp (NJ)	856	1.48
20		Valero Energy Cv Pfd $3.125	840	1.45
1000	10-01-01	Genzyme Cv 6.75%	840	1.45
20		Catellus Development B Cv Pfd	790	1.36
50		Long Island Lighting	769	1.33

Composition % 12-31-94

Cash	7.7	Preferreds	0.0
Stocks	12.4	Convertibles	68.4
Bonds	11.5	Other	0.0

Tax Analysis

	Tax-Adj Historical Return %	% Pretax Return
3 Yr Avg	4.81	60.5
5 Yr Avg	5.81	62.2
10 Yr Avg	---	---

Potential Capital Gain Exposure (% of assets)   -2%

Most Similar Funds in MF500

Seligman Income A	Weak Fit
SBSF	Weak Fit
Fidelity Balanced	Weak Fit

Coupon Range

	% of Bonds	Rel Obj
0%	0.0	0.00
0% to 6%	13.2	0.39
6% to 7%	11.0	0.74
7% to 8.5%	24.0	2.05
More than 8.5%	10.0	1.83
Not applicable	41.8	1.62

Credit Analysis 12-31-94
% of Bonds

US Govt	36	BB	1
AAA	3	B	13
AA	4	Below B	0
A	10	NR/NA	29
BBB	4		

SBSF

	Ticker	Load	NAV	Yield	SEC Yield	Assets	Objective
	SBFFX	None	13.82	1.4%	1.64%	108.0	Growth/Inc.

SBSF Fund seeks total return from dividend and interest income and capital appreciation, consistent with reasonable risk.

The fund may invest in common stocks, preferred stocks, convertible securities, and fixed-income securities. It may shift assets between equity and debt securities to take advantage of relative periods of market strength and weakness. The fund emphasizes growth in rising markets, and preservation of capital during periods of market weakness.

Prior to June 21, 1993, the fund was named SBSF Growth.

Manager's Investment Style

Management rarely holds more than three fourths of assets in stocks; instead, it holds between 10% and 20% in bonds due to mature within two years, and about 10% in convertibles. The fund is nevertheless willing to take substantial positions in individual stocks and sectors. The stocks management buys are often out-of-favor blue chips, but it also picks up smaller-cap names that hold value. The fund has also held gold, on occasion.

Fund Manager(s)

Louis R. Benzak, since 10-83. Birthdate: 08-39.
BA, Pennsylvania State U. 1961

Manager Experience

	Dates Managed	Invest Obj	Std Dev	+/- Index
Louis R. Benzak				
SBSF Convertible Secs	04/88 - 12/94	CV	6.79	0.96

Historical Profile

Return	Average
Risk	Low
Rating	★★★
	Neutral

Investment Style History
Equity
Average % Stocks Held in Portfolio

68% 65% 75% 69% 67% 75% 74% 75%

Growth of $10,000
|||| Value of Fund ($000)
— Value of Index ($000)
S&P 500
▼ Manager Change
▽ Partial Manager Change
► Mgr Unknown After
◄ Mgr Unknown Before

Performance Quartile (Within Objective)

1983	1984	1985	1986	1987	1988	1989	1990	1991	1992	1993	1994	History
10.09	11.08	13.75	12.72	11.49	12.97	16.26	14.83	15.46	15.07	15.71	13.82	NAV
0.60 *	11.84	28.33	4.42	-0.48	17.23	34.04	-2.68	19.04	6.69	20.41	-5.64	Total Return %
2.79 *	5.58	-3.41	-14.26	-5.73	0.62	2.36	0.44	-11.45	-0.93	10.36	-6.95	+/- S&P 500
---	8.79	-4.23	-11.68	-2.84	-0.71	4.87	3.51	-15.17	-2.28	9.13	-5.57	+/- Wilshire 5000
0.00	2.03	4.23	2.76	3.61	3.73	3.71	3.72	3.69	2.71	1.91	1.44	Income Return %
0.60	9.81	24.10	1.66	-4.08	13.50	30.33	-6.39	15.35	3.98	18.51	-7.08	Capital Return %
---	18	32	97	63	20	8	63	46	61	17	69	Total Rtn % Rank All
---	13	44	96	72	35	7	38	93	62	6	90	Total Rtn % Rank Obj
0.00	0.18	0.40	0.38	0.46	0.42	0.51	0.59	0.56	0.40	0.30	0.21	Income $
0.00	0.00	0.00	1.25	0.76	0.07	0.58	0.41	1.60	1.00	2.11	0.79	Capital Gains $
---	1.37	1.40	1.17	1.10	1.16	1.20	1.15	1.15	1.16	1.15	1.19	Expense Ratio %
---	4.11	1.96	1.80	1.67	3.12	3.12	3.66	3.11	2.68	2.05	1.46	Income Ratio %
---	87	80	65	66	47	44	42	50	45	70	---	Turnover Rate %
2.0	23.5	60.7	86.6	84.6	81.0	98.8	92.0	107.6	110.5	120.8	108.0	Net Assets ($mil)

Performance 12-31-94

	1st Qtr	2nd Qtr	3rd Qtr	4th Qtr	Total
1987	15.04	1.37	5.97	-19.47	-0.48
1988	6.79	5.26	4.41	-0.11	17.23
1989	7.25	9.06	9.82	4.36	34.04
1990	-3.75	5.23	-7.50	3.88	-2.68
1991	8.56	-1.53	6.00	5.05	19.04
1992	-5.24	1.07	7.05	4.05	6.69
1993	5.31	3.72	6.70	3.32	20.41
1994	-3.25	-0.86	1.14	-2.73	-5.64

Bear Market Performance

Decile Rank (5-year period)

Worst .... Best

	Worst 3 Mo Period 1985-89	Worst 3 Mo Period 1990-94
SBSF	-22.86	-8.52
+/- S&P 500	6.72	5.32
+/- Best Fit Index : S&P 500	6.72	5.32

Trailing Returns

	Total Return %	+/- S&P 500	+/- Wil 5000	% Rank All	% Rank Obj	Growth of $10,000
3 Mo	-2.73	-2.72	-1.96	80	80	9,727
6 Mo	-1.63	-6.49	-6.25	83	95	9,837
1 Yr	-5.64	-6.95	-5.57	69	90	9,436
3 Yr Avg	6.63	0.36	0.01	29	35	12,122
5 Yr Avg	7.03	-1.66	-1.79	49	72	14,044
10 Yr Avg	11.40	-2.98	-2.46	43	65	29,432
15 Yr Avg	---	---	---	---	---	---

Operations

Address and Telephone	45 Rockefeller Plaza
	New York, NY 10111
	800-422-7273 / 212-903-1200
Advisor	Spears Benzak Salomon & Farrell
Subadvisor	None
Distributor	SBSF Funds
States Available	All except ID,MO,NM,ND,SD
Report Grade	D
Income Distrib	Paid Semiannually
* Date of Inception	10-17-83
Fiscal Year End	November

Risk Analysis

Time Period	Load-Adj Return %	Risk % Rank All	Risk % Rank Obj	Morningstar [2] Return	Morningstar Risk	Morningstar Risk-Adj Rating
1 Yr	-5.64					
3 Yr	6.63	56	18	0.91 [3]	0.61	★★★
5 Yr	7.03	55	12	0.56 [3]	0.61	★★★
10 Yr	11.40	45	12	0.77	0.66	★★★

Average Historical Rating (99 months) 3.6 ★s

[1] 1 = low, 100 = high [2] 1.00 = Equity Avg [3] 1.00 = 90-day T-bill return

Other Measures

	Standard S&P 500	Best Fit S&P 500
Standard Deviation	7.23	Alpha 1.2	1.2
Mean	6.69	Beta 0.68	0.68
Sharpe Ratio	0.44	R-Squared 55	55

Investment Style

	Stock Portfolio Avg	Relative S&P 500
Price/Earnings Ratio	22.8	1.23
Price/Book Ratio	2.1	0.63
5 Yr Earnings Gr %	10.2	1.83
Return on Assets %	4.2	0.57
Debt % Total Cap	35.9	1.27
Med Mkt Cap ($mil)	3058	0.24

Style
Value Blend Growth
Size: Large Med Small

Diversification Value for Portfolio Types

Large Cap: Low | Small Cap: High | Bond: Medium | Balanced: Low | Diversified: Low

Expenses & Fees

Sales Fees	
	0.00% front
	0.00% deferred
	0.00% 12b-1
Management Fee	0.75% flat fee, 0.25%A
3-,5-,10-yr Expense Projections	$38, $65, $144
Annual Brokerage Cost	0.21%

Min Initial Purchase	$5000 (Addt'l: $100)
Min IRA Purchase	$500 (Addt'l: $100)
Min Auto Invest Plan	$100 (Systematic Inv: $100)

Portfolio 12-31-94

Share Chg (05-94)000	Amount 000	Total Stocks: 45 / Total Fixed-Income: 6	Value $000	% Net Assets
0	76	American International Group	7399	6.86
0	119	Avatar	4535	4.21
-12	213	USX-Marathon Group	3488	3.24
-25	150	Tele-Communications Cl A	3263	3.03
50	50	Intel	3194	2.96
	2825	American City Bus Jrnls Cv 6%	3023	2.80
	3065	US Treasury Note 5.625%	2905	2.70
-43	355	Santa Fe Energy Resources	2841	2.64
0	78	Genetics Institute	2808	2.61
60	60	Boeing	2805	2.60
25	50	JP Morgan	2800	2.60
15	115	Standard Federal Bank (MI)	2746	2.55
100	100	Unocal	2725	2.53
172	172	System Software Associates	2701	2.51
0	150	Hanson (ADR)	2700	2.50
75	75	Echo Bay Finl A Cv Pfd $1.75	2466	2.29
0	151	Comcast Special Cl A	2368	2.20
81	81	Tosco	2359	2.19
13	175	Horsham	2231	2.07
0	75	Pacific Telesis Group	2138	1.98
25	100	PartnerRe Holdings	2075	1.93
25	125	Shawmut National	2047	1.90
75	175	Beazer Homes USA	2034	1.89
0	38	Gannett	1997	1.85
0	15	General Re	1856	1.72

Composition % 12-31-94

Cash	9.5	Preferreds	0.0
Stocks	82.0	Convertibles	7.0
Bonds	1.5	Other	0.0

Tax Analysis

	Tax-Adj Historical Return %	% Pretax Return
3 Yr Avg	3.60	52.8
5 Yr Avg	3.99	53.5
10 Yr Avg	8.59	65.8
Potential Capital Gain Exposure (% of assets)		7%

Most Similar Funds in MF500

CGM Mutual	Weak Fit
Flag Inv Telephone Income A	Weak Fit
T. Rowe Price Balanced	Weak Fit

Index Allocation

	% of Stocks
S&P 500	56.4
S&P MidCap 400	4.4
U.S. Small Cap	29.7
Foreign	9.5

Sector Weightings

	% of Stocks	Relative S&P 500
Utilities	2.5	0.20
Energy	14.7	1.45
Financials	33.6	3.18
Industrial Cyclicals	17.3	1.06
Consumer Durables	0.4	0.06
Consumer Staples	1.6	0.13
Services	18.1	2.22
Retail	0.6	0.11
Health	1.7	0.20
Technology	9.5	1.04

Morningstar **1995 Mutual Fund 500**

Schafer Value

	Ticker	Load	NAV	Yield	SEC Yield	Assets	Objective
	SCHVX	None	33.23	0.9%	N/A	73.5	Growth

Schafer Value Fund seeks long-term capital appreciation. Current income is secondary.

The fund invests in securities of established companies with market capitalizations of at least $250 million and low stock-market valuations relative to their intrinsic investment value. Securities are generally held until they no longer meet the fund's financial or valuation criteria. The fund may invest up to 20% of its assets in foreign securities. It rarely engages in market timing.

Manager's Investment Style

Manager David Schafer is a stringent value manager who emphasizes individual stock selection. He looks for companies selling at discounts to their potential earnings, which has led to very low price multiples relative to other mid-cap, value strategies. He also looks for companies that can be expected to grow faster than the average S&P 500 company over a several-year period. He also limits the number of holdings to about 35.

Fund Manager(s)

David K. Schafer, since 10-85. Birthdate: 04-39.
BA, DePauw U. 1963 MBA, New York U. 1966

Manager Experience

	Dates Managed	Invest Obj	Std Dev	+/- Index
David K. Schafer				
Chubb Growth & Income	05/93 - 12/94	GI	10.29	-1.63
Chubb Total Return	05/93 - 12/94	B	7.62	-1.77

Performance 12-31-94

	1st Qtr	2nd Qtr	3rd Qtr	4th Qtr	Total
1987	20.21	3.33	9.12	-26.52	-0.40
1988	12.48	3.16	-0.90	2.60	17.98
1989	11.31	4.49	14.68	-2.51	30.05
1990	-3.04	4.80	-16.64	6.16	-10.07
1991	22.52	-4.65	10.69	8.98	40.92
1992	3.35	2.70	2.70	8.87	18.67
1993	7.33	2.46	7.26	5.11	23.98
1994	-2.50	-0.81	2.73	-3.65	-4.28

Bear Market Performance

Decile Rank (5-year period)

Worst ———————————————— Best

	Worst 3 Mo Period 1985-89	Worst 3 Mo Period 1990-94
Schafer Value	---	-21.43
+/- S&P 500	---	-7.59
+/- Best Fit Index : SPMid400	---	-3.01

Trailing Returns

	Total Return %	+/- S&P 500	+/- Wil 5000	% Rank All	% Rank Obj	Growth of $10,000
3 Mo	-3.65	-3.63	-2.88	87	85	9,635
6 Mo	-1.02	-5.88	-5.64	74	93	9,898
1 Yr	-4.28	-5.59	-4.21	56	71	9,572
3 Yr Avg	12.09	5.83	5.48	8	10	14,083
5 Yr Avg	12.28	3.59	3.47	8	12	17,848
10 Yr Avg	---	---	---	---	---	---
15 Yr Avg	---	---	---	---	---	---

Operations

Address and Telephone	645 Fifth Avenue
	New York, NY 10022
	800-343-0481 / 212-644-1800
Advisor	Schafer Capital Management
Subadvisor	None
Distributor	Lazard Freres
States Available	All
Report Grade	B+
Income Distrib	Paid Annually
* Date of Inception	10-22-85
Fiscal Year End	September

Historical Profile

Return	Above Average
Risk	Average
Rating ★★★★	Above Average

	114%				97%	96%	97%	100%

Investment Style History
Equity

Average % Stocks Held in Portfolio

Growth of $10,000
- |||| Value of Fund ($000)
- — Value of Index ($000) SPMid400
- ▼ Manager Change
- ▽ Partial Manager Change
- ► Mgr Unknown After
- ◄ Mgr Unknown Before

Performance Quartile (Within Objective)

	1983	1984	1985	1986	1987	1988	1989	1990	1991	1992	1993	1994	History
NAV	---	---	20.73	22.51	22.42	24.86	30.28	24.91	28.98	30.70	36.78	33.23	
Total Return %	---	---	3.55 *	10.06	-0.40	17.98	30.05	-10.07	40.92	18.67	23.98	-4.28	
+/- S&P 500	---	---	-9.94 *	-8.62	-5.66	1.37	-1.63	-6.95	10.43	11.05	13.92	-5.59	
+/- Wilshire 5000	---	---		-6.03	-2.76	0.04	0.88	-3.89	6.71	9.70	12.69	-4.21	
Income Return %	---	---	0.00	1.48	0.00	1.02	5.49	2.24	1.86	1.29	0.54	0.98	
Capital Return %	---	---	3.55	8.59	-0.40	16.96	24.57	-12.30	39.06	17.38	23.44	-5.26	
Total Rtn % Rank All	---	---		84	63	18	13	84	13	6	12	56	
Total Rtn % Rank Obj	---	---		81	70	36	35	81	31	8	8	71	
Income $	---	---	0.00	0.31	0.00	0.22	1.26	0.58	0.52	0.39	0.19	0.33	
Capital Gains $	---	---	0.00	0.00	0.00	1.18	0.60	1.73	5.48	3.27	1.08	1.64	
Expense Ratio %	---	---		2.05	1.96	1.82	2.09	2.00	2.00	2.08	1.74	1.48	
Income Ratio %	---	---		1.80	1.20	2.32	1.81	1.45	1.26	1.20	0.79	0.99	
Turnover Rate %	---	---		20	47	43	42	36	55	53	33	28	
Net Assets ($mil)	---	---			8.8	12.5	9.0	12.0	10.0	10.3	13.6	25.8	73.5

Risk Analysis

Time Period	Load-Adj Return %	Risk % Rank [1] All	Obj	Morningstar [2] Return	Morningstar Risk	Morningstar Risk-Adj Rating
1 Yr	-4.28					
3 Yr	12.09	64	23	2.67 [3]	0.72	★★★★
5 Yr	12.28	77	53	2.03 [3]	0.93	★★★★
10 Yr	---	---	---	---	---	---

Average Historical Rating (75 months) 3.9 ★s

[1] 1 = low, 100 = high [2] 1.00 = Equity Avg [3] 1.00 = 90-day T-bill return

Other Measures

			Standard S&P 500	Best Fit SPMid400
Standard Deviation	9.29	Alpha	5.8	5.4
Mean	11.90	Beta	0.96	0.80
Sharpe Ratio	0.90	R-Squared	67	73

Investment Style

	Stock Portfolio Avg	Relative S&P 500
Price/Earnings Ratio	13.3	0.72
Price/Book Ratio	2.1	0.61
5 Yr Earnings Gr %	10.1	1.81
Return on Assets %	5.7	0.76
Debt % Total Cap	30.1	1.06
Med Mkt Cap ($mil)	2522	0.19

Style: Value Blend Growth — Size Large Med Small

Diversification Value for Portfolio Types

Large Cap: Low	Small Cap: Low	Bond: High	Balanced: Low	Diversified: Low

Portfolio 09-30-94

Total Stocks: 36
Total Fixed-Income: 0

Share Chg (03-94)	Amount 000		Value $000	% Net Assets
67	91	Fingerhut	2098	3.07
80	162	National Health Lab Hldgs	2091	3.06
16	35	American Home Products	2082	3.04
31	53	Cummins Engine	2079	3.04
41	41	Burlington Northern	2060	3.01
33	43	General Motors	2030	2.97
21	44	First Chicago	2014	2.94
50	103	Fleet Mortgage Group	2012	2.94
52	79	Ultramar	2004	2.93
31	60	Owens-Corning	1997	2.92
22	57	Polaroid	1985	2.90
29	54	Avnet	1985	2.90
32	32	Philip Morris	1980	2.90
65	65	Inco	1967	2.88
46	109	K mart	1952	2.85
76	135	PaineWebber Group	1946	2.85
56	56	Merrill Lynch	1939	2.83
34	80	FirstFed Michigan	1926	2.82
17	54	Progressive	1917	2.80
22	46	E-Systems	1916	2.80
19	67	Baxter International	1896	2.77
15	34	Mellon Bank	1884	2.75
90	166	Toll Brothers	1884	2.75
94	146	Sotheby's Holdings Cl A	1880	2.75
23	43	Boeing	1863	2.72

Composition % 12-31-94

Cash	0.3	Preferreds	0.0	
Stocks	99.7	Convertibles	0.0	
Bonds	0.0	Other	0.0	

Tax Analysis

	Tax-Adj Historical Return %	% Pretax Return
3 Yr Avg	9.96	80.7
5 Yr Avg	9.28	71.2
10 Yr Avg	---	---
Potential Capital Gain Exposure (% of assets)		-2%

Most Similar Funds in MF500

Fundamental Investors	Fair Fit
Neuberger&Berman Partners	Fair Fit
Fidelity Stock Selector	Fair Fit

Index Allocation

	% of Stocks
S&P 500	56.0
S&P MidCap 400	17.6
U.S. Small Cap	20.9
Foreign	8.5

Sector Weightings

	% of Stocks	Relative S&P 500
Utilities	2.6	0.21
Energy	5.6	0.55
Financials	27.0	2.55
Industrial Cyclicals	23.7	1.44
Consumer Durables	8.5	1.37
Consumer Staples	5.4	0.43
Services	11.6	1.42
Retail	2.9	0.50
Health	6.0	0.69
Technology	6.9	0.76

Min Purchase

Min Initial Purchase	$2000 (Addt'l: $1000)
Min IRA Purchase	$2000 (Addt'l: $1000)
Min Auto Invest Plan	$500 (Systematic Inv: $100)

Expenses & Fees

Sales Fees	0.00% front
	0.00% deferred
	0.00% 12b-1
Management Fee	1.00% flat fee
3-,5-,10-yr Expense Projections	$55, $94, $205
Annual Brokerage Cost	0.27%

Schooner

Schooner Fund seeks long-term growth of capital.
The fund invests at least 50% of its assets in undervalued equity-related securities issued by companies with market capitalization of less than $1 billion. It primarily considers a company's assets and earning power when purchasing a security; dividend income matters little. The balance of fund assets may be invested in nonconvertible preferred stocks and long-term debt obligations that may offer capital appreciation. At least 75% of the debt obligations are high quality; the remainder may be low quality. The fund may invest up to 25% of its assets in foreign equity and debt instruments.

Manager's Investment Style

Management displays a willingness to take on the market's ugly ducklings--out-of-favor stocks with depressed values. In order to allow these picks time to appreciate, management will hold its choices for the long term.

	Ticker	Load	NAV	Yield	SEC Yield	Assets	Objective
	N/A	None	25.25	0.9%	N/A	4.7	Small Company

Historical Profile
Return ---
Risk ---
Rating   Not Rated

24%   50%

Investment Style History
Equity
Average % Stocks Held
in Portfolio

Growth of $10,000
|||| Value of Fund ($000)
— Value of Index ($000)
S&P 500
▼ Manager Change
▽ Partial Manager Change
► Mgr Unknown After
◄ Mgr Unknown Before

Performance Quartile
(Within Objective)

	1983	1984	1985	1986	1987	1988	1989	1990	1991	1992	1993	1994	History
	---	---	---	---	---	---	---	---	---	---	25.56	25.25	NAV
	---	---	---	---	---	---	---	---	---	---	2.71 *	0.32	Total Return %
	---	---	---	---	---	---	---	---	---	---	-3.39 *	-0.99	+/- S&P 500
	---	---	---	---	---	---	---	---	---	---	---	2.98	+/- Wilshire 4500
	---	---	---	---	---	---	---	---	---	---	0.45	0.90	Income Return %
	---	---	---	---	---	---	---	---	---	---	2.26	-0.58	Capital Return %
	---	---	---	---	---	---	---	---	---	---	---	17	Total Rtn % Rank All
	---	---	---	---	---	---	---	---	---	---	---	38	Total Rtn % Rank Obj
	---	---	---	---	---	---	---	---	---	---	0.11	0.23	Income $
	---	---	---	---	---	---	---	---	---	---	0.01	0.16	Capital Gains $
	---	---	---	---	---	---	---	---	---	---	1.50	1.50	Expense Ratio %
	---	---	---	---	---	---	---	---	---	---	1.14	1.39	Income Ratio %
	---	---	---	---	---	---	---	---	---	---	1	15	Turnover Rate %
	---	---	---	---	---	---	---	---	---	---	2.2	4.7	Net Assets ($mil)

Fund Manager(s)

James H. Gipson, since 06-93. Birthdate: 10-42.
MA, U. of California-Los Angeles 1964   MBA, Harvard 1973
Douglas Grey, since 01-94. Birthdate: 10-60. BE, Vanderbilt U. 1983   MBA, U. of Chicago 1986

Manager Experience	Dates Managed	Invest Obj	Std Dev	+/- Index
James H. Gipson				
Clipper	02/84 - 12/94	G	12.75	-0.11

Performance 12-31-94

	1st Qtr	2nd Qtr	3rd Qtr	4th Qtr	Total
1987	---	---	---	---	---
1988	---	---	---	---	---
1989	---	---	---	---	---
1990	---	---	---	---	---
1991	---	---	---	---	---
1992	---	---	---	---	---
1993	---	---	0.24	2.47	2.71 *
1994	-1.68	-0.24	0.52	1.76	0.32

Bear Market Performance

Decile Rank (5-year period)

Worst _____ Best

	Worst 3 Mo Period 1985-89	Worst 3 Mo Period 1990-94
Schooner	---	---
+/- S&P 500	---	---
+/- Best Fit Index :	---	---

Trailing Returns

	Total Return %	+/- S&P 500	+/- Wil 4500	% Rank All	% Rank Obj	Growth of $10,000
3 Mo	1.76	1.77	4.26	4	21	10,176
6 Mo	2.28	-2.58	-1.91	24	79	10,228
1 Yr	0.32	-0.99	2.98	17	38	10,032
3 Yr Avg	---	---	---	---	---	---
5 Yr Avg	---	---	---	---	---	---
10 Yr Avg	---	---	---	---	---	---
15 Yr Avg	---	---	---	---	---	---

Risk Analysis

Time Period	Load-Adj Return %	Risk % Rank All	Risk % Rank Obj	Morningstar Return	Morningstar Risk	Morningstar Risk-Adj Rating
1 Yr	0.32					
3 Yr	---	---	---	---	---	---
5 Yr	---	---	---	---	---	---
10 Yr	---	---	---	---	---	---

Average Historical Rating ---

[1] 1 = low, 100 = high   [2] 1.00 = Equity Avg   [3] 1.00 = 90-day T-bill return

Other Measures

		Standard S&P 500	Best Fit
Standard Deviation	Alpha	---	---
Mean	Beta	---	---
Sharpe Ratio	R-Squared	---	---

Investment Style

	Stock Portfolio Avg	Relative S&P 500
Price/Earnings Ratio	11.8	0.64
Price/Book Ratio	1.9	0.57
5 Yr Earnings Gr %	18.1	3.25
Return on Assets %	7.7	1.02
Debt % Total Cap	30.6	1.08
Med Mkt Cap ($mil)	289	0.02

Style
Value Blend Growth
Size Large/Med/Small

Diversification Value for Portfolio Types

Large Cap: Small Cap: Bond: Balanced: Diversified:

Portfolio 09-30-94

Total Stocks: 21
Total Fixed-Income: 1

Share Chg (08-94) 000	Amount 000		Value $000	% Net Assets
	1559	US Treasury Note 7.25%	1497	31.52
3	13	Boston Acoustics	189	3.98
0	5	Stanhome	164	3.45
6	28	Michael Anthony Jewelers	161	3.39
0	11	Russ Berrie	152	3.21
0	6	TCA Cable Television	149	3.13
0	18	Carr-Gottstein Foods	137	2.89
0	5	Quick & Reilly Group	135	2.83
0	5	Alex Brown	134	2.82
0	10	Cone Mills	129	2.71
4	8	Scotts Cl A	119	2.51
0	5	Inter-Regional Financial Grp	115	2.43
0	4	Eaton Vance	108	2.27
0	17	Service Merchandise	107	2.26
0	8	Leslie's Poolmart	106	2.23
0	5	John Nuveen Cl A	105	2.21
0	5	MacFrugals Bargains	89	1.88
0	5	Lillian Vernon	89	1.87
0	6	Home State Holdings	81	1.71
12	12	Central Garden & Pet	78	1.64
0	2	First Brands	67	1.41
0	3	MagneTek	43	0.91

Composition % 12-31-94

Cash	21.6	Preferreds	0.0
Stocks	72.4	Convertibles	0.0
Bonds	6.0	Other	0.0

Tax Analysis

	Tax-Adj Historical Return %	% Pretax Return
3 Yr Avg	---	---
5 Yr Avg	---	---
10 Yr Avg	---	---

Potential Capital Gain Exposure
(% of assets)   0%

Most Similar Funds in MF500

Fund lacks three-year record

Index Allocation

	% of Stocks
S&P 500	0.0
S&P MidCap 400	25.2
U.S. Small Cap	74.8
Foreign	0.0

Sector Weightings

	% of Stocks	Relative S&P 500
Utilities	0.0	0.00
Energy	0.0	0.00
Financials	27.6	2.61
Industrial Cyclicals	6.6	0.40
Consumer Durables	28.4	4.57
Consumer Staples	6.7	0.53
Services	6.1	0.74
Retail	24.7	4.24
Health	0.0	0.00
Technology	0.0	0.00

Operations

Address and Telephone	9601 Wilshire Boulevard Beverly Hills, CA 90210 800-420-7556
Advisor	Pacific Financial Research
Subadvisor	None
Distributor	Schooner
States Available	Selected states
Report Grade	A-
Income Distrib	Paid Annually
* Date of Inception	06-24-93
Fiscal Year End	December

Min Initial Purchase	$5000 (Addt'l: $1000)
Min IRA Purchase	$1000 (Addt'l: $200)
Min Auto Invest Plan	N/A

Expenses & Fees
Sales Fees	0.00% front
	0.00% deferred
	0.00% 12b-1
Management Fee	1.00% flat fee
3-,5-,10-yr Expense Projections	$48, N/A, N/A
Annual Brokerage Cost	

MORNINGSTAR 1995 Mutual Fund 500

Scudder Global

	Ticker	Load	NAV	Yield	SEC Yield	Assets	Objective
	SCOBX	None	23.33	0.5%	N/A	1117.7	World Stock

Scudder Global Fund seeks long-term growth of capital; income is incidental.

The fund invests in companies expected to benefit from global economic trends, promising technologies, or specific country opportunities. It is expected that investments will be spread broadly around the world, including the United States, in companies of varying size as measured by assets, sales, or capitalization. It generally invests in the equity securities of established companies listed on foreign securities exchanges. The fund may purchase and sell options on any of its securities.

Manager's Investment Style

As with other funds in this family, management follows a complex strategy, pinpointing global or regional themes, while also focusing on markets where the themes are likely to play out and where prices are cheap. Management will also resort to bonds for defensiveness, and favors a risk-lowering diversified portfolio. Overall, management follows a value discipline with a focus on the long term.

Fund Manager(s)

William E. Holzer, since 07-86.
Nicholas Bratt, since 03-94.
Alice Ho, since 03-94.

Manager Experience	Dates Managed	Invest Obj	Std Dev	+/- Index
William E. Holzer				
Managers Intl Equity	12/89 - 12/94	WF	12.71	0.73
Cambridge Global B	03/94 - 12/94	WW	7.62	-8.12

Historical Profile
Return	Average
Risk	Below Average
Rating	★★★ Neutral

Average % Stocks Held in Portfolio: 86% 87% 81% 71% 82% 86% 81% 84%

Investment Style History Equity

Growth of $10,000
- IIII Value of Fund ($000)
- — Value of Index ($000) MSEASEA
- ▼ Manager Change
- ▽ Partial Manager Change
- ► Mgr Unknown After
- ◄ Mgr Unknown Before

Performance Quartile (Within Objective)

	1983	1984	1985	1986	1987	1988	1989	1990	1991	1992	1993	1994	History
	---	---	---	12.43	12.56	14.74	19.48	17.06	18.96	19.32	24.80	23.33	NAV
	---	---	---	3.58 *	3.03	19.19	37.41	-6.40	17.07	4.55	31.10	-4.20	Total Return %
	---	---	---	0.36 *	-2.23	2.58	5.72	-3.29	-13.41	-3.07	21.05	-5.52	+/- S&P 500
	---	---	---	---	-13.14	-4.10	20.80	10.62	-1.21	9.77	8.60	-9.28	+/- MSCI World
	---	---	---	0.00	0.17	0.69	0.61	3.40	1.77	0.83	1.14	0.44	Income Return %
	---	---	---	3.58	2.86	18.50	36.80	-9.80	15.30	3.71	29.96	-4.64	Capital Return %
	---	---	---	---	35	16	5	75	50	79	8	55	Total Rtn % Rank All
	---	---	---	---	52	24	5	20	45	16	47	64	Total Rtn % Rank Obj
	---	---	---	0.00	0.03	0.09	0.11	0.62	0.31	0.16	0.24	0.11	Income $
	---	---	---	0.00	0.28	0.13	0.64	0.58	0.66	0.34	0.26	0.34	Capital Gains $
	---	---	---	---	1.84	1.71	1.98	1.81	1.70	1.59	1.48	1.45	Expense Ratio %
	---	---	---	---	0.63	1.23	1.22	1.77	2.21	1.09	0.90	0.97	Income Ratio %
	---	---	---	---	32	54	31	38	85	45	65	60	Turnover Rate %
	---	---	---	41.0	115.0	74.5	145.0	237.6	298.8	400.5	963.0	1117.7	Net Assets ($mil)

Performance 12-31-94

	1st Qtr	2nd Qtr	3rd Qtr	4th Qtr	Total
1987	15.93	7.01	8.37	-23.37	3.03
1988	9.39	5.24	-1.56	5.17	19.19
1989	9.84	8.96	11.95	2.56	37.41
1990	-0.36	4.89	-13.99	4.12	-6.40
1991	8.68	-2.59	6.74	3.61	17.07
1992	-0.84	4.04	0.51	0.82	4.55
1993	6.63	5.00	8.61	7.82	31.10
1994	-3.06	-0.29	3.70	-4.42	-4.20

Bear Market Performance

Decile Rank (5-year period)

	Worst 3 Mo Period 1985-89	Worst 3 Mo Period 1990-94
Scudder Global	---	-13.99
+/- S&P 500	---	-0.24
+/- Best Fit Index : MSEASEA	---	2.63

Trailing Returns

	Total Return %	+/- S&P 500	+/- MSCI World	% Rank All	% Rank Obj	Growth of $10,000
3 Mo	-4.42	-4.41	-3.69	90	46	9,558
6 Mo	-0.88	-5.75	-2.28	71	62	9,912
1 Yr	-4.20	-5.52	-9.28	55	64	9,580
3 Yr Avg	9.50	3.24	2.65	15	30	13,130
5 Yr Avg	7.55	-1.14	3.88	40	22	14,388
10 Yr Avg	---	---	---	---	---	---
15 Yr Avg	---	---	---	---	---	---

Operations

Address and Telephone	Two International Place Boston, MA 02110 800-225-2470 / 617-439-4640
Advisor	Scudder Stevens & Clark
Subadvisor	None
Distributor	Scudder Investor Services
States Available	All
Report Grade	A
Income Distrib	Paid Annually
* Date of Inception	07-23-86
Fiscal Year End	June

Risk Analysis

Time Period	Load-Adj Return %	Risk % Rank [1] All	Obj	Morningstar [2] Return	Morningstar Risk	Morningstar Risk-Adj Rating
1 Yr	-4.20					
3 Yr	9.50	58	2	1.81 [3]	0.64	★★★★
5 Yr	7.55	61	5	0.69 [3]	0.73	★★★
10 Yr	---	---	---			

Average Historical Rating (66 months)   4.2 ★s

[1] 1 = low, 100 = high [2] 1.00 = Equity Avg [3] 1.00 = 90-day T-bill return

Other Measures

				Standard S&P 500	Best Fit MSEASEA
Standard Deviation	8.65	Alpha		3.9	2.4
Mean	9.48	Beta		0.72	0.57
Sharpe Ratio	0.69	R-Squared		44	75

Investment Style

	Stock Portfolio Avg	Rel MSCI EAFE	Rel Obj	Style
Price/Earnings Ratio	27.6	0.75	1.12	
Price/Cash Flow	12.3	0.79	0.91	
Price/Book Ratio	2.2	0.85	0.75	
5 Yr Earnings Gr %	0.4#		0.09	
Return on Assets %	5.0	1.11	0.73	
Debt % Total Cap	30.6	0.90	1.06	
Med Mkt Cap ($mil)	7604	0.64	1.51	

Style: V B G / Size L M S
figure is based on 50% or less of stocks

Diversification Value for Portfolio Types

Large Cap: Medium	Small Cap: Medium	Bond: Medium	Balanced: Low	Diversified: Low

Tax Analysis

	Tax-Adj Historical Return %	% Pretax Return
3 Yr Avg	8.78	91.8
5 Yr Avg	6.34	82.0
10 Yr Avg	---	---
Potential Capital Gain Exposure (% of assets)	10%	

Most Similar Funds in MF500

Templeton Growth	Strong Fit
Putnam Global Growth A	Strong Fit
Templeton Smaller Comp Grth	Strong Fit

Portfolio 06-30-94

Share Chg (12-93) 000	Amount 000	Total Stocks: 168 Total Fixed-Income: 14	Value $000	% Net Assets
633	1018	Canon	17854	1.63
0	372	Intl Nederlanden Group	15943	1.46
288	481	Enron	15756	1.44
4	18	BBC Brown Boveri (Br)	15720	1.43
230	591	WMX Technologies	15667	1.43
255	1490	Hitachi	15558	1.42
1037	1037	Canadian Pacific	15292	1.40
360	1823	Toshiba	14933	1.36
191	191	Kyocera	14271	1.30
109	775	Matsushita Electric Indl	14221	1.30
	9770	United Kingdom Treasury 7.75%	14006	1.28
111	284	Boeing	13144	1.20
189	189	Secom	13125	1.20
166	213	Sony	13064	1.19
146	230	Ito-Yokado	12708	1.16
	84400	US Treasury Bond 0%	12706	1.16
1910	6067	Lasmo	12596	1.15
310	716	SKF Cl B Free (Sweden)	12570	1.15
855	3711	Woodside Petroleum	12473	1.14
249	973	RTZ	12340	1.13

Regional Exposure 12-31-94
% of Stocks

Europe	33	Pacific Rim	17
Japan	12	U.S.	32
Latin Amer	3	Other	3

Composition % 12-31-94
Cash	-0.2	Preferred	1.6
Stocks	87.1	Convertibles	1.9
Bonds	9.6	Other	0.0

Top 5 Countries 12-31-94
% of Stocks

U.S.	31
Japan	11
Switzerland	7
Germany	6
South Korea	5

Total Number of Countries: 28
Hedging Policy: Occasional

Sector Weightings

	% of Stocks	Relative S&P 500
Utilities	12.7	1.53
Energy	7.5	1.55
Financials	14.4	0.87
Industrial Cyclicals	24.6	1.06
Consumer Durables	6.3	0.61
Consumer Staples	2.6	0.52
Services	15.0	1.27
Retail	4.0	0.69
Health	3.9	0.75
Technology	8.9	1.00

Expenses & Fees

Sales Fees	0.00% front 0.00% deferred 0.00% 12b-1
Management Fee	1.00% flat fee
3-,5-,10-yr Expense Projections	$47, $81, $177
Annual Brokerage Cost	0.24%

Min Initial Purchase	$1000 (Addt'l: $100)
Min IRA Purchase	$500 (Addt'l: $50)
Min Auto Invest Plan	$50 (Systematic Inv: $50)

Scudder GNMA

	Ticker	Load	NAV	Yield	SEC Yield	Assets	Objective
	SGMSX	None	13.66	6.8%	6.93%	417.0	Gvt Mortgage

Scudder GNMA Fund seeks high current income.

The fund invests primarily in mortgage securities issued or backed by the U.S. government or its agencies or instrumentalities. In addition, it may invest in bills, notes, and bonds issued by the U.S. Treasury or by various U.S. government agencies or instrumentalities. The fund may purchase or sell options on any of these securities or enter into repurchase agreements secured by U.S. government obligations. For hedging purposes, the fund may use futures contracts and put and call options on such contracts.

The fund used to be named Scudder Government Mortgage Securities Fund.

Manager's Investment Style

Historically, management has favored slight-premium Ginnie Maes for their high payouts. It has also used dollar rolls--at times, extending the fund's assets by 20%--in an attempt to bolster yield. The fund has, however, made some uncharacteristic moves. In 1994, in particular, management moved into current-coupon Ginnie Maes to play falling rates; when rates rose unexpectedly, however, management raised cash to a record 20% level. The fund's recent yield has thus eroded from pre-1994 levels.

Fund Manager(s)

David H. Glen CFA(1985), since 07-85. Birthdate: 05-57. BBA, U. of Michigan 1978 MBA, Indiana U. 1981
Robert E. Pruyne, since 07-85. Birthdate: 08-34. BA, Amherst C. 1956 MA, Princeton U. 1958

Manager Experience	Dates Managed	Invest Obj	Std Dev	+/- Index
Robert E. Pruyne				
AARP GNMA & U.S. Treas	11/84 - 12/94	GG	3.57	-1.71
David H. Glen				
AARP GNMA & U.S. Treas	01/85 - 12/94	GG	3.57	-1.31

Historical Profile
Return	Above Average
Risk	Average
Rating	★★★
	Neutral

75	63	65	62	60	11	10	48

Investment Style History
Fixed Income
Income Rtn % Rank Obj

Growth of $10,000
‖‖‖ Value of Fund ($000)
— Value of Index ($000)
   LB Mtg
▼ Manager Change
▽ Partial Manager Change
► Mgr Unknown After
◄ Mgr Unknown Before

Performance Quartile
(Within Objective)

	1983	1984	1985	1986	1987	1988	1989	1990	1991	1992	1993	1994	History
	---	---	15.34	15.50	14.43	14.09	14.56	14.72	15.62	15.36	15.06	13.66	NAV
	---	---	8.42 *	11.34	1.32	6.76	12.84	10.15	15.01	6.96	6.00	-3.10	Total Return %
	---	---	---	-3.91	-1.44	-1.12	-1.70	1.20	-0.99	-0.28	-3.75	-0.19	+/- LB Aggregate
	---	---	---	-2.09	-2.97	-1.96	-2.51	-0.58	-0.71	0.01	-0.84	-1.50	+/- LB Mortgage
	---	---	4.35	9.79	8.21	9.11	9.50	9.05	8.89	8.63	7.95	6.19	Income Return %
	---	---	4.07	1.56	-6.89	-2.36	3.34	1.10	6.11	-1.66	-1.95	-9.30	Capital Return %
	---	---	---	78	48	82	54	5	58	58	88	44	Total Rtn % Rank All
	---	---	---	43	70	73	54	33	50	22	71	62	Total Rtn % Rank Obj
	---	---	0.62	1.42	1.26	1.29	1.26	1.23	1.21	1.29	1.20	0.94	Income $
	---	---	0.00	0.08	0.00	0.00	0.00	0.00	0.00	0.00	0.00	0.00	Capital Gains $
	---	---	---	1.02	1.05	1.04	1.04	1.05	1.04	0.99	0.93	0.87	Expense Ratio %
	---	---	---	10.11	8.63	8.93	8.95	8.74	8.49	8.24	8.36	7.35	Income Ratio %
	---	---	---	124	59	92	128	71	52	87	87	272	Turnover Rate %
	---	---	96.7	248.2	234.4	248.0	259.4	252.1	329.0	512.0	610.3	417.0	Net Assets ($mil)

Performance 12-31-94

	1st Qtr	2nd Qtr	3rd Qtr	4th Qtr	Total
1987	1.76	-2.10	-2.69	4.50	1.32
1988	3.54	1.40	1.82	-0.13	6.76
1989	0.68	7.11	0.94	3.67	12.84
1990	-0.20	3.48	1.44	5.13	10.15
1991	2.63	1.58	5.19	4.87	15.01
1992	-1.41	4.36	3.46	0.48	6.96
1993	3.15	1.63	1.03	0.09	6.00
1994	-3.31	-1.01	0.79	0.44	-3.11

Bear Market Performance

Decile Rank (5-year period)

Worst — Best

	Worst 3 Mo Period 1985-89	Worst 3 Mo Period 1990-94
Scudder GNMA	---	-5.23
+/- LB Aggregate	---	-0.29
+/- Best Fit Index : LB Mtg	---	-1.23

Trailing Returns

	Total Return %	+/- LB Aggregate	+/- LB Mortgage	% Rank All	% Rank Obj	Growth of $10,000
3 Mo	0.44	0.07	0.02	12	21	10,044
6 Mo	1.24	0.25	-0.07	34	15	10,124
1 Yr	-3.10	-0.19	-1.50	44	62	9,690
3 Yr Avg	3.18	-1.36	-0.80	83	66	10,986
5 Yr Avg	6.83	-0.79	-0.74	54	46	13,916
10 Yr Avg	---	---	---	---	---	---
15 Yr Avg	---	---	---	---	---	---

Operations

Address and Telephone	Two International Place
	Boston, MA 02110
	800-225-2470 / 617-439-4640
Advisor	Scudder Stevens & Clark
Subadvisor	None
Distributor	Scudder Investor Services
States Available	All
Report Grade	A
Income Distrib	Paid Monthly
* Date of Inception	07-05-85
Fiscal Year End	March

Risk Analysis

Time Period	Load-Adj Return %	Risk % Rank[1] All	Obj	Morningstar[2] Return	Morningstar Risk	Morningstar Risk-Adj Rating
1 Yr	-3.10					
3 Yr	3.18	24	72	-0.11[3]	1.02	★★★
5 Yr	6.83	18	62	0.51[3]	0.92	★★★
10 Yr	---	---	---	---	---	

Average Historical Rating (78 months) 3.5 ★s

[1] 1 = low, 100 = high [2] 1.00 = Taxable Avg [3] 1.00 = 90-day T-bill return

Other Measures

			Standard LB Agg	Best Fit LB Mtg
Standard Deviation	3.89	Alpha	-1.2	-0.8
Mean	3.21	Beta	0.91	1.16
Sharpe Ratio	-0.08	R-Squared	89	94

Investment Style

Interest-Rate Stance
Avg Effective Duration	6.2 Yrs**
Avg Effective Maturity	8.6 Yrs

Maturity
Short Intm Long

Quality
Avg Credit Quality	AAA
Avg Weighted Coupon	8.50%
Avg Weighted Price	99.41% of Par

**figure provided by fund

Diversification Value for Portfolio Types

Large Cap: Medium	Small Cap: High	Bond: None	Balanced: Medium	Diversified: Medium

Portfolio 09-30-94

Amount 000	Date of Maturity	Total Stocks: 0 / Total Fixed-Income: 15	Value $000	% Net Assets
87929	08-15-24	GNMA 9%	90198	19.98
86114	07-15-24	GNMA 8%	83530	18.50
82662	08-15-24	GNMA 8.5%	82532	18.28
36784	08-15-24	GNMA 9.5%	38691	8.57
39951	12-15-23	GNMA 7.5%	37529	8.31
36171	03-15-24	GNMA 7%	32780	7.26
28905	07-15-24	GNMA 10%	30966	6.86
20421	06-15-24	GNMA 6.5%	17830	3.95
4459	02-20-16	GNMA 12%	5027	1.11
1575	02-15-16	GNMA 11.5%	1768	0.39
1045	10-15-15	GNMA 13%	1212	0.27
660	08-20-19	GNMA 10.5%	706	0.16
333	10-20-13	GNMA 12.5%	374	0.08
247	08-15-14	GNMA 13.5%	287	0.06
33	07-15-12	GNMA 15%	39	0.01

Composition % 12-31-94

Cash	12.0	Preferreds	0.0
Stocks	0.0	Convertibles	0.0
Bonds	88.0	Other	0.0

Tax Analysis

	Tax-Adj Historical Return %	% Pretax Return
3 Yr Avg	0.38	11.7
5 Yr Avg	4.04	55.8
10 Yr Avg	---	---
Potential Capital Gain Exposure (% of assets)		-13%

Most Similar Funds in MF500

Gradison-McDonald Govt Inc	Strong Fit
American Cap Govt Secs A	Strong Fit
Lexington GNMA Income	Strong Fit

Coupon Range

	% of Bonds	Rel Obj
0%	0.0	0.00
0% to 8%	40.5	0.74
8% to 9%	40.8	1.87
9% to 10%	16.4	1.91
More than 10%	2.2	0.34
Not applicable	0.0	0.00

Sector Analysis 09-30-94
% of Bonds

US Treas	0	CMOs	0
GNMA mtgs	100	ARMs	0
FNMA mtgs	0	Other	0
FHLMC mtgs	0		

Expenses & Fees

Min Initial Purchase	$1000 (Addt'l: $100)
Min IRA Purchase	$500 (Addt'l: $50)
Min Auto Invest Plan	$50 (Systematic Inv: $50)

Sales Fees	0.00% front
	0.00% deferred
	0.00% 12b-1
Management Fee	0.65% max./0.55% min.
3-,5-,10-yr Expense Projections	$28, $48, $107

MORNINGSTAR 1995 Mutual Fund 500

Scudder Growth & Income

	Ticker	Load	NAV	Yield	SEC Yield	Assets	Objective
	SCDGX	None	16.27	2.9%	N/A	1994.2	Growth/Inc.

Scudder Growth and Income Fund seeks growth of capital, current income, and growth of income.

The fund invests primarily in dividend-paying common stocks, preferred stocks, and convertible securities with growth potential. In addition, it may purchase non-dividend-paying common stocks and bonds. The fund may invest in foreign securities.

The fund absorbed the approximately $215 million in assets of closed-end Niagara Shares on July 24, 1992. In Oct. 1991, Scudder Equity-Income Fund merged into this fund. Prior to Nov. 13, 1984, the fund was named Scudder Common Stock and long-term capital growth was its primary objective.

Manager's Investment Style

The management team fullfills both the growth and income parts of its objective. Income requirements are satisfied by following a bottom-up style of investing. Management first ranks stocks by their dividend yields, only selecting those issues with yields that are greater than 120% of those of the S&P 500. From this universe they determine which companies have the best fundamentals and opportunities for growth. Such a strategy produces a portfolio of mostly out-of-favor industries, as lower stock prices give way to higher yields.

Fund Manager(s)

Robert T. Hoffman, since 1990.
Benjamin W. Thorndike CFA(1987), since 1987.
Kathleen T. Millard CFA(1986), since 1993.

Manager Experience	Dates Managed	Invest Obj	Std Dev	+/- Index
Benjamin W. Thorndike				
AARP Growth & Income	11/84 - 12/94	GI	12.82	-1.09
Robert T. Hoffman				
AARP Growth & Income	01/90 - 12/94	GI	10.60	1.11

Historical Profile

Return	Above Average
Risk	Below Average
Rating ★★★★	
	Above Average

62% 73% 83% 79% 84% 86% 82% 87%

Investment Style History
Equity
Average % Stocks Held in Portfolio

Growth of $10,000

IIII Value of Fund ($000)
— Value of Index ($000) S&P 500
▼ Manager Change
▽ Partial Manager Change
► Mgr Unknown After
◄ Mgr Unknown Before

Performance Quartile (Within Objective)

	1983	1984	1985	1986	1987	1988	1989	1990	1991	1992	1993	1994	History
	---	11.90	15.35	15.02	12.31	13.17	14.14	12.77	15.76	16.20	17.24	16.27	NAV
	---	---	34.55	18.30	3.50	11.93	26.45	-2.33	28.16	9.57	15.59	2.60	Total Return %
	---	---	2.82	-0.38	-1.76	-4.69	-5.23	0.79	-2.33	1.95	5.53	1.29	+/- S&P 500
	---	---	1.99	2.21	1.13	-6.02	-2.72	3.85	-6.05	0.60	4.31	2.67	+/- Wilshire 5000
	---	---	5.56	4.55	4.38	4.94	4.96	5.12	4.74	3.44	2.71	3.00	Income Return %
	---	---	28.99	13.75	-0.88	6.99	21.49	-7.45	23.41	6.13	12.88	-0.40	Capital Return %
	---	---	13	31	32	46	30	63	30	26	27	8	Total Rtn % Rank All
	---	---	7	34	38	71	38	37	50	32	18	9	Total Rtn % Rank Obj
	---	0.00	0.58	0.68	0.68	0.59	0.69	0.67	0.55	0.53	0.45	0.51	Income $
	---	0.00	0.00	2.28	2.64	0.00	1.77	0.34	0.00	0.50	1.01	0.91	Capital Gains $
	---	---	0.84	0.83	0.89	0.92	0.87	0.95	0.97	0.94	0.86	0.87	Expense Ratio %
	---	---	4.35	4.19	4.24	4.63	4.47	5.03	4.03	3.60	2.93	2.81	Income Ratio %
	---	---	73	45	60	48	77	65	45	28	36	48	Turnover Rate %
	---	223.6	302.1	384.5	329.7	400.9	490.0	490.8	723.4	1168.9	1631.3	1994.2	Net Assets ($mil)

Performance 12-31-94

	1st Qtr	2nd Qtr	3rd Qtr	4th Qtr	Total
1987	14.95	2.17	6.46	-17.23	3.50
1988	4.86	2.90	-0.23	3.96	11.93
1989	7.74	9.61	8.17	-1.01	26.45
1990	-5.58	5.73	-9.78	8.45	-2.33
1991	10.65	-1.23	8.17	8.41	28.16
1992	0.00	2.54	1.27	5.51	9.57
1993	5.68	1.30	5.45	2.40	15.59
1994	-3.34	3.14	5.85	-2.78	2.60

Bear Market Performance

Decile Rank (5-year period)

Worst ... Best

	Worst 3 Mo Period 1985-89	Worst 3 Mo Period 1990-94
Scudder Growth & Income	-23.70	-9.78
+/- S&P 500	5.88	3.96
+/- Best Fit Index : S&P 500	5.88	3.96

Trailing Returns

	Total Return %	+/- S&P 500	+/- Wil 5000	% Rank All	% Rank Obj	Growth of $10,000
3 Mo	-2.78	-2.76	-2.01	80	81	9,722
6 Mo	2.91	-1.95	-1.71	21	45	10,291
1 Yr	2.60	1.29	2.67	8	9	10,260
3 Yr Avg	9.12	2.86	2.51	17	15	12,994
5 Yr Avg	10.22	1.53	1.40	16	12	16,266
10 Yr Avg	14.26	-0.12	0.40	16	12	37,927
15 Yr Avg	---	---	---	---	---	---

Risk Analysis

Time Period	Load-Adj Return %	Risk % Rank [1] All	Risk % Rank [1] Obj	Morningstar [2] Return	Morningstar [2] Risk	Morningstar Risk-Adj Rating
1 Yr	2.60					
3 Yr	9.12	57	19	1.69 [3]	0.62	★★★★
5 Yr	10.22	57	15	1.42 [3]	0.65	★★★★
10 Yr	14.26	49	24	1.33	0.70	★★★★

Average Historical Rating (85 months)   4.0 ★s

[1] 1 = low, 100 = high [2] 1.00 = Equity Avg [3] 1.00 = 90-day T-bill return

Other Measures

			Standard S&P 500	Best Fit S&P 500
Standard Deviation	8.19	Alpha	2.9	2.9
Mean	9.10	Beta	0.93	0.93
Sharpe Ratio	0.68	R-Squared	81	81

Investment Style

	Stock Portfolio Avg	Relative S&P 500
Price/Earnings Ratio	21.8	1.18
Price/Book Ratio	3.3	0.97
5 Yr Earnings Gr %	-2.7	-0.48
Return on Assets %	5.8	0.77
Debt % Total Cap	30.8	1.09
Med Mkt Cap ($mil)	4289	0.33

Style Value Blend Growth
Size Large Med Small

Diversification Value for Portfolio Types

Large Cap: None	Small Cap: Medium	Bond: High	Balanced: None	Diversified: None

Portfolio 06-30-94

Total Stocks: 109
Total Fixed-Income: 24

Share Chg (12-93) 000	Amount 000		Value $000	% Net Assets
-1	739	United Technologies	47487	2.63
92	441	Xerox	43127	2.39
174	946	Parker-Hannifin	40332	2.24
602	1151	Halliburton	38850	2.16
47	598	TRW	38590	2.14
-238	920	Chemical Banking	35412	1.96
	341	Ford Motor Cl A Cv Pfd $4.20	33096	1.83
626	855	British Telecom (ADR)	32811	1.82
309	526	Eli Lilly	29899	1.66
532	532	American Cyanamid	29764	1.65
152	424	Dow Chemical	27726	1.54
184	471	Avon Products	27701	1.54
-31	470	El duPont de Nemours	27436	1.52
453	907	Dana	25838	1.43
102	386	Warner-Lambert	25450	1.41
258	1007	Lyondell Petrochemical	24802	1.38
144	541	Betz Laboratories	22921	1.27
60	558	Telefonica de Espana (ADR)	22451	1.25
472	883	McDermott International	22080	1.22
0	599	First Bank System	21871	1.21
0	578	Rockwell International	21603	1.20
276	403	Bristol-Myers Squibb	21600	1.20
349	349	Schering-Plough	21364	1.19
253	375	American Home Products	21293	1.18
64	346	Thomas & Betts	21254	1.18

Composition % 12-31-94

Cash	1.8	Preferreds	0.3
Stocks	89.6	Convertibles	7.8
Bonds	0.5	Other	1.0

Tax Analysis

	Tax-Adj Historical Return %	% Pretax Return
3 Yr Avg	6.61	70.7
5 Yr Avg	7.91	73.9
10 Yr Avg	10.80	64.1
Potential Capital Gain Exposure (% of assets)		8%

Most Similar Funds in MF500

Merrill Lynch Capital A	Strong Fit
Putnam Fund for Grth & Inc A	Strong Fit
Lexington Corporate Leaders	Fair Fit

Index Allocation

	% of Stocks
S&P 500	62.9
S&P MidCap 400	10.1
U.S. Small Cap	11.0
Foreign	16.7

Sector Weightings

	% of Stocks	Relative S&P 500
Utilities	7.7	0.62
Energy	12.5	1.24
Financials	14.8	1.40
Industrial Cyclicals	27.0	1.65
Consumer Durables	3.3	0.53
Consumer Staples	7.3	0.58
Services	5.9	0.72
Retail	4.4	0.75
Health	14.0	1.61
Technology	3.2	0.35

Operations

Address and Telephone	Two International Place
	Boston, MA 02110
	800-225-2470 / 617-439-4640
Advisor	Scudder Stevens & Clark
Subadvisor	None
Distributor	Scudder Investor Services
States Available	All
Report Grade	A+
Income Distrib	Paid Quarterly
* Date of Inception	12-31-84
Fiscal Year End	December

Min Initial Purchase	$1000 (Addt'l: $100)
Min IRA Purchase	$500 (Addt'l: $50)
Min Auto Invest Plan	$50 (Systematic Inv: $50)

Expenses & Fees

Sales Fees	0.00% front
	0.00% deferred
	0.00% 12b-1
Management Fee	0.65% max./0.50% min.
3-,5-,10-yr Expense Projections	$27, $47, $105
Annual Brokerage Cost	0.14%

Scudder High-Yield Tax-Free

	Ticker	Load	NAV	Yield	SEC Yield	Assets	Objective
	SHYTX	None	10.86	6.1%	6.52%	259.8	Muni Nat

Scudder High-Yield Tax-Free Fund seeks income exempt from federal income taxes.

The fund normally invests at least 65% of its assets in investment-grade municipal securities, including general obligation and revenue bonds and notes. The balance of assets may be invested in lower-rated securities. The fund expects to invest principally in securities with maturities longer than 10 years. It may also invest up to 20% of its assets in securities subject to the Alternative Minimum Tax.

Historical Profile

Return	Above Average
Risk	Above Average
Rating	★★★
	Neutral

Investment Style History
Fixed Income
Income Rtn % Rank Obj

---	12	52	36	29	32	38	29

Growth of $10,000

- |||| Value of Fund ($000)
- — Value of Index ($000)
  LB Muni
- ▼ Manager Change
- ▽ Partial Manager Change
- ► Mgr Unknown After
- ◄ Mgr Unknown Before

Performance Quartile
(Within Objective)

Manager's Investment Style

Management invests mostly in credits with ratings at the lower end of the investment-grade spectrum, while also keeping a fairly high interest-rate exposure, relative to its peers. Large weightings in discount and noncallable bonds have contributed to the portfolio's rate sensitivity.

Fund Manager(s)

Philip P. Condon, since 01-87. Birthdate: 08-50.
BA, U. of Massachusetts 1973 MA, U. of Massachusetts 1976
Kimberley R. Manning, since 01-87. Birthdate: 11-58. BA, Miami U. 1980

Manager Experience

	Dates Managed	Invest Obj	Std Dev	+/- Index
Kimberley R. Manning				
Scudder PA Tax-Free	05/87 - 12/94	MS	5.65	-1.09
Philip P. Condon				
Scudder CA Tax-Free	01/89 - 07/90	MC	4.75	-4.16

	1983	1984	1985	1986	1987	1988	1989	1990	1991	1992	1993	1994	History
	---	---	---	---	10.52	11.06	11.35	11.19	11.67	11.90	12.55	10.86	NAV
	---	---	---	---	-5.81 *	13.49	10.32	6.02	13.46	10.88	13.85	-8.38	Total Return %
	---	---	---	---	---	5.61	-4.22	-2.92	-2.54	3.63	4.10	-5.46	+/- LB Aggregate
	---	---	---	---	---	3.33	-0.46	-1.28	1.32	2.06	1.57	-2.78	+/- LB Muni
	---	---	---	---	6.52	8.35	7.14	7.04	7.19	6.49	5.83	5.08	Income Return %
	---	---	---	---	-12.33	5.13	3.18	-1.02	6.27	4.39	8.01	-13.47	Capital Return %
	---	---	---	---	---	34	70	34	65	18	34	87	Total Rtn % Rank All
	---	---	---	---	---	11	27	64	9	4	11	90	Total Rtn % Rank Obj
	---	---	---	---	0.78	0.83	0.76	0.77	0.76	0.72	0.67	0.66	Income $
	---	---	---	---	0.00	0.00	0.06	0.05	0.21	0.27	0.28	0.00	Capital Gains $
	---	---	---	---	0.40	0.67	1.00	1.00	1.00	0.98	0.92	0.80	Expense Ratio %
	---	---	---	---	8.45	7.65	6.72	6.88	6.65	6.10	5.38	5.62	Income Ratio %
	---	---	---	---	132	37	76	33	46	57	56	29	Turnover Rate %
	---	---	---	---	36.2	73.5	113.3	127.9	159.1	203.1	315.9	259.8	Net Assets ($mil)

Performance 12-31-94

	1st Qtr	2nd Qtr	3rd Qtr	4th Qtr	Total
1987	---	-5.81	-1.96	2.61	-5.81 *
1988	2.59	3.80	3.48	2.98	13.49
1989	1.27	5.77	-0.72	3.74	10.32
1990	-0.10	2.37	-0.15	3.83	6.02
1991	2.23	3.12	3.91	3.59	13.46
1992	0.56	5.15	2.68	2.13	10.88
1993	4.29	3.74	3.82	1.36	13.85
1994	-6.37	0.82	0.29	-3.24	-8.38

Bear Market Performance

Decile Rank (5-year period)

Worst ————————————— Best

	Worst 3 Mo Period 1985-89	Worst 3 Mo Period 1990-94
Scudder High-Yield Tax-Free	---	-7.56
+/- LB Aggregate	---	-2.63
+/- Best Fit Index : LB Muni	---	-1.80

Trailing Returns

	Total Return %	+/- LB Aggregate	+/- LB Muni	% Rank All	% Rank Obj	Growth of $10,000
3 Mo	-3.24	-3.62	-1.80	85	99	9,676
6 Mo	-2.95	-3.94	-1.71	94	98	9,705
1 Yr	-8.38	-5.46	-2.78	87	90	9,162
3 Yr Avg	4.97	0.42	0.10	49	30	11,565
5 Yr Avg	6.83	-0.80	0.05	54	17	13,912
10 Yr Avg	---	---	---	---	---	---
15 Yr Avg	---	---	---	---	---	---

Operations

Address and Telephone
Two International Place
Boston, MA 02110
800-225-2470 / 617-439-4640

Advisor	Scudder Stevens & Clark
Subadvisor	None
Distributor	Scudder Investor Services
States Available	All
Report Grade	A+
Income Distrib	Paid Monthly
* Date of Inception	01-22-87
Fiscal Year End	December

Risk Analysis

Time Period	Load-Adj Return %	Risk % Rank [1] All	Obj	Morningstar [2] Return	Morningstar Risk	Morningstar Risk-Adj Rating
1 Yr	-8.38					
3 Yr	4.97	44	76	1.28	1.21	★★★
5 Yr	6.83	33	68	1.18	1.20	★★★
10 Yr	---	---	---	---	---	---

Average Historical Rating (60 months)   3.3 ★ s

[1] 1 = low, 100 = high   [2] 1.00 = Muni Avg   [3] 1.00 = 90-day T-bill return

Other Measures

			Standard LB Agg	Best Fit LB Muni
Standard Deviation	6.82	Alpha	0.3	-0.1
Mean	5.09	Beta	1.29	1.21
Sharpe Ratio	0.23	R-Squared	57	94

Investment Style

Interest-Rate Stance
Avg Effective Maturity   18.0 Yrs

Quality
Avg Credit Quality   A
Avg Weighted Coupon   6.14%
Avg Weighted Price   94.95% of Par

Diversification Value for Portfolio Types

Large Cap: Medium	Small Cap: High	Bond: Low	Balanced: Medium	Diversified: Medium

Portfolio 06-30-94

Total Stocks: 0
Total Fixed-Income: 93

Amount 000	Date of Maturity		Value $000	% Net Assets
29000	01-01-13	CA San Joaquin Hills Transp Toll Rd 0%	16783	5.60
8275	11-15-13	CO Denver Arpt Sys 7.75%	8323	2.78
8650	11-15-13	CO Denver Arpt Sys 6.75%	7741	2.58
14295	11-15-05	CO Denver Arpt Sys 0%	7648	2.55
7000	03-01-07	LA Bastrop Indl Dev Brd Poll Cntrl 6.9%	7493	2.50
6500	10-01-18	VI GO Pub Fin Matching Loan 7.25%	6855	2.29
6000	01-01-16	NJ Tpk 6.5%	6262	2.09
5485	07-01-08	OH Hamilton Providence Hosp 6.8%	5470	1.82
5000	01-01-09	AZ Salt Rvr Agri Impr/Pwr Dist 6%	5014	1.67
5500	07-01-12	PA Mont Redev Multi-Fam Hsg 6.375%	5010	1.67
5000	04-01-17	IN Indianapolis Arpt Fac Proj 6.85%	4996	1.67
5000	12-15-18	TX Retama Dev Spcl Fac Racetrack 8.75%	4980	1.66
5500	07-01-07	WA Pub Pwr Sply Sys Proj #3 5.1%	4965	1.66
5000	01-01-16	IL Chicago GO Brd Educ Lease 6%	4813	1.61
5000	11-01-30	TX Dallas/Ft Worth Intl Arpt Impr 7.25%	4778	1.59
5000	07-01-13	PA Philadelphia Hosp/Higher Educ 6.25%	4639	1.55
4500	01-01-13	DC COP 7.3%	4623	1.54
4475	09-01-09	IL Hlth Fac Franciscan Sisters Care 6%	4405	1.47
4685	07-01-07	MA Muni Whlse Elec Pwr Sply Sys 5.1%	4296	1.43
4300	06-01-05	DC GO 5.875%	4240	1.41

Credit Analysis % of Bonds 12-31-94

US Govt	0	BB	14
AAA	16	B	0
AA	12	Below B	0
A	14	NR/NA	26
BBB	18		

Composition % of Assets 12-31-94

Cash	3.7	Preferreds	0.0
Stocks	0.0	Convertibles	0.0
Bonds	96.3	Other	0.0

Tax Analysis

	Tax-Adj Historical Return %	% Pretax Return
3 Yr Avg	4.54	91.0
5 Yr Avg	6.44	93.6
10 Yr Avg	---	---

Potential Capital Gain Exposure (% of assets)   -7%

Most Similar Funds in MF500

Van Kampen Ins T/F Income A	Strong Fit
General Municipal Bond	Strong Fit
MFS Municipal Bond A	Strong Fit

Coupon Range

	% Bonds	Rel Obj
0%	9.0	3.60
0% to 6.8%	49.8	0.82
6.8% to 7.5%	25.3	1.63
7.5% to 8.3%	8.6	0.97
More than 8.3%	5.2	0.59
Not applicable	2.0	0.52

Sector Weightings

	% Bonds	Rel Obj
General Obl	9.99	0.47
Utilities	11.51	0.92
Health	23.56	1.79
Water/Waste	0.94	0.15
Housing	5.38	0.73
Education	1.12	0.18
Transportation	24.08	2.36
COP/Lease	5.32	1.67
Private	18.09	1.55
Misc Revenue	0.00	0.00
Demand	0.00	0.00

Top 5 States % of Bonds

CO	10.89	MA	7.93
CA	10.40	IL	7.85
TX	8.59		

Min Initial Purchase / Expenses & Fees

Min Initial Purchase	$1000 (Addt'l: $100)
Min IRA Purchase	$500 (Addt'l: $50)
Min Auto Invest Plan	$50 (Systematic Inv: $50)

Expenses & Fees

Sales Fees	0.00% front
	0.00% deferred
	0.00% 12b-1
Management Fee	0.70% max./0.65% min.
3-,5-,10-yr Expense Projections	$29, $51, $113

446

Scudder Income

	Ticker	Load	NAV	Yield	SEC Yield	Assets	Objective
	SCSBX	None	12.32	6.2%	7.15%	464.1	Corp Hi Qlty

Scudder Income Fund seeks income consistent with prudent investment of capital.

The fund invests primarily in a broad range of high-quality intermediate- and longer-term fixed-income securities. These may include investment-grade corporate bonds, convertible bonds, and government obligations. Municipal obligations, mortgage-backed securities, and zero-coupon bonds may also be held. No more than 25% of the fund's assets may be invested in debt rated BBB. The fund's average portfolio maturity is usually longer than eight years. It may also invest in foreign securities and engage in options and futures activities.

Manager's Investment Style

Management keeps duration within a 3.5-year to 6.5-year range. The fund has, nevertheless, been one of the more-aggressive funds in the corporate high-quality group during the past few years, keeping its duration near the long end of its range. To extend duration, the fund has invested in volatile Treasury zeros; government bonds have also taken up more than a third of the portfolio. The fund dabbles in international bond markets for yield pickup. These tactics have contributed to the fund's above-average yield.

Fund Manager(s)

William M. Hutchinson, since 09-86. Birthdate: 09-47. BS, Lehigh U. 1969 MBA, U. of Michigan 1971
Stephen Wohler CFA(1984), since 06-94. Birthdate: 12-48. BS, Naval Academy 1971 MBA, U. of

Manager Experience	Dates Managed	Invest Obj	Std Dev	+/- Index
William M. Hutchinson				
AARP High-Quality Bond	10/87 - 12/94	CQ	4.57	-0.60
Scudder Balanced	01/93 - 12/94	B	8.14	-4.62

Historical Profile

Return	Above Average
Risk	Above Average
Rating	★★★★ Above Average

Investment Style History
Fixed Income
Income Rtn % Rank Obj

	1983	1984	1985	1986	1987	1988	1989	1990	1991	1992	1993	1994	History
	11.64	11.70	12.82	13.41	12.40	12.41	12.89	12.82	13.91	13.48	13.72	12.32	NAV
	10.88	12.27	21.80	14.75	0.67	8.99	12.75	8.32	17.32	6.74	12.66	-4.50	Total Return %
	2.51	-2.89	-0.33	-0.50	-2.09	1.11	-1.79	-0.62	1.32	-0.51	2.91	-1.58	+/- LB Aggregate
	1.61	-4.36	-2.27	-1.79	-1.89	-0.23	-1.23	1.17	-1.19	-1.96	0.50	-0.57	+/- LB Corporate
	11.14	11.75	12.22	10.14	8.20	8.91	8.88	8.86	7.84	6.99	6.53	5.59	Income Return %
	-0.26	0.52	9.57	4.60	-7.53	0.08	3.87	-0.54	9.47	-0.25	6.13	-10.08	Capital Return %
	75	16	61	56	54	68	55	13	50	61	44	58	Total Rtn % Rank All
	10	65	18	21	79	8	25	37	13	36	8	81	Total Rtn % Rank Obj
	1.25	1.25	1.29	1.22	1.09	1.08	1.06	1.09	0.94	0.93	0.87	0.76	Income $
	0.00	0.00	0.00	0.00	0.00	0.00	0.00	0.00	0.12	0.40	0.57	0.02	Capital Gains $
	0.97	1.02	0.91	0.88	0.94	0.94	0.93	0.95	0.97	0.93	0.92	0.96	Expense Ratio %
	10.61	11.04	10.57	9.12	8.37	8.53	8.23	8.21	7.13	7.05	6.32	5.95	Income Ratio %
	40	40	30	24	34	20	63	48	110	121	131	39	Turnover Rate %
	110.5	122.9	171.7	197.0	243.0	244.7	271.5	301.2	404.1	456.2	508.9	464.1	Net Assets ($mil)

Growth of $10,000
|||| Value of Fund ($000)
— Value of Index ($000) LB Corp
▼ Manager Change
▽ Partial Manager Change
► Mgr Unknown After
◄ Mgr Unknown Before

Performance Quartile (Within Objective)

Performance 12-31-94

	1st Qtr	2nd Qtr	3rd Qtr	4th Qtr	Total
1987	2.09	-2.72	-3.51	5.06	0.67
1988	3.68	0.95	2.73	1.36	8.99
1989	1.13	6.75	1.54	2.85	12.75
1990	-0.93	3.54	0.38	5.20	8.32
1991	2.81	1.61	6.33	5.61	17.32
1992	-2.16	4.14	4.46	0.28	6.74
1993	4.56	3.47	3.48	0.63	12.66
1994	-3.86	-1.91	0.63	0.65	-4.50

Bear Market Performance

Decile Rank (5-year period)

	Worst 3 Mo Period 1985-89	Worst 3 Mo Period 1990-94
Scudder Income	-4.95	-6.72
+/- LB Aggregate	-1.40	-1.78
+/- Best Fit Index : LB Corp	-0.84	-0.45

Trailing Returns

	Total Return %	+/- LB Aggregate	+/- LB Corporate	% Rank All	% Rank Obj	Growth of $10,000
3 Mo	0.65	0.27	0.21	9	18	10,065
6 Mo	1.28	0.29	0.11	33	16	10,128
1 Yr	-4.50	-1.58	-0.57	58	81	9,550
3 Yr Avg	4.72	0.18	-0.69	54	17	11,485
5 Yr Avg	7.85	0.23	-0.41	35	8	14,595
10 Yr Avg	9.70	-0.25	-0.93	61	18	25,233
15 Yr Avg	10.27	-0.54	-1.05	73	28	43,351

Risk Analysis

Time Period	Load-Adj Return %	Risk % Rank All	Obj	Morningstar Return	Morningstar Risk	Morningstar Risk-Adj Rating
1 Yr	-4.50					
3 Yr	4.72	35	79	0.33 [3]	1.18	★★★★
5 Yr	7.85	31	77	0.77 [3]	1.11	★★★★
10 Yr	9.70	22	62	1.03 [3]	1.07	★★★★
Average Historical Rating (109 months)					3.7	★ s

[1] 1 = low, 100 = high   [2] 1.00 = Taxable Avg   [3] 1.00 = 90-day T-bill return

Other Measures

				Standard LB Agg	Best Fit LB Corp
Standard Deviation	5.04	Alpha		0.0	-0.6
Mean	4.75	Beta		1.22	0.98
Sharpe Ratio	0.24	R-Squared		94	96

Investment Style

Interest-Rate Stance
Avg Effective Duration	6.1 Yrs
Avg Effective Maturity	11.0 Yrs

Quality
Avg Credit Quality	AA
Avg Weighted Coupon	6.59%
Avg Weighted Price	86.97% of Par

Diversification Value for Portfolio Types

Large Cap: Medium   Small Cap: High   Bond: None   Balanced: Medium   Diversified: Medium

Portfolio 06-30-94

Amount 000	Date of Maturity	Total Stocks: 0 Total Fixed-Income: 53	Value $000	% Net Assets
75000	02-15-04	US Treasury Note 5.875%	67418	13.51
35000	09-30-97	US Treasury Note 5.5%	33901	6.79
29265	06-01-23	Govt of Canada 8%	18186	3.64
15000	02-01-22	Coca-Cola Enterprises 8.5%	15263	3.06
15000	02-25-23	Prudential Hm Mtg Secs CMO 7%	14700	2.95
15000	04-15-03	HSBC Finance Nederland 7.4%	14194	2.84
15000	12-01-02	RJR Nabisco 8.625%	13008	2.61
41750	08-15-09	US Treasury Bond 0%	12897	2.58
12000	01-15-22	Ford Motor 8.875%	12425	2.49
14797	04-15-19	FHLMC Debenture 0%	11421	2.29
12000	01-15-13	Time Warner 9.125%	11200	2.24
35000	05-15-09	US Treasury Bond 0%	11033	2.21
10000	04-01-12	McDonnell Douglas 9.75%	10819	2.17
10000	04-01-21	Dow Chemical 9%	10680	2.14
10000		Kingdom of Thailand 8.7%	10349	2.07
10000	02-01-13	News America Holdings 9.25%	9942	1.99
10000	06-15-24	Loral 8.375%	9574	1.92
10000	04-01-23	NOVA Gas Transmission 7.875%	9154	1.83
8500	07-15-11	MLMI 9.85%	8811	1.77
7500	12-15-00	KFW Intl Finance 9.5%	8259	1.65
10000	10-15-43	Boeing 6.875%	8231	1.65
7000	06-07-96	Standard CC Master Tr 8.5%	7230	1.45
38000	02-15-16	US Treasury Bond 0%	6932	1.39
33750	05-15-16	US Treasury Bond 0%	6044	1.21
4425	08-31-00	Govt of Hungary 10.5%	4956	0.99

Composition % 12-31-94

Cash	10.0	Preferreds	0.0
Stocks	0.0	Convertibles	1.0
Bonds	89.0	Other	0.0

Tax Analysis

	Tax-Adj Historical Return %	% Pretax Return
3 Yr Avg	1.71	35.2
5 Yr Avg	4.94	59.4
10 Yr Avg	6.29	55.2
Potential Capital Gain Exposure (% of assets)		-8%

Coupon Range

	% of Bonds	Rel Obj
0%	14.9	6.50
0% to 8.5%	56.2	0.80
8.5% to 9.5%	18.3	1.40
9.5% to 11%	8.7	1.90
More than 11%	1.9	0.83
Not applicable	0.0	0.00

Credit Analysis 12-31-94

% of Bonds

US Govt	44	BB	0
AAA	11	B	0
AA	11	Below B	0
A	16	NR/NA	2
BBB	16		

Most Similar Funds in MF500

Fidelity Government Secs	Strong Fit
PaineWebber Invmt Grade Inc	Strong Fit
New England Bond Income A	Strong Fit

Operations

Address and Telephone	Two International Place Boston, MA 02110 800-225-2470 / 617-439-4640
Advisor	Scudder Stevens & Clark
Subadvisor	None
Distributor	Scudder Investor Services
States Available	All
Report Grade	A+
Income Distrib	Paid Quarterly
Date of Inception	05-10-28
Fiscal Year End	December

Min Initial Purchase	$1000 (Addt'l: $100)
Min IRA Purchase	$500 (Addt'l: $50)
Min Auto Invest Plan	$50 (Systematic Inv: $50)

Expenses & Fees

Sales Fees	0.00% front 0.00% deferred 0.00% 12b-1
Management Fee	0.65% max./0.55% min.
3-,5-,10-yr Expense Projections	$29, $51, $113

Scudder International Bond

	Ticker	Load	NAV	Yield	SEC Yield	Assets		Objective
	SCIBX	None	11.38	8.7%	8.88%	1086.2		World Bond

Scudder International Bond Fund seeks income. Secondarily, the fund seeks protection and possible enhancement of principal value.

The fund invests primarily in a managed portfolio of high-quality international bonds. It intends to have investments from a minimum of three different countries; however, it may invest substantially all of its assets in one country. Under normal circumstances, it may not invest more than 35% of its assets in U.S. securities. The fund actively manages currency, bond-market, and maturity exposure.

It may also engage in a variety of options and futures transactions.

Manager's Investment Style

Management is constantly searching for bargains. This strategy has led the fund to invest heavily in European markets. More than 70% of assets have been devoted to these markets, where, in management's opinion, bonds have been hit hard by sell-offs and inflation is in check. The fund is partial to peripheral markets that have been beat up and offer attractive yields. Management is also on the lookout for cheap foreign currencies, but typically remains hedged into the dollar.

Fund Manager(s)

Lawrence Teitelbaum, since 03-93. Birthdate:
11-51. BA, Tufts U. 1973 MBA, U. of Colorado 1981
Adam M. Greshin CFA(1990), since 07-88.
Birthdate: 09-60. BA, Bowdoin C. 1982 M, Tufts U. 1984

Manager Experience	Dates Managed	Invest Obj	Std Dev	+/- Index
Adam M. Greshin				
Scudder S-T Global Inc	03/91 - 03/93	SW	2.67	-4.36
Lawrence Teitelbaum				
Merrill Lynch Global Bd B	12/88 - 03/93	WB	7.31	-1.31

Historical Profile

Return	Above Average
Risk	Below Average
Rating	★★★★ Above Average

Growth of $10,000

|||| Value of Fund ($000)
— Value of Index ($000) LB Int
▼ Manager Change
▽ Partial Manager Change
► Mgr Unknown After
◄ Mgr Unknown Before

Investment Style History
Fixed Income

Income Rtn % Rank Obj

Performance Quartile (Within Objective)

	1983	1984	1985	1986	1987	1988	1989	1990	1991	1992	1993	1994	History
	---	---	---	---	---	12.21	11.97	12.90	13.53	12.83	13.50	11.38	NAV
	---	---	---	---	---	5.72 *	7.23	21.11	22.14	7.62	15.83	-8.61	Total Return %
	---	---	---	---	---	---	-7.31	12.17	6.14	0.37	6.08	-5.69	+/- LB Aggregate
	---	---	---	---	---	---	10.66	5.82	5.90	2.85	0.71	-15.30	+/- SB World Govt
	---	---	---	---	---	4.22	9.20	10.68	10.04	8.30	7.44	7.10	Income Return %
	---	---	---	---	---	1.50	-1.97	10.43	12.10	-0.68	8.39	-15.70	Capital Return %
	---	---	---	---	---	---	92	1	41	50	26	89	Total Rtn % Rank All
	---	---	---	---	---	---	41	9	1	6	36	74	Total Rtn % Rank Obj
	---	---	---	---	---	0.49	1.05	1.16	1.16	1.06	0.92	0.99	Income $
	---	---	---	---	---	0.00	0.00	0.29	0.81	0.62	0.39	0.00	Capital Gains $
	---	---	---	---	---	---	1.00	1.25	1.25	1.25	1.25	1.27	Expense Ratio %
	---	---	---	---	---	---	8.58	9.57	9.48	8.31	7.69	6.86	Income Ratio %
	---	---	---	---	---	---	104	216	260	148	250	233	Turnover Rate %
	---	---	---	---	---	6.9	31.6	190.6	296.8	741.9	1365.0	1086.2	Net Assets ($mil)

Performance 12-31-94

	1st Qtr	2nd Qtr	3rd Qtr	4th Qtr	Total
1987	---	---	---	---	---
1988	---	---	---	5.81	5.72 *
1989	-2.64	-1.00	4.40	6.56	7.23
1990	-1.07	6.85	6.51	7.57	21.11
1991	1.52	-1.24	11.06	9.69	22.14
1992	-3.83	9.48	2.99	-0.74	7.62
1993	5.04	4.45	3.55	1.95	15.83
1994	-3.39	-4.72	0.12	-0.83	-8.61

Bear Market Performance

Decile Rank (5-year period)

	Worst 3 Mo Period 1985-89	Worst 3 Mo Period 1990-94
Scudder International Bond	---	-5.65
+/- LB Aggregate	---	-0.71
+/- Best Fit Index : LB Int	---	-1.42

Trailing Returns

	Total Return %	+/- LB Aggregate	+/- SB World	% Rank All	Obj	Growth of $10,000
3 Mo	-0.83	-1.21	-1.40	41	69	9,917
6 Mo	-0.71	-1.71	-2.94	69	77	9,929
1 Yr	-8.61	-5.69	-15.30	89	74	9,139
3 Yr Avg	4.44	-0.10	-4.33	60	38	11,392
5 Yr Avg	11.00	3.38	-0.51	12	1	16,852
10 Yr Avg	---	---	---	---	---	---
15 Yr Avg	---	---	---	---	---	---

Operations

Address and Telephone	Two International Place Boston, MA 02110 800-225-2470 / 617-439-4640
Advisor	Scudder Stevens & Clark
Subadvisor	None
Distributor	Scudder Investor Services
States Available	All
Report Grade	A+
Income Distrib	Paid Monthly
* Date of Inception	07-06-88
Fiscal Year End	June

Risk Analysis

Time Period	Load-Adj Return %	Risk % Rank All	Obj	Morningstar Return	Morningstar Risk	Morningstar Risk-Adj Rating
1 Yr	-8.61	---	---	---	---	---
3 Yr	4.44	55	54	0.25[3]	0.77	★★★
5 Yr	11.00	44	42	1.64[3]	0.54	★★★★★
10 Yr	---	---	---	---	---	---

Average Historical Rating (42 months) 4.7 ★s

[1] 1 = low, 100 = high [2] 1.00 = Hybrid Avg [3] 1.00 = 90-day T-bill return

Other Measures

			Standard LB Agg	Best Fit LB Int
Standard Deviation	6.22	Alpha	-0.1	0.3
Mean	4.55	Beta	1.09	1.28
Sharpe Ratio	0.16	R-Squared	49	51

Investment Style

Interest-Rate Stance

Avg Effective Maturity 8.0 Yrs

Maturity: Short Intm Long

Quality

Avg Credit Quality	AA	
Avg Weighted Coupon	7.44%	

Quality: High Med Low

Diversification Value for Portfolio Types

Large Cap: High	Small Cap: High	Bond: Medium	Balanced: High	Diversified: High

Portfolio 06-30-94

Total Stocks: 0
Total Fixed-Income: 70

Amount 000	Date of Maturity		Value $000	% Net Assets
645000	12-15-04	Kingdom of Denmark 7%	93962	7.63
140330	06-01-23	Govt of Canada 8%	87158	7.08
652000	02-09-05	Kingdom of Sweden 6%	62753	5.10
32205	06-10-03	United Kingdom Treasury 8%	47425	3.85
70300000	01-02-02	Republic of Italy 12%	46658	3.79
220000	10-25-03	Govt of France 6.75%	38220	3.10
68500	01-18-24	Baden-Wuerttemberg 6.5%	35356	2.87
52365	03-15-02	Govt of New Zealand 10%	35206	2.86
228300	05-15-18	US Treasury Bond 0%	35056	2.85
24100	11-06-01	United Kingdom Treasury 7%	33838	2.75
32500	02-16-04	Republic of Portugal 6%	33522	2.72
184000	11-15-00	Kingdom of Denmark 9%	30689	2.49
3300000	08-30-96	Kingdom of Spain 11.85%	26183	2.13
21700	04-25-22	Govt of France 8.25%	25744	2.09
175000	01-21-99	Kingdom of Sweden 11%	24025	1.95
42000	05-01-06	New So Wales Treasury 6.5%	22883	1.86
32520	09-15-04	Commonwealth Australia 9%	22686	1.84
39700	06-14-05	Queensland Treasury 6.5%	22087	1.79
17000	03-15-02	Govt of France 8.5%	21113	1.71
32200000	08-01-98	Republic of Italy 10%	20051	1.63
35000	03-31-23	Republic of Argentina 4.25%	17369	1.41
107800	10-01-06	Byggeriets Realkreditfond 9%	17218	1.40
2150000	06-15-97	Kingdom of Spain 11%	16809	1.37
26000	12-31-19	United Mexican States A 6.25%	16445	1.34
13100	06-04-07	Eurofima 8.5%	15879	1.29

Composition % 12-31-94

Cash	1.7	Preferreds	0.0
Stocks	0.0	Convertibles	0.0
Bonds	98.3	Other	0.0

Tax Analysis

	Tax-Adj Historical Return %	% Pretax Return
3 Yr Avg	0.87	18.9
5 Yr Avg	7.07	59.4
10 Yr Avg	---	---
Potential Capital Gain Exposure (% of assets)		-17%

Most Similar Funds in MF500

Putnam Global Govtl Inc A	Weak Fit
Fidelity Global Bond	Weak Fit
Templeton Income	Weak Fit

Country Exposure 12-31-94

	% of Bonds
Denmark	14
Australia	14
Italy	12
Germany	9
Spain	8

Currency Exposure 12-31-94

	% of Net Assets
Denmark	14
Australia	14
U.S.	14
E.C.	12
Italy	11

Expenses & Fees

Min Initial Purchase	$1000 (Addt'l: $100)
Min IRA Purchase	$500 (Addt'l: $50)
Min Auto Invest Plan	$50 (Systematic Inv: $50)

Sales Fees
0.00% front
0.00% deferred
0.00% 12b-1
Management Fee 0.85% flat fee
3-,5-,10-yr Expense Projections $41, $70, $155

Scudder International

	Ticker	Load	NAV	Yield	SEC Yield	Assets	Objective
	SCINX	None	40.37	0.0%	N/A	2271.8	Foreign Stock

Scudder International Fund seeks long-term growth of capital.
The fund invests in companies, wherever located, that do business primarily outside of the United States. It generally invests in equity securities of established companies that are listed on foreign exchanges. It may also invest in fixed-income securities of foreign governments and companies. The fund attempts to diversify investments among several countries and does not concentrate investments in any particular industry.

Historical Profile
Return	Above Average
Risk	Average
Rating	★★★★
	Above Average

Investment Style History
Equity

90% 90% 87% 77% 84% 85% 88% 92%

Average % Stocks Held in Portfolio

Growth of $10,000
- |||| Value of Fund ($000)
- — Value of Index ($000) S&P 500
- ▼ Manager Change
- ▽ Partial Manager Change
- ► Mgr Unknown After
- ◄ Mgr Unknown Before

Performance Quartile
(Within Objective)

	1983	1984	1985	1986	1987	1988	1989	1990	1991	1992	1993	1994	History
NAV	22.15	21.32	31.03	39.79	30.60	33.10	38.20	32.15	35.53	32.93	44.10	40.37	NAV
	29.72	-0.92	49.01	50.69	0.85	18.84	26.95	-8.92	11.78	-2.64	36.50	-2.99	Total Return %
	7.25	-7.19	17.27	32.01	-4.41	2.23	-4.73	-5.81	-18.71	-10.26	26.45	-4.30	+/- S&P 500
	6.03	-8.30	-7.16	-18.75	-23.78	-9.43	16.41	14.53	-0.35	9.54	3.94	-10.77	+/- MSCI EAFE
	1.90	0.44	2.43	1.35	2.84	0.56	1.18	2.14	0.00	2.38	1.06	0.00	Income Return %
	27.81	-1.36	46.58	49.34	-1.99	18.28	25.77	-11.06	11.78	-5.02	35.44	-2.99	Capital Return %
	11	68	3	3	52	17	19	82	77	93	5	43	Total Rtn % Rank All
	36	16	37	35	80	34	26	28	49	37	53	58	Total Rtn % Rank Obj
	0.31	0.10	0.41	0.49	0.99	0.19	0.43	0.74	0.00	0.83	0.39	0.00	Income $
	0.00	0.58	0.13	5.93	9.22	3.00	3.15	1.98	0.40	0.86	0.39	2.42	Capital Gains $
	1.13	1.05	1.04	0.99	1.09	1.21	1.22	1.18	1.24	1.30	1.26	1.21	Expense Ratio %
	2.23	1.02	2.34	2.60	1.19	1.16	1.20	1.33	2.22	1.25	1.13	0.75	Income Ratio %
	39	17	20	36	67	55	48	49	70	50	29	40	Turnover Rate %
	110.8	188.9	323.9	710.8	471.7	537.2	767.2	802.3	965.9	1049.0	2069.0	2271.8	Net Assets ($mil)

Manager's Investment Style

Management takes a multilayered approach, searching for markets with attractive valuations and economic factors, while also evaluating country factors, including the political, economic, and valuation histories. Management also looks at broader regional or global trends, with an emphasis on how they may affect individual stocks, and finally choosing stocks based on relative valuations and other fundamentals.

Fund Manager(s)

Carol L. Franklin CFA(1985), since 1989.
Nicholas Bratt, since 1976.
Irene T. Cheng, since 06-93.
Francisco S. "Kit" Rodrigo III, since 1994.

Manager Experience	Dates Managed	Invest Obj	Std Dev	+/- Index
Nicholas Bratt				
Korea Fund	01/85 - 12/94	WP	26.50	12.53
Brazil Fund	01/89 - 12/94	WL	57.09	11.54

Performance 12-31-94

	1st Qtr	2nd Qtr	3rd Qtr	4th Qtr	Total
1987	10.93	6.62	11.06	-23.22	0.85
1988	9.25	1.04	-3.38	11.43	18.84
1989	4.98	2.80	13.41	3.71	26.95
1990	-3.12	10.46	-18.08	3.88	-8.92
1991	7.90	-3.14	6.29	0.62	11.78
1992	-3.32	4.42	-2.00	-1.59	-2.64
1993	8.38	4.73	10.53	8.80	36.50
1994	-2.61	1.83	2.56	-4.62	-2.99

Bear Market Performance

Decile Rank (5-year period)

Worst .... Best

	Worst 3 Mo Period 1985-89	Worst 3 Mo Period 1990-94
Scudder International	-26.86	-18.08
+/- S&P 500	2.72	-4.34
+/- Best Fit Index : MSAIlCtry	----	0.88

Trailing Returns

	Total Return %	+/- S&P 500	+/- MSCI EAFE	% Rank All	% Rank Obj	Growth of $10,000
3 Mo	-4.62	-4.61	-3.60	91	45	9,538
6 Mo	-2.19	-7.05	-1.26	89	66	9,781
1 Yr	-2.99	-4.30	-10.77	43	58	9,701
3 Yr Avg	8.84	2.57	0.98	18	45	12,893
5 Yr Avg	5.59	-3.10	4.09	83	44	13,125
10 Yr Avg	16.19	1.81	-1.36	6	43	44,844
15 Yr Avg	14.04	-0.45	-0.70	23	20	71,710

Operations

Address and Telephone	Two International Place
	Boston, MA 02110
	800-225-2470 / 617-439-4640
Advisor	Scudder Stevens & Clark
Subadvisor	None
Distributor	Scudder Investor Services
States Available	All
Report Grade	A+
Income Distrib	Paid Irregularly
Date of Inception	01-16-57
Fiscal Year End	March

Min Initial Purchase	$1000 (Addt'l: $100)
Min IRA Purchase	$500 (Addt'l: $50)
Min Auto Invest Plan	$50 (Systematic Inv: $50)

Expenses & Fees
Sales Fees	0.00% front
	0.00% deferred
	0.00% 12b-1
Management Fee	1.00% max./0.80% min.
3-,5-,10-yr Expense Projections	$38, $66, $146
Annual Brokerage Cost	0.20%

Risk Analysis

Time Period	Load-Adj Return %	Risk % Rank [1] All	Obj	Morningstar [2] Return	Risk	Morningstar Risk-Adj Rating
1 Yr	-2.99					
3 Yr	8.84	81	22	1.60[3]	0.98	★★★★
5 Yr	5.59	86	42	0.20[3]	1.78	★★
10 Yr	16.19	68	18	1.77	0.90	★★★★★

Average Historical Rating (109 months) 4.1 ★s

[1] 1 = low, 100 = high [2] 1.00 = Equity Avg [3] 1.00 = 90-day T-bill return

Other Measures

			Standard S&P 500	Best Fit MSAIlCtry
Standard Deviation	11.73	Alpha	3.8	3.1
Mean	9.18	Beta	0.68	1.00
Sharpe Ratio	0.48	R-Squared	21	81

Investment Style

	Stock Portfolio Avg	Rel MSCI EAFE	Rel Obj
Price/Earnings Ratio	33.9	0.92	1.21
Price/Cash Flow	13.6	0.87	1.01
Price/Book Ratio	2.7	1.05	0.92
5 Yr Earnings Gr %	-1.0	---	-0.25
Return on Assets %	5.1	1.13	0.71
Debt % Total Cap	30.3	0.89	1.09
Med Mkt Cap ($mil)	6251	0.52	1.22

Style: V B G / Size L M S

Diversification Value for Portfolio Types

Large Cap: High	Small Cap: High	Bond: High	Balanced: Medium	Diversified: Low

Portfolio 09-30-94

Total Stocks: 142
Total Fixed-Income: 14

Share Chg (03-94) 000	Amount 000		Value $000	% Net Assets
	70	SAP Pfd	35902	1.50
0	1933	Canon	33957	1.42
1678	1678	Outokumpu Cl A	33954	1.42
0	550	Sony	31984	1.34
	152060	Vale do Rio Doce Pfd	31731	1.32
200	3196	Hitachi	30847	1.29
3	4	Orix	30530	1.27
0	427	Kyocera	30522	1.27
650	3670	Toshiba	27604	1.15
0	82	Veba	27083	1.13
765	1965	NGK Spark Plug	26385	1.10
-1	237	Keyence	26320	1.10
500	2500	Fujitsu	26249	1.10
-100	340	Mabuchi Motor	25710	1.07
300	1385	Takuma	25449	1.06
0	6036	Technology Resources	24722	1.03
0	28	BBC Brown Boveri (Br)	23804	0.99
0	1271	Sumitomo Forestry	23611	0.99
0	1659	RTZ	22959	0.96
2110	9495	LASMO	22873	0.95

Regional Exposure 12-31-94
% of Stocks
Europe	28	Pacific Rim	16
Japan	10	Other	2
Latin Amer	9		

Composition % 12-31-94
Cash	6.7	Preferreds	2.4
Stocks	88.7	Convertibles	2.2
Bonds	0.0	Other	0.0

Tax Analysis
	Tax-Adj Historical Return %	% Pretax Return
3 Yr Avg	7.51	83.9
5 Yr Avg	4.20	73.0
10 Yr Avg	13.36	71.9
Potential Capital Gain Exposure (% of assets)		10%

Most Similar Funds in MF500
T. Rowe Price Intl Stock	Strong Fit
Vanguard Intl Growth	Strong Fit
Putnam Global Growth A	Fair Fit

Country Exposure 12-31-94
	% of Stocks
Japan	28
United Kingdom	10
Germany	9
France	6
Switzerland	6

Total Number of Countries: 26
Hedging Policy: Occasional

Sector Weightings
	% of Stocks	Relative S&P 500
Utilities	8.0	0.89
Energy	8.0	1.97
Financials	13.1	0.70
Industrial Cyclicals	27.1	1.08
Consumer Durables	13.2	1.23
Consumer Staples	4.7	0.68
Services	10.2	0.93
Retail	4.5	0.76
Health	3.6	1.02
Technology	7.6	1.48

Scudder Latin America

	Ticker	Load	NAV	Yield	SEC Yield	Assets	Objective
	SLAFX	None	18.88	0.0%	N/A	649.6	Foreign Stock

Scudder Latin America Fund seeks long-term capital appreciation.

The fund normally invests at least 65% of its assets in Mexico, Central America, South America, and the Spanish-speaking islands of the Caribbean; Latin American equity securities comprise 50% of assets. The fund intends to focus on the developed capital markets of Latin America: Argentina, Brazil, Chile, Mexico, and Venezuela. Debt obligations may also be considered when their potential for capital appreciation outstrips equities. The rest of assets may be invested in non-Latin American equities.

Manager's Investment Style

Management often strays from country weightings of major indexes to take advantage of themes, and the fund can thus behave differently than its benchmark and other Latin American-focused funds. It is also willing to raise cash as a buffer during market turmoil. Although this fund's history is brief, Scudder's international funds generally take thematic approaches to their markets of choice, but they aren't rapid traders. Instead, they play long-term themes and stick with high-quality companies.

Fund Manager(s)

Edmund B. Games, Jr., since 01-93.
William F. Truscott, since 01-93.
Joyce E. Cornell, since 1994.

Manager Experience	Dates Managed	Invest Obj	Std Dev	+/- Index
William F. Truscott				
Argentina Fund	02/92 - 12/94	WL	24.04	-2.47
Brazil Fund	10/93 - 12/94	WL	40.63	57.84

Performance 12-31-94

	1st Qtr	2nd Qtr	3rd Qtr	4th Qtr	Total
1987	---	---	---	---	---
1988	---	---	---	---	---
1989	---	---	---	---	---
1990	---	---	---	---	---
1991	---	---	---	---	---
1992	---	---	---	---	4.17 *
1993	10.24	6.82	16.58	26.98	74.32
1994	-0.60	-7.66	26.83	-22.19	-9.41

Bear Market Performance

Decile Rank (5-year period)

Worst |———|———|———|———|———|———|———|———|———| Best

	Worst 3 Mo Period 1985-89	Worst 3 Mo Period 1990-94
Scudder Latin America	---	---
+/- S&P 500	---	---
+/- Best Fit Index :	---	---

Trailing Returns

	Total Return %	+/- S&P 500	+/- MSCI Latin Am	% Rank All	% Rank Obj	Growth of $10,000
3 Mo	-22.19	-22.17	-0.42	100	97	7,781
6 Mo	-1.31	-6.17	0.87	79	51	9,869
1 Yr	-9.41	-10.73	-1.11	92	85	9,059
3 Yr Avg	---	---	---	---	---	---
5 Yr Avg	---	---	---	---	---	---
10 Yr Avg	---	---	---	---	---	---
15 Yr Avg	---	---	---	---	---	---

Operations

Address and Telephone	Two International Place
	Boston, MA 02110
	800-225-2470 / 617-439-4640
Advisor	Scudder Stevens & Clark
Subadvisor	None
Distributor	Scudder Investor Services
States Available	All
Report Grade	A+
Income Distrib	Paid Annually
* Date of Inception	12-08-92
Fiscal Year End	October

Historical Profile

Return	---
Risk	---
Rating	Not Rated

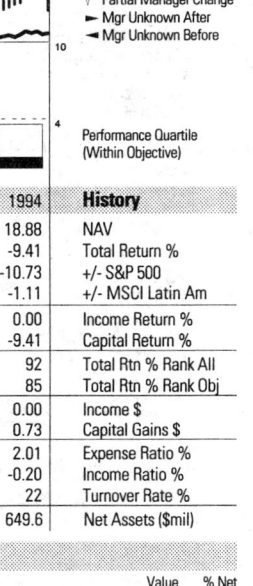

	Investment Style History Equity
	Average % Stocks Held in Portfolio
	55% 85% 86%

Growth of $10,000

IIII Value of Fund ($000)
— Value of Index ($000) S&P 500
▼ Manager Change
▽ Partial Manager Change
◄— Mgr Unknown After
—◄ Mgr Unknown Before

Performance Quartile (Within Objective)

	1983	1984	1985	1986	1987	1988	1989	1990	1991	1992	1993	1994	History
	---	---	---	---	---	---	---	---	---	12.50	21.68	18.88	NAV
	---	---	---	---	---	---	---	---	---	4.17 *	74.32	-9.41	Total Return %
	---	---	---	---	---	---	---	---	---	4.25 *	64.26	-10.73	+/- S&P 500
	---	---	---	---	---	---	---	---	---	---	25.24	-1.11	+/- MSCI Latin Am
	---	---	---	---	---	---	---	---	---	0.00	0.35	0.00	Income Return %
	---	---	---	---	---	---	---	---	---	4.17	73.97	-9.41	Capital Return %
	---	---	---	---	---	---	---	---	---	---	2	92	Total Rtn % Rank All
	---	---	---	---	---	---	---	---	---	---	5	85	Total Rtn % Rank Obj
	---	---	---	---	---	---	---	---	---	0.00	0.06	0.00	Income $
	---	---	---	---	---	---	---	---	---	0.00	0.06	0.73	Capital Gains $
	---	---	---	---	---	---	---	---	---	---	2.00	2.01	Expense Ratio %
	---	---	---	---	---	---	---	---	---	---	0.44	-0.20	Income Ratio %
	---	---	---	---	---	---	---	---	---	---	5	22	Turnover Rate %
	---	---	---	---	---	---	---	---	---	4.2	409.1	649.6	Net Assets ($mil)

Risk Analysis

Time Period	Load-Adj Return %	Risk % Rank[1] All	Obj	Morningstar[2] Return	Morningstar Risk	Morningstar Risk-Adj Rating
1 Yr	-11.41					
3 Yr	---	---	---	---	---	---
5 Yr	---	---	---	---	---	---
10 Yr	---	---	---	---	---	---
Average Historical Rating ---				---		

[1] = low, 100 = high   [2] 1.00 = Equity Avg   [3] 1.00 = 90-day T-bill return

Other Measures

			Standard S&P 500	Best Fit
Standard Deviation	---	Alpha	---	---
Mean	---	Beta	---	---
Sharpe Ratio	---	R-Squared	---	---

Investment Style

	Stock Portfolio Avg	Rel MSCI EAFE	Rel Obj	Style V B G
Price/Earnings Ratio	23.5#	0.63	0.84	
Price/Cash Flow	18.3#	1.18	1.37	
Price/Book Ratio	4.6#	1.78	1.57	
5 Yr Earnings Gr %	---	---	---	
Return on Assets %	---	---	---	
Debt % Total Cap	---	---	---	
Med Mkt Cap ($mil)	2944#	0.25	0.57	

figure is based on 50% or less of stocks

Diversification Value for Portfolio Types

Large Cap: Small Cap: Bond: Balanced: Diversified:

Portfolio 10-31-94

Total Stocks: 60
Total Fixed-Income: 14

Share Chg (04-94) 000	Amount 000		Value $000	% Net Assets
160	600	Telefonos de Mexico L (ADR)	33075	4.09
100	350	Telefonos de Chile (ADR)	32944	4.07
500	2800	Grupo Carso Cl A1	29776	3.68
1640	5182	Perez Cl B	27990	3.46
	53500	Telecomunicacoes do Parana Pfd	27257	3.37
190	1120	YPF Cl D (ADR)	27020	3.34
2200	10002	Cifra Cl C	26947	3.33
	122000	Vale do Rio Doce Pfd	26525	3.28
	167000	Petrobras Pfd	25723	3.18
100	1296	Kimberly-Clark de Mexico A	25716	3.18
	216200	Energetica Minas Gerais Pfd	22030	2.72
	58475	Cervejaria Brahma Pfd	20577	2.54
	11600000	Usinas Siderurgicas Minas Pfd	19104	2.36
230	600	Empresas ICA (ADR)	17775	2.20
	50540	Banco Itau Pfd	16228	2.01
	10440	Sadia Concordia Pfd	15895	1.96
310300	310300	Siderurigica Nacional	14265	1.76
145	500	Quilmes Industrial	13125	1.62
120	368	Panamerican Beverages Cl A	12689	1.57
-50	1250	Apasco Cl A	11638	1.44

Regional Exposure 12-31-94

% of Stocks

Europe	34	Pacific Rim	0
Japan	29	Other	0
Latin Amer	17		

Composition % 12-31-94

Cash	10.4	Preferreds	0.0
Stocks	89.6	Convertibles	0.0
Bonds	0.0	Other	0.0

Tax Analysis

	Tax-Adj Historical Return %	% Pretax Return
3 Yr Avg	---	---
5 Yr Avg	---	---
10 Yr Avg	---	---
Potential Capital Gain Exposure (% of assets)		-7%

Most Similar Funds in MF500

Fund lacks three-year record

Country Exposure 12-31-94

	% of Stocks
Brazil	34
Mexico	29
Argentina	17
Chile	7
Peru	3

Total Number of Countries: 8
Hedging Policy: Never

Sector Weightings

	% of Stocks	Relative S&P 500
Utilities	23.7	2.66
Energy	0.0	0.00
Financials	2.6	0.14
Industrial Cyclicals	24.6	0.98
Consumer Durables	3.4	0.31
Consumer Staples	33.8	4.90
Services	0.0	0.00
Retail	11.8	2.03
Health	0.0	0.00
Technology	0.0	0.00

Min Initial Purchase / Expenses & Fees

Min Initial Purchase	$1000 (Addt'l: $100)
Min IRA Purchase	$500 (Addt'l: $50)
Min Auto Invest Plan	$50 (Systematic Inv: $50)

Expenses & Fees

Sales Fees	
	0.00% front
	0.00% deferred
	0.00% 12b-1
Management Fee	1.25% flat fee
3-,5-,10-yr Expense Projections	$68, $116, $250
Annual Brokerage Cost	---

MORNINGSTAR 1995 Mutual Fund 500

Scudder Medium-Term Tax-Fr

	Ticker	Load	NAV	Yield	SEC Yield	Assets	Objective
	SCMTX	None	10.39	5.3%	5.29%	703.1	Muni Nat

Scudder Medium-Term Tax-Free Fund seeks income exempt from federal income taxes and low principal fluctuation.

The fund invests at least 80% of its assets in high-quality intermediate-term municipal bonds. The portfolio's average weighted maturity ranges between five and 10 years. The fund may not invest in bonds subject to Alternative Minimum Tax.

Prior to Nov. 1, 1990, the fund was named Scudder Tax-Free Target Fund 1990 Portfolio and followed a different investment objective. On May 15, 1992, Scudder Tax-Free Target 1993 Fund and Scudder Tax-Free Target 1996 Fund merged into this fund.

Manager's Investment Style

Management typically keeps the fund's maturity between six and 8.5 years. Management nevertheless gets a good dose of interest-rate exposure within those parameters by favoring noncallable bonds and a number of zero-coupon bonds. The fund favors higher-quality names, stuffing two thirds of assets into the top two rungs of the investment-grade ladder. Management has installed fee caps to keep the fund's expenses low.

Fund Manager(s)

Donald M. Carleton, since 1986. BA, Brown U. 1956 MBA, Harvard 1958
M. Ashton Patton CFA(1991), since 11-90. Birthdate: 10-63. BA, Duke U. 1985

Manager Experience	Dates Managed	Invest Obj	Std Dev	+/- Index
Donald M. Carleton				
Atlas CA Municipal Bond A	01/90 - 11/91	MC	5.20	-1.91
Atlas National Muni Bd A	01/90 - 11/91	MN	5.44	-2.06

Historical Profile

Return	Average
Risk	Low
Rating	★★★★ Above Average

	89	99	97	99	38	38	42	41

Investment Style History
Fixed Income
Income Rtn % Rank Obj

Growth of $10,000

- |||| Value of Fund ($000)
- — Value of Index ($000) LB Muni
- ▼ Manager Change
- ▽ Partial Manager Change
- ◄ Mgr Unknown After
- ◄ Mgr Unknown Before

Performance Quartile (Within Objective)

	1983	1984	1985	1986	1987	1988	1989	1990	1991	1992	1993	1994	History
	9.65	9.67	10.03	10.34	10.07	10.02	10.04	10.11	10.62	10.86	11.36	10.39	NAV
	3.87 *	8.11	11.10	10.61	3.73	4.92	6.00	6.29	12.13	8.93	10.94	-3.50	Total Return %
	---	-7.05	-11.03	-4.64	0.98	-2.96	-8.54	-2.65	-3.88	1.69	1.19	-0.58	+/- LB Aggregate
	---	-2.45	-8.93	-8.70	2.23	-5.24	-4.79	-1.01	-0.02	0.11	-1.33	2.11	+/- LB Muni
	4.49	7.90	7.37	6.46	5.86	5.42	5.80	5.59	7.03	6.36	5.75	4.84	Income Return %
	-0.62	0.21	3.72	4.16	-2.12	-0.50	0.20	0.70	5.10	2.57	5.19	-8.33	Capital Return %
	---	37	96	82	29	92	95	30	75	34	60	48	Total Rtn % Rank All
	---	71	86	89	5	99	98	48	32	35	64	27	Total Rtn % Rank Obj
	0.43	0.73	0.68	0.62	0.59	0.54	0.56	0.54	0.67	0.65	0.60	0.55	Income $
	0.00	0.00	0.00	0.10	0.05	0.00	0.00	0.00	0.01	0.03	0.06	0.03	Capital Gains $
	1.00	0.83	0.85	0.82	0.80	0.79	0.91	0.97	0.00	0.00	0.14	0.56	Expense Ratio %
	7.03	7.66	6.76	6.00	5.37	5.05	5.62	5.37	6.44	6.07	5.35	5.10	Income Ratio %
	97	96	132	44	33	31	16	117	14	22	37	37	Turnover Rate %
	13.5	30.2	58.8	104.0	110.0	99.0	54.8	26.2	267.1	649.5	1012.0	703.1	Net Assets ($mil)

Performance 12-31-94

	1st Qtr	2nd Qtr	3rd Qtr	4th Qtr	Total
1987	2.22	-0.15	-0.96	2.62	3.73
1988	2.43	0.83	0.84	0.75	4.92
1989	0.79	2.13	1.42	1.53	6.00
1990	1.38	1.36	1.26	2.16	6.29
1991	2.11	2.32	3.99	3.19	12.13
1992	0.06	3.95	2.84	1.83	8.93
1993	3.27	2.66	3.30	1.32	10.94
1994	-4.02	1.10	0.45	-1.00	-3.50

Bear Market Performance

Decile Rank (5-year period)

	Worst 3 Mo Period 1985-89	Worst 3 Mo Period 1990-94
Scudder Medium-Term Tax-Fr	-2.55	-4.49
+/- LB Aggregate	1.01	0.45
+/- Best Fit Index : LB Muni	3.95	1.27

Trailing Returns

	Total Return %	+/- LB Aggregate	+/- LB Muni	% Rank All	% Rank Obj	Growth of $10,000
3 Mo	-1.00	-1.37	0.44	44	30	9,900
6 Mo	-0.55	-1.54	0.70	66	34	9,945
1 Yr	-3.50	-0.58	2.11	48	27	9,650
3 Yr Avg	5.26	0.72	0.39	43	18	11,663
5 Yr Avg	6.81	-0.82	0.03	55	18	13,900
10 Yr Avg	7.02	-2.93	-2.41	94	86	19,706
15 Yr Avg	---	---	---	---	---	---

Operations

Address and Telephone	Two International Place
	Boston, MA 02110
	800-225-2470 / 617-439-4640
Advisor	Scudder Stevens & Clark
Subadvisor	None
Distributor	Scudder Investor Services
States Available	All
Report Grade	A+
Income Distrib	Paid Monthly
* Date of Inception	04-12-83
Fiscal Year End	December

Risk Analysis

Time Period	Load-Adj Return %	Risk % Rank[1] All	Obj	Morningstar[2] Return	Morningstar[2] Risk	Morningstar Risk-Adj Rating
1 Yr	-3.50					
3 Yr	5.26	16	29	1.33	0.81	★★★★
5 Yr	6.81	5	13	1.11	0.64	★★★★★
10 Yr	7.02	3	14	0.63	0.55	★★★

Average Historical Rating (106 months) 3.5 ★s

[1] 1 = low, 100 = high   [2] 1.00 = Muni Avg   [3] 1.00 = 90-day T-bill return

Other Measures

		Standard LB Agg	Best Fit LB Muni
Standard Deviation	4.69	Alpha	0.8	0.6
Mean	5.25	Beta	0.87	0.84
Sharpe Ratio	0.37	R-Squared	56	97

Investment Style

Interest-Rate Stance

Avg Effective Maturity	8.5 Yrs

Maturity Short Intm Long
Quality High Med Low

Quality

Avg Credit Quality	AA
Avg Weighted Coupon	5.21%
Avg Weighted Price	94.54% of Par

Diversification Value for Portfolio Types

Large Cap: Medium	Small Cap: High	Bond: Low	Balanced: Medium	Diversified: Medium

Expenses & Fees

Sales Fees	0.00% front
	0.00% deferred
	0.00% 12b-1
Management Fee	0.60% max./0.50% min.
3-,5-,10-yr Expense Projections	$16, $28, $63

Min Initial Purchase	$1000 (Addt'l: $100)
Min IRA Purchase	$500 (Addt'l: $50)
Min Auto Invest Plan	$50 (Systematic Inv: $50)

Portfolio 06-30-94

Amount 000	Date of Maturity	Total Stocks: 0 Total Fixed-Income: 227	Value $000	% Net Assets
21040	12-01-00	CO Denver Arpt Sys 10.5%	21606	2.50
25915	06-01-01	MA State GO 0%	19033	2.20
19210	07-01-05	WA Pub Pwr Sply Sys Proj #3 5%	18045	2.09
25605	07-01-06	AZ Maricopa GO USD #41 Gilbert 0%	14124	1.64
13825	03-01-02	MA New England Educ Loan Mktg 5.8%	13815	1.60
17800	06-30-03	AK North Slope GO 0%	11627	1.35
10880	05-01-99	NY Med Care Fac Fin Mt Sinai Hosp 5.95%	10772	1.25
10200	10-01-03	NY New York City GO 6.6%	10687	1.24
10635	07-01-03	CT Bristol Resource Rec Ogden Sys 6.125%	10242	1.19
10000	07-01-03	WA Pub Pwr Sply Sys Proj #1 Ser A 5.25%	9748	1.13
10355	01-01-05	NY Urban Dev Crtnl Fac 5.3%	9727	1.13
9495	07-01-04	PA Philadelphia Gas Wks 5.5%	9374	1.09
10000	12-01-03	CA Pub Wks Brd Dept Crtns Lease 4.7%	9244	1.07
15100	07-01-03	AZ Maricopa GO Sch Dist #28 Kyrene 0%	9182	1.06
9250	07-01-03	NY Dorm City Univ 5.5%	9127	1.06
8500	10-15-14	IL Dev Fin Poll Cntrl Edison 11.375%	8861	1.03
9500	07-01-05	VA SE Pub Svc Regl Solid Waste 4.8%	8721	1.01
12995	07-01-02	UT Intermountain Pwr Sply 0%	8706	1.01
9500	02-01-04	NE Omaha Pub Pwr Dist Elec Sys 4.5%	8517	0.99
13180	07-01-05	AZ Maricopa GO USD #97 Deer Vlly 0%	7862	0.91

Credit Analysis % of Bonds 12-31-94

US Govt	0	BB	4
AAA	57	B	0
AA	11	Below B	0
A	15	NR/NA	5
BBB	8		

Composition % of Assets 12-31-94

Cash	1.7	Preferreds	0.0
Stocks	0.0	Convertibles	0.0
Bonds	98.3	Other	0.0

Tax Analysis

	Tax-Adj Historical Return %	% Pretax Return
3 Yr Avg	5.16	97.9
5 Yr Avg	6.74	98.7
10 Yr Avg	6.95	98.7
Potential Capital Gain Exposure (% of assets)		-4%

Most Similar Funds in MF500

SteinRoe Intermediate Munis	Strong Fit
American Cap Muni Bond A	Strong Fit
USAA Tax-Exempt Int-Term	Strong Fit

Coupon Range

	% Bonds	Rel Obj
0%	16.9	6.74
0% to 6.8%	67.3	1.11
6.8% to 7.5%	5.2	0.34
7.5% to 8.3%	2.1	0.23
More than 8.3%	8.5	0.96
Not applicable	0.0	0.00

Sector Weightings

	% Bonds	Rel Obj
General Obl	31.61	1.50
Utilities	19.66	1.57
Health	14.47	1.10
Water/Waste	2.03	0.32
Housing	2.84	0.39
Education	6.14	0.96
Transportation	9.64	0.95
COP/Lease	4.98	1.56
Private	6.53	0.56
Misc Revenue	2.11	0.42
Demand	0.00	0.00

Top 5 States % of Bonds

NY	13.42	IL	8.91
WA	11.04	DC	6.11
MA	10.95		

Scudder Short-Term Bond

	Ticker	Load	NAV	Yield	SEC Yield	Assets	Objective
	SCSTX	None	10.92	6.9%	7.70%	2138.8	Corp Hi Qlty

Scudder Short-Term Bond Fund seeks income consistent with principal stability.

The fund normally invests at least 65% of its assets in U.S. government obligations, corporate debt securities, mortgage-backed securities, or other asset-backed securities rated AA or above (or of similar quality). Its average weighted maturity may not exceed three years. The fund may not purchase debt rated below BBB.

On June 26, 1992, Scudder Zero Coupon 1995 Fund was merged into this fund. Prior to July 1989, the fund was named Scudder General Target Fund of 1994 and invested in municipal securities maturing in that year.

Manager's Investment Style

Within its credit-quality and maturity parameters, management enhances yield by dedicating a substantial portion of assets to high-coupon mortgage-backeds and asset-backeds. It has also dabbled in derivatives--specifically, inverse floaters and principal-only strips. Foreign issues round out the portfolio. By investing in less-conventional fare, the fund has been able to offer one of the highest yields among all short-term funds, but not without added risk.

Fund Manager(s)

Thomas M. Poor CFA(1975), since 07-89.
Christopher L. Gootkind CFA(1989), since 07-89.
Scott E. Dolan, since 02-94.

Manager Experience	Dates Managed	Invest Obj	Std Dev	+/- Index
Thomas M. Poor				
Sierra S-T Hi-Qual A	11/93 - 12/94	CQ	2.08	0.61

Historical Profile
Return	Average
Risk	Below Average
Rating	★★★★★ Highest

| | 94 | 91 | 91 | 5 | 7 | 9 | 26 | 16 | Investment Style History Fixed Income |

Income Rtn % Rank Obj

Growth of $10,000

|||| Value of Fund ($000)
— Value of Index ($000) LB Int
▼ Manager Change
▽ Partial Manager Change
► Mgr Unknown After
◄ Mgr Unknown Before

Performance Quartile (Within Objective)

	1983	1984	1985	1986	1987	1988	1989	1990	1991	1992	1993	1994	History
	---	10.26	11.35	11.92	11.23	11.19	11.71	11.72	12.24	11.93	12.01	10.92	NAV
	---	11.28 *	20.91	14.66	1.25	6.31	13.28	9.88	14.28	5.52	7.87	-2.87	Total Return %
	---	---	-1.22	-0.59	-1.50	-1.57	-1.26	0.94	-1.72	-1.73	-1.88	0.05	+/- LB Aggregate
	---	---	-3.15	-1.88	-1.30	-2.92	-0.70	2.73	-4.22	-3.18	-4.30	1.05	+/- LB Corporate
	---	7.85	10.29	7.61	6.21	6.66	7.82	9.80	9.85	8.05	6.61	6.20	Income Return %
	---	3.43	10.62	7.05	-4.95	-0.36	5.46	0.09	4.44	-2.53	1.26	-9.08	Capital Return %
	---	---	67	57	48	86	53	5	61	73	80	42	Total Rtn % Rank All
	---	---	37	28	67	80	19	2	56	80	59	51	Total Rtn % Rank Obj
	---	0.73	0.96	0.81	0.73	0.73	0.83	1.09	1.08	0.96	0.77	0.76	Income $
	---	0.00	0.00	0.21	0.11	0.00	0.09	0.00	0.00	0.00	0.07	0.00	Capital Gains $
	---	1.00	1.27	1.45	1.45	1.50	0.36	0.16	0.44	0.75	0.68	0.72	Expense Ratio %
	---	9.69	8.82	6.89	6.34	6.48	7.97	9.36	8.96	8.01	7.21	6.74	Income Ratio %
	---	---	58	16	29	24	40	53	41	84	66	81	Turnover Rate %
	---	1.8	4.8	7.9	9.7	10.3	70.4	335.7	2234.8	2854.4	3196.7	2138.8	Net Assets ($mil)

Performance 12-31-94

	1st Qtr	2nd Qtr	3rd Qtr	4th Qtr	Total
1987	2.57	-1.85	-4.60	5.42	1.25
1988	3.52	0.49	1.64	0.54	6.31
1989	0.44	6.97	2.11	3.26	13.28
1990	0.35	3.32	2.88	3.01	9.88
1991	3.32	2.82	3.66	3.78	14.28
1992	-0.16	2.39	2.94	0.27	5.52
1993	2.98	2.03	1.79	0.86	7.87
1994	-1.53	-0.79	1.01	-1.57	-2.87

Bear Market Performance

Decile Rank (5-year period)

Worst — Best

	Worst 3 Mo Period 1985-89	Worst 3 Mo Period 1990-94
Scudder Short-Term Bond	-4.60	-2.77
+/- LB Aggregate	-1.87	2.16
+/- Best Fit Index : LB Int	-3.31	1.45

Trailing Returns

	Total Return %	+/- LB Aggregate	+/- LB Corporate	% Rank All	% Rank Obj	Growth of $10,000
3 Mo	-1.57	-1.95	-2.01	58	98	9,843
6 Mo	-0.58	-1.57	-1.75	66	95	9,942
1 Yr	-2.87	0.05	1.05	42	51	9,713
3 Yr Avg	3.40	-1.14	-2.01	81	80	11,055
5 Yr Avg	6.78	-0.84	-1.48	55	53	13,883
10 Yr Avg	8.91	-1.04	-1.72	74	48	23,469
15 Yr Avg	---	---	---	---	---	---

Operations

Address and Telephone	Two International Place Boston, MA 02110 800-225-2470 / 617-439-4640
Advisor	Scudder Stevens & Clark
Subadvisor	None
Distributor	Scudder Investor Services
States Available	All
Report Grade	A+
Income Distrib	Paid Monthly
* Date of Inception	04-02-84
Fiscal Year End	December

Risk Analysis

Time Period	Load-Adj Return %	Risk % Rank [1] All	Obj	Morningstar [2] Return	Risk	Morningstar Risk-Adj Rating
1 Yr	-2.87					
3 Yr	3.40	7	27	-0.05 [3]	0.67	★★★★
5 Yr	6.78	4	23	0.50 [3]	0.55	★★★★★
10 Yr	8.91	5	14	0.79 [3]	0.75	★★★★★

Average Historical Rating (93 months) 4.2 ★s

[1] = low, 100 = high   [2] 1.00 = Taxable Avg   [3] 1.00 = 90-day T-bill return

Other Measures

			Standard LB Agg	Best Fit LB Int
Standard Deviation	2.51	Alpha	-0.7	-0.5
Mean	3.38	Beta	0.51	0.62
Sharpe Ratio	-0.06	R-Squared	64	70

Investment Style

Interest-Rate Stance

		Maturity Short Intm Long	Quality
Avg Effective Duration	0.8 Yrs**		High Med Low
Avg Effective Maturity	1.5 Yrs		

Quality

Avg Credit Quality	AA
Avg Weighted Coupon	6.87%
Avg Weighted Price	96.51% of Par

**figure provided by fund

Diversification Value for Portfolio Types

Large Cap: High	Small Cap: High	Bond: Low	Balanced: Medium	Diversified: High

Portfolio 06-30-94

Amount 000	Date of Maturity	Total Stocks: 0 Total Fixed-Income: 177	Value $000	% Net Assets
137963	01-15-23	GNMA 9.5%	145359	5.42
121853	07-28-94	Associates North Amer 4.4%	121853	4.55
97978	12-15-21	GNMA 10%	104877	3.91
82643	05-15-21	GNMA 11%	92003	3.43
118285	05-15-99	FHLMC CMO P/O 0%	91301	3.41
78000	09-15-97	Commonwealth Australia 12.5%	63142	2.36
68482	10-28-98	FHLMC CMO IFRN COF	55726	2.08
52400	12-29-97	FNMA CMO IFRN	55151	2.06
58259	03-25-94	Countrywide Funding CMO 6.25%	54727	2.04
65767	05-15-01	FHLMC CMO REMIC P/O 0%	49188	1.84
39388	04-15-19	GNMA 11.5%	44458	1.66
44625	09-15-95	RJR Nabisco 5.5%	43355	1.62
45000	03-15-98	Lockheed 5.875%	43146	1.61
41700	08-07-96	Standard CC Trust 5.875%	41661	1.55
39772	08-18-94	United Mexican States N/A	39401	1.47
245000	02-15-18	US Treasury Bond 0%	38316	1.43
37337	02-15-18	TMS Home Equity Loan Tr 5.075%	36077	1.35
38846	11-25-24	Chase Mortgage Fin CMO 6.75%	35496	1.32
35414	01-01-99	FHLMC 5yr 6%	34263	1.28
34747	03-25-24	Countrywide Funding CMO 6.75%	32999	1.23
34700	03-07-99	Standard CC Trust 4.65%	32889	1.23
32000	07-28-94	United Mexican States N/A	31829	1.19
31469	07-25-24	Chase Mortgage Fin CMO 7.25%	30528	1.14
31102	02-15-04	Green Tree Financial 6.9%	30499	1.14
30966	12-08-94	United Mexican States N/A	29942	1.12

Composition % 12-31-94

Cash	7.0	Preferreds	0.0
Stocks	0.0	Convertibles	0.0
Bonds	93.0	Other	0.0

Tax Analysis

	Tax-Adj Historical Return %	% Pretax Return
3 Yr Avg	0.77	22.2
5 Yr Avg	3.97	55.4
10 Yr Avg	5.86	56.9
Potential Capital Gain Exposure (% of assets)		-10%

Most Similar Funds in MF500

Fidelity Short-Term Bond	Strong Fit
T. Rowe Price Short-Trm Bond	Fair Fit
Prudential Struct Maturity A	Fair Fit

Min Purchase

Min Initial Purchase	$1000 (Addt'l: $100)
Min IRA Purchase	$500 (Addt'l: $50)
Min Auto Invest Plan	$50 (Systematic Inv: $50)

Expenses & Fees

Sales Fees	0.00% front
	0.00% deferred
	0.00% 12b-1
Management Fee	0.60% flat fee
3-,5-,10-yr Expense Projections	$22, $38, $85

Coupon Range

	% of Bonds	Rel Obj
0%	9.0	3.96
0% to 8.5%	50.4	0.72
8.5% to 9.5%	13.3	1.02
9.5% to 11%	9.7	2.12
More than 11%	4.1	1.78
Not applicable	13.4	1.76

Credit Analysis 12-31-94
% of Bonds

US Govt	28	BB	0
AAA	30	B	0
AA	10	Below B	0
A	18	NR/NA	0
BBB	14		

MORNINGSTAR 1995 Mutual Fund 500

Scudder Short-Term Global Income

	Ticker	Load	NAV	Yield	SEC Yield	Assets	Objective
	SSTGX	None	10.54	8.2%	8.26%	496.9	S/T World Inc

Scudder Short-Term Global Income Fund seeks high current income.

The fund invests primarily in high-quality money-market instruments and short-term bonds denominated in foreign currencies and the U.S. dollar. It may also invest in mortgage-backed securities. Portfolio securities generally have an average life that does not exceed three years. The fund engages in various options and futures strategies for hedging purposes, to manage portfolio duration, or to enhance potential gain.

Historical Profile

Return	Average
Risk	Below Average
Rating	★★★★ Above Average

Investment Style History
Fixed Income

Income Rtn % Rank Obj

Manager's Investment Style

Within its maturity parameters, management focuses primarily on yield. It has also stuck with the world's highest-yielding bond markets, including a foray in developing-market debt. Active currency hedging is a staple of this fund.

Growth of $10,000

|||| Value of Fund ($000)
— Value of Index ($000)
LB Int
▼ Manager Change
▽ Partial Manager Change
► Mgr Unknown After
◄ Mgr Unknown Before

Performance Quartile
(Within Objective)

	1983	1984	1985	1986	1987	1988	1989	1990	1991	1992	1993	1994	History
	---	---	---	---	---	---	---	---	12.13	11.70	11.53	10.54	NAV
	---	---	---	---	---	---	---	---	9.40 *	5.49	6.74	-1.13	Total Return %
	---	---	---	---	---	---	---	---	---	-1.76	-3.01	1.78	+/- LB Aggregate
	---	---	---	---	---	---	---	---	---	0.72	-8.38	-7.83	+/- SB World Govt
	---	---	---	---	---	---	---	---	8.32	8.87	8.20	7.45	Income Return %
	---	---	---	---	---	---	---	---	1.08	-3.39	-1.45	-8.59	Capital Return %
	---	---	---	---	---	---	---	---	---	74	85	27	Total Rtn % Rank All
	---	---	---	---	---	---	---	---	---	1	48	26	Total Rtn % Rank Obj
	---	---	---	---	---	---	---	---	0.95	1.05	0.94	0.86	Income $
	---	---	---	---	---	---	---	---	0.00	0.02	0.00	0.00	Capital Gains $
	---	---	---	---	---	---	---	---	1.00	1.00	1.00	1.00	Expense Ratio %
	---	---	---	---	---	---	---	---	9.97	8.94	8.10	7.60	Income Ratio %
	---	---	---	---	---	---	---	---	26	274	260	290	Turnover Rate %
	---	---	---	---	---	---	---	---	348.0	1109.2	940.0	496.9	Net Assets ($mil)

Fund Manager(s)

Margaret R. Craddock, since 10-91.
Lawrence Teitelbaum, since 03-93.
Gary P. Johnson, since 11-92.

Manager Experience	Dates Managed	Invest Obj	Std Dev	+/- Index
Margaret R. Craddock				
Sierra S-T Glob GovtA	02/92 - 12/94	SW	2.91	-0.93
Lawrence Teitelbaum				
Merrill Lynch Global Bd B	12/88 - 03/93	WB	7.31	-1.31

Performance 12-31-94

	1st Qtr	2nd Qtr	3rd Qtr	4th Qtr	Total
1987	---	---	---	---	---
1988	---	---	---	---	---
1989	---	---	---	---	---
1990	---	---	---	---	---
1991	---	0.39	5.08	3.59	9.40 *
1992	0.28	3.82	1.22	0.10	5.49
1993	1.60	4.14	0.14	0.75	6.74
1994	-1.71	0.46	0.51	-0.38	-1.13

Bear Market Performance

Decile Rank (5-year period)

Worst ———————————————— Best

	Worst 3 Mo Period 1985-89	Worst 3 Mo Period 1990-94
Scudder Short-Term Global Inc	---	---
+/- LB Aggregate	---	---
+/- Best Fit Index :	---	---

Trailing Returns

	Total Return %	+/- LB Aggregate	+/- SB World	% Rank All	Obj	Growth of $10,000
3 Mo	-0.38	-0.76	-0.95	32	36	9,962
6 Mo	0.12	-0.87	-2.11	55	31	10,012
1 Yr	-1.13	1.78	-7.83	27	26	9,887
3 Yr Avg	3.64	-0.91	-5.13	77	1	11,132
5 Yr Avg	---	---	---	---	---	---
10 Yr Avg	---	---	---	---	---	---
15 Yr Avg	---	---	---	---	---	---

Operations

Address and Telephone	Two International Place
	Boston, MA 02110
	800-225-2470 / 617-439-4640
Advisor	Scudder Stevens & Clark
Subadvisor	None
Distributor	Scudder Investor Services
States Available	All
Report Grade	A+
Income Distrib	Paid Monthly
* Date of Inception	03-01-91
Fiscal Year End	October

Risk Analysis

Time Period	Load-Adj Return %	Risk % Rank All	Obj	Morningstar Return	Morningstar Risk	Morningstar Risk-Adj Rating
1 Yr	-1.13	---	---	---	---	---
3 Yr	3.64	6	1	0.02³	0.62	★★★★
5 Yr	---	---	---	---	---	---
10 Yr	---	---	---	---	---	---

Average Historical Rating (10 months)   3.9 ★s

¹ 1 = low, 100 = high   ² 1.00 = Taxable Avg   ³ 1.00 = 90-day T-bill return

Other Measures

				Standard LB Agg	Best Fit LB Int
Standard Deviation	2.43	Alpha		-0.2	-0.1
Mean	3.61	Beta		0.31	0.37
Sharpe Ratio	0.04	R-Squared		26	27

Investment Style

Interest-Rate Stance

Avg Effective Maturity   27.6 Mos.

Quality

Avg Credit Quality   AA

Avg Weighted Coupon   8.84%

Maturity: Short Intm Long
Quality: High Med Low

Diversification Value for Portfolio Types

Large Cap: High	Small Cap: High	Bond: High	Balanced: High	Diversified: High
●	●	●	●	●

Portfolio 10-31-94

Total Stocks: 0
Total Fixed-Income: 47

Amount 000	Date of Maturity		Value $000	% Net Assets
240000	10-12-96	Govt of France 6.5%	46108	8.21
53625	01-15-98	Commonwealth Australia 12.5%	42839	7.63
915000	06-23-95	New South Wales 8%	36442	6.49
28000	01-21-97	United Kingdom Treasury 5.25%	33727	6.00
46525	07-15-97	Govt of New Zealand 10%	29427	5.24
154000	02-10-96	Kingdom of Denmark 6%	25643	4.57
40000000	04-01-97	Republic of Italy 8.5%	24546	4.37
37000000	01-01-97	Republic of Italy 8.5%	22878	4.07
2500000	08-30-96	Kingdom of Spain 11.85%	20472	3.65
106800	11-15-96	Kingdom of Denmark 9%	18465	3.29
17300	06-12-97	Home Savings of America 10.5%	17701	3.15
17319	04-20-95	United Mexican States N/A	16704	2.97
24000	07-21-97	Republic of Germany 8.25%	16550	2.95
15785	09-01-97	Argentina Bonos Del Tesoro FRN	15110	2.69
61200	08-15-97	Republic of South Africa 14%	14539	2.59
17300	08-03-95	United Mexican States N/A	14099	2.51
105000	06-21-95	Kingdom of Sweden N/A	13892	2.47
10500	01-23-96	United Kingdom Treasury 8%	13447	2.39
12500	04-21-95	Itt Financial 6.3%	12224	2.18
11900	07-08-95	Queensland Treasury 12.1%	11900	2.12
11000	08-31-97	US Treasury Note 5.625%	10591	1.89
267281	01-27-95	New South Wales Note	10499	1.87
10000	05-15-98	United Svgs Asso Texas 9.05%	9475	1.69
54000	08-16-95	Kingdom of Sweden N/A	7041	1.25
7047	07-25-14	United Co Financial 6.075%	6680	1.19

Composition % 12-31-94

Cash	8.3	Preferreds	0.0
Stocks	0.0	Convertibles	0.0
Bonds	91.7	Other	0.0

Tax Analysis

	Tax-Adj Historical Return %	% Pretax Return
3 Yr Avg	0.57	15.1
5 Yr Avg	---	---
10 Yr Avg	---	---
Potential Capital Gain Exposure (% of assets)	-14%	

Most Similar Funds in MF500

PaineWebber Global Inc B	Weak Fit
Fidelity Short-Term Bond	Weak Fit
Scudder Short-Term Bond	Weak Fit

Country Exposure 12-31-94

	% of Bonds
U.S.	17
Australia	14
Mexico	13
Denmark	10
Italy	10

Currency Exposure 12-31-94

	% of Net Assets
U.S.	30
E.C.	10
Denmark	10
Italy	10
Australia	8

Expenses & Fees

Sales Fees	0.00% front
	0.00% deferred
	0.00% 12b-1
Management Fee	0.75% max./0.70% min.
3-,5-,10-yr Expense Projections	$32, $55, $122

Min Initial Purchase	$1000 (Addt'l: $100)
Min IRA Purchase	$500 (Addt'l: $50)
Min Auto Invest Plan	$50 (Systematic Inv: $50)

Selected American

Selected American Shares seeks growth of capital and income.
The fund normally invests at least 65% of its assets in securities of U.S. companies, including common stocks, convertibles, fixed-income, and short-term instruments. It invests chiefly in blue-chip firms with capitalizations of more than $1 billion. Although the portfolio is biased toward equity securities, the fund maintains no restrictions on percentage holdings of asset types.

Selected Financial Services (formerly Prescott Asset Management) managed the fund from Jan. 1, 1983, to May 1, 1993.

	Ticker	Load	NAV	Yield	SEC Yield	Assets	Objective
	SLASX	None	13.09	1.6%	1.91%	527.9	Growth/Inc.

Historical Profile
Return Average
Risk Average
Rating ★★★
Neutral

Investment Style History
Equity

Average % Stocks Held in Portfolio

78% 98% 77% 87% 88% 90% 89% 93%

Growth of $10,000
|||| Value of Fund ($000)
— Value of Index ($000) S&P 500
▼ Manager Change
▽ Partial Manager Change
► Mgr Unknown After
◄ Mgr Unknown Before

Performance Quartile
(Within Objective)

Manager's Investment Style
Manager Shelby Davis' current overweighting in financials illustrates his stock-picking criteria. He believes these stocks will benefit from positive demographic trends, while they are also good businesses to be in. He may buy on price weakness, and may use dividend-paying stocks and convertibles to generate income. Davis' style, similar to that he uses in running New York Venture, makes a distinct contrast with prior fund management.

1983	1984	1985	1986	1987	1988	1989	1990	1991	1992	1993	1994	History
9.69	10.54	13.35	12.65	11.43	13.67	13.81	12.79	18.43	17.13	14.60	13.09	NAV
21.54	14.86	33.34	17.15	0.23	22.04	20.07	-3.90	46.26	5.80	5.50	-3.26	Total Return %
-0.93	8.60	1.61	-1.53	-5.03	5.43	-11.61	-0.79	-15.77	-1.82	-4.56	-4.58	+/- S&P 500
-1.93	11.81	0.78	1.06	-2.13	4.10	-9.10	2.28	12.05	-3.18	-5.79	-3.19	+/- Wilshire 5000
7.40	6.09	4.30	3.79	4.34	2.41	3.18	3.19	2.16	1.09	1.66	1.56	Income Return %
14.13	8.77	29.05	13.36	-4.10	19.63	16.90	-7.09	44.10	4.71	3.83	-4.82	Capital Return %
34	6	15	38	58	10	35	67	9	71	90	46	Total Rtn % Rank All
45	8	11	45	66	15	71	53	3	72	87	74	Total Rtn % Rank Obj
0.56	0.53	0.40	0.48	0.58	0.26	0.45	0.43	0.24	0.19	0.26	0.22	Income $
0.00	0.00	0.17	2.29	0.76	0.00	2.10	0.04	0.00	2.19	3.22	0.82	Capital Gains $
0.94	0.99	0.87	0.85	1.11	1.11	1.08	1.35	1.19	1.17	1.01	1.32	Expense Ratio %
5.80	4.58	4.42	3.07	2.38	2.07	3.06	2.04	1.41	0.95	1.37	1.26	Income Ratio %
66	49	33	40	45	35	46	48	21	50	79	---	Turnover Rate %
81.3	84.3	122.6	160.4	264.3	284.7	361.0	400.6	705.6	581.9	451.9	527.9	Net Assets ($mil)

Fund Manager(s)
Shelby M. C. Davis, since 04-93. Birthdate: 03-37. BA, Princeton U. 1958

Manager Experience

	Dates Managed	Invest Obj	Std Dev	+/- Index
Shelby M. C. Davis				
Retirement Plan Growth B	05/84 - 01/87	G	11.33	-8.93
Selected Special	05/93 - 11/94	SC	9.35	-1.60

Performance 12-31-94

	1st Qtr	2nd Qtr	3rd Qtr	4th Qtr	Total
1987	16.12	3.25	3.38	-19.13	0.23
1988	9.01	5.99	4.39	1.19	22.04
1989	9.07	9.16	5.51	-4.42	20.07
1990	-5.29	7.46	-13.95	9.72	-3.90
1991	26.04	-1.94	6.59	11.02	46.26
1992	-4.34	-0.05	3.70	6.70	5.80
1993	0.70	0.81	6.03	-2.00	5.50
1994	-3.79	-0.23	1.14	-0.37	-3.26

Bear Market Performance
Decile Rank (5-year period)

Worst ▬ Best

	Worst 3 Mo Period 1985-89	Worst 3 Mo Period 1990-94
Selected American	-25.85	-18.84
+/- S&P 500	3.73	-5.00
+/- Best Fit Index : S&P 500	3.73	-5.00

Trailing Returns

	Total Return %	+/- S&P 500	+/- Wil 5000	% Rank All	% Rank Obj	Growth of $10,000
3 Mo	-0.36	-0.35	0.41	32	30	9,964
6 Mo	0.77	-4.09	-3.85	42	80	10,077
1 Yr	-3.26	-4.58	-3.19	46	74	9,674
3 Yr Avg	2.59	-3.68	-4.02	88	85	10,797
5 Yr Avg	8.70	0.01	-0.12	26	32	15,174
10 Yr Avg	13.29	-1.10	-0.57	24	28	34,818
15 Yr Avg	14.15	-0.33	0.17	22	24	72,809

Operations

Address and Telephone	P.O. Box 1688
	Santa Fe, NM 87504
	800-243-1575 / 505-983-4335
Advisor	Selected/Venture Advisers
Subadvisor	None
Distributor	Selected/Venture Advisers
States Available	All
Report Grade	D
Income Distrib	Paid Quarterly
Date of Inception	02-20-33
Fiscal Year End	December

Risk Analysis

Time Period	Load-Adj Return %	Risk % Rank All [1]	Risk % Rank Obj	Morningstar [2] Return	Morningstar Risk	Morningstar Risk-Adj Rating
1 Yr	-3.26					
3 Yr	2.59	84	96	-0.28 [3]	1.04	★★
5 Yr	8.70	84	96	0.99 [3]	1.03	★★★
10 Yr	13.29	67	78	1.12	0.90	★★★

Average Historical Rating (109 months) 4.1 ★ s

[1] = low, 100 = high [2] 1.00 = Equity Avg [3] 1.00 = 90-day T-bill return

Other Measures

			Standard S&P 500	Best Fit S&P 500
Standard Deviation	9.87	Alpha	-3.5	-3.5
Mean	3.05	Beta	1.07	1.07
Sharpe Ratio	-0.05	R-Squared	74	74

Investment Style

	Stock Portfolio Avg	Relative S&P 500
Price/Earnings Ratio	14.8	0.80
Price/Book Ratio	2.8	0.83
5 Yr Earnings Gr %	11.4	2.06
Return on Assets %	6.0	0.80
Debt % Total Cap	26.0	0.92
Med Mkt Cap ($mil)	6623	0.51

Style
Value Blend Growth — Size Large/Med/Small

Diversification Value for Portfolio Types

Large Cap: Low | Small Cap: Medium | Bond: High | Balanced: Low | Diversified: Low

Expenses & Fees

Sales Fees	0.00% front
	0.00% deferred
	0.25% 12b-1
Management Fee	0.65% max./0.55% min.
3-,5-,10-yr Expense Projections	$39, $67, $148
Annual Brokerage Cost	0.22%

Min Initial Purchase	$1000 (Addt'l: $100)
Min IRA Purchase	$500 (Addt'l: $100)
Min Auto Invest Plan	$1000 (Systematic Inv: $100)

Portfolio 11-30-94

Share Chg (06-94)000	Amount 000	Total Stocks: 55 Total Fixed-Income: 15	Value $000	% Net Assets
0	125	Wells Fargo	18063	3.56
0	130	General Re	15282	3.01
40	240	Intel	15150	2.99
29	254	Morgan Stanley Group	14994	2.96
35	210	Chubb	14753	2.91
0	235	JP Morgan	13806	2.72
0	150	American International Group	13744	2.71
0	275	FHLMC	13716	2.70
0	402	First Bank System	13372	2.64
0	403	Travelers	13260	2.61
22	464	Archer-Daniels-Midland	12813	2.53
0	250	Coca-Cola	12781	2.52
0	250	Tribune	12531	2.47
0	600	MCI Communications	11700	2.31
0	150	Warner-Lambert	11606	2.29
0	150	Pfizer	11606	2.29
42	342	Vornado Realty Trust	10770	2.12
0	90	Citicorp Cv Pfd	10247	2.02
334	334	Illinois Central	10091	1.99
218	218	Tandy	10037	1.98
0	200	Sears Roebuck	9450	1.86
0	300	Lubrizol	9450	1.86
0	532	Equitable	9312	1.84
55	255	Burlington Resources	9116	1.80
0	265	SLMA	9076	1.79

Composition % 12-31-94

				% of Stocks
Cash	0.7	Preferreds	0.0	
Stocks	91.6	Convertibles	7.8	
Bonds	0.0	Other	0.0	

Tax Analysis

	Tax-Adj Historical Return %	% Pretax Return
3 Yr Avg	-1.38	---
5 Yr Avg	5.82	63.2
10 Yr Avg	9.98	64.1
Potential Capital Gain Exposure (% of assets)		6%

Most Similar Funds in MF500

Enterprise Capital Apprec	Fair Fit
Janus Growth & Income	Fair Fit
Liberty All-Star	Fair Fit

Index Allocation

	% of Stocks
S&P 500	70.3
S&P MidCap 400	13.5
U.S. Small Cap	16.2
Foreign	0.0

Sector Weightings

	% of Stocks	Relative S&P 500
Utilities	2.6	0.21
Energy	3.1	0.30
Financials	55.2	5.22
Industrial Cyclicals	3.1	0.19
Consumer Durables	3.5	0.57
Consumer Staples	7.6	0.60
Services	7.0	0.86
Retail	6.3	1.09
Health	6.9	0.79
Technology	4.7	0.51

MORNINGSTAR 1995 Mutual Fund 500

Seligman High-Yield Bond A

	Ticker	Load	NAV	Yield	SEC Yield	Assets	Objective
	SHYBX	4.75%	6.35	10.1%	10.31%	59.0	Corp Hi Yld

Seligman High-Yield Bond Series -- Class A seeks maximum current income.

The fund normally invests at least 80% of its assets in high-yielding, income-producing corporate bonds generally unrated or rated BBB or lower. The remaining 20% of assets may be invested in a range of high-yield, medium- and lower-quality corporate notes, short-term money-market instruments, U.S. government obligations, and cash. The fund may invest in zero-coupon bonds and payment-in-kind bonds. Also, the fund may invest in foreign debt in the form of ADRs.

Class A shares have front loads and 12b-1 fees; Class D shares have level loads.

Manager's Investment Style

This fund plays it safe while delivering consistent yields. Management prefers B rated bonds--80% of the portfolio is invested in these issues. This helps deliver a decent yield without significant default risk. The fund is heavily invested in cyclicals and plans to stay that way as long as management holds the opinion that, on an absolute basis, rates are low.

Fund Manager(s)

Daniel J. Charleston, since 01-89. Birthdate: 11-59. BS, Kean C. 1983

Manager Experience	Dates Managed	Invest Obj	Std Dev	+/- Index
Not available.				

Historical Profile
Return	Above Average
Risk	Low
Rating	★★★★★ Highest

Investment Style History
Fixed Income
Income Rtn % Rank Obj

	52	71	11	74	52	32	31	13

Growth of $10,000
|||| Value of Fund ($000)
— Value of Index ($000)
LB Agg
▼ Manager Change
▽ Partial Manager Change
► Mgr Unknown After
◄ Mgr Unknown Before

Performance Quartile (Within Objective)

1983	1984	1985	1986	1987	1988	1989	1990	1991	1992	1993	1994	History
---	---	7.59	7.83	7.07	7.02	6.40	5.21	5.96	6.42	6.94	6.35	NAV
---	---	18.43 *	15.39	3.36	11.38	3.84	-7.28	30.70	20.07	19.19	0.78	Total Return %
---	---		0.14	0.60	3.50	-10.70	-16.22	14.70	12.83	9.44	3.70	+/- LB Aggregate
---	---		-0.24	-3.17	-0.06	3.45	-0.90	-13.05	3.41	0.29	1.76	+/- FB High-Yield
---	---	12.13	12.23	11.25	12.08	12.67	11.32	16.31	12.36	11.09	9.28	Income Return %
---	---	6.30	3.16	-7.89	-0.71	-8.83	-18.59	14.40	7.72	8.10	-8.50	Capital Return %
---	---		52	33	51	96	78	25	5	18	15	Total Rtn % Rank All
---	---		29	27	79	18	32	75	23	40	6	Total Rtn % Rank Obj
---	---	0.80	0.89	0.84	0.83	0.89	0.75	0.77	0.69	0.66	0.64	Income $
---	---	0.00	0.00	0.17	0.00	0.00	0.00	0.00	0.00	0.00	0.00	Capital Gains $
---	---		1.08	1.20	1.14	1.13	1.21	1.29	1.21	1.20	1.23	Expense Ratio %
---	---		11.32	10.64	11.41	13.02	13.40	13.36	10.82	9.68	9.28	Income Ratio %
---	---			110	103	95	135	118	181	146	194	---	Turnover Rate %
---	---	32.6	71.9	66.0	62.3	45.5	27.6	32.3	40.8	61.3	59.0	Net Assets ($mil)

Performance 12-31-94

	1st Qtr	2nd Qtr	3rd Qtr	4th Qtr	Total
1987	4.87	-2.59	-2.91	4.22	3.36
1988	4.79	2.34	1.41	2.41	11.38
1989	1.90	3.84	0.05	-1.91	3.84
1990	-3.72	3.44	-4.27	-2.74	-7.28
1991	12.22	5.49	6.42	3.75	30.70
1992	9.15	2.90	5.48	1.36	20.07
1993	7.00	4.22	1.76	5.04	19.19
1994	-0.60	-0.10	0.45	1.03	0.78

Bear Market Performance

Decile Rank (5-year period)

Worst | Best

	Worst 3 Mo Period 1985-89	Worst 3 Mo Period 1990-94
Seligman High-Yield Bond A	---	-10.69
+/- LB Aggregate	---	-11.43
+/- Best Fit Index : FB HY	---	3.42

Trailing Returns

	Total Return %	+/- LB Aggregate	+/- FB High-Yield	% Rank All	% Rank Obj	Growth of $10,000
3 Mo	1.03	0.66	1.08	6	1	10,103
6 Mo	1.49	0.50	-0.07	31	7	10,149
1 Yr	0.78	3.70	1.76	15	6	10,078
3 Yr Avg	12.99	8.44	1.83	6	15	14,424
5 Yr Avg	11.82	4.19	-1.26	10	26	17,480
10 Yr Avg	---	---	---	---	---	---
15 Yr Avg	---	---	---	---	---	---

Operations

Address and Telephone	100 Park Avenue New York, NY 10017 800-221-2783 / 212-850-1864
Advisor	J.& W. Seligman
Subadvisor	None
Distributor	Seligman Financial Services
States Available	Selected states
Report Grade	B
Income Distrib	Paid Monthly
* Date of Inception	03-11-85
Fiscal Year End	December

Risk Analysis

Time Period	Load-Adj Return %	Risk % Rank [1] All	Obj	Morningstar [2] Return	Morningstar Risk	Morningstar Risk-Adj Rating
1 Yr	-4.01					
3 Yr	11.17	4	10	2.36 [3]	0.27	★★★★★
5 Yr	10.73	34	11	1.56 [3]	0.42	★★★★★
10 Yr	---	---	---	---	---	

Average Historical Rating (82 months)   3.5 ★ s

[1] 1 = low, 100 = high   [2] 1.00 = Hybrid Avg   [3] 1.00 = 90-day T-bill return

Other Measures

			Standard LB Agg	Best Fit FB HY
Standard Deviation	4.71	Alpha	8.6	1.5
Mean	12.38	Beta	0.56	1.02
Sharpe Ratio	1.88	R-Squared	23	89

Investment Style

Interest-Rate Stance
Avg Effective Duration	4.5 Yrs
Avg Effective Maturity	8.2 Yrs

Maturity
Short Intm Long

Quality
High Med Low

Quality
Avg Credit Quality	B
Avg Weighted Coupon	10.44%
Avg Weighted Price	94.71% of Par

Diversification Value for Portfolio Types

Large Cap: High	Small Cap: High	Bond: High	Balanced: High	Diversified: High

Portfolio 10-31-94

Amount 000	Date of Maturity	Total Stocks: 0 Total Fixed-Income: 47	Value $000	% Net Assets
2180	10-01-04	Aztar 13.75%	2147	3.73
1744	11-01-01	Delaval Imo Industries 12%	1774	3.08
1744	08-01-03	Pilgrim's Pride 10.875%	1674	2.91
1744	11-01-04	Flagstar 11.25%	1417	2.46
2180	04-15-98	Marvel 0%	1384	2.40
1308	05-15-02	OrNda HealthCorp 12.25%	1383	2.40
1308	06-15-02	Silgan 11.75%	1354	2.35
2616	11-15-99	United International 0%	1328	2.31
1308	02-01-03	Kaiser Aluminium/Chem 12.75%	1319	2.29
1308	08-15-04	Allbritton Comm 11.5%	1315	2.28
1308	06-01-07	Continental Cablevision 11%	1315	2.28
1308	11-01-00	Crown Packaging 10.75%	1308	2.27
1308	10-01-00	SFX Broadcasting 11.375%	1308	2.27
1308	10-01-04	Stone Container 11.5%	1298	2.25
1308	04-01-05	Applied Extrusion Tech 11.5%	1295	2.25
1308	04-01-04	Cablevision Systems 10.75%	1295	2.25
1308	06-01-02	SPX 11.75%	1295	2.25
1308	02-15-03	Di Giorgio 12%	1288	2.24
1308	08-01-99	Continental Homes Holding 12%	1282	2.23
1308	05-01-01	Arcadian Partner 10.75%	1275	2.21
1308	07-15-12	Comcast 10.625%	1275	2.21
1308	08-15-99	Stone Container 11%	1275	2.21
1308	10-01-02	Bell & Howell 10.75%	1249	2.17
1308	06-15-04	Plitt Theaters 10.875%	1233	2.14
1308	02-01-04	Allied Waste Industry 10.75%	1216	2.11

Composition % 11-25-94

Cash	1.7	Preferreds	0.0
Stocks	0.0	Convertibles	1.8
Bonds	96.5	Other	0.0

Tax Analysis

	Tax-Adj Historical Return %	% Pretax Return
3 Yr Avg	9.02	66.9
5 Yr Avg	7.64	59.5
10 Yr Avg	---	---
Potential Capital Gain Exposure (% of assets)		-22%

Most Similar Funds in MF500

Merrill Lynch Corp Hi-Inc A	Strong Fit
Fidelity Adv High-Yield A	Strong Fit
AIM High-Yield A	Strong Fit

Coupon Range

	% of Bonds	Rel Obj
0%, PIK	8.6	1.16
0% to 11%	35.0	0.71
11% to 13%	48.5	1.45
13% to 14.5%	6.1	1.12
More than 14.5%	1.8	1.09
Not applicable	0.0	0.00

Credit Analysis 11-25-94
% of Bonds

US Govt	0	BB	4
AAA	0	B	91
AA	0	Below B	5
A	0	NR/NA	0
BBB	0		

Expenses & Fees

Sales Fees	4.75% front
	0.00% deferred
	0.25% 12b-1
Management Fee	0.50% flat fee
3-,5-,10-yr Expense Projections	$84, $110, $186

Min Initial Purchase	$1000 (Addt'l: $50)
Min IRA Purchase	$1000 (Addt'l: $50)
Min Auto Invest Plan	$1000 (Systematic Inv: $50)

Seligman Income A

Ticker	Load	NAV	Yield	SEC Yield	Assets	Objective
SINFX	4.75%	13.05	5.7%	5.58%	286.3	Income

Seligman Income Fund - Class A seeks current income consistent with prudent risk; growth of income and capital value are secondary.

The fund normally invests at least 80% of its assets in fixed-income securities, convertible bonds, common stocks, and money-market instruments. At least 25% of its assets are invested in cash, fixed-income securities, and/or preferred stocks. The fund does not expect to invest more than 5% of its assets in nonconvertible debt securities rated below BBB.

Class A shares have front loads and 12b-1 fees; Class D shares have level loads.

Manager's Investment Style

Despite its broad mandate, management has favored straight bonds and convertibles. Its bond exposure barbells medium-to-low quality corporates with governments. Stocks are typically from high-yielding sectors, such as utilities, oils, and natural resources. Foreign stocks have, at times, made up a significant portion of the equity exposure.

Historical Profile
Return	Average
Risk	Below Average
Rating	★★★★ Above Average

Investment Style History
Fixed Income
Income Rtn % Rank Obj

Growth of $10,000
- IIII Value of Fund ($000)
- — Value of Index ($000) S&P 500
- ▼ Manager Change
- ▽ Partial Manager Change
- ► Mgr Unknown After
- ◄ Mgr Unknown Before

Performance Quartile (Within Objective)

	1983	1984	1985	1986	1987	1988	1989	1990	1991	1992	1993	1994	History
	11.66	11.51	13.21	13.44	11.80	12.04	12.44	10.38	12.45	13.69	14.58	13.05	NAV
	10.72	12.11	27.07	17.10	-3.99	10.53	15.11	-8.30	30.12	17.54	16.03	-5.44	Total Return %
	-11.75	5.85	-4.67	-1.58	-9.25	-6.08	-16.58	-5.19	-0.36	9.92	5.98	-6.75	+/- S&P 500
	2.35	-3.04	4.94	1.86	-6.75	2.65	0.57	-17.25	14.12	10.29	6.28	-2.52	+/- LB Aggregate
	10.02	11.51	11.08	8.52	7.37	8.50	8.84	8.26	10.18	7.58	5.57	5.06	Income Return %
	0.69	1.06	15.99	8.59	-11.37	2.03	6.27	-16.56	19.94	9.96	10.46	-10.49	Capital Return %
	76	17	37	39	85	57	46	80	27	7	25	68	Total Rtn % Rank All
	58	46	28	25	61	69	37	85	8	7	12	67	Total Rtn % Rank Obj
	1.14	1.16	1.16	1.09	1.01	0.99	1.03	1.06	0.97	0.89	0.75	0.75	Income $
	0.45	0.27	0.11	0.85	0.13	0.00	0.34	0.00	0.00	0.00	0.51	0.00	Capital Gains $
	0.79	0.78	0.77	0.73	0.79	0.80	0.75	0.76	0.85	0.84	1.03	0.99	Expense Ratio %
	9.58	10.65	9.47	7.75	7.77	7.99	8.35	8.79	8.24	6.88	5.29	5.24	Income Ratio %
	25	49	84	72	80	74	83	53	67	70	61	---	Turnover Rate %
	76.8	81.7	105.0	162.9	165.8	160.4	159.2	127.9	153.5	213.0	321.0	286.3	Net Assets ($mil)

Fund Manager(s)

Charles C. Smith et al. Birthdate: 05-56 BA, Hamilton C. 1978

Manager Experience	Dates Managed	Invest Obj	Std Dev	+/- Index
Stacey Navin				
Seligman Common Stock A	01/88 - 12/94	GI	12.30	-1.71
Charles C. Smith				
Seligman Common Stock A	06/89 - 12/94	GI	12.82	-0.32

Performance 12-31-94

	1st Qtr	2nd Qtr	3rd Qtr	4th Qtr	Total
1987	3.33	-2.65	-1.85	-2.77	-3.99
1988	5.65	3.18	0.81	0.57	10.53
1989	3.42	6.73	1.95	2.29	15.11
1990	-0.80	0.58	-10.77	3.00	-8.30
1991	10.98	3.09	8.78	4.55	30.12
1992	5.14	3.90	4.73	2.74	17.54
1993	6.51	2.51	3.51	2.67	16.03
1994	-4.01	-1.61	2.01	-1.85	-5.44

Bear Market Performance

Decile Rank (5-year period)

Worst ———————————— Best

	Worst 3 Mo Period 1985-89	Worst 3 Mo Period 1990-94
Seligman Income A	-7.61	-13.79
+/- S&P 500	21.97	0.05
+/- Best Fit Index : FB HY	---	0.32

Trailing Returns

	Total Return %	+/- S&P 500	+/- LB Aggregate	% Rank All	% Rank Obj	Growth of $10,000
3 Mo	-1.85	-1.84	-2.23	65	63	9,815
6 Mo	0.12	-4.74	-0.87	55	51	10,012
1 Yr	-5.44	-6.75	-2.52	68	67	9,456
3 Yr Avg	8.85	2.58	4.30	18	10	12,896
5 Yr Avg	9.00	0.31	1.38	24	26	15,388
10 Yr Avg	10.83	-3.55	0.89	49	35	27,968
15 Yr Avg	12.03	-2.45	1.22	54	50	54,973

Operations

Address and Telephone	100 Park Avenue New York, NY 10017 800-221-2783 / 212-850-1864
Advisor	J.& W. Seligman
Subadvisor	Seligman Henderson
Distributor	Seligman Financial Services
States Available	All
Report Grade	B+
Income Distrib	Paid Quarterly
Date of Inception	07-27-47
Fiscal Year End	December

Min Initial Purchase	$1000 (Addt'l: $50)
Min IRA Purchase	$1000 (Addt'l: $50)
Min Auto Invest Plan	$1000 (Systematic Inv: $50)

Expenses & Fees
Sales Fees	4.75% front
	0.00% deferred
	0.25% 12b-1
Management Fee	0.50% max./0.44% min.
3-,5-,10-yr Expense Projections	$79, $102, $167
Annual Brokerage Cost	---

Risk Analysis

Time Period	Load-Adj Return %	Risk % Rank All	Risk % Rank Obj	Morningstar Return	Morningstar Risk	Morningstar Risk-Adj Rating
1 Yr	-9.93					
3 Yr	7.10	30	57	1.05[3]	0.56	★★★★
5 Yr	7.95	50	82	0.80[3]	0.68	★★★★
10 Yr	10.29	38	57	0.71	0.59	★★★

Average Historical Rating (109 months) 3.3 ★ s

[1] = low, 100 = high [2] 1.00 = Hybrid Avg [3] 1.00 = 90-day T-bill return

Other Measures
	Standard S&P 500		Best Fit FB HY
Standard Deviation	5.71	Alpha	3.8	-2.0
Mean	8.67	Beta	0.49	1.00
Sharpe Ratio	0.90	R-Squared	45	58

Investment Style

Stocks	Port Avg	Rel S&P 500
Price/Earnings Ratio	17.0	0.92
Price/Book Ratio	1.9	0.57
5 Yr Earnings Gr %	-3.8#	-0.69
Med Mkt Cap ($mil)	11209	0.86

Style V B G, Size L M S

figure is based on 50% or less of stocks

Bonds
Avg Effective Duration	5.0 Yrs
Avg Effective Maturity	7.5 Yrs
Avg Credit Quality	BBB
Avg Weighted Coupon	7.52%

Maturity S I L, Quality H M L

Diversification Value for Portfolio Types
Large Cap: Medium	Small Cap: Medium	Bond: Medium	Balanced: Low	Diversified: Medium

Portfolio 09-30-94

Share Chg (06-94)000	Amount 000	Total Stocks: 33 Total Fixed-Income: 112	Date of Maturity	Value $000	% Net Assets
	9587	GNMA 10%	01-15-21	10276	3.32
	8144	US Treasury Note 8.5%	05-15-97	8472	2.74
	4196	FHLMC CMO REMIC 10%	05-15-97	4430	1.43
	2117	Carlton Communications Cv 7.5%	08-14-07	4255	1.38
	4151	GNMA 8.5%	08-15-24	4151	1.34
	4072	US Treasury Note 7.25%	11-15-96	4121	1.33
	4072	GMAC FRN	07-19-96	4072	1.32
	4072	FNMA CMO 6.75%	08-25-99	3933	1.27
	4072	FHLMC CMO REMIC 7%	05-15-05	3902	1.26
	33	Citicorp Cv Pfd $5.375		3868	1.25
	4072	FNMA CMO 7%	07-25-07	3699	1.20
	3257	General Motors 9.125%	07-15-01	3410	1.10
	3257	Unifi Cv 6%	03-15-02	3270	1.06
	3257	USX 9.25%	01-15-13	3201	1.03
	3257	Aegon 8%	08-15-06	3156	1.02
	2850	Sears Roebuck 9.375%	11-01-11	3045	0.98
	3257	First USA Bank 5.75%	01-15-99	2996	0.97
	49	Ceridian Cv Pfd 5.5%		2938	0.95
	3257	News America Holdings 8.25%	08-10-18	2875	0.93
	13010	IBM Cv 5.75%	01-01-98	2809	0.91

Index Allocation
	% of Stocks
S&P 500	48.6
S&P MidCap 400	0.0
U.S. Small Cap	7.5
Foreign	43.9

Composition % 11-14-94
Cash	4.0	Preferreds	0.0
Stocks	16.3	Convertibles	41.3
Bonds	38.4	Other	0.0

Tax Analysis
	Tax-Adj Historical Return %	% Pretax Return
3 Yr Avg	6.32	69.7
5 Yr Avg	6.29	66.2
10 Yr Avg	7.39	57.9
Potential Capital Gain Exposure (% of assets)		-3%

Most Similar Funds in MF500
Putnam Convert Income Gr A	Fair Fit
Lindner	Fair Fit
Evergreen Foundation	Fair Fit

Bond Credit Analysis 11-15-94
% of Bonds
US Govt	20	BB	12
AAA	0	B	18
AA	2	Below B	0
A	11	NR/NA	7
BBB	30		

Stock Sector Weightings
	% of Stocks	Relative S&P 500
Utilities	42.2	3.40
Energy	11.8	1.17
Financials	16.7	1.58
Industrial Cyclicals	5.2	0.32
Consumer Durables	5.1	0.81
Consumer Staples	4.0	0.32
Services	9.2	1.13
Retail	3.4	0.58
Health	2.4	0.28
Technology	0.0	0.00

Sentinel Balanced

	Ticker	Load	NAV	Yield	SEC Yield	Assets	Objective
	SEBLX	5.00%	14.09	4.1%	4.05%	228.0	Balanced

Sentinel Balanced Fund seeks a conservative combination of stability, income, and growth.

The fund invests in both stocks and investment-grade fixed-income securities. At least 25% of its assets are invested in fixed-income senior securities. Management not only selects the securities in the portfolio, but it also determines, within conservative limits, the proportion of assets to be invested in each type of security.

On March 1, 1993, ProvidentMutual Total Return Trust merged into the fund.

Manager's Investment Style

Management typically maintains a 10% to 15% cash position, and balances remaining assets between stocks and bonds almost equally. Stock selection focuses on large caps trading at moderate multiples. Its bond exposure is primarily intermediate-term, high-quality issues.

Fund Manager(s)

Rodney A. Buck CFA(1977), since 01-82. Birthdate: 01-48. BA, Colby C. 1970 MBA, Dartmouth C. 1972

Richard A. Pender CFA(1987), since 10-94. Birthdate: 07-57. BA, Dartmouth C. 1979 MBA, Boston U. 1983

Manager Experience	Dates Managed	Invest Obj	Std Dev	+/- Index
Richard A. Pender				
Sentinel Common Stock	09/94 - 12/94	GI	9.56	-1.37

Historical Profile
Return	Average
Risk	Below Average
Rating	★★★ Neutral

Investment Style History
Equity
Average % Stocks Held in Portfolio

56% 51% 47% 48% 49% 46% 50% 48%

Growth of $10,000
- ||| Value of Fund ($000)
- — Value of Index ($000) S&P 500
- ▼ Manager Change
- ▽ Partial Manager Change
- ► Mgr Unknown After
- ◄ Mgr Unknown Before

Performance Quartile (Within Objective)

	1983	1984	1985	1986	1987	1988	1989	1990	1991	1992	1993	1994	History
	9.17	9.60	11.30	12.35	11.72	12.09	13.21	12.59	14.65	14.63	15.22	14.09	NAV
	14.59	14.79	28.04	19.07	0.63	9.86	19.35	1.91	23.29	6.19	9.63	-3.56	Total Return %
	-7.88	8.52	-3.70	0.40	-4.63	-6.75	-12.34	5.02	-7.20	-1.43	-0.43	-4.87	+/- S&P 500
	6.22	-0.37	5.91	3.83	-2.13	1.98	4.81	-7.04	7.29	-1.06	-0.12	-0.64	+/- LB Aggregate
	8.19	8.47	7.74	5.97	5.73	6.36	6.97	6.24	6.63	4.88	3.91	3.78	Income Return %
	6.40	6.32	20.30	13.11	-5.10	3.50	12.37	-4.33	16.66	1.31	5.72	-7.34	Capital Return %
	60	6	33	25	55	63	36	50	39	67	69	49	Total Rtn % Rank All
	60	3	53	27	63	71	51	17	58	61	66	65	Total Rtn % Rank Obj
	0.70	0.70	0.69	0.68	0.77	0.73	0.82	0.80	0.76	0.69	0.56	0.58	Income $
	0.30	0.14	0.21	0.41	0.00	0.04	0.35	0.05	0.03	0.21	0.23	0.01	Capital Gains $
	0.80	0.83	0.75	0.68	0.67	0.97	0.96	0.91	0.85	0.81	1.14	1.16	Expense Ratio %
	7.24	7.66	6.49	5.44	5.38	5.74	6.16	6.17	5.70	4.86	3.88	3.68	Income Ratio %
	39	32	71	58	32	52	71	40	32	38	72	---	Turnover Rate %
	13.7	13.6	21.5	94.0	65.1	66.5	75.9	76.2	98.7	125.5	230.2	228.0	Net Assets ($mil)

Performance 12-31-94

	1st Qtr	2nd Qtr	3rd Qtr	4th Qtr	Total
1987	10.58	1.11	1.64	-11.45	0.63
1988	3.56	3.26	1.98	0.74	9.86
1989	3.90	6.85	4.68	2.68	19.35
1990	-1.66	3.61	-6.45	6.91	1.91
1991	7.65	1.38	5.78	6.79	23.29
1992	-2.41	3.52	4.11	0.96	6.19
1993	4.82	1.07	3.33	0.15	9.63
1994	-3.70	-0.41	1.54	-0.96	-3.56

Bear Market Performance

Decile Rank (5-year period)

Worst ____ Best

	Worst 3 Mo Period 1985-89	Worst 3 Mo Period 1990-94
Sentinel Balanced	-17.71	-6.45
+/- S&P 500	11.87	7.30
+/- Best Fit Index : S&P 500	11.87	7.30

Trailing Returns

	Total Return %	+/- S&P 500	+/- LB Aggregate	% Rank All	% Rank Obj	Growth of $10,000
3 Mo	-0.96	-0.94	-1.34	43	50	9,904
6 Mo	0.56	-4.30	-0.43	46	73	10,056
1 Yr	-3.56	-4.87	-0.64	49	65	9,644
3 Yr Avg	3.93	-2.33	-0.61	71	69	11,227
5 Yr Avg	7.12	-1.57	-0.50	47	68	14,106
10 Yr Avg	10.99	-3.39	1.05	47	57	28,373
15 Yr Avg	12.54	-1.94	1.73	48	56	58,851

Operations

Address and Telephone	National Life Drive Montpelier, VT 05604 800-282-3863 / 802-229-3900	
Advisor	Sentinel Advisors	
Subadvisor	None	
Distributor	Sentinel Financial Services	
States Available	All	
Report Grade	C+	
Income Distrib	Paid Quarterly	
Date of Inception	11-15-38	
Fiscal Year End	November	

Min Initial Purchase	$500 (Addt'l: $50)
Min IRA Purchase	$500 (Addt'l: $50)
Min Auto Invest Plan	$50 (Systematic Inv: $50)

Expenses & Fees
Sales Fees	5.00% front
	0.00% deferred
	0.30% 12b-1
Management Fee	0.70% max./0.55% min.
3-,5-,10-yr Expense Projections	$85, $110, $183
Annual Brokerage Cost	0.03%

Risk Analysis

Time Period	Load-Adj Return %	Risk % Rank[1] All	Obj	Morningstar[2] Return	Morningstar Risk	Morningstar Risk-Adj Rating
1 Yr	-8.38					
3 Yr	2.17	46	38	-0.40[3]	0.68	★★
5 Yr	6.03	47	16	0.31[3]	0.62	★★★
10 Yr	10.42	40	21	0.74	0.65	★★★

Average Historical Rating (109 months) 3.8 ★s

[1] 1 = low, 100 = high [2] 1.00 = Hybrid Avg [3] 1.00 = 90-day T-bill return

Other Measures

				Standard S&P 500	Best Fit S&P 500
Standard Deviation	5.45	Alpha		-1.2	-1.2
Mean	4.01	Beta		0.60	0.60
Sharpe Ratio	0.09	R-Squared		75	75

Investment Style

Stocks	Port Avg	Rel S&P 500
Price/Earnings Ratio	17.9	0.97
Price/Book Ratio	3.3	0.97
5 Yr Earnings Gr %	1.7	0.30
Med Mkt Cap ($mil)	12983	1.00

Bonds	
Avg Effective Duration	5.7 Yrs
Avg Effective Maturity	8.4 Yrs
Avg Credit Quality	AA
Avg Weighted Coupon	7.62%

Diversification Value for Portfolio Types

Large Cap: Low Small Cap: High Bond: Low Balanced: None Diversified: Low

Portfolio 12-31-94

Total Stocks: 67
Total Fixed-Income: 39

Share Chg (05-94)000	Amount 000		Date of Maturity	Value $000	% Net Assets
	11000	US Treasury Note 7.5%	11-15-01	10808	4.74
	8700	US Treasury Note 8%	05-15-01	8772	3.85
	6700	US Treasury Note 7.875%	04-15-98	6709	2.94
	6000	US Treasury Note 6%	11-30-97	5723	2.51
	5000	US Treasury Note 7.25%	08-15-04	4806	2.11
	4000	US Treasury Bond 10.375%	11-15-09	4651	2.04
	3000	US Treasury Note 7.25%	05-15-04	2882	1.26
	2562	FNMA 15yr 8.5%	09-01-07	2581	1.13
0	24	Royal Dutch Petroleum		2580	1.13
0	55	JC Penney		2454	1.08
0	38	Emerson Electric		2375	1.04
0	46	General Electric		2346	1.03
26	52	Chevron		2321	1.02
28	40	Motorola		2315	1.02
40	40	WW Grainger		2310	1.01
	2321	GNMA 8.5%	09-15-17	2299	1.01
	40	General Motors Cv Pfd 6.5%		2295	1.01
	2000	Tenneco 10%	03-15-08	2250	0.99
	2500	Heller Financial 5.625%	03-15-00	2213	0.97
12	40	Dun & Bradstreet		2200	0.96

Index Allocation

	% of Stocks
S&P 500	90.8
S&P MidCap 400	6.5
U.S. Small Cap	0.0
Foreign	5.1

Composition % 12-31-94

Cash	11.4	Preferreds	0.0
Stocks	48.3	Convertibles	2.3
Bonds	38.0	Other	0.0

Tax Analysis

	Tax-Adj Historical Return %	% Pretax Return
3 Yr Avg	2.12	53.0
5 Yr Avg	5.20	70.2
10 Yr Avg	8.48	68.4
Potential Capital Gain Exposure (% of assets)		5%

Most Similar Funds in MF500

Keystone Custodian K-1	Strong Fit
George Putnam of Boston A	Strong Fit
Vanguard/Wellesley Income	Strong Fit

Bond Credit Analysis 12-31-94
% of Bonds

US Govt	63	BB	0
AAA	1	B	0
AA	0	Below B	0
A	6	NR/NA	0
BBB	30		

Stock Sector Weightings

	% of Stocks	Relative S&P 500
Utilities	10.8	0.87
Energy	14.1	1.39
Financials	10.2	0.97
Industrial Cyclicals	17.7	1.08
Consumer Durables	3.9	0.63
Consumer Staples	10.0	0.80
Services	16.6	2.04
Retail	4.2	0.72
Health	8.5	0.98
Technology	4.0	0.43

Sentinel Common Stock

	Ticker	Load	NAV	Yield	SEC Yield	Assets	Objective
	SENCX	5.00%	27.38	2.9%	2.73%	842.0	Growth/Inc.

Sentinel Common Stock Fund seeks growth of principal and income, current return, and relatively low risk.

The fund invests primarily in common stocks of well-established companies, which are selected for their quality and the fund's appraisal of their price position relative to their value. It may also hold preferred stocks or debentures convertible into common stocks.

On March 1, 1993, ProvidentMutual Investment Shares and ProvidentMutual Value Shares merged into the fund.

Historical Profile
Return Average
Risk   Below Average
Rating ★★★
        Neutral

Investment Style History
Equity
Average % Stocks Held in Portfolio

Growth of $10,000
|||| Value of Fund ($000)
— Value of Index ($000) S&P 500
▼ Manager Change
▽ Partial Manager Change
► Mgr Unknown After
◄ Mgr Unknown Before

Performance Quartile (Within Objective)

	1983	1984	1985	1986	1987	1988	1989	1990	1991	1992	1993	1994	History
	16.93	17.01	20.65	23.61	21.26	21.93	25.68	23.26	28.90	28.53	29.69	27.38	NAV
	20.30	12.40	29.81	23.63	0.03	13.37	27.57	-2.70	30.79	5.78	9.33	-1.24	Total Return %
	-2.16	6.13	-1.93	4.95	-5.23	-3.24	-4.12	0.41	0.31	-1.84	-0.73	-2.56	+/- S&P 500
	-3.16	9.35	-2.76	7.53	-2.34	-4.58	-1.61	3.48	-3.42	-3.19	-1.96	-1.17	+/- Wilshire 5000
	6.05	5.74	5.58	3.78	3.55	4.41	4.14	4.13	3.92	3.20	2.80	2.90	Income Return %
	14.25	6.66	24.23	19.85	-3.53	8.96	23.43	-6.84	26.87	2.58	6.53	-4.14	Capital Return %
	38	15	27	11	59	35	17	63	25	72	71	28	Total Rtn % Rank All
	55	12	37	6	69	64	30	38	31	73	67	56	Total Rtn % Rank Obj
	0.92	0.90	0.89	0.83	0.94	0.94	0.93	1.01	0.88	0.90	0.78	0.83	Income $
	0.78	1.00	0.40	1.08	1.55	1.20	1.27	0.70	0.50	1.12	0.65	1.11	Capital Gains $
	0.71	0.72	0.68	0.64	0.62	0.87	0.80	0.76	0.74	0.72	0.93	1.01	Expense Ratio %
	5.38	5.20	4.76	3.49	3.28	3.75	3.69	3.82	3.41	3.13	2.68	2.65	Income Ratio %
	40	10	15	8	9	7	11	6	9	5	---		Turnover Rate %
	333.6	334.3	396.0	487.3	482.0	500.5	600.5	550.3	683.3	687.8	904.6	842.0	Net Assets ($mil)

Manager's Investment Style
A recent management change to a team approach makes future management style open for alteration. Historically, management has been characterized by long-term commitments to individual holdings, a very low turnover rate, and a preference for stocks with below-market multiples and above-average yields. Management has consistently favored a large-cap, blend strategy, which is not atypical of this objective.

Fund Manager(s)
Keniston P. Merrill, since 09-94.
Robert L. Lee CFA(1985), since 09-94.
Richard A. Pender CFA(1987), since 09-94.

Manager Experience
	Dates Managed	Invest Obj	Std Dev	+/- Index
Richard A. Pender				
Sentinel Balanced	10/94 - 12/94	B	6.65	0.77
Robert L. Lee				
Shawmut Growth Equity Tr	12/92 - 11/93	G	10.91	-6.82

Performance 12-31-94
	1st Qtr	2nd Qtr	3rd Qtr	4th Qtr	Total
1987	17.47	2.96	3.80	-20.33	0.03
1988	5.32	3.22	1.75	2.49	13.37
1989	6.53	7.07	8.68	2.91	27.57
1990	-3.53	4.66	-11.26	8.61	-2.70
1991	13.32	-0.03	6.14	8.77	30.79
1992	-3.23	3.64	3.42	1.98	5.78
1993	4.40	0.24	3.96	0.49	9.33
1994	-4.70	0.93	4.11	-1.39	-1.24

Bear Market Performance
Decile Rank (5-year period)

Worst _____ Best

	Worst 3 Mo Period 1985-89	Worst 3 Mo Period 1990-94
Sentinel Common Stock	-27.83	-11.68
+/- S&P 500	1.75	2.17
+/- Best Fit Index : S&P 500	1.75	2.17

Trailing Returns
	Total Return %	+/- S&P 500	+/- Wil 5000	% Rank All	% Rank Obj	Growth of $10,000
3 Mo	-1.39	-1.37	-0.62	54	49	9,861
6 Mo	2.67	-2.19	-1.96	22	48	10,267
1 Yr	-1.24	-2.56	-1.17	28	56	9,876
3 Yr Avg	4.53	-1.74	-2.09	58	70	11,420
5 Yr Avg	7.76	-0.93	-1.05	36	54	14,533
10 Yr Avg	12.93	-1.45	-0.93	28	35	33,737
15 Yr Avg	14.57	0.09	0.59	18	17	76,921

Operations
Address and Telephone	National Life Drive
	Montpelier, VT 05604
	800-282-3863 / 802-229-3900
Advisor	Sentinel Advisors
Subadvisor	None
Distributor	Sentinel Financial Services
States Available	All
Report Grade	C+
Income Distrib	Paid Quarterly
Date of Inception	01-01-34
Fiscal Year End	November

Risk Analysis
Time Period	Load-Adj Return %	Risk % Rank¹ All	Obj	Morningstar² Return	Risk	Morningstar Risk-Adj Rating
1 Yr	-6.18					
3 Yr	2.75	67	57	-0.24³	0.75	★★
5 Yr	6.66	63	36	0.47³	0.75	★★★
10 Yr	12.35	61	59	0.94	0.85	★★★

Average Historical Rating (109 months) 4.0 ★s

¹ 1 = low, 100 = high ² 1.00 = Equity Avg ³ 1.00 = 90-day T-bill return

Other Measures
			Standard S&P 500	Best Fit S&P 500
Standard Deviation	7.66	Alpha	-1.4	-1.4
Mean	4.73	Beta	0.92	0.92
Sharpe Ratio	0.16	R-Squared	90	90

Investment Style
	Stock Portfolio Avg	Relative S&P 500
Price/Earnings Ratio	17.8	0.96
Price/Book Ratio	3.2	0.94
5 Yr Earnings Gr %	1.4	0.24
Return on Assets %	6.3	0.85
Debt % Total Cap	30.0	1.06
Med Mkt Cap ($mil)	13720	1.06

Style Value Blend Growth — Size Large/Med/Small

Diversification Value for Portfolio Types
Large Cap: None	Small Cap: High	Bond: Medium	Balanced: None	Diversified: Low

Portfolio 12-30-94
Total Stocks: 69
Total Fixed-Income: 1

Share Chg (05-94) 000	Amount 000		Value $000	% Net Assets
0	559	General Electric	28499	3.38
0	350	Emerson Electric	21875	2.60
0	197	Royal Dutch Petroleum	21201	2.52
0	405	Kimberly-Clark	20453	2.43
0	350	Philip Morris	20125	2.39
0	269	Gillette	20076	2.38
0	318	American Home Products	19973	2.37
0	315	Exxon	19161	2.28
0	350	Coca-Cola	18025	2.14
0	210	Mobil	17693	2.10
0	700	Sara Lee	17675	2.10
0	295	JP Morgan	16503	1.96
0	260	Amoco	15349	1.82
0	370	Citicorp	15309	1.82
0	400	American Brands	14985	1.78
0	255	El duPont de Nemours	14349	1.70
0	320	JC Penney	14280	1.70
28	185	IBM	13575	1.61
230	230	Motorola	13311	1.58
0	371	US West	13209	1.57
0	257	AT & T	12911	1.53
420	420	Enron	12810	1.52
-80	165	Warner-Lambert	12705	1.51
130	360	FPL Group	12645	1.50
0	254	Sears Roebuck	11661	1.38

Composition % 12-31-94
Cash	4.2	Preferreds	0.0
Stocks	95.5	Convertibles	0.3
Bonds	0.0	Other	0.0

Tax Analysis
	Tax-Adj Historical Return %	% Pretax Return
3 Yr Avg	2.51	54.3
5 Yr Avg	5.72	70.7
10 Yr Avg	10.27	69.9
Potential Capital Gain Exposure (% of assets)		38%

Most Similar Funds in MF500
Massachusetts Inv A	Strong Fit
Vanguard Index 500	Strong Fit
Investment Comp of America	Fair Fit

Index Allocation
	% of Stocks
S&P 500	93.7
S&P MidCap 400	4.8
U.S. Small Cap	0.0
Foreign	4.1

Sector Weightings
	% of Stocks	Relative S&P 500
Utilities	14.7	1.19
Energy	14.3	1.41
Financials	13.0	1.23
Industrial Cyclicals	16.2	0.99
Consumer Durables	3.0	0.48
Consumer Staples	10.1	0.81
Services	9.6	1.18
Retail	4.6	0.80
Health	10.5	1.21
Technology	4.0	0.44

Min Initial Purchase	$500 (Addt'l: $50)
Min IRA Purchase	$500 (Addt'l: $50)
Min Auto Invest Plan	$50 (Systematic Inv: $50)

Expenses & Fees
Sales Fees	5.00% front
	0.00% deferred
	0.30% 12b-1
Management Fee	0.55% flat fee
3-,5-,10-yr Expense Projections	$80, $101, $164
Annual Brokerage Cost	0.03%

MORNINGSTAR 1995 Mutual Fund 500

Sequoia

	Ticker	Load	NAV	Yield	SEC Yield	Assets	Objective
	SEQUX	Clsd	55.59	1.1%	N/A	1548.3	Growth

Sequoia Fund seeks growth of capital.

The fund emphasizes investment in common stocks that management feels are undervalued, with the hope that growth of capital will result. No weight is given to technical stock-market studies, nor are such techniques as borrowing, hedging, or short sales used. Extensive study is made of balance sheets and earning-power factors to appraise the fundamental worth of investments. The fund may also invest to a limited extent in restricted securities and special situations, and may invest up to 15% of its assets in foreign securities.

Manager's Investment Style

As a former student of Ben Graham's, comanager Bill Ruane and his partner Rick Cunniff focus on strong franchise values, committed management teams, clean balance sheets, and easily understood operations. They then try to purchase these firms for less than they are actually worth. Ruane's investment thinking is in synch with that of Warren Buffet, which is why this fund holds a large stake in Buffet's firm, Berkshire Hathaway. The duo does intensive research on each holding and holds for the long term. When they have not found the qualities and values that they seek, Ruane and Cunniff have been willing to hold large cash stakes.

Fund Manager(s)

William J. Ruane, since 07-70. Birthdate: 10-25.
BS, U. of Minnesota 1945   MBA, Harvard 1949
Richard Cunniff, since 07-70. BA, Colgate U. 1945
MBA, Harvard 1950

Manager Experience	Dates Managed	Invest Obj	Std Dev	+/- Index

Not available.

Historical Profile

Return	Above Average
Risk	Below Average
Rating	★★★★
	Closed

Average % Stocks Held in Portfolio: 49% 49% 60% 62% 63% 72% 69% 85%

Investment Style History
Equity

Growth of $10,000

|||| Value of Fund ($000)
— Value of Index ($000)
S&P 500
▼ Manager Change
▽ Partial Manager Change
► Mgr Unknown After
◄ Mgr Unknown Before

Performance Quartile (Within Objective)

	1983	1984	1985	1986	1987	1988	1989	1990	1991	1992	1993	1994	History
	37.11	39.26	44.01	39.29	38.43	38.81	46.86	41.94	53.31	56.66	54.84	55.59	NAV
	27.31	18.50	27.96	13.37	7.41	11.05	27.91	-3.80	40.00	9.36	12.60	3.71	Total Return %
	4.85	12.23	-3.78	-5.31	2.15	-5.56	-3.78	-0.68	9.52	1.74	2.54	2.39	+/- S&P 500
	3.85	15.45	-4.60	-2.72	5.04	-6.90	-1.27	2.38	5.80	0.39	1.32	3.78	+/- Wilshire 5000
	5.76	4.29	4.08	3.89	5.45	3.76	3.04	3.06	3.03	1.82	2.87	1.12	Income Return %
	21.55	14.21	23.88	9.48	1.96	7.29	24.87	-6.86	36.98	7.54	9.73	2.59	Capital Return %
	16	2	33	65	15	53	17	67	14	28	45	6	Total Rtn % Rank All
	21	1	61	64	22	68	46	45	34	41	45	11	Total Rtn % Rank Obj
	1.64	1.43	1.51	1.61	2.21	1.39	1.28	1.38	1.36	0.93	1.58	0.62	Income $
	1.30	2.58	3.77	8.54	1.59	2.23	1.43	1.78	3.58	0.63	7.20	0.66	Capital Gains $
	1.00	1.00	1.00	1.00	1.00	1.00	1.00	1.00	1.00	1.00	1.00	1.00	Expense Ratio %
	5.00	4.30	3.80	3.90	3.30	3.60	2.80	3.10	2.80	1.80	1.10	0.90	Income Ratio %
	17	39	44	40	43	39	44	29	36	28	24	---	Turnover Rate %
	350.7	443.2	599.6	696.7	720.6	714.2	924.4	870.2	1251.4	1389.3	1512.1	1548.3	Net Assets ($mil)

Performance 12-31-94

	1st Qtr	2nd Qtr	3rd Qtr	4th Qtr	Total
1987	14.02	2.77	2.21	-10.32	7.41
1988	4.28	2.70	1.81	1.85	11.05
1989	8.32	9.99	8.90	-1.42	27.91
1990	-1.26	6.80	-14.05	6.14	-3.80
1991	15.87	1.64	6.55	11.57	40.00
1992	-1.99	0.73	4.67	5.82	9.36
1993	3.66	7.24	1.90	-0.60	12.60
1994	-1.62	2.89	3.50	-1.01	3.71

Bear Market Performance

Decile Rank (5-year period)

Worst — Best

	Worst 3 Mo Period 1985-89	Worst 3 Mo Period 1990-94
Sequoia	-15.16	-16.23
+/- S&P 500	14.42	-2.39
+/- Best Fit Index : S&P 500	14.42	-2.39

Trailing Returns

	Total Return %	+/- S&P 500	+/- Wil 5000	% Rank All	% Rank Obj	Growth of $10,000
3 Mo	-1.01	-0.99	-0.24	44	44	9,899
6 Mo	2.46	-2.41	-2.17	24	67	10,246
1 Yr	3.71	2.39	3.78	6	11	10,371
3 Yr Avg	8.49	2.23	1.88	19	26	12,771
5 Yr Avg	11.46	2.77	2.64	11	16	17,200
10 Yr Avg	14.30	-0.08	0.44	16	25	38,068
15 Yr Avg	16.83	2.34	2.85	3	8	103,063

Risk Analysis

Time Period	Load-Adj Return %	Risk % Rank[1] All	Obj	Morningstar[2] Return	Risk	Morningstar Risk-Adj Rating
1 Yr	3.71					
3 Yr	8.49	61	17	1.49[3]	0.67	★★★★
5 Yr	11.46	61	11	1.78[3]	0.73	★★★★
10 Yr	14.30	44	3	1.33	0.61	★★★★

Average Historical Rating (109 months) 5.0 ★s

[1] 1 = low, 100 = high   [2] 1.00 = Equity Avg   [3] 1.00 = 90-day T-bill return

Other Measures

				Standard S&P 500	Best Fit S&P 500
Standard Deviation	8.81	Alpha		2.5	2.5
Mean	8.56	Beta		0.88	0.88
Sharpe Ratio	0.57	R-Squared		63	63

Investment Style

	Stock Portfolio Avg	Relative S&P 500
Price/Earnings Ratio	17.4	0.94
Price/Book Ratio	2.3	0.66
5 Yr Earnings Gr %	16.5	2.98
Return on Assets %	5.3	0.71
Debt % Total Cap	15.5#	0.55
Med Mkt Cap ($mil)	9240	0.71

figure is based on 50% or less of stocks

Style Value Blend Growth — Size Large/Med/Small

Diversification Value for Portfolio Types

Large Cap: Low	Small Cap: High	Bond: High	Balanced: Low	Diversified: Medium

Portfolio 12-31-94

Total Stocks: 19
Total Fixed-Income: 0

Share Chg (06-94) 000	Amount 000		Value $000	% Net Assets
0	21	Berkshire Hathaway	429094	27.71
0	3550	FHLMC	179275	11.58
518	4400	Progressive	154000	9.95
0	3763	Hasbro	110056	7.11
1827	1827	Fifth Third Bancorp	87020	5.62
-335	1380	Johnson & Johnson	75555	4.88
-367	1880	Salomon	70500	4.55
0	700	Capital Cities/ABC	59675	3.85
429	1283	First Bank System	42660	2.76
185	1566	Bancorp Hawaii	39745	2.57
148	1038	Banc One	26347	1.70
0	757	Toys 'R' Us	23101	1.49
678	678	First Virginia Banks	21709	1.40
0	697	C-TEC	13764	0.89
-1270	330	The Limited	5981	0.39
0	160	Regions Financial	4970	0.32
0	170	Sturm Ruger	4812	0.31
0	225	Mercantile Bankshares (MD)	4444	0.29
37	154	Valley National Bancorp (NJ)	4148	0.27

Composition % 12-31-94

Cash	10.4	Preferreds	0.0
Stocks	89.6	Convertibles	0.0
Bonds	0.0	Other	0.0

Tax Analysis

	Tax-Adj Historical Return %	% Pretax Return
3 Yr Avg	6.37	73.5
5 Yr Avg	9.07	75.5
10 Yr Avg	11.21	67.4
Potential Capital Gain Exposure (% of assets)		32%

Most Similar Funds in MF500

American Leaders A	Weak Fit
Vanguard Index 500	Weak Fit
Liberty All-Star	Weak Fit

Index Allocation

	% of Stocks
S&P 500	40.6
S&P MidCap 400	26.1
U.S. Small Cap	33.3
Foreign	0.0

Sector Weightings

	% of Stocks	Relative S&P 500
Utilities	0.0	0.00
Energy	0.0	0.00
Financials	46.8	4.43
Industrial Cyclicals	0.0	0.00
Consumer Durables	8.5	1.36
Consumer Staples	5.6	0.44
Services	37.0	4.55
Retail	2.1	0.37
Health	0.0	0.00
Technology	0.0	0.00

Operations

Address and Telephone	767 Fifth Avenue New York, NY 10153 212-245-4500
Advisor	Ruane Cunniff & Company
Subadvisor	None
Distributor	Ruane Cunniff & Company
States Available	All except AK,AR,ID,MS,WV
Report Grade	A-
Income Distrib	Paid Annually
Date of Inception	07-15-70
Fiscal Year End	December

Min Initial Purchase	Closed (Addt'l: $50)
Min IRA Purchase	None (Addt'l: None)
Min Auto Invest Plan	N/A

Expenses & Fees

Sales Fees	0.00% front
	0.00% deferred
	0.00% 12b-1
Management Fee	1.00% flat fee
3-,5-,10-yr Expense Projections	$32, $56, $124
Annual Brokerage Cost	0.03%

Seven Seas Growth & Income

	Ticker	Load	NAV	Yield	SEC Yield	Assets	Objective
	SSGWX	None	9.89	1.8%	N/A	26.1	Growth/Inc.

Seven Seas Growth and Income Fund seeks long-term capital growth, current income and growth of income.

The fund normally invests at least 65% of its assets in equity securities. It generally invests in well-established companies, but may invest up to 5% of its assets in securities of issuers that have been in operation for less than three years. The fund may invest in American Depositary Receipts. It may also invest in investment-grade corporate debt securities having an average weighted maturity of 10 years or less; debt securities purchased by the fund may include dollar-denominated foreign securities.

Historical Profile
Return ---
Risk ---
Rating
Not Rated

Investment Style History
Equity
Average % Stocks Held in Portfolio — 97%

Growth of $10,000
|||| Value of Fund ($000)
— Value of Index ($000) S&P 500
▼ Manager Change
▽ Partial Manager Change
► Mgr Unknown After
◄ Mgr Unknown Before

Performance Quartile (Within Objective)

Manager's Investment Style

Management maintains a fairly concentrated portfolio of large-cap stocks. Within that portfolio, it attempts to maximize its exposure to different industries, as well as including a number of standard growth names and some cyclicals. While the fund's portfolio statistics are similar to those of the S&P 500, its performance tends to be more volatile.

	1983	1984	1985	1986	1987	1988	1989	1990	1991	1992	1993	1994	History
	---	---	---	---	---	---	---	---	---	---	10.09	9.89	NAV
	---	---	---	---	---	---	---	---	---	---	1.30 *	-0.26	Total Return %
	---	---	---	---	---	---	---	---	---	---	-0.32 *	-1.57	+/- S&P 500
	---	---	---	---	---	---	---	---	---	---	---	-0.19	+/- Wilshire 5000
	---	---	---	---	---	---	---	---	---	---	0.40	1.72	Income Return %
	---	---	---	---	---	---	---	---	---	---	0.90	-1.98	Capital Return %
	---	---	---	---	---	---	---	---	---	---	---	21	Total Rtn % Rank All
	---	---	---	---	---	---	---	---	---	---	---	44	Total Rtn % Rank Obj
	---	---	---	---	---	---	---	---	---	---	0.04	0.18	Income $
	---	---	---	---	---	---	---	---	---	---	0.00	0.00	Capital Gains $
	---	---	---	---	---	---	---	---	---	---	---	0.95	Expense Ratio %
	---	---	---	---	---	---	---	---	---	---	---	1.75	Income Ratio %
	---	---	---	---	---	---	---	---	---	---	---	36	Turnover Rate %
	---	---	---	---	---	---	---	---	---	---	15.1	26.1	Net Assets ($mil)

Fund Manager(s)

Management Team

Manager Experience

	Dates Managed	Invest Obj	Std Dev	+/- Index
Management Team				
SteinRoe Total Return	08/49 - 01/81	EI	13.51	-2.34
SteinRoe Stock	07/58 - 01/89	G	19.99	-2.42

Performance 12-31-94

	1st Qtr	2nd Qtr	3rd Qtr	4th Qtr	Total
1987	---	---	---	---	---
1988	---	---	---	---	---
1989	---	---	---	---	---
1990	---	---	---	---	---
1991	---	---	---	---	---
1992	---	---	---	---	---
1993	---	---	---	2.11	1.30 *
1994	-2.90	-0.83	6.14	-2.41	-0.26

Bear Market Performance

Decile Rank (5-year period)

	Worst	Best
	Worst 3 Mo Period 1985-89	Worst 3 Mo Period 1990-94
Seven Seas Growth & Income	---	---
+/- S&P 500	---	---
+/- Best Fit Index :	---	---

Trailing Returns

	Total Return %	+/- S&P 500	+/- Wil 5000	% Rank All	% Rank Obj	Growth of $10,000
3 Mo	-2.41	-2.39	-1.64	76	76	9,759
6 Mo	3.58	-1.28	-1.04	17	35	10,358
1 Yr	-0.26	-1.57	-0.19	21	44	9,974
3 Yr Avg	---	---	---	---	---	---
5 Yr Avg	---	---	---	---	---	---
10 Yr Avg	---	---	---	---	---	---
15 Yr Avg	---	---	---	---	---	---

Operations

Address and Telephone	2 International Place
	Boston, MA 02110
	617-654-6089 / 800-647-7327
Advisor	State Street Bank & Trust
Subadvisor	None
Distributor	Russell Fund Distributors
States Available	All
Report Grade	N/A
Income Distrib	Paid Quarterly
* Date of Inception	09-01-93
Fiscal Year End	September

Risk Analysis

Time Period	Load-Adj Return %	Risk % Rank All	Risk % Rank Obj	Morningstar Return	Morningstar Risk	Morningstar Risk-Adj Rating
1 Yr	-0.26					
3 Yr	---	---	---	---	---	---
5 Yr	---	---	---	---	---	---
10 Yr	---	---	---	---	---	---
Average Historical Rating ---					---	

[1] 1 = low, 100 = high   [2] 1.00 = Equity Avg   [3] 1.00 = 90-day T-bill return

Other Measures

			Standard S&P 500	Best Fit
Standard Deviation	---	Alpha	---	---
Mean	---	Beta	---	---
Sharpe Ratio	---	R-Squared	---	---

Investment Style

	Stock Portfolio Avg	Relative S&P 500
Price/Earnings Ratio	19.5	1.05
Price/Book Ratio	3.0	0.87
5 Yr Earnings Gr %	6.9	1.25
Return on Assets %	7.0	0.93
Debt % Total Cap	26.8	0.95
Med Mkt Cap ($mil)	8122	0.63

Style Value Blend Growth
Size Large Med Small

Diversification Value for Portfolio Types

Large Cap:	Small Cap:	Bond:	Balanced:	Diversified:

Expenses & Fees

Min Initial Purchase	$1000 (Addt'l: $500)
Min IRA Purchase	$1000 (Addt'l: $250)
Min Auto Invest Plan	N/A
Sales Fees	0.00% front
	0.00% deferred
	0.25% 12b-1
Management Fee	0.85% flat fee, 0.06%A
3-,5-,10-yr Expense Projections	$30, N/A, N/A
Annual Brokerage Cost	---

Portfolio 12-31-94

Total Stocks: 38
Total Fixed-Income: 0

Share Chg (08-94) 000	Amount 000		Value $000	% Net Assets
0	27	Vodafone Group (ADR)	908	3.48
0	25	Halliburton	841	3.23
0	14	Motorola	828	3.17
19	19	General Motors	803	3.08
-64	8	American International Group	784	3.01
0	12	Intel	764	2.93
2	16	Boeing	748	2.87
17	17	Reuters Holdings (ADR)	746	2.86
0	23	Panamerican Beverages Cl A	727	2.79
0	41	Brush Wellman	718	2.75
14	14	Kimberly-Clark	707	2.71
3	25	American General	706	2.71
0	12	Automatic Data Processing	702	2.69
0	19	United Asset Management	701	2.69
12	12	Exxon	699	2.68
0	17	US Healthcare	689	2.64
5	31	Ryder System	682	2.62
0	14	Eastman Kodak	669	2.56
0	13	AT & T	668	2.56
0	13	CPC International	666	2.55
0	12	Bristol-Myers Squibb	666	2.55
26	26	Tele Danmark Cl B (ADR)	663	2.54
4	29	Masco	656	2.52
-1	9	Warner-Lambert	655	2.51
0	33	Worthington Industries	654	2.51

Composition % 12-31-94

Cash	1.2	Preferreds	0.0
Stocks	98.8	Convertibles	0.0
Bonds	0.0	Other	0.0

Tax Analysis

	Tax-Adj Historical Return %	% Pretax Return
3 Yr Avg	---	---
5 Yr Avg	---	---
10 Yr Avg	---	---
Potential Capital Gain Exposure (% of assets)		-11%

Most Similar Funds in MF500

Fund lacks three-year record

Index Allocation

	% of Stocks
S&P 500	82.7
S&P MidCap 400	2.8
U.S. Small Cap	5.7
Foreign	8.8

Sector Weightings

	% of Stocks	Relative S&P 500
Utilities	7.2	0.58
Energy	8.2	0.81
Financials	11.1	1.05
Industrial Cyclicals	23.7	1.45
Consumer Durables	11.4	1.84
Consumer Staples	5.5	0.44
Services	10.6	1.30
Retail	2.4	0.42
Health	10.4	1.20
Technology	9.4	1.03

M✪**RNINGSTAR** **1995 Mutual Fund 500**

Sit Growth

	Ticker	Load	NAV	Yield	SEC Yield	Assets	Objective
	NBNGX	None	11.51	0.0%	N/A	303.1	Growth

Sit Growth Fund seeks long-term growth of capital.

The fund normally invests at least 85% of its assets in a diversified group of small- to medium-size growth companies. It may also invest in larger companies with restructured management, product changes, or other developments that stimulate earnings growth.

The fund began operations on Oct. 19, 1981, but shares did not become effectively registered until Sept. 2, 1982. Prior to Dec. 31, 1987, the fund was named New Beginning Growth Fund. From that date until Nov. 1, 1993, the fund was named Sit "New Beginning" Growth Fund.

Manager's Investment Style

Management has a high-growth investment strategy that targets niche companies that sustain an annual 15% to 20% growth rate, and boast expanding unit-volume sales and efficient operations.

Historical Profile

Return	Above Average
Risk	Above Average
Rating	★★★★ Above Average

Investment Style History
Equity
Average % Stocks Held in Portfolio

93% 95% 94% 88% 87% 86% 93% 93%

Growth of $10,000
|||| Value of Fund ($000)
— Value of Index ($000)
SPMid400
▼ Manager Change
▽ Partial Manager Change
► Mgr Unknown After
◄ Mgr Unknown Before

Performance Quartile (Within Objective)

	1983	1984	1985	1986	1987	1988	1989	1990	1991	1992	1993	1994	History
	5.10	4.79	6.60	6.34	6.09	6.33	8.11	7.48	12.29	11.96	12.66	11.51	NAV
	26.75	-3.21	43.66	8.35	5.49	9.78	35.15	-2.04	65.49	-2.13	8.55	-0.47	Total Return %
	4.29	-9.48	11.92	-10.33	0.23	-6.83	3.47	1.08	35.00	-9.75	-1.51	-1.78	+/- S&P 500
	3.29	-6.26	11.10	-7.74	3.13	-8.16	5.98	4.15	31.28	-11.10	-2.74	-0.40	+/- Wilshire 5000
	0.35	0.88	1.08	0.19	0.10	1.49	1.12	1.02	0.62	0.37	0.15	0.00	Income Return %
	26.40	-4.09	42.58	8.16	5.40	8.29	34.03	-3.06	64.86	-2.51	8.40	-0.47	Capital Return %
	17	76	4	90	20	63	7	62	3	92	76	23	Total Rtn % Rank All
	23	57	2	88	31	74	16	36	5	94	66	38	Total Rtn % Rank Obj
	0.02	0.04	0.06	0.01	0.01	0.09	0.09	0.08	0.06	0.05	0.02	0.00	Income $
	0.25	0.10	0.19	0.82	0.74	0.25	0.36	0.39	0.04	0.02	0.29	1.04	Capital Gains $
	1.50	1.50	1.50	1.32	1.20	1.21	1.19	1.10	1.03	0.83	0.80	0.82	Expense Ratio %
	0.85	1.18	2.65	0.19	0.09	0.57	1.85	0.75	0.96	0.52	0.35	-0.08	Income Ratio %
	67	80	130	99	81	78	88	55	37	25	45	47	Turnover Rate %
	22.1	15.4	30.7	33.9	35.7	49.3	58.6	68.6	209.0	335.0	332.3	303.1	Net Assets ($mil)

Fund Manager(s)

Eugene C. Sit CFA(1968), since 09-82. Birthdate: 08-38. BS, De Paul U. 1960 Finance Program, U. of Chicago
Erik S. Anderson CFA(1990), since 04-93. BS, U. of Minnesota

Manager Experience	Dates Managed	Invest Obj	Std Dev	+/- Index
Eugene C. Sit				
IDS New Dimensions	06/69 - 10/76	G	16.18	-8.26
IDS Growth	03/72 - 10/76	G	14.86	-6.22

Performance 12-31-94

	1st Qtr	2nd Qtr	3rd Qtr	4th Qtr	Total
1987	29.56	1.97	2.41	-22.03	5.49
1988	10.60	3.69	-2.22	-2.09	9.78
1989	10.06	8.75	15.17	-1.96	35.15
1990	-1.73	9.16	-18.34	11.83	-2.04
1991	28.88	-3.04	13.25	16.93	65.49
1992	-6.28	-8.67	1.36	12.81	-2.13
1993	-0.46	0.07	7.18	1.68	8.55
1994	-4.98	-7.90	13.18	0.48	-0.47

Bear Market Performance

Decile Rank (5-year period)

Worst _____ Best

	Worst 3 Mo Period 1985-89	Worst 3 Mo Period 1990-94
Sit Growth	-32.44	-18.34
+/- S&P 500	-2.86	-4.59
+/- Best Fit Index : SPMid400	-3.64	-0.56

Trailing Returns

	Total Return %	+/- S&P 500	+/- Wil 5000	% Rank All	% Rank Obj	Growth of $10,000
3 Mo	0.48	0.50	1.25	12	15	10,048
6 Mo	13.72	8.86	9.10	3	3	11,372
1 Yr	-0.47	-1.78	-0.40	23	38	9,953
3 Yr Avg	1.88	-4.39	-4.74	92	81	10,573
5 Yr Avg	11.38	2.69	2.56	11	16	17,141
10 Yr Avg	15.37	0.98	1.51	9	12	41,762
15 Yr Avg	---	---	---	---	---	---

Risk Analysis

Time Period	Load-Adj Return %	Risk % Rank All	Risk % Rank Obj	Morningstar Return	Morningstar Risk	Morningstar Risk-Adj Rating
1 Yr	-0.47					
3 Yr	1.88	95	95	-0.49[3]	1.39	★★
5 Yr	11.38	91	90	1.75[3]	1.18	★★★★
10 Yr	15.37	89	88	1.57	1.16	★★★★
Average Historical Rating (109 months)				3.3 ★s		

[1] = low, 100 = high   [2] 1.00 = Equity Avg   [3] 1.00 = 90-day T-bill return

Other Measures

				Standard S&P 500	Best Fit SPMid400
Standard Deviation	13.28	Alpha		-4.1	-5.3
Mean	2.74	Beta		1.18	1.21
Sharpe Ratio	-0.06	R-Squared		50	82

Investment Style

	Stock Portfolio Avg	Relative S&P 500
Price/Earnings Ratio	28.9	1.56
Price/Book Ratio	5.2	1.53
5 Yr Earnings Gr %	21.8	3.92
Return on Assets %	12.8	1.71
Debt % Total Cap	22.4	0.79
Med Mkt Cap ($mil)	1225	0.09

Style
Value Blend Growth
Size Large/Med/Small

Diversification Value for Portfolio Types

Large Cap: Low	Small Cap: Low	Bond: High	Balanced: Low	Diversified: Medium

Portfolio 12-31-94

Total Stocks: 66
Total Fixed-Income: 1

Share Chg (06-94) 000	Amount 000		Value $000	% Net Assets
-9	224	DSC Communications	8036	2.65
16	193	Paychex	7796	2.57
-25	177	Oracle Systems	7788	2.57
-22	209	cisco Systems	7324	2.42
0	207	Parametric Technology	7142	2.36
10	191	HEALTHSOUTH Rehabilitation	7049	2.33
129	264	Coventry	6458	2.13
33	160	Integrated Health Services	6300	2.08
14	105	Xilinx	6221	2.05
17	151	TCF Financial	6208	2.05
107	218	Harley-Davidson	6104	2.01
114	114	Cellular Communications Cl A	6072	2.00
161	264	Mid-Atlantic Medical Svcs	6039	1.99
168	168	Sensormatic Electronics	6030	1.99
-25	96	First Financial Management	5885	1.94
110	310	Federated Department Stores	5803	1.91
-76	202	Mercury General	5793	1.91
52	104	Medtronic	5785	1.91
-65	73	Oxford Health Plans	5746	1.90
-6	71	Chiron	5707	1.88
189	189	T Rowe Price Associates	5682	1.87
20	164	HBO	5658	1.87
7	155	Varity	5615	1.85
42	204	Ceridian	5485	1.81
68	181	Integrated Device Technology	5340	1.76

Composition % 12-31-94

Cash	7.7	Preferreds	0.0
Stocks	92.3	Convertibles	0.0
Bonds	0.0	Other	0.0

Index Allocation

	% of Stocks
S&P 500	14.5
S&P MidCap 400	38.8
U.S. Small Cap	45.1
Foreign	3.6

Tax Analysis

	Tax-Adj Historical Return %	% Pretax Return
3 Yr Avg	0.80	42.0
5 Yr Avg	10.19	87.5
10 Yr Avg	13.60	81.2
Potential Capital Gain Exposure (% of assets)		18%

Most Similar Funds in MF500

Value Line Leveraged Gr Inv	Fair Fit
Enterprise Capital Apprec	Fair Fit
AIM Weingarten	Fair Fit

Sector Weightings

	% of Stocks	Relative S&P 500
Utilities	0.0	0.00
Energy	6.3	0.62
Financials	12.7	1.20
Industrial Cyclicals	5.1	0.31
Consumer Durables	5.2	0.84
Consumer Staples	0.0	0.00
Services	12.7	1.56
Retail	4.2	0.72
Health	19.7	2.26
Technology	34.2	3.73

Operations

Address and Telephone	4600 Norwest Center 90 S. 7th St Minneapolis, MN 55402-4130 800-332-5580 / 612-334-5888
Advisor	Sit Investment Associates
Subadvisor	None
Distributor	SIA Securities
States Available	All except NE
Report Grade	A-
Income Distrib	Paid Annually
Date of Inception	09-02-82
Fiscal Year End	June

Min Initial Purchase	$2000 (Addt'l: $100)
Min IRA Purchase	None (Addt'l: None)
Min Auto Invest Plan	$2000 (Systematic Inv: $100)

Expenses & Fees

Sales Fees	0.00% front
	0.00% deferred
	0.00% 12b-1
Management Fee	1.00% flat fee
3-,5-,10-yr Expense Projections	$27, $47, $104
Annual Brokerage Cost	0.10%

Sit Tax-Free Income

Sit Tax-Free Income Fund seeks current income exempt from federal income tax, consistent with preservation of capital.

The fund ordinarily invests 100% of its net assets in investment-grade municipal securities. It has no restrictions on portfolio maturity.

Prior to Nov. 1, 1993, the fund was named Sit "New Beginning" Tax-Free Income Fund.

	Ticker	Load	NAV	Yield	SEC Yield	Assets	Objective
	SNTIX	None	9.43	6.0%	6.34%	243.3	Muni Nat

Historical Profile
Return	Above Average
Risk	Low
Rating	★★★★★ Highest

Investment Style History
Fixed Income

Income Rtn % Rank Obj
---	---	4	1	14	15	23	10

Growth of $10,000
- IIII Value of Fund ($000)
- — Value of Index ($000) LB Muni
- ▼ Manager Change
- ▽ Partial Manager Change
- ► Mgr Unknown After
- ◄ Mgr Unknown Before

Manager's Investment Style
In an attempt to bolster yield, management favors high-coupon or high-imputed-yield securities with short effective lives. The fund thus often features large positions in high-yielding health, housing, and private-activity bonds. Additionally, the portfolio's names tend to land in the two lower tiers of the investment-grade ladder. The fund's duration is thus relatively short, and its yield is relatively high.

Performance Quartile
(Within Objective)

	1983	1984	1985	1986	1987	1988	1989	1990	1991	1992	1993	1994	History
NAV	---	---	---	---	---	9.67	9.68	9.57	9.72	9.76	10.08	9.43	NAV
	---	---	---	---	---	2.19 *	8.38	7.29	9.25	7.76	10.42	-0.63	Total Return %
	---	---	---	---	---	---	-6.16	-1.66	-6.75	0.52	0.67	2.29	+/- LB Aggregate
	---	---	---	---	---	---	-2.41	-0.01	-2.89	-1.06	-1.86	4.98	+/- LB Muni
	---	---	---	---	---	1.98	8.28	8.42	7.68	6.93	6.18	5.63	Income Return %
	---	---	---	---	---	0.21	0.10	-1.14	1.57	0.83	4.24	-6.25	Capital Return %
	---	---	---	---	---	---	88	19	93	49	63	24	Total Rtn % Rank All
	---	---	---	---	---	---	75	7	90	71	71	7	Total Rtn % Rank Obj
	---	---	---	---	---	0.19	0.77	0.79	0.70	0.65	0.58	0.56	Income $
	---	---	---	---	---	0.00	0.00	0.00	0.00	0.04	0.09	0.02	Capital Gains $
	---	---	---	---	---	---	0.80	0.80	0.80	0.80	0.80	0.77	Expense Ratio %
	---	---	---	---	---	---	8.08	8.16	7.62	7.02	6.17	5.68	Income Ratio %
	---	---	---	---	---	---	---	87	74	80	58	48	Turnover Rate %
	---	---	---	---	---	7.5	20.3	47.9	133.6	278.2	340.8	243.3	Net Assets ($mil)

Fund Manager(s)
Michael C. Brilley, since 09-88. Birthdate: 05-45. BS, Millikin U. 1967
Debra A. Sit CFA(1990), since 11-91. Birthdate: 08-60. BA, U. of Minnesota 1982 MBA, U. of Chicago 1987

Manager Experience	Dates Managed	Invest Obj	Std Dev	+/- Index
Michael C. Brilley				
Sit U.S. Government Secs	06/87 - 12/94	GG	3.43	-0.17
Sit MN Tax-Free Income	12/93 - 12/94	MS	4.30	3.55

Performance 12-31-94
	1st Qtr	2nd Qtr	3rd Qtr	4th Qtr	Total
1987	---	---	---	---	---
1988	---	---	---	2.30	2.19 *
1989	1.54	2.65	1.86	2.07	8.38
1990	1.61	1.78	1.84	1.87	7.29
1991	1.67	2.17	2.76	2.35	9.25
1992	0.70	3.00	2.02	1.83	7.76
1993	2.85	2.81	3.05	1.33	10.42
1994	-3.09	1.77	0.93	-0.17	-0.63

Bear Market Performance
Decile Rank (5-year period)

		Best
Worst		

	Worst 3 Mo Period 1985-89	Worst 3 Mo Period 1990-94
Sit Tax-Free Income	---	-3.09
+/- LB Aggregate	---	-0.21
+/- Best Fit Index : LB Muni	---	2.40

Trailing Returns
	Total Return %	+/- LB Aggregate	+/- LB Muni	% Rank All	% Rank Obj	Growth of $10,000
3 Mo	-0.17	-0.54	1.27	27	8	9,983
6 Mo	0.76	-0.23	2.01	42	7	10,076
1 Yr	-0.63	2.29	4.98	24	7	9,938
3 Yr Avg	5.74	1.20	0.88	36	9	11,824
5 Yr Avg	6.75	-0.88	-0.03	56	22	13,859
10 Yr Avg	---	---	---	---	---	---
15 Yr Avg	---	---	---	---	---	---

Operations
Address and Telephone	4600 Norwest Center 90 S. 7th St Minneapolis, MN 55402-4130 800-332-5580 / 612-334-5888
Advisor	Sit Investment Associates
Subadvisor	None
Distributor	SIA Securities
States Available	All except NE
Report Grade	A
Income Distrib	Paid Monthly
* Date of Inception	09-29-88
Fiscal Year End	March

Risk Analysis
Time Period	Load-Adj Return %	Risk % Rank All	Risk % Rank Obj	Morningstar[2] Return	Morningstar Risk	Morningstar Risk-Adj Rating
1 Yr	-0.62					
3 Yr	5.74	5	11	1.57	0.54	★★★★★
5 Yr	6.75	2	8	1.24	0.42	★★★★★
10 Yr	---	---	---	---	---	---

Average Historical Rating (40 months) 5.0 ★ s

[1] 1 = low, 100 = high [2] 1.00 = Muni Avg [3] 1.00 = 90-day T-bill return

Other Measures
		Standard LB Agg	Best Fit LB Muni
Standard Deviation	3.77	Alpha	1.4	1.2
Mean	5.67	Beta	0.70	0.67
Sharpe Ratio	0.57	R-Squared	55	96

Investment Style
Interest-Rate Stance
Avg Effective Maturity 14.3 Yrs

Quality
Avg Credit Quality A
Avg Weighted Coupon 6.24%
Avg Weighted Price 91.69% of Par

Diversification Value for Portfolio Types
Large Cap: Medium	Small Cap: High	Bond: Low	Balanced: Medium	Diversified: Medium

Min Initial Purchase
Min Initial Purchase	$2000 (Addt'l: $100)
Min IRA Purchase	None (Addt'l: None)
Min Auto Invest Plan	$2000 (Systematic Inv: $100)

Expenses & Fees
Sales Fees	0.00% front
	0.00% deferred
	0.00% 12b-1
Management Fee	0.80% flat fee
3-,5-,10-yr Expense Projections	$25, $44, $98

Portfolio 12-31-94
Total Stocks: 0
Total Fixed-Income: 219

Amount 000	Date of Maturity		Value $000	% Net Assets
10615	01-01-00	CA San Joaquin Hills Transp Toll Rd 0%	7146	2.94
5910	12-01-08	FL Broward Resource Rec South 7.95%	6371	2.62
6000	01-01-12	PA Montgomery Indl Dev Resrc Rec 7.5%	6108	2.51
5000	07-01-15	MA Hlth/Educ Fac Goddard Hosp 9%	5358	2.20
5100	05-01-11	IL Hlth Fac Galesburg Cottage Hosp 6.25%	4797	1.97
5000	04-01-07	WY Sweetwater Poll Cntrl Idaho Pwr 6%	4782	1.97
3135	09-01-11	TX Baytown Hsg Fin Sngl Fam Mtg 8.5%	3380	1.39
3000	11-01-16	LA Pub Fac Multi-Fam Hsg 7.75%	3133	1.29
3000	03-01-20	IL Hsg Dev Elderly Vlg Ctr Sect 8 6.85%	2892	1.19
2655	09-15-03	OH Cleveland Parking Fac Impr 7.6%	2889	1.19
2595	03-01-11	AR Saline Resid Hsg Fac Sngl Fam 7.875%	2735	1.12
2750	10-01-12	MI Troy Econ Dev Drury Inn Proj 6.75%	2672	1.10
2750	10-01-10	IN Indianapolis Econ Dev Impr 7.25%	2647	1.09
2900	06-01-11	PA Erie Higher Educ Bldg Univ 5.9%	2607	1.07
2860	10-01-08	PA McKean Bradford Hosp 5.95%	2503	1.03
2540	11-01-12	OK Tulsa Pub Fac Assembly Ctr Lease 6.2%	2447	1.01
2350	02-01-00	WY Cheyenne Indl Dev Plaza 6.9%	2417	0.99
2231	11-01-11	LA Bossier Pub Trust Fin Mtg 8.5%	2338	0.96
2500	07-01-14	WA Hsg Fin Com Nonprofit Crista 6.2%	2274	0.93
5765	09-01-08	CA Los Angeles COP Disney Parking 0%	2262	0.93

Credit Analysis % of Bonds 12-31-94
US Govt	0	BB	1
AAA	7	B	0
AA	11	Below B	0
A	41	NR/NA	0
BBB	40		

Composition % of Assets 12-31-94
Cash	0.1	Preferreds	0.0
Stocks	0.0	Convertibles	0.0
Bonds	99.9	Other	0.0

Tax Analysis
	Tax-Adj Historical Return %	% Pretax Return
3 Yr Avg	5.60	97.3
5 Yr Avg	6.66	98.5
10 Yr Avg	---	---
Potential Capital Gain Exposure (% of assets)		-3%

Most Similar Funds in MF500
Nuveen Municipal Bond	Strong Fit
Nuv Muni Value	Strong Fit
Franklin High-Yld T/F Income	Strong Fit

Coupon Range
	% Bonds	Rel Obj
0%	13.2	5.28
0% to 6.8%	28.5	0.47
6.8% to 7.5%	30.1	1.94
7.5% to 8.3%	16.9	1.90
More than 8.3%	11.3	1.28
Not applicable	0.0	0.00

Sector Weightings
	% Bonds	Rel Obj
General Obl	1.01	0.05
Utilities	0.00	0.00
Health	29.61	2.24
Water/Waste	0.77	0.12
Housing	35.96	4.91
Education	3.54	0.55
Transportation	2.94	0.29
COP/Lease	4.52	1.42
Private	16.97	1.46
Misc Revenue	4.68	0.94
Demand	0.00	0.00

Top 5 States % of Bonds
IL	13.56	CA	7.66
TX	10.44	PA	7.29
IN	7.90		

MORNINGSTAR 1995 Mutual Fund 500

Skyline Special Equities

	Ticker	Load	NAV	Yield	SEC Yield	Assets	Objective
	SKSEX	Clsd	15.64	0.0%	N/A	202.8	Small Company

Skyline Fund Special Equities Portfolio seeks capital appreciation.

The fund normally invests at least 65% of its assets in equity securities of companies with market capitalizations under $400 million. These include: 1) companies with below-average price/earnings ratios but above-average revenues or earnings-growth prospects; 2) companies with temporarily depressed stock prices but improving operations; or 3) companies that are undervalued because of special circumstances.

Manager's Investment Style

Manager Bill Dutton looks for issues that are cheap based on existing earnings, but that he expects will post 15% or greater future annual earnings growth. He prefers very small stocks that are easily overlooked by most investors, and tends to sell his winners (and thus lock in his profits) quickly.

Fund Manager(s)

William M. Dutton, since 04-87. Birthdate: 12-53. BA, Princeton U. 1976 MAS, U. of Illinois 1980

Manager Experience

	Dates Managed	Invest Obj	Std Dev	+/- Index

Not available.

Historical Profile
Return	High
Risk	Below Average
Rating	★★★★★
	Closed

Investment Style History
Equity

Average % Stocks Held in Portfolio

Growth of $10,000
|||| Value of Fund ($000)
— Value of Index ($000)
Russ 2000
▼ Manager Change
▽ Partial Manager Change
◄ Mgr Unknown After
◄ Mgr Unknown Before

Performance Quartile (Within Objective)

	1983	1984	1985	1986	1987	1988	1989	1990	1991	1992	1993	1994	History
					71%	88%	88%	85%	93%	94%	96%	96%	
	---	---	---	---	7.99	10.32	11.49	10.32	12.67	17.12	17.83	15.64	NAV
	---	---	---	---	-16.86 *	29.74	24.01	-9.28	47.38	42.41	22.85	-1.17	Total Return %
	---	---	---	---	-5.07 *	13.13	-7.67	-6.17	16.90	34.80	12.79	-2.48	+/- S&P 500
	---	---	---	---	---	9.20	0.07	4.28	3.93	30.66	8.31	1.49	+/- Wilshire 4500
	---	---	---	---	0.00	0.58	1.21	0.90	0.14	0.00	0.00	0.00	Income Return %
	---	---	---	---	-16.86	29.16	22.80	-10.18	47.25	42.41	22.84	-1.17	Capital Return %
	---	---	---	---	---	3	26	83	9	1	13	28	Total Rtn % Rank All
	---	---	---	---	---	9	45	44	56	1	23	48	Total Rtn % Rank Obj
	---	---	---	---	0.00	0.05	0.14	0.10	0.02	0.00	0.00	0.00	Income $
	---	---	---	---	0.00	0.00	1.16	0.00	2.39	0.91	3.14	1.93	Capital Gains $
	---	---	---	---	1.60	1.70	1.60	1.59	1.55	1.51	1.48	1.50	Expense Ratio %
	---	---	---	---	0.20	0.61	1.30	0.95	0.09	-0.19	-0.54	-0.45	Income Ratio %
	---	---	---	---	173	68	90	98	104	87	104	81	Turnover Rate %
	---	---	---	---	6.6	11.4	20.8	22.2	37.4	168.3	227.7	202.8	Net Assets ($mil)

Performance 12-31-94

	1st Qtr	2nd Qtr	3rd Qtr	4th Qtr	Total
1987			4.01	-23.03	-16.86 *
1988	18.52	9.19	-1.06	1.33	29.74
1989	10.47	5.53	9.64	-2.97	24.01
1990	2.96	4.99	-20.54	5.62	-9.28
1991	27.81	-0.08	7.66	7.19	47.38
1992	12.31	-1.97	5.81	22.25	42.41
1993	7.65	0.87	5.38	7.36	22.85
1994	-0.84	-3.34	4.62	-1.44	-1.17

Bear Market Performance

Decile Rank (5-year period)

Worst   Best

	Worst 3 Mo Period 1985-89	Worst 3 Mo Period 1990-94
Skyline Special Equities	---	-24.40
+/- S&P 500	---	-10.56
+/- Best Fit Index : Russ 2000	---	1.50

Trailing Returns

	Total Return %	+/- S&P 500	+/- Wil 4500	% Rank All	% Rank Obj	Growth of $10,000
3 Mo	-1.44	-1.43	1.06	55	58	9,856
6 Mo	3.11	-1.75	-1.08	20	72	10,311
1 Yr	-1.17	-2.48	1.49	28	48	9,883
3 Yr Avg	20.02	13.76	12.42	1	2	17,291
5 Yr Avg	18.25	9.56	9.15	2	9	23,118
10 Yr Avg	---	---	---	---	---	---
15 Yr Avg	---	---	---	---	---	---

Operations

Address and Telephone	350 N. Clark Street
	Chicago, IL 60610
	800-458-5222 / 312-670-6035
Advisor	Mesirow Asset Management
Subadvisor	None
Distributor	Mesirow Financial
States Available	All plus PR
Report Grade	B-
Income Distrib	Paid Annually
* Date of Inception	04-23-87
Fiscal Year End	December

Risk Analysis

Time Period	Load-Adj Return %	Risk % Rank [1] All	Risk % Rank [1] Obj	Morningstar [2] Return	Morningstar Risk	Morningstar Risk-Adj Rating
1 Yr	-1.17					
3 Yr	20.02	52	8	5.55 [3]	0.56	★★★★
5 Yr	18.25	72	19	4.06 [3]	0.87	★★★★★
10 Yr	---	---	---	---		

Average Historical Rating (57 months)   4.5 ★s

[1] = low, 100 = high   [2] 1.00 = Equity Avg   [3] 1.00 = 90-day T-bill return

Other Measures

				Standard S&P 500	Best Fit Russ 2000
Standard Deviation	11.46	Alpha		14.2	9.0
Mean	19.03	Beta		0.75	0.86
Sharpe Ratio	1.35	R-Squared		27	78

Investment Style

	Stock Portfolio Avg	Relative S&P 500
Price/Earnings Ratio	12.6	0.68
Price/Book Ratio	2.5	0.74
5 Yr Earnings Gr %	15.0#	2.70
Return on Assets %	7.7	1.02
Debt % Total Cap	33.6	1.19
Med Mkt Cap ($mil)	218	0.02

figure is based on 50% or less of stocks

Style
Value Blend Growth
Size Large/Med/Small

Diversification Value for Portfolio Types

Large Cap: Medium	Small Cap: Low	Bond: High	Balanced: Medium	Diversified: Medium

Min Initial Purchase	Closed (Addt'l: Closed)
Min IRA Purchase	$1000 (Addt'l: $100)
Min Auto Invest Plan	$1000 (Systematic Inv: $50)

Expenses & Fees

Sales Fees	0.00% front
	0.00% deferred
	0.00% 12b-1
Management Fee	1.50% max./1.35% min.
3-,5-,10-yr Expense Projections	$49, $86, $195
Annual Brokerage Cost	---

Portfolio 12-30-94

Share Chg (09-94) 000	Amount 000	Total Stocks: 85 Total Fixed-Income: 0	Value $000	% Net Assets
44	196	Exar	4795	2.36
-9	210	Belden	4670	2.30
-10	231	Libbey	4034	1.99
-8	185	Kellwood	3879	1.91
-8	193	US Can	3661	1.81
-9	209	Scotsman Industries	3581	1.77
-7	163	Life Partners	3566	1.76
-11	247	Primark	3235	1.60
-5	243	PennCorp Financial Group	3188	1.57
-4	104	CMAC Investment	2991	1.48
-4	82	United Wisconsin Services	2956	1.46
-7	156	Digi International	2931	1.45
-5	231	Rhodes	2889	1.42
29	151	American Heritage Life	2880	1.42
-3	75	Barnes Group	2842	1.40
-5	125	Security-Connecticut	2806	1.38
67	374	Ryan's Family Steak Houses	2805	1.38
-5	109	Applied Power Cl A	2758	1.36
29	200	North Fork Bancorp	2743	1.35
117	117	Carmike Cinemas Cl A	2680	1.32
-4	99	Komag	2597	1.28
36	120	Charter Medical	2578	1.27
25	87	Ameron	2528	1.25
-8	177	ALLIED Life Financial	2515	1.24
-30	199	Citation	2493	1.23

Composition % 12-31-94

Cash	3.4	Preferreds	0.0
Stocks	96.6	Convertibles	0.0
Bonds	0.0	Other	0.0

Tax Analysis

	Tax-Adj Historical Return %	% Pretax Return
3 Yr Avg	16.55	80.0
5 Yr Avg	15.06	77.5
10 Yr Avg	---	---
Potential Capital Gain Exposure (% of assets)		3%

Most Similar Funds in MF500

Oppenheimer Main St Inc&Gr	Fair Fit
Strong Common Stock	Weak Fit
Fidelity Low-Priced Stock	Weak Fit

Index Allocation

	% of Stocks
S&P 500	1.6
S&P MidCap 400	1.3
U.S. Small Cap	97.1
Foreign	0.0

Sector Weightings

	% of Stocks	Relative S&P 500
Utilities	0.0	0.00
Energy	1.0	0.10
Financials	18.8	1.78
Industrial Cyclicals	29.9	1.83
Consumer Durables	16.0	2.58
Consumer Staples	0.7	0.05
Services	8.2	1.01
Retail	7.4	1.27
Health	7.0	0.81
Technology	11.0	1.20

MORNINGSTAR 1995 Mutual Fund 500   463

Skyline Special Equities II

	Ticker	Load	NAV	Yield	SEC Yield	Assets	Objective
	SPEQX	None	10.14	0.2%	N/A	100.1	Small Company

Skyline Fund Special Equities II seeks capital appreciation.

The fund normally invests at least 65% of its assets in equities of companies with market capitalizations from $400 million to $2 billion. These include: 1) companies with below-average price/earnings ratios but above-average revenues or earnings-growth prospects; 2) companies with temporarily depressed stock prices but improving operations; or 3) companies that are undervalued because of special circumstances.

On June 7, 1993, Skyline Value Portfolio merged into the fund. Skyline Europe Portfolio merged into the fund on Dec. 30, 1994.

Manager's Investment Style

Rather than making sector bets or macroeconomic calls, management picks individual stocks of strong-growth firms that are selling at low multiples. This fund was launched shortly after its immensely successful smaller-cap sibling, Skyline Special Equities, closed its doors to new investors.

Historical Profile
Return ---
Risk ---
Rating
Not Rated

Investment Style History
Equity

94% 92%   Average % Stocks Held in Portfolio

Growth of $10,000
|||| Value of Fund ($000)
— Value of Index ($000)
S&P 500
▼ Manager Change
▽ Partial Manager Change
► Mgr Unknown After
◄ Mgr Unknown Before

Performance Quartile (Within Objective)

Fund Manager(s)

Kenneth S. Kailin CFA(1992), since 02-93.
Birthdate: 12-58. BS, Indiana U. 1982 MBA, U. of Chicago 1989

Manager Experience

	Dates Managed	Invest Obj	Std Dev	+/- Index
Not available.				

	1983	1984	1985	1986	1987	1988	1989	1990	1991	1992	1993	1994	History
	---	---	---	---	---	---	---	---	---	---	10.79	10.14	NAV
	---	---	---	---	---	---	---	---	---	---	10.08 *	-1.52	Total Return %
	---	---	---	---	---	---	---	---	---	---	2.54 *	-2.83	+/- S&P 500
	---	---	---	---	---	---	---	---	---	---	---	1.13	+/- Wilshire 4500
	---	---	---	---	---	---	---	---	---	---	0.00	0.16	Income Return %
	---	---	---	---	---	---	---	---	---	---	10.08	-1.68	Capital Return %
	---	---	---	---	---	---	---	---	---	---	---	30	Total Rtn % Rank All
	---	---	---	---	---	---	---	---	---	---	---	54	Total Rtn % Rank Obj
	---	---	---	---	---	---	---	---	---	---	0.00	0.02	Income $
	---	---	---	---	---	---	---	---	---	---	0.22	0.46	Capital Gains $
	---	---	---	---	---	---	---	---	---	---	1.51	1.50	Expense Ratio %
	---	---	---	---	---	---	---	---	---	---	0.10	0.02	Income Ratio %
	---	---	---	---	---	---	---	---	---	---	---	84	Turnover Rate %
	---	---	---	---	---	---	---	---	---	---	58.6	100.1	Net Assets ($mil)

Performance 12-31-94

	1st Qtr	2nd Qtr	3rd Qtr	4th Qtr	Total
1987	---	---	---	---	---
1988	---	---	---	---	---
1989	---	---	---	---	---
1990	---	---	---	---	---
1991	---	---	---	---	---
1992	---	---	---	---	---
1993	---	-0.10	3.58	5.75	10.08 *
1994	-1.58	-1.98	6.24	-3.92	-1.52

Bear Market Performance

Decile Rank (5-year period)

Worst ——————————————— Best

	Worst 3 Mo Period 1985-89	Worst 3 Mo Period 1990-94
Skyline Special Equities II		
+/- S&P 500	---	---
+/- Best Fit Index :	---	---

Trailing Returns

	Total Return %	+/- S&P 500	+/- Wil 4500	% Rank All	% Rank Obj	Growth of $10,000
3 Mo	-3.92	-3.91	-1.42	89	89	9,608
6 Mo	2.08	-2.79	-2.12	26	81	10,208
1 Yr	-1.52	-2.83	1.13	30	54	9,848
3 Yr Avg	---	---	---	---	---	---
5 Yr Avg	---	---	---	---	---	---
10 Yr Avg	---	---	---	---	---	---
15 Yr Avg	---	---	---	---	---	---

Risk Analysis

Time Period	Load-Adj Return %	Risk % Rank [1] All	Obj	Morningstar [2] Return	Morningstar Risk	Morningstar Risk-Adj Rating
1 Yr	-1.52					
3 Yr	---	---	---	---	---	---
5 Yr	---	---	---	---	---	---
10 Yr	---	---	---	---	---	---

Average Historical Rating ---

[1] 1 = low, 100 = high [2] 1.00 = Equity Avg [3] 1.00 = 90-day T-bill return

Other Measures

		Standard S&P 500	Best Fit
Standard Deviation	---	Alpha	---	---
Mean	---	Beta	---	---
Sharpe Ratio	---	R-Squared	---	---

Investment Style

	Stock Portfolio Avg	Relative S&P 500
Price/Earnings Ratio	12.6	0.68
Price/Book Ratio	2.8	0.83
5 Yr Earnings Gr %	7.1#	1.28
Return on Assets %	5.9	0.79
Debt % Total Cap	35.1	1.24
Med Mkt Cap ($mil)	585	0.05

figure is based on 50% or less of stocks

Style Value Blend Growth — Size Large/Med/Small

Diversification Value for Portfolio Types

Large Cap: Small Cap: Bond: Balanced: Diversified:

Operations

Address and Telephone	350 N. Clark Street Chicago, IL 60610 800-458-5222 / 312-670-6035
Advisor	Mesirow Asset Management
Subadvisor	None
Distributor	Mesirow Financial
States Available	All
Report Grade	B-
Income Distrib	Paid Annually
* Date of Inception	02-09-93
Fiscal Year End	December

Min Initial Purchase	$1000 (Addt'l: $100)
Min IRA Purchase	$1000 (Addt'l: $100)
Min Auto Invest Plan	$1000 (Systematic Inv: $50)

Expenses & Fees

Sales Fees	0.00% front
	0.00% deferred
	0.00% 12b-1
Management Fee	1.50% max./1.35% min.
3-,5-,10-yr Expense Projections	$50, $88, $199
Annual Brokerage Cost	0.55%

Portfolio 12-30-94

Share Chg (09-94) 000	Amount 000	Total Stocks: 40 Total Fixed-Income: 0	Value $000	% Net Assets
12	94	Sterling Software	3436	3.43
14	140	Belden	3119	3.12
15	87	United Wisconsin Services	3103	3.10
155	155	Mark IV Industries	3051	3.05
101	101	Echlin	3030	3.03
100	100	AGCO	3030	3.03
24	97	Banta	2933	2.93
7	76	Stratus Computer	2888	2.88
20	115	Elsag Bailey Process Auto	2820	2.82
0	116	Ethan Allen Interiors	2813	2.81
4	114	Alberto-Culver Cl A	2781	2.78
41	75	Cleveland-Cliffs	2757	2.75
24	131	Kellwood	2741	2.74
32	89	Illinois Central	2740	2.74
8	128	Dial	2726	2.72
0	123	Life Partners	2699	2.70
16	101	Komag	2626	2.62
0	107	AO Smith Cl B	2609	2.61
19	99	Lyondell Petrochemical	2549	2.55
60	193	PennCorp Financial Group	2533	2.53
1	63	Beneficial	2457	2.45
23	113	Charter Medical	2419	2.42
27	109	Caldor	2414	2.41
0	126	Southern National (NC)	2414	2.41
0	129	SouthTrust	2322	2.32

Composition % 12-31-94

Cash	6.6	Preferreds	0.0
Stocks	93.4	Convertibles	0.0
Bonds	0.0	Other	0.0

Index Allocation

	% of Stocks
S&P 500	9.1
S&P MidCap 400	21.4
U.S. Small Cap	69.5
Foreign	0.0

Tax Analysis

	Tax-Adj Historical Return %	% Pretax Return
3 Yr Avg	---	---
5 Yr Avg	---	---
10 Yr Avg	---	---
Potential Capital Gain Exposure (% of assets)		0%

Most Similar Funds in MF500

Fund lacks three-year record

Sector Weightings

	% of Stocks	Relative S&P 500
Utilities	0.0	0.00
Energy	0.0	0.00
Financials	28.5	2.70
Industrial Cyclicals	16.6	1.01
Consumer Durables	14.1	2.27
Consumer Staples	6.1	0.49
Services	8.5	1.05
Retail	7.0	1.20
Health	2.7	0.31
Technology	16.5	1.80

MORNINGSTAR 1995 Mutual Fund 500

Smith Barney Appreciation A

	Ticker	Load	NAV	Yield	SEC Yield	Assets	Objective
	SHAPX	5.00%	10.15	1.7%	N/A	1573.9	Growth

Smith Barney Appreciation Fund - Class A seeks long-term growth of capital.

The fund invests primarily in equities issued by blue chip companies that are dominant in their industry and companies with earnings growth.

A shares have front loads; B shares have deferred loads, higher 12b-1 fees, and conversion features; C shares have level loads; Y shares are designed for institutions; Z shares are designed for 401(k) plans. On Nov. 20, 1992, Shearson Lehman Brothers Appreciation merged into this fund. Prior to Nov. 7, 1994, the fund was named Smith Barney Shearson Appreciation Fund A; prior to that, it went through several other name changes.

Manager's Investment Style

Management takes a large-cap blend approach that often highlights slightly tarnished blue chips. Defensive posturing is characteristic as well, with 10% to 20% typically in cash, and a dedication to keeping price multiples at reasonable levels. Further, management favors less-volatile large caps, while underweighting riskier sectors such as technology. Specifically, managers are buy-and-hold investors who surround a core of classic growth stocks with slightly more-opportunistic picks.

Fund Manager(s)

Hersh Cohen, since 01-79. Birthdate: 12-40. Case Western Reserve U. 1962 PhD, Tufts U. 1966

Manager Experience	Dates Managed	Invest Obj	Std Dev	+/- Index
Not available.				

Historical Profile

Return	Average
Risk	Below Average
Rating	★★★ Neutral

Average % Stocks Held in Portfolio: 85% 84% 85% 83% 88% 87% 90% 85%

Growth of $10,000

|||| Value of Fund ($000)
— Value of Index ($000) S&P 500
▼ Manager Change
▽ Partial Manager Change
► Mgr Unknown After
◄ Mgr Unknown Before

Performance Quartile (Within Objective)

Investment Style History Equity

	1983	1984	1985	1986	1987	1988	1989	1990	1991	1992	1993	1994	History
	4.52	4.45	5.82	6.54	6.49	7.04	8.66	8.30	10.26	10.66	11.01	10.15	NAV
	23.14	1.77	33.96	19.93	6.95	13.45	29.55	-0.27	26.94	6.29	8.12	-0.77	Total Return %
	0.67	-4.50	2.22	1.25	1.69	-3.16	-2.13	2.85	-3.55	-1.33	-1.94	-2.08	+/- S&P 500
	-0.32	-1.28	1.40	3.83	4.59	-4.49	0.38	5.91	-7.27	-2.68	-3.16	-0.70	+/- Wilshire 5000
	2.00	1.45	0.64	0.00	3.90	2.77	3.11	2.94	2.37	1.51	1.43	1.73	Income Return %
	21.14	0.32	33.32	19.93	3.05	10.68	26.44	-3.20	24.57	4.78	6.69	-2.50	Capital Return %
	30	61	14	20	16	35	56	32	66	78	25		Total Rtn % Rank All
	42	31	25	17	24	58	37	24	77	62	67	41	Total Rtn % Rank Obj
	0.07	0.06	0.04	0.00	0.26	0.19	0.24	0.25	0.20	0.15	0.16	0.18	Income $
	0.12	0.09	0.09	0.41	0.25	0.13	0.22	0.08	0.07	0.09	0.36	0.60	Capital Gains $
	1.10	1.00	1.00	1.00	0.93	0.89	0.90	0.80	0.80	0.88	1.03	1.02	Expense Ratio %
	3.60	3.30	2.40	2.10	2.20	2.70	3.20	2.90	2.20	1.58	1.35	1.51	Income Ratio %
	74	62	62	30	26	25	24	30	19	21	52	---	Turnover Rate %
	116.9	114.9	178.9	315.6	391.2	470.7	954.5	1103.4	1750.1	1712.9	1511.1	1573.9	Net Assets ($mil)

Performance 12-31-94

	1st Qtr	2nd Qtr	3rd Qtr	4th Qtr	Total
1987	18.74	4.38	6.92	-19.29	6.95
1988	4.29	5.47	0.56	2.57	13.45
1989	6.61	7.95	10.96	1.45	29.55
1990	-2.19	6.85	-10.90	7.10	-0.27
1991	12.29	-0.54	5.18	8.06	26.94
1992	-3.02	1.01	3.28	5.06	6.29
1993	3.10	-0.55	2.38	3.00	8.12
1994	-2.82	0.84	2.04	-0.77	-0.77

Bear Market Performance

Decile Rank (5-year period)

	Worst 3 Mo Period 1985-89	Worst 3 Mo Period 1990-94
Smith Barney Appreciation A	-26.29	-11.31
+/- S&P 500	3.29	2.53
+/- Best Fit Index : S&P 500	3.29	2.53

Trailing Returns

	Total Return %	+/- S&P 500	+/- Wil 5000	% Rank All	% Rank Obj	Growth of $10,000
3 Mo	-0.77	-0.75	0.00	39	38	9,923
6 Mo	1.25	-3.61	-3.37	33	78	10,125
1 Yr	-0.77	-2.08	-0.70	25	41	9,923
3 Yr Avg	4.48	-1.79	-2.14	59	61	11,404
5 Yr Avg	7.62	-1.07	-1.20	38	66	14,437
10 Yr Avg	13.81	-0.57	-0.05	19	30	36,461
15 Yr Avg	14.69	0.21	0.71	17	32	78,142

Operations

Address and Telephone	388 Greenwich Street 37th Floor	
	New York, NY 10013	
	800-451-2010 / 212-720-9218	
Advisor	Smith Barney Mutual Funds Managemt	
Subadvisor	None	
Distributor	Smith Barney	
States Available	All plus PR	
Report Grade	B+	
Income Distrib	Paid Annually	
Date of Inception	02-01-70	
Fiscal Year End	December	

Risk Analysis

Time Period	Load-Adj Return %	Risk % Rank[1] All	Obj	Morningstar[2] Return	Risk	Morningstar Risk-Adj Rating
1 Yr	-5.73					
3 Yr	2.70	62	18	-0.25[3]	0.68	★★
5 Yr	6.52	60	9	0.43[3]	0.71	★★★
10 Yr	13.23	53	11	1.11	0.76	★★★★

Average Historical Rating (109 months) 4.2 ★s

[1] = low, 100 = high [2] 1.00 = Equity Avg [3] 1.00 = 90-day T-bill return

Other Measures

				Standard S&P 500	Best Fit S&P 500
Standard Deviation	6.91	Alpha		-1.3	-1.3
Mean	4.63	Beta		0.85	0.85
Sharpe Ratio	0.16	R-Squared		95	95

Investment Style

	Stock Portfolio Avg	Relative S&P 500
Price/Earnings Ratio	18.7	1.01
Price/Book Ratio	3.6	1.06
5 Yr Earnings Gr %	3.2	0.57
Return on Assets %	6.8	0.91
Debt % Total Cap	28.3	1.00
Med Mkt Cap ($mil)	12845	0.99

Style Value Blend Growth / Size Large Med Small

Diversification Value for Portfolio Types

Large Cap: None	Small Cap: Medium	Bond: High	Balanced: None	Diversified: Low

Expenses & Fees

Sales Fees	5.00% front
	0.00% deferred
	0.25% 12b-1
Management Fee	0.55% max./0.37% min., 0.20%A
3-,5-,10-yr Expense Projections	$81, $104, $170
Annual Brokerage Cost	0.10%

Min Initial Purchase	$1000 (Addt'l: $50)
Min IRA Purchase	$250 (Addt'l: $50)
Min Auto Invest Plan	$100 (Systematic Inv: $100)

Portfolio 08-05-94

Share Chg (06-94) 000	Amount 000	Total Stocks: 109 Total Fixed-Income: 1	Value $000	% Net Assets
49	763	Minnesota Mining & Mfg	41189	2.95
49	864	Eastman Kodak	41169	2.95
23	737	AT & T	39908	2.86
-52	458	El duPont de Nemours	27573	1.98
-1	305	FNMA	26010	1.86
2	231	Xerox	23686	1.70
-1	254	Mobil	20976	1.50
42	188	Hercules	20534	1.47
-1	292	Gillette	20211	1.45
0	178	Royal Dutch Petroleum	19955	1.43
-1	407	Johnson & Johnson	19476	1.40
-90	369	Burlington Northern	19124	1.37
-2	648	RR Donnelley & Sons	18883	1.35
-1	509	Time Warner	18687	1.34
-26	356	General Motors	17887	1.28
-1	407	Coca-Cola	17747	1.27
50	356	General Electric	17486	1.25
25	356	UNUM	17130	1.23
50	280	Amoco	16466	1.18
0	178	American International Group	16418	1.18
-1	305	Procter & Gamble	16399	1.18
-1	305	Microsoft	16018	1.15
-1	305	Amerada Hess	15941	1.14
-5	102	Wells Fargo	15916	1.14
-1	254	Texaco	15795	1.13

Composition % 12-31-94

Cash	11.4	Preferreds	0.0
Stocks	87.7	Convertibles	0.0
Bonds	1.0	Other	0.0

Tax Analysis

	Tax-Adj Historical Return %	% Pretax Return
3 Yr Avg	2.99	65.9
5 Yr Avg	6.26	80.0
10 Yr Avg	12.25	82.2
Potential Capital Gain Exposure (% of assets)		9%

Most Similar Funds in MF500

Vanguard Index 500	Strong Fit
Investment Comp of America	Strong Fit
Massachusetts Inv A	Strong Fit

Index Allocation

	% of Stocks
S&P 500	93.4
S&P MidCap 400	3.0
U.S. Small Cap	2.8
Foreign	2.5

Sector Weightings

	% of Stocks	Relative S&P 500
Utilities	4.5	0.37
Energy	10.4	1.02
Financials	15.6	1.48
Industrial Cyclicals	26.8	1.64
Consumer Durables	6.6	1.06
Consumer Staples	7.2	0.58
Services	14.5	1.78
Retail	3.9	0.66
Health	5.3	0.61
Technology	5.2	0.57

Smith Barney Income & Growth A

	Ticker	Load	NAV	Yield	SEC Yield	Assets	Objective
	SBCIX	5.00%	12.18	3.6%	N/A	550.4	Growth/Inc.

Smith Barney Funds Income and Growth Portfolio - Class A seeks current income and long-term growth of income and capital.

The fund invests primarily in common stocks offering current income from dividends; the portfolio may also include debt securities. Stocks with established dividend records, as well as growth potential, are emphasized. Non-dividend-paying common stocks may be purchased.

Class A shares have front loads; Class C shares have level loads.

Smith Barney Equity Portfolio - Class A merged into this fund on March 11, 1994.

Manager's Investment Style

Ayako Weissman joins long-time manager Bruce Sargent in continuing the fund's income-and-growth strategy. To produce the yield for which the fund's objective calls, management focuses on out-of-favor large-cap stocks and higher-yielding convertibles. Neglected stocks with low price multiples, decent fundamentals, and potential for earnings growth fulfill the equity side of the fund's portfolio. To be selected, these issues must have yields at least equal to that of the S&P 500's. To further support payouts, management will sell stocks if their rising price causes yield to sink below 75% of the S&P 500's.

Fund Manager(s)

Bruce D. Sargent CFA, since 01-74. MBA, Columbia U. BA, Columbia U.

Ayako Weissman CFA(1989), since 03-94. BA, International Christian University 1989

Manager Experience	Dates Managed	Invest Obj	Std Dev	+/- Index
Ayako Weissman				
Inefficient Market	05/94 - 12/94	DE	10.74	-4.94

Historical Profile

Return	Below Average
Risk	Below Average
Rating	★★★
	Neutral

| | 67% | 72% | 77% | 73% | 77% | 78% | 78% | 84% |

Investment Style History
Equity
Average % Stocks Held in Portfolio

Growth of $10,000
- |||| Value of Fund ($000)
- — Value of Index ($000) S&P 500
- ▼ Manager Change
- ▽ Partial Manager Change
- ◄— Mgr Unknown After
- ◄ Mgr Unknown Before

Performance Quartile (Within Objective)

1983	1984	1985	1986	1987	1988	1989	1990	1991	1992	1993	1994	History
9.84	8.69	10.10	11.40	10.05	11.00	12.69	10.54	12.51	12.48	13.31	12.18	NAV
17.35	10.33	27.34	21.00	-3.14	17.42	24.71	-9.78	26.35	7.19	16.39	-4.21	Total Return %
-5.12	4.06	-4.40	2.32	-8.40	0.81	-6.97	-6.67	-4.14	-0.43	6.33	-5.53	+/- S&P 500
-6.12	7.28	-5.22	4.90	-5.51	-0.52	-4.46	-3.60	-7.86	-1.78	5.10	-4.14	+/- Wilshire 5000
7.28	7.99	7.89	6.52	4.09	6.11	6.18	5.44	7.10	4.19	3.63	3.29	Income Return %
10.07	2.34	19.45	14.48	-7.23	11.30	18.53	-15.22	19.25	3.00	12.75	-7.50	Capital Return %
50	25	36	16	81	20	24	84	33	55	24	56	Total Rtn % Rank All
75	19	51	18	85	34	46	84	65	55	14	81	Total Rtn % Rank Obj
0.64	0.65	0.66	0.67	0.50	0.63	0.71	0.71	0.72	0.51	0.46	0.44	Income $
0.00	1.35	0.22	0.13	0.63	0.17	0.31	0.25	0.05	0.40	0.73	0.14	Capital Gains $
1.50	1.00	0.74	0.56	0.45	0.49	0.44	0.45	0.84	0.92	0.91	0.96	Expense Ratio %
6.12	7.54	7.19	5.99	5.90	5.58	5.65	5.69	4.80	3.97	3.42	3.38	Income Ratio %
44	18	25	54	51	26	38	48	45	39	46	---	Turnover Rate %
5.5	12.5	85.6	379.5	547.0	517.9	590.0	513.6	583.7	572.9	627.9	550.4	Net Assets ($mil)

Performance 12-31-94

	1st Qtr	2nd Qtr	3rd Qtr	4th Qtr	Total
1987	12.16	1.71	2.61	-17.26	-3.14
1988	7.44	6.61	-0.25	2.76	17.42
1989	5.75	7.73	7.54	1.79	24.71
1990	-3.62	1.76	-11.67	4.14	-9.78
1991	11.68	1.49	6.52	4.65	26.35
1992	0.15	3.25	1.66	1.97	7.19
1993	7.55	2.42	4.01	1.59	16.39
1994	-4.52	0.53	2.61	-2.75	-4.21

Bear Market Performance

Decile Rank (5-year period)

Worst ———————————————— Best

	Worst 3 Mo Period 1985-89	Worst 3 Mo Period 1990-94
Smith Barney Income & Growth	-22.99	-12.64
+/- S&P 500	6.59	1.20
+/- Best Fit Index : S&P 500	6.59	1.20

Trailing Returns

	Total Return %	+/- S&P 500	+/- Wil 5000	% Rank All	% Rank Obj	Growth of $10,000
3 Mo	-2.75	-2.73	-1.98	80	81	9,725
6 Mo	-0.21	-5.07	-4.83	60	90	9,979
1 Yr	-4.21	-5.53	-4.14	56	81	9,579
3 Yr Avg	6.12	-0.15	-0.49	32	46	11,950
5 Yr Avg	6.38	-2.31	-2.44	67	83	13,622
10 Yr Avg	11.53	-2.86	-2.33	42	63	29,767
15 Yr Avg	14.15	-0.33	0.18	21	21	72,834

Operations

Address and Telephone	388 Greenwich Street 37th Floor New York, NY 10013 800-544-7835 / 212-698-5349
Advisor	Smith Barney Advisers
Subadvisor	None
Distributor	Smith Barney Shearson
States Available	All
Report Grade	B
Income Distrib	Paid Quarterly
Date of Inception	05-01-67
Fiscal Year End	December

Risk Analysis

Time Period	Load-Adj Return %	Risk % Rank[1] All	Obj	Morningstar[2] Return	Morningstar Risk	Morningstar Risk-Adj Rating
1 Yr	-9.00					
3 Yr	4.32	59	25	0.21[3]	0.65	★★★
5 Yr	5.29	60	25	0.13[3]	0.71	★★
10 Yr	10.95	46	14	0.70	0.66	★★★
Average Historical Rating (109 months)					3.8	★s

[1] 1 = low, 100 = high   [2] 1.00 = Equity Avg   [3] 1.00 = 90-day T-bill return

Other Measures

			Standard S&P 500	Best Fit S&P 500
Standard Deviation	7.30	Alpha	0.2	0.2
Mean	6.22	Beta	0.85	0.85
Sharpe Ratio	0.37	R-Squared	85	85

Investment Style

	Stock Portfolio Avg	Relative S&P 500
Price/Earnings Ratio	16.4	0.88
Price/Book Ratio	3.1	0.93
5 Yr Earnings Gr %	-2.5	-0.45
Return on Assets %	5.6	0.75
Debt % Total Cap	31.1	1.10
Med Mkt Cap ($mil)	8999	0.69

Style Value Blend Growth — Size Large/Med/Small

Diversification Value for Portfolio Types

Large Cap: None	Small Cap: Medium	Bond: Medium	Balanced: None	Diversified: Low

Expenses & Fees

Sales Fees	5.00% front
	0.00% deferred
	0.25% 12b-1
Management Fee	0.60% max./0.50% min.
3-,5-,10-yr Expense Projections	$73, $93, $152
Annual Brokerage Cost	0.13%

Min Initial Purchase $3000 (Addt'l: $50)
Min IRA Purchase $1000 (Addt'l: $50)
Min Auto Invest Plan $3000 (Systematic Inv: $50)

Portfolio 06-30-94

Total Stocks: 68
Total Fixed-Income: 14

Share Chg (12-93) 000	Amount 000		Value $000	% Net Assets
-4	244	Royal Dutch Petroleum	25538	3.79
33	373	Texaco	22539	3.35
41	431	Sears Roebuck	20676	3.07
-5	287	United Technologies	18450	2.74
226	421	Chevron	17637	2.62
-71	172	Xerox	16842	2.50
165	335	Minnesota Mining & Mfg	16584	2.46
-5	287	Exxon	16261	2.41
134	335	Eastman Kodak	16123	2.39
-5	287	Tenneco	13317	1.98
44	258	Philip Morris	13310	1.98
142	239	Dun & Bradstreet	13281	1.97
-3	191	Dow Chemical	12516	1.86
-3	191	Norfolk Southern	12061	1.79
-7	383	GTE	12061	1.79
-2	144	Marsh & McLennan	11971	1.78
239	239	Imperial Chemical Inds (ADR)	11367	1.69
-4	258	Barnett Banks	11307	1.68
84	191	Avon Products	11271	1.67
191	191	El duPont de Nemours	11176	1.66
	177	Banc One Cl C Cv Pfd $3.50	11068	1.64
	354	USAir Group Cl B Cv Pfd $4.375	10669	1.58
-71	153	Lockheed	10013	1.49
144	144	AMP	9943	1.48
-4	239	Chemical Banking	9213	1.37

Composition % 09-30-94

Cash	8.4	Preferreds	4.9
Stocks	82.6	Convertibles	0.0
Bonds	4.1	Other	0.0

Tax Analysis

	Tax-Adj Historical Return %	% Pretax Return
3 Yr Avg	3.82	61.1
5 Yr Avg	4.00	59.9
10 Yr Avg	8.62	65.1
Potential Capital Gain Exposure (% of assets)		9%

Most Similar Funds in MF500

Dean Witter Dividend Growth	Strong Fit
Vanguard Index 500	Strong Fit
Washington Mutual Investors	Strong Fit

Index Allocation

	% of Stocks
S&P 500	90.6
S&P MidCap 400	3.7
U.S. Small Cap	3.1
Foreign	7.6

Sector Weightings

	% of Stocks	Relative S&P 500
Utilities	9.4	0.76
Energy	16.5	1.63
Financials	10.2	0.96
Industrial Cyclicals	32.5	1.99
Consumer Durables	0.6	0.09
Consumer Staples	8.6	0.69
Services	13.9	1.71
Retail	4.6	0.79
Health	0.0	0.00
Technology	3.7	0.41

MORNINGSTAR 1995 Mutual Fund 500

Smith Barney Tax-Ex Inc B

	Ticker	Load	NAV	Yield	SEC Yield	Assets	Objective
	SXMTX	4.50%d	16.33	5.9%	5.89%	731.3	Muni Nat

Smith Barney Tax-Exempt Income Fund - Class B seeks income exempt from federal income tax.

The fund invests at least 80% of its net assets in municipal obligations. It invests primarily in investment-grade securities, but may invest up to 35% of its assets in securities rated BB or below.

Class A shares have front loads; Class B shares have deferred loads, higher 12b-1 fees, and conversion features; Class C shares have level loads; Class Y shares are designed for institutions. Prior to Nov. 7, 1994, the fund was named Smith Barney Shearson Tax-Exempt Income Fund A; prior to that it went through several other name changes.

Manager's Investment Style

Management barbells insured bonds with issues from investment-grade's two lowest tiers and an occasional touch of nonrated paper. For yield pickup, management targets premium-coupon issues hailing from the long end of the yield curve, and it also holds an overweighted position in higher-paying private-activity bonds.

Historical Profile

Return	Average
Risk	Average
Rating	★★★
	Neutral

73	60	67	61	46	43	25	28

Investment Style History
Fixed Income
Income Rtn % Rank Obj

Growth of $10,000
- ||| Value of Fund ($000)
- — Value of Index ($000) LB Muni
- ▼ Manager Change
- ▽ Partial Manager Change
- ▶ Mgr Unknown After
- ◀ Mgr Unknown Before

Performance Quartile (Within Objective)

History

	1983	1984	1985	1986	1987	1988	1989	1990	1991	1992	1993	1994	
	---	---	15.74	17.20	16.07	16.77	17.10	16.71	17.30	17.59	18.48	16.33	NAV
	---	---	7.54 *	16.88	0.31	11.81	9.05	5.08	11.17	8.73	11.78	-6.53	Total Return %
	---	---	---	1.63	-2.45	3.93	-5.49	-3.87	-4.83	1.48	2.03	-3.61	+/- LB Aggregate
	---	---	---	-2.44	-1.20	1.65	-1.74	-2.23	-0.97	-0.09	-0.50	-0.93	+/- LB Muni
	---	---	2.61	7.60	6.54	7.36	6.90	6.72	6.84	6.27	6.16	5.10	Income Return %
	---	---	4.93	9.28	-6.24	4.45	2.15	-1.65	4.34	2.46	5.62	-11.63	Capital Return %
	---	---	---	42	57	47	84	43	83	37	52	76	Total Rtn % Rank All
	---	---	---	66	44	32	62	91	60	43	47	67	Total Rtn % Rank Obj
	---	---	0.38	1.13	1.11	1.13	1.12	1.11	1.09	1.04	1.04	0.96	Income $
	---	---	0.00	0.00	0.06	0.01	0.03	0.11	0.13	0.13	0.09	0.00	Capital Gains $
	---	---	---	1.53	1.57	1.43	1.44	1.47	1.45	1.46	1.38	1.33	Expense Ratio %
	---	---	---	6.88	6.43	6.99	6.70	6.57	6.48	5.96	5.52	5.34	Income Ratio %
	---	---	---	---	16	12	21	29	44	61	34	39	Turnover Rate %
	---	---	152.9	434.3	410.2	486.2	563.9	581.0	695.1	963.3	1162.5	731.3	Net Assets ($mil)

Fund Manager(s)

Lawrence T. McDermott, since 09-85.

Manager Experience

	Dates Managed	Invest Obj	Std Dev	+/- Index
Lawrence T. McDermott				
Smith Barney Mngd Munis	03/81 - 11/88	MN	10.81	-0.98
Smith Barney CA Munis A	04/84 - 11/88	MC	8.04	-3.31

Performance 12-31-94

	1st Qtr	2nd Qtr	3rd Qtr	4th Qtr	Total
1987	2.55	-4.24	-2.67	4.95	0.31
1988	3.42	2.17	3.01	2.72	11.81
1989	0.82	5.52	-0.17	2.68	9.05
1990	0.10	1.68	-0.14	3.38	5.08
1991	2.04	2.15	3.44	3.11	11.17
1992	0.79	3.53	2.43	1.73	8.73
1993	3.81	3.16	3.20	1.15	11.78
1994	-5.68	0.56	0.45	-1.89	-6.53

Bear Market Performance

Decile Rank (5-year period)

Worst ———————————————— Best

	Worst 3 Mo Period 1985-89	Worst 3 Mo Period 1990-94
Smith Barney Tax-Ex Inc B	---	-6.16
+/- LB Aggregate	---	-1.23
+/- Best Fit Index : LB Muni	---	-0.40

Trailing Returns

	Total Return %	+/- LB Aggregate	+/- LB Muni	% Rank All	% Rank Obj	Growth of $10,000
3 Mo	-1.89	-2.27	-0.46	66	78	9,811
6 Mo	-1.46	-2.45	-0.21	81	74	9,854
1 Yr	-6.53	-3.61	-0.93	76	67	9,347
3 Yr Avg	4.34	-0.20	-0.53	62	60	11,360
5 Yr Avg	5.82	-1.80	-0.95	80	69	13,270
10 Yr Avg	---	---	---	---	---	---
15 Yr Avg	---	---	---	---	---	---

Operations

Address and Telephone	388 Greenwich Street 37th Floor
	New York, NY 10013
	800-451-2010 / 212-720-9218
Advisor	Smith Barney Mutual Funds Management
Subadvisor	None
Distributor	Smith Barney
States Available	All plus PR
Report Grade	B
Income Distrib	Paid Monthly
* Date of Inception	09-16-85
Fiscal Year End	July

Min Initial Purchase	$1000 (Addt'l: $50)
Min IRA Purchase	N/A
Min Auto Invest Plan	$100 (Systematic Inv: $100)

Expenses & Fees

Sales Fees	0.00% front
	4.50% deferred
	0.65% 12b-1
Management Fee	0.40% flat fee, 0.20%A
3-,5-,10-yr Expense Projections	$72, $83, $147

Risk Analysis

Time Period	Load-Adj Return %	Risk % Rank [1] All	Risk % Rank [1] Obj	Morningstar [2] Return	Morningstar [2] Risk	Morningstar Risk-Adj Rating
1 Yr	-10.07					
3 Yr	3.76	30	49	0.96	1.01	★★★
5 Yr	5.82	20	48	0.94	1.01	★★★
10 Yr	---	---	---	---	---	

Average Historical Rating (76 months) 3.3 ★s

[1] 1 = low, 100 = high [2] 1.00 = Muni Avg [3] 1.00 = 90-day T-bill return

Other Measures

			Standard LB Agg	Best Fit LB Muni
Standard Deviation	5.65	Alpha	-0.2	-0.5
Mean	4.42	Beta	1.05	1.02
Sharpe Ratio	0.16	R-Squared	56	97

Investment Style

Interest-Rate Stance

Avg Effective Maturity 18.8 Yrs

Maturity		
Short	Intm	Long

Quality

Avg Credit Quality AA

Avg Weighted Coupon 7.12%

Avg Weighted Price 102.00% of Par

Diversification Value for Portfolio Types

Large Cap: Medium	Small Cap: High	Bond: Low	Balanced: Medium	Diversified: Medium

Portfolio 07-31-94

Amount 000	Date of Maturity	Total Stocks: 0 Total Fixed-Income: 470	Value $000	% Net Assets
9345	04-01-24	RI Hsg/Mtg Fin 7.1%	9345	0.87
8558	01-01-08	NC East Muni Pwr Sys 7%	9253	0.87
9000	01-01-32	CA San Joaquin Hills Transp Toll 6.75%	8539	0.80
7869	04-01-24	VA Isle of Wight Indl Dev 6.55%	7899	0.74
7377	05-01-09	MI Detroit Econ Dev Resource Rec 6.875%	7829	0.73
7869	05-01-19	GA Burke Dev Poll Cntrl Pwr 6.35%	7741	0.72
6885	09-01-15	GA Monroe Dev Poll Cntrl Pwr 10.5%	7436	0.70
7722	02-15-23	MA Boston Hosp 5.75%	7177	0.67
6885	05-01-24	TN Humphreys Indl Dev Brd 6.7%	7040	0.66
6885	01-01-23	GA Muni Elec Pwr 6.4%	7015	0.66
6207	11-01-15	GA Burke Dev Poll Cntrl Pwr 10.5%	6773	0.63
6885	07-01-14	NY Dorm City Univ Sys 6%	6687	0.63
6246	12-13-08	MI Detroit Resource Rec Ser B 9.25%	6660	0.62
6197	04-01-12	NJ Mercer Impr Solid Waste 6.7%	6607	0.62
5902	01-01-07	MD NE Waste Disp SW Resource Rec 7.2%	6462	0.60
5666	10-01-04	PR Urban Renewal/Hsg 7.875%	6331	0.59
6394	07-01-24	NJ Educ Fac Inst Tech 6%	6298	0.59
5902	10-01-22	NV Clark Indl Dev Poll Cntrl 7.2%	6108	0.57
5902	01-01-07	NC Muni Pwr #1 Catawba Elec IFRN	5902	0.55
5394	08-15-28	AZ Navajo Poll Cntrl Pub Svc 5.875%	5730	0.54

Credit Analysis % of Bonds 12-31-94

US Govt	0	BB	4
AAA	41	B	1
AA	9	Below B	4
A	20	NR/NA	0
BBB	21		

Composition % of Assets 12-31-94

Cash	0.3	Preferreds	0.0
Stocks	0.0	Convertibles	0.0
Bonds	99.7	Other	0.0

Tax Analysis

	Tax-Adj Historical Return %	% Pretax Return
3 Yr Avg	4.22	97.1
5 Yr Avg	5.66	96.9
10 Yr Avg	---	---
Potential Capital Gain Exposure (% of assets)		-4%

Most Similar Funds in MF500

Fortress Municipal Income	Strong Fit
SteinRoe Managed Municipal	Strong Fit
Colonial Tax-Exempt A	Strong Fit

Coupon Range

	% Bonds	Rel Obj
0%	0.0	0.00
0% to 6.8%	54.9	0.91
6.8% to 7.5%	18.6	1.20
7.5% to 8.3%	8.6	0.97
More than 8.3%	15.6	1.76
Not applicable	2.3	0.59

Sector Weightings

	% Bonds	Rel Obj
General Obl	7.40	0.35
Utilities	7.87	0.63
Health	14.01	1.06
Water/Waste	4.66	0.73
Housing	7.59	1.04
Education	5.22	0.82
Transportation	12.66	1.24
COP/Lease	4.79	1.50
Private	33.40	2.86
Misc Revenue	1.91	0.38
Demand	0.48	0.20

Top 5 States % of Bonds

PA	9.47	NY	5.73
TX	9.28	NJ	5.41
GA	5.84		

SoGen Gold

	Ticker	Load	NAV	Yield	SEC Yield	Assets	Objective
	SGGDX	3.75%	11.20	0.3%	N/A	47.8	Sp.-Metals

SoGen Gold Fund seeks growth of capital.

The fund normally invests at least 65% of its assets in securities issued by companies engaged in gold operations, including gold mining finance companies. It may invest up to 35% of its assets in equity and debt securities unrelated to the precious metals industry. The fund may invest in sponsored and unsponsored American Depositary Receipts and European Depositary Receipts. It may also invest up to 20% of its assets in debt securities, including those rated below investment grade. A substantial portion of the fund's assets may be invested in foreign securities.

Manager's Investment Style

Remarkably successful international money manager Jean-Marie Eveillard applies his value-driven approach to gold-mining and gold-related stocks around the world. He begins his investment process by looking at macroeconomic factors, and then he examines price levels of stocks. He is a buy-and-hold investor whose investment horizon lies in the three- to five-year range. He isn't afraid to hold cash: This fund's famous sibling, SoGen International, typically holds between 10% and 30% in cash when good values are scarce.

Fund Manager(s)

Jean-Marie Eveillard, since 08-93. Birthdate: 01-40. BA, Lycee Descartes 1957 MBA, Ecole des Hautes Etudes Commerciale 1962

Manager Experience	Dates Managed	Invest Obj	Std Dev	+/- Index
Jean-Marie Eveillard				
SoGen International	01/79 - 12/94	AA	10.57	2.32
ONE Fund International	04/93 - 12/94	WF	12.44	17.64

Historical Profile

Return	---
Risk	---
Rating	---
	Not Rated

Growth of $10,000

- |||| Value of Fund ($000)
- — Value of Index ($000) S&P 500
- ▼ Manager Change
- ▽ Partial Manager Change
- ◄ Mgr Unknown After
- ► Mgr Unknown Before

Performance Quartile (Within Objective)

	1983	1984	1985	1986	1987	1988	1989	1990	1991	1992	1993	1994	History
	---	---	---	---	---	---	---	---	---	---	11.42	11.20	NAV
	---	---	---	---	---	---	---	---	---	---	14.20 *	-0.84	Total Return %
	---	---	---	---	---	---	---	---	---	---	12.67 *	-2.16	+/- S&P 500
	---	---	---	---	---	---	---	---	---	---	---	-17.60	+/- S&P Metals
	---	---	---	---	---	---	---	---	---	---	0.00	0.33	Income Return %
	---	---	---	---	---	---	---	---	---	---	14.20	-1.17	Capital Return %
	---	---	---	---	---	---	---	---	---	---	---	26	Total Rtn % Rank All
	---	---	---	---	---	---	---	---	---	---	---	3	Total Rtn % Rank Obj
	---	---	---	---	---	---	---	---	---	---	0.00	0.04	Income $
	---	---	---	---	---	---	---	---	---	---	0.00	0.08	Capital Gains $
	---	---	---	---	---	---	---	---	---	---	---	2.27	Expense Ratio %
	---	---	---	---	---	---	---	---	---	---	---	-0.32	Income Ratio %
	---	---	---	---	---	---	---	---	---	---	---	---	Turnover Rate %
	---	---	---	---	---	---	---	---	---	---	11.1	47.8	Net Assets ($mil)

Investment Style History Equity

Average % Stocks Held in Portfolio 87% 80%

Performance 12-31-94

	1st Qtr	2nd Qtr	3rd Qtr	4th Qtr	Total
1987	---	---	---	---	---
1988	---	---	---	---	---
1989	---	---	---	---	---
1990	---	---	---	---	---
1991	---	---	---	---	---
1992	---	---	---	---	---
1993	---	---	---	13.97	14.20 *
1994	0.00	-4.20	14.90	-9.92	-0.84

Bear Market Performance

Decile Rank (5-year period)

Worst | Best

	Worst 3 Mo Period 1985-89	Worst 3 Mo Period 1990-94
SoGen Gold	---	---
+/- S&P 500	---	---
+/- Best Fit Index :	---	---

Trailing Returns

	Total Return %	+/- S&P 500	+/- S&P Metals	% Rank All	% Rank Obj	Growth of $10,000
3 Mo	-9.92	-9.90	-3.57	98	2	9,008
6 Mo	3.51	-1.35	-2.59	18	17	10,351
1 Yr	-0.84	-2.16	-17.60	26	3	9,916
3 Yr Avg	---	---	---	---	---	---
5 Yr Avg	---	---	---	---	---	---
10 Yr Avg	---	---	---	---	---	---
15 Yr Avg	---	---	---	---	---	---

Operations

Address and Telephone	1221 Ave of the Americas 8th Fl New York, NY 10020 800-628-0252
Advisor	Societe Generale Asset Management
Subadvisor	None
Distributor	Societe Generale Securities
States Available	All
Report Grade	B-
Income Distrib	Paid Annually
* Date of Inception	08-31-93
Fiscal Year End	March

Risk Analysis

Time Period	Load-Adj Return %	Risk % Rank [1] All	Obj	Morningstar [2] Return	Risk	Morningstar Risk-Adj Rating
1 Yr	-4.56					
3 Yr	---	---	---	---	---	---
5 Yr	---	---	---	---	---	---
10 Yr	---	---	---	---	---	---

Average Historical Rating ---

[1] 1 = low, 100 = high   [2] 1.00 = Equity Avg   [3] 1.00 = 90-day T-bill return

Other Measures

			Standard S&P 500	Best Fit
Standard Deviation	---	Alpha	---	---
Mean	---	Beta	---	---
Sharpe Ratio	---	R-Squared	---	---

Investment Style

	Stock Portfolio Avg	Relative S&P 500
Price/Earnings Ratio	23.8	1.29
Price/Book Ratio	2.6	0.78
5 Yr Earnings Gr %	14.4#	2.59
Return on Assets %	8.9#	1.19
Debt % Total Cap	27.3#	0.97
Med Mkt Cap ($mil)	2342	0.18

figure is based on 50% or less of stocks

Style: Value Blend Growth / Size: Large Med Small

Diversification Value for Portfolio Types

Large Cap: Small Cap: Bond: Balanced: Diversified:

Portfolio 09-30-94

Share Chg (03-94) 000	Amount 000	Total Stocks: 38 Total Fixed-Income: 9	Value $000	% Net Assets
0	0	Bank For Intl Settlement Reg	3673	8.71
85	85	Santa Fe Pacific	1923	4.56
	70	Freeport-McMoran Cop/Gld D Pfd	1540	3.65
300	300	Newcrest Mining	1512	3.59
16	33	Newmont Mining	1463	3.47
	38	Freeport-McMoran Cop/Gld C Pfd	1406	3.34
15	65	Homestake Mining	1381	3.28
12	21	Franco-Nevada Mining	1335	3.17
165	615	Lonrho	1275	3.02
160	425	Industrias Penoles Cl A	1201	2.85
20	45	Minorco (ADR)	1176	2.79
22	45	Terra Mines	1172	2.78
	29	Freeport-McMoran Cop/Gld B Pfd	1094	2.59
23	35	Euro-Nevada Mining	1076	2.55
24	40	Placer Dome	1005	2.38
	1000	Coeur d'Alene Mines Cv 6.375%	983	2.33
25	50	Free State Consld Gold (ADR)	866	2.05
0	50	Kloof Gold Mining (ADR)	844	2.00
5	50	Driefontein Consld Mines ADR	800	1.90
0	1	Case Pomeroy Cl A	798	1.89
25	50	Cambior	782	1.86
75	250	Eltin	777	1.84
25	60	Battle Mountain Gold	765	1.81
25	70	Harmony Gold Mining (ADR)	754	1.79
16	26	Johannesburg Consld Inv ADR	633	1.50

Composition % 12-31-94

Cash	9.2	Preferreds	11.5
Stocks	71.6	Convertibles	7.8
Bonds	0.0	Other	0.0

Tax Analysis

	Tax-Adj Historical Return %	% Pretax Return
3 Yr Avg	---	---
5 Yr Avg	---	---
10 Yr Avg	---	---
Potential Capital Gain Exposure (% of assets)		-3%

Most Similar Funds in MF500

Fund lacks three-year record

Index Allocation

	% of Stocks
S&P 500	18.9
S&P MidCap 400	2.5
U.S. Small Cap	2.8
Foreign	81.6

Regional Exposure 12-31-94

	% of Stocks
N. America	48
S. Africa	14
Australia	11
Other	28
Bullion	0

Min Initial Purchase	$1000 (Addt'l: $100)
Min IRA Purchase	$1000 (Addt'l: $100)
Min Auto Invest Plan	$100 (Systematic Inv: $100)

Expenses & Fees

Sales Fees	3.75% front
	0.00% deferred
	0.25% 12b-1
Management Fee	0.75% flat fee
3-,5-,10-yr Expense Projections	$106, $154, $288
Annual Brokerage Cost	

MORNINGSTAR 1995 Mutual Fund 500

SoGen International

	Ticker	Load	NAV	Yield	SEC Yield	Assets	Objective
	SGENX	Clsd	22.68	0.6%	N/A	1822.5	Asset Alloc.

SoGen International Fund seeks long-term growth of capital and income.

The fund invests primarily in foreign and domestic common stock and convertibles. Fixed-income instruments may be purchased if they provide a potential for capital appreciation. With regard to debt, the fund maintains no restrictions on credit quality; it may purchase debt upon which the issuer has defaulted. The fund normally invests in at least three countries. It may invest up to 10% of its assets in illiquid or restricted securities.

Manager's Investment Style

Famed manager Jean-Marie Eveillard emphasizes smaller issues in this fund's stock portfolio, and places 60% of stocks in foreign issues. On the bond side, Eveillard holds mostly junk bonds. He attempts to balance his more-aggressive security choices with what is typically a 10% to 30% cash stake, low turnover, and high diversification.

Historical Profile
Return High
Risk Low
Rating ★★★★★
Closed

Investment Style History
Equity
Average % Stocks Held in Portfolio

70% 60% 53% 44% 45% 43% 52% 58%

Growth of $10,000

Fund Manager(s)

Jean-Marie Eveillard, since 01-79. Birthdate: 01-40. BA, Lycee Descartes 1957 MBA, Ecole des Hautes Etudes Commerciale 1962

Manager Experience	Dates Managed	Invest Obj	Std Dev	+/- Index
Jean-Marie Eveillard				
ONE Fund International	04/93 - 12/94	WF	12.44	17.64
SoGen Gold	08/93 - 12/94	SP	14.31	7.63

1983	1984	1985	1986	1987	1988	1989	1990	1991	1992	1993	1994	History
16.48	14.01	16.52	17.71	15.98	16.68	17.83	16.41	18.11	18.65	22.82	22.68	NAV
24.32	2.78	32.86	25.03	13.77	14.20	17.23	-1.29	18.82	8.80	26.17	2.52	Total Return %
1.85	-3.49	1.12	6.35	8.51	-2.42	-14.46	1.83	-11.66	1.18	16.11	1.21	+/- S&P 500
15.94	-12.37	10.73	9.78	11.01	6.32	2.69	-10.23	2.82	1.56	16.42	5.44	+/- LB Aggregate
5.60	5.40	4.77	3.60	5.15	4.92	4.12	4.16	5.99	3.90	2.41	0.67	Income Return %
18.71	-2.62	28.09	21.43	8.61	9.27	13.11	-5.45	12.83	4.90	23.76	1.86	Capital Return %
26	57	17	9	6	30	42	59	46	35	11	9	Total Rtn % Rank All
25	33	25	25	17	7	47	66	60	23	6	7	Total Rtn % Rank Obj
0.85	0.76	0.63	0.60	0.84	0.80	0.71	0.71	0.98	0.71	0.47	0.15	Income $
1.76	2.03	1.15	2.22	3.33	0.77	1.01	0.47	0.37	0.34	0.23	0.56	Capital Gains $
1.50	1.24	1.34	1.39	1.47	1.36	1.39	1.38	1.30	1.37	1.31	1.28	Expense Ratio %
6.69	4.71	4.26	3.71	2.71	3.09	4.23	4.32	4.84	4.00	3.69	2.34	Income Ratio %
78	64	58	59	41	43	33	31	24	24	18	24	Turnover Rate %
38.8	43.1	47.7	73.7	77.8	105.6	162.3	209.4	313.2	531.3	1427.4	1822.5	Net Assets ($mil)

Performance 12-31-94

	1st Qtr	2nd Qtr	3rd Qtr	4th Qtr	Total
1987	21.34	-0.09	9.50	-14.30	13.77
1988	5.82	4.02	-0.06	3.80	14.20
1989	3.78	3.18	6.16	3.13	17.23
1990	-0.67	3.44	-5.29	1.44	-1.29
1991	6.70	0.97	5.37	4.66	18.82
1992	1.82	4.18	2.39	0.17	8.80
1993	7.88	4.22	5.39	6.47	26.17
1994	2.19	-0.94	4.81	-3.36	2.52

Bear Market Performance

Decile Rank (5-year period)

Worst — Best

	Worst 3 Mo Period 1985-89	Worst 3 Mo Period 1990-94
SoGen International	-16.59	-8.31
+/- S&P 500	12.99	5.53
+/- Best Fit Index : MSAllCtry	---	4.09

Trailing Returns

	Total Return %	+/- S&P 500	+/- LB Aggregate	% Rank All	% Rank Obj	Growth of $10,000
3 Mo	-3.36	-3.35	-3.74	85	84	9,664
6 Mo	1.28	-3.58	0.29	33	49	10,128
1 Yr	2.52	1.21	5.44	9	7	10,252
3 Yr Avg	12.07	5.80	7.52	8	1	14,074
5 Yr Avg	10.54	1.85	2.92	14	8	16,507
10 Yr Avg	15.37	0.98	5.42	9	1	41,760
15 Yr Avg	16.57	2.09	5.76	5	1	99,698

Operations

Address and Telephone	1221 Ave of the Americas 8th Fl New York, NY 10020 800-628-0252 / 212-399-1141
Advisor	Societe Generale Asset Management
Subadvisor	None
Distributor	Societe Generale Securities
States Available	All
Report Grade	B-
Income Distrib	Paid Annually
Date of Inception	04-28-70
Fiscal Year End	March

Risk Analysis

Time Period	Load-Adj Return %	Risk % Rank All	Obj	Morningstar Return	Morningstar Risk	Morningstar Risk-Adj Rating
1 Yr	-1.32					
3 Yr	10.65	10	1	2.18[3]	0.38	★★★★★
5 Yr	9.70	40	2	1.27[3]	0.47	★★★★
10 Yr	14.93	35	1	1.77	0.49	★★★★★

Average Historical Rating (109 months) 4.7 ★s

[1] = low, 100 = high [2] 1.00 = Hybrid Avg [3] 1.00 = 90-day T-bill return

Other Measures

			Standard S&P 500	Best Fit MSAllCtry
Standard Deviation	5.29	Alpha	7.2	7.4
Mean	11.58	Beta	0.36	0.37
Sharpe Ratio	1.52	R-Squared	29	53

Investment Style

Stocks	Port Avg	Rel S&P 500
Price/Earnings Ratio	23.9	1.29
Price/Book Ratio	2.8	0.82
5 Yr Earnings Gr %	1.4#	0.25
Med Mkt Cap ($mil)	817	0.06

figure is based on 50% or less of stocks

Bonds	
Avg Effective Duration	NMF
Avg Effective Maturity	---
Avg Credit Quality	---
Avg Weighted Coupon	7.81%

Not Available

Diversification Value for Portfolio Types

Large Cap: Medium	Small Cap: High	Bond: High	Balanced: Medium	Diversified: Low

Portfolio 09-30-94

Share Chg (03-94)000	Amount 000	Total Stocks: 298 Total Fixed-Income: 137	Date of Maturity	Value $000	% Net Assets
0	5	Bank For Intl Settlement		38868	2.04
250	8558	Carter Holt Harvey		19423	1.02
28	36	SAP		18487	0.97
1175	8750	Lonrho		18134	0.95
7500	40000	CDL Hotels International		17290	0.91
	415	Freeport-McMor Cp/Gd B Cv Pfd		15926	0.84
80	600	Enterra		13350	0.70
14	59	Bayer		13212	0.69
0	10	Schindler Holding (Br)		13210	0.69
0	1000	Lawter International		13000	0.68
28	279	Greif Brothers Cl A		12115	0.64
50	225	Ito-Yokado		12017	0.63
20	395	Philips (ADR)		11998	0.63
475	7250	Shaw Brothers (Hong Kong)		11728	0.62
75	4075	Industrias Penoles Cl A		11516	0.60
7	195	Saint Joe Paper		11115	0.58
90	385	Dole Food		10684	0.56
-10	215	Randstad Holding		10651	0.56
60	405	Minorco (ADR)		10581	0.56
265	515	Noranda		10409	0.55

Index Allocation
	% of Stocks
S&P 500	10.0
S&P MidCap 400	7.4
U.S. Small Cap	22.8
Foreign	60.2

Composition % 12-31-94
Cash	16.5	Preferreds	3.4
Stocks	59.8	Convertibles	5.1
Bonds	15.3	Other	0.0

Tax Analysis
	Tax-Adj Historical Return %	% Pretax Return
3 Yr Avg	10.72	87.7
5 Yr Avg	8.79	80.6
10 Yr Avg	12.31	69.0
Potential Capital Gain Exposure (% of assets)		9%

Most Similar Funds in MF500
Merrill Lynch Global Alloc B	Weak Fit
Fidelity Puritan	Weak Fit
Fidelity Asset Manager	Weak Fit

Bond Credit Analysis 12-31-94
% of Bonds
US Govt	41	BB	11
AAA	30	B	6
AA	3	Below B	0
A	4	NR/NA	0
BBB	6		

Stock Sector Weightings
	% of Stocks	Relative S&P 500
Utilities	2.0	0.16
Energy	2.8	0.28
Financials	9.6	0.91
Industrial Cyclicals	36.0	2.20
Consumer Durables	9.1	1.46
Consumer Staples	9.0	0.72
Services	19.3	2.37
Retail	5.7	0.98
Health	1.9	0.21
Technology	4.6	0.50

Min Initial Purchase	Closed (Addt'l: $100)
Min IRA Purchase	$1000 (Addt'l: $100)
Min Auto Invest Plan	$100 (Systematic Inv: $100)

Expenses & Fees
Sales Fees	0.00% front
	0.00% deferred
	0.25% 12b-1
Management Fee	1.00% max./0.75% min.
3-,5-,10-yr Expense Projections	$77, $105, $186
Annual Brokerage Cost	0.17%

SoGen Overseas

SoGen Overseas Fund seeks long-term capital appreciation.
The fund normally invests at least 75% of its assets in small- and medium-size foreign companies, domiciled in developed or emerging markets. These companies are characterized by growth potential, financial strength, stability, strong management and fundamental value. The fund does not set prescribed limits on geographical allocation; but, it normally invests in at least three countries. The fund may invest in any type of security, although it concentrates on equity securities. Up to 20% of assets may be invested in debt; these obligations may include debt rated BB or lower.

Manager's Investment Style

Renowned international money manager Jean-Marie Eveillard begins his investment process by first looking at macroeconomic considerations, and then examines valuations. He favors underfollowed and underpriced regions and individual stocks, and holds them for a long time: His time horizon lies in the three- to five-year range. If there aren't any attractive values around, Eveillard isn't skittish about holding cash: Cash in this fund's famous and currently closed sibling, SoGen International, typically hovers between 10% and 30% of assets.

Fund Manager(s)

Jean-Marie Eveillard, since 08-93. Birthdate: 01-40. BA, Lycee Descartes 1957 MBA, Ecole des Hautes Etudes Commerciale 1962

Manager Experience

	Dates Managed	Invest Obj	Std Dev	+/- Index
Jean-Marie Eveillard				
SoGen International	01/79 - 12/94	AA	10.57	2.32
ONE Fund International	04/93 - 12/94	WF	12.44	17.64

Ticker	Load	NAV	Yield	SEC Yield	Assets	Objective
SGOVX	3.75%	11.70	0.4%	N/A	437.9	Foreign Stock

Historical Profile
Return ---
Risk ---
Rating
Not Rated

68% 55%

Investment Style History
Equity
Average % Stocks Held in Portfolio

Growth of $10,000
|||| Value of Fund ($000)
— Value of Index ($000)
S&P 500
▼ Manager Change
▽ Partial Manager Change
► Mgr Unknown After
◄ Mgr Unknown Before

Performance Quartile (Within Objective)

	1983	1984	1985	1986	1987	1988	1989	1990	1991	1992	1993	1994	History
	---	---	---	---	---	---	---	---	---	---	10.92	11.70	NAV
	---	---	---	---	---	---	---	---	---	---	9.20 *	7.79	Total Return %
	---	---	---	---	---	---	---	---	---	---	7.67 *	6.47	+/- S&P 500
	---	---	---	---	---	---	---	---	---	---	---	0.01	+/- MSCI EAFE
	---	---	---	---	---	---	---	---	---	---	0.00	0.48	Income Return %
	---	---	---	---	---	---	---	---	---	---	9.20	7.31	Capital Return %
	---	---	---	---	---	---	---	---	---	---	---	3	Total Rtn % Rank All
	---	---	---	---	---	---	---	---	---	---	---	6	Total Rtn % Rank Obj
	---	---	---	---	---	---	---	---	---	---	0.00	0.05	Income $
	---	---	---	---	---	---	---	---	---	---	0.00	0.02	Capital Gains $
	---	---	---	---	---	---	---	---	---	---	---	1.72	Expense Ratio %
	---	---	---	---	---	---	---	---	---	---	---	-0.23	Income Ratio %
	---	---	---	---	---	---	---	---	---	---	---	---	Turnover Rate %
	---	---	---	---	---	---	---	---	---	---	35.9	437.9	Net Assets ($mil)

Performance 12-31-94

	1st Qtr	2nd Qtr	3rd Qtr	4th Qtr	Total
1987	---	---	---	---	---
1988	---	---	---	---	---
1989	---	---	---	---	---
1990	---	---	---	---	---
1991	---	---	---	---	---
1992	---	---	---	---	---
1993	---	---	---	9.31	9.20 *
1994	5.68	0.26	3.89	-2.08	7.79

Bear Market Performance

Decile Rank (5-year period)

Worst ——————————————— Best

	Worst 3 Mo Period 1985-89	Worst 3 Mo Period 1990-94
SoGen Overseas	---	---
+/- S&P 500	---	---
+/- Best Fit Index :	---	---

Trailing Returns

	Total Return %	+/- S&P 500	+/- MSCI EAFE	% Rank All	% Rank Obj	Growth of $10,000
3 Mo	-2.08	-2.06	-1.06	70	13	9,792
6 Mo	1.73	-3.13	2.66	29	17	10,173
1 Yr	7.79	6.47	0.01	3	6	10,779
3 Yr Avg	---	---	---	---	---	---
5 Yr Avg	---	---	---	---	---	---
10 Yr Avg	---	---	---	---	---	---
15 Yr Avg	---	---	---	---	---	---

Operations

Address and Telephone	1221 Ave of the Americas 8th Fl New York, NY 10020 800-628-0252
Advisor	Societe Generale Asset Management
Subadvisor	None
Distributor	Societe Generale Securities
States Available	All
Report Grade	B-
Income Distrib	Paid Annually
* Date of Inception	08-31-93
Fiscal Year End	March

Risk Analysis

Time Period	Load-Adj Return %	Risk % Rank[1] All	Risk % Rank[1] Obj	Morningstar[2] Return	Morningstar[2] Risk	Morningstar Risk-Adj Rating
1 Yr	3.75					
3 Yr	---	---	---	---	---	---
5 Yr	---	---	---	---	---	---
10 Yr	---	---	---	---	---	---

Average Historical Rating ---

[1] 1 = low, 100 = high   [2] 1.00 = Equity Avg   [3] 1.00 = 90-day T-bill return

Other Measures

			Standard S&P 500	Best Fit
Standard Deviation	---	Alpha	---	---
Mean	---	Beta	---	---
Sharpe Ratio	---	R-Squared	---	---

Investment Style

	Stock Portfolio Avg	Rel MSCI EAFE	Rel Obj	Style
Price/Earnings Ratio	23.7	0.64	0.84	
Price/Cash Flow	11.0	0.70	0.82	
Price/Book Ratio	2.4#	0.92	0.81	
5 Yr Earnings Gr %	0.6#	---	0.15	
Return on Assets %	7.5#	1.64	1.04	
Debt % Total Cap	23.3#	0.68	0.84	
Med Mkt Cap ($mil)	1747	0.15	0.34	

Style V B G Size L M S

figure is based on 50% or less of stocks

Diversification Value for Portfolio Types

Large Cap: Small Cap: Bond: Balanced: Diversified:

Portfolio 09-30-94

Total Stocks: 131
Total Fixed-Income: 34

Share Chg (03-94) 000	Amount 000		Value $000	% Net Assets
1	1	Bank For Intl Settlement ADR	6389	1.75
13	13	Buderus	5426	1.49
150	195	Minorco (ADR)	5094	1.40
215	215	Assid-Man	5083	1.39
-38	23	Bayer	5082	1.39
-6050	2450	Lonrho	5077	1.39
-9	4	Schindler Holding	4962	1.36
205	245	Noranda	4952	1.36
5	6	Legrand	4801	1.32
6800	10750	CDL Hotels International	4647	1.28
60	85	Ito-Yokado	4540	1.25
32	45	Hitachi (ADR)	4376	1.20
685	1876	Carter Holt Harvey	4257	1.17
295	650	Antofagasta Holdings (UK)	3872	1.06
1700	2350	Shaw Brothers (Hong Kong)	3802	1.04
-200	200	Canadian Pacific	3350	0.92
50	75	Carlsberg Cl B	3243	0.89
145	145	Freeport-McMoRan	3190	0.88
-1825	175	Dofasco	3048	0.84
3750	3750	Siderca	2786	0.76

Regional Exposure 12-31-94

% of Stocks

Europe	11	Pacific Rim	16
Japan	8	Other	23
Latin Amer	6		

Composition % 12-31-94

Cash	34.1	Preferreds	3.1
Stocks	55.1	Convertibles	0.0
Bonds	7.8	Other	0.0

Country Exposure 12-31-94

% of Stocks

France	11
Germany	8
Switzerland	6
Japan	6
Canada	5

Total Number of Countries: 29
Hedging Policy: Occasional

Sector Weightings

	% of Stocks	Relative S&P 500
Utilities	3.6	0.40
Energy	3.3	0.81
Financials	5.7	0.30
Industrial Cyclicals	31.8	1.27
Consumer Durables	10.8	1.00
Consumer Staples	10.6	1.53
Services	23.5	2.15
Retail	5.9	1.02
Health	3.8	1.06
Technology	1.0	0.19

Expenses & Fees

Sales Fees	3.75% front
	0.00% deferred
	0.25% 12b-1
Management Fee	0.75% flat fee
3-,5-,10-yr Expense Projections	$90, $127, $233
Annual Brokerage Cost	---

Min Purchases

Min Initial Purchase	$1000 (Addt'l: $100)
Min IRA Purchase	$1000 (Addt'l: $100)
Min Auto Invest Plan	$100 (Systematic Inv: $100)

Tax Analysis

	Tax-Adj Historical Return %	% Pretax Return
3 Yr Avg	---	---
5 Yr Avg	---	---
10 Yr Avg	---	---

Potential Capital Gain Exposure (% of assets)   0%

Most Similar Funds in MF500

Fund lacks three-year record

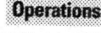 1995 Mutual Fund 500

Sound Shore

	Ticker	Load	NAV	Yield	SEC Yield	Assets	Objective
	SSHFX	None	15.46	1.3%	N/A	56.7	Growth

Sound Shore Fund seeks growth of capital. Income is a secondary consideration.

The fund intends to invest in equity securities selected on the basis of fundamental value. Factors such as price, earnings expectations, earnings and price histories, balance-sheet characteristics, and perceived management skills play a large role in security selection. Changes in economic and political outlooks, as well as individual corporate developments, are also considered. It may invest up to 10% of its assets in the securities of other investment companies.

Manager's Investment Style

Management practices a moderate-value, bottom-up discipline that targets out-of-favor stocks. It looks at a stock's valuation relative to the market, as well as to the issue's own historical price. This approach leads the fund to high-quality contrarian stocks.

Fund Manager(s)

T. Gibbs Kane, Jr. CFA(1977), since 05-85.
Birthdate: 05-47. BS, U. of Pennsylvania 1969
Harry Burn III CFA(1981), since 05-85. Birthdate:
01-44. BA, U. of Virginia 1966 MBA, U. of Virginia 1975

Manager Experience	Dates Managed	Invest Obj	Std Dev	+/- Index
Not available.				

Historical Profile
Return Above Average
Risk Below Average
Rating ★★★★ Above Average

Investment Style History
Equity
Average % Stocks Held in Portfolio

	89%	92%	86%	76%	83%	83%	77%	80%

Growth of $10,000
‖‖ Value of Fund ($000)
— Value of Index ($000) SPMid400
▼ Manager Change
▽ Partial Manager Change
► Mgr Unknown After
◄ Mgr Unknown Before

Performance Quartile (Within Objective)

1983	1984	1985	1986	1987	1988	1989	1990	1991	1992	1993	1994	History
---	---	11.55	13.31	11.58	12.67	13.73	11.77	15.17	16.24	16.50	15.46	NAV
---	---	15.62 *	20.59	-3.71	21.14	22.46	-10.64	32.24	21.17	11.97	0.30	Total Return %
---	---	-4.98 *	1.91	-8.97	4.53	-9.23	-7.53	1.76	13.55	1.91	-1.02	+/- S&P 500
---	---	---	4.50	-6.07	3.20	-6.72	-4.46	-1.96	12.20	0.68	0.37	+/- Wilshire 5000
---	---	0.00	1.78	1.36	1.40	2.52	3.63	2.41	1.11	0.84	1.38	Income Return %
---	---	15.62	18.82	-5.07	19.74	19.94	-14.28	29.83	20.05	11.12	-1.08	Capital Return %
---	---	---	17	83	11	30	86	23	4	51	17	Total Rtn % Rank All
---	---	---	14	83	20	71	84	60	5	48	29	Total Rtn % Rank Obj
---	---	0.00	0.22	0.18	0.18	0.35	0.52	0.29	0.18	0.14	0.22	Income $
---	---	0.00	0.39	1.21	1.18	1.42	0.00	0.10	1.95	1.54	0.87	Capital Gains $
---	---	1.48	1.36	1.40	1.24	1.33	1.30	1.37	1.27	1.25		Expense Ratio %
---	---	2.55	1.06	1.57	2.37	3.55	2.10	1.10	0.88	1.14		Income Ratio %
---	---	---	85	134	91	105	100	88	91	---		Turnover Rate %
---	---	9.6	22.5	23.8	28.6	42.4	28.3	31.8	36.0	58.2	56.7	Net Assets ($mil)

Performance 12-31-94

	1st Qtr	2nd Qtr	3rd Qtr	4th Qtr	Total
1987	19.98	-5.36	5.27	-19.45	-3.71
1988	6.56	5.83	5.08	2.22	21.14
1989	10.34	7.85	6.08	-3.00	22.46
1990	-1.53	4.28	-15.21	2.62	-10.64
1991	16.48	2.48	6.04	4.47	32.24
1992	4.22	0.06	4.83	10.83	21.17
1993	5.97	-0.87	0.71	5.84	11.97
1994	-0.55	-1.04	3.47	-1.51	0.30

Bear Market Performance

Decile Rank (5-year period)

	Worst 3 Mo Period 1985-89	Worst 3 Mo Period 1990-94
Sound Shore	---	-18.53
+/- S&P 500	---	-4.69
+/- Best Fit Index : SPMid400	---	-0.12

Trailing Returns

	Total Return %	+/- S&P 500	+/- Wil 5000	% Rank All	% Rank Obj	Growth of $10,000
3 Mo	-1.51	-1.50	-0.74	57	55	9,849
6 Mo	1.90	-2.96	-2.72	27	72	10,190
1 Yr	0.30	-1.02	0.37	17	29	10,030
3 Yr Avg	10.81	4.55	4.20	11	14	13,607
5 Yr Avg	9.96	1.27	1.15	17	30	16,079
10 Yr Avg	---	---	---	---	---	---
15 Yr Avg	---	---	---	---	---	---

Operations

Address and Telephone	61 Broadway Suite 2770
	New York, NY 10006
	800-551-1980 / 203-629-1980
Advisor	Sound Shore Management
Subadvisor	None
Distributor	Sound Shore Fund
States Available	All
Report Grade	D
Income Distrib	Paid Semiannually
* Date of Inception	05-03-85
Fiscal Year End	December

Min Initial Purchase	$10000 (Addt'l: None)
Min IRA Purchase	$250 (Addt'l: None)
Min Auto Invest Plan	N/A

Expenses & Fees
Sales Fees	0.00% front
	0.00% deferred
	0.00% 12b-1
Management Fee	0.75% flat fee, 0.25%A
3-,5-,10-yr Expense Projections	$40, $70, $153
Annual Brokerage Cost	---

Risk Analysis

Time Period	Load-Adj Return %	Risk % Rank All	Obj	Morningstar Return	Morningstar Risk	Morningstar Risk-Adj Rating
1 Yr	0.30					
3 Yr	10.81	50	5	2.24[3]	0.54	★★★★
5 Yr	9.96	63	14	1.34[3]	0.76	★★★★
10 Yr	---	---	---	---	---	---

Average Historical Rating (80 months) 3.6 ★s

[1] = low, 100 = high [2] 1.00 = Equity Avg [3] 1.00 = 90-day T-bill return

Other Measures

			Standard S&P 500	Best Fit SPMid400
Standard Deviation	7.94	Alpha	4.9	4.5
Mean	10.62	Beta	0.80	0.70
Sharpe Ratio	0.89	R-Squared	63	76

Investment Style

	Stock Portfolio Avg	Relative S&P 500	Style Value Blend Growth
Price/Earnings Ratio	15.6	0.84	
Price/Book Ratio	3.1	0.92	
5 Yr Earnings Gr %	6.9	1.24	
Return on Assets %	5.7	0.76	
Debt % Total Cap	33.1	1.17	
Med Mkt Cap ($mil)	1376	0.11	

Size Large Med Small

Diversification Value for Portfolio Types

Large Cap: Low	Small Cap: Low	Bond: High	Balanced: Low	Diversified: Medium

Portfolio 06-30-94

Share Chg (12-93) 000	Amount 000	Total Stocks: 42 Total Fixed-Income: 2	Value $000	% Net Assets
18	39	Mellon Bank	2194	3.71
8	26	FNMA	2171	3.67
20	42	Philip Morris	2163	3.65
-5	201	ADT	2030	3.43
33	33	MBIA	1893	3.20
25	89	PartnerRe Holdings	1802	3.05
16	76	Allstate	1793	3.03
0	38	Republic New York	1753	2.96
24	102	Vons	1734	2.93
2	20	Loews	1705	2.88
18	45	Tambrands	1654	2.79
8	51	BCE	1651	2.79
27	27	Avon Products	1560	2.64
33	52	Warnaco Group Cl A	1528	2.58
0	88	SafeCard Services	1507	2.55
0	39	SLMA	1386	2.34
74	74	Ogden Projects	1283	2.17
0	38	Stanhome	1254	2.12
-14	34	First Brands	1245	2.10
51	51	CR Bard	1218	2.06
80	80	Lehman Brothers Holdings	1210	2.04
-13	69	Gerber Scientific	1070	1.81
0	39	Dean Foods	1053	1.78
0	78	Interstate Bakeries	975	1.65
7	25	Fred Meyer	909	1.54

Composition % 09-30-94

Cash	6.9	Preferreds	0.0
Stocks	85.3	Convertibles	0.0
Bonds	7.8	Other	0.0

Tax Analysis

	Tax-Adj Historical Return %	% Pretax Return
3 Yr Avg	7.87	70.7
5 Yr Avg	7.73	74.2
10 Yr Avg	---	---
Potential Capital Gain Exposure (% of assets)		-2%

Most Similar Funds in MF500

SteinRoe Special	Fair Fit
Neuberger&Berman Guardian	Fair Fit
Neuberger&Berman Partners	Fair Fit

Index Allocation

	% of Stocks
S&P 500	23.2
S&P MidCap 400	17.9
U.S. Small Cap	46.6
Foreign	12.3

Sector Weightings

	% of Stocks	Relative S&P 500
Utilities	3.3	0.26
Energy	0.0	0.00
Financials	31.3	2.96
Industrial Cyclicals	1.7	0.10
Consumer Durables	7.0	1.12
Consumer Staples	17.8	1.42
Services	25.2	3.09
Retail	6.1	1.05
Health	3.8	0.43
Technology	3.9	0.43

Source Capital

	Ticker	NAV	Mkt Price	Prem/Disc	Yield	Objective
	SOR	$38.52	$37.00	-3.9%	3.7%	Domestic Eq

Source Capital seeks capital appreciation for its common stockholders consistent with current income to meet the dividend on its preferred stock.

The fund invests primarily in common stocks and convertibles. It also uses fixed-income securities that offer attractive yields or appreciation potential. Management concentrates on medium-sized companies with established earnings records, high earnings-growth rates, high returns on invested capital, strong market positions, and low debt-to-equity levels. The fund seeks such characteristics at reasonable prices.

The fund has a 10% annual-payout policy. It pays out $3.60 per share per year based on management's ability to maintain a $36.00 NAV.

The fund is leveraged with cumulative preferred stock.

-3.8	7.2	10.0	13.8	9.4	1.9	1.6	5.0	10.9	15.4	17.4	10.5
-12.4	-6.5	5.4	3.1	-9.5	-7.2	-5.7	-1.7	1.1	2.4	3.3	-3.9

Highest Prem/Disc
Lowest Prem/Disc

Historical Profile

Return Average
Risk Low
Rating ★★★
Neutral

Growth of $10,000
— at NAV ($000)
— at Market Price ($000)

Premium
Discount %

1983	1984	1985	1986	1987	1988	1989	1990	1991	1992	1993	1994	History
32.62	32.88	37.97	38.04	35.16	37.38	41.95	36.94	41.23	42.87	41.85	38.52	NAV
21.95	12.48	27.25	13.20	1.88	16.52	24.01	-3.40	22.17	13.27	6.30	0.65	NAV Total Return %
-0.51	6.21	-4.49	-5.48	-3.38	-0.09	-7.68	-0.28	-8.32	5.66	-3.75	-0.67	+/- S&P 500
-4.14	11.30	-8.33	-3.01	3.92	-4.35	-11.53	1.72	-27.90	1.37	-7.63	4.24	+/- S&P Mid 400
9.65	10.21	6.89	5.87	5.59	5.91	6.36	4.67	5.70	3.24	3.07	3.59	Income Return %
12.31	2.26	20.37	7.33	-3.71	10.61	17.65	-8.07	16.47	10.03	3.23	-2.95	Capital Return %
25	39	31	58	55	27	21	69	40	22	93	12	Total Rtn % Rank All
54	1	53	50	50	46	48	44	77	25	70	27	Total Rtn % Rank Obj
26.16	27.92	30.51	10.96	-12.29	24.30	26.92	-5.78	32.70	17.56	-1.37	-6.08	Market Total Rtn %
-7.2	-0.9	7.0	7.6	-2.1	-2.4	-2.8	1.2	4.7	9.3	11.6	3.1	Avg Prem/Disc %
2.67	3.10	2.40	2.28	2.19	2.07	2.31	1.85	2.04	1.30	1.26	1.44	Income $
0.94	0.50	1.49	2.78	1.56	1.43	1.79	1.75	1.56	2.30	2.34	2.16	Capital Gains $
0.96	0.97	0.97	0.97	0.96	1.00	0.96	0.97	0.97	0.94	0.95	1.01	Expense Ratio %
6.46	6.36	5.57	4.70	4.51	5.07	5.01	5.10	4.22	3.93	3.86	3.41	Income Ratio %
96	67	85	82	76	43	36	43	41	69	74	---	Turnover Rate %
196.7	198.3	227.8	231.4	214.8	275.5	259.6	232.3	263.6	278.4	276.3	275.3	Net Assets ($mil)
54.5	54.5	54.2	54.2	54.2	54.2	54.2	54.2	54.2	54.2	54.2	54.2	Pfd/Debt Leverage ($mil)

Manager's Investment Style

Manager George Michaelis is regarded as one of the best value managers around--and he's available to small investors only through Source Capital. Michaelis blends stocks and bonds--typically in a 60/40 mix--to achieve low risk and respectable returns. His value leaning means the portfolio typically features staid, debt-free blue chips. Two of his several value criteria include consistently achievable ROEs of 20, and the ability to internally finance capital requirements. He employs a strategy that overlooks market whims, focusing instead on the economic value of businesses as the driving force in stock returns.

Fund Manager(s)

George Michaelis. Since 1977. BS'58 U. of California-Los Angeles; MBA'60 Harvard.

Manager Experience

	Dates Managed	Invest Obj	Std Dev	+/- Index
Not available.				

NAV Performance % 12-30-94

	1st Qtr	2nd Qtr	3rd Qtr	4th Qtr	Total
1987	11.87	1.62	3.38	-13.31	1.88
1988	11.03	4.00	-0.54	1.45	16.52
1989	7.68	7.86	6.87	-0.09	24.01
1990	-1.82	4.31	-12.32	7.58	-3.40
1991	11.56	-0.19	2.88	6.65	22.17
1992	3.36	0.73	4.77	3.85	13.27
1993	2.57	-0.66	1.43	2.85	6.30
1994	-2.50	-0.33	3.18	0.39	0.65

Bear Market Performance

Decile Rank (5-year period)

Worst ▬ Best

	Worst 3 Mo Period 1985-89	Worst 3 Mo Period 1990-94
Source Capital	-18.94	-13.17
+/- S&P 500	10.65	0.67

Trailing Returns

	NAV Total Return %	+/- S&P 500	+/- S&P Mid 400	% Rank All	% Rank Obj	Mkt Total Return %
3 Mo	0.39	0.40	2.97	16	20	-9.30
6 Mo	3.58	-1.28	-0.43	12	31	-5.56
1 Yr	0.65	-0.67	4.24	12	27	-6.08
3 Yr Avg	6.62	0.35	-0.50	39	28	2.88
5 Yr Avg	7.42	-1.27	-4.42	61	62	6.37
10 Yr Avg	11.73	-2.65	-4.30	25	46	10.56

Operations

Address and Telephone	11400 W. Olympic Blvd., Ste. 1200 Los Angeles, CA 90064 310-473-0225 / 800-982-4372
Advisor	First Pacific Advisors, Inc.
Subadvisor	N/A
Administrator	N/A
Transfer Agent	Chemical Bank N.A.
Custodian	State Street Bank and Trust Co.
Auditor	Ernst & Young LLP
Legal Counsel	O'Melveny & Myers

Income Distrib Schedule	Paid Quarterly
Management Fee	0.73%
Reinvestment Plan	Yes
Direct Purchase Plan	No
Shares Outstanding	7,145,470
Exchange	NYSE
Date of Inception	10-24-68
Shareholder Report	A

Risk Analysis

	Risk % Rank[1]		Morningstar[2]		Morningstar
	All	Obj	Return	Risk	Risk-Adj Rating
3 Yr	43	9	0.40	0.33	★★★
5 Yr	61	10	0.50	0.44	★★★
10 Yr	51	1	0.57	0.44	★★★
Average Historical Rating (144 months)					4.1 ★s

[1] 1 = Low, 100 = High [2] 1.00 = Equity Avg [3] 1.00 = 90-day T-bill Return

Other Measures

				S&P 500
Standard Deviation	5.89	Alpha		1.30
Mean	6.60	Beta		0.62
Sharpe Ratio	0.52	R-Squared		69

Investment Style

	Stock Portfolio Avg	Relative S&P 500
Price/Earnings Ratio	15.2	0.82
Price/Cash Flow Ratio	13.6	1.18
Price/Book Ratio	3.0	0.88
5 Yr Earnings Gr %	8.7	1.57
Return on Assets %	10.2	1.36
Debt % Total Cap	12.9	0.45
Med Mkt Cap ($mil)	2162	0.17

figure is based on less than 50% of stocks

Style: Value Blend Growth / Size Large Med Small

Index Allocation

	% of Stocks
Dow 30	6.5
S&P 500	47.4
S&P Mid-Cap 400	24.6
US Small-Cap	23.8
Foreign	4.3

Diversification Value for Portfolio Types

Large Cap: Low | Small Cap: Low | Bond: High | Balanced: Low | Diversified: Low

Portfolio 12-31-94

Share Chg (06-94)	Amount	Total Equity: 42 / Total Fixed-Income: 29	Value $000	% Total Invest
27100	202800	Bandag Cl A	10850	3.29
18400	134900	Marsh & McLennan	10691	3.25
0	6700	First Natl Bank of Anchorage	10318	3.13
-27800	173400	Johnson & Johnson	9494	2.88
47600	263200	Lubrizol	8916	2.71
-10300	185500	Loctite	8626	2.62
-6200	158400	Minnesota Mining & Mfg	8455	2.57
---	8000000	US Treasury Note 6.25%	7238	2.20
85600	164000	Walgreen	7175	2.18
---	8550000	Dr Pepper/Seven-Up 0/11.5%	6755	2.05
---	6900000	Plantronics 10%	6590	2.00
500	80500	Pfizer	6219	1.89
0	127900	VF	6219	1.89
18000	186300	Abbott Laboratories	6078	1.85
0	168800	Golden West Financial	5950	1.81
---	2540000	Liebert Cv 8%	5899	1.79
12000	199200	Cedar Fair	5876	1.78
-13400	293650	Mercantile Bankshares (MD)	5800	1.76
---	5972000	Primark 8.75%	5670	1.72
-18300	195300	Devon Group	5615	1.70
16000	137400	EXEL	5427	1.65
---	10655000	United Intl Holdings 0%	5412	1.64
0	305927	Washington Fed S & L (WA)	5335	1.62
0	246000	Expeditors Intl Washington	5258	1.60
0	179400	Hasbro	5247	1.59

Composition % 12-31-94

Cash	7.7	Preferreds	0.0
Stocks	66.4	Convertibles	10.0
Bonds	15.9	Other	0.0
Leverage factor: 1.20			

Tax Analysis

	Tax-Adj Historical Return %	% Pretax Return
3 Yr Avg	3.90	55.9
5 Yr Avg	4.57	57.3
10 Yr Avg	8.35	60.1
Potential Capital Gain Exposure (% of assets)		10

Most Similar Funds in MF500

FPA Perennial	Strong Fit
Delaware A	Fair Fit
Quest for Value A	Fair Fit

Sector Weightings

	% of Stocks	Relative S&P 500
Utilities	2.2	0.18
Energy	0.0	0.00
Financials	14.5	1.37
Industrial Cyclicals	16.8	1.02
Consumer Durables	18.6	3.00
Consumer Staples	8.1	0.65
Services	22.0	2.71
Retail	5.4	0.93
Health	10.6	1.22
Technology	1.8	0.20

Stagecoach Asset Allocation A

	Ticker	Load	NAV	Yield	SEC Yield	Assets	Objective
	SFAAX	4.50%	16.73	4.4%	N/A	897.2	Asset Alloc.

Stagecoach Asset Allocation Fund - Class A seeks long-term total return consistent with reasonable risk.

The fund pursues an asset-allocation strategy, using an investment model to regularly determine the optimum mix of common stocks, U.S. Treasury bonds, and money-market instruments. The equity portion consists of nearly all the stocks in the S&P 500 in approximately the same weighting as in the Index. The fund's bond portion generally maintains an average maturity between 22 and 28 years.

Prior to Jan. 2, 1992, the fund was named Wells Fargo Asset Allocation Fund.

Manager's Investment Style

Management uses a proprietary quantitative model to determine the relative risks and rewards of holding stocks, bonds, and cash. A neutral allocation is 60% stocks, 40% bonds. Dramatic allocation changes over a short period of time aren't out of the ordinary for this fund. The stock portfolio indexes the S&P 500, while the bond portfolio shadows long-term Treasuries.

Fund Manager(s)

Janice L. Deringer, since 11-86. BS, Willamette U. 1983 MBA, U. of California-Berkeley 1988
Ross Sakamoto, since 01-91. BS, U. of California-Berkeley

Manager Experience	Dates Managed	Invest Obj	Std Dev	+/- Index
Janice L. Deringer				
Stagecoach U.S. Gov All A	03/87 - 12/94	GT	5.96	-0.33
Overland Exp Asset All A	04/88 - 12/94	AA	6.48	-3.09

Historical Profile
Return	Above Average
Risk	Below Average
Rating	★★★★ Above Average

Equity average % Stocks Held in Portfolio: 31% 11% 20% --- 27% 29% 52% 48%

Investment Style History

Average % Stocks Held in Portfolio

Growth of $10,000
- |||| Value of Fund ($000)
- — Value of Index ($000) LB L-T
- ▼ Manager Change
- ▽ Partial Manager Change
- ◄ Mgr Unknown After
- ◄ Mgr Unknown Before

Performance Quartile (Within Objective)

	1983	1984	1985	1986	1987	1988	1989	1990	1991	1992	1993	1994	History
	---	---	---	10.07	10.93	11.99	13.42	14.49	17.65	17.90	18.80	16.73	NAV
	---	---	---	0.70 *	8.54	9.70	11.93	7.97	21.81	7.01	14.91	-2.82	Total Return %
	---	---	---	0.49 *	3.28	-6.91	-19.76	11.09	-8.68	-0.61	4.85	-4.14	+/- S&P 500
	---	---	---	---	5.78	1.82	-2.61	-0.97	5.81	-0.24	5.15	0.10	+/- LB Aggregate
	---	---	---	0.00	0.00	0.00	0.00	0.00	0.00	5.21	4.27	4.33	Income Return %
	---	---	---	0.70	8.54	9.70	11.93	7.97	21.81	1.80	10.63	-7.15	Capital Return %
	---	---	---	---	12	64	59	15	42	58	29	41	Total Rtn % Rank All
	---	---	---	---	41	44	73	1	47	45	41	53	Total Rtn % Rank Obj
	---	---	---	0.00	0.00	0.00	0.00	0.00	0.00	0.87	0.77	0.77	Income $
	---	---	---	0.00	0.00	0.00	0.00	0.00	0.00	0.07	0.97	0.76	Capital Gains $
	---	---	---	---	1.04	1.00	1.02	0.96	0.95	0.95	0.86	0.82	Expense Ratio %
	---	---	---	---	6.79	6.23	7.35	6.59	5.88	5.22	4.20	3.84	Income Ratio %
	---	---	---	---	81	94	117	88	25	5	40	---	Turnover Rate %
	---	---	---	---	111.0	172.3	229.3	253.7	367.3	542.4	1048.7	897.2	Net Assets ($mil)

Performance 12-31-94

	1st Qtr	2nd Qtr	3rd Qtr	4th Qtr	Total
1987	6.95	-1.67	-4.15	7.68	8.54
1988	4.30	2.63	0.43	2.04	9.70
1989	2.42	2.77	3.72	2.52	11.93
1990	0.60	2.81	-1.30	5.77	7.97
1991	5.38	-0.13	7.80	7.36	21.81
1992	-3.66	3.19	5.34	2.19	7.01
1993	5.64	3.42	4.44	0.71	14.91
1994	-4.22	-1.63	1.85	1.27	-2.82

Bear Market Performance

Decile Rank (5-year period)

Worst | | | | | | | | | | Best

	Worst 3 Mo Period 1985-89	Worst 3 Mo Period 1990-94
Stagecoach Asset Allocation A	---	-6.96
+/- S&P 500	---	-1.21
+/- Best Fit Index : LB L-T	---	2.43

Trailing Returns

	Total Return %	+/- S&P 500	+/- LB Aggregate	% Rank All	% Rank Obj	Growth of $10,000
3 Mo	1.27	1.28	0.89	5	2	10,127
6 Mo	3.14	-1.72	2.15	20	18	10,314
1 Yr	-2.82	-4.14	0.10	41	53	9,718
3 Yr Avg	6.11	-0.15	1.57	33	39	11,948
5 Yr Avg	9.46	0.77	1.84	20	22	15,715
10 Yr Avg	---	---	---	---	---	---
15 Yr Avg	---	---	---	---	---	---

Operations

Address and Telephone	111 Center Street
	Little Rock, AR 72201
	800-222-8222
Advisor	Wells Fargo Bank
Subadvisor	Wells Fargo Nikko Investment Advisors
Distributor	Stephens
States Available	All
Report Grade	C
Income Distrib	Paid Quarterly
• Date of Inception	11-13-86
Fiscal Year End	December

Risk Analysis

Time Period	Load-Adj Return %	Risk % Rank All [1]	Obj	Morningstar [2] Return	Morningstar Risk	Morningstar Risk-Adj Rating
1 Yr	-7.20					
3 Yr	4.50	55	63	0.27 [3]	0.78	★★★
5 Yr	8.46	43	12	0.93 [3]	0.53	★★★★
10 Yr	---	---	---			

Average Historical Rating (62 months) 4.0 ★s

[1] 1 = low, 100 = high [2] 1.00 = Hybrid Avg [3] 1.00 = 90-day T-bill return

Other Measures
			Standard S&P 500	Best Fit LB L-T
Standard Deviation	6.81	Alpha	0.6	1.0
Mean	6.18	Beta	0.70	0.81
Sharpe Ratio	0.39	R-Squared	67	84

Investment Style

Stocks
	Port Avg	Rel S&P 500
Price/Earnings Ratio	18.1	0.98
Price/Book Ratio	3.3	0.97
5 Yr Earnings Gr %	5.2	0.94
Med Mkt Cap ($mil)	12713	0.98

Style V B G

Bonds
Avg Effective Duration	10.5 Yrs
Avg Effective Maturity	25.0 Yrs
Avg Credit Quality	AAA
Avg Weighted Coupon	8.49%

Maturity S I L

Diversification Value for Portfolio Types

Large Cap: Low	Small Cap: High	Bond: Low	Balanced: Low	Diversified: Low

Portfolio 06-30-94

Share Chg (12-93)000	Amount 000	Total Stocks: 500 Total Fixed-Income: 20	Date of Maturity	Value $000	% Net Assets
	50883	US Treasury Bond 7.25%	05-15-16	48323	4.64
	46000	US Treasury Bond 8%	11-15-21	47509	4.56
	38082	US Treasury Bond 8.75%	05-15-17	42128	4.05
	33525	US Treasury Bond 8.75%	08-15-20	37255	3.58
	27215	US Treasury Bond 8.875%	02-15-19	30523	2.93
	21100	US Treasury Bond 12.5%	08-15-14	30127	2.89
	27500	US Treasury Bond 8.5%	02-15-20	29777	2.86
	28549	US Treasury Bond 8.125%	08-15-19	29691	2.85
	22810	US Treasury Bond 9.875%	11-15-15	27885	2.68
	28700	US Treasury Bond 7.125%	02-15-23	26852	2.58
	20824	US Treasury Bond 9.25%	02-15-16	24097	2.31
	24300	US Treasury Bond 6.25%	08-15-23	20412	1.96
	18100	US Treasury Bond 8.125%	05-15-21	18881	1.81
	16050	US Treasury Bond 8.125%	08-15-21	16782	1.61
	14449	US Treasury Bond 9%	11-15-18	16395	1.57
	15200	US Treasury Bond 7.875%	02-15-21	15428	1.48
	15500	US Treasury Bond 7.25%	08-15-22	14735	1.41
	12250	US Treasury Bond 9.125%	05-15-18	14068	1.35
	13700	US Treasury Bond 7.625%	11-15-22	13610	1.31
92	282	General Electric		13155	1.26

Index Allocation
	% of Stocks
S&P 500	98.8
S&P MidCap 400	0.0
U.S. Small Cap	1.2
Foreign	3.6

Composition % 11-15-94
Cash	0.0	Preferreds	0.0
Stocks	40.0	Convertibles	0.0
Bonds	60.0	Other	0.0

Tax Analysis
	Tax-Adj Historical Return %	% Pretax Return
3 Yr Avg	3.52	56.1
5 Yr Avg	7.85	80.3
10 Yr Avg	---	---
Potential Capital Gain Exposure (% of assets)		-6%

Most Similar Funds in MF500
Vanguard Asset Allocation	Strong Fit
Overland Exp Asset Alloc A	Strong Fit
Vanguard/Wellesley Income	Strong Fit

Bond Credit Analysis 11-15-94
% of Bonds
US Govt	100	BB	0
AAA	0	B	0
AA	0	Below B	0
A	0	NR/NA	0
BBB	0		

Stock Sector Weightings
	% of Stocks	Relative S&P 500
Utilities	13.0	1.05
Energy	10.4	1.03
Financials	11.6	1.10
Industrial Cyclicals	16.4	1.03
Consumer Durables	6.4	1.03
Consumer Staples	11.6	0.93
Services	8.4	1.03
Retail	6.3	1.07
Health	7.9	1.01
Technology	8.1	0.88

Min Initial Purchase	$1000 (Addt'l: $100)
Min IRA Purchase	$250 (Addt'l: $100)
Min Auto Invest Plan	$100 (Systematic Inv: $100)

Expenses & Fees
Sales Fees	4.50% front
	0.00% deferred
	0.30% 12b-1
Management Fee	0.50% max./0.30% min., 0.03%A
3-,5-,10-yr Expense Projections	$71, $91, $147
Annual Brokerage Cost	0.00%

SteinRoe Income

SteinRoe Income Fund seeks current income; capital appreciation and capital preservation are secondary objectives.

The fund normally invests at least 65% of its assets in convertible and nonconvertible bonds and debentures; the balance may be invested in other debt, preferred or common stock, or municipal securities. It maintains at least 60% of its assets in investment-grade debt securities; to a lesser extent, it may hold securities rated as low as C.

Prior to Nov. 6, 1989, the fund was named SteinRoe High-Yield Bonds.

Manager's Investment Style

Management focuses its efforts on improving credit situations. The portfolio thus typically features an above-average stake in below-investment-grade securities that management thinks are poised for upgrades. Management is, however, willing to retreat to higher-quality paper, depending on its economic outlook. The fund has, at times, had a modest position in U.S. dollar-denominated debt. Duration typically hovers around the group average.

Fund Manager(s)

Ann H. Benjamin, since 01-90. Birthdate: 02-58.
Economics, Chatham C. 1980 MBA, Carnegie Mellon U. 1985

Manager Experience

	Dates Managed	Invest Obj	Std Dev	+/- Index
Not available.				

	Ticker	Load	NAV	Yield	SEC Yield	Assets	Objective
	SRHBX	None	9.06	7.5%	8.28%	152.8	Corp General

Historical Profile

Return	High
Risk	Average
Rating	★★★★
	Above Average

Investment Style History
Fixed Income
Income Rtn % Rank Obj

Growth of $10,000

- |||| Value of Fund ($000)
- — Value of Index ($000) LB Corp
- ▼ Manager Change
- ▽ Partial Manager Change
- ◄— Mgr Unknown After
- —◄ Mgr Unknown Before

Performance Quartile (Within Objective)

	1983	1984	1985	1986	1987	1988	1989	1990	1991	1992	1993	1994	History
NAV	---	---	---	9.96	9.37	9.47	9.17	8.85	9.53	9.60	10.14	9.06	NAV
	---	---	---	5.21 *	6.63	11.56	7.11	6.15	17.18	9.10	13.38	-4.06	Total Return %
	---	---	---		3.88	3.68	-7.43	-2.80	1.18	1.86	3.63	-1.14	+/- LB Aggregate
	---	---	---		4.08	2.33	-6.87	-1.01	-1.33	0.41	1.21	-0.13	+/- LB Corporate
	---	---	---	5.61	12.56	10.49	10.27	9.63	9.50	8.37	7.75	6.59	Income Return %
	---	---	---	-0.40	-5.92	1.07	-3.17	-3.49	7.68	0.73	5.63	-10.65	Capital Return %
	---	---	---		17	49	93	32	50	31	37	54	Total Rtn % Rank All
	---	---	---		7	9	89	60	36	16	15	59	Total Rtn % Rank Obj
	---	---	---	0.55	1.21	0.95	0.96	0.85	0.77	0.76	0.71	0.68	Income $
	---	---	---	0.00	0.00	0.00	0.00	0.00	0.00	0.00	0.00	0.00	Capital Gains $
	---	---	---	1.00	0.96	0.91	0.90	0.93	0.95	0.90	0.82	0.82	Expense Ratio %
	---	---	---	10.07	9.90	10.08	9.97	10.02	8.98	8.20	7.62	6.94	Income Ratio %
	---	---	---		153	158	94	90	77	76	39	53	Turnover Rate %
	---	---	---		71.5	94.5	102.5	94.4	88.8	105.9	118.0	161.8	152.8	Net Assets ($mil)

Performance 12-31-94

	1st Qtr	2nd Qtr	3rd Qtr	4th Qtr	Total
1987	3.91	-1.47	-2.95	7.32	6.63
1988	4.82	2.40	2.31	1.59	11.56
1989	1.28	5.50	0.85	-0.61	7.11
1990	-1.34	3.67	-0.25	4.04	6.15
1991	3.31	1.99	5.31	5.61	17.18
1992	-0.12	3.82	5.34	-0.12	9.10
1993	5.31	3.46	3.26	0.78	13.38
1994	-3.37	-1.25	0.82	-0.27	-4.06

Bear Market Performance

Decile Rank (5-year period)

Worst ▬ Best

	Worst 3 Mo Period 1985-89	Worst 3 Mo Period 1990-94
SteinRoe Income	---	-5.68
+/- LB Aggregate	---	-0.75
+/- Best Fit Index : LB Corp	---	0.58

Trailing Returns

	Total Return %	+/- LB Aggregate	+/- LB Corp	% Rank All	% Rank Obj	Growth of $10,000
3 Mo	-0.27	-0.65	-0.71	29	72	9,973
6 Mo	0.54	-0.45	-0.63	46	45	10,054
1 Yr	-4.06	-1.14	-0.13	54	59	9,594
3 Yr Avg	5.87	1.33	0.46	35	12	11,868
5 Yr Avg	8.10	0.47	-0.16	32	18	14,761
10 Yr Avg	---	---	---	---	---	---
15 Yr Avg	---	---	---	---	---	---

Operations

Address and Telephone	P.O. Box 804058
	Chicago, IL 60680
	800-338-2550 / 312-368-7800
Advisor	Stein Roe & Farnham
Subadvisor	None
Distributor	Liberty Securities
States Available	All plus PR,VI,GU
Report Grade	B-
Income Distrib	Paid Monthly
* Date of Inception	03-05-86
Fiscal Year End	June

Min Initial Purchase	$2500 (Addt'l: $100)
Min IRA Purchase	$500 (Addt'l: $50)
Min Auto Invest Plan	$1000 (Systematic Inv: $50)

Expenses & Fees

Sales Fees	
	0.00% front
	0.00% deferred
	0.00% 12b-1
Management Fee	0.65% max./0.60% min.
3-,5-,10-yr Expense Projections	$26, $46, $101

Risk Analysis

Time Period	Load-Adj Return %	Risk % Rank [1] All	Obj	Morningstar [2] Return	Morningstar Risk	Morningstar Risk-Adj Rating
1 Yr	-4.06					
3 Yr	5.87	23	51	0.68 [3]	1.01	★★★★★
5 Yr	8.10	24	44	0.84 [3]	0.99	★★★★
10 Yr	---					

Average Historical Rating (70 months) 3.7 ★s

[1] 1 = low, 100 = high [2] 1.00 = Taxable Avg [3] 1.00 = 90-day T-bill return

Other Measures

	Standard LB Agg	Best Fit LB Corp
Standard Deviation	4.63	Alpha 1.2	0.6
Mean	5.83	Beta 1.11	0.90
Sharpe Ratio	0.50	R-Squared 93	94

Investment Style

Interest-Rate Stance

Avg Effective Duration	5.1 Yrs
Avg Effective Maturity	7.1 Yrs

Quality

Avg Credit Quality	BBB
Avg Weighted Coupon	8.71%
Avg Weighted Price	97.53% of Par

Diversification Value for Portfolio Types

Large Cap: Medium	Small Cap: High	Bond: None	Balanced: Medium	Diversified: Medium

Portfolio 12-31-94

Amount 000	Date of Maturity	Total Stocks: 0 / Total Fixed-Income: 78	Value $000	% Net Assets
10000	04-15-00	US Treasury Note 5.5%	9010	5.89
3000	02-15-01	US Treasury Note 7.75%	2988	1.95
3000	01-15-98	Prime CC Trust 7.55%	2932	1.92
3000	08-31-99	US Treasury Note 6.875%	2887	1.89
3000	06-01-02	North Atlantic Energy 9.05%	2814	1.84
3000	07-15-99	Korea Development Bank 7%	2808	1.84
2000	03-01-04	RBSG Capital 10.125%	2188	1.43
2000	07-01-02	Rexnord 10.75%	2184	1.43
2000	11-15-00	Texas Eastern Transmsn 10.375%	2166	1.42
2000	03-15-11	Occidental Petroleum 11.75%	2162	1.41
2000	05-01-02	MGM Grand Hotel Finance 12%	2160	1.41
2000	05-15-02	Ford Capital BV 9.875%	2129	1.39
2000	12-15-99	Chrysler Financial 9.5%	2084	1.36
2000	08-01-00	CSX 9.5%	2084	1.36
2000	06-15-97	Circus Circus Enterp 10.625%	2078	1.36
2000	05-01-21	Texas Utilities Elec 9.75%	2061	1.35
2000	12-15-06	Govt of New Zealand 8.75%	2052	1.34
2000	09-15-01	Viacom International 10.25%	2040	1.33
2000	09-04-03	Lyondell Petrochemical 9.75%	2037	1.33
2000	06-01-02	Hook-SupeRx 10.125%	2035	1.33
2000	07-15-97	Texas Gas Transmission 9.625%	2034	1.33
2000	04-15-97	NorAm Energy 9.875%	2030	1.33
2000	11-01-01	Rogers Cantel Mobile 10.75%	2025	1.32
2000	05-21-01	Kentucky Power 8.9%	2019	1.32
2000	11-15-04	US Treasury Note 7.875%	2007	1.31

Composition % 12-31-94

Cash	6.3	Preferreds	0.0
Stocks	0.0	Convertibles	0.0
Bonds	93.7	Other	0.0

Tax Analysis

	Tax-Adj Historical Return %	% Pretax Return
3 Yr Avg	3.09	51.2
5 Yr Avg	5.23	60.9
10 Yr Avg	---	---
Potential Capital Gain Exposure (% of assets)		-9%

Most Similar Funds in MF500

Bond Fund of America	Strong Fit
New England Bond Income A	Strong Fit
Columbia Fixed-Income Secs	Strong Fit

Coupon Range

	% of Bonds	Rel Obj
0%	0.0	0.00
0% to 8.5%	42.2	0.67
8.5% to 9.5%	25.4	1.56
9.5% to 11%	28.7	3.10
More than 11%	3.8	0.97
Not applicable	0.0	0.00

Credit Analysis 12-31-94

% of Bonds

US Govt	15	BB	26
AAA	4	B	4
AA	3	Below B	2
A	17	NR/NA	0
BBB	30		

MORNINGSTAR 1995 Mutual Fund 500

SteinRoe Intermediate Municipals

	Ticker	Load	NAV	Yield	SEC Yield	Assets	Objective
	SRIMX	None	10.70	4.8%	5.14%	215.6	Muni Nat

SteinRoe Intermediate Municipals seeks current yield exempt from federal income tax, consistent with the preservation of capital.

The fund normally invests at least 65% of its assets in municipal securities; at least 75% of the fund's municipal securities are high quality. It primarily purchases debt obligations with a maturity of 10 years or less; the dollar-weighted average maturity generally ranges between three and 10 years. No more than 20% of the fund's holdings are subject to the Alternative Minimum Tax.

Manager's Investment Style

High credit quality is this fund's mantra: More than half of its assets are held in AAA rated issues, and there's modest exposure to BBBs. The fund is similarly conservative in its sector allocations: GOs, transportation, and water and waste bonds consume the most assets. Finally, management is willing to pull the trigger on issues or sectors that show signs of weakness. The fund has, however, pushed the envelope of its maturity constraints; in 1993, for example, management kept the fund a bit longer than its average intermediate-term rival.

Fund Manager(s)

Joanne Costopoulos, since 09-91. Birthdate: 1947.
BS, Elmhurst C. 1985

Manager Experience

	Dates Managed	Invest Obj	Std Dev	+/- Index

Not available.

Historical Profile
Return	Average
Risk	Below Average
Rating	★★★
	Neutral

Investment Style History
Fixed Income
Income Rtn % Rank Obj

	63	90	88	86	93	87	83	66

Growth of $10,000
- Value of Fund ($000)
- Value of Index ($000) LB Muni
▼ Manager Change
▽ Partial Manager Change
► Mgr Unknown After
◄ Mgr Unknown Before

Performance Quartile (Within Objective)

1983	1984	1985	1986	1987	1988	1989	1990	1991	1992	1993	1994	History
---	---	10.14	10.77	10.37	10.39	10.55	10.65	10.99	11.13	11.62	10.70	NAV
---	---	1.40 *	12.11	3.15	6.10	8.14	7.51	10.67	7.63	10.91	-3.51	Total Return %
---	---	---	-3.14	0.40	-1.78	-6.40	-1.43	-5.33	0.39	1.16	-0.59	+/- LB Aggregate
---	---	---	-7.21	1.65	-4.06	-2.65	0.21	-1.47	-1.19	-1.37	2.10	+/- LB Muni
---	---	0.00	5.90	6.76	5.91	6.27	6.24	5.83	5.23	4.78	4.41	Income Return %
---	---	1.40	6.21	-3.60	0.19	1.87	1.27	4.84	2.40	6.13	-7.92	Capital Return %
---	---	---	73	34	88	90	17	87	50	60	48	Total Rtn % Rank All
---	---	---	85	9	90	80	4	73	73	65	27	Total Rtn % Rank Obj
---	---	0.00	0.57	0.71	0.60	0.63	0.63	0.59	0.55	0.52	0.52	Income $
---	---	0.00	0.00	0.01	0.00	0.03	0.03	0.17	0.12	0.18	0.00	Capital Gains $
---	---	0.80	0.80	0.80	0.80	0.80	0.80	0.80	0.79	0.72	0.71	Expense Ratio %
---	---	5.82	5.45	5.47	5.66	5.96	5.96	5.79	5.23	4.79	4.63	Income Ratio %
---	---	---	10	49	22	83	141	96	109	96	55	Turnover Rate %
---	---	23.0	104.7	96.1	91.2	96.7	104.5	148.9	201.6	258.5	215.6	Net Assets ($mil)

Performance 12-31-94

	1st Qtr	2nd Qtr	3rd Qtr	4th Qtr	Total
1987	1.96	-2.26	-1.43	5.01	3.15
1988	2.12	1.14	1.36	1.35	6.10
1989	0.18	3.81	0.73	3.23	8.14
1990	0.37	2.40	0.74	3.84	7.51
1991	1.82	1.59	3.17	3.70	10.67
1992	-0.45	3.58	2.32	2.01	7.63
1993	3.52	2.66	3.06	1.27	10.91
1994	-4.36	1.19	0.48	-0.77	-3.51

Bear Market Performance

Decile Rank (5-year period)

Worst — Best

	Worst 3 Mo Period 1985-89	Worst 3 Mo Period 1990-94
SteinRoe Intermediate Municip	---	-4.53
+/- LB Aggregate	---	0.40
+/- Best Fit Index : LB Muni	---	1.23

Trailing Returns

	Total Return %	+/- LB Aggregate	+/- LB Muni	% Rank All	% Rank Obj	Growth of $10,000
3 Mo	-0.77	-1.15	0.67	40	21	9,923
6 Mo	-0.29	-1.28	0.95	62	25	9,971
1 Yr	-3.51	-0.59	2.10	48	27	9,649
3 Yr Avg	4.83	0.28	-0.04	52	38	11,519
5 Yr Avg	6.51	-1.12	-0.27	63	31	13,705
10 Yr Avg	---	---	---	---	---	---
15 Yr Avg	---	---	---	---	---	---

Operations

Address and Telephone	P.O. Box 804058
	Chicago, IL 60680
	800-338-2550 / 312-368-7800
Advisor	Stein Roe & Farnham
Subadvisor	None
Distributor	Liberty Securities
States Available	All plus PR,VI,GU
Report Grade	B
Income Distrib	Paid Monthly
* Date of Inception	10-09-85
Fiscal Year End	June

Min Initial Purchase	$2500 (Addt'l: $100)
Min IRA Purchase	N/A
Min Auto Invest Plan	$1000 (Systematic Inv: $50)

Expenses & Fees
Sales Fees	0.00% front
	0.00% deferred
	0.00% 12b-1
Management Fee	0.60% max./0.50% min.
3-,5-,10-yr Expense Projections	$23, $40, $89

Risk Analysis

Time Period	Load-Adj Return %	Risk % Rank All	Risk % Rank Obj	Morningstar Return	Morningstar Risk	Morningstar Risk-Adj Rating
1 Yr	-3.51					
3 Yr	4.83	18	31	1.07	0.84	★★★★
5 Yr	6.51	13	33	0.97	0.85	★★★
10 Yr	---	---	---	---	---	

Average Historical Rating (75 months) 3.1 ★s

[1] 1 = low, 100 = high [2] 1.00 = Muni Avg [3] 1.00 = 90-day T-bill return

Other Measures
				Standard LB Agg	Best Fit LB Muni
Standard Deviation	4.80	Alpha		0.4	0.1
Mean	4.84	Beta		0.89	0.86
Sharpe Ratio	0.27	R-Squared		55	96

Investment Style

Interest-Rate Stance
Avg Effective Maturity 8.7 Yrs

Quality
Avg Credit Quality AA
Avg Weighted Coupon 6.72%
Avg Weighted Price 102.66% of Par

Diversification Value for Portfolio Types

Large Cap: Medium	Small Cap: High	Bond: Low	Balanced: Medium	Diversified: High

Portfolio 12-30-94

Amount 000	Date of Maturity	Total Stocks: 0 Total Fixed-Income: 123	Value $000	% Net Assets
5000	07-01-12	NY Dorm City Univ Sys 8.125%	5379	2.50
5000	11-15-14	NY Envir Fac Wtr Poll Cntrl Fund 6.3%	5131	2.38
3700	10-01-13	OR Morrow Port DMD	3700	1.72
3600	01-01-05	NC Muni Pwr #1 Catawba Elec 6%	3518	1.63
3700	12-01-03	IL Chicago GO Pub Bldg Com 5.25%	3453	1.60
2655	07-01-14	IN Toll Rd Fin 9%	3336	1.55
3000	06-30-98	AK North Slope GO 8.35%	3241	1.50
3410	12-01-11	MA Wtr Resource 6%	3206	1.49
3000	05-15-01	TX San Antonio Wtr Sys 6%	3031	1.41
3000	10-01-22	LA St Charles Poll Cntrl DMD	3000	1.39
2500	09-01-03	CA Los Angeles Dept Wtr/Pwr Elec 9%	2982	1.38
2750	10-01-08	FL Orlando Aviation Arpt Fac 8.25%	2939	1.36
3000	08-01-07	CA San Jose Redev Merged Area Tax 6%	2937	1.36
3000	10-01-03	OH Bldg 5.85%	2884	1.34
2750	01-01-10	TN Nashville/Davidson Metro Govt 6.5%	2783	1.29
2540	12-01-00	WA Snohomish GO Sch Dist #2 7.25%	2727	1.27
2700	04-01-20	FL St Lucie Poll Cntrl Pwr/Lt 6.5%	2700	1.25
2580	11-15-02	AR Beaver Wtr Dist 5.2%	2613	1.21
2500	11-01-16	CA Oakland Port 7.6%	2576	1.19
2500	07-01-02	AZ Pima GO 6.3%	2575	1.19

Credit Analysis % of Bonds 12-31-94
US Govt	0	BB	0
AAA	57	B	0
AA	16	Below B	0
A	24	NR/NA	0
BBB	4		

Composition % of Assets 12-31-94
Cash	8.3	Preferreds	0.0
Stocks	0.0	Convertibles	0.0
Bonds	91.7	Other	0.0

Tax Analysis
	Tax-Adj Historical Return %	% Pretax Return
3 Yr Avg	4.57	94.4
5 Yr Avg	6.24	95.4
10 Yr Avg	---	---
Potential Capital Gain Exposure (% of assets)	-1%	

Most Similar Funds in MF500
USAA Tax-Exempt Int-Term	Strong Fit
Dreyfus Intermediate Muni	Strong Fit
Scudder Medium-Term T-F	Strong Fit

Coupon Range
	% Bonds	Rel Obj
0%	0.0	0.00
0% to 6.8%	66.5	1.10
6.8% to 7.5%	15.4	0.99
7.5% to 8.3%	5.6	0.64
More than 8.3%	9.1	1.03
Not applicable	3.4	0.88

Sector Weightings
	% Bonds	Rel Obj
General Obl	28.62	1.36
Utilities	7.21	0.58
Health	7.28	0.55
Water/Waste	14.81	2.32
Housing	1.61	0.22
Education	8.32	1.30
Transportation	12.49	1.23
COP/Lease	0.90	0.28
Private	10.23	0.88
Misc Revenue	3.20	0.64
Demand	5.33	2.17

Top 5 States % of Bonds
TX	9.44	AZ	7.13
IL	8.99	CA	7.08
NY	7.23		

SteinRoe Managed Municipals

	Ticker	Load	NAV	Yield	SEC Yield	Assets	Objective
	SRMMX	None	8.36	5.8%	5.83%	604.7	Muni Nat

SteinRoe Managed Municipals seeks current income exempt from federal income tax, consistent with the preservation of capital.

The fund invests primarily in a diversified portfolio of long-term municipal securities. At least 75% of these municipal securities have a high-quality credit rating or are backed by the U.S. government. No more than 20% of assets may be invested in bonds subject to the Alternative Minimum Tax.

The fund was formerly named SteinRoe Tax-Exempt Bond Fund.

Manager's Investment Style

Credit quality is management's top concern; it typically favors the upper tiers of investment grade, and largely shuns BBBs. Management doesn't go out on an interest-rate limb, either: Duration is typically equal to or less than the average muni-bond fund.

Fund Manager(s)

M. Jane McCart, since 09-91. Birthdate: 10-55.
BS, Lawrence Technological University 1983

Manager Experience	Dates Managed	Invest Obj	Std Dev	+/- Index
M. Jane McCart				
SteinRoe Interm Munis	10/85 - 09/91	MN	4.09	-3.31

Historical Profile

Return	Above Average
Risk	Above Average
Rating	★★★★ Above Average

	1983	1984	1985	1986	1987	1988	1989	1990	1991	1992	1993	1994	History
	7.71	7.89	8.93	9.22	8.50	8.76	8.80	8.76	9.01	9.04	9.36	8.36	NAV
	10.75	11.29	23.43	23.35	2.08	10.88	10.60	7.00	13.76	8.29	11.08	-5.55	Total Return %
	2.38	-3.86	1.31	8.10	-0.68	3.00	-3.94	-1.94	-2.24	1.05	1.33	-2.63	+/- LB Aggregate
	2.70	0.74	3.41	4.03	0.58	0.72	-0.19	-0.30	1.62	-0.53	-1.20	0.05	+/- LB Muni
	8.77	8.96	9.83	9.17	8.61	7.47	7.18	6.87	8.52	6.21	5.61	5.13	Income Return %
	1.98	2.33	13.60	14.18	-6.53	3.41	3.42	0.13	5.24	2.08	5.47	-10.68	Capital Return %
	76	20	52	11	54	54	67	64	64	42	59	69	Total Rtn % Rank All
	33	6	4	1	19	51	20	19	6	57	63	51	Total Rtn % Rank Obj
	0.65	0.64	0.69	0.78	0.77	0.61	0.60	0.58	0.71	0.54	0.49	0.49	Income $
	0.00	0.00	0.03	0.92	0.14	0.03	0.25	0.05	0.20	0.15	0.17	0.00	Capital Gains $
	0.65	0.64	0.65	0.65	0.65	0.65	0.65	0.66	0.66	0.64	0.64	0.65	Expense Ratio %
	8.15	8.74	8.11	7.04	6.99	7.03	7.00	6.66	6.39	6.17	5.65	5.45	Income Ratio %
	114	190	113	92	113	28	102	95	203	94	63	36	Turnover Rate %
	214.9	242.8	357.2	524.0	458.2	475.1	553.8	613.9	713.0	741.5	781.4	604.7	Net Assets ($mil)

Investment Style History
Fixed Income
Income Rtn % Rank Obj

| 2 | 54 | 49 | 48 | 3 | 48 | 53 | 26 |

Growth of $10,000
- |||| Value of Fund ($000)
- — Value of Index ($000) LB Muni
- ▼ Manager Change
- ▽ Partial Manager Change
- ► Mgr Unknown After
- ◄ Mgr Unknown Before

Performance Quartile (Within Objective)

Performance 12-31-94

	1st Qtr	2nd Qtr	3rd Qtr	4th Qtr	Total
1987	2.83	-4.85	-2.95	7.50	2.08
1988	2.40	2.24	2.95	2.87	10.88
1989	0.18	6.22	-0.34	4.29	10.60
1990	-0.12	2.28	0.37	4.36	7.00
1991	1.81	2.16	3.63	5.55	13.76
1992	-0.11	4.20	2.13	1.87	8.29
1993	3.72	2.67	3.17	1.10	11.08
1994	-5.38	0.85	0.41	-1.42	-5.55

Bear Market Performance
Decile Rank (5-year period)

	Worst 3 Mo Period 1985-89	Worst 3 Mo Period 1990-94
SteinRoe Managed Municipals	-7.45	-5.91
+/- LB Aggregate	-3.90	-0.98
+/- Best Fit Index : LB Muni	-0.96	-0.15

Trailing Returns

	Total Return %	+/- LB Aggregate	+/- LB Muni	% Rank All	Obj	Growth of $10,000
3 Mo	-1.42	-1.80	0.02	55	54	9,858
6 Mo	-1.02	-2.01	0.23	74	55	9,898
1 Yr	-5.55	-2.63	0.05	69	51	9,445
3 Yr Avg	4.34	-0.20	-0.52	62	59	11,361
5 Yr Avg	6.70	-0.93	-0.07	58	23	13,829
10 Yr Avg	10.18	0.23	0.75	56	2	26,357
15 Yr Avg	9.13	-1.67	0.66	86	10	37,104

Operations

Address and Telephone	P.O. Box 804058 Chicago, IL 60680 800-338-2550 / 312-368-7800
Advisor	Stein Roe & Farnham
Subadvisor	None
Distributor	Liberty Securities
States Available	All plus PR,VI,GU
Report Grade	B
Income Distrib	Paid Monthly
Date of Inception	02-23-77
Fiscal Year End	June

Min Initial Purchase	$2500 (Addt'l: $100)
Min IRA Purchase	N/A
Min Auto Invest Plan	$1000 (Systematic Inv: $50)

Expenses & Fees
Sales Fees	0.00% front
	0.00% deferred
	0.00% 12b-1
Management Fee	0.60% max./0.45% min.
3-,5-,10-yr Expense Projections	$20, $36, $80

Risk Analysis

Time Period	Load-Adj Return %	Risk % Rank All	Obj	Morningstar Return	Morningstar Risk	Morningstar Risk-Adj Rating
1 Yr	-5.55					
3 Yr	4.34	31	50	1.08	1.03	★★★
5 Yr	6.70	24	54	1.16	1.05	★★★
10 Yr	10.18	29	88	1.38	1.25	★★★★
Average Historical Rating (109 months)				3.0 ★s		

[1] = low, 100 = high   [2] 1.00 = Muni Avg   [3] 1.00 = 90-day T-bill return

Other Measures		Standard LB Agg	Best Fit LB Muni
Standard Deviation	5.70	Alpha	-0.2	-0.5
Mean	4.42	Beta	1.06	1.02
Sharpe Ratio	0.16	R-Squared	56	95

Investment Style

Interest-Rate Stance
Avg Effective Maturity   16.7 Yrs

Quality
Avg Credit Quality   AA
Avg Weighted Coupon   6.96%
Avg Weighted Price   98.17% of Par

Diversification Value for Portfolio Types

Large Cap: Medium	Small Cap: High	Bond: Low	Balanced: Medium	Diversified: High

Portfolio 12-30-94

Total Stocks: 0
Total Fixed-Income: 133

Amount 000	Date of Maturity		Value $000	% Net Assets
25000	12-01-16	TX GO Vet 8.3%	27182	4.40
16600	06-01-10	IL Metro Fair/Expo Dedicated Tax 8%	17564	2.84
15000	06-01-26	IL Hsg Dev Multi-Fam 8%	15168	2.45
14100	01-01-18	GA Muni Elec Pwr 6.6%	13629	2.20
13700	01-01-14	GA Fulton Wtr/Swr 6.375%	13512	2.19
12840	01-01-19	NY New York City Indl Dev Spcl Fac 6%	11301	1.83
10000	07-01-11	TN Hsg Dev Homeownshp Prog 7.3%	10050	1.63
10950	11-01-16	IN Transp Fin Aircraft Maint Fac 6.25%	10012	1.62
9000	05-01-09	GA Cartersville Dev Wtr/Wastewtr 7.375%	9584	1.55
10000	06-15-12	IL Sales Tax 6%	9300	1.50
9825	03-01-16	MA GO Bay Transp 6.2%	9217	1.49
8715	01-01-12	NY Triborough Bridge/Tunnel Genl 6.625%	8797	1.42
8000	11-01-20	KY Trimble Poll Cntrl Gas/Elec 7.625%	8425	1.36
8795	10-01-03	IN Michigan City Poll Cntrl Pub Svc 5.7%	8263	1.34
8250	10-01-08	WA Longview Solid Wst Disp Port 6.875%	8225	1.33
8285	01-01-17	IN Indianapolis GO Local Pub Impr 6.7%	7969	1.29
7260	11-01-15	MI Hosp Fin St Mary Daughter Charity 10%	7690	1.24
7825	08-15-24	TX Hurst/Euless/Bedford GO ISD 6.5%	7565	1.22
7500	01-01-11	IL Toll Hwy 6.3%	7178	1.16
7365	07-01-24	MA Hlth/Educ Fac Brigham/Women's 6.75%	7004	1.13

Credit Analysis % of Bonds 12-31-94

US Govt	0	BB	0
AAA	34	B	0
AA	37	Below B	0
A	26	NR/NA	1
BBB	2		

Composition % of Assets 12-31-94

Cash	3.8	Preferreds	0.0
Stocks	0.0	Convertibles	0.0
Bonds	96.2	Other	0.0

Tax Analysis

	Tax-Adj Historical Return %	% Pretax Return
3 Yr Avg	4.01	92.0
5 Yr Avg	6.33	93.7
10 Yr Avg	9.62	92.0
Potential Capital Gain Exposure (% of assets)		-2%

Most Similar Funds in MF500

Smith Barney T-E IncB	Strong Fit
Dreyfus Muni Bond	Strong Fit
USAA Tax-Exempt Long-Term	Strong Fit

Coupon Range

	% Bonds	Rel Obj
0%	3.9	1.57
0% to 6.8%	52.1	0.86
6.8% to 7.5%	11.0	0.71
7.5% to 8.3%	21.3	2.40
More than 8.3%	10.8	1.23
Not applicable	0.8	0.20

Sector Weightings

	% Bonds	Rel Obj
General Obl	21.26	1.01
Utilities	12.22	0.98
Health	6.15	0.47
Water/Waste	10.54	1.65
Housing	14.44	1.97
Education	3.13	0.49
Transportation	13.08	1.28
COP/Lease	0.61	0.19
Private	16.01	1.37
Misc Revenue	2.55	0.51
Demand	0.00	0.00

Top 5 States % of Bonds

TX	12.11	NY	8.17
IL	11.16	MA	6.30
GA	10.35		

Morningstar   1995 Mutual Fund 500

SteinRoe Prime Equities

	Ticker	Load	NAV	Yield	SEC Yield	Assets	Objective
	SRPEX	None	13.78	1.3%	N/A	121.5	Growth/Inc.

SteinRoe Prime Equities seeks growth of capital.

The fund invests at least 65% of its assets in companies with market capitalizations in excess of $1 billion. It believes that stock prices of such companies are less volatile than smaller-company issues because of well-reputed management, broader and more-diversified product lines, better resources, and easier access to credit.

On June 29, 1990, SteinRoe Growth and Income Fund merge into this fund. On Sept. 30, 1992, Allegro Growth Fund merged into this fund.

Historical Profile

Return	Above Average
Risk	Below Average
Rating	★★★★
	Above Average

Manager's Investment Style

A new management team took control of the fund in August. It plans to continue the same bottom-up, growth-oriented approach practiced by previous manager Ralph Segall. SteinRoe, as a firm, usually favors strong-growing stocks with reasonable P/Es. Segall, however, surrounded a core of classic growth stocks with undervalued restructuring plays, financials, and cyclicals.

Fund Manager(s)

Robert A. Christensen, since 08-94. Birthdate: 10-33. BA, Vanderbilt U. 1955 MBA, Harvard 1962
Millie Adams Hurwitz, since 08-94. Birthdate: 12-62. BA, Northwestern U. 1985 MM, Northwestern U. 1989

Manager Experience	Dates Managed	Invest Obj	Std Dev	+/- Index
Robert A. Christensen				
SteinRoe Total Return	01/81 - 12/94	EI	10.98	-3.38
Liberty Financial Util	10/91 - 12/94	SU	7.31	-1.10

Investment Style History
Equity
Average % Stocks Held in Portfolio

78%	88%	86%	83%	84%	89%	87%	89%	

Growth of $10,000

|||| Value of Fund ($000)
— Value of Index ($000) SPMid400
▼ Manager Change
▽ Partial Manager Change
► Mgr Unknown After
◄ Mgr Unknown Before

Performance Quartile (Within Objective)

	1983	1984	1985	1986	1987	1988	1989	1990	1991	1992	1993	1994	History
NAV	---	---	---	---	8.33	8.89	11.39	10.54	13.32	13.71	14.58	13.78	NAV
Total Return %	---	---	---	---	-15.91 *	9.02	31.00	-1.72	32.42	10.01	12.86	-0.14	Total Return %
+/- S&P 500	---	---	---	---	-0.13 *	-7.59	-0.69	1.40	1.94	2.39	2.80	-1.46	+/- S&P 500
+/- Wilshire 5000	---	---	---	---	---	-8.93	1.82	4.46	-1.79	1.04	1.58	-0.07	+/- Wilshire 5000
Income Return %	---	---	---	---	0.79	2.29	2.88	2.61	2.15	1.27	1.15	1.28	Income Return %
Capital Return %	---	---	---	---	-16.70	6.72	28.12	-4.33	30.27	8.73	11.70	-1.42	Capital Return %
Total Rtn % Rank All	---	---	---	---	---	68	12	61	23	22	42	20	Total Rtn % Rank All
Total Rtn % Rank Obj	---	---	---	---	---	84	15	29	23	29	36	42	Total Rtn % Rank Obj
Income $	---	---	---	---	0.08	0.19	0.23	0.29	0.23	0.17	0.16	0.18	Income $
Capital Gains $	---	---	---	---	0.00	0.00	0.00	0.36	0.35	0.76	0.71	0.59	Capital Gains $
Expense Ratio %	---	---	---	---	1.91	1.47	1.24	1.08	1.00	0.97	0.88	0.90	Expense Ratio %
Income Ratio %	---	---	---	---	1.43	2.03	2.28	2.40	2.27	1.46	1.23	1.18	Income Ratio %
Turnover Rate %	---	---	---	---	---	105	63	51	48	40	50	85	Turnover Rate %
Net Assets ($mil)	---	---	---	---	33.9	23.7	33.3	46.7	62.5	77.1	108.7	121.5	Net Assets ($mil)

Performance 12-31-94

	1st Qtr	2nd Qtr	3rd Qtr	4th Qtr	Total
1987	---	3.98	3.34	-20.07	-15.91 *
1988	1.32	6.20	0.12	1.20	9.02
1989	8.22	8.89	9.54	1.49	31.00
1990	-2.89	9.31	-12.06	5.27	-1.72
1991	11.59	-1.38	7.13	12.31	32.42
1992	-1.36	-1.15	4.11	8.37	10.01
1993	3.58	-0.35	5.47	3.67	12.86
1994	-3.23	0.28	3.41	-0.49	-0.14

Bear Market Performance

Decile Rank (5-year period)

Worst — Best

	Worst 3 Mo Period 1985-89	Worst 3 Mo Period 1990-94
SteinRoe Prime Equities	---	-12.97
+/- S&P 500	---	0.87
+/- Best Fit Index : SPMid400	---	5.45

Trailing Returns

	Total Return %	+/- S&P 500	+/- Wil 5000	% Rank All	% Rank Obj	Growth of $10,000
3 Mo	-0.49	-0.47	0.28	34	32	9,951
6 Mo	2.90	-1.96	-1.72	21	45	10,290
1 Yr	-0.14	-1.46	-0.07	20	42	9,986
3 Yr Avg	7.43	1.16	0.81	24	26	12,398
5 Yr Avg	10.04	1.35	1.22	17	13	16,135
10 Yr Avg	---	---	---	---	---	---
15 Yr Avg	---	---	---	---	---	---

Operations

Address and Telephone	P.O. Box 804058
	Chicago, IL 60680
	800-338-2550 / 312-368-7800
Advisor	Stein Roe & Farnham
Subadvisor	None
Distributor	Liberty Securities
States Available	All plus PR,VI,GU
Report Grade	B-
Income Distrib	Paid Quarterly
* Date of Inception	03-23-87
Fiscal Year End	September

Min Initial Purchase	$2500 (Addt'l: $100)
Min IRA Purchase	$500 (Addt'l: $50)
Min Auto Invest Plan	$1000 (Systematic Inv: $50)

Expenses & Fees

Sales Fees	0.00% front
	0.00% deferred
	0.00% 12b-1
Management Fee	0.60% max./0.50% min.
3-,5-,10-yr Expense Projections	$28, $49, $108
Annual Brokerage Cost	0.16%

Risk Analysis

Time Period	Load-Adj Return %	Risk % Rank [1] All	Risk % Rank [1] Obj	Morningstar [2] Return	Morningstar [2] Risk	Morningstar Risk-Adj Rating
1 Yr	-0.14	---	---	---	---	---
3 Yr	7.43	59	26	1.15 [3]	0.65	★★★★
5 Yr	10.04	59	21	1.36 [3]	0.69	★★★★
10 Yr	---	---	---	---	---	---
Average Historical Rating (58 months)					3.9	★s

[1] 1 = low, 100 = high [2] 1.00 = Equity Avg [3] 1.00 = 90-day T-bill return

Other Measures

				Standard S&P 500	Best Fit SPMid400
Standard Deviation	7.32	Alpha		1.7	1.4
Mean	7.45	Beta		0.79	0.67
Sharpe Ratio	0.54	R-Squared		73	81

Investment Style

	Stock Portfolio Avg	Relative S&P 500
Price/Earnings Ratio	22.0	1.19
Price/Book Ratio	3.4	1.00
5 Yr Earnings Gr %	8.4	1.51
Return on Assets %	8.0	1.07
Debt % Total Cap	22.2	0.79
Med Mkt Cap ($mil)	5033	0.39

Style
Value Blend Growth
Size Large Med Small

Diversification Value for Portfolio Types

Large Cap: Low	Small Cap: Low	Bond: High	Balanced: Low	Diversified: Low

Portfolio 12-30-94

Total Stocks: 60
Total Fixed-Income: 2

Share Chg (09-94) 000	Amount 000		Value $000	% Net Assets
0	47	First Financial Management	2896	2.38
0	93	Enron	2821	2.32
0	1	Roche Holding (Div Cert)	2421	1.99
0	30	British Petroleum (ADR)	2414	1.99
0	38	Alco Standard	2385	1.96
-11	39	Microsoft	2384	1.96
58	58	Viacom Cl B	2364	1.95
0	80	AirTouch Communications	2330	1.92
0	71	Abbott Laboratories	2300	1.89
6	44	General Electric	2244	1.85
7	72	Equity Residential Ppty Tr	2160	1.78
0	54	General Motors Cl E	2079	1.71
0	35	Amoco	2069	1.70
4	64	Interpublic Group	2056	1.69
-3	27	NIKE Cl B	2015	1.66
3	29	First Interstate Bancorp	1961	1.61
2	35	Tribune	1916	1.58
-17	83	Perceptron	1909	1.57
-3	25	Gillette	1891	1.56
0	100	Camco International	1888	1.55
56	56	Goodyear Tire & Rubber	1883	1.55
0	30	Emerson Electric	1875	1.54
0	100	Petroleum Geo-Services (ADR)	1863	1.53
95	95	National Semiconductor	1853	1.52
0	118	Comcast Special Cl A	1851	1.52

Composition % 12-31-94

Cash	13.6	Preferreds	1.2
Stocks	84.0	Convertibles	1.2
Bonds	0.0	Other	0.0

Tax Analysis

	Tax-Adj Historical Return %	% Pretax Return
3 Yr Avg	5.57	73.7
5 Yr Avg	8.20	78.7
10 Yr Avg	---	---
Potential Capital Gain Exposure (% of assets)		15%

Most Similar Funds in MF500

Quantitative Grth & Inc Ord	Fair Fit
SteinRoe Special	Fair Fit
Massachusetts Inv A	Fair Fit

Index Allocation

	% of Stocks
S&P 500	55.2
S&P MidCap 400	8.4
U.S. Small Cap	20.9
Foreign	15.6

Sector Weightings

	% of Stocks	Relative S&P 500
Utilities	4.7	0.38
Energy	16.0	1.58
Financials	14.0	1.33
Industrial Cyclicals	11.7	0.71
Consumer Durables	5.6	0.90
Consumer Staples	3.1	0.25
Services	15.3	1.88
Retail	5.0	0.86
Health	10.7	1.23
Technology	13.8	1.51

SteinRoe Special

Ticker	Load	NAV	Yield	SEC Yield	Assets	Objective
SRSPX	None	21.72	0.6%	N/A	1167.7	Growth

SteinRoe Special Fund seeks maximum capital growth.

The fund invests primarily in common stocks, and favors securities of companies expected to benefit from special factors or trends. These may include established companies, small companies, new issues, securities with limited marketability, or securities of companies with managerial changes, new technology, new products or services, or changes in demand. The fund may invest up to 35% of its assets in debt securities, and up to 25% of its assets in foreign securities.

Historical Profile
Return	Above Average
Risk	Average
Rating	★★★★ Above Average

Investment Style History: Equity
Average % Stocks Held in Portfolio: 86% 85% 84% 76% 83% 87% 84% 90%

Growth of $10,000
- |||| Value of Fund ($000)
- — Value of Index ($000) SPMid400
- ▼ Manager Change
- ▽ Partial Manager Change
- ►◄ Mgr Unknown After / Mgr Unknown Before

Performance Quartile (Within Objective)

1983	1984	1985	1986	1987	1988	1989	1990	1991	1992	1993	1994	History
17.73	14.88	18.41	16.95	12.83	15.14	18.31	15.58	20.16	21.63	24.00	21.72	NAV
33.20	-1.01	29.42	14.70	4.27	20.25	37.84	-5.81	34.04	14.05	20.42	-3.35	Total Return %
10.73	-7.28	-2.32	-3.98	-0.99	3.64	6.15	-2.69	3.56	6.43	10.36	-4.66	+/- S&P 500
9.73	-4.06	-3.15	-1.40	1.91	2.31	8.66	0.37	-0.17	5.08	9.14	-3.28	+/- Wilshire 5000
1.80	1.61	1.27	1.89	3.71	1.73	2.29	2.14	2.26	0.86	0.93	0.67	Income Return %
31.39	-2.63	28.14	12.81	0.56	18.51	35.54	-7.95	31.78	13.19	19.49	-4.02	Capital Return %
7	68	28	56	26	13	5	73	21	11	17	47	Total Rtn % Rank All
8	43	50	49	41	25	11	60	54	19	15	63	Total Rtn % Rank Obj
0.23	0.23	0.19	0.34	0.57	0.22	0.39	0.34	0.37	0.18	0.21	0.15	Income $
0.57	2.29	0.54	3.80	3.90	0.06	2.08	1.32	0.31	1.16	1.77	1.31	Capital Gains $
0.93	0.96	0.92	0.92	0.96	0.99	0.96	1.02	1.04	0.99	0.97	0.96	Expense Ratio %
1.88	1.99	2.07	1.75	1.32	1.31	2.12	2.33	2.11	0.99	0.92	0.91	Income Ratio %
81	89	96	116	103	42	85	70	50	40	42	58	Turnover Rate %
145.1	152.1	278.1	253.7	188.0	229.7	320.5	388.3	590.4	718.3	1167.2	1167.7	Net Assets ($mil)

Manager's Investment Style

Management's bottom-up, long-term strategy hinges on knowing and understanding a firm's management. It places a premium on firms with managers who are proven money makers and looks for lesser-followed businesses at attractive prices. Management targets financially strong small- and mid-cap firms that can support real growth, favoring low-cost producers or firms with competitive advantages. Management sells once a stock reaches a predetermined valuation target.

Fund Manager(s)

E. Bruce Dunn, since 03-91. Birthdate: 03-34.
BA, Yale 1956 MBA, Harvard 1958
Richard B. Peterson CFA, since 06-91. Birthdate: 10-40. BA, Carleton C. 1962 MPA, Princeton U. 1964

Manager Experience	Dates Managed	Invest Obj	Std Dev	+/- Index
E. Bruce Dunn				
SteinRoe Capital Opport	03/91 - 10/94	AG	14.34	6.23
SteinRoe Stock	01/89 - 03/91	G	16.52	4.81

Performance 12-31-94

	1st Qtr	2nd Qtr	3rd Qtr	4th Qtr	Total
1987	19.30	2.51	5.93	-19.51	4.27
1988	9.91	6.17	1.07	1.96	20.25
1989	8.06	14.12	11.36	0.38	37.84
1990	0.60	7.76	-16.17	3.64	-5.81
1991	19.00	-0.54	7.75	5.10	34.04
1992	1.49	-2.39	4.66	10.01	14.05
1993	6.20	2.79	6.06	4.02	20.42
1994	-6.71	-0.67	5.85	-1.46	-3.35

Bear Market Performance

Decile Rank (5-year period)

	Worst 3 Mo Period 1985-89	Worst 3 Mo Period 1990-94
SteinRoe Special	-28.91	-17.37
+/- S&P 500	0.67	-3.53
+/- Best Fit Index : SPMid400	-0.10	1.05

Trailing Returns

	Total Return %	+/- S&P 500	+/- Wil 5000	% Rank All	Obj	Growth of $10,000
3 Mo	-1.46	-1.44	-0.69	56	53	9,854
6 Mo	4.30	-0.56	-0.32	14	45	10,430
1 Yr	-3.35	-4.66	-3.28	47	63	9,665
3 Yr Avg	9.90	3.63	3.29	13	19	13,274
5 Yr Avg	10.88	2.19	2.06	13	21	16,758
10 Yr Avg	15.70	1.32	1.84	7	9	42,991
15 Yr Avg	16.93	2.45	2.95	3	6	104,417

Risk Analysis

Time Period	Load-Adj Return %	Risk % Rank [1] All	Obj	Morningstar [2] Return	Risk	Morningstar Risk-Adj Rating
1 Yr	-3.35					
3 Yr	9.90	65	24	1.94 [3]	0.73	★★★★
5 Yr	10.88	72	33	1.61 [3]	0.85	★★★★
10 Yr	15.70	69	39	1.65	0.90	★★★★

Average Historical Rating (109 months) 4.6 ★s

[1] 1 = low, 100 = high [2] 1.00 = Equity Avg [3] 1.00 = 90-day T-bill return

Other Measures

		Standard S&P 500	Best Fit SPMid400
Standard Deviation	9.22	Alpha	3.8	3.1
Mean	9.90	Beta	0.93	0.86
Sharpe Ratio	0.69	R-Squared	63	85

Investment Style

	Stock Portfolio Avg	Relative S&P 500
Price/Earnings Ratio	23.8	1.29
Price/Book Ratio	3.2	0.95
5 Yr Earnings Gr %	17.8#	3.20
Return on Assets %	7.5	1.0
Debt % Total Cap	26.3	0.93
Med Mkt Cap ($mil)	1064	0.08

figure is based on 50% or less of stocks

Diversification Value for Portfolio Types

Large Cap: Low
Small Cap: Low
Bond: High
Balanced: Low
Diversified: Low

Portfolio 12-30-94

Total Stocks: 68
Total Fixed-Income: 3

Share Chg (09-94) 000	Amount 000		Value $000	% Net Assets
0	1627	Revco Drug Stores	38437	3.29
50	1081	Olsten	34334	2.94
200	1958	Boston Scientific	34020	2.91
0	1118	Unifi	28521	2.44
0	1012	Harley-Davidson	28336	2.43
180	1006	Superior Industries Intl	26533	2.27
90	810	Interpublic Group	26021	2.23
40	840	AirTouch Communications	24450	2.09
0	385	Alco Standard	24159	2.07
138	689	Molex Cl A	21361	1.83
80	756	A Schulman	20788	1.78
29	592	Progressive	20731	1.78
80	600	Stewart & Stevenson Services	20700	1.77
0	863	Allstate	20388	1.75
120	700	Shanghai Petrochemical (ADR)	20125	1.72
220	562	Burlington Resources	19684	1.69
115	1125	Westpac Banking (ADR)	19125	1.64
	250	Nokia Pfd	18750	1.61
0	635	Littelfuse	18574	1.59
43	268	First Interstate Bancorp	18124	1.55
0	444	Viacom Cl B	18017	1.54
100	400	First Fidelity Bancorp (NJ)	17950	1.54
40	594	Minerals Technologies	17380	1.49
90	705	Interim Services	17361	1.49
3500	26000	National Mutual Asia	17138	1.47

Composition % 12-31-94

Cash	5.0	Preferreds	0.1
Stocks	93.9	Convertibles	0.1
Bonds	0.9	Other	0.0

Tax Analysis

	Tax-Adj Historical Return %	% Pretax Return
3 Yr Avg	7.80	77.2
5 Yr Avg	8.69	76.5
10 Yr Avg	12.44	67.6
Potential Capital Gain Exposure (% of assets)		14%

Most Similar Funds in MF500

Vanguard Index Extended Mkt	Strong Fit
Neuberger&Berman Partners	Fair Fit
William Blair Growth	Fair Fit

Index Allocation

	% of Stocks
S&P 500	15.9
S&P MidCap 400	27.7
U.S. Small Cap	43.5
Foreign	12.8

Sector Weightings

	% of Stocks	Relative S&P 500
Utilities	0.0	0.00
Energy	11.2	1.10
Financials	16.0	1.51
Industrial Cyclicals	15.8	0.96
Consumer Durables	15.0	2.42
Consumer Staples	0.6	0.04
Services	16.1	1.98
Retail	8.1	1.39
Health	7.8	0.90
Technology	9.6	1.05

Operations

Address and Telephone	P.O. Box 804058 Chicago, IL 60680 800-338-2550 / 312-368-7800
Advisor	Stein Roe & Farnham
Subadvisor	None
Distributor	Liberty Securities
States Available	All plus PR,VI,GU
Report Grade	B-
Income Distrib	Paid Annually
Date of Inception	05-22-68
Fiscal Year End	September

Min Initial Purchase	$2500 (Addt'l: $100)
Min IRA Purchase	$500 (Addt'l: $50)
Min Auto Invest Plan	$1000 (Systematic Inv: $50)

Expenses & Fees

Sales Fees	
	0.00% front
	0.00% deferred
	0.00% 12b-1
Management Fee	0.75% flat fee
3-,5-,10-yr Expense Projections	$31, $54, $119
Annual Brokerage Cost	0.13%

MORNINGSTAR 1995 Mutual Fund 500

SteinRoe Total Return

	Ticker	Load	NAV	
	SRFBX	None	24.30	4.8%

SteinRoe Total Return Fund seeks current income and capital appreciation consistent with reasonable risk.

The fund invests in a combination of equity, fixed-income, and convertible securities in accordance with the fund's forecast of economic conditions, interest rates, and the outlook for common stocks. The equity portion consists chiefly of common stocks selected for long-term growth potential. For its fixed-income investments, the fund favors investment-grade securities.

Through mid-1989, the fund was marketed as a balanced fund and required a 25% minimum investment in bonds.

Historical Profile

Return	Average
Risk	Low
Rating	★★★ Neutral

Manager's Investment Style

Management puts a high priority on yield and safety. The fund's portfolio is designed around limiting downside risk. It places more than 30% of assets in convertible securities, as these issues report less volatility than common stocks and their payout is of a greater priority. Management holds a similar amount of assets in common stocks. By choosing growth-oriented issues with P/E ratios that are slightly below the market's, the fund hopes to cut price risk while adding additional yield. This strategy is effective in lowering risk and producing dividends, but tends to fall short in capital appreciation.

Fund Manager(s)

Robert A. Christensen, since 01-81. Birthdate: 10-33. BA, Vanderbilt U. 1955 MBA, Harvard 1962

Manager Experience

	Dates Managed	Invest Obj	Std Dev	+/- Index
Robert A. Christensen				
Liberty Financial Util	10/91 - 12/94	SU	7.31	-1.10
Liberty Financial G & I	08/92 - 12/94	GI	7.21	-2.66

Growth of $10,000

- |||| Value of Fund ($000)
- — Value of Index ($000) S&P 500
- ▼ Manager Change
- ▽ Partial Manager Change
- ► Mgr Unknown After
- ◄ Mgr Unknown Before

Average % in Portfolio: 35% 36% 44% 49% 48% 45% 36% 39%

Performance Quartile (Within Objective)

1983	1984	1985	1986	1987	1988	1989	1990	1991	1992	1993	1994	History
23.40	21.37	25.04	25.07	22.25	22.15	24.41	22.16	26.62	25.69	26.85	24.30	NAV
13.52	4.85	25.78	17.11	0.72	7.87	20.34	-1.72	29.59	7.89	12.34	-4.12	Total Return %
-8.95	-1.42	-5.96	-1.57	-4.54	-8.74	-11.35	1.40	-0.90	0.27	2.28	-5.44	+/- S&P 500
-9.95	1.80	-6.78	1.01	-1.65	-10.07	-8.84	4.46	-4.62	-1.09	1.06	-4.05	+/- Wilshire 5000
5.93	6.92	7.44	5.51	6.46	6.04	6.52	4.62	6.18	5.04	4.91	4.42	Income Return %
7.59	-2.08	18.34	11.60	-5.74	1.83	13.82	-6.34	23.41	2.84	7.43	-8.54	Capital Return %
64	51	43	38	54	74	35	60	27	47	48	55	Total Rtn % Rank All
84	66	62	52	34	90	56	22	30	64	59	74	Total Rtn % Rank Obj
1.26	1.41	1.42	1.35	1.63	1.31	1.40	1.07	1.32	1.30	1.23	1.19	Income $
0.00	1.55	0.19	2.70	1.45	0.50	0.73	0.73	0.62	1.67	0.71	0.28	Capital Gains $
0.73	0.73	0.77	0.79	0.80	0.87	0.90	0.88	0.87	0.85	0.81	0.83	Expense Ratio %
5.55	6.94	6.30	5.21	5.12	5.68	5.83	5.36	5.50	4.94	4.69	4.53	Income Ratio %
79	50	100	108	86	85	93	75	71	59	53	29	Turnover Rate %
93.0	95.7	128.7	149.8	140.3	130.8	142.4	128.3	156.5	180.9	226.5	215.1	Net Assets ($mil)

Performance 12-31-94

	1st Qtr	2nd Qtr	3rd Qtr	4th Qtr	Total
1987	10.94	0.37	2.36	-11.63	0.72
1988	3.63	2.64	0.14	1.28	7.87
1989	4.70	6.78	6.70	0.88	20.34
1990	-3.01	5.13	-9.49	6.49	-1.72
1991	12.40	1.25	7.00	6.42	29.59
1992	-1.34	2.11	3.66	3.31	7.89
1993	5.44	0.46	4.70	1.30	12.34
1994	-2.98	-1.47	3.63	-3.22	-4.12

Bear Market Performance

Decile Rank (5-year period)

Worst — Best

	Worst 3 Mo Period 1985-89	Worst 3 Mo Period 1990-94
SteinRoe Total Return	-17.25	-11.16
+/- S&P 500	12.33	2.68
+/- Best Fit Index : S&P 500	12.33	2.68

Trailing Returns

	Total Return %	+/- S&P 500	+/- Wil 5000	% Rank All	% Rank Obj	Growth of $10,000
3 Mo	-3.22	-3.20	-2.45	84	67	9,678
6 Mo	0.30	-4.56	-4.33	51	71	10,030
1 Yr	-4.12	-5.44	-4.05	55	74	9,588
3 Yr Avg	5.13	-1.13	-1.48	45	71	11,620
5 Yr Avg	8.16	-0.54	-0.66	31	30	14,800
10 Yr Avg	11.04	-3.34	-2.82	47	56	28,500
15 Yr Avg	10.75	-3.74	-3.23	69	76	46,225

Operations

Address and Telephone	P.O. Box 804058 Chicago, IL 60680 800-338-2550 / 312-368-7800
Advisor	Stein Roe & Farnham
Subadvisor	None
Distributor	Liberty Securities
States Available	All plus PR,VI,GU
Report Grade	B-
Income Distrib	Paid Quarterly
Date of Inception	08-25-49
Fiscal Year End	September

Risk Analysis

Time Period	Load-Adj Return %	Risk % Rank [1] All	Risk % Rank [1] Obj	Morningstar [2] Return	Morningstar Risk	Morningstar Risk-Adj Rating
1 Yr	-4.12					
3 Yr	5.13	51	23	0.45 [3]	0.55	★★★
5 Yr	8.16	53	4	0.85 [3]	0.57	★★★★
10 Yr	11.04	43	6	0.71	0.58	★★★

Average Historical Rating (109 months)   3.2 ★s

[1] 1 = low, 100 = high [2] 1.00 = Equity Avg [3] 1.00 = 90-day T-bill return

Other Measures

				Standard S&P 500	Best Fit S&P 500
Standard Deviation	6.00	Alpha		-0.2	-0.2
Mean	5.20	Beta		0.65	0.65
Sharpe Ratio	0.28	R-Squared		72	72

Investment Style

	Stock Portfolio Avg	Relative S&P 500
Price/Earnings Ratio	20.0	1.08
Price/Book Ratio	3.2	0.94
5 Yr Earnings Gr %	5.9	1.06
Return on Assets %	7.2	0.97
Debt % Total Cap	32.8	1.16
Med Mkt Cap ($mil)	12482	0.96

Style: Value Blend Growth; Size Large/Med/Small

Diversification Value for Portfolio Types

Large Cap: Low	Small Cap: Medium	Bond: Medium	Balanced: None	Diversified: Low

Portfolio 12-30-94

Total Stocks: 29
Total Fixed-Income: 55

Share Chg (09-94) 000	Amount 000		Value $000	% Net Assets
0	293	United Dominion Realty Trust	4212	1.96
0	78	General Electric	3978	1.85
	3000	Integrated Health Svcs Cv 6%	3810	1.77
	188	James River Cv Pfd DECS	3797	1.76
	2000	LM Ericsson Cv Pfd 3.125%	3750	1.74
	65	General Motors C Cv Pfd $3.25	3729	1.73
0	62	Bristol-Myers Squibb	3588	1.67
	64	Sears Roebuck Cv PERCS $3.75	3560	1.65
0	56	Emerson Electric	3500	1.63
-10	92	Kimco Realty	3485	1.62
0	112	Enron	3416	1.59
0	104	Abbott Laboratories	3393	1.58
-5	42	British Petroleum (ADR)	3382	1.57
125	125	Atlantic Richfield	3266	1.52
	3500	Nationwide Hlth Pptys Cv 6.25%	3185	1.48
0	155	Plum Creek Timber	3100	1.44
	2500	Staples Cv 5%	3094	1.44
0	170	Hanson (ADR)	3060	1.42
0	56	Minnesota Mining & Mfg	2989	1.39
	26	Citicorp Cv Pfd $5.3750	2974	1.38
	3000	Roadmaster Industries Cv 8%	2970	1.38
	2500	SFP Pipeline Holdings Cv FRN	2950	1.37
0	125	Borden Chemicals/Plastics	2875	1.34
	3000	Consolidated Nat Gas Cv 7.25%	2869	1.33
0	88	Fleet Financial Group	2860	1.33

Composition % 12-31-94

Cash	4.1
Stocks	39.7
Bonds	11.4
Preferreds	6.4
Convertibles	38.4
Other	0.0

Index Allocation

	% of Stocks
S&P 500	56.9
S&P MidCap 400	0.0
U.S. Small Cap	25.2
Foreign	17.9

Tax Analysis

	Tax-Adj Historical Return %	% Pretax Return
3 Yr Avg	2.42	45.9
5 Yr Avg	5.48	63.7
10 Yr Avg	7.80	60.5
Potential Capital Gain Exposure (% of assets)		7%

Most Similar Funds in MF500

American Cap Harbor A	Strong Fit
Oppenheimer Equity-Inc A	Strong Fit
Evergreen Total Return	Strong Fit

Sector Weightings

	% of Stocks	Relative S&P 500
Utilities	14.9	1.20
Energy	12.5	1.23
Financials	24.8	2.35
Industrial Cyclicals	20.4	1.25
Consumer Durables	0.0	0.00
Consumer Staples	3.3	0.26
Services	3.3	0.40
Retail	8.7	1.50
Health	12.1	1.40
Technology	0.0	0.00

Operations (continued)

Min Initial Purchase	$2500 (Addt'l: $100)
Min IRA Purchase	$500 (Addt'l: $50)
Min Auto Invest Plan	$1000 (Systematic Inv: $50)

Expenses & Fees

Sales Fees	
	0.00% front
	0.00% deferred
	0.00% 12b-1
Management Fee	0.63% max./0.50% min.
3-,5-,10-yr Expense Projections	$26, $45, $100
Annual Brokerage Cost	0.09%

	Ticker	Load	NAV	Yield	SEC Yield	Assets	Objective
	SRYIX	None	10.66	N/A	N/A	12.0	Growth

...g term capital

...nally invests at least 65% of its assets in ...curities issued by companies that affect the lives of teenagers or children. These typically include companies that produce products or services that children or teenagers use, are aware of, or could potentially have an interest in. The fund may invest up to 35% of its assets in debt securities. Up to 25% of the fund's assets may be invested in foreign securities. The fund also attempts to educate young investors about personal finance and investing.

Manager's Investment Style

Management follows in SteinRoe's conservative tradition of investing in large-cap stocks for the long term. The group's bottom-up approach includes doing its homework on the management of prospective holdings. It then tries to buy good businesses that fall within its investment parameters at reasonable prices.

Fund Manager(s)

Kenneth W. Corba CFA(1987), since 05-94.
Lawson E. Whitesides, Jr. CFA(1978), since 05-94.
Daniel K. Cantor CFA, since 05-94.

Manager Experience

	Dates Managed	Invest Obj	Std Dev	+/- Index
Lawson E. Whitesides, Jr.				
SteinRoe Stock	07/91 - 12/94	G	11.95	-1.58
Kenneth W. Corba				
SteinRoe Stock	01/89 - 12/94	G	14.03	1.39

Performance 12-31-94

	1st Qtr	2nd Qtr	3rd Qtr	4th Qtr	Total
1987	---	---	---	---	---
1988	---	---	---	---	---
1989	---	---	---	---	---
1990	---	---	---	---	---
1991	---	---	---	---	---
1992	---	---	---	---	---
1993	---	---	---	---	---
1994	---	---	5.57	4.87	7.49 *

Bear Market Performance

Decile Rank (5-year period)

Worst |————————————| Best

	Worst 3 Mo Period 1985-89	Worst 3 Mo Period 1990-94
SteinRoe Young Investor	---	---
+/- S&P 500	---	---
+/- Best Fit Index :	---	---

Trailing Returns

	Total Return %	+/- S&P 500	+/- Wil 5000	% Rank All	% Rank Obj	Growth of $10,000
3 Mo	4.87	4.89	5.64	1	1	10,487
6 Mo	10.71	5.85	6.08	4	7	11,071
1 Yr	---	---	---			---
3 Yr Avg	---	---	---			---
5 Yr Avg	---	---	---			---
10 Yr Avg	---	---	---			---
15 Yr Avg	---	---	---			---

Operations

Address and Telephone	P.O. Box 804058
	Chicago, IL 60680
	800-338-2550 / 312-368-7800
Advisor	Stein Roe & Farnham
Subadvisor	None
Distributor	Liberty Securities
States Available	All plus PR,VI,GU
Report Grade	N/A
Income Distrib	Paid Annually
* Date of Inception	05-02-94
Fiscal Year End	October

Historical Profile

Return	---
Risk	---
Rating	
	Not Rated

Investment Style History
Equity

Average % Stocks Held in Portfolio — 81%

Growth of $10,000
- |||| Value of Fund ($000)
- — Value of Index ($000) S&P 500
- ▼ Manager Change
- ▽ Partial Manager Change
- ► Mgr Unknown After
- ◄ Mgr Unknown Before

Performance Quartile (Within Objective)

1983	1984	1985	1986	1987	1988	1989	1990	1991	1992	1993	1994	History
---	---	---	---	---	---	---	---	---	---	---	10.66	NAV
---	---	---	---	---	---	---	---	---	---	---	7.49 *	Total Return %
---	---	---	---	---	---	---	---	---	---	---	4.01 *	+/- S&P 500
---	---	---	---	---	---	---	---	---	---	---	---	+/- Wilshire 5000
---	---	---	---	---	---	---	---	---	---	---	0.79	Income Return %
---	---	---	---	---	---	---	---	---	---	---	6.71	Capital Return %
---	---	---	---	---	---	---	---	---	---	---	---	Total Rtn % Rank All
---	---	---	---	---	---	---	---	---	---	---	---	Total Rtn % Rank Obj
---	---	---	---	---	---	---	---	---	---	---	0.08	Income $
---	---	---	---	---	---	---	---	---	---	---	0.00	Capital Gains $
---	---	---	---	---	---	---	---	---	---	---	0.99	Expense Ratio %
---	---	---	---	---	---	---	---	---	---	---	1.07	Income Ratio %
---	---	---	---	---	---	---	---	---	---	---	---	Turnover Rate %
---	---	---	---	---	---	---	---	---	---	---	12.0	Net Assets ($mil)

Risk Analysis

Time Period	Load-Adj Return %	Risk % Rank All	Risk % Rank Obj	Morningstar[2] Return	Morningstar Risk	Morningstar Risk-Adj Rating
1 Yr	---					
3 Yr	---	---	---	---	---	
5 Yr	---	---	---	---	---	
10 Yr	---	---	---	---	---	
Average Historical Rating ---				---		

[1] 1 = low, 100 = high [2] 1.00 = Equity Avg [3] 1.00 = 90-day T-bill return

Other Measures

			Standard S&P 500	Best Fit
Standard Deviation	---	Alpha	---	---
Mean	---	Beta	---	---
Sharpe Ratio	---	R-Squared	---	---

Investment Style

	Stock Portfolio Avg	Relative S&P 500
Price/Earnings Ratio	27.2	1.47
Price/Book Ratio	5.0	1.48
5 Yr Earnings Gr %	15.0#	2.70
Return on Assets %	11.5	1.53
Debt % Total Cap	23.3	0.83
Med Mkt Cap ($mil)	5250	0.40

figure is based on 50% or less of stocks

Style: Value Blend Growth / Size: Large Med Small

Diversification Value for Portfolio Types

Large Cap: Small Cap: Bond: Balanced: Diversified:

Min Initial Purchase	$2500 (Addt'l: $50)
Min IRA Purchase	$500 (Addt'l: $50)
Min Auto Invest Plan	$1000 (Systematic Inv: $50)

Expenses & Fees

Sales Fees	
	0.00% front
	0.00% deferred
	0.00% 12b-1
Management Fee	0.75% max./0.60% min.
3-,5-,10-yr Expense Projections	$32, N/A, N/A
Annual Brokerage Cost	---

Portfolio 12-30-94

Share Chg (09-94) 000	Amount 000	Total Stocks: 41 / Total Fixed-Income: 0	Value $000	% Net Assets
2	8	Microsoft	458	3.81
2	8	Motorola	434	3.61
1	8	Coca-Cola	386	3.21
1	6	Procter & Gamble	372	3.09
2	14	Learning	343	2.85
5	7	Broderbund Software	327	2.72
2	8	Duracell International	325	2.70
10	15	Carnival Cl A	319	2.65
4	8	Department 56	318	2.64
1	4	Gillette	299	2.49
1	9	Barnes & Noble	281	2.34
8	8	Coleman	281	2.34
0	6	Intl Flavors & Fragrances	278	2.31
2	6	Walt Disney	277	2.30
0	6	Home Depot	276	2.29
5	5	Johnson & Johnson	274	2.28
1	6	United HealthCare	271	2.25
0	8	Sensormatic Electronics	270	2.24
4	4	Nokia (ADR)	263	2.18
6	6	Walgreen	263	2.18
0	8	Abbott Laboratories	261	2.17
0	5	Whirlpool	254	2.11
5	5	AT & T	251	2.09
6	6	Viacom Cl B	244	2.03
6	6	Integrated Health Services	237	1.97

Composition % 12-31-94

Cash	14.1	Preferreds	0.0
Stocks	86.0	Convertibles	0.0
Bonds	0.0	Other	0.0

Tax Analysis

	Tax-Adj Historical Return %	% Pretax Return
3 Yr Avg	---	---
5 Yr Avg	---	---
10 Yr Avg	---	---
Potential Capital Gain Exposure (% of assets)		5%

Most Similar Funds in MF500

Fund lacks three-year record

Index Allocation

	% of Stocks
S&P 500	55.7
S&P MidCap 400	4.4
U.S. Small Cap	35.0
Foreign	4.8

Sector Weightings

	% of Stocks	Relative S&P 500
Utilities	4.9	0.39
Energy	0.0	0.00
Financials	0.0	0.00
Industrial Cyclicals	7.7	0.47
Consumer Durables	17.2	2.77
Consumer Staples	14.8	1.19
Services	15.9	1.95
Retail	15.6	2.67
Health	10.8	1.24
Technology	13.2	1.44

MORNINGSTAR 1995 Mutual Fund 500

Stratton Monthly Dividend

	Ticker	Load	NAV	Yield	SEC Yield	Assets	Objective
	STMDX	None	23.78	8.1%	7.48%	121.9	Equity-Inc.

Stratton Monthly Dividend Shares seeks return from dividend and interest income.

The fund normally invests at least 80% of its assets in common stock and securities convertible into, or exchangeable for, common stock. At least 25% of its assets are invested in securities of public utility companies engaged in the production, transmission, or distribution of electric, energy, gas, water, or telephone service. The fund may also invest in real estate investment trusts.

The fund was named Energy and Utility Shares prior to 1985, and prior to Nov. 1981, it operated as a closed-end fund.

Manager's Investment Style

Management sets lofty goals for income distributions. In an effort to maintain its 8% yield, the fund holds more than 60% of assets in high-paying electric utilities. While utilities do offer high yields, they are dragged down by rising interest rates and a tightening regulatory environment. To combat this volitility, management also buys REITs and convertibles. Utilities remain a favorite though, as management continues to reposition itself toward more-favorable parts of this sector.

Fund Manager(s)

Gerard E. Heffernan CFA(1967), since 05-80.
Birthdate: 12-37. BS, U. of Pennsylvania 1959
James W. Stratton, since 05-80. Birthdate: 12-36.
BS, Pennsylvania State U. 1958 MBA, Harvard 1960

Manager Experience	Dates Managed	Invest Obj	Std Dev	+/- Index
James W. Stratton Stratton Growth	09/72 - 12/94	G	16.49	-0.47

Historical Profile

Return	Below Average
Risk	Low
Rating	★★ Below Average

Average % Stocks Held in Portfolio: 58% 56% 59% 79% 86% 87% 94% 89%

Investment Style History
Equity

Growth of $10,000

||| Value of Fund ($000)
— Value of Index ($000) LB L-T
▼ Manager Change
▽ Partial Manager Change
► Mgr Unknown After
◄ Mgr Unknown Before

Performance Quartile (Within Objective)

	1983	1984	1985	1986	1987	1988	1989	1990	1991	1992	1993	1994	History
	20.49	22.42	26.62	29.21	23.44	23.63	25.88	22.66	28.31	29.16	29.17	23.78	NAV
	11.87	21.19	29.90	20.47	-11.40	9.76	18.77	-3.83	35.10	10.33	6.61	-12.13	Total Return %
	-10.60	14.93	-1.84	1.79	-16.66	-6.85	-12.92	-0.71	4.61	2.71	-3.45	-13.44	+/- S&P 500
	-11.60	18.14	-2.66	4.37	-13.77	-8.18	-10.41	2.36	0.89	1.36	-4.68	-12.06	+/- Wilshire 5000
	9.72	11.77	11.17	8.73	6.70	8.95	9.25	8.62	10.16	7.33	6.57	6.35	Income Return %
	2.14	9.42	18.73	11.74	-18.11	0.81	9.52	-12.44	24.93	3.00	0.03	-18.48	Capital Return %
	71	1	26	18	97	63	38	67	19	20	85	97	Total Rtn % Rank All
	92	1	31	21	95	87	63	34	8	31	94	99	Total Rtn % Rank Obj
	1.92	2.04	2.16	2.28	2.09	2.08	2.05	2.20	1.95	1.92	1.95	1.92	Income $
	0.00	0.00	0.00	0.50	0.65	0.00	0.00	0.00	0.00	0.00	0.00	0.00	Capital Gains $
	1.98	1.74	1.72	1.49	1.24	1.21	1.21	1.25	1.27	1.23	1.10	0.99	Expense Ratio %
	10.33	9.03	9.77	8.36	6.90	7.52	8.54	8.19	8.79	7.63	6.74	6.12	Income Ratio %
	33	30	28	14	15	24	15	39	14	44	36	19	Turnover Rate %
	9.0	10.3	19.7	48.4	33.8	32.7	34.7	30.6	43.2	88.5	176.4	121.9	Net Assets ($mil)

Performance 12-31-94

	1st Qtr	2nd Qtr	3rd Qtr	4th Qtr	Total
1987	5.92	-4.59	-2.63	-9.96	-11.40
1988	9.01	2.65	-1.19	-0.74	9.76
1989	4.86	7.92	4.78	0.16	18.77
1990	-4.56	1.40	-6.66	6.47	-3.83
1991	11.70	1.19	9.08	9.57	35.10
1992	-2.75	4.29	3.95	4.65	10.33
1993	9.04	0.97	3.59	-6.53	6.61
1994	-6.93	-7.26	1.50	0.30	-12.13

Bear Market Performance

Decile Rank (5-year period)

	Worst		Best

	Worst 3 Mo Period 1985-89	Worst 3 Mo Period 1990-94
Stratton Monthly Dividend	-11.61	-7.64
+/- S&P 500	17.97	-7.96
+/- Best Fit Index : LB L-T	-14.20	-6.12

Trailing Returns

	Total Return %	+/- S&P 500	+/- Wil 5000	% Rank All	% Rank Obj	Growth of $10,000
3 Mo	0.30	0.32	1.07	15	5	10,030
6 Mo	1.81	-3.06	-2.82	28	41	10,181
1 Yr	-12.13	-13.44	-12.06	97	99	8,787
3 Yr Avg	1.11	-5.16	-5.51	94	95	10,335
5 Yr Avg	6.07	-2.62	-2.74	74	72	13,429
10 Yr Avg	9.27	-5.11	-4.59	68	93	24,272
15 Yr Avg	11.02	-3.46	-2.96	65	69	47,974

Operations

Address and Telephone	610 W. Germantown Pike Suite 300 Plymouth Meeting, PA 19462-1050 800-634-5726 / 215-941-0255
Advisor	Stratton Management
Subadvisor	None
Distributor	Fund/Plan Broker Services
States Available	All
Report Grade	A-
Income Distrib	Paid Monthly
Date of Inception	04-01-72
Fiscal Year End	January

Min Initial Purchase	$2000 (Addt'l: $100)
Min IRA Purchase	None (Addt'l: $100)
Min Auto Invest Plan	$2000 (Systematic Inv: $100)

Expenses & Fees

Sales Fees	0.00% front
	0.00% deferred
	0.00% 12b-1
Management Fee	0.63% flat fee
3-,5-,10-yr Expense Projections	$31, $54, $120
Annual Brokerage Cost	0.14%

Risk Analysis

Time Period	Load-Adj Return %	Risk % Rank All	Risk % Rank Obj	Morningstar[1] Return	Morningstar[2] Risk	Morningstar Risk-Adj Rating
1 Yr	-12.13					
3 Yr	1.11	77	97	-0.70[3]	0.89	★★
5 Yr	6.07	57	37	0.32[3]	0.66	★★★
10 Yr	9.27	47	25	0.44	0.67	★★
Average Historical Rating (109 months)					3.6	★s

[1] 1 = low, 100 = high   [2] 1.00 = Equity Avg   [3] 1.00 = 90-day T-bill return

Other Measures

			Standard S&P 500	Best Fit LB L-T
Standard Deviation	8.57	Alpha	-3.5	-3.5
Mean	1.47	Beta	0.53	0.76
Sharpe Ratio	-0.24	R-Squared	24	47

Investment Style

	Stock Portfolio Avg	Relative S&P 500
Price/Earnings Ratio	17.1	0.93
Price/Book Ratio	1.3	0.38
5 Yr Earnings Gr %	-4.1	-0.73
Return on Assets %	3.9	0.52
Debt % Total Cap	45.5	1.61
Med Mkt Cap ($mil)	1242	0.10

Style Value Blend Growth
Size Large Med Small

Diversification Value for Portfolio Types

Large Cap: High	Small Cap: High	Bond: Medium	Balanced: Medium	Diversified: High

Portfolio 12-30-94

Total Stocks: 29
Total Fixed-Income: 6

Share Chg (10-94) 000	Amount 000		Value $000	% Net Assets
0	245	Public Service Enterprise	6493	5.33
0	310	Health Care REIT	6235	5.12
0	180	Oklahoma Gas & Electric	5963	4.89
0	300	Delmarva Power & Light	5400	4.43
	5000	US Treasury Note 5.875%	4893	4.02
200	200	Boston Edison	4775	3.92
0	220	Rochester Gas & Electric	4593	3.77
0	225	American Health Property	4434	3.64
0	230	Ohio Edison	4255	3.49
0	160	National Health Investors	4180	3.43
200	200	Nevada Power	4075	3.34
150	213	Pennsylvania Power & Light	4043	3.32
0	200	Puget Sound Power & Light	4025	3.30
0	170	CINergy	3974	3.26
237	237	SCEcorp	3463	2.84
122	255	Crown American Realty Tr	3443	2.82
0	150	Allegheny Power System	3263	2.68
100	100	Texas Utilities	3200	2.63
0	102	Meditrust	3086	2.53
0	100	Public Service Colorado	2938	2.41
0	100	Pacific Telesis Group	2850	2.34
0	105	Central Hudson Gas/Electric	2793	2.29
0	110	IES Industries	2778	2.28
0	100	General Public Utilities	2625	2.15
0	116	Colonial Properties Trust	2599	2.13

Composition % 12-31-94

Cash	6.2	Preferreds	0.0
Stocks	85.5	Convertibles	0.0
Bonds	8.3	Other	0.0

Tax Analysis

	Tax-Adj Historical Return %	% Pretax Return
3 Yr Avg	-1.45	---
5 Yr Avg	3.38	52.8
10 Yr Avg	6.01	55.5
Potential Capital Gain Exposure (% of assets)		-23%

Most Similar Funds in MF500

Franklin Utilities	Strong Fit
Prudential Utility B	Weak Fit
Fortress Utility	Weak Fit

Index Allocation

	% of Stocks
S&P 500	24.8
S&P MidCap 400	27.7
U.S. Small Cap	47.4
Foreign	0.0

Sector Weightings

	% of Stocks	Relative S&P 500
Utilities	74.7	6.03
Energy	0.0	0.00
Financials	25.3	2.39
Industrial Cyclicals	0.0	0.00
Consumer Durables	0.0	0.00
Consumer Staples	0.0	0.00
Services	0.0	0.00
Retail	0.0	0.00
Health	0.0	0.00
Technology	0.0	0.00

Strong Advantage

	Ticker	Load	NAV	Yield	SEC Yield	Assets	Objective
	STADX	None	9.98	5.5%	6.82%	910.5	Corp General

Strong Advantage Fund seeks current income consistent with minimum fluctuation of principal.

The fund invests primarily in investment-grade fixed-income securities. These may include corporate debt securities, bank obligations, commercial paper, repurchase agreements, convertible securities, preferred stock, U.S. government obligations, and mortgage-related securities. The fund may invest up to 25% of its assets in BB-rated securities. It may also invest up to 25% of its assets directly in foreign securities, and may invest without limit in American Depositary Receipts. The average weighted maturity may not exceed one year.

Manager's Investment Style

In 1994, the fund tightened its maturity constraints: Average effective maturity previously stayed between 90 and 365 days; now, the 90-day floor has been eliminated. Instead of depending on duration to boost income, management relies mostly on credit plays: It generally buys high-yielding issues of low or middling quality that are trading to their nearest call dates. The fund does carry exposure to non-investment-grade debt. The fund also invests in floating-rate securities.

Fund Manager(s)

Jeffrey A. Koch CFA(1994), since 07-91.
Birthdate: 06-64. BA, U. of Minnesota-Morris 1987 MBA, Washington U. 1989

Manager Experience

	Dates Managed	Invest Obj	Std Dev	+/- Index
Jeffrey A. Koch				
Strong Government Secs	03/91 - 10/93	GG	3.88	2.54
Strong Short-Term Bond	07/91 - 10/93	CG	2.18	-2.02

Historical Profile

Return	Above Average
Risk	Low
Rating	★★★★★ Highest

	1983	1984	1985	1986	1987	1988	1989	1990	1991	1992	1993	1994	History
	---	---	---	---	---	10.00	9.87	9.67	9.90	10.01	10.19	9.98	NAV
	---	---	---	---	---	1.00 *	9.51	6.61	10.58	8.43	8.12	3.55	Total Return %
	---	---	---	---	---		-5.03	-2.33	-5.42	1.19	-1.64	6.47	+/- LB Aggregate
	---	---	---	---	---		-4.47	-0.54	-7.92	-0.27	-4.05	7.48	+/- LB Corporate
	---	---	---	---	---	0.90	10.76	8.64	8.21	7.32	6.32	5.47	Income Return %
	---	---	---	---	---	0.10	-1.25	-2.03	2.38	1.11	1.80	-1.91	Capital Return %
	---	---	---	---	---		79	26	88	40	78	6	Total Rtn % Rank All
	---	---	---	---	---		75	55	97	23	78	1	Total Rtn % Rank Obj
	---	---	---	---	---	0.09	1.04	0.83	0.75	0.70	0.61	0.55	Income $
	---	---	---	---	---	0.00	0.00	0.00	0.00	0.00	0.00	0.02	Capital Gains $
	---	---	---	---	---		1.10	1.10	1.20	1.20	1.00	0.90	0.80	Expense Ratio %
	---	---	---	---	---		11.10	10.00	8.50	7.80	7.00	5.80	5.00	Income Ratio %
	---	---	---	---	---		232	211	274	503	316	305	241	Turnover Rate %
	---	---	---	---	---	7.6	142.8	119.2	143.2	272.3	415.5	910.5	Net Assets ($mil)

Investment Style History
Fixed Income
Income Rtn % Rank Obj

Growth of $10,000
|||| Value of Fund ($000)
— Value of Index ($000) FB HY
▼ Manager Change
▽ Partial Manager Change
► Mgr Unknown After
◄ Mgr Unknown Before

Performance Quartile (Within Objective)

Performance 12-31-94

	1st Qtr	2nd Qtr	3rd Qtr	4th Qtr	Total
1987	---	---	---	---	---
1988	---	---	---	---	1.00 *
1989	3.02	3.05	1.65	1.47	9.51
1990	1.08	2.21	2.09	1.09	6.61
1991	2.18	2.31	2.73	2.98	10.58
1992	2.46	2.07	2.76	0.90	8.43
1993	2.50	1.79	1.61	1.98	8.12
1994	0.72	0.38	1.51	0.91	3.56

Bear Market Performance

Decile Rank (5-year period)

Worst ———— Best

	Worst 3 Mo Period 1985-89	Worst 3 Mo Period 1990-94
Strong Advantage	---	-0.20
+/- LB Aggregate	---	3.06
+/- Best Fit Index : FB HY	---	3.50

Trailing Returns

	Total Return %	+/- LB Aggregate	+/- LB Corp	% Rank All	% Rank Obj	Growth of $10,000
3 Mo	0.91	0.53	0.47	7	7	10,091
6 Mo	2.43	1.44	1.26	24	1	10,243
1 Yr	3.55	6.47	7.48	6	1	10,355
3 Yr Avg	6.68	2.13	1.26	29	6	12,140
5 Yr Avg	7.43	-0.19	-0.83	41	39	14,312
10 Yr Avg	---	---	---	---	---	---
15 Yr Avg	---	---	---	---	---	---

Operations

Address and Telephone	P.O. Box 2936
	Milwaukee, WI 53201-2936
	800-368-1030 / 414-359-1400
Advisor	Strong Capital Management
Subadvisor	None
Distributor	Strong Funds Distributors
States Available	All plus PR,GU
Report Grade	B-
Income Distrib	Paid Monthly
* Date of Inception	11-25-88
Fiscal Year End	December

Risk Analysis

Time Period	Load-Adj Return %	Risk % Rank All [1]	Obj	Morningstar [2] Return	Morningstar Risk	Morningstar Risk-Adj Rating
1 Yr	3.55					
3 Yr	6.68	1	1	0.92 [3]	0.14	★★★★★
5 Yr	7.43	1	1	0.66 [3]	0.19	★★★★★
10 Yr	---					

Average Historical Rating (38 months)   4.7 ★s

[1] 1 = low, 100 = high   [2] 1.00 = Taxable Avg   [3] 1.00 = 90-day T-bill return

Other Measures

			Standard LB Agg	Best Fit FB HY
Standard Deviation	1.17	Alpha	2.8	1.5
Mean	6.49	Beta	0.19	0.20
Sharpe Ratio	2.54	R-Squared	38	52

Investment Style

Interest-Rate Stance
Avg Effective Duration	0.4 Yrs **
Avg Effective Maturity	0.5 Yrs

Quality
Avg Credit Quality	BBB
Avg Weighted Coupon	7.96%
Avg Weighted Price	99.52% of Par

Maturity Short Intrm Long
Quality High Med Low

**figure provided by fund

Diversification Value for Portfolio Types

Large Cap: High	Small Cap: High	Bond: Medium	Balanced: High	Diversified: High

Portfolio 12-31-94

Total Stocks: 0
Total Fixed-Income: 93

Amount 000	Date of Maturity		Value $000	% Net Assets
44750	12-15-01	Fleming FRN	44733	4.91
44360	09-01-29	Resolution Trust CMO FRN	44083	4.84
32000	10-14-49	Okobank FRN	31760	3.49
30700	02-28-01	Bank of Boston 5%	30086	3.30
30000	07-13-99	Health & Rehab Ppty 6.345%	29739	3.27
30270	12-30-09	Chase Manhattan 5.25%	29059	3.19
27350	05-01-99	Texas Utilities Elec FRN	27200	2.99
24985	11-25-30	Ryland Mortgage Sec CMO 7.65%	24103	2.65
23002	06-22-98	Time Warner FRN	23002	2.53
21990	09-30-43	Kansallis-Osake-Pankki FRN	22232	2.44
18250	07-01-00	Public Svc New Hamp 15.23%	21574	2.37
21460	12-31-09	Marine Midland Bank FRN	20494	2.25
20470	03-15-25	The Money Store Tr 6.425%	20444	2.25
18329	06-01-01	INTERCO 10%	18466	2.03
15000	03-11-98	News America Holdings 7.375%	15035	1.65
14763	05-15-01	Viacom International 8.75%	14837	1.63
13906	05-15-04	Citicorp FRN	13934	1.53
13041	01-15-02	Magma Copper 11.5%	13791	1.51
14509	08-17-23	Merrill Lynch Hm CMO 6.4375%	13711	1.51
13293	05-31-96	Republic of Argentina FRN	12734	1.40
14022	03-15-24	MLMI CMO 6.375%	12704	1.40
12500	12-20-00	Marine Midland Bank FRN	12234	1.34
10960	05-25-24	Resolution Trust CMO 9.4%	10864	1.19
10000	06-18-07	DLJ Mortgage CMO FRN	10188	1.12
10000	07-15-99	Essar Gujarat FRN	10072	1.11

Composition % 12-31-94

Cash	12.3	Preferreds	0.0
Stocks	0.0	Convertibles	0.0
Bonds	87.7	Other	0.0

Tax Analysis

	Tax-Adj Historical Return %	% Pretax Return
3 Yr Avg	4.35	63.7
5 Yr Avg	4.96	63.5
10 Yr Avg	---	---
Potential Capital Gain Exposure (% of assets)		-1%

Most Similar Funds in MF500

Overland Exp Var Rate Govt A	Weak Fit
Fidelity Spartan Lim Mat Gov	Weak Fit
FPA New Income	Weak Fit

Coupon Range

	% of Bonds	Rel Obj
0%	3.4	1.56
0% to 8.5%	40.3	0.64
8.5% to 9.5%	3.0	0.18
9.5% to 11%	5.7	0.61
More than 11%	17.3	4.44
Not applicable	30.4	6.08

Credit Analysis 12-31-94
% of Bonds

US Govt	1	BB	14
AAA	14	B	0
AA	7	Below B	0
A	8	NR/NA	28
BBB	29		

Min Initial Purchase / Expenses & Fees

Min Initial Purchase	$1000 (Addt'l: $50)
Min IRA Purchase	$250 (Addt'l: $50)
Min Auto Invest Plan	$50 (Systematic Inv: $50)

Expenses & Fees
Sales Fees	0.00% front
	0.00% deferred
	0.00% 12b-1
Management Fee	0.60% flat fee
3-,5-,10-yr Expense Projections	$28, $48, $107

MORNINGSTAR 1995 Mutual Fund 500

Strong Asia Pacific

	Ticker	Load	NAV	Yield	SEC Yield	Assets	Objective
	SASPX	None	9.35	0.1%	N/A	57.7	Pacific Stock

Strong Asia Pacific Fund seeks capital appreciation.

The fund normally invests at least 65% of its assets in equities issued by companies domiciled in Asia or the Pacific Basin. The balance of assets may be invested in equity securities issued in other parts of the world, including the United States, or in debt obligations of foreign governments. The fund may not invest more than 25% of its assets in bank obligations. It may invest up to 5% of its assets in debt securities rated below investment grade. The fund may engage in forward foreign currency contracts, options, and futures contracts.

Manager's Investment Style

Management diversifies assets broadly across most of the Pacific Rim's markets--including some exposure to Japan, but certainly not a market-weighted position. It takes a thematic approach to the region, and pays modest multiples for its holdings. It also invests in some lesser-known names.

Historical Profile
Return ---
Risk ---
Rating
Not Rated

Investment Style History
Equity
Average % Stocks Held in Portfolio

88%

Growth of $10,000
|||| Value of Fund ($000)
— Value of Index ($000)
S&P 500
▼ Manager Change
▽ Partial Manager Change
► Mgr Unknown After
◄ Mgr Unknown Before

Performance Quartile
(Within Objective)

Fund Manager(s)

Anthony L. T. Cragg, since 12-93. Birthdate: 01-56. MA, Oxford U. 1979

Manager Experience	Dates Managed	Invest Obj	Std Dev	+/- Index
Anthony L. T. Cragg				
Strong Intrnational Stock	08/93 - 12/94	WF	16.28	10.88

	1983	1984	1985	1986	1987	1988	1989	1990	1991	1992	1993	1994	History
	---	---	---	---	---	---	---	---	---	---	10.00	9.35	NAV
	---	---	---	---	---	---	---	---	---	---	---	-5.27	Total Return %
	---	---	---	---	---	---	---	---	---	---	---	-6.59	+/- S&P 500
	---	---	---	---	---	---	---	---	---	---	---	-18.10	+/- MSCI Pacific
	---	---	---	---	---	---	---	---	---	---	---	0.06	Income Return %
	---	---	---	---	---	---	---	---	---	---	---	-5.33	Capital Return %
	---	---	---	---	---	---	---	---	---	---	---	66	Total Rtn % Rank All
	---	---	---	---	---	---	---	---	---	---	---	35	Total Rtn % Rank Obj
	---	---	---	---	---	---	---	---	---	---	0.00	0.01	Income $
	---	---	---	---	---	---	---	---	---	---	0.00	0.12	Capital Gains $
	---	---	---	---	---	---	---	---	---	---	---	1.90	Expense Ratio %
	---	---	---	---	---	---	---	---	---	---	---	-0.20	Income Ratio %
	---	---	---	---	---	---	---	---	---	---	---	123	Turnover Rate %
	---	---	---	---	---	---	---	---	---	---	---	57.7	Net Assets ($mil)

Performance 12-31-94

	1st Qtr	2nd Qtr	3rd Qtr	4th Qtr	Total
1987	---	---	---	---	---
1988	---	---	---	---	---
1989	---	---	---	---	---
1990	---	---	---	---	---
1991	---	---	---	---	---
1992	---	---	---	---	---
1993	---	---	---	---	---
1994	-3.70	2.18	2.80	-6.36	-5.27

Bear Market Performance

Decile Rank (5-year period)

Worst | Best

	Worst 3 Mo Period 1985-89	Worst 3 Mo Period 1990-94
Strong Asia Pacific	---	---
+/- S&P 500	---	---
+/- Best Fit Index :	---	---

Trailing Returns

	Total Return %	+/- S&P 500	+/- MSCI Pacific	% Rank All	% Rank Obj	Growth of $10,000
3 Mo	-6.36	-6.34	-3.82	95	38	9,364
6 Mo	-3.73	-8.60	1.67	96	57	9,627
1 Yr	-5.27	-6.59	-18.10	66	35	9,473
3 Yr Avg	---	---	---	---	---	---
5 Yr Avg	---	---	---	---	---	---
10 Yr Avg	---	---	---	---	---	---
15 Yr Avg	---	---	---	---	---	---

Operations

Address and Telephone	P.O. Box 2936
	Milwaukee, WI 53201-2936
	800-368-1030 / 414-359-1400
Advisor	Strong Capital Management
Subadvisor	None
Distributor	Strong Funds Distributors
States Available	All plus PR,GU
Report Grade	B-
Income Distrib	Paid Quarterly
* Date of Inception	12-31-93
Fiscal Year End	December

Risk Analysis

Time Period	Load-Adj Return %	Risk % Rank All	Risk % Rank Obj	Morningstar Return	Morningstar Risk	Morningstar Risk-Adj Rating
1 Yr	-5.27					
3 Yr	---	---	---	---	---	---
5 Yr	---	---	---	---	---	---
10 Yr	---	---	---	---	---	---

Average Historical Rating ---

[1] 1 = low, 100 = high   [2] 1.00 = Equity Avg   [3] 1.00 = 90-day T-bill return

Other Measures

			Standard S&P 500	Best Fit
Standard Deviation	---	Alpha	---	---
Mean	---	Beta	---	---
Sharpe Ratio	---	R-Squared	---	---

Investment Style

	Stock Portfolio Avg	Rel MSCI EAFE	Rel Obj
Price/Earnings Ratio	26.5#	0.72	0.83
Price/Cash Flow	13.3#	0.86	0.69
Price/Book Ratio	2.1#	0.80	0.72
5 Yr Earnings Gr %	-0.7#	---	-0.07
Return on Assets %	6.9#	1.51	0.85
Debt % Total Cap	29.8#	0.88	1.25
Med Mkt Cap ($mil)	2616	0.22	0.64

Style: V B G / Size L M S

figure is based on 50% or less of stocks

Diversification Value for Portfolio Types

Large Cap: | Small Cap: | Bond: | Balanced: | Diversified:

Expenses & Fees

Min Initial Purchase	$1000 (Addt'l: $50)
Min IRA Purchase	$250 (Addt'l: $50)
Min Auto Invest Plan	$50 (Systematic Inv: $50)

Sales Fees	0.00% front
	0.00% deferred
	0.00% 12b-1
Management Fee	1.00% flat fee
3-,5-,10-yr Expense Projections	$63, N/A, N/A
Annual Brokerage Cost	---

Tax Analysis

	Tax-Adj Historical Return %	% Pretax Return
3 Yr Avg	---	---
5 Yr Avg	---	---
10 Yr Avg	---	---
Potential Capital Gain Exposure (% of assets)		-10%

Most Similar Funds in MF500

Fund lacks three-year record

Portfolio 11-30-94

Share Chg (06-94) 000	Amount 000	Total Stocks: 109 Total Fixed-Income: 2	Value $000	% Net Assets
39	39	Indosat (ADR)	1482	2.51
5	59	Toc	1163	1.97
-50	498	Carter Holt Harvey	1104	1.87
-52	73	SM Prime Holdings (144A)	1099	1.86
32	306	Woodside Petroleum	1096	1.86
0	0	East Japan Railway	1062	1.80
38	38	Bajaj Auto (144A)	979	1.66
-25	475	MIM Holdings	891	1.51
13	363	Burns Philip	873	1.48
0	130	Tube Investment (144A)	862	1.46
0	1300	Walker	840	1.42
-22	74	Fraser & Neave	821	1.39
0	0	Nippon Telegraph & Telephone	790	1.34
-55	63	Lend Lease	767	1.30
0	329	Poseidon Gold	743	1.26
533	1799	CDL Hotels International New	734	1.24
71	71	Benpress Holdings (144A)	726	1.23
5	50	Broken Hill Proprietary	717	1.22
-669	1607	CDL Hotels International	686	1.16
-235	485	Putra Surya Perkasa (Reg)	668	1.13

Index Allocation

	% of Stocks
S&P 500	0.0
S&P MidCap 400	0.0
U.S. Small Cap	1.7
Foreign	98.3

Composition % 12-31-94

Cash	10.1	Preferreds	0.0
Stocks	89.0	Convertibles	0.0
Bonds	1.0	Other	0.0

Country Exposure 12-31-94

	% of Stocks
Australia	21
Japan	21
New Zealand	9
Singapore	8
Thailand	7

Total Number of Countries: 16
Hedging Policy: ---

Sector Weightings

	% of Stocks	Relative S&P 500
Utilities	6.2	1.00
Energy	3.7	2.11
Financials	18.9	0.74
Industrial Cyclicals	26.8	1.21
Consumer Durables	14.1	1.02
Consumer Staples	10.1	3.75
Services	14.8	1.15
Retail	3.5	0.65
Health	2.1	1.21
Technology	0.0	0.00

Strong Asset Allocation

	Ticker	Load	NAV	Yield	SEC Yield	Assets	Objective
	STAAX	None	17.91	3.9%	N/A	248.6	Asset Alloc.

Strong Asset Allocation Fund seeks total return consistent with the preservation of capital.

The fund invests in a flexible combination of equities, debt, and money-market securities. Under neutral conditions, it allocates its assets to 40% equities, 40% debt obligations, and 20% short-term fixed-income obligations. The equity portion may comprise 0% to 65% of assets, depending on market conditions. The bond portion may comprise 0% to 100% of assets; this portion maintains a duration of two years or more. The fund may invest up to 15% of its assets directly in foreign securities.

Prior to Jan. 10, 1995, the fund was named Strong Investment Fund.

Manager's Investment Style

Prior to 1993, the fund was managed by Strong/Corneliuson head Bill Corneliuson, who regularly moved large portions of the fund's assets among stocks, bonds, and cash. When Corneliuson left the fund in early 1993, the new management took on a more consistent approach: Stocks, bonds, and cash remain near a 40/40/20 mix. Equity allocation is fairly diversified among sectors and higher- and lower-yielding stocks. In the bond portfolio, duration is kept near the short end of the Lehman Brothers Corporate Index.

Fund Manager(s)

Jay N. Mueller CFA(1994), since 01-93.
Andrew C. Stephens, since 01-93.
Bradley C. Tank, since 01-93.

Manager Experience

	Dates Managed	Invest Obj	Std Dev	+/- Index
Bradley C. Tank				
Strong Income	06/90 - 10/93	CG	4.30	-0.74
Strong Advantage	06/90 - 10/93	CG	1.14	-3.30

Historical Profile
Return Average
Risk Low
Rating ★★★
Neutral

Investment Style History Equity
Average % Stocks Held in Portfolio

40% 41% 30% 21% 42% 30% 37% 33%

Growth of $10,000
||||| Value of Fund ($000)
— Value of Index ($000) S&P 500
▼ Manager Change
▽ Partial Manager Change
► Mgr Unknown After
◄ Mgr Unknown Before

Performance Quartile (Within Objective)

	1983	1984	1985	1986	1987	1988	1989	1990	1991	1992	1993	1994	History
	17.48	17.62	20.12	22.18	17.60	17.57	18.41	17.50	19.68	18.49	19.06	17.91	NAV
	45.23	9.77	19.31	17.77	-0.31	9.19	11.20	2.78	19.64	3.23	14.53	-1.51	Total Return %
	22.76	3.50	-12.43	-0.91	-5.57	-7.42	-20.48	5.90	-10.85	-4.39	4.47	-2.82	+/- S&P 500
	36.86	-5.39	-2.82	2.52	-3.06	1.31	-3.34	-6.17	3.63	-4.02	4.78	1.41	+/- LB Aggregate
	3.80	1.96	4.83	5.08	8.79	9.36	5.59	7.72	5.94	4.57	4.49	3.72	Income Return %
	41.43	7.81	14.48	12.69	-9.09	-0.17	5.61	-4.94	13.70	-1.34	10.04	-5.23	Capital Return %
	1	28	77	34	62	67	63	49	45	83	30	30	Total Rtn % Rank All
	1	1	50	41	88	48	76	22	58	82	47	29	Total Rtn % Rank Obj
	0.43	0.31	0.74	0.95	1.78	1.61	0.97	1.38	0.97	0.87	0.82	0.70	Income $
	0.90	1.10	0.04	0.42	2.95	0.00	0.14	0.00	0.20	0.94	1.24	0.16	Capital Gains $
	1.70	1.20	1.10	1.10	1.10	1.20	1.30	1.30	1.30	1.20	1.20	1.20	Expense Ratio %
	5.40	8.40	5.40	4.70	4.20	7.50	6.60	6.10	5.10	4.40	4.20	3.50	Income Ratio %
	162	77	144	80	337	426	207	320	418	320	348	325	Turnover Rate %
	23.1	146.0	222.7	339.4	272.9	256.1	240.5	203.6	215.0	208.4	254.4	248.6	Net Assets ($mil)

Performance 12-31-94

	1st Qtr	2nd Qtr	3rd Qtr	4th Qtr	Total
1987	6.87	-2.27	1.87	-6.29	-0.31
1988	2.79	1.51	2.20	2.39	9.19
1989	4.97	2.87	3.88	-0.86	11.20
1990	-1.41	1.99	-0.67	2.91	2.78
1991	5.08	0.04	5.17	8.21	19.64
1992	-1.02	0.06	2.98	1.21	3.23
1993	5.17	2.07	4.71	1.90	14.53
1994	-2.14	-1.85	2.14	0.39	-1.51

Bear Market Performance

Decile Rank (5-year period)

Worst ─────────── Best

	Worst 3 Mo Period 1985-89	Worst 3 Mo Period 1990-94
Strong Asset Allocation	-7.64	-4.68
+/- S&P 500	21.95	1.08
+/- Best Fit Index : S&P 500	21.95	1.08

Trailing Returns

	Total Return %	+/- S&P 500	+/- LB Aggregate	% Rank All	% Rank Obj	Growth of $10,000
3 Mo	0.39	0.41	0.02	13	12	10,039
6 Mo	2.55	-2.32	1.55	23	28	10,255
1 Yr	-1.51	-2.82	1.41	30	29	9,849
3 Yr Avg	5.21	-1.06	0.66	44	56	11,644
5 Yr Avg	7.44	-1.25	-0.18	41	54	14,318
10 Yr Avg	9.31	-5.07	-0.64	67	50	24,353
15 Yr Avg	---	---	---	---	---	---

Operations

Address and Telephone	P.O. Box 2936
	Milwaukee, WI 53201-2936
	800-368-1030 / 414-359-1400
Advisor	Strong Capital Management
Subadvisor	None
Distributor	Strong Funds Distributors
States Available	All plus PR,GU
Report Grade	B
Income Distrib	Paid Quarterly
Date of Inception	12-30-81
Fiscal Year End	December

Risk Analysis

Time Period	Load-Adj Return %	Risk % Rank All	Obj	Morningstar Return	Risk	Morningstar Risk-Adj Rating
1 Yr	-1.51					
3 Yr	5.21	37	23	0.48[3]	0.61	★★★
5 Yr	7.44	43	8	0.66[3]	0.52	★★★★
10 Yr	9.31	35	12	0.53	0.50	★★★
Average Historical Rating (109 months)				3.7 ★s		

[1] 1 = low, 100 = high [2] 1.00 = Hybrid Avg [3] 1.00 = 90-day T-bill return

Other Measures

			Standard S&P 500	Best Fit S&P 500
Standard Deviation	4.82	Alpha	0.2	0.2
Mean	5.20	Beta	0.50	0.50
Sharpe Ratio	0.35	R-Squared	68	68

Investment Style

Stocks
	Port Avg	Rel S&P 500
Price/Earnings Ratio	20.5	1.11
Price/Book Ratio	3.2	0.93
5 Yr Earnings Gr %	13.5	2.43
Med Mkt Cap ($mil)	3822	0.29

Bonds
Avg Effective Duration	4.2 Yrs
Avg Effective Maturity	---
Avg Credit Quality	AA
Avg Weighted Coupon	7.76%

Not Available

Diversification Value for Portfolio Types

Large Cap: Low | Small Cap: Medium | Bond: Low | Balanced: None | Diversified: Low

Portfolio 12-31-94

Share Chg (09-94)000	Amount 000	Total Stocks: 95 Total Fixed-Income: 70	Date of Maturity	Value $000	% Net Assets
	6450	Resolution Trust CMO 9.4%	05-25-24	6394	2.57
	6000	Rogers Cablesystems 9.625%	08-01-02	5745	2.31
	5000	CCP Insurance 10.5%	12-15-04	4977	2.00
	4463	Manufactured Housing 6.075%	04-25-11	4460	1.79
	4100	Tosco 9%	03-15-97	4146	1.67
	5645	FNMA CMO IFRN	02-25-23	4020	1.62
	3900	Hook-SuperRx 10.125%	06-01-02	3968	1.60
	5412	GNMA 6%	01-16-24	3903	1.57
	4000	US Treasury Bond 6.25%	08-15-23	3250	1.31
	3000	American Re 10.875%	09-15-04	3191	1.28
	3004	MLMI CMO 10.1%	11-15-07	3133	1.26
	2975	Citicorp FRN	05-01-04	2981	1.20
	24625	Small Bus Adm I/O 2.5312%	02-15-18	2870	1.15
	3000	Marine Midland Banks FRN	12-31-09	2865	1.15
	2831	CMO Trust 8.25%	06-20-96	2835	1.14
	3029	First Bost Mtg Secs CMO 7.5%	03-25-33	2753	1.11
	2716	Citicorp FRN	05-01-04	2721	1.09
	3000	MLMI CMO 6.375%	03-15-24	2718	1.09
	2700	Resolution Trust 7.125%	09-01-29	2699	1.09
	2711	FNMA 6.5%	09-01-08	2572	1.03

Index Allocation
	% of Stocks
S&P 500	58.6
S&P MidCap 400	9.6
U.S. Small Cap	21.1
Foreign	12.2

Composition % 12-31-94
Cash	7.5	Preferreds	0.0
Stocks	36.6	Convertibles	0.8
Bonds	55.1	Other	0.0

Tax Analysis
	Tax-Adj Historical Return %	% Pretax Return
3 Yr Avg	2.50	46.9
5 Yr Avg	4.88	62.3
10 Yr Avg	6.22	57.7
Potential Capital Gain Exposure (% of assets)		-2%

Most Similar Funds in MF500
Prudential Alloc Cons Mgd B	Strong Fit
Sentinel Balanced	Fair Fit
Connecticut Mutual Total Ret	Fair Fit

Bond Credit Analysis 12-31-94
% of Bonds
US Govt	28	BB	0
AAA	23	B	0
AA	4	Below B	0
A	18	NR/NA	0
BBB	28		

Stock Sector Weightings
	% of Stocks	Relative S&P 500
Utilities	8.7	0.70
Energy	10.2	1.01
Financials	8.3	0.79
Industrial Cyclicals	12.9	0.79
Consumer Durables	7.2	1.17
Consumer Staples	7.5	0.60
Services	15.1	1.86
Retail	4.9	0.84
Health	9.9	1.14
Technology	15.3	1.67

Expenses & Fees
Sales Fees	
	0.00% front
	0.00% deferred
	0.00% 12b-1
Management Fee	0.85% max./0.80% min.
3-,5-,10-yr Expense Projections	$37, $64, $141
Annual Brokerage Cost	0.28%

Min Initial Purchase — $250 (Addt'l: $50)
Min IRA Purchase — $250 (Addt'l: $50)
Min Auto Invest Plan — $50 (Systematic Inv: $50)

Strong Common Stock

Strong Common Stock Fund seeks growth of capital; current income is not a consideration.

The fund normally invests at least 80% of its assets in common stocks. The balance may be invested in other equity-type securities, including preferred stocks, warrants, and securities convertible into common or preferred stocks. The fund may also invest up to 20% of its assets in short-term fixed-income securities as a temporary defensive measure. It may engage in substantial short-term trading. It may also invest up to 15% of its assets directly in foreign securities, and may invest without limit in ADRs.

Ticker	Load	NAV	Yield	SEC Yield	Assets
STCSX	Clsd	16.74	0.3%	N/A	790.1

Objective
Small Company

Historical Profile
Return   High
Risk   Below Average
Rating   ★★★★★
            Closed

Manager's Investment Style

Management attempts to buy a stock when it is selling below its private-market value, and then sells when the price exceeds that value. They typically hold a number of overlooked firms with turnaround potential. Although the fund is not highly concentrated, management will load up on sectors it finds compelling.

Investment Style History
Equity
Average % Stocks Held in Portfolio

92% 84% 87% 86% 89%

Growth of $10,000
|||| Value of Fund ($000)
— Value of Index ($000)
   Wil 4500
▼ Manager Change
▽ Partial Manager Change
► Mgr Unknown After
◄ Mgr Unknown Before

Performance Quartile (Within Objective)

	1983	1984	1985	1986	1987	1988	1989	1990	1991	1992	1993	1994	History
	---	---	---	---	---	---	10.00	10.02	12.84	15.07	17.94	16.74	NAV
	---	---	---	---	---	---	---	1.00 *	57.07	20.78	25.17	-0.50	Total Return %
	---	---	---	---	---	---	---	4.12 *	26.59	13.16	15.11	-1.81	+/- S&P 500
	---	---	---	---	---	---	---	14.56	13.62	9.02	10.63	2.16	+/- Wilshire 4500
	---	---	---	---	---	---	---	0.80	19.99	2.03	0.24	0.26	Income Return %
	---	---	---	---	---	---	---	0.20	37.08	18.75	24.92	-0.76	Capital Return %
	---	---	---	---	---	---	---	52	5	4	11	23	Total Rtn % Rank All
	---	---	---	---	---	---	---	15	28	19	13	44	Total Rtn % Rank Obj
	---	---	---	---	---	---	0.00	0.08	1.86	0.22	0.04	0.04	Income $
	---	---	---	---	---	---	0.00	0.00	0.73	0.16	0.86	1.06	Capital Gains $
	---	---	---	---	---	---	---	2.00	2.00	1.40	1.40	1.30	Expense Ratio %
	---	---	---	---	---	---	---	0.90	-0.50	0.10	0.20	0.20	Income Ratio %
	---	---	---	---	---	---	---	291	2461	292	81	102	Turnover Rate %
	---	---	---	---	---	---	---	2.4	48.5	179.1	762.1	790.1	Net Assets ($mil)

Fund Manager(s)

Richard T. Weiss, since 03-91. Birthdate: 05-51.
BS, U. of Southern California 1973   MBA, Harvard 1975
Marina T. Carlson CFA, since 12-93. BA, Drake U.
MBA, DePaul U.

Manager Experience	Dates Managed	Invest Obj	Std Dev	+/- Index
Richard T. Weiss				
SteinRoe Special	11/90 - 03/91	G	7.55	3.34
SteinRoe Capital Opport	11/90 - 03/91	AG	8.80	7.36

Performance 12-31-94

	1st Qtr	2nd Qtr	3rd Qtr	4th Qtr	Total
1987	---	---	---	---	---
1988	---	---	---	---	---
1989	---	---	---	---	---
1990	0.74	7.83	-16.17	10.92	1.00
1991	22.72	3.96	17.27	4.98	57.07
1992	6.03	-7.50	8.49	13.51	20.78
1993	9.60	1.43	8.12	4.13	25.17
1994	-2.83	-0.29	5.70	-2.84	-0.50

Bear Market Performance

Decile Rank (5-year period)

Worst ———————————— Best

	Worst 3 Mo Period 1985-89	Worst 3 Mo Period 1990-94
Strong Common Stock	---	-16.17
+/- S&P 500		-2.43
+/- Best Fit Index : Wil 4500	---	2.05

Trailing Returns

	Total Return %	+/- S&P 500	+/- Wil 4500	% Rank All	% Rank Obj	Growth of $10,000
3 Mo	-2.84	-2.83	-0.34	81	82	9,716
6 Mo	2.70	-2.17	-1.50	22	75	10,270
1 Yr	-0.50	-1.81	2.16	23	44	9,950
3 Yr Avg	14.58	8.31	6.97	4	19	15,042
5 Yr Avg	19.00	10.31	9.91	2	6	23,863
10 Yr Avg	---	---	---	---	---	---
15 Yr Avg	---	---	---	---	---	---

Risk Analysis

Time Period	Load-Adj Return %	Risk % Rank [1] All	Obj	Morningstar [2] Return	Risk	Morningstar Risk-Adj Rating
1 Yr	-0.50					
3 Yr	14.58	65	18	3.53 [3]	0.73	★★★★★
5 Yr	19.00	69	14	4.34 [3]	0.82	★★★★★
10 Yr	---					

Average Historical Rating (25 months)   5.0 ★s

[1] 1 = low, 100 = high   [2] 1.00 = Equity Avg   [3] 1.00 = 90-day T-bill return

Other Measures

			Standard S&P 500	Best Fit Wil 4500
Standard Deviation	10.44	Alpha	8.5	6.6
Mean	14.23	Beta	0.88	0.99
Sharpe Ratio	1.03	R-Squared	45	86

Investment Style

	Stock Portfolio Avg	Relative S&P 500
Price/Earnings Ratio	22.8	1.23
Price/Book Ratio	3.2	0.94
5 Yr Earnings Gr %	5.5#	1.00
Return on Assets %	6.8	0.91
Debt % Total Cap	32.2	1.14
Med Mkt Cap ($mil)	1375	0.11

figure is based on 50% or less of stocks

Style
Value Blend Growth
Size Large Med Small

Diversification Value for Portfolio Types

Large Cap: Medium	Small Cap: None	Bond: High	Balanced: Low	Diversified: Low

Operations

Address and Telephone	P.O. Box 2936
	Milwaukee, WI 53201-2936
	800-368-1030 / 414-359-1400
Advisor	Strong Capital Management
Subadvisor	None
Distributor	Strong Funds Distributors
States Available	All plus PR,GU
Report Grade	B-
Income Distrib	Paid Quarterly
* Date of Inception	12-31-89
Fiscal Year End	December

Min Initial Purchase	Closed (Addt'l: $50)
Min IRA Purchase	$250 (Addt'l: $50)
Min Auto Invest Plan	$50 (Systematic Inv: $50)

Expenses & Fees
Sales Fees	0.00% front
	0.00% deferred
	0.00% 12b-1
Management Fee	1.00% flat fee
3-,5-,10-yr Expense Projections	$43, $75, $165
Annual Brokerage Cost	0.37%

Portfolio 12-31-94

Share Chg (09-94) 000	Amount 000	Total Stocks: 96 Total Fixed-Income: 0	Value $000	% Net Assets
120	310	Autodesk	12284	1.55
0	115	Tempest Reinsurance	11515	1.46
-5	135	Capital Cities/ABC	11509	1.46
10	350	US Cellular	11463	1.45
20	425	American Stores	11422	1.45
0	332	Paging Network	11298	1.43
31	468	Kroger	11291	1.43
0	385	AirTouch Communications	11213	1.42
-52	415	Marshall Industries	11101	1.41
-35	525	Union Texas Petroleum	10894	1.38
0	500	Tele-Communications Cl A	10875	1.38
0	81	LIN Broadcasting	10814	1.37
68	390	IHOP	10628	1.35
-25	475	Belden	10569	1.34
740	740	National Medical Enterprises	10453	1.32
54	330	Times Mirror Cl A	10354	1.31
5	360	Cabot	10215	1.29
-16	214	Nestle (Reg) (ADR)	10196	1.29
-42	243	Wisconsin Central Transport	10003	1.27
-4	152	Eli Lilly	9975	1.26
35	385	FHP International	9914	1.25
50	900	Battle Mountain Gold	9900	1.25
0	219	JC Penney	9773	1.24
25	130	Texas Instruments	9734	1.23
-10	547	Sonat Offshore Drilling	9709	1.23

Composition % 12-31-94

Cash	10.6	Preferreds	0.0
Stocks	89.4	Convertibles	0.0
Bonds	0.0	Other	0.0

Tax Analysis

	Tax-Adj Historical Return %	% Pretax Return
3 Yr Avg	13.09	88.5
5 Yr Avg	16.73	84.2
10 Yr Avg	---	---
Potential Capital Gain Exposure (% of assets)		7%

Most Similar Funds in MF500

Acorn	Fair Fit
Strong Opportunity	Fair Fit
Vista Capital Growth A	Fair Fit

Index Allocation

	% of Stocks
S&P 500	32.5
S&P MidCap 400	16.9
U.S. Small Cap	37.2
Foreign	14.9

Sector Weightings

	% of Stocks	Relative S&P 500
Utilities	1.5	0.12
Energy	10.2	1.00
Financials	4.2	0.39
Industrial Cyclicals	16.9	1.03
Consumer Durables	4.6	0.73
Consumer Staples	4.4	0.35
Services	21.0	2.58
Retail	9.8	1.68
Health	7.8	0.90
Technology	19.6	2.14

Strong Discovery

	Ticker	Load	NAV	Yield	SEC Yield	Assets	Objective
	STDIX	None	15.67	4.2%	N/A	388.4	Aggr. Growth

Strong Discovery Fund seeks capital appreciation.

The fund may invest substantially all of its assets in common stocks, convertible securities, and warrants. It may also invest all of its assets in nonconvertible corporate debt and intermediate- to long-term government debt securities if the fund perceives a greater opportunity for capital appreciation. The fund intends to engage in short-term trading, and it may invest a substantial portion of its assets in small, unseasoned companies. The fund may invest up to 15% of its assets directly in foreign securities, and may invest without limit in ADRs.

Manager's Investment Style

Management has a strategy of aggressive opportunism, dabbling in a variety of asset classes, sectors, and markets to meet its goals. Management will venture into sectors where few of its peers go. In 1990, the fund held cash and bonds. In 1993, it held three times the objective average in financials and nearly a fourth of assets in Hong Kong.

Fund Manager(s)

Richard S. Strong, since 12-87. Birthdate: 05-42.
BA, Baldwin-Wallace C. 1963 MBA, U. of Wisconsin 1966

Manager Experience	Dates Managed	Invest Obj	Std Dev	+/- Index
Richard S. Strong				
Strong Total Return	12/81 - 04/93	GI	12.12	-0.76
Strong Asset Allocation	12/81 - 01/93	AA	9.46	-1.79

Performance 12-31-94

	1st Qtr	2nd Qtr	3rd Qtr	4th Qtr	Total
1987	---	---	---	---	---
1988	19.19	3.77	2.14	-1.49	24.45
1989	6.48	19.54	7.73	-9.56	24.01
1990	-4.32	10.49	-10.31	2.57	-2.75
1991	27.95	-3.31	18.26	14.57	67.61
1992	-1.60	-6.83	-5.63	17.83	1.94
1993	3.87	0.12	6.14	10.72	22.21
1994	-5.37	-5.83	9.56	-3.39	-5.68

Bear Market Performance

Decile Rank (5-year period)

	Worst 3 Mo Period 1985-89	Worst 3 Mo Period 1990-94
Strong Discovery	---	-10.39
+/- S&P 500	---	3.45
+/- Best Fit Index : Wil 4500	---	9.01

Trailing Returns

	Total Return %	+/- S&P 500	+/- Wil 4500	% Rank All	% Rank Obj	Growth of $10,000
3 Mo	-3.39	-3.38	-0.89	85	88	9,661
6 Mo	5.84	0.98	1.65	9	62	10,584
1 Yr	-5.68	-7.00	-3.03	70	67	9,432
3 Yr Avg	5.52	-0.74	-2.08	38	57	11,750
5 Yr Avg	13.88	5.19	4.79	5	25	19,154
10 Yr Avg	---	---	---	---	---	---
15 Yr Avg	---	---	---	---	---	---

Operations

Address and Telephone	P.O. Box 2936	
	Milwaukee, WI 53201-2936	
	800-368-1030 / 414-359-1400	
Advisor	Strong Capital Management	
Subadvisor	None	
Distributor	Strong Funds Distributors	
States Available	All plus PR,GU	
Report Grade	B-	
Income Distrib	Paid Quarterly	
* Date of Inception	12-31-87	
Fiscal Year End	December	

Min Initial Purchase	$1000 (Addt'l: $50)
Min IRA Purchase	$250 (Addt'l: $50)
Min Auto Invest Plan	$50 (Systematic Inv: $50)

Expenses & Fees

Sales Fees	
	0.00% front
	0.00% deferred
	0.00% 12b-1
Management Fee	1.00% flat fee
3-,5-,10-yr Expense Projections	$46, $80, $176
Annual Brokerage Cost	1.71%

Historical Profile

Return	Above Average
Risk	Average
Rating	★★★★ Above Average

	1983	1984	1985	1986	1987	1988	1989	1990	1991	1992	1993	1994	History
						51%	66%	62%	92%	91%	95%	79%	Average % Stocks Held in Portfolio
NAV	---	---	---	---	10.00	11.44	13.18	12.51	17.49	16.01	18.05	15.67	NAV
	---	---	---	---	---	24.45	24.01	-2.75	67.61	1.94	22.21	-5.68	Total Return %
	---	---	---	---	---	7.84	-7.67	0.37	37.13	-5.68	12.15	-7.00	+/- S&P 500
	---	---	---	---	---	3.91	0.07	10.81	24.16	-9.82	7.67	-3.03	+/- Wilshire 4500
	---	---	---	---	---	9.72	2.21	2.34	5.30	9.64	3.25	4.19	Income Return %
	---	---	---	---	---	14.73	21.80	-5.08	62.31	-7.70	18.96	-9.87	Capital Return %
	---	---	---	---	---	6	26	63	2	87	14	70	Total Rtn % Rank All
	---	---	---	---	---	19	57	27	27	75	26	67	Total Rtn % Rank Obj
	---	---	---	---	0.00	0.97	0.28	0.31	0.83	1.50	0.50	0.69	Income $
	---	---	---	---	0.00	0.03	0.71	0.00	2.60	0.15	0.93	0.68	Capital Gains $
	---	---	---	---	---	2.00	1.90	1.90	1.60	1.50	1.50	1.40	Expense Ratio %
	---	---	---	---	---	11.90	2.40	2.10	0.00	-0.40	-0.20	0.00	Income Ratio %
	---	---	---	---	---	442	550	494	1060	1259	668	409	Turnover Rate %
	---	---	---	---	---	13.6	57.9	56.3	162.5	193.3	301.8	388.4	Net Assets ($mil)

Investment Style History
Equity

Growth of $10,000
- Value of Fund ($000)
- Value of Index ($000) Wil 4500
- ▼ Manager Change
- ▽ Partial Manager Change
- ► Mgr Unknown After
- ◄ Mgr Unknown Before

Performance Quartile (Within Objective)

Risk Analysis

Time Period	Load-Adj Return %	Risk % Rank [1] All	Risk % Rank [1] Obj	Morningstar [2] Return	Morningstar Risk	Morningstar Risk-Adj Rating
1 Yr	-5.68					
3 Yr	5.52	90	36	0.57 [3]	1.20	★★★
5 Yr	13.88	82	16	2.53 [3]	1.00	★★★★★
10 Yr	---	---	---	---	---	

Average Historical Rating (49 months)   4.4 ★s

[1] 1 = low, 100 = high   [2] 1.00 = Equity Avg   [3] 1.00 = 90-day T-bill return

Other Measures

			Standard S&P 500	Best Fit Wil 4500
Standard Deviation	13.36	Alpha	-0.4	-2.2
Mean	6.27	Beta	1.09	1.16
Sharpe Ratio	0.21	R-Squared	42	72

Investment Style

	Stock Portfolio Avg	Relative S&P 500
Price/Earnings Ratio	26.0	1.40
Price/Book Ratio	3.8	1.11
5 Yr Earnings Gr %	20.3#	3.65
Return on Assets %	8.7	1.16
Debt % Total Cap	23.9	0.84
Med Mkt Cap ($mil)	1757	0.14

figure is based on 50% or less of stocks

Style
Value Blend Growth
Size Large/Med Small

Diversification Value for Portfolio Types

Large Cap: Medium	Small Cap: Low	Bond: High	Balanced: Low	Diversified: Low

Portfolio 12-31-94

Share Chg (09-94) 000	Amount 000	Total Stocks: 163 Total Fixed-Income: 1	Value $000	% Net Assets
999	1440	Santa Fe Pacific Gold	18540	4.77
593	677	National Medical Enterprises	9563	2.46
156	156	Motorola	9029	2.32
120	220	Value Health	8195	2.11
18	180	Telebras (ADR)	8055	2.07
370	370	EMC	8001	2.06
-118	370	Danka Business Systems (ADR)	8001	2.06
1	63	HSBC Holdings (ADR)	6799	1.75
92	342	Federated Department Stores	6584	1.69
107	420	Fingerhut	6510	1.68
131	244	Movie Gallery	6339	1.63
-44	174	Compuware	6264	1.61
-287	451	OrNda Healthcorp	5638	1.45
-109	228	Office Depot	5472	1.41
	895	RJR Nabisco PERCS 9.25%	5370	1.38
90	90	Exide	5063	1.30
34	84	Nucor	4662	1.20
120	120	Micro Warehouse	4200	1.08
12	150	Harley-Davidson	4200	1.08
130	130	Informix	4176	1.08
-19	130	Times Mirror Cl A	4079	1.05
143	143	Service International	3968	1.02
0	1454	Citic Pacific	3505	0.90
92	92	Canandaigua Wine Cl A	3496	0.90
0	1552	Consolidated Elec Power Asia	3410	0.88

Composition % 12-31-94

Cash	10.8	Preferreds	0.0
Stocks	87.8	Convertibles	1.4
Bonds	0.0	Other	0.0

Tax Analysis

	Tax-Adj Historical Return %	% Pretax Return
3 Yr Avg	2.66	46.8
5 Yr Avg	10.76	72.9
10 Yr Avg	---	---
Potential Capital Gain Exposure (% of assets)		-4%

Most Similar Funds in MF500

CGM Capital Development	Fair Fit
Oppenheimer Discovery A	Weak Fit
Alger Small Capitalization	Weak Fit

Index Allocation

	% of Stocks
S&P 500	35.0
S&P MidCap 400	14.8
U.S. Small Cap	35.3
Foreign	16.1

Sector Weightings

	% of Stocks	Relative S&P 500
Utilities	0.0	0.00
Energy	2.5	0.25
Financials	12.3	1.16
Industrial Cyclicals	23.5	1.44
Consumer Durables	8.4	1.35
Consumer Staples	1.6	0.13
Services	18.9	2.32
Retail	5.6	0.96
Health	11.3	1.30
Technology	15.9	1.74

Strong Government Securities

	Ticker	Load	NAV	Yield	SEC Yield	Assets	Objective
	STVSX	None	9.63	6.5%	7.41%	276.8	Gvt General

Strong Government Securities Fund seeks current income.

The fund normally invests at least 80% of its assets in U.S. government securities. In addition to Treasury obligations, these may include securities issued by agencies such as the Federal Housing Administration, Government National Mortgage Association, Federal Home Loan Banks, and the Student Loan Marketing Association; these agency securities are backed by differing levels of government support. The balance of assets may be invested in other investment-grade fixed-income securities. The fund maintains no restrictions on average maturity.

Historical Profile
Return: High
Risk: Below Average
Rating: ★★★★★ Highest

Manager's Investment Style

Management keeps the fund's duration within a four- to six-year range. To add value, management churns the portfolio rapidly (as its enormous turnover ratio suggests) to take advantage of inefficiencies in the market. In 1994, for example, the fund bought downtrodden mortgages and CMOs--and even some municipal bonds--for their high yields and turnaround potential. The fund actively uses interest-rate futures, as well, to take advantage of under- or overvalued yield-curve positions. Finally, inverse floaters and interest-only strips have played small roles in the portfolio.

Fund Manager(s)

Bradley C. Tank, since 06-90. Birthdate: 09-57.
BS, U. of Wisconsin 1980 MBA, U. of Wisconsin 1982

Manager Experience	Dates Managed	Invest Obj	Std Dev	+/- Index
Bradley C. Tank				
Strong Income	06/90 - 10/93	CG	4.30	-0.74
Strong Advantage	06/90 - 10/93	CG	1.14	-3.30

Investment Style History
Fixed Income
Income Rtn % Rank Obj

Growth of $10,000
||| Value of Fund ($000)
— Value of Index ($000) LB Corp
▼ Manager Change
▽ Partial Manager Change
► Mgr Unknown After
◄ Mgr Unknown Before

Performance Quartile (Within Objective)

	1983	1984	1985	1986	1987	1988	1989	1990	1991	1992	1993	1994	History
	---	---	---	10.09	9.75	9.98	10.08	10.10	10.77	10.39	10.61	9.63	NAV
	---	---	---	2.20 *	3.46	10.50	9.97	8.71	16.68	9.19	12.78	-3.37	Total Return %
	---	---	---	---	0.70	2.62	-4.57	-0.24	0.68	1.95	3.03	-0.45	+/- LB Aggregate
	---	---	---	---	1.27	3.47	-4.25	-0.01	1.37	1.96	2.13	0.01	+/- LB Government
	---	---	---	1.30	6.83	7.17	8.37	7.53	8.25	8.08	6.54	5.87	Income Return %
	---	---	---	0.90	-3.37	3.33	1.60	1.18	8.43	1.11	6.25	-9.24	Capital Return %
	---	---	---	---	32	57	74	11	52	30	43	47	Total Rtn % Rank All
	---	---	---	---	24	3	90	55	11	4	6	51	Total Rtn % Rank Obj
	---	---	---	0.13	0.65	0.68	0.81	0.72	0.77	0.80	0.66	0.63	Income $
	---	---	---	0.00	0.00	0.09	0.06	0.10	0.17	0.48	0.41	0.00	Capital Gains $
	---	---	---	0.60	1.00	0.40	1.30	1.30	0.80	0.70	0.80	0.90	Expense Ratio %
	---	---	---	7.20	6.60	6.90	7.60	7.20	7.50	7.70	6.00	5.90	Income Ratio %
	---	---	---	0	715	1728	422	254	293	629	521	472	Turnover Rate %
	---	---	---	0.9	11.4	25.4	35.1	41.1	51.9	82.2	222.0	276.8	Net Assets ($mil)

Performance 12-31-94

	1st Qtr	2nd Qtr	3rd Qtr	4th Qtr	Total
1987	1.69	-7.93	2.00	8.34	3.46
1988	4.31	1.39	2.10	2.33	10.50
1989	2.80	5.96	-1.16	2.15	9.97
1990	1.08	2.07	1.75	3.55	8.71
1991	2.03	1.73	5.61	6.44	16.68
1992	-1.01	4.06	4.72	1.22	9.19
1993	5.58	3.04	3.34	0.31	12.78
1994	-2.50	-1.93	1.01	0.05	-3.37

Bear Market Performance

Decile Rank (5-year period)

Worst ———— Best

	Worst 3 Mo Period 1985-89	Worst 3 Mo Period 1990-94
Strong Government Securities	---	-5.20
+/- LB Aggregate	---	-0.27
+/- Best Fit Index : LB Corp	---	1.07

Trailing Returns

	Total Return %	+/- LB Aggregate	+/- LB Govt	% Rank All	Rank Obj	Growth of $10,000
3 Mo	0.05	-0.33	-0.31	20	49	10,005
6 Mo	1.06	0.07	0.28	36	14	10,106
1 Yr	-3.37	-0.45	0.01	47	51	9,663
3 Yr Avg	5.97	1.43	1.31	34	1	11,900
5 Yr Avg	8.58	0.96	1.06	27	1	15,095
10 Yr Avg	---	---	---	---	---	---
15 Yr Avg	---	---	---	---	---	---

Operations

Address and Telephone	P.O. Box 2936
	Milwaukee, WI 53201-2936
	800-368-1030 / 414-359-1400
Advisor	Strong Capital Management
Subadvisor	None
Distributor	Strong Funds Distributors
States Available	All plus PR,GU
Report Grade	B-
Income Distrib	Paid Monthly
* Date of Inception	10-29-86
Fiscal Year End	December

Risk Analysis

Time Period	Load-Adj Return %	Risk % Rank All	Obj	Morningstar Return	Morningstar Risk	Morningstar Risk-Adj Rating
1 Yr	-3.37					
3 Yr	5.97	22	45	0.71[3]	0.99	★★★★★
5 Yr	8.58	11	28	0.96[3]	0.79	★★★★★
10 Yr	---	---	---			

Average Historical Rating (63 months)   4.9 ★s

[1] 1 = low, 100 = high [2] 1.00 = Taxable Avg [3] 1.00 = 90-day T-bill return

Other Measures

				Standard LB Agg	Best Fit LB Corp
Standard Deviation	4.40	Alpha		1.3	0.8
Mean	5.91	Beta		1.07	0.86
Sharpe Ratio	0.54	R-Squared		94	94

Investment Style

Interest-Rate Stance
Avg Effective Duration   4.9 Yrs**
Avg Effective Maturity   7.5 Yrs

Maturity: Short Intm Long
Quality: High Med Low

Quality
Avg Credit Quality   AAA
Avg Weighted Coupon   7.52%
Avg Weighted Price   91.84% of Par

**figure provided by fund

Diversification Value for Portfolio Types

Large Cap: Medium	Small Cap: High	Bond: None	Balanced: Medium	Diversified: Medium

Portfolio 12-31-94

Total Stocks: 0
Total Fixed-Income: 75

Amount 000	Date of Maturity		Value $000	% Net Assets
33535	08-15-02	US Treasury Note 6.375%	30726	11.10
15737	05-01-21	FHA Project Loan 7.43%	14979	5.41
10355	12-01-24	GNMA TBA 7%	10132	3.66
10000	06-21-14	NWA 10.23%	10038	3.63
9434	12-01-24	FNMA 9%	9501	3.43
9877	09-25-21	FNMA CMO Z 8.5%	9465	3.42
11000	07-16-24	GNMA CMO REMIC 5%	9089	3.28
10216	11-15-08	FHLMC CMO 6.5%	8682	3.14
9656	05-25-20	FNMA CMO PAC IFRN	8362	3.02
8316	08-01-11	FHLMC 9%	8353	3.02
8525	11-01-24	GNMA TBA 6.5%	8213	2.97
9844	11-01-06	FHA Project Loan 3.025%	7808	2.82
6400	12-15-04	CCP Insurance 10.5%	6371	2.30
5000	03-15-02	Tosco 9.625%	5151	1.86
5045	04-25-21	FNMA CMO PAC FRN	4963	1.79
5350	08-15-05	Citicorp 6.75%	4642	1.68
5287	10-25-16	American Savings Bank 7.43%	4600	1.66
4145	01-01-16	FNMA 12%	4548	1.64
4518	09-01-08	FNMA 6.5%	4287	1.55
4194	11-25-20	FNMA CMO 8.5%	4118	1.49
3923	08-01-02	FHLMC 9.75%	3999	1.44
3943	05-01-16	FHLMC 8.5%	3861	1.39
4750	12-15-13	FHLMC CMO 6.5%	3827	1.38
5946	08-25-22	FNMA CMO P/O 0%	3518	1.27
3477	07-01-08	FHLMC 7.25%	3334	1.20

Composition % 12-31-94

Cash	11.2	Preferreds	3.6	
Stocks	0.0	Convertibles	0.0	
Bonds	85.2	Other	0.0	

Tax Analysis

	Tax-Adj Historical Return %	% Pretax Return
3 Yr Avg	2.68	43.5
5 Yr Avg	5.45	59.7
10 Yr Avg	---	---

Potential Capital Gain Exposure (% of assets)   -9%

Most Similar Funds in MF500

SteinRoe Income	Strong Fit
J Hancock Inc	Strong Fit
Bond Fund of America	Strong Fit

Coupon Range

	% of Bonds	Rel Obj
0%	2.9	2.12
0% to 8%	53.9	0.85
8% to 9%	15.9	1.03
9% to 10%	4.5	0.56
More than 10%	14.4	2.31
Not applicable	8.5	1.43

Sector Analysis 12-31-94
% of Bonds

US Treas	14	CMOs	31
GNMA mtgs	10	ARMs	0
FNMA mtgs	8	Other	25
FHLMC mtgs	11		

Min Initial Purchase / Expenses & Fees

Min Initial Purchase	$1000 (Addt'l: $50)
Min IRA Purchase	$250 (Addt'l: $50)
Min Auto Invest Plan	$50 (Systematic Inv: $50)

Expenses & Fees

Sales Fees	0.00% front
	0.00% deferred
	0.00% 12b-1
Management Fee	0.60% flat fee
3-,5-,10-yr Expense Projections	$31, $53, $118

Strong Growth

	Ticker	Load	NAV	Yield	SEC Yield	Assets	Objective
	SGROX	None	11.61	0.9%	N/A	106.0	Growth

Strong Growth Fund seeks capital appreciation.
The fund normally invests at least 65% of its assets in equity securities. Factors considered in selecting equities include prospects for above-average sales and earnings growth per share, high return on invested capital, a sound balance sheet, financial and accounting policies, and overall financial strength. Up to 35% of the fund's assets may be invested in intermediate- to long-term U.S. government- or corporate-debt securities. The fund may invest up to 15% of its assets directly in foreign securities; it may invest in American Depositary Receipts without limit.

Manager's Investment Style

Management takes a bottom-up approach to picking stocks. High P/E, small- and mid-cap growth stocks fill the portfolio. Management trades frequently to capture gains and jump into new opportunities, and it isn't afraid to keep plenty of cash on hand.

Fund Manager(s)

Ronald C. Ognar CFA(1983), since 12-93.
Birthdate: 10-42. BS, U. of Illinois 1968

Manager Experience

Manager Experience	Dates Managed	Invest Obj	Std Dev	+/- Index
Ronald C. Ognar				
Kemper Growth A	01/89 - 06/91	G	17.15	8.97
Kemper Retirement I	02/90 - 06/91	B	12.06	4.67

Historical Profile

Return	---
Risk	---
Rating	
	Not Rated

Investment Style History
Equity

Average % Stocks Held in Portfolio 75%

Growth of $10,000

|||| Value of Fund ($000)
— Value of Index ($000)
S&P 500
▼ Manager Change
▽ Partial Manager Change
► Mgr Unknown After
◄ Mgr Unknown Before

Performance Quartile (Within Objective)

History

	1983	1984	1985	1986	1987	1988	1989	1990	1991	1992	1993	1994	History
	---	---	---	---	---	---	---	---	---	---	10.00	11.61	NAV
	---	---	---	---	---	---	---	---	---	---		17.27	Total Return %
	---	---	---	---	---	---	---	---	---	---		15.95	+/- S&P 500
	---	---	---	---	---	---	---	---	---	---		17.34	+/- Wilshire 5000
	---	---	---	---	---	---	---	---	---	---		1.17	Income Return %
	---	---	---	---	---	---	---	---	---	---		16.10	Capital Return %
	---	---	---	---	---	---	---	---	---	---		1	Total Rtn % Rank All
	---	---	---	---	---	---	---	---	---	---		1	Total Rtn % Rank Obj
	---	---	---	---	---	---	---	---	---	---	0.00	0.11	Income $
	---	---	---	---	---	---	---	---	---	---	0.00	0.00	Capital Gains $
	---	---	---	---	---	---	---	---	---	---		1.60	Expense Ratio %
	---	---	---	---	---	---	---	---	---	---		0.30	Income Ratio %
	---	---	---	---	---	---	---	---	---	---		629	Turnover Rate %
	---	---	---	---	---	---	---	---	---	---		106.0	Net Assets ($mil)

Performance 12-31-94

	1st Qtr	2nd Qtr	3rd Qtr	4th Qtr	Total
1987	---	---	---	---	---
1988	---	---	---	---	---
1989	---	---	---	---	---
1990	---	---	---	---	---
1991	---	---	---	---	---
1992	---	---	---	---	---
1993	---	---	---	---	---
1994	8.80	-2.24	7.69	2.38	17.27

Bear Market Performance

Decile Rank (5-year period)

Worst ———————————————— Best

	Worst 3 Mo Period 1985-89	Worst 3 Mo Period 1990-94
Strong Growth	---	---
+/- S&P 500	---	---
+/- Best Fit Index :	---	---

Trailing Returns

	Total Return %	+/- S&P 500	+/- Wil 5000	% Rank All	% Rank Obj	Growth of $10,000
3 Mo	2.38	2.40	3.15	3	4	10,238
6 Mo	10.26	5.39	5.63	4	8	11,026
1 Yr	17.27	15.95	17.34	1	1	11,727
3 Yr Avg	---	---	---	---	---	---
5 Yr Avg	---	---	---	---	---	---
10 Yr Avg	---	---	---	---	---	---
15 Yr Avg	---	---	---	---	---	---

Operations

Address and Telephone	P.O. Box 2936	
	Milwaukee, WI 53201-2936	
	800-368-1030 / 414-359-1400	
Advisor	Strong Capital Management	
Subadvisor	None	
Distributor	Strong Funds Distributors	
States Available	All plus PR,GU	
Report Grade	B-	
Income Distrib	Paid Quarterly	
* Date of Inception	12-31-93	
Fiscal Year End	December	

Risk Analysis

Time Period	Load-Adj Return %	Risk % Rank [1] All	Risk % Rank [1] Obj	Morningstar [2] Return	Morningstar Risk	Morningstar Risk-Adj Rating
1 Yr	17.27					
3 Yr	---	---	---	---	---	---
5 Yr	---	---	---	---	---	---
10 Yr	---	---	---	---	---	---

Average Historical Rating ---

[1] 1 = low, 100 = high   [2] 1.00 = Equity Avg   [3] 1.00 = 90-day T-bill return

Other Measures

			Standard S&P 500	Best Fit
Standard Deviation	---	Alpha	---	---
Mean	---	Beta	---	---
Sharpe Ratio	---	R-Squared	---	---

Investment Style

	Stock Portfolio Avg	Relative S&P 500
Price/Earnings Ratio	28.8	1.56
Price/Book Ratio	6.1	1.79
5 Yr Earnings Gr %	18.1#	3.25
Return on Assets %	13.1	1.75
Debt % Total Cap	18.8	0.67
Med Mkt Cap ($mil)	1777	0.14

figure is based on 50% or less of stocks

Diversification Value for Portfolio Types

Large Cap: Small Cap: Bond: Balanced: Diversified:

Min Initial Purchase / Expenses & Fees

Min Initial Purchase	$1000 (Addt'l: $50)
Min IRA Purchase	$250 (Addt'l: $50)
Min Auto Invest Plan	$50 (Systematic Inv: $50)

Expenses & Fees

Sales Fees	0.00% front
	0.00% deferred
	0.00% 12b-1
Management Fee	1.00% flat fee
3-,5-,10-yr Expense Projections	$47, N/A, N/A
Annual Brokerage Cost	---

Portfolio 12-31-94

Total Stocks: 94
Total Fixed-Income: 5

Share Chg (09-94)000	Amount 000		Value $000	% Net Assets
17	34	Motorola	1968	1.86
50	50	cisco Systems	1756	1.66
42	52	MGIC Investment	1723	1.62
50	50	Informix	1606	1.52
35	35	Microtouch Systems	1575	1.49
3	28	Tellabs	1561	1.47
44	44	StrataCom	1540	1.45
17	27	Exide	1519	1.43
4	24	Alco Standard	1506	1.42
20	40	DSC Communications	1435	1.35
30	80	Circa Pharmaceuticals	1430	1.35
12	27	3Com	1392	1.31
13	25	Medtronic	1391	1.31
12	27	Coca-Cola	1391	1.31
30	30	RP Scherer	1361	1.28
75	75	Just For Feet	1284	1.21
17	17	Nokia (ADR)	1275	1.20
55	55	Sunglass Hut International	1265	1.19
16	16	Pfizer	1236	1.17
32	57	EMC	1233	1.16
5	22	Nucor	1221	1.15
25	50	Intl Rectifier	1213	1.14
6	31	Gartner Group	1209	1.14
12	22	Johnson & Johnson	1205	1.14
27	27	Walgreen	1181	1.11

Composition % 12-31-94

Cash	12.0	Preferreds	0.0
Stocks	85.1	Convertibles	3.1
Bonds	0.0	Other	-0.2

Tax Analysis

	Tax-Adj Historical Return %	% Pretax Return
3 Yr Avg	---	---
5 Yr Avg	---	---
10 Yr Avg	---	---

Potential Capital Gain Exposure (% of assets) 5%

Most Similar Funds in MF500

Fund lacks three-year record

Index Allocation

	% of Stocks
S&P 500	33.5
S&P MidCap 400	15.1
U.S. Small Cap	47.8
Foreign	3.7

Sector Weightings

	% of Stocks	Relative S&P 500
Utilities	0.0	0.00
Energy	0.0	0.00
Financials	4.5	0.42
Industrial Cyclicals	12.4	0.76
Consumer Durables	9.9	1.60
Consumer Staples	5.0	0.40
Services	4.1	0.50
Retail	11.0	1.90
Health	21.4	2.47
Technology	31.7	3.46

Strong International Stock

	Ticker	Load	NAV	Yield	SEC Yield	Assets	Objective
	STISX	None	12.65	0.0%	N/A	257.8	Foreign Stock

Strong International Stock Fund seeks long-term capital appreciation.

The fund expects to invest 90% of its assets, but at least 65%, in equity securities of issuers located in countries other than the United States. It normally invests in at least three countries, expecting to focus initially on Japan, the United Kingdom, Germany, France, Indonesia, Malaysia, the Netherlands, Italy, Singapore, Switzerland, Spain, and Mexico. The fund may, at times, invest up to 35% of its assets in U.S. securities and in debt securities issued by foreign governments. It may invest up to 5% of its assets in ADRs and EDRs.

Manager's Investment Style

Management takes a thematic approach to international investing, showing most interest in underappreciated regions and stocks. The portfolio thus carries modest price multiples. To dampen risk, management has a self-imposed 10% ceiling on emerging-markets exposure.

Historical Profile
Return ---
Risk ---
Rating ---
Not Rated

Investment Style History
Equity
Average % Stocks Held in Portfolio

87% 89% 88%

Growth of $10,000
|||| Value of Fund ($000)
— Value of Index ($000) S&P 500
▼ Manager Change
▽ Partial Manager Change
► Mgr Unknown After
◄ Mgr Unknown Before

Performance Quartile (Within Objective)

History	1992	1993	1994
NAV	9.77	14.18	12.65
Total Return %	-1.81 *	47.13	-1.56
+/- S&P 500	-10.95 *	37.08	-2.87
+/- MSCI EAFE	---	14.57	-9.34
Income Return %	0.49	0.19	0.03
Capital Return %	-2.30	46.94	-1.58
Total Rtn % Rank All	---	3	30
Total Rtn % Rank Obj	---	22	51
Income $	0.05	0.02	0.00
Capital Gains $	0.00	0.17	1.31
Expense Ratio %	2.00	1.90	1.60
Income Ratio %	0.80	-0.30	0.10
Turnover Rate %	25	140	163
Net Assets ($mil)	12.7	128.4	257.8

Fund Manager(s)

Anthony L. T. Cragg, since 08-93. Birthdate: 01-56. MA, Oxford U. 1979

Manager Experience	Dates Managed	Invest Obj	Std Dev	+/- Index
Anthony L. T. Cragg				
Strong Asia Pacific	12/93 - 12/94	WP	13.51	-6.59

Performance 12-31-94

	1st Qtr	2nd Qtr	3rd Qtr	4th Qtr	Total
1987	---	---	---	---	---
1988	---	---	---	---	---
1989	---	---	---	---	---
1990	---	---	---	---	---
1991	---	---	---	---	---
1992	---	4.09	-5.20	1.65	-1.81 *
1993	9.83	3.63	9.37	18.20	47.13
1994	-2.38	1.92	2.92	-3.87	-1.56

Bear Market Performance

Decile Rank (5-year period)

Worst   Best

	Worst 3 Mo Period 1985-89	Worst 3 Mo Period 1990-94
Strong International Stock	---	---
+/- S&P 500	---	---
+/- Best Fit Index :	---	---

Trailing Returns

	Total Return %	+/- S&P 500	+/- MSCI EAFE	% Rank All	% Rank Obj	Growth of $10,000
3 Mo	-3.87	-3.85	-2.85	88	36	9,613
6 Mo	-1.06	-5.92	-0.13	75	45	9,894
1 Yr	-1.56	-2.87	-9.34	30	51	9,844
3 Yr Avg	---	---	---	---	---	---
5 Yr Avg	---	---	---	---	---	---
10 Yr Avg	---	---	---	---	---	---
15 Yr Avg	---	---	---	---	---	---

Operations

Address and Telephone	P.O. Box 2936
	Milwaukee, WI 53201-2936
	800-368-1030 / 414-359-1400
Advisor	Strong Capital Management
Subadvisor	Dillon Read International Asset Mgmt
Distributor	Strong Funds Distributors
States Available	All plus PR,GU
Report Grade	B-
Income Distrib	Paid Quarterly
* Date of Inception	03-04-92
Fiscal Year End	December

Risk Analysis

Time Period	Load-Adj Return %	Risk % Rank [1] All	Obj	Morningstar [2] Return	Risk	Morningstar Risk-Adj Rating
1 Yr	-1.56					
3 Yr	---	---	---	---	---	---
5 Yr	---	---	---	---	---	---
10 Yr	---	---	---	---	---	---

Average Historical Rating ---

[1] 1 = low, 100 = high [2] 1.00 = Equity Avg [3] 1.00 = 90-day T-bill return

Other Measures

			Standard S&P 500	Best Fit
Standard Deviation	---	Alpha	---	---
Mean	---	Beta	---	---
Sharpe Ratio	---	R-Squared	---	---

Investment Style

	Stock Portfolio Avg	Rel MSCI EAFE	Rel Obj
Price/Earnings Ratio	27.0	0.73	0.96
Price/Cash Flow	12.5#	0.80	0.93
Price/Book Ratio	2.0	0.77	0.68
5 Yr Earnings Gr %	-1.9#	---	-0.50
Return on Assets %	5.5#	1.21	0.77
Debt % Total Cap	31.7	0.93	1.14
Med Mkt Cap ($mil)	2789	0.23	0.54

figure is based on 50% or less of stocks

Style
V B G
Size L M S

Diversification Value for Portfolio Types

Large Cap: Small Cap: Bond: Balanced: Diversified:

Tax Analysis

	Tax-Adj Historical Return %	% Pretax Return
3 Yr Avg	---	---
5 Yr Avg	---	---
10 Yr Avg	---	---
Potential Capital Gain Exposure (% of assets)		-6%

Most Similar Funds in MF500

Fund lacks three-year record

Expenses & Fees

Sales Fees	0.00% front
	0.00% deferred
	0.00% 12b-1
Management Fee	1.00% flat fee
3-,5-,10-yr Expense Projections	$61, $105, $226
Annual Brokerage Cost	1.35%

Min Purchase

Min Initial Purchase	$1000 (Addt'l: $50)
Min IRA Purchase	$250 (Addt'l: $50)
Min Auto Invest Plan	$50 (Systematic Inv: $50)

Portfolio 11-30-94

Share Chg (06-94) 000	Amount 000	Total Stocks: 129 / Total Fixed-Income: 4	Value $000	% Net Assets
50	204	Investor CI B Free	5196	1.94
-250	2316	Carter Holt Harvey	5135	1.92
600	1425	Woodside Petroleum	5106	1.91
29	254	Toc	5008	1.87
0	1	East Japan Railway	5006	1.87
207	707	Sensonor	4718	1.76
-6	19	Chargeurs	4528	1.69
-28	264	Arjo Wiggins Appleton	4405	1.65
76	76	Anglo-American	4263	1.59
-41	1698	Burns Philip	4086	1.53
-240	565	Coca-Cola Amatil	3691	1.38
-227	281	Lend Lease	3433	1.28
100	1780	MIM Holdings	3340	1.25
0	0	Nippon Telegraph & Telephone	3270	1.22
-200	240	Mitsubishi	3203	1.20
30	141	YPF CI D (ADR)	3183	1.19
700	1213	Lonrho	2993	1.12
125	125	Lagardere Groupe	2981	1.11
207	207	Broken Hill Proprietary	2970	1.11
66	66	PolyGram	2787	1.04

Regional Exposure 12-31-94

% of Stocks

Europe	18	Pacific Rim	34
Japan	13	Other	8
Latin Amer	12		

Country Exposure 12-31-94

% of Stocks

Japan	18
Australia	13
United Kingdom	12
France	6
Norway	5

Total Number of Countries: 27
Hedging Policy: Occasional

Composition % 12-31-94

Cash	9.7	Preferreds	0.8
Stocks	87.6	Convertibles	0.9
Bonds	0.0	Other	1.0

Sector Weightings

	% of Stocks	Relative S&P 500
Utilities	5.9	0.66
Energy	4.1	1.00
Financials	16.9	0.90
Industrial Cyclicals	25.0	1.00
Consumer Durables	14.5	1.34
Consumer Staples	7.9	1.14
Services	17.3	1.59
Retail	4.3	0.74
Health	2.2	0.62
Technology	1.9	0.37

Historical years: 1983 1984 1985 1986 1987 1988 1989 1990 1991 1992 1993 1994 (NAV, Total Return %, +/- S&P 500, +/- MSCI EAFE, Income Return %, Capital Return %, etc. with --- for 1983–1991)

Strong Municipal Bond

	Ticker	Load	NAV	Yield	SEC Yield	Assets	Objective
	SXFIX	None	9.23	6.0%	6.23%	279.8	Muni Nat

Strong Municipal Bond Fund seeks current income exempt from federal income taxes.

The fund invests primarily in investment-grade municipal securities. It may, however, invest up to 5% of its assets in securities rated as low as CC. The fund does not maintain maturity restrictions on its investments. It may also invest without limit in private-activity bonds subject to the Alternative Minimum Tax. The fund may also engage in hedging activities involving futures and options contracts.

Prior to Jan. 27, 1989, the fund was named Strong Tax-Free Income Fund.

Manager's Investment Style

Management actively adjusts the portfolio's duration to reflect its interest-rate outlook. Management has been preparing for rising rates since 1992, when it minimized the fund's rate sensitivity by focusing on premium-coupon issues and avoiding zero-coupon and other discount fare. A premium-coupon focus has resulted in overweighted exposure to high-paying health-care issues.

Fund Manager(s)

Thomas J. Conlin CFA(1983), since 10-91.
Birthdate: 03-54. BS, Illinois State U. 1976 MBA, Indiana U. 1978

Mary-Kay H. Bourbulas, since 10-91.

Manager Experience	Dates Managed	Invest Obj	Std Dev	+/- Index
Thomas J. Conlin				
SteinRoe Managed Munis	08/90 - 09/91	MN	1.84	-2.84
SteinRoe High-Yield Munis	01/91 - 09/91	MN	1.21	-0.83

Historical Profile

Return	High
Risk	Average
Rating	★★★★
	Above Average

Investment Style History
Fixed Income
Income Rtn % Rank Obj

| 59 | 97 | 96 | 21 | 21 | 12 | 30 | 18 |

Growth of $10,000

- ‖‖ Value of Fund ($000)
- — Value of Index ($000)
  LB Muni
- ▼ Manager Change
- ▽ Partial Manager Change
- ► Mgr Unknown After
- ◄ Mgr Unknown Before

Performance Quartile
(Within Objective)

	1983	1984	1985	1986	1987	1988	1989	1990	1991	1992	1993	1994	History
	---	*	---	10.00	9.16	9.35	9.47	9.22	9.76	10.00	10.25	9.23	NAV
	---	*	---	1.20 *	-1.63	7.60	7.10	4.63	13.36	12.19	11.73	-4.55	Total Return %
	---	---	---	---	-4.38	-0.28	-7.44	-4.31	-2.64	4.95	1.98	-1.63	+/- LB Aggregate
	---	---	---	---	-3.13	-2.56	-3.69	-2.67	1.22	3.38	-0.55	1.05	+/- LB Muni
	---	---	---	1.20	6.78	5.53	5.82	7.27	7.51	6.98	6.02	5.40	Income Return %
	---	---	---	0.00	-8.40	2.07	1.28	-2.64	5.86	5.21	5.71	-9.95	Capital Return %
	---	---	---	---	72	76	93	44	66	15	53	59	Total Rtn % Rank All
	---	---	---	---	74	79	92	94	10	1	48	38	Total Rtn % Rank Obj
	---	---	---	0.12	0.68	0.49	0.53	0.66	0.65	0.65	0.59	0.56	Income $
	---	---	---	0.00	0.00	0.00	0.00	0.00	0.00	0.26	0.31	0.00	Capital Gains $
	---	---	---	0.40	1.00	1.30	1.70	0.30	0.10	0.10	0.70	0.80	Expense Ratio %
	---	---	---	6.40	7.00	5.30	5.60	7.20	6.90	6.40	5.60	5.70	Income Ratio %
	---	---	---	116	284	344	243	586	465	324	157	271	Turnover Rate %
	---	---	---	2.2	19.1	18.3	18.7	31.6	115.2	289.8	398.9	279.8	Net Assets ($mil)

Performance 12-31-94

	1st Qtr	2nd Qtr	3rd Qtr	4th Qtr	Total
1987	3.64	-7.75	-0.67	3.59	-1.63
1988	2.42	1.40	2.01	1.57	7.60
1989	1.66	2.78	0.10	2.41	7.10
1990	-0.57	0.96	-0.09	4.33	4.63
1991	1.69	2.08	5.51	3.50	13.36
1992	0.86	5.78	3.30	1.80	12.19
1993	3.83	3.00	3.01	1.42	11.73
1994	-5.13	0.73	1.03	-1.14	-4.55

Bear Market Performance

Decile Rank (5-year period)

		Worst 3 Mo Period 1985-89	Worst 3 Mo Period 1990-94
Strong Municipal Bond		---	-5.77
+/- LB Aggregate		---	-0.84
+/- Best Fit Index : LB Muni		---	-0.01

Trailing Returns

	Total Return %	+/- LB Aggregate	+/- LB Muni	% Rank All	% Rank Obj	Growth of $10,000
3 Mo	-1.14	-1.52	0.29	47	37	9,886
6 Mo	-0.12	-1.11	1.13	59	20	9,988
1 Yr	-4.55	-1.63	1.05	59	38	9,545
3 Yr Avg	6.16	1.62	1.29	32	5	11,964
5 Yr Avg	7.25	-0.37	0.48	44	7	14,192
10 Yr Avg	---	---	---	---	---	---
15 Yr Avg	---	---	---	---	---	---

Operations

Address and Telephone	P.O. Box 2936
	Milwaukee, WI 53201-2936
	800-368-1030 / 414-359-1400
Advisor	Strong Capital Management
Subadvisor	None
Distributor	Strong Funds Distributors
States Available	All plus PR,GU
Report Grade	C
Income Distrib	Paid Monthly
* Date of Inception	10-23-86
Fiscal Year End	December

Risk Analysis

Time Period	Load-Adj Return %	Risk % Rank [1] All	Risk % Rank [1] Obj	Morningstar [2] Return	Morningstar [2] Risk	Morningstar Risk-Adj Rating
1 Yr	-4.55					
3 Yr	6.16	25	42	1.68	0.95	★★★★★
5 Yr	7.25	25	55	1.31	1.06	★★★★
10 Yr	---					

Average Historical Rating (63 months)   3.0 ★s

[1] 1 = low, 100 = high   [2] 1.00 = Muni Avg   [3] 1.00 = 90-day T-bill return

Other Measures

				Standard LB Agg	Best Fit LB Muni
Standard Deviation	6.00	Alpha		1.6	1.2
Mean	6.17	Beta		1.09	1.03
Sharpe Ratio	0.44	R-Squared		53	90

Investment Style

Interest-Rate Stance
Avg Effective Maturity   19.4 Yrs

Quality
Avg Credit Quality   A

Avg Weighted Coupon   5.93%
Avg Weighted Price   86.30% of Par

Maturity: Short Intm Long
Quality: High Med Low

Diversification Value for Portfolio Types

Large Cap: Medium	Small Cap: High	Bond: Low	Balanced: Medium	Diversified: High

Min Initial Purchase	$2500 (Addt'l: $50)
Min IRA Purchase	N/A
Min Auto Invest Plan	$50 (Systematic Inv: $50)

Expenses & Fees

Sales Fees	0.00% front
	0.00% deferred
	0.00% 12b-1
Management Fee	0.60% flat fee
3-,5-,10-yr Expense Projections	$26, $46, $101

Portfolio 12-31-94

Amount 000	Date of Maturity	Total Stocks: 0 / Total Fixed-Income: 74	Value $000	% Net Assets
26160	11-01-19	NY Battery Park City 4.75%	19228	6.87
10000	05-01-21	TX North Central Hlth Fac Dev 9.5%	10600	3.79
9240	11-01-24	UT Emery Poll Cntrl Pwr/Lt 4.4%	9240	3.30
10000	12-01-23	MT Forsyth Poll Cntrl 5.9%	8775	3.14
10000	09-01-13	CA State GO 4.75%	7775	2.78
7790	02-15-22	IN Hlth Fac Fin Schneck Meml Hosp 7.5%	7381	2.64
9710	05-15-18	CA Los Angeles Dept Wtr/Pwr Elec 4.5%	7317	2.62
10000	12-01-23	MA Wtr Resource 4.75%	7288	2.60
8805	01-01-20	CA South Pub Pwr San Juan Unit #3 5%	6877	2.46
6000	07-01-09	PA Blair Hosp Altoona 7.875%	6113	2.18
6000	06-01-08	IL Granite City St Elizabeth Hosp 8.125%	5865	2.10
6000	06-15-07	NY NY City Muni Wtr Fin Swr 5.375%	5543	1.98
5300	06-01-24	TX Gulf Coast Waste Disp DMD	5300	1.89
5000	02-01-08	UT Salt Lake Poll Cntrl DMD	5000	1.79
6000	08-15-16	TX Harris Toll Rd 5%	4778	1.71
6000	07-01-11	MA Muni Whlse Elec Pwr Sply Sys 4.75%	4733	1.69
4500	12-01-15	LA Pub Fac Multi-Fam Mtg DMD	4500	1.61
5000	10-01-13	WA Hlth Care Fac Providence 6.25%	4456	1.59
5000	08-01-07	MI Pontiac Genl Hosp 6%	4431	1.58
6650	10-01-23	MA Hlth/Educ Fac 6%	4223	1.51

Credit Analysis % of Bonds 12-31-94

US Govt	0	BB	0
AAA	44	B	3
AA	17	Below B	0
A	3	NR/NA	13
BBB	20		

Composition % of Assets 12-31-94

Cash	18.1	Preferreds	0.0
Stocks	0.0	Convertibles	0.0
Bonds	81.9	Other	0.0

Tax Analysis

	Tax-Adj Historical Return %	% Pretax Return
3 Yr Avg	5.62	90.8
5 Yr Avg	6.93	94.9
10 Yr Avg	---	---
Potential Capital Gain Exposure (% of assets)		-9%

Most Similar Funds in MF500

Flagship All-American T/E A	Strong Fit
USAA Tax-Exempt Long-Term	Strong Fit
Putnam Municipal Income A	Strong Fit

Coupon Range

	% Bonds	Rel Obj
0%	1.8	0.73
0% to 6.8%	38.1	0.63
6.8% to 7.5%	19.7	1.27
7.5% to 8.3%	29.7	3.35
More than 8.3%	10.7	1.21
Not applicable	0.0	0.00

Sector Weightings

	% Bonds	Rel Obj
General Obl	6.97	0.33
Utilities	7.34	0.59
Health	26.73	2.03
Water/Waste	11.95	1.88
Housing	14.38	1.96
Education	0.00	0.00
Transportation	3.33	0.33
COP/Lease	1.27	0.40
Private	14.86	1.27
Misc Revenue	3.90	0.78
Demand	9.29	3.78

Top 5 States % of Bonds

NY	11.61	TX	8.58
CA	11.31	IL	6.16
MA	11.27		

MORNINGSTAR **1995 Mutual Fund 500**

Strong Opportunity

	Ticker	Load	NAV	Yield	SEC Yield	Assets	Objective
	SOPFX	None	27.71	0.5%	N/A	805.7	Growth

Strong Opportunity Fund seeks capital appreciation. Current income is not a factor in selecting investments.

The fund normally invests at least 70% of its assets in equities, including common stocks, convertible debentures, preferred stocks, convertible preferred stocks, and warrants. The balance of assets may be invested in nonconvertible corporate and government intermediate- to long-term debt securities when these securities have capital-appreciation potential. The fund may engage in substantial short-term trading. It may invest up to 15% of its assets directly in foreign securities, and may invest without limit in ADRs.

Manager's Investment Style

The recent departure of former comanager Carlene Murphy Ziegler casts some uncertainty over strategy, but with Dick Weiss still on board, things might not change much. Management typically looks for undiscovered growth stories or turnaround plays, but won't pay high multiples for them. This discipline limits the fund's downside and makes it a player in both growth- and value-driven markets.

Fund Manager(s)

Richard T. Weiss, since 03-91. Birthdate: 05-51.
BS, U. of Southern California 1973 MBA, Harvard 1975
Marina T. Carlson CFA, since 12-93. BA, Drake U.
MBA, DePaul U.

Manager Experience	Dates Managed	Invest Obj	Std Dev	+/- Index
Richard T. Weiss				
SteinRoe Special	11/90 - 03/91	G	7.55	3.34
SteinRoe Capital Opport	11/90 - 03/91	AG	8.80	7.36

Historical Profile

Return	Above Average	
Risk	Below Average	
Rating	★★★★ Above Average	

	1983	1984	1985	1986	1987	1988	1989	1990	1991	1992	1993	1994	History
	---	---	10.00	15.99	15.87	16.90	19.21	16.29	21.24	24.70	28.23	27.71	NAV
	---	---	---	59.90	11.85	16.47	18.49	-11.30	31.69	17.35	21.16	3.18	Total Return %
	---	---	---	41.22	6.59	-0.14	-13.19	-8.19	1.21	9.73	11.11	1.87	+/- S&P 500
	---	---	---	43.80	9.49	-1.47	-10.68	-5.12	-2.51	8.38	9.88	3.25	+/- Wilshire 5000
	---	---	---	0.00	1.35	9.98	3.79	3.72	1.31	0.28	0.23	0.47	Income Return %
	---	---	---	59.90	10.49	6.49	14.70	-15.03	30.39	17.07	20.93	2.71	Capital Return %
	---	---	---	2	8	23	38	87	24	7	15	7	Total Rtn % Rank All
	---	---	---	1	9	43	82	85	62	11	12	14	Total Rtn % Rank Obj
	---	---	0.00	0.00	0.24	1.55	0.68	0.74	0.19	0.06	0.06	0.13	Income $
	---	---	0.00	0.00	1.80	0.00	0.16	0.04	0.00	0.16	1.56	1.28	Capital Gains $
	---	---	---	1.70	1.50	1.60	1.60	1.70	1.70	1.50	1.40	1.40	Expense Ratio %
	---	---	---	0.70	1.70	7.40	4.30	3.30	1.10	0.30	0.20	0.40	Income Ratio %
	---	---	---	170	371	352	306	275	271	139	109	66	Turnover Rate %
	---	---	---	43.6	153.6	157.4	205.0	131.9	159.7	193.2	443.5	805.7	Net Assets ($mil)

Investment Style History
Equity
Average % Stocks Held in Portfolio

Growth of $10,000
|||| Value of Fund ($000)
— Value of Index ($000) SPMid400
▼ Manager Change
▽ Partial Manager Change
► Mgr Unknown After
◄ Mgr Unknown Before

Performance Quartile (Within Objective)

Performance 12-31-94

	1st Qtr	2nd Qtr	3rd Qtr	4th Qtr	Total
1987	24.54	4.11	7.26	-19.58	11.85
1988	8.79	3.73	1.69	1.49	16.47
1989	10.06	10.41	5.42	-7.51	18.49
1990	-4.67	4.22	-12.93	2.54	-11.30
1991	14.74	-1.30	10.31	5.41	31.69
1992	1.39	-1.71	6.30	10.78	17.35
1993	7.61	1.90	7.54	2.75	21.16
1994	-1.55	1.85	5.89	-2.82	3.18

Bear Market Performance

Decile Rank (5-year period)

Worst									Best

	Worst 3 Mo Period 1985-89	Worst 3 Mo Period 1990-94
Strong Opportunity	---	-12.93
+/- S&P 500	---	0.81
+/- Best Fit Index : SPMid400	---	4.84

Trailing Returns

	Total Return %	+/- S&P 500	+/- Wil 5000	% Rank All	% Rank Obj	Growth of $10,000
3 Mo	-2.82	-2.81	-2.05	81	78	9,718
6 Mo	2.90	-1.97	-1.73	21	63	10,290
1 Yr	3.18	1.87	3.25	7	14	10,318
3 Yr Avg	13.63	7.36	7.02	5	6	14,671
5 Yr Avg	11.37	2.68	2.56	11	17	17,137
10 Yr Avg	---	---	---	---	---	---
15 Yr Avg	---	---	---	---	---	---

Risk Analysis

Time Period	Load-Adj Return %	Risk % Rank[1] All	Obj	Morningstar[2] Return	Morningstar Risk	Morningstar Risk-Adj Rating
1 Yr	3.18					
3 Yr	13.63	62	20	3.19[3]	0.69	★★★★★
5 Yr	11.37	64	17	1.75[3]	0.77	★★★★
10 Yr	---	---	---	---	---	---

Average Historical Rating (73 months)   3.6 ★s

[1] = low, 100 = high   [2] 1.00 = Equity Avg   [3] 1.00 = 90-day T-bill return

Other Measures

	Standard S&P 500	Best Fit SPMid400
Standard Deviation	9.53	Alpha	7.2	6.4
Mean	13.30	Beta	0.96	0.91
Sharpe Ratio	1.03	R-Squared	63	89

Investment Style

	Stock Portfolio Avg	Relative S&P 500
Price/Earnings Ratio	22.1	1.20
Price/Book Ratio	2.8	0.83
5 Yr Earnings Gr %	8.2	1.47
Return on Assets %	6.5	0.86
Debt % Total Cap	31.4	1.11
Med Mkt Cap ($mil)	1914	0.15

Style Value Blend Growth — Size Large/Med/Small

Diversification Value for Portfolio Types

Large Cap: Low	Small Cap: Low	Bond: High	Balanced: Low	Diversified: Low

Portfolio 12-31-94

Share Chg (09-94) 000	Amount 000	Total Stocks: 96 Total Fixed-Income: 2	Value $000	% Net Assets
144	307	Autodesk	12165	1.51
11	113	American International Group	11103	1.38
-5	130	Capital Cities/ABC	11083	1.38
96	350	Times Mirror Cl A	10981	1.36
226	226	Tyco International	10754	1.33
114	445	Kroger	10736	1.33
38	290	Newmont Mining	10440	1.30
124	124	Mobil	10405	1.29
290	290	Arrow Electronics	10404	1.29
27	387	American Stores	10401	1.29
30	190	AMR	10118	1.26
41	340	NIPSCO Industries	10115	1.26
7	377	Marshall Industries	10074	1.25
29	335	Mallinckrodt Group	10008	1.24
297	297	Goodyear Tire & Rubber	9987	1.24
139	281	Sun Microsystems	9976	1.24
60	455	Tele-Communications Cl A	9896	1.23
13	277	Raychem	9868	1.22
3	150	Eli Lilly	9844	1.22
37	300	US Cellular	9825	1.22
25	485	Bell Cablemedia (ADR)	9821	1.22
75	588	Dallas Semiconductor	9776	1.21
14	335	AirTouch Communications	9757	1.21
53	325	Vigoro	9750	1.21
-34	520	Petroleum Geo-Services (ADR)	9685	1.20

Composition % 12-31-94

Cash	11.4	Preferreds	0.0
Stocks	88.1	Convertibles	0.6
Bonds	0.0	Other	0.0

Tax Analysis

	Tax-Adj Historical Return %	% Pretax Return
3 Yr Avg	12.40	89.9
5 Yr Avg	10.24	88.1
10 Yr Avg	---	---
Potential Capital Gain Exposure (% of assets)		8%

Most Similar Funds in MF500

Strong Common Stock	Strong Fit
Fidelity Contrafund	Strong Fit
SteinRoe Special	Fair Fit

Index Allocation

	% of Stocks
S&P 500	44.8
S&P MidCap 400	11.4
U.S. Small Cap	27.0
Foreign	16.9

Sector Weightings

	% of Stocks	Relative S&P 500
Utilities	4.2	0.34
Energy	10.1	1.00
Financials	9.3	0.88
Industrial Cyclicals	11.6	0.71
Consumer Durables	5.5	0.89
Consumer Staples	4.4	0.35
Services	19.9	2.45
Retail	12.6	2.16
Health	6.8	0.79
Technology	15.5	1.70

Operations

Address and Telephone	P.O. Box 2936 Milwaukee, WI 53201-2936 800-368-1030 / 414-359-1400
Advisor	Strong Capital Management
Subadvisor	None
Distributor	Strong Funds Distributors
States Available	All plus PR,GU
Report Grade	B-
Income Distrib	Paid Quarterly
* Date of Inception	12-31-85
Fiscal Year End	December

Min Initial Purchase	$1000 (Addt'l: $50)
Min IRA Purchase	$250 (Addt'l: $50)
Min Auto Invest Plan	$50 (Systematic Inv: $50)

Expenses & Fees

Sales Fees	0.00% front
	0.00% deferred
	0.00% 12b-1
Management Fee	1.00% flat fee
3-,5-,10-yr Expense Projections	$44, $76, $166
Annual Brokerage Cost	0.41%

Strong Short-Term Bond

Ticker	Load	NAV	Yield	SEC Yield	Assets	Objective
SSTBX	None	9.42	6.7%	8.25%	1041.1	Corp General

Strong Short-Term Bond Fund seeks income consistent with minimum fluctuation of principal value and current liquidity.
The fund normally invests at least 65% of its assets in corporate and U.S. government debt securities; it attempts to invest at least 95% of its assets in investment-grade fixed-income securities. The fund may invest up to 25% of its assets directly in foreign securities and may invest without limit in American Depositary Receipts. The average weighted maturity ranges from one to three years.

Investment Style History
Fixed Income
Income Rtn % Rank Obj

Historical Profile
Return	Average
Risk	Below Average
Rating	★★★★
	Above Average

Boxes: --- 55 12 55 59 23 32 29

Growth of $10,000
||||| Value of Fund ($000)
— Value of Index ($000) LB Corp
▼ Manager Change
▽ Partial Manager Change
► Mgr Unknown After
◄ Mgr Unknown Before

Performance Quartile (Within Objective)

Manager's Investment Style
Management positions the portfolio so that duration falls between 1.5 and 2.5 years, and that average credit quality never dips far below BBB. Such a stance protects the fund against damage from interest-rate shocks. This strategy may seem constrictive, but management does a fair bit of maneuvering in order to take advantage of changing interest-rate climates.

	1983	1984	1985	1986	1987	1988	1989	1990	1991	1992	1993	1994	History
NAV	---	---	---	---	10.03	10.09	9.86	9.53	10.12	9.99	10.23	9.42	
Total Return %	---	---	---	---	3.18 *	10.12	8.22	5.28	14.61	6.68	9.32	-1.79	
+/- LB Aggregate	---	---	---	---	---	2.24	-6.32	-3.66	-1.39	-0.57	-0.43	1.13	
+/- LB Corporate	---	---	---	---	---	0.90	-5.76	-1.87	-3.89	-2.02	-2.85	2.14	
Income Return %	---	---	---	---	2.78	8.87	10.25	8.63	8.42	7.96	6.92	6.13	
Capital Return %	---	---	---	---	0.40	1.25	-2.03	-3.35	6.19	-1.28	2.40	-7.92	
Total Rtn % Rank All	---	---	---	---	---	61	89	41	60	62	72	32	
Total Rtn % Rank Obj	---	---	---	---	---	23	85	76	69	65	61	22	
Income $	---	---	---	---	0.28	0.86	1.01	0.81	0.75	0.78	0.67	0.63	
Capital Gains $	---	---	---	---	0.01	0.07	0.03	0.00	0.00	0.00	0.00	0.00	
Expense Ratio %	---	---	---	---	0.10	1.00	1.10	1.30	1.00	0.60	0.80	0.90	
Income Ratio %	---	---	---	---	8.80	8.50	9.70	8.60	7.80	7.30	6.30	6.30	
Turnover Rate %	---	---	---	---	136	461	177	314	398	353	445	311	
Net Assets ($mil)	---	---	---	---	17.1	102.2	130.0	80.1	165.0	756.9	1531.6	1041.1	

Fund Manager(s)
Bradley C. Tank, since 06-90. Birthdate: 09-57.
BS, U. of Wisconsin 1980 MBA, U. of Wisconsin 1982

Manager Experience
	Dates Managed	Invest Obj	Std Dev	+/- Index
Bradley C. Tank				
Strong Income	06/90 - 10/93	CG	4.30	-0.74
Strong Advantage	06/90 - 10/93	CG	1.14	-3.30

Performance 12-31-94
	1st Qtr	2nd Qtr	3rd Qtr	4th Qtr	Total
1987	---	---	---	2.72	3.18 *
1988	4.35	1.55	2.08	1.79	10.12
1989	2.38	4.03	0.81	0.79	8.22
1990	-1.17	1.45	2.12	2.82	5.28
1991	2.96	2.24	3.59	5.11	14.61
1992	1.35	2.55	2.48	0.16	6.68
1993	3.69	1.92	1.79	1.63	9.32
1994	-0.83	-1.31	1.10	-0.74	-1.79

Bear Market Performance
Decile Rank (5-year period)

	Worst 3 Mo Period 1985-89	Worst 3 Mo Period 1990-94
Strong Short-Term Bond	---	-3.12
+/- LB Aggregate	---	1.81
+/- Best Fit Index : LB Corp	---	3.14

Trailing Returns
	Total Return %	+/- LB Aggregate	+/- LB Corp	% Rank All	% Rank Obj	Growth of $10,000
3 Mo	-0.74	-1.12	-1.18	39	85	9,926
6 Mo	0.35	-0.64	-0.82	50	59	10,035
1 Yr	-1.79	1.13	2.14	32	22	9,821
3 Yr Avg	4.63	0.08	-0.79	56	39	11,453
5 Yr Avg	6.69	-0.94	-1.58	58	74	13,821
10 Yr Avg	---	---	---	---	---	---
15 Yr Avg	---	---	---	---	---	---

Operations
Address and Telephone	P.O. Box 2936
	Milwaukee, WI 53201-2936
	800-368-1030 / 414-359-1400
Advisor	Strong Capital Management
Subadvisor	None
Distributor	Strong Funds Distributors
States Available	All plus PR,GU
Report Grade	B-
Income Distrib	Paid Monthly
* Date of Inception	08-31-87
Fiscal Year End	December

Min Initial Purchase $1000 (Addt'l: $50)
Min IRA Purchase $250 (Addt'l: $50)
Min Auto Invest Plan $50 (Systematic Inv: $50)

Expenses & Fees
Sales Fees 0.00% front
  0.00% deferred
  0.00% 12b-1
Management Fee 0.63% flat fee
3-,5-,10-yr Expense Projections $29, $50, $111

Risk Analysis
Time Period	Load-Adj Return %	Risk % Rank All	Obj	Morningstar Return	Morningstar Risk	Morningstar Risk-Adj Rating
1 Yr	-1.79					
3 Yr	4.63	4	7	0.31 [3]	0.56	★★★★★
5 Yr	6.69	4	7	0.47 [3]	0.57	★★★★
10 Yr	---	---	---	---	---	

Average Historical Rating (53 months) 4.0 ★ s

[1] = low, 100 = high [2] 1.00 = Taxable Avg [3] 1.00 = 90-day T-bill return

Other Measures
			Standard LB Agg	Best Fit LB Corp
Standard Deviation	2.43	Alpha	0.5	0.3
Mean	4.56	Beta	0.50	0.41
Sharpe Ratio	0.43	R-Squared	66	67

Investment Style
Interest-Rate Stance
Avg Effective Duration 2.1 Yrs **
Avg Effective Maturity 2.5 Yrs

Quality
Avg Credit Quality A
Avg Weighted Coupon 7.44%
Avg Weighted Price 90.04% of Par

** figure provided by fund

Diversification Value for Portfolio Types
Large Cap: High Small Cap: High Bond: Low Balanced: Medium Diversified: High

Portfolio 12-31-94
Total Stocks: 0
Total Fixed-Income: 111

Amount 000	Date of Maturity		Value $000	% Net Assets
39785	04-01-02	FNMA Note 8.733%	39934	3.84
41600	03-25-33	First Boston Mtg CMO 7.5%	39624	3.81
35789	01-01-14	FHA Reilly 7.43%	33954	3.26
35470	08-15-02	Time Warner 0%	33519	3.22
37270	07-07-06	Viacom 8%	32006	3.07
30000	03-11-98	News America Holdings 7.375%	30069	2.89
28913	05-01-04	Citicorp FRN	28971	2.78
27600	03-15-97	Tosco 9%	27911	2.68
115		Norwest 18.6%	23000	2.21
23600	03-08-99	Petroleos Mexicanos FRN	21712	2.09
19114	08-15-18	FHA Reilly 7.43%	18086	1.74
16920	09-15-04	American Re 10.875%	17999	1.73
89772	01-26-95	United Mexican States 0%	17944	1.72
58000	12-17-12	Time Warner Cv 0%	17763	1.71
17000	07-15-05	GMAC 8.75%	17398	1.67
16836	09-01-99	Kaufman & Broad Home 10.375%	16920	1.63
17000	05-12-97	Deere 8.38%	16727	1.61
17150	11-12-97	Empresas La Moderna 10.25%	15435	1.48
19489	07-25-17	Merrill Lynch Trust P/O 0%	14836	1.43
14900	10-02-95	South African Tran Line 8.207%	14695	1.41
14985	08-01-14	FHA Project Loan 6.9%	14666	1.41
15001	07-25-29	Resolution Trust 8%	14626	1.40
13050	12-15-01	News America Holdings 12%	14535	1.40
14500	10-25-95	Cemex Trust 6.25%	14210	1.36
13993	08-17-23	Merrill Lynch Hm Eq CMO 5.75%	13223	1.27

Composition % 12-31-94
Cash	4.2	Preferred	2.2
Stocks	0.0	Convertibles	1.7
Bonds	91.8	Other	0.1

Coupon Range
	% of Bonds	Rel Obj
0%	7.3	3.34
0% to 8.5%	42.3	0.67
8.5% to 9.5%	14.8	0.91
9.5% to 11%	12.4	1.33
More than 11%	4.8	1.23
Not applicable	18.5	3.70

Tax Analysis
	Tax-Adj Historical Return %	% Pretax Return
3 Yr Avg	2.05	43.2
5 Yr Avg	4.06	57.7
10 Yr Avg	---	---

Potential Capital Gain Exposure (% of assets) -11%

Credit Analysis 12-31-94
% of Bonds
US Govt	21	BB	11
AAA	17	B	4
AA	3	Below B	0
A	7	NR/NA	18
BBB	21		

Most Similar Funds in MF500
Fidelity Short-Term Bond	Fair Fit
Scudder Short-Term Bond	Fair Fit
Prudential Struct Maturity A	Fair Fit

MORNINGSTAR 1995 Mutual Fund 500

SunAmerica Tax-Exempt Insured A

	Ticker	Load	NAV	Yield	SEC Yield	Assets	Objective
	STEAX	4.75%	11.56	5.6%	5.29%	135.9	Muni Nat

SunAmerica Tax Exempt Insured Fund - Class A seeks income exempt from federal income taxes.

The fund normally invests at least 80% of its assets in municipal bonds; it invests at least 65% of its assets in insured municipal bonds. A portion of the fund's assets may be invested in municipal housing bonds.

Class A shares have front loads and lower 12b-1 fees; Class B shares have deferred loads and conversion features. Prior to March 1, 1990, the fund was named Integrated Tax-Free Portfolios STRIPES Portfolio. Then until Feb. 3, 1992, the fund was named SunAmerica Tax-Free Portfolios STRIPES Portfolio.

Manager's Investment Style

Management has traditionally emphasized housing issues--at times, to the virtual exclusion of all other sectors. These high-yielding bonds have allowed the fund to boast one of the highest yields among all insured muni funds. And because housing bonds are prone to prepayments, the fund's interest-rate sensitivity has been minimal. An influx of new assets during the past few years--and a dearth of new housing bonds--has led to a slight increase in sector diversification, and, as a result, a slightly longer duration than before.

Fund Manager(s)

John C. Mooney, since 08-94. Birthdate: 08-65.
BA, Denison U. 1987

Manager Experience	Dates Managed	Invest Obj	Std Dev	+/- Index
Not available.				

Historical Profile

Return	Low
Risk	Below Average
Rating	★★ Below Average

46	64	63	25	62	19	52	30

Investment Style History
Fixed Income
Income Rtn % Rank Obj

Growth of $10,000

IIII Value of Fund ($000)
— Value of Index ($000)
    LB Muni
▼ Manager Change
▽ Partial Manager Change
◄─ Mgr Unknown After
─► Mgr Unknown Before

Performance Quartile
(Within Objective)

1983	1984	1985	1986	1987	1988	1989	1990	1991	1992	1993	1994	History
---	---	12.14	12.52	11.73	12.13	12.34	12.21	12.43	12.44	12.71	11.56	NAV
---	---	1.93 *	11.28	0.65	10.67	8.70	6.17	8.45	6.81	7.79	-3.99	Total Return %
---	---	---	-3.97	-2.11	2.79	-5.84	-2.78	-7.55	-0.43	-1.96	-1.07	+/- LB Aggregate
---	---	---	-8.03	-0.86	0.51	-2.08	-1.14	-3.69	-2.00	-4.49	1.61	+/- LB Muni
---	---	0.00	8.15	6.96	7.26	6.97	7.22	6.65	6.73	5.62	5.06	Income Return %
---	---	1.93	3.13	-6.31	3.41	1.73	-1.05	1.80	0.08	2.17	-9.05	Capital Return %
---	---	---	78	54	56	87	32	94	60	80	53	Total Rtn % Rank All
---	---	---	87	36	54	72	56	95	88	91	32	Total Rtn % Rank Obj
---	---	0.00	0.95	0.86	0.82	0.81	0.87	0.78	0.81	0.68	0.65	Income $
---	---	0.00	0.00	0.00	0.00	0.00	0.00	0.00	0.00	0.00	0.00	Capital Gains $
---	---	---	0.77	0.98	1.30	1.32	1.31	1.32	1.25	1.10	1.28	Expense Ratio %
---	---	---	7.12	7.06	6.85	6.68	6.70	6.57	6.26	5.56	4.99	Income Ratio %
---	---	---	---	23	20	18	0	16	21	26	52	Turnover Rate %
---	---	38.3	131.5	113.4	110.4	100.0	90.3	95.4	113.2	185.7	135.9	Net Assets ($mil)

Performance 12-31-94

	1st Qtr	2nd Qtr	3rd Qtr	4th Qtr	Total
1987	1.61	-2.76	-1.41	3.32	0.65
1988	3.27	2.19	2.60	2.20	10.67
1989	1.16	3.13	1.17	3.00	8.70
1990	1.30	1.67	0.87	2.18	6.17
1991	1.97	2.07	2.36	1.79	8.45
1992	0.86	2.91	1.78	1.11	6.81
1993	1.34	3.52	2.48	0.26	7.79
1994	-4.80	0.51	0.96	-0.63	-3.99

Bear Market Performance

Decile Rank (5-year period)

Worst ——————————————————— Best

	Worst 3 Mo Period 1985-89	Worst 3 Mo Period 1990-94
SunAmerica Tax-Exempt Insure	---	-5.47
+/- LB Aggregate	---	-0.53
+/- Best Fit Index : LB Muni	---	0.30

Trailing Returns

	Total Return %	+/- LB Aggregate	+/- LB Muni	% Rank All	% Rank Obj	Growth of $10,000
3 Mo	-0.63	-1.00	0.81	37	16	9,937
6 Mo	0.33	-0.66	1.58	50	10	10,033
1 Yr	-3.99	-1.07	1.61	53	32	9,601
3 Yr Avg	3.40	-1.15	-1.47	81	93	11,054
5 Yr Avg	4.94	-2.69	-1.83	90	95	12,727
10 Yr Avg	---	---	---	---	---	---
15 Yr Avg	---	---	---	---	---	---

Operations

Address and Telephone	733 Third Avenue
	New York, NY 10017-3204
	800-858-8850 / 212-551-5353
Advisor	SunAmerica Asset Management
Subadvisor	Wellington Management
Distributor	SunAmerica Capital Services
States Available	All
Report Grade	C
Income Distrib	Paid Monthly
* Date of Inception	11-22-85
Fiscal Year End	March

Risk Analysis

Time Period	Load-Adj Return %	Risk % Rank [1] All	Risk % Rank [1] Obj	Morningstar [2] Return	Morningstar Risk	Morningstar Risk-Adj Rating
1 Yr	-8.55					
3 Yr	1.73	16	29	0.38	0.82	★★
5 Yr	3.92	7	19	0.54	0.72	★★
10 Yr	---	---	---	---	---	

Average Historical Rating (74 months)   3.1 ★s

[1] 1 = low, 100 = high   [2] 1.00 = Muni Avg   [3] 1.00 = 90-day T-bill return

Other Measures

				Standard LB Agg	Best Fit LB Muni
Standard Deviation	4.42	Alpha		-0.9	-1.1
Mean	3.44	Beta		0.82	0.77
Sharpe Ratio	-0.02	R-Squared		56	92

Investment Style

Interest-Rate Stance

Avg Effective Maturity	17.0 Yrs

Maturity Short Intm Long

Quality

Avg Credit Quality	AAA
Avg Weighted Coupon	6.61%
Avg Weighted Price	100.31% of Par

Diversification Value for Portfolio Types

Large Cap: Medium | Small Cap: High | Bond: Low | Balanced: Medium | Diversified: Medium

Expenses & Fees

Sales Fees	4.75% front
	0.00% deferred
	0.35% 12b-1
Management Fee	0.50% max./0.45% min.
3-,5-,10-yr Expense Projections	$86, $114, $195

Min Initial Purchase	$500 (Addt'l: $100)
Min IRA Purchase	$250 (Addt'l: $25)
Min Auto Invest Plan	$500 (Systematic Inv: $25)

Portfolio 12-31-94

Total Stocks: 0
Total Fixed-Income: 94

Amount 000	Date of Maturity		Value $000	% Net Assets
6571	08-01-11	CA San Jose Redev Merged Area Tax 6%	6381	4.70
4779	12-01-13	TX GO Vet Land 7.625%	5071	3.73
4502	07-01-04	NJ Econ Dev 7%	4831	3.55
4587	07-01-14	MA Hsg Fin 6.6%	4450	3.27
4267	11-01-02	CA State GO 6.3%	4391	3.23
3883	01-01-03	MD NE Waste Disp SW Resource Rec 7.1%	4136	3.04
4267	06-01-10	DC GO 6%	3974	2.92
5073	04-01-16	NV Hsg Div Sngl Fam Prog 0%	3658	2.69
3413	08-15-19	TX Bexar Hlth Fac Dev Baptist Meml 6.75%	3389	2.49
3413	11-01-10	MA Wtr Resource 6.25%	3363	2.47
3413	02-01-07	NY Suffolk Indl Dev 6%	3350	2.47
2987	08-15-07	OH Lucas St Vincent M/C 6.5%	3064	2.25
2722	07-01-14	AZ Phoenix Civic Impr Wastewtr 6.125%	2816	2.07
2748	07-01-04	GA State GO 6%	2804	2.06
2901	06-01-11	WA State GO 6%	2776	2.04
2560	05-15-12	MD Comnty Dev Ad Multi-Fam Hsg 8.75%	2657	1.95
2560	05-01-17	WV Hsg Dev Fund 7.25%	2637	1.94
2560	11-15-03	OH Cleveland Pub Pwr Sys Impr 6.1%	2590	1.91
2560	08-15-14	NY Med Care Fin Hosp/Nurs Home 6.75%	2560	1.88
2560	08-15-13	NY GO Med Care Fac Fin Mental Hlth 6.1%	2424	1.78

Credit Analysis % of Bonds 12-31-94

US Govt	0	BB	0
AAA	77	B	0
AA	16	Below B	0
A	2	NR/NA	5
BBB	1		

Composition % of Assets 12-31-94

Cash	-4.9	Preferreds	0.0
Stocks	0.0	Convertibles	0.0
Bonds	104.9	Other	0.0

Tax Analysis

	Tax-Adj Historical Return %	% Pretax Return
3 Yr Avg	3.40	100.0
5 Yr Avg	4.94	100.0
10 Yr Avg	---	---
Potential Capital Gain Exposure (% of assets)		-9%

Most Similar Funds in MF500

First Invest Insured T/E A	Strong Fit
IDS High-Yield Tax-Exempt	Strong Fit
Colonial Tax-Exempt A	Strong Fit

Coupon Range

	% Bonds	Rel Obj
0%	2.5	1.01
0% to 6.8%	52.5	0.87
6.8% to 7.5%	23.7	1.53
7.5% to 8.3%	11.1	1.10
More than 8.3%	9.7	1.10
Not applicable	0.4	0.11

Sector Weightings

	% Bonds	Rel Obj
General Obl	26.55	1.26
Utilities	4.73	0.38
Health	14.60	1.11
Water/Waste	6.60	1.04
Housing	23.20	3.17
Education	1.99	0.31
Transportation	2.36	0.23
COP/Lease	2.68	0.84
Private	15.91	1.36
Misc Revenue	1.37	0.28
Demand	0.00	0.00

Top 5 States % of Bonds

NY	10.80	MA	6.71
CA	10.06	MD	5.90
TX	9.26		

MORNINGSTAR 1995 Mutual Fund 500

Swiss Helvetia

Swiss Helvetia Fund seeks long-term capital appreciation. The fund invests primarily in equity and debt securities of Swiss companies. The fund does not enter into transactions to reduce currency risk.

The fund's antitakeover provisions include staggered board terms and supermajority voting requirements (75%) for mergers and liquidation.

	Ticker	NAV	Mkt Price	Prem/Disc	Yield	Objective
	SWZ	$19.79	$18.88	-4.6%	1.4%	Europe Stock

3.9	0.7	16.0	15.3	8.7	5.6	8.5	6.4	Highest Prem/Disc
-23.0	-16.2	-16.4	-13.1	-11.8	-11.6	-8.1	-8.6	Lowest Prem/Disc

Historical Profile
Return Average
Risk Below Average
Rating ★★★★ Above Average

Growth of $10,000
■ at NAV ($000)
— at Market Price ($000)

Premium Discount %

	1983	1984	1985	1986	1987	1988	1989	1990	1991	1992	1993	1994	History
	---	---	---	---	12.34	10.99	13.04	13.17	13.80	14.62	20.96	19.79	NAV
	---	---	---	---	-11.54*	-10.76	18.65	1.42	5.03	7.23	45.54	1.10	NAV Total Return %
	---	---	---	---	12.87*	-27.37	-13.03	4.53	-25.45	-0.39	35.49	-0.21	+/- S&P 500
	---	---	---	---	---	-39.02	8.12	24.87	-7.10	19.41	12.98	-6.68	+/- MSCI EAFE
	---	---	---	---	---	-16.94	-7.56	7.65	-10.74	-10.00	-0.25	-2.44	+/- MSCI Switzerland
	---	---	---	---	0.00*	0.19	0.00	0.42	0.25	0.17	0.45	1.50	Income Return %
	---	---	---	---	-11.54*	-10.94	18.65	1.00	4.78	7.07	45.09	-0.40	Capital Return %
	---	---	---	---	---	97	25	60	92	64	9	11	Total Rtn % Rank All
	---	---	---	---	---	75	50	22	31	5	10	42	Total Rtn % Rank Obj
	---	---	---	---	-36.67*	1.53	57.14	-21.16	11.84	6.45	66.45	-11.16	Market Total Rtn %
	---	---	---	---	---	-10.0	-7.6	-4.0	-2.3	-3.8	-0.3	-3.2	Avg Prem/Disc %
	---	---	---	---	0.00	0.02	0.00	0.05	0.03	0.03	0.08	0.27	Income $
	---	---	---	---	0.00	0.00	0.00	0.00	0.00	0.00	0.25	0.99	Capital Gains $
	---	---	---	---	1.85	1.83	1.80	1.77	1.85	1.69	1.50	1.48	Expense Ratio %
	---	---	---	---	0.39	-0.14	0.07	0.49	0.07	0.39	0.29	1.79	Income Ratio %
	---	---	---	---	28	64	30	44	41	13	20	--	Turnover Rate %
	---	---	---	---	98.8	185.1	104.5	105.4	110.5	125.9	184.7	181.8	Net Assets ($mil)

Manager's Investment Style
Tied to the Swiss economy by charter, the portfolio is a blend of Switzerland's multinationals and more-local concerns. Due to the makeup of the Swiss market, the fund typically shows a large weighting in financials and pharmaceuticals, though management adjusts this exposure according to the current outlook. In addition, management attempts to thwart risk by diversifying the portfolio beyond the handful of firms that dominate the market. Although management practices a buy-and-hold strategy, it is willing to tinker with holdings based on its economic outlook.

Fund Manager(s)
Georges L. de Montebello. Since 8-87. BA'56 Harvard.

Manager Experience

	Dates Managed	Invest Obj	Std Dev	+/- Index
Not available.				

NAV Performance % 12-30-94

	1st Qtr	2nd Qtr	3rd Qtr	4th Qtr	Total
1987	---	---	-1.65*	-10.06	-11.54*
1988	-4.78	-6.81	-2.17	2.81	-10.76
1989	-4.91	10.14	11.29	1.80	18.65
1990	-2.99	16.92	-14.86	5.02	1.42
1991	-0.30	-4.27	3.98	5.83	5.03
1992	-2.46	11.49	8.35	-8.99	7.23
1993	6.63	9.30	10.45	13.06	45.54
1994	-0.19	0.43	0.19	0.67	1.10

Bear Market Performance

Decile Rank (5-year period)

Worst [bar] Best

	Worst 3 Mo Period 1985-89	Worst 3 Mo Period 1990-94
Swiss Helvetia	---	-14.86
+/- S&P 500	---	-1.11

Trailing Returns

	NAV Total Return %	+/- S&P 500	+/- MSCI Swiss	% Rank All	% Rank Obj	Mkt Total Return %
3 Mo	0.67	0.69	-0.56	14	25	-0.19
6 Mo	0.86	-4.00	-1.45	29	47	-0.19
1 Yr	1.10	-0.21	-2.44	11	42	-11.16
3 Yr Avg	16.42	10.15	-4.54	7	5	16.33
5 Yr Avg	10.94	2.25	-3.01	21	1	6.78
Incept Avg	6.37*	---	---	---	---	4.71*

Operations

Address and Telephone	630 Fifth Ave., Suite 915 New York, NY 10111 212-332-7930	
Advisor	Hottinger Capital Corp.	
Subadvisor	N/A	
Administrator	Investor Company Capital Corp.	
Transfer Agent	Provident Financial Process. Corp.	
Custodian	PNC Bank N.A.	
Auditor	Deloitte & Touche	
Legal Counsel	Kelley Drye & Warren	

Income Distrib Schedule	Paid Annually
Management Fee	1.00%, 0.20%A
Reinvestment Plan	Yes
Direct Purchase Plan	No
Shares Outstanding	9,186,692
Exchange	NYSE
*Date of Inception	08-27-87
Shareholder Report	A

Risk Analysis

	Risk % Rank[1]		Morningstar[2]		Morningstar
	All	Obj	Return	Risk	Risk-Adj Rating
3 Yr	71	1	1.86	0.55	★★★★
5 Yr	77	1	1.22	0.66	★★★★
10 Yr	---	---	---	---	---

Average Historical Rating (53 months) 2.6 ★s

[1] 1 = Low, 100 = High [2] 1.00 = Equity Avg [3] 1.00 = 90-day T-bill Return

Other Measures

				S&P 500
Standard Deviation	13.34	Alpha		11.51
Mean	16.18	Beta		0.59
Sharpe Ratio	0.95	R-Squared		13

Investment Style

	Stock Portfolio Avg	Rel WS SwitzrInd	Rel WS Foreign
Price/Earnings Ratio	19.6	0.96	0.40
Price/Cash Flow Ratio	10.2	1.03	0.70
Price/Book Ratio	1.9	0.84	0.63
5 Yr Earnings Gr %	6.9	0.57	NMF
Return on Assets %	5.4#	0.77	1.17
Debt % Total Cap	29.4	1.01	0.91
Med Mkt Cap ($mil)	8657	0.61	1.37

figure is based on less than 50% of stocks

Country Exposure (top five) 12-31-94

	Securities %		Currency %
Switzerland	98	Switzerland	100

Diversification Value for Portfolio Types

Large Cap: High	Small Cap: High	Bond: High	Balanced: High	Diversified: Medium

Portfolio 09-30-94

Share Chg (06-94)	Amount	Total Equity: 47 Total Fixed-Income: 0	Value $000	% Total Invest
4000	30000	Nestle (Reg)	27283	14.1
-900	5400	Roche Holding (Div Cert)	24324	13.23
0	21800	Union Bank of Switz (Br)	20334	11.06
0	22875	Sandoz (Reg)	11611	6.31
3500	18000	Ciba-Geigy (Reg)	10144	5.52
1000	10000	BBC Brown Boveri (Br)	8628	4.69
0	100000	CS Holdings (Reg)	7812	4.25
0	7800	Zurich Insurance (Reg)	7197	3.91
0	20000	Swiss Bank (Br)	5705	3.10
2800	7500	Holderbank Fin Glarus (Br)	5509	3.00
-2900	8600	Swiss Reinsurance (Reg)	4185	2.28
6345	13000	Merkur Holding (Reg)	3517	1.91
0	3200	Financiere Richemont (Br)	3010	1.64
-2500	5500	Winterthur Insurance (Reg)	2629	1.43
700	5000	Alusuisse-Lonza (Reg)	2620	1.42
0	3000	Sulzer Gebruder (Reg)	2073	1.13
0	7200	Generale de Surveill (Reg)	2071	1.13
200	1000	Baloise Holding (Reg)	1998	1.09
400	1000	Forbo Holdings (Reg)	1920	1.04
500	1500	Bobst (Br)	1912	1.04
1500	1800	AFG Arbonia-Forster (Br)	1889	1.03
1550	1550	Ascom Holding (Br)	1837	1.00
0	3000	Landis & Gyr (Reg)	1796	0.98
300	1800	Schweizer Ind Ges (Reg)	1777	0.97
0	200	Bank for Intl Settlement Reg	1648	0.90

Composition % 12-31-94

Cash	2.0	Preferreds	0.0
Stocks	98.0	Convertibles	0.0
Bonds	0.0	Other	0.0

Tax Analysis

	Tax-Adj Historical Return %	% Pretax Return
3 Yr Avg	15.74	91.6
5 Yr Avg	10.51	91.9
10 Yr Avg	---	---

Potential Capital Gain Exposure (% of assets) 28

Most Similar Funds in MF500

Vanguard Intl Growth	Weak Fit
Harbor International	Weak Fit
T. Rowe Price Intl Stock	Weak Fit

Sector Weightings

	% of Stocks
Utilities	5.8
Energy	0.0
Financials	29.4
Industrial Cyclicals	20.0
Consumer Durables	0.4
Consumer Staples	18.3
Services	1.5
Retail	2.6
Health	20.0
Technology	2.1

Taiwan Fund

	Ticker	NAV	Mkt Price	Prem/Disc	Yield	Objective
	TWN	$31.76	$28.88	-9.1%	0.1%	Pacific/Asia

Taiwan Fund seeks long-term capital appreciation.

Normally, the fund will invest at least 75% of its assets in stocks listed on the Taiwan Stock Exchange. The fund may raise cash for defensive purposes.

The fund has had six public offerings: December 1986, approximately 2.3 million shares; May 1988, 505,560 shares; February 1990, 1.1 million shares; June 1991, 2.1 million shares; November 1991, 1.7 million shares; and December 1993, 3.2 million shares.

172.0	108.0	28.7	45.0	37.5	37.6	51.2	32.1	Highest Prem/Disc
-6.2	-25.0	-13.7	-15.5	0.7	-15.9	-2.3	-13.9	Lowest Prem/Disc

Historical Profile

Return: Below Average
Risk: Above Average
Rating: ★★ Below Average

Growth of $10,000
■ at NAV ($000)
— at Market Price ($000)

Premium Discount %

1983	1984	1985	1986	1987	1988	1989	1990	1991	1992	1993	1994	History
---	---	---	11.16	19.44	22.32	39.12	16.50	20.89	19.03	25.87	31.76	NAV
---	---	---	0.00*	74.19	50.65	219.01	-54.67	26.61	-8.33	36.60	22.85	NAV Total Return %
---	---	---	3.31*	68.94	34.04	187.33	-51.55	-3.88	-15.95	26.54	21.54	+/- S&P 500
---	---	---	---	49.56	22.38	208.47	-31.22	14.48	3.84	4.04	15.08	+/- MSCI EAFE
---	---	---	---	N/A	-66.60	135.48	0.77	14.80	16.30	-45.72	3.15	+/- MSCI Taiwan
---	---	---	0.00*	0.00	5.08	43.93	0.00	0.00	0.57	0.66	0.09	Income Return %
---	---	---	0.00*	74.19	45.57	175.08	-54.67	26.61	-8.90	35.94	22.77	Capital Return %
---	---	---	1	3	1	99	28	93	12	2		Total Rtn % Rank All
---	---	---	1	16	1	90	13	73	70	16		Total Rtn % Rank Obj
---	---	---	58.33*	65.13	45.33	160.58	-55.72	20.12	-23.38	109.67	-26.15	Market Total Rtn %
---	---	---	---	80.9	36.4	7.8	22.4	17.2	3.4	17.4	5.2	Avg Prem/Disc %
---	---	---	0.00	0.00	1.85	8.50	0.00	0.00	0.12	0.13	0.02	Income $
---	---	---	0.00	0.00	7.26	14.75	1.69	0.00	0.00	0.00	0.00	Capital Gains $
---	---	---	---	3.75	2.50	2.11	2.34	3.47	2.94	2.67	2.49	Expense Ratio %
---	---	---	---	-2.03	-1.31	-0.69	2.80	-0.79	0.29	1.05	-1.01	Income Ratio %
---	---	---	---	203	141	169	226	298	129	163	· 267	Turnover Rate %
---	---	---	26.3	41.2	264.4	73.1	69.6	167.9	153.0	162.8	289.5	Net Assets ($mil)

Manager's Investment Style

Management attempts to move quickly in the fast-paced Taiwan market. It often takes large positions in favored stocks or sectors, and often times the market by building up large cash stakes when management is defensive.

Fund Manager(s)

Michael Chen. Since 7-92.

Manager Experience

Not available.

	Dates Managed	Invest Obj	Std Dev	+/- Index

NAV Performance % 12-30-94

	1st Qtr	2nd Qtr	3rd Qtr	4th Qtr	Total
1987	21.95	21.68	125.00	-47.83	74.19
1988	33.84	37.77	59.26	-48.70	50.65
1989	72.69	30.13	11.15	27.72	219.01
1990	-36.30	-24.74	-7.79	2.55	-54.67
1991	19.03	13.80	-6.85	0.34	26.61
1992	4.50	-1.37	-10.17	-0.99	-8.33
1993	7.20	-5.59	-5.56	42.91	36.60
1994	-8.31	6.31	22.74	2.68	22.85

Bear Market Performance

Decile Rank (5-year period)

Worst ———————————— Best

	Worst 3 Mo Period 1985-89	Worst 3 Mo Period 1990-94
Taiwan Fund	---	-36.30
+/- S&P 500	---	-33.30

Trailing Returns

	NAV Total Return %	+/- S&P 500	+/- MSCI Taiwan	% Rank All	% Rank Obj	Mkt Total Return %
3 Mo	2.68	2.70	1.70	4	8	-5.33
6 Mo	26.03	21.17	1.49	1	1	7.44
1 Yr	22.85	21.54	3.15	2	16	-26.15
3 Yr Avg	15.44	9.17	-2.61	8	60	5.86
5 Yr Avg	-2.46	-11.15	1.44	97	90	-8.79
Incept Avg	28.11*	---	---	---	---	25.48*

Operations

Address and Telephone	82 Devonshire Street Boston, MA 02109 800-426-5523	
Advisor	China Securities Investment Trust	
Subadvisor	N/A	
Administrator	N/A	
Transfer Agent	State Street Bank and Trust Co.	
Custodian	State Street Bank and Trust Co.	
Auditor	Coopers & Lybrand	
Legal Counsel	Rogers & Wells	

Income Distrib Schedule	Paid Irregularly
Management Fee	1.50%, 0.50%P, 0.10%A
Reinvestment Plan	Yes
Direct Purchase Plan	Yes
Shares Outstanding	11,274,365
Exchange	NYSE
*Date of Inception	12-05-86
Shareholder Report	C+

Risk Analysis

	Risk % Rank¹		Morningstar²		Morningstar
	All	Obj	Return	Risk	Risk-Adj Rating
3 Yr	86	13	1.70	0.93	★★★★
5 Yr	96	60	-1.09	1.45	★
10 Yr	---	---	---	---	

Average Historical Rating (61 months)   2.4 ★s

¹1 = Low, 100 = High ²1.00 = Equity Avg   ³1.00 = 90-day T-bill Return

Other Measures

			S&P 500
Standard Deviation	26.11	Alpha	12.31
Mean	17.43	Beta	0.78
Sharpe Ratio	0.53	R-Squared	6

Investment Style

	Stock Portfolio Avg	Rel WS Taiwan	Rel WS Foreign
Price/Earnings Ratio	27.2#	0.66	0.55
Price/Cash Flow Ratio	15.2#	1.07	1.04
Price/Book Ratio	3.3#	0.80	1.09
5 Yr Earnings Gr %			
Return on Assets %			
Debt % Total Cap	12.4#	0.84	0.38
Med Mkt Cap ($mil)	3446#	1.00	0.55

figure is based on less than 50% of stocks

Country Exposure (top five) 12-31-94

	Securities %		Currency %
Taiwan	78	Taiwan	100

Diversification Value for Portfolio Types

Large Cap: High	Small Cap: High	Bond: High	Balanced: High	Diversified: High

Portfolio 12-31-94

Share Chg (08-94)	Amount	Total Equity: 55 Total Fixed-Income: 0	Value $000	% Total Invest
2800000	13379761	Formosa Chemical & Fiber	22496	6.26
1906000	6799373	Delta Electrical Industries	19529	5.43
724000	6554112	Nan Ya Plastic	15956	4.44
9000000	9000000	Far Eastern Textile	15304	4.26
-2400000	5600000	Taiwan Glass Industrial	13527	3.76
-3000000	10000000	China Steel	12553	3.49
2000000	2000000	Taiwan Secom	11869	3.30
1000000	8137457	Formosa Taffeta	11051	3.07
6010000	6010000	U Ming Marine	9511	2.65
-200000	2927650	Electronic Industries Comp	9188	2.56
-1616000	4097280	Formosa Plastic	8806	2.45
3700000	3700000	Uniglory Marine	8586	2.39
-6544000	5740800	Sampo	8451	2.35
-930504	3388392	First Intl Computer	8314	2.31
5000000	5000000	China Petrochemical Dev	8198	2.28
3500000	3650000	Evergreen Marine (Taiwan)	7984	2.22
4065000	4065000	Chung Hwa Pulp	7886	2.19
4500000	4500000	Yang Ming Marine	7429	2.07
-200000	1936000	Yageo	7328	2.04
1700000	3554500	Everlight Chemical Industry	6896	1.92
-1695887	1977873	Teco Electric & Machinery	5718	1.59
3090000	3090000	Shinkong Synthetic	5583	1.55
-1596000	2504000	Taiwan Synthetic Rubber	5191	1.44
-1349000	2314245	China Synthetic Rubber	4666	1.30
700000	2600000	Kenda Rubber Industrial	4649	1.29

Composition % 12-31-94

Cash	22.4	Preferreds	0.0
Stocks	77.6	Convertibles	0.0
Bonds	0.0	Other	0.0

Tax Analysis

	Tax-Adj Historical Return %	% Pretax Return
3 Yr Avg	15.30	98.9
5 Yr Avg	-2.99	NMF
10 Yr Avg	---	---

Potential Capital Gain Exposure (% of assets)   29

Most Similar Funds in MF500

Dreyfus Global Growth	Weak Fit
Invesco European	Weak Fit
Strong Discovery	Weak Fit

Sector Weightings

	% of Stocks
Utilities	0.0
Energy	0.0
Financials	0.6
Industrial Cyclicals	49.7
Consumer Durables	19.8
Consumer Staples	0.8
Services	7.9
Retail	0.2
Health	0.0
Technology	21.0

Templeton Developing Markets

	Ticker	Load	NAV	Yield	SEC Yield	Assets	Objective
	TEDMX	5.75%	13.42	0.9%	N/A	2000.9	Foreign Stock

Templeton Developing Markets Trust seeks capital appreciation over the long term.

The fund normally invests at least 65% of its assets in equity securities of countries with developing markets. It may not necessarily seek to diversify investments among geographic regions or levels of economic development in any particular country. For capital appreciation, the fund may invest up to 35% of its assets in debt securities rated at least C or judged to be of comparable quality. It may also leverage its portfolio. The fund usually expects that its annual turnover rate will not exceed 50%.

Manager's Investment Style

Manager J. Mark Mobius applies Sir John Templeton's modest-turnover, bottom-up, value-driven approach to the world's emerging markets. His research-driven strategy emphasizes stock selection, not sector or country rotation. Mobius looks for companies that are cheap relative to their historical valuations, to their markets, or to similar emerging-markets concerns. In the past, cash has swelled to 50% of assets at times, when management couldn't find good values.

Fund Manager(s)

J. Mark Mobius, since 10-91. MA, Boston U. PhD, MIT 1964

Manager Experience	Dates Managed	Invest Obj	Std Dev	+/- Index
J. Mark Mobius				
Templtn Em Mkts	02/87 - 12/94	WW	19.33	13.15
Templeton Instl Emerg Mkt	05/93 - 12/94	WF	15.28	6.61

Historical Profile

Return	Above Average
Risk	Average
Rating	★★★★
	Above Average

Investment Style History
Equity

Average % Stocks Held in Portfolio

Growth of $10,000

- |||| Value of Fund ($000)
- — Value of Index ($000) MSPacxJp
- ▼ Manager Change
- ▽ Partial Manager Change
- ► Mgr Unknown After
- ◄ Mgr Unknown Before

Performance Quartile (Within Objective)

	1983	1984	1985	1986	1987	1988	1989	1990	1991	1992	1993	1994	History
	---	---	---	---	---	---	---	---	10.02	8.86	15.26	13.42	NAV
	---	---	---	---	---	---	---	---	0.25 *	-9.77	74.50	-8.58	Total Return %
	---	---	---	---	---	---	---	---	-7.01 *	-17.38	64.44	-9.90	+/- S&P 500
	---	---	---	---	---	---	---	---	---	-12.37	8.99	-6.17	+/- MSCI Emerging
	---	---	---	---	---	---	---	---	0.15	0.82	0.50	0.86	Income Return %
	---	---	---	---	---	---	---	---	0.10	-10.59	73.99	-9.44	Capital Return %
	---	---	---	---	---	---	---	---	---	98	2	88	Total Rtn % Rank All
	---	---	---	---	---	---	---	---	---	81	4	82	Total Rtn % Rank Obj
	---	---	---	---	---	---	---	---	0.02	0.08	0.06	0.12	Income $
	---	---	---	---	---	---	---	---	0.00	0.11	0.12	0.43	Capital Gains $
	---	---	---	---	---	---	---	---	2.25	2.25	2.20	2.17	Expense Ratio %
	---	---	---	---	---	---	---	---	0.86	1.30	0.57	1.02	Income Ratio %
	---	---	---	---	---	---	---	---	---	---	22	16	---	Turnover Rate %
	---	---	---	---	---	---	---	---	---	22.3	179.7	1391.5	2000.9	Net Assets ($mil)

Performance 12-31-94

	1st Qtr	2nd Qtr	3rd Qtr	4th Qtr	Total
1987	---	---	---	---	---
1988	---	---	---	---	---
1989	---	---	---	---	---
1990	---	---	---	---	---
1991	---	---	---	---	0.25 *
1992	-1.00	2.62	-5.99	-5.52	-9.77
1993	12.36	13.71	12.68	21.21	74.50
1994	-4.21	-5.64	10.57	-8.53	-8.58

Bear Market Performance

Decile Rank (5-year period)

Worst _____ Best

	Worst 3 Mo Period 1985-89	Worst 3 Mo Period 1990-94
Templeton Developing Markets	---	---
+/- S&P 500	---	---
+/- Best Fit Index :	---	---

Trailing Returns

	Total Return %	+/- S&P 500	+/- MSCI Emerging	% Rank All	% Rank Obj	Growth of $10,000
3 Mo	-8.53	-8.51	3.59	97	76	9,147
6 Mo	1.14	-3.72	-4.89	35	20	10,114
1 Yr	-8.58	-9.90	-6.17	88	82	9,142
3 Yr Avg	12.91	6.64	-5.43	6	15	14,394
5 Yr Avg	---	---	---	---	---	---
10 Yr Avg	---	---	---	---	---	---
15 Yr Avg	---	---	---	---	---	---

Operations

Address and Telephone	700 Central Avenue St. Petersburg, FL 33701-3628 800-292-9293 / 813-823-8712	Min Initial Purchase	$100 (Addt'l: $25)
		Min IRA Purchase	None (Addt'l: None)
		Min Auto Invest Plan	$25 (Systematic Inv: $25)
Advisor	Templeton Investment Mgmt Hong K	**Expenses & Fees**	
Subadvisor	None	Sales Fees	5.75% front
Distributor	Franklin/Templeton Distributors		0.00% deferred
States Available	All plus PR		0.35% 12b-1
Report Grade	A-	Management Fee	1.25% flat fee, 0.15%A
Income Distrib	Paid Annually	3-,5-,10-yr Expense Projections	$122, $169, $296
* Date of Inception	10-17-91	Annual Brokerage Cost	0.58%
Fiscal Year End	December		

Risk Analysis

Time Period	Load-Adj Return %	Risk % Rank [1] All	Risk % Rank [1] Obj	Morningstar [2] Return	Morningstar Risk	Morningstar Risk-Adj Rating
1 Yr	-13.84					
3 Yr	10.70	83	29	2.20 [3]	1.02	★★★★
5 Yr	---	---	---	---	---	
10 Yr	---	---	---	---	---	

Average Historical Rating (3 months)   4.0 ★s

[1] 1 = low, 100 = high   [2] 1.00 = Equity Avg   [3] 1.00 = 90-day T-bill return

Other Measures

				Standard S&P 500	Best Fit MSPacxJp
Standard Deviation	13.41	Alpha		8.4	3.0
Mean	13.08	Beta		0.51	0.43
Sharpe Ratio	0.71	R-Squared		9	44

Investment Style

	Stock Portfolio Avg	Rel MSCI EAFE	Rel Obj	Style V B G
Price/Earnings Ratio	23.4	0.63	0.83	
Price/Cash Flow	13.5#	0.87	1.01	
Price/Book Ratio	6.9	2.67	2.34	
5 Yr Earnings Gr %	9.3#	---	2.44	
Return on Assets %	---			
Debt % Total Cap	18.4#	0.54	0.66	
Med Mkt Cap ($mil)	1532	0.13	0.30	

figure is based on 50% or less of stocks

Diversification Value for Portfolio Types

Large Cap: High	Small Cap: High	Bond: High	Balanced: High	Diversified: High

Portfolio 09-30-94

Share Chg (03-94) 000	Amount 000	Total Stocks: 331 Total Fixed-Income: 6	Value $000	% Net Assets
176	942	Telefonos de Mexico L (ADR)	58881	2.74
0	121632	Centrais Eletricas Brasil	52301	2.44
3578	8950	Cheung Kong Holdings	43550	2.03
0	213165	Petrobras	42206	1.97
-12	601	Philippine Long Dist Tel	33632	1.57
2641	2641	HSBC Holdings (HK)	29480	1.37
139	1151	Banco Bilbao Vizcaya (Reg)	28311	1.32
52	289	Banco Interconti Espnl (Reg)	26281	1.22
-2385	37367	Investimentos Itau	26268	1.22
140	1654	Grupo Industrial Alfa CI A	23350	1.09
2410	6709	New World Development	23138	1.08
53	1460	Philippine National Bank	22802	1.06
-344560	451592	Telebras	22222	1.04
355058	355058	Telebras New	22131	1.03
95	520	Credit Bank	22027	1.03
3800	11888	Hang Lung Development	21923	1.02
15627	99284	Vale Do Rio Doce	20705	0.96
618	2647	Sun Hung Kai Properties	19696	0.92
99	1303	Banco Comercial Port (Reg)	17892	0.83
1382	5128	Malaysian Intl Shipping For	17103	0.80

Regional Exposure 12-31-94

% of Stocks

Europe	20	Pacific Rim	37
Japan	18	Other	12
Latin Amer	8		

Composition % 12-31-94

Cash	35.9	Preferreds	0.0
Stocks	63.9	Convertibles	0.0
Bonds	0.0	Other	0.2

Tax Analysis

	Tax-Adj Historical Return %	% Pretax Return
3 Yr Avg	12.10	93.0
5 Yr Avg	---	---
10 Yr Avg	---	---
Potential Capital Gain Exposure (% of assets)		3%

Most Similar Funds in MF500

Templtn Em Mkts	Weak Fit
Jakarta Growth	Weak Fit
T. Rowe Price New Asia	Weak Fit

Country Exposure 12-31-94

% of Stocks

Hong Kong	20
Brazil	18
Portugal	8
Turkey	7
Mexico	6

Total Number of Countries: 27
Hedging Policy: Never

Sector Weightings

	% of Stocks	Relative S&P 500
Utilities	18.0	2.02
Energy	4.8	1.17
Financials	41.9	2.22
Industrial Cyclicals	15.0	0.60
Consumer Durables	6.7	0.62
Consumer Staples	3.7	0.54
Services	5.4	0.50
Retail	3.3	0.56
Health	0.0	0.00
Technology	1.3	0.24

MORNINGSTAR 1995 Mutual Fund 500

Templeton Emerging Markets

	Ticker	NAV	Mkt Price	Prem/Disc	Yield	Objective
	EMF	$17.86	$19.50	9.2%	0.4%	World Stock

Templeton Emerging Markets Fund seeks long-term capital appreciation.

Under normal conditions, the fund will invest at least 75% of its assets in emerging countries with low- or middle-income economies (as determined by the World Bank). The fund may employ options, futures, and forward foreign-currency exchange contracts for hedging purposes.

To discourage takeover attempts, directors serve staggered terms, and 75% of outstanding shares are required to remove a director from office, merge or liquidate the fund, or sell off fund assets.

Options on the fund are traded on the American Stock Exchange.

Historical Profile
Return High
Risk Average
Rating ★★★★ Highest

| | | | | | 17.1 | -3.7 | 13.2 | 7.9 | 31.3 | 35.6 | 43.7 | 31.0 | Highest Prem/Disc |
| | | | | | -20.2 | -20.9 | -11.9 | -14.2 | -1.2 | 8.6 | 10.6 | -0.6 | Lowest Prem/Disc |

Growth of $10,000
■ at NAV ($000)
— at Market Price ($000)

Premium Discount %

1983	1984	1985	1986	1987	1988	1989	1990	1991	1992	1993	1994	History
---	---	---	---	7.52	9.39	13.47	11.93	16.94	12.32	22.90	17.86	NAV
---	---	---	---	-14.92*	27.43	49.65	2.15	69.75	2.76	96.97	-11.45	NAV Total Return %
---	---	---	---	-4.77*	10.82	17.96	5.26	39.27	-4.86	86.91	-12.77	+/- S&P 500
---	---	---	---	---	-0.84	39.11	25.59	57.62	14.93	64.41	-19.23	+/- MSCI EAFE
---	---	---	---	---	-47.68	-0.96	35.17	40.64	0.15	31.47	-9.03	+/- MSCI Emerging
---	---	---	---	3.03*	0.93	2.49	1.93	0.36	2.56	1.95	0.43	Income Return %
---	---	---	---	-17.96*	26.50	47.16	0.22	69.39	0.20	95.02	-11.88	Capital Return %
---	---	---	---		10	7	57	4	79	3	71	Total Rtn % Rank All
---	---	---	---		1	20	1	1	25	10	75	Total Rtn % Rank Obj
---	---	---	---	-36.87*	33.94	102.01	-2.63	106.60	-7.92	102.80	-20.22	Market Total Rtn %
---	---	---	---	2.5	-14.8	-4.2	-1.6	9.3	19.1	23.2	16.9	Avg Prem/Disc %
---	---	---	---	0.20	0.07	0.23	0.24	0.08	0.39	0.29	0.10	Income $
---	---	---	---	0.10	0.10	0.25	1.64	3.96	5.68	0.85	3.06	Capital Gains $
---	---	---	---	1.67	2.07	2.03	1.89	1.91	1.91	1.84	1.78	Expense Ratio %
---	---	---	---	3.16	1.73	1.44	1.67	1.43	2.34	2.07	0.46	Income Ratio %
---	---	---	---		12	13	24	34	53	22	7	Turnover Rate %
---	---	---	---	86.9	108.0	155.0	138.4	198.6	243.3	285.4	288.9	Net Assets ($mil)

Manager's Investment Style

Known as the emerging-markets pioneer, manager J. Mark Mobius employs his signature value-based discipline. By focusing on emerging-markets bargains, management helps to keep risk at bay. Further, Mobius is known for a hands-on approach to stock selection, whereby he personally investigates many potential buys. Management will also employ cash as a buffer, or if there are not enough appealing value stocks to buy.

Fund Manager(s)

J. Mark Mobius. Since 2-87. MA Boston U.; PhD'64 MIT.

Manager Experience

	Dates Managed	Invest Obj	Std Dev	+/- Index
J. Mark Mobius				
Templeton Developing Mar	10/91 - 12/94	WF	13.06	4.08
Templeton Instl Emerg Mkt	05/93 - 12/94	WF	15.28	6.61

NAV Performance % 12-30-94

	1st Qtr	2nd Qtr	3rd Qtr	4th Qtr	Total
1987	-0.11*	3.77	8.40	-24.28	-14.92*
1988	11.30	12.19	-2.77	4.96	27.43
1989	9.96	9.66	24.91	-0.65	49.65
1990	5.35	13.60	-14.14	-0.59	2.15
1991	28.08	3.40	15.00	11.46	69.75
1992	11.98	2.21	-3.82	-6.66	2.76
1993	13.23	18.49	17.24	25.21	96.97
1994	-8.25	-6.62	17.53	-12.06	-11.45

Bear Market Performance

Decile Rank (5-year period)

Worst ▮ Best

	Worst 3 Mo Period 1985-89	Worst 3 Mo Period 1990-94
Templtn Em Mkts	---	-18.65
+/- S&P 500	---	-4.81

Trailing Returns

	NAV Total Return %	+/- S&P 500	+/- MSCI Emerging	% Rank All	% Rank Obj	Mkt Total Return %
3 Mo	-12.07	-12.05	0.05	96	83	-14.44
6 Mo	3.35	-1.51	-2.67	13	44	-5.28
1 Yr	-11.45	-12.77	-9.03	71	75	-20.22
3 Yr Avg	21.47	15.20	3.13	5	12	14.21
5 Yr Avg	25.45	16.76	17.99	2	1	24.55
Incept Avg	22.90*	---	---	---	---	23.14*

Operations

Address and Telephone	700 Central Avenue St. Petersburg, FL 33701 813-823-8712 / 800-292-9293	Income Distrib Schedule	Paid Annually
Advisor	Templeton Investment Management	Management Fee	1.40%
Subadvisor	Templeton, Galbraith & Hansberger	Reinvestment Plan	Yes
Administrator	N/A	Direct Purchase Plan	No
Transfer Agent	Mellon Financial Services	Shares Outstanding	16,181,993
Custodian	Chase Manhattan Bank N.A.	Exchange	NYSE
Auditor	McGladrey & Pullen	*Date of Inception	02-26-87
Legal Counsel	Dechert Price & Rhoads	Shareholder Report	A-

Risk Analysis

	Risk % Rank[1]		Morningstar[2]		Morningstar
	All	Obj	Return	Risk	Risk-Adj Rating
3 Yr	83	62	2.71	0.87	★★★★
5 Yr	81	20	5.36	0.73	★★★★★
10 Yr	---	---	---	---	---

Average Historical Rating (59 months)   4.8 ★s

[1] 1 = Low, 100 = High   [2] 1.00 = Equity Avg   [3] 1.00 = 90-day T-bill Return

Other Measures

			S&P 500
Standard Deviation	18.52	Alpha	17.07
Mean	21.29	Beta	0.66
Sharpe Ratio	0.96	R-Squared	8

Investment Style

	Stock Portfolio Avg	Rel WS Foreign	Rel WS World
Price/Earnings Ratio	37.7	0.77	0.92
Price/Cash Flow Ratio	13.7#	0.94	0.98
Price/Book Ratio	6.9	2.29	2.21
5 Yr Earnings Gr %	8.2#	NMF	NMF
Return on Assets %	43.1#	9.34	7.67
Debt % Total Cap	12.5#	0.39	0.39
Med Mkt Cap ($mil)	746	0.12	0.10

figure is based on less than 50% of stocks

Country Exposure (top five) 12-31-94

	Securities %		Currency %
Brazil	19	Brazil	19
Philippines	11	US	13
Turkey	11	Philippines	11
Portugal	9	Turkey	11
Greece	7	Portugal	9

Diversification Value for Portfolio Types

Large Cap: High	Small Cap: High	Bond: High	Balanced: High	Diversified: High

Tax Analysis

	Tax-Adj Historical Return %	% Pretax Return
3 Yr Avg	16.00	70.5
5 Yr Avg	19.79	69.4
10 Yr Avg	---	---
Potential Capital Gain Exposure (% of assets)		35

Most Similar Funds in MF500

Templeton Developing	Fair Fit
Morgan Stan Em Mkts	Weak Fit
Jakarta Growth	Weak Fit

Portfolio 08-31-94

Share Chg (05-94)	Amount	Total Equity: 150 Total Fixed-Income: 3	Value $000	% Total Invest
0	108.179M	Petrobras	19148	5.27
64076	885556	Philippine National Bank	16071	4.42
200006	200006	Philippine Long Dist Tel (Br)	13200	3.63
5357906	209.358M	Telebras PN	12344	3.40
0	196700	Telefonos de Mexico L (ADR)	12343	3.40
0	28376204	Centrais Eletricas Brasil B	11965	3.29
0	633896	Banco Comercial Portugues	9016	2.48
0	1688000	Cheung Kong Holdings	8541	2.35
-16.000M	73391054	Energetica de Minas Gerais	8440	2.32
0	903600	Singapore Bus Service (For)	8253	2.27
1348000	1685000	Antofagasta Holdings (Chile)	7974	2.19
5145828	15832463	Arcelik	6924	1.90
482667	1930667	Malaysian Intl Shipping	6451	1.77
0	1088000	Oriental Holdings	6038	1.66
0	8854346	Investimentos Itau	5890	1.62
16831324	16831324	Akbank	5889	1.62
0	3179000	Hang Lung Development	5780	1.59
0	32992300	Vale do Rio Doce	5133	1.41
0	134800	Ergo Bank	4904	1.35
26940	148640	Portuguesa Radio Marconi	4755	1.31
0	6592800	Copene-Petro do Nordeste	4608	1.27
0	20707000	Eregil Demir Ve Celik Fabrik	4347	1.20
0	97620	Alpha Credit Bank	4111	1.13
121700	401789	Portuguesa Radio Marconi (Br)	3984	1.10
0	401789	Philippine Comm Intl Bank	3722	1.02

Composition % 12-31-94

Cash	13.3	Preferreds	0.0
Stocks	86.7	Convertibles	0.0
Bonds	0.0	Other	0.8

Sector Weightings

	% of Stocks
Utilities	18.6
Energy	8.3
Financials	30.6
Industrial Cyclicals	19.8
Consumer Durables	6.0
Consumer Staples	5.1
Services	7.0
Retail	1.3
Health	0.0
Technology	3.4

Templeton Foreign

Templeton Foreign Fund seeks long-term capital growth. Any realized income is incidental.

The fund invests primarily in stocks and debt securities of companies and governments outside the United States. It maintains a flexible investment policy and can invest in all types of securities and in any foreign country, developed or underdeveloped. While common stocks are the usual form of investment, the fund is authorized to invest up to 5% of its assets in medium-quality or high-risk lower-quality debt securities rated between BBB and CCC.

Ticker	**Load**	**NAV**	**Yield**	**SEC Yield**	**Assets**	**Objective**		
TEMFX	5.75%	8.82	1.7%	N/A	5305.8	Foreign Stock		

Manager's Investment Style

Management follows the traditional value-driven Templeton strategy by investing in companies selling cheap relative to either their assets or to their long-term earnings. Management tries to buy the world's best bargains. Owing to high prices, the fund generally avoids Japan, but is willing to invest in value-priced emerging-markets stocks.

Historical Profile
Return: Above Average
Risk: Below Average
Rating: ★★★★ Above Average

Investment Style History
Equity
Average % Stocks Held in Portfolio: 85% 84% 87% 77% 79% 77% 73% 65%

Growth of $10,000
IIII Value of Fund ($000)
— Value of Index ($000) MSEASEA
▼ Manager Change
▽ Partial Manager Change
► Mgr Unknown After
◄ Mgr Unknown Before

Performance Quartile (Within Objective)

	1983	1984	1985	1986	1987	1988	1989	1990	1991	1992	1993	1994	History
	3.73	3.57	4.38	5.14	5.78	6.43	7.77	6.99	7.63	7.10	9.43	8.82	NAV
	36.52	-1.19	26.86	28.79	24.73	22.01	30.52	-3.01	18.26	0.09	36.81	0.35	Total Return %
	14.05	-7.46	-4.88	10.11	19.47	5.40	-1.16	0.11	-12.23	-7.53	26.75	-0.96	+/- S&P 500
	12.83	-8.57	-29.30	-40.65	0.10	-6.26	19.99	20.44	6.13	12.26	4.25	-7.43	+/- MSCI EAFE
	1.86	2.31	3.51	2.60	3.60	3.54	3.70	3.50	3.23	2.68	1.66	1.68	Income Return %
	34.65	-3.50	23.35	26.19	21.13	18.47	26.82	-6.51	15.03	-2.59	35.15	-1.33	Capital Return %
	5	70	39	7	3	10	12	64	48	89	5	17	Total Rtn % Rank All
	9	33	81	85	1	11	9	2	21	19	49	35	Total Rtn % Rank Obj
	0.05	0.08	0.12	0.12	0.19	0.21	0.25	0.26	0.23	0.19	0.13	0.16	Income $
	0.01	0.03	0.01	0.36	0.41	0.39	0.33	0.30	0.39	0.33	0.14	0.52	Capital Gains $
	1.44	0.84	0.90	0.79	0.77	0.81	0.81	0.77	0.80	0.94	1.12	1.14	Expense Ratio %
	3.67	3.36	3.32	2.99	2.89	3.29	3.55	3.95	3.59	2.92	2.11	1.84	Income Ratio %
	4	4	4	21	14	20	17	11	19	22	21	37	Turnover Rate %
	23.5	67.0	94.2	197.5	261.2	320.9	564.1	934.3	1300.6	1709.2	3528.8	5305.8	Net Assets ($mil)

Fund Manager(s)

Mark G. Holowesko CFA, since 01-87. BA, C. of the Holy Cross   MBA, Babson C.

Manager Experience

	Dates Managed	Invest Obj	Std Dev	+/- Index
Mark G. Holowesko				
Templeton Smaller Co Gr	01/87 - 12/92	WW	18.64	-4.68
Templeton Real Est Sec	01/91 - 12/92	S	11.05	-4.33

Performance 12-31-94

	1st Qtr	2nd Qtr	3rd Qtr	4th Qtr	Total
1987	18.88	13.69	10.90	-16.79	24.73
1988	9.86	2.42	2.04	6.27	22.01
1989	5.96	1.81	13.33	6.77	30.52
1990	1.89	6.94	-11.65	0.75	-3.01
1991	7.83	-1.25	8.33	2.52	18.26
1992	1.13	7.57	-6.51	-1.59	0.09
1993	8.21	4.39	8.07	12.07	36.81
1994	-0.03	-0.32	4.79	-3.90	0.35

Bear Market Performance

Decile Rank (5-year period)

Worst ——————— Best

	Worst 3 Mo Period 1985-89	Worst 3 Mo Period 1990-94
Templeton Foreign	-22.28	-13.79
+/- S&P 500	7.30	0.06
+/- Best Fit Index : MSEASEA	2.04	0.41

Trailing Returns

	Total Return %	+/- S&P 500	+/- MSCI EAFE	% Rank All	% Rank Obj	Growth of $10,000
3 Mo	-3.90	-3.88	-2.88	88	36	9,610
6 Mo	0.70	-4.16	1.63	43	23	10,070
1 Yr	0.35	-0.96	-7.43	17	35	10,035
3 Yr Avg	11.18	4.91	3.32	10	30	13,741
5 Yr Avg	9.53	0.84	8.03	20	14	15,761
10 Yr Avg	17.73	3.35	0.18	4	12	51,152
15 Yr Avg	---	---	---	---	---	---

Risk Analysis

Time Period	Load-Adj Return %	Risk % Rank[1] All	Obj	Morningstar[2] Return	Risk	Morningstar Risk-Adj Rating
1 Yr	-5.42					
3 Yr	9.00	73	5	1.65[3]	0.83	★★★★
5 Yr	8.24	63	1	0.87[3]	0.76	★★★
10 Yr	17.03	46	1	1.99	0.67	★★★★★

Average Historical Rating (109 months)   4.5 ★s

[1] 1 = low, 100 = high   [2] 1.00 = Equity Avg   [3] 1.00 = 90-day T-bill return

Other Measures

			Standard S&P 500	Best Fit MSEASEA
Standard Deviation	10.37	Alpha	5.7	3.0
Mean	11.17	Beta	0.71	0.74
Sharpe Ratio	0.74	R-Squared	29	89

Investment Style

	Stock Portfolio Avg	Rel MSCI EAFE	Rel Obj	Style V B G
Price/Earnings Ratio	18.6	0.50	0.66	
Price/Cash Flow	9.7	0.62	0.72	
Price/Book Ratio	1.9	0.74	0.65	
5 Yr Earnings Gr %	-1.8	---	-0.47	
Return on Assets %	5.5	1.22	0.77	
Debt % Total Cap	32.4	0.95	1.17	
Med Mkt Cap ($mil)	4812	0.40	0.94	

Size L M S

Diversification Value for Portfolio Types

Large Cap: Medium
Small Cap: High
Bond: High
Balanced: Medium
Diversified: Low

Portfolio 09-30-94

Total Stocks: 205
Total Fixed-Income: 10

Share Chg (06-94) 000	Amount 000		Value $000	% Net Assets
	73000	US Treasury Note 6.375%	70060	1.39
	72500	US Treasury Note 6.375%	69931	1.39
	73000	US Treasury Note 6%	69112	1.37
0	770	DSM (Netherlands)	65405	1.30
500	3962	Telefonica de Espana	53493	1.06
500	4627	HSBC Holdings (Plc) (HK)	51643	1.02
250	825	Total Petroleum Cl B	48514	0.96
4298	16898	Hillsdown Holdings	46101	0.91
0	5175	Vitro Cl A	45098	0.89
25	80	Ciba-Geigy (Reg)	45011	0.89
3	23	Baloise Holding (Reg)	44983	0.89
0	1451	Philips Electronics	44370	0.88
0	373	Akzo	43889	0.87
0	600	Nationale Elf Aquitaine	43096	0.85
0	4372	Singapore Airlines (For)	42762	0.85
1983	2341	Volvo Cl B Free	42702	0.85
0	5805	British Aerospace	41424	0.82
0	700	Sony	40727	0.81
3000	8000	Cheung Kong Holdings	38927	0.77
160	1560	Banco Bilbao Vizcaya (Reg)	38373	0.76

Regional Exposure 12-31-94
% of Stocks

Europe	11	Pacific Rim	21
Japan	10	Other	12
Latin Amer	9		

Composition % 12-31-94

Cash	26.1	Preferreds	0.0
Stocks	66.7	Convertibles	0.0
Bonds	7.2	Other	0.0

Tax Analysis

	Tax-Adj Historical Return %	% Pretax Return
3 Yr Avg	9.28	81.5
5 Yr Avg	7.38	74.2
10 Yr Avg	15.19	75.7
Potential Capital Gain Exposure (% of assets)		5%

Most Similar Funds in MF500

EuroPacific Growth	Strong Fit
20th Century Intl Equity	Strong Fit
Putnam Global Growth A	Strong Fit

Country Exposure 12-31-94
% of Stocks

	% of Stocks
United Kingdom	11
Hong Kong	10
Netherlands	9
U.S.	8
Australia	7

Total Number of Countries: 33
Hedging Policy: Never

Sector Weightings

	% of Stocks	Relative S&P 500
Utilities	11.4	1.27
Energy	6.6	1.61
Financials	24.4	1.29
Industrial Cyclicals	21.6	0.86
Consumer Durables	12.2	1.13
Consumer Staples	2.9	0.42
Services	9.6	0.88
Retail	5.0	0.86
Health	4.8	1.35
Technology	1.5	0.30

Operations

Address and Telephone	700 Central Avenue
	St. Petersburg, FL 33701-3628
	800-292-9293 / 813-823-8712
Advisor	Templeton Galbraith & Hansberger
Subadvisor	None
Distributor	Franklin/Templeton Distributors
States Available	All
Report Grade	A-
Income Distrib	Paid Annually
Date of Inception	10-05-82
Fiscal Year End	August

Min Initial Purchase	$100 (Addt'l: $25)
Min IRA Purchase	None (Addt'l: None)
Min Auto Invest Plan	$25 (Systematic Inv: $25)

Expenses & Fees

Sales Fees	5.75% front
	0.00% deferred
	0.25% 12b-1
Management Fee	0.75% max./0.60% min., 0.15%A
3-,5-,10-yr Expense Projections	$93, $120, $195
Annual Brokerage Cost	0.13% (aggregate)

MORNINGSTAR 1995 Mutual Fund 500

Templeton Growth

	Ticker	Load	NAV	Yield	SEC Yield	Assets	Objective
	TEPLX	5.75%	16.23	1.7%	N/A	5475.7	World Stock

Templeton Growth Fund seeks long-term capital growth. Any income realized is incidental.

The fund maintains a flexible investment policy that allows it to invest in all types of securities in any nation. Generally, common stocks are the fund's primary holding. Annual portfolio turnover is generally well below 50%.

On Dec. 31, 1986, the fund reorganized into two parts: the existing Canadian corporation and a newly formed U.S. fund, in order to lessen the tax consequences for non-Canadian shareholders. Expenses prior to 1987 included taxes on income imposed on non-Canadians.

Manager's Investment Style

Management is on a staunch pursuit of value. The portfolio is dominated by issues that are undervalued relative to their underlying assets or projected earnings growth. This strategy tends to keep the fund out of the pricier, booming markets. Instead, it remains invested in countries where price multiples are low. Despite management's adversity to risk, it does not hedge the portfolio for currency fluctuations. This has proved irrelevant in recent history, because the fund has been heavily invested in the U.S.

Fund Manager(s)

Mark G. Holowesko CFA, since 01-87. BA, C. of the Holy Cross MBA, Babson C.

Manager Experience

	Dates Managed	Invest Obj	Std Dev	+/- Index
Mark G. Holowesko				
Templeton Smaller Co Gr	01/87 - 12/92	WW	18.64	-4.68
Templeton Real Estate Sec	01/91 - 12/92	S	11.05	-4.33

Historical Profile

Return	Above Average
Risk	Below Average
Rating ★★★★	
	Above Average

	83%	83%	92%	91%	88%	82%	81%	79%

Investment Style History
Equity

Average % Stocks Held in Portfolio

Growth of $10,000
IIII Value of Fund ($000)
— Value of Index ($000)
MSEASEA
▼ Manager Change
▽ Partial Manager Change
► Mgr Unknown After
◄ Mgr Unknown Before

Performance Quartile (Within Objective)

	1983	1984	1985	1986	1987	1988	1989	1990	1991	1992	1993	1994	History
	9.84	9.53	11.36	12.87	11.73	13.75	15.76	13.10	15.43	14.38	17.62	16.23	NAV
	32.94	2.17	27.79	21.24	3.08	23.60	22.56	-9.06	31.33	4.21	32.70	0.82	Total Return %
	10.47	-4.10	-3.95	2.56	-2.18	6.99	-9.12	-5.94	0.85	-3.40	22.64	-0.50	+/- S&P 500
	11.01	-2.55	-12.78	-20.65	-13.09	0.31	5.95	7.96	13.05	9.44	10.19	-4.26	+/- MSCI World
	2.60	2.15	2.55	3.38	3.69	4.00	4.32	3.86	3.19	2.53	1.80	1.72	Income Return %
	30.33	0.02	25.23	17.86	-0.62	19.60	18.24	-12.92	28.14	1.68	30.89	-0.90	Capital Return %
	7	59	34	16	35	7	30	82	24	80	7	15	Total Rtn % Rank All
	20	16	87	70	47	10	47	37	12	20	39	27	Total Rtn % Rank Obj
	0.18	0.19	0.24	0.40	0.44	0.48	0.62	0.54	0.44	0.36	0.29	0.29	Income $
	0.00	0.29	0.48	0.48	1.08	0.25	0.47	0.68	1.22	1.27	1.10	1.29	Capital Gains $
	2.62	2.48	2.97	2.40	0.66	0.69	0.66	0.67	0.75	0.88	1.03	1.10	Expense Ratio %
	2.45	2.10	2.66	1.76	2.99	3.50	4.20	3.70	3.09	2.62	2.10	1.76	Income Ratio %
	10	3	20	10	18	11	12	19	30	24	29	27	Turnover Rate %
	797.3	865.4	1026.6	1132.7	1285.3	1691.2	2451.5	2330.0	3079.4	3347.2	4625.3	5475.7	Net Assets ($mil)

Performance 12-31-94

	1st Qtr	2nd Qtr	3rd Qtr	4th Qtr	Total
1987	14.84	4.80	10.14	-22.24	3.08
1988	9.80	6.13	3.29	2.68	23.60
1989	6.04	3.50	10.27	1.27	22.56
1990	-2.35	6.37	-15.52	3.64	-9.06
1991	14.81	0.60	7.67	5.61	31.33
1992	1.10	4.62	-3.37	1.97	4.21
1993	7.16	4.67	7.81	9.73	32.70
1994	-1.02	0.40	5.77	-4.08	0.82

Bear Market Performance

Decile Rank (5-year period)

Worst ———————— Best

	Worst 3 Mo Period 1985-89	Worst 3 Mo Period 1990-94
Templeton Growth	-26.44	-18.89
+/- S&P 500	3.14	-5.05
+/- Best Fit Index : MSEASEA	-2.12	-4.70

Trailing Returns

	Total Return %	+/- S&P 500	+/- MSCI World	% Rank All	% Rank Obj	Growth of $10,000
3 Mo	-4.08	-4.06	-3.35	89	42	9,592
6 Mo	1.45	-3.41	0.06	31	35	10,145
1 Yr	0.82	-0.50	-4.26	15	27	10,082
3 Yr Avg	11.71	5.45	4.86	9	16	13,942
5 Yr Avg	10.74	2.05	7.07	13	5	16,652
10 Yr Avg	14.95	0.57	0.11	11	25	40,280
15 Yr Avg	14.49	0.01	---	19	37	76,103

Operations

Address and Telephone	700 Central Avenue		
	St. Petersburg, FL 33701-3628		
	800-292-9293 / 813-823-8712		
Advisor	Templeton Galbraith & Hansberger		
Subadvisor	None		
Distributor	Franklin/Templeton Distributors		
States Available	All		
Report Grade	B+		
Income Distrib	Paid Annually		
Date of Inception	11-29-54		
Fiscal Year End	August		

Risk Analysis

Time Period	Load-Adj Return %	Risk % Rank [1] All	Obj	Morningstar [2] Return	Morningstar Risk	Morningstar Risk-Adj Rating
1 Yr	-4.98					
3 Yr	9.53	66	9	1.82 [3]	0.73	★★★★
5 Yr	9.43	65	8	1.20 [3]	0.79	★★★★
10 Yr	14.27	53	12	1.33	0.77	★★★★
Average Historical Rating (109 months)					3.8	★s

[1] 1 = low, 100 = high [2] 1.00 = Equity Avg [3] 1.00 = 90-day T-bill return

Other Measures

				Standard S&P 500	Best Fit MSEASEA
Standard Deviation	9.60	Alpha		5.7	4.0
Mean	11.58	Beta		0.88	0.65
Sharpe Ratio	0.84	R-Squared		53	79

Investment Style

	Stock Portfolio Avg	Rel MSCI EAFE	Rel Obj	Style V B G
Price/Earnings Ratio	18.7	0.51	0.76	
Price/Cash Flow	9.6	0.62	0.71	
Price/Book Ratio	2.0	0.78	0.70	
5 Yr Earnings Gr %	2.1	---	0.43	
Return on Assets %	4.6	1.01	0.66	
Debt % Total Cap	31.8	0.94	1.10	
Med Mkt Cap ($mil)	5843	0.49	1.16	

Size L M S

Diversification Value for Portfolio Types

Large Cap: Low	Small Cap: Medium	Bond: High	Balanced: Low	Diversified: Low

Expenses & Fees

Sales Fees	5.75% front
	0.00% deferred
	0.25% 12b-1
Management Fee	0.75% max./0.60% min., 0.15%A
3-,5-,10-yr Expense Projections	$90, $114, $183
Annual Brokerage Cost	0.12%

Min Initial Purchase, etc.

Min Initial Purchase	$100 (Addt'l: $25)
Min IRA Purchase	$100 (Addt'l: $25)
Min Auto Invest Plan	$25 (Systematic Inv: $25)

Portfolio 09-30-94

Share Chg (06-94) 000	Amount 000	Total Stocks: 230 / Total Fixed-Income: 12	Value $000	% Net Assets
0	6618	HSBC Holdings (Plc) (HK)	73866	1.33
0	950	Georgia-Pacific	72675	1.31
0	2093	Merrill Lynch	72463	1.30
0	1125	Total Petroleum Cl B	66193	1.19
	60000	US Treasury Note 4.25%	59803	1.08
	60000	US Treasury Note 3.875%	59635	1.07
0	700	DSM (Netherlands)	59459	1.07
0	658	American International Group	58435	1.05
0	730	FNMA	57488	1.03
0	1250	Boeing	53906	0.97
0	625	ALCOA	52969	0.95
50	730	Nationale Elf Aquitaine	52434	0.94
0	900	Sony	52364	0.94
0	1650	Philips Electronics	50455	0.91
200	3610	Telefonica de Espana	48744	0.88
0	214	Bayer	48405	0.87
0	775800	Telebras	48357	0.87
0	838	Reynolds Metals	47441	0.85
0	800	Nike Cl B	47100	0.85
0	396	Akzo	46537	0.84

Regional Exposure 12-31-94
% of Stocks

Europe	34	Pacific Rim	14
Japan	2	U.S.	44
Latin Amer	4	Other	2

Composition % 12-31-94

Cash	10.5	Preferreds	0.6
Stocks	80.8	Convertibles	1.2
Bonds	6.9	Other	0.0

Tax Analysis

	Tax-Adj Historical Return %	% Pretax Return
3 Yr Avg	8.78	72.9
5 Yr Avg	7.74	67.9
10 Yr Avg	12.09	70.3
Potential Capital Gain Exposure (% of assets)		12%

Most Similar Funds in MF500

EuroPacific Growth	Strong Fit
Templeton Foreign	Strong Fit
New Perspective	Strong Fit

Top 5 Countries 12-31-94
% of Stocks

U.S.	44
Hong Kong	7
United Kingdom	7
France	5
Netherlands	5

Total Number of Countries: 32
Hedging Policy: Never

Sector Weightings

	% of Stocks	Relative S&P 500
Utilities	8.8	1.06
Energy	6.9	1.43
Financials	28.4	1.72
Industrial Cyclicals	24.8	1.07
Consumer Durables	11.3	1.10
Consumer Staples	1.4	0.27
Services	7.5	0.63
Retail	5.1	0.88
Health	3.9	0.75
Technology	1.8	0.20

MORNINGSTAR **1995 Mutual Fund 500**

Templeton Income

	Ticker	Load	NAV	Yield	SEC Yield	Assets	Objective
	TPINX	4.25%	8.82	7.6%	7.72%	198.6	World Bond

Templeton Income Fund seeks current income.
　　The fund can invest any amount of its assets in any kind of income-producing security, including, but not limited to, debt obligations of companies and governments, convertible securities, preferred stocks, and common stocks. It may invest anywhere in the world. The fund may also engage in options and futures portfolio strategies, lend its portfolio securities, and borrow money for investment purposes.

Manager's Investment Style

　　This fund is a conservative vehicle for international exposure. Management tends to steer clear of volatile emerging markets, preferring instead the U.S., Canadian, and Australian markets. The fund, for the most part, has also kept modest holdings in Europe. This investment style causes the fund to miss out on some short term gains, but keeps it above its peers in down markets.

Fund Manager(s)

Samuel J. Forester, Jr., since 05-90. BS, U. of Arkansas 1970

Manager Experience	Dates Managed	Invest Obj	Std Dev	+/- Index
Samuel J. Forester, Jr.				
Franklin/Templtn Hard Cur	11/93 - 12/94	WB	5.06	17.11
Franklin/Templtn Glob Cur	11/93 - 12/94	WB	3.08	9.65

Historical Profile
Return: Below Average
Risk: Below Average
Rating: ★★★
Neutral

	50	53	25	57	32	38	45	17

Investment Style History
Fixed Income
Income Rtn % Rank Obj

Growth of $10,000
|||| Value of Fund ($000)
— Value of Index ($000) LB Agg
▼ Manager Change
▽ Partial Manager Change
►◄ Mgr Unknown After
◄ Mgr Unknown Before

Performance Quartile (Within Objective)

	1983	1984	1985	1986	1987	1988	1989	1990	1991	1992	1993	1994	History
NAV	---	---	---	10.20	10.22	10.08	9.94	9.91	10.45	9.65	9.88	8.82	NAV
	---	---	---	3.22 *	8.44	7.07	8.54	9.89	14.91	3.11	10.36	-3.58	Total Return %
	---	---	---	---	5.69	-0.81	-6.00	0.94	-1.09	-4.13	0.60	-0.67	+/- LB Aggregate
	---	---	---	---	-26.71	4.72	11.97	-5.40	-1.33	-1.66	-4.76	-10.28	+/- SB World Govt
	---	---	---	1.01	7.86	7.26	9.64	9.89	9.46	8.03	7.97	6.84	Income Return %
	---	---	---	2.20	0.59	-0.19	-1.10	0.00	5.45	-4.91	2.38	-10.42	Capital Return %
	---	---	---	---	13	80	87	5	58	84	64	49	Total Rtn % Rank All
	---	---	---	---	80	26	20	75	37	38	81	37	Total Rtn % Rank Obj
	---	---	---	0.10	0.78	0.72	0.94	0.93	0.86	0.82	0.74	0.68	Income $
	---	---	---	0.02	0.04	0.12	0.03	0.03	0.00	0.30	0.00	0.04	Capital Gains $
	---	---	---	---	1.00	1.10	1.10	1.04	1.05	0.98	1.01	1.18	Expense Ratio %
	---	---	---	---	6.68	7.12	8.63	9.50	9.23	8.14	8.45	7.50	Income Ratio %
	---	---	---	---	---	158	89	86	408	234	267	139	Turnover Rate %
	---	---	---	68.0	123.2	125.3	115.9	117.4	144.6	180.6	217.0	198.6	Net Assets ($mil)

Performance 12-31-94

	1st Qtr	2nd Qtr	3rd Qtr	4th Qtr	Total
1987	6.20	-0.17	0.76	1.51	8.44
1988	3.27	-0.40	1.05	3.00	7.07
1989	1.28	1.61	4.00	1.41	8.54
1990	-1.72	4.46	3.65	3.27	9.89
1991	0.32	1.54	6.81	5.61	14.91
1992	-2.98	7.43	-1.59	0.52	3.11
1993	4.51	1.72	1.94	1.84	10.36
1994	-3.51	-2.38	1.91	0.44	-3.58

Bear Market Performance

Decile Rank (5-year period)

Worst ------- Best

	Worst 3 Mo Period 1985-89	Worst 3 Mo Period 1990-94
Templeton Income	---	-6.38
+/- LB Aggregate	---	-1.45
+/- Best Fit Index : MSAllCtry	---	-2.51

Trailing Returns

	Total Return %	+/- LB Aggregate	+/- SB World	% Rank All	% Rank Obj	Growth of $10,000
3 Mo	0.44	0.07	-0.12	12	43	10,044
6 Mo	2.36	1.37	0.13	24	20	10,236
1 Yr	-3.58	-0.67	-10.28	49	37	9,642
3 Yr Avg	3.14	-1.41	-5.63	84	62	10,971
5 Yr Avg	6.74	-0.89	-4.78	57	63	13,853
10 Yr Avg	---	---	---	---	---	---
15 Yr Avg	---	---	---	---	---	---

Operations

Address and Telephone	700 Central Avenue	
	St. Petersburg, FL 33701-3628	
	800-292-9293 / 813-823-8712	
Advisor	Templeton Global Bond Managers	
Subadvisor	None	
Distributor	Franklin/Templeton Distributors	
States Available	All	
Report Grade	B+	
Income Distrib	Paid Monthly	
* Date of Inception	09-24-86	
Fiscal Year End	August	

Risk Analysis

Time Period	Load-Adj Return %	Risk % Rank [1] All	Obj	Morningstar [2] Return	Risk	Morningstar Risk-Adj Rating
1 Yr	-7.68					
3 Yr	1.66	56	58	-0.55[3]	0.78	★★
5 Yr	5.81	44	30	0.26[3]	0.54	★★★
10 Yr	---					

Average Historical Rating (64 months)　　3.4 ★s

[1] 1 = low, 100 = high　[2] 1.00 = Hybrid Avg　[3] 1.00 = 90-day T-bill return

Other Measures

			Standard LB Agg	Best Fit MSAllCtry
Standard Deviation	5.96	Alpha	-1.1	-1.2
Mean	3.27	Beta	0.88	0.37
Sharpe Ratio	-0.04	R-Squared	35	44

Investment Style

Interest-Rate Stance

Avg Effective Maturity　6.8 Yrs

Quality

Avg Credit Quality　---

Avg Weighted Coupon　8.03%

Not Available

Diversification Value for Portfolio Types

Large Cap: High	Small Cap: High	Bond: Medium	Balanced: Medium	Diversified: Medium

Expenses & Fees

Sales Fees	4.25% front
	0.00% deferred
	0.25% 12b-1
Management Fee	0.50% flat fee, 0.15%A
3-,5-,10-yr Expense Projections	$78, $101, $170

Min Initial Purchase / Min IRA / Min Auto

Min Initial Purchase	$100 (Addt'l: $25)
Min IRA Purchase	$100 (Addt'l: $25)
Min Auto Invest Plan	$25 (Systematic Inv: $25)

Portfolio 09-30-94

Amount 000	Date of Maturity	Total Stocks: 5 / Total Fixed-Income: 52	Value $000	% Net Assets
8060	09-08-06	United Kingdom Treasury 7.75%	11737	5.78
15000	07-26-99	Republic of Italy 5%	9633	4.74
12500	11-15-95	Govt of New Zealand 8%	7493	3.69
11500	07-15-99	Republic of Portugal 5%	7400	3.64
13270	04-15-04	Govt of New Zealand 8%	7362	3.63
4000	08-06-97	United Kingdom Treasury 7%	6142	3.03
8600	10-15-03	Victoria Treasury 8.25%	5505	2.71
6350	04-01-02	Govt of Canada 8.5%	4686	2.31
7000000	10-01-95	Republic of Italy 12%	4543	2.24
5000	08-01-12	AMR 9%	4527	2.23
24000	06-01-08	Eskom 11%	3889	1.92
5000	08-23-13	Province Brit Columbia 8.5%	3491	1.72
4000	12-08-03	Sud Americana Vapores 7.375%	3420	1.68
400000	01-15-97	Govt of Spain 11.6%	3175	1.56
5250	07-15-05	Commonwealth Australia 7.5%	3170	1.56
3150	04-01-22	Province Nova Scotia 8.75%	3066	1.51
3000	10-27-96	Henderson Capital Intl 4%	2944	1.45
3085	08-15-03	US Treasury Note 5.75%	2720	1.34
4000	06-01-23	Govt of Canada 8%	2666	1.31
3000	06-15-99	Republic of Turkey 9%	2640	1.30
4000000	01-20-98	Republic of Italy 12%	2614	1.29
3900	05-14-03	Queensland Treasury 8%	2486	1.22
3000	12-20-03	Republic of Argentina 8.375%	2468	1.22
300000	07-15-96	Govt of Spain 11.9%	2396	1.18
70		Texas Utilities	2284	1.12

Composition % 12-31-94

Cash	13.9	Preferreds	0.0
Stocks	5.3	Convertibles	0.0
Bonds	80.8	Other	0.0

Tax Analysis

	Tax-Adj Historical Return %	% Pretax Return
3 Yr Avg	0.00	---
5 Yr Avg	3.62	50.6
10 Yr Avg	---	---

Potential Capital Gain Exposure (% of assets)　　-14%

Most Similar Funds in MF500

PaineWebber Global Inc B	Weak Fit
Fidelity Global Bond	Weak Fit
Global Income Plus	Weak Fit

Country Exposure 09-30-94

	% of Bonds
Italy	14
U.S.	13
Canada	12
United Kingdom	10
Australia	9

Currency Exposure 09-30-94

	% of Net Assets
U.S.	49
United Kingdom	9
Canada	9
New Zealand	7
Italy	7

 **1995 Mutual Fund 500**

Templeton Real Estate Secs

	Ticker	Load	NAV	Yield	SEC Yield	Assets	Objective
	TEMRX	5.75%	12.49	1.7%	N/A	128.5	Specialty

Templeton Real Estate Securities Fund seeks long-term capital growth; current income is secondary.

The fund normally invests at least 65% of its assets in U.S. or listed foreign issues of companies engaged in the real-estate industry. It may invest the balance of its assets in the equity and debt securities of non-real-estate businesses, but it may not buy debt securities rated below A.

Prior to March 12, 1990, the fund was named Templeton Real Estate Trust. On Dec. 17, 1990, National Real Estate merged into the fund.

Historical Profile
Return	Average
Risk	Below Average
Rating	★★★
	Neutral

Investment Style History
Equity
Average % Stocks Held in Portfolio

87%	87%	83%	82%	67%

Growth of $10,000
IIII Value of Fund ($000)
— Value of Index ($000) MSPacxJp
▼ Manager Change
▽ Partial Manager Change
► Mgr Unknown After
◄ Mgr Unknown Before

Manager's Investment Style
Management follows the Templeton value strategy by targeting real-estate concerns from around the world that are cheap relative to projected earnings or cash flow. Unlike many other real-estate funds, this fund doesn't own many REITs. Instead, it favors foreign builders, mortgage lenders, and real-estate holding companies, while also dabbling in emerging markets.

Performance Quartile (Within Objective)

1983	1984	1985	1986	1987	1988	1989	1990	1991	1992	1993	1994	History
---	---	---	---	---	---	9.93	8.16	10.45	10.52	13.76	12.49	NAV
---	---	---	---	---	---	0.10 *	-13.08	34.41	4.15	32.98	-7.70	Total Return %
---	---	---	---	---	---	-2.35 *	-9.97	3.92	-3.47	22.92	-9.01	+/- S&P 500
---	---	---	---	---	---	---	-6.90	0.20	-4.82	21.69	-7.63	+/- Wilshire 5000
---	---	---	---	---	---	0.80	3.98	6.34	3.48	2.18	1.53	Income Return %
---	---	---	---	---	---	-0.70	-17.06	28.06	0.67	30.80	-9.23	Capital Return %
---	---	---	---	---	---	---	90	20	80	7	84	Total Rtn % Rank All
---	---	---	---	---	---	---	55	52	77	27	56	Total Rtn % Rank Obj
---	---	---	---	---	---	0.08	0.37	0.48	0.35	0.22	0.22	Income $
---	---	---	---	---	---	0.00	0.09	0.00	0.00	0.00	0.00	Capital Gains $
---	---	---	---	---	---	---	1.25	1.25	1.69	1.68	1.58	Expense Ratio %
---	---	---	---	---	---	---	3.59	5.48	3.64	2.60	1.97	Income Ratio %
---	---	---	---	---	---	---	---	25	32	20	32	Turnover Rate %
---	---	---	---	---	---	9.9	29.1	34.7	39.3	83.9	128.5	Net Assets ($mil)

Fund Manager(s)
Jeffrey A. Everett et al. BS, Pennsylvania State U.

Manager Experience
	Dates Managed	Invest Obj	Std Dev	+/- Index
Not available.

Performance 12-31-94
	1st Qtr	2nd Qtr	3rd Qtr	4th Qtr	Total
1987	---	---	---	---	---
1988	---	---	---	---	---
1989	---	---	---	0.10	0.10 *
1990	-3.02	4.36	-18.31	5.13	-13.08
1991	22.06	0.20	2.81	6.90	34.41
1992	0.96	2.75	-3.04	3.56	4.15
1993	13.50	1.26	6.37	8.78	32.98
1994	-2.11	-3.56	3.85	-5.85	-7.70

Bear Market Performance
Decile Rank (5-year period)

Worst — Best

	Worst 3 Mo Period 1985-89	Worst 3 Mo Period 1990-94
Templeton Real Estate Secs	---	-19.07
+/- S&P 500	---	-5.22
+/- Best Fit Index : MSPacxJp	---	-1.75

Trailing Returns
	Total Return %	+/- S&P 500	+/- Wil 5000	% Rank All	Obj	Growth of $10,000
3 Mo	-5.85	-5.83	-5.08	94	85	9,415
6 Mo	-2.23	-7.09	-6.85	89	70	9,777
1 Yr	-7.70	-9.01	-7.63	84	56	9,230
3 Yr Avg	8.53	2.27	1.92	19	59	12,784
5 Yr Avg	8.35	-0.34	-0.47	29	61	14,934
10 Yr Avg	---	---	---	---	---	---
15 Yr Avg	---	---	---	---	---	---

Operations
Address and Telephone	700 Central Avenue St. Petersburg, FL 33701-3628 800-292-9293 / 813-823-8712
Advisor	Templeton Galbraith & Hansberger
Subadvisor	None
Distributor	Franklin/Templeton Distributors
States Available	All
Report Grade	B+
Income Distrib	Paid Annually
* Date of Inception	09-12-89
Fiscal Year End	August

Min Initial Purchase	$100 (Addt'l: $25)
Min IRA Purchase	$100 (Addt'l: $25)
Min Auto Invest Plan	$25 (Systematic Inv: $25)

Expenses & Fees
Sales Fees	5.75% front 0.00% deferred 0.25% 12b-1
Management Fee	0.75% flat fee, 0.15%A
3-,5-,10-yr Expense Projections	$110, $147, $253
Annual Brokerage Cost	0.34%

Risk Analysis
Time Period	Load-Adj Return %	Risk % Rank [1] All	Obj	Morningstar [2] Return	Morningstar Risk	Morningstar Risk-Adj Rating
1 Yr	-13.00					
3 Yr	6.41	66	13	0.84 [3]	0.74	★★★
5 Yr	7.08	67	11	0.57 [3]	0.80	★★★
10 Yr	---	---	---	---	---	---
Average Historical Rating (28 months)				3.3 ★s		

[1] 1 = low, 100 = high [2] 1.00 = Equity Avg [3] 1.00 = 90-day T-bill return

Other Measures
			Standard S&P 500	Best Fit MSPacxJp
Standard Deviation	9.03	Alpha	3.4	0.4
Mean	8.62	Beta	0.60	0.31
Sharpe Ratio	0.56	R-Squared	28	49

Investment Style
	Stock Portfolio Avg	Relative S&P 500
Price/Earnings Ratio	19.4	1.05
Price/Book Ratio	2.0	0.59
5 Yr Earnings Gr %	1.0#	0.17
Return on Assets %	5.0	0.67
Debt % Total Cap	36.3	1.28
Med Mkt Cap ($mil)	647	0.05

figure is based on 50% or less of stocks

Style: Value Blend Growth / Size Large Med Small

Diversification Value for Portfolio Types
Large Cap: Medium	Small Cap: Medium	Bond: High	Balanced: Medium	Diversified: Medium

Portfolio 08-31-94
Total Stocks: 77
Total Fixed-Income: 10

Share Chg (06-94) 000	Amount 000		Value $000	% Net Assets
0	1066	Patten	3731	2.84
	3500	Empresas ICA Cv 5%	3658	2.78
0	226	LTC Properties	3164	2.41
0	156	Rouse	2970	2.26
35	135	McArthur/Glen Realty	2539	1.93
50	124	Property Trust America	2238	1.70
	2800	Revenue Properties Cv 6%	2184	1.66
0	70	Empresas ICA (ADR)	2065	1.57
0	542	Canlan Investment	1908	1.45
0	40	Weyerhaeuser	1835	1.39
90	90	Weeks	1811	1.38
150	818	Parkway Holdings	1800	1.37
0	150	HSBC Holdings	1766	1.34
105	1160	Tai Cheung Holdings	1682	1.28
0	46	Nationwide Health Properties	1662	1.26
0	105	Kaufman & Broad Home	1628	1.24
	2570	ARBED Cv 2.5%	1611	1.22
0	137	Uralita	1594	1.21
0	58	Fleetwood Enterprises	1530	1.16
0	17	FNMA	1511	1.15
0	20	TH Wessel/Vett Magasin Cl C	1508	1.15
0	20	Georgia-Pacific	1488	1.13
0	9	Bail Investissement	1457	1.11
0	652	Taylor Woodrow	1453	1.10
0	64	American Health Property	1447	1.10

Composition % 12-31-94
Cash	19.1	Preferreds	0.0
Stocks	73.1	Convertibles	1.5
Bonds	6.3	Other	0.0

Tax Analysis
	Tax-Adj Historical Return %	% Pretax Return
3 Yr Avg	7.70	89.5
5 Yr Avg	7.17	83.8
10 Yr Avg	---	---
Potential Capital Gain Exposure (% of assets)		-6%

Most Similar Funds in MF500
Templeton Smaller Comp Grth	Strong Fit
G.T. Global Worldwide Grth A	Weak Fit
Scudder Global	Weak Fit

Index Allocation
	% of Stocks
S&P 500	11.3
S&P MidCap 400	0.0
U.S. Small Cap	49.8
Foreign	39.0

Sector Weightings
	% of Stocks	Relative S&P 500
Utilities	1.7	0.13
Energy	2.4	0.24
Financials	53.7	5.08
Industrial Cyclicals	34.8	2.13
Consumer Durables	2.0	0.33
Consumer Staples	0.0	0.00
Services	3.4	0.42
Retail	2.0	0.34
Health	0.0	0.00
Technology	0.0	0.00

Templeton Smaller Co Growth

	Ticker	Load	NAV	Yield	SEC Yield	Assets	Objective
	TEMGX	5.75%	7.43	1.4%	N/A	1275.9	World Stock

Templeton Smaller Companies Growth Fund seeks long-term growth of capital.

The fund invests primarily in equity securities of companies with market capitalizations of less than $1 billion. Stocks of both foreign and domestic companies may be held.

Prior to Dec. 31, 1990, the fund was named Templeton Global Fund. On Dec. 16, 1988, Templeton Global Fund (then with $276.5 million in assets) and Templeton Global II Fund ($458.3 million in assets) were merged. The performance record on this page that predates the merger belongs to the smaller Templeton Global Fund. On Oct. 25, 1993, Templeton Value Fund merged into this fund.

Historical Profile
Return	Average
Risk	Average
Rating	★★★ Neutral

Investment Style History
Equity

Average % Stocks Held in Portfolio

Stocks held: 86%, 88%, 85%, 89%, 80%, 77%, 86%, 86%

Growth of $10,000
- ‖‖ Value of Fund ($000)
- — Value of Index ($000) MSEASEA
- ▼ Manager Change
- ▽ Partial Manager Change
- ► Mgr Unknown After
- ◄ Mgr Unknown Before

Performance Quartile (Within Objective)

Manager's Investment Style

As in most Templeton funds, management seeks stocks selling at a discount to their projected five-year earnings. This fund targets small-cap stocks from around the world, including issues from the United States. Management takes a bottom-up approach, and has invested in emerging-markets stocks.

Fund Manager(s)

Daniel L. Jacobs CFA(1983), since 12-92.
Birthdate: 05-52. BA, Miami U. 1974 MBA, Emory U. 1976

	1983	1984	1985	1986	1987	1988	1989	1990	1991	1992	1993	1994	History
	6.83	6.32	7.44	8.16	6.53	7.29	8.01	5.99	7.52	6.14	7.99	7.43	NAV
	38.95	0.41	30.70	18.84	-11.61	28.81	17.85	-15.67	39.52	3.69	31.85	-4.59	Total Return %
	16.48	-5.86	-1.04	0.16	-16.87	12.20	-13.83	-12.55	9.03	-3.93	21.79	-5.90	+/- S&P 500
	17.02	-4.31	-9.87	-23.05	-27.78	5.53	1.25	1.35	21.23	8.92	9.35	-9.66	+/- MSCI World
	2.70	2.49	2.67	2.85	3.27	3.06	2.68	2.70	2.16	2.47	1.12	1.32	Income Return %
	36.25	-2.08	28.02	15.99	-14.89	25.75	15.18	-18.37	37.35	1.22	30.73	-5.91	Capital Return %
	3	64	22	27	97	3	40	93	15	82	7	59	Total Rtn % Rank All
	1	33	68	76	95	3	67	71	2	23	45	66	Total Rtn % Rank Obj
	0.17	0.16	0.17	0.22	0.23	0.22	0.21	0.17	0.15	0.15	0.07	0.11	Income $
	0.74	0.37	0.56	0.44	0.45	0.90	0.38	0.58	0.65	1.44	0.03	0.09	Capital Gains $
	1.09	0.79	0.83	0.51	0.47	0.52	0.95	0.96	0.97	1.33	1.29	1.36	Expense Ratio %
	2.66	2.36	2.37	2.76	2.13	2.07	2.25	2.13	2.33	1.96	1.70	1.17	Income Ratio %
	21	13	6	4	13	7	24	27	34	49	29	28	Turnover Rate %
	240.6	237.2	265.1	296.9	236.4	732.5	896.8	685.3	912.9	936.5	1345.2	1275.9	Net Assets ($mil)

Manager Experience

	Dates Managed	Invest Obj	Std Dev	+/- Index
Not available.				

Performance 12-31-94

	1st Qtr	2nd Qtr	3rd Qtr	4th Qtr	Total
1987	15.12	2.36	2.00	-26.46	-11.61
1988	18.18	5.98	-7.97	11.75	28.81
1989	6.04	6.86	7.39	-3.14	17.85
1990	-1.00	4.67	-21.33	3.45	-15.67
1991	24.21	2.15	6.32	3.43	39.52
1992	3.46	2.19	-4.65	2.87	3.69
1993	10.91	1.91	7.64	8.37	31.85
1994	-0.13	-3.63	6.11	-6.58	-4.59

Bear Market Performance

Decile Rank (5-year period)

Worst ——————————————— Best

	Worst 3 Mo Period 1985-89	Worst 3 Mo Period 1990-94
Templeton Smaller Co Growth	-31.55	-21.95
+/- S&P 500	-1.96	-8.11
+/- Best Fit Index : MSEASEA	-7.23	-7.76

Trailing Returns

	Total Return %	+/- S&P 500	+/- MSCI World	% Rank All	% Rank Obj	Growth of $10,000
3 Mo	-6.58	-6.56	-5.84	95	80	9,342
6 Mo	-0.87	-5.73	-2.26	71	61	9,913
1 Yr	-4.59	-5.90	-9.66	59	66	9,541
3 Yr Avg	9.26	3.00	2.41	16	37	13,044
5 Yr Avg	8.94	0.25	5.28	24	11	15,347
10 Yr Avg	12.33	-2.05	-2.51	34	68	31,985
15 Yr Avg	---	---	---	---	---	---

Operations

Address and Telephone	700 Central Avenue St. Petersburg, FL 33701-3628 800-292-9293 / 813-823-8712
Advisor	Templeton Investment Counsel
Subadvisor	None
Distributor	Franklin/Templeton Distributors
States Available	All
Report Grade	A-
Income Distrib	Paid Annually
Date of Inception	06-01-81
Fiscal Year End	August

Risk Analysis

Time Period	Load-Adj Return %	Risk % Rank [1] All	Obj	Morningstar [2] Return	Morningstar Risk	Morningstar Risk-Adj Rating
1 Yr	-10.07					
3 Yr	7.13	72	29	1.06 [3]	0.81	★★★
5 Yr	7.66	75	25	0.72 [3]	0.89	★★★
10 Yr	11.67	64	37	0.82	0.88	★★★

Average Historical Rating (109 months) 3.2 ★s

[1] 1 = low, 100 = high [2] 1.00 = Equity Avg [3] 1.00 = 90-day T-bill return

Other Measures

			Standard S&P 500	Best Fit MSEASEA
Standard Deviation	9.79	Alpha	3.7	2.2
Mean	9.37	Beta	0.77	0.58
Sharpe Ratio	0.60	R-Squared	38	62

Investment Style

	Stock Portfolio Avg	Rel MSCI EAFE	Rel Obj
Price/Earnings Ratio	17.3	0.47	0.70
Price/Cash Flow	11.1	0.72	0.82
Price/Book Ratio	2.2	0.86	0.77
5 Yr Earnings Gr %	7.4	---	1.55
Return on Assets %	7.2	1.58	1.04
Debt % Total Cap	25.1	0.74	0.87
Med Mkt Cap ($mil)	539	0.05	0.11

Style: V B G / Size L M S

Diversification Value for Portfolio Types

Large Cap: Medium	Small Cap: Medium	Bond: High	Balanced: Medium	Diversified: Low

Expenses & Fees

Sales Fees	5.75% front
	0.00% deferred
	0.25% 12b-1
Management Fee	0.75% flat fee, 0.15%A
3-,5-,10-yr Expense Projections	$100, $131, $218
Annual Brokerage Cost	0.21%

Min Initial Purchase	$100 (Addt'l: $25)
Min IRA Purchase	$100 (Addt'l: $25)
Min Auto Invest Plan	$25 (Systematic Inv: $25)

Portfolio 09-30-94

Share Chg (06-94) 000	Amount 000	Total Stocks: 241 Total Fixed-Income: 6	Value $000	% Net Assets
0	594	Telebras (ADR)	36923	2.66
0	7888	News International (Spcl Nv)	30227	2.18
0	137	Hollandsche Beton Groep	21932	1.58
0	11067	Sime Darby (Hong Kong)	17187	1.24
0	382	Gas & Electricidad	17140	1.24
0	261	Telefonos de Mexico L (ADR)	16326	1.18
0	140	Fives-Lille	14819	1.07
-27	265	Fairfax Financial	14626	1.06
0	4593	Telefonos de Mexico Cl L	14334	1.03
0	600	IHC Caland	14270	1.03
100	400	First USA	14050	1.01
0	375	Mercantile Bancorp	13828	1.00
0	122	Banco de Andalucia (Reg)	13298	0.96
0	8814	National Foods	12725	0.92
0	6	Schweizer Industrie Ges (Br)	12485	0.90
-30	570	Stolt-Nielsen	12255	0.88
20	102	Ecco	12185	0.88
0	200	Kemper	12175	0.88
0	90	Banco Popular Espanol (Reg)	10681	0.77
0	496	Shorewood Packaging	10660	0.77

Regional Exposure 12-31-94
% of Stocks

Europe	28	Pacific Rim	15
Japan	0	U.S.	44
Latin Amer	9	Other	3

Composition % 12-31-94

Cash	12.9	Preferreds	0.0
Stocks	84.5	Convertibles	0.0
Bonds	2.4	Other	0.2

Tax Analysis

	Tax-Adj Historical Return %	% Pretax Return
3 Yr Avg	6.59	69.3
5 Yr Avg	5.92	62.3
10 Yr Avg	9.15	63.7
Potential Capital Gain Exposure (% of assets)		16%

Most Similar Funds in MF500

Templeton Real Estate Secs	Fair Fit
G.T. Global Worldwide Grth A	Fair Fit
Templeton Growth	Fair Fit

Top 5 Countries 12-31-94
% of Stocks

U.S.	44
Netherlands	8
Hong Kong	8
Spain	5
Australia	5

Total Number of Countries: 29
Hedging Policy: Never

Sector Weightings

	% of Stocks	Relative S&P 500
Utilities	7.8	0.94
Energy	1.8	0.36
Financials	23.4	1.42
Industrial Cyclicals	23.0	0.99
Consumer Durables	8.9	0.86
Consumer Staples	3.8	0.75
Services	15.8	1.34
Retail	4.4	0.75
Health	3.4	0.66
Technology	7.6	0.86

MORNINGSTAR 1995 Mutual Fund 500

Thai Fund

	Ticker	NAV	Mkt Price	Prem/Disc	Yield	Objective
	TTF	$28.29	$22.38	-20.9%	1.3%	Pacific/Asia

Thai Fund seeks long-term capital appreciation.

Normally, the fund invests at least 80% of its assets in equity securities of Thai companies. It may invest the remainder in baht-denominated debt and money-market instruments.

To qualify for certain tax exemptions and benefits not available to foreign direct investors in Thai securities, the fund invests as a Thai national through a special investment plan approved by the Thai government. No more than 20% of assets may be in non-baht-denominated investments under this structure.

If for any fiscal quarter after February 1993 the fund's average discount is substantial, the board will consider repurchasing shares or proposing to open-end the fund. The Thai government has indicated, however, that it would not grant approval to permit the investment plan to distribute capital to the fund in the event of open-ending.

Manager's Investment Style

Management plays sectors in the Thai market. When interest rates were falling, for example, it overweighted rate-sensitive bank stocks. It has also maintained a bulky stake in telecommunications issues to take part in that market segment's growth. Prescient sector plays have resulted in market-besting results.

Fund Manager(s)

Seah Kiat Seng, CFA. Since 8-91.

Manager Experience

	Dates Managed	Invest Obj	Std Dev	+/- Index
Not available.

Historical Profile

Return Above Average
Risk Above Average
Rating ★★★★
Above Average

													Highest Prem/Disc	Lowest Prem/Disc
				74.5	70.9	87.5	26.3	14.1	9.5	4.1	Highest Prem/Disc			
				12.2	11.5	-6.2	-3.0	-15.2	-12.4	-22.2	Lowest Prem/Disc			

Growth of $10,000
■ at NAV ($000)
— at Market Price ($000)

Premium Discount %

1983	1984	1985	1986	1987	1988	1989	1990	1991	1992	1993	1994	History
---	---	---	---	---	10.24	18.87	13.08	15.41	20.72	39.42	28.29	NAV
---	---	---	---	---	-5.60*	109.76	-20.40	22.53	34.46	98.18	-13.66	NAV Total Return %
---	---	---	---	---	-16.31*	78.07	-17.28	-7.95	26.84	88.12	-14.98	+/- S&P 500
---	---	---	---	---	---	99.22	3.05	10.40	46.63	65.62	-21.44	+/- MSCI EAFE
---	---	---	---	---	---	3.68	9.34	4.48	4.04	0.34	-2.52	+/- MSCI Thailand
---	---	---	---	---	2.65*	2.28	1.59	1.31	0.00	2.37	1.20	Income Return %
---	---	---	---	---	-8.24*	107.47	-21.99	21.23	34.46	95.81	-14.87	Capital Return %
---	---	---	---	---	---	1	89	38	2	2	79	Total Rtn % Rank All
---	---	---	---	---	---	12	60	33	6	20	56	Total Rtn % Rank Obj
---	---	---	---	---	0.74*	212.42	-44.81	8.20	16.28	104.86	-27.00	Market Total Rtn %
---	---	---	---	---	31.1	29.7	18.8	11.8	-3.3	-2.4	-10.1	Avg Prem/Disc %
---	---	---	---	---	0.29	0.36	0.21	0.21	0.00	0.36	0.35	Income $
---	---	---	---	---	0.00	2.09	1.68	0.47	0.00	0.51	4.63	Capital Gains $
---	---	---	---	---	1.50	1.51	1.78	1.69	1.70	1.38	1.33	Expense Ratio %
---	---	---	---	---	2.88	2.32	1.89	2.45	1.83	1.42	1.68	Income Ratio %
---	---	---	---	---	---	---	51	18	10	24	22	Turnover Rate %
---	---	---	---	---	307.9	181.1	135.7	154.3	209.1	401.0	343.8	Net Assets ($mil)

NAV Performance % 12-30-94

	1st Qtr	2nd Qtr	3rd Qtr	4th Qtr	Total
1987	---	---	---	---	---
1988	-0.54*	5.50	-1.02	-9.10	-5.60*
1989	11.52	28.55	14.71	27.55	109.76
1990	-4.24	24.24	-31.00	-3.03	-20.40
1991	35.93	-11.53	-9.60	12.71	22.53
1992	12.98	-7.70	16.80	10.39	34.46
1993	1.20	0.94	9.65	76.93	98.18
1994	-23.24	6.01	19.04	-10.87	-13.66

Bear Market Performance

Decile Rank (5-year period)

	Worst 3 Mo Period 1985-89	Worst 3 Mo Period 1990-94
Worst		Best
Thai Fund	---	-35.40
+/- S&P 500	---	-21.56

Trailing Returns

	NAV Total Return %	+/- S&P 500	+/- MSCI Thailand	% Rank All	% Rank Obj	Mkt Total Return %
3 Mo	-10.87	-10.85	-4.06	94	73	-20.84
6 Mo	6.10	1.24	-3.00	8	23	-6.42
1 Yr	-13.66	-14.98	-2.52	79	56	-27.00
3 Yr Avg	32.01	25.75	0.15	2	13	20.25
5 Yr Avg	17.54	8.85	3.83	4	10	0.76
Incept Avg	24.23*	---	---	---	---	18.80*

Risk Analysis

	Risk % Rank[1]		Morningstar[2]		Morningstar
	All	Obj	Return	Risk	Risk-Adj Rating
3 Yr	92	53	4.74	1.28	★★★★★
5 Yr	95	50	2.86	1.43	★★★★
10 Yr					
Average Historical Rating (47 months)				4.1 ★s	

[1] 1 = Low, 100 = High [2] 1.00 = Equity Avg [3] 1.00 = 90-day T-bill Return

Other Measures

			S&P 500
Standard Deviation	31.82	Alpha	30.50
Mean	32.76	Beta	0.81
Sharpe Ratio	0.92	R-Squared	4

Investment Style

	Stock Portfolio Avg	Rel WS Thailand	Rel WS Foreign
Price/Earnings Ratio	33.5#	0.91	0.68
Price/Cash Flow Ratio	---	---	---
Price/Book Ratio	6.1#	1.17	2.02
5 Yr Earnings Gr %	---	---	---
Return on Assets %	---	---	---
Debt % Total Cap	---	---	---
Med Mkt Cap ($mil)	6502#	1.42	1.03

figure is based on less than 50% of stocks

Country Exposure (top five) 12-31-94

Securities %		Currency %	
Thailand	90	Thailand	90
		US	10

Diversification Value for Portfolio Types

Large Cap: High	Small Cap: High	Bond: High	Balanced: High	Diversified: High

Portfolio 09-30-94

Share Chg (06-94)	Amount	Total Equity: 60 Total Fixed-Income: 0	Value $000	% Total Invest
120000	4220000	Bangkok Bank	34808	8.86
214000	4774000	Thai Farmers Bank (For)	31349	7.98
-17000	523000	Siam Cement	25967	6.61
221700	2600000	Siam Commercial Bank	21862	5.57
-53710	631800	Shinawatra Computer	19125	4.87
-476500	4503500	Telecom Asia	18393	4.68
465519	836000	National Finance/Securities	16067	4.09
-5000	529038	Dhana Siam Financ/Security	15252	3.88
0	759600	Land & House	14112	3.59
0	759000	Finance One	13797	3.51
-45000	1221000	Intl Engineering	11636	2.96
95500	1014000	PTT	9094	2.32
0	526000	Advanced Information Svcs	8635	2.20
0	311000	United Communication Inds	8567	2.18
74200	445200	Siam City Cement	8236	2.10
0	209000	Thai Investment & Securities	8134	2.07
-247700	1120000	Charoen Pokphand Feedmill	7355	1.87
0	331287	Intl Cosmetics	6367	1.62
0	502000	Asia Credit	6030	1.54
0	1247000	MDX	5542	1.41
0	712800	Quality House	5337	1.36
0	161804	Bangkok Insurance	3784	0.96
2692	356692	Serm Suk	3685	0.94
0	334875	Singer Thailand	3486	0.89
280400	560800	Swedish Motors (Thailand)	3379	0.86

Composition % 12-31-94

Cash	9.5	Preferreds	0.0
Stocks	90.4	Convertibles	0.0
Bonds	0.0	Other	0.0

Tax Analysis

	Tax-Adj Historical Return %	% Pretax Return
3 Yr Avg	29.22	88.9
5 Yr Avg	14.78	79.7
10 Yr Avg	---	---
Potential Capital Gain Exposure (% of assets)		50

Sector Weightings

	% of Stocks
Utilities	0.0
Energy	0.0
Financials	64.5
Industrial Cyclicals	9.9
Consumer Durables	2.3
Consumer Staples	6.8
Services	0.6
Retail	0.0
Health	0.3
Technology	15.6

Most Similar Funds in MF500

Asia Pacific	Weak Fit
T. Rowe Price New Asia	Weak Fit
Newport Tiger	Weak Fit

Operations

Address and Telephone	126 High St.
	Boston, MA 02110
	617-557-8000 / 212-296-7200
Advisor	Morgan Stanley Asset Management
Subadvisor	Mutual Fund Co., Ltd. (The)
Administrator	United States Trust Co. New York
Transfer Agent	First National Bank of Boston
Custodian	Morgan Guaranty Trust Co. of New York
Auditor	Price Waterhouse LLP
Legal Counsel	Sullivan & Cromwell

Income Distrib Schedule	Paid Irregularly
Management Fee	1.30%, 0.05%A
Reinvestment Plan	Yes
Direct Purchase Plan	Yes
Shares Outstanding	10,322,771
Exchange	NYSE
*Date of Inception	02-16-88
Shareholder Report	B

Third Avenue Value

	Ticker	Load	NAV	Yield	SEC Yield	Assets	Objective
	TAVFX	4.50%	16.97	1.5%	N/A	180.1	Growth

Third Avenue Value Fund seeks long-term capital appreciation. The fund invests in domestic and foreign securities, including common and preferred stocks and high-risk, high-yield debt securities. A substantial portion of the fund's assets may be invested in securities having relatively inactive markets. The fund employs investment techniques that involve a high degree of risk. It may leverage its portfolio with up to 50% of its net assets. New purchases are likely to be made in the securities of companies in depressed industries.

Prior to May 19, 1992, the fund was named Third Avenue Fund.

Manager's Investment Style

Manager Martin Whitman looks for deeply undervalued issues selling at a 50% discount from private-market value. More specifically, he seeks firms with cash reserves exceeding their liabilities. Once he buys a stock, he will rummage through its sector looking for further values. Whitman has also invested in illiquid stocks and typically maintains a dense portfolio, preferring to put his faith in his market knowledge rather than broad-market diversification.

Fund Manager(s)

Martin J. Whitman CFA, since 11-90. BS, Syracuse U. MA, New School for Social Research

Manager Experience

	Dates Managed	Invest Obj	Std Dev	+/- Index
Not available.				

Historical Profile
Return: Above Average
Risk: Low
Rating: ★★★★★ Highest

							68%	65%	55%	74%

Investment Style History
Equity

Average % Stocks Held in Portfolio

Growth of $10,000
||| Value of Fund ($000)
— Value of Index ($000)
Russ 2000
▼ Manager Change
▽ Partial Manager Change
► Mgr Unknown After
◄ Mgr Unknown Before

Performance Quartile (Within Objective)

	1983	1984	1985	1986	1987	1988	1989	1990	1991	1992	1993	1994	History
NAV	---	---	---	---	---	---	---	10.86	12.47	14.67	17.62	16.97	NAV
	---	---	---	---	---	---	---	8.60 *	34.41	21.29	23.66	-1.46	Total Return %
	---	---	---	---	---	---	---	0.25 *	3.93	13.67	13.60	-2.78	+/- S&P 500
	---	---	---	---	---	---	---	---	0.21	12.32	12.38	-1.39	+/- Wilshire 5000
	---	---	---	---	---	---	---	0.00	1.36	1.49	1.67	1.43	Income Return %
	---	---	---	---	---	---	---	8.60	33.05	19.80	21.99	-2.90	Capital Return %
	---	---	---	---	---	---	---	---	20	4	12	30	Total Rtn % Rank All
	---	---	---	---	---	---	---	---	52	4	8	47	Total Rtn % Rank Obj
	---	---	---	---	---	---	---	0.00	0.17	0.20	0.26	0.25	Income $
	---	---	---	---	---	---	---	0.00	1.89	0.25	0.25	0.14	Capital Gains $
	---	---	---	---	---	---	---	---	2.50	2.32	1.42	1.15	Expense Ratio %
	---	---	---	---	---	---	---	---	1.71	1.71	1.45	1.94	Income Ratio %
	---	---	---	---	---	---	---	---	67	31	17	---	Turnover Rate %
	---	---	---	---	---	---	---	3.1	18.9	38.7	137.6	180.1	Net Assets ($mil)

Performance 12-31-94

	1st Qtr	2nd Qtr	3rd Qtr	4th Qtr	Total
1987	---	---	---	---	---
1988	---	---	---	---	---
1989	---	---	---	---	---
1990	---	---	---	---	8.60 *
1991	26.98	4.95	1.13	-0.26	34.41
1992	7.38	-2.54	4.52	10.88	21.29
1993	14.38	0.89	5.72	1.36	23.66
1994	-2.89	-1.05	5.97	-3.22	-1.46

Bear Market Performance

Decile Rank (5-year period)

Worst — Best

	Worst 3 Mo Period 1985-89	Worst 3 Mo Period 1990-94
Third Avenue Value	---	---
+/- S&P 500	---	---
+/- Best Fit Index :	---	---

Trailing Returns

	Total Return %	+/- S&P 500	+/- Wil 5000	% Rank All	% Rank Obj	Growth of $10,000
3 Mo	-3.22	-3.21	-2.45	84	82	9,678
6 Mo	2.55	-2.31	-2.07	23	67	10,255
1 Yr	-1.46	-2.78	-1.39	30	47	9,854
3 Yr Avg	13.91	7.64	7.29	5	6	14,779
5 Yr Avg	---	---	---	---	---	---
10 Yr Avg	---	---	---	---	---	---
15 Yr Avg	---	---	---	---	---	---

Operations

Address and Telephone	767 Third Avenue Fifth Floor
	New York, NY 10017
	800-443-1021 / 212-888-6685
Advisor	EQSF Advisers
Subadvisor	None
Distributor	M.J. Whitman
States Available	Selected states
Report Grade	A
Income Distrib	Paid Annually
* Date of Inception	11-01-90
Fiscal Year End	October

Risk Analysis

Time Period	Load-Adj Return %	Risk % Rank [1] All	Obj	Morningstar [2] Return	Morningstar Risk	Morningstar Risk-Adj Rating
1 Yr	-5.90	---	---	---	---	---
3 Yr	12.17	48	4	2.69 [3]	0.53	★★★★★
5 Yr	---	---	---	---	---	---
10 Yr	---	---	---	---	---	---

Average Historical Rating (14 months)   4.3 ★s

[1] 1 = low, 100 = high   [2] 1.00 = Equity Avg   [3] 1.00 = 90-day T-bill return

Other Measures

			Standard S&P 500	Best Fit Russ 2000
Standard Deviation	9.05	Alpha	8.4	5.4
Mean	13.49	Beta	0.65	0.58
Sharpe Ratio	1.10	R-Squared	32	57

Investment Style

	Stock Portfolio Avg	Relative S&P 500
Price/Earnings Ratio	16.7	0.90
Price/Book Ratio	1.3	0.38
5 Yr Earnings Gr %	23.8#	4.28
Return on Assets %	4.6	0.61
Debt % Total Cap	19.8#	0.70
Med Mkt Cap ($mil)	217	0.02

figure is based on 50% or less of stocks

Style: Value Blend Growth
Size: Large Med Small

Diversification Value for Portfolio Types

Large Cap: Medium	Small Cap: Low	Bond: High	Balanced: Medium	Diversified: Medium

Expenses & Fees

Sales Fees	4.50% front
	0.00% deferred
	0.00% 12b-1
Management Fee	0.75% max./0.50% min.
3-,5-,10-yr Expense Projections	$88, $120, $208
Annual Brokerage Cost	---

Min Initial Purchase / IRA / Auto

Min Initial Purchase	$1000 (Addt'l: $1000)
Min IRA Purchase	$500 (Addt'l: $200)
Min Auto Invest Plan	$1000 (Systematic Inv: $200)

Portfolio 10-31-94

Share Chg (07-94)000	Amount 000	Total Stocks: 70 Total Fixed-Income: 3	Value $000	% Net Assets
116	500	First American Financial	9313	4.97
0	525	Raymond James Financial	7875	4.21
0	175	Apple Computer	7558	4.04
0	220	Digital Equipment	6738	3.60
0	260	American Prem Underwriters	6500	3.47
0	804	Danielson Holding	6429	3.43
0	310	Stewart Information Services	5270	2.82
78	318	Capital Guaranty	4816	2.57
23	81	MBIA	4406	2.35
0	130	Brooklyn Bancorp	4323	2.31
0	165	CoreStates Financial	4282	2.29
0	480	Koger Equity	4023	2.15
0	200	USLICO	4000	2.14
0	100	SunAmerica	3888	2.08
0	80	Security Capital	3620	1.93
60	300	Interphase	3600	1.92
131	300	Piper Jaffray	3488	1.86
0	118	Alex Brown	3263	1.74
0	66	Policy Management Systems	3121	1.67
0	54	Saint Joe Paper	3087	1.65
0	43	Fund American Enterpr Hldg	3023	1.61
0	131	GP Financial	2931	1.57
0	100	Photronics	2700	1.44
	3385	USTrails 12%	2403	1.28
0	61	Saint Jude Medical	2254	1.20

Composition % 12-31-94

Cash	3.5	Preferreds	0.0
Stocks	85.4	Convertibles	1.9
Bonds	2.9	Other	6.3

Tax Analysis

	Tax-Adj Historical Return %	% Pretax Return
3 Yr Avg	12.91	92.0
5 Yr Avg	---	---
10 Yr Avg	---	---

Potential Capital Gain Exposure (% of assets)   6%

Most Similar Funds in MF500

Strong Common Stock	Weak Fit
Acorn	Weak Fit
Royce Equity-Income	Weak Fit

Index Allocation

	% of Stocks
S&P 500	15.0
S&P MidCap 400	8.3
U.S. Small Cap	76.8
Foreign	0.0

Sector Weightings

	% of Stocks	Relative S&P 500
Utilities	0.0	0.00
Energy	0.0	0.00
Financials	67.4	6.37
Industrial Cyclicals	4.4	0.27
Consumer Durables	1.3	0.20
Consumer Staples	0.3	0.02
Services	1.2	0.15
Retail	1.3	0.23
Health	4.2	0.48
Technology	19.9	2.18

MORNINGSTAR 1995 Mutual Fund 500

Thornburg Ltd-Term Muni Natl A

	Ticker	Load	NAV	Yield	SEC Yield	Assets	Objective
	LTMFX	2.50%	12.92	4.9%	4.73%	1019.2	Muni Nat

Thornburg Limited-Term Municipal Fund National Portfolio - Class A seeks income exempt from federal income tax consistent with preservation of capital.

The fund normally invests at least 80% of its assets in investment-grade municipal obligations with an average weighted maturity of less than five years. The balance of assets may be invested in taxable obligations. Some investments may be subject to the Alternative Minimum Tax.

Class A shares have front loads and lower 12b-1 fees; Class B shares have deferred loads and conversion features; Class C shares have level loads. Prior to Nov. 1, 1992, the fund was named Limited-Term Municipal Fund National Portfolio.

Historical Profile

Return	Below Average
Risk	Low
Rating	★★★★★ Highest

Investment Style History
Fixed Income

Income Rtn % Rank Obj

Growth of $10,000

IIII Value of Fund ($000)
— Value of Index ($000)
  LB Muni
▼ Manager Change
▽ Partial Manager Change
► Mgr Unknown After
◄ Mgr Unknown Before

Performance Quartile (Within Objective)

Manager's Investment Style

Within its five-year average weighted maturity mandate, management employs a laddering strategy. It ladders securities that mature within three years or less, four to six years, and six years or more; the portfolio's average weighted maturity still lands around five years, yet it has varied rate exposure. Additionally, because part of the portfolio is always maturing, there's always cash on hand to take advantage of new opportunities. To minimize overall risk, management sticks with high-quality credits, favors more-staid sectors--including GOs--and holds an immense number of issues in the portfolio.

Fund Manager(s)

Brian J. McMahon, since 09-84. Birthdate: 11-55. BA, U. of Virginia 1977 MBA, Dartmouth C. 1979

Manager Experience

	Dates Managed	Invest Obj	Std Dev	+/- Index
Brian J. McMahon				
Thornburg Ltd-T Muni CA	02/87 - 12/94	MC	2.42	-1.86
Thornburg NM Int Muni A	06/91 - 12/94	MS	3.88	-0.51

History	1983	1984	1985	1986	1987	1988	1989	1990	1991	1992	1993	1994
NAV	---	11.93	12.44	12.90	12.59	12.72	12.82	12.76	13.01	13.25	13.75	12.92
Total Return %	---	2.04 *	12.89	11.09	4.15	7.89	7.79	6.48	8.61	7.74	8.81	-1.49
+/- LB Aggregate	---	---	-9.24	-4.16	1.39	0.01	-6.75	-2.46	-7.39	0.50	-0.94	1.43
+/- LB Muni	---	---	-7.14	-8.23	2.64	-2.27	-2.99	-0.82	-3.53	-1.08	-3.46	4.11
Income Return %	---	1.79	8.61	7.32	6.55	6.86	7.01	6.95	6.65	5.90	5.04	4.55
Capital Return %	---	0.25	4.27	3.77	-2.40	1.03	0.79	-0.47	1.96	1.84	3.77	-6.04
Total Rtn % Rank All	---	---	95	79	27	74	91	28	94	49	75	30
Total Rtn % Rank Obj	---	---	79	88	3	79	84	41	94	71	86	10
Income $	---	0.21	0.97	0.87	0.83	0.84	0.86	0.86	0.81	0.74	0.65	0.63
Capital Gains $	---	0.00	0.00	0.01	0.00	0.00	0.00	0.00	0.00	0.00	0.00	0.00
Expense Ratio %	---	---	0.70	1.00	1.00	1.10	1.15	1.11	1.07	1.04	1.01	0.95
Income Ratio %	---	---	6.80	6.92	6.27	6.58	6.66	6.73	6.58	5.96	5.03	4.60
Turnover Rate %	---	---	---	53	47	66	70	68	32	28	19	16
Net Assets ($mil)	---	10.0	30.7	60.2	128.7	172.8	201.1	236.7	384.2	719.2	911.6	1019.2

Performance 12-31-94

	1st Qtr	2nd Qtr	3rd Qtr	4th Qtr	Total
1987	2.17	-0.67	0.21	2.40	4.15
1988	3.19	1.40	1.83	1.27	7.89
1989	1.11	2.91	1.39	2.18	7.79
1990	0.89	1.87	1.23	2.35	6.48
1991	1.96	1.86	2.21	2.33	8.61
1992	0.91	2.72	2.22	1.69	7.74
1993	2.76	2.27	2.45	1.07	8.81
1994	-2.12	0.88	0.49	-0.72	-1.49

Bear Market Performance

Decile Rank (5-year period)

Worst — Best

	Worst 3 Mo Period 1985-89	Worst 3 Mo Period 1990-94
Thornburg Ltd-Term Muni Natl .	-1.60	-2.45
+/- LB Aggregate	1.95	2.48
+/- Best Fit Index : LB Muni	4.89	3.31

Trailing Returns

	Total Return %	+/- LB Aggregate	+/- LB Muni	% Rank All	% Rank Obj	Growth of $10,000
3 Mo	-0.72	-1.10	0.72	38	19	9,928
6 Mo	-0.24	-1.23	1.01	61	24	9,976
1 Yr	-1.49	1.43	4.11	30	10	9,851
3 Yr Avg	4.92	0.37	0.05	50	32	11,549
5 Yr Avg	5.96	-1.67	-0.81	77	61	13,356
10 Yr Avg	7.33	-2.61	-2.10	92	82	20,286
15 Yr Avg	---	---	---	---	---	---

Operations

Address and Telephone	119 E. Marcy Street Suite 202
	Santa Fe, NM 87501
	800-847-0200 / 505-984-0200
Advisor	Thornburg Management
Subadvisor	None
Distributor	Thornburg Securities
States Available	All
Report Grade	C+
Income Distrib	Paid Monthly
* Date of Inception	09-28-84
Fiscal Year End	June

Risk Analysis

Time Period	Load-Adj Return %	Risk % Rank [1] All	Obj	Morningstar [2] Return	Morningstar Risk	Morningstar Risk-Adj Rating
1 Yr	-3.95					
3 Yr	4.03	3	7	0.90	0.43	★★★★
5 Yr	5.42	2	7	0.79	0.38	★★★★
10 Yr	7.06	2	8	0.68	0.31	★★★★★

Average Historical Rating (88 months) 5.0 ★s

[1] = low, 100 = high [2] 1.00 = Muni Avg [3] 1.00 = 90-day T-bill return

Other Measures

			Standard LB Agg	Best Fit LB Muni
Standard Deviation	2.96	Alpha	0.8	0.6
Mean	4.85	Beta	0.57	0.53
Sharpe Ratio	0.45	R-Squared	58	93

Investment Style

Interest-Rate Stance

Avg Effective Maturity   4.4 Yrs

Quality

Avg Credit Quality   AA

Avg Weighted Coupon   5.42%

Avg Weighted Price 99.82% of Par

Maturity: Short Intm Long
Quality: High Med Low

Diversification Value for Portfolio Types

Large Cap: Medium	Small Cap: High	Bond: Low	Balanced: Medium	Diversified: High

Expenses & Fees

Sales Fees	2.50% front
	0.00% deferred
	0.13% 12b-1
Management Fee	0.75% flat fee
3-,5-,10-yr Expense Projections	$55, $77, $140

Min Initial Purchase $5000 (Addt'l: $100)
Min IRA Purchase N/A
Min Auto Invest Plan $5000 (Systematic Inv: $100)

Portfolio 05-31-94

Amount 000	Date of Maturity	Total Stocks: 0 / Total Fixed-Income: 532	Value $000	% Net Assets
11430	07-01-02	WA Pub Pwr Sply Sys Proj #2 5.3%	11282	1.18
10095	08-01-13	TX GO Palo Duro Rvr 7.6%	11138	1.17
13260	09-01-00	CA San Marcos Pub Fac Impr 0%	10144	1.06
10000	03-01-02	MS Perry Poll Cntrl Leaf Rvr Forest DMD	10000	1.05
10000	02-01-19	CA Sacramento GO USD 4.6%	9988	1.05
12400	06-30-02	AK North Slope GO 0%	9623	1.01
9000	11-01-07	FL Hsg Fin 5.5%	9092	0.95
9000	10-01-23	TX Bell Hlth Fac Dev 4.75%	8741	0.92
8300	02-15-99	CA Orange Local Transp Sales Tax DMD	8300	0.87
8355	12-01-97	PA State COP 4.6%	8290	0.87
7440	07-01-16	CA Hlth Fac Fin Catholic Care West 6.5%	8048	0.84
6500	10-01-18	CA Simi Vlly COP Comnty Dev 6.05%	6665	0.70
6570	04-01-98	MI Hsg Dev Rental Multi-Fam 5.4%	6621	0.69
5465	02-01-02	LA East Baton Rouge Sales/Use Tax 8%	6260	0.66
6230	06-01-00	DC GO 4.9%	6038	0.63
6000	01-01-00	HI State GO 5%	6005	0.63
5880	02-01-98	TX Pub Fin Bldg 5.25%	5991	0.63
8000	07-01-00	UT Intermountain Pwr Sply 0%	5837	0.61
6705	07-01-00	AZ Maricopa GO USD #97 Deer Vlly 0%	5808	0.61
5730	09-01-02	CO Student Loan Obl 5.9%	5752	0.60

Credit Analysis % of Bonds 12-31-94

US Govt	0	BB	0
AAA	38	B	0
AA	18	Below B	0
A	29	NR/NA	5
BBB	10		

Composition % of Assets 12-31-94

Cash	0.0	Preferreds	0.0
Stocks	0.0	Convertibles	0.0
Bonds	100.0	Other	0.0

Tax Analysis

	Tax-Adj Historical Return %	% Pretax Return
3 Yr Avg	4.92	100.0
5 Yr Avg	5.96	100.0
10 Yr Avg	7.33	100.0
Potential Capital Gain Exposure (% of assets)		-2%

Most Similar Funds in MF500

Nuv Muni Value	Strong Fit
Sit Tax-Free Income	Strong Fit
Fidelity Spartan Sh-Int Muni	Strong Fit

Coupon Range

	% Bonds	Rel Obj
0%	11.0	4.38
0% to 6.8%	59.1	0.98
6.8% to 7.5%	13.1	0.84
7.5% to 8.3%	9.3	1.05
More than 8.3%	4.6	0.52
Not applicable	3.0	0.77

Sector Weightings

	% Bonds	Rel Obj
General Obl	22.90	1.09
Utilities	8.67	0.69
Health	13.79	1.05
Water/Waste	4.39	0.69
Housing	9.91	1.35
Education	8.01	1.25
Transportation	3.34	0.33
COP/Lease	7.44	2.33
Private	11.23	0.96
Misc Revenue	8.17	1.64
Demand	2.15	0.87

Top 5 States % of Bonds

CA	9.96	OH	7.12
PA	8.16	MA	5.55
TX	7.59		

Transamerica Income

	Ticker	NAV	Mkt Price	Prem/Disc	Yield	Objective
	TAI	$22.47	$21.13	-6.0%	9.1%	Corp General

Transamerica Income Shares seeks high current income consistent with prudent investment. Capital appreciation is a secondary objective.

The fund invests at least 65% of assets in investment-grade securities, securities issued or guaranteed by the U.S. government, commercial paper, and/or cash or cash equivalents. It may hold no more than 35% in nonrated and below-investment-grade securities.

The fund completed a rights offering in December 1992, which raised $22.9 million and added about 1.05 million shares.

11.7	14.0	3.3	5.0	9.3	11.2	4.9	2.8	Highest Prem/Disc
1.5	-2.8	-5.3	-7.1	-5.1	-3.4	-5.0	-6.6	Lowest Prem/Disc

Historical Profile
Return Average
Risk Below Average
Rating ★★★
Neutral

Growth of $10,000
■ at NAV ($000)
— at Market Price ($000)

Premium Discount %

Manager's Investment Style

In its quest for yield, management targets the long end of the yield curve. Indeed, the fund typically touts one of the longest average weighted maturities among all closed-end corporate-bond funds. Management also targets issues with upgrade potential. Unlike many of its corporate-bond rivals, this portfolio typically sticks with corporate bonds, shunning Treasuries and mortgage-backeds. The fund has on occasion held Yankee bonds, though.

Fund Manager(s)

Sharon Kilmer, CFA. Since 1987. BA'80 U. of Southern California; MBA'82 U. of Southern California.

1983	1984	1985	1986	1987	1988	1989	1990	1991	1992	1993	1994	History
---	---	---	23.60	21.82	22.24	23.11	22.56	24.48	24.18	25.63	22.47	NAV
---	---	---	---	2.43	11.95	14.31	7.46	18.72	9.07	14.47	-4.45	NAV Total Return %
---	---	---	---	-0.33	4.07	-0.23	-1.48	2.71	1.83	4.72	-1.53	+/- LB Aggregate
---	---	---	---	-0.13	2.73	0.33	0.31	0.21	0.37	2.31	-0.52	+/- LB Corp
---	---	---	---	9.97	10.03	10.40	9.84	10.21	8.47	8.17	7.68	Income Return %
---	---	---	---	-7.54	1.93	3.91	-2.38	8.51	0.60	6.31	-12.12	Capital Return %
---	---	---	---	51	52	34	21	47	52	58	34	Total Rtn % Rank All
---	---	---	---	50	23	20	16	60	53	22	55	Total Rtn % Rank Obj
15.29	15.19	30.87	22.10	7.37	0.54	20.81	4.29	26.42	8.36	10.14	-10.58	Market Total Rtn %
---	---	---	---	6.6	7.7	-1.3	-1.2	2.3	4.6	0.9	-1.7	Avg Prem/Disc %
2.16	2.17	2.23	2.28	2.48	2.26	2.16	2.16	2.16	2.05	1.96	1.93	Income $
0.00	0.00	0.00	0.00	0.00	0.00	0.00	0.00	0.00	0.00	0.07	0.06	Capital Gains $
0.67	0.69	0.68	0.66	0.67	0.68	0.71	0.69	0.68	0.60	0.69	0.66•	Expense Ratio %
11.19	12.11	10.77	9.45	9.86	9.93	9.53	9.58	8.98	8.27	7.60	8.26•	Income Ratio %
84	142	206	167	38	15	30	17	30	32	15	---	Turnover Rate %
103.4	96.6	100.7	124.1	126.7	117.1	121.7	118.8	128.9	152.8	161.9	142.0	Net Assets ($mil)

• ratio annualized by Morningstar

Manager Experience

	Dates Managed	Invest Obj	Std Dev	+/- Index
Not available.				

NAV Performance % 12-30-94

	1st Qtr	2nd Qtr	3rd Qtr	4th Qtr	Total
1987	4.21	-3.27	-3.04	4.80	2.43
1988	6.37	0.73	2.67	1.77	11.95
1989	1.62	7.53	1.68	2.87	14.31
1990	-1.24	3.72	0.05	4.86	7.46
1991	4.97	2.56	5.31	4.71	18.72
1992	0.12	3.76	4.49	0.48	9.07
1993	6.03	3.71	5.00	-0.86	14.47
1994	-3.87	-2.47	0.71	1.19	-4.45

Bear Market Performance

Decile Rank (5-year period)

Worst — Best

	Worst 3 Mo Period 1985-89	Worst 3 Mo Period 1990-94
Transamerica Income	---	-7.44
+/- LB Aggregate	---	-2.51

Trailing Returns

	NAV Total Return %	+/- LB Agg	+/- LB Corp	% Rank All	% Rank Obj	Mkt Total Return %
3 Mo	1.19	0.81	0.76	9	26	-5.26
6 Mo	1.91	0.92	0.74	20	17	-6.32
1 Yr	-4.45	-1.53	-0.52	34	55	-10.58
3 Yr Avg	6.06	1.52	0.65	50	50	2.19
5 Yr Avg	8.76	1.14	0.50	37	32	7.07
10 Yr Avg	---	---	---	---	---	11.36

Operations

Address and Telephone	1150 S. Olive St. Los Angeles, CA 90015 213-742-4141
Advisor	Transamerica Investment Services
Subadvisor	N/A
Administrator	N/A
Transfer Agent	Mellon Securities Trust Co.
Custodian	State Street Bank and Trust Co.
Auditor	Ernst & Young LLP
Legal Counsel	Orrick, Herrington, Rowley & Sutcliffe

Income Distrib Schedule	Paid Monthly
Management Fee	0.50%
Reinvestment Plan	Yes
Direct Purchase Plan	No
Shares Outstanding	6,318,771
Exchange	NYSE
Date of Inception	02-28-72
Shareholder Report	B+

Risk Analysis

	Risk % Rank[1] All	Obj	Morningstar[2] Return	Risk	Morningstar Risk-Adj Rating
3 Yr	34	69	0.73[3]	0.83	★★★
5 Yr	28	32	1.01[3]	0.75	★★★
10 Yr					

Average Historical Rating (61 months) 4.3 ★s

[1] = Low, 100 = High [2] 1.00 = Fixed-Inc Avg [3] 1.00 = 90-day T-bill Return

Other Measures

			LB Aggregate
Standard Deviation	5.41	Alpha	1.35
Mean	6.04	Beta	1.17
Sharpe Ratio	0.47	R-Squared	75

Investment Style

Interest-Rate Stance

	Fund	Relative Objective
Avg Eff Duration	8.2 Yrs**	1.29
Avg Eff Maturity	22.7 Yrs	1.44
Avg Wtd Coupon	9.36%	1.05
Avg Wtd Price	100.1% Par	1.02

Duration: Short Intm Long
Quality: High Med Low

Quality

Avg Cred Quality BBB

** figure provided by fund

Credit Analysis 12-31-94

	% of Bonds		% of Bonds
US Govt	0	BB	5
AAA	1	B	1
AA	10	Below B	0
A	26	NR/NA	0
BBB	57		

Diversification Value for Portfolio Types

Large Cap: Medium
Small Cap: High
Bond: Low
Balanced: Medium
Diversified: Medium

Portfolio 09-30-94

Total Equity: 0
Total Fixed-Income: 70

Amount 000		Maturity	Value $000	% Total Invest
5000	Occidental Petroleum 11.75%	03-15-11	5499	3.83
4000	Commonwealth Australia 9.625%	02-01-06	4404	3.07
4000	Texas Utilities Elec 10.625%	09-01-20	4380	3.05
3750	General Motors 9.4%	07-15-21	3950	2.75
4000	Phillips Petroleum 8.49%	01-01-23	3755	2.62
4000	United Air Lines 9.75%	08-15-21	3642	2.54
3500	Scott Paper 8.8%	05-15-22	3441	2.40
3250	Arkansas Power & Light 10%	02-01-20	3430	2.39
4000	Time Warner 8.375%	07-15-33	3411	2.38
3000	GTE 10.75%	09-15-17	3373	2.35
3000	Barclays N American Cap 10.5%	12-15-17	3346	2.33
3000	ConAgra 9.75%	03-01-21	3228	2.25
3000	Georgia-Pacific 9.625%	03-15-22	3053	2.13
3000	GMAC 8.5%	01-01-03	3029	2.11
2800	Dayton Hudson 9.25%	08-15-11	2906	2.02
3000	Pacific Bell 8.5%	08-15-31	2882	2.01
3000	Tele-Communications 9.25%	01-15-23	2824	1.97
3000	Hydro-Quebec 8%	02-01-13	2775	1.93
3000	Georgia-Pacific 8.25%	03-01-23	2716	1.89
2500	Caterpillar 9.75%	06-01-19	2652	1.85
3000	Kansas City Sthrn Inds 6.625%	03-01-05	2627	1.83
2500	Eastman Kodak 9.2%	06-01-21	2625	1.83
2500	Tele-Communications 9.8%	02-01-12	2560	1.78
2250	Arizona Public Service 10.25%	05-15-20	2500	1.74
2500	Federal Express 9.625%	10-15-19	2497	1.74

Composition % 12-31-94

Cash	0.3	Preferreds	0.0
Stocks	0.0	Convertibles	0.7
Bonds	99.0	Other	0.0

Coupon Range

	% of Bonds	Relative Objective
0%, PIK	0.0	0.0
0% to 8.5%	28.5	0.8
8.5% to 9.5%	26.2	1.0
9.5% to 11%	39.7	1.8
More than 11%	5.6	0.6
Not applicable	0.0	0.0

1.0 = Objective Average

Tax Analysis

	Tax-Adj Historical Return %	% Pretax Return
3 Yr Avg	3.51	47.8
5 Yr Avg	5.85	58.1
10 Yr Avg	---	---

Potential Capital Gain Exposure (% of assets) -2

Most Similar Funds in MF500

Vanguard F/I L/T Corp Bond	Strong Fit
MFS Bond A	Fair Fit
Scudder Income	Fair Fit

MORNINGSTAR 1995 Mutual Fund 500

Tweedy, Browne American Value

	Ticker	Load	NAV	Yield	SEC Yield	Assets	Objective
	TWEBX	None	9.82	0.7%	N/A	35.7	Growth

Tweedy, Browne American Value Fund seeks long-term growth of capital.

The fund invests primarily in undervalued equity securities issued by domestic companies of various sizes. It may invest up to 20% of its assets in foreign securities. The fund may also invest a portion of its assets in nonconvertible debt securities issued by governments, companies, and supranational organizations; no more than 15% of assets may be invested in debt securities rated below BBB.

Prior to Oct. 4, 1994, the fund was named Tweedy, Browne Value Fund.

Manager's Investment Style

Management uses a proven value strategy to produce above-average results. They first screen a universe of 10,000 stocks and flag the most inexpensive ones. Then, those issues with low prices relative to current and projected earnings are singled out. This stock-picking method has resulted in a portfolio heavy in financial companies. Management strategy favors investors with a long time horizon.

Fund Manager(s)

Christopher H. Browne, since 12-93.
William H. Browne, since 12-93.
James M. Clark, Jr., since 12-93.
John D. Spears, since 12-93.

Manager Experience	Dates Managed	Invest Obj	Std Dev	+/- Index
John D. Spears				
Tweedy, Browne Global Va	06/93 - 12/94	WW	11.95	9.17
James M. Clark, Jr.				
Tweedy, Browne Global Va	06/93 - 12/94	WW	11.95	9.17

Performance 12-31-94

	1st Qtr	2nd Qtr	3rd Qtr	4th Qtr	Total
1987	---	---	---	---	---
1988	---	---	---	---	---
1989	---	---	---	---	---
1990	---	---	---	---	---
1991	---	---	---	---	---
1992	---	---	---	---	---
1993	---	---	---	---	-0.60 *
1994	-2.31	1.13	4.48	-3.66	-0.56

Bear Market Performance

Decile Rank (5-year period)

Worst — Best

	Worst 3 Mo Period 1985-89	Worst 3 Mo Period 1990-94
Tweedy, Browne American Val	---	---
+/- S&P 500	---	---
+/- Best Fit Index :	---	---

Trailing Returns

	Total Return %	+/- S&P 500	+/- Wil 5000	% Rank All	% Rank Obj	Growth of $10,000
3 Mo	-3.66	-3.65	-2.89	87	86	9,634
6 Mo	0.65	-4.21	-3.97	44	84	10,065
1 Yr	-0.56	-1.88	-0.49	24	38	9,944
3 Yr Avg	---	---	---	---	---	---
5 Yr Avg	---	---	---	---	---	---
10 Yr Avg	---	---	---	---	---	---
15 Yr Avg	---	---	---	---	---	---

Operations

Address and Telephone	52 Vanderbilt Avenue New York, NY 10017 800-432-4789
Advisor	Tweedy Browne
Subadvisor	None
Distributor	Tweedy Browne
States Available	All plus PR
Report Grade	B
Income Distrib	Paid Annually
* Date of Inception	12-08-93
Fiscal Year End	March

Min Initial Purchase	$2500 (Addt'l: $500)
Min IRA Purchase	$500 (Addt'l: $500)
Min Auto Invest Plan	$2500 (Systematic Inv: $500)

Expenses & Fees

Sales Fees	
	0.00% front
	0.00% deferred
	0.00% 12b-1
Management Fee	1.25% flat fee, 0.16%A
3-,5-,10-yr Expense Projections	$71, N/A, N/A
Annual Brokerage Cost	---

Historical Profile

Return	---
Risk	---
Rating	Not Rated

Investment Style History Equity

Average % Stocks Held in Portfolio — 59% / 78%

Growth of $10,000
|||| Value of Fund ($000)
— Value of Index ($000) S&P 500
▼ Manager Change
▽ Partial Manager Change
► Mgr Unknown After
◄ Mgr Unknown Before

Performance Quartile (Within Objective)

	1983	1984	1985	1986	1987	1988	1989	1990	1991	1992	1993	1994	History
	---	---	---	---	---	---	---	---	---	---	9.94	9.82	NAV
	---	---	---	---	---	---	---	---	---	---	-0.60 *	-0.56	Total Return %
	---	---	---	---	---	---	---	---	---	---	-0.83 *	-1.88	+/- S&P 500
	---	---	---	---	---	---	---	---	---	---		-0.49	+/- Wilshire 5000
	---	---	---	---	---	---	---	---	---	---	0.00	0.64	Income Return %
	---	---	---	---	---	---	---	---	---	---	-0.60	-1.21	Capital Return %
	---	---	---	---	---	---	---	---	---	---		24	Total Rtn % Rank All
	---	---	---	---	---	---	---	---	---	---		38	Total Rtn % Rank Obj
	---	---	---	---	---	---	---	---	---	---	0.00	0.06	Income $
	---	---	---	---	---	---	---	---	---	---	0.00	0.00	Capital Gains $
	---	---	---	---	---	---	---	---	---	---		2.26	Expense Ratio %
	---	---	---	---	---	---	---	---	---	---		0.64	Income Ratio %
	---	---	---	---	---	---	---	---	---	---		0	Turnover Rate %
	---	---	---	---	---	---	---	---	---	---	3.1	35.7	Net Assets ($mil)

Risk Analysis

Time Period	Load-Adj Return %	Risk % Rank [1] All	Obj	Morningstar [2] Return	Morningstar Risk	Morningstar [3] Risk-Adj Rating
1 Yr	-0.56					
3 Yr	---	---	---	---	---	
5 Yr	---	---	---	---	---	
10 Yr	---	---	---	---	---	

Average Historical Rating ---

[1] 1 = low, 100 = high   [2] 1.00 = Equity Avg   [3] 1.00 = 90-day T-bill return

Other Measures

			Standard S&P 500	Best Fit
Standard Deviation	---	Alpha	---	---
Mean	---	Beta	---	---
Sharpe Ratio	---	R-Squared	---	---

Investment Style

	Stock Portfolio Avg	Relative S&P 500
Price/Earnings Ratio	13.8	0.75
Price/Book Ratio	1.6	0.46
5 Yr Earnings Gr %	4.8#	0.86
Return on Assets %	4.3	0.57
Debt % Total Cap	27.8#	0.98
Med Mkt Cap ($mil)	1451	0.11

Style: Value Blend Growth / Size Large Med Small

figure is based on 50% or less of stocks

Diversification Value for Portfolio Types

Large Cap: Small Cap: Bond: Balanced: Diversified:

Portfolio 09-30-94

Total Stocks: 75
Total Fixed-Income: 1

Share Chg (03-94) 000	Amount 000		Value $000	% Net Assets
23	42	Great Atlantic & Pacific Tea	1072	3.55
16	31	American Express	949	3.15
7	15	Philip Morris	930	3.08
13	26	Polaroid	922	3.06
24	30	Hasbro	880	2.92
8	25	Chase Manhattan	865	2.87
8	17	Johnson & Johnson	862	2.86
9	18	American National Insurance	849	2.81
9	21	Salomon	836	2.77
4	7	Heineken Holding Cl A	798	2.65
11	28	Comerica	788	2.61
21	43	K mart	772	2.56
4	21	Household International	758	2.51
4	17	First Chicago	757	2.51
6	16	Nestle (Reg) (ADR)	742	2.46
3	13	FHLMC	719	2.38
2	19	Reebok International	676	2.24
66	72	Continental Medical Systems	644	2.13
10	24	Digital Equipment	636	2.11
9	15	National Western Life Ins A	566	1.88
16	16	Value Line	527	1.75
6	15	BanPonce	503	1.67
7	21	USLICO	428	1.42
49	53	Syms	407	1.35
12	12	Coca-Cola Bottling	357	1.18

Composition % 12-31-94

Cash	13.0	Preferreds	0.1
Stocks	87.0	Convertibles	0.0
Bonds	0.0	Other	0.0

Tax Analysis

	Tax-Adj Historical Return %	% Pretax Return
3 Yr Avg	---	---
5 Yr Avg	---	---
10 Yr Avg	---	---
Potential Capital Gain Exposure (% of assets)		-3%

Most Similar Funds in MF500

Fund lacks three-year record

Index Allocation

	% of Stocks
S&P 500	49.9
S&P MidCap 400	7.0
U.S. Small Cap	34.8
Foreign	8.3

Sector Weightings

	% of Stocks	Relative S&P 500
Utilities	0.0	0.00
Energy	0.0	0.00
Financials	50.3	4.76
Industrial Cyclicals	7.5	0.46
Consumer Durables	6.7	1.08
Consumer Staples	13.3	1.06
Services	4.2	0.52
Retail	12.0	2.06
Health	2.7	0.31
Technology	3.3	0.36

Tweedy, Browne Global Value

	Ticker	Load	NAV	Yield	SEC Yield	Assets	Objective
	TBGVX	None	11.88	0.0%	N/A	565.7	World Stock

Tweedy, Browne Global Value Fund seeks long-term growth of capital.

The fund invests nearly all of its assets in equities. It focuses on foreign issues, but may also invest in the United States. The fund generally purchases equities issued by established, but undervalued, companies with at least three years of operations. These securities are selling at a substantial discount to the company's underlying assets, earning power, or private market value. The fund may invest in government and supranational organization debt; up to 15% of assets may be invested in debt securities rated below investment grade.

Manager's Investment Style

Management uses computer screens to choose stocks from developed nations worldwide. Its stays away from emerging markets reasoning that political volatility and the lack of reliable data makes these areas too risky. Instead, management opts to make value plays in developed nations. They seek out companies that show a discount to book value or earning power. This strategy has led management to obscure firms that other investors have overlooked. Management eliminates currency risk by remaining fully hedged at all times.

Fund Manager(s)

Christopher H. Browne, since 06-93.
William H. Browne, since 06-93.
James M. Clark, Jr., since 06-93.
John D. Spears, since 06-93.

Manager Experience

	Dates Managed	Invest Obj	Std Dev	+/- Index
John D. Spears				
Tweedy, Browne Amer Val	12/93 - 12/94	G	7.45	-1.88
James M. Clark, Jr.				
Tweedy, Browne Amer Val	12/93 - 12/94	G	7.45	-1.88

Historical Profile
Return ---
Risk ---
Rating
Not Rated

History	1993	1994
NAV	11.54	11.88
Total Return %	15.40 *	4.36
+/- S&P 500	9.22 *	3.05
+/- MSCI World	---	-0.71
Income Return %	0.00	0.00
Capital Return %	15.40	4.36
Total Rtn % Rank All		5
Total Rtn % Rank Obj		3
Income $	0.00	0.00
Capital Gains $	0.00	0.16
Expense Ratio %		1.73
Income Ratio %		0.00
Turnover Rate %		---
Net Assets ($mil)	157.9	565.7

Investment Style History Equity
Average % Stocks Held in Portfolio: 86% 88%

Growth of $10,000

Performance 12-31-94

	1st Qtr	2nd Qtr	3rd Qtr	4th Qtr	Total
1987	---	---	---	---	---
1988	---	---	---	---	---
1989	---	---	---	---	---
1990	---	---	---	---	---
1991	---	---	---	---	---
1992	---	---	---	---	---
1993	---	---	3.31	11.93	15.40 *
1994	6.24	-0.41	0.74	-2.09	4.36

Bear Market Performance
Decile Rank (5-year period)

	Worst 3 Mo Period 1985-89	Worst 3 Mo Period 1990-94
Tweedy, Browne Global Value	---	---
+/- S&P 500	---	---
+/- Best Fit Index	---	---

Trailing Returns

	Total Return %	+/- S&P 500	+/- MSCI World	% Rank All	Obj	Growth of $10,000
3 Mo	-2.09	-2.07	-1.36	70	19	9,791
6 Mo	-1.37	-6.23	-2.76	80	70	9,863
1 Yr	4.36	3.05	-0.71	5	3	10,436
3 Yr Avg	---	---	---	---	---	---
5 Yr Avg	---	---	---	---	---	---
10 Yr Avg	---	---	---	---	---	---
15 Yr Avg	---	---	---	---	---	---

Operations

Address and Telephone	52 Vanderbilt Avenue, New York, NY 10017, 800-432-4789
Advisor	Tweedy Browne
Subadvisor	None
Distributor	Tweedy Browne
States Available	All plus PR
Report Grade	A-
Income Distrib	Paid Annually
* Date of Inception	06-15-93
Fiscal Year End	March

Min Initial Purchase	$2500 (Addt'l: $500)
Min IRA Purchase	$500 (Addt'l: $500)
Min Auto Invest Plan	$2500 (Systematic Inv: $500)

Expenses & Fees
Sales Fees	0.00% front / 0.00% deferred / 0.00% 12b-1
Management Fee	1.25% flat fee, 0.20%A
3-,5-,10-yr Expense Projections	$55, N/A, N/A
Annual Brokerage Cost	---

Risk Analysis

Time Period	Load-Adj Return %	Risk % Rank All	Risk % Rank Obj	Morningstar Return	Morningstar Risk	Morningstar Risk-Adj Rating
1 Yr	4.36					
3 Yr	---	---	---	---	---	
5 Yr	---	---	---	---	---	
10 Yr	---	---	---	---	---	

Average Historical Rating ---
1 = low, 100 = high 2 1.00 = Equity Avg 3 1.00 = 90-day T-bill return

Other Measures
			Standard S&P 500	Best Fit
Standard Deviation	---	Alpha	---	---
Mean	---	Beta	---	---
Sharpe Ratio	---	R-Squared	---	---

Investment Style
	Stock Portfolio Avg	Rel MSCI EAFE	Rel Obj
Price/Earnings Ratio	20.2	0.55	0.82
Price/Cash Flow	9.4	0.60	0.70
Price/Book Ratio	1.6	0.61	0.54
5 Yr Earnings Gr %	-3.1	---	-0.65
Return on Assets %	5.1	1.11	0.73
Debt % Total Cap	20.9	0.61	0.72
Med Mkt Cap ($mil)	1298	0.11	0.26

Diversification Value for Portfolio Types
Large Cap: Small Cap: Bond: Balanced: Diversified:

Tax Analysis
	Tax-Adj Historical Return %	% Pretax Return
3 Yr Avg	---	---
5 Yr Avg	---	---
10 Yr Avg	---	---
Potential Capital Gain Exposure (% of assets)		0%

Most Similar Funds in MF500
Fund lacks three-year record

Portfolio 09-30-94

Total Stocks: 182
Total Fixed-Income: 3

Share Chg (03-94) 000	Amount 000		Value $000	% Net Assets
134	162	Unilever (Netherlands)	18507	3.56
7	20	Nestle (Reg)	17786	3.42
18	121	Heineken Holding Cl A	14812	2.85
18	18	Swissair (Reg)	11951	2.30
214	253	Salomon	10001	1.92
286	429	Fuji Photo Film	9654	1.86
104	104	Alcatel Alsthom Genl D'Elec	9617	1.85
307	820	Kesko	9557	1.84
25	25	Eurafrance	8736	1.68
350	1183	Guinness	8497	1.64
45	622	Kirin Brewery	7218	1.39
65	65	Kone Cl B	6876	1.32
150	221	American Express	6713	1.29
16	16	Axel Springer Verlag Cl A	6525	1.26
150	496	Zeneca Group	6298	1.21
12	29	Sinn	6087	1.17
260	757	Nissan Fire & Marine Ins	5683	1.09
118	118	Financiere de Suez	5617	1.08
211	469	Franco Tosi	5566	1.07
1120	1120	Lloyds Chemists	5333	1.03

Regional Exposure 12-31-94
% of Stocks
Europe	0	Pacific Rim	0
Japan	0	U.S.	0
Latin Amer	0	Other	0

Composition % 12-31-94
Cash	8.3	Preferreds	0.0
Stocks	91.5	Convertibles	0.2
Bonds	0.0	Other	0.0

Top 5 Countries 12-31-94
% of Stocks

Total Number of Countries: 18
Hedging Policy: Active

Sector Weightings
	% of Stocks	Relative S&P 500
Utilities	0.0	0.00
Energy	0.0	0.00
Financials	27.2	1.64
Industrial Cyclicals	26.0	1.12
Consumer Durables	4.3	0.42
Consumer Staples	21.6	4.24
Services	4.9	0.41
Retail	8.2	1.42
Health	3.6	0.68
Technology	4.2	0.47

MORNINGSTAR 1995 Mutual Fund 500

20th Century Balanced Investors

	Ticker	Load	NAV	Yield	SEC Yield	Assets	Objective
	TWBIX	None	15.27	2.8%	3.34%	689.5	Balanced

Twentieth Century Balanced Investors seeks capital growth and current income.

The fund normally invests approximately 60% of its assets in common stocks with above-average growth potential. A minimum of 25% of assets are held in fixed-income senior securities. The fund may only purchase stocks of companies that have operating histories of at least three years and whose securities are readily marketable. The average weighted maturity of the fixed-income portion ranges between three and 10 years. At least 80% of the fund's fixed-income investments are rated A or above; the remaining 20% may be rated BBB or of comparable quality.

Manager's Investment Style

Management invests boldly in equities and conservatively in bonds. On the stock side, the fund is not afraid of hefty sector overweightings, provided that the issues' earnings are promising. In order to temper the risk of the equity portfolio, management chooses a stable group of bonds. With a low average effective maturity, currently two years less than its peers', the fund keeps its interest-rate risk low.

Fund Manager(s)

Management Team

Historical Profile

Return	Average
Risk	Above Average
Rating	★★ Below Average

Investment Style History
Equity
Average % Stocks Held in Portfolio

			57%	59%	58%	59%	58%	54%

Growth of $10,000
- |||| Value of Fund ($000)
- — Value of Index ($000) SPMid400
- ▼ Manager Change
- ▽ Partial Manager Change
- ► Mgr Unknown After
- ◄ Mgr Unknown Before

Performance Quartile (Within Objective)

1983	1984	1985	1986	1987	1988	1989	1990	1991	1992	1993	1994	History
---	---	---	---	---	10.04	11.83	11.62	16.64	15.28	16.00	15.27	NAV
---	---	---	---	---	0.97 *	25.50	1.82	46.86	-6.06	7.22	-0.07	Total Return %
---	---	---	---	---	-2.11 *	-6.19	4.93	16.38	-13.68	-2.83	-1.38	+/- S&P 500
---	---	---	---	---	---	10.96	-7.13	30.86	-13.30	-2.53	2.85	+/- LB Aggregate
---	---	---	---	---	0.57	4.27	3.59	3.66	2.11	2.51	2.79	Income Return %
---	---	---	---	---	0.40	21.23	-1.78	43.20	-8.17	4.71	-2.86	Capital Return %
---	---	---	---	---	---	22	51	9	96	82	20	Total Rtn % Rank All
---	---	---	---	---	---	8	19	1	99	79	13	Total Rtn % Rank Obj
---	---	---	---	---	0.06	0.42	0.42	0.36	0.34	0.38	0.44	Income $
---	---	---	---	---	0.00	0.32	0.00	0.00	0.00	0.00	0.27	Capital Gains $
---	---	---	---	---	1.00	1.00	1.00	1.00	1.00	1.00	1.00	Expense Ratio %
---	---	---	---	---	4.80	4.20	3.80	3.10	2.40	2.40	2.40	Income Ratio %
---	---	---	---	---	274	171	104	116	100	95	101	Turnover Rate %
---	---	---	---	---	10.8	35.2	74.3	351.2	700.5	684.8	689.5	Net Assets ($mil)

Manager Experience

	Dates Managed	Invest Obj	Std Dev	+/- Index
Robert C. Puff, Jr.				
20th Century Select Inv	01/83 - 12/94	G	17.53	-1.91
20th Century Heritage Inv	11/87 - 12/94	G	15.48	1.03

Performance 12-31-94

	1st Qtr	2nd Qtr	3rd Qtr	4th Qtr	Total
1987	---	---	---	---	---
1988	---	---	---	0.97	0.97 *
1989	2.42	7.56	9.87	3.68	25.50
1990	-2.09	9.52	-11.11	6.81	1.82
1991	15.77	-2.81	12.57	15.95	46.86
1992	-6.73	-3.65	1.75	2.74	-6.06
1993	0.90	2.70	4.37	-0.86	7.22
1994	-0.94	-2.24	2.99	0.19	-0.07

Bear Market Performance

Decile Rank (5-year period)

Worst ———————————————— Best

	Worst 3 Mo Period 1985-89	Worst 3 Mo Period 1990-94
20th Century Balanced Investor	---	-11.11
+/- S&P 500	---	2.64
+/- Best Fit Index : SPMid400	---	6.67

Trailing Returns

	Total Return %	+/- S&P 500	+/- LB Aggregate	% Rank All	% Rank Obj	Growth of $10,000
3 Mo	0.19	0.21	-0.19	17	10	10,019
6 Mo	3.18	-1.68	2.19	19	13	10,318
1 Yr	-0.07	-1.38	2.85	20	13	9,993
3 Yr Avg	0.22	-6.05	-4.33	96	96	10,066
5 Yr Avg	8.52	-0.17	0.89	28	28	15,051
10 Yr Avg	---	---	---	---	---	---
15 Yr Avg	---	---	---	---	---	---

Risk Analysis

Time Period	Load-Adj Return %	Risk % Rank All	Obj	Morningstar[2] Return	Morningstar Risk	Morningstar[2] Risk-Adj Rating
1 Yr	-0.07					
3 Yr	0.22	79	99	-0.94[3]	1.22	★
5 Yr	8.52	65	94	0.95[3]	1.07	★★★
10 Yr	---	---	---	---	---	---

Average Historical Rating (40 months) 3.6 ★s

[1] 1 = low, 100 = high [2] 1.00 = Hybrid Avg [3] 1.00 = 90-day T-bill return

Other Measures

			Standard S&P 500	Best Fit SPMid400
Standard Deviation	7.78	Alpha	-5.1	-5.4
Mean	0.52	Beta	0.78	0.67
Sharpe Ratio	-0.39	R-Squared	62	72

Investment Style

Stocks

	Port Avg	Rel S&P 500
Price/Earnings Ratio	23.3	1.26
Price/Book Ratio	3.4	1.01
5 Yr Earnings Gr %	5.4	0.97
Med Mkt Cap ($mil)	12284	0.95

Style V B G / Size L M S

Bonds

Avg Effective Duration	3.1 Yrs
Avg Effective Maturity	4.2 Yrs
Avg Credit Quality	AA
Avg Weighted Coupon	6.89%

Maturity S I L / Quality H M L

Diversification Value for Portfolio Types

Large Cap: Low	Small Cap: Low	Bond: High	Balanced: Low	Diversified: Low

Portfolio 09-30-94

Total Stocks: 53 Total Fixed-Income: 49

Share Chg (06-94)000	Amount 000		Date of Maturity	Value $000	% Net Assets
	20000	US Treasury Note 8%	01-15-97	20552	2.97
	15000	US Treasury Note 8.875%	11-15-97	15808	2.28
9	47	Veba		15583	2.25
0	255	Microsoft		14328	2.07
394	394	BCE (Canada)		14146	2.04
40	200	IBM		13900	2.01
0	240	United HealthCare		12720	1.84
0	230	Motorola		12106	1.75
230	280	Oracle Systems		12075	1.74
110	220	Caterpillar		11908	1.72
-130	360	Compaq Computer		11745	1.70
0	255	Columbia/HCA Healthcare		11093	1.60
230	345	Vodafone Group (ADR)		10824	1.56
	10800	FNMA CMO REMIC PAC 0%		10343	1.49
0	240	Citicorp		10200	1.47
	10000	US Treasury Note 6.25%	08-31-96	9943	1.44
0	210	General Motors		9844	1.42
	10000	Puget Sound Pwr & Lt 6.5%	09-15-99	9525	1.38
0	2000	Hutchison Whampoa		9447	1.36
365	365	Mylan Laboratories		9308	1.34

Index Allocation

	% of Stocks
S&P 500	63.7
S&P MidCap 400	4.6
U.S. Small Cap	2.4
Foreign	30.3

Composition % 12-31-94

Cash	9.3	Preferreds	0.0
Stocks	55.3	Convertibles	0.0
Bonds	35.4	Other	0.0

Tax Analysis

	Tax-Adj Historical Return %	% Pretax Return
3 Yr Avg	-0.85	---
5 Yr Avg	7.44	85.4
10 Yr Avg	---	---

Potential Capital Gain Exposure (% of assets) 5%

Most Similar Funds in MF500

AIM Weingarten	Fair Fit
Janus Twenty	Fair Fit
Janus Growth & Income	Fair Fit

Bond Credit Analysis 12-31-94

% of Bonds

US Govt	34	BB	0
AAA	0	B	0
AA	14	Below B	0
A	38	NR/NA	0
BBB	15		

Stock Sector Weightings

	% of Stocks	Relative S&P 500
Utilities	3.6	0.29
Energy	2.2	0.22
Financials	5.9	0.56
Industrial Cyclicals	17.4	1.06
Consumer Durables	16.4	2.64
Consumer Staples	2.9	0.23
Services	8.2	1.00
Retail	4.2	0.71
Health	13.4	1.54
Technology	25.8	2.82

Operations

Address and Telephone	4500 Main Street P.O. Box 419200
	Kansas City, MO 64141-6200
	800-345-2021 / 816-531-5575
Advisor	Investors Research
Subadvisor	None
Distributor	Twentieth Century Investors
States Available	All
Report Grade	C
Income Distrib	Paid Quarterly
* Date of Inception	09-30-88
Fiscal Year End	October

Min Initial Purchase	$2500 (Addt'l: $50)
Min IRA Purchase	None (Addt'l: $50)
Min Auto Invest Plan	$50 (Systematic Inv: $50)

Expenses & Fees

Sales Fees	0.00% front
	0.00% deferred
	0.00% 12b-1
Management Fee	1.00% flat fee
3-,5-,10-yr Expense Projections	$32, $55, $122
Annual Brokerage Cost	---

20th Century Growth Investors

	Ticker	Load	NAV	Yield	SEC Yield	Assets	Objective
	TWCGX	None	18.74	0.2%	N/A	4158.0	Growth

Twentieth Century Growth Investors seeks capital appreciation. The fund primarily purchases equity securities of large, established companies that meet its standards of earnings and revenue trends. The fund intends to remain fully invested in such securities, as long as viable candidates are present. Up to 10% of the fund's assets may be held in cash. The fund may only purchase securities of companies with at least three years of operations. The fund also emphasizes securities with a high degree of liquidity.

Historical Profile
Return Average
Risk Above Average
Rating ★★★
Neutral

99% 97% 98% 95% 95% 95% 94% 96%

Investment Style History
Equity
Average % Stocks Held in Portfolio

Growth of $10,000
|||| Value of Fund ($000)
— Value of Index ($000)
SPMid400
▼ Manager Change
▽ Partial Manager Change
► Mgr Unknown After
◄ Mgr Unknown Before

Performance Quartile (Within Objective)

Manager's Investment Style
Management follows a bottom-up strategy of growth, favoring large, established companies with a high level of earnings. Companies must be in operation for more than three years and highly liquid to be considered for purchase. Management invests in both domestic and foreign markets, and looks for companies that have survived tough markets.

	1983	1984	1985	1986	1987	1988	1989	1990	1991	1992	1993	1994	History
	15.65	12.25	16.21	14.06	12.30	12.31	16.95	15.29	25.83	24.36	22.40	18.74	NAV
	24.45	-11.21	33.98	18.85	13.12	2.72	43.13	-3.85	69.02	-4.29	3.76	-1.49	Total Return %
	1.99	-17.48	2.24	0.17	7.86	-13.89	11.45	-0.74	38.54	-11.90	-6.30	-2.80	+/- S&P 500
	0.99	-14.26	1.42	2.75	10.76	-15.22	13.96	2.33	34.82	-13.26	-7.53	-1.42	+/- Wilshire 5000
	0.44	0.38	1.65	1.17	0.98	2.64	0.49	0.72	0.09	0.00	0.26	0.27	Income Return %
	24.01	-11.59	32.33	17.68	12.14	0.08	42.65	-4.57	68.93	-4.29	3.50	-1.76	Capital Return %
	25	91	14	27	7	96	3	67	2	95	95	30	Total Rtn % Rank All
	36	91	24	24	8	94	4	45	2	97	83	47	Total Rtn % Rank Obj
	0.05	0.05	0.15	0.18	0.13	0.32	0.08	0.11	0.01	0.00	0.06	0.05	Income $
	0.00	1.82	0.00	5.08	3.46	0.00	0.59	0.89	0.00	0.37	2.77	3.22	Capital Gains $
	1.02	1.01	1.01	1.01	1.00	1.00	1.00	1.00	1.00	1.00	1.00	1.00	Expense Ratio %
	0.50	1.40	1.30	0.60	0.20	2.40	0.50	0.60	0.20	-0.10	0.20	-0.10	Income Ratio %
	98	132	116	105	114	143	98	118	69	53	94	85	Turnover Rate %
	659.1	678.2	759.9	928.4	1231.9	1193.8	1642.0	1914.7	3879.1	4853.4	4552.5	4158.0	Net Assets ($mil)

Fund Manager(s)
James E. Stowers III, since 1981.
Christopher K. Boyd CFA, since 01-91.
Derek V. Felske CFA, since 09-93.

Manager Experience
	Dates Managed	Invest Obj	Std Dev	+/- Index
James E. Stowers III				
20th Century Ultra Inv	11/81 - 12/94	AG	26.08	1.88
20th Century Vista Inv	11/83 - 12/94	SC	26.92	-1.68

Performance 12-31-94
	1st Qtr	2nd Qtr	3rd Qtr	4th Qtr	Total
1987	31.95	4.50	12.87	-27.32	13.12
1988	-0.57	9.48	-8.66	3.31	2.72
1989	11.94	12.92	16.58	-2.87	43.13
1990	-0.47	11.62	-19.44	7.43	-3.85
1991	28.45	-6.42	15.07	22.19	69.02
1992	-6.62	-6.67	4.09	5.52	-4.29
1993	-1.89	-0.33	6.51	-0.37	3.76
1994	-0.40	-4.26	3.60	-0.29	-1.49

Bear Market Performance
Decile Rank (5-year period)

Worst —————————————————— Best

	Worst 3 Mo Period 1985-89	Worst 3 Mo Period 1990-94
20th Century Growth Investors	-34.55	-19.44
+/- S&P 500	-4.97	-5.69
+/- Best Fit Index : SPMid400	-5.75	-1.66

Trailing Returns
	Total Return %	+/- S&P 500	+/- Wil 5000	% Rank All	% Rank Obj	Growth of $10,000
3 Mo	-0.29	-0.27	0.48	30	26	9,971
6 Mo	3.31	-1.55	-1.32	19	58	10,331
1 Yr	-1.49	-2.80	-1.42	30	47	9,851
3 Yr Avg	-0.73	-6.99	-7.34	98	92	9,783
5 Yr Avg	9.72	1.03	0.90	19	33	15,899
10 Yr Avg	15.46	1.08	1.60	8	11	42,105
15 Yr Avg	15.16	0.68	1.19	11	22	83,106

Operations
Address and Telephone	4500 Main Street P.O. Box 419200	
	Kansas City, MO 64141-6200	
	800-345-2021 / 816-531-5575	
Advisor	Investors Research	
Subadvisor	None	
Distributor	Twentieth Century Investors	
States Available	All	
Report Grade	C	
Income Distrib	Paid Annually	
Date of Inception	10-31-58	
Fiscal Year End	October	

Min Initial Purchase	$2500 (Addt'l: $50)
Min IRA Purchase	None (Addt'l: $50)
Min Auto Invest Plan	$50 (Systematic Inv: $50)

Expenses & Fees
Sales Fees	0.00% front
	0.00% deferred
	0.00% 12b-1
Management Fee	1.00% flat fee
3-,5-,10-yr Expense Projections	$32, $55, $122
Annual Brokerage Cost	---

Risk Analysis
Time Period	Load-Adj Return %	Risk % Rank [1] All	Risk % Rank [1] Obj	Morningstar [2] Return	Morningstar Risk	Morningstar Risk-Adj Rating
1 Yr	-1.49					
3 Yr	-0.73	94	92	-1.19 [3]	1.32	★
5 Yr	9.72	90	89	1.27 [3]	1.17	★★★
10 Yr	15.46	91	93	1.60	1.23	★★★★

Average Historical Rating (109 months) 3.8 ★s

[1] = low, 100 = high [2] 1.00 = Equity Avg [3] 1.00 = 90-day T-bill return

Other Measures
			Standard S&P 500	Best Fit SPMid400
Standard Deviation	11.80	Alpha	-6.7	-7.3
Mean	-0.03	Beta	1.15	1.04
Sharpe Ratio	-0.30	R-Squared	60	76

Investment Style
	Stock Portfolio Avg	Relative S&P 500
Price/Earnings Ratio	22.7	1.23
Price/Book Ratio	3.4	1.00
5 Yr Earnings Gr %	0.4	0.08
Return on Assets %	7.5	1.00
Debt % Total Cap	28.1	0.99
Med Mkt Cap ($mil)	12350	0.95

Style Value Blend Growth
Size Large/Med/Small

Diversification Value for Portfolio Types
Large Cap: Low
Small Cap: Low
Bond: High
Balanced: Low
Diversified: Low

Portfolio 09-30-94
Total Stocks: 82
Total Fixed-Income: 0

Share Chg (06-94) 000	Amount 000		Value $000	% Net Assets
1200	2700	IBM	187650	4.45
-20	2255	LM Ericsson Telephone (ADR)	120935	2.86
-14	1456	Capital Cities/ABC	119359	2.83
679	2104	Motorola	110997	2.63
1600	1800	Philip Morris	110025	2.61
946	1996	AT & T	107757	2.55
-175	425	Mannesmann (ADR)	106613	2.53
-1	1349	British Petroleum (ADR)	102181	2.42
1766	3566	General Instrument	101631	2.41
-20	2330	Citicorp	99012	2.35
-2200	3000	Compaq Computer	97875	2.32
-20	2180	Columbia/HCA Healthcare	94830	2.25
0	5800	Daiwa Securities	84907	2.01
-14	1486	Microsoft	83495	1.98
1300	2850	AirTouch Communications	81581	1.93
800	800	Atlantic Richfield	80700	1.91
1310	2542	Vodafone Group (ADR)	79740	1.89
730	1350	El DuPont de Nemours	78300	1.85
2600	2600	WMX Technologies	75075	1.78
-8	917	Monsanto	73712	1.75
391	916	Mobil	72447	1.72
-1498	2847	Humana	67260	1.59
-200	1400	General Motors	65625	1.55
-17	1808	Union Carbide	61482	1.46
950	950	Telefonos de Mexico L (ADR)	59375	1.41

Composition % 12-31-94
Cash	1.2	Preferreds	0.0
Stocks	98.8	Convertibles	0.0
Bonds	0.0	Other	0.0

Tax Analysis
	Tax-Adj Historical Return %	% Pretax Return
3 Yr Avg	-3.30	NMF
5 Yr Avg	7.55	74.5
10 Yr Avg	12.59	70.8
Potential Capital Gain Exposure (% of assets)		7%

Most Similar Funds in MF500
Kemper Growth A	Fair Fit
Enterprise Capital Apprec	Fair Fit
Janus Twenty	Fair Fit

Index Allocation
	% of Stocks
S&P 500	68.0
S&P MidCap 400	2.7
U.S. Small Cap	5.5
Foreign	26.3

Sector Weightings
	% of Stocks	Relative S&P 500
Utilities	4.4	0.36
Energy	8.2	0.81
Financials	8.0	0.75
Industrial Cyclicals	20.9	1.28
Consumer Durables	9.6	1.55
Consumer Staples	5.7	0.45
Services	9.9	1.22
Retail	2.5	0.42
Health	7.3	0.84
Technology	23.5	2.57

MORNINGSTAR 1995 Mutual Fund 500

20th Century Heritage Invest

	Ticker	Load	NAV	Yield	SEC Yield	Assets	Objective
	TWHIX	None	9.35	0.3%	N/A	851.6	Growth

Twentieth Century Heritage Investors seeks capital growth.

The fund purchases equities with growth potential and a stated commitment to paying dividends. The fund tends to invest in smaller companies, whose issues are less liquid. Therefore, the fund may exhibit relatively high short-term risk. The fund may hold up to 10% of its assets in cash. It may purchase only securities issued by companies with at least three years of operations.

Historical Profile

Return	Average
Risk	Average
Rating	★★★ Neutral

Investment Style History
Equity

Average % Stocks Held in Portfolio

98%	96%	92%	91%	90%	94%	94%

Growth of $10,000

- IIII Value of Fund ($000)
- — Value of Index ($000) SPMid400
- ▼ Manager Change
- ▽ Partial Manager Change
- ► Mgr Unknown After
- ◄ Mgr Unknown Before

Performance Quartile (Within Objective)

Manager's Investment Style

As in most Twentieth Century funds, management follows a bottom-up approach, seeking firms growing at sustainable rates. Management also looks for solid balance sheets and shareholder-minded management among smaller firms that issue dividend-paying stocks. These criteria have often led to a heavy industrial weighting.

Fund Manager(s)

Robert C. Puff, Jr. CFA, since 11-87.
Charles M. Duboc CFA, since 04-93.
Nancy Prial CFA, since 02-94.

Manager Experience	Dates Managed	Invest Obj	Std Dev	+/- Index
Robert C. Puff, Jr.				
20th Century Select Inv	01/83 - 12/94	G	17.53	-1.91
20th Century Balanced Inv	09/88 - 12/94	B	11.36	-1.37

History	1983	1984	1985	1986	1987	1988	1989	1990	1991	1992	1993	1994	
NAV	---	---	---	---	5.40	6.22	7.64	6.83	9.17	9.31	10.61	9.35	
Total Return %	---	---	---	---	9.36 *	16.43	35.06	-9.16	35.98	10.14	20.43	-6.32	
+/- S&P 500	---	---	---	---	5.33 *	-0.18	3.38	-6.04	5.50	2.52	10.37	-7.63	
+/- Wilshire 5000	---	---	---	---	---	-1.51	5.89	-2.98	1.77	1.17	9.14	-6.25	
Income Return %	---	---	---	---	0.27	1.25	0.87	1.44	1.72	1.02	0.68	0.36	
Capital Return %	---	---	---	---	9.09	15.19	34.19	-10.60	34.26	9.12	19.75	-6.68	
Total Rtn % Rank All	---	---	---	---	---	23	7	82	18	21	16	74	
Total Rtn % Rank Obj	---	---	---	---	---	45	17	80	44	36	15	81	
Income $	---	---	---	---	0.01	0.07	0.07	0.11	0.11	0.09	0.07	0.03	
Capital Gains $	---	---	---	---	0.00	0.00	0.69	0.00	0.00	0.68	0.51	0.54	
Expense Ratio %	---	---	---	---	---	1.00	1.00	1.00	1.00	1.00	1.00	1.00	
Income Ratio %	---	---	---	---	---	1.40	1.30	1.60	1.50	1.10	0.70	0.70	
Turnover Rate %	---	---	---	---	---	130	159	127	146	119	116	124	
Net Assets ($mil)	---	---	---	---	7.4	58.7	144.2	210.7	292.2	425.5	721.5	851.6	

Performance 12-31-94

	1st Qtr	2nd Qtr	3rd Qtr	4th Qtr	Total
1987	---	---	---	---	9.36 *
1988	7.59	9.12	-2.84	2.07	16.43
1989	7.40	10.78	15.00	-1.28	35.06
1990	-3.53	8.82	-17.08	4.36	-9.16
1991	17.28	-3.37	9.69	9.39	35.98
1992	2.40	-7.88	4.86	11.35	10.14
1993	8.81	0.39	9.73	0.46	20.43
1994	-3.96	-4.22	5.12	-3.12	-6.32

Bear Market Performance

Decile Rank (5-year period)

Worst ———————— Best

	Worst 3 Mo Period 1985-89	Worst 3 Mo Period 1990-94
20th Century Heritage Invest	---	-17.51
+/- S&P 500	---	-3.66
+/- Best Fit Index : SPMid400	---	0.91

Trailing Returns

	Total Return %	+/- S&P 500	+/- Wil 5000	% Rank All	% Rank Obj	Growth of $10,000
3 Mo	-3.12	-3.10	-2.35	84	81	9,688
6 Mo	1.84	-3.02	-2.78	28	73	10,184
1 Yr	-6.32	-7.63	-6.25	74	81	9,368
3 Yr Avg	7.51	1.24	0.90	23	35	12,426
5 Yr Avg	8.95	0.26	0.13	24	46	15,349
10 Yr Avg	---	---	---	---	---	---
15 Yr Avg	---	---	---	---	---	---

Operations

Address and Telephone	4500 Main Street P.O. Box 419200 Kansas City, MO 64141-6200 800-345-2021 / 816-531-5575
Advisor	Investors Research
Subadvisor	None
Distributor	Twentieth Century Investors
States Available	All
Report Grade	C
Income Distrib	Paid Annually
* Date of Inception	11-10-87
Fiscal Year End	October

Risk Analysis

Time Period	Load-Adj Return %	Risk % Rank [1] All	Risk % Rank [1] Obj	Morningstar [2] Return	Morningstar Risk	Morningstar Risk-Adj Rating
1 Yr	-6.32					
3 Yr	7.51	87	77	1.18 [3]	1.11	★★★
5 Yr	8.95	85	78	1.06 [3]	1.05	★★★
10 Yr	---	---	---	---	---	

Average Historical Rating (50 months)   3.7 ★ s

[1] 1 = low, 100 = high   [2] 1.00 = Equity Avg   [3] 1.00 = 90-day T-bill return

Other Measures

			Standard S&P 500	Best Fit SPMid400
Standard Deviation	11.87	Alpha	1.2	0.2
Mean	7.96	Beta	1.11	1.11
Sharpe Ratio	0.37	R-Squared	55	85

Investment Style

	Stock Portfolio Avg	Relative S&P 500
Price/Earnings Ratio	24.5	1.32
Price/Book Ratio	3.1	0.92
5 Yr Earnings Gr %	4.2	0.76
Return on Assets %	8.0	1.07
Debt % Total Cap	27.1	0.96
Med Mkt Cap ($mil)	1456	0.11

Style
Value Blend Growth
Size Large Med Small

Diversification Value for Portfolio Types

Large Cap: Low	Small Cap: Low	Bond: High	Balanced: Low	Diversified: Low

Expenses & Fees

Sales Fees	0.00% front
	0.00% deferred
	0.00% 12b-1
Management Fee	1.00% flat fee
3-,5-,10-yr Expense Projections	$32, $55, $122
Annual Brokerage Cost	---

Portfolio 09-30-94

Total Stocks: 72
Total Fixed-Income: 2

Share Chg (06-94) 000	Amount 000		Value $000	% Net Assets
950	1150	Mylan Laboratories	29325	3.27
100	1350	Brunswick	27169	3.03
0	750	HBO	25594	2.85
0	8250	STET	25545	2.84
125	375	Alco Standard	23297	2.59
0	600	Varian Associates	21900	2.44
0	800	Manor Care	21300	2.37
75	600	Pep Boys-Manny Moe & Jack	20850	2.32
0	775	Mori Seiki	20656	2.30
-50	350	Rohm & Haas	19994	2.23
	125	Dell Computers Pfd $7.	19813	2.21
-175	375	AGCO	18797	2.09
300	300	Nokia (ADR)	17550	1.95
0	325	Millipore	17469	1.95
50	550	Lyondell Petrochemical	17119	1.91
325	650	Kennametal	16981	1.89
200	2300	Itochu	16835	1.87
-150	600	Shared Medical Systems	16575	1.85
221	422	Wabash National	15512	1.73
75	425	La Quinta Inns	15247	1.70
475	475	Federal Paper Board	14963	1.67
350	350	York International	14569	1.62
375	375	Tektronix	14531	1.62
550	550	Circuit City Stores	14231	1.58
325	325	Potash of Saskatchewan	13284	1.48

Composition % 12-31-94

Cash	3.1	Preferreds	4.2
Stocks	92.0	Convertibles	0.0
Bonds	0.7	Other	0.0

Tax Analysis

	Tax-Adj Historical Return %	% Pretax Return
3 Yr Avg	5.60	73.2
5 Yr Avg	7.59	82.5
10 Yr Avg	---	---
Potential Capital Gain Exposure (% of assets)		4%

Most Similar Funds in MF500

Founders Frontier	Strong Fit
MainStay Capital Apprec B	Fair Fit
Founders Special	Fair Fit

Index Allocation

	% of Stocks
S&P 500	37.2
S&P MidCap 400	31.6
U.S. Small Cap	13.2
Foreign	18.0

Sector Weightings

	% of Stocks	Relative S&P 500
Utilities	4.0	0.32
Energy	3.7	0.36
Financials	3.2	0.30
Industrial Cyclicals	39.0	2.38
Consumer Durables	10.8	1.74
Consumer Staples	1.9	0.15
Services	6.3	0.78
Retail	5.6	0.96
Health	7.4	0.85
Technology	18.3	2.00

Min Purchase

Min Initial Purchase	$2500 (Addt'l: $50)
Min IRA Purchase	None (Addt'l: $50)
Min Auto Invest Plan	$50 (Systematic Inv: $50)

20th Century Intl Equity

	Ticker	Load	NAV	Yield	SEC Yield	Assets	Objective
	TWIEX	None	6.96	0.0%	N/A	1272.4	Foreign Stock

Twentieth Century International Equity seeks capital growth. The fund invests primarily in common stocks of foreign companies that meet certain fundamental and technical standards and have potential for capital appreciation; these criteria come before considerations of the economic and political situation of the issuer's country or region. However, to maintain diversity, the fund invests at least 65% of its assets in common stocks of issuers from at least three countries outside the United States. The fund may enter into forward foreign-currency-exchange contracts.

Manager's Investment Style

Management follows an aggressive growth strategy, using a bottom-up style of investing in companies with rapid, yet sustainable, growth rates. While management may shy away from emerging markets in favor of more-established regions, it will consider companies in underdeveloped countries when the companies exhibit sustainable growth.

Fund Manager(s)

Management Team

Manager Experience

	Dates Managed	Invest Obj	Std Dev	+/- Index
Theodore J. Tyson				
20th Century Intl Emrg Gr	03/94 - 12/94	WF	12.47	2.30
Mark S. Kopinski				
20th Century Intl Emrg Gr	03/94 - 12/94	WF	12.47	2.30

Historical Profile

Return	Above Average
Risk	Average
Rating	★★★★ Above Average

Investment Style History
Equity

Average % Stocks Held in Portfolio

95% 92% 93% 93%

Growth of $10,000

IIII Value of Fund ($000)
— Value of Index ($000)
MSEASEA

▼ Manager Change
▽ Partial Manager Change
► Mgr Unknown After
◄ Mgr Unknown Before

Performance Quartile (Within Objective)

	1983	1984	1985	1986	1987	1988	1989	1990	1991	1992	1993	1994	History
	---	---	---	---	---	---	---	---	5.61	5.69	7.70	6.96	NAV
	---	---	---	---	---	---	---	---	10.14 *	4.83	42.65	-4.76	Total Return %
	---	---	---	---	---	---	---	---	-1.18 *	-2.79	32.59	-6.07	+/- S&P 500
	---	---	---	---	---	---	---	---	---	17.00	10.09	-12.53	+/- MSCI EAFE
	---	---	---	---	---	---	---	---	0.14	3.40	0.00	0.00	Income Return %
	---	---	---	---	---	---	---	---	10.00	1.43	42.65	-4.76	Capital Return %
	---	---	---	---	---	---	---	---	---	77	4	61	Total Rtn % Rank All
	---	---	---	---	---	---	---	---	---	2	33	64	Total Rtn % Rank Obj
	---	---	---	---	---	---	---	---	0.01	0.19	0.00	0.00	Income $
	---	---	---	---	---	---	---	---	0.00	0.00	0.40	0.37	Capital Gains $
	---	---	---	---	---	---	---	---	1.87	1.91	1.90	1.90	Expense Ratio %
	---	---	---	---	---	---	---	---	0.43	0.95	-0.34	-0.38	Income Ratio %
	---	---	---	---	---	---	---	---	113	180	255	282	Turnover Rate %
	---	---	---	---	---	---	---	---	48.8	222.8	944.5	1272.4	Net Assets ($mil)

Performance 12-31-94

	1st Qtr	2nd Qtr	3rd Qtr	4th Qtr	Total
1987	---	---	---	---	---
1988	---	---	---	---	---
1989	---	---	---	---	---
1990	---	---	---	---	---
1991	---	---	6.61	5.59	10.14 *
1992	5.70	6.07	-4.13	-2.48	4.83
1993	8.61	4.21	6.52	18.32	42.65
1994	-3.64	1.35	3.59	-5.86	-4.76

Bear Market Performance

Decile Rank (5-year period)

Worst ———————————————— Best

	Worst 3 Mo Period 1985-89	Worst 3 Mo Period 1990-94
20th Century Intl Equity	---	---
+/- S&P 500	---	---
+/- Best Fit Index :	---	---

Trailing Returns

	Total Return %	+/- S&P 500	+/- MSCI EAFE	% Rank All	% Rank Obj	Growth of $10,000
3 Mo	-5.86	-5.84	-4.84	94	59	9,414
6 Mo	-2.48	-7.34	-1.55	91	70	9,752
1 Yr	-4.76	-6.07	-12.53	61	64	9,524
3 Yr Avg	12.51	6.24	4.65	7	18	14,242
5 Yr Avg	---	---	---	---	---	---
10 Yr Avg	---	---	---	---	---	---
15 Yr Avg	---	---	---	---	---	---

Operations

Address and Telephone	4500 Main Street P.O. Box 419200
	Kansas City, MO 64141-6200
	800-345-2021 / 816-531-5575
Advisor	Investors Research
Subadvisor	None
Distributor	Twentieth Century Investors
States Available	All
Report Grade	B
Income Distrib	Paid Annually
* Date of Inception	05-09-91
Fiscal Year End	November

Risk Analysis

Time Period	Load-Adj Return %	Risk % Rank [1] All	Obj	Morningstar [2] Return	Morningstar Risk	Morningstar Risk-Adj Rating
1 Yr	-4.76					
3 Yr	12.51	77	8	2.81 [3]	0.89	★★★★
5 Yr	---	---	---	---	---	
10 Yr	---	---	---	---	---	

Average Historical Rating (8 months) 4.8 ★s

[1] 1 = low, 100 = high [2] 1.00 = Equity Avg [3] 1.00 = 90-day T-bill return

Other Measures

	Standard S&P 500	Best Fit MSEASEA
Standard Deviation	12.03	
Mean	12.55	
Sharpe Ratio	0.75	
Alpha	7.1	3.9
Beta	0.73	0.82
R-Squared	23	82

Investment Style

	Stock Portfolio Avg	Rel MSCI EAFE	Rel Obj
Price/Earnings Ratio	34.7	0.94	1.23
Price/Cash Flow	13.6#	0.87	1.01
Price/Book Ratio	2.4	0.92	0.81
5 Yr Earnings Gr %	-2.0#	---	-0.51
Return on Assets %	4.0#	0.88	0.56
Debt % Total Cap	34.0	1.00	1.23
Med Mkt Cap ($mil)	4737	0.40	0.92

Style V B G — Size L M S

figure is based on 50% or less of stocks

Diversification Value for Portfolio Types

Large Cap: High	Small Cap: High	Bond: High	Balanced: High	Diversified: Medium

Expenses & Fees

Sales Fees	0.00% front
	0.00% deferred
	0.00% 12b-1
Management Fee	1.90% flat fee
3-,5-,10-yr Expense Projections	$60, $102, $222
Annual Brokerage Cost	---

Min Initial Purchase	$2500 (Addt'l: $50)
Min IRA Purchase	None (Addt'l: $50)
Min Auto Invest Plan	$50 (Systematic Inv: $50)

Portfolio 09-30-94

Share Chg (06-94) 000	Amount 000	Total Stocks: 121 Total Fixed-Income: 1	Value $000	% Net Assets
0	600	Lyonnaise Des Eaux-Dumez	53220	3.94
1500	6000	Mitsubishi Heavy Industries	46643	3.45
10	136	Veba	45091	3.33
1400	5500	Itochu	40257	2.98
1750	12000	STET	37157	2.75
1601	2001	Volvo Cl B	36517	2.70
50	456	Wolters Kluwer	32368	2.39
0	110	Mannesmann (Germany)	27594	2.04
1200	2000	Mitsubishi Estate	24028	1.78
2004	2004	Grupo Carso	22743	1.68
21800	FHLMC 10%		21725	1.61
-1315	685	Philips Electronics (ADR)	20804	1.54
800	800	Bell Cablemedia	20600	1.52
15	80	Man	20300	1.50
200	2700	NTN	19790	1.46
11049	11049	TNT	19550	1.45
200	3400	Sanyo Electric	19291	1.43
0	2200	Sasol	18544	1.37
500	500	BCE (Canada)	17970	1.33
-700	2300	Toray Industries	17880	1.32

Regional Exposure 06-30-94

% of Stocks

Europe	35	Pacific Rim	9
Japan	10	Other	10
Latin Amer	10		

Composition % 12-31-94

Cash	5.0	Preferreds	0.5
Stocks	93.6	Convertibles	0.0
Bonds	0.9	Other	0.0

Tax Analysis

	Tax-Adj Historical Return %	% Pretax Return
3 Yr Avg	11.08	87.4
5 Yr Avg	---	---
10 Yr Avg	---	---
Potential Capital Gain Exposure (% of assets)		1%

Most Similar Funds in MF500

T. Rowe Price Intl Stock	Strong Fit
Vanguard Intl Growth	Fair Fit
Templeton Foreign	Fair Fit

Country Exposure 06-30-94

% of Stocks

Japan	35
Netherlands	10
Germany	10
Sweden	7
United Kingdom	6

Total Number of Countries: 23
Hedging Policy: Occasional

Sector Weightings

	% of Stocks	Relative S&P 500
Utilities	6.6	0.74
Energy	0.9	0.21
Financials	10.9	0.58
Industrial Cyclicals	42.5	1.70
Consumer Durables	11.2	1.04
Consumer Staples	1.5	0.22
Services	19.0	1.74
Retail	3.7	0.64
Health	1.4	0.40
Technology	2.3	0.44

512

20th Century Ultra Investors

	Ticker	Load	NAV	Yield	SEC Yield	Assets	Objective
	TWCUX	None	19.95	0.0%	N/A	9850.8	Aggr. Growth

Twentieth Century Ultra Investors seeks capital growth.

The fund typically invests at least 90% of its assets in equity securities selected for their appreciation potential. The majority of these securities are common stocks issued by mid-cap companies that meet management's standards for earnings and revenue trends. The fund may purchase securities only of companies that have operated continuously for three or more years.

Historical Profile

Return	High
Risk	High
Rating	★★★★ Above Average

Investment Style History
Equity
Average % Stocks Held in Portfolio

99% 99% 99% 99% 97% 94% 93% 92%

Growth of $10,000

|||| Value of Fund ($000)
— Value of Index ($000) S&P 500
▼ Manager Change
▽ Partial Manager Change
► Mgr Unknown After
◄ Mgr Unknown Before

Performance Quartile (Within Objective)

Manager's Investment Style

The management team follows a strict bottom-up approach, investing in issues with high, sustainable growth rates. The fund holds a hefty stake in technology stocks, for which management pays a high premium. The fund has avoided large losses in bear markets by remaining well diversified in the technology sector. Management also spices up the fund's portfolio with foreign stocks, holding upwards of 30% of assets in foreign companies chosen from the 20th Century International Equity portfolio.

Fund Manager(s)

James E. Stowers III, since 11-81.
Christopher K. Boyd CFA, since 01-91.
Derek V. Felske CFA, since 09-93.

Manager Experience

	Dates Managed	Invest Obj	Std Dev	+/- Index
James E. Stowers III				
20th Century Growth Inv	01/81 - 12/94	G	21.37	-1.04
20th Century Vista Inv	11/83 - 12/94	SC	26.92	-1.68

1983	1984	1985	1986	1987	1988	1989	1990	1991	1992	1993	1994	History
8.21	6.41	8.10	8.92	6.23	7.06	8.53	9.30	17.34	17.56	21.39	19.95	NAV
26.89	-19.45	26.37	10.26	6.69	13.32	36.94	9.36	86.45	1.27	21.81	-3.62	Total Return %
4.43	-25.71	-5.37	-8.42	1.43	-3.29	5.25	12.48	55.97	-6.35	11.75	-4.93	+/- S&P 500
---	---	-17.73	-5.65	-1.50	10.20	-7.21	12.99	22.92	43.00	-10.49	7.27	-0.96	+/- Wilshire 4500
0.00	0.00	0.00	0.14	0.08	0.00	2.37	0.00	0.00	0.00	0.00	0.00	Income Return %
26.89	-19.45	26.37	10.12	6.61	13.32	34.57	9.36	86.45	1.27	21.81	-3.62	Capital Return %
17	97	41	84	17	36	6	7	1	88	14	50	Total Rtn % Rank All
10	71	66	57	20	47	16	2	2	77	32	58	Total Rtn % Rank Obj
0.00	0.00	0.00	0.01	0.01	0.00	0.20	0.00	0.00	0.00	0.00	0.00	Income $
0.00	0.26	0.00	0.00	3.26	0.00	0.95	0.03	0.00	0.00	0.00	0.65	Capital Gains $
1.02	1.01	1.01	1.01	1.00	1.00	1.00	1.00	1.00	1.00	1.00	1.00	Expense Ratio %
-0.40	-0.30	0.10	0.00	-0.50	-0.30	2.21	-0.30	-0.50	-0.40	-0.60	-0.50	Income Ratio %
58	93	100	99	137	140	132	141	42	59	53	65	Turnover Rate %
506.0	445.6	385.4	286.9	247.8	255.6	345.5	458.3	2939.7	5299.3	8353.2	9850.8	Net Assets ($mil)

Performance 12-31-94

	1st Qtr	2nd Qtr	3rd Qtr	4th Qtr	Total
1987	40.80	-3.82	7.46	-26.68	6.69
1988	10.59	10.16	-7.77	0.86	13.32
1989	18.13	10.43	11.40	-5.77	36.94
1990	-4.34	16.05	-16.16	17.49	9.36
1991	40.75	-6.19	18.57	19.09	86.45
1992	-6.92	-11.03	2.65	19.13	1.27
1993	-0.11	14.03	10.25	-2.99	21.81
1994	-1.82	-8.29	5.14	1.81	-3.62

Bear Market Performance

Decile Rank (5-year period)

Worst — Best

	Worst 3 Mo Period 1985-89	Worst 3 Mo Period 1990-94
20th Century Ultra Investors	-38.54	-16.25
+/- S&P 500	-8.96	-2.41
+/- Best Fit Index : Wil 4500	-8.40	3.15

Trailing Returns

	Total Return %	+/- S&P 500	+/- Wil 4500	% Rank All	% Rank Obj	Growth of $10,000
3 Mo	1.81	1.83	4.31	4	20	10,181
6 Mo	7.04	2.18	2.85	7	56	10,704
1 Yr	-3.62	-4.93	-0.96	50	58	9,638
3 Yr Avg	5.94	-0.33	-1.67	34	53	11,889
5 Yr Avg	19.38	10.68	10.28	1	4	24,243
10 Yr Avg	18.78	4.40	6.15	2	3	55,922
15 Yr Avg	---	---	---	---	---	---

Operations

Address and Telephone	4500 Main Street P.O. Box 419200
	Kansas City, MO 64141-6200
	800-345-2021 / 816-531-5575
Advisor	Investors Research
Subadvisor	None
Distributor	Twentieth Century Investors
States Available	All
Report Grade	C
Income Distrib	Paid Annually
Date of Inception	11-02-81
Fiscal Year End	October

Min Initial Purchase	$2500 (Addt'l: $50)
Min IRA Purchase	None (Addt'l: None)
Min Auto Invest Plan	$50 (Systematic Inv: $50)

Expenses & Fees

Sales Fees	0.00% front
	0.00% deferred
	0.00% 12b-1
Management Fee	1.00% flat fee
3-,5-,10-yr Expense Projections	$32, $55, $122
Annual Brokerage Cost	---

Risk Analysis

Time Period	Load-Adj Return %	Risk % Rank[1] All	Risk % Rank[1] Obj	Morningstar[2] Return	Morningstar Risk	Morningstar Risk-Adj Rating
1 Yr	-3.62					
3 Yr	5.94	98	85	0.70[3]	1.67	★★
5 Yr	19.38	96	76	4.49[3]	1.43	★★★★★
10 Yr	18.78	97	88	2.49	1.52	★★★★★
Average Historical Rating (109 months)				3.2 ★s		

[1] 1 = low, 100 = high   [2] 1.00 = Equity Avg   [3] 1.00 = 90-day T-bill return

Other Measures

			Standard S&P 500	Best Fit Wil 4500
Standard Deviation	17.08	Alpha	-0.1	-2.9
Mean	7.23	Beta	1.31	1.55
Sharpe Ratio	0.22	R-Squared	37	79

Investment Style

	Stock Portfolio Avg	Relative S&P 500
Price/Earnings Ratio	30.7	1.66
Price/Book Ratio	5.0	1.48
5 Yr Earnings Gr %	13.7#	2.47
Return on Assets %	11.8	1.58
Debt % Total Cap	20.5	0.72
Med Mkt Cap ($mil)	7360	0.57

figure is based on 50% or less of stocks

Style Value Blend Growth
Size Large Med Small

Diversification Value for Portfolio Types

Large Cap: Medium	Small Cap: Low	Bond: High	Balanced: Medium	Diversified: Medium

Portfolio 09-30-94

Total Stocks: 148
Total Fixed-Income: 0

Share Chg (06-94) 000	Amount 000		Value $000	% Net Assets
150	9150	Oracle Systems	394594	3.97
0	350	BBC Brown Boveri (Reg)	301280	3.03
120	4795	Microsoft	269419	2.71
-1095	10760	Nomura Securities	222696	2.24
0	10750	Toyota Motor	220318	2.22
3089	5800	3Com	217500	2.19
0	3900	United HealthCare	206700	2.08
-1900	4400	Applied Materials	204600	2.06
6600	6600	Philips Electronics	200475	2.02
3650	3650	Motorola	192538	1.94
2400	3600	Amgen	191945	1.93
-1200	5800	Compaq Computer	189225	1.90
0	3950	Sybase	181206	1.82
1100	3100	AT & T	167400	1.68
1975	3875	Home Depot	162750	1.64
1900	31400	Hutchison Whampoa	148320	1.49
700	8450	Matsushita Electric Indl	134791	1.36
2550	2550	Johnson & Johnson	131644	1.32
5700	7125	Volvo Cl B	130025	1.31
46000	46000	Telecom Italia	129619	1.30
925	1100	Royal Dutch Petroleum	118113	1.19
117	2650	Computer Associates Intl	117925	1.19
3050	3050	Dell Computer	114184	1.15
-1000	2750	Murata Manufacturing	106335	1.07
2735	3735	Ford Motor	103646	1.04

Composition % 12-31-94

Cash	4.2	Preferreds	0.0
Stocks	95.8	Convertibles	0.0
Bonds	0.0	Other	0.0

Tax Analysis

	Tax-Adj Historical Return %	% Pretax Return
3 Yr Avg	5.63	94.5
5 Yr Avg	19.14	98.3
10 Yr Avg	17.00	82.9
Potential Capital Gain Exposure (% of assets)		17%

Most Similar Funds in MF500

Alger Small Capitalization	Fair Fit
Berger 100	Fair Fit
MainStay Capital Apprec B	Fair Fit

Index Allocation

	% of Stocks
S&P 500	36.4
S&P MidCap 400	17.2
U.S. Small Cap	15.7
Foreign	33.6

Sector Weightings

	% of Stocks	Relative S&P 500
Utilities	6.6	0.53
Energy	3.4	0.33
Financials	8.5	0.81
Industrial Cyclicals	5.1	0.31
Consumer Durables	14.9	2.40
Consumer Staples	1.6	0.13
Services	6.4	0.78
Retail	2.3	0.39
Health	10.4	1.20
Technology	40.9	4.47

20th Century Value

	Ticker	Load	NAV	Yield	SEC Yield	Assets	Objective
	TWVLX	None	4.92	2.4%	2.49%	153.1	Growth/Inc.

Twentieth Century Value Fund seeks long-term capital appreciation. Income is a secondary objective.

The fund usually invests at least 80% of its assets in equity securities issued by well-established medium- and large-size companies. These securities are characterized by lower price/cash-flow and/or price/book ratios relative to the equity market. Up to 25% of fund assets may be invested in foreign issues, including government obligations and American depositary receipts. The fund may also invest up to 15% of its assets in convertible securities rated at least BB. It may also invest a portion of its assets in investment-grade straight debt.

Manager's Investment Style

Management seeks out stocks that fulfill at least two of four criteria: low P/E ratio, low price/book ratio, low price/cash flow ratio, or a high yield. This method, ideally, gives the portfolio low price risk and above-average yields, which can help dampen volatility. Management also tries to diversify across all market caps and sectors. Management has also shown a willingness to invest in convertible bonds.

Fund Manager(s)

Peter A. Zuger CFA(1980), since 09-93. Birthdate: 06-48. BA, C. of William & Mary 1970 BS, Virginia Commonwealth U. 1974

Philip N. Davidson CFA(1994), since 09-93.

Manager Experience	Dates Managed	Invest Obj	Std Dev	+/- Index
Philip N. Davidson				
20th Century Equity-Inc	08/94 - 12/94	EI	11.05	-0.51
Peter A. Zuger				
20th Century Equity-Inc	08/94 - 12/94	EI	11.05	-0.51

Historical Profile

Return ---
Risk ---
Rating
Not Rated

	1983	1984	1985	1986	1987	1988	1989	1990	1991	1992	1993	1994	History
	---	---	---	---	---	---	---	---	---	---	5.12	4.92	NAV
	---	---	---	---	---	---	---	---	---	---	3.07 *	3.99	Total Return %
	---	---	---	---	---	---	---	---	---	---	1.45 *	2.68	+/- S&P 500
	---	---	---	---	---	---	---	---	---	---		4.06	+/- Wilshire 5000
	---	---	---	---	---	---	---	---	---	---	0.87	2.50	Income Return %
	---	---	---	---	---	---	---	---	---	---	2.20	1.50	Capital Return %
	---	---	---	---	---	---	---	---	---	---		5	Total Rtn % Rank All
	---	---	---	---	---	---	---	---	---	---		5	Total Rtn % Rank Obj
	---	---	---	---	---	---	---	---	---	---	0.04	0.12	Income $
	---	---	---	---	---	---	---	---	---	---	0.00	0.27	Capital Gains $
	---	---	---	---	---	---	---	---	---	---		1.00	Expense Ratio %
	---	---	---	---	---	---	---	---	---	---		3.37	Income Ratio %
	---	---	---	---	---	---	---	---	---	---		---	Turnover Rate %
	---	---	---	---	---	---	---	---	---	---	61.3	153.1	Net Assets ($mil)

Investment Style History Equity
Average % Stocks Held in Portfolio

96% 87%

Growth of $10,000
||| Value of Fund ($000)
— Value of Index ($000) S&P 500
▼ Manager Change
▽ Partial Manager Change
► Mgr Unknown After
◄ Mgr Unknown Before

Performance Quartile (Within Objective)

Performance 12-31-94

	1st Qtr	2nd Qtr	3rd Qtr	4th Qtr	Total
1987	---	---	---	---	---
1988	---	---	---	---	---
1989	---	---	---	---	---
1990	---	---	---	---	---
1991	---	---	---	---	---
1992	---	---	---	---	---
1993	---	---	---	3.07	3.07 *
1994	-2.17	1.85	4.59	-0.22	3.99

Bear Market Performance

Decile Rank (5-year period)

Worst — Best

	Worst 3 Mo Period 1985-89	Worst 3 Mo Period 1990-94
20th Century Value	---	---
+/- S&P 500	---	---
+/- Best Fit Index :	---	---

Trailing Returns

	Total Return %	+/- S&P 500	+/- Wil 5000	% Rank All	% Rank Obj	Growth of $10,000
3 Mo	-0.22	-0.20	0.55	28	26	9,978
6 Mo	4.37	-0.50	-0.26	14	24	10,437
1 Yr	3.99	2.68	4.06	5	5	10,399
3 Yr Avg	---	---	---	---	---	---
5 Yr Avg	---	---	---	---	---	---
10 Yr Avg	---	---	---	---	---	---
15 Yr Avg	---	---	---	---	---	---

Operations

Address and Telephone	4500 Main Street P.O. Box 419200 Kansas City, MO 64141-6200 800-345-2021 / 816-531-5575
Advisor	Twentieth Century Investors
Subadvisor	None
Distributor	Twentieth Century Capital
States Available	All
Report Grade	D
Income Distrib	Paid Quarterly
* Date of Inception	09-01-93
Fiscal Year End	March

Risk Analysis

Time Period	Load-Adj Return %	Risk % Rank [1] All	Risk % Rank [1] Obj	Morningstar [2] Return	Morningstar Risk	Morningstar Risk-Adj Rating
1 Yr	3.99					
3 Yr	---	---	---	---	---	
5 Yr	---	---	---	---	---	
10 Yr	---	---	---	---	---	

Average Historical Rating ---

[1] 1 = low, 100 = high [2] 1.00 = Equity Avg [3] 1.00 = 90-day T-bill return

Other Measures

			Standard S&P 500	Best Fit
Standard Deviation	---	Alpha	---	---
Mean	---	Beta	---	---
Sharpe Ratio	---	R-Squared	---	---

Investment Style

	Stock Portfolio Avg	Relative S&P 500
Price/Earnings Ratio	20.1	1.09
Price/Book Ratio	1.7	0.49
5 Yr Earnings Gr %	0.7	0.12
Return on Assets %	4.5	0.60
Debt % Total Cap	29.5	1.04
Med Mkt Cap ($mil)	2884	0.22

Style
Value Blend Growth
Size Large Med Small

Diversification Value for Portfolio Types

Large Cap: Small Cap: Bond: Balanced: Diversified:

Expenses & Fees

Sales Fees	0.00% front
	0.00% deferred
	0.00% 12b-1
Management Fee	1.00% flat fee
3-,5-,10-yr Expense Projections	$32, $55, $122
Annual Brokerage Cost	---

Portfolio 09-30-94

Total Stocks: 42
Total Fixed-Income: 5

Share Chg (06-94) 000	Amount 000		Value $000	% Net Assets
	102	Sears Roebuck Cv Pfd $3.75	5729	4.36
28	74	Union Pacific	3968	3.02
58	146	Dillard Department Stores A	3895	2.97
30	68	Exxon	3890	2.96
40	180	Giant Food Cl A	3868	2.95
	95	Tenneco Cv Pfd $2.80	3863	2.94
133	133	General Public Utilities	3294	2.51
25	124	Archer-Daniels-Midland	3219	2.45
	59	Unocal Cv Pfd $3.50	3193	2.43
10	53	American Home Products	3180	2.42
4	106	Argonaut Group	3152	2.40
111	111	Ball	3138	2.39
12	52	Texaco	3126	2.38
28	85	Melville	3028	2.31
19	138	CMS Energy	2997	2.28
53	53	MAPCO	2974	2.26
6	33	Loews	2943	2.24
95	95	Boatmen's Bancshares	2942	2.24
8	103	Florida Progress	2904	2.21
7	45	CNA Financial	2860	2.18
-46	61	Security Capital	2809	2.14
13	139	Sierra Pacific Resources	2763	2.10
70	146	Baker Hughes	2725	2.08
0	73	Seafield Capital	2712	2.07
54	177	Gerber Scientific	2672	2.04

Composition % 12-31-94

Cash	2.3	Preferreds	5.2
Stocks	90.6	Convertibles	0.0
Bonds	1.9	Other	0.0

Tax Analysis

	Tax-Adj Historical Return %	% Pretax Return
3 Yr Avg	---	---
5 Yr Avg	---	---
10 Yr Avg	---	---
Potential Capital Gain Exposure (% of assets)		-4%

Most Similar Funds in MF500

Fund lacks three-year record

Index Allocation

	% of Stocks
S&P 500	51.8
S&P MidCap 400	14.3
U.S. Small Cap	32.8
Foreign	1.2

Sector Weightings

	% of Stocks	Relative S&P 500
Utilities	10.8	0.87
Energy	15.8	1.55
Financials	24.3	2.30
Industrial Cyclicals	10.0	0.61
Consumer Durables	4.6	0.74
Consumer Staples	8.2	0.66
Services	8.8	1.09
Retail	9.7	1.67
Health	5.3	0.61
Technology	2.4	0.26

Min Purchase

Min Initial Purchase	$2500 (Addt'l: $50)
Min IRA Purchase	None (Addt'l: $50)
Min Auto Invest Plan	$50 (Systematic Inv: $50)

514

U.S. Government Securities

Ticker	Load	NAV	Yield	SEC Yield	Assets	Objective
AMUSX	4.75%	12.69	8.0%	6.49%	1290.1	Gvt General

U.S. Government Securities Fund seeks current income, consistent with prudent investment risk and preservation of capital.

The fund invests primarily in securities guaranteed by the U.S. government, including (but not limited to) Government National Mortgage Association (GNMA) mortgage-backed securities. The fund is not required to maintain any particular average effective portfolio maturity, and its average maturity varies according to current and anticipated market conditions.

Prior to November 15, 1990, the fund was named U.S. Government Guaranteed Securities Fund.

Manager's Investment Style

This fund produces high yields at a price. Management produces lofty yields by buying premium bonds with 10% coupons. To further bump up its payouts, the fund refrains from fully amortizing these coupons when making distributions. This is not a problem as long as the securities appreciate enough to maintain NAV, but during periods of rising interest rates the fund loses its cushion against depreciating premiums.

Fund Manager(s)

Abner D. Goldstine, since 10-85.
John H. Smet, since 01-87.
John Ressner, since 10-92.
Richard T. Schotte, since 1993.

Manager Experience	Dates Managed	Invest Obj	Std Dev	+/- Index
Abner D. Goldstine				
Income Fund of America	11/73 - 12/94	I	9.53	-0.15
Bond Fund of America	05/74 - 12/94	CG	6.62	0.65

Historical Profile

Return Average
Risk Average
Rating ★★★
Neutral

	24	12	11	10	14	6	9	5

Growth of $10,000

|||| Value of Fund ($000)
— Value of Index ($000)
LB Govt
▼ Manager Change
▽ Partial Manager Change
► Mgr Unknown After
◄ Mgr Unknown Before

Performance Quartile
(Within Objective)

Investment Style History
Fixed Income
Income Rtn % Rank Obj

	1983	1984	1985	1986	1987	1988	1989	1990	1991	1992	1993	1994	History
	---	---	14.76	14.96	13.74	13.34	13.53	13.50	14.13	13.99	14.37	12.69	NAV
	---	---	4.83 *	12.08	0.97	6.92	11.71	9.59	14.16	7.60	10.45	-4.65	Total Return %
	---	---	---	-3.17	-1.78	-0.96	-2.83	0.65	-1.84	0.35	0.70	-1.73	+/- LB Aggregate
	---	---	---	-3.23	-1.22	-0.11	-2.51	0.88	-1.16	0.37	-0.21	-1.27	+/- LB Government
	---	---	1.55	10.32	9.13	9.83	10.29	9.82	9.49	8.59	7.73	7.04	Income Return %
	---	---	3.29	1.76	-8.16	-2.91	1.42	-0.22	4.67	-0.99	2.72	-11.69	Capital Return %
	---	---	---	73	51	81	60	6	62	51	63	60	Total Rtn % Rank All
	---	---	---	46	66	37	52	18	52	12	14	72	Total Rtn % Rank Obj
	---	---	0.22	1.44	1.34	1.33	1.30	1.25	1.18	1.16	1.05	1.02	Income $
	---	---	0.00	0.06	0.00	0.00	0.00	0.00	0.00	0.00	0.00	0.00	Capital Gains $
	---	---	---	1.00	1.00	0.97	0.87	0.95	0.88	0.83	0.78		Expense Ratio %
	---	---	---	9.33	9.80	9.68	9.73	9.07	8.63	7.54	7.35		Income Ratio %
	---	---	---	68	89	101	50	53	45	35	72		Turnover Rate %
	---	---	37.4	295.0	371.0	442.9	555.4	734.8	1157.1	1359.6	1573.8	1290.1	Net Assets ($mil)

Performance 12-31-94

	1st Qtr	2nd Qtr	3rd Qtr	4th Qtr	Total
1987	1.53	-2.60	-3.96	6.31	0.97
1988	4.09	0.89	1.41	0.40	6.92
1989	0.94	5.77	1.48	3.10	11.71
1990	0.04	3.26	1.71	4.31	9.59
1991	1.94	1.50	4.99	5.09	14.16
1992	-1.63	3.55	5.16	0.44	7.60
1993	4.17	3.17	3.16	-0.38	10.45
1994	-3.91	-1.45	0.41	0.28	-4.65

Bear Market Performance

Decile Rank (5-year period)

Worst ———————— Best

	Worst 3 Mo Period 1985-89	Worst 3 Mo Period 1990-94
U.S. Government Securities	---	-6.08
+/- LB Aggregate	---	-1.15
+/- Best Fit Index : LB Govt	---	-1.00

Trailing Returns

	Total Return %	+/- LB Aggregate	+/- LB Govt	% Rank All	% Rank Obj	Growth of $10,000
3 Mo	0.28	-0.10	-0.08	15	30	10,028
6 Mo	0.69	-0.30	-0.10	43	30	10,069
1 Yr	-4.65	-1.73	-1.27	60	72	9,535
3 Yr Avg	4.25	-0.29	-0.41	64	14	11,331
5 Yr Avg	7.23	-0.40	-0.30	45	17	14,177
10 Yr Avg	---	---	---	---	---	---
15 Yr Avg	---	---	---	---	---	---

Operations

Address and Telephone	333 S. Hope Street
	Los Angeles, CA 90071
	800-421-4120 / 213-486-9200
Advisor	Capital Research & Management
Subadvisor	None
Distributor	American Funds Distributors
States Available	All plus GU,PR,VI
Report Grade	A
Income Distrib	Paid Monthly
* Date of Inception	10-17-85
Fiscal Year End	August

Risk Analysis

Time Period	Load-Adj Return %	Risk % Rank [1] All	Risk % Rank [1] Obj	Morningstar [2] Return	Morningstar Risk	Morningstar Risk-Adj Rating
1 Yr	-9.18					
3 Yr	2.58	28	59	-0.29 [3]	1.08	★★★
5 Yr	6.19	18	41	0.35 [3]	0.92	★★★
10 Yr	---	---	---	---	---	

Average Historical Rating (75 months) 2.9 ★s

[1] 1 = low, 100 = high [2] 1.00 = Taxable Avg [3] 1.00 = 90-day T-bill return

Other Measures

			Standard LB Agg	Best Fit LB Govt
Standard Deviation	4.43	Alpha	-0.3	-0.4
Mean	4.27	Beta	1.09	1.01
Sharpe Ratio	0.17	R-Squared	96	97

Investment Style

Interest-Rate Stance

Avg Effective Duration	5.3 Yrs
Avg Effective Maturity	6.2 Yrs

Maturity Short Intm Long
Quality High Med Low

Quality

Avg Credit Quality	AAA
Avg Weighted Coupon	10.33%
Avg Weighted Price	112.22% of Par

Diversification Value for Portfolio Types

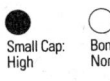 Large Cap: Medium   Small Cap: High Bond: None Balanced: Medium   Diversified: Medium

Tax Analysis

	Tax-Adj Historical Return %	% Pretax Return
3 Yr Avg	1.37	31.3
5 Yr Avg	4.30	56.1
10 Yr Avg	---	---
Potential Capital Gain Exposure (% of assets)		-10%

Most Similar Funds in MF500

Columbia Fixed-Income Secs	Strong Fit
Portico Bond Immdex Ret	Strong Fit
New England Bond Income A	Strong Fit

Portfolio 08-31-94

Total Stocks: 0
Total Fixed-Income: 113

Amount 000	Date of Maturity		Value $000	% Net Assets
85500	1995	US Treasury Note 11.5%	91178	6.64
71000	01-15-97	US Treasury Note 8%	73685	5.37
39000	2002	US Treasury Note 14.25%	55234	4.02
42000	11-15-02	US Treasury Note 11.625%	53648	3.91
39000	05-15-01	US Treasury Note 13.125%	51730	3.77
45000	04-15-97	US Treasury Note 8.5%	47313	3.45
49119	2024	GNMA ARM	46390	3.38
38000	04-15-96	US Treasury Note 9.375%	39959	2.91
28500	2001	US Treasury Note 13.375%	38444	2.80
26000	08-15-13	US Treasury Bond 12%	35990	2.62
35000	04-30-96	US Treasury Note 7.625%	35908	2.62
23500	11-15-11	US Treasury Bond 14%	35834	2.61
25500	11-15-04	US Treasury Bond 11.625%	33477	2.44
20500	11-15-09	US Treasury Bond 10.375%	24856	1.81
25182	2024	GNMA 7.5%	24306	1.77
21000	08-15-17	US Treasury Bond 8.875%	23786	1.73
24396	03-25-19	FNMA CMO PAC Z 6.5%	21522	1.57
16000	02-15-10	US Treasury Bond 11.75%	21037	1.53
20000	02-15-98	US Treasury Note 8.125%	20953	1.53
20095	2022	GNMA 9%	20871	1.52
19000	08-15-98	US Treasury Note 9.25%	20680	1.51
17250	10-15-97	US Treasury Note 8.75%	18331	1.34
17042	2023	FNMA 8.5%	17356	1.26
12500	11-15-14	US Treasury Bond 11.75%	17246	1.26
15000	05-15-09	US Treasury Bond 9.125%	16765	1.22

Composition % 12-31-94

Cash	10.7	Preferreds	0.0
Stocks	0.0	Convertibles	0.0
Bonds	89.3	Other	0.0

Coupon Range

	% of Bonds	Rel Obj
0%	0.7	0.52
0% to 8%	17.5	0.28
8% to 9%	19.3	1.26
9% to 10%	9.4	1.17
More than 10%	47.8	7.64
Not applicable	5.3	0.90

Sector Analysis 08-31-94

% of Bonds

US Treas	68	CMOs	6
GNMA mtgs	10	ARMs	4
FNMA mtgs	5	Other	2
FHLMC mtgs	6		

Min Initial Purchase / Expenses

Min Initial Purchase	$1000 (Addt'l: $50)
Min IRA Purchase	$250 (Addt'l: $50)
Min Auto Invest Plan	$50 (Systematic Inv: $50)

Expenses & Fees

Sales Fees	4.75% front
	0.00% deferred
	0.30% 12b-1
Management Fee	0.30% max./0.16% min.+3.00%I
3-,5-,10-yr Expense Projections	$71, $89, $140

UMB Stock

Ticker	Load	NAV	Yield	SEC Yield	Assets	Objective
UMBSX	None	15.01	2.4%	N/A	120.9	Growth

UMB Stock Fund seeks long-term growth of capital and dividend income; current yield is a secondary consideration.

The fund normally invests at least 80% of its assets (exclusive of cash) in common stocks. In selecting securities, the primary emphasis is on progressive, well-managed companies that are in growing industries and that have demonstrated a consistent and above-average ability to increase their earnings and dividends. The fund may at times invest in convertible securities, preferred stocks, or high-quality bonds. A portion of the fund's assets is typically maintained in cash or short-term instruments, including repurchase agreements.

Manager's Investment Style

Management follows a strategy that keeps the fund out of the red. By holding large amounts of cash and paying close attention to dividends, the fund is well positioned to survive a bearish market. Management seeks out companies that have been able to consistently increase both earnings and dividends. The resulting portfolio is a blend of both growth and value stocks. While this approach may not yield the highest short-term returns, it certainly does guarantee a smoother ride.

Fund Manager(s)

David B. Anderson, since 11-82. Birthdate: 11-47.
BS, U. of Missouri 1969 MA, Central Missouri State U. 1972

Manager Experience

	Dates Managed	Invest Obj	Std Dev	+/- Index
Not available.				

Historical Profile

Return	Average
Risk	Below Average
Rating	★★★ Neutral

Average % Stocks Held in Portfolio: 77% 78% 72% 70% 74% 74% 79% 76%

Investment Style History
Equity
Average % Stocks Held in Portfolio

Growth of $10,000

IIII Value of Fund ($000)
— Value of Index ($000) S&P 500
▼ Manager Change
▽ Partial Manager Change
► Mgr Unknown After
◄ Mgr Unknown Before

Performance Quartile (Within Objective)

1983	1984	1985	1986	1987	1988	1989	1990	1991	1992	1993	1994	History
11.34	11.20	12.74	12.78	11.87	12.62	13.87	12.76	15.40	15.77	16.24	15.01	NAV
23.73	5.90	23.20	12.36	5.53	13.87	19.06	-2.38	24.76	7.11	10.65	2.76	Total Return %
1.27	-0.36	-8.54	-6.32	0.27	-2.74	-12.62	0.73	-5.73	-0.51	0.60	1.44	+/- S&P 500
0.27	2.86	-9.37	-3.74	3.16	-4.07	-10.11	3.80	-9.45	-1.86	-0.63	2.83	+/- Wilshire 5000
8.84	2.56	4.77	4.07	4.85	3.94	4.61	4.22	4.01	2.59	2.16	2.57	Income Return %
14.89	3.34	18.42	8.29	0.68	9.94	14.45	-6.60	20.75	4.52	8.50	0.19	Capital Return %
28	47	53	72	20	32	37	63	36	56	62	8	Total Rtn % Rank All
39	19	81	71	31	56	81	37	84	57	54	15	Total Rtn % Rank Obj
0.86	0.26	0.50	0.51	0.63	0.47	0.58	0.58	0.48	0.39	0.34	0.39	Income $
0.00	0.47	0.45	1.01	1.12	0.41	0.53	0.21	0.01	0.31	0.82	1.26	Capital Gains $
0.85	0.87	0.88	0.87	0.87	0.86	0.87	0.88	0.85	0.86	0.87	0.87	Expense Ratio %
3.95	4.38	4.36	3.75	3.08	3.41	4.08	4.23	4.03	2.91	2.30	2.22	Income Ratio %
76	80	65	38	50	33	17	9	8	12	21	22	Turnover Rate %
11.8	14.6	23.8	34.3	39.6	41.0	45.3	45.1	65.3	85.7	114.6	120.9	Net Assets ($mil)

Performance 12-31-94

	1st Qtr	2nd Qtr	3rd Qtr	4th Qtr	Total
1987	17.83	2.90	6.96	-18.63	5.53
1988	5.56	4.31	1.04	2.36	13.87
1989	5.78	5.13	6.99	0.07	19.06
1990	-1.37	2.85	-9.72	6.58	-2.38
1991	12.15	0.64	4.24	6.05	24.76
1992	0.19	0.11	2.78	3.89	7.11
1993	3.68	0.57	1.52	4.53	10.65
1994	-1.72	1.01	3.89	-0.36	2.76

Bear Market Performance

Decile Rank (5-year period)

Worst ———————————————— Best

	Worst 3 Mo Period 1985-89	Worst 3 Mo Period 1990-94
UMB Stock	-24.98	-11.56
+/- S&P 500	4.60	2.28
+/- Best Fit Index : S&P 500	4.60	2.28

Trailing Returns

	Total Return %	+/- S&P 500	+/- Wil 5000	% Rank All	% Rank Obj	Growth of $10,000
3 Mo	-0.36	-0.35	0.41	31	29	9,964
6 Mo	3.51	-1.35	-1.11	18	55	10,351
1 Yr	2.76	1.44	2.83	8	15	10,276
3 Yr Avg	6.79	0.53	0.18	28	41	12,179
5 Yr Avg	8.20	-0.49	-0.61	31	58	14,832
10 Yr Avg	11.38	-3.01	-2.48	44	74	29,373
15 Yr Avg	---	---	---	---	---	---

Operations

Address and Telephone	Three Crown Ctr 2440 Pershing Rd
	Kansas City, MO 64108
	800-422-2766 / 816-471-5200
Advisor	Jones & Babson
Subadvisor	United Missouri Bank of Kansas City
Distributor	Jones & Babson
States Available	Selected states
Report Grade	C+
Income Distrib	Paid Semiannually
Date of Inception	11-18-82
Fiscal Year End	June

Risk Analysis

Time Period	Load-Adj Return %	Risk % Rank [1] All	Obj	Morningstar [2] Return	Morningstar Risk	Morningstar Risk-Adj Rating
1 Yr	2.76					
3 Yr	6.79	52	6	0.96 [3]	0.56	★★★
5 Yr	8.20	56	4	0.86 [3]	0.62	★★★★
10 Yr	11.38	50	8	0.77	0.72	★★★

Average Historical Rating (109 months) 3.2 ★s

[1] = low, 100 = high [2] 1.00 = Equity Avg [3] 1.00 = 90-day T-bill return

Other Measures

			Standard S&P 500	Best Fit S&P 500
Standard Deviation	6.39	Alpha	1.1	1.1
Mean	6.79	Beta	0.77	0.77
Sharpe Ratio	0.51	R-Squared	91	91

Investment Style

	Stock Portfolio Avg	Relative S&P 500
Price/Earnings Ratio	19.2	1.04
Price/Book Ratio	2.5	0.73
5 Yr Earnings Gr %	0.4	0.07
Return on Assets %	5.9	0.79
Debt % Total Cap	29.5	1.04
Med Mkt Cap ($mil)	4566	0.35

Style
Value Blend Growth — Large Med Small

Diversification Value for Portfolio Types

Large Cap: None	Small Cap: Medium	Bond: High	Balanced: Low	Diversified: Low

Expenses & Fees

Sales Fees	0.00% front
	0.00% deferred
	0.00% 12b-1
Management Fee	0.85% flat fee
3-,5-,10-yr Expense Projections	$28, $48, $107
Annual Brokerage Cost	---

Min Initial Purchase	$1000 (Addt'l: $100)
Min IRA Purchase	$500 (Addt'l: None)
Min Auto Invest Plan	$100 (Systematic Inv: $100)

Tax Analysis

	Tax-Adj Historical Return %	% Pretax Return
3 Yr Avg	4.47	64.3
5 Yr Avg	6.16	72.1
10 Yr Avg	8.68	67.1
Potential Capital Gain Exposure (% of assets)		5%

Most Similar Funds in MF500

Smith Barney Appreciation A	Strong Fit
Investment Comp of America	Strong Fit
Dean Witter Dividend Growth	Strong Fit

Portfolio 11-30-94

Share Chg (09-94) 000	Amount 000	Total Stocks: 134 / Total Fixed-Income: 6	Value $000	% Net Assets
-3	47	Archer-Daniels-Midland	1298	1.06
-2	18	IBM	1274	1.04
3	24	Dun & Bradstreet	1269	1.04
0	20	CIGNA	1268	1.04
2	12	Atlantic Richfield	1242	1.02
9	24	Bell Atlantic	1203	0.99
5	38	Snap-On	1197	0.98
3	25	Gannett	1184	0.97
0	25	Kerr-McGee	1181	0.97
0	36	Texas Utilities	1175	0.96
-3	18	American Home Products	1172	0.96
0	65	USX-Marathon Group	1170	0.96
15	65	Baker Hughes	1170	0.96
0	20	Bristol-Myers Squibb	1155	0.95
5	30	Weyerhaeuser	1151	0.94
7	32	US West	1128	0.93
0	100	Calgon Carbon	1125	0.92
1	16	Chubb	1124	0.92
-5	30	Merck	1118	0.92
0	30	Dominion Resources	1114	0.91
8	35	Aon	1107	0.91
0	40	Perkin-Elmer	1105	0.91
-2	18	Amoco	1094	0.90
2	17	Deere	1092	0.90
0	18	Norfolk Southern	1089	0.89

Composition % 12-31-94

Cash	21.0	Preferreds	0.0
Stocks	76.0	Convertibles	2.0
Bonds	1.0	Other	0.0

Index Allocation

	% of Stocks
S&P 500	88.3
S&P MidCap 400	8.5
U.S. Small Cap	3.2
Foreign	0.0

Sector Weightings

	% of Stocks	Relative S&P 500
Utilities	12.3	0.99
Energy	13.2	1.31
Financials	8.1	0.76
Industrial Cyclicals	17.2	1.05
Consumer Durables	7.6	1.22
Consumer Staples	8.2	0.66
Services	15.7	1.93
Retail	3.3	0.57
Health	8.1	0.93
Technology	6.4	0.70

MORNINGSTAR **1995 Mutual Fund 500**

United Income

	Ticker	Load	NAV	Yield	SEC Yield	Assets	Objective
	UNCMX	5.75%	23.34	1.5%	N/A	3144.3	Equity-Inc.

United Income Fund seeks current income.

The fund invests at least 65% of its assets in income-producing securities. It invests primarily in common stocks or securities convertible into common stocks that have the potential for capital growth or that may be expected to resist market decline. If market conditions warrant, the fund may invest primarily in debt and preferred stock. The fund may hold up to 5% of its assets in non-investment grade debt securities.

Historical Profile

Return	Above Average
Risk	Average
Rating	★★★★ Above Average

Investment Style History
Equity

Average % Stocks Held in Portfolio

60% 80% 82% 83% 89% 88% 90% 91%

Growth of $10,000

||| Value of Fund ($000)
— Value of Index ($000)
S&P 500
▼ Manager Change
▽ Partial Manager Change
► Mgr Unknown After
◄ Mgr Unknown Before

Performance Quartile
(Within Objective)

Manager's Investment Style

Management's top-down approach takes both the current phase of the economy and future business trends into consideration. By emphasizing industrial and consumer cyclicals that increased their earnings as rates declined, management produced strong returns in the early 1990's. Management doesn't pay much attention to yield, which makes the fund more growth-oriented than most of its equity-income peers.

Fund Manager(s)

Russell E. Thompson CFA(1974), since 02-79.
Birthdate: 03-40. BS, U. of Missouri 1967 MBA, U. of Missouri 1968

Manager Experience	Dates Managed	Invest Obj	Std Dev	+/- Index
Russell E. Thompson				
Waddell & Reed Total Ret	09/92 - 12/94	GI	8.63	0.94

1983	1984	1985	1986	1987	1988	1989	1990	1991	1992	1993	1994	History
13.53	13.11	16.20	17.03	15.08	16.76	18.69	16.46	20.44	22.05	24.77	23.34	NAV
31.55	6.06	34.04	22.15	7.30	19.83	27.49	-5.43	29.64	10.75	16.06	-1.80	Total Return %
9.09	-0.20	2.30	3.47	2.04	3.22	-4.19	-2.31	-0.85	3.14	6.00	-3.12	+/- S&P 500
8.09	3.01	1.48	6.05	4.94	1.89	-1.68	0.75	-4.57	1.78	4.78	-1.73	+/- Wilshire 5000
6.28	5.30	5.06	2.78	3.73	4.39	3.62	3.43	3.29	2.34	1.82	1.43	Income Return %
25.28	0.76	28.98	19.37	3.58	15.44	23.87	-8.86	26.34	8.42	14.23	-3.23	Capital Return %
8	47	14	13	15	14	18	72	27	18	25	32	Total Rtn % Rank All
7	60	1	10	4	35	12	43	28	28	26	47	Total Rtn % Rank Obj
0.64	0.64	0.61	0.49	0.66	0.67	0.65	0.63	0.54	0.46	0.40	0.36	Income $
0.00	0.48	0.52	2.28	2.60	0.60	1.96	0.60	0.29	0.10	0.39	0.63	Capital Gains $
0.61	0.70	0.66	0.62	0.63	0.67	0.64	0.68	0.66	0.65	0.66	0.72	Expense Ratio %
5.16	5.32	4.09	2.70	3.99	3.65	3.41	3.44	2.71	2.19	1.70	1.47	Income Ratio %
30	21	38	30	58	49	61	31	25	19	22	16	Turnover Rate %
550.9	533.8	675.3	836.6	963.7	1149.3	1548.9	1578.1	2151.7	2538.8	3061.4	3144.3	Net Assets ($mil)

Performance 12-31-94

	1st Qtr	2nd Qtr	3rd Qtr	4th Qtr	Total
1987	17.75	0.77	1.80	-11.17	7.30
1988	7.86	6.09	1.61	3.05	19.83
1989	6.45	9.54	10.60	-1.14	27.49
1990	0.16	5.70	-17.35	8.09	-5.43
1991	15.31	1.62	4.06	6.31	29.64
1992	2.18	1.42	0.45	6.39	10.75
1993	4.45	2.58	3.04	5.13	16.06
1994	-0.95	-1.48	3.24	-2.53	-1.80

Bear Market Performance

Decile Rank (5-year period)

Worst ———————————————— Best

	Worst 3 Mo Period 1985-89	Worst 3 Mo Period 1990-94
United Income	-19.54	-17.96
+/- S&P 500	10.05	-4.12
+/- Best Fit Index : S&P 500	10.05	-4.12

Trailing Returns

	Total Return %	+/- S&P 500	+/- Wil 5000	% Rank All	% Rank Obj	Growth of $10,000
3 Mo	-2.53	-2.51	-1.76	78	47	9,747
6 Mo	0.63	-4.24	-4.00	44	68	10,063
1 Yr	-1.80	-3.12	-1.73	32	47	9,820
3 Yr Avg	8.07	1.81	1.46	21	32	12,622
5 Yr Avg	9.12	0.43	0.31	22	20	15,474
10 Yr Avg	15.30	0.92	1.44	10	6	41,530
15 Yr Avg	15.80	1.32	1.83	7	7	90,310

Operations

Address and Telephone	6300 Lamar Avenue P.O. Box 29217
	Shawnee Mission, KS 66201-9217
	800-366-5465 / 913-236-2000
Advisor	Waddell & Reed Investment Mngmt
Subadvisor	None
Distributor	Waddell & Reed
States Available	All
Report Grade	B-
Income Distrib	Paid Quarterly
Date of Inception	10-09-40
Fiscal Year End	December

Min Initial Purchase	$500 (Addt'l: $25)
Min IRA Purchase	$50 (Addt'l: $25)
Min Auto Invest Plan	$500 (Systematic Inv: $25)

Expenses & Fees

Sales Fees	5.75% front
	0.00% deferred
	0.25% 12b-1
Management Fee	0.05% flat fee+0.51%G
3-,5-,10-yr Expense Projections	$84, $104, $161
Annual Brokerage Cost	0.07%

Risk Analysis

Time Period	Load-Adj Return %	Risk % Rank All	Risk % Rank Obj	Morningstar Return	Morningstar Risk	Morningstar Risk-Adj Rating
1 Yr	-7.45					
3 Yr	5.96	61	69	0.70[3]	0.67	★★★
5 Yr	7.84	71	93	0.77[3]	0.84	★★★
10 Yr	14.62	63	93	1.40	0.86	★★★★
Average Historical Rating (109 months)					4.1 ★s	

[1] = low, 100 = high [2] 1.00 = Equity Avg [3] 1.00 = 90-day T-bill return

Other Measures

				Standard S&P 500	Best Fit S&P 500
Standard Deviation	8.38	Alpha		1.9	1.9
Mean	8.14	Beta		0.94	0.94
Sharpe Ratio	0.55	R-Squared		78	78

Investment Style

	Stock Portfolio Avg	Relative S&P 500
Price/Earnings Ratio	17.7	0.96
Price/Book Ratio	3.1	0.93
5 Yr Earnings Gr %	3.0	0.54
Return on Assets %	7.3	0.98
Debt % Total Cap	31.9	1.13
Med Mkt Cap ($mil)	8503	0.65

Style
Value Blend Growth
Size Large/Med/Small

Diversification Value for Portfolio Types

Large Cap: Low	Small Cap: Low	Bond: High	Balanced: Low	Diversified: Low

Portfolio 09-30-94

Share Chg (03-94)000	Amount 000	Total Stocks: 106 Total Fixed-Income: 7	Value $000	% Net Assets
850	1700	Motorola	89675	2.78
800	1600	Caterpillar	86600	2.69
100	750	ITT	62548	1.94
600	1200	General Electric	57750	1.79
350	1150	Air Products & Chemicals	53763	1.67
950	1900	Ford Motor	52725	1.64
625	1250	PPG Industries	49531	1.54
0	1100	Chrysler	49363	1.53
0	1400	Polaroid	49175	1.53
0	765	Intel	47143	1.46
200	600	Intl Paper	47100	1.46
0	685	Deere	47008	1.46
290	1000	General Motors	46875	1.45
0	50000	US Treasury Note 5.75%	44086	1.37
0	550	AMP	42556	1.32
0	1600	Circuit City Stores	41400	1.28
0	865	Applied Materials	40223	1.25
0	1000	May Department Stores	39375	1.22
0	1000	General Motors Cl E	38000	1.18
0	1650	Southwest Airlines	37125	1.15
700	1400	McDonald's	36750	1.14
0	600	Procter & Gamble	35775	1.11
0	500	Gillette	35375	1.10
0	676	JC Penney	34899	1.08
0	600	El DuPont de Nemours	34800	1.08

Composition % 09-30-94

Cash	4.6	Preferreds	0.7
Stocks	90.6	Convertibles	0.0
Bonds	4.2	Other	0.0

Tax Analysis

	Tax-Adj Historical Return %	% Pretax Return
3 Yr Avg	6.94	85.1
5 Yr Avg	7.67	81.7
10 Yr Avg	12.43	70.6
Potential Capital Gain Exposure (% of assets)		27%

Most Similar Funds in MF500

Fundamental Investors	Fair Fit
Vanguard Index 500	Fair Fit
Neuberger&Berman Partners	Fair Fit

Index Allocation

	% of Stocks
S&P 500	87.5
S&P MidCap 400	3.9
U.S. Small Cap	1.4
Foreign	7.2

Sector Weightings

	% of Stocks	Relative S&P 500
Utilities	3.5	0.28
Energy	0.0	0.00
Financials	7.0	0.66
Industrial Cyclicals	31.5	1.92
Consumer Durables	17.5	2.81
Consumer Staples	5.1	0.41
Services	10.4	1.28
Retail	11.1	1.91
Health	3.2	0.37
Technology	10.8	1.17

United Municipal High-Income

Ticker	Load	NAV	Yield	SEC Yield	Assets	Objective
UMUHX	4.25%	4.93	6.8%	N/A	339.5	Muni Nat

United Municipal High-Income Fund seeks income exempt from federal taxation.

The fund normally invests at least 75% of its assets in medium- and lower-quality municipal bonds. This is not a fundamental policy, however, and it may invest more than 25% of its assets in higher-quality municipal bonds at times when yield spreads are narrow or when the fund perceives a lack of medium- and lower-quality security candidates. Up to one half of the dividend payouts may be subject to the Alternative Minimum Tax.

Historical Profile

Return	Above Average
Risk	Low
Rating	★★★★★
	Highest

Investment Style History
Fixed Income
Income Rtn % Rank Obj

Growth of $10,000

‖‖ Value of Fund ($000)
— Value of Index ($000)
    LB Muni
▼ Manager Change
▽ Partial Manager Change
► Mgr Unknown After
◄ Mgr Unknown Before

Performance Quartile (Within Objective)

Manager's Investment Style

In its quest for high yield, management stuffs this portfolio with nonrated munis. In addition to fattening yield, these issues have provided the fund with a cushion against interest-rate fluctuations. Liquidity risk is a concern, though. The fund has also held reasonable positions in higher-yielding issues subject to the alternative minimum tax.

Fund Manager(s)

John M. Holliday CFA(1973), since 01-86.
Birthdate: 06-35. BA, Dartmouth C. 1957 MBA, Wharton 1959

Manager Experience

	Dates Managed	Invest Obj	Std Dev	+/- Index
John M. Holliday				
United Government Secs	04/84 - 01/88	GG	7.27	-1.85

Historical data by year (top row shows Investment Style History ranks: 4 4 2 2 6 5 4 3):

	1983	1984	1985	1986	1987	1988	1989	1990	1991	1992	1993	1994	History
	---	---	---	5.30	4.85	4.87	4.97	4.92	5.11	5.21	5.46	4.93	NAV
	---	---	---	14.95 *	0.53	9.43	10.79	7.20	11.90	10.15	13.20	-3.11	Total Return %
	---	---	---	-2.23	1.55	-3.75	-1.75	-4.10	2.91	3.45	-0.19	+/- LB Aggregate
	---	---	---	-0.97	-0.74	0.01	-0.11	-0.24	1.33	0.92	2.49	+/- LB Muni
	---	---	---	8.57	8.41	9.01	8.74	8.20	8.04	7.34	6.89	6.19	Income Return %
	---	---	---	6.39	-7.88	0.41	2.05	-1.01	3.86	2.81	6.30	-9.30	Capital Return %
	---	---	---		56	66	66	20	77	21	39	44	Total Rtn % Rank All
	---	---	---		38	70	14	11	39	8	21	23	Total Rtn % Rank Obj
	---	---	---	0.40	0.44	0.42	0.41	0.39	0.37	0.36	0.34	0.34	Income $
	---	---	---	0.02	0.04	0.00	0.00	0.00	0.00	0.04	0.07	0.02	Capital Gains $
	---	---	---	0.86	0.80	0.75	0.75	0.77	0.72	0.70	0.76		Expense Ratio %
	---	---	---	8.42	8.76	8.36	7.97	7.63	7.08	6.49	6.39		Income Ratio %
	---	---	---		57	44	39	27	61	54	26	26	Turnover Rate %
	---	---	---	27.9	79.4	129.6	177.4	200.7	233.3	269.2	337.2	339.5	Net Assets ($mil)

Performance 12-31-94

	1st Qtr	2nd Qtr	3rd Qtr	4th Qtr	Total
1987	1.99	-1.90	-0.43	0.92	0.53
1988	2.71	1.02	2.59	2.80	9.43
1989	1.21	5.49	1.47	2.26	10.79
1990	0.93	2.41	0.19	3.53	7.20
1991	2.06	2.31	3.94	3.10	11.90
1992	1.31	3.77	2.48	2.24	10.15
1993	3.63	3.29	3.97	1.72	13.20
1994	-3.93	1.49	0.88	-1.50	-3.11

Bear Market Performance

Decile Rank (5-year period)

Worst   Best

	Worst 3 Mo Period 1985-89	Worst 3 Mo Period 1990-94
United Municipal High-Income	---	-4.67
+/- LB Aggregate	---	0.26
+/- Best Fit Index : LB Muni	---	1.09

Trailing Returns

	Total Return %	+/- LB Aggregate	+/- LB Muni	% Rank All	% Rank Obj	Growth of $10,000
3 Mo	-1.50	-1.87	-0.06	57	58	9,850
6 Mo	-0.63	-1.62	0.61	67	39	9,937
1 Yr	-3.11	-0.19	2.49	44	23	9,689
3 Yr Avg	6.50	1.96	1.63	30	1	12,080
5 Yr Avg	7.70	0.07	0.93	37	2	14,490
10 Yr Avg	---	---	---	---	---	---
15 Yr Avg	---	---	---	---	---	---

Operations

Address and Telephone	6300 Lamar Avenue P.O. Box 29217
	Shawnee Mission, KS 66201-9217
	800-366-5465 / 913-236-2000
Advisor	Waddell & Reed Investment Mgmnt
Subadvisor	None
Distributor	Waddell & Reed
States Available	All
Report Grade	C
Income Distrib	Paid Monthly
* Date of Inception	01-21-86
Fiscal Year End	September

Risk Analysis

Time Period	Load-Adj Return %	Risk % Rank All	Obj	Morningstar Return	Morningstar Risk	Morningstar Risk-Adj Rating
1 Yr	-7.23					
3 Yr	4.97	10	18	1.44	0.71	★★★★★
5 Yr	6.77	6	14	1.29	0.67	★★★★★
10 Yr	---	---	---	---	---	---

Average Historical Rating (72 months)   5.0 ★s

[1] 1 = low, 100 = high   [2] 1.00 = Muni Avg   [3] 1.00 = 90-day T-bill return

Other Measures

			Standard LB Agg	Best Fit LB Muni
Standard Deviation	4.78	Alpha	2.0	1.7
Mean	6.43	Beta	0.87	0.85
Sharpe Ratio	0.61	R-Squared	54	95

Investment Style

Interest-Rate Stance
Avg Effective Maturity   21.6 Yrs

Not Available

Quality
Avg Credit Quality   ---
Avg Weighted Coupon   7.49%
Avg Weighted Price   97.52% of Par

Diversification Value for Portfolio Types

Large Cap: Medium	Small Cap: High	Bond: Low	Balanced: Medium	Diversified: Medium

Expenses & Fees

Sales Fees	4.25% front
	0.00% deferred
	0.25% 12b-1
Management Fee	0.10% flat fee+0.51%G
3-,5-,10-yr Expense Projections	$71, $93, $154

Portfolio 09-30-94

Amount 000	Date of Maturity	Total Stocks: 0 Total Fixed-Income: 186	Value $000	% Net Assets
6000	11-15-23	CO Denver Arpt Sys 8.75%	6330	1.93
4500	12-01-11	TX Alliance Arpt Spcl Fac American 7%	4298	1.31
4000	05-01-21	NH Indl Dev Poll Cntrl Pub Svc 7.65%	4105	1.25
4000	09-01-32	NV Clark Indl Dev SW Gas 7.5%	4080	1.25
3500	12-15-18	TX Retama Dev 8.75%	3456	1.05
3500	09-01-24	OR Klamath Falls Intercomnty Hosp 7.1%	3434	1.05
3000	07-01-15	MA Indl Fin Resource Rec Semass 9.25%	3338	1.02
3000	04-01-22	MO Econ Dev Export/Infrastructure 8.75%	3274	1.00
3000	02-15-21	CO Hlth Fac PSL Sys 8.5%	3255	0.99
3000	08-15-20	IN Hlth Fac Fin Hancock Meml Hosp 8.3%	3218	0.98
3000	06-01-10	MO Bi-State Dev MO/IL Metro Dist 7.75%	3210	0.98
5255	01-01-02	CA San Joaquin Hills Transp Toll Rd 0%	3184	0.97
3180	01-01-23	GA Savannah Hosp Candler Genl 7%	3136	0.96
3000	01-01-13	DC COP 7.3%	3030	0.92
3000	01-01-07	SC Charleston Indl Massey Coal Term DMD	3000	0.92
3000	12-01-09	NJ Camden Poll Cntrl Solid Waste 7.5%	2993	0.91
3000	10-01-10	Guam Arpt 6.6%	2966	0.91
2790	09-01-11	KS Dev Fin Comnty Provider Loan 8.875%	2930	0.89
3000	08-01-24	CA Huntington Beach Pub Fin Redev 7%	2921	0.89
3000	12-01-19	PA Allegheny Indl Dev 6.7%	2891	0.88

Credit Analysis % of Bonds 11-01-94

US Govt	0	BB	4
AAA	2	B	0
AA	1	Below B	0
A	3	NR/NA	57
BBB	33		

Composition % of Assets 11-01-94

Cash	2.5	Preferreds	0.0
Stocks	0.0	Convertibles	0.0
Bonds	97.5	Other	0.0

Tax Analysis

	Tax-Adj Historical Return %	% Pretax Return
3 Yr Avg	6.24	95.7
5 Yr Avg	7.54	97.6
10 Yr Avg	---	---
Potential Capital Gain Exposure (% of assets)		-3%

Most Similar Funds in MF500

T. Rowe Price Tax-Fr Hi-Yld	Strong Fit
Putnam H/Y Muni	Strong Fit
Franklin Insured T/F Income	Strong Fit

Coupon Range

	% Bonds	Rel Obj
0%	4.1	1.62
0% to 6.8%	19.1	0.32
6.8% to 7.5%	25.7	1.66
7.5% to 8.3%	15.5	1.75
More than 8.3%	33.4	3.78
Not applicable	2.2	0.56

Sector Weightings

	% Bonds	Rel Obj
General Obl	7.49	0.36
Utilities	0.38	0.03
Health	32.74	2.48
Water/Waste	2.19	0.34
Housing	5.74	0.78
Education	2.58	0.40
Transportation	10.27	1.01
COP/Lease	2.92	0.92
Private	30.09	2.58
Misc Revenue	4.66	0.94
Demand	0.95	0.39

Top 5 States % of Bonds

CO	8.87	IL	5.08
MO	7.40	NH	4.82
PA	7.10		

Min Initial Purchase $500 (Addt'l: $25)
Min IRA Purchase   N/A
Min Auto Invest Plan $500 (Systematic Inv: $25)

518

MORNINGSTAR   1995 Mutual Fund 500

USAA Investment Balanced

	Ticker	Load	NAV	Yield	SEC Yield	Assets	Objective
	USBLX	None	11.64	3.9%	4.48%	124.7	Balanced

USAA Investment Trust Balanced Portfolio Fund seeks a conservative balance between tax-exempt income and the potential for long-term growth of capital.

The fund typically allocates its assets within the following ranges: 27% to 33% in short-term tax-exempt securities; 27% to 33% in long-term tax-exempt securities; and 36% to 44% in common stocks and convertible securities of U.S. companies. The fund targets stocks that are undervalued as measured by factors such as low price/earnings ratios and high dividend yields. At least 95% of the fund's long-term fixed-income investments are rated A or higher.

Historical Profile
Return: Average
Risk: Below Average
Rating: ★★★ Neutral

Investment Style History
Equity

Average % Stocks Held in Portfolio

---	---	42%	41%	43%	41%	41%	41%	

Growth of $10,000
|||| Value of Fund ($000)
— Value of Index ($000) S&P 500
▼ Manager Change
▽ Partial Manager Change
► Mgr Unknown After
◄ Mgr Unknown Before

Performance Quartile (Within Objective)

Manager's Investment Style

Management follows a three-pronged investment strategy. Separate individuals manage value equities, short-term munis, and long-term munis. The portfolio is adjusted on a quarterly basis to ensure that the muni portion accounts for 60% of assets. The muni choices are fairly conservative, sporting an average weighted maturity of about five years. Management of the equity side is also wary of risk, using a top-down strategy to choose issues with low price multiples and high dividends.

Fund Manager(s)

Kenneth E. Willmann CFA(1978), since 01-89.
Stephan J. Klaffke CFA(1987), since 01-94.
Clifford A. Gladson CFA(1990), since 04-94.
John W. Saunders, Jr. CFA(1976), since 01-89.

Manager Experience	Dates Managed	Invest Obj	Std Dev	+/- Index
Kenneth E. Willmann				
USAA Tax-Exempt CA Bnd	08/89 - 04/94	MC	5.79	-1.64
USAA Tax-Exempt VA Bnd	10/90 - 04/94	MS	5.06	-1.17

	1983	1984	1985	1986	1987	1988	1989	1990	1991	1992	1993	1994	History
NAV	---	---	---	---	---	---	11.18	10.78	11.82	11.92	12.71	11.64	NAV
	---	---	---	---	---	---	16.18 *	1.37	14.68	4.93	13.72	-2.62	Total Return %
	---	---	---	---	---	---	-13.50 *	4.48	-15.81	-2.69	3.66	-3.93	+/- S&P 500
	---	---	---	---	---	---		-7.58	-1.33	-2.32	3.97	0.30	+/- LB Aggregate
	---	---	---	---	---	---	4.15	4.94	5.03	3.99	3.79	3.79	Income Return %
	---	---	---	---	---	---	12.02	-3.58	9.65	0.93	9.92	-6.41	Capital Return %
	---	---	---	---	---	---		52	60	77	35	40	Total Rtn % Rank All
	---	---	---	---	---	---		29	99	72	24	50	Total Rtn % Rank Obj
	---	---	---	---	---	---	0.40	0.54	0.51	0.46	0.45	0.47	Income $
	---	---	---	---	---	---	0.02	0.00	0.00	0.01	0.37	0.27	Capital Gains $
	---	---	---	---	---	---	1.29	1.00	1.00	0.92	0.86	0.84	Expense Ratio %
	---	---	---	---	---	---	4.90	5.05	4.91	4.31	3.81	3.56	Income Ratio %
	---	---	---	---	---	---		106	81	107	99	171	Turnover Rate %
	---	---	---	---	---	---	27.9	39.8	61.5	91.2	127.4	124.7	Net Assets ($mil)

Performance 12-31-94

	1st Qtr	2nd Qtr	3rd Qtr	4th Qtr	Total
1987	---	---	---	---	---
1988	---	---	---	---	---
1989	---	6.40	3.45	3.38	16.18 *
1990	-1.97	1.48	-2.58	4.59	1.37
1991	4.82	-0.09	4.25	5.03	14.68
1992	-1.52	2.95	2.12	1.35	4.93
1993	4.28	4.06	2.36	2.38	13.72
1994	-3.47	0.99	2.30	-2.35	-2.62

Bear Market Performance

Decile Rank (5-year period)

	Worst 3 Mo Period 1985-89	Worst 3 Mo Period 1990-94
USAA Investment Balanced	---	-4.48
+/- S&P 500	---	-0.60
+/- Best Fit Index : S&P 500	---	-0.60

Trailing Returns

	Total Return %	+/- S&P 500	+/- LB Aggregate	% Rank All	% Rank Obj	Growth of $10,000
3 Mo	-2.35	-2.33	-2.73	75	88	9,765
6 Mo	-0.10	-4.96	-1.10	59	89	9,990
1 Yr	-2.62	-3.93	0.30	40	50	9,738
3 Yr Avg	5.13	-1.13	0.59	45	54	11,619
5 Yr Avg	6.20	-2.50	-1.43	71	85	13,507
10 Yr Avg	---	---	---	---	---	---
15 Yr Avg	---	---	---	---	---	---

Operations

Address and Telephone	USAA Building
	San Antonio, TX 78288
	800-382-8722
Advisor	USAA Investment Management
Subadvisor	None
Distributor	USAA Investment Management
States Available	All
Report Grade	B
Income Distrib	Paid Quarterly
* Date of Inception	01-11-89
Fiscal Year End	May

Risk Analysis

Time Period	Load-Adj Return %	Risk % Rank [1] All	Obj	Morningstar [2] Return	Morningstar Risk	Morningstar Risk-Adj Rating
1 Yr	-2.62					
3 Yr	5.13	37	13	0.45 [3]	0.61	★★★
5 Yr	6.20	45	6	0.35 [3]	0.57	★★★
10 Yr	---	---	---			

Average Historical Rating (36 months)   3.0 ★s

[1] 1 = low, 100 = high   [2] 1.00 = Hybrid Avg   [3] 1.00 = 90-day T-bill return

Other Measures

		Standard S&P 500	Best Fit S&P 500
Standard Deviation	5.08	Alpha	0.1	0.1
Mean	5.14	Beta	0.53	0.53
Sharpe Ratio	0.32	R-Squared	67	67

Investment Style

Stocks	Port Avg	Rel S&P 500
Price/Earnings Ratio	15.9	0.86
Price/Book Ratio	2.0	0.59
5 Yr Earnings Gr %	-3.1	-0.57
Med Mkt Cap ($mil)	7074	0.54

Style: V B G

Bonds	
Avg Effective Duration	NMF
Avg Effective Maturity	5.3 Yrs
Avg Credit Quality	AA
Avg Weighted Coupon	6.29%

Maturity: S I L

Diversification Value for Portfolio Types

Large Cap: Low	Small Cap: High	Bond: Low	Balanced: Low	Diversified: Low

Min Initial Purchase	$1000 (Addt'l: $50)
Min IRA Purchase	$1000 (Addt'l: $50)
Min Auto Invest Plan	$1000 (Systematic Inv: $50)

Expenses & Fees

Sales Fees	0.00% front
	0.00% deferred
	0.00% 12b-1
Management Fee	0.50% flat fee
3-,5-,10-yr Expense Projections	$27, $48, $106
Annual Brokerage Cost	0.05%

Portfolio 12-31-94

Share Chg (05-94)000	Amount 000	Total Stocks: 46 Total Fixed-Income: 19	Date of Maturity	Value $000	% Net Assets
	8495	CA San Joaquin Hills Transp 5%	01-01-33	5330	4.27
	5200	RI Hsg/Mtg Fin 6.85%	10-01-24	5027	4.03
	5000	ME Hsg Mtg Purch 6.5%	11-15-11	4792	3.84
	5000	TX San Antonio Elec/Gas Sys 6%	02-01-14	4591	3.68
	4785	PA Philadelphia Gas Wks 6.375%	07-01-26	4329	3.47
	4400	IL Chicago O'Hare Arpt 6.375%	01-01-15	4206	3.37
	4200	TX Grapevine Indl Dev DMD	12-01-24	4200	3.37
	4200	FL Dade Hlth Fac DMD	09-01-20	4200	3.37
	3355	VI GO Pub Fin Matching Ln 7.3%	10-01-18	3571	2.86
	3000	FL Sarasota Hlth Fac 6.05%	12-01-15	3000	2.41
	3000	MA State GO 4%	01-01-96	2960	2.37
0	50	Boeing		2338	1.87
	2100	FL Hillsborough Indl Dev DMD	05-15-18	2100	1.68
36	72	Ford Motor		2016	1.62
0	27	Dow Chemical		1816	1.46
5	40	BF Goodrich		1735	1.39
	1900	NV Las Vegas Dwtwn Tax 6.1%	06-15-14	1658	1.33
0	25	Deere		1656	1.33
0	44	NYNEX		1617	1.30
0	43	American Brands		1613	1.29

Index Allocation

	% of Stocks
S&P 500	89.4
S&P MidCap 400	10.6
U.S. Small Cap	0.0
Foreign	0.0

Composition % 10-31-94

Cash	27.0	Preferreds	0.0
Stocks	41.0	Convertibles	0.0
Bonds	32.0	Other	0.0

Tax Analysis

	Tax-Adj Historical Return %	% Pretax Return
3 Yr Avg	3.21	61.4
5 Yr Avg	4.41	68.8
10 Yr Avg	---	---
Potential Capital Gain Exposure (% of assets)		0%

Most Similar Funds in MF500

George Putnam of Boston A	Strong Fit
American Balanced	Fair Fit
Sentinel Balanced	Fair Fit

Bond Credit Analysis 09-30-94

% of Bonds			
US Govt	0	BB	0
AAA	25	B	0
AA	43	Below B	0
A	30	NR/NA	0
BBB	2		

Stock Sector Weightings

	% of Stocks	Relative S&P 500
Utilities	12.1	0.98
Energy	13.1	1.29
Financials	5.3	0.50
Industrial Cyclicals	38.4	2.34
Consumer Durables	6.8	1.09
Consumer Staples	7.5	0.60
Services	6.2	0.76
Retail	5.9	1.01
Health	4.7	0.54
Technology	0.0	0.00

USAA Investment Cornerstone

	Ticker	Load	NAV	Yield	SEC Yield	Assets	Objective
	USCRX	None	21.24	2.6%	N/A	841.3	Asset Alloc.

USAA Investment Trust Cornerstone Fund seeks to hedge against inflation consistent with a stable share value.

The fund allocates its assets among five categories: gold stocks, foreign stocks, real-estate stocks, U.S. government securities, and basic-value stocks. It intends to invest 0% to 10% of its assets in gold stocks; each of the remaining sectors receives 22% to 28% of the fund's assets.

Historical Profile

Return	Above Average
Risk	Below Average
Rating	★★★★
	Above Average

Investment Style History
Equity
Average % Stocks Held in Portfolio

82% 81% 79% 77% 80% 79% 77% 76%

Growth of $10,000

|||| Value of Fund ($000)
— Value of Index ($000) S&P 500
▼ Manager Change
▽ Partial Manager Change
◄— Mgr Unknown After
—► Mgr Unknown Before

Performance Quartile (Within Objective)

Manager's Investment Style

Management's main goal is to stave off the forces of inflation. One main weapon it uses is gold. As gold prices have become more unpredictable, however, management has cut back on its holdings. The fund's new charter states that it can only hold up to 8% of assets in gold. Management now uses more value-oriented, foreign, and real-estate equities as well as government bonds.

1983	1984	1985	1986	1987	1988	1989	1990	1991	1992	1993	1994	History
---	9.89	10.97	14.92	15.87	16.54	19.44	16.98	19.12	19.69	23.46	21.24	NAV
---	-0.50 *	14.85	40.81	9.00	8.39	21.94	-9.20	16.23	6.35	23.73	-1.05	Total Return %
---	-5.23 *	-16.89	22.13	3.74	-8.23	-9.75	-6.08	-14.26	-1.27	13.67	-2.36	+/- S&P 500
---		-7.28	25.56	6.24	0.51	7.40	-18.14	0.23	-0.89	13.98	1.87	+/- LB Aggregate
---	0.42	3.30	2.52	2.48	4.16	4.40	3.46	3.62	3.37	2.91	2.68	Income Return %
---	-0.91	11.55	38.29	6.51	4.22	17.53	-12.65	12.60	2.98	20.82	-3.73	Capital Return %
---	---	92	4	12	71	31	83	53	65	12	27	Total Rtn % Rank All
---	---	62	8	35	51	21	85	74	55	9	26	Total Rtn % Rank Obj
---	0.04	0.32	0.30	0.36	0.66	0.71	0.65	0.59	0.63	0.59	0.58	Income $
---	0.02	0.06	0.21	0.02	0.00	0.00	0.00	0.00	0.00	0.29	1.38	Capital Gains $
---	1.90	1.50	1.50	1.07	1.21	1.21	1.21	1.18	1.18	1.18	1.11	Expense Ratio %
---	6.98	5.03	3.68	3.41	3.54	3.57	3.50	3.58	3.25	2.92	2.68	Income Ratio %
---	---	15	70	15	28	33	41	28	33	45	31	Turnover Rate %
---	3.3	13.6	49.4	587.3	519.9	549.9	551.7	603.7	578.1	762.8	841.3	Net Assets ($mil)

Fund Manager(s)

John W. Saunders, Jr. CFA(1976), since 10-85.
Stephan J. Klaffke CFA(1987), since 01-94.
W. Travis Selmier II CFA(1990), since 01-94.
Mark W. Johnson CFA(1978), since 01-94.

Manager Experience

	Dates Managed	Invest Obj	Std Dev	+/- Index
John W. Saunders, Jr.				
USAA Investment Gold	08/84 - 10/85	SP	21.65	-42.88
W. Travis Selmier II				
USAA Investment Emerg	11/94 - 12/94	WF	0.00	-5.46

Performance 12-31-94

	1st Qtr	2nd Qtr	3rd Qtr	4th Qtr	Total
1987	21.25	2.76	6.35	-17.74	9.00
1988	4.98	2.64	-2.28	2.94	8.39
1989	4.59	3.99	7.34	4.44	21.94
1990	-4.27	-0.59	-7.08	2.69	-9.20
1991	6.07	0.22	3.16	5.99	16.23
1992	-2.35	3.80	2.89	1.98	6.35
1993	10.06	3.46	4.50	3.98	23.73
1994	-2.43	0.00	3.58	-2.09	-1.05

Bear Market Performance

Decile Rank (5-year period)

Worst — Best

	Worst 3 Mo Period 1985-89	Worst 3 Mo Period 1990-94
USAA Investment Cornerstone	-21.54	-11.29
+/- S&P 500	-1.15	2.55
+/- Best Fit Index : MSAIICtry	---	1.11

Trailing Returns

	Total Return %	+/- S&P 500	+/- LB Aggregate	% Rank All	Obj	Growth of $10,000
3 Mo	-2.09	-2.07	-2.46	70	66	9,791
6 Mo	1.42	-3.44	0.43	31	48	10,142
1 Yr	-1.05	-2.36	1.87	27	26	9,895
3 Yr Avg	9.20	2.93	4.65	16	9	13,021
5 Yr Avg	6.56	-2.13	-1.06	61	66	13,742
10 Yr Avg	12.34	-2.04	2.39	34	25	32,012
15 Yr Avg	---	---	---	---	---	---

Operations

Address and Telephone	USAA Building San Antonio, TX 78288 800-382-8722
Advisor	USAA Investment Management
Subadvisor	None
Distributor	USAA Investment Management
States Available	All
Report Grade	B
Income Distrib	Paid Annually
* Date of Inception	08-15-84
Fiscal Year End	May

Risk Analysis

Time Period	Load-Adj Return %	Risk % Rank [1] All	Obj	Morningstar [2] Return	Risk	Morningstar Risk-Adj Rating
1 Yr	-1.05					
3 Yr	9.20	52	48	1.71 [3]	0.73	★★★★
5 Yr	6.56	56	72	0.44 [3]	0.85	★★★
10 Yr	12.34	42	50	1.13	0.71	★★★★

Average Historical Rating (89 months) 3.8 ★s

[1] 1 = low, 100 = high [2] 1.00 = Hybrid Avg [3] 1.00 = 90-day T-bill return

Other Measures

	Standard S&P 500	Best Fit MSAIICtry
Standard Deviation	7.37	Alpha 3.8 4.2
Mean	9.10	Beta 0.64 0.58
Sharpe Ratio	0.76	R-Squared 47 69

Investment Style

Stocks

	Port Avg	Rel S&P 500
Price/Earnings Ratio	24.7	1.34
Price/Book Ratio	2.4	0.69
5 Yr Earnings Gr %	1.1#	0.21
Med Mkt Cap ($mil)	2421	0.19

figure is based on 50% or less of stocks

Bonds

Avg Effective Duration	8.0 Yrs
Avg Effective Maturity	5.1 Yrs
Avg Credit Quality	AAA
Avg Weighted Coupon	7.57%

Diversification Value for Portfolio Types

Large Cap: Medium	Small Cap: Medium	Bond: Medium	Balanced: Low	Diversified: Low

Portfolio 12-31-94

Total Stocks: 212
Total Fixed-Income: 14

Share Chg (06-94)000	Amount 000		Date of Maturity	Value $000	% Net Assets
	40000	US Treasury Bond 7.875%	02-15-21	39475	4.69
	23933	GNMA 7%	08-15-23	21495	2.55
	14111	GNMA 6.5%	08-15-23	12237	1.45
-50	600	United Dominion Realty Trust		8625	1.03
0	375	Glimcher Realty Trust		8203	0.98
0	250	Post Properties		7875	0.94
0	250	Developers Diversified Rlty		7813	0.93
0	350	Merry Land & Investment		7656	0.91
-50	200	Weingarten Realty		7575	0.90
-50	200	Kimco Realty		7575	0.90
0	250	Health Care Pptys Invst Tr		7531	0.90
0	250	Equity Residential Ppty Tr		7500	0.89
	7233	GNMA 9.5%	08-15-17	7475	0.89
0	300	Camden Property Trust		7463	0.89
20	370	Manufactured Home Community		7354	0.87
0	600	South West Property Trust		7350	0.87
-21	325	Colonial Properties Trust		7313	0.87
0	100	Monsanto		7050	0.84
0	150	Boeing		7013	0.83
250	250	Storage USA		6875	0.82

Index Allocation

	% of Stocks
S&P 500	34.7
S&P MidCap 400	3.7
U.S. Small Cap	28.4
Foreign	34.7

Composition % 12-31-94

Cash	12.0	Preferreds	0.0
Stocks	76.0	Convertibles	0.0
Bonds	12.0	Other	0.0

Tax Analysis

	Tax-Adj Historical Return %	% Pretax Return
3 Yr Avg	7.38	78.8
5 Yr Avg	5.04	74.5
10 Yr Avg	10.85	81.9

Potential Capital Gain Exposure (% of assets) 4%

Most Similar Funds in MF500

Scudder Global	Fair Fit
Templeton Real Estate Secs	Fair Fit
Scudder Growth & Income	Weak Fit

Bond Credit Analysis 12-31-94

% of Bonds

US Govt	100	BB	0
AAA	0	B	0
AA	0	Below B	0
A	0	NR/NA	0
BBB	0		

Stock Sector Weightings

	% of Stocks	Relative S&P 500
Utilities	7.5	0.60
Energy	5.5	0.54
Financials	31.8	3.01
Industrial Cyclicals	26.6	1.62
Consumer Durables	6.6	1.06
Consumer Staples	4.7	0.38
Services	7.5	0.92
Retail	4.7	0.81
Health	3.9	0.45
Technology	1.2	0.13

Min Initial Purchase

Min Initial Purchase	$1000 (Addt'l: $50)
Min IRA Purchase	$1000 (Addt'l: $50)
Min Auto Invest Plan	$100 (Systematic Inv: $50)

Expenses & Fees

Sales Fees	0.00% front
	0.00% deferred
	0.00% 12b-1
Management Fee	0.75% flat fee
3-,5-,10-yr Expense Projections	$37, $65, $143
Annual Brokerage Cost	0.16%

MORNINGSTAR 1995 Mutual Fund 500

USAA Mutual Income

	Ticker	Load	NAV	Yield	SEC Yield	Assets	Objective
	USAIX	None	11.19	7.7%	7.69%	1611.8	Income

USAA Mutual Income Fund seeks current income without undue risk to principal.

The fund invests primarily in investment-grade debt securities. These securities may include U.S. government obligations, mortgage-backed securities, corporate debt, U.S. bank obligations and asset-backed securities. It may also purchase convertible securities, common stocks, and preferred stocks. For temporary purposes, the fund may invest up to 100% of its assets in high-quality, short-term debt instruments.

Manager's Investment Style

Management is more conservative than most, investing 85% of assets in high-quality bonds. The remainder is tucked away in value-priced electric utilities. The fund's bond portfolio, with a maturity of more than 11 years, is feeling the pinch of rising rates. Its utilities have been hurt as well. Management plans to move its equities into other high-yielding stocks, such as oil companies.

Fund Manager(s)

John W. Saunders, Jr. CFA(1976), since 10-85.
Birthdate: 01-35. BS, Portland State U. 1965

Manager Experience

	Dates Managed	Invest Obj	Std Dev	+/- Index
John W. Saunders, Jr.				
USAA Investment Gold	08/84 - 10/85	SP	21.65	-42.88

Historical Profile

Return Average
Risk Low
Rating ★★★★ Above Average

Investment Style History
Fixed Income

Income Rtn % Rank Obj

| 14 | 15 | 24 | 35 | 57 | 42 | 47 | 36 |

Growth of $10,000

‖‖‖ Value of Fund ($000)
— Value of Index ($000)
LB L-T
▼ Manager Change
▽ Partial Manager Change
◄ Mgr Unknown After
◄ Mgr Unknown Before

Performance Quartile (Within Objective)

1983	1984	1985	1986	1987	1988	1989	1990	1991	1992	1993	1994	History
10.79	11.12	11.89	11.98	10.97	10.96	11.61	11.41	12.55	12.61	12.71	11.19	NAV
10.68	14.24	19.18	12.74	3.43	9.98	16.30	7.69	19.38	8.37	9.91	-5.22	Total Return %
-11.79	7.98	-12.56	-5.94	-1.83	-6.63	-15.39	10.80	-11.10	0.75	-0.15	-6.53	+/- S&P 500
2.31	-0.91	-2.95	-2.51	0.68	2.11	1.76	-1.26	3.38	1.12	0.16	-2.30	+/- LB Aggregate
10.09	11.19	12.07	11.47	9.80	10.07	10.08	9.41	9.29	7.89	7.09	6.74	Income Return %
0.58	3.06	7.10	1.27	-6.37	-0.09	6.22	-1.72	10.09	0.48	2.82	-11.96	Capital Return %
76	9	77	69	32	62	43	16	45	41	67	66	Total Rtn % Rank All
66	30	57	50	28	76	31	8	77	47	79	58	Total Rtn % Rank Obj
1.04	1.07	1.20	1.28	1.13	1.07	1.03	1.03	0.96	0.94	0.88	0.86	Income $
0.12	0.00	0.02	0.06	0.26	0.00	0.03	0.00	0.01	0.00	0.25	0.00	Capital Gains $
1.09	0.75	0.68	0.65	0.61	0.61	0.57	0.53	0.47	0.42	0.41	0.41	Expense Ratio %
10.58	10.97	10.96	9.69	9.13	9.57	9.36	9.19	8.61	7.78	7.00	6.98	Income Ratio %
166	116	79	38	36	11	14	12	15	22	45	25	Turnover Rate %
39.0	92.1	138.8	213.0	255.2	288.2	356.0	481.8	1004.3	1452.1	1945.8	1611.8	Net Assets ($mil)

Performance 12-31-94

	1st Qtr	2nd Qtr	3rd Qtr	4th Qtr	Total
1987	3.11	-2.16	-3.36	6.09	3.43
1988	4.19	1.74	2.74	0.98	9.98
1989	0.63	8.99	1.82	4.13	16.30
1990	-1.20	2.98	-0.64	6.52	7.69
1991	3.80	1.47	6.65	6.29	19.38
1992	-1.91	4.25	4.63	1.29	8.37
1993	4.75	2.95	2.13	-0.20	9.91
1994	-5.09	-2.04	0.77	1.17	-5.22

Bear Market Performance

Decile Rank (5-year period)

Worst ———————————————— Best

	Worst 3 Mo Period 1985-89	Worst 3 Mo Period 1990-94
USAA Mutual Income	-3.50	-6.07
+/- S&P 500	-6.36	-0.32
+/- Best Fit Index : LB L-T	4.19	3.32

Trailing Returns

	Total Return %	+/- S&P 500	+/- LB Aggregate	% Rank All	% Rank Obj	Growth of $10,000
3 Mo	1.17	1.19	0.79	6	1	10,117
6 Mo	1.95	-2.91	0.96	27	7	10,195
1 Yr	-5.22	-6.53	-2.30	66	58	9,478
3 Yr Avg	4.13	-2.14	-0.42	67	78	11,289
5 Yr Avg	7.73	-0.96	0.11	37	55	14,513
10 Yr Avg	9.94	-4.44	0.00	58	64	25,798
15 Yr Avg	11.03	-3.46	0.22	65	58	48,011

Operations

Address and Telephone	USAA Building San Antonio, TX 78288 800-382-8722	
Advisor	USAA Investment Management	
Subadvisor	None	
Distributor	USAA Investment Management	
States Available	All	
Report Grade	C+	
Income Distrib	Paid Monthly	
Date of Inception	03-04-74	
Fiscal Year End	July	

Risk Analysis

Time Period	Load-Adj Return %	Risk % Rank¹ All	Risk % Rank¹ Obj	Morningstar² Return	Morningstar Risk	Morningstar Risk-Adj Rating
1 Yr	-5.22					
3 Yr	4.13	41	71	0.16³	0.63	★★★
5 Yr	7.73	38	26	0.74³	0.45	★★★★
10 Yr	9.94	28	7	0.65	0.42	★★★★
Average Historical Rating (109 months)					3.9	★ s

¹ 1 = low, 100 = high   ² 1.00 = Hybrid Avg   ³ 1.00 = 90-day T-bill return

Other Measures

			Standard S&P 500	Best Fit LB L-T
Standard Deviation	5.25	Alpha	-0.5	-0.6
Mean	4.19	Beta	0.40	0.65
Sharpe Ratio	0.13	R-Squared	36	91

Investment Style

Stocks

	Port Avg	Rel S&P 500
Price/Earnings Ratio	12.9	0.70
Price/Book Ratio	1.3	0.38
5 Yr Earnings Gr %	-1.1	-0.20
Med Mkt Cap ($mil)	2746	0.21

Style: V B G / L M S (Size)

Bonds

Avg Effective Duration	6.5 Yrs
Avg Effective Maturity	11.0 Yrs
Avg Credit Quality	AAA
Avg Weighted Coupon	7.52%

Maturity: S I L / H M L (Quality)

Diversification Value for Portfolio Types

Large Cap: Medium | Small Cap: High | Bond: None | Balanced: Low | Diversified: Medium

Portfolio 12-31-94

Share Chg (07-94)000	Amount 000	Total Stocks: 13 / Total Fixed-Income: 44	Date of Maturity	Value $000	% Net Assets
	237817	FNMA 7.5%	02-01-23	222285	13.79
	224237	GNMA 7.5%	07-15-23	208190	12.92
	196027	GNMA 6.5%	02-15-24	169992	10.55
	119055	US Treasury Bond 7.875%	02-15-21	117492	7.29
	102686	GNMA 7%	09-15-23	92225	5.72
	98135	FNMA 6.5%	12-01-99	86420	5.36
	89686	FNMA 7%	07-01-23	81474	5.05
	68380	GNMA 8%	01-15-24	65431	4.06
	57726	FNMA 8%	12-01-22	55363	3.43
	50121	FHLMC 8%	04-01-21	47787	2.96
0	1000	Public Service Enterprise		26500	1.64
0	800	American Electric Power		26300	1.63
0	1200	Allegheny Power System		26100	1.62
0	1100	CINergy		25713	1.60
	28593	FNMA CMO 6.5%	09-25-23	25179	1.56
0	1100	Northeast Utilities		23788	1.48
0	650	Houston Industries		23156	1.44
	22814	FHLMC 8.5%	09-01-20	22336	1.39
	18206	GNMA 8.5%	02-15-17	17898	1.11
	16894	FHLMC 10%	09-01-20	17649	1.10

Index Allocation

	% of Stocks
S&P 500	55.3
S&P MidCap 400	31.4
U.S. Small Cap	13.3
Foreign	0.0

Composition % 12-31-94

Cash	1.0	Preferreds	0.0
Stocks	14.0	Convertibles	0.0
Bonds	85.0	Other	0.0

Tax Analysis

	Tax-Adj Historical Return %	% Pretax Return
3 Yr Avg	1.25	29.6
5 Yr Avg	4.85	59.2
10 Yr Avg	6.25	52.8
Potential Capital Gain Exposure (% of assets)		-9%

Most Similar Funds in MF500

Fidelity Government Secs	Strong Fit
Scudder Income	Strong Fit
Vanguard F/I L/T Corp Bond	Strong Fit

Bond Credit Analysis 12-31-94

% of Bonds

US Govt	96	BB	0
AAA	1	B	0
AA	0	Below B	0
A	2	NR/NA	0
BBB	1		

Stock Sector Weightings

	% of Stocks	Relative S&P 500
Utilities	95.1	7.67
Energy	4.9	0.48
Financials	0.0	0.00
Industrial Cyclicals	0.0	0.00
Consumer Durables	0.0	0.00
Consumer Staples	0.0	0.00
Services	0.0	0.00
Retail	0.0	0.00
Health	0.0	0.00
Technology	0.0	0.00

Min / Expenses

Min Initial Purchase	$1000 (Addt'l: $50)
Min IRA Purchase	$1000 (Addt'l: $50)
Min Auto Invest Plan	$1000 (Systematic Inv: $50)

Expenses & Fees

Sales Fees	0.00% front
	0.00% deferred
	0.00% 12b-1
Management Fee	0.24% flat fee
3-,5-,10-yr Expense Projections	$13, $23, $52
Annual Brokerage Cost	0.02%

USAA Mutual Income Stock

	Ticker	Load	NAV	Yield	SEC Yield	Assets	Objective
	USISX	None	13.06	5.6%	N/A	1171.7	Equity-Inc.

USAA Mutual Fund Income Stock Fund seeks current income consistent with potential for increasing dividend income and capital gains.

The fund invests primarily in above-average dividend-paying common stocks of well-established, large companies. It is structured to provide a yield greater than the composite yield of the S&P 500 Index. Criteria for selection include level and safety of dividend, prospects for dividend increases, and potential for capital appreciation. The fund may write covered calls on up to 5% of its portfolio.

Manager's Investment Style

Management uses many tools to produce hefty yields. Preferred convertibles are central in the fund's portfolio, taking up 25% of assets. Electric-utilities holdings, growing to as much as 30% of assets, have also played an important part. When management is wary of rising rates, it will trim utilities holdings accordingly. REITs, diversified among many different issues, fill in the gaps, and give the portfolio less downside risk.

Historical Profile
Return — Average
Risk — Low
Rating — ★★★★ Above Average

Investment Style History
Equity

| 91% | 95% | 94% | 95% | 90% | 90% | 82% | 76% |

Average % Stocks Held in Portfolio

Growth of $10,000
IIII Value of Fund ($000)
— Value of Index ($000) S&P 500
▼ Manager Change
▽ Partial Manager Change
► Mgr Unknown After
◄ Mgr Unknown Before

Performance Quartile (Within Objective)

	1983	1984	1985	1986	1987	1988	1989	1990	1991	1992	1993	1994	History
	---	---	---	---	9.03	10.28	11.85	11.01	13.27	13.48	14.13	13.06	NAV
	---	---	---	---	-7.78 *	19.43	27.14	-1.42	27.33	7.80	11.56	-0.70	Total Return %
	---	---	---	---	5.01 *	2.82	-4.55	-3.16	0.18	0.18	1.50	-2.02	+/- S&P 500
	---	---	---	---	---	1.49	-2.04	4.76	-6.88	-1.17	0.27	-0.63	+/- Wilshire 5000
	---	---	---	---	1.75	5.59	5.54	5.67	6.80	5.50	5.28	5.47	Income Return %
	---	---	---	---	-9.53	13.84	21.59	-7.09	20.53	2.30	6.28	-6.17	Capital Return %
	---	---	---	---	---	15	19	59	31	48	55	25	Total Rtn % Rank All
	---	---	---	---	---	38	14	20	40	66	70	32	Total Rtn % Rank Obj
	---	---	---	---	0.19	0.48	0.57	0.65	0.68	0.70	0.71	0.75	Income $
	---	---	---	---	0.02	0.00	0.58	0.00	0.00	0.09	0.19	0.22	Capital Gains $
	---	---	---	---	1.00	1.00	1.00	1.00	0.83	0.74	0.70	0.73	Expense Ratio %
	---	---	---	---	5.22	4.72	5.10	5.75	6.30	5.99	5.43	5.25	Income Ratio %
	---	---	---	---	---	28	72	49	27	16	27	25	Turnover Rate %
	---	---	---	---	20.9	33.3	65.7	92.0	243.4	592.4	1129.9	1171.7	Net Assets ($mil)

Fund Manager(s)
Harry W. Miller CFA(1968), since 01-89.
Birthdate: 06-34. BS, Rider U. 1957 MBA, U. of Southern California 1968

Manager Experience

	Dates Managed	Invest Obj	Std Dev	+/- Index
Harry W. Miller				
USAA Mutual Growth	12/84 - 01/89	G	19.02	-7.35
USAA Invst Cornerstone	10/85 - 04/88	AA	18.08	6.71

Performance 12-31-94

	1st Qtr	2nd Qtr	3rd Qtr	4th Qtr	Total
1987	---	---	3.67	-14.38	-7.78 *
1988	7.86	6.06	1.99	2.36	19.43
1989	5.74	8.00	7.50	3.56	27.14
1990	-4.89	2.16	-8.30	10.64	-1.42
1991	10.81	-0.82	7.28	7.99	27.33
1992	-1.43	3.72	1.58	3.80	7.80
1993	7.12	1.33	4.77	-1.91	11.56
1994	-3.99	0.00	5.91	-2.35	-0.70

Bear Market Performance
Decile Rank (5-year period)

Worst — Best

	Worst 3 Mo Period 1985-89	Worst 3 Mo Period 1990-94
USAA Mutual Income Stock	---	-8.30
+/- S&P 500	---	5.44
+/- Best Fit Index : S&P 500	---	5.44

Trailing Returns

	Total Return %	+/- S&P 500	+/- Wil 5000	% Rank All	% Rank Obj	Growth of $10,000
3 Mo	-2.35	-2.34	-1.58	75	44	9,765
6 Mo	3.42	-1.45	-1.21	18	10	10,342
1 Yr	-0.70	-2.02	-0.63	25	32	9,930
3 Yr Avg	6.09	-0.18	-0.52	33	62	11,941
5 Yr Avg	8.43	-0.26	-0.39	29	27	14,987
10 Yr Avg	---	---	---	---	---	---
15 Yr Avg	---	---	---	---	---	---

Operations

Address and Telephone	USAA Building
	San Antonio, TX 78288
	800-382-8722
Advisor	USAA Investment Management
Subadvisor	None
Distributor	USAA Investment Management
States Available	All
Report Grade	C+
Income Distrib	Paid Quarterly
* Date of Inception	05-04-87
Fiscal Year End	July

Min Initial Purchase	$1000 (Addt'l: $50)
Min IRA Purchase	$1000 (Addt'l: $100)
Min Auto Invest Plan	$100 (Systematic Inv: $50)

Expenses & Fees
Sales Fees	0.00% front
	0.00% deferred
	0.00% 12b-1
Management Fee	0.50% flat fee
3-,5-,10-yr Expense Projections	$22, $39, $87
Annual Brokerage Cost	0.17%

Risk Analysis

Time Period	Load-Adj Return %	Risk % Rank [1] All	Obj	Morningstar [2] Return	Morningstar Risk	Morningstar Risk-Adj Rating
1 Yr	-0.70					
3 Yr	6.09	61	67	0.74 [3]	0.67	★★★
5 Yr	8.43	57	32	0.92 [3]	0.64	★★★★
10 Yr	---	---	---	---	---	

Average Historical Rating (56 months) 4.2 ★ s

[1] = low, 100 = high [2] 1.00 = Equity Avg [3] 1.00 = 90-day T-bill return

Other Measures
			Standard S&P 500	Best Fit S&P 500
Standard Deviation	7.71	Alpha	0.2	0.2
Mean	6.22	Beta	0.85	0.85
Sharpe Ratio	0.35	R-Squared	77	77

Investment Style
	Stock Portfolio Avg	Relative S&P 500
Price/Earnings Ratio	18.2	0.98
Price/Book Ratio	2.2	0.65
5 Yr Earnings Gr %	0.9	0.16
Return on Assets %	6.2	0.82
Debt % Total Cap	34.3	1.21
Med Mkt Cap ($mil)	5416	0.42

Style
Value Blend Growth
Size Large Med Small

Diversification Value for Portfolio Types
Large Cap: Low	Small Cap: Medium	Bond: Medium	Balanced: Low	Diversified: Low

Portfolio 12-31-94

Total Stocks: 56
Total Fixed-Income: 12

Share Chg (07-94) 000	Amount 000		Value $000	% Net Assets
	1000	Sears Roebuck A Cv Pfd $3.75	55625	4.75
0	900	Bristol-Myers Squibb	52088	4.45
0	1300	American Brands	48750	4.16
-165	700	Dow Chemical	47075	4.02
75	800	Philip Morris	46000	3.93
605	700	American Home Products	43925	3.75
0	2150	Occidental Petroleum	41388	3.53
	400	Ford Motor Cl A Cv Pfd 8.40%	36800	3.14
0	1200	GTE	36450	3.11
0	1500	Allegheny Power System	32625	2.78
	1200	Atlantic Richfield Cv DECS 9%	31350	2.68
300	300	Atlantic Richfield	30525	2.61
	950	Unisys Cl A Cv Pfd $3.75	30163	2.57
0	1000	Sun	28750	2.45
0	1050	Public Service Enterprise	27825	2.37
	571	First Chicago B Cv Pfd $5.75	26984	2.30
1000	1000	CINergy	23500	2.01
0	831	National Fuel Gas	21191	1.81
1000	1000	James River	20250	1.73
0	300	Deere	19875	1.70
	850	Quanex Cv Pfd 6.88%	18594	1.59
0	427	BF Goodrich	18521	1.58
0	300	Texaco	17963	1.53
-113	500	Nationwide Health Properties	17875	1.53
	1344	Westinghouse Elec Cv Pfd $1.53	17812	1.52

Composition % 12-31-94
Cash	3.0	Preferreds	0.0
Stocks	72.0	Convertibles	25.0
Bonds	0.0	Other	0.0

Tax Analysis
	Tax-Adj Historical Return %	% Pretax Return
3 Yr Avg	3.74	60.0
5 Yr Avg	6.25	71.0
10 Yr Avg	---	---

Potential Capital Gain Exposure (% of assets) -3%

Most Similar Funds in MF500
Evergreen Total Return	Strong Fit
Vanguard Equity-Income	Fair Fit
Washington Mutual Investors	Fair Fit

Index Allocation
	% of Stocks
S&P 500	70.6
S&P MidCap 400	13.9
U.S. Small Cap	15.5
Foreign	0.0

Sector Weightings
	% of Stocks	Relative S&P 500
Utilities	25.2	2.03
Energy	17.1	1.69
Financials	17.9	1.69
Industrial Cyclicals	15.8	0.96
Consumer Durables	0.0	0.00
Consumer Staples	11.2	0.90
Services	0.0	0.00
Retail	0.0	0.00
Health	12.8	1.48
Technology	0.0	0.00

M⊙RNINGSTAR 1995 Mutual Fund 500

USAA Tax-Exempt Interm-Term

Ticker	Load	NAV	Yield	SEC Yield	Assets	Objective
USATX	None	12.02	5.7%	5.89%	1416.1	Muni Nat

USAA Tax-Exempt Fund Intermediate-Term Fund seeks interest income exempt from federal income tax.

The fund invests primarily in municipal obligations. At least 80% of its annual interest income is typically exempt from regular federal income tax and the Alternative Minimum Tax. At least 75% of the municipal securities purchased by the fund are rated A or higher; none may be rated below investment grade. The average weighted maturity ranges between three and 10 years.

Historical Profile

Return	Average
Risk	Below Average
Rating	★★★★ Above Average

Investment Style History
Fixed Income

| 57 | 58 | 38 | 31 | 32 | 42 | 42 | 25 |

Income Rtn % Rank Obj

Growth of $10,000

||| Value of Fund ($000)
— Value of Index ($000) LB Muni
▼ Manager Change
▽ Partial Manager Change
► Mgr Unknown After
◄ Mgr Unknown Before

Performance Quartile (Within Objective)

Manager's Investment Style

Management favors GOs and essential-services bonds because of their more-dedicated revenue streams; it thus avoids lease-backed issues. It also generally sticks with issues rated at least A. The fund is, however, willing to push the envelope of its 10-year maturity constraint, depending on its interest-rate outlook. Additionally, management has overweighted sectors and individual states for yield pickup.

Fund Manager(s)

Clifford A. Gladson CFA(1990), since 04-93.
Birthdate: 11-50. BS, Marquette U. 1985 MS, U. of Wisconsin 1987

History	1983	1984	1985	1986	1987	1988	1989	1990	1991	1992	1993	1994
NAV	11.06	11.00	11.75	12.35	11.61	11.76	11.98	11.93	12.41	12.68	13.26	12.02
Total Return %	9.67	8.86	16.40	13.24	0.95	8.72	9.24	6.72	11.14	8.49	11.47	-4.03
+/- LB Aggregate	1.30	-6.30	-5.73	-2.01	-1.81	0.84	-5.30	-2.23	-4.87	1.25	1.72	-1.11
+/- LB Muni	1.63	-1.70	-3.62	-6.08	-0.56	-1.44	-1.55	-0.58	-1.01	-0.33	-0.81	1.58
Income Return %	9.13	9.40	9.58	8.13	6.81	7.43	7.37	7.14	7.11	6.31	5.77	5.16
Capital Return %	0.55	-0.54	6.82	5.11	-5.86	1.29	1.87	-0.42	4.02	2.18	5.70	-9.18
Total Rtn % Rank All	81	32	89	66	51	69	82	25	83	39	55	54
Total Rtn % Rank Obj	47	54	77	80	33	74	55	28	61	50	53	33
Income $	0.98	0.99	0.99	0.91	0.83	0.84	0.83	0.82	0.81	0.75	0.70	0.69
Capital Gains $	0.00	0.00	0.00	0.00	0.02	0.00	0.00	0.00	0.00	0.00	0.13	0.03
Expense Ratio %	1.18	0.73	0.64	0.57	0.60	0.56	0.49	0.46	0.43	0.44	0.42	0.40
Income Ratio %	8.84	8.84	9.09	8.36	7.07	7.16	7.10	6.95	6.91	6.45	5.85	5.30
Turnover Rate %	38	49	127	80	91	139	113	62	66	67	74	69
Net Assets ($mil)	33.5	90.1	113.8	201.2	320.3	393.4	453.1	536.9	818.3	1205.8	1660.9	1416.1

Manager Experience

	Dates Managed	Invest Obj	Std Dev	+/- Index
Clifford A. Gladson				
USAA Tax-Exempt Sh-Ter	04/94 - 12/94	MN	1.14	0.78
USAA Investment Balncd	04/94 - 12/94	B	4.95	-4.07

Performance 12-31-94

	1st Qtr	2nd Qtr	3rd Qtr	4th Qtr	Total
1987	1.92	-2.87	-1.62	3.65	0.95
1988	3.28	1.87	1.62	1.69	8.72
1989	0.76	4.81	0.46	2.97	9.24
1990	0.81	1.83	0.96	2.98	6.72
1991	2.30	1.99	3.37	3.04	11.14
1992	0.56	3.37	2.46	1.87	8.49
1993	3.15	3.08	3.28	1.51	11.47
1994	-4.63	1.10	0.98	-1.42	-4.03

Bear Market Performance

Decile Rank (5-year period)

Worst .... Best

	Worst 3 Mo Period 1985-89	Worst 3 Mo Period 1990-94
USAA Tax-Exempt Interm-Term	-5.48	-5.11
+/- LB Aggregate	-1.93	-0.17
+/- Best Fit Index : LB Muni	1.01	0.65

Trailing Returns

	Total Return %	+/- LB Aggregate	+/- LB Muni	% Rank All	% Rank Obj	Growth of $10,000
3 Mo	-1.42	-1.80	0.01	55	55	9,858
6 Mo	-0.46	-1.45	0.79	64	32	9,954
1 Yr	-4.03	-1.11	1.58	54	33	9,597
3 Yr Avg	5.09	0.55	0.22	46	24	11,606
5 Yr Avg	6.60	-1.03	-0.17	60	27	13,766
10 Yr Avg	8.08	-1.86	-1.35	86	74	21,752
15 Yr Avg	---	---	---	---	---	---

Operations

Address and Telephone	USAA Building
	San Antonio, TX 78288
	800-382-8722
Advisor	USAA Investment Management
Subadvisor	None
Distributor	USAA Investment Management
States Available	All
Report Grade	B-
Income Distrib	Paid Monthly
Date of Inception	12-07-81
Fiscal Year End	March

Min Initial Purchase	$3000 (Addt'l: $50)
Min IRA Purchase	N/A
Min Auto Invest Plan	$3000 (Systematic Inv: $50)

Expenses & Fees

Sales Fees	0.00% front
	0.00% deferred
	0.00% 12b-1
Management Fee	0.28% flat fee
3-,5-,10-yr Expense Projections	$13, $22, $51

Risk Analysis

Time Period	Load-Adj Return %	Risk % Rank [1] All	Risk % Rank [1] Obj	Morningstar [2] Return	Morningstar Risk	Morningstar Risk-Adj Rating
1 Yr	-4.03					
3 Yr	5.09	15	28	1.30	0.81	★★★★
5 Yr	6.60	8	22	1.12	0.77	★★★★
10 Yr	8.08	4	17	0.91	0.73	★★★★
Average Historical Rating (109 months)					3.9	★s

[1] 1 = low, 100 = high [2] 1.00 = Muni Avg [3] 1.00 = 90-day T-bill return

Other Measures

				Standard LB Agg	Best Fit LB Muni
Standard Deviation	4.89	Alpha		0.7	0.3
Mean	5.10	Beta		0.91	0.88
Sharpe Ratio	0.32	R-Squared		55	98

Investment Style

Interest-Rate Stance
Avg Effective Maturity 8.8 Yrs

Maturity Short Intm Long

Quality
Avg Credit Quality A
Avg Weighted Coupon 5.69%
Avg Weighted Price 94.77% of Par

Diversification Value for Portfolio Types

 Large Cap: Medium   Small Cap: High    Bond: Low   Balanced: Medium   Diversified: High

Portfolio 12-31-94

Total Stocks: 0
Total Fixed-Income: 156

Amount 000	Date of Maturity		Value $000	% Net Assets
60000	03-01-02	MA New England Educ Loan Mktg 5.8%	59443	4.20
54460	06-01-04	OK Grand Rvr Dam 4%	46195	3.26
32260	01-01-03	NJ Tpk 6.5%	33373	2.36
34035	01-01-05	TX Lower CO Rvr 5.25%	31655	2.24
26305	01-01-07	GA Muni Elec Pwr 7%	27210	1.92
27750	06-01-04	DC GO 5.8%	25627	1.81
27665	06-15-06	NY New York City Muni Wtr Fin Swr 5.3%	24787	1.75
27775	02-01-05	MA State GO 5.1%	24596	1.74
29395	01-01-05	IL Toll Hwy 3.5%	24131	1.70
25195	09-02-05	CA Pleasanton Jt Pwrs Fin 6%	24031	1.70
24950	07-01-05	PR GO Pub Impr 5.375%	22230	1.57
38325	07-01-04	UT Intermountain Pwr Sply 0%	22011	1.55
20000	12-01-06	PR Hsg Bank/Fin 7.5%	21986	1.55
23780	06-01-06	DC GO 5.75%	21096	1.49
21235	01-01-07	IL Chicago O'Hare Intl Arpt VAR	20935	1.48
21000	01-01-03	NC East Muni Pwr 6.25%	20715	1.46
20920	11-15-04	CA Sacramento MUD Elec 5.25%	19266	1.36
20300	11-01-05	IN Hlth Fac Fin 5.4%	18987	1.34
18110	12-01-15	LA Pub Fac DMD	18843	1.33
17175	08-01-99	MA Indl Fin Biomed Rsrch 7.1%	17849	1.26

Credit Analysis % of Bonds 12-31-94

US Govt	0	BB	0
AAA	18	B	0
AA	15	Below B	0
A	57	NR/NA	0
BBB	10		

Composition % of Assets 12-31-94

Cash	1.0	Preferreds	0.0
Stocks	0.0	Convertibles	0.0
Bonds	99.0	Other	0.0

Tax Analysis

	Tax-Adj Historical Return %	% Pretax Return
3 Yr Avg	4.98	97.6
5 Yr Avg	6.53	98.8
10 Yr Avg	8.04	99.3

Potential Capital Gain Exposure (% of assets) -3%

Most Similar Funds in MF500

Dreyfus Intermediate Muni	Strong Fit
SteinRoe Intermediate Munis	Strong Fit
T. Rowe Price Tax-Fr Hi-Yld	Strong Fit

Coupon Range

	% Bonds	Rel Obj
0%	5.9	2.36
0% to 6.8%	64.9	1.07
6.8% to 7.5%	15.4	0.99
7.5% to 8.3%	4.4	0.50
More than 8.3%	1.0	0.11
Not applicable	8.5	2.18

Sector Weightings

	% Bonds	Rel Obj
General Obl	24.22	1.15
Utilities	17.36	1.39
Health	11.61	0.88
Water/Waste	3.30	0.52
Housing	7.10	0.97
Education	6.70	1.05
Transportation	8.11	0.80
COP/Lease	0.03	0.01
Private	11.38	0.98
Misc Revenue	4.47	0.90
Demand	5.72	2.33

Top 5 States % of Bonds

NY	10.68	TX	8.38
MA	8.64	CA	8.02
IL	8.45		

USAA Tax-Exempt Long-Term

	Ticker	Load	NAV	Yield	SEC Yield	Assets	Objective
	USTEX	None	12.22	6.3%	6.46%	1661.2	Muni Nat

USAA Tax-Exempt Fund Long-Term Fund seeks tax-exempt interest income.

The fund invests primarily in municipal securities, so that at least 80% of its annual income is exempt from federal income tax and the Alternative Minimum Tax. At least 75% of the fund's securities are rated A or higher; the remainder may be rated no lower than BBB at the time of purchase. The fund typically maintains an average weighted maturity of 10 years or more.

Prior to Aug. 1, 1992, the fund was named USAA Tax-Exempt Fund High-Yield Fund.

Manager's Investment Style

Management's top priority is yield. As a result, management has decided not to shorten maturity just to decrease price volatility. Instead, management will accept some losses in order to keep payouts at their current level. In an effort to combat price risk while preserving yield, management has decided to invest in bonds with lower credit ratings. The portfolio now holds 17% of assets in BBB bonds and has a slightly lower credit quality than its average peer.

Fund Manager(s)

Kenneth E. Willmann CFA(1978), since 06-82.
Birthdate: 08-46. BA, U. of Texas 1968 MBA, U. of Texas 1973

Manager Experience	Dates Managed	Invest Obj	Std Dev	+/- Index
Kenneth E. Willmann				
USAA Tax-Ex CA Bond	08/89 - 04/94	MC	5.79	-1.64
USAA Tax-Ex VA Bond	10/90 - 04/94	MS	5.06	-1.17

Historical Profile
Return	Above Average
Risk	Average
Rating	★★★ Neutral

Investment Style History
Fixed Income
Income Rtn % Rank Obj

	19	15	18	14	21	17	19	17

Growth of $10,000
- ‖‖ Value of Fund ($000)
- — Value of Index ($000) LB Muni
- ▼ Manager Change
- ▽ Partial Manager Change
- ► Mgr Unknown After
- ◄ Mgr Unknown Before

Performance Quartile (Within Objective)

1983	1984	1985	1986	1987	1988	1989	1990	1991	1992	1993	1994	History
11.69	11.73	12.81	13.79	12.31	12.84	13.21	13.09	13.73	13.90	14.18	12.22	NAV
11.43	10.49	19.74	17.31	-1.87	12.53	10.62	6.56	12.38	10.18	12.51	-7.93	Total Return %
3.06	-4.66	-2.38	2.06	-4.63	4.65	-3.92	-2.39	-3.62	2.94	2.76	-5.01	+/- LB Aggregate
3.38	-0.06	-0.28	-2.01	-3.38	2.37	-0.16	-0.75	0.24	1.36	0.23	-2.32	+/- LB Muni
9.69	10.15	10.54	8.92	7.44	8.23	7.74	7.46	7.49	6.84	6.27	5.41	Income Return %
1.74	0.34	9.21	8.39	-9.31	4.31	2.88	-0.91	4.89	3.34	6.24	-13.33	Capital Return %
72	24	74	38	74	41	67	27	72	21	46	85	Total Rtn % Rank All
29	16	51	59	78	24	18	38	24	8	35	85	Total Rtn % Rank Obj
1.08	1.11	1.14	1.07	0.98	0.96	0.95	0.95	0.92	0.89	0.84	0.78	Income $
0.00	0.00	0.00	0.09	0.22	0.00	0.00	0.00	0.00	0.28	0.56	0.09	Capital Gains $
1.09	0.68	0.56	0.50	0.49	0.51	0.45	0.43	0.40	0.40	0.39	0.38	Expense Ratio %
9.33	9.34	9.78	8.94	7.64	7.75	7.58	7.23	7.22	6.83	6.35	5.69	Income Ratio %
18	64	150	122	83	169	124	92	91	76	88	109	Turnover Rate %
50.3	148.2	272.8	648.0	791.6	950.2	1145.2	1360.2	1637.1	1784.3	2014.0	1661.2	Net Assets ($mil)

Performance 12-31-94

	1st Qtr	2nd Qtr	3rd Qtr	4th Qtr	Total
1987	3.10	-5.99	-3.54	4.96	-1.87
1988	3.01	2.75	3.15	3.08	12.53
1989	0.46	6.71	-0.12	3.31	10.62
1990	0.30	2.21	-0.21	4.17	6.56
1991	2.08	2.03	4.16	3.59	12.38
1992	0.27	5.55	2.70	1.38	10.18
1993	3.81	3.81	3.22	1.14	12.51
1994	-5.55	0.00	0.15	-2.66	-7.93

Bear Market Performance

Decile Rank (5-year period)

Worst | | | | | | | | | | Best

	Worst 3 Mo Period 1985-89	Worst 3 Mo Period 1990-94
USAA Tax-Exempt Long-Term	-9.00	-6.48
+/- LB Aggregate	-5.44	-4.70
+/- Best Fit Index : LB Muni	-2.50	-1.04

Trailing Returns

	Total Return %	+/- LB Aggregate	+/- LB Muni	% Rank All	% Rank Obj	Growth of $10,000
3 Mo	-2.66	-3.04	-1.23	79	96	9,734
6 Mo	-2.52	-3.51	-1.27	92	94	9,748
1 Yr	-7.93	-5.01	-2.32	85	85	9,207
3 Yr Avg	4.51	-0.04	-0.36	59	52	11,414
5 Yr Avg	6.45	-1.18	-0.32	64	36	13,668
10 Yr Avg	8.90	-1.05	-0.53	74	44	23,452
15 Yr Avg	---	---	---	---	---	---

Operations

Address and Telephone	USAA Building San Antonio, TX 78288 800-382-8722
Advisor	USAA Investment Management
Subadvisor	None
Distributor	USAA Investment Management
States Available	All
Report Grade	B-
Income Distrib	Paid Monthly
Date of Inception	12-07-81
Fiscal Year End	March

Risk Analysis

Time Period	Load-Adj Return %	Risk % Rank [1] All	Risk % Rank [1] Obj	Morningstar [2] Return	Morningstar Risk	Morningstar Risk-Adj Rating
1 Yr	-7.93					
3 Yr	4.51	38	61	1.21	1.12	★★★
5 Yr	6.45	27	58	1.14	1.10	★★★
10 Yr	8.90	16	47	1.13	1.06	★★★
Average Historical Rating (109 months)					3.6	★s

[1] = low, 100 = high [2] 1.00 = Muni Avg [3] 1.00 = 90-day T-bill return

Other Measures

	Standard LB Agg	Best Fit LB Muni
Standard Deviation	6.21	Alpha	-0.1	-0.4
Mean	4.61	Beta	1.19	1.10
Sharpe Ratio	0.17	R-Squared	59	95

Investment Style

Interest-Rate Stance
Avg Effective Maturity   23.2 Yrs

Maturity Short Intm Long

Quality
Avg Credit Quality   AA

Quality High Med Low

Avg Weighted Coupon   6.88%
Avg Weighted Price   95.27% of Par

Diversification Value for Portfolio Types

Large Cap: Medium	Small Cap: High	Bond: Low	Balanced: Medium	Diversified: Medium

Portfolio 12-31-94

Amount 000	Date of Maturity	Total Stocks: 0 Total Fixed-Income: 109	Value $000	% Net Assets
68500	01-01-32	WA Seattle Swr 6.2%	62190	3.74
74505	01-01-32	CA San Joaquin Hills Transp Toll 6.75%	61929	3.73
51420	02-01-14	LA Orleans GO Sch Brd 7.65%	51651	3.11
50000	08-15-19	NY New York City GO 7.25%	50345	3.03
41485	01-01-34	WA King GO 6.25%	37648	2.27
40900	02-01-20	TX San Antonio Elec/Gas Sys 6%	37604	2.26
36275	08-15-34	NY Med Care Fac Fin 6.9%	36449	2.19
32705	07-01-20	UT Intermountain Pwr Sply 8%	33292	2.00
36195	01-01-20	TX Tpk Dallas North Tollway 6%	32380	1.95
35000	08-01-24	GA Burke Dev Poll Cntrl Pwr 6.375%	32079	1.93
30000	06-01-13	MA State GO 6.5%	29649	1.78
33735	06-01-33	WY Comnty Dev Sngl Fam Mtg 6.1%	29346	1.77
30100	04-01-13	NM Lordsburg Poll Cntrl Phelps 6.5%	28265	1.70
24000	06-01-08	MA GO Consolid Loan 7.625%	26780	1.61
25730	08-15-22	LA Lake Charles Harbor/Term Dist 7.75%	25915	1.56
25000	07-01-13	VA Hsg Dev Mtg 6.9%	24974	1.50
23500	07-01-11	AZ Maricopa Indl Dev Hlth Fac 9.25%	24464	1.47
26000	04-01-17	IN Indianapolis Arpt Fac 6.8%	24340	1.47
26215	07-01-12	PR Pub Bldg Educ/Hlth Fac 6%	24290	1.46
25000	10-01-24	RI Hsg/Mtg Fin 6.85%	24167	1.45

Credit Analysis % of Bonds 12-31-94

US Govt	0	BB	0	
AAA	21	B	0	
AA	29	Below B	0	
A	34	NR/NA	0	
BBB	17			

Composition % of Assets 12-31-94

Cash	2.0	Preferreds	0.0
Stocks	0.0	Convertibles	0.0
Bonds	98.0	Other	0.0

Tax Analysis

	Tax-Adj Historical Return %	% Pretax Return
3 Yr Avg	3.89	85.9
5 Yr Avg	6.07	93.5
10 Yr Avg	8.64	95.9
Potential Capital Gain Exposure (% of assets)		-6%

Most Similar Funds in MF500

Dreyfus Muni Bond	Strong Fit
General Municipal Bond	Strong Fit
MFS Municipal Bond A	Strong Fit

Coupon Range

	% Bonds	Rel Obj
0%	6.6	2.64
0% to 6.8%	57.8	0.96
6.8% to 7.5%	17.0	1.09
7.5% to 8.3%	10.9	1.24
More than 8.3%	5.3	0.60
Not applicable	2.4	0.63

Sector Weightings

	% Bonds	Rel Obj
General Obl	14.27	0.68
Utilities	9.75	0.78
Health	23.14	1.75
Water/Waste	5.54	0.87
Housing	14.55	1.98
Education	1.57	0.25
Transportation	14.05	1.38
COP/Lease	0.00	0.00
Private	13.64	1.17
Misc Revenue	0.73	0.15
Demand	2.76	1.12

Top 5 States % of Bonds

TX	11.64	WA	6.84
IL	8.50	LA	5.18
NY	7.13		

Expenses & Fees

Sales Fees	0.00% front 0.00% deferred 0.00% 12b-1
Management Fee	0.28% flat fee
3-,5-,10-yr Expense Projections	$12, $21, $48

Min Initial Purchase $3000 (Addt'l: $50)
Min IRA Purchase   N/A
Min Auto Invest Plan $3000 (Systematic Inv: $50)

MORNINGSTAR 1995 Mutual Fund 500

USAA Tax-Exempt Short-Term

	Ticker	Load	NAV	Yield	SEC Yield	Assets	Objective
	USSTX	None	10.33	4.4%	4.77%	810.8	Muni Nat

USAA Tax-Exempt Fund Short-Term Fund seeks tax-exempt interest income.

The fund invests primarily in municipal securities, so that at least 80% of its annual income is exempt from federal income tax and the Alternative Minimum Tax. At least 75% of the fund's securities are rated A or higher; the remainder may be rated no lower than BBB at the time of purchase. The fund typically maintains an average weighted maturity of three years or less.

Historical Profile
Return Low
Risk Low
Rating ★★★★★ Highest

Investment Style History
Fixed Income
Income Rtn % Rank Obj

| 92 | 87 | 73 | 66 | 84 | 91 | 90 | 75 |

Growth of $10,000
|||| Value of Fund ($000)
— Value of Index ($000)
LB Muni
▼ Manager Change
▽ Partial Manager Change
► Mgr Unknown After
◄ Mgr Unknown Before

Performance Quartile
(Within Objective)

Manager's Investment Style
The fund creates an environment of stability and safety akin to CDs. One of the reasons that the fund is so stable is that the portfolio regularly holds about one fourth of assets in cash equivalents. With the rest of assets, management buys demand notes, laddering them up to five-year notes with an average maturity of no greater than three years. In order to boost yield, the fund holds some issues on the low side of high quality.

Fund Manager(s)
Clifford A. Gladson CFA(1990), since 04-94.
Birthdate: 11-50. BS, Marquette U. 1985 MS, U. of Wisconsin 1987

Manager Experience	Dates Managed	Invest Obj	Std Dev	+/- Index
Clifford A. Gladson				
USAA Tax-Exempt Int-Trm	04/93 - 12/94	MN	4.99	0.60
USAA Investment Bal	04/94 - 12/94	B	4.95	-4.07

	1983	1984	1985	1986	1987	1988	1989	1990	1991	1992	1993	1994	History
	10.21	10.24	10.47	10.71	10.36	10.35	10.42	10.34	10.50	10.59	10.70	10.33	NAV
	6.37	7.69	9.50	8.70	2.82	6.07	7.40	5.87	7.70	5.96	5.49	0.82	Total Return %
	-2.00	-7.47	-12.62	-6.55	0.06	-1.81	-7.14	-3.07	-8.30	-1.28	-4.26	3.74	+/- LB Aggregate
	-1.68	-2.87	-10.52	-10.61	1.32	-4.09	-3.39	-1.43	-4.44	-2.86	-6.79	6.43	+/- LB Muni
	6.95	7.39	7.26	6.41	5.74	6.17	6.73	6.64	6.15	5.11	4.45	4.28	Income Return %
	-0.58	0.29	2.25	2.29	-2.92	-0.10	0.68	-0.77	1.55	0.86	1.04	-3.46	Capital Return %
	95	39	97	88	92	88	92	36	95	70	90	15	Total Rtn % Rank All
	85	75	88	94	11	91	89	71	97	96	97	3	Total Rtn % Rank Obj
	0.70	0.73	0.72	0.65	0.60	0.62	0.67	0.67	0.61	0.52	0.46	0.45	Income $
	0.00	0.00	0.00	0.00	0.04	0.00	0.00	0.00	0.00	0.00	0.00	0.00	Capital Gains $
	1.15	0.85	0.70	0.65	0.57	0.56	0.51	0.52	0.50	0.48	0.43	0.43	Expense Ratio %
	7.56	6.67	7.19	6.85	5.78	5.81	6.14	6.47	6.48	5.59	4.75	4.25	Income Ratio %
	57	56	159	101	142	148	146	87	96	107	138	102	Turnover Rate %
	20.5	62.2	85.1	139.4	226.9	250.7	258.4	360.7	602.8	840.2	954.8	810.8	Net Assets ($mil)

Performance 12-31-94
	1st Qtr	2nd Qtr	3rd Qtr	4th Qtr	Total
1987	1.32	-0.30	-0.31	2.10	2.82
1988	2.07	0.99	1.52	1.35	6.07
1989	0.83	3.19	1.34	1.86	7.40
1990	1.31	1.03	1.43	1.98	5.87
1991	1.68	1.64	2.08	2.08	7.70
1992	1.11	1.97	1.39	1.36	5.96
1993	1.50	1.49	1.44	0.96	5.49
1994	-1.05	0.89	0.91	0.08	0.82

Bear Market Performance
Decile Rank (5-year period)

Worst ... Best

	Worst 3 Mo Period 1985-89	Worst 3 Mo Period 1990-94
USAA Tax-Exempt Short-Term	-1.33	-1.32
+/- LB Aggregate	2.22	3.61
+/- Best Fit Index : LB Muni	5.16	4.44

Trailing Returns
	Total Return %	+/- LB Aggregate	+/- LB Muni	% Rank All	% Rank Obj	Growth of $10,000
3 Mo	0.08	-0.29	1.52	19	4	10,008
6 Mo	0.99	0.00	2.24	37	4	10,099
1 Yr	0.82	3.74	6.43	15	3	10,082
3 Yr Avg	4.06	-0.48	-0.80	68	73	11,270
5 Yr Avg	5.14	-2.48	-1.63	88	94	12,851
10 Yr Avg	6.00	-3.94	-3.42	97	91	17,917
15 Yr Avg	---	---	---	---	---	---

Operations
Address and Telephone	USAA Building
	San Antonio, TX 78288
	800-382-8722
Advisor	USAA Investment Management
Subadvisor	None
Distributor	USAA Investment Management
States Available	All
Report Grade	B-
Income Distrib	Paid Monthly
Date of Inception	12-07-81
Fiscal Year End	March

Min Initial Purchase	$3000 (Addt'l: $50)
Min IRA Purchase	N/A
Min Auto Invest Plan	$3000 (Systematic Inv: $50)

Expenses & Fees
Sales Fees	0.00% front
	0.00% deferred
	0.00% 12b-1
Management Fee	0.28% flat fee
3-,5-,10-yr Expense Projections	$14, $24, $54

Risk Analysis
Time Period	Load-Adj Return %	Risk % Rank All [1]	Risk % Rank Obj [1]	Morningstar[2] Return	Morningstar[2] Risk	Morningstar Risk-Adj Rating
1 Yr	0.82					
3 Yr	4.06	1	3	0.83	0.22	★★★★★
5 Yr	5.14	1	3	0.68	0.19	★★★★★
10 Yr	6.01	1	7	0.46	0.23	★★★★

Average Historical Rating (109 months) 4.0 ★s

[1] 1 = low, 100 = high [2] 1.00 = Muni Avg [3] 1.00 = 90-day T-bill return

Other Measures
			Standard LB Agg	Best Fit LB Muni
Standard Deviation	1.66	Alpha	0.2	0.1
Mean	4.00	Beta	0.30	0.30
Sharpe Ratio	0.29	R-Squared	51	93

Investment Style
Interest-Rate Stance
Avg Effective Maturity 2.8 Yrs

Maturity Short Intm Long
Quality High Med Low

Quality
Avg Credit Quality AA
Avg Weighted Coupon 5.55%
Avg Weighted Price 99.32% of Par

Diversification Value for Portfolio Types
Large Cap: Medium
Small Cap: High
Bond: Low
Balanced: Medium
Diversified: High

Portfolio 12-31-94
Total Stocks: 0
Total Fixed-Income: 110

Amount 000	Date of Maturity		Value $000	% Net Assets
37695	04-25-96	CA State GO 5.75%	37642	4.64
25805	06-15-99	NY Envir Fac Wtr Poll Cntrl Fund 5.5%	25784	3.18
22480	01-01-28	IL Dev Fin DMD	21623	2.67
20000	08-15-99	Guam GO Govt 5.75%	19967	2.46
20400	09-01-97	TX Muni Pwr 4.25%	19896	2.45
18550	08-01-05	CA San Bernardino Multi-Fam 6%	18550	2.29
17290	12-01-00	PA Higher Educ Assist Student Loan 6.8%	18028	2.22
18790	06-01-99	DC GO DMD	17399	2.15
16050	05-01-98	WA Seattle Muni Lt/Pwr 4.3%	15328	1.89
15300	01-01-08	CA Fremont Multi-Fam Hsg DMD	15300	1.89
15100	08-01-16	CA Irvine Ranch Wtr Dist Jt Pwrs DMD	15100	1.86
15000	06-01-99	OK Grand Rvr Dam 5%	14653	1.81
15000	12-01-98	TN Clarksville GO Pub Bldg 4.4%	14387	1.77
14700	07-01-01	IN Hlth Fac Fin St Francis VAR	14205	1.75
14675	12-01-99	MA New England Educ Loan Mktg 4.75%	13847	1.71
13480	07-01-00	WV GO Sch Bldg Cap Impr 6%	13486	1.66
14000	07-01-98	PR GO Pub Impr 4.55%	13337	1.64
13000	06-15-96	CO GO Centennial Wtr/San Dist 6.5%	13201	1.63
13625	12-01-96	PA Mont Redev Multi-Fam Hsg DMD	13111	1.62
12000	11-01-09	PA Pooled Fin Educ Fac Clg/Univ 8%	12791	1.58

Credit Analysis % of Bonds 12-31-94
US Govt	0	BB	0
AAA	17	B	0
AA	33	Below B	0
A	43	NR/NA	0
BBB	7		

Composition % of Assets 12-31-94
Cash	11.0	Preferreds	0.0
Stocks	0.0	Convertibles	0.0
Bonds	89.0	Other	0.0

Tax Analysis
	Tax-Adj Historical Return %	% Pretax Return
3 Yr Avg	4.06	100.0
5 Yr Avg	5.14	100.0
10 Yr Avg	5.99	99.8
Potential Capital Gain Exposure (% of assets)	-2%	

Most Similar Funds in MF500
Dreyfus Short-Intrm Muni Bd	Strong Fit
T. Rowe Price Tax-Fr Sh-Intm	Strong Fit
Vanguard Muni Limited-Term	Strong Fit

Coupon Range
	% Bonds	Rel Obj
0%	1.2	0.49
0% to 6.8%	55.6	0.92
6.8% to 7.5%	9.5	0.62
7.5% to 8.3%	3.3	0.37
More than 8.3%	0.3	0.03
Not applicable	30.0	7.72

Sector Weightings
	% Bonds	Rel Obj
General Obl	27.78	1.32
Utilities	12.42	0.99
Health	8.62	0.65
Water/Waste	1.35	0.21
Housing	2.59	0.35
Education	11.50	1.80
Transportation	5.41	0.53
COP/Lease	0.53	0.17
Private	7.41	0.64
Misc Revenue	1.19	0.24
Demand	21.21	8.62

Top 5 States % of Bonds
CA	14.00	TX	7.62
NY	10.08	IL	7.25
PA	8.59		

MORNINGSTAR 1995 Mutual Fund 500

525

Value Line Convertible

	Ticker	Load	NAV	Yield	SEC Yield	Assets	Objective
	VALCX	None	11.01	6.6%	N/A	45.1	Convrt. Bond

Value Line Convertible Fund seeks high current income together with capital appreciation.

The fund normally invests at least 70% of its assets in bonds, debentures, or other securities that are convertible into common stocks. The balance may be invested in nonconvertible debt or equities, warrants, U.S. government debt, or repurchase agreements. The fund is not required to sell securities if, due to conversions, it does not hold 70% of its assets in convertibles. To select holdings, the fund uses the Value Line Ranking System for convertible securities. This system evaluates the underlying common stock.

Historical Profile

Return	Above Average
Risk	Average
Rating	★★★★ Above Average

Income Rtn % Rank Obj: 1 78 45 38 39 33 16 1

Growth of $10,000

- |||| Value of Fund ($000)
- — Value of Index ($000) Wil 4500
- ▼ Manager Change
- ▽ Partial Manager Change
- ► Mgr Unknown After
- ◄ Mgr Unknown Before

Performance Quartile (Within Objective)

Manager's Investment Style

Management has turned its attention toward limiting downside risk. By purchasing bonds selling below par, the fund has avoided a correction in covertibles that grounded prices. Management has also loaded the portfolio with B rated bonds. These more-illiquid securities are less affected by sell-offs sparked by interest-rate rises. The fund does not offer stellar returns, but its low risk has allowed it to be a consistent performer.

Fund Manager(s)

Management Team

Manager Experience

	Dates Managed	Invest Obj	Std Dev	+/- Index

Not available.

1983	1984	1985	1986	1987	1988	1989	1990	1991	1992	1993	1994	History
---	---	10.97	11.53	9.66	10.70	11.12	10.04	12.25	13.25	12.85	11.01	NAV
---	---	10.58 *	16.24	-6.11	15.98	10.72	-3.72	28.71	13.83	14.83	-5.28	Total Return %
---	---	---	0.99	-8.86	8.10	-3.82	-12.67	12.71	6.59	5.08	-2.36	+/- LB Aggregate
---	---	0.53 *	-2.44	-11.37	-0.63	-20.96	-0.60	-1.77	6.21	4.77	-6.59	+/- S&P 500
---	---	1.20	4.55	7.14	5.21	6.80	5.99	6.70	5.67	5.00	6.02	Income Return %
---	---	9.37	11.69	-13.25	10.77	3.93	-9.71	22.01	8.16	9.83	-11.29	Capital Return %
---	---	---	47	91	25	66	67	29	12	29	66	Total Rtn % Rank All
---	---	---	14	54	7	60	33	39	29	44	53	Total Rtn % Rank Obj
---	---	0.12	0.51	0.82	0.48	0.72	0.66	0.61	0.64	0.66	0.76	Income $
---	---	0.00	0.71	0.48	0.00	0.00	0.00	0.00	1.67	0.43	Capital Gains $
---	---	---	1.31	1.04	1.06	1.03	1.05	1.19	1.14	1.10	1.07	Expense Ratio %
---	---	---	5.37	5.12	4.78	6.32	5.81	5.50	5.45	4.80	5.32	Income Ratio %
---	---	---	234	257	112	105	216	140	146	142	Turnover Rate %
---	---	49.8	60.3	62.7	61.9	54.0	34.8	38.1	41.1	51.8	45.1	Net Assets ($mil)

Performance 12-31-94

	1st Qtr	2nd Qtr	3rd Qtr	4th Qtr	Total
1987	11.61	-2.34	5.16	-18.08	-6.11
1988	4.14	8.39	1.59	1.13	15.98
1989	4.96	2.83	6.51	-3.69	10.72
1990	-0.36	5.60	-11.10	2.93	-3.72
1991	10.15	2.38	7.44	6.24	28.71
1992	2.93	-2.48	5.09	7.91	13.83
1993	6.49	3.30	4.56	-0.17	14.83
1994	-0.97	-3.44	1.65	-2.55	-5.28

Bear Market Performance

Decile Rank (5-year period)

Worst .... Best

	Worst 3 Mo Period 1985-89	Worst 3 Mo Period 1990-94
Value Line Convertible	---	-14.13
+/- LB Aggregate	---	-14.87
+/- Best Fit Index : Wil 4500	---	5.27

Trailing Returns

	Total Return %	+/- LB Aggregate	+/- S&P 500	% Rank All	% Rank Obj	Growth of $10,000
3 Mo	-2.55	-2.92	-2.53	78	37	9,745
6 Mo	-0.94	-1.93	-5.80	72	60	9,906
1 Yr	-5.28	-2.36	-6.59	66	53	9,472
3 Yr Avg	7.38	2.84	1.12	24	41	12,382
5 Yr Avg	8.94	1.31	0.25	24	47	15,344
10 Yr Avg	---	---	---	---	---	---
15 Yr Avg	---	---	---	---	---	---

Operations

Address and Telephone	220 E. 42nd Street New York, NY 10017-5891 800-223-0818 / 212-907-1500		
Advisor	Value Line		
Subadvisor	None		
Distributor	Value Line Securities		
States Available	All		
Report Grade	C+		
Income Distrib	Paid Quarterly		
* Date of Inception	06-03-85		
Fiscal Year End	April		

Risk Analysis

Time Period	Load-Adj Return %	Risk % Rank All	Risk % Rank Obj	Morningstar[2] Return	Morningstar[2] Risk	Morningstar Risk-Adj Rating
1 Yr	-5.28					
3 Yr	7.38	52	58	1.14[3]	0.74	★★★★
5 Yr	8.94	56	57	1.06[3]	0.85	★★★★
10 Yr	---	---	---	---	---	

Average Historical Rating (79 months) 2.8 ★s

[1] 1 = low, 100 = high [2] 1.00 = Hybrid Avg [3] 1.00 = 90-day T-bill return

Other Measures

	Standard LB Agg	Best Fit Wil 4500
Standard Deviation	6.38	Alpha	3.2	1.5
Mean	7.35	Beta	0.69	0.55
Sharpe Ratio	0.60	R-Squared	18	69

Investment Style

Interest-Rate Stance

Avg Effective Maturity 9.9 Yrs

Not Applicable

Quality

Avg Credit Quality	BB
Avg Weighted Coupon	5.73%
Avg Weighted Price	88.09% of Par

Diversification Value for Portfolio Types

Large Cap: Medium	Small Cap: Low	Bond: High	Balanced: Low	Diversified: Medium

Portfolio 09-30-94

Total Stocks: 1
Total Fixed-Income: 48

Amount 000	Date of Maturity		Value $000	% Net Assets
7500	02-15-09	US Treasury Bond 0%	2384	4.99
2250	01-10-15	Time Warner Cv 8.75%	2244	4.70
2250	01-15-03	Air Express Intl Cv 6%	2183	4.57
2750	03-01-01	Hanson America Cv 2.39%	2014	4.21
2000	07-15-00	Pioneer Financial Svcs Cv 8%	1945	4.07
2000	01-15-01	Alexander Haagen Pptys Cv 7.5%	1883	3.94
1500	12-15-03	Raymond Cv 6.5%	1860	3.89
1500	01-15-04	CenterPoint Pptys Cv 8.22%	1633	3.42
1750	03-15-02	Albany International Cv 5.25%	1523	3.19
2000	11-15-00	Bell Sports Cv 4.25%	1470	3.08
1750	01-15-00	NovaCare Cv 5.5%	1461	3.06
1750	03-01-02	Conner Peripherals Cv 6.5%	1374	2.87
30		Delta Air Lines Cv Pfd	1350	2.82
1250	07-01-02	Waban Cv 6.5%	1225	2.56
1950	05-15-11	National Education Cv 6.5%	1131	2.37
1000	04-15-01	Thermo Electron Cv 5%	1115	2.33
1450	12-15-03	Waterhouse Investor Svcs Cv 6%	1098	2.30
19		General Motors Cl C Cv Pfd	1087	2.27
1000	03-15-03	Beverly Enterprises Cv 7.625%	1013	2.12
20		WHX Cl B Cv Pfd	1008	2.11
1000	07-15-04	Malan Realty Investors Cv 9.5%	954	2.00
950	04-01-02	Quantum Cv 6.375%	933	1.95
1250	09-27-13	Motorola Cv 0%	838	1.75
2000	02-20-12	Automatic Data Process Cv 0%	818	1.71
700	03-15-03	Big B Cv 6.5%	767	1.60

Composition % 12-31-94

Cash	6.2	Preferreds	0.0
Stocks	6.3	Convertibles	87.5
Bonds	0.0	Other	0.0

Coupon Range

	% of Bonds	Rel Obj
0%	8.9	1.05
0% to 6%	32.1	0.95
6% to 7%	18.7	1.26
7% to 8.5%	18.7	1.60
More than 8.5%	8.9	1.63
Not applicable	12.6	0.49

Tax Analysis

	Tax-Adj Historical Return %	% Pretax Return
3 Yr Avg	3.83	50.1
5 Yr Avg	5.99	63.2
10 Yr Avg	---	---

Potential Capital Gain Exposure (% of assets) -13%

Credit Analysis 11-30-94

% of Bonds

US Govt	5	BB	18
AAA	0	B	38
AA	6	Below B	9
A	12	NR/NA	1
BBB	10		

Most Similar Funds in MF500

Vista Growth & Income A	Fair Fit
American Cap Harbor A	Weak Fit
MainStay Convertible B	Weak Fit

Min Initial Purchase / Expenses

Min Initial Purchase	$1000 (Addt'l: $250)
Min IRA Purchase	$1000 (Addt'l: $100)
Min Auto Invest Plan	$40 (Systematic Inv: $40)

Expenses & Fees

Sales Fees	0.00% front
	0.00% deferred
	0.00% 12b-1
Management Fee	0.75% flat fee
3-,5-,10-yr Expense Projections	$34, $59, $131

526

Value Line Income

	Ticker	Load	NAV	Yield	SEC Yield	Assets	Objective
	VALIX	None	6.21	3.4%	N/A	131.6	Income

Value Line Income Fund seeks income. Capital growth is a secondary objective.

The fund invests primarily in common stocks or securities convertible into common stocks. There are no limitations, however, on proportions of assets that must be invested in common stocks, preferred stocks, or bonds. To select issues, the fund uses the Value Line Ranking System for timeliness. This system is based on historical and reported earnings, recent earnings and price momentum, and the degree to which the latest earnings deviate from estimated earnings.

Historical Profile

Return	Average
Risk	Below Average
Rating	★★★
	Neutral

Investment Style History
Fixed Income

Income Rtn % Rank Obj

| 38 | 65 | 68 | 85 | 85 | 89 | 91 | 92 |

Growth of $10,000

▌▐ Value of Fund ($000)
— Value of Index ($000)
S&P 500
▼ Manager Change
▽ Partial Manager Change
► Mgr Unknown After
◄ Mgr Unknown Before

Performance Quartile
(Within Objective)

1983	1984	1985	1986	1987	1988	1989	1990	1991	1992	1993	1994	History
6.77	6.16	7.09	6.81	5.57	5.84	6.66	6.39	7.86	7.29	6.77	6.21	NAV
6.74	2.65	23.86	16.78	-2.37	12.19	22.53	2.00	28.50	1.75	8.26	-4.36	Total Return %
-15.72	-3.62	-7.88	-1.90	-7.63	-4.42	-9.15	5.11	-5.87	-1.98	-1.80	-5.67	+/- S&P 500
-1.63	-12.50	1.73	1.53	-5.13	4.31	7.99	-6.95	12.50	-5.49	-1.49	-1.44	+/- LB Aggregate
8.14	7.98	8.76	7.06	7.74	7.34	8.49	6.05	5.50	3.75	2.99	3.17	Income Return %
-1.40	-5.34	15.10	9.72	-10.11	4.85	14.04	-4.05	23.00	-2.00	5.27	-7.53	Capital Return %
93	58	50	43	77	44	30	50	29	87	77	57	Total Rtn % Rank All
91	92	35	31	57	50	6	41	11	94	89	46	Total Rtn % Rank Obj
0.56	0.48	0.48	0.48	0.48	0.40	0.46	0.39	0.31	0.28	0.22	0.21	Income $
0.14	0.26	0.00	0.91	0.59	0.00	0.00	0.00	0.00	0.42	0.89	0.05	Capital Gains $
0.78	0.89	0.83	0.77	0.76	0.80	0.75	0.77	0.74	0.89	0.88	0.91	Expense Ratio %
5.52	7.17	7.62	6.43	5.95	6.76	7.38	5.59	4.37	3.69	2.82	2.85	Income Ratio %
72	114	148	167	96	83	108	57	67	85	165	---	Turnover Rate %
126.0	177.9	134.4	162.8	140.2	133.1	148.1	141.0	172.2	163.3	162.9	131.6	Net Assets ($mil)

Manager's Investment Style

The fund does not behave like most income funds. While the majority dabble in equities, this fund often commits 60% of assets to stocks. Management uses its own Value Line Timeliness Ranking System, which favors earnings momentum, to choose its purchases. This strategy has generally resulted in a portfolio heavy in large-cap growth stocks. On the bond side, management takes few chances, investing in mostly U.S. government issues and steering clear of junk. The result has been low yield with steady growth.

Fund Manager(s)

Management Team

Manager Experience

	Dates Managed	Invest Obj	Std Dev	+/- Index
Management Team				
SteinRoe Total Return	08/49 - 01/81	EI	13.51	-2.34
SteinRoe Stock	07/58 - 01/89	G	19.99	-2.42

Performance 12-31-94

	1st Qtr	2nd Qtr	3rd Qtr	4th Qtr	Total
1987	10.94	0.59	3.97	-15.86	-2.37
1988	5.21	3.48	1.89	1.13	12.19
1989	4.48	6.67	7.32	2.45	22.53
1990	-3.44	4.26	-6.17	7.98	2.00
1991	10.82	-0.87	7.17	9.14	28.50
1992	-5.29	1.44	3.03	2.79	1.75
1993	3.71	3.34	1.04	-0.03	8.26
1994	-5.49	-0.57	3.42	-1.58	-4.36

Bear Market Performance

Decile Rank (5-year period)

Worst ▬ Best

	Worst 3 Mo Period 1985-89	Worst 3 Mo Period 1990-94
Value Line Income	-21.36	-7.10
+/- S&P 500	8.22	-1.35
+/- Best Fit Index : S&P 500	8.22	-1.35

Trailing Returns

	Total Return %	+/- S&P 500	+/- LB Aggregate	% Rank All	% Rank Obj	Growth of $10,000
3 Mo	-1.58	-1.57	-1.96	59	55	9,842
6 Mo	1.78	-3.08	0.79	28	9	10,178
1 Yr	-4.36	-5.67	-1.44	57	46	9,564
3 Yr Avg	1.75	-4.51	-2.79	92	92	10,536
5 Yr Avg	6.67	-2.02	-0.96	58	85	13,809
10 Yr Avg	10.36	-4.02	0.42	54	50	26,806
15 Yr Avg	12.20	-2.28	1.39	51	41	56,201

Operations

Address and Telephone	220 E. 42nd Street
	New York, NY 10017-5891
	800-223-0818 / 212-907-1500
Advisor	Value Line
Subadvisor	None
Distributor	Value Line Securities
States Available	All
Report Grade	B-
Income Distrib	Paid Quarterly
Date of Inception	10-01-52
Fiscal Year End	December

Risk Analysis

Time Period	Load-Adj Return %	Risk % Rank All	Risk % Rank Obj[1]	Morningstar[2] Return	Morningstar Risk	Morningstar Risk-Adj Rating
1 Yr	-4.36					
3 Yr	1.75	60	92	-0.52[3]	0.87	★★
5 Yr	6.67	53	91	0.47[3]	0.78	★★★
10 Yr	10.36	44	78	0.73	0.75	★★★
Average Historical Rating (109 months)					3.6	★s

[1] 1 = low, 100 = high [2] 1.00 = Hybrid Avg [3] 1.00 = 90-day T-bill return

Other Measures

			Standard S&P 500	Best Fit S&P 500
Standard Deviation	6.52	Alpha	-3.5	-3.5
Mean	1.95	Beta	0.70	0.70
Sharpe Ratio	-0.24	R-Squared	72	72

Investment Style

Stocks

	Port Avg	Rel S&P 500
Price/Earnings Ratio	18.8	1.02
Price/Book Ratio	3.6	1.05
5 Yr Earnings Gr %	9.2	1.65
Med Mkt Cap ($mil)	4499	0.35

Style
V B G

Bonds

Avg Effective Duration	5.7 Yrs
Avg Effective Maturity	10.4 Yrs
Avg Credit Quality	AA
Avg Weighted Coupon	6.35%

Diversification Value for Portfolio Types

Large Cap: Low	Small Cap: Medium	Bond: Medium	Balanced: Low	Diversified: Low

Portfolio 09-30-94

Total Stocks: 36
Total Fixed-Income: 15

Share Chg (06-94)000	Amount 000		Date of Maturity	Value $000	% Net Assets
	10000	US Treasury Note 3.875%	09-30-95	9800	6.97
	5600	Federal Farm Credit Bk 3.83%	12-21-95	5577	3.97
	5000	McDonnell Douglas 7.375%	11-15-05	4546	3.23
	5291	FNMA CMO REMIC 7.5%	07-25-22	4174	2.97
	4000	FNMA CMO REMIC 8.7%	12-25-19	4040	2.87
0	150	American Barrick Resources		3994	2.84
0	75	Coca-Cola		3647	2.59
0	150	Hong Kong Telecom (ADR)		3019	2.15
0	100	Equifax		2963	2.11
0	60	SCANA		2663	1.89
	125	Texaco Capital Pfd 6.875%		2594	1.85
0	60	Citicorp		2550	1.81
0	50	Telecom New Zealand (ADR)		2544	1.81
0	75	Abbott Laboratories		2353	1.67
0	100	New Plan Realty Trust		2138	1.52
18	60	Chemed		2130	1.52
0	50	Southwestern Bell		2125	1.51
0	40	Motorola		2110	1.50
0	30	Briggs & Stratton		2108	1.50
0	70	Illinois Central		2100	1.49

Index Allocation

	% of Stocks
S&P 500	54.7
S&P MidCap 400	14.7
U.S. Small Cap	19.2
Foreign	17.3

Composition % 12-31-94

Cash	12.1	Preferreds	2.7
Stocks	57.2	Convertibles	2.6
Bonds	25.5	Other	0.0

Tax Analysis

	Tax-Adj Historical Return %	% Pretax Return
3 Yr Avg	-1.13	---
5 Yr Avg	4.19	59.8
10 Yr Avg	6.98	57.4
Potential Capital Gain Exposure (% of assets)		-2%

Most Similar Funds in MF500

AIM Charter	Fair Fit
MIMLIC Asset Allocation A	Fair Fit
Sentinel Common Stock	Fair Fit

Bond Credit Analysis 09-30-94

% of Bonds

US Govt	64	BB	5
AAA	0	B	11
AA	0	Below B	0
A	5	NR/NA	4
BBB	11		

Stock Sector Weightings

	% of Stocks	Relative S&P 500
Utilities	15.5	1.25
Energy	6.4	0.63
Financials	18.5	1.75
Industrial Cyclicals	14.9	0.91
Consumer Durables	9.4	1.51
Consumer Staples	15.7	1.26
Services	6.4	0.78
Retail	1.6	0.28
Health	3.5	0.41
Technology	8.2	0.89

Min Initial Purchase / Expenses & Fees

Min Initial Purchase	$1000 (Addt'l: $100)
Min IRA Purchase	$1000 (Addt'l: $100)
Min Auto Invest Plan	$40 (Systematic Inv: $40)

Expenses & Fees

Sales Fees	0.00% front
	0.00% deferred
	0.00% 12b-1
Management Fee	0.70% max./0.65% min.
3-,5-,10-yr Expense Projections	$28, $49, $108
Annual Brokerage Cost	---

Value Line Leveraged Gr Inv

	Ticker	Load	NAV	Yield	SEC Yield	Assets	Objective
	VALLX	None	23.18	0.5%	N/A	264.8	Aggr. Growth

Value Line Leveraged Growth Investors Fund seeks capital appreciation.

The fund invests substantially all of its assets in common stocks or convertible securities. It uses the Value Line Ranking System for timeliness in selecting securities for purchase or sale. The fund may borrow up to 50% of the value of its net assets in order to purchase securities. It may also write covered call options, purchase call options, and enter repurchase agreements.

Manager's Investment Style

Management takes a cautious approach to investing in growth sectors. Despite the option to leverage up to 50% of assets, management tends to keep the fund debt free. During bullish markets, management has been known to leverage in order to gain a larger position in technology or financial stocks.

Fund Manager(s)

Management Team

Manager Experience

	Dates Managed	Invest Obj	Std Dev	+/- Index

Not available.

Historical Profile
Return	Above Average
Risk	Above Average
Rating	★★★ Neutral

Investment Style History
Equity
Average % Stocks Held in Portfolio

99%	83%	86%	87%	90%	90%	95%	89%

Growth of $10,000
- |||| Value of Fund ($000)
- — Value of Index ($000) SPMid400
- ▼ Manager Change
- ▽ Partial Manager Change
- ► Mgr Unknown After
- ◄ Mgr Unknown Before

Performance Quartile (Within Objective)

1983	1984	1985	1986	1987	1988	1989	1990	1991	1992	1993	1994	History
19.66	16.56	20.90	22.80	18.15	18.87	23.10	21.16	25.64	22.15	24.67	23.18	NAV
8.00	-8.88	27.11	23.13	2.81	6.43	32.31	-1.65	46.35	-2.46	16.20	-3.71	Total Return %
-14.47	-15.14	-4.63	4.45	-2.45	-10.08	0.63	1.47	15.87	-10.08	6.14	-5.02	+/- S&P 500
---	-7.16	-4.91	11.37	6.32	-14.11	8.37	11.91	2.90	-14.22	1.66	-1.05	+/- Wilshire 4500
3.42	1.88	0.90	1.55	2.21	2.46	1.78	1.69	0.99	0.69	0.25	0.49	Income Return %
4.57	-10.75	26.21	21.58	0.60	3.97	30.53	-3.34	45.36	-3.15	15.95	-4.20	Capital Return %
88	88	37	11	36	85	10	60	9	92	25	50	Total Rtn % Rank All
84	19	62	14	38	73	38	20	65	85	63	60	Total Rtn % Rank Obj
0.65	0.31	0.13	0.34	0.46	0.46	0.39	0.36	0.23	0.15	0.11		Income $
0.02	0.99	0.00	2.60	4.93	0.00	1.45	1.18	4.61	2.69	0.98	0.45	Capital Gains $
0.80	0.86	0.80	0.96	0.95	0.97	0.96	0.96	0.92	0.93	0.92	0.90	Expense Ratio %
2.24	0.90	1.51	0.98	1.05	1.99	1.47	1.51	0.84	0.62	0.22	0.25	Income Ratio %
105	89	121	115	148	143	122	94	250	208	80	---	Turnover Rate %
216.1	181.5	228.6	251.5	282.9	235.2	254.5	236.1	346.4	290.8	303.2	264.8	Net Assets ($mil)

Performance 12-31-94

	1st Qtr	2nd Qtr	3rd Qtr	4th Qtr	Total
1987	22.07	1.71	8.45	-23.65	2.81
1988	3.97	4.98	-4.48	2.08	6.43
1989	7.63	7.29	13.91	0.59	32.31
1990	-3.81	10.22	-15.68	10.02	-1.65
1991	22.31	-2.13	8.01	13.19	46.35
1992	-6.98	-9.35	4.26	10.95	-2.46
1993	3.97	3.82	11.00	-3.02	16.20
1994	-5.27	-5.56	7.39	0.23	-3.71

Bear Market Performance

Decile Rank (5-year period)

Worst   Best

	Worst 3 Mo Period 1985-89	Worst 3 Mo Period 1990-94
Value Line Leveraged Gr Inv	-30.44	-15.68
+/- S&P 500	-0.85	-1.93
+/- Best Fit Index : SPMid400	-1.63	2.10

Trailing Returns

	Total Return %	+/- S&P 500	+/- Wil 4500	% Rank All	% Rank Obj	Growth of $10,000
3 Mo	0.23	0.25	2.74	16	35	10,023
6 Mo	7.64	2.78	3.44	6	54	10,764
1 Yr	-3.71	-5.02	-1.05	50	60	9,629
3 Yr Avg	2.96	-3.31	-4.65	86	73	10,914
5 Yr Avg	9.45	0.76	0.36	20	58	15,709
10 Yr Avg	13.54	-0.85	0.90	21	59	35,589
15 Yr Avg	13.59	-0.89	---	29	33	67,611

Operations

Address and Telephone	220 E. 42nd Street	Min Initial Purchase	$1000 (Addt'l: $100)
	New York, NY 10017-5891	Min IRA Purchase	$1000 (Addt'l: $100)
	800-223-0818 / 212-907-1500	Min Auto Invest Plan	$40 (Systematic Inv: $40)
Advisor	Value Line	**Expenses & Fees**	
Subadvisor	None	Sales Fees	0.00% front
Distributor	Value Line Securities		0.00% deferred
States Available	All		0.00% 12b-1
Report Grade	B-	Management Fee	0.75% flat fee
Income Distrib	Paid Annually	3-,5-,10-yr Expense Projections	$29, $51, $113
Date of Inception	03-20-72	Annual Brokerage Cost	0.20%
Fiscal Year End	December		

Risk Analysis

Time Period	Load-Adj Return %	Risk % Rank [1] All	Risk % Rank [1] Obj	Morningstar [2] Return	Morningstar [2] Risk	Morningstar Risk-Adj Rating
1 Yr	-3.71					
3 Yr	2.96	94	59	-0.18 [3]	1.31	★★
5 Yr	9.45	88	30	1.20 [3]	1.11	★★★
10 Yr	13.54	87	18	1.17	1.10	★★★

Average Historical Rating (109 months)   3.3 ★ s

[1] 1 = low, 100 = high   [2] 1.00 = Equity Avg   [3] 1.00 = 90-day T-bill return

Other Measures

			Standard S&P 500	Best Fit SPMid400
Standard Deviation	12.04	Alpha	-3.0	-4.0
Mean	3.64	Beta	1.11	1.09
Sharpe Ratio	0.01	R-Squared	54	80

Investment Style

	Stock Portfolio Avg	Relative S&P 500
Price/Earnings Ratio	19.1	1.03
Price/Book Ratio	4.1	1.20
5 Yr Earnings Gr %	20.2	3.64
Return on Assets %	10.2	1.36
Debt % Total Cap	21.1	0.75
Med Mkt Cap ($mil)	3698	0.28

Style: Value Blend Growth — Size: Large Med Small

Diversification Value for Portfolio Types

Large Cap:	Small Cap:	Bond:	Balanced:	Diversified:
Low	Low	High	Low	Low

Portfolio 09-30-94

Share Chg (06-94) 000	Amount 000	Total Stocks: 73 / Total Fixed-Income: 1	Value $000	% Net Assets
0	200	Computer Associates Intl	8900	3.28
0	300	DSC Communications	8550	3.15
0	380	EMC	7648	2.82
0	150	US Healthcare	6984	2.57
0	100	Nucor	6963	2.57
0	100	Deere	6863	2.53
0	150	Citicorp	6375	2.35
0	160	Loral	6300	2.32
0	225	Midlantic	6216	2.29
0	188	CUC International	6188	2.28
0	100	Intel	6150	2.27
0	150	Best Buy	5869	2.16
0	140	SunAmerica	5828	2.15
0	100	First Financial Management	5750	2.12
0	135	Arrow Electronics	5063	1.87
0	250	Clayton Homes	4750	1.75
0	120	Olsten	4530	1.67
0	80	Motorola	4220	1.56
0	80	Fifth Third Bancorp	4180	1.54
0	50	Capital Cities/ABC	4100	1.51
0	82	SunTrust Banks	3973	1.46
0	150	Office Depot	3900	1.44
50	100	3Com	3738	1.38
0	150	Atlantic Southeast Airlines	3488	1.29
0	50	IBM	3475	1.28

Composition % 12-31-94

Cash	8.0	Preferreds	0.0
Stocks	88.4	Convertibles	0.0
Bonds	3.6	Other	0.0

Tax Analysis

	Tax-Adj Historical Return %	% Pretax Return
3 Yr Avg	1.21	40.1
5 Yr Avg	6.88	69.1
10 Yr Avg	10.72	69.1
Potential Capital Gain Exposure (% of assets)		22%

Most Similar Funds in MF500

Sit Growth	Strong Fit
Enterprise Capital Apprec	Fair Fit
Kemper Growth A	Fair Fit

Index Allocation

	% of Stocks
S&P 500	56.8
S&P MidCap 400	29.1
U.S. Small Cap	13.3
Foreign	0.8

Sector Weightings

	% of Stocks	Relative S&P 500
Utilities	0.0	0.00
Energy	0.0	0.00
Financials	18.4	1.74
Industrial Cyclicals	19.8	1.21
Consumer Durables	3.9	0.62
Consumer Staples	1.5	0.12
Services	11.6	1.42
Retail	5.0	0.86
Health	9.8	1.12
Technology	30.1	3.28

 **1995 Mutual Fund 500**

Value Line Tax-Exempt Hi-Yld

	Ticker	Load	NAV	Yield	SEC Yield	Assets	Objective
	VLHYX	None	9.89	5.7%	5.93%	225.9	Muni Nat

Value Line Tax-Exempt Fund High-Yield Portfolio seeks income exempt from federal income taxes, while avoiding undue risk to principal. Capital appreciation is secondary.

The fund invests primarily in investment-grade municipal bonds. It expects to maintain an average weighted maturity of between 10 and 40 years.

Investment Style History
Fixed Income
Income Rtn % Rank Obj

| | 7 | 10 | 9 | 7 | 25 | 51 | 48 | 33 |

Historical Profile

Return	Average
Risk	Average
Rating	★★★
	Neutral

Growth of $10,000

- ‖‖‖ Value of Fund ($000)
- — Value of Index ($000) LB Muni
- ▼ Manager Change
- ▽ Partial Manager Change
- ► Mgr Unknown After
- ◄ Mgr Unknown Before

Performance Quartile (Within Objective)

Manager's Investment Style

Although this fund has a history of low volatility and high payout, management has recently taken a greater interest in predicting and preparing for interest-rate swings, which has given the fund a more-volatile flavor.

Fund Manager(s)

Management Team

Manager Experience

	Dates Managed	Invest Obj	Std Dev	+/- Index
Management Team				
SteinRoe Total Return	08/49 - 01/81	EI	13.51	-2.34
SteinRoe Stock	07/58 - 01/89	G	19.99	-2.42

1983	1984	1985	1986	1987	1988	1989	1990	1991	1992	1993	1994	History
---	9.82	10.70	10.81	9.99	10.26	10.30	10.17	10.68	10.86	11.27	9.89	NAV
---	6.17 *	19.76	13.66	0.71	11.10	8.35	6.55	12.29	7.86	11.45	-6.91	Total Return %
---	---	-2.37	-1.59	-2.05	3.22	-6.19	-2.39	-3.71	0.61	1.70	-3.99	+/- LB Aggregate
---	---	-0.27	-5.66	-0.80	0.94	-2.43	-0.75	0.15	-0.96	-0.82	-1.31	+/- LB Muni
---	7.97	10.80	9.10	7.90	8.40	7.96	7.81	7.28	6.17	5.69	5.00	Income Return %
---	-1.80	8.96	4.55	-7.19	2.70	0.39	-1.26	5.01	1.69	5.76	-11.91	Capital Return %
---	---	74	63	54	52	89	27	73	47	56	79	Total Rtn % Rank All
---	---	49	78	35	46	76	40	25	69	54	71	Total Rtn % Rank Obj
---	0.75	0.98	0.91	0.82	0.81	0.79	0.77	0.70	0.63	0.60	0.57	Income $
---	0.00	0.00	0.36	0.05	0.00	0.00	0.00	0.00	0.00	0.20	0.04	Capital Gains $
---	---	0.17	0.66	0.68	0.64	0.63	0.62	0.60	0.58	0.60	0.58	Expense Ratio %
---	---	10.49	9.36	8.20	7.98	7.77	7.70	7.47	6.50	5.89	5.30	Income Ratio %
---	---	---	187	254	79	76	73	63	122	122	101	55	Turnover Rate %
---	30.0	36.8	133.9	228.4	254.6	274.9	278.7	300.7	288.7	290.1	225.9	Net Assets ($mil)

Performance 12-31-94

	1st Qtr	2nd Qtr	3rd Qtr	4th Qtr	Total
1987	3.33	-3.41	-2.11	3.07	0.71
1988	3.60	2.34	2.50	2.24	11.10
1989	1.15	4.13	0.63	2.23	8.35
1990	0.67	2.02	-0.20	3.96	6.55
1991	1.82	2.31	4.21	3.44	12.29
1992	-0.05	4.23	1.76	1.74	7.86
1993	3.43	3.27	3.48	0.83	11.45
1994	-6.57	0.59	0.27	-1.22	-6.91

Bear Market Performance

Decile Rank (5-year period)

Worst | Best

	Worst 3 Mo Period 1985-89	Worst 3 Mo Period 1990-94
Value Line Tax-Exempt Hi-Yld	-5.92	-7.57
+/- LB Aggregate	-2.36	-2.63
+/- Best Fit Index : LB Muni	0.58	-1.81

Trailing Returns

	Total Return %	+/- LB Aggregate	+/- LB Muni	% Rank All	% Rank Obj	Growth of $10,000
3 Mo	-1.22	-1.60	0.22	50	41	9,878
6 Mo	-0.95	-1.94	0.30	73	52	9,905
1 Yr	-6.91	-3.99	-1.31	79	71	9,309
3 Yr Avg	3.82	-0.73	-1.05	74	84	11,190
5 Yr Avg	6.01	-1.62	-0.76	76	59	13,388
10 Yr Avg	8.25	-1.69	-1.18	84	67	22,093
15 Yr Avg	---	---	---	---	---	---

Operations

Address and Telephone	220 E. 42nd Street
	New York, NY 10017-5891
	800-223-0818 / 212-907-1500
Advisor	Value Line
Subadvisor	None
Distributor	Value Line Securities
States Available	All
Report Grade	C
Income Distrib	Paid Monthly
* Date of Inception	03-23-84
Fiscal Year End	February

Min Initial Purchase	$1000 (Addt'l: $250)
Min IRA Purchase	N/A
Min Auto Invest Plan	$40 (Systematic Inv: $40)

Expenses & Fees

Sales Fees	0.00% front
	0.00% deferred
	0.00% 12b-1
Management Fee	0.50% flat fee
3-,5-,10-yr Expense Projections	$19, $32, $73

Risk Analysis

Time Period	Load-Adj Return %	Risk % Rank [1] All	Risk % Rank [1] Obj	Morningstar [2] Return	Morningstar [2] Risk	Morningstar Risk-Adj Rating
1 Yr	-6.91					
3 Yr	3.82	47	82	0.93	1.24	★★
5 Yr	6.01	31	65	1.00	1.16	★★
10 Yr	8.25	10	33	1.01	0.95	★★★

Average Historical Rating (94 months) 4.3 ★s

[1] = low, 100 = high [2] 1.00 = Muni Avg [3] 1.00 = 90-day T-bill return

Other Measures

		Standard LB Agg	Best Fit LB Muni
Standard Deviation	6.53	Alpha	-0.8	-1.2
Mean	3.97	Beta	1.21	1.17
Sharpe Ratio	0.07	R-Squared	55	96

Investment Style

Interest-Rate Stance

Avg Effective Maturity 18.8 Yrs

Maturity: Short Intm Long
Quality: High Med Low

Quality

Avg Credit Quality AA

Avg Weighted Coupon 6.54%

Avg Weighted Price 101.54% of Par

Diversification Value for Portfolio Types

| Large Cap: Medium | Small Cap: High | Bond: Low | Balanced: Medium | Diversified: Medium |

Portfolio 08-31-94

Total Stocks: 0
Total Fixed-Income: 83

Amount 000	Date of Maturity		Value $000	% Net Assets
10000	12-01-23	AK Hsg Fin Vet Mtg Prog 5.4%	8453	3.39
8850	08-15-13	NY Med Care Fac Fin St Luke Hosp 5.6%	8290	3.33
7200	07-01-09	WA Pub Pwr Sply Sys Proj #1 7.25%	8067	3.24
8200	03-20-28	CA Stockton Hsg Fac O'Connor Woods 5.6%	7147	2.87
7000	12-01-10	TX Houston Hsg Fin Sngl Fam Mtg 5.95%	6691	2.68
6000	06-01-11	WI Clean Wtr Fund 6.875%	6457	2.59
5700	02-01-04	NY New York City GO 7.5%	6265	2.51
5500	06-01-10	NV Clark GO Sch Dist 7%	6061	2.43
5800	07-01-23	NY Dorm Oxford Univ DMD	5800	2.33
5000	01-01-08	NC East Muni Pwr 7%	5331	2.14
5000	03-01-12	GA State GO 6%	5142	2.06
5000	10-01-09	TX GO Pub Fin 6%	5124	2.06
5000	07-01-14	VA Hsg Dev Mtg 6.85%	5070	2.03
5000	01-01-12	GA Muni Elec Pwr 6.25%	5031	2.02
5000	11-01-10	MA Wtr Resource 6.25%	5022	2.01
4500	07-01-16	IL Hsg Dev Multi-Fam 8.25%	4898	1.96
5000	05-01-13	WA State GO 5.75%	4806	1.93
5000	06-01-13	FL GO Brd Educ Cap 5.3%	4551	1.83
3900	11-15-04	NY New York City GO 8.2%	4468	1.79
4055	08-01-10	CO Denver Sngl Fam Mtg 7%	4371	1.75

Credit Analysis % of Bonds 12-31-94

US Govt	0	BB	1
AAA	37	B	0
AA	28	Below B	0
A	19	NR/NA	10
BBB	4		

Composition % of Assets 12-31-94

Cash	8.5	Preferreds	0.0
Stocks	0.0	Convertibles	0.0
Bonds	91.5	Other	0.0

Tax Analysis

	Tax-Adj Historical Return %	% Pretax Return
3 Yr Avg	3.61	94.3
5 Yr Avg	5.88	97.6
10 Yr Avg	8.10	97.6
Potential Capital Gain Exposure (% of assets)		-7%

Most Similar Funds in MF500

Fidelity Municipal Bond	Strong Fit
Lord Abbett T/F Income Natl	Strong Fit
Safeco Municipal Bond	Strong Fit

Coupon Range

	% Bonds	Rel Obj
0%	0.0	0.00
0% to 6.8%	52.6	0.87
6.8% to 7.5%	26.2	1.69
7.5% to 8.3%	8.4	0.95
More than 8.3%	3.1	0.35
Not applicable	9.7	2.49

Sector Weightings

	% Bonds	Rel Obj
General Obl	20.44	0.97
Utilities	16.02	1.28
Health	11.01	0.83
Water/Waste	2.08	0.33
Housing	27.58	3.76
Education	0.56	0.09
Transportation	3.83	0.38
COP/Lease	0.38	0.12
Private	6.78	0.58
Misc Revenue	0.44	0.09
Demand	10.89	4.43

Top 5 States % of Bonds

TX	14.52	IL	6.25
NY	12.26	MA	5.05
WA	6.46		

Van Kampen Insured T/F Income A

	Ticker	Load	NAV	Yield	SEC Yield	Assets	Objective
	VKMTX	4.65%	17.57	6.0%	5.44%	1186.6	Muni Nat

Van Kampen Merritt Insured Tax-Free Income Fund - Class A seeks current income exempt from federal income taxes, with liquidity and safety of principal.

The fund invests in insured municipal securities of any maturity. All of the fund's municipal holdings are insured by municipal-bond insurers whose claims-paying ability is rated AAA on the date of purchase. The fund may invest in bonds that are subject to the Alternative Minimum Tax.

Class A shares have front loads; Class B shares have deferred loads, higher 12b-1 fees, and conversion features; Class C shares have level loads; Class D shares are designed for institutions.

Manager's Investment Style

Management finds creative ways to make this fund tamer than its peers. Buying insured paper in sectors where bonds are of lower quality is one way that management has boosted yield while reducing interest-rate risk. Also, by reducing zero-coupon holdings and using shorts, the fund has historically positioned itself to resist rate hikes.

Fund Manager(s)

Joseph A. Piraro, since 04-92. Birthdate: 07-48. BS, De Paul U. 1970

Manager Experience

	Dates Managed	Invest Obj	Std Dev	+/- Index
Joseph A. Piraro				
VanKamp CA Muni	01/92 - 12/94	MS	7.72	1.20
VanKamp Tr Ins Muni	04/92 - 12/94	MN	11.22	1.11

Performance 12-31-94

	1st Qtr	2nd Qtr	3rd Qtr	4th Qtr	Total
1987	2.62	-5.19	-2.07	5.49	0.51
1988	2.62	1.98	3.52	2.91	11.48
1989	-0.09	5.83	-0.66	4.14	9.40
1990	0.41	1.29	-0.17	5.45	7.07
1991	1.98	1.69	3.33	3.24	10.63
1992	0.57	3.99	3.01	1.66	9.52
1993	3.93	3.44	3.62	0.83	12.32
1994	-6.08	1.11	0.06	-1.40	-6.31

Bear Market Performance

Decile Rank (5-year period)

Worst _____ Best

	Worst 3 Mo Period 1985-89	Worst 3 Mo Period 1990-94
Van Kampen Insured T/F Incom	-7.24	-6.79
+/- LB Aggregate	-3.68	-1.85
+/- Best Fit Index : LB Muni	-0.75	-1.03

Trailing Returns

	Total Return %	+/- LB Aggregate	+/- LB Muni	% Rank All	% Rank Obj	Growth of $10,000
3 Mo	-1.40	-1.78	0.04	54	52	9,860
6 Mo	-1.34	-2.33	-0.10	79	69	9,866
1 Yr	-6.31	-3.39	-0.70	74	63	9,369
3 Yr Avg	4.84	0.30	-0.02	51	36	11,525
5 Yr Avg	6.42	-1.20	-0.35	65	40	13,652
10 Yr Avg	9.34	-0.61	-0.09	66	24	24,418
15 Yr Avg	---	---	---	---	---	---

Operations

Address and Telephone	One Parkview Plaza
	Oakbrook Terrace, IL 60181
	800-225-2222 / 708-684-6000
Advisor	Van Kampen Merritt Investment Adv
Subadvisor	None
Distributor	Van Kampen Merritt
States Available	All
Report Grade	C+
Income Distrib	Paid Monthly
* Date of Inception	12-14-84
Fiscal Year End	December

Historical Profile

Return	Average
Risk	Above Average
Rating	★★★
	Neutral

Investment Style History
Fixed Income
Income Rtn % Rank Obj

| | 18 | 60 | 58 | 46 | 42 | 35 | 20 | 23 |

Growth of $10,000

- |||| Value of Fund ($000)
- — Value of Index ($000) LB Muni
- ▼ Manager Change
- ▽ Partial Manager Change
- ► Mgr Unknown After
- ◄ Mgr Unknown Before

Performance Quartile (Within Objective)

	1983	1984	1985	1986	1987	1988	1989	1990	1991	1992	1993	1994	History
	---	14.47	16.19	17.95	16.70	17.39	17.80	17.83	18.48	18.72	19.86	17.57	NAV
	---	1.26 *	21.96	19.64	0.51	11.48	9.40	7.07	10.63	9.52	12.32	-6.31	Total Return %
	---	---	-0.17	4.40	-2.25	3.61	-5.14	-1.88	-5.37	2.27	2.57	-3.39	+/- LB Aggregate
	---	---	1.94	0.33	-1.00	1.32	-1.39	-0.23	-1.51	0.70	0.05	-0.70	+/- LB Muni
	---	0.00	10.07	8.03	7.46	7.35	7.04	6.90	6.87	6.42	6.23	5.22	Income Return %
	---	1.26	11.89	11.61	-6.95	4.13	2.36	0.17	3.77	3.09	6.09	-11.53	Capital Return %
	---	---	60	22	56	50	80	21	87	27	48	74	Total Rtn % Rank All
	---	---	13	23	39	40	52	15	75	18	38	63	Total Rtn % Rank Obj
	---	0.00	1.33	1.24	1.31	1.17	1.17	1.17	1.16	1.14	1.12	1.06	Income $
	---	0.00	0.00	0.11	0.00	0.00	0.00	0.00	0.02	0.32	0.00	0.00	Capital Gains $
	---	0.66	0.89	0.76	0.71	0.85	0.88	0.87	0.88	0.83	0.84	0.79	Expense Ratio %
	---	9.59	8.00	7.07	7.04	6.92	6.73	6.63	6.39	6.14	5.69	5.64	Income Ratio %
	---	---	98	31	120	133	81	108	113	112	79	---	Turnover Rate %
	---	14.9	188.2	418.1	501.1	554.3	632.5	699.0	829.4	987.4	1225.9	1186.6	Net Assets ($mil)

Risk Analysis

Time Period	Load-Adj Return %	Risk % Rank All	Risk % Rank Obj	Morningstar Return	Morningstar Risk	Morningstar Risk-Adj Rating
1 Yr	-10.66					
3 Yr	3.19	47	82	0.80	1.25	★★
5 Yr	5.41	34	74	0.85	1.22	★★
10 Yr	8.82	22	64	1.06	1.15	★★★

Average Historical Rating (85 months)   2.6 ★s

[1] 1 = low, 100 = high   [2] 1.00 = Muni Avg   [3] 1.00 = 90-day T-bill return

Other Measures

			Standard LB Agg	Best Fit LB Muni
Standard Deviation	6.84	Alpha	0.2	-0.3
Mean	4.97	Beta	1.23	1.22
Sharpe Ratio	0.21	R-Squared	52	97

Investment Style

Interest-Rate Stance

Avg Effective Maturity   22.2 Yrs

Maturity: Short Intm Long

Quality

Avg Credit Quality   AAA

Avg Weighted Coupon   6.29%
Avg Weighted Price   96.79% of Par

Diversification Value for Portfolio Types

Large Cap: Medium	Small Cap: High	Bond: Low	Balanced: Medium	Diversified: High

Portfolio 06-30-94

Total Stocks: 0
Total Fixed-Income: 351

Amount 000	Date of Maturity		Value $000	% Net Assets
35267	06-01-31	KS Burlington Poll Cntrl Gas/Elec 7%	37998	3.27
34051	12-01-24	IL Dev Fin Poll Cntrl Pwr Proj 7.4%	36600	3.15
18942	01-01-06	IL Cook COP Comnty Clg Dist #508 8.75%	23258	2.00
17512	08-15-21	RI Hlth/Educ Bldg Hosp IFRN	18694	1.61
19769	06-01-20	CA Los Angeles Wastewtr Sys 5.6%	17918	1.54
19458	06-01-15	CA Pub Wks Brd Dept Crtns Lease 5.25%	17018	1.46
14496	11-15-22	CO Univ Hosp 6.4%	14681	1.26
14788	01-01-22	IL Chicago Brd Educ Lease 6%	14120	1.21
13377	12-01-16	CA Pub Wks Brd State Univ Lease 6.4%	13682	1.18
12404	02-15-16	CO Hlth Fac PSL Sys 7.25%	13615	1.17
13241	03-01-19	CA Norco Redev Proj #1 Tax Alloc 6.25%	13092	1.13
12438	07-01-08	HI Arpt Sys 6.4%	12962	1.11
13426	07-01-16	CA San Bernardino COP IFRN	11970	1.03
52541	02-15-16	TX Dallas GO Util/Reclamation Dist 0%	11708	1.01
10001	07-01-18	CA Concord Redev Central Tax Preref 8%	11257	0.97
12258	06-15-15	PA Intergovt Coop Spcl Tax 5.6%	11161	0.96
12526	03-01-20	CA State GO 5.5%	11098	0.95
9179	07-01-08	WA Pub Pwr Sply Sys Proj #1 7.75%	10255	0.88
11300	02-01-24	IL Dev Fin Poll Cntrl Mtg 7.3%	10241	0.88
8999	06-01-16	MO Hlth/Educ Fac 7.75%	10021	0.86

Credit Analysis % of Bonds 09-30-94

US Govt	0	BB	0
AAA	100	B	0
AA	0	Below B	0
A	0	NR/NA	0
BBB	0		

Composition % of Assets 12-31-94

Cash	3.1	Preferreds	0.0
Stocks	0.0	Convertibles	0.0
Bonds	96.9	Other	0.0

Tax Analysis

	Tax-Adj Historical Return %	% Pretax Return
3 Yr Avg	4.68	96.4
5 Yr Avg	6.32	98.1
10 Yr Avg	9.27	98.9

Potential Capital Gain Exposure (% of assets)   -1%

Most Similar Funds in MF500

Vanguard Muni Insured L/T	Strong Fit
Lord Abbett T/F Income Natl	Strong Fit
General Municipal Bond	Strong Fit

Coupon Range

	% Bonds	Rel Obj
0%	8.2	3.15
0% to 6.8%	47.2	0.78
6.8% to 7.5%	14.3	0.92
7.5% to 8.3%	16.1	1.82
More than 8.3%	8.1	0.91
Not applicable	6.1	1.57

Sector Weightings

	% Bonds	Rel Obj
General Obl	10.90	0.52
Utilities	7.00	0.57
Health	26.30	1.98
Water/Waste	6.90	1.08
Housing	4.60	0.63
Education	3.40	0.53
Transportation	4.40	0.43
COP/Lease	13.90	4.34
Private	17.20	1.48
Misc Revenue	5.40	1.08
Demand	0.00	0.00

Top 5 States % of Bonds

CA	21.15	GA	3.90
IL	15.97	CO	3.88
TX	6.76		

Min Initial Purchase / Expenses & Fees

Min Initial Purchase	$1000 (Addt'l: $100)
Min IRA Purchase	N/A
Min Auto Invest Plan	$1000 (Systematic Inv: $100)

Expenses & Fees

Sales Fees	4.65% front
	0.00% deferred
	0.30% 12b-1
Management Fee	0.50% max./0.40% min.
3-,5-,10-yr Expense Projections	$72, $91, $145

MORNINGSTAR 1995 Mutual Fund 500

Vanguard Asset Allocation

	Ticker	Load	NAV	Yield	SEC Yield	Assets	Objective
	VAAPX	None	13.54	4.2%	N/A	1125.5	Asset Alloc.

Vanguard Asset Allocation Fund seeks maximum total return. The fund allocates assets among a common-stock portfolio, a bond portfolio, and money-market instruments. It varies its mix according to the relative attractiveness of the asset classes; there is no limitation as to the amount of assets in each class. Common stocks are evaluated using a dividend-discount model, a mathematical model that evaluates stocks according to the projected worth of their dividends. Bonds will consist primarily of long-term U.S. Treasuries or securities issued by other government agencies.

Manager's Investment Style

The fund has definite guidelines for its allocation of assets. On the bond side, management invests solely in long Treasuries, while mimicking the S&P 500 on the stock side. Management determines the portfolio's mix by employing a customized model that predicts expected return. Management also uses cash to temper risk but requires an environment of a flattening yield curve to do so.

Fund Manager(s)

William L. Fouse CFA, since 11-88.
Thomas F. Loeb, since 11-88.
Thomas B. Hazuka, since 11-88.

Manager Experience	Dates Managed	Invest Obj	Std Dev	+/- Index
Thomas B. Hazuka				
Preferred Asset Alloc	06/92 - 12/94	AA	7.00	-1.88

Performance 12-31-94

	1st Qtr	2nd Qtr	3rd Qtr	4th Qtr	Total
1987	---	---	---	---	---
1988	---	---	---	---	3.20 *
1989	3.89	9.48	5.58	2.99	23.68
1990	-3.75	4.99	-8.31	8.88	0.89
1991	9.25	-0.10	7.14	7.40	25.59
1992	-3.06	2.88	4.71	2.95	7.51
1993	5.65	2.10	3.93	1.23	13.49
1994	-4.57	-1.04	2.45	0.96	-2.32

Bear Market Performance

Decile Rank (5-year period)

Worst 3 Mo Period 1985-89	Worst 3 Mo Period 1990-94
Vanguard Asset Allocation	---	-8.31
+/- S&P 500	---	5.44
+/- Best Fit Index : S&P 500	---	5.44

Trailing Returns

	Total Return %	+/- S&P 500	+/- LB Aggregate	% Rank All	% Rank Obj	Growth of $10,000
3 Mo	0.96	0.98	0.58	7	5	10,096
6 Mo	3.44	-1.42	2.45	18	14	10,344
1 Yr	-2.32	-3.63	0.60	37	46	9,768
3 Yr Avg	6.03	-0.24	1.48	33	41	11,919
5 Yr Avg	8.59	-0.10	0.97	27	35	15,102
10 Yr Avg	---	---	---	---	---	---
15 Yr Avg	---	---	---	---	---	---

Operations

Address and Telephone	Vanguard Fin Ctr. P.O. Box 2600
	Valley Forge, PA 19482
	800-662-7447 / 610-669-1000
Advisor	Mellon Capital Management
Subadvisor	None
Distributor	Vanguard Group
States Available	All plus PR,VI,GU
Report Grade	A-
Income Distrib	Paid Semiannually
* Date of Inception	11-03-88
Fiscal Year End	September

Historical Profile

Return	Above Average
Risk	Average
Rating	★★★★
	Above Average

Investment Style History Equity

Average % Stocks Held in Portfolio

| | | | 50% | 62% | 49% | 47% | 66% | 60% |

Growth of $10,000

|||| Value of Fund ($000)
— Value of Index ($000) S&P 500
▼ Manager Change
▽ Partial Manager Change
► Mgr Unknown After
◄ Mgr Unknown Before

Performance Quartile (Within Objective)

	1983	1984	1985	1986	1987	1988	1989	1990	1991	1992	1993	1994	History
NAV	---	---	---	---	---	10.27	12.01	11.35	13.41	13.64	14.45	13.54	
Total Return %	---	---	---	---	---	3.20 *	23.68	0.89	25.59	7.51	13.49	-2.32	
+/- S&P 500	---	---	---	---	---	2.99 *	-8.01	4.01	-4.90	-0.11	3.43	-3.63	
+/- LB Aggregate	---	---	---	---	---	---	9.14	-8.06	9.59	0.27	3.74	0.60	
Income Return %	---	---	---	---	---	0.50	5.10	5.35	5.44	4.52	3.50	3.98	
Capital Return %	---	---	---	---	---	2.70	18.58	-4.46	20.14	3.00	9.99	-6.30	
Total Rtn % Rank All	---	---	---	---	---	---	27	53	35	52	37	37	
Total Rtn % Rank Obj	---	---	---	---	---	---	2	41	31	34	51	46	
Income $	---	---	---	---	---	0.05	0.51	0.62	0.59	0.59	0.48	0.57	
Capital Gains $	---	---	---	---	---	0.00	0.15	0.13	0.19	0.17	0.53	0.00	
Expense Ratio %	---	---	---	---	---	---	0.49	0.50	0.44	0.52	0.49	0.50	
Income Ratio %	---	---	---	---	---	---	5.53	5.53	5.28	4.95	4.07	3.68	
Turnover Rate %	---	---	---	---	---	---	---	12	44	18	31	51	
Net Assets ($mil)	---	---	---	---	---	---	129.0	179.1	341.2	585.2	1125.8	1125.5	

Risk Analysis

Time Period	Load-Adj Return %	Risk % Rank All	Risk % Rank Obj	Morningstar[2] Return	Morningstar Risk	Morningstar Risk-Adj Rating
1 Yr	-2.32					
3 Yr	6.03	57	67	0.72[3]	0.82	★★★
5 Yr	8.59	53	64	0.97[3]	0.78	★★★★
10 Yr	---	---	---	---	---	---

Average Historical Rating (38 months)   4.0 ★s

[1] 1 = low, 100 = high   [2] 1.00 = Hybrid Avg   [3] 1.00 = 90-day T-bill return

Other Measures

			Standard S&P 500	Best Fit S&P 500
Standard Deviation	6.95	Alpha	0.3	0.3
Mean	6.11	Beta	0.79	0.79
Sharpe Ratio	0.37	R-Squared	82	82

Investment Style

Stocks

	Port Avg	Rel S&P 500
Price/Earnings Ratio	18.5	1.00
Price/Book Ratio	3.4	1.00
5 Yr Earnings Gr %	5.6	1.00
Med Mkt Cap ($mil)	12983	1.00

Style
V B G
Size L/M/S

Bonds

Avg Effective Duration	10.8 Yrs
Avg Effective Maturity	25.8 Yrs
Avg Credit Quality	AAA
Avg Weighted Coupon	8.30%

Maturity S I L
Quality H/M/L

Diversification Value for Portfolio Types

Large Cap: None	Small Cap: High	Bond: Low	Balanced: None	Diversified: Low

Min Initial Purchase	$3000 (Addt'l: $100)
Min IRA Purchase	$500 (Addt'l: $100)
Min Auto Invest Plan	$3000 (Systematic Inv: $50)

Expenses & Fees

Sales Fees	0.00% front
	0.00% deferred
	0.00% 12b-1
Management Fee	0.20% max./0.15% min.+(-)0.05%P
3-,5-,10-yr Expense Projections	$16, $28, $63
Annual Brokerage Cost	0.04%

Portfolio 12-31-94

Total Stocks: 499
Total Fixed-Income: 19

Share Chg (10-94)000	Amount 000		Date of Maturity	Value $000	% Net Assets
	67	US Treasury Bond 7.625%	11-15-22	64806	5.76
	64	US Treasury Bond 8%	11-15-21	64250	5.71
	53	US Treasury Bond 8.125%	08-15-21	53543	4.76
	51	US Treasury Bond 7.125%	02-15-23	46087	4.09
	42	US Treasury Bond 8.75%	05-15-20	45413	4.03
	40	US Treasury Bond 8.5%	02-15-20	42538	3.78
	38	US Treasury Bond 8.75%	08-15-20	41153	3.66
	37	US Treasury Bond 8.875%	02-15-19	40197	3.57
	39	US Treasury Bond 8.125%	05-15-21	39576	3.52
	29	US Treasury Bond 8.125%	08-15-19	29446	2.62
	24	US Treasury Bond 8.875%	08-15-17	25831	2.30
7	289	General Electric		14749	1.31
	13	US Treasury Bond 8.75%	05-15-17	13577	1.21
7	265	AT & T		13320	1.18
6	210	Exxon		12745	1.13
6	218	Coca-Cola		11222	1.00
2	91	Royal Dutch Petroleum		9740	0.87
	9	US Treasury Bond 7.5%	11-15-16	8921	0.79
4	147	Philip Morris		8464	0.75
8	386	Wal-Mart Stores		8209	0.73

Index Allocation

	% of Stocks
S&P 500	99.8
S&P MidCap 400	0.0
U.S. Small Cap	0.2
Foreign	3.7

Composition % 09-30-94

Cash	2.0	Preferreds	0.0
Stocks	49.0	Convertibles	0.0
Bonds	49.0	Other	0.0

Tax Analysis

	Tax-Adj Historical Return %	% Pretax Return
3 Yr Avg	4.10	66.8
5 Yr Avg	6.60	73.8
10 Yr Avg	---	---
Potential Capital Gain Exposure (% of assets)		-1%

Most Similar Funds in MF500

Overland Exp Asset Alloc A	Strong Fit
Stagecoach Asset Alloc A	Strong Fit
Investment Comp of America	Strong Fit

Bond Credit Analysis 05-10-94

% of Bonds

US Govt	100	BB	0
AAA	0	B	0
AA	0	Below B	0
A	0	NR/NA	0
BBB	0		

Stock Sector Weightings

	% of Stocks	Relative S&P 500
Utilities	12.4	1.00
Energy	10.2	1.00
Financials	10.5	0.99
Industrial Cyclicals	16.4	1.00
Consumer Durables	6.2	1.00
Consumer Staples	12.6	1.01
Services	8.1	1.00
Retail	5.8	1.00
Health	8.7	1.00
Technology	9.2	1.00

Vanguard Bond Idx Total Bond Mkt

	Ticker	Load	NAV	Yield	SEC Yield	Assets	Objective
	VBMFX	None	9.17	6.8%	7.82%	1730.7	Corp General

Vanguard Bond Index Fund Total Bond Market Portfolio seeks to replicate the total return of the Lehman Brothers Aggregate Bond Index.

The fund normally invests at least 80% of its assets in securities listed on the index. It attempts to keep its portfolio weightings in line with the weightings of the index. The fund may invest the balance of assets in short-term money-market instruments, and in bond futures contracts and options.

Shareholders are charged a $10 annual account-maintenance fee. Prior to April 23, 1993, the fund was named Vanguard Bond Market Fund. From that date until Jan. 19, 1994, it was called Vanguard Bond Index Fund.

Manager's Investment Style

The fund endeavors to track the performance of the Lehman Brothers Aggregate Bond Index. Instead of holding all 4,700 issues in the index, management chooses about 400 bonds that match the cash flows of the benchmark. Management believes that such a strategy helps the portfolio to copy the duration and yield-curve position of its bogy.

Historical Profile

Return	Above Average
Risk	Average
Rating	★★★★ Above Average

	32	36	41	26	26	33	25	16

Investment Style History
Fixed Income
Income Rtn % Rank Obj

Growth of $10,000

- |||| Value of Fund ($000)
- — Value of Index ($000) LB Agg
- ▼ Manager Change
- ▽ Partial Manager Change
- ► Mgr Unknown After
- ◄ Mgr Unknown Before

Performance Quartile (Within Objective)

	1983	1984	1985	1986	1987	1988	1989	1990	1991	1992	1993	1994	History
	---	---	---	9.94	9.20	9.05	9.44	9.41	9.99	9.88	10.06	9.17	NAV
	---	---	---	-0.60 *	1.54	7.35	13.64	8.65	15.25	7.14	9.68	-2.65	Total Return %
	---	---	---	---	-1.22	-0.53	-0.90	-0.30	-0.76	-0.10	-0.07	0.26	+/- LB Aggregate
	---	---	---	---	-1.02	-1.87	-0.34	1.50	-3.26	-1.55	-2.48	1.27	+/- LB Corporate
	---	---	---	0.00	8.98	8.98	9.33	8.97	8.80	7.32	6.62	6.18	Income Return %
	---	---	---	-0.60	-7.44	-1.63	4.31	-0.32	6.44	-0.18	3.06	-8.83	Capital Return %
	---	---	---	---	46	78	51	11	56	56	69	40	Total Rtn % Rank All
	---	---	---	---	61	41	15	24	42	20	38	49	Total Rtn % Rank Obj
	---	---	---	0.00	0.87	0.81	0.80	0.80	0.77	0.70	0.64	0.62	Income $
	---	---	---	0.00	0.00	0.00	0.00	0.00	0.02	0.09	0.12	0.00	Capital Gains $
	---	---	---	0.00	0.14	0.30	0.24	0.21	0.16	0.20	0.18	0.18	Expense Ratio %
	---	---	---	6.82	9.01	8.84	8.49	8.60	7.95	7.06	6.24	6.28	Income Ratio %
	---	---	---	---	77	21	33	29	31	49	50	50	Turnover Rate %
	---	---	---	2.7	43.3	58.1	138.6	276.7	848.8	1059.9	1540.2	1730.7	Net Assets ($mil)

Fund Manager(s)

Ian A. MacKinnon, since 12-86. Birthdate: 04-48. BA, Lafayette C. 1970 MBA, Pennsylvania State U. 1974
Kenneth Volpert CFA(1984), since 11-92. Birthdate: 11-59. BS, U. of Illinois 1981 MBA, U. of Chicago 1985

Manager Experience	Dates Managed	Invest Obj	Std Dev	+/- Index
Ian A. MacKinnon				
Vanguard Muni Short-Term	11/81 - 12/94	MN	1.18	-5.52
Vanguard Muni Long-Term	11/81 - 12/94	MN	8.35	-0.62

Performance 12-31-94

	1st Qtr	2nd Qtr	3rd Qtr	4th Qtr	Total
1987	1.19	-2.21	-3.12	5.91	1.54
1988	3.12	1.13	1.89	1.04	7.35
1989	0.50	7.64	1.02	3.99	13.64
1990	-1.08	3.56	0.76	5.26	8.65
1991	2.61	1.61	5.47	4.81	15.25
1992	-1.27	3.91	4.21	0.22	7.14
1993	4.17	2.70	2.72	-0.19	9.68
1994	-2.71	-1.01	0.52	0.55	-2.65

Bear Market Performance

Decile Rank (5-year period)

Worst ▭ Best

	Worst 3 Mo Period 1985-89	Worst 3 Mo Period 1990-94
Vanguard Bond Idx Total Bond I	---	-4.84
+/- LB Aggregate	---	0.10
+/- Best Fit Index : LB Agg	---	0.10

Trailing Returns

	Total Return %	+/- LB Aggregate	+/- LB Corp	% Rank All	% Rank Obj	Growth of $10,000
3 Mo	0.55	0.17	0.11	11	25	10,055
6 Mo	1.07	0.08	-0.10	36	26	10,107
1 Yr	-2.65	0.26	1.27	40	49	9,735
3 Yr Avg	4.59	0.04	-0.83	57	23	11,440
5 Yr Avg	7.45	-0.17	-0.81	41	20	14,324
10 Yr Avg	---	---	---	---	---	---
15 Yr Avg	---	---	---	---	---	---

Operations

Address and Telephone	Vanguard Fin Ctr. P.O. Box 2600 Valley Forge, PA 19482 800-662-7447 / 610-669-1000
Advisor	Vanguard's Fixed-Income Group
Subadvisor	None
Distributor	Vanguard Group
States Available	All plus PR,VI,GU
Report Grade	B+
Income Distrib	Paid Monthly
Date of Inception	12-11-86
Fiscal Year End	December

Risk Analysis

Time Period	Load-Adj Return %	Risk % Rank All	Risk % Rank Obj	Morningstar Return	Morningstar Risk	Morningstar Risk-Adj Rating
1 Yr	-2.65					
3 Yr	4.59	19	51	0.29 [3]	0.94	★★★★
5 Yr	7.45	18	49	0.67 [3]	0.92	★★★★
10 Yr	---	---	---	---	---	

Average Historical Rating (61 months)   3.8 ★ s

[1] 1 = low, 100 = high [2] 1.00 = Taxable Avg [3] 1.00 = 90-day T-bill return

Other Measures

				Standard LB Agg	Best Fit LB Agg
Standard Deviation	3.91	Alpha		0.1	0.1
Mean	4.57	Beta		0.97	0.97
Sharpe Ratio	0.27	R-Squared		100	100

Investment Style

Interest-Rate Stance

		Maturity Short Intm Long
Avg Effective Duration	5.3 Yrs	
Avg Effective Maturity	8.9 Yrs	Quality High Med Low

Quality

Avg Credit Quality	AA
Avg Weighted Coupon	8.02%
Avg Weighted Price	99.15% of Par

Diversification Value for Portfolio Types

Large Cap: Medium	Small Cap: High	Bond: None	Balanced: Medium	Diversified: Medium

Portfolio 12-31-94

Amount 000	Date of Maturity	Total Stocks: 0 / Total Fixed-Income: 403	Value $000	% Net Assets
39610	08-15-17	US Treasury Bond 8.875%	43150	2.49
44249	07-01-24	FNMA 7%	40764	2.36
38670	02-15-20	US Treasury Bond 8.5%	40755	2.35
43029	07-01-24	FHLMC 7%	39944	2.31
37125	02-15-99	US Treasury Note 8.875%	38424	2.22
41393	07-01-24	FHLMC 6.5%	37550	2.17
40030	07-01-24	FNMA 6.5%	36151	2.09
31710	09-15-24	GNMA 8%	30615	1.77
32609	04-15-24	GNMA 7%	29530	1.71
29175	07-15-96	US Treasury Note 7.875%	29293	1.69
29055	11-01-24	FNMA 8%	28249	1.63
29724	08-01-24	FNMA 7.5%	28215	1.63
29293	08-15-24	GNMA 7.5%	27367	1.58
27912	09-01-24	FHLMC 7.5%	26603	1.54
26020	08-15-19	US Treasury Bond 8.125%	26366	1.52
26310	04-15-99	US Treasury Note 7%	25496	1.47
20344	12-15-24	GNMA 9%	20542	1.19
20255	11-01-24	FHLMC 8%	19656	1.14
19710	07-31-99	US Treasury Note 6.875%	18971	1.10
18000	08-15-97	US Treasury Note 8.625%	18340	1.06
18000	08-15-21	US Treasury Bond 8.125%	18304	1.06
17550	02-15-00	US Treasury Note 8.5%	18030	1.04
18000	01-15-98	US Treasury Note 7.875%	18023	1.04
18500	05-15-04	US Treasury Note 7.25%	17766	1.03
16485	02-15-21	US Treasury Bond 7.875%	16279	0.94

Composition % 09-30-94

Cash	2.0	Preferreds	0.0
Stocks	0.0	Convertibles	0.0
Bonds	98.0	Other	0.0

Tax Analysis

	Tax-Adj Historical Return %	% Pretax Return
3 Yr Avg	1.91	40.5
5 Yr Avg	4.72	60.0
10 Yr Avg	---	---
Potential Capital Gain Exposure (% of assets)		-6%

Most Similar Funds in MF500

Portico Bond Immdex Ret	Strong Fit
American Cap Govt Secs A	Strong Fit
T. Rowe Price New Income	Strong Fit

Coupon Range

	% of Bonds	Rel Obj
0%	0.0	0.02
0% to 8.5%	65.4	1.03
8.5% to 9.5%	24.0	1.48
9.5% to 11%	8.0	0.87
More than 11%	2.6	0.67
Not applicable	0.0	0.00

Credit Analysis 07-31-94
% of Bonds

US Govt	70	BB	0
AAA	6	B	0
AA	3	Below B	0
A	18	NR/NA	0
BBB	4		

Expenses & Fees

Sales Fees	0.00% front
	0.00% deferred
	0.00% 12b-1
Management Fee	Provided at cost.
3-,5-,10-yr Expense Projections	$36, $60, $122

Min Initial Purchase / IRA / Auto Invest

Min Initial Purchase	$3000 (Addt'l: $100)
Min IRA Purchase	$500 (Addt'l: $50)
Min Auto Invest Plan	$3000 (Systematic Inv: $50)

MORNINGSTAR 1995 Mutual Fund 500

Vanguard Convertible Securities

	Ticker	Load	NAV	Yield	SEC Yield	Assets	Objective
	VCVSX	None	10.55	4.8%	5.71%	170.7	Convrt. Bond

Vanguard Convertible Securities Fund seeks a high level of current income as well as long-term capital appreciation.

The fund normally invests at least 80% of its assets in convertible securities. The balance may be invested in non-convertible corporate debt, U.S. government debt, common stocks, and money markets. It seeks companies whose earnings are expected to grow faster than those of the S&P 500. The fund intends to maintain at least 70% of its convertibles in credit ratings of BB or better. Up to 15% of assets may be invested in foreign issues.

Historical Profile
Return	Above Average
Risk	Above Average
Rating	★★★★
	Above Average

Income Rtn % Rank Obj: 63 28 60 47 34 37 32 30

Manager's Investment Style
This fund does not fit in with the convertible-fund norm. Management seeks appreciation from rapidly growing, small-cap companies. The fund has a lower average coupon and conversion rate than its peers', giving it a profile more befitting of a growth-oriented equity fund. The fund is not easily enticed by market temptations. Instead, management sticks to its guns in the belief that the current portfolio has great long-term potential.

Growth of $10,000
Value of Fund ($000); Value of Index ($000) Wil 4500; Manager Change; Partial Manager Change; Mgr Unknown After; Mgr Unknown Before

Performance Quartile (Within Objective)

Fund Manager(s)
Rohit M. Desai et al. BS, U. of Bombay 1958
MBA, Harvard 1964

	1983	1984	1985	1986	1987	1988	1989	1990	1991	1992	1993	1994	History
	---	---	---	9.68	8.04	8.72	9.52	8.19	10.40	11.80	11.91	10.55	NAV
	---	---	---	-0.55 *	-10.62	15.71	15.85	-8.18	34.34	19.00	13.54	-5.68	Total Return %
	---	---	---		-13.38	7.83	1.31	-17.12	18.34	11.75	3.79	-2.76	+/- LB Aggregate
	---	---	---	-6.24 *	-15.88	-0.90	-15.84	-5.06	3.85	11.38	3.49	-6.99	+/- S&P 500
	---	---	---	2.65	5.25	7.25	6.67	5.79	7.35	5.54	4.59	4.34	Income Return %
	---	---	---	-3.20	-15.87	8.46	9.17	-13.97	26.98	13.46	8.95	-10.02	Capital Return %
	---	---	---		96	26	44	80	20	5	36	70	Total Rtn % Rank All
	---	---	---		90	21	40	71	26	16	56	61	Total Rtn % Rank Obj
	---	---	---	0.26	0.56	0.57	0.56	0.57	0.54	0.53	0.53	0.51	Income $
	---	---	---	0.00	0.12	0.00	0.00	0.00	0.00	0.00	0.91	0.18	Capital Gains $
	---	---	---	0.80	0.85	0.88	0.84	0.88	0.81	0.85	0.71	0.73	Expense Ratio %
	---	---	---	6.02	6.13	6.52	5.60	6.35	5.72	4.80	4.44	4.37	Income Ratio %
	---	---	---			45	24	55	55	57	55	81	52	Turnover Rate %
	---	---	---	72.8	72.6	68.3	57.7	45.4	60.4	134.3	204.4	170.7	Net Assets ($mil)

Manager Experience — Dates Managed / Invest Obj / Std Dev / +/- Index. Not available.

Performance 12-31-94
	1st Qtr	2nd Qtr	3rd Qtr	4th Qtr	Total
1987	10.83	-3.59	0.70	-16.94	-10.62
1988	10.32	3.56	-0.55	1.85	15.71
1989	3.45	7.87	6.68	-2.68	15.85
1990	-0.11	3.53	-16.01	5.72	-8.18
1991	14.65	1.19	8.77	6.46	34.34
1992	4.41	0.48	6.38	6.62	19.00
1993	4.09	1.16	4.36	3.34	13.54
1994	-3.40	-3.52	4.32	-2.98	-5.68

Bear Market Performance
Decile Rank (5-year period)

	Worst 3 Mo Period 1985-89	Worst 3 Mo Period 1990-94
Vanguard Convertible Secur	---	-17.76
+/- LB Aggregate	---	-18.50
+/- Best Fit Index : Wil 4500	---	1.64

Trailing Returns
	Total Return %	+/- LB Aggregate	+/- S&P 500	% Rank All	% Rank Obj	Growth of $10,000
3 Mo	-2.98	-3.36	-2.97	83	48	9,702
6 Mo	1.21	0.21	-3.66	34	17	10,121
1 Yr	-5.68	-2.76	-6.99	70	61	9,432
3 Yr Avg	8.42	3.87	2.15	19	29	12,744
5 Yr Avg	9.47	1.84	0.78	20	38	15,721
10 Yr Avg	---	---	---	---	---	---
15 Yr Avg	---	---	---	---	---	---

Operations
Address and Telephone	Vanguard Fin Ctr. P.O. Box 2600, Valley Forge, PA 19482, 800-662-7447 / 610-669-1000
Advisor	Desai Capital Management
Subadvisor	None
Distributor	Vanguard Group
States Available	All plus PR,VI,GU
Report Grade	B+
Income Distrib	Paid Quarterly
* Date of Inception	06-17-86
Fiscal Year End	November

Risk Analysis
Time Period	Load-Adj Return %	Risk % Rank All	Risk % Rank Obj	Morningstar Return	Morningstar Risk	Morningstar Risk-Adj Rating
1 Yr	-5.68					
3 Yr	8.42	61	79	1.46 [3]	0.88	★★★★
5 Yr	9.47	64	80	1.21 [3]	1.05	★★★★
10 Yr	---					

Average Historical Rating (67 months) 2.8 ★s

[1] 1 = low, 100 = high [2] 1.00 = Hybrid Avg [3] 1.00 = 90-day T-bill return

Other Measures
			Standard LB Agg	Best Fit Wil 4500
Standard Deviation	8.04	Alpha	4.4	1.9
Mean	8.43	Beta	0.59	0.71
Sharpe Ratio	0.61	R-Squared	9	75

Investment Style
Interest-Rate Stance
Avg Effective Maturity 8.6 Yrs

Not Applicable

Quality
Avg Credit Quality ---
Avg Weighted Coupon 5.21%
Avg Weighted Price 98.40% of Par

Diversification Value for Portfolio Types
Large Cap: Medium; Small Cap: Low; Bond: High; Balanced: Low; Diversified: Medium

Portfolio 12-31-94
Total Stocks: 3 — Total Fixed-Income: 43

Amount 000	Date of Maturity		Value $000	% Net Assets
7000	02-15-97	Home Depot Cv 4.5%	8400	4.92
6500	01-01-03	Integrated Health Svcs Cv 6%	8255	4.84
6000	07-01-04	Inco Cv 5.75%	6675	3.91
5000	11-01-99	Staples Cv 5%	6150	3.60
120		BancOne Cl C Cv Pfd $3.50	5955	3.49
95		General Motors Cv Pfd $3.25	5451	3.19
115		Corning Glass Cv Pfd	5405	3.17
10050	11-26-05	Rogers Communications Cv 0%	5327	3.12
7500	06-15-03	Delta Air Lines Cv 3.23%	5269	3.09
6700	09-09-05	Comcast Cv 3.375%	5260	3.08
4500	09-01-13	Amoco Canada Petro A Cv 7.375%	5141	3.01
120		Arkansas Best Cv Pfd 5.75%	4860	2.85
6250	05-15-03	Synoptics Cv 5.25%	4750	2.78
4250	10-01-02	Vencor Cv 6%	4739	2.78
100		Northern Trust Cv Pfd $3.125	4725	2.77
120		TJX Cl C Cv Pfd $6.25	4590	2.69
6000	09-27-13	Motorola Cv	4200	2.46
4000	12-15-99	First Financial Mgmt	4200	2.46
4450	09-15-12	Guilford Mills Cv 6%	3938	2.31
80		Reynolds Metals Cv Pfd $3.00	3870	2.27
4000	08-15-99	Developers Div Realty Cv 7%	3840	2.25
4000	07-01-01	Liberty Property Tr Cv 8%	3800	2.23
3250	01-15-03	Pennzoil Cv 6.5%	3656	2.14
3500	06-01-03	Varlen Cv 6.5%	3640	2.13
3310	03-15-02	Albany International Cv 5.25%	2863	1.68

Composition % 09-30-94
Cash	9.0	Preferreds	0.0
Stocks	0.0	Convertibles	91.0
Bonds	0.0	Other	0.0

Coupon Range
	% of Bonds	Rel Obj
0%	3.1	0.36
0% to 6%	57.2	1.70
6% to 7%	10.4	0.70
7% to 8.5%	8.4	0.72
More than 8.5%	0.0	0.00
Not applicable	21.0	0.81

Tax Analysis
	Tax-Adj Historical Return %	% Pretax Return
3 Yr Avg	5.82	67.4
5 Yr Avg	7.07	71.2
10 Yr Avg	---	---

Potential Capital Gain Exposure (% of assets) -8%

Credit Analysis 05-31-94
% of Bonds
US Govt	0	BB	29
AAA	0	B	33
AA	7	Below B	0
A	18	NR/NA	0
BBB	13		

Most Similar Funds in MF500
Vanguard Index Extended Mkt	Fair Fit
Babson Enterprise II	Fair Fit
Fidelity OTC	Weak Fit

Expenses & Fees
Sales Fees	0.00% front / 0.00% deferred / 0.00% 12b-1
Management Fee	0.45% max./0.30% min.
3-,5-,10-yr Expense Projections	$23, $40, $88

Min Initial Purchase	$3000 (Addt'l: $100)
Min IRA Purchase	$500 (Addt'l: $50)
Min Auto Invest Plan	$3000 (Systematic Inv: $50)

MORNINGSTAR 1995 Mutual Fund 500

Vanguard Equity-Income

Vanguard Equity-Income Fund seeks current income. Capital appreciation potential is also considered.

The fund normally invests at least 80% of its assets in dividend-paying equity securities. The average income yield of the fund's portfolio is expected to be at least 50% greater than that of the S&P 500 Index. The fund expects that its shares demonstrate less price volatility than the S&P 500. The balance of assets may be invested in cash and fixed-income securities; this portion of the portfolio consists primarily of higher-grade debt securities.

Ticker	Load	NAV	Yield	SEC Yield	Assets	Objective
VEIPX	None	12.77	4.5%	4.86%	859.0	Equity-Inc.

Historical Profile
Return	Average
Risk	Below Average
Rating	★★★
	Neutral

Investment Style History
Equity

Average % Stocks Held in Portfolio

96% 74% 93% 94% 96% 97% 99%

Growth of $10,000
IIII Value of Fund ($000)
— Value of Index ($000) S&P 500
▼ Manager Change
▽ Partial Manager Change
► Mgr Unknown After
◄ Mgr Unknown Before

Performance Quartile (Within Objective)

Manager's Investment Style

Management's strategy lives up to the fund's name. While many other funds use nonequities to produce yields, this fund buys nothing but stocks. The manager's approach is a simple one: No stock is considered unless its yield is at least 125% of the S&P 400 Industrials Index's. The stock's yield must also be at or near its historical high. Since yields and share prices are inversely related, management buys mostly value plays. After the stock is bought, it will be held while its yield remains within a predetermined range.

Fund Manager(s)

Roger D. Newell, since 03-88. Birthdate: 11-26.
BA, U. of Minnesota 1949 JD, Harvard 1952

Manager Experience

	Dates Managed	Invest Obj	Std Dev	+/- Index
Not available.				

1983	1984	1985	1986	1987	1988	1989	1990	1991	1992	1993	1994	History
---	---	---	---	---	10.78	12.86	10.54	12.40	12.92	13.66	12.77	NAV
---	---	---	---	---	11.12 *	26.50	-11.92	25.38	9.18	14.65	-1.59	Total Return %
---	---	---	---	---	4.57 *	-5.18	-8.80	-5.10	1.56	4.59	-2.91	+/- S&P 500
---	---	---	---	---	---	-2.67	-5.74	-8.82	0.21	3.37	-1.52	+/- Wilshire 5000
---	---	---	---	---	3.10	6.89	5.69	6.57	4.98	4.69	4.30	Income Return %
---	---	---	---	---	8.01	19.62	-17.60	18.81	4.19	9.96	-5.90	Capital Return %
---	---	---	---	---	---	20	88	35	31	30	30	Total Rtn % Rank All
---	---	---	---	---	---	19	79	61	51	39	42	Total Rtn % Rank Obj
---	---	---	---	---	0.30	0.70	0.73	0.65	0.59	0.61	0.58	Income $
---	---	---	---	---	0.02	0.03	0.07	0.10	0.00	0.52	0.09	Capital Gains $
---	---	---	---	---	0.72	0.44	0.48	0.46	0.44	0.40	0.43	Expense Ratio %
---	---	---	---	---	4.82	6.01	5.67	5.52	4.74	4.39	4.41	Income Ratio %
---	---	---	---	---	3	8	5	3	13	15	18	Turnover Rate %
---	---	---	---	---	63.8	334.1	398.9	569.8	835.8	1067.9	859.0	Net Assets ($mil)

Performance 12-31-94

	1st Qtr	2nd Qtr	3rd Qtr	4th Qtr	Total
1987	---	---	---	---	---
1988	---	6.95	3.39	2.64	11.12 *
1989	7.35	7.88	8.39	0.78	26.50
1990	-3.81	1.80	-15.12	5.98	-11.92
1991	13.38	-0.60	5.87	5.09	25.38
1992	-1.14	4.79	3.11	2.21	9.18
1993	7.51	2.56	5.74	-1.67	14.65
1994	-6.56	1.96	4.41	-1.07	-1.59

Bear Market Performance

Decile Rank (5-year period)

Worst ——————————————— Best

	Worst 3 Mo Period 1985-89	Worst 3 Mo Period 1990-94
Vanguard Equity-Income	---	-16.52
+/- S&P 500	---	-2.68
+/- Best Fit Index : S&P 500	---	-2.68

Trailing Returns

	Total Return %	+/- S&P 500	+/- Wil 5000	% Rank All	% Rank Obj	Growth of $10,000
3 Mo	-1.07	-1.06	-0.30	46	18	9,893
6 Mo	3.29	-1.57	-1.33	19	14	10,329
1 Yr	-1.59	-2.91	-1.52	30	42	9,841
3 Yr Avg	7.20	0.93	0.58	26	49	12,318
5 Yr Avg	6.35	-2.34	-2.47	67	69	13,604
10 Yr Avg	---	---	---	---	---	---
15 Yr Avg	---	---	---	---	---	---

Operations

Address and Telephone	Vanguard Fin Ctr. P.O. Box 2600
	Valley Forge, PA 19482
	800-662-7447 / 610-669-1000
Advisor	Newell Associates
Subadvisor	Spare Kaplan & Bischel/John A. Levin
Distributor	Vanguard Group
States Available	All plus PR,VI,GU
Report Grade	A
Income Distrib	Paid Quarterly
* Date of Inception	03-21-88
Fiscal Year End	September

Min Initial Purchase	$3000 (Addt'l: $100)
Min IRA Purchase	$500 (Addt'l: $100)
Min Auto Invest Plan	$3000 (Systematic Inv: $50)

Expenses & Fees
Sales Fees	0.00% front
	0.00% deferred
	0.00% 12b-1
Management Fee	0.20% max./0.08% min.
3-,5-,10-yr Expense Projections	$13, $22, $51
Annual Brokerage Cost	0.07%

Risk Analysis

Time Period	Load-Adj Return %	Risk % Rank [1] All	Risk % Rank [1] Obj	Morningstar [2] Return	Morningstar Risk	Morningstar Risk-Adj Rating
1 Yr	-1.59					
3 Yr	7.20	59	58	1.08 [3]	0.64	★★★★
5 Yr	6.35	66	86	0.39 [3]	0.79	★★★
10 Yr	---	---	---	---	---	

Average Historical Rating (46 months) 3.0 ★s

[1] = low, 100 = high [2] 1.00 = Equity Avg [3] 1.00 = 90-day T-bill return

Other Measures
		Standard S&P 500	Best Fit S&P 500
Standard Deviation	7.82	Alpha	1.2	1.2
Mean	7.27	Beta	0.87	0.87
Sharpe Ratio	0.48	R-Squared	79	79

Investment Style
	Stock Portfolio Avg	Relative S&P 500
Price/Earnings Ratio	17.8	0.96
Price/Book Ratio	2.5	0.74
5 Yr Earnings Gr %	-2.7	-0.49
Return on Assets %	5.6	0.75
Debt % Total Cap	32.4	1.15
Med Mkt Cap ($mil)	10862	0.84

Style Value Blend Growth
Size Large Med Small

Diversification Value for Portfolio Types
Large Cap: Low	Small Cap: High	Bond: Medium	Balanced: Low	Diversified: Low

Portfolio 12-31-94

Total Stocks: 97
Total Fixed-Income: 0

Share Chg (11-94)000	Amount 000		Value $000	% Net Assets
-72	396	Bristol-Myers Squibb	22942	2.67
-21	389	Philip Morris	22362	2.60
-15	343	American Home Products	21492	2.50
-106	314	Eli Lilly	20633	2.40
-13	343	Texaco	20543	2.39
-20	199	Atlantic Richfield	20208	2.35
-39	321	Exxon	19507	2.27
-28	518	NYNEX	19033	2.22
-48	421	Chevron	18783	2.19
-108	612	GTE	18583	2.16
-102	478	American Brands	17918	2.09
-118	399	Ameritech	16126	1.88
-29	523	Upjohn	16079	1.87
-75	191	Mobil	16058	1.87
-29	230	Dow Chemical	15494	1.80
-32	311	Bell Atlantic	15447	1.80
-47	240	CIGNA	15199	1.77
-15	417	US West	14841	1.73
-1	312	ARCO Chemical	13715	1.60
-26	243	Dun & Bradstreet	13376	1.56
-59	1009	K Mart	13120	1.53
-70	264	Eastman Kodak	12589	1.47
-41	207	BellSouth	11209	1.30
-91	589	Ogden	11040	1.29
-261	571	PacifiCorp	10355	1.21

Composition % 11-30-94
Cash	1.1	Preferreds	0.0
Stocks	98.9	Convertibles	0.0
Bonds	0.0	Other	0.0

Tax Analysis
	Tax-Adj Historical Return %	% Pretax Return
3 Yr Avg	5.06	68.8
5 Yr Avg	4.19	63.3
10 Yr Avg	---	
Potential Capital Gain Exposure (% of assets)		5%

Most Similar Funds in MF500
Washington Mutual Investors	Strong Fit
American Mutual	Strong Fit
USAA Mutual Income Stock	Strong Fit

Index Allocation
	% of Stocks
S&P 500	91.9
S&P MidCap 400	4.4
U.S. Small Cap	2.4
Foreign	2.0

Sector Weightings
	% of Stocks	Relative S&P 500
Utilities	28.7	2.31
Energy	16.2	1.60
Financials	16.2	1.53
Industrial Cyclicals	8.1	0.50
Consumer Durables	0.2	0.03
Consumer Staples	7.5	0.60
Services	4.9	0.60
Retail	3.6	0.61
Health	13.4	1.55
Technology	1.2	0.14

MORNINGSTAR 1995 Mutual Fund 500

Vanguard Fixed-Inc GNMA

	Ticker	Load	NAV	Yield	SEC Yield	Assets	Objective
	VFIIX	None	9.58	7.1%	7.41%	5777.8	Gvt Mortgage

Vanguard Fixed-Income Securities GNMA Portfolio seeks current income consistent with safety of principal and maintenance of liquidity.

The fund normally invests at least 80% of its assets in Government National Mortgage Association (GNMA) certificates, which are mortgage-backed securities representing part ownership of a pool of mortgage loans. The balance of the fund's assets are invested in other U.S. government securities as well as in repurchase agreements secured by U.S. government securities.

Historical Profile
Return: Above Average
Risk: Below Average
Rating: ★★★★★ Highest

43	38	25	50	33	37	64	29

Investment Style History
Fixed Income
Income Rtn % Rank Obj

Growth of $10,000
|||| Value of Fund ($000)
— Value of Index ($000)
LB Mtg
▼ Manager Change
▽ Partial Manager Change
► Mgr Unknown After
◄ Mgr Unknown Before

Performance Quartile (Within Objective)

Manager's Investment Style
The fund's new manager, Paul Kaplan, is taking over where longtime head Paul Sullivan left off. As before, management will take a plain-vanilla approach to investing in GNMAs. Only simple pass-throughs are allowed; CMOs, options, and futures are prohibited. The fund's goals have not changed, either. Low expenses and consistent returns remain the primary objectives.

Fund Manager(s)
Paul D. Kaplan, since 03-94. Birthdate: 11-46.
BA, Dickinson U. 1968 MS, MIT 1974

Manager Experience
	Dates Managed	Invest Obj	Std Dev	+/- Index
Paul D. Kaplan				
North American Inv Qual A	05/91 - 04/94	CG	5.16	-0.46

1983	1984	1985	1986	1987	1988	1989	1990	1991	1992	1993	1994	History
9.13	9.23	9.94	10.05	9.35	9.27	9.70	9.79	10.52	10.42	10.37	9.58	NAV
9.65	14.03	20.68	11.69	2.15	8.81	14.77	10.32	16.77	6.85	5.90	-0.95	Total Return %
1.28	-1.12	-1.45	-3.56	-0.61	0.93	0.23	1.38	0.77	-0.39	-3.85	1.97	+/- LB Aggregate
-0.48	-1.76	-4.53	-1.74	-2.15	0.09	-0.58	-0.40	1.05	-0.11	-0.94	0.65	+/- LB Mortgage
12.42	12.94	12.99	10.59	9.06	9.67	10.13	9.39	9.31	7.80	6.38	6.60	Income Return %
-2.77	1.10	7.69	1.11	-6.92	-0.86	4.64	0.93	7.46	-0.95	-0.48	-7.56	Capital Return %
81	9	69	75	41	69	47	4	51	59	88	26	Total Rtn % Rank All
12	22	9	25	48	12	10	24	10	25	72	16	Total Rtn % Rank Obj
1.11	1.07	1.08	0.99	0.89	0.88	0.88	0.85	0.84	0.79	0.65	0.68	Income $
0.00	0.00	0.00	0.00	0.01	0.00	0.00	0.00	0.00	0.00	0.00	0.01	Capital Gains $
0.57	0.58	0.58	0.50	0.38	0.35	0.35	0.31	0.34	0.29	0.29	0.28	Expense Ratio %
11.89	11.31	11.90	10.16	9.41	9.35	9.35	9.25	8.95	8.22	7.38	6.19	Income Ratio %
41	21	23	32	28	22	8	9	1	1	7	2	Turnover Rate %
84.7	172.4	298.9	2214.1	1864.2	1882.2	2149.3	2598.0	5297.5	6920.6	7073.2	5777.8	Net Assets ($mil)

Performance 12-31-94
	1st Qtr	2nd Qtr	3rd Qtr	4th Qtr	Total
1987	2.18	-2.65	-3.82	6.76	2.15
1988	4.39	1.73	2.14	0.31	8.81
1989	1.07	7.82	1.26	4.00	14.77
1990	-0.15	3.55	1.29	5.35	10.32
1991	2.80	1.71	5.91	5.44	16.77
1992	-1.58	4.26	3.28	0.82	6.85
1993	2.67	1.65	0.64	0.82	5.90
1994	-2.28	-0.36	0.88	0.83	-0.95

Bear Market Performance
Decile Rank (5-year period)

Worst _____ Best

	Worst 3 Mo Period 1985-89	Worst 3 Mo Period 1990-94
Vanguard Fixed-Inc GNMA	-4.15	-3.49
+/- LB Aggregate	-0.60	1.44
+/- Best Fit Index : LB Mtg	-0.88	0.50

Trailing Returns
	Total Return %	+/- LB Aggregate	+/- LB Mortgage	% Rank All	% Rank Obj	Growth of $10,000
3 Mo	0.83	0.46	0.41	8	2	10,083
6 Mo	1.72	0.73	0.42	29	2	10,172
1 Yr	-0.95	1.97	0.65	26	16	9,905
3 Yr Avg	3.87	-0.67	-0.11	72	17	11,208
5 Yr Avg	7.62	0.00	0.05	38	4	14,438
10 Yr Avg	9.52	-0.43	-0.83	64	1	24,824
15 Yr Avg	---	---	---	---	---	---

Operations
Address and Telephone	Vanguard Fin Ctr. P.O. Box 2600 Valley Forge, PA 19482 800-662-7447 / 610-669-1000
Advisor	Wellington Management
Subadvisor	None
Distributor	Vanguard Group
States Available	All plus PR,VI,GU
Report Grade	A-
Income Distrib	Paid Monthly
Date of Inception	06-27-80
Fiscal Year End	January

Risk Analysis
Time Period	Load-Adj Return %	Risk % Rank All	Obj	Morningstar[2] Return	Risk	Morningstar Risk-Adj Rating
1 Yr	-0.95					
3 Yr	3.87	11	23	0.08[3]	0.79	★★★★
5 Yr	7.62	10	33	0.71[3]	0.78	★★★★★
10 Yr	9.52	10	27	0.97[3]	0.89	★★★★★

Average Historical Rating (109 months)   4.2 ★s

[1] 1 = low, 100 = high   [2] 1.00 = Taxable Avg   [3] 1.00 = 90-day T-bill return

Other Measures
			Standard LB Agg	Best Fit LB Mtg
Standard Deviation	3.29	Alpha	-0.4	-0.1
Mean	3.86	Beta	0.73	0.99
Sharpe Ratio	0.10	R-Squared	79	95

Investment Style
Interest-Rate Stance
Avg Effective Duration   5.5 Yrs
Avg Effective Maturity   9.0 Yrs

Quality
Avg Credit Quality   AAA
Avg Weighted Coupon   8.30%
Avg Weighted Price   97.89% of Par

Maturity: Short Intm Long
Quality: High Med Low

Diversification Value for Portfolio Types
Large Cap: High
Small Cap: High
Bond: Low
Balanced: Medium
Diversified: High

Min Initial Purchase / Fees
Min Initial Purchase	$3000 (Addt'l: $100)
Min IRA Purchase	$500 (Addt'l: $50)
Min Auto Invest Plan	$3000 (Systematic Inv: $50)

Expenses & Fees
Sales Fees	0.00% front
	0.00% deferred
	0.00% 12b-1
Management Fee	0.13% max./0.05% min.
3-,5-,10-yr Expense Projections	$9, $16, $36

Portfolio 12-31-94
Total Stocks: 0
Total Fixed-Income: 36

Amount 000	Date of Maturity		Value $000	% Net Assets
866021	09-15-23	GNMA 7.5%	817722	14.15
697010	07-15-23	GNMA 8%	675221	11.69
608093	04-15-32	GNMA 8.5%	602056	10.42
547096	02-15-23	GNMA 9%	552640	9.56
324116	02-15-30	GNMA 9.5%	334011	5.78
263606	10-15-23	GNMA 7%	241654	4.18
73277	03-15-21	GNMA 10.5%	77974	1.35
11179	07-15-01	GNMA 15yr 9%	11376	0.20
8729	07-15-08	GNMA 8.25%	8589	0.15
7810	07-15-22	GNMA 10%	8031	0.14
3956	05-15-18	GNMA GPM 9.25%	4015	0.07
3728	01-20-16	GNMA 12%	3967	0.07
2495	07-20-15	GNMA 12.5%	2662	0.05
1518	02-20-16	GNMA 11%	1608	0.03
1441	05-20-15	GNMA 13%	1575	0.03
1807	11-15-23	GNMA 6.5%	1570	0.03
1344	08-15-13	GNMA GPM 11.5%	1440	0.02
1083	02-20-16	GNMA GPM 11.25%	1156	0.02
1137	05-15-08	GNMA 15yr 7.5%	1096	0.02
832	11-20-15	GNMA 11.5%	882	0.02
659	12-15-14	GNMA 13.5%	732	0.01
434	09-15-10	GNMA 11%	461	0.01
394	01-15-15	GNMA GPM 12.75%	426	0.01
365	01-15-13	GNMA GPM 13%	399	0.01
345	03-15-01	GNMA 15yr 9.5%	357	0.01

Composition % 09-30-94
Cash	3.0	Preferreds	0.0
Stocks	0.0	Convertibles	0.0
Bonds	97.0	Other	0.0

Tax Analysis
	Tax-Adj Historical Return %	% Pretax Return
3 Yr Avg	1.32	33.2
5 Yr Avg	4.94	61.4
10 Yr Avg	6.05	53.9
Potential Capital Gain Exposure (% of assets)		-5%

Most Similar Funds in MF500
Benham GNMA Income	Strong Fit
Dreyfus GNMA	Strong Fit
T. Rowe Price GNMA	Strong Fit

Coupon Range
	% of Bonds	Rel Obj
0%	0.0	0.04
0% to 8%	67.2	1.22
8% to 9%	24.2	1.11
9% to 10%	6.9	0.80
More than 10%	1.7	0.26
Not applicable	0.0	0.00

Sector Analysis 12-31-94
% of Bonds
US Treas	0	CMOs	0
GNMA mtgs	100	ARMs	0
FNMA mtgs	0	Other	0
FHLMC mtgs	0		

Vanguard Fixed-Inc High-Yld Corp

Ticker	Load	NAV	Yield	SEC Yield	Assets	Objective
VWEHX	None	7.20	9.4%	10.43%	2120.7	Corp Hi Yld

Vanguard Fixed-Income Securities High-Yield Corporate seeks high current income without assuming undue risk.

The fund normally invests at least 80% of its assets in high-yielding, income-producing debt securities and debt securities rated B or better. Normally, no more than 20% of the fund's assets may include debt securities rated below B, convertible securities, preferred stocks, and money-market instruments.

Prior to Oct. 28, 1991, the fund was named Vanguard Fixed-Income Securities High-Yield Bond.

Manager's Investment Style

This fund achieves high yield without assuming credit risk. Unlike most high-yield bond funds, this one is devoid of zero coupons and PIKs, and holds very few below B or non rated issues. In fact, the portfolio sports an average credit quality of BB. Management has been able to produce relatively high yields by purchasing bonds with longer-than-average maturities.

Fund Manager(s)

Earl E. McEvoy, since 01-84. Birthdate: 03-48.
BA, Dartmouth C. 1970 MBA, Columbia U. 1972

Manager Experience

	Dates Managed	Invest Obj	Std Dev	+/- Index
Earl E. McEvoy				
Vanguard/Wellesley Inc	10/82 - 12/94	I	7.48	-1.81
Vanguard Preferred Stock	10/82 - 12/94	I	7.41	-4.13

Performance 12-31-94

	1st Qtr	2nd Qtr	3rd Qtr	4th Qtr	Total
1987	6.29	-2.23	-2.85	1.67	2.65
1988	6.19	2.63	2.04	2.12	13.56
1989	1.65	3.14	-0.74	-2.09	1.89
1990	-2.30	4.25	-9.03	1.62	-5.84
1991	9.78	5.56	5.96	5.06	29.01
1992	4.88	3.38	4.65	0.68	14.24
1993	6.71	4.51	2.35	3.59	18.24
1994	-3.22	-0.76	1.75	0.57	-1.71

Bear Market Performance

Decile Rank (5-year period)

Worst   Best

	Worst 3 Mo Period 1985-89	Worst 3 Mo Period 1990-94
Vanguard Fixed-Inc High-Yld	-6.47	-12.50
+/- LB Aggregate	-7.29	-13.25
+/- Best Fit Index : FB HY	---	1.60

Trailing Returns

	Total Return %	+/- LB Aggregate	+/- FB High-Yield	% Rank All	% Rank Obj	Growth of $10,000
3 Mo	0.57	0.19	0.61	10	6	10,057
6 Mo	2.33	1.34	0.78	24	2	10,233
1 Yr	-1.71	1.21	-0.74	32	22	9,829
3 Yr Avg	9.91	5.36	-1.25	13	59	13,277
5 Yr Avg	10.03	2.40	-3.04	17	59	16,127
10 Yr Avg	10.57	0.62	---	52	35	27,306
15 Yr Avg	11.15	0.35	---	64	45	48,847

Operations

Address and Telephone	Vanguard Fin Ctr. P.O. Box 2600
	Valley Forge, PA 19482
	800-662-7447 / 610-669-1000
Advisor	Wellington Management
Subadvisor	None
Distributor	Vanguard Group
States Available	All plus PR,VI,GU
Report Grade	A-
Income Distrib	Paid Monthly
Date of Inception	12-27-78
Fiscal Year End	January

Historical Profile

Return	Above Average
Risk	Low
Rating	★★★★
	Above Average

Investment Style History
Fixed Income
Income Rtn % Rank Obj

| 54 | 50 | 52 | 57 | 80 | 77 | 67 | 44 |

Growth of $10,000

||| Value of Fund ($000)
— Value of Index ($000)
LB Agg
▼ Manager Change
▽ Partial Manager Change
► Mgr Unknown After
◄ Mgr Unknown Before

Performance Quartile
(Within Objective)

1983	1984	1985	1986	1987	1988	1989	1990	1991	1992	1993	1994	History
8.92	8.33	8.86	9.20	8.32	8.39	7.55	6.22	7.16	7.41	8.02	7.20	NAV
15.87	7.74	21.99	16.86	2.65	13.56	1.89	-5.84	29.01	14.24	18.24	-1.71	Total Return %
7.50	-7.42	-0.14	1.61	-0.11	5.68	-12.65	-14.79	13.01	7.00	8.49	1.21	+/- LB Aggregate
---	---	---	1.23	-3.88	2.13	1.50	-14.74	-2.42	-0.66	-0.74	+/- FB High-Yield
15.20	14.35	15.63	13.02	11.17	12.71	11.90	11.77	13.89	10.75	10.01	8.51	Income Return %
0.68	-6.61	6.36	3.84	-8.52	0.84	-10.01	-17.62	15.11	3.49	8.23	-10.22	Capital Return %
54	39	60	42	38	34	97	73	28	11	20	32	Total Rtn % Rank All
41	65	45	8	36	41	32	26	80	85	54	22	Total Rtn % Rank Obj
1.28	1.20	1.18	1.09	1.01	1.02	1.01	0.92	0.78	0.73	0.70	0.68	Income $
0.00	0.00	0.00	0.00	0.12	0.00	0.00	0.00	0.00	0.00	0.00	0.00	Capital Gains $
0.71	0.68	0.65	0.60	0.45	0.41	0.41	0.38	0.40	0.34	0.34	0.32	Expense Ratio %
13.58	12.75	13.61	12.51	11.43	11.47	12.07	12.56	13.35	11.13	9.82	8.81	Income Ratio %
52	82	71	61	67	82	48	41	61	44	83	51	Turnover Rate %
51.2	116.8	252.5	634.3	1369.0	1164.3	895.3	693.8	1452.2	2021.0	2529.8	2120.7	Net Assets ($mil)

Risk Analysis

Time Period	Load-Adj Return %	Risk % Rank All	Risk % Rank Obj [1]	Morningstar [2] Return	Morningstar Risk	Morningstar Risk-Adj Rating
1 Yr	-2.71					
3 Yr	9.91	12	66	1.94 [3]	0.41	★★★★★
5 Yr	10.03	42	31	1.36 [3]	0.51	★★★★
10 Yr	10.57	28	16	0.76	0.41	★★★★

Average Historical Rating (109 months) 3.6 ★s

[1] 1 = low, 100 = high   [2] 1.00 = Hybrid Avg   [3] 1.00 = 90-day T-bill return

Other Measures

			Standard LB Agg	Best Fit FB HY
Standard Deviation	5.03	Alpha	5.3	-1.3
Mean	9.61	Beta	0.89	1.02
Sharpe Ratio	1.21	R-Squared	51	78

Investment Style

Interest-Rate Stance

Avg Effective Duration	5.0 Yrs
Avg Effective Maturity	9.2 Yrs

Quality

Avg Credit Quality	BB
Avg Weighted Coupon	9.67%
Avg Weighted Price	95.39% of Par

Maturity
Short Intm Long

Quality High Med Low

Diversification Value for Portfolio Types

Large Cap: High	Small Cap: High	Bond: Low	Balanced: Medium	Diversified: High

Portfolio 12-31-94

Total Stocks: 0
Total Fixed-Income: 151

Amount 000	Date of Maturity		Value $000	% Net Assets
49500	03-15-01	Fort Howard 9.25%	46283	2.18
40000	04-15-03	Container of America 9.75%	37900	1.79
35000	02-01-23	Time Warner 9.15%	30840	1.45
30000	02-01-01	Stone Container 9.875%	28200	1.33
30000	01-15-13	Time Warner 9.125%	27028	1.27
30000	09-01-08	Continental Cablevision 9%	27000	1.27
27000	07-15-12	Comcast 10.625%	26460	1.25
30000	11-01-22	Long Island Lighting 9%	24812	1.17
30000	07-01-13	Turner Broadcasting Sys 8.375%	24392	1.15
25000	03-31-96	US Treasury Note 5.125%	24301	1.15
25000	02-29-96	US Treasury Note 4.625%	24238	1.14
25000	01-31-96	US Treasury Note 4%	24137	1.14
25000	08-15-96	US Treasury Note 4.375%	23785	1.12
25000	09-30-97	US Treasury Note 5.5%	23598	1.11
25000	07-23-05	Midland Funding 11.75%	22836	1.08
23000	04-01-99	Owens-Illinois 10.25%	22770	1.07
25000	09-30-98	US Treasury Note 4.75%	22524	1.06
22000	04-01-04	AK Steel 10.75%	21780	1.03
25000	12-15-03	Playtex Family Products 9%	21750	1.03
20000	12-15-01	Magma Copper 12%	21600	1.02
22000	08-01-02	Owens-Illinois 10%	21505	1.01
20000	10-15-12	News America Holdings 10.125%	20849	0.98
21000	05-01-03	Uniroyal Chemical 11%	20685	0.98
20000	05-14-04	American Standard 11.375%	20500	0.97
20000	12-15-04	Schuller Intl 10.875%	20450	0.96

Composition % 09-30-94

Cash	7.0	Preferreds	0.0
Stocks	0.0	Convertibles	0.0
Bonds	93.0	Other	0.0

Tax Analysis

	Tax-Adj Historical Return %	% Pretax Return
3 Yr Avg	6.34	61.8
5 Yr Avg	6.20	57.2
10 Yr Avg	5.94	45.1

Potential Capital Gain Exposure
(% of assets) -10%

Most Similar Funds in MF500

Invesco High-Yield	Strong Fit
American High-Income	Strong Fit
Phoenix High-Yield A	Strong Fit

Coupon Range

	% of Bonds	Rel Obj
0%, PIK	0.0	0.00
0% to 11%	85.3	1.74
11% to 13%	13.1	0.39
13% to 14.5%	0.5	0.10
More than 14.5%	1.0	0.60
Not applicable	0.0	0.00

Credit Analysis 11-30-94
% of Bonds

US Govt	0	BB	28
AAA	14	B	52
AA	0	Below B	0
A	1	NR/NA	0
BBB	5		

Min Initial Purchase / Expenses & Fees

Min Initial Purchase	$3000 (Addt'l: $100)
Min IRA Purchase	$500 (Addt'l: $50)
Min Auto Invest Plan	$3000 (Systematic Inv: $50)

Expenses & Fees

Sales Fees	0.00% front
	0.00% deferred
	0.00% 12b-1
Management Fee	0.13% max./0.05% min.
3-,5-,10-yr Expense Projections	$10, $18, $41

MORNINGSTAR 1995 Mutual Fund 500

Vanguard Fixed-Inc I/T US Treas

Ticker	Load	NAV	Yield	SEC Yield	Assets	Objective
VFITX	None	9.63	6.2%	7.83%	844.2	Gvt Treasury

Vanguard Fixed-Income Securities Fund Intermediate-Term U.S. Treasury Portfolio seeks current income consistent with the maintenance of principal and liquidity.

The fund normally invests at least 85% of its assets in intermediate-term U.S. Treasury notes and bonds and other guaranteed U.S. government obligations. The balance of assets may be invested in other U.S. government securities, including repurchase agreements on such securities. The average weighted maturity of the portfolio is expected to range from five to 10 years.

Historical Profile

Return	Above Average
Risk	Above Average
Rating	★★★ Neutral

Investment Style History
Fixed Income
Income Rtn % Rank Obj

Growth of $10,000

IIII Value of Fund ($000)
— Value of Index ($000)
  LB Govt
▼ Manager Change
▽ Partial Manager Change
► Mgr Unknown After
◄ Mgr Unknown Before

Performance Quartile
(Within Objective)

Manager's Investment Style

Like all Vanguard funds, this one is a straight shooter. Management maintains a neutral duration of 5.5 years but will shorten it when faced with rising rates. The fund does add a bit of spice, though, by investing about 15% of assets in non-Treasury government-backed paper and dabbling in futures contracts. The extra returns from these holdings, coupled with low expenses, give the fund an edge over its peers.

Fund Manager(s)

Ian A. MacKinnon, since 10-91. Birthdate: 04-48.
BA, Lafayette C. 1970 MBA, Pennsylvania State U. 1974
Robert F. Auwaerter, since 10-91. Birthdate:
08-55. BS, U. of Pennsylvania 1977 MBA, Northwestern U.

Manager Experience	Dates Managed	Invest Obj	Std Dev	+/- Index
Ian A. MacKinnon				
Vanguard Muni Short-Term	11/81 - 12/94	MN	1.18	-5.52
Vanguard Muni Long-Term	11/81 - 12/94	MN	8.35	-0.62

	1983	1984	1985	1986	1987	1988	1989	1990	1991	1992	1993	1994	History
	---	---	---	---	---	---	---	---	10.47	10.56	10.71	9.63	NAV
	---	---	---	---	---	---	---	---	5.87 *	7.78	11.43	-4.33	Total Return %
	---	---	---	---	---	---	---	---	---	0.53	1.68	-1.41	+/- LB Aggregate
	---	---	---	---	---	---	---	---	---	0.55	0.78	-0.96	+/- LB Government
	---	---	---	---	---	---	---	---	1.17	6.76	5.98	5.54	Income Return %
	---	---	---	---	---	---	---	---	4.70	1.02	5.45	-9.87	Capital Return %
	---	---	---	---	---	---	---	---	---	48	56	57	Total Rtn % Rank All
	---	---	---	---	---	---	---	---	---	12	38	58	Total Rtn % Rank Obj
	---	---	---	---	---	---	---	---	0.12	0.67	0.63	0.59	Income $
	---	---	---	---	---	---	---	---	0.00	0.02	0.41	0.03	Capital Gains $
	---	---	---	---	---	---	---	---		0.26	0.26	0.26	Expense Ratio %
	---	---	---	---	---	---	---	---		6.47	6.44	5.55	Income Ratio %
	---	---	---	---	---	---	---	---		32	123	118	Turnover Rate %
	---	---	---	---	---	---	---	---	139.1	604.8	984.9	844.2	Net Assets ($mil)

Performance 12-31-94

	1st Qtr	2nd Qtr	3rd Qtr	4th Qtr	Total
1987	---	---	---	---	---
1988	---	---	---	---	---
1989	---	---	---	---	---
1990	---	---	---	---	---
1991	---	---	---	---	5.87 *
1992	-2.54	4.63	6.12	-0.40	7.78
1993	5.74	2.91	2.93	-0.51	11.43
1994	-3.60	-1.08	0.19	0.15	-4.33

Bear Market Performance

Decile Rank (5-year period)

Worst			Best

		Worst 3 Mo Period 1985-89	Worst 3 Mo Period 1990-94
Vanguard Fixed-Inc I/T US Tr		---	---
+/- LB Aggregate		---	---
+/- Best Fit Index :		---	---

Trailing Returns

	Total Return %	+/- LB Aggregate	+/- LB Govt	% Rank All	% Rank Obj	Growth of $10,000
3 Mo	0.15	-0.23	-0.21	18	47	10,015
6 Mo	0.33	-0.66	-0.45	50	63	10,033
1 Yr	-4.33	-1.41	-0.96	57	58	9,567
3 Yr Avg	4.74	0.19	0.08	54	7	11,490
5 Yr Avg	---	---	---	---	---	---
10 Yr Avg	---	---	---	---	---	---
15 Yr Avg	---	---	---	---	---	---

Operations

Address and Telephone	Vanguard Fin Ctr. P.O. Box 2600
	Valley Forge, PA 19482
	800-662-7447 / 610-669-1000
Advisor	Vanguard's Fixed-Income Group
Subadvisor	None
Distributor	Vanguard Group
States Available	All plus PR,VI,GU
Report Grade	A-
Income Distrib	Paid Monthly
* Date of Inception	10-28-91
Fiscal Year End	January

Min Initial Purchase	$3000 (Addt'l: $100)
Min IRA Purchase	$500 (Addt'l: $50)
Min Auto Invest Plan	$3000 (Systematic Inv: $50)

Expenses & Fees

Sales Fees	0.00% front
	0.00% deferred
	0.00% 12b-1
Management Fee	Provided at cost.
3-,5-,10-yr Expense Projections	$8, $15, $33

Risk Analysis

Time Period	Load-Adj Return %	Risk % Rank All	Obj	Morningstar Return	Morningstar Risk	Morningstar Risk-Adj Rating
1 Yr	-4.33					
3 Yr	4.74	38	48	0.34 [3]	1.22	★★★
5 Yr	---	---	---	---	---	
10 Yr	---	---	---	---	---	

Average Historical Rating (3 months)   3.7 ★s

[1] 1 = low, 100 = high   [2] 1.00 = Taxable Avg   [3] 1.00 = 90-day T-bill return

Other Measures

		Standard LB Agg	Best Fit LB Govt
Standard Deviation	5.11	Alpha	0.0	-0.1
Mean	4.77	Beta	1.25	1.16
Sharpe Ratio	0.24	R-Squared	96	98

Investment Style

Interest-Rate Stance

Avg Effective Duration	4.6 Yrs
Avg Effective Maturity	8.6 Yrs

Quality

Avg Credit Quality	AAA
Avg Weighted Coupon	9.00%
Avg Weighted Price	108.92% of Par

Diversification Value for Portfolio Types

Large Cap: Medium	Small Cap: High	Bond: None	Balanced: Medium	Diversified: High

Portfolio 12-31-94

Total Stocks: 0
Total Fixed-Income: 23

Amount 000	Date of Maturity		Value $000	% Net Assets
183000	11-15-12	US Treasury Bond 10.375%	217770	25.80
103000	08-15-02	US Treasury Note 6.375%	94309	11.17
82000	08-15-01	US Treasury Note 7.875%	82166	9.73
49000	08-15-13	US Treasury Bond 12%	65155	7.72
51250	11-15-02	US Treasury Bond 11.625%	62301	7.38
36826	12-14-00	Guaranteed Export Trust 7.46%	35311	4.18
27300	11-15-04	US Treasury Bond 11.625%	34193	4.05
20700	11-15-03	US Treasury Bond 11.875%	25888	3.07
22800	04-15-99	Overseas Private Invsmt 5.735%	20614	2.44
21354	05-01-99	Govt Trust Certificate 6%	19299	2.29
19525	11-30-98	US Treasury Note 5.125%	17762	2.10
19425	02-15-03	US Treasury Note 6.25%	17567	2.08
20000	12-19-01	Overseas Private Invsmt 5.94%	17428	2.06
17500	12-01-99	Guaranteed Trade Trust 7.02%	16584	1.96
16860	05-31-99	US Treasury Note 6.75%	16167	1.92
12600	07-15-99	US Treasury Note 6.375%	11905	1.41
10762	02-14-97	Guaranteed Export Trust 7.8%	10495	1.24
7600	05-15-01	US Treasury Note 8%	7659	0.91
5100	05-15-03	US Treasury Bond 10.75%	5985	0.71
6000	08-15-03	US Treasury Bond 5.75%	5214	0.62
5000	11-15-98	US Treasury Note 8.875%	5167	0.61
4000	02-15-03	US Treasury Bond 10.75%	4675	0.55
5000	09-15-00	Aid to Israel 5.25%	4358	0.52

Composition % 09-30-94

Cash	3.0	Preferreds	0.0
Stocks	0.0	Convertibles	0.0
Bonds	97.0	Other	0.0

Tax Analysis

	Tax-Adj Historical Return %	% Pretax Return
3 Yr Avg	2.09	42.9
5 Yr Avg	---	---
10 Yr Avg	---	---
Potential Capital Gain Exposure (% of assets)		-10%

Most Similar Funds in MF500

Fidelity Government Secs	Strong Fit
New England Bond Income A	Strong Fit
Columbia Fixed-Income Secs	Strong Fit

Coupon Range

	% of Bonds	Rel Obj
0%	0.0	0.00
0% to 8%	62.4	1.23
8% to 9%	3.5	0.52
9% to 10%	0.0	0.00
More than 10%	34.1	4.13
Not applicable	0.0	0.00

Maturity Breakdown 12-31-94

% of Bonds

1 to 3 Yrs	0	10 to 15 Yrs	4
3 to 5 Yrs	24	15 to 20 Yrs	17
5 to 7 Yrs	11	20 to 30 Yrs	0
7 to 10 Yrs	27	Non-Treas	16

Vanguard Fixed-Inc L/T Corp Bond

Ticker	Load	NAV	Yield	SEC Yield	Assets	Objective
VWESX	None	8.05	7.6%	8.32%	2552.3	Corp Hi Qlty

Vanguard Fixed-Income Long-Term Corporate Bond Fund seeks current income consistent with maintenance of principal and liquidity.

The fund typically invests at least 70% of its assets in high-quality corporate bonds; it invests at least 80% of its assets in a combination of U.S. government securities and investment-grade corporate bonds. The average weighted maturity generally ranges from 15 to 25 years.

Prior to October 28, 1991, the fund was named Vanguard Fixed-Income Securities Investment Grade Bond. From that date until November 1, 1993, the fund was named Vanguard Fixed-Income Securities Investment Grade Corporate Portfolio.

Manager's Investment Style

By charter, this fund must keep average weighted maturity between 15 and 25 years. Furthermore, management is not allowed to invest in derivatives and therefore has few instruments with which to hedge duration. Given this stance, the fund is highly sensitive to interest-rate changes.

Fund Manager(s)

Earl E. McEvoy, since 03-94. Birthdate: 03-48.
BA, Dartmouth C. 1970 MBA, Columbia U. 1972

Manager Experience

	Dates Managed	Invest Obj	Std Dev	+/- Index
Earl E. McEvoy				
Vanguard/Wellesley Inc	10/82 - 12/94	I	7.48	-1.81
Vanguard Preferred Stock	10/82 - 12/94	I	7.41	-4.13

Performance 12-31-94

	1st Qtr	2nd Qtr	3rd Qtr	4th Qtr	Total
1987	2.61	-3.63	-5.79	7.55	0.20
1988	4.13	1.00	2.80	1.47	9.70
1989	1.18	9.56	0.79	3.09	15.18
1990	-2.20	4.36	-2.26	6.47	6.21
1991	4.15	1.45	7.20	6.74	20.90
1992	-1.54	4.76	5.79	0.61	9.78
1993	6.26	3.86	4.43	-0.67	14.49
1994	-4.01	-2.31	-0.21	1.21	-5.30

Bear Market Performance

Decile Rank (5-year period)

Worst ———————————— Best

	Worst 3 Mo Period 1985-89	Worst 3 Mo Period 1990-94
Vanguard Fixed-Inc L/T Corp	-5.82	-7.05
+/- LB Aggregate	-2.26	-2.11
+/- Best Fit Index : LB Corp	-1.71	-0.78

Trailing Returns

	Total Return %	+/- LB Aggregate	+/- LB Corporate	% Rank All	% Rank Obj	Growth of $10,000
3 Mo	1.21	0.83	0.77	5	2	10,121
6 Mo	0.99	0.00	-0.18	37	29	10,099
1 Yr	-5.30	-2.38	-1.37	66	88	9,470
3 Yr Avg	5.98	1.43	0.57	34	2	11,903
5 Yr Avg	8.86	1.23	0.59	25	1	15,285
10 Yr Avg	10.41	0.46	-0.22	54	1	26,917
15 Yr Avg	11.06	0.26	-0.26	65	1	48,267

Operations

Address and Telephone	Vanguard Fin Ctr. P.O. Box 2600
	Valley Forge, PA 19482
	800-662-7447 / 610-669-1000
Advisor	Wellington Management
Subadvisor	None
Distributor	Vanguard Group
States Available	All plus PR,VI,GU
Report Grade	A-
Income Distrib	Paid Monthly
Date of Inception	07-09-73
Fiscal Year End	January

Min Initial Purchase	$3000 (Addt'l: $100)
Min IRA Purchase	$500 (Addt'l: $100)
Min Auto Invest Plan	$3000 (Systematic Inv: $50)

Expenses & Fees

Sales Fees	
	0.00% front
	0.00% deferred
	0.00% 12b-1
Management Fee	0.13% max./0.05% min.
3-,5-,10-yr Expense Projections	$10, $17, $38

Historical Profile

Return	High
Risk	High
Rating	★★★★ Above Average

29	10	10	14	6	7	8	5

Growth of $10,000

‖‖‖ Value of Fund ($000)
— Value of Index ($000) LB Corp
▶ Manager Change
▽ Partial Manager Change
▶ Mgr Unknown After
◀ Mgr Unknown Before

Performance Quartile (Within Objective)

1983	1984	1985	1986	1987	1988	1989	1990	1991	1992	1993	1994	History
7.84	7.88	8.46	8.73	7.84	7.83	8.24	7.99	8.87	8.86	9.22	8.05	NAV
6.98	14.67	21.66	14.33	0.20	9.70	15.18	6.21	20.90	9.78	14.49	-5.30	Total Return %
-1.39	-0.49	-0.46	-0.92	-2.56	1.82	0.64	-2.74	4.90	2.54	4.74	-2.38	+/- LB Aggregate
-2.29	-1.96	-2.40	-2.20	-2.36	0.48	1.20	-0.94	2.40	1.08	2.33	-1.37	+/- LB Corporate
11.95	14.16	14.30	11.14	9.24	9.83	9.94	9.24	9.89	8.14	7.37	6.76	Income Return %
-4.97	0.51	7.36	3.19	-9.04	-0.13	5.24	-3.03	11.01	1.64	7.13	-12.05	Capital Return %
92	7	62	58	58	64	46	31	43	24	31	66	Total Rtn % Rank All
73	17	25	35	88	2	2	87	1	1	1	88	Total Rtn % Rank Obj
0.96	1.01	1.01	0.88	0.77	0.74	0.73	0.72	0.71	0.68	0.64	0.62	Income $
0.00	0.00	0.00	0.00	0.12	0.00	0.00	0.00	0.00	0.15	0.26	0.07	Capital Gains $
0.75	0.67	0.62	0.55	0.41	0.37	0.38	0.34	0.37	0.31	0.31	0.30	Expense Ratio %
12.16	11.80	12.50	10.78	9.41	9.40	9.40	9.07	9.16	8.46	7.68	6.71	Income Ratio %
122	62	55	56	47	63	60	70	62	72	50	77	Turnover Rate %
62.5	68.6	106.5	697.8	587.2	711.8	987.1	1192.7	2006.2	2619.2	3168.4	2552.3	Net Assets ($mil)

Investment Style History
Fixed Income
Income Rtn % Rank Obj

Risk Analysis

Time Period	Load-Adj Return %	Risk % Rank [1] All	Risk % Rank [1] Obj	Morningstar [2] Return	Morningstar Risk	Morningstar Risk-Adj Rating
1 Yr	-5.30					
3 Yr	5.98	47	94	0.71 [3]	1.36	★★★★
5 Yr	8.86	43	96	1.04 [3]	1.42	★★★
10 Yr	10.41	35	92	1.25 [3]	1.35	★★★★

Average Historical Rating (109 months)   3.6 ★s

[1] 1 = low, 100 = high   [2] 1.00 = Taxable Avg   [3] 1.00 = 90-day T-bill return

Other Measures

			Standard LB Agg	Best Fit LB Corp
Standard Deviation	6.12	Alpha	1.0	0.2
Mean	6.01	Beta	1.49	1.20
Sharpe Ratio	0.41	R-Squared	95	98

Investment Style

Interest-Rate Stance

Avg Effective Duration	7.9 Yrs
Avg Effective Maturity	20.7 Yrs

Quality

Avg Credit Quality	AA
Avg Weighted Coupon	8.13%
Avg Weighted Price	96.35% of Par

Maturity Short Intm Long
Quality High Med Low

Diversification Value for Portfolio Types

Large Cap: Medium	Small Cap: High	Bond: None	Balanced: Medium	Diversified: Medium

Portfolio 12-31-94

Amount 000	Date of Maturity	Total Stocks: 0 Total Fixed-Income: 131	Value $000	% Net Assets
153000	02-15-23	US Treasury Bond 7.125%	139230	5.46
87126	07-15-24	GNMA 6.5%	75732	2.97
75000	05-15-16	US Treasury Bond 7.25%	69352	2.72
65000	08-15-19	US Treasury Bond 8.125%	65863	2.58
48000	12-01-05	Bank of Boston 6.625%	40463	1.59
40000	12-31-31	AT & T 8.625%	39111	1.53
35000	04-01-20	United Parcel Svc Amer 8.375%	35088	1.37
35000	11-15-01	US Treasury Note 7.5%	34360	1.35
30000	01-01-21	Procter & Gamble 9.36%	32364	1.27
30000	11-01-21	Georgia-Pacific 9.875%	30875	1.21
35000	02-15-04	US Treasury Note 5.875%	30521	1.20
30000	05-15-12	General Electric Cap 8.125%	29475	1.15
30000	01-15-22	El DuPont de Nemours 8.25%	28848	1.13
30000	10-01-22	Amoco Canada Petroleum 7.95%	27686	1.08
35000	09-27-23	Republic of Italy 6.875%	27570	1.08
25000	02-01-20	ARCO Chemical 9.8%	27569	1.08
20000	05-01-20	Auburn Hills Trust 15.375%	26922	1.05
27250	01-15-97	Ford Cred Auto Ln Mstr 6.875%	26628	1.04
25000	06-01-02	European Investment Bk 9.125%	26232	1.03
25000	06-01-16	Chevron 9.375%	25819	1.01
25000	11-01-24	Johnson & Johnson 8.72%	25293	0.99
25000	09-15-21	Phillips Petroleum 9.18%	24900	0.98
25000	04-15-17	Archer-Daniels-Midland 8.375%	24813	0.97
25000	05-08-97	GMAC 7.85%	24661	0.97
25000	06-01-06	KFW Intl Finance 8.2%	24562	0.96

Composition % 09-30-94

Cash	4.0	Preferreds	0.0
Stocks	0.0	Convertibles	0.0
Bonds	96.0	Other	0.0

Coupon Range

	% of Bonds	Rel Obj
0%	0.0	0.00
0% to 8.5%	62.4	0.89
8.5% to 9.5%	26.8	2.05
9.5% to 11%	8.8	1.91
More than 11%	2.1	0.90
Not applicable	0.0	0.00

Tax Analysis

	Tax-Adj Historical Return %	% Pretax Return
3 Yr Avg	2.73	44.3
5 Yr Avg	5.72	60.7
10 Yr Avg	6.59	52.8
Potential Capital Gain Exposure (% of assets)		-5%

Credit Analysis 07-31-94

% of Bonds

US Govt	18	BB	0
AAA	16	B	0
AA	14	Below B	0
A	37	NR/NA	0
BBB	15		

Most Similar Funds in MF500

Fidelity Government Secs	Strong Fit
Scudder Income	Strong Fit
Vanguard F/I Interm-Term US	Strong Fit

MORNINGSTAR 1995 Mutual Fund 500

Vanguard Fixed-Inc S/T Corporate

	Ticker	Load	NAV	Yield	SEC Yield	Assets	Objective
	VFSTX	None	10.30	5.7%	7.74%	2905.8	Corp General

Vanguard Fixed-Income Securities Short-Term Corporate Portfolio seeks income consistent with liquidity and minimum principal fluctuation.

The fund invests in short-term investment-grade bonds and other fixed-income securities. It is expected to maintain an average weighted maturity between one and three years. Not more than 30% of the fund's assets may be invested in debt securities rated BBB. The fund may also invest in U.S. government securities, bank obligations, commercial paper, repurchase agreements, and foreign securities.

Prior to Oct. 28, 1991, the fund was named Vanguard Fixed-Income Securities Short-Term Bond.

Historical Profile

Return	Above Average
Risk	Low
Rating	★★★★★ Highest

Manager's Investment Style

Management's focus on investment-grade corporates with an average weighted maturity of one to three years doesn't keep it from reaping healthy returns. To boost yield, management invests 11% of assets in Yankee bonds and stakes twice as much capital in A and BBB issues than the norm. Management is also very active in shifting duration in reponse to interest-rate changes.

Fund Manager(s)

Ian A. MacKinnon, since 10-82. Birthdate: 04-48.
BA, Lafayette C. 1970 MBA, Pennsylvania State U. 1974
Robert F. Auwaerter, since 01-84. Birthdate: 08-55. BS, U. of Pennsylvania 1977 MBA, Northwestern U.

Manager Experience	Dates Managed	Invest Obj	Std Dev	+/- Index
Ian A. MacKinnon				
Vanguard Muni Short-Term	11/81 - 12/94	MN	1.18	-5.52
Vanguard Muni Long-Term	11/81 - 12/94	MN	8.35	-0.62

Investment Style History
Fixed Income
Income Rtn % Rank Obj

76	63	49	31	43	61	61	52

Growth of $10,000

|||| Value of Fund ($000)
— Value of Index ($000) LB Int
▼ Manager Change
▽ Partial Manager Change
►◄ Mgr Unknown After
◄ Mgr Unknown Before

Performance Quartile (Within Objective)

1983	1984	1985	1986	1987	1988	1989	1990	1991	1992	1993	1994	History
9.87	10.12	10.55	10.82	10.33	10.20	10.43	10.47	10.97	10.86	10.90	10.30	NAV
9.11	14.22	14.90	11.42	4.45	6.95	11.46	9.23	13.08	7.19	7.07	-0.08	Total Return %
0.74	-0.93	-7.23	-3.83	1.69	-0.93	-3.09	0.28	-2.92	-0.05	-2.68	2.84	+/- LB Aggregate
-0.16	-2.40	-9.16	-5.12	1.89	-2.27	-2.53	2.08	-5.43	-1.50	-5.10	3.84	+/- LB Corporate
10.61	11.69	10.65	8.86	7.38	8.21	9.20	8.85	8.30	6.67	5.78	5.42	Income Return %
-1.50	2.53	4.25	2.56	-2.93	-1.26	2.25	0.38	4.78	0.52	1.28	-5.50	Capital Return %
84	9	92	77	25	81	62	8	68	55	83	20	Total Rtn % Rank All
42	21	81	71	23	58	52	11	73	17	62	25	Total Rtn % Rank Obj
1.02	1.06	1.01	0.89	0.76	0.83	0.89	0.88	0.81	0.70	0.61	0.59	Income $
0.00	0.00	0.00	0.00	0.18	0.00	0.00	0.00	0.00	0.16	0.10	0.00	Capital Gains $
0.51	0.56	0.62	0.49	0.38	0.33	0.34	0.28	0.31	0.26	0.27	0.26	Expense Ratio %
10.33	10.23	11.26	9.50	7.79	7.36	8.17	8.70	8.48	7.44	6.33	5.48	Income Ratio %
65	121	270	460	278	258	165	121	107	99	71	61	Turnover Rate %
64.1	135.9	119.1	375.0	410.4	498.3	597.2	796.4	1866.4	2696.1	3482.9	2905.8	Net Assets ($mil)

Performance 12-31-94

	1st Qtr	2nd Qtr	3rd Qtr	4th Qtr	Total
1987	1.51	-0.22	-0.11	3.24	4.45
1988	2.70	1.31	1.67	1.11	6.95
1989	1.47	5.01	1.61	2.94	11.46
1990	0.75	2.82	2.24	3.12	9.23
1991	2.42	2.25	3.83	3.98	13.08
1992	-0.13	3.76	3.70	-0.25	7.19
1993	3.04	1.50	1.65	0.71	7.07
1994	-1.00	0.06	0.93	-0.06	-0.08

Bear Market Performance

Decile Rank (5-year period)

Worst _____ Best

	Worst 3 Mo Period 1985-89	Worst 3 Mo Period 1990-94
Vanguard Fixed-Inc S/T Corp	-1.65	-2.18
+/- LB Aggregate	1.90	2.76
+/- Best Fit Index : LB Int	0.49	2.05

Trailing Returns

	Total Return %	+/- LB Aggregate	+/- LB Corp	% Rank All	% Rank Obj	Growth of $10,000
3 Mo	-0.06	-0.44	-0.50	24	69	9,994
6 Mo	0.87	-0.12	-0.31	40	35	10,087
1 Yr	-0.08	2.84	3.84	20	25	9,992
3 Yr Avg	4.67	0.13	-0.74	55	18	11,468
5 Yr Avg	7.21	-0.42	-1.05	45	28	14,164
10 Yr Avg	8.48	-1.46	-2.14	80	66	22,576
15 Yr Avg	---	---	---	---	---	---

Operations

Address and Telephone	Vanguard Fin Ctr. P.O. Box 2600
	Valley Forge, PA 19482
	800-662-7447 / 610-669-1000
Advisor	Vanguard's Fixed-Income Group
Subadvisor	None
Distributor	Vanguard Group
States Available	All plus PR,VI,GU
Report Grade	A-
Income Distrib	Paid Monthly
Date of Inception	10-29-82
Fiscal Year End	January

Risk Analysis

Time Period	Load-Adj Return %	Risk % Rank All	Risk % Rank Obj	Morningstar Return[2]	Morningstar Risk	Morningstar Risk-Adj Rating
1 Yr	-0.08					
3 Yr	4.67	4	21	0.32[3]	0.57	★★★★★
5 Yr	7.21	3	17	0.61[3]	0.48	★★★★★
10 Yr	8.48	2	7	0.68[3]	0.48	★★★★★

Average Historical Rating (109 months) 4.9 ★s

[1] 1 = low, 100 = high [2] 1.00 = Taxable Avg [3] 1.00 = 90-day T-bill return

Other Measures

			Standard LB Agg	Best Fit LB Int
Standard Deviation	2.45	Alpha	0.5	0.7
Mean	4.60	Beta	0.57	0.69
Sharpe Ratio	0.44	R-Squared	84	93

Investment Style

Interest-Rate Stance
Avg Effective Duration 2.4 Yrs**
Avg Effective Maturity 2.4 Yrs

Maturity: Short Intm Long
Quality: High Med Low

Quality
Avg Credit Quality A
Avg Weighted Coupon 7.03%
Avg Weighted Price 97.62% of Par

**figure provided by fund

Diversification Value for Portfolio Types

Large Cap: High	Small Cap: High	Bond: None	Balanced: Medium	Diversified: High

Portfolio 12-31-94

Total Stocks: 0
Total Fixed-Income: 163

Amount 000	Date of Maturity		Value $000	% Net Assets
132000	11-30-99	US Treasury Note 7.75%	131505	4.53
90000	04-28-99	FNMA Note Step 6.5%	86754	2.99
74866	02-28-00	Mobil Oil 9.17%	76504	2.63
49635	03-15-97	General Electric Cap 6.2%	48590	1.67
50000	05-16-97	Federal Home Loan Bank Step 6%	48510	1.67
43000	11-15-97	Banc One 7.55%	42395	1.46
44200	10-14-96	Huntington National Bk 4.48%	41718	1.44
42630	02-15-97	CIT Group Holdings 6%	41688	1.43
42500	12-16-96	NationsBank 4.75%	40043	1.38
40000	11-08-99	RR Donnelley & Sons 7.96%	39507	1.36
40000	03-01-98	Gannett 5.25%	36733	1.26
38500	03-15-99	Compaq Computer 6.5%	35850	1.23
38000	11-19-96	General Electric Cap 4.7%	35840	1.23
35000	08-15-97	Sears Roebuck 7.36%	34515	1.19
34400	12-01-95	WR Grace Cv 6.5%	33948	1.17
35000	02-15-96	AT & T 4.5%	33810	1.16
32000	03-15-97	Carco Auto Loan Mstr Tr 7.875%	31760	1.09
29500	08-01-98	Tenneco 10%	30807	1.06
33650	12-01-99	GTE Southwest 5.82%	30310	1.04
32000	02-24-97	PepsiCo 5%	30090	1.04
30000	11-01-97	Ford Motor FRN	29963	1.03
30000	05-06-96	GMAC FRN	29939	1.03
30000	06-27-97	FNMA Note Step 6%	29153	1.00
30000	06-30-97	Texaco Capital 6.87%	29112	1.00
30565	07-15-97	Kellogg 5.9%	29047	1.00

Composition % 12-12-94

Cash	4.0	Preferreds	0.0
Stocks	0.0	Convertibles	0.0
Bonds	96.0	Other	0.0

Tax Analysis

	Tax-Adj Historical Return %	% Pretax Return
3 Yr Avg	2.26	47.1
5 Yr Avg	4.69	61.8
10 Yr Avg	5.37	54.6
Potential Capital Gain Exposure (% of assets)		-5%

Most Similar Funds in MF500

Vanguard F/I Short-Trm US Tr	Strong Fit
Vanguard F/I Short-Trm Fed	Strong Fit
Prudential Struct Maturity A	Strong Fit

Coupon Range

	% of Bonds	Rel Obj
0%	0.0	0.00
0% to 8.5%	76.7	1.21
8.5% to 9.5%	13.2	0.81
9.5% to 11%	7.1	0.77
More than 11%	0.4	0.09
Not applicable	2.5	0.51

Credit Analysis 12-12-94

% of Bonds

US Govt	6	BB	19
AAA	9	B	0
AA	12	Below B	0
A	21	NR/NA	0
BBB	34		

Expenses & Fees

Sales Fees	0.00% front
	0.00% deferred
	0.00% 12b-1
Management Fee	Provided at cost.
3-,5-,10-yr Expense Projections	$8, $15, $33

Min Initial Purchase $3000 (Addt'l: $100)
Min IRA Purchase $500 (Addt'l: $50)
Min Auto Invest Plan $3000 (Systematic Inv: $50)

Vanguard Fixed-Inc S/T Federal

	Ticker	Load	NAV	Yield	SEC Yield	Assets	Objective
	VSGBX	None	9.69	5.6%	7.49%	1504.8	Gvt General

Vanguard Fixed-Income Securities Short-Term Federal Bond Portfolio seeks current income consistent with the maintenance of principal and liquidity.

The fund invests primarily in short-term U.S. government agency securities; it also invests in U.S. Treasury obligations and repurchase agreements collateralized by government securities. The fund's average weighted maturity typically ranges between one and three years.

Prior to Oct. 28, 1991, the fund was named Vanguard Fixed-Income Securities Short-Term Government Bond.

Historical Profile
Return	Average
Risk	Below Average
Rating	★★★★
	Above Average

Investment Style History
Fixed Income
Income Rtn % Rank Obj

	68	55	57	73	75	78	61

Growth of $10,000
- |||| Value of Fund ($000)
- — Value of Index ($000)
  LB Int
- ▼ Manager Change
- ▽ Partial Manager Change
- ► Mgr Unknown After
- ◄ Mgr Unknown Before

Performance Quartile
(Within Objective)

Manager's Investment Style
Management is restricted to an average weighted maturity between one and three years, and may not invest in derivatives beyond CMOs. Despite these limitations, the fund does make some creative choices. Instead of holding primarily Treasuries, management stocks up on other agency bonds. Government-guaranteed debt and agency debentures have helped to boost yield without prepayment or credit worries.

1983	1984	1985	1986	1987	1988	1989	1990	1991	1992	1993	1994	History
---	---	---	---	10.00	9.76	9.98	10.06	10.43	10.27	10.34	9.69	NAV
---	---	---	---	---	5.73	11.34	9.31	12.24	6.19	7.00	-0.94	Total Return %
---	---	---	---	---	-2.15	-3.20	0.37	-3.76	-1.05	-2.75	1.98	+/- LB Aggregate
---	---	---	---	---	-1.30	-2.88	0.60	-3.07	-1.04	-3.65	2.43	+/- LB Government
---	---	---	---	---	8.13	9.09	8.51	7.75	6.16	5.23	5.26	Income Return %
---	---	---	---	---	-2.40	2.25	0.80	4.49	0.03	1.77	-6.20	Capital Return %
---	---	---	---	---	90	62	8	73	67	84	26	Total Rtn % Rank All
---	---	---	---	---	81	62	29	81	46	68	14	Total Rtn % Rank Obj
---	---	---	---	0.00	0.80	0.84	0.81	0.73	0.62	0.53	0.54	Income $
---	---	---	---	0.00	0.00	0.00	0.00	0.08	0.16	0.11	0.01	Capital Gains $
---	---	---	---	---	---	---	0.32	0.28	0.30	0.26	0.27	0.26	Expense Ratio %
---	---	---	---	---	---	8.50	8.59	8.06	6.98	5.88	4.98	Income Ratio %
---	---	---	---	---	---	228	133	141	111	70	49	Turnover Rate %
---	---	---	---	---	142.3	205.5	456.8	1179.5	1622.5	1921.8	1504.8	Net Assets ($mil)

Fund Manager(s)
Ian A. MacKinnon, since 12-87. Birthdate: 04-48. BA, Lafayette C. 1970 MBA, Pennsylvania State U. 1974
Robert F. Auwaerter, since 12-87. Birthdate: 08-55. BS, U. of Pennsylvania 1977 MBA, Northwestern U.

Manager Experience
	Dates Managed	Invest Obj	Std Dev	+/- Index
Ian A. MacKinnon				
Vanguard Muni Short-Term	11/81 - 12/94	MN	1.18	-5.52
Vanguard Muni Long-Term	11/81 - 12/94	MN	8.35	-0.62

Performance 12-31-94
	1st Qtr	2nd Qtr	3rd Qtr	4th Qtr	Total
1987	---	---	---	---	---
1988	2.08	0.93	1.59	1.02	5.73
1989	1.16	5.48	1.30	3.01	11.34
1990	0.54	2.79	2.15	3.55	9.31
1991	1.89	1.95	3.83	4.06	12.24
1992	-0.59	3.49	3.71	-0.48	6.19
1993	3.17	1.53	1.77	0.38	7.00
1994	-0.98	-0.46	0.70	-0.20	-0.94

Bear Market Performance
Decile Rank (5-year period)

Worst ———————————————— Best

	Worst 3 Mo Period 1985-89	Worst 3 Mo Period 1990-94
Vanguard Fixed-Inc S/T Federal	---	-2.42
+/- LB Aggregate	---	2.51
+/- Best Fit Index : LB Int	---	1.80

Trailing Returns
	Total Return %	+/- LB Aggregate	+/- LB Govt	% Rank All	% Rank Obj	Growth of $10,000
3 Mo	-0.20	-0.57	-0.55	27	68	9,980
6 Mo	0.50	-0.49	-0.28	47	42	10,050
1 Yr	-0.94	1.98	2.43	26	14	9,906
3 Yr Avg	4.02	-0.52	-0.64	69	24	11,256
5 Yr Avg	6.67	-0.96	-0.86	58	38	13,810
10 Yr Avg	---	---	---	---	---	---
15 Yr Avg	---	---	---	---	---	---

Risk Analysis
Time Period	Load-Adj Return %	Risk % Rank [1] All	Obj	Morningstar [2] Return	Morningstar Risk	Morningstar Risk-Adj Rating
1 Yr	-0.94	---	---	---	---	---
3 Yr	4.02	6	11	0.13 [3]	0.66	★★★★
5 Yr	6.67	4	9	0.47 [3]	0.55	★★★★
10 Yr	---	---	---	---	---	---

Average Historical Rating (49 months)   4.7 ★s

[1] 1 = low, 100 = high [2] 1.00 = Taxable Avg [3] 1.00 = 90-day T-bill return

Other Measures
			Standard LB Agg	Best Fit LB Int
Standard Deviation	2.53	Alpha	-0.1	0.1
Mean	3.98	Beta	0.59	0.72
Sharpe Ratio	0.18	R-Squared	85	94

Investment Style

Interest-Rate Stance
Avg Effective Duration   2.9 Yrs**
Avg Effective Maturity   2.3 Yrs

Maturity Short Intm Long
Quality High Med Low

Quality
Avg Credit Quality   AAA
Avg Weighted Coupon   6.43%
Avg Weighted Price   96.65% of Par

**figure provided by fund

Diversification Value for Portfolio Types
Large Cap: High	Small Cap: High	Bond: None	Balanced: Medium	Diversified: High

Operations
Address and Telephone
Vanguard Fin Ctr. P.O. Box 2600
Valley Forge, PA 19482
800-662-7447 / 610-669-1000

Advisor	Vanguard's Fixed-Income Group
Subadvisor	None
Distributor	Vanguard Group
States Available	All plus PR,VI,GU
Report Grade	A-
Income Distrib	Paid Monthly
* Date of Inception	12-31-87
Fiscal Year End	January

Min Initial Purchase	$3000 (Addt'l: $100)
Min IRA Purchase	$500 (Addt'l: $50)
Min Auto Invest Plan	$3000 (Systematic Inv: $50)

Expenses & Fees
Sales Fees	0.00% front
	0.00% deferred
	0.00% 12b-1
Management Fee	Provided at cost.
3-,5-,10-yr Expense Projections	$8, $15, $33

Portfolio 12-31-94
Total Stocks: 0
Total Fixed-Income: 89

Amount 000	Date of Maturity		Value $000	% Net Assets
70315	12-20-01	FNMA Debenture 0%	57637	3.83
49450	10-14-97	FNMA Debenture 7.09%	48441	3.22
45000	05-15-97	US Treasury Note 8.5%	45668	3.03
41000	04-15-97	US Treasury Note 8.5%	41615	2.77
40000	02-11-95	FNMA CMO 7%	38079	2.53
36000	02-28-97	US Treasury Note 6.75%	35291	2.35
35000	04-28-99	FNMA Debenture Step 6.5%	33738	2.24
30000	06-27-97	FNMA Debenture Step 6%	29153	1.94
29800	03-16-96	FNMA CMO 5.5%	27724	1.84
29352	01-15-97	Banco Nacional de Mexico 4.91%	27546	1.83
26960	11-15-97	Govt Trust Certificate 8.5%	27175	1.81
26500	01-01-96	FNMA Debenture IFRN	26707	1.77
28550	03-15-00	FHLMC CMO TAC 6.5%	26240	1.74
27000	09-29-97	FHLMC Debenture 6.83%	26196	1.74
25000	07-25-97	FNMA CMO 8.8%	25727	1.71
25000	07-15-97	US Treasury Note 8.5%	25402	1.69
25000	06-10-96	FNMA Debenture 8.5%	25227	1.68
25000	05-11-98	FNMA Debenture 8.15%	25125	1.67
25000	10-20-95	Federal Home Loan Bank FRN	24963	1.66
25000	12-10-96	FNMA Debenture 7.7%	24891	1.65
27000	07-13-98	FNMA Debenture Step 3%	24881	1.65
25000	07-25-00	Federal Home Loan Bank FRN	24625	1.64
25000	05-19-99	FNMA Debenture Step 6.875%	24272	1.61
25000	05-16-97	Federal Home Loan Bank Step 6%	24255	1.61
25000	04-21-99	Federal Home Ln Bk Step 6.25%	23848	1.58

Composition % 09-30-94
Cash	8.0	Preferreds	0.0
Stocks	0.0	Convertibles	0.0
Bonds	92.0	Other	0.0

Tax Analysis
	Tax-Adj Historical Return %	% Pretax Return
3 Yr Avg	1.72	41.9
5 Yr Avg	4.23	60.4
10 Yr Avg	---	---

Potential Capital Gain Exposure (% of assets)   -6%

Most Similar Funds in MF500
Prudential Struct Maturity A	Strong Fit
Vanguard F/I Short-Trm US Tr	Strong Fit
Vanguard F/I Short-Trm Corp	Strong Fit

Coupon Range
	% of Bonds	Rel Obj
0%	4.7	3.44
0% to 8%	70.8	1.12
8% to 9%	18.6	1.21
9% to 10%	0.6	0.08
More than 10%	0.0	0.00
Not applicable	5.2	0.88

Sector Analysis 12-31-94
% of Bonds
US Treas	15	CMOs	12
GNMA mtgs	0	ARMs	0
FNMA mtgs	0	Other	72
FHLMC mtgs	1		

MORNINGSTAR 1995 Mutual Fund 500

Vanguard Fixed-Inc S/T US Treas

	Ticker	Load	NAV	Yield	SEC Yield	Assets	Objective
	VFISX	None	9.79	0.0%	7.59%	704.0	Gvt Treasury

Vanguard Fixed-Income Securities Fund Short-Term U.S. Treasury Portfolio seeks current income consistent with the maintenance of principal and liquidity.

The fund invests at least 85% of its assets in U.S. Treasury bills, notes, bonds, and other guaranteed U.S. government obligations. The remainder of assets may be invested in U.S. Treasury or U.S. government agency securities, including repurchase agreements on such securities. The fund expects to maintain an average weighted portfolio maturity between one and three years.

Historical Profile

Return	Above Average
Risk	Below Avg
Rating	★★★★ Above Avg

Investment Style History
Fixed Income

Income Rtn % Rank Obj

		76	55	41

Growth of $10,000

- |||| Value of Fund ($000)
- — Value of Index ($000)
  LB Int
- ▼ Manager Change
- ▽ Partial Manager Change
- ► Mgr Unknown After
- ◄ Mgr Unknown Before

Performance Quartile
(Within Objective)

Manager's Investment Style

The fund is limited to a maximum average weighted maturity of three years, but often keeps it much shorter. Management does not only invest in short-term securities, though. The fund employs intermediate-term issues and Government Export Trust bonds to boost yield and give return a push when rates fall. Such digressions give the fund an aggressive slant but do not carry enough risk to scare away timid investors.

1983	1984	1985	1986	1987	1988	1989	1990	1991	1992	1993	1994	History
---	---	---	---	---	---	---	---	10.21	10.31	10.38	9.79	NAV
---	---	---	---	---	---	---	---	3.08 *	6.75	6.31	-0.48	Total Return %
---	---	---	---	---	---	---	---	---	-0.50	-3.45	2.44	+/- LB Aggregate
---	---	---	---	---	---	---	---	---	-0.48	-4.35	2.89	+/- LB Government
---	---	---	---	---	---	---	---	0.98	5.35	4.85	5.03	Income Return %
---	---	---	---	---	---	---	---	2.10	1.40	1.45	-5.51	Capital Return %
---	---	---	---	---	---	---	---	---	61	87	23	Total Rtn % Rank All
---	---	---	---	---	---	---	---	---	41	75	28	Total Rtn % Rank Obj
---	---	---	---	---	---	---	---	0.10	0.53	0.49	0.52	Income $
---	---	---	---	---	---	---	---	0.00	0.04	0.08	0.02	Capital Gains $
---	---	---	---	---	---	---	---	---	0.26	0.26	0.26	Expense Ratio %
---	---	---	---	---	---	---	---	---	5.22	5.12	4.64	Income Ratio %
---	---	---	---	---	---	---	---	---	---	71	86	Turnover Rate %
---	---	---	---	---	---	---	---	65.1	483.4	705.5	704.0	Net Assets ($mil)

Fund Manager(s)

Ian A. MacKinnon, since 10-91. Birthdate: 04-48.
BA, Lafayette C. 1970 MBA, Pennsylvania State U. 1974
John Hollyer CFA(1993), since 10-93. Birthdate: 1963. BS, U. of Pennsylvania

Manager Experience

	Dates Managed	Invest Obj	Std Dev	+/- Index
Ian A. MacKinnon				
Vanguard Muni Short-Term	11/81 - 12/94	MN	1.18	-5.52
Vanguard Muni Long-Term	11/81 - 12/94	MN	8.35	-0.62

Performance 12-31-94

	1st Qtr	2nd Qtr	3rd Qtr	4th Qtr	Total
1987	---	---	---	---	---
1988	---	---	---	---	---
1989	---	---	---	---	---
1990	---	---	---	---	---
1991	---	---	---	---	3.08 *
1992	-0.47	3.38	3.86	-0.11	6.75
1993	2.94	1.29	1.45	0.50	6.31
1994	-1.09	-0.13	0.84	-0.08	-0.48

Bear Market Performance

Decile Rank (5-year period)

Worst ——————————— Best

	Worst 3 Mo Period 1985-89	Worst 3 Mo Period 1990-94
Vanguard Fixed-Inc S/T US Trea	---	---
+/- LB Aggregate	---	---
+/- Best Fit Index :	---	---

Trailing Returns

	Total Return %	+/- LB Aggregate	+/- LB Govt	% Rank All	% Rank Obj	Growth of $10,000
3 Mo	-0.08	-0.46	-0.44	24	54	9,992
6 Mo	0.76	-0.23	-0.03	42	36	10,076
1 Yr	-0.48	2.44	2.89	23	28	9,952
3 Yr Avg	4.14	-0.41	-0.53	66	43	11,294
5 Yr Avg	---	---	---	---	---	---
10 Yr Avg	---	---	---	---	---	---
15 Yr Avg	---	---	---	---	---	---

Operations

Address and Telephone	Vanguard Fin Ctr. P.O. Box 2600 Valley Forge, PA 19482 800-662-7447 / 610-669-1000
Advisor	Vanguard's Fixed-Income Group
Subadvisor	None
Distributor	Vanguard Group
States Available	All plus PR,VI,GU
Report Grade	A-
Income Distrib	Paid Monthly
* Date of Inception	10-28-91
Fiscal Year End	January

Min Initial Purchase	$3000 (Addt'l: $100)
Min IRA Purchase	$500 (Addt'l: $100)
Min Auto Invest Plan	$3000 (Systematic Inv: $50)

Expenses & Fees

Sales Fees	
	0.00% front
	0.00% deferred
	0.00% 12b-1
Management Fee	Provided at cost.
3-,5-,10-yr Expense Projections	$8, $15, $33

Risk Analysis

Time Period	Load-Adj Return %	Risk % Rank All	Risk % Rank Obj	Morningstar[2] Return	Morningstar[2] Risk	Morningstar Risk-Adj Rating
1 Yr	-0.48					
3 Yr	4.14	6	12	0.16T[3]	0.63	★★★★
5 Yr	---	---	---	---	---	---
10 Yr	4.90					

Average Historical Rating (3 months)   4.0 ★s

[1] = low, 100 = high   [2] 1.00 = Taxable Avg   [3] 1.00 = 90-day T-bill return

Other Measures

			Standard LB Agg	Best Fit LB Int
Standard Deviation	2.45	Alpha	0.0	0.2
Mean	4.09	Beta	0.57	0.69
Sharpe Ratio	0.23	R-Squared	84	93

Investment Style

Interest-Rate Stance

Avg Effective Duration	1.9 Yrs
Avg Effective Maturity	2.5 Yrs

Maturity: Short Intm Long
Quality: High Med Low

Quality

Avg Credit Quality	AAA
Avg Weighted Coupon	6.36%
Avg Weighted Price	95.93% of Par

Diversification Value for Portfolio Types

Large Cap: High	Small Cap: High	Bond: None	Balanced: Medium	Diversified: High

Portfolio 12-31-94

Total Stocks: 0
Total Fixed-Income: 31

Amount 000	Date of Maturity		Value $000	% Net Assets
167500	06-30-98	US Treasury Note 5.125%	153760	21.84
80000	07-31-98	US Treasury Note 5.25%	73600	10.46
69400	04-15-97	US Treasury Note 8.5%	70441	10.01
53800	03-31-98	US Treasury Note 5.125%	49681	7.06
45389	02-15-96	US Treasury Note 7.875%	45587	6.48
41000	08-15-97	US Treasury Note 6.5%	39757	5.65
24576	04-15-96	US Treasury Note 9.375%	25121	3.57
20000	10-15-97	US Treasury Note 8.75%	20450	2.91
20800	06-14-96	Guaranteed Export Trust 4.743%	19597	2.78
18500	02-29-96	US Treasury Note 7.5%	18520	2.63
18000	04-30-96	US Treasury Note 7.625%	18031	2.56
18000	06-30-99	US Treasury Note 6.75%	17260	2.45
17300	05-31-96	US Treasury Note 5.875%	16924	2.40
16000	10-15-96	Banco Nacional de Mexico 4.62%	14970	2.13
14900	04-30-96	US Treasury Note 5.5%	14525	2.06
13333	10-01-97	Govt Trust Certificate 7.75%	13167	1.87
8400	11-01-95	Govt Trust Certificate 5.69%	8122	1.15
7000	12-31-97	US Treasury Note 6%	6670	0.95
6429	01-14-96	Banque Nationale Com 6.82%	6240	0.89
7140	03-15-03	Private Export Funding 5.65%	6084	0.86
6000	06-01-97	Small Business Admin 6.95%	5830	0.83
5400	01-14-95	Banque Nationale Com 5.95%	5271	0.75
4800	10-15-96	Banco Nacional de Mexico 4.91%	4505	0.64
4000	01-31-96	US Treasury Note 7.5%	4007	0.57
4020	08-01-96	Guaranteed Trade Trust 4.77%	3827	0.54

Composition % 09-30-94

Cash	3.0	Preferreds	0.0
Stocks	0.0	Convertibles	0.0
Bonds	97.0	Other	0.0

Tax Analysis

	Tax-Adj Historical Return %	% Pretax Return
3 Yr Avg	2.13	51.6
5 Yr Avg	---	---
10 Yr Avg	---	---

Potential Capital Gain Exposure
(% of assets)   -5%

Most Similar Funds

Vanguard F/I Shrt-Trm Fed	Strong Fit
Vanguard F/I S-T Corp	Strong Fit
Prudential Struct Mat A	Strong Fit

Coupon Range

	% of Bonds	Rel Obj
0%	0.0	0.00
0% to 8%	81.6	1.61
8% to 9%	14.7	2.15
9% to 10%	3.8	0.56
More than 10%	0.0	0.00
Not applicable	0.0	0.00

Maturity Breakdown 12-31-94

% of Bonds

1 to 3 Yrs	68	10 to 15 Yrs	0
3 to 5 Yrs	20	15 to 20 Yrs	0
5 to 7 Yrs	0	20 to 30 Yrs	0
7 to 10 Yrs	0	Non-Treas	12

Vanguard Index Extended Market

	Ticker	Load	NAV	Yield	SEC Yield	Assets	Objective
	VEXMX	None	18.52	1.5%	1.65%	967.3	Small Company

Vanguard Index Trust Extended Market Portfolio seeks to replicate the performance of the Wilshire 4500 Index.

The fund invests in a statistically selected sample of the stocks included in the Wilshire 4500 Index. This index consists of 4,500 primarily smaller- to medium-size U.S. common stocks traded on the New York Stock Exchange, the American Stock Exchange, or NASDAQ. These stocks are not included in the S&P 500 Index.

Fund shares are subject to a 1% transaction fee, paid to the fund to defray the costs of investing in smaller stocks. Shareholders are charged an annual account maintenance fee of $10.

Manager's Investment Style

The fund's manager seeks a representative sample of the Wilshire 4500. The Fund holds approximately 1600 issues, but has sector weightings similar to the index, and owns the 800 largest stocks in the Wilshire 4500, while staying away for the smaller, more illiquid issues. This strategy gives the portfolio a slightly mid-cap slant compared with the index.

Fund Manager(s)

George U. Sauter, since 12-87. Birthdate: 07-54.
BA, Dartmouth C. 1976   MBA, U. of Chicago 1980

Manager Experience

	Dates Managed	Invest Obj	Std Dev	+/- Index
George U. Sauter				
Vanguard Index 500	10/87 - 12/94	GI	12.68	-0.23
Vanguard Idx Sm Cap Stk	09/89 - 12/94	SC	16.32	0.07

Historical Profile

Return	Above Average
Risk	Average
Rating	★★★
	Neutral

Investment Style History Equity
Average % Stocks Held in Portfolio

Growth of $10,000
|||| Value of Fund ($000)
— Value of Index ($000) Wil 4500
▼ Manager Change
▽ Partial Manager Change
► Mgr Unknown After
◄ Mgr Unknown Before

Performance Quartile (Within Objective)

History	1983	1984	1985	1986	1987	1988	1989	1990	1991	1992	1993	1994
NAV	---	---	---	---	9.99	11.60	13.91	11.48	15.82	17.35	19.43	18.52
Total Return %	---	---	---	---	-0.10 *	19.75	24.01	-13.98	41.85	12.47	14.49	-1.76
+/- S&P 500	---	---	---	---	0.59 *	3.14	-7.68	-10.87	11.37	4.85	4.43	-3.08
+/- Wilshire 4500	---	---	---	---	---	-0.79	0.07	-0.43	-1.60	0.71	-0.05	0.89
Income Return %	---	---	---	---	0.00	1.89	1.84	2.54	1.97	1.55	1.27	1.50
Capital Return %	---	---	---	---	-0.10	17.85	22.17	-16.52	39.88	10.92	13.22	-3.26
Total Rtn % Rank All	---	---	---	---	---	15	26	91	12	14	31	32
Total Rtn % Rank Obj	---	---	---	---	---	51	46	70	70	57	58	55
Income $	---	---	---	---	0.00	0.20	0.23	0.33	0.25	0.25	0.23	0.28
Capital Gains $	---	---	---	---	0.00	0.16	0.23	0.16	0.20	0.18	0.20	0.20
Expense Ratio %	---	---	---	---	0.00	0.24	0.23	0.23	0.19	0.20	0.20	0.20
Income Ratio %	---	---	---	---	0.00	2.90	2.92	2.68	2.14	1.73	1.48	1.44
Turnover Rate %	---	---	---	---	3	26	14	9	11	9	13	23
Net Assets ($mil)	---	---	---	---	5.3	34.6	146.3	178.8	372.4	583.5	927.9	967.3

Investment Style box: 97% 98% 97% 98% 97% 99% 98%

Performance 12-31-94

	1st Qtr	2nd Qtr	3rd Qtr	4th Qtr	Total
1987	---	---	---	---	-0.10 *
1988	12.81	6.04	-0.59	0.69	19.75
1989	8.37	8.00	8.96	-2.76	24.01
1990	-4.53	3.18	-18.87	7.63	-13.98
1991	20.64	-0.65	8.44	9.14	41.85
1992	1.51	-3.50	2.92	11.56	12.47
1993	4.04	1.33	7.00	1.50	14.49
1994	-3.13	-2.68	6.60	-2.25	-1.76

Bear Market Performance

Decile Rank (5-year period)

Worst ————————— Best

	Worst 3 Mo Period 1985-89	Worst 3 Mo Period 1990-94
Vanguard Index Extended Mark	---	-19.91
+/- S&P 500	---	-6.07
+/- Best Fit Index : Wil 4500	---	-0.51

Trailing Returns

	Total Return %	+/- S&P 500	+/- Wil 4500	% Rank All	% Rank Obj	Growth of $10,000
3 Mo	-2.25	-2.23	0.26	73	72	9,775
6 Mo	4.20	-0.66	0.01	15	61	10,420
1 Yr	-1.76	-3.08	0.89	32	55	9,824
3 Yr Avg	8.15	1.88	0.54	20	57	12,649
5 Yr Avg	9.07	0.38	-0.02	23	71	15,434
10 Yr Avg	---	---	---	---	---	---
15 Yr Avg	---	---	---	---	---	---

Operations

Address and Telephone	Vanguard Fin Ctr. P.O. Box 2600 Valley Forge, PA 19482 800-662-7447 / 610-669-1000
Advisor	Vanguard's Core Management Group
Subadvisor	None
Distributor	Vanguard Group
States Available	All plus PR,VI,GU
Report Grade	B+
Income Distrib	Paid Annually
* Date of Inception	12-21-87
Fiscal Year End	December

Min Initial Purchase	$3000 (Addt'l: $100)
Min IRA Purchase	$500 (Addt'l: $100)
Min Auto Invest Plan	$3000 (Systematic Inv: $50)

Expenses & Fees
Sales Fees	0.00% front
	0.00% deferred
	0.00% 12b-1
Management Fee	Provided at cost.
3-,5-,10-yr Expense Projections	$46, $71, $134
Annual Brokerage Cost	0.20%

Risk Analysis

Time Period	Load-Adj Return %	Risk % Rank All[1]	Risk % Rank Obj	Morningstar Return[2]	Morningstar Risk	Morningstar Risk-Adj Rating
1 Yr	-1.76					
3 Yr	8.15	75	35	1.38[3]	0.86	★★★★
5 Yr	9.07	79	33	1.09[3]	0.96	★★★
10 Yr	---					
Average Historical Rating (49 months)				3.0 ★s		

[1] 1 = low, 100 = high   [2] 1.00 = Equity Avg   [3] 1.00 = 90-day T-bill return

Other Measures

			Standard S&P 500	Best Fit Wil 4500
Standard Deviation	9.59	Alpha	2.1	0.6
Mean	8.32	Beta	0.93	0.98
Sharpe Ratio	0.50	R-Squared	59	100

Investment Style

	Stock Portfolio Avg	Relative S&P 500
Price/Earnings Ratio	21.1	1.14
Price/Book Ratio	3.0	0.87
5 Yr Earnings Gr %	10.0	1.81
Return on Assets %	7.1	0.94
Debt % Total Cap	28.1	1.00
Med Mkt Cap ($mil)	813	0.06

Style: Value Blend Growth / Size Large Med Small

Diversification Value for Portfolio Types

Large Cap: Low	Small Cap: None	Bond: High	Balanced: Low	Diversified: Low

Portfolio 12-31-94

Total Stocks: 1535
Total Fixed-Income: 3

Share Chg (11-94) 000	Amount 000		Value $000	% Net Assets
0	1	Berkshire Hathaway	15463	1.60
0	165	General Motors Cl E	6337	0.66
0	853	RJR Nabisco	4690	0.48
0	33	LIN Broadcasting	4413	0.46
90	180	Carnival Cl A	3828	0.40
0	174	Marion Merrell Dow	3555	0.37
0	72	Reader's Digest Assn Cl A	3547	0.37
0	40	Loews	3475	0.36
0	120	Bank of New York	3472	0.36
0	74	Genentech	3336	0.34
0	75	Duracell International	3239	0.33
0	86	Rhone-Poulenc Rorer	3128	0.32
0	50	Morgan Stanley Group	2961	0.31
0	89	Silicon Graphics	2746	0.28
0	41	CNA Financial	2660	0.27
0	60	ARCO Chemical	2636	0.27
0	121	EMC	2608	0.27
0	55	Microtouch Systems	2477	0.26
0	73	First Bank System	2420	0.25
0	39	First Financial Management	2412	0.25
0	72	CUC International	2401	0.25
5	95	Office Depot	2290	0.24
0	63	Newmont Gold	2262	0.23
0	100	Humana	2260	0.23
0	74	General Instrument	2229	0.23

Composition % 09-30-94

Cash	2.0	Preferreds	0.0
Stocks	98.0	Convertibles	0.0
Bonds	0.0	Other	0.0

Tax Analysis

	Tax-Adj Historical Return %	% Pretax Return
3 Yr Avg	7.26	88.3
5 Yr Avg	8.05	87.0
10 Yr Avg	---	---
Potential Capital Gain Exposure (% of assets)		12%

Most Similar Funds in MF500

Columbia Growth	Strong Fit
Vista Capital Growth A	Strong Fit
Fidelity Growth Company	Strong Fit

Index Allocation

	% of Stocks
S&P 500	0.1
S&P MidCap 400	33.9
U.S. Small Cap	64.7
Foreign	1.4

Sector Weightings

	% of Stocks	Relative S&P 500
Utilities	7.7	0.62
Energy	3.6	0.30
Financials	19.1	1.80
Industrial Cyclicals	14.0	0.85
Consumer Durables	5.8	0.94
Consumer Staples	4.1	0.32
Services	15.7	1.93
Retail	5.2	0.89
Health	8.2	0.94
Technology	16.7	1.82

MORNINGSTAR   1995 Mutual Fund 500

Vanguard Index 500

	Ticker	Load	NAV	Yield	SEC Yield	Assets	Objective
	VFINX	None	42.97	2.7%	2.88%	9356.4	Growth/Inc.

Vanguard Index Trust 500 Portfolio seeks investment results that correspond to the price and yield performance of the S&P 500 Index.

The fund allocates the percentage of net assets each company receives on the basis of the stock's relative total-market value: its market price per share multiplied by the number of shares outstanding.

Shareholders are charged an annual account-maintenance fee of $10.

Prior to Dec. 21, 1987, the fund was named Vanguard Index Trust. Prior to 1980, it was named First Index Investment Trust.

Manager's Investment Style

The fund's manager strives to replicate the performance of the S&P 500. By owning all 500 issues in the index, he rarely strays from this strategy, even in poor markets. The fund's very low expenses also boost performance.

Fund Manager(s)

George U. Sauter, since 10-87. Birthdate: 07-54.
BA, Dartmouth C. 1976 MBA, U. of Chicago 1980

Manager Experience

	Dates Managed	Invest Obj	Std Dev	+/- Index
George U. Sauter				
Vanguard Index Ext Mkt	12/87 - 12/94	SC	13.09	-0.26
Vanguard Idx Sm Cap Stk	09/89 - 12/94	SC	16.32	0.07

Historical Profile

Return	Above Average
Risk	Average
Rating	★★★★
	Above Average

Average % Stocks Held in Portfolio: 99% 97% 97% 97% 100% 99% 100% 98%

Growth of $10,000
|||| Value of Fund ($000)
— Value of Index ($000) S&P 500
▼ Manager Change
▽ Partial Manager Change
► Mgr Unknown After
◄ Mgr Unknown Before

Performance Quartile (Within Objective)

Investment Style History
Equity

	1983	1984	1985	1986	1987	1988	1989	1990	1991	1992	1993	1994	History
	19.70	19.52	22.99	24.27	24.65	27.18	33.64	31.24	39.32	40.97	43.83	42.97	NAV
	21.29	6.21	31.23	18.06	4.71	16.22	31.37	-3.33	30.22	7.42	9.89	1.18	Total Return %
	-1.17	-0.05	-0.51	-0.62	-0.55	-0.39	-0.32	-0.21	-0.26	-0.20	-0.16	-0.14	+/- S&P 500
	-2.17	3.16	-1.34	1.96	2.34	-1.72	2.19	2.86	-3.98	-1.55	-1.39	1.25	+/- Wilshire 5000
	4.78	4.67	4.54	3.69	2.42	4.56	4.33	3.54	3.87	2.96	2.83	2.69	Income Return %
	16.51	1.55	26.69	14.37	2.28	11.66	27.04	-6.86	26.35	4.46	7.06	-1.52	Capital Return %
	35	46	21	32	24	24	11	66	26	53	67	12	Total Rtn % Rank All
	49	38	26	35	26	45	14	46	37	49	54	20	Total Rtn % Rank Obj
	0.87	0.88	0.91	0.89	0.69	1.10	1.20	1.17	1.15	1.12	1.13	1.17	Income $
	0.71	0.48	1.61	2.02	0.17	0.32	0.75	0.10	0.12	0.10	0.03	0.20	Capital Gains $
	0.28	0.27	0.28	0.28	0.26	0.22	0.21	0.22	0.20	0.19	0.19	0.19	Expense Ratio %
	4.22	4.53	4.09	3.40	3.15	4.08	3.62	3.60	3.07	2.81	2.65	2.68	Income Ratio %
	35	14	36	29	15	10	8	23	5	4	6	7	Turnover Rate %
	233.7	289.7	394.3	485.1	826.3	1055.1	1803.8	2173.0	4345.3	6517.7	8272.7	9356.4	Net Assets ($mil)

Performance 12-31-94

	1st Qtr	2nd Qtr	3rd Qtr	4th Qtr	Total
1987	21.13	5.06	6.46	-22.71	4.71
1988	5.64	6.47	0.34	2.98	16.22
1989	7.04	8.79	10.58	2.02	31.37
1990	-3.07	6.24	-13.78	8.88	-3.33
1991	14.47	-0.29	5.28	8.36	30.22
1992	-2.57	1.87	3.08	5.00	7.42
1993	4.33	0.43	2.52	2.30	9.89
1994	-3.84	0.40	4.86	-0.05	1.18

Bear Market Performance

Decile Rank (5-year period)

Worst ▬ Best

	Worst 3 Mo Period 1985-89	Worst 3 Mo Period 1990-94
Vanguard Index 500	-29.78	-13.84
+/- S&P 500	-0.19	0.01
+/- Best Fit Index : S&P 500	-0.19	0.01

Trailing Returns

	Total Return %	+/- S&P 500	+/- Wil 5000	% Rank All	% Rank Obj	Growth of $10,000
3 Mo	-0.05	-0.03	0.72	23	18	9,995
6 Mo	4.80	-0.06	0.18	12	12	10,480
1 Yr	1.18	-0.14	1.25	12	20	10,118
3 Yr Avg	6.10	-0.17	-0.51	33	46	11,944
5 Yr Avg	8.50	-0.19	-0.32	28	35	15,036
10 Yr Avg	14.05	-0.33	0.19	17	14	37,239
15 Yr Avg	14.13	-0.36	0.15	22	25	72,573

Operations

Address and Telephone	Vanguard Fin Ctr. P.O. Box 2600
	Valley Forge, PA 19482
	800-662-7447 / 610-669-1000
Advisor	Vanguard's Core Management Group
Subadvisor	None
Distributor	Vanguard Group
States Available	All plus PR,VI,GU
Report Grade	B+
Income Distrib	Paid Quarterly
Date of Inception	08-31-76
Fiscal Year End	December

Min Initial Purchase	$3000 (Addt'l: $100)
Min IRA Purchase	$500 (Addt'l: $50)
Min Auto Invest Plan	$3000 (Systematic Inv: $50)

Expenses & Fees

Sales Fees	0.00% front
	0.00% deferred
	0.00% 12b-1
Management Fee	None
3-,5-,10-yr Expense Projections	$36, $60, $123
Annual Brokerage Cost	0.02%

Risk Analysis

Time Period	Load-Adj Return %	Risk % Rank[1] All	Obj	Morningstar[2] Return	Risk	Morningstar Risk-Adj Rating
1 Yr	1.18					
3 Yr	6.10	66	49	0.75[3]	0.74	★★★
5 Yr	8.50	67	56	0.94[3]	0.80	★★★
10 Yr	14.05	63	67	1.28	0.86	★★★★
Average Historical Rating (109 months)					4.0	★s

[1] 1 = low, 100 = high [2] 1.00 = Equity Avg [3] 1.00 = 90-day T-bill return

Other Measures

				Standard S&P 500	Best Fit S&P 500
Standard Deviation	7.94	Alpha		-0.2	-0.2
Mean	6.25	Beta		1.00	1.00
Sharpe Ratio	0.34	R-Squared		100	100

Investment Style

	Stock Portfolio Avg	Relative S&P 500
Price/Earnings Ratio	18.5	1.00
Price/Book Ratio	3.4	1.00
5 Yr Earnings Gr %	5.6	1.00
Return on Assets %	7.5	1.00
Debt % Total Cap	28.3	1.00
Med Mkt Cap ($mil)	12983	1.00

Style
Value Blend Growth
Size Large Med Small

Diversification Value for Portfolio Types

Large Cap: None	Small Cap: Medium	Bond: Medium	Balanced: None	Diversified: Low

Portfolio 12-31-94

Total Stocks: 502
Total Fixed-Income: 0

Share Chg (11-94)000	Amount 000		Value $000	% Net Assets
239	4776	General Electric	243597	2.60
208	4367	AT & T	219435	2.35
178	3468	Exxon	210706	2.25
174	3592	Coca-Cola	184991	1.98
77	1498	Royal Dutch Petroleum	161000	1.72
92	2401	Philip Morris	138058	1.48
329	6421	Wal-Mart Stores	136442	1.46
176	3516	Merck	134031	1.43
95	1640	IBM	120571	1.29
103	1915	Procter & Gamble	118718	1.27
99	1902	El duPont de Nemours	107002	1.14
101	1627	Microsoft	99454	1.06
91	1795	Johnson & Johnson	98294	1.05
139	1638	Motorola	94797	1.01
55	1110	Mobil	93548	1.00
118	2105	General Motors	88948	0.95
44	883	American International Group	86535	0.92
77	1427	Bristol-Myers Squibb	82570	0.88
72	1388	Amoco	82079	0.88
153	2688	GTE	81638	0.87
94	1821	Chevron	81246	0.87
113	2213	PepsiCo	80212	0.86
178	2852	Ford Motor	79844	0.85
71	1386	BellSouth	75037	0.80
46	1158	Intel	73659	0.79

Composition % 09-30-94

Cash	4.0	Preferreds	0.0
Stocks	96.0	Convertibles	0.0
Bonds	0.0	Other	0.0

Tax Analysis

	Tax-Adj Historical Return %	% Pretax Return
3 Yr Avg	5.00	81.1
5 Yr Avg	7.33	84.3
10 Yr Avg	12.17	79.1
Potential Capital Gain Exposure (% of assets)		11%

Most Similar Funds in MF500

Massachusetts Inv A	Strong Fit
Investment Comp of America	Strong Fit
Smith Barney Appreciation A	Strong Fit

Index Allocation

	% of Stocks
S&P 500	99.7
S&P MidCap 400	0.0
U.S. Small Cap	0.3
Foreign	3.7

Sector Weightings

	% of Stocks	Relative S&P 500
Utilities	12.4	1.00
Energy	10.1	1.00
Financials	10.6	1.00
Industrial Cyclicals	16.4	1.00
Consumer Durables	6.2	1.00
Consumer Staples	12.5	1.00
Services	8.1	1.00
Retail	5.8	1.00
Health	8.7	1.00
Technology	9.2	1.00

Vanguard Index Total Stock Mkt

	Ticker	Load	NAV	Yield	SEC Yield	Assets	Objective
	VTSMX	None	11.37	2.4%	2.45%	785.7	Growth/Inc.

Vanguard Index Trust Total Stock Market Portfolio seeks to replicate the aggregate price and yield of the Wilshire 5000 Index.

The fund purchases approximately 1,000 of the largest securities in the Wilshire 5000 Index (all U.S. stocks that trade regularly on the NYSE, AMEX, or OTC markets), and a representative sample of the rest; its portfolio consists of 1,400 or 1,500 issues. The fund may also invest in futures contracts.

Fund shares are sold at net asset value plus a 0.25% portfolio-transaction fee. Shareholders are also charged a $10 annual account-maintenance fee.

Manager's Investment Style

Management aspires to mimic the Wilshire 5000 Index. The portfolio consists of the largest 1,000 companies in the Wilshire 5000, and a representative sample of the balance of the index's stocks. The fund, therefore, has a decidedly large-cap slant that resembles the S&P 500. Management keeps turnover extremely low, resulting in low expenses and deferred taxation.

Historical Profile

Return ---
Risk ---
Rating Not Rated

Investment Style History
Equity

Average % Stocks Held in Portfolio: 97% 98% 98%

Growth of $10,000

IIII Value of Fund ($000)
— Value of Index ($000) S&P 500
▼ Manager Change
▽ Partial Manager Change
▶ Mgr Unknown After
◀ Mgr Unknown Before

Performance Quartile (Within Objective)

Fund Manager(s)

George U. Sauter, since 04-92. Birthdate: 07-54.
BA, Dartmouth C. 1976 MBA, U. of Chicago 1980

Manager Experience	Dates Managed	Invest Obj	Std Dev	+/- Index
George U. Sauter				
Vanguard Index 500	10/87 - 12/94	GI	12.68	-0.23
Vanguard Index Ext Mkt	12/87 - 12/94	SC	13.09	-0.26

	1983	1984	1985	1986	1987	1988	1989	1990	1991	1992	1993	1994	History
	---	---	---	---	---	---	---	---	---	10.84	11.69	11.37	NAV
	---	---	---	---	---	---	---	---	---	10.41 *	10.63	-0.17	Total Return %
	---	---	---	---	---	---	---	---	---	1.29 *	0.57	-1.48	+/- S&P 500
	---	---	---	---	---	---	---	---	---	---	-0.66	-0.10	+/- Wilshire 5000
	---	---	---	---	---	---	---	---	---	2.33	2.48	2.32	Income Return %
	---	---	---	---	---	---	---	---	---	8.08	8.14	-2.49	Capital Return %
	---	---	---	---	---	---	---	---	---	---	62	21	Total Rtn % Rank All
	---	---	---	---	---	---	---	---	---	---	48	43	Total Rtn % Rank Obj
	---	---	---	---	---	---	---	---	---	0.23	0.26	0.27	Income $
	---	---	---	---	---	---	---	---	---	0.00	0.03	0.03	Capital Gains $
	---	---	---	---	---	---	---	---	---	0.21	0.20	0.20	Expense Ratio %
	---	---	---	---	---	---	---	---	---	2.42	2.31	2.31	Income Ratio %
	---	---	---	---	---	---	---	---	---	---	1	3	Turnover Rate %
	---	---	---	---	---	---	---	---	---	275.4	512.3	785.7	Net Assets ($mil)

Performance 12-31-94

	1st Qtr	2nd Qtr	3rd Qtr	4th Qtr	Total
1987	---	---	---	---	---
1988	---	---	---	---	---
1989	---	---	---	---	---
1990	---	---	---	---	---
1991	---	---	---	---	---
1992	---	---	2.99	7.10	10.41 *
1993	3.98	0.73	3.66	1.90	10.63
1994	-3.71	-0.90	5.62	-0.95	-0.17

Bear Market Performance

Decile Rank (5-year period)

Worst | Best

	Worst 3 Mo Period 1985-89	Worst 3 Mo Period 1990-94
Vanguard Index Total Stock Mk	---	---
+/- S&P 500	---	---
+/- Best Fit Index :	---	---

Trailing Returns

	Total Return %	+/- S&P 500	+/- Wil 5000	% Rank All	% Rank Obj	Growth of $10,000
3 Mo	-0.95	-0.93	-0.18	43	41	9,905
6 Mo	4.62	-0.24	-0.01	13	19	10,462
1 Yr	-0.17	-1.48	-0.10	21	43	9,983
3 Yr Avg	---	---	---	---	---	---
5 Yr Avg	---	---	---	---	---	---
10 Yr Avg	---	---	---	---	---	---
15 Yr Avg	---	---	---	---	---	---

Risk Analysis

Time Period	Load-Adj Return %	Risk % Rank [1] All Obj		Morningstar [2] Return	Morningstar Risk	Morningstar Risk-Adj Rating
1 Yr	-0.17					
3 Yr	---	---	---	---	---	---
5 Yr	---	---	---	---	---	---
10 Yr	---	---	---	---	---	---

Average Historical Rating ---

[1] 1 = low, 100 = high [2] 1.00 = Equity Avg [3] 1.00 = 90-day T-bill return

Other Measures

			Standard S&P 500	Best Fit
Standard Deviation	---	Alpha	---	---
Mean	---	Beta	---	---
Sharpe Ratio	---	R-Squared	---	---

Investment Style

	Stock Portfolio Avg	Relative S&P 500
Price/Earnings Ratio	19.1	1.04
Price/Book Ratio	3.3	0.97
5 Yr Earnings Gr %	7.1	1.27
Return on Assets %	7.4	0.99
Debt % Total Cap	28.3	1.00
Med Mkt Cap ($mil)	6546	0.50

Style Value Blend Growth
Size Large Med Small

Diversification Value for Portfolio Types

Large Cap: Small Cap: Bond: Balanced: Diversified:

Portfolio 12-31-94

Total Stocks: 1686
Total Fixed-Income: 1

Share Chg (11-94) 000	Amount 000		Value $000	% Net Assets
7	280	General Electric	14259	1.81
6	256	AT & T	12847	1.64
5	203	Exxon	12337	1.57
5	210	Coca-Cola	10827	1.38
1	140	Philip Morris	8076	1.03
4	370	Wal-Mart Stores	7860	1.00
5	206	Merck	7849	1.00
3	96	IBM	7071	0.90
3	112	Procter & Gamble	6960	0.89
3	112	El duPont de Nemours	6284	0.80
3	95	Microsoft	5806	0.74
2	105	Johnson & Johnson	5731	0.73
5	95	Motorola	5525	0.70
1	65	Mobil	5450	0.69
3	123	General Motors	5185	0.66
1	52	American International Group	5062	0.64
3	84	Bristol-Myers Squibb	4851	0.62
2	82	Amoco	4826	0.61
3	107	Chevron	4778	0.61
4	157	GTE	4756	0.61
3	129	PepsiCo	4675	0.60
5	166	Ford Motor	4653	0.59
2	81	BellSouth	4382	0.56
1	68	Intel	4340	0.55
1	132	Abbott Laboratories	4291	0.55

Composition % 09-30-94

Cash	2.0	Preferreds	0.0
Stocks	98.0	Convertibles	0.0
Bonds	0.0	Other	0.0

Tax Analysis

	Tax-Adj Historical Return %	% Pretax Return
3 Yr Avg	---	---
5 Yr Avg	---	---
10 Yr Avg	---	---
Potential Capital Gain Exposure (% of assets)	4%	

Most Similar Funds in MF500

Fund lacks three-year record

Index Allocation

	% of Stocks
S&P 500	69.2
S&P MidCap 400	10.8
U.S. Small Cap	19.8
Foreign	0.4

Sector Weightings

	% of Stocks	Relative S&P 500
Utilities	11.3	0.91
Energy	7.1	0.70
Financials	14.2	1.34
Industrial Cyclicals	15.4	0.94
Consumer Durables	6.0	0.97
Consumer Staples	9.5	0.75
Services	10.5	1.29
Retail	5.7	0.97
Health	8.8	1.02
Technology	11.6	1.27

Operations

Address and Telephone	Vanguard Fin Ctr. P.O. Box 2600 Valley Forge, PA 19482 800-662-7447 / 610-669-1000
Advisor	Vanguard's Core Management Group
Subadvisor	None
Distributor	Vanguard Group
States Available	All plus PR,VI,GU
Report Grade	B+
Income Distrib	Paid Quarterly
* Date of Inception	04-27-92
Fiscal Year End	December

Min Initial Purchase	$3000 (Addt'l: $100)
Min IRA Purchase	$500 (Addt'l: $100)
Min Auto Invest Plan	$3000 (Systematic Inv: $50)

Expenses & Fees

Sales Fees	0.00% front
	0.00% deferred
	0.00% 12b-1
Management Fee	Provided at cost.
3-,5-,10-yr Expense Projections	$39, $63, $127
Annual Brokerage Cost	0.02%

MORNINGSTAR 1995 Mutual Fund 500

Vanguard Intl Growth

	Ticker	Load	NAV	Yield	SEC Yield	Assets	Objective
	VWIGX	None	13.43	1.3%	N/A	2927.7	Foreign Stock

Vanguard International Growth Portfolio seeks capital appreciation; income is incidental.

The fund invests in a broadly diversified array of non-U.S. equity securities, primarily common stocks of seasoned companies.

Prior to Sept. 30, 1985, Vanguard World Fund U.S. Growth Portfolio and this fund were united and known as Ivest Fund. Results on this page from 1982 to Sept. 1985 have been adjusted to reflect only the international holdings of Ivest Fund. From Sept. 1985 until May 3, 1993, the fund was named Vanguard World Fund.

Manager's Investment Style

The fund's manager takes a large-cap approach to international investing. Foulkes weighs the fund heavily in the Pacific Rim based on the belief that it holds tremendous opportunites for long-term growth. He tends to seek out bargains as part of an overall value slant.

Fund Manager(s)

Richard R. Foulkes, since 09-81. Birthdate: 10-45. BA, Cambridge U. 1967 MA, Cambridge U. 1968

Manager Experience

	Dates Managed	Invest Obj	Std Dev	+/- Index

Not available.

Historical Profile

Return	Above Average
Risk	Average
Rating	★★★★ Above Average

	1983	1984	1985	1986	1987	1988	1989	1990	1991	1992	1993	1994	History
% Stocks Held			97%	96%	95%	92%	95%	97%		94%		99%	Average % Stocks Held in Portfolio
NAV	6.11	5.56	7.79	11.26	10.34	10.30	12.42	10.05	10.21	9.41	13.51	13.43	NAV
	43.06	-1.02	56.95	56.71	12.48	11.61	24.76	-12.05	4.74	-5.79	44.74	0.76	Total Return %
	20.60	-7.29	25.21	38.03	7.22	-5.00	-6.92	-8.93	-25.75	-13.40	34.69	-0.56	+/- S&P 500
	19.37	-8.41	0.79	-12.73	-12.15	-16.66	14.22	11.40	-7.40	6.39	12.18	-7.02	+/- MSCI EAFE
	1.79	1.88	1.52	0.70	1.07	1.57	1.30	1.89	1.91	2.05	1.17	1.35	Income Return %
	41.27	-2.90	55.43	56.00	11.41	10.05	23.47	-13.94	2.82	-7.84	43.57	-0.59	Capital Return %
	1	68	2	2	7	48	24	88	98	96	3	15	Total Rtn % Rank All
	1	25	18	15	19	71	34	52	92	64	30	33	Total Rtn % Rank Obj
	0.09	0.11	0.09	0.07	0.13	0.16	0.15	0.20	0.19	0.21	0.11	0.18	Income $
	0.12	0.38	0.65	0.80	2.43	1.07	0.28	0.68	0.12	0.00	0.00	0.00	Capital Gains $
	1.07	0.88	1.04	0.78	0.66	0.67	0.64	0.68	0.67	0.58	0.59	0.46	Expense Ratio %
	2.16	2.53	2.10	1.10	1.00	1.39	1.27	3.01	1.80	2.04	1.27	1.37	Income Ratio %
	95	70	61	39	77	71	50	45	49	58	51	28	Turnover Rate %
	182.4	180.4	211.3	443.6	472.2	462.0	685.2	733.6	869.4	880.1	2127.3	2927.7	Net Assets ($mil)

Investment Style History Equity

Growth of $10,000

‖‖‖ Value of Fund ($000)
— Value of Index ($000) MSEASEA
▼ Manager Change
▽ Partial Manager Change
► Mgr Unknown After
◄ Mgr Unknown Before

Performance Quartile (Within Objective)

Performance 12-31-94

	1st Qtr	2nd Qtr	3rd Qtr	4th Qtr	Total
1987	7.99	7.40	11.41	-12.95	12.48
1988	6.96	-2.08	-1.75	8.47	11.61
1989	-0.10	0.78	17.94	5.07	24.76
1990	-8.29	10.18	-18.25	6.47	-12.05
1991	4.98	-3.60	4.92	-1.35	4.74
1992	-5.09	7.43	-4.61	-3.13	-5.79
1993	7.76	7.30	11.31	12.47	44.74
1994	-1.78	2.03	3.18	-2.56	0.76

Bear Market Performance

Decile Rank (5-year period)

	Worst 3 Mo Period 1985-89	Worst 3 Mo Period 1990-94
Vanguard Intl Growth	-19.56	-18.25
+/- S&P 500	10.02	-4.50
+/- Best Fit Index : MSEASEA	4.76	-1.63

Trailing Returns

	Total Return %	+/- S&P 500	+/- MSCI EAFE	% Rank All	% Rank Obj	Growth of $10,000
3 Mo	-2.56	-2.55	-1.54	78	20	9,744
6 Mo	0.53	-4.33	1.46	46	24	10,053
1 Yr	0.76	-0.56	-7.02	15	33	10,076
3 Yr Avg	11.17	4.91	3.31	10	31	13,740
5 Yr Avg	4.83	-3.87	3.33	91	54	12,657
10 Yr Avg	17.17	2.78	-0.38	5	25	48,758
15 Yr Avg	---	---	---	---	---	---

Operations

Address and Telephone	Vanguard Fin Ctr. P.O. Box 2600 Valley Forge, PA 19482 800-662-7447 / 610-669-1000
Advisor	Schroder Capital Management Intl
Subadvisor	None
Distributor	Vanguard Group
States Available	All plus PR,VI,GU
Report Grade	A-
Income Distrib	Paid Annually
Date of Inception	09-30-81
Fiscal Year End	August

Min Initial Purchase	$3000 (Addt'l: $100)
Min IRA Purchase	$500 (Addt'l: $100)
Min Auto Invest Plan	$3000 (Systematic Inv: $50)

Expenses & Fees

Sales Fees	
	0.00% front
	0.00% deferred
	0.00% 12b-1
Management Fee	0.85% max./0.12% min.
3-,5-,10-yr Expense Projections	$13, $22, $51
Annual Brokerage Cost	0.29%

Risk Analysis

Time Period	Load-Adj Return %	Risk % Rank All	Risk % Rank Obj	Morningstar Return	Morningstar Risk	Morningstar Risk-Adj Rating
1 Yr	0.76					
3 Yr	11.17	81	18	2.36[3]	0.97	★★★★
5 Yr	4.83	90	76	0.02[3]	1.16	★★
10 Yr	17.17	75	50	2.03	0.97	★★★★★

Average Historical Rating (109 months) 4.3 ★s

[1] 1 = low, 100 = high   [2] 1.00 = Equity Avg   [3] 1.00 = 90-day T-bill return

Other Measures

			Standard S&P 500	Best Fit MSEASEA
Standard Deviation	12.75	Alpha	6.0	2.3
Mean	11.43	Beta	0.72	0.89
Sharpe Ratio	0.62	R-Squared	20	85

Investment Style

	Stock Portfolio Avg	Rel MSCI EAFE	Rel Obj	Style
Price/Earnings Ratio	30.6	0.83	1.09	
Price/Cash Flow	13.4	0.86	1.00	
Price/Book Ratio	2.5	0.95	0.83	
5 Yr Earnings Gr %	1.2	---	0.32	
Return on Assets %	5.5	1.22	0.77	
Debt % Total Cap	30.0	0.88	1.09	
Med Mkt Cap ($mil)	8353	0.70	1.63	

Diversification Value for Portfolio Types

Large Cap: High	Small Cap: High	Bond: High	Balanced: High	Diversified: Low

Portfolio 11-30-94

Share Chg (10-94) 000	Amount 000	Total Stocks: 185 Total Fixed-Income: 11	Value $000	% Net Assets
0	1795	Intl Nederlander Groep	84246	2.86
0	1500	Ito-Yokado	79465	2.70
0	502	Heineken (Netherlands)	72476	2.46
0	26712	SIP	69002	2.34
0	3200	Matsushita Electric Indl	49405	1.68
0	7000	Toshiba	48880	1.66
0	3750	Sekisui House	43517	1.48
0	2200	Nomura Securities	43068	1.46
0	2000	Toyota Motor	42583	1.44
0	4300	Hitachi	42393	1.44
0	14453	STET	42115	1.43
0	45	Nestle (Reg)	41684	1.41
0	110	Veba	36055	1.22
0	2100	Bridgestone	32634	1.11
0	4047	Genting	32118	1.09
0	792	Murata Manufacturing	31968	1.08
0	651	East Japan Railway	30678	1.04
0	3480	Mitsui	30165	1.02
0	400	Mabuchi Motor	29263	0.99
0	4500	Sun Hung Kai Properties	28923	0.98

Regional Exposure 08-31-94

% of Stocks

Europe	31	Pacific Rim	19
Japan	15	Other	0
Latin Amer	8		

Composition % 09-30-94

Cash	1.0	Preferreds	0.0
Stocks	99.0	Convertibles	0.0
Bonds	0.0	Other	0.0

Tax Analysis

	Tax-Adj Historical Return %	% Pretax Return
3 Yr Avg	10.61	94.4
5 Yr Avg	3.76	76.3
10 Yr Avg	14.89	77.6
Potential Capital Gain Exposure (% of assets)		12%

Most Similar Funds in MF500

T. Rowe Price Intl Stock	Strong Fit
Scudder International	Strong Fit
Putnam Global Growth A	Fair Fit

Country Exposure 03-31-94

	% of Stocks
Japan	31
United Kingdom	15
Netherlands	8
Hong Kong	6
Italy	5

Total Number of Countries: 24
Hedging Policy: Occasional

Sector Weightings

	% of Stocks	Relative S&P 500
Utilities	9.6	1.07
Energy	2.6	0.63
Financials	18.9	1.00
Industrial Cyclicals	23.5	0.94
Consumer Durables	8.8	0.82
Consumer Staples	7.0	1.01
Services	10.6	0.97
Retail	6.1	1.04
Health	3.9	1.10
Technology	9.1	1.77

Vanguard Muni Bond Hi-Yld

	Ticker	Load	NAV	Yield	SEC Yield	Assets	Objective
	VWAHX	None	9.66	6.4%	6.58%	1572.6	Muni Nat

Vanguard Municipal Bond Fund High-Yield Portfolio seeks income exempt from federal income tax, consistent with preservation of capital.

The fund invests at least 80% of its assets in investment-grade municipal securities. It expects to maintain an average weighted maturity of 15 to 25 years. Up to 20% of the fund's assets may be invested in bonds subject to the Alternative Minimum Tax.

Historical Profile

Return	High
Risk	Above Average
Rating	★★★★ Above Average

Investment Style History
Fixed Income
Income Rtn % Rank Obj

	20	14	14	13	8	11	14	8

Growth of $10,000

|||| Value of Fund ($000)
— Value of Index ($000)
  LB Muni
▼ Manager Change
▽ Partial Manager Change
► Mgr Unknown After
◄ Mgr Unknown Before

Performance Quartile
(Within Objective)

1983	1984	1985	1986	1987	1988	1989	1990	1991	1992	1993	1994	History
9.04	8.99	10.00	10.67	9.52	10.05	10.26	9.96	10.53	10.57	11.01	9.66	NAV
10.38	9.70	21.65	19.67	-1.57	13.81	11.07	5.91	14.75	9.88	12.66	-5.07	Total Return %
2.01	-5.45	-0.47	4.42	-4.33	5.93	-3.47	-3.03	-1.25	2.64	2.91	-2.15	+/- LB Aggregate
2.33	-0.85	1.63	0.36	-3.08	3.65	0.28	-1.39	2.61	1.06	0.39	0.54	+/- LB Muni
9.72	10.25	10.42	8.76	7.43	8.24	7.84	7.49	7.88	7.02	6.39	5.77	Income Return %
0.67	-0.55	11.23	10.91	-9.01	5.57	3.23	-1.58	6.87	2.86	6.28	-10.84	Capital Return %
77	28	62	22	72	33	64	36	59	23	44	64	Total Rtn % Rank All
41	33	16	22	72	8	9	70	2	12	31	45	Total Rtn % Rank Obj
0.85	0.87	0.85	0.83	0.77	0.74	0.75	0.73	0.74	0.71	0.65	0.63	Income $
0.00	0.00	0.00	0.39	0.20	0.00	0.11	0.14	0.11	0.25	0.21	0.17	Capital Gains $
0.46	0.41	0.39	0.33	0.26	0.29	0.27	0.25	0.25	0.23	0.20	0.20	Expense Ratio %
9.05	9.69	9.37	8.32	7.55	7.74	7.43	7.30	7.34	6.83	6.15	5.83	Income Ratio %
206	90	41	38	83	40	80	82	58	64	34	50	Turnover Rate %
156.2	238.9	451.9	794.5	654.3	739.6	941.2	1016.9	1341.8	1609.4	1903.6	1572.6	Net Assets ($mil)

Manager's Investment Style

Management finds ways to produce competitive yields without sacrificing credit quality. Unlike other high-yield funds, this offering does not invest large chunks of assets in lower-grade or nonrated bonds. Instead, management owes its favorable payouts to Vanguard's typically low expenses. Thanks to its long maturity, the fund has historically enjoyed positive capital returns; faced with rising rates, however, management has pulled back a bit.

Fund Manager(s)

Ian A. MacKinnon, since 11-81. Birthdate: 04-48.
BA, Lafayette C. 1970 MBA, Pennsylvania State U. 1974
Jerome J. Jacobs CFA, since 08-88. Birthdate: 08-58. BS, U. of Pennsylvania 1980

Manager Experience

	Dates Managed	Invest Obj	Std Dev	+/- Index
Ian A. MacKinnon				
Vanguard Muni Short-Term	11/81 - 12/94	MN	1.18	-5.52
Vanguard Muni Long-Term	11/81 - 12/94	MN	8.35	-0.62

Performance 12-31-94

	1st Qtr	2nd Qtr	3rd Qtr	4th Qtr	Total
1987	3.05	-5.86	-3.85	5.53	-1.57
1988	3.17	2.86	3.92	3.20	13.81
1989	0.85	6.86	-0.57	3.65	11.07
1990	-0.56	2.66	-1.35	5.17	5.91
1991	2.42	2.73	5.04	3.83	14.75
1992	-0.10	4.85	2.22	2.63	9.88
1993	3.83	3.86	3.15	1.29	12.66
1994	-5.11	1.20	-0.03	-1.11	-5.07

Bear Market Performance

Decile Rank (5-year period)

Worst ———————————————— Best

	Worst 3 Mo Period 1985-89	Worst 3 Mo Period 1990-94
Vanguard Muni Bond Hi-Yld	-8.70	-6.18
+/- LB Aggregate	-5.15	-4.41
+/- Best Fit Index : LB Muni	-2.21	-0.75

Trailing Returns

	Total Return %	+/- LB Aggregate	+/- LB Muni	% Rank All	% Rank Obj	Growth of $10,000
3 Mo	-1.11	-1.49	0.32	47	36	9,889
6 Mo	-1.14	-2.14	0.10	76	59	9,886
1 Yr	-5.07	-2.15	0.54	64	45	9,493
3 Yr Avg	5.53	0.98	0.66	38	11	11,752
5 Yr Avg	7.39	-0.24	0.62	42	6	14,283
10 Yr Avg	9.97	0.03	0.54	58	3	25,871
15 Yr Avg	8.59	-2.22	0.11	89	18	34,400

Operations

Address and Telephone	Vanguard Fin Ctr. P.O. Box 2600 Valley Forge, PA 19482 800-662-7447 / 610-669-1000
Advisor	Vanguard's Fixed-Income Group
Subadvisor	None
Distributor	Vanguard Group
States Available	All plus PR,VI,GU
Report Grade	A-
Income Distrib	Paid Monthly
Date of Inception	12-27-78
Fiscal Year End	August

Risk Analysis

Time Period	Load-Adj Return %	Risk % Rank [1] All	Risk % Rank [1] Obj	Morningstar [2] Return	Morningstar Risk	Morningstar Risk-Adj Rating
1 Yr	-5.07					
3 Yr	5.53	44	76	1.53	1.20	★★★★
5 Yr	7.39	39	88	1.38	1.32	★★★
10 Yr	9.97	27	82	1.37	1.22	★★★★
Average Historical Rating (109 months)				3.2	★s	

[1] = low, 100 = high [2] 1.00 = Muni Avg [3] 1.00 = 90-day T-bill return

Other Measures

			Standard LB Agg	Best Fit LB Muni
Standard Deviation	6.76	Alpha	0.9	0.4
Mean	5.62	Beta	1.19	1.19
Sharpe Ratio	0.31	R-Squared	50	94

Investment Style

Interest-Rate Stance

Avg Effective Maturity   17.8 Yrs

Quality

Avg Credit Quality   A
Avg Weighted Coupon   6.75%
Avg Weighted Price   94.26% of Par

Maturity Short Intm Long / Quality High Med Low

Diversification Value for Portfolio Types

Large Cap: Medium	Small Cap: High	Bond: Low	Balanced: Medium	Diversified: High

Portfolio 12-31-94

Amount 000	Date of Maturity	Total Stocks: 0 Total Fixed-Income: 153	Value $000	% Net Assets
44340	01-01-16	NJ Tpk 6.5%	43716	2.78
43700	07-15-19	MA Wtr Resource 6.5%	42194	2.68
46595	07-01-05	MI Pub Pwr 5.5%	40622	2.58
43710	01-01-20	WA Snohomish PUD #1 Elec 5.5%	36243	2.30
40000	07-01-09	PA State COP 5.4%	35649	2.27
40050	04-01-20	TX State GO 5.5%	34534	2.20
35575	02-15-08	MA State GO 5.25%	31264	1.99
28660	06-01-16	AZ Univ Brd Regents Sys 6.2%	27322	1.74
25660	07-01-11	IN COP Office Bldg Com Cap Complex 6.9%	26271	1.67
25220	08-01-24	CA San Bernardino COP M/C Cap 6.875%	26014	1.65
25690	07-01-20	NY GO Metro Transp Transit Fac 6.375%	24767	1.57
22870	07-01-08	NY GO Metro Transp Transit Fac 7.375%	24020	1.53
24000	02-01-20	IN Indianapolis GO Local Pub Impr 6.75%	23686	1.51
21000	12-01-14	MS Claiborne Poll Cntrl Engy 9.875%	23508	1.49
21500	06-15-11	PA Philadelphia Wtr/Swr 7%	22755	1.45
20000	10-01-17	TX Brazos Rvr Poll Cntrl Util 9.875%	22267	1.42
22000	11-15-21	FL Cape Coral Hlth Fac M/C 7.5%	21452	1.36
21095	05-22	FL Dade Wtr/Swr Sys DMD	21095	1.34
25000	06-15-20	NY New York City Muni Wtr Fin Swr 5.5%	20521	1.30
22000	10-01-11	KY GO Ppty/Bldg Com 5.75%	20015	1.27

Credit Analysis % of Bonds 11-04-94

US Govt	0	BB	1
AAA	34	B	1
AA	14	Below B	0
A	25	NR/NA	10
BBB	16		

Composition % of Assets 11-04-94

Cash	12.2	Preferreds	0.0
Stocks	0.0	Convertibles	0.0
Bonds	87.8	Other	0.0

Tax Analysis

	Tax-Adj Historical Return %	% Pretax Return
3 Yr Avg	4.94	88.9
5 Yr Avg	6.87	92.1
10 Yr Avg	9.53	93.6
Potential Capital Gain Exposure (% of assets)		-5%

Most Similar Funds in MF500

Vanguard Muni Insured L/T	Strong Fit
Van Kampen Ins T/F Income A	Strong Fit
General Municipal Bond	Strong Fit

Coupon Range

	% Bonds	Rel Obj
0%	0.9	0.37
0% to 6.8%	56.2	0.93
6.8% to 7.5%	19.8	1.28
7.5% to 8.3%	3.4	0.38
More than 8.3%	14.4	1.64
Not applicable	5.2	1.35

Sector Weightings

	% Bonds	Rel Obj
General Obl	20.65	0.98
Utilities	9.05	0.72
Health	13.04	0.99
Water/Waste	9.81	1.54
Housing	3.14	0.43
Education	3.20	0.50
Transportation	9.21	0.90
COP/Lease	10.99	3.45
Private	13.06	1.12
Misc Revenue	2.13	0.43
Demand	5.72	2.33

Top 5 States % of Bonds

PA	13.71	CA	8.86
NY	13.32	TX	5.79
MA	9.96		

Operations (continued)

Min Initial Purchase	$3000 (Addt'l: $100)
Min IRA Purchase	$500 (Addt'l: $100)
Min Auto Invest Plan	$3000 (Systematic Inv: $50)

Expenses & Fees

Sales Fees	0.00% front
	0.00% deferred
	0.00% 12b-1
Management Fee	Provided at cost.
3-,5-,10-yr Expense Projections	$6, $11, $26

MORNINGSTAR 1995 Mutual Fund 500

Vanguard Muni Bond Insd L/T

	Ticker	Load	NAV	Yield	SEC Yield	Assets	Objective
	VILPX	None	11.23	6.1%	6.22%	1738.0	Muni Nat

Vanguard Municipal Bond Fund Insured Long-Term Portfolio seeks income exempt from federal income tax.

The fund normally maintains at least 80% of its assets in insured tax-free municipal securities. The balance of the fund's assets may be invested in municipal bonds rated a minimum of A. The fund expects to maintain an average weighted maturity of 15 to 25 years. The overall quality of the portfolio is expected to be AAA.

Historical Profile
Return	Above Average
Risk	Above Average
Rating	★★★
	Neutral

Investment Style History
Fixed Income
Income Rtn % Rank Obj

	32	27	28	29	31	30	26	13

Growth of $10,000

IIII Value of Fund ($000)
— Value of Index ($000)
LB Muni
▼ Manager Change
▽ Partial Manager Change
► Mgr Unknown After
◄ Mgr Unknown Before

Performance Quartile
(Within Objective)

Manager's Investment Style

This fund is typical of the Vanguard group. While its insured status and high-credit quality mean that it holds lower coupons than average, its low expenses keep yield competitive. By positioning the fund for long duration, management has historically reaped the gains of falling interest rates. Even though rates are now rising, management is maintaining a slightly long posture.

1983	1984	1985	1986	1987	1988	1989	1990	1991	1992	1993	1994	History
---	9.99	10.94	11.86	10.92	11.45	11.64	11.50	12.03	12.14	12.81	11.23	NAV
---	2.19 *	19.35	18.62	0.12	12.79	10.59	7.04	12.49	9.17	13.09	-5.59	Total Return %
---	---	-2.78	3.37	-2.63	4.92	-3.95	-1.90	-3.52	1.92	3.34	-2.67	+/- LB Aggregate
---	---	-0.67	-0.69	-1.38	2.63	-0.20	-0.26	0.34	0.35	0.82	0.02	+/- LB Muni
---	2.29	9.84	8.52	7.26	7.94	7.56	7.18	7.16	6.52	6.05	5.53	Income Return %
---	-0.10	9.51	10.10	-7.14	4.85	3.03	-0.13	5.32	2.65	7.05	-11.12	Capital Return %
---	---	76	28	59	39	67	21	71	31	40	69	Total Rtn % Rank All
---	---	57	44	48	20	20	17	21	27	23	52	Total Rtn % Rank Obj
---	0.23	0.91	0.89	0.84	0.82	0.83	0.79	0.78	0.75	0.71	0.70	Income $
---	0.00	0.00	0.17	0.10	0.10	0.15	0.12	0.08	0.20	0.18	0.17	Capital Gains $
---	---	0.36	0.33	0.26	0.29	0.27	0.25	0.25	0.23	0.20	0.20	Expense Ratio %
---	---	8.70	7.99	7.35	7.50	7.24	6.99	6.77	6.34	5.77	5.62	Income Ratio %
---	---	16	20	50	28	36	47	33	42	30	16	Turnover Rate %
---	46.0	472.4	709.6	685.8	806.8	1018.5	1250.8	1701.6	1997.6	2161.7	1738.0	Net Assets ($mil)

Fund Manager(s)

Ian A. MacKinnon, since 10-84. Birthdate: 04-48.
BA, Lafayette C. 1970 MBA, Pennsylvania State U. 1974
David E. Hamlin, since 02-86. Birthdate: 02-58.
BS, Emory U. MA, U. of Delaware

Manager Experience
	Dates Managed	Invest Obj	Std Dev	+/- Index
Ian A. MacKinnon				
Vanguard Muni Short-Term	11/81 - 12/94	MN	1.18	-5.52
Vanguard Muni Long-Term	11/81 - 12/94	MN	8.35	-0.62

Performance 12-31-94

	1st Qtr	2nd Qtr	3rd Qtr	4th Qtr	Total
1987	2.60	-4.55	-2.73	5.10	0.12
1988	3.41	2.50	3.05	3.27	12.79
1989	0.85	6.38	-0.61	3.72	10.59
1990	-0.06	2.56	-1.43	5.95	7.04
1991	2.01	1.75	4.41	3.79	12.49
1992	-0.32	4.76	2.02	2.47	9.17
1993	4.25	3.52	3.56	1.19	13.09
1994	-6.03	1.29	0.11	-0.91	-5.59

Bear Market Performance

Decile Rank (5-year period)

Worst | | Best

	Worst 3 Mo Period 1985-89	Worst 3 Mo Period 1990-94
Vanguard Muni Bond Insd L/T	-7.77	-6.50
+/- LB Aggregate	-4.21	-1.56
+/- Best Fit Index : LB Muni	-1.28	-0.74

Trailing Returns

	Total Return %	+/- LB Aggregate	+/- LB Muni	% Rank All	% Rank Obj	Growth of $10,000
3 Mo	-0.91	-1.29	0.52	42	26	9,909
6 Mo	-0.81	-1.80	0.44	70	45	9,919
1 Yr	-5.59	-2.67	0.02	69	52	9,441
3 Yr Avg	5.24	0.70	0.37	43	19	11,656
5 Yr Avg	7.01	-0.61	0.24	50	13	14,035
10 Yr Avg	9.52	-0.43	0.09	64	17	24,817
15 Yr Avg	---	---	---	---	---	---

Operations

Address and Telephone	Vanguard Fin Ctr. P.O. Box 2600
	Valley Forge, PA 19482
	800-662-7447 / 610-669-1000
Advisor	Vanguard's Fixed-Income Group
Subadvisor	None
Distributor	Vanguard Group
States Available	All plus PR,VI,GU
Report Grade	A-
Income Distrib	Paid Monthly
* Date of Inception	10-01-84
Fiscal Year End	August

Min Initial Purchase	$3000 (Addt'l: $100)
Min IRA Purchase	$500 (Addt'l: $100)
Min Auto Invest Plan	$3000 (Systematic Inv: $50)

Expenses & Fees
Sales Fees	0.00% front
	0.00% deferred
	0.00% 12b-1
Management Fee	Provided at cost.
3-,5-,10-yr Expense Projections	$6, $11, $26

Risk Analysis

Time Period	Load-Adj Return %	Risk % Rank[1] All	Obj	Morningstar[2] Return	Morningstar Risk	Morningstar Risk-Adj Rating
1 Yr	-5.59					
3 Yr	5.24	49	86	1.39	1.28	★★★
5 Yr	7.01	41	95	1.23	1.40	★★
10 Yr	9.52	28	86	1.23	1.23	★★★
Average Historical Rating (88 months)					3.2	★ s

[1] 1 = low, 100 = high   [2] 1.00 = Muni Avg   [3] 1.00 = 90-day T-bill return

Other Measures
			Standard LB Agg	Best Fit LB Muni
Standard Deviation	7.00	Alpha	0.6	0.1
Mean	5.36	Beta	1.24	1.24
Sharpe Ratio	0.26	R-Squared	51	94

Investment Style

Interest-Rate Stance
Avg Effective Maturity 16.7 Yrs

Maturity: Short Intm Long

Quality
Avg Credit Quality AAA
Avg Weighted Coupon 6.32%
Avg Weighted Price 97.09% of Par

Diversification Value for Portfolio Types

Large Cap: Medium	Small Cap: High	Bond: Low	Balanced: Medium	Diversified: High

Portfolio 12-31-94

Total Stocks: 0
Total Fixed-Income: 246

Amount 000	Date of Maturity		Value $000	% Net Assets
30350	07-01-16	FL Orlando/Orange Expwy 8.25%	36609	2.11
35000	01-01-16	NJ Tpk 6.5%	35129	2.02
32250	07-01-09	MA State GO 7%	34249	1.97
31500	06-15-11	PA Philadelphia Wtr/Swr 7%	33352	1.92
29930	10-01-12	FL Tampa Util Tax/Spcl 6.75%	31257	1.80
35470	12-01-19	PA Tpk Com 5.5%	30455	1.75
30000	09-29-95	CA Sacramento Transp 4.5%	29825	1.72
35500	01-01-22	SC Piedmont Muni Pwr 5%	28014	1.61
27485	10-01-08	MA Hsg Fin Proj 5.95%	25883	1.49
25000	09-01-22	MI Monroe Econ Dev Detroit Edison 6.95%	25843	1.49
24000	11-01-20	IL Regl Transp 7.2%	25218	1.45
23515	01-01-20	SC Piedmont Muni Pwr 6.75%	23714	1.36
23885	11-01-10	KY Dev Fin St Elizabeth M/C 6%	22848	1.31
25000	08-01-24	CA State GO 6%	22669	1.30
25000	11-15-16	TX Austin Combined Util Sys 5.75%	22292	1.28
21500	01-01-20	IL Chicago GO Pub Bldg Com 7%	22277	1.28
20000	06-01-15	FL Palm Beach Criminal Justice Fac 7.2%	22026	1.27
21005	08-01-15	NJ Hoboken/Union City GO Swr 6.25%	20474	1.18
22250	09-01-21	LA New Orleans GO Pub Impr 6%	20324	1.17
20225	10-01-22	CA Modesto Irr Dist Fin 6.5%	19865	1.14

Credit Analysis % of Bonds 11-04-94
US Govt	0	BB	0
AAA	97	B	0
AA	3	Below B	0
A	0	NR/NA	0
BBB	0		

Composition % of Assets 11-04-94
Cash	9.8	Preferreds	0.0
Stocks	0.0	Convertibles	0.0
Bonds	90.2	Other	0.0

Tax Analysis
	Tax-Adj Historical Return %	% Pretax Return
3 Yr Avg	4.80	91.2
5 Yr Avg	6.63	93.8
10 Yr Avg	9.22	95.5
Potential Capital Gain Exposure (% of assets)		-2%

Most Similar Funds in MF500
Vanguard Muni High-Yield	Strong Fit
Van Kampen Ins T/F Income A	Strong Fit
MFS Municipal Bond A	Strong Fit

Coupon Range
	% Bonds	Rel Obj
0%	1.9	0.75
0% to 6.8%	61.9	1.03
6.8% to 7.5%	23.5	1.52
7.5% to 8.3%	5.6	0.63
More than 8.3%	2.5	0.29
Not applicable	4.6	1.18

Sector Weightings
	% Bonds	Rel Obj
General Obl	17.60	0.84
Utilities	18.25	1.46
Health	14.31	1.08
Water/Waste	10.88	1.71
Housing	3.36	0.46
Education	1.12	0.18
Transportation	15.05	1.48
COP/Lease	3.64	1.14
Private	8.95	0.77
Misc Revenue	2.53	0.51
Demand	4.31	1.75

Top 5 States % of Bonds
CA	17.74	FL	7.80
PA	8.93	TX	6.79
MA	7.99		

Vanguard Muni Bond Int-Term

Vanguard Municipal Bond Fund Intermediate-Term Portfolio seeks income exempt from federal income tax, consistent with preservation of capital.

The fund typically invests at least 65% of its assets in municipal securities. At least 95% of these securities are ordinarily rated BBB or better; at least 80% are rated A or better. The fund may invest in high-quality short-term municipal obligations. It does not usually invest in securities subject to the Alternative Minimum Tax. The fund expects to maintain an average weighted maturity of seven to 12 years.

Ticker	Load	NAV	Yield	SEC Yield	Assets	Objective
VWITX	None	12.39	5.5%	5.68%	4585.0	Muni Nat

Historical Profile

Return	Above Average
Risk	Below Average
Rating	★★★★★ Highest

Investment Style History
Fixed Income
Income Rtn % Rank Obj

52 65 36 39 45 59 51 25

Growth of $10,000

- |||| Value of Fund ($000)
- — Value of Index ($000) LB Muni
- ▼ Manager Change
- ▽ Partial Manager Change
- ► Mgr Unknown After
- ◄ Mgr Unknown Before

Performance Quartile (Within Objective)

Manager's Investment Style

The fund plays it safe while keeping yields competitive. Management has a loyalty to highly rated bonds; the fund has about 50% of assets in AAA issues. Management is also wary of interest-rate sensitivity. Despite the fact that its charter allows management to stretch average maturity to 12 years, it typically keeps it under 10 years. Typically low expenses keep this fund's yield up to par.

1983	1984	1985	1986	1987	1988	1989	1990	1991	1992	1993	1994	History
10.50	10.54	11.39	12.29	11.56	11.88	12.12	12.05	12.61	12.84	13.52	12.39	NAV
6.48	9.53	17.33	16.22	1.64	10.00	10.00	7.20	12.16	8.86	11.56	-2.12	Total Return %
-1.89	-5.62	-4.80	0.97	-1.12	2.12	-4.54	-1.75	-3.84	1.61	1.80	0.80	+/- LB Aggregate
-1.57	-1.02	-2.69	-3.10	0.14	-0.16	-0.78	-0.10	0.02	0.04	-0.72	3.48	+/- LB Muni
8.26	9.15	9.27	8.12	6.87	7.23	7.41	6.99	6.85	6.05	5.63	5.14	Income Return %
-1.78	0.38	8.06	8.09	-5.23	2.77	2.59	0.20	5.31	2.81	5.92	-7.26	Capital Return %
94	29	85	47	45	62	73	20	74	35	55	35	Total Rtn % Rank All
83	37	71	71	23	66	34	10	30	38	51	14	Total Rtn % Rank Obj
0.87	0.91	0.91	0.87	0.82	0.81	0.84	0.81	0.78	0.73	0.70	0.69	Income $
0.00	0.00	0.00	0.02	0.09	0.04	0.07	0.09	0.09	0.12	0.08	0.16	Capital Gains $
0.46	0.41	0.39	0.33	0.26	0.29	0.27	0.25	0.25	0.23	0.20	0.20	Expense Ratio %
7.85	8.58	8.53	7.66	6.94	6.88	7.03	6.83	6.49	5.91	5.41	5.15	Income Ratio %
117	55	26	13	57	89	56	54	27	32	15	18	Turnover Rate %
150.1	209.1	411.8	811.9	762.9	851.8	1113.1	1411.6	2459.7	3491.3	5238.1	4585.0	Net Assets ($mil)

Fund Manager(s)

Ian A. MacKinnon, since 11-81. Birthdate: 04-48. BA, Lafayette C. 1970 MBA, Pennsylvania State U. 1974
Christopher M. Ryon, since 09-91. BS, Villanova U. MBA, Drexel U.

Manager Experience

	Dates Managed	Invest Obj	Std Dev	+/- Index
Ian A. MacKinnon				
Vanguard Muni Short-Term	11/81 - 12/94	MN	1.18	-5.52
Vanguard Muni Long-Term	11/81 - 12/94	MN	8.35	-0.62

Performance 12-31-94

	1st Qtr	2nd Qtr	3rd Qtr	4th Qtr	Total
1987	2.66	-3.60	-2.14	4.95	1.64
1988	3.07	1.96	2.70	1.92	10.00
1989	0.74	5.14	0.43	3.41	10.00
1990	0.46	2.31	0.02	4.28	7.20
1991	2.56	2.19	3.83	3.07	12.16
1992	0.10	3.82	2.38	2.31	8.86
1993	3.54	3.04	3.13	1.39	11.56
1994	-3.21	1.32	0.47	-0.66	-2.12

Bear Market Performance

Decile Rank (5-year period)

Worst ████ Best

	Worst 3 Mo Period 1985-89	Worst 3 Mo Period 1990-94
Vanguard Muni Bond Int-Term	-6.79	-3.68
+/- LB Aggregate	-3.23	-1.90
+/- Best Fit Index : LB Muni	-0.30	1.76

Trailing Returns

	Total Return %	+/- LB Aggregate	+/- LB Muni	% Rank All	% Rank Obj	Growth of $10,000
3 Mo	-0.66	-1.04	0.77	37	18	9,934
6 Mo	-0.20	-1.19	1.05	60	22	9,980
1 Yr	-2.12	0.80	3.48	35	14	9,788
3 Yr Avg	5.93	1.38	1.06	35	6	11,886
5 Yr Avg	7.40	-0.22	0.63	42	5	14,291
10 Yr Avg	9.13	-0.81	-0.29	70	32	23,966
15 Yr Avg	7.70	-3.11	-0.78	95	70	30,413

Operations

Address and Telephone	Vanguard Fin Ctr. P.O. Box 2600 Valley Forge, PA 19482 800-662-7447 / 610-669-1000
Advisor	Vanguard's Fixed-Income Group
Subadvisor	None
Distributor	Vanguard Group
States Available	All plus PR,VI,GU
Report Grade	A-
Income Distrib	Paid Monthly
Date of Inception	09-01-77
Fiscal Year End	August

Risk Analysis

Time Period	Load-Adj Return %	Risk % Rank All	Risk % Rank Obj[1]	Morningstar[2] Return	Morningstar Risk	Morningstar Risk-Adj Rating
1 Yr	-2.12					
3 Yr	5.93	13	24	1.51	0.78	★★★★★
5 Yr	7.40	11	29	1.27	0.82	★★★★★
10 Yr	9.13	7	26	1.10	0.87	★★★★

Average Historical Rating (109 months) 3.1 ★s

[1] 1 = low, 100 = high [2] 1.00 = Muni Avg [3] 1.00 = 90-day T-bill return

Other Measures

			Standard LB Agg	Best Fit LB Muni
Standard Deviation	4.89	Alpha	1.5	1.2
Mean	5.89	Beta	0.85	0.86
Sharpe Ratio	0.48	R-Squared	48	92

Investment Style

Interest-Rate Stance
Avg Effective Maturity 8.4 Yrs

Maturity: Short Intm Long / Quality: High Med Low

Quality
Avg Credit Quality AA
Avg Weighted Coupon 6.23%
Avg Weighted Price 100.13% of Par

Diversification Value for Portfolio Types

Large Cap: Medium | Small Cap: High | Bond: Medium | Balanced: Medium | Diversified: High

Portfolio 12-31-94

Total Stocks: 0
Total Fixed-Income: 437

Amount 000	Date of Maturity		Value $000	% Net Assets
65000	08-31-95	TX State GO 5%	65114	1.42
59325	01-01-10	NY Triborough Bridge/Tunnel Genl 6.6%	60458	1.32
62650	02-01-05	HI State GO 5%	59735	1.30
59095	04-12-95	NY New York City GO 4.5%	59099	1.29
50000	10-01-07	TX State GO 8%	58133	1.27
57770	07-01-10	CA Los Angeles Metro Transp Tax 6.5%	57569	1.26
50410	11-01-07	GA State GO 7%	54853	1.20
50000	01-01-09	NJ Tpk 6.5%	50921	1.11
47335	05-01-08	WI State GO 6.25%	47526	1.04
47100	12-01-15	DE Econ Dev Hosp Bill/Collection Svc DMD	47100	1.03
47515	07-15-21	MA Wtr Resource 6.5%	46762	1.02
117725	09-01-03	NJ Camden Muni Util Swr 0%	46325	1.01
46490	04-15-08	PA State GO 5%	41080	0.90
37405	03-01-08	TX Houston GO 7%	39548	0.86
42550	09-01-06	CT Spcl Tax Obl Infrastructure 5.25%	38370	0.84
30560	10-01-09	HI Honolulu GO 8%	35370	0.77
35750	01-01-05	NC Muni Pwr #1 Catawba Elec 6%	34531	0.75
32840	09-01-09	TX Muni Pwr 6.1%	32123	0.70
32065	01-01-06	NJ Tpk 4.75%	30894	0.67
31480	08-15-03	NY GO Med Care Fac Fin Mental Hlth 6%	30710	0.67

Credit Analysis % of Bonds 10-31-94

US Govt	0	BB	0
AAA	46	B	0
AA	17	Below B	0
A	29	NR/NA	0
BBB	8		

Composition % of Assets 10-31-94

Cash	12.0	Preferreds	0.0
Stocks	0.0	Convertibles	0.0
Bonds	88.0	Other	0.0

Tax Analysis

	Tax-Adj Historical Return %	% Pretax Return
3 Yr Avg	5.66	95.2
5 Yr Avg	7.15	96.1
10 Yr Avg	8.96	97.3
Potential Capital Gain Exposure (% of assets)		-1%

Most Similar Funds in MF500

Scudder Medium-Term T-F	Strong Fit
Franklin Insured T/F Income	Strong Fit
Dreyfus Intermediate Muni	Strong Fit

Coupon Range

	% Bonds	Rel Obj
0%	2.2	0.86
0% to 6.8%	62.1	1.03
6.8% to 7.5%	18.5	1.19
7.5% to 8.3%	7.3	0.83
More than 8.3%	3.9	0.44
Not applicable	6.1	1.56

Sector Weightings

	% Bonds	Rel Obj
General Obl	41.46	1.97
Utilities	9.86	0.79
Health	2.65	0.20
Water/Waste	7.37	1.16
Housing	0.01	0.00
Education	3.59	0.56
Transportation	13.56	1.33
COP/Lease	4.84	1.52
Private	7.45	0.64
Misc Revenue	4.97	1.00
Demand	4.25	1.73

Top 5 States % of Bonds

NY	11.88	PA	7.32
TX	11.25	MA	7.07
CA	9.07		

Expenses & Fees

Sales Fees	0.00% front
	0.00% deferred
	0.00% 12b-1
Management Fee	Provided at cost.
3-,5-,10-yr Expense Projections	$6, $11, $26

Purchase

Min Initial Purchase	$3000 (Addt'l: $100)
Min IRA Purchase	$500 (Addt'l: $50)
Min Auto Invest Plan	$3000 (Systematic Inv: $50)

MORNINGSTAR 1995 Mutual Fund 500

Vanguard Muni Bond Ltd-Trm

	Ticker	Load	NAV	Yield	SEC Yield	Assets	Objective
	VMLTX	None	10.37	4.4%	4.85%	1629.5	Muni Nat

Vanguard Municipal Bond Fund Limited-Term Portfolio seeks income exempt from federal income tax, consistent with preservation of capital.

The fund invests primarily in tax-exempt municipal obligations; at least 95% of these securities are rated A or better. It expects to maintain an average weighted maturity of two to five years, and purchases securities with effective maturities of 10 years or less. The fund may invest in bond futures contracts and options to a limited extent.

Historical Profile

Return	Below Average
Risk	Low
Rating	★★★★★ Highest

Investment Style History
Fixed Income
Income Rtn % Rank Obj

		88	75	73	88	92	88	77

Growth of $10,000
|||| Value of Fund ($000)
— Value of Index ($000)
LB Muni
▼ Manager Change
▽ Partial Manager Change
► Mgr Unknown After
◄ Mgr Unknown Before

Performance Quartile
(Within Objective)

Manager's Investment Style

This fund falls between its intermediate- and short-term siblings. With an average weighted maturity of less than three years, the fund is well positioned to stave off interest-rate risk. On the performance side, management has pumped up yield by purchasing premium bonds and keeping expenses low. Overall, the fund offers solid protection along with decent returns.

Fund Manager(s)

Ian A. MacKinnon, since 09-87. Birthdate: 04-48.
BA, Lafayette C. 1970 MBA, Pennsylvania State U. 1974
Christopher M. Ryon, since 08-88. BS, Villanova U. MBA, Drexel U.

Manager Experience	Dates Managed	Invest Obj	Std Dev	+/- Index
Ian A. MacKinnon				
Vanguard Muni Short-Term	11/81 - 12/94	MN	1.18	-5.52
Vanguard Muni Long-Term	11/81 - 12/94	MN	8.35	-0.62

1983	1984	1985	1986	1987	1988	1989	1990	1991	1992	1993	1994	History
---	---	---	---	10.07	10.09	10.22	10.27	10.56	10.65	10.82	10.37	NAV
---	---	---	---	2.71 *	6.40	8.07	7.04	9.48	6.39	6.31	0.07	Total Return %
---	---	---	---	---	-1.48	-6.47	-1.91	-6.52	-0.86	-3.44	2.99	+/- LB Aggregate
---	---	---	---	---	-3.76	-2.71	-0.26	-2.67	-2.43	-5.97	5.67	+/- LB Muni
---	---	---	---	2.01	6.14	6.68	6.50	6.03	5.07	4.51	4.23	Income Return %
---	---	---	---	0.70	0.26	1.40	0.54	3.45	1.32	1.80	-4.16	Capital Return %
---	---	---	---	---	85	90	21	92	64	87	19	Total Rtn % Rank All
---	---	---	---	---	89	82	17	88	93	96	5	Total Rtn % Rank Obj
---	---	---	---	0.20	0.61	0.65	0.64	0.59	0.52	0.47	0.46	Income $
---	---	---	---	0.00	0.01	0.01	0.01	0.06	0.05	0.02	0.00	Capital Gains $
---	---	---	---	---	0.29	0.27	0.25	0.25	0.23	0.20	0.20	Expense Ratio %
---	---	---	---	---	5.91	6.33	6.31	5.91	5.08	4.50	4.24	Income Ratio %
---	---	---	---	---	122	88	55	57	37	20	21	Turnover Rate %
---	---	---	---	79.0	175.1	193.8	270.1	547.0	1084.0	1817.7	1629.5	Net Assets ($mil)

Performance 12-31-94

	1st Qtr	2nd Qtr	3rd Qtr	4th Qtr	Total
1987	---	---	---	2.86	2.71 *
1988	2.57	1.36	1.23	1.10	6.40
1989	0.46	3.35	1.44	2.61	8.07
1990	0.88	1.99	1.28	2.72	7.04
1991	2.19	1.54	2.69	2.75	9.48
1992	0.30	2.52	1.87	1.56	6.39
1993	1.87	1.58	1.65	1.07	6.31
1994	-1.17	0.79	0.69	-0.22	0.07

Bear Market Performance

Decile Rank (5-year period)

Worst _____ Best

	Worst 3 Mo Period 1985-89	Worst 3 Mo Period 1990-94
Vanguard Muni Bond Ltd-Trm	---	-1.43
+/- LB Aggregate	---	3.50
+/- Best Fit Index : LB Muni	---	4.33

Trailing Returns

	Total Return %	+/- LB Aggregate	+/- LB Muni	% Rank All	Obj	Growth of $10,000
3 Mo	-0.22	-0.60	1.22	28	8	9,978
6 Mo	0.47	-0.52	1.71	47	9	10,047
1 Yr	0.07	2.99	5.67	19	5	10,007
3 Yr Avg	4.21	-0.33	-0.66	65	67	11,318
5 Yr Avg	5.81	-1.82	-0.96	80	69	13,263
10 Yr Avg	---	---	---	---	---	---
15 Yr Avg	---	---	---	---	---	---

Operations

Address and Telephone	Vanguard Fin Ctr. P.O. Box 2600
	Valley Forge, PA 19482
	800-662-7447 / 610-669-1000
Advisor	Vanguard's Fixed-Income Group
Subadvisor	None
Distributor	Vanguard Group
States Available	All plus PR,VI,GU
Report Grade	A-
Income Distrib	Paid Monthly
* Date of Inception	09-01-87
Fiscal Year End	August

Risk Analysis

Time Period	Load-Adj Return %	Risk % Rank [1] All	Obj	Morningstar [2] Return	Morningstar Risk	Morningstar Risk-Adj Rating
1 Yr	0.07					
3 Yr	4.21	2	5	0.87	0.29	★★★★★
5 Yr	5.81	2	6	0.81	0.30	★★★★★
10 Yr	---					

Average Historical Rating (53 months)   4.5 ★ s

[1] 1 = low, 100 = high   [2] 1.00 = Muni Avg   [3] 1.00 = 90-day T-bill return

Other Measures

			Standard LB Agg	Best Fit LB Muni
Standard Deviation	2.09	Alpha	0.2	0.1
Mean	4.16	Beta	0.38	0.36
Sharpe Ratio	0.30	R-Squared	51	83

Investment Style

Interest-Rate Stance
Avg Effective Maturity   2.6 Yrs

Quality
Avg Credit Quality   AA

Avg Weighted Coupon   6.17%
Avg Weighted Price 101.39% of Par

Diversification Value for Portfolio Types

Large Cap: Medium	Small Cap: High	Bond: Low	Balanced: Medium	Diversified: High

Operations (continued)

Min Initial Purchase	$3000 (Addt'l: $100)
Min IRA Purchase	$500 (Addt'l: $50)
Min Auto Invest Plan	$3000 (Systematic Inv: $50)

Expenses & Fees
Sales Fees	0.00% front
	0.00% deferred
	0.00% 12b-1
Management Fee	Provided at cost.
3-,5-,10-yr Expense Projections	$6, $11, $26

Portfolio 12-31-94

Total Stocks: 0
Total Fixed-Income: 240

Amount 000	Date of Maturity		Value $000	% Net Assets
31505	11-15-00	PA Philadelphia GO 6%	31835	1.95
33625	11-01-98	WI State GO 4.125%	31470	1.93
30470	11-15-96	CT Spcl Assmt Unemp Comp Fund 4%	29634	1.82
28000	09-29-95	CA Sacramento Transp 4.5%	27836	1.71
19600	04-01-98	CA State GO 10%	22022	1.35
21700	06-30-95	NY New York City GO 4.75%	21702	1.33
19600	07-01-98	FL Dade GO Sch Dist Unltd Tax 7.375%	21289	1.31
20000	06-30-00	AK North Slope GO 7.25%	21242	1.30
20000	09-01-99	PA GO Conv Ctr 5.75%	19606	1.20
19170	08-15-97	NY New York City GO 5.6%	18958	1.16
17000	06-01-95	FL GO Brd Educ Cap 8.4%	17602	1.08
17695	06-15-96	NJ Transp Trust Fund Sys 3.8%	17291	1.06
17500	06-01-98	OK Grand Rvr Dam 4.9%	17049	1.05
16500	02-01-96	HI State GO 3.85%	16171	0.99
15500	10-01-14	FL Jacksonville Elec St John Rvr 7.5%	16011	0.98
15435	09-15-97	PA State GO 6%	15642	0.96
14500	07-01-98	MA State GO 7.25%	15459	0.95
14250	08-01-96	GA Gwinnett GO Wtr/Swr 8.75%	15260	0.94
15000	01-01-98	NJ Tpk 5.2%	14832	0.91
15000	08-01-98	NY New York City GO 5.5%	14648	0.90

Credit Analysis % of Bonds 10-31-94

US Govt	0	BB	1
AAA	49	B	0
AA	28	Below B	0
A	19	NR/NA	0
BBB	3		

Composition % of Assets 10-31-94

Cash	20.7	Preferreds	0.0
Stocks	0.0	Convertibles	0.0
Bonds	79.3	Other	0.0

Tax Analysis

	Tax-Adj Historical Return %	% Pretax Return
3 Yr Avg	4.15	98.4
5 Yr Avg	5.73	98.5
10 Yr Avg	---	---
Potential Capital Gain Exposure (% of assets)		-2%

Most Similar Funds in MF500

T. Rowe Price Tax-Fr Sh-Intm	Strong Fit
Fidelity Spartan Sh-Int Muni	Strong Fit
Dreyfus Short-Intrm Muni Bd	Fair Fit

Coupon Range

	% Bonds	Rel Obj
0%	0.3	0.13
0% to 6.8%	63.9	1.06
6.8% to 7.5%	12.6	0.81
7.5% to 8.3%	3.7	0.42
More than 8.3%	15.1	1.71
Not applicable	4.3	1.10

Sector Weightings

	% Bonds	Rel Obj
General Obl	46.87	2.23
Utilities	10.63	0.85
Health	1.23	0.09
Water/Waste	8.14	1.28
Housing	0.18	0.02
Education	3.53	0.55
Transportation	12.31	1.21
COP/Lease	3.08	0.97
Private	5.39	0.46
Misc Revenue	7.29	1.47
Demand	1.34	0.54

Top 5 States % of Bonds

TX	13.40	PA	8.23
NY	10.09	FL	7.08
CA	8.28		

Vanguard Muni Bond S-T

	Ticker	Load	NAV	Yield	SEC Yield	Assets	Objective
	VWSTX	None	15.33	3.6%	4.50%	1483.5	Muni Nat

Vanguard Municipal Bond Fund Short-Term Portfolio seeks income exempt from federal income tax, consistent with preservation of capital.

The fund invests primarily in tax-exempt municipal obligations; at least 95% of these securities are rated A or better. It expects to maintain an average weighted maturity of one to two years, and purchases securities with an effective maturity of five years or less. The fund may invest in bond futures contracts and options to a limited extent.

Manager's Investment Style

Management has positioned this fund for a smooth ride. The fund's average maturity of one to two years should quell even the most interest-rate-wary investors' fears. In addition, management focuses its attentions on the fund's credit rating. The fully investment-grade portfolio includes a large stake in Treasury-backed prerefunded issues as well as general-obligation utility bonds. Along with a worry-free portfolio, the fund offers extremely low expenses, which benefit shareholders in the form of higher yields.

Fund Manager(s)

Ian A. MacKinnon, since 11-81. Birthdate: 04-48.
BA, Lafayette C. 1970 MBA, Pennsylvania State U. 1974
Christopher M. Ryon, since 08-88. BS, Villanova U. MBA, Drexel U.

Manager Experience	Dates Managed	Invest Obj	Std Dev	+/- Index
Ian A. MacKinnon				
Vanguard Muni Long-Term	11/81 - 12/94	MN	8.35	-0.62
Vanguard Muni Inter-Term	11/81 - 12/94	MN	6.37	-1.53

Historical Profile

Return	Low
Risk	Low
Rating	★★★★ Above Average

	97	99	91	91	98	100	97	95

Investment Style History
Fixed Income
Income Rtn % Rank Obj

Growth of $10,000
|||| Value of Fund ($000)
— Value of Index ($000)
LB Muni
▼ Manager Change
▽ Partial Manager Change
► Mgr Unknown After
◄ Mgr Unknown Before

Performance Quartile
(Within Objective)

	1983	1984	1985	1986	1987	1988	1989	1990	1991	1992	1993	1994	History
	15.12	15.14	15.22	15.44	15.19	15.21	15.36	15.43	15.63	15.64	15.63	15.33	NAV
	5.06	6.80	6.96	7.39	4.11	5.61	7.08	6.57	7.20	4.71	3.82	1.63	Total Return %
	-3.31	-8.36	-15.17	-7.86	1.35	-2.27	-7.46	-2.37	-8.80	-2.53	-5.93	4.55	+/- LB Aggregate
	-2.99	-3.75	-13.07	-11.93	2.61	-4.56	-3.71	-0.73	-4.94	-4.10	-8.45	7.23	+/- LB Muni
	5.85	6.67	6.43	5.87	5.06	5.47	6.09	6.12	5.50	4.37	3.76	3.54	Income Return %
	-0.79	0.13	0.53	1.51	-0.95	0.13	0.99	0.46	1.70	0.34	0.06	-1.91	Capital Return %
	98	43	98	92	27	90	93	27	96	78	94	11	Total Rtn % Rank All
	95	90	96	100	4	95	93	37	98	99	100	1	Total Rtn % Rank Obj
	0.87	0.98	0.95	0.87	0.76	0.81	0.90	0.91	0.82	0.67	0.58	0.55	Income $
	0.00	0.00	0.00	0.01	0.10	0.00	0.00	0.00	0.06	0.04	0.02	0.00	Capital Gains $
	0.46	0.41	0.39	0.33	0.26	0.29	0.27	0.25	0.25	0.23	0.20	0.20	Expense Ratio %
	5.99	6.08	6.47	5.81	5.12	5.13	5.77	5.90	5.55	4.58	3.88	3.42	Income Ratio %
	136	102	55	57	120	113	54	78	104	60	46	27	Turnover Rate %
	346.8	353.9	536.3	1051.4	834.4	806.5	704.8	751.7	874.2	1109.5	1464.9	1483.5	Net Assets ($mil)

Performance 12-31-94

	1st Qtr	2nd Qtr	3rd Qtr	4th Qtr	Total
1987	1.58	0.65	0.04	1.78	4.11
1988	2.08	1.09	1.18	1.15	5.61
1989	0.78	2.69	1.41	2.02	7.08
1990	1.21	1.75	1.37	2.09	6.57
1991	1.74	1.41	1.69	2.18	7.20
1992	0.55	1.64	1.35	1.10	4.71
1993	1.00	1.02	0.77	0.98	3.82
1994	-0.07	0.67	0.70	0.32	1.63

Bear Market Performance

Decile Rank (5-year period)

Worst | Best

	Worst 3 Mo Period 1985-89	Worst 3 Mo Period 1990-94
Vanguard Muni Bond S-T	-0.34	-0.24
+/- LB Aggregate	-1.16	4.69
+/- Best Fit Index : LB Muni	2.78	5.52

Trailing Returns

	Total Return %	+/- LB Aggregate	+/- LB Muni	% Rank All	Obj	Growth of $10,000
3 Mo	0.32	-0.06	1.75	15	2	10,032
6 Mo	1.02	0.03	2.26	37	3	10,102
1 Yr	1.63	4.55	7.23	11	1	10,163
3 Yr Avg	3.38	-1.16	-1.49	81	94	11,049
5 Yr Avg	4.77	-2.86	-2.00	91	96	12,622
10 Yr Avg	5.49	-4.45	-3.94	98	97	17,067
15 Yr Avg	6.03	-4.78	-2.45	98	97	24,054

Operations

Address and Telephone	Vanguard Fin Ctr. P.O. Box 2600
	Valley Forge, PA 19482
	800-662-7447 / 610-669-1000
Advisor	Vanguard's Fixed-Income Group
Subadvisor	None
Distributor	Vanguard Group
States Available	All plus PR,VI,GU
Report Grade	A-
Income Distrib	Paid Monthly
Date of Inception	09-01-77
Fiscal Year End	August

Risk Analysis

Time Period	Load-Adj Return %	Risk % Rank All	Obj	Morningstar Return	Morningstar Risk	Morningstar Risk-Adj Rating
1 Yr	1.63					
3 Yr	3.38	1	1	0.53	0.10	★★★★
5 Yr	4.77	1	1	0.52	0.09	★★★★★
10 Yr	5.49	1	2	0.33	0.13	★★★★
Average Historical Rating (109 months)					3.8	★ s

[1] 1 = low, 100 = high   [2] 1.00 = Muni Avg   [3] 1.00 = 90-day T-bill return

Other Measures

		Standard LB Agg	Best Fit LB Muni
Standard Deviation	0.91	Alpha	-0.4	-0.4
Mean	3.33	Beta	0.16	0.14
Sharpe Ratio	-0.21	R-Squared	47	62

Investment Style

Interest-Rate Stance
Avg Effective Maturity   1.2 Yrs

Maturity: Short Intm Long
Quality: High Med Low

Quality
Avg Credit Quality   AAA
Avg Weighted Coupon   7.00%
Avg Weighted Price 102.35% of Par

Diversification Value for Portfolio Types

Large Cap: High	Small Cap: High	Bond: Medium	Balanced: Medium	Diversified: High

Expenses & Fees

Sales Fees	
	0.00% front
	0.00% deferred
	0.00% 12b-1
Management Fee	Provided at cost.
3-,5-,10-yr Expense Projections	$6, $11, $26

Min Initial Purchase	$3000 (Addt'l: $100)
Min IRA Purchase	$500 (Addt'l: $100)
Min Auto Invest Plan	$3000 (Systematic Inv: $50)

Portfolio 12-31-94

Total Stocks: 0
Total Fixed-Income: 203

Amount 000	Date of Maturity		Value $000	% Net Assets
37000	09-01-08	TX Sam Rayburn Muni Pwr 9.25%	38793	2.61
28000	06-01-26	AR Hsg Fin DMD	28000	1.89
24395	11-15-12	TX Austin Combined Util Sys 10.25%	25985	1.75
25000	09-29-95	CA Sacramento Transp 4.5%	24854	1.68
23300	12-01-15	DE Econ Dev Hosp Bill/Collection Svc DMD	23300	1.57
23170	08-15-95	NY New York City GO 4.9%	23013	1.55
22870	11-01-97	HI State GO 5%	22702	1.53
21695	09-01-05	WA State GO 8%	22651	1.53
22400	07-01-24	GA Burke Dev Poll Cntrl Pwr DMD	22400	1.51
20185	10-05-22	FL Dade Wtr/Swr Sys DMD	20185	1.36
19100	09-01-28	CT Dev Poll Cntrl Lt/Pwr DMD	19100	1.29
17105	06-01-14	IL Metro Fair/Expo 10.375%	18017	1.21
17970	07-31-95	CA San Bernardino COP M/C Cap Fac 4.5%	17611	1.19
16130	08-01-14	TX Harris GO Toll Rd Unltd Tax 9.25%	16677	1.12
16525	06-30-95	NY New York City GO 4.75%	16526	1.11
15555	11-01-95	TX Dallas/Ft Worth Regl Arpt 3.4%	15229	1.03
15000	07-31-95	CA Santa Barbara 4.25%	14893	1.00
15000	09-29-95	CA San Diego Transp 4.5%	14625	0.99
13980	10-01-09	FL Orlando Util Com Wtr/Elec 8.5%	14614	0.99
13450	07-01-15	MD Transp 9%	14011	0.94

Credit Analysis % of Bonds 10-31-94

US Govt	0	BB	0
AAA	75	B	0
AA	12	Below B	0
A	11	NR/NA	0
BBB	2		

Composition % of Assets 10-31-94

Cash	60.6	Preferreds	0.0
Stocks	0.0	Convertibles	0.0
Bonds	39.4	Other	0.0

Tax Analysis

	Tax-Adj Historical Return %	% Pretax Return
3 Yr Avg	3.34	98.8
5 Yr Avg	4.72	98.9
10 Yr Avg	5.45	99.0
Potential Capital Gain Exposure (% of assets)		-1%

Most Similar Funds in MF500

Merrill Lynch Muni Ltd Mat A	Strong Fit
USAA Tax-Exempt Short-Term	Weak Fit
Dreyfus Short-Intrm Muni Bd	Weak Fit

Coupon Range

	% Bonds	Rel Obj
0%	0.0	0.00
0% to 6.8%	39.6	0.66
6.8% to 7.5%	5.8	0.38
7.5% to 8.3%	11.3	1.27
More than 8.3%	26.6	3.01
Not applicable	16.6	4.29

Sector Weightings

	% Bonds	Rel Obj
General Obl	31.03	1.47
Utilities	20.13	1.61
Health	4.26	0.32
Water/Waste	5.88	0.92
Housing	0.00	0.00
Education	1.20	0.19
Transportation	12.26	1.20
COP/Lease	3.60	1.13
Private	2.80	0.24
Misc Revenue	3.51	0.71
Demand	15.33	6.23

Top 5 States % of Bonds

TX	13.09	FL	7.02
CA	8.50	WA	6.02
NY	7.60		

 **MORNINGSTAR** 1995 Mutual Fund 500

Vanguard Preferred Stock

	Ticker	Load	NAV	Yield	SEC Yield	Assets	Objective
	VQIIX	None	8.15	8.0%	8.27%	278.9	Income

Vanguard Preferred Stock Fund seeks dividend income from investments that qualify for the 70% corporate dividends-received deduction under federal tax laws.

The fund normally invests more than 75% of its assets in cumulative, investment-grade preferred stocks of domestic corporations. The balance of assets may be invested in preferred stocks with lower ratings, convertibles, and money-market instruments. The fund may not invest in common stocks.

Prior to Oct. 20, 1987, the fund was named Qualified Dividend II.

Manager's Investment Style

Management uses preferred stocks to reap fat yields. Management, aware of the interest-rate risk that holding only preferreds represents, attempts to take other steps to cushion the blow of rate hikes. It focuses most of its efforts on thwarting credit risk. Although preferred stocks tend not to be highly rated, management tries to find the most-stable markets in which to invest and rarely strays from investment grades.

Fund Manager(s)

Earl E. McEvoy, since 10-82. Birthdate: 03-48. BA, Dartmouth C. 1970 MBA, Columbia U. 1972

Manager Experience

	Dates Managed	Invest Obj	Std Dev	+/- Index
Earl E. McEvoy				
Vanguard/Wellesley Inc	10/82 - 12/94	I	7.48	-1.81
Vanguard F/I Hi-Yld Corp	01/84 - 12/94	CY	6.34	-0.14

Historical Profile
Return	Average
Risk	Low
Rating	★★★★
	Above Average

Investment Style History: Fixed Income

Income Rtn % Rank Obj

		57	19	20	29	48	39	27	41

Growth of $10,000
- |||| Value of Fund ($000)
- — Value of Index ($000) LB L-T
- ▼ Manager Change
- ▽ Partial Manager Change
- ► Mgr Unknown After
- ◄ Mgr Unknown Before

Performance Quartile (Within Objective)

1983	1984	1985	1986	1987	1988	1989	1990	1991	1992	1993	1994	History
7.42	7.20	8.36	9.52	8.05	7.89	8.29	9.22	9.23	9.54	8.15		NAV
7.86	10.39	29.82	24.66	-7.71	8.01	18.72	6.40	20.96	8.42	13.04	-7.95	Total Return %
-14.60	4.12	-1.92	5.99	-12.97	-8.60	-12.97	9.51	-9.53	0.81	2.99	-9.26	+/- S&P 500
-0.51	-4.77	7.69	9.42	-10.47	0.14	4.18	-2.55	4.95	1.18	3.29	-5.03	+/- LB Aggregate
11.87	13.35	13.71	10.11	6.65	10.00	10.23	9.55	9.74	8.32	8.11	6.62	Income Return %
-4.01	-2.96	16.11	14.55	-14.36	-1.99	8.49	-3.15	11.22	0.11	4.93	-14.57	Capital Return %
89	24	27	9	93	73	38	29	43	40	41	85	Total Rtn % Rank All
75	53	1	1	90	84	17	14	68	44	62	93	Total Rtn % Rank Obj
0.93	0.93	0.89	0.80	0.65	0.78	0.75	0.78	0.73	0.74	0.72	0.65	Income $
0.00	0.00	0.00	0.05	0.12	0.00	0.00	0.00	0.00	0.00	0.14	0.00	Capital Gains $
0.66	0.66	0.59	0.58	0.64	0.66	0.67	0.65	0.63	0.58	0.53	0.45	Expense Ratio %
11.50	13.16	11.01	9.07	8.60	9.40	9.11	8.69	7.96	7.43	6.77	7.06	Income Ratio %
56	73	34	48	67	52	42	15	18	33	45	37	Turnover Rate %
62.7	47.7	85.5	154.0	94.7	73.8	63.7	56.1	100.6	185.8	386.4	278.9	Net Assets ($mil)

Performance 12-31-94

	1st Qtr	2nd Qtr	3rd Qtr	4th Qtr	Total
1987	3.95	-6.58	-4.86	-0.11	-7.71
1988	4.90	-1.08	3.03	1.02	8.01
1989	1.56	10.19	2.46	3.54	18.72
1990	-2.04	4.07	-1.89	6.38	6.40
1991	4.96	1.94	8.07	4.61	20.96
1992	0.15	3.53	4.44	0.12	8.42
1993	5.21	3.10	4.11	0.10	13.04
1994	-3.71	-2.35	-0.93	-1.18	-7.95

Bear Market Performance

Decile Rank (5-year period)

Worst ———— Best

	Worst 3 Mo Period 1985-89	Worst 3 Mo Period 1990-94
Vanguard Preferred Stock	-9.04	-6.90
+/- S&P 500	-11.89	-1.14
+/- Best Fit Index : LB L-T	-1.35	2.50

Trailing Returns

	Total Return %	+/- S&P 500	+/- LB Aggregate	% Rank All	% Rank Obj	Growth of $10,000
3 Mo	-1.18	-1.16	-1.56	49	47	9,882
6 Mo	-2.10	-6.97	-3.10	89	93	9,790
1 Yr	-7.95	-9.26	-5.03	85	93	9,205
3 Yr Avg	4.10	-2.16	-0.44	67	81	11,283
5 Yr Avg	7.74	-0.95	0.12	37	52	14,520
10 Yr Avg	10.77	-3.61	0.82	49	42	27,809
15 Yr Avg	10.94	-3.54	0.13	66	66	47,457

Operations

Address and Telephone	Vanguard Fin Ctr. P.O. Box 2600 Valley Forge, PA 19482 800-662-7447 / 610-669-1000
Advisor	Wellington Management
Subadvisor	None
Distributor	Vanguard Group
States Available	All plus PR,VI,GU
Report Grade	B+
Income Distrib	Paid Quarterly
Date of Inception	12-03-75
Fiscal Year End	October

Risk Analysis

Time Period	Load-Adj Return %	Risk % Rank¹ All	Obj	Morningstar² Return	Morningstar Risk	Morningstar Risk-Adj Rating
1 Yr	-7.95					
3 Yr	4.10	40	68	0.15³	0.62	★★★
5 Yr	7.74	42	47	0.74³	0.50	★★★★
10 Yr	10.77	35	28	0.80	0.50	★★★★
Average Historical Rating (109 months)						3.7 ★s

¹ 1 = low, 100 = high ² 1.00 = Hybrid Avg ³ 1.00 = 90-day T-bill return

Other Measures

			Standard S&P 500	Best Fit LB L-T
Standard Deviation	4.84	Alpha	-0.3	-0.4
Mean	4.15	Beta	0.32	0.52
Sharpe Ratio	0.13	R-Squared	26	69

Investment Style

Stocks
	Port Avg	Rel S&P 500
Price/Earnings Ratio	---	---
Price/Book Ratio	---	---
5 Yr Earnings Gr %	---	---
Med Mkt Cap ($mil)	---	---

Not Available

Bonds
Avg Effective Duration	NMF
Avg Effective Maturity	39.3 Yrs
Avg Credit Quality	A
Avg Weighted Coupon	7.61%

Maturity S I L
Quality H M L

Diversification Value for Portfolio Types

Large Cap: Medium	Small Cap: High	Bond: Low	Balanced: Medium	Diversified: Medium

Portfolio 12-31-94

Total Stocks: 0
Total Fixed-Income: 93

Share Chg ---000	Amount 000		Date of Maturity	Value $000	% Net Assets
	450	Ford Holdings Cl A Pfd		10294	3.69
	400	PSI Energy Pfd 7.44%		8550	3.07
	343	Bankamerica Cl M Pfd 7.875%		7706	2.76
	325	Chemical Banking H Pfd 8.375%		7638	2.74
	350	Household Intl Cl A Pfd 7.35%		7088	2.54
	300	AON Pfd 8%		7013	2.51
	280	General Motors Cl G Pfd 9.12%		6965	2.50
	85	Pennsylvania Pwr/Lt Pfd 6.75%		6917	2.48
	75	Florida Power & Lt Pfd 6.98%		6338	2.27
	280	Bank of Boston Pfd 7.875%		6230	2.23
	300	Pacific Gas & Elec Pfd 7.04%		6225	2.23
	300	Arizona Public Svc Pfd 7.25%		5963	2.14
	250	Pacificorp Pfd 7.92%		5813	2.08
	259	Great Western Finl Pfd 8.3%		5804	2.08
	225	McDonald's Cl E Pfd 7.72%		5428	1.95
	63	Unicom Pfd $7.24		4886	1.75
	225	Detroit Edison Pfd 7.75%		4809	1.72
	240	Washington Nat Gas Pfd 7.45%		4800	1.72
	50	Monongahela Power Pfd 7.73%		4719	1.69
	200	Mellon Bank Cl K Pfd 8.2%		4700	1.69

Index Allocation
	% of Stocks
S&P 500	---
S&P MidCap 400	---
U.S. Small Cap	---
Foreign	---

Composition % 10-31-94
Cash	2.4	Preferreds	97.0
Stocks	0.0	Convertibles	0.0
Bonds	0.6	Other	0.0

Tax Analysis
	Tax-Adj Historical Return %	% Pretax Return
3 Yr Avg	1.14	26.9
5 Yr Avg	4.77	58.1
10 Yr Avg	7.23	56.7
Potential Capital Gain Exposure (% of assets)		-17%

Most Similar Funds in MF500
PaineWebber Invmt Grade Inc	Fair Fit
Fidelity Government Secs	Fair Fit
Bond Fund of America	Fair Fit

Bond Credit Analysis 10-31-94
US Govt	1	BB	0
AAA	0	B	0
AA	9	Below B	0
A	53	NR/NA	0
BBB	38		

Stock Sector Weightings
	% of Stocks	Relative S&P 500
Utilities	---	---
Energy	---	---
Financials	---	---
Industrial Cyclicals	---	---
Consumer Durables	---	---
Consumer Staples	---	---
Services	---	---
Retail	---	---
Health	---	---
Technology	---	---

Operations (continued)

Min Initial Purchase	$3000 (Addt'l: $100)
Min IRA Purchase	$500 (Addt'l: $100)
Min Auto Invest Plan	$3000 (Systematic Inv: $50)

Expenses & Fees
Sales Fees	0.00% front
	0.00% deferred
	0.00% 12b-1
Management Fee	0.33% max./0.15% min.
3-,5-,10-yr Expense Projections	$17, $30, $66
Annual Brokerage Cost	0.00%

Vanguard Special Energy

Ticker	Load	NAV	Yield	SEC Yield	Assets	Objective
VGENX	None	14.29	1.6%	1.64%	445.5	Sp.-Nat. Res.

Vanguard Specialized Portfolios - Energy seeks long-term growth of capital.

The fund normally invests at least 80% of its assets in equity securities of traditional or emerging companies engaged in energy-related activities; these companies may be involved in the production, transmission, marketing, control, or measurement of energy or energy fuels. The fund may not invest in electric-utility companies, although it may invest in natural-gas distributors and pipelines.

The fund levies a 1% redemption fee; this fee is paid to the portfolio.

Manager's Investment Style

Manager Ernst von Metzsch doesn't take huge bets, but instead remains well diversified in energy sectors, while buying heavily only in areas that have been unfairly beat up by the market. Von Metzsch avoids downside risk by following a mild contrarian strategy.

Fund Manager(s)

Ernst H. von Metzsch CFA, since 05-84. Birthdate: 12-39.

Manager Experience

Not available.

Historical Profile
Return: Average
Risk: Above Average
Rating: ★★ Below Average

% Stocks Held: 83% 92% 87% 92% 94% 97% 93% 96%

	1983	1984	1985	1986	1987	1988	1989	1990	1991	1992	1993	1994	History
	---	9.34	10.46	11.18	9.69	11.39	15.40	13.84	13.03	13.29	15.06	14.29	NAV
	---	-6.60*	14.43	12.70	6.13	21.37	43.45	-1.37	0.28	6.18	26.42	-1.63	Total Return %
	---	-19.32*	-17.31	-5.98	0.88	4.76	11.77	1.75	-30.20	-1.44	16.37	-2.94	+/- S&P 500
	---	---	---	---	-3.74	2.65	3.75	-4.52	-7.24	4.14	10.70	-5.46	+/- S&P Energy
	---	0.00	1.49	5.19	7.36	3.82	2.68	3.23	3.24	2.78	2.05	1.64	Income Return %
	---	-6.60	12.94	7.51	-1.23	17.54	40.77	-4.60	-2.95	3.41	24.37	-3.26	Capital Return %
	---	---	93	69	18	11	2	59	99	67	10	31	Total Rtn % Rank All
	---	---	42	33	54	1	11	11	73	40	21	33	Total Rtn % Rank Obj
	---	0.00	0.14	0.44	0.76	0.37	0.36	0.46	0.42	0.36	0.29	0.24	Income $
	---	0.00	0.08	0.05	1.41	0.00	0.57	0.88	0.42	0.18	1.38	0.29	Capital Gains $
	---	---	0.55	0.92	0.65	0.38	0.40	0.38	0.35	0.30	0.21	0.17	Expense Ratio %
	---	---	3.75	4.40	3.43	3.70	3.07	3.05	3.24	2.78	2.47	1.87	Income Ratio %
	---	---	34	156	34	84	46	44	40	42	37	41	Turnover Rate %
	---	0.7	1.0	28.6	32.0	38.7	72.1	119.4	116.3	155.7	269.6	445.5	Net Assets ($mil)

Performance 12-31-94

	1st Qtr	2nd Qtr	3rd Qtr	4th Qtr	Total
1987	26.19	7.55	2.29	-23.55	6.13
1988	16.10	1.16	-2.46	5.95	21.37
1989	13.35	6.66	7.77	10.10	43.45
1990	0.99	1.43	3.84	-7.27	-1.37
1991	5.20	-2.51	6.35	-8.06	0.28
1992	-4.76	6.38	8.35	-3.26	6.18
1993	21.29	7.82	6.16	-8.93	26.42
1994	-2.70	7.76	0.00	-6.17	-1.63

Bear Market Performance

Decile Rank (5-year period)

	Worst 3 Mo Period 1985-89	Worst 3 Mo Period 1990-94
Vanguard Special Energy	-31.70	-11.59
+/- S&P 500	-2.12	-11.91
+/- Best Fit Index : MSAIICtry	---	-7.37

Trailing Returns

	Total Return %	+/- S&P 500	+/- S&P Energy	% Rank All	% Rank Obj	Growth of $10,000
3 Mo	-6.17	-6.15	-8.05	94	37	9,383
6 Mo	-6.17	-11.03	-9.68	98	70	9,383
1 Yr	-1.63	-2.94	-5.46	31	33	9,837
3 Yr Avg	9.71	3.45	2.68	14	20	13,206
5 Yr Avg	5.49	-3.20	-0.86	85	16	13,062
10 Yr Avg	12.02	-2.36	---	37	1	31,124
15 Yr Avg	---	---	---	---	---	---

Operations

Address and Telephone	Vanguard Fin Ctr. P.O. Box 2600 Valley Forge, PA 19482 800-662-7447 / 610-669-1000
Advisor	Wellington Management
Subadvisor	None
Distributor	Vanguard Group
States Available	All plus PR,VI,GU
Report Grade	B+
Income Distrib	Paid Annually
Date of Inception	05-23-84
Fiscal Year End	January

Risk Analysis

Time Period	Load-Adj Return %	Risk % Rank All	Risk % Rank Obj	Morningstar Return	Morningstar Risk	Morningstar Risk-Adj Rating
1 Yr	-2.63					
3 Yr	9.71	93	75	1.88[3]	1.27	★★★★
5 Yr	5.49	90	72	0.18[3]	1.15	★★
10 Yr	12.02	82	28	0.88	1.05	★★

Average Historical Rating (92 months) 3.5 ★s

[1] 1 = low, 100 = high [2] 1.00 = Equity Avg [3] 1.00 = 90-day T-bill return

Other Measures

	Standard S&P 500	Best Fit MSAIICtry
Standard Deviation	15.29	Alpha 3.8 / 4.4
Mean	10.47	Beta 1.11 / 1.04
Sharpe Ratio	0.45	R-Squared 33 / 52

Investment Style

	Stock Portfolio Avg	Relative S&P 500
Price/Earnings Ratio	27.2	1.47
Price/Book Ratio	2.2	0.65
5 Yr Earnings Gr %	3.0#	0.54
Return on Assets %	4.5	0.60
Debt % Total Cap	35.4	1.25
Med Mkt Cap ($mil)	2001	0.15

figure is based on 50% or less of stocks

Diversification Value for Portfolio Types

Large Cap: Medium / Small Cap: High / Bond: Medium / Balanced: Medium / Diversified: Low

Expenses & Fees

Sales Fees	0.00% front
	0.00% deferred
	0.00% 12b-1
Management Fee	0.30% max./0.10% min.
3-,5-,10-yr Expense Projections	$9, $15, $34
Annual Brokerage Cost	0.20%

Min Initial Purchase: $3000 (Addt'l: $100)
Min IRA Purchase: $500 (Addt'l: $100)
Min Auto Invest Plan: $3000 (Systematic Inv: $50)

Portfolio 12-31-94

Total Stocks: 92 / Total Fixed-Income: 0

Share Chg (08-94) 000	Amount 000		Value $000	% Net Assets
0	310	Exxon	18833	4.23
0	546	Unocal	14879	3.34
30	140	Atlantic Richfield	14245	3.20
50	850	USX-Marathon Group	13919	3.12
100	300	Kerr-McGee	13800	3.10
10	380	Ashland Oil	13110	2.94
-10	210	Amoco	12416	2.79
30	270	Amerada Hess	12319	2.76
250	850	Oryx Energy	10094	2.27
0	160	Texaco	9580	2.15
-60	280	Phillips Petroleum	9170	2.06
0	231	Norsk Hydro (ADR)	9042	2.03
5	305	TOTAL CI B (ADR)	9010	2.02
0	3857	LASMO	8929	2.00
0	375	DEKALB Energy CI B	7875	1.77
0	420	Baker Hughes	7665	1.72
0	400	Pogo Producing	7100	1.59
0	2000	Maxus Energy	6750	1.52
200	600	Transtexas Gas	6750	1.52
0	150	Chevron	6694	1.50
0	150	Pennzoil	6619	1.49
0	300	Union Texas Petroleum	6225	1.40
0	270	Overseas Shipholding Group	6210	1.39
0	240	Vastar Resources	5970	1.34
0	497	Home Oil	5272	1.18

Composition % 09-30-94

Cash	3.0	Preferreds	0.0
Stocks	97.0	Convertibles	0.0
Bonds	0.0	Other	0.0

Tax Analysis

	Tax-Adj Historical Return %	% Pretax Return
3 Yr Avg	7.75	78.3
5 Yr Avg	3.36	58.6
10 Yr Avg	9.58	70.9
Potential Capital Gain Exposure (% of assets)		-5%

Most Similar Funds in MF500

Prudential Utility B	Weak Fit
Fidelity Utilities	Weak Fit
Fortress Utility	Weak Fit

Index Allocation

	% of Stocks
S&P 500	48.0
S&P MidCap 400	10.8
U.S. Small Cap	13.6
Foreign	27.7

Sector Weightings

	% of Stocks	Relative S&P 500
Utilities	1.7	0.14
Energy	91.6	9.04
Financials	0.0	0.00
Industrial Cyclicals	2.2	0.14
Consumer Durables	0.0	0.00
Consumer Staples	0.0	0.00
Services	4.5	0.55
Retail	0.0	0.00
Health	0.0	0.00
Technology	0.0	0.00

MORNINGSTAR 1995 Mutual Fund 500

Vanguard Special Gold & Prec Met

	Ticker	Load	NAV	Yield	SEC Yield	Assets	Objective
	VGPMX	None	12.72	2.4%	N/A	639.2	Sp.-Metals

Vanguard Specialized Portfolios - Gold and Precious Metals seeks long-term capital appreciation.

The fund typically invests at least 80% of its assets in equity securities of companies involved in the exploration, mining, processing, or distribution of gold and other precious metals. It may also invest up to 20% of its assets directly in gold, silver, or other precious-metal bullion and coins. The fund may invest a substantial portion of its assets in foreign securities.

The fund levies a 1% redemption fee.

Manager's Investment Style

The fund's manager uses diversification as a guideline in gold investments, and buys mostly senior mines in North America, North Africa, and Australia. Hutchins seeks potential improvement in production and earnings, and helps hedge the portfolio by investing in polymetallics, which are mines that produce more than just gold.

Fund Manager(s)

David J. Hutchins, since 01-87. Birthdate: 10-60.

Manager Experience

	Dates Managed	Invest Obj	Std Dev	+/- Index
Not available.				

Historical Profile
Return	Average
Risk	High
Rating	★★ Below Average

Investment Style History
Equity

Average % Stocks Held in Portfolio

77%	78%	81%	85%	83%	83%	86%	89%

Growth of $10,000
- |||| Value of Fund ($000)
- — Value of Index ($000) S&P 500
- ▼ Manager Change
- ▽ Partial Manager Change
- ► Mgr Unknown After
- ◄ Mgr Unknown Before

Performance Quartile (Within Objective)

1983	1984	1985	1986	1987	1988	1989	1990	1991	1992	1993	1994	History
---	6.73	6.33	9.22	11.11	9.27	11.73	9.07	9.21	7.24	13.78	12.72	NAV
---	-32.70 *	-5.03	49.88	38.73	-14.19	30.40	-19.86	4.37	-19.41	93.36	-5.42	Total Return %
---	-45.42 *	-36.77	31.20	33.47	-30.80	-1.29	-16.75	-26.11	-27.03	83.30	-6.74	+/- S&P 500
---	---	---	57.16	-37.13	-46.00	15.31	-14.85	-8.46	-26.70	81.95	-22.19	+/- S&P Metals
---	0.00	0.91	4.22	4.79	2.37	3.86	2.81	2.83	1.98	3.03	2.27	Income Return %
---	-32.70	-5.94	45.66	33.94	-16.56	26.54	-22.68	1.54	-21.39	90.33	-7.69	Capital Return %
---		99	3	1	99	13	97	98	100	33	67	Total Rtn % Rank All
---		38	6	36	30	23	26	7	72	23	18	Total Rtn % Rank Obj
---	0.00	0.06	0.21	0.48	0.26	0.34	0.32	0.25	0.18	0.21	0.31	Income $
---	0.00	0.00	0.00	1.14	0.00	0.00	0.00	0.00	0.00	0.00	0.00	Capital Gains $
---	---	0.87	0.73	0.59	0.47	0.48	0.45	0.42	0.35	0.36	0.26	Expense Ratio %
---	---	3.25	3.86	3.36	2.71	2.67	3.01	2.78	2.54	2.50	2.04	Income Ratio %
---	---	11	40	32	44	18	17	10	3	2	14	Turnover Rate %
---	6.0	6.9	53.2	158.3	124.2	191.6	129.1	170.4	173.9	609.6	639.2	Net Assets ($mil)

Performance 12-31-94

	1st Qtr	2nd Qtr	3rd Qtr	4th Qtr	Total
1987	52.89	-3.44	21.47	-22.64	38.73
1988	-8.31	0.30	-10.83	4.65	-14.19
1989	3.77	-0.10	8.49	15.95	30.40
1990	-7.59	-9.69	3.17	-6.93	-19.86
1991	-2.21	9.36	-3.71	1.36	4.37
1992	-4.02	2.26	-8.63	-10.14	-19.41
1993	25.83	31.28	-10.79	31.20	93.36
1994	-6.99	-0.94	17.47	-12.62	-5.42

Bear Market Performance

Decile Rank (5-year period)

Worst | Best

	Worst 3 Mo Period 1985-89	Worst 3 Mo Period 1990-94
Vanguard Special Gold & Prec	-27.63	-21.36
+/- S&P 500	-7.23	-22.73
+/- Best Fit Index : JSE Gold	---	-0.87

Trailing Returns

	Total Return %	+/- S&P 500	+/- S&P Metals	% Rank All	% Rank Obj	Growth of $10,000
3 Mo	-12.62	-12.61	-6.28	99	25	8,738
6 Mo	2.64	-2.22	-3.46	23	20	10,264
1 Yr	-5.42	-6.74	-22.19	67	18	9,458
3 Yr Avg	13.80	7.53	2.05	5	31	14,737
5 Yr Avg	4.27	-4.42	-4.11	92	7	12,327
10 Yr Avg	10.54	-3.84	---	52	7	27,236
15 Yr Avg	---	---	---	---	---	---

Operations

Address and Telephone	Vanguard Fin Ctr. P.O. Box 2600
	Valley Forge, PA 19482
	800-662-7447 / 610-669-1000
Advisor	M&G Investment Management
Subadvisor	None
Distributor	Vanguard Group
States Available	All plus PR,VI,GU
Report Grade	B+
Income Distrib	Paid Annually
* Date of Inception	05-23-84
Fiscal Year End	January

Risk Analysis

Time Period	Load-Adj Return %	Risk % Rank[1] All	Obj	Morningstar[2] Return	Morningstar Risk	Morningstar Risk-Adj Rating
1 Yr	-6.42					
3 Yr	13.80	99	6	3.25[3]	1.89	★★★★
5 Yr	4.27	99	11	-0.10[3]	1.70	★
10 Yr	10.54	99	23	0.63[3]	1.75	★

Average Historical Rating (92 months) 2.0 ★s

[1] 1 = low, 100 = high [2] 1.00 = Equity Avg [3] 1.00 = 90-day T-bill return

Other Measures

			Standard S&P 500	Best Fit JSE Gold
Standard Deviation	25.10	Alpha	11.9	4.2
Mean	16.04	Beta	0.42	0.59
Sharpe Ratio	0.50	R-Squared	2	76

Investment Style

	Stock Portfolio Avg	Relative S&P 500
Price/Earnings Ratio	34.5#	1.87
Price/Book Ratio	3.1#	0.92
5 Yr Earnings Gr %	-1.5#	-0.27
Return on Assets %	8.9#	1.19
Debt % Total Cap	20.4#	0.72
Med Mkt Cap ($mil)	1029#	0.08

figure is based on 50% or less of stocks

Style: Value Blend Growth — Size: Large Med Small

Diversification Value for Portfolio Types

Large Cap: High	Small Cap: High	Bond: High	Balanced: High	Diversified: High

Portfolio 12-31-94

Share Chg (08-94) 000	Amount 000	Total Stocks: 65 / Total Fixed-Income: 4	Value $000	% Net Assets
-50	1825	Free State Consld Gold (ADR)	27603	4.32
75	1800	Randfontein Estate Gold ADR	20475	3.20
125	2125	Vaal Reefs Expl & Mng (ADR)	19258	3.01
0	4000	Newcrest Mining	17842	2.79
350	775	American Barrick Resources	17244	2.70
-50	700	Impala Platinum Hldgs (ADR)	16975	2.66
-25	600	Rustenberg Platinum (ADR)	16350	2.56
25	700	DeBeers Consold Mines (ADR)	16188	2.53
0	275	Anglo American of SA (ADR)	15744	2.46
0	1000	Driefontein Consld Mines ADR	15125	2.37
0	350	Western Deep Levels (ADR)	14044	2.20
3000	15000	Highland Gold	13963	2.18
0	2000	TVX Gold	13548	2.12
0	275	Franco-Nevada Mining	13506	2.11
500	3500	Renison Goldfields Consolid	13304	2.08
250	2250	Western Mining	13021	2.04
0	850	Kloof Gold Mining (ADR)	12431	1.94
0	400	Gold Fields So Africa (ADR)	12400	1.94
0	500	Placer Dome	10875	1.70
0	500	Euro-Nevada Mining	10518	1.65
0	2300	Hartebeestfontein Gold (ADR)	10063	1.57
0	2250	Plutonic Resources	10036	1.57
0	1500	Elandsrand Gold Mining (ADR)	9938	1.55
25	275	Newmont Mining	9900	1.55
0	3500	Placer Pacific	9774	1.53

Composition % 09-30-94

Cash	10.0	Preferreds	0.0
Stocks	90.0	Convertibles	0.0
Bonds	0.0	Other	0.0

Tax Analysis

	Tax-Adj Historical Return %	% Pretax Return
3 Yr Avg	12.93	92.9
5 Yr Avg	3.39	77.9
10 Yr Avg	9.24	82.4
Potential Capital Gain Exposure (% of assets)		12%

Most Similar Funds in MF500

Dreyfus Global Growth	Weak Fit
Value Line Income	Weak Fit
Warburg Pincus Growth & Inc	Weak Fit

Index Allocation

	% of Stocks
S&P 500	9.9
S&P MidCap 400	0.0
U.S. Small Cap	3.1
Foreign	92.3

Regional Exposure 04-15-94

	% of Stocks
N. America	32
S. Africa	31
Australia	26
Other	5
Bullion	6

Expenses & Fees

Sales Fees	
	0.00% front
	0.00% deferred
	0.00% 12b-1
Management Fee	0.30% max./0.20% min.
3-,5-,10-yr Expense Projections	$11, $19, $42
Annual Brokerage Cost	0.20%

Min Initial Purchase	$3000 (Addt'l: $100)
Min IRA Purchase	$500 (Addt'l: $100)
Min Auto Invest Plan	$3000 (Systematic Inv: $50)

Vanguard Special Health Care

	Ticker	Load	NAV	Yield	SEC Yield	Assets	Objective
	VGHCX	None	35.47	1.5%	1.45%	708.1	Sp.-Health

Vanguard Specialized Portfolios - Health Care seeks long-term growth of capital.

The fund normally invests at least 80% of its assets in equity securities of companies engaged in the development, production, or distribution of products and services related to the treatment or prevention of diseases and other medical infirmities. These companies include pharmaceutical firms, medical-supply firms, and companies that operate hospitals and other health-care facilities. Research companies such as biotech firms may be considered.

The fund levies a 1% redemption fee; this fee is paid to the portfolio.

Manager's Investment Style

This fund's manager follows a low-turnover approach to health-care investing. Owens avoids big losses by seeking established companies in all areas of the industry, while overlooking the more speculative biotech firms. He adds to the portfolio's range by investing upward of 20% of assets in European and Japanese stocks.

Fund Manager(s)

Edward P. Owens CFA, since 05-84. Birthdate: 09-46. BS, U. of Virginia 1968 MBA, Harvard 1974

Manager Experience

	Dates Managed	Invest Obj	Std Dev	+/- Index
Not available.				

Historical Profile
Return: High
Risk: Average
Rating: ★★★★★ Highest

Investment Style History
Equity
Average % Stocks Held in Portfolio

	92%	93%	88%	89%	88%	95%	96%	95%

Growth of $10,000
IIII Value of Fund ($000)
— Value of Index ($000) SPMid400
▼ Manager Change
▽ Partial Manager Change
► Mgr Unknown After
◄ Mgr Unknown Before

Performance Quartile (Within Objective)

1983	1984	1985	1986	1987	1988	1989	1990	1991	1992	1993	1994	History
---	10.66	15.31	17.64	15.70	18.43	23.21	25.69	36.50	34.01	35.07	35.47	NAV
---	6.60 *	45.76	21.42	-0.50	28.41	32.95	16.80	46.32	-1.57	11.81	9.54	Total Return %
---	-6.12 *	14.02	2.74	-5.76	11.80	1.27	19.91	15.84	-9.19	1.75	8.22	+/- S&P 500
---	---	---	---	---	15.87	-12.68	-0.66	-7.69	14.72	20.21	-3.58	+/- S&P Health
---	0.00	0.68	0.83	3.25	1.94	2.41	2.29	1.82	2.03	2.26	1.63	Income Return %
---	6.60	45.08	20.59	-3.75	26.46	30.54	14.51	44.51	-3.59	9.54	7.91	Capital Return %
---	---	4	15	63	4	9	1	9	91	52	2	Total Rtn % Rank All
---	---	20	28	37	1	66	30	60	18	7	33	Total Rtn % Rank Obj
---	0.00	0.07	0.13	0.57	0.34	0.49	0.55	0.53	0.70	0.76	0.57	Income $
---	0.00	0.11	0.80	1.39	1.29	0.72	0.84	0.53	1.20	1.97	2.31	Capital Gains $
---	---	0.59	0.83	0.61	0.51	0.62	0.39	0.36	0.30	0.22	0.19	Expense Ratio %
---	---	2.41	1.52	1.47	1.65	1.85	2.34	2.54	1.98	2.06	2.37	Income Ratio %
---	---	23	59	27	41	19	28	17	7	15	19	Turnover Rate %
---	1.8	2.7	43.4	47.4	54.5	78.6	163.6	547.6	607.1	609.1	708.1	Net Assets ($mil)

Performance 12-31-94

	1st Qtr	2nd Qtr	3rd Qtr	4th Qtr	Total
1987	23.68	3.56	4.40	-25.59	-0.50
1988	17.77	5.20	1.52	2.09	28.41
1989	9.84	4.11	11.46	4.30	32.95
1990	-0.68	12.31	-11.04	17.69	16.80
1991	18.88	-0.26	9.66	12.54	46.32
1992	-7.11	-2.16	1.94	6.25	-1.57
1993	-7.85	5.97	3.94	10.15	11.81
1994	-5.32	0.43	14.66	0.47	9.54

Bear Market Performance

Decile Rank (5-year period)

Worst ▬ Best

	Worst 3 Mo Period 1985-89	Worst 3 Mo Period 1990-94
Vanguard Special Health Care	-31.22	-11.31
+/- S&P 500	-1.64	-14.77
+/- Best Fit Index : SPMid400	-2.42	-14.49

Trailing Returns

	Total Return %	+/- S&P 500	+/- S&P Health	% Rank All	% Rank Obj	Growth of $10,000
3 Mo	0.47	0.49	-2.73	12	37	10,047
6 Mo	15.20	10.34	-3.69	2	43	11,520
1 Yr	9.54	8.22	-3.58	2	33	10,954
3 Yr Avg	6.43	0.16	11.06	30	18	12,055
5 Yr Avg	15.55	6.86	6.13	4	30	20,601
10 Yr Avg	20.00	5.62	---	1	40	61,935
15 Yr Avg	---	---	---	---	---	---

Operations

Address and Telephone	Vanguard Fin Ctr. P.O. Box 2600 Valley Forge, PA 19482 800-662-7447 / 610-669-1000	
Advisor	Wellington Management	
Subadvisor	None	
Distributor	Vanguard Group	
States Available	All plus PR,VI,GU	
Report Grade	B+	
Income Distrib	Paid Annually	
* Date of Inception	05-23-84	
Fiscal Year End	January	

Min Initial Purchase	$3000 (Addt'l: $100)
Min IRA Purchase	$500 (Addt'l: $100)
Min Auto Invest Plan	$3000 (Systematic Inv: $50)

Expenses & Fees

Sales Fees	0.00% front
	0.00% deferred
	0.00% 12b-1
Management Fee	0.30% max./0.10% min.
3-,5-,10-yr Expense Projections	$12, $20, $46
Annual Brokerage Cost	0.17%

Risk Analysis

Time Period	Load-Adj Return %	Risk % Rank [1] All	Obj	Morningstar [2] Return	Risk	Morningstar Risk-Adj Rating
1 Yr	8.44					
3 Yr	6.43	89	1	0.85 [3]	1.16	★★★
5 Yr	15.55	76	1	3.09 [3]	0.90	★★★★★
10 Yr	20.00	66	1	2.88	0.89	★★★★★
Average Historical Rating (92 months)				4.7	★s	

[1] 1 = low, 100 = high [2] 1.00 = Equity Avg [3] 1.00 = 90-day T-bill return

Other Measures

				Standard S&P 500	Best Fit SPMid400
Standard Deviation	12.92	Alpha		0.4	0.0
Mean	7.07	Beta		1.10	0.93
Sharpe Ratio	0.27	R-Squared		46	51

Investment Style

	Stock Portfolio Avg	Relative S&P 500
Price/Earnings Ratio	21.8	1.18
Price/Book Ratio	3.4	0.99
5 Yr Earnings Gr %	9.6	1.72
Return on Assets %	9.3	1.24
Debt % Total Cap	18.4	0.65
Med Mkt Cap ($mil)	3548	0.27

Style: Value Blend Growth
Size: Large Med Small

Diversification Value for Portfolio Types

Large Cap: Medium
Small Cap: Medium
Bond: High
Balanced: Medium
Diversified: Medium

Tax Analysis

	Tax-Adj Historical Return %	% Pretax Return
3 Yr Avg	4.25	64.8
5 Yr Avg	13.55	83.7
10 Yr Avg	17.82	80.0
Potential Capital Gain Exposure (% of assets)		16%

Most Similar Funds in MF500

Fidelity Sel Health Care	Weak Fit
Dreyfus Appreciation	Weak Fit
T. Rowe Price New America G	Weak Fit

Portfolio 12-31-94

Total Stocks: 80
Total Fixed-Income: 1

Share Chg (08-94) 000	Amount 000		Value $000	% Net Assets
0	650	Johnson & Johnson	35588	5.03
-30	460	Pfizer	35535	5.02
0	795	Zeneca Group (ADR)	32675	4.61
80	430	Bristol-Myers Squibb	24886	3.51
0	41	Ciba-Geigy (Br)	24306	3.43
0	845	Beckman Instruments	23554	3.33
280	750	Mallinckrodt Group	22406	3.16
328	565	Rhone-Poulenc Rorer	20615	2.91
40	620	Abbott Laboratories	20228	2.86
0	300	Eli Lilly	19688	2.78
0	848	AL Pharma Cl A	17166	2.42
-10	220	Warner-Lambert	16940	2.39
0	730	Humana	16525	2.33
-100	350	Biogen	14438	2.04
-10	21	Schering	14002	1.98
185	405	McKesson	13207	1.87
0	661	Advanced Technology Labs	11902	1.68
30	314	Columbia/HCA Healthcare	11474	1.62
0	450	FHP International	11363	1.60
85	170	American Home Products	10668	1.51
10	380	DEKALB Genetics Cl B	9881	1.40
325	735	National Health Lab Hldgs	9736	1.38
0	340	Allergan	9605	1.36
0	592	Pharmacia Cl A Free	9478	1.34
50	267	Genetics Institute	9477	1.34

Composition % 09-30-94

Cash	7.0	Preferreds	0.0
Stocks	93.0	Convertibles	0.0
Bonds	0.0	Other	0.0

Index Allocation

	% of Stocks
S&P 500	37.8
S&P MidCap 400	16.0
U.S. Small Cap	23.8
Foreign	22.4

Sector Weightings

	% of Stocks	Relative S&P 500
Utilities	0.0	0.00
Energy	0.0	0.00
Financials	0.0	0.00
Industrial Cyclicals	3.9	0.24
Consumer Durables	0.8	0.13
Consumer Staples	7.7	0.61
Services	3.5	0.43
Retail	0.3	0.05
Health	79.0	9.10
Technology	5.0	0.54

MORNINGSTAR 1995 Mutual Fund 500

Vanguard Special Utilities Inc

	Ticker	Load	NAV	Yield	SEC Yield	Assets	Objective
	VGSUX	None	9.94	5.9%	5.98%	560.5	Sp.-Util

Vanguard Specialized Portfolios - Utilities Income seeks current income. It also seeks moderate growth of capital and income.

The fund invests in equity and debt securities of utility companies. These include companies engaged in the generation, transmission, or distribution of electricity, gas, water, or telecommunications.

Manager's Investment Style

The fund's management team splits its responsibilities into two categories, equity and bonds. Both managers, though, follow a similar strategy. The fund has a definite contrarian approach to investing, often staying ashore while the masses dive in. This has not produced stellar returns, but has resulted in low price multiples and high yields. Management continues to support its mainstay, electric utilities. Reasoning that regulation laws will never fully be implemented, management continues to pick up reasonably priced electric companies in California and New York.

Fund Manager(s)

John R. Ryan CFA, since 05-92. Birthdate: 02-49.
BS, Lehigh U. 1971 MBA, U. of Virginia 1981
Paul D. Kaplan, since 05-94. Birthdate: 11-46.
BA, Dickinson U. 1968 MS, MIT 1974

Manager Experience

	Dates Managed	Invest Obj	Std Dev	+/- Index
John R. Ryan				
Global Utility A	01/90 - 05/92	SU	10.39	0.02
Paul D. Kaplan				
North American Inv Qual A	05/91 - 04/94	CG	5.16	-0.46

Performance 12-31-94

	1st Qtr	2nd Qtr	3rd Qtr	4th Qtr	Total
1987	---	---	---	---	---
1988	---	---	---	---	---
1989	---	---	---	---	---
1990	---	---	---	---	---
1991	---	---	---	---	---
1992	---	---	7.56	3.55	12.16 *
1993	9.88	2.88	5.63	-3.64	15.06
1994	-6.96	-2.29	1.40	-0.79	-8.56

Bear Market Performance

Decile Rank (5-year period)

Worst ———————————— Best

	Worst 3 Mo Period 1985-89	Worst 3 Mo Period 1990-94
Vanguard Special Utilities Inc	---	---
+/- S&P 500	---	---
+/- Best Fit Index :	---	---

Trailing Returns

	Total Return %	+/- S&P 500	+/- S&P Util	% Rank All	% Rank Obj	Growth of $10,000
3 Mo	-0.79	-0.78	-0.69	40	32	9,921
6 Mo	0.60	-4.26	0.23	45	55	10,060
1 Yr	-8.55	-9.87	-0.61	88	50	9,145
3 Yr Avg	---	---	---	---	---	---
5 Yr Avg	---	---	---	---	---	---
10 Yr Avg	---	---	---	---	---	---
15 Yr Avg	---	---	---	---	---	---

Operations

Address and Telephone	Vanguard Fin Ctr. P.O. Box 2600
	Valley Forge, PA 19482
	800-662-7447 / 610-669-1000
Advisor	Wellington Management
Subadvisor	None
Distributor	Vanguard Group
States Available	All plus PR,VI,GU
Report Grade	B+
Income Distrib	Paid Quarterly
* Date of Inception	05-15-92
Fiscal Year End	January

Historical Profile

Return	---
Risk	---
Rating	
	Not Rated

			1992	1993	1994	History
78%	78%	83%				Average % Stocks Held in Portfolio

1983	1984	1985	1986	1987	1988	1989	1990	1991	1992	1993	1994	History
---	---	---	---	---	---	---	---	---	10.95	11.63	9.94	NAV
---	---	---	---	---	---	---	---	---	12.16 *	15.06	-8.55	Total Return %
---	---	---	---	---	---	---	---	---	3.64 *	5.00	-9.87	+/- S&P 500
---	---	---	---	---	---	---	---	---	---	0.62	-0.61	+/- S&P Util
---	---	---	---	---	---	---	---	---	2.44	5.01	5.16	Income Return %
---	---	---	---	---	---	---	---	---	9.72	10.05	-13.71	Capital Return %
---	---	---	---	---	---	---	---	---	---	28	88	Total Rtn % Rank All
---	---	---	---	---	---	---	---	---	---	42	50	Total Rtn % Rank Obj
---	---	---	---	---	---	---	---	---	0.24	0.56	0.59	Income $
---	---	---	---	---	---	---	---	---	0.02	0.40	0.12	Capital Gains $
---	---	---	---	---	---	---	---	---	0.45	0.42		Expense Ratio %
---	---	---	---	---	---	---	---	---	4.70	4.82		Income Ratio %
---	---	---	---	---	---	---	---	---	---	---	46	Turnover Rate %
---	---	---	---	---	---	---	---	---	312.3	774.1	560.5	Net Assets ($mil)

Investment Style History Equity

Growth of $10,000

|||| Value of Fund ($000)
—	Value of Index ($000) S&P 500
▼	Manager Change
▽	Partial Manager Change
►	Mgr Unknown After
◄	Mgr Unknown Before

Performance Quartile (Within Objective)

Risk Analysis

Time Period	Load-Adj Return %	Risk % Rank [1] All	Obj	Morningstar [2] Return	Morningstar Risk	Morningstar Risk-Adj Rating
1 Yr	-8.55					
3 Yr	---	---	---	---	---	---
5 Yr	---	---	---	---	---	---
10 Yr	---	---	---	---	---	---
Average Historical Rating ---				---		

[1] = low, 100 = high [2] 1.00 = Equity Avg [3] 1.00 = 90-day T-bill return

Other Measures

	Standard S&P 500	Best Fit
Standard Deviation	---	Alpha	---	---
Mean	---	Beta	---	---
Sharpe Ratio	---	R-Squared	---	---

Investment Style

	Stock Portfolio Avg	Relative S&P 500
Price/Earnings Ratio	13.9	0.75
Price/Book Ratio	1.8	0.54
5 Yr Earnings Gr %	-1.7	-0.31
Return on Assets %	4.2	0.56
Debt % Total Cap	42.1	1.49
Med Mkt Cap ($mil)	4694	0.36

Style Value Blend Growth
Size Large Med Small

Diversification Value for Portfolio Types

Large Cap: Small Cap: Bond: Balanced: Diversified:

Expenses & Fees

Sales Fees	0.00% front
	0.00% deferred
	0.00% 12b-1
Management Fee	0.30% max./0.10% min.
3-,5-,10-yr Expense Projections	$13, $24, $53
Annual Brokerage Cost	0.16%

Min Initial Purchase	$3000 (Addt'l: $100)
Min IRA Purchase	$500 (Addt'l: $100)
Min Auto Invest Plan	$3000 (Systematic Inv: $50)

Portfolio 12-31-94

Share Chg (08-94) 000	Amount 000	Total Stocks: 61 / Total Fixed-Income: 38	Value $000	% Net Assets
134	638	US West	22715	4.05
-50	674	GTE	20476	3.65
-184	530	NYNEX	19485	3.48
0	383	Bell Atlantic	19054	3.40
-40	360	AT & T	18085	3.23
-100	627	Pacific Gas & Electric	15276	2.73
-30	447	DQE	13228	2.36
220	220	BellSouth	11908	2.12
449	449	Unicom	10778	1.92
0	572	Comsat	10650	1.90
90	530	Pinnacle West Capital	10471	1.87
-52	322	Southern New England Telecom	10335	1.84
-330	256	Southwestern Bell	10324	1.84
-100	525	Sierra Pacific Resources	9907	1.77
0	308	BCE	9882	1.76
0	337	Pacific Telesis Group	9613	1.72
40	351	General Public Utilities	9206	1.64
40	407	Entergy	8894	1.59
0	9000	US Treasury Note 5.5%	8096	1.44
199	294	Equitable Resources	7980	1.42
-120	301	Detroit Edison	7864	1.40
20	265	Public Service Colorado	7773	1.39
100	212	Consolidated Natural Gas	7522	1.34
321	321	CINergy	7499	1.34
250	250	Sprint	6906	1.23

Composition % 09-30-94

Cash	1.6	Preferreds	0.0
Stocks	78.2	Convertibles	0.0
Bonds	20.2	Other	0.0

Tax Analysis

	Tax-Adj Historical Return %	% Pretax Return
3 Yr Avg	---	---
5 Yr Avg	---	---
10 Yr Avg	---	---
Potential Capital Gain Exposure (% of assets)		-15%

Most Similar Funds in MF500

Fund lacks three-year record

Index Allocation

	% of Stocks
S&P 500	58.4
S&P MidCap 400	18.7
U.S. Small Cap	17.5
Foreign	5.4

Sector Weightings

	% of Stocks	Relative S&P 500
Utilities	83.7	6.75
Energy	4.1	0.40
Financials	5.7	0.54
Industrial Cyclicals	0.0	0.00
Consumer Durables	2.6	0.41
Consumer Staples	0.0	0.00
Services	2.4	0.29
Retail	0.0	0.00
Health	0.0	0.00
Technology	1.7	0.18

Vanguard STAR

	Ticker	Load	NAV	Yield	SEC Yield	Assets	Objective
	VGSTX	None	12.60	4.0%	4.58%	3766.2	Balanced

Vanguard STAR Fund seeks total return.

The fund normally allocates its assets in the following proportions: 47.5% in value-oriented equity funds, namely the Vanguard/Windsor and Vanguard/Windsor II Funds; 25% in fixed-income, split between Vanguard F/I GNMA and Vanguard F/I Long Term Corporate Bond; and 15% in growth-oriented funds, including Vanguard Explorer, Vanguard/Primecap, Vanguard U.S. Growth, and Vanguard/Morgan Growth. The fund also invests 12.5% in Vanguard Prime Portfolio. If at any time the fund owns 10% of the shares in its individual equity components, it has the option to invest in Vanguard Index Trust 500.

Manager's Investment Style

This fund of funds has a very simple strategy--low expenses, low turnover, and a consistent approach. Of the assets divided between the seven Vanguard funds in the portfolio, 50% are devoted to value-oriented large-cap stock funds. The remainder is split between bond funds, growth-stock funds, and cash. With no expense ratio of its own and an extremely low turnover rate, the fund preserves almost all real returns for its shareholders.

Fund Manager(s)

Multiple Managers

Manager Experience

	Dates Managed	Invest Obj	Std Dev	+/- Index
Not available.				

Historical Profile

Return	Average
Risk	Below Average
Rating	★★★ Neutral

Equity Average % Stocks Held in Portfolio: 46% 72% 62% 75% 62% 62% 62% 61%

Investment Style History

Growth of $10,000

‖‖ Value of Fund ($000)
— Value of Index ($000) S&P 500
▼ Manager Change
▽ Partial Manager Change
◄— Mgr Unknown After
—◄ Mgr Unknown Before

Performance Quartile (Within Objective)

	1983	1984	1985	1986	1987	1988	1989	1990	1991	1992	1993	1994	History
	---	---	11.45	11.34	9.98	11.12	12.04	10.72	12.30	12.88	13.41	12.60	NAV
	---	---	15.04 *	13.93	1.66	19.04	18.70	-3.63	24.29	10.42	10.97	-0.29	Total Return %
	---	---	-5.61 *	-4.75	-3.60	2.43	-12.98	-0.51	-6.19	2.81	0.91	-1.60	+/- S&P 500
	---	---	---	-1.32	-1.09	11.16	4.16	-12.57	8.29	3.18	1.22	2.63	+/- LB Aggregate
	---	---	0.54	8.31	7.41	7.28	6.80	6.13	5.73	4.19	3.67	3.96	Income Return %
	---	---	14.50	5.62	-5.75	11.75	11.90	-9.76	18.57	6.24	7.30	-4.25	Capital Return %
	---	---	---	61	45	16	38	66	37	20	60	22	Total Rtn % Rank All
	---	---	---	63	58	4	54	79	51	18	50	16	Total Rtn % Rank Obj
	---	---	0.05	0.86	0.85	0.69	0.77	0.73	0.62	0.51	0.47	0.52	Income $
	---	---	0.00	0.71	0.75	0.03	0.38	0.16	0.37	0.18	0.40	0.25	Capital Gains $
	---	---	0.00	0.00	0.00	0.00	0.00	0.00	0.00	0.00	0.00	0.00	Expense Ratio %
	---	---	7.04	5.44	6.08	5.87	6.42	6.65	5.48	4.36	3.67	3.29	Income Ratio %
	---	---	0	17	21	7	12	11	3	3	6		Turnover Rate %
	---	---	112.3	454.9	567.4	681.5	949.2	1038.3	1574.3	2482.8	3628.2	3766.2	Net Assets ($mil)

Performance 12-31-94

	1st Qtr	2nd Qtr	3rd Qtr	4th Qtr	Total
1987	11.09	1.32	1.39	-10.92	1.66
1988	7.60	6.17	2.56	1.60	19.04
1989	5.49	6.99	5.80	-0.59	18.70
1990	-2.33	2.81	-10.71	7.49	-3.63
1991	12.31	0.00	5.13	5.27	24.29
1992	0.24	3.24	3.01	3.58	10.42
1993	4.74	1.29	3.95	0.63	10.97
1994	-3.06	1.05	2.33	-0.53	-0.29

Bear Market Performance

Decile Rank (5-year period)

Worst | | | | | | | | | | Best

	Worst 3 Mo Period 1985-89	Worst 3 Mo Period 1990-94
Vanguard STAR	---	-11.15
+/- S&P 500	---	2.69
+/- Best Fit Index : S&P 500	---	2.69

Trailing Returns

	Total Return %	+/- S&P 500	+/- LB Aggregate	% Rank All	% Rank Obj	Growth of $10,000
3 Mo	-0.53	-0.52	-0.91	35	35	9,947
6 Mo	1.78	-3.08	0.79	28	45	10,178
1 Yr	-0.29	-1.60	2.63	22	16	9,971
3 Yr Avg	6.91	0.64	2.36	27	26	12,218
5 Yr Avg	7.91	-0.78	0.29	34	51	14,635
10 Yr Avg	---	---	---	---	---	---
15 Yr Avg	---	---	---	---	---	---

Operations

Address and Telephone	Vanguard Fin Ctr. P.O. Box 2600 Valley Forge, PA 19482 800-662-7447 / 610-669-1000
Advisor	Vanguard Group
Subadvisor	None
Distributor	Vanguard Group
States Available	All plus PR,VI,GU
Report Grade	B+
Income Distrib	Paid Semiannually
* Date of Inception	03-29-85
Fiscal Year End	December

Risk Analysis

Time Period	Load-Adj Return %	Risk % Rank [1] All	Risk % Rank [1] Obj	Morningstar [2] Return	Morningstar [2] Risk	Morningstar Risk-Adj Rating
1 Yr	-0.29					
3 Yr	6.91	40	19	0.99 [3]	0.63	★★★★
5 Yr	7.91	53	52	0.79 [3]	0.77	★★★
10 Yr	---	---	---	---	---	

Average Historical Rating (82 months)   3.8 ★s

[1] 1 = low, 100 = high   [2] 1.00 = Hybrid Avg   [3] 1.00 = 90-day T-bill return

Other Measures

		Standard S&P 500	Best Fit S&P 500
Standard Deviation	5.50	Alpha	1.5	1.5
Mean	6.85	Beta	0.65	0.65
Sharpe Ratio	0.60	R-Squared	86	86

Investment Style

Stocks

	Port Avg	Rel S&P 500
Price/Earnings Ratio	17.3	0.94
Price/Book Ratio	2.6	0.76
5 Yr Earnings Gr %	3.0	0.54
Med Mkt Cap ($mil)	9448	0.73

Not Available

Bonds

Avg Effective Duration	6.7 Yrs
Avg Effective Maturity	12.0 Yrs
Avg Credit Quality	AA
Avg Weighted Coupon	0.00%

Not Available

Diversification Value for Portfolio Types

Large Cap: None	Small Cap: Medium	Bond: Medium	Balanced: None	Diversified: Low

Portfolio 12-31-94

Total Stocks: 7
Total Fixed-Income: 2

Share Chg (10-94)000	Amount 000		Date of Maturity	Value $000	% Net Assets
7250	99372	Vanguard/Windsor II Fund		1572071	41.74
-8527	472382	Vanguard Prime Portfolio Fd		472382	12.54
	49281	Vanguard F/I GNMA Fund		472109	12.54
	58560	Vanguard F/I L-T Corp Fund		471411	12.52
1680	20812	Vanguard/Windsor Fund		262029	6.96
153	13193	Vanguard US Growth Fund		202251	5.37
130	5695	Vanguard/Primecap Fund		113781	3.02
0	9556	Vanguard/Morgan Growth Fund		108555	2.88
128	2325	Vanguard Explorer Fund		99658	2.65

Index Allocation

	% of Stocks
S&P 500	85.6
S&P MidCap 400	3.7
U.S. Small Cap	8.7
Foreign	2.3

Composition % 11-10-94

Cash	17.9	Preferreds	0.0
Stocks	56.6	Convertibles	0.0
Bonds	25.5	Other	0.0

Tax Analysis

	Tax-Adj Historical Return %	% Pretax Return
3 Yr Avg	4.85	68.9
5 Yr Avg	5.63	68.0
10 Yr Avg	---	---
Potential Capital Gain Exposure (% of assets)		1%

Most Similar Funds in MF500

MFS Total Return A	Strong Fit
George Putnam of Boston A	Strong Fit
IDS Mutual	Strong Fit

Bond Credit Analysis 11-10-94

% of Bonds

US Govt	59	BB	0
AAA	8	B	0
AA	7	Below B	0
A	19	NR/NA	0
BBB	7		

Stock Sector Weightings

	% of Stocks	Relative S&P 500
Utilities	7.7	0.62
Energy	12.9	1.27
Financials	21.8	2.06
Industrial Cyclicals	10.8	0.66
Consumer Durables	4.8	0.77
Consumer Staples	10.6	0.85
Services	7.3	0.90
Retail	6.0	1.03
Health	9.2	1.06
Technology	8.9	0.97

Min Initial Purchase	$500 (Addt'l: $100)
Min IRA Purchase	$500 (Addt'l: $100)
Min Auto Invest Plan	$500 (Systematic Inv: $50)

Expenses & Fees

Sales Fees	0.00% front
	0.00% deferred
	0.00% 12b-1
Management Fee	Provided at cost.
3-,5-,10-yr Expense Projections	$12, $21, $48
Annual Brokerage Cost	---

 **1995 Mutual Fund 500**

Vanguard U.S. Growth

	Ticker	Load	NAV	Yield	SEC Yield	Assets	Objective
	VWUSX	None	15.33	1.2%	1.64%	2109.3	Growth

Vanguard U.S. Growth Portfolio seeks capital appreciation; income is incidental.

The fund invests primarily in the equity securities of seasoned U.S. companies. It seeks common stocks selling at attractive prices.

On Sept. 30, 1985, the Ivest Fund divided into this fund and Vanguard World International Growth Fund. The Ivest Fund invested in U.S. securities before Sept. 30, 1981, and both domestic and foreign stocks after that date.

Lincoln Capital became the fund's advisor in 1987. From Sept. 1985 until May 3, 1993, the fund was named Vanguard World Fund U.S. Growth Portfolio.

Manager's Investment Style

This management team rises and falls with the growth market, picking the best 40 to 60 classic large-cap stocks. Criteria for selection include liquidity, consistent earnings and revenue growth, as well as above-average profitability. The fund is heavily weighted in health, retail, and technology sectors. Management will liquidate one fourth of a position if earnings estimates fall by more than 5%.

Fund Manager(s)

J. Parker Hall III, since 08-87. Birthdate: 06-33. Swarthmore C. 1955 MBA, Harvard 1957
David Fowler, since 1987. Birthdate: 1951. Loyola U. of Chicago 1971 MBA, Northwestern U. 1972

Manager Experience	Dates Managed	Invest Obj	Std Dev	+/- Index
Not available.				

Historical Profile
Return	Average
Risk	Average
Rating	★★★
	Neutral

Investment Style History
Equity
Average % Stocks Held in Portfolio

Growth of $10,000
- IIII Value of Fund ($000)
- — Value of Index ($000) S&P 500
- ▼ Manager Change
- ▽ Partial Manager Change
- ► Mgr Unknown After
- ◄ Mgr Unknown Before

Performance Quartile (Within Objective)

1983	1984	1985	1986	1987	1988	1989	1990	1991	1992	1993	1994	History
10.01	9.49	11.69	10.32	6.96	7.51	10.21	10.49	15.20	15.36	14.93	15.33	NAV
23.94	1.20	36.52	7.84	-6.07	8.76	37.70	4.60	46.76	2.76	-1.45	3.88	Total Return %
1.47	-5.06	4.79	-10.84	-11.33	-7.85	6.01	7.72	16.27	-4.86	-11.50	2.57	+/- S&P 500
0.48	-1.85	3.96	-8.26	-8.43	-9.18	8.52	10.79	12.55	-6.22	-12.73	3.95	+/- Wilshire 5000
2.32	3.19	2.76	2.75	3.31	0.86	1.74	1.86	1.86	1.18	1.35	1.20	Income Return %
21.62	-1.99	33.76	5.09	-9.39	7.90	35.95	2.74	44.90	1.58	-2.80	2.68	Capital Return %
27	62	9	91	91	69	5	44	9	85	99	6	Total Rtn % Rank All
38	33	10	89	90	78	11	5	19	83	96	10	Total Rtn % Rank Obj
0.24	0.31	0.26	0.28	0.31	0.06	0.13	0.19	0.19	0.18	0.21	0.18	Income $
1.86	0.33	0.82	1.94	3.26	0.00	0.00	0.00	0.00	0.08	0.00	0.00	Capital Gains $
1.07	0.88	1.04	0.80	0.65	0.88	0.95	0.74	0.56	0.49	0.49	0.52	Expense Ratio %
2.16	2.53	2.10	2.27	2.41	1.23	1.44	1.77	1.82	1.52	1.50	1.30	Income Ratio %
95	70	61	44	142	38	48	49	30	24	37	47	Turnover Rate %
182.4	180.4	211.3	161.6	135.0	132.2	198.2	355.9	978.1	1813.9	1847.2	2109.3	Net Assets ($mil)

Performance 12-31-94

	1st Qtr	2nd Qtr	3rd Qtr	4th Qtr	Total
1987	18.70	-0.57	2.38	-22.27	-6.07
1988	3.59	5.41	0.00	-0.40	8.76
1989	8.26	9.10	14.66	1.68	37.70
1990	0.59	12.76	-15.63	9.31	4.60
1991	20.31	-1.35	8.11	14.37	46.76
1992	-4.93	-1.11	4.48	4.61	2.76
1993	-2.99	-2.28	0.62	3.33	-1.45
1994	-2.81	0.48	4.60	1.70	3.88

Bear Market Performance

Decile Rank (5-year period)

Worst — Best

	Worst 3 Mo Period 1985-89	Worst 3 Mo Period 1990-94
Vanguard U.S. Growth	-29.93	-15.92
+/- S&P 500	-0.34	-2.07
+/- Best Fit Index : S&P 500	-0.34	-2.07

Trailing Returns

	Total Return %	+/- S&P 500	+/- Wil 5000	% Rank All	% Rank Obj	Growth of $10,000
3 Mo	1.70	1.72	2.47	4	7	10,170
6 Mo	6.38	1.52	1.75	8	23	10,638
1 Yr	3.88	2.57	3.95	6	10	10,388
3 Yr Avg	1.70	-4.56	-4.91	93	82	10,520
5 Yr Avg	10.06	1.37	1.24	17	29	16,150
10 Yr Avg	12.83	-1.55	-1.03	29	52	33,446
15 Yr Avg	13.49	-0.99	-0.48	31	47	66,776

Risk Analysis

Time Period	Load-Adj Return %	Risk % Rank [1] All	Risk % Rank [1] Obj	Morningstar [2] Return	Morningstar [2] Risk	Morningstar Risk-Adj Rating
1 Yr	3.88					
3 Yr	1.70	74	41	-0.53 [3]	0.84	★★
5 Yr	10.06	72	33	1.37 [3]	0.86	★★★★
10 Yr	12.83	72	46	1.03	0.93	★★★
Average Historical Rating (109 months)					3.2	★s

[1] 1 = low, 100 = high [2] 1.00 = Equity Avg [3] 1.00 = 90-day T-bill return

Other Measures

				Standard S&P 500	Best Fit S&P 500
Standard Deviation	7.90	Alpha		-3.9	-3.9
Mean	2.00	Beta		0.84	0.84
Sharpe Ratio	-0.19	R-Squared		71	71

Investment Style

	Stock Portfolio Avg	Relative S&P 500	Style Value Blend Growth
Price/Earnings Ratio	19.8	1.07	
Price/Book Ratio	4.8	1.41	
5 Yr Earnings Gr %	12.8	2.31	
Return on Assets %	10.3	1.37	
Debt % Total Cap	22.5	0.80	
Med Mkt Cap ($mil)	21177	1.63	

Diversification Value for Portfolio Types

Large Cap: Low	Small Cap: Medium	Bond: High	Balanced: Low	Diversified: Medium

Portfolio 12-31-94

Total Stocks: 51
Total Fixed-Income: 0

Share Chg (11-94)000	Amount 000		Value $000	% Net Assets
0	2173	General Electric	110823	5.25
-33	1920	Coca-Cola	98880	4.69
709	4260	Wal-Mart Stores	90525	4.29
0	1469	Automatic Data Processing	85937	4.07
0	1325	Procter & Gamble	82150	3.89
43	1106	FNMA	80600	3.82
-45	801	American International Group	78498	3.72
0	949	Gillette	70938	3.36
0	1357	FHLMC	68529	3.25
65	1013	Intel	64452	3.06
0	820	Pfizer	63345	3.00
0	1602	General Motors Cl E	61677	2.92
41	1199	AT & T	60250	2.86
58	1642	PepsiCo	59523	2.82
144	1996	McDonald's	58383	2.77
0	872	Minnesota Mining & Mfg	46543	2.21
21	432	Hewlett-Packard	43146	2.05
111	1165	Chemical Banking	41794	1.98
0	1083	cisco Systems	37905	1.80
27	1157	Abbott Laboratories	37747	1.79
30	511	AMP	37175	1.76
75	1239	Morton International	35312	1.67
0	761	Home Depot	35006	1.66
0	720	Walt Disney	33210	1.57
0	989	Toys 'R' Us	30165	1.43

Composition % 11-30-94

Cash	8.4	Preferreds	0.0
Stocks	91.6	Convertibles	0.0
Bonds	0.0	Other	0.0

Index Allocation
	% of Stocks
S&P 500	91.1
S&P MidCap 400	3.9
U.S. Small Cap	2.6
Foreign	3.1

Tax Analysis

	Tax-Adj Historical Return %	% Pretax Return
3 Yr Avg	1.19	69.6
5 Yr Avg	9.52	93.6
10 Yr Avg	10.49	73.0
Potential Capital Gain Exposure (% of assets)		12%

Most Similar Funds in MF500
Dreyfus Appreciation	Strong Fit
Dreyfus	Fair Fit
AIM Weingarten	Fair Fit

Sector Weightings
	% of Stocks	Relative S&P 500
Utilities	4.5	0.36
Energy	1.1	0.11
Financials	15.0	1.42
Industrial Cyclicals	12.7	0.78
Consumer Durables	0.0	0.00
Consumer Staples	16.5	1.32
Services	7.1	0.88
Retail	10.8	1.85
Health	13.1	1.51
Technology	19.2	2.09

Operations

Address and Telephone	Vanguard Fin Ctr. P.O. Box 2600 Valley Forge, PA 19482 800-662-7447 / 610-669-1000
Advisor	Lincoln Capital Management
Subadvisor	None
Distributor	Vanguard Group
States Available	All plus PR,VI,GU
Report Grade	A
Income Distrib	Paid Annually
Date of Inception	01-06-59
Fiscal Year End	August

Min Initial Purchase	$3000 (Addt'l: $100)
Min IRA Purchase	$500 (Addt'l: $100)
Min Auto Invest Plan	$3000 (Systematic Inv: $50)

Expenses & Fees
Sales Fees	0.00% front
	0.00% deferred
	0.00% 12b-1
Management Fee	0.40% flat fee
3-,5-,10-yr Expense Projections	$17, $29, $65
Annual Brokerage Cost	---

Vanguard/Wellesley Income

	Ticker	Load	NAV	Yield	SEC Yield	Assets	Objective
	VWINX	None	17.05	6.4%	7.11%	5680.6	Income

Vanguard/Wellesley Income Fund seeks current income consistent with reasonable risk.

The fund invests in both fixed-income securities and common stocks. Fixed-income securities normally account for approximately 60% of fund assets and may include government and corporate bonds and preferred stocks. Bond holdings are usually rated no lower than BBB. The balance of the fund's assets may be invested in common stocks chosen primarily for their income characteristics.

Prior to May 3, 1993, the fund was named Wellesley Income Fund.

Manager's Investment Style

Management devotes 60% to 70% of assets to bonds, while investing the balance in equities. The fund is always invested in long-term bonds, as its effective maturity of more than 15 years illustrates. Management attempts to fight off the interest-rate sensitivity of these bonds by focusing on the credit quality of new investments. On the equity side, management only purchases stocks with a 35% yield premium to the S&P 500.

Fund Manager(s)

Earl E. McEvoy, since 10-82. Birthdate: 03-48.
BA, Dartmouth C. 1970 MBA, Columbia U. 1972

Manager Experience

	Dates Managed	Invest Obj	Std Dev	+/- Index
Earl E. McEvoy				
Vanguard Preferred Stock	10/82 - 12/94	I	7.41	-4.13
Vanguard F/I Hi-Yld Corp	01/84 - 12/94	CY	6.34	-0.14

Performance 12-31-94

	1st Qtr	2nd Qtr	3rd Qtr	4th Qtr	Total
1987	3.79	-2.48	-1.52	-1.60	-1.92
1988	5.47	3.43	2.80	1.31	13.61
1989	3.41	8.77	3.50	3.88	20.93
1990	-2.03	2.80	-3.79	7.09	3.76
1991	5.25	1.03	6.93	6.92	21.57
1992	-3.43	5.31	5.57	1.22	8.67
1993	6.83	3.00	5.11	-0.87	14.65
1994	-4.47	-0.35	0.74	-0.35	-4.44

Bear Market Performance

Decile Rank (5-year period)

Worst ———————————————— Best

	Worst 3 Mo Period 1985-89	Worst 3 Mo Period 1990-94
Vanguard/Wellesley Income	-5.79	-6.17
+/- S&P 500	-8.65	-0.42
+/- Best Fit Index : LB L-T	1.89	3.22

Trailing Returns

	Total Return %	+/- S&P 500	+/- LB Aggregate	% Rank All	% Rank Obj	Growth of $10,000
3 Mo	-0.35	-0.33	-0.73	31	19	9,965
6 Mo	0.39	-4.48	-0.61	49	42	10,039
1 Yr	-4.44	-5.75	-1.52	58	51	9,556
3 Yr Avg	5.99	-0.28	1.44	34	39	11,907
5 Yr Avg	8.47	-0.22	0.85	28	35	15,018
10 Yr Avg	11.80	-2.58	1.86	40	14	30,516
15 Yr Avg	13.09	-1.39	2.28	38	25	63,287

Operations

Address and Telephone	Vanguard Fin Ctr. P.O. Box 2600
	Valley Forge, PA 19482
	800-662-7447 / 610-669-1000
Advisor	Wellington Management
Subadvisor	None
Distributor	Vanguard Group
States Available	All plus PR,VI,GU
Report Grade	B+
Income Distrib	Paid Quarterly
Date of Inception	07-01-70
Fiscal Year End	December

Historical Profile

Return	Average
Risk	Below Average
Rating	★★★★ Above Average

71	42	55	58	62	55	60	60

Investment Style History
Fixed Income
Income Rtn % Rank Obj

Growth of $10,000

- IIII Value of Fund ($000)
- — Value of Index ($000) LB L-T
- ▼ Manager Change
- ▽ Partial Manager Change
- ► Mgr Unknown After
- ◄ Mgr Unknown Before

Performance Quartile
(Within Objective)

1983	1984	1985	1986	1987	1988	1989	1990	1991	1992	1993	1994	History
12.66	13.28	15.31	16.27	14.57	15.26	16.82	16.02	18.08	18.16	19.24	17.05	NAV
18.60	16.64	27.41	18.34	-1.92	13.61	20.93	3.76	21.57	8.67	14.65	-4.44	Total Return %
-3.86	10.38	-4.32	-0.34	-7.18	-3.00	-10.75	6.87	-8.92	1.06	4.59	-5.75	+/- S&P 500
10.23	1.49	5.29	3.09	-4.68	5.74	6.39	-5.19	5.57	1.43	4.90	-1.52	+/- LB Aggregate
11.50	11.74	11.27	8.90	6.34	8.88	8.99	8.06	8.71	7.04	6.37	5.84	Income Return %
7.11	4.90	16.14	9.44	-8.26	4.74	11.94	-4.31	12.86	1.63	8.28	-10.28	Capital Return %
45	3	35	30	75	34	33	47	42	38	30	58	Total Rtn % Rank All
25	1	21	18	52	38	10	32	60	42	37	51	Total Rtn % Rank Obj
1.31	1.37	1.38	1.33	1.04	1.23	1.31	1.30	1.27	1.21	1.14	1.11	Income $
0.00	0.00	0.10	0.47	0.38	0.00	0.24	0.08	0.00	0.21	0.40	0.24	Capital Gains $
0.70	0.71	0.60	0.58	0.49	0.51	0.45	0.45	0.40	0.35	0.33	0.35	Expense Ratio %
10.23	10.68	9.36	7.74	7.83	8.14	7.68	7.77	7.08	6.50	5.79	5.94	Income Ratio %
43	36	20	32	41	20	11	19	29	21	21	31	Turnover Rate %
105.4	114.6	224.0	510.1	495.0	567.1	787.8	1021.9	1934.1	3177.7	6011.5	5680.6	Net Assets ($mil)

Risk Analysis

Time Period	Load-Adj Return %	Risk % Rank All[1]	Risk % Rank Obj[1]	Morningstar[2] Return	Morningstar[2] Risk	Morningstar Risk-Adj Rating
1 Yr	-4.44					
3 Yr	5.99	48	81	0.71[3]	0.70	★★★★
5 Yr	8.47	46	64	0.93[3]	0.57	★★★★
10 Yr	11.80	36	35	1.02	0.53	★★★★

Average Historical Rating (109 months)   4.4 ★s

[1] = low, 100 = high   [2]1.00 = Hybrid Avg   [3]1.00 = 90-day T-bill return

Other Measures

			Standard S&P 500	Best Fit LB L-T
Standard Deviation	6.28	Alpha	0.8	1.0
Mean	6.03	Beta	0.58	0.75
Sharpe Ratio	0.40	R-Squared	53	85

Investment Style

Stocks	Port Avg	Rel S&P 500
Price/Earnings Ratio	17.3	0.93
Price/Book Ratio	1.9	0.56
5 Yr Earnings Gr %	-0.4	-0.07
Med Mkt Cap ($mil)	7530	0.58

Style
V B G

Bonds	
Avg Effective Duration	7.3 Yrs
Avg Effective Maturity	15.7 Yrs
Avg Credit Quality	AA
Avg Weighted Coupon	7.26%

Maturity S I L

Diversification Value for Portfolio Types

Large Cap: Low	Small Cap: High	Bond: None	Balanced: Low	Diversified: Medium

Portfolio 12-31-94

Total Stocks: 87
Total Fixed-Income: 192

Share Chg (10-94)000	Amount 000		Date of Maturity	Value $000	% Net Assets
	392320	GNMA 6.5%	10-15-24	341765	6.02
	225000	US Treasury Bond 7.25%	05-15-16	208055	3.66
	129489	GNMA 7%	05-15-24	117028	2.06
	100000	US Treasury Bond 8.125%	08-15-19	101328	1.78
	100000	US Treasury Bond 7.125%	02-15-23	91000	1.60
0	100000	US Treasury Note 5.75%	08-15-03	86906	1.53
0	1404	Texaco		84076	1.48
0	3209	CoreStates Financial		83424	1.47
0	887	Mobil		74721	1.32
0	660	Royal Dutch Petroleum		70896	1.25
50	1540	BankAmerica		60830	1.07
	61769	GNMA 7.5%	08-15-22	58057	1.02
0	1027	Bankers Trust New York		56842	1.00
140	1004	El DuPont de Nemours		56498	0.99
0	518	Atlantic Richfield		52707	0.93
0	1432	NYNEX		52618	0.93
0	877	Bristol-Myers Squibb		50756	0.89
0	2029	KeyCorp		50726	0.89
0	1930	Pacific Gas & Electric		47049	0.83
0	820	JP Morgan		45900	0.81

Index Allocation

	% of Stocks
S&P 500	80.1
S&P MidCap 400	6.8
U.S. Small Cap	10.8
Foreign	5.8

Composition % 10-31-94

Cash	1.0	Preferreds	0.0
Stocks	38.0	Convertibles	1.0
Bonds	60.0	Other	0.0

Tax Analysis

	Tax-Adj Historical Return %	% Pretax Return
3 Yr Avg	3.20	52.1
5 Yr Avg	5.73	64.0
10 Yr Avg	8.44	60.9
Potential Capital Gain Exposure (% of assets)		-6%

Most Similar Funds in MF500

Stagecoach Asset Alloc A	Strong Fit
Vanguard Asset Allocation	Strong Fit
Vanguard F/I L/T Corp Bond	Strong Fit

Bond Credit Analysis 10-31-94

% of Bonds

US Govt	32	BB	0
AAA	12	B	0
AA	18	Below B	0
A	26	NR/NA	0
BBB	12		

Stock Sector Weightings

	% of Stocks	Relative S&P 500
Utilities	24.9	2.01
Energy	19.9	1.96
Financials	29.4	2.78
Industrial Cyclicals	12.4	0.76
Consumer Durables	0.3	0.05
Consumer Staples	2.6	0.21
Services	3.5	0.43
Retail	2.5	0.44
Health	4.5	0.52
Technology	0.0	0.00

Expenses & Fees

Sales Fees	0.00% front
	0.00% deferred
	0.00% 12b-1
Management Fee	0.15% max./0.05% min.
3-,5-,10-yr Expense Projections	$11, $19, $42
Annual Brokerage Cost	0.05%

Min Initial Purchase

Min Initial Purchase	$3000 (Addt'l: $100)
Min IRA Purchase	$500 (Addt'l: $50)
Min Auto Invest Plan	$3000 (Systematic Inv: $50)

MORNINGSTAR 1995 Mutual Fund 500

Vanguard/Wellington

	Ticker	Load	NAV	Yield	SEC Yield	Assets	Objective
	VWELX	None	19.39	4.5%	4.96%	8809.4	Balanced

Vanguard/Wellington Fund seeks conservation of capital and reasonable income.

The fund typically invests 60% to 70% of its assets in common stocks. The balance may be invested in preferred stocks and debt securities. The amount held in each class varies according to business, economic, and market conditions. The fund may invest up to 10% of its assets in foreign securities.

Prior to May 3, 1993, the fund was named Wellington Fund. The performance fee is contingent on preceding 36 months' performance; the fund must outperform the index (65% S&P 500, 35% Salomon Brothers High Grade Index) by at least 6%.

Manager's Investment Style

Management's strategy has withstood the test of time. 65% of assets are invested in large-cap, low-multiple stocks. Such value plays help to reduce the overall price risk of the portfolio. The remainder of the portfolio is filled with investment-grade long bonds. Management is willing to accept the high interest-rate risk that such a long portfolio represents, looking instead toward future bond-market rallies. This strategy, combined with low expenses, has given investors consistent returns.

Fund Manager(s)

Vincent Bajakian CFA, since 10-72. Birthdate: 06-30. BA, Queens C. 1951 MBA, New York U. 1953

Manager Experience

	Dates Managed	Invest Obj	Std Dev	+/- Index
Not available.				

Historical Profile
Return	Above Average
Risk	Average
Rating	★★★★ Above Average

Investment Style History
Equity
Average % Stocks Held in Portfolio

71% 65% 63% 70% 61% 58% 59% 64%

Growth of $10,000
|||| Value of Fund ($000)
— Value of Index ($000)
S&P 500
▼ Manager Change
▽ Partial Manager Change
► Mgr Unknown After
◄ Mgr Unknown Before

Performance Quartile (Within Objective)

1983	1984	1985	1986	1987	1988	1989	1990	1991	1992	1993	1994	History
12.46	12.32	14.50	15.85	15.15	16.01	17.78	16.26	18.81	19.16	20.40	19.39	NAV
23.57	10.70	28.53	18.40	2.28	16.11	21.61	-2.81	23.65	7.93	13.52	-0.49	Total Return %
1.11	4.44	-3.21	-0.28	-2.98	-0.50	-10.08	0.31	-6.84	0.31	3.46	-1.80	+/- S&P 500
15.20	-4.45	6.40	3.15	-0.48	8.23	7.07	-11.75	7.65	0.68	3.77	2.43	+/- LB Aggregate
8.16	7.87	7.94	6.54	5.84	6.42	6.44	5.74	6.26	5.19	4.93	4.32	Income Return %
15.42	2.83	20.59	11.87	-3.57	9.69	15.17	-8.55	17.38	2.74	8.59	-4.81	Capital Return %
28	22	31	30	40	24	32	64	38	46	36	23	Total Rtn % Rank All
14	28	46	42	44	21	32	72	55	42	27	20	Total Rtn % Rank Obj
0.91	0.92	0.92	0.94	0.98	0.96	1.02	1.01	0.96	0.94	0.92	0.88	Income $
0.44	0.48	0.30	0.34	0.14	0.58	0.60	0.00	0.23	0.16	0.38	0.03	Capital Gains $
0.64	0.59	0.64	0.53	0.43	0.47	0.42	0.43	0.35	0.33	0.34	0.39	Expense Ratio %
7.09	7.52	6.84	5.88	5.56	5.88	5.77	5.99	5.39	4.98	4.55	4.21	Income Ratio %
30	27	27	25	27	28	30	33	35	24	34	41	Turnover Rate %
617.3	604.2	778.5	1134.8	1331.4	1526.9	2099.2	2449.2	3818.4	5559.2	8075.8	8809.4	Net Assets ($mil)

Performance 12-31-94

	1st Qtr	2nd Qtr	3rd Qtr	4th Qtr	Total
1987	13.96	2.05	0.36	-12.37	2.28
1988	6.98	5.18	1.12	2.05	16.11
1989	6.15	6.85	5.51	1.63	21.61
1990	-3.40	3.01	-9.48	7.90	-2.81
1991	9.42	1.23	5.33	5.97	23.65
1992	-1.61	3.83	2.94	2.63	7.93
1993	5.20	2.82	2.86	2.03	13.52
1994	-3.86	1.48	3.39	-1.34	-0.49

Bear Market Performance

Decile Rank (5-year period)

Worst ———————————— Best

	Worst 3 Mo Period 1985-89	Worst 3 Mo Period 1990-94
Vanguard/Wellington	-19.61	-10.21
+/- S&P 500	9.97	3.64
+/- Best Fit Index : S&P 500	9.97	3.64

Trailing Returns

	Total Return %	+/- S&P 500	+/- LB Aggregate	% Rank All	% Rank Obj	Growth of $10,000
3 Mo	-1.34	-1.32	-1.71	53	63	9,866
6 Mo	2.00	-2.86	1.01	26	40	10,200
1 Yr	-0.49	-1.80	2.43	23	20	9,951
3 Yr Avg	6.83	0.56	2.28	28	27	12,192
5 Yr Avg	7.94	-0.75	0.31	34	43	14,652
10 Yr Avg	12.40	-1.98	2.46	33	28	32,197
15 Yr Avg	13.76	-0.72	2.96	28	20	69,198

Operations

Address and Telephone	Vanguard Fin Ctr. P.O. Box 2600
	Valley Forge, PA 19482
	800-662-7447 / 610-669-1000
Advisor	Wellington Management
Subadvisor	None
Distributor	Vanguard Group
States Available	All plus PR,VI,GU
Report Grade	A-
Income Distrib	Paid Quarterly
Date of Inception	07-01-29
Fiscal Year End	November

Risk Analysis

Time Period	Load-Adj Return %	Risk % Rank All	Risk % Rank Obj	Morningstar Return	Morningstar Risk	Morningstar Risk-Adj Rating
1 Yr	-0.49					
3 Yr	6.83	53	57	0.97[3]	0.75	★★★★
5 Yr	7.94	56	69	0.79[3]	0.84	★★★
10 Yr	12.40	44	67	1.15	0.79	★★★★

Average Historical Rating (109 months) 4.1 ★s

[1] = low, 100 = high [2] 1.00 = Hybrid Avg [3] 1.00 = 90-day T-bill return

Other Measures

		Standard S&P 500	Best Fit S&P 500
Standard Deviation	6.55	Alpha	1.1	1.1
Mean	6.84	Beta	0.76	0.76
Sharpe Ratio	0.51	R-Squared	84	84

Investment Style

Stocks	Port Avg	Rel S&P 500
Price/Earnings Ratio	16.8	0.91
Price/Book Ratio	2.5	0.74
5 Yr Earnings Gr %	-0.4	-0.08
Med Mkt Cap ($mil)	9716	0.75

Style: V B G / Size L M S

Bonds	
Avg Effective Duration	7.7 Yrs
Avg Effective Maturity	17.8 Yrs
Avg Credit Quality	AA
Avg Weighted Coupon	7.64%

Maturity: S I L / Quality H M L

Diversification Value for Portfolio Types

Large Cap: None	Small Cap: High	Bond: Low	Balanced: None	Diversified: Low

Portfolio 12-31-94

Total Stocks: 85
Total Fixed-Income: 137

Share Chg (10-94)000	Amount 000		Date of Maturity	Value $000	% Net Assets
	273725	GNMA 6.5%	06-15-24	238010	2.70
	230000	US Treasury Bond 7.5%	11-15-16	218284	2.48
0	2571	Pfizer		198579	2.25
	200000	US Treasury Bond 7.25%	05-15-16	184938	2.10
0	3589	General Electric		183054	2.08
0	1200	General Re		148500	1.69
75	4725	Bank of New York		137025	1.56
	150000	US Treasury Note 6.25%	02-15-03	135656	1.54
	148500	US Treasury Bond 7.125%	02-15-23	135135	1.53
0	2000	Exxon		121500	1.38
140	2915	Citicorp		120608	1.37
93	2093	El DuPont de Nemours		117731	1.34
189	3489	First Bank System		116009	1.32
100	2700	General Motors		114075	1.29
50	1150	Xerox		113850	1.29
250	2250	Kimberly-Clark		113625	1.29
56	1306	ALCOA		113106	1.28
50	2629	Northrop Grumman		110410	1.25
0	2000	Johnson & Johnson		109500	1.24
100	4300	Banc One		109113	1.24

Index Allocation
	% of Stocks
S&P 500	84.2
S&P MidCap 400	6.7
U.S. Small Cap	2.2
Foreign	7.9

Composition % 10-31-94
Cash	3.3	Preferreds	0.0
Stocks	64.6	Convertibles	0.0
Bonds	32.1	Other	0.0

Tax Analysis
	Tax-Adj Historical Return %	% Pretax Return
3 Yr Avg	4.80	69.0
5 Yr Avg	5.89	71.2
10 Yr Avg	9.65	68.2
Potential Capital Gain Exposure (% of assets)		8%

Most Similar Funds in MF500
American Mutual	Strong Fit
IDS Mutual	Strong Fit
Overland Exp Asset Alloc A	Strong Fit

Min Initial Purchase / Expenses

Min Initial Purchase	$3000 (Addt'l: $100)
Min IRA Purchase	$500 (Addt'l: $50)
Min Auto Invest Plan	$3000 (Systematic Inv: $50)

Expenses & Fees
Sales Fees	
	0.00% front
	0.00% deferred
	0.00% 12b-1
Management Fee	0.13% max./0.04% min.+(-)0.02%P
3-,5-,10-yr Expense Projections	$11, $19, $43
Annual Brokerage Cost	0.05%

Bond Credit Analysis 10-31-94
% of Bonds			
US Govt	38	BB	1
AAA	12	B	0
AA	15	Below B	0
A	23	NR/NA	0
BBB	11		

Stock Sector Weightings
	% of Stocks	Relative S&P 500
Utilities	4.4	0.36
Energy	14.3	1.41
Financials	21.6	2.05
Industrial Cyclicals	32.0	1.95
Consumer Durables	3.7	0.59
Consumer Staples	2.8	0.23
Services	6.2	0.76
Retail	3.7	0.63
Health	10.8	1.24
Technology	0.5	0.06

Vanguard/Windsor

	Ticker	Load	NAV	Yield	SEC Yield	Assets	Objective
	VWNDX	Clsd	12.59	3.3%	3.58%	10672.9	Growth/Inc.

Vanguard/Windsor Fund seeks long-term growth of capital and income; current income is secondary.

The fund invests primarily in equity securities selected on the basis of fundamental value. Key to the valuation process is the relationship of a company's underlying earning power and dividend payout to the market price of its stock. In addition to low price/earnings ratios, the fund looks for meaningful income yields.

On April 17, 1991, Vanguard High-Yield Stock Fund merged into this fund. Prior to May 17, 1993, the fund was named Windsor Fund.

Manager's Investment Style

John Neff, manager of this fund since 1964, will be retiring at the end of 1995. Throughout his career, Neff has been known as the quintessential value investor. He seeks misunderstood or ignored stocks that are capable of strong growth, and maintains a six- to 18-month time frame. He commonly holds concentrated stock and sector positions. He does not actively manage for yield, and the fund often carries a market-like payout.

Fund Manager(s)

John B. Neff, since 06-64. Birthdate: 1931. BBA, U. of Toledo MBA, Case Western Reserve U.

Manager Experience	Dates Managed	Invest Obj	Std Dev	+/- Index
John B. Neff				
Gemini II Inc	02/85 - 12/94	I	2.88	-0.63
Gemini II Cap	02/85 - 12/94	DE	23.63	-1.01

Performance 12-31-94

	1st Qtr	2nd Qtr	3rd Qtr	4th Qtr	Total
1987	16.27	6.17	0.77	-18.63	1.23
1988	10.17	13.19	1.92	1.26	28.70
1989	6.89	6.95	8.61	-7.36	15.03
1990	-2.91	1.37	-20.34	7.78	-15.50
1991	18.25	0.74	5.59	2.20	28.55
1992	4.27	5.55	-2.62	8.70	16.50
1993	8.87	1.40	7.36	0.72	19.37
1994	-1.80	3.79	1.14	-3.15	-0.15

Bear Market Performance

Decile Rank (5-year period)

Worst —————————————————— Best

	Worst 3 Mo Period 1985-89	Worst 3 Mo Period 1990-94
Vanguard/Windsor	-26.80	-22.18
+/- S&P 500	2.78	-8.34
+/- Best Fit Index : S&P 500	2.78	-8.34

Trailing Returns

	Total Return %	+/- S&P 500	+/- Wil 5000	% Rank All	% Rank Obj	Growth of $10,000
3 Mo	-3.15	-3.13	-2.38	84	87	9,685
6 Mo	-2.04	-6.90	-6.66	88	96	9,796
1 Yr	-0.15	-1.46	-0.08	21	42	9,985
3 Yr Avg	11.56	5.30	4.95	9	5	13,886
5 Yr Avg	8.57	-0.12	-0.25	27	33	15,083
10 Yr Avg	13.28	-1.10	-0.58	24	29	34,803
15 Yr Avg	16.13	1.65	2.16	7	2	94,241

Operations

Address and Telephone	Vanguard Fin Ctr. P.O. Box 2600
	Valley Forge, PA 19482
	800-662-7447 / 610-669-1000
Advisor	Wellington Management
Subadvisor	None
Distributor	Vanguard Group
States Available	All plus PR,VI,GU
Report Grade	A
Income Distrib	Paid Semiannually
Date of Inception	10-23-58
Fiscal Year End	October

Historical Profile

Return	Average
Risk	Average
Rating	★★★
	Closed

Average % Stocks Held in Portfolio: 82% 91% 83% 87% 73% 77% 78% 85%

Investment Style History
Equity

Growth of $10,000

||||| Value of Fund ($000)
— Value of Index ($000) S&P 500
▼ Manager Change
▽ Partial Manager Change
► Mgr Unknown After
◄ Mgr Unknown Before

Performance Quartile (Within Objective)

1983	1984	1985	1986	1987	1988	1989	1990	1991	1992	1993	1994	History
11.69	12.64	14.50	13.95	11.11	13.07	13.41	10.30	11.72	12.74	13.91	12.59	NAV
30.06	19.47	28.03	20.27	1.23	28.70	15.03	-15.50	28.55	16.50	19.37	-0.15	Total Return %
7.60	13.21	-3.71	1.60	-4.03	12.09	-16.66	-12.38	-1.93	8.88	9.31	-1.46	+/- S&P 500
6.60	16.43	-4.54	4.18	-1.14	10.76	-14.15	-9.32	-5.66	7.53	8.09	-0.08	+/- Wilshire 5000
6.50	6.83	6.49	5.94	6.77	5.62	5.71	5.79	5.34	4.27	2.84	3.28	Income Return %
23.56	12.64	21.54	14.33	-5.54	23.07	9.31	-21.29	23.21	12.23	16.53	-3.43	Capital Return %
10	1	33	19	49	4	46	93	29	8	18	21	Total Rtn % Rank All
10	2	46	20	55	4	87	96	49	6	7	42	Total Rtn % Rank Obj
0.70	0.76	0.79	0.85	0.87	0.63	0.75	0.74	0.57	0.49	0.37	0.44	Income $
1.03	0.48	0.74	2.59	2.21	0.55	0.85	0.32	0.84	0.38	0.89	0.86	Capital Gains $
0.67	0.63	0.53	0.52	0.43	0.46	0.41	0.37	0.30	0.26	0.40	0.45	Expense Ratio %
6.31	6.72	6.19	5.28	4.86	5.08	5.07	5.82	4.84	3.89	2.68	3.11	Income Ratio %
48	23	23	51	46	24	34	21	36	32	25	34	Turnover Rate %
1665.9	2337.6	3814.3	4893.8	4565.2	5826.1	8062.6	6523.8	7822.3	8832.6	10610.8	10672.9	Net Assets ($mil)

Risk Analysis

Time Period	Load-Adj Return %	Risk % Rank [1] All	Risk % Rank [1] Obj	Morningstar [2] Return	Morningstar [2] Risk	Morningstar Risk-Adj Rating
1 Yr	-0.15					
3 Yr	11.56	65	44	2.49 [3]	0.73	★★★★
5 Yr	8.57	81	93	0.96 [3]	0.98	★★★
10 Yr	13.28	70	84	1.12	0.92	★★★
Average Historical Rating (109 months)					4.3	★s

[1] = low, 100 = high   [2] 1.00 = Equity Avg   [3] 1.00 = 90-day T-bill return

Other Measures

				Standard S&P 500	Best Fit S&P 500
Standard Deviation	9.88	Alpha		5.3	5.3
Mean	11.48	Beta		0.98	0.98
Sharpe Ratio	0.81	R-Squared		62	62

Investment Style

	Stock Portfolio Avg	Relative S&P 500
Price/Earnings Ratio	16.0	0.87
Price/Book Ratio	1.5	0.44
5 Yr Earnings Gr %	4.3	0.78
Return on Assets %	3.2	0.43
Debt % Total Cap	37.5	1.33
Med Mkt Cap ($mil)	5153	0.40

Style Value Blend Growth / Size Large Med Small

Diversification Value for Portfolio Types

Large Cap: Low	Small Cap: Medium	Bond: High	Balanced: Low	Diversified: Low

Tax Analysis

	Tax-Adj Historical Return %	% Pretax Return
3 Yr Avg	8.74	73.6
5 Yr Avg	5.55	61.0
10 Yr Avg	9.19	56.8
Potential Capital Gain Exposure (% of assets)		0%

Most Similar Funds in MF500

American Leaders A	Weak Fit
Vanguard/Windsor II	Weak Fit
United Income	Weak Fit

Portfolio 12-31-94

Share Chg (11-94)000	Amount 000	Total Stocks: 73 Total Fixed-Income: 4	Value $000	% Net Assets
0	15971	Citicorp	660808	6.19
0	13031	Chrysler	638529	5.98
1083	21372	Ford Motor	598427	5.61
0	5799	Atlantic Richfield	590089	5.53
	355	US Treasury Bond 12%	472040	4.42
0	8599	Aetna Life & Casualty	405208	3.80
0	6269	CIGNA	396483	3.71
0	24027	USX-Marathon Group	393445	3.69
0	6496	Bankers Trust New York	359695	3.37
0	8449	First Union	349569	3.28
0	9842	Burlington Resources	344467	3.23
0	3910	ALCOA	338660	3.17
0	8189	BankAmerica	323468	3.03
	240	US Treasury Bond 10.375%	285600	2.68
0	11221	Unicom	269316	2.52
0	5263	Reynolds Metals	257872	2.42
	245	US Treasury Note 7.25%	242590	2.27
0	6222	Golden West Financial	219340	2.06
1022	4838	NationsBank	218310	2.05
0	6010	Chemical Banking	215605	2.02
184	13257	Great Western Financial	212108	1.99
0	2903	Intel	184703	1.73
0	10859	HF Ahmanson	175104	1.64
492	7010	Advanced Micro Devices	174384	1.63
1043	7358	Allstate	173840	1.63

Composition % 09-30-94

Cash	7.0	Preferreds	0.0
Stocks	93.0	Convertibles	0.0
Bonds	0.0	Other	0.0

Index Allocation

	% of Stocks
S&P 500	88.8
S&P MidCap 400	3.4
U.S. Small Cap	6.8
Foreign	1.0

Sector Weightings

	% of Stocks	Relative S&P 500
Utilities	3.8	0.31
Energy	18.1	1.79
Financials	41.3	3.90
Industrial Cyclicals	11.0	0.67
Consumer Durables	14.0	2.26
Consumer Staples	0.0	0.00
Services	3.7	0.45
Retail	2.2	0.38
Health	0.0	0.00
Technology	6.0	0.65

Min Initial Purchase	Closed (Addt'l: $100)
Min IRA Purchase	$500 (Addt'l: $100)
Min Auto Invest Plan	$10000 (Systematic Inv: $50)

Expenses & Fees

Sales Fees	0.00% front
	0.00% deferred
	0.00% 12b-1
Management Fee	0.35% max./0.15% min.+(-)0.10%P
3-,5-,10-yr Expense Projections	$13, $22, $51
Annual Brokerage Cost	0.09%

MORNINGSTAR 1995 Mutual Fund 500

Vanguard/Windsor II

	Ticker	Load	NAV	Yield	SEC Yield	Assets	Objective
	VWNFX	None	15.82	3.4%	3.61%	7959.0	Growth/Inc.

Vanguard/Windsor II seeks long-term growth of capital and income; current income is secondary.

The fund invests primarily in undervalued, income-producing stocks, characterized by above-average income yields and below-average price/earnings ratios relative to the stock market. Barrow Hanley Mewhinney & Strauss supervises approximately 75% of assets, Equinox and Tukman each supervise approximately 9%, and Vanguard supervises the remainder.

Prior to May 17, 1993, the fund was named Windsor II. Equinox and Tukman replaced Invesco as advisors in Oct. 1991.

Manager's Investment Style

Management seeks value in large-cap issues, and targets yield premiums similiar to that of the S&P 500, but at discount multiples. Management tends to stockpile issues in favorable sectors, with financials, consumer staples, and energy stocks as favorites.

Fund Manager(s)

James P. Barrow et al. Birthdate: 08-40 BS, U. of South Carolina 1962

Manager Experience

	Dates Managed	Invest Obj	Std Dev	+/- Index
Not available.				

Historical Profile

Return	Average
Risk	Average
Rating	★★★
	Neutral

Investment Style History
Equity
Average % Stocks Held in Portfolio

Growth of $10,000

- ‖‖ Value of Fund ($000)
- — Value of Index ($000) S&P 500
- ▼ Manager Change
- ▽ Partial Manager Change
- ► Mgr Unknown After
- ◄ Mgr Unknown Before

Performance Quartile (Within Objective)

	1983	1984	1985	1986	1987	1988	1989	1990	1991	1992	1993	1994	History
	---	---	10.99	12.39	10.75	12.81	14.96	12.46	14.89	15.91	17.04	15.82	NAV
	---	---	11.12 *	21.41	-2.14	24.73	27.83	-9.99	28.70	11.99	13.60	-1.17	Total Return %
	---	---	-3.29 *	2.73	-7.40	8.12	-3.86	-6.87	-1.79	4.37	3.55	-2.48	+/- S&P 500
	---	---	---	5.31	-4.50	6.78	-1.35	-3.80	-5.51	3.02	2.32	-1.10	+/- Wilshire 5000
	---	---	1.22	3.71	5.05	5.56	5.70	5.12	4.95	3.57	3.20	3.32	Income Return %
	---	---	9.90	17.70	-7.19	19.16	22.13	-15.10	23.75	8.42	10.40	-4.49	Capital Return %
	---	---	---	15	76	6	17	84	29	15	36	28	Total Rtn % Rank All
	---	---	---	17	82	8	28	86	48	19	31	56	Total Rtn % Rank Obj
	---	---	0.11	0.43	0.61	0.57	0.74	0.73	0.61	0.52	0.51	0.55	Income $
	---	---	0.00	0.52	0.80	0.00	0.61	0.28	0.44	0.22	0.50	0.47	Capital Gains $
	---	---	0.80	0.65	0.49	0.58	0.53	0.52	0.48	0.41	0.39	0.39	Expense Ratio %
	---	---	4.56	4.33	4.11	4.94	5.29	4.93	4.51	3.72	3.11	3.26	Income Ratio %
	---	---	---	50	46	25	22	20	41	23	26	24	Turnover Rate %
	---	---	133.0	901.6	1235.0	1502.6	2298.8	2334.5	3626.6	5407.4	7616.3	7959.0	Net Assets ($mil)

Performance 12-31-94

	1st Qtr	2nd Qtr	3rd Qtr	4th Qtr	Total
1987	16.38	2.17	4.13	-20.97	-2.14
1988	9.12	7.18	4.29	2.26	24.73
1989	9.52	7.83	8.98	-0.68	27.83
1990	-4.41	1.41	-15.05	9.31	-9.99
1991	17.90	-1.73	4.85	5.95	28.70
1992	0.13	3.98	3.99	3.44	11.99
1993	6.66	0.85	5.38	0.22	13.60
1994	-4.46	2.62	2.85	-1.98	-1.17

Bear Market Performance

Decile Rank (5-year period)

Worst ▬▬ Best

	Worst 3 Mo Period 1985-89	Worst 3 Mo Period 1990-94
Vanguard/Windsor II	---	-15.47
+/- S&P 500	---	-1.63
+/- Best Fit Index : S&P 500	---	-1.63

Trailing Returns

	Total Return %	+/- S&P 500	+/- Wil 5000	% Rank All	% Rank Obj	Growth of $10,000
3 Mo	-1.98	-1.97	-1.21	68	63	9,802
6 Mo	0.81	-4.06	-3.82	41	79	10,081
1 Yr	-1.17	-2.48	-1.10	28	56	9,884
3 Yr Avg	7.93	1.67	1.32	21	22	12,574
5 Yr Avg	7.81	-0.88	-1.00	36	52	14,567
10 Yr Avg	---	---	---	---	---	---
15 Yr Avg	---	---	---	---	---	---

Risk Analysis

Time Period	Load-Adj Return %	Risk % Rank¹ All	Risk % Rank¹ Obj	Morningstar² Return	Morningstar Risk	Morningstar Risk-Adj Rating
1 Yr	-1.17					
3 Yr	7.93	62	35	1.31³	0.69	★★★★
5 Yr	7.81	70	68	0.76³	0.83	★★★
10 Yr	---	---	---	---		

Average Historical Rating (79 months) 3.7 ★s

¹ 1 = low, 100 = high ² 1.00 = Equity Avg ³ 1.00 = 90-day T-bill return

Other Measures

			Standard S&P 500	Best Fit S&P 500
Standard Deviation	7.77	Alpha	1.8	1.8
Mean	7.96	Beta	0.91	0.91
Sharpe Ratio	0.57	R-Squared	86	86

Investment Style

	Stock Portfolio Avg	Relative S&P 500
Price/Earnings Ratio	16.3	0.88
Price/Book Ratio	2.3	0.69
5 Yr Earnings Gr %	-0.8	-0.14
Return on Assets %	5.3	0.70
Debt % Total Cap	32.8	1.16
Med Mkt Cap ($mil)	10213	0.79

Style Value Blend Growth — Size Large Med Small

Diversification Value for Portfolio Types

Large Cap: None	Small Cap: Medium	Bond: Medium	Balanced: None	Diversified: Low

Portfolio 12-31-94

Total Stocks: 180
Total Fixed-Income: 1

Share Chg (11-94)000	Amount 000		Value $000	% Net Assets
0	5626	Anheuser-Busch	286207	3.60
96	3579	Bristol-Myers Squibb	207158	2.60
0	3180	Exxon	193179	2.43
0	5369	Chase Manhattan	184544	2.32
-328	5092	Chemical Banking	182690	2.30
0	3030	Amoco	179149	2.25
0	3092	Philip Morris	177813	2.23
-672	4839	PepsiCo	175399	2.20
0	2778	American Home Products	174294	2.19
0	5125	Phillips Petroleum	167831	2.11
-257	3502	First Chicago	167210	2.10
0	5137	Travelers	166941	2.10
0	3525	Aetna Life & Casualty	166101	2.09
3	2551	Raytheon	162932	2.05
-204	3511	Sears Roebuck	161520	2.03
-734	5447	American Express	160687	2.02
0	2675	Texaco	160136	2.01
0	5591	Pacific Telesis Group	159341	2.00
0	2426	Eli Lilly	159213	2.00
0	3959	BankAmerica	156388	1.96
0	3491	JC Penney	155790	1.96
-50	3051	Schlumberger	153684	1.93
2675	6628	Entergy	144985	1.82
0	5163	Ford Motor	144553	1.82
15	2990	Eastman Kodak	142782	1.79

Composition % 09-30-94

				% of Stocks
Cash	7.0	Preferreds	0.0	
Stocks	93.0	Convertibles	0.0	
Bonds	0.0	Other	0.0	

Index Allocation

	% of Stocks
S&P 500	94.7
S&P MidCap 400	1.3
U.S. Small Cap	2.8
Foreign	1.6

Tax Analysis

	Tax-Adj Historical Return %	% Pretax Return
3 Yr Avg	6.01	74.3
5 Yr Avg	5.69	69.9
10 Yr Avg	---	---
Potential Capital Gain Exposure (% of assets)		4%

Most Similar Funds in MF500

Washington Mutual Investors	Strong Fit
Vanguard Equity-Income	Strong Fit
Investment Comp of America	Strong Fit

Sector Weightings

	% of Stocks	Relative S&P 500
Utilities	10.1	0.82
Energy	15.9	1.57
Financials	22.3	2.11
Industrial Cyclicals	11.0	0.67
Consumer Durables	3.3	0.53
Consumer Staples	13.3	1.06
Services	5.4	0.66
Retail	6.4	1.10
Health	9.4	1.08
Technology	3.0	0.33

Operations

Address and Telephone	Vanguard Fin Ctr. P.O. Box 2600 Valley Forge, PA 19482 800-662-7447 / 610-669-1000
Advisor	Barrow/Vanguard's Core Mngmnt
Subadvisor	None
Distributor	Vanguard Group
States Available	All plus PR,VI,GU
Report Grade	A
Income Distrib	Paid Semiannually
* Date of Inception	06-24-85
Fiscal Year End	October

Min Initial Purchase	$3000 (Addt'l: $100)
Min IRA Purchase	$500 (Addt'l: $50)
Min Auto Invest Plan	$3000 (Systematic Inv: $50)

Expenses & Fees

Sales Fees	0.00% front
	0.00% deferred
	0.00% 12b-1
Management Fee	0.63% max./0.12% min.+(-)0.03%P
3-,5-,10-yr Expense Projections	$13, $22, $49
Annual Brokerage Cost	0.10%

Vista Capital Growth A

	Ticker	Load	NAV	Yield	SEC Yield	Assets	Objective
	VCAGX	4.75%	30.53	0.3%	0.73%	543.2	Growth

Vista Capital Growth Fund - Class A seeks long-term capital growth; dividend income is incidental.

The fund ordinarily invests at least 80% of its assets in common stocks. It seeks both domestic and foreign companies that may benefit from changes brought about by social, economic, demographic, or legislative developments. The fund typically emphasizes small- and medium-size companies.

Shares of the fund can be purchased at the NAV by registered investment advisers and fee-based financial planners. Class A shares have front loads; Class B shares have deferred loads, higher 12b-1 fees, and conversion features. On July 19, 1993, Olympus Growth Fund merged into this fund.

Manager's Investment Style

Management invests in stocks that are cheap relative to cash flows, yet show signs of building momentum. High earnings suprises serve as a flag to buy. Management has also been disciplined in making profits, selling stocks at peak prices and then repurchasing at discounts. Sometimes it uses large cash holdings to help temper risk.

Historical Profile
Return High
Risk Average
Rating ★★★★★ Highest

Investment Style History
Equity
Average % Stocks Held in Portfolio

| | | 45% | 64% | 91% | 75% | 79% | 83% |

Growth of $10,000

|||| Value of Fund ($000)
— Value of Index ($000)
Wil 4500
▼ Manager Change
▽ Partial Manager Change
► Mgr Unknown After
◄ Mgr Unknown Before

Performance Quartile (Within Objective)

Fund Manager(s)

Mark A. Tincher CFA(1981), since 05-91.
Birthdate: 10-55. BBA, U. of Toledo 1977 MBA, U. of Toledo 1978
David Klassen CFA(1987), since 01-93. Birthdate:
07-58. BA, Franklin and Marshall C. 1980

Manager Experience	Dates Managed	Invest Obj	Std Dev	+/- Index
Mark A. Tincher				
Vista Growth & Income A	09/91 - 12/94	GI	10.08	1.27
Vista Equity-Income	07/93 - 12/94	EI	8.45	-4.51

	1983	1984	1985	1986	1987	1988	1989	1990	1991	1992	1993	1994	History
	---	---	---	---	10.00	11.47	15.39	14.15	24.16	26.97	31.71	30.53	NAV
	---	---	---	---	0.00 *	23.23	44.41	-5.98	70.74	12.95	20.18	-1.31	Total Return %
	---	---	---	---	22.19 *	6.62	12.73	-2.86	40.26	5.33	10.12	-2.63	+/- S&P 500
	---	---	---	---		5.29	15.24	0.21	36.54	3.98	8.89	-1.24	+/- Wilshire 5000
	---	---	---	---	0.00	1.58	4.34	2.08	0.00	0.23	0.22	0.29	Income Return %
	---	---	---	---	0.00	21.65	40.07	-8.06	70.74	12.72	19.95	-1.60	Capital Return %
	---	---	---	---		8	2	73	2	13	17	29	Total Rtn % Rank All
	---	---	---	---		12	3	62	1	23	16	45	Total Rtn % Rank Obj
	---	---	---	---	0.00	0.18	0.56	0.34	0.00	0.06	0.07	0.09	Income $
	---	---	---	---	0.00	0.68	0.60	0.00	0.00	0.26	0.63	0.68	Capital Gains $
	---	---	---	---	0.00	0.00	0.00	1.04	1.27	1.40	1.49	1.49	Expense Ratio %
	---	---	---	---	0.00	1.55	3.87	2.82	-0.09	0.32	0.12	0.33	Income Ratio %
	---	---	---	---		229	189	139	83	67	43	60	Turnover Rate %
	---	---	---	---	0.5	0.6	4.6	5.3	11.4	55.5	263.7	543.2	Net Assets ($mil)

Performance 12-31-94

	1st Qtr	2nd Qtr	3rd Qtr	4th Qtr	Total
1987	---	---	---	0.00	0.00 *
1988	4.50	11.63	0.34	5.28	23.23
1989	18.05	12.70	11.62	-2.75	44.41
1990	-1.62	5.50	-18.11	10.62	-5.98
1991	26.78	-3.12	19.04	16.77	70.74
1992	2.98	-6.32	3.99	12.59	12.95
1993	7.30	1.73	9.36	0.67	20.18
1994	-1.36	-3.00	6.46	-3.12	-1.31

Bear Market Performance

Decile Rank (5-year period)

Worst ▬▬ Best

	Worst 3 Mo Period 1985-89	Worst 3 Mo Period 1990-94
Vista Capital Growth A	---	-18.51
+/- S&P 500	---	-4.66
+/- Best Fit Index : Wil 4500	---	0.90

Trailing Returns

	Total Return %	+/- S&P 500	+/- Wil 5000	% Rank All	% Rank Obj	Growth of $10,000
3 Mo	-3.12	-3.11	-2.35	84	81	9,688
6 Mo	3.14	-1.73	-1.49	20	60	10,314
1 Yr	-1.31	-2.63	-1.24	29	45	9,869
3 Yr Avg	10.24	3.97	3.62	13	17	13,396
5 Yr Avg	16.55	7.86	7.73	3	4	21,505
10 Yr Avg	---	---	---	---	---	---
15 Yr Avg	---	---	---	---	---	---

Operations

Address and Telephone	Vista Svc Center P.O. Box 419392 Kansas City, MO 64179 800-648-4782
Advisor	Chase Manhattan Bank
Subadvisor	None
Distributor	Vista Broker-Dealer Services
States Available	All plus PR
Report Grade	C
Income Distrib	Paid Semiannually
* Date of Inception	09-23-87
Fiscal Year End	October

Min Initial Purchase	$2500 (Addt'l: $100)
Min IRA Purchase	$1000 (Addt'l: $100)
Min Auto Invest Plan	$2500 (Systematic Inv: $100)

Expenses & Fees

Sales Fees	4.75% front
	0.00% deferred
	0.25% 12b-1
Management Fee	0.40% flat fee, 0.05%A
3-,5-,10-yr Expense Projections	$93, $125, $218
Annual Brokerage Cost	0.26%

Risk Analysis

Time Period	Load-Adj Return %	Risk % Rank [1] All	Risk % Rank [1] Obj	Morningstar [2] Return	Morningstar Risk	Morningstar Risk-Adj Rating
1 Yr	-6.00					
3 Yr	8.46	78	53	1.48 [3]	0.91	★★★★
5 Yr	15.42	81	66	3.04 [3]	0.99	★★★★★
10 Yr	---	---	---	---	---	---

Average Historical Rating (52 months) 5.0 ★s

[1] 1 = low, 100 = high [2] 1.00 = Equity Avg [3] 1.00 = 90-day T-bill return

Other Measures

		Standard S&P 500	Best Fit Wil 4500
Standard Deviation	10.61	Alpha	4.3	2.4
Mean	10.35	Beta	0.89	1.04
Sharpe Ratio	0.64	R-Squared	45	91

Investment Style

	Portfolio Avg	Relative S&P 500
Price/Earnings Ratio	16.0	0.86
Price/Book Ratio	2.2	0.66
5 Yr Earnings Gr %	8.5	1.53
Return on Assets %	6.7	0.89
Debt % Total Cap	31.8	1.12
Med Mkt Cap ($mil)	750	0.06

Style
Value Blend Growth
Size Large Med Small

Diversification Value for Portfolio Types

Large Cap: Medium Small Cap: None Bond: High Balanced: Low Diversified: Medium

Portfolio 11-30-94

Share Chg (04-94) 000	Amount 000	Total Stocks: 194 Total Fixed-Income: 12	Value $000	% Net Assets
	9668	Goldman Sachs FRN	9607	1.77
170	262	FHP International	7070	1.30
92	161	Triton Energy	5821	1.07
58	242	Black & Decker	5801	1.07
102	121	Danaher	5634	1.04
262	262	Comdisco	5597	1.03
242	242	CMS Energy	5378	0.99
322	322	LTV	5076	0.93
3	141	SunAmerica	5005	0.92
110	201	Standard Federal Bank (MI)	4985	0.92
104	242	Kellwood	4955	0.91
57	149	Lancaster Colony	4918	0.90
119	242	Amcast Industrial	4894	0.90
161	161	DQE	4874	0.90
6	121	GATX	4834	0.89
36	105	Computer Sciences	4831	0.89
92	161	Signet Banking	4814	0.88
69	161	HealthCare COMPARE	4773	0.88
24	161	Caldor	4693	0.86
181	181	Diamond Shamrock	4668	0.86
46	161	Informix	4632	0.85
206	206	CINergy	4584	0.84
60	60	Michigan National	4570	0.84
322	322	Countrywide Credit Industry	4552	0.84
121	121	AnnTaylor Stores	4532	0.83

Composition % 12-31-94

Cash	2.0	Preferreds	0.0
Stocks	97.0	Convertibles	0.0
Bonds	1.0	Other	0.0

Tax Analysis

	Tax-Adj Historical Return %	% Pretax Return
3 Yr Avg	9.62	93.4
5 Yr Avg	15.98	95.4
10 Yr Avg	---	---
Potential Capital Gain Exposure (% of assets)		0%

Most Similar Funds in MF500

Vanguard Index Extended Mkt	Strong Fit
Columbia Special	Fair Fit
Meridian	Fair Fit

Index Allocation

	% of Stocks
S&P 500	14.2
S&P MidCap 400	27.5
U.S. Small Cap	56.4
Foreign	3.0

Sector Weightings

	% of Stocks	Relative S&P 500
Utilities	4.3	0.34
Energy	6.9	0.68
Financials	14.9	1.41
Industrial Cyclicals	15.9	0.97
Consumer Durables	14.4	2.31
Consumer Staples	0.7	0.05
Services	10.4	1.27
Retail	7.9	1.36
Health	6.2	0.71
Technology	18.6	2.03

MORNINGSTAR **1995 Mutual Fund 500**

Vista Growth & Income A

	Ticker	Load	NAV	Yield	SEC Yield	Assets	Objective
	VGRIX	4.75%	29.09	1.8%	2.02%	1340.8	Growth/Inc.

Vista Growth and Income Fund - Class A seeks long-term capital appreciation; current income is secondary.

The fund normally invests at least 80% of its assets in common stocks issued by companies representing a broad range of market capitalizations. It selects undervalued securities that display relatively low price/earnings or price/book ratios, or underlying asset values that are not fully reflected in the current market price.

Shares of the fund can be purchased at the NAV by registered investment advisors and fee-based financial planners. On July 19, 1993, Olympus Growth Fund merged into this fund.

Manager's Investment Style

Management follows a custom quantitative model for picking stocks, targeting points that include growth and value variables and macroeconomic trends. Tincher holds up to 20% cash as a defense against market weakness.

Fund Manager(s)

Mark A. Tincher CFA(1981), since 09-91.
Birthdate: 10-55. BBA, U. of Toledo 1977   MBA, U. of Toledo 1978

Manager Experience	Dates Managed	Invest Obj	Std Dev	+/- Index
Mark A. Tincher				
Vista Capital Growth A	05/91 - 12/94	G	14.38	9.27
Vista Equity-Income	07/93 - 12/94	EI	8.45	-4.51

Performance 12-31-94

	1st Qtr	2nd Qtr	3rd Qtr	4th Qtr	Total
1987	---	---	---	0.00	0.00 *
1988	7.22	24.92	6.59	-1.88	40.08
1989	9.04	17.75	14.26	6.91	56.85
1990	3.38	8.93	-13.65	3.01	0.17
1991	33.98	1.82	8.45	7.52	59.07
1992	5.95	-3.13	2.33	9.60	15.11
1993	5.71	3.30	2.59	0.86	13.00
1994	-2.68	-1.39	3.06	-2.35	-3.41

Bear Market Performance

Decile Rank (5-year period)

Worst ———————————— Best

	Worst 3 Mo Period 1985-89	Worst 3 Mo Period 1990-94
Vista Growth & Income A	---	-13.82
+/- S&P 500	---	0.02
+/- Best Fit Index : Wil 4500	---	5.58

Trailing Returns

	Total Return %	+/- S&P 500	+/- Wil 5000	% Rank All	% Rank Obj	Growth of $10,000
3 Mo	-2.35	-2.33	-1.58	75	75	9,765
6 Mo	0.64	-4.22	-3.98	44	82	10,064
1 Yr	-3.41	-4.73	-3.34	48	75	9,659
3 Yr Avg	7.90	1.64	1.29	22	22	12,562
5 Yr Avg	14.89	6.20	6.07	4	1	20,016
10 Yr Avg	---	---	---	---	---	---
15 Yr Avg	---	---	---	---	---	---

Operations

Address and Telephone	Vista Svc Center P.O. Box 419392 Kansas City, MO 64179 800-648-4782
Advisor	Chase Manhattan Bank
Subadvisor	None
Distributor	Vista Broker-Dealer Services
States Available	All plus PR
Report Grade	C
Income Distrib	Paid Quarterly
* Date of Inception	09-23-87
Fiscal Year End	October

Historical Profile

Return	Above Average
Risk	Below Average
Rating	★★★★
	Above Average

Investment Style History Equity

Average % Stocks Held in Portfolio

| | | --- | --- | 46% | 50% | 90% | 75% | 76% | 74% |

Growth of $10,000

||||| Value of Fund ($000)
— Value of Index ($000)
Wil 4500
▼ Manager Change
▽ Partial Manager Change
► Mgr Unknown After
◄ Mgr Unknown Before

Performance Quartile (Within Objective)

	1983	1984	1985	1986	1987	1988	1989	1990	1991	1992	1993	1994	History
	---	---	---	---	10.00	12.67	18.02	16.83	24.93	27.73	30.65	29.09	NAV
	---	---	---	---	0.00 *	40.08	56.85	0.17	59.07	15.11	13.00	-3.41	Total Return %
	---	---	---	---	22.19 *	23.47	25.16	3.28	28.59	7.49	2.94	-4.73	+/- S&P 500
	---	---	---	---	---	22.14	27.67	6.35	24.86	6.14	1.71	-3.34	+/- Wilshire 5000
	---	---	---	---	0.00	2.62	5.05	3.66	1.05	1.28	1.16	1.68	Income Return %
	---	---	---	---	0.00	37.46	51.80	-3.50	58.02	13.82	11.84	-5.09	Capital Return %
	---	---	---	---	---	1	1	55	5	10	41	48	Total Rtn % Rank All
	---	---	---	---	---	1	1	18	2	8	35	75	Total Rtn % Rank Obj
	---	---	---	---	0.00	0.32	0.71	0.66	0.23	0.32	0.33	0.52	Income $
	---	---	---	---	0.00	1.02	1.06	0.57	1.59	0.62	0.35	0.00	Capital Gains $
	---	---	---	---	---	0.00	0.00	1.09	1.25	1.43	1.39	1.40	Expense Ratio %
	---	---	---	---	---	2.64	4.56	3.65	1.24	1.19	1.07	1.60	Income Ratio %
	---	---	---	---	---	109	319	160	103	56	41	57	Turnover Rate %
	---	---	---	---	---	1.2	9.1	18.9	45.4	190.2	1032.0	1340.8	Net Assets ($mil)

Risk Analysis

Time Period	Load-Adj Return %	Risk % Rank All	Obj	Morningstar Return	Morningstar Risk	Morningstar Risk-Adj Rating
1 Yr	-8.00					
3 Yr	6.16	61	31	0.77 [3]	0.67	★★★
5 Yr	13.78	62	33	2.49 [3]	0.75	★★★★★
10 Yr	---					
Average Historical Rating (52 months)				4.9		★ s

[1] = low, 100 = high   [2] 1.00 = Equity Avg   [3] 1.00 = 90-day T-bill return

Other Measures

			Standard S&P 500	Best Fit Wil 4500
Standard Deviation	8.10	Alpha	2.2	1.2
Mean	7.96	Beta	0.78	0.74
Sharpe Ratio	0.55	R-Squared	59	80

Investment Style

	Stock Portfolio Avg	Relative S&P 500	Style
Price/Earnings Ratio	15.9	0.86	
Price/Book Ratio	2.6	0.76	
5 Yr Earnings Gr %	5.9	1.06	
Return on Assets %	5.8	0.77	
Debt % Total Cap	33.3	1.18	
Med Mkt Cap ($mil)	3641	0.28	

Diversification Value for Portfolio Types

Large Cap: Low	Small Cap: Low	Bond: High	Balanced: Low	Diversified: Low

---

Portfolio 11-30-94

Share Chg (10-94) 000	Amount 000	Total Stocks: 162 Total Fixed-Income: 43	Value $000	% Net Assets
	22232	FNMA 6.5%	19453	1.45
-2	200	Schering-Plough	14982	1.12
	13339	Aegon Cv 4.75%	13779	1.03
	13562	Time Warner Cv 8.75%	12917	0.96
-2	151	Mobil	12888	0.96
-2	156	Texas Instruments	11756	0.88
-2	200	United Technologies	11705	0.87
-3	267	Citicorp	11105	0.83
	1601	RJR Nabisco Cl C Cv Pfd 9.25%	10805	0.81
-4	356	American Express	10538	0.79
-1	89	General Re	10438	0.78
-3	267	Compaq Computer	10438	0.78
-1	111	American International Group	10185	0.76
-3	267	Varity	9938	0.74
-2	200	AT & T	9829	0.73
	10360	Renong Berhad Cv 2.5%	9816	0.73
-2	222	Chevron	9699	0.72
	222	Catellus Dev B Cv Pfd $3.625	9671	0.72
-1	133	Georgia-Pacific	9538	0.71
-3	267	PepsiCo	9438	0.70
-3	311	Echlin	9415	0.70
-4	356	American Stores	9382	0.70
-2	178	Conrail	9249	0.69
-3	281	Travelers	9234	0.69
-2	178	Tribune	8915	0.66

Composition % 12-31-94

Cash	5.0	Preferreds	0.0
Stocks	77.0	Convertibles	7.0
Bonds	11.0	Other	0.0

Tax Analysis

	Tax-Adj Historical Return %	% Pretax Return
3 Yr Avg	7.04	88.4
5 Yr Avg	13.36	87.1
10 Yr Avg	---	---
Potential Capital Gain Exposure (% of assets)	0%	

Most Similar Funds in MF500

Vanguard Index Extended Mkt	Strong Fit
Neuberger&Berman Partners	Fair Fit
Fidelity Stock Selector	Fair Fit

Index Allocation

	% of Stocks
S&P 500	76.2
S&P MidCap 400	12.7
U.S. Small Cap	7.8
Foreign	4.5

Sector Weightings

	% of Stocks	Relative S&P 500
Utilities	7.5	0.61
Energy	9.0	0.89
Financials	15.1	1.42
Industrial Cyclicals	20.6	1.26
Consumer Durables	10.8	1.73
Consumer Staples	4.4	0.35
Services	10.5	1.29
Retail	5.6	0.96
Health	4.8	0.55
Technology	11.8	1.29

Expenses & Fees

Min Initial Purchase	$2500 (Addt'l: $100)
Min IRA Purchase	$1000 (Addt'l: $100)
Min Auto Invest Plan	$250 (Systematic Inv: $200)

Sales Fees	4.75% front
	0.00% deferred
	0.25% 12b-1
Management Fee	0.40% flat fee, 0.05%A
3-,5-,10-yr Expense Projections	$90, $120, $207
Annual Brokerage Cost	0.23%

MORNINGSTAR   **1995 Mutual Fund 500**

Vista Tax-Free Income A

	Ticker	Load	NAV	Yield	SEC Yield	Assets	Objective
	VTFIX	4.50%	11.05	5.2%	5.45%	82.1	Muni Nat

Vista Tax-Free Income Fund - Class A seeks dividend income exempt from federal income taxes consistent with capital preservation.

The fund normally invests at least 80% of its assets in municipal obligations whose interest is exempt from federal taxes, including the Alternative Minimum Tax.

Shares of the fund can be purchased at the NAV by registered investment advisers and fee-based financial planners. Class A shares have front loads; Class B shares have deferred loads, higher 12b-1 fees, and conversion features. On July 19, 1993, Olympus National Tax-Free Fund merged into this fund.

Manager's Investment Style

This potentially risky fund has pulled in the reins. With its long duration, the fund has benefited from the falling rates of the last few years, but it has suffered in the face of rate hikes. In response, management has begun to barbell the portfolio in order to shorten duration to under eight years. One end will consist of bonds maturing in less than two years, while the other end will hold issues that mature within 12 to 16 years. The fund has also begun to invest in higher-quality bonds, while pulling out of its volatile solid-waste-recovery position.

Fund Manager(s)

Pamela Hunter, since 09-87. Birthdate: 12-53.
Business Admin./Finance, Edison State U.

Manager Experience	Dates Managed	Invest Obj	Std Dev	+/- Index
Pamela Hunter				
Vista NY Tax-Free Inc A	09/87 - 12/94	MY	5.47	-0.88
Vista CA Intermediate T/F	07/93 - 12/94	MC	4.36	0.70

Performance 12-31-94

	1st Qtr	2nd Qtr	3rd Qtr	4th Qtr	Total
1987	---	---	---	3.85	3.85 *
1988	1.91	2.10	3.42	2.64	10.44
1989	0.74	6.04	-1.09	4.17	10.07
1990	0.01	2.21	-0.19	5.10	7.22
1991	2.02	2.12	4.63	4.62	14.04
1992	0.19	5.57	3.57	3.01	12.83
1993	5.49	3.77	3.98	1.06	15.02
1994	-6.53	0.67	0.19	-2.03	-7.64

Bear Market Performance

Decile Rank (5-year period)

	Worst 3 Mo Period 1985-89	Worst 3 Mo Period 1990-94
Vista Tax-Free Income A	---	-7.42
+/- LB Aggregate	---	-2.49
+/- Best Fit Index : LB Muni	---	-1.66

Trailing Returns

	Total Return %	+/- LB Aggregate	+/- LB Muni	% Rank All	% Rank Obj	Growth of $10,000
3 Mo	-2.03	-2.41	-0.60	69	83	9,797
6 Mo	-1.85	-2.84	-0.60	86	84	9,816
1 Yr	-7.64	-4.72	-2.03	84	81	9,236
3 Yr Avg	6.23	1.68	1.36	32	4	11,987
5 Yr Avg	7.95	0.32	1.17	34	1	14,658
10 Yr Avg	---	---	---	---	---	---
15 Yr Avg	---	---	---	---	---	---

Operations

Address and Telephone	Vista Svc Center P.O. Box 419392
	Kansas City, MO 64179
	800-648-4782
Advisor	Chase Manhattan Bank
Subadvisor	None
Distributor	Vista Broker-Dealer Services
States Available	All
Report Grade	C
Income Distrib	Paid Monthly
* Date of Inception	09-08-87
Fiscal Year End	October

Historical Profile	
Return	Above Average
Risk	Above Average
Rating	★★★
	Neutral

1983	1984	1985	1986	1987	1988	1989	1990	1991	1992	1993	1994	History
				54	31	32	22	21	45	63		
---	---	---	---	10.19	10.44	10.65	10.66	11.21	11.65	12.57	11.05	NAV
---	---	---	---	3.85 *	10.44	10.07	7.22	14.04	12.83	15.02	-7.64	Total Return %
---	---	---	---		2.56	-4.48	-1.72	-1.96	5.59	5.27	-4.72	+/- LB Aggregate
---	---	---	---		0.28	-0.72	-0.08	1.90	4.02	2.75	-2.03	+/- LB Muni
---	---	---	---	1.95	7.45	7.52	7.13	7.35	6.70	5.72	4.45	Income Return %
---	---	---	---	1.90	2.99	2.55	0.09	6.70	6.13	9.30	-12.09	Capital Return %
---	---	---	---		58	73	19	62	13	28	84	Total Rtn % Rank All
---	---	---	---		58	32	9	4	1	4	81	Total Rtn % Rank Obj
---	---	---	---	0.20	0.73	0.75	0.72	0.74	0.71	0.64	0.57	Income $
---	---	---	---	0.00	0.05	0.06	0.00	0.16	0.24	0.15	0.00	Capital Gains $
---	---	---	---	0.00	0.00	0.00	0.12	0.04	0.00	0.23	0.48	Expense Ratio %
---	---	---	---	7.35	7.50	7.06	6.86	6.71	6.26	5.25	4.72	Income Ratio %
---	---	---	---	---	422	257	89	211	266	149	---	Turnover Rate %
---	---	---	---	0.1	1.5	3.4	4.2	5.9	19.4	92.7	82.1	Net Assets ($mil)

Investment Style History
Fixed Income
Income Rtn % Rank Obj

Growth of $10,000

|||| Value of Fund ($000)
— Value of Index ($000) LB Muni
▼ Manager Change
▽ Partial Manager Change
► Mgr Unknown After
◄ Mgr Unknown Before

Performance Quartile (Within Objective)

Risk Analysis

Time Period	Load-Adj Return %	Risk % Rank [1] All	Obj	Morningstar [2] Return	Morningstar Risk	Morningstar Risk-Adj Rating
1 Yr	-11.79					
3 Yr	4.61	40	65	1.13	1.14	★★★
5 Yr	6.96	34	75	1.19	1.22	★★★
10 Yr	---					

Average Historical Rating (52 months) 2.5 ★s

[1] = low, 100 = high [2] 1.00 = Muni Avg [3] 1.00 = 90-day T-bill return

Other Measures

			Standard LB Agg	Best Fit LB Muni
Standard Deviation	6.91	Alpha	1.5	1.1
Mean	6.29	Beta	1.30	1.23
Sharpe Ratio	0.40	R-Squared	57	96

Investment Style

Interest-Rate Stance

Avg Effective Maturity 17.2 Yrs

Quality

Avg Credit Quality AA
Avg Weighted Coupon 6.35%
Avg Weighted Price 92.62% of Par

Diversification Value for Portfolio Types

Large Cap: Medium	Small Cap: High	Bond: Low	Balanced: Medium	Diversified: High

Portfolio 11-30-94

Amount 000	Date of Maturity	Total Stocks: 0 Total Fixed-Income: 71	Value $000	% Net Assets
4846	12-13-08	MI Detroit Resource Rec 9.25%	5058	6.05
4405	01-01-17	GA Muni Elec Spcl Obl 6.5%	4169	4.99
4846	10-01-21	MI State GO 5.5%	3919	4.69
4405	10-01-14	CA Contra Costa Wtr Dist 5.75%	3800	4.55
4057	11-01-15	CA San Francisco GO 6%	3662	4.38
3524	11-15-24	OH Cleveland Pub Pwr Sys Impr 7%	3533	4.23
3370	12-15-11	MD Stadium Sports Fac Lease 5.875%	3042	3.64
2643	04-01-23	MI Hsg Dev Rental Multi-Fam 7.55%	2671	3.20
2731	07-01-00	DC Metro Washington Transp 4.4%	2516	3.01
2643	10-01-20	NY Mtg 6.125%	2488	2.98
2643	07-01-06	PR Muni Fin 5.875%	2458	2.94
2643	01-01-15	NY New York City Indl Dev Spcl Fac 6%	2290	2.74
2467	09-01-13	CA South Orange Pub Fin Spcl Tax A 6.2%	2282	2.73
2643	07-01-07	DC Metro Washington Transp 5.25%	2174	2.60
2643	08-01-18	MI Pontiac Hosp Fin North Oakland 6%	2012	2.41
2203	07-01-19	NJ Educ Fac Trenton State Clg 6%	1969	2.36
2203	07-01-22	WI Transp 5.5%	1776	2.12
1762	05-01-29	AZ Maricopa Poll Cntrl NM Pub Svc DMD	1762	2.11
1674	09-02-20	CA Irvine Assmnt Dist DMD	1674	2.00
1674	09-01-18	CA Orange 1915 Act Assmnt Dist DMD	1674	2.00

Credit Analysis % of Bonds 12-31-94

US Govt	0	BB	1
AAA	45	B	0
AA	18	Below B	0
A	21	NR/NA	13
BBB	2		

Composition % of Assets 12-31-94

Cash	2.0	Preferreds	0.0
Stocks	0.0	Convertibles	0.0
Bonds	98.0	Other	0.0

Tax Analysis

	Tax-Adj Historical Return %	% Pretax Return
3 Yr Avg	5.91	94.6
5 Yr Avg	7.67	96.0
10 Yr Avg	---	---
Potential Capital Gain Exposure (% of assets)		-11%

Most Similar Funds in MF500

Vanguard Muni Insured L/T	Strong Fit
Vanguard Muni High-Yield	Strong Fit
MFS Municipal Bond A	Strong Fit

Coupon Range

	% Bonds	Rel Obj
0%	0.0	0.00
0% to 6.8%	58.5	0.97
6.8% to 7.5%	17.8	1.15
7.5% to 8.3%	7.3	0.82
More than 8.3%	6.3	0.72
Not applicable	10.1	2.59

Sector Weightings

	% Bonds	Rel Obj
General Obl	19.15	0.91
Utilities	9.98	0.80
Health	4.96	0.38
Water/Waste	6.65	1.04
Housing	7.85	1.07
Education	7.95	1.24
Transportation	10.77	1.06
COP/Lease	1.06	0.33
Private	11.28	0.97
Misc Revenue	9.65	1.94
Demand	10.71	4.35

Top 5 States % of Bonds

CA	19.78	NY	7.90
MI	17.72	DC	5.82
GA	8.52		

Min Initial Purchase / Expenses

Min Initial Purchase	$2500 (Addt'l: $100)
Min IRA Purchase	$1000 (Addt'l: $100)
Min Auto Invest Plan	$2500 (Systematic Inv: $100)

Expenses & Fees

Sales Fees	4.50% front
	0.00% deferred
	0.25% 12b-1
Management Fee	0.30% flat fee, 0.10%A
3-,5-,10-yr Expense Projections	$68, $85, $134

MORNINGSTAR 1995 Mutual Fund 500

Warburg Pincus Captl Appr Comm

	Ticker	Load	NAV	Yield	SEC Yield	Assets	Objective
	CUCAX	None	12.66	0.1%	0.37%	145.3	Growth

Warburg Pincus Capital Appreciation Fund - Common Shares seeks long-term capital appreciation.

The fund invests principally in the securities of financially strong companies that demonstrate increased earnings power and improved utilization of or recognition of assets; these companies may be of any size. The fund may invest up to 10% of its assets in foreign issues.

Series 2 shares are also available; they are subject to 12b-1 fees that are distributed to Service Organizations for services provided. Prior to Feb. 26, 1992, the fund was named Counsellors Capital Appreciation Fund.

Manager's Investment Style

Former manager Andrew Massie looked at broad economic trends and selected growth companies selling at or below market price multiples. He held half of assets in small and medium-cap stocks, and preferred to invest in issues with very high management ownership. He was not adverse to building up a concentration in a favored sector. It is not yet clear how a recent change in management will affect the fund's strategy.

Fund Manager(s)

Susan L. Black, since 09-94.

Manager Experience

	Dates Managed	Invest Obj	Std Dev	+/- Index

Not available.

Historical Profile

Return	Average
Risk	Average
Rating	★★★
	Neutral

Average % Stocks Held in Portfolio: 83% 89% 88% 91% 97% 93% 91%

Investment Style History: Equity

Average % Stocks Held in Portfolio

Growth of $10,000

- Value of Fund ($000)
- Value of Index ($000) SPMid400
- ▼ Manager Change
- ▽ Partial Manager Change
- ► Mgr Unknown After
- ◄ Mgr Unknown Before

Performance Quartile (Within Objective)

	1983	1984	1985	1986	1987	1988	1989	1990	1991	1992	1993	1994	History
	---	---	---	---	8.01	9.39	11.31	10.48	13.06	13.24	14.06	12.66	NAV
	---	---	---	---	-19.17 *	21.38	26.79	-5.47	26.29	7.61	15.87	-2.74	Total Return %
	---	---	---	---	5.86 *	4.77	-4.89	-2.35	-4.19	-0.01	5.81	-4.05	+/- S&P 500
	---	---	---	---	---	3.44	-2.38	0.72	-7.91	-1.36	4.59	-2.67	+/- Wilshire 5000
	---	---	---	---	0.65	2.31	3.55	1.87	1.08	0.42	0.51	0.13	Income Return %
	---	---	---	---	-19.82	19.07	23.24	-7.34	25.21	7.19	15.36	-2.87	Capital Return %
	---	---	---	---	---	11	19	72	33	50	25	41	Total Rtn % Rank All
	---	---	---	---	---	18	52	58	80	53	29	58	Total Rtn % Rank Obj
	---	---	---	---	0.07	0.20	0.35	0.22	0.11	0.05	0.07	0.02	Income $
	---	---	---	---	0.00	0.14	0.24	0.00	0.05	0.76	1.19	0.98	Capital Gains $
	---	---	---	---	1.00	1.07	1.10	1.04	1.08	1.06	1.01	1.05	Expense Ratio %
	---	---	---	---	1.88	2.00	1.90	2.07	1.27	0.41	0.30	0.26	Income Ratio %
	---	---	---	---	---	33	37	37	40	56	48	52	Turnover Rate %
	---	---	---	---	17.9	31.4	57.8	83.0	122.5	120.3	158.9	145.3	Net Assets ($mil)

Performance 12-31-94

	1st Qtr	2nd Qtr	3rd Qtr	4th Qtr	Total
1987	---	---	---	-18.35	-19.17 *
1988	11.99	6.07	-0.53	2.73	21.38
1989	7.88	9.36	9.18	-1.57	26.79
1990	-3.45	5.85	-12.23	5.38	-5.47
1991	12.31	-1.55	3.73	10.11	26.29
1992	-3.29	0.50	2.45	8.08	7.61
1993	6.80	0.90	6.53	0.94	15.87
1994	-5.62	-0.25	6.81	-3.28	-2.74

Bear Market Performance

Decile Rank (5-year period)

Worst — Best

	Worst 3 Mo Period 1985-89	Worst 3 Mo Period 1990-94
Warburg Pincus Captl Appr	---	-13.98
+/- S&P 500	---	-0.14
+/- Best Fit Index : SPMid400	---	4.43

Trailing Returns

	Total Return %	+/- S&P 500	+/- Wil 5000	% Rank All	% Rank Obj	Growth of $10,000
3 Mo	-3.28	-3.26	-2.51	85	82	9,672
6 Mo	3.31	-1.55	-1.32	19	58	10,331
1 Yr	-2.74	-4.05	-2.67	41	58	9,726
3 Yr Avg	6.64	0.37	0.03	29	43	12,127
5 Yr Avg	7.68	-1.01	-1.14	37	65	14,478
10 Yr Avg	---	---	---	---	---	---
15 Yr Avg	---	---	---	---	---	---

Operations

Address and Telephone	466 Lexington Avenue	
	New York, NY 10017-3147	
	800-257-5614	
Advisor	Warburg Pincus Counsellors	
Subadvisor	None	
Distributor	Counsellors Securities	
States Available	All plus PR	
Report Grade	C	
Income Distrib	Paid Annually	
* Date of Inception	08-17-87	
Fiscal Year End	October	

Min Initial Purchase	$2500 (Addt'l: $500)
Min IRA Purchase	$500 (Addt'l: $500)
Min Auto Invest Plan	$2500 (Systematic Inv: $50)

Expenses & Fees

Sales Fees	0.00% front
	0.00% deferred
	0.00% 12b-1
Management Fee	0.70% flat fee, 0.22%A
3-,5-,10-yr Expense Projections	$32, $56, $124
Annual Brokerage Cost	---

Risk Analysis

Time Period	Load-Adj Return %	Risk % Rank All	Risk % Rank Obj	Morningstar[2] Return	Morningstar Risk	Morningstar Risk-Adj Rating
1 Yr	-2.74					
3 Yr	6.64	76	48	0.91[3]	0.88	★★★
5 Yr	7.68	75	44	0.73[3]	0.89	★★★
10 Yr	---					

Average Historical Rating (53 months): 3.3 ★s

[1] 1 = low, 100 = high [2] 1.00 = Equity Avg [3] 1.00 = 90-day T-bill return

Other Measures

			Standard S&P 500	Best Fit SPMid400
Standard Deviation	9.76	Alpha	0.3	0.0
Mean	6.92	Beta	1.08	0.88
Sharpe Ratio	0.35	R-Squared	77	79

Investment Style

	Stock Portfolio Avg	Relative S&P 500
Price/Earnings Ratio	27.6	1.49
Price/Book Ratio	3.8	1.11
5 Yr Earnings Gr %	22.6#	4.07
Return on Assets %	7.7	1.03
Debt % Total Cap	28.5	1.01
Med Mkt Cap ($mil)	2911	0.22

figure is based on 50% or less of stocks

Style: Value Blend Growth — Size Large Med Small

Diversification Value for Portfolio Types

Large Cap: Low	Small Cap: Low	Bond: Medium	Balanced: None	Diversified: Low

Portfolio 12-31-94

Share Chg (04-94) 000	Amount 000	Total Stocks: 59 / Total Fixed-Income: 1	Value $000	% Net Assets
2	131	Harcourt General	4631	3.19
91	91	Wal-Mart Stores	4190	2.88
2	110	Paging Network	3737	2.57
34	120	Singer	3552	2.44
-31	7	Alco Standard	3408	2.35
1	73	Telephone & Data Systems	3375	2.32
1	67	Tandy	3360	2.31
1	71	Thermo Electron	3190	2.20
2	119	Noble Affiliates	2944	2.03
29	129	Tele-Communications Cl A	2811	1.93
-20	80	Molex	2758	1.90
39	39	Scott Paper	2726	1.88
1	85	Olsten	2697	1.86
-1	53	FHLMC	2666	1.83
23	23	Hercules	2625	1.81
-29	40	Intel	2561	1.76
-18	38	PacifiCare Health Sys Cl B	2527	1.74
1	80	Health Care & Retirement	2410	1.66
-44	78	AirTouch Communications	2275	1.57
109	109	Bell CableMedia (ADR)	2209	1.52
-3	77	Manpower	2159	1.49
66	66	Informix	2135	1.47
8	37	Motorola	2133	1.47
1	62	AlliedSignal	2101	1.45
6	56	Columbia/HCA Healthcare	2041	1.40

Composition % 12-31-94

Cash	20.8	Preferreds	0.5
Stocks	78.8	Convertibles	0.0
Bonds	0.0	Other	0.0

Tax Analysis

	Tax-Adj Historical Return %	% Pretax Return
3 Yr Avg	4.47	66.0
5 Yr Avg	6.14	77.5
10 Yr Avg	---	---
Potential Capital Gain Exposure (% of assets)		15%

Most Similar Funds in MF500

IDS New Dimensions	Strong Fit
Liberty All-Star	Fair Fit
20th Century Heritage Invest	Fair Fit

Index Allocation

	% of Stocks
S&P 500	50.2
S&P MidCap 400	19.1
U.S. Small Cap	23.0
Foreign	7.8

Sector Weightings

	% of Stocks	Relative S&P 500
Utilities	0.0	0.00
Energy	6.9	0.68
Financials	10.5	0.99
Industrial Cyclicals	7.0	0.42
Consumer Durables	7.7	1.23
Consumer Staples	2.4	0.19
Services	20.2	2.48
Retail	8.5	1.47
Health	8.1	0.94
Technology	28.8	3.14

Warburg Pincus Emerging Gr Comm

	Ticker	Load	NAV	Yield	SEC Yield	Assets	Objective
	CUEGX	None	21.99	0.0%	-0.58%	222.8	Small Company

Warburg Pincus Emerging Growth Fund - Common Shares seeks capital appreciation.

The fund normally invests at least 65% of its assets in common stocks of small- and medium-size companies that show positive earnings and prospects of achieving significant gain in a relatively short time period. It may invest up to 20% of its assets in investment-grade debt securities. Up to 10% of fund assets may be invested in foreign securities.

Common shares are available to individual investors; Series 2 shares are offered only to institutions. Prior to Feb. 26, 1992, the fund was named Counsellors Emerging Growth Fund.

Manager's Investment Style

Management focuses on small, rapidly growing companies with able management. Many of these stocks fall into the media and communications and biotech sectors. Management reduces volatility by holding cash and seeking out lower than average price/earnings or price/book ratios.

Historical Profile

Return	Above Average
Risk	Above Average
Rating	★★★★ Above Average

Investment Style History
Equity

Average % Stocks Held in Portfolio: 81% 83% 81% 86% 89% 90% 93%

Growth of $10,000

|||| Value of Fund ($000)
— Value of Index ($000) Russ 2000
▼ Manager Change
▽ Partial Manager Change
► Mgr Unknown After
◄ Mgr Unknown Before

Performance Quartile (Within Objective)

Fund Manager(s)

Elizabeth B. Dater CFA(1975), since 01-88.
Birthdate: 05-45. BFA, Boston U. 1966
Stephen J. Lurito, since 07-93. Birthdate: 07-62.
BA, U. of Virginia 1983 MBA, Wharton 1985

Manager Experience	Dates Managed	Invest Obj	Std Dev	+/- Index
Not available.				

	1983	1984	1985	1986	1987	1988	1989	1990	1991	1992	1993	1994	History
	---	---	---	---	---	11.42	13.37	11.92	18.23	20.07	22.31	21.99	NAV
	---	---	---	---	---	16.99 *	21.82	-9.93	56.13	12.13	18.11	-1.43	Total Return %
	---	---	---	---	---	-1.51 *	-9.86	-6.81	25.65	4.52	8.05	-2.75	+/- S&P 500
	---	---	---	---	---		-2.12	3.63	12.68	0.38	3.57	1.22	+/- Wilshire 4500
	---	---	---	---	---	0.92	3.24	0.92	1.25	0.00	0.00	0.00	Income Return %
	---	---	---	---	---	16.07	18.58	-10.85	54.88	12.13	18.11	-1.43	Capital Return %
	---	---	---	---	---		31	84	6	15	21	29	Total Rtn % Rank All
	---	---	---	---	---		55	49	32	58	45	52	Total Rtn % Rank Obj
	---	---	---	---	---	0.10	0.39	0.13	0.18	0.00	0.00	0.00	Income $
	---	---	---	---	---	0.18	0.16	0.00	0.20	0.37	1.36	0.00	Capital Gains $
	---	---	---	---	---	1.25	1.25	1.25	1.25	1.24	1.23	1.22	Expense Ratio %
	---	---	---	---	---	1.10	1.38	1.05	0.32	-0.25	-0.60	-0.58	Income Ratio %
	---	---	---	---	---		100	107	98	63	68	60	Turnover Rate %
	---	---	---	---	---	12.8	26.8	23.9	75.4	110.5	183.1	222.8	Net Assets ($mil)

Performance 12-31-94

	1st Qtr	2nd Qtr	3rd Qtr	4th Qtr	Total
1987	---	---	---	---	---
1988	---	8.81	-1.63	1.68	16.99 *
1989	9.90	10.34	5.00	-4.33	21.82
1990	-2.77	6.98	-19.16	7.12	-9.93
1991	26.51	-6.08	12.23	17.09	56.13
1992	0.77	-8.87	5.14	16.15	12.13
1993	1.49	4.66	13.04	-1.64	18.11
1994	-5.15	-5.43	9.25	0.59	-1.43

Bear Market Performance

Decile Rank (5-year period)

Worst — Best

	Worst 3 Mo Period 1985-89	Worst 3 Mo Period 1990-94
Warburg Pincus Emerging Gr	---	-19.24
+/- S&P 500	---	-5.40
+/- Best Fit Index : Russ 2000	---	6.66

Trailing Returns

	Total Return %	+/- S&P 500	+/- Wil 4500	% Rank All	% Rank Obj	Growth of $10,000
3 Mo	0.59	0.61	3.10	10	29	10,059
6 Mo	9.90	5.03	5.70	5	34	10,990
1 Yr	-1.43	-2.75	1.22	29	52	9,857
3 Yr Avg	9.29	3.02	1.68	16	47	13,054
5 Yr Avg	12.92	4.23	3.83	7	35	18,358
10 Yr Avg	---	---	---	---	---	---
15 Yr Avg	---	---	---	---	---	---

Operations

Address and Telephone	466 Lexington Avenue New York, NY 10017-3147 800-257-5614
Advisor	Warburg Pincus Counsellors
Subadvisor	None
Distributor	Counsellors Securities
States Available	All plus PR
Report Grade	C
Income Distrib	Paid Annually
* Date of Inception	01-21-88
Fiscal Year End	October

Risk Analysis

Time Period	Load-Adj Return %	Risk % Rank [1] All	Risk % Rank [1] Obj	Morningstar [2] Return	Morningstar [2] Risk	Morningstar Risk-Adj Rating
1 Yr	-1.43					
3 Yr	9.29	90	60	1.74 [3]	1.19	★★★★
5 Yr	12.92	91	60	2.22 [3]	1.18	★★★★
10 Yr	---	---	---	---	---	

Average Historical Rating (48 months)   3.6 ★s

[1] 1 = low, 100 = high [2] 1.00 = Equity Avg [3] 1.00 = 90-day T-bill return

Other Measures

				Standard S&P 500	Best Fit Russ 2000
Standard Deviation	13.60	Alpha		3.9	-2.0
Mean	9.84	Beta		0.87	1.04
Sharpe Ratio	0.46	R-Squared		26	81

Investment Style

	Stock Portfolio Avg	Relative S&P 500
Price/Earnings Ratio	28.8	1.56
Price/Book Ratio	4.2	1.22
5 Yr Earnings Gr %	32.9#	5.92
Return on Assets %	10.9	1.46
Debt % Total Cap	19.4#	0.69
Med Mkt Cap ($mil)	521	0.04

Style: Value Blend Growth / Size Large Med Small

figure is based on 50% or less of stocks

Diversification Value for Portfolio Types

Large Cap: Medium	Small Cap: Low	Bond: High	Balanced: Medium	Diversified: Medium

Portfolio 12-31-94

Share Chg (04-94) 000	Amount 000	Total Stocks: 73 / Total Fixed-Income: 1	Value $000	% Net Assets
114	244	Maxim Integrated Products	8544	3.83
34	235	Solectron	6473	2.90
49	126	Synopsys	5514	2.47
19	315	Methode Electronics Cl A	5353	2.40
34	134	Integrated Health Services	5292	2.37
24	154	Paging Network	5246	2.35
50	88	Catalina Marketing	4922	2.21
115	115	Altera	4813	2.16
82	206	PLATINUM technology	4663	2.09
136	136	HealthCare COMPARE	4654	2.09
25	155	Lincare Holdings	4495	2.02
-12	106	Healthsource	4347	1.95
-6	72	Xilinx	4251	1.91
138	138	Viking Office Products	4212	1.89
11	82	Scholastic	4158	1.87
-110	204	American Freightways	4063	1.82
7	70	Glenayre Technologies	4049	1.82
-5	148	Worthen Banking	4024	1.81
43	121	Infinity Broadcasting Cl A	3800	1.71
110	110	PETsMART	3796	1.70
96	96	California Microwave	3510	1.57
54	179	GMIS	3489	1.57
67	378	NutraMax Products	3447	1.55
157	157	Mariner Health Group	3388	1.52
226	226	Foothill Group Cl A	3386	1.52

Composition % 12-31-94

Cash	5.4	Preferred	0.0
Stocks	94.6	Convertibles	0.0
Bonds	0.0	Other	0.0

Tax Analysis

	Tax-Adj Historical Return %	% Pretax Return
3 Yr Avg	8.51	90.9
5 Yr Avg	12.22	93.3
10 Yr Avg	---	---
Potential Capital Gain Exposure (% of assets)		17%

Most Similar Funds in MF500

Hancock Emerging Growth B	Fair Fit
MainStay Capital Apprec B	Fair Fit
Founders Frontier	Fair Fit

Index Allocation

	% of Stocks
S&P 500	0.0
S&P MidCap 400	7.8
U.S. Small Cap	90.2
Foreign	2.0

Sector Weightings

	% of Stocks	Relative S&P 500
Utilities	0.0	0.00
Energy	5.8	0.58
Financials	4.5	0.43
Industrial Cyclicals	1.1	0.06
Consumer Durables	8.9	1.44
Consumer Staples	0.0	0.00
Services	19.4	2.38
Retail	6.2	1.06
Health	15.4	1.78
Technology	38.7	4.22

Expenses & Fees

Sales Fees	0.00% front
	0.00% deferred
	0.00% 12b-1
Management Fee	0.90% flat fee, 0.22%A
3-,5-,10-yr Expense Projections	$39, $68, $149
Annual Brokerage Cost	---

Min Initial Purchase	$2500 (Addt'l: $500)
Min IRA Purchase	$500 (Addt'l: $500)
Min Auto Invest Plan	$2500 (Systematic Inv: $50)

 **M**ORNINGSTAR **1995 Mutual Fund 500**

Warburg Pincus Growth & Inc

	Ticker	Load	NAV	Yield	SEC Yield	Assets	Objective
	RBEGX	None	13.64	0.8%	N/A	628.0	Growth/Inc.

Warburg Pincus Growth & Income Fund seeks long-term growth of capital and income and a reasonable current return.

The fund invests primarily in dividend-paying common stocks, convertibles, and readily marketable securities, such as rights and warrants, that derive their value from common stocks. It may also purchase ADRs without limitation. Normally, the fund will invest virtually all of its assets in equity securities.

Prior to Dec. 3, 1991, the fund was named SafeGuard Equity Growth and Income Portfolio. From that date until July 30, 1993, the fund was named RBB Equity Growth & Income Portfolio.

Manager's Investment Style

An aggressive manager that focuses more on growth than income, Anthony Orphanos ignores yield when buying stocks, resulting in beefy holdings in technology and medium-cap issues. He targets sectors that will benefit from long-term secular trends, but is quick to realize gains. Such a strategy results in a concentrated portfolio with a high turnover rate. Orphanos also stows a high percentage of assets in cash to avoid market woes.

Fund Manager(s)

Anthony G. Orphanos, since 01-92. Birthdate: 09-45. BA, Harvard 1968 MBA, New York U. 1977

Manager Experience

	Dates Managed	Invest Obj	Std Dev	+/- Index
Anthony G. Orphanos				
Counsellors Tandem	07/90 - 12/94	DE	15.38	-5.01

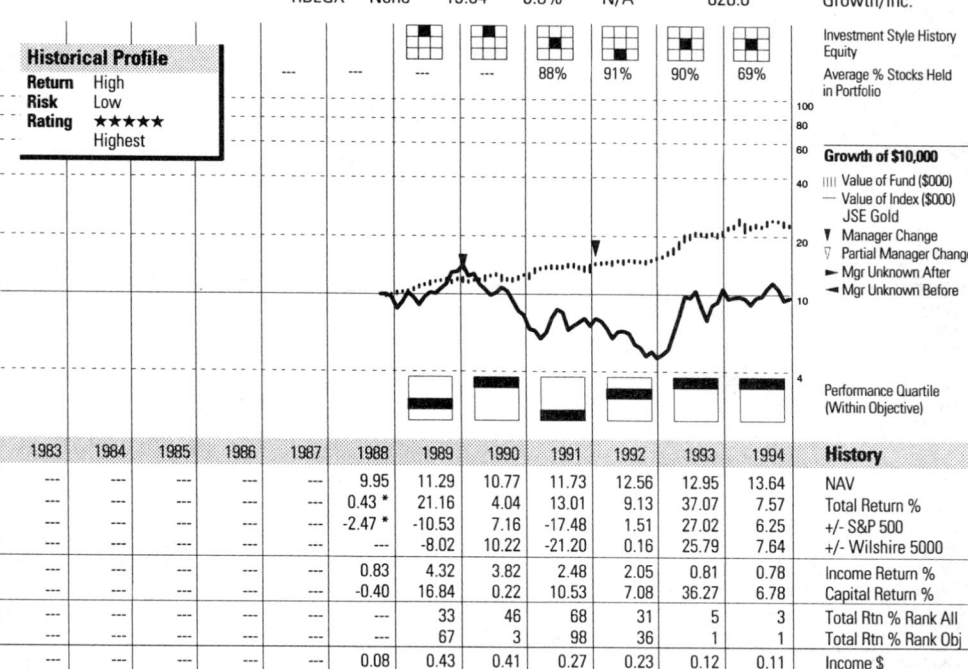

Historical Profile
Return High
Risk Low
Rating ★★★★★ Highest

Investment Style History
Equity
Average % Stocks Held in Portfolio

Growth of $10,000
‖‖ Value of Fund ($000)
— Value of Index ($000)
    JSE Gold
▼ Manager Change
▽ Partial Manager Change
► Mgr Unknown After
◄ Mgr Unknown Before

Performance Quartile (Within Objective)

	1983	1984	1985	1986	1987	1988	1989	1990	1991	1992	1993	1994	History
	---	---	---	---	---	9.95	11.29	10.77	11.73	12.56	12.95	13.64	NAV
	---	---	---	---	---	0.43 *	21.16	4.04	13.01	9.13	37.07	7.57	Total Return %
	---	---	---	---	---	-2.47 *	-10.53	7.16	-17.48	1.51	27.02	6.25	+/- S&P 500
	---	---	---	---	---	---	-8.02	10.22	-21.20	0.16	25.79	7.64	+/- Wilshire 5000
	---	---	---	---	---	0.83	4.32	3.82	2.48	2.05	0.81	0.78	Income Return %
	---	---	---	---	---	-0.40	16.84	0.22	10.53	7.08	36.27	6.78	Capital Return %
	---	---	---	---	---	---	33	46	68	31	5	3	Total Rtn % Rank All
	---	---	---	---	---	---	67	3	98	36	1	1	Total Rtn % Rank Obj
	---	---	---	---	---	0.08	0.43	0.41	0.27	0.23	0.12	0.11	Income $
	---	---	---	---	---	0.00	0.31	0.55	0.16	0.00	3.97	0.18	Capital Gains $
	---	---	---	---	---	---	1.40	1.40	1.30	1.25	1.14	1.28	Expense Ratio %
	---	---	---	---	---	---	4.32	3.32	3.42	1.66	0.30	0.41	Income Ratio %
	---	---	---	---	---	---	---	98	41	175	344	150	Turnover Rate %
	---	---	---	---	---	---	1.1	1.0	22.1	30.7	34.5	628.0	Net Assets ($mil)

Performance 12-31-94

	1st Qtr	2nd Qtr	3rd Qtr	4th Qtr	Total
1987	---	---	---	---	---
1988	---	---	---	---	0.43 *
1989	4.12	6.53	6.56	2.51	21.16
1990	-1.98	5.15	-5.11	6.38	4.04
1991	7.99	-0.26	2.14	2.72	13.01
1992	1.79	1.60	0.67	4.82	9.13
1993	11.80	17.94	-2.13	6.22	37.07
1994	8.25	-3.79	8.10	-4.46	7.57

Bear Market Performance

Decile Rank (5-year period)

Worst   Best

	Worst 3 Mo Period 1985-89	Worst 3 Mo Period 1990-94
Warburg Pincus Growth & Inc	---	-8.99
+/- S&P 500	---	-4.62
+/- Best Fit Index : JSE Gold	---	-23.47

Trailing Returns

	Total Return %	+/- S&P 500	+/- Wil 5000	% Rank All	% Rank Obj	Growth of $10,000
3 Mo	-4.46	-4.44	-3.69	90	94	9,554
6 Mo	3.29	-1.57	-1.34	19	39	10,329
1 Yr	7.57	6.25	7.64	3	1	10,757
3 Yr Avg	17.18	10.91	10.57	2	1	16,090
5 Yr Avg	13.60	4.91	4.78	5	2	18,917
10 Yr Avg	---	---	---	---	---	---
15 Yr Avg	---	---	---	---	---	---

Operations

Address and Telephone	466 Lexington Avenue
	New York, NY 10017-3147
	800-257-5614
Advisor	Warburg Pincus Counsellors
Subadvisor	None
Distributor	Counsellors Securities
States Available	All except LA,NV,NH,NM,NC,ND
Report Grade	C+
Income Distrib	Paid Quarterly
* Date of Inception	10-06-88
Fiscal Year End	August

Risk Analysis

Time Period	Load-Adj Return %	Risk % Rank[1] All	Risk % Rank[1] Obj	Morningstar[2] Return	Morningstar Risk	Morningstar Risk-Adj Rating
1 Yr	7.57					
3 Yr	17.18	57	20	4.47[3]	0.63	★★★★★
5 Yr	13.60	57	14	2.44[3]	0.64	★★★★★
10 Yr	---	---	---	---	---	

Average Historical Rating (39 months)   4.1 ★s

[1] 1 = low, 100 = high [2] 1.00 = Equity Avg [3] 1.00 = 90-day T-bill return

Other Measures

			Standard S&P 500	Best Fit JSE Gold
Standard Deviation	10.94	Alpha	11.9	10.8
Mean	16.55	Beta	0.58	0.19
Sharpe Ratio	1.19	R-Squared	18	40

Investment Style

	Stock Portfolio Avg	Relative S&P 500
Price/Earnings Ratio	21.8	1.18
Price/Book Ratio	2.5	0.73
5 Yr Earnings Gr %	3.5#	0.63
Return on Assets %	5.3	0.71
Debt % Total Cap	28.6	1.01
Med Mkt Cap ($mil)	3333	0.26

figure is based on 50% or less of stocks

Diversification Value for Portfolio Types

Large Cap: High	Small Cap: High	Bond: High	Balanced: High	Diversified: Medium

Expenses & Fees

Sales Fees	0.00% front
	0.00% deferred
	0.00% 12b-1
Management Fee	0.75% flat fee, 0.20%A
3-,5-,10-yr Expense Projections	$36, $63, $139
Annual Brokerage Cost	1.54%

Min Initial Purchase	$1000 (Addt'l: $100)
Min IRA Purchase	$500 (Addt'l: $100)
Min Auto Invest Plan	$1000 (Systematic Inv: $50)

Portfolio 12-31-94

Share Chg (08-94) 000	Amount 000	Total Stocks: 36 Total Fixed-Income: 0	Value $000	% Net Assets
273	594	Honeywell	18711	2.98
470	470	BankAmerica	18565	2.96
358	358	FHLMC	18079	2.88
249	505	Stone & Webster	16778	2.67
756	1155	Acclaim Entertainment	16603	2.64
365	365	Tenneco	15513	2.47
556	601	CBI Industries	15393	2.45
507	507	Corning	15147	2.41
170	470	Inco	13454	2.14
269	558	Allstate	13183	2.10
368	368	Rockwell International	13156	2.09
82	432	Storage Technology	12514	1.99
278	878	USF & G	11964	1.91
90	340	Time Warner	11943	1.90
151	151	Chubb	11653	1.86
417	1000	Pegasus Gold	11375	1.81
334	334	AlliedSignal	11342	1.81
365	365	Foster Wheeler	10871	1.73
36	280	Newmont Mining	10080	1.61
104	454	Tele-Communications Cl A	9875	1.57
110	450	Placer Dome	9788	1.56
300	300	Trinity Industries	9459	1.51
86	530	Homestake Mining	9143	1.46
464	1226	Prime Resources	8852	1.41
265	265	Halliburton	8778	1.40

Composition % 12-31-94

Cash	38.0	Preferreds	0.0
Stocks	62.0	Convertibles	0.0
Bonds	0.0	Other	0.0

Tax Analysis

	Tax-Adj Historical Return %	% Pretax Return
3 Yr Avg	13.99	79.0
5 Yr Avg	10.87	75.7
10 Yr Avg	---	---
Potential Capital Gain Exposure (% of assets)		-2%

Most Similar Funds in MF500

T. Rowe Price Intl Stock	Weak Fit
Fidelity Magellan	Weak Fit
USAA Invstmnt Cornerstone	Weak Fit

Index Allocation

	% of Stocks
S&P 500	66.2
S&P MidCap 400	13.5
U.S. Small Cap	14.0
Foreign	12.3

Sector Weightings

	% of Stocks	Relative S&P 500
Utilities	4.1	0.33
Energy	7.2	0.71
Financials	20.5	1.94
Industrial Cyclicals	41.1	2.51
Consumer Durables	7.4	1.18
Consumer Staples	0.0	0.00
Services	15.4	1.89
Retail	0.0	0.00
Health	1.1	0.12
Technology	3.3	0.36

Wasatch Aggressive Equity

	Ticker	Load	NAV	Yield	SEC Yield	Assets	Objective
	WAAEX	None	19.06	0.0%	N/A	55.5	Aggr. Growth

Wasatch Aggressive Equity Fund seeks long-term growth of capital. Income is a secondary objective.

The fund normally invests at least 65% of its assets in common stocks of growth companies. It may also invest in preferred stocks and convertible bonds or bonds with attached warrants. The fund may invest up to 10% of its assets in foreign securities and up to 5% of its assets in special situations.

Historical Profile
Return High
Risk Above Average
Rating ★★★★★ Highest

Investment Style History
Equity
Average % Stocks Held in Portfolio

98% 98% 97% 95%

Growth of $10,000
|||| Value of Fund ($000)
— Value of Index ($000) Wil 4500
▼ Manager Change
▽ Partial Manager Change
► Mgr Unknown After
◄ Mgr Unknown Before

Performance Quartile (Within Objective)

Manager's Investment Style

The fund's manager takes a prudent approach to aggressive investing by seeking companies that he believes will meet their earnings projections. He also invests not more than 50% of assets in emerging-growth stocks. He holds risk down by only buying issues with low price multiples, yet manages to purchase stocks with high earnings-growth rates.

Fund Manager(s)

Samuel S. Stewart, Jr. CFA(1978), since 12-86.
Birthdate: 08-42. MBA, Stanford U. 1969 PhD, Stanford U. 1970

Manager Experience

	Dates Managed	Invest Obj	Std Dev	+/- Index
Samuel S. Stewart, Jr.				
Wasatch Mid-Cap	08/92 - 12/94	G	17.42	-0.71

	1983	1984	1985	1986	1987	1988	1989	1990	1991	1992	1993	1994	History
	---	---	---	9.99	8.44	8.27	10.92	11.78	16.82	16.95	19.50	19.06	NAV
	---	---	---	-0.10 *	-4.89	-1.45	32.04	7.88	50.42	4.73	23.37	5.50	Total Return %
	---	---	---	3.21 *	-10.14	-18.06	0.36	10.99	19.94	-2.88	13.31	4.18	+/- S&P 500
	---	---	---	-1.37	-21.98	8.10	21.43	6.97	-7.02	8.83	8.15	+/- Wilshire 4500
	---	---	---	0.00	0.15	0.57	0.00	0.00	5.75	0.00	0.74	0.00	Income Return %
	---	---	---	-0.10	-5.04	-2.01	32.04	7.88	44.68	4.73	22.63	5.50	Capital Return %
	---	---	---		88	98	10	15	7	78	13	4	Total Rtn % Rank All
	---	---	---		55	92	40	4	61	63	20	3	Total Rtn % Rank Obj
	---	---	---	0.00	0.01	0.05	0.00	0.00	0.72	0.00	0.13	0.00	Income $
	---	---	---	0.00	1.05	0.00	0.00	0.00	0.18	0.66	1.22	1.51	Capital Gains $
	---	---	---		1.26	1.50	1.50	1.56	1.51	1.51	1.50	1.50	Expense Ratio %
	---	---	---		0.16	0.30	-0.12	0.08	-0.36	-0.41	-0.77	-0.67	Income Ratio %
	---	---	---		58	71	82	74	41	32	70	64	Turnover Rate %
	---	---	---	0.1	0.8	1.8	3.7	9.5	15.7	29.0	55.5	Net Assets ($mil)

Performance 12-31-94

	1st Qtr	2nd Qtr	3rd Qtr	4th Qtr	Total
1987	20.32	1.00	-3.13	-19.20	-4.89
1988	10.78	3.10	-5.91	-8.29	-1.45
1989	7.86	9.75	11.54	0.00	32.04
1990	7.23	11.96	-25.48	20.57	7.88
1991	30.56	-2.67	9.69	7.92	50.42
1992	3.69	-11.98	-0.78	15.67	4.73
1993	3.72	4.08	9.48	4.39	23.37
1994	-2.15	-4.98	10.09	3.07	5.50

Bear Market Performance

Decile Rank (5-year period)

Worst ▮▯▯▯▯▯▯▯▯▯ Best

	Worst 3 Mo Period 1985-89	Worst 3 Mo Period 1990-94
Wasatch Aggressive Equity	---	-25.48
+/- S&P 500		-11.73
+/- Best Fit Index : Wil 4500	---	-7.25

Trailing Returns

	Total Return %	+/- S&P 500	+/- Wil 4500	% Rank All	% Rank Obj	Growth of $10,000
3 Mo	3.07	3.08	5.57	3	14	10,307
6 Mo	13.47	8.61	9.28	3	23	11,347
1 Yr	5.50	4.18	8.15	4	3	10,550
3 Yr Avg	10.88	4.61	3.27	11	22	13,631
5 Yr Avg	17.21	8.52	8.12	2	13	22,120
10 Yr Avg	---	---	---			---
15 Yr Avg	---	---	---			---

Operations

Address and Telephone	68 S. Main Street
	Salt Lake City, UT 84101
	800-345-7460 / 801-533-0777
Advisor	Wasatch Advisors
Subadvisor	None
Distributor	Wasatch Advisors
States Available	Selected states
Report Grade	D
Income Distrib	Paid Annually
* Date of Inception	12-06-86
Fiscal Year End	September

Risk Analysis

Time Period	Load-Adj Return %	Risk % Rank¹ All	Obj	Morningstar² Return	Risk	Morningstar Risk-Adj Rating
1 Yr	5.50					
3 Yr	10.88	88	28	2.26³	1.13	★★★★
5 Yr	17.21	90	32	3.67³	1.14	★★★★★
10 Yr	---					

Average Historical Rating (61 months)   3.7 ★s

¹ 1 = low, 100 = high ² 1.00 = Equity Avg ³ 1.00 = 90-day T-bill return

Other Measures

			Standard S&P 500	Best Fit Wil 4500
Standard Deviation	13.44	Alpha	5.4	2.9
Mean	11.26	Beta	0.85	1.13
Sharpe Ratio	0.58	R-Squared	25	68

Investment Style

	Stock Portfolio Avg	Relative S&P 500
Price/Earnings Ratio	27.6	1.49
Price/Book Ratio	4.1	1.22
5 Yr Earnings Gr %	22.2#	4.00
Return on Assets %	10.3	1.37
Debt % Total Cap	18.8#	0.67
Med Mkt Cap ($mil)	322	0.02

figure is based on 50% or less of stocks

Style
Value Blend Growth (Size: Large Med Small)

Diversification Value for Portfolio Types

Large Cap: High Small Cap: Low Bond: High Balanced: Medium Diversified: High

Expenses & Fees

Sales Fees	0.00% front
	0.00% deferred
	0.00% 12b-1
Management Fee	1.00% flat fee, 0.20%A
3-,5-,10-yr Expense Projections	$47, $82, $179
Annual Brokerage Cost	0.32%

Min Initial Purchase	$2000 (Addt'l: $100)
Min IRA Purchase	$1000 (Addt'l: $250)
Min Auto Invest Plan	$1000 (Systematic Inv: $100)

Portfolio 12-30-94

Share Chg (09-94) 000	Amount 000	Total Stocks: 63 / Total Fixed-Income: 1	Value $000	% Net Assets
19	131	Loewen Group	3481	6.27
15	94	US Cellular	3083	5.55
4	77	United Asset Management	2832	5.10
29	110	Heilig-Meyers	2770	4.99
60	159	Washington Fed S & L (WA)	2754	4.96
4	65	Century Telephone Enterprise	1926	3.47
22	131	REN-USA	1742	3.14
27	100	Barrett Business Services	1399	2.52
10	50	Concord EFS	1238	2.23
-14	43	Saint John Knits	1229	2.21
36	52	World Acceptance	1210	2.18
27	81	BMC West	1134	2.04
17	81	Barefoot Grass Lawn Service	1113	2.00
-4	51	Expeditors Intl Washington	1112	2.00
31	102	INTERCEL	1111	2.00
18	32	Wonderware	1070	1.93
5	63	Lattice Semiconductor	1062	1.91
52	52	Hummingbird Communications	1055	1.90
14	64	American Power Conversion	1046	1.88
5	41	O'Reilly Automotive	1017	1.83
18	32	Duracraft	1017	1.83
-3	22	Synopsys	983	1.77
6	26	Express Scripts Cl A	958	1.73
77	121	Interpore International	940	1.69
48	48	Communications Central	893	1.61

Composition % 12-31-94

Cash	7.2	Preferreds	0.0
Stocks	92.8	Convertibles	0.0
Bonds	0.0	Other	0.0

Tax Analysis

	Tax-Adj Historical Return %	% Pretax Return
3 Yr Avg	9.02	81.5
5 Yr Avg	15.67	88.3
10 Yr Avg	---	---
Potential Capital Gain Exposure (% of assets)		7%

Most Similar Funds in MF500

Hancock Emerging Growth B	Fair Fit
Loomis Sayles Small Cap	Weak Fit
Kaufmann	Weak Fit

Index Allocation

	% of Stocks
S&P 500	0.0
S&P MidCap 400	13.4
U.S. Small Cap	78.8
Foreign	7.9

Sector Weightings

	% of Stocks	Relative S&P 500
Utilities	3.7	0.30
Energy	0.0	0.00
Financials	13.2	1.25
Industrial Cyclicals	3.4	0.21
Consumer Durables	3.1	0.49
Consumer Staples	0.0	0.00
Services	27.3	3.35
Retail	14.0	2.40
Health	8.8	1.01
Technology	26.6	2.91

MORNINGSTAR 1995 Mutual Fund 500

Washington Mutual Investors

	Ticker	Load	NAV	Yield	SEC Yield	Assets	Objective
	AWSHX	5.75%	16.84	3.6%	3.39%	12668.3	Growth/Inc.

Washington Mutual Investors Fund seeks to provide income and an opportunity for growth of principal, consistent with sound common-stock investment.

The fund's charter limits its investments to common stocks or equivalent securities that are legal for the investment of trust funds in the District of Columbia. It intends to be fully invested and well diversified. It tries to select a portfolio that an investor with fiduciary responsibility might select under the Prudent Investor Rule of the Superior Court of the District of Columbia.

Manager's Investment Style

Management follows a consistant strategy of blue-chip investing. The fund travels this path for many reasons. Primarily, investing in blue chips complies with the District of Columbia Prudent Investor Rule. But the fund also reaps rich rewards from its portfolio. Many of the issues produce a long, consistent line of dividend payments. In addition, this collection of old-guard stocks can withstand a down market, and therefore help the fund stay fully invested. An added bonus to some is that management does not invest in any sin stocks, such as tobacco and alcohol companies.

Fund Manager(s)

Management Team

Manager Experience

	Dates Managed	Invest Obj	Std Dev	+/- Index
James K. Dunton				
American Mutual	04/71 - 12/94	GI	12.02	1.75
Stephen E. Bepler				
New Perspective	01/77 - 12/94	WW	13.65	3.03

Performance 12-31-94

	1st Qtr	2nd Qtr	3rd Qtr	4th Qtr	Total
1987	14.51	5.00	4.15	-19.01	1.42
1988	7.53	6.42	0.40	2.41	17.66
1989	7.21	8.93	9.43	0.91	28.96
1990	-3.70	2.46	-13.13	12.20	-3.82
1991	10.96	0.38	4.90	5.69	23.49
1992	-1.27	3.55	3.07	3.54	9.10
1993	7.00	1.95	3.76	-0.12	13.05
1994	-5.04	2.60	3.92	-0.75	0.49

Bear Market Performance

Decile Rank (5-year period)

	Worst 3 Mo Period 1985-89	Worst 3 Mo Period 1990-94
Washington Mutual Investors	-25.38	-13.13
+/- S&P 500	4.20	0.62
+/- Best Fit Index : S&P 500	4.20	0.62

Trailing Returns

	Total Return %	+/- S&P 500	+/- Wil 5000	% Rank All	% Rank Obj	Growth of $10,000
3 Mo	-0.75	-0.74	0.02	39	37	9,925
6 Mo	3.14	-1.73	-1.49	20	41	10,314
1 Yr	0.49	-0.83	0.56	16	34	10,049
3 Yr Avg	7.42	1.15	0.80	24	26	12,394
5 Yr Avg	8.04	-0.65	-0.78	33	47	14,721
10 Yr Avg	13.87	-0.51	0.01	19	19	36,666
15 Yr Avg	15.78	1.29	1.80	8	4	90,000

Operations

Address and Telephone	1101 Vermont Avenue N.W.	
	Washington, DC 20005	
	800-421-4120 / 202-842-5665	
Advisor	Capital Research & Management	
Subadvisor	None	
Distributor	American Funds Distributors	
States Available	All plus GU,PR,VI	
Report Grade	B+	
Income Distrib	Paid Quarterly	
Date of Inception	07-31-52	
Fiscal Year End	April	

Historical Profile

Return	Average
Risk	Below Average
Rating	★★★★ Above Average

Investment Style History
Equity

Average % Stocks Held in Portfolio

Growth of $10,000

|||| Value of Fund ($000)
— Value of Index ($000)
S&P 500
▼ Manager Change
▽ Partial Manager Change
► Mgr Unknown After
◄ Mgr Unknown Before

Performance Quartile
(Within Objective)

1983	1984	1985	1986	1987	1988	1989	1990	1991	1992	1993	1994	History
10.07	9.40	11.04	12.30	11.45	12.62	14.89	13.63	15.90	16.58	17.78	16.84	NAV
26.18	8.28	32.13	22.50	1.42	17.66	28.96	-3.82	23.49	9.10	13.05	0.49	Total Return %
3.72	2.02	0.39	3.82	-3.84	1.05	-2.72	-0.70	-6.99	1.48	3.00	-0.83	+/- S&P 500
2.72	5.23	-0.43	6.40	-0.94	-0.29	-0.21	2.36	-10.71	0.13	1.77	0.56	+/- Wilshire 5000
5.38	5.28	5.48	4.63	3.98	5.04	4.85	4.30	4.24	3.65	3.36	3.53	Income Return %
20.80	3.00	26.65	17.87	-2.56	12.62	24.11	-8.12	19.26	5.45	9.70	-3.04	Capital Return %
20	36	18	12	47	20	15	67	39	31	40	16	Total Rtn % Rank All
22	26	17	8	54	33	24	51	79	37	34	34	Total Rtn % Rank Obj
0.46	0.47	0.48	0.51	0.52	0.56	0.62	0.62	0.56	0.56	0.56	0.62	Income $
0.51	0.89	0.67	0.66	0.59	0.24	0.68	0.06	0.30	0.18	0.39	0.41	Capital Gains $
0.58	0.56	0.56	0.52	0.54	0.58	0.67	0.69	0.77	0.74	0.70	0.69	Expense Ratio %
5.34	4.83	5.38	4.78	4.03	4.25	4.54	4.01	4.24	3.58	3.33	3.29	Income Ratio %
27	26	26	13	12	12	21	7	11	10	19	24	Turnover Rate %
528.0	537.8	668.6	1906.3	2468.6	2758.4	4481.8	5606.9	8215.4	10100.4	12638.5	12668.3	Net Assets ($mil)

Risk Analysis

Time Period	Load-Adj Return %	Risk % Rank [1] All	Obj	Morningstar [2] Return	Morningstar Risk	Morningstar Risk-Adj Rating
1 Yr	-5.29					
3 Yr	5.32	60	28	0.51 [3]	0.65	★★★
5 Yr	6.77	63	*38	0.49 [3]	0.76	★★★
10 Yr	13.20	53	37	1.11	0.85	★★★★
Average Historical Rating (109 months)					4.0	★s

[1] = low, 100 = high   [2] 1.00 = Equity Avg   [3] 1.00 = 90-day T-bill return

Other Measures

			Standard S&P 500	Best Fit S&P 500
Standard Deviation	7.79	Alpha	1.4	1.4
Mean	7.48	Beta	0.90	0.90
Sharpe Ratio	0.51	R-Squared	84	84

Investment Style

	Stock Portfolio Avg	Relative S&P 500
Price/Earnings Ratio	16.5	0.90
Price/Book Ratio	2.7	0.79
5 Yr Earnings Gr %	-0.2	-0.04
Return on Assets %	5.5	0.73
Debt % Total Cap	28.3	1.00
Med Mkt Cap ($mil)	9994	0.77

Style Value Blend Growth   Size Large Med Small

Diversification Value for Portfolio Types

Large Cap: None	Small Cap: High	Bond: Medium	Balanced: Low	Diversified: Low
◯	⬤	◍	◍	◍

Portfolio 10-31-94

Total Stocks: 110
Total Fixed-Income: 3

Share Chg (09-94) 000	Amount 000		Value $000	% Net Assets
0	5950	Eli Lilly	368900	2.82
0	11065	GTE	340249	2.60
0	3280	Xerox	336200	2.57
0	4205	Warner-Lambert	320631	2.45
0	5045	Amoco	319727	2.44
0	5175	Bristol-Myers Squibb	302091	2.31
0	4800	El duPont de Nemours	286200	2.18
0	4380	American Home Products	278130	2.12
1185	6850	US West	257731	1.97
0	8236	American Express	253266	1.93
-550	3990	United Technologies	251370	1.92
0	6725	Merck	240419	1.83
0	4013	Dun & Bradstreet	235262	1.80
-150	2735	Mobil	235210	1.80
0	3440	Bankers Trust New York	229620	1.75
0	3440	Texaco	224890	1.72
0	3535	Norfolk Southern	222705	1.70
0	5485	Ameritech	221457	1.69
0	6600	Bank of New York	209550	1.60
0	4775	BankAmerica	207712	1.59
858	3858	General Electric	188570	1.44
0	3419	AT & T	188045	1.44
200	5652	Pacific Telesis Group	178759	1.36
0	1761	American Cyanamid	173928	1.33
0	3245	Bell Atlantic	169957	1.30

Composition % 12-31-94

Cash	2.8	Preferreds	0.0
Stocks	97.0	Convertibles	0.2
Bonds	0.0	Other	0.0

Tax Analysis

	Tax-Adj Historical Return %	% Pretax Return
3 Yr Avg	5.57	73.8
5 Yr Avg	6.25	75.0
10 Yr Avg	11.35	72.4
Potential Capital Gain Exposure (% of assets)		15%

Most Similar Funds in MF500

Vanguard Equity-Income	Strong Fit
American Mutual	Strong Fit
Smith Barney Inc & Grth A	Strong Fit

Index Allocation

	% of Stocks
S&P 500	92.7
S&P MidCap 400	3.9
U.S. Small Cap	3.4
Foreign	0.0

Sector Weightings

	% of Stocks	Relative S&P 500
Utilities	20.9	1.69
Energy	9.6	0.95
Financials	22.8	2.15
Industrial Cyclicals	14.4	0.88
Consumer Durables	1.8	0.29
Consumer Staples	2.8	0.22
Services	9.5	1.16
Retail	0.7	0.12
Health	15.8	1.82
Technology	1.8	0.19

Min Initial Purchase / Expenses & Fees

Min Initial Purchase	$250 (Addt'l: $50)
Min IRA Purchase	$250 (Addt'l: $50)
Min Auto Invest Plan	$50 (Systematic Inv: $50)

Expenses & Fees

Sales Fees	5.75% front
	0.00% deferred
	0.25% 12b-1
Management Fee	0.25% max./0.20% min., 0.25%A
3-,5-,10-yr Expense Projections	$78, $94, $138
Annual Brokerage Cost	0.10%

Weitz Value

	Ticker	Load	NAV	Yield	SEC Yield	Assets	Objective
	WVALX	None	14.43	0.0%	0.50%	107.7	Growth

Weitz Series Fund Value Portfolio seeks capital appreciation; current income is secondary.

The fund invests primarily in equity securities. It seeks securities trading at a price below their intrinsic value, that is, the price per share that an informed buyer would pay if buying the entire company. Little weight is given to technical stock-market analysis. Any convertible securities the fund holds carry a rating of investment grade. The fund may also invest in foreign securities and securities that are not readily marketable, and may write covered call options.

Manager's Investment Style

Management emphasizes low capital needs, dependable cash flows, and strong pricing power when purchasing a stock. Using this strategy, management has built up large stakes in the financial sector and in services such as cable and communications. Management combats the up-and-down nature of these sectors by holding cash and sticking with mostly low-price-multiple issues. The fund also takes advantage of down times by purchasing shares where the market has overreacted.

Fund Manager(s)

Wallace R. Weitz CFA(1978), since 05-86.
Birthdate: 04-49. BA, Carleton C. 1970

Manager Experience	Dates Managed	Invest Obj	Std Dev	+/- Index
Wallace R. Weitz				
Weitz Fixed-Income	12/88 - 12/94	CG	2.56*	-2.06

Historical Profile

Return	Average
Risk	Low
Rating	★★★
	Neutral

Average % Stocks Held in Portfolio: 31% 58% 61% --- 53% 60% 65% 76%

Investment Style History: Equity

Growth of $10,000

- |||| Value of Fund ($000)
- — Value of Index ($000) S&P 500
- ▼ Manager Change
- ▽ Partial Manager Change
- ► Mgr Unknown After
- ◄ Mgr Unknown Before

Performance Quartile (Within Objective)

	1983	1984	1985	1986	1987	1988	1989	1990	1991	1992	1993	1994	History
	---	---	---	10.35	9.70	10.97	12.30	11.22	13.58	14.54	16.80	14.43	NAV
	---	---	---	3.45*	-0.55	16.43	21.85	-5.16	27.59	13.63	20.01	-9.82	Total Return %
	---	---	---	-0.71*	-5.81	-0.19	-9.83	-2.05	-2.90	6.01	9.96	-11.13	+/- S&P 500
	---	---	---	---	-2.91	-1.52	-7.32	1.02	-6.62	4.66	8.73	-9.75	+/- Wilshire 5000
	---	---	---	0.00	4.71	3.34	3.76	3.13	2.69	2.02	0.15	0.00	Income Return %
	---	---	---	3.45	-5.26	13.08	18.09	-8.29	24.90	11.61	19.86	-9.82	Capital Return %
	---	---	---	---	64	23	31	71	31	12	17	93	Total Rtn % Rank All
	---	---	---	---	71	45	74	56	74	21	16	93	Total Rtn % Rank Obj
	---	---	---	0.00	0.49	0.32	0.43	0.38	0.32	0.28	0.02	0.00	Income $
	---	---	---	0.00	0.11	0.00	0.63	0.07	0.40	0.55	0.59	0.73	Capital Gains $
	---	---	---	---	1.50	1.50	1.50	1.46	1.49	1.40	1.35	1.41	Expense Ratio %
	---	---	---	---	3.72	3.47	3.30	3.71	2.71	2.75	1.66	0.64	Income Ratio %
	---	---	---	---	55	68	25	49	29	35	23	23	Turnover Rate %
	---	---	---	4.0	8.6	11.5	24.4	23.5	32.3	49.5	106.7	107.7	Net Assets ($mil)

Performance 12-31-94

	1st Qtr	2nd Qtr	3rd Qtr	4th Qtr	Total
1987	4.32	-0.15	2.97	-7.27	-0.55
1988	8.44	4.45	2.29	0.49	16.43
1989	7.29	8.20	5.23	-0.26	21.85
1990	-3.63	4.70	-9.69	4.07	-5.16
1991	14.46	0.14	6.07	4.94	27.59
1992	2.61	1.81	0.35	8.40	13.63
1993	6.81	1.52	6.95	3.49	20.01
1994	-6.67	0.89	0.84	-5.02	-9.82

Bear Market Performance

Decile Rank (5-year period)

Worst ─────────── Best

	Worst 3 Mo Period 1985-89	Worst 3 Mo Period 1990-94
Weitz Value	---	-12.27
+/- S&P 500	---	1.57
+/- Best Fit Index : S&P 500	---	1.57

Trailing Returns

	Total Return %	+/- S&P 500	+/- Wil 5000	% Rank All	% Rank Obj	Growth of $10,000
3 Mo	-5.03	-5.01	-4.26	92	94	9,498
6 Mo	-4.23	-9.09	-8.85	97	98	9,577
1 Yr	-9.82	-11.13	-9.75	93	93	9,018
3 Yr Avg	7.14	0.87	0.53	26	38	12,298
5 Yr Avg	8.27	-0.42	-0.55	30	56	14,877
10 Yr Avg	---	---	---	---	---	---
15 Yr Avg	---	---	---	---	---	---

Operations

Address and Telephone	One Pacific Place 1125 S. 103 St Omaha, NE 68124-6008 800-232-4161 / 402-391-1980
Advisor	Wallace R. Weitz & Company
Subadvisor	None
Distributor	Weitz Securities
States Available	All except MA,WI
Report Grade	A
Income Distrib	Paid Annually
*Date of Inception	05-09-86
Fiscal Year End	March

Risk Analysis

Time Period	Load-Adj Return %	Risk % Rank [1] All	Risk % Rank [1] Obj	Morningstar [2] Return	Morningstar Risk	Morningstar Risk-Adj Rating
1 Yr	-9.82					
3 Yr	7.14	63	20	1.06[3]	0.69	★★★
5 Yr	8.27	58	8	0.88[3]	0.67	★★★
10 Yr	---	---	---			
Average Historical Rating (68 months)					4.2	★s

[1] = low, 100 = high [2] 1.00 = Equity Avg [3] 1.00 = 90-day T-bill return

Other Measures

				Standard S&P 500	Best Fit S&P 500
Standard Deviation	8.48	Alpha		1.3	1.3
Mean	7.27	Beta		0.84	0.84
Sharpe Ratio	0.44	R-Squared		61	61

Investment Style

	Stock Portfolio Avg	Relative S&P 500
Price/Earnings Ratio	21.4	1.16
Price/Book Ratio	2.2	0.64
5 Yr Earnings Gr %	14.3#	2.58
Return on Assets %	2.1	0.28
Debt % Total Cap	39.6#	1.40
Med Mkt Cap ($mil)	2934	0.23

figure is based on 50% or less of stocks

Style: Value Blend Growth / Size Large Med Small

Diversification Value for Portfolio Types

Large Cap: Low	Small Cap: Medium	Bond: Medium	Balanced: Low	Diversified: Medium

Expenses & Fees

Sales Fees	0.00% front
	0.00% deferred
	0.00% 12b-1
Management Fee	1.00% flat fee
3-,5-,10-yr Expense Projections	$45, $77, $169
Annual Brokerage Cost	0.22%

Min Initial Purchase	$25000 (Addt'l: $5000)
Min IRA Purchase	N/A
Min Auto Invest Plan	N/A

Portfolio 12-31-94

Total Stocks: 59
Total Fixed-Income: 9

Share Chg (09-94) 000	Amount 000		Value $000	% Net Assets
0	270	Tele-Communications Cl A	5873	5.45
0	220	Bank of Boston	5693	5.29
330	330	Comcast Special Cl A	5177	4.81
0	140	SLMA	4550	4.23
0	120	Salomon	4455	4.14
80	330	Countrywide Credit Industry	4249	3.95
0	50	FNMA	3644	3.38
30	530	Catellus Development	3114	2.89
0	50	Berkshire Hathaway	3060	2.84
80	100	Brooklyn Bancorp	3025	2.81
	3	US Treasury Note 7.625%	3003	2.79
30	175	Centennial Cellular	2975	2.76
0	130	Union Texas Petroleum	2681	2.49
0	65	BankAmerica	2568	2.38
0	75	Business Records	2438	2.26
	3	FNMA 7.55%	2351	2.18
5	15	Wells Fargo	2175	2.02
0	338	Falcon Cable Systems	2114	1.96
0	136	Valassis Communications	2040	1.89
0	55	Time Warner	1932	1.79
	210	Forest Oil Cv Pfd $.75	1890	1.76
0	33	FHLMC	1667	1.55
0	100	Shawmut National	1638	1.52
0	33	Telephone & Data Systems	1531	1.42
	60	Riggs National Pfd 10.75%	1499	1.39

Composition % 12-31-94

Cash	8.6	Preferreds	1.9
Stocks	80.4	Convertibles	2.7
Bonds	6.4	Other	0.0

Tax Analysis

	Tax-Adj Historical Return %	% Pretax Return
3 Yr Avg	5.73	79.2
5 Yr Avg	6.82	80.1
10 Yr Avg	---	---
Potential Capital Gain Exposure (% of assets)		0%

Most Similar Funds in MF500

Clipper	Fair Fit
Warburg Pincus Cap Appr	Fair Fit
American Leaders A	Weak Fit

Index Allocation

	% of Stocks
S&P 500	48.5
S&P MidCap 400	3.4
U.S. Small Cap	46.4
Foreign	1.7

Sector Weightings

	% of Stocks	Relative S&P 500
Utilities	1.2	0.09
Energy	3.6	0.36
Financials	54.5	5.16
Industrial Cyclicals	1.0	0.06
Consumer Durables	0.0	0.00
Consumer Staples	0.4	0.03
Services	29.5	3.63
Retail	0.0	0.00
Health	0.8	0.09
Technology	9.1	0.99

MORNINGSTAR 1995 Mutual Fund 500

Westcore Midco Growth Ret

	Ticker	Load	NAV	Yield	SEC Yield	Assets	Objective
	WMGRX	4.50%	16.07	0.0%	N/A	22.0	Growth

Westcore Trust Midco Growth Fund - Retail Shares seeks long-term capital appreciation.

The fund invests primarily in medium-size companies, using valuation techniques that emphasize earnings growth. It may also invest in larger companies that offer improved growth possibilities because of rejuvenated management, product changes, or some other development that might stimulate earnings growth, and in smaller companies that have limited product lines, markets, or financial resources.

Institutional shares have no loads; Retail shares have front loads and 12b-1 fees.

Manager's Investment Style

Management emphasizes growth when picking stocks. Not settling for slow growers, management chooses companies with expected earnings-per-share growth of more than 30%. Management avoids price risk by remaining well diversified, owning in excess of 120 stocks. While management's strategy is risky, it has paid off in long term-returns.

Fund Manager(s)

Todger Anderson CFA, since 10-93. Birthdate: 1944. BA, Colby C.   MBA, U. of Denver

Manager Experience

	Dates Managed	Invest Obj	Std Dev	+/- Index
Todger Anderson				
PaineWebber Cap Apprec	07/92 - 12/94	G	13.30	4.32

Historical Profile
Return ---
Risk ---
Rating Not Rated

93% 95%

Investment Style History
Equity
Average % Stocks Held in Portfolio

Growth of $10,000
|||| Value of Fund ($000)
— Value of Index ($000)
  S&P 500
▼ Manager Change
▽ Partial Manager Change
► Mgr Unknown After
◄ Mgr Unknown Before

Performance Quartile
(Within Objective)

	1983	1984	1985	1986	1987	1988	1989	1990	1991	1992	1993	1994	History
	---	---	---	---	---	---	---	---	---	---	16.80	16.07	NAV
	---	---	---	---	---	---	---	---	---	---	3.09 *	-1.13	Total Return %
	---	---	---	---	---	---	---	---	---	---	1.08 *	-2.44	+/- S&P 500
	---	---	---	---	---	---	---	---	---	---	---	-1.06	+/- Wilshire 5000
	---	---	---	---	---	---	---	---	---	---	0.00	0.00	Income Return %
	---	---	---	---	---	---	---	---	---	---	3.09	-1.13	Capital Return %
	---	---	---	---	---	---	---	---	---	---	---	27	Total Rtn % Rank All
	---	---	---	---	---	---	---	---	---	---	---	44	Total Rtn % Rank Obj
	---	---	---	---	---	---	---	---	---	---	0.00	0.00	Income $
	---	---	---	---	---	---	---	---	---	---	1.03	0.53	Capital Gains $
	---	---	---	---	---	---	---	---	---	---	1.10	Expense Ratio %	
	---	---	---	---	---	---	---	---	---	---	-0.37	Income Ratio %	
	---	---	---	---	---	---	---	---	---	---	---	---	Turnover Rate %
	---	---	---	---	---	---	---	---	---	---	40.9	22.0	Net Assets ($mil)

Performance 12-31-94

	1st Qtr	2nd Qtr	3rd Qtr	4th Qtr	Total
1987	---	---	---	---	---
1988	---	---	---	---	---
1989	---	---	---	---	---
1990	---	---	---	---	---
1991	---	---	---	---	---
1992	---	---	---	---	---
1993	---	---	---	---	3.09 *
1994	-4.35	-5.10	10.69	-1.60	-1.13

Bear Market Performance

Decile Rank (5-year period)

Worst _____ Best

	Worst 3 Mo Period 1985-89	Worst 3 Mo Period 1990-94
Westcore Midco Growth Ret	---	---
+/- S&P 500	---	---
+/- Best Fit Index :	---	---

Trailing Returns

	Total Return %	+/- S&P 500	+/- Wil 5000	% Rank All	% Rank Obj	Growth of $10,000
3 Mo	-1.60	-1.58	-0.83	59	57	9,840
6 Mo	8.92	4.06	4.30	5	11	10,892
1 Yr	-1.13	-2.44	-1.06	27	44	9,887
3 Yr Avg	---	---	---	---	---	---
5 Yr Avg	---	---	---	---	---	---
10 Yr Avg	---	---	---	---	---	---
15 Yr Avg	---	---	---	---	---	---

Operations

Address and Telephone	600 Seventeenth Street Ste 1605S Denver, CO 80202 800-392-2673 / 303-623-2577
Advisor	First Interstate Bank of Denver
Subadvisor	Denver Investment Advisors
Distributor	Alps Mutual Funds Services
States Available	All except MO
Report Grade	A-
Income Distrib	Paid Quarterly
* Date of Inception	10-08-93
Fiscal Year End	May

Risk Analysis

Time Period	Load-Adj Return %	Risk % Rank All	Risk % Rank Obj	Morningstar [2] Return	Morningstar Risk	Morningstar Risk-Adj Rating
1 Yr	-5.58					
3 Yr	---	---	---	---	---	
5 Yr	---	---	---	---	---	
10 Yr	---	---	---	---	---	

Average Historical Rating ---   ---

[1] 1 = low, 100 = high   [2] 1.00 = Equity Avg   [3] 1.00 = 90-day T-bill return

Other Measures

				Standard S&P 500	Best Fit
Standard Deviation	---	Alpha		---	---
Mean	---	Beta		---	---
Sharpe Ratio	---	R-Squared		---	---

Investment Style

	Stock Portfolio Avg	Relative S&P 500
Price/Earnings Ratio	27.8	1.50
Price/Book Ratio	5.0	1.47
5 Yr Earnings Gr %	28.0#	5.04
Return on Assets %	10.9	1.46
Debt % Total Cap	24.7	0.88
Med Mkt Cap ($mil)	1620	0.12

figure is based on 50% or less of stocks

Style
Value Blend Growth
Size: Large Med Small

Diversification Value for Portfolio Types

Large Cap: Small Cap: Bond: Balanced: Diversified:

Expenses & Fees

Sales Fees	4.50% front
	0.00% deferred
	0.35% 12b-1
Management Fee	0.65% flat fee, 0.05%A
3-,5-,10-yr Expense Projections	$81, $108, $184
Annual Brokerage Cost	---

Min Initial Purchase $1000 (Addt'l: $50)
Min IRA Purchase $250 (Addt'l: $50)
Min Auto Invest Plan $50 (Systematic Inv: $50)

Portfolio 12-30-94

Share Chg (10-94) 000	Amount 000	Total Stocks: 134 Total Fixed-Income: 0	Value $000	% Net Assets
1	11	Oxford Health Plans	900	4.09
1	12	Oracle Systems	550	2.50
1	16	CUC International	534	2.43
0	11	United HealthCare	515	2.34
1	12	US Healthcare	496	2.26
1	7	First Financial Management	442	2.01
1	16	Loewen Group	419	1.91
0	5	Capital Cities/ABC	391	1.78
1	19	LDDS Communications Cl A	371	1.69
1	14	Hospitality Franchise System	362	1.65
1	12	Silicon Graphics	357	1.62
1	14	Coventry	339	1.54
0	6	Sybase	328	1.49
1	15	Newell	313	1.42
1	10	Storage Technology	285	1.30
2	7	Georgia Gulf	284	1.29
2	11	Apache	273	1.24
1	13	Tele-Communications Cl A	272	1.24
1	9	Dollar General	256	1.16
0	5	3Com	254	1.15
1	9	Geon	250	1.14
1	11	Mid-Atlantic Medical Svcs	249	1.13
0	6	Duracell International	248	1.13
1	19	Mercury Finance	246	1.12
1	11	La Quinta Inns	236	1.07

Composition % 12-31-94

Cash	3.6	Preferreds	0.0
Stocks	94.8	Convertibles	0.0
Bonds	1.6	Other	0.0

Tax Analysis

	Tax-Adj Historical Return %	% Pretax Return
3 Yr Avg	---	---
5 Yr Avg	---	---
10 Yr Avg	---	---
Potential Capital Gain Exposure (% of assets)		15%

Most Similar Funds in MF500

Fund lacks three-year record

Index Allocation

	% of Stocks
S&P 500	24.1
S&P MidCap 400	29.3
U.S. Small Cap	42.6
Foreign	4.4

Sector Weightings

	% of Stocks	Relative S&P 500
Utilities	0.8	0.06
Energy	2.3	0.23
Financials	12.9	1.22
Industrial Cyclicals	13.2	0.81
Consumer Durables	5.7	0.92
Consumer Staples	0.0	0.00
Services	16.5	2.03
Retail	7.2	1.24
Health	13.8	1.59
Technology	27.6	3.01

WPG Government Securities

Ticker	Load	NAV	Yield	SEC Yield	Assets	Objective
WPGVX	None	8.82	7.3%	7.21%	216.4	Gvt General

WPG Government Securities Fund seeks current return consistent with capital preservation.

The fund invests at least 65% of its assets in U.S. government securities having remaining maturities of one or more years except when prevailing market or economic conditions warrant a temporary defensive position. During these periods, the fund may invest more heavily in cash or money-market instruments. The balance of assets are normally invested in shorter-term U.S. government securities, other debt instruments, and cash or cash equivalents, such as liquid high-grade debt obligations and high-grade commercial paper.

Manager's Investment Style

Management is not afraid to take chances. Although more than half of assets are invested safely in U.S. Treasuries, other portions are sprinkled among derivatives such as IOs and POs. These securities have helped to boost yields but hindered the fund's 1994 performance. Management adequately prepared the portfolio for imminent interest-rate hikes, but ran into problems when a flooded market reduced the demand for IOs. Management plans to trim the portfolio's derivative holdings when the CMO market becomes more liquid.

Fund Manager(s)

David W. Hoyle, since 02-86. Birthdate: 07-47.
BS, Georgetown U. 1974   MBA, Harvard 1976

Manager Experience

	Dates Managed	Invest Obj	Std Dev	+/- Index
David W. Hoyle				
Smith Barney Inv Gr Bd B	01/82 - 01/84	CG	6.27	-4.41

Historical Profile

Return	Below Average
Risk	Above Average
Rating ★★	
	Below Average

	77	62	40	55	48	19	9	29

Growth of $10,000

|||| Value of Fund ($000)
— Value of Index ($000)
   LB Corp
▼ Manager Change
▽ Partial Manager Change
► Mgr Unknown After
◄ Mgr Unknown Before

Performance Quartile (Within Objective)

Investment Style History
Fixed Income

Income Rtn % Rank Obj

	1983	1984	1985	1986	1987	1988	1989	1990	1991	1992	1993	1994	History
	---	---	---	10.33	9.77	9.74	10.18	10.22	10.79	10.40	10.37	8.82	NAV
	---	---	---	10.85 *	2.44	7.94	13.91	8.95	13.97	7.89	8.96	-8.81	Total Return %
	---	---	---	---	-0.32	0.07	-0.63	0.00	-2.04	0.64	-0.80	-5.89	+/- LB Aggregate
	---	---	---	---	0.24	0.91	-0.31	0.23	-1.35	0.66	-1.70	-5.44	+/- LB Government
	---	---	---	5.77	7.25	8.25	9.39	8.55	8.39	7.67	7.79	6.02	Income Return %
	---	---	---	5.08	-4.81	-0.31	4.52	0.39	5.58	0.22	1.17	-14.83	Capital Return %
	---	---	---	---	39	73	50	10	62	47	74	90	Total Rtn % Rank All
	---	---	---	---	39	11	16	46	57	11	31	97	Total Rtn % Rank Obj
	---	---	---	0.56	0.72	0.78	0.86	0.82	0.80	0.77	0.79	0.64	Income $
	---	---	---	0.17	0.07	0.00	0.00	0.00	0.00	0.41	0.15	0.02	Capital Gains $
	---	---	---	1.16	0.87	0.82	0.76	0.75	0.81	0.78	0.81	0.78	Expense Ratio %
	---	---	---	6.09	7.41	7.97	8.64	8.13	7.64	7.36	7.43	6.78	Income Ratio %
	---	---	---	203	108	130	159	184	190	137	98	132	Turnover Rate %
	---	---	---	48.7	74.3	78.9	90.2	130.2	193.1	263.8	334.9	216.4	Net Assets ($mil)

Performance 12-31-94

	1st Qtr	2nd Qtr	3rd Qtr	4th Qtr	Total
1987	1.56	-1.57	-2.88	5.51	2.44
1988	3.26	1.77	1.70	1.00	7.94
1989	1.02	7.61	1.23	3.52	13.91
1990	-0.42	3.20	1.44	4.51	8.95
1991	2.42	1.28	5.54	4.10	13.97
1992	-0.63	3.68	4.33	0.37	7.89
1993	3.22	3.23	2.55	-0.29	8.96
1994	-3.39	-4.63	-0.58	-0.45	-8.81

Bear Market Performance

Decile Rank (5-year period)

Worst — Best

	Worst 3 Mo Period 1985-89	Worst 3 Mo Period 1990-94
WPG Government Securities	---	-6.66
+/- LB Aggregate	---	-3.40
+/- Best Fit Index : LB Corp	---	-2.31

Trailing Returns

	Total Return %	+/- LB Aggregate	+/- LB Govt	% Rank All	% Rank Obj	Growth of $10,000
3 Mo	-0.45	-0.82	-0.80	33	88	9,955
6 Mo	-1.02	-2.01	-1.80	74	96	9,898
1 Yr	-8.81	-5.89	-5.44	90	97	9,119
3 Yr Avg	2.34	-2.20	-2.32	90	88	10,719
5 Yr Avg	5.88	-1.74	-1.64	79	78	13,309
10 Yr Avg	---	---	---	---	---	---
15 Yr Avg	---	---	---	---	---	---

Operations

Address and Telephone	One New York Plaza
	New York, NY 10004
	800-223-3332 / 212-908-9582
Advisor	Weiss Peck & Greer
Subadvisor	None
Distributor	WPG Mutual Funds
States Available	All
Report Grade	C+
Income Distrib	Paid Monthly
* Date of Inception	02-20-86
Fiscal Year End	December

Risk Analysis

Time Period	Load-Adj Return %	Risk % Rank [1] All	Obj	Morningstar [2] Return	Morningstar Risk	Morningstar Risk-Adj Rating
1 Yr	-8.81					
3 Yr	2.34	44	87	-0.35 [3]	1.32	★★
5 Yr	5.88	32	72	0.28 [3]	1.12	★★
10 Yr	---	---	---	---	---	

Average Historical Rating (71 months)   4.1 ★ s

[1] 1 = low, 100 = high   [2] 1.00 = Taxable Avg   [3] 1.00 = 90-day T-bill return

Other Measures

				Standard LB Agg	Best Fit LB Corp
Standard Deviation	4.62	Alpha		-2.2	-2.7
Mean	2.43	Beta		1.07	0.87
Sharpe Ratio	-0.24	R-Squared		85	88

Investment Style

Interest-Rate Stance

		Maturity Short Intm Long
Avg Effective Duration	7.4 Yrs**	
Avg Effective Maturity	6.5 Yrs	

Quality

Avg Credit Quality	AAA
Avg Weighted Coupon	9.87%
Avg Weighted Price	112.93% of Par

**figure provided by fund

Diversification Value for Portfolio Types

Large Cap: High	Small Cap: High	Bond: None	Balanced: Medium	Diversified: High

Portfolio 12-31-94

Total Stocks: 0
Total Fixed-Income: 65

Amount 000	Date of Maturity		Value $000	% Net Assets
33135	08-15-13	US Treasury Bond 12%	44059	20.36
16200	11-15-11	US Treasury Bond 14%	23581	10.90
16500	08-15-04	US Treasury Bond 13.75%	22930	10.60
13319	04-01-21	FNMA ARM	12804	5.92
10000		FNMA Note 11.875%	11709	5.41
10000	11-01-99	FNMA Note 11.5%	11411	5.27
30500	05-15-08	US Treasury Bond 0%	10677	4.93
10000	11-30-98	US Treasury Note 5.125%	9097	4.20
8400	02-10-99	FNMA Note 4.5%	7639	3.53
7190	02-15-24	GNMA 7.5%	6672	3.08
5000	08-10-20	FNMA Debenture 9.65%	5334	2.47
5195	04-01-06	Govt Backed Trust Cert 8.5%	5276	2.44
5000	01-15-97	US Treasury Note 8%	5026	2.32
4500	10-01-99	World Bank Global 8.375%	4615	2.13
3565	02-15-16	US Treasury Bond 9.25%	4011	1.85
5000	05-15-98	US Treasury Note 0%	3862	1.78
3610	03-15-24	GNMA Forward 8.5%	3455	1.60
3000	12-22-97	FNMA Note 6.26%	2868	1.33
3000		FNMA Note N/A	2747	1.27
2760	10-31-97	US Treasury Note 5.75%	2616	1.21
2372	12-01-14	FHLMC 9%	2374	1.10
2040	12-16-96	Federal Home Loan Bank 7.69%	2033	0.94
1660	09-10-98	FNMA Debenture 7.85%	1666	0.77
1481	04-20-21	GNMA 10%	1530	0.71
750	06-10-03	FNMA Debenture 6.45%	660	0.31

Composition % 09-30-94

Cash	0.6	Preferreds	0.0
Stocks	0.0	Convertibles	0.0
Bonds	99.4	Other	0.0

Tax Analysis

	Tax-Adj Historical Return %	% Pretax Return
3 Yr Avg	-0.83	
5 Yr Avg	2.91	46.7
10 Yr Avg	---	---

Potential Capital Gain Exposure (% of assets)   -22%

Coupon Range

	% of Bonds	Rel Obj
0%	7.0	5.08
0% to 8%	18.8	0.30
8% to 9%	8.3	0.54
9% to 10%	5.4	0.67
More than 10%	53.1	8.49
Not applicable	7.4	1.25

Sector Analysis 12-31-94

% of Bonds

US Treas	61	CMOs	0
GNMA mtgs	6	ARMs	6
FNMA mtgs	17	Other	9
FHLMC mtgs	2		

Expenses & Fees

Sales Fees	0.00% front
	0.00% deferred
	0.00% 12b-1
Management Fee	0.60% max./0.50% min., 0.03%A
3-,5-,10-yr Expense Projections	$26, $45, $100

Min Purchase

Min Initial Purchase	$2500 (Addt'l: $100)
Min IRA Purchase	$250 (Addt'l: $100)
Min Auto Invest Plan	$50 (Systematic Inv: $50)

Most Similar Funds in MF500

Scudder Income	Strong Fit
PaineWebber Invmt Grade Inc	Fair Fit
American Cap Corp Bond A	Fair Fit

 **1995 Mutual Fund 500**

Yacktman

	Ticker	Load	NAV	Yield	SEC Yield	Assets	Objective
	YACKX	None	10.05	2.2%	2.90%	295.1	Growth

Yacktman Fund seeks long-term growth of capital. Current income is a secondary objective.

The fund invests primarily in equities, including convertibles. It may also invest in money-markets for income and longer-term, high-quality debt for growth. There is no limitation on the percentage of assets that it may invest in any particular type of security. The fund focuses on companies with at least $1 billion in market capitalization that have records of earnings growth and dividends.

The fund pays dealers an annual fee of 0.65% on shares purchased prior to December 31, 1992. These distribution fees are charged over the entire asset base.

Manager's Investment Style

Management seeks highly profitable, large-cap companies with a high ROA and earnings-growth rate. The stock price must be low, and the company's management must be shareholder-oriented. Management veers away from capital-intensive companies, reasoning that their high reinvestment rates hinder returns. Management's strong commitment to this strategy is enforced by a self-proclaimed 10 year time horizon.

Fund Manager(s)

Donald A. Yacktman CFA(1976), since 07-92.
Birthdate: 09-41. BS, U. of Utah 1965   MBA, Harvard 1967

Manager Experience

	Dates Managed	Invest Obj	Std Dev	+/- Index
Donald A. Yacktman				
Selected American	01/83 - 03/92	GI	15.55	1.21

Historical Profile

Return	---
Risk	---
Rating	
	Not Rated

Investment Style History
Equity

Average % Stocks Held in Portfolio: 60% 91% 92%

Growth of $10,000
IIII Value of Fund ($000)
— Value of Index ($000) S&P 500
▼ Manager Change
▽ Partial Manager Change
► Mgr Unknown After
◄ Mgr Unknown Before

Performance Quartile (Within Objective)

	1983	1984	1985	1986	1987	1988	1989	1990	1991	1992	1993	1994	History
	---	---	---	---	---	---	---	---	---	10.39	9.56	10.05	NAV
	---	---	---	---	---	---	---	---	---	4.72 *	-6.58	8.80	Total Return %
	---	---	---	---	---	---	---	---	---	-2.67 *	-16.63	7.48	+/- S&P 500
											-17.86	8.87	+/- Wilshire 5000
	---	---	---	---	---	---	---	---	---	0.52	1.41	2.37	Income Return %
	---	---	---	---	---	---	---	---	---	4.20	-7.99	6.43	Capital Return %
	---	---	---	---	---	---	---	---	---	---	100	2	Total Rtn % Rank All
											99	3	Total Rtn % Rank Obj
	---	---	---	---	---	---	---	---	---	0.05	0.14	0.22	Income $
	---	---	---	---	---	---	---	---	---	0.03	0.00	0.12	Capital Gains $
	---	---	---	---	---	---	---	---	---	1.18	1.18	1.12	Expense Ratio %
	---	---	---	---	---	---	---	---	---	1.49	1.61	2.34	Income Ratio %
										---	61	---	Turnover Rate %
	---	---	---	---	---	---	---	---	---	74.7	143.0	295.1	Net Assets ($mil)

Performance 12-31-94

	1st Qtr	2nd Qtr	3rd Qtr	4th Qtr	Total
1987	---	---	---	---	---
1988	---	---	---	---	---
1989	---	---	---	---	---
1990	---	---	---	---	---
1991	---	---	---	---	---
1992	---	---	---	4.47	4.72 *
1993	-3.81	-6.89	-3.50	8.10	-6.58
1994	-2.24	1.10	9.48	0.55	8.80

Bear Market Performance

Decile Rank (5-year period)

Worst   Best

	Worst 3 Mo Period 1985-89	Worst 3 Mo Period 1990-94
Yacktman	---	---
+/- S&P 500	---	---
+/- Best Fit Index :	---	---

Trailing Returns

	Total Return %	+/- S&P 500	+/- Wil 5000	% Rank All	% Rank Obj	Growth of $10,000
3 Mo	0.55	0.57	1.32	11	14	10,055
6 Mo	10.08	5.22	5.45	4	8	11,008
1 Yr	8.80	7.48	8.87	2	3	10,880
3 Yr Avg	---	---	---	---	---	---
5 Yr Avg	---	---	---	---	---	---
10 Yr Avg	---	---	---	---	---	---
15 Yr Avg	---	---	---	---	---	---

Operations

Address and Telephone	303 W. Madison Street
	Chicago, IL 60606
	800-525-8258 / 312-201-1200
Advisor	Yacktman Asset Management
Subadvisor	None
Distributor	Yacktman Fund
States Available	All
Report Grade	A-
Income Distrib	Paid Quarterly
* Date of Inception	07-02-92
Fiscal Year End	December

Risk Analysis

Time Period	Load-Adj Return %	Risk % Rank [1] All	Risk % Rank [1] Obj	Morningstar [2] Return	Morningstar Risk	Morningstar [3] Risk-Adj Rating
1 Yr	8.80					
3 Yr	---	---	---	---	---	---
5 Yr	---	---	---	---	---	---
10 Yr	---	---	---	---	---	---
Average Historical Rating ---						---

[1] 1 = low, 100 = high   [2] 1.00 = Equity Avg   [3] 1.00 = 90-day T-bill return

Other Measures

	Standard S&P 500	Best Fit
Standard Deviation	---	Alpha	---	---
Mean	---	Beta	---	---
Sharpe Ratio	---	R-Squared	---	---

Investment Style

	Stock Portfolio Avg	Relative S&P 500
Price/Earnings Ratio	16.5	0.89
Price/Book Ratio	5.1	1.49
5 Yr Earnings Gr %	10.0	1.81
Return on Assets %	11.3	1.51
Debt % Total Cap	28.5	1.01
Med Mkt Cap ($mil)	4189	0.32

Style: Value Blend Growth / Size Large Med Small

Diversification Value for Portfolio Types

Large Cap: Small Cap: Bond: Balanced: Diversified:

Expenses & Fees

Sales Fees	0.00% front
	0.00% deferred
	0.25% 12b-1
Management Fee	0.65% max./0.55% min., 0.15%A
3-,5-,10-yr Expense Projections	$39, $67, $147
Annual Brokerage Cost	0.42%

Portfolio 12-31-94

Share Chg (11-94) 000	Amount 000	Total Stocks: 35 / Total Fixed-Income: 0	Value $000	% Net Assets
70	360	Philip Morris	20700	7.01
265	480	Quaker Oats	14760	5.00
10	250	Bristol-Myers Squibb	14469	4.90
18	410	Torchmark	14299	4.84
50	475	Fruit of the Loom Cl A	12836	4.35
30	390	SLMA	12675	4.29
0	135	Loews	11728	3.97
50	420	UST (Inc)	11655	3.95
0	300	Merck	11438	3.88
19	300	United Asset Management	11063	3.75
60	350	Dow Jones	10850	3.68
0	130	Pfizer	10043	3.40
0	170	Clorox	10009	3.39
15	265	Salomon Brothers	9938	3.37
0	180	Johnson & Johnson	9855	3.34
40	250	Tambrands	9656	3.27
0	165	General Mills	9405	3.19
0	200	Ralston-Purina Group	8925	3.02
135	1493	RJR Nabisco	8212	2.78
-30	105	NIKE Cl B	7836	2.65
80	370	Liz Claiborne	6244	2.12
10	410	Valassis Communications	6150	2.08
15	190	Interpublic Group	6104	2.07
24	326	American Media Cl A	5293	1.79
0	80	American Home Products	5020	1.70

Composition % 12-31-94

Cash	2.6	Preferreds	0.0
Stocks	97.4	Convertibles	0.0
Bonds	0.0	Other	0.0

Tax Analysis

	Tax-Adj Historical Return %	% Pretax Return
3 Yr Avg	---	---
5 Yr Avg	---	---
10 Yr Avg	---	---
Potential Capital Gain Exposure (% of assets)		2%

Most Similar Funds in MF500

Fund lacks three-year record

Index Allocation

	% of Stocks
S&P 500	67.1
S&P MidCap 400	12.5
U.S. Small Cap	20.4
Foreign	0.0

Sector Weightings

	% of Stocks	Relative S&P 500
Utilities	0.0	0.00
Energy	0.0	0.00
Financials	17.9	1.70
Industrial Cyclicals	0.0	0.00
Consumer Durables	13.7	2.21
Consumer Staples	38.4	3.07
Services	13.8	1.69
Retail	0.0	0.00
Health	16.2	1.86
Technology	0.0	0.00

Min Initial Purchase etc.

Min Initial Purchase	$2500 (Addt'l: $100)
Min IRA Purchase	$500 (Addt'l: $100)
Min Auto Invest Plan	$500 (Systematic Inv: $100)

Zweig Managed Assets A

	Ticker	Load	NAV	Yield	SEC Yield	Assets	Objective
	ZMAAX	5.50%	11.76	2.2%	N/A	154.4	Asset Alloc.

Zweig Series Trust Managed Assets Fund - Class A seeks total return.

The fund normally invests in a mixture of 30% stocks, 40% bonds, and 30% short-term instruments. It may weight the portfolio within the following parameters: 0-50% in stocks, 0-60% in bonds, and 0-100% in short-term instruments. Stocks purchased may include any type of equity security; the fund seeks a group of companies in each country in which it invests whose performance in the aggregate closely parallels that country's major stock index. Fixed-income securities and short-term instruments consist of high-quality obligations.

Class A shares have front loads and lower 12b-1 fees; Class B shares have deferred loads.

Manager's Investment Style

Management uses a custom-made model to help time market movements. Key focal points include monetary conditions, institutional buying patterns, and investor sentiment. Management simultaneously tracks the markets in eight major countries. If the economy appears promising and liquidity is increasing, management will buy a market-like portfolio of stocks. If commodity prices point to falling interest rates, management will accquire a representative collection of bonds. In the event of market instability, assets are moved into cash.

Fund Manager(s)

Timothy Clark, since 02-93. Birthdate: 03-63.
BA, Harvard 1985   MBA, New York U. 1990

Manager Experience

	Dates Managed	Invest Obj	Std Dev	+/- Index
Timothy Clark				
Zweig Government Secs C	02/92 - 12/94	GG	4.05	-0.97

Historical Profile

Return	---
Risk	---
Rating	Not Rated

Investment Style History
Equity
30% 15%

Average % Stocks Held in Portfolio

Growth of $10,000

‖‖‖ Value of Fund ($000)
— Value of Index ($000)
   S&P 500
▼ Manager Change
▽ Partial Manager Change
► Mgr Unknown After
◄ Mgr Unknown Before

Performance Quartile (Within Objective)

	1983	1984	1985	1986	1987	1988	1989	1990	1991	1992	1993	1994	History
	---	---	---	---	---	---	---	---	---	---	12.38	11.76	NAV
	---	---	---	---	---	---	---	---	---	---	11.98 *	-2.93	Total Return %
	---	---	---	---	---	---	---	---	---	---	5.04 *	-4.24	+/- S&P 500
	---	---	---	---	---	---	---	---	---	---	---	-0.01	+/- LB Aggregate
	---	---	---	---	---	---	---	---	---	---	1.22	2.08	Income Return %
	---	---	---	---	---	---	---	---	---	---	10.76	-5.01	Capital Return %
	---	---	---	---	---	---	---	---	---	---	---	43	Total Rtn % Rank All
	---	---	---	---	---	---	---	---	---	---	---	58	Total Rtn % Rank Obj
	---	---	---	---	---	---	---	---	---	---	0.14	0.26	Income $
	---	---	---	---	---	---	---	---	---	---	0.17	0.00	Capital Gains $
	---	---	---	---	---	---	---	---	---	---	1.67	1.60	Expense Ratio %
	---	---	---	---	---	---	---	---	---	---	1.93	2.26	Income Ratio %
	---	---	---	---	---	---	---	---	---	---	---	336	Turnover Rate %
	---	---	---	---	---	---	---	---	---	---	121.6	154.4	Net Assets ($mil)

Performance 12-31-94

	1st Qtr	2nd Qtr	3rd Qtr	4th Qtr	Total
1987	---	---	---	---	---
1988	---	---	---	---	---
1989	---	---	---	---	---
1990	---	---	---	---	---
1991	---	---	---	---	---
1992	---	---	---	---	---
1993	---	2.48	4.27	1.48	11.98 *
1994	-1.30	-1.07	-0.42	-0.17	-2.93

Bear Market Performance

Decile Rank (5-year period)

	Worst		Best
		Worst 3 Mo Period 1985-89	Worst 3 Mo Period 1990-94
Zweig Managed Assets A		---	---
+/- S&P 500		---	---
+/- Best Fit Index :		---	---

Trailing Returns

	Total Return %	+/- S&P 500	+/- LB Aggregate	% Rank All	Obj	Growth of $10,000
3 Mo	-0.17	-0.15	-0.55	27	24	9,983
6 Mo	-0.59	-5.45	-1.58	66	80	9,941
1 Yr	-2.93	-4.24	-0.01	43	58	9,707
3 Yr Avg	---	---	---	---	---	---
5 Yr Avg	---	---	---	---	---	---
10 Yr Avg	---	---	---	---	---	---
15 Yr Avg	---	---	---	---	---	---

Operations

Address and Telephone	5 Hanover Square 17th Floor
	New York, NY 10004
	800-444-2706 / 212-635-9800
Advisor	Zweig/Glaser Advisers
Subadvisor	None
Distributor	Zweig Securities
States Available	All
Report Grade	B
Income Distrib	Paid Quarterly
* Date of Inception	02-08-93
Fiscal Year End	December

Risk Analysis

Time Period	Load-Adj Return %	Risk % Rank [1] All	Obj	Morningstar [2] Return	Morningstar Risk	Morningstar Risk-Adj Rating
1 Yr	-8.27	---	---	---	---	---
3 Yr	---	---	---	---	---	---
5 Yr	---	---	---	---	---	---
10 Yr	---	---	---	---	---	---

Average Historical Rating ---

[1] 1 = low, 100 = high   [2] 1.00 = Hybrid Avg   [3] 1.00 = 90-day T-bill return

Other Measures

			Standard S&P 500	Best Fit
Standard Deviation	---	Alpha	---	---
Mean	---	Beta	---	---
Sharpe Ratio	---	R-Squared	---	---

Investment Style

Stocks

	Port Avg	Rel S&P 500
Price/Earnings Ratio	24.1	1.30
Price/Book Ratio	2.9	0.86
5 Yr Earnings Gr %	5.3	0.95
Med Mkt Cap ($mil)	8655	0.67

Bonds

Avg Effective Duration	---
Avg Effective Maturity	6.6 Yrs
Avg Credit Quality	AAA
Avg Weighted Coupon	6.68%

Diversification Value for Portfolio Types

Large Cap: Small Cap: Bond: Balanced: Diversified:

Portfolio 12-31-94

Total Stocks: 237
Total Fixed-Income: 28

Share Chg (06-94)000	Amount 000		Date of Maturity	Value $000	% Net Assets
	12630	US Treasury Bond 7.125%	02-15-23	11489	7.44
	4824	Export-Import Bk Japan 4.375%	10-01-03	4744	3.07
	4907	US Treasury Note 5.5%	04-15-00	4426	2.87
	4323	US Treasury Bond 7.5%	11-15-24	4134	2.68
	2137	United Kingdom Treasury 6.75%	11-26-04	2915	1.89
	14387	Govt of France 8.25%	02-27-04	2700	1.75
	2577	US Treasury Bond 8.125%	08-15-19	2609	1.69
	2982	US Treasury Note 5.875%	02-15-04	2602	1.68
	1874	Republic of Austria 4.5%	09-28-05	1839	1.19
	2715	Republic of Germany 6.75%	09-22-97	1647	1.07
	1818	FHLMC Debenture 7.05%	03-24-04	1643	1.06
	2513	Republic of Germany 7.25%	10-20-97	1605	1.04
	1641	US Treasury Note 5.75%	08-15-03	1427	0.92
	1508	FNMA Debenture 6.85%	04-05-04	1385	0.90
	1281	FNMA Debenture 7.6%	04-14-04	1208	0.78
	1776	Commonwealth Australia 7.5%	07-15-05	1154	0.75
3	22	Columbia/HCA Healthcare		812	0.53
	708	US Treasury Note 7.25%	08-15-04	680	0.44
	650	General Electric Cap 8.375%	03-01-01	655	0.42
	645	Exxon Capital 7.875%	08-15-97	643	0.42

Index Allocation

	% of Stocks
S&P 500	27.3
S&P MidCap 400	3.3
U.S. Small Cap	7.5
Foreign	62.1

Composition % 12-31-94

Cash	87.4	Preferreds	0.0
Stocks	14.2	Convertibles	0.0
Bonds	34.0	Other	-35.6

Tax Analysis

	Tax-Adj Historical Return %	% Pretax Return
3 Yr Avg	---	---
5 Yr Avg	---	---
10 Yr Avg	---	---
Potential Capital Gain Exposure (% of assets)		-3%

Most Similar Funds in MF500

Fund lacks three-year record

Bond Credit Analysis 12-31-94

% of Bonds

US Govt	100	BB	0
AAA	0	B	0
AA	0	Below B	0
A	0	NR/NA	0
BBB	0		

Stock Sector Weightings

	% of Stocks	Relative S&P 500
Utilities	11.0	0.89
Energy	7.5	0.74
Financials	19.2	1.81
Industrial Cyclicals	18.2	1.11
Consumer Durables	5.5	0.88
Consumer Staples	12.7	1.02
Services	9.9	1.22
Retail	4.6	0.79
Health	6.5	1.01
Technology	4.8	0.53

Min Initial Purchase $1000 (Addt'l: $100)
Min IRA Purchase $250 (Addt'l: None)
Min Auto Invest Plan $1000 (Systematic Inv: $100)

Expenses & Fees

Sales Fees	5.50% front
	0.00% deferred
	0.30% 12b-1
Management Fee	1.00% flat fee
3-,5-,10-yr Expense Projections	$105, $141, $242
Annual Brokerage Cost	---

MORNINGSTAR 1995 Mutual Fund 500

Indexes

423	Quantitative Growth & Inc Ord	476	SteinRoe Managed Municipals	539	Vanguard Fixed-Inc S/T Corporate
424	Quantitative Numeric Ord	477	SteinRoe Prime Equities	540	Vanguard Fixed-Inc S/T Federal
425	• Quest For Val Cap	478	SteinRoe Special	541	Vanguard Fixed-Inc S/T US Treas
426	Quest For Value A	479	SteinRoe Total Return	542	Vanguard Index Extended Market
427	Quest For Value Opportunity A	480	SteinRoe Young Investor	543	Vanguard Index 500
		481	Stratton Monthly Dividend	544	Vanguard Index Total Stock Mkt
428	Reich & Tang Equity	482	Strong Advantage	545	Vanguard Intl Growth
429	Robertson Stephens Contrarian	483	Strong Asia Pacific	546	Vanguard Muni Bond High-Yield
430	Robertson Stephens Value + Grth	484	Strong Asset Allocation	547	Vanguard Muni Bond Insured L/T
431	Royce Equity-Income	485	Strong Common Stock	548	Vanguard Muni Bond Interm-Term
432	Royce Premier	486	Strong Discovery	549	Vanguard Muni Bond Limited-Term
433	• Royce Value	487	Strong Government Securities	550	Vanguard Muni Bond Short-Term
434	Rydex Nova	488	Strong Growth	551	Vanguard Preferred Stock
		489	Strong International Stock	552	Vanguard Special Energy
435	Safeco Equity	490	Strong Municipal Bond	553	Vanguard Special Gold & Prec Met
436	Safeco Income	491	Strong Opportunity	554	Vanguard Special Health Care
437	Safeco Municipal Bond	492	Strong Short-Term Bond	555	Vanguard Special Utilities Inc
438	Salomon Bros Opportunity	493	SunAmerica Tax-Exempt Insured A	556	Vanguard STAR
439	SBSF Convertible Securities	494	• Swiss Helvetia	557	Vanguard U.S. Growth
440	SBSF			558	Vanguard/Wellesley Income
441	Schafer Value	495	• Taiwan Fund	559	Vanguard/Wellington
442	Schooner	496	Templeton Developing Markets	560	Vanguard/Windsor
443	Scudder Global	497	• Templtn Em Mkts	561	Vanguard/Windsor II
444	Scudder GNMA	498	Templeton Foreign	562	Vista Capital Growth A
445	Scudder Growth & Income	499	Templeton Growth	563	Vista Growth & Income A
446	Scudder High-Yield Tax-Free	500	Templeton Income	564	Vista Tax-Free Income A
447	Scudder Income	501	Templeton Real Estate Securities		
448	Scudder International Bond	502	Templeton Smaller Company Growth	565	Warburg Pincus Captl Appr Comm
449	Scudder International	503	• Thai Fund	566	Warburg Pincus Emerging Gr Comm
450	Scudder Latin America	504	Third Avenue Value	567	Warburg Pincus Growth & Income
451	Scudder Medium-Term Tax-Free	505	Thornburg Ltd-Term Muni Natl A	568	Wasatch Aggressive Equity
452	Scudder Short-Term Bond	506	• Transamerica Income	569	Washington Mutual Investors
453	Scudder Short-Term Global Income	507	Tweedy, Browne American Value	570	Weitz Value
454	Selected American	508	Tweedy, Browne Global Value	571	Westcore Midco Growth Ret
455	Seligman High-Yield Bond A	509	20th Century Balanced Investors	572	WPG Government Securities
456	Seligman Income A	510	20th Century Growth Investors		
457	Sentinel Balanced	511	20th Century Heritage Investors	573	Yacktman
458	Sentinel Common Stock	512	20th Century Intl Equity		
459	Sequoia	513	20th Century Ultra Investors	574	Zweig Managed Assets A
460	Seven Seas Growth & Income	514	20th Century Value		
461	Sit Growth				
462	Sit Tax-Free Income	515	U.S. Government Securities		
463	Skyline Special Equities	516	UMB Stock		
464	Skyline Special Equities II	517	United Income		
465	Smith Barney Appreciation A	518	United Municipal High-Income		
466	Smith Barney Income & Growth A	519	USAA Investment Balanced		
467	Smith Barney Tax-Exempt Income B	520	USAA Investment Cornerstone		
468	SoGen Gold	521	USAA Mutual Income		
469	SoGen International	522	USAA Mutual Income Stock		
470	SoGen Overseas	523	USAA Tax-Exempt Interm-Term		
471	Sound Shore	524	USAA Tax-Exempt Long-Term		
472	• Source Capital	525	USAA Tax-Exempt Short-Term		
473	Stagecoach Asset Allocation A				
474	SteinRoe Income	526	Value Line Convertible		
475	SteinRoe Intermediate Municipals	527	Value Line Income		
		528	Value Line Leveraged Growth Inv		
		529	Value Line Tax-Exempt High-Yield		
		530	Van Kampen Insured T/F Income A		
		531	Vanguard Asset Allocation		
		532	Vanguard Bond Idx Total Bond Mkt		
		533	Vanguard Convertible Securities		
		534	Vanguard Equity-Income		
		535	Vanguard Fixed-Inc GNMA		
		536	Vanguard Fixed-Inc High-Yld Corp		
		537	Vanguard Fixed-Inc I/T US Treas		
		538	Vanguard Fixed-Inc L/T Corp Bond		

Mahoney, Michael J.	
222	G.T. Global Telecommunications A
Mair, James E.	
372	Pasadena Balanced Return A
373	Pasadena Growth A
Management Team,	
384	PIMCo Adv Growth C
385	PIMCo Adv Opportunity C
386	PIMCo Adv Target A
460	Seven Seas Growth & Income
527	Value Line Income
529	Value Line Tax-Exempt High-Yield
Mangum, Charles	
183	Fidelity Select Health Care
Manning, Howard	
420	•Putnam Mgd Muni Inc
Manning, Kimberley R.	
446	Scudder High-Yield Tax-Free
Manning, Robert J.	
324	MFS High-Income A
Marsico, Thomas F.	
275	Janus Growth & Income
277	Janus Twenty
Martin, Edward L.	
86	Babson Bond L
Martini, Reno J.	
103	Calvert Tax-Free Res Lim-Term A
Marx III, Lawrence	
340	Neuberger & Berman Guardian
Matlack, Paul A.	
127	Delaware Delchester A
Maunder, Rachael	
238	Govett Emerging Markets
Mayer, Charles P.	
266	Invesco Industrial Income
McCart, M. Jane	
476	SteinRoe Managed Municipals
McClennen, James C.A.	
294	•Liberty All-Star
McCormick, Walter T.	
287	Keystone Custodian K-1
McDermott, Kelly	
135	Dreyfus Global Growth
McDermott, Lawrence T.	
467	Smith Barney Tax-Exempt Income B
McEvoy, Earl E.	
536	Vanguard Fixed-Inc High-Yld Corp
538	Vanguard Fixed-Inc L/T Corp Bond
551	Vanguard Preferred Stock
558	Vanguard/Wellesley Income
McKissack, Eric T.	
83	Ariel Appreciation A
McMahon, Brian J.	
505	Thornburg Ltd-Term Muni Natl A

McNamara, Michael A.	
285	Kemper High-Yield A
Medcalf, Thomas W.	
260	IDS Mutual
Meeder, Jr., Robert S.	
197	Flex-funds Muirfield
Meyer, Robert	
289	•Latin Amer Discover
Michael, Thomas G.	
434	Rydex Nova
Milans, Gonzalo	
243	•Growth Fund Spain
Millard, Kathleen T.	
445	Scudder Growth & Income
Miller, George A.	
72	American Balanced
262	Income Fund of America
269	Investment Company of America
Miller, Harry W.	
522	USAA Mutual Income Stock
Miller, James A.	
90	Bartlett Basic Value
Miller, Jeffrey J.	
143	Enterprise Capital Appreciation
294	•Liberty All-Star
Miller, Mary J.	
407	T. Rowe Price Tax-Fr Short-Intrm
Miller, Neal P.	
179	Fidelity New Millennium
Miller, Timothy J.	
267	Invesco Strategic Leisure
Miller III, William H.	
290	Legg Mason Special Invmnt Prim
291	Legg Mason Total Return
Milnamow, Robert	
383	Phoenix Total Return A
Mobius, J. Mark	
496	Templeton Developing Markets
497	•Templtn Em Mkts
Molumphy, Christopher J.	
210	Franklin AGE High-Income
Monrad, Bruce H.	
352	Northeast Investors
Monrad, Ernest E.	
352	Northeast Investors
Mooney, John C.	
493	SunAmerica Tax-Exempt Insured A
Moorhead, James T.	
248	Hancock Sovereign Investors A
Morris, Charles A.	
402	T. Rowe Price Science & Tech
Mousseau, John	
305	Lord Abbett Tax-Free Income Natl

Moynihan, Richard J.	
138	Dreyfus Municipal Bond
Mueller, Jay N.	
484	Strong Asset Allocation
Mulally, James R.	
106	Capital World Bond
Mullarkey, Michael J.	
336	Mutual Benefit
Mullin, Hugh	
411	Putnam Convertible Income Grth A
Mullins, Bert J.	
133	Dreyfus Disciplined Stock Inv
Multiple Managers,	
556	Vanguard STAR
Muresianu, John	
190	Fidelity Utilities
Murphy, David L.	
188	Fidelity Spartan Sh-Interm Muni
Mussey, John M.	
347	Newport Tiger
Nanberg, Leslie J.	
327	MFS World Governments A
Navin, Stacey	
456	Seligman Income A
Neff, John B.	
232	•Gemini II Cap
233	•Gemini II Inc
560	Vanguard/Windsor
Negri, David P.	
362	Oppenheimer Strategic Income A
Neill, Jane	
270	•Irish Investment
Neuharth, Chris J.	
198	Fortis Advantage Asset Alloc A
Newell, Roger D.	
534	Vanguard Equity-Income
Newton, William C.	
242	Growth Fund of America
269	Investment Company of America
345	New Perspective
Nguyen, Triet M.	
418	•Putnam H/Y Muni
Nicholas, Albert O.	
348	Nicholas
350	Nicholas Income
Nicholas, David O.	
349	Nicholas II
351	Nicholas Limited Edition
Nichols, Gerald T.	
127	Delaware Delchester A
Nichols, John P.	
103	Calvert Tax-Free Res Lim-Term A
Nicklin, Jr., Edmund H.	
147	Evergreen Growth & Income

Sachnowitz, Lanny H.
61 AIM Charter

Sakamoto, Ross
473 Stagecoach Asset Allocation A

Sams, William M.
207 FPA Paramount

Sanborn, Robert J.
356 Oakmark

Sandler, Michael C.
113 Clipper

Sargent, Bruce D.
466 Smith Barney Income & Growth A

Sarofim, Fayez
132 Dreyfus Appreciation

Saunders, Jr., John W.
519 USAA Investment Balanced
520 USAA Investment Cornerstone
521 USAA Mutual Income

Sauter, George U.
542 Vanguard Index Extended Market
543 Vanguard Index 500
544 Vanguard Index Total Stock Mkt

Schafer, David K.
441 Schafer Value

Schliemann, Peter C.
87 Babson Enterprise
88 Babson Enterprise II

Schmidt, James K.
247 Hancock Regional Bank B

Schoolar, Jonathan C.
62 AIM Constellation
65 AIM Weingarten

Schotte, Richard T.
79 American High-Income
97 Bond Fund of America
262 Income Fund of America
515 U.S. Government Securities

Schroeder, David W.
92 Benham Treasury Note

Schwartz, Robert D.
296 •Lincoln Natl Convert

Scullion, Rodger
104 Calvert World Values Glob Eqty A

Segalas, Spiros
252 Harbor Capital Appreciation

Selfslagh, Serge
223 G.T. Global Worldwide Growth A

Selmier II, W. Travis
520 USAA Investment Cornerstone

Shanahan, R. Michael
81 American Mutual
242 Growth Fund of America
269 Investment Company of America

Simon, Jeff
310 MainStay Value B

Simons, Kent
340 Neuberger & Berman Guardian

Single, Paul
365 Overland Express Var Rate Govt A

Sit, Debra A.
462 Sit Tax-Free Income

Sit, Eugene C.
461 Sit Growth

Smet, John H.
97 Bond Fund of America
515 U.S. Government Securities

Smith, Bonnie L.
313 Merger

Smith, Catherine A.
254 •High Yield Plus

Smith, Charles C.
456 Seligman Income A

Smith, Charles P.
401 T. Rowe Price New Income

Smith, Irwin F.
294 •Liberty All-Star

Smith, Scott E.
89 •Baker Fentress

Snyder III, John F.
248 Hancock Sovereign Investors A

Spalding, Thomas C.
353 Nuveen Municipal Bond
354 •Nuv Muni Value

Speaker, Ronald V.
273 Janus Flexible Income

Spears, John D.
507 Tweedy, Browne American Value
508 Tweedy, Browne Global Value

Spelman, Edmund C.
306 MainStay Capital Appreciation B
309 MainStay Total Return B

Spitz, Warren E.
410 Prudential Utility B

Stanek, Mary Ellen
389 Portico Bond Immdex Ret

Stansky, Robert E.
172 Fidelity Growth Company

Stauffer, Susann
59 Advantage Income

Steinmetz, Arthur P.
362 Oppenheimer Strategic Income A

Stellmacher, Ralph W.
360 Oppenheimer High-Yield A

Stephens, Andrew C.
484 Strong Asset Allocation

Stephens, Paul H.
429 Robertson Stephens Contrarian

Stewart, Scott
167 Fidelity Fifty

Stewart, Jr., Samuel S.
568 Wasatch Aggressive Equity

Stonberg, Peter
423 Quantitative Growth & Inc Ord

Stone, John R.
336 Mutual Benefit

Stowers III, James E.
510 20th Century Growth Investors
513 20th Century Ultra Investors

Strabo, Henrik
512 20th Century Intl Equity

Strathearn, Michael C.
121 Connecticut Mutual Total Return

Stratton, James W.
481 Stratton Monthly Dividend

Stromberg, William J.
392 T. Rowe Price Dividend Growth

Strong, Richard S.
486 Strong Discovery

Stumpp, Mark
408 Prudential Allocation Conserv B

Suarez, Eduardo
243 •Growth Fund Spain

Sudweeks, Bryan
330 Montgomery Emerging Markets

Swanberg, Charles H.
422 Putnam Voyager A

Swayze, Gary
177 Fidelity Municipal Bond

Tananbaum, Steven
308 MainStay Hi-Yield Corp Bond B

Tank, Bradley C.
484 Strong Asset Allocation
487 Strong Government Securities
492 Strong Short-Term Bond

Taubes, Kenneth J.
414 George Putnam Fund of Boston A
419 Putnam Income A

Taylor, Donald G.
184 Fidelity Short-Term Bond

Taylor, Morais A.
304 Lord Abbett Bond-Debenture

Teitelbaum, Lawrence
448 Scudder International Bond
453 Scudder Short-Term Global Income

Tern, Joseph
311 •Malaysia Fund

Terrana, Beth F.
168 Fidelity

Testa, M. David
396 T. Rowe Price Intl Stock

Nuts and Bolts: Introductory Information for the New Investor

Putting Yourself in the Investment Picture

Before selecting a mutual fund or a portfolio of funds, you need first to answer some questions about yourself: What specifically do you hope to achieve by investing? What kinds of risks are you willing and able to take on? By assessing your own investment goals and your tolerance for risk, you pave the way to intelligently choosing the fund mix right for you.

Too often people approach investing as a search for the perfect fund—that is, one that can be considered a good buy for any investor. Unfortunately, there are no great, blanket investments, nor are there shortcuts to the process of building a diversified portfolio. If there are no one-size-fits-all winners, then what constitutes a good fund? The best answer to this question is a personal one: A fund is a good investment if it fulfills the goal or goals you have set.

There are also no guaranteed approaches to building a suitable mutual-fund portfolio. Therefore we don't provide ready-made models to guide you in picking funds. Instead, we offer here some broad guidelines outlining the questions to ask yourself when trying to determine an appropriate fund mix for you.

What are your specific investment goals?

Are you investing with a specific goal in mind—such as financing the purchase of a car or house—or do you have several goals, ranging from the short to the long term? Short-term goals are those that fall within roughly three years. Accumulating the down payment for an upcoming home purchase could be considered a short-term goal. Intermediate goals fall between three and 10 years; this could include the financing of a child's college education. Long-term goals, such as planning for retirement, are those 10 or more years in the future. Clearly defining your investment objectives based on the time over which you wish to invest will help you devise an effective fund mix.

Based on your goals, how much risk can you prudently assume?

The greater the time you have to invest, the greater amount of risk you're probably willing to tolerate. If an investment goal lies far in the future, you can ride out the periods of downward fluctuation in an aggressive fund that offers the potential for high growth; such investments emphasize capital growth over preservation of initial investments. If your need for the money is sooner rather than later, though, you're better sticking with more stable investments that emphasize capital preservation. Otherwise, your need for the capital may very well coincide with a period of depressed fund performance.

Based on your personality, how much risk can you tolerate?

After objectively evaluating your investment goals, it's important not to forget that investing is a personal process. You should not select funds purely on the basis of dispassionate, objective criteria. You also need to think about your own personality and how it relates to investing. For example, if you are someone who lies awake nights worrying about the fate of any but the most cautious investment, then perhaps your portfolio should tend toward more conservative funds. If you have a longer investment horizon, though, you may still want to venture into stock funds by choosing those that are specifically geared toward cautious investors. This would allow you to enjoy some of the long-term growth potential of the equity market with less relative risk.

On the other hand, if you enjoy taking chances, yet your investment goals are rather short-term, you could allocate a modest percentage of your portfolio to more-volatile offerings. This lets you venture into riskier, more exciting areas without betting your future on them.

Considering the factors of goals, risk, and personality, what should your portfolio look like?

After identifying goals and the investment framework that feels most comfortable, you can begin to look at the different types of funds offered to see how each might fit into your portfolio. You'll need to decide how many funds to hold; just remember there is no optimal number. On one hand, the more funds into which your assets are divided, the less harm any single fund's losses can inflict. On the other hand, too many funds are difficult to follow conscientiously. Further, if one of your fund choices enjoys a period of outstanding returns, you want to have enough invested in it to make the gains significant.

In assessing a fund, it's important to consider its place in a broader portfolio. A diversified portfolio is one that offers potential for growth in a variety of market conditions. For example, an international stock fund with highly fluctuating returns could alone be considered quite volatile and risky. When added to a portfolio of domestic funds, though, it could help offset potential declines in the U.S. market.

Any decisions you make regarding your portfolio should be re-evaluated periodically as the time horizon on your investments changes. For example, retirement investing for a 20-year-old is clearly a long-term concern, so such a portfolio can emphasize many aggressive funds. As retirement draws near, however, it would be prudent to shift into more-conservative funds or into a guaranteed savings account. Putting short-term dollars into funds that seek primarily to preserve capital will help ensure having money available when you need it, though it does mean sacrificing growth potential.

Morningstar Mutual Fund 500 Categories

Welcome to the the world of the *Morningstar Mutual Fund 500*—a compendium of 450 open-end and 50 closed-end funds. With a universe of more than 5,000 mutual funds to choose from, making selections for this book was not an easy process. We feel, however, that the 500 funds shown here represent the most consistently successful funds in the mutual-fund industry today.

In order to narrow down the fund universe to 500, we have eliminated all institutional funds not available for purchase by individual investors from the *Morningstar Mutual Fund 500*. We have also excluded funds closed to new investors and clones, or highly similar funds. We thought it important that the *Morningstar Mutual Fund 500* list represent a wide array of funds, even if funds of a specific type had relatively low ratings. Thus, we have included gold and foreign funds, even though traditionally these funds earned lower star ratings than our core selections.

We have also had to make some judgment calls. For example, we included a list of 50 rookie funds, believing it was necessary to give investors information on some young, promising prospects. This is especially true of our selection of closed-end funds. The closed-end universe has expanded so rapidly the past few years that we thought it negligent to exclude interesting candidates simply on the basis of their newness.

The investment categories for the *Morningstar Mutual Fund 500* break down as follows:

Taxable Bond

The taxable-bond fund category for the *Morningstar Mutual Fund 500* is comprised of 50 funds—our picks for the best taxable-bond funds in the mutual-fund universe. These selections represent a wide array of taxable-bond objectives: corporate bond–general, corporate bond–high quality, government bond–adjustable-rate mortgage (ARM), government bond–general, and government bond–Treasury.

When evaluating these funds, keep in mind that only corporate funds face credit risk, because the U.S. government does not allow any of its securities to default. All funds in this category, however, face interest-rate risk; the lower their average weighted coupon, the higher the interest-rate sensitivity. Additionally, as the average weighted maturity increases, so does the fund's volatility. Such risk is more greatly felt in time of rising interest rates.

Municipal Bond

Municipal-bond funds hold bonds issued by state, city, or other local governments. They are all exempt from federal taxes, and many are also exempt from state and local taxes. (It should be noted that there are no single-state municipal bonds listed in the *Morningstar Mutual Fund 500*. We exclude single-state municipal-bond funds because they are of interest primarily to investors who live in the state where a particular fund invests.) Municipal-bond funds are attractive for investors who want tax-exempt earnings, and for those who depend on current income. Yields here tend to be higher than those from taxable—bond funds because of their longer bond maturities. This increased maturity does lead to greater interest-rate sensitivity.

Specialty Bond

We group the most-aggressive bond funds under the name of Specialty-bond funds. These funds are not appropriate as corner-stones for any but the most aggressive fixed-income portfolios. They can, however, add an aggressive edge to a diversified portfolio.

Specialty-bond funds are similar to other bond funds in that they provide regular income. They become more aggressive, however, by taking on specific forms of additional risk. High-yield (sometimes called junk) and convertible bonds, for example, are directly or indirectly linked to the performance of an issuer's stock; they therefore contain an element of equity exposure. International bonds are denominated in foreign currency, exposing them to changes in valuation relative to the dollar. The strategic income funds included in the *Morningstar Mutual Fund 500* seek to balance bond-market exposure by combining a percentage of aggressive international, junk, or convertible bonds with investment-grade bonds or cash.

Hybrid

Hybrid funds are those that generally invest in a combination of stocks and bonds. Some funds in this category may be useful for those who can invest in only one or a very few mutual funds. The hybrid category includes three objectives: asset allocation, balanced, and income. Because hybrid funds include exposure to both bonds and stocks, changes in either market affect these funds less dramatically than they do funds invested largely in one market or the other. Hybrid funds rarely offer chart-topping returns, but their diversification protects them from the biggest losses as well. Not all hybrid funds are as stable as others, however. When evaluating hybrid funds, look at their composition and fund-objective information, as well as their Morningstar risk score.

Conservative

We group stock funds in the conservative category if they have a 3-year Morningstar risk score of less than 0.75, indicating low or below-average risk. Such funds provide a solid foundation on which to build a portfolio. Conservative funds may include the following objectives: equity income, foreign stock, growth, growth and income, specialty-utility, and world stock. Funds in this category often moderate their stock exposure with some bonds or cash. Their stock holdings tend toward those of large or medium-size companies and of low or moderate price. The total returns of these funds are derived more from distributions (stock dividends or capital gains) than are those of more-aggressive stock funds. As a result, the returns, on average, fluctuate less dramatically than those of core or aggressive funds.

Core

Core stock funds are those that are appropriate as equity holdings for the portfolios of the broadest range of our readers. Three-year Morningstar risk scores for funds in this category will generally fall between 0.75 and 1.00, indicating near-average risk. Core funds typically include the following objectives: aggressive growth, equity income, foreign stock, specialty–financial, specialty–health, specialty–natural resources, and world stock. Funds in the core category demonstrate greater volatility of yearly total returns than do those in the conservative category, but in the long term they offer higher average returns.

Aggressive

In the aggressive stock funds group you'll find the most volatile mutual-fund offerings in the *Morningstar Mutual Fund 500* (excluding some closed-end funds). These funds are best-suited for long-term investing or for adding diversification and strong growth potential to your portfolio. Such funds carry a Morningstar risk score of more than 1.00, indicating high or above-average risk. Aggressive funds typically include the following objectives: aggressive growth, growth, Europe stock, Pacific stock, foreign stock, world stock, small company, specialty–financial, specialty–health, specialty–precious metals, and specialty–technology.

Because this category comprises an array of fund objectives, you should look closely at the objectives, style boxes, and sector weightings to get a clearer picture of what each fund is setting out to accomplish. The returns of many of these funds fluctuate in opposition to those of more-conservative funds—for example, a gold fund may rally when other equity funds are lagging. Aggressive funds can therefore reduce the overall volatility of an investor's portfolio.

Closed-End

Unlike mutual funds, which sell unlimited shares that are redeemable at their net asset value (NAV), closed-end funds have a limited number of shares and they are traded on an exchange. Prices of closed-end shares may rise above or fall below NAV, based on demand. We've divided the closed-end funds in the *Morningstar Mutual Fund 500* into equity and income groupings. The equity offerings range from domestic-equity funds to those that invest in international regions and individual countries. Closed-end income funds include both domestic and international funds as well.

When evaluating closed-end funds, consider the percentage premium or discount. This figure denotes whether market sentiment is causing the fund to trade above or below its net asset value. Additionally, the Morningstar risk scores vary greatly in these groupings: You'll find higher- and lower-risk funds grouped together on the same page.

Two other important fund categories separate some funds not by how they invest, but by a characteristic of the fund itself: its availability to new investors or its age.

Closed Fund Hall of Fame

The Closed Fund Hall of Fame tracks funds that have closed their doors to new investors usually because of their large asset size. Included here are some of the most successful and well-known funds in the mutual-fund industry.

Rookie Funds

Rookie funds are those investment vehicles too young to earn their stars. In order to be rated by Morningstar, a fund must have a three-year history. Thus, these funds have been chosen by Morningstar based on criterion (other than performance) that we think will make the fund stand out, such as the fund company's past success, for example, or a manager's unique investment style. Once the fund attains a three-year history, it is then evaluated as to whether it should join the rest of the *Morningstar Mutual Fund 500* or be dropped from the list completely.

Glossary of Terms

All items labeled on the page are listed below alphabetically and defined. Entries for items not explicitly labeled on the page include the following: fund name (top left), investment criteria (block of text at top left), style box (in the Investment Style section at the center of the page), and performance indexes (+/– items in History and Trailing Returns sections).

A

Address
Usually the location of the fund's distributor, this address is where to write to receive a prospectus.

Administrative Fees
see Fees

Administrator
(Closed-end funds only)
This is the company responsible for the fund's administrative functions which may include fund accounting and preparation of shareholder reports and mailings.

Advisor
This is the company that takes primary responsibility for managing the fund.

Alpha
see Modern Portfolio Theory Statistics

Amount
see Portfolio

Annual Brokerage Cost
The most recent annual brokerage cost (not shown for fixed-income funds) is a ratio representing the percentage of assets spent by a fund on stock transactions. In each fund's Statement of Additional Information, the dollar amount paid in brokerage fees is listed. That number is divided by the fund's average net assets for the same period. It is important to remember that brokerage fees are not calculated into a fund's expense ratio. Some trading costs are omitted, however, such as those of non-exchange-listed stocks, for which higher trading costs are built into the bid-ask spread. Accordingly, the true trading costs of some international and small-company funds are understated. Because trading costs for bonds are incorporated into bond prices, we do not calculate brokerage costs for bond funds.

Assets
The assets of the fund, listed at the top of the page, are listed in millions of dollars, reflecting the total dollars in the fund at the end of the most recently reported month.

Auditor
(Closed-end funds only)
This is the independent accountant employed by the fund to audit the fund's official shareholder reports.

Average Credit Quality
see also Credit Analysis
Average credit quality gives a snapshot of the portfolio's overall credit quality. It is an average of each bond's credit rating, weighted by the relative size in the portfolio.

Average Effective Duration
Average effective duration provides a measure of a fund's interest-rate sensitivity—the longer a fund's duration, the more sensitive the fund is to shifts in interest rates. The relationship between funds with different durations is straightforward: a fund with a duration of 10 years is twice as volatile as a fund with a five-year duration. Duration also gives an indication of how a fund's NAV will change as interest rates change. A fund with a five-year duration would be expected to lose 5% from its NAV if interest rates rose by one percentage point or gain 5% if interest rates fell by one percentage point.

Because fund companies use various methods to calculate duration, Morningstar calculates bond portfolio durations in-house using data provided by Capital Management Sciences in order to provide direct comparisons of different funds' durations. Morningstar prints an average effective duration statistic that incorporates call, put, and prepayment possibilities. When it is impossible to calculate duration (often because of inadequate bond labeling in a shareholder report), Morningstar will sometimes substitute a fund company's calculation of duration. Such substitutions are denoted with a double asterisk (**). These fund-company numbers may provide some indication of a fund's interest-rate sensitivity, but they are not necessarily directly comparable to Morningstar's calculations.

For closed-end funds, the ratio of the fund's average effective duration to the average effective duration of all the funds in the same objective appears to the right in the Rel Obj column. The objective average is set to 1.0. For example, a figure of 1.2 means that the fund's average effective duration is 20% greater than the average effective duration for the objective.

Average Effective Maturity
Average effective maturity, used for taxable fixed-income funds only, is a weighted average of all the maturities of the bonds in a portfolio, computed by weighting each maturity date (the

date the security comes due) by the market value of the security. Average effective maturity takes into consideration all mortgage prepayments, puts, and adjustable coupons; it does not, however, account for call provisions. Longer-maturity funds are generally considered more interest-rate sensitive than their shorter counterparts.

For closed-end funds, the ratio of the fund's average effective maturity to the average effective maturity of all the funds in the same objective appears to the right in the Rel Obj column. The objective average is set to 1.0. For example, a figure of 1.2 means that the fund's average effective maturity is 20% greater than the average effective maturity for the objective.

Average Historical Rating

The figure at the bottom of the performance/risk section is the fund's average historical rating, the mean of the fund's overall star ratings (as they appear in the historical profile box) for all of the months in which a fund received a rating. This statistic provides a broader context in which to evaluate a fund's current rating. A 5-star fund that also posts an average rating between 4 and 5 stars has consistently been highly rated in Morningstar's system. Alternatively, a 5-star fund that carries an average rating of only 3.2 stars has likely fluctuated among various star ratings over the time it has been rated.

Also, this statistic reflects fund performance in time periods that may have temporarily fallen out of consideration for the star rating. Funds that are more than five but less than 10 years old, for example, have only their most-recent five years' performance enter into the overall star rating. That portion of its history beyond five years will not re-enter the equation until the fund is 10 years old, because the overall risk-adjusted rating is a weighted average of the fund's three-, five-, and 10-year histories.

The average historical rating is followed by the number of months for which the fund has been rated. This statistic provides additional context for the star rating. If, for example, a fund with a 5.0 average star rating has been rated for only six months, the conclusions an investor can draw about the fund's resilience in various market climates are somewhat limited. On the other hand, an investor can be fairly confident that a 4-star fund with a 3.6 average rating over 90 months historically has been able to manage risk effectively in a variety of markets.

Average Reset Interval

Average reset interval is the average time it takes for a portfolio of adjustable-rate mortgages (ARMs) to adjust their coupons to their respective indexes. The price of an ARM that resets its coupon monthly will typically be more stable than one that adjusts semiannually or annually because monthly adjustments allow an ARM's coupon to more closely mirror current market interest rates.

Average Weighted Coupon

Average weighted coupon is computed by weighting each bond's rate of interest by its relative size in the portfolio. This figure indicates whether the fund is opting for a high- or low-coupon strategy, and serves as an indicator of interest-rate sensitivity, particularly for mortgage-backed funds or other funds with callable bonds. A high coupon frequently indicates less sensitivity to interest rates; a low coupon, the opposite. (Refer to the overview pages for an objective average). Because the coupons are constantly changing in adjustable-rate mortgage funds, this statistic is omitted for these funds.

The ratio of the fund's average weighted coupon to the average weighted coupon of all the funds in the same objective appears to the right in the Rel Obj column. The objective average is set to 1.0. For example, a figure of 1.2 means that the fund's average weighted coupon is 20% greater than the average weighted coupon for the objective.

Average Weighted Maturity

Average weighted maturity, listed only for municipal-bond funds, is computed by weighting the nominal maturity of each security in the portfolio by the market value of the security, then averaging these weighted figures. Unlike Morningstar's duration figure, it does not take prepayments, puts, calls, or adjustable coupons into account.

Average Weighted Price

Average weighted price is computed for most bond funds by weighting the price of each bond by its relative size in the portfolio. This number reveals whether the fund favors bonds selling at prices above or below face value (premium or discount securities, respectively). This statistic is expressed as a percentage of par (face) value. This statistic is not calculated for world bond and short-term world income funds, as those funds' holdings are often expressed in terms of foreign currencies.

The ratio of the fund's average weighted price to the average weighted price of all the funds in the same objective appears to the right in the Rel Obj column. The objective average is set to 1.0. For example, a figure of 1.2 means that the fund's average weighted price is 20% greater than the average weighted price for the objective.

B

Bear Market Ranking

This statistic enables investors to gauge a fund's performance during a bear market. As a standard measure, we compare all equity funds in the Morningstar mutual-fund universe against the S&P 500 index and all fixed-income funds against the Lehman Brothers Aggregate Bond Index. Morningstar defines a bear market for equities as any month during the last five years that the S&P 500 lost more than 3.00%. Morningstar defines a bear market for bonds as any month in the past five years that the Lehman Brothers index lost more than 1.00%. Morningstar adds together a fund's performance during each bear market month to reach a cumulative bear market return. Based on these returns, equity funds are compared against other equity funds and bond funds are compared against other bond funds. They are then assigned a decile ranking; the higher the ranking the better the fund performed during bear markets. Because Morningstar employs the trailing five-year time period for this statistic, only funds with five years of history are given a bear market performance number.

Bear Market Ranking

Equity			Bond		
Month	S&P 500	Fund X	Month	LB Agg	Fund Y
1/90	−6.71	−14.51	1/90	−1.19	−1.18
8/90	−9.04	−8.10	8/90	−1.34	−2.11
9/90	−4.87	−9.54	1/92	−1.36	−0.46
6/91	−4.58	−1.80	10/92	−1.33	−1.74
11/91	−4.03	−1.84	2/94	−1.74	−2.07
3/94	−4.35	−6.78	3/94	−2.74	−3.26
11/94	−3.63	−4.40	9/94	−1.47	−0.93
Total		**−46.67**	**Total**		**−11.75**

The total is then compared to all similar funds (Equity or Bonds) and ranked on a scale of 1 to 10. The highest 10% get a score of 1, the second 10% get a score of 2, etc.

$$\frac{\text{Absolute Rank} \times 10}{\text{\# of Funds}} = \text{Decile Rank}$$

For example, if the decile is 3:

Decile Rank (5-year period)

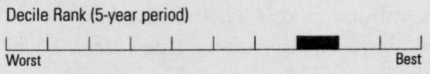

Worst | Best

+/− Benchmark Index

A benchmark index gives the investor a point of reference for evaluating a fund's performance. In all cases where such comparisons are made, Morningstar uses the S&P 500 as the basic benchmark for equity funds, including asset-allocation, balanced, and income funds, and the Lehman Brothers Aggregate Bond Index (an overall bond benchmark) as the benchmark index for fixed-income funds, including convertible, high-yield, and world bond funds.

For all funds except certain domestic-equity and hybrid funds, the column to the right of the benchmark index provides a comparison with a secondary, specialized benchmark. Because the S&P 500 is composed almost entirely of straight domestic-equity securities, it is fine for measuring domestic-equity funds. Comparing a foreign stock fund with the S&P 500, however, does not tell the reader much about how the fund has done compared with foreign stock markets. Therefore, in this column, a fund's total return is compared with that of one of the following indexes that track investment performance relevant to that fund's objective.

FB H-Y Bond
(First Boston High-Yield Bond Index)
This index tracks the returns of all new publicly offered debt of more than $75 million rated below BBB.

JSE Gold
(Johannesburg Stock Exchange Gold Index)
This index tracks the performance of gold on the Johannesburg stock exchange.

LB ARM
(Lehman Brothers Adjustable-Rate Mortgage Index)
This index serves as a benchmark for the performance of adjustable-rate mortgage securities issued by GNMA, FNMA, and FHLMC.

LB Corp
(Lehman Brothers Corporate Bond Index)
This index tracks the returns of all publicly issued, fixed-rate, nonconvertible, dollar-denominated, SEC-registered, investment-grade corporate debt.

LB Govt
(Lehman Brothers Government Bond Index)
This index tracks the returns of U.S. Treasuries, agency bonds, and one- to three-year U.S. government obligations.

LB Int
(Lehman Brothers Intermediate-term Treasury)
This index tracks the performance of U.S. Treasury Bonds with maturities up to 10 years.

LB L-T
(Lehman Brothers Long-term Treasury Index)
This index measures the returns of U.S. Treasury Bonds with maturities greater than 10 years.

LB Mtg
(Lehman Brothers Mortgage-Backed Securities Index)
This index includes 15- and 30-year fixed-rate securities backed by mortgage pools issued by GNMA, FNMA, and FHLMC.

LB Muni
(Lehman Brothers Municipal Bond Index)
This index serves as a benchmark for the performance of long-term, investment-grade, tax-exempt municipal bonds.

MSAllCtry
(Morgan Stanley Capital International All Country Index)
This index tracks the performance of stock markets in 43 countries, including the United States and Japan.

MSCI Emerging
(Morgan Stanley Capital International Emerging Markets Index)
This index is composed of 20 of the world's emerging markets: Argentina, Brazil, Chile, Columbia, Greece, India, Indonesia, Jordan, Korea, Malaysia, Mexico, Pakistan, Peru, the Philippines, Portugal, Sri Lanka, Taiwan, Thailand, Turkey, and Venezuela.

MSCI Europe
(Morgan Stanley Capital International Europe Index)
This index measures the performance of stock markets in Austria, Belgium, Denmark, Finland, France, Germany, Ireland, Italy, the Netherlands, Norway, Spain, Sweden, Switzerland, and the United Kingdom.

MSCI EAFE
(Morgan Stanley Capital International Europe, Australia, and Far East Index)
Widely accepted as a benchmark for international stock performance, the EAFE Index is an aggregate of 20 individual country indexes that collectively represent many of the major markets of the world, excluding Canada and the United States.

MSCI FE ex Japan
(Morgan Stanley Capital International Far East excluding Japan Index)
This is an index of Far Eastern markets, excluding Japan.

MSCI Japan
(Morgan Stanley Capital International Japan Index)
This index measures the performance of Japan's stock market.

MSCI Latin Am
(Morgan Stanley Capital International Latin America Index)
This index tracks the performance of Latin American markets.

MSCI Pacific
(Morgan Stanley Capital International Pacific Index)
This index measures the performance of stock markets in Australia, Hong Kong, Japan, New Zealand, Singapore, and Malaysia.

MSPacxJp
(Morgan Stanley Capital International Pacific Index excluding Japan)
This index follows the performance of stock markets in Australia, Hong Kong, New Zealand, Singapore, and Malaysia.

MSCI World
(Morgan Stanley Capital International World Index)
This index measures the performance of stock markets in 22 nations, including Australia, Hong Kong, Germany, the United Kingdom, Canada, and the United States.

MSWdxUS
(Morgan Stanley Capital International World Index excluding U.S.)
This index follows the performance of stock markets in 21 countries excluding the United States.

Russell 2000
(Russell 2000 Index)
This commonly cited small-cap index tracks the returns of the smallest 2,000 firms in the Russell 3000 Index, which is composed of the 3,000 largest companies in the United States, as measured by market capitalization.

SB World
(Salomon Brothers Non-U.S.-Dollar World Government Bond Index)
This index measures total-return performance of government bonds with a maturity of one year or more in 12 countries other than the United States. The index weights bonds based on market capitalization, so that large debt-issuing countries such as Japan and Germany have larger representations than do smaller issuing countries.

S&P 400
(Standard and Poor's 400 Index)
This mid-cap index measures the performance of the largest 400 stocks outside of the S&P 500.

S&P Energy
(Standard and Poor's Energy Composite Index)
This specialty index measures the performance of energy stocks, including oil, drilling, and exploration companies.

S&P Financial
(Standard and Poor's Financial Index)
This specialty index measures the performance of the financial stocks, including banks, S&Ls and insurance companies.

S&P Health
(Standard and Poor's Health-Care Composite Index)
This specialty index measures the performance of health-care stocks, including drug, hospital management, and medical supply companies.

S&P Metals
(Standard and Poor's Metals Index)
This specialty index measures the performance of the precious metals stocks.

S&P Tech
(Standard and Poor's High-Technology Composite Index)
This specialty index measures the performance of high-technology stocks, including computer, aerospace, and electronics companies.

S&P Utility
(Standard and Poor's Utilities Index)
This specialty index measures the performance of utilities stocks, including electric, gas, and telephone companies.

Wil 4500
(Wilshire 4500 Index)
This index measures the performance of all U.S. common-stocks excluding those in the S&P 500.

Wil 5000
(Wilshire 5000 Index)
This index measures the performance of all U.S. common-stocks including those in the S&P 500.

Wil REIT
(Wilshire Real-Estate Investment Trust Index)
This is an index of real-estate investment trusts.

Closed-end funds may also feature the following:

Wil
(Wilshire Equity Indexes)
A collection of six equity indexes covering three ranges of company sizes (small-, mid-, and large-cap) and two company types (value and growth).

Best-Fit Index
A market index that has the best monthly returns correlation with a fund in the last 36 consecutive months. Morningstar regresses the fund's monthly excess returns against monthly excess returns of several well-known market indices. "Best-Fit" signifies the index that provides the highest R-squared.

Beta
see Modern Portfolio Theory Statistics

C

Capital Gains
Capital gains are the profits received and distributed from the sale of securities within the portfolio. This line shows a summary of the fund's annual capital-gains distributions expressed in per-share dollar amounts. Options premiums and distributions from paid-in capital are also recorded here.

Capital Return
see also Total Return
Here, Morningstar provides the amount of total returns that was generated by both realized and unrealized increases in the value of securities in the portfolio.

Composition Percentages
The composition percentages provide a simple breakdown of the fund's portfolio holdings, as of the date listed in its banner, into general investment classes. Cash encompasses both the actual cash and the cash equivalents (fixed-income securities with a maturity of one year or less) held by the portfolio. Negative percentages of cash indicate that the portfolio is leveraged, meaning it has borrowed against its own assets to buy more securities. The percentage listed as stocks incorporates only the portfolio's straight common stocks. Bonds include every fixed-income security with a maturity of more than one year, from government notes to high-yield corporate bonds. Preferreds show preferred stocks (equity securities that pay dividends at a specified rate) but do not include convertible preferreds. Convertible bonds and convertible preferreds are considered corporate securities that are exchangeable for a set number of another form of security (usually common shares) at a prestated price. Other denotes all those not-so-neatly categorized securities, such as warrants and options. With these composition figures, investors can glean information about the portfolio's investment strategy. A portfolio with a large percentage of its assets in cash, for example, might indicate a defensive position, while a heavy bond exposure in a balanced fund may reveal a solid income orientation. A gold fund's significant weighting in the other category might indicate a tendency to hold defensive gold bullion.

Country Exposure
The country exposure table, which appears for Europe and Pacific stock funds as well as world-bond and short-term world-income funds, displays the five countries in which the fund invests most heavily and the percentage of the portfolio's bonds each country represents. Some funds invest in the European Currency Unit (ECU), a currency substitute that includes the European Economic Community currencies. The information given here is the most recent available; the date is listed at the top of the table.

Coupon Range

Fixed-income funds feature a table listing the statistical breakdown of each portfolio's bond coupons, or rates of interest. The coupon range is designed to help an investor complete the picture suggested by the average weighted coupon statistic. Coupon ranges are not provided for adjustable-rate mortgage funds because these bonds' coupon rates are constantly changing.

These numbers are calculated by sorting bonds' coupons into five ranges. These ratings differ according to fund objective. For example, coupon rates for all general, mortgage, and Treasury government-bond funds are currently divided into the following ranges: 0%; 0% to 8%; 8% to 9%; 9% to 10%; and over 10%.

Because of changing interest rates, these ranges are subject to alteration over time. Whatever the breakdown may be, the first number is always exclusive and the second number is always inclusive. A range of 8% to 9%, for example, would exclude bonds that have a weighted coupon rate of exactly 8.0% but would include bonds with a weighted coupon rate of 9.0%. High-yield bond funds include PIKs in their coupon breakdown, which are payment-in-kind issues that make interest payments in the form of additional securities rather than cash.

The final category in the coupon range is Not Applicable, which covers any holding without a stated coupon rate—variable or adjustable-rate securities or certain mortgage derivatives, for example.

The overall percentage of bond assets that fall within each coupon range is noted in the % of Bonds column. Next to the percentage of bonds is the relative objective (Rel Obj) column, which compares a fund with others in its objective class. In this column's scale, the objective average is set at 1.00.

Credit Analysis

For corporate- and municipal-bond funds, this section contains a credit analysis depicting the quality of bonds in the portfolio. The credit analysis is a table showing the percentage of fixed-income securities that fall within each credit-quality rating. Bond ratings appear on the lefthand side of the table and the percentage of bonds shows up on the righthand side, next to each rating category.

At the top of the ratings are U.S. government bonds. Bonds issued and backed by the government are of extremely high quality and thus are considered separate from but equal to bonds rated AAA, which is the highest possible rating a corporate issue can receive. Morningstar gives U.S. government bonds a credit rating separate from AAA securities to allow a more accurate credit analysis of a portfolio's holdings. Bonds with a BBB rating are the lowest bonds that are still considered to be of investment grade. Bonds that are rated BB or lower (often called junk bonds or high-

yield bonds) are considered to be quite speculative. Any bonds that appear in the NR/NA category are either not rated or did not have a rating available at the time of publication.

Currency Exposure Graph

The currency-exposure table features the five currencies to which a fund has the greatest exposure, and appears on the page for all world-bond and short-term world-income funds. Morningstar has included this table because many foreign-bond funds routinely alter their profiles through currency hedging.

A fund's currency exposure is calculated as a percentage of its net assets. That way, cash that is denominated in other currencies can be included in the graph. Cross-hedges aren't included in the graph. In other words, if a manager hedges his British pound exposure by shorting the Spanish peseta, the pound will still show up in the currency exposure graph. Negative currency exposures do not appear on the graph.

Custodian

For closed-end funds: This is the company that maintains the fund's assets and securities. By law, the advisor of a fund may not serve as its custodian. While many funds contract this service out to large banks, some large investment advisors set up independent divisions to serve as custodian.

D

Date of Inception

The date of inception gives the date on which the fund commenced operations. If an asterisk appears next to the date, then returns for that partial year appear in the history section of the page. (Those returns are also marked with an asterisk.)

Debt Leverage Amount

see Leverage Amount

Debt Percent of Total Capital

This is the weighted average calculation of the amount of capital (assets) that companies derive from long-term debt (as opposed to equity). Companies with relatively low debt ratios and high returns on assets are generally considered to be of high quality. This figure can be useful for identifying fund managers who are careful about the balance sheets of the companies in which they invest.

This statistic is displayed in comparison with the Vanguard Index Trust 500 Portfolio (a fund that serves as a surrogate for the S&P 500 Index), such that 1.00 equals the market level. A figure of 0.43, for example, indicates that the fund's statistic is 57% lower than that of the market average. Similarly, a score of 1.15 indicates that the fund's statistic is 15% greater than the equivalent calculation for the index.

Direct Purchase Plan

For closed-end funds: This indicates whether or not the fund has a plan through which shareholders may purchase additional shares of a fund directly from the fund's management.

Discount

see Premium/Discount

Distributor

The distributor, also known as the fund underwriter, is the company that distributes the shares of the fund. This task usually includes promoting the fund and preparing and sending out fund literature.

Diversification Value

For diversification value, Morningstar developed five hypothetical portfolios comprised of a variety of indexes—each portfolio represents a basic investment style. By regressing the funds in the Mutual Fund 500 against each of the five portfolios, an R-squared, or correlation, measure is derived. The lower the correlation, the better the diversification value of that particular fund.

The five hypothetical portfolios that comprise diversification value are as follows.

Large-cap	S&P 500
Small-cap	Russell 2000
Bond	Lehman Brothers Aggregate
Balanced	60% Wilshire 5000 / 40% Lehman Brothers Aggregate
Diversified Stock	70% Wilshire 5000 / 30% EAFE

If the R-squared is below 25, a rating of High ● is bestowed upon the fund. If the R-squared falls between 25 and 50, the fund receives a Medium ◕ rating. An R-squared in the 50 to 80 range earns the fund a Low ◔ rating and a correlation over 80 merits a rating of None ○.

E

Earnings Growth

(5-Year)

The five-year earnings-growth rate is a measure of the trailing five-year annualized earnings growth record of the stocks currently in the portfolio. This number is weighted such that larger positions in the portfolio count proportionately more than lesser positions. Stocks with losses during the past five years, or stocks that lack a five-year track record, are excluded from this calculation. Growth-oriented managers are more likely than

are value managers to pay for stocks with high historical earnings-growth rates. This statistic is displayed in comparison with the Vanguard Index Trust 500 Portfolio (a fund that serves as a surrogate for the S&P 500 Index), such that 1.00 equals the market level. A figure of 0.43, for example, indicates that the fund's statistic is 57% lower than that of the market average. Similarly, a score of 1.15 indicates that the fund's statistic is 15% greater than the equivalent calculation for the index.

Economic Sensitivity

The stock market is prone to cyclical increases and decreases. In a downturn, also known as a bear market, stock investments generally lose value. In bull markets, or times of market growth, stock investments in general flourish. Stocks related to markets that are strongly affected by the health of the economy, such as luxury items, real estate, and industrial goods, will be more prone to such cyclical fluctuations.

Exchange

For closed-end funds: This is the exchange or exchanges on which the fund is traded. The most common exchanges for closed-end funds are the New York Stock Exchange (NYSE) and the American Stock Exchange (AMEX). Other exchanges that may be listed include NASDAQ, the Chicago Stock Exchange (CSE), the Toronto Stock Exchange (TSE), the Pacific Stock Exchange (PSE), the Osaka Stock Exchange (OSE), and the over-the-counter (OTC) market.

Expense Projections

(Three-, Five-, and 10-Year)

Found in the fund's prospectus, these figures show how much an investor would expect to pay in expenses—sales charges (loads) and fees—over the next three, five, and 10 years, assuming a $1,000 investment that grows by 5% per year.

Expense Ratio

The annual expense ratio expresses the percentage of assets deducted each fiscal year for fund operating expenses, including 12B-1 fees, management fees, administrative fees, operating costs, and all other asset-based costs incurred by the fund, except brokerage costs. Sales charges are not included in the expense ratio. The expense ratio, which is deducted from the fund's average net assets, is accrued on a daily basis. If the fund's assets, listed in the bottom row of the history section, are small, the expense ratio can be quite high because the fund must meet its expenses from a restricted asset base. Conversely, as the net assets of the fund grow, the expense percentage should ideally diminish as expenses are spread across the wider base.

For closed-end funds, if an annualized ratio is not available from the fund, Morningstar will calculate an annualized figure from whatever data are available and mark it on the page with a bullet [•].

F

Fees

Administrative
The maximum administrative fee is the fund's maximum allowable charge for costs like management-fee structures, excluding advisor fees. Other costs associated with SEC compliance may also be included under this banner. Administrative fees often operate on a sliding scale. The costs of basic fund operations, such as leasing office space are included. Investors should note that there is not necessarily a total expense differential between funds with disclosed administrative fees and funds without disclosed administrative fees. Most funds roll administrative costs into their management fees; other funds, especially those with out-of-house administration, prefer to break them out.

Management
The management fee is the percentage deducted from a fund's average net assets to pay an advisor or subadvisor. Often, as the fund's net assets grow, the percentage deducted for management fees decreases. For example, a particular fund may report a management fee of 0.40% on the first $500 million in assets, 0.35% on all assets between $500 million and $1 billion, and 0.30% on assets in excess of $1 billion. Thus, if the fund contains $1.5 billion in total net assets, the advisor scales back its management fees accordingly. Alternatively, the fund may compute the fee as a flat percentage of average net assets. A portion of the management fee may also be charged in the form of a group fee (G), which normally operates on a sliding scale. To determine the group fee, the fund family creates a sliding scale for the family's total net assets and determines a percentage applied to each fund's asset base. The management fee might also come in the form of a performance fee (P), which raises or lowers the management fee based on the fund's returns as they compare with an established index (we list the maximum by which the fee can increase or decrease); or a gross income fee (I), a percentage based on the total amount of income generated by the investment portfolio.

Sales, or Load
Sales charges note the maximum level of initial and deferred sales charges (also known as loads) and 12B-1 and redemption fees imposed by a fund. The scales of minimum and maximum charges are taken from a fund's prospectus. Because fees change frequently and are sometimes waived, it is wise to examine the fund's prospectus carefully for specific information before investing.

L (Load)
The initial sales charge or front-end load is a deduction made from each investment in the fund. The amount is generally based on the amount of the investment, so large investments may receive quantity discounts.

B (12B-1)
The 12B-1 fee represents the maximum annual charge deducted from fund assets to pay for distribution and marketing costs. Although occasionally a flat dollar amount, this fee is almost always a percentage. Some funds may be permitted to impose 12B-1 fees but are not doing so at present. Only active 12B-1 plans are represented here. Total distribution charges, excluding loads, are capped at 1.00% of average net assets annually. Of this, a 12B-1 fee may account for up to 0.75%.

S (Service)
Closely related to the 12B-1 fee, the service fee is part of the total distribution cost. Capped at a maximum 0.25%, the service fee is designed to compensate financial planners or brokers for continued as shareholder liaison, services which may include responding to customer inquiries and providing information on investments. An integral component to level-load and deferred-load funds, the fees were previously known as a trail commission. Despite the implication of its name, service fees do not include any transfer agency or custodial services.

R (Redemption)
The redemption fee is an amount charged when money is withdrawn from the fund. This fee does not go back into the pockets of the fund company, but rather into the fund itself and thus does not represent a net cost to shareholders. Also, unlike deferred charges, redemption fees typically operate only in short, specific time clauses, often 30 or 60 days. However, some redemption fees exist for up to four years. Charges are not imposed after the stated time has passed. These fees are typically imposed to discourage market timers, whose quick movements into and out of funds can be disruptive. The charge is normally imposed on the ending share value, appreciated or depreciated from the original value.

Fund Name
The fund name that appears in the banner is a shortened version of the fund's legal name.

G

Graphs
see also Performance Quartile Graph
The dotted line on the graph charts the growth of $10,000 for the fund over the past 12 years; the solid line shows the growth of $10,000 of the Best-Fit index.

For closed-end funds, the graph shows the growth of $10,000 in terms of both NAVs and market prices. The heavy line represents the growth of a $10,000 investment based on NAV performance and the light line represents the growth of the same investment based on market-price performance. The starting date for each line is set to the earliest month from which Morningstar has continuous monthly return data, or to the leftmost point on the chart—January 1983.

Both lines are plotted on a logarithmic scale, so that identical percentage changes in the value of an investment have the same vertical distance on the graph. For example, the vertical distance between $10,000 and $20,000 is the same as the distance between $100,000 and $200,000 because both represent a 100% increase in investment value. This provides a more accurate representation of a fund's performance than would a simple arithmetic graph. All the graphs are scaled so that the full length of the vertical axis represents a tenfold increase in investment value. For funds whose returns have exhibited greater than a tenfold increase over the period shown in the graph, the vertical axis has been compressed accordingly.

Growth of $10,000
The last column in the performance/risk section shows the current value of a $10,000 investment made at the beginning of each of the time periods listed. These calculations are not load- or tax-adjusted.

H

Historical Profile
see also Morningstar Rating Components
The historical profile, found within the graph at the center top of the page, provides Morningstar's overall assessment of a fund's historical returns and risk, and its overall risk-adjusted star rating. The return and risk assessments are based on a fund's historical performance relative to other funds in its broad investment category (equity, taxable-bond, municipal-bond, or hybrid). The three time periods are combined in a weighted average: The 10-year rating accounts for 50% of the overall rating, the five-year figure for 30%, and the three-year rating for 20%. If only five years of history are available, the five-year period is weighted 60% and the three-year period 40%. If only three years of data are available, the three-year figure is also the overall rating.

The Historical Profile section also provides Morningstar's overall assessment of a fund's historical return and risk. The same bell curve that is used in the calculation of the risk-adjusted star rating is used in determining a fund's three-, five-, and 10-year return and risk profiles. Return or risk that falls in the top 10% of those of all funds in the investment category are labeled High; the next

22.5% are considered Above Average; the middle 35% are Average; the next 22.5% are labeled Below Average; and the bottom 10% are considered Low.

The return and risk profiles for the three time periods are then combined as weighted averages: The 10-year return or risk profile accounts for 50% of the overall rating, the five-year profile for 30%, and the three-year profile for 20%. If only five years of history are available, the five-year period is weighted 60% and the three-year period 40%. If only three years of data are available, the three-year figure is also the overall profile. Because the overall return or risk assessments are weighted averages of profiles from different time periods, it does not follow that the overall assessments will follow the same percentage breakdowns as profiles from a single time period. In other words, it is not a given that 10% of funds in a particular category will have an overall assessment of High, 22.5% a rating of Above Average, and so on.

I

Income
The dividends and interest generated by a fund's holdings. This line shows a fund's yearly income distribution expressed in per-share dollar amounts.

Income Ratio
The fund's income ratio reveals the percentage of current income earned per share. It is calculated by dividing the fund's net investment income by its average net assets. The net investment income is the total income of the fund, less operating expenses. An income ratio can be negative if a fund's expenses exceed its income, which can occur with funds that tend to emphasize capital gains rather than income. Because the income ratio is based on a fund's fiscal year and is taken directly from the fund's prospectus, it may not exactly correspond with other calendar-year information on the page.

For closed-end funds, income ratios annualized by Morningstar will be marked with a bullet [•].

Income Return
see also Total Returns
This figure shows the portion of the fund's total returns that was derived from the reinvestment of income distributions.

Index Allocation

For closed-end funds: This table shows what portion of the fund's equity assets belong to various market indexes or foreign exchanges. The first percentage reveals a fund's concentration in the 30 Dow Jones Industrial stocks. Likewise, the next two figures show a fund's exposure to the S&P 500 stocks and to those in the S&P Mid-Cap 400. The fourth category, U.S. Small Stocks, represents all U.S. companies not included in the two S&P indexes.

The last percentage is the portion of equity assets in foreign stocks. American Depositary Receipts (ADRs) are treated as foreign stocks, even though they are foreign stocks that are packaged for trade on U.S. exchanges.

Investment Criteria

Located in the upper lefthand corner, the investment criteria section describes the investment policies and objectives of the mutual fund. This information is not an analysis of the fund's current investment patterns or strategies; rather it is derived from the description of objectives and strategies found in the fund's prospectus.

L

Legal Counsel

This is the law firm or attorneys responsible for the fund's legal affairs.

Leverage Amount

For closed-end funds: This shows the dollar amount by which a fund has increased its asset base, whether through borrowing, issuance of classes of preferred shares, or both. Data may be from the fiscal- rather than the calendar-year-end. The greater the proportion of the leverage dollar amount to the net assets, the greater the effect changes in the value of the portfolio will have on shareholders' NAV.

Leverage Factor

For closed-end funds: This is an indication of how leverage can amplify the effect that a fund's portfolio has on returns. It is calculated by adding the current dollar amount of leverage to the current net assets applicable to common shareholders, and then dividing the sum by the current net assets applicable to common shareholders. For example, a fund with $100 million in net assets that has borrowed $50 million in leverage would have a factor of 1.5. By applying this factor to the percentages in the composition, or any of the portfolio-related breakdowns, one can get a truer sense of the potential impact different portions of the portfolio might have on the fund's returns. Using the above example, if a portfolio holding that represented 10% of a fund's investments were to drop in value to zero, the impact on

the common shareholder's NAV would be a drop of 10% times 1.5, or 15%. Of course, upward swings in a portfolio's value would be similarly amplified.

Load

see also Fees

Load denotes a fund's maximum initial or deferred sales charge. This figure is expressed as a percentage of the initial investment payable for front-end loads (sales charges incurred upon purchase of shares). If the fund does not have a load and remains open to investors, None appears. If the fund no longer offers shares to new investors, Closed is listed here. A percentage followed by a w indicates that, at the time of publication, the fund is waiving its load for the general public.

Load-Adjusted Total Return

For this statistic, listed in the Rating section, total returns are adjusted downward to account for sales charges and are listed for the trailing one-, five-, and 10-year periods. For funds with front-end loads, the full amount of the load is deducted. For deferred loads, the percentage charged declines the longer shares are held. This charge, often coupled with a 12B-1 fee, usually disappears entirely after several years. For funds that lack a 10-year history, Morningstar provides a load-adjusted return figure for the period since the fund's inception.

M

Management Fee

see Fees

Manager Experience

This feature shows management's track record for at least two other funds the manager has previously led. Morningstar first looks for funds the manager has headed in the past. If none of exist, funds currently under the manager's direction are singled out. In the case of a team or multiple-managed fund, management is ordered by tenure: Morningstar databases search for the manager with the longest history first. If no data is found, the next manager's history is examined. Under the manager name, the fund name, dates of management, objective, excess return, and annualized standard deviation are reported. If the manager's history is less than one year, Morningstar reports the actual excess return for that period; otherwise this figure is annualized. All equity-managed funds are compared against the S&P 500 and all fixed-income-managed funds are compared to the Lehman Brothers Aggregate.

Manager Investment Style

This feature describes the investment style of a mutual fund's management. Unlike the criterion section (above Manager Investment Style on the page), which elucidates the broad investment parameters as stated in the fund's prospectus, this feature specifically focuses on the investment strategies that management has employed in the past to achieve total return.

Manager Profile

Information about the individual or individuals responsible for choosing what securities make up the fund's portfolio. Each manager's name is followed by the date he or she began managing the fund, and any degrees he or she has obtained. If a fund provides a list of several managers' names, Morningstar will list them as space permits. Management teams may consist of many people, but if one manager is considered a central figure, that individual's name will be printed first.

Investors often wonder whether they should redeem their shares in a fund when it changes managers. This question usually arises when a manager with a great reputation leaves a fund. First and foremost, investors should not hastily sell their shares. While it's easy to feel that it's necessary to make an immediate decision, in fact, the departing manager's imprint will usually remain on the fund for some time after his or her departure. The new manager will inherit a portfolio and only slowly begin to replace the securities with ones of his or her own choosing. Therefore, hasty judgments are unnecessary; shareholders often have plenty of time to consider what, if any, action the manager change necessitates.

Market Price

see also NAV

For closed-end funds: The price at which closed-end funds may be bought or sold. The price at the top of the fund review page is the closing price as of 12/31/94. The market price of a closed-end fund share generally differs from the NAV; the existence of this price difference is the main feature separating closed-end funds from open-end mutual funds. The label Market Price in the legend of the performance graph indicates returns calculated on the basis of market prices as opposed to NAVs.

Market Total Return

see Total Return

Maturity

see Portfolio

Maturity Breakdown

Instead of a sector analysis, Treasury funds feature a maturity breakdown table. This table shows the percentage of Treasuries that fall within the following maturity ranges:

one to three years; three to five years; five to seven years; seven to 10 years; 10 to 15 years; 15 to 20 years; and 20 to 30 years. In each case, the first number is always exclusive and the second number is always inclusive.

Mean

see Standard Deviation

Median Market Capitalization

The median market capitalization of an equity portfolio gives the reader a measure of the size of the companies in which the fund invests. Half of the fund's assets are invested in the stocks of companies larger than the median market capitalization statistic, and half is invested in smaller issues. The advantage of a median over an average is that the median is not disproportionately affected by one or two extremely large or small holdings. For example, a small-company fund that holds a small position in General Electric for liquidity purposes won't have its market cap unduly skewed by the median figure.

For closed-end domestic equity and closed-end income funds, this statistic is displayed in comparison with the Vanguard Index Trust 500 Portfolio (a fund that serves as a surrogate for the S&P 500 Index), such that 1.00 equals the market level. A figure of 0.43, for example, indicates that the fund's median is 57% smaller than that of the market average. Similarly, a score of 1.15 indicates that the fund's statistic is 15% greater than the equivalent calculation for the index.

Minimum Initial Purchase

The minimum initial purchase indicates the smallest investment accepted for establishing a new account. Noted in parentheses is the smallest additional purchase a fund will accept in an existing account.

Minimum IRA Purchase

Minimum IRA purchase indicates the smallest permissible initial investment in an Individual Retirement Account. If the fund does not offer an IRA program, N/A will appear.

Minimum Automatic Investment Plan

This indicates the smallest amount with which one may enter a fund's automatic-investment plan—an arrangement where the fund takes money on a monthly, quarterly, semiannual, or annual basis from the shareholder's checking account. Often, the normal minimum initial purchase requirements are waived in lieu of this systematic investment plan. Studies indicate that regular automatic investment, also known as dollar-cost-averaging, is perhaps the most successful investment plan for long-term investors.

Modern Portfolio Theory Statistics

The next three statistics, alpha, beta, and R-squared, are components of Modern Portfolio Theory (MPT), which is a standard financial and academic method for assessing the risk of a fund, relative to a benchmark. To understand how to use MPT stats, readers unfamiliar to them may want to begin with the explanation of R-squared (below), then move to beta, and finally to alpha. Read on here to understand how the statistics are calculated: Morningstar bases alpha, beta, and R-squared on a least-squared regression of the fund's excess return over T-bills compared with the excess returns of the fund's benchmark index. These calculations are computed for the trailing 36-month period. Morningstar also shows a separate alpha, beta, and R-squared based on a regression against the "best-fit" index. The best-fit index for each fund is selected based on the highest R-squared result from separate regressions on a number indexes. If the standard index already has the highest R-squared, it will be shown again as the best fit.

For example, many Corporate High-Yield funds show low R-squared results when regressed against the standard bond index, the Lehman Brothers Aggregate. These low R-squared results indicate that the Aggregate index does not explain well the behavior of most High-Yield funds. However, most High-Yield funds show significantly higher R-squared results when regressed against the First Boston High-Yield index.

For closed-end funds, only one set of MPT statistics is shown. Equity funds are run against the S&P 500 Index, taxable-bond funds against the Lehman Brothers Aggregate Bond Index, and municipal-bond funds against the Lehman Brothers Municipal Bond Index.

Alpha

Alpha measures the difference between a fund's actual returns and its expected performance, given its level of risk (as measured by beta). A positive alpha figure indicates the fund has performed better than its beta would predict. In contrast, a negative alpha indicates a fund has underperformed, given the expectations established by the fund's beta. Many investors see alpha as a measurement of the value added or subtracted by a fund's manager.

There are limitations to alpha's ability to accurately depict a fund's added or subtracted value. In some cases, a negative alpha can result from the expenses that are present in the fund figures but are not present in the figures of the comparison index. Alpha is completely dependent on the accuracy of beta: If the investor accepts beta as a conclusive definition of risk, a positive alpha would be a conclusive indicator of good fund performance.

The exact mathematical definition of alpha that Morningstar uses is given at the top of the opposite page. Morningstar deducts the current return of the 90-day T-bill from the total return of both the fund and the benchmark index. The difference is called the fund's excess return.

Beta

Beta is a measure of a fund's sensitivity to market movements. It measures the relationship between a fund's excess return over T-bills and the excess return of the benchmark index. Morningstar calculates beta using the same regression equation as the one used for alpha, which may differ slightly from other methodologies that rely on a regression of raw returns.

By definition, the beta of the benchmark index is 1.00. Accordingly, a fund with a 1.10 beta is expected to perform 10% better, after deducting the T-bill rate, than the index in up markets and 10% worse in down markets, assuming all other economic factors remain constant. Conversely, a beta of 0.85 indicates that the fund is expected to perform 15% worse than the index in up markets and 15% better in down markets. A low fund beta does not imply that the fund has a low level of volatility, though; rather, a low beta means only that the fund's market-related risk is low. A specialty fund that invests primarily in gold, for example, will usually have a low beta, as its performance is tied more closely to the price of gold and gold-mining stocks than to the overall stock market. Thus, though the specialty fund might fluctuate wildly because of rapid changes in gold prices, its beta will remain low.

R-squared

R-squared reflects the percentage of a fund's movements that are explained by movements in its benchmark index. An R-squared of 100 means that all movements of a fund are completely explained by movements in the index. Thus, index funds that invest only in S&P 500 stocks will have an R-squared very close to 100. Conversely, a low R-squared indicates that very few of the fund's movements are explained by movements in its benchmark index. An R-squared measure of 35, for example, means that only 35% of the fund's movements can be explained by movements in its benchmark index.

Therefore, R-squared can be used to ascertain the significance of a particular beta or alpha. Generally, a higher R-squared will indicate a more reliable beta figure. If the R-squared is lower, then the beta is less relevant to the fund's performance.

Morningstar Rating Components

In this section, a fund's relative returns and risk are measured separately, then used to calculate risk-adjusted ratings for specific time periods, and then combined in the overall Morningstar risk-adjusted rating (which appears in the Historical Profile box). For each rating component, Morningstar separates open-end funds into four broad investment categories: equity, taxable-bond, municipal-bond, and hybrid. Separately, closed-end equity funds are evaluated against a universe of closed-end equity funds; closed-end fixed-income funds against all closed-end fixed-income funds; and closed-end hybrid funds are rated against the taxable closed-end fund universe. The first three of these are scored within the single class, while hybrid funds (asset-allocation, balanced, convertible-bond, income, high-yield corporate-bond, and world-bond funds) are scored against the combined universe of equity, taxable-bond, and hybrid funds. The category average is set at 1.00 for each time period, and individual fund returns and risk are rated relative to that average. (For return averages, 1.00 can sometimes represent the return for 90-day Treasury Bills; see below for further details on Morningstar Return.) Morningstar does not rate any fund that has less than three years of performance data.

Tax Considerations for Municipal-Bond Fund Ratings

Morningstar adjusts the basic rating calculation to reflect the tax treatment of municipal-bond funds.

Capital-gain distributions from municipal-bond funds are left unadjusted because they are already on a pretax basis. Total pretax returns are then calculated for each municipal fund using the adjusted dividends. These pretax returns are used in the calculation of both the Morningstar Return and Morningstar Risk scores. The municipal returns are adjusted upward to pretax levels in order to be consistent with the other three categories, which are all measured on a pretax return basis; to distinguish between tax-exempt dividends and taxable capital gains; and to allow investors to directly compare single-state and national muni funds.

The star ratings for single-state funds assume that the investor lives in that state. Residents of other states will typically not receive the state-tax benefit of out-of-state municipal bonds, so when using star ratings, investors should focus on single-state funds for their state of residence or national funds, but not single-state funds from other states. For all types of municipal-bond funds, the tax benefits are based on a federal tax bracket of 36%.

Morningstar Return

The Morningstar Return figures rate a fund's performance relative to other funds in its investment category after adjusting for maximum front-end loads, applicable deferred loads, and redemption fees.

After fund returns are adjusted, Morningstar calculates the excess return for each fund, defined as the fund's load-adjusted return minus the return for 90-day T-bills over the same period. The use of excess instead of raw returns reflects our belief that mutual funds should be rated highly for only those returns earned beyond those of T-bills, which are available to investors essentially risk-free. The excess returns are then compared with the higher of the average excess return of the fund's broad investment class or the ninety-day T-bill return. This last adjustment prevents distortions caused by low or negative excess returns, as might occur during a protracted down market, which could distort the return component of the star rating. The equation is:

$$\frac{\text{Return on Fund* } - \text{ T-bill}}{\text{Higher of (Category Return* } - \text{ T-bill) or T-bill}}$$

*Fund returns are adjusted for loads. Category average is based on load-adjusted returns.

The Morningstar Return figure is listed relative to the benchmark average—the higher of either the excess return of the investment category or the T-bill, which is set at 1.00. A figure of 1.10 means that the fund outperformed the category average (or T-bills) by 10 percent, while 0.90 means that the fund underperformed by 10 percent. In periods of low excess returns, most funds could hypothetically underperform T-bill returns.

Morningstar Risk

The Morningstar Risk statistic evaluates the fund's downside volatility relative to that of other funds in its investment category. Morningstar uses a proprietary risk measure that operates differently from traditional risk measures, such as beta and standard deviation, which see both greater- and less-than-expected returns as added volatility. Morningstar believes that most investors' greatest fear is losing money—defined as underperforming the risk-free rate of return an investor can earn from the 90-day Treasury bill—so our risk measure focuses only on that downside risk.

To calculate the risk score, we plot monthly fund returns in relation to T-bill returns. We add up the amounts by which the fund trails the T-bill return and divide that total by the period's total number of months. This number, the average monthly underperformance statistic, is then compared with those of other funds in the same broad investment category to assign our risk ratings. The resulting risk rating expresses how risky the fund is relative to the average fund in its category. The average risk rating for the category is set equal to 1.00; a Morningstar Risk

Defining Morningstar Risk

Month	Fund return	T-Bill return	Underperformance (loss)
1	3.0	0.5	—
2	−1.5	0.5	2.0
3	0.5	0.6	0.1
4	4.0	0.7	—
5	−2.0	0.5	2.5
6	3.0	0.5	—
Total			**4.6**

$$\frac{\text{Total loss}}{\text{Total \# months}} = \frac{4.6}{6} = 0.77 \text{ (Average monthly loss)}$$

$$\text{Morningstar Risk} = \frac{\text{average monthly loss}}{\text{average monthly loss of investment category}}$$

rating of 1.35 for a taxable-bond fund means that the fund has been 35% riskier than the average taxable-bond fund for the period considered.

Morningstar Risk-Adjusted Rating

A rating, expressed on a scale of 1 to 5 stars, that incorporates both performance and risk measures into one comprehensive evaluation. To determine a fund's star rating for a given period (three, five, or 10 years), Morningstar subtracts the fund's comparative Risk score from its Return score. The resulting number is plotted along a bell curve to determine the fund's rating for each time period: If the fund scores in the top 10% of its category (equity, hybrid, taxable-bond, or municipal-bond), it receives 5 stars (Highest); if it falls in the next 22.5% it receives 4 stars (Above Average); a place in the middle 35% earns it 3 stars (Neutral or Average); those in the next 22.5% receive 2 stars (Below Average); and the bottom 10% get 1 star (Lowest). Because hybrids are rated against both other hybrids and non-hybrid funds, these percentage breakdowns may not be reflected in the actual hybrid-fund ratings. The star ratings are recalculated monthly.

The rating displayed in the Historical Profile section provides a fund's overall risk-adjusted star rating. The ratings for the three time periods are combined as a weighted average: The 10-year rating accounts for 50% of the overall rating, the five-year figure for 30%, and the three-year rating for 20%. If only five years of history are available, the five-year period is weighted 60% and the three-year period 40%. If only three years of data are available, the three-year figure is also the overall rating. Because the overall star ratings are weighted averages of ratings from different time periods, the overall ratings will not necessarily follow the same percentage breakdowns as ratings from a single time period. In other words, it is not a given that 10% of funds in a particular category will have an overall rating of five stars, 22.5% a rating of four stars, and so on.

While the risk-adjusted rating is a useful tool in considering funds in which to invest, it is best used only as an initial screen, not as a conclusion. It's important that investors not place too much emphasis on this rating when evaluating funds. The Morningstar rating system is designed to help investors cut down on the amount of time spent trying to select funds. Because there are so many funds now available, it can be hard to know where to start to make an investment decision. The ratings, which are Morningstar's proprietary measure of historical risk-adjusted performance, give investors a way to narrow down the group of funds that they want to look at in more depth.

The star rating is neither a predictive measure nor a buy/sell recommendation. It is a purely descriptive representation of how well a fund has balanced risk and return in the past. It views funds individually, not as part of an overall portfolio. While investors seeking to hold only one fund would be likely to prefer a higher-rated fund, in a larger portfolio many investors may want to hold a 2- or even 1-star fund. For example, there are good reasons—diversification is one, hedging against inflation another—that some investors may want to have a small stake in an European-equity fund, but currently all rated funds in that category earn fewer than 4 stars. Choosing funds purely on the basis of rating in this case would deny an investor access to all funds in a specific category.

Nonetheless, funds with 3, 4, and 5 stars often make the most sense for many investors. This may be particularly true for those who are making their first investments outside of bank savings, because high-risk funds—just the type that such investors would seek to avoid—have difficulty shining in this system, as their returns must be very high to offset their risk. Few investors are able to tolerate the volatility inherent in high-risk funds, and we have geared our rating system accordingly. That doesn't mean, however, that lower-rated funds don't have a place in some portfolios; we just want to emphasize that they don't belong in every portfolio, and that anyone investing in these funds should be very sure of his or her ability to withstand the risks involved.

Morningstar Risk Percentile Rank

To the left of the Morningstar Risk and Return scores, the Morningstar Risk percentile rank column lists the fund's risk rating relative to two groups. In the column headed by All, a fund's risk rating is ranked against the risk ratings for all funds tracked by Morningstar; the Obj column makes the same comparison within the fund's investment objective.

The most favorable ranking is one, and the least favorable is 100. This system reverses the raw calculation used to rank returns, but enables investors to recognize both favorable risk and return information by low numbers.

Most Similar Funds

The most similar funds section identifies the three funds that have exhibited similar performance characteristics based on historical total returns. It does not measure similarity of current or historical portfolio holdings. This statistic is calculated only among those funds with three or more years of performance history.

To determine the similarity of a fund, Morningstar calculates a linear regression line for each fund against every other fund covered in *Morningstar Mutual Fund 500* (except municipal bond funds, which are run separately). The linear regression, based on the trailing 36 monthly total returns, generates an alpha and beta coefficient and an R-squared statistic. (Note: these are not the same as the statistics covered in the section on Modern Portfolio Theory.) Adjusted alpha, beta, and R-squared figures are then combined to produce an overall similarity statistic.

R-squared measures the percent of the movements of one fund that is explained by the movement in the other fund. A perfect correlation would produce an R-squared of 1.00. Since any number less than 1.00 indicates less-than-perfect correlation, we subtract the R-squared from 1.00. We then multiply this result by two in order to weigh the correlation more heavily than the alpha and beta components.

The beta coefficient measures the relative volatility of one fund versus the other. A perfect match would produce a beta of 1.00. Because any deviation from 1.00 (positive or negative) would indicate less-than-perfect relative volatility, we subtract beta from 1.00 and take the absolute value.

The alpha coefficient measures relative performance. A fund that performs just as well (or poorly) as another fund (adjusting for beta), will have an alpha of zero. Because any deviation from zero (positive or negative) would indicate a difference in performance, we use the absolute value of alpha in the calculation process.

Adding the three components produces a similarity statistic, as shown below:

$$2(1 - \text{R-squared}) + |1 - \text{beta}| + |\text{alpha}|$$

If R-squared or beta are different from one or if alpha is different from zero (or any combination of these), the similarity statistic will be greater than zero. High results thus indicate a poor fit, while a low result indicates a good fit. The similarity statistics are

classified into three grades of how well the two funds fit each other: strong fit, fair fit and weak fit. The top three matches are always listed, even if all three are weak fits.

N

NAV

A fund's net asset value (NAV) represents its per-share price. A fund's NAV is derived by dividing the total net assets of the fund by the number of shares outstanding.

Net Assets

The final row of the table in the history section lists a fund's assets, both for the year-end and the most-recent-month-end. The figure is recorded in millions of dollars.

For closed-end funds: These figures represent year-end assets net of liabilities and expenses, applicable to common shareholders of the fund.

Net Asset Value

see NAV

No-Load

see also Loads and Fees

This label denotes the fund as a true no-load fund, charging no sales or 12B-1 fees.

O

Objective

The objective indicates the investment goals of a particular fund. Morningstar usually bases a fund's objective on the wording in the prospectus issued by the fund's advisor, but may adjust that categorization to better reflect the fund's actual investment practices.

Aggressive Growth (AG)

seeks rapid growth of capital, often through investment in smaller companies and with investment techniques involving greater-than-average risk, such as frequent trading, leveraging, and short-selling.

Asset Allocation (AA)

seeks both income and capital appreciation by determining the optimal percentage of assets to place in stocks, bonds, and cash. A high priority of managers of these funds is determining the correct allocation of assets to these sectors, a decision often based on an analysis of business-cycle trends.

Balanced (B)

seeks both income and capital appreciation by investing in a generally fixed combination of both stocks and bonds. In general, these funds hold a minimum of 25% of their assets in stocks and 25% in bonds at any time.

Convertible Bond (CV)

invests primarily in bonds and preferred stocks that can be converted into common stocks.

Corporate Bond–General (CG)

seeks income by investing in fixed-income securities, primarily corporate bonds of various quality ratings.

Corporate Bond–High Quality (CQ)

seeks income by investing in corporate fixed-income securities, at least 65% of which are rated A or higher.

Corporate Bond–High Yield (CY)

seeks income by generally investing 65% or more of its assets in bonds rated below investment grade. The price of these issues generally is affected more by the condition of the issuing company (similar to a stock) than by the interest-rate fluctuation that usually causes bond prices to move up and down.

Equity-Income (EI)

seeks current income by investing at least 65% of its assets in equity securities with above-average yields.

Europe Stock (WE)

generally invests at least 65% of assets in equity securities of European issuers.

Foreign Stock (WF)

invests primarily in equity securities of issuers located outside the United States.

Government Bond—Adj-Rate Mortgage (GA)

invests at least 65% of its assets in mortgage or mortgage-related securities with adjustable coupons. These securities are usually backed by the U.S. government.

Government Bond–General (GG)

seeks income by investing in a combination of mortgage-backed securities, Treasuries, and agency securities.

Government Bond–Mortgage (GM)

seeks income by generally investing at least 65% of its assets in securities backed by mortgages, such as securities issued by the Government National Mortgage Association (GNMA), the Federal National Mortgage Association (FNMA), and the Federal Home Loan Mortgage Corporation (FHLMC).

Government Bond–Treasury (GT)

seeks income by generally investing at least 80% of its assets in U.S. Treasury securities.

Growth (G)

seeks capital appreciation by investing primarily in equity securities. Current income, if considered at all, is a secondary objective.

Growth and Income (GI)

seeks growth of capital and current income as near-equal objectives, primarily by investing in equity securities with above-average yields and some potential for appreciation.

Income (I)

invests in both equity and fixed-income securities primarily for the purpose of realizing current income. Although they may invest in equity securities, these funds invest primarily in domestic and foreign debt obligations. The percentages of assets in stocks and bonds typically aren't fixed by charter, as they are in balanced funds.

Municipal Bond-National (MN)

seeks income that is exempt from federal income tax by investing primarily in bonds issued by any state or municipality.

Pacific Stock (WP)

invests primarily in issuers located in countries in the Pacific Rim, including Japan, China, Hong Kong, Malaysia, Singapore, New Zealand, and Australia.

Short-Term World Income (SW)

seeks income and a stable net asset value (NAV) by investing primarily in a portfolio of various non-U.S.-currency-denominated bonds, usually with maturities of three years or less. Funds in this category seek higher yield than a money-market fund and less fluctuation of NAV than a world bond fund. These funds may engage in substantial hedging strategies to reduce NAV fluctuation.

Small Company (SC)
seeks capital appreciation by investing primarily in stocks of companies with market capitalizations of less than $1 billion. Income is unlikely.

Specialty (S)
seeks capital appreciation by concentrating its investments in a single industry or sector other than those described below.

Specialty–Financial (SF)
seeks capital appreciation by investing primarily in equity securities of financial-services companies, including banks, brokerage firms, and insurance companies.

Specialty–Health (SH)
seeks capital appreciation by investing primarily in equity securities of health-care companies, including drug manufacturers, hospitals, and biotechnology firms.

Specialty–Natural Resources (SN)
seeks capital appreciation by investing primarily in equity securities of companies involved in the exploration, distribution, or processing of natural resources.

Specialty–Precious Metals (SP)
seeks capital appreciation by investing primarily in equity securities of companies engaged in the mining, distribution, or processing of precious metals.

Specialty–Technology (ST)
seeks capital appreciation by investing primarily in equity securities of companies engaged in the development, distribution, or servicing of technology-related equipment or processes.

Specialty–Utilities (SU)
seeks capital appreciation by investing primarily in equity securities of public utilities.

World Bond (WB)
seeks current income with capital appreciation as a secondary objective by investing primarily in debt obligations issued throughout the world. These bonds are frequently foreign government issues.

World Stock (WW)
invests primarily in equity securities of issuers located throughout the world, maintaining a percentage of assets (normally 25% to 50%) in the United States.

The following closed-end fund objectives may also appear:

Latin America Stock (WL)
seeks capital appreciation by investing primarily in Latin American equity securities.

Domestic Equity (DE)
seeks capital appreciation by investing primarily in U.S. equity securities. This category includes everything from traditional growth-stock funds to small-company funds to specialty-sector funds (for example, financial, health, natural resources, precious metals, or utilities). Funds in this objective may engage in aggressive techniques such as short-selling and leveraging their assets, or they may have relatively conservative charters calling for growth and income characteristics.

Government Bond (GB)
invests in a blend of mortgage-backed securities, Treasuries, and agency securities.

International Bond (IB)
invests primarily in foreign-currency-denominated bonds.

Multisector Bond (MB)
invests in a variety of fixed-income securities, including corporate bonds, government bonds, and international bonds. Equity securities are also sometimes used.

P

Percentile Rank
These measure how the total returns or Risk scores of a fund compare to those of other funds in its objective or in the closed-end universe as a whole. In the Trailing Returns and History sections, funds are ranked by returns on a scale from 1 to 100 where 1 represents the fund with the highest returns and 100 represents the fund with the lowest returns. In the Risk-Adjusted Rating section, funds are ranked by their Risk scores on a scale from 1 to 100 where 1 represents with the lowest risk and 100 represents the fund with the highest risk.

Percent of Total Investments
For closed-end funds: The percentage of the fund's total investments in a given security; calculated by dividing the market value of the security by the fund's total investments.

Portfolio

Occupying much of the right side of the page is the portfolio. Prominent in this section are the fund's most recently reported top 25 securities (excluding cash and cash equivalents except for short-term bond funds), ranked in descending order by the percentage of the portfolio's net assets they occupy. With this information, investors can more clearly identify exactly what drives the fund's performance.

Morningstar makes every effort to gather the most up-to-date portfolio information from a fund. By law, however, funds need only report this information two times during a calendar year. Therefore, we print the date the portfolio was reported. Portfolios older than six months should not be disregarded, however; although the list may not represent the exact current holdings of the fund, it may still provide a good picture of the overall nature of the fund's management style.

Amount

The amount column refers to the size of the portfolio's investment. The size is enumerated in the thousands for a given security and marked with the date the portfolio was recorded. For equities, this figure gives the number of shares of a particular stock currently held by the fund. For fixed-income securities, this figure reflects the principal value of the security in thousands of dollars. Funds that hold both stocks and bonds will list share amounts and principal value (both in thousands), respectively, in the amount column.

For closed-end equity funds, the amount shown is the actual number of shares or par value of the holding; it is not expressed in thousands. For very large numbers of shares or values, the amount may be expressed in millions and followed by an M. (Some funds supply the par amounts for non-U.S. bonds in the bond's local currency rather than in U.S. dollars. Morningstar does not convert these amounts to U.S. dollars.)

Maturity

Maturity, located in the portfolio section for bond funds only, indicates the date on which a bond or note comes due. Because the maturity dates listed here are not adjusted for calls, which are rights an issuer may have to redeem outstanding bonds before their scheduled maturities, or the likelihood of mortgage prepayments, they might not accurately state the actual time to repayment of a bond, thus possibly overstating a portfolio's sensitivity to interest-rate changes.

Security

The middle column lists the names of the equity or fixed-income securities held as of the portfolio date. For equity holdings, this line will simply display the name of the issuing company. Fixed-income holdings, however, will usually include more information to differentiate among the many types of bonds available. For most bonds, the coupon rate is listed as a percentage figure after the name of the bond. Adjustable-rate and floating-rate bonds will have ARM or FRN listed after the name of the bond to indicate that the coupon rate is variable. Some adjustable-rate bond listings will include the formula by which the coupon rate is calculated, which is usually a fixed percentage plus some benchmark value. Some securities followed by abbreviations, such as IO or PO, would indicate an interest-only security, one that consists only of the interest portion of a security, not the principal portion. PO would indicate a principal-only security that sells at a discount to par and carries a coupon rate of zero.

Share Change

Found only on equity fund pages, the share change entry indicates the change in the number of shares of each stock from the previously reported portfolio.

For closed-end equity funds, the share change shown is the actual amount by which the number of shares changed; it is not expressed in thousands. For very large share changes, the amount may be expressed in millions and followed by an M.

Total Stocks/Total Fixed-Income

The portfolio section lists both equity and fixed-income holdings that are among a fund's 25 largest holdings. The total stocks heading indicates the total number of equity securities in a fund's portfolio, and total fixed income denotes the total number of fixed-income securities a fund holds. These do not simply refer to the stocks or bonds listed on the page; rather, they represent all stocks and bonds in the portfolio. These listings can be quite useful for gaining greater insight into the portfolio's per-issue diversification, as well as for getting a sense of how many securities the fund's management is currently investing in.

Value/Percentage of Net Assets

Value and percentage of net assets appear in the portfolio section of the page and are most meaningful to investors when considered together. Value simply gives the market value of a particular security in thousands of dollars as of the portfolio date. Adding to the significance of the value figure, the net assets column indicates what percentage of the portfolio's net assets a given security constitutes. Morningstar calculates the percentage of net assets figure by dividing the market value of the security by the fund's total net assets. If a given security makes up a large percentage of the fund's net assets, the fund uses a concentrated portfolio strategy, at least with respect to the security in question. If, however, the percentage figure is low, then the manager is either maintaining per-issue diversification or is simply not willing to bet heavily on that particular security. The value column also allows investors to gauge whether a fixed-income security is selling at a premium or a discount to its face value, as reflected in the amount column.

Portfolio Date

The securities are current as of the date (listed at the top right) that the portfolio was reported.

Portfolio Manager

The portfolio manager is the individual or individuals responsible for the overall fund strategy and buying and selling decisions of the securities in a fund's portfolio. If a fund provides a list of several managers names, Morningstar will list them as space permits. Management teams may consist of many people, but if one manager is considered a central figure, that individual's name will be printed. We also note the year in which the manager began managing the fund. This information is useful for determining whether a specific year's performance is attributable to a fund's current manager.

Potential Capital Gains Exposure

see Tax Analysis

Preferred Leverage Amount

see Leverage Amount

Premium/Discount

For the closed-end funds: The amount by which a fund's market price as of a particular date was greater or less than the NAV, expressed as a percentage of the NAV. A negative number indicates that the fund's shares sold at a discount to NAV, and a positive number indicates the shares sold at a premium. For example, if the number shown is –10.0, the shares sold at a 10% discount to NAV. The premium or discount at the top of the page represents data as of 12/31/94. Along the top of the performance graph are the highest and lowest premiums and discounts for the fund on a yearly basis. Weekly data is used when available; otherwise, monthly data is used to calculate these maximum and minimum values. At the bottom of the performance graph is a bar graph charting the month-end premiums or discounts of the fund. The History section contains a row showing the average premium or discount for the fund on a yearly basis. Again, weekly data is used when available to calculate these average values; otherwise, monthly data is used.

Price/Book Ratio

The price/book (P/B) ratio of a fund is the weighted average of the price/book ratios of all the stocks in a fund's portfolio. The P/B ratio of a company is a comparison of the cost of the company's stock and its book value, or the historical value of the company's tangible assets, which is calculated by dividing the market price of its stock by the company's per-share book value. (Stocks with negative book values are excluded from this calculation.) In computing the average, Morningstar weights each portfolio holding by the percentage of equity assets it represents, so that larger positions have proportionately greater influence on the final P/B. A fund with a higher-than-average P/B ratio may

indicate that the average price of stocks in the portfolio exceeds the recorded value of the company's assets. A low P/B may indicate that the stocks are bargains, priced below what the companies' assets could be worth if liquidated.

For closed-end domestic equity and closed-end income funds, this statistic is displayed in comparison with the Vanguard Index Trust 500 Portfolio (a fund that serves as a surrogate for the s&p 500 Index), such that 1.00 equals the market level. A figure of 0.43, for example, indicates that the fund's statistic is 57% lower than that of the market average. Similarly, a score of 1.15 indicates that the fund's statistic is 15% greater than the equivalent calculation for the index.

Price/Cash Flow

Price/cash flow, which is listed for international-stock funds, is a weighted average of the price/cash flow ratios of the stocks in a fund's portfolio. Price/cash flow represents the amount of money an investor is willing to pay for a dollar of cash generated from a particular company's operations. Price/cash flow shows the ability of a business to generate cash and can be an effective gauge of liquidity and solvency. This is not a stand-alone statistic, however, and should be used in conjunction with a fund's P/E ratio.

For closed-end domestic equity and closed-end income funds, this statistic is displayed in comparison with the Vanguard Index Trust 500 Portfolio (a fund that serves as a surrogate for the s&p 500 Index), such that 1.00 equals the market level. A figure of 0.43, for example, indicates that the fund's statistic is 57% lower than that of the market average. Similarly, a score of 1.15 indicates that the fund's statistic is 15% greater than the equivalent calculation for the index.

Price/Earnings Ratio

The price/earnings (or P/E) ratio of a fund is the weighted average of the price/earnings ratios of the stocks in a fund's portfolio. The P/E ratio of a company is a comparison of the cost of the company's stock and its trailing 12 months' earnings per share, which is calculated by dividing these two figures. In computing the average, Morningstar weights each portfolio holding by the percentage of equity assets it represents, so that larger positions have proportionately greater influence on the fund's final P/E. A high P/E indicates that the market will pay more to obtain the company's earnings because it believes in the firm's ability to increase its earnings. A low P/E indicates the market has less confidence the company's earnings will increase; however, a fund manager or an individual with a "value investing" approach may believe the stocks have an overlooked or undervalued potential for appreciation.

For closed-end domestic equity and closed-end income funds, this statistic is displayed in comparison with the Vanguard Index Trust 500 Portfolio (a fund that serves as a surrogate for the s&p 500 Index), such that 1.00 equals the market level. A figure of 0.43, for example, indicates that the fund's statistic is 57% lower than that of the market average. Similarly, a score of 1.15 indicates that the fund's statistic is 15% greater than the equivalent calculation for the index.

R

Regional Exposure

Foreign and world stock funds, as well as precious-metals funds, feature a country exposure table. For most foreign and world stock funds, this table displays the percentage of the fund's equity assets invested in the U.S., Europe, Japan, the Pacific Rim (including Australia, Hong Kong, and Singapore), and other regions. Because the table takes into account all equity assets, these percentages should add up to 100%. For precious-metals funds, the table shows the percentage of assets invested in stocks from issuers in North America, South Africa, Australia, and in other regions, or in bullion. Again, the percentages—representing assets in gold-related investments—should add up to 100%.

For closed-end funds: This bar graph for international-equity and international-bond funds shows the top countries represented in the fund's portfolio and its currency exposure. This measure is helpful in determining a fund's stake in a particular country or currency.

Reinvestment Plan

A plan whereby a shareholder can reinvest dividends automatically, and therefore acquire additional shares of a fund without having to go through a broker for the transaction.

Relative Strength

see Graphs

Relative Comparisons

Objective (for bond funds)
This column appears in the Portfolio section of the page for Coupon Range and Sector Weightings. Portfolio statistics are listed under this column, showing how an individual fund compares to the average of all funds within its Morningstar objective. The objective average is always set equal to 1.00, thus: The higher the number over 1.00, the greater the fund's overweighting for that statistic relative to other funds in its objective; the lower the number under 1.00, the bigger the fund's underweighting for that statistic relative to other funds within its objective. For example, a municipal bond fund with a Utility weighting of 1.50 is 50% more overweighted than

its objective peers. On the other hand, a municipal bond fund with a Utility weighting of 0.50 is 50% underweighted compared to its objective peers.

S&P 500 (for equity and hybrid funds)
This column appears in the Portfolio section of the page for Sector Weightings. Portfolio statistics are listed under this column, showing how an individual fund compares to the s&p 500 index. The portfolio statistics relative to the s&p 500; the lower the number under 1.00, the bigger the fund's under-weighting for that statistic relative to the s&p500. For example, a conservative stock fund with a Utility weighting of 1.50 is 50% more overweighted than the s&p 500 index. On the other hand, a conservative stock fund with a Utility weighting of 0.50 is 50% underweighted compared to the s&p 500 index.

Return

see Morningstar Return and Total Return

Return on Assets

Return on assets is the measure of the after-tax and after debt-service profitability of a company. The number listed is the portfolio's weighted average, calculated from the companies' net earnings over the trailing 12 months and their total assets. Usually, but not always, funds that score well by this measure are those with high earnings-growth rates as well.

For closed-end domestic equity and closed-end income funds, this statistic is displayed in comparison with the Vanguard Index Trust 500 Portfolio (a fund that serves as a surrogate for the s&p 500 Index), such that 1.00 equals the market level. A figure of 0.43, for example, indicates that the fund's statistic is 57% lower than that of the market average. Similarly, a score of 1.15 indicates that the fund's statistic is 15% greater than the equivalent calculation for the index.

Risk

see Morningstar Risk, Standard Deviation, and Beta

Risk % Rank

see Morningstar Risk Percentile Rank

R-Squared

see Modern Portfolio Statistics

Sector Analysis

For government-bond funds, which generally invest most of their assets in AAA rated securities, a sector analysis replaces the credit analysis shown for other bond funds. The table indicates the percentage of bond assets held in various types of government bonds, including Treasuries, mortgage pass-throughs, collateralized mortgage obligations, and adjustable-rate mortgages. Because the government-bond market has become a virtual alphabet soup of acronyms, we've listed some definitions below:

ARMs

Adjustable-rate mortgages are backed by loans that reset periodically based on movements in market interest rates.

CMOs

Collateralized mortgage obligation are created by chopping up mortgage pass-throughs or whole loans into various slices in order to redistribute the cash flows (both principal and interest payments) from the underlying bonds. The CMO category includes planned amortization class bonds (PACs), floating- and inverse floating-rate CMOs, and accrual or z-tranche bonds, among other varieties.

FHLMC mortgages

Mortgage pass-through securities issued by the Federal Home Loan Mortgage Corporation. Like FNMA issues, FHLMC pass-throughs are not guaranteed by the U.S. Government.

FNMA mortgages

Mortgage pass-through securities issued by the Federal National Mortgage Association. FNMA mortgage pass-throughs are not explicitly backed by the U.S. Government.

GNMA mortgages

Mortgage pass-through securities issued by the Government National Mortgage Association. These bonds are backed by the full faith and credit of the U.S. Government.

Inverse Floater

A mortgage-backed derivative with a coupon that changes inversely with fluctuations in interest rates.

Other

Other includes anything that doesn't fall into one of the six categories listed above. This category incorporates agency debentures—bonds that are issued by the FNMA and FHLMC to finance their activities and are not backed by pools of mortgages.

U.S. Treasuries

U.S. Treasuries includes any bond or note issued by the United States Treasury.

Sector Weightings

Sector weightings are calculated for all equity and municipal-bond funds based on the securities in the fund's most recent portfolio. For domestic-equity funds, this statistic shows the percentage of the fund's equity assets invested in each of 10 major industry classifications (% of stocks) and how this weighting compares with the S&P 500 index's current weighting of the same sector relative to the S&P 500, as determined by the S&P 500-surrogate Vanguard Index Trust 500 Portfolio. For international stock funds, the portfolio average is compared with other funds in the same objective (Relative Obj), not with the S&P 500. Sector weightings appear only if 25% or more of a fund's holdings can be categorized into sectors.

Sector-weighting statistics are useful because they reveal the areas a fund is favoring and the areas it's avoiding. Quite often, a look at the sector weightings of two funds in the same category will reveal that the funds pursue their common objective in markedly different ways. Sector weightings are also a valuable tool for explaining why certain funds have bettered the market while others have lagged behind.

Because the individual funds may vary in how they categorize a particular security, Morningstar calculates the sector weightings in-house, using uniform categorizations that allow an investor to make meaningful sector-weighting comparisons between funds. Sectors are listed on the page beginning with the cheapest, lowest-risk sectors and progressing to the priciest and most volatile.

For closed-end municipal-bond funds, percentages of bond assets in prefunded bonds and bonds subject to the Alternative Minimum Tax (AMT) will also appear here. These percentages are independent of the percentages for the 11 sectors described above; they will not add up with the other percentages to 100%.

The major industries within each sector, listed alphabetically here, are as follows:

Consumer Durables

autos, housewares, recreation/luxury, multi-industry

Consumer Staples

foods, beverages, tobaccos, household goods

Energy

oil, natural gas

Financials
banks, thrifts, insurance, real estate

Health
pharmaceuticals, health-care services, medical devices, drug
wholesalers

Industrial Cyclicals
aerospace, construction, machinery, machine tools, chemicals,
metals, papers, building materials

Retail
all retail (except drug wholesalers)

Services
media, entertainment, personal and business services, waste
management, transportation

Technology
computer hardware, software, electronics, electrical equipment

Utilities
telephones, electrics, gas utilities

Sector weightings are also calculated in-house for municipal-bond
funds. They represent the percentage of bond assets (% of Bonds)
invested in each of 10 revenue types and one catch-all category,
along with a comparison of the fund's weighting in each category
with those of other funds in the same objective (Rel Obj).

The municipal-bond classifications are as follows:

COP/Lease
certificates of participation and leases

Demand
short-term municipal securities

Education
colleges and universities, independent and unified school districts,
student loans, tuition

Gen Obl
general obligation bonds, which are repaid from general revenue
and borrowings rather than from the revenue of a specific project
or facility

Health
hospitals, nursing homes, retirement facilities

Housing
single and multifamily housing

Misc Rev
miscellaneous revenue bonds

Private
private-activity bonds involving economic and industrial
development, pollution control, fairs and expositions, stadiums,
hotels

Trans
transportation by air, water, road, or railroad

Utility
electricity, gas, nuclear power, dams, telephones

Wtr/Waste
water, sewers, sanitation, irrigation, drainage

Security
see Portfolio

SEC Yield
SEC yield is a standardized figure that the Securities and
Exchange Commission requires funds to calculate rates of income
return on a fund's capital investment. SEC yield is an annualized
calculation that is based on a trailing 30-day period. This figure
will often differ significantly from Morningstar's other yield
figure, which reflects trailing 12-month distributed yield, because
of differing time periods as well as differing accounting policies.
For example, SEC yield is based on a bond's yield to maturity,
which takes into account amortization of premiums and
discounts, while distributed yield (see Yield) is often based on
bonds' declared yields.

Share Change
see Portfolio

Shareholder Report Grade
With the shareholder report grade, Morningstar evaluates the
quality of a report the fund sends to its shareholders. The
scale runs from A+ to F. The following criteria are taken into
consideration: the letter to shareholders, the frequency of
the report, its timeliness and completeness, its orientation toward
providing relevant investment information (rather than
toward marketing the fund), any special features, and overall
presentation and organization.

Shares Outstanding

For closed-end funds: The number of common shares held by investors.

Sharpe Ratio

The Sharpe ratio is a risk-adjusted measure developed by Nobel Laureate William Sharpe. It is calculated using standard deviation and excess return to determine reward per unit of risk. First, the 12-month return of the 90-day Treasury bill is subtracted from the fund's 12-month total return. The difference in total return represents the fund's excess return beyond that of the 90-day Treasury bill, a risk-free investment. To show a relationship between excess return and risk, this number is then divided by the fund's standard deviation. The higher the Sharpe ratio, the better the fund's historical risk-adjusted performance.

Standard Deviation

see also Modern Portfolio Theory

When a fund has a high standard deviation, the range of performance is very wide, meaning that there is a greater potential for volatility. Approximately 68% of the time, the total returns of any given fund will differ from its mean total return by no more than plus or minus the standard deviation figure. Ninety-five percent of the time, a fund's total returns will be within a range of plus or minus two times the standard deviation from its mean. These ranges assume that a fund's returns fall in a typical bell-shaped distribution. In any case, the greater the standard deviation, the greater the fund's volatility.

Mean

The mean represents the annualized average monthly return from which the standard deviation is calculated. The mean will not be the same as the total annual return figure for the same year. (Technically, the mean is an annualized arithmetic average while the total return figure is an annualized geometric average.)

States Available

This is a list of the states and U.S. territories in which the fund is registered and available for sale. ALL appears for those funds available in all states. Puerto Rico, Guam, and the U.S. Virgin Islands are listed separately.

Stock Exchange/Index Allocation

This section, located directly below the portfolio holdings, shows what portion of the fund's equity assets are invested in the S&P 500 Index and the S&P MidCap 400 Index, as well as the percentage in U.S. small-company stocks and foreign stocks. The S&P 500 measures the performance of 500 widely held stocks and serves as a proxy for the stock market. The S&P MidCap 400 tracks 400 midsize domestic companies. U.S. Small Cap represents all U.S. companies not included in the two S&P indexes.

Standard Deviation

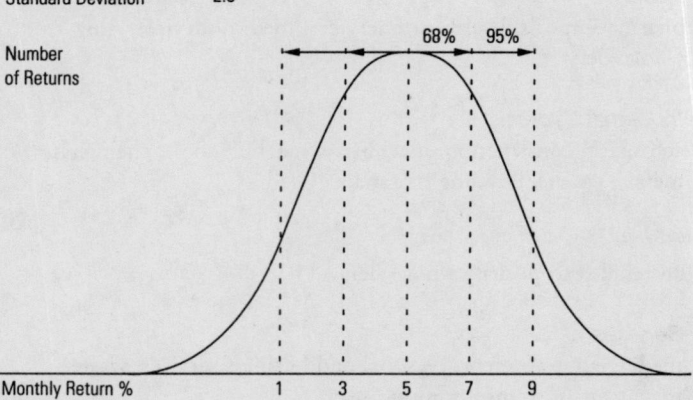

Fund B

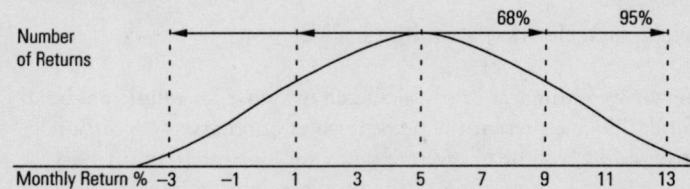

A fund with a higher standard deviation has a wider range of returns. The smaller a fund's standard deviation, the more consistent its returns.

The final category, foreign stocks, includes American Depositary Receipts which are foreign stocks packaged for trade on U.S. exchanges.

The composition, sector weightings, coupon range, credit analysis, and top five states graph may be located in different areas of this section or may not even appear at all, depending upon the specific fund type and objective. For example, a graph that provides a portfolio's bond credit ratings would not appear for an equity fund, which may hold no bonds.

Style Box

At one point fund categories made sense. There were stock funds and bond funds. Over time, with the explosion in the mutual-fund industry, that simplicity has disappeared as fund companies have created new categories for an ever-growing variety of investment styles and types. Even with some pruning, Morningstar still lists more than 20 separate fund objectives, and fund companies continue to promote new ones. This trend greatly enhances the chance that a fund may lead its category, but it doesn't necessarily help an investor make informed decisions. For example, three funds with identical small-cap, technology-oriented portfolios—but different names and marketing campaigns—could find themselves in three supposedly distinct categories: aggressive growth, small company, and specialty—technology. Categorizing funds can be perplexing: They may be grouped by their aims, as in growth and income or equity-income. Or they may be considered by the types of securities they own, such as international bond, utilities, or small company. And they may be described by the features of the stocks in their portfolio, as with the terms growth or value.

Such terminology carries the potential for confusion, as the three approaches use differing starting points. Complicating the issue is that many of these phrases have assumed multiple meanings. For example, growth has come to mean both a goal, as in growth of capital, and an investment style, that of buying rapidly growing companies by allowing a systematic way to look at what is being held in the funds' portfolios.

Morningstar has designed the style box to help investors cut through the confusion and profusion of fund categories. It is designed to help investors better understand a fund's true investment strategy.

Equity Style Box

The equity style box is a nine-box matrix that displays both the fund's investment methodology and the size of the companies in which it invests. Combining these two variables offers a broad view of a fund's holdings and risk.

Along the horizontal axis of the equity style box are the three types of investment styles. Morningstar categorizes a fund's style as being growth-oriented (G), value-oriented (V), or a blend of the two (B). Generally speaking, a growth-oriented portfolio will mostly contain companies that its portfolio manager believes have the potential to increase earnings faster than the rest of the market. A value orientation, on the other hand, focuses on stocks that the manager thinks are currently undervalued in price and believes will eventually see their worth recognized by the market. A blend fund will mix the two philosophies: The portfolio may contain growth stocks and value stocks, or it may contain stocks that exhibit both characteristics.

In order to classify funds by investment style, Morningstar takes a stock portfolio's average price/earnings ratio (the ratio of a company's stock price to its actual earnings) relative to the average of the S&P 500 Index, and adds to it the portfolio's average price/book figure relative to that of the S&P 500. (The S&P 500 average in each case is set equal to 1.00) This emphasis on relative, rather than absolute, numbers is quite important for equity funds.

For example, a price/earnings ratio of 15 could be cheap in one market, but expensive in another; what is truly useful is seeing how that number compares with the overall market and with other funds. The sum of the relative ratios is then placed into one of the three style categories. Funds with a combined relative price/earnings and price/book figure of less than 1.75 are considered to be value funds. Portfolios with combined ratios from 1.75 to 2.25 are considered to be blend funds (by definition, the S&P 500 scores 2.00), and any funds with a sum greater than 2.25 are classified as growth funds.

Morningstar also categorizes funds by size. All funds with median market capitalizations of less than $1 billion are grouped in the small-company, or small-cap (S), box. Funds with median market capitalizations equal to or greater than $1 billion but less than or equal to $5 billion are labeled as medium-cap (M) offerings, and funds with median market capitalizations exceeding $5 billion qualify for the large-cap (L) designation. This information is plotted along the vertical axis of the style box.

International equity style boxes are analogous to the style boxes on the domestic-equity pages. On the vertical axis, funds are grouped by median market cap as small, medium, or large cap with the same parameters as domestic funds.

On the horizontal axis, international funds, like their domestic counterparts, are separated into value, blend, or growth funds. For international funds, however, the style box determination is made on the basis of price/cash flow and price/book relative to the EAFE Index. If the sum of the relative price/cash flow and the relative price/book is less than 1.75, it is defined as a value fund; if the sum lands from 1.75 to 2.25, the fund is classified as a blend vehicle; if the sum is greater than 2.25, the fund falls into the growth category. Thus, funds that pay low price multiples for their stocks land toward the value side; those that pay high price multiples in hope of greater future gains tend toward the growth end.

Fixed-Income Style Box

Domestic and international fixed-income funds feature their own style boxes, which focus on the two pillars of fixed-income performance; interest-rate sensitivity and credit quality. Morningstar splits fixed-income funds into three maturity groups (short, intermediate, and long) and three credit-quality groups (high, medium, and low). These groupings graphically display a portfolio's effective maturity and credit quality. As with equity funds, nine possible combinations exist, ranging from short maturity/high quality for the safest funds to long maturity/low quality for the most risky.

Along the horizontal axis of the style box lies the average term length of a fund's bond portfolio based on average effective maturity (average weighted maturity for municipal-bond funds). This statistic is calculated by weighting each bond's maturity by its relative size within the portfolio. Average effective maturity provides a more accurate description of a bond's true life than does a simple weighted maturity; the former takes into consideration all mortgage prepayments, puts, and adjustable coupons. Funds with an average effective maturity of less than four years qualify as short-term (s). Funds whose bonds have an average effective maturity greater than or equal to four years but less than or equal to 10 years are categorized as intermediate (I), and those with maturity that exceeds 10 years are long-term (L).

Along the vertical axis of a fixed-income style box lies the average quality rating of a bond portfolio. Funds that have an average credit rating of AAA or AA are categorized as high quality (H). Bond portfolios with average ratings of A, BB, or BBB are medium quality (M), and those rated below BBB are categorized as low quality (L). For the purposes of Morningstar's calculations, U.S. government securities are considered AAA bonds, nonrated municipal bonds are classified as BB, and all other nonrated bonds are labeled B.

For closed-end fixed-income funds, Morningstar uses duration to designate funds as short, intermediate, and long. For asset-allocation, balanced, and income funds, both equity and fixed-income style boxes appear on the page.

Subadvisor

In some cases, the advisor employs another company, called the subadvisor, to handle the fund's day-to-day management. If the fund employs a subadvisor, the portfolio manager probably works for the fund's subadvisor, not the fund's advisor.

Equity Style Box

Risk		Median Market Capitalization	Investment Style		
			Value	Blend	Growth
Low	○	Large	Large-cap Value	Large-cap Blend	Large-cap Growth
Moderate	◍	Medium	Mid-cap Value	Mid-cap Blend	Mid-cap Growth
High	●	Small	Small-cap Value	Small-cap Blend	Small-cap Growth

Within the equity style box grid, nine possible combinations exist, ranging from Large-Cap–Value for the safest funds to Small-Cap–Growth for the riskiest.

Fixed-Income Style Box

Risk		Quality	Maturity		
			Short-term	Intermediate-term	Long-term
Low	○	High	Short-term High Quality	Interm-term High Quality	Long-term High Quality
Moderate	◍	Medium	Short-term Medium Quality	Interm-term Medium Quality	Long-term Medium Quality
High	●	Low	Short-term Low Quality	Interm-term Low Quality	Long-term Low Quality

Within the equity style box grid, nine possible combinations exist, ranging from Short Maturity–High Quality for the safest funds to Long Maturity-Low Quality for the riskiest.

T

Tax-Adjusted Historical Returns

Tax-adjusted historical return shows the fund's annualized after-tax total return for the three-, five-, and 10-year periods, excluding any capital-gains effects from selling the fund at the end of the period. To determine this figure, all income and capital gain distributions are reinvested at their full value and allowed to compound until year-end, at which time the maximum tax rate is used to exact a tax penalty. (For current taxes, Morningstar continues to use the 31% federal rate.) State and local taxes are ignored, and only the capital gains are adjusted for tax-exempt funds, as the income from these funds is nontaxable.

Percentage Pretax Return

The percentage pretax return provides a contrast to historical tax-adjusted return. While the latter measures the bottom-line after-tax results of a fund, without regard to pretax performance, the percentage pretax return statistic measures tax efficiency. This statistic, which excluded the investor's taxes upon selling the fund, is derived by dividing after-tax returns by pretax returns. The highest possible score would be 100%, which would apply to a fund that had no taxable distributions whatsoever (as do many municipal-bond funds). While it may seem that the lowest possible score would be 100% minus the average tax rate (which would represent the total if all of a fund's total returns were paid out in distributions), funds that erode capital can score even lower as their taxable income distributions actually exceed total returns.

For closed-end funds: All income and capital gains distributions are taxed at the time of distribution rather than at year-end.

Tax Analysis

Potential Capital Gain Exposure: Morningstar calculates potential capital gain exposure to give investors some idea of the potential tax consequences of their investment in a fund. We cannot predict what a fund's taxable distributions might be, but we can offer some clues based on a fund's liquidation liability. The figure we provide is useful for making comparisons between funds and in determining their appropriateness for one's investment portfolio.

A mutual fund's assets are composed of paid-in (investment) capital, appreciation or depreciation of this capital, and any undistributed net income. Paid-in capital is simply the monies investors have put into the fund (and can decrease should shareholders decide to redeem their shares). Any appreciation of this capital may eventually be taxed. Our potential capital gain exposure figure shows what percentage of a fund's total assets represent capital appreciation. We don't take into account undistributed net income in our calculation, because it would

greatly increase the complexity of the calculation but would have negligible impact on the outcome. (Funds rarely have much undistributed income.)

Capital appreciation can be either unrealized or realized. In the first case, the fund's holdings have increased in value, but the fund has not yet sold these holdings; taxes are not due until the fund does so. Realized net appreciation (commonly called realized gains) represents actual gains achieved by the sale of holdings; taxes must be paid on these capital gains. Unrealized appreciation may turn into realized gains at any time, should the fund's management decide to sell the profitable holdings. Thus, our formula includes unrealized appreciation as part of the potential capital gain exposure.

A negative potential capital gain exposure figure means that the fund has greater net losses than it has gains. This likely indicates that the fund has or will have a tax-loss carryforward, which would mean that some amount of future gains could be offset by past losses.

To keep our calculation current, we update the information between shareholder reports by accounting for a fund's market losses or gains, the sale or redemption of shares, and the payment of capital gains. This updated figure is not quite as precise as the one stated in the shareholder report, but it is more current and therefore more relevant to the investor.

Because the fund's asset base serves as the denominator in this calculation, a change in assets from the sale or redemption of shares can greatly influence a fund's potential capital gain exposure. As a fund's asset base grows, the tax impact of previous gains to shareholders is diminished. Conversely, a shrinking asset base amplifies the tax impact of past performance.

Telephone Numbers

These are the local and toll-free (if available) numbers that an investor may use to contact the fund.

Ticker

A ticker is the symbol assigned to the fund by the National Association of Securities Dealers Automated Quotation (NASDAQ) system. The ticker is commonly used to locate a fund on electronic price-quoting systems.

For closed-end funds: The ticker is the symbol assigned to the fund by the exchange on which it trades.

Top Five Countries
see Country Exposure

Top Five States
The portfolio analysis of municipal-bond funds includes a chart that displays the five states or U.S. territories in which the fund invests most heavily and the percentage of the portfolio each state or territory represents. This information reflects the holdings of the portfolio on the page.

Total Number of Countries
Listed below the top five countries or country exposure graph for international stock funds, this statistic represents the total number of countries (including the United States) in which a fund is invested. Morningstar calculates this number from the fund's portfolio.

Total Return
The first section of quarterly information shows a fund's total return, which represents a fund's gains over a specified period of time. The figure takes into account income (in the form of dividends and interest payments) and capital gains (the increase in the value of a security). Morningstar calculates total return by taking the change in NAV, assuming the reinvestment of all income (on the actual reinvestment date used by the fund) and capital-gains distributions during the period, and dividing by the initial NAV.

Unless marked as load-adjusted total returns, Morningstar does not adjust total return for sales charges or for redemption fees. (Morningstar Return, Morningstar risk-adjusted ratings, and the load-adjusted returns in the top right-hand corner of the page do incorporate those fees.) Total returns do account for management, administrative, and 12B-1 fees and other costs automatically deducted from fund assets. The quarterly returns express the fund's return for each individual quarter; the total shown on the right is the compounded return for the four quarters of that year. An asterisk next to the total return number indicates that the return is calculated for a partial quarter or partial year because the fund began operations during that time period.

For closed-end funds: Total returns are also calculated using market prices instead of NAVs.

Total Stocks/Total Fixed-Income
see Portfolio

Transfer Agent
The company (often a bank) that handles the purchase and redemption of shares of the fund; also responsible for dividend-reinvestment plans.

Turnover Ratio
The turnover ratio represents the fund's level of trading activity. This publicly reported figure is calculated by the funds in accordance with SEC regulations, and Morningstar gathers the information from fund shareholder reports. A fund divides the lesser of purchases or sales (expressed in dollars and excluding all securities with maturities of less than one year) by the fund's average monthly assets. The resulting percentage can be loosely interpreted to represent the percentage of the portfolio's holdings that have changed over the past year.

V

Value/Percentage of Net Assets
For closed-end funds, the percentages are based on the fund's total investments rather than the net assets.

W

Worst 3 Months
Morningstar's bear market return ranking identifies funds that perform well in a down market, but it does not show how funds behave during more-stable market climates. To provide an idea of how widely a fund's returns have fluctuated in the past, a Worst 3 Months figure is included with the bear-market bar graph on the page. For the past two consecutive five-year time periods, Morningstar highlights the fund's worst three-month period of performance and shows how that performance compares to either the S&P 500 or Lehman Brothers Aggregate Index for the same time period. Morningstar also shows how the fund's Worst 3 Month return stacks up next to the fund's best fit index.

Y

Yield
Yield, expressed as a percentage, represents a fund's income return on capital investment for the past 12 months. This figure refers only to distributions of interest from fixed-income securities and dividends from stocks. Monies generated from the sale of securities or from options and futures transactions are considered capital gains, not income. (Realized gains from currency transactions are considered income, though.) Return of capital is also not considered income. NMF—or No Meaningful Figure—appears in this space for those funds that do not properly label their distributions.

Morningstar computes yield by dividing the sum of the fund's income distributions for the past 12 months by the previous month's NAV (for open-end funds) and the previous month's market price (for closed-end funds) adjusting upward for any capital gains distributed over the same period.

Index of Terms

Follow the Morningstar 500 funds every month in the *5-Star Investor* newsletter.

Morningstar's *5-Star Investor* newsletter helps you create and maintain your own winning mutual-fund portfolio. Every month you get updated performance, risk, portfolio, and operations information on the open- and closed-end funds in the *Morningstar Mutual Fund 500*. In addition, we provide you with the industry news you need to make informed investment decisions.

In each 44-page issue:

- *Lead Articles* examine in detail important issues in the market— and how they can affect your investment strategy.

- *Data Overview* allows you to spot the top-performing sectors, see which investment styles are reaping the greatest rewards, and check the performance of a number of market indexes.

- *Fund News* updates you on recent developments in the mutual-fund industry.

- *Planners' Corner* examines and rebuilds an individual's fund portfolio to achieve the combination of return and risk appropriate for the investor.

- *Fund Profile* spotlights a mutual fund that merits special attention or that illustrates a broader market trend, helping you better understand the ideas that are paying off in the market.

- *The Last Word,* a candid editorial that discusses any of a broad range of market topics, concludes every issue.

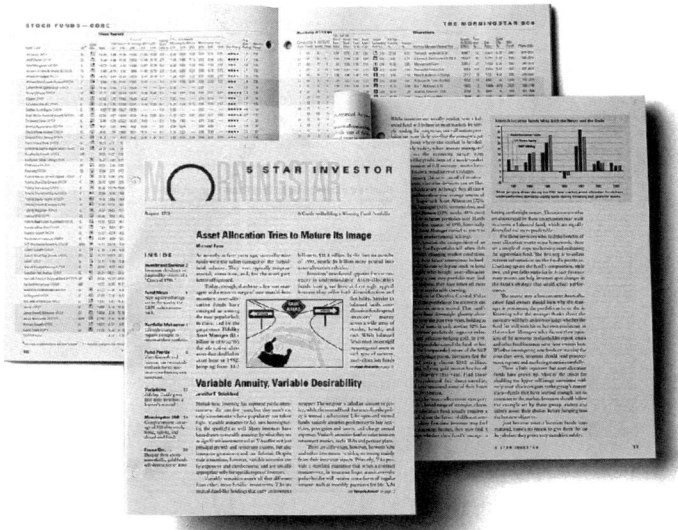

Used together, *Morningstar Mutual Fund 500* and *5-Star Investor* give you a potent combination of background data and up-to-date results on leading mutual funds. An annual subscription to *5-Star Investor* is only $79.

For your free sample issue, return the attached card or call 800-876-5005 (Monday through Thursday 7:30 a.m. to 7 p.m., Friday 7:30 a.m. to 6 p.m., Saturday 9 a.m. to 4 p.m., Central Time). Please mention code HFS5 when calling.

Please send me a free sample copy of *5-Star Investor.*

For your free sample issue, return this completed card or fax it to us at 312-696-6001. Please allow four to six weeks for delivery.

NAME

ADDRESS

CITY   STATE   ZIP CODE

DAYTIME TELEPHONE   •HFS5

Attn: Marketing—HFS5

BUSINESS REPLY MAIL
FIRST CLASS MAIL   PERMIT NO. 15474   CHICAGO, IL

Postage will be paid by addressee

Morningstar, Inc.
225 W Wacker Dr Ste 400
Chicago IL 60606-9629